TIME
ALMANAC
2002

with **INFORMATION PLEASE**®

BORGNA BRUNNER
EDITOR IN CHIEF

Information Please
www.infoplease.com
Part of **LEARNING** NETWORK

Information Please
www.infoplease.com
Part of **LEARNING** NETWORK

Editor in Chief *Borgna Brunner*

Editor *Ann-Marie Imbornoni*

Senior Contributing Editors
David P. Johnson, Jr., Beth Rowen

Contributing Editors *Susanna Brougham
(Religion), Christine Frantz (Sports),
Arthur Reed (Current Events),
Aimee Roebuck (Science)*

Contributors *Holly Hartman,
Laura Hayes, George Kane, Michael Rozett,
Ricco Villanueva Siasoco*

Senior Vice President
Elizabeth Buckley Kubik

Production Director
Susan Hyde

Production Editor *Christine Frantz*

Proofreading and Fact-checking
Katie Blatt

Editorial Assistants *Megan Handley,
Elizabeth Olson, Adam M. Shire*

Graphics *Sean M. Dessureau*

Technical Support *Karl DeBisschop*

Time Inc.
HOME ENTERTAINMENT

Contributing Editor *Kelly Knauer*

Design *Anthony Kosner*

Pictures *Patricia Cadley*

President *Rob Gursha*

Vice President, Branded Businesses
David Arfine

Executive Director, Marketing Services
Carol Pittard

Director, Retail & Special Sales
Tom Mifsud

Director of Finance *Tricia Griffin*

Marketing Director *Kenneth Maehlum*

Assistant Director *Ann Marie Ross*

Editorial Operations Manager
John Calvano

Retention/Centralized Marketing Manager
Meredith Shelley

Associate Product Manager
Jennifer Dowell

Assistant Product Manager
Michelle Kuhr

Special thanks to: *Suzanne DeBenedetto, Robert Dente, Gina Di Meglio, Peter Harper,
Roberta Harris, Natalie McCrea, Jessica McGrath, Jonathan Polsky, Emily Rabin, Mary Jane Rigoroso,
Steven Sandonato, Tara Sheehan, Bozena Szwagulinski, Marina Weinstein, Niki Whelan*

The *TIME Almanac* welcomes comments and suggestions from readers. Although the editors carefully consider each suggestion, because of the volume of correspondence we receive we cannot respond personally to each writer. The *TIME Almanac* does not rule on bets or wagers.

Editorial Office
Information Please
20 Park Plaza, Suite 1220
Boston, MA 02116
Email: ipa@infoplease.com

Customer Service
Attention: TIME Almanac
PO Box 11016
Des Moines, IA 50336-1016

ISBN: 1-929049-29-3 Paperback
ISBN: 1-929049-28-5 Hardcover
ISSN: 0073-7860

If you would like to order copies of TIME's hardcover Collector's Edition books, please call us at 1-800-327-6388 (Monday through Friday, 7:00 A.M.–8:00 P.M. or Saturday, 7:00 A.M.–6:00 P.M. Central Time), or visit our website at www.TimeBookstore.com.

Printed in the United States of America.
WP Pa BP Hbd 10 9 8 7 6 5 4 3 2 1

Keyword Index

Section Index

Page numbers followed by "n" indicate information in footnotes.

The News of 2001: Nation

(through Oct. 31, 2001)

The transition from the 42nd to 43rd president was troubled on both sides. George W. Bush was inaugurated on Jan. 20, 2001, following one of the most disputed presidential elections in the nation's history (see p. 53). Scandal trailed his predecessor to the very end: on his final day in office, Bill Clinton struck a deal that gained him immunity from criminal liability in the Whitewater probe in exchange for admitting that he had given false testimony under oath during the investigation. His departure was further tarnished by a series of highly controversial last-minute pardons.

Economic Downturn and a Tax Cut

The top item on Bush's domestic agenda, a $1.6 trillion tax cut, was the subject of bitter partisan debate in Congress, with Democrats arguing that the bill heavily favored the rich and would squander the unprecedented budget surplus. The Senate eventually trimmed the tax cut to $1.35 trillion over 11 years, and Bush signed it into law on June 7. The tax-cut victory was somewhat marred by the defection of Vermont senator James Jeffords, who changed his party affiliation from Republican to Independent—a major blow for the president, since it resulted in the Democrats' gaining control of the Senate.

By the time Americans began receiving their tax rebate checks in August (up to $300 for individuals and $600 for married couples), the country's budget surplus had indeed withered. The Congressional Budget Office attributed this rapid change in the nation's fortunes to the slowing economy and the Bush tax cut. By the fall, most analysts believed that the country was heading toward a full-blown recession, the result of sluggish growth and the stock market plunge, which had been exacerbated by the repercussions of the Sept. 11 terrorist attacks. Republicans proposed a stimulus plan that they hoped would infuse billions into the economy over the next year, primarily through tax breaks to businesses.

Missile Defense Shield

President Bush also championed an antimissile defense system, meant to intercept long-range missiles lobbed at U.S. shores. Opponents of the plan have argued that it is technologically unfeasible, astronomically expensive, and largely superfluous (see pp. 366–367). The proposed missile shield strained relations with U.S. allies and former cold-war adversaries Russia and China, who feared that the system could spark a new arms race. Its implementation would require the U.S. to pull out of the 1972 Antiballistic Missile Treaty (which bans missile defense), the basis for the last three decades of nuclear stability. But Russian president Vladimir Putin eventually expressed willingness to modify the ABM treaty if it also led to reductions in the nuclear arsenals of both countries. Sino-American relations, already shaky, had deteriorated in April after a standoff over a downed U.S. spy plane in Chinese territory, as well as the sale of arms to Taiwan later that month. China thus greeted the proposed missile shield with unequivocal hostility.

Foreign Policy

During his first seven months in office, Bush's foreign policy decisions were viewed by much of the world as starkly unilateralist. In addition to sounding the death knell on the ABM treaty, Bush refused to back a UN-proposed international criminal court and walked away from a conference to regulate the global small-arms trade. Most disturbing to the international community was the U.S.'s abandonment in March of the Kyoto treaty on global warming, which Bush contended would harm the economy. In July, 178 nations hammered out a modified and more realistic version of the treaty without the participation of the United States, the largest emitter of greenhouse gases (25%). The U.S. also rejected the biological weapons convention banning germ warfare, claiming that the proposed inspections would be too burdensome on the legitimate biotechnology industry. The administration also announced a new hands-off policy toward Israeli-Palestinian negotiations and put a sharp halt to the previous administration's nascent diplomatic overtures to North Korea, which in 2000 had been instrumental in narrowing the divide between the two Koreas.

September 11

The terrorist attacks on the World Trade Center and the Pentagon on Sept. 11 irrevocably scarred the nation. That morning, two commercial planes, en route from Boston to Los Angeles, were hijacked and flown minutes apart into the north and south towers of the World Trade Center in New York City. Shortly afterward, another plane, en route from Washington, DC, to Los Angeles, crashed into the Pentagon. A fourth hijacked plane, headed from Newark to San Francisco, crashed in a field near Shanksville, Pa.—investigators have speculated that the plane's intended target was Washington, DC, and that passengers aboard the flight may have thwarted the hijackers. Both World Trade Center towers collapsed, and a section of the Pentagon was destroyed. All 266 passengers and crew aboard the planes were killed; total dead from the Trade Center and Pentagon were estimated in the thousands. The country reeled from the world's deadliest act of terrorism, which caused the largest single-day loss of life in American history.

Nineteen hijackers, all Islamic extremists, were identified, and within days the attacks were linked to Osama bin Laden (see p. 45 for bio), a millionaire fundamentalist Saudi whose stated goals are the destruction of the U.S., Israel, and the Saudi monarchy. After the bombings he issued a videotape praising the hijackers and announcing that "America will not live in peace before peace reigns in Palestine, and before all the army of infidels depart the land of

Muhammad." His extensive but loosely knit terrorist network, al-Qaeda ("the base"), which is believed to have operations in more than 60 countries, has been implicated in numerous terrorist acts against Americans. These include the bombings of U.S. barracks in Saudi Arabia, the U.S. embassies in Kenya and Tanzania, and the USS *Cole* in Yemen, among others (*see* p. 46).

Fighting Terrorism

Bush immediately shored up an international coalition to fight terrorism worldwide and demanded that Afghanistan's Taliban government, which has harbored bin Laden since 1996 and is host to al-Qaeda training camps, surrender the terrorists or risk military attack. In a televised address on Sept. 20, Bush warned Americans that the war against terrorism would be a lengthy campaign, involving covert action as well as air strikes that will not only target terrorists but the groups and governments that abet them. Following the speech, polls showed that the president's approval rating had soared to 90%. On Oct. 7, after the Taliban repeatedly and defiantly refused to turn over bin Laden, the U.S. and its close ally Britain began air strikes against Afghan military installations and terrorist training camps. The immediate goal was to destroy Afghanistan's military resources and capture bin Laden and al-Qaeda members. "Today we focus on Afghanistan," Bush contended, but "the battle is broader." How much broader and in what way was a matter for speculation at the end of October. Differences within the Bush administration over its antiterrorism strategy rose almost immediately. Hawks such as Deputy Defense Secretary Paul Wolfowitz advocated expanding the military response to include strikes against Iraq because of its sponsorship of terrorism—despite the fact that there was no evidence of Iraq's involvement in the Sept. 11 bombings. Secretary of State Colin Powell, the administration's most dovish influence, has urged that a concert of military, diplomatic, intelligence, and financial tactics be engaged.

A new White House agency, the Office of Homeland Security, under former Pennsylvania governor Tom Ridge, was formed to coordinate a national strategy to safeguard the country against terrorism. Almost immediately a new menace surfaced: anthrax-contaminated mail, which was sent to major newspapers and television networks, as well as to mail facilities for the White House, Congress, the CIA, and the Supreme Court, causing temporary shutdowns. As the number of cases multiplied, the threat of bioterrorism further undermined the country's sense of security.

The New Multilateralism

Bush has announced that the global war against terrorism "will be the focus of my administration from now on." His new calling has already transformed his presidency from its domestic focus and narrowly defined foreign policy to one demonstrating a heightened appreciation for international coalition-building. The U.S. rapidly began repairing its neglected relations with the UN and resumed a more active diplomatic role in the Middle East. In October Bush delayed missile defense testing in an effort to shore up good will with Russia and other nations. As Colin Powell quipped in mid-October, "Nobody is calling us unilateral anymore . . . We're so multilateral, it keeps me up 24 hours a day."

The News of 2001: World

Afghanistan

The ultimatum issued to the Taliban after Sept. 11 to turn over bin Laden was the last of several such demands made by the U.S. and the UN after bin Laden was implicated in the 1998 U.S. embassy bombings in East Africa (the U.S. also responded then by launching retaliatory missile attacks on Sudan and an Al-Qaeda training camp in Afghanistan). Binding their fate to bin Laden's, the Taliban became the target of daily air strikes by the U.S. and Britain in October. The Pentagon has warned that the military conflict may be difficult and prolonged; Afghanistan has famously thwarted invasions by powerful enemies in the past.

The Taliban, a group of militant Islamic fundamentalists, came to power in 1996 after a six-year civil war between various factions of Islamic guerrillas (mujahideen), who, no longer united in their long struggle against a brutal Soviet invasion (1979–1989), turned on each other. The Taliban brought a measure of stability to the impoverished and war-torn land, but its harsh and puritanical interpretation of Islamic law, oppression of women, and active support of terrorism turned the regime into an international pariah. Only three countries—Saudi Arabia, Pakistan, and the United Arab Emirates— have ever recognized the Taliban as Afghanistan's legitimate government.

Afghanistan served as a cold-war battleground for the U.S., which spent a reported $3 billion training and equipping the mujahideen to fight the Soviet occupation. Once the Soviets were defeated, however, the U.S. withdrew, abandoning the anarchic and exhausted country to its own devices. The CIA-funded mujahideen of the Soviet era became the fractious groups engaged in the civil war that followed, producing a fertile ground for Islamic extremism. Under the assumption that the Taliban will be removed from power, the U.S. and the international community have vowed to see the country through its reconstruction. Such "nation-building," formerly derided by the Bush administration, has become of paramount importance. Complex sectarian and ethnic differences, however, deepened by decades of war and internecine conflict, have made it challenging for the international community to establish a representative government that would be acceptable to the diverse populace.

Three years of severe drought have resulted in a growing famine in Afghanistan. Before Sept. 11, an estimated 3.5 million Afghan refugees were already subsisting in bordering countries; another million had been internally displaced. And now, eviscerated by decades of nearly constant war and poverty, Afghanistan's 26 million people find themselves caught between the might of a superpower and the ruthlessness of an extremist jihad.

Pakistan, India, and Kashmir

Close ties with Afghanistan's Taliban government thrust Pakistan into a difficult position following the Sept. 11 terrorist attacks. Under U.S. pressure, Pakistan broke with its neighbor to become the United States' chief ally in the region. In return, President Bush ended sanctions (instituted after Pakistan's testing of nuclear weapons in 1998), rescheduled its debt, and helped to bolster the legitimacy of Pervez Musharraf's rule—the general came to power in a military coup in 1999 and appointed himself president in 2001.

But strong ideological and cultural links to the Taliban have spawned virulent anti-American feeling in the country, and a percentage of the population consider Musharraf's pro-American stance collaborationist and a betrayal of Islam. Another source of widespread resentment is the U.S.'s desertion of Pakistan after it helped the U.S. drive the Soviets from Afghanistan. As Pakistan's current UN representative bluntly put it, "you left us in the lurch with all the problems stemming from the war: an influx of refugees, the drug and gun running, a Kalashnikov culture."

Two of the three wars that India and Pakistan have fought since their partition 54 years ago—as well as countless smaller skirmishes—have centered on the disputed territory of Kashmir. Pakistan has fought India for control of predominantly Muslim Kashmir with support of mujahideen from various parts of the world. While Pakistan refers to these troops as Kashmiri freedom fighters, India denounces them as Islamic terrorists. In the last decade alone, more than 30,000 deaths have resulted from the chronic fighting, and in 1998 the seemingly regional conflict evolved into a global threat after both India and Pakistan demonstrated their nuclear weapons capabilities.

In October violence again broke out in the region when a suicide bombing by a Pakistan-based militant organization killed 38 in India-controlled Kashmir. India retaliated on Oct. 15 with heavy shelling across the "line of control" that divides the region. India, angered by Washington's sudden coziness to Pakistan, took the opportunity to point out that while Pakistan might be helping the U.S. fight terrorism on the Afghan front, it was simultaneously supporting terrorism on its own borders with India. The timing was unfortunate for the U.S.—the escalation of the fighting in Kashmir threatened to weaken Musharraf's somewhat tenuous hold on power, crucial to the U.S.'s military strategy against Afghanistan. At the same time, the U.S., in its global fight against terrorism, could hardly ignore India's terrorist problems.

Middle East

The renewal of violence in the Middle East since the fall of 2000 (more than 800 people have been killed between Sept. 2000 and Sept. 2001, most of them Palestinians) and the collapse of the peace process paved the way for the stunning landslide victory of right-wing Likud leader Ariel Sharon over incumbent Labour Party leader Ehud Barak in Feb. 2001. With the Barak-brokered peace negotiations in shambles and Palestinian-Israeli relations deteriorating, Sharon's uncompromising stance on Israeli security became a powerful draw. Since the election, violence has continued at an alarming rate. Palestinians have carried out some of the most horrific suicide bombings in years, and Israeli F-16 fighter jets have bombed Palestinian territory. Unable to sustain a cease-fire, both sides seem further away from new peace negotiations than ever.

Macedonia and the Balkans

The long-simmering resentment of Macedonia's ethnic Albanians erupted into violence in March, prompting the government to send troops into the heavily Albanian western section of the country. The rebels sought greater autonomy within Macedonia, including official recognition of the Albanian language. The more radical aspired to create a greater Albania, one that would unite the ethnic Albanians of Macedonia, Kosovo, and Albania proper, but there was little enthusiasm for pan-Albanianism among Macedonia's war-weary neighbors. On Aug. 13, after six months of fighting, the rebels and the Macedonian government signed a peace agreement that allowed a British-led NATO force to enter the country and disarm the guerrillas. The guerrillas handed over weapons in exchange for the promise of constitutional amendments granting greater rights to Macedonia's Albanians. The ending of the conflict was one of the most placid in the recent troubled history of the Balkans.

In June, Yugoslavia turned over disgraced former president Slobodan Milosevic to the United Nations International Criminal Tribunal, which charged him with crimes against humanity and genocide. Milosevic is the first former head of state to face an international war-crimes court. As a result, the UN Security Council lifted the arms embargo on Yugoslavia, removing the last sanction against the country.

Northern Ireland

After issuing one last ultimatum to the IRA to begin destroying its weapons stores, in July Ulster Unionist leader David Trimble resigned his post as first minister of the Northern Ireland coalition government. As had been the case in the past year-and-a-half, Sinn Fein, the political wing of the IRA, continued to stall on disarmament. Trimble concluded he had exhausted his political viability: while Sinn Fein continued to dangle the promise of disarmament just out of reach, many hard-line Protestants perceived Trimble as a dupe of the IRA. Trimble's resignation threatened to topple the Northern Ireland assembly and return rule to the British—the government had in fact already been suspended twice since its formation in Dec. 1999.

Following Trimble's departure, the IRA offered another vague and open-ended disarmament plan, only to withdraw it. But on Oct. 23, days before Britain was to suspend the assembly, Sinn Fein leader Gerry Adams dramatically announced that the IRA had indeed begun disarming. Partially in response to the Sept. 11 attacks, which made the IRA's claim to weapons of terror seem even more senselessly brutal, Sinn Fein chose to embrace the promise of a political solution to the Northern Irish troubles.

What Happened in 2001: Month by Month

Highlights of key events of the year, organized month by month, in three categories for easy reference. For a detailed account of the Sept. 11, 2001, bombings and background on terrorism, see pp. 44–47. For the year's major Supreme Court decisions, see pp. 97–98. "Countries of the World" covers specific international events, country by country. See also "People in the News," pp. 1031–1034 and "2001 Deaths," pp. 1035–1039 for more current events coverage.

January 2001

WORLD

Israelis Rally in Jerusalem (Jan. 8): Religious and nationalist groups gather to "pledge allegiance" to the Holy City and protest an American plan for its division.

Iran Sentences Reformists (Jan. 13): Metes harsh jail terms to several leaders and a prominent journalist for attending "un-Islamic" conference in Germany.

Congo President Assassinated (Jan. 16): Laurent Kabila shot dead by bodyguard. He had overthrown dictator Mobutu Sese Seko in 1997 but led country into increasing instability and a brutal civil war.

Britain Outlaws Fox Hunting (Jan. 17): Parliament votes to ban traditional sport despite opposition.

Pope Appoints New Cardinals (Jan. 21): John Paul II names a record 37, including three Americans, in move to shape future of Roman Catholic Church. **(Jan. 28):** In unexpected move, pontiff appoints seven more cardinals.

Libyan Convicted in Flight 103 Bombing (Jan. 31): Scottish court finds Abdelbaset Ali Mohmed al-Megrahi, an intelligence officer, guilty of murder in deaths of 270 over Lockerbie, Scotland, in 1988. Court convened in Netherlands. A second defendant is released. In Washington, White House says verdict will not end sanctions on Libya.

NATION

Bush Names Democrat to Cabinet (Jan. 2): Fills cabinet by picking Norman Mineta, Clinton's commerce secretary, to head Department of Transportation.

INS Moves to Protect Jailed Immigrants (Jan. 2): Agency sets new standards in response to complaints and lawsuits concerning alleged mental abuse of prisoners.

Logging of Oldest Trees Banned (Jan. 8): Head of Clinton's Forest Service halts harvesting of old-growth timber on public lands.

Bush Cabinet Choice Withdraws (Jan. 9): Linda Chavez withdraws her nomination to be labor secretary after admitting to providing shelter and financial assistance to an illegal immigrant in the early 1990s.

Clinton Presents Final Message (Jan. 14): Departing president urges Congress to enact broad program to promote racial unity between whites and minorities.

Clinton Settles Long Legal Battle (Jan. 19): Forges deal with Independent Counsel Robert W. Ray to avoid a possible indictment by admitting that he gave false testimony about relationship with White House intern. He also agrees to give up law license for five years.

In Final Days, Clinton Issues 140 Pardons (Jan. 20): List includes Marc Rich, billionaire fugitive financier, and other prominent figures.

George W. Bush Sworn In as 43rd President (Jan. 20): In inaugural speech he plans to unite nation after one of most-disputed elections in history. He says "civility is not a tactic or a sentiment" but "a choice of trust over cynicism."

Bush Bars Abortion Aid Overseas (Jan. 22): Moves to deny federal funds to groups that provide abortion counseling or help women to have abortions.

Gore Says He Plans to Teach (Jan. 24): Defeated Democratic candidate to take posts at three universities—Middle Tennessee State, Fisk, and Columbia. He also plans to write book with his wife, Tipper.

Bush Seeks to Fund Church Groups that Offer Social Services (Jan. 28): Sets up first federal office to promote integration of religious and government programs.

BUSINESS/SCIENCE/SOCIETY

Federal Reserve Cuts Rates (Jan. 3): Alan Greenspan reduces rates by one half a percentage point to stem an economic slowdown. **(Jan. 31):** Fed slashes rates another half a percentage point. More cuts expected.

Louisiana Ex-Governor Sentenced (Jan. 8): U.S. judge sentences Edwin W. Edwards, 73, to 10 years in prison and fines him $250,000 for extortion from casinos.

AOL–Time Warner Merger Approved (Jan. 11): F.C.C. sanctions creation of world's largest media business but imposes conditions to prevent monopoly.

Earthquake Rocks Central America (Jan. 13 et seq.): Landslide buries hundreds of houses in El Salvador. **(Jan. 17):** Death toll reaches 700. Hundreds missing.

Oil Spill Threatens Pacific Wildlife (Jan. 16 et seq.): Tanker rams reef off San Cristobal Island in the Galápagos. Spill estimated 144,000 gallons. Rescue crews struggle to prevent environmental disaster.

Power Crisis Hurts California Business (Jan. 19): Workers and consumers also suffer from wide interruptions at major electrical plants.

Earthquake Kills Thousands in India (Jan. 26 et seq.): Massive temblor, registering 6.9 on scientific scale, rocks subcontinent. Thousands missing. **(Jan. 29):** Search for survivors gives way to excavating the dead. Homes and other buildings in ruins.

February 2001

WORLD

Congo's New President Addresses UN (Feb. 2): Joseph Kabila, son of slain president Laurent Kabila, promises Security Council he will open dialogue with opponents in an effort to end his nation's long civil war.

Russia Frees Chechnya Relief Worker (Feb. 4): Releases Kenneth Gluck, a director of Doctors Without Borders. He was held for three weeks and emerges in good health.

Ariel Sharon Wins Election in Israel (Feb. 6): Right-wing leader chosen overwhelmingly as nation's fifth prime minister in just over five years. Sharon, 72, victorious amid worst Israeli-Palestinian violence in years. Takes 62.5% of vote to Ehud Barak's 37.4%.

Russia Vows to Destroy Chemical Weapons (Feb. 8): Promises to begin destruction of 40,000 tons of lethal weapons, largest stockpile in the world.

Errant Bus Kills Eight Israelis (Feb. 14): Palestinian driver plows into crowd of soldiers and civilians at bus stop in Azur, Israel. Seventeen wounded. Rush-hour assault thought to be terrorist attack.

Europe Approves Strict Food Controls (Feb. 14): Union Parliament tightens rules governing genetically modified organisms. Vote is 338–52.

U.S. and Britain Attack Iraq (Feb. 16): Planes target radar stations and air defense command centers, including sites near Baghdad. Calls action a necessary response to Iraqi provocation.

Britain Fights Foot-and-Mouth Disease (Feb. 21): Suspends all exports of live animals, milk, and meat.

Ehud Barak Quits Politics (Feb. 21): Resigns as Israeli Labor Party chairman, leaves Parliament seat, and refuses invitation by prime minister–elect Ariel Sharon to become defense minister.

Three Serbs Convicted in Wartime Rapes (Feb. 22): UN war crimes tribunal, in first trial dealing solely with sex crimes, finds former Bosnian Serb soldiers guilty of attacking and torturing Muslim women and girls.

Israel Laborites Vote to Join Cabinet (Feb. 26): Party leaders agree to support unity government led by rightist prime minister Ariel Sharon.

NATION

Senate Confirms Attorney General, 58–42 (Feb. 1): Approves John Ashcroft, President Bush's nominee. Vote ends hostile five-week battle in which many Democrats criticized Ashcroft for his conservative views and legislative record.

Clintons to Reimburse 27 Gift Donors (Feb. 2): Former president and wife to pay $86,000 following a storm of criticism from both Democrats and Republicans.

Bush Orders Nuclear Arms Review (Feb. 8): President takes first step toward unilateral cut in weapons that he outlined during campaign.

Bush Drops Clinton's Mideast Peace Plan (Feb. 8): Administration calls former president's proposals out of date and out of step with regime of Ariel Sharon, new Israeli prime minister.

Bush Asks Increased Benefits for Military (Feb. 12): Seeks to shift $5.7 billion in Pentagon spending for increased pay, improved health care, and better housing.

President Plans to Introduce New Weapons (Feb. 13): Intends to break with Pentagon convention and invest "in a new architecture for the defense of America and our allies." in existing systems.

Social Security Agency Criticized (Feb. 18): Federal advisory panel reports deterioration of service in recent years that is likely to grow worse with retirement of millions of baby boomers.

Clinton Defense of Pardons Attacked (Feb. 18): Leaders of House and Senate investigating committees critical of article by former president defending his actions and say it merits investigation.

FBI Agent Charged as Spy for Russia (Feb. 20): Robert Hanssen accused of handing over highly classified information to Moscow for 15 years. As a senior agent he had worked as a counterintelligence supervisor.

President Outlines Agenda and Budget (Feb. 27): In televised address, Bush calls his proposed $1.6 trillion tax cut reasonable and responsible. **(Feb. 28):** In budget message he presents $1.96 trillion budget for next year that would reduce taxes and increase spending on education, medical research, and military. Scaled-back programs include corporate subsidies, health-care grants for poor areas, and agricultural research.

BUSINESS/SCIENCE/SOCIETY

California Votes Power Purchase (Feb. 1): Legislature approves $10 billion outlay as shortage of electricity reaches 17th day. Long-term contracts planned.

Reagan, 90, Celebrates Birthday Quietly (Feb. 6): Former president has simple observance because of Alzheimer's disease and recovery from a broken hip.

U.S. Submarine Sinks Japanese Ship (Feb. 9): Nuclear vessel, the *Greeneville*, strikes fishing trawler when surfacing during drill off Honolulu. Many on ship rescued, nine missing after search. Civilian visitors sat at sub's controls. **(Feb. 15):** Navy tightens rules governing civilians on submarines. **(Feb. 17):** Navy plans court of inquiry to investigate collision. **(Feb. 28):** Scott Waddle, commander of sub, sends letters of apology to victims' families.

Court Backs Curb on Music Copying (Feb. 12): Federal appeals judges in San Francisco deliver blow to Napster, a software program that has shaken record industry by allowing millions to share music for free over the Internet.

New Earthquake Rocks El Salvador (Feb. 13): More than 100 killed, and more than 1,000 injured by massive disaster, second within a month.

Stock Car Racing Star Killed in Crash (Feb. 18): Dale Earnhardt, 49, swerves into wall in last lap of sport's premier event, Daytona 500, at Daytona Beach, Fla.

Bush Dedicates Oklahoma City Museum (Feb. 19): Views mementos of explosion on April 19, 1995, worst act of domestic terrorism in American history.

Pope Elevates 44 as Cardinals (Feb. 21): Promotes largest number in history in Vatican ceremony. John Paul II has now appointed 155 cardinals.

Earthquake Jolts Pacific Northwest (Feb. 28): Tremor lasting 40 seconds is worst for area in 52 years. Damages heavy in Seattle and elsewhere.

March 2001

WORLD

Suicide Bomber Kills Three Israelis (March 4): Attack in Netanya, town north of Tel Aviv, follows slaying by Israelis of six Palestinians. Tension builds in area.

Israel Restores Parliamentary System (March 7): Legislature votes overwhelmingly to abandon direct election of prime minister and have legislators make choice.

Bomb Kills Six in Kuwait (March 12): Five Americans die when the U.S. Navy, in a training drill, drops a 500-pound missile and hits observation post filled with military personnel. A New Zealander also dies.

Russia to Resume Arms Sales to Iran (March 12): President Putin agrees to provide conventional weapons after five-year interval.

Albanian Rebels Fight in Macedonia (March 15): Battle police in Tetovo. Some civilian casualties.

OPEC to Cut Oil Output (March 17): Members of Organization of Petroleum Exporting Countries agree to trim production by 4 percent to stem falling prices.

Russia Convicts Six in Bombing (March 19): Islamic extremists sentenced for 1999 blast in Dagestan region that killed 68 and sparked popular support for war in Chechnya.

Bush Meets with Israeli Prime Minister (March 20): Discussion with Ariel Sharon appears to indicate desire to shun peace talks while violence continues.

Russian Diplomats Expelled from U.S. (March 21): Move follows arrest of FBI agent Robert Hanssen, who allegedly spied for Moscow for 15 years.

British Livestock Epidemic Spreads (March 23): Foot-and-mouth disease reaches crisis levels and government intensifies efforts to eradicate it.

Bush Abandons Global-Warming Treaty (March 30): International session in Montreal breaks up after Bush balks at Kyoto Protocol, which calls on industrialized nations to reduce emissions of heat-trapping gases. **(March 31):** European leaders angered by Bush's decision to abandon international treaty.

NATION

Census Bureau Rejects Tally Revision (March 1): Urges commerce secretary not to adjust 2000 population figures to make up for persons not counted.

Pentagon Reveals a New Weapon (March 1): Military officials say device uses electronic magnetic waves to disperse crowds without injury.

Aides Say Clinton Rejected Pardon Advice (March 1): Three senior advisers tell House panel that president overruled them and granted a pardon to Marc Rich on last day in office.

Cheney Hospitalized (March 5): Doctors clear an obstructed artery. Second angioplasty in four months.

Congress Repeals Clinton Work Rules (March 6): Senate votes, 56–44, to rescind new regulations designed to reduce injuries, especially those from repetitive stress. **(March 7):** House by narrow margin, 223–206, also votes for repeal.

Increase in U.S. Hispanic Population (March 7): Census Bureau reports Hispanic population grew by more than 60 percent over last decade.

Bush Bars Talks with North Korea (March 7): Tells South Korean president Kim Dae Jung that he will not discuss missile negotiations any time soon, shelving Clinton effort toward normal relations.

Senate Toughens Bankruptcy Rules (March 15): Votes, 83–15, to make debt reduction more difficult.

Rule on Arsenic in Water to End (March 20): EPA plans to rescind Clinton administration order to reduce arsenic level in drinking water.

ABA Role on Judgeships to End (March 22): White House tells bar association it will no longer seek its evaluation of nominees for federal bench.

Senate Blocks Campaign Finance Reform Foes (March 27): Defeats, 60–40, proposal that would have limited but not banned unregulated donations to parties.

BUSINESS/SCIENCE/SOCIETY

Ruling Expands Reach of Cable Companies (March 2): Appeals court strikes down federal regulations that prevent big organizations from expanding and broadcasting more of their own shows.

Crash of Guard Plane Kills 21 (March 3): C-23 Sherpa plunges to ground in heavy rain in Georgia.

Student Kills Two Others in California (March 5): Charles Andrew Williams, 15, also wounds 13 others at high school in Santee. Incident called worst episode of school violence since Columbine in 1999.

U.S. Bans Meat from Europe (March 13): Blocks imports of animals and animal products after foot-and-mouth disease spreads from Britain to France.

Four Blasts Kill 108 in China (March 16): Coordinated explosions shake Shijiazhuang. Dozens reported injured. Investigation focuses on a resident of one of bombed buildings who is also wanted for murder.

Federal Reserve Acts to Bolster Markets (March 20): Lowers interest rates half a percentage point to stimulate economy after sharp plunges in stock market and Nasdaq technology index.

Rolling Blackouts in California (March 20): Hundreds of thousands lose power as industry managers move to counter energy production crisis.

Study Links Estrogen to Cancer (March 21): Researchers find that risk of ovarian cancer is greater among those who took hormone for ten or more years.

Defects Result in Cloning Animals (March 24): Scientists report mounting evidence of random genetic errors that threaten similar efforts to duplicate humans.

Fire Kills 58 Youths in Kenya (March 26): Sleeping students perish in dormitory blaze.

Suspect in Anti-Abortion Killing Seized (March 29): French police arrest James Charles Kopp, activist charged in 1998 sniper shooting in Amherst, N.Y.

Stem Cells Thought to Yield Benefits (March 30): Scientists see use in repairing damaged heart tissue.

April 2001

WORLD

Serbs Arrest Slobodan Milosevic (April 1): Former Yugoslav president held at Belgrade's Central Prison. He surrenders after receiving a guarantee of a fair trial.

U.S. Plane and Chinese Jet Collide (April 2): Navy surveillance craft on routine mission near China coast hit by fighter craft that was closely trailing it. Damaged U.S. plane, with 24 crew members and secret equipment, makes emergency landing at military base on Chinese island of Hainan. Chinese pilot, Wang Wei, is missing and presumed dead. **(April 3):** Chinese government blames United States for midair collision and hints that release of crew depends on apology from Washington. **(April 10):** United States issues formal statement of regret to Beijing for collision with Chinese

fighter. **(April 12):** China releases all 24 U.S. crew members after 11 days in custody. Crew later reports having destroyed much of the plane's secret equipment.

Mubarak Seeks Greater U.S. Role in Middle East (April 2): But President Bush, in a meeting with the Egyptian president, defends policy of allowing Israelis and Palestinians to seek peace independently.

Putin Pledges Major Shake up (April 3): Russian president promises government-wide moves to make business work, reverse capital flight, and sustain economic growth.

Israel Strikes Deep into Lebanon (April 16): Air attack destroys Syrian radar installation. Move further unsettles Arab world.

Israel Occupies Part of Gaza (April 17): Plans to use area for border buffer zone. Troops withdraw after strong rebuke from U.S. secretary of state Colin L. Powell.

Peru Downs U.S. Missionary Plane (April 20): Peruvian Air Force, aided by CIA contract workers, shoots down private aircraft carrying American Baptists reportedly misidentified as drug traffickers. Veronica Bowers and her infant daughter are killed.

Hemisphere Summit Adjourns (April 22): Thirty-four leaders of Western nations close Quebec conference with pledge of equal support to democracy and free trade. Commit to Free Trade Treaty that will share benefits with all 800 million residents of area.

Bush Pledges Defense of Taiwan (April 25): Says U.S. would do "whatever it took" to protect island if attacked by China.

Ukraine Political Crisis Deepens (April 26): Parliament delivers blow to reform movement, voting to oust Prime Minister Viktor Yushchenko and his government.

U.S. Scholar Convicted in Russia (April 27): John Tobin, Fulbright scholar, found guilty of minor marijuana violation and sentenced to 37 months in penal colony.

NATION

U.S. Population Up Sharply (April 2): Census Bureau reports increase of 32.7 million people in 1990s, greater than in any other ten-year period in nation's history.

Senate Approves Campaign Finance Bill (April 2): Passes, 59–41, wide-ranging overhaul of law to ban "soft money"—unrestricted political contributions.

Senate Passes Budget Measure (April 6): GOP hails approval, 65–35, of bill allowing $1.2 trillion tax reduction over ten years, $85 billion this year.

Rioting Breaks Out in Cincinnati (April 7): Rioting breaks out in Cincinnati following the shooting death of an unarmed African-American man by a white police officer. Violence continues for several days.

Bush Offers First Budget (April 9): President proposes increased aid for education and cuts to farm subsidies.

Bush Accepts Medical Privacy Rules (April 12): Approves sweeping provisions on patients' records but hints at future revision.

No Court-Martial Urged for Sub's Captain (April 14): Navy court of inquiry recommends that Commander Scott D. Waddle not be tried for February's deadly collision between U.S. submarine and Japanese fishing vessel. **(April 23):** Waddle reprimanded and resigns from Navy. Will receive full pension and retain his rank.

EPA Supports Wetlands Ruling (April 16): Leaves standing Clinton administration order to expand protection to tens of thousands of acres.

House Approves Fetus Protection (April 26): Bill calls for charging a criminal with murder or manslaughter if a fetus dies after an attack on a pregnant woman.

Naval Bombing in Puerto Rico Approved (April 26): U.S. judge permits resumption on island of Vieques, but offers encouragement to opponents.

Census Finds Big-City Whites in Minority (April 29): Reports nearly half of 100 largest cities have more blacks, Hispanics, and other minorities than whites.

U.S. Asks Limit on Painkiller (April 30): DEA calls on maker to curb distribution of Oxy-Contin, drug blamed for more than 100 fatal overdoses.

BUSINESS/SCIENCE/SOCIETY

Helicopter Crash Kills 16 in Vietnam (April 8): Bodies recovered from wreckage. Victims were seven Americans and nine Vietnamese in group seeking remains of American soldiers missing in the Vietnam War.

Fed Cuts Interest Rate Again (April 18): Reduces benchmark by half a percentage point to spur flagging economy. Wall Street rally follows.

Robot Arm Linked to Space Station (April 22): Canadian device joined to International Space Station by two Canadian spacewalking astronauts.

Ill Man Rescued from Antarctica (April 24): Dr. Ronald Shemenski, suffering from pancreatitis, evacuated by plane from South Pole research station.

Space Tourist Lifts Off (April 28): Dennis Tito, taking off aboard a Russian booster from the Baikonur Cosmodrome in Kazakhstan, to visit the International Space Station in an eight-day trip that cost him $20 million.

May 2001

WORLD

Pope Visits Middle East (May 5 et seq.): John Paul II greeted in Syria by new president, Bashar al-Assad, who publicly accuses Israel of torturing and murdering Palestinians.

U.S. Resumes Spy Flights off China Coast (May 7): First mission since Navy plane and Chinese fighter jet collided in April. Flight completed without incident.

China Bars Flight by Stranded U.S. Plane (May 8): Refuses to allow damaged surveillance aircraft to be repaired and flown from Hainan Island.

Conservatives Win Italian Election (May 14): Coalition behind media magnate Silvio Berlusconi wins majority in each house of parliament. Berlusconi elected to a second, non-consecutive term as prime minister.

Israelis and Palestinians Clash (May 18): Suicide bomber kills five Israelis and wounds more than 100 at crowded shopping mall in Netanya. By evening Israeli warplanes retaliate by attacking West Bank and Gaza Strip for first time since 1967 war.

U.S. Broadens Role in Middle East (May 21): Senior State Department aide urged to actively help Israelis and Palestinians take steps to resume peace talks.

Israeli Building Collapse Kills at Least 25 (May 25): Crowded dance floor in Jerusalem falls onto packed floor below. More than 300 severely injured.

Ethnic Albanians Flee Attacks in Macedonia (May 25 et seq.): Thousands escape on foot in face of Macedonian government offensive against rebels in northern hills.

Russia Stands Firm on Missile Treaty (May 28): Kremlin says U.S. offer to use Russian missiles and radar in new antimissile system will not affect its opposition to scrapping 1972 antiballistic missile treaty.

China to Return Downed U.S. Plane (May 29): American surveillance aircraft will be partially dismantled and shipped to the U.S. on Russian-designed cargo plane.

NATION

FBI Director Plans to Resign (May 1): Louis J. Freeh will leave post in June after eight years in which he expanded agency's world activity but faced criticism for recent high-profile missteps.

U.S. Spending Agreement Reached (May 2): White House and congressional negotiators settle on nearly 5% budget increase for next year.

Chairman of SEC Appointed (May 7): White House names Harvey L. Pitt, prominent corporate lawyer and critic of agency he will regulate.

Bush Chooses Pro-Business Advocates (May 9): Fills several environmental-related jobs with representatives of various industries that have faced off against federal government, especially during Clinton era.

McVeigh Files Withheld (May 10): FBI discovers several thousand pages of documents related to Oklahoma City bombing that agency never turned over to lawyers for Timothy McVeigh. **(May 11):** Citing FBI's failure to hand over all documents to McVeigh's lawyers, Attorney General John Ashcroft postpones McVeigh's execution until June 11.

Congress Approves Major Tax Cut (May 10): Final action on budget clears way for biggest reduction in 20 years. Senate votes 53–47, with five Democrats approving budget. Previous House vote was also on party lines. Tax reduction would total $1.35 trillion over 11 years.

U.S. to Help Fight AIDS (May 11): President Bush says nation will contribute $200 million to a global fund that is also battling malaria and tuberculosis.

Bush Outlines Energy Program (May 16): Plan calls for easing regulations on oil and gas exploration, conservation efforts, and $4 billion tax credit for highly fuel-efficient cars. President also proposes rethinking the 25-year ban on reprocessing of nuclear fuel.

Former FBI Agent Indicted on Spy Charges (May 16): Federal grand jury alleges Robert P. Hanssen aided Moscow for more than 15 years.

GOP Loses Control of Senate (May 24): Vermont senator James Jeffords bolts Republican Party to become an Independent. Democrats move to revamp agenda.

Congress Completes Tax-Cut Bill (May 27): Negotiators from both houses agree on biggest reduction in 20 years. Rebate checks due to everyone who filed an income tax return in 2000.

Bush Signs World War II Memorial Bill (May 28): Approves building for Washington Mall. Veterans cheer president at Memorial Day addresses.

BUSINESS/SCIENCE/SOCIETY

Birmingham Bomber Convicted (May 1): Alabama jury finds former klansman Thomas E. Blanton, Jr. guilty of murder in 1963 deaths of four black girls in bombing of Baptist church.

Cincinnati Chief Quits After Racial Unrest (May 2): City Manager John Shirey resigns amid criticism of his handling of rioting over shooting death of unarmed black man by police.

Transformation by Gays Called Possible (May 9): Columbia Univ. psychiatrist Robert Spitzer reports that some "motivated" homosexuals can become heterosexual.

Dozens Dead in Ghana Soccer Stampede (May 9): Toll reaches 120; more deaths expected from disaster at Accra stadium.

New Cancer Drug Approved (May 10): FDA sanctions Gleevec after swift review of clinical data. Promising results in treatment of myelogenous leukemia.

Fed Lowers Rates Fifth Time This Year (May 15): Half-point cut intended to revive weakened economy.

Fuel Economy of Vehicles Drops (May 17): U.S. reports average level for new cars and trucks drops to 24.5 miles per gallon, lowest since 1980.

Firestone Bars Sale of Tires to Ford (May 21): Company charges auto maker with raising safety issue to divert attention from Explorer model.

New Study Doubts Placebo Effect (May 23): Two Danish researchers report clinical research shows no support for common belief that, in general, about a third of patients will improve if they take a placebo that they are told is cause of improvement. Researchers cite uneven course of diseases as cause of improvement.

Disabled Golfer May Use Cart on Tour (May 29): In 7–2 decision, Supreme Court rules that Casey Martin, who has a degenerative disease, has legal right under Americans with Disabilities Act to ride during tournaments.

Four Guilty in Terrorist Bombings (May 29): Convicted by U.S. jury in New York for conspiring to destroy embassies in Kenya and Tanzania in 1998. Two defendants found guilty of murder and can face death penalty.

June 2001

WORLD

Blast Kills 17 in Tel Aviv (June 1): Dozens injured in powerful blast by suicide bomber outside crowded disco. Most deadly attack since Israeli-Palestinian violence began last fall.

Peru Elects New President (June 3): Alejandro Toledo, who ran for the office last year, defeats former president Alan García.

Former Argentine President Arrested (June 7): Carlos Saúl Menem detained by judge investigating conspiracy to smuggle arms to Croatia and Ecuador.

British Labor Party Wins Election (June 8): Prime Minister Tony Blair hands once-dominant Conservatives second major defeat. Win marks Labor's first reelection to full term in office.

Irish Voters Reject European Union Expansion (June 8): Oppose treaty designed to admit 12 new members, mostly former Communist countries.

Iran's President Reelected (June 9): Mohammad Khatami draws sweeping support for his drive toward greater democracy and social freedom.

Bush Visits Europe on First Overseas Trip (June 12): In Madrid, president promotes plan to build missile defense shield, terming 1972 arms treaty obsolete.

Mideast Foes Accept U.S. Cease-Fire Plan (June 13): Israel and Palestinians agree on plan after six days of mediation by CIA director George Tenet.

Putin Warns of Arms Buildup (June 18): Russian president says that if U.S. constructs own missile defense system, Russia would upgrade its strategic nuclear arsenal with multiple warheads.

Syria Evacuates Beirut Area (June 19): In six days withdraws 6,000 troops. Action ends decades of military presence loathed by Lebanese Christians.

Compensation Begins for Nazi-Era Slave Labor (June 19): Thousands receive payment from $4.5 billion German fund after years of legal squabbles and delays.

U.S. Indicts 14 in 1996 Saudi Blast (June 21): Charges 13 Saudis and one Lebanese man with truck bombing that killed 19 American airmen and wounded nearly 400 at Khobar Towers apartments.

Factions Clash in Northern Ireland (June 21): Roman Catholics and Protestants fight in Belfast for second consecutive night. **(June 22):** Peace talks falter and power-sharing government on brink of collapse.

Macedonians Attack Albanian Rebels (June 22): Launch heavy offensive just north of Skopje. Action breaks fragile cease-fire.

Yugoslav Cabinet Backs Hague Trial for Milosevic (June 23): Commits to send former president to United Nations tribunal to face charges of war crimes.

Former Peru Spy Chief Captured (June 24): Vladimiro Montesinos seized in Venezuela. Longtime CIA agent accused of gun running, money laundering, and collaborating with drug traffickers.

Bush and Sharon Disagree on Mideast (June 26): In White House meeting, leaders of U.S. and Israel divided on steps to end violence.

UN Maps Battle Against AIDS (June 27): General Assembly ends three-day special session by outlining strategy. Views epidemic as political, human rights, and economic threat. Calls on nations and private industry to provide billions to pay for fight against pandemic.

Milosevic Delivered to UN (June 29): Former Yugoslav president imprisoned at Hague to await war-crimes trial on charges involving blame for starting four Balkan wars and isolating and ravaging his country.

UN Head Begins Second Term (June 29): Kofi Annan reelected secretary-general by 189 member countries.

NATION

Democrats Take Control of Senate (June 5): First time in history that balance of power shifts because of a senator's switch in party affiliation.

Bush Signs New Tax Law (June 7): President approves legislation in White House ceremony. Politicians quickly begin to discuss possible revisions.

Senate Votes for Annual School Testing (June 14): Bill, passed overwhelmingly, calls for annual testing and will penalize schools that do not improve.

Navy Resumes Vieques Bombing (June 18): Jet fighters return to disputed Puerto Rico island after arrest of several protesters against military maneuvers.

Affirmative Action Foe Nominated (June 26): Administration picks Gerald A. Reynolds, a lawyer, to head education department's Office of Civil Rights.

Senate Passes Patients' Rights Bill (June 29): Approves, 59–36, measure to establish wide range of standards for millions with health insurance. Nine Republicans join 50 Democrats to defy veto threat.

Vice President Gets Pacemaker (June 30): Doctors place pacemaker and defibrillator to remedy Cheney's abnormal heart rate. Patient returns home within hours. It is Cheney's third major heart procedure since his election.

BUSINESS/SCIENCE/SOCIETY

Global Warming Reported on Rise (June 6): Leading scientists reaffirm mainstream view that human activity is largely responsible.

Smoker Wins Record Award (June 6): Los Angeles jury levies more than $3 billion damages against Philip Morris tobacco company in suit brought by man who said he had smoked Marlboro cigarettes 40 years.

Study Finds Heart Rejuvenates Cells (June 8): Experts report that some muscle regrowth in humans can follow a heart attack. Findings rebut old dogma.

Tropical Storm Batters Two States (June 10): Heavy toll of deaths and damage recorded in Texas and Louisiana.

Oklahoma City Bomber Dies (June 11): Timothy J. McVeigh executed in Indiana federal prison for deaths of 168 persons on April 19, 1995. He dies by lethal injection without word of regret.

Bridge Collapse Kills 59 in India (June 22): Passenger train plunges into Kadalundi River in Kerala state after 120-year-old span gives way.

Fed Cuts Interest Rate Sixth Time in Year (June 27): Reserve decrees quarter point reduction.

Microsoft Breakup Overruled (June 28): U.S. Appeals Court voids lower court's order, but finds that corporation had abused monopoly power in software business. District judge, Thomas Penfield Jackson, is rebuked.

July 2001

WORLD

David Trimble Resigns (July 1): First minister of the Northern Ireland Assembly steps down as IRA continues to balk at disarmament.

Russians Raid Two Chechen Villages (July 3 et seq.): Russian troops storm area after Chechen mine blasts kill four Russian soldiers.

Pinochet Found Too Ill for Trial (July 9): Former Chilean dictator, 85, charged with covering up execution of political opponents after seizing power in 1973.

Russian General Rebukes Troops (July 11): Commander in Chechnya says forces committed "widespread crimes" during two-day spree of terror against civilians.

Russia and China Sign Friendship Treaty (July 16): Twenty-year agreement binds nations in their opposition to U.S.-proposed missile shield.

India and Pakistan End Talks (July 17): Leaders fail in two-day summit to make progress on intractable conflict over Kashmir, which both nations claim, or on reducing risks of nuclear clash.

Bush and Putin Agree on Arms Cuts (July 22): At Genoa meeting leaders agree to link talks on U.S. plans for antimissile system with cuts in both nuclear stockpiles.

178 Nations Reach Accord on Climate (July 23): World's leaders, without U.S., reach compromise on treaty that, for first time, would require industrialized nations to cut emissions of gases linked to global warming. Accord saves, though dilutes, 1997 Kyoto Protocol.

Seven Killed in Macedonia Fighting (July 23): Dozens of villagers wounded as government forces battle Albanian rebels in western town of Tetovo.

Chinese Free U.S.-Based Scholar (July 26): Release Gao Zhan, 39, who had been sentenced to ten years in prison on espionage charges.

Israelis Kill Eight Palestinians (July 31): Army helicopters fire missiles into West Bank offices of militant Islamic group Hamas. Two small boys among victims.

NATION

Bush Modifies Oil-Drilling Plan (July 2): Scales back proposal to let companies seek oil and natural gas in Gulf of Mexico. President retreats on issue his brother, Florida governor Jeb Bush, has opposed.

Bush Nominates FBI Director (July 5): President selects Robert S. Mueller III, seasoned criminal prosecutor, to head troubled agency.

Ex-FBI Agent Pleads Guilty to Espionage (July 6): Robert P. Hanssen admits passing highly sensitive U.S. secrets to Russians. He avoids death penalty.

Campaign Bill Collapses in House (July 12): Finance reform measure dropped after bitter battle over procedure. Speaker J. Dennis Hastert says he has no plans to reintroduce measure any time soon. Each party blames the other for leaving bill's future in doubt.

Equipment Missing Within FBI (July 17): Check finds loss or theft of 449 firearms and 184 laptop computers, including one containing classified data.

Senate Votes to Extend Sanctions (July 25): Approves, 96–2, retention of penalties against Iran and Libya for an additional five years. Vote rejects Bush administration push to limit duration of sanctions to allow for diplomatic flexibility.

Vieques Votes to End Bombing (July 29): In nonbinding referendum, residents of small Puerto Rican island demand by more than two to one that U.S. Navy end practice maneuvers.

House Votes to Ban Human Cloning (July 31): Rejects cloning, 265–162, in bipartisan vote.

BUSINESS/SCIENCE/SOCIETY

Russian Airliner Crashes in Siberia (July 3): Death toll of 143 passengers and crew members reported.

Artificial Heart Implanted in Human (July 3): Surgeons in Louisville, Ky., report success of first operation for self-contained organ. **(July 4):** Patient, man in 50s, reported to be recovering.

Embryos Created to Harvest Cells (July 10): Scientists at Virginia clinic mix donated eggs and sperm to create embryonic stem cells. Move breaks medical taboo and stirs national debate.

Four Firefighters Killed in Northwest (July 11): Fifth seriously injured. Group trapped when flames explode, engulfing 2,500 acres in Washington's North Cascades.

Microsoft Makes Concession (July 12): Announces it will give personal computer makers more flexibility in which software and services they package on their machines.

Prescription Drug Aid Proposed (July 12): Five major health-care companies agree to work with president to help Medicare beneficiaries receive discounts.

World's Third Set of Septuplets Born (July 13): Five boys and two girls delivered at Georgetown University Hospital. Babies weigh 2 to 2.4 pounds. Mother reported to be in good condition.

Beijing Awarded Olympics (July 13): Will host 2008 Summer Games. Despite criticism of China's human rights practices and its environmental record, the International Olympic Committee gave Beijing the simple majority it needed in the second round of voting.

Boy Sentenced for Killing Teacher (July 27): Nathaniel Brazill, 14, denied chance of parole by Florida court.

August 2001

WORLD

Bosnian Serb Convicted by Hague Court (Aug. 2): International war-crimes tribunal finds former general Radislav Krstic guilty of genocide for role in execution of some 7,000 unarmed Muslim men and boys in July 1995. He's the first European convicted of genocide.

Russians Free Fulbright Scholar (Aug. 3): District court releases John E. Tobin, 24, American imprisoned on marijuana charges. Russians had earlier suspected him of training to become a U.S. spy.

IRA Arms Proposal Rejected (Aug. 7): North Ireland Protestant leader David Trimble brands as inadequate disarmament plan backed by British and Irish governments.

President of Iran Inaugurated (Aug. 8): Mohammad Khatami promises to enact reforms in his second term.

Suicide Bomber Strikes Jerusalem (Aug. 10): Kills 14 and wounds 130 in crowded Israeli restaurant located in heart of city.

U.S. and British Planes Bomb Iraq (Aug. 10): Hits three air defense sites in retaliation for Saddam Hussein's increasing aggression toward allied pilots.

Britain Suspends Northern Ireland Government (Aug. 10): In temporary move, London hopes to buy time for continued effort to end 30 years of conflict.

China Rejects U.S. Compensation Offer (Aug. 12): Says payment to help cover expenses after U.S. spy plane and Chinese jet collided is inadequate.

Fighting Ends in Macedonia (Aug. 13): Macedonian government sign peace agreement with Albanian rebels. British-led NATO force enters country to disarm guerrillas.

Japanese Reject History Textbook (Aug. 15): Most school districts refuse to adopt text accused of glossing over nation's wartime atrocities.

Coal Mine Blast Kills 36 in Ukraine (Aug. 19): Underground explosion injures 44. Most serious accident of year in Ukraine's treacherous coal mines.

China Reports AIDS Epidemic (Aug. 23): In policy shift, senior official admits that lax government efforts to control disease led to epidemic.

Israeli Troops Raid Palestinian Town (Aug. 28): Tanks and soldiers seize parts of Beit Jala on West Bank in first foray into Palestinian-ruled zone. **(Aug. 30):** Israeli forces begin withdrawal after two days, longest stay in a Palestinian-ruled area.

Milosevic to Face Added Charges (Aug. 30): UN tribunal to try former Yugoslav president on expanded accusations, including genocide in Bosnia massacres and war crimes in Croatia.

NATION

House Passes Patients' Rights Bill (Aug. 2): Votes, 218–213, for compromise with president. Democrats say bill favors health maintenance organizations.

Product Safety Nomination Blocked (Aug. 2): Senate committee rejects Mary Sheila Gall, president's choice to head Consumer Product Safety Commission. Vote, 12–11, on party lines.

Senate Approves Farm Subsidy Bill (Aug. 3): Democrats yield to veto threat and accept aid measure containing $2 billion less than they sought.

Bush Allows Stem Cell Research (Aug. 9): In address to nation, president approves use of federal funds for studies on human embryos. But he says research with such funds must be limited to cells that have already been extracted. He declares government will not finance destruction of new embryos.

Budget Surplus Dwindling (Aug. 22): Projections by Bush administration show sharp decline outside of Social Security. Tax cut and economic lag blamed.

Bush Confirms Missile Treaty Withdrawal (Aug. 23): Declares U.S. will abandon 1972 antiballistic missile pact "at a time convenient to America."

Bush Stands Firm on Spending Goals (Aug. 29): Pledges not to let economic slowdown or diminishing surplus prevent him from increasing military budget, developing missile shield, or increasing education spending.

Bush Agrees to Protect Endangered Species (Aug. 29): In compromise with environmentalists, administration pledges action to protect 29 plant and animal groups.

B U S I N E S S / S C I E N C E / S O C I E T Y

Clinton Agrees to Sell Memoirs (Aug. 7): Accepts advance of more than $10 million from Alfred A. Knopf, Inc. Amount believed to be record for nonfiction book.

Anticholesterol Drug Withdrawal (Aug. 8): Bayer A. G., German manufacturer, removes Baycol from U.S. market, reporting 31 deaths among users.

Patent Complicates Stem Cell Policy (Aug. 16): Patent of the human embryonic stem cell, held by a University of Wisconsin foundation, likely to complicate plan for U.S. financing of limited research.

Ford Cuts 5,000 Salaried Jobs (Aug. 17): Also discloses plans to cut back auto production.

Balloonist Ends World Flight (Aug. 17): Steve Fossett, American millionaire, calls off fifth attempt to be first to complete around the world balloon trip.

Five in Family Slain on West Coast (Aug. 20): Ukrainian immigrant, Nikolay Soltys, 27, stabs wife to death, then drives to home and kills four other relatives.

Federal Reserve Cuts Key Rate (Aug. 21): Reduces basic interest level by another quarter of percentage point.

Condit Defends Record (Aug. 23): In national TV interview, California representative repeats statements that he has no knowledge about the disappearance of former federal intern Chandra Levy. Also admits he had a "very close relationship" with her.

September 2001

W O R L D

U.S. Accepts China's Missile Program (Sept. 1): Plans to drop objections to China's arms buildup in compromise to overcome objections to American missile-defense program.

Race Conference Reaches Accord (Sept. 3): U.S. and Israel quit Durban talks, protesting condemnation of Israel in draft declaration. **(Sept. 8):** Participating nations condemn slave trade and express concern over "plight of the Palestinians under foreign occupation." Final document does not single out Israel as racist state.

NATO Supports U.S. (Sept. 13): NATO secretary-general George Robertson says the organization will invoke a clause stating that an attack on one of its 19 member states is an attack on the whole alliance.

Pakistan Vows to Support U.S. (Sept. 13): Country's military ruler, Gen. Pervez Musharraf, promises full cooperation with the U.S. in its fight against terrorism.

China Clears Trade Obstacle (Sept. 14): Agreement with U.S. and Europe will allow China to enter World Trade Organization by early 2002, ending 15-year effort.

Arafat Orders Cease-Fire (Sept. 18): Palestinian leader orders security forces not to shoot even in self-defense. Israel responds by barring offensive action and moves troops out of Palestinian-controlled zones. Actions pave way for resumption of peace talks.

Europe Moves Against Terrorism (Sept. 19): Commission proposes drastic new enforcement measures in wake of terrorist attacks on U.S.

Former Communists Win Polish Election (Sept. 23): Democratic Left Alliance ousts Solidarity to gain decisive majority of seats in Warsaw's parliament.

Russia Offers Help to U.S. (Sept. 24): Promises broad support, including opening Russian airspace, to antiterrorist actions in Afghanistan.

Middle East Leaders Meet (Sept. 26): Yasir Arafat and Shimon Peres, Israeli foreign minister, agree to resume pursuit of peace. Gaza conference tarnished by nearby clash that injures three Israeli soldiers.

Canada Backs U.S. Antiterrorist Move (Sept. 26): Freezes assets of groups linked to violent actions.

UN Adopts Antiterror Campaign (Sept. 28): Security Council unanimously passes U.S. resolution requiring all 189 members to act against the financing, training, and movement of terrorist groups.

Swiss Examine Firearms Rules (Sept. 29): Killing of 14 lawmakers and government officials by man with army rifle spurs review of gun-possession policies.

N A T I O N

Congress and President Return to Work (Sept. 2): Back from vacations, leaders face potentially bruising battles over budget surplus, spending, and taxes.

Mexico President Visits White House (Sept. 5): Vicente Fox urges Bush to commit to quick agreement on status of millions of illegal Mexican immigrants.

Terrorists Attack U.S. (Sept. 11): Hijackers ram jetliners into twin towers of New York City's World Trade Center and the Pentagon. A fourth hijacked plane crashes 80 miles outside of Pittsburgh. Toll of dead and injured in thousands. U.S. moves to reassure financial markets and prevent global economic slowdown. **(Sept. 12 et seq.):** Rescuers comb mountains of rubble in grim and daunting search for survivors.

Chief Bombing Suspect Named (Sept. 13): Administration reports radical Islamic militant Osama bin Laden is prime suspect in terrorist attacks on U.S. Bush pledges to wipe out terrorist networks with military action.

President Visits Scene of Bombings (Sept. 14): Leads nation in day of mourning for victims of terrorist attacks. In Washington, Senate votes, 98–0, to give president "all necessary and appropriate force" to respond to terrorist attacks.

U.S. Warns Arab Countries (Sept. 14): Senior state department official gives representatives from 15 Arab countries ultimatum to either join international coalition against terrorism or face isolation in global conflict.

Looser Rules on CIA Urged (Sept. 15): Lawmakers see need for U.S. intelligence agency to be more aggressive in battling terrorism.

U.S. Promises to Aid Airlines (Sept. 18): Projects billions in financial help to ease impact of losses following terrorist attacks. Major carriers have already laid off 44,000 employees.

Curbs on Immigrants Expanded (Sept. 18): Administration extends powers of detention. New rules prompted by terrorist attacks on the U.S.

Bush Demands Taliban Hand Over bin Laden (Sept. 20): In address to Congress, president insists that Afghan leaders surrender bin Laden and close down terrorist training camps.

Senate Passes Airline Bailout (Sept. 21): Approves, 96–1, $15 billion package to aid struggling airlines. Also votes, 96–1, to establish federal fund to compensate victims of terrorist attacks.

Bush Orders Freeze of Terrorists' Assets (Sept. 24): Also gives treasury secretary power to impose sanctions on banks abroad that provide terrorists access to international financial system.

National Guard to Protect Airports (Sept. 27): Bush announces greater U.S. role in security.

Bush Approves Aid to Taliban Foes (Sept. 30): Moves to strengthen groups opposing Afghanistan leaders.

BUSINESS/SCIENCE/SOCIETY

Sharks Attack Eastern Beaches (Sept. 5): Virginia begins inquiry after two fatal attacks over Labor Day weekend. Florida considers curbs on divers feeding sharks.

U.S. Drops Case to Break Up Microsoft (Sept. 6): In reversal, government says it will also abandon part of its antitrust lawsuit. Will seek less drastic regulation of company.

U.S. Jobless Rate Rises Sharply (Sept. 7): Bureau of Labor Statistics reports unemployment rate jumped to 4.9% in August from 4.5% in July. Highest one-month rise since 1995.

Bigger Supply of Stem Cells Urged (Sept. 10): Experts conclude that more embryonic material is needed to advance research.

Stock Markets Plummet 14% (Sept. 21): Prices plunge in second-largest decline in history as investors seek safe havens following terrorist attacks on U.S.

October 2001

WORLD

Suicide Bombers Kill Dozens in Kashmir (Oct. 1): Car bomb kills at least 38 in Srinagar, increasing Indian-Pakistani tension. Pakistan-based Islamic militants claim responsibility.

Russian Airliner Crashes in Black Sea (Oct. 4): Casualties include 64 passengers and 12 crew members; stray Ukranian missile is suspected and later confirmed.

Attacks on Afghanistan Begin (Oct. 7): U.S. and British air forces attack Taliban military installations and terrorist training camps. Bombings continue on a daily basis. Food and medicine is dropped for civilians in areas not controlled by Taliban.

Hurricane Iris Socks Central America (Oct. 8): Storm kills approximately 18 people in Belize, mostly American tourists who drowned when their diving boat sank. Some 13,000 people are left homeless.

U.S. Forces in Uzbekistan (Oct. 13): Uzbekistan agrees to allow U.S. forces to be stationed there in fight against Taliban in neighboring Afghanistan.

Israeli Official Assassinated (Oct. 17): Right-wing cabinet member Rehavam Zeevi is shot in a hotel corridor. Popular Front for the Liberation of Palestine claims responsibility. **(Oct. 18):** Israeli forces begin to occupy Palestinian-controlled towns and villages in response to assassination of Zeevi.

U.S. Embassy Bombers Get Life Sentences (Oct. 18): Four members of Osama bin Laden's al-Qaeda network receive life without parole for their roles in the 1998 bombings of the U.S. embassies in Kenya and Tanzania.

President Bush Arrives in Shanghai (Oct. 18): Attends the Asia-Pacific Economic Cooperation Summit of 21 nations. Participants issue a statement condemning terrorist attacks on U.S. **(Oct. 21):** Bush and Russian president Vladimir Putin announce they could agree to amend the 1972 antiballistic missile treaty, thus allowing the U.S. to proceed with a missile defense shield.

IRA Begins to Disarm (Oct. 23): Irish Republican Army announces that it has begun to dismantle its weapons arsenal, marking a dramatic leap forward in fragile Northern Ireland peace process.

NATION

Anthrax Scare Rivets Nation (Oct. 5 et. seq.): Photo editor at Florida's American Media becomes first person to die from illness in U.S. since 1976. **(Oct. 9):** FBI joins investigation after second case of anthrax exposure confirmed at American Media. **(Oct. 15):** Letter sent to office of Senate Majority Leader Tom Daschle tests positive for anthrax. Contaminated mail has also been received by NBC News in New York and a Microsoft office in Reno, Nevada. **(Oct. 16):** A 7-month-old boy who had visited the offices of ABC News in New York is hospitalized with anthrax, while a second case of anthrax is confirmed in Florida. **(Oct. 18):** An employee of CBS News in New York and a New Jersey postal worker have been infected with anthrax, for a total of six people with the disease, while about 37 people in New York, Washington, New Jersey, and Florida have been exposed. **(Oct. 22):** Two postal workers in Washington, DC, die of anthrax.

Anti-Terror Chief Sworn In (Oct. 8): Former Pennsylvania governor Tom Ridge takes the helm of the recently created Office of Homeland Security. He's charged with coordinating 40 federal agencies to prevent future terrorist attacks.

BUSINESS/SCIENCE/SOCIETY

Federal Reserve Board Cuts Interest Rates (Oct. 2): Key federal rate drops one-half point to 2.5 percent; ninth cut of year brings rates to a 39-year low.

Russian Nuclear Submarine Raised (Oct 8): *Kursk* is brought to surface more than a year after it sank, killing its 118-man crew.

Polaroid Files for Bankruptcy (Oct. 12): Huge debts, declining market share cited.

Retail Sales Plunge (Oct. 12): Commerce Dept. announces sales fell 2.4% in September, the worst monthly drop in nearly a decade.

2001 Nobel Prize Winners

Peace: United Nations and Kofi Annan, secretary-general of the UN, were cited "for their work for a better organized and more peaceful world."

Literature: Sir V. S. Naipaul (UK) "for having united perceptive narrative and incorruptible scrutiny in works that compel us to see the presence of suppressed histories." Naipaul explores alienation and the hardships of postcolonial countries in his works of fiction, nonfiction, and the occasional blend of the two.

Physics: Wolfgang Ketterle (Germany), Eric A. Cornell, and Carl E. Wieman (both U.S.) "for the achievement of Bose-Einstein condensation in dilute gases of alkali atoms, and for early fundamental studies of the properties of the condensates." In discovering the Bose-Einstein condensate, a new state of matter, the laureates have explained "the secrets of the microworld of quantum physics."

Chemistry: One-half jointly to William S. Knowles (U.S.) and Ryoji Noyori (Japan) "for their work on chirally catalyzed hydrogenation reactions," and one-half to K. Barry Sharpless (U.S.) "for his work on chirally catalyzed oxidation reactions." They "have opened up a new field of research in which it is possible to synthesize molecules and material with new properties."

Medicine: Leland H. Hartwell (U.S.), R. Timothy Hunt, and Paul M. Nurse (both UK) for their discoveries of "key regulators of the cell cycle." Their discoveries concerning control of the cell cycle "may in the long term open new possibilities for cancer treatment."

Economics: George A. Akerlof, A. Michael Spence, and Joseph E. Stiglitz (all U.S.) for "their analyses of markets with asymmetric information." "The laureates' contributions form the core of modern information economics."

Terrorism 2001

September 11, 2001: Timeline of Terrorism

(all times are eastern daylight time)

An American Airlines Boeing 767 and a United Airlines Boeing 767, both en route from Boston to Los Angeles, were hijacked and flown only minutes apart into the north and south towers of the World Trade Center in New York City. Shortly afterward, an American Airlines Boeing 757, en route from Washington, DC, to Los Angeles, crashed into the Pentagon. A fourth hijacked plane, operated by United and headed from Newark to San Francisco, crashed in a field near Shanksville, Pa. Both World Trade Center towers collapsed, and a section of the Pentagon was destroyed. All 266 passengers and crew aboard the planes were killed; the total deaths were in the thousands. The names of the 19 hijackers, all Islamic radicals, were released a few days after the attacks.

8:45 A.M.—American Airlines Flight 11, Boston to Los Angeles, with 92 people aboard, crashes into the north tower of the World Trade Center in New York City.

9:03 A.M.—United Airlines Flight 175, Boston to Los Angeles, with 65 people aboard, flies into the south tower of the World Trade Center.

9:40 A.M.—American Flight 77, en route from Dulles Airport, Washington, DC, to Los Angeles, with 64 people aboard, crashes into the Pentagon.

9:48 A.M.—The U.S. Capitol and the West Wing of the White House are evacuated.

9:49 A.M.—The Federal Aviation Administration orders all aircraft grounded in the United States.

9:50 A.M.—South tower of the World Trade Center collapses.

9:58 A.M.—Emergency operator in Pennsylvania receives a call from a passenger on United Flight 93, Newark to San Francisco, with 45 people aboard, stating the plane was being hijacked.

10:00 A.M.—United Flight 93 crashes about 80 miles southeast of Pittsburgh.

10:29 A.M.—North tower of the World Trade Center collapses.

2:51 P.M.—U.S. military deploys missile destroyers and other equipment in New York and Washington.

5:20 P.M.—Another World Trade Center building collapses.

For photos of the bombings, *see* pp. 505–507.

Boston, MA
American Airlines Flight 11 and United Airlines Flight 175 depart Logan Airport

Newark, NJ
United Airlines Flight 93 departs Newark International

New York City, NY
8:45 A.M.
American Airlines Flight 11 crashes into the north tower of the World Trade Center

9:03 A.M.
United Airlines Flight 175 flies into south tower of World Trade Center

Somerset County, PA
10:00 A.M.
United Airlines Flight 93 crashes 80 miles southeast of Pittsburgh

Arlington, VA
9:40 A.M.
American Airlines Flight 77 crashes into the Pentagon

Washington, DC
American Airlines Flight 77 departs Dulles International

Map by Sean M. Dessureau, Information Please

Who Is Osama bin Laden?

Considered the world's foremost terrorist, Osama bin Laden is the leading suspect in the horrific Sept. 11, 2001, attacks that destroyed the World Trade Center, damaged part of the Pentagon, and resulted in a plane crash in Pennsylvania. Although he has denied involvement in the attack, he referred to it, through an aide, as "punishment from Allah."

Bin Laden has been implicated in a string of deadly attacks on the United States and its allies: the 1993 World Trade Center bombing; the 1998 bombings at the U.S. embassies in Kenya and Tanzania that killed more than 200; and the 2000 bombing of the USS *Cole* in Yemen. Bin Laden also claims responsibility for a 1993 gunfight that killed 18 U.S. troops in Somalia and the 1996 bombing of the Khobar military complex in Saudi Arabia that left 19 U.S. soldiers dead.

Born with a Silver Spoon

Bin Laden was born in Saudi Arabia in 1957 to a father of Yemeni origins and a Syrian mother. His father, Muhammad bin Laden, founded a construction company and with royal patronage became a billionaire. The company's connections won it such important commissions as rebuilding mosques in the holy cities of Mecca and Medina.

Muhammad bin Laden took numerous wives and fathered about 50 children. Osama was the 17th son, the only child of his mother, who was a later wife. In a society where status within a family is highly important, bin Laden would therefore have been of relatively low rank.

Bin Laden studied management and economics at King Abdul Aziz University in Jedda, Saudi Arabia, coming under the influence of religious teachers who introduced him to the wider world of Islamic politics.

USSR Invades Afghanistan

The 1979 Soviet invasion of Afghanistan galvanized bin Laden. He supported the Afghan resistance, which became a jihad, or holy war. Ironically, the U.S. was a major supporter of the Afghan resistance, or mujahideen, supplying them with arms and money, and working with Saudi Arabia and Pakistan to set up Islamic schools in Pakistan for Afghan refugees. These schools later evolved into virtual training centers for Islamic radicals.

By the mid-1980s, bin Laden had moved to Afghanistan, where he established an organization, Maktab al-Khidimat (MAK), to recruit Islamic soldiers from around the world who later formed the basis of an international network. The MAK maintained recruiting offices in Detroit and Brooklyn in the 1980s.

The Taliban, the current rulers of Afghanistan, arose from the religious schools set up during the mujahideen's war against the Soviet invasion. After the Soviet army withdrew in 1989, fighting erupted among mujahideen factions. In response to the chaos, the fundamentalist Taliban was formed and within two years it captured most of the country. The Taliban has given bin Laden sanctuary since 1996.

An International Network

After the Soviet withdrawal in 1989, bin Laden returned to Saudi Arabia and worked in his family's construction business. He founded an organization to help veterans of the Afghan war, many of whom went on to fight in Bosnia, Chechnya, Somalia, and the Philippines. Scholars have suggested these loosely connected bands of seasoned soldiers, ready to fight for Islamic causes, form the basis of bin Laden's current support.

In 1990, in response to the Iraqi invasion of Kuwait, the Saudi government allowed American troops to be stationed in Saudi Arabia. Bin Laden was incensed that nonbelievers (American soldiers) were stationed in the birthplace of Islam. He also charged the Saudi regime with deviating from true Islam.

Bin Laden was expelled from Saudi Arabia in 1991 because of his antigovernment activities. He eventually wound up in Sudan, where he worked with Egyptian radical groups in exile.

Anti-U.S. Attacks

In 1992 bin Laden claimed responsibility for attempting to bomb U.S. soldiers in Yemen and for attacking U.S. troops in Somalia the following year. In 1994 pressure from the U.S. and Saudi Arabia prompted Sudan to expel bin Laden, and he returned to Afghanistan.

In 1998 bin Laden called for all Americans and Jews, including children, to be killed. He has since been accused of increasing his terrorist activities, such as the 1998 bombings at the U.S. embassies in Kenya and Tanzania. The date, Aug. 7, was the anniversary of the deployment of U.S. troops to Saudi Arabia.

U.S. cruise missile attacks against targets in Sudan and Afghanistan in Aug. 1998 are not believed to have seriously hampered bin Laden's network. Bin Laden continues to call for the destruction of the U.S., Israel, and the Saudi monarchy, stating that with these obstacles removed, Islam's three holiest sites, Mecca, Medina, and Jerusalem, would then be liberated.

International Terrorist Network

Yet, even as he is reviled in the West, bin Laden is a hero in parts of the Islamic world, according to intelligence reports. His organization is called al-Qaeda, "the base," and has approximately 3,000 followers, which he funds with his estimated $250 million fortune. Experts have said that bin Laden could represent a new trend in terrorism—privatization. Until his emergence, most large-scale terrorist organizations are believed to have been connected to governments. With his money and disciplined followers, however, bin Laden is believed to have the ability to launch even more devastating terrorist attacks. He has not denied that he is seeking to buy nuclear or chemical weapons.

Al-Qaeda

After the terrorist attacks of Sept. 11, 2001, al-Qaeda (pronounced al-KYE-da) surpassed the IRA, Hamas, and Hezbollah as the world's most infamous terrorist organization. Al-Qaeda ("the base" in Arabic) is the network of extremists organized by Osama bin Laden.

Origins in the Mujahideen

Al-Qaeda had its origins in the uprising against the Soviet occupation of Afghanistan. Thousands of volunteers from around the Middle East came to Afghanistan as mujahideen, warriors fighting to defend fellow Muslims. In the mid-1980s, Osama bin Laden became the prime financier for an organization that recruited Muslims from mosques around the world. These "Afghan Arab" mujahideen, which numbered in the thousands, were crucial in defeating Soviet forces.

After the Soviets withdrew from Afghanistan, bin Laden returned to his native Saudi Arabia. He founded an organization to help veterans of the Afghan war, many of whom went on to fight elsewhere (including Bosnia) and now form the basis of al-Qaeda. Bin Laden also studied with radical Islamic thinkers and may have already been organizing al-Qaeda when Iraq invaded Kuwait in 1990. Bin Laden was outraged when the government allowed U.S. troops to be stationed in Saudi Arabia, the birthplace of Islam.

The Rise of al-Qaeda

Expelled from Saudi Arabia in 1991 for anti-government activities, bin Laden moved the headquarters for al-Qaeda to Khartoum, Sudan. The first actions of al-Qaeda against American interests were attacks on U.S. servicemen in Somalia. A string of terrorist actions suspected to have been orchestrated by al-Qaeda followed (*see* box), and in Aug. 1996 bin Laden issued a *fatwa* against the U.S.

Al-Qaeda also worked to forge alliances with other radical groups. In Feb. 1998, bin Laden announced a coalition of terrorist organizations—the "International Islamic Front for Jihad Against the Jews and Crusaders"—that included Egypt's al-Gama'a al-Islamiyya and Pakistan's Harakat ul-Ansar (*see* p. 47), among others. Al-Qaeda supports terrorist organizations from such diverse regions as the Philippines, Algeria, Eritrea, Chechnya, Tajikistan, Yemen, and Kashmir.

In 1994 Sudan, under pressure from Saudi Arabia and the U.S., expelled bin Laden, who moved his base of operations to Afghanistan. Since 1996 bin Laden has been a "guest" of the Taliban.

Leadership and Structure

Although al-Qaeda and Osama bin Laden have become virtually synonymous, bin Laden does not run the organization single-handedly. Dr. Ayman al-Zawahiri is al-Qaeda's theological leader and bin Laden's probable successor. Al-Zawahiri, an Egyptian surgeon from an upper-class family, served

Suspected al-Qaeda Acts

1993—Killing of U.S. soldiers in Somalia.
1993—Bombing of World Trade Center; 6 killed.
1994—Investigation of the WTC bombing reveals that it was only a small part of a massive attack plan that included hijacking a plane and crashing it into CIA headquarters.
1995–1996—Bombing of U.S. barracks in Saudi Arabia; 22 soldiers killed.
1998—Bombing of U.S. embassies in East Africa; 224 killed, including 12 Americans.
1999—Jordanian police arrested members of a cell planning attacks against Western tourists.
1999—Plot to bomb millennium celebrations in Seattle foiled when customs agents arrest an Algerian smuggling explosives into the U.S. Other Algerians subsequently arrested were "Afghan alumni."
2000—Bombing of the USS *Cole* in port in Yemen; 17 U.S. sailors killed.
2001—Destruction of WTC, Pentagon attack.

three years in prison on charges connected to the assassination of Anwar Sadat, during which time he was tortured. After his release he went to Afghanistan, where he met bin Laden and became his personal physician and adviser. Al-Zawahiri is suspected of helping organize the 1997 massacre of 58 foreign tourists in the Egyptian town of Luxor and was indicted in connection with the bombing of U.S. embassies in Tanzania and Kenya.

Muhammed Atef is al-Qaeda's military commander. Atef joined al-Zawahiri in Afghanistan in the 1980s. He is suspected of having planned the Sept. 11 attack as well as the 1998 embassy bombings. Other key members of al-Qaeda include Mustafa Hamza, Rifie Ahmed Taha, and Mohammed Islambouli, the brother of Khaled Islambouli, Sadat's assassin.

Sheikh Omar Abdel Rahman, who is serving a life sentence in a Minnesota prison in connection with the 1993 World Trade Center bombing, is revered as a spiritual leader. Both bin Laden and al-Zawahiri have vowed revenge against the U.S. if Rahman, a diabetic, dies in prison.

The al-Qaeda leadership oversees and supports a loosely tied network of local cells. Each cell operates independently with its members not knowing the identity of other cells. Therefore, if members of one group are arrested they will not be able to betray other cells. In addition, it is difficult to trace the local cells back to al-Qaeda's leadership.

Ideology and Goals

The principal aims of al-Qaeda are to drive Americans and American influence out of all Muslim nations, especially Saudi Arabia, destroy Israel, and topple pro-Western dictatorships around the Middle East. Furthermore, it is bin Laden's goal to unite all Muslims and establish, by force, an Islamic nation adhering to the rule of the first caliphs.

State-Sponsored Terrorism

The U.S. State Department has labeled the following countries state sponsors of international terrorism: Cuba, Iran, Iraq, Libya, North Korea, Sudan, and Syria.

International Terrorist Organizations

Source: U.S. Department of State

The secretary of state has formally designated 28 groups as terrorist organizations (Foreign Terrorist Organizations [FTOs]). This is a partial list of those groups. For a detailed overview of al-Qaeda, the organization believed to be responsible for the Sept. 11, 2001, bombings, *see* p. 46.

Abu Nidal Organization (ANO) Formerly part of the Palestinian Liberation Organization. Has launched attacks in 20 countries, killing or injuring almost 900 persons. Led by Sabri al-Banna, AKA Abu Nidal. **Activities:** Attacks in Rome and Vienna airports (1995); Pan Am Flight 73 hijacking (1986).

Abu Sayyaf Group (ASG) The smallest and most radical of the Islamic separatist groups operating in the southern Philippines. Some ASG members have developed ties to the mujahideen while fighting in Afghanistan. **Activities:** Bombings, assassinations, kidnappings, and extortion to promote an independent Islamic state in western Mindanao and the Sulu Archipelago.

Al-Gama'a al-Islamiyya (Islamic Group, IG) Egypt's largest militant group. Issued a cease-fire in March 1999, but its spiritual leader, Sheik Umar Abd al-Rahman, denounced it in June 2000. IG's primary goal is to replace Egyptian government with an Islamic state. **Activities:** Armed attacks against Egyptian government officials, Coptic Christians, and Egyptian opponents of Islamic extremism. Launched the 1997 attack at Luxor that killed 58 foreign tourists. Attempted to assassinate Egyptian president Hosni Mubarak in 1995.

Armed Islamic Group (GIA)/Salafi Group for Call and Combat (GSPC) An Islamic extremist group that aims to replace the secular Algerian regime with an Islamic state. The Salafi Group for Call and Combat (GSPC) splinter faction appears to have eclipsed the GIA and is considered to be the most effective armed group inside Algeria. **Activities:** Between 1992 and 1998 the GIA conducted a campaign of civilian massacres.

Aum Supreme Truth (Aum) Religious group that aims to take over Japan and the rest of the world. Based in Japan but has operated in Europe, the U.S., and elsewhere in Asia. Established in 1987 by Shoko Asahara. **Activities:** Sarin nerve gas attack that killed 12 persons and injured more than 5,000 on a Tokyo subway in March 1995.

Basque Fatherland and Liberty (ETA) Spanish separatist group created in 1959 with the aim of establishing an independent Basque homeland. **Activities:** Bombings and assassinations of Spanish government officials. Appears to have ties to the Irish Republican Army.

Hamas Formed in late 1987 to establish an Islamic Palestinian state in place of Israel. Some elements work through mosques and social service institutions. Militant elements advocate and use violence. **Activities:** Many attacks, including suicide bombings, against Israeli civilian and military targets, suspected Palestinian collaborators, and Fatah rivals.

Harakat ul-Mujahidin (HUM) Islamic militant group based in Pakistan that operates primarily in Kashmir and trains in eastern Afghanistan. Former leader Fazlur Rehman Khalil has been linked to Osama bin Laden and in 1998 called for attacks on the U.S. and western interests. Farooq Kashmiri is the current leader. **Activities:** Attacks against Indian troops, western tourists, and civilian targets in Kashmir. Linked to the Kashmiri militant group al-Faran. Tied to hijacking of an Indian airliner in Dec. 2000.

Hezbollah Seeks the creation of Iranian-style Islamic republic in Lebanon and removal of all non-Islamic influences from the area. Strongly anti-West and anti-Israel. **Activities:** Anti-U.S. terrorist attacks, including the suicide truck bombing of the U.S. Marine barracks and embassy in Beirut in 1983 and the U.S. embassy annex in Beirut in 1984. Attack on Israeli embassy in Argentina in 1992.

Irish Republican Army (IRA) Radical terrorist group formed in 1969 as clandestine armed wing of Sinn Fein. Formally stopped its campaign to abolish Northern Ireland and its British links in July 1997. **Activities:** Bombings, assassinations, kidnappings, and extortion of British targets.

Kurdistan Workers' Party (PKK) Established in 1974 as a Marxist-Leninist insurgent group primarily composed of Turkish Kurds. Seeks an independent Kurdish state in southeast Turkey. **Activities:** Attacks on Turkish diplomatic and commercial facilities in dozens of West European cities in 1993 and 1995. Attacks on tourists and tourist sites.

The Liberation Tigers of Tamil Eelam (LTTE) The most powerful Tamil group in Sri Lanka. Seeks to create an independent Tamil state. Began its armed conflict with the Sri Lankan government in 1983. **Activities:** Political assassinations of Sri Lankan president Ranasinghe Remadasa in 1993 and Indian prime minister Rajiv Gandhi in 1991. Massive truck bombings.

The Palestine Islamic Jihad (PIJ) Loosely affiliated factions committed to the creation of an Islamic Palestinian state and the destruction of Israel through holy war. **Activities:** Suicide bombing attacks against Israeli targets in the West Bank, Gaza Strip, and Israel.

Popular Front for the Liberation of Palestine (PFLP) Marxist-Leninist group founded in 1967 by PLO member George Habash. Joined the Alliance of Palestinian Forces (APF) to oppose 1993's Declaration of Principles and has suspended participation in the PLO. **Activities:** International terrorist attacks in the 1970s and attacks against Israeli and moderate Arab targets.

Revolutionary Armed Forces of Colombia (FARC) Best-trained and best-equipped guerrilla organization in Colombia. Established in 1966 as military wing of Colombian Communist Party, seeks to overthrow the government. Anti-U.S. since its inception. **Activities:** Armed attacks against Colombian political and military targets. Traffics in drugs.

Sendero Luminoso (Shining Path, or SL) Formed by Maoist professor Abimael Guzman in the late 1960s. Seeks to replace Peruvian institutions with a communist peasant revolutionary regime. **Activities:** One the most ruthless terrorist groups in the West, SL has killed about 30,000 people since 1980.

The One Hundred Seventh Congress
Composition of the 106th and 107th Congresses

107th Congress	Rep.	Dem.	Ind.	Vacant	Male	Female	106th Congress	Rep.	Dem.	Ind.	Male	Female
Senate	49	50	1	—	87	13	Senate	54	46	0	91	9
House	219	210	2	4	369	62	House	223	210	2	377	58

NOTE: As of Sept. 2001.

The Senate

Dates in left column indicate term in office; birth dates are given in parentheses after party affiliation. All terms are for six years and expire in January. Senators listed in italics were elected or reelected in 2000.

Alabama
1987–2005 Richard Shelby (R) (1934)
1997–2003 Jeff Sessions (R) (1946)
Alaska
1969–2003 Ted Stevens (R) (1923)
1981–2005 Frank H. Murkowski (R) (1933)
Arizona
1987–2005 John McCain (R) (1936)
1995–2007 Jon Kyl (R) (1942)
Arkansas
1997–2003 Tim Hutchinson (R) (1949)
1999–2005 Blanche Lincoln (D) (1960)
California
1993–2007 Dianne Feinstein (D) (1933)
1993–2005 Barbara Boxer (D) (1940)
Colorado
1993–2005 Ben Nighthorse Campbell (R) (1933)
1997–2003 Wayne Allard (R) (1943)
Connecticut
1981–2005 Christopher J. Dodd (D) (1944)
1989–2007 Joseph I. Lieberman (D) (1942)
Delaware
1973–2003 Joseph R. Biden, Jr. (D) (1942)
2001–2007 Thomas R. Carper (D) (1947)
Florida
1987–2005 Bob Graham (D) (1936)
2001–2007 Bill Nelson (D) (1942)
Georgia
1997–2003 Max Cleland (D) (1942)
2000–2005[1] Zell Miller (D) (1932)
Hawaii
1963–2005 Daniel K. Inouye (D) (1924)
1990–2007 Daniel K. Akaka (D) (1924)
Idaho
1991–2003 Larry E. Craig (R) (1945)
1999–2005 Mike Crapo (R) (1951)
Illinois
1997–2003 Richard J. Durbin (D) (1944)
1999–2005 Peter G. Fitzgerald (R) (1960)
Indiana
1977–2007 Richard G. Lugar (R) (1932)
1999–2005 Evan Bayh (D) (1955)
Iowa
1981–2005 Chuck Grassley (R) (1933)
1985–2003 Tom Harkin (D) (1939)
Kansas
1997–2005 Sam Brownback (R) (1956)
1997–2003 Pat Roberts (R) (1936)
Kentucky
1985–2003 Mitch McConnell (R) (1942)
1999–2005 Jim Bunning (R) (1931)
Louisiana
1987–2005 John B. Breaux (D) (1944)
1997–2003 Mary L. Landrieu (D) (1955)
Maine
1995–2007 Olympia J. Snowe (R) (1947)
1997–2003 Susan M. Collins (R) (1952)

Maryland
1977–2007 Paul S. Sarbanes (D) (1933)
1987–2005 Barbara A. Mikulski (D) (1936)
Massachusetts
1963–2007 Edward M. Kennedy (D) (1932)
1985–2003 John F. Kerry (D) (1943)
Michigan
1979–2003 Carl Levin (D) (1934)
2001–2007 Debbie A. Stabenow (D) (1950)
Minnesota
1991–2003 Paul Wellstone (D) (1944)
2001–2007 Mark Dayton (D) (1947)
Mississippi
1979–2003 Thad Cochran (R) (1937)
1989–2007 Trent Lott (R) (1941)
Missouri
1987–2005 Christopher S. "Kit" Bond (R) (1939)
2001–2007 Jean Carnahan (D) (1933)
Montana
1978–2003 Max Baucus (D) (1941)
1989–2007 Conrad Burns (R) (1935)
Nebraska
1997–2003 Charles Hagel (R) (1946)
2001–2007 Ben Nelson (D) (1941)
Nevada
1987–2005 Harry Reid (D) (1939)
2001–2007 John Ensign (R) (1958)
New Hampshire
1991–2003 Bob Smith (R) (1941)
1993–2005 Judd Gregg (R) (1947)
New Jersey
1997–2003 Robert Torricelli (D) (1951)
2001–2007 Jon Corzine (D) (1947)
New Mexico
1973–2003 Pete V. Domenici (R) (1932)
1983–2007 Jeff Bingaman (D) (1943)
New York
1999–2005 Charles E. Schumer (D) (1950)
2001–2007 Hillary Rodham Clinton (D) (1947)
North Carolina
1973–2003 Jesse Helms (R) (1921)
1999–2005 John Edwards (D) (1953)
North Dakota
1987–2007 Kent Conrad (D) (1948)
1993–2005 Byron L. Dorgan (D) (1942)
Ohio
1995–2007 Mike DeWine (R) (1947)
1999–2005 George Voinovich (R) (1936)
Oklahoma
1989–2005 Don Nickles (R) (1948)
1994–2003 James M. Inhofe (R) (1934)
Oregon
1996–2005 Ron Wyden (D) (1949)
1997–2003 Gordon Smith (R) (1952)
Pennsylvania
1981–2005 Arlen Specter (R) (1930)
1995–2007 Rick Santorum (R) (1958)

Rhode Island
1997–2003 Jack Reed (D) (1949)
1999–2007 Lincoln Chafee (R) (1953)
South Carolina
1957–2003 Strom Thurmond (R) (1902)
1966–2005 Ernest Hollings (D) (1922)
South Dakota
1987–2005 Thomas A. Daschle (D) (1947)
1997–2003 Tim Johnson (D) (1946)
Tennessee
1995–2003 Fred Thompson (R) (1942)
1995–2007 William Frist (R) (1952)
Texas
1985–2003 Phil Gramm (R) (1942)
1995–2007 Kay Bailey Hutchison (R) (1943)
Utah
1977–2007 Orrin G. Hatch (R) (1934)
1993–2005 Robert F. Bennett (R) (1933)

Vermont
1975–2005 Patrick Leahy (D) (1940)
1989–2007 James M. Jeffords (I) (1934)
Virginia
1979–2003 John Warner (R) (1927)
2001–2007 George Allen (R) (1952)
Washington
1993–2005 Patty Murray (D) (1950)
2001–2007 Maria Cantwell (D) (1958)
West Virginia
1959–2007 Robert C. Byrd (D) (1917)
1985–2003 John D. "Jay" Rockefeller IV (D) (1937)
Wisconsin
1989–2007 Herbert Kohl (D) (1935)
1993–2005 Russ Feingold (D) (1953)
Wyoming
1995–2007 Craig Thomas (R) (1933)
1997–2003 Michael B. Enzi (R) (1944)

1. Zell Miller was appointed and then elected to serve out the remaining term of Paul Coverdell, who died in July 2000.

The House of Representatives

In the following lists, the numeral indicates the congressional district represented; AL is for representatives at large. All terms run from Jan. 2001 to Jan. 2003. Vacancies are as of Sept. 2001.

Alabama
1. Sonny Callahan (R)
2. Terry Everett (R)
3. Bob Riley (R)
4. Robert B. Aderholt (R)
5. Robert E. "Bud" Cramer, Jr. (D)
6. Spencer Bachus (R)
7. Earl F. Hilliard (D)

Alaska
AL Don Young (R)

Arizona
1. Jeff Flake (R)
2. Ed Pastor (D)
3. Bob Stump (R)
4. John B. Shadegg (R)
5. Jim Kolbe (R)
6. J. D. Hayworth (R)

Arkansas
1. Marion Berry (D)
2. Vic Snyder (D)
3. Vacant
4. Mike Ross (D)

California
1. Mike Thompson (D)
2. Wally Herger (R)
3. Doug Ose (R)
4. John T. Doolittle (R)
5. Robert T. Matsui (D)
6. Lynn C. Woolsey (D)
7. George Miller (D)
8. Nancy Pelosi (D)
9. Barbara Lee (D)
10. Ellen O. Tauscher (D)
11. Richard W. Pombo (R)
12. Tom Lantos (D)
13. Fortney Pete Stark (D)
14. Anna G. Eshoo (D)
15. Mike Honda (D)
16. Zoe Lofgren (D)
17. Sam Farr (D)
18. Gary A. Condit (D)
19. George P. Radanovich (R)
20. Calvin M. Dooley (D)
21. William M. Thomas (R)
22. Lois Capps (D)
23. Elton Gallegly (R)
24. Brad Sherman (D)
25. Howard P. "Buck" McKeon (R)
26. Howard L. Berman (D)
27. Adam Schiff (D)
28. David Dreier (R)
29. Henry A. Waxman (D)
30. Xavier Becerra (D)
31. Hilda L. Solis (D)
32. Diane E. Watson (D)
33. Lucille Roybal-Allard (D)
34. Grace F. Napolitano (D)
35. Maxine Waters (D)
36. Jane Harman (D)
37. Juanita Millender-McDonald (D)
38. Steve Horn (R)
39. Edward R. Royce (R)
40. Jerry Lewis (R)
41. Gary G. Miller (R)
42. Joe Baca (D)
43. Ken Calvert (R)
44. Mary Bono (R)
45. Dana Rohrabacher (R)
46. Loretta Sanchez (D)
47. Christopher Cox (R)
48. Darrell Issa (R)
49. Susan A. Davis (D)
50. Bob Filner (D)
51. Randy "Duke" Cunningham (R)
52. Duncan Hunter (R)

Colorado
1. Diana DeGette (D)
2. Mark Udall (D)
3. Scott McInnis (R)
4. Bob Schaffer (R)
5. Joel Hefley (R)
6. Thomas G. Tancredo (R)

Connecticut
1. John B. Larson (D)
2. Rob Simmons (R)
3. Rosa L. DeLauro (D)
4. Christopher Shays (R)
5. James H. Maloney (D)
6. Nancy L. Johnson (R)

Delaware
AL Michael N. Castle (R)

Florida
1. Vacant
2. Allen Boyd (D)
3. Corrine Brown (D)
4. Ander Crenshaw (R)
5. Karen L. Thurman (D)
6. Cliff Stearns (R)
7. John L. Mica (R)
8. Richard "Ric" Keller (R)
9. Michael Bilirakis (R)
10. C. W. Bill Young (R)
11. Jim Davis (D)
12. Adam Putnam (R)
13. Dan Miller (R)
14. Porter J. Goss (R)
15. Dave Weldon (R)
16. Mark Foley (R)
17. Carrie P. Meek (D)
18. Ileana Ros-Lehtinen (R)
19. Robert Wexler (D)
20. Peter Deutsch (D)
21. Lincoln Diaz-Balart (R)
22. E. Clay Shaw, Jr. (R)
23. Alcee L. Hastings (D)

Georgia
1. Jack Kingston (R)
2. Sanford D. Bishop, Jr. (D)
3. Mac Collins (R)
4. Cynthia A. McKinney (D)
5. John Lewis (D)
6. Johnny Isakson (R)
7. Bob Barr (R)
8. Saxby Chambliss (R)
9. Nathan Deal (R)
10. Charlie Norwood (R)
11. John Linder (R)

Hawaii
1. Neil Abercrombie (D)
2. Patsy T. Mink (D)

Idaho
1. C. L. "Butch" Otter (R)
2. Michael K. Simpson (R)

Illinois
1. Bobby L. Rush (D)
2. Jesse L. Jackson, Jr. (D)
3. William O. Lipinski (D)
4. Luis V. Gutierrez (D)
5. Rod R. Blagojevich (D)
6. Henry J. Hyde (R)
7. Danny K. Davis (D)
8. Philip M. Crane (R)
9. Janice D. Schakowsky (D)
10. Mark Steven Kirk (R)
11. Jerry Weller (R)
12. Jerry F. Costello (D)
13. Judy Biggert (R)
14. J. Dennis Hastert (R)
15. Timothy V. Johnson (R)
16. Donald A. Manzullo (R)

17. Lane Evans (D)
18. Ray LaHood (R)
19. David D. Phelps (D)
20. John Shimkus (R)

Indiana
1. Peter J. Visclosky (D)
2. Mike Pence (R)
3. Tim Roemer (D)
4. Mark E. Souder (R)
5. Steve Buyer (R)
6. Dan Burton (R)
7. Brian D. Kerns (R)
8. John N. Hostettler (R)
9. Baron P. Hill (D)
10. Julia Carson (D)

Iowa
1. James A. Leach (R)
2. Jim Nussle (R)
3. Leonard L. Boswell (D)
4. Greg Ganske (R)
5. Tom Latham (R)

Kansas
1. Jerry Moran (R)
2. Jim Ryun (R)
3. Dennis Moore (D)
4. Todd Tiahrt (R)

Kentucky
1. Edward Whitfield (R)
2. Ron Lewis (R)
3. Anne M. Northup (R)
4. Ken Lucas (D)
5. Harold Rogers (R)
6. Ernie Fletcher (R)

Louisiana
1. David Vitter (R)
2. William J. Jefferson (D)
3. W. J. "Billy" Tauzin (R)
4. Jim McCrery (R)
5. John Cooksey (R)
6. Richard H. Baker (R)
7. Christopher John (D)

Maine
1. Thomas H. Allen (D)
2. John E. Baldacci (D)

Maryland
1. Wayne T. Gilchrest (R)
2. Robert L. Ehrlich, Jr. (R)
3. Benjamin L. Cardin (D)
4. Albert Russell Wynn (D)
5. Steny H. Hoyer (D)
6. Roscoe G. Bartlett (R)
7. Elijah E. Cummings (D)
8. Constance A. Morella (R)

Massachusetts
1. John W. Olver (D)
2. Richard E. Neal (D)
3. James P. McGovern (D)
4. Barney Frank (D)
5. Martin T. Meehan (D)
6. John F. Tierney (D)
7. Edward J. Markey (D)
8. Michael E. Capuano (D)
9. Vacant
10. William D. Delahunt (D)

Michigan
1. Bart Stupak (D)
2. Peter Hoekstra (R)
3. Vernon J. Ehlers (R)
4. Dave Camp (R)
5. James A. Barcia (D)
6. Fred Upton (R)

7. Nick Smith (R)
8. Mike Rogers (R)
9. Dale E. Kildee (D)
10. David E. Bonior (D)
11. Joe Knollenberg (R)
12. Sander M. Levin (D)
13. Lynn N. Rivers (D)
14. John Conyers, Jr. (D)
15. Carolyn C. Kilpatrick (D)
16. John D. Dingell (D)

Minnesota
1. Gil Gutknecht (R)
2. Mark Kennedy (R)
3. Jim Ramstad (R)
4. Betty McCollum (D)
5. Martin Olav Sabo (D)
6. Bill Luther (D)
7. Collin C. Peterson (D)
8. James L. Oberstar (D)

Mississippi
1. Roger F. Wicker (R)
2. Bennie G. Thompson (D)
3. Charles W. "Chip" Pickering (R)
4. Ronnie Shows (D)
5. Gene Taylor (D)

Missouri
1. William Lacy Clay, Jr. (D)
2. Todd Akin (R)
3. Richard A. Gephardt (D)
4. Ike Skelton (D)
5. Karen McCarthy (D)
6. Samuel Graves (R)
7. Roy Blunt (R)
8. Jo Ann Emerson (R)
9. Kenny C. Hulshof (R)

Montana
AL Dennis Rehberg (R)

Nebraska
1. Doug Bereuter (R)
2. Lee Terry (R)
3. Tom Osborne (R)

Nevada
1. Shelley Berkley (D)
2. Jim Gibbons (R)

New Hampshire
1. John E. Sununu (R)
2. Charles F. Bass (R)

New Jersey
1. Robert E. Andrews (D)
2. Frank A. LoBiondo (R)
3. Jim Saxton (R)
4. Christopher H. Smith (R)
5. Marge Roukema (R)
6. Frank Pallone, Jr. (D)
7. Mike Ferguson (R)
8. Bill Pascrell, Jr. (D)
9. Steven R. Rothman (D)
10. Donald M. Payne (D)
11. Rodney P. Frelinghuysen (R)
12. Rush Holt (D)
13. Robert Menendez (D)

New Mexico
1. Heather Wilson (R)
2. Joe Skeen (R)
3. Tom Udall (D)

New York
1. Felix J. Grucci, Jr. (R)
2. Steven J. Israel (D)
3. Peter T. King (R)
4. Carolyn McCarthy (D)
5. Gary L. Ackerman (D)

6. Gregory W. Meeks (D)
7. Joseph Crowley (D)
8. Jerrold Nadler (D)
9. Anthony D. Weiner (D)
10. Edolphus Towns (D)
11. Major R. Owens (D)
12. Nydia M. Velázquez (D)
13. Vito Fossella (R)
14. Carolyn B. Maloney (D)
15. Charles B. Rangel (D)
16. José E. Serrano (D)
17. Eliot L. Engel (D)
18. Nita M. Lowey (D)
19. Sue W. Kelly (R)
20. Benjamin A. Gilman (R)
21. Michael R. McNulty (D)
22. John E. Sweeney (R)
23. Sherwood L. Boehlert (R)
24. John M. McHugh (R)
25. James T. Walsh (R)
26. Maurice D. Hinchey (D)
27. Thomas M. Reynolds (R)
28. Louise McIntosh Slaughter (D)
29. John J. LaFalce (D)
30. Jack Quinn (R)
31. Amo Houghton (R)

North Carolina
1. Eva M. Clayton (D)
2. Bob Etheridge (D)
3. Walter B. Jones (R)
4. David E. Price (D)
5. Richard Burr (R)
6. Howard Coble (R)
7. Mike McIntyre (D)
8. Robin Hayes (R)
9. Sue Wilkins Myrick (R)
10. Cass Ballenger (R)
11. Charles H. Taylor (R)
12. Melvin L. Watt (D)

North Dakota
AL Earl Pomeroy (D)

Ohio
1. Steve Chabot (R)
2. Rob Portman (R)
3. Tony P. Hall (D)
4. Michael G. Oxley (R)
5. Paul E. Gillmor (R)
6. Ted Strickland (D)
7. David L. Hobson (R)
8. John A. Boehner (R)
9. Marcy Kaptur (D)
10. Dennis J. Kucinich (D)
11. Stephanie Tubbs Jones (D)
12. Pat Tiberi (R)
13. Sherrod Brown (D)
14. Tom Sawyer (D)
15. Deborah Pryce (R)
16. Ralph Regula (R)
17. James A. Traficant, Jr. (D)
18. Robert W. Ney (R)
19. Steven C. LaTourette (R)

Oklahoma
1. Steve Largent (R)
2. Brad Carson (D)
3. Wes Watkins (R)
4. J. C. Watts, Jr. (R)
5. Ernest J. Istook, Jr. (R)
6. Frank D. Lucas (R)

Oregon
1. David Wu (D)
2. Greg Walden (R)
3. Earl Blumenauer (D)
4. Peter A. DeFazio (D)
5. Darlene Hooley (D)

Pennsylvania
1. Robert A. Brady (D)
2. Chaka Fattah (D)
3. Robert A. Borski (D)
4. Melissa Hart (R)
5. John E. Peterson (R)
6. Tim Holden (D)
7. Curt Weldon (R)
8. James C. Greenwood (R)
9. Bill Shuster (R)
10. Don Sherwood (R)
11. Paul E. Kanjorski (D)
12. John P. Murtha (D)
13. Joseph M. Hoeffel (D)
14. William J. Coyne (D)
15. Patrick J. Toomey (R)
16. Joseph R. Pitts (R)
17. George W. Gekas (R)
18. Michael F. Doyle (D)
19. Todd Platts (R)
20. Frank Mascara (D)
21. Phil English (R)

Rhode Island
1. Patrick J. Kennedy (D)
2. James R. Langevin (D)

South Carolina
1. Henry Brown (R)
2. Vacant
3. Lindsey O. Graham (R)
4. Jim DeMint (R)
5. John M. Spratt, Jr. (D)
6. James E. Clyburn (D)

South Dakota
AL John R. Thune (R)

Tennessee
1. William L. Jenkins (R)
2. John J. Duncan, Jr. (R)
3. Zach Wamp (R)
4. Van Hilleary (R)

5. Bob Clement (D)
6. Bart Gordon (D)
7. Ed Bryant (R)
8. John S. Tanner (D)
9. Harold E. Ford, Jr. (D)

Texas
1. Max Sandlin (D)
2. Jim Turner (D)
3. Sam Johnson (R)
4. Ralph M. Hall (D)
5. Pete Sessions (R)
6. Joe Barton (R)
7. John Culberson (R)
8. Kevin Brady (R)
9. Nick Lampson (D)
10. Lloyd Doggett (D)
11. Chet Edwards (D)
12. Kay Granger (R)
13. William "Mac" Thornberry (R)
14. Ron Paul (R)
15. Rubén Hinojosa (D)
16. Silvestre Reyes (D)
17. Charles W. Stenholm (D)
18. Sheila Jackson-Lee (D)
19. Larry Combest (R)
20. Charles A. Gonzalez (D)
21. Lamar S. Smith (R)
22. Tom DeLay (R)
23. Henry Bonilla (R)
24. Martin Frost (D)
25. Ken Bentsen (D)
26. Richard K. Armey (R)
27. Solomon P. Ortiz (D)
28. Ciro D. Rodriguez (D)
29. Gene Green (D)
30. Eddie Bernice Johnson (D)

Utah
1. James V. Hansen (R)
2. Jim Matheson (D)
3. Christopher B. Cannon (R)

Vermont
AL Bernard Sanders (I)

Virginia
1. Jo Ann S. Davis (R)
2. Edward L. Schrock (R)
3. Robert C. Scott (D)
4. J. Randy Forbes (R)
5. Virgil H. Goode, Jr. (I)
6. Robert W. Goodlatte (R)
7. Eric I. Cantor (R)
8. James P. Moran (D)
9. Rick Boucher (D)
10. Frank R. Wolf (R)
11. Thomas M. Davis (R)

Washington
1. Jay Inslee (D)
2. Rick Larsen (D)
3. Brian Baird (D)
4. Richard "Doc" Hastings (R)
5. George R. Nethercutt, Jr. (R)
6. Norman D. Dicks (D)
7. Jim McDermott (D)
8. Jennifer Dunn (R)
9. Adam Smith (D)

West Virginia
1. Alan B. Mollohan (D)
2. Shelley Moore Capito (R)
3. Nick J. Rahall II (D)

Wisconsin
1. Paul D. Ryan (R)
2. Tammy Baldwin (D)
3. Ron Kind (D)
4. Gerald D. Kleczka (D)
5. Thomas M. Barrett (D)
6. Thomas E. Petri (R)
7. David R. Obey (D)
8. Mark Green (R)
9. F. James Sensenbrenner, Jr. (R)

Wyoming
AL Barbara Cubin (R)

The Governors of the Fifty States

State	Governor	Current term[1]	State	Governor	Current term[1]
Ala.	Don Siegelman (D)	1999–2003	Mont.	Judy Martz (R)	2001–2005
Alaska	Tony Knowles (D)	1998–2002[2]	Nebr.	Mike Johanns (R)	1999–2003
Ariz.	Jane Dee Hull (R)	1999–2003	Nev.	Kenny Guinn (R)	1999–2003
Ark.	Mike Huckabee (R)	1999–2003	N.H.	Jeanne Shaheen (D)	2001–2005
Calif.	Gray Davis (D)	1999–2003	N.J.	Donald T. DiFrancesco (R)[5]	2000–2002
Colo.	Bill Owens (R)	1999–2003	N.M.	Gary E. Johnson (R)	1999–2003
Conn.	John G. Rowland (R)	1999–2003	N.Y.	George E. Pataki (R)	1999–2003
Del.	Ruth Ann Minner (D)	2001–2005	N.C.	Mike Easley (D)	2001–2005
Fla.	Jeb Bush (R)	1999–2003	N.D.	John Hoeven (R)	2001–2005
Ga.	Roy E. Barnes (D)	1999–2003	Ohio	Bob Taft (R)	1999–2003
Hawaii	Benjamin J. Cayetano (D)	1998–2002[2]	Okla.	Frank Keating (R)	1999–2003
Idaho	Dirk Kempthorne (R)	1999–2003	Ore.	John Kitzhaber (D)	1999–2003
Ill.	George H. Ryan (R)	1999–2003	Pa.	Mark S. Schweiker (R)[3]	2001–2003
Ind.	Frank O'Bannon (D)	2001–2005	R.I.	Lincoln C. Almond (R)	1999–2003
Iowa	Tom Vilsack (D)	1999–2003	S.C.	Jim Hodges (D)	1999–2003
Kans.	Bill Graves (R)	1999–2003	S.D.	William J. Janklow (R)	1999–2003
Ky.	Paul E. Patton (D)	1999–2003[2]	Tenn.	Don Sundquist (R)	1999–2003
La.	Mike Foster (R)	2000–2004	Tex.	Rick Perry (R)[3]	2000–2003
Maine	Angus S. King, Jr. (I)	1999–2003	Utah	Michael O. Leavitt (R)	2001–2005
Md.	Parris N. Glendening (D)	1999–2003	Vt.	Howard Dean (D)	2001–2005
Mass.	Jane Swift (R) [3]	2001–2003	Va.	James S. Gilmore (R)	1998–2002
Mich.	John Engler (R)	1999–2003	Wash.	Gary Locke (D)	2001–2005
Minn.	Jesse Ventura (IP)[4]	1999–2003	W. Va.	Bob Wise (D)	2001–2005
Miss.	Ronnie Musgrove (D)	2000–2004	Wis.	Scott McCallum (R)[3]	2001–2003
Mo.	Bob Holden (D)	2001–2005	Wyo.	Jim Geringer (R)	1999–2003

NOTE: Governors listed in italics were elected or reelected in 2000. 1. Except where indicated, all terms begin and end in January. 2. Term begins and ends in December. 3. Lieutenant governor serving out the remaining term of governor. 4. Independence Party. 5. New Jersey State Senate president serving out the remaining term of governor.

Presidential Election of 2000, Electoral and Popular Vote Summary

Principal Candidates for President and Vice President:
Republican—George W. Bush; Richard B. Cheney (winner)
Democratic—Albert A. Gore, Jr.; Joseph I. Lieberman
Green—Ralph Nader; Winona LaDuke

	George W. Bush		Albert A. Gore, Jr.		Ralph Nader		Electoral votes		
	Popular vote	%	Popular vote	%	Popular vote	%	R	D	G
Alabama	941,173	56%	692,611	42%	18,323	1%	9		
Alaska	167,398	59	79,004	28	28,747	10	3		
Arizona	781,652	51	685,341	45	45,645	3	8		
Arkansas	472,940	51	422,768	46	13,421	1	6		
California	4,567,429	42	5,861,203	53	418,707	4		54	
Colorado	883,748	51	738,227	42	91,434	5	8		
Connecticut	561,094	38	816,015	56	64,452	4		8	
Delaware	137,288	42	180,068	55	8,307	3		3	
DC	18,073	9	171,923	85	10,576	5		2[1]	
Florida	2,912,790	49	2,912,253	49	97,488	2	25		
Georgia	1,419,720	55	1,116,230	43	13,432[2]	.5	13		
Hawaii	137,845	37	205,286	56	21,623	6		4	
Idaho	336,937	67	138,637	28	12,292[2]	2	4		
Illinois	2,019,421	43	2,589,026	55	103,759	2		22	
Indiana	1,245,836	57	901,980	41	18,531[2]	.8	12		
Iowa	634,373	48	638,517	49	29,374	2		7	
Kansas	622,332	58	399,276	37	36,086	3	6		
Kentucky	872,492	57	638,898	41	23,192	2	8		
Louisiana	927,871	53	792,344	45	20,473	1	9		
Maine	286,616	44	319,951	49	37,127	6		4	
Maryland	813,797	40	1,140,782	56	53,768	3		10	
Massachusetts	878,502	33	1,616,487	60	173,564	6		12	
Michigan	1,953,139	46	2,170,418	51	84,165	2		18	
Minnesota	1,109,659	46	1,168,266	48	126,696	5		10	
Mississippi	572,844	58	404,614	41	8,122	.8	7		
Missouri	1,189,924	50	1,111,138	47	38,515	2	11		
Montana	240,178	58	137,126	33	24,437	6	3		
Nebraska	433,862	62	231,780	33	24,540	4	5		
Nevada	301,575	50	279,978	46	15,008	2	4		
New Hampshire	273,559	48	266,348	47	22,198	4	4		
New Jersey	1,284,173	40	1,788,850	56	94,554	3		15	
New Mexico	286,417	48	286,783	48	21,251	4		5	
New York	2,403,374	35	4,107,697	60	244,030	4		33	
North Carolina	1,631,163	56	1,257,692	43	—	—	14		
North Dakota	174,852	61	95,284	33	9,486	3	3		
Ohio	2,350,363	50	2,183,628	46	117,799	3	21		
Oklahoma	744,337	60	474,276	38	—	—	8		
Oregon	713,577	47	720,342	47	77,357	5		7	
Pennsylvania	2,281,127	46	2,485,967	51	103,392	2		23	
Rhode Island	130,555	32	249,508	61	25,052	6		4	
South Carolina	785,937	57	565,561	41	20,200	1	8		
South Dakota	190,700	60	118,804	38	—	—	3		
Tennessee	1,061,949	51	981,720	47	19,781	1	11		
Texas	3,799,639	59	2,433,746	38	137,994	2	32		
Utah	515,096	67	203,053	26	35,850	5	5		
Vermont	119,775	41	149,022	51	20,374	7		3	
Virginia	1,437,490	52	1,217,290	44	59,398	2	13		
Washington	1,108,864	45	1,247,652	50	103,002	4		11	
West Virginia	336,475	52	295,497	46	10,680	2	5		
Wisconsin	1,237,279	48	1,242,987	48	94,070	4		11	
Wyoming	147,947	68	60,481	28	4,625[2]	2	3		
Total	**50,455,156**	**47.87%**	**50,992,335**	**48.38%**	**2,882,897**	**2.74%**	**271**	**266**	

NOTE: Total electoral votes = 538. Total electoral votes needed to win = 270. Dash (—) indicates not on ballot. 1. The District of Columbia has 3 votes. There was 1 abstention. 2. Write-in votes. *Source:* Federal Election Commission.

Voting age population (Census Bureau Population Survey for Nov. 2000): 205,815,000
Percentage of voting age population casting a vote for president: 51.21%

2000 Election Chronology

Tuesday, Nov. 7—Election Day. Pundits have predicted a tight race between Texas governor George W. Bush and Vice President Al Gore, but few expect one of the closest elections in U.S. history. By early evening, it's clear the election hinges on Florida.

Wednesday, Nov. 8—Gore calls Bush at approximately 3 A.M. to concede, but retracts the concession shortly after, because Bush's razor-slim lead prompts an automatic recount. He leads Gore by about 1,210 votes out of nearly 6 million cast in Florida. Meanwhile Gore leads in both the national popular count and the electoral college. An unusual amount of votes for third-party candidates in Palm Beach County leads to disputes over the county's "butterfly ballots." A number of ballots in other counties are disqualified because the chad—the small piece of paper punched out of punch-card ballots—did not fully detach from the ballot.

Thursday, Nov. 9—Gore's camp requests a hand recount of the approximately 1.8 million ballots cast in Palm Beach, Miami-Dade, Broward, and Volusia counties, Democratic strongholds.

Friday, Nov. 10—Florida's automatic recount is completed. The Associated Press reports that Bush has retained his lead but only by 327 votes.

Saturday, Nov. 11—The Bush team, led by former secretary of state James Baker, files suit in federal court to block Gore's request for a recount.

Monday, Nov. 13—Florida secretary of state Katherine Harris announces she will not extend the Nov. 14 deadline for the submission of all state results, excluding absentee ballots from overseas.

A federal judge in Miami rejects Bush's efforts to halt manual recounts. Bush appeals the decision.

Tuesday, Nov. 14—Harris postpones certification of the state's votes until Nov. 15, so Miami-Dade, Palm Beach, and Broward counties have time to prepare an explanation of why they should hand count their ballots.

Wednesday, Nov. 15—Harris decides that no county offered adequate evidence to justify further hand recounts.

Florida Supreme Court denies a request from Harris to stop the hand recounts. Certification is again postponed.

Thursday, Nov. 16—Bush's lawyers present written arguments to the U.S. federal appeals court in Atlanta to end the manual recounts. Gore's team files a counter motion.

Friday, Nov. 17—The Florida Supreme Court blocks Harris from certifying election until it rules on the Democrats' motion to include hand recounts.

The 11th Circuit Court of Appeals denies the Republicans' motion to stop manual recounts on constitutional grounds.

Saturday, Nov. 18—With a tally of absentee ballots, uncertified count has Bush ahead of Gore by 930 votes.

Tuesday, Nov. 21—Florida Supreme Court rules that results of hand counts of ballots in Miami-Dade, Palm Beach, and Broward counties must be included in the vote tally if the counts are completed by Nov. 26.

Sunday, Nov. 26—Harris certifies Bush as the winner of Florida's 25 electoral votes, with a 537-vote lead over Gore. Gore pledges to challenge certification in court. The tally does not include results from Palm Beach County, which finished its hand recount hours after the deadline.

Monday, Nov. 27—Gore contests the Florida results in a circuit court in Tallahassee.

Wednesday, Nov. 29—Leon County Circuit Court judge N. Sanders Sauls orders that all ballots from Palm Beach and Miami-Dade counties be sent to Tallahassee for a hearing on whether the hand count, which was incomplete at the time of the court-ordered Nov. 26 deadline, should be included in the final vote tally.

Thursday, Nov. 30—Florida lawmakers, voting along party lines, recommend holding a special session to name the state's 25 electors if the election dispute is not resolved by Dec. 12, six days before the electoral college meets.

Friday, Dec. 1—The U.S. Supreme Court hears arguments on whether the Florida Supreme Court acted properly when it forced the Florida secretary of state to accept manual recounts submitted after the legal deadline.

The Florida Supreme Court denies Gore's appeal to immediately begin recounting ballots and rejects motion filed by some Palm Beach County citizens who questioned the integrity of the "butterfly ballot."

Gore requests of approximately 14,000 "undervotes" from Palm Beach and Miami-Dade counties.

Monday, Dec. 4—Judge Sauls rejects Gore's contest of the election results, saying the vice president failed to prove that hand recounts would have altered the results. Gore appeals to the Florida Supreme Court.

U.S. Supreme Court asks Florida Supreme Court to explain why it ordered Harris to accept results submitted after the Nov. 14 deadline mandated by state law, thus returning the case to Tallahassee.

Thursday, Dec. 7—Gore's legal team appeals Sauls's ruling. Bush's lawyers argue that the decision should stand.

Friday, Dec. 8—The Florida Supreme Court, ruling on Gore's appeal, orders manual recounts in counties with large numbers of undervotes. Bush appeals to the U.S. Supreme Court and seeks injunction to stop recounts.

In two separate lawsuits, Leon County Circuit Court judges refuse to throw out absentee ballots from Seminole and Martin counties that had been disputed by Gore.

Saturday, Dec. 9—The U.S. Supreme Court votes 5–4 to halt the hand recounts and sets a hearing for Dec. 11.

Florida Supreme Court hears appeal on whether absentee ballots in Martin and Seminole counties should be counted.

Tuesday, Dec. 12—The U.S. Supreme Court rules 7–2 to reverse the Florida Supreme Court, which had ordered manual recounts in certain counties. The Court contends that the recount was not treating all ballots equally, and was thus a violation of the Constitution's equal protection and due process guarantees. The Supreme Court of Florida would be required to set up new voting standards and carry them out in a recount. The justices, however, split 5–4 along partisan lines about implementing their remedy. Five justices maintain that this process and the recount must adhere to the official deadline for certifying electoral college votes: midnight, Dec. 12. Since the Court makes its ruling just hours before the deadline, it in effect ensures that it is too late for a recount. The decision means that the Supreme Court, not the electorate, has determined the outcome of the presidential election. In a scathing dissent, Justice John Paul Stevens writes, "Although we may never know with complete certainty the identity of the winner of this year's presidential election, the identity of the loser is perfectly clear. It is the nation's confidence in the judge as an impartial guardian of the rule of law."

Wednesday, Dec. 13—In another decision, Florida Supreme Court decides not to hear an appeal from Gore asking that absentee ballots from Martin and Seminole counties be thrown out.

In televised speeches, Gore concedes, and Bush accepts the presidency.

Monday, Dec. 18—Electoral college representatives meet in state capitals and cast votes to select president.

Wednesday, Jan. 5—Congress meets to tally electoral college results.

Saturday, Jan. 20—George W. Bush sworn in as 43rd president of the United States.

How a President Is Nominated and Elected

The Conventions

The national conventions of both major parties are held during the summer of a presidential election year. Earlier, each party selects delegates by primaries, conventions, committees, etc.

At each convention, a temporary chairman is chosen. After a credentials committee seats the delegates, a permanent chairman is elected. The convention then votes on a platform, drawn up by the platform committee.

By the third or fourth day, presidential nominations begin. The chairman calls the roll of states alphabetically. A state may place a candidate in nomination or yield to another state.

Voting, again alphabetically by roll call of states, begins after all nominations have been made and seconded. A simple majority is required in each party, although this may require many ballots.

Finally, the vice-presidential candidate is selected. Although there is no law saying that the candidates *must* come from different states, it is, practically, necessary for this to be the case. Otherwise, according to the Constitution (*see* the 12th Amendment), electors from that state could vote for only one of the candidates and would have to cast their other vote for some person of another state. This could result in a presidential candidate's receiving a majority electoral vote and his or her running mate's failing to do so.

The Electoral College

The next step in the process is the nomination of electors in each state, according to its laws. These electors must not be federal office holders. In the November election, the voters cast their votes for electors, not for president. In some states, the ballots include only the names of the presidential and vice-presidential candidates; in others, they include only names of the electors. Nowadays, it is rare for electors to be split between parties. The last such occurrence was in North Carolina in 1968;[1] the last before that, in Tennessee in 1948. On four occasions (1824, 1876, 1888, and 2000), the presidential candidate with the largest popular vote failed to obtain an electoral vote majority.

Each state has as many electors as it has senators and representatives. For the 2000 election, the total electors were 538, based on 100 senators and 435 representatives, plus 3 electoral votes from the District of Columbia as a result of the 23rd Amendment to the Constitution.

On the first Monday after the second Wednesday in December, the electors cast their votes in their respective state capitols. Constitutionally they may vote for someone other than the party candidate but usually they do not since they are pledged to one party and its candidate on the ballot. Should the presidential or vice-presidential candidate die between the November election and the December meetings, the electors pledged to vote for him or her could vote for whomever they pleased. However, it seems certain that the national committee would attempt to get an agreement among the state party leaders for a replacement candidate.

The votes of the electors, certified by the states, are sent to Congress, where the president of the Senate opens the certificates and has them counted in the presence of both houses on Jan. 6. The new president is inaugurated at noon on Jan. 20.

Should no candidate receive a majority of the electoral vote for president, the House of Representatives chooses a president from among the three highest candidates, voting, not as individuals, but as states, with a majority (now 26) needed to elect. Should no vice-presidential candidate obtain the majority, the Senate, voting as individuals, chooses from the highest two.

1. In 1956, one of Alabama's 11 electoral votes was cast for Walter B. Jones. In 1960, six of Alabama's 11 electoral votes and one of Oklahoma's eight electoral votes were cast for Harry Flood Byrd. (Byrd also received all eight of Mississippi's electoral votes.)

Electoral College Votes by State, 2000 Presidential Elections

(total electoral votes: 538; majority needed to elect: 270)

State	Votes	State	Votes	State	Votes
Alabama	9	Kentucky	8	North Dakota	3
Alaska	3	Louisiana	9	Ohio	21
Arizona	8	Maine	4	Oklahoma	8
Arkansas	6	Maryland	10	Oregon	7
California	54	Massachusetts	12	Pennsylvania	23
Colorado	8	Michigan	18	Rhode Island	4
Connecticut	8	Minnesota	10	South Carolina	8
Delaware	3	Mississippi	7	South Dakota	3
District of Columbia	3	Missouri	11	Tennessee	11
Florida	25	Montana	3	Texas	32
Georgia	13	Nebraska	5	Utah	5
Hawaii	4	Nevada	4	Vermont	3
Idaho	4	New Hampshire	4	Virginia	13
Illinois	22	New Jersey	15	Washington	11
Indiana	12	New Mexico	5	West Virginia	5
Iowa	7	New York	33	Wisconsin	11
Kansas	6	North Carolina	14	Wyoming	3

National Political Conventions Since 1856

Opening date	Party	Where held	Opening date	Party	Where held
June 17, 1856	Republican	Philadelphia	June 14, 1932	Republican	Chicago
June 2, 1856	Democratic	Cincinnati	June 27, 1932	Democratic	Chicago
May 16, 1860	Republican	Chicago	June 9, 1936	Republican	Cleveland
April 23, 1860	Democratic	Charleston and Baltimore	June 23, 1936	Democratic	Philadelphia
June 7, 1864	Republican[1]	Baltimore	June 24, 1940	Republican	Philadelphia
Aug. 29, 1864	Democratic	Chicago	July 15, 1940	Democratic	Chicago
May 20, 1868	Republican	Chicago	June 26, 1944	Republican	Chicago
July 4, 1868	Democratic	New York City	July 19, 1944	Democratic	Chicago
June 5, 1872	Republican	Philadelphia	June 21, 1948	Republican	Philadelphia
June 9, 1872	Democratic	Baltimore	July 12, 1948	Democratic	Philadelphia
June 14, 1876	Republican	Cincinnati	July 17, 1948	(3)	Birmingham
June 28, 1876	Democratic	St. Louis	July 22, 1948	Progressive	Philadelphia
June 2, 1880	Republican	Chicago	July 7, 1952	Republican	Chicago
June 23, 1880	Democratic	Cincinnati	July 21, 1952	Democratic	Chicago
June 3, 1884	Republican	Chicago	Aug. 20, 1956	Republican	San Francisco
July 11, 1884	Democratic	Chicago	Aug. 13, 1956	Democratic	Chicago
June 19, 1888	Republican	Chicago	July 25, 1960	Republican	Chicago
June 6, 1888	Democratic	St. Louis	July 11, 1960	Democratic	Los Angeles
June 7, 1892	Republican	Minneapolis	July 13, 1964	Republican	San Francisco
June 21, 1892	Democratic	Chicago	Aug. 24, 1964	Democratic	Atlantic City
June 16, 1896	Republican	St. Louis	Aug. 5, 1968	Republican	Miami Beach
July 7, 1896	Democratic	Chicago	Aug. 26, 1968	Democratic	Chicago
June 19, 1900	Republican	Philadelphia	July 10, 1972	Democratic	Miami Beach
July 4, 1900	Democratic	Kansas City	Aug. 21, 1972	Republican	Miami Beach
June 21, 1904	Republican	Chicago	July 12, 1976	Democratic	New York City
July 6, 1904	Democratic	St. Louis	Aug. 16, 1976	Republican	Kansas City, Mo.
June 16, 1908	Republican	Chicago	Aug. 11, 1980	Democratic	New York City
July 7, 1908	Democratic	Denver	July 14, 1980	Republican	Detroit
June 18, 1912	Republican	Chicago	Aug. 20, 1984	Republican	Dallas
June 25, 1912	Democratic	Baltimore	July 16, 1984	Democratic	San Francisco
June 7, 1916	Republican	Chicago	July 18, 1988	Democratic	Atlanta
June 14, 1916	Democratic	St. Louis	Aug. 15, 1988	Republican	New Orleans
June 8, 1920	Republican	Chicago	July 13, 1992	Democratic	New York City
June 28, 1920	Democratic	San Francisco	Aug. 17, 1992	Republican	Houston
June 10, 1924	Republican	Cleveland	Aug. 10, 1996	Republican	San Diego
June 24, 1924[2]	Democratic	New York City	Aug. 26, 1996	Democratic	Chicago
June 12, 1928	Republican	Kansas City	July 29, 2000	Republican	Philadelphia
June 26, 1928	Democratic	Houston	Aug. 14, 2000	Democratic	Los Angeles

1. The convention adopted name Union Party to attract War Democrats and others favoring prosecution of war. 2. In session until July 10, 1924. 3. States' Rights delegates from 13 southern states.

National Committee Chairs Since 1944

Chairman and (state)	Term	Chairman and (state)	Term
Republican		**Democratic**	
Herbert Brownell, Jr. (N.Y.)	1944–1946	Robert E. Hannegan (Mo.)	1944–1947
Carroll Reece (Tenn.)	1946–1948	J. Howard McGrath (R.I.)	1947–1949
Hugh D. Scott, Jr. (Pa.)	1948–1949	William M. Boyle, Jr. (Mo.)	1949–1951
Guy G. Gabrielson (N.J.)	1949–1952	Frank E. McKinney (Ind.)	1951–1952
Arthur E. Summerfield (Mich.)	1952–1953	Stephen A. Mitchell (Ill.)	1952–1954
Wesley Roberts (Kan.)	1953	Paul M. Butler (Ind.)	1955–1960
Leonard W. Hall (N.Y.)	1953–1957	Henry M. Jackson (Wash.)	1960–1961
Meade Alcorn (Conn.)	1957–1959	John M. Bailey (Conn.)	1961–1968
Thruston B. Morton (Ky.)	1959–1961	Lawrence F. O'Brien (Mass.)	1968–1969
William E. Miller (N.Y.)	1961–1964	Fred R. Harris (Okla.)	1969–1970
Dean Burch (Ariz.)	1964–1965	Lawrence F. O'Brien (Mass.)	1970–1972
Ray C. Bliss (Ohio)	1965–1969	Jean Westwood (Utah)	1972
Rogers C. B. Morton (Md.)	1969–1971	Robert S. Strauss (Tex.)	1972–1977
Robert Dole (Kan.)	1971–1973	Kenneth M. Curtis (Me.)	1977
George H. Bush (Tex.)	1973–1974	John C. White (Tex.)	1977–1981
Mary Louise Smith (Iowa)	1974–1977	Charles T. Manatt (Calif.)	1981–1985
William E. Brock III (Tenn.)	1977–1981	Paul G. Kirk, Jr. (Mass.)	1985–1989
Richard Richards (Utah)	1981–1983	Ronald H. Brown (D.C.)	1989–1993
Frank J. Fahrenkopf, Jr. (Nevada)	1983–1989	David Wilhelm (Ill.)	1993–1994
Lee Atwater (S.C.)	1989–1991	Christopher J. Dodd (Conn.)	1995–1996
Clayton K. Yeutter (Neb.)	1991–1992	Steven Grossman (Mass.)	1996–1999
Richard Bond (N.Y.)	1992–1993	Joe Andrew (Ind.)	1999–2001
Haley Barbour (Miss.)	1993–1997	Terry McAuliffe (Va.)	2001–
Jim Nicholson (Colo.)	1997–2001		
Jim Gilmore (Va.)	2001–		

Republican National Committee: 310 First St., SE, Washington, DC 20003. *Democratic National Committee:* 430 South Capitol St., SE, Washington, DC 20003.

Presidential Elections, 1789–2000

For the original method of electing the president and the vice president (elections of 1789, 1792, 1796, and 1800), *see* Article II, Section 1, of the Constitution. The election of 1804 was the first one in which the electors voted for president and vice president on separate ballots. (See Amendment XII to the Constitution.)

Year	Presidential candidate	Party	Electoral votes	Year	Presidential candidate	Party	Electoral votes
1789[1]	George Washington	(no party)	69	1796	John Adams	Federalist	71
	John Adams	(no party)	34		Thomas Jefferson	Dem.-Rep.	68
	Scattering	(no party)	35		Thomas Pinckney	Federalist	59
	Votes not cast		8		Aaron Burr	Dem.-Rep.	30
					Scattering		48
1792	George Washington	Federalist	132				
	John Adams	Federalist	77	1800[2]	Thomas Jefferson	Dem.-Rep.	73
	George Clinton	Anti-Federalist	50		Aaron Burr	Dem.-Rep.	73
	Thomas Jefferson	Anti-Federalist	4		John Adams	Federalist	65
	Aaron Burr	Anti-Federalist	1		Charles C. Pinckney	Federalist	64
	Votes not cast		6		John Jay	Federalist	1

Year	Presidential candidate	Party	Electoral votes	Vice-presidential candidate	Party	Electoral votes
1804	Thomas Jefferson	Dem.-Rep.	162	George Clinton	Dem.-Rep.	162
	Charles C. Pinckney	Federalist	14	Rufus King	Federalist	14
1808	James Madison	Dem.-Rep.	122	George Clinton	Dem.-Rep.	113
	Charles C. Pinckney	Federalist	47	Rufus King	Federalist	47
	George Clinton	Dem.-Rep.	6	John Langdon	Ind. (no party)	9
	Votes not cast		1	James Madison	Dem.-Rep.	3
				James Monroe	Dem.-Rep.	3
				Votes not cast		1
1812	James Madison	Dem.-Rep.	128	Elbridge Gerry	Dem.-Rep.	131
	De Witt Clinton	Federalist	89	Jared Ingersoll	Federalist	86
	Votes not cast		1	Votes not cast		1
1816	James Monroe	Dem.-Rep.	183	Daniel D. Tompkins	Dem.-Rep.	183
	Rufus King	Federalist	34	John E. Howard	Federalist	22
	Votes not cast		4	James Ross	Ind (no party)	5
				John Marshall	Federalist	4
				Robert G. Harper	Ind. (no party)	3
				Votes not cast		4
1820	James Monroe	Dem-Rep	231	Daniel D. Tompkins	Dem.-Rep.	218
	John Quincy Adams	Ind. (no party)	1	Richard Stockton	Ind. (no party)	8
	Votes not cast		3	Daniel Rodney	Ind. (no party)	4
				Richard Rush	Ind. (no party)	1
				Robert G. Harper	Ind. (no party)	1
				Votes not cast		3
1824[3]	John Quincy Adams	(no party)	84	John C. Calhoun	(no party)	182
	Andrew Jackson	(no party)	99	Nathan Sanford	(no party)	30
	William H. Crawford	(no party)	41	Nathaniel Macon	(no party)	24
	Henry Clay	(no party)	37	Andrew Jackson	(no party)	13
				Martin Van Buren	(no party)	9
				Henry Clay	(no party)	2
				Votes not cast		1
1828	Andrew Jackson	Democratic	178	John C. Calhoun	Democratic	171
	John Quincy Adams	Natl. Rep.	83	Richard Rush	Natl. Rep.	83
				William Smith	Democratic	7
1832	Andrew Jackson	Democratic	219	Martin Van Buren	Democratic	189
	Henry Clay	Natl. Rep.	49	John Sergeant	Natl. Rep.	49
	John Floyd	Ind. (no party)	11	Henry Lee	Ind. (no party)	11
	William Wirt	Antimasonic[4]	7	Amos Ellmaker	Antimasonic	7
	Votes not cast		2	William Wilkins	Ind. (no party)	30
				Votes not cast		2
1836	Martin Van Buren	Democratic	170	Richard M. Johnson[5]	Democratic	147
	William H. Harrison	Whig	73	Francis Granger	Whig	77
	Hugh L. White	Whig	26	John Tyler	Whig	47
	Daniel Webster	Whig	14	William Smith	Ind. (no party)	23
	W. P. Mangum	Ind. (no party)	11			

Year	Presidential candidate	Party	Electoral votes	Vice-presidential candidate	Party	Electoral votes
1840	William H. Harrison[6]	Whig	234	John Tyler	Whig	234
	Martin Van Buren	Democratic	60	Richard M. Johnson	Democratic	48
				L. W. Tazewell	Ind. (no party)	11
				James K. Polk	Democratic	1
1844	James K. Polk	Democratic	170	George M. Dallas	Democratic	170
	Henry Clay	Whig	105	Theo. Frelinghuysen	Whig	105
1848	Zachary Taylor[7]	Whig	163	Millard Fillmore	Whig	163
	Lewis Cass	Democratic	127	William O. Butler	Democratic	127
1852	Franklin Pierce	Democratic	254	William R. King	Democratic	254
	Winfield Scott	Whig	42	William A. Graham	Whig	42
1856	James Buchanan	Democratic	174	John C. Breckinridge	Democratic	174
	John C. Fremont	Republican	114	William L. Dayton	Republican	114
	Millard Fillmore	American[8]	8	A. J. Donelson	American[8]	8
1860	Abraham Lincoln	Republican	180	Hannibal Hamlin	Republican	180
	John C. Breckinridge	Democratic	72	Joseph Lane	Democratic	72
	John Bell	Const. Union	39	Edward Everett	Const. Union	39
	Stephen A. Douglas	Democratic	12	H. V. Johnson	Democratic	12
1864	Abraham Lincoln[9]	Union[10]	212	Andrew Johnson	Union[15]	212
	George B. McClellan	Democratic	21	G. H. Pendleton	Democratic	21
1868	Ulysses S. Grant	Republican	214	Schuyler Colfax	Republican	214
	Horatio Seymour	Democratic	80	Francis P. Blair, Jr.	Democratic	80
	Votes not counted[11]		23	Votes not counted[11]		23

NOTE: Due to the communications constrictions of the time and the lack of formal political party organizations, the framers of the Constitution specified that the president and vice president be chosen based upon the votes cast by members of an electoral college rather than by a direct popular vote. Eventually, states began to change the method by which electors cast their votes. Today, all but two states, Maine and Nebraska, have a winner-take-all system in which a popular vote decides which candidates will be given all of a given state's electoral votes. The number of popular votes won by each presidential candidate are listed here for elections beginning in 1872.

Year	Presidential candidate	Party	Electoral votes	Popular votes	Vice-presidential candidate and party
1872	Ulysses S. Grant	Republican	286	3,597,132	Henry Wilson—R
	Horace Greeley	Dem., Liberal Rep.	([12])	2,834,125	B. Gratz Brown—D, LR—(47)
	Thomas A. Hendricks	Democratic	42		Scattering—(19)
	B. Gratz Brown	Dem., Liberal Rep.	18		Vote not counted—(14)
	Charles J. Jenkins	Democratic	2		
	David Davis	Democratic	1		
	Votes not counted		17		
1876[13]	Rutherford B. Hayes	Republican	185	4,033,768	William A. Wheeler—R
	Samuel J. Tilden	Democratic	184	4,285,992	Thomas A. Hendricks—D
	Peter Cooper	Greenback	0	81,737	Samuel F. Cary—G
1880	James A. Garfield[14]	Republican	214	4,449,053	Chester A. Arthur—R
	Winfield S. Hancock	Democratic	155	4,442,035	William H. English—D
	James B. Weaver	Greenback	0	308,578	B. J. Chambers—G
1884	Grover Cleveland	Democratic	219	4,911,017	Thomas A. Hendricks—D
	James G. Blaine	Republican	182	4,848,334	John A. Logan—R
	Benjamin F. Butler	Greenback	0	175,370	A. M. West—G
	John P. St. John	Prohibition	0	150,369	William Daniel—P
1888	Benjamin Harrison	Republican	233	5,440,216	Levi P. Morton—R
	Grover Cleveland	Democratic	168	5,538,233	A. G. Thurman—D
	Clinton B. Fisk	Prohibition	0	249,506	John A. Brooks—P
	Alson J. Streeter	Union Labor	0	146,935	Charles E. Cunningham—UL
1892	Grover Cleveland	Democratic	277	5,556,918	Adlai E. Stevenson—D
	Benjamin Harrison	Republican	145	5,176,108	Whitelaw Reid—R
	James B. Weaver	People's[15]	22	1,041,028	James G. Field—Peo
	John Bidwell	Prohibition	0	264,133	James B. Cranfill—P
1896	William McKinley	Republican	271	7,035,638	Garret A. Hobart—R
	William J. Bryan	Dem., People's[15]	176	6,467,946	Arthur Sewall—D—(149)
					Thomas E. Watson—Peo—(27)
	John M. Palmer	Natl. Dem.	0	133,148	Simon B. Buckner—ND
	Joshua Levering	Prohibition	0	132,007	Hale Johnson—P

Year	Presidential candidate	Party	Electoral votes	Popular votes	Vice-presidential candidate and party
1900	William McKinley[16]	Republican	292	7,219,530	Theodore Roosevelt—R
	William J. Bryan	Dem., People's[15]	155	6,358,071	Adlai E. Stevenson—D, Peo
	Eugene V. Debs	Social Democratic	0	94,768	Job Harriman—SD
1904	Theodore Roosevelt	Republican	336	7,628,834	Charles W. Fairbanks—R
	Alton B. Parker	Democratic	140	5,084,491	Henry G. Davis—D
	Eugene V. Debs	Socialist	0	402,400	Benjamin Hanford—S
1908	William H. Taft	Republican	321	7,679,006	James S. Sherman—R
	William J. Bryan	Democratic	162	6,409,106	John W. Kern—D
	Eugene V. Debs	Socialist	0	402,820	Benjamin Hanford—S
1912	Woodrow Wilson	Democratic	435	6,286,214	Thomas R. Marshall—D
	Theodore Roosevelt	Progressive	88	4,126,020	Hiram Johnson—Prog
	William H. Taft	Republican	8	3,483,922	Nicholas M. Butler—R[17]
	Eugene V. Debs	Socialist	0	897,011	Emil Seidel—S
1916	Woodrow Wilson	Democratic	277	9,129,606	Thomas R. Marshall—D
	Charles E. Hughes	Republican	254	8,538,221	Charles W. Fairbanks—R
	A. L. Benson	Socialist	0	585,113	G. R. Kirkpatrick—S
1920	Warren G. Harding[18]	Republican	404	16,152,200	Calvin Coolidge—R
	James M. Cox	Democratic	127	9,147,353	Franklin D. Roosevelt—D
	Eugene V. Debs	Socialist	0	917,799	Seymour Stedman—S
1924	Calvin Coolidge	Republican	382	15,725,016	Charles G. Dawes—R
	John W. Davis	Democratic	136	8,385,586	Charles W. Bryan—D
	Robert M. LaFollette	Progressive, Socialist	13	4,822,856	Burton K. Wheeler—Prog, S
1928	Herbert Hoover	Republican	444	21,392,190	Charles Curtis—R
	Alfred E. Smith	Democratic	87	15,016,443	Joseph T. Robinson—D
	Norman Thomas	Socialist	0	267,420	James H. Maurer—S
1932	Franklin D. Roosevelt	Democratic	472	22,821,857	John N. Garner—D
	Herbert Hoover	Republican	59	15,761,841	Charles Curtis—R
	Norman Thomas	Socialist	0	884,781	James H. Maurer—S
1936	Franklin D. Roosevelt	Democratic	523	27,751,597	John N. Garner—D
	Alfred M. Landon	Republican	8	16,679,583	Frank Knox—R
	Norman Thomas	Socialist	0	187,720	George Nelson—S
1940	Franklin D. Roosevelt	Democratic	449	27,244,160	Henry A. Wallace—D
	Wendell L. Willkie	Republican	82	22,305,198	Charles L. McNary—R
	Norman Thomas	Socialist	0	99,557	Maynard C. Krueger—S
1944	Franklin D. Roosevelt[19]	Democratic	432	25,602,504	Harry S. Truman—D
	Thomas E. Dewey	Republican	99	22,006,285	John W. Bricker—R
	Norman Thomas	Socialist	0	80,518	Darlington Hoopes—S
1948	Harry S. Truman	Democratic	303	24,179,345	Alben W. Barkley—D
	Thomas E. Dewey	Republican	189	21,991,291	Earl Warren—R
	J. Strom Thurmond	States' Rights Dem.	39	1,176,125	Fielding L. Wright—SR
	Henry A. Wallace	Progressive	0	1,157,326	Glen Taylor—Prog
	Norman Thomas	Socialist	0	139,572	Tucker P. Smith—S
1952	Dwight D. Eisenhower	Republican	442	33,936,234	Richard M. Nixon—R
	Adlai E. Stevenson	Democratic	89	27,314,992	John J. Sparkman—D
1956	Dwight D. Eisenhower	Republican	457	35,590,472	Richard M. Nixon—R
	Adlai E. Stevenson	Democratic	73[20]	26,022,752	Estes Kefauver—D
1960	John F. Kennedy[21]	Democratic	303	34,226,731	Lyndon B. Johnson—D
	Richard M. Nixon	Republican	219[22]	34,108,157	Henry Cabot Lodge—R
1964	Lyndon B. Johnson	Democratic	486	43,129,484	Hubert H. Humphrey—D
	Barry M. Goldwater	Republican	52	27,178,188	William E. Miller—R
1968	Richard M. Nixon	Republican	301	31,785,480	Spiro T. Agnew—R
	Hubert H. Humphrey	Democratic	191	31,275,166	Edmund S. Muskie—D
	George C. Wallace	American Independent	46	9,906,473	Curtis F. LeMay—AI
1972	Richard M. Nixon[23]	Republican	520[24]	47,169,911	Spiro T. Agnew—R
	George McGovern	Democratic	17	29,170,383	Sargent Shriver—D
	John G. Schmitz	American	0	1,099,482	Thomas J. Anderson—A
1976	Jimmy Carter	Democratic	297	40,830,763	Walter F. Mondale—D
	Gerald R. Ford	Republican	240[25]	39,147,973	Robert J. Dole—R
	Eugene J. McCarthy	Independent	0	756,631	None

Year	Presidential candidate	Party	Electoral votes	Popular votes	Vice-presidential candidate and party
1980	Ronald Reagan	Republican	489	43,899,248	George Bush—R
	Jimmy Carter	Democratic	49	36,481,435	Walter F. Mondale—D
	John B. Anderson	Independent	0	5,719,437	Patrick J. Lucey—I
1984	Ronald Reagan	Republican	525	54,455,075	George Bush—R
	Walter F. Mondale	Democratic	13	37,577,185	Geraldine A. Ferraro—D
1988	George H. Bush	Republican	426	48,886,097	J. Danforth Quayle—R
	Michael S. Dukakis	Democratic	111[26]	41,809,074	Lloyd Bentsen—D
1992	William J. Clinton	Democratic	370	44,909,889	Albert A. Gore, J.—D
	George H. Bush	Republican	168	39,104,545	J. Danforth Quayle—R
	H. Ross Perot	Independent	0	19,742,267	James B. Stockdale—I
1996	William J. Clinton	Democratic	379	47,402,357	Albert A. Gore, Jr.—D
	Robert J. Dole	Republican	159	39,198,755	Jack F. Kemp—R
	H. Ross Perot	Reform Party[27]	0	8,085,402	Pat Choate—RP[27]
2000	George W. Bush	Republican	271	50,455,156	Richard B. Cheney—R
	Albert A. Gore	Democratic	266[28]	50,992,335	Joseph I. Lieberman—D
	Ralph Nader	Green Party	0	2,882,897	Winona LaDuke—GP

1. Only 10 states participated in the election. The New York legislature chose no electors, and North Carolina and Rhode Island had not yet ratified the Constitution. 2. As Jefferson and Burr were tied, the House of Representatives chose the president. In a vote by states, 10 votes were cast for Jefferson, 4 for Burr; 2 votes were not cast. 3. As no candidate had an electoral-vote majority, the House of Representatives chose the president from the first three. In a vote by states, 13 votes were cast for Adams, 7 for Jackson, and 4 for Crawford. 4. The Antimasonic Party on Sept. 26, 1831, was the first party to hold a nominating convention to choose candidates for president and vice president. 5. As Johnson did not have an electoral-vote majority, the Senate chose him 33–14 over Granger, the others being legally out of the race. 6. Harrison died April 4, 1841, and Tyler succeeded him April 6. 7. Taylor died July 9, 1850, and Fillmore succeeded him July 10. 8. Also known as the Know-Nothing Party. 9. Lincoln died April 15, 1865, and Johnson succeeded him the same day. 10. Name adopted by the Republican National Convention of 1864. Johnson was a War Democrat. 11. 23 Southern electoral votes were excluded. 12. See Election of 1872 in Unusual Voting Results. 13. See Election of 1876 in Unusual Voting Results. 14. Garfield died Sept. 19, 1881, and Arthur succeeded him Sept. 20. 15. Members of People's Party were called Populists. 16. McKinley died Sept. 14, 1901, and Roosevelt succeeded him the same day. 17. James S. Sherman, Republican candidate for vice president, died Oct. 30, 1912, and the Republican electoral votes were cast for Butler. 18. Harding died Aug. 2, 1923, and Coolidge succeeded him Aug. 3. 19. Roosevelt died April 12, 1945, and Truman succeeded him the same day. 20. One electoral vote from Alabama was cast for Walter B. Jones. 21. Kennedy died Nov. 22, 1963, and Johnson succeeded him the same day. 22. Sen. Harry F. Byrd received 15 electoral votes. 23. Nixon resigned Aug. 9, 1974, and Gerald R. Ford succeeded him the same day. 24. One electoral vote from Virginia was cast for John Hospers, Libertarian Party. 25. One electoral vote from Washington was cast for Ronald Reagan. 26. One electoral vote from West Virginia was cast for Lloyd Bentsen. 27. Perot helped establish the Reform Party following his defeat in the 1992 election. 28. In the electoral college vote on Dec. 18, 2000, one Gore elector from the District of Columbia left her ballot blank to protest the city's lack of representation in Congress, leaving Gore with 266 electoral votes instead of 267.

The Closest Presidential Races

Although the 2000 presidential race was extremely close, there have been others that were also too close to call immediately after the election. Indeed, the results of the Nov. 7 election in 1876 were not known until March 2, 1877, just three days before the inauguration. More recently, John F. Kennedy's defeat of Richard M. Nixon in 1960 wasn't official until noon the following day.

President	Electoral votes	Popular votes
1800[1]		
Thomas Jefferson (Dem.-Rep.)	73	—
Aaron Burr (Dem.-Rep.)	73	—
John Adams (Federalist)	65	—
Charles C. Pinckney (Federalist)	64	—
John Jay (Federalist)	1	—
1824[2]		
John Quincy Adams[3]	84	—
Andrew Jackson[3]	99	—
William H. Crawford[3]	41	—
Henry Clay[3]	37	—
1876		
Rutherford B. Hayes (R)	185	4,033,768
Samuel J. Tilden (D)	184	4,285,992

President	Electoral votes	Popular votes
1880		
James A. Garfield (R)	214	4,449,053
Winfield S. Hancock (D)	155	4,442,035
1916		
Woodrow Wilson (D)	277	9,129,606
Charles E. Hughes (R)	254	8,538,221
1960		
John F. Kennedy (D)	303	34,226,731
Richard M. Nixon (R)	219	34,108,157
1968		
Richard M. Nixon (R)	301	31,785,480
Hubert H. Humphrey (R)	191	31,275,166
George C. Wallace[4]	46	9,906,473
1976		
Jimmy Carter (D)	297	40,830,763
Gerald R. Ford (R)	240	39,147,973

1. As Jefferson and Burr were tied, the House of Representatives chose the president. In a vote by states, 10 votes were cast for Jefferson, 4 for Burr; 2 votes were not cast. For the original method of electing the president and vice president (elections of 1789, 1792, 1796, and 1800), see Article II, Section 1, of the Constitution. 2. As no candidate had an electoral vote majority, the House of Representatives chose the president from the first three. In a vote by states, 13 votes were cast for Adams, 7 for Jackson, and 4 for Crawford. 3. No party. 4. American Independent.

Plurality and Majority

In order to win a plurality, a candidate must receive a greater number of votes than anyone running against him. If he receives 50 votes, for example, and two other candidates receive 49 and 2, he will have a plurality of one vote over his closest opponent.

However, a candidate does not have a majority unless he receives more than 50% of the total votes cast. In the example above, the candidate does not have a majority, because his 50 votes are less than 50% of the 101 votes cast.

Presidents Elected Without a Majority

Fifteen candidates (three of them twice) have become president of the United States with a popular vote less than 50% of the total cast. It should be noted, however, that in elections before 1872, presidential electors were not chosen by popular vote in all states. Adams's election in 1824 was by the House of Representatives, which chose him over Jackson, who had a plurality of both electoral and popular votes, but not a majority in the electoral college.

The "minority" presidents are listed below.

Year	President	Electoral percent	Popular percent	Year	President	Electoral percent	Popular percent
1824	John Q. Adams	31.8%	29.8%	1892	Grover Cleveland (D)	62.4%	46.0%
1844	James K. Polk (D)	61.8	49.3	1912	Woodrow Wilson (D)	81.9	41.8
1848	Zachary Taylor (W)	56.2	47.3	1916	Woodrow Wilson (D)	52.1	49.3
1856	James Buchanan (D)	58.7	45.3	1948	Harry S. Truman (D)	57.1	49.5
1860	Abraham Lincoln (R)	59.4	39.9	1960	John F. Kennedy (D)	56.4	49.7
1876	Rutherford B. Hayes (R)	50.1	47.9	1968	Richard M. Nixon (R)	56.1	43.4
1880	James A. Garfield (R)	57.9	48.3	1992	William J. Clinton (D)	68.8	43.0
1884	Grover Cleveland (D)	54.6	48.8	1996	William J. Clinton (D)	70.4	49.0
1888	Benjamin Harrison (R)	58.1	47.8	2000	George W. Bush (R)	50.3	47.8

National Voter Turnout in Federal Elections: 1960–2000

Year	Voting-age population	Voter registration	Voter turnout	Turnout of voting-age population (percent)
2000	205,815,000	n.a.	105,399,313	51.2%
1998	200,929,000	141,850,558	73,117,022	36.4
1996	196,511,000	146,211,960	96,456,345	49.1
1994	193,650,000	130,292,822	75,105,860	38.8
1992	189,529,000	133,821,178	104,405,155	55.1
1990	185,812,000	121,105,630	67,859,189	36.5
1988	182,778,000	126,379,628	91,594,693	50.1
1986	178,566,000	118,399,984	64,991,128	36.4
1984	174,466,000	124,150,614	92,652,680	53.1
1982	169,938,000	110,671,225	67,615,576	39.8
1980	164,597,000	113,043,734	86,515,221	52.6
1978	158,373,000	103,291,265	58,917,938	37.2
1976	152,309,190	105,037,986	81,555,789	53.6
1974	146,336,000	96,199,020[1]	55,943,834	38.2
1972	140,776,000	97,328,541	77,718,554	55.2
1970	124,498,000	82,496,747[2]	58,014,338	46.6
1968	120,328,186	81,658,180	73,211,875	60.8
1966	116,132,000	76,288,283[3]	56,188,046	48.4
1964	114,090,000	73,715,818	70,644,592	61.9
1962	112,423,000	65,393,751[4]	53,141,227	47.3
1960	109,159,000	64,833,096[5]	68,838,204	63.1

n.a. = not available. NOTE: Presidential election years are in boldface. 1. Registrations from Iowa not included. 2. Registrations from Iowa and Mo. not included. 3. Registrations from Iowa, Kans., Miss., Mo., Nebr., and Wyo. not included. D.C. did not have independent status. 4. Registrations from Ala., Alaska, D.C., Iowa, Kans., Ky., Miss., Mo., Nebr., N.C., N.D., Okla., S.D., Wis., and Wyo. not included. 5. Registrations from Ala., Alaska, D.C., Iowa, Kans., Ky., Miss., Mo., Nebr., N.M., N.C., N.D., Okla., S.D., Wis., and Wyo. not included. Source: Federal Election Commission. Data drawn from Congressional Research Service reports, Election Data Services Inc., and State Election Offices.

Facts About Elections

Candidate with highest popular vote: Reagan (1984), 54,455,075.

Candidate with highest electoral vote: Reagan (1984), 525.

Candidate carrying most states: Nixon (1972) and Reagan (1984), 49.

Candidate running most times: Norman Thomas (Socialist Party), six (1928, 1932, 1936, 1940, 1944, 1948).

Candidate elected, defeated, then reelected: Cleveland (1884, 1888, 1892).

Presidents

	Name and (party)[1][2]	Term	State of birth	Born	Died	Religion	Age at inaug.	Age at death
1.	Washington (F)[2]	1789–1797	Va.	2/22/1732	12/14/1799	Episcopalian	57	67
2.	J. Adams (F)	1797–1801	Mass.	10/30/1735	7/4/1826	Unitarian	61	90
3.	Jefferson (DR)	1801–1809	Va.	4/13/1743	7/4/1826	Deist	57	83
4.	Madison (DR)	1809–1817	Va.	3/16/1751	6/28/1836	Episcopalian	57	85
5.	Monroe (DR)	1817–1825	Va.	4/28/1758	7/4/1831	Episcopalian	58	73
6.	J. Q. Adams (DR)	1825–1829	Mass.	7/11/1767	2/23/1848	Unitarian	57	80
7.	Jackson (D)	1829–1837	S.C.	3/15/1767	6/8/1845	Presbyterian	61	78
8.	Van Buren (D)	1837–1841	N.Y.	12/5/1782	7/24/1862	Reformed Dutch	54	79
9.	W. H. Harrison (W)[3]	1841	Va.	2/9/1773	4/4/1841	Episcopalian	68	68
10.	Tyler (W)	1841–1845	Va.	3/29/1790	1/18/1862	Episcopalian	51	71
11.	Polk (D)	1845–1849	N.C.	11/2/1795	6/15/1849	Methodist	49	53
12.	Taylor (W)[3]	1849–1850	Va.	11/24/1784	7/9/1850	Episcopalian	64	65
13.	Fillmore (W)	1850–1853	N.Y.	1/7/1800	3/8/1874	Unitarian	50	74
14.	Pierce (D)	1853–1857	N.H.	11/23/1804	10/8/1869	Episcopalian	48	64
15.	Buchanan (D)	1857–1861	Pa.	4/23/1791	6/1/1868	Presbyterian	65	77
16.	Lincoln (R)[4]	1861–1865	Ky.	2/12/1809	4/15/1865	Liberal	52	56
17.	A. Johnson (U)[5]	1865–1869	N.C.	12/29/1808	7/31/1875	[6]	56	66
18.	Grant (R)	1869–1877	Ohio	4/27/1822	7/23/1885	Methodist	46	63
19.	Hayes (R)	1877–1881	Ohio	10/4/1822	1/17/1893	Methodist	54	70
20.	Garfield (R)[4]	1881	Ohio	11/19/1831	9/19/1881	Disciples of Christ	49	49
21.	Arthur (R)	1881–1885	Vt.	10/5/1830	11/18/1886	Episcopalian	50	56
22.	Cleveland (D)	1885–1889	N.J.	3/18/1837	6/24/1908	Presbyterian	47	71
23.	B. Harrison (R)	1889–1893	Ohio	8/20/1833	3/13/1901	Presbyterian	55	67
24.	Cleveland (D)[7]	1893–1897	—	—	—	—	55	—
25.	McKinley (R)[4]	1897–1901	Ohio	1/29/1843	9/14/1901	Methodist	54	58
26.	T. Roosevelt (R)	1901–1909	N.Y.	10/27/1858	1/6/1919	Reformed Dutch	42	60
27.	Taft (R)	1909–1913	Ohio	9/15/1857	3/8/1930	Unitarian	51	72
28.	Wilson (D)	1913–1921	Va.	12/28/1856	2/3/1924	Presbyterian	56	67
29.	Harding (R)[3]	1921–1923	Ohio	11/2/1865	8/2/1923	Baptist	55	57
30.	Coolidge (R)	1923–1929	Vt.	7/4/1872	1/5/1933	Congregationalist	51	60
31.	Hoover (R)	1929–1933	Iowa	8/10/1874	10/20/1964	Quaker	54	90
32.	F. D. Roosevelt (D)[3]	1933–1945	N.Y.	1/30/1882	4/12/1945	Episcopalian	51	63
33.	Truman (D)	1945–1953	Mo.	5/8/1884	12/26/1972	Baptist	60	88
34.	Eisenhower (R)	1953–1961	Tex.	10/14/1890	3/28/1969	Presbyterian	62	78
35.	Kennedy (D)[4]	1961–1963	Mass.	5/29/1917	11/22/1963	Roman Catholic	43	46
36.	L. B. Johnson (D)	1963–1969	Tex.	8/27/1908	1/22/1973	Disciples of Christ	55	64
37.	Nixon (R)[8]	1969–1974	Calif.	1/9/1913	4/22/1994	Quaker	56	81
38.	Ford (R)	1974–1977	Neb.	7/14/1913	—	Episcopalian	61	—
39.	Carter (D)	1977–1981	Ga.	10/1/1924	—	Southern Baptist	52	—
40.	Reagan (R)	1981–1989	Ill.	2/6/1911	—	Disciples of Christ	69	—
41.	G. H. W. Bush (R)	1989–1993	Mass.	6/12/1924	—	Episcopalian	64	—
42.	Clinton (D)	1993–2001	Ark.	8/19/1946	—	Baptist	46	—
43.	G. W. Bush (R)	2001–2005	Conn.	7/6/46	—	Methodist	54	—

1. F—Federalist; DR—Democratic-Republican; D—Democratic; W—Whig; R—Republican; U—Union. 2. No party for first election. The party system in the U.S. made its appearance during Washington's first term. 3. Died in office. 4. Assassinated in office. 5. The Republican National Convention of 1864 adopted the name Union Party. It renominated Lincoln for president; for vice president it nominated Johnson, a War Democrat. Although frequently listed as a Republican vice president and president, Johnson undoubtedly considered himself strictly a member of the Union Party. When that party broke apart after 1868, he returned to the Democratic Party. 6. Johnson was not a professed church member; however, he admired the Baptist principles of church government. 7. Second nonconsecutive term. 8. Resigned Aug. 9, 1974.

Vice Presidents

	Name and (party)[1][2]	Term	State of birth	Birth and death dates	President served under
1.	John Adams (F)[2]	1789–1797	Massachusetts	1735–1826	Washington
2.	Thomas Jefferson (DR)	1797–1801	Virginia	1743–1826	J. Adams
3.	Aaron Burr (DR)	1801–1805	New Jersey	1756–1836	Jefferson
4.	George Clinton (DR)[3]	1805–1812	New York	1739–1812	Jefferson and Madison
5.	Elbridge Gerry (DR)[3]	1813–1814	Massachusetts	1744–1814	Madison
6.	Daniel D. Tompkins (DR)	1817–1825	New York	1774–1825	Monroe
7.	John C. Calhoun[4]	1825–1832	South Carolina	1782–1850	J. Q. Adams and Jackson
8.	Martin Van Buren (D)	1833–1837	New York	1782–1862	Jackson
9.	Richard M. Johnson (D)	1837–1841	Kentucky	1780–1850	Van Buren
10.	John Tyler (W)[5]	1841	Virginia	1790–1862	W. H. Harrison
11.	George M. Dallas (D)	1845–1849	Pennsylvania	1792–1864	Polk
12.	Millard Fillmore (W)[5]	1849–1850	New York	1800–1874	Taylor
13.	William R. King (D)[3]	1853	North Carolina	1786–1853	Pierce

Name and (party)[1]	Term	State of birth	Birth and death dates	President served under
14. John C. Breckinridge (D)	1857–1861	Kentucky	1821–1875	Buchanan
15. Hannibal Hamlin (R)	1861–1865	Maine	1809–1891	Lincoln
16. Andrew Johnson (U)[5]	1865	North Carolina	1808–1875	Lincoln
17. Schuyler Colfax (R)	1869–1873	New York	1823–1885	Grant
18. Henry Wilson (R)[3]	1873–1875	New Hampshire	1812–1875	Grant
19. William A. Wheeler (R)	1877–1881	New York	1819–1887	Hayes
20. Chester A. Arthur (R)[5]	1881	Vermont	1830–1886	Garfield
21. Thomas A. Hendricks (D)[3]	1885	Ohio	1819–1885	Cleveland
22. Levi P. Morton (R)	1889–1893	Vermont	1824–1920	B. Harrison
23. Adlai E. Stevenson (D)	1893–1897	Kentucky	1835–1914	Cleveland
24. Garrett A. Hobart (R)[3]	1897–1899	New Jersey	1844–1899	McKinley
25. Theodore Roosevelt (R)[5]	1901	New York	1858–1919	McKinley
26. Charles W. Fairbanks (R)	1905–1909	Ohio	1852–1918	T. Roosevelt
27. James S. Sherman (R)[3]	1909–1912	New York	1855–1912	Taft
28. Thomas R. Marshall (D)	1913–1921	Indiana	1854–1925	Wilson
29. Calvin Coolidge (R)[5]	1921–1923	Vermont	1872–1933	Harding
30. Charles G. Dawes (R)	1925–1929	Ohio	1865–1951	Coolidge
31. Charles Curtis (R)	1929–1933	Kansas	1860–1936	Hoover
32. John N. Garner (D)	1933–1941	Texas	1868–1967	F. D. Roosevelt
33. Henry A. Wallace (D)	1941–1945	Iowa	1888–1965	F. D. Roosevelt
34. Harry S. Truman (D)[5]	1945	Missouri	1884–1972	F. D. Roosevelt
35. Alben W. Barkley (D)	1949–1953	Kentucky	1877–1956	Truman
36. Richard M. Nixon (R)	1953-1961	California	1913–1994	Eisenhower
37. Lyndon B. Johnson (D)[5]	1961–1963	Texas	1908–1973	Kennedy
38. Hubert H. Humphrey (D)	1965–1969	South Dakota	1911–1978	L. B. Johnson
39. Spiro T. Agnew (R)[6]	1969–1973	Maryland	1918–1996	Nixon
40. Gerald R. Ford (R)[7]	1973–1974	Nebraska	1913–	Nixon
41. Nelson A. Rockefeller (R)[8]	1974–1977	Maine	1908–1979	Ford
42. Walter F. Mondale (D)	1977–1981	Minnesota	1928–	Carter
43. George Bush (R)	1981–1989	Massachusetts	1924–	Reagan
44. J. Danforth Quayle (R)	1989–1993	Indiana	1947–	G. H. W. Bush
45. Albert A. Gore, Jr. (D)	1993– 2001	Washington, D.C.	1948–	Clinton
46. Richard B. Cheney (R)	2001–2005	Nebraska	1941–	G. W. Bush

1. F—Federalist; DR—Democratic-Republican; D—Democratic; W—Whig; R—Republican; U—Union. 2. No party for first election. The party system in the U.S. made its appearance during Washington's first term as president. 3. Died in office. 4. Democratic-Republican with J. Q. Adams; Democratic with Jackson. Calhoun resigned in 1832 to become a U.S. senator. 5. Succeeded to presidency on death of president. Prior to the passage of the 25th Amendment (ratified Feb. 10, 1967), there were no provisions for filling a vacancy in the vice presidency. In the event of a vacancy, the president pro tempore took over most of the vice president's duties. 6. Resigned Oct. 10, 1973, after pleading no contest to federal income tax evasion charges. 7. Nominated by Nixon on Oct. 12, 1973, under provisions of 25th Amendment. Confirmed by Congress on Dec. 6, 1973, and was sworn in same day. He became president Aug. 9, 1974, upon Nixon's resignation. 8. Nominated by Ford Aug. 20, 1974; confirmed by Congress on Dec. 19, 1974, and was sworn in same day.

Presidential Libraries

These are not traditional libraries, but rather repositories for preserving and making available the papers, records, and other historical materials of the presidents since Herbert Hoover. The presidential library system formally began in 1939, when President Franklin Roosevelt donated his personal and presidential papers to the federal government.

Hoover Library
210 Parkside Drive
P.O. Box 488
West Branch, IA 52358-0488
http://hoover.nara.gov

Roosevelt Library
4079 Albany Post Road
Hyde Park, NY 12538-1999
http://www.fdrlibrary.marist.edu/

Truman Library
500 West U.S. Highway 24
Independence, MO 64050-1798
http://www.trumanlibrary.org

Eisenhower Library
200 SE 4th Street
Abilene, KS 67410-2900
http://www.eisenhower.utexas.edu

Kennedy Library
Columbia Point
Boston, MA 02125-3398
http://www.jfklibrary.org

Johnson Library
2313 Red River Street
Austin, TX 78705-5702
http://www.lbjlib.utexas.edu

The Nixon Project[1]
National Archives at College Park
8601 Adelphi Road
College Park, MD 20740-6001
http://www.nara.gov/nixon/

Ford Library
1000 Beal Avenue
Ann Arbor, MI 48109-2114
http://www.ford.utexas.edu

Carter Library
441 Freedom Parkway
Atlanta, GA 30307-1498
http://carterlibrary.galileo.peachnet.edu

Reagan Library
40 Presidential Drive
Simi Valley, CA 93065-0666
http://www.reagan.utexas.edu

Bush Library
1000 George Bush Drive West
College Station, TX 77845
http://bushlibrary.tamu.edu/

1. The Nixon Project is not affiliated with the Richard Nixon Library and Birthplace in Yorba Linda, Calif., a private institution that was established by Nixon in 1990. *Source:* National Archives and Records Administration; Web: www.nara.gov/nara/president.

Wives and Children of the Presidents

President	Wife's name	Year and place of wife's birth	Married	Wife died	Children[1] Sons	Daughters
Washington	Martha Dandridge Custis	1732, Va.	1759	1802	—	—
John Adams	Abigail Smith	1744, Mass.	1764	1818	3	2
Jefferson [2]	Martha Wayles Skelton	1748, Va.	1772	1782	1	5
Madison	Dorothy "Dolley" Payne Todd	1768, N.C.	1794	1849	—	—
Monroe	Elizabeth "Eliza" Kortright	1768, N.Y.	1786	1830	—	2
J. Q. Adams	Louisa Catherine Johnson	1775, England	1797	1852	3	1
Jackson	Rachel Donelson Robards	1767, Va.	1791	1828	—	—
Van Buren	Hannah Hoes	1788, N.Y.	1807	1819	4	—
W. H. Harrison	Anna Symmes	1775, N.J.	1795	1864	6	4
Tyler	Letitia Christian	1790, Va.	1813	1842	3	4
	Julia Gardiner	1820, N.Y.	1844	1889	5	2
Polk	Sarah Childress	1803, Tenn.	1824	1891	—	—
Taylor	Margaret Smith	1788, Md.	1810	1852	1	5
Fillmore	Abigail Powers	1798, N.Y.	1826	1853	1	1
	Caroline Carmichael McIntosh	1813, N.J.	1858	1881	—	—
Pierce	Jane Means Appleton	1806, N.H.	1834	1863	3	—
Buchanan	(Unmarried)	—	—	—	—	—
Lincoln	Mary Todd	1818, Ky.	1842	1882	4	—
A. Johnson	Eliza McCardle	1810, Tenn.	1827	1876	3	2
Grant	Julia Dent	1826, Mo.	1848	1902	3	1
Hayes	Lucy Ware Webb	1831, Ohio	1852	1889	7	1
Garfield	Lucretia Rudolph	1832, Ohio	1858	1918	5	2
Arthur	Ellen Lewis Herndon	1837, Va.	1859	1880	2	1
Cleveland	Frances Folsom	1864, N.Y.	1886	1947	2	3
B. Harrison	Caroline Lavinia Scott	1832, Ohio	1853	1892	1	1
	Mary Scott Lord Dimmick	1858, Pa.	1896	1948	—	1
McKinley	Ida Saxton	1847, Ohio	1871	1907	—	2
T. Roosevelt	Alice Hathaway Lee	1861, Mass.	1880	1884	—	1
	Edith Kermit Carow	1861, Conn.	1886	1948	4	1
Taft	Helen Herron	1861, Ohio	1886	1943	2	1
Wilson	Ellen Louise Axson	1860, Ga.	1885	1914	—	3
	Edith Bolling Galt	1872, Va.	1915	1961	—	—
Harding	Florence Kling DeWolfe	1860, Ohio	1891	1924	—	—
Coolidge	Grace Anna Goodhue	1879, Vt.	1905	1957	2	—
Hoover	Lou Henry	1875, Iowa	1899	1944	2	—
F. D. Roosevelt	(Anna) Eleanor Roosevelt	1884, N.Y.	1905	1962	5	1
Truman	Bess Wallace	1885, Mo.	1919	1982	—	1
Eisenhower	Mamie Geneva Doud	1896, Iowa	1916	1979	2	—
Kennedy	Jacqueline Lee Bouvier	1929, N.Y.	1953	1994	2	1
L. B. Johnson	Claudia Alta "Lady Bird" Taylor	1912, Tex.	1934	—	—	2
Nixon	Thelma Catherine "Pat" Ryan	1912, Nev.	1940	1993	—	2
Ford	Elizabeth "Betty" Bloomer Warren	1918, Ill.	1948	—	3	1
Carter	Rosalynn Smith	1928, Ga.	1946	—	3	1
Reagan	Jane Wyman	1914, Mo.	1940[3]	—	1[4]	1
	Nancy Davis	1921 (?)[5], N.Y.	1952	—	1	1
G. H. W. Bush	Barbara Pierce	1925, N.Y.	1945	—	4	2
Clinton	Hillary Rodham	1947, Ill.	1975	—	—	1
G. W. Bush	Laura Welch	1946, Tex.	1977	—	—	2

1. Includes children who died in infancy. 2. Number of children listed here reflects only children Jefferson had with Martha Wayles Skelton. Scientists and historians agree, based on DNA evidence, that Jefferson probably fathered at least one child with slave Sally Hemings. 3. Divorced in 1948. 4. Adopted. 5. Birthday officially given as 1923 but her high school and college records show 1921 for year of birth.

Biographies of the Presidents

GEORGE WASHINGTON was born on Feb. 22, 1732 (Feb. 11, 1731/2, old style) in Westmoreland County, Va. While in his teens, he trained as a surveyor, and at the age of 20 he was appointed adjutant in the Va. militia. For the next three years, he fought in the wars against the French and Indians, serving as Gen. Edward Braddock's aide in the disastrous campaign against Ft. Duquesne. In 1759, he resigned from the militia, married Martha Dandridge Custis, a widow with children, and settled down as a gentleman farmer at Mount Vernon, Va.

As a militiaman, Washington had been exposed to the arrogance of the British officers, and his experience as a planter with British commercial restrictions increased his anti-British sentiment. He opposed the Stamp Act of 1765 and after 1770 became increasingly prominent in organizing resistance. A delegate to the Continental Congress, Washington was selected as commander in chief of the Continental Army and took command at Cambridge, Mass., on July 3, 1775.

Inadequately supported and sometimes covertly sabotaged by the Congress, in charge of troops who were inexperienced, badly equipped, and impatient of discipline, Washington conducted the war on the policy of avoiding major engagements with the British and wearing them down by harassing tactics. His able generalship, along with the French alliance and the growing weariness within Britain, brought the war to a conclusion with the surrender of Cornwallis at Yorktown, Va., on Oct. 19, 1781.

The chaotic years under the Articles of Confederation led Washington to return to public life in the hope of promoting the formation of a strong central government. He presided over the Constitutional Convention and yielded to the universal demand that he serve as first president. He was inaugurated on April 30, 1789, in New York, the first national capital. In office, he sought to unite the nation and establish the authority of the new government at home and abroad. Greatly distressed by the emergence of the Hamilton-Jefferson rivalry, Washington worked to maintain neutrality but actually sympathized more with Hamilton. Following his unanimous re-election in 1792, his second term was dominated by the Federalists. His Farewell Address on Sept. 17, 1796 (published but never delivered) rebuked party spirit and warned against "permanent alliances" with foreign powers.

He died at Mount Vernon on Dec. 14, 1799.

JOHN ADAMS born on Oct. 30 (Oct. 19, old style), 1735, at Braintree (now Quincy), Mass. A Harvard graduate, he considered teaching and the ministry but finally turned to law and was admitted to the bar in 1758. Six years later, he married Abigail Smith. He opposed the Stamp Act, served as lawyer for patriots indicted by the British, and by the time of the Continental Congresses, was in the vanguard of the movement for independence. In 1778, he went to France as commissioner. Subsequently he helped negotiate the peace treaty with Britain, and in 1785 became envoy to London. Resigning in 1788, he was elected vice president under Washington and was re-elected in 1792.

Though a Federalist, Adams did not get along with Hamilton, who sought to prevent his election to the presidency in 1796 and thereafter intrigued against his administration. In 1798, Adams's independent policy averted a war with France but completed the break with Hamilton and the right-wing Federalists; at the same time, the enactment of the Alien and Sedition Acts, directed against foreigners and against critics of the government, exasperated the Jeffersonian opposition. The split between Adams and Hamilton resulted in Jefferson's becoming the next president. Adams retired to his home in Quincy. He and Jefferson died on the same day, July 4, 1826, the 50th anniversary of the adoption of the Declaration of Independence.

His *Defence of the Constitutions of Government of the United States* (1787) contains original and striking, if conservative, political ideas.

THOMAS JEFFERSON was born on April 13 (April 2, old style), 1743, at Shadwell in Goochland (now Albemarle) County, Va. A William and Mary graduate, he studied law, but from the start showed an interest in science and philosophy. His literary skill and political clarity brought him to the forefront of the revolutionary movement in Virginia. As delegate to the Continental Congress, he drafted the Declaration of Independence. In 1776, he entered the Virginia House of Delegates and initiated a comprehensive reform program for the abolition of feudal survivals in land tenure and the separation of church and state.

In 1779, he became governor, but constitutional limitations on his power, combined with his own lack of executive energy, caused an unsatisfactory administration, culminating in Jefferson's virtual abdication when the British invaded Virginia in 1781. He retired to his beautiful home at Monticello, Va., to his family. His wife, Martha Wayles Skelton, whom he married in 1772, died in 1782.

Jefferson's *Notes on Virginia* (1784–85) illustrate his many-faceted interests, his limitless intellectual curiosity, his deep faith in agrarian democracy. Sent to Congress in 1783, he helped lay down the decimal system and drafted basic reports on the organization of the western lands. In 1785 he was appointed minister to France, where the Anglo-Saxon liberalism he had drawn from John Locke, the British philosopher, was stimulated by contact with the thought that would soon ferment in the French Revolution. In 1789, Washington appointed him Secretary of State. While favoring the Constitution and a strengthened central government, Jefferson came to believe that Hamilton contemplated the establishment of a monarchy. Growing differences resulted in Jefferson's resignation on Dec. 31, 1793.

Elected vice president in 1796, Jefferson continued to serve as spiritual leader of the opposition to Federalism, particularly to the repressive Alien and Sedition Acts. He was elected president in 1801 by the House of Representatives as a result of Hamilton's decision to throw the Federalist votes to him rather than to Aaron Burr, who had tied him in electoral votes. He was the first president to be inaugurated in Washington, which he had helped to design.

The purchase of Louisiana from France in 1803, though in violation of Jefferson's earlier constitutional scruples, was the most notable act of his administration. Re-elected in 1804, with the Federalist Charles C. Pinckney opposing him, Jefferson tried desperately to keep the United States out of the Napoleonic Wars in Europe, employing to this end the unpopular embargo policy.

After his retirement to Monticello in 1809, he developed his interest in education, founding the University of Virginia and watching its development with never-flagging interest. He died at Monticello on July 4, 1826. Jefferson had an enormous variety of interests and skills, ranging from education and science to architecture and music.

JAMES MADISON was born in Port Conway, Va., on March 16, 1751 (March 5, 1750/1, old style). A Princeton graduate, he joined the struggle for independence on his return to Virginia in 1771. In the 1770s and 1780s he was active in state politics, where he championed the Jefferson reform program, and in the Continental Congress. Madison was influential in the Constitutional Convention as leader of the group favoring a strong central government and as recorder of the debates; and he subsequently wrote, in collaboration with Alexander Hamilton and John Jay, the *Federalist* papers to aid the campaign for the adoption of the Constitution.

Serving in the new Congress, Madison soon emerged as the leader in the House of the men who opposed Hamilton's financial program and his pro-British leanings in foreign policy. Retiring from Congress in 1797, he continued to be active in Virginia and drafted the Virginia Resolution protesting the Alien and Sedition Acts. His intimacy with Jefferson made him the natural choice for Secretary of State in 1801.

In 1809, Madison succeeded Jefferson as president, defeating Charles C. Pinckney. His wife, Dolley Payne Todd, whom he married in 1794, brought a new social sparkle to the executive mansion. In the meantime, increasing tension with Britain culminated in the War of 1812—a war for which the United States was unprepared and for which Madison lacked the executive talent to clear out incompetence and mobilize the nation's energies. Madison was re-elected in 1812, running against the Federalist De Witt Clinton. In 1814, the British actually captured Washington and forced Madison to flee to Virginia.

Madison's domestic program capitulated to the Hamiltonian policies that he had resisted 20 years before and he now signed bills to establish a United States Bank and a higher tariff.

After his presidency, he remained in retirement in Virginia until his death on June 28, 1836.

JAMES MONROE

JAMES MONROE was born on April 28, 1758, in Westmoreland County, Va. A William and Mary graduate, he served in the army during the first years of the Revolution and was wounded at Trenton. He then entered Virginia politics and later national politics under the sponsorship of Jefferson. In 1786, he married Elizabeth (Eliza) Kortright.

Fearing centralization, Monroe opposed the adoption of the Constitution and, as senator from Virginia, was highly critical of the Hamiltonian program. In 1794, he was appointed minister to France, where his ardent sympathies with the Revolution exceeded the wishes of the State Department. His troubled diplomatic career ended with his recall in 1796. From 1799 to 1802, he was governor of Virginia. In 1803, Jefferson sent him to France to help negotiate the Louisiana Purchase and for the next few years he was active in various negotiations on the Continent.

In 1808, Monroe flirted with the radical wing of the Republican Party, which opposed Madison's candidacy; but the presidential boom came to naught and, after a brief term as governor of Virginia in 1811, Monroe accepted Madison's offer to become Secretary of State. During the War of 1812, he vainly sought a field command and instead served as Secretary of War from September 1814 to March 1815.

Elected president in 1816 over the Federalist Rufus King, and re-elected without opposition in 1820, Monroe, the last of the Virginia dynasty, pursued the course of systematic tranquilization that won for his administrations the name "the era of good feeling." He continued Madison's surrender to the Hamiltonian domestic program, signed the Missouri Compromise, acquired Florida, and with the able assistance of his Secretary of State, John Quincy Adams, promulgated the Monroe Doctrine in 1823, declaring against foreign colonization or intervention in the Americas. He died in New York

City on July 4, 1831, the third president to die on the anniversary of Independence.

JOHN QUINCY ADAMS

JOHN QUINCY ADAMS was born on July 11, 1767, at Braintree (now Quincy), Mass., the son of John Adams, the second president. He spent his early years in Europe with his father, graduated from Harvard, and entered law practice. His anti-Paine newspaper articles won him political attention. In 1794, he became minister to the Netherlands, the first of several diplomatic posts that occupied him until his return to Boston in 1801. In 1797, he married Louisa Catherine Johnson.

In 1803, Adams was elected to the Senate, nominally as a Federalist, but his repeated displays of independence on such issues as the Louisiana Purchase and the embargo caused his party to demand his resignation and ostracize him socially. In 1809, Madison rewarded him for his support of Jefferson by appointing him minister to St. Petersburg. He helped negotiate the Treaty of Ghent in 1814, and in 1815 became minister to London. In 1817 Monroe appointed him Secretary of State where he served with great distinction, gaining Florida from Spain without hostilities and playing an equal part with Monroe in formulating the Monroe Doctrine.

When no presidential candidate received a majority of electoral votes in 1824, Adams, with the support of Henry Clay, was elected by the House in 1825 over Andrew Jackson, who had the original plurality. Adams had ambitious plans of government activity to foster internal improvements and promote the arts and sciences, but congressional obstructionism, combined with his own unwillingness or inability to play the role of a politician, resulted in little being accomplished. After being defeated for re-election by Jackson in 1828, he successfully ran for the House of Representatives in 1830. There, though nominally a Whig, he pursued as ever an independent course. He led the fight to force Congress to receive antislavery petitions and fathered the Smithsonian Institution.

Adams had a stroke while on the floor of the House, and died two days later on Feb. 23, 1848. His long and detailed *Diary* gives a unique picture of the personalities and politics of the times.

ANDREW JACKSON

ANDREW JACKSON was born on March 15, 1767, in what is now generally agreed to be Waxhaw, S.C. After a turbulent boyhood as an orphan and a British prisoner, he moved west to Tennessee, where he soon qualified for law practice but found time for such frontier pleasures as horse racing, cockfighting, and dueling. His marriage to Rachel Donelson Robards in 1791 was complicated by subsequent legal uncertainties about the status of her divorce. During the 1790s, Jackson served in the Tennessee Constitutional Convention, the United States House of Representatives and Senate, and on the Tennessee Supreme Court.

After some years as a country gentleman, living at the Hermitage near Nashville, Jackson in 1812 was given command of Tennessee troops sent against the Creeks. He defeated the Indians at Horseshoe Bend in 1814; subsequently he became a major general and won the Battle of New Orleans over veteran British troops, though after the treaty of peace had been signed at Ghent. In 1818, Jackson invaded Florida, captured Pensacola, and hanged two

Englishmen named Arbuthnot and Ambrister, creating an international incident. A presidential boom began for him in 1821, and to foster it, he returned to the Senate (1823–25). Though he won a plurality of electoral votes in 1824, he lost in the House when Clay threw his strength to Adams. Four years later, he easily defeated Adams.

As president, Jackson greatly expanded the power and prestige of the presidential office and carried through an unprecedented program of domestic reform, vetoing the bill to extend the United States Bank, moving toward a hard-money currency policy, and checking the program of federal internal improvements. He also vindicated federal authority against South Carolina with its doctrine of nullification and against France on the question of debts. The support given his policies by the workingmen of the East as well as by the farmers of the East, West, and South resulted in his triumphant re-election in 1832 over Clay.

After watching the inauguration of his handpicked successor, Martin Van Buren, Jackson retired to the Hermitage, where he maintained a lively interest in national affairs until his death on June 8, 1845.

MARTIN VAN BUREN was born on Dec. 5, 1782, at Kinderhook, N.Y. After graduating from the village school, he became a law clerk, entered practice in 1803, and soon became active in state politics as state senator and attorney general. In 1820, he was elected to the United States Senate. He threw the support of his efficient political organization, known as the Albany Regency, to William H. Crawford in 1824 and to Jackson in 1828. After leading the opposition to Adams's administration in the Senate, he served briefly as governor of New York (1828–1829) and resigned to become Jackson's Secretary of State. He was soon on close personal terms with Jackson and played an important part in the Jacksonian program.

In 1832, Van Buren became vice president; in 1836, president. The Panic of 1837 overshadowed his term. He attributed it to the overexpansion of the credit and favored the establishment of an independent treasury as repository for the federal funds. In 1840, he established a 10-hour day on public works. Defeated by Harrison in 1840, he was the leading contender for the Democratic nomination in 1844 until he publicly opposed immediate annexation of Texas, and was subsequently beaten by the Southern delegations at the Baltimore convention. This incident increased his growing misgivings about the slave power.

After working behind the scenes among the antislavery Democrats, Van Buren joined in the movement that led to the Free-Soil Party and became its candidate for president in 1848. He subsequently returned to the Democratic Party while continuing to object to its pro-Southern policy. He died in Kinderhook on July 24, 1862. His *Autobiography* throws valuable sidelights on the political history of the times.

His wife, Hannah Hoes, whom he married in 1807, died in 1819.

WILLIAM HENRY HARRISON was born in Charles City County, Va., on Feb. 9, 1773. Joining the army in 1791, he was active in Indian fighting in the Northwest, became secretary of the Northwest

Territory in 1798 and governor of Indiana in 1800. He married Anna Symmes in 1795. Growing discontent over white encroachments on Indian lands led to the formation of an Indian alliance under Tecumseh to resist further aggressions. In 1811, Harrison won a nominal victory over the Indians at Tippecanoe and in 1813 a more decisive one at the Battle of the Thames, where Tecumseh was killed.

After resigning from the army in 1814, Harrison had an obscure career in politics and diplomacy, ending up 20 years later as a county recorder in Ohio. Nominated for president in 1835 as a military hero whom the conservative politicians hoped to be able to control, he ran surprisingly well against Van Buren in 1836. Four years later, he defeated Van Buren but caught pneumonia and died in Washington on April 4, 1841, a month after his inauguration. Harrison was the first president to die in office.

JOHN TYLER was born in Charles City County, Va., on March 29, 1790. A William and Mary graduate, he entered law practice and politics, serving in the House of Representatives (1817–21), as governor of Virginia (1825–27), and as senator (1827–36). A strict constructionist, he supported Crawford in 1824 and Jackson in 1828, but broke with Jackson over his United States Bank policy and became a member of the Southern state-rights group that cooperated with the Whigs. In 1836, he resigned from the Senate rather than follow instructions from the Virginia legislature to vote for a resolution expunging censure of Jackson from the Senate record.

Elected vice president on the Whig ticket in 1840, Tyler succeeded to the presidency on Harrison's death. His strict-constructionist views soon caused a split with the Henry Clay wing of the Whig party and a stalemate on domestic questions. Tyler's more considerable achievements were his support of the Webster-Ashburton Treaty with Britain and his success in bringing about the annexation of Texas.

After his presidency he lived in retirement in Virginia until the outbreak of the Civil War, when he emerged briefly as chairman of a peace convention and then as delegate to the provisional Congress of the Confederacy. He died on Jan. 18, 1862. He married Letitia Christian in 1813 and, two years after her death in 1842, Julia Gardiner.

JAMES KNOX POLK was born in Mecklenburg County, N.C., on Nov. 2, 1795. A graduate of the University of North Carolina, he moved west to Tennessee, was admitted to the bar, and soon became prominent in state politics. In 1825, he was elected to the House of Representatives, where he opposed Adams and, after 1829, became Jackson's floor leader in the fight against the Bank. In 1835, he became Speaker of the House. Four years later, he was elected governor of Tennessee, but was beaten in tries for re-election in 1841 and 1843.

The supporters of Van Buren for the Democratic nomination in 1844 counted on Polk as his running mate, but when Van Buren's stand on Texas alienated Southern support, the convention swung to Polk on the ninth ballot. He was elected over Henry Clay, the Whig candidate. Rapidly disillusioning those who thought that he would not run his own administration, Polk proceeded steadily and precisely to achieve four major objectives—the acquisition of California, the settlement of the Oregon question, the reduction of the tariff, and the establishment of the independent treasury. He also enlarged the Monroe Doctrine to exclude all non-American intervention in American affairs, whether forcible or not, and he forced Mexico into a war that he waged to a successful conclusion.

His wife, Sarah Childress, whom he married in 1824, was a woman of charm and ability. Polk died in Nashville, Tenn., on June 15, 1849.

ZACHARY TAYLOR

ZACHARY TAYLOR was born at Montebello, Orange County, Va., on Nov. 24, 1784. Embarking on a military career in 1808, Taylor fought in the War of 1812, the Black Hawk War, and the Seminole War, meanwhile holding garrison jobs on the frontier or desk jobs in Washington. A brigadier general as a result of his victory over the Seminoles at Lake Okeechobee (1837), Taylor held a succession of Southwestern commands and in 1846 established a base on the Rio Grande, where his forces engaged in hostilities that precipitated the war with Mexico. He captured Monterrey in September 1846 and, disregarding Polk's orders to stay on the defensive, defeated Santa Anna at Buena Vista in February 1847, ending the war in the northern provinces.

Though Taylor had never cast a vote for president, his party affiliations were Whiggish and his availability was increased by his difficulties with Polk. He was elected president over the Democrat Lewis Cass. During the revival of the slavery controversy, which was to result in the Compromise of 1850, Taylor began to take an increasingly firm stand against appeasing the South; but he died in Washington on July 9, 1850, during the fight over the Compromise. He married Margaret Mackall Smith in 1810. His bluff and simple soldierly qualities won him the name Old Rough and Ready.

MILLARD FILLMORE

MILLARD FILLMORE was born at Locke, Cayuga County, N.Y., on Jan. 7, 1800. A lawyer, he entered politics with the Anti-Masonic Party under the sponsorship of Thurlow Weed, editor and party boss, and subsequently followed Weed into the Whig Party. He served in the House of Representatives (1833–35 and 1837–43) and played a leading role in writing the tariff of 1842. Defeated for governor of New York in 1844, he became State comptroller in 1848, was put on the Whig ticket with Taylor as a concession to the Clay wing of the party, and became president upon Taylor's death in 1850.

As president, Fillmore broke with Weed and William H. Seward and associated himself with the pro-Southern Whigs, supporting the Compromise of 1850. Defeated for the Whig nomination in 1852, he ran for president in 1856 as candidate of the American, or Know-Nothing, Party, which sought to unite the country against foreigners in the alleged hope of diverting it from the explosive slavery issue. Fillmore opposed Lincoln during the Civil War. He died in Buffalo on March 8, 1874.

He was married in 1826 to Abigail Powers, who died in 1853, and in 1858 to Caroline Carmichael McIntosh.

FRANKLIN PIERCE

FRANKLIN PIERCE was born at Hillsboro, N.H., on Nov. 23, 1804. A Bowdoin graduate, lawyer, and Jacksonian Democrat, he won rapid political advancement in the party, in part because of the prestige of his father, Gov. Benjamin Pierce. By 1831 he was Speaker of the New Hampshire House of Representatives; from 1833 to 1837, he served in the federal House and from 1837 to 1842 in the Senate. His wife, Jane Means Appleton, whom he married in 1834, disliked Washington and the somewhat dissipated life led by Pierce; in 1842 Pierce resigned from the Senate and began a successful law practice in Concord, N.H. During the Mexican War, he was a brigadier general.

Thereafter Pierce continued to oppose antislavery tendencies within the Democratic Party. As a result, he was the Southern choice to break the deadlock at the Democratic convention of 1852 and was nominated on the 49th ballot. In the election, Pierce overwhelmed Gen. Winfield Scott, the Whig candidate.

As president, Pierce followed a course of appeasing the South at home and of playing with schemes of territorial expansion abroad. The failure of his foreign and domestic policies prevented his renomination. He died in Concord on Oct. 8, 1869, in relative obscurity.

JAMES BUCHANAN

JAMES BUCHANAN was born near Mercersburg, Pa., on April 23, 1791. A Dickinson graduate and a lawyer, he entered Pennsylvania politics as a Federalist. With the disappearance of the Federalist Party, he became a Jacksonian Democrat. He served with ability in the House (1821–31), as minister to St. Petersburg (1832–33), and in the Senate (1834–45), and in 1845 became Polk's Secretary of State. In 1853, Pierce appointed Buchanan minister to Britain, where he participated with other American diplomats in Europe in drafting the expansionist Ostend Manifesto.

He was elected president in 1856, defeating John C. Frémont, the Republican candidate, and former President Millard Fillmore of the American Party. The growing crisis over slavery presented Buchanan with problems he lacked the will to tackle. His appeasement of the South alienated the Stephen Douglas wing of the Democratic Party without reducing Southern militancy on slavery issues. While denying the right of secession, Buchanan also denied that the federal government could do anything about it. He supported the administration during the Civil War and died in Lancaster, Pa., on June 1, 1868.

The only president to remain a bachelor throughout his term, Buchanan used his charming niece, Harriet Lane, as White House hostess.

ABRAHAM LINCOLN

ABRAHAM LINCOLN was born in Hardin (now Larue) County, Ky., on Feb. 12, 1809. His family moved to Indiana and then to Illinois, and Lincoln gained what education he could along the way. While reading law, he worked in a store, managed a mill, surveyed, and split rails. In 1834, he went to the Illinois legislature as a Whig and became the party's floor leader. For the next 20 years he practiced law in Springfield, except for a single term (1847–49) in Congress, where he denounced the Mexican War. In 1855, he was a candidate for senator and the next year he joined the new Republican Party.

A leading but unsuccessful candidate for the vice-presidential nomination with Frémont, Lincoln gained national attention in 1858 when, as Republican candidate for senator from Illinois, he engaged in a series of debates with Stephen A. Douglas, the

Democratic candidate. He lost the election, but continued to prepare the way for the 1860 Republican convention and was rewarded with the presidential nomination on the third ballot. He won the election over three opponents.

From the start, Lincoln made clear that, unlike Buchanan, he believed the national government had the power to crush the rebellion. Not an abolitionist, he held the slavery issue subordinate to that of preserving the Union, but soon perceived that the war could not be brought to a successful conclusion without freeing the slaves. His administration was hampered by the incompetence of many Union generals, the inexperience of the troops, and the harassing political tactics both of the Republican Radicals, who favored a hard policy toward the South, and the Democratic Copperheads, who desired a negotiated peace. The Gettysburg Address of Nov. 19, 1863, marks the high point in the record of American eloquence. Lincoln's long search for a winning combination finally brought Generals Ulysses S. Grant and William T. Sherman to the top; and their series of victories in 1864 dispelled the mutterings from both Radicals and Peace Democrats that at one time seemed to threaten Lincoln's re-election. He was re-elected in 1864, defeating Gen. George B. McClellan, the Democratic candidate. His inaugural address urged leniency toward the South: "With malice toward none, with charity for all . . . let us strive on to finish the work we are in; to bind up the nation's wounds . . ." This policy aroused growing opposition on the part of the Republican Radicals, but before the matter could be put to the test, Lincoln was shot by the actor John Wilkes Booth at Ford's Theater, Washington, on April 14, 1865. He died the next morning.

Lincoln's marriage to Mary Todd in 1842 was often unhappy and turbulent, in part because of his wife's pronounced instability.

ANDREW JOHNSON was born at Raleigh, N.C., on Dec. 29, 1808. Self-educated, he became a tailor in Greeneville, Tenn., but soon went into politics, where he rose steadily. He served in the House of Representatives (1843–54), as governor of Tennessee (1853–57), and as a senator (1857–62). Politically he was a Jacksonian Democrat and his specialty was the fight for a more equitable land policy. Alone among the Southern Senators, he stood by the Union during the Civil War. In 1862, he became war governor of Tennessee and carried out a thankless and difficult job with great courage. Johnson became Lincoln's running mate in 1864 as a result of an attempt to give the ticket a nonpartisan and nonsectional character. Succeeding to the presidency on Lincoln's death, Johnson sought to carry out Lincoln's policy, but without his political skill. The result was a hopeless conflict with the Radical Republicans who dominated Congress, passed measures over Johnson's vetoes, and attempted to limit the power of the executive concerning appointments and removals. The conflict culminated with Johnson's impeachment for attempting to remove his disloyal Secretary of War in defiance of the Tenure of Office Act which required senatorial concurrence for such dismissals. The opposition failed by one vote to get the two thirds necessary for conviction.

After his presidency, Johnson maintained an interest in politics and in 1875 was again elected to the Senate. He died near Carter Station, Tenn., on July 31, 1875. He married Eliza McCardle in 1827.

ULYSSES SIMPSON GRANT was born (as Hiram Ulysses Grant) at Point Pleasant, Ohio, on April 27, 1822. He graduated from West Point in 1843 and served without particular distinction in the Mexican War. In 1848 he married Julia Dent. He resigned from the army in 1854, after warnings from his commanding officer about his drinking habits, and for the next six years held a wide variety of jobs in the Middle West. With the outbreak of the Civil War, he sought a command and soon, to his surprise, was made a brigadier general. His continuing successes in the western theaters, culminating in the capture of Vicksburg, Miss., in 1863, brought him national fame and soon the command of all the Union armies. Grant's dogged, implacable policy of concentrating on dividing and destroying the Confederate armies brought the war to an end in 1865. The next year, he was made full general.

In 1868, as Republican candidate for president, Grant was elected over the Democrat, Horatio Seymour. From the start, Grant showed his unfitness for the office. His Cabinet was weak, his domestic policy was confused, and many of his intimate associates were corrupt. The notable achievement in foreign affairs was the settlement of controversies with Great Britain in the Treaty of London (1871), negotiated by his able Secretary of State, Hamilton Fish.

Running for re-election in 1872, he defeated Horace Greeley, the Democratic and Liberal Republican candidate. The Panic of 1873 graft scandals close to the presidency created difficulties for his second term.

After retiring from office, Grant toured Europe for two years and returned in time to accede to a third-term boom, but was beaten in the convention in 1880. Illness and bad business judgment darkened his last years, but he worked steadily at the *Personal Memoirs,* which were to be successful when published after his death at Mount McGregor, near Saratoga, N.Y., on July 23, 1885.

RUTHERFORD BIRCHARD HAYES was born in Delaware, Ohio, on Oct. 4, 1822. A graduate of Kenyon College and the Harvard Law School, he practiced law in Lower Sandusky (now Fremont) and then in Cincinnati. In 1852 he married Lucy Webb. A Whig, he joined the Republican party in 1855. During the Civil War he rose to major general. He served in the House of Representatives from 1865 to 1867 and then confirmed a reputation for honesty and efficiency in two terms as Governor of Ohio (1868–72). His election to a third term in 1875 made him the logical candidate for those Republicans who wished to stop James G. Blaine in 1876, and he was nominated.

The result of the election was in doubt for some time and hinged upon disputed returns from South Carolina, Louisiana, Florida, and Oregon. Samuel J. Tilden, the Democrat, had the larger popular vote but was adjudged by the strictly partisan decisions of the Electoral Commission to have one fewer electoral vote, 185 to 184. The national acceptance of this result was due in part to the general understanding that Hayes would pursue a conciliatory policy toward the South. He withdrew the troops from the South, took a conservative position on financial and labor issues, and urged civil service reform.

Hayes served only one term by his own wish and spent the rest of his life in various humanitarian endeavors. He died in Fremont on Jan. 17, 1893.

JAMES ABRAM GARFIELD, the last president to be born in a log cabin, was born in Cuyahoga County, Ohio, on Nov. 19, 1831. A Williams graduate, he taught school for a time and entered Republican politics in Ohio. In 1858, he married Lucretia Rudolph. During the Civil War, he had a promising career, rising to major general of volunteers; but he resigned in 1863, having been elected to the House of Representatives, where he served until 1880. His oratorical and parliamentary abilities soon made him the leading Republican in the House, though his record was marred by his unorthodox acceptance of a fee in the DeGolyer paving contract case and by suspicions of his complicity in the Crédit Mobilier scandal.

In 1880, Garfield was elected to the Senate, but instead became the presidential candidate on the 36th ballot as a result of a deadlock in the Republican convention. In the election, he defeated Gen. Winfield Scott Hancock, the Democratic candidate. Garfield's administration was barely under way when he was shot by Charles J. Guiteau, a disappointed office seeker, in Washington on July 2, 1881. He died in Elberton, N.J., on Sept. 19.

CHESTER ALAN ARTHUR was born at Fairfield, Vt., on Oct. 5, 1830. A graduate of Union College, he became a successful New York lawyer. In 1859, he married Ellen Herndon. During the Civil War, he held administrative jobs in the Republican state administration and in 1871 was appointed collector of the Port of New York by Grant. This post gave him control over considerable patronage. Though not personally corrupt, Arthur managed his power in the interests of the New York machine so openly that President Hayes in 1877 called for an investigation and the next year Arthur was suspended.

In 1880 Arthur was nominated for vice president in the hope of conciliating the followers of Grant and the powerful New York machine. As president upon Garfield's death, Arthur, stepping out of his familiar role as spoilsman, backed civil service reform, reorganized the Cabinet, and prosecuted political associates accused of post office graft. Losing machine support and failing to gain the reformers, he was not nominated for a full term in 1884. He died in New York City on Nov. 18, 1886.

(STEPHEN) GROVER CLEVELAND was born at Caldwell, N.J., on March 18, 1837. He was admitted to the bar in Buffalo, N.Y., in 1859 and lived there as a lawyer, with occasional incursions into Democratic politics, for more than 20 years. He did not participate in the Civil War. As mayor of Buffalo in 1881, he carried through a reform program so ably that the Democrats ran him successfully for governor in 1882. In 1884 he won the Democratic nomination for president. The campaign contrasted Cleveland's spotless public career with the uncertain record of James G. Blaine, the Republican candidate, and Cleveland received enough Mugwump (independent Republican) support to win.

As president, Cleveland pushed civil service reform, opposed the pension grab and attacked the high tariff rates. While in the White House, he married Frances Folsom in 1886. Renominated in 1888, Cleveland was defeated by Benjamin Harrison, polling more popular but fewer electoral votes. In 1892, he was elected over Harrison. When the Panic of 1893 burst upon the country, Cleveland's attempts to solve it by sound-money measures alienated the free-silver wing of the party, while his tariff policy alienated the protectionists. In 1894, he sent troops to break the Pullman strike. In foreign affairs, his firmness caused Great Britain to back down in the Venezuela border dispute.

In his last years Cleveland was an active and much-respected public figure. He died in Princeton, N.J., on June 24, 1908.

BENJAMIN HARRISON was born in North Bend, Ohio, on Aug. 20, 1833, the grandson of William Henry Harrison, the ninth president. A graduate of Miami University in Ohio, he took up the law in Indiana and became active in Republican politics. In 1853, he married Caroline Lavinia Scott. During the Civil War, he rose to brigadier general. A sound-money Republican, he was elected senator from Indiana in 1880. In 1888, he received the Republican nomination for president on the eighth ballot. Though behind on the popular vote, he won over Grover Cleveland in the electoral college by 233 to 168.

As president, Harrison failed to please either the bosses or the reform element in the party. In foreign affairs he backed Secretary of State Blaine, whose policy foreshadowed later American imperialism. Harrison was renominated in 1892 but lost to Cleveland. His wife died in the White House in 1892 and Harrison married her niece, Mary Scott (Lord) Dimmick, in 1896. After his presidency, he resumed law practice. He died in Indianapolis on March 13, 1901.

WILLIAM McKINLEY was born in Niles, Ohio, on Jan. 29, 1843. He taught school, then served in the Civil War, rising from the ranks to become a major. Subsequently he opened a law office in Canton, Ohio, and in 1871 married Ida Saxton. Elected to Congress in 1876, he served there until 1891, except for 1883–85. His faithful advocacy of business interests culminated in the passage of the highly protective McKinley Tariff of 1890. With the support of Mark Hanna, a shrewd Cleveland businessman interested in safeguarding tariff protection, McKinley became governor of Ohio in 1892 and Republican presidential candidate in 1896. The business community, alarmed by the progressivism of William Jennings Bryan, the Democratic candidate, spent considerable money to assure McKinley's victory.

The chief event of McKinley's administration was the war with Spain, which resulted in the United States' acquisition of the Philippines and other islands. With imperialism an issue, McKinley defeated Bryan again in 1900. On Sept. 6, 1901, he was shot at Buffalo, N.Y., by Leon F. Czolgosz, an anarchist, and he died there eight days later.

THEODORE ROOSEVELT was born in New York City on Oct. 27, 1858. A Harvard graduate, he was early interested in ranching, in politics, and in writing picturesque historical narratives. He was a Republican member of the New York Assembly in 1882–84, an unsuccessful candidate for mayor of

New York in 1886, a U.S. Civil Service Commissioner under Benjamin Harrison, Police Commissioner of New York City in 1895, and Assistant Secretary of the Navy under McKinley in 1897. He resigned in 1898 to help organize a volunteer regiment, the Rough Riders, and take a more direct part in the war with Spain. He was elected governor of New York in 1898 and vice president in 1900, in spite of lack of enthusiasm on the part of the bosses.

Assuming the presidency of the assassinated McKinley in 1901, Roosevelt embarked on a wide-ranging program of government reform and conservation of natural resources. He ordered antitrust suits against several large corporations, threatened to intervene in the anthracite coal strike of 1902, which prompted the operators to accept arbitration, and, in general, championed the rights of the "little man" and fought the "malefactors of great wealth." He was also responsible for such progressive legislation as the Elkins Act of 1901, which outlawed freight rebates by railroads; the bill establishing the Department of Commerce and Labor; the Hepburn Act, which gave the I.C.C. greater control over the railroads; the Meat Inspection Act; and the Pure Food and Drug Act.

In foreign affairs, Roosevelt pursued a strong policy, permitting the instigation of a revolt in Panama to dispose of Colombian objections to the Panama Canal and helping to maintain the balance of power in the East by bringing the Russo-Japanese War to an end, for which he won the Nobel Peace Prize, the first American to achieve a Nobel prize in any category. In 1904, he decisively defeated Alton B. Parker, his conservative Democratic opponent.

Roosevelt's increasing coldness toward his successor, William Howard Taft, led him to overlook his earlier disclaimer of third-term ambitions and to re-enter politics. Defeated by the machine in the Republican convention of 1912, he organized the Progressive Party (Bull Moose) and polled more votes than Taft, though the split brought about the election of Woodrow Wilson. From 1915 on, Roosevelt strongly favored intervention in the European war. He became deeply embittered at Wilson's refusal to allow him to raise a volunteer division. He died in Oyster Bay, N.Y., on Jan. 6, 1919. He was married twice: in 1880 to Alice Hathaway Lee, who died in 1884, and in 1886 to Edith Kermit Carow.

WILLIAM HOWARD TAFT was born in Cincinnati on Sept. 15, 1857. A Yale graduate, he entered Ohio Republican politics in the 1880s. In 1886 he married Helen Herron. From 1887 to 1890, he served on the Ohio Superior Court; 1890–92, as solicitor general of the United States; 1892–1900, on the federal circuit court. In 1900 McKinley appointed him president of the Philippine Commission and in 1901 governor general. Taft had great success in pacifying the Filipinos, solving the problem of the church lands, improving economic conditions, and establishing limited self-government. His period as Secretary of War (1904–08) further demonstrated his capacity as administrator and conciliator, and he was Roosevelt's hand-picked successor in 1908. In the election, he polled 321 electoral votes to 162 for William Jennings Bryan, who was running for the presidency for the third time.

Though he carried on many of Roosevelt's policies, Taft got into increasing trouble with the progressive wing of the party and displayed mounting irritability and indecision. After his defeat in 1912, he became professor of constitutional law at Yale. In 1921 he was appointed Chief Justice of the United States Supreme Court. He died in Washington, D.C., on March 8, 1930.

(THOMAS) WOODROW WILSON was born in Staunton, Va., on Dec. 28, 1856. A Princeton graduate, he turned from law practice to post-graduate work in political science at Johns Hopkins University, receiving his Ph.D. in 1886. He taught at Bryn Mawr, Wesleyan, and Princeton, and in 1902 was made president of Princeton. After an unsuccessful attempt to democratize the social life of the university, he welcomed an invitation in 1910 to be the Democratic gubernatorial candidate in New Jersey, and was elected. His success in fighting the machine and putting through a reform program attracted national attention.

In 1912, at the Democratic convention in Baltimore, Wilson won the nomination on the 46th ballot and went on to defeat Roosevelt and Taft in the election. Wilson proceeded under the standard of the New Freedom to enact a program of domestic reform, including the Federal Reserve Act, the Clayton Antitrust Act, the establishment of the Federal Trade Commission, and other measures designed to restore competition in the face of the great monopolies. In foreign affairs, while privately sympathetic with the Allies, he strove to maintain neutrality in the European war and warned both sides against encroachments on American interests.

Re-elected in 1916 as a peace candidate, he tried to mediate between the warring nations; but when the Germans resumed unrestricted submarine warfare in 1917, Wilson brought the United States into what he now believed was a war to make the world safe for democracy. He supplied the classic formulations of Allied war aims and the armistice of Nov. 11, 1918 was negotiated on the basis of Wilson's Fourteen Points. In 1919 he strove at Versailles to lay the foundations for enduring peace. He accepted the imperfections of the Versailles Treaty in the expectation that they could be remedied by action within the League of Nations. He probably could have secured ratification of the treaty by the Senate if he had adopted a more conciliatory attitude toward the mild reservationists; but his insistence on all or nothing eventually caused the diehard isolationists and diehard Wilsonites to unite in rejecting a compromise.

In September 1919 Wilson suffered a paralytic stroke that limited his activity. After leaving the presidency he lived on in retirement in Washington, dying on Feb. 3, 1924. He was married twice—in 1885 to Ellen Louise Axson, who died in 1914, and in 1915 to Edith Bolling Galt.

WARREN GAMALIEL HARDING was born in Morrow County, Ohio, on Nov. 2, 1865. After attending Ohio Central College, Harding became interested in journalism and in 1884 bought the *Marion* (Ohio) *Star.* In 1891 he married a wealthy widow, Florence Kling De Wolfe. As his paper prospered, he entered Republican politics, serving as state senator (1899–1903) and as lieutenant governor (1904–06). In 1910, he was defeated for governor, but in 1914 was elected to the Senate. His reputation as an orator made him the keynoter at the 1916 Republican convention.

When the 1920 convention was deadlocked between Leonard Wood and Frank O. Lowden, Harding became the dark-horse nominee on his solemn affirmation that there was no reason in his past that he should not be. Straddling the League question, Harding was easily elected over James M. Cox, his Democratic opponent. His Cabinet contained some able men, but also some manifestly unfit for public office. Harding's own intimates were mediocre when they were not corrupt. The impending disclosure of the Teapot Dome scandal in the Interior Department and illegal practices in the Justice Department and Veterans' Bureau, as well as political setbacks, profoundly worried him. On his return from Alaska in 1923, he died unexpectedly in San Francisco on Aug. 2.

(JOHN) CALVIN COOLIDGE was born in Plymouth, Vt., on July 4, 1872. An Amherst graduate, he went into law practice at Northampton, Mass., in 1897. He married Grace Anna Goodhue in 1905. He entered Republican state politics, becoming successively mayor of Northampton, state senator, lieutenant governor and, in 1919, governor. His use of the state militia to end the Boston police strike in 1919 won him a somewhat undeserved reputation for decisive action and brought him the Republican vice-presidential nomination in 1920. After Harding's death Coolidge handled the Washington scandals with care and finally managed to save the Republican Party from public blame for the widespread corruption.

In 1924, Coolidge was elected without difficulty, defeating the Democrat, John W. Davis, and Robert M. La Follette running on the Progressive ticket. His second term, like his first, was characterized by a general satisfaction with the existing economic order. He stated that he did not choose to run in 1928.

After his presidency, Coolidge lived quietly in Northampton, writing an unilluminating autobiography and conducting a syndicated column. He died there on Jan. 5, 1933.

HERBERT CLARK HOOVER was born at West Branch, Iowa, on Aug. 10, 1874, the first president to be born west of the Mississippi. A Stanford graduate, he worked from 1895 to 1913 as a mining engineer and consultant throughout the world. In 1899, he married Lou Henry. During World War I, he served with distinction as chairman of the American Relief Committee in London, as chairman of the Commission for Relief in Belgium, and as U.S. Food Administrator. His political affiliations were still too indeterminate for him to be mentioned as a possibility for either the Republican or Democratic nomination in 1920, but after the election he served Harding and Coolidge as Secretary of Commerce.

In the election of 1928, Hoover overwhelmed Gov. Alfred E. Smith of New York, the Democratic candidate and the first Roman Catholic to run for the presidency. He soon faced the worst depression in the nation's history, but his attacks upon it were hampered by his devotion to the theory that the forces that brought the crisis would soon bring the revival and then by his belief that there were too many areas in which the federal government had no power to act. In a succession of vetoes, he struck down measures proposing a national employment system or national relief, he reduced income tax rates, and only at the end of his term did he yield to popular pressure and set up agencies such as the Reconstruction Finance Corporation to make emergency loans to assist business.

After his 1932 defeat, Hoover returned to private business. In 1946, President Truman charged him with various world food missions; and from 1947 to 1949 and 1953 to 1955, he was head of the Commission on Organization of the Executive Branch of the Government. He died in New York City on Oct. 20, 1964.

FRANKLIN DELANO ROOSEVELT was born in Hyde Park, N.Y., on Jan. 30, 1882. A Harvard graduate, he attended Columbia Law School and was admitted to the New York bar. In 1910, he was elected to the New York State Senate as a Democrat. Reelected in 1912, he was appointed Assistant Secretary of the Navy by Woodrow Wilson the next year. In 1920, his radiant personality and his war service resulted in his nomination for vice president as James M. Cox's running mate. After his defeat, he returned to law practice in New York. In August 1921, Roosevelt was stricken with infantile paralysis while on vacation at Campobello, New Brunswick. After a long and gallant fight, he recovered partial use of his legs. In 1924 and 1928, he led the fight at the Democratic national conventions for the nomination of Gov. Alfred E. Smith of New York, and in 1928 Roosevelt was himself induced to run for governor of New York. He was elected, and was reelected in 1930.

In 1932, Roosevelt received the Democratic nomination for president and immediately launched a campaign that brought new spirit to a weary and discouraged nation. He defeated Hoover by a wide margin. His first term was characterized by an unfolding of the New Deal program, with greater benefits for labor, the farmers, and the unemployed, and the progressive estrangement of most of the business community.

At an early stage, Roosevelt became aware of the menace to world peace posed by totalitarian fascism, and from 1937 on he tried to focus public attention on the trend of events in Europe and Asia. As a result, he was widely denounced as a warmonger. He was re-elected in 1936 over Gov. Alfred M. Landon of Kansas by the overwhelming electoral margin of 523 to 8, and the gathering international crisis prompted him to run for an unprecedented third term in 1940. He defeated Wendell L. Willkie.

Roosevelt's program to bring maximum aid to Britain and, after June 1941, to Russia was opposed, until the Japanese attack on Pearl Harbor restored national unity. During the war, Roosevelt shelved the New Deal in the interests of conciliating the business community, both in order to get full production during the war and to prepare the way for a united acceptance of the peace settlements after the war. A series of conferences with Winston Churchill and Joseph Stalin laid down the bases for the postwar world. In 1944 he was elected to a fourth term, running against Gov. Thomas E. Dewey of New York.

On April 12, 1945, Roosevelt died of a cerebral hemorrhage at Warm Springs, Ga., shortly after his return from the Yalta Conference. His wife, (Anna) Eleanor Roosevelt, whom he married in 1905, was a woman of great ability who made significant contributions to her husband's policies.

HARRY S. TRUMAN was born on a farm near Lamar, Mo., on May 8, 1884. During World War I, he served in France as a captain with the 129th Field Artillery. He married Bess Wallace in 1919. After engaging briefly and unsuccessfully in the haberdashery business in Kansas City, Mo., Truman entered local politics. Under the sponsorship of Thomas Pendergast, Democratic boss of Missouri, he held a number of local offices, preserving his personal honesty in the midst of a notoriously corrupt political machine. In 1934, he was elected to the Senate and was re-elected in 1940. During his first term he was a loyal but quiet supporter of the New Deal, but in his second term, an appointment as head of a Senate committee to investigate war production brought out his special qualities of honesty, common sense, and hard work, and he won widespread respect.

Elected vice president in 1944, Truman became president upon Roosevelt's sudden death in April 1945 and was immediately faced with the problems of winding down the war against the Axis and preparing the nation for postwar adjustment. Germany surrendered on May 8, and in July Truman attended the Potsdam Conference to discuss the settlement plans for postwar Europe. To end the war with Japan, he authorized the dropping of atomic bombs on Hiroshima and Nagasaki on Aug. 6 and Aug. 9, 1945. Japan surrendered on Aug. 14. Although the action undoubtedly saved many American lives by bringing the war to an end, the morality of the decision is still debated.

The years 1947–48 were distinguished by civil-rights proposals, the Truman Doctrine to contain the spread of Communism, and the Marshall Plan to aid in the economic reconstruction of war-ravaged nations. Truman's general record, highlighted by a vigorous Fair Deal campaign, brought about his unexpected election in 1948 over the heavily favored Thomas E. Dewey.

Truman's second term was primarily concerned with the Cold War with the Soviet Union, the implementing of the North Atlantic Pact, the United Nations police action in Korea, and the vast rearmament program with its accompanying problems of economic stabilization.

On March 29, 1952, Truman announced that he would not run again for the presidency. After leaving the White House, he returned to his home in Independence, Mo., to write his memoirs. He further busied himself with the Harry S. Truman Library there. He died in Kansas City, Mo., on Dec. 26, 1972.

DWIGHT DAVID EISENHOWER was born in Denison, Tex., on Oct. 14, 1890. His ancestors lived in Germany and emigrated to America, settling in Pennsylvania, early in the 18th century. His father, David, had a general store in Hope, Kans., which failed. After a brief time in Texas, the family moved to Abilene, Kan.

After graduating from Abilene High School in 1909, Eisenhower did odd jobs for almost two years. He won an appointment to the Naval Academy at Annapolis, but was too old for admittance. Then he received an appointment in 1910 to West Point, from which he graduated as a second lieutenant in 1915.

He did not see service in World War I, having been stationed at Fort Sam Houston, Tex. There he met Mamie Geneva Doud, whom he married in Denver on July 1, 1916, and by whom he had two sons: Doud Dwight (died in infancy) and John Sheldon Doud.

Eisenhower served in the Philippines from 1935 to 1939 with Gen. Douglas MacArthur. Afterward, Gen. George C. Marshall, the Army Chief of Staff, brought him into the War Department's General Staff and in 1942 placed him in command of the invasion of North Africa. In 1944, he was made Supreme Allied Commander for the invasion of Europe.

After the war, Eisenhower served as Army Chief of Staff from November 1945 until February 1948, when he was appointed president of Columbia University.

In December 1950, President Truman recalled Eisenhower to active duty to command the North Atlantic Treaty Organization forces in Europe. He held his post until the end of May 1952.

At the Republican convention of 1952 in Chicago, Eisenhower won the presidential nomination on the first ballot in a close race with Senator Robert A. Taft of Ohio. In the election, he defeated Gov. Adlai E. Stevenson of Illinois.

Through two terms, Eisenhower hewed to moderate domestic policies. He sought peace through Free World strength in an era of new nationalisms, nuclear missiles, and space exploration. He fostered alliances pledging the United States to resist "Red" aggression in Europe, Asia, and Latin America. The Eisenhower Doctrine of 1957 extended commitments to the Middle East.

At home, the popular president lacked Republican Congressional majorities after 1954, but he was re-elected in 1956 by 457 electoral votes to 73 for Stevenson.

While retaining most Fair Deal programs, he stressed "fiscal responsibility" in domestic affairs. A moderate in civil rights, he sent troops to Little Rock, Ark., to enforce court-ordered school integration.

With his wartime rank restored by Congress, Eisenhower returned to private life and the role of elder statesman, with his vigor hardly impaired by a heart attack, an ileitis operation, and a mild stroke suffered while in office. He died in Washington, D.C., on March 28, 1969.

JOHN FITZGERALD KENNEDY was born in Brookline, Mass., on May 29, 1917. His father, Joseph P. Kennedy, was Ambassador to Great Britain from 1937 to 1940.

Kennedy was graduated from Harvard University in 1940 and joined the Navy the next year. He became skipper of a PT boat that was sunk in the Pacific by a Japanese destroyer. Although given up for lost, he swam to a safe island, towing an injured enlisted man.

After recovering from a war-aggravated spinal injury, Kennedy entered politics in 1946 and was elected to Congress. In 1952, he ran against Senator Henry Cabot Lodge, Jr., of Massachusetts, and won.

Kennedy was married on Sept. 12, 1953, to Jacqueline Lee Bouvier, by whom he had three children: Caroline, John Fitzgerald, Jr. (died in a 1999 plane crash), and Patrick Bouvier (died in infancy).

In 1957 Kennedy won the Pulitzer Prize for a book he had written earlier, *Profiles in Courage.*

After strenuous primary battles, Kennedy won the Democratic presidential nomination on the first ballot at the 1960 Los Angeles convention. With a plurality of only 118,574 votes, he carried the election over Vice President Richard M. Nixon and became the first Roman Catholic president.

Kennedy brought to the White House the dynamic idea of a "New Frontier" approach in dealing with problems at home, abroad, and in the dimensions of space. Out of his leadership in his first few months in office came the 10-year Alliance for Progress to aid Latin America, the Peace Corps, and accelerated programs that brought the first Americans into orbit in the race in space.

Failure of the U.S.-supported Cuban invasion in April 1961 led to the entrenchment of the Communist-backed Castro regime, only 90 miles from United States soil. When it became known that Soviet offensive missiles were being installed in Cuba in 1962, Kennedy ordered a naval "quarantine" of the island and moved troops into position to eliminate this threat to U.S. security. The world seemed on the brink of a nuclear war until Soviet Premier Khrushchev ordered the removal of the missiles.

A sudden "thaw," or the appearance of one, in the cold war came with the agreement with the Soviet Union on a limited test-ban treaty signed in Moscow on Aug. 6, 1963.

In his domestic policies, Kennedy's proposals for medical care for the aged and aid to education were defeated, but on minimum wage, trade legislation, and other measures he won important victories.

Widespread racial disorders and demonstrations led to Kennedy's proposing sweeping civil rights legislation. As his third year in office drew to a close, he also recommended an $11-billion tax cut to bolster the economy. Both measures were pending in Congress when Kennedy, looking forward to a second term, journeyed to Texas for a series of speeches.

While riding in an automobile procession in Dallas on Nov. 22, 1963, he was shot to death by an assassin firing from an upper floor of a building. The alleged assassin, Lee Harvey Oswald, was killed two days later in the Dallas city jail by Jack Ruby, owner of a strip-tease place.

At 46 years of age, Kennedy became the fourth president to be assassinated and the eighth to die in office.

LYNDON BAINES JOHNSON was born in
Stonewall, Tex., on Aug. 27, 1908. On both sides of his family he had a political heritage mingled with a Baptist background of preachers and teachers. Both his father and his paternal grandfather served in the Texas House of Representatives.

After his graduation from Southwest Texas State Teachers College, Johnson taught school for two years. He went to Washington in 1932 as secretary to Rep. Richard M. Kleberg. During this time, he married Claudia Alta Taylor, known as "Lady Bird." They had two children: Lynda Bird and Luci Baines.

In 1935, Johnson became Texas administrator for the National Youth Administration. Two years later,

he was elected to Congress as an all-out supporter of Franklin D. Roosevelt, and served until 1949. He was the first member of Congress to enlist in the armed forces after the attack on Pearl Harbor. He served in the Navy in the Pacific and won a Silver Star.

Johnson was elected to the Senate in 1948 after he had captured the Democratic nomination by only 87 votes. He was 40 years old. He became the Senate Democratic leader in 1953. A heart attack in 1955 threatened to end his political career, but he recovered fully and resumed his duties.

At the height of his power as Senate leader, Johnson sought the Democratic nomination for president in 1960. When he lost to John F. Kennedy, he surprised even some of his closest associates by accepting second place on the ticket.

Johnson was riding in another car in the motorcade when Kennedy was assassinated in Dallas on Nov. 22, 1963. He took the oath of office in the presidential jet on the Dallas airfield.

With Johnson's insistent backing, Congress finally adopted a far-reaching civil-rights bill, a voting-rights bill, a Medicare program for the aged, and measures to improve education and conservation. Congress also began what Johnson described as "an all-out war" on poverty.

Amassing a record-breaking majority of nearly 16 million votes, Johnson was elected president in his own right in 1964, defeating Senator Barry Goldwater of Arizona.

The double tragedy of a war in Southeast Asia and urban riots at home marked Johnson's last two years in office. Faced with disunity in the nation and challenges within his own party, Johnson surprised the country on March 31, 1968, with the announcement that he would not be a candidate for re-election. He died of a heart attack suffered at his LBJ Ranch on Jan. 22, 1973.

RICHARD MILHOUS NIXON was born in Yorba
Linda, Calif., on Jan. 9, 1913, to Midwestern-bred parents, Francis A. and Hannah Milhous Nixon, who raised their five sons as Quakers.

Nixon was a high school debater and was undergraduate president at Whittier College in California, where he was graduated in 1934. As a scholarship student at Duke University Law School in North Carolina, he graduated third in his class in 1937.

After five years as a lawyer, Nixon joined the Navy in August 1942. He was an air transport officer in the South Pacific and a legal officer stateside before his discharge in 1946 as a lieutenant commander.

Running for Congress in California as a Republican in 1946, Nixon defeated Rep. Jerry Voorhis. As a member of the House Un-American Activities Committee, he made a name as an investigator of Alger Hiss, a former high State Department official, who was later jailed for perjury. In 1950, Nixon defeated Rep. Helen Gahagan Douglas, a Democrat, for the Senate. He was criticized for portraying her as a Communist dupe.

Nixon's anti-Communism ideals, his Western roots, and his youth figured into his selection in 1952 to run for vice president on the ticket headed by Dwight D. Eisenhower. Demands for Nixon's withdrawal followed disclosure that California businessmen had paid some of his Senate office expenses. His televised rebuttal, known as "the

Checkers speech" (named for a cocker spaniel given to the Nixons), brought him support from the public and from Eisenhower. The ticket won easily in 1952 and again in 1956.

Eisenhower gave Nixon substantive assignments, including missions to 56 countries. In Moscow in 1959, Nixon won acclaim for his defense of U.S. interests in an impromptu "kitchen debate" with Soviet Premier Nikita S. Khrushchev.

Nixon lost the 1960 race for the presidency to John F. Kennedy.

In 1962, Nixon failed in a bid for California's governorship and seemed to be finished as a national candidate. He became a Wall Street lawyer, but kept his old party ties and developed new ones through constant travels to speak for Republicans.

Nixon won the 1968 Republican presidential nomination after a shrewd primary campaign, then made Gov. Spiro T. Agnew of Maryland his surprise choice for vice president. In the election, they edged out the Democratic ticket headed by Vice President Hubert H. Humphrey by 510,314 votes out of 73,212,065 cast.

Committed to winding down the U.S. role in the Vietnamese War, Nixon pursued "Vietnamization"—training and equipping South Vietnamese to do their own fighting. American ground combat forces in Vietnam fell steadily from 540,000 when Nixon took office to none in 1973 when the military draft was ended. But there was heavy continuing use of U.S. air power.

Nixon improved relations with Moscow and reopened the long-closed door to mainland China with a good-will trip there in February 1972. In May of that year, he visited Moscow and signed agreements on arms limitation and trade expansion and approved plans for a joint U.S.–Soviet space mission in 1975.

Inflation was a campaign issue for Nixon, but he failed to master it as president. On Aug. 15, 1971, with unemployment edging up, Nixon abruptly announced a new economic policy: a 90-day wage-price freeze, stimulative tax cuts, a temporary 10% tariff, and spending cuts. A second phase, imposing guidelines on wage, price, and rent boosts, was announced October 7.

The economy responded in time for the 1972 campaign, in which Nixon played up his foreign-policy achievements. Played down was the burglary on June 17, 1972, of Democratic national headquarters in the Watergate apartment complex in Washington. The Nixon–Agnew re-election campaign cost a record $60 million and swamped the Democratic ticket headed by Senator George McGovern of South Dakota with a plurality of 17,999,528 out of 77,718,554 votes. Only Massachusetts, with 14 electoral votes, and the District of Columbia, with 3, went for McGovern.

In January 1973, hints of a cover-up emerged at the trial of six men found guilty of the Watergate burglary. With a Senate investigation under way, Nixon announced on April 30 the resignations of his top aides, H. R. Haldeman and John D. Ehrlichman, and the dismissal of White House counsel John Dean III. Dean was the star witness at televised Senate hearings that exposed both a White House cover-up of Watergate and massive illegalities in Republican fund-raising in 1972.

The hearings also disclosed that Nixon had routinely tape-recorded his office meetings and telephone conversations.

On Oct. 10, 1973, Agnew resigned as vice president, then pleaded no-contest to a negotiated federal charge of evading income taxes on alleged bribes. Two days later, Nixon nominated the House minority leader, Rep. Gerald R. Ford of Michigan, as the new vice president. Congress confirmed Ford on Dec. 6, 1973.

In June 1974, Nixon visited Israel and four Arab nations. Then he met in Moscow with Soviet leader Leonid I. Brezhnev and reached preliminary nuclear arms limitation agreements.

But, in the month after his return, Watergate ended the Nixon regime. On July 24 the Supreme Court ordered Nixon to surrender subpoenaed tapes. On July 30, the Judiciary Committee referred three impeachment articles to the full membership. On August 5, Nixon bowed to the Supreme Court and released tapes showing he halted an FBI probe of the Watergate burglary six days after it occurred. It was in effect an admission of obstruction of justice, and impeachment appeared inevitable.

Nixon resigned on Aug. 9, 1974, the first president ever to do so. A month later, President Ford issued an unconditional pardon for any offenses Nixon might have committed as president, thus forestalling possible prosecution.

In 1940, Nixon married Thelma Catherine (Pat) Ryan. They had two daughters, Patricia (Tricia) and Julie, who married Dwight David Eisenhower II, grandson of the former president.

He died on April 22, 1994, in New York City of a massive stroke.

GERALD RUDOLPH FORD was born Leslie King Jr. in Omaha, Neb., on July 14, 1913, the only child of Leslie and Dorothy Gardner King. His parents were divorced in 1915. His mother moved to Grand Rapids, Mich., and married Gerald R. Ford. The boy was renamed for his stepfather.

Ford captained his high school football team in Grand Rapids, and a football scholarship took him to the University of Michigan, where he starred as varsity center before his graduation in 1935. A job as assistant football coach at Yale gave him an opportunity to attend Yale Law School, from which he graduated in the top third of his class in 1941.

He returned to Grand Rapids to practice law, but entered the Navy in April 1942. He saw wartime service in the Pacific on the light aircraft carrier *Monterey* and was a lieutenant commander when he returned to Grand Rapids early in 1946 to resume law practice and dabble in politics.

Ford was elected to Congress in 1948 for the first of his 13 terms in the House. He was soon assigned to the influential Appropriations Committee and rose to become the ranking Republican on the subcommittee on Defense Department appropriations.

As a legislator, Ford described himself as "a moderate on domestic issues, a conservative in fiscal affairs, and a dyed-in-the-wool internationalist." He carried the ball for Pentagon appropriations, was a hawk on the war in Vietnam, and kept a low profile on civil-rights issues.

Ford was also dependable and hard-working and popular with his colleagues. In 1963, he was elected chairman of the House Republican Conference. He served in 1963-1964 as a member of the Warren Commission, which investigated the assassination of John F. Kennedy. A revolt by dissatisfied younger Republicans in 1965 made him minority leader.

Ford shelved his hopes for the speakership on Oct. 12, 1973, when Nixon nominated him to fill the vice presidency left vacant by Agnew's resignation under fire. It was the first use of the procedures for filling vacancies in the vice presidency laid down in the 25th Amendment to the Constitution, which Ford had helped enact.

Congress confirmed Ford as vice president on Dec. 6, 1973. Once in office, he said he did not believe Nixon had been involved in the Watergate scandals, but criticized his stubborn court battle against releasing tape recordings of Watergate-related conversations for use as evidence.

The scandals led to Nixon's unprecedented resignation on Aug. 9, 1974, and Ford was sworn in immediately as the 38th president, the first to enter the White House without winning a national election.

Ford assured the nation when he took office that "our long national nightmare is over" and pledged "openness and candor" in all his actions. He won a warm response from the Democratic 93rd Congress when he said he wanted "a good marriage" rather than a honeymoon with his former colleagues. In December 1974 Congressional majorities backed his choice of former New York Gov. Nelson A. Rockefeller as his successor in the again-vacant vice presidency.

The cordiality was chilled by Ford's announcement on Sept. 8, 1974, that he had granted an unconditional pardon to Nixon for any crimes he might have committed as president. Although no formal charges were pending, Ford said he feared "ugly passions" would be aroused if Nixon were brought to trial. The pardon was widely criticized.

To fight inflation, the new president first proposed fiscal restraints and spending curbs and a 5% tax surcharge that got nowhere in the Senate and House. Congress again rebuffed Ford in the spring of 1975 when he appealed for emergency military aid to help the governments of South Vietnam and Cambodia resist massive Communist offensives.

In November 1974, Ford visited Japan, South Korea, and the Soviet Union, where he and Soviet leader Leonid I. Brezhnev conferred in Vladivostok and reached a tentative agreement to limit the number of strategic offensive nuclear weapons. It was Ford's first meeting as president with Brezhnev, who planned a return visit to Washington in the fall of 1975.

Politically, Ford's fortunes improved steadily in the first half of 1975. Badly divided Democrats in Congress were unable to muster votes to override his vetoes of spending bills that exceeded his budget. He faced some right-wing opposition in his own party, but moved to pre-empt it with an early announcement—on July 8, 1975—of his intention to be a candidate in 1976.

Early state primaries in 1976 suggested an easy victory for Ford despite Ronald Reagan's bitter attacks on administration foreign policy and defense programs. But later Reagan primary successes threatened the President's lead. At the Kansas City convention, Ford was nominated by the narrow margin of 1,187 to 1,070. But Reagan had moved the party to the right, and Ford himself was regarded as a caretaker president lacking in strength and vision. He was defeated in November by Jimmy Carter.

In 1948, Ford married Elizabeth Anne (Betty) Bloomer. They had four children, Michael Gerald, John Gardner, Steven Meigs, and Susan Elizabeth.

JAMES EARL CARTER, JR., was born in the tiny village of Plains, Ga., Oct. 1, 1924, and grew up on the family farm at nearby Archery. Both parents were fifth-generation Georgians. His father, James Earl Carter, was known as a segregationist, but treated his black and white workers equally. Carter's mother, Lillian Gordy, was a matriarchal presence in home and community and opposed the then-prevailing code of racial inequality. The future president was baptized in 1935 in the conservative Southern Baptist Church and spoke often of being a "born again" Christian, although committed to the separation of church and state.

Carter married Rosalynn Smith, a neighbor, in 1946. Their first child, John William, was born a year later in Portsmouth, Va. Their other children are James Earl III, born in Honolulu in 1950; Donnel Jeffrey, born in New London, Conn., in 1952; and Amy Lynn, born in Plains in 1967.

In 1946 Carter was graduated from the U.S. Naval Academy at Annapolis and served in the nuclear-submarine program under Adm. Hyman G. Rickover. In 1954, after his father's death, he resigned from the Navy to take over the family's flourishing warehouse and cotton gin, with several thousand acres for growing seed peanuts.

Carter was elected to the Georgia Senate in 1962. In 1966 he lost the race for Governor, but was elected in 1970. His term brought a state government reorganization, sharply reduced agencies, increased economy and efficiency, and new social programs, all with no general tax increase. In 1972 the peanut farmer–politician set his sights on the presidency and in 1974 built a base for himself as he criss-crossed the country as chairman of the Democratic Campaign Committee, appealing for revival and reform. In 1975 his image as a typical Southern white was erased when he won support of most of the old Southern civil-rights coalition after endorsement by Rep. Andrew Young, black Democrat from Atlanta, who had been the closest aide to the Rev. Martin Luther King, Jr. At Carter's 1971 inauguration as Governor he had called for an end to all forms of racial discrimination.

In the 1976 spring primaries, he won 19 out of 31 with a broad appeal to conservatives and liberals, black and white, poor and well-to-do. Throughout his campaigning Carter set forth his policies in his soft Southern voice, and with his electric-blue stare faced down skeptics who joked about "Jimmy Who?" He defeated Gerald R. Ford in Nov. 1976. Likewise, in 1980 he was renominated on the first ballot after vanquishing Senator Edward M. Kennedy of Massachusetts in the primaries. In the election campaign, Carter attacked his rivals, Ronald Reagan and John B. Anderson, independent, with the warning that a Reagan Republican victory would heighten the risk of war and impede civil rights and economic opportunity. In November Carter lost to Reagan, who won 489 Electoral College votes and 51% of the popular tally, to 49 electoral votes and 41% for Carter.

In his one term, Carter fought hard for his programs against resistance from an independent-minded Democratic Congress that frustrated many pet projects although it overrode only two vetoes. Observers generally viewed public dissatisfaction with the "stagflation" economy as a principal factor in his defeat. Others included his jittery performance in the debate Oct. 28 with Reagan, staff problems, friction with Congress, long gasoline lines, and the months-long Iranian crisis, including the abortive sally in April 1980 to free the hostages. Yet, assessments of his record noted many positive elements. There was, for one thing, peace throughout his term, with no American combat deaths and with a brake on the advocates of force. Regarded as perhaps his greatest personal achievements were the Camp David accords between Israel and Egypt and the resulting treaty—the first between Israel and an Arab neighbor. The treaty with China and the Panama Canal treaties were also major achievements. Carter worked for nuclear-arms control. His concern for international human rights was credited with saving lives and reducing torture, and he supported the British policy that ended internecine warfare in Rhodesia, now Zimbabwe. Domestically, his environmental record was a major accomplishment. His judicial appointments won acclaim; the Southerner who had forsworn racism made 265 choices for the Federal bench that included minority members and women. He also ended the U.S. practice of holding petroleum prices far below world levels with price decontrols.

RONALD WILSON REAGAN rode to the presidency in 1980 on a tide of resurgent right-wing sentiment among an electorate battered by winds of unwanted change, longing for a distant, simpler era.

He left office in Jan. 1989 with two-thirds of the American people approving his performance during his two terms. It was the highest rating for any retiring president since World War II.

His place in history will rest, perhaps, on the short- and intermediate-range missile treaty consummated on a cordial visit to the Soviet Union that he had once reviled as an "evil empire." Its provisions, including a ground-breaking agreement on verification inspection, were formulated in four days of summit talks in Moscow in May 1988 with the Soviet leader, Mikhail S. Gorbachev.

Reagan can point to numerous domestic achievements as well: sharp cuts in income tax rates, sweeping tax reform, creating economic growth without inflation, and reducing the unemployment rate, among others. He failed, however, to win the "Reagan Revolution" on such issues as abortion and school prayer, and he seemed aloof from "sleazy" conduct by some top officials.

In his final months Reagan campaigned aggressively to win election as president for his two-term vice president, George Bush.

Reagan's popularity with the public dipped sharply in 1986 when the Iran-Contra scandal broke, shortly after the Democrats gained control of the Senate. Observers agreed that Reagan's presidency had been weakened, if temporarily, by the two unrelated events. Then the weeks-long Congressional hearings in the summer of 1987 heard an array of Administration officials, present and former, tell their tales of a White House riven by deceit and undercover maneuvering. Yet no breath of illegality touched the President's personal reputation; on Aug. 12, 1987, he told the nation that he had not known of questionable activities but agreed that he was "ultimately accountable."

Ronald Reagan, actor turned politician, New Dealer turned conservative, came to films and politics from a thoroughly Middle-American background—middle class, Middle West, and small town. He was born in Tampico, Ill., Feb. 6, 1911, the second son of John Edward Reagan and Nelle Wilson Reagan, and the family later moved to Dixon, Ill. The father, of Irish descent, was a shop clerk and merchant with Democratic sympathies. It was an impoverished family; young Ronald sold homemade popcorn at high school games and worked as a lifeguard to earn money for his college tuition. When the father got a New Deal WPA job, the future president became an ardent Roosevelt Democrat.

Reagan won a B.A. degree in 1932 from Eureka (Ill.) College, where a photographic memory aided in his studies and in debating and college theatricals. In a Depression year, he was making $100 a week as a sports announcer for radio station WHO in Des Moines, Iowa, from 1932 to 1937. His career as a film and TV actor stretched from 1937 to 1966, and his salary climbed to $3,500 a week. As a World War II captain in Army film studios, Reagan recoiled from what he saw as the laziness of Civil Service workers, and moved to the Right. As president of the Screen Actors Guild, he resisted what he considered a Communist plot to subvert the film industry. With advancing age, Reagan left leading-man roles and became a television spokesman for the General Electric Company.

With oratorical skill his trademark, Reagan became an active Republican. At the behest of a small group of conservative Southern California businessmen, he ran for governor with a pledge to cut spending, and was elected by almost a million votes over the political veteran, Democratic Gov. Edmund G. Brown, father of later governor Jerry Brown.

In the 1980 election battle against Jimmy Carter, Reagan broadened his appeal by espousing moderate policies, gaining much of his support from disaffected Democrats and blue-collar workers. The incoming Administration immediately set out to "turn the government around" with a new economic program. Over strenuous Congressional opposition, Reagan triumphed on his "supply side" theory to stimulate production and control inflation through tax cuts and sharp reductions in government spending.

The president won high acclaim for his nomination of Sandra Day O'Connor as the first woman on the Supreme Court. His later nominations met increasing opposition but did much to tilt the Court's orientation to the Right.

In 1982, the President's popularity had slipped as the economy declined into the worst recession in 40 years, with persistent high unemployment and interest rates. Initial support for "supply side" economics faded but the President won crucial battles in Congress.

Internationally, Reagan confronted numerous critical problems in his first term. The successful invasion of Grenada accomplished much diplomatically. But the intervention in Lebanon and the withdrawal of Marines after a disastrous terrorist attack were regarded as military failures.

The popular president won reelection in the 1984 landslide, with the economy improving and inflation under control. Domestically, a tax reform bill that Reagan backed became law. But the constantly growing budget deficit remained a constant irritant, with the President and Congress persistently at odds over priorities in spending for defense and domestic programs. His foreign policy met stiffening opposition, with Congress increasingly reluctant to increase spending for the Nicaraguan "Contras" and the Pentagon and to expand the development of the MX missile. But even severe critics praised Reagan's restrained but decisive handling of the crisis following the hijacking of an American plane in Beirut by Muslim extremists. The attack on Libya in April 1986 galvanized the nation, although it drew scathing disapproval from the NATO alliance.

Barely three months into his first term, Reagan was the target of an assassin's bullet; his courageous comeback won public admiration.

Reagan is devoted to his wife, Nancy, whom he married after his divorce from the screen actress Jane Wyman. The children from his first marriage are Maureen, his daughter by Wyman, and Michael, an adopted son. He had two children by Nancy: Patricia and Ron. Reagan continues to struggle with Alzheimer's disease, which he developed in the years following his presidency.

GEORGE HERBERT WALKER BUSH was born June 12, 1924, in Milton, Mass., to Prescott and Dorothy Bush. The family later moved to Connecticut. The youth studied at the elite Phillips Academy in Andover, Mass.

The future president joined the Navy after war broke out and at 18 became the Navy's youngest commissioned pilot, serving from 1942 to 1945. The man later derided by some as a "wimp" fought the Japanese on 58 missions and was shot down once. He won the Distinguished Flying Cross.

After the war, Bush earned an economics degree and a Phi Beta Kappa key in two and a half years at Yale University. While there he captained the baseball team and was initiated into "Skull and Bones," the prestigious Yale secret society.

In 1945 Bush married Barbara Pierce of Rye, N.Y., daughter of a magazine publisher. With his bride, Bush moved to Texas instead of entering his father's investment banking business. There he founded his oil company and by 1980 reported an estimated wealth of $1.4 million.

Throughout his whole career, Bush had the backing of an established family, headed by his father, Prescott Bush, who was elected to the Senate from Connecticut in 1952. The family helped the young patrician become established in his early business ventures, a rich uncle raising most of the capital required for founding the oil company.

In the 1960s, Bush won two contests for a Texas Republican seat in the House of Representatives, but lost two bids for a Senate seat and one for the presidency. After Bush's second race for the Senate, President Nixon appointed him U.S. delegate to the United Nations with the rank of Ambassador and he later became Republican National Chairman. He headed the United States liaison office in Beijing before becoming Director of Central Intelligence.

In 1980 Bush became Reagan's running mate despite earlier criticism of Reagan "voodoo economics" and by the 1984 election had won acclaim for devotion to Reagan's conservative agenda despite his own reputation as somewhat more liberally inclined. Nevertheless, die-hard right-wingers could find satisfaction in Bush's war record and his government service, particularly with the C.I.A. Throughout he remained influential in White House decisions, particularly in foreign affairs.

In the 1988 campaign, Bush's choice of Senator Dan Quayle of Indiana for vice president surprised his friends and provoked criticism and ridicule that continued even after the Administration was established in office. Nonetheless Bush strongly defended his choice.

George Herbert Walker Bush became president on Jan. 20, 1989, with his theme harmony and conciliation after the often-turbulent Reagan years. With his calm and unassuming manner, he emerged from his subordinate vice-presidential role with an air of quiet authority. His Inaugural address emphasized "A new breeze is blowing, and the old bipartisanship must be made new again."

In his first months, the president, the nation's 41st, established himself as his own man and all but erased memories of what many had regarded as his fiercely abrasive presidential election campaign of 1988 and questionable tactics against his Democratic opponent. People liked his easy style and readiness to compromise even as he remained a staunch conservative, although that readiness had disconcerted some conservatives.

Bush's early Cabinet choices reflected a pragmatic desire for an efficient, nonideological government. And with his usual cautious instinct, in 1990 he nominated to the Supreme Court the scholarly David H. Souter, with broadly conservative views. Souter was confirmed without a bruising battle.

In his first year, Bush, a World War II hero, had won plaudits at home and abroad for his confident, competent conduct at the NATO 40th anniversary summit meeting in Brussels, the Paris economic conference, on his tour of Eastern Europe, and at the Malta conference with Gorbachev. Grave challenges in that year were the Lebanese hostage crisis and the ongoing war against drug trafficking.

Domestically, Bush had to cope with such issues as the *Exxon Valdez* oil spill in Alaska and the dispute over flag-burning restrictions, which was resolved, if only for a time, in mid-1990.

But in his second year, 1990, the president confronted a mounting array of problems, chief among them the staggering budget deficit and the savings and loan crisis. The president's popularity dipped sharply from its near-record public approval following the invasion of Panama in late 1989. This plunge followed Bush's recantation of his campaign "no new taxes" pledge as he sat down with Congressional leaders to tame the budget deficit and deal with a faltering economy.

In 1991, the 67-year-old president emerged as the leader of an international coalition of Western democracies, Japan, and even some Arab states that freed invaded Kuwait and vanquished, at least for a time, Iraq's President Saddam Hussein and his armies.

A nation grateful at feeling the end of the "Vietnam syndrome" gave the president an overall rating of 89 percent in a Gallup poll in March after the end of the war. The approval rate fell as the year went on, but a solid majority continued to approve the president's performance, although with growing concern about the faltering economy and other domestic problems. And there were nagging doubts about the Persian Gulf war, its motives and conduct, and about the ensuing refugee crisis.

A major Bush accomplishment in 1991 was the Strategic Arms Reduction Treaty (START), signed in July with Soviet president Mikhail S. Gorbachev at their fourth summit conference, marking the end of the long weapons buildup. Succeeding events in the Soviet Union and the disintegration of the Communist empire could only enhance his status.

The year also saw the president undergoing treatment for Graves' disease, a thyroid disorder, from which he suffered serious side effects.

In the 1992 presidential election, Bush was defeated by Gov. Bill Clinton of Arkansas.

The Bushes have lived in 17 cities and more than a score of homes and have traveled in as many countries. In her husband's frequent absences during the early years, Mrs. Bush was matriarch of a family of four boys (George, Jeb, Neil, and Marvin) and a girl (Dorothy).

After the Clinton inauguration in January, the Bushes returned to Houston, Texas.

WILLIAM JEFFERSON CLINTON was born William Jefferson Blythe IV in Hope, Ark., on Aug. 19, 1946. He was named for his father, who was killed in an automobile accident before Clinton's birth. Virginia Kelley, his mother, eventually married Roger Clinton, a car dealer, whose surname the future president later adopted.

In high school in Hot Springs, Ark., Clinton considered becoming a doctor, but politics beckoned after a meeting with President John F. Kennedy in Washington, D.C., on a Boys' Nation trip. He earned a B.S. in international affairs in 1968 at Georgetown University, having spent his junior year working for Arkansas Senator J. William Fulbright. He was a Rhodes scholar at Oxford between 1968 and 1970. He then attended Yale Law School, where he met his future wife, Hillary Rodham, a Wellesley graduate. The couple has one child, Chelsea.

Clinton taught at the University of Arkansas (1974–1976), was elected state attorney general (1976), and in 1979 became the nation's youngest governor. But he was defeated for reelection in 1980 by voters irate at a rise in the state's automobile license fees. In 1982 he was elected again. This time he reined in liberal tendencies to accommodate the conservative bent of the voters.

Clinton became the 42nd U.S. president following a turbulent political campaign. He overcame vigorous personal attacks on his character and on his actions during the Vietnam War, which he actively opposed. The "character issue" stemmed from allegations of infidelity, which Clinton refuted in a television interview in which he and Hillary avowed their relationship was solid. Throughout his term in office, Clinton was dogged by allegations relating to the Whitewater real estate deal in which he and Hillary were involved prior to the 1992 election. Though the Clintons were never accused of any wrongdoing, partners in the venture were convicted of fraud and conspiracy in a trial in 1996.

The problems faced by the new president were as daunting as they were varied. In January 1993 he became embroiled with the military leadership over his campaign pledge to allow homosexuals to serve openly in the armed services. He ultimately agreed to a compromise, dubbed the "don't ask, don't tell" policy. Clinton's first year also saw him wrangling with Congress over the Federal budget and economic policy.

In his second year, Clinton faced persistent troubles on the domestic front, with acrimonious battles raging over health care, welfare reform, and crime prevention. A health care reform package crafted by his wife failed to gain sufficient support. Clinton had to reduce his objective from massive overhaul to incremental reform.

Clinton won major victories with the passage of the North American Free Trade Agreement (NAFTA), which took effect Jan. 1, 1994, and the Global Agreement on Tariffs and Trade (GATT), which led to the establishment in 1995 of the World Trade Organization (WTO). Congress also approved a deficit reduction bill, rules allowing abortion counseling in federally funded clinics, a waiting period for handgun purchases (the Brady Bill), and a national service program.

Foreign affairs, once a weak point for a man elected on a domestic economic agenda, became a proving ground for Clinton. He improved his international image when the Israel–Jordan peace agreement was signed at the White House in the summer of 1994 by Israeli prime minister Yitzhak Rabin and Jordan's King Hussein. In the fall of that year, the administration succeeded in restoring Haiti's ousted president, Jean-Bertrand Aristide, to power. Clinton scored again by bolstering Russian president Boris Yeltsin's popularity with promises of economic aid.

The problems in Eastern Europe were Clinton's next big challenge. Though he wanted desperately to end the brutal ethnic cleansing in Bosnia, he did not want to commit American ground troops to do so. A peace accord involving American peacekeeping troops was ultimately signed in Dayton, Ohio, in November 1995.

The 1994 elections resulted in a Republican-controlled Congress, and 1995 was largely a tug-of-war between the White House and Capitol Hill over budget-balancing and other key points of the G.O.P.'s "Contract with America," crafted by Speaker of the House Newt Gingrich.

In 1996, aided by a booming economy, Clinton won reelection to a second term, becoming the first Democratic president since Franklin D. Roosevelt to do so. The country's general prosperity also made it possible in 1997 for Clinton and the Republicans to reach an agreement to balance the federal budget in three decades.

However, the character issues that had followed Clinton for years soon began to emerge once again. A series of investigations was begun to determine whether Clinton and Vice President Gore had participated in questionable fund-raising practices in their 1996 campaign.

As his tenure wore on, Clinton came under increasing pressure from Kenneth Starr, the independent counsel who in 1994 took over the investigation of the Clintons' involvement in the Whitewater land deal. Over time, Starr's brief was expanded to include other matters, such as the death of White House lawyer Vincent Foster, the handling of firings in the White House travel office, and shocking allegations of sexual misconduct by Clinton.

In Jan. 1998, Clinton was called to testify in a long-pending sexual harassment suit brought against him by Paula Corbin Jones, a former Arkansas state employee. In his testimony, Clinton denied that he had had a sexual relationship with a young White House intern, Monica Lewinsky, and that he had attempted to cover it up. Although a federal judge in Arkansas threw out the Jones sexual harassment suit in April 1998, by this time the Lewinsky affair had become the focus of Kenneth Starr's investigation as well as a national obsession.

Finally, on Aug. 17, 1998, after relentless media attention, leaks, and news of Lewinsky's upcoming testimony, Clinton made history by becoming the first U.S. president to testify in front of a grand jury in an investigation of his own possibly criminal conduct. In an address to the nation that evening, he admitted to having had an "inappropriate relationship" with Lewinsky, but reaffirmed that he did not ask anyone to lie about or cover up the affair.

Paradoxically, however, in spite of the scandalous outcome of events, Clinton's overall popularity among Americans remained high. The country seemed willing to ignore his weaknesses in character, much as they did in the 1992 elections, as long as the economy was good, his policies were popular, and the United States remained strong abroad.

On Sept. 9, Starr—a conservative Republican whose investigation was seen by Clinton supporters as a politically inspired vendetta—delivered his report to the House of Representatives. While the report outlined 11 possible grounds for impeachment, none stemmed from the initial subjects of the investigation, including the Whitewater real estate deal. The real focus of the accusations seemed to be Clinton's moral conduct, and the "Starr Report" graphically detailed his sexual affair.

Despite the American population's general disapproval of a trial (which was reflected in poll after poll), Congress moved forward in its highly partisan impeachment proceedings and on Dec. 19, Clinton became the second president in American history to be impeached. Two of the four articles of impeachment passed (Article I, grand jury perjury, and Article III, obstruction of justice), the votes drawn along party lines. After a Senate trial in Jan.–Feb. 1999, Clinton was acquitted on both counts.

While the impeachment trial overshadowed all other activity in Washington for a good portion of 1998, Clinton was forced to respond to continued problems with Iraq at the end of the year. In December, Saddam Hussein blocked a weapons inspection by the United Nations. The U.N. responded with airstrikes that would continue on a nearly daily basis for the next three months, and then off and on through the spring and summer, as Iraq taunted the U.S. and its allies further by shooting at jets patrolling the no-fly zones set up after the Persian Gulf war.

In the spring of 1999, reports of continued ethnic cleansing in the Serbian province of Kosovo were growing. Clinton and his British counterpart, Tony Blair, led the push for NATO intervention, which resulted in a 78-day bombing campaign against Serbia that began in March. Although Clinton received some sharp criticism for holding back on the deployment of NATO ground troops, he was ultimately justified, as Serbian president Slobodan Milosevic finally agreed to a peace treaty, signed June 9.

In his final year of office, the president maintained a relatively low profile but took several major trips overseas, to South Asia, Europe, and Africa. He also prepared for the 2000 elections, lending his support not only to presidential hopeful Al Gore, but also to his wife, Hillary Clinton, who successfully ran for U.S. senator from New York.

On Jan. 19, 2001, the day before he left office, Clinton agreed to a five-year suspension of his Arkansas law license and his payment of a $25,000 fine to the Arkansas Bar Association. In exchange, Kenneth Starr's successor, Robert Ray, agreed to close the Whitewater probe, ending the threat of criminal liability for Mr. Clinton after he left office.

GEORGE WALKER BUSH

GEORGE WALKER BUSH was born on July 6, 1946, in New Haven, Conn., the first child of President George Bush, who was then still a student at Yale. In 1948, the family moved to Odessa, Tex., where the senior Bush went to work in the oil business. George W. grew up mainly in Midland, Tex., and Houston and later attended two of his father's alma maters, Phillips Academy in Andover, Mass., and Yale.

After graduating from Yale with a history degree in 1968, Bush joined the Texas Air National Guard. He underwent two years of flight training and subsequently served as a part-time fighter pilot until 1973, when he entered Harvard Business School. After receiving an MBA in 1975, he returned to Texas, where he established his own oil and gas business in the late 1970s. In 1977 he met and married his wife, Laura Welch, a librarian. The couple has twin daughters, Jenna and Barbara, born in 1981.

Coming from a prominent political family—his grandfather Prescott Bush had been a senator from Connecticut and his father a U.S. congressman and political appointee—George W. had been immersed in politics since childhood, and by 1977 he had worked on several political campaigns, including three of his father's. In that year Bush finally entered the fray himself, running for U.S. Congress from the West Texas district that included his hometown of Midland. Although he won the Republican primary, he ultimately lost in the general election to his Democratic opponent.

Following his defeat, Bush returned to the oil business. In 1985, however, oil prices fell sharply, and Bush's company verged on collapse until it was acquired by a Dallas firm. It was a lucky break for Bush, and also something of a turning point. Having finalized the buyout of his oil company in September, he headed to Washington to become a paid adviser to his father's 1988 presidential campaign. It was while working on his father's campaign that Bush began to weigh the possibility of running for governor of Texas.

After the 1988 election, Bush returned to Texas and assembled a group of investors to buy the Texas Rangers for $86 million. Although Bush invested only $606,302, he was named managing partner, a position that allowed him to build his reputation in the public eye as a Texas businessman. A baseball enthusiast from his childhood, Bush preferred to sit in the stands among the other fans rather than in the owners' box.

The younger Bush's political turn at bat finally came in 1993, when, in the wake of his father's unsuccessful bid for reelection, he announced his plans to run for the Texas governorship. Although he had a tough opponent in the immensely popular incumbent Ann Richards, he created a clear agenda focused on issues such as education and juvenile justice and won with 53% of the vote.

He was reelected in 1998, not long before he announced plans to run for president. At this point the Rangers partners decided to sell the team for $250 million. The timing was fortuitous—Bush made $14.9 million (on his $606,302 investment), which helped fund his presidential campaign as well as his new 1,500-acre ranch near Crawford, Tex.

During the campaign leading up to the 2000 election, Bush characterized himself as a "compassionate conservative," a somewhat vague description meant to evoke a kinder, gentler Republican. On the core issues, however, Bush adhered closely to the traditional conservative line, favoring small government, tax cuts, a strong military, and opposing gun control and abortion. He won plaudits for his choice of running mate, Dick Cheney, who had served as secretary of defense during his father's administration and had commanded the Pentagon during the Persian Gulf War. Bush had been faulted for his lack of Washington political experience and gravitas, qualities that Cheney brought to the ticket in abundance.

With the country in a state of general prosperity and the candidates divided primarily along ideological lines, the 2000 election between George W. Bush and Vice President Al Gore was perceived to be one of the least dynamic on issues, and the party conventions and presidential debates drew smaller audiences than in previous elections. The race was expected to be close, with polls showing the candidates neck-and-neck in the weeks leading up to the Nov. 7 election. Few, however, would have predicted the contest would come down to a few hundred votes in a single state.

Bush officially became the president-elect on Dec. 13, after the U.S. Supreme Court reversed a decision by the Florida Supreme Court to allow manual recounts of ballots in some Florida counties. With Florida in his column, Bush won the presidency with 271 electoral votes, just one more than he needed, although he lost the popular vote by half a million. Bush accepted the presidency in a televised speech and promised to bring the nation together. (*See* p. 53 for an election chronology.)

Despite the delay in finding out the election results, Bush was able to effect a smooth transition, with all cabinet officers except attorney general in place ten days after the Jan. 20 inauguration. The new administration lost no time moving on a number of initiatives that Bush had campaigned on, including an education bill and legislation aimed at increasing the availability of federal funds to religious groups that provide social programs.

The top item on Bush's domestic agenda, a $1.6 trillion tax cut, was the subject of bitter partisan debate in Congress, with opponents (mostly Democratic) arguing that the bill primarily favored the wealthy and would not provide the desired economic stimulus. The Senate eventually trimmed the tax cut to $1.35 trillion over 11 years, and Bush signed it into law in early June. Eligible Americans began receiving their refund checks, $300 for individuals and $600 for married couples, in August. Victory over the tax cut was somewhat marred, however, by the defection of Sen. James Jeffords (I-Vt.) from the Republican Party—a major blow for the president, since it resulted in the Democrats' gaining control of the Senate.

Although Bush came into the White House focused on domestic issues, he soon was forced to turn his attention to foreign affairs. In April a tense situation with China over a downed U.S. spy plane on Chinese territory ended peacefully through diplomatic means. Then in June, on his first official trip to Europe, Bush faced strong criticism from European leaders on a number of issues, including the administration's proposal for a missile defense system and its refusal to back the Kyoto treaty on global warming. Specifically, the Europeans feared that a missile defense system, which would violate the 1972 Anti-Ballistic Missile Treaty (ABM), might potentially lead to a new arms race. The administration was also criticized for its disengagement from the Middle East as well as its perceived unilateralism.

With the nation's economy in the doldrums and the federal budget surplus dwindling, the Bush team in early September was gearing up for a major battle in Congress over spending for Bush's domestic programs. The surprise terrorist attack on the World Trade Center and the Pentagon on Sept. 11, however, instantly moved all pending issues to the back burner. In the hours and days following the catastophe, congressional partisans united behind the president, approving a $40 billion emergency aid package and working to hammer out comprehensive antiterrorism legislation.

In a televised address on Sept. 20, Bush warned Americans that the war against terrorism that would be waged by the U.S. and its allies would be a lengthy campaign, involving covert action as well as air strikes and potentially resulting in numerous casualties. Bush also announced the creation of a new White House agency, the Office of Homeland Security, to oversee and coordinate a national strategy to safeguard the country against future attacks. Following the speech, polls showed that the president's approval rating had soared to 90%.

The Presidential Oath of Office

The oath to be taken by the president on first entering office is specified in Article II, Section 1, of the Constitution:

I do solemnly swear (or affirm) that I will faithfully execute the office of President of the United States, and will to the best of my ability, preserve, protect, and defend the Constitution of the United States.

Senate and House Standing Committees, 107th Congress

Committees of the Senate

Aging (21 members)
Chairman: John B. Breaux (La.)
Ranking Rep.: Larry Craig (Idaho)

Agriculture, Nutrition, and Forestry (21 members)
Chairman: Tom Harkin (Iowa)
Ranking Rep.: Richard G. Lugar (Ind.)

Appropriations (29 members)
Chairman: Robert C. Byrd (W.Va.)
Ranking Rep.: Ted Stevens (Alaska)

Armed Services (25 members)
Chairman: Carl Levin (Mich.)
Ranking Rep.: John Warner (Va.)

Banking, Housing, and Urban Affairs (21 members)
Chairman: Paul S. Sarbanes (Md.)
Ranking Rep.: Phil Gramm (Tex.)

Budget (23 members)
Chairman: Kent Conrad (N.D.)
Ranking Rep.: Pete V. Domenici (N.M.)

Commerce, Science, and Transportation (23 members)
Chairman: Ernest F. Hollings (S.C.)
Ranking Rep.: John McCain (Ariz.)

Energy and Natural Resources (23 members)
Chairman: Jeff Bingaman (N.M.)
Ranking Rep.: Frank H. Murkowski (Alaska)

Environment and Public Works (19 members)
Chairman: James M. Jeffords (Vt.)
Ranking Rep.: Robert C. Smith (N.H.)

Ethics (6 members)
Chairman: Harry Reid (Nev.)
Ranking Rep.: Pat Roberts (Kans.)

Finance (21 members)
Chairman: Max Baucus (Mont.)
Ranking Rep.: Charles E. Grassley (Iowa)

Foreign Relations (19 members)
Chairman: Joseph R. Biden, Jr. (Del.)
Ranking Rep.: Jesse Helms (N.C.)

Governmental Affairs (17 members)
Chairman: Joseph Lieberman (Conn.)
Ranking Rep.: Fred Thompson (Tenn.)

Health, Education, Labor, and Pensions (21 members)
Chairman: Edward M. Kennedy (Mass.)
Ranking Rep.: Judd Gregg (N.H.)

Indian Affairs (15 members)
Chairman: Daniel K. Inouye (Hawaii)
Ranking Rep.: Ben Nighthorse Campbell (Colo.)

Intelligence (17 members)
Chairman: Bob Graham (Fla.)
Ranking Rep.: Richard C. Shelby (Ala.)

Judiciary (19 members)
Chairman: Patrick J. Leahy (Vt.)
Ranking Rep.: Orrin G. Hatch (Utah)

Rules and Administration (19 members)
Chairman: Christopher Dodd (Conn.)
Ranking Rep.: Mitch McConnell (Ky.)

Small Business (19 members)
Chairman: John Kerry (Mass.)
Ranking Rep.: Christopher S. Bond (Mo.)

Veterans' Affairs (15 members)
Chairman: John D. Rockefeller IV (W.Va.)
Ranking Rep: Arlen Specter (Pa.)

Committees of the House

Agriculture (51 members)
Chairman: Larry Combest (Tex.)
Ranking Dem.: Charles W. Stenholm (Tex.)

Appropriations (65 members)
Chairman: C. W. Bill Young (Fla.)
Ranking Dem.: David R. Obey (Wis.)

Armed Services (60 members)
Chairman: Bob Stump (Ariz.)
Ranking Dem.: Ike Skelton (Mo.)

Budget (43 members)
Chairman: Jim Nussle (Iowa)
Ranking Dem.: John M. Spratt, Jr. (S.C.)

Education and the Workforce (49 members)
Chairman: John A. Boehner (Ohio)
Ranking Dem.: George Miller (Calif.)

Financial Services (70 members)
Chairman: Michael G. Oxley (Ohio)
Ranking Dem.: John J. LaFalce (N.Y.)

Government Reform (44 members)
Chairman: Dan Burton (Ind.)
Ranking Dem.: Henry A. Waxman (Calif.)

House Administration (9 members)
Chairman: Robert W. Ney (Ohio)
Ranking Dem.: Steny H. Hoyer (Md.)

International Relations (49 members)
Chairman: Henry J. Hyde (Ill.)
Ranking Dem.: Tom Lantos (Calif.)

Judiciary (37 members)
Chairman: F. James Sensenbrenner, Jr. (Wis.)
Ranking Dem.: John Conyers, Jr. (Mich.)

Resources (52 members)
Chairman: James V. Hansen (Utah)
Ranking Dem.: Nick J. Rahall II (W. Va.)

Rules (13 members)
Chairman: David Dreier (Calif.)
Ranking Dem.: Martin Frost (Tex.)

Science (47 members)
Chairman: Sherwood L. Boehlert (N.Y.)
Ranking Dem.: Ralph M. Hall (Tex.)

Small Business (36 members)
Chairman: Donald A. Manzullo (Ill.)
Ranking Dem.: Nydia M. Velázquez (N.Y.)

Standards of Official Conduct (10 members)
Chairman: Joel Hefley (Colo.)
Ranking Dem.: Howard L. Berman (Calif.)

Transportation and Infrastructure (75 members)
Chairman: Don Young (Alaska)
Ranking Dem.: James L. Oberstar (Minn.)

Veterans' Affairs (31 members)
Chairman: Christopher H. Smith (N.J.)
Ranking Dem.: Lane Evans (Ill.)

Ways and Means (41 members)
Chairman: William M. Thomas (Calif.)
Ranking Dem.: Charles B. Rangel (N.Y.)

Speakers of the House of Representatives

Dates served	Congress	Name and state	Dates served	Congress	Name and state
1789–1791	1	Frederick A. C. Muhlenberg (Pa.)	1869–1875	41–43	James G. Blaine (Maine)
1791–1793	2	Jonathan Trumbull (Conn.)	1875–1876	44	Michael C. Kerr (Ind.)[6]
1793–1795	3	Frederick A. C. Muhlenberg (Pa.)	1876–1881	44–46	Samuel J. Randall (Pa.)
1795–1799	4–5	Jonathan Dayton (N.J.)[1]	1881–1883	47	J. Warren Keifer (Ohio)
1799–1801	6	Theodore Sedgwick (Mass.)	1883–1889	48–50	John G. Carlisle (Ky.)
1801–1807	7–9	Nathaniel Macon (N.C.)	1889–1891	51	Thomas B. Reed (Maine)
1807–1811	10–11	Joseph B. Varnum (Mass.)	1891–1895	52–53	Charles F. Crisp (Ga.)
1811–1814	12–13	Henry Clay (Ky.)[2]	1895–1899	54–55	Thomas B. Reed (Maine)
1814–1815	13	Langdon Cheves (S.C.)	1899–1903	56–57	David B. Henderson (Iowa)
1815–1820	14–16	Henry Clay (Ky.)[3]	1903–1911	58–61	Joseph G. Cannon (Ill.)
1820–1821	16	John W. Taylor (N.Y.)	1911–1919	62–65	Champ Clark (Mo.)
1821–1823	17	Philip P. Barbour (Va.)	1919–1925	66–68	Frederick H. Gillett (Mass.)
1823–1825	18	Henry Clay (Ky.)	1925–1931	69–71	Nicholas Longworth (Ohio)
1825–1827	19	John W. Taylor (N.Y.)	1931–1933	72	John N. Garner (Tex.)
1827–1834	20–23	Andrew Stevenson (Va.)[4]	1933–1934	73	Henry T. Rainey (Ill.)[7]
1834–1835	23	John Bell (Tenn.)	1935–1936	74	Joseph W. Byrns (Tenn.)[8]
1835–1839	24–25	James K. Polk (Tenn.)	1936–1940	74–76	William B. Bankhead (Ala.)[9]
1839–1841	26	Robert M. T. Hunter (Va.)	1940–1947	76–79	Sam Rayburn (Tex.)
1841–1843	27	John White (Ky.)	1947–1949	80	Joseph W. Martin, Jr. (Mass.)
1843–1845	28	John W. Jones (Va.)	1949–1953	81–82	Sam Rayburn (Tex.)
1845–1847	29	John W. Davis (Ind.)	1953–1955	83	Joseph W. Martin, Jr. (Mass.)
1847–1849	30	Robert C. Winthrop (Mass.)	1955–1961	84–87	Sam Rayburn (Tex.)[10]
1849–1851	31	Howell Cobb (Ga.)	1963–1971	87–91	John W. McCormack (Mass.)[11]
1851–1855	32–33	Linn Boyd (Ky.)	1971–1977	92–94	Carl Albert (Okla.)[12]
1855–1857	34	Nathaniel P. Banks (Mass.)	1977–1987	95–99	Thomas P. O'Neill, Jr. (Mass.)[13]
1857–1859	35	James L. Orr (S.C.)	1987–1989	100–101	James C. Wright, Jr. (Tex.)[14]
1859–1861	36	Wm. Pennington (N.J.)	1989–1995	101–103	Thomas S. Foley (Wash.)
1861–1863	37	Galusha A. Grow (Pa.)	1995–1999	104–105	Newt Gingrich (Ga.)[15]
1863–1869	38–40	Schuyler Colfax (Ind.)	1999–	106–	Dennis Hastert (Ill.)
1869–1869	40	Theodore M. Pomeroy (N.Y.)[5]			

1. George Dent (Md.) was elected Speaker pro tempore for April 20 and May 28, 1798. 2. Resigned during second session of 13th Congress. 3. Resigned between first and second sessions of 16th Congress. 4. Resigned during first session of 23rd Congress. 5. Elected Speaker and served the day of adjournment. 6. Died between first and second sessions of 44th Congress. During first session, there were two Speakers pro tempore: Samuel S. Cox (N.Y.), appointed for Feb. 17, May 12, and June 19, 1876, and Milton Sayler (Ohio), appointed for June 4, 1876. 7. Died in 1934 after adjournment of second session of 73rd Congress. 8. Died during second session of 74th Congress. 9. Died during third session of 76th Congress. 10. Died between first and second sessions of 87th Congress. 11. Not a candidate in 1970 election. 12. Not a candidate in 1976 election. 13. Not a candidate in 1986 election. 14. Resigned during first session of 101st Congress. 15. Resigned Jan. 3, 1999, three days before the first session of the 106th Congress. *Source: Congressional Directory.*

Floor Leaders of the Senate

Democratic	Republican
Gilbert M. Hitchcock, Neb. (Min. 1919–20)	Charles Curtis, Kan. (Maj. 1925–29)
Oscar W. Underwood, Ala. (Min. 1920–23)	James E. Watson, Ind. (Maj. 1929–33)
Joseph T. Robinson, Ark. (Min. 1923–33, Maj. 1933–37)	Charles L. McNary, Ore. (Min. 1933–44)
Alben W. Barkley, Ky. (Maj. 1937–46, Min. 1947–48)	Wallace H. White, Jr., Maine (Min. 1944–47, Maj. 1947–48)
Scott W. Lucas, Ill. (Maj. 1949–50)	Kenneth S. Wherry, Neb. (Min. 1949–51)
Ernest W. McFarland, Ariz. (Maj. 1951–52)	Styles Bridges, N.H. (Min. 1951–52)
Lyndon B. Johnson, Tex. (Min. 1953–54, Maj. 1955–60)	Robert A. Taft, Ohio (Maj. 1953)
Mike Mansfield, Mont. (Maj. 1961–77)	William F. Knowland, Calif. (Maj. 1953–54, Min. 1955–58)
Robert C. Byrd, W. Va. (Maj. 1977–81, Min. 1981–86, Maj. 1987–88)	Everett M. Dirksen, Ill. (Min. 1959–69)
George John Mitchell, Maine (Maj. 1989–1994)	Hugh Scott, Pa. (Min. 1969–1977)
Thomas A. Daschle, S.D. (Min. 1995–2001, Maj. 2001–)	Howard H. Baker, Jr., Tenn. (Min. 1977–81, Maj. 1981–84)
	Robert J. Dole, Kan. (Maj. 1985–86, Min. 1987–94, Maj. 1995–96)
	Trent Lott, Miss. (Maj. 1996–2001, Min. 2001–)

NOTE: Min. = Minority Leader; Maj. = Majority Leader. *Source:* United States Senate, Secretary for the Majority.

Composition of Congress, by Political Party, 1855–2001

Congress	Years	Senate					House				
		Total	Dems	Reps	Others	Vacant	Total	Dems	Reps	Others	Vacant
34th	1855–1857	62	42	15	5	—	234	83	108	43	—
35th	1857–1859	64	39	20	5	—	237	131	92	14	—
36th	1859–1861	66	38	26	2	—	237	101	113	23	—
37th	1861–1863	50	11	31	7	1	178	42	106	28	2
38th	1863–1865	51	12	39	—	—	183	80	103	—	—
39th	1865–1867	52	10	42	—	—	191	46	145	—	—
40th	1867–1869	53	11	42	—	—	193	49	143	—	1
41st	1869–1871	74	11	61	—	2	243	73	170	—	—
42nd	1871–1873	74	17	57	—	—	243	104	139	—	—
43rd	1873–1875	74	19	54	—	1	293	88	203	—	2
44th	1875–1877	76	29	46	—	1	293	181	107	3	2
45th	1877–1879	76	36	39	1	—	293	156	137	—	—
46th	1879–1881	76	43	33	—	—	293	150	128	14	1
47th	1881–1883	76	37	37	2	—	293	130	152	11	—
48th	1883–1885	76	36	40	—	—	325	200	119	6	—
49th	1885–1887	76	34	41	—	1	325	182	140	2	1
50th	1887–1889	76	37	39	—	—	325	170	151	4	—
51st	1889–1891	84	37	47	—	—	330	156	173	1	—
52nd	1891–1893	88	39	47	2	—	333	231	88	14	—
53rd	1893–1895	88	44	38	3	3	356	220	126	10	—
54th	1895–1897	88	39	44	5	—	357	104	246	7	—
55th	1897–1899	90	34	46	10	—	357	134	206	16	1
56th	1899–1901	90	26	53	11	—	357	163	185	9	—
57th	1901–1903	90	29	56	3	2	357	153	198	5	1
58th	1903–1905	90	32	58	—	—	386	178	207	—	1
59th	1905–1907	90	32	58	—	—	386	136	250	—	—
60th	1907–1909	92	29	61	—	2	386	164	222	—	—
61st	1909–1911	92	32	59	—	1	391	172	219	—	—
62nd	1911–1913	92	42	49	—	1	391	228	162	1	—
63rd	1913–1915	96	51	44	1	—	435	290	127	18	—
64th	1915–1917	96	56	39	1	—	435	231	193	8	3
65th	1917–1919	96	53	42	1	—	435	210[1]	216	9	—
66th	1919–1921	96	47	48	1	—	435	191	237	7	—
67th	1921–1923	96	37	59	—	—	435	132	300	1	2
68th	1923–1925	96	43	51	2	—	435	207	225	3	—
69th	1925–1927	96	40	54	1	1	435	183	247	5	—
70th	1927–1929	96	47	48	1	—	435	195	237	3	—
71st	1929–1931	96	39	56	1	—	435	163	267	1	4
72nd	1931–1933	96	47	48	1	—	435	216[2]	218	1	—
73rd	1933–1935	96	59	36	1	—	435	313	117	5	—
74th	1935–1937	96	69	25	2	—	435	322	103	10	—
75th	1937–1939	96	75	17	4	—	435	333	89	13	—
76th	1939–1941	96	69	23	4	—	435	262	169	4	—
77th	1941–1943	96	66	28	2	—	435	267	162	6	—
78th	1943–1945	96	57	38	1	—	435	222	209	4	—
79th	1945–1947	96	57	38	1	—	435	243	190	2	—
80th	1947–1949	96	45	51	—	—	435	188	246	1	—
81st	1949–1951	96	54	42	—	—	435	263	171	1	—
82nd	1951–1953	96	48	47	1	—	435	234	199	2	—
83rd	1953–1955	96	46	48	2	—	435	213	221	1	—
84th	1955–1957	96	48	47	1	—	435	232	203	—	—
85th	1957–1959	96	49	47	—	—	435	234	201	—	—
86th	1959–1961	98	64	34	—	—	436[3]	283	153	—	—
87th	1961–1963	100	64	36	—	—	437[4]	262	175	—	—
88th	1963–1965	100	67	33	—	—	435	258	176	—	1
89th	1965–1967	100	68	32	—	—	435	295	140	—	—
90th	1967–1969	100	64	36	—	—	435	248	187	—	—
91st	1969–1971	100	58	42	—	—	435	243	192	—	—
92nd	1971–1973	100	54	44	2	—	435	255	180	—	—
93rd	1973–1975	100	56	42	2	—	435	242	192	1	—
94th	1975–1977	100	61	37	2	—	435	291	144	—	—
95th	1977–1979	100	61	38	1	—	435	292	143	—	—
96th	1979–1981	100	58	41	1	—	435	277	158	—	—
97th	1981–1983	100	46	53	1	—	435	242	192	1	—
98th	1983–1985	100	46	54	—	—	435	269	166	—	—
99th	1985–1987	100	47	53	—	—	435	253	182	—	—
100th	1987–1989	100	55	45	—	—	435	258	177	—	—
101st	1989–1991	100	55	45	—	—	435	260	175	—	—

Congress	Years	Senate					House				
		Total	Dems	Reps	Others	Vacant	Total	Dems	Reps	Others	Vacant
102nd	1991–1993	100	56	44	—	—	435	267	167	1	—
103rd	1993–1995	100	57	43	—	—	435	258	176	1	—
104th	1995–1997	100	48	52	—	—	435	204	230	1	—
105th	1997–1999	100	45	55	—	—	435	206	228	1	—
106th	1999–2001	100	45	55	—	—	435	211	222	2	—
107th	2001–2003	100	50	50	—	—	435	212	221	2	—

NOTE: All figures reflect immediate results of elections. 1. Democrats organized House with help of other parties. 2. Democrats organized House due to Republican deaths. 3. Proclamation declaring Alaska a state issued Jan 3., 1959. 4. Proclamation declaring Hawaii a state issued Aug. 21, 1959. *Source:* Office of the Clerk of the House of Representatives. Web: http://clerkweb.house.gov/histrecs/history.htm.

Congressional Apportionment, 2000

Source: U.S. Census Bureau

Apportionment is the process of dividing the 435 seats in the House of Representatives among the 50 states. The number of seats, or representatives, each state is entitled to is apportioned according to the new census figures that are compiled every 10 years. States with larger populations have more representatives than states with smaller populations. Each state must have at least one representative.

Once the number of seats is assigned to each state, it is up to the individual state legislatures to redraw new congressional districts. Each representative is elected by voters from a congressional district within their state.

Who Counts?

The population figure used to calculate the apportionment of House seats is based on the total resident population of the United States, including citizens and noncitizens, plus U.S. military personnel and federal civilian employees and their dependents living overseas. It excludes the populations of the District of Columbia, Puerto Rico, and other U.S. territories that do not have voting seats in the House of Representatives. The Census 2000 apportionment population was 281,424,177.

Congressional District Size

The number of representatives in the U.S. House of Representatives has remained constant at 435 since 1911, except for a temporary increase to 437 at the time of admission of Alaska and Hawaii as states in 1959. However, the apportionment based on the 1960 census, which took effect for the election of 1962, reverted to 435 seats.

The average size of a congressional district based on the Census 2000 apportionment population will be 646,952, more than triple the average district size of 193,167 based on the 1900 census apportionment, and about 74,486 more than the average size of 572,466 based on the 1990 census.

Congressional Seats Gained/Loss in the 108th Congress[1]

Seats gained		Seats lost	
+ 2 seats	**+1 seat**	**−1 seat**	**−2 seats**
Arizona (8)	California (53)	Connecticut (5)	New York (29)
Florida (25)	Colorado (7)	Illinois (19)	Pennsylvania (19)
Georgia (13)	Nevada (3)	Indiana (9)	
Texas (32)	North Carolina (13)	Michigan (15)	
		Mississippi (4)	
		Ohio (18)	
		Oklahoma (5)	
		Wisconsin (8)	

NOTE: The number of representatives based on Census 2000 is given in parentheses after each state. 1. Based on Census 2000. *Source:* U.S. Census Bureau, Census 2000. Web: www.census.gov.

Salaries of the President, Vice President, and Other U.S. Officials, 2001

(per year)

Position	Salary	Position	Salary
President		Vice President	$186,300[2]
1789	$ 25,000	Senator	145,100
1873	50,000	Representative	145,100
1909	75,000	Majority and Minority Leaders	161,200
1949	100,000[1]	Speaker of the House	186,300
1969	200,000[1]	Chief Justice, U.S. Supreme Court	186,300
2001	400,000[1]	Assoc. Justice, U.S. Supreme Court	178,300

1. Plus $50,000 non-taxable expense allowance to assist in defraying expenses relating to or resulting from the discharge of his official duties. 2. Plus $10,000 taxable expense allowance. *Source:* Office of Personnel Management. Web: www.opm.gov/.

How a Bill Becomes a Law

When a senator or a representative introduces a bill, he or she sends it to the clerk of his house, who gives it a number and title. This is the *first reading,* and the bill is referred to the proper committee.

The committee may decide the bill is unwise or unnecessary and *table* it, thus killing it at once. Or it may decide the bill is worthwhile and hold hearings to listen to facts and opinions presented by experts and other interested persons. After members of the committee have debated the bill and perhaps offered amendments, a vote is taken; and if the vote is favorable, the bill is sent back to the floor of the house.

The clerk reads the bill sentence by sentence to the house, and this is known as the *second reading.* Members may then debate the bill and offer amendments. In the House of Representatives, the time for debate is limited by a *cloture rule,* but there is no such restriction in the Senate for cloture, where 60 votes are required. This makes possible a *filibuster,* in which one or more opponents hold the floor to defeat the bill.

The *third reading* is by title only, and the bill is put to a vote, which may be by voice or roll call, depending on the circumstances and parliamentary rules. Members who must be absent at the time but who wish to record their vote may be paired if each negative vote has a balancing affirmative one.

The bill then goes to the other house of Congress, where it may be defeated, or passed with or without amendments. If the bill is defeated, it dies. If it is passed with amendments, a joint congressional committee must be appointed by both houses to iron out the differences.

After its final passage by both houses, the bill is sent to the president. If he approves, he signs it, and the bill becomes a law. However, if he disapproves, he *vetoes* the bill by refusing to sign it and sending it back to the house of origin with his reasons for the veto. The objections are read and debated, and a roll-call vote is taken. If the bill receives less than a two-thirds vote, it is defeated and goes no further. But if it receives a two-thirds vote or greater, it is sent to the other house for a vote. If that house also passes it by a two-thirds vote, the president's veto is *overridden,* and the bill becomes a law.

Should the president desire neither to sign nor to veto the bill, he may retain it for ten days, Sundays excepted, after which time it automatically becomes a law without signature. However, if Congress has adjourned within those ten days, the bill is automatically killed, that process of indirect rejection being known as a *pocket veto.*

Presidential Vetoes, 1789–1999

President	Coincident Congresses	Regular vetoes	Pocket vetoes	Total vetoes	Vetoes overridden
Washington	1st–4th	2	—	2	—
Adams	5th–6th	—	—	—	—
Jefferson	7th–10th	—	—	—	—
Madison	11th–14th	5	2	7	—
Monroe	15th–18th	1	—	1	—
J. Q. Adams	19th–20th	—	—	—	—
Jackson	21st–24th	5	7	12	—
Van Buren	25th–26th	—	1	1	—
W. H. Harrison	27th	—	—	—	—
Tyler	27th–28th	6	4	10	1
Polk	29th–30th	2	1	3	—
Taylor	31st	—	—	—	—
Fillmore	31st–32nd	—	—	—	—
Pierce	33rd–34th	9	—	9	5
Buchanan	35th–36th	4	3	7	—
Lincoln	37th–39th	2	5	7	—
A. Johnson	39th–40th	21	8	29	15
Grant	41st–44th	45	48	93	4
Hayes	45th–46th	12	1	13	1
Garfield	47th	—	—	—	—
Arthur	47th–48th	4	8	12	1
Cleveland	49th–50th	304	110	414	2
B. Harrison	51st–52nd	19	25	44	1
Cleveland	53rd–54th	42	128	170	5
McKinley	55th–57th	6	36	42	—
T. Roosevelt	57th–60th	42	40	82	1
Taft	61st–62nd	30	9	39	1
Wilson	63rd–66th	33	11	44	6
Harding	67th	5	1	6	—
Coolidge	68th–70th	20	30	50	4
Hoover	71st–72nd	21	16	37	3
F. D. Roosevelt	73rd–79th	372	263	635	9
Truman	79th–82nd	180	70	250	12
Eisenhower	83rd–86th	73	108	181	2
Kennedy	87th–88th	12	9	21	—
L. B. Johnson	88th–90th	16	14	30	—

President	Coincident Congresses	Regular vetoes	Pocket vetoes	Total vetoes	Vetoes overridden
Nixon	91st–93rd	26	17	43	7
Ford	93rd–94th	48	18	66	12
Carter	95th–96th	13	18	31	2
Reagan	97th–100th	39	39	78	9
G. H. W. Bush[1]	101st–102nd	29	15	44	1
Clinton	103rd–106th	33	4	37	2
Total		**1,481**	**1,069**	**2,550**	**106**

1. President Bush attempted to pocket veto two bills during intrasession recess periods. Congress considered the two bills enacted into law because of the president's failure to return the legislation. The bills are not counted as pocket vetoes in this table. *Source: Presidential Vetoes, 1789–Present: A Summary Overview*, Nov. 4, 2000.

Order of Presidential Succession

The procedure for filling vacancies in the presidency and vice presidency is outlined by the 20th and 25th amendments to the Constitution. The Presidential Succession Act of 1792 had placed the Senate president pro tempore[1] and the Speaker of the House next in the line of succession, but in 1886 Congress replaced them with the cabinet officers. The Presidential Succession Act of 1947, signed by President Harry Truman, changed the order again to what it is today.

1. The Vice President
2. Speaker of the House
3. President pro tempore of the Senate[1]
4. Secretary of State
5. Secretary of the Treasury
6. Secretary of Defense
7. Attorney General
8. Secretary of the Interior
9. Secretary of Agriculture
10. Secretary of Commerce
11. Secretary of Labor
12. Secretary of Health and Human Services
13. Secretary of Housing and Urban Development
14. Secretary of Transportation
15. Secretary of Energy
16. Secretary of Education
17. Secretary of Veterans Affairs

NOTE: An official cannot succeed to the Presidency unless that person meets the Constitutional requirements. 1. The president pro tempore presides over the Senate when the vice president is absent. By tradition the position is held by the senior member of the majority party.

Executive Departments and Agencies

Source: United States Government Manual, 2001–2002

Unless otherwise indicated, addresses shown are in Washington, D.C.

White House Offices and Agencies

Office of Administration
Eisenhower Executive Office Bldg., 725 17th St., N.W. (20503)
   Established: Dec. 12, 1977
   Director: Phillip D. Larsen
Office of National Drug Control Policy
Executive Office of the President (20503)
   Established: Jan. 29, 1989
   Director: Edward H. Jurith, Acting
Council of Economic Advisers (CEA)
Old Executive Office Bldg. (20502)
   Members: 3
   Established: Feb. 20, 1946
   Chair: R. Glenn Hubbard
Council on Environmental Quality
Room 360, Eisenhower Executive Office Bldg. (20501)
   Established: 1969
   Chair: Vacant
Office of Homeland Security
   Established: 2001
   Chair: Tom Ridge
Office of Management and Budget
Executive Office Bldg. (20503)
   Established: July 1, 1939
   Director: Mitchell Daniels, Jr.
Office of Science and Technology Policy
Eisenhower Executive Office Building (20502)
   Established: May 11, 1976
   Director: Rosina Bierbaum, Acting

National Security Council (NSC)
Eisenhower Executive Office Bldg. (20504)
   Members: 4
   Established: July 26, 1947
   Chair: The President
   National Security Adviser: Condoleezza Rice
   Other members: Vice President; Secretary of State; Secretary of Defense
Office of the United States Trade Representative
600 17th St., N.W. (20508)
   Established: Jan. 15, 1963
   Trade Representative: Robert Zoellick

Executive Departments

Department of Agriculture
1400 Independence Ave., S.W. (20250)
   Established: May 15, 1862. Administered by Commissioner of Agriculture until 1889, when it was made executive department.
   Secretary: Ann Veneman
Department of Commerce
14th St. and Constitution Ave., N.W. (20230)
   Established: Department of Commerce and Labor was created Feb. 14, 1903. On March 4, 1913, all labor activities were transferred out of Department of Commerce and Labor and it was renamed Department of Commerce.
   Secretary: Donald L. Evans
Department of Defense
Office of the Secretary, The Pentagon (20301-1155)
   Established: July 26, 1947, as National Military Establishment; name changed to Department of Defense on Aug. 10, 1949. Subordinate to Secretary of Defense are Secretaries of Army, Navy, Air Force.
   Secretary: Donald H. Rumsfeld

Deputy Secretary: Paul D. Wolfowitz
Secretary of Army: Thomas E. White
Secretary of Navy: Gordon R. Englandz
Secretary of Air Force: James G. Roche
Commandant of Marine Corps: Gen. James L. Jones
Joint Chiefs of Staff: Gen. Richard B. Myers, Air Force, Chairman; Gen. Peter Pace, Marine Corps, Vice Chairman; Gen. Eric K. Shinseki, Army; Adm. Vernon E. Clark, Navy; Gen. Michael E. Ryan, Air Force; Gen. James L. Jones, Marine Corps.

Department of Education
400 Maryland Ave., S.W. (20202)
Established: Oct. 17, 1979
Secretary: Roderick R. Paige

Department of Energy
1000 Independence Ave., S.W. (20585)
Established: Oct. 1, 1977
Secretary: Spencer Abraham

Department of Health and Human Services
200 Independence Ave., S.W. (20201)
Established: Department of Health, Education, and Welfare was created April 11, 1953, replacing Federal Security Agency created in 1939. On Oct. 17, 1979, the Department of Education became a separate department.
Secretary: Tommy G. Thompson
Surgeon General: David Satcher

Department of Housing and Urban Development
451 7th St., S.W. (20410)
Established: Nov. 9, 1965, replacing Housing and Home Finance Agency created in 1947
Secretary: Melquiades R. Martinez

Department of the Interior
1849 C St., N.W. (20240)
Established: March 3, 1849
Secretary: Gale A. Norton

Department of Justice
950 Pennsylvania Ave., N.W. (20530)
Established: Office of Attorney General was created Sept. 24, 1789. Although one of the original cabinet members, the attorney general was not an executive department head until June 22, 1870, when the Department of Justice was established.
Attorney General: John Ashcroft
Solicitor General: Theodore B. Olson
Director of FBI: Robert S. Mueller, III

Department of Labor
200 Constitution Ave., N.W. (20210)
Established: Bureau of Labor was created in 1884 under Department of the Interior; later became independent department without executive rank. Returned to bureau status in Department of Commerce and Labor, but on March 4, 1913, became independent executive department under its present name.
Secretary: Elaine L. Chao

Department of State
2201 C St., N.W. (20520)
Established: 1781 as Department of Foreign Affairs; reconstituted, 1789, following adoption of Constitution; name changed to Department of State Sept. 15, 1789.
Secretary: Colin L. Powell
UN Ambassador: John D. Negroponte
Deputy UN Ambassador: James Cunningham

Department of Transportation
400 7th St., S.W. (20590)
Established: Oct. 15, 1966, as result of Department of Transportation Act, which became effective April 1, 1967.
Secretary: Norman Y. Mineta

Department of the Treasury
1500 Pennsylvania Ave., N.W. (20220)
Established: Sept. 2, 1789
Secretary: Paul H. O'Neill
Treasurer of the U.S.: Rosario Marin

Department of Veterans' Affairs
810 Vermont Ave., N.W. (20420)
Established: March 15, 1989, replacing Veterans Administration created in 1930
Secretary: Anthony J. Principi

Major Independent Agencies

Central Intelligence Agency (CIA)
Washington, D.C. (20505)
Established: 1947
Director of Central Intelligence: George J. Tenet

U.S. Commission on Civil Rights
624 9th St., N.W. (20425)
Established: 1957
Chair: Mary Frances Berry

Consumer Product Safety Commission
East West Towers, 4330 East West Highway, Bethesda, Md. 20814
Established: Oct. 27, 1972
Chair: Ann Brown

Corporation for National and Community Service
1201 New York Ave., N.W. (20525)
Established: Sept. 1993
CEO: Wendy Zenker, Acting

Environmental Protection Agency (EPA)
1200 Pennsylvania Ave., N.W. (20460)
Established: Dec. 2, 1970
Administrator: Christine Todd Whitman

Equal Employment Opportunity Commission (EEOC)
1801 L St., N.W. (20507)
Members: 5
Established: July 2, 1965
Chair: Ida L. Castro

Farm Credit Administration (FCA)
1501 Farm Credit Dr., McLean, Va. 22102-5090
Members: 13
Established: March 27, 1933
Chair: Michael M. Reyna

Federal Communications Commission (FCC)
445 Twelfth Street, S.W. (20554)
Established: 1934
Chair: Michael Powell

Federal Deposit Insurance Corporation (FDIC)
550 17th St., N.W. (20429)
Established: June 16, 1933
Chair: Donald E. Powell

Federal Election Commission (FEC)
999 E St., N.W. (20463)
Members: 6
Established: 1975
Chair: Danny L. McDonald

Federal Maritime Commission
800 North Capitol St., N.W. (20573-0001)
Members: 5
Established: Aug. 12, 1961
Chair: Harold J. Creel, Jr.

Federal Mediation and Conciliation Service (FMCS)
2100 K St., N.W. (20427)
Established: 1947
Director: C. Richard Barnes

Federal Reserve System (FRS), Board of Governors of
20th St. & Constitution Ave., N.W. (20551)
Members: 7
Established: Dec. 23, 1913
Chair: Alan Greenspan

Federal Trade Commission (FTC)
600 Pennsylvania Ave., N.W. (20580)
Members: 5
Established: Sept. 26, 1914
Chair: Timothy J. Muris

General Services Administration (GSA)
1800 F St., N.W. (20405)
Established: July 1, 1949
Administrator: Stephen A. Perry

U.S. Information Agency
301 Fourth St., S.W. (20547)
 Established: Aug. 1, 1953. Reorganized April 1, 1978.
 Director: Theodore C. Streibert
U.S. International Trade Commission
500 E St., S.W. (20436)
 Members: 6
 Established: Sept. 8, 1916
 Chair: Stephen Koplan
National Aeronautics and Space Administration (NASA)
300 E St., S.W. (20546)
 Established: 1958
 Administrator: Daniel S. Goldin
National Archives and Records Administration (NARA)
8601 Adelphi Road, College Park, Md. 20740-6001
 Established: Oct. 19, 1984. NARA is the successor agency to the National Archives Establishment, which was created in 1934 and later incorporated into the General Services Administration as the National Archives and Records Service in 1949.
 Archivist of the U.S.: John W. Carlin
National Foundation on the Arts and the Humanities
1100 Pennsylvania Ave., N.W. (20506-0001)
 Established: 1965
 Chairs: National Endowment for the Arts, Chair, William Ivey; National Endowment for the Humanities, Chair, Bruce Cole
National Labor Relations Board (NLRB)
1099 14th St., N.W. (20570)
 Members: 5
 Established: July 5, 1935
 Chair: John C. Truesdale
National Mediation Board
Suite 250 East, 1301 K St., N.W. (20572)
 Established: June 21, 1934
 Chair: Francis J. Duggan
National Science Foundation (NSF)
4201 Wilson Blvd., Arlington, Va. 22230
 Established: 1950
 Director: Rita R. Colwell
National Transportation Safety Board
490 L'Enfant Plaza, S.W. (20594)
 Members: 5
 Established: April 1, 1967, as an independent agency supported by the Dept. of Transportation. Ties with Dept. of Transportation officially ended in 1975.
 Chair: Marion Blakey
Nuclear Regulatory Commission (NRC)
Washington, D.C. 20555
 Members: 5
 Established: Jan. 19, 1975
 Chair: Richard A. Meserve
Office of Personnel Management (OPM)
1900 E St., N.W. (20415-0001)
 Established: Jan. 1, 1979
 Director: Kay Coles James
U.S. Postal Service
475 L'Enfant Plaza West, S.W. (20260-0010)
 Established: In 1775 with the appointment of Benjamin Franklin as the first postmaster general under the Continental Congress. In 1970 became independent agency headed by 11-member board of governors.
 Postmaster General: John E. Potter
Securities and Exchange Commission (SEC)
450 5th St., N.W. (20549)
 Members: 5
 Established: July 2, 1934
 Chair: Harvey L. Pitt
Selective Service System (SSS)
National Headquarters, Arlington, Va., 22209-2425
 Established: Sept. 16, 1940

 Director: Alfred Rascon
Small Business Administration (SBA)
409 3rd St., S.W. (20416)
 Established: July 30, 1953
 Administrator: Hector V. Barreto
Tennessee Valley Authority (TVA)
400 West Summit Hill Drive, Knoxville, Tenn. 37902. Washington office: One Massachusetts Ave., N.W. (20444-0001)
 Members of Board of Directors: 3
 Established: May 18, 1933
 Chairman: Glenn L. McCullough, Jr.

Other Independent Agencies

American Battle Monuments Commission—Casimir Pulaski Bldg., 20 Massachusetts Ave., N.W. (20314)
Appalachian Regional Commission—1666 Connecticut Ave., N.W., Suite 700 (20235)
Commission of Fine Arts—441 F St., N.W., Ste. 312 (20001)
Commodity Futures Trading Commission—1155 21st St., N.W. (20581)
Export-Import Bank of the United States—811 Vermont Ave., N.W. (20571)
Federal Emergency Management Agency—500 C St., S.W. (20472)
Federal Housing Finance Board—1777 F St., N.W. (20006)
Federal Labor Relations Authority—607 14th St., N.W. (20424-0001)
Inter-American Foundation—901 N. Stuart St., Arlington, Va. 22203
National Commission on Libraries and Information Science—1110 Vermont Ave., N.W., Ste. 820 (20005-3552)
National Credit Union Administration—1775 Duke St., Alexandria, Va. 22314-3428
Occupational Safety and Health Review Commission—1120 20th St., N.W. (20036-3419)
U.S. Parole Commission—Dept. of Justice, 5550 Friendship Blvd., Ste. 420, Chevy Chase, Md. 20815
Peace Corps—1111 20th St., N.W. (20526)
Pension Benefit Guaranty Corporation—1200 K St., N.W. (20005-4026)
Postal Rate Commission—1333 H St., N.W. (20268-0001)
President's Council on Physical Fitness and Sports—Dept. W, 200 Independence Ave., S.W., Room 738-H (20201-0004)
Railroad Retirement Board (RRB)—844 N. Rush St., Ninth Floor, Chicago, Ill. 60611-2092; Office of Legislative Affairs: 1310 G St., N.W, Ste. 500 (20005-3004).

Legislative Department

Architect of the Capitol—U.S. Capitol Building (20515)
General Accounting Office (GAO)—441 G St., N.W. (20548)
Government Printing Office (GPO)—732 North Capitol St., N.W. (20401)
Library of Congress—101 Independence Ave., S.E. (20540)
United States Botanic Garden—Office of Executive Director, 245 1st St., S.W. (20024)

Quasi-Official Agencies

American National Red Cross—430 17th St., N.W. (20006)
Legal Services Corporation—750 1st St., N.E. (20002-4250)
National Academy of Sciences, National Academy of Engineering, National Research Council, Institute of Medicine—2101 Constitution Ave., N.W. (20418)
National Railroad Passenger Corporation (Amtrak)—60 Massachusetts Ave., N.E. (20002)
Smithsonian Institution—1000 Jefferson Dr., S.W. (20560)

Government Officials

Cabinet Members with Dates of Appointment

Although the Constitution made no provision for a president's advisory group, the heads of the three executive departments (State, Treasury, and War) and the attorney general were organized by Washington into such a group; and by about 1793, the name "cabinet" was applied to it. With the exception of the attorney general up to 1870 and the postmaster general from 1829 to 1872, cabinet members have been heads of executive departments.

Cabinet members are appointed by the president, subject to the confirmation of the Senate; and as their terms are not fixed, they may be replaced at any time by the president. At a change in administration, it is customary for cabinet members to resign, but they remain in office until successors are appointed.

The table of cabinet members lists only those members who actually served after being duly commissioned. The dates shown are those of appointment. "Cont." indicates that the term continued from the previous administration for a substantial amount of time.

Washington

Secretary of State	Thomas Jefferson, 1789
	Edmund Randolph, 1794
	Timothy Pickering, 1795
Secretary of the Treasury	Alexander Hamilton, 1789
	Oliver Wolcott, Jr., 1795
Secretary of War	Henry Knox, 1789
	Timothy Pickering, 1795
	James McHenry, 1796
Attorney General	Edmund Randolph, 1789
	William Bradford, 1794
	Charles Lee, 1795

J. Adams

Secretary of State	Timothy Pickering (Cont.)
	John Marshall, 1800
Secretary of the Treasury	Oliver Wolcott, Jr. (Cont.)
	Samuel Dexter, 1801
Secretary of War	James McHenry (Cont.)
	Samuel Dexter, 1800
Attorney General	Charles Lee (Cont.)
Secretary of the Navy	Benjamin Stoddert, 1798

Jefferson

Secretary of State	James Madison, 1801
Secretary of the Treasury	Samuel Dexter (Cont.)
	Albert Gallatin, 1801
Secretary of War	Henry Dearborn, 1801
Attorney General	Levi Lincoln, 1801
	Robert Smith, 1805
	John Breckinridge, 1805
	Caesar A. Rodney, 1807
Secretary of the Navy	Benjamin Stoddert (Cont.)
	Robert Smith, 1801

Madison

Secretary of State	Robert Smith, 1809
	James Monroe, 1811
Secretary of the Treasury	Albert Gallatin (Cont.)
	George W. Campbell, 1814
	Alexander J. Dallas, 1814
	William H. Crawford, 1816
Secretary of War	William Eustis, 1809
	John Armstrong, 1813
	James Monroe, 1814
	William H. Crawford, 1815
Attorney General	Caesar A. Rodney (Cont.)
	William Pinckney, 1811
	Richard Rush, 1814
Secretary of the Navy	Paul Hamilton, 1809
	William Jones, 1813
	B. W. Crowninshield, 1814

Monroe

Secretary of State	John Quincy Adams, 1817
Secretary of the Treasury	William H. Crawford (Cont.)
Secretary of War	John C. Calhoun, 1817
Attorney General	Richard Rush (Cont.)
	William Wirt, 1817
Secretary of the Navy	B. W. Crowninshield (Cont.)
	Smith Thompson, 1818
	Samuel L. Southard, 1823

J. Q. Adams

Secretary of State	Henry Clay, 1825
Secretary of the Treasury	Richard Rush, 1825
Secretary of War	James Barbour, 1825
	Peter B. Porter, 1828
Attorney General	William Wirt (Cont.)
Secretary of the Navy	Samuel L. Southard (Cont.)

Jackson

Secretary of State	Martin Van Buren, 1829
	Edward Livingston, 1831
	Louis McLane, 1833
	John Forsyth, 1834
Secretary of the Treasury	Samuel D. Ingham, 1829
	Louis McLane, 1831
	William J. Duane, 1833
	Roger B. Taney[1], 1833
	Levi Woodbury, 1834
Secretary of War	John H. Eaton, 1829
	Lewis Cass, 1831
Attorney General	John M. Berrien, 1829
	Roger B. Taney, 1831
	Benjamin F. Butler, 1833
Postmaster General[2]	William T. Barry, 1829
	Amos Kendall, 1835
Secretary of the Navy	John Branch, 1829
	Levi Woodbury, 1831
	Mahlon Dickerson, 1834

1. Not confirmed by the Senate. 2. The postmaster general did not become a cabinet member until 1829. Earlier postmasters general were: Samuel Osgood (1789), Timothy Pickering (1791), Joseph Habersham (1795), Gideon Granger (1801), Return J. Meigs, Jr. (1814), and John McLean (1823).

Van Buren

Secretary of State	John Forsyth (Cont.)
Secretary of the Treasury	Levi Woodbury (Cont.)
Secretary of War	Joel R. Poinsett, 1837
Attorney General	Benjamin F. Butler (Cont.)
	Felix Grundy, 1838
	Henry D. Gilpin, 1840
Postmaster General	Amos Kendall (Cont.)
	John M. Niles, 1840
Secretary of the Navy	Mahlon Dickerson (Cont.)
	James K. Paulding, 1838

W. H. Harrison

Secretary of State	Daniel Webster, 1841
Secretary of the Treasury	Thomas Ewing, 1841
Secretary of War	John Bell, 1841
Attorney General	John J. Crittenden, 1841
Postmaster General	Francis Granger, 1841
Secretary of the Navy	George E. Badger, 1841

Tyler

Secretary of State	Daniel Webster (Cont.)
	Abel P. Upshur, 1843
	John C. Calhoun, 1844
Secretary of the Treasury	Thomas Ewing (Cont.)
	Walter Forward, 1841
	John C. Spencer[1], 1843
	George M. Bibb, 1844
Secretary of War	John Bell (Cont.)
	John C. Spencer, 1841
	James M. Porter[1], 1843
	William Wilkins, 1844
Attorney General	John J. Crittenden (Cont.)
	Hugh S. Legaré, 1841
	John Nelson, 1843
Postmaster General	Francis Granger (Cont.)
	Charles A. Wickliffe, 1841
Secretary of the Navy	George E. Badger (Cont.)
	Abel P. Upshur, 1841
	David Henshaw[1], 1843
	Thomas W. Gilmer, 1844
	John Y. Mason, 1844

1. Not confirmed by the Senate.

Polk

Secretary of State	James Buchanan, 1845
Secretary of the Treasury	Robert J. Walker, 1845
Secretary of War	William L. Marcy, 1845
Attorney General	John Y. Mason, 1845
	Nathan Clifford, 1846
	Isaac Toucey, 1848
Postmaster General	Cave Johnson, 1845
Secretary of the Navy	George Bancroft, 1845
	John Y. Mason, 1846

Taylor

Secretary of State	John M. Clayton, 1849
Secretary of the Treasury	William M. Meredith, 1849
Secretary of War	George W. Crawford, 1849
Attorney General	Reverdy Johnson, 1849
Postmaster General	Jacob Collamer, 1849
Secretary of the Navy	William B. Preston, 1849
Secretary of the Interior	Thomas Ewing, 1849

Fillmore

Secretary of State	Daniel Webster, 1850
	Edward Everett, 1852
Secretary of the Treasury	Thomas Corwin, 1850
Secretary of War	Charles M. Conrad, 1850
Attorney General	John J. Crittenden, 1850
Postmaster General	Nathan K. Hall, 1850
	Samuel D. Hubbard, 1852
Secretary of the Navy	William A. Graham, 1850
	John P. Kennedy, 1852
Secretary of the Interior	Thos. M. T. McKennan, 1850
	Alex. H. H. Stuart, 1850

Pierce

Secretary of State	William L. Marcy, 1853
Secretary of the Treasury	James Guthrie, 1853
Secretary of War	Jefferson Davis, 1853
Attorney General	Caleb Cushing, 1853
Postmaster General	James Campbell, 1853
Secretary of the Navy	James C. Dobbin, 1853
Secretary of the Interior	Robert McClelland, 1853

Buchanan

Secretary of State	Lewis Cass, 1857
	Jeremiah S. Black, 1860
Secretary of the Treasury	Howell Cobb, 1857
	Philip F. Thomas, 1860
	John A. Dix, 1861
Secretary of War	John B. Floyd, 1857
	Joseph Holt, 1861
Attorney General	Jeremiah S. Black, 1857
	Edwin M. Stanton, 1860
Postmaster General	Aaron V. Brown, 1857
	Joseph Holt, 1859
	Horatio King, 1861
Secretary of the Navy	Isaac Toucey, 1857
Secretary of the Interior	Jacob Thompson, 1857

Lincoln

Secretary of State	William H. Seward, 1861
Secretary of the Treasury	Salmon P. Chase, 1861
	William P. Fessenden, 1864
	Hugh McCulloch, 1865
Secretary of War	Simon Cameron, 1861
	Edwin M. Stanton, 1862
Attorney General	Edward Bates, 1861
	James Speed, 1864
Postmaster General	Montgomery Blair, 1861
	William Dennison, 1864
Secretary of the Navy	Gideon Welles, 1861
Secretary of the Interior	Caleb B. Smith, 1861
	John P. Usher, 1863

A. Johnson

Secretary of State	William H. Seward (Cont.)
Secretary of the Treasury	Hugh McCulloch (Cont.)
Secretary of War	Edwin M. Stanton (Cont.)
	John M. Schofield, 1868
Attorney General	James Speed (Cont.)
	Henry Stanbery, 1866
	William M. Evarts, 1868
Postmaster General	William Dennison (Cont.)
	Alexander W. Randall, 1866
Secretary of the Navy	Gideon Welles (Cont.)
Secretary of the Interior	John P. Usher (Cont.)
	James Harlan, 1865
	Orville H. Browning, 1866

Grant

Secretary of State	Elihu B. Washburne, 1869
	Hamilton Fish, 1869
	George S. Boutwell, 1869
	William A. Richardson, 1873
	Benjamin H. Bristow, 1874
	Lot M. Morrill, 1876
Secretary of War	John A. Rawlins, 1869
	William W. Belknap, 1869
	Alphonso Taft, 1876
	James D. Cameron, 1876
Attorney General	Ebenezer R. Hoar, 1869
	Amos T. Akerman, 1870
	George H. Williams, 1871
	Edwards Pierrepont, 1875
	Alphonso Taft, 1876
Postmaster General	John A. J. Creswell, 1869
	Marshall Jewell, 1874
	James N. Tyner, 1876
Secretary of the Navy	Adolph E. Borie, 1869
	George M. Robeson, 1869
Secretary of the Interior	Jacob D. Cox, 1869
	Columbus Delano, 1870
	Zachariah Chandler, 1875

Hayes

Secretary of State	William M. Evarts, 1877
Secretary of the Treasury	John Sherman, 1877
Secretary of War	George W. McCrary, 1877
	Alexander Ramsey, 1879
Attorney General	Charles Devens, 1877
Postmaster General	David M. Key, 1877
	Horace Maynard, 1880
	Richard W. Thompson, 1877
	Nathan Goff, Jr., 1881
Secretary of the Interior	Carl Schurz, 1877

Garfield

Secretary of State	James G. Blaine, 1881
Secretary of the Treasury	William Windom, 1881
Secretary of War	Robert T. Lincoln, 1881
Attorney General	Wayne MacVeagh, 1881
Postmaster General	Thomas L. James, 1881
Secretary of the Navy	William H. Hunt, 1881
Secretary of the Interior	Samuel J. Kirkwood, 1881

Arthur

Secretary of State	James G. Blaine (Cont.)
	F. T. Frelinghuysen, 1881
Secretary of the Treasury	William Windom (Cont.)
	Charles J. Folger, 1881
	Walter Q. Gresham, 1884
	Hugh McCulloch, 1884
Secretary of War	Robert T. Lincoln (Cont.)
Attorney General	Wayne MacVeagh (Cont.)
	Benjamin H. Brewster, 1881
Postmaster General	Thomas L. James (Cont.)
	Timothy O. Howe, 1881
	Walter Q. Gresham, 1883
	Frank Hatton, 1884
Secretary of the Navy	William H. Hunt (Cont.)
	William E. Chandler, 1882
Secretary of the Interior	Samuel J. Kirkwood (Cont.)
	Henry M. Teller, 1882

Cleveland

Secretary of State	Thomas F. Bayard, 1885
Secretary of the Treasury	Daniel Manning, 1885
	Charles S. Fairchild, 1887
Secretary of War	William C. Endicott, 1885
Attorney General	Augustus H. Garland, 1885
Postmaster General	William F. Vilas, 1885
	Don M. Dickinson, 1888
Secretary of the Navy	William C. Whitney, 1885
Secretary of the Interior	Lucius Q. C. Lamar, 1885
	William F. Vilas, 1888
Secretary of Agriculture	Norman J. Colman, 1889

B. Harrison

Secretary of State	James G. Blaine, 1889
	John W. Foster, 1892
Secretary of the Treasury	William Windom, 1889
	Charles Foster, 1891
Secretary of War	Redfield Proctor, 1889
	Stephen B. Elkins, 1891
Attorney General	William H. H. Miller, 1889
Postmaster General	John Wanamaker, 1889
Secretary of the Navy	Benjamin F. Tracy, 1889
Secretary of the Interior	John W. Noble, 1889
Secretary of Agriculture	Jeremiah M. Rusk, 1889

Cleveland

Secretary of State	Walter Q. Gresham, 1893
	Richard Olney, 1895
Secretary of the Treasury	John G. Carlisle, 1893
Secretary of War	Daniel S. Lamont, 1893
Attorney General	Richard Olney, 1893
	Judson Harmon, 1895
Postmaster General	Wilson S. Bissell, 1893
	William L. Wilson, 1895
Secretary of the Navy	Hilary A. Herbert, 1893
Secretary of the Interior	Hoke Smith, 1893
	David R. Francis, 1896
Secretary of Agriculture	Julius Sterling Morton, 1893

McKinley

Secretary of State	John Sherman, 1897
	William R. Day, 1898
	John Hay, 1898
Secretary of the Treasury	Lyman J. Gage, 1897
Secretary of War	Russell A. Alger, 1897
	Elihu Root, 1899
Attorney General	Joseph McKenna, 1897
	John W. Griggs, 1898
	Philander C. Knox, 1901
Postmaster General	James A. Gary, 1897
	Charles E. Smith, 1898
Secretary of the Navy	John D. Long, 1897
Secretary of the Interior	Cornelius N. Bliss, 1897
	Ethan A. Hitchcock, 1898
Secretary of Agriculture	James Wilson, 1897

T. Roosevelt

Secretary of State	John Hay (Cont.)
	Elihu Root, 1905
	Robert Bacon, 1909
Secretary of the Treasury	Lyman J. Gage (Cont.)
	Leslie M. Shaw, 1902
	George B. Cortelyou, 1907
Secretary of War	Elihu Root (Cont.)
	William H. Taft, 1904
	Luke E. Wright, 1908
Attorney General	Philander C. Knox (Cont.)
	William H. Moody, 1904
	Charles J. Bonaparte, 1906
Postmaster General	Charles E. Smith (Cont.)
	Henry C. Payne, 1902
	Robert J. Wynne, 1904
	George B. Cortelyou, 1905
	George von L. Meyer, 1907
Secretary of the Navy	John D. Long (Cont.)
	William H. Moody, 1902
	Paul Morton, 1904
	Charles J. Bonaparte, 1905
	Victor H. Metcalf, 1906
	Truman H. Newberry, 1908
Secretary of the Interior	Ethan A. Hitchcock (Cont.)
	James R. Garfield, 1907
Secretary of Agriculture	James Wilson (Cont.)
Secretary of Commerce and Labor	George B. Cortelyou, 1903
	Victor H. Metcalf, 1904
	Oscar S. Straus, 1906

Taft

Secretary of State	Philander C. Knox, 1909
Secretary of the Treasury	Franklin MacVeagh, 1909
Secretary of War	Jacob M. Dickinson, 1909
	Henry L. Stimson, 1911
Attorney General	George W. Wickersham, 1909
Postmaster General	Frank H. Hitchcock, 1909
Secretary of the Navy	George von L. Meyer, 1909
Secretary of the Interior	Richard A. Ballinger, 1909
	Walter L. Fisher, 1911
Secretary of Agriculture	James Wilson (Cont.)
Secretary of Commerce and Labor	Charles Nagel, 1909

Wilson

Secretary of State	William J. Bryan, 1913
	Robert Lansing, 1915
	Bainbridge Colby, 1920
Secretary of the Treasury	William G. McAdoo, 1913
	Carter Glass, 1918
	David F. Houston, 1920
Secretary of War	Lindley M. Garrison, 1913
	Newton D. Baker, 1916
Attorney General	James C. McReynolds, 1913
	Thomas W. Gregory, 1914
	A. Mitchell Palmer, 1919
Postmaster General	Albert S. Burleson, 1913
Secretary of the Navy	Josephus Daniels, 1913
Secretary of the Interior	Franklin K. Lane, 1913
	John B. Payne, 1920
Secretary of Agriculture	David F. Houston, 1913
	Edwin T. Meredith, 1920
Secretary of Commerce	William C. Redfield, 1913
	Joshua W. Alexander, 1919
Secretary of Labor	William B. Wilson, 1913

Harding

Secretary of State	Charles E. Hughes, 1921
Secretary of the Treasury	Andrew W. Mellon, 1921
Secretary of War	John W. Weeks, 1921
Attorney General	Harry M. Daugherty, 1921
Postmaster General	Will H. Hays, 1921
	Hubert Work, 1922
	Harry S. New, 1923
Secretary of the Navy	Edwin Denby, 1921
Secretary of the Interior	Albert B. Fall, 1921
	Hubert Work, 1923
Secretary of Agriculture	Henry C. Wallace, 1921
Secretary of Commerce	Herbert Hoover, 1921
Secretary of Labor	James J. Davis, 1921

Coolidge

Secretary of State	Charles E. Hughes (Cont.)
	Frank B. Kellogg, 1925
Secretary of the Treasury	Andrew W. Mellon (Cont.)
Secretary of War	John W. Weeks (Cont.)
	Dwight F. Davis, 1925
Attorney General	Harry M. Daughtery (Cont.)
	Harlan F. Stone, 1924
	John G. Sargent, 1925
Postmaster General	Harry S. New (Cont.)
Secretary of the Navy	Edwin Denby (Cont.)
	Curtis D. Wilbur, 1924
Secretary of the Interior	Hubert Work (Cont.)
	Roy O. West, 1928
Secretary of Agriculture	Henry C. Wallace (Cont.)
	Howard M. Gore, 1924
	William M. Jardine, 1925
Secretary of Commerce	Herbert Hoover (Cont.)
	William F. Whiting, 1928
Secretary of Labor	James J. Davis (Cont.)

Hoover

Secretary of State	Frank B. Kellogg (Cont.)
	Henry L. Stimson, 1929
Secretary of the Treasury	Andrew W. Mellon (Cont.)
	Ogden L. Mills, 1932
Secretary of War	James W. Good, 1929
	Patrick J. Hurley, 1929
Attorney General	William D. Mitchell, 1929
Postmaster General	Walter F. Brown, 1929
Secretary of the Navy	Charles F. Adams, 1929
Secretary of the Interior	Ray Lyman Wilbur, 1929
Secretary of Agriculture	Arthur M. Hyde, 1929
Secretary of Commerce	Robert P. Lamont, 1929
	Roy D. Chapin, 1932
Secretary of Labor	James J. Davis (Cont.)
	William N. Doak, 1930

F. D. Roosevelt

Secretary of State	Cordell Hull, 1933
	E. R. Stettinius, Jr., 1944
Secretary of the Treasury	William H. Woodin, 1933
	Henry Morgenthau, Jr., 1934
Secretary of War	George H. Dern, 1933
	Harry H. Woodring, 1936
	Henry L. Stimson, 1940
Attorney General	Homer S. Cummings, 1933
	Frank Murphy, 1939
	Robert H. Jackson, 1940
	Francis Biddle, 1941
Postmaster General	James A. Farley, 1933
	Frank C. Walker, 1940
Secretary of the Navy	Claude A. Swanson, 1933
	Charles Edison, 1940
	Frank Knox, 1940
	James Forrestal, 1944
Secretary of the Interior	Harold L. Ickes, 1933
Secretary of Agriculture	Henry A. Wallace, 1933
	Claude R. Wickard, 1940

Secretary of Commerce	Daniel C. Roper, 1933
	Harry L. Hopkins, 1938
	Jesse H. Jones, 1940
	Henry A. Wallace, 1945
Secretary of Labor	Frances Perkins, 1933

Truman

Secretary of State	E. R. Stettinius, Jr. (Cont.)
	James F. Byrnes, 1945
	George C. Marshall, 1947
	Dean Acheson, 1949
Secretary of the Treasury	Henry Morgenthau, Jr. (Cont.)
	Frederick M. Vinson, 1945
	John W. Snyder, 1946
Secretary of Defense	James Forrestal, 1947
	Louis A. Johnson, 1949
	George C. Marshall, 1950
	Robert A. Lovett, 1951
Attorney General	Francis Biddle (Cont.)
	Tom C. Clark, 1945
	J. Howard McGrath, 1949
	James P. McGranery, 1952
Postmaster General	Frank C. Walker (Cont.)
	Robert E. Hannegan, 1945
	Jesse M. Donaldson, 1947
Secretary of the Interior	Harold L. Ickes (Cont.)
	Julius A. Krug, 1946
	Oscar L. Chapman, 1949
Secretary of Agriculture	Claude R. Wickard (Cont.)
	Clinton P. Anderson, 1945
	Charles F. Brannan, 1948
Secretary of Commerce	Henry A. Wallace (Cont.)
	W. Averell Harriman, 1946
	Charles Sawyer, 1948
Secretary of Labor	Frances Perkins (Cont.)
	Lewis B. Schwellenbach, 1945
	Maurice J. Tobin, 1948
Secretary of War[1]	Henry L. Stimson (Cont.)
	Robert P. Patterson, 1945
	Kenneth C. Royall, 1947
Secretary of the Navy[1]	James Forrestal (Cont.)

1. On July 26, 1947, the Departments of War and of the Navy were incorporated into the Department of Defense.

Eisenhower

Secretary of State	John Foster Dulles, 1953
	Christian A. Herter, 1959
Secretary of the Treasury	George M. Humphrey, 1953
	Robert B. Anderson, 1957
Secretary of Defense	Charles E. Wilson, 1953
	Neil H. McElroy, 1957
	Thomas S. Gates, Jr., 1959
Attorney General	Herbert Brownell, Jr., 1953
	William P. Rogers, 1958
Postmaster General	Arthur E. Summerfield, 1953
Secretary of the Interior	Douglas McKay, 1953
	Frederick A. Seaton, 1956
Secretary of Agriculture	Ezra Taft Benson, 1953
Secretary of Commerce	Sinclair Weeks, 1953
	Lewis L. Strauss[1], 1958
	Frederick H. Mueller, 1959
Secretary of Health, Education, and Welfare	Oveta Culp Hobby, 1953
	Marion B. Folsom, 1955
	Arthur S. Flemming, 1958
Secretary of Labor	Martin P. Durkin, 1953
	James P. Mitchell, 1953

1. Not confirmed by the Senate.

Kennedy

Secretary of State	Dean Rusk, 1961
Secretary of the Treasury	C. Douglas Dillon, 1961
Secretary of Defense	Robert S. McNamara, 1961
Attorney General	Robert F. Kennedy, 1961
Postmaster General	J. Edward Day, 1961
	John A. Gronouski, 1963

Secretary of the Interior	Stewart L. Udall, 1961
Secretary of Agriculture	Orville L. Freeman, 1961
Secretary of Commerce	Luther H. Hodges, 1961
Secretary of Labor	Arthur J. Goldberg, 1961
	W. Willard Wirtz, 1962
Secretary of Health, Education, and Welfare	Abraham A. Ribicoff, 1961
	Anthony J. Celebrezze, 1962

L. B. Johnson

Secretary of State	Dean Rusk (Cont.)
Secretary of the Treasury	C. Douglas Dillon (Cont.)
	Henry H. Fowler, 1965
	Joseph W. Barr[1], 1968
Secretary of Defense	Robert S. McNamara (Cont.)
	Clark M. Clifford, 1968
Attorney General	Robert F. Kennedy (Cont.)
	N. de B. Katzenbach, 1965
	Ramsey Clark, 1967
Postmaster General	John A. Gronouski (Cont.)
	Lawrence F. O'Brien, 1965
	W. Marvin Watson, 1968
Secretary of the Interior	Stewart L. Udall (Cont.)
Secretary of Agriculture	Orville L. Freeman (Cont.)
Secretary of Commerce	Luther H. Hodges (Cont.)
	John T. Connor, 1964
	A. B. Trowbridge, 1967
	C. R. Smith, 1968
Secretary of Labor	W. Willard Wirtz (Cont.)
Secretary of Health, Education, and Welfare	Anthony J. Celebrezze (Cont.)
	John W. Gardner, 1965
	Wilbur J. Cohen, 1968
Secretary of Housing and Urban Development	Robert C. Weaver, 1966
	Robert C. Wood[1], 1969
Secretary of Transportation	Alan S. Boyd, 1966

1. Recess appointment.

Nixon

Secretary of State	William P. Rogers, 1969
	Henry A. Kissinger, 1973
Secretary of the Treasury	David M. Kennedy, 1969
	John B. Connally, 1971
	George P. Shultz, 1972
	William E. Simon, 1974
Secretary of Defense	Melvin R. Laird, 1969
	Elliot L. Richardson, 1973
	James R. Schlesinger, 1973
Attorney General	John N. Mitchell, 1969
	Richard G. Kleindienst, 1972
	Elliot L. Richardson, 1973
	William B. Saxbe, 1974
Postmaster General[1]	William M. Blount, 1969
Secretary of the Interior	Walter J. Hickel, 1969
	Rogers C. B. Morton, 1971
Secretary of Agriculture	Clifford M. Hardin, 1969
	Earl L. Butz, 1971
Secretary of Commerce	Maurice H. Stans, 1969
	Peter G. Peterson, 1972
	Frederick B. Dent, 1973
Secretary of Labor	George P. Shultz, 1969
	James D. Hodgson, 1970
	Peter J. Brennan, 1973
Secretary of Health, Education, and Welfare	Robert H. Finch, 1969
	Elliot L. Richardson, 1970
	Caspar W. Weinberger, 1973
Secretary of Housing and Urban Development	George Romney, 1969
	James T. Lynn, 1973
Secretary of Transportation	John A. Volpe, 1969
	Claude S. Brinegar, 1973

1. The postmaster general is no longer a cabinet member.

Ford

Secretary of State	Henry A. Kissinger (Cont.)
Secretary of the Treasury	William E. Simon (Cont.)
Secretary of Defense	James R. Schlesinger (Cont.)
	Donald H. Rumsfeld, 1975
Attorney General	William B. Saxbe (Cont.)
	Edward H. Levi, 1975
Secretary of the Interior	Rogers C. B. Morton (Cont.)
	Stanley K. Hathaway, 1975
	Thomas S. Kleppe, 1975
Secretary of Agriculture	Earl L. Butz (Cont.)
	John Knebel, 1976
Secretary of Commerce	Frederick B. Dent (Cont.)
	Rogers C. B. Morton, 1975
	Elliot L. Richardson, 1976
Secretary of Labor	Peter J. Brennan (Cont.)
	John T. Dunlop, 1975
	William J. Usery, Jr., 1976
Secretary of Health, Education, and Welfare	Caspar W. Weinberger (Cont.)
	F. David Mathews, 1975
Secretary of Housing and Urban Development	James T. Lynn (Cont.)
	Carla A. Hills, 1975
Secretary of Transportation	Claude S. Brinegar (Cont.)
	William T. Coleman, Jr., 1975

Carter

Secretary of State	Cyrus R. Vance, 1977
	Edmund S. Muskie, 1980
Secretary of the Treasury	W. Michael Blumenthal, 1977
	G. William Miller, 1979
Secretary of Defense	Harold Brown, 1977
Attorney General	Griffin B. Bell, 1977
	Benjamin R. Civiletti, 1979
Secretary of the Interior	Cecil D. Andrus, 1977
Secretary of Agriculture	Bob S. Bergland, 1977
Secretary of Commerce	Juanita M. Kreps, 1977
	Philip M. Klutznick, 1979
Secretary of Labor	F. Ray Marshall, 1977
Secretary of Health and Human Services[1]	Joseph A. Califano, Jr., 1977
	Patricia Roberts Harris, 1979
Secretary of Housing and Urban Development	Patricia Roberts Harris, 1977
	Moon Landrieu, 1979
Secretary of Transportation	Brock Adams, 1977
	Neil B. Goldschmidt, 1979
Secretary of Energy	James R. Schlesinger, 1977
	Charles W. Duncan, Jr., 1979
Secretary of Education	Shirley Mount Hufstedler, 1979

1. Known as Department of Health, Education, and Welfare until May 1980.

Reagan

Secretary of State	Alexander M. Haig, Jr., 1981
	George P. Shultz, 1982
Secretary of the Treasury	Donald T. Regan, 1981
	James A. Baker 3rd, 1985
	Nicholas F. Brady, 1988
Secretary of Defense	Caspar W. Weinberger, 1981
	Frank C. Carlucci, 1987
Attorney General	William French Smith, 1981
	Edwin Meese 3rd, 1985
	Richard L. Thornburgh, 1988
Secretary of the Interior	James G. Watt, 1981
	William P. Clark, 1983
	Donald P. Hodel, 1985
Secretary of Agriculture	John R. Block, 1981
	Richard E. Lyng, 1986
Secretary of Commerce	Malcolm Baldrige, 1981
	C. William Verity, Jr., 1987
Secretary of Labor	Raymond J. Donovan, 1981
	William E. Brock, 1985
	Ann Dore McLaughlin, 1987
Secretary of Health and Human Services	Richard S. Schweiker, 1981
	Margaret M. Heckler, 1983
	Otis R. Bowen, 1985
Secretary of Housing and Urban Development	Samuel R. Pierce, Jr., 1981
Secretary of Transportation	Andrew L. Lewis, Jr., 1981
	Elizabeth H. Dole, 1983
	James H. Burnley 4th, 1987

Secretary of Energy	James B. Edwards, 1981
	Donald P. Hodel, 1983
	John S. Herrington, 1985
Secretary of Education	T. H. Bell, 1981
	William J. Bennett, 1985
	Lauro F. Cavazos, 1988

G. H. W. Bush

Secretary of State	James A. Baker 3d, 1989
	Lawrence S. Eagleburger, 1992
Secretary of the Treasury	Nicholas F. Brady (Cont.)
Secretary of Defense	Richard Cheney, 1989
Attorney General	Richard L. Thornburgh (Cont.)
	William P. Barr, 1992
Secretary of the Interior	Manuel Lujan Jr., 1989
Secretary of Agriculture	Clayton K. Yeutter, 1989
	Edward Madigan, 1991
Secretary of Commerce	Robert A. Mosbacher Sr., 1989
	Barbara H. Franklin, 1992
Secretary of Labor	Elizabeth H. Dole, 1989
	Lynn Martin, 1991
Secretary of Health and Human Services	Louis W. Sullivan, 1989
Secretary of Housing and Urban Development	Jack F. Kemp, 1989
Secretary of Transportation	Samuel K. Skinner, 1989
	Andrew Card, 1992
Secretary of Energy	James D. Watkins, 1989
Secretary of Education	Lauro F. Cavazos (Cont.)
	Lamar Alexander, 1991
Secretary of Veterans' Affairs	Edward J. Derwinski, 1989

Clinton

Secretary of State	Warren M. Christopher, 1993
	Madeleine Albright, 1996
Secretary of the Treasury	Lloyd Bentsen, 1993
	Robert E. Rubin, 1995–1999
	Lawrence H. Summers, 1999
Secretary of Defense	Les Aspin, 1993
	William J. Perry, 1994
	William S. Cohen, 1997
Attorney General	Janet Reno, 1993

Secretary of the Interior	Bruce Babbitt, 1993
Secretary of Agriculture	Mike Espy, 1993
	Dan Glickman, 1995
Secretary of Commerce	Ronald H. Brown, 1993
	Mickey Kantor, 1996
	William M. Daley, 1997
	Norman Y. Mineta, 2000
Secretary of Labor	Robert B. Reich, 1993
	Alexis Herman, 1997
Secretary of Health and Human Services	Donna E. Shalala, 1993
Secretary of Housing and Urban Development	Henry G. Cisneros, 1993
	Andrew M. Cuomo, 1997
Secretary of Transportation	Federico F. Pena, 1993
	Rodney Slater, 1997
Secretary of Energy	Hazel R. O'Leary, 1993
	Frederico F. Pena, 1997
	Bill Richardson, 1998
Secretary of Education	Richard W. Riley, 1993
Secretary of Veterans' Affairs	Jesse Brown, 1993
	Togo D. West, Jr., 1998

G. W. Bush

Secretary of State	Gen. Colin L. Powell, 2001
Secretary of the Treasury	Paul H. O'Neill, 2001
Secretary of Defense	Donald H. Rumsfeld, 2001
Attorney General	John Ashcroft, 2001
Secretary of the Interior	Gale A. Norton, 2001
Secretary of Agriculture	Ann M. Veneman, 2001
Secretary of Commerce	Donald L. Evans, 2001
Secretary of Labor	Elaine L. Chao, 2001
Secretary of Health and Human Services	Tommy G. Thompson, 2001
Secretary of Housing and Urban Development	Melquiades R. Martinez, 2001
Secretary of Transportation	Norman Y. Mineta, 2001
Secretary of Energy	Spencer Abraham, 2001
Secretary of Education	Roderick R. Paige, 2001
Secretary of Veterans' Affairs	Anthony Principi, 2001

Impeachments of Federal Officials

Source: Congressional Directory

The procedure for the impeachment of federal officials is detailed in Article I, Section 3, of the Constitution. The Senate has sat as a court of impeachment in the following cases:

William Blount, Senator from Tennessee; charges dismissed for want of jurisdiction, Jan. 14, 1799.

John Pickering, Judge of the U.S. District Court for New Hampshire; removed from office March 12, 1804.

Samuel Chase, Associate Justice of the Supreme Court; acquitted March 1, 1805.

James H. Peck, Judge of the U.S. District Court for Missouri; acquitted Jan. 31, 1831.

West H. Humphreys, Judge of the U.S. District Court for the middle, eastern, and western districts of Tennessee; removed from office June 26, 1862.

Andrew Johnson, President of the United States; acquitted May 26, 1868.

William W. Belknap, Secretary of War; acquitted Aug. 1, 1876.

Charles Swayne, Judge of the U.S. District Court for the northern district of Florida; acquitted Feb. 27, 1905.

Robert W. Archbald, Associate Judge, U.S. Commerce Court; removed Jan. 13, 1913.

George W. English, Judge of the U.S. District Court for eastern district of Illinois; resigned Nov. 4, 1926; proceedings dismissed.

Harold Louderback, Judge of the U.S. District Court for the northern district of California; acquitted May 24, 1933.

Halsted L. Ritter, Judge of the U.S. District Court for the southern district of Florida; removed from office April 17, 1936.

Harry E. Claiborne, Judge of the U.S. District Court for the district of Nevada; removed from office Oct. 9, 1986.

Alcee L. Hastings, Judge of the U.S. District Court for the southern district of Florida; removed from office Oct. 20, 1988.

Walter L. Nixon, Judge of the U.S. District Court for Mississippi; removed from office Nov. 3, 1989.

William J. Clinton, President of the United States; acquitted Feb. 12, 1999.

Members of the Supreme Court of the United States

Mailing address for the Supreme Court: U.S. Supreme Court Building, 1 First Street NE Washington, DC 20543

Name, state	Service Term	Yrs	Birth Place	Date	Died	Religion
Chief Justices						
John Jay, N.Y.	1789–1795	5	N.Y.	1745	1829	Episcopal
John Rutledge, S.C.	1795	0	S.C.	1739	1800	Church of England
Oliver Ellsworth, Conn.	1796–1800	4	Conn.	1745	1807	Congregational
John Marshall, Va.	1801–1835	34	Va.	1755	1835	Episcopal
Roger B. Taney, Md.	1836–1864	28	Md.	1777	1864	Roman Catholic
Salmon P. Chase, Ohio	1864–1873	8	N.H.	1808	1873	Episcopal
Morrison R. Waite, Ohio	1874–1888	14	Conn.	1816	1888	Episcopal
Melville W. Fuller, Ill.	1888–1910	21	Maine	1833	1910	Episcopal
Edward D. White, La.	1910–1921	10	La.	1845	1921	Roman Catholic
William H. Taft, Conn.	1921–1930	8	Ohio	1857	1930	Unitarian
Charles E. Hughes, N.Y.	1930–1941	11	N.Y.	1862	1948	Baptist
Harlan F. Stone, N.Y.	1941–1946	4	N.H.	1872	1946	Episcopal
Frederick M. Vinson, Ky.	1946–1953	7	Ky.	1890	1953	Methodist
Earl Warren, Calif.	1953–1969	15	Calif.	1891	1974	Protestant
Warren E. Burger, Va.	1969–1986	17	Minn.	1907	1995	Presbyterian
William H. Rehnquist, Ariz.	1986–	—	Wis.	1924	—	Lutheran
Associate Justices						
James Wilson, Pa.	1789–1798	8	Scotland	1742	1798	Episcopal
John Rutledge, S.C.	1790–1791	1	S.C.	1739	1800	Church of England
William Cushing, Mass.	1790–1810	20	Mass.	1732	1810	Unitarian
John Blair, Va.	1790–1796	5	Va.	1732	1800	Presbyterian
James Iredell, N.C.	1790–1799	9	England	1751	1799	Episcopal
Thomas Johnson, Md.	1792–1793	0	Md.	1732	1819	Episcopal
William Paterson, N.J.	1793–1806	13	Ireland	1745	1806	Protestant
Samuel Chase, Md.	1796–1811	15	Md.	1741	1811	Episcopal
Bushrod Washington, Va.	1799–1829	30	Va.	1762	1829	Episcopal
Alfred Moore, N.C.	1800–1804	3	N.C.	1755	1810	Episcopal
William Johnson, S.C.	1804–1834	30	S.C.	1771	1834	Presbyterian
Brockholst Livingston, N.Y.	1807–1823	16	N.Y.	1757	1823	Presbyterian
Thomas Todd, Ky.	1807–1826	18	Va.	1765	1826	Presbyterian
Gabriel Duval, Md.	1811–1835	23	Md.	1752	1844	French Protestant
Joseph Story, Mass.	1812–1845	33	Mass.	1779	1845	Unitarian
Smith Thompson, N.Y.	1823–1843	20	N.Y.	1768	1843	Presbyterian
Robert Trimble, Ky.	1826–1828	2	Va.	1777	1828	Protestant
John McLean, Ohio	1830–1861	31	N.J.	1785	1861	Methodist-Epis.
Henry Baldwin, Pa.	1830–1844	14	Conn.	1780	1844	Trinity Church
James M. Wayne, Ga.	1835–1867	32	Ga.	1790	1867	Protestant
Philip P. Barbour, Va.	1836–1841	4	Va.	1783	1841	Episcopal
John Catron, Tenn.	1837–1865	28	Pa.	1786	1865	Presbyterian
John McKinley, Ala.	1837–1852	14	Va.	1780	1852	Protestant
Peter V. Daniel, Va.	1841–1860	18	Va.	1784	1860	Episcopal
Samuel Nelson, N.Y.	1845–1872	27	N.Y.	1792	1873	Protestant
Levi Woodbury, N.H.	1845–1851	5	N.H.	1789	1851	Protestant
Robert C. Grier, Pa.	1846–1870	23	Pa.	1794	1870	Presbyterian
Benjamin R. Curtis, Mass.	1851–1857	5	Mass.	1809	1874	(2)
John A. Campbell, Ala.	1853–1861	8	Ga.	1811	1889	Episcopal
Nathan Clifford, Maine	1858–1881	23	N.H.	1803	1881	(1)
Noah H. Swayne, Ohio	1862–1881	18	Va.	1804	1884	Quaker
Samuel F. Miller, Iowa	1862–1890	28	Ky.	1816	1890	Unitarian
David Davis, Ill.	1862–1877	14	Md.	1815	1886	(4)
Stephen J. Field, Calif.	1863–1897	34	Conn.	1816	1899	Episcopal
William Strong, Pa.	1870–1880	10	Conn.	1808	1895	Presbyterian
Joseph P. Bradley, N.J.	1870–1892	21	N.Y.	1813	1892	Presbyterian
Ward Hunt, N.Y.	1872–1882	9	N.Y.	1810	1886	Episcopal
John M. Harlan, Ky.	1877–1911	33	Ky.	1833	1911	Presbyterian
William B. Woods, Ga.	1880–1887	6	Ohio	1824	1887	Protestant
Stanley Matthews, Ohio	1881–1889	7	Ohio	1824	1889	Presbyterian
Horace Gray, Mass.	1882–1902	20	Mass.	1828	1902	(3)
Samuel Blatchford, N.Y.	1882–1893	11	N.Y.	1820	1893	Presbyterian
Lucius Q. C. Lamar, Miss.	1888–1893	5	Ga.	1825	1893	Methodist
David J. Brewer, Kan.	1889–1910	20	Asia Minor	1837	1910	Protestant
Henry B. Brown, Mich.	1890–1906	15	Mass.	1836	1913	Protestant

Name, state	Service Term	Yrs	Birth Place	Date	Died	Religion
George Shiras, Jr., Pa.	1892–1903	10	Pa.	1832	1924	Presbyterian
Howell E. Jackson, Tenn.	1893–1895	2	Tenn.	1832	1895	Baptist
Edward D. White, La.*	1894–1910	16	La.	1845	1921	Roman Catholic
Rufus W. Peckham, N.Y.	1895–1909	13	N.Y.	1838	1909	Episcopal
Joseph McKenna, Calif.	1898–1925	26	Pa.	1843	1926	Roman Catholic
Oliver W. Holmes, Mass.	1902–1932	29	Mass.	1841	1935	Unitarian
William R. Day, Ohio	1903–1922	19	Ohio	1849	1923	Protestant
William H. Moody, Mass.	1906–1910	3	Mass.	1853	1917	Episcopal
Horace H. Lurton, Tenn.	1909–1914	4	Ky.	1844	1914	Episcopal
Charles E. Hughes, N.Y.*	1910–1916	5	N.Y.	1862	1948	Baptist
Willis Van Devanter, Wyo.	1910–1937	26	Ind.	1859	1941	Episcopal
Joseph R. Lamar, Ga.	1910–1916	4	Ga.	1857	1916	Ch. of Disciples
Mahlon Pitney, N.J.	1912–1922	10	N.J.	1858	1924	Presbyterian
James C. McReynolds, Tenn.	1914–1941	26	Ky.	1862	1946	Disciples of Christ
Louis D. Brandeis, Mass.	1916–1939	22	Ky.	1856	1941	Jewish
John H. Clarke, Ohio	1916–1922	5	Ohio	1857	1945	Protestant
George Sutherland, Utah	1922–1938	15	England	1862	1942	Episcopal
Pierce Butler, Minn.	1923–1939	16	Minn.	1866	1939	Roman Catholic
Edward T. Sanford, Tenn.	1923–1930	7	Tenn.	1865	1930	Episcopal
Harlan F. Stone, N.Y.*	1925–1941	16	N.H.	1872	1946	Episcopal
Owen J. Roberts, Pa.	1930–1945	15	Pa.	1875	1955	Episcopal
Benjamin N. Cardozo, N.Y.	1932–1938	6	N.Y.	1870	1938	Jewish
Hugo L. Black, Ala.	1937–1971	34	Ala.	1886	1971	Baptist
Stanley F. Reed, Ky.	1938–1957	19	Ky.	1884	1980	Protestant
Felix Frankfurter, Mass.	1939–1962	23	Austria	1882	1965	Jewish
William O. Douglas, Conn.	1939–1975	36	Minn.	1898	1980	Presbyterian
Frank Murphy, Mich.	1940–1949	9	Mich.	1890	1949	Roman Catholic
James F. Byrnes, S.C.	1941–1942	1	S.C.	1879	1972	Episcopal
Robert H. Jackson, Pa.	1941–1954	13	N.Y.	1892	1954	Episcopal
Wiley B. Rutledge, Iowa	1943–1949	6	Ky.	1894	1949	Unitarian
Harold H. Burton, Ohio	1945–1958	13	Mass.	1888	1964	Unitarian
Tom C. Clark, Tex.	1949–1967	17	Tex.	1899	1977	Presbyterian
Sherman Minton, Ind.	1949–1956	7	Ind.	1890	1965	Roman Catholic
John M. Harlan, N.Y.	1955–1971	16	Ill.	1899	1971	Presbyterian
William J. Brennan, Jr., N.J.	1956–1990	33	N.J.	1906	1997	Roman Catholic
Charles E. Whittaker, Mo.	1957–1962	5	Kan.	1901	1973	Methodist
Potter Stewart, Ohio	1958–1981	23	Mich.	1915	1985	Episcopal
Byron R. White, Colo.	1962–1993	31	Colo.	1917	—	Episcopal
Arthur J. Goldberg, Ill.	1962–1965	2	Ill.	1908	1990	Jewish
Abe Fortas, Tenn.	1965–1969	3	Tenn.	1910	1982	Jewish
Thurgood Marshall, N.Y.	1967–1991	24	Md.	1908	1993	Episcopal
Harry A. Blackmun, Minn.	1970–1994	24	Ill.	1908	—	Methodist
Lewis F. Powell, Jr., Va.	1972–1987	15	Va.	1907	1998	Presbyterian
William H. Rehnquist, Ariz.*	1972–1986	14	Wis.	1924	—	Lutheran
John Paul Stevens, Ill.	1975–	—	Ill.	1920	—	Protestant
Sandra Day O'Connor, Ariz.	1981–	—	Tex.	1930	—	Episcopal
Antonin Scalia, D.C.	1986–	—	N.J.	1936	—	Roman Catholic
Anthony M. Kennedy, Calif.	1988–	—	Calif.	1936	—	Roman Catholic
David H. Souter, N.H.	1990–	—	Mass.	1939	—	Episcopal
Clarence Thomas, D.C.	1991–	—	Ga.	1948	—	Roman Catholic
Ruth Bader Ginsburg, D.C.	1993–	—	N.Y.	1933	—	Jewish
Stephen G. Breyer, Mass.	1994–	—	Calif.	1938	—	n.a.

NOTE: n.a. = not available. *Served as both chief justice and associate justice. 1. Congregational; later Unitarian. 2. Unitarian; then Episcopal. 3. Unitarian or Congregational. 4. Not a member of any church.

Supreme Court Facts

Youngest justice appointed: Joseph Story (age 32)

Oldest justice appointed: Horace Lurton (age 65)

Oldest justice to serve: Oliver Wendell Holmes (retired at age 90)

Shortest term: John Rutledge (1 year associate justice; 4 months chief justice)

Longest term: William O. Douglas (36 years, 209 days)

First African-American justice: Thurgood Marshall

First woman justice: Sandra Day O'Connor

President to appoint the most justices: George Washington (11)

President to appoint the most justices in the 20th century: Franklin Roosevelt (9)

Presidents to appoint current justices: Nixon (Rehnquist); Ford (Stevens); Reagan (O'Connor, Scalia, Kennedy); G. H. W. Bush (Souter, Thomas); Clinton (Ginsburg, Breyer)

Milestone Cases in Supreme Court History

1803 *Marbury v. Madison* was the first instance in which a law passed by Congress was declared unconstitutional. The decision greatly expanded the power of the Court by establishing its right to overturn acts of Congress, a power not explicitly granted by the Constitution. Initially the case involved Secretary of State James Madison, who refused to seat four judicial appointees although they had been confirmed by the Senate.

1819 *McCulloch v. Maryland* upheld the right of Congress to create a Bank of the United States, ruling that it was a power implied but not enumerated by the Constitution. The case is significant because it advanced the doctrine of implied powers, or a loose construction of the Constitution. The Court, Chief Justice John Marshall wrote, would sanction laws reflecting "the letter and spirit" of the Constitution.

1857 *Dred Scott v. Sanford* was a highly controversial case that intensified the national debate over slavery. The case involved Dred Scott, a slave, who was taken from a slave state to a free territory. Scott filed a lawsuit claiming that because he had lived on free soil he was entitled to his freedom. Chief Justice Roger B. Taney disagreed, ruling that blacks were not citizens and therefore could not sue in federal court. Taney further inflamed antislavery forces by declaring that Congress had no right to ban slavery from U.S. territories.

1896 *Plessy v. Ferguson* was the infamous case that asserted that "equal but separate accommodations" for blacks on railroad cars did not violate the "equal protection under the laws" clause of the 14th Amendment. By defending the constitutionality of racial segregation, the Court paved the way for the repressive Jim Crow laws of the South. The lone dissenter on the Court, Justice John Marshall Harlan, protested, "The thin disguise of 'equal' accommodations . . . will not mislead anyone."

1954 *Brown v. Board of Education of Topeka* invalidated racial segregation in schools and led to the unraveling of de jure segregation in all areas of public life. In the unanimous decision spearheaded by Chief Justice Earl Warren, the Court invalidated the Plessy ruling, declaring "in the field of public education, the doctrine of 'separate but equal' has no place" and contending that "separate educational facilities are inherently unequal." Future Supreme Court justice Thurgood Marshall was one of the NAACP lawyers who successfully argued the case.

1963 *Gideon v. Wainwright* guaranteed a defendant's right to legal counsel. The Supreme Court overturned the Florida felony conviction of Clarence Earl Gideon, who had defended himself after having been denied a request for free counsel. The Court held that the state's failure to provide counsel for a defendant charged with a felony violated the Fourteenth Amendment's due process clause. Gideon was given another trial, and with a court-appointed lawyer defending him, he was acquitted. The decision was one of many made by the Court under Chief Justice Earl Warren that protected the rights of the accused.

1966 *Miranda v. Arizona* was another case that helped define the due process clause of the 14th Amendment. At the center of the case was Ernesto Miranda, who had confessed to a crime during police questioning without knowing he had a right to have an attorney present. Based on his confession, Miranda was convicted. The Supreme Court overturned the conviction, ruling that criminal suspects must be warned of their rights before they are questioned by police. These rights are: the right to remain silent, to have an attorney present, and, if the suspect cannot afford an attorney, to have one appointed by the state. The police must also warn suspects that any statements they make can be used against them in court. Miranda was retried without the confession and convicted.

1973 *Roe v. Wade* legalized abortion and is at the center of the current controversy between "pro-life" and "pro-choice" advocates. The Court ruled that a woman has the right to an abortion without interference from the government in the first trimester of pregnancy, contending that it is part of her "right to privacy." The Court maintained that right to privacy is not absolute, however, and granted states the right to intervene in the second and third trimesters of pregnancy.

Notable Decisions of the U.S. Supreme Court, 2000–2001 Term

Highway Checkpoints for Drugs (Nov. 28, 2000): Court, 6–3, finds highway checkpoints with the primary purpose of detecting illegal drugs violates Fourth Amendment's prohibition of suspicionless seizures.

Presidential Election (Dec. 12, 2000): Court reverses Florida Supreme Court decision ordering manual recount of ballots. Majority of justices (7–2) agree that recount violates Constitution's equal protection and due process guarantees, since counting standards varied among counties. Court remands case to Florida Supreme Court for remedy but, in 5-4 split, maintains that deadline for recount ends at midnight. *See also* p. 53.

Clean Water Act Limited (Jan. 9, 2001): Justices rule, 5–4, that law does not authorize federal government to regulate dredging and filling of isolated ponds and wetlands.

States Allowed to Hold Sex Offenders (Jan. 17, 2001): Justices, 8–1, overturn lower court verdict and rule that sexually violent predators can be confined in civil commitment centers upon release from prison.

Court Rules Against Disabled Workers (Feb. 21, 2001): Decides, 5–4, that state employees cannot seek damages under the federal Americans with Disabilities Act.

Attack on Clean Air Act Rejected (Feb. 27, 2001): Justices rule unanimously against industry in important environmental decision. Court declares that Environmental Protection Agency may not consider implementation costs in setting air quality standards.

Fifth Amendment Right Upheld (March 19, 2001): Court rules unanimously that a witness does not lose his right to avoid self-incrimination by claiming to have had no involvement in a crime.

Hospital Drug Testing Limited (March 21, 2001): Ruling, 6–3, says hospital workers cannot test maternity patients for illegal drug use without their consent.

Right to Counsel Rule Modified (April 2, 2001): Decision, 5–4, holds that under Constitution, police may question a suspect without a lawyer if suspect is already represented by one in a closely related crime.

Race Permitted in Redistricting (April 18, 2001): In crucial 5–4 ruling, justices reverse lower court finding that North Carolina legislature had violated the Constitution by using race as a predominant factor in drawing boundaries of congressional district. Because state's black voters vote overwhelmingly Democratic, Court could not determine definitively that redistricting was based on unconstitutional racial considerations rather than permissible political considerations.

Arrests Backed for Minor Offenses (April 24, 2001): Court rules, 5–4, that full custodial arrest for a minor offense (in this case failure to use a seat belt) does not violate Fourth Amendment ban on unreasonable seizure.

Medical Use of Marijuana Limited (May 14, 2001): Court, 8–0, rules that federal law does not allow exception to use of substance. Ruling does not overturn state laws giving patients access.

Golf Carts for Disabled Persons on the PGA (May 29, 2001): By a majority of 7–2, the Court found that the Americans with Disabilities Act requires the PGA to allow disabled golfers to use golf carts during qualification rounds on PGA tour.

Texas Death Sentence Reversed (June 4, 2001): Justices, 6–3, rule that jurors received flawed instructions in case of retarded man, Johnny Paul Penry. In 20 years on death row, he became a symbol in growing national debate over execution of mentally retarded.

Religious Activities for Schools Approved (June 11, 2001): Justices rule, 6–3, that public schools must be open to after-hours religious programs on same basis as any other after-hours activity that school policy permits.

Heat-Sensing Police Surveillance (June 11, 2001): Justices, 5–4, disallow the use without a warrant of a thermal imaging device to determine whether a home is radiating abnormal heat (which might indicate the presence of high-intensity lamps used for growing marijuana indoors).

Citizenship of Children Born Abroad to Unwed Parents (June 11, 2001): In a 5–4 decision, Court validated a citizenship law that treats children born out of wedlock to noncitizen mothers abroad differently from those born to noncitizen fathers abroad.

Protection for Police Increased (June 18, 2001): In 6–3 decision, Court gives extra safeguard to officers in lawsuit alleging use of excessive force.

Immigrants Upheld on Challenges (June 25, 2001): Justices decide, 5–4, against automatic deportation of those convicted of crimes before new stringent legal provisions took effect in 1996.

Writers Upheld in Copyright Case (June 25, 2001): Court finds, 7–2, that newspaper and magazine publishers infringed on the rights of freelance contributors by making their work accessible to electronic databases without permission.

Local Regulation of Tobacco Ads Limited (June 28, 2001): All nine justices agree that smoking is a health problem but invoke statutory and constitutional reasons to invalidate sweeping Massachusetts restrictions on the advertising of tobacco products.

Assassinations and Attempts in U.S. Since 1865

Lincoln, Abraham (president of U.S.): Shot April 14, 1865, in Washington, D.C., by John Wilkes Booth; died April 15.

Seward, William H. (secretary of state): Escaped assassination (though injured) April 14, 1865, in Washington, D.C., by Lewis Powell (or Paine), accomplice of John Wilkes Booth.

Garfield, James A. (president of U.S.): Shot July 2, 1881, in Washington, D.C., by Charles J. Guiteau; died Sept. 19.

McKinley, William (president of U.S.): Shot Sept. 6, 1901, in Buffalo by Leon Czolgosz; died Sept. 14.

Roosevelt, Theodore (ex-president of U.S.): Escaped assassination (though shot) Oct. 14, 1912, in Milwaukee while campaigning for president.

Cermak, Anton J. (mayor of Chicago): Shot Feb. 15, 1933, in Miami by Giuseppe Zangara, who attempted to assassinate Franklin D. Roosevelt; Cermak died March 6.

Roosevelt, Franklin D. (president-elect of U.S.): Escaped assassination unhurt Feb. 15, 1933, in Miami.

Long, Huey P. (U.S. senator from Louisiana): Shot Sept. 8, 1935, in Baton Rouge by Dr. Carl A. Weiss; died Sept. 10.

Truman, Harry S. (president of U.S.): Escaped assassination attempt Nov. 1, 1950, in Washington, D.C., as 2 Puerto Rican nationalists attempted to shoot their way into Blair House.

Kennedy, John F. (president of U.S.): Shot Nov. 22, 1963, in Dallas, Tex., allegedly by Lee Harvey Oswald; died same day. Injured was Gov. John B. Connally of Texas. Oswald was shot and killed two days later by Jack Ruby.

Malcolm X, also known as El-Hajj Malik El-Shabazz (black activist): Shot and killed in a New York City auditorium, Feb. 21, 1965; his killer(s) were never positively identified.

King, Martin Luther, Jr. (civil rights leader): Shot April 4, 1968, in Memphis by James Earl Ray; died same day.

Kennedy, Robert F. (U.S. senator from New York): Shot June 5, 1968, in Los Angeles by Sirhan Bishara Sirhan; died June 6.

Wallace, George C. (governor of Alabama): Shot and critically wounded in assassination attempt May 15, 1972, at Laurel, Md., by Arthur Herman Bremer. Wallace paralyzed from waist down.

Ford, Gerald R. (president of U.S.): Escaped assassination attempt Sept. 5, 1975, in Sacramento, Calif., by Lynette Alice (Squeaky) Fromme, who pointed but did not fire .45-caliber pistol. Escaped assassination attempt in San Francisco, Calif., Sept. 22, 1975, by Sara Jane Moore, who fired one shot from a .38-caliber pistol that was deflected.

Jordan, Vernon E., Jr. (civil rights leader): Shot and critically wounded in assassination attempt May 29, 1980, in Fort Wayne, Ind.

Reagan, Ronald (president of U.S.): Shot in left lung in Washington by John W. Hinckley, Jr., on March 30, 1981; three others also wounded.

The Early Congresses

At the urging of Massachusetts and Virginia, the First Continental Congress met in Philadelphia on Sept. 5, 1774, and was attended by representatives of all the colonies except Georgia. Patrick Henry of Virginia declared: "The distinctions between Pennsylvanians, New Yorkers, and New Englanders are no more. I am not a Virginian but an American." This Congress, which adjourned Oct. 26, 1774, passed intercolonial resolutions calling for extensive boycott by the colonies against British trade.

The following year, most of the delegates from the colonies were chosen by popular election to attend the Second Continental Congress, which assembled in Philadelphia on May 10. As war had already begun between the colonies and England, the chief problems before the Congress were the procuring of military supplies, the establishment of an army and proper defenses, the issuing of continental bills of credit, etc. On June 15, 1775, George Washington was elected to command the Continental army. Congress adjourned Dec. 12, 1776.

Other Continental Congresses were held in Baltimore (1776–1777), Philadelphia (1777), Lancaster, Pa. (1777), York, Pa. (1777–1778), and Philadelphia (1778–1781).

In 1781, the Articles of Confederation, although establishing a league of the thirteen states rather than a strong central government, provided for the continuance of Congress. Known thereafter as the Congress of the Confederation, it held sessions in Philadelphia (1781–1783), Princeton, N.J. (1783), Annapolis, Md. (1783–1784), and Trenton, N.J. (1784). Five sessions were held in New York City between the years 1785 and 1789.

The Congress of the United States, established by the ratification of the Constitution, held its first meeting on March 4, 1789, in New York City. Several sessions of Congress were held in Philadelphia, and the first meeting in Washington, DC, was on Nov. 17, 1800.

Presidents of the Continental Congresses

Name	Elected	Birth and death dates	Name	Elected	Birth and death dates
Peyton Randolph, Va.	9/5/1774	c.1721–1775	John Hanson, Md.	11/5/1781	1715–1783
Henry Middleton, S.C.	10/22/1774	1717–1784	Elias Boudinot, N.J.	11/4/1782	1740–1821
Peyton Randolph, Va.	5/10/1775	c.1721–1775	Thomas Mifflin, Pa.	11/3/1783	1744–1800
John Hancock, Mass.	5/24/1775	1737–1793	Richard Henry Lee, Va.	11/30/1784	1732–1794
Henry Laurens, S.C.	11/1/1777	1724–1792	John Hancock, Mass.[1]	11/23/1785	1737–1793
John Jay, N.Y.	12/10/1778	1745–1829	Nathaniel Gorham, Mass.	6/6/1786	1738–1796
Samuel Huntington, Conn.	9/28/1779	1731–1796	Arthur St. Clair, Pa.	2/2/1787	1734–1818
Thomas McKean, Del.	7/10/1781	1734–1817	Cyrus Griffin, Va.	1/22/1788	1748–1810

1. Resigned May 29, 1786, never having served, because of continued illness.

States by Order of Entry into Union

State	Entered Union	Year settled	State	Entered Union	Year settled
1. Delaware	Dec. 7, 1787	1638	26. Michigan	Jan. 26, 1837	1668
2. Pennsylvania	Dec. 12, 1787	1682	27. Florida	Mar. 3, 1845	1565
3. New Jersey	Dec. 18, 1787	1660	28. Texas	Dec. 29, 1845	1682
4. Georgia	Jan. 2, 1788	1733	29. Iowa	Dec. 28, 1846	1788
5. Connecticut	Jan. 9, 1788	1634	30. Wisconsin	May 29, 1848	1766
6. Massachusetts	Feb. 6, 1788	1620	31. California	Sept. 9, 1850	1769
7. Maryland	Apr. 28, 1788	1634	32. Minnesota	May 11, 1858	1805
8. South Carolina	May 23, 1788	1670	33. Oregon	Feb. 14, 1859	1811
9. New Hampshire	June 21, 1788	1623	34. Kansas	Jan. 29, 1861	1727
10. Virginia	June 25, 1788	1607	35. West Virginia	June 20, 1863	1727
11. New York	July 26, 1788	1614	36. Nevada	Oct. 31, 1864	1849
12. North Carolina	Nov. 21, 1789	1660	37. Nebraska	Mar. 1, 1867	1823
13. Rhode Island	May 29, 1790	1636	38. Colorado	Aug. 1, 1876	1858
14. Vermont	Mar. 4, 1791	1724	39. North Dakota	Nov. 2, 1889	1812
15. Kentucky	June 1, 1792	1774	40. South Dakota	Nov. 2, 1889	1859
16. Tennessee	June 1, 1796	1769	41. Montana	Nov. 8, 1889	1809
17. Ohio	Mar. 1, 1803	1788	42. Washington	Nov. 11, 1889	1811
18. Louisiana	Apr. 30, 1812	1699	43. Idaho	July 3, 1890	1842
19. Indiana	Dec. 11, 1816	1733	44. Wyoming	July 10, 1890	1834
20. Mississippi	Dec. 10, 1817	1699	45. Utah	Jan. 4, 1896	1847
21. Illinois	Dec. 3, 1818	1720	46. Oklahoma	Nov. 16, 1907	1889
22. Alabama	Dec. 14, 1819	1702	47. New Mexico	Jan. 6, 1912	1610
23. Maine	Mar. 15, 1820	1624	48. Arizona	Feb. 14, 1912	1776
24. Missouri	Aug. 10, 1821	1735	49. Alaska	Jan. 3, 1959	1784
25. Arkansas	June 15, 1836	1686	50. Hawaii	Aug. 21, 1959	1820

Source: Compiled from various sources by the editors.

The Confederate States of America

State	Seceded from Union	Readmitted to Union[1]		State	Seceded from Union	Readmitted to Union[1]
1. South Carolina	Dec. 20, 1860	July 9, 1868	7.	Texas	March 2, 1861	March 30, 1870
2. Mississippi	Jan. 9, 1861	Feb. 23, 1870	8.	Virginia	April 17, 1861	Jan. 26, 1870
3. Florida	Jan. 10, 1861	June 25, 1868	9.	Arkansas	May 6, 1861	June 22, 1868
4. Alabama	Jan. 11, 1861	July 13, 1868	10.	North Carolina	May 20, 1861	July 4, 1868
5. Georgia	Jan. 19, 1861	July 15, 1870[2]	11.	Tennessee	June 8, 1861	July 24, 1866
6. Louisiana	Jan. 26, 1861	July 9, 1868				

NOTE: Four other slave states—Delaware, Maryland, Kentucky, and Missouri—remained in the Union. The latter two were actually represented on the Confederate flag, which, like the Stars and Stripes, featured a star for every state. 1. Date of readmission to representation in U.S. House of Representatives. 2. Second readmission date. First date was July 21, 1868, but the representatives were unseated March 5, 1869.

Territorial Expansion

Accession	Date	Area[1]	Accession	Date	Area[1]
United States	—	3,717,796	Other territory		
Territory in 1790	—	891,364	Philippines[2]	1898	115,600
Louisiana Purchase	1803	831,321	Puerto Rico	1899	3,508
Florida	1819	69,866	Guam	1899	217
Texas	1845	384,958	American Samoa	1900	90
Oregon	1846	283,439	Canal Zone[3]	1904	553
Mexican Cession	1848	530,706	Virgin Islands of U.S.	1917	171
Gadsden Purchase	1853	29,640	Trust Territory of Pacific Islands[4]	1947	241
Alaska	1867	591,004	Northern Mariana Islands	1986	189
Hawaii	1898	6,471	All other	—	16
			Total, 1990	—	**3,722,228**

1. Total area (land and water), in square miles. 2. Became independent in 1946. 3. Reverted to Panama in 1979. 4. Palau, the last remaining trust territory, became a sovereign state in 1994. *Source:* U.S. Bureau of the Census, Web: www.census.gov.

The Monroe Doctrine

The Monroe Doctrine was announced in President James Monroe's message to Congress, during his second term on Dec. 2, 1823, in part as follows:

"In the discussions to which this interest has given rise, and in the arrangements by which they may terminate, the occasion has been deemed proper for asserting as a principle in which rights and interests of the United States are involved, that the American continents, by the free and independent condition which they have assumed and maintain, are henceforth not to be considered as subjects for future colonization by any European power. . . . We owe it, therefore, to candor and to the amicable relations existing between the United States and those powers to declare that we should consider any attempt on their part to extend their system to any portion of this hemisphere as dangerous to our peace and safety. With the existing colonies or dependencies of any European power we have not interfered and shall not interfere. But with the governments who have declared their independence and maintain it, and whose independence we have, on great consideration and on just principles, acknowledged, we could not view any interposition for the purpose of oppressing them or controlling in any other manner their destiny by any European power in any other light than as the manifestation of an unfriendly disposition toward the United States."

Figures and Legends in American Folklore

Appleseed, Johnny (John Chapman, 1774–1847): Massachusetts-born nurseryman; reputed to have spread seeds and seedlings out of which grew the apple orchards of the Midwest.

Billy the Kid (William H. Bonney, 1859–1881): Desperado who killed his first man before he reached his teens; after short life of crime in Wild West was gunned down by Sheriff Pat Garrett; symbol of lawless West.

Boone, Daniel (1734–1820): Frontiersman and Indian fighter, about whom legends of early America have been built; figured in Byron's *Don Juan.*

Buffalo Bill (William F. Cody, 1846–1917): Buffalo hunter and Indian scout; many of the legends about him stem from his own Wild West show, which he operated in late 19th century.

Bunyan, Paul: Mythical lumberjack; subject of tall tales throughout timber country (that he dug Grand Canyon, for example).

Crockett, Davy (1786–1836): Frontiersman, congressman, and defender of the Alamo, his backwoods humor and larger-than-life adventures made him synonymous with the Wild West.

Jones, Casey (John Luther Jones, 1863–1900): Example of heroic locomotive engineer given to feats of prowess; died in wreck when his Illinois Central "Cannonball" express hit a freight train at Vaughan, Miss.

Uncle Sam: Personification of U.S. and its people; origin uncertain; may be based on inspector of government supplies in Revolutionary War and War of 1812.

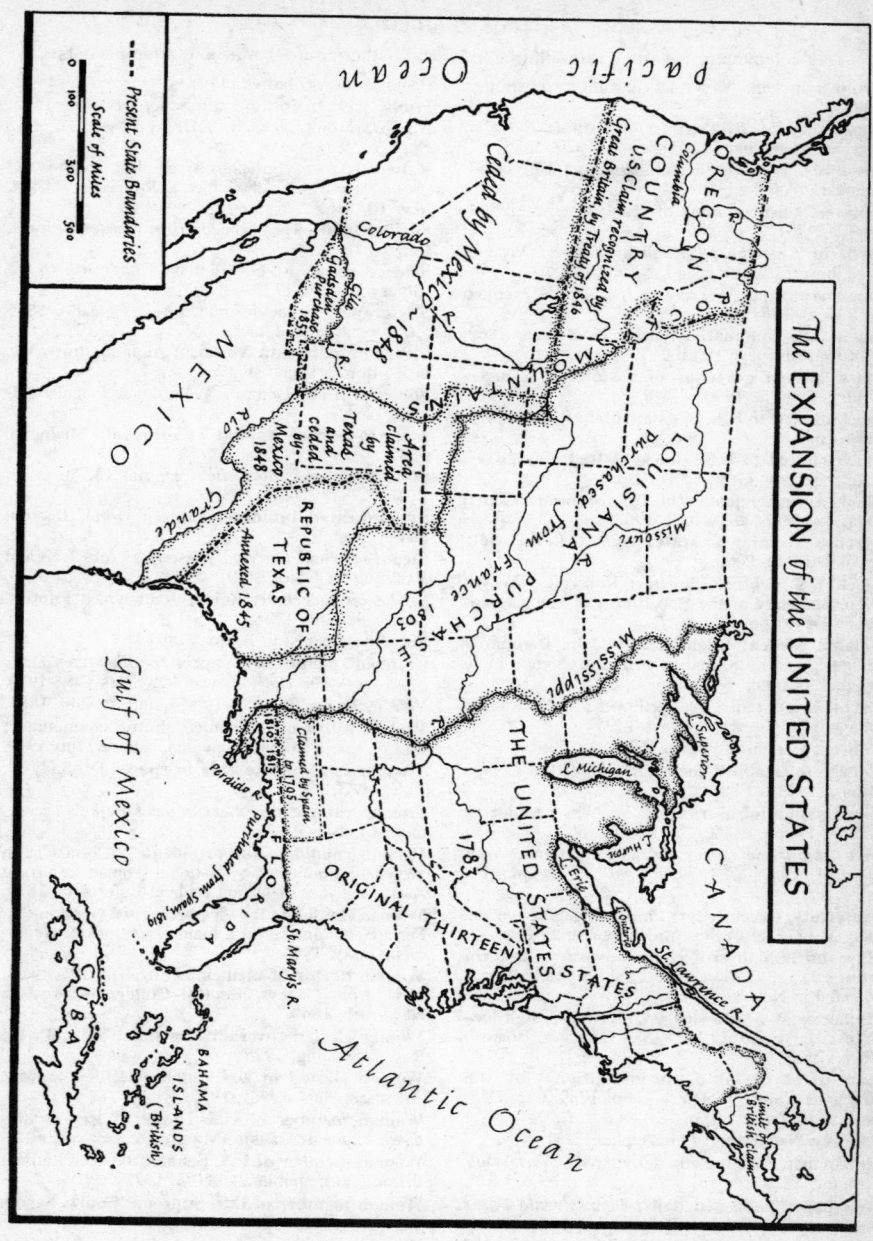

The EXPANSION of the UNITED STATES

Firsts in America

This selection is based on our editorial judgment. Other sources may list different firsts.

Admiral in U.S. Navy: David Glasgow Farragut, 1866.

Airmail route, first transcontinental: Between New York City and San Francisco, 1920.

Assembly, representative: House of Burgesses, founded in Virginia, 1619.

Bank established: Bank of North America, Philadelphia, 1781.

Birth in America to English parents: Virginia Dare, born Roanoke Island, N.C., 1587. .

Black newspaper: *Freedom's Journal,* 1827, edited by John B. Russworm.

Black U.S. diplomat: Ebenezer D. Bassett, 1869, minister-resident to Haiti.

Black elected governor of a state: L. Douglas Wilder, Virginia, 1990.

Black elected to U.S. Senate: Hiram Revels, 1870, Mississippi.

Black elected to U.S. House of Representatives: Jefferson Long, Georgia, 1870.

Black associate justice of U.S. Supreme Court: Thurgood Marshall, Oct. 2, 1967.

Black secretary of state: Gen. Colin Powell, appointed Dec. 2000.

Black U.S. cabinet minister: Robert C. Weaver, 1966, Secretary of the Department of Housing and Urban Development.

Botanic garden: Established by John Bartram in Philadelphia, 1728, and is still in existence in its original location.

Cartoon, colored: "The Yellow Kid," by Richard Outcault, in *New York World,* 1895.

College: Harvard, founded 1636.

College to establish coeducation: Oberlin College (Ohio), 1833.

Electrocution of a criminal: William Kemmler in Auburn Prison, Auburn, N.Y., Aug. 6, 1890.

Five and Dime store: Founded by Frank Woolworth, Utica, N.Y., 1879 (moved to Lancaster, Pa., same year).

Fraternity, Greek-letter: Phi Beta Kappa; founded Dec. 5, 1776, at College of William and Mary.

Gay and lesbian civil rights advocacy organization: National Gay and Lesbian Task Force, founded in New York City, 1973.

Homosexual, acknowledged, elected to high local office: Harvey Milk, 1977, San Francisco Board of Supervisors.

Law to be declared unconstitutional by U.S. Supreme Court: Judiciary Act of 1789. Case: *Marbury* v. *Madison,* 1803.

Library, circulating: Philadelphia, 1731.

Newspaper, illustrated daily: *New York Daily Graphic,* 1873.

Newspaper published daily: *Pennsylvania Packet and General Advertiser,* Philadelphia, Sept. 1784.

Newspaper published over a continuous period: *The Boston News-Letter,* April 1704.

Oil well, commercial: Titusville, Pa., 1859.

Panel quiz show on radio: *Information Please,* May 17, 1938.

Postage stamps issued: 1847.

Public school: Boston Latin School, Boston, 1635.

Radio station licensed: KDKA, Pittsburgh, Pa., Oct. 27, 1920.

Railroad, transcontinental: Central Pacific and Union Pacific railroads, joined at Promontory, Utah, May 10, 1869.

Savings bank: The Provident Institute for Savings, Boston, 1816.

Science museum: Founded by Charleston (S.C.) Library Society, 1773.

Skyscraper: Home Insurance Co., Chicago, 1885 (10 floors, 2 added later).

Slaves brought into America: At Jamestown, Va., 1619, from a Dutch ship.

Sorority: Alpha Delta Pi, at Wesleyan Female College, 1851.

State to abolish capital punishment: Michigan, 1847.

State to enter Union after original 13: Vermont, 1791.

Steam-heated building: Eastern Hotel, Boston, 1845.

Steam railroad (carried passengers and freight): Baltimore & Ohio, 1830.

Strike on record by union: Journeymen Printers, New York City, 1776.

Subway: Opened in Boston, 1897.

"Tabloid" picture newspaper: *The Illustrated Daily News* (now *The Daily News*), New York City, 1919.

Vaudeville theater: Gaiety Museum, Boston, 1883.

Woman astronaut appointed shuttle commander: Lt. Col. Eileen Collins, *Columbia,* launched July 1999.

Woman astronaut to ride in space: Dr. Sally K. Ride, 1983.

Woman cabinet member: Frances Perkins, Secretary of Labor, 1933.

Woman candidate for president: Victoria Claflin Woodhull, nominated by National Woman's Suffrage Assn. on ticket of Nation Radical Reformers, 1872.

Woman candidate for vice president: Geraldine A. Ferraro, nominated on a major party ticket, Democratic Party, 1984.

Woman doctor of medicine: Elizabeth Blackwell; M.D. from Geneva Medical College of Western New York, 1849.

Woman elected governor of a state: Nellie Tayloe Ross, Wyoming, 1925.

Woman elected to U.S. Senate: Hattie Caraway, Arkansas; elected Nov. 1932.

Woman member of U.S. House of Representatives: Jeannette Rankin (Mont.); elected Nov. 1916.

Woman member of U.S. Senate: Rebecca Latimer Felton (Ga.); appointed Oct. 3, 1922.

Woman member of U.S. Supreme Court: Sandra Day O'Connor; appointed July 1981.

Woman secretary of state: Madeleine Albright, appointed Dec. 1996.

Woman suffrage granted: Wyoming Territory, 1869.

Written constitution: *Fundamental Orders of Connecticut,* 1639.

The Great Seal of the U.S.

On July 4, 1776, the Continental Congress appointed a committee consisting of Benjamin Franklin, John Adams, and Thomas Jefferson "to bring in a device for a seal of the United States of America." After many delays, a verbal description of a design by William Barton was finally approved by Congress on June 20, 1782. The seal shows an American bald eagle with a ribbon in its mouth bearing the device *E pluribus unum* (One out of many). In its talons are the arrows of war and an olive branch of peace. On the reverse side it shows an unfinished pyramid with an eye (the eye of Providence) above it. Although this description was adopted in 1782, the first drawing was not made until four years later, and no die has ever been cut.

The Star-Spangled Banner

Francis Scott Key, 1814

O say, can you see, by the dawn's early light,
What so proudly we hail'd at the twilight's last gleaming?
Whose broad stripes and bright stars, thro' the perilous fight,
O'er the ramparts we watch'd, were so gallantly streaming?
And the rockets' red glare, the bombs bursting in air,
Gave proof thro' the night that our flag was still there.
O say, does that star-spangled banner yet wave
O'er the land of the free and the home of the brave?

On the shore dimly seen thro' the mists of the deep,
Where the foe's haughty host in dread silence reposes,
What is that which the breeze, o'er the towering steep,
As it fitfully blows, half conceals, half discloses?
Now it catches the gleam of the morning's first beam,
In full glory reflected, now shines on the stream:
'Tis the star-spangled banner: O, long may it wave
O'er the land of the free and the home of the brave!

And where is that band who so vauntingly swore
That the havoc of war and the battle's confusion,
A home and a country should leave us no more?
Their blood has wash'd out their foul footsteps' pollution.
No refuge could save the hireling and slave
From the terror of flight or the gloom of the grave:
And the star-spangled banner in triumph doth wave
O'er the land of the free and the home of the brave.

O thus be it ever when free-men shall stand
Between their lov'd home and the war's desolation;
Blest with vict'ry and peace, may the heav'n-rescued land
Praise the Pow'r that hath made and preserv'd us a nation!
Then conquer we must, when our cause it is just,
And this be our motto: "In God is our trust!"
And the star-spangled banner in triumph shall wave
O'er the land of the free and the home of the brave!

On Sept. 13, 1814, Francis Scott Key visited the British fleet in Chesapeake Bay to secure the release of Dr. William Beanes, who had been captured after the burning of Washington, DC. The release was secured, but Key was detained on ship overnight during the shelling of Fort McHenry, one of the forts defending Baltimore. In the morning, he was so delighted to see the American flag still flying over the fort that he began a poem to commemorate the occasion. First published under the title "Defense of Fort M'Henry," the poem soon attained wide popularity as sung to the tune "To Anacreon in Heaven." The origin of this tune is obscure, but it may have been written by John Stafford Smith, a British composer born in 1750. "The Star-Spangled Banner" was officially made the national anthem by Congress in 1931, although it already had been adopted as such by the army and the navy.

History of the American Flag

According to popular legend, the first American flag was made by Betsy Ross, a Philadelphia seamstress who was acquainted with George Washington, leader of the Continental Army, and other influential Philadelphians. In May 1776, so the story goes, General Washington and two representatives from the Continental Congress visited Ross at her upholstery shop and showed her a rough design of the flag. Although Washington initially favored using a star with six points, Ross advocated for a five-pointed star, which could be cut with just one quick snip of the scissors, and the gentlemen were won over.

Unfortunately, historians have never been able to verify this charming version of events, although it is known that Ross made flags for the navy of Pennsylvania. The story of Washington's visit to the flagmaker became popular about the time of the country's first centennial, after William Canby, a grandson of Ross, told about her role in shaping U.S. history in a speech given at the Philadelphia Historical Society in March 1870.

What is known is that the first unofficial national flag, called the Grand Union Flag or the Continental Colours, was raised at the behest of General Washington near his headquarters outside Boston, Mass., on Jan. 1, 1776. The flag had 13 alternating red and white horizontal stripes and the British Union Flag (a predecessor of the Union Jack) in the canton. Another early flag had a rattlesnake on a background of 13 red and white stripes with the motto "Don't Tread on Me."

The first official national flag, also known as the Stars and Stripes, or Old Glory, was approved by the Continental Congress on June 14, 1777. The blue canton contained 13 stars, representing the original 13 colonies, but the layout varied. Although nobody knows for sure who designed the flag, it may have been Continental Congress member Francis Hopkinson.

After Vermont and Kentucky were admitted to the Union in 1791 and 1792, respectively, two more stars and two more stripes were added in 1795. This 15-star, 15-stripe flag was the "star-spangled banner" that inspired lawyer Francis Scott Key to write the poem that later became the U.S. national anthem.

In 1818, after five more states had gained admittance, Congress passed legislation fixing the number of stripes at 13 and requiring that the number of stars equal the number of states. The last new star, bringing the total to 50, was added on July 4, 1960, after Hawaii became a state.

The Pledge of Allegiance to the Flag[1]

I pledge allegiance to the Flag of the United States of America, and to the Republic for which it stands, one Nation under God,[2] indivisible, with liberty and justice for all.

1. The original pledge was published in the Sept. 8, 1892, issue of *The Youth's Companion* in Boston. For years, the authorship was in dispute between James B. Upham and Francis Bellamy of the magazine's staff. In 1939, after a study of the controversy, the United States Flag Association decided that authorship be credited to Bellamy.
2. The phrase "under God" was added to the pledge on June 14, 1954.

The Statue of Liberty

The Statue of Liberty ("Liberty Enlightening the World") is a 225-ton, steel-reinforced copper female figure, 152 ft in height, facing the ocean from Liberty Island[1] in New York Harbor. The right hand holds aloft a torch, and the left hand carries a tablet upon which is inscribed: "July IV MDCCLXXVI."

The statue was designed by Frédéric Auguste Bartholdi of Alsace as a gift to the United States from the people of France to memorialize the alliance of the two countries in the American Revolution and their abiding friendship. The French people contributed the $250,000 cost.

The 150-foot pedestal was designed by Richard M. Hunt and built by Gen. Charles P. Stone, both Americans. It contains steel underpinnings designed by Alexander Eiffel of France to support the statue. The $270,000 cost was borne by popular subscription in this country. President Grover Cleveland accepted the statue for the United States on Oct. 28, 1886.

The Statue of Liberty was designated a National Monument in 1924 and a World Heritage Site in 1984.

On Sept. 26, 1972, President Richard M. Nixon dedicated the American Museum of Immigration, housed in structural additions to the base of the statue. In 1984 scaffolding went up for a major restoration and the torch was extinguished on July 4. It was relit with much ceremony July 4, 1986, to mark its centennial.

On a tablet inside the pedestal is engraved the following sonnet, written by Emma Lazarus (1849–1887):

The New Colossus

Not like the brazen giant of Greek fame.
With conquering limbs astride from land to land;
Here at our sea-washed, sunset gates shall stand
A mighty woman with a torch, whose flame
Is the imprisoned lightning, and her name
Mother of Exiles. From her beacon-hand
Glows world-wide welcome; her mild eyes command
The air-bridged harbor that twin cities frame.
"Keep, ancient lands, your storied pomp!" cries she
With silent lips. "Give me your tired, your poor,
Your huddled masses yearning to breathe free,
The wretched refuse of your teeming shore.
Send these, the homeless, tempest-tost to me,
I lift my lamp beside the golden door!"

1. Called Bedloe's Island prior to 1956.

The White House

Source: Department of the Interior, U.S. National Park Service

The White House, the official residence of the president, is at 1600 Pennsylvania Avenue in Washington, DC 20500. The site, covering about 18 acres, was selected by President Washington and city planner Pierre Charles L'Enfant, and the architect was James Hoban. The design appears to have been influenced by Leinster House, Dublin, and James Gibb's *Book of Architecture*. The cornerstone was laid Oct. 13, 1792, and the first residents were President John Adams and First Lady Abigail Adams in Nov. 1800.

The White House has a fascinating history. The main building was burned by the British in 1814 during the War of 1812. Afterward, when the building was being restored, the smoke-stained gray stone walls were painted white. The name "White House," however, was not used officially until President Theodore Roosevelt had it engraved on his stationery in 1901. Prior to that, the building was known variously as the "President's Palace," the "President's House," and the "Executive Mansion."

Over the years, there have been several additions made to the main building, including the west wing (1902), the east wing (1942), and a penthouse and a bomb shelter (1952). The west wing, which contains the president's oval office and the offices of his staff, is the center of activity at the White House. During Harry Truman's presidency, from Dec. 1948 to March 1952, the interior of the White House was rebuilt, and the outer walls were strengthened. Nevertheless, the exterior stone walls are the same ones that were first put in place when the White House was constructed two centuries ago.

The rooms for public functions are on the first floor; the second and third floors are used as the residence of the president and first family. The most celebrated public room is the East Room, where formal receptions take place. Other public rooms are the Red Room, the Green Room, and the Blue Room. The State Dining Room is used for formal dinners. In all, there are 132 rooms, 35 bathrooms, 28 fireplaces, 8 staircases, and 3 elevators.

U.S. Capitol

When the French architect and engineer Maj. Pierre Charles L'Enfant first began to lay out the plans for a new federal city (now Washington, DC), he noted that Jenkins' Hill, overlooking the area, seemed to be "a pedestal waiting for a monument." It was here that the U.S. Capitol would be built. The basic structure as we know it today evolved over a period of more than 150 years. In 1792 a competition was held for the design of a capitol building. Dr. William Thornton, a physician and amateur architect, submitted the winning plan, a simple, low-lying structure of classical proportions with a shallow dome. Later, internal modifications were made by Benjamin Henry Latrobe. After the building was burned by the British in 1814, Latrobe and architect Charles Bulfinch were responsible for its reconstruction. Finally, under Thomas Walter, who was Architect of the Capitol from 1851 to 1865, the House and Senate wings and the imposing cast-iron dome topped with the Statue of Freedom were added, and the Capitol assumed the form we see today.

The Capitol building is rich in historic associations. It was in the old Senate chamber that Daniel Webster cried out, "Liberty and union, now and forever, one and inseparable!" In Statuary Hall, which used to be the old House chamber, a small disk on the floor marks the spot where John Quincy Adams was fatally stricken after more than 50 years of service to his country. A whisper from one side of this room can be heard across the vast space of the hall. Visitors can see the original Supreme Court chamber a floor below the Rotunda.

The Capitol Building is also a vast artistic treasure house. The works of such famous artists as Gilbert Stuart, Rembrandt Peale, and John Trumbull are displayed on the walls. The Great Rotunda, with its 180-foot- (54.9-meter-) high dome, is decorated with a fresco by Constantino Brumidi, which extends some 300 ft (90 m) in circumference. Throughout the building are many paintings of events in U.S. history and sculptures of outstanding Americans. The 68-acre (27.5-hectare) park that the Capitol is situated on was designed by the 19th-century landscape architect Frederick Law Olmsted.

There are free guided tours of the Capitol, which include admission to the House and Senate galleries. Those who wish to visit the visitors' gallery in either wing without taking the tour may obtain passes from their senators or representatives. Visitors may ride on the monorail subway that joins the House and Senate wings of the Capitol with the congressional office buildings.

Washington Monument

Construction of this magnificent Washington, DC, monument, which draws some two million visitors a year, took nearly a century of planning, building, and controversy. Provision for a large equestrian statue of George Washington was made in the original city plan, but the project was soon dropped. After Washington's death it was taken up again, and a number of false starts and changes of design were made. Finally, in 1848, work was begun on the monument that stands today. The design, by architect Robert Mills, then featured an ornate base. In 1854, however, political squabbling and a lack of money brought construction to a halt. Work was resumed in 1880, and the monument was completed in 1884 and opened to the public in 1888. The tapered shaft, faced with white marble and rising from walls 15 ft (4.6 m) thick at the base, was modeled after the obelisks of ancient Egypt. The monument, one of the tallest masonry constructions in the world, stands just over 555 ft (169 m). Memorial stones from the 50 states, foreign countries, and organizations line the interior walls. The top, reached only by elevator, commands a panoramic view of the city.

The Liberty Bell

The Liberty Bell was cast in England in 1752 for the Pennsylvania Statehouse (now named Independence Hall) in Philadelphia. It was recast in Philadelphia in 1753. It is inscribed with the words, "Proclaim liberty throughout all the land unto all the inhabitants thereof" (Lev. 25:10). The bell was rung on July 8, 1776, for the first public reading of the Declaration of Independence. Hidden in Allentown during the British occupation of Philadelphia, it was re-placed in Independence Hall in 1778. The bell cracked on July 8, 1835, while tolling the death of Chief Justice John Marshall. In 1976 the Liberty Bell was moved to a special exhibition building near Independence Hall.

The Declaration of Independence

On April 12, 1776, the legislature of North Carolina authorized its delegates to the Continental Congress to join with others in a declaration of separation from Great Britain; the first colony to instruct its delegates to take the actual initiative was Virginia on May 15. On June 7, 1776, Richard Henry Lee of Virginia offered a resolution to the Congress to the effect "that these United Colonies are, and of right ought to be, free and independent States. . . ." A committee consisting of Thomas Jefferson, John Adams, Benjamin Franklin, Robert R. Livingston, and Roger Sherman was organized to "prepare a declaration to the effect of the said first resolution." The Declaration of Independence was adopted on July 4, 1776. Most delegates signed the Declaration August 2, but George Wythe (Va.) signed August 27; Richard Henry Lee (Va.), Elbridge Gerry (Mass.), and Oliver Wolcott (Conn.) in September; Matthew Thornton (N.H.), not a delegate until September, in November; and Thomas McKean (Del.), although present on July 4, not until 1781 by special permission, having served in the army in the interim.

In Congress, July 4, 1776

The unanimous Declaration of the thirteen United States of America

When in the Course of human events it becomes necessary for one people to dissolve the political bands which have connected them with another, and to assume among the powers of the earth, the separate and equal station to which the Laws of Nature and of Nature's God entitle them, a decent respect to the opinions of mankind requires that they should declare the causes which impel them to the separation.

We hold these truths to be self-evident, that all men are created equal, that they are endowed by their Creator with certain unalienable Rights, that among these are Life, Liberty and the pursuit of Happiness.—That to secure these rights, Governments are instituted among Men, deriving their just powers from the consent of the governed.—That whenever any Form of Government becomes destructive of these ends, it is the Right of the People to alter or to abolish it, and to institute new Government, laying its foundation on such principles and organizing its powers in such form, as to them shall seem most likely to effect their Safety and Happiness. Prudence, indeed, will dictate that Governments long established should not be changed for light and transient causes; and accordingly all experience hath shewn that mankind are more disposed to suffer, while evils are sufferable, than to right themselves by abolishing the forms to which they are accustomed. But when a long train of abuses and usurpations, pursuing invariably the same Object evinces a design to reduce them under absolute Despotism, it is their right, it is their duty, to throw off such Government, and to provide new Guards for their future security.—Such has been the patient sufferance of these Colonies; and such is now the necessity which constrains them to alter their former Systems of Government. The history of the present King of Great Britain is a history of repeated injuries and usurpations, all having in direct object the establishment of an absolute Tyranny over these States. To prove this, let Facts be submitted to a candid world.

He has refused his Assent to Laws, the most wholesome and necessary for the public good.

He has forbidden his Governors to pass Laws of immediate and pressing importance, unless suspended in their operation till his Assent should be obtained; and when so suspended, he has utterly neglected to attend to them.

He has refused to pass other Laws for the accommodation of large districts of people, unless those people would relinquish the right of Representation in the Legislature, a right inestimable to them and formidable to tyrants only.

He has called together legislative bodies at places unusual, uncomfortable, and distant from the depository of their Public Records, for the sole purpose of fatiguing them into compliance with his measures.

He has dissolved Representative Houses repeatedly, for opposing with manly firmness his invasions on the rights of the people.

He has refused for a long time, after such dissolutions, to cause others to be elected; whereby the Legislative Powers, incapable of Annihilation, have returned to the People at large for their exercise; the State remaining in the mean time exposed to all the dangers of invasion from without, and convulsions within.

He has endeavoured to prevent the population of these States; for that purpose obstructing the Laws for Naturalization of Foreigners; refusing to pass others to encourage their migrations hither, and raising the conditions of new Appropriations of Lands.

He has obstructed the Administration of Justice, by refusing his Assent to Laws for establishing Judiciary Powers.

He has made Judges dependent on his Will alone, for the tenure of their offices, and the amount and payment of their salaries.

He has erected a multitude of New Offices, and sent hither swarms of Officers to harass our people, and eat out their substance.

He has kept among us, in times of peace, Standing Armies without the Consent of our legislatures.

He has affected to render the Military independent of and superior to the Civil Power.

He has combined with others to subject us to a jurisdiction foreign to our constitution, and unacknowledged by our laws; giving his Assent to their Acts of pretended Legislation:

For quartering large bodies of armed troops among us:

For protecting them, by a mock Trial, from punishment for any Murders which they should commit on the Inhabitants of these States:

For cutting off our Trade with all parts of the world:

For imposing Taxes on us without our Consent:

For depriving us in many cases, of the benefits of Trial by Jury:

For transporting us beyond Seas to be tried for pretended offences:

For abolishing the free System of English Laws in a neighbouring Province, establishing therein an Arbitrary government, and enlarging its Boundaries so as to render it at once an example and fit instrument for introducing the same absolute rule into these Colonies:

For taking away our Charters, abolishing our most valuable Laws and altering fundamentally the Forms of our Governments:

For suspending our own Legislatures, and declaring themselves invested with power to legislate for us in all cases whatsoever.

He has abdicated Government here, by declaring us out of his Protection and waging War against us.

He has plundered our seas, ravaged our Coasts, burnt our towns, and destroyed the lives of our people.

He is at this time transporting large Armies of foreign Mercenaries to compleat the works of death, desolation, and tyranny, already begun with circumstances of Cruelty & Perfidy scarcely paralleled in the most barbarous ages, and totally unworthy the Head of a civilized nation.

He has constrained our fellow Citizens taken Captive on the high Seas to bear Arms against their Country, to become the executioners of their friends and Brethren, or to fall themselves by their Hands.

He has excited domestic insurrections amongst us, and has endeavoured to bring on the inhabitants of our frontiers, the merciless Indian Savages, whose known rule of warfare, is an undistinguished destruction of all ages, sexes and conditions.

In every stage of these Oppressions We have Petitioned for Redress in the most humble terms: Our repeated Petitions have been answered only by repeated injury. A Prince, whose character is thus marked by every act which may define a Tyrant, is unfit to be the ruler of a free people.

Nor have We been wanting in attentions to our British brethren. We have warned them from time to time of attempts by their legislature to extend an unwarrantable jurisdiction over us. We have reminded them of the circumstances of our emigration and settlement here. We have appealed to their native justice and magnanimity, and we have conjured them by the ties of our common kindred to disavow these usurpations, which would inevitably interrupt our connections and correspondence. They too have been deaf to the voice of justice and of consanguinity. We must, therefore, acquiesce in the necessity, which denounces our Separation, and hold them, as we hold the rest of mankind, Enemies in War, in Peace Friends.

We, therefore, the Representatives of the United States of America, in General Congress, Assembled, appealing to the Supreme Judge of the world for the rectitude of our intentions, do, in the Name, and by Authority of the good People of these Colonies, solemnly publish and declare, That these United Colonies are, and of Right ought to be Free and Independent States; that they are Absolved from all Allegiance to the British Crown, and that all political connection between them and the State of Great Britain, is and ought to be totally dissolved; and that as Free and Independent States, they have full Power to levy War, conclude Peace, contract Alliances, establish Commerce, and to do all other Acts and Things which Independent States may of right do.—And for the support of this Declaration, with a firm reliance on the protection of Divine Providence, we mutually pledge to each other our Lives, our Fortunes and our sacred Honor.

—John Hancock

New Hampshire
Josiah Bartlett
Wm. Whipple
Matthew Thornton

Rhode Island
Step. Hopkins
William Ellery

Connecticut
Roger Sherman
Sam'el Huntington
Wm. Williams
Oliver Wolcott

New York
Wm. Floyd
Phil. Livingston
Frans. Lewis
Lewis Morris

New Jersey
Richd. Stockton
Jno. Witherspoon
Fras. Hopkinson
John Hart
Abra. Clark

Pennsylvania
Robt. Morris
Benjamin Rush
Benj. Franklin
John Morton
Geo. Clymer
Jas. Smith
Geo. Taylor
James Wilson
Geo. Ross

Massachusetts-Bay
Saml. Adams

John Adams
Robt. Treat Paine
Elbridge Gerry

Delaware
Caesar Rodney
Geo. Read
Tho. M'Kean

Maryland
Samuel Chase
Wm. Paca
Thos. Stone
Charles Carroll of Carrollton

Virginia
George Wythe
Richard Henry Lee
Th. Jefferson

Benj. Harrison
Ths. Nelson, Jr.
Francis Lightfoot Lee
Carter Braxton

North Carolina
Wm. Hooper
Joseph Hewes
John Penn

South Carolina
Edward Rutledge
Thos. Heyward, Junr.
Thomas Lynch, Junr.
Arthur Middleton

Georgia
Button Gwinnett
Lyman Hall
Geo. Walton

Constitution of the United States of America

(Historical text has been edited to conform to contemporary American usage. The bracketed words are designations for your convenience; they are not part of the Constitution.)

The oldest federal constitution in existence was framed by a convention of delegates from twelve of the thirteen original states in Philadelphia in May 1787, Rhode Island failing to send a delegate. George Washington presided over the session, which lasted until September 17, 1787. The draft (originally a preamble and seven Articles) was submitted to all thirteen states and was to become effective when ratified by nine states. It went into effect on the first Wednesday in March 1789, having been ratified by New Hampshire, the ninth state to approve, on June 21, 1788. The states ratified the Constitution in the following order:

Delaware	December 7, 1787	South Carolina	May 23, 1788
Pennsylvania	December 12, 1787	New Hampshire	June 21, 1788
New Jersey	December 18, 1787	Virginia	June 25, 1788
Georgia	January 2, 1788	New York	July 26, 1788
Connecticut	January 9, 1788	North Carolina	November 21, 1789
Massachusetts	February 6, 1788	Rhode Island	May 29, 1790
Maryland	April 28, 1788		

[Preamble]

We the people of the United States, in order to form a more perfect Union, establish justice, insure domestic tranquility, provide for the common defence, promote the general welfare, and secure the blessings of liberty to ourselves and our posterity, do ordain and establish this Constitution for the United States of America.

Article I

Section 1

[Legislative powers vested in Congress.] All legislative powers herein granted shall be vested in a Congress of the United States, which shall consist of a Senate and House of Representatives.

Section 2

[Composition of the House of Representatives.—1.] The House of Representatives shall be composed of members chosen every second year by the people of the several States, and the electors in each State shall have the qualifications requisite for electors of the most numerous branch of the State Legislature.

[Qualifications of Representatives.—2.] No Person shall be a Representative who shall not have attained to the age of twenty-five years, and been seven years a citizen of the United States, and who shall not, when elected, be an inhabitant of that State in which he shall be chosen.

[Apportionment of Representatives and direct taxes—census.[1]—3.] (Representatives and direct taxes shall be apportioned among the several States which may be included within this Union, according to their respective numbers, which shall be determined by adding to the whole number of free persons, including those bound to service for a term of years, and excluding Indians not taxed, three fifths of all other persons.) The actual enumeration shall be made within three years after the first meeting of the Congress of the United States, and within every subsequent term of ten years, in such manner as they shall by law direct. The number of Representatives shall not exceed one for every thirty thousand, but each State shall have at least one Representa-

tive; and until such enumeration shall be made, the State of New Hampshire shall be entitled to choose three, Massachusetts eight, Rhode-Island and Providence Plantations one, Connecticut five, New York six, New Jersey four, Pennsylvania eight, Delaware one, Maryland six, Virginia ten, North Carolina five, South Carolina five, and Georgia three.

[Filling of vacancies in representation.—4.] When vacancies happen in the representation from any State, the Executive Authority thereof shall issue writs of election to fill such vacancies.

[Selection of officers; power of impeachment.—5.] The House of Representatives shall choose their Speaker and other officers; and shall have the sole power of impeachment

Section 3[2]

[The Senate.—1.] The Senate of the United States shall be composed of two Senators from each State, chosen by the Legislature thereof, for six years; and each Senator shall have one vote.

[Classification of Senators; filling of vacancies.—2.] Immediately after they shall be assembled in consequence of the first election, they shall be divided as equally as may be into three classes. The seats of the Senators of the first class shall be vacated at the expiration of the second year, of the second class at the expiration of the fourth year, and of the third class at the expiration of the sixth year, so that one-third may be chosen every second year; and if vacancies happen by resignation, or otherwise, during the recess of the Legislature of any State, the Executive thereof may make temporary appointments (until the next meeting of the Legislature, which shall then fill such vacancies.

[Qualification of Senators.—3.] No person shall be a Senator who shall not have attained to the age of thirty years, and been nine years a citizen of the United States, and who shall not, when elected, be an inhabitant of that State for which he shall be chosen.

[Vice President to be President of Senate.—4.] The Vice President of the United States shall be President of the Senate, but shall have no vote, unless they be equally divided.

[Selection of Senate officers; President pro tempore.—5.] The Senate shall choose their other

---

1. The clause included in parentheses is amended by the 14th Amendment, Section 2. 2. The first paragraph of this section and the part of the second paragraph included in parentheses are amended by the 17th Amendment.

officers, and also a President pro tempore, in the absence of the Vice President, or when he shall exercise the office of President of the United States.

[Senate to try impeachments.—6.] The Senate shall have the sole power to try all impeachments. When sitting for that purpose, they shall be on oath or affirmation. When the President of the United States is tried, the Chief Justice shall preside: and no person shall be convicted without the concurrence of two thirds of the members present.

[Judgment in cases of Impeachment.—7.] Judgment in cases of impeachment shall not extend further than to removal from office, and disqualification to hold and enjoy any office of honor, trust, or profit under the United States: but the party convicted shall nevertheless be liable and subject to indictment, trial, judgment and punishment, according to Law.

Section 4

[Control of congressional elections.—1.] The times, places, and manner of holding elections for Senators and Representatives, shall be prescribed in each State by the Legislature thereof; but the Congress may at any time by law make or alter such regulations, except as to the places of choosing Senators.

[Time for assembling of Congress³—2.] The Congress shall assemble at least once in every year, and such meeting shall be on the first Monday in December, unless they shall by law appoint a different day.

Section 5

[Each house to be the judge of the election and qualifications of its members; regulations as to quorum.—1.] Each House shall be the judge of the elections, returns, and qualifications of its own members, and a majority of each shall constitute a quorum to do business; but a smaller number may adjourn from day to day, and may be authorized to compel the attendance of absent members, in such manner, and under such penalties as each House may provide.

[Each house to determine its own rules.—2.] Each House may determine the rules of its proceedings, punish its members for disorderly behavior, and, with the concurrence of two thirds, expel a member.

[Journals and yeas and nays.—3.] Each House shall keep a journal of its proceedings, and from time to time publish the same, excepting such parts as may in their judgment require secrecy; and the yeas and nays of the members of either House on any question shall, at the desire of one fifth of those present, be entered on the journal.

[Adjournment.—4.] Neither House, during the session of Congress, shall, without the consent of the other, adjourn for more than three days, nor to any other place than that in which the two Houses shall be sitting.

Section 6

[Compensation and privileges of members of Congress.—1.] The Senators and Representatives shall receive a compensation for their services, to be ascertained by law, and paid out of the Treasury of the United States. They shall in all cases, except treason, felony, and breach of the peace, be privileged from arrest during their attendance at the session of their respective Houses, and in going to and returning from the same; and for any speech or debate in either House, they shall not be questioned in any other place.

[Incompatible offices; exclusions.—2.] No Senator or Representative shall, during the time for which he was elected, be appointed to any civil office under the authority of the United States, which shall have been created, or the emoluments whereof shall have been increased during such time; and no person holding any office under the United States shall be a member of either House during his continuance in office.

Section 7

[Revenue bills to originate in House.—1.] All bills for raising revenue shall originate in the House of Representatives; but the Senate may propose or concur with amendments as on other bills.

[Manner of passing bills; veto power of President.—2.] Every bill which shall have passed the House of Representatives and the Senate, shall, before it becomes a law, be presented to the President of the United States; if he approve he shall sign it, but if not he shall return it, with his objections to that House in which it shall have originated, who shall enter the objections at large on their journal, and proceed to reconsider it. If after such reconsideration two thirds of that House shall agree to pass the bill, it shall be sent, together with the objections, to the other House, by which it shall likewise be reconsidered, and if approved by two thirds of that House, it shall become a law. But in all such cases the votes of both Houses shall be determined by yeas and nays, and the names of the persons voting for and against the bill shall be entered on the journal of each house, respectively. If any bill shall not be returned by the President within ten days (Sundays excepted) after it shall have been presented to him, the same shall be a law, in like manner as if he had signed it, unless the Congress by their adjournment prevent its return, in which case it shall not be a law.

[Concurrent orders or resolutions, to be passed by President.—3.] Every order, resolution, or vote to which the concurrence of the Senate and House of Representatives may be necessary (except on a question of adjournment) shall be presented to the President of the United States; and before the same shall take effect, shall be approved by him, or being disapproved by him, shall be repassed by two thirds of the Senate and House of Representatives, according to the rules and limitations prescribed in the case of a bill.

Section 8

[General powers of Congress.⁴]
[Taxes, duties, imposts, and excises.—1.] The Congress shall have power to lay and collect taxes, duties, imposts and excises, to pay the debts and provide for the common defense and general welfare of the United States; but all duties, imposts and excises shall be uniform throughout the United States;

---

3. Amended by the 20th Amendment, Section 2. 4. By the 16th Amendment, Congress is given the power to lay and collect taxes on income.

[Borrowing of money.—2.] To borrow money on the credit of the United States;

[Regulation of commerce.—3.] To regulate commerce with foreign nations, and among the several States, and with the Indian tribes;

[Naturalization and bankruptcy.—4.] To establish a uniform rule of naturalization, and uniform laws on the subject of bankruptcies throughout the United States;

[Money, weights and measures.—5.] To coin money, regulate the value thereof, and of foreign coin, and fix the standard of weights and measures;

[Counterfeiting.—6.] To provide for the punishment of counterfeiting the securities and current coin of the United States;

[Post offices.—7.] To establish post offices and post roads;

[Patents and copyrights.—8.] To promote the progress of science and useful arts, by securing for limited times to authors and inventors the exclusive right to their respective writings and discoveries;

[Inferior courts.—9.] To constitute tribunals inferior to the Supreme Court;

[Piracies and felonies.—10.] To define and punish piracies and felonies committed on the high seas, and offences against the law of nations;

[War; marque and reprisal.—11.] To declare war, grant letters of marque and reprisal, and make rules concerning captures on land and water;

[Armies.—12.] To raise and support armies, but no appropriation of money to that use shall be for a longer term than two years;

[Navy.—13.] To provide and maintain a navy;

[Land and naval forces.—14.] To make rules for the government and regulation of the land and naval forces;

[Calling out militia.—15.] To provide for calling forth the militia to execute the laws of the Union, suppress insurrections, and repel invasions;

[Organizing, arming, and disciplining militia. —16.] To provide for organizing, arming, and disciplining, the militia, and for governing such part of them as may be employed in the service of the United States, reserving to the States, respectively, the appointment of the officers, and the authority of training the militia according to the discipline prescribed by Congress;

[Exclusive legislation over District of Columbia.—17.] To exercise exclusive legislation in all cases whatsoever, over such district (not exceeding ten miles square) as may, by cession of particular States, and the acceptance of Congress, become the seat of the Government of the United States, and to exercise like authority over all places purchased by the consent of the Legislature of the State in which the same shall be, for the erection of forts, magazines, arsenals, dock-yards, and other needful buildings;—And

[To enact laws necessary to enforce Constitution.—18.] To make all laws which shall be necessary and proper for carrying into execution the foregoing powers, and all other powers vested by this Constitution in the Government of the United States, or in any department or officer thereof.

Section 9

[Migration or importation of certain persons not to be prohibited before 1808.—1.] The migration or importation of such persons as any of the States now existing shall think proper to admit, shall not be prohibited by the Congress prior to the year one thousand eight hundred and eight, but a tax or duty may be imposed on such importation, not exceeding ten dollars for each person.

[Writ of habeas corpus not to be suspended; exception.—2.] The privilege of the writ of habeas corpus shall not be suspended, unless when in cases of rebellion or invasion the public safety may require it.

[Bills of attainder and ex post facto laws prohibited.—3.] No bill of attainder or ex post facto law shall be passed.

[Capitation and other direct taxes.—4.] No capitation, or other direct, tax shall be laid, unless in proportion to the census or enumeration herein before directed to be taken.[5]

[Exports not to be taxed.—5.] No tax or duty shall be laid on articles exported from any State.

[No preference to be given to ports of any States; interstate shipping.—6.] No preference shall be given by any regulation of commerce or revenue to the ports of one State over those of another: nor shall vessels bound to, or from, one State, be obliged to enter, clear, or pay duties in another.

[Money, how drawn from treasury; financial statements to be published.—7.] No money shall be drawn from the Treasury, but in consequence of appropriations made by law; and a regular statement and account of the receipts and expenditures of all public money shall be published from time to time.

[Titles of nobility not to be granted; acceptance by government officers of favors from foreign powers.—8.] No title of nobility shall be granted by the United States: and no person holding any office of profit or trust under them, shall, without the consent of the Congress, accept of any present, emolument, office, or title, of any kind whatever, from any king, prince, or foreign state.

Section 10

[Limitations of the powers of the several States.—1.] No State shall enter into any treaty, alliance, or confederation; grant letters of marque and reprisal; coin money; emit bills of credit; make any thing but gold and silver coin a tender in payment of debts; pass any bill of attainder, ex post facto law, or law impairing the obligation of contracts, or grant any title of nobility.

[State imposts and duties.—2.] No State shall, without the consent of the Congress, lay any imposts or duties on imports or exports, except what may be absolutely necessary for executing its inspection laws; and the net produce of all duties and imposts, laid by any State on imports or exports, shall be for the use of the Treasury of the United States; and all such laws shall be subject to the revision and control of the Congress.

[Further restrictions on powers of States.—3.] No State shall, without the consent of Congress, lay any duty of tonnage, keep troops, or ships of war in time of peace, enter into any agreement or compact

---

5. *See* the 16th Amendment.

with another state, or with a foreign power, or engage in war, unless actually invaded, or in such imminent danger as will not admit of delay.

Article II

Section 1

[The president; the executive power.—1.] The executive power shall be vested in a President of the United States of America. He shall hold his office during the term of four years, and, together with the Vice President, chosen for the same term, be elected, as follows

[Appointment and qualifications of presidential electors.—2.] Each State shall appoint, in such manner as the Legislature thereof may direct, a number of electors, equal to the whole number of Senators and Representatives to which the State may be entitled in the Congress: but no Senator or Representative, or person holding an office of trust or profit under the United States, shall be appointed an elector.

[Original method of electing the president and vice president.[6]] (The electors shall meet in their respective States, and vote by ballot for two persons, of whom at least one shall not be an inhabitant of the same State with themselves. And they shall make a list of all the persons voted for, and of the number of votes for each; which list they shall sign and certify, and transmit sealed to the seat of the Government of the United States, directed to the President of the Senate. The President of the Senate shall, in the presence of the Senate and House of Representatives, open all the certificates, and the votes shall then be counted. The person having the greatest number of votes shall be the President, if such number be a majority of the whole number of electors appointed; and if there be more than one who have such majority, and have an equal number of votes, then the House of Representatives shall immediately choose by ballot one of them for President; and if no person have a majority, then from the five highest on the list the said House shall in like manner choose the President. But in choosing the President, the votes shall be taken by States, the representation from each State having one vote; A quorum for this purpose shall consist of a member or members from two thirds of the States, and a majority of all the states shall be necessary to a choice. In every case, after the choice of the President, the person having the greatest number of votes of the electors shall be the Vice President. But if there should remain two or more who have equal votes, the Senate should choose from them by ballot the Vice President.)

[Congress may determine time of choosing electors and day for casting their votes.—3.] The Congress may determine the time of choosing the electors, and the day on which they shall give their votes; which day shall be the same throughout the United States.

[Qualifications for the office of president.[7]—4.] No person except a natural born citizen, or a citizen of the United States, at the time of the adoption of this Constitution, shall be eligible to the office of President; neither shall any person be eligible to that office who shall not have attained to the age of thirty-five years, and been fourteen years a resident within the United States.

[Filling vacancy in the office of president.[8]—5.] In case of the removal of the President from office, or of his death, resignation, or inability to discharge the powers and duties of the said office, the same shall devolve on the Vice President, and the Congress may by law provide for the case of removal, death, resignation or inability, both of the President and Vice President, declaring what officer shall then act as President, and such officer shall act accordingly, until the disability be removed, or a President shall be elected.

[Compensation of the president.—6.] The President shall, at stated times, receive for his services, a compensation, which shall neither be increased nor diminished during the period for which he shall have been elected, and he shall not receive within that period any other emolument from the United States, or any of them.

[Oath to be taken by the president.—7.] Before he enter on the execution of his office, he shall take the following oath or affirmation:—"I do solemnly swear (or affirm) that I will faithfully execute the office of President of the United States, and will to the best of my ability, preserve, protect, and defend the Constitution of the United States."

Section 2

[The president to be commander in chief of army and navy and head of executive departments; may grant reprieves and pardons.—1.] The President shall be Commander in Chief of the Army and Navy of the United States, and of the militia of the several States, when called into the actual service of the United States; he may require the opinion, in writing, of the principal officer in each of the executive departments, upon any subject relating to the duties of their respective offices, and he shall have power to grant reprieves and pardons for offences against the United States, except in cases of impeachment.

[President may, with concurrence of Senate, make treaties, appoint ambassadors, etc.; appointment of inferior officers, authority of Congress over.—2.] He shall have power, by and with the advice and consent of the Senate, to make treaties, provided two thirds of the Senators present concur; and he shall nominate, and by and with the advice and consent of the Senate, shall appoint ambassadors, other public ministers and consuls, judges of the Supreme Court, and all other officers of the United States, whose appointments are not herein otherwise provided for, and which shall be established by law: but the Congress may by law vest the appointment of such inferior officers, as they think proper, in the President alone, in the courts of law, or in the heads of departments.

[President may fill vacancies in office during recess of Senate.—3.] The President shall have power to fill up all vacancies that may happen during the recess of the Senate, by granting commissions which shall expire at the end of their session.

---

6. This clause has been superseded by the 12th Amendment. 7. For qualifications of the vice president, *see* the 12th Amendment. 8. Amended by the 20th Amendment, Sections 3 and 4.

Section 3

[**President to give advice to Congress; may convene or adjourn it on certain occasions; to receive ambassadors, etc.; have laws executed and commission all officers.**] He shall from time to time give to the Congress information of the state of the Union, and recommend to their consideration such measures as he shall judge necessary and expedient; he may, on extraordinary occasions, convene both Houses, or either of them, and in case of disagreement between them, with respect to the time of adjournment, he may adjourn them to such time as he shall think proper; he shall receive ambassadors and other public ministers: he shall take care that the laws be faithfully executed, and shall commission all the officers of the United States.

Section 4

[**All civil officers removable by impeachment.**] The President, Vice President, and all civil officers of the United States shall be removed from office on impeachment for, and conviction of, treason, bribery, or other high crimes and misdemeanors.

Article III

Section 1

[**Judicial powers; how vested; term of office and compensation of judges.**] The judicial Power of the United States, shall be vested in one Supreme Court, and in such inferior courts as the Congress may from time to time ordain and establish. The judges, both of the supreme and inferior courts, shall hold their offices during good behavior, and shall, at stated times, receive for their services, a compensation, which shall not be diminished during their continuance in office.

Section 2

[**Jurisdiction of federal courts[9]—1.**] The judicial power shall extend to all cases, in law and equity, arising under this Constitution, the laws of the United States, and treaties made, or which shall be made, under their authority; to all cases affecting ambassadors, other public ministers and consuls; to all cases of admiralty and maritime jurisdiction; to controversies to which the United States, shall be a party; to controversies between two or more States; between a State and citizens of another State; between citizens of different States; between citizens of the same State claiming lands under grants of different states, and between a State, or the citizens thereof, and foreign states, citizens, or subjects.

[**Original and appellate jurisdiction of Supreme Court.—2.**] In all cases affecting ambassadors, other public ministers and consuls, and those in which a State shall be party, the Supreme Court shall have original jurisdiction. In all the other cases before mentioned, the Supreme Court shall have appellate jurisdiction, both as to law and fact, with such exceptions, and under such regulations, as the Congress shall make.

[**Trial of all crimes, except impeachment, to be by jury.—3.**] The trial of all crimes, except in cases of impeachment, shall be by jury; and such trial shall be held in the State where the said crimes shall have been committed; but when not committed within any State, the trial shall be at such place or places as the Congress may by law have directed.

Section 3

[**Treason defined; conviction of.—1.**] Treason against the United States, shall consist only in levying war against them, or, in adhering to their enemies, giving them aid and comfort. No person shall be convicted of treason unless on the testimony of two witnesses to the same overt act, or on confession in open court.

[**Congress to declare punishment for treason; proviso.—2.**] The Congress shall have power to declare the punishment of treason, but no attainder of treason shall work corruption of blood, or forfeiture except during the life of the person attained.

Article IV

Section 1

[**Each state to give full faith and credit to the public acts and records of other states.**] Full faith and credit shall be given in each State to the public acts, records, and judicial proceedings of every other State. And the Congress may by general laws prescribe the manner in which such acts, records, and proceedings shall be proved, and the effect thereof.

Section 2

[**Privileges of citizens.—1.**] The citizens of each State shall be entitled to all privileges and immunities of citizens in the several States.

[**Extradition between the several states.—2.**] A person charged in any State with treason, felony, or other crime, who shall flee from justice, and be found in another State, shall on demand of the Executive authority of the State from which he fled, be delivered up, to be removed to the State having jurisdiction of the crime.

[**Persons held to labor or service in one state, fleeing to another, to be returned.—3.**] No person held to service or labor in one State, under the laws thereof, escaping into another, shall, in consequence of any law or regulation therein, be discharged from such service or labor, but shall be delivered up on claim of the party to whom such service or labor may be due.

Section 3

[**New states.—1.**] New States may be admitted by the Congress into this Union; but no new State shall be formed or erected within the jurisdiction of any other State; nor any State be formed by the junction of two or more States, or parts of States, without the consent of the Legislatures of the States concerned as well as of the Congress.

[**Regulations concerning territory.—2.**] The Congress shall have power to dispose of and make all needful rules and regulations respecting the territory or other property belonging to the United States; and nothing in this Constitution shall be so construed as to prejudice any claims of the United States, or of any particular State.

Section 4

[**Republican form of government and protection guaranteed the several states.**] The United States shall guarantee to every State in this Union a Republican form of government, and shall protect each of them against invasion; and on application of the Legislature, or of the Executive (when the Legislature cannot be convened) against domestic violence.

9. This section is abridged by the 11th Amendment.

Article V

[Ways in which the Constitution can be amended.] The Congress, whenever two thirds of both Houses shall deem it necessary, shall propose amendments to this Constitution, or, on the application of the Legislatures of two thirds of the several States shall call a convention for proposing amendments, which, in either case, shall be valid to all intents and purposes, as part of this Constitution, when ratified by the Legislatures of three fourths of the several States, or by conventions in three fourths thereof, as the one or the other mode of ratification may be proposed by the Congress; provided that no amendment which may be made prior to the year one thousand eight hundred and eight shall in any manner affect the first and fourth clauses in the ninth Section of the first Article; and that no State, without its consent, shall be deprived of its equal suffrage in the Senate.

Article VI

[Debts contracted under the confederation secured.—1.] All debts contracted and engagements entered into, before the adoption of this Constitution, shall be as valid against the United States under this Constitution, as under the Confederation.

[Constitution, laws, and treaties of the United States to be supreme.—2.] This Constitution, and the laws of the United States which shall be made in pursuance thereof; and all treaties made, or which shall be made, under the authority of the United States, shall be the supreme law of the land; and the judges in every State shall be bound thereby, any thing in the Constitution or laws of any State to the contrary notwithstanding.

[Who shall take constitutional oath; no religious test as to official qualification.—3.] The Senators and Representatives before mentioned, and the members of the several State Legislatures, and all executive and judicial officers, both of the United States and of the several States, shall be bound by oath or affirmation, to support this Constitution; but no religious test shall ever be required as a qualification to any office or public trust under the United States.

Article VII

[Constitution to be considered adopted when ratified by nine states.] The ratification of the conventions of nine States shall be sufficient for the establishment of this Constitution between the States so ratifying the same.

Done in convention by the unanimous consent of the States present the seventeenth day of September in the year of our Lord one thousand seven hundred and eighty seven and of the independence of the United States of America the Twelfth. In witness whereof we have hereunto subscribed our names.

George Washington
President and Deputy from Virginia

New Hampshire	David Brearley	John Dickinson	**South Carolina**
John Langdon	Jona. Dayton	Richard Bassett	J. Rutledge
Nicholas Gilman		Jaco. Broom	Charles Cotesworth
	Pennsylvania		Pinckney
Massachusetts	B. Franklin	**Maryland**	Charles Pinckney
Nathaniel Gorham	Thomas Mifflin	James McHenry	Pierce Butler
Rufus King	Robt. Morris	Dan. of St. Thos. Jenifer	
	Geo. Clymer	Danl. Carroll	**Georgia**
Connecticut	Thos. FitzSimons		William Few
Wm. Saml. Johnson	Jared Ingersoll	**Virginia**	Abr. Baldwin
Roger Sherman	James Wilson	John Blair	Attest: William Jackson,
	Gouv. Morris	James Madison, Jr.	Secretary
New York			
Alexander Hamilton	**Delaware**	**North Carolina**	
	Geo. Read	Wm. Blount	
New Jersey	Gunning Bedford Jun.	Richd Dobbs Spaight	
Wil. Livingston		Hu. Williamson	
Wm. Paterson			

Amendments to the Constitution of the United States

(Amendments I to X inclusive, popularly known as the Bill of Rights, were proposed and sent to the states by the first session of the First Congress. They were ratified Dec. 15, 1791.)

Amendment I

[Freedom of religion, speech, of the press, and right of petition.] Congress shall make no law respecting an establishment of religion, or prohibiting the free exercise thereof; or abridging the freedom of speech, or of the press; or the right of the people peaceably to assemble, and to petition the Government for a redress of grievances.

Amendment II

[Right of people to bear arms not to be infringed.] A well regulated militia, being necessary to the security of a free State, the right of the people to keep and bear arms, shall not be infringed.

Amendment III

[Quartering of troops.] No soldier shall, in time of peace be quartered in any house, without the consent of the owner, nor in time of war, but in a manner to be prescribed by law.

Amendment IV

[Persons and houses to be secure from unreasonable searches and seizures.] The right of the people to be secure in their persons, houses, papers, and effects, against unreasonable searches and seizures, shall not be violated, and no warrants shall issue, but upon probable cause, supported by oath or affirmation, and particularly describing the place to be searched, and the persons or things to be seized.

Amendment V

[Trials for crimes; just compensation for private property taken for public use.] No person shall be held to answer for a capital, or otherwise infamous crime, unless on a presentment or indictment of a Grand Jury, except in cases arising in the land or naval forces, or in the militia, when in actual service in time of war or public danger; nor shall any person be subject for the same offence to be twice put in jeopardy of life or limb; nor shall be compelled in any criminal case to be a witness, against himself, nor be deprived of life, liberty, or property, without due process of law; nor shall private property be taken for public use, without just compensation.

Amendment VI

[Civil rights in trials for crimes enumerated.] In all criminal prosecutions, the accused shall enjoy the right to a speedy and public trial, by an impartial jury of the State and district wherein the crime shall have been committed, which district shall have been previously ascertained by law, and to be informed of the nature and cause of the accusation; to be confronted with the witnesses against him; to have compulsory process for obtaining witnesses in his favor, and to have the assistance of counsel for his defense.

Amendment VII

[Civil rights in civil suits.] In suits at common law, where the value in controversy shall exceed twenty dollars, the right of trial by jury shall be preserved, and no fact tried by a jury, shall be otherwise re-examined in any court of the United States, than according to the rules of the common law.

Amendment VIII

[Excessive bail, fines, and punishments prohibited.] Excessive bail shall not be required, nor excessive fines imposed, nor cruel and unusual punishments inflicted.

Amendment IX

[Reserved rights of people.] The enumeration in the Constitution, of certain rights, shall not be construed to deny or disparage others retained by the people.

Amendment X

[Powers not delegated, reserved to states and people respectively.] The powers not delegated to the United States by the Constitution, nor prohibited by it to the States, are reserved to the States, respectively, or to the people.

Amendment XI

(The proposed amendment was sent to the states Mar. 5, 1794, by the Third Congress. It was ratified Feb. 7, 1795.)

[Judicial power of United States not to extend to suits against a state.] The judicial power of the United States shall not be construed to extend to any suit in law or equity, commenced or prosecuted against one of the United States by citizens of another State, or by citizens or subjects of any foreign state.

Amendment XII

(The proposed amendment was sent to the states Dec. 12, 1803, by the Eighth Congress. It was ratified July 27, 1804.)

[Present mode of electing president and vice president by electors.[1]]

The electors shall meet in their respective states, and vote by ballot for President and Vice President, one of whom, at least, shall not be an inhabitant of the same state with themselves; they shall name in their ballots the person voted for as President, and in distinct ballots the person voted for as Vice President, and they shall make distinct lists of all persons voted for as President, and of all persons voted for as Vice President, and of the number of votes for each, which lists they shall sign and certify, and transmit sealed to the seat of the government of the United States, directed to the President of the Senate; the President of the Senate shall, in the presence of the Senate and House of Representatives, open all the certificates and the votes shall then be counted; the person having the greatest number of votes for President, shall be the President, if such number be a majority of the whole number of electors appointed; and if no person have such majority, then from the persons having the highest numbers not exceeding three on the list of those voted for as President, the House of Representatives shall choose immediately, by ballot, the President. But in choosing the President, the votes shall be taken by states, the representation from each State having one vote; a quorum for this purpose shall consist of a member or members from two thirds of the states, and a majority of all the states shall be necessary to a choice. And if the House of Representatives shall not choose a President whenever the right of choice shall devolve upon them, before the fourth day of March next following, then the Vice President shall act as President, as in the case of the death or other constitutional disability of the President. The person having the greatest number of votes as Vice President, shall be the Vice President, if such number be a majority of the whole number of electors appointed, and if no person have a majority, then from the two highest numbers on the list, the Senate shall choose the Vice President; a quorum for the purpose shall consist of two thirds of the whole

---

1. Amended by the 20th Amendment, Sections 3 and 4.

number of Senators, and a majority of the whole number shall be necessary to a choice. But no person constitutionally ineligible to the office of President shall be eligible to that of Vice President of the United States.

Amendment XIII

(The proposed amendment was sent to the states Feb. 1, 1865, by the Thirty-eighth Congress. It was ratified Dec. 6, 1865.)

Section 1

[Slavery prohibited.] Neither slavery nor involuntary servitude, except as a punishment for crime whereof the party shall have been duly convicted, shall exist within the United States, or any place subject to their jurisdiction.

Section 2

[Congress given power to enforce this article.] Congress shall have power to enforce this article by appropriate legislation.

Amendment XIV

(The proposed amendment was sent to the states June 16, 1866, by the Thirty-ninth Congress. It was ratified July 9, 1868.)

Section 1

[Citizenship defined; privileges of citizens.] All persons born or naturalized in the United States, and subject to the jurisdiction thereof, are citizens of the United States and of the State wherein they reside. No State shall make or enforce any law which shall abridge the privileges or immunities of citizens of the United States; nor shall any State deprive any person of life, liberty, or property, without due process of law; nor deny to any person within its jurisdiction the equal protection of the laws.

Section 2

[Apportionment of Representatives.] Representatives shall be apportioned among the several States according to their respective numbers, counting the whole number of persons in each State, excluding Indians not taxed. But when the right to vote at any election for the choice of electors for President and Vice President of the United States, Representatives in Congress, the executive and judicial officers of a State, or the members of the Legislature thereof, is denied to any of the male inhabitants of such State, being twenty-one years of age, and citizens of the United States, or in any way abridged, except for participation in rebellion, or other crime, the basis of representation therein shall be reduced in the proportion which the number of such male citizens shall bear to the whole number of male citizens twenty-one years of age in such State.

Section 3

[Disqualification for office; removal of disability.] No person shall be a Senator or Representative in Congress, or elector of President and Vice President, or hold any office, civil or military, under the United States, or under any State, who, having previously taken an oath, as a member of Congress, or as an officer of the United States, or as a member of any State Legislature, or as an executive or judicial officer of any State, to support the Constitution of the United States, shall have engaged in insurrection or rebellion against the same, or given aid or comfort to the enemies thereof. But Congress may, by a vote of two thirds of each House, remove such disability.

Section 4

[Public debt not to be questioned; payment of debts and claims incurred in aid of rebellion forbidden.] The validity of the public debt of the United States, authorized by law, including debts incurred for payment of pensions and bounties for services in suppressing insurrection or rebellion, shall not be questioned. But neither the United States nor any State shall assume or pay any debt or obligation incurred in aid of insurrection or rebellion against the United States, or any claim for the loss or emancipation of any slave; but all such debts, obligations, and claims shall be held illegal and void.

Section 5

[Congress given power to enforce this article.] The Congress shall have power to enforce, by appropriate legislation, the provisions of this article.

Amendment XV

(The proposed amendment was sent to the states Feb. 27, 1869, by the Fortieth Congress. It was ratified Feb. 3, 1870.)

Section 1

[Right of certain citizens to vote established.] The right of citizens of the United States to vote shall not be denied or abridged by the United States or by any State on account of race, color, or previous condition of servitude.

Section 2

[Congress given power to enforce this article.] The Congress shall have power to enforce this article by appropriate legislation.

Amendment XVI

(The proposed amendment was sent to the states July 12, 1909, by the Sixty-first Congress. It was ratified Feb. 3, 1913.)

[Taxes on income; Congress given power to lay and collect.] The Congress shall have power to lay and collect taxes on incomes, from whatever source derived, without apportionment among the several States, and without regard to any census or enumeration.

Amendment XVII

(The proposed amendment was sent to the states May 16, 1912, by the Sixty-second Congress. It was ratified April 8, 1913.)

[Election of U.S. senators; filling of vacancies; qualifications of electors.] The Senate of the United States shall be composed of two Senators from each State, elected by the people thereof, for six years; and each Senator shall have one vote. The electors in each State shall have the qualifications requisite for electors of the most numerous branch of the State Legislatures.

When vacancies happen in the representation of any State in the Senate, the executive authority of such State shall issue writs of election to fill such vacancies: Provided, that the legislature of any State may empower the executive thereof to make temporary appointment until the people fill the vacancies by election as the legislature may direct.

This amendment shall not be so construed as to affect the election or term of any Senator chosen before it becomes valid as part of the Constitution.

Amendment XVIII[2]

(**The proposed amendment was sent to the states Dec. 18, 1917, by the Sixty-fifth Congress. It was ratified by three quarters of the states by Jan. 16, 1919, and became effective Jan. 16, 1920.**)

Section 1

[**Manufacture, sale, or transportation of intoxicating liquors, for beverage purposes, prohibited.**] After one year from the ratification of this article the manufacture, sale, or transportation of intoxicating liquors within, the importation thereof into, or the exportation thereof from the United States and all territory subject to the jurisdiction thereof for beverage purposes is hereby prohibited.

Section 2

[**Congress and the several states given concurrent power to pass appropriate legislation to enforce this article.**] The Congress and the several States shall have concurrent power to enforce this article by appropriate legislation.

Section 3

[**Provisions of article to become operative, when adopted by three fourths of the states.**] This article shall be inoperative unless it shall have been ratified as an amendment to the Constitution by the legislatures of the several States, as provided in the Constitution, within seven years from the date of the submission hereof to the States by Congress.

Amendment XIX

(**The proposed amendment was sent to the states June 4, 1919, by the Sixty-sixth Congress. It was ratified Aug. 18, 1920.**)

[**The right of citizens to vote shall not be denied because of sex.**] The right of citizens of the United States to vote shall not be denied or abridged by the United States or by any State on account of sex.

[**Congress given power to enforce this article.**] Congress shall have power to enforce this article by appropriate legislation.

Amendment XX

(**The proposed amendment, sometimes called the "Lame Duck Amendment," was sent to the states Mar. 3, 1932, by the Seventy-second Congress. It was ratified Jan. 23, 1933; but, in accordance with Section 5, Sections 1 and 2, did not go into effect until Oct. 15, 1933.**)

Section 1

[**Terms of president, vice president, senators, and representatives.**] The terms of the President and Vice President shall end at noon on the twentieth day of January, and the terms of Senators and Representatives at noon on the third day of January, of the years in which such terms would have ended if this article had not been ratified; and the terms of their successors shall then begin.

Section 2

[**Time of assembling Congress.**] The Congress shall assemble at least once in every year, and such meeting shall begin at noon on the third day of January, unless they shall by law appoint a different day.

Section 3

[**Filling vacancy in office of president.**] If, at the time fixed for the beginning of the term of the President, the President-elect shall have died, the Vice President-elect shall become President. If a President shall not have been chosen before the time fixed for the beginning of his term, or if the President-elect shall have failed to qualify, then the Vice President shall have qualified; and the Congress may by law provide for the case wherein neither a President-elect nor a Vice President-elect shall have qualified, declaring who shall then act as President, or the manner in which one who is to act shall be selected, and such person shall act accordingly until a President or Vice President shall have qualified.

Section 4

[**Power of Congress in presidential succession.**] The Congress may by law provide for the case of the death of any of the persons from whom the House of Representatives may choose a President whenever the right of choice shall have devolved upon them, and for the case of the death of any of the persons from whom the Senate may choose a Vice President whenever the right of choice shall have devolved upon them.

Section 5

[**Time of taking effect.**] Sections 1 and 2 shall take effect on the 15th day of October following the ratification of this article.

Section 6

[**Ratification.**] This article shall be inoperative unless it shall have been ratified as an amendment to the Constitution by the legislatures of three fourths of the several States within seven years from the date of its submission.

Amendment XXI

(**The proposed amendment was sent to the states Feb. 20, 1933, by the Seventy-second Congress. It was ratified Dec. 5, 1933.**)

Section 1

[**Repeal of Prohibition Amendment.**] The eighteenth article of amendment to the Constitution of the United States is hereby repealed.

Section 2

[**Transportation of intoxicating liquors.**] The transportation or importation into any State, territory, or possession of the United States for delivery or use therein of intoxicating liquors, in violation of the laws thereof, is hereby prohibited.

Section 3

[**Ratification.**] This article shall be inoperative unless it shall have been ratified as an amendment to the Constitution by convention in the several States, as provided in the Constitution, within seven years from the date of the submission thereof to the States by the Congress.

Amendment XXII

(**The proposed amendment was sent to the states Mar. 21, 1947, by the Eightieth Congress. It was ratified Feb. 27, 1951.**)

---

2. Repealed by the 21st Amendment.

Section 1

[Limit to number of terms a president may serve.] No person shall be elected to the office of the President more than twice, and no person who has held the office of President, or acted as President, for more than two years of a term to which some other person was elected President shall be elected to the office of the President more than once. But this article shall not apply to any person holding the office of President when this article was proposed by the Congress, and shall not prevent any person who may be holding the office of President, or acting as President, during the term within which this article becomes operative from holding the office of President or acting as President during the remainder of such term.

Section 2

[Ratification.] This article shall be inoperative unless it shall have been ratified as an amendment to the Constitution by the legislatures of three fourths of the several States within seven years from the date of its submission to the States by the Congress.

Amendment XXIII

(The proposed amendment was sent to the states June 16, 1960, by the Eighty-sixth Congress. It was ratified March 29, 1961.)

Section 1

[Electors for the District of Columbia.] The District constituting the seat of Government of the United States shall appoint in such manner as the Congress may direct: A number of electors of President and Vice President equal to the whole number of Senators and Representatives in Congress to which the District would be entitled if it were a State, but in no event more than the least populous State; they shall be in addition to those appointed by the States, but they shall be considered, for the purposes of the election of President and Vice President, to be electors appointed by a State; and they shall meet in the District and perform such duties as provided by the twelfth article of amendment.

Section 2

[Congress given power to enforce this article.] The Congress shall have the power to enforce this article by appropriate legislation.

Amendment XXIV

(The proposed amendment was sent to the states Aug. 27, 1962, by the Eighty-seventh Congress. It was ratified Jan. 23, 1964.)

Section 1

[Payment of poll tax or other taxes not to be prerequisite for voting in federal elections.] The right of citizens of the United States to vote in any primary or other election for President or Vice President, for electors for President or Vice President, or for Senator or Representative in Congress, shall not be denied or abridged by the United States or any State by reasons of failure to pay any poll tax or other tax.

Section 2

[Congress given power to enforce this article.] The Congress shall have the power to enforce this article by appropriate legislation.

Amendment XXV

(The proposed amendment was sent to the states July 6, 1965, by the Eighty-ninth Congress. It was ratified Feb. 10, 1967.)

Section 1

[Succession of vice president to presidency.] In case of the removal of the President from office or of his death or resignation, the Vice President shall become President.

Section 2

[Vacancy in office of vice president.] Whenever there is a vacancy in the office of the Vice President, the President shall nominate a Vice President who shall take office upon confirmation by a majority vote of both Houses of Congress.

Section 3

[Vice president as acting president.] Whenever the President transmits to the President pro tempore of the Senate and the Speaker of the House of Representatives his written declaration that he is unable to discharge the powers and duties of his office, and until he transmits to them a written declaration to the contrary, such powers and duties shall be discharged by the Vice President as Acting President.

Section 4

[Vice president as acting president.] Whenever the Vice President and a majority of either the principal officers of the executive departments or of such other body as Congress may by law provide, transmit to the President pro tempore of the Senate and the Speaker of the House of Representatives their written declaration that the President is unable to discharge the powers and duties of his office, the Vice President shall immediately assume the powers and duties of the office as Acting President.

Thereafter, when the President transmits to the President pro tempore of the Senate and the Speaker of the House of Representatives his written declaration that no inability exists, he shall resume the powers and duties of his office unless the Vice President and a majority of either the principal officers of the executive department or of such other body as Congress may by law provide, transmit within four days to the President pro tempore of the Senate and the Speaker of the House of Representatives their written declaration that the President is unable to discharge the powers and duties of his office. Thereupon Congress shall decide the issue, assembling within forty-eight hours for that purpose if not in session. If the Congress, within twenty-one days after receipt of the latter written declaration, or, if Congress is not in session, within twenty-one days after Congress is required to assemble, determines by two thirds vote of both Houses that the President is unable to discharge the powers and duties of his office, the Vice President shall continue to discharge the same as Acting President; otherwise, the President shall resume the powers and duties of his office.

Amendment XXVI

(The proposed amendment was sent to the states Mar. 23, 1971, by the Ninety-second Congress. It was ratified July 1, 1971.)

Section 1

[Voting for 18-year-olds.] The right of citizens of the United States, who are 18 years of age or older, to vote shall not be denied or abridged by the United States or by any state on account of age.

Section 2
[Congress given power to enforce this article.] The Congress shall have power to enforce this article by appropriate legislation.

Amendment XXVII
(Ratified May 7, 1992.)
[Congressional raises.] No law, varying the compensation for the services of the Senators and Representatives, shall take effect, until an election of Representatives shall have intervened.

Lincoln's Gettysburg Address

The Battle of Gettysburg, one of the most noted battles of the Civil War, was fought on July 1–3, 1863. On Nov. 19, 1863, the field was dedicated as a national cemetery by President Lincoln in a two-minute speech that was to become immortal. At the time of its delivery the speech was relegated to the inside pages of the papers, while a two-hour address by Edward Everett, the leading orator of the time, caught the headlines.

The following is the text of the address revised by President Lincoln from his own notes:

> Fourscore and seven years ago our fathers brought forth on this continent a new nation conceived in liberty and dedicated to the proposition that all men are created equal. Now we are engaged in a great civil war testing whether that nation, or any nation so conceived and so dedicated, can long endure. We are met on a great battlefield of that war. We have come to dedicate a portion of that field as a final resting-place for those who here gave their lives that that nation might live. It is altogether fitting and proper that we should do this. But, in a larger sense, we cannot dedicate, we cannot consecrate, we cannot hallow this ground. The brave men, living and dead, who struggled here have consecrated it far above our poor power to add or detract. The world will little note nor long remember what we say here, but it can never forget what they did here. It is for us the living rather to be dedicated here to the unfinished work which they who fought here have thus far so nobly advanced. It is rather for us to be here dedicated to the great task remaining before us—that from these honored dead we take increased devotion to that cause for which they gave the last full measure of devotion—that we here highly resolve that these dead shall not have died in vain, that this nation under God shall have a new birth of freedom, and that government of the people, by the people, for the people shall not perish from the earth.

"In God We Trust"

"In God We Trust" first appeared on U.S. coins after April 22, 1864, when Congress passed an act authorizing the coinage of a 2-cent piece bearing this motto. Thereafter, Congress extended its use to other coins. On July 30, 1956, it became the national motto.

Arlington National Cemetery

Arlington National Cemetery occupies 612 acres in Virginia on the Potomac River, directly opposite Washington. This land was part of the estate of John Parke Custis, Martha Washington's son. His son, George Washington Parke Custis, built the mansion which later became the home of Robert E. Lee. In 1864, Arlington became a military cemetery. More than 240,000 service members and their dependents are buried there. Expansion of the cemetery began in 1966, using a 180-acre tract of land directly east of the present site.

Among the many famous and distinguished people buried in the cemetery are presidents William Howard Taft and John F. Kennedy; a number of supreme court justices, including Chief Justice Earl Warren, Oliver Wendell Holmes, Jr., and Thurgood Marshall; explorers Robert Peary and Matthew Henson; civil rights leader Medgar Evers; band leader Glenn Miller; and mystery writer Dashiell Hammett. There are also 3,800 Civil War "contrabands" (fugitive and liberated slaves) buried there, their headstones engraved only with "Civilian" or "Citizen."

In 1921, an Unknown American Soldier of World War I was buried in the cemetery; the monument at the Tomb of the Unknown Soldier was opened to the public without ceremony in 1932. Two additional Unknowns, one from World War II and one from the Korean War, were buried May 30, 1958.

The Unknown Serviceman of Vietnam was buried on May 28, 1984. In June 1998 his body was disinterred and recent DNA-testing technology was used to identify him as First Lt. Michael Blassie, an Air Force pilot from St. Louis. It is possible that technology will prevent there from ever being another "unknown" buried in the tomb.

The inscription carved on the Tomb of the Unknowns reads:

> HERE RESTS IN
> HONORED GLORY
> AN AMERICAN
> SOLDIER
> KNOWN BUT TO GOD

Profile of the United States

This profile was created by the editors of the almanac from many data sources. Most figures are approximate. For additional details about the U.S., please refer to the appropriate sections of the almanac.

Geography

Number of states: 50
Area (1990): total: 3,717,796 sq mi (9,629,091 sq km), land only: 3,536,278 sq mi (9,158,960 sq km), water: 181,518 sq mi (470,131 sq km). Share of world land area (1990): 6.2%
Population density (2000): 79.6 people per sq mi
Northernmost point: Point Barrow, Alaska
Easternmost point: West Quoddy Head, Maine
Southernmost point: Ka Lae (South Cape), Hawaii
Westernmost point: Cape Wrangell, Alaska[1]
Geographic center (50 states): in Butte County, S.D. (44' 58' N. lat., 103° 46' W. long.)
Highest point: Mt. McKinley, Alaska (20,320 ft)
Lowest point: Death Valley, Calif. (282 ft below sea level)
1. The extreme points are measured from the geographic center of the United States (incl. Alaska and Hawaii), west of Castle Rock, S.D., 44° 58' N. lat., 103° 46' W. long. If measured from the prime meridian in Greenwich, England, Cape Wrangell, Alaska, would be the easternmost point.

Population

(Based on Census 2000 data unless otherwise noted.)

Total Resident Pop.[1]: 281,421,906
Mean center of population: 3 mi east of Edgar Springs in Phelps County, Mo.
Males: 138,053,563 (49.1% of pop.)
Females: 143,368,343 (50.9% of pop.)
White: 211,460,626 (75.1% of pop.)
Black: 34,658,190 (12.3% of pop.)
Asian: 10,242,998 (3.6% of pop.)
American Indian and Alaska Native: 2,475,956 (0.9% of pop.)
Hispanic/Latino[2]: 35,305,818 (12.5% of pop.)
Native Hawaiian and Other Pacific Islander: 398,835 (0.1% of pop.)
Median age: 35.3
Metropolitan population: 225,981,679
Nonmetropolitan population: 55,440,227
Families: 71,787,347
Average family size: 3.14
Homeownership (2000): 67.4% of pop.
Married couples (1999): 55,849,000
Unmarried couples (1999): 4,486,000
Never married (1999): 47,600,000
Divorced (1999): 19,700,000
Widowed (1999): 13,500,000
Single parents (1999): female, 12,789,000; male, 3,976,000
1. Excludes the U.S. Armed Forces overseas. 2. People of Hispanic or Latino origin may be of any race.

Vital Statistics

Births (1999): 3,959,417 (14.5 per 1,000 pop.)
Deaths (1999): 2,391,630 (8.7 per 1,000 pop.)
Marriages (1999): 2,358,000 (8.6 per 1,000 pop.)
Divorces (1997): 1,163,000 (4.3 per 1,000 pop.)
Infant mortality rate (1998): 7.2 per 1,000 live births
Legal abortions (1997): 1,186,039
Life expectancy (1999)[1]: Total U.S., both sexes, 76.7; total men, 73.9; total women, 79.4; white men, 74.6; white women, 79.9; black men, 67.8; black women, 74.7
1. Preliminary.

Civilian Labor Force

All (2000): 140,863,000 (4.0% unemployed)
Males (2000): 75,247,000 (3.9% unemployed)
Females (2000): 65,616,000 (4.1% unemployed)
Work at home (1997 est.): 21.5 million
Farms (2000): 2,172,080; total acres (2000): 942,990,000
Avg. hourly earnings of workers (2000): $13.75
Avg. weekly hours of workers (2000): 34.5

Income and Credit

Gross Domestic Product (2000): $9,872.90 billion[1]
Federal budget (2000): total receipts, $2,025,218 million; total outlays, $1,788,826 million; (est. 2001): total receipts, $2,136,946 million; total outlays, $1,856,238 million
Personal income per capita (2000): $30,205
Median four-person family income (1999): $59,981
Families with stockholdings (1998): 48.8%
Number below poverty level (1999): total, 32,258,000; white, 21,922,000; black, 8,360,000; Hispanic, 7,439,000
1. Preliminary.

Education

Elementary school pupils, grades K–8 (2002)[1]: 38,157,000
Secondary school pupils, grades 9–12 (2002)[1]: 15,130,000
High school dropout rate, ages 16–24 (1999): 11.2%
College and university enrollment (2002)[1]: 15,500,000
Total expenditures for public elementary and secondary education (1997–1998): $334,321,587,000
Public school teachers (1999)[1]: 2,887,000; elementary, 1,733,000; secondary, 1,154,000
Private school teachers (1999)[1]: 397,000; elementary, 281,000; secondary, 116,000
Average salary for public school teachers (1998–1999 est.): $40,582
1. Projected.

Conveniences

Radio stations (Sept. 1999): AM, 4,783; FM, 5,766
Television stations (Sept. 1999): 1,616
Registered automobiles (1998): 131,800,000
Daily newspaper circulation (1998): 55,900,000
Cable TV households (1998): 66,000,000
Total TV households (1998): 98,000,000
Avg. number TV sets per household (1998): 2.4
Percent TV households with VCRs (1998): 84.6%
Percent households with Internet access (1998): 26.2

Crime

Total arrests (1999): 9,141,201
State and federal prison inmates (2000): 1,381,892
Prisoners under sentence of death (1998): 3,452
Persons executed under civil authority (1999): 98
Law enforcement officers killed (1998): 142
Total murder victims (1999): 12,658
Violent crimes per 1,000 people (2000): 27.4
Property crimes per 1,000 people (2000): 178.1
Homicides per 100,000 people (1999): 5.7
Hate crime victims (1999): 7,271

First Results of Census 2000 Released

On Dec. 28, 2000, the U.S. Census Bureau released the first data from Census 2000, the country's 22nd decennial census. The new figures show that the nation's resident population on Census Day, April 1, 2000, was 281,421,906, a 13.2% increase over the 1990 count of 248,709,873. The resident population includes both citizens and noncitizens living in the 50 states and the District of Columbia.

West and South Grew Fastest

According to the new census figures, all the states increased their populations, but the most dramatic gains were seen in the southeast and western parts of the country. Nevada had the largest population gain, up 66.3% from 1990.

California remains the most populous state with 33.8 million people, up 13.8% from 1990. Texas, however, surpassed New York to become the second most populous state, with a population increase of 22.8% for a total of 20.8 million people.

Other states with population gains of more than 20% were Arizona, Colorado, Utah, Idaho, Georgia, Florida, North Carolina, Washington, Oregon, and New Mexico.

Other Highlights

Census briefs released during the early part of 2001 highlighted a number of significant findings.

- The overall population growth of 32.7 million people between 1990 and 2000 was the largest census-to-census increase in American history.
- Nearly 7 million people, or 2.4% of the population, identified themselves as belonging to more than one racial group, a category that appeared for the first time on the 2000 Census questionnaire.
- The Hispanic population grew by more than 60%, up from 22.4 million in 1990 to 35.3 million in 2000. The number of Hispanics is now roughly equal to the number of blacks, with each group making up approximately 12% of the population.
- The median age of the U.S. population in 2000 was 35.3 years, the highest it has ever been. The increase reflects the aging of the baby boomers.

A Good Census

Employing nearly 1 million temporary workers and costing more than $6 billion, Census 2000 was the largest peacetime mobilization of resources and personnel—and it looks like the effort paid off. Kenneth Prewitt, the former director of the Census Bureau, has called Census 2000 the most accurate headcount in the nation's history. And the final national response rate of 67% marked not only an improvement on the response rate of 65% in 1990, but also a reversal of a 30-year decline in public cooperation with the census. Officials had predicted only a 61% response rate when the 2000 count began.

Prewitt credited the census's success to the bureau's extensive outreach campaign, which included its first-ever paid advertising, for getting the message out that the count was important. Also, in an effort to reach everyone, Census 2000 used forms printed in English, Spanish, Korean, Chinese, Vietnamese, and Tagalog (spoken in the Philippines).

Officials Oppose Adjustment

Despite the overall accuracy of the count, it is estimated that Census 2000 missed a total of 3.3 million people, including a disproportionate number of minorities. Nevertheless, census officials have argued against using adjusted figures, saying they could not guarantee that those numbers would be more accurate than the original results. The use of adjusted census data is an issue that has been hotly debated by Republicans and Democrats in Congress, as census numbers are used to redraw voting districts among other things.

The Census Bureau will continue to release Census 2000 data through 2003.

Colonial Population Estimates

(in round numbers)

Year	Population	Year	Population
1610	350	1700	250,900
1620	2,300	1710	331,700
1630	4,600	1720	466,200
1640	26,600	1730	629,400
1650	50,400	1740	905,600
1660	75,100	1750	1,170,800
1670	111,900	1760	1,593,600
1680	151,500	1770	2,148,100
1690	210,400	1780	2,780,400

Covers years before the establishment of the U.S. Census in 1790.

National Censuses[1]

Year	Resident population[2]	Land area, sq mi	Pop. per sq mi	Year	Resident population[2]	Land area, sq mi	Pop. per sq mi
1790	3,929,214	864,746	4.5	1900	75,994,575	2,969,834	25.6
1800	5,308,483	864,746	6.1	1910	91,972,266	2,969,565	31.0
1810	7,239,881	1,681,828	4.3	1920	105,710,620	2,969,451	35.6
1820	9,638,453	1,749,462	5.5	1930	122,775,046	2,977,128	41.2
1830	12,866,020	1,749,462	7.4	1940	131,669,275	2,977,128	44.2
1840	17,069,453	1,749,462	9.8	1950	150,697,361	2,974,726	50.7
1850	23,191,876	2,940,042	7.9	1960	179,323,175	3,540,911	50.6
1860	31,443,321	2,969,640	10.6	1970	203,302,031	3,540,023	57.4
1870	39,818,449	2,969,640	13.4	1980	226,545,805	3,539,289	64.0
1880	50,155,783	2,969,640	16.9	1990	248,709,873	3,536,278	70.3
1890	62,947,714	2,969,640	21.2	2000	281,421,906	3,537,441	79.6

1. Beginning with 1960, figures include Alaska and Hawaii. 2. Excludes armed forces overseas. *Source:* U.S. Bureau of the Census; Web: www.census.gov.

Profile of General Demographic Characteristics, 2000

Subject	Number	Percent
Total population	**281,421,906**	**100.0%**
Sex and age		
Male	138,053,563	49.1
Female	143,368,343	50.9
Under 5 years	19,175,798	6.8
5 to 9 years	20,549,505	7.3
10 to 14 years	20,528,072	7.3
15 to 19 years	20,219,890	7.2
20 to 24 years	18,964,001	6.7
25 to 34 years	39,891,724	14.2
35 to 44 years	45,148,527	16.0
45 to 54 years	37,677,952	13.4
55 to 59 years	13,469,237	4.8
60 to 64 years	10,805,447	3.8
65 to 74 years	18,390,986	6.5
75 to 84 years	12,361,180	4.4
85 years and over	4,239,587	1.5
Median age (years)	35.3	n.a.
18 years and over	209,128,094	74.3
Male	100,994,367	35.9
Female	108,133,727	38.4
21 years and over	196,899,193	70.0
62 years and over	41,256,029	14.7
65 years and over	34,991,753	12.4
Male	14,409,625	5.1
Female	20,582,128	7.3
Race		
One race	274,595,678	97.6
White	211,460,626	75.1
Black or African American	34,658,190	12.3
American Indian and Alaska Native	2,475,956	0.9
Asian	10,242,998	3.6
Asian Indian	1,678,765	0.6
Chinese	2,432,585	0.9
Filipino	1,850,314	0.7
Japanese	796,700	0.3
Korean	1,076,872	0.4
Vietnamese	1,122,528	0.4
Other Asian[1]	1,285,234	0.5
Native Hawaiian and Other Pacific Islander	398,835	0.1
Native Hawaiian	140,652	—
Guamanian or Chamorro	58,240	—
Samoan	91,029	—
Other Pacific Islander[2]	108,914	—
Some other race	15,359,073	5.5
Two or more races	6,826,228	2.4
Race alone or in combination with one or more other races:[3]		
White	216,930,975	77.1
Black or African American	36,419,434	12.9
American Indian and Alaska Native	4,119,301	1.5
Asian	11,898,828	4.2
Native Hawaiian and Other Pacific Islander	874,414	0.3
Some other race	18,521,486	6.6

Subject	Number	Percent
Hispanic or Latino and race		
Total population	**281,421,906**	**100.0%**
Hispanic or Latino (of any race)	35,305,818	12.5
Mexican	20,640,711	7.3
Puerto Rican	3,406,178	1.2
Cuban	1,241,685	0.4
Other Hispanic or Latino	10,017,244	3.6
Not Hispanic or Latino	246,116,088	87.5
White alone	194,552,774	69.1
Relationship		
Total population	**281,421,906**	**100.0%**
In households	273,643,273	97.2
Householder	105,480,101	37.5
Spouse	54,493,232	19.4
Child	83,393,392	29.6
Own child under 18	64,494,637	22.9
Other relatives	15,684,318	5.6
Under 18	6,042,435	2.1
Nonrelatives	14,592,230	5.2
Unmarried partner	5,475,768	1.9
In group quarters	7,778,633	2.8
Institutionalized pop.	4,059,039	1.4
Noninstitutionalized pop.	3,719,594	1.3
Household by type		
Total households	**105,480,101**	**100.0**
Family households (families)	71,787,347	68.1
With own children under 18	34,588,368	32.8
Married-couple family	54,493,232	51.7
With own children under 18	24,835,505	23.5
Female householder, no husband present	12,900,103	12.2
With own children under 18	7,561,874	7.2
Nonfamily households	33,692,754	31.9
Householder living alone	27,230,075	25.8
Householder 65 and over	9,722,857	9.2
Households with individuals under 18	38,022,115	36.0
Households with individuals 65 and over	24,672,708	23.4
Average household size	2.59	n.a.
Average family size	3.14	n.a.
Housing occupancy		
Total housing units	**115,904,641**	**100.0**
Occupied housing units	105,480,101	91.0
Vacant housing units	10,424,540	9.0
For seasonal, recreational, or occasional use	3,578,718	3.1
Homeowner vacancy rate (%)	1.7	n.a.
Rental vacancy rate (%)	6.8	n.a.
Housing tenure		
Occupied housing units	**105,480,101**	**100.0**
Owner-occupied housing units	69,815,753	66.2
Renter-occupied housing units	35,664,348	33.8
Average household size of owner-occupied units	2.69	n.a.
Average household size of renter-occupied units	2.40	n.a.

NOTES: (—) represents zero or rounds to zero; n.a. = not applicable. 1. Other Asian alone, or two or more Asian categories. 2. Other Pacific Islander alone, or two or more Native Hawaiian and Other Pacific Islander categories. 3. In combination with one or more of the other races listed. The six numbers may add to more than the total population and the six percentages may add to more than 100% because individuals may report more than one race. Source: U.S. Census Bureau, Census 2000. Web: www.census.gov.

Population by State

State	2000	Percent change, 1990–2000	Pop. per sq mi, 2000	Pop. rank, 2000	1990	1950	1900	1790
Alabama	4,447,100	10.1%	87.6	23	4,040,587	3,061,743	1,828,697	—
Alaska	626,932	14.0	1.1	48	550,043	128,643	63,592	—
Arizona	5,130,632	40.0	45.2	20	3,665,228	749,587	122,931	—
Arkansas	2,673,400	13.7	51.3	33	2,350,725	1,909,511	1,311,564	—
California	33,871,648	13.8	217.2	1	29,760,021	10,586,223	1,485,053	—
Colorado	4,301,261	30.6	41.5	24	3,294,394	1,325,089	539,700	—
Connecticut	3,405,565	3.6	702.9	29	3,287,116	2,007,280	908,420	237,946
Delaware	783,600	17.6	401.0	45	666,168	318,085	184,735	59,096
DC	572,059	-5.7	9,378.0	—	606,900	802,178	278,718	—
Florida	15,982,378	23.5	296.4	4	12,937,926	2,771,305	528,542	—
Georgia	8,186,453	26.4	141.4	10	6,478,216	3,444,578	2,216,331	82,548
Hawaii	1,211,537	9.3	188.6	42	1,108,229	499,794	154,001	—
Idaho	1,293,953	28.5	15.6	39	1,006,749	588,637	161,772	—
Illinois	12,419,293	8.6	223.4	5	11,430,602	8,712,176	4,821,550	—
Indiana	6,080,485	9.7	169.5	14	5,544,159	3,934,224	2,516,462	—
Iowa	2,926,324	5.4	52.4	30	2,776,755	2,621,073	2,231,853	—
Kansas	2,688,418	8.5	32.9	32	2,477,574	1,905,299	1,470,495	—
Kentucky	4,041,769	9.7	101.7	25	3,685,296	2,944,806	2,147,174	73,677
Louisiana	4,468,976	5.9	102.6	22	4,219,973	2,683,516	1,381,625	—
Maine	1,274,923	3.8	41.3	40	1,227,928	913,774	694,466	96,540
Maryland	5,296,486	10.8	541.9	19	4,781,468	2,343,001	1,188,044	319,728
Massachusetts	6,349,097	5.5	809.8	13	6,016,425	4,690,514	2,805,346	378,787
Michigan	9,938,444	6.9	175.0	8	9,295,297	6,371,766	2,420,982	—
Minnesota	4,919,479	12.4	61.8	21	4,375,099	2,982,483	1,751,394	—
Mississippi	2,844,658	10.5	60.6	31	2,573,216	2,178,914	1,551,270	—
Missouri	5,595,211	9.3	81.2	17	5,117,073	3,954,653	3,106,665	—
Montana	902,195	12.9	6.2	44	799,065	591,024	243,329	—
Nebraska	1,711,263	8.4	22.3	38	1,578,385	1,325,510	1,066,300	—
Nevada	1,998,257	66.3	18.2	35	1,201,833	160,083	42,335	—
New Hampshire	1,235,786	11.4	137.8	41	1,109,252	533,242	411,588	141,885
New Jersey	8,414,350	8.9	1,134.5	9	7,730,188	4,835,329	1,883,669	184,139
New Mexico	1,819,046	20.1	15.0	36	1,515,069	681,187	195,310	—
New York	18,976,457	5.5	401.9	3	17,990,455	14,830,192	7,268,894	340,120
North Carolina	8,049,313	21.4	165.2	11	6,628,637	4,061,929	1,893,810	393,751
North Dakota	642,200	0.5	9.3	47	638,800	619,636	319,146	—
Ohio	11,353,140	4.7	277.3	7	10,847,115	7,946,627	4,157,545	—
Oklahoma	3,450,654	9.7	50.3	27	3,145,585	2,233,351	790,391[1]	—
Oregon	3,421,399	20.4	35.6	28	2,842,321	1,521,341	413,536	—
Pennsylvania	12,281,054	3.4	274.0	6	11,881,643	10,498,012	6,302,115	434,373
Rhode Island	1,048,319	4.5	1,003.2	43	1,003,464	791,896	428,556	68,825
South Carolina	4,012,012	15.1	133.2	26	3,486,703	2,117,027	1,340,316	249,073
South Dakota	754,844	8.5	9.9	46	696,004	652,740	401,570	—
Tennessee	5,689,283	16.7	138.0	16	4,877,185	3,291,718	2,020,616	35,691
Texas	20,851,820	22.8	79.6	2	16,986,510	7,711,194	3,048,710	—
Utah	2,233,169	29.6	27.2	34	1,722,850	688,862	276,749	—
Vermont	608,827	8.2	65.8	49	562,758	377,747	343,641	85,425
Virginia	7,078,515	14.4	178.8	12	6,187,358	3,318,680	1,854,184	747,610[2]
Washington	5,894,121	21.1	88.6	15	4,866,692	2,378,963	518,103	—
West Virginia	1,808,344	0.8	75.1	37	1,793,477	2,005,552	958,800	—
Wisconsin	5,363,675	9.6	98.8	18	4,891,769	3,434,575	2,069,042	—
Wyoming	493,782	8.9	5.1	50	453,588	290,529	92,531	—
Total U.S.	**281,421,906**	**13.2**	—	—	**248,709,873**	**151,325,798**	**76,212,168**	**3,929,214**

1. Includes population of Indian Territory, 1900: 392,960. 2. Until 1863, Virginia included what is now West Virginia. *Source:* U.S. Bureau of the Census; Web: www.census.gov.

Total U.S. Population

Area	2000	1990	1980	Area	2000	1990	1980
50 states[1]	281,421,906	248,709,873	226,545,805	N. Mariana Is.[3]	69,221	43,345	([4])
48 coterminous[1]	279,583,437	247,051,601	225,179,263	Puerto Rico	3,808,610	3,522,037	3,196,520
Alaska	626,932	550,043	401,851	Trust Ter. of Pac. Is.	([7])	15,122[6]	132,929[5]
Hawaii	1,211,537	1,108,229	964,691	Virgin Is. of U.S.	108,612	101,809	96,569
American Samoa	57,291	46,773	32,297	Wake Island	([2])	([2])	302
Guam	154,805	133,152	105,979	Population abroad	576,367[8]	922,819	995,546
Johnston Atoll	([2])	([2])	327	Armed forces	n.a.	910,611	515,408
Midway	([2])	([2])	453	**Total**	**286,196,812**	**253,451,585**	**231,106,727**

NOTE: n.a. = not available. 1. Includes the District of Columbia. 2. No indigenous population. 3. The Commonwealth of the Northern Mariana Islands (CNMI) became part of the United States in 1986. 4. Included under trust territory of the Pacific Islands. 5. Includes Northern Mariana Islands. 6. Palau only trust territory remaining. 7. Palau, the last remaining trust territory, became an independent country in 1994. 8. Includes overseas U.S. military and federal civilian employees and their dependents living with them. *Source:* U.S. Bureau of the Census; Web: www.census.gov.

U.S. Population by Region, 1990–2000

	Population		Change, 1990–2000	
Area	April 1, 1990	April 1, 2000	Number	Percent
United States	**248,709,873**	**281,421,906**	**32,712,033**	**13.2%**
Region[1]				
Northeast	50,809,229	53,594,378	2,785,149	5.5
Midwest	59,668,632	64,392,776	4,724,144	7.9
South	85,445,930	100,236,820	14,790,890	17.3
West	52,786,082	63,197,932	10,411,850	19.7

1. The Northeast region includes Connecticut, Maine, Massachusetts, New Hampshire, New Jersey, New York, Pennsylvania, Rhode Island, and Vermont. The Midwest includes Illinois, Indiana, Iowa, Kansas, Michigan, Minnesota, Missouri, Nebraska, North Dakota, Ohio, South Dakota, and Wisconsin. The South includes Alabama, Arkansas, Delaware, the District of Columbia, Florida, Georgia, Kentucky, Louisiana, Maryland, Mississippi, North Carolina, Oklahoma, South Carolina, Tennessee, Texas, Virginia, and West Virginia. The West includes Alaska, Arizona, California, Colorado, Hawaii, Idaho, Montana, Nevada, New Mexico, Oregon, Utah, Washington, and Wyoming. *Source:* U.S. Census Bureau, Census 2000; 1990 Census. Web: www.census.gov.

Resident Population—Selected Characteristics, 1790–2000

(in thousands)

						Other		
Date	Male	Female	White	Black	Total other	American Indian, Eskimo, Aleut	Asian and Pacific Islanders	Hispanic origin[1]
1790 (Aug. 2)[2]	n.a.	n.a.	3,172	757	n.a.	n.a.	n.a.	n.a.
1800 (Aug. 4)[2]	n.a.	n.a.	4,306	1,002	n.a.	n.a.	n.a.	n.a.
1850 (June 1)[2]	11,838	11,354	19,553	3,639	n.a.	n.a.	n.a.	n.a.
1900 (June 1)[2]	38,816	37,178	66,809	8,834	351	n.a.	n.a.	n.a.
1910 (Apr. 15)[2]	47,332	44,640	81,732	9,828	413	n.a.	n.a.	n.a.
1920 (Jan. 1)[2]	53,900	51,810	94,821	10,463	427	n.a.	n.a.	n.a.
1930 (Apr. 1)[2]	62,137	60,638	110,287	11,891	597	n.a.	n.a.	n.a.
1940 (Apr. 1)[2]	66,062	65,608	118,215	12,866	589	n.a.	n.a.	n.a.
1950 (Apr. 1)[2]	74,833	75,864	134,942	15,042	713	n.a.	n.a.	n.a.
1950 (Apr. 1)	75,187	76,139	135,150	15,045	1,131	n.a.	n.a.	n.a.
1960 (Apr. 1)	88,331	90,992	158,832	18,872	1,620	n.a.	n.a.	n.a.
1970 (Apr. 1)[3]	98,926	104,309	178,098	22,581	2,557	n.a.	n.a.	n.a.
1980 (Apr. 1)[4, 5]	110,053	116,493	194,713	26,683	5,150	1,420	3,729	14,609
1990 (Apr. 1)[4, 6]	121,271	127,494	208,727	30,511	9,527	2,065	7,462	22,372
2000 (Apr. 1)[4]	138,054	143,368	211,461	34,658	13,118	2,476	10,642	35,306

NOTES: n.a. = not available. 1. Persons of Hispanic origin may be of any race. 2. Excludes Alaska and Hawaii. 3. The revised 1970 resident population count is 203,302,031, which incorporates changes due to errors found after tabulations were completed. The race and sex data shown here reflect the official 1970 census count. 4. The race data shown have been modified to be consistent with the guidelines in Federal Statistical Directive No. 15 issued by the Office of Management and Budget and are not comparable to data for earlier years. 5. Total population count has been revised since the 1980 census publications. Numbers by age, race, Hispanic origin, and sex have not been corrected. 6. The April 1, 1990, census count (248,765,170) includes count resolution corrections processed through Aug. 1997, and does not include adjustments for census coverage errors except for adjustments estimated for the 1995 Census Test in Oakland, Calif.; Paterson, N.J.; and six Louisiana parishes. These adjustments amounted to a total of 55,297 persons. *Source: Statistical Abstract of the United States* and Census 2000. Web (Census 2000): www.census.gov.

Ratio of Males to Females, by Age Group, 1950–2025

(number of males per 100 females, total resident population)

							Projections	
Age	1950	1960	1970	1980	1990[1]	1998	2000	2025
All ages	**98.6**	**97.1**	**94.8**	**94.5**	**95.1**	**95.5**	**95.5**	**96.0**
Under 14 years	103.7	103.4	103.9	104.6	104.9	104.8	104.8	105.1
14 to 24 years	98.2	98.7	98.7	101.9	104.6	104.8	104.1	104.2
25 to 44 years	96.4	95.7	95.5	97.4	98.9	98.6	98.9	97.7
45 to 64 years	100.1	95.7	91.6	90.7	92.5	93.7	93.8	93.5
65 years and over	89.6	82.8	72.1	67.6	67.2	70.3	70.4	82.9

NOTES: As of April 1 for 1950–1990. As of July 1 for 1998–2025. 1. The April 1, 1990, census count (248,765,170) includes count resolution corrections processed through August 1997, and does not include adjustments for census coverage errors except for adjustments estimated for the 1995 Census Test in Oakland, Calif.; and six Louisiana parishes. These adjustments amounted to a total of 55,297 persons. *Source:* U.S. Census Bureau, *Current Population Reports,* P25-1095 and P25-1130; and unpublished data. From *Statistical Abstract of the United States 1999.*

Population Distribution by Age, Race, Nativity, and Sex Ratio

| | | | Age | | | | Race and Nativity | | | | |
| | | | | | | | | White[1] | | | |
Year	Total	Under 5	5–19	20–44	45–64	65 and over	Total	Native born	Foreign born	Black	Other races[1]
Percent Distribution											
1860[2]	100.0%	15.4%	35.8%	35.7%	10.4%	2.7%	85.6%	72.6%	13.0%	14.1%	0.3%
1870[2]	100.0	14.3	35.4	35.4	11.9	3.0	87.1	72.9	14.2	12.7	0.2
1880[2]	100.0	13.8	34.3	35.9	12.6	3.4	86.5	73.4	13.1	13.1	0.3
1890[3]	100.0	12.2	33.9	36.9	13.1	3.9	87.5	73.0	14.5	11.9	0.3
1900	100.0	12.1	32.3	37.7	13.7	4.1	87.9	74.5	13.4	11.6	0.5
1910	100.0	11.6	30.4	39.0	14.6	4.3	88.9	74.4	14.5	10.7	0.4
1920	100.0	10.9	29.8	38.4	16.1	4.7	89.7	76.7	13.0	9.9	0.4
1930	100.0	9.3	29.5	38.3	17.4	5.4	89.8	78.4	11.4	9.7	0.5
1940	100.0	8.0	26.4	38.9	19.8	6.8	89.8	81.1	8.7	9.8	0.4
1950	100.0	10.7	23.2	37.6	20.3	8.1	89.5	82.8	6.7	10.0	0.5
1960	100.0	11.3	27.1	32.2	20.1	9.2	88.6	83.4	5.2	10.5	0.9
1970[2]	100.0	8.4	29.5	31.7	20.6	9.8	87.6	83.4	4.3	11.1	1.4
1980	100.0	7.2	24.8	37.1	19.6	11.3	83.1	—	—	11.7	5.2
1990	100.0	7.6	21.3	40.1	18.6	12.5	83.9	—	—	12.3	3.8
Males per 100 Females											
1860[2]	104.7	102.4	101.2	107.9	111.5	98.3	105.3	103.7	115.1	99.6	260.8
1870[2]	102.2	102.9	101.2	99.2	114.5	100.5	102.8	100.6	115.3	96.2	400.7
1880[2]	103.6	103.0	101.3	104.0	110.2	101.4	104.0	102.1	115.9	97.8	362.2
1890[3]	105.0	103.6	101.4	107.3	108.3	104.2	105.4	102.9	118.7	99.5	165.2
1900	104.4	102.1	100.9	105.8	110.7	102.0	104.9	102.8	117.4	98.6	185.2
1910	106.0	102.5	101.3	108.1	114.4	101.1	106.6	102.7	129.2	98.9	185.6
1920	104.0	102.5	100.8	102.8	115.2	101.3	104.4	101.7	121.7	99.2	156.6
1930	102.5	103.0	101.4	100.5	109.1	100.5	102.9	101.1	115.8	97.0	150.6
1940	100.7	103.2	102.0	98.1	105.2	95.5	101.2	100.1	111.1	95.0	140.5
1950	98.6	103.9	102.5	96.2	100.1	89.6	99.0	98.8	102.0	93.7	129.7
1960	97.1	103.4	102.7	95.6	95.7	82.8	97.4	97.6	94.2	93.3	109.7
1970[2]	94.8	104.0	103.3	95.1	91.6	72.1	95.3	95.9	83.8	90.8	100.2
1980	94.5	104.7	104.0	98.1	90.7	67.6	94.8	—	—	89.6	100.3
1990	95.1	104.8	105.0	99.8	92.5	67.2	95.9	—	—	89.8	96.5

NOTES: Data exclude armed forces overseas. Beginning in 1960, includes Alaska and Hawaii. (—) Data not available. 1. The 1980 and 1990 census data for white and other race categories are not directly comparable to those shown for the preceding years because of changes in the way some persons reported their race, as well as changes in procedures relating to racial classification. 2. Excludes persons for whom age is not available. 3. Excludes persons enumerated in the Indian Territory and on Indian reservations. *Source:* U.S. Bureau of the Census; Web: www.census.gov.

Households by Size, 1790–2000

| | Number of households (in thousands) | Percent distribution of number of households | | | | | | |
Year		1 person	2 persons	3 persons	4 persons	5 persons	6 persons	7 or more persons
1790 (Mar.)	558	3.7%	7.8%	11.7%	13.8%	13.9%	13.2%	35.8%
1890 (June)	12,690	3.6	13.2	16.7	16.8	15.1	11.6	23.0
1900 (Mar.)	15,964	5.1	15.0	17.6	16.9	14.2	10.9	20.4
1930 (Apr.)	29,905	7.9	23.4	20.8	17.5	12.0	7.6	10.9
1940 (Apr.)	34,949	7.1	24.8	22.4	18.1	11.5	6.8	9.3
1950 (Apr.)[1]	43,468	10.9	28.8	22.6	17.8	10.0	5.1	4.9
1955 (Mar.)	47,788	10.9	28.5	20.4	18.9	11.1	5.4	4.9
1960 (Mar.)[2]	52,610	13.1	27.8	18.9	17.6	11.5	5.7	5.4
1965 (Mar.)	57,251	15.0	28.1	17.9	16.1	11.0	5.8	6.1
1970 (Mar.)	62,874	17.0	28.8	17.3	15.8	10.4	5.6	5.1
1975 (Mar.)	71,120	19.6	30.6	17.4	15.6	9.0	4.3	3.5
1980 (Mar.)	80,776	22.7	31.3	17.5	15.7	7.5	3.1	2.2
1985 (Mar.)	86,789	23.7	31.6	17.8	15.7	7.0	2.6	1.5
1990 (Mar.)	93,347	24.6	32.2	17.2	15.5	6.7	2.3	1.4
1995 (Mar.)	98,990	25.0	32.1	17.0	15.5	6.7	2.3	1.4
2000 (Mar.)	104,705	25.5	33.1	16.4	14.6	6.7	2.3	1.4

1. Covers related persons only; therefore, not strictly comparable with other years. 2. Denotes first year for which figures include Alaska and Hawaii. *Source:* U.S. Census Bureau; Web: www.census.gov.

Population Explosion Among Older Americans

The United States saw a rapid growth in its elderly population during the 20th century. The number of Americans aged 65 and older climbed above 34.6 million in 1999, compared with 3.1 million in 1900. For the same years, the ratio of elderly Americans to the total population jumped from one in 25 to one in eight. The trend is guaranteed to continue in the coming century as the baby-boom generation grows older. Between 1990 and 2020, the population aged 65 to 74 is projected to grow 74%.

The elderly population explosion is a result of impressive increases in life expectancy. When the nation was founded, the average American could expect to live to the age of 35. Life expectancy at birth had increased to 47.3 by 1900 and in 1997 stood at 76.5.

Along with the growth of the general elderly population has come a remarkable increase in the number of Americans reaching age 100. The 1990 census found that there were 37,306 centenarians in the U.S. Current projections estimate that the number will reach 131,000 in the year 2010 and as many as 834,000 by 2050.

Source: Based on U.S. Census Bureau data.

Persons 65 Years Old and Over—Characteristics by Sex, 1980–1999

Characteristic	Total			Male			Female		
	1980	1990	1999	1980	1990	1999	1980	1990	1999
Total[1] (million)	24.2	29.6	32.4	9.9	12.3	13.7	14.2	17.2	18.7
White (million)	21.9	26.5	n.a.	9.0	11.0	n.a.	12.9	15.4	n.a.
Black (million)	2.0	2.5	n.a.	0.8	1.0	n.a.	1.2	1.5	n.a.
Percent below poverty level[2]	15.2%	11.4%	10.5%	11.1%	7.8%	7.2%	17.9%	13.9%	12.8%
Percent distribution									
Marital status:									
Single	5.5%	4.6%	3.8%	4.9%	4.2%	3.6%	5.9%	4.9%	4.0%
Married	55.4	56.1	57.7	78.0	76.5	75.9	39.5	41.4	44.3
Spouse present	53.6	54.1	55.3	76.1	74.2	73.6	37.9	39.7	41.8
Spouse absent	1.8	2.0	2.4	1.9	2.3	2.3	1.7	1.7	2.5
Widowed	35.7	34.2	31.8	13.5	14.2	14.0	51.2	48.6	44.9
Divorced	3.5	5.0	6.7	3.6	5.0	6.5	3.4	5.1	6.8
Years of school completed:									
8 years or fewer	43.1%	28.5%	17.6%	45.3%	30.0%	18.3%	41.6%	27.5%	17.1%
1 to 3 years of high school	16.2	16.1	14.3[3]	15.5	15.7	12.9[3]	16.7	16.4	15.4[3]
4 years of high school	24.0	32.9	34.9[4]	21.4	29.0	29.9[4]	25.8	35.6	38.5[4]
1 to 3 years of college	8.2	10.9	17.8[5]	7.5	10.8	18.1[5]	8.6	11.0	17.7[5]
4 years or more of college	8.6	11.6	15.3[6]	10.3	14.5	20.9[6]	7.4	9.5	11.3[6]
Labor force participation[7]:									
Employed	12.2%	11.5%	12.0%	18.4%	15.9%	16.4%	7.8%	8.4%	8.7%
Unemployed	0.4	0.4	0.4	0.6	0.5	0.5	0.3	0.3	0.3
Not in labor force	87.5	88.1	87.7	81.0	83.6	83.1	91.9	91.3	91.1

NOTES: n.a. = not available. (—) Represents zero. 1. Includes other races, not shown separately. 2. Poverty status based on income in preceding year. 3. Represents those who completed 9th to 12th grade, but have no high school diploma. 4. High school graduate. 5. Some college or associate degree. 6. Bachelor's or advanced degree. 7. Annual averages of monthly figures (from U.S. Bureau of Labor Statistics, *Employment and Earnings*, January issues. Data beginning 1994 not directly comparable with earlier years). *Source:* Except as noted, U.S. Bureau of the Census, *Current Population Reports.* From *Statistical Abstract of the United States 2000.*

Population Aged 100 and Over, 1990

	Total	White	Black	American Indian, Eskimo, and Aleut	Asian and Pacific Islander	Other	Hispanic[1]	Non-Hispanic	
								White	All other races
Both sexes	37,306	30,105	5,874	264	492	571	1,642	29,130	6,534
100 to 104 years	30,947	25,881	4,208	180	357	321	1,051	25,186	4,710
105 years and over	6,359	4,224	1,666	84	135	250	591	3,944	1,824
Males	7,901	5,799	1,587	99	175	241	581	5,490	1,830
100 to 104 years	5,944	4,616	1,025	68	122	113	317	4,421	1,206
105 years and over	1,957	1,183	562	31	53	128	264	1,069	624
Females	29,405	24,306	4,287	165	317	330	1,061	23,640	4,704
100 to 104 years	25,003	21,265	3,183	112	235	208	734	20,765	3,504
105 years and over	4,402	3,041	1,104	53	82	122	327	2,875	1,200

1. Persons of Hispanic origin may be of any race. *Source:* U.S. Bureau of the Census, *1990 Census of Population—General Population Characteristics, United States.*

Marital Status and Household Characteristics

Marriages and Divorces, 1900–1999

Year	Marriage Number	Marriage Rate[2]	Divorce[1] Number	Divorce[1] Rate[2]	Year	Marriage Number	Marriage Rate[2]	Divorce[1] Number	Divorce[1] Rate[2]
1900	709,000	9.3	55,751	0.7	1986	2,400,000	10.0	1,159,000	4.8
1910	948,166	10.3	83,045	0.9	1987	2,421,000	9.9	1,157,000	4.8
1920	1,274,476	12.0	170,505	1.6	1988	2,389,000	9.7	1,183,000	4.8
1930	1,126,856	9.2	195,961	1.6	1989	2,404,000	9.7	1,163,000	4.7
1940	1,595,879	12.1	264,000	2.0	1990	2,448,000	9.8	1,175,000	4.7
1950	1,667,231	11.1	385,144	2.6	1991	2,371,000	9.4	1,187,000	4.7
1960	1,523,000	8.5	393,000	2.2	1992	2,362,000	9.2	1,215,000	4.8
1965	1,800,000	9.3	479,000	2.5	1993	2,334,000	9.0	1,187,000	4.6
1970	2,158,802	10.6	708,000	3.5	1994	2,362,000	9.1	1,191,000	4.6
1975	2,152,662	10.1	1,036,000	4.9	1995	2,336,000	8.9	1,169,000	4.4
1980	2,406,708	10.6	1,182,000	5.2	1996	2,344,000	8.8	1,150,000	4.3
1982	2,495,000	10.8	1,180,000	5.1	1997	2,384,000	8.9	1,163,000	4.3
1983	2,444,000	10.5	1,179,000	5.0	1998	2,256,000	8.4	—	4.2
1984	2,487,000	10.5	1,155,000	4.9	1999	2,358,000	8.6	—	4.1
1985	2,425,000	10.2	1,187,000	5.0					

NOTE: (—) Data not available. Marriage and divorce figures for most years include some estimated data. Alaska is included beginning 1959, Hawaii beginning 1960. 1. Includes annulments. 2. Per 1,000 population. *Source:* U.S. Dept. of Health and Human Services, National Center for Health Statistics; Web: www.cdc.gov/nchs/.

Median Age at First Marriage

Year	Males	Females	Year	Males	Females	Year	Males	Females
1890	26.1	22.0	1950	22.8	20.3	1996	27.1	24.8
1900	25.9	21.9	1960	22.8	20.3	1997	26.8	25.0
1910	25.1	21.6	1970	23.2	20.8	1998	26.7	25.0
1920	24.6	21.2	1980	24.7	22.0	1999	26.9	25.1
1930	24.3	21.3	1990	26.1	23.9	2000	26.8	25.1
1940	24.3	21.5	1995	26.9	24.5			

Source: U.S. Bureau of the Census; Web: www.census.gov.

Marital Status of the Population, 1980–1999

(numbers are in millions)

Marital status	Total 1999	Total 1995	Total 1990	Total 1980	Male 1999	Male 1995	Male 1990	Male 1980	Female 1999	Female 1995	Female 1990	Female 1980
Total	199.7	191.6	181.8	159.5	95.9	92.0	86.9	75.7	103.9	99.6	95.0	83.8
Never married	47.6	43.9	40.4	32.3	25.8	24.6	22.4	18.0	21.9	19.3	17.9	14.3
Married	118.9	116.7	112.6	104.6	59.0	57.7	55.8	51.8	59.9	58.9	56.7	52.8
Widowed	13.5	13.4	13.8	12.7	2.5	2.3	2.3	2.0	10.9	11.1	11.5	10.8
Divorced	19.7	17.6	15.1	9.9	8.5	7.4	6.3	3.9	11.1	10.3	8.8	6.0
Percent of total	100.0%	100.0%	100.0%	100.0%	100.0%	100.0%	100.0%	100.0%	100.0%	100.0%	100.0%	100.0%
Never married	23.9	22.9	22.2	20.3	26.9	26.8	25.8	23.8	21.0	19.4	18.9	17.1
Married	59.5	60.9	61.9	65.5	61.5	62.7	64.3	68.4	57.7	59.2	59.7	63.0
Widowed	6.7	7.0	7.6	8.0	2.7	2.5	2.7	2.6	10.5	11.1	12.1	12.8
Divorced	9.9	9.2	8.3	6.2	8.9	8.0	7.2	5.2	10.7	10.3	9.3	7.1

Source: U.S. Bureau of the Census, *Current Population Reports*, P20-491, and earlier reports; and unpublished data. From *Statistical Abstract of the United States 2000.*

Percent Never Married, 1970 and 1999

Age	1970	1999	Age	1970	1999
Male:			**Female:**		
20 to 24 years	35.8%	83.2%	20 to 24 years	54.7%	72.3%
25 to 29 years	10.5	52.1	25 to 29 years	19.1	38.9
30 to 34 years	6.2	30.7	30 to 34 years	9.4	22.1
35 to 39 years	5.4	21.1	35 to 39 years	7.2	15.2
40 to 44 years	4.9	15.8	40 to 44 years	6.3	10.9

NOTE: Data apply to the U.S. *Source:* U.S. Bureau of the Census. From *Statistical Abstract of the United States 2000.*

Persons Living Alone, by Sex and Age

(in thousands)

Sex and Age	1999 Number	1999 Percent	1995 Number	1995 Percent	1990 Number	1990 Percent	1980 Number	1980 Percent
Both sexes								
15 to 24 years	1,313	5%	1,196	5%	1,210	5%	1,726	9%
25 to 34 years	3,714	14	3,653	15	3,972	17	4,729[1]	26[1]
35 to 44 years	4,074	15	3,663	15	3,138	14	([1])	([1])
45 to 64 years	7,757	29	6,377	26	5,502	24	4,514	25
65 to 74 years	4,125	16	4,374	18	4,350	19	3,851	21
75 years and over	5,622	21	5,470	22	4,825	21	3,477	19
Total, 15 years and over	**26,606**	**100**	**24,732**	**100**	**22,999**	**100**	**18,296**	**100**
Male								
15 to 24 years	644	2	623	3	674	3	947	5
25 to 34 years	2,166	8	2,213	9	2,395	10	2,920[1]	16[1]
35 to 44 years	2,521	9	2,263	9	1,836	8	([1])	([1])
45 to 64 years	3,380	13	2,787	11	2,203	10	1,613	9
65 to 74 years	1,127	4	1,134	5	1,042	5	775	4
75 years and over	1,127	4	1,120	5	901	4	711	4
Total, 15 years and over	**10,966**	**41**	**10,140**	**41**	**9,049**	**39**	**6,966**	**38**
Female								
15 to 24 years	668	3	572	2	536	2	779	4
25 to 34 years	1,549	6	1,440	6	1,578	7	1,809[1]	10[1]
35 to 44 years	1,553	6	1,399	6	1,303	6	([1])	([1])
45 to 64 years	4,377	16	3,589	15	3,300	14	2,901	16
65 to 74 years	2,998	11	3,240	13	3,309	14	3,076	17
75 years and over	4,495	17	4,351	18	3,924	17	2,766	15
Total, 15 years and over	**15,640**	**59**	**14,592**	**59**	**13,950**	**61**	**11,330**	**62**

NOTE: As of March. 1. Data for persons 35 to 44 years old included with persons 25 to 34 years old. *Source:* U.S. Bureau of the Census, *Current Population Reports,* P20-491, and earlier reports; and unpublished data. From *Statistical Abstract of the United States 2000.*

Singles in the United States
(The ratio of unmarried men per 100 unmarried women in U.S. Metro Areas, 1990)

Highest Ratio Men to Women

Rank	Metro Area	Ratio
1	Jacksonville, N.C. MSA	223.64
2	Killeen–Temple, Tex. MSA	122.75
3	Fayetteville, N.C. MSA	117.66
4	Brazoria, Tex. PMSA	116.71
5	Lawton, Okla. MSA	115.63
6	State College, Pa. MSA	112.98
7	Clarksville–Hopkinsville, Tenn.–Ky. MSA	112.71
8	Anchorage, Alaska MSA	112.45
9	Salinas–Seaside–Monterey, Calif. MSA	112.01
10	Bryan–College Station, Tex. MSA	111.40
11	Bremerton, Wash. MSA	108.30
12	San Diego, Calif. MSA	105.33
13	Honolulu, Hawaii MSA	105.22
14	Las Vegas, Nev. MSA	104.65
15	Yuma, Ariz. MSA	104.64
16	Grand Forks, N.D. MSA	104.19
17	San Jose, Calif. PMSA	103.63
18	Reno, Nev. MSA	103.52
19	Lafayette–West Lafayette, Ind. MSA	102.01
20	Fort Walton Beach, Fla. MSA	101.70
21	Vallejo–Fairfield–Napa, Calif. PMSA	101.68
22	Lake County, Ill. PMSA	101.56
23	Champaign–Urbana–Rantoul, Ill. MSA	101.33
24	Jackson, Miss. MSA	101.24
25	Colorado Springs, Colo. MSA	99.42

Lowest Ratio Men to Women

Rank	Metro Area	Ratio
1	Sarasota, Fla. MSA	65.57
2	Bradenton, Fla. MSA	68.41
3	Altoona, Pa. MSA	69.42
4	Springfield, Ill. MSA	69.63
5	Jacksonville, Tenn. MSA	69.72
6	Gadsden, Ala. MSA	69.86
7	Wheeling, W.Va.–Ohio MSA	70.48
8	Charleston, W.Va. MSA	70.65
9	St. Joseph, Mo. MSA	70.93
10	Lynchburg, Va. MSA	71.04
11	Roanoke, Va. MSA	71.09
12	Asheville, N.C. MSA	71.14
13	Shreveport, La. MSA	71.54
14	Birmingham, Ala. MSA	71.63
15	Danville, Va. MSA	71.72
16	Pittsburgh, Pa. PMSA	72.04
17	Monroe, La. MSA	72.06
18	Owensboro, Ky. MSA	72.14
19	Pittsburgh–Beaver Valley, Pa. (CMSA)	72.16
20	Florence, Ala. MSA	72.20
21	Sherman–Denison, Tex. MSA	72.27
22	Florence, S.C. MSA	72.32
23	Huntington–Ashland, W.Va.–Ky.–Ohio MSA	72.67
24	Cumberland, Md.–W.Va. MSA	72.73
25	Steubenville–Weirton, Ohio–W.Va. MSA	72.87

NOTE: Unmarried includes never-married, widowed, and divorced persons, 15 years or older. Metro Areas as defined June 30, 1990. The presence of a military base, college or university, etc. in a metropolitan area may have a significant impact on the size of the ratio. MSA—Metropolitan Statistical Area. CMSA—Consolidated Metropolitan Statistical Area. PMSA—Primary Metropolitan Statistical Area. *Source:* U.S. Bureau of the Census; Web: www.census.gov.

Characteristics of Unmarried Partners and Married Spouses, 2000

(in thousands)

	Number				Percent			
	Unmarried partners		Married spouses		Unmarried partners		Married spouses	
Characteristic	Men	Women	Men	Women	Men	Women	Men	Women
Total	3,822	3,822	56,497	56,497	100.0%	100.0%	100.0%	100.0%
Age:								
15 to 24 years old	597	937	1,321	2,386	15.6	24.5	2.3	4.2
25 to 34 years old	1,413	1,269	9,296	10,964	37.0	33.2	16.5	19.4
35 years old and over	1,811	1,616	45,881	43,146	47.4	42.3	81.2	76.4
Race and Hispanic origin								
White	3,127	3,147	49,668	49,581	81.8	82.3	87.9	87.8
Non-Hispanic	2,710	2,742	44,350	44,142	70.9	71.7	78.5	78.1
Black	562	498	4,294	4,097	14.7	13.0	7.6	7.3
Asian and Pacific Islander	63	105	2,118	2,393	1.6	2.7	3.7	4.2
Hispanic (of any race)	453	433	5,550	5,671	11.9	11.3	9.8	10.0
Education								
Less than high school	683	599	8,314	7,160	17.9	15.7	14.7	12.7
High school graduate	1,441	1,357	17,506	19,950	37.7	35.5	31.0	35.3
Some college	996	1,223	14,002	14,968	26.1	32.0	24.8	26.5
College graduate	702	643	16,674	14,419	18.4	16.8	29.5	25.5
Labor force status								
Employed	3,179	2,894	42,854	34,067	83.2	75.7	75.9	60.3
Unemployed	187	178	992	961	4.9	4.7	1.8	1.7
Not in labor force	453	747	12,650	21,468	11.9	19.5	22.4	38.0
Personal earnings								
Without earnings	402	642	11,353	19,368	10.5	16.8	20.1	34.3
With earnings	3,419	3,178	45,144	37,132	89.5	83.2	79.9	65.7
Under $5,000	184	373	1,874	4,683	4.8	9.8	3.3	8.3
$5,000 to $9,999	286	395	1,665	4,183	7.5	10.3	2.9	7.4
$10,000 to $14,999	360	445	2,401	4,497	9.4	11.6	4.2	8.0
$15,000 to $19,999	410	441	3,101	4,427	10.7	11.5	5.5	7.8
$20,000 to $24,999	401	397	3,561	4,249	10.5	10.4	6.3	7.5
$25,000 to $29,999	336	315	3,595	3,429	8.8	8.2	6.4	6.1
$30,000 to $39,999	548	405	7,492	4,954	14.3	10.6	13.3	8.8
$40,000 to $49,999	337	201	6,096	2,976	8.8	5.3	10.8	5.3
$50,000 to $74,999	370	137	8,703	2,683	9.7	3.6	15.4	4.7
$75,000 and over	187	69	6,656	1,051	4.9	1.8	11.8	1.9
Presence of children								
With children[1]	1,563	1,563	25,771	25,771	40.9	40.9	45.6	45.6

NOTE: Data are not shown separately for the American Indian and Alaska Native population because of the small sample size in the Current Population Survey in March 2000. 1. May be own children of either partner or both partners. Excludes ever married children under 18 years. *Source:* U.S. Census Bureau, Current Population Survey, March 2000.

Married Couples of Same or Mixed Races and Origins, 1980–1999

(in thousands)

Race and origin of spouse	1980	1990	1995	1998	1999[1]
Married couples, total	49,714	53,256	54,937	55,305	55,849
Race					
White/white	44,910	47,202	48,030	48,050	42,669
Black/black	3,354	3,687	3,703	3,839	3,765
Black/white	167	211	328	330	307
Black husband/white wife	122	150	206	210	215
White husband/black wife	45	61	122	120	92
White/other race[2]	450	720	988	975	983
Black/other race[2]	34	33	76	43	27
All other couples[2]	799	1,401	1,811	2,068	1,972
Hispanic origin					
Hispanic/Hispanic	1,906	3,085	3,857	4,279	4,480
Hispanic/other origin (not Hispanic)	891	1,193	1,434	1,662	1,647
All other couples (not of Hispanic origin)	46,917	48,979	49,646	49,363	49,722

NOTE: Persons 15 years old and over. Persons of Hispanic origin may be of any race. 1. Race categories exclude persons of Hispanic origin. 2. Excluding white and black. *Source:* U.S. Census Bureau, *Current Population Reports.* From *Statistical Abstract of the United States 2000.*

Births

Births, Birth Rates, and Fertility Rates by State, 1999

State	Number of births	Birth rate[1]	Fertility rate[2]	State	Number of births	Birth rate[1]	Fertility rate[2]
United States[3]	3,959,417	14.5	65.9	Nebraska	23,907	14.3	66.6
Alabama	62,122	14.2	63.3	Nevada	29,362	16.2	78.3
Alaska	9,950	16.1	74.3	New Hampshire	14,041	11.7	50.8
Arizona	81,145	17.0	81.1	New Jersey	114,105	14.0	64.5
Arkansas	36,729	14.4	67.7	New Mexico	27,191	15.6	72.2
California	518,508	15.6	69.5	New York	255,612	14.0	63.6
Colorado	62,167	15.3	69.8	North Carolina	113,795	14.9	67.6
Connecticut	43,310	13.2	61.9	North Dakota	7,639	12.1	57.3
Delaware	10,676	14.2	61.7	Ohio	152,584	13.6	61.4
District of Columbia	7,522	14.5	60.0	Oklahoma	49,010	14.6	68.9
Florida	197,023	13.0	65.1	Oregon	45,204	13.6	64.8
Georgia	126,717	16.3	68.8	Pennsylvania	145,347	12.1	57.4
Hawaii	17,038	14.4	68.7	Rhode Island	12,366	12.5	57.2
Idaho	19,872	15.9	73.2	South Carolina	54,948	14.1	62.1
Illinois	182,068	15.0	68.0	South Dakota	10,524	14.4	67.7
Indiana	86,031	14.5	65.2	Tennessee	77,803	14.2	63.5
Iowa	37,558	13.1	62.3	Texas	349,245	17.4	77.6
Kansas	38,782	14.6	67.5	Utah	46,290	21.7	93.1
Kentucky	54,403	13.7	61.5	Vermont	6,567	11.1	49.2
Louisiana	67,136	15.4	67.7	Virginia	95,469	13.9	59.6
Maine	13,616	10.9	49.4	Washington	79,586	13.8	62.1
Maryland	71,967	13.9	60.4	West Virginia	20,728	11.5	54.7
Massachusetts	80,939	13.1	58.5	Wisconsin	68,208	13.0	59.3
Michigan	133,607	13.5	60.7	Wyoming	6,129	12.8	60.8
Minnesota	65,970	13.8	62.6	Puerto Rico	59,563	15.3	65.3
Mississippi	42,684	15.4	67.9	Virgin Islands	1,671	14.0	64.3
Missouri	75,432	13.8	63.0	Guam	4,021	26.5	129.2
Montana	10,785	12.2	59.8				

NOTE: Data by place of residence. 1. Total births per 1,000 total population. 2. Total births per 1,000 women aged 15–44. 3. Excludes data for Puerto Rico, Virgin Islands, and Guam. *Source:* National Center for Health Statistics, *National Vital Statistics Reports,* vol. 49, no. 1, April 17, 2001. Web: www.cdc.gov/nchs.

Live Births by Age and Race of Mother, 1940–1999

Year[1]/race	Total	Age of Mother							
		Under 15	15–19	20–24	25–29	30–34	35–39	40–44	45–49[2]
1940	2,558,647	3,865	332,667	799,537	693,268	431,468	222,015	68,269	7,558
1945	2,858,449	4,028	298,868	832,746	785,299	554,906	296,852	78,853	6,897
1950	3,631,512	5,413	432,911	1,155,167	1,041,360	610,816	302,780	77,743	5,322
1955	4,014,112	6,181	493,770	1,290,939	1,133,155	732,540	352,320	89,777	5,430
1960	4,257,850	6,780	586,966	1,426,912	1,092,816	687,722	359,908	91,564	5,182
1965	3,760,358	7,768	590,894	1,337,350	925,732	529,376	282,908	81,716	4,614
1970	3,731,386	11,752	644,708	1,418,874	994,904	427,806	180,244	49,952	3,146
1975	3,144,198	12,642	582,238	1,093,676	936,786	375,500	115,409	26,319	1,628
1980	3,612,258	10,169	552,161	1,226,200	1,108,291	550,354	140,793	23,090	1,200
1985	3,760,561	10,220	467,485	1,141,320	1,201,350	696,354	214,336	28,334	1,162
1990	4,158,212	11,657	521,826	1,093,730	1,277,108	886,063	317,583	48,607	1,638
1995	3,899,589	12,242	499,873	965,547	1,063,539	904,666	383,745	67,250	2,727
1996	3,914,953	11,242	494,272	951,247	1,078,411	904,329	400,810	71,663	2,980
1997	3,880,894	10,121	483,220	942,048	1,069,436	886,798	409,710	76,084	3,333
1998	3,941,553	9,462	484,895	965,122	1,083,010	889,365	424,890	81,027	3,782[2]
1999	3,959,417	9,054	476,050	981,929	1,078,252	892,400	434,294	83,090	4,348[2]
White	3,132,501	4,739	337,888	748,371	873,654	739,948	356,959	67,419	3,523[2]
Black	605,970	3,977	121,166	193,211	138,868	91,486	47,277	9,564	421[2]
American Indian[3]	40,170	198	7,915	13,225	9,641	5,701	2,844	621	25[2]
Asian or Pacific Islander	180,776	140	9,081	27,122	56,089	55,265	27,214	5,486	379[2]
Hispanic origin[4]	764,339	2,725	124,677	231,475	203,985	131,369	58,146	11,440	522[2]

NOTE: Data refer only to births occurring within the U.S. 1. Data for 1940–1955 are adjusted for under-registration. Beginning 1960, only registered births are shown. Data for 1960–1970 based on a 50% sample of births. For 1972–1984, based on 100% of births in selected states and on 50% sample in all other states. Beginning 1989, births are tabulated by race of mother; previously based on race of child. 2. Beginning 1998, ages 45–54. 3. Includes births to Aleuts and Eskimos. 4. Persons of Hispanic origin may be any race. *Source:* National Center for Health Statistics, *National Vital Statistics Reports,* vol. 49, no. 1, April 17, 2001. Web: www.cdc.gov/nchs.

Live Births by Sex and Sex Ratio

	Total[1,2]			White			Black		
Year	Male	Female	Males per 1,000 females	Male	Female	Males per 1,000 females	Male	Female	Males per 1,000 females
1985	1,927,983	1,832,578	1,052	1,536,646	1,454,727	1,056	308,575	299,618	1,030
1986	1,924,868	1,831,679	1,051	1,523,914	1,446,525	1,053	315,788	305,433	1,034
1987	1,951,153	1,858,241	1,050	1,535,517	1,456,971	1,054	325,259	316,308	1,028
1988	2,002,424	1,907,086	1,050	1,562,675	1,483,487	1,053	341,441	330,535	1,033
1989	2,069,490	1,971,468	1,050	1,606,757	1,525,234	1,053	360,131	349,264	1,031
1990	2,129,495	2,028,717	1,050	1,654,928	1,570,415	1,054	367,455	357,121	1,029
1991	2,101,518	2,009,389	1,046	1,659,077	1,582,196	1,049	346,455	336,147	1,031
1992	2,082,097	1,982,917	1,050	1,641,811	1,559,867	1,053	342,726	330,907	1,036
1993	2,048,861	1,951,379	1,050	1,616,332	1,533,501	1,054	333,984	324,891	1,028
1994	2,022,589	1,930,178	1,048	1,599,803	1,521,401	1,051	322,554	313,837	1,028
1995	1,996,355	1,930,234	1,049	1,588,427	1,510,458	1,052	308,115	297,024	1,031
1996	1,990,480	1,901,014	1,047	—	—	1,050	—	—	1,028
1997	1,985,596	1,895,298	1,048	—	—	1,052	—	—	1,031
1998	2,016,205	1,925,348	1,047	—	—	1,052	—	—	1,034
1999	2,026,854	1,932,563	1,049	—	—	1,052	—	—	1,031

NOTE: (—) Data not available. 1. Excludes births to nonresidents of U.S. 2. Includes races other than white and black. *Source:* National Center for Health Statistics, *National Vital Statistics Reports*, vol. 49, no. 1, April 17, 2001. Web: www.cdc.gov/nchs.

Selected Characteristics of Births by Race of Mother, 1999

Characteristic	All races	White	Black	American Indian[1]	Asian or Pacific Islander	Hispanic origin[2]
Percentage of mothers who:						
Had prenatal care beginning in the first trimester	83.2%	85.1%	74.1%	69.5%	83.7%	74.4%
Had late or no prenatal care	3.8	3.2	6.6	8.2	3.5	6.3
Were tobacco users[3]	12.6	13.6	9.3	20.2	2.9	3.7
Were alcohol users[4]	1.0	1.0	1.2	3.5	0.3	0.6
Gained less than 16 lbs[5]	11.8	10.8	17.0	15.9	9.7	13.8
Median weight gain[5]	30.5	30.7	30.0	30.1	30.1	29.8
Had cesarean births	22.0	21.9	23.2	18.9	20.2	21.2
Percentage of infants who:						
Were born prior to 37 full weeks	11.8	10.7	17.5	12.9	10.4	11.4
Weighed less than 1,500 grams (3 lb 4 oz.)	1.5	1.2	3.1	1.3	1.1	1.1
Weighed less than 2,500 grams (5 lb 8 oz.)	7.6	6.6	13.1	7.1	7.4	6.4
Weighed 4,000 grams (8 lb 14 oz.) or more	9.9	11.0	5.4	12.2	5.8	9.0
Had five-minute Apgar scores of less than 7[6]	1.4	1.2	2.4	1.5	1.0	1.1

1. Includes births to Aleuts and Eskimos. 2. Hispanic origin may be of any race. 3. Excludes data for Calif. and S.D., which did not report tobacco use on birth certificate. 4. Excludes data for Calif. and S.D., which did not report alcohol use on birth certificate. 5. Excludes data for Calif., which did not report weight gain on birth certificate. Median weight gain shown in pounds. 6. Excludes data for Calif. and Tex., which did not report Apgar scores on birth certificate. Apgar scores are derived from evaluations of five major signs at one minute and five minutes after birth. Each sign is given a score of 0–2 for a total of ten possible points; scores of 7–10 are considered normal, 4–7 may require resuscitative measures, and 0–3 require immediate resuscitation. The signs and scores (0-1-2) are as follows: Activity or muscle tone (absent—arms and legs flexed—active movement); Pulse (absent—below 100 bpm—above 100 bpm); Grimace or reflex irritability (no response—grimace—sneeze, cough, pulls away); Appearance or skin color (blue-gray, pale all over—normal, except for extremities—normal over entire body); Respiration (absent—slow, irregular—good, crying). *Source:* National Center for Health Statistics, *National Vital Statistics Reports*, vol. 49, no. 1, April 17, 2001. Web: www.cdc.gov/nchs.

Births: Other Data for 1999

The source for the data on U.S. births, birth rates, and fertility rates in this section is the *National Vital Statistics Reports* series published by the National Center for Health Statistics, a part of the Centers for Disease Control and Prevention. The report issued on April 17, 2001, showing final birth data for 1999 also highlighted these findings:

Births in the United States increased less than 1% in 1999, to 3,959,417, the second consecutive increase following a 7% decline from 1990 to 1997. The **birth rate** declined slightly in 1999 to 14.5 births per 1,000 total population, matching the

record low reached in 1997. The **fertility rate,** which relates births to the number of women of childbearing age, increased less than 1% to 65.9 births per 1,000 women aged 15–44 years.

The **birth rate for teenagers** declined again in 1999, falling 3% to 49.6 births per 1,000 women aged 15–19 years. The rate has declined 20% since 1991. (*See also* p. 340.)

The **birth rates for women in their twenties** have changed relatively little since the early to mid-1970s. However, **birth rates for women in their thirties** increased to 89.6 per 1,000 aged 30–34 years, and to 38.3 per 1,000 aged 35–39 years, up 2% to 3% each. The rates for these age groups are at their highest in more than three decades. The birth rate for women aged 40–44 years increased again in 1999 to 7.4 per 1,000.

In 1999, the **median age at first birth** increased to 24.5 years. The median has risen slowly but steadily since 1972.

Cigarette smoking during pregnancy declined again in 1999, to 12.6%. The overall rate has fallen steadily since 1989. However, tobacco use by pregnant teenagers continued to increase in 1999. Infant birth weight is seriously compromised by maternal smoking: In 1999, 12.1% of infants born to smokers weighed less than 2,500 grams (5 lbs, 8 oz), compared with 7.2% of infants born to nonsmokers.

After falling steadily from 1989 to 1996, the rate of **cesarean delivery** increased again in 1999, up 4% from 1998. Twenty-two percent of all births were by cesarean delivery in 1999. The 1999 rate is 6% higher than the recent low point in 1996

(20.7%). (A total of 862,086 infants were born by cesarean delivery in 1999, compared to 3,063,870 vaginal births.)

Twin births continued to rise in 1999, but for the first year in over a decade, **triplet and higher multiple births** declined. The number and rate of twin births was up 3% to 114,307, or 28.9 per 1,000 live births between 1998 and 1999. The twinning rate has risen by more than 50% since 1980. The number of triplet-plus births, however, was down to 7,321 for 1999, from 7,625 in 1998. The rate for triplet-plus births declined 4%, from 193.5 to 184.9 per 100,000 live births. An estimated two-thirds of triplet-plus births are the result of fertility treatments.

Nearly 12% of all births were delivered preterm (less than 37 completed weeks of gestation). The percent of **infants born preterm** has risen 11% since 1990.

Source: National Center for Health Statistics, *National Vital Statistics Reports,* vol. 49, no. 1, April 17, 2001.

Contraceptive Use by Women, 15 to 44 Years Old, 1995

Contraceptive status and method	All women	Age 15–24 years	Age 25–34 years	Age 35–44 years	Marital status Never married	Marital status Currently married	Marital status Formerly married
All women (in thousands)	60,201	18,002	20,758	21,440	22,679	29,673	7,849
Percent distribution							
Sterile[1]	29.7%	2.6%	25.0%	57.0%	6.9%	43.2%	45.1%
Surgically sterile	27.9	1.8	23.6	54.0	5.7	41.1	42.5
Nonsurgically sterile[2]	1.7	0.7	1.3	2.8	1.1	2.0	2.2
Pill	17.3	23.1	23.7	6.3	20.4	15.6	14.6
IUD	0.5	0.1	0.6	0.8	0.3	0.7	0.4
Diaphragm	1.2	0.2	1.2	2.0	0.5	1.8	0.9
Condom	13.1	13.9	15.0	10.7	13.9	13.3	10.1
Periodic abstinence	1.5	0.5	1.8	2.0	0.6	2.3	0.7
Withdrawal	2.0	1.6	2.3	1.9	1.5	2.3	1.8
Other methods[3]	3.9	5.6	4.2	2.1	4.6	3.3	3.9

1. Total sterile includes male sterile for unknown reasons. 2. Persons sterile from illness, accident, or congenital conditions. 3. Includes implants, injectables, morning-after-pill, suppository, Today™ sponge, and less frequently used methods. *Source:* U.S. National Center for Health Statistics. From *Statistical Abstract of the United States 2000.*

Abortion Statistics, 1972–1997

	1972	1980	1985	1990	1995	1997
Reported no. legal abortions	586,760	1,297,606	1,328,570	1,429,577	1,210,883	1,186,039
Abortion ratio[1]	180	359	354	345	311	306
Abortion rate[2]	13	25	24	24	20	20
Percentage distribution						
Age group (yrs)						
≤19	32.6%	29.2%	26.3%	22.4%	20.1%	20.1%
20–24	32.5	35.5	34.7	33.2	32.5	31.7
≥25	34.9	35.3	39.0	44.4	47.4	48.2
Marital status						
Married	29.7	23.1	19.3	21.7	19.7	19.0
Unmarried	70.3	76.9	80.7	78.3	80.3	81.0

NOTE: The number of areas reporting a given characteristic varied. 1. Number of legal induced abortions per 1,000 live births. 2. Number of legal induced abortions per 1,000 women aged 15–44 years. *Source:* U.S. Centers for Disease Control and Prevention. *Abortion Surveillance: Preliminary Analysis—United States, 1997.* Jan. 7, 2000.

Mortality

10 Leading Causes of Death in the U.S., 1999[1]

Leading causes of death differ somewhat by age, sex, and race. In 1999 as in previous years, accidents were the leading cause of death for those under 44 years, while in older age groups malignant neoplasms (cancer) and heart disease were the leading causes. HIV, which was the leading cause of death in 1995 for those aged 25–44, dropped to fifth rank for that age group in 1997 and remained there in 1998 and 1999. However, in 1999 HIV was still the leading cause of death for black males aged 25–44.

Trends also vary according to place. In 1999 Hawaii had the lowest mortality, with an age-adjusted death rate of 680.3 deaths per 100,000 people. (The age-adjusted rate for the U.S. overall was 881.9.) The state with the highest rate, Mississippi, had an age-adjusted death rate of 1,064.9 deaths per 100,000 people.

Rank[2]	Causes of death	Number	Deaths per 100,000 population	Percent of total deaths
	All causes	**2,391,630**	**877.0**	**100.0%**
1	Diseases of heart	724,915	265.8	30.3
2	Malignant neoplasms (cancer)	549,787	201.6	23.0
3	Cerebrovascular diseases (stroke)	167,340	61.4	7.0
4	Chronic lower respiratory diseases	124,153	45.5	5.2
5	Accidents (unintentional injuries)	97,298	35.7	4.1
	Motor vehicle accidents	42,437	15.6	1.8
	All other accidents	54,862	20.1	2.3
6	Diabetes mellitus	68,379	25.1	2.9
7	Pneumonia and influenza	63,686	23.4	2.7
8	Alzheimer's disease	44,507	16.3	1.9
9	Nephritis, nephrotic syndrome, and nephrosis	35,524	13.0	1.5
10	Septicemia	30,670	11.2	1.3
	All other causes	485,371	178.0	20.2

1. Preliminary. 2. Rank based on number of deaths. *Source:* U.S. National Center for Health Statistics, *National Vital Statistics Reports,* vol. 49, no. 3, June 26, 2001. Web: www.cdc.gov/nchs.

Life Expectancy at Birth by Race and Sex, 1940–1999

	All races			White			Black		
Year	Both sexes	Male	Female	Both sexes	Male	Female	Both sexes	Male	Female
1999[1]	76.7	73.9	79.4	77.3	74.6	79.9	71.4	67.8	74.7
1998	76.7	73.8	79.5	77.3	74.5	80.0	71.3	67.6	74.8
1997	76.5	73.6	79.4	77.1	74.3	79.9	71.1	67.2	74.7
1996	76.1	73.1	79.1	76.8	73.9	79.7	70.2	66.1	74.2
1995	75.8	72.5	78.9	76.5	73.4	79.6	69.6	65.2	73.9
1994	75.7	72.4	79.0	76.5	73.3	79.6	69.5	64.9	73.9
1993	75.5	72.2	78.8	76.3	73.1	79.5	69.2	64.6	73.7
1992	75.8	72.3	79.1	76.5	73.2	79.8	69.6	65.0	73.9
1991	75.5	72.0	78.9	76.3	72.9	79.6	69.3	64.6	73.8
1990	75.4	71.8	78.8	76.1	72.7	79.4	69.1	64.5	73.6
1989	75.1	71.7	78.5	75.9	72.5	79.2	68.8	64.3	73.3
1988	74.9	71.4	78.3	75.6	72.2	78.9	68.9	64.4	73.2
1987	74.9	71.4	78.3	75.6	72.1	78.9	69.1	64.7	73.4
1986	74.7	71.2	78.2	75.4	71.9	78.8	69.1	64.8	73.4
1985	74.7	71.1	78.2	75.3	71.8	78.7	69.3	65.0	73.4
1984	74.7	71.1	78.2	75.3	71.8	78.7	69.5	65.3	73.6
1983	74.6	71.0	78.1	75.2	71.6	78.7	69.4	65.2	73.5
1982	74.5	70.8	78.1	75.1	71.5	78.7	69.4	65.1	73.6
1981	74.1	70.4	77.8	74.8	71.1	78.4	68.9	64.5	73.2
1980	73.7	70.0	77.4	74.4	70.7	78.1	68.1	63.8	72.5
1979	73.9	70.0	77.8	74.6	70.8	78.4	68.5	64.0	72.9
1978	73.5	69.6	77.3	74.1	70.4	78.0	68.1	63.7	72.4
1977	73.3	69.5	77.2	74.0	70.2	77.9	67.7	63.4	72.0
1976	72.9	69.1	76.8	73.6	69.9	77.5	67.2	62.9	71.6
1975	72.6	68.8	76.6	73.4	69.5	77.3	66.8	62.4	71.3
1974	72.0	68.2	75.9	72.8	69.0	76.7	66.0	61.7	70.3
1973	71.4	67.6	75.3	72.2	68.5	76.1	65.0	60.9	69.3
1972[2]	71.2	67.4	75.1	72.0	68.3	75.9	64.7	60.4	69.1
1971	71.1	67.4	75.0	72.0	68.3	75.8	64.6	60.5	68.9
1970	70.8	67.1	74.7	71.7	68.0	75.6	64.1	60.0	68.3
1960	69.7	66.6	73.1	70.6	67.4	74.1	—	—	—
1950	68.2	65.6	71.1	69.1	66.5	72.2	—	—	—
1940	62.9	60.8	65.2	64.2	62.1	66.6	—	—	—

(—) Data not available. 1. Preliminary. 2. Deaths based on a 50% sample. *Source:* National Center for Health Statistics, *National Vital Statistics Reports,* vol. 49, no. 3, June 26, 2001. Web: www.cdc.gov/nchs.

Life Expectancy by Age, 1850–1999

The expectation of life at a specified age is the average number of years that members of a hypothetical group of people of the same age would continue to live if they were subject throughout the remainder of their lives to the same mortality rate.

Calendar period	Age								
	0	10	20	30	40	50	60	70	80
White males									
1850[1]	38.3	48.0	40.1	34.0	27.9	21.6	15.6	10.2	5.9
1890[1]	42.50	48.45	40.66	34.05	27.37	20.72	14.73	9.35	5.40
1900–1902[2]	48.23	50.59	42.19	34.88	27.74	20.76	14.35	9.03	5.10
1909–1911[2]	50.23	51.32	42.71	34.87	27.43	20.39	13.98	8.83	5.09
1919–1921[3]	56.34	54.15	45.60	37.65	29.86	22.22	15.25	9.51	5.47
1929–1931	59.12	54.96	46.02	37.54	29.22	21.51	14.72	9.20	5.26
1939–1941	62.81	57.03	47.76	38.80	30.03	21.96	15.05	9.42	5.38
1949–1951	66.31	58.98	49.52	40.29	31.17	22.83	15.76	10.07	5.88
1959–1961[5]	67.55	59.78	50.25	40.98	31.73	23.22	16.01	10.29	5.89
1969–1971[6]	67.94	59.69	50.22	41.07	31.87	23.34	16.07	10.38	6.18
1979–1981	70.82	61.98	52.45	43.31	34.04	25.26	17.56	11.35	6.76
1990	72.7	63.5	54.0	44.7	35.6	26.7	18.7	12.1	7.1
1999[7]	74.6	65.3	55.6	46.2	36.9	28.0	19.8	12.9	7.5
White females									
1850[1]	40.5	47.2	40.2	35.4	29.8	23.5	17.0	11.3	6.4
1890[1]	44.46	49.62	42.03	35.36	28.76	22.09	15.70	10.15	5.75
1900–1902[2]	51.08	52.15	43.77	36.42	29.17	21.89	15.23	9.59	5.50
1909–1911[2]	53.62	53.57	44.88	36.96	29.26	21.74	14.92	9.38	5.35
1919–1921[3]	58.53	55.17	46.46	38.72	30.94	23.12	15.93	9.94	5.70
1929–1931	62.67	57.65	48.52	39.99	31.52	23.41	16.05	9.98	5.63
1939–1941	67.29	60.85	51.38	42.21	33.25	24.72	17.00	10.50	5.88
1949–1951	72.03	64.26	54.56	45.00	35.64	26.76	18.64	11.68	6.59
1959–1961[5]	74.19	66.05	56.29	46.63	37.13	28.08	19.69	12.38	6.67
1969–1971[6]	75.49	66.97	57.24	47.60	38.12	29.11	20.79	13.37	7.59
1979–1981	78.22	69.21	59.44	49.76	40.16	30.96	22.45	14.89	8.65
1990	79.4	70.1	60.3	50.6	41.0	31.6	23.0	15.4	9.0
1999[7]	79.9	70.5	60.6	50.9	41.3	31.9	23.2	15.5	9.0
All other males[4]									
1900–1902[2]	32.54	41.90	35.11	29.25	23.12	17.34	12.62	8.33	5.12
1909–1911[2]	34.05	40.65	33.46	27.33	21.57	16.21	11.67	8.00	5.53
1919–1921[3]	47.14	45.99	38.36	32.51	26.53	20.47	14.74	9.58	5.83
1929–1931	47.55	44.27	35.95	29.45	23.36	17.92	13.15	8.78	5.42
1939–1941	52.33	48.54	39.74	32.25	25.23	19.18	14.38	10.06	6.46
1949–1951	58.91	52.96	43.73	35.31	27.29	20.25	14.91	10.74	7.07
1959–1961[5]	61.48	55.19	45.78	37.05	28.72	21.28	15.29	10.81	6.87
1969–1971[6]	60.98	53.67	44.37	36.20	28.29	21.24	15.35	10.68	7.57
1979–1981	65.63	57.40	47.87	39.13	30.64	22.92	16.54	11.36	7.22
1990	67.0	58.5	49.0	40.3	31.9	23.9	17.0	11.4	7.0
1999[7]	67.8	59.2	49.6	40.7	31.9	24.0	17.2	11.6	7.2
All other females[4]									
1900–1902[2]	35.04	43.02	36.89	30.70	24.37	18.67	13.60	9.62	6.48
1909–1911[2]	37.67	42.84	36.14	29.61	23.34	17.65	12.78	9.22	6.05
1919–1921[3]	46.92	44.54	37.15	31.48	25.60	19.76	14.69	10.25	6.58
1929–1931	49.51	45.33	37.22	30.67	24.30	18.60	14.22	10.38	6.90
1939–1941	55.51	50.83	42.14	34.52	27.31	21.04	16.14	11.81	8.00
1949–1951	62.70	56.17	46.77	38.02	29.82	22.67	16.95	12.29	8.15
1959–1961[5]	66.47	59.72	50.07	40.83	32.16	24.31	17.83	12.46	7.66
1969–1971[6]	69.05	61.49	51.85	42.61	33.87	25.97	19.02	13.30	9.01
1979–1981	74.00	65.64	55.88	46.39	37.16	28.59	20.49	14.44	9.17
1990	75.2	66.6	56.8	47.3	38.1	29.2	21.3	14.5	8.8
1999[7]	74.7	66.0	56.2	46.6	37.4	28.7	20.9	14.0	8.6

1. Massachusetts only; white and nonwhite combined, the latter being about 1% of the total. *Source:* U.S. Dept. of Commerce, Bureau of the Census, *Historical Statistics of the United States.* 2. Original Death Registration States. 3. Death Registration States of 1920. 4. Data for periods 1900–1902, 1929–1931, 1998, and 1999 relate to blacks only. 5. Alaska and Hawaii included beginning in 1959. 6. Deaths of nonresidents of the United States excluded starting in 1970. 7. Preliminary. *Sources:* Department of Health and Human Services, National Center for Health Statistics; Web: www.dhhs.gov.

U.S. Annual Death Rates per 1,000 Population

Year	Rate	Year	Rate	Year	Rate	Year	Rate	Year	Rate	Year	Rate	Year	Rate
1900	17.2	1935	10.9	1946	10.0	1957	9.6	1969	9.5	1980	8.7	1991	8.5
1905	15.9	1936	11.6	1947	10.1	1958	9.5	1970[1]	9.5	1981	8.6	1992	8.5
1910	14.7	1937	11.3	1948	9.9	1959	9.4	1971	9.3	1982	8.5	1993	8.8
1915	13.2	1938	10.6	1949	9.7	1960	9.5	1972	9.4	1983	8.6	1994	8.8
1920	13.0	1939	10.6	1950	9.6	1962	9.5	1973	9.3	1984	8.6	1995	8.8
1925	11.7	1940	10.8	1951	9.7	1963	9.6	1974	9.1	1985	8.7	1996	8.8
1930	11.3	1941	10.5	1952	9.6	1964	9.4	1975	8.8	1986	8.7	1997	8.6
1931	11.1	1942	10.3	1953	9.6	1965	9.4	1976	8.8	1987	8.7	1998	8.6
1932	10.9	1943	10.9	1954	9.2	1966	9.5	1977	8.6	1988	8.8	1999[2]	8.8
1933	10.7	1944	10.6	1955	9.3	1967	9.4	1978	8.7	1989	8.7		
1934	11.1	1945	10.6	1956	9.4	1968	9.7	1979	8.5	1990	8.6		

NOTES: Includes only deaths occurring within the registration states. Beginning with 1933, area includes entire U.S.; with 1959 includes Alaska, and with 1960 includes Hawaii. Excludes fetal deaths. Rates as of April 1 for 1940, 1950, 1960, 1970, and 1980, and estimated as of July 1 for all other years. 1. First year for which deaths of nonresidents are excluded. 2. Preliminary. *Sources:* Department of Health and Human Services, National Center for Health Statistics. Web: www.dhhs.gov.

Infant Mortality Rates, 1950–1998

Year	Infant	Deaths per 1,000 live births		Postneonatal	Fetal mortality rate[1]	Late fetal mortality rate[2]
		Neonatal				
		Under 28 days	Under 7 days			
1950[3]	29.2	20.5	17.8	8.7	18.4	14.9
1960[3]	26.0	18.7	16.7	7.3	15.8	12.1
1970	20.0	15.1	13.6	4.9	14.0	9.5
1980	12.6	8.5	7.1	4.1	9.1	6.2
1985	10.6	7.0	5.8	3.7	7.8	4.9
1990	9.2	5.8	4.8	3.4	7.5	4.3
1991	8.9	5.6	4.6	3.4	7.3	4.1
1992	8.5	5.4	4.4	3.1	7.4	4.1
1993	8.4	5.3	4.3	3.1	7.1	3.8
1994	8.0	5.1	4.2	2.9	7.0	3.7
1995	7.6	4.9	4.0	2.7	7.0	3.6
1996	7.3	4.8	3.8	2.5	6.9	3.6
1997	7.2	4.8	3.8	2.5	6.8	3.5
1998	7.2	4.8	3.8	2.4	—	—

NOTES: "Infant" is defined as under 1 year of age; "neonatal" is under 28 days; "postneonatal" is 28–365 days. (—) Data not available. 1. Number of fetal deaths of 20 weeks or more gestation per 1,000 live births plus fetal deaths. 2. Number of fetal deaths of 28 weeks or more gestation per 1,000 live births plus late fetal deaths. 3. Includes birth and deaths of persons who were not residents of the 50 states and the District of Columbia. *Sources:* Centers for Disease Control and Prevention, National Center for Health Statistics. From *Health, United States, 2000.*

Deaths and Death Rates from Accidents, by Type: 1980–1996

Type of accident	Deaths (number)					Rate per 100,000 population				
	1980	1990	1994	1995	1996	1980	1990	1994	1995	1996
Motor vehicle accidents	53,172	46,814	42,524	43,363	43,649	23.5	18.8	16.3	16.5	16.5
Traffic	51,930	45,827	41,507	42,331	42,522	22.9	18.4	15.9	16.1	16.0
Nontraffic	1,242	987	1,017	1,032	1,127	0.5	0.4	0.4	0.4	0.4
Water-transport accidents	1,429	923	723	762	675	0.6	0.4	0.3	0.3	0.3
Air and space transport accidents	1,494	941	1,075	851	1,061	0.7	0.4	0.4	0.3	0.4
Railway accidents	632	663	635	569	565	0.3	0.3	0.2	0.2	0.2
Accidental falls	13,294	12,313	13,450	13,986	14,986	5.9	5.0	5.2	5.3	5.6
Accidental drowning	6,043	3,979	3,404	3,790	3,488	2.7	1.6	1.3	1.4	1.3
Accidents caused by—										
Fires and flames	5,822	4,175	3,986	3,761	3,741	2.6	1.7	1.5	1.4	1.4
Firearms, unspecified and other	1,667	1,175	1,123	992	947	0.7	0.5	0.4	0.4	0.4
Handguns	288	241	233	233	187	0.1	0.1	0.1	0.1	0.1
Electric current	1,095	670	561	559	482	0.5	0.3	0.2	0.2	0.2
Accidental poisoning by—										
Drugs and medicines	2,492	4,506	7,828	8,000	8,431	1.1	1.8	3.0	3.0	3.2
Other solid and liquid substances	597	549	481	461	441	0.3	0.2	0.2	0.2	0.2
Gases and vapors	1,242	748	685	611	638	0.5	0.3	0.3	0.2	0.2
Complications due to medical procedures	2,282	2,669	2,616	2,712	2,919	1.0	1.1	1.0	1.0	1.1
Inhalation and ingestion of objects	3,249	3,303	3,065	3,185	3,206	1.4	1.3	1.2	1.2	1.2

NOTE: Excludes deaths of nonresidents of the United States. *Source: Statistical Abstract of the United States 2000.*

Deaths by Firearms, 1979–1998

(per 100,000 population in specified group)

Year	All races		White		Black	
	Number of deaths	Death rate[1]	Number of deaths	Death rate[1]	Number of deaths	Death rate[1]
1979	33,019	14.7	24,234	12.5	8,304	31.6
1980	33,780	14.9	24,849	12.8	8,505	31.9
1981	34,050	14.8	25,237	12.8	8,324	30.7
1982	32,957	14.2	25,071	12.7	7,415	27.0
1983	31,099	13.3	24,038	12.1	6,589	23.6
1984	31,331	13.3	24,419	12.2	6,449	22.9
1985	31,566	13.3	24,507	12.1	6,565	23.0
1986	33,373	13.9	25,339	12.5	7,494	25.9
1987	32,895	13.6	24,789	12.1	7,586	25.9
1988	33,989	13.9	24,892	12.1	8,475	28.5
1989	34,776	14.1	25,023	12.1	9,077	30.1
1990	37,155	14.9	26,299	12.6	10,175	33.4
1991	38,317	15.2	26,455	12.5	11,025	35.4
1992	37,776	14.8	26,120	12.3	10,906	34.5
1993	39,595	15.4	26,948	12.5	11,763	36.6
1994	38,505	14.8	26,403	12.2	11,223	34.4
1995	35,957	13.7	25,438	11.7	9,643	29.1
1996	34,040	12.8	24,114	11.0	9,175	27.4
1997	32,436	12.1	23,270	10.5	8,389	24.7
1998	30,708	11.4	22,480	10.1	7,503	21.8

1. On an annual basis, per 100,000 population in specified group. *Source:* Centers for Disease Control and Prevention, *National Vital Statistics Reports,* vol. 48, no. 11, July 24, 2000.

Death Rates for Suicide, 1950–1998

(deaths per 100,000 resident population)

Characteristic	1950[1]	1960[1]	1970	1980	1990	1996	1997	1998
All ages[2]	11.0	10.6	11.8	11.4	11.5	10.8	10.6	10.4
5 to 14 years	0.2	0.3	0.3	0.4	0.8	0.8	0.8	0.8
15 to 24 years	4.5	5.2	8.8	12.3	13.2	12.0	11.4	11.1
25 to 34 years	9.1	10.0	14.1	16.0	15.2	14.5	14.3	13.8
35 to 44 years	14.3	14.2	16.9	15.4	15.3	15.5	15.3	15.4
45 to 54 years	20.9	20.7	20.0	15.9	14.8	14.9	14.7	14.8
55 to 64 years	27.0	23.7	21.4	15.9	16.0	13.7	13.5	13.1
65 to 74 years	29.3	23.0	20.8	16.9	17.9	15.0	14.4	14.1
75 to 84 years	31.1	27.9	21.2	19.1	24.9	20.0	19.3	19.7
85 years and over	28.8	26.0	19.0	19.2	22.2	20.2	20.8	21.0
Male, all ages[2]	17.3	16.6	17.3	18.0	19.0	18.0	17.4	17.2
Female, all ages[2]	4.9	5.0	6.8	5.4	4.5	4.0	4.1	4.0

1. Includes deaths of persons who were not residents of the 50 states and the District of Columbia. 2. Data are age-adjusted. *Sources:* Centers for Disease Control and Prevention, National Center for Health Statistics. From *Health, United States, 2000.*

Miscellaneous

Most Common Last Names in the U.S.

Rank	Name	Frequency[1]	Rank	Name	Frequency[1]	Rank	Name	Frequency[1]
1.	Smith	1.01%	11.	Anderson	0.31	21.	Clark	0.23
2.	Johnson	0.81	12.	Thomas	0.31	22.	Rodriguez	0.23
3.	Williams	0.70	13.	Jackson	0.31	23.	Lewis	0.23
4.	Jones	0.62	14.	White	0.28	24.	Lee	0.22
5.	Brown	0.62	15.	Harris	0.28	25.	Walker	0.22
6.	Davis	0.48	16.	Martin	0.27	26.	Hall	0.20
7.	Miller	0.42	17.	Thompson	0.27	27.	Allen	0.20
8.	Wilson	0.34	18.	Garcia	0.25	28.	Young	0.19
9.	Moore	0.31	19.	Martinez	0.23	29.	Hernandez	0.19
10.	Taylor	0.31	20.	Robinson	0.23	30.	King	0.19

NOTE: Based on 1990 Census data. Numbers are rounded. 1. Percent of U.S. population sample. *Source:* U.S. Census Bureau. Web: www.census.gov/genealogy/names/dist.all.last.

Most Popular Given Names, 1880–2000

Boys

1880: John, William, Charles, George, James, Joseph, Frank, Henry, Thomas, Harry

1890: John, William, James, George, Charles, Joseph, Frank, Harry, Henry, Edward

1900: John, William, James, George, Charles, Joseph, Frank, Henry, Robert, Harry

1910: John, William, James, Robert, Joseph, Charles/George (tie), Edward, Frank, Henry

1920: John, William, James, Robert, Joseph, Charles, George, Edward, Thomas, Frank

1930: Robert, James, John, William, Richard, Charles, Donald, George, Joseph, Edward

1940: James, Robert, John, William, Richard, Charles, David, Thomas, Donald, Ronald

1950: John, James, Robert, William, Michael, David, Richard, Thomas, Charles, Gary

1960: David, Michael, John, James, Robert, Mark, William, Richard, Thomas, Steven

1970: Michael, David, John, James, Robert, Christopher, William, Mark, Richard, Brian

1980: Michael, Jason, Christopher, David, James, Matthew, John, Joshua, Robert, Daniel

1990: Michael, Christopher, Joshua, Matthew, David, Daniel, Andrew, Joseph, Justin, James

2000: Jacob, Michael, Matthew, Joshua, Christopher, Nicholas, Andrew, Joseph, Daniel, Tyler

Girls

1880: Mary, Anna, Elizabeth, Margaret, Minnie, Emma, Martha, Alice, Marie, Annie/Sarah (tie)

1890: Mary, Anna, Elizabeth, Emma, Margaret, Rose, Ethel, Florence, Ida, Bertha/Helen (tie)

1900: Mary, Helen, Anna, Margaret, Ruth, Elizabeth, Marie, Rose, Florence, Bertha

1910: Mary, Helen, Margaret, Dorothy, Ruth, Anna, Mildred, Elizabeth, Alice, Ethel

1920: Mary, Dorothy, Helen, Margaret, Ruth, Virginia, Elizabeth, Anna, Mildred, Betty

1930: Mary, Betty, Dorothy, Helen, Barbara, Margaret, Maria, Patricia, Doris, Joan/Ruth (tie)

1940: Mary, Barbara, Patricia, Carol, Judith, Betty, Nancy, Maria, Margaret, Linda

1950: Linda, Mary, Patricia, Barbara, Susan, Maria, Sandra, Nancy, Deborah, Kathleen

1960: Mary, Susan, Maria, Karen, Lisa, Linda, Donna, Patricia, Debra, Deborah

1970: Jennifer, Lisa, Kimberly, Michelle, Angela, Maria, Amy, Melissa, Mary, Tracy

1980: Jennifer, Jessica, Amanda, Melissa, Sarah, Nicole, Heather, Amy, Michelle, Elizabeth

1990: Jessica, Ashley, Brittany, Amanda, Stephanie, Jennifer, Samantha, Sarah, Megan, Lauren

2000: Emily, Hannah, Madison, Ashley, Sarah, Alexis, Samantha, Jessica, Taylor, Elizabeth

NOTE: Represents the most frequently used given names for births, based on a sampling of Social Security Number card applications. *Source:* Social Security Administration. Web: www.ssa.gov/OACT/NOTES/note139/note139.html.

Most Popular Pet Names

The American Society for the Prevention of Cruelty to Animals (ASPCA) has conducted a veterinarian survey to find out which pet names are most popular in the United States today. Here are the top 30:

1. Max	7. Kitty	13. Misty	19. Samantha	25. Sheba
2. Sam	8. Molly	14. Missy	20. Lucky	26. Rocky
3. Lady	9. Buddy	15. Pepper	21. Muffin	27. Patches
4. Bear	10. Brandy	16. Jake	22. Princess	28. Tigger
5. Smokey	11. Ginger	17. Bandit	23. Maggie	29. Rusty
6. Shadow	12. Baby	18. Tiger	24. Charlie	30. Buster

Household Pet Ownership, 1996

Item	Dog	Cat	Pet bird	Horse
Households owning companion pets[1] (millions)	31.20	27.00	4.60	1.50
Percent of all households	31.60%	27.30%	4.60%	1.50%
Average number owned	1.70	2.20	2.70	2.70
Total companion pet population[1] (millions)	52.90	59.10	12.60	4.00
Households obtaining veterinary care[2]	88.70%	72.90%	15.80%	66.30%
Average visits per household per year	2.60	1.90	0.20	2.30
Average annual costs per household	$ 186.80	$ 112.24	$10.95	$226.26
Total expenditures (millions)	$5,828.00	$3,030.00	$50.00	$339.00
Percent distribution of households owning pets				
Annual household income:				
Under $12,500	12.70%	13.90%	17.30%	9.50%
$12,500 to $24,999	19.10	19.70	20.90	20.30
$25,000 to $39,999	21.60	21.50	22.00	21.80
$40,000 to $59,999	21.50	21.20	17.50	23.10
$60,000 and over	25.20	23.70	22.30	25.40
Family size:[1]				
One person	13.20%	16.80%	12.70%	12.10%
Two persons	31.00	32.60	27.90	29.10
Three persons	21.40	20.60	20.40	22.00
Four or more persons	34.50	29.90	38.90	36.70

NOTE: Based on a sample survey of 80,000 households in 1996. 1. As of December. 2. During 1996. *Source:* American Veterinary Medical Association, Schaumburg, Ill., *U.S. Pet Ownership and Demographics Sourcebook, 1997.* Reprinted with permission.

Hunger Still a Problem in U.S.

Source: Economic Research Service, U.S. Dept. of Agriculture, *Household Food Security in the United States, 1999*

According to a report released by the U.S. Department of Agriculture, 10.1% of U.S. households, 31 million Americans, were food insecure during the 12 months ending April 1999. "Food insecure" means that at some time during the previous year they were uncertain of having or unable to acquire adequate food sufficient to meet basic needs. Of these, about 3 million households were food insecure to the extent that one or more household members were hungry due to inadequate resources at least some time during the year.

The prevalence of food insecurity and hunger varied considerably among household types, and some groups, including 29.7% of households with children headed by a single woman, 21.2% of black households, and 20.8% of Hispanic households, experienced rates of food insecurity greater than the national average. Overall, households with children experienced food insecurity at double the rate for households without children (14.8% versus 7.4%).

Food Insecurity and Hunger, 1999
(numbers in thousands)

| Category | Total number[1] | Food secure | | Food insecure | | | | | |
| | | | | Total | | Without hunger | | With hunger | |
		Number	Percent	Number	Percent	Number	Percent	Number	Percent
All households	104,684	94,154	89.9%	10,529	10.1%	7,420	7.1%	3,109	3.0%
All persons in households	270,318	239,304	88.5	31,015	11.5	23,237	8.6	7,779	2.9
Adults in households	198,900	179,960	90.5	18,941	9.5	13,869	7.0	5,072	2.5
Children in households	71,418	59,344	83.1	12,074	16.9	9,368	13.1	2,707	3.8
Household composition:									
With children < 18	37,884	32,290	85.2	5,594	14.8	4,340	11.5	1,254	3.3
Married couple families	26,303	23,771	90.4	2,532	9.6	2,105	8.0	428	1.6
Female head, no spouse	8,744	6,146	70.3	2,598	29.7	1,890	21.6	709	8.1
Male head, no spouse	2,187	1,817	83.1	370	16.9	280	12.8	89	4.1
Other household with child[2]	650	556	85.6	94	14.4	66	10.1	28	4.3
With no children < 18	66,800	61,865	92.6	4,935	7.4	3,080	4.6	1,855	2.8
More than one adult	39,568	37,380	94.5	2,188	5.5	1,470	3.7	718	1.8
Women living alone	16,046	14,473	90.2	1,573	9.8	908	5.7	665	4.1
Men living alone	11,187	10,013	89.5	1,174	10.5	701	6.3	473	4.2
Households with elderly	24,704	23,265	94.2	1,439	5.8	1,055	4.3	385	1.6
Elderly living alone	10,049	9,413	93.7	636	6.3	423	4.2	214	2.1
Race/ethnicity of households:									
White non-Hispanic	78,998	73,451	93.0	5,546	7.0	3,873	4.9	1,673	2.1
Black non-Hispanic	12,616	9,936	78.8	2,680	21.2	1,866	14.8	814	6.4
Hispanic[3]	9,192	7,285	79.2	1,907	20.8	1,406	15.3	502	5.5
Other non-Hispanic	3,878	3,482	89.8	396	10.2	275	7.1	121	3.1

1. Total households in each category exclude households whose food security status is unknown. 2. Households with children in complex living arrangements, e.g., children of other relatives or unrelated roommate or boarder. 3. Hispanics may be of any race. *Source:* Economic Research Service, U.S. Dept. of Agriculture, *Household Food Security in the United States, 1999.* Fall, 2000. Web: www.ers.usda.gov/briefing/foodsecurity/.

Food Stamp Households, 1998
(for year ending Sept. 30)

Household type	Households Number (1,000)	Percent	Sex, race, and Hispanic origin	Participants Number (1,000)	Percent
Total	8,246	100.0%	**Total**	19,969	100.0%
With children	4,803	58.2	Male	7,926	39.7
Single-parent households	3,264	39.6	Female	11,967	59.9
Married-couple households	712	8.6	White, non-Hispanic	8,008	40.1
Other	830	10.0	Black, non-Hispanic	7,248	36.3
With elderly	1,500	18.2	Hispanic	3,652	18.3
Living alone	1,184	14.4	Asian	605	3.0
Not living alone	316	3.8	Native American	311	1.6
Disabled	2,015	24.4	Other	145	0.7
Living alone	1,113	13.5			
Not living alone	903	10.9			

Source: U.S. Dept. of Agriculture, Food and Nutrition Service, *Characteristics of Food Stamp Households: Fiscal Year 1998 (Advance Report),* July 1999. From: *Statistical Abstract of the United States, 2000.*

U.S. Charities Receiving Highest Donations in 1999

1999 Rank	Charity	Private support	Year Ending	1998 rank
1.	Salvation Army[1]	$1,396,877,000	9/30/1999	1
2.	YMCA of the USA[1,2]	693,271,000	12/31/1999	2
3.	American Red Cross[1]	678,320,787	6/30/1999	5
4.	American Cancer Society[1]	620,033,000	8/31/1999	4
5.	Fidelity Investments Charitable Gift Fund	573,426,582	6/30/1999	3
6.	Lutheran Services in America[1]	559,041,141	6/30/1999	42
7.	United Jewish Communities[3]	524,262,231	6/30/1999	n.a.
8.	America's Second Harvest	471,816,003	6/30/1999	10
9.	Habitat for Humanity International[1]	466,716,000	6/30/1999	22
10.	Harvard University	451,672,023	6/30/1999	6
11.	Catholic Charities USA[1]	446,266,726	12/31/1998	7
12.	Nature Conservancy[4]	403,484,807	6/30/1999	14
13.	Boys and Girls Clubs of America[1]	362,336,978	12/31/1999	8
14.	American Heart Association[1]	357,769,173	6/30/1999	11
15.	Gifts in Kind International	346,533,993	12/31/1999	15
16.	Cornell University	341,359,263	6/30/1999	20
17.	World Vision[1]	331,449,000	9/30/1999	13
18.	Duke University	330,991,502	6/30/1999	19
19.	Stanford University	319,590,155	8/31/1999	12
20.	Campus Crusade for Christ International[1]	314,959,000	8/31/1999	18
21.	Larry Jones Ministries/Feed the Children	312,141,593	9/30/1999	28
22.	Columbia University	284,486,570	6/30/1999	17
23.	Boy Scouts of America[1]	273,827,000	12/31/1999	16
24.	University of Pennsylvania	270,060,684	6/30/1999	29
25.	AmeriCares Foundation	267,036,324	6/30/1999	30

1. Includes affiliates. 2. Affiliates have different fiscal years. 3. United Jewish Communities formed from merger in 1999 of United Jewish Appeal, United Israel Appeal, and Council of Jewish Federations. Figures include full year of data from the United Jewish Appeal and six months from United Israel Appeal; 1999 figures are not available for Council of Jewish Federations. 4. Another $251,050,949 was spent to purchase land, which is not included in program services. An additional $184,060,000 was put into an endowment to be used for future land acquisitions and land management. *Source: The Chronicle of Philanthropy*, Nov. 2, 2000. Reprinted with permission.

Percent of Adult Population Doing Volunteer Work, 1998

Age, sex, race, and Hispanic origin	Percent of population volunteering	Average hours volunteered per week	Educational attainment and household income	Percent of population volunteering	Average hours volunteered per week
Total	55.5%	3.5	Elementary school	29.4%	(B)
			Some high school	43.0	3.9
18–24 years	48.5	3.0	High-school graduate	43.2	2.8
25–34 years	54.9	3.5	Technical, trade, or		
35–44 years	67.3	3.7	business school	53.5	3.5
45–54 years	62.7	3.8	Some college	67.2	4.8
55–64 years	50.3	3.3	College graduate	67.7	3.1
65–74 years	46.6	3.6			
75 years and over	43.0	3.1	Under $10,000	42.1	3.4
			$10,000–19,999	42.2	2.9
Male	49.4	3.6	$20,000–29,999	43.7	4.0
Female	61.7	3.4	$30,000–39,999	54.4	3.4
			$40,000–49,999	67.5	3.6
White	58.6	3.5	$50,000–59,999	62.8	4.3
Black	46.6	4.7	$60,000–74,999	71.2	2.9
Hispanic[1]	46.4	2.1	$75,000–99,999	64.2	3.5
			$100,000 or more	70.5	3.5

Type of activity	Percent of population involved in activity	Type of activity	Percent of population involved in activity
Arts, culture, humanities	8.6%	Political organizations	4.6%
Education	17.3	Private, community foundations	3.4
Environment	9.2	Public and societal benefit	7.9
Health	11.4	Recreation—adults	8.6
Human services	15.9	Religion	22.8
Informal	24.4	Work-related organizations	10.3
International, foreign	2.5	Youth development	17.5

(B) = Base figure too small to meet statistical standards for reliability. 1. Hispanic persons may be of any race. NOTE: Covers persons 18 years and over. Volunteers are persons who worked in some way to help others for no monetary pay during the previous year. Based on a sample survey conducted during the spring of the following year and subject to sampling variability. *Source: Statistical Abstract of the United States 2000.*

Homeownership Rates by Race and Ethnicity of Householder

	1994	1995	1996	1997	1998	1999	2000
U.S. total	64.0	64.7	65.4	65.7	66.3	66.8	67.4
White, total	67.7	68.7	69.1	69.3	70.0	70.5	71.1
White, non-Hispanic	70.0	70.9	71.7	72.0	72.6	73.2	73.8
Black, total	42.3	42.7	44.1	44.8	45.6	46.3	47.2
Other race[1]	47.7	47.2	51.0	52.5	53.0	53.7	53.5
American Indian, Aleut, Eskimo	51.7	55.8	51.6	51.7	54.3	56.1	56.2
Asian or Pacific Islander	51.3	50.8	50.8	52.8	52.6	53.1	52.8
Other	36.1	37.4	n.a.	n.a.	n.a.	n.a.	n.a.
Hispanic	41.2	42.1	42.8	43.3	44.7	45.5	46.3
Non-Hispanic	65.9	66.7	67.4	67.4	67.8	68.3	69.5

NOTE: n.a. = not applicable. 1. Beginning in 1996, those answering "other" for race were allocated to one of the 4 race categories—white, black, American Indian, Aleut, or Eskimo (one category), or Asian or Pacific Islander. *Source:* U.S. Census Bureau. Web: www.census.gov.

Homeownership by State, 1990 and 2000

State	Homeownership rate (%) 1990	2000	State	Homeownership rate (%) 1990	2000	State	Homeownership rate (%) 1990	2000
U.S. total	63.9%	67.4%	Kentucky	65.8%	73.4%	Ohio	68.7%	71.3%
Alabama	68.4	73.2	Louisiana	67.8	68.1	Oklahoma	70.3	72.7
Alaska	58.4	66.4	Maine	74.2	76.5	Oregon	64.4	65.3
Arizona	64.5	68.0	Maryland	64.9	69.9	Pennsylvania	73.8	74.7
Arkansas	67.8	68.9	Massachusetts	58.6	59.9	Rhode Island	58.5	61.5
California	53.8	57.1	Michigan	72.3	77.2	South Carolina	71.4	76.5
Colorado	59.0	68.3	Minnesota	68.0	76.1	South Dakota	66.2	71.2
Connecticut	67.9	70.0	Mississippi	69.4	75.2	Tennessee	68.3	70.9
Delaware	67.7	72.0	Missouri	64.0	74.2	Texas	59.7	63.8
DC	36.4	41.9	Montana	69.1	70.2	Utah	70.1	72.7
Florida	65.1	68.4	Nebraska	67.3	70.2	Vermont	72.6	68.7
Georgia	64.3	69.8	Nevada	55.8	64.0	Virginia	69.8	73.9
Hawaii	55.5	55.2	New Hampshire	65.0	69.2	Washington	61.8	63.6
Idaho	69.4	70.5	New Jersey	65.0	66.2	West Virginia	72.0	75.9
Illinois	63.0	67.9	New Mexico	68.6	73.7	Wisconsin	68.3	71.8
Indiana	67.0	74.9	New York	53.3	53.4	Wyoming	68.9	71.0
Iowa	70.7	75.2	North Carolina	69.0	71.1			
Kansas	69.0	69.3	North Dakota	67.2	70.7			

Source: U.S. Census Bureau. Web: www.census.gov.

Characteristics of the Homeless, 1996

Characteristic	U.S. adult population (1996)	All homeless persons	Persons in homeless families	Single homeless persons
Sex:				
Male	48%	68%	16%	77%
Female	52	32	84	23
Race/ethnicity:				
White non-Hispanic	75	41	38	41
Black non-Hispanic	11	40	43	40
Hispanic	10	11	15	10
Native American	1	8	3	8
Marital status:				
Never married	23	48	41	50
Married	60	9	23	7
Separated	(2)	15	23	14
Divorced	10	24	13	26
Widowed	7	3	0	4
Educational attainment:				
Less than high school	25	38	53	37
High school graduate/G.E.D.	30	34	21	36
More than high school	45	28	27	28
Veteran	13	23	5	26

NOTE: Numbers do not add up to 100% due to rounding. 1. Denotes percentage less than 0.5 percent but greater than 0. 2. Included in "married." *Source:* U.S. Bureau of the Census. From Interagency Council on the Homeless, *Homelessness: Programs and the People They Serve,* 1999.

States

Data for state populations are the latest available from the U.S. Census Bureau. NOTE: Persons of Hispanic origin can be of any race. "American Indian" includes American Indians, Eskimos, and Aleuts. "Asian" includes Asian Indians, Chinese, Filipino, Japanese, Korean, and Vietnamese. Largest cities include incorporated places only, as defined by the U.S. Census Bureau. They do not include adjacent or suburban areas. Population data for U.S. cities are also the latest available from the U.S. Census Bureau.

For secession and readmission dates of the former Confederate states, *see* U.S. Government & History: The Confederate States of America. For a separate list of governors, and lists of senators and representatives elected to terms beginning in 2001, *see* U.S. Government & History: The Governors of the Fifty States, The Senate, and The House of Representatives. For U.S. Territories, *see* Countries of the World: United States.

Alabama

Capital: Montgomery
Governor: Don Siegelman, D (to Jan. 2003)
Lieut. Governor: Steve Windom, D (to Jan. 2003)
Senators: Jeff Sessions, R (to Jan. 2003); Richard C. Shelby, R (to Jan. 2005)
Secy. of State: Jim Bennett, R (to Jan. 2003)
Treasurer: Lucy Baxley, D (to Jan. 2003)
Atty. General: William Pryor, R (to Jan. 2003)
Auditor: Susan D. Parker, D (to Jan. 2003)
Organized as territory: March 3, 1817
Entered Union (rank): Dec. 14, 1819 (22)
Present constitution adopted: 1901
Motto: *Audemus jura nostra defendere* (We dare defend our rights)
State Symbols: flower, camellia (1959); **bird,** yellowhammer (1927); **song,** "Alabama" (1931); **tree,** Southern longleaf pine (1949, 1997); **salt water fish,** fighting tarpon (1955); **fresh water fish,** largemouth bass (1975); **horse,** racking horse (1975); **mineral,** hematite (1967); **rock,** marble (1969); **game bird,** wild turkey (1980); **dance,** square dance (1981); **nut,** pecan (1982); **fossil,** species *Basilosaurus Cetoides* (1984); **official mascot and butterfly,** eastern tiger swallowtail (1989); **insect,** monarch butterfly (1989); **reptile,** Alabama red-bellied turtle (1990); **gemstone,** star blue quartz (1990); **shell,** *scaphella junonia johnstoneae* (1990);
Nickname: Yellowhammer State
Origin of name: May come from Choctaw meaning "thicket-clearers" or "vegetation-gatherers"
10 largest cities (2000): Birmingham, 242,820; Montgomery, 201,568; Mobile, 198,915; Huntsville, 158,216; Tuscaloosa, 77,906; Hoover, 62,742; Dothan, 57,737; Decatur, 53,929; Auburn, 42,987; Gadsden, 38,978
Land area: 50,750 sq mi. (131,443 sq km)
Geographic center: In Chilton Co., 12 mi. SW of Clanton
Number of counties: 67
Largest county by population and area: Jefferson, 662,047 (2000); Baldwin, 1,596 sq mi.
State forests: 21 (48,000 ac.)
State parks: 22 (45,614 ac.)
Residents: Alabamian, Alabaman
2000 resident census population (rank): 4,447,100 (23). **Male:** 2,146,504 (48.3%); **Female:** 2,300,596 (51.7%). **White:** 3,162,808 (71.1%); **Black:** 1,155,930 (26.0%); **American Indian:** 22,430 (0.5%); **Asian:** 31,346 (0.7%); **Other race:** 28,998 (0.7%); **Two or more races:** 44,179 (1.0%); **Hispanic/Latino:** 75,830 (1.7%). **2000 percent population 18 and over:** 74.7; **65 and over:** 13.0; **median age:** 35.8.

Spanish explorers are believed to have arrived at Mobile Bay in 1519, and the territory was visited in 1540 by the explorer Hernando de Soto. The first permanent European settlement in Alabama was founded by the French at Fort Louis de la Mobile in 1702. The British gained control of the area in 1763 by the Treaty of Paris but had to cede almost all the Alabama region to the U.S. and Spain after the American Revolution. The Confederacy was founded at Montgomery in Feb. 1861, and, for a time, the city was the Confederate capital.

During the last part of the 19th century, the economy of the state slowly improved. At Tuskegee Institute, founded in 1881 by Booker T. Washington, Dr. George Washington Carver carried out his famous agricultural research.

In the 1950s and '60s, Alabama was the site of such landmark civil-rights actions as the bus boycott in Montgomery (1955–56) and the "Freedom March" from Selma to Montgomery (1965).

Today paper, chemicals, rubber and plastics, apparel and textiles, primary metals, and automobile manufacturing constitute the leading industries of Alabama. Continuing as a major manufacturer of coal, iron, and steel, Birmingham is also noted for its world-renowned medical center. The state ranks high in the production of poultry, soybeans, milk, vegetables, livestock, wheat, cattle, cotton, peanuts, fruits, hogs, and corn.

Points of interest include the Helen Keller birthplace at Tuscumbia, the Space and Rocket Center at Huntsville, the White House of the Confederacy, the restored state Capitol, the Civil Rights Memorial, the Rosa Parks Museum & Library, and the Shakespeare Festival Theater Complex in Montgomery; the Civil Rights Institute and the McWane Center in Birmingham; the Russell Cave near Bridgeport; the Bellingrath Gardens at Theodore; the USS *Alabama* at Mobile; Mound State Monument near Tuscaloosa; and the Gulf Coast area.

Famous natives and residents: Hank Aaron, baseball player; Ralph Abernathy, civil rights activist; Tallulah Bankhead, actress; Hugo L. Black, jurist; George Washington Carver, educator, agricultural chemist; Nat "King" Cole, entertainer; Lionel Hampton, jazz musician; W. C. Handy, composer; Courtney Cox, actress; Helen Keller, author and educator; Coretta Scott King, civil rights leader; Harper Lee, writer; Joe Louis, boxer; Willie Mays, baseball player; Jim Nabors, actor; Jesse Owens, athlete; Rosa Parks, civil rights activist; Wayne Rogers, actor; Tascaluza, Choctaw chief; George Wallace, former governor; William Weatherford (Red Eagle), Creek leader; Heather Whitestone, Miss America (1995).

Alaska

Capital: Juneau
Governor: Tony Knowles, D (to Dec. 2002)
Lieut. Governor: Fran Ulmer, D (to Dec. 2002)
Senators: Frank H. Murkowski, R (to Jan. 2005); Ted Stevens, R (to Jan. 2003)
Commissioner of Administration: Jim Duncan
Atty. General: Bruce M. Bothelho, D
Organized as territory: 1912
Entered Union (rank): Jan. 3, 1959 (49)
Constitution ratified: April 24, 1956
Motto: North to the Future
State Symbols: flower, forget-me-not (1949); **tree,** sitka spruce (1962); **bird,** willow ptarmigan (1955); **fish,** king salmon (1962); **song,** "Alaska's Flag" (1955); **gem,** jade (1968); **marine mammal,** bowhead whale (1983); **fossil,** woolly mammoth (1986); **mineral,** gold (1968); **sport,** dog mushing (1972);
Nickname: The state is commonly called "The Last Frontier" or "Land of the Midnight Sun"
Origin of name: Corruption of Aleut word meaning "great land" or "that which the sea breaks against"
10 largest cities (2000): Anchorage, 260,283; Juneau, 30,711; Fairbanks, 30,224; Sitka, 8,835; Ketchikan, 7,922; Kenai, 6,942; Kodiak, 6,334; Bethel, 5,471; Wasilla, 5,469; Barrow, 4,581
Land area: 570,374 sq mi. (1,477,267 sq km)
Geographic center: 60 mi. NW of Mt. McKinley
Number of boroughs: 16
Largest borough by population and area: Anchorage, 260,283 (2000); Yukon-Koyukuk, 157,121 sq mi.
State parks: more than 100 (3.5 million acres)
Residents: Alaskan
2000 resident census population (rank): 626,932 (48).
Male: 324,112 (51.7%); **Female:** 302,820 (48.3%).
White: 434,534 (69.3%); **Black:** 21,787 (3.5%); **American Indian and Alaska Native:** 98,043 (15.6%); **Asian:** 25,116 (4.0%); **Other race:** 9,997 (1.6%); **Two or more races:** 34,146 (5.4%); **Hispanic/Latino:** 25,852 (4.1%).
2000 percent population 18 and over: 69.6; **65 and over:** 5.7; **median age:** 32.4.

Vitus Bering, a Dane working for the Russians, and Alexei Chirikov discovered the Alaskan mainland and the Aleutian Islands in 1741. The tremendous land mass of Alaska—equal to one-fifth of the continental U.S.—was unexplored in 1867 when Secretary of State William Seward arranged for its purchase from the Russians for $7,200,000. The transfer of the territory took place on Oct. 18, 1867. Despite a price of about two cents an acre, the purchase was widely ridiculed as "Seward's Folly." The first official census (1880) reported a total of 33,426 Alaskans, all but 430 being of aboriginal stock. The Gold Rush of 1898 resulted in a mass influx of more than 30,000 people. Since then, Alaska has contributed billions of dollars' worth of products to the U.S. economy.

In 1968, a large oil and gas reservoir near Prudhoe Bay on the Arctic Coast was found. The Prudhoe Bay reservoir, with an estimated recoverable 10 billion barrels of oil and 27 trillion cubic feet of gas, is twice as large as any other oil field in North America. The Trans-Alaska pipeline was completed in 1977 at a cost of $7.7 billion. On June 20, oil started flowing through the 800-mile-long pipeline from Prudhoe Bay to the port of Valdez.

Other important industries are fisheries, wood and wood products, furs, and tourism.

Denali National Park and Mendenhall Glacier in North Tongass National Forest are of interest, as is the large totem pole collection at Sitka National Historical Park. The Katmai National Park includes the "Valley of Ten Thousand Smokes," an area of active volcanoes.

The Alaska Native population, the indigenous peoples of Alaska, include Eskimos, Indians, and Aleuts. More than half of all Alaska Natives are Eskimos. (*Eskimo* is used for Alaska Natives; *Inuit* is used for Eskimos living in Canada.) The two main Eskimo groups, Inupiat and Yupik, are distinguished by their language and geography. The former live in the north and northwest parts of Alaska and speak Inupiaq, while the latter live in the south and southwest and speak Yupik.

About 36% of Alaska Natives are American Indians. The major tribes are the Alaskan Athabaskan (11,696) in the central part of the state, and the Tlingit (9,448), Tsimshian (1,653), and Haida (1,083) in the southeast.

The Aleuts, native to the Aleutian Islands, Kodiak Island, the lower Alaska and Kenai Peninsulas, and Prince William Sound, are physically and culturally related to the Eskimos. About 12% of Alaska Natives are Aleuts, and in 1990, they made up 10,052 of the indigenous population.

Famous natives and residents: Clarence L. Andrews, author; Aleksandr Baranov, first governor of Russian America; Margaret Elizabeth Bell, author; Benny Benson, designed state flag at age 13; Vitus Bering, explorer; Charles E. Bunnell, educator; Susan Butcher, sled-dog racer; William A. Egan, first state governor; Carl Ben Eielson, pioneer pilot; Henry E. Gruennig, political leader; B. Frank Heintzleman, territorial governor; Walter J. Hickel, former governor; Sheldon Jackson, educator and missionary; Joe Juneau, prospector; Austin Lathrop, industrialist; Sydney Lawrence, painter; Ray Mala, actor; Virgil F. Partch, cartoonist; Joe Redington, Sr., sled-dog musher and promoter; Peter Trinble Rowe, first Episcopal bishop; Ivan Popov-Veniaminov (St. Innocent), Russian Orthodox missionary; Ferdinand Wrangel, educator; Samuel Hall Young, founder of first American church.

Arizona

Capital: Phoenix
Governor: Jane Dee Hull, R (to Jan. 2003)
Senators: Jon Kyl, R (to Jan. 2007); John McCain, R (to Jan. 2005)
Secy. of State: Betsey Bayless, R (to Jan. 2003)
Atty. General: Janet Napolitano, D (to Jan. 2003)
Treasurer: Carol Springer, R (to Jan. 2003))
Organized as territory: Feb. 24, 1863
Entered Union (rank): Feb. 14, 1912 (48)
Present constitution adopted: 1911
Motto: *Ditat Deus* (God enriches)
State Symbols: flower, flower of saguaro cactus (1931); **bird,** cactus wren (1931); **colors,** blue and old gold (1915); **song,** "Arizona" (1919); **tree,** palo verde (1954); **neckwear,** bola tie (1971); **fossil,** petrified wood (1988); **gemstone,** turquoise (1974); **mammal,** ringtail (1986); **reptile,** Arizona ridgenose rattlesnake (1986); **fish,** Arizona trout (1986); **amphibian,** Arizona tree frog (1986); **butterfly,** two-tailed swallowtail (2001);
Nickname: Grand Canyon State
Origin of name: From the Indian "Arizonac," meaning "little spring" or "young spring"
10 largest cities (2000): Phoenix, 1,321,045; Tucson, 486,699; Mesa, 396,375; Glendale, 218,812; Scottsdale, 202,705; Chandler, 176,581; Tempe, 158,625; Gilbert, 109,697; Peoria, 108,364; Yuma, 77,515
Land area: 113,642 sq mi. (296,400 sq km)
Geographic center: In Yavapai Co., 55 mi. ESE of Prescott

Number of counties: 15
Largest county by population and area: Maricopa, 3,072,149 (2000); Coconino, 18,562 sq mi.
State parks: 28
Residents: Arizonan, Arizonian
2000 resident census population (rank): 5,130,632 (20). **Male:** 2,561,057 (49.9%); **Female:** 2,569,575 (50.1%). **White:** 3,873,611 (75.5%); **Black:** 158,873 (3.1%); **American Indian:** 255,879 (5.0%); **Asian:** 92,236 (1.8%); **Other race:** 596,774 (11.6%); **Two or more races:** 146,526 (2.9%); **Hispanic/Latino:** 1,295,617 (25.3%). **2000 percent population 18 and over:** 73.4; **65 and over:** 13.0; **median age:** 34.2.

Marcos de Niza, a Spanish Franciscan friar, was the first European to explore Arizona. He entered the area in 1539 in search of the mythical Seven Cities of Gold. Although he was followed a year later by another gold seeker, Francisco Vásquez de Coronado, most of the early settlement was for missionary purposes. In 1775 the Spanish established Fort Tucson. In 1848, after the Mexican War, most of the Arizona territory became part of the U.S., and the southern portion of the territory was added by the Gadsden Purchase in 1853.

Arizona history is rich in legends of America's Old West. It was here that the great Indian chiefs Geronimo and Cochise led their people against the frontiersmen. Tombstone, Ariz., was the site of the West's most famous shoot-out—the gunfight at the O.K. Corral. Today, Arizona has one of the largest U.S. Indian populations; more than 14 tribes are represented on 20 reservations.

Manufacturing has become Arizona's most important industry. Principal products include electrical, communications, and aeronautical items. The state produces over half of the country's copper. Agriculture is also important to the state's economy. In 1973 one of the world's most massive dams, the New Cornelia Tailings, was completed near Ajo.

State attractions include the Grand Canyon, the Petrified Forest, the Painted Desert, Hoover Dam, Lake Mead, Fort Apache, and the reconstructed London Bridge at Lake Havasu City.

Famous natives and residents: Apache Kid, Indian outlaw; Erma Bombeck, humorist and writer; Glen Campbell, singer; Lynda Carter, actress; Cesar Chavez, labor leader; Cochise, Apache chief; Alice Cooper, singer and songwriter; Wyatt Earp, marshall; Max Ernst, painter; Geronimo (Goyathlay), Apache chief; Barry Goldwater, politician; Zane Grey, novelist; Carl Trumbull Hayden, politician; George W. P. Hunt, first state governor; Bill Keane, cartoonist; Eusebio Kino, missionary; Percival Lowell, astronomer; Frank Luke, Jr., WWI fighter ace; Charles Mingus, jazz musician and composer; Carlos Montezuma, doctor and Indian spokesman; Stevie Nicks, singer; Sandra Day O'Connor, jurist; William O'Neill, frontier sheriff; Alexander M. Patch, general; William H. Pickering, astronomer; Linda Ronstadt, singer; Paolo Soleri, architect; Clyde W. Tombaugh, astronomer; Tanya Tucker, singer; Stewart Udall, former secretary of the Interior; Frank Lloyd Wright, architect.

Arkansas

Capital: Little Rock
Governor: Mike Huckabee, R (to Jan. 2003)
Lieut. Governor: Winthrop Rockefeller, R (to Jan. 2002)
Senators: Tim Hutchinson, R (to Jan. 2003);
  Blanche Lambert Lincoln, D (to Jan. 2005)
Secy. of State: Sharon Priest, D (to Jan. 2003)
Atty. General: Mark Pryor (to Jan. 2003)
Auditor of State: Gus Wingfield, D (to Jan. 2003)
Treasurer of State: Jimmie Lou Fisher, D
  (to Jan. 2003)

Land Commissioner: Charles Daniels, D
  (to Jan. 2003)
Organized as territory: March 2, 1819
Entered Union (rank): June 15, 1836 (25)
Present constitution adopted: 1874
Motto: *Regnat populus* (The people rule)
State Symbols: flower, apple blossom (1901); **tree,** pine (1939); **bird,** mockingbird (1929); **insect,** honeybee (1973); **song,** "Arkansas" (1963);
Nickname: The Natural State
Origin of name: From the Quapaw Indians
10 largest cities (2000): Little Rock, 183,133; Fort Smith, 80,268; North Little Rock, 60,433; Fayetteville, 58,047; Jonesboro, 55,515; Pine Bluff, 55,085; Springdale, 45,798; Conway, 43,167; Rogers, 38,829; Hot Springs, 35,750
Land area: 52,075 sq mi. (134,874 sq km)
Geographic center: In Pulaski Co., 12 mi. NW of Little Rock
Number of counties: 75
Largest county by population and area: Pulaski, 361,474 (2000); Union, 1,039 sq mi.
State parks: 50
Residents: Arkansan
2000 resident census population (rank): 2,673,400 (33). **Male:** 1,304,693 (48.8%); **Female:** 1,368,707 (51.2%). **White:** 2,138,598 (80.0%); **Black:** 418,950 (15.7%); **American Indian:** 17,808 (0.7%); **Asian:** 20,220 (0.8%); **Other race:** 40,412 (1.5%); **Two or more races:** 35,744 (1.3%); **Hispanic/Latino:** 86,866 (3.2%). **2000 percent population 18 and over:** 74.6; **65 and over:** 14.0; **median age:** 36.0.

Spaniard Hernando de Soto, in 1541, was among the early European explorers to visit the territory, but it was a Frenchman, Henri de Tonti, who in 1686 founded the first permanent white settlement—the Arkansas Post. In 1803 the area was acquired by the U.S. as part of the Louisiana Purchase.

Part of the Territory of Missouri from 1812, the area became a separate entity in 1819 after the first large wave of settlers arrived. The next several decades were marked by the development of the cotton industry and the spread of the Southern plantation system west into Arkansas. Arkansas joined the Confederacy in 1861, but from 1863 the northern part of the state was occupied by Union troops.

Food products are the state's largest employing sector, with lumber and wood products a close second. Arkansas is also a leader in the production of cotton, rice, and soybeans. It also has the country's only active diamond mine; located near Murfreesboro, it is operated as a tourist attraction.

Hot Springs National Park and Buffalo National River in the Ozarks are major state attractions. Blanchard Springs Caverns, the Arkansas Territorial Restoration at Little Rock, and the Arkansas Folk Center in Mountain View are also of interest.

Famous natives and residents: G. M. "Broncho Billy" Anderson, actor; Maya Angelou, author and poet; Katharine Susan Anthony, author; Helen Gurley Brown, editor; Glen Campbell, singer; Hattie Caraway, first elected woman senator; Johnny Cash, singer; Eldridge Cleaver, black activist; William Jefferson Clinton, 42nd President; Dizzy Dean, baseball player; Orval Faubus, former governor; John Gould Fletcher, writer; James W. Fulbright, former senator; John H. Johnson, publisher; Alan Ladd, actor; Douglas MacArthur, 5-star general; John Paul McConnell, U.S. Air Force officer; Ben Murphy, actor; Frank Pace, Jr., public official; Ben Piazza, actor; Albert Pike, pioneer teacher and lawyer; Dick Powell, actor; Opie P. Read, writer; Jenny D. Rice-Meyrowitz, painter; Brehon Burke Somervell, World Wars I and II U.S. Army officer; Mary Steenburgen, actress; Edward Durell Stone, architect; William C. Warfield, concert singer and actor.

California

Capital: Sacramento
Governor: Gray Davis, D (to Jan. 2003)
Lieut. Governor: Cruz M. Bustamante, D (to Jan. 2003)
Senators: Barbara Boxer, D (to Jan. 2005);
  Dianne Feinstein, D (to Jan. 2007)
Secy. of State: Bill Jones, R (to Jan. 2003)
Controller: Kathleen Connell, D (to Jan. 2003)
Atty. General: Bill Lockyer, D (to Jan. 2003)
Treasurer: Phil Angelides, D (to Jan. 2003)
Supt. of Public Instruction: Delaine Eastin
Entered Union (rank): Sept. 9, 1850 (31)
Present constitution adopted: 1879
Motto: *Eureka* (I have found it)
State Symbols: flower, golden poppy (1903); **tree,** California redwoods (*Sequoia sempervirens & Sequoia gigantea*) (1937, 1953); **bird,** California valley quail (1931); **animal,** California grizzly bear (1953); **fish,** California golden trout (1947); **colors,** blue and gold (1951); **song,** "I Love You, California" (1951);
Nickname: Golden State
Origin of name: From a book, *Las Sergas de Esplandián*, by Garcia Ordóñez de Montalvo, c. 1500
10 largest cities (2000): Los Angeles, 3,694,820; San Diego, 1,223,400; San Jose, 894,943; San Francisco, 776,733; Long Beach, 461,522; Fresno, 427,652; Sacramento, 407,018; Oakland, 399,484; Santa Ana, 337,977; Anaheim, 328,014
Land area: 155,973 sq mi. (403,970 sq km)
Geographic center: In Madera Co., 35 mi. NE of Madera
Number of counties: 58
Largest county by population and area: Los Angeles, 9,519,338 (2000); San Bernardino, 20,062 sq mi.
National forests: 18
State parks and beaches: 264
Residents: Californian
2000 resident census population (rank): 33,871,648 (1). **Male:** 16,874,892 (49.8%); **Female:** 16,996,756 (50.2%). **White:** 20,170,059 (59.5%); **Black:** 2,263,882 (6.7%); **American Indian:** 333,346 (1.0%); **Asian:** 3,697,513 (10.9%); **Other race:** 5,682,241 (16.8%); **Two or more races:** 1,607,646 (4.7%); **Hispanic/Latino:** 10,966,556 (32.4%). **2000 percent population 18 and over:** 72.7; **65 and over:** 10.6; **median age:** 33.3.

Although California was sighted by Spanish navigator Juan Rodríguez Cabrillo in 1542, its first Spanish mission (at San Diego) was not established until 1769. California became a U.S. territory in 1847 when Mexico surrendered it to John C. Frémont. On Jan. 24, 1848, James W. Marshall discovered gold at Sutter's Mill, starting the California Gold Rush and bringing settlers to the state in large numbers. In 1964, the U.S. Census Bureau estimated that California had become the most populous state, surpassing New York. One reason for this may be that more immigrants settle in California than any other state—more than one-third of the nation's total in 1994. Asians and Pacific Islanders led the influx.

Leading industries include agriculture, manufacturing (transportation equipment, machinery, and electronic equipment), biotechnology, aerospace-defense, and tourism. Principal natural resources include timber, petroleum, cement, and natural gas.

Death Valley, in the southeast, is 282 ft below sea level, the lowest point in the nation. Mt. Whitney (14,491 ft) is the highest point in the contiguous 48 states. Lassen Peak is one of two active U.S. volca-noes outside of Alaska and Hawaii; its last eruptions were recorded in 1917.

Other points of interest include Yosemite National Park, Disneyland, Hollywood, the Golden Gate Bridge, Sequoia National Park, San Simeon State Park, and Point Reyes National Seashore.

Famous natives and residents: Gertrude Atherton, author; David Belasco, playwright and producer; Shirley Temple Black, actress, ambassador; Dave Brubeck, musician; Luther Burbank, horticulturalist; Julia Child, chef; Joe DiMaggio, baseball player; James H. Doolittle, air force general; Isadora Duncan, dancer; John Frémont, explorer; Robert Frost, poet; Henry George, economist; Richard "Pancho" Gonzales, tennis player; George E. Hale, astronomer; Bret Harte, writer; William Randolph Hearst, publisher; Sidney Howard, playwright; Collis Potter Huntington, financier; Helen Hunt Jackson, writer; Robinson Jeffers, poet; Anthony M. Kennedy, jurist; Jack London, author; James W. Marshall, first discovered gold; Aimee Semple McPherson, evangelist; Marilyn Monroe, actress; John Muir, naturalist; Richard M. Nixon, President; Isamu Noguchi, sculptor; Frank Norris, novelist; Kathleen Norris, novelist; George S. Patton, Jr., general; Robert Redford, actor; Sally K. Ride, astronaut; William Saroyan, author; Junípero Serra, missionary; Upton Sinclair, novelist; Leland Stanford, railroad magnate; Lincoln Steffens, journalist, author; John Steinbeck, author; Adlai Stevenson, statesman; Johann Sutter, pioneer; Michael Tilson Thomas, conductor; Earl Warren, jurist.

Colorado

Capital: Denver
Governor: Bill Owens, R (to Jan. 2003)
Lieut. Governor: Joe Rogers, D (to Jan. 2003)
Senators: Wayne A. Allard, R (to Jan. 2003);
  Ben Nighthorse Campbell, R (to Jan. 2005)
Secy. of State: Donetta Davidson, R (to Jan. 2003)
Treasurer: Mike Coffman, R (to Jan. 2003)
Controller: Arthur Barnhart
Atty. General: Ken Salazar, D (to Jan. 2003)
Organized as territory: Feb. 28, 1861
Entered Union (rank): Aug. 1, 1876 (38)
Present constitution adopted: 1876
Motto: *Nil sine Numine* (Nothing without Providence)
State Symbols: flower, Rocky Mountain columbine (1899); **tree,** Colorado blue spruce (1939); **bird,** lark bunting (1931); **animal,** Rocky Mountain bighorn sheep (1961); **gemstone,** aquamarine (1971); **colors,** blue and white (1911); **song,** "Where the Columbines Grow" (1915); **fossil,** stegosaurus (1991);
Nickname: Centennial State
Origin of name: From the Spanish, "ruddy" or "red"
10 largest cities (2000): Denver, 554,636; Colorado Springs, 360,890; Aurora, 276,393; Lakewood, 144,126; Fort Collins, 118,652; Arvada, 102,153; Pueblo, 102,121; Westminster, 100,940; Boulder, 94,673; Thornton, 82,384
Land area: 103,730 sq mi. (268,660 sq km)
Geographic center: In Park Co., 30 mi. NW of Pikes Peak
Number of counties: 63
Largest county by population and area: Denver, 554,636 (2000); Las Animas, 4,773 sq mi.
State forests: 1 (71,000 ac.)
State parks: 44 (160,000 ac.)
Residents: Coloradan, Coloradoan
2000 resident census population (rank): 4,301,261 (24). **Male:** 2,165,983 (50.4%); **Female:** 2,135,278 (49.6%). **White:** 3,560,005 (82.8%); **Black:** 165,063 (3.8%); **American Indian:** 44,241 (1.0%); **Asian:** 95,213 (2.2%); **Other race:** 309,931 (7.2%); **Two or more races:** 122,187 (2.8%); **Hispanic/Latino:** 735,601 (17.1%). **2000 percent population 18 and over:** 74.4; **65 and over:** 9.7; **median age:** 34.3.

First visited by Spanish explorers in the 1500s, the territory was claimed for Spain by Juan de Ulibarri in 1706. The U.S. obtained eastern Colorado as part of the Louisiana Purchase in 1803, the central portion in 1845 with the admission of Texas as a state, and the western part in 1848 as a result of the Mexican War.

Colorado has the highest mean elevation of any state, with more than 1,000 Rocky Mountain peaks over 10,000 ft high and 54 towering above 14,000 ft. Pikes Peak, the most famous of these mountains, was discovered by U.S. Army lieutenant Zebulon M. Pike in 1806.

Once primarily a mining and agricultural state, Colorado's economy is now driven by the service industries, including medical providers and other business and professional services. Colorado's economy also has a strong manufacturing base. The primary manufactures are food products, printing and publishing, machinery, and electrical instruments. The state is also a communications and transportation hub for the Rocky Mountain region.

Breathtaking scenery and world-class skiing make Colorado a prime tourist destination. The main tourist attractions in the state include Rocky Mountain National Park, Mesa Verde National Park, the Great Sand Dunes and Dinosaur National Monuments, Colorado National Monument, and the Black Canyon of the Gunnison National Monument.

The farm industry, which is primarily concentrated in livestock, is also an important element of the state's economy. The primary crops in Colorado are corn, hay, and wheat.

Famous natives and residents: Tim Allen, actor and comedian; William E. Barrett, writer; William Bent, fur trader and pioneer; Charles F. Brannan, lawyer and public official; M. Scott Carpenter, astronaut; Lon Chaney, actor; Mary Coyle Chase, playwright; Jack Dempsey, boxer; John Evans, physician, educator; Douglas Fairbanks, actor; Eugene Fodor, violinist; Gene Fowler, writer; Erick Hawkins, choreographer; Homer Lea, soldier, writer; Ted Mack, TV host; Jaye P. Morgan, singer; Peg Murray, actress; Ouray, Ute Indian chief; Anne Parrish, writer; Barbara Rush, actress; Horace A. Tabor, silver king and lieut. governor; Lowell Thomas, commentator and author; Dalton Trumbo, screenwriter, novelist; Byron R. White, jurist; Paul Whiteman, conductor; Don Wilson, announcer.

Connecticut

Capital: Hartford
Governor: John G. Rowland, R (to Jan. 2003)
Lieut. Governor: M. Jodi Rell, R (to Jan. 2003)
Senators: Christopher J. Dodd, D (to Jan. 2005); Joseph I. Lieberman, D (to Jan. 2007)
Secy. of the State: Susan Bysiewicz, D (to Jan. 2003)
Comptroller: Nancy Wyman, D (to Jan. 2003)
Treasurer: Denise Nappier, D (to Jan. 2003)
Atty. General: Richard Blumenthal, D (to Jan. 2003)
Entered Union (rank): Jan. 9, 1788 (5)
Present constitution adopted: Dec. 30, 1965
Motto: *Qui transtulit sustinet* (He who transplanted still sustains)
State Symbols: flower, mountain laurel (1907); **tree,** white oak (1947); **animal,** sperm whale (1975); **bird,** American robin (1943); **hero,** Nathan Hale (1985); **heroine,** Prudence Crandall (1995); **insect,** praying mantis (1977); **mineral,** garnet (1977); **song,** "Yankee Doodle" (1978); **ship,** USS *Nautilus* (1983); **shellfish,** eastern oyster (1989); **fossil,** *Eubrontes Giganteus* (1991); **composer,** Charles Edward Ives (1991);
Nickname: Constitution State (official, 1959); Nutmeg State

Origin of name: From an Indian word (Quinnehtukqut) meaning "beside the long tidal river"
10 largest cities (2000): Bridgeport, 139,529; New Haven, 123,626; Hartford, 121,578; Stamford, 117,083; Waterbury, 107,271; Norwalk, 82,951; Danbury, 74,848; New Britain, 71,538; West Hartford, 63,589; Greenwich, 61,101
Land area: 4,845 sq mi. (12,550 sq km)
Geographic center: In Hartford Co., at East Berlin
Number of counties: 8
Largest county by population and area: Fairfield, 882,567 (2000); Litchfield, 920 sq mi.
State forests: 30 (149,352 ac.)
State parks: 93 (32,868 ac.)
Residents: Connecticuter; Nutmegger
2000 resident census population (rank): 3,405,565 (29). **Male:** 1,649,319 (48.4%); **Female:** 1,756,246 (51.6%). **White:** 2,780,355 (81.6%); **Black:** 309,843 (9.1%); **American Indian:** 9,639 (0.3%); **Asian:** 82,313 (2.4%); **Other race:** 147,201 (4.3%); **Two or more races:** 74,848 (2.2%); **Hispanic/Latino:** 320,323 (9.4%). **2000 percent population 18 and over:** 75.3; **65 and over:** 13.8; **median age:** 37.4.

The Dutch navigator, Adriaen Block, was the first European of record to explore the area, sailing up the Connecticut River in 1614. In 1633, Dutch colonists built a fort and trading post near present-day Hartford but soon lost control to English Puritans from the Massachusetts Bay Colony. English settlements, established in the 1630s at Windsor, Wethersfield, and Hartford, united in 1639 to form the Connecticut Colony and adopted the *Fundamental Orders.*

Connecticut played a prominent role in the Revolutionary War, serving as the Continental Army's major supplier. Sometimes called the "Arsenal of the Nation," the state became one of the most industrialized in the nation.

Today, Connecticut factories produce weapons, sewing machines, jet engines, helicopters, motors, hardware and tools, cutlery, clocks, locks, silverware, and submarines. Hartford has the oldest U.S. newspaper still being published—the *Hartford Courant,* established 1764—and is the insurance capital of the nation.

Connecticut leads New England in the production of eggs, pears, peaches, and mushrooms, and its oyster crop is the nation's second largest. Poultry and dairy products also account for a large portion of farm income.

Connecticut is a popular resort area with its 250-mile Long Island Sound shoreline and many inland lakes. Among the major points of interest are Yale University's Gallery of Fine Arts and Peabody Museum. Other famous museums include the P. T. Barnum, Winchester Gun, and American Clock and Watch. The town of Mystic features a recreated 19th-century New England seaport and the Mystic Marinelife Aquarium.

Famous natives and residents: Dean Acheson, statesman; Ethan Allan, American Revolutionary soldier; Benedict Arnold, American Revolutionary general; P. T. Barnum, showman; Henry Ward Beecher, clergyman; John Brown, abolitionist; Oliver Ellsworth, jurist; Eileen Farrell, soprano; Charles Goodyear, inventor; Nathan Hale, American Revolutionary officer; Dorothy Hamill, ice skater; Katharine Hepburn, actress; Charles Ives, composer; Edwin H. Land, inventor; John Pierpont Morgan, financier; Frederick Law Olmsted, landscape designer; Rosa Ponselle, soprano; Adam Clayton Powell, Jr., congressman; Benjamin Spock, pediatrician; Harriet Beecher Stowe, author; Mark Twain, author; Morris R. Waite, jurist; Noah Webster, lexicographer.

Delaware

Capital: Dover
Governor: Ruth Ann Minner, D (to Jan. 2005)
Lieut. Governor: John C. Carney, Jr., D (to Jan. 2005)
Senators: Joseph R. Biden, Jr., D (to Jan. 2003);
Thomas R. Carper, D (to Jan. 2007)
Secy. of State: Edward J. Freel, D (pleasure
of governor)
State Treasurer: Jack Markell, D (to Jan. 2002)
Atty. General: M. Jane Brady, R (to Jan. 2002)
Entered Union (rank): Dec. 7, 1787 (1)
Present constitution adopted: 1897
Motto: Liberty and independence
State Symbols: colors, colonial blue and buff; **flower,**
peach blossom (1895); **tree,** American holly (1939);
bird, blue hen chicken (1939); **insect,** ladybug (1974);
fish, weakfish, *cynoscion regalis* (1981); **song,** "Our
Delaware";
Nicknames: Diamond State; First State; Small Wonder
Origin of name: From Delaware River and Bay; named
in turn for Sir Thomas West, Baron De La War
10 largest cities (2000): Wilmington, 72,664; Dover,
32,135; Newark, 28,547; Milford, 6,732; Seaford,
6,699; Middletown, 6,161; Elsmere, 5,800; Smyrna,
5,679; New Castle, 4,862; Georgetown, 4,643
Land area: 1,955 sq mi. (5,153 sq km)
Geographic center: In Kent Co., 11 mi. S of Dover
Number of counties: 3
Largest county by population and area: New Castle,
500,265 (2000); Sussex, 938 sq mi.
State forests: 3 (9,353 ac.)
State parks: 13
Residents: Delawarean
2000 resident census population (rank): 783,600 (45).
Male: 380,541 (48.6%); **Female:** 403,059 (51.4%).
White: 584,773 (74.6%); **Black:** 150,666 (19.2%);
American Indian: 2,731 (0.3%); **Asian:** 16,259 (2.1%);
Other race: 15,855 (2.0%); **Two or more races:**
13,033 (1.7%); **Hispanic/Latino:** 37,277 (4.8%). **2000
percent population 18 and over:** 75.2; **65 and over:**
13.0; **median age:** 36.0.

Henry Hudson, sailing under the Dutch flag, is
credited with Delaware's discovery in 1609. The
following year, Capt. Samuel Argall of Virginia
named Delaware for his colony's governor, Thomas
West, Baron De La Warr. An attempted Dutch settlement failed in 1631. Swedish colonization began at
Fort Christina (now Wilmington) in 1638, but New
Sweden fell to Dutch forces led by New Netherlands' governor Peter Stuyvesant in 1655.

England took over the area in 1664, and it was
transferred to William Penn as the southern Three
Counties in 1682. Semiautonomous after 1704,
Delaware fought as a separate state in the American
Revolution and became the first state to ratify the
Constitution in 1787.

During the Civil War, although a slave state,
Delaware did not secede from the Union.

In 1802, Éleuthère Irénée du Pont established a
gunpowder mill near Wilmington that laid the foundation for Delaware's huge chemical industry. Delaware's manufactured products now also include vul-
canized fiber, textiles, paper, medical supplies, metal
products, machinery, machine tools, and automobiles.

Delaware also grows a great variety of fruits and
vegetables and is a U.S. pioneer in the food-canning
industry. Corn, soybeans, potatoes, and hay are
important crops. Delaware's broiler-chicken farms
supply the big Eastern markets, and fishing and
dairy products are other important industries.

Points of interest include the Fort Christina
Monument, Hagley Museum, Holy Trinity Church
(erected in 1698, the oldest Protestant church in the
United States still in use), and Winterthur Museum,
in and near Wilmington; central New Castle, an
almost unchanged late 18th-century capital; and the
Delaware Museum of Natural History.

Popular recreation areas include Cape Henlopen,
Delaware Seashore, Trapp Pond State Park, and
Rehoboth Beach.

Famous natives and residents: Richard Allen, founder of
the African Methodist Episcopal Church; Valerie Bertinelli,
actress; Robert Montgomery Bird, writer and artist; Henry
S. Canby, editor and author; Annie Jump Cannon,
astronomer; Elizabeth Margaret Chandler, author; Felix
Darley, artist; John Dickinson, statesman; E. I. du Pont,
industrialist; Oliver Evans, inventor; Thomas Garrett,
abolitionist; Henry Heimlich, surgeon, inventor; William
Julius "Judy" Johnson, baseball player; J. P. Marquand,
novelist; Howard Pyle, artist and author; George Read,
jurist, signer of Declaration of Independence; Jay
Saunders Redding, educator and author; Caesar Rodney,
patriot, signer of Declaration of Independence; Frank
Stephens, sculptor; Estelle Taylor, actress; George Alfred
Townsend, journalist and author.

District of Columbia

See Washington, D.C., listing in U.S. Cities.

Florida

Capital: Tallahassee
Governor: Jeb Bush, R (to Jan. 2003)
Lieut. Governor: Frank Brogan, R (to Jan. 2003)
Senators: Bob Graham, D (to Jan. 2005); Bill Nelson, D
(to Jan. 2007)
Secy. of State: Katherine Harris, R (to Jan. 2003)
Comptroller: Bob Milligan, R (to Jan. 2003)
Commissioner of Agriculture: Charles H. Bronson, R
(to Jan. 2003)
Atty. General: Bob Butterworth, D (to Jan. 2003)
Organized as territory: March 30, 1821
Entered Union (rank): March 3, 1845 (27)
Present constitution adopted: 1969
Motto: In God we trust (1868)
State Symbols: flower, orange blossom (1909); **bird,**
mockingbird (1927); **song,** "Suwannee River" (1935);
Nickname: Sunshine State (1970)
Origin of name: From the Spanish, meaning "feast of
flowers" (Easter)
10 largest cities (2000): Jacksonville, 735,617; Miami,
362,470; Tampa, 303,447; St. Petersburg, 248,232;
Hialeah, 226,419; Orlando, 185,951; Fort Lauderdale,
152,397; Tallahassee, 150,624; Hollywood, 139,357;
Pembroke Pines, 137,427
Land area: 54,153 sq mi. (140,256 sq km)
Geographic center: In Hernando Co., 12 mi. NNW of
Brooksville
Number of counties: 67
Largest county by population and area: Miami-Dade,
2,253,362 (2000); Palm Beach, 2,034 sq mi.
State forests: 31 (more than 890,000 ac.)
State parks: 151 (523,920 ac.)
Residents: Floridian, Florida
2000 resident census population (rank): 15,982,378
(4). **Male:** 7,797,715 (48.8%); **Female:** 8,184,663
(51.2%). **White:** 12,465,029 (78.0%); **Black:**
2,335,505 (14.6%); **American Indian:** 53,541 (0.3%);
Asian: 266,256 (1.7%); **Other race:** 477,107 (3.0%);
Two or more races: 376,315 (2.4%); **Hispanic/
Latino:** 2,682,715 (16.8%). **2000 percent population
18 and over:** 77.2; **65 and over:** 17.6; **median age:**
38.7.

In 1513, Ponce de León, seeking the mythical
"Fountain of Youth," discovered and named Florida,

claiming it for Spain. Later, Florida would be held at different times by Spain and England until Spain finally sold it to the United States in 1819. (Incidentally, France established a colony named Fort Caroline in 1564 in the state that was to become Florida.)

Florida's history in the early 19th century was marked by wars with the Seminole Indians, which did not end until 1842.

Florida's economy rests on a solid base of tourism, manufacturing, and agriculture. Leading the manufacturing sector are electrical equipment and electronics, printing and publishing, transportation equipment, food processing, and machinery. Oranges, grapefruit, and other citrus fruits lead Florida's agricultural products list, followed by potatoes, melons, strawberries, sugar cane, peanuts, dairy products, and cattle.

Major tourist attractions are Miami Beach, Palm Beach, St. Augustine (founded in 1565, thus the oldest permanent city in the U.S.), Daytona Beach, and Fort Lauderdale on the East Coast; Sarasota, Tampa, and St. Petersburg on the West Coast; and Key West off the southern tip of Florida. The Orlando area, where Disney World is located on a 27,000-acre site, is Florida's most popular tourist destination. Also drawing many visitors are the NASA Kennedy Space Center's Spaceport USA, Everglades National Park, and the Epcot Center.

Famous natives and residents: Julian "Cannonball" Adderley, jazz saxophonist; Pat Boone, singer; Fernando Bujones, ballet dancer; Steve Carlton, baseball player; Faye Dunaway, actress; Stepin Fetchit (Lincoln Theodore Perry), comedian; Lue Gim Gong, horticulturist; Dwight Gooden, baseball player; Zora Neale Hurston, writer; Daniel James, four-star general; James Weldon Johnson, author and educator; Frances Langford, singer; Butterfly McQueen, actress; Jim Morrison, singer; Osceola, Seminole Indian leader; Sidney Poitier, actor; A. Philip Randolph, labor leader; Marjorie Kinnan Rawlings, author; Burt Reynolds, actor; Charles and John Ringling, circus entrepreneurs; Joseph W. Stilwell, army general; Norman E. Thargard, astronaut; Clarence Thomas, jurist; Ben Vereen, actor.

Georgia

Capital: Atlanta
Governor: Roy E. Barnes, D (to Jan. 2003)
Lieut. Governor: Mark Taylor, D (to Jan. 2003)
Senators: Max Cleland, D (to Jan. 2003);
Zell Miller, D (to Jan. 2005)
Secy. of State: Cathy Cox, D (to Jan. 2003)
Insurance Commissioner: John Oxendine, R (to Jan. 2003)
Atty. General: Thurbert Baker, D (to Jan. 2003)
Entered Union (rank): Jan. 2, 1788 (4)
Present constitution adopted: 1977
Motto: Wisdom, justice, and moderation
State Symbols: flower, Cherokee rose (1916); **tree,** live oak (1937); **bird,** brown thrasher (1935); **song,** "Georgia on My Mind" (1922);
Nicknames: Peach State, Empire State of the South
Origin of name: In honor of George II of England
10 largest cities (2000): Atlanta, 416,474; Augusta-Richmond County[1], 199,775; Columbus[1], 186,291; Savannah, 131,510; Athens-Clarke County[1], 101,489; Macon, 97,255; Roswell, 79,334; Albany, 76,939; Marietta, 58,748; Warner Robins, 48,804
Land area: 57,919 sq mi. (150,010 sq km)
Geographic center: In Twiggs Co., 18 mi. SE of Macon
Number of counties: 159
Largest county by population and area: Fulton, 816,006 (2000); Ware, 903 sq mi.

State forests: 25,258,000 ac. (67% of total state area)
State parks: 53 (42,600 ac.)
Residents: Georgian
2000 resident census population (rank): 8,186,453 (10). **Male:** 4,027,113 (49.2%); **Female:** 4,159,340 (50.8%). **White:** 5,327,281 (65.1%); **Black:** 2,349,542 (28.7%); **American Indian:** 21,737 (0.3%); **Asian:** 173,170 (2.1%); **Other race:** 196,289 (2.4%); **Two or more races:** 114,188 (1.4%); **Hispanic/Latino:** 435,227 (5.3%). **2000 percent population 18 and over:** 73.5; **65 and over:** 9.6; **median age:** 33.4.

1. The city is part of a consolidated city-county government; the city and county are coextensive.

Hernando de Soto, the Spanish explorer, first traveled parts of Georgia in 1540. British claims later conflicted with those of Spain. After obtaining a royal charter, Gen. James Oglethorpe established the first permanent settlement in Georgia in 1733 as a refuge for English debtors. In 1742, Oglethorpe defeated Spanish invaders in the Battle of Bloody Marsh.

A Confederate stronghold, Georgia was the scene of extensive military action during the Civil War. Union general William T. Sherman burned Atlanta and destroyed a 60-mile-wide path to the coast, where he captured Savannah in 1864.

The largest state east of the Mississippi, Georgia is typical of the changing South with an ever-increasing industrial development. Atlanta, largest city in the state, is the communications and transportation center for the Southeast and the area's chief distributor of goods.

Georgia leads the nation in the production of paper and board, tufted textile products, and processed chicken. Other major manufactured products are transportation equipment, food products, apparel, and chemicals.

Important agricultural products are corn, cotton, tobacco, soybeans, eggs, and peaches. Georgia produces twice as many peanuts as the next leading state. From its vast stands of pine come more than half of the world's resins and turpentine and 74.4 percent of the U.S. supply. Georgia is a leader in the production of marble, kaolin, barite, and bauxite.

Principal tourist attractions in Georgia include the Okefenokee National Wildlife Refuge, Andersonville Prison Park and National Cemetery, Chickamauga and Chattanooga National Military Park, the Little White House at Warm Springs where Pres. Franklin D. Roosevelt died in 1945, Sea Island, the enormous Confederate Memorial at Stone Mountain, Kennesaw Mountain National Battlefield Park, and Cumberland Island National Seashore.

Famous natives and residents: Conrad Aiken, poet; James Bowie, soldier; James Brown, singer; Jim Brown, actor and athlete; Erskine Caldwell, writer; James E. Carter, former president; Ray Charles, singer; Lucius D. Clay, banker and former general; Ty Cobb, baseball player; Ossie Davis, actor and writer; James Dickey, poet; Melvyn Douglas, actor; Rebecca Latimer Felton, first appointed woman U.S. senator; Roosevelt Grier, entertainer and former athlete; Oliver Hardy, comedian; Joel Chandler Harris, journalist and author; Larry Holmes, boxer; Miriam Hopkins, actress; Harry James, trumpeter; Jasper Johns, painter and sculptor; Bobby Jones, golfer; Stacy Keach, actor; DeForest Kelley, actor; Martin Luther King, Jr., civil rights leader; Gladys Knight, singer; Joseph R. Lamar, jurist; Little Richard, singer; Juliette Gordon Low, U.S. Girl Scouts founder; Carson McCullers, novelist; Johnny Mercer, songwriter; Margaret Mitchell, novelist; Elijah Muhammad, religious leader; Jessye Norman, soprano; Otis Redding, singer; Burt Reynolds, actor; Jackie Robinson, baseball player; Dean Rusk, former secretary of state; Nipsey Russell, comedian; Alice Walker, author; Joanne Woodward, actress.

Hawaii

Capital: Honolulu (on Oahu)
Governor: Benjamin Cayetano, D (to Dec. 2002)
Lieut. Governor: Mazie Hirono, D
Senators: Daniel K. Akaka, D (to Jan. 2007); Daniel K. Inouye, D (to Jan. 2005)
Comptroller: Wayne Kimura (to Dec. 2002)
Atty. General: Earl Anzai (to Dec. 2002)
Organized as territory: 1900
Entered Union (rank): Aug. 21, 1959 (50)
Motto: *Ua Mau Ke Ea O Ka Aina I Ka Pono* (The life of the land is perpetuated in righteousness)
State Symbols: flower, hibiscus (yellow) (1988); **song,** "Hawaii Ponoi" (1967); **bird,** nene (hawaiian goose) (1957); **tree,** kukui (candlenut) (1959);
Nickname: Aloha State (1959)
Origin of name: Uncertain. The islands may have been named by Hawaii Loa, their traditional discoverer. Or they may have been named after Hawaii or Hawaiki, the traditional home of the Polynesians.
10 largest cities[1] (2000): Honolulu, 371,657; Hilo, 40,759; Kailua, 36,513; Kaneohe, 34,970; Waipahu, 33,108; Pearl City, 30,976; Waimalu, 29,371; Mililani Town, 28,608; Kahului, 20,146; Kihei, 16,749
Land area: 6,423 sq mi. (16,637 sq km)
Geographic center: Between islands of Hawaii and Maui
Number of counties: Five (Kalawao non-functioning)
Largest county by population and area: Honolulu, 876,156 (2000); Hawaii, 4,028 sq mi.
State parks and historic sites: 69
Residents: Hawaiian, also kamaaina (native-born nonethnic Hawaiian), malihini (newcomer)
2000 resident census population (rank): 1,211,537 (42). **Male:** 608,671 (50.2%); **Female:** 602,866 (49.8%). **White:** 294,102 (24.3%); **Black:** 22,003 (1.8%); **American Indian:** 3,535 (0.3%); **Asian:** 503,868 (41.6%); **Native Hawaiian and Other Pacific Islander:** 113,539 (9.4%); **Other race:** 15,147 (1.3%); **Two or more races:** 259,343 (21.4%); **Hispanic/Latino:** 87,699 (7.2%). **2000 percent population 18 and over:** 75.6; **65 and over:** 13.3; **median age:** 36.2.

1. Census Designated Places. There are no political boundaries to Honolulu or any other place, but statistical boundaries are assigned under state law.

First settled by Polynesians sailing from other Pacific islands between A.D. 300 and 600, Hawaii was visited in 1778 by British captain James Cook, who called the group the Sandwich Islands.

Hawaii was a native kingdom throughout most of the 19th century, when the expansion of the sugar industry (pineapple came after 1898) meant increasing U.S. business and political involvement. In 1893, Queen Liliuokalani was deposed, and a year later the Republic of Hawaii was established with Sanford B. Dole as president. Following annexation (1898), Hawaii became a U.S. territory in 1900.

The Japanese attack on the naval base at Pearl Harbor on Dec. 7, 1941, was directly responsible for U.S. entry into World War II.

Hawaii, 2,397 mi west-southwest of San Francisco, is a 1,523-mile chain of islets and eight main islands—Hawaii, Kahoolawe, Maui, Lanai, Molokai, Oahu, Kauai, and Niihau. The Northwestern Hawaiian Islands, other than Midway, are administratively part of Hawaii.

The temperature is mild, and cane sugar, pineapple, and flowers and nursery products are the chief products. Hawaii also grows coffee beans, bananas, and macadamia nuts. The tourist business is Hawaii's largest source of outside income.

Hawaii's highest peak is Mauna Kea (13,796 ft). Mauna Loa (13,679 ft) is the largest volcanic mountain in the world by volume.

Among the major points of interest are Hawaii Volcanoes National Park (Hawaii), Haleakala National Park (Maui), Puuhonua o Honaunau National Historical Park (Hawaii), Polynesian Cultural Center (Oahu), the USS *Arizona* and USS *Missouri* Memorial at Pearl Harbor, The National Memorial Cemetery of the Pacific (Oahu), and Iolani Palace (the only royal palace in the U.S.), Bishop Museum, and Waikiki Beach (all in Honolulu).

Famous natives and residents: Salevaa Atisanoe (Konishiki), sumo wrestler; George Ariyoshi, first Japanese-American elected governor; Angela Perez Baraquio, Miss America (2001); Tia Carrere, singer, actress; Steve Case, business executive; Father Damien, priest; Hiram L. Fong, first Chinese-American senator; Don Ho, entertainer; Kaahumanu, Hawaiian queen; Duke Paoa Kahanamoku, Olympic swimming champion; Kamehameha I, first Hawaiian king; Kamehameha V, last of the dynasty; Liliuokalani, queen, last Hawaiian monarch; Bette Midler, singer; Ellison Onizuka, astronaut; Chad Rowan (Akebono), sumo wrestler; Harold Sakata, actor; Carolyn Suzanne Sapp, Miss America (1991); James Shigeta, actor; Don Stroud, actor; John Waihee, first Hawaiian elected governor.

Idaho

Capital: Boise
Governor: Dirk Kempthorne, R (to Jan. 2003)
Lieut. Governor: Jack T. Riggs, MD, R (to Jan. 2003)
Senators: Larry E. Craig, R (to Jan. 2003); Mike Crapo, R (to Jan. 2005)
Secy. of State: Pete T. Cenarrusa, R (to Jan. 2003)
State Controller: J. D. Williams, D (to Jan. 2003)
Atty. General: Alan G. Lance, R (to Jan. 2003)
Treasurer: Ron G. Crane, R (to Jan. 2003)
Organized as territory: March 3, 1863
Entered Union (rank): July 3, 1890 (43)
Present constitution adopted: 1890
Motto: *Esto perpetua* (It is forever)
State Symbols: flower, syringa (1931); **tree,** white pine (1935); **bird,** mountain bluebird (1931); **horse,** Appaloosa (1975); **gem,** star garnet (1967); **song,** "Here We Have Idaho"; **folk dance,** square dance; **fish,** cutthroat trout (1990); **fossil,** Hagerman horse fossil (1988);
Nickname: Gem State
Origin of name: Though popularly believed to be an Indian word, it is an invented name whose meaning is unknown.
10 largest cities (2000): Boise, 185,787; Nampa, 51,867; Pocatello, 51,466; Idaho Falls, 50,730; Meridian, 34,919; Coeur d'Alene, 34,514; Twin Falls, 34,469; Lewiston, 30,904; Caldwell, 25,967; Moscow, 21,291
Land area: 82,751 sq mi. (214,325 sq km)
Geographic center: In Custer Co., at Custer, SW of Challis
Number of counties: 44, plus small part of Yellowstone National Park
Largest county by population and area: Ada, 300,904 (2000); Idaho, 8,485 sq mi.
State forests: 881,000 ac.
State parks: 27
Residents: Idahoan
2000 resident census population (rank): 1,293,953 (39). **Male:** 648,660 (50.1%); **Female:** 645,293 (49.9%). **White:** 1,177,304 (91.0%); **Black:** 5,456 (0.4%); **American Indian:** 17,645 (1.4%); **Asian:** 11,889 (0.9%); **Other race:** 54,742 (4.2%); **Two or more races:** 25,609 (2.0%); **Hispanic/Latino:** 101,690 (7.9%). **2000 percent population 18 and over:** 71.5; **65 and over:** 11.3; **median age:** 33.2.

After its acquisition by the U.S. as part of the Louisiana Purchase in 1803, the region was explored by Meriwether Lewis and William Clark in 1805–1806. Northwest boundary disputes with Great Britain were settled by the Oregon Treaty in 1846, and the first permanent U.S. settlement in Idaho was established by the Mormons at Franklin in 1860.

After gold was discovered at Orofino Creek in 1860, prospectors swarmed into the territory, but they left little more than a number of ghost towns.

In the 1870s, growing white occupation of Indian lands led to a series of battles between U.S. forces and the Nez Percé, Bannock, and Sheepeater tribes.

Mining and lumbering have been important for years. Idaho ranks high among the states in silver, antimony, lead, cobalt, garnet, phosphate rock, vanadium, zinc, and mercury.

Agriculture is a major industry: The state produces about one fourth of the nation's potato crop, as well as wheat, apples, corn, barley, sugar beets, and hops.

The 1990s have seen a remarkable growth in the high technology industries, concentrated in the metropolitan Boise area.

With the growth of winter sports, tourism now outranks other industries in revenue. Idaho's many streams and lakes provide fishing, camping, and boating sites. The nation's largest elk herds draw hunters from all over the world, and the famed Sun Valley resort attracts thousands of visitors to its swimming, golfing, and skiing facilities.

Points of interest are the Craters of the Moon National Monument; Nez Percé National Historic Park, which includes many sites visited by Lewis and Clark; and the State Historical Museum in Boise. Other attractions are the Snake River Birds of Prey National Conservation Area south of Boise, Hells Canyon on the Idaho-Oregon border, and the Sawtooth National Recreation Area in south-central Idaho.

Famous natives and residents: Joe Albertson, grocery chain founder; Cecil Andrus, former governor; T. H. Bell, educator; Ezra Taft Benson, former secretary of Agriculture, pres. LDS church, marketing specialist; William E. Borah, former senator; Gutzon Borglum, Mt. Rushmore sculptor; Carol R. Brink, author; Frank F. Church, former senator; Fred Dubois, senator; Vardis Fisher, novelist; Lawrence H. Gipson, historian; Ernest Hemingway, author; Mariel Hemingway, actress; Chief Joseph, Nez Percé chief; Harmon Killebrew, baseball player; Jerry Kramer, football player, author; Ezra Pound, poet; Sacagawea, Shoshonean guide; J. R. Simplot, industrialist; Robert E. Smylie, political leader; Henry Spalding, missionary; Frank Steunenberg, former governor; Picabo Street, skier; David Tompson, founded first trading post; Lana Turner, actress.

Illinois

Capital: Springfield
Governor: George H. Ryan, R (to Jan. 2003)
Lieut. Governor: Corinne G. Wood, R (to Jan. 2003)
Senators: Richard J. Durbin, D (to Jan. 2003); Peter G. Fitzgerald, R (to Jan. 2005)
Atty. General: Jim Ryan, R (to Jan. 2003)
Secy. of State: Jesse White, D (to Jan. 2003)
Comptroller: Daniel W. Hynes, D (to Jan. 2003)
Treasurer: Judith Barr Topinka, R (to Jan. 2003)
Organized as territory: Feb. 3, 1809
Entered Union (rank): Dec. 3, 1818 (21)
Present constitution adopted: 1970
Motto: State sovereignty, national union

State Symbols: flower, violet (1908); **tree,** white oak (1973); **bird,** cardinal (1929); **animal,** white-tailed deer (1982); **fish,** bluegill (1987); **insect,** monarch butterfly (1975); **song,** "Illinois" (1925); **mineral,** fluorite (1965);
Nickname: Prairie State
Origin of name: Algonquin for "tribe of superior men"
10 largest cities (2000): Chicago, 2,896,016; Rockford, 150,115; Aurora, 142,990; Naperville, 128,358; Peoria, 112,936; Springfield, 111,454; Joliet, 106,221; Elgin, 94,487; Waukegan, 87,901; Cicero, 85,616
Land area: 55,593 sq mi. (143,987 sq km)
Geographic center: Chestnut, on Illinois route 54 between Mt. Pulaski and Clinton.
Number of counties: 102
Largest county by population and area: Cook, 5,376,741 (2000); McLean, 1,184 sq mi.
Public use areas: 187 (275,000 ac.), incl. state parks, memorials, forests and conservation areas
Residents: Illinoisan
2000 resident census population (rank): 12,419,293 (5). **Male:** 6,080,336 (49.0%); **Female:** 6,338,957 (51.0%). **White:** 9,125,471 (73.5%); **Black:** 1,876,875 (15.1%); **American Indian:** 31,006 (0.2%); **Asian:** 423,603 (3.4%); **Other race:** 722,712 (5.8%); **Two or more races:** 235,016 (1.9%); **Hispanic/Latino:** 1,530,262 (12.3%). **2000 percent population 18 and over:** 73.9; **65 and over:** 12.1; **median age:** 34.7.

French explorers Jacques Marquette and Louis Joliet, in 1673, were the first Europeans of record to visit the region. In 1699 French settlers established the first permanent settlement at Cahokia, near present-day East St. Louis.

Great Britain obtained the region at the end of the French and Indian Wars in 1763. The area figured prominently in frontier struggles during the Revolutionary War and in Indian wars during the early 19th century.

Significant episodes in the state's early history include the influx of settlers following the opening of the Erie Canal in 1825; the Black Hawk War, which virtually ended the Indian troubles in the area; and the rise of Abraham Lincoln from farm laborer to president.

Today, Illinois stands high in manufacturing, coal mining, agriculture, and oil production. The sprawling Chicago district (including a slice of Indiana) is a great iron and steel producer, meat packer, grain exchange, and railroad center. Chicago is also famous as a Great Lakes port.

The state manufactures a great variety of industrial and consumer products: railroad cars, clothing, furniture, tractors, liquor, watches, and farm implements are just some of the items made in its factories and plants.

Illinois ranks third in the nation in the sale of agricultural products, second in corn and soybeans, and fourth in hog production.

Central Illinois is noted for shrines and memorials associated with the life of Abraham Lincoln. In Springfield are the Lincoln Home, the Lincoln Tomb, and the restored Old State Capitol. Other points of interest are the home of Mormon leader Joseph Smith in Nauvoo and, in Chicago: the Art Institute, Field Museum, Museum of Science and Industry, Shedd Aquarium, Adler Planetarium, Merchandise Mart, and Chicago Portage National Historic Site.

Famous natives and residents: Franklin Pierce Adams, author; Jane Addams, social worker; Mary Astor, actress; Jack Benny, comedian; Black Hawk, Sauk Indian chief; Harry A. Blackmun, jurist; Ray Bradbury, author; William Jennings Bryan, orator and politician; Edgar Rice Burroughs, novelist;

Gower Champion, choreographer; John Chancellor, TV commentator; Raymond Chandler, writer; Jimmy Connors, tennis champion; James Gould Cozzens, novelist; Richard J. Daley, former mayor of Chicago; Miles Davis, musician; Peter DeVries, novelist; Walt Disney, film animator and producer; John Dos Passos, author; James T. Farrell, novelist; Betty Friedan, feminist; Benny Goodman, musician; John Gunther, author; Ernest Hemingway, author; Charlton Heston, actor; Wild Bill Hickok, scout; William Holden, actor; Rock Hudson, actor; Burl Ives, singer; James Jones, novelist; John Jones, civil rights leader; Quincy Jones, composer; Keokuk (Watchful Fox), chief of the Sac and Fox Indians; Walter Kerr, drama critic; Shelley Long, actress; Archibald MacLeish, poet; David Mamet, playwright; Robert A. Millikan, physicist; Sherrill Milnes, baritone; Bill Murray, actor; Bob Newhart, actor and comedian; William S. Paley, broadcasting executive; Drew Pearson, columnist; Richard Pryor, comedian and actor; Ronald Reagan, former president and actor; Carl Sandburg, poet; Sam Shepard, playwright; William L. Shirer, author and historian; John Paul Stevens, jurist; McLean Stevenson, actor; Preston Sturges, director; Gloria Swanson, actress; Carl Van Doren, writer and educator; Melvin Van Peebles, playwright; Irving Wallace, novelist; Alfred Wallenstein, conductor; Raquel Welch, actress; Oprah Winfrey, television talk show host and actress; Florenz Ziegfield, theatrical producer.

Indiana

Capital: Indianapolis
Governor: Frank O'Bannon, D (to Jan. 2005)
Lieut. Governor: Joseph E. Kernan, D (to Jan. 2005)
Senators: Evan Bayh, D (to Jan. 2005); Richard G. Lugar, R (to Jan. 2007)
Secy. of State: Sue Anne Gilroy, R (to Dec. 2002)
Treasurer: Tim Berry, R (to Feb. 2003)
Atty. General: Karen Freeman-Wilson, D (to Jan. 2001)
Auditor: Connie Kay Nass, R (to Dec. 2002)
Organized as territory: May 7, 1800
Entered Union (rank): Dec. 11, 1816 (19)
Present constitution adopted: 1851
Motto: The Crossroads of America
State Symbols: flower, peony (1957); **tree,** tulip tree (1931); **bird,** cardinal (1933); **song,** "On the Banks of the Wabash, Far Away" (1913); **river,** Wabash; **stone,** limestone;
Official language: English
Nickname: Hoosier State
Origin of name: Meaning "land of Indians"
10 largest cities (2000): Indianapolis, 791,926; Fort Wayne, 205,727; Evansville, 121,582; South Bend, 107,789; Gary, 102,746; Hammond, 83,048; Bloomington, 69,291; Muncie, 67,430; Anderson, 59,734; Terre Haute, 59,614
Land area: 35,870 sq mi. (92,904 sq km)
Geographic center: In Boone Co., 14 mi. NNW of Indianapolis
Number of Counties: 92
Largest county by population and area: Marion, 860,454 (2000); Allen, 657 sq mi.
State parks: 23 (56,409 ac.)
State historic sites: 17 (2,007 ac.)
Residents: Indianan, Indianian
2000 resident census population (rank): 6,080,485 (14). **Male:** 2,982,474 (49.0%); **Female:** 3,098,011 (51.0%); **White:** 5,320,022 (87.5%); **Black:** 510,034 (8.4%); **American Indian:** 15,815 (0.3%); **Asian:** 59,126 (1.0%); **Other race:** 97,811 (1.6%); **Two or more races:** 75,672 (1.2%); **Hispanic/Latino:** 214,536 (3.5%). **2000 percent population 18 and over:** 74.1; **65 and over:** 12.4; **median age:** 35.2.

First explored for France by Robert Cavelier, Sieur de la Salle, in 1679–1680, the region figured importantly in the Franco-British struggle for North America that culminated with British victory in 1763.

George Rogers Clark led American forces against the British in the area during the Revolutionary War and, prior to becoming a state, Indiana was the scene of frequent Indian uprisings until the victory of Gen. William Henry Harrison at Tippecanoe in 1811.

Indiana's 41-mile Lake Michigan waterfront—one of the world's great industrial centers—turns out iron, steel, and oil products. Products include automobile parts and accessories, mobile homes and recreational vehicles, truck and bus bodies, aircraft engines, farm machinery, and fabricated structural steel. Wood office furniture and pharmaceuticals are also manufactured.

The state is a leader in agriculture with corn the principal crop. Hogs, soybeans, wheat, oats, rye, tomatoes, onions, and poultry also contribute heavily to Indiana's agricultural output. Much of the building limestone used in the U.S. is quarried in Indiana, which is also a large producer of coal.

Wyandotte Cave, one of the largest in the U.S., is located in Crawford County in southern Indiana, and West Baden and French Lick are well known for their mineral springs. Other attractions include Indiana Dunes National Lakeshore, Indianapolis Motor Speedway, Lincoln Boyhood National Memorial, and the George Rogers Clark National Historical Park.

Famous natives and residents: George Ade, humorist; Leon Ames, actor; Anne Baxter, actress; Albert J. Beveridge, political leader; Larry Bird, basketball player; Bill Blass, fashion designer; Frank Borman, astronaut; Hoagy Carmichael, songwriter; James Dean, actor; Eugene V. Debs, Socialist leader; Lloyd C. Douglas, author; Theodore Dreiser, writer; Bernard F. Gimbel, merchant; Virgil Grissom, astronaut; Phil Harris, actor and band leader; John Milton Hay, statesman; James R. Hoffa, labor leader; Michael Jackson, singer; Buck Jones, actor; Alfred C. Kinsey, zoologist; David Letterman, TV host and comedian; Eli Lilly, pharmaceuticals manufacturer; Carole Lombard, actress; Shelley Long, actress; Marjorie Main, actress; James McCracken, tenor; Joaquin Miller, poet; Paul Osborn, playwright; Cole Porter, songwriter; Gene Stratton Porter, naturalist and author; Ernest Taylor Pyle, journalist; J. Danforth Quayle, former vice president; James Whitcomb Riley, poet; Knute Rockne, football coach; Ned Rorem, composer; Red Skelton, comedian; Rex Stout, mystery writer; Booth Tarkington, author; Twyla Tharp, dancer and choreographer; Forrest Tucker, actor; Harold C. Urey, physicist; Kurt Vonnegut, Jr., author; Dan Wakefield, author; Robert Wise, director; Jessamyn West, novelist; Wendell Willkie, lawyer; Wilbur Wright, inventor.

Iowa

Capital: Des Moines
Governor: Tom Vilsack, D (to Jan. 2003)
Lieut. Governor: Sally Pederson, D (to Jan. 2003)
Senators: Chuck Grassley, R (to Jan. 2005); Tom Harkin, D (to Jan. 2003)
Secy. of State: Chet Culver, D (to Jan. 2003)
Treasurer: Michael L. Fitzgerald, D (to Jan. 2003)
Atty. General: Tom Miller, D (to Jan. 2003)
Organized as territory: June 12, 1838
Entered Union (rank): Dec. 28, 1846 (29)
Present constitution adopted: 1857
Motto: Our liberties we prize and our rights we will maintain
State Symbols: flower, wild rose (1897); **bird,** eastern goldfinch (1933); **colors,** red, white, and blue (in state flag); **song,** "Song of Iowa";
Nickname: Hawkeye State
Origin of name: Probably from an Indian word meaning "this is the place" or "the Beautiful Land"

10 largest cities (2000): Des Moines, 198,682; Cedar Rapids, 120,758; Davenport, 98,359; Sioux City, 85,013; Waterloo, 68,747; Iowa City, 62,220; Council Bluffs, 58,268; Dubuque, 57,686; Ames, 50,731; West Des Moines, 46,403
Land area: 55,875 sq mi. (144,716 sq km)
Geographic center: In Story Co., 5 mi. NE of Ames
Number of counties: 99
Largest county by population and area: Polk, 374,601 (2000); Kossuth, 973 sq mi.
State forests: 8 (40,706 ac.)
State parks: 83 (53,000 ac.)
Residents: Iowan
2000 resident census population (rank): 2,926,324 (30). **Male:** 1,435,515 (49.1%); **Female:** 1,490,809 (50.9%). **White:** 2,748,640 (93.9%); **Black:** 61,853 (2.1%); **American Indian:** 8,989 (0.3%); **Asian:** 36,635 (1.3%); **Other race:** 37,420 (1.3%); **Two or more races:** 31,778 (1.1%); **Hispanic/Latino:** 82,473 (2.8%). **2000 percent population 18 and over:** 74.9; **65 and over:** 14.9; **median age:** 36.6.

The first Europeans to visit the area were the French explorers Jacques Marquette and Louis Joliet in 1673. The U.S. obtained control of the area in 1803 as part of the Louisiana Purchase.

During the first half of the 19th century, there was heavy fighting between white settlers and Indians. Lands were taken from the Indians after the Black Hawk War in 1832 and again in 1836 and 1837.

When Iowa became a state in 1846, its capital was Iowa City; the more centrally located Des Moines became the new capital in 1857. At that time, the state's present boundaries were also drawn.

Although Iowa produces a tenth of the nation's food supply, the value of Iowa's manufactured products is twice that of its agriculture. Major industries are food and associated products, non-electrical machinery, electrical equipment, printing and publishing, and fabricated products.

Iowa stands in a class by itself as an agricultural state. Its farms sell over $10 billion worth of crops and livestock annually. Iowa leads the nation in all corn, soybean, and hog marketings, and comes in third in total livestock sales. Iowa's forests produce hardwood lumber, particularly walnut, and its mineral products include cement, limestone, sand, gravel, gypsum, and coal.

Tourist attractions include the Herbert Hoover birthplace and library near West Branch; the Amana Colonies; Fort Dodge Historical Museum, Fort, and Stockade; the Iowa State Fair at Des Moines in August; and the Effigy Mounds National Monument, a prehistoric Indian burial site at Marquette.

Famous natives and residents: Bix Beiderbecke, jazz musician; Norman Borlaug, plant pathologist, geneticist, and Nobel Peace Prize winner; William "Buffalo Bill" F. Cody, scout; Johnny Carson, TV entertainer; Gardner Cowles, Jr., publisher; Simon Estes, bass-baritone; William Frawley, actor; George H. Gallup, poll taker; Susan Glaspell, writer; Herbert Hoover, former president; MacKinlay Kantor, novelist; Charles A. Kettering, inventor; Ann Landers, columnist; Cloris Leachman, actress; John L. Lewis, labor leader; Glenn L. Martin, aviator and manufacturer; Elsa Maxwell, writer; Frederick L. Maytag, inventor and manufacturer; Glenn Miller, bandleader; Kate Mulgrew, actress; Harriet Nelson, actress; Nathan M. Pusey, educator; David Rabe, playwright; Harry Reasoner, TV commentator; Donna Reed, actress; Lillian Russell, soprano; Robert Schuller, evangelist; Wallace Stegner, novelist and critic; Billy Sunday, evangelist; James A. Van Allen, space physicist; Abigail Van Buren, columnist; Henry A. Wallace, statesman and vice president; John Wayne, actor; Andy Williams, singer; Meredith Willson, composer; Grant Wood, painter.

Kansas

Capital: Topeka
Governor: Bill Graves, R (to Jan. 2003)
Lieut. Governor: Gary Sherrer, R (to Jan. 2003)
Senators: Sam Brownback, R (to Jan. 2005); Pat Roberts, R (to Jan. 2003)
Secy. of State: Ron Thornburgh, R (to Jan. 2003)
Treasurer: Tim Shallenburger, R (to Jan. 2003)
Atty. General: Carla Stovall, R (to Jan. 2003)
Commission of Insurance: Kathleen Sebelius, D (to Jan. 2003)
Organized as territory: May 30, 1854
Entered Union (rank): Jan. 29, 1861 (34)
Present constitution adopted: 1859
Motto: *Ad astra per aspera* (To the stars through difficulties)
State Symbols: flower, sunflower (1903); **tree,** cottonwood (1937); **bird,** western meadowlark (1937); **animal,** buffalo (1955); **song,** "Home on the Range" (1947);
Nicknames: Sunflower State; Jayhawk State
Origin of name: From a Sioux word meaning "people of the south wind"
10 largest cities (2000): Wichita, 344,284; Overland Park, 149,080; Kansas City, 146,866; Topeka, 122,377; Olathe, 92,962; Lawrence, 80,098; Shawnee, 47,996; Salina, 45,679; Manhattan, 44,831; Hutchinson, 40,787
Land area: 81,823 sq mi. (211,922 sq km)
Geographic center: In Barton Co., 15 mi. NE of Great Bend
Number of counties: 105
Largest county by population and area: Sedgwick, 452,869 (2000); Butler, 1,428 sq mi.
State parks: 22 (14,394 ac.)
Residents: Kansan
2000 resident census population (rank): 2,688,418 (32). **Male:** 1,328,474 (49.4%); **Female:** 1,359,944 (50.6%). **White:** 2,313,944 (86.1%); **Black:** 154,198 (5.7%); **American Indian:** 24,936 (0.9%); **Asian:** 46,806 (1.7%); **Other race:** 90,725 (3.4%); **Two or more races:** 56,496 (2.1%); **Hispanic/Latino:** 188,252 (7.0%). **2000 percent population 18 and over:** 73.5; **65 and over:** 13.3; **median age:** 35.2.

Spanish explorer Francisco de Coronado, in 1541, is considered the first European to have traveled this region. Sieur de la Salle's extensive land claims for France (1682) included present-day Kansas. Ceded to Spain by France in 1763, the territory reverted to France in 1800 and was sold to the U.S. as part of the Louisiana Purchase in 1803.

Lewis and Clark, Zebulon Pike, and Stephen H. Long explored the region between 1803 and 1819. The first permanent white settlements in Kansas were outposts—Fort Leavenworth (1827), Fort Scott (1842), and Fort Riley (1853)—established to protect travelers along the Santa Fe and Oregon Trails.

Just before the Civil War, the conflict between the pro- and anti-slavery forces earned the region the grim title of Bleeding Kansas.

Today, wheat fields, oil-well derricks, herds of cattle, and grain-storage elevators are chief features of the Kansas landscape. A leading wheat-growing state, Kansas also raises corn, sorghum, oats, barley, soybeans, and potatoes. Kansas stands high in petroleum production and mines zinc, coal, salt, and lead. It is also the nation's leading producer of helium.

Wichita is one of the nation's leading aircraft-manufacturing centers, ranking first in production of private aircraft. Kansas City is an important transportation, milling, and meat-packing center.

Points of interest include the Kansas History Center at Topeka, the Eisenhower boyhood home and the Eisenhower Memorial Museum and Presidential Library at Abilene, John Brown's cabin at Osawatomie, re-created Front Street in Dodge City, Fort Larned (once the most important military post on the Santa Fe Trail), Fort Leavenworth and Fort Riley.

Famous natives and residents: Roscoe "Fatty" Arbuckle, actor; Clarence D. Batchelor, political cartoonist; Gwendolyn Brooks, poet; Walter P. Chrysler, auto manufacturer; Clark M. Clifford, former secretary of defense; John Steuart Curry, painter; Charles Curtis, U.S. vice president; Robert Dole, senator; Amelia Earhart, aviator; Dwight D. Eisenhower, U.S. general and president; Milton S. Eisenhower, educator; Gary Hart, politician; William Inge, playwright; Walter Johnson, baseball pitcher; Osa L. Johnson, documentary film producer; Buster Keaton, comedian; Emmett Kelly, clown; Stan Kenton, jazz musician; James Lehrer, broadcast journalist; Edgar Lee Masters, poet; Mary McCarthy, actress; Hattie McDaniel, actress; Karl Menninger, psychiatrist; Carry A. Nation, temperance leader; Gordon Parks, film director; Zasu Pitts, actress; Samuel Ramey, opera singer; Charles Robinson, statesman and first governor; Charles (Buddy) Rogers, actor; Damon Runyon, journalist; Gale Sayers, football player; Eugene W. Smith, photojournalist; Milburn Stone, actor; John Cameron Swayze, news commentator; William Allen White, journalist; Charles E. Whittaker, jurist; Jess Willard, boxer.

Kentucky

Capital: Frankfort
Governor: Paul E. Patton, D (to Dec. 2003)
Lieut. Governor: Stephen L. Henry, D (to Dec. 2003)
Senators: Jim Bunning, R (to Jan. 2005);
   Mitch McConnell, R (to Jan. 2003)
Secy. of State: John Y. Brown III, D (to Dec. 2003)
Treasurer: Jonathan Miller, D (to Dec. 2003)
Auditor: Ed Hatchett, D (to Dec. 2003)
Atty. General: A. B. "Ben" Chandler III, D (to Dec. 2003)
Entered Union (rank): June 1, 1792 (15)
Present constitution adopted: 1891
Motto: United we stand, divided we fall
State Symbols: tree, tulip poplar (1994); **flower,** goldenrod; **bird,** Kentucky cardinal; **song,** "My Old Kentucky Home";
Nickname: Bluegrass State
Origin of name: From an Iroquoian word "Ken-tah-ten" meaning "land of tomorrow"
10 largest cities (2000): Lexington-Fayette[1], 260,512; Louisville, 256,231; Owensboro, 54,067; Bowling Green, 49,296; Covington, 43,370; Hopkinsville, 30,089; Frankfort, 27,741; Henderson, 27,373; Richmond, 27,152; Jeffersontown, 26,633
Land area: 39,732 sq mi. (102,907 sq km)
Geographic center: In Marion Co., 3 mi. NNW of Lebanon
Number of counties: 120
Largest county by population and area: Jefferson, 693,604 (2000); Pike, 787 sq mi.
State forests: 9 (44,173 ac.)
State parks: 49
Residents: Kentuckian
2000 resident census population (rank): 4,041,769 (25). **Male:** 1,975,368 (48.9%); **Female:** 2,066,401 (51.1%). **White:** 3,640,889 (90.1%); **Black:** 295,994 (7.3%); **American Indian:** 8,616 (0.2%); **Asian:** 29,744 (0.7%); **Other race:** 22,623 (0.6%); **Two or more races:** 42,443 (1.1%); **Hispanic/Latino:** 59,939 (1.5%). **2000 percent population 18 and over:** 75.4; **65 and over:** 12.5; **median age:** 35.9.

1. Coextensive with Fayette County.
   Kentucky was the first region west of the Allegheny Mountains to be settled by American pioneers. James Harrod established the first permanent settlement at Harrodsburg in 1774; the following year Daniel Boone, who had explored the area in 1767, blazed the Wilderness Trail and founded Boonesboro.

Politically, the Kentucky region was originally part of Virginia, but statehood was gained in 1792. As a slaveholding state with a considerable abolitionist population, Kentucky was caught in the middle during the Civil War, supplying both Union and Confederate forces with thousands of troops.

Kentucky prides itself on producing some of the nation's best tobacco, horses, and whiskey. Corn, soybeans, wheat, fruit, hogs, cattle, and dairy products are among the agricultural items produced.

Among the manufactured items produced in the state are motor vehicles, furniture, aluminum ware, brooms, apparel, lumber products, machinery, textiles, and iron and steel products. Kentucky also produces significant amounts of petroleum, natural gas, fluorspar, clay, and stone. However, coal accounts for 85% of the total mineral income.

Louisville, the largest city, famed for the Kentucky Derby at Churchill Downs, is also the location of a large state university, whiskey distilleries, and cigarette factories. The Bluegrass country around Lexington is the home of some of the world's finest race horses. Other attractions are Mammoth Cave, the George S. Patton, Jr., Military Museum at Fort Knox, and Old Fort Harrod State Park.

Famous natives and residents: John Adair, pioneer and political leader; Muhammad Ali, boxer; Alben W. Barkley, former vice president; Louis D. Brandeis, jurist; John Mason Brown, critic; Kit Carson, scout; Champ Clark, politician; George Clooney, actor; Rosemary Clooney, singer; Irvin S. Cobb, humorist; Jefferson Davis, president of the Confederacy; Johnny Depp, actor; Irene Dunne, actress; Crystal Gayle, singer; David W. Griffith, film producer; John M. Harlan, jurist; Elizabeth Hardwick, writer; Casey Jones, celebrated locomotive engineer; Naomi Judd, singer; Wynona Judd, singer; Barbara Kingsolver, writer; Abraham Lincoln, former president; Loretta Lynn, singer; Bill Monroe, bluegrass musician; Carry A. Nation, temperance leader; Patricia Neal, actress; George Reeves, actor; Wiley B. Rutledge, jurist; Diane Sawyer, broadcast journalist; Phil Simms, football player; Adlai Stevenson, former vice president; Allen Tate, poet and critic; Hunter Thompson, writer; Frederick M. Vinson, jurist; Robert Penn Warren, novelist.

Louisiana

Capital: Baton Rouge
Governor: Murphy J. "Mike" Foster, R (to Jan. 2004)
Lieut. Governor: Kathleen Blanco, D (to Jan. 2004)
Senators: John B. Breaux, D (to Jan. 2005);
   Mary Landrieu, D (to Jan. 2003)
Secy. of State: W. Fox McKeithen, R (to Jan. 2004)
Treasurer: John Neely Kennedy, D (to Jan. 2004)
Atty. General: Richard P. Ieyoub, D (to Jan. 2004)
Organized as territory: March 26, 1804
Entered Union (rank): April 30, 1812 (18)
Present constitution adopted: 1974
Motto: Union, justice, and confidence
State Symbols: flower, magnolia (1900); **tree,** bald cypress (1963); **bird,** eastern brown pelican (1958); **songs,** "Give Me Louisiana" and "You Are My Sunshine";
Nickname: Pelican State
Origin of name: In honor of Louis XIV of France
10 largest cities (2000): New Orleans, 484,674; Baton Rouge, 227,818; Shreveport, 200,145; Lafayette, 110,257; Lake Charles, 71,757; Kenner, 70,517; Bossier City, 56,461; Monroe, 53,107; Alexandria, 46,342; New Iberia, 32,623
Land area: 43,566 sq mi. (112,836 sq km)

Geographic center: In Avoyelles Parish, 3 mi. SE of Marksville
Number of parishes (counties): 64
Largest parish by population and area: Orleans, 484,674 (2000); Vernon, 1,328 sq mi.
State forests: 1 (8,000 ac.)
State parks: 30 (13,932 ac.)
Residents: Louisianan, Louisianian
2000 resident census population (rank): 4,468,976 (22). **Male:** 2,162,903 (48.4%); **Female:** 2,306,073 (51.6%). **White:** 2,856,161 (63.9%); **Black:** 1,451,944 (32.5%); **American Indian:** 25,477 (0.6%); **Asian:** 54,758 (1.2%); **Other race:** 31,131 (0.7%); **Two or more races:** 48,265 (1.1%); **Hispanic/Latino:** 107,738 (2.4%). **2000 percent population 18 and over:** 72.7; **65 and over:** 11.6; **median age:** 34.0.

Louisiana has a rich, colorful historical background. Early Spanish explorers were Alvárez Piñeda, 1519; Álvar Núñez Cabeza de Vaca, 1528; and Hernando De Soto in 1541. Sieur de la Salle reached the mouth of the Mississippi and claimed all the land drained by it and its tributaries for Louis XIV of France in 1682.

Louisiana became a French crown colony in 1731, was ceded to Spain in 1763, returned to France in 1800, and was sold by Napoléon to the U.S. as part of the Louisiana Purchase (with large territories to the north and northwest) in 1803.

In 1815, Gen. Andrew Jackson's troops defeated a larger British army in the Battle of New Orleans, neither side aware that the treaty ending the War of 1812 had been signed.

Louisiana is a leader in natural gas, salt, petroleum, and sulfur production. Much of the oil and sulfur comes from offshore deposits. The state also produces large crops of sweet potatoes, rice, sugar cane, pecans, soybeans, corn, and cotton.

Leading manufactured items include chemicals, processed food, petroleum and coal products, paper, lumber and wood products, transportation equipment, and apparel.

Louisiana marshes supply most of the nation's muskrat fur as well as that of opossum, raccoon, mink, and otter, and large numbers of game birds.

Major points of interest include New Orleans with its French Quarter and Superdome, plantation homes near Natchitoches and New Iberia, Cajun country in the Mississippi Delta region, Chalmette National Historical Park, and the state capital at Baton Rouge.

Famous natives and residents: Louis Armstrong, musician; Geoffrey Beene, fashion designer; Truman Capote, writer; Kitty Carlisle, singer and actress; Van Cliburn, concert pianist; Michael De Bakey, heart surgeon; Fats Domino, musician; Louis Moreau Gottschalk, pianist and composer; Bryant Gumbel, TV newscaster; Lillian Hellman, playwright; Al Hirt, trumpeter; Mahalia Jackson, gospel singer; Jean Laffite, privateer; Dorothy Lamour, actress; John A. Lejeune, Marine Corps general; Elmore Leonard, author; Jerry Lee Lewis, singer; Huey P. Long, politician; Wynton Marsalis, musician; Jelly Roll Morton, jazz musician and composer; Huey Newton, black activist; Paul Prudhomme, chef; Howard K. Smith, TV commentator; Ben Turpin, comedian; Ray Walston, actor; Edward Douglas White, jurist.

Maine

Capital: Augusta
Governor: Angus S. King, Jr., I (to Jan. 2003)
Senators: Susan Collins, R (to Jan. 2003); Olympia J. Snowe, R (to Jan. 2007)
Secy. of State: Dan A. Gwadosky, D (to Jan. 2003)
Treasurer: Dale McCormick (to Jan. 2003)

Auditor: Gail M. Chase (to Jan. 2005)
Atty. General: G. Steven Rowe (to Jan. 2003)
Entered Union (rank): March 15, 1820 (23)
Present constitution adopted: 1820
Motto: *Dirigo* (I lead)
State Symbols: flower, white pine cone and tassel (1895); **tree,** white pine tree (1945); **bird,** chickadee (1927); **fish,** landlocked salmon (1969); **mineral,** tourmaline (1971); **song,** "State of Maine Song" (1937); **animal,** moose (1979); **cat,** Maine coon cat (1985); **fossil,** *pertica quadrifaria* (1985); **insect,** honeybee (1975);
Nickname: Pine Tree State
Origin of name: First used to distinguish the mainland from the offshore islands. It has been considered a compliment to Henrietta Maria, queen of Charles I of England. She was said to have owned the province of Mayne in France.
10 largest cities (2000): Portland, 64,249; Lewiston, 35,690; Bangor, 31,473; South Portland, 23,324; Auburn, 23,203; Brunswick, 21,172; Biddeford, 20,942; Sanford, 20,806; Augusta, 18,560; Scarborough, 16,970
Largest town (1990 census): Brunswick, 20,906
Land area: 30,865 sq mi. (79,939 sq km)
Geographic center: In Piscataquis Co., 18 mi. N of Dover-Foxcroft
Number of counties: 16
Largest county by population and area: Cumberland, 265,612 (2000); Aroostook, 6,672 sq mi.
State forests: 1 (21,000 ac.)
State parks: 26 (247,627 ac.)
State historic sites: 18 (403 ac.)
Residents: Mainer
2000 resident census population (rank): 1,274,923 (40). **Male:** 620,309 (48.7%); **Female:** 654,614 (51.3%). **White:** 1,236,014 (96.9%); **Black:** 6,760 (0.5%); **American Indian:** 7,098 (0.6%); **Asian:** 9,111 (0.7%); **Other race:** 2,911 (0.2%); **Two or more races:** 12,647 (1.0%); **Hispanic/Latino:** 9,360 (0.7%); **2000 percent population 18 and over:** 76.4; **65 and over:** 14.4; **median age:** 38.6.

John Cabot and his son, Sebastian, are believed to have visited the Maine coast in 1498. However, the first permanent English settlements were not established until more than a century later, in 1623.

The first naval action of the Revolutionary War occurred in 1775 when colonials captured the British sloop *Margaretta* off Machias on the Maine coast. In that same year, the British burned Falmouth (now Portland).

Long governed by Massachusetts, Maine became the 23rd state as part of the Missouri Compromise in 1820.

Maine produces 98% of the nation's low-bush blueberries. Farm income is also derived from apples, potatoes, dairy products, and vegetables, with poultry and eggs the largest selling items.

The state is one of the world's largest pulp-paper producers. With almost 89% of its area forested, Maine turns out wood products from boats to toothpicks.

Maine leads the world in the production of the familiar flat tins of sardines, producing more than 75 million of them annually. Lobstermen normally catch 50% of the nation's total of lobsters. The 1996 catch was 16,435 metric tons, the second-largest lobster catch in history.

A scenic seacoast, beaches, lakes, mountains, and resorts make Maine a popular vacationland. There are more than 2,500 lakes and 5,000 streams, plus 26 state parks to attract hunters, fishermen, skiers, and campers.

Major points of interest are Bar Harbor, Acadia National Park, Allagash National Wilderness Waterway, the Wadsworth-Longfellow House in Portland, Roosevelt Campobello International Park, and the St. Croix Island National Monument.

Famous natives and residents: F. Lee Bailey, defense attorney; Charles F. Browne (Artemus Ward), humorist; Cyrus Curtis, publisher; Dorothea Dix, civil rights reformer; John Ford, film director; Melville Fuller, jurist; Marsden Hartley, painter; Henry Wadsworth Longfellow, poet; Sarah Orne Jewett, author; Stephen King, writer; Linda Lavin, actress; Edna St. Vincent Millay, poet; Marston Morse, mathematician; Frank Munsey, publisher; Walter Piston, composer; George Putnam, publisher; Kenneth Roberts, historical novelist; Edwin Arlington Robinson, poet; Margaret Chase Smith, politician; Samantha Smith, peacemaker and actress; John Hay Whitney, publisher.

Maryland

Capital: Annapolis
Governor: Parris N. Glendening, D (to Jan. 2003)
Lieut. Gov.: Kathleen Kennedy Townsend, D (to Jan. 2003)
Senators: Barbara A. Mikulski, D (to Jan. 2005); Paul S. Sarbanes, D (to Jan. 2007)
Secy. of State: John T. Willis, D (to Jan. 2003)
Comptroller of the Treasury: William Donald Schaefer, D (to Jan. 2003)
Treasurer: Richard N. Dixon, D (to Jan. 2003)
Atty. General: J. Joseph Curran, Jr., D (to Jan. 2003)
Entered Union (rank): April 28, 1788 (7)
Present constitution adopted: 1867
Motto: *Fatti maschii, parole femine* (Manly deeds, womanly words)
State Symbols: bird, Baltimore oriole (1947); **boat,** skipjack (1985); **crustacean,** Maryland blue crab (1989); **dinosaur,** Astrodon johnstoni (1998); **dog,** Chesapeake Bay retriever (1964); **beverage,** milk (1998); **flower,** black-eyed susan (1918); **fish,** rockfish (1965); **folk dance,** square dance (1994); **fossil shell,** *ecphora gardnerae gardnerae* (Wilson) (1994); **insect,** Baltimore checkerspot butterfly (1973); **reptile,** Diamondback terrapin (1994); **song,** "Maryland! My Maryland!" (1939); **sport,** jousting (1962); **tree,** white oak (1941);
Nicknames: Free State; Old Line State
Origin of name: In honor of Henrietta Maria (queen of Charles I of England)
10 largest cities (2000): Baltimore, 651,154; Frederick, 52,767; Gaithersburg, 52,613; Bowie, 50,269; Rockville, 47,388; Hagerstown, 36,687; Annapolis, 35,838; College Park, 24,657; Salisbury, 23,743; Cumberland, 21,518
Land area: 9,775 sq mi. (25,316 sq km)
Geographic center: In Prince Georges Co., 4½ mi. NW of Davidsonville
Number of counties: 23, and 1 independent city
Largest county by population and area: Montgomery, 873,341 (2000); Frederick, 663 sq mi.
State forests: 13 (132,944 ac.)
State parks: 47 (87,670 ac.)
Residents: Marylander
2000 resident census population (rank): 5,296,486 (19). **Male:** 2,557,794 (48.3%); **Female:** 2,738,692 (51.7%). **White:** 3,391,308 (64.0%); **Black:** 1,477,411 (27.9%); **American Indian:** 15,423 (0.3%); **Asian:** 210,929 (4.0%); **Other race:** 95,525 (1.8%); **Two or more races:** 103,587 (2.0%); **Hispanic/Latino:** 227,916 (4.3%). **2000 percent population 18 and over:** 74.4; **65 and over:** 11.3; **median age:** 36.0.

Maryland was inhabited by Indians as early as circa 10,000 B.C. Permanent Indian villages were established by circa A.D. 1000.

In 1608, Capt. John Smith explored Chesapeake Bay. Charles I granted a royal charter for Maryland to Cecil Calvert, Lord Baltimore, in 1632, and English settlers, many of whom were Roman Catholic, landed on St. Clement's (now Blakistone) Island in 1634. Religious freedom, granted all Christians in the Toleration Act passed by the Maryland assembly in 1649, was ended by a Puritan revolt, 1654–1658.

From 1763 to 1767, Charles Mason and Jeremiah Dixon surveyed Maryland's northern boundary line with Pennsylvania. In 1791, Maryland ceded land to form the District of Columbia.

In 1814, when the British attempted to capture Baltimore, the bombardment of Fort McHenry inspired Francis Scott Key to write the words to "The Star-Spangled Banner." During the Civil War, Maryland was a slave state but remained in the Union. Consequently, Marylanders fought on both sides and many families were divided.

Maryland's Eastern Shore and Western Shore embrace the Chesapeake Bay, and the many estuaries and rivers create one of the longest waterfronts of any state. The Bay produces more seafood—oysters, crabs, clams, fin fish—than any comparable body of water. Important agricultural products are greenhouse and nursery products, chickens, dairy products, eggs, vegetables, and soybeans. Stone, coal, sand, gravel, cement, and clay are the chief mineral products.

Manufacturing industries include food products, chemicals, computer and electronic products, transportation equipment, and primary metals. Baltimore, home of the Johns Hopkins University and Hospital, ranks as the nation's second port in foreign tonnage. Annapolis, site of the U.S. Naval Academy, has one of the earliest state houses (1772–1779) still in regular use by a state government.

Among the popular attractions in Maryland are the Fort McHenry National Monument; Harpers Ferry and Chesapeake and Ohio Canal National Historic Parks; Antietam National Battlefield; National Aquarium, USS *Constellation*, and Maryland Science Center at Baltimore's Inner Harbor; Historic St. Mary's City; Jefferson Patterson Historical Park and Museum at St. Leonard; U.S. Naval Academy in Annapolis; Goddard Space Flight Center at Greenbelt; Assateague Island National Park Seashore; Ocean City beach resort; and Catoctin Mountain, Fort Frederick, and Piscataway parks.

Famous natives and residents: Benjamin Banneker, mathematician and astronomer; John Barth, writer; Eubie Blake, musician; John Wilkes Booth, actor and Lincoln assassin; Francis X. Bushman, actor; James M. Cain, writer; Samuel Chase, jurist; Frederick Douglass, abolitionist; John Hurst Fletcher, Methodist bishop and educator; Christopher Gist, frontiersman; Philip Glass, composer; Matthew Henson, polar explorer; Billie Holiday, jazz-blues singer; Johns Hopkins, financier; Reverdy Johnson, lawyer and statesman; Thomas Johnson, political leader; Francis Scott Key, lawyer and poet; Thurgood Marshall, jurist; H. L. Mencken, writer; Hezekiah Niles, journalist; Charles Willson Peale, painter; Frank Perdue, farmer, businessman; James R. Randall, journalist and writer of the state song; Babe Ruth, baseball player; Upton Sinclair, novelist; Roger B. Taney, jurist; George Alfred Townsend (Gath), journalist; Harriet Tubman, abolitionist; Leon Uris, novelist; Frank Zappa, singer.

Massachusetts

Capital: Boston
Acting Governor: Jane Swift, R (to Jan. 2003)
Lieut. Governor: vacant
Senators: Edward M. Kennedy, D (to Jan. 2007);
  John F. Kerry, D (to Jan. 2003)
Secy. of the Commonwealth: William F. Galvin, D
  (to Jan. 2003)
Treasurer & Receiver-General: Shannon P. O'Brien, D
  (to Jan. 2003)
Auditor of the Commonwealth: A. Joseph DeNucci, D
  (to Jan. 2003)
Atty. General: Thomas F. Reilly, D (to Jan. 2003)
Present constitution drafted: 1780 (oldest U.S. state
  constitution in effect today)
Entered Union (rank): Feb. 6, 1788 (6)
Motto: *Ense petit placidam sub libertate quietem*
  (By the sword we seek peace, but peace only
  under liberty)
State Symbols: flower, mayflower (1918); **tree,**
  American elm (1941); **bird,** chickadee (1941); **song,**
  "All Hail to Massachusetts" (1966); **beverage,**
  cranberry juice (1970); **insect,** ladybug (1974);
  cookie, chocolate chip (1997); **muffin,** corn muffin
  (1986); **dessert,** Boston cream pie (1996);
Nicknames: Bay State; Old Colony State
Origin of name: From Massachusett tribe of Native
  Americans, meaning "at or about the great hill"
10 largest cities (2000): Boston, 589,141; Worcester,
  172,648; Springfield, 152,082; Lowell, 105,167;
  Cambridge, 101,355; Brockton, 94,304; New Bedford,
  93,768; Fall River, 91,938; Lynn, 89,050; Quincy,
  88,025
Land area: 7,838 sq mi. (20,300 sq km)
Geographic center: In Worcester Co., in S part of city
  of Worcester
Number of counties: 14
Largest county by population and area: Middlesex,
  1,465,396 (2000); Worcester, 1,513 sq mi.
State forests and parks: 129 (242,000 ac.)[1]
Residents: Bay Stater
2000 resident census population (rank): 6,349,097
  (13). **Male:** 3,058,816 (48.2%); **Female:** 3,290,281
  (51.8%). **White:** 5,367,286 (84.5%); **Black:** 343,454
  (5.4%); **American Indian:** 15,015 (0.2%); **Asian:**
  238,124 (3.8%); **Other race:** 236,724 (3.7%); **Two or
  more races:** 146,005 (2.3%); **Hispanic/Latino:**
  428,729 (6.8%). **2000 percent population 18 and
  over:** 76.4; **65 and over:** 13.5; **median age:** 36.5.

1. The Metropolitan District Commission, an agency of
the Commonwealth serving municipalities in the Boston
area, has about 14,000 acres of parkways and reservations under its jurisdiction.

Massachusetts has played a significant role in
American history since the Pilgrims, seeking religious freedom, founded Plymouth Colony in 1620.
As one of the most important of the 13 colonies,
Massachusetts became a leader in resisting British
oppression. In 1773, the Boston Tea Party protested
unjust taxation. The Minute Men started the American Revolution by battling British troops at Lexington and Concord on April 19, 1775.

During the 19th century, Massachusetts was
famous for the intellectual activity of its writers and
educators and for its expanding commercial fishing,
shipping, and manufacturing interests. Massachusetts pioneered the manufacture of textiles and
shoes. Today, these industries have been replaced in
importance by the electronics and communications
equipment fields.

The state's cranberry crop is the nation's largest.
Also important are dairy and poultry products, nursery and greenhouse produce, vegetables, and fruit.

Tourism has become an important factor in the
economy of the state because of its numerous recreational areas and historical landmarks. Cape Cod
has summer theaters, water sports, and an artists'
colony at Provincetown. Tanglewood, in the Berk-
shires, features the summer concerts of the Boston
Symphony.

Among the many other points of interest are Old
Sturbridge Village in Sturbridge, Minute Man
National Historical Park between Lexington and
Concord, and Plimoth Plantation in Plymouth. In
Boston there are many places of historical interest,
including Old North Church, Old State House,
Faneuil Hall, the USS *Constitution,* and the John F.
Kennedy Library and Museum.

Famous natives and residents: John Adams, former
president; John Quincy Adams, former president; Samuel
Adams, patriot; Bronson Alcott, educator and social
reformer; Louisa May Alcott, writer; Horatio Alger, novelist;
Susan B. Anthony, woman suffragist; Clara Barton,
American Red Cross founder; Leonard Bernstein,
conductor; George Bush, former president; William Cullen
Bryan, poet and editor; Luther Burbank, horticulturalist;
John Cheever, novelist; John Singleton Copley, painter;
e.e. cummings, poet; Jacques d'Amboise, ballet dancer;
Bette Davis, actress; Cecil B. DeMille, film director; Emily
Dickinson, poet; Ralph Waldo Emerson, philosopher and
poet; Geraldine Farrar, soprano, actress; Benjamin
Franklin, statesman and scientist; Buckminster Fuller,
architect and educator; Robert Goddard, father of modern
rocketry; John Hancock, statesman; Nathaniel Hawthorne,
novelist; Oliver Wendell Holmes, jurist; Winslow Homer,
painter; Elias Howe, inventor; John F. Kennedy, former
president; Amy Lowell, poet; James Russell Lowell, poet;
Robert Lowell, poet; Horace Mann, educator; Cotton
Mather, clergyman; Samuel F. B. Morse, painter and
inventor; Edgar Allan Poe, writer; Paul Revere, silversmith
and Revolutionary War figure; Dr. Seuss (Theodore
Geisel), author and illustrator; David Souter, jurist; Lucy
Stone, woman suffragist; Louis Henry Sullivan, architect;
Henry David Thoreau, author; Barbara Walters, TV
commentator; James McNeill Whistler, painter; Eli Whitney,
inventor; John Greenleaf Whittier, poet.

Michigan

Capital: Lansing
Governor: John Engler, R (to Jan. 2003)
Lieut. Governor: Dick Posthumus, R (to Jan. 2003)
Senators: Carl Levin, D (to Jan. 2003);
  Debbie A. Stabenow, D (to Jan. 2007)
Secy. of State: Candace S. Miller, R (to Jan. 2003)
Atty. General: Jennifer Granholm, D (to Jan. 2003)
Organized as territory: Jan. 11, 1805
Entered Union (rank): Jan. 26, 1837 (26)
Present constitution adopted: April 1, 1963, (effective
  Jan. 1, 1964)
Motto: *Si quaeris peninsulam amoenam circumspice*
  (If you seek a pleasant peninsula, look around you)
State Symbols: flower, apple blossom (1897); **bird,**
  robin (1931); **mammal,** white-tailed deer (1997);
  fishes, trout (1965), brook trout (1988); **gem,** isle
  royal greenstone (chlorastrolite) (1972); **stone,**
  petoskey stone (1965); **tree,** white pine (1955); **soil,**
  kalkaska soil series (1990); **reptile,** painted turtle
  (1995); **flag,** "Blue charged with the arms of the state"
  (1911); **wildflower,** Dwarf Lake iris (1998);
Nickname: Wolverine State
Origin of name: From Indian word "Michigana" meaning
  "great or large lake"
10 largest cities (2000): Detroit, 951,270; Grand
  Rapids, 197,800; Warren, 138,247; Flint, 124,943;
  Sterling Heights, 124,471; Lansing, 119,128; Ann

Arbor, 114,024; Livonia, 100,545; Dearborn, 97,775; Westland, 86,602
Land area: 56,809 sq mi.
Geographic center: In Wexford Co., 5 mi. NNW of Cadillac
Number of counties: 83
Largest county by population and area: Wayne, 2,061,162 (2000); Marquette, 1,821 sq mi.
State parks and recreation areas: 96 (265,000 ac.)
Residents: Michigander, Michiganite
2000 resident census population (rank): 9,938,444 (8). **Male:** 4,873,095 (49.0%); **Female:** 5,065,349 (51.0%). **White:** 7,966,053 (80.2%); **Black:** 1,412,742 (14.2%); **American Indian:** 58,479 (0.6%); **Asian:** 176,510 (1.8%); **Other race:** 129,552 (1.3%); **Two or more races:** 192,416 (1.9%); **Hispanic/Latino:** 323,877 (3.3%). **2000 percent population 18 and over:** 73.9; **65 and over:** 12.3; **median age:** 35.5.

Indian tribes were living in the Michigan region when the first European, Etienne Brulé of France, arrived in 1618. Other French explorers, including Jacques Marquette, Louis Joliet, and Sieur de la Salle, followed, and the first permanent settlement was established in 1668 at Sault Ste. Marie. France was ousted from the territory by Great Britain in 1763, following the French and Indian Wars.

After the Revolutionary War, the U.S. acquired most of the region, which remained the scene of constant conflict between the British and U.S. forces and their respective Indian allies through the War of 1812.

Bordering on four of the five Great Lakes, Michigan is divided into Upper and Lower peninsulas by the Straits of Mackinac, which link lakes Michigan and Huron. The two parts of the state are connected by the Mackinac Bridge, one of the world's longest suspension bridges. To the north, connecting lakes Superior and Huron, are the busy Sault Ste. Marie Canals.

While Michigan ranks first among the states in production of motor vehicles and parts, it is also a leader in many other manufacturing and processing lines, including prepared cereals, machine tools, airplane parts, refrigerators, hardware, steel springs, and furniture.

The state produces important amounts of iron, copper, iodine, gypsum, bromine, salt, lime, gravel, and cement. Michigan's farms grow apples, cherries, beans, pears, grapes, potatoes, and sugar beets. Michigan's forests contribute significantly to the state's economy, supporting thousands of jobs in the wood-product, tourism, and recreation industries. With 10,083 inland lakes and 3,288 mi of Great Lakes shoreline, Michigan is a prime area for both commercial and sport fishing.

Points of interest are the automobile plants in Dearborn, Detroit, Flint, Lansing, and Pontiac; Mackinac Island; Pictured Rocks and Sleeping Bear Dunes National Lakeshores; Greenfield Village in Dearborn; and the many summer resorts along both the inland lakes and Great Lakes.

Famous natives and residents: Nelson Algren, novelist; Tim Allen, actor and comedian; Ralph J. Bunche, statesman; Ellen Burstyn, actress; Bruce Catton, historian; Roger Chaffee, astronaut; Francis Ford Coppola, film director; Thomas E. Dewey, politician; Edna Ferber, novelist; Gerald Ford, former president; Henry Ford, industrialist; Ali Haji-Sheikh, football player; Julie Harris, actress; Earvin "Magic" Johnson, basketball player; Ring Lardner, writer; Charles A. Lindbergh, aviator; Madonna, singer; Dick Martin, comedian; Terry McMillan, author; John N. Mitchell, former attorney general; Ted Nugent, singer; Gilda Radner, comedienne; Della Reese, singer; Jason Robards, Sr., actor; Diana Ross, singer; Steven Seagal, actor; Bob Seger, singer; Tom Selleck, actor; Thomas Schippers, conductor; Potter Stewart, jurist; Lily Tomlin, actress; Danny Thomas, entertainer; Margaret Whiting, singer; Robin Williams, comedian and actor; Stevie Wonder, singer.

Minnesota

Capital: St. Paul
Governor: Jesse Ventura, IP[1] (to Jan. 2003)
Lieut. Governor: Mae Schunk, IP[1] (to Jan. 2003)
Senators: Paul Wellstone, D (to Jan. 2003)
  Mark Dayton, D (to Jan. 2007)
Secy. of State: Mary Kiffmeyer, R
  (to Jan. 2003)
State Auditor: Judi Dutcher, D (to Jan. 2003)
Atty. General: Mike Hatch, D
  (to Jan. 2003)
State Treasurer: Carol Johnson, D (to Jan. 2003)
Organized as territory: March 3, 1849
Entered Union (rank): May 11, 1858 (32)
Present constitution adopted: 1858
Motto: L'Étoile du Nord (The North Star)
State Symbols: flower, lady slipper (1902); **tree,** red (or Norway) pine (1953); **bird,** common loon (also called great northern diver) (1961); **song,** "Hail Minnesota" (1945); **fish,** walleye (1965); **mushroom,** morel (1984);
Nicknames: North Star State; Gopher State; Land of 10,000 Lakes
Origin of name: From a Dakota Indian word meaning "sky-tinted water"
10 largest cities (2000): Minneapolis, 382,618; St. Paul, 287,151; Duluth, 86,918; Rochester, 85,806; Bloomington, 85,172; Brooklyn Park, 67,338; Plymouth, 65,894; Eagan, 63,557; Coon Rapids, 61,607; Burnsville, 60,220
Land area: 79,617 sq mi. (206,207 sq km)
Geographic center: In Crow Wing Co., 10 mi. SW of Brainerd
Number of counties: 87
Largest county by population and area: Hennepin, 1,116,200 (2000); St. Louis, 6,226 sq mi.
State forests: 55
State parks: 66 (226,000 ac.)
Residents: Minnesotan
2000 resident census population (rank): 4,919,479 (21). **Male:** 2,435,631 (49.5%); **Female:** 2,483,848 (50.5%). **White:** 4,400,282 (89.4%); **Black:** 171,731 (3.5%); **American Indian:** 54,967 (1.1%); **Asian:** 141,968 (2.9%); **Other race:** 65,810 (1.3%); **Two or more races:** 82,742 (1.7%); **Hispanic/Latino:** 143,382 (2.9%). **2000 percent population 18 and over:** 73.8; **65 and over:** 12.1; **median age:** 35.4.

1. Independence Party.

Following the visits of several French explorers, fur traders, and missionaries, including Jacques Marquette, Louis Joliet, and Robert Cavelier, Sieur de la Salle, the region was claimed for Louis XIV by Daniel Greysolon, Sieur Duluth, in 1679.

The U.S. acquired eastern Minnesota from Great Britain after the Revolutionary War and 20 years later bought the western part from France in the Louisiana Purchase of 1803. Much of the region was explored by U.S. Army lieutenant Zebulon M. Pike before the northern strip of Minnesota bordering Canada was ceded by Britain in 1818.

The state is rich in natural resources. A few square miles of land in the north in the Mesabi, Cuyuna, and Vermillion ranges produce more than 75% of the nation's iron ore. The state's farms rank high in yields of corn, wheat, rye, alfalfa, and sugar beets. Other leading farm products include butter, eggs, milk, potatoes, green peas, barley, soybeans, oats, and livestock.

Minnesota's factory production includes nonelectrical machinery, fabricated metals, flour-mill products, plastics, electronic computers, scientific instruments, and processed foods. It is also one of the nation's leaders in the printing and paper-products industries.

Minneapolis is the trade center of the Midwest, and the headquarters of the world's largest supercomputer and grain distributor. St. Paul is the nation's biggest publisher of calendars and law books. These "twin cities" are the nation's third-largest trucking center. Duluth has the nation's largest inland harbor and now handles a significant amount of foreign trade. Rochester is home to the Mayo Clinic, a world-famous medical center.

Tourism is a major revenue producer in Minnesota, with arts, fishing, hunting, water sports, and winter sports bringing in millions of visitors each year.

Among the most popular attractions are the St. Paul Winter Carnival; the Tyrone Guthrie Theatre, the Institute of Arts, Walker Art Center, and Minnehaha Park, in Minneapolis; Boundary Waters Canoe Area; Voyageurs National Park; North Shore Drive; the Minnesota Zoological Gardens; and the state's more than 10,000 lakes.

Famous natives and residents: LaVerne, Maxene, and Patti Andrews, singers; Warren E. Burger, jurist; William E. Colby, former director of the CIA; William Demarest, actor; William O. Douglas, jurist; Bob Dylan, singer and composer; F. Scott Fitzgerald, novelist; Judy Garland, singer and actress; J. Paul Getty, oil executive; Cass Gilbert, architect; Duane Hanson, sculptor; Hubert H. Humphrey, senator and vice president; Jessica Lange, actress; Sinclair Lewis, novelist; Cornell MacNeil, baritone; Roger Maris, baseball player; E. G. Marshall, actor; Charles H. Mayo, surgeon; William J. Mayo, surgeon; Eugene J. McCarthy, former senator; Kate Millett, feminist; Walter F. Mondale, former U.S. vice president; Gen. Lauris Norstad, former commander of NATO forces; Westbrook Pegler, columnist; John Sargent Pillsbury, businessman; Marion Ross, actress; Jane Russell, actress; Harrison E. Salisbury, journalist; Charles M. Schulz, cartoonist; Max Shulman, novelist; Maurice H. Stans, former secretary of commerce; Harold E. Stassen, former government official; Michael Todd, producer; Frederick Weyerhaeuser, businessman; Gig Young, actor.

Mississippi

Capital: Jackson
Governor: Ronnie Musgrove, D (to Jan. 2004)
Lieut. Governor: Amy Tuck, D (to Jan. 2004)
Senators: Thad Cochran, R (to Jan. 2003); Trent Lott, R (to Jan. 2007)
Secy. of State: Eric Clark, D (to Jan. 2004)
Treasurer: Marshall Bennett, D (to Jan. 2004)
Auditor: Phil Bryant, R (to Jan. 2004)
Atty. General: Mike Moore, D (to Jan. 2004)
Agriculture and Commerce Commissioner: Lester Spell, Jr., D (to Jan. 2004)
Insurance Commissioner: George Dale, D (to Jan. 2004)
Organized as territory: April 7, 1798
Entered Union (rank): Dec. 10, 1817 (20)
Present constitution adopted: 1890
Motto: *Virtute et armis* (By valor and arms)
State Symbols: flower, flower or bloom of the magnolia or evergreen magnolia (1952); **wildflower,** coreopsis (1991); **tree,** magnolia (1938); **bird,** mockingbird (1944); **song,** "Go, Mississippi" (1962); **stone,** petrified wood (1976); **fish,** largemouth or black bass (1974); **insect,** honeybee (1980); **shell,** oyster shell (1974); **water mammal,** bottlenosed dolphin or porpoise (1974);

fossil, prehistoric whale (1981); **land mammal,** white-tailed deer (1974), red fox (1997); **waterfowl,** wood duck (1974); **beverage,** milk (1984); **butterfly,** spicebush swallowtail (1991); **dance,** square dance (1995);
Nickname: Magnolia State
Origin of name: From an Indian word meaning "Father of Waters"
10 largest cities (2000): Jackson, 184,256; Gulfport, 71,127; Biloxi, 50,644; Hattiesburg, 44,779; Greenville, 41,663; Meridian, 39,968; Tupelo, 34,211; Southhaven, 28,977; Vicksburg, 26,407; Pascagoula, 26,200
Land area: 46,914 sq mi. (121,506 sq km)
Geographic center: In Leake Co., 9 mi. WNW of Carthage
Number of counties: 82
Largest county by population and area: Hinds, 250,800 (2000); Yazoo, 920 sq mi.
State forests: 1 (1,760 ac.)
State parks: 29 (24,521 ac.)
Residents: Mississippian
2000 resident census population (rank): 2,844,658 (31). **Male:** 1,373,554 (48.3%); **Female:** 1,471,104 (51.7%). **White:** 1,746,099 (61.4%); **Black:** 1,033,809 (36.3%); **American Indian:** 11,652 (0.4%); **Asian:** 18,626 (0.7%); **Other race:** 13,784 (0.5%); **Two or more races:** 20,021 (0.7%); **Hispanic/Latino:** 39,569 (1.4%). **2000 percent population 18 and over:** 72.7; **65 and over:** 12.1; **median age:** 33.8.

First explored for Spain by Hernando De Soto, who discovered the Mississippi River in 1540, the region was later claimed by France. In 1699, a French group under Sieur d'Iberville established the first permanent settlement near present-day Ocean Springs.

Great Britain took over the area in 1763 after the French and Indian Wars, ceding it to the U.S. in 1783 after the Revolution. Spain did not relinquish its claims until 1798, and in 1810 the U.S. annexed West Florida from Spain, including what is now southern Mississippi.

For a little more than one hundred years, from shortly after the state's founding through the Great Depression, cotton was the undisputed king of Mississippi's largely agrarian economy. Over the last half-century, however, Mississippi has diversified its economy by balancing agricultural output with increased industrial activity.

Today, agriculture continues as a major segment of the state's economy. For almost four decades soybeans have occupied the most acreage, while cotton has remained the largest cash crop. In 2001, however, more acres of cotton were planted than soybeans, and Mississippi has jumped to second in the nation in cotton production (exceeded only by Texas). The state's farmlands yield important harvests of corn, peanuts, pecans, rice, sugar cane, sweet potatoes, and food grains as well as poultry, eggs, meat animals, dairy products, feed crops, and horticultural crops. Mississippi remains the world's leading producer of pond-raised catfish.

The state abounds in historical landmarks and is the home of the Vicksburg National Military Park. Other National Park Service areas are Brices Cross Roads National Battlefield Site, Tupelo National Battlefield, and part of Natchez Trace National Parkway. Pre–Civil War mansions are the special pride of Natchez, Oxford, Columbus, Vicksburg, and Jackson.

Famous natives and residents: Red Barber, sportscaster; Jimmy Buffett, singer and songwriter; Craig Claiborne, columnist and restaurant critic; Bo Diddley, guitarist;

Charles Evers, civil rights leader; Medgar Evers, civil rights leader; William Faulkner, novelist; Shelby Foote, historian; Richard Ford, novelist; John Grisham, novelist; Barry Hannah, novelist; Beth Henley, playwright and actress; Jim Henson, puppeteer; James Earl Jones, actor; B. B. King, guitarist; Steve McNair, football player; Mary Ann Mobley, actress; Willie Morris, writer; Elvis Presley, singer and actor; Leontyne Price, soprano; William Raspberry, columnist; Jerry Rice, football player; Jimmie Rodgers, singer; Sela Ward, actress; Muddy Waters, singer and guitarist; Eudora Welty, novelist; Tennessee Williams, playwright; Oprah Winfrey, talk-show host and actress; Richard Wright, novelist; Tammy Wynette, singer.

Missouri

Capital: Jefferson City
Governor: Bob Holden, D (to Jan. 2005)
Lieut. Governor: Joe Maxwell, D (to Jan. 2005)
Senators: Christopher S. Bond, R (to Jan. 2005); Jean Carnahan, D (to Jan. 2003)
Secy. of State: Matt Blunt, R (to Jan. 2005)
Auditor: Claire C. McCaskill, D (to Jan. 2003)
Treasurer: Nancy Farmer, D (to Jan. 2005)
Atty. General: Jeremiah "Jay" W. Nixon, D (to Jan. 2005)
Organized as territory: June 4, 1812
Entered Union (rank): Aug. 10, 1821 (24)
Present constitution adopted: 1945
Motto: *Salus populi suprema lex esto* (The welfare of the people shall be the supreme law)
State Symbols: flower, hawthorn (1923); **bird,** bluebird (1927); **fish,** paddlefish (1997), channel catfish (1997); **song,** "Missouri Waltz" (1949); **fossil,** crinoid (1989); **musical instrument,** fiddle (1987); **rock,** mozarkite (1967); **mineral,** galena (1967); **insect,** honeybee (1985); **tree,** flowering dogwood (1955); **tree nut,** eastern black walnut (1990); **animal,** mule (1995); **dance,** square dance (1995); **Missouri Day,** third Wednesday in October (1969);
Nickname: Show-me State
Origin of name: Named after the Missouri Indian tribe. "Missouri" means "town of the large canoes."
10 largest cities (2000): Kansas City, 441,545; St. Louis, 348,189; Springfield, 151,580; Independence, 113,288; Columbia, 84,531; St. Joseph, 73,990; Lee's Summit, 70,700; St. Charles, 60,321; St. Peter's, 51,381; Florissant, 50,497
Land area: 68,898 sq mi. (178,446 sq km)
Geographic center: In Miller Co., 20 mi. SW of Jefferson City
Number of counties: 114, plus 1 independent city
Largest county by population and area: St. Louis, 1,016,315 (2000); Texas, 1,179 sq mi.
Conservation areas[1]: leased, 251 (199,587 ac.); owned, 551 (759,189 ac.)
Conservation accesses: leased, 77; owned, 237
State parks and historic sites: 81
Residents: Missourian
2000 resident census population (rank): 5,595,211 (17). **Male:** 2,720,177 (48.6%); **Female:** 2,875,034 (51.4%). **White:** 4,748,083 (84.9%); **Black:** 629,391 (11.2%); **American Indian:** 25,076 (0.4%); **Asian:** 61,595 (1.1%); **Other race:** 45,827 (0.8%); **Two or more races:** 82,061 (1.5%); **Hispanic/Latino:** 118,592 (2.1%). **2000 percent population 18 and over:** 74.5; **65 and over:** 13.5; **median age:** 36.1.

1. Includes wildlife areas, natural history areas, state forests, and tower sites.

Hernando De Soto visited the Missouri area in 1541. France's claim to the entire region was based on Sieur de la Salle's travels in 1682. French fur traders established Ste. Genevieve in 1735, and St. Louis was first settled in 1764.

The U.S. gained Missouri from France as part of the Louisiana Purchase in 1803, and the territory was admitted as a state following the Missouri Compromise of 1820. Throughout the pre–Civil War period and during the war, Missourians were sharply divided in their opinions about slavery and in their allegiances, supplying both Union and Confederate forces with troops. However, the state itself remained in the Union.

Historically, Missouri played a leading role as a gateway to the West, St. Joseph being the eastern starting point of the Pony Express, while the much-traveled Santa Fe and Oregon trails began in Independence.

Missouri's economy is highly diversified. Service industries provide more income and jobs than any other segment, and include a growing tourism and travel sector. Wholesale and retail trade, manufacturing, and agriculture also play significant roles in the state's economy.

Missouri is a leading producer of transportation equipment (including automobile manufacturing and auto parts), beer and beverages, and defense and aerospace technology. Food processing is the state's fastest-growing industry, well suited to the state's blend of agricultural, natural, energy, and transportation resources.

Missouri mines produce 90% of the nation's principal (non-recycled) lead supply. Other natural resources include iron ore, zinc, barite, limestone, and timber.

The state's top agricultural products include grain, sorghum, hay, corn, soybeans, and rice. Missouri also ranks high among the states in cattle and calves, hogs, and turkeys and broilers. A well-established grape and wine program brings together aspects of agriculture, manufacturing, and tourism to support a vibrant vintner industry.

Tourism draws hundreds of thousands of visitors to a number of Missouri points of interest: the country-music shows of Branson; Bass Pro Shops national headquarters (Springfield); the Gateway Arch at the Jefferson National Expansion (St. Louis); Mark Twain's boyhood home (Hannibal); the Harry S Truman home and library (Independence); the scenic beauty of the Ozark National Scenic Riverways; and the Pony Express and Jesse James museums (St. Joseph). The state's different lake regions also attract fishermen and sun-seekers from throughout the Midwest.

Famous natives and residents: Robert Altman, film director; Burt Bacharach, songwriter; Josephine Baker, singer and dancer; Wallace Beery, actor; Robert Russell Bennett, composer; Yogi Berra, baseball player; Thomas Hart Benton, painter; Bill Bradley, basketball player and former N.J. senator; Omar N. Bradley, five-star general; Grace Bumbry, soprano; William Burroughs, writer; Sarah Caldwell, opera director and conductor; Martha Jane Canary (Calamity Jane), frontierswoman; George Washington Carver, scientist; Walter Cronkite, TV newscaster; Robert Cummings, actor; Jane Darwell, actress; Walt Disney, artist; T. S. Eliot, poet; Redd Foxx, actor and comedian; Betty Grable, actress; Dick Gregory, comic and activist; Jean Harlow, actress; Coleman Hawkins, jazz musician; George Hearn, actor; Edwin Hubble, astronomer; Langston Hughes, poet; John Huston, film director; Jesse James, outlaw; Scott Joplin, composer; Marianne Moore, poet; Geraldine Page, actress; James C. Penney, merchant; John Joseph Pershing, general; Vincent Price, actor; Joseph Pulitzer, journalist; Ginger Rogers, dancer and actress; Casey Stengel, baseball player; Gladys Swarthout, soprano; Sara Teasdale, poet; Virgil Thomson, composer; Harry S Truman, former president; Mark Twain, author; Dick Van Dyke, actor; Ruth Warrick, actress; Dennis Weaver, actor; Mary Wickes, actress; Laura Ingalls Wilder, author; Roy Wilkins, civil rights leader.

Montana

Capital: Helena
Governor: Judy Martz, R (to Jan. 2005)
Lieut. Governor: Karl Ohs, R (to Jan. 2005)
Senators: Max Baucus, D (to Jan. 2003);
    Conrad R. Burns, R (to Jan. 2007)
Secy. of State: Bob Brown, R (to Jan. 2005)
Auditor: John Morrison, D (to Jan. 2005)
Atty. General: Mike McGrath, D (to Jan. 2005)
Organized as territory: May 26, 1864
Entered Union (rank): Nov. 8, 1889 (41)
Present constitution adopted: 1972
Motto: *Oro y plata* (Gold and silver)
State Symbols: flower, bitterroot (1895); **tree,**
    ponderosa pine (1949); **stones,** sapphire and agate
    (1969); **bird,** Western meadowlark (1981); **song,**
    "Montana" (1945);
Nickname: Treasure State
Origin of name: Chosen from Latin dictionary by J. M.
    Ashley. It is a Latinized Spanish word meaning
    "mountainous."
10 largest cities (2000): Billings, 89,847; Missoula,
    57,053; Great Falls, 56,690; Butte-Silver Bow[1],
    34,606; Bozeman, 27,509; Helena, 25,780; Kalispell,
    14,223; Havre, 9,621; Anaconda–Deer Lodge County,
    9,417; Miles City, 8,487
Land area: 145,556 sq mi. (376,991 sq km)
Geographic center: In Fergus Co., 12 mi. W
    of Lewistown
Number of counties: 56
Largest county by population and area: Yellowstone,
    129,352 (2000); Beaverhead, 5,543 sq mi.
State forests: 7 (214,000 ac.)
State parks and recreation areas: 110 (18,273 ac.)
Residents: Montanan
2000 resident census population (rank): 902,195 (44).
    Male: 449,480 (49.8%); **Female:** 452,715 (50.2%).
    White: 817,229 (90.6%); **Black:** 2,692 (0.3%); **Ameri-
    can Indian:** 56,068 (6.2%); **Asian:** 4,691 (0.5%); **Other
    race:** 5,315 (0.6%); **Two or more races:** 15,730 (1.7%);
    Hispanic/Latino: 18,081 (2.0%). **2000 percent popu-
    lation 18 and over:** 74.5; **65 and over:** 13.4; **median
    age:** 37.5.

1. The city is part of a consolidated city-county government and is coextensive with Silver Bow County.

First explored for France by François and Louis-
Joseph Verendrye in the early 1740s, much of the
region was acquired by the U.S. from France as part
of the Louisiana Purchase in 1803. Before western
Montana was obtained from Great Britain in the
Oregon Treaty of 1846, American trading posts and
forts had been established in the territory.

The major Indian Wars (1867–1877) included the
famous 1876 Battle of the Little Big Horn, better
known as "Custer's Last Stand," in which Cheyenne
and Sioux defeated George A. Custer and more than
200 of his men in southeast Montana.

Much of Montana's early history was concerned
with mining, with copper, lead, zinc, silver, coal,
and oil as principal products. Butte is the center of
the area that once supplied half of the U.S. copper.

Fields of grain cover much of Montana's plains. It
ranks high among the states in wheat and barley,
with rye, oats, flaxseed, sugar beets, and potatoes as
other important crops. Sheep and cattle raising make
significant contributions to the economy.

Tourist attractions include hunting, fishing, skiing,
and dude ranching. Glacier National Park, on the
Continental Divide, has 60 glaciers, 200 lakes, and
many streams with good trout fishing. Other major
points of interest include the Little Bighorn Battlefield National Monument, Virginia City, Yellowstone National Park, Fort Union Trading Post and
Grant-Kohr's Ranch National Historic Sites, and the
Museum of the Plains Indians at Browning.

Famous natives and residents: Dorothy Baker, author; Dirk
Benedict, actor; W. A. (Tony) Boyle, labor union official;
Gary Cooper, actor; John Cowan, prospector and founder
of Last Chance Gulch (now Helena); Alfred Bertram
Guthrie, Pulitzer Prize–winning author; Chet Huntley, TV
newscaster; Will James, writer and artist; Dorothy
Johnson, author; Evel Knievel, daredevil motorcyclist;
Myrna Loy, actress; David Lynch, filmmaker; Mike
Mansfield, former senator; George Montgomery, actor;
Jeannette Rankin, first woman elected to Congress;
Martha Raye, actress; Charles M. Russell, Old West
painter; Michael Smuin, choreographer; Lester C. Thurow,
economist and educator.

Nebraska

Capital: Lincoln
Governor: Mike Johanns, R (to Jan. 2003)
Lieut. Governor: Dave Maurstad, R (to Jan. 2003)
Senators: Chuck Hagel, R (to Jan. 2003);
    Ben Nelson, D (to Jan. 2007)
Secy. of State: Scott Moore, R (to Jan. 2003)
Atty. General: Don Stenberg, R (to Jan. 2003)
Auditor: Kate Witek, R (to Jan. 2003)
Treasurer: David Heineman, R (to Jan. 2003)
Organized as territory: May 30, 1854
Entered Union (rank): March 1, 1867 (37)
Present constitution adopted: Oct. 12, 1875 (exten-
    sively amended 1919–20)
Motto: Equality before the law
State Symbols: flower, goldenrod (1895); **fish,** channel
    catfish (1997); **American folk dance,** square dance
    (1997); **ballad,** "A Place Like Nebraska" (1997); **tree,**
    cottonwood (1972); **bird,** Western meadowlark (1929);
    insect, honeybee (1975); **gemstone,** blue agate
    (1967); **rock,** prairie agate (1967); **fossil,** mammoth
    (1967); **song,** "Beautiful Nebraska" (1967); **soil,** typic
    argiustolls, holdreges series (1979); **mammal,** whitetail
    deer (1981); **grass,** little bluestem (1969); **beverage,**
    milk (1998);
Nicknames: Cornhusker State (1945); Beef State
Origin of name: From an Oto Indian word meaning
    "flat water"
10 largest cities (2000): Omaha, 390,007; Lincoln,
    225,581; Bellevue, 44,382; Grand Island, 42,940;
    Kearney, 27,431; Fremont, 25,174; Hastings, 24,064;
    North Platte, 23,878; Norfolk, 23,516; Columbus,
    20,971
Land area: 76,878 sq mi. (199,113 sq km)
Geographic center: In Custer Co., 10 mi. NW of
    Broken Bow
Number of counties: 93
Largest county by population and area: Douglas,
    463,585 (2000); Cherry, 5,961 sq mi.
State parks: 85 areas, historical and recreational;
    8 major areas
Residents: Nebraskan
2000 resident census population (rank): 1,711,263
    (38). **Male:** 843,351 (49.3%); **Female:** 867,912
    (50.7%). **White:** 1,533,261 (89.6%); **Black:** 68,541
    (4.0%); **American Indian:** 14,896 (0.9%); **Asian:**
    21,931 (1.3%); **Other race:** 47,845 (2.8%); **Two or
    more races:** 23,953 (1.4%); **Hispanic/Latino:** 94,425
    (5.5%). **2000 percent population 18 and over:** 73.7;
    65 and over: 13.6; **median age:** 35.3.

French fur traders first visited Nebraska in the late
1600s. Part of the Louisiana Purchase in 1803, eastern Nebraska was explored by Lewis and Clark in
1804–1806.

Robert Stuart pioneered the Oregon Trail across
Nebraska in 1812–1813, and the first permanent

white settlement was established at Bellevue in 1823. Western Nebraska was acquired by treaty following the Mexican War in 1848. The Union Pacific began its transcontinental railroad at Omaha in 1865. In 1937, Nebraska became the only state in the Union to have a unicameral (one-house) legislature. Members are elected to it without party designation.

Nebraska is a leading grain-producer with bumper crops of grain, sorghum, corn, and wheat. More varieties of grass, valuable for forage, grow in this state than in any other in the nation. The state's sizable cattle and hog industries make Dakota City and Lexington among the nation's largest meat-packing centers.

Manufacturing has become diversified in Nebraska, strengthening the state's economic base. Firms making electronic components, auto accessories, pharmaceuticals, and mobile homes have joined such older industries as clothing, farm machinery, chemicals, and transportation equipment. Oil was discovered in 1939 and natural gas in 1949.

Among the principal attractions are Agate Fossil Beds, Homestead, and Scotts Bluff National Monuments; Chimney Rock National Historic Site; a re-created pioneer village at Minden; SAC Museum near Ashland; the Stuhr Museum of the Prairie Pioneer with 57 original 19th-century buildings near Grand Island; Boys Town; the Sheldon Memorial Art Gallery and the Lied Center for the Performing Arts located on the University of Nebraska campus in Lincoln; the State Capitol in Lincoln; the Joslyn Art Museum in Omaha; the Henry Doorly Zoo in Omaha; Museum of Nebraska Art in Kearney; Museum of Nebraska History in Lincoln; and the University of Nebraska State Museum in Lincoln.

Famous natives and residents: Grace Abbott, social worker; Bess Streeter Aldrich, author; Grover Cleveland Alexander, Hall of Fame pitcher; Fred Astaire, dancer and actor; Max Baer, boxer; Bil Baird, puppeteer; George Beadle, geneticist; Marlon Brando, actor; William Jennings Bryan, three-time U.S. presidential candidate; Warren Buffett, investor; Johnny Carson, TV host; Willa Cather, author; Dick Cavett, TV entertainer; Richard B. Cheney, vice president; Montgomery Clift, actor; James Coburn, actor; Sandy Dennis, actress; Mignon Eberhart, author; Harold "Doc" Edgerton, inventor; Ruth Etting, singer and actress; Fr. Edward J. Flanagan, founder of Boys Town; Henry Fonda, actor; Gerald Ford, former president; Bob Gibson, baseball player; Howard Hanson, conductor; Leland Hayward, producer; Robert Henri, painter; David Janssen, actor; Francis La Flesche, ethnologist; Melvin Laird, politician; Frank W. Leahy, football coach; Harold Lloyd, actor; Malcolm X, civil rights advocate; Dorothy McGuire, actress; Julius Sterling Morton, politician and journalist; John G. Neihardt, epic poet; Nick Nolte, actor; George W. Norris, senator; John J. Pershing, army general; Nathan Roscoe Pound, dean of Harvard Law School and botanist; Red Cloud, Indian rights advocate; Mari Sandoz, author; Standing Bear, Indian rights advocate; Robert Taylor, actor; Susette La Flesche Tibbles, Omaha Indian activist; Paul Williams, singer, composer, and actor; Julie Wilson, singer and actress; Darryl F. Zanuck, film producer.

Nevada

Capital: Carson City
Governor: Kenny Guinn, R (to Jan. 2003)
Lieut. Governor: Lorraine Hunt, R (to Jan. 2003)
Senators: Harry Reid, D (to Jan. 2005);
  John Ensign, R (to Jan. 2007)
Secy. of State: Dean Heller, R (to Jan. 2003)
Treasurer: Brian Krolicki, R (to Jan. 2003)
Controller: Kathy Augustine, R (to Jan. 2003)
Atty. General: Frankie Sue Del Papa, D (to Jan. 2003)

Organized as territory: March 2, 1861
Entered Union (rank): Oct. 31, 1864 (36)
Present constitution adopted: 1864
Motto: All for Our Country
State Symbols: flower, sagebrush (1959); **trees,** single-leaf pinon (1953) and bristlecone pine (1987); **bird,** mountain bluebird (1967); **animal,** desert bighorn sheep (1973); **colors,** silver and blue (1983); **song,** "Home Means Nevada" (1933); **rock,** sandstone (1987); **precious gemstone,** virgin valley black fire opal (1987); **semiprecious gemstone,** Nevada turquoise (1987); **grass,** Indian ricegrass (1977); **metal,** silver (1977); **fossil,** ichthyosaur (1977); **fish,** lahontan cutthroat trout (1981); **reptile,** desert tortoise (1989); **state artifact,** tule duck decoy (1995);
Nicknames: Sagebrush State; Silver State; Battle Born State
Origin of name: Spanish: "snowcapped"
10 largest cities (2000): Las Vegas, 478,434; Reno, 180,480; Henderson, 175,381; North Las Vegas, 115,488; Sparks, 66,346; Carson City, 52,457; Elko, 16,708; Boulder City, 14,966; Mesquite, 9,389; Fallon, 7,536
Land area: 109,806 sq mi. (284,397 sq km)
Geographic center: In Lander Co., 26 mi. SE of Austin
Number of counties: 16, plus 1 independent city
Largest county by population and area: Clark, 1,375,765 (2000); Nye, 18,147 sq mi.
State parks: 20 (150,000 ac., including leased lands)
Residents: Nevadan, Nevadian
2000 resident census population (rank): 1,998,257 (35). **Male:** 1,018,051 (50.9%); **Female:** 980,206 (49.1%). **White:** 1,501,886 (75.2%); **Black:** 135,477 (6.8%); **American Indian:** 26,420 (1.3%); **Asian:** 90,266 (4.5%); **Other race:** 159,354 (8.0%); **Two or more races:** 76,428 (3.8%); **Hispanic/Latino:** 393,970 (19.7%). **2000 percent population 18 and over:** 74.4; **65 and over:** 11.0; **median age:** 35.0.

Trappers and traders, including Jedediah Smith and Peter Skene Ogden, entered the Nevada area in the 1820s. In 1843–1845, John C. Frémont and Kit Carson explored the Great Basin and Sierra Nevada.

In 1848 following the Mexican War, the U.S. obtained the region, and the first permanent settlement was a Mormon trading post near present-day Genoa.

The driest state in the nation, with an average annual rainfall of only about 7 in., much of Nevada is uninhabited, sagebrush-covered desert. The wettest part of the state receives about 40 in. of precipitation per year, while the driest spot has less than 4 in. per year.

Nevada was made famous by the discovery of the Comstock Lode, the richest known U.S. silver deposit, in 1859, and its mines have produced large quantities of gold, silver, copper, lead, zinc, mercury, barite, and tungsten. Oil was discovered in 1954. Gold now far exceeds all other minerals in value of production.

In 1931, the state created two industries, divorce and gambling. For many years, Reno and Las Vegas were the "divorce capitals of the nation." More liberal divorce laws in many states have ended this distinction, but Nevada is still the gambling capital of the U.S. and a leading entertainment center. State gambling taxes account for 35.2% of general fund tax revenues. Although Nevada leads the nation in per capita gambling revenue, it ranks only tenth in total gambling revenue.

The state's leading agricultural industry is cattle and calves. Agricultural crops consist mainly of hay, alfalfa seed, barley, wheat, and potatoes.

Nevada manufactures gaming equipment; lawn and garden irrigation devices; titanium products; seismic and machinery monitoring devices; and specialty printing.

Lake Tahoe, Reno, and Las Vegas are major resorts. Recreation areas include Pyramid Lake, Lake Tahoe, and Lake Mead and Lake Mohave, both in Lake Mead National Recreation Area. Other attractions are Hoover Dam, Virginia City, and Great Basin National Park (includes Lehman Caves).

Famous natives and residents: Eva Adams, former director of U.S. Mint; Andre Agassi, tennis player; Raymond T. Baker, former director of U.S. Mint; Helen Delich Bentley, government official and newspaperwoman; Robert Caples, painter; Walter Van Tilburg Clark, writer; Henry Comstock, prospector; Abby Dalton, actress; Michele Greene, actress; Sarah Winnemucca Hopkins, author and Paiute interpreter and peacemaker; Jack Kramer, tennis player; Paul Laxalt, politician; Robert Laxalt, writer; William Lear, aviation inventor; Robert C. Lynch, surgeon; John W. Mackay, benefactor, one of Big Four of Comstock Lode; Emma Nevada, opera singer; Thelma "Pat" Nixon, former first lady; James W. Nye, territory governor and former senator; Lute Pease, cartoonist and Pulitzer Prize winner; Edna Purviance, actress; Patty Sheehan, golfer; Jack Wilson, Paiute Indian prophet; George Wingfield, mining millionaire.

New Hampshire

Capital: Concord
Governor: Jeanne Shaheen, D (to Jan. 2005)
Senators: Judd Gregg, R (to Jan. 2005); Bob Smith, R (to Jan. 2003)
Treasurer: Georgie A. Thomas, R (to Dec. 2002)
Secy. of State: William M. Gardner, D (to Dec. 2002)
Atty. General: Philip T. McLaughlin (to March 2001)
Entered Union (rank): June 21, 1788 (9)
Present constitution adopted: 1784
Motto: Live free or die
State Symbols: flower, purple lilac (1919); **tree,** white birch (1947); **animal,** white-tailed deer (1983); **insect,** ladybug (1977); **saltwater fish,** striped bass (1994); **freshwater fish,** brook trout (1995); **amphibian,** spotted newt (1985); **butterfly,** karner blue (1992); **bird,** purple finch (1957); **songs,** "Old New Hampshire" (1949) and "New Hampshire, My New Hampshire" (1963);
Nickname: Granite State
Origin of name: From the English county of Hampshire
10 largest cities (2000): Manchester, 107,006; Nashua, 86,605; Concord, 40,687; Derry, 34,021; Rochester, 28,461; Salem, 28,112; Dover, 26,884; Merrimack, 25,119; Londonderry, 23,236; Hudson, 22,928
Land area: 8,969 sq mi. (23,231 sq km)
Geographic center: In Belknap Co., 3 mi. E of Ashland
Number of counties: 10
Largest county by population and area: Hillsborough, 380,841 (2000); Coos, 1,801 sq mi.
State parks: 42 (50,000+ ac.)
Residents: New Hampshirite
2000 resident census population (rank): 1,235,786 (41). **Male:** 607,687 (49.2%); **Female:** 628,099 (50.8%). **White:** 1,186,851 (96.0%); **Black:** 9,035 (0.7%); **American Indian:** 2,964 (0.2%); **Asian:** 15,931 (1.3%); **Other race:** 7,420 (0.6%); **Two or more races:** 13,214 (1.1%); **Hispanic/Latino:** 20,489 (1.7%). **2000 percent population 18 and over:** 75.0; **65 and over:** 12.0; **median age:** 37.1.

Under an English land grant, Capt. John Smith sent settlers to establish a fishing colony at the mouth of the Piscataqua River, near present-day Rye and Dover, in 1623. Capt. John Mason, who participated in the founding of Portsmouth in 1630, gave New Hampshire its name.

After a 38-year period of union with Massachusetts, New Hampshire was made a separate royal colony in 1679. As leaders in the revolutionary cause, New Hampshire delegates received the honor of being the first to vote for the Declaration of Independence on July 4, 1776. New Hampshire gained a measure of international attention in 1905 when Portsmouth Naval Base played host to the signing of the treaty ending the Russo-Japanese War, known as the Treaty of Portsmouth.

Abundant water power turned New Hampshire into an industrial state early on, and manufacturing is the principal source of income. The most important industrial products are electrical and other machinery, textiles, pulp and paper products, and stone and clay products. Dairy and poultry, and growing fruit, truck vegetables, corn, potatoes, and hay are the major agricultural pursuits.

Because of New Hampshire's scenic and recreational resources, tourism now brings over $3.5 billion into the state annually.

Vacation attractions include Lake Winnipesaukee, largest of 1,300 lakes and ponds; the 724,000-acre White Mountain National Forest; Daniel Webster's birthplace near Franklin; Strawbery Banke, restored buildings of the original settlement at Portsmouth; and the famous "Old Man of the Mountain" granite head profile, the state's official emblem, at Franconia.

Famous natives and residents: Sherman Adams, former governor and presidential advisor; Salmon P. Chase, jurist; Charles Anderson Dana, editor; Mary Baker Eddy, founder of the Christian Science Church; Dustin Farnum, actor; Thomas Green Fessenden, journalist and satirical poet; Daniel Chester French, sculptor; Robert Frost, poet; Horace Greeley, journalist and politician; Sarah J. Hale, editor; John Irving, writer; Benjamin F. Keith, theater entrepreneur; Jackson Hall Kelly, promoter of Oregon settlement; John Langdon, political leader; Sharon Christa McAuliffe, teacher and astronaut; Franklin Pierce, former president; Augustus Saint-Gaudens, sculptor; Alan Shepard, astronaut; Harlan F. Stone, jurist; Daniel Webster, statesman; Henry Wilson, politician and former vice president; Noah Worcester, clergyman and pacifist.

New Jersey

Capital: Trenton
Senate President and Acting Governor: Donald T. DiFrancesco, R (to Jan. 2002)
Senators: Robert Torricelli, D (to Jan. 2003); Jon Corzine, D (to Jan. 2007)
Secy. of State: DeForest B. Soaries, Jr., R (to Jan. 2002)
Acting Treasurer: Peter R. Lawrance (to Jan. 2002)
Atty. General: John Farmer, Jr., R (to Jan. 2002)
Chief Justice: Deborah T. Poritz, R
Entered Union (rank): Dec. 18, 1787 (3)
Present constitution adopted: 1947
Motto: Liberty and prosperity
State Symbols: flower, purple violet (1913); **bird,** eastern goldfinch (1935); **insect,** honeybee (1974); **tree,** red oak (1950); **animal,** horse (1977); **colors,** buff and blue (1965); **folk dance,** square dance; **dinosaur,** hadrosaurus foulkii; **fish,** brook trout; **shell,** knobbed whelk;
Nickname: Garden State
Origin of name: From the Channel Isle of Jersey

10 largest cities (2000): Newark, 273,546; Jersey City, 240,055; Paterson, 149,222; Elizabeth, 120,568; Edison, 97,687; Woodbridge, 97,203; Dover, 89,706; Hamilton, 87,109; Trenton, 85,403; Camden, 79,904
Land area: 7,419 sq mi. (19,215 sq km)
Geographic center: In Mercer Co., 5 mi. SE of Trenton
Number of counties: 21
Largest county by population and area: Bergen, 884,118 (2000); Burlington, 805 sq mi.
State forests: 11
State parks: 35 (67,111 ac.)
Residents: New Jerseyite, New Jerseyan
2000 resident census population (rank): 8,414,350 (9). **Male:** 4,082,813 (48.5%); **Female:** 4,331,537 (51.5%). **White:** 6,104,705 (72.6%); **Black:** 1,141,821 (13.6%); **American Indian:** 19,492 (0.2%); **Asian:** 480,276 (5.7%); **Other race:** 450,972 (5.4%); **Two or more races:** 213,755 (2.5%); **Hispanic/Latino:** 1,117,191 (13.3%). **2000 percent population 18 and over:** 75.2; **65 and over:** 13.2; **median age:** 36.7.

New Jersey's early colonial history was involved with that of New York (New Netherlands), of which it was a part. One year after the Dutch surrender to England in 1664, New Jersey was organized as an English colony under Gov. Philip Carteret.

In 1676 the colony was divided between Carteret and a company of English Quakers who had obtained the rights belonging to John, Lord Berkeley. New Jersey became a united crown colony in 1702, administered by the royal governor of New York. Finally, in 1738, New Jersey was separated from New York under its own royal governor, Lewis Morris. Because of its key location between New York City and Philadelphia, New Jersey saw much fighting during the American Revolution.

Today, New Jersey, an area of wide industrial diversification, is known as the Crossroads of the East. Products from over 15,000 factories can be delivered overnight to almost 60 million people, representing 12 states and the District of Columbia. The greatest single industry is chemicals; New Jersey is one of the foremost research centers in the world. Many large oil refineries are located in northern New Jersey. Other important manufactured items are pharmaceuticals, instruments, machinery, electrical goods, and apparel.

Productive farmland covers nearly one million acres, about 20% of New Jersey's land area. The state ranks high in the production of almost all garden vegetables, as well as cranberries, blueberries, and peaches. Poultry, dairy products, and seafood are also top commodities.

Tourism is the second-largest industry in New Jersey. The state has numerous resort areas on 127 mi of Atlantic coastline. In 1977, New Jersey voters approved legislation allowing legalized casino gambling in Atlantic City. Points of interest include the Delaware Water Gap, the Edison National Historic Site in West Orange, Princeton University, Liberty State Park, Jersey City, and the N.J. State Aquarium in Camden.

Famous natives and residents: Bud Abbott, comedian; Charles Addams, cartoonist; Edwin Aldrin, astronaut; Count Basie, band leader; Joan Bennett, actress; Jon Bon Jovi, musician; William J. Brennan, jurist; Aaron Burr, political leader; James Fenimore Cooper, novelist; Lou Costello, comedian; Stephen Crane, writer; Helen Gahagan Douglas, former representative; Allen Ginsberg, poet; William Frederick Halsey, Jr., admiral; Alfred Joyce Kilmer, poet; Ernie Kovacs, comedian; Jerry Lewis, comedian and film director; Anne Morrow Lindbergh, author; Norman Mailer, novelist; Patricia McBride, ballerina; Richard Nixon, former president; Dorothy Parker, author; Joe Piscopo, comedian and actor; Paul Robeson, singer and actor; Philip Roth, novelist; Ruth St. Denis, dancer and choreographer; Antonin Scalia, jurist; H. Norman Schwarzkopf, general; Frank Sinatra, singer and actor; Bruce Springsteen, musician; Alfred Stieglitz, photographer; Albert Payson Terhune, journalist and novelist; Sarah Vaughan, singer; William Carlos Williams, physician and poet; Edmund Wilson, literary critic and author.

New Mexico

Capital: Santa Fe
Governor: Gary E. Johnson, R (to Jan. 2003)
Lieut. Governor: Walter Bradley, R (to Jan. 2003)
Senators: Jeff Bingaman, D (to Jan. 2007); Pete V. Domenici, R (to Jan. 2003)
Secy. of State: Rebecca Vigil-Giron, D (to Jan. 2003)
Atty. General: Patricia A. Madrid, D (to Jan. 2003)
State Auditor: Domingo P. Martinez, D (to Jan. 2003)
State Treasurer: Michael A. Montoya, D (to Jan. 2003)
Commissioner of Public Lands: Ray Powell, D (to Jan. 2003)
Organized as territory: Sept. 9, 1850
Entered Union (rank): Jan. 6, 1912 (47)
Present constitution adopted: 1911
Motto: *Crescit eundo* (It grows as it goes)
State Symbols: flower, yucca (1927); **tree,** pinon (1949); **animal,** black bear (1963); **bird,** roadrunner (1949); **fish,** cutthroat trout (1955); **vegetables,** chili and frijol (1965); **gem,** turquoise (1967); **song,** "O Fair New Mexico" (1917); **Spanish-language song,** "Asi Es Nuevo Méjico" (1971); **poem,** A Nuevo México (1991); **grass,** blue gramma (1973); **fossil,** coelophysis (1981); **cookie,** bizcochito (1989); **insect,** tarantula hawk wasp (1989); **ballad,** "Land of Enchantment" (1989); **bilingual song,** "New Mexico—Mi Lindo Nuevo Mexico", (1995); **question,** "Red or Green?" (1999);
Nickname: Land of Enchantment (1999)
Origin of name: From the country of Mexico
10 largest cities (2000): Albuquerque, 448,607; Las Cruces, 74,267; Santa Fe, 62,203; Rio Rancho, 51,765; Roswell, 45,293; Farmington, 37,844; Alamogordo, 35,582; Clovis, 32,667; Hobbs, 28,657; Carlsbad, 25,625
Land area: 121,365 sq mi. (314,334 sq km)
Geographic center: In Torrance Co., 12 mi. SSW of Willard
Number of counties: 33
Largest county by population and area: Bernalillo, 556,678 (2000); Catron, 6,928 sq mi.
State-owned forested land: 933,000 ac.
State parks: 31 (267,302 ac.)
Residents: New Mexican
2000 resident census population (rank): 1,819,046 (36). **Male:** 894,317 (49.2%); **Female:** 924,729 (50.8%). **White:** 1,214,253 (66.8%); **Black:** 34,343 (1.9%); **American Indian:** 173,483 (9.5%); **Asian:** 19,255 (1.1%); **Other race:** 309,882 (17.0%); **Two or more races:** 66,327 (3.6%); **Hispanic/Latino:** 765,386 (42.1%). **2000 percent population 18 and over:** 72.0; **65 and over:** 11.7; **median age:** 34.6.

Francisco Vásquez de Coronado, a Spanish explorer searching for gold, traveled the region that became New Mexico in 1540–1542. In 1598 the first Spanish settlement was established on the Rio Grande River by Juan de Onate; in 1610 Santa Fe was founded and made the capital of New Mexico.

The U.S. acquired most of New Mexico in 1848, as a result of the Mexican War, and the remainder in the 1853 Gadsden Purchase. Union troops captured the territory from the Confederates during the Civil

War. With the surrender of Geronimo in 1886, the Apache Wars and most of the Indian conflicts in the area were ended.

Since 1945, New Mexico has been a leader in energy research and development with extensive experiments conducted at Los Alamos Scientific Laboratory and Sandia Laboratories in the nuclear, solar, and geothermal areas.

Minerals are the state's richest natural resource, and New Mexico is one of the U.S. leaders in output of uranium and potassium salts. Petroleum, natural gas, copper, gold, silver, zinc, lead, and molybdenum also contribute heavily to the state's income.

The principal manufacturing industries include food products, chemicals, transportation equipment, lumber, electrical machinery, and stone-clay-glass products. More than two-thirds of New Mexico's farm income comes from livestock products, especially sheep. Cotton, pecans, and sorghum are the most important field crops. Corn, peanuts, beans, onions, chilies, and lettuce are also grown.

Tourist attractions include the Carlsbad Caverns National Park, Inscription Rock at El Morro National Monument, the ruins at Fort Union, Billy the Kid mementos at Lincoln, the White Sands and Gila Cliff Dwellings National Monuments, and the Chaco Culture National Historical Park.

Famous natives and residents: Kathy Baker, actress; Notah Begay III, golfer; Judy Blume, author; Ernest L. Blumenshein, artist; William "Billy the Kid" Bonney, outlaw; Richard Bradford, author; Ralph Bunche, Nobel Peace Prize winner; Bruce Cabot, actor; Glen Campbell, singer; Kit Carson, army scout and trapper; Dennis Chavez, former senator; John Chisum, cattle king; Mangus Coloradas, Apache leader; Edward Condon, physicist; Bill Daily, actor; John Denver, singer; Bo Diddley, blues guitarist; Patrick Garrett, lawman; Greer Garson, actress; Sid Gutierrez, astronaut; William Hanna, animator; Neil Patrick Harris, actor; Carl Hatch, former senator; Tony Hillerman, author; Conrad Hilton, hotel executive; Dennis Hopper, actor; Peter Hurd, artist; Preston Jones, playwright and actor; Ralph Kiner, baseball player and sportscaster; Nancy Lopez, golfer; Maria Martínez, San Ildefonso Pueblo potter; Demi Moore, actress; Jim Morrison, singer and songwriter; Bill Mauldin, political cartoonist; Popé, San Juan Pueblo medicine man and leader; Georgia O'Keeffe, painter; Harrison Schmitt, astronaut and U.S. representative; Kim Stanley, actress; Slim Summerville, actor; Clyde Tombaugh, astronomer; Al Unser, Bobby Unser, auto racers; Victorio, Apache chief; Linda Wertheimer, NPR correspondent; Kathy Whitworth, golfer.

New York

Capital: Albany
Governor: George E. Pataki, R (to Jan. 2003)
Lieut. Governor: Mary Donohue, R (to Jan. 2003)
Senators: Charles E. Schumer, D (to Jan. 2005); Hillary Rodham Clinton, D (to Jan. 2007)
Secy. of State: Randy A. Daniels, R (apptd. by governor)
Comptroller: Carl McCall, D (to Jan. 2003)
Atty. General: Eliot Spitzer, D (to Jan. 2003)
Entered Union (rank): July 26, 1788 (11)
Present constitution adopted: 1777 (last revised 1938)
Motto: *Excelsior* (Ever upward)
State Symbols: animal, beaver (1975); **fish,** brook trout (1975); **gem,** garnet (1969); **flower,** rose (1955); **tree,** sugar maple (1956); **bird,** bluebird (1970); **insect,** ladybug (1989); **song,** "I Love New York" (1980);
Nickname: Empire State
Origin of name: In honor of the Duke of York
10 largest cities (2000): New York, 8,008,278; Buffalo, 292,648; Rochester, 219,773; Yonkers, 196,086; Syracuse, 147,306; Albany, 95,658; New Rochelle, 72,182; Mount Vernon, 68,381; Schenectady, 61,821; Utica, 60,651

Land area: 47,224 sq mi. (122,310 sq km)
Geographic center: In Madison Co., 12 mi. S of Oneida and 26 mi. SW of Utica
Number of counties: 62
Largest county by population and area: Kings, 2,465,326 (2000); St. Lawrence, 2,686 sq mi.
State forest preserves: Adirondacks, 2,500,000 ac.; Catskills, 250,000 ac.
State parks: 152
Residents: New Yorker
2000 resident census population (rank): 18,976,457 (3). **Male:** 9,146,748 (48.2%); **Female:** 9,829,709 (51.8%). **White:** 12,893,689 (67.9%); **Black:** 3,014,385 (15.9%); **American Indian:** 82,461 (0.4%); **Asian:** 1,044,976 (5.5%); **Other race:** 1,341,946 (7.1%); **Two or more races:** 590,182 (3.1%); **Hispanic/Latino:** 2,867,583 (15.1%). **2000 percent population 18 and over:** 75.3; **65 and over:** 12.9; **median age:** 35.9.

Giovanni da Verrazano, an Italian-born navigator sailing for France, discovered New York Bay in 1524. Henry Hudson, an Englishman employed by the Dutch, reached the bay and sailed up the river now bearing his name in 1609, the same year that northern New York was explored and claimed for France by Samuel de Champlain.

In 1624 the first permanent Dutch settlement was established at Fort Orange (now Albany); one year later Peter Minuit is said to have purchased Manhattan Island from the Indians for trinkets worth about $24 and founded the Dutch colony of New Amsterdam (now New York City), which was surrendered to the English in 1664.

For a short time, New York City was the U.S. capital, and George Washington was inaugurated there as the first president on April 30, 1789.

New York's extremely rapid commercial growth may be partly attributed to Gov. De Witt Clinton, who pushed through the construction of the Erie Canal (Buffalo to Albany), which was opened in 1825. Today, the 641-mile Gov. Thomas E. Dewey Thruway connects New York City with Buffalo and with Connecticut, Massachusetts, and Pennsylvania express highways. Two toll-free superhighways, the Adirondack Northway (linking Albany with the Canadian border) and the North-South Expressway (crossing central New York from the Pennsylvania border to the Thousand Islands), have been opened.

The great metropolis of New York City is the nerve center of the nation. It is a leader in manufacturing, foreign trade, commerce and banking, book and magazine publishing, and theatrical production. A leading seaport, its John F. Kennedy International Airport is one of the busiest airports in the world. New York is also home to the New York Stock Exchange, the largest in the world. The printing and publishing industry is the city's largest manufacturing employer, with the apparel industry second.

Nearly all the rest of the state's manufacturing is done on Long Island, along the Hudson River north to Albany, and through the Mohawk Valley, Central New York, and Southern Tier regions to Buffalo. The St. Lawrence seaway and power projects have opened the North Country to industrial expansion and have given the state a second seacoast.

The state ranks seventh in the nation in manufacturing, with 874,200 employees in 2000. The principal industries are printing and publishing, industrial machinery and equipment, electronic equipment, and instruments. The convention and tourist business is also an important source of income.

New York farms produce cattle and calves, corn and poultry, and vegetables and fruits. The state is a leading wine producer.

Major points of interest are Castle Clinton, Fort Stanwix, and Statue of Liberty National Monuments; Niagara Falls; U.S. Military Academy at West Point; National Historic Sites that include homes of Franklin D. Roosevelt at Hyde Park and Theodore Roosevelt in Oyster Bay and New York City; the Women's Rights National Historical Park in Seneca Falls; National Memorials, including Grant's Tomb and Federal Hall in New York City; Fort Ticonderoga; the Baseball Hall of Fame in Cooperstown; and the United Nations, skyscrapers, museums, theaters, and parks in New York City.

Famous natives and residents: Kareem Abdul-Jabbar, basketball player; Lucille Ball, actress; Humphrey Bogart, actor; James Cagney, actor; Maria Callas, soprano; Benjamin N. Cardozo, jurist; Paddy Chayefsky, playwright; Peter Cooper, industrialist and philanthropist; Aaron Copland, composer; Sammy Davis, Jr., actor and singer; Agnes de Mille, choreographer; Eamon De Valera, former president of Ireland; George Eastman, inventor; Millard Fillmore, former president; Lou Gehrig, baseball player; George Gershwin, composer; Learned Hand, jurist; Edward Hopper, painter; Julia Ward Howe, poet and reformer; Charles Evans Hughes, jurist; Washington Irving, author; Henry James, novelist; John Jay, jurist; Michael Jordan, basketball player; Jerome Kern, composer; Rockwell Kent, painter; Vince Lombardi, football coach; Chico, Groucho, Harpo, and Zeppo Marx, comedians; Herman Melville, author; Ethel Merman, singer and actress; Ogden Nash, poet; Eugene O'Neill, playwright; Red Jacket, Seneca chief; John D. Rockefeller, industrialist; Norman Rockwell, painter and illustrator; Mickey Rooney, actor; Anna Eleanor Roosevelt, reformer and humanitarian; Franklin D. Roosevelt, former president; Theodore Roosevelt, former president; Jonas Salk, polio researcher; Margaret Sanger, birth control leader; Barbara Stanwyck, actress; Risë Stevens, mezzo-soprano; Joe Torre, baseball player and manager; Richard Tucker, tenor; Martin Van Buren, former president; Mae West, actress; Walt Whitman, poet; Edith Wharton, novelist.

North Carolina

Capital: Raleigh
Governor: Mike Easley, D (to Jan. 2005)
Lieut. Governor: Beverly Perdue, D (to Jan. 2005)
Senators: John Edwards, D (to Jan. 2005); Jesse Helms, R (to Jan. 2003)
Secy. of State: Elaine F. Marshall, D (to Jan. 2005)
Treasurer: Richard H. Moore, D (to Jan. 2005)
Auditor: Ralph Campbell, D (to Jan. 2005)
Atty. General: Roy Cooper, D (to Jan. 2005)
Entered Union (rank): Nov. 21, 1789 (12)
Present constitution adopted: 1971
Motto: *Esse quam videri* (To be rather than to seem)
State Symbols: flower, dogwood (1941); **tree,** pine (1963); **bird,** cardinal (1943); **mammal,** gray squirrel (1969); **insect,** honeybee (1973); **reptile,** eastern box turtle (1979); **gemstone,** emerald (1973); **shell,** scotch bonnet (1965); **historic boat,** shad boat (1987); **beverage,** milk (1987); **rock,** granite (1979); **dog,** plott hound (1989); **song,** "The Old North State" (1927); **colors,** red and blue (1945);
Nickname: Tar Heel State
Origin of name: In honor of Charles I of England
10 largest cities (2000): Charlotte, 540,828; Raleigh, 276,093; Greensboro, 223,891; Durham, 187,035; Winston-Salem, 185,776; Fayetteville, 121,015; Cary, 94,536; High Point, 85,839; Wilmington, 75,838; Asheville, 68,889
Land area: 48,718 sq mi. (126,180 sq km)
Geographic center: In Chatham Co., 10 mi. NW of Sanford
Number of counties: 100

Largest county by population and area: Mecklenburg, 695,454 (2000); Robeson, 949 sq mi.
State forests: 1
State parks: 30 (125,000 ac.)
Residents: North Carolinian
2000 resident census population (rank): 8,049,313 (11). **Male:** 3,942,695 (49.0%); **Female:** 4,106,618 (51.0%). **White:** 5,804,656 (72.1%); **Black:** 1,737,545 (21.6%); **American Indian:** 99,551 (1.2%); **Asian:** 113,689 (1.4%); **Other race:** 186,629 (2.3%); **Two or more races:** 103,260 (1.3%); **Hispanic/Latino:** 378,963 (4.7%). **2000 percent population 18 and over:** 75.6; **65 and over:** 12.0; **median age:** 35.3.

English colonists, sent by Sir Walter Raleigh, unsuccessfully attempted to settle Roanoke Island in 1585 and 1587. Virginia Dare, born there in 1587, was the first child of English parentage born in America.

In 1653 the first permanent settlements were established by English colonists from Virginia near the Roanoke and Chowan rivers. The region was established as an English proprietary colony in 1663–1665 and in its early history was the scene of Culpepper's Rebellion (1677), the Quaker-led Cary Rebellion (1708), the Tuscarora Indian War (1711–1713), and many pirate raids.

During the American Revolution, there was relatively little fighting within the state, but many North Carolinians saw action elsewhere. Despite considerable pro-Union, anti-slavery sentiment, North Carolina joined the Confederacy during the Civil War.

North Carolina is the nation's largest furniture, tobacco, brick, and textile producer. It holds second place in the Southeast in population and first place in the value of its industrial and agricultural production. This production is highly diversified, with metalworking, chemicals, and paper constituting enormous industries. Tobacco, corn, cotton, hay, peanuts, and vegetable crops are of major importance. It is the country's leading producer of mica and lithium.

Tourism is also important, with visitors spending more than $1 billion annually. Sports include year-round golfing, skiing at mountain resorts, both fresh- and salt-water fishing, and hunting.

Among the major attractions are the Great Smoky Mountains, the Blue Ridge National Parkway, the Cape Hatteras and Cape Lookout National Seashores, the Wright Brothers National Memorial at Kitty Hawk, Guilford Courthouse and Moores Creek National Military Parks, Carl Sandburg's home near Hendersonville, and the Old Salem Restoration in Winston-Salem.

Famous natives and residents: David Brinkley, TV newscaster; Howard Cosell, sportscaster; Virginia Dare, first person born in America to English parents; James B. Duke, industrialist; Donna Fargo, singer; Roberta Flack, singer; Ava Gardner, actress; Richard Gatling, inventor; Billy Graham, evangelist; Kathryn Grayson, singer and actress; Andy Griffith, actor; Jesse Helms, politician; O. Henry, writer; Barbara Howar, broadcaster and writer; Andrew Johnson, former president; Charles Kuralt, TV journalist; Sugar Ray Leonard, boxer; Dolley Madison, former first lady; Ronnie Milsap, singer; Thelonious Monk, pianist; Alfred Moore, jurist; Edward R. Murrow, commentator and government official; Walter Hines Page, journalist and ambassador; Floyd Patterson, boxer; Richard Petty, auto racer; James K. Polk, former president; Soupy Sales, comedian; Earl Scruggs, bluegrass musician; Randy Travis, musician; John Scott Trotter, orchestra leader; Thomas Wolfe, novelist.

North Dakota

Capital: Bismarck
Governor: John Hoeven, R (to Dec. 15, 2004)
Lieut. Governor: Jack Dalrymple, R (to Dec. 15, 2004)
Senators: Kent Conrad, D (to Jan. 2007);
Byron L. Dorgan, D (to Jan. 2005)
Secy. of State: Alvin A. Jaeger, R (to Dec. 31, 2004)
Auditor: Robert R. Peterson, R (to Dec. 31, 2004)
Treasurer: Kathi Gilmore, D (to Dec. 31, 2004)
Atty. General: Wayne Stenehjem, R (to Dec. 31, 2004)
Organized as territory: March 2, 1861
Entered Union (rank): Nov. 2, 1889 (39)
Present constitution adopted: 1889
Motto: Liberty and union, now and forever: one and inseparable
State Symbols: tree, American elm (1947); **bird,** western meadowlark (1947); **song,** "North Dakota Hymn" (1947); **fish,** northern pike (1969); **grass,** western wheatgrass (1977); **fossil,** teredo petrified wood (1967); **beverage,** milk (1983); **state march,** Spirit of the Land (1975); **flower,** wild prairie rose (1907); **equine,** Nokota horse (1993); **dance,** square dance (1995);
Nickname: Sioux State; Flickertail State; Peace Garden State; Rough Rider State
Origin of name: From the Sioux tribe, meaning "allies"
10 largest cities (2000): Fargo, 90,599; Bismarck, 55,532; Grand Forks, 49,321; Minot, 36,567; Mandan, 16,718; Dickinson, 16,010; Jamestown, 15,527; West Fargo, 14,940; Williston, 12,512; Wahpeton, 8,586
Land area: 70,704 sq mi. (183,123 sq km)
Geographic center: In Sheridan Co., 5 mi. SW of McClusky
Number of counties: 53
Largest county by population and area: Cass, 123,138 (2000); McKenzie, 2,742 sq mi.
State parks: 20 (14,822 ac.)
Residents: North Dakotan
2000 resident census population (rank): 642,200 (47). **Male:** 320,524 (49.9%); **Female:** 321,676 (50.1%). **White:** 593,181 (92.4%); **Black:** 3,916 (0.6%); **American Indian:** 31,329 (4.9%); **Asian:** 3,606 (0.6%); **Other race:** 2,540 (0.4%); **Two or more races:** 7,398 (1.2%); **Hispanic/Latino:** 7,786 (1.2%). **2000 percent population 18 and over:** 75.0; **65 and over:** 14.7; **median age:** 36.2.

North Dakota was explored in 1738–1740 by French Canadians led by Sieur de la Verendrye. In 1803, the U.S. acquired most of North Dakota from France in the Louisiana Purchase. Lewis and Clark explored the region in 1804–1806, and the first settlements were made at Pembina in 1812 by Scottish and Irish families while this area was still in dispute between the U.S. and Great Britain. In 1818, the U.S. obtained the northeast part of North Dakota by treaty with Great Britain and took possession of Pembina in 1823.

North Dakota is the most rural of all the states, with farms covering more than 90% of the land. North Dakota ranks first in the nation's production of spring and durum wheat, and the state's coal and oil reserves are plentiful.

Other agricultural products include barley, rye, sunflowers, dry edible beans, honey, oats, flaxseed, sugar beets, hay, beef cattle, sheep, and hogs.

Recently, manufacturing industries have grown, especially food processing and farm equipment. The state also produces natural gas, lignite, salt, clay, sand, and gravel.

The Garrison Dam on the Missouri River provides extensive irrigation and produces 400,000 kilowatts of electricity for the Missouri Basin areas.

Known for its waterfowl, grouse, and deer hunting and bass, trout, and pike fishing, North Dakota has 20 state parks and recreation areas. Points of interest include the International Peace Garden near Dunseith, Fort Union Trading Post National Historic Site near Williston, Knife River Indian Villages National Historic Site in Stanton, the State Capitol at Bismarck, the Badlands, Theodore Roosevelt National Park, and Fort Abraham Lincoln State Park.

Famous natives and residents: Lynn Anderson, singer; Maxwell Anderson, playwright; Elizabeth Bodine, humanitarian; Dr. Anne Carlsen, educator; Warren Christopher, statesman; Ronald N. Davies, jurist; Angie Dickinson, actress; Dr. Leon O. Jacobson, researcher and educator; Harold K. Johnson, general; David C. Jones, general; Louis L'Amour, author; Peggy Lee, singer; William Lemke, former representative; Roger Maris, baseball player; Marquis de Mores, cattleman who established Medora; Gerald P. Nye, former senator; Casper Oimoen, skier; Arthur Peterson, radio and TV actor; Cliff (Fido) Purpur, hockey player and coach; James Rosenquist, painter; Harold Schafer, founder of Gold Seal Co.; Eric Sevareid, TV commentator; Ann Sothern, actress; Dorothy Stickney, actress; Edward K. Thompson, editor; Era Bell Thompson, editor; Tommy Tucker, band leader; Bobby Vee, entertainer; Lawrence Welk, band leader; Larry Woiwode, writer.

Ohio

Capital: Columbus
Governor: Bob Taft, R (to Jan. 2003)
Lieut. Governor: Maureen O'Connor, R (to Jan. 2003)
Senators: Mike DeWine, R (to Jan. 2007);
George V. Voinovich, R (to Jan. 2005)
Secy. of State: J. Kenneth Blackwell, R (to Jan. 2003)
Auditor: Jim Petro, R (to Jan. 2003)
Treasurer: Joseph T. Deters, R (to Jan. 2003)
Atty. General: Betty D. Montgomery, R (to Jan. 2003)
Entered Union (rank): March 1, 1803 (17)
Present constitution adopted: 1851
Motto: With God all things are possible
State Symbols: flower, scarlet carnation (1904); **tree,** buckeye (1953); **bird,** cardinal (1933); **insect,** ladybug (1975); **gemstone,** flint (1965); **song,** "Beautiful Ohio" (1969); **beverage,** tomato juice (1965); **fossil,** trilobite (1985); **animal,** white-tailed deer (1988); **wildflower,** large white trillium (1987);
Nickname: Buckeye State
Origin of name: From an Iroquoian word meaning "great river"
10 largest cities (2000): Columbus, 711,470; Cleveland, 478,403; Cincinnati, 331,285; Toledo, 313,619; Akron, 217,074; Dayton, 166,179; Parma, 85,655; Youngstown, 82,026; Canton, 80,806; Lorain, 68,652
Land area: 40,953 sq mi. (106,067 sq km)
Geographic center: In Delaware Co., 25 mi. NNE of Columbus
Number of counties: 88
Largest county by population and area: Cuyahoga, 1,393,978 (2000); Ashtabula, 703 sq mi.
State forests: 20 (more than 183,000 ac.)
State parks: 73 (more than 204,000 ac.)
Residents: Ohioan
2000 resident census population (rank): 11,353,140 (7). **Male:** 5,512,262 (48.6%); **Female:** 5,840,878 (51.4%). **White:** 9,645,453 (85.0%); **Black:** 1,301,307 (11.5%); **American Indian:** 24,486 (0.2%); **Asian:** 132,633 (1.2%); **Other race:** 88,627 (0.8%); **Two or more races:** 157,885 (1.4%); **Hispanic/Latino:** 217,123 (1.9%). **2000 percent population 18 and over:** 74.6; **65 and over:** 13.3; **median age:** 36.2.

First explored for France by Robert Cavelier, Sieur de la Salle in 1669, the Ohio region became British property after the French and Indian Wars. Ohio was acquired by the U.S. after the Revolutionary War in 1783. In 1788, the first permanent settlement was established at Marietta, capital of the Northwest Territory.

The 1790s saw severe fighting with the Indians in Ohio; a major battle was won by Maj. Gen. Anthony Wayne at Fallen Timbers in 1794. In the War of 1812, Commodore Oliver H. Perry defeated the British in the Battle of Lake Erie on Sept. 10, 1813.

Ohio is one of the nation's industrial leaders, ranking third in the value of manufactured products. Important manufacturing centers are located in or near Ohio's major cities. Akron is known for rubber; Canton for roller bearings; Cincinnati for jet engines and machine tools; Cleveland for auto assembly, auto parts, and steel; Dayton for office machines, refrigeration, and heating and auto equipment; Youngstown and Steubenville for steel; and Toledo for glass and auto parts.

The state's fertile soil produces soybeans, corn, oats, grapes, and clover. More than half of Ohio's farm receipts come from dairy farming and sheep and hog raising. Ohio is the top state in lime production and among the leaders in coal, clay, salt, sand, and gravel. Petroleum, gypsum, cement, and natural gas are also important.

Tourism is a valuable revenue producer, bringing in $27 billion in 1999. (In 1999 Ohio ranked 7th among the 50 states as a destination for U.S. travelers.) Attractions include the Rock and Roll Hall of Fame, Indian burial grounds at Mound City Group National Monument, Perry's Victory International Peace Memorial, the Pro Football Hall of Fame at Canton, and the homes of presidents Grant, Taft, Hayes, Harding, and Garfield.

Famous natives and residents: Neil Armstrong, astronaut; Kathleen Battle, soprano; George Bellows, painter and lithographer; Ambrose Bierce, journalist; Erma Bombeck, columnist; Bill Boyd (Hopalong Cassidy), actor; Milton Caniff, cartoonist; Hart Crane, poet; George Armstrong Custer, army officer; Dorothy Dandridge, actress; Doris Day, singer and actress; Clarence Darrow, lawyer; Ruby Dee, actress; Rita Dove, poet; Hugh Downs, TV broadcaster; Thomas A. Edison, inventor; Clark Gable, actor; James A. Garfield, former president; Lillian Gish, actress; John Glenn, astronaut and senator; Ulysses S. Grant, former president; Warren G. Harding, former president; Rutherford Hayes, former president; Benjamin Harrison, former president; William Dean Howells, novelist and critic; Zane Grey, author; Robert Henri, painter; Kenisaw Mountain Landis, first baseball commissioner; Dean Martin, singer and actor; William McKinley, former president; Paul Newman, actor; Jack Nicklaus, golfer; Annie Oakley, markswoman; Norman Vincent Peale, clergyman; Tyrone Power, actor; Judith Resnik, astronaut; Eddie Rickenbacker, aviator; Arthur M. Schlesinger, Jr., historian; William Tecumseh Sherman, army general; Gloria Steinem, feminist; William H. Taft, former president; Tecumseh, Shawnee Indian chief; Lowell Thomas, explorer and commentator; James Thurber, author and cartoonist; Orville Wright, inventor; Cy Young, baseball player.

Oklahoma

Capital: Oklahoma City
Governor: Frank Keating, R (to Jan. 2003)
Lieut. Governor: Mary Fallin, R (to Jan. 2003)
Senators: James M. Inhofe, R (to Jan. 2003); Don Nickles, R (to Jan. 2005)
Secy. of State: Mike Hunter, R (to Jan. 2003)
Treasurer: Robert Butkin, D (to Jan. 2003)

Atty. General: Drew Edmondson, D (to Jan. 2003)
Organized as territory: May 2, 1890
Entered Union (rank): Nov. 16, 1907 (46)
Present constitution adopted: 1907
Motto: *Labor omnia vincit* (Labor conquers all things)
State Symbols: flower, mistletoe (1893); **tree,** redbud (1937); **bird,** scissor-tailed flycatcher (1951); **animal,** bison (1972); **reptile,** mountain boomer lizard (1969); **stone,** rose rock (barite rose) (1968); **colors,** green and white (1915); **song,** "Oklahoma" (1953); **beverage,** milk; **butterfly,** black swallowtail; **fish,** white or sand bass; **folk dance,** square dance; **furbearer,** raccoon; **game animal,** white-tailed deer; **grass,** Indiangrass; **insect,** honeybee; **musical instrument,** fiddle; **poem,** "Howdy Folks," David Randolph Milsten; **waltz,** "Oklahoma Wind"; **wildflower,** Indian blanket;
Nickname: Sooner State
Origin of name: From two Choctaw Indian words meaning "red people"
10 largest cities (2000): Oklahoma City, 506,132; Tulsa, 393,049; Norman, 95,694; Lawton, 92,757; Broken Arrow, 74,859; Edmond, 68,315; Midwest City, 54,088; Enid, 47,045; Moore, 41,138; Stillwater, 39,065
Land area: 68,679 sq mi. (177,877 sq km)
Geographic center: In Oklahoma Co., 8 mi. N of Oklahoma City
Number of counties: 77
Largest county by population and area: Oklahoma, 660,448 (2000); Osage, 2,251 sq mi.
State parks: 51 (72,000 ac.)
Residents: Oklahoman
2000 resident census population (rank): 3,450,654 (27). **Male:** 1,696,895 (49.1%); **Female:** 1,754,759 (50.9%). **White:** 2,628,434 (76.2%); **Black:** 260,968 (7.6%); **American Indian:** 273,230 (7.9%); **Asian:** 46,767 (1.4%); **Other race:** 82,898 (2.4%); **Two or more races:** 155,985 (4.5%); **Hispanic/Latino:** 179,304 (5.2%). **2000 percent population 18 and over:** 74.1; **65 and over:** 13.2; **median age:** 35.5.

Francisco Vásquez de Coronado first explored the region for Spain in 1541. The U.S. acquired most of Oklahoma in 1803 in the Louisiana Purchase from France; the Western Panhandle region became U.S. territory with the annexation of Texas in 1845.

Set aside as Indian Territory in 1834, the region was divided into Indian Territory and Oklahoma Territory on May 2, 1890. The two were combined to make a new state, Oklahoma, on Nov. 16, 1907.

On April 22, 1889, the first day homesteading was permitted, 50,000 people swarmed into the area. Those who tried to beat the noon starting gun were called "Sooners," hence the state's nickname.

Oil made Oklahoma a rich state, but natural-gas production has now surpassed it. Oil refining, meat packing, food processing, and machinery manufacturing (especially construction and oil equipment) are important industries. Minerals produced in Oklahoma include helium, gypsum, zinc, cement, coal, copper, and silver.

Oklahoma's rich plains produce bumper yields of wheat, as well as large crops of sorghum, hay, cotton, and peanuts. More than half of Oklahoma's annual farm receipts are contributed by livestock products, including cattle, dairy products, swine, and broilers.

Tourist attractions include the National Cowboy Hall of Fame in Oklahoma City, the Will Rogers Memorial in Claremore, the Cherokee Cultural Center with a restored Cherokee village, the restored Fort Gibson Stockade near Muskogee, the Lake

Texoma recreation area, Pari-Mutual horse racing at Remington Park in Oklahoma City, and Blue Ribbon Downs in Sallisaw.

Famous natives and residents: Johnny Bench, baseball player; John Berryman, poet; Garth Brooks, singer; Iron Eyes Cody, Cherokee actor; L. Gordon Cooper, astronaut; Ralph Ellison, writer; James Garner, actor; Owen K. Garriott, astronaut; Vince Gill, singer; Chester Gould, cartoonist; Woody Guthrie, singer and composer; Roy Harris, composer; Paul Harvey, broadcaster; Van Heflin, actor; Ron Howard, actor and director; Ben Johnson, actor; Jennifer Jones, actress; Jeane Kirkpatrick, educator and public-affairs spokesperson; Shannon Lucid, astronaut; Wilma P. Mankiller, principal chief of the Cherokee Nation of Oklahoma; Mickey Mantle, baseball player; Reba McEntire, singer; Shannon Miller, Olympic gymnast; Bill Moyers, journalist; Daniel Patrick Moynihan, N.Y. senator; Patti Page, singer; Mary Kay Place, actress and writer; Tony Randall, actor; Oral Roberts, evangelist; Dale Robertson, actor; Will Rogers, humorist; Dan Rowan, comedian; Thomas P. Stafford, astronaut; Maria Tallchief, ballerina; Jim Thorpe, athlete; Alfre Woodard, actress.

Oregon

Capital: Salem
Governor: John A. Kitzhaber, D (to Jan. 2003)
Senators: Gordon Smith, R (to Jan. 2003); Ron Wyden, D (to Jan. 2005)
Secy. of State: Bill Bradbury, D (to Jan. 2005)
Treasurer: Randall Edwards, D (to Jan. 2005)
Atty. General: Hardy Myers, D (to Jan. 2005)
Organized as territory: Aug. 14, 1848
Entered Union (rank): Feb. 14, 1859 (33)
Present constitution adopted: 1859
Motto: *Alis volat Propriis* (She flies with her own wings) (1987)
State Symbols: flower, Oregon grape (1899); **tree,** douglas fir (1939); **animal,** beaver (1969); **bird,** western meadowlark (1927); **fish,** chinook salmon (1961); **rock,** thunderegg (1965); **colors,** navy blue and gold (1959); **song,** "Oregon, My Oregon" (1927); **insect,** swallowtail butterfly (1979); **dance,** square dance (1977); **nut,** hazelnut (1989); **gemstone,** sunstone (1987); **seashell,** Oregon hairy triton (1991); **beverage,** milk (1997); **mushroom,** Pacific golden chanterelle (1999);
Nickname: Beaver State
Origin of name: Unknown. However, it is generally accepted that the name, first used by Jonathan Carver in 1778, was taken from the writings of Maj. Robert Rogers, an English army officer.
10 largest cities (2000): Portland, 529,121; Eugene, 137,893; Salem, 136,924; Gresham, 90,205; Beaverton, 76,129; Hillsboro, 70,186; Medford, 63,154; Springfield, 52,864; Bend, 52,029; Corvallis, 49,322
Land area: 96,003 sq mi. (248,647 sq km)
Geographic center: In Crook Co., 25 mi. SSE of Prineville
Number of counties: 36
Largest county by population and area: Multnomah, 660,486 (2000); Harney, 10,135 sq mi.
State forests: 820,000 ac.
State parks: 240 (93,330 ac.)
Residents: Oregonian
2000 resident census population (rank): 3,421,399 (28). **Male:** 1,696,550 (49.6%); **Female:** 1,724,849 (50.4%). **White:** 2,961,623 (86.6%); **Black:** 55,662 (1.6%); **American Indian:** 45,211 (1.3%); **Asian:** 101,350 (3.0%); **Other race:** 144,832 (4.2%); **Two or more races:** 104,745 (3.1%); **Hispanic/Latino:** 275,314 (8.0%). **2000 percent population 18 and over:** 75.3; **65 and over:** 12.8; **median age:** 36.3.

Spanish and English sailors are believed to have sighted the Oregon coast in the 1500s and 1600s. Capt. James Cook, seeking the Northwest Passage, charted some of the coastline in 1778. In 1792, Capt. Robert Gray, in the *Columbia,* discovered the river named after his ship and claimed the area for the U.S.

In 1805 the Lewis and Clark expedition explored the area. John Jacob Astor's fur depot, Astoria, was founded in 1811. Disputes for control of Oregon between American settlers and the Hudson Bay Company were finally resolved in the 1846 Oregon Treaty, in which Great Britain gave up claims to the region.

Oregon has a $3.3 billion lumber and wood products industry, and an $859 million paper and allied manufacturing industry. Its salmon-fishing industry is one of the world's largest.

In agriculture, the state leads in growing peppermint, cover seed crops, blackberries, boysenberries, loganberries, black raspberries, and hazelnuts. It is second in raising hops, raspberries, sweet cherries, prunes, snap beans, and onions. Oregon has the only nickel smelter in the United States.

With the low-cost electric power provided by dams, Oregon has developed steadily as a manufacturing state. Leading manufactured items are lumber and plywood, metalwork, machinery, aluminum, chemicals, paper, food packing, and electronic equipment.

Crater Lake National Park, Mount Hood, and Bonneville Dam on the Columbia are major tourist attractions. Other points of interest include the Oregon Dunes National Recreation Area, Oregon Caves National Monument, Cape Perpetua in Siuslaw National Forest, Columbia River Gorge between The Dalles and Troutdale, Hells Canyon, Newberry Volcanic National Monument, and John Day Fossil Beds National Monument.

Famous natives and residents: James Beard, food expert; Raymond Carver, writer and poet; Homer C. Davenport, political cartoonist; David Douglas, botanist; Abigail Scott Duniway, women's suffrage advocate; Robert Gray, sea captain and discoverer of Columbia River; Matt Groening, cartoonist; Mark Hatfield, senator; Donald P. Hodel, former secretary of the Interior; Chief Joseph, Nez Percé chief; Dave Kingman, baseball player; Ursula LeGuin, writer; Edwin Markham, poet; Phyllis McGinley, author; Linus Pauling, chemist; Jane Powell, actress and singer; John Reed, poet and author; Harvey W. Scott, editor; Doc Severinsen, band leader; Norton Simon, business executive; Paul M. Simon, Illinois senator; William E. Stafford, poet; Sally Struthers, actress.

Pennsylvania

Capital: Harrisburg
Governor: Mark Schweiker, R (to Jan. 2003)
Lieut. Governor: Robert Jubelirer, R (to Jan. 2003)
Senators: Rick Santorum, R (to Jan. 2007); Arlen Specter, R (to Jan. 2005)
Acting Secy. of the Commonwealth: Kim Pizzingrilli, R (at the pleasure of the governor)
Auditor General: Robert P. Casey, Jr., D (to Jan. 2005)
Atty. General: Mike Fisher, R (to Jan. 2005)
Entered Union (rank): Dec. 12, 1787 (2)
Present constitution adopted: 1968
Motto: Virtue, liberty, and independence
State Symbols: flower, mountain laurel (1933); **tree,** hemlock (1931); **bird,** ruffed grouse (1931); **dog,** Great Dane (1965); **colors,** blue and gold (1907); **song,** "Pennsylvania" (1990);
Nickname: Keystone State
Origin of name: In honor of Adm. Sir William Penn, father of William Penn. It means "Penn's Woodland."

10 largest cities (2000): Philadelphia, 1,517,550; Pittsburgh, 334,563; Allentown, 106,632; Erie, 103,717; Upper Darby, 81,821; Reading, 81,207; Scranton, 76,415; Bethlehem, 71,329; Lower Merion, 59,850; Bensalem, 58,434
Land area: 44,820 sq mi. (116,083 sq km)
Geographic center: In Centre Co., 2½ mi. SW of Bellefonte
Number of counties: 67
Largest county by population and area: Philadelphia, 1,517,550 (2000); Lycoming, 1,235 sq mi.
State forests: over 2 mil. ac.
State parks: 116
Residents: Pennsylvanian
2000 resident census population (rank): 12,281,054 (6). **Male:** 5,929,663 (48.3%); **Female:** 6,351,391 (51.7%). **White:** 10,484,203 (85.4%); **Black:** 1,224,612 (10.0%); **American Indian:** 18,348 (0.1%); **Asian:** 219,813 (1.8%); **Other race:** 188,437 (1.5%); **Two or more races:** 142,224 (1.2%); **Hispanic/Latino:** 394,088 (3.2%). **2000 percent population 18 and over:** 76.2; **65 and over:** 15.6; **median age:** 38.0.

Rich in historic lore, Pennsylvania territory was disputed in the early 1600s among the Dutch, the Swedes, and the English. England acquired the region in 1664 with the capture of New York, and in 1681 Pennsylvania was granted to William Penn, a Quaker, by King Charles II.

Philadelphia was the seat of the federal government almost continuously from 1776 to 1800; there the Declaration of Independence was signed in 1776 and the U.S. Constitution drawn up in 1787. Valley Forge, of Revolutionary War fame, and Gettysburg, site of the pivotal battle of the Civil War, are both in Pennsylvania. The Liberty Bell is located in a glass pavilion across from Independence Hall in Philadelphia.

With the decline of the coal, steel, and railroad industries, Pennsylvania's industry has diversified, although the state still leads the country in the production of specialty steel. Pennsylvania is a leader in the production of chemicals, food, and electrical machinery and produces 10% of the nation's cement. Also important are brick and tiles, glass, limestone, and slate. Data processing is also increasingly important.

Pennsylvania's 59,000 farms (occupying nearly 8 million acres) are the backbone of the state's economy, producing a wide variety of crops. Leading commodities are dairy products, cattle and calves, mushrooms, greenhouse and nursery products, poultry and eggs, a variety of fruits, sweet corn, potatoes, maple syrup, and Christmas trees.

Pennsylvania's rich heritage draws billions of tourist dollars annually. Among the chief attractions are the Gettysburg National Military Park, Valley Forge National Historical Park, Independence National Historical Park in Philadelphia, the Pennsylvania Dutch region, the Eisenhower farm near Gettysburg, and the Delaware Water Gap National Recreation Area.

Famous natives and residents: Louisa May Alcott, novelist; Marian Anderson, contralto; Maxwell Anderson, dramatist; Samuel Barber, composer; John Barrymore, actor; Donald Barthelme, author; Stephen Vincent Benet, poet and story writer; Daniel Boone, frontiersman; Ed Bradley, TV anchorman; James Buchanan, former president; Alexander Calder, sculptor; Rachel Carson, biologist and author; Mary Cassatt, painter; Henry Steele Commager, historian; Bill Cosby, actor; Stuart Davis, painter; Jimmy and Tommy Dorsey, band leaders; W. C. Fields, comedian; Stephen Foster, composer; Robert Fulton, inventor; Grace, Princess of Monaco; Martha Graham, choreographer; Alexander Haig, former secretary of state; Marilyn Horne, mezzo-soprano; Lee Iacocca, auto executive; Reggie Jackson, baseball player; Gene Kelly, dancer and actor; Gelsey Kirkland, ballerina; S. S. Kresge, merchant; Mario Lanza, actor and singer; George C. Marshall, five-star general; George McClellan, former general; Margaret Mead, anthropologist; Andrew Mellon, financier; Tom Mix, actor; Arnold Palmer, golfer; Robert E. Peary, explorer; Man Ray, painter; Mary Roberts Rinehart, novelist; Betsy Ross, flagmaker; B. F. Skinner, psychologist; John Sloan, painter; Gertrude Stein, author; James Stewart, actor; John Updike, novelist; Honus Wagner, baseball player; Fred Waring, band leader; Ethel Waters, singer and actress; Anthony Wayne, military officer; August Wilson, poet, writer, and playwright; Wallis Warfield, Duchess of Windsor; Andrew Wyeth, painter.

Rhode Island

Capital: Providence
Governor: Lincoln C. Almond, R (to Jan. 2003)
Lieut. Governor: Charles J. Fogarty, D (to Jan. 2003)
Senators: Jack Reed, D (to Jan. 2003); Lincoln Chafee, R (to Jan. 2007)
Secy. of State: Jim Langevin, D (to Jan. 2003)
Atty. General: Sheldon Whitehouse, D (to Jan. 2003)
General Treasurer: Paul J. Tavares, D (to Jan. 2003)
Entered Union (rank): May 29, 1790 (13)
Present constitution adopted: 1843
Motto: Hope
State Symbols: flower, violet (unofficial) (1968); **tree,** red maple (official) (1964); **bird,** Rhode Island red hen (official) (1954); **shell,** quahog (official); **mineral,** bowenite (1966); **stone,** cumberlandite (1966); **colors,** blue, white, and gold (in state flag); **song,** "Rhode Island" (1946);
Nickname: The Ocean State
Origin of name: From the Greek Island of Rhodes
10 largest cities (2000): Providence, 173,618; Warwick, 85,808; Cranston, 79,269; Pawtucket, 72,958; East Providence, 48,688; Woonsocket, 43,224; Coventry, 33,668; North Providence, 32,411; Cumberland, 31,840; West Warwick, 29,581
Land area: 1,045 sq mi. (2,706 sq km)
Geographic center: In Kent Co., 1 mi. SSW of Compton
Number of counties: 5
Largest county by population and area: Providence, 621,602 (2000); Providence, 413 sq mi.
State forests: 11 (20,900 ac.)
State parks: 14
Residents: Rhode Islander
2000 resident census population (rank): 1,048,319 (43). **Male:** 503,635 (48.0%); **Female:** 544,684 (52.0%). **White:** 891,191 (85.0%); **Black:** 46,908 (4.5%); **American Indian:** 5,121 (0.5%); **Asian:** 23,665 (2.3%); **Other race:** 52,616 (5.0%); **Two or more races:** 28,251 (2.7%); **Hispanic/Latino:** 90,820 (8.7%). **2000 percent population 18 and over:** 76.4; **65 and over:** 14.5; **median age:** 36.7.

From its beginnings, Rhode Island has been distinguished by its support for freedom of conscience and action: Clergyman Roger Williams founded the present state capital, Providence, after being exiled by the Massachusetts Bay Colony Puritans in 1636. Williams was followed by other religious exiles who founded Pocasset, now Portsmouth, in 1638 and Newport in 1639.

Rhode Island's rebellious, authority-defying nature was further demonstrated by the burnings of the British revenue cutters *Liberty* and *Gaspee* prior to the Revolution, by its early declaration of independence from Great Britain in May 1776, by its refusal to participate actively in the War of 1812, and by Dorr's Rebellion of 1842, which protested property requirements for voting.

Rhode Island, smallest of the fifty states, is densely populated and highly industrialized. It is a major center for jewelry manufacturing. Electronics, metal, plastic products, and boat and ship construction are other important industries. Non-manufacturing employment includes research in health, medicine, and the ocean environment. Providence is a wholesale distribution center for New England.

Fishing ports are at Galilee and Newport. Rural areas of the state support small-scale farming, including grapes for local wineries, turf grass, and nursery stock. Tourism generates over a billion dollars a year in revenue.

Newport became famous as the summer capital of high society in the mid-19th century. Touro Synagogue (1763) is the oldest in the U.S. Other points of interest include the Roger Williams National Memorial in Providence, Samuel Slater's Mill in Pawtucket, the General Nathanael Greene Homestead in Coventry, and Block Island.

Famous natives and residents: Harry Anderson, actor; George M. Cohan, actor and dramatist; Eddie Dowling, actor and stage producer; Nelson Eddy, baritone and actor; Ann Smith Franklin, printer and almanac publisher; Charles Gorham, silversmith; Spalding Gray, writer, performance artist; Bobby Hackett, trumpeter; David Hartman, TV newscaster; Ruth Hussey, actress; Anne Hutchinson, religious leader; Thomas H. Ince, film producer; Wilbur John, Quaker leader; Van Johnson, actor; Clarence King, first director of the U.S. Geological Survey; Galway Kinnell, poet; Oliver LaFarge, writer; Irving R. Levine, news correspondent; H. P. Lovecraft, author; Ida Lewis, lighthouse keeper; John McLaughlin, political commentator, broadcaster; Dana C. Munro, educator and historian; Matthew C. Perry, naval officer; Oliver Hazard Perry, naval officer; King Philip (Metacomet), Indian leader; Anthony Quinn, actor; Gilbert Stuart, painter; Sarah Helen (Power) Whitman, poet; Jemima Wilkinson, religious leader; Roger Williams, clergyman and founder of Rhode Island; Leonard Woodcock, labor union official; James Woods, actor.

South Carolina

Capital: Columbia
Governor: Jim Hodges, D (to Jan. 2003)
Lieut. Governor: Robert L. Peeler, R (to Jan. 2003)
Senators: Ernest Hollings, D (to Jan. 2005); Strom Thurmond, R (to Jan. 2003)
Secy. of State: Jim Miles, R (to Jan. 2003)
Comptroller General: Jim Lander, D (to Jan. 2003)
Atty. General: Charles M. Condon, R (to Jan. 2003)
Entered Union (rank): May 23, 1788 (8)
Present constitution adopted: 1895
Mottoes: *Animis opibusque parati* (Prepared in mind and resources) and *Dum spiro spero* (While I breathe, I hope)
State Symbols: flower, Carolina yellow jessamine (1924); **tree,** palmetto tree (1939); **bird,** Carolina wren (1948); **song,** "Carolina" (1911);
Nickname: Palmetto State
Origin of name: In honor of Charles I of England
10 largest cities (2000): Columbia, 116,278; Charleston, 96,650; North Charleston, 79,641; Greenville, 56,002; Rock Hill, 49,765; Mount Pleasant, 47,609; Spartanburg, 39,673; Sumter, 39,643; Hilton Head Island, 33,862; Florence, 30,248
Land area: 30,111 sq mi. (77,988 sq km)
Geographic center: In Richland Co., 13 mi. SE of Columbia
Number of counties: 46
Largest county by population and area: Greenville,

379,616 (2000); Horry, 1,134 sq mi.
State forests: 4 (124,052 ac.)
State parks: 50 (61,726 ac.)
Residents: South Carolinian
2000 resident census population (rank): 4,012,012 (26). **Male:** 1,948,929 (48.6%); **Female:** 2,063,083 (51.4%). **White:** 2,695,560 (67.2%); **Black:** 1,185,216 (29.5%); **American Indian:** 13,718 (0.3%); **Asian:** 36,014 (0.9%); **Other race:** 39,926 (1.0%); **Two or more races:** 39,950 (1.0%); **Hispanic/Latino:** 95,076 (2.4%). **2000 percent population 18 and over:** 74.8; **65 and over:** 12.1; **median age:** 35.4.

Following exploration of the coast in 1521 by Francisco de Gordillo, the Spanish tried unsuccessfully to establish a colony near present-day Georgetown in 1526, and the French also failed to colonize Parris Island near Fort Royal in 1562.

The first English settlement was made in 1670 at Albemarle Point on the Ashley River, but poor conditions drove the settlers to the site of Charleston (originally called Charles Town). South Carolina, officially separated from North Carolina in 1729, was the scene of extensive military action during the Revolution and again during the Civil War. The Civil War began in 1861 as South Carolina troops fired on federal Fort Sumter in Charleston Harbor, and the state was the first to secede from the Union.

Once primarily agricultural, South Carolina today has many large textile and other mills that produce eight times the output of its farms in cash value. Charleston makes asbestos, wood, pulp, steel products, chemicals, machinery, and apparel.

Farms have become fewer but larger in recent years. South Carolina grows more peaches than any other state except California; it ranks fifth in overall tobacco production. Other top agricultural commodities include nursery and greenhouse products, watermelons, peanuts, broilers and turkeys, and cattle and calves. The only commercial tea plantation in America is 20 mi south of Charleston on Wadmalaw Island.

Points of interest include Fort Sumter National Monument, Fort Moultrie, Fort Johnson, and aircraft carrier USS *Yorktown* in Charleston Harbor; the Middleton, Magnolia, and Cypress Gardens in Charleston; Cowpens National Battlefield; the Hilton Head resorts; and the Riverbanks 200 and Botanical Garden in Columbia.

Famous natives and residents: Bernard Baruch, statesman; Mary McLeod Bethune, educator; James F. Byrnes, senator, jurist and secretary of state; John C. Calhoun, statesman; Mark Clark, general; Joe Frazier, prize fighter; Althea Gibson, tennis champion; Dizzy Gillespie, jazz trumpeter; DuBose Heyward, poet, playwright, and novelist; Andrew Jackson, former president; Jesse Jackson, civil rights leader; Eartha Kitt, singer; Francis Marion ("Swamp Fox"), Revolutionary general; Ronald McNair, astronaut; John Rutledge, jurist; Strom Thurmond, politician; Charles Townes, physicist; William Westmoreland, general; Vanna White, TV personality.

South Dakota

Capital: Pierre
Governor: William J. Janklow, R (to Jan. 2003)
Lieut. Governor: Carole Hillard, R (to Jan. 2003)
Senators: Thomas A. Daschle, D (to Jan. 2005); Tim Johnson, D (to Jan. 2003)
Atty. General: Mark Barnett, R (to Jan. 2003)
Secy. of State: Joyce Hazeltine, R (to Jan. 2003)
Auditor: Vern Larson, R (to Jan. 2003)
Treasurer: Richard Butler, D (to Jan. 2003)

Organized as territory: March 2, 1861
Entered Union (rank): Nov. 2, 1889 (40)
Present constitution adopted: 1889
Motto: Under God the people rule
State Symbols: flower, American pasqueflower (1903); **grass,** Western wheat grass (1970); **soil,** houdek (1990); **tree,** black hills spruce (1947); **bird,** ring-necked pheasant (1943); **insect,** honeybee (1978); **animal,** coyote (1949); **mineral stone,** rose quartz (1966); **gemstone,** fairburn agate (1966); **colors,** blue and gold (in state flag); **song,** "Hail! South Dakota" (1943); **fish,** walleye (1982); **musical instrument,** fiddle (1989); **dessert,** kuchen (2000):
Nicknames: Mount Rushmore State; Coyote State
Origin of name: From the Sioux tribe, meaning "allies"
10 largest cities (2000): Sioux Falls, 123,975; Rapid City, 59,607; Aberdeen, 24,658; Watertown, 20,237; Brookings, 18,504; Mitchell, 14,558; Pierre, 13,876; Yankton, 13,528; Huron, 11,893; Vermillion, 9,765
Land area: 75,898 sq mi. (196,575 sq km)
Geographic center: In Hughes Co., 8 mi. NE of Pierre
Number of counties: 67 (64 county governments)
Largest county by population and area: Minnehaha, 148,281 (2000); Meade, 3,471 sq mi.
State forests: None[1]
State parks: 12 plus 39 recreational areas (87,269 ac.)[2]
Residents: South Dakotan
2000 resident census population (rank): 754,844 (46). **Male:** 374,558 (49.6%); **Female:** 380,286 (50.4%). **White:** 669,404 (88.7%); **Black:** 4,685 (0.6%); **American Indian:** 62,283 (8.3%); **Asian:** 4,378 (0.6%); **Other race:** 3,677 (0.5%); **Two or more races:** 10,156 (1.3%); **Hispanic/Latino:** 10,903 (1.4%). **2000 percent population 18 and over:** 73.2; **65 and over:** 14.3; **median age:** 35.6.

1. No designated state forests; about 13,000 ac. of state land is forestland. 2. Acreage includes 39 recreation areas and 80 roadside parks, in addition to 12 state parks.

Exploration of this area began in 1743 when Louis-Joseph and François Verendrye came from France in search of a route to the Pacific.

The U.S. acquired the region as part of the Louisiana Purchase in 1803, and it was explored by Lewis and Clark in 1804–1806. Fort Pierre, the first permanent settlement, was established in 1817.

Settlement of South Dakota did not begin in earnest until the arrival of the railroad in 1873 and the discovery of gold in the Black Hills in 1874.

Agriculture is a cultural and economic mainstay, but it no longer leads the state in employment or share of gross state product. Durable-goods manufacturing and private services have evolved as the drivers of the economy. Tourism is also a booming industry in the state, generating approximately $1.25 billion worth of economic activity each year.

South Dakota is the second-largest producer of flaxseed and sunflower seed in the nation. It is the third-largest producer of hay and rye.

South Dakota is the nation's second leading producer of gold, and the Homestake Mine is the richest in the U.S. Other minerals include berylium, bentonite, granite, silver, and uranium.

The Black Hills are the highest mountains east of the Rockies. Mt. Rushmore, in this group, is famous for the likenesses of Washington, Jefferson, Lincoln, and Theodore Roosevelt, which were carved in granite by Gutzon Borglum. A memorial to Crazy Horse is also being carved in granite near Custer.

Other tourist attractions include the Badlands; the World's Only Corn Palace, in Mitchell; and the city of Deadwood, where Wild Bill Hickok was killed in 1876 and where gambling was recently legalized.

Famous natives and residents: Sparky Anderson, baseball manager; Gertrude Bonnin (Zitkala-Sa), Sioux writer and pan-Indian activist; Tom Brokaw, TV newscaster; Robert Casey, writer; Myron Floren, accordionist; Joseph J. Foss, WW II Marine fighter ace; Mary Hart, TV host; Crazy Horse, Oglala chief; Oscar Howe, Sioux artist; Hubert H. Humphrey, former vice president; Cheryl Ladd, actress; Ernest Orlando Lawrence, physicist; Russell Means, American Indian activist; George McGovern, politician; Arthur C. Mellette, first governor; Dorothy Provine, actress; Rain-in-the-Face, Hunkpapa Sioux chief; Red Cloud, chief of the Oglala Sioux; Ben Reifel, Brulé Sioux congressman; Ole Edvart Rölvaag, writer; Sitting Bull, chief of Hunkpappa Sioux; Norm Van Brocklin, football player; Mamie Van Doren, actress.

Tennessee

Capital: Nashville
Governor: Don Sundquist, R (to Jan. 2003)
Lieut. Governor: John S. Wilder, D (to Jan. 2005)
Senators: Fred Thompson, R (to Jan. 2003); William Frist, R (to Jan. 2007)
Secy. of State: Riley C. Darnell, D (to Jan. 2005)
Atty. General: Paul G. Summers, D (to Aug. 2005)
Treasurer: Steve Adams, D (to Jan. 2003)
Comptroller: John G. Morgan (to Jan. 2003)
Entered Union (rank): June 1, 1796 (16)
Present constitution adopted: 1870; amended 1953, 1960, 1966, 1972, 1978
Motto: Agriculture and Commerce (1987)
Slogan: Tennessee—America at its best! (1965)
State Symbols: flower, iris (1933); **tree,** tulip poplar (1947); **bird,** mockingbird (1933); **horse,** Tennessee walking horse; **animal,** raccoon (1971); **wild flower,** passion flower (1973); **songs,** "Tennessee Waltz" (1965); "My Homeland, Tennessee" (1925); "When It's Iris Time in Tennessee" (1935); "My Tennessee" (1955); "Rocky Top" (1982); "Tennessee" (1992);
Nickname: Volunteer State
Origin of name: Of Cherokee origin; the exact meaning is unknown
10 largest cities (2000): Memphis, 650,100; Nashville-Davidson [1], 569,891; Knoxville, 173,890; Chattanooga, 155,554; Clarksville, 103,455; Murfreesboro, 68,816; Jackson, 59,643; Johnson City, 55,469; Kingsport, 44,905; Franklin, 41,842
Land area: 41,220 sq mi. (106,759 sq km)
Geographic center: In Rutherford Co., 5 mi. NE of Murfreesboro
Number of counties: 95
Largest county by population and area: Shelby, 897,472 (2000); Shelby, 755 sq mi.
State forests: 5[·]
State parks: 80
Residents: Tennessean, Tennesseean
2000 resident census population (rank): 5,689,283 (16). **Male:** 2,770,275 (48.7%); **Female:** 2,919,008 (51.3%). **White:** 4,563,310 (80.2%); **Black:** 932,809 (16.4%); **American Indian:** 15,152 (0.3%); **Asian:** 56,662 (1.0%); **Other race:** 56,036 (1.0%); **Two or more races:** 63,109 (1.1%); **Hispanic/Latino:** 123,838 (2.2%). **2000 percent population 18 and over:** 75.4; **65 and over:** 12.4; **median age:** 35.9.

1. The city is part of a consolidated city-county government and is coextensive with Davidson County.

First visited by the Spanish explorer Hernando de Soto in 1540, the Tennessee area would later be claimed by both France and England as a result of the 1670s and 1680s explorations of Jacques Marquette and Louis Joliet, Sieur de la Salle, and James Needham and Gabriel Arthur. Great Britain obtained the area after the French and Indian Wars in 1763.

During 1784–1787, the settlers formed the "state" of Franklin, which was disbanded when the region was allowed to send representatives to the North Carolina legislature. In 1790 Congress organized the territory south of the Ohio River, and Tennessee joined the Union in 1796.

Although Tennessee joined the Confederacy during the Civil War, there was much pro-Union sentiment in the state, which was the scene of extensive military action.

The state is now predominantly industrial; the majority of its population lives in urban areas. Among the most important products are chemicals, textiles, apparel, electrical machinery, furniture, and leather goods. Other lines include food processing, lumber, primary metals, and metal products. The state is known as the U.S. hardwood-flooring center and ranks first in the production of marble, zinc, pyrite, and ball clay.

Tennessee is a leading tobacco-producing state. Other farming income is derived from livestock and dairy products, as well as greenhouse and nursery products and cotton.

With six other states, Tennessee shares the extensive federal reservoir developments on the Tennessee and Cumberland River systems. The Tennessee Valley Authority operates a number of dams and reservoirs in the state.

Among the major points of interest are the Andrew Johnson National Historic Site at Greenville, the American Museum of Atomic Energy at Oak Ridge, Great Smoky Mountains National Park, the Hermitage (home of Andrew Jackson near Nashville), Rock City Gardens near Chattanooga, and three National Military Parks.

Famous natives and residents: James Agee, writer; Eddy Arnold, singer; Chet Atkins, guitarist; Julian Bond, Georgia legislator; Davy Crockett, frontiersman; David G. Farragut, first American admiral; Lester Flatt, bluegrass musician; Tennessee Ernie Ford, singer; Abe Fortas, jurist; Aretha Franklin, singer; Nikki Giovanni, poet; Al Gore, Jr., former vice president; Red Grooms, artist; Isaac Hayes, composer; Benjamin L. Hooks, civil rights activist; Cordell Hull, former secretary of state; Andrew Jackson, former president; Andrew Johnson, former president; Estes Kefauver, legislator; Anita Kerr, singer; Grace Moore, soprano; Dolly Parton, singer; Minnie Pearl, singer and comedienne; James K. Polk, president; Grantland Rice, sportswriter; Carl Rowan, journalist; Wilma Rudolph, sprinter; Sequoia, Cherokee scholar and educator; Cybil Shepherd, actress; Dinah Shore, actress and singer; Tina Turner, singer; Alvin York, World War I hero.

Texas

Capital: Austin
Governor: Rick Perry, R (to Jan. 2003)
Lieut. Governor: Bill Ratliff, R (to Jan. 2003)
Senators: Phil Gramm, R (to Jan. 2003);
    Kay Bailey Hutchison, R (to Jan. 2003)
Secy. of State: Henry Cuellar (apptd. by gov.)
Comptroller: Carole Keeton Rylander, R (to Jan. 2003)
Atty. General: John Cornyn, R (to Jan. 2003)
Entered Union (rank): Dec. 29, 1845 (28)
Present constitution adopted: 1876
Motto: Friendship
State Symbols: flower, bluebonnet (1901); **tree,** pecan (1919); **bird,** mockingbird (1927); **song,** "Texas, Our Texas" (1929); **fish,** guadalupe bass (1989); **seashell,** lightning whelk (1987); **dish,** chili (1977); **folk dance,** square dance (1991); **fruit,** Texas red grapefruit (1993); **gem,** Texas blue topaz (1969); **gemstone cut,** Lone Star cut (1977); **grass,** sideoats grass (1971);

reptile, horned lizard (1993); **stone,** petrified palmwood (1969); **plant,** prickly pear cactus; **insect,** monarch butterfly; **pepper,** jalapeño pepper; **mammal,** longhorn; **small mammal,** armadillo; **flying mammal,** Mexican free-tailed bat;
Nickname: Lone Star State
Origin of name: From an Indian word meaning "friends"
10 largest cities (2000): Houston, 1,953,631; Dallas, 1,188,580; San Antonio, 1,144,646; Austin, 656,562; El Paso, 563,662; Fort Worth, 534,694; Arlington, 332,969; Corpus Christi, 277,454; Plano, 222,030; Garland, 215,768
Land area: 261,914 sq mi. (678,358 sq km)
Geographic center: In McCulloch Co., 15 mi. NE of Brady
Number of counties: 254
Largest county by population and area: Harris, 3,400,578 (2000); Brewster, 6,193 sq mi.
State forests: 5 (7,314 ac.)
State parks[1]: 125 (587,216 ac.)
Residents: Texan
2000 resident census population (rank): 20,851,820 (2). **Male:** 10,352,910 (49.6%); **Female:** 10,498,910 (50.4%). **White:** 14,799,505 (71.0%); **Black:** 2,404,566 (11.5%); **American Indian:** 118,362 (0.6%); **Asian:** 562,319 (2.7%); **Other race:** 2,438,001 (11.7%); **Two or more races:** 514,633 (2.5%); **Hispanic/Latino:** 6,669,666 (32.0%). **2000 percent population 18 and over:** 71.8; **65 and over:** 9.9; **median age:** 32.3.

1. Includes state parks and natural areas, two state fishing piers, and one county park.

Spanish explorers, including Álvar Núñez Cabeza de Vaca and Francisco Vásquez de Coronado, were the first to visit the region in the 16th and 17th centuries, settling at Ysleta near El Paso in 1682. In 1685, Robert Cavelier, Sieur de la Salle, established a short-lived French colony at Matagorda Bay.

Americans, led by Stephen F. Austin, began to settle along the Brazos River in 1821 when Texas was controlled by Mexico, recently independent from Spain. In 1836, following a brief war between the American settlers in Texas and the Mexican government, the Independent Republic of Texas was proclaimed with Sam Houston as president. This war was famous for the battles of the Alamo and San Jacinto. After Texas became the 28th U.S. state in 1845, border disputes led to the Mexican War of 1846–1848.

Possessing enormous natural resources, Texas is a major agricultural state and an industrial giant. Second only to Alaska in land area, it leads all other states in such categories as oil, cattle, sheep, and cotton. Texas ranches and farms also produce poultry and eggs, dairy products, greenhouse and nursery products, wheat, hay, rice, sugar cane, and peanuts, and a variety of fruits and vegetables.

Sulfur, salt, helium, asphalt, graphite, bromine, natural gas, cement, and clays are among the state's valuable resources. Chemicals, oil refining, food processing, machinery, and transportation equipment are among the major Texas manufacturing industries.

Millions of tourists spend well over $20.6 billion annually visiting more than 100 state parks, recreation areas, and points of interest such as the Gulf Coast resort area, the Lyndon B. Johnson Space Center in Houston, the Alamo in San Antonio, the state capital in Austin, and the Big Bend and Guadalupe Mountains National Park.

Famous natives and residents: Alvin Ailey, choreographer; Mary Kay Ash, cosmetics entrepreneur; Steven Fuller Austin, founding father of Texas; Gene Autry, singer and actor; Carol Burnett, comedienne; George W. Bush, president and governor; Cyd Charisse, actress and dancer; Denton A. Cooley, heart surgeon; Joan Crawford, actress; Dwight David Eisenhower, president and general; A. J. Foyt, auto racer; Ben Hogan, golfer; Sam Houston, general and statesman; Howard Hughes, industrialist and film producer; Jack Johnson, boxer; Lyndon B. Johnson, former president; George Jones, singer; Tommy Lee Jones, actor; Scott Joplin, composer; Trini Lopez, singer; Mary Martin, singer and actress; Spanky McFarland, actor; Audie Murphy, actor and war hero; Chester Nimitz, admiral; Sandra Day O'Connor, jurist; Buck Owens, singer; Selena Pérez, singer; Lou Diamond Phillips, actor; Katherine Anne Porter, novelist; Wiley Post, aviator; Dan Rather, TV newscaster; Robert Rauschenberg, painter; Tex Ritter, singer; Rip Torn, actor and director; Tommy Tune, dancer and choreographer; Lupe Velez, actress; Dooley Wilson, actor and musician; Babe Didrikson Zaharias, athlete and golfer.

Utah

Capital: Salt Lake City
Governor: Michael O. Leavitt, R (to Jan. 2005)
Lieut. Governor: Olene Walker, R (to Jan. 2005)
Senators: Robert F. Bennett, R (to Jan. 2005);
    Orrin G. Hatch, R (to Jan. 2007)
Treasurer: Edward T. Alter, R. (Jan. 2005)
Auditor: Auston G. Johnson, R (Jan. 2005)
Atty. General: Mark Shurtleff, R (to Jan. 2005)
Organized as territory: Sept. 9, 1850
Entered Union (rank): Jan. 4, 1896 (45)
Present constitution adopted: 1896
Motto: Industry
State Symbols: flower, sego lily (1911); **tree,** blue spruce (1933); **bird,** California gull (1955); **emblem,** beehive (1959); **song,** "Utah, We Love Thee" (1953); **gem,** topaz; **animal,** Rocky Mountain elk (1971); **insect,** honeybee (1983); **grass,** Indian rice grass (1990); **fossil,** allosaurus (1988); **cooking pot,** dutch oven (1997); **fish,** Bonneville cutthroat trout (1997); **fruit,** cherry (1997); **mineral,** copper; **rock,** coal (1991);
Nickname: Beehive State
Origin of name: From the Ute tribe, meaning "people of the mountains"
10 largest cities (2000): Salt Lake City, 181,743; West Valley City, 108,896; Provo, 105,166; Sandy, 88,418; Orem, 84,324; Ogden, 77,226; West Jordan, 68,336; Layton, 58,474; Taylorsville, 57,439; St. George, 49,663
Land area: 82,168 sq mi. (212,816 sq km)
Geographic center: In Sanpete Co., 3 mi. N. of Manti
Number of counties: 29
Largest county by population and area: Salt Lake, 898,387 (2000); San Juan, 7,821 sq mi.
National parks: 5
National monuments: 7
State parks/forests: 45 (64,097 ac.)
Residents: Utahan, Utahn
2000 resident census population (rank): 2,233,169 (34). **Male:** 1,119,031 (50.1%); **Female:** 1,114,138 (49.9%). **White:** 1,992,975 (89.2%); **Black:** 17,657 (0.8%); **American Indian:** 29,684 (1.3%); **Asian:** 37,108 (1.7%); **Other race:** 93,405 (4.2%); **Two or more races:** 47,195 (2.1%); **Hispanic/Latino:** 201,559 (9.0%). **2000 percent population 18 and over:** 67.8; **65 and over:** 8.5; **median age:** 27.1.

The region was first explored for Spain by Franciscan friars Escalante and Dominguez in 1776. In 1824 the famous American frontiersman Jim Bridger discovered the Great Salt Lake.

Fleeing religious persecution in the East and Midwest, the Mormons arrived in 1847 and began to build Salt Lake City. The U.S. acquired the Utah region in the treaty ending the Mexican War in 1848, and the first transcontinental railroad was completed with the driving of a golden spike at Promontory Summit in 1869.

Mormon difficulties with the federal government about polygamy did not end until the Mormon Church renounced the practice in 1890, six years before Utah became a state.

Rich in natural resources, Utah has long been a leading producer of copper, gold, silver, lead, zinc, and molybdenum. Oil has also become a major product. Utah shares rich oil shale deposits with Colorado and Wyoming. Utah also has large deposits of low sulphur coal.

The state's top agricultural commodities include cattle and calves, dairy products, hay, greenhouse and nursery products, and hogs.

Utah's traditional industries of agriculture and mining are complemented by increased tourism and growing aerospace, biomedical, and computer-related businesses.

Utah is a great vacationland with 11,000 mi of fishing streams and 147,000 acres of lakes and reservoirs. Among the many tourist attractions are Arches, Bryce Canyon, Canyonlands, Capitol Reef, and Zion National Parks; Cedar Breaks, Dinosaur, Hovenweep, Natural Bridges, Rainbow Bridge, Timpanogos Cave, and Grand Staircase (Escalante) National Monuments; the Mormon Tabernacle in Salt Lake City; and Monument Valley. Salt Lake City will be the site of the 2002 Winter Olympics.

Famous natives and residents: Maude Adams, actress; Roseanne, actress; Frank Borzage, film director and producer; John M. Browning, inventor; Butch Cassidy, outlaw; Laraine Day, actress; Bernard De Voto, writer; Avard Fairbanks, sculptor; Philo Farnsworth, television pioneer; Jake Garn, senator; John Gilbert, actor; J. Willard Marriott, restaurant and hotel chain founder; Peter Skene Ogden, fur trader and trapper; Merlin Olsen, football player; Donny Osmond, Marie Osmond, singers; Ivy Baker Priest, former U.S. treasurer; Lee Greene Richards, painter; Leroy Robertson, composer; Brent Scowcroft, business executive and consultant; Reed Smoot, first Mormon elected to U.S. Senate; Mack Swain, actor; Everett Thorpe, painter; Robert Walker, actor; James Woods, actor; Brigham Young, territory governor and religious leader; Loretta Young, actress.

Vermont

Capital: Montpelier
Governor: Howard Dean, D (to Jan. 2003)
Lieut. Governor: Douglas A. Racine, D (to Jan. 2003)
Senators: James M. Jeffords, I (to Jan. 2007);
    Patrick Leahy, D (to Jan. 2005)
Secy. of State: Deborah L. Markowitz, D (to Jan. 2003)
Treasurer: James H. Douglas, R (to Jan. 2003)
Auditor of Accounts: Elizabeth M. Ready, D
    (to Jan. 2003)
Atty. General: William Sorrell, D (to Jan. 2003)
Entered Union (rank): March 4, 1791 (14)
Present constitution adopted: 1793
Motto: Vermont, Freedom and Unity
State Symbols: flower, red clover (1894); **tree,** sugar maple (1949); **bird,** hermit thrush (1941); **animal,** Morgan horse (1961); **insect,** honeybee (1978); **song,** "These Green Mountains" (2000);
Nickname: Green Mountain State
Origin of name: From the French "vert mont," meaning "green mountain"
10 largest cities (2000): Burlington, 38,889; Essex, 18,626; Rutland, 17,292; Colchester, 16,986; South Burlington, 15,814; Bennington, 15,737; Brattleboro, 12,005; Hartford, 10.367; Milton, 9,479; Barre, 9,291
Land area: 9,249 sq mi. (23,956 sq km)

Geographic center: In Washington Co., 3 mi. E of Roxbury
Number of counties: 14
Largest county by population and area: Chittenden, 146,571 (2000); Windsor, 971 sq mi.
State forests: 34 (113,953 ac.)
State parks: 45 (31,325 ac.)
Residents: Vermonter
2000 resident census population (rank): 608,827 (49). **Male:** 298,337 (49.0%); **Female:** 310,490 (51.0%). **White:** 589,208 (96.8%); **Black:** 3,063 (0.5%); **American Indian:** 2,420 (0.4%); **Asian:** 5,217 (0.9%); **Other race:** 1,443 (0.2%); **Two or more races:** 7,335 (1.2%); **Hispanic/Latino:** 5,504 (0.9%). **2000 percent population 18 and over:** 75.8; **65 and over:** 12.7; **median age:** 37.7.

The Vermont region was explored and claimed for France by Samuel de Champlain in 1609, and the first French settlement was established at Fort Ste. Anne in 1666. The first English settlers moved into the area in 1724 and built Fort Dummer on the site of present-day Brattleboro. England gained control of the area in 1763 after the French and Indian Wars.

First organized to drive settlers from New York out of Vermont, the Green Mountain Boys, led by Ethan Allen, won fame by capturing Fort Ticonderoga from the British on May 10, 1775, in the early days of the Revolutionary War. In 1777 Vermont adopted its first constitution, abolishing slavery and providing for universal male suffrage without property qualifications.

Vermont leads the nation in the production of monument granite, marble, and maple syrup. It is also a leader in the production of talc. Vermont's rugged, rocky terrain discourages extensive agricultural farming, but is well suited to raising fruit trees, and to dairy farming.

Principal industrial products include electrical equipment, fabricated metal products, printing and publishing, and paper and allied products.

Tourism is a major industry in Vermont. Vermont's many famous ski areas include Stowe, Killington, Mt. Snow, Bromley, Jay Peak, and Sugarbush. Hunting and fishing also attract many visitors to Vermont each year. Among the many points of interest are the Green Mountain National Forest, Bennington Battle Monument, the Calvin Coolidge Homestead at Plymouth, and the Marble Exhibit in Proctor.

Famous natives and residents: Chester A. Arthur, former president; Orson Bean, actor; Calvin Coolidge, former president; George Dewey, admiral; John Dewey, philosopher and educator; Stephen A. Douglas, politician; James Fisk, financial speculator; Wilbur Fisk, clergyman and educator; Richard Morris Hunt, architect; William Morris Hunt, painter; Elisha Otis, inventor; Moses Pendleton, choreographer; Joseph Smith, religious leader; Ernest Thompson, actor and writer; Rudy Vallee, singer and band leader; Henry Wells, pioneer entrepreneur (Wells Fargo & Co.); Brigham Young, religious leader.

Virginia

Capital: Richmond
Governor: James S. Gilmore, R (to Jan. 2002)
Lieut. Governor: John H. Hager, R (to Jan. 2002)
Senators: John Warner, R (to Jan. 2003); George Allen, R (to Jan. 2007)
Secy. of the Commonwealth: Anne P. Petera (apptd. by governor)
Comptroller: William E. Landsidle (apptd. by governor)
Atty. General: Mark L. Earley
Entered Union (rank): June 25, 1788 (10)
Present constitution adopted: 1970

Motto: *Sic semper tyrannis* (Thus always to tyrants)
State Symbols: flower, American dogwood (1918); **bird,** cardinal (1950); **dog,** American foxhound (1966); **shell,** oyster shell (1974); **tree,** dogwood (1956);
Nicknames: The Old Dominion; Mother of Presidents
Origin of name: In honor of Elizabeth "Virgin Queen" of England
10 largest cities (2000): Virginia Beach, 425,257; Norfolk, 234,403; Chesapeake, 199,184; Richmond, 197,790; Newport News, 180,150; Hampton, 146,437; Alexandria, 128,283; Portsmouth, 100,565; Roanoke, 94,911; Lynchburg, 65,269
Land area: 39,598 sq mi. (102,558 sq km)
Geographic center: In Buckingham Co., 5 mi. SW of Buckingham
Number of counties: 95, plus 40 independent cities
Largest county by population and area: Fairfax, 969,749 (2000); Augusta, 972 sq mi.
State forests: 15 (45,393 ac.)
State parks: 34 (plus 31 natural areas)
Residents: Virginian
2000 resident census population (rank): 7,078,515 (12). **Male:** 3,471,895 (49.0%); **Female:** 3,606,620 (51.0%). **White:** 5,120,110 (72.3%); **Black:** 1,390,293 (19.6%); **American Indian:** 21,172 (0.3%); **Asian:** 261,025 (3.7%); **Other race:** 138,900 (2.0%); **Two or more races:** 143,069 (2.0%); **Hispanic/Latino:** 329,540 (4.7%). **2000 percent population 18 and over:** 75.4; **65 and over:** 11.2; **median age:** 35.7.

The history of America is closely tied to that of Virginia, particularly during the Colonial period. Jamestown, founded in 1607, was the first permanent English settlement in North America and slavery was introduced there in 1619. The surrenders ending both the American Revolution (Yorktown) and the Civil War (Appomattox) occurred in Virginia. The state is called the "Mother of Presidents" because eight U.S. presidents were born there.

Today, the service sector provides one-third of all jobs in Virginia, generating as much income as the manufacturing and retail industries combined in 1998 and accounting for 22% of gross state product. (The largest component of the service sector is business services, which includes computer and data processing services.)

Virginia has a large number of manufacturing industries, including transportation equipment, textiles, food processing, electronic and other electrical equipment, chemicals, apparel, lumber and wood products, and furniture.

Although Virginia's economy is no longer agrarian-based, agriculture remains an important sector, and the state ranks among the top ten in the production of tomatoes, tobacco, peanuts, apples, summer potatoes, sweet potatoes, and turkeys and broilers. Virginia also has a large dairy industry.

Coal accounts for roughly 70% of Virginia's mineral value; lime, kyanite, and stone are also mined.

Points of interest include Mt. Vernon, home of George Washington; Monticello, home of Thomas Jefferson; Stratford, home of the Lees; Richmond, capital of the Confederacy and of Virginia; and Williamsburg, the restored Colonial capital.

Other attractions are the Shenandoah National Park, Colonial National Historical Park, Fredericksburg and Spotsylvania National Military Park, the Booker T. Washington birthplace near Roanoke, Arlington House (the Robert E. Lee Memorial), the Skyline Drive, and the Blue Ridge National Parkway.

Famous natives and residents: Richard Arlen, actor; Arthur Ashe, tennis player; Pearl Bailey, singer; Russell Baker, columnist; Warren Beatty, actor; George Bingham, painter; Richard E. Byrd, polar explorer; Willa Cather, novelist; Roy Clark, country music artist; William Clark, explorer; Henry Clay, statesman; Joseph Cotten, actor; Ella Fitzgerald, singer; William H. Harrison, former president; Patrick Henry, statesman; Sam Houston, political leader; Thomas Jefferson, former president; Robert E. Lee, Confederate general; Meriwether Lewis, explorer; Shirley MacLaine, actress; James Madison, former president; John Marshall, jurist; Cyrus McCormick, inventor; James Monroe, former president; Opechancanough, Powhatan leader; John Payne, actor; Walter Reed, army surgeon; Matthew Ridgway, general; Bill "Bojangles" Robinson, dancer; George C. Scott, actor; Sam Snead, golfer; James "Jeb" Stuart, Confederate army officer; Zachary Taylor, former president; Nat Turner, leader of slave uprising; John Tyler, former president; Booker T. Washington, educator; George Washington, first president; Woodrow Wilson, former president; Tom Wolfe, journalist.

Washington

Capital: Olympia
Governor: Gary Locke, D (to Jan. 2005)
Lieut. Governor: Brad Owen, D (to Jan. 2005)
Senators: Patty Murray, D (to Jan. 2005);
   Maria Cantwell, D (to Jan. 2007)
Secy. of State: Sam Reed, R (to Jan. 2005)
Treasurer: Michael J. Murphy (to Jan. 2005)
Atty. General: Christine Gregoire, D (to Jan. 2005)
Auditor: Brian Sonntag, D (to Jan. 2005)
Organized as territory: March 2, 1853
Entered Union (rank): Nov. 11, 1889 (42)
Present constitution adopted: 1889
Motto: *Al-Ki* (Indian word meaning "by and by")
State Symbols: flower, coast rhododendron (1892); **tree,** western hemlock (1947); **bird,** willow goldfinch (1951); **fish,** steelhead trout (1969); **gem,** petrified wood (1975); **colors,** green and gold (1925); **song,** "Washington, My Home" (1959); **folk song,** "Roll On Columbia, Roll On" (1987); **dance,** square dance (1979); **grass,** bluebunch wheatgrass (1989); **insect,** blue darner dragonfly (1997); **fossil,** Columbian mammoth (1998); **fruit,** apple (1989);
Nicknames: Evergreen State
Origin of name: In honor of George Washington
10 largest cities (2000): Seattle, 563,374; Spokane, 195,629; Tacoma, 193,556; Vancouver, 143,560; Bellevue, 109,569; Everett, 91,488; Federal Way, 83,259; Kent, 79,524; Yakima, 71,845; Bellingham, 67,171
Land area: 66,582 sq mi. (172,447 sq km)
Geographic center: In Chelan Co., 10 mi. WSW of Wenatchee
Number of counties: 39
Largest county by population and area: King, 1,737,034 (2000); Okanogan, 5,268 sq mi.
State forest lands: 2.1 million ac.
State parks: 215 (260,000 ac.)[1]
Residents: Washingtonian
2000 resident census population (rank): 5,894,121 (15). **Male:** 2,934,300 (49.8%); **Female:** 2,959,821 (50.2%). **White:** 4,821,823 (81.8%); **Black:** 190,267 (3.2%); **American Indian:** 93,301 (1.6%); **Asian:** 322,335 (5.5%); **Other race:** 228,923 (3.9%); **Two or more races:** 213,519 (3.6%); **Hispanic/Latino:** 441,509 (7.5%). **2000 percent population 18 and over:** 74.3; **65 and over:** 11.2; **median age:** 35.3.

1. Parks and undeveloped areas administered by State Parks and Recreation Commission. Dept. of Wildlife administers wildlife and recreation areas totaling 428,989.5 acres.

As part of the vast Oregon Country, Washington territory was visited by Spanish, American, and British explorers—Bruno Heceta for Spain in 1775, the American Capt. Robert Gray in 1792, and Capt. George Vancouver for Britain in 1792–1794. Lewis and Clark explored the Columbia River region and coastal areas for the U.S. in 1805–1806.

Rival American and British settlers and conflicting territorial claims threatened war in the early 1840s. However, in 1846 the Oregon Treaty set the boundary at the 49th parallel and war was averted.

Washington is a leading lumber producer. Its rugged surface is rich in stands of Douglas fir, hemlock, ponderosa and white pine, spruce, larch, and cedar. The state holds first place in apples, lentils, dry edible peas, hops, pears, red raspberries, spearmint oil, and sweet cherries, and ranks high in apricots, asparagus, grapes, peppermint oil, and potatoes. Livestock and livestock products make important contributions to total farm revenue and the commercial fishing catch of salmon, halibut, and bottomfish makes a significant contribution to the state's economy.

Manufacturing industries in Washington include aircraft and missiles, shipbuilding and other transportation equipment, lumber, food processing, metals and metal products, chemicals, and machinery.

Washington has over 1,000 dams, including the Grand Coulee, built for a variety of purposes including irrigation, power, flood control, and water storage. Its abundance of electrical power makes Washington one of the nation's major producers of refined aluminum.

Among the major points of interest: Mt. Rainier, Olympic, and North Cascades National Parks. Mount St. Helens, a peak in the Cascade Range, erupted in May 1980. Also of interest are Whitman Mission and Fort Vancouver National Historic Sites; and the Pacific Science Center and the Space Needle, in Seattle.

Famous natives and residents: Earl Anthony, professional bowler; Mildred Bailey, singer; Bob Barker, TV host; Dyan Cannon, actress; Raymond Carver, writer; Carol Channing, actress; Ray Charles, singer and musician; Kurt Cobain, rock musician; Judy Collins, singer; Chris Cornell, rock musician; Fred Couples, professional golfer; Bing Crosby, singer and actor; Bob Crosby, musician; Merce Cunningham, choreographer; Howard Duff, actor; Frances Farmer, actress; Kenny G., saxophonist; Bill Gates, software executive; Jimi Hendrix, guitarist; Frank Herbert, writer; Robert Joffrey, choreographer; Chuck Jones, animator; Quincy Jones, music producer; Hank Ketcham, cartoonist; Gary Larson, cartoonist; Gypsy Rose Lee, entertainer; Kenny Loggins, rock musician; Mary McCarthy, novelist; Guthrie McClintic, theatrical producer and director; John McIntire, actor; Steve Miller, rock musician; Robert Motherwell, artist; Patrice Munsel, soprano; Craig T. Nelson, actor; Ella Raines, actress; Ahmad Rashad, football player; Ann Reinking, dancer and actress; Tom Robbins, novelist; Ann Rule, writer; Francis Scobee, astronaut; Seattle, Dwamish, Suquamish chief; Smohalla, Indian prophet and chief; Hillary Swank, actress; Julia Sweeney, actress; Adam West, actor; Audrey Wurdemann, poet.

West Virginia

Capital: Charleston
Governor: Bob Wise, D (to Jan. 2005)
Senators: Robert C. Byrd, D (to Jan. 2007);
   John D. "Jay" Rockefeller IV, D (to Jan. 2003)
Secy. of State: Joe Manchin, D (to Jan. 2005)
Treasurer: John D. Perdue, D (to Jan. 2005)
Auditor: Glen B. Gainer III, D (to Jan. 2005)
Atty. General: Darrell McGraw, D (to Jan. 2005)
Entered Union (rank): June 20, 1863 (35)
Present constitution adopted: 1872
Motto: *Montani semper liberi* (Mountaineers are always free)

State Symbols: flower, rhododendron (1903); **tree,** sugar maple (1949); **bird,** cardinal (1949); **animal,** black bear (1973); **colors,** blue and gold (official) (1863); **songs,** "West Virginia, My Home Sweet Home," "The West Virginia Hills," and "This Is My West Virginia" (adopted by Legislature in 1947, 1961, and 1963 as official state songs);
Nickname: Mountain State
Origin of name: In honor of Elizabeth, "Virgin Queen" of England
10 largest cities (2000): Charleston, 53,421; Huntington, 51,475; Parkersburg, 33,099; Wheeling, 31,419; Morgantown, 26,809; Weirton, 20,411; Fairmont, 19,097; Beckley, 17,254; Clarksburg, 16,743; Martinsburg, 14,972
Land area: 24,087 sq mi. (62,384 sq km)
Geographic center: In Braxton Co., 4 mi. E of Sutton
Number of counties: 55
Largest county by population and area: Kanawha, 200,073 (2000); Randolph, 1,040 sq mi.
State forests: 9 (79,502 ac.)
State parks: 35 (74,508 ac.)
Residents: West Virginian
2000 resident census population (rank): 1,808,344 (37). **Male:** 879,170 (48.6%); **Female:** 929,174 (51.4%). **White:** 1,718,777 (95.0%); **Black:** 57,232 (3.2%); **American Indian:** 3,606 (0.2%); **Asian:** 9,434 (0.5%); **Other race:** 3,107 (0.2%); **Two or more races:** 15,788 (0.9%); **Hispanic/Latino:** 12,279 (0.7%). **2000 percent population 18 and over:** 77.7; **65 and over:** 15.3; **median age:** 38.9.

West Virginia's early history from 1609 until 1863 is largely shared with Virginia, of which it was a part until Virginia seceded from the Union in 1861. The delegates of the 40 western counties who opposed secession formed their own government, which was granted statehood in 1863.

In 1731 Morgan Morgan established the first permanent white settlement on Mill Creek in present-day Berkeley County. Coal, a mineral asset that would figure significantly in West Virginia's history, was discovered in 1742. Other important natural resources are oil, natural gas, and hardwood forests, which cover about 75% of the state's area.

The state's rapid industrial expansion began in the 1870s, drawing thousands of European immigrants and African Americans into the region. Miners' strikes between 1912 and 1921 required the intervention of state and federal troops to quell the violence.

Today, the state ranks second in total coal production, with about 15% of the U.S. total. It is also a leader in steel, glass, aluminum, and chemical manufactures. Major agricultural commodities are poultry and eggs, dairy products, and apples.

Tourism is increasingly popular in mountainous West Virginia. More than a million acres have been set aside in 35 state parks and recreation areas and in 9 state forests and national forests. Major points of interest include Harpers Ferry and New River Gorge National River, The Greenbrier and Berkeley Springs resorts, the scenic railroad at Cass, and the historic homes in the Eastern Panhandle.

Famous natives and residents: George Brett, baseball player; Pearl S. Buck, author; Phyllis Curtin, soprano; Martin R. Delany, first black army major; Billy Dixon, frontiersman and scout; Joanne Dru, actress; Thomas "Stonewall" Jackson, Confederate general; John S. Knight, publisher; Don Knotts, actor; Peter Marshall, TV host; Kathy Mattea, singer; Whitney D. Morrow, banker and diplomat; Mary Lou Retton, gymnast; Walter Reuther, labor leader; Eleanor Steber, soprano; Lewis L. Strauss, naval officer and scientist;

Cyrus Vance, government official; William Lyne Wilson, legislator and university president; Chuck Yeager, test pilot and Air Force general.

Wisconsin

Capital: Madison
Governor: Scott McCallum, R (to Jan. 2003)
Lieut. Governor: Margaret Farrow, R (to Jan. 2003)
Senators: Russell D. Feingold, D (to Jan. 2005); Herbert Kohl, D (to Jan. 2007)
Secy. of State: Douglas J. La Follette, D (to Jan. 2003)
State Treasurer: Jack C. Voight, R (to Jan. 2003)
Atty. General: James E. Doyle, D (to Jan. 2003)
Superintendent of Public Instruction: Elizabeth Burmaster, Nonpartisan (to July 2005)
Organized as territory: July 4, 1836
Entered Union (rank): May 29, 1848 (30)
Present constitution adopted: 1848
Motto: Forward
State Symbols: flower, wood violet (1949); **tree,** sugar maple (1949); **grain,** corn (1990); **bird,** robin (1949); **animal,** badger; **wild life animal,** white-tailed deer (1957); **domestic animal,** dairy cow (1971); **insect,** honeybee (1977); **fish,** musky (muskellunge) (1955); **song,** "On Wisconsin"; **mineral,** galena (1971); **rock,** red granite (1971); **symbol of peace,** mourning dove (1971); **soil,** antigo silt loam (1983); **fossil,** trilobite (1985); **dog,** American Water Spaniel (1986); **beverage,** milk (1988); **dance,** polka (1994);
Nickname: Badger State
Origin of name: French corruption of an Indian word whose meaning is disputed
10 largest cities (2000): Milwaukee, 596,974; Madison, 208,054; Green Bay, 102,313; Kenosha, 90,352; Racine, 81,855; Appleton, 70,087; Waukesha, 64,825; Oshkosh, 62,916; Eau Claire, 61,704; West Allis, 61,254
Land area: 54,314 sq mi. (140,673 sq km)
Geographic center: In Wood Co., 9 mi. SE of Marshfield
Number of counties: 72
Largest county by population and area: Milwaukee, 940,164 (2000); Marathon, 1,545 sq mi.
State forests: 9 (476,004 ac.)
State parks & scenic trails: 45 parks, 14 trails (66,185 ac.)
Residents: Wisconsinite
2000 resident census population (rank): 5,363,675 (18). **Male:** 2,649,041 (49.4%); **Female:** 2,714,634 (50.6%). **White:** 4,769,857 (88.9%); **Black:** 304,460 (5.7%); **American Indian:** 47,228 (0.9%); **Asian:** 88,763 (1.7%); **Other race:** 84,842 (1.6%); **Two or more races:** 66,895 (1.2%); **Hispanic/Latino:** 192,921 (3.6%). **2000 percent population 18 and over:** 74.5; **65 and over:** 13.1; **median age:** 36.0.

The Wisconsin region was first explored for France by Jean Nicolet, who landed at Green Bay in 1634. In 1660 a French trading post and Roman Catholic mission were established near present-day Ashland.

Great Britain obtained the region in settlement of the French and Indian Wars in 1763; the U.S. acquired it in 1783 after the Revolutionary War. However, Great Britain retained actual control until after the War of 1812. The region was successively governed as part of the territories of Indiana, Illinois, and Michigan between 1800 and 1836, when it became a separate territory.

Wisconsin is a leading state in milk and cheese production. In 1999 the state ranked second in the number of milk cows (1,360,000) and produced 27% of the nation's total output of cheese. Other important farm products are peas, beans, beets, corn, potatoes, oats, hay, and cranberries.

The chief industrial products of the state are automobiles, machinery, furniture, paper, beer, and processed foods. Wisconsin ranks second among the 47 paper-producing states.

Wisconsin is a pioneer in social legislation, providing pensions for the blind (1907), aid to dependent children (1913), and old-age assistance (1925). In labor legislation, the state was the first to enact an unemployment compensation law (1932) and the first in which a workman's compensation law actually took effect. In 1984, Wisconsin became the first state to adopt the Uniform Marital Property Act.

The state has over 14,000 lakes, of which Winnebago is the largest. Water sports, ice-boating, and fishing are popular, as are skiing and hunting. Public parks and forests take up one-seventh of the land, with 45 state parks, 9 state forests, 14 state trails, 3 recreational areas, and 2 national forests.

Among the many points of interest are the Apostle Islands National Lakeshore; Ice Age National Scientific Reserve; the Circus World Museum at Baraboo; the Wolf, St. Croix, and Lower St. Croix national scenic riverways; and the Wisconsin Dells.

Famous natives and residents: Don Ameche, actor; Ray Chapman Andrews, naturalist and explorer; Walter Annenberg, media tycoon and philanthropist; Carrie Catt, woman suffragist; John R. Commons, economist; Tyne Daly, actress; August Derleth, author; Jeanne Dixon, seer; Zona Gale, novelist; Eric Heiden, skater; Woody Herman, band leader; Hildegarde, singer; Harry Houdini, magician; Hans V. Kaltenborne, journalist; Pee Wee King, singer; George F. Kennan, diplomat; Robert La Follette, politician; William D. Leahy, admiral; Liberace, pianist; Charles Litel, actor; Allen Ludden, TV host; Alfred Lunt, actor; Frederic March, actor; Jackie Mason, comedian; John Ringling North, circus director; Pat O'Brien, actor; Georgia O'Keeffe, painter; Charlotte Rae, actress; William H. Rehnquist, jurist; Gena Rowlands, actress; Tom Snyder, newscaster; Spencer Tracy, actor; Thorstein Veblen, economist; Orson Welles, actor and producer; Thornton Wilder, author; Charles Winninger, actor; Frank Lloyd Wright, architect.

Wyoming

Capital: Cheyenne
Governor: Jim Geringer, R (to Jan. 2003)
Senators: Michael B. Enzi, R (to Jan. 2003); Craig Thomas, R (to Jan. 2007)
Secy. of State: Joe Meyer, R (to Jan. 2003)
Auditor: Max Maxfield, R (to Jan. 2003)
Supt. of Public Instruction: Judy Catchpole, R (to Jan. 2003)
Treasurer: Cynthia M. Lummis, R (to Jan. 2003)
Atty. General: Gay Woodhouse, R
Organized as territory: May 19, 1869
Entered Union (rank): July 10, 1890 (44)
Present constitution adopted: 1890
Motto: Equal rights (1955)
State Symbols: flower, Indian paintbrush (1917); **tree,** cottonwood (1947); **bird,** meadowlark (1927); **gemstone,** jade (1967); **insignia,** bucking horse (unofficial); **song,** "Wyoming" (1955);
Nickname: Equality State
Origin of name: From the Delaware Indian word, meaning "mountains and valleys alternating"; the same as the Wyoming Valley in Pennsylvania
10 largest cities (2000): Cheyenne, 53,011; Casper, 49,644; Laramie, 27,204; Gillette, 19,646; Rock Springs, 18,708; Sheridan, 15,804; Green River, 11,808; Evanston, 11,507; Riverton, 9,310; Cody, 8,835
Land area: 97,105 sq mi. (251,501 sq km)
Geographic center: In Fremont Co., 58 mi. ENE of Lander
Number of counties: 23, plus Yellowstone National Park
Largest county by population and area: Laramie, 81,607 (2000); Sweetwater, 10,426 sq mi.
State parks and historic sites: 23 (58,498 ac.)
Residents: Wyomingite
2000 resident census population (rank): 493,782 (50). **Male:** 248,374 (50.3%); **Female:** 245,408 (49.7%). **White:** 454,670 (92.1%); **Black:** 3,722 (0.8%); **American Indian:** 11,133 (2.3%); **Asian:** 2,771 (0.6%); **Other race:** 12,301 (2.5%); **Two or more races:** 8,883 (1.8%); **Hispanic/Latino:** 31,669 (6.4%). **2000 percent population 18 and over:** 73.9; **65 and over:** 11.7; **median age:** 36.2.

The U.S. acquired the land comprising Wyoming from France as part of the Louisiana Purchase in 1803. John Colter, a fur-trapper, is the first white man known to have entered the region. In 1807 he explored the Yellowstone area and brought back news of its geysers and hot springs.

Robert Stuart pioneered the Oregon Trail across Wyoming in 1812–1813 and, in 1834, Fort Laramie, the first permanent trading post in Wyoming, was built. Western Wyoming was obtained by the U.S. in the 1846 Oregon Treaty with Great Britain and as a result of the treaty ending the Mexican War in 1848.

When the Wyoming Territory was organized in 1869, Wyoming women became the first in the nation to obtain the right to vote. In 1925 Mrs. Nellie Tayloe Ross was elected first woman governor in the United States.

Wyoming's towering mountains and vast plains provide spectacular scenery, grazing lands for sheep and cattle, and rich mineral deposits.

Mining, particularly oil and natural gas, is the most important industry. Wyoming has the world's largest sodium carbonate (natrona) deposits and has the nation's second largest uranium deposits.

In 2000 Wyoming ranked second among the states in wool production (exceeded only by Texas) and third in sheep and lambs (exceeded only by Texas and California); it also had 1,580,000 cattle. Principal crops include wheat, oats, sugar beets, corn, barley, and alfalfa.

Second in mean elevation to Colorado, Wyoming has many attractions for the tourist trade, notably Yellowstone National Park. Cheyenne is famous for its annual "Frontier Days" celebration. Flaming Gorge, the Fort Laramie National Historic Site, and Devils Tower and Fossil Butte National Monuments are other points of interest.

Famous natives and residents: James Bridger, trapper, guide, and storyteller; Dick Cheney, vice president; Buffalo Bill Cody, scout; John Colter, trader and first white man to enter Wyoming; June E. Downey, educator; Thomas Fitzpatrick, mountain man and guide; Curt Gowdy, sportscaster; Tom Horn, detective; Isabel Jewell, actress; Velma Linford, writer; Esther Morris, first woman judge; Ted Olson, writer; John "Portugee" Phillips, frontiersman; Jackson Pollock, painter; Nellie Tayloe Ross, first woman elected governor of a state; Alan K. Simpson, senator; Jedediah S. Smith, mountain man and first American to reach California from the East; Alan Swallow, publisher and author; Willis Van Devanter, jurist; Francis E. Warren, first state governor; Chief Washakie, chief of the Shoshone; James G. Watt, former secretary of the Interior.

Tabulated Data on State Governments

State	Governor		Legislature[1]						Highest Court[2]		
	Term, years	Annual salary	Membership U[3]	L[4]	Term, years U[3]	L[4]	Salaries of members[5]		Members	Term, years	Annual salary
Alabama	4[6]	$ 94,655	35	105	4	4	$ 10	per diem	9	6	$175,726[7]
Alaska	4	83,281	20	40	4	2	24,012[8]	per annum	5	3[9]	109,908[7]
Arizona	4	95,000	30	60	2	2	24,000	per annum	5	6	126,525[7]
Arkansas	4	60,000	35	100	4	2	12,500	per annum	7	8	95,216[7]
California	4	165,000	40	80	4	2	99,000	per annum	7	12	162,409[7]
Colorado	4	90,000	35	65	4	2	30,000	per annum	7	10	79,500[7]
Connecticut	4	78,000	36	151	2	2	21,788[8]	per annum	7	8	124,683[7]
Delaware	4[10]	107,000	21	41[1]	4	2	28,300	per annum	5	12	121,200[7]
Florida	4[6]	110,962	40	120	4[6]	2[11]	26,388	per annum	7	6	137,314
Georgia	4[6]	119,416	56	180	2	2	11,348	per annum	7	6	143,601
Hawaii	4	94,780	25	51	4	2	32,000[8]	per annum	5	10	115,547[7]
Idaho	4	95,500	35	70	2	2	15,646[8]	per annum	5	6	102,125[7]
Illinois	4	145,900	59	118	4-2	2	55,778	per annum	7	10	159,235
Indiana	4[6]	95,000	50	100	4	2	11,600	per annum	5	2[9]	115,000
Iowa	4	104,352	50	100	4	2	20,758	per annum	9	8	109,900[7]
Kansas	4	94,036	40	125	4	2	76	per diem[12]	7	6	109,756[7]
Kentucky	4	99,657	38	100	4	2	158	per diem[13]	7	8	114,373[7]
Louisiana	4	95,000	39	105	4	4	16,800	per annum	7	10	85,000
Maine	4	70,000	35	151	2	2	18,540	per biennium	7	7	96,000
Maryland	4[6]	120,000	47	141	4	4	29,700	per annum	7	10	107,300[7]
Massachusetts	4	135,000	40	160	2	2	46,410	per annum	7	(14)	95,880[7]
Michigan	4	172,000	38	110	4	2	77,400	per annum	7	8	159,960
Minnesota	4	120,303	67	134	4[15]	2	31,140	per annum	7	6	110,998[7]
Mississippi	4	83,160	52	122	4	4	10,000	per session	9	8	90,800[7]
Missouri	4[10]	119,982	34	163	4[16]	2	31,246	per annum	7	12	120,000[7]
Montana	4	83,672	50	100	4	2	55	per diem	7	8	83,550
Nebraska	4[6]	85,000	49[17]	—	4[17]	—	12,000	per biennium	7	6	111,003
Nevada	4[6]	117,000	21	42	4	2	7,800	per biennium	7	6	107,600
New Hampshire	2	96,060	24	(18)	2	2	200	per biennium	5	(14)	109,848[7]
New Jersey	4[6]	130,000	40	80	4[15]	2	35,000[8]	per annum	7	7[19]	152,191[7]
New Mexico	4[6]	90,000	42	70	4	2	136	per diem	5	8	96,283[7]
New York	4	179,000	61	150	2	2	79,500	per annum	7	14	151,200[7]
North Carolina	4[6]	118,430	50	120	2	2	13,951	per annum	7	8	115,336[7]
North Dakota	4	83,013	49	98	4	4	111	per diem[20]	5	10	83,107[7]
Ohio	4	115,752	33	99	4	2	51,674[8]	per annum	7	6	120,750[7]
Oklahoma	4	101,140	48	101	4	2	38,400	per annum	(21)	6	97,807[7]
Oregon	4[6]	80,000	30	60	4	2	1,092	per month	7	6	83,700
Pennsylvania	4[6]	125,000	50	203	4	2	47,000	per annum	7	10	119,750[7]
Rhode Island	4	69,900	50	100	2	2	10,000	per annum	5	(22)	104,403
South Carolina	4	106,078	46	124	4	2	10,400	per annum	5	10	106,061[7]
South Dakota	4[6]	92,564	35	70	2	2	6,000	per annum	5	3[23]	94,887[7]
Tennessee	4	85,000	33	99	4	2	16,500	per annum	5	8	101,820
Texas	4	99,122	31	150	4	2	7,200	per annum	9	6	94,686[7]
Utah	4	100,600	29	75	4	2	120[8]	per diem	5	3	109,650[7]
Vermont	2	115,763	30	150	2	2	536[24]	per week	5	6	99,489[7]
Virginia	4	124,855	40	100	4	2	17,640[25]	per annum	7	12	132,523[7]
Washington	4[26]	135,960	49	98	4[11]	2	32,064	per annum	9	6	123,600
West Virginia	4[6]	72,000	34	100	4	2	15,000	per annum	5	12	72,000
Wisconsin	4	122,406	33	99	4	2	44,233	per annum	7	10	118,824[7]
Wyoming	4	95,000	30	60	4	2	125	per diem	5	8	93,000

NOTE: Salaries are rounded to nearest dollar. 1. Known as *General Assembly* in Ark., Colo., Conn., Del., Ga., Ill., Iowa, Ind., Ky., Md., Mo., N.C., Ohio, Pa., R.I., S.C., Tenn., Vt., Va.; *Legislative Assembly* in N.D., Ore.; *General Court* in Mass., N.H.; *Legislature* in other states. Meets biennially in Ark., Ky., Mont., Nev., N.D., Ore., Texas. Wyoming Legislature has regular general session on odd-numbered years and a budget session on even-numbered years. Arkansas General Assembly meets every other year for 60 days in odd numbered years. Ohio General Assembly meets when deemed necessary. Legislative bodies meet annually in other states. 2. Known as *Court of Appeals* in Md., N.Y.; *Supreme Court of Virginia* in Va.; *Supreme Judicial Court* in Maine, Mass.; *Supreme Court* in other states. 3. Upper house: *Senate* in all states except Neb., which has a single-house legislative body, "the Legislature." 4. Lower house: *Assembly* in Calif., Nev., N.Y., Wis.; *House of Delegates* in Md., Va., W.Va.; *General Assembly* in N.J.; *House of Representatives* in other states. 5. Base salary. Does not include additional payments for expenses, mileage, special sessions, etc., or additional per diem payments. 6. May not serve third consecutive term. 7. Chief justice receives a higher salary. 8. Leaders receive a higher salary. 9. Initial term; thereafter elected popularly for 10-year term. 10. May serve only two terms, consecutive or otherwise. 11. Have term limitations. 12. When in session, plus $85 per day for expenses. There is also an out-of-session expense allowance of $5,400. The total annual compensation for members of the legislature is $21,867. Leaders receive an additional sum. 13. Plus $1,503 per month when not in session. 14. Until 70 years old. 15. Every 10 years (the year after census) term is only for 2 years. 16. Legislators may serve only 8 years in each house, 16 combined. 17. Unicameral legislature. 18. Constitutional number: 375-400. 19. Second term receive tenure, mandatory retirement at 70. 20. When in session, plus $250 per month when not in session. 21. Nine members in Supreme Court, highest in civil cases; five in Court of Criminal Appeals. 22. Term of good behavior. 23. Subsequent terms, eight years. 24. To limit of $13,000 per biennium; $105 per diem for Special Session. 25. Upper house receives higher salary. 26. No person is eligible who would have served during 8 of the previous 14 years. *Source:* questionnaires to the states.

Land and Water Area of States, 1990

(in square miles)

State	Rank (total area)	Land[1] area	Water[2] area	Total area	State	Rank (total area)	Land[1] area	Water[2] area	Total area
Alabama	30	50,750.23	1,672.71	52,422.94	Montana	4	145,556.34	1,489.82	147,046.16
Alaska	1	570,373.55	86,050.59	656,424.14	Nebraska	16	76,877.73	480.67	77,358.40
Arizona	6	113,642.26	364.00	114,006.26	Nevada	7	109,805.89	761.02	110,566.91
Arkansas	29	52,075.29	1,107.07	53,182.36	New Hampshire	46	8,969.36	381.57	9,350.93
California	3	155,973.09	7,734.06	163,707.15	New Jersey	47	7,418.84	1,303.11	8,721.95
Colorado	8	103,729.54	370.78	104,100.32	New Mexico	5	121,364.54	233.69	123,598.23
Connecticut	48	4,845.39	698.26	5,543.65	New York	27	47,223.85	7,250.71	54,474.56
Delaware	49	1,954.62	534.76	2,489.38	North Carolina	28	48,718.08	5,103.27	53,821.35
Dist. of Columbia	—	61.41	6.95	68.36	North Dakota	19	68,994.24	1,709.59	70,703.83
Florida	22	53,997.08	11,761.00	65,758.08	Ohio	34	40,952.59	3,874.94	44,827.53
Georgia	24	57,918.73	1,522.49	59,441.22	Oklahoma	20	68,678.57	1,224.33	69,902.90
Hawaii	43	6,423.34	4,508.24	10,931.58	Oregon	9	96,002.58	2,383.17	98,385.75
Idaho	14	82,750.93	822.84	83,573.77	Pennsylvania	33	44,819.61	1,238.63	46,058.24
Illinois	25	55,593.29	2,324.55	57,917.84	Rhode Island	50	1,044.98	500.12	1,545.10
Indiana	38	35,870.18	549.91	36,420.09	South Carolina	40	30,111.12	1,895.99	32,007.11
Iowa	26	55,874.90	400.64	56,275.54	South Dakota	17	75,897.74	1,223.72	77,121.46
Kansas	15	81,823.02	458.98	82,282.00	Tennessee	36	41,219.52	926.49	42,146.01
Kentucky	37	39,732.31	678.93	40,411.24	Texas	2	261,914.26	6,686.70	268,600.96
Louisiana	31	43,566.03	8,277.44	51,843.47	Utah	13	82,168.15	2,735.97	84,904.12
Maine	39	30,864.55	4,522.78	35,387.33	Vermont	45	9,249.33	365.67	9,615.00
Maryland	42	9,774.65	2,632.80	12,407.45	Virginia	35	39,597.79	3,171.09	42,768.88
Massachusetts	44	7,837.98	2,716.81	10,554.79	Washington	18	66,581.95	4,720.70	71,302.65
Michigan	11	56,809.18	40,001.04	96,810.22	West Virginia	41	24,086.55	144.89	24,231.44
Minnesota	12	79,616.66	7,326.05	86,942.71	Wisconsin	23	54,313.71	11,189.50	65,503.21
Mississippi	32	46,913.64	1,519.95	48,433.59	Wyoming	10	97,104.55	713.56	97,818.11
Missouri	21	68,898.01	810.80	69,708.81	**U.S. Total**		**3,536,341.73**	**251,083.35**	**3,787,425.08**

1. Dry land and land temporarily or partially covered by water, such as marshland, swamps, etc.; streams and canals under one-eighth statute mile wide; and lakes, reservoirs, and ponds under 40 acres. 2. Permanent inland water surface, such as lakes, reservoirs, and ponds having an area of 40 acres or more; streams, sloughs, estuaries, and canals one-eighth statute mile or more in width; deeply indented embayments and sounds, and other coastal waters behind or sheltered by headlands or islands separated by less than 1 nautical mile of water, and islands under 40 acres in area. Excludes areas of oceans, bays, sounds, etc. lying within U.S. jurisdiction but not defined as inland water. *Source:* Department of Commerce, Bureau of the Census.

State Capitals and Largest Cities

State	Capital	Largest city	State	Capital	Largest city
Alabama	Montgomery	Birmingham	Montana	Helena	Billings
Alaska	Juneau	Anchorage	Nebraska	Lincoln	Omaha
Arizona	Phoenix	Phoenix	Nevada	Carson City	Las Vegas
Arkansas	Little Rock	Little Rock	New Hampshire	Concord	Manchester
California	Sacramento	Los Angeles	New Jersey	Trenton	Newark
Colorado	Denver	Denver	New Mexico	Santa Fe	Albuquerque
Connecticut	Hartford	Bridgeport	New York	Albany	New York City
Delaware	Dover	Wilmington	North Carolina	Raleigh	Charlotte
Florida	Tallahassee	Jacksonville	North Dakota	Bismarck	Fargo
Georgia	Atlanta	Atlanta	Ohio	Columbus	Columbus
Hawaii	Honolulu	Honolulu	Oklahoma	Oklahoma City	Oklahoma City
Idaho	Boise	Boise	Oregon	Salem	Portland
Illinois	Springfield	Chicago	Pennsylvania	Harrisburg	Philadelphia
Indiana	Indianapolis	Indianapolis	Rhode Island	Providence	Providence
Iowa	Des Moines	Des Moines	South Carolina	Columbia	Columbia
Kansas	Topeka	Wichita	South Dakota	Pierre	Sioux Falls
Kentucky	Frankfort	Lexington	Tennessee	Nashville	Memphis
Louisiana	Baton Rouge	New Orleans	Texas	Austin	Houston
Maine	Augusta	Portland	Utah	Salt Lake City	Salt Lake City
Maryland	Annapolis	Baltimore	Vermont	Montpelier	Burlington
Massachusetts	Boston	Boston	Virginia	Richmond	Virginia Beach
Michigan	Lansing	Detroit	Washington	Olympia	Seattle
Minnesota	St. Paul	Minneapolis	West Virginia	Charleston	Charleston
Mississippi	Jackson	Jackson	Wisconsin	Madison	Milwaukee
Missouri	Jefferson City	Kansas City	Wyoming	Cheyenne	Cheyenne

Source: U.S. Bureau of the Census, 2000 figures.

50 Largest Cities of the United States

(According to Census 2000 data)

Data supplied by U.S. Census Bureau and by the cities in response to questionnaires. Per capita personal income data are given for the Metropolitan Statistical Area (MSA), the Primary Metropolitan Statistical Area (PMSA), the New England County Metropolitan Area (NECMA), or the Consolidated Metropolitan Statistical Area (CMSA), as noted. Average daily temperature data are from *County and City Data Book*. NOTE: Persons of Hispanic origin may be of any race.

Albuquerque, N.M.

Mayor: Jim Baca (to Dec. 2001)
2000 census population (rank): 448,607 (35); **% change:** 16.6; **Male:** 217,887 (48.6%); **Female:** 230,720 (51.4%); **White:** 321,179 (71.6%); **Black:** 13,854 (3.1%); **American Indian and Alaska Native:** 17,444 (3.9%); **Asian:** 10,068 (2.2%); **Other race:** 66,292 (14.8%); **Two or more races:** 19,318 (4.3%); **Hispanic/Latino:** 179,075 (39.9%). **2000 percent population 18 and over:** 75.5%; **65 and over:** 12.0%; **median age:** 34.9.
Land area: 163 sq mi. (422 sq km); **Alt.:** 4,958 ft.
Avg. daily temp. (1998): Jan., 34.8° F; July, 78.8° F
Churches: 211; **City-owned parks:** 189; **Radio stations:** 43 (AM, 17; FM, 26); **Television stations:** 11
Civilian Labor Force (MSA) 2001: 374,200; **Unemployed:** 14,700, **Percent:** 3.9; **Per capita personal income (MSA) 1999:** $25,619
Chamber of Commerce: Greater Albuquerque Chamber of Commerce, 401 2nd St. N.W., Albuquerque, N.M. 87125. Albuquerque Hispanic Chamber of Commerce, 202 Central Ave. S.E., Albuquerque, N.M. 87102

Albuquerque is the largest city in New Mexico and the seat of Bernalillo County. It is situated in west-central New Mexico on the upper Rio Grande River.

Spanish settlers arrived in the mid-1600s, but they retreated from the area in 1680 after the Pueblo revolt. The old town was founded in 1706 by Don Francisco Cuervo y Valdés, the governor of New Mexico, and named after the Duke of Albuquerque, the viceroy of New Spain.

The opening of the Santa Fe Trail in the early 19th century brought an influx of settlers, and an army post was established following U.S. occupation in 1846. Albuquerque remained loyal to the Union during the Civil War, although it was briefly occupied by Confederate forces in 1862. The new town was laid out in 1880 after the Santa Fe Railroad was built one mile east of the original plaza. The Spanish old town and the mission church of San Felipe de Neri (1706) were soon enveloped by the new construction and survive today.

The city is noted as a center for health and medical services in the region, and government agencies, nuclear research, banking, and tourism are important to the economy. There is a growing high-tech center in Albuquerque, and Intel Corp.'s largest manufacturing facility is located there.

Albuquerque is the seat of the University of New Mexico (1889) and the headquarters for the Cibola National Forest. Its numerous attractions include the National Atomic Museum, Petroglyph National Monument, Coronado State Park, many pueblos, and the Sandia Mountains.

Famous natives: Pete Domenici, U.S. senator; Erna Fergusson, author; Annabeth Gish, actress; Fred Haney, baseball player, executive; Ernie Pyle, World War II war correspondent; Slim Summerville, actor; Al and Bobby Unser, auto racers.

Atlanta, Ga.

Mayor: Bill Campbell (to Jan. 2002)
2000 census population (rank): 416,474 (39); **% change:** 5.7; **Male:** 206,725 (49.6%); **Female:** 209,749 (50.4%); **White:** 138,352 (33.2%); **Black:** 255,689 (61.4%); **American Indian and Alaska Native:** 765 (0.2%); **Asian:** 8,046 (1.9%); **Other race:** 8,272 (2.0%); **Two or more races:** 5,177 (1.2%); **Hispanic/Latino:** 18,720 (4.5%). **2000 percent population 18 and over:** 77.7%; **65 and over:** 9.7%; **median age:** 31.9.
City land area: 136 sq mi. (352.2 sq km); **Alt.:** Highest, 1,050 ft.; lowest, 940 ft.
Avg. daily temp.: Jan., 41.9° F; July, 78.6° F
Churches: 1,500; **City-owned parks:** 277 (3,178 ac.); **Radio stations:** AM, 7; FM, 20; **Television stations:** 8 commercial; 2 PBS
Civilian Labor Force (MSA) 2001: 2,289,700; **Unemployed:** 67,700, **Percent:** 3.0; **Per capita personal income (MSA) 1999:** $32,486
Chamber of Commerce: Metro Atlanta Chamber of Commerce, 235 International Blvd., Atlanta, Ga. 30303

Atlanta, the largest city and capital of Georgia, is the seat of Fulton County. It is situated in the northwest part of the state at the base of the Blue Ridge Mountains near the Chattahoochee River. The first European settler was Hardy Ivy, who built a cabin there in 1833.

Founded as Terminus in 1837, the town served as the end of the Georgia railroad line (Western and Atlantic Railroad) and later became incorporated as Marthasville in 1843 in honor of ex-governor Lumpkin's daughter Martha. It was renamed Atlanta in 1845 and incorporated as a city in 1847. The name was suggested by the railroad's chief engineer, J. Edgar Thomson, and was derived from its location at the end of the Georgia and Atlantic railroad line. The city became the capital of Georgia in 1868.

During the Civil War, the city was burned and almost completely destroyed while occupied by Gen. William T. Sherman's troops in Nov. 1864. It was quickly rebuilt after the war, and it grew rapidly due to the expansion of the railroads in the southwest.

Today, Atlanta is the major commercial and transportation hub of the southeast United States, and its international airport is one of the busiest in the world. The city's economy is led by the service, communications, retail trade, manufacturing, finance, and insurance industries. The convention business is also important, and Atlanta is home to many major corporations, including Coca-Cola, which was founded there in 1892.

Atlanta is also a major educational center, with many prestigious universities and colleges, including Emory University (1836), Georgia Institute of Technology (1885), and Georgia State University (1913). Morehouse College (1867), Spelman College (1881), and Clark Atlanta University (1865; 1869) are important historically black colleges.

Major attractions include Martin Luther King, Jr., National Historic Site, Grant Park, and the Carter Presidential Center. The 1996 Summer Olympics were held in Atlanta.

Famous natives: Hank Aaron, baseball player; Arrested Development, recording artists; Jimmy Carter, former president; Ray Charles, singer; James Dickey, poet; Mattivilda Dobbs, soprano; Walt Frazier, basketball player; Oliver Hardy, comedian; Evander Holyfield, boxer; Allan Jackson, singer; Bobby Jones, golfer; DeForest Kelley, actor; Martin Luther King, Jr., civil rights leader and Nobel Peace Prize winner; Margaret Mitchell, novelist; Bert Parks, entertainer; Eric Roberts, actor; Julia Roberts, actress; Doug Stone, singer; Gwen Torrence, Olympic athlete; Lee Tracy, actor; Travis Tritt, singer; Ted Turner, TBS and CNN founder; Jane Withers, actress; Joanne Woodward, actress; Andrew Young, civil rights activist.

Austin, Tex.

Mayor: Kirk Watson (to June 2003)
2000 census population (rank): 656,562
(16); **% change:** 41.0; **Male:** 337,569 (51.4%);
Female: 318,993 (48.6%); **White:** 429,100 (65.4%);
Black: 65,956 (10.0%); **American Indian and Alaska Native:** 3,889 (0.6%); **Asian:** 30,960 (4.7%); **Other race:** 106,538 (16.2%); **Two or more races:** 19,650 (3.0%); **Hispanic/Latino:** 200,579 (30.5%). **2000 percent population 18 and over:** 77.5%; **65 and over:** 6.7%; **median age:** 29.6
Land area: 252.3 sq mi. (653 sq km); **Alt.:** From 425 ft. to over 1000 ft.
Avg. daily temp.: Jan., 49.1° F; July, 84.7° F
Churches: 353 churches, representing 45 denominations; **City-owned parks and playgrounds:** 169 (11,800 ac.); **Radio stations:** AM, 12; FM, 27; **Television stations:** 7 commercial; 1 PBS; 1 independent
Civilian Labor Force (MSA) 2001: 759,500[1];
Unemployed: 25,000, **Percent:** 3.3; **Per capita personal income (MSA) 1999:** $31,794[1]
Chamber of Commerce: Greater Austin Chamber of Commerce, P.O. Box 1967, Austin, Tex. 78767

1. Austin–San Marcos, Tex.

Austin, the state capital of Texas and seat of Travis County, is the fourth-largest city in Texas. It is situated in the south-central part of the state on the Colorado River.

The site was called Waterloo in 1838, and in 1839 it was incorporated as a city and chosen as the capital of the independent Republic of Texas. Waterloo was renamed Austin in honor of Stephen F. Austin, the founder of the Texas Republic. It became the permanent capital of the state of Texas in 1870.

Austin's growth was spurred by several developments after the Civil War—the railroads reached the city in the 1870s; it was crossed by the important Chisholm cattle trail; and it became the seat of the state university in 1883.

Austin has a growing commercial and diversified manufacturing sector. Civilian government employment is 20% of the labor force and is important to

the economy. As home to the University of Texas, Austin is a major center for research and development and is nationally recognized as a high-technology center. The city has a new convention center downtown.

Famous natives: Don Baylor, baseball player and manager; Earl Campbell, football player; Liz Carpenter, author; Dabney Coleman, actor; Ben Crenshaw, golfer; Michael Dell, founder Dell Computer Corp.; Tobe Hooper, film director; Lady Bird Johnson, former first lady; Tom Kite, golfer; James Michener, author; Willie Nelson, musician; Amado Pena, artist; Darrell Royal, football coach; Zachary Scott, actor; Jerry Jeff Walker, musician; Dalhart Windberg, artist.

Baltimore, Md.

Mayor: Martin O'Malley (to Dec. 2003)
2000 census population (rank): 651,154
(17); **% change:** −11.5; **Male:** 303,687 (46.6%);
Female: 347,467 (53.4%); **White:** 205,982 (31.6%);
Black: 418,951 (64.3%); **American Indian and Alaska Native:** 2,097 (0.3%); **Asian:** 9,985 (1.5%); **Other race:** 4,363 (0.7%); **Two or more races:** 9,554 (1.5%); **Hispanic/Latino:** 11,061 (1.7%). **2000 percent population 18 and over:** 75.2%; **65 and over:** 13.2%; **Median age:** 35.0.
Land area: 80.3 sq mi. (208 sq km); **Alt.:** Highest, 490 ft.; lowest, sea level
Avg. daily temp.: Jan., 35.5° F; July, 79.9° F
Churches: Roman Catholic, 72; Jewish, 50; Protestant and others, 344; **City-owned parks:** 347 park areas and tracts (6,314 ac.); **Radio stations:** AM, 10; FM, 11; **Television stations:** 7 (including Home Shopping Network)
Civilian Labor Force (PMSA) 2001: 1,341,400;
Unemployed: 55,000, **Percent:** 4.1; **Per capita personal income (PMSA) 1999:** $31,434
Chamber of Commerce: Greater Baltimore Committee, 111 S. Calvert St., Ste. 1700, Baltimore, Md. 21202

Baltimore, the largest city in Maryland, is situated in the northern part of the state on the Patapsco River estuary, an arm of Chesapeake Bay. The city is independent and does not fall within any county.

The site was settled in the early 17th century and founded as a town in 1729. The town was named after Lord Baltimore, the founder of Maryland, and was incorporated as a city in 1797. It has an excellent harbor and has been a principal port since the 18th century. Baltimore was a pioneer shipbuilding center, and the Baltimore clipper was used extensively in world trade.

The city has been greatly affected by the nation's wars. During the War of 1812, the British bombarded nearby Fort McHenry, inspiring Francis Scott Key to write the *Star-Spangled Banner*. And although Maryland never seceded from the Union, Baltimore was occupied by Union troops throughout the Civil War.

An important shipbuilding and supply center during the World Wars, the city center later underwent a period of urban decay followed by major redevelopment in the 1970s and 1980s.

Baltimore's economy is very diverse, with strong financial, legal, and nonprofit service industries. The city also leads in scientific research and development through two highly acclaimed medical institutions, Johns Hopkins Hospital and University of Maryland Hospital. There is also a significant tourist sector. Major attractions include the Edgar Allan Poe House, Fort McHenry National Monument, and Pimlico Race Course, site of the Preakness.

Famous natives: Larry Adler, musician; John Astin, actor; Eubie Blake, pianist; Francis X. Bushman, actor; Charlie Chase, actor; Hans Conried, actor; Mildred Dunnock, actress; "Mama" Cass Elliot, singer; Barry Farber, broadcaster; Paul Ford, actor; Philip Glass, composer; Billie Holiday, singer; Barry Levinson, director; H. L. Mencken, writer; Babe Ruth, baseball player; Upton Sinclair, novelist; Leon Uris, novelist; John Waters, film director, writer, and actor; Frank Zappa, musician.

Boston, Mass.

Mayor: Thomas Menino (to Dec. 2001)
2000 census population (rank): 589,141 (20); **% change:** 2.6; **Male:** 283,588 (48.1%); **Female,** 305,553 (51.9%); **White:** 320,944 (54.5%); **Black:** 149,202 (25.3%); **American Indian and Alaska Native:** 2,365 (0.4%); **Asian:** 44,284 (7.5%); **Other race:** 46,102 (7.8%); **Two or more races:** 25,878 (4.4%); **Hispanic/Latino:** 85,089 (14.4%). **2000 percent population 18 and over:** 80.2%; **65 and over:** 10.4%; **median age:** 31.1.
Land area: 47.2 sq mi. (122 sq km); **Alt.:** Highest, 330 ft.; lowest, sea level
Avg. daily temp.: Jan., 29.6° F; July, 73.5° F
Churches: Protestant, 187; Roman Catholic, 70; Jewish, 13; others, 100; **City-owned parks, playgrounds, etc.:** 2,260 ac.; **Radio stations**[1]**:** AM, 24; FM, 22; **Television stations**[1]**:** 27
Civilian Labor Force (PMSA) 2001: 1,850,700; **Unemployed:** 53,000, **Percent:** 2.9; **Per capita personal income (NECMA) 1999:** $36,285[2]
Chamber of Commerce: Boston Chamber of Commerce, 600 Atlantic Ave., Boston, Mass. 02210

1. Metropolitan area. 2. Boston–Worcester–Lawrence–Lowell–Brockton, Mass.–N.H.

Boston is the state capital, the seat of Suffolk County, and the largest city in Massachusetts. It is located in the eastern part of the state on Massachusetts Bay. It was incorporated as a city in 1822. No city in the U.S. is richer in historical associations than Boston, and no city has retained more of its original buildings as memorials to America's past.

The first European settler was Rev. William Blackstone, who arrived in 1623, just three years after the Pilgrims had landed at Plymouth in 1620. He was joined by Puritans from England in 1630. They named their new town Boston, after the former home of many of them in Lincolnshire, England. Fourteen years later, the pioneer Bostonians set aside the first public park in the U.S.—the Boston Common. The following year, 1635, they opened the first free public school in America. Today, the Boston metropolitan area is home to 68 colleges and universities.

Boston is a major industrial, financial, and educational hub and has one of the finest ports in the world. The port of Boston handled more than 17.1 million tons of cargo in 2000.

The city's banking and financial services, insurance, and real estate sectors continue to drive Boston's economy. Boston is also a leading city in health care, with 25 inpatient hospitals and numerous community health centers. The city's unique cultural and historic heritage makes it a center of tourism, and its hotel industry ranks first in the nation in occupancy. Boston's other businesses are in high technology, biotechnology, software, and electronics.

Famous natives: Samuel Adams, patriot; Louisa May Alcott, author; John Singleton Copley, painter; Ralph Waldo Emerson, philosopher and poet; Arthur Fiedler, conductor; Benjamin Franklin, statesman and scientist; Edward Everett Hale, clergyman and author; Oliver Wendell Holmes, Supreme Court justice; Winslow Homer, painter; Joseph P. Kennedy, financier; Jack Lemmon, actor; Robert Lowell, poet; Edgar Allan Poe, writer; Paul Revere, patriot and silversmith; John L. Sullivan, boxer; Barbara Walters, TV journalist.

Charlotte, N.C.

Mayor: Pat McCrory (to Nov. 2001)
2000 census population (rank): 540,828 (26); **% change:** 36.6; **Male:** 264,978 (49.0%); **Female:** 275,850 (51.0%); **White:** 315,061 (58.3%); **Black:** 176,964 (32.7%); **American Indian and Alaska Native:** 1,863 (0.3%); **Asian:** 18,418 (3.4%); **Other race:** 19,242 (3.6%); **Two or more races:** 8,997 (1.7%); **Hispanic/Latino:** 39,800 (7.4%). **2000 percent population 18 and over:** 75.3%; **65 and over:** 8.8%; **median age:** 32.7.
Land area: 234 sq mi. (606.2 sq km); **Alt.:** 765 ft.
Avg. daily temp.: Jan., 40.5° F; July, 78.5° F
Churches: Protestant, over 500; Roman Catholic, 13; Jewish, 3; Greek Orthodox, 1; **City-owned parks and parkways:** 130; **Radio stations:** AM, 10; FM, 19; **Television stations:** 6 commercial; 1 PBS
Civilian Labor Force (MSA) 2001: 838,400[1]; **Unemployed:** 44,900, **Percent:** 5.4; **Per capita personal income (MSA) 1999:** $30,340[1]
Chamber of Commerce: Charlotte Chamber, P.O. Box 32785, Charlotte, N.C., 28232

1. Charlotte–Gastonia–Rock Hill, N.C.–S.C.

Charlotte, North Carolina's largest city and the seat of Mecklenburg County, is located in the southern part of the state near the South Carolina border. It was named for King George III of England's wife, Charlotte Sophia of Mecklenburg-Strelitz.

Settled about 1750, Charlotte was incorporated as a city in 1768 and made the county seat in 1774. From 1800 to 1848, Charlotte was the center of U.S. gold production. A branch of the U.S. mint operated there from 1837 to 1913. Charlotte was a leading Confederate city during the Civil War and was the last meeting place of the full Confederate cabinet.

Charlotte is the second-largest banking center in the United States, and two of the nation's top banks, First Union Corporation and Bank of America, are headquartered there. Other major employers are the education, health care, government, technology, and communications sectors. The city is also a hub for US Airways.

Charlotte is the seat of the University of North Carolina and home to two professional sports teams, the Carolina Panthers (football) and the Charlotte Hornets (basketball).

Famous natives: Romare Bearden, artist; Richard G. Darman, government official; Billy Graham, evangelist; Charles Gwathmey, architect; Hamilton Jordan, government official; Donald Schollander, swimmer; Randolph Scott, actor.

Chicago, Ill.

Mayor: Richard M. Daley (to April 2003)
2000 census population (rank): 2,896,016 (3); **% change:** 4.0; **Male:** 1,405,107 (48.5%); **Female:** 1,490,909 (51.5%); **White:** 1,215,315 (42.0%); **Black:** 1,065,009 (36.8%); **American Indian and Alaska Native:** 10,290 (0.4%); **Asian:** 125,974 (4.3%); **Other race:** 393,203 (13.6%); **Two or more races:** 84,437 (2.9%); **Hispanic/Latino:** 753,644 (26.0%). **2000 percent population 18 and over:** 73.8%; **65 and over:** 10.3%; **median age:** 31.5.
Land area: 228.443 sq mi. (592 sq km); **Alt.:** Highest, 672 ft.; lowest, 578.5 ft.
Avg. daily temp. (1998): Jan., 29.6° F; July, 74.5° F

Churches: Protestant, 850; Roman Catholic, 252; Jewish, 51; **City-owned parks:** 551; **Radio stations (1999):** AM, 16; FM, 28; **Television stations:** 14
Civilian Labor Force (PMSA): 4,258,700;
  Unemployed: 212,900, **Percent:** 5.0; **Per capita personal income (PMSA) 1999:** $34,743
Chamber of Commerce: Chicagoland Chamber of Commerce, 330 N. Wabash, One IBM Plaza, Suite 2800, Chicago, Ill. 60611

Chicago is the largest city in Illinois and the seat of Cook County. Built directly on the lake front, it stretches for 22 mi along the southwest shore of Lake Michigan.

The first white men known to have visited the region were Louis Joliet and Jacques Marquette in 1673. The first permanent white settler was John Kinzie, who is sometimes called the Father of Chicago. He took over a trading post in 1796 that had been established in 1791 by Jean-Baptiste Point du Sable, a black fur trapper. Fort Dearborn, a blockhouse and stockade, was built in 1804 but was evacuated in 1812, at which time more than half of its garrison was massacred by Potawatomi and Ottawa Indians loyal to the British.

The name Chicago is thought to come from the Algonquian word "Chicagou" meaning strong or powerful. Some early Frenchmen believed that the name was derived from the Algonquian word for "onion place" because wild onions grew there.

Laid out in 1830, Chicago was incorporated as a village in 1833 and as a city in 1837. In the Great Chicago Fire of 1871, an area of the city about 4 mi long and nearly a mile wide—more than two thousand acres—was totally destroyed. However, much of the city, including the railroads and stockyards, survived intact, and from the ashes of the old wooden structures there arose more modern constructions in steel and stone.

Today, Chicago is a major Great Lakes port and the commercial, financial, industrial, and cultural center of the Midwest. The manufacturing industries dominate the wholesale and retail trade, and trade in agricultural commodities is important to the economy. The Chicago Board of Trade is the largest agricultural futures market in the world.

Among Chicago's many attractions are the Art Institute of Chicago, the Field Museum of Natural History, the Jane Addams–Hull House Museum, Navy Pier, and numerous architectural landmarks such as the Sears Tower and Frank Lloyd Wright's Robie House.

Famous natives: Jack Benny, comedian; Edgar Rice Burroughs, author; Raymond Chandler, author; Hillary Rodham Clinton, lawyer and former first lady; Michael Crichton, author; Walt Disney, filmmaker; John Dos Passos, author; Bobby Fischer, chess player; Bob Fosse, choreographer and director; Benny Goodman, clarinetist; Dorothy Hamill, figure skater; Quincy Jones, composer; Gene Krupa, drummer; David Mamet, playwright; Bob Newhart, comedian; Kim Novak, actress; Donald O'Connor, actor; William L. Shirer, journalist and historian; Gloria Swanson, actress; Melvin Van Peebles, playwright; Alfred Wallenstein, conductor; Robin Williams, comedian and actor; Robert Young, actor.

Cleveland, Ohio

Mayor: Michael R. White (to Dec. 2001)
2000 census population (rank): 478,403 (33);
  % change: –5.4; **Male:** 226,550 (47.4%); **Female:** 251,853 (52.6%); **White:** 198,510 (41.5%); **Black:** 243,939 (51.0%); **American Indian and Alaska**

Native: 1,458 (0.3%); **Asian:** 6,444 (1.3%); **Other race:** 17,173 (3.6%); **Two or more races:** 10,701 (2.2%); **Hispanic/Latino:** 34,728 (7.3%). **2000 percent population 18 and over:** 71.5%; **65 and over:** 12.5%; **median age:** 33.0.
Land area: 79 sq mi. (205 sq km); **Alt.:** Highest, 1048 ft.; lowest, 573 ft.
Avg. daily temp.: Jan., 25.5° F; July, 71.6° F
Churches[1]: Protestant, 980; Roman Catholic, 187; Jewish, 31; Eastern Orthodox, 22; **City-owned parks:** 41 (1,930 ac.); **Radio stations:** AM, 15; FM, 17; **Television stations:** 7
Civilian Labor Force (PMSA) 2001: 1,139,000[1];
  Unemployed: 43,000, **Percent:** 3.8; **Per capita personal income (PMSA) 1999:** $30,472[1]
Chamber of Commerce: Greater Cleveland Growth Association, 200 Tower City Center, Cleveland, Ohio 44113

1. Cleveland–Lorain–Elyria, Ohio.

Cleveland is the second-largest city in Ohio and the seat of Cuyahoga County. It is located in the northeast part of the state on Lake Erie.

In the colonial era, the Cleveland area was known as the Connecticut Western Reserve, part of a land grant made to Connecticut by King Charles II in 1662. The city was founded in 1796 by Gen. Moses Cleaveland, who was the head surveyor of the Connecticut Land Company. This company had bought 3 million acres in what is now northern Ohio. A permanent settlement was founded in 1799, named after the general, and the spelling was shortened to Cleveland. The city was incorporated in 1836.

Cleveland's industrial growth was stimulated by the opening of the Ohio and Erie canals in 1832 and, later, by the advent of the Civil War, with the increasing demand for machinery, railroad equipment, ships, and other items.

The port of Cleveland is the largest overseas general cargo port on Lake Erie. Greater Cleveland has long been famous as a diversified durable goods manufacturing area. Following the national trend, Cleveland has been shifting to a more services-based economy. Greater Cleveland is a world corporate center for leading national and multinational companies in industries ranging from transportation, insurance, retailing, and utilities, to commercial banking and finance.

Famous natives: Jim Backus, actor; Drew Carey, actor and comedian; Dorothy Dandridge, actress; Ruby Dee, actress; Phil Donahue, talk-show host; Joel Grey, actor; Arsenio Hall, talk-show host; Margaret Hamilton, actress; Philip Johnson, architect; Henry Mancini, composer; Burgess Meredith, actor; Paul Newman, actor; Carl Stokes, jurist.

Colorado Springs, Colo.

Mayor: Mary Lou Makepeace (to April 2005)
2000 census population (rank): 360,890 (48); **% change:** 28.4; **Male:** 178,469 (49.5%); **Female:** 182,421 (50.5%); **White:** 291,095 (80.7%); **Black:** 23,677 (6.6%); **American Indian and Alaska Native:** 3,175 (0.9%); **Asian:** 10,179 (2.8%); **Other race:** 18,091 (5.0%); **Two or more races:** 13,909 (3.9%); **Hispanic/Latino:** 43,330 (12.0%). **2000 percent population 18 and over:** 75.3%; **65 and over:** 9.6%; **median age:** 33.6.
Land area: 183.2 sq mi. (474.49 sq km); **Alt.:** 6,035 ft.
Avg. daily temp.: Jan., 28.8° F; July, 71.2° F
Churches: Protestant, 400+; Roman Catholic, 20; Jewish, 3; others, **City parks and playgrounds:** 156 (10,762 ac.); **Radio stations:** AM, 7; FM, 17; **Television stations:** 7

Civilian Labor Force (MSA) 2001: 262,300;
Unemployed: 8,000, **Percent:** 3.0; **Per capita personal income (MSA) 1999:** $27,255
Chamber of Commerce: Colorado Springs Chamber of Commerce, 2 N. Cascade Ave., Suite 110, Colorado Springs, Colo. 80903

Colorado Springs is the second-largest city in Colorado, after Denver. It is the seat of El Paso County, making up about three-quarters of the county's population. It is located on the edge of the Rocky Mountains, with Pikes Peak (14,110 ft) towering beside it to the west. To the east begin the Great Plains.

The city was founded in 1871. Gen. William Jackson Palmer, a Pennsylvania-born Civil War veteran, came across the scenic spot in his railroad travels and was inspired to begin a new resort community there. The subsequent development of Colorado Springs was influenced in part by an influx of English tourists later in the 1870s and by the discovery of gold in nearby Cripple Creek in the 1890s. Millionaire businessmen and philanthropists, such as Spencer Penrose, Charles Tutt, and Winfield Scott Stratton, helped to establish the city's infrastructure and shape its popularity as a tourist destination.

During World War II, Colorado Springs sold a large amount of land just south of the city to the military. The U.S. Army established Fort Carson as a training facility. The military presence in Colorado Springs would continue to grow, with the establishment of the United States Air Force Academy there in the 1950s, and later, the construction of Peterson Air Force Base, Falcon Air Force Base, and Cheyenne Mountain Air Force Base. The bases are all home to space command centers (with Cheyenne Mountain housing the headquarters for the North American Aerospace Defense Command [NORAD]) and have collectively earned Colorado Springs its national reputation as the leading center for military space operations.

The city's economy is still based heavily on tourism. In more recent years, Colorado Springs has gained a strong foothold in the electronics, high-technology, and manufacturing industries. The city is also a large center for amateur sports, as it is home to the headquarters of the U.S. Olympic Committee and Olympic Training Center facility.

Famous natives: Bert Andrews, journalist; Kelly Bishop, actress; Spring Byington, actress; Lon Chaney, actor; Marjorie Daw, actress; Marceline Day, actress; Rich "Goose" Gossage, baseball player; Helen Hunt Jackson, writer and poet; Chase Masterson, actress; Sherry Stringfield, actress.

Columbus, Ohio

Mayor: Michael B. Coleman (to Nov. 2003)
2000 census population (rank): 711,470 (15);
% change: 12.4; **Male:** 345,878 (48.6%); **Female:** 365,592 (51.4%); **White:** 483,332 (67.9%); **Black:** 174,065 (24.5%); **American Indian and Alaska Native:** 2,090 (0.3%); **Asian:** 24,495 (3.4%); **Other race:** 8,292 (1.2%); **Two or more races:** 18,829 (2.6%); **Hispanic/Latino:** 17,471 (2.5%). **2000 percent population 18 and over:** 75.8%; **65 and over:** 8.9%; **median age:** 30.6.
Land area: 211 sq mi. (546.4 sq km); **Alt.:** Highest, 902 ft.; lowest, 702 ft.
Avg. daily temp.: Jan., 27.1° F; July, 73.8° F
Churches: Protestant, 436; Roman Catholic, 62; Jewish,

5; Other, 8; **City-owned parks:** 203 (12,891 ac.);
Radio stations: AM, 10; FM, 16; **Television stations:** 9 commercial, 3 PBS
Civilian Labor Force (MSA) 2001: 874,100;
Unemployed: 20,400, **Percent:** 2.3; **Per capita personal income (MSA) 1999:** $29,777
Chamber of Commerce: Columbus Area Chamber of Commerce, P.O. Box 1527, Columbus, Ohio 43216

Columbus, the largest city in Ohio, is the state capital and the seat of Franklin County. It is located in central Ohio on the Scioto River.

The first structures near the site of downtown Columbus were earthen mounds constructed by Indian tribes known as Mound Builders. Native Americans lived undisturbed in Central Ohio until the 1700s, when the first explorers entered the Midwest. The first permanent settlement in the area was founded by a surveyor from Kentucky, Lucas Sullivant, in 1797 and was named Franklinton. The state capital was laid out nearby in 1812 and named after Christopher Columbus. It became the capital in 1816. Columbus was chartered as a city in 1834 and annexed Franklinton in 1870. The city's growth was stimulated by the development of transportation facilities—a feeder to the Ohio Canal completed in 1832, the National Road in 1833, and the arrival of the railroad in 1850.

Columbus is a port of entry and a major industrial, commercial, manufacturing, and cultural center. It is the seat of Ohio State University. The city has enjoyed steady growth over the years due to its economic diversity—no single activity dominates the economy.

Famous natives: Warner Baxter, actor; George Bellows, painter; Michael Feinstein, singer and pianist; Eileen Heckart, actress; Jack Nicklaus, golfer; Tom Poston, actor; Eddie Rickenbacker, aviator; Arthur M. Schlesinger, historian; James Thurber, writer; Nancy Wilson, singer.

Dallas, Tex.

Mayor: Ron Kirk (to May 2001)
City Manager: Teodoro J. Benavides
2000 census population (rank): 1,188,580 (8);
% change: 18.0; **Male:** 598,991 (50.4%); **Female:** 589,589 (49.6%); **White:** 604,209 (50.8%); **Black:** 307,957 (25.9%); **American Indian and Alaska Native:** 6,472 (0.5%); **Asian:** 32,118 (2.7%); **Other race:** 204,883 (17.2%); **Two or more races:** 32,351 (2.7%); **Hispanic/Latino:** 422,587 (35.6%). **2000 percent population 18 and over:** 73.4%; **65 and over:** 8.6%; **median age:** 30.5.
Land area: 378 sq mi. (979 sq km); **Alt.:** Highest, 750 ft.; lowest, 375 ft.
Avg. daily temp.: Jan., 45.0° F; July, 86.3° F
Churches: 1,974 (in Dallas Co.); **City-owned parks:** 296 (47,025 ac.); **Radio stations:** AM, 19; FM, 30; **Television stations:** 10 commercial, 1 PBS
Civilian Labor Force (PMSA) 2001: 2,032,500;
Unemployed: 79,300, **Percent:** 3.9; **Per capita personal income (PMSA) 1999:** $34,690
Chamber of Commerce: Dallas Chamber of Commerce, 1201 Elm, Dallas, Tex. 75270

Dallas is the second-largest city in Texas and is the seat of Dallas County. It is situated 185 mi northeast of Austin on the Trinity River near the junction of its three forks.

Dallas was first settled by Tennessee lawyer John Neely Bryan as a trading post on the Trinity River in 1841. Many historians believe that Bryan named the city after George Mifflin Dallas, vice president under James K. Polk, but there is no official agreement on this. It was incorporated as a town in 1856 and as a city in 1871. Located in the chief cotton-producing region of Texas, the city developed as a cotton market in the 1870s.

The economy is highly diversified, and the city is the leading commercial, marketing, and industrial center of the southwest. The insurance business is important, and the service sector has experienced rapid growth. Dallas is also a popular tourist and convention city.

Famous natives: Tex Avery, animator and director; Robby Benson, actor; Ernie Banks, baseball player; Bebe Daniels, actress; Linda Darnell, actress; Lee Elder, golfer; Morgan Fairchild, actress; Trini Lopez, singer; Aaron Spelling, producer; Stephen Stills, singer; Sharon Tate, actress; Lee Trevino, golfer.

Denver, Colo.

Mayor: Wellington Webb (to June 30, 2003)
2000 census population (rank): 554,636 (25);
% change: 18.6; **Male:** 280,207 (50.5%); **Female:** 274,429 (49.5%); **White:** 362,180 (65.3%); **Black:** 61,649 (11.1%); **American Indian and Alaska Native:** 7,290 (1.3%); **Asian:** 15,611 (2.8%); **Other race:** 86,464 (15.6%); **Two or more races:** 20,794 (3.7%); **Hispanic/Latino:** 175,704 (31.7%); **2000 percent population 18 and over:** 78.0%; **65 and over:** 11.3%; **median age:** 33.1.
Land area: 154.63 sq mi. (400.5 sq km); **Alt.:** Highest, 5,494 ft.; lowest, 5,140 ft.
Avg. daily temp.: Jan., 29.5° F; July, 73.3° F
Churches[1]**:** Protestant, 859; Roman Catholic, 60; Jewish, 13; **City-owned parks:** 205 (4,166 ac.); **City-owned mountain parks:** 40 (13,600 ac.); **Radio stations**[1]**:** AM, 23; FM, 20; **Television stations**[1]**:** 17
Civilian Labor Force (PMSA) 2001: 1,176,200; **Unemployed:** 26,300; **Percent:** 2.2; **Per capita personal income (PMSA) 1999:** $36,058
Chamber of Commerce: Greater Denver Chamber of Commerce, 1445 Market Street, Denver, Colo. 80202

1. Metropolitan area.

Denver is the largest city in Colorado, the state capital, and the seat of Denver County. It lies at the foot of the Rocky Mountains and is situated at the junction of the South Platte River and Cherry Creek.

The city was born in 1858, when gold was discovered in the sands of Cherry Creek, at first just a tough village of cabins, shacks, and tents. It was incorporated as a city in 1861 and became the territorial capital in 1867. The city is named for James W. Denver, governor of the Kansas Territory, which included part of Colorado. The city prospered from the famous gold and silver mines of the 1870s and 1880s.

Denver is an important cultural, industrial, transportation, tourist, and marketing center. It is also a regional center for many federal government agencies and a leader in the development of western energy resources. Denver's fastest-growing industries include contract construction, real estate, retail trade, and government.

Denver International Airport, the first major new airport constructed in the U.S. in 21 years, opened to passenger traffic on Feb. 28, 1995, at a cost of $4.9 billion. At 53 sq mi, it is the largest airport in North America.

Famous natives: Tim Allen, comedian and actor; Ward Bond, actor; Douglas Fairbanks, Sr., actor; John Hart, newsman; Pat Hingle, actor; Ted Mack, TV host; Barbara Rush, actress; Alan K. Simpson, senator; Paul Whiteman, bandleader; Don Wilson, announcer.

Detroit, Mich.

Mayor: Dennis W. Archer (to Dec. 2001)
2000 census population (rank): 951,270 (10);
% change: −7.5; **Male:** 448,319 (47.1%); **Female:** 502,951 (52.9%); **White:** 116,599 (12.3%); **Black:** 775,772 (81.6%); **American Indian and Alaska Native:** 3,140 (0.3%); **Asian:** 9,268 (1.0%); **Other race:** 24,199 (2.5%); **Two or more races:** 22,041 (2.3%); **Hispanic/Latino:** 47,167 (5.0%). **2000 percent population 18 and over:** 68.9%; **65 and over:** 10.4%; **median age:** 30.9.
Land area: 143 sq mi. (370 sq km); **Alt.:** Highest, 685 ft.; lowest, 574 ft.
Avg. daily temp.: Jan., 23.4° F; July, 71.9° F
Churches[1]**:** Protestant, 1,165; Roman Catholic, 89; Jewish, 2; **City-owned parks:** 56 parks (3,843 ac.); 393 sites (5,838 ac.); **Radio stations:** AM, 27; FM, 30 (includes 3 in Windsor, Ont.); **Television stations:** 8[2] (includes 1 in Windsor, Ont.)
Civilian Labor Force (PMSA) 2001: 2,337,900; **Unemployed:** 104,700; **Percent:** 4.5; **Per capita personal income (PMSA) 1999:** $31,472
Chamber of Commerce: Detroit Regional Chamber of Commerce, One Woodward Avenue, P.O. Box 33840, Detroit MI 48232-0840

1. Six-county metropolitan area. 2. Within four counties of Metro Detroit.

Detroit, the largest city in Michigan, is situated in the southeast part of the state on the Detroit River. It is the seat of Wayne County. Detroit was incorporated as a city in 1815 and reincorporated in 1824.

Detroit is the oldest city of any size west of the seaboard colonies, having been founded by Antoine de la Mothe Cadillac on July 24, 1701, more than a century before Chicago was founded. The French were the first settlers, and they gave the city its name from their word meaning "strait," referring to the 27-mile-long Detroit River, which connects Lake Erie and Lake St. Clair. The river forms part of the international boundary, and marks the only point where Canada lies directly south of U.S. territory.

Because of its strategic location, Detroit was fought over by the French, the British, and the Indians. It was the headquarters for the British forces in the Northwest Territory during the American Revolutionary War.

The first steam vessel, the *Walk-in-the-Water*, made its appearance on the Great Lakes in 1818, and Detroit was the western terminus for most of its voyages from Buffalo. Its link to all the important cities on the Great Lakes made it a major exporting center.

Detroit is one of the largest manufacturing cities in the U.S. and is the center of the automobile manufacturing industry, which has experienced a decline due to foreign competition in the past decade. The health and medical care sector is important to the economy, and employment in the finance, insurance, and real-estate industries has inched up in the Detroit metropolitan area since 1991.

Famous natives: Anita Baker, singer; Sonny Bono, congressman and singer; Ralph Bunche, statesman; Ellen Burstyn, actress; Francis Ford Coppola, director; Aretha Franklin, singer; Casey Kasem, radio personality; Charles Lindbergh, aviator; Madonna, singer and actress; John Mitchell, former U.S. attorney general; Harry Morgan, actor; Rosa Parks, activist; George Peppard, actor; Gilda Radner, comedian; Della Reese, singer; Smokey Robinson, singer; Sugar Ray Robinson, boxer; Diana Ross, singer; George C. Scott, actor; Tom Selleck, actor; Lily Tomlin, comedian and actress; Margaret Whiting, singer.

El Paso, Tex.

Mayor: Raymond C. Caballero (to May 2003)
2000 census population (rank): 563,662 (23);
   % change: 9.4; **Male:** 267,651 (47.5%); **Female:** 296,011 (52.5%); **White:** 413,061 (73.3%); **Black:** 17,586 (3.1%); **American Indian and Alaska Native:** 4,601 (0.8%); **Asian:** 6,321 (1.1%); **Other race:** 102,320 (18.2%); **Two or more races:** 19,190 (3.4%); **Hispanic/Latino:** 431,875 (76.6%). **2000 percent population 18 and over:** 69.0%; **65 and over:** 10.7%; **median age:** 31.1
Land area: 250.9 sq mi. (649.8 sq km); **Alt.:** 4,000 ft.
Avg. daily temp.: Jan., 44.2° F; July, 82.5° F
Churches: Protestant, 320; Roman Catholic, 39; Jewish, 3; others, 20; **City-owned parks:** 145 (2,150 ac.)[1]; **Radio Stations:** AM, 18; FM, 17; **Television stations:** 6
Civilian Labor Force (MSA) 2001: 285,200;
   Unemployed: 21,800, **Percent:** 7.7; **Per capita personal income (MSA) 1999:** $17,216
Chamber of Commerce: El Paso Chamber of Commerce, Hispanic Chamber of Commerce, Black Chamber of Commerce, and Korean Chamber of Commerce, 10 Civic Center Plaza, El Paso, Tex. 79944

1. Includes 129 developed and 16 undeveloped parks.

El Paso, the fifth-largest city in Texas and the seat of El Paso County, is located in the far western part of the state on the north bank of the Rio Grande River, opposite the Mexican city of Ciudad Juárez on the south bank.

On April 30, 1598, Juan de Onate took formal possession of the area for King Philip II of Spain and subsequently crossed the Rio Grande River near a site west of present downtown El Paso that he called "El Paso del Rio del Norte," meaning the crossing of the river—the first use of the name "El Paso." In 1659, the mission of Nuestra Senora de Guadalupe was founded on a site that is present-day downtown Ciudad Juárez; the mission is still in use today. In 1682, Spanish colonists from Mexico founded the settlement of Ysleta on the site of the present-day city. However, it wasn't until 1827 that the first permanent settlement at El Paso was established by Juan María Ponce de León. The city's real growth started with the arrival of the Southern Pacific Railroad in 1881. El Paso was incorporated as a city in 1873.

In 1888, Mexico changed the name of Paso del Norte to Ciudad Juárez in honor of Benito Juárez. Later, in 1967, the U.S. agreed to cede a long-disputed part of El Paso to Mexico due to changes in the course of the Rio Grande, which forms the international boundary between the two countries. El Paso and its sister city of Ciudad Juárez across the U.S./Mexico border are inexorably joined by culture and economy. El Paso and Juárez make up the largest international metroplex in the world.

El Paso is an important port of entry to the U.S. from Mexico. The high technology, medical device manufacturing, plastics, refining, automotive, food processing, and defense-related industries are important to the economy. El Paso's service sector has experienced healthy growth since the 1980s. El Paso is also a major tourist resort.

Famous natives: Manuel Acosta, artist; Don Bluth, animation director; Vicki Carr, singer; Jose Cisneros, artist; Sam Donaldson, newsman; Albert Fall, government official; Judith Ivey, actress; Guy Kibbee, actor; Sandra Day O'Connor, Supreme Court justice; Debbie Reynolds, actress; Irene Ryan, actress.

Fort Worth, Tex.

Mayor: Kenneth Barr (to May 2002)
City Manager: Gary W. Jackson
2000 census population (rank): 534,694 (27);
   % change: 19.5; **Male:** 263,720 (49.3%); **Female:** 270,974 (50.7%); **White:** 319,159 (59.7%); **Black:** 108,310 (20.3%); **American Indian and Alaska Native:** 3,144 (0.6%); **Asian:** 14,105 (2.6%); **Other race:** 75,100 (14.0%); **Two or more races:** 14,535 (2.7%); **Hispanic/Latino:** 159,368 (29.8%). **2000 percent population 18 and over:** 71.7%; **65 and over:** 9.6%; **median age:** 30.9.
Land area: 303 sq mi. (784.7 sq km); **Alt.:** Highest, 780 ft.; lowest, 520 ft.
Avg. daily temp.: Jan., 44.2° F; July, 82.5° F
Churches: 941, representing 72 denominations; **City-owned parks:** 200 (9,906.7 ac.); **Radio stations:** AM, 12; FM, 18; **Television stations:** 13
Civilian Labor Force (PMSA) 2001: 944,100[1];
   Unemployed: 33,000, **Percent:** 3.5; **Per capita personal income (PMSA) 1999:** $28,035[1]
Chamber of Commerce: Fort Worth Chamber of Commerce, 777 Taylor Street, Suite 900, Fort Worth, Tex. 76102

1. Fort Worth–Arlington, Tex.

Fort Worth, seat of Tarrant County, is situated in the north-central part of Texas on the Trinity River.

The city was founded by Maj. Ripley Arnold in 1849 as a military outpost on the Trinity River to protect settlers moving westward from frequent Indian attacks. It was named after Gen. William J. Worth, the commander of the Texas army. Fort Worth was incorporated in 1873. Its growth was stimulated in the 1870s by its proximity to the Chisholm cattle trail. It prospered as a meat-packing and shipping center when the Texas and Pacific Railway arrived in 1876 and later experienced a new boom when oil was discovered nearby in 1917. The establishment of military installations in the area during both world wars also spurred the economy.

Fort Worth has traditionally been a diverse center of manufacturing and is not dependent on the oil or financial sectors. The city's industries range from clothing and food products to jet fighters, helicopters, computers, pharmaceuticals, and plastics. Fort Worth is a national leader in aviation products, electronic equipment, and refrigeration equipment. It is home to a multitude of major corporate headquarters, offices, and distribution centers.

Famous natives: Robert Bass, financier; Mark Brooks, golfer; Betty Buckley, singer and actress; Kate Capshaw, actress; Ornette Coleman, composer; Sandra Haynie, golfer; Patricia Highsmith, writer; Spanky McFarland, actor; R. Bruce Merrifield, Nobelist in chemistry; Roger Miller, singer; Fess Parker, actor; Bill Paxton, actor; Rex Reed, critic; Johnny Rutherford, auto racer; Liz Smith, columnist.

Fresno, Calif.

Mayor: Alan Autry (to Jan. 2005)
City Manager: Daniel G. Hobbs
2000 census population (rank): 427,652 (37);
   % change: 20.7; **Male:** 210,107 (49.1%); **Female:** 217,545 (50.9%); **White:** 214,556 (50.2%); **Black:** 35,763 (8.4%); **American Indian and Alaska Native:** 6,763 (1.6%); **Asian:** 48,028 (11.2%); **Other race:** 99,898 (23.4%); **Two or more races:** 22,061 (5.2%); **Hispanic/Latino:** 170,520 (39.9%). **2000 percent population 18 and over:** 67.1%; **65 and over:** 9.3%; **median age:** 28.5.
Land area: 99.38 sq mi. (257.39 sq km); **Alt.:** 328 ft.
Avg. daily temp.: Jan., 45.5° F; July, 81.0° F

Churches: 450 (approximate); **City-owned parks:** 38 (690 ac.); **Radio stations:** AM, 11[1]; FM, 13[1]; Bilingual 1; **Television stations:** 8[1]
Civilian Labor Force (CMSA) 2001: 447,800;
   Unemployed: 56,200, **Percent:** 12.6; **Per capita personal income (MSA) 1999:** $20,776
Chamber of Commerce: Fresno County and City Chamber of Commerce, P.O. Box 1469, 2331 Fresno St., Fresno, Calif. 93716

1. Metropolitan area.

Fresno is located in central California, 184 mi southeast of San Francisco and 222 mi northwest of Los Angeles. It is the seat of Fresno County. Fresno was incorporated as a city in 1885.

Fresno began as a station for the Central Pacific Railroad in 1872 and was made the seat of Fresno County in 1874. The city's name is Spanish for the ash trees that the early explorers found in the area.

Fresno is a leading agribusiness hub, with 250 different crops produced by 7,500 farmers on 1.9 million irrigated acres, worth $3 billion a year. Fresno County's top five agricultural products are grapes, cotton, tomatoes, cattle and calves, and turkeys.

The city is also a distribution and manufacturing center. Its diverse industries include agricultural chemicals, farm equipment, canned fruit and vegetables, clothing, computer software, electric wire, pumps, glass, and plastic products.

Famous natives: Mike Connors, actor; Maynard Dixon, painter; Bruce Furniss, swimmer; Jon Hall, actor; Daryle Lamonica, football player; Sam Peckinpah, director; William Saroyan, novelist; Tom Seaver, baseball player.

Honolulu, Hawaii

Mayor: Jeremy Harris (to Jan. 2005)
2000 census population (rank)[1]: 371,657 (46);
   % change: 1.7; **Male:** 182,628 (49.1%); **Female:** 189,029 (50.9%); **White:** 73,093 (19.7%); **Black:** 6,038 (1.6%); **American Indian and Alaska Native:** 689 (0.2%); **Asian:** 207,588 (55.9%); **Native Hawaiian and Other Pacific Islander:** 25,457 (6.8%); **Other race:** 3,318 (0.9%); **Two or more races:** 55,474 (14.9%); **Hispanic/Latino:** 16,229 (4.4%). **2000 percent population 18 and over:** 80.8%; **65 and over:** 17.8%; **median age:** 39.7
Land area: 85.7 sq mi. (221.9 sq km)[1]; **Alt.:** Highest, 2,013 ft.[1]; lowest, sea level
Avg. daily temp.: Jan., 72.6° F; July, 81° F
Churches: Roman Catholic, 39; Buddhist, 51; Jewish, 2; Protestant and others, 402; **City-owned parks**[1]: 2,056 ac.; **Radio stations**[1]: AM, 17[1]; FM, 11; **Television stations**[1]: 12
Civilian Labor Force (MSA) 2001: 425,700[2];
   Unemployed: 15,500[2], **Percent:** 3.6[2]; **Per capita personal income (MSA) 1999:** $29,465[2]
Chamber of Commerce: Chamber of Commerce of Hawaii, 1132 Bishop St., Suite 200, Honolulu, Hawaii 96813

1. Census Designated Place, approximately Salt Lake to Hawaii Kai. 2. City and county.

Honolulu is the capital and largest city of Hawaii, on the southeast coast of Oahu. The city is legally coextensive with the county of Honolulu, which includes the entire island of Oahu and most of the Northwest Hawaiian Islands, from Nihoa to Kure Atoll, except Midway. The population of Oahu makes up 73% of the state's total population. It is situated in the central Pacific Ocean 2,397 mi westsouthwest of San Francisco. Honolulu's name means "sheltered harbor" and derives from the native words *hono,* meaning "a bay," and *lulu,* meaning "sheltered."

Honolulu's early history was one of turbulence and conflict. One of the last areas on the globe to be explored and exploited by Europeans (it was first visited by British captain James Cook in 1778), Hawaii was subject to strong pressures from many forces, including American missionaries, who arrived in 1820, and opportunistic whalers. These whalers were among those who built Honolulu originally, bringing trade, commerce, and prosperity that led to expansion into the sugar and pineapple industries.

As early as 1814, Russia tried to move in, and Russian soldiers built a bastion at the harbor's edge. The British flag was raised in 1843 and French forces occupied Honolulu in 1849. Each time control was returned to the independent native kingdom without bloodshed. In 1898, a group of Americans completed a project attempted at intervals during the previous 65 years—annexation to the United States. Honolulu was incorporated as a city in 1907.

The Honolulu area was bombed by Japan in a surprise attack on the unprepared U.S. naval base at Pearl Harbor on Dec. 7, 1941. This action forced the United States to enter World War II. "Remember Pearl Harbor" became a famous American wartime slogan.

Hawaiian statehood in 1959 and the viability of commercial air travel to the island brought boom times to Honolulu. Tourism is the city's principal industry, followed by federal defense expenditures and agricultural exports (chiefly pineapples).

Famous natives: Hiram Bingham, explorer; Jean Erdman, dancer and choreographer; Hiram Fong, senator; Daniel Inouye, senator; Duke Kahanamoku, surfer and Olympian swimmer; Bette Midler, actress and singer; Kelly Preston, actress; Louise Morgan Sill, author; Don Stroud, actor; Merlin D. Tuttle, biologist and wildlife photographer.

Houston, Tex.

Mayor: Lee P. Brown (to Dec. 2001)
2000 census population (rank): 1,953,631 (4);
   % change: 19.8; **Male:** 975,551 (49.9%); **Female:** 978,080 (50.1%); **White:** 962,610 (49.3%); **Black:** 494,496 (25.3%); **American Indian and Alaska Native:** 8,568 (0.4%); **Asian:** 103,694 (5.3%); **Other race:** 321,603 (16.5%); **Two or more races:** 61,478 (3.1%); **Hispanic/Latino:** 730,865 (37.4%). **2000 percent population 18 and over:** 72.5%; **65 and over:** 8.4%; **median age:** 30.9.
Land area: 618.89 sq mi. (1,603 sq km); **Alt.:** Highest, 120 ft.; lowest, sea level
Avg. daily temp.: Jan., 50.4° F; July, 82.6° F
Churches[1]: 1,750; **City-owned parks:** 293 (32,733 ac.); **Radio stations**[1]: AM, 23; FM, 32; **Television stations:** 15 commercial, 1 PBS
Civilian Labor Force (PMSA) 2001: 2,196,700;
   Unemployed: 84,700, **Percent:** 3.9; **Per capita personal income (PMSA) 1999:** $32,386
Chamber of Commerce: Greater Houston Partnership, 1200 Smith, Suite 700, Houston, Tex. 77002-4400

1. Harris County.

Houston, the largest city in Texas and seat of Harris County, is located in the southeast part of the state near the Gulf of Mexico.

Sam Houston was the commander-in-chief of the Texas troops who fought a successful war of rebellion against domination by Mexico, which had been in possession of Texas. On April 21, 1836, Houston's men won a decisive victory in which the

Mexican dictator, Gen. Santa Anna, was taken prisoner and forced to sign the treaty that launched the Republic of Texas. In September, a constitution was ratified, and Houston was elected president. The Texas Republic was recognized by the U.S. and by the major European powers. The present city of Houston was incorporated in 1837 and named after Sam Houston; it was the Republic's first capital.

The port of Houston ranks first among U.S. ports in foreign tonnage handled. The city is a major business, financial, science, and technology center. Houston is outstanding in oil and natural-gas production and is the energy capital of the world. It is the home of one of the largest medical facilities in the world—the Texas Medical Center—and the focus of the aerospace industry. The Lyndon B. Johnson Space Center is the nation's headquarters for staffed spaceflight.

Famous natives: Debbie Allen, choreographer; Lance Alworth, football player; Denton Cooley, heart surgeon; Jim Demaret, golfer; Allen Drury, novelist; Shelly Duvall, actress; A. J. Foyt, auto racer; Howard Hughes, industrialist and film producer; Barbara C. Jordan, educator, lawyer, and politician; Barbara Mandrell, singer; Annette O'Toole, actress; Dennis and Randy Quaid, actors; Kenny Rogers, singer; Patrick Swayze, actor and dancer.

Indianapolis, Ind.

Mayor: Bart Peterson (to Dec. 31, 2003)
2000 census population (rank): 781,870 (12);
  % change: 6.7; **Male:** 378,310 (48.4%); **Female:** 403,560 (51.6%); **White:** 540,212 (69.1%); **Black:** 199,412 (25.5%); **American Indian and Alaska Native:** 1,985 (0.3%); **Asian:** 11,161 (1.4%); **Other race:** 15,921 (2.0%); **Two or more races:** 12,857 (1.6%); **Hispanic/Latino:** 30,636 (3.9%). **2000 percent population 18 and over:** 74.3%; **65 and over:** 11.0%; **median age:** 33.5.
Land area: 352 sq mi. (912 sq km); **Alt.:** Highest, 840 ft.; lowest, 700 ft.
Avg. daily temp.: Jan., 25.5 F; July, 75.4° F
Churches[1]: 1,191; **City-owned parks:** 172 (10,174 ac.); **Radio stations[2]:** AM, 8; FM, 17; **Television stations[1]:** 7
Civilian Labor Force (MSA) 2001: 869,800;
  Unemployed: 19,600, **Percent:** 2.2; **Per capita personal income (MSA) 1999:** $30,523
Chamber of Commerce: Indianapolis Chamber of Commerce, 320 N. Meridian St., Indianapolis, Ind. 46204

1. Marion County. 2. Metropolitan area.

Indianapolis, the largest city in Indiana and seat of Marion County, is located in the central part of the state on the West Fork of the White River. Its name derives from combining "Indiana" with "polis," the Greek word for city.

Indianapolis was settled in 1820, and five years later it was chosen as the state capital. It was incorporated as a city in 1832 and reincorporated in 1838. The city's growth began when the railroad reached it in 1847. Toward the end of the 19th century, the discovery of nearby natural gas and the start of the automobile industry hastened its industrial expansion. On Jan. 1, 1970, Indianapolis merged with surrounding Marion County.

Indianapolis is at the center of a rich agricultural region and is a major grain and livestock market. It is also a focal point of commerce, transportation, and manufacturing for the region. Some leading industries are electronics, pharmaceuticals, and food processing. The financial sector and service and insurance industries are growing rapidly.

Indianapolis is the site of the world-famous 500-mile automobile race and the Indiana State Fair.

Famous natives: Monte Blue, actor; David Letterman, TV host; Steve McQueen, actor; Jane Pauley, TV newscaster; Booth Tarkington, author; Kurt Vonnegut, Jr., author; Harry Von Zell, announcer; Clifton Webb, actor.

Jacksonville, Fla.

Mayor: John Delaney (to June 30, 2003)
2000 census population (rank): 735,617 (14);
  % change: 15.8; **Male:** 356,284 (48.4%); **Female:** 379,333 (51.6%); **White:** 474,307 (64.5%); **Black:** 213,514 (29.0%); **American Indian and Alaska Native:** 2,474 (0.3%); **Asian:** 20,427 (2.8%); **Other race:** 9,816 (1.3%); **Two or more races:** 14,631 (2.0%); **Hispanic/Latino:** 30,594 (4.2%). **2000 percent population 18 and over:** 73.3%; **65 and over:** 10.3%; **median age:** 33.8.
Land area: 759.6 sq mi. (1,967 sq km); **Alt.:** Highest, 71 ft.; lowest, sea level
Avg. daily temp.: Jan., 53.2° F; July, 81.3° F
Churches: Protestant, 794; Roman Catholic, 21; Jewish, 5; others, 22; **City-owned parks and playgrounds:** 19 (7,404 ac.); **Radio stations:** AM, 14; FM, 16; **Television stations:** 6 commercial, 1 PBS, 1 religious
Civilian Labor Force (MSA) 2001: 580,100;
  Unemployed: 20,100, **Percent:** 3.5; **Per capita personal income (MSA) 1999:** $27,625
Chamber of Commerce: Jacksonville Area Chamber of Commerce, Jacksonville, Fla. 32202

Jacksonville, Florida's largest city, is located in Duval County in the northeast corner of Florida, on the banks of the St. Johns River and adjacent to the Atlantic Ocean. It is the largest metropolitan area in northeast Florida and southeast Georgia.

Starting in the 16th century, French, Spanish, and English explorers and colonists were attracted to the region by the St. Johns River. The site was settled by Lewis Hogans in 1816. Jacksonville was laid out in 1822 and was named after Gen. Andrew Jackson, the first military governor of Florida. It was incorporated as a city in 1832.

During the Civil War, much of the city was destroyed by Union forces, who occupied Jacksonville four times. The city was rebuilt and, following the development of its harbor and the railroads, quickly became the transportation hub and leading industrial city in Florida by the 1880s. In 1968, city and county governments consolidated.

Jacksonville is the leading transportation and distribution hub in the state. However, the strength of the city's economy lies in its broad diversification. The area's economy is balanced among distribution, financial services, biomedical technology, consumer goods, information services, manufacturing, and other industries. Jacksonville has the largest deep-water port in the South Atlantic and is the leading port in the U.S. for automobile imports.

Famous natives: Mae Axton, songwriter; Pat Boone, singer; Judy Canova, comedian; Harold Carmichael, football player; Merion C. Cooper, producer and director; Billy Daniels, vocalist; Storm Davis, athlete; Bob Hayes, athlete; Wanda Hendrix, actress; James Weldon Johnson, author and educator; John Rosamond Johnson, musician and composer; Mark McCumber, pro golfer; Ray Mercer, boxer; Charles "Hoss" Singleton, songwriter; Bill Terry, member of Baseball Hall of Fame; Donnie Van Zant, rock musician; Ronnie Van Zant, rock musician; Leeroy Yarbrough, auto racer.

Kansas City, Mo.

Mayor: Kay Barnes (to April 2003)
City Manager: Robert L. Collins (apptd. July 1997)
2000 census population (rank): 441,545 (36);
   % change: 1.5; **Male:** 213,141 (48.3%); **Female:**
   228,404 (51.7%); **White:** 267,931 (60.7%); **Black:**
   137,879 (31.2%); **American Indian and Alaska
   Native:** 2,122 (0.5%); **Asian:** 8,182 (1.9%); **Other
   race:** 14,158 (3.2%); **Two or more races:** 10,780
   (2.4%); **Hispanic/Latino:** 30,604 (6.9%). **2000 percent population 18 and over:** 74.6%; **65 and over:**
   11.7%; **median age:** 34.0.
Land area: 317 sq mi. (821 sq km); **Alt.:** Highest, 1,014
   ft.; lowest, 722 ft.
Avg. daily temp.: Jan., 28.4° F; July, 80.9 F
Churches: 1,100 churches of all denominations[1]; **City-
   owned parks and playgrounds:** 189 (10,647 ac.);
   Radio stations[1]**:** AM, 14; FM, 19; **Television
   stations**[1]**:** 7
Civilian Labor Force (MSA) 2001: 1,046,900[2];
   Unemployed: 38,100, **Percent:** 3.6; **Per capita per-
   sonal income (MSA) 1999:** $30,225[2]
Chamber of Commerce: Chamber of Commerce of
   Greater Kansas City, 911 Main St., Kansas
   City, Mo. 64105

1. Metropolitan area. 2. Kansas City, Mo.–Kan.

Kansas City is the largest city in Missouri. It is
located in the western part of the state, at the junction of the Missouri and Kansas rivers. Kansas City
is located in Jackson, Clay, Platte, and Cass counties.

In 1821, the year Missouri entered the Union,
French trader François Chouteau came from St.
Louis to establish a trading post on the site of the
present city to take advantage of the growing fur
trade with the Kansa, Osage, Wyandotte, and other
tribes. In 1833, a settlement, called the town of Westport Landing, was laid out by John Calvin McCoy
and developed. The community became the Town of
Kansas and was incorporated as a city in 1850 and
renamed Kansas City in 1889. The city's name
reflects its Native American heritage—its site was
within the territory of the Kansa, or Kaw, Indians.

The city grew rapidly in the mid-1880s as the
starting point for gold prospectors and settlers heading westward. The coming of the Missouri-Pacific
Railroad in 1865 and the spanning of the Missouri
River by the Hannibal Bridge in 1869 also contributed to the city's growth. It also prospered as a center for the nation's cattle business.

The Kansas City metropolitan area, once known
primarily for agriculture and manufacturing, has
expanded its economic base to include strong
growth in areas of telecommunications, banking and
finance, and the service industry. A transportation
hub since the 1800s, the area enjoys a national and
regional prominence as a distribution and manufacturing center. Kansas City ranks nationally as first in
greeting-card publishing, frozen food storage and
distribution, and hard winter-wheat marketing; second in wheat flour production; and third in auto and
truck assembly. The area is one of ten federal
regional centers and employs over 25,000 in local,
state, and federal government. The city is also a
regional center for health care, employing over
55,000 in this industry.

Famous natives: Robert Altman, director; Edward Asner,
actor; Burt Bacharach, composer; Noah and Wallace
Beery, actors; Robert Russell Bennett, composer; Jeanne
Eagels, actress; Jean Harlow, actress; Ted Shawn, dancer
and choreographer; Casey Stengel, baseball player; Virgil
Thompson, composer; Tom Watson, golfer.

Las Vegas, Nev.

Mayor: Oscar Goodman (to May 2003)
2000 census population (rank): 478,434 (32);
   % change: 85.2; **Male:** 243,077 (50.8%); **Female:**
   235,357 (49.2%); **White:** 334,230 (69.9%); **Black:**
   49,570 (10.4%); **American Indian and Alaska Native:**
   3,570 (0.7%); **Asian:** 22,879 (4.8%); **Other race:**
   46,643 (9.7%); **Two or more races:** 19,397 (4.1%);
   Hispanic/Latino: 112,962 (23.6%); **2000 percent
   population 18 and over:** 74.1%; **65 and over:**
   11.6%; **median age:** 34.5.
Land area: 83.3 sq mi. (1,215.7 sq km); **Alt.:** 2,174 ft.
Avg. daily temp.: Jan., 45.5° F; July, 91° F
Churches: over 500 churches and synagogues; **Radio
   stations:** AM, 8; FM, 18; **Television stations:** 7
Civilian Labor Force (MSA) 2001: 794,000[1];
   Unemployed: 32,700, **Percent:** 4.1; **Per capita per-
   sonal income 1999:** $29,486[1]
Chamber of Commerce: 3720 Howard Hughes Park-
   way, Las Vegas, NV 89109

1. Las Vegas, Nev.–Ariz.

Las Vegas, seat of Clark County in southeast
Nevada, is the largest city in the state and one of the
fastest-growing cities in the United States. Between
April 1990 and April 2000, the Las Vegas metropolitan area population increased by 83%, growing
from 852,737 to 1,563,282.

The area was discovered by Spanish explorers in
1829. The site of Las Vegas ("The Meadows" in
Spanish) was originally a watering place for travelers on their way to southern California. It was
first settled by Mormons in 1855, who were
attracted by its artesian springs. They abandoned
their settlement two years later in 1857, and the
U.S. Army established Fort Baker there in 1864. In
1867, Las Vegas was detached from the Arizona
Territory and joined with Nevada.

The town was established and started to grow
with the arrival of the railroad in 1905. However, its
growth did not really take off until shortly after
1931, when the Nevada legislature legalized gambling in an effort to lift the state from the Great
Depression. The construction of nearby Hoover
Dam economically aided the area as well.

The Las Vegas that we know today basically
began after World War II, when the idea of large
hotels along the brand new "strip" was developed.
Las Vegas is the "marriage capital" of America;
there are 50 wedding chapels in the city. Tourism
and the convention industry are the city's major
sources of income. In addition, manufacturing, government, warehousing, and trucking are major
sources of employment. Many high-technology
companies are also located in Las Vegas, in close
proximity to sophisticated military technology centers like Nellis Air Force Base, the top-secret
Nuclear Testing Grounds, and the College of Engineering at the University of Nevada, Las Vegas.

Las Vegas has a favorable business climate: taxes
are relatively low, and there are neither city nor state
income taxes. This is because gambling and sales
taxes, paid by tourists, have allowed the city and
state governments to avoid personal and corporate
income taxes.

Popular nearby tourist attractions are Hoover
Dam and Lake Mead (the largest man-made lake in
the U.S.), Lake Mojave, the Mt. Charleston Recreation Area, Red Rock Canyon, and the Death Valley
National Monument.

Famous natives: Andre Agassi, tennis player; Clara Bow, actress; Jack Kramer, tennis player; Phyllis McGuire, singer; Benjamin Siegel, hotel-casino promoter; Orson Welles, actor and producer; Joe Williams, jazz singer.

Long Beach, Calif.

Mayor: Beverly O'Neill (to April 2002)
City Manager: Henry Taboada
2000 census population (rank): 461,522 (34);
　% change: 7.5; **Male:** 226,718 (49.1%); **Female:** 234,804 (50.9%); 1996 est. population breakdown:
White: 208,410 (45.2%); **Black:** 68,618 (14.9%);
American Indian and Alaska Native: 3,881 (0.8%);
Asian: 55,591 (12.0%); **Other race:** 95,107 (20.6%);
Two or more races: 24,310 (5.3%); **Hispanic/Latino:** 165,092 (35.8%). **2000 percent population 18 and over:** 70.8%; **65 and over:** 9.1%; **median age:** 30.8.
Land area: 49.8 sq mi. (129 sq km); **Alt.:** Highest, 170 ft.; lowest, sea level
Avg. daily temp.: Jan., 55.2° F; July, 72.8° F
Churches: 236; **City-owned parks:** 58 (plus 5 golf courses); **Radio stations:** AM, 2; FM, 2; **Television stations:** 8 (metro area)
Civilian Labor Force (PMSA) 2001: 4,818,100[1];
　Unemployed: 234,300, **Percent:** 4.9; **Per capita personal income (PMSA) 1999:** $28,276[1]
Chamber of Commerce: Long Beach Area Chamber of Commerce, One World Trade Center, Suite 350, Long Beach, Calif. 90831-0350

1. Los Angeles–Long Beach, Calif.

Long Beach is the fifth-largest city in California and is situated on San Pedro Bay, south of Los Angeles, in Los Angeles County.

The town was laid out and settled in 1881 by developer W. E. Willmore, who sold lots in the site as a seaside resort community called Willmore City. It was renamed Long Beach for its 8½-mile beach in 1884. The city was incorporated in 1888 and reincorporated in 1897.

Long Beach is a major industrial port, ranked second-busiest in the U.S. and eighth-busiest in the world. The services and manufacturing industries together account for over 50% of the local economy. Retail trade and government are the next largest sectors, accounting for an additional 30% of employment. Minor industries include transportation, communication and utilities, wholesale trade, finance, insurance, and real estate.

Tourism is also important to the economy. Major attractions are the RMS *Queen Mary*, the Aquarium of the Pacific, whale watching tours, and water sports.

Famous natives: Jack Anderson, journalist; Jennifer Bartlett, artist; Barbara Britton, actress; Nicholas Cage, actor; Spike Jones, orchestra leader; Sally Kellerman, actress; Billie Jean King, tennis player; Martha Rae Watson, track star; Heather Watts, dancer.

Los Angeles, Calif.

Mayor: James K. Hahn (to June 2005)
2000 census population (rank): 3,694,820 (2);
　% change: 6.0; **Male:** 1,841,805 (49.8%); **Female:** 1,853,015 (50.2%); **White:** 1,734,036 (46.9%); **Black:** 415,195 (11.2%); **American Indian and Alaska Native:** 29,412 (0.8%); **Asian:** 369,254 (10.0%);
Other race: 949,720 (25.7%); **Two or more races:** 191,288 (5.2%); **Hispanic/Latino:** 1,719,073 (46.5%).
2000 percent population 18 and over: 73.4%; **65 and over:** 9.7%; **median age:** 31.6.
Land area: 467.4 sq mi. (1,210.57 sq km); **Alt.:** Highest, 5,081 ft.; lowest, sea level

Avg. daily temp.: Jan., 57.2° F; July, 74.1° F
Churches: 2,000 of all denominations; **City-owned parks:** 355 (15,357 ac.); **Radio stations:** AM, 35; FM, 53; **Television stations:** 19
Civilian Labor Force (PMSA) 2001: 4,818,100[1];
　Unemployed: 234,300, **Percent:** 4.9; **Per capita personal income (PMSA) 1999:** $28,276[1]
Chamber of Commerce: Los Angeles Chamber of Commerce, 404 S. Bixel St., Los Angeles, Calif. 90017

1. Los Angeles–Long Beach, Calif.

Los Angeles is the largest city in California and the second-largest urban area in the nation. It is located in the southern part of the state on the Pacific Ocean. It is the seat of Los Angeles County. Geographically, it extends more than 40 mi from the mountains to the sea.

The Spanish explorer Gaspar de Portolá visited the site in 1769. On Sept. 4, 1781, the Mexican provincial governor, Filipe de Neve, founded "El Pueblo de Nuestra Señora la Reina de Los Angeles," meaning "The Village of Our Lady, the Queen of the Angels." The pueblo became the capital of the Mexican province, Alta California, and it was the last place to surrender to the United States at the time of the American occupation in 1847. By the Treaty of Guadalupe Hidalgo in 1848, Mexico ceded California to the United States, and Los Angeles was incorporated as a city in 1850.

The city's phenomenal growth was brought about by its equable climate, which attracted people and industry from all parts of the nation; the development of its citrus-fruit industry; the discovery of oil in the area during the early 1890s; the development of its man-made harbor—its port is one of the busiest in the United States; and the growth of the motion picture industry in the early 20th century. Today, Hollywood is a suburb of Los Angeles.

Los Angeles is a major hub of shipping, manufacturing, industry, and finance, and is world-renowned in the entertainment and communications fields. It is a favorite vacation destination and attracts millions of tourists to the area each year from all over the world. Points of interest include the J. Paul Getty Museum, the Los Angeles County Museum of Art, the La Brea Tar Pits (famous for Ice Age fossils), Disneyland (Anaheim), and the Santa Anita and Hollywood racetracks.

Los Angeles County is the nation's largest manufacturing center, and the ports of Los Angeles and Long Beach are second only to New York as the largest customs district in the United States. Major employers in the Los Angeles Five-County area are in the business and management sector. Growth in the key wholesale industries—apparel and textiles, furniture, jewelry, and toys—and the boom in industrial trade were the trend for the region in the 1990s. Other important sectors are health services and international trade and investment. After some lean years, the aerospace industry is making a modest comeback as a result of increased federal defense spending.

Famous natives: Busby Berkeley, choreographer and director; Marge Champion, dancer and choreographer; Jackie Coogan, actor; Jackie Cooper, actor; Linda Fratianne, figure skater; Jodie Foster, actress and director; John Gavin, actor and diplomat; Pancho Gonzalez, tennis player; Cynthia Gregory, ballerina; Jerome Hines, basso; Dustin Hoffman, actor; Theodore Harold Maiman, laser inventor; Marilyn Monroe, actress; Isamu Noguchi, sculptor; Leonard Slotkin, conductor; Duke Snider, baseball player; Adlai E. Stevenson, statesman; Madeleine Stowe, actress; Darryl Strawberry, baseball player.

Memphis, Tenn.

Mayor: W. W. Herenton (to Dec. 2003)
2000 census population (rank): 650,100 (18);
% change: 6.5; **Male:** 307,643 (47.3%); **Female:**
342,457 (52.7%); **White:** 223,728 (34.4%); **Black:**
399,208 (61.4%); **American Indian and Alaska
Native:** 1,217 (0.2%); **Asian:** 9,482 (1.5%); **Other
race:** 9,438 (1.5%); **Two or more races:** 6,788
(1.0%); **Hispanic/Latino:** 19,317 (3.0%). **2000 percent population 18 and over:** 72.1%; **65 and over:**
10.9%; **median age:** 31.9.
Land area: 277 sq mi. (702 sq km); **Alt.:** Highest, 417 ft.
Avg. daily temp.: Jan., 39.6° F; July, 82.1° F
Churches: 2000+; **Parks and playgrounds:** 230
(13,291 ac.); **Radio stations:** AM, 14; FM, 15;
Television stations: 6
Civilian Labor Force (MSA) 2001: 570,600[1];
Unemployed: 19,000, **Percent:** 3.3; **Per capita per-
sonal income (MSA) 1999:** $28,828[1]
Chamber of Commerce: Memphis Area Chamber of
Commerce, P.O. Box 224, Memphis, Tenn. 38103

1. Memphis, Tenn.–Ark.–Miss.

Memphis, the largest city in Tennessee and the
seat of Shelby County, is located in the southwest
corner of the state, on the Mississippi River near the
borders of Arkansas and Mississippi.

The first settlers of Memphis were the Chickasaw
Indians, who had a village named Chisca there on
the bluffs overlooking the Mississippi River. Hernando de Soto, in 1541, is said to have had his first
glimpse of the Mississippi from the site of Memphis; in the next century, Louis Joliet and Jacques
Marquette stopped there to trade with the Indians.
The French explorer Robert Cavelier, Sieur de La
Salle, tried to claim the region for France in 1682
and built Fort Prudhomme on the site.

The area was ceded to the United States by the
Chickasaw Indians in 1818. Memphis was officially
established in 1819 by three enterprising businessmen from Nashville, James Winchester, John Overton, and future president Andrew Jackson. Jackson
named it after the ancient Egyptian city because of
its site on the Nile-like Mississippi River. Memphis
was incorporated as a city in 1826 and became an
important Mississippi River port.

During the Civil War, Memphis was a Confederate military center. In 1862, Federal forces won a
gunboat battle on the river at Memphis, and General
Sherman was able to take the city.

Memphis's population was devastated by several
yellow-fever epidemics during the 1870s. As a
result, the city fell into decline and went bankrupt,
losing its charter in 1879. However, owing to its
superior location, the city was destined to recover
economically, and a new city charter was granted in
1893.

Memphis is one of the country's largest inland
ports and is known as "America's Distribution Center," serving the northeast, southeast, and southwest
regions of the country. Memphis is a leader in agribusiness, and the city is the world's largest trading
center for spot cotton, handling over 40% of the
nation's crops annually. It is the largest hardwood
lumber trading and processing center in the world
and is estimated to be the nation's third-largest total
food processor.

Health care and related activities such as medical
education and biomedical research are Memphis's
largest industries, bringing over $2.5 billion a year

to the local economy. Also important are high-
technology communications.

Famous natives: Kathy Bates, actress; Dixie Carter,
actress; Rosalind Cash, singer; Aretha Franklin, singer;
Morgan Freeman, actor; Al Green, singer; George
Hamilton, actor; Anfernee "Penny" Hardaway, basketball
player; Isaac Hayes, singer; Hal Holbrook, actor; Benjamin
Hooks, organization official; Hal Needham, director;
Charlie Rich, singer; Cybill Shepherd, actress; Robert
Siodmak, director; Fred Smith, business executive; Rufus
Thomas, singer; Kemmons Wilson, business executive.

Mesa, Ariz.

Mayor: Keno Hawker (to June 2004)
City Manager: Mike Hutchinson
2000 census population (rank): 396,375 (42);
% change: 37.6; **Male:** 196,378 (49.5%); **Female:**
199,997 (50.5%); **White:** 323,655 (81.7%); **Black:**
9,977 (2.5%); **American Indian and Alaska Native:**
6,572 (1.7%); **Asian:** 5,917 (1.5%); **Other race:**
38,271 (9.7%); **Two or more races:** 11,051 (2.8%);
Hispanic/Latino: 78,281 (19.7%). **2000 percent
population 18 and over:** 72.7%; **65 and over:**
13.3%; **median age:** 32.0
Land area: 124.62 sq mi. (319 sq km); **Alt.:** 1,241 ft.
Avg. daily temp.: Jan., 52.9° F; July, 84.9° F
City-owned parks: 52; **Radio stations:** AM, 20;
FM, 17; **Television stations:** 7
Civilian Labor Force (MSA) 2001: 1,625,900[1];
Unemployed: 53,700, **Percent:** 3.3; **Per capita per-
sonal income (MSA) 1999:** $27,617[1]
Chamber of Commerce: 120 N. Center St., P.O. Box
5820, Mesa, Ariz. 85211–5820

1. Phoenix–Mesa, Ariz.

Mesa is the third-largest city in Arizona and is
located in the south-central portion of the state in
Maricopa County. Sitting atop a plateau overlooking
the Valley of the Sun, the city gets its name from the
Spanish word for "tabletop."

Prior to the arrival of Europeans, the area had
been inhabited for centuries by native peoples,
including the Hohokam and later the Pima. The
Hohokam culture developed an extensive system of
irrigation canals, some of which are still used today.

Controlled by Spain and then by Mexico, the area
was ceded to the U.S. following the Mexican War
(1846–1848). Mormon settlers arrived on the site in
1878 and used the old irrigation canals for farming
in the Salt River valley. Mesa was incorporated as a
town in 1883 and as a city in 1930.

Falcon Field Airport and Williams Air Force Base
were built in 1941 to train fighter pilots during
World War II. After the war, the city grew rapidly,
as many military families decided to settle in Mesa
permanently, and tourism also became a major
force. Williams AFB closed in the early 1990s, but
Falcon Field has become one of the ten largest U.S.
airports in terms of based aircraft and supports more
than 30 aviation-related businesses.

Currently Mesa is one of the fastest-growing cities in the United States, due to its excellent climate
and strong local economy, which boasts some of the
country's top manufacturers. Electronics, automotive testing, propulsion equipment, aerospace, and
heavy machinery firms are among the most significant in the region.

With 313 days of sunshine a year, Mesa has been
an ideal choice for several major-league baseball
spring training camps.

Famous natives: Danielle Fishel, actress; Liz Reney,
actress; John J. Rhodes, politician; Keri Russell, actress.

Miami, Fla.

Mayor: Joe Carollo (to Nov. 2001)
City Manager: Carlos Gimenez (apptd. May 2000)
2000 census population (rank): 362,470 (47);
% change: 1.1; **Male:** 180,194 (49.7%); **Female:**
182,276 (50.3%); **White:** 241,470 (66.6%); **Black:**
80,858 (22.3%); **American Indian and Alaska
Native:**, 810 (0.2%); **Asian:** 2,376 (0.7%); **Other
race:** 19,644 (5.4%); **Two or more races:** 17,182
(4.7%); **Hispanic/Latino:** 238,351 (65.8%). **2000 percent population 18 and over:** 78.3%; **65 and over:**
17.0%; **median age:** 37.7.
Land area: 34.3 sq mi. (89 sq km); **Water area:** 19.5 sq
mi.; **Alt.:** Average, 12 ft.
Avg. daily temp.: Jan., 67.1° F; July, 82.4° F
Churches[1]: Protestant, 850; Roman Catholic, 61; Jewish, 64; **City-owned parks:** 109; **Radio stations[1]:**
29; **Television stations[1]:** 9 TV, 1 Cable
Civilian Labor Force (PMSA) 2001: 1,083,100;
Unemployed: 62,300, **Percent:** 5.8; **Per capita per-
sonal income (PMSA) 1999:** $24,733
Chamber of Commerce: Greater Miami Chamber of
Commerce, 1601 Biscayne Blvd., Miami, Fla. 33132

1. Dade County.

Miami, the second-largest city in Florida and seat
of Dade County, is located in the southeast part of
the state, on Biscayne Bay.

The area was once the home of the Tequesta Indians until they were nearly wiped out by European
diseases and warfare brought on by two centuries of
Spanish control of Florida. Miami was founded in
1870 near the site of Ft. Dallas, built in 1835 during
the Seminole Indian wars. The city's name is probably derived from "Mayaimi," an Indian word for
"big water."

Miami is the only U.S. city to have been planned
by a woman. Julia Tuttle, a Clevelander, arrived
there in 1891 and bought several hundred acres on
the bank of the Miami River. She convinced New
York financier Henry M. Flagler of the area's vast
potential and persuaded him to extend his Florida
East Coast Railroad to Miami in 1896, the year the
city was incorporated. Flagler dredged Miami Harbor, built the renowned Royal Palm Hotel, which
opened Jan. 1, 1897, and promoted the area as a
winter playground. Tourists flocked there, and by
1910 the city was a thriving recreational area.
Miami survived the collapse of a land speculation
boom in the 1920s and severe hurricanes in 1926
and 1935, and it continued to grow in the aftermath
of these disasters.

Miami experienced a monumental population
boost during the 1960s, when about 260,000 Cuban
refugees arrived on its shore. They made a great
impact on Miami, which is now a bilingual
metropolis.

Miami is an international banking and finance
center, and the city has the greatest concentration of
international and Edge Act banks (banks making
only foreign loans and deposits) in North America;
these constitute a major employment base. Greater
Miami has a highly diversified economy with over
170 multinational Miami-based companies, a bevy
of Fortune 500 companies, and rapidly growing
manufacturing and distribution industries. Miami
ranks number one in Florida for total manufacturing
income, employment, and number of manufacturing
establishments. Greater Miami is the nation's leader
in biomedical technology, and the health care sector

is a major industry. It is also part of an area known
as the Computer Coast of Florida, and its growing
technologies include computers, electrical engineering, and plastics manufacturing.

Miami is one of the world's leading year-round
resort centers with tourism contributing over 60% of
the area's economy. The city is a major transportation hub, and the port of Miami is the world's largest cruise port and a major seaport for cargo. The
famous island resort of Miami Beach, incorporated
in 1915, is part of Greater Miami and is connected
to Miami by four causeways.

Famous natives: Fernando Bujones, dancer; Steve
Carlton, baseball player; Debbie Harry, singer; Dick
Howser, baseball player and manager; Sidney Poitier,
actor; Janet Reno, former attorney general of the U.S.;
Ben Vereen, actor; Ellen Zwilich, composer.

Milwaukee, Wis.

Mayor: John O. Norquist (to April 2004)
2000 census population (rank): 596,974 (19);
% change: –5.0; **Male:** 285,363 (47.8%); **Female:**
311,611 (52.2%); **White:** 298,379 (50.0%); **Black:**
222,933 (37.3%); **American Indian and Alaska
Native:** 5,212 (0.9%); **Asian:** 17,571 (2.9%); **Other
race:** 36,428 (6.1%); **Two or more races:** 16,150
(2.7%); **Hispanic/Latino:** 71,646 (12.0%). **2000 percent population 18 and over:** 71.4%; **65 and over:**
10.9%; **median age:** 30.6.
Land area: 95.8 sq mi. (248 sq km); **Alt.:** 580.60 ft.
Avg. daily temp.: Jan., 26.9° F; July, 72.4° F
Churches: 411; **County-owned parks:** 14,785 ac.;
Radio stations: AM, 6; FM, 13; **Television
stations:** 11
Civilian Labor Force (PMSA) 2001: 817,900[1];
Unemployed: 34,600; **Percent:** 4.2; **Per capita per-
sonal income (PMSA) 1999:** $31,805[1]
Chamber of Commerce: Metropolitan Milwaukee Asso-
ciation of Commerce, 756 N. Milwaukee St., Milwau-
kee, Wis. 53202; Milwaukee Minority Chamber of
Commerce, 509 W. Wisconsin Ave. #606, Milwaukee,
Wis. 53203; Hispanic Chamber of Commerce, 816
W. National Ave., Milwaukee, Wis. 53204

1. Milwaukee–Waukesha, Wis.

Milwaukee, the largest city in Wisconsin and seat
of Milwaukee County, is located in the southeast
part of the state on Lake Michigan.

French missionaries visited the site of Milwaukee
in the 17th century, but it was not until 1795 that
Jacques Vieau established a fur-trading post there.
The first permanent white settler, Vieau's son-in-
law, Solomon Juneau, an agent of the American Fur
Company, made his home there in 1818. The settlement merged with several neighboring villages in
1838 to form Milwaukee, and the city was incorporated in 1846. A large wave of German immigrants
arrived after 1848 and contributed greatly to the
city's political, economic, and cultural development.

The origins of the word "Milwaukee" are disputed; it may come from the Potawatomi "Mahn-ah-
wauk," meaning council grounds of the Potawatomi;
"Mah-an-wauk-seepe," meaning gathering place of
rivers; or the Algonquian "Milo-aki," meaning beautiful land.

Milwaukee is one of the great industrial centers in
the country and one of the largest Great Lakes ports.
Currently, port commerce runs almost 3 million tons
per year. Manufacturing remains strong, and Milwaukee manufacturers are national leaders in litho-
graphic commercial printing and the production of

medical diagnostic instruments, small gasoline engines, malt beverages, iron and steel forgings, mining and construction machinery, robotics, speed changers and drives, and electronic controls. Milwaukee's high-tech manufacturing community is the ninth-largest among the nation's 31 major metropolitan areas.

Though Milwaukee was once known as a "beer town," less than 1% of its workforce is now involved in beer production. However, beer still plays an important role, and almost 11% of the nation's malt beverage is produced there.

Famous natives: Donald Gramm, bass-baritone; Woody Herman, band leader; Al Jarreau, singer; Kristen Johnston, actress; George F. Kennan, diplomat; Alfred Lunt, actor; Douglas MacArthur, army general; Pat O'Brien, actor; Tom Snyder, TV personality; Speech, member of the rap group "Arrested Development;" Spencer Tracy, actor; Gene Wilder, actor; Jerry and David Zucker, film producers.

Minneapolis, Minn.

Mayor: Sharon Sayles Belton (to Jan. 2002)
2000 census population (rank): 382,618 (45);
 % change: 3.9; **Male:** 192,232 (50.2%); **Female:** 190,386 (49.8%); **White:** 249,186 (65.1%); **Black:** 68,818 (18.0%); **American Indian and Alaska Native:** 8,378 (2.2%); **Asian:** 23,455 (6.1%); **Other race:** 15,798 (4.1%); **Two or more races:** 16,694 (4.4%); **Hispanic/Latino:** 29,175 (7.6%). **2000 percent population 18 and over:** 78.0%; **65 and over:** 9.1%; **median age:** 31.2
Land area: 58.7 sq mi. (143 sq km); **Alt.:** Highest, 945 ft.; lowest, 695 ft.
Avg. daily temp.: Jan., 11.2° F; July, 73.1° F
Churches: 419; **City-owned parks:** 153; **Radio stations**[1]: AM, 17; FM, 15; **Television stations**[1]: 6
Civilian Labor Force (MSA) 2001: 1,765,600[2];
 Unemployed: 52,100, **Percent:** 3.0; **Per capita personal income (MSA) 1999:** $35,250[2]
Chamber of Commerce: Greater Minneapolis Chamber of Commerce, Young Quinlan Building, 81 S. Ninth Street, Suite 200, Minneapolis, Minn. 55402-3223

1. Metropolitan area. 2. Minneapolis–St. Paul, Minn.–Wis.

Minneapolis, the largest city in Minnesota and the seat of Hennepin County, is located in the southeast central part of the state on the Mississippi River. It is adjacent to its "twin city" of St. Paul. The Minneapolis–St. Paul Metropolitan Statistical Area is the 15th-largest in the United States.

In 1680, Father Louis Hennepin visited the future site of Minneapolis and gave the Falls of St. Anthony their name. Lt. Zebulon Pike made a treaty with the Sioux Indians in 1805–1806, by which they ceded to the whites much land, including the Falls of St. Anthony and the site of Minneapolis. Fort Snelling was built in 1819–1820, and in 1823 the government built a lumber and flour mill. Flour milling became the major industry of early Minneapolis and made the city the milling capital of the world. The town of St. Anthony was established on the east bank of the Mississippi in 1848, and the town of Minneapolis grew up on the opposite bank of the river. The name Minneapolis is a combination of the Dakota Sioux word "minna," for water, and the Greek word "polis," for city. Minneapolis was incorporated as a city in 1867, and in 1872 the city of St. Anthony (chartered in 1860) was annexed to it. After the spread of the railroads in the 1870s, Minneapolis became the gateway to the Northern Great Plains.

Minneapolis is a center of industry and commerce serving a large agricultural region. During the 20th

century, manufacturing, food processing, milling, computers, health services, and graphic arts developed as Minneapolis's major industries. Fifteen Fortune 500 companies are headquartered in the Minneapolis–St. Paul metropolitan area. The city is the home of the world's largest cash grain market and is the headquarters of the Ninth Federal Reserve Bank.

Famous natives: La Verne, Maxene, and Patti Andrews, singers; James Arness, actor; Lew Ayres, actor; Patty Berg, golfer; Virginia Bruce, actress; J. Paul Getty, oil executive; Peter Graves, actor; George Roy Hill, director; Cornell MacNeil, baritone; Ralph Meeker, actor; Westbrook Pegler, columnist; Prince, singer; Harrison Salisbury, journalist; Charles Schulz, cartoonist; Anne Tyler, writer; Bud Wilkinson, football coach; David Winfield, baseball player.

Nashville-Davidson, Tenn.

Mayor: Bill Purcell (to Oct. 2003)
2000 census population (rank)[1]: 545,524 (22);
 % change: 11.6; **Male:** 264,095 (48.4%); **Female:** 281,429 (51.6%); **White:** 359,581 (65.9%); **Black:** 146,235 (26.8%); **American Indian and Alaska Native:** 1,639 (0.3%); **Asian:** 12,992 (2.4%); **Other race:** 13,677 (2.5%); **Two or more races:** 11,000 (2.0%); **Hispanic/Latino:** 25,774 (4.7%). **2000 percent population 18 and over:** 77.9%; **65 and over:** 11.0%; **median age:** 33.9.
Land area: 533 sq mi. (1,380 sq km); **Altitude:** Highest, 1,100 ft.; lowest, approx. 400 ft.
Avg. daily temp.: Jan., 36.7° F; July, 76.6° F
Churches: Protestant, 781; Roman Catholic, 18; Jewish, 3; **City-owned parks:** 76 (6,650 ac.); **Radio stations:** AM, 15; FM, 19; **Television stations:** 11
Civilian Labor Force (MSA) 2001: 679,400;
 Unemployed: 18,400, **Percent:** 2.7; **Per capita personal income 1999:** $30,510[1]
Chamber of Commerce: Nashville Area Chamber of Commerce, 211 Commerce Street, Suite 100, Nashville, Tenn. 37201

1. Nashville-Davidson city is consolidated with Davidson County.

Nashville-Davidson is the state capital and second-largest city in Tennessee and is located in the north-central part of the state on the Cumberland River. It is coextensive with Davidson County.

During the winter of 1779–1780, James Robertson and John Donelson founded a settlement at Big Salt Lick by the Cumberland River at the present site of the city. They built forts on both sides of the river, naming one of them Fort Nashborough in honor of Francis Nash, a Revolutionary War general. In 1784, the town was named Nashville, and it was incorporated as a city in 1806.

Nashville became the capital of Tennessee in 1843 and was the seat of Davidson County until 1963, when it merged with the county to become Nashville-Davidson.

The city is a port of entry and an important industrial and commercial center serving the Upper South. Its economy is based on a number of industries, including automobiles, apparel, publishing, insurance, and banking. Health care services are the largest sector, but Nashville is best known for its music industry. It is a major recording center, especially for country music.

Nashville is home to several religious organizations and is a major tourist attraction and convention center. Its many institutions of higher education include Vanderbilt University, Fisk University, and the University of Tennessee.

Famous natives: Roy Acuff, singer; Gregg Allman, singer; Pat Boone, singer; Rita Coolidge, singer; Jeff Gordon, race car driver; Al Gore, former vice president; Red Grooms, artist; Alex Haley, author; Barbara Howar, hostess and writer; Brenda Lee, singer; Minnie Pearl, comedienne; Annie Potts, actress; Paula Robeson, flutist; Wilma Rudolph, athlete; Dinah Shore, actress and singer; Tina Turner, singer; Oprah Winfrey, entertainer.

New Orleans, La.

Mayor: Marc H. Morial (to Feb. 2002)
2000 census population (rank): 484,674 (31);
  % change: −2.5; **Male:** 227,094 (46.9%); **Female:** 257,580 (53.1%); **White:** 135,956 (28.1%); **Black:** 325,947 (67.3%); **American Indian and Alaska Native:** 991 (0.2%); **Asian:** 10,972 (2.3%); **Other race:** 4,498 (0.9%); **Two or more races:** 6,201 (1.3%); **Hispanic/Latino:** 14,826 (3.1%). **2000 percent population 18 and over:** 73.3%; **65 and over:** 11.7%; **median age:** 33.1.
Land area: 199.4 sq mi. (516 sq km); **Alt.:** Highest, 15 ft.; lowest, −4 ft.
Avg. daily temp.: Jan., 52.4° F; July, 77° F
Churches: 712; **City-owned parks:** 165 (299 ac.); **Radio stations:** AM, 12; FM, 14; **Television stations:** 7
Civilian Labor Force (MSA) 2001: 604,900;
  Unemployed: 26,000, **Percent:** 4.3; **Per capita personal income (MSA) 1999:** $25,960
Chamber of Commerce: The Chamber/New Orleans and the River Region, 301 Camp Street, New Orleans, La. 70130

New Orleans, the largest city in Louisiana, is located in the southeast part of the state, between the Mississippi River and Lake Ponchartrain. It is coextensive with Orleans Parish.

One of the few cities of the nation that has been under three flags, New Orleans has belonged to Spain, France, and the United States. The French founded it in 1718 and named it in honor of the Duke of Orleans. In 1762, France ceded the city and the territory to Spain. In 1800, the territory was returned to France, but government authorities did not take over until 1803, only 20 days before the region became part of the United States in the Louisiana Purchase.

New Orleans is famous for its French Quarter, with its mixture of French, Spanish, and native architectural styles. The Mardi Gras—a week of carnival held in New Orleans before the beginning of Lent—is the most spectacular festival in the U.S. and is a popular tourist attraction. Tourism has grown rapidly in recent years, and New Orleans hosts more than seven million visitors annually.

New Orleans has one of the world's greatest international ports, one of the largest in the nation, and it is a major focus of the city's economy. New Orleans is home to the corporate offices of oil companies with major offshore operations in the Gulf of Mexico, as well as the distribution and service centers of offshore equipment suppliers and fabricators.

The manufacturing industry is a significant part of the economy, with petroleum, petrochemical, shipbuilding, and aerospace industries all playing a role. The New Orleans region also functions as a mining, processing, and transportation center for other minerals, principally sulfur. Service industries are playing a larger role, with health care and telecommunications leading the way. The information services sector is one of the fastest-growing, and the New

Orleans region is widely regarded as a leading center of medicine and health care in the South.

Famous natives: Louis Armstrong, musician; Truman Capote, author; Fats Domino, musician; Louis Gottschalk, pianist and composer; Bryant Gumbel, TV personality; Lillian Hellman, playwright and author; Al Hirt, musician; Mahalia Jackson, singer; Dorothy Lamour, actress; Wynton Marsalis, musician; Huey Newton, activist; Marguerite Piazza, soprano; Rusty Staub, baseball player; Ben Turpin, comedian; Shirley Verrett, mezzo-soprano; Carl Weathers, actor; Del Williams, football player.

New York, N.Y.

Mayor: Rudolph W. Giuliani (to Dec. 2001)
Borough Presidents: Bronx, Fernando Ferrer; Brooklyn, Howard Golden; Manhattan, C. Virginia Fields; Queens, Claire Shulman; Staten Island, Guy V. Molinari
2000 census population (rank): 8,008,278 (1);
  % change: 9.4; **Male:** 3,794,204 (47.4%); **Female:** 4,214,074 (52.6%); **White:** 3,576,385 (44.7%); **Black:** 2,129,762 (26.6%); **American Indian and Alaska Native:** 41,289 (0.5%); **Asian:** 787,047 (9.8%); **Other race:** 1,074,406 (13.4%); **Two or more races:** 393,959 (4.9%); **Hispanic/Latino:** 2,160,554 (27.0%). **2000 percent population 18 and over:** 75.8%; **65 and over:** 11.7%; **median age:** 34.2.
Land area: 321.8 sq mi. (826.68 sq km) (Queens, 112.1; Brooklyn, 81.8; Staten Island, 60.2; Bronx, 44.0; Manhattan, 23.7); **Alt.:** Highest, 426 ft.; lowest, sea level
Avg. daily temp.: Jan., 31.8° F; July, 76.7° F
Churches: Protestant, 1,766; Jewish, 1,256; Roman Catholic, 437; Orthodox, 66; **City-owned parks:** 1,701 (28,312 ac.); **Radio stations:** AM, 19; FM, 18; **Television stations:** 6 commercial, 1 public
Civilian Labor Force (PMSA) 2001: 4,137,900;
  Unemployed: 188,000, **Percent:** 4.5; **Per capita personal income (PMSA) 1999:** $38,814
Chamber of Commerce: New York Chamber of Commerce and Industry, One Battery Park Plaza, New York, N.Y. 10004

New York City is the largest city in the United States. It is located in the southern part of New York State, at the mouth of the Hudson River (also known as North River as it passes Manhattan Island).

In 1609, Henry Hudson, who worked for the Dutch East India Company, sailed up the river that now bears his name and went as far as Albany. Five years later, a permanent settlement was established at what is now New York, but it was originally called New Amsterdam by the Dutch governors. One of them, Peter Minuit, was said to have bought Manhattan Island from the Indians for $24 worth of beads, buttons, and trinkets. In 1664, Great Britain's Duke of York sent a fleet that quietly seized the settlement from the Dutch without bloodshed and rechristened the colony in honor of the duke.

Control of New York passed to the young U.S. at the end of the Revolutionary War, and George Washington was inaugurated president in New York's old City Hall. Congress met in New York from 1785 to 1790.

In 1898, when Greater New York was chartered, the city expanded to include the following five boroughs, which are also counties in New York State: Manhattan (New York County); Brooklyn (Kings County); Bronx (Bronx County); Queens (Queens County); and Staten Island (Richmond County). There are recurrent efforts among Staten Island residents to separate from Greater New York and become the independent city of Staten Island.

"The Big Apple" is a major world capital and a world leader in finance, the arts, and communications. The port of New York is one of the finest in the world. The city is the home of the United Nations and is headquarters for some of the world's largest corporations. The city is also the center of advertising, fashion, publishing, and radio broadcasting in the United States.

The city suffered incredible devastation in Sept. 2001, when terrorist hijackers crashed two commercial jets into the World Trade Center in lower Manhattan, causing the complete destruction of the twin towers and major loss of life.

Famous natives: Kareem Abdul-Jabbar, basketball player; Woody Allen, actor and director; Lauren Bacall, actress; James Baldwin, novelist; Harry Belafonte, singer and actor; Humphrey Bogart, actor; James Cagney, actor; Maria Callas, soprano; Aaron Copland, composer; Sammy Davis, Jr., singer and actor; Agnes de Mille, choreographer; Robert De Niro, actor; Eamon De Valera, former president of Ireland; Gertrude Elion, Nobel Prize winner in medicine; Lou Gehrig, baseball player; George Gershwin, composer; Ira Gershwin, lyricist; Jackie Gleason, actor; Rita Hayworth, actress; Lena Horne, singer; Julia Ward Howe, poet and reformer; Washington Irving, author; Henry James, novelist; Michael Jordan, basketball player; Sandy Koufax, baseball player; Roy Lichtenstein, painter; Vince Lombardi, football player and coach; Chico, Groucho, Harpo, and Zeppo Marx, comedians; Herman Melville, novelist; Yehudi Menuhin, violinist; James Michener, novelist; Arthur Miller, playwright; Eugene O'Neill, playwright; J. Robert Oppenheimer, nuclear physicist; Al Pacino, actor; Jerome Robbins, choreographer; Eleanor Roosevelt, reformer and humanitarian; Theodore Roosevelt, former president; Jonas Salk, polio researcher; Beverly Sills, soprano; Neil Simon, playwright; Barbra Streisand, singer and actress; Ed Sullivan, TV personality; Mae West, actress; Edith Wharton, novelist.

Oakland, Calif.

Mayor: Jerry Brown (to 2003)
City Manager: Robert C. Bobb
2000 census popultion (rank): 399,484 (41);
  % change: 7.3; **Male:** 192,757 (48.3%); **Female:** 206,727 (51.7%); **White:** 125,013 (31.3%); **Black:** 142,460 (35.7%); **American Indian and Alaska Native:** 2,655 (0.7%); **Asian:** 60,851 (15.2%); **Other race:** 46,592 (11.7%); **Two or more races:** 19,911 (5.0%); **Hispanic/Latino:** 87,467 (21.9%). **2000 percent population 18 and over:** 75.0%; **65 and over:** 10.5%; **median age:** 33.3.
Land area: 53.9 sq mi. (140 sq km); **Alt.:** Highest, 1,700 ft.; lowest, sea level
Avg. daily temp.: Jan., 49.0° F; July, 63.7° F
Churches: 374, representing over 78 denominations in the city; over 500 churches in Alameda County; **City-owned parks:** 2,196 ac.; **Radio stations:** AM, 1; **Television stations:** 1 commercial, 1 government access, 2 education access, 1 local
Civilian Labor Force (PMSA) 2001: 1,266,200;
  Unemployed: 42,000, **Percent:** 3.3; **Per capita personal income (PMSA) 1999:** $35,666
Chamber of Commerce: Oakland Chamber of Commerce, 475 Fourteenth St., Oakland, Calif. 94612

Oakland is located in the west-central part of California on the east side of San Francisco Bay. It is the seat of Alameda County.

Don Luis Peralta first settled the site of Oakland in 1820 when he established the Rancho San Antonio. The gold rush of 1849 attracted more people to the area and the city's population continued to grow after a ferry service to San Francisco was started in 1851. Oakland was incorporated as a town in 1852 and as a city in 1854. It was named after the numer-

ous oak trees found in the area. Oakland became the western terminus of the Central Pacific Railroad in 1869 and the seat of Alameda County in 1873.

In the latter part of the 19th century and also in 1910, additional territory was annexed to Oakland and the city assumed its present size. In 1906, thousands of people fled to Oakland in the aftermath of the San Francisco earthquake and settled there permanently, furthering the city's growth. Oakland's economic development continued to rise with the opening of the San Francisco–Oakland Bay Bridge in 1936.

Oakland is a major center of culture and commerce. It is an important container shipping port and the terminus of three transcontinental railroads. Oakland's industries include food processing, chemicals, pharmaceuticals, and electrical and high technology manufacturing. Oakland is also a leading importer of foreign cars. The city is the headquarters of many national and international corporations.

Famous natives: Buster Crabbe, actor; Frederick Cottrell, inventor; Dennis Eckersley, athlete; Hammer, singer, dancer, and songwriter; Rod McKuen, singer and composer; Russ Meyer, producer and director; Eddie (Anderson) Rochester, actor; George Stevens, director; Amy Tan, writer; Jo Van Fleet, actress.

Oklahoma City, Okla.

Mayor: Kirk Humphreys (to April 2002)
City Manager: Glen E. Deck
2000 census population (rank): 506,132 (29);
  % change: 13.8; **Male:** 247,313 (48.9%); **Female:** 258,819 (51.1%); **White:** 346,226 (68.4%); **Black:** 77,810 (15.4%); **American Indian and Alaska Native:** 17,743 (3.5%); **Asian:** 17,595 (3.5%); **Other race:** 26,705 (5.3%); **Two or more races:** 19,693 (3.9%); **Hispanic/Latino:** 51,368 (10.1%). **2000 percent population 18 and over:** 74.5%; **65 and over:** 11.5%; **median age:** 34.0.
Land area: 608.2 sq mi. (1,575 sq km); **Alt.:** Highest, 1,320 ft.; lowest, 1,140 ft.
Avg. daily temp.: Jan., 35.9° F; July, 82.1° F
Churches: Roman Catholic, 25; Jewish, 4; Protestant and others, 741; **City-owned parks:** 144 (5,225 ac.); **Radio stations:** AM, 10; FM, 14; **Television stations:** 8
Civilian Labor Force (MSA) 2001: 548,700;
  Unemployed: 14,400; **Percent:** 2.6; **Per capita personal income (MSA) 1999:** $24,437
Chamber of Commerce: Greater Oklahoma City Chamber of Commerce, 123 Park Ave., Oklahoma City, Okla. 73102

Oklahoma City, the state capital and seat of Oklahoma County, is the largest city in Oklahoma. It is located in the central part of the state on the North Canadian River.

Oklahoma City sprang into being almost overnight. On April 22, 1889, the U.S. government threw open the territory for settlement, and there was a rush across the line to stake claims. A sprawling tent city sprang up near the Santa Fe railroad tracks, and within a short time Oklahoma City was a bustling town of 10,000. The city was incorporated in 1890 and replaced Guthrie as the state capital in 1910. Oil was discovered in the city in 1928, and petroleum production became a mainstay of the city's economy.

Oklahoma City is the wholesale and distributing center for the state, and the city's stockyards are the largest stocker and feeder cattle market in the world. Following the decline of the energy sector, Oklahoma City is fostering a private entrepreneurial environment and a more diversified economy. Within the service sector, health services are projected to grow, followed by retail trade and business services. Nearby Tinker Air Force Base, one of the world's largest air depots, is a major city employer.

In 1995 the city was the scene of the worst terrorist attack on U.S. soil up till that time, when a bomb destroyed a federal office building, killing 168 people.

Famous natives: Johnny Bench, baseball; Lon Chaney, Jr., actor; Ralph Ellison, writer; Kay Francis, actress; Dale Robertson, actor; Ted Shackleford, actor; Pamela Tiffin, actress; Vince Gill, country singer.

Omaha, Neb.

Mayor: Michael Fahey (to June 2005)
2000 census population (rank): 390,007 (44);
  % change: 16.1; **Male:** 190,032 (48.7%); **Female:**
  199,975 (51.3%); **White:** 305,745 (78.4%); **Black:**
  51,917 (13.3%); **American Indian and Alaska Native:**
  2,616 (0.7%); **Asian:** 6,773 (1.7%); **Other race:**
  15,250 (3.9%); **Two or more races:** 7,478 (1.9%);
  Hispanic/Latino: 29,397 (7.5%). **2000 percent population 18 and over:** 74.4%; **65 and over:** 11.8%;
  median age: 33.5.
Land area: 118.5 sq mi. (303 sq km); **Alt.:** Highest,
  1,270 ft.
Avg. daily temp.: Jan., 20.2° F; July, 77.7° F
Churches: Protestant, 192; Roman Catholic, 44; Jewish,
  4; **City-owned parks:** 192 (over 8,000 ac.); **Radio**
  stations: AM, 7; FM, 13; **Television stations:** 4
Civilian Labor Force (MSA) 2001: 399,800[1];
  Unemployed: 11,400, **Percent:** 2.9; **Per capita personal income (MSA) 1999:** $30,692[1]
Chamber of Commerce: Omaha Chamber of Commerce, 1301 Harney St., Omaha, Neb. 68102

1. Omaha, Neb.–Iowa.

Omaha, the largest city in Nebraska and the seat of Douglas County, is located in the eastern part of the state on the west bank of the Missouri River, opposite Council Bluffs, Iowa.

The Lewis and Clark expedition visited the area in 1804, and the U.S. Army built Ft. Atkinson nearby in 1819. Pierre Cabanne established a fur-trading post at the site in 1825. The first Mormon migrants wintered there in 1846–1847 on their way to Utah. The city grew rapidly as the most northerly supply point for overland wagons to the Far West.

The city was officially founded in 1854 after the Nebraska Territory was opened for settlement. It was named for the Omaha Indians living nearby, whose tribal name means "those who go upstream or against the current." Omaha was incorporated as a city in 1857 and was the capital of the Nebraska Territory from 1855 to 1867. The city continued to thrive as a point of entry and a major transportation center when the Union Pacific transcontinental railroad arrived in 1869.

Omaha is a major market for grain and livestock, food processing, telecommunications, and insurance. Other important industries include electrical equipment and finance as well as printing and publishing. It continues to be a major railroad hub.

Famous natives: Fred Astaire, dancer and actor; Max Baer, boxer; Ronald Boone, former NBA professional; Robert Boozer, former NBA professional; Marlon Brando, actor; Montgomery Clift, actor; Gerald Ford, former president; Bob Gibson, baseball player; Swoosie Kurtz, actress; Melvin Laird, former secretary of defense; Dorothy McGuire, actress; Nick Nolte, actor; Gale Sayers, football player; Malcolm X, political activist; Paul Williams, singer and composer.

Philadelphia, Pa.

Mayor: John F. Street (to Jan. 2004)
2000 census population (rank): 1,517,550 (5);
  % change: –4.3; **Male:** 705,107 (46.5%); **Female:**
  812,443 (53.5%); **White:** 683,267 (45.0%); **Black:**
  655,824 (43.2%); **American Indian and Alaska**
  Native: 4,073 (0.3%); **Asian:** 67,654 (4.5%); **Other**
  race: 72,429 (4.8%); **Two or more races:** 33,574
  (2.2%); **Hispanic/Latino:** 128,928 (8.5%). **2000 percent population 18 and over:** 74.7%; **65 and over:**
  14.1%; **median age:** 34.2.
Land area: 136 sq mi. (352 sq km); **Alt.:** Highest, 440
  ft.; lowest, sea level
Avg. daily temp.: Jan., 31.2° F; July, 76.5° F
Churches: Roman Catholic, 133; Jewish, 55; Protestant
  and others, 830; **City-owned parks:** 630 (10,252 ac.);
  Radio stations[1]: AM, 40; FM, 43; **Television**
  stations: 14
Civilian Labor Force (PMSA) 2001: 2,529,100[2];
  Unemployed: 108,000, **Percent:** 4.3; **Per capita personal income (PMSA) 1999:** $32,627[2]
Chamber of Commerce: Philadelphia Chamber of Commerce, 1234 Market Street, Suite 1800, Philadelphia,
  Pa. 19107

1. Metropolitan area. 2. Philadelphia, Pa.–N.J.

Philadelphia, the largest city in Pennsylvania, is located in the southeast part of the state at the junction of the Schuylkill and Delaware Rivers. It is coextensive with Philadelphia County.

Philadelphia, the City of Brotherly Love, was settled in 1681 by Capt. William Markham, who, with a small band of colonists, had been sent out by his cousin, William Penn. Penn arrived the following year with the intention of creating a refuge for the Quakers.

In the period before the American Revolution, the city outstripped all others in the colonies in education, arts, science, industry, and commerce. In 1774–1776, the First and Second Continental Congresses met in Philadelphia; and, from 1781–1783, the city was the capital of the United States under the Articles of Confederation. In 1790, it became the nation's capital under the Constitution and remained so until the seat of the federal government moved to Washington in 1800.

Within a half-century of the founding of the nation at Independence Hall, Philadelphia had emerged as a leader in America's Industrial Revolution. The steam locomotives and hat factories of the 19th century have been replaced by diverse manufacturing specialties such as chemicals (including pharmaceuticals), medical devices, transportation equipment, and printing and publishing. In the services sector, Philadelphia leads in subsectors such as health services, insurance carriers, legal services, and architecture and engineering services. Philadelphia is also home to branches of the U.S. Mint, the Federal Reserve System, and the Internal Revenue Service.

The city's harbor, one of the largest freshwater ports in the world, is the centerpiece of the Ameri-Port facility in south Philadelphia, a major shipping center with rail links to the Midwest and Canada.

The city abounds in landmarks of early American history, including Independence Hall, where the Declaration of Independence was signed, and the Liberty Bell. Other significant tourist attractions are the Philadelphia Museum of Art, the Franklin Institute Science Museum, and the Philadelphia Zoological Gardens.

Famous natives: Marian Anderson, contralto; Frankie Avalon, singer and actor; John, Lionel, and Ethel Barrymore, actors; Kevin Bacon, actor; Boyz II Men, R&B group; Mary Cassatt, artist; Wilt Chamberlain, basketball player; Chubby Checker, singer; Bill Cosby, actor; Stuart Davis, painter; Thomas Eakins, painter and sculptor; W. C. Fields, comedian; Benjamin Franklin, inventor and statesman; Grace (Kelly), actress and princess of Monaco; Walt Kelly, cartoonist; Patti LaBelle, singer; Mario Lanza, singer and actor; George McClellan, general; Margaret Mead, anthropologist; Edgar Allen Poe, author; Anna Quindlen, writer and Pulitzer Prize winner; Man Ray, painter; Betsy Ross, flagmaker; Will Smith, actor; Jacqueline Susann, novelist; Robert Venturi, architect.

Phoenix, Ariz.

Mayor: Skip Rimsza (to Oct. 2003)
2000 census population (rank): 1,321,045 (6);
% change: 34.3; **Male:** 671,760 (50.9%); **Female:** 649,285 (49.1%); **White:** 938,853 (71.1%); **Black:** 67,416 (5.1%); **American Indian and Alaska Native:** 26,696 (2.0%); **Asian:** 26,449 (2.0%); **Other race:** 216,589 (16.4%); **Two or more races:** 43,276 (3.3%); **Hispanic/Latino:** 449,972 (34.1%). **2000 percent population 18 and over:** 71.1%; **65 and over:** 8.1%; **median age:** 30.7.
Land area: 476.7 sq mi. (1,216.8 sq km); **Alt.:** Highest, 2,740 ft.; lowest, 1,017 ft.
Avg. daily temp.: Jan., 53.6° F; July, 93.5° F
City-owned parks: 170 (25,235 ac.); **Radio stations:** AM, 20; FM, 20; **Television stations:** 9 commercial; 1 PBS
Civilian Labor Force (MSA) 2001: 1,625,900[1];
Unemployed: 53,700, **Percent:** 3.3; **Per capita personal income (MSA) 1999:** $27,617[1]
Chamber of Commerce: Phoenix Chamber of Commerce, 201 N. Central, Phoenix, Ariz. 85073

1. Phoenix–Mesa, Ariz.

Phoenix, the capital of Arizona and seat of Maricopa County, is the largest city in the state. It is located in the center of Arizona, on the Salt River.

The prehistoric Hohokam Indians first settled the area about 300 B.C. and dug a system of extensive irrigation canals for farming. The Indian culture mysteriously broke up in the 1400s.

The site was permanently resettled by Jack Swilling and "Lord Darrell" Duppa about 1867. Because the city was founded on the ruins of the ancient civilization, it was named Phoenix after the legendary Phoenix bird that could regenerate itself. The irrigation canals were restored for farming, and ranching and prospecting began in the surrounding area. The city quickly grew as an important trading center.

Phoenix was incorporated as a city in 1881 and was made the territorial capital in 1889. It became the state capital when Arizona was admitted to the Union in 1912.

Partly owing to its warm, dry climate, the city developed rapidly in the decades after World War II. Between 1950 and 1990 the population increased from 100,000 to 980,000.

Phoenix is a commercial and manufacturing center in an agricultural region. Major industries include government, agricultural products, aerospace technology, electronics, air-conditioning, leather goods, and Indian arts and crafts. Mining, timbering, and tourism also contribute to the economy.

The city of Phoenix is renowned as a leader in local government management and received the 1993 Bertelsmann Foundation award for the best-managed city in the world.

Famous natives: Lynda Carter, actress; Joan Ganz Cooney, TV executive; Alice Cooper, musician; Arthur A. Fletcher, government official; Barry Goldwater, politician; Stevie Nicks, musician; Charles S. Robb, politician; Mare Winningham, actress.

Portland, Ore.

Mayor: Vera Katz (to Dec. 2004)
2000 census population (rank): 529,121 (28);
% change: 21.0; **Male:** 261,565 (49.4%); **Female:** 267,556 (50.6%); **White:** 412,241 (77.9%); **Black:** 35,115 (6.6%); **American Indian and Alaska Native:** 5,587 (1.1%); **Asian:** 33,470 (6.3%); **Other race:** 18,760 (3.5%); **Two or more races:** 21,955 (4.1%); **Hispanic/Latino:** 36,058 (6.8%). **2000 percent population 18 and over:** 78.9%; **65 and over:** 11.6%; **median age:** 35.2.
Land area: 146.6 sq mi. (379.7 sq km); **Alt.:** Highest, 1073 ft.; lowest, sea level
Avg. daily temp.: Jan., 38.9° F; July, 67.7° F
Churches: Protestant, 450; Roman Catholic, 48; Jewish, 9; Buddhist, 6; other, 190; **City-owned parks:** 200 (over 9,400 ac.); **Radio stations:** AM: 14, FM: 14; **Television stations:** 5 commercial, 1 public
Civilian Labor Force (PMSA) 2001: 1,068,400[1];
Unemployed: 48,900, **Percent:** 4.6; **Per capita personal income (PMSA) 1999:** $30,672[1]
Chamber of Commerce: Portland Chamber of Commerce, 221 NW 2nd Ave., Portland, Ore. 97209

1. Portland–Vancouver, Ore.–Wash.

Portland, the largest city in Oregon and seat of Multnomah County, is located in the northwest part of the state on the Willamette River.

Lewis and Clark camped at the site of Portland in 1805 on their expedition across the continent. Portland was founded in 1845 and was almost called Boston after the city in Massachusetts. Founders Amos Lovejoy from Massachusetts and Francis Pettygrove from Maine flipped a coin to decide the name of the new town. Pettygrove won the toss and named the place Portland after his hometown. Portland was incorporated as a city in 1851.

In the 1850s Portland served as a supply base for the California gold rush, and it grew with the development of its salmon and lumber industries and the arrival of the railroad in 1883. The city continued to grow from 1879 to 1900 as a supply point for the Alaska gold rush and as the site of the Lewis and Clark Centennial Exposition in 1905.

The port of Portland leads the West in grain exports and is among the top five auto-import centers in the United States. The port ranks third in overall volume behind Los Angeles and Long Beach.

Portland has a diverse economy with a broad base of manufacturing, distribution, wholesale and retail trade, regional government, and business services. Major manufacturing industries include machinery, electronics, metals, transportation equipment, and lumber and wood products. Technology is a thriving part of Portland's economy, with over 500 high-tech companies located in the metropolitan area. Tourism is also important to Portland's economy, drawing more than 7 million visitors annually.

Famous natives: James Beard, food expert; Pietro Belluschi, architect; Richard Fosbury, high jumper; Matt Groening, cartoonist; Margaux Hemingway, actress; Phil Knight, founder of Nike; Terrance Knox, actor; Jeff Lorber, jazz musician; Linus Pauling, chemist; Jane Powell, singer and actress; Ahmad Rashad, football player and sportscaster; Susan Ruttan, actress; Doc Severinson, band leader; Norton Simon, business executive; Sally Ann Struthers, actress; Gus Van Sant, film director; Lindsay Wagner, actress; Mitch Williams, baseball pitcher.

Sacramento, Calif.

Mayor: Heather Fargo (to Nov. 2004)
2000 census population (rank): 407,018 (40);
  % change: 10.2; **Male:** 197,784 (48.6%); **Female:**
209,234 (51.4%); **White:** 196,549 (48.3%); **Black:**
62,968 (15.5%); **American Indian and Alaska Native:**
5,300 (1.3%); **Asian:** 67,635 (16.6%); **Other race:**
44,627 (11.0%); **Two or more races:** 26,078 (6.4%);
Hispanic/Latino: 87,974 (21.6%). **2000 percent**
population 18 and over: 72.7%; **65 and over:**
11.4%; **median age:** 32.8.
Land area: 123 sq mi. (318.7 sq km)
Avg. daily temp.: Jan., 53.5° F; July, 88.4° F
City park & recreational facilities: 134+ (1,427+ ac.);
  Television stations: 7
Civilian Labor Force (PMSA) 2001: 1,538,700;
  Unemployed: 67,200, **Percent:** 4.4; **Per capita per-**
sonal income (PMSA) 1999: $28,718
Chamber of Commerce: Sacramento Chamber of Com-
merce, 917 7th St., Sacramento, Calif. 95814; West
Sacramento Chamber of Commerce, 834-C Jefferson
Blvd., Sacramento, Calif. 95691

Sacramento is the capital of California and the seat
of Sacramento County. It is located in the north-
central part of the state at the confluence of the Sacramento and American rivers.

In 1839, German-born Swiss citizen John Augustus Sutter obtained a grant from the Mexican governor to establish a colony for fellow Swiss emigrants
on a large tract of land that he named New Helvetia
(New Switzerland). He established Fort Sutter there
as a trading post.

After gold was discovered on Sutter's property in
1848, the settlement rapidly expanded as the prominent supply point for gold prospectors coming from
the East. Sacramento was laid out in 1848 and named
after California's principal river, which ran beside it.
The river's name in Spanish honors the Holy Sacra-
ment. It became incorporated as a city in 1849 and
was made the state capital in 1854. Sacramento was
the terminus of the first railroad in 1856 and the western terminus of the Pony Express in 1860.

The city has always been a hub of river transportation and is a major deep-water port connected to
the Pacific Ocean. Sacramento's economy is highly
diversified and, along with state government and
military installations, its industries include aerospace, high technology, furniture, chemicals, pharmaceuticals, meat packing, and food processing of
crops from the Central Valley.

The defense sector of the economy declined and
Mather Air Force Base and the Army Depot were
closed in 1995.

Famous natives: Joan Didion, author; Mark Goodson, TV
producer; Tom Hanks, actor; Henry Hathaway, director;
Anthony M. Kennedy, Supreme Court justice; Molly
Ringwald, actress.

San Antonio, Tex.

Mayor: Ed Garza (to May 2003)
City Manager: Terry M. Brechtel
2000 census population (rank): 1,144,646 (9);
  % change: 22.3; **Male:** 553,245 (48.3%); **Female:**
591,401 (51.7%); **White:** 774,708 (67.7%); **Black:**
78,120 (6.8%); **American Indian and Alaska Native:**
9,584 (0.8%); **Asian:** 17,934 (1.6%); **Other race:**
221,362 (19.3%); **Two or more races:** 41,871 (3.7%);
Hispanic/Latino: 671,394 (58.7%). **2000 percent**
population 18 and over: 71.5%; **65 and over:**
10.4%; **median age:** 31.7.

Land area: 430 sq mi. (1,113.7 sq km); **Alt.:** 700 ft.
Avg. daily temp.: Jan., 51.2° F; July, 86.1° F
City-owned parks: 6,717 ac.; **Radio stations:** AM, 20;
  FM, 22; **Television stations:** 9
Civilian Labor Force (MSA) 2001: 789,300;
  Unemployed: 26,400, **Percent:** 3.3; **Per capita per-**
sonal income (MSA) 1999: $24,716
Chamber of Commerce: Greater San Antonio Chamber
of Commerce, P.O. Box 1628, 602 E. Commerce, San
Antonio, Tex. 78296

San Antonio, the third-largest city in Texas and
the seat of Bexar County, is located in the south-
central part of the state, on the San Antonio River.

The site of San Antonio was first visited in 1691
by a Franciscan friar on the feast day of St. Anthony
and was named San Antonio de Padua in his honor.
San Antonio was permanently settled on May 1,
1718, when the Spanish governor of Coahuila and
Texas, Martin de Alarcón, founded the presidio (a
fort) of San Antonio de Bejar (Bexar) and the mission of San Antonio de Valero (later called the
Alamo) on the site of a Coahuiltecan Indian village.
San Antonio remained almost continuously under
Spanish rule until 1812, when Mexico won its independence from Spain.

During the outbreak of the Texas revolution
(1835) against the tyranny of Mexican dictator General Santa Anna, San Antonio was captured by a
small band of rebels who occupied the fortified mission of the Alamo in Dec. 1835. The historic battle
of the Alamo was fought there (Feb. 24 to March 6,
1836), and its 183 besieged defenders were massacred by Santa Anna's troops. Their heroism aroused
the anger and fighting spirit of Texans and led them
to shout their famous battle cry "Remember the
Alamo!" and defeat the Mexicans six weeks later
(April 21, 1836) at the battle of San Jacinto. Texas
became an independent republic in 1836, and San
Antonio was incorporated as a city on Jan. 5, 1837.

After the Civil War, with the arrival of the railroad in 1877, San Antonio prospered as a major
shipping point for cattle. The city has been an
important military center since World War II and is
the home to five of the largest military installations
in the nation, including Fort Sam Houston, constructed in 1876. San Antonio is a leading livestock
center and one of the largest produce exchange markets. The city's industries are highly diversified, and
tourism is also important to the economy.

Famous natives: Carol Burnett, comedienne; Cody Carlson,
football player; Henry G. Cisneros, secretary of HUD; Joan
Crawford, actress; Cito Gaston, baseball manager; Ann
Harding, actress; Jesse James Leija, boxer; Emilio Navaira,
Tejano music singer; Oliver North, military officer and
government official; Suzy Parker, model and actress; Paula
Prentiss, actress; Kyle Rote, football player; David R. Scott,
astronaut; John Silber, university president; Patsy Torres,
Tejano music singer; Edward H. White, astronaut.

San Diego, Calif.

Mayor: Dick Murphy (to Dec. 2004)
City Manager: Michael Uberuaga (apptd. Nov. 1997)
2000 census population (rank): 1,223,400 (7);
  % change: 10.2; **Male:** 616,884 (50.4%); **Female:**
606,516 (49.6%); **White:** 736,207 (60.2%); **Black:**
96,216 (7.9%); **American Indian and Alaska Native:**
7,543 (0.6%); **Asian:** 166,968 (13.6%); **Other race:**
151,532 (12.4%); **Two or more races:** 59,081 (4.8%);
Hispanic/Latino: 310,752 (25.4%). **2000 percent**
population 18 and over: 76.0%; **65 and over:**
10.5%; **median age:** 32.5.

Land area: 330.7 sq miles (857 sq km); **Alt.:** Highest, 1,591 ft.; lowest, sea level
Avg. daily temp.: Jan., 56.8° F; July, 70.3° F
Churches: Roman Catholic, 39; Jewish, 9; Protestant, 334; Eastern Orthodox, 8; other, 18; **City park and recreation facilities:** 164 (17,207 ac.); **Radio stations:** AM, 14; FM, 25; **Television stations:** 9
Civilian Labor Force (MSA) 2001: 1,421,800; **Unemployed:** 39,300, **Percent:** 2.8; **Per capita personal income (MSA) 1999:** $29,489
Chamber of Commerce: San Diego Chamber of Commerce, 402 West Broadway, Suite 1000, San Diego, Calif. 92101

San Diego is the second-largest city in California. It is located in the southwest part of the state, on San Diego Bay.

Portuguese navigator Juan Rodríguez Cabrillo claimed the bay for Spain in 1542. The site was named San Miguel by Cabrillo. On Nov. 12, 1602, Don Sebastian de Viscaíno came ashore with his party on the day of St. Didacus (San Diego in Spanish) and celebrated a mass in the saint's honor. By coincidence, Viscaíno's flagship was named *San Diego*. He renamed the place San Diego after the 15th-century saint.

In 1769, Franciscan father Junípero Serra established the first California mission there—San Diego del Alcala. In 1822, Mexico won control of the town after it declared its independence from Spain. In 1846, during the Mexican War, San Diego was seized by the U.S. and incorporated as a city in 1850, just after California joined the Union.

Today, San Diego's excellent natural harbor is a busy commercial port and a hub of U.S. naval operations (although the naval training center at San Diego has closed due to defense cutbacks). Other leading industries are electronics, aerospace and missiles, medical and scientific research, oceanography, and agriculture. Its magnificent climate and proximity to Mexico have made tourism a significant part of the city's economy.

Famous natives: Billy Casper, golfer; Florence Chadwick, swimmer; Dennis Conner, yacht racer; Ted Danson, actor; Robert Duvall, actor; Nanette Fabray, actress; Margaret O'Brien, actress; Carol Vaness, soprano; Ted Williams, baseball player; Mickey Wright, golfer.

San Francisco, Calif.

Mayor: Willie L. Brown, Jr. (to Jan. 2004)
2000 census population (rank): 776,733 (13); **% change:** 7.3; **Male:** 394,828 (50.8%); **Female:** 381,905 (49.2%); **White:** 385,728 (49.7%); **Black:** 60,515 (7.8%); **American Indian and Alaska Native:** 3,458 (0.4%); **Asian:** 239,565 (30.8%); **Other race:** 50,368 (6.5%); **Two or more races:** 33,255 (4.3%); **Hispanic/Latino:** 109,504 (14.1%). **2000 percent population 18 and over:** 85.5%; **65 and over:** 13.7%; **median age:** 36.5.
Land area: 46.1 sq mi. (120 sq km); **Alt.:** Highest, 925 ft.; lowest, sea level
Avg. daily temp.: Jan., 48.5° F; July, 62.2° F
Churches: 540 of all denominations; **City-owned parks and squares:** 225; **Radio stations:** 29; **Television stations:** 10
Civilian Labor Force (PMSA) 2001: 1,004,000; **Unemployed:** 31,800, **Percent:** 3.2; **Per capita personal income (PMSA) 1999:** $49,695
Chamber of Commerce: Greater San Francisco Chamber of Commerce, 465 California St., San Francisco, Calif. 94104

San Francisco, the fourth-largest city in California, is coextensive with San Francisco County. It is located in the northern part of the state between the Pacific Ocean and San Francisco Bay. A narrow arm of land embraces San Francisco Bay, the largest land-locked harbor in the world, and shelters it from the Pacific Ocean. On this arm of land is San Francisco, a city on hills, almost surrounded by water.

A Franciscan father who was sailing with Sebastián Rodríguez Cermeño named the bay San Francisco on Nov. 7, 1595. In 1776, the Spaniards established a presidio, or military post, and a Franciscan mission on the end of the beautiful peninsula. In the following year, a little town was founded around the mission. It was called Yerba Buena, Spanish for "Good Herb," because mint grew in abundance there. In 1846, during the Mexican War, Yerba Buena was taken over by the United States. It was renamed San Francisco in 1847 and became incorporated as a city in 1850.

When gold was discovered in California in 1848, the city's population jumped to 10,000, and it experienced turbulent years until order was established by Vigilance Committees, first in 1851, and again in 1856. Then followed a period of more orderly growth, and the foundations of the great commerce and industry of today were laid.

In 1906, San Francisco experienced the nation's most destructive earthquake, which, together with the fire that followed, practically destroyed the city. The city was quickly rebuilt and grew rapidly as a leading transportation, industrial, and cultural center. In the 19th century, the American explorer and soldier John C. Frémont, known as The Pathfinder, named the entrance to the bay the Golden Gate, and the famous bright orange Golden Gate Bridge was dedicated in May 1937.

A vital part of the economic and cultural fabric of northern California, the port of San Francisco covers 7½ mi of waterfront. The port is home to a broad range of commercial, maritime, and public activities. Its major shipping terminals serve shipping lines from around the world. Fisherman's Wharf, Alcatraz, Hyde St. Pier, and Pier 39 all make the port of San Francisco one of the world's leading visitor destinations.

Small businesses have a very important place in the economy. More than 80% of the city's 33,800 businesses have fewer than 15 employees. The high-technology industries of electronics and biotechnology are well represented throughout the Bay Area. With nearly 30% of the worldwide biotechnology labor force, and 360 biotech firms, the Bay Area has been appropriately called "Bionic Bay." Tourism is one of San Francisco's largest industries and the largest employer of city residents. Nearly 13.4 million people visit San Francisco each year, and annual visitor spending is $231 million, providing 66,400 jobs.

The military has played an important role in San Francisco and the Bay Area's economies, but its impact will decline due to defense cutbacks. San Francisco is also the banking and financial center of the West and is home to a Federal Reserve Bank and a United States Mint. More than 60 foreign banks maintain offices there.

Famous natives: Gracie Allen, comedienne; Luis Walter Alvarez, Nobel Prize winner in physics; David Belasco, dramatist and producer; Mel Blanc, actor and voice specialist; Rosemary Casals, tennis player; Isadora Duncan, dancer; Clint Eastwood, actor; Robert Frost, poet; Rube Goldberg, cartoonist; William Randolph Hearst, publisher; Bruce Lee, actor; Mervyn LeRoy, director; Jack London, novelist; Johnny Mathis, singer; Lloyd Nolan, actor; O. J. Simpson, football player; Robert G. Sproul, educator; Irving Stone, novelist; Natalie Wood, actress.

San Jose, Calif.

Mayor: Ron Gonzales (to Dec. 31, 2002)
Acting City Manager: Debra Figone
2000 census population (rank): 894,943 (11);
  % change: 14.4; **Male:** 454,798 (50.8%); **Female:**
  440,145 (49.2%); **White:** 425,017 (47.5%); **Black:**
  31,349 (3.5%); **American Indian and Alaska Native:**
  6,865 (0.8%); **Asian:** 240,375 (26.9%); **Other race:**
  142,691 (15.9%); **Two or more races:** 45,062 (5.0%);
  Hispanic/Latino: 269,989 (30.2%). **2000 percent**
  population 18 and over: 73.6%; **65 and over:** 8.3%;
  median age: 32.6.
Land area: 180.8 sq mi. (468.27 sq km); **Alt.:** Highest,
  4,372 ft.; lowest, sea level
Avg. daily temp.: Jan., 49.5° F; July, 68.8° F
Churches: 403; **City-owned parks and playgrounds:**
  152 (3,136 ac.); **Radio stations:** 14; **Television**
  stations: 4
Civilian Labor Force (PMSA) 2001: 1,013,200;
  Unemployed: 33,400, **Percent:** 3.3; **Per capita per-**
  sonal income (PMSA) 1999: $46,649
Chamber of Commerce: San Jose Chamber of Com-
  merce, One Paseo de San Antonio, San Jose,
  Calif. 95113

San Jose, the third-largest city in California and seat of Santa Clara County, is located in the north-ern part of the state in the Santa Clara Valley, 50 mi south of downtown San Francisco.

San Jose was founded on Nov. 29, 1777, by Span-ish colonizers who named the settlement Pueblo de San José de Guadalupe in honor of Saint Joseph and after the Guadalupe River on which the pueblo (town) was situated. San Jose was the first city to be established in California.

After California became a U.S. territory in 1847, San Jose was the state capital from 1849 to 1852 and was incorporated as a city in 1850. It developed commercially as a supply base for gold prospectors and, when the railroad connected it with San Fran-cisco in 1864, it became the distribution point for agricultural products from the Santa Clara Valley.

Today, the city continues to be the distribution and food-processing center for the surrounding rich agricultural region, which produces seasonal fruits and grapes. More than 50 wineries grace the valley.

San Jose is the capital of Silicon Valley (Santa Clara), where more than 3,000 high-tech companies are located. Silicon Valley is also one of the world's leading centers for medical treatment and research. Heart transplants, gene splicing, and transportable baby incubators were developed there.

San Jose has healthy retail, transportation, and tourism industries and is the primary center for real estate and industrial development in the area.

Famous natives: "Fatty" Arbuckle, actor; Chuck Berry, singer and guitarist; Cesar Chavez, labor leader; Peggy Fleming, figure skater; Farley Granger, actor; Edmund Lowe, actor; Jim Plunkett, football player.

Seattle, Wash.

Mayor: Paul Schell (to Dec. 31, 2001)
2000 census population (rank): 563,374 (24);
  % change: 9.1; **Male:** 280,973 (49.9%); **Female:**
  282,401 (50.1%); **White:** 394,889 (70.1%); **Black:**
  47,541 (8.4%); **American Indian and Alaska Native:**
  5,659 (1.0%); **Asian:** 73,910 (13.1%); **Other race:**

13,423 (2.4%); **Two or more races:** 25,148 (4.5%);
Hispanic/Latino: 29,719 (5.3%). **2000 percent popu-**
lation 18 and over: 84.4%; **65 and over:** 12.0%;
median age: 35.4.
Land area: 144.6 sq mi. (375 sq km); **Alt.:** Highest, 521
  ft.; lowest, sea level
Avg. daily temp.: Jan., 42.2° F; July, 67.6° F
Churches: Roman Catholic, 35; Jewish, 12; Protestant,
  447; others, 42; **City-owned parks, playgrounds,**
  etc.: 397 (6,000+ ac.); **Radio stations:** AM, 15; FM,
  22; **Television stations:** 6
Civilian Labor Force (PMSA) 2001: 1,425,400[1];
  Unemployed: 60,500, **Percent:** 4.2; **Per capita per-**
  sonal income (PMSA) 1999: $39,880[1]
Chamber of Commerce: Greater Seattle Chamber of
  Commerce, 1301 5th Ave., Suite 2400, Seattle, Wash.
  98101-2603

1. Seattle–Bellevue–Everett, Wash.

Seattle is the largest city in Washington and the seat of King County. A city of steep hills, Seattle lies in western Washington between two bodies of water—Puget Sound on the west and Lake Washing-ton on the east. Its fine landlocked harbor has made Seattle one of the major ports in the United States.

Seattle was first settled by five pioneer families from Illinois at Alki Point at the south end of Elliott Bay in 1851. They moved in 1852 to the eastern shore of the bay and laid out a town in 1853. It was named Seattle after a friendly Suquamish Indian chief (Seattle is only an approximation of his name).

Seattle successfully withstood an Indian attack in 1856 and was incorporated as a city in 1869. A disastrous fire almost destroyed the entire business district in 1889. When the Great Northern Railway arrived in 1893, the city became a major rail termi-nus and it grew rapidly. It was a boom town during the Alaska gold rush of 1897 and continued to pros-per as a major Pacific port of entry with the opening of the Panama Canal in 1914.

Seattle is the region's commercial and transporta-tion hub and the center of manufacturing, trade, and finance. Its important diversified industries include aircraft, lumber and forest products, fishing, high technology, food processing, boat building, machin-ery, fabricated metals, chemicals, pharmaceuticals, and apparel.

Famous natives: Chester Carlson, Xerox inventor; Carol Channing, actress; Judy Collins, singer; Fred Couples, golfer; Gail Devers, athlete; Frances Farmer, actress; William Gates, Microsoft founder; June Havoc, actress; Jimi Hendrix, guitarist; Robert Joffrey, choreographer; Gypsy Rose Lee, entertainer; Mary Livingstone, comedienne; Kevin McCarthy, actor; Mary McCarthy, novelist; Jeff Smith, food expert; Martha Wright, singer.

Tucson, Ariz.

Mayor: Bob Walkup (to Dec. 2003)
2000 census population (rank): 486,699 (30);
  % change: 20.1; **Male:** 238,408 (49.0%); **Female:**
  248,291 (51.0%); **White:** 341,424 (70.2%); **Black:**
  21,057 (4.3%); **American Indian and Alaska Native:**
  11,038 (2.3%); **Asian:** 11,959 (2.5%); **Other race:**
  81,988 (16.8%); **Two or more races:** 18,437 (3.8%);
  Hispanic/Latino: 173,868 (35.7%). **2000 percent**
  population 18 and over: 75.4%; **65 and over:**
  11.9%; **median age:** 32.1.
Land area: 162 sq mi. (419 sq km); **Alt.:** 2,400 ft.
Avg. daily temp.: Jan., 51.1° F; July, 86.2° F
Churches: Protestant, 340; Roman Catholic, 42; other,
  150; **City-owned parks and parkways:** (25,349 ac.);
  Radio stations: AM, 15; FM, 17; **Television stations:**
  3 commercial; 1 educational; 3 other

Civilian Labor Force (MSA) 2001): 398,300;
  Unemployed: 11,200, **Percent:** 2.8; **Per capita personal income (MSA) 1999:** $23,911
Chamber of Commerce: Tucson Metropolitan Chamber of Commerce, P.O. Box 991, Tucson, Ariz. 85702

Tucson is the second-largest city in Arizona and the seat of Pima County. It is located in the southeast part of the state on the Santa Cruz River.

The site was originally settled by the prehistoric Hohokam Indians (300 B.C.–A.D.1400s). The first Europeans to visit the area were Spanish missionaries in the 17th century. In 1700, the Jesuit missionary explorer Father Eusebio Francisco Kino founded the mission of San Xavier del Bac close by the Papago Indian village of Stjukshon (later called Tucson). Stjukshon is an Indian word meaning "village of the dark spring at the foot of the mountain." The Papago Indians are descendants of the ancient Hohokam peoples.

In 1776, Spanish colonists from Mexico constructed a presidio (fort) at Tucson as protection against the hostile Apache Indians and also established the mission of San Jose de Tucson nearby. Tucson remained a military outpost under Spanish and later Mexican control until the area was sold to the United States as part of the Gadsden Purchase in 1853. Tucson was the capital of the Arizona Territory from 1867 to 1877. It was incorporated as a city in 1877. The town grew rapidly when the Southern Pacific Railroad arrived in 1880 and silver and copper deposits were discovered nearby.

Tucson is a popular vacation and health resort due to its sunny, mild, dry climate and unique desert location. Tourism is important to the city's economy. Major industries include aerospace and missile production, high technology, optics, biotechnology, environmental technology, software, and electronics. Tucson is also the commercial center for the surrounding area's agricultural and mining industries. The city is the home of the University of Arizona.

Famous natives: Rose E. Bird, jurist; Dennis De Concini, senator; Barbara Eden, actress; Linda Ronstadt, singer.

Tulsa, Okla.

Mayor: M. Susan Savage (to May 2002)
2000 census population (rank): 393,049 (43);
  % change: 7.0; **Male:** 189,937 (48.3%); **Female:** 203,112 (51.7%); **White:** 275,488 (70.1%); **Black:** 60,794 (15.5%); **American Indian and Alaska Native:** 18,551 (4.7%); **Asian:** 7,150 (1.8%); **Other race:** 13,564 (3.5%); **Two or more races:** 17,300 (4.4%); **Hispanic/Latino:** 28,111 (7.2%). **2000 percent population 18 and over:** 75.2%; **65 and over:** 12.9%; **median age:** 34.5.
Land area: 186.9 sq mi. (484 sq km); **Alt.:** 674 ft.
Avg. daily temp.: Jan., 35.2° F; July, 83.2° F
Churches: Protestant, 290; Roman Catholic, 40; Jewish, 3; others, 4; **City parks and playgrounds:** 131 (6,000 ac.); **Radio stations:** AM, 10; FM, 16; **Television stations:** 7 commercial; 1 PBS; 123 cable
Civilian Labor Force (MSA) 2001: 414,600;
  Unemployed: 11,300, **Percent:** 2.7; **Per capita personal income (MSA) 1999:** $27,654
Chamber of Commerce: Metropolitan Tulsa Chamber of Commerce, 616 S. Boston, Tulsa, Okla. 74119

Tulsa, the second-largest city in Oklahoma and seat of Tulsa County, is located in the northeast part of the state on the Arkansas River.

Tulsa was settled in the 1830s by Creek Indians from Alabama who were forcibly sent to the area (then part of Indian Territory) under the Indian Removal Act of 1830. Creek medicine men planted ashes from their old home at the new site, and the Creeks named their new village "Tulsy," meaning old town, in memory of their former home in Tallassee, Ala. In time, the village became the town of Tulsa.

The coming of the first railroad in 1882 attracted white settlers to Tulsa, and the town developed into a cattle-shipping center. When enormous oil deposits were discovered at nearby Red Fork in 1901 and at Glenn Pool in 1905, the city experienced rapid growth as a center of a booming petroleum industry. Tulsa was incorporated as a city in 1898 and chartered in 1908.

Tulsa is the center of the state's petroleum industry and has a diversified economy. Important industries include aerospace, chemicals, computer parts, automobile glass, fabricated metals, and industrial machinery. The city became a major inland port when the Tulsa port of Catoosa opened in 1971.

Famous natives: Garth Brooks, singer; Blake Edwards, director; Paul Harvey, commentator; Jennifer Jones, actress; Henry R. Kravis, investment banker; Daniel Patrick Moynihan, senator; Tony Randall, actor; Alfre Woodard, actress; Judy Woodruff, journalist.

Virginia Beach, Va.

Mayor: Meyera E. Oberndorf (to June 2004)
2000 census population (rank): 425,257 (38);
  % change: 8.2; **Male:** 210,524 (49.5%); **Female:** 214,733 (50.5%); **White:** 303,681 (71.4%); **Black:** 80,593 (19.0%); **American Indian and Alaska Native:** 1,619 (0.4%); **Asian:** 20,869 (4.9%); **Other race:** 6,402 (1.5%); **Two or more races:** 11,677 (2.7%); **Hispanic/Latino:** 17,770 (4.2%); **2000 percent population 18 and over:** 72.5%; **65 and over:** 8.4%; **median age:** 32.7.
Land area: 258.7 sq mi. (670 sq km); **Alt.:** 12 ft.
Avg. daily temp.: Jan., 39.9° F; July, 78.4° F
Churches: Protestant, 235; Catholic, 13; Jewish, 5;
City-owned parks: 182 (1,748 ac.); **Radio stations:** AM 13, FM 31; **Television stations:** 8 commercial, 1 PBS, 1 cable
Civilian Labor Force (MSA) 2001: 758,600[1];
  Unemployed: 23,200, **Percent:** 3.1; **Per capita personal income (MSA) 1999:** $24,979[1]
Chamber of Commerce: Hampton Roads Chamber of Commerce, 4512 Virginia Beach Blvd., Virginia Beach, Va., 23463

1. Norfolk–Virginia Beach–Newport News, Va.–N.C.

Virginia Beach, the most populous city in Virginia, is located in the southeast part of the state on the Atlantic coastline. It is independent and is not part of any county.

The first English settlers to set foot in America landed at Cape Henry at the tip of Virginia Beach on April 29, 1607. They were led by John Smith on his way to establishing Jamestown. The first permanent settlement within the city limits was made at Lynnhaven Bay in 1621. Cape Henry became an important port for British merchant ships calling on America, and it was here that the French fleet led by Admiral Comte de Grasse blockaded the British fleet during the American Revolution.

Virginia Beach gained its reputation as a famous vacation resort in the 19th century, following the building of a railroad connecting its oceanfront with Norfolk and the construction of its first hotel in 1883. Virginia Beach was incorporated as a town in 1906 and as a city in 1952. In 1963, Princess Anne County and Virginia Beach merged, giving the present city an area of 310 sq mi bordered by the Atlantic Ocean and the Chesapeake Bay.

Tourism is a mainstay of the economy, and 2.9 million people visit Virginia Beach overnight each year. Virginia Beach's economy is supported by four military bases and diverse industries, including agriculture (165 farms), computer software, engineering, and technical services.

Famous natives and residents: V. C. Andrews, novelist; Raymond Brian Buckland, occult writer; Ann Woodruff Compton, news correspondent; D. J. Dozier, football and baseball player; George Eastman, inventor; Juice Newton, singer; Kenneth S. Reightler, Jr., astronaut; Pat Robertson, evangelist; Henry Walke, naval officer in Mexican and Civil wars; Pernell "Sweet Pea" Whitaker, boxer; Skip Wilkins, wheelchair athlete.

Washington, DC

Created municipal corporation: Feb. 21, 1871
Mayor: Anthony Williams (to Jan. 2003)
Motto: Justitia omnibus (Justice to all)
Flower: American beauty rose; **Tree:** Scarlet oak
2000 census population (rank): 572,059 (21);
% change: –5.7; **Male:** 269,366 (47.1%); **Female:** 302,693 (52.9%); **White:** 176,101 (30.8%); **Black:** 343,312 (60.0%); **American Indian and Alaska Native:** 1,713 (0.3%); **Asian:** 15,189 (2.7%); **Other race:** 21,950 (3.8%); **Two or more races:** 13,446 (2.4%); **Hispanic/Latino:** 44,953 (7.9%); **2000 percent population 18 and over:** 79.9%; **65 and over:** 12.2%; **median age:** 34.6.
Land area: 68.25 sq mi. (177 sq km); **Alt.:** Highest, 420 ft.; lowest, sea level
Avg. daily temp.: Jan., 35.2° F; July, 78.9° F
Churches: Protestant, 610; Roman Catholic, 132; Jewish, 9; **City parks:** 753 (7,725 ac.); **Radio stations:** AM, 9; FM, 38; **Television stations:** 19
Civilian Labor Force (PMSA) 2001: 2,784,700[1];
Unemployed: 67,800, **Percent:** 2.4; **Per capita personal income (PMSA) 1999:** $38,403[1]
Board of Trade: Greater Washington Board of Trade, 1129 20th Street, N.W., Washington, D.C. 20036
Chamber of Commerce: D.C. Chamber of Commerce, 1319 F St., NW, Washington, D.C. 20004

1. Washington, D.C.–Md.–Va.–W.Va.

The District of Columbia—identical with the City of Washington—is the capital of the United States. It is located between Virginia and Maryland on the Potomac River. The district is named after Columbus.

DC history began in 1790 when Congress directed selection of a new capital site, 100 sq mi, along the Potomac. When the site was determined, it included 30.75 sq mi on the Virginia side of the river. In 1846, however, Congress returned that area to Virginia, leaving the 68.25 sq mi ceded by Maryland in 1788. The seat of government was transferred from Philadelphia to Washington on Dec. 1, 1800, and President John Adams became the first resident in the White House.

The city was planned and partly laid out by Maj. Pierre Charles L'Enfant, a French engineer. This work was perfected and completed by Maj. Andrew Ellicott and Benjamin Banneker, a freeborn black man who was an astronomer and mathematician. In 1814, during the War of 1812, a British force burned the capital including the White House.

Until Nov. 3, 1967, the District of Columbia was administered by three commissioners appointed by the president. On that day, a government consisting of a mayor-commissioner and a 9-member council, all appointed by the president with the approval of the Senate, took office. On May 7, 1974, the citizens

of the District of Columbia approved a Home Rule Charter, giving them an elected mayor and 13-member council—their first elected municipal government in more than a century. The district also has one nonvoting member in the House of Representatives and an elected Board of Education.

On Aug. 22, 1978, Congress passed a proposed constitutional amendment to give Washington, DC, voting representation in the Congress. The amendment had to be ratified by at least 38 state legislatures within seven years to become effective. It died in 1985. A petition asking for the district's admission to the Union as the 51st state was filed in Congress on Sept. 9, 1983, and new statehood bills were introduced in 1993. The district is continuing this drive for statehood.

The federal government and tourism are the mainstays of the city's economy, and many unions, business, professional, and nonprofit organizations are headquartered there. Among the city's many educational institutions are the Catholic University of America, Georgetown University, Howard University, and Gallaudet University. Cultural attractions include the National Gallery of Art, the Smithsonian Institution, the John F. Kennedy Center for the Performing Arts, and the Folger Shakespeare Library.

Famous natives: Edward Albee, playwright; Billie Burke, comedienne; Ina Claire, actress; John Foster Dulles, statesman; Duke Ellington, musician; Jane Greer, actress; Goldie Hawn, actress; Helen Hayes, actress; J. Edgar Hoover, former director of the F.B.I.; Michael Learned, actress; Roger Mudd, newscaster; Eleanor Holmes Norton, government official; Chita Rivera, dancer and actress; Leonard Rose, cellist; John Philip Sousa, composer; Frances Sternhagen, actress.

Wichita, Kans.

Mayor: Bob Knight (to April 2003)
City Manager: Chris Cherches
2000 census population (rank): 344,284 (50);
% change: 13.2; **Male:** 169,604 (49.3%); **Female:** 174,680 (50.7%); **White:** 258,900 (75.2%); **Black:** 39,325 (11.4%); **American Indian and Alaska Native:** 3,986 (1.2%); **Asian:** 13,647 (4.0%); **Other race:** 17,566 (5.1%); **Two or more races:** 10,662 (3.1%); **Hispanic/Latino:** 33,112 (9.6%); **2000 percent population 18 and over:** 72.9%; **65 and over:** 11.9%; **median age:** 33.4.
Land area: 140 sq mi. (362.6 sq km); **Alt.:** 1,332 ft.
Avg. daily temp.: Jan., 30°F; July, 81°F
Churches: Protestant, 512; Roman Catholic, 20; Jewish, 2; other, 66; **City parks:** 90 (4,190 ac.); **Radio stations:** 22; **Television stations:** 7
Civilian Labor Force (MSA) 2001: 289,300;
Unemployed: 9,400, **Percent:** 3.2; **Per capita personal income (MSA) 1999:** $26,916
Chamber of Commerce: Wichita Chamber of Commerce, 350 W. Douglas, Wichita, Kans. 67202

Wichita is the largest city in Kansas and the seat of Sedgwick County. It is located in the south-central part of the state, at the confluence of the Arkansas and Little Arkansas rivers. Incorporated as a city in 1870, Wichita is the chief commercial and industrial center of southern Kansas.

More or less uninhabited at the time of Kansas's entry into the Union in 1861, the area was first settled by Wichita Indians, who came north from Texas and Oklahoma during the Civil War. At about the same time (during the mid-1860s) a number of trading posts were established at or near the river junction. One of the traders, Jesse Chisholm, pioneered the Chisholm Trail, which passed through Wichita and was the main cattle-drive route from Texas to the railroad in Abilene. After the railroad was extended to Wichita in 1872, the city boomed first as a cow town and then later as the trading center in an agricultural and livestock region. Although the city experienced an economic slump at the end of the 19th century, oil was discovered nearby in 1915, and subsequently the population almost doubled.

Aircraft manufacturing began in the 1920s, and Wichita remains a center of the aircraft industry today. In addition, the city also has flour mills, meatpacking plants, and oil refineries. Major manufactures include camping equipment, heaters and air conditioners, and electronics. Wichita has a number of art and historical museums, a zoo, and a planetarium. It is the site of several universities, including Wichita State University (1895). McConnell Air Force Base is nearby.

Famous natives: Kirstie Alley, actress; Alan Fudge, actor; Dan Glickman, former congressman and U.S. secretary of agriculture; Laurel Goodwin, actress; Stan Kenton, musician; Jim Lehrer, news anchor; Fred, Thomas, and Edwin McConnell, WWII pilots; Hattie McDaniel, actress; Gale Sayers, football player; Arlen Specter, U.S. senator from Pennsylvania; Ron Wyden, U.S. senator from Oregon.

Top 50 Cities in the U.S. by Population and Rank, 1990 and 2000

	4/1/2000 census population	4/1/1990 census population	Numeric population change 1990–2000	Percent population change 1990–2000	Size rank 1990	Size rank 2000
New York, N.Y.	8,008,278	7,322,564	685,714	9.4	1	1
Los Angeles, Calif.	3,694,820	3,485,398	209,422	6.0	2	2
Chicago, Ill.	2,896,016	2,783,726	112,290	4.0	3	3
Houston, Tex.	1,953,631	1,630,553	323,078	19.8	4	4
Philadelphia, Pa.	1,517,550	1,585,577	−68,027	−4.3	5	5
Phoenix, Ariz.	1,321,045	983,403	337,642	34.3	10	6
San Diego, Calif.	1,223,400	1,110,549	112,851	10.2	6	7
Dallas, Tex.	1,188,580	1,006,877	181,703	18.0	8	8
San Antonio, Tex.	1,144,646	935,933	208,713	22.3	9	9
Detroit, Mich.	951,270	1,027,974	−76,704	−7.5	7	10
San Jose, Calif.	894,943	782,248	112,695	14.4	11	11
Indianapolis, Ind.	791,926	741,952	49,974	6.7	13	12
San Francisco, Calif.	776,733	723,959	52,774	7.3	14	13
Jacksonville, Fla.	735,617	635,230	100,387	15.8	16	14
Columbus, Ohio	711,470	632,910	78,560	12.4	15	15
Austin, Tex.	656,562	465,622	190,940	41.0	25	16
Baltimore, Md.	651,154	736,014	−84,860	−11.5	12	17
Memphis, Tenn.	650,100	610,337	39,763	6.5	18	18
Milwaukee, Wis.	596,974	628,088	−31,114	−5.0	17	19
Boston, Mass.	589,141	574,283	14,858	2.6	20	20
Washington, DC	572,059	606,900	−34,841	−5.7	19	21
Nashville-Davidson, Tenn.[1]	569,891	510,784	59,107	11.6	26	22
El Paso, Tex.	563,662	515,342	48,320	9.4	22	23
Seattle, Wash.	563,374	516,259	47,115	9.1	21	24
Denver, Colo.	554,636	467,610	87,026	18.6	28	25
Charlotte, N.C.	540,828	395,934	144,894	36.6	33	26
Fort Worth, Tex.	534,694	447,619	87,075	19.5	29	27
Portland, Ore.	529,121	437,319	91,802	21.0	27	28
Oklahoma City, Okla.	506,132	444,719	61,413	13.8	30	29
Tucson, Ariz.	486,699	405,390	81,309	20.1	34	30
New Orleans, La.	484,674	496,938	−12,264	−2.5	24	31
Las Vegas, Nev.	478,434	258,295	220,139	85.2	63	32
Cleveland, Ohio	478,403	505,616	−27,213	−5.4	23	33
Long Beach, Calif.	461,522	429,433	32,089	7.5	32	34
Albuquerque, N.M.	448,607	384,736	63,871	16.6	40	35
Kansas City, Mo.	441,545	435,146	6,399	1.5	31	36
Fresno, Calif.	427,652	354,202	73,450	20.7	48	37
Virginia Beach, Va.	425,257	393,069	32,188	8.2	39	38
Atlanta, Ga.	416,474	394,017	22,457	5.7	38	39
Sacramento, Calif.	407,018	369,365	37,653	10.2	37	40
Oakland, Calif.	399,484	372,242	27,242	7.3	35	41
Mesa, Ariz.	396,375	288,091	108,284	37.6	53	42
Tulsa, Okla.	393,049	367,302	25,747	7.0	44	43
Omaha, Neb.	390,007	335,795	54,212	16.1	47	44
Minneapolis, Minn.	382,618	368,383	14,235	3.9	43	45
Honolulu CDP,[2] Hawaii	371,657	365,272	6,385	1.7	41	46
Miami, Fla.	362,470	358,548	3,922	1.1	46	47
Colorado Springs, Colo.	360,890	281,140	79,750	28.4	54	48
St. Louis, Mo.	348,189	396,685	−48,496	−12.2	42	49
Wichita, Kans.	344,284	304,011	40,273	13.2	51	50

NOTE: 1990 population figures in this table reflect most recent revisions by the Census Bureau. 1. Nashville-Davidson city is consolidated with Davidson County. 2. Honolulu Census Designated Place; by agreement with the State of Hawaii, the Census Bureau does not show data separately for the city of Honolulu, which is coextensive with Honolulu County. *Source:* U.S. Census Bureau; Web: www.census.gov.

Tabulated Data on City Governments

City	Mayor		City manager's salary[1,2]	Council or Commission			
	Term, years	Salary[1]		Name	Members	Term, years	Salary[1,3]
Albuquerque, N.M.	4	$ 83,491	$109,096	Council	9	4	$ 7,028
Atlanta, Ga.	4	141,490	—	Council	18	4	32,474
Austin, Tex.	3	35,006	188,115	Council	7	3	45,011
Baltimore, Md.	4	125,000	—	Council	19	4	48,000
Boston, Mass.	4	125,000	—	Council	13	2	62,500
Charlotte, N.C.	2	18,262	153,773	Council	11	2	13,044
Chicago, Ill.	4	192,100	—	Council	50	4	85,000
Cleveland, Ohio	4	101,286	—	Council	21	4	47,751
Colorado Springs, Colo.	4	6,250	137,000	Council	9	4	6,200
Columbus, Ohio	4	110,300	—	Council	7	4	25,000
Dallas, Tex.	4	60,000	179,001	Council	15[5]	2	37,500
Denver, Colo.	4	113,184	—	Council	13	4	57,432
Detroit, Mich.	4	176,176	—	Council	9	4	81,312
El Paso, Tex.	2	25,000	—	Council	9[5]	2	15,000
Fort Worth, Tex.	2	75[4]	170,112	Council	9[5]	2	75[4]
Fresno, Calif.	4	99,369	120,000	Council	7	4	44,511
Honolulu, Hawaii	4	112,200	107,100[6]	Council	9	4	48,450
Houston, Tex.	2	165,816	—	Council	14	2	44,218
Indianapolis, Ind.	4	95,000	—	Council	29	4	11,400
Jacksonville, Fla.	2	110,000	105,000[7]	Council	19	4	24,000
Kansas City, Mo.	4	83,208	153,408	Council	13[5]	4	41,592
Las Vegas, Nev.	4	75,800	112,499	Council	4	4	33,480
Long Beach, Calif.	4	93,238	181,500	Council	9	4	23,310
Los Angeles, Calif.	4[8]	139,607	193,224[6]	Council	15	4	107,390
Memphis, Tenn.	4	140,000	107,000[6]	Council	13	4	20,100
Mesa, Ariz.	4	33,600	144,860	Council	6	4	16,800
Miami, Fla.	4	97,000	100,000	Commission	5	4	5,000
Milwaukee, Wis.	4	124,625	—	Council	17	4	61,934
Minneapolis, Minn.	4	84,096	114,283	Council	13	4	63,997
Nashville, Tenn.	4	75,000	8,900[9]	Council	40	4	6,900
New Orleans, La.	4	90,000	57,900	Council	7	4	42,500
New York, N.Y.	4	195,000	156,000[9]	Council	51	4	90,000
Oakland, Calif.	4	97,740	207,505[10]	Council	9[5]	4	60,000[8,11]
Oklahoma City, Okla.	4	24,000	133,500	Council	8	4	12,000
Omaha, Neb.	4	92,883	—	Council	7	4	27,135
Philadelphia, Pa.	4	130,000	140,000[7]	Council	17	4	80,000
Phoenix, Ariz.	4	56,000	183,810	Council	9[5]	4	35,999
Portland, Ore.	4	95,950	—	Council	4	4	80,808
Sacramento, Calif.	4	3,325[12]	151,715	Council	9	4	2,300[12]
St. Louis, Mo.	4	97,422	—	Board of Alderman	29	4	28,745
San Antonio, Tex.	2	3,000[13]	160,422	Council	11[5]	2	20[4]
San Diego, Calif.	4	86,982	189,255	Council	8	4	65,269
San Francisco, Calif.	4	155,688	155,052	Bd. of Supvrs.	11	4	37,584
San Jose, Calif.	4	87,550	158,000	Council	10	4	58,240
Seattle, Wash.	4	122,691	—	Council	9	4	75,505
Tucson, Ariz.	4	42,000	127,000	Council	7[5]	4	24,000
Tulsa, Okla.	4	70,000	—	Council	9	2	12,000
Virginia Beach, Va.	4	20,000	160,000	Council	11[5]	4	18,000
Washington, D.C.	4	90,705	115,700	Council	13	4	71,885
Wichita, Kans.	4	65,240	141,260	Council	7[5]	4	19,850

1. Annual salary unless otherwise indicated; does not include additional payments for expenses, special sessions, etc. 2. City manager's term is indefinite and at will of council (or mayor). 3. In some cities, leaders receive a higher salary. 4. Per council meeting, with an annual cap. 5. Including mayor. 6. Appointed by mayor, approved by council. 7. Appointed by mayor; not subject to council confirmation. 8. At mayor's request; limited to 2 terms. 9. No city manager; salary is for deputy or vice mayor. 10. Denotes average based on range. 11. Council also serves as the Redevelopment Agency for which there is additional compensation. 12. Per month. 13. Plus council pay. *Source:* Questionnaires to the cities.

U.S. Cities and Metro Areas: Census 2000

Source: U.S. Census Bureau

Overall, cities have expanded rapidly over the last decade, growing nearly twice as fast in the 1990s as in the 1980s. Western and southern cities grew the fastest, while urban industrial centers in the Midwest and Northeast declined in population. New York remained the country's largest city, however, passing the 8 million mark (see table p. 201).

In 2000, 80.3% of Americans (226 million people) lived in metropolitan areas, up slightly from

79.8% (198.4 million people) in 1990. (A metropolitan area is a city plus the adjacent communities to which it is linked economically.) All of the metropolitan areas with populations of at least 5 million grew over the period, ranging from 29% for the Dallas metropolitan area to 5% for Philadelphia. The total population within metropolitan areas increased by 14%, while the nonmetropolitan population grew by 10%.

Top Ten U.S. Cities by Percent Population Change, 1990–2000

Rank	Place name	Population		Change, 1990 to 2000	
		April 1, 2000	April 1, 1990	Number	Percent
1.	Augusta-Richmond County[1], Ga.	199,775	44,639	155,136	347.5%
2.	Gilbert, Ariz.	109,697	29,188	80,509	275.8
3.	Vancouver, Wash.	143,560	46,380	97,180	209.5
4.	Henderson, Nev.	175,381	64,942	110,439	170.1
5.	North Las Vegas, Nev.	115,488	47,707	67,781	142.1
6.	Athens-Clark County[2], Ga.	101,489	45,734	55,755	121.9
7.	Peoria, Ariz.	108,364	50,618	57,746	114.1
8.	Pembroke Pines, Fla.	137,427	65,452	71,975	110.0
9.	Chandler, Ariz.	176,581	90,533	86,048	95.0
10.	Las Vegas, Nev.	478,434	258,295	220,139	85.2

1. In 2000, Richmond County and the incorporated place of Augusta-Richmond County are coextensive. The 1990 population is for the incorporated place of Augusta city before consolidation of the city and county governments. 2. In 2000, Clarke County and the incorporated place of Athens-Clarke County are coextensive. The 1990 population is for the incorporated place of Athens city before consolidation of the city and county governments. *Source:* U.S. Census Bureau, Census 2000; 1990 Census; Web: www.census.gov.

The Ten Fastest-Growing Metropolitan Areas, 1990–2000

Metropolitan area	Population		Change, 1990–2000	
	April 1, 1990	April 1, 2000	Number	Percent
Las Vegas, Nev., Ariz.	852,737	1,563,282	710,545	83.3%
Naples, Fla.	152,099	251,377	99,278	65.3
Yuma, Ariz.	106,895	160,026	53,131	49.7
McAllen-Edinburg-Mission, Tex.	383,545	569,463	185,918	48.5
Austin-San Marcos, Tex.	846,227	1,249,763	403,536	47.7
Fayetteville-Springdale-Rogers, Ark.	210,908	311,121	100,213	47.5
Boise, Idaho	295,851	432,345	136,494	46.1
Phoenix-Mesa, Ariz.	2,238,480	3,251,876	1,013,396	45.3
Laredo, Tex.	133,239	193,117	59,878	44.9
Provo-Orem, Utah	263,590	368,536	104,946	39.8

Source: U.S. Census Bureau, Census 2000; 1990 Census; Web: www.census.gov.

Metropolitan Areas with Population of 5,000,000 or More

Metropolitan area	Population		Percent change, 1990 to 2000	2000 share of U.S. total
	April 1, 1990	April 1, 2000		
Total for metropolitan areas of 5,000,000 or more	75,874,152	84,064,274	10.8%	29.9%
New York-Northern New Jersey-Long Island, N.Y., N.J., Conn., Pa.	19,549,649	21,199,865	8.4	7.5
Los Angeles-Riverside-Orange County, Calif.	14,531,529	16,373,645	12.7	5.8
Chicago-Gary-Kenosha, Ill., Ind., Wis.	8,239,820	9,157,540	11.1	3.3
Washington-Baltimore, D.C., Md., Va., W.Va.	6,727,050	7,608,070	13.1	2.7
San Francisco-Oakland-San Jose, Calif.	6,253,311	7,039,362	12.6	2.5
Philadelphia-Wilmington-Atlantic City, Pa., N.J., Del., Md.	5,892,937	6,188,463	5.0	2.2
Boston-Worcester-Lawrence, Mass., N.H., Maine, Conn.	5,455,403	5,819,100	6.7	2.1
Detroit-Ann Arbor-Flint, Mich.	5,187,171	5,456,428	5.2	1.9
Dallas-Fort Worth, Tex.	4,037,282	5,221,801	29.3	1.9

Source: U.S. Census Bureau, Census 2000; 1990 Census; Web: www.census.gov.

U.S. Cities with Population over 100,000

ZIP codes provided below indicate the primary ZIP code for each city; please consult a ZIP code directory to find the appropriate ZIP code for a particular address.

City	2000 Pop.	2000 Rank	ZIP Code	City	2000 Pop.	2000 Rank	ZIP Code
Alabama				San Jose	894,943	11	95101
Birmingham	242,820	72	35203	Santa Ana	337,977	52	92711
Huntsville	158,216	130	35813	Santa Clara	102,361	232	95050
Mobile	198,915	94	36601	Santa Clarita	151,088	137	91355
Montgomery	201,568	89	36119	Santa Rosa	147,595	144	95402
Alaska				Simi Valley	111,351	206	93065
Anchorage	260,283	66	99599	Stockton	243,771	71	95208
Arizona				Sunnyvale	131,760	165	94086
Chandler	176,581	116	85225	Thousand Oaks	117,005	192	91362
Gilbert	109,697	208	85296	Torrance	137,946	159	90503
Glendale	218,812	81	85302	Vallejo	116,760	193	94590
Mesa	396,375	43	85201	West Covina	105,080	224	91793
Peoria	108,364	214	85381	**Colorado**			
Phoenix	1,321,045	6	85026	Arvada	102,153	235	80004
Scottsdale	202,705	88	85251	Aurora	276,393	62	80017
Tempe	158,625	129	85282	Colorado Springs	360,890	49	80903
Tucson	486,699	30	85726	Denver	554,636	25	80202
Arkansas				Fort Collins	118,652	189	80525
Little Rock	183,133	112	72202	Lakewood	144,126	148	80202
California				Pueblo	102,121	236	81003
Anaheim	328,014	56	92803	Westminster	100,940	239	80030
Bakersfield	247,057	70	93380	**Connecticut**			
Berkeley	102,743	231	94704	Bridgeport	139,529	156	06602
Burbank	100,316	243	91505	Hartford	121,578	183	06101
Chula Vista	173,556	122	91910	New Haven	123,626	179	06511
Concord	121,780	181	94520	Stamford	117,083	191	06904
Corona	124,966	174	91718	Waterbury	107,271	217	06702
Costa Mesa	108,724	213	92628	**District of Columbia**			
Daly City	103,621	227	94015	Washington[1]	572,059	21	20090
Downey	107,323	216	90241	**Florida**			
El Monte	115,965	196	91734	Cape Coral	102,286	234	33909
Escondido	133,559	164	92025	Clearwater	108,787	212	33990
Fontana	128,929	167	92335	Coral Springs	117,549	190	33075
Fremont	203,413	87	94537	Fort Lauderdale	152,397	134	33310
Fresno	427,652	37	93706	Hialeah	226,419	76	33010
Fullerton	126,003	173	92834	Hollywood	139,357	157	33022
Garden Grove	165,196	127	92842	Jacksonville	735,617	14	32203
Glendale	194,973	100	91205	Miami	362,470	48	33152
Hayward	140,030	154	94544	Orlando	185,951	107	32802
Huntington Beach	189,594	103	92647	Pembroke Pines	137,427	161	33024
Inglewood	112,580	204	90301	St. Petersburg	248,232	69	33730
Irvine	143,072	150	92619	Tallahassee	150,624	139	32301
Lancaster	118,718	188	93534	Tampa	303,447	58	33630
Long Beach	461,522	34	90802	**Georgia**			
Los Angeles	3,694,820	2	90052	Athens-Clarke County[2]	101,489	237	30608
Modesto	188,856	104	95350	Atlanta	416,474	40	30304
Moreno Valley	142,381	152	92553	Augusta-Richmond County[3]	199,775	91	30901
Norwalk	103,298	229	90650	Columbus	186,291	106	31908
Oakland	399,484	42	94612	Savannah	131,510	166	31402
Oceanside	161,029	128	92054	**Hawaii**			
Ontario	158,007	131	91761	Honolulu CDP[4]	371,657	47	96820
Orange	128,821	168	92863	**Idaho**			
Oxnard	170,358	124	93030	Boise	185,787	108	83708
Palmdale	116,670	194	93550	**Illinois**			
Pasadena	133,936	163	91103	Aurora	142,990	151	60505
Pomona	149,473	141	91769	Chicago	2,896,016	3	60607
Rancho Cucamonga	127,743	171	91729	Joliet	106,221	221	60436
Riverside	255,166	68	92507	Naperville	128,358	169	60540
Sacramento	407,018	41	95813	Peoria	112,936	203	61601
Salinas	151,060	138	93907	Rockford	150,115	140	61125
San Bernardino	185,401	110	92401	Springfield	111,454	205	62703
San Buenaventura (Ventura)	100,916	240	93001	**Indiana**			
San Diego	1,223,400	7	92199	Evansville	121,582	182	47708
San Francisco	776,733	13	94188	Fort Wayne	205,727	85	46802

City	2000 Pop.	2000 Rank	ZIP Code	City	2000 Pop.	2000 Rank	ZIP Code
Gary	102,746	230	46401	**North Carolina**			
Indianapolis	791,926	12	46206	Charlotte	540,828	26	28228
South Bend	107,789	215	46624	Durham	187,035	105	27701
Iowa				Fayetteville	121,015	184	28302
Cedar Rapids	120,758	185	52401	Greensboro	223,891	78	27420
Des Moines	198,682	95	50318	Raleigh	276,093	63	27613
Kansas				Winston-Salem	185,776	109	27102
Kansas City	146,866	146	66106	**Ohio**			
Overland Park	149,080	143	66204	Akron	217,074	82	44309
Topeka	122,377	180	66603	Cincinnati	331,285	55	45225
Wichita	344,284	51	67276	Cleveland	478,403	33	44101
Kentucky				Columbus	711,470	15	43216
Lexington-Fayette	260,512	65	40511	Dayton	166,179	126	45401
Louisville	256,231	67	40231	Toledo	313,619	57	43601
Louisiana				**Oklahoma**			
Baton Rouge	227,818	75	70826	Oklahoma City	506,132	29	73125
Lafayette	110,257	207	70509	Tulsa	393,049	44	74107
New Orleans	484,674	31	70113	**Oregon**			
Shreveport	200,145	90	71102	Eugene	137,893	160	97401
Maryland				Portland	529,121	28	97208
Baltimore	651,154	17	21202	Salem	136,924	162	97309
Massachusetts				**Pennsylvania**			
Boston	589,141	20	02205	Allentown	106,632	219	18101
Cambridge	101,355	238	02139	Erie	103,717	226	16515
Lowell	105,167	222	01853	Philadelphia	1,517,550	5	19104
Springfield	152,082	135	01101	Pittsburgh	334,563	53	15290
Worcester	172,648	123	01613	**Rhode Island**			
Michigan				Providence	173,618	121	02904
Ann Arbor	114,024	199	48104	**South Carolina**			
Detroit	951,270	10	48233	Columbia	116,278	195	29201
Flint	124,943	175	48502	**South Dakota**			
Grand Rapids	197,800	96	49501	Sioux Falls	123,975	178	57104
Lansing	119,128	187	48924	**Tennessee**			
Livonia	100,545	242	48150	Chattanooga	155,554	132	37421
Sterling Heights	124,471	177	48311	Clarksville	103,455	228	37043
Warren	138,247	158	48090	Knoxville	173,890	119	37950
Minnesota				Memphis	650,100	18	38101
Minneapolis	382,618	46	55401	Nashville-Davidson[5]	569,891	22	37230
St. Paul	287,151	60	55109	**Texas**			
Mississippi				Abilene	115,930	197	79604
Jackson	184,256	111	39205	Amarillo	173,627	120	79120
Missouri				Arlington	332,969	54	76004
Independence	113,288	202	64052	Austin	656,562	16	78710
Kansas City	441,545	36	64108	Beaumont	113,866	200	77707
St. Louis	348,189	50	63155	Brownsville	139,722	155	78520
Springfield	151,580	136	65801	Carrollton	109,576	209	75006
Nebraska				Corpus Christi	277,454	61	78469
Lincoln	225,581	77	68501	Dallas	1,188,580	8	75260
Omaha	390,007	45	68108	El Paso	563,662	23	79910
Nevada				Fort Worth	534,694	27	76161
Henderson	175,381	118	89015	Garland	215,768	83	75040
Las Vegas	478,434	32	89199	Grand Prairie	127,427	172	75051
North Las Vegas	115,488	198	89030	Houston	1,953,631	4	77201
Reno	180,480	114	89510	Irving	191,615	102	75061
New Hampshire				Laredo	176,576	117	78041
Manchester	107,006	218	03103	Lubbock	199,564	92	79402
New Jersey				McAllen	106,414	220	78501
Elizabeth	120,568	186	07208	Mesquite	124,523	176	75149
Jersey City	240,055	73	07302	Pasadena	141,674	153	77501
Newark	273,546	64	07102	Plano	222,030	79	75074
Paterson	149,222	142	07510	San Antonio	1,144,646	9	78284
New Mexico				Waco	113,726	201	76702
Albuquerque	448,607	35	87101	Wichita Falls	104,197	225	76307
New York				**Utah**			
Buffalo	292,648	59	14240	Provo	105,166	223	84601
New York	8,008,278	1	10199	Salt Lake City	181,743	113	84199
Rochester	219,773	80	14692	West Valley City	108,896	211	84199
Syracuse	147,306	145	13220	**Virginia**			
Yonkers	196,086	98	10701	Alexandria	128,283	170	22314

City	2000 Pop.	2000 Rank	ZIP Code	City	2000 Pop.	2000 Rank	ZIP Code
Chesapeake	199,184	93	23320	Seattle	563,374	24	98108
Hampton	146,437	147	23670	Spokane	195,629	99	99201
Newport News	180,150	115	23607	Tacoma	193,556	101	98413
Norfolk	234,403	74	23501	Vancouver	143,560	149	98668
Portsmouth	100,565	241	23707	**Wisconsin**			
Richmond	197,790	97	23232	Green Bay	102,313	233	54303
Virginia Beach	425,257	38	23450	Madison	208,054	84	53714
Washington				Milwaukee	596,974	19	53203
Bellevue	109,569	210	98009				

1. Washington city is coextensive with the District of Columbia. 2. In 2000, Clarke County and the incorporated place of Athens-Clarke County are coextensive. 3. In 2000, Richmond County and the incorporated place of Augusta-Richmond County are coextensive. 4. Honolulu Census Designated Place; data are not given separately for the city of Honolulu, which is coextensive with Honolulu County. 5. Nashville-Davidson city is consolidated with Davidson County. *Source:* U.S. Census Bureau; Web: www.census.gov.

Area Codes: United States, Canada, Caribbean

Area codes	Selected cities
UNITED STATES	
Alabama	
205	Birmingham, Tuscaloosa
251	Jackson, Mobile
256	Huntsville, Florence
334	Montgomery, Dothan
Alaska	
907	Anchorage, Fairbanks, Juneau
250	Hyder
Arizona	
480	Chandler
520	Tucson, Flagstaff
602	Phoenix
623	Buckeye, Peoria
928	Flagstaff, Yuma
Arkansas	
501	Little Rock, Fayetteville
870	Jonesboro, Texarkana
California	
209	Stockton
213, 323	Los Angeles
310	Malibu, Torrance
408	San Jose
415	San Francisco, San Rafael
510	Oakland
530	Redding
559	Fresno
562	Long Beach
619	San Diego
626	Pasadena
650	Palo Alto
661	Bakersfield
707	Vallejo, Eureka
714	Orange
760	Bishop
805	San Luis Obispo
818	San Fernando
831	Santa Cruz, Salinas
858	Solana Beach
909	Pomona
916	Sacramento
925	Concord
949	Irvine
Colorado	
303, 720	Denver, Boulder
719	Colorado Springs, Pueblo
970	Aspen, Fort Collins

Area codes	Selected cities
Connecticut	
203	Bridgeport, New Haven
860	Hartford, Norwich
Delaware	
302	Entire state
District of Columbia	
202	
Florida	
305	Miami, Key West
321	Orlando, Cape Canaveral
352	Gainesville, Ocala
386	Daytona Beach
407	Kissimmee, Orlando
561	West Palm Beach
727	Clearwater
786	Miami
813	Tampa
850	Tallahassee, Pensacola
863	Avon Park, Clewiston
904	Jacksonville
941	Fort Myers
954, 754	Ft. Lauderdale
Georgia	
229	Albany
404	Atlanta, Decatur
478	Macon
678	Atlanta, Roswell
706	Athens, Augusta
770	Marietta
912	Savannah
Hawaii	
808	Entire state
Idaho	
208	Entire state
Illinois	
217	Springfield, Champaign
309	Peoria
312, 773	Chicago
618	Carbondale
630	Aurora, Naperville
708	Chicago Heights, Cicero
815	Rockford
847	Waukegan
Indiana	
219	Fort Wayne, Gary
317	Indianapolis
765	Muncie
812	Bloomington, Terre Haute

Area codes	Selected cities
Iowa	
319	Cedar Rapids
515	Des Moines
563	Dubuque, Davenport
641	Mason City
712	Sioux City
Kansas	
316	Wichita
620	Fort Scott
785	Topeka
913	Kansas City
Kentucky	
270	Owensboro
502	Frankfort, Louisville
606	Morehead
859	Lexington
Louisiana	
225	Baton Rouge
318	Shreveport
337	Lafayette
504	New Orleans
985	Hammond
Maine	
207	Entire state
Maryland	
240, 301	Frederick, Hagerstown
410, 443	Baltimore, Salisbury
Massachusetts	
413	Springfield
508, 774	Worcester
617, 857	Boston
781, 339	Waltham
978, 351	Lowell
Michigan	
231	Traverse City
248	Troy
313	Detroit
517	Lansing
616	Grand Rapids
734	Ann Arbor
810	Flint
906	Sault Ste. Marie
989	Saginaw
Minnesota	
218	Duluth
320	St.Cloud
507	Rochester
612	Minneapolis

Area codes	Selected cities
651	St. Paul
763	Maple Grove
952	Bloomington
Mississippi	
228	Gulfport
601	Jackson
662	Tupelo
Missouri	
314	St. Louis
417	Springfield
573	Jefferson City
636	Chesterfield
660	Sedalia, Maryville
816	Kansas City, Independence
Montana	
406	Entire state
Nebraska	
308	Grand Island, Scottsbluff
402	Lincoln, Omaha
Nevada	
702	Las Vegas
775	Carson City, Reno
New Hampshire	
603	Entire state
New Jersey	
201	Jersey City
609	Trenton, Atlantic City
732	New Brunswick
856	Cherry Hill, Vineland
908	Elizabeth
973	Newark, Paterson
New Mexico	
505	Entire state
New York	
212	Manhattan
315	Syracuse
347, 718	Bronx, Brooklyn, Queens, Staten Island
516	Mineola
518	Albany
607	Binghamton
631	Riverhead
646	Manhattan
716	Buffalo, Rochester
845	Poughkeepsie
914	White Plains
917	Manhattan, Bronx, Queens, Staten Island, Brooklyn
North Carolina	
252	Greenville
336	Winston-Salem
704, 980	Charlotte
828	Asheville
910	Fayetteville
919	Raleigh
North Dakota	
701	Entire state
Ohio	
216	Cleveland
234, 330	Akron, Youngstown
419	Toledo
440	Ashtabula
513	Cincinnati
614	Columbus
740	Marion, Jackson
937	Dayton

Area codes	Selected cities
Oklahoma	
405	Oklahoma City
580	Enid, Lawton
918	Tulsa
Oregon	
503	Salem, Portland, Astoria
541	Eugene
971	Salem, Portland
Pennsylvania	
215, 267, 445	Philadelphia
412	Pittsburgh
484, 610, 835	Allentown
570	Scranton
717	Harrisburg
724	Uniontown
814	Erie
Rhode Island	
401	Entire state
South Carolina	
803	Columbia
843	Charleston
864	Greenville
South Dakota	
605	Entire state
Tennessee	
423	Chattanooga
615	Nashville
731	Jackson
865	Knoxville
901	Memphis
931	Columbia
Texas	
210	San Antonio
214	Dallas
254	Waco
281, 713, 832	Houston
361	Corpus Christi
409	Galveston
469, 972	Dallas, Plano
512	Austin
682, 817	Fort Worth
806	Lubbock
830	Uvalde
903	Tyler, Texarkana
915	El Paso
936	Huntsville
940	Wichita Falls
956	Laredo
979	Bryan
Utah	
435	Moab
801	Salt Lake City, Provo
Vermont	
802	Entire state
Virginia	
540	Roanoke
571, 703	Alexandria
757	Norfolk
804	Virginia Beach
Washington	
206	Seattle
253	Tacoma
360	Olympia
425	Bellevue
509	Spokane

Area codes	Selected cities
West Virginia	
304	Entire state
Wisconsin	
262	Racine
414	Milwaukee
608	Madison
715	Eau Claire
920	Green Bay
Wyoming	
307	Entire state
U.S. TERRITORIES	
684	American Samoa
671	Guam
670	Marianas Islands
787	Puerto Rico
340	U.S. Virgin Islands
CANADA	
Alberta	
403	Calgary
780	Edmonton
British Columbia	
250	Victoria
604	Vancouver
Manitoba	
204	Entire province
New Brunswick	
506	Entire province
Newfoundland	
709	Entire province
Nova Scotia	
902	Nova Scotia, Prince Edward Island
Ontario	
416, 647	Toronto
519	Windsor
613	Ottawa
705	Sudbury
807	Thunder Bay
905	Hamilton
Quebec	
418	Quebec
450	Laval
514	Montreal
819	Trois-Rivieres
Saskatchewan	
306	Entire province
Yukon & Northwest Territories	
867	Both provinces
CARIBBEAN AND ATLANTIC ISLANDS	
264	Anguilla
268	Antigua and Barbuda
242	Bahamas
246	Barbados
441	Bermuda
284	British Virgin Islands
345	Cayman Islands
809	Dominican Republic
767	Dominica
473	Grenada
876	Jamaica
664	Montserrat
869	St. Kitts & Nevis
758	St. Lucia
784	St. Vincent & the Grenadines
868	Trinidad & Tobago
649	Turks & Caicos

The Unfrozen North

Who needs sun and surf? With its thermal springs and hopping club scene, Iceland is the hot getaway

By THOMAS SANCTON TIME

It may be the marketing coup of the century: take a frozen lava field on the edge of the Arctic Circle, where the skiing is not great, the food is overpriced, and the capital city is a windswept collection of multicolored concrete boxes, and turn it into one of the world's hottest winter vacation spots. How does Iceland do it? By touting its reputation for swinging nightclubs packed with platinum-haired babes and hearty Nordic men, its unspoiled natural wonders and, not least, the low-priced winter deals offered by Icelandair, which enjoys a monopoly on air service to the 40,000-sq-mi North Atlantic island. Off-season round trips from the U.S. to Reykjavik can be had for as little as $250, and two-day package tours for under $300.

Cheap Fares Fuel Boom

Many tourists who come for the cheap fares—a lot of them students and budget travelers who first used Reykjavik as a stopover on flights to Europe—get hooked on the place and become regulars. "I've been here five times," says Karin Ciescik, 45, a New York insurance broker. "I'm a polar buff. I just love the cold." Jeff Warren, managing director of Britain's Windrush Management, chose Iceland for a company holiday. Why? "If we went to Tenerife, we'd just hang around on the beach and drink, mon, so we decided to branch out," says this burly, dreadlocked native of Jamaica after a day of snowboarding in the Arctic cold. "This is one of the few places I've ever been where you're planning to return even before you leave."

Such enthusiastic word of mouth has helped give the local tourist industry growth figures that a lot of Fortune 500 companies would envy: more than 53,000 Americans visited in 2000, up 20% from the year before, and the U.S. is now Iceland's No. 1 tourist market. Tourism generates 13.6% of Iceland's foreign earnings, making it the second biggest industry after fishing.

Wild Nights

For those in their 20s and 30s, the biggest draw is the weekend nightlife. With more than 60 clubs packed into central Reykjavik, the drinking, danc-ing, and nuzzling go on past 6 A.M. "The winters are long and hard here, and people get depressed, so we let it all hang out on the weekend," says Birgir Orn Steinarsson, 25, lead singer for an up-and-coming Icelandic rock group called Maus. Most revelers go from club to club in a giant pub crawl that can jam Reykjavik's narrow streets with up to 5,000 drunken kids every Friday and Saturday night. Some clubs feature deejays and techno rock, while others offer live bands playing anything from R & B to the alternative Icelandic rock that singer-actress Bjork made world famous. But music is hardly the only attraction. "Icelandic girls are just gorgeous," raves Mark Mascarenhas, 27, a medical student from New Jersey, sounding a little like a refugee from MTV Spring Break.

Aside from the club scene and first-rate restaurants like Laekjarbrekka, with its renowned game menu featuring wild reindeer, puffin, and gannet, Reykjavik (pop. 170,000) does not exactly offer world-class attractions. Its main shopping street has more Chinese restaurants than chic boutiques, and everything is expensive (a beer in a club costs about $7). "We are not a country that offers high-class tourism," admits Oddny Oladottir of the Iceland Tourist Board. "But for people interested in nature and geology, you can see a lot of things in a small area."

Natural Wonders

Indeed, once outside the capital city, visitors find an unspoiled geological wonderland: a moonscape of lava fields covered with ice and snow; mountains, glaciers, and volcanoes that still erupt periodically; waterfalls, geysers, and hot springs, which provide 85% of the population with heating. Activities in the winter (when temperatures average around 35°F—higher than in New York) include dogsledding, horseback riding, snowmobiling—and swimming. No one ever goes in the frigid ocean, even in the summer, but numerous public pools filled with warm, sulfurous springwater offer indoor and outdoor swimming—not to mention soaking in cozy and convivial hot tubs.

And while all these foreigners are frolicking in Iceland's frigid winterscapes, where do the natives go on holiday? "We head for the sun and sand," says the tourist board's Oladottir. Their favorite destination: Spain. □

Iceland's Glaciers

Glaciers cover approximately one-ninth of Iceland's land surface. Vatnajökull, located in the southeast part of the country, measures 3,300 sq mi (8,500 sq km) and is the largest glacier in Europe. Other famous Icelandic glaciers include Snaefellsjökull, the legendary abode of elves, fairies, and trolls on the western Snaefellsnes Peninsula, Mýrdalsjökull on the south coast, and Langjökull, the glacier closest to the capital.

Current Travel Warnings

(for U.S. citizens; as of Sept. 2001)

Travel Warnings are issued when the State Department recommends that Americans avoid a certain country. The countries listed below are currently on that list. In addition to this list, the State Department issues Consular Information Sheets for every country of the world with information on such matters as the health conditions, crime, unusual currency or entry requirements, any areas of instability, and the location of the nearest U.S. embassy or consulate in the subject country.

Country	Most recent warning issued	Country	Most recent warning issued
Afghanistan	12/12/00	Lebanon	8/28/00
Albania	6/12/00	Liberia	5/31/01
Algeria	5/31/01	Libya	6/6/01
Angola	9/8/00	Macedonia	9/5/01
Bosnia and Herzegovina	4/13/01	Nigeria	4/7/00
Burundi	12/7/00	Pakistan	9/17/01
Central African Republic	5/30/01	Sierra Leone	8/20/01
Colombia	4/17/01	Solomon Islands	5/1/01
Republic of Congo (Brazzaville)	5/3/00	Somalia	2/16/01
Dem. Rep. of the Congo (formerly Zaire)	4/11/01	Sri Lanka	7/24/01
Guinea-Bissau	4/30/01	Sudan	12/12/00
Fiji	4/10/00	Tajikistan	6/29/01
Indonesia	8/10/01	Turkmenistan	9/19/01
Iran	8/24/01	Yemen	9/19/01
Iraq	7/20/01	Yugoslavia	2/13/01
Israel	8/10/01		

NOTE: In the wake of the terrorist attacks on the World Trade Center and the Pentagon on Sept. 11, 2001, the State Department issued a worldwide caution for U.S. citizens traveling abroad. *Source:* U.S. Department of State. Web: http://travel.state.gov.

U.S. Passport Information

Source: Department of State, Bureau of Consular Affairs. Web: http://travel.state.gov.

With a few exceptions, a passport is required for all U.S. citizens to depart and enter the United States and to enter most foreign countries. Persons who travel to a country where a U.S. passport is not required should be in possession of documentary evidence of their U.S. citizenship and identity to facilitate reentry into the United States. Travelers should check passport and visa requirements with consular officials of the countries to be visited well in advance of their departure date.

Application for a passport may be made at a passport agency, many federal and state courts, probate courts, some county and municipal offices, and some post offices. The thirteen major cities with

U.S. passport agencies are Boston, Chicago, Honolulu, Houston, Los Angeles, Miami, New Orleans, New York, Philadelphia, San Francisco, Seattle, Stamford, Conn., and Washington, D.C.

All persons are required to obtain individual passports in their own names. Neither spouses nor children may be included in each other's passports. Applicants age 13 years and older must appear in person before the clerk or agent executing the application if it is their first time applying. For children under the age of 13, a parent or legal guardian may execute an application for them.

First-time passport applicants must apply in person. Applicants must present the following items at a passport facility:

• Completed Form DSP-11, Application for Passport (available at passport agencies, many travel agencies, or on the Web). This form may be completed in advance; however, it must be signed by you in person before a passport agent.

• Proof of U.S. citizenship. You may use one of the following: previous U.S. passport; certified birth certificate issued by the city, county, or state; Consular Report of Birth Abroad; Naturalization Certificate; or Certificate of Citizenship.

• Proof of identity. Acceptable proof includes: previous U.S. passport; Naturalization Certificate; Certificate of Citizenship; current, valid driver's license; government ID (city, state, or federal); military ID (military and dependents); work ID (must be currently employed by the company); student ID (must be currently enrolled); Merchant Marines card (also known as a "Seamen's" or "Z" card); pilot or flight attendant ID. *Note:* Social Security cards are NOT acceptable as identification.

Travel Websites

Adventurous Traveler Bookstore:
www.adventuroustraveler.com
Amtrak: www.amtrak.com
Bureau of Consular Affairs: travel.state.gov
CIA World Factbook:
www.odci.gov/cia/publications/factbook
Exchange Rates: www.x-rates.com
Expedia Travel (Microsoft): www.expedia.com
Fodor's Travel Online: www.fodors.com
Frommer's: www.frommers.com
Greyhound: www.greyhound.com
Hostelling International: www.iyhf.org
Lonely Planet: www.lonelyplanet.com
National Park Service ParkNet: www.nps.gov
Preview Travel: www.previewtravel.com
Priceline: www.priceline.com
Rail Connection (Europe): www.railconnection.com
Travelocity: www.travelocity.com
Zagat (restaurants): www.zagat.com

• Two passport photographs. Photographs must be 2 × 2 inches in size. The image size from the bottom of the chin to the top of the head should be between 1 inch and 1⅜ inches. They may be in color or black and white. They must be full face, front view with a plain white or off-white background. Photographs should be taken in normal street attire, without a hat or headgear that obscures the hair or hairline.

• The applicable fee. A fee of $45 plus a $15 execution fee is charged for adults 16 years and older for a passport valid for ten years from the date of issue. The fee for children under 16 years of age is $25 for a five-year passport plus $15 for the execution of the application. Persons of all ages born outside the U.S. are required to pay an additional $100 complex case fee. The fee for passport renewals by mail is $40 (there is no execution fee added).

• DSP-64 Lost or Stolen Passport Form (if necessary). In addition to the items listed above, if your passport was lost or stolen, you will need to complete and submit this form (available at passport facilities and on the Web).

Passport renewals can be handled through the mail in some instances. You may apply by mail if: (1) you can submit your most recent passport and it is not mutilated, altered, or damaged; (2) you were at least 16 years old when your most recent passport was issued; (3) you were issued your most recent passport less than 15 years ago; and (4) you use the same name as on your most recent passport, OR, you have had your name changed by marriage or court order and can submit proper documentation to reflect your name changes.

In order to apply for a renewal by mail, you must fill out and submit Form DSP-82, which can be obtained at a passport facility or downloaded from the Web site. Attach to it the following: (1) your most recent passport; (2) two identical passport photographs; and (3) the $40 fee. If your name changed, enclose a certified copy of the Court Order, Adop-

tion Decree, Marriage Certificate, or Divorce Decree specifying another name for you to use. Mail the above items to: National Passport Center; P.O. Box 371971, Pittsburgh, PA 15250-7971.

Normal processing time for a passport application is 25 working days. However, it is recommended that you apply for your passport several months in advance of your planned departure. If you will need visas from foreign embassies, allow more time. If you need to leave in a hurry, you may expedite the process for an additional fee of $35 per passport. When requesting expedited service, two-way overnight mail for each application is strongly suggested. If you are applying by mail and wish to have your processing expedited, clearly mark the envelope EXPEDITED. You should receive your passport in 7–10 business days if using expedited service and two-way overnight delivery, depending upon the reliability of your overnight service.

If your passport is lost or stolen, report the loss on Form DSP-64 when you apply, in person, for your new passport. If you are abroad, report the loss immediately to local police authorities and the nearest U.S. embassy or consulate. Remember to write your current address in the space provided in your passport, so that, if it is found, it can be returned to you.

The State Dept. suggests you make two copies of the identification page—one to leave with a friend or relative at home in case of an emergency, and one to keep with you in the event that your passport is lost or stolen while abroad. This will make it easier to get a new passport, should it be necessary. It is also a good idea to carry two extra passport-size photos with you.

If you have questions or would like more information about obtaining or renewing a passport, visit the State Dept. website (http://travel.state.gov) or call the National Passport Information Center, 1-888-362-8668.

State Tourism Offices

The following is a selected list of state tourism office Web addresses and phone numbers. Where a toll-free 800 or 888 number is available, it is given. However, the numbers are subject to change.

Alabama
1-800-ALABAMA
www.touralabama.org

Alaska
907-465-2010
www.travelalaska.com

Arizona
1-888-520-3433
www.arizonaguide.com

Arkansas
1-800-NATURAL
www.arkansas.com

California
1-800-GOCALIF
www.gocalif.ca.gov

Colorado
1-800-COLORADO
www.colorado.com

Connecticut
1-800-CT-BOUND
www.ctbound.org

Delaware
1-866-2-VISITOR
www.state.de.us/tourism

District of Columbia (Washington, D.C.)
202-789-7000
www.washington.org

Florida
888-7FLA-USA
www.flausa.com

Georgia
1-800-VISIT-GA
www.georgia.com

Hawaii
1-800-GO-HAWAII
www.gohawaii.com

Idaho
1-800-635-7820
www.visitid.org

Illinois
1-800-2-CONNECT
www.enjoyillinois.com

Indiana
1-800-ENJOY-IN
www.enjoyindiana.com

Iowa
1-888-472-6035
www.traveliowa.com/

Kansas
1-800-2-KANSAS
www.travelks.com

Kentucky
1-800-225-TRIP
www.tourky.com

Louisiana
1-800-677-4082
www.louisianatravel.com

Maine
1-888-MAINE-45
www.visitmaine.com

Average Daily Temperatures (°F) in Tourist Cities

(For U.S. cities, *see* Climate of Selected U.S. Cities, pp. 606–607)

Location	January High	January Low	April High	April Low	July High	July Low	October High	October Low
Acapulco (Mexico)	87	72	87	73	89	77	89	77
Amsterdam (Netherlands)	41	34	53	40	69	55	57	46
Athens (Greece)	54	42	67	52	90	72	74	60
Auckland (New Zealand)	73	60	67	56	56	46	63	52
Bangkok (Thailand)	89	69	94	78	91	77	89	76
Beijing (China)	35	15	68	44	87	71	67	44
Belgrade (Yugoslavia)	38	28	62	43	81	60	64	46
Berlin (Germany)	35	26	55	38	74	55	55	41
Bombay (India)	83	67	89	76	85	77	89	76
Cairo (Egypt)	65	47	83	57	96	70	86	65
Calcutta (India)	80	55	97	75	89	79	89	74
Cape Town (South Africa)	69	56	66	54	60	50	65	53
Caracas (Venezuela)	75	56	81	60	78	61	79	61
Copenhagen (Denmark)	36	29	50	37	72	55	53	42
Dublin (Ireland)	47	35	54	38	67	51	57	43
Glasgow (Scotland)	43	34	53	38	66	52	54	43
Hamilton (Bermuda)	68	58	71	59	85	73	79	69
Helsinki (Finland)	27	17	43	31	71	57	45	37
Hong Kong (China)	67	51	79	67	90	78	84	70
Istanbul (Turkey)	48	36	59	45	78	64	66	53
Jerusalem (Israel)	55	41	73	50	87	63	81	59
Kingston (Jamaica)	86	67	87	70	90	73	88	73
Lagos (Nigeria)	88	74	89	77	82	74	85	74
Lisbon (Portugal)	56	46	64	52	79	63	69	57
London (United Kingdom)	44	35	56	40	73	55	58	44
Madrid (Spain)	50	34	63	43	89	61	67	48
Mexico City (Mexico)	66	42	77	51	73	53	70	50
Montreal (Canada)	22	6	51	33	79	60	56	39
Moscow (Russia)	21	9	47	31	76	55	46	34
Nairobi (Kenya)	77	53	75	57	69	51	77	54
Nassau (Bahamas)	77	65	81	69	88	75	85	73
Oslo (Norway)	30	20	50	34	73	56	49	37
Paris (France)	42	32	60	41	76	55	59	44
Prague (Czech Republic)	34	25	55	40	74	58	54	44
Quebec (Canada)	19	3	45	30	77	58	51	37
Rio de Janeiro (Brazil)	84	73	80	69	75	63	77	66
Rome (Italy)	54	39	68	46	88	64	73	53
San José (Costa Rica)	75	58	79	62	77	62	77	60
San Juan (Puerto Rico)	81	70	83	72	86	76	86	75
Seoul (Korea)	33	17	62	42	84	70	67	47
Singapore	86	73	89	75	87	75	88	74
Stockholm (Sweden)	31	23	45	32	70	55	48	39
Sydney (Australia)	79	65	73	57	62	44	72	55
Taipei (Taiwan)	66	54	77	63	92	76	81	67
Tokyo (Japan)	48	31	64	48	84	71	70	56
Toronto (Canada)	30	17	51	35	79	60	57	42
Vancouver (Canada)	42	32	55	41	71	55	57	44
Vienna (Austria)	34	26	57	41	75	59	55	44
Zurich (Switzerland)	36	26	60	41	77	56	57	43

New York
1-800-CALL-NYS
www.iloveny.state.ny.us

North Carolina
1-800-VISIT-NC
www.visitnc.com

North Dakota
1-800-HELLO-ND
www.ndtourism.com

Ohio
1-800-BUCKEYE
www.ohiotourism.com

Oklahoma
1-800-654-8240
www.touroklahoma.com

Oregon
1-800-547-7842
www.traveloregon.com

Pennsylvania
1-800-VISIT-PA
www.experiencepa.com

Rhode Island
1-800-556-2484
www.visitrhodeisland.com

South Carolina
803-734-1700
www.travelsc.com

South Dakota
1-800-S-DAKOTA
www.travelsd.com

Tennessee
1-800-836-6200
www.tourism.state.tn.us/

Texas
1-800-452-9292
www.state.tx.us/Travel

Utah
1-800-200-1160
www.state.ut.us/visiting/
travel.html

Vermont
1-800-VERMONT
www.1-800-vermont.com

Virginia
1-800-932-5827
www.virginia.org

Washington
360-586-2088
www.tourism.wa.gov

Washington, D.C.
See District of Columbia

West Virginia
1-800-CALL-WVA
www.state.wv.us/tourism

Wisconsin
1-800-432-TRIP
www.travelwisconsin.com

Wyoming
1-800-225-5996
www.wyomingtourism.org

The World's Top Tourism Destinations[1]
(international tourist arrivals)

1999 rank	Country	Arrivals (million) 1998	1999	% change 1998/1999	1999 market share	1999 rank	Country	Arrivals (million) 1998	1999	% change 1998/1999	1999 market share
1.	France	70.0	73.0	4.3%	11.0	9.	Russian Fed.	15.8	18.5	17.0%	2.8
2.	Spain	47.4	51.8	9.2	7.8	10.	Poland	18.8	18.0	−4.4	2.7
3.	United States	46.4	48.5	4.5	7.3	11.	Austria	17.4	17.5	0.7	2.6
4.	Italy	34.9	36.1	3.3	5.4	12.	Germany	16.5	17.1	3.7	2.6
5.	China	25.1	27.0	7.9	4.1	13.	Czech Rep.	16.3	16.0	−1.8	2.4
6.	United Kingdom	25.7	25.7	0.0	3.9	14.	Hungary	15.0	12.9	−13.8	1.9
7.	Canada	18.9	19.6	3.7	2.9	15.	Greece	10.9	12.0	9.9	1.8
8.	Mexico	19.8	19.2	−2.9	2.9						

1. Preliminary data as of Aug. 2000. *Source:* World Tourism Organization (WTO). Web: www.world-tourism.org.

Top International Destinations of American Tourists
(numbers in thousands)

1999 rank	Country[1]	1999 travelers	1999 rank	Country[1]	1999 travelers	1999 rank	Country[1]	1999 travelers
1.	Mexico	17,743	9.	Netherlands	1,032	16.	Belgium	492
2.	Canada	16,036	10.	Spain	909	17.	India	467
3.	United Kingdom	4,129	11.	Hong Kong	787	18.	Austria	442
4.	France	2,728	11.	Switzerland	787	18.	Ireland	442
5.	Germany	1,966	12.	South Korea	688	19.	Singapore	418
6.	Italy	1,893	13.	Taiwan	590	20.	Thailand	369
7.	Jamaica	1,499	13.	Australia	590	20.	New Zealand	369
8.	Japan	1,254	14.	China	565	20.	Greece	369
8.	Bahamas	1,254	15.	Brazil	541	20.	Bermuda	369

1. Ranked by 1999 visitation volume. *Source:* U.S. Dept. of Commerce, International Trade Administration. Web: www.tinet.ita.doc.gov/research/reports.

Top Nationalities of Travelers to the U.S.

2000 rank	Country of residence	2000 total	% of total travelers to U.S.	2000 rank	Country of residence	2000 total	% of total travelers to U.S.
1.	Canada	14,594,000	29%	9.	Italy	612,357	1%
2.	Mexico	10,322,000	20	10.	Venezuela	576,663	1
3.	Japan	5,061,377	10	11.	Netherlands	553,297	1
4.	United Kingdom	4,703,008	9	12.	Australia	539,559	1
5.	Germany	1,786,045	4	13.	Argentina	533,936	1
6.	France	1,087,087	2	14.	Taiwan	457,302	—
7.	Brazil	737,245	1	15.	Colombia	417,065	—
8.	South Korea	661,844	1				

NOTE: (—) = less than 1%. *Source:* U.S. Dept. of Commerce, International Trade Administration. Web: www.tinet.ita.doc.gov/research/reports.

Transportation

Consumer Complaints Against Top U.S. Airlines by Airline[1]

Rank	Airline	Complaints	System-wide enplanements	Complaints per 100,000 enplanements
1.	America West	1,499	19,972,168	7.51
2.	United	4,482	84,520,683	5.30
3.	American	3,055	86,312,806	3.54
4.	TWA	918	26,443,877	3.47
5.	Continental	1,291	45,409,245	2.84
6.	Northwest	1,538	58,822,847	2.61
7.	U.S. Airways	1,549	59,826,406	2.59
8.	Alaska	276	13,524,685	2.04
9.	Delta	2,125	105,564,802	2.01
10.	Southwest	339	72,710,320	0.47
	Total	**17,072**	**573,107,839**	**2.98**

NOTE: Data for Jan. 2000–Dec. 2000. 1. Includes U.S. airlines with at least 1% of total domestic scheduled-service passenger revenues. *Source:* Office of Aviation Enforcement and Proceedings, U.S. Dept. of Transportation, *Air Travel Consumer Report;* Web: www.dot.gov/airconsumer/index1.htm.

Consumer Complaints Against Top U.S. Airlines by Category

Complaint category	1990	1991	1992	1993	1994	1995	1996	1997	1998	1999	2000
TOTAL	7,703	6,106	5,639	4,438	5,179	4,629	5,782	6,394	7,994	17,381	20,564
Flight problems[1]	3,034	1,877	1,624	1,211	1,586	1,133	1,628	1,699	2,277	6,469	8,698
Customer service[2]	758	714	695	599	805	667	999	1,418	1,715	3,664	4,074
Baggage	1,329	883	752	627	761	628	882	826	1,108	2,353	2,753
Reservations/ticketing/ boarding[3]	624	659	680	577	598	666	857	904	1,137	1,328	1,405
Refunds	701	783	721	482	393	576	521	531	602	940	803
Oversales[4]	399	301	265	257	301	263	353	414	388	673	759
Fares[5]	312	388	573	398	267	185	180	195	277	584	708
Disability[3]	n.a.	n.a.	n.a.	n.a.	n.a.	n.a.	n.a.	n.a.	n.a.	526	612
Advertising	96	96	54	51	94	66	61	57	40	57	42
Tours	29	23	12	16	127	18	16	13	23	28	25
Smoking[6]	74	30	25	30	20	15	13	5	4	n.a.	n.a.
Credit[6]	5	10	10	4	2	4	3	1	1	n.a.	n.a.
Other[6]	342	342	228	186	225	408	269	331	422	759	675
Animals[7]	n.a.	n.a.	n.a.	n.a.	n.a.	n.a.	n.a.	n.a.	n.a.	0	1

1. Cancellations, delays, and other deviations from schedule. 2. Rude or unhelpful employees, inadequate meals or cabin service, treatment of delayed passengers. 3. Effective with the Sept. 1999 report, "disability" complaints are listed as a separate category. Previously, disability complaints were included in the "Reservations/ticketing/boarding" category. 4. All bumping problems, whether or not airline complied with DOT regulations. 5. Incorrect or incomplete information about fares, discount fare conditions and availability, overcharges, fare increases, and level of fares in general. 6. Complaints about "smoking" and "credit," which were formerly separate categories, are now included in the "other" category. 7. Effective with the Oct. 2000 report, "Animals" was added as a new category. *Source:* Office of Aviation Enforcement and Proceedings, U.S. Dept. of Transportation, *Air Travel Consumer Report;* Web: www.dot.gov/airconsumer/index1.htm.

Passengers Denied Boarding by Top U.S. Airlines,[1] 2000

Rank Airline		Denied boardings (DBs)		Enplaned passengers	Involuntary DBs per 10,000 passengers
		Voluntary	Involuntary		
1.	TWA	65,061	6,385	25,138,095	2.54
2.	Southwest	90,352	13,741	72,568,399	1.89
3.	Continental	66,391	7,259	40,270,205	1.80
4.	United	119,306	11,101	77,624,771	1.43
5.	Alaska	33,113	1,910	13,512,111	1.41
6.	America West	57,935	2,274	20,229,421	1.12
7.	U.S. Airways	94,259	3,740	57,481,514	0.65
8.	Northwest	108,501	3,011	53,112,324	0.57
9.	American	210,427	3,274	78,229,763	0.42
10.	Delta	212,050	3,327	102,031,565	0.33
	Total	**1,057,395**	**56,022**	**540,198,168**	**1.04**

NOTE: Data for Jan. 2000–Sept. 2000. 1. Includes U.S. airlines with at least 1% of total domestic scheduled-service passenger revenues. *Source:* Office of Aviation Enforcement and Proceedings, U.S. Dept. of Transportation, *Air Travel Consumer Report;* Web: www.dot.gov/airconsumer/index1.htm.

World's 25 Busiest Airports by Passengers and Cargo, 2000

Airport	Total passengers[1]	1999–2000 percent change	Airport	Total cargo[1]	1999–2000 percent change
1. Atlanta, Hartsfield (ATL)	80,171,036	2.8%	Memphis (MEM)	2,489,070	3.2%
2. Chicago, O'Hare (ORD)	72,135,887	−0.7	Hong Kong (HKG)	2,267,175	13.3
3. Los Angeles (LAX)	68,477,689	5.1	Los Angeles (LAX)	2,054,212	5.9
4. London, Heathrow (LHR)	64,607,185	3.8	Tokyo, Narita (NRT)	1,932,694	4.9
5. Dallas/Ft. Worth (DFW)	60,687,122	1.1	Anchorage (ANC)[2]	1,883,825	10.0
6. Tokyo, Haneda (HND)	56,402,206	3.8	Seoul (SEL)	1,874,228	13.2
7. Frankfurt-Main (FRA)	49,360,620	7.6	New York (JFK)	1,825,906	5.7
8. Paris, Charles de Gaulle (CDG)	48,240,137	11.6	Frankfurt-Main (FRA)	1,710,144	11.1
9. San Francisco (SFO)	41,173,983	2.1	Singapore (SIN)	1,705,410	12.0
10. Amsterdam, Schiphol (AMS)	39,604,589	7.7	Miami (MIA)	1,642,484	−0.5
11. Denver (DEN)	38,748,781	1.9	Louisville (SDF)	1,519,558	5.5
12. Las Vegas (LAS)	36,856,186	9.5	Chicago, O'Hare (ORD)	1,463,941	−4.6
13. Seoul (SEL)	36,727,124	10.1	London, Heathrow (LHR)	1,402,088	3.4
14. Minneapolis/St. Paul (MSP)	36,688,159	5.3	Paris, Charles de Gaulle (CDG)	1,380,068	14.5
15. Phoenix, Sky Harbor (PHX)	35,889,933	7.0	Amsterdam, Schiphol (AMS)	1,267,386	3.4
16. Detroit (DTW)	35,535,080	4.6	Taipei (TPE)	1,208,838	14.0
17. Houston (IAH)	35,246,176	6.5	Indianapolis (IND)	1,173,967	12.4
18. Newark (EWR)	34,194,788	1.7	Newark (EWR)	1,082,668	−1.0
19. Miami (MIA)	33,569,625	−1.0	Osaka (KIX)	1,000,693	15.8
20. New York (JFK)	32,779,428	3.5	Dallas/Ft. Worth (DFW)	904,994	9.0
21. Madrid (MAD)	32,765,820	18.2	Atlanta, Hartsfield (ATL)	871,602	−1.3
22. Hong Kong (HKG)	32,746,737	10.2	Bangkok (BKK)	871,000	7.6
23. London, Gatwick (LGW)	32,056,942	4.9	San Francisco (SFO)	870,113	3.3
24. Orlando (MCO)	30,822,580	5.6	Dayton (DAY)	832,205	−7.0
25. St. Louis (STL)	30,546,698	1.2	Tokyo, Haneda (HND)	769,733	6.3

NOTES: Total passengers enplaned and deplaned, passengers in transit counted once. Total cargo loaded and unloaded, freight and mail (in metric tons). 1. Results are preliminary. 2. Includes transit freight. *Source:* Airports Council International World Headquarters, Geneva, Switzerland; Web: www.airports.org.

Getting to Work in the City
Commuting characteristics for the 15 largest U.S. cities by population, 1990

1990 rank	City of residence	Total workers 16 years and over	Means of transportation (%)				Average travel time to work (min.)
			Drove alone	Carpool	Public transit	Other means[1]	
1.	New York, N.Y.	3,183,088	24.0%	8.5%	53.4%	14.0%	36.5
2.	Los Angeles, Calif.	1,629,096	65.2	15.4	10.5	8.9	26.5
3.	Chicago, Ill.	1,181,677	46.3	14.8	29.7	9.2	31.5
4.	Houston, Tex.	772,957	71.7	15.5	6.5	6.3	24.7
5.	Philadelphia, Pa.	640,577	44.7	13.2	28.7	13.5	27.4
6.	San Diego, Calif.	560,913	70.7	12.8	4.2	12.2	20.4
7.	Detroit, Mich.	325,054	67.8	16.1	10.7	5.3	24.7
8.	Dallas, Tex.	500,566	72.5	15.2	6.7	5.7	24.0
9.	Phoenix, Ariz.	473,966	73.7	15.1	3.3	7.9	23.0
10.	San Antonio, Tex.	395,551	73.4	15.5	4.9	6.2	21.7
11.	San Jose, Calif.	400,932	76.9	14.6	3.5	5.1	25.5
12.	Indianapolis, Ind.	362,777	78.0	13.4	3.3	5.2	20.8
13.	Baltimore, Md.	307,679	50.9	16.8	22.0	10.2	26.0
14.	San Francisco, Calif.	382,309	38.5	11.5	33.5	16.5	26.9
15.	Jacksonville, Fla.	312,958	75.5	14.2	2.7	7.6	21.6
	Total for U.S.	115,070,274	73.2%	13.4%	5.3%	0.7%	n.a.

NOTES: n.a. = not available. 1. Percentages may not add up to 100%, due to rounding. 1. Includes commuting by motorcycle, bicycle, walking, and all other means. Also includes those who worked at home. *Source:* U.S. Bureau of the Census; Web: www.census.gov/population/socdemo/journey/city.txt.

World's Largest Subway Systems
(by 1997 usage)

City	Date system completed	Number of riders in 1997 (in millions)	Length (km)	City	Date system completed	Number of riders in 1997 (in millions)	Length (km)
Moscow	1935	3,160	200+	Paris	1900	1,120	200.9
Tokyo	1927	2,740	169.3	Osaka	1933	1,000	99.1
Mexico City	n.a.	1,420	178.0	Hong Kong	n.a.	779	28.2
Seoul	n.a.	1,390	n.a.	London	1863	770	391.0
New York City	1904	1,130	320.0	São Paulo	n.a.	701	n.a.

NOTE: n.a. = not available.

Eisenhower and the U.S. Interstate System

What could be more emblematic of America than the open road? From Jack Kerouac to *Thelma and Louise,* an unbroken expanse of land with a solitary road calls forth images of romantic waywardness and infinite grandeur.

Yet at the beginning of the 20th century, a national, uninterrupted system of highways was merely a dream. A National Road was built in 1815 that ran between Maryland and St. Louis and facilitated immigration to the central United States. This road, however, fell into disrepair. It wasn't until the late 1930s that Dwight D. Eisenhower advocated for the transcontinental system of highways that now links Portland to Pensacola and all the cities and rural towns in between.

Two-Month Cross-Country Trip

In 1919 Eisenhower was a young army colonel. As part of a program to encourage the national government to invest in a national interstate system for defense purposes, he traveled from Washington, DC, to San Francisco. Like most Americans, he traveled on dirt roads and crumbling bridges. It took him about two months to cross the country.

The Federal-Aid Highway Act of 1938 was the first serious attempt to develop a national roadway system. Under the auspices of the Bureau of Public Roads, the goal of this act was to study the feasibility of a toll-financed system of three east-west and three north-south superhighways. From this study officials determined that this system could not be self-supporting. They advocated for a 26,700-mile network instead.

Interstate System Takes Shape

Congress passed further legislation in the form of the Federal-Aid Highway Act of 1944. The act chartered a national system of interstate highways and expanded the network to 40,000 mi. Soon state highway agencies and the Department of Defense planned nationwide routes. However, because no specific funds were authorized for construction, progress was slow.

In 1952, President Eisenhower authorized the first funding of the interstate system. The Federal-Aid Highway Act of 1952 provided a token amount of $25 million a year for two years, and then an additional $175 million after. Four years later, the expanded Federal-Aid Highway Act of 1956 provided:
- an extended length of 41,000 mi
- nationwide design standards
- a new system of apportioning funds among the states
- the official name, "National System of Interstate and Defense Highways"
- the federal government's share of costs at 90%

A Standard Design

The legislation of 1956 called for national design standards. All interstates were to feature:
- design speeds of 50–70 mph
- a minimum of two lanes in each direction
- lanes that were 12 ft in width
- 10-foot right paved shoulder
- 4-foot left paved shoulder

Further legislation continued to expand the total length of the system. In 1968, Congress authorized a length of 42,500 mi; in 1973, another 500 mi; and in 1978, full funding for the construction of routes designated by previous system adjustments.

Naming the Interstates

The procedure for naming the highways is systematic. Major routes are designated by single- or two-digit numbers. If a route runs north-south, it is given an odd number, and if a route runs east-west, an even number. For north-south routes, numbering conventions begin in the western part of the country. Thus I-5 runs north and south along the West Coast, while I-95 runs north and south along the East Coast. For east-west routes, numbers begin in the southern part of the country.

Major routes usually traverse cities and are the shortest and most direct line of travel. Connecting interstate routes that ordinarily travel around a city carry three-digit numbers.

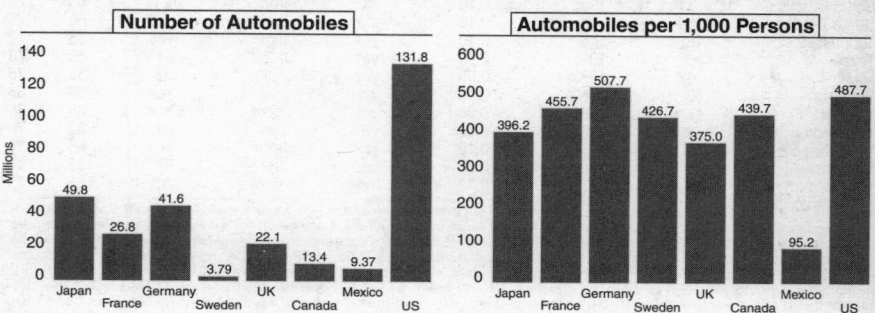

Automobile Registrations for Selected Countries, 1998

Number of Automobiles (Millions)

Japan	France	Germany	Sweden	UK	Canada	Mexico	US
49.8	26.8	41.6	3.79	22.1	13.4	9.37	131.8

Automobiles per 1,000 Persons

Japan	France	Germany	Sweden	UK	Canada	Mexico	US
396.2	455.7	507.7	426.7	375.0	439.7	95.2	487.7

Source: Office of Highway Policy Information, Federal Highway Administration, *Highway Statistics 1999*; Web: www.fhwa.dot.gov.

Driving Laws, 2001

Currently all states plus D.C. have child safety seat laws and enforce a drinking age of 21. A national speed limit of 55 mph was imposed in 1974, and in 1987 it was modified to allow 65-mile-per-hour speeds on some rural freeways. The federal law was entirely repealed in 1995, giving states the right to set their own limits. Montana, which had been the only state with no speed limit, imposed a 75-mile-an-hour limit in 1999. As of Jan. 2000, graduated licensing laws were in effect in 40 states, 30 of which prohibit young drivers from driving during high-risk nighttime and early morning hours.

State	Age for driver's license[1]	License revocation for alcohol offenses since	Blood alcohol concentration limit[2]	Alcohol ignition interlock device[3]	Mandatory belt-use law seating positions	Motorcycle helmet law[4]	Maximum allowable speed limit 1995[5]	1999
Alabama	17	1996	0.08	no	front	yes	65	70
Alaska	16	1983	0.10	yes	all	18[6]	—	65
Arizona	18	1992	0.10	yes	front	18	55	75
Arkansas	16	1995	0.10	yes	front	21	65	70
California	17	1989	0.08	yes	all	yes	55	70
Colorado	17	1983	0.10	yes	front	no	65	75
Connecticut	16 + 6 mo.	1990	0.10	no	front[7]	18	55	65
Delaware	16 + 10 mo.	yes	0.10	yes	front	19[8]	—	65
D.C.	18	yes	0.08	no	all	yes	—	—
Florida	18	1990	0.08	yes	front	yes	65	70
Georgia	18	1995	0.10	yes	front[7]	yes	55	70
Hawaii	15 + 3 mo.	1990	0.08	no	front	18	—	55
Idaho	16	1994	0.08	yes	front	18	65	75
Illinois	17	1986	0.08	yes	front	no	65	65
Indiana	18	yes	0.10	yes	front	18	65	65
Iowa	17	1982	0.10	yes	front	no	55	65
Kansas	16	1988	0.08	yes	front	18	65	70
Kentucky	18	no	0.10	no	all	21[9,10,11]	65	65
Louisiana	17	1984	0.10	yes	front[7]	18[9]	65	70
Maine	16	1984	0.08	yes	all	15	65	65
Maryland	18	1989	0.10	yes	front[7]	yes	55	65
Massachusetts	18	1994	0.08	no	all	yes	55	65
Michigan	17	no	0.10	yes	front[7]	yes	55	70
Minnesota	16	1976	0.10	no	front[7]	18	65	70
Mississippi	16	1983	0.10	yes	front	yes	65	70
Missouri	18	1987	0.10	yes	front[7]	yes	70	70
Montana	15	no	0.10	yes	all	18	65	75
Nebraska	18	1993	0.10	yes	front[7]	yes	65	75
Nevada	16	1983	0.10	yes	all	yes	55	75
New Hampshire	18	1994	0.08	no	—	18	65	65
New Jersey	18	no	0.10	yes	front	yes	—	65
New Mexico	16 + 6 mo.	1984	0.08	yes	front	18	65	75
New York	17	1994	0.10	yes	front[7]	yes	55	65
North Carolina	16 + 6 mo.	1983	0.08	yes	front[7]	yes	55	70
North Dakota	18	1983	0.10	yes	front	18	65	70
Ohio	17	1993	0.10	yes	front	18[11]	65	65
Oklahoma	16	1983	0.10	yes	front	18	65	75
Oregon	18	1983	0.08	yes	all	yes	65	65
Pennsylvania	18	no	0.10	no	front	yes	55	65
Rhode Island	17 + 6 mo.	no	0.10	yes	all	21[6,11]	55	65
South Carolina	16 + 3 mo.	1998	0.10	no	front[7]	21	65	70
South Dakota	16	no	0.10	no	front	18	65	75
Tennessee	16	no	0.10	yes	front[7]	yes	65	70
Texas	16	1995	0.08	yes	front[7]	21[9]	55	70
Utah	16	1983	0.08	yes	all	18	65	75
Vermont	18	1969	0.08	no	all	yes	65	65
Virginia	17	1995	0.08	yes	front	yes	65	65
Washington	18	1998	0.08	yes	all	yes	55	70
West Virginia	17	1981	0.10	yes	front[7]	yes	65	70
Wisconsin	19	1988	0.10[12]	yes	front	18[10]	65	65
Wyoming	16	1973	0.10	no	front	18	65	75

NOTES: A driver's license is required in every state. 1. Refers to minimum age for unrestricted driver's license. 2. Blood alcohol concentration that constitutes the threshold of legal intoxication. 3. Legislation for instruments designed to prevent drivers from starting their cars when breath alcohol content is at or above a set point. 4. Presence of law, or age below which riders are required to wear helmet. 5. In 1995, Congress repealed the national 55-miles-per-hour speed limit. 6. All passengers required to wear helmet. 7. Required for certain ages at all seating positions. 8. Helmet must also be carried on the motorcycle, whether or not it is worn, for persons 19 and older. 9. Helmet optional for those over listed age if they have proper insurance. 10. Helmets must be worn by cyclists holding learners' permits. 11. First-year novices required to wear helmet. 12. 0.08 after second DUI conviction. *Sources:* National Safety Council, *Injury Facts, 2000 Edition;* Web: www.nsc.org. U.S. Dept. of Transportation, National Highway Traffic Safety Administration, *Traffic Safety Facts, 1999;* Web: www.nhtsa.dot.gov. Insurance Institute for Highway Safety; Web: www.hwysafety.org.

Traffic Congestion in U.S. Cities, 1999

Urban area	Travel Rate Index[1] TRI	Rank	Annual delay per eligible driver Hours	Rank	Annual congestion cost Total	Rank	Per eligible driver	Rank
Los Angeles, Calif.	1.55	1	56	1	12,570	1	1,000	1
San Francisco-Oakland, Calif.	1.45	2	42	10	3,055	4	760	8
Seattle-Everett, Wash.	1.44	3	53	2	1,860	12	930	2
Washington, D.C.-Md.-Va.	1.42	4	46	5	2,730	6	780	6
Chicago, Ill.-Northwestern Ind.	1.40	5	34	23	4,605	3	570	28
San Diego, Calif.	1.40	5	37	19	1,820	13	675	18
Boston, Mass.	1.37	7	42	10	2,155	9	715	12
Portland-Vancouver, Ore.-Wash.	1.36	8	34	23	910	22	610	22
Atlanta, Ga.	1.35	9	53	2	2,620	8	915	3
Las Vegas, Nev.	1.35	9	21	45	465	37	370	45
Denver, Colo.	1.34	11	45	7	1,415	17	760	8
Houston, Tex.	1.33	12	50	4	2,665	7	850	4
New York, N.Y.-Northeastern N.J.	1.32	13	34	23	9,745	2	595	24
Miami-Hialeah, Fla.	1.32	13	42	10	1,485	16	705	14
Detroit, Mich.	1.31	15	41	16	2,810	5	700	16
Minneapolis-St. Paul, Minn.	1.31	15	38	17	1,565	14	670	19
San Jose, Calif.	1.31	15	42	10	1,250	19	750	10
Sacramento, Calif.	1.31	15	34	23	830	23	605	23
San Bernardino-Riverside, Calif.	1.31	15	38	17	965	21	685	17
Phoenix, Ariz.	1.30	20	31	31	1,385	18	540	31

NOTE: Study conducted in 68 urbanized areas. 1. The Travel Rate Index is defined as the travel rate (in minutes per mile) during the peak period divided by the rate in the off-peak. A TRI of 1.30 indicates the average peak trip takes 30% longer than in uncongested conditions—a 20-minute trip becomes a 26-minute trip. *Source:* Texas Transportation Institute, the Texas A&M University System. *The 2001 Urban Mobility Report,* David Schrank and Tim Lomax; Web: http://mobility.tamu.edu.

Improper Driving as a Factor in Accidents

Kind of improper driving	Fatal accidents 1999	1998	1995	Injury accidents 1999	1998	1995	All accidents 1999	1998	1995
Improper driving	**72.6%**	**60.0%**	**68.1%**	**67.2%**	**62.3%**	**73.5%**	**62.2%**	**61.5%**	**75.5%**
Speed too fast or unsafe	23.0	16.8	19.8	13.0	12.8	13.9	10.6	13.3	14.0
Right of way	20.1	16.0	15.2	25.8	21.9	25.5	22.9	18.4	22.9
Failed to yield	10.8	11.1	10.2	19.2	15.9	18.1	13.8	13.8	17.0
Disregarded signal	4.7	2.3	3.0	4.9	1.8	5.0	5.9	1.5	4.0
Passed stop sign	4.6	2.6	2.2	1.7	4.2	2.4	3.2	3.1	1.9
Drove left of center	9.6	7.3	9.1	1.7	1.7	2.4	1.3	1.6	2.2
Made improper turn	1.2	4.1	2.3	2.4	4.0	2.8	3.0	5.0	4.2
Improper overtaking	1.1	1.2	1.5	0.9	0.6	1.3	1.2	1.0	1.5
Followed too closely	0.5	0.5	0.5	3.4	4.3	7.0	6.3	5.4	7.2
Other improper driving	17.1	14.1	19.7	20.3	17.0	20.7	16.9	16.8	23.6
No improper driving stated	27.4	40.0	31.9	32.8	37.7	26.5	37.8	38.5	24.5
Total	**100.0%**	**100.0%**	**100.0%**	**100.0%**	**100.0%**	**100.0%**	**100.0%**	**100.0%**	**100.0%**

NOTE: Based on reports from 12 state traffic authorities. *Source:* National Safety Council, *Injury Facts, 2000 Edition;* Web: www.nsc.org.

Alcohol-Related Traffic Fatalities on Holidays, 1999

Holiday 1999	Total traffic fatalities	Total fatalities alcohol-related	Percent fatalities alcohol-related	Time period monitored
New Year's Eve	117	43	36.5%	12/31/98
New Year's Day	149	98	65.7	1/1/99
St. Patrick's Day	128	58	44.9	6 p.m. 3/17/99–5:59 a.m. 3/18/99
Memorial Day weekend	500	249	49.8	6 p.m. 5/28/99–5:59 a.m. 6/1/99
Fourth of July weekend	510	227	44.6	6 p.m. 7/2/99–5:59 a.m. 7/6/99
Labor Day weekend	484	229	47.2	6 p.m. 9/3/99–5:59 a.m. 9/7/99
Halloween	279	112	40.1	6 p.m. 10/31/99–5:59 a.m. 11/1/99
Thanksgiving weekend	578	252	43.6	6 p.m. 11/24/99–5:59 a.m. 11/29/99
Thanksgiving—New Year's	4,444	1,610	36.0	11/24/99–12/31/99
Christmas weekend	479	221	46.1	6 p.m. 12/23/99–5:59 a.m. 12/27/99
New Year's Eve (2000)	147	75	51.2	12/31/99

Source: Mothers Against Drunk Driving (MADD).

Fatalities by Transportation Mode, 1970–1999

Mode	1970	1980	1990	1998	1999[1]	Mode	1970	1980	1990	1998	1999[1]
Passenger car	n.a.	n.a.	n.a.	21,194	20,818	Railroad[2]	785	584	599	577	530
Light truck	n.a.	n.a.	n.a.	10,705	11,243	Heavy rail transit[3]	n.a.	n.a.	339	54	84
Motorcycle	n.a.	n.a.	n.a.	2,294	2,472	Bus[4]	n.a.	n.a.	n.a.	38	58
Large truck	n.a.	n.a.	n.a.	742	758	Waterborne					
Large air carrier	146	1	39	1	12	Vessel casualties	178	206	85	59	44
Commuter air	n.a.	37	7	0	12	Nonvessel	420	281	101	76	67
On-demand air taxi	n.a.	105	50	45	38	casualties					
General aviation	1,310	1,239	765	623	628	Recreational boating	1,418	1,360	865	815	734

NOTES: n.a. = not available. 1. Preliminary data. 2 Includes fatalities from nontrain incidents, as well as train incidents and accidents. Also includes train occupants and nonoccupants, except motor vehicle occupants at grade crossings. 3. Subway. 4. School, intercity, and transit. *Source:* U.S. Dept. of Transportation, Bureau of Transportation Statistics, *National Transportation Statistics, 2000.*

Most Popular Car Colors, 1998–2000

(percentage of vehicles manufactured during 2000 model year in North America)

Luxury (1999 rank)	2000	1999	1998	Sport compact (1999 rank)	2000	1999	1998
1. White Met. (1)	19.8%	15.8%	12.3%	1. Silver (1)	22.3%	16.2%	10.4%
2. Silver (2)	17.2	14.8	9.2	2. Black (2)	14.4	14.7	15.0
3. Black (5)	10.8	9.4	12.3	3. White (3)	11.4	14.0	14.7
4. Lt. Brown (3)	8.6	12.9	17.7	4. Lt. Brown (3)	9.9	8.5	7.0
5. White (4)	7.1	10.3	11.3	5. Med./Dk. Green (4)	9.7	12.4	15.9
6. Med./Dk. Blue (10)	7.1	4.9	4.8	6. Med. Red (8)	8.3	7.0	6.4
7. Med. Gray (6)	6.6	8.3	5.3	7. Bright Red (7)	7.5	7.5	9.5
8. Med. Red (8)	6.1	6.0	7.5	8. Med./Dk. Blue (5)	5.0	8.5	5.3
9. Gold (7)	5.3	7.0	4.8	9. Teal (n.a.)	2.6	n.a.	n.a.
10. Med./Dk. Green (9)	4.3	6.1	10.0	10. Bright Blue (n.a.)	2.1	n.a.	n.a.

Full/Intermediate (1999 rank)	2000	1999	1998	SUV/Truck/Van (1999 rank)	2000	1999	1998
1. Silver (2)	21.5%	14.1%	11.0%	1. White (1)	23.1%	26.2%	22.5%
2. White (1)	13.0	15.4	15.6	2. Silver (5)	14.1	7.7	6.2
3. Black (5)	11.5	11.7	8.9	3. Med./Dk. Blue (4)	11.1	8.4	4.7
4. Med./Dk. Green (4)	10.7	13.9	16.4	4. Black (2)	10.6	11.2	15.5
5. Lt. Brown (3)	8.5	14.0	14.1	5. Med./Dk. Green (3)	8.3	11.0	7.2
6. Med./Dk. Blue (6)	7.0	6.4	6.0	6. Med. Red (6)	6.2	7.4	7.2
7. Med. Red (7)	6.9	5.7	6.5	7. Bright Red (8)	5.4	6.1	7.1
8. Med. Gray (9)	4.3	4.3	n.a.	8. Gold (n.a.)	4.1	n.a.	n.a.
9. Bright Red (8)	3.8	4.9	n.a.	9. Med. Gray (n.a.)	3.9	n.a.	n.a.
10. Gold (10)	3.5	1.8	n.a.	10. Dk. Red (10)	3.2	3.1	4.5

Source: DuPont Herberts Automotive Systems, Troy, Mich. 2000 DuPont Automotive Color Popularity Survey Results. Web: www.dupont.com.

Two Centuries of Railroading

Source: Association of American Railroads. Web: www.aar.org.

1797 The steam locomotive is invented in England.

1823 The first public railway in the world opens in England.

1827 The first railroad in North America—the Baltimore & Ohio—is chartered by Baltimore merchants.

1830 The first regularly scheduled steam-powered rail passenger service in the U.S. begins operation in South Carolina, utilizing the U.S.-built locomotive *The Best Friend of Charleston.*

1833 Andrew Jackson travels from Baltimore to Ellicott's Mills, becoming the first sitting U.S. president to ride the rails.

1838 Five of the six New England states have rail service, as do such frontier states as Kentucky and Indiana.

1840 More than 2,800 miles of track are in operation.

1850 More than 9,000 miles of track are in operation in the U.S., as much as in the rest of the world combined.

1860 More than 30,000 miles of track are in operation in the U.S.

1862 President Abraham Lincoln signs the Pacific Railroad Act for the construction of the transcontinental railroad that will ultimately link California with the rest of the nation.

1865 The "golden age" of railroads begins. For nearly half a century, no other mode of transportation challenges railroads. During these years, the rail network grows from 35,000 to a peak of 254,000 miles in 1916.

1869 On May 10, at Promontory, in the Utah Territory, the "Golden Spike" joins the Union Pacific and Central Pacific railroads, marking completion of the first transcontinental railroad.

1917 The federal government seizes control of the railroads for the duration of World War I.

1900–1940 By the eve of World War II, automobiles, large buses, trucks, planes, and pipelines—supported by government subsidies and less burdened by regulation than railroads—have become full-fledged competitors to railroads.

1945–1970 Railroads enter the postwar era with a new sense of optimism that leads them to invest billions of dollars in new locomotives, freight equipment, and passenger trains. That investment would see retirement of the last steam locomotive by the late 1950s in favor of diesel engines. In spite of this modernization, the decline in rail market share that began before the war resumes.

1970–1975   Burdened by regulation and faced with subsidized competition, nine Class I railroads, representing almost one-quarter of the industry's trackage, file for bankruptcy protection.

1970   The Rail Passenger Service Act creates Amtrak to take over intercity rail passenger service.

1971   Amtrak officially begins service on May 1.

1980   The Staggers Rail Act reduces the Interstate Commerce Commission's regulatory jurisdiction over railroads and sparks competition that stimulates advances in technology and a restructuring of the industry.

1987   Conrail is privatized in what—at that time—was the largest share offering in U.S. history as investors pay $1.9 billion to buy shares in the railroad.

1998   U.S. freight railroads move 1.38 trillion ton-miles of freight, more than ever before, setting new safety records in the process.

Railroad Ridership, 1988–2000

(millions)

	1988	1989	1990	1991	1992	1993	1994	1995	1996	1997	1998	1999	2000
Amtrak system	21.5	21.4	22.2	22.0	21.3	22.1	21.2	20.7	19.7	20.2	21.1	21.5	22.5
Northeast Corridor	11.2	11.1	11.2	10.9	10.1	10.3	11.7	11.6	11.0	11.1	11.9	12.3	12.9
Intercity + West	10.3	10.3	11.0	11.1	11.2	11.8	9.4	9.1	8.7	9.1	9.2	9.2	9.6
Commuter trains[1]	15.4	17.4	18.0	18.1	20.3	32.9	39.5	42.2	45.9	48.5	54.0	58.3	61.6
Total	**36.9**	**38.8**	**40.2**	**40.1**	**41.6**	**55.0**	**60.7**	**62.9**	**65.6**	**68.7**	**75.1**	**79.8**	**84.1**

1. Includes only commuter trains run by Amtrak under contract. *Source:* National Assoc. of Railroad Passengers. Based on Amtrak annual reports. Web: www.narprail.org.

Ten Famous Trains

Trans-Siberian Express

Traveling between Moscow and Vladivostok, the *Trans-Siberian Express* makes the longest regular train trip in the world, covering 5,778 mi and making 91 stops over the course of nine days. During the Cold War, Westerners could travel only in compartments, where they were subject to Stalinist propaganda played on loudspeakers.

Blue Train

The *Blue Train* has run between Cape Town and Pretoria, South Africa, since 1939 and derives its name from its blue locomotives, railroad cars, and leather seats. It is still considered one of the most luxurious trains running, having been upgraded in 1997 to include televisions and phones in all of its suites.

Indian Pacific

Connecting the east and west coasts of Australia, the *Indian Pacific* runs from Sydney to Perth in three days, over a distance of 2,461 mi. This route has the world's longest stretch of straight track, which lasts for 297 mi.

Super Chief

Originally operated by the Santa Fe Railroad beginning in 1936, the *Super Chief* ran from Chicago to Los Angeles. It was considered one of the best long-distance trains in the U.S. and was renowned for its gourmet food and Hollywood clientele. Amtrak currently operates a version of this train.

TGV

The French *TGV* (train à grande vitesse, or high speed train) is an electric train that runs between Paris and Lyon, regularly traveling at an average speed of 132 mph, with top speeds as high as 186 mph. A modified *TGV* set a world speed record in 1990 when it hit 320 mph in trial runs.

Orient Express

In 1883 the *Orient Express* began service from Paris to Istanbul, crossing six countries. The train was famous for its five-course French meals and for its passengers, who were often diplomats, royalty, or government couriers.

20th Century Limited

The *20th Century Limited* debuted in 1902 as the New York Central's luxury train, operating between New York and Chicago. It traveled the smooth "water level route" alongside the Hudson River and the shores of Lake Erie. The railroad would roll out a crimson carpet to welcome passengers to the train, giving rise to the phrase the "red carpet treatment."

The Flying Scotsman

Running between King's Cross station in London and Edinburgh, Scotland, the *Flying Scotsman* was a luxury express train full of amenities. It featured a hairdressing salon, a Louis the XVI–style restaurant and bar, and, for a short time, a cinema coach.

Peruvian Central Railway

The highest railway in the world, the Peruvian Central Railway is an engineering marvel, climbing 13,000 ft on its trip from La Oroya to Lima, Peru. The railroad, which features 66 tunnels and 59 bridges, zigzags across valleys in order to minimize the steepness of its climb. There is an onboard doctor who administers oxygen to passengers who get altitude sickness.

Bullet Train

The Japanese *Shinkansen*, or *Bullet Train*, runs at speeds of more than 100 mph over special tracks with minimal curves. In 1997, a newer version of the *Bullet Train* became the fastest scheduled train in the world, regularly reaching speeds of up to 186 mph.

Many public figures not listed here may be found elsewhere in the almanac.

U.S. Presidents
U.S. Vice Presidents
Families of U.S. Presidents
U.S. Governors
U.S. Congress
U.S. Supreme Court Justices
U.S. Government Officials

British Prime Ministers
Rulers of England
Rulers of France
Rulers of Judah and Israel
Rulers of Prussia
Rulers of Russia
Sports Personalities

Names in parentheses indicate a person's original name or nickname. Locations in parentheses are the present-day name of the birthplace. Dates of birth appear as month/day/year. **Boldface** years in parentheses are dates of **(birth–death).**

Information has been gathered from many sources, including the individuals themselves. However, the almanac cannot guarantee the accuracy of every item.

A

Aalto, Alvar (architect); Kuortane, Finland **(1898–1976)**
Abbado, Claudio (orchestra conductor); Milan, Italy, 6/26/33
Abbott, Bud (William Abbott) (comedian); Asbury Park, N.J. **(1898–1974)**
Abbott, George (stage producer); Forestville, N.Y. **(1887–1995)**
Abelard, Peter (theologian); nr. Nantes, France **(1079–1142)**
Abernathy, Ralph (civil rights leader); Linden, Ala. **(1926–1990)**
Abraham, F(ahrid) Murray (actor); Pittsburgh, 10/24/39
Achebe, Chinua (writer); Ogidi, Nigeria, 11/16/30
Acheson, Dean (statesman); Middletown, Conn. **(1893–1971)**
Acuff, Roy Claxton (musician); nr. Maynardsville, Tenn. **(1903–1992)**
Adams, Abigail (First Lady, writer); Weymouth, Mass. **(1744–1818)**
Adams, Bryan (singer, songwriter); Kingston, Ont., Canada, 11/5/59
Adams, Charles Francis (diplomat); Boston **(1807–1886)**
Adams, Don (actor); New York City, 4/19/26
Adams, Edie (Edie Enke) (actress); Kingston, Pa., 4/16/29
Adams, Franklin Pierce (columnist, author); Chicago **(1881–1960)**
Adams, Gerry (political leader); West Belfast, Northern Ireland, 10/6/48
Adams, Henry Brooks (historian); Boston **(1838–1918)**
Adams, Joey (comedian); New York City **(1911–1999)**
Adams, John (2nd U.S. president); Braintree (Quincy), Mass. **(1735–1826)**
Adams, John Quincy (6th U.S. president); Braintree (Quincy), Mass. **(1767–1848)**
Adams, Maude (Maude Kiskadden) (actress); Salt Lake City **(1872–1953)**
Adams, Samuel (American Revolutionary patriot); Boston **(1722–1803)**
Adams, Scott (cartoonist); Catskill, N.Y., 6/8/57
Adamson, Joy (naturalist, writer); Troppau, Silesia **(1910–1980)**
Addams, Charles (cartoonist); Westfield, N.J. **(1912–1988)**
Addams, Jane (social worker, Nobel laureate); Cedarville, Ill. **(1860–1935)**
Adderley, Julian "Cannonball" (jazz saxophonist); Tampa, Fla. **(1928–1975)**
Ade, George (humorist); Kentland, Ind. **(1866–1944)**
Adenauer, Konrad (statesman); Cologne, Germany **(1876–1967)**
Adler, Alfred (psychoanalyst); Vienna **(1870–1937)**
Adler, Larry (musician); Baltimore **(1914–2001)**
Adler, Richard (songwriter); New York City, 8/3/21
Aeschylus (dramatist); Eleusis, Greece **(525–456 B.C.)**
Aesop (fabulist); Samos?, Greece, fl. c. 500 B.C.
Agnew, Spiro (political figure); Baltimore **(1905–1996)**
Aiello, Danny (actor); New York City, 6/20/33
Aiken, Conrad (poet); Savannah, Ga. **(1889–1973)**
Ailey, Alvin (choreographer); Rogers, Tex. **(1931–1989)**
Akhmatova, Anna (poet); Odessa, Ukraine **(1889–1966)**
Akihito, Tsugunomiya (Emperor of Japan); Tokyo, 12/23/33
Albanese, Licia (operatic soprano); Bari, Italy, 7/22/13
Albee, Edward (playwright); Washington, D.C., 3/12/28
Albers, Josef (painter); Bottrop, Germany **(1888–1976)**
Albert, Eddie (Edward Albert Heimberger) (actor); Rock Island, Ill., 4/22/08
Albert, Edward (actor); Los Angeles, 2/20/51
Albertson, Jack (actor); Malden, Mass. **(1907–1981)**
Albright, Madeleine (diplomat, U.S. secretary of state); Prague, Czechoslovakia, 5/15/37

Alcott, Louisa May (novelist); Germantown, Pa. **(1832–1888)**
Alda, Alan (actor); New York City, 1/28/36
Alden, John (American Pilgrim); England **(c. 1599–1687)**
Alexander, Jane (Quigley) (actress); Boston, 10/28/39
Alexander, Jason (Jay Scott Greenspan) (actor); Newark, N.J., 9/23/59
Alexander the Great (monarch, conqueror); Pella, Macedonia, Greece **(356–323 B.C.)**
Alger, Horatio (author); Revere, Mass. **(1834–1899)**
Algren, Nelson (novelist); Detroit **(1909–1981)**
Allen, Debbie (dancer-choreographer, actress); Houston, 1/16/50
Allen, Ethan (American Revolutionary soldier); Litchfield, Conn. **(1738–1789)**
Allen, Fred (John Florence Sullivan) (comedian); Cambridge, Mass. **(1894–1956)**
Allen, Gracie (Grace Ethel Cecile Rosalie Allen) (comedienne); San Francisco **(1906–1964)**
Allen, Joan (actress); Rochelle, Ill., 8/20/56
Allen, Mel (Melvin Israel) (sportscaster); Birmingham, Ala. **(1913–1996)**
Allen, Peter (actor, songwriter); Tenterfield, Australia **(1944–1992)**
Allen, Steve (TV entertainer); New York City, 12/26/21
Allen, Woody (Allen Stewart Konigsberg) (actor, writer, director); Brooklyn, N.Y., 12/1/35
Allende, Isabel (novelist); Lima, Peru, 8/2/42
Alley, Kirstie (actress); Wichita, Kans., 1/12/55
Allison, Fran (actress); LaPorte City, Iowa **(1908?–1989)**
Allman, Gregg (singer); Nashville, Tenn., 12/8/47
Allyson, June (Ella Geisman) (actress); New York City, 10/7/17
Alonso, Alicia (ballet dancer); Havana, 12/21/21?
Alpert, Herb (band leader); Los Angeles, 3/31/35?
Alsop, Joseph W., Jr. (journalist); Avon, Conn. **(1910–1989)**
Alsop, Stewart (journalist); Avon, Conn. **(1914–1974)**
Alt, Carol (model); Flushing, New York, 12/1/60
Altman, Robert (director); Kansas City, Mo., 2/20/25
Amanpour, Christiane (broadcast journalist); London, 1958
Amati, Nicola (violin maker); Cremona, Italy **(1596–1684)**
Ambler, Eric (suspense writer); London **(1909–1998)**
Ameche, Don (Dominic Amici) (actor); Kenosha, Wis. **(1908–1993)**
Amis, Kingsley (novelist); London **(1922–1995)**
Amis, Martin (novelist); Oxford, England, 8/25/49
Amory, Cleveland (writer, conservationist); Nahant, Mass. **(1917–1998)**
Amos (Freeman F. Gosden) (radio comedian); Richmond, Va. **(1899–1982)**
Amos, John (actor); Newark, N.J., 12/27/41
Amos, Tori (singer); Newton, N.C., 8/22/63
Amsterdam, Morey (actor); Chicago **(1914–1996)**
Andersen, Hans Christian (author of fairy tales); Odense, Denmark **(1805–1875)**
Anderson, Eddie (Rochester) (actor); Oakland, Calif. **(1905–1977)**
Anderson, Gillian (actress); Chicago, 8/9/68
Anderson, Harry (actor); Newport, R.I., 10/14/52
Anderson, Ib (ballet dancer); Copenhagen, 12/14/54
Anderson, Jack (journalist); Long Beach, Calif., 10/19/22
Anderson, Dame Judith (actress); Adelaide, Australia **(1898–1992)**
Anderson, Lindsay (Gordon) (director); Bangalore, India **(1923–1994)**
Anderson, Loni (actress); St. Paul, Minn., 8/5/45

Anderson, Lynn (singer); Grand Forks, N.D., 9/26/47
Anderson, Marian (contralto); Philadelphia **(1897–1993)**
Anderson, Maxwell (dramatist); Atlantic, Pa. **(1888–1959)**
Anderson Lee, Pamela (Pamela Anderson) (model, actress); Ladysmith, B.C., Canada, 7/1/67
Anderson, Richard Dean (actor); Minneapolis, Minn., 1/23/50
Anderson, Robert (playwright); New York City, 4/28/17
Anderson, Sherwood (novelist); Camden, Ohio **(1876–1941)**
Andress, Ursula (actress); Bern, Switzerland, 3/19/38
Andrews, Julie (Julia Wells) (actress, singer); Walton-on-Thames, England, 10/1/35
Andrews, La Verne (singer); Minneapolis **(1916–1967)**
Andrews, Maxene (singer); Minneapolis **(1918–1995)**
Andrews, Patti (singer); Minneapolis, 2/16/20
Andy (Charles J. Correll) (radio comedian); Peoria, Ill. **(1890–1972)**
Angelico, Fra (Guido di Pietro; Giovanni de Fiesole) (painter); nr. Florence **(c. 1400–1455)**
Angelou, Maya (Marguerite Johnson) (poet, novelist); St. Louis, 4/4/28
Aniston, Jennifer (Jennifer Anistonapoulos) (actress); Sherman Oaks, Calif., 2/11/69
Anka, Paul (singer, composer); Ottawa, Ont., Canada, 7/30/41
Annan, Kofi (diplomat, UN secretary general); Kumasi, Ghana, 4/8/38
Ann-Margret (Ann-Margaret Olsson) (actress); Valsjobyn, Sweden, 4/28/41
Anouilh, Jean (playwright); Bordeaux, France **(1910–1987)**
Anthony, Susan Brownell (woman suffragist); Adams, Mass. **(1820–1906)**
Antonioni, Michelangelo (director); Ferrara, Italy, 9/29/12
Antony, Mark (Marcus Antonius) (statesman); Rome **(c. 83–30 B.C.)**
Anuszkiewicz, Richard (painter); Erie, Pa., 5/23/30
Apple, Fiona (singer); New York City, 4/8/68
Applegate, Christina (actress); Los Angeles, Calif., 11/25/71
Aquinas, St. Thomas (philosopher); nr. Aquino, Italy **(1225–1274)**
Arafat, Yasir (Mohammed Abdel-Raouf Arafat al Qudwa al Husseini) (chairman of the Palestine Liberation Organization); Cairo, Egypt, 8/24/29
Arbuckle, Roscoe "Fatty" (actor, director); Smith Center, Kans. **(1887–1933)**
Archimedes (physicist, mathematician); Syracuse, Sicily **(287–212 B.C.)**
Archipenko, Alexandre (sculptor); Kiev, Ukraine **(1887–1964)**
Arden, Elizabeth (Florence Nightingale Graham) (cosmetics executive); Woodbridge, Canada **(1878–1966)**
Arden, Eve (Eunice Quedens) (actress); Mill Valley, Calif. **(1912–1990)**
Arendt, Hannah (historian); Hanover, Germany **(1906–1975)**
Aristophanes (dramatist); Athens **(c. 448–c. 385 B.C.)**
Aristotle (philosopher); Stagirus, Macedonia **(384–322 B.C.)**
Arkin, Adam (actor); New York City, 8/19/57
Arkin, Alan (actor, director); New York City, 3/26/34
Arledge, Roone (TV executive); Forest Hills, N.Y., 7/8/31
Arlen, Harold (Hyman Arluck) (composer); Buffalo, N.Y. **(1905–1986)**
Armani, Georgio (fashion designer); Piacenza, Italy, 7/11/34
Armstrong, Louis ("Satchmo") (musician); New Orleans **(1900–1971)**
Arnaz, Desi (Desiderio Alberto Araz y de Acha III) (actor, producer); Santiago, Cuba **(1917–1986)**
Arness, James (James Aurness) (actor); Minneapolis, 5/26/23
Arno, Peter (cartoonist); New York City **(1904–1968)**
Arnold, Benedict (American Revolutionary War general, charged with treason); Norwich, Conn. **(1741–1801)**
Arnold, Matthew (poet, critic); Laleham, England **(1822–1888)**
Arp, Jean (sculptor, painter); Strasbourg, France **(1887–1966)**
Arquette, Cliff (actor); Toledo, Ohio **(1905–1974)**
Arquette, Patricia (actress); Chicago, 4/8/68
Arquette, Rosanna (actress); New York City, 8/10/59
Arrau, Claudio (pianist); Chillán, Chile **(1903–1991)**
Arroyo, Martina (soprano); New York City, 2/2/40
Arthur, Bea (Bernice Frankel) (actress); New York City, 5/13/23
Arthur, Chester Alan (21st U.S. president); Fairfield, Vt. **(1830–1886)**
Ashcroft, Dame Peggy (actress); Croydon, England **(1907–1991)**
Ashkenazy, Vladimir (concert pianist); Gorki, U.S.S.R., 7/6/37
Ashley, Elizabeth (actress); Ocala, Fla., 8/30/39
Ashton, Sir Frederick William Mallandaine (choreographer); Guayaquil, Ecuador **(1904–1988)**
Asimov, Isaac (author); Petrovichi, Russia **(1920–1992)**
Asner, Edward (actor); Kansas City, Mo., 11/15/29
Assante, Armand (actor); New York City, 10/4/49

Astaire, Fred (Frederick Austerlitz) (dancer, actor); Omaha, Neb. **(1899–1987)**
Astin, John (actor, director); Baltimore, 3/30/30
Astor, Brooke (socialite, philanthropist); Portsmouth, N.H., 3/16/05
Astor, John Jacob (financier); Waldorf, Germany **(1763–1848)**
Astor, Mary (Lucile Langhanke) (actress); Quincy, Ill. **(1906–1987)**
Ataturk, Kemal (Mustafa Kemal) (Turkish soldier, statesman); Salonika, Greece **(1881–1938)**
Atkins, Chet (guitarist); nr. Luttrell, Tenn. **(1924–2001)**
Atkinson, Rowan (actor); Newcastle-Upon-Tyne, England, 1/6/55
Attenborough, Richard (actor, director); Cambridge, England, 8/29/23
Attila (King of Huns); **(406?–453)**
Attucks, Crispus (American Revolutionary patriot); Boston **(c. 1723–1770)**
Auberjonois, Rene (actor); New York City, 6/1/40
Auchincloss, Louis (author); Lawrence, N.Y., 9/27/17
Auden, W(ystan) H(ugh) (poet); York, England **(1907–1973)**
Audubon, John James (naturalist, painter); Haiti **(1785–1851)**
Auer, Leopold (violinist, teacher); Veszprém, Hungary **(1845–1930)**
Augustine, Saint (Aurelius Augustinus) (theologian); Tagaste, Numidia, Algeria **(354–430)**
Augustus (Gaius Octavius) (Roman emperor); Rome **(63 B.C.– A.D. 14)**
Aung San Suu Kyi (human rights activist); Rangoon, Burma, 6/19/45
Austen, Jane (novelist); Steventon, England **(1775–1817)**
Autry, Gene (singer, actor); Tioga, Tex. **(1907–1998)**
Avalon, Frankie (singer); Philadelphia, 9/18/39
Avedon, Richard (photographer); New York City, 5/15/23
Avery, Milton (painter); Altmar, N.Y. **(1893–1965)**
Ax, Emanuel (pianist); Lvov, Ukraine, 6/8/49
Axelrod, George (playwright); New York City, 6/9/22
Ayckbourn, Alan (playwright); London, 4/12/39
Aykroyd, Dan (actor); Ottawa, Ont., Canada, 7/1/52
Ayres, Lew (actor); Minneapolis **(1908–1996)**

B

Bacall, Lauren (Betty Joan Perske) (actress); New York City, 9/16/24
Bach, Carl Phillipp Emanuel (composer); Weimar, Germany **(1714–1788)**
Bach, Johann Sebastian (composer); Eisenach, Germany **(1685–1750)**
Bacharach, Burt (songwriter); Kansas City, Mo., 5/12/29
Backus, Jim (actor); Cleveland **(1913–1989)**
Bacon, Francis (philosopher, essayist); London **(1561–1626)**
Bacon, Francis (painter); Dublin **(1910–1992)**
Bacon, Kevin (actor); Philadelphia, 7/8/58
Bacon, Roger (philosopher, scientist); Ilchester, England **(c. 1214–1294?)**
Badu, Erykah (Erykah Wright) (singer); Dallas, 1971
Baez, Joan (folk singer); Staten Island, N.Y., 1/9/41
Bailey, F. Lee (lawyer); Waltham, Mass., 6/10/33
Bailey, Pearl (singer); Newport News, Va. **(1918–1990)**
Bain, Conrad (actor); Lethbridge, Alba., Canada, 2/4/23
Baio, Scott (actor); Brooklyn, N.Y., 9/22/61
Baird, Bil (William B. Baird) (puppeteer); Grand Island, Neb. **(1904–1987)**
Baker, Anita (singer); Toledo, Ohio, 1958
Baker, Carroll (actress); Johnstown, Pa., 5/28/31
Baker, Josephine (singer, dancer); St. Louis **(1906–1975)**
Baker, Russell (columnist); Loudoun County, Va., 8/14/25
Balanchine, George (choreographer); St. Petersburg, Russia **(1904–1983)**
Balboa, Vasco Nuñez de (explorer); Jerez de los Caballeros, Spain **(1475–1517)**
Baldwin, Alec (actor); Massapequa, N.Y., 4/3/58
Baldwin, James (novelist); New York City **(1924–1987)**
Bale, Christian (actor); Pembrokeshire, Wales, 1/30/74
Balenciaga, Cristóbal (fashion designer); Guetaria, Spain **(1895–1972)**
Ball, Lucille (Lucille Désirée Ball) (actress, producer); Celoron (nr. Jamestown), N.Y. **(1911–1989)**
Balsam, Martin (actor); Bronx, New York **(1919–1996)**
Balzac, Honoré de (novelist); Tours, France **(1799–1850)**
Bancroft, Anne (Annemarie Italiano) (actress); New York City, 9/17/31
Banderas, Antonio (José Antonio Dominguez Banderas) (actor, model); Málaga, Spain, 8/10/60
Bankhead, Tallulah (actress); Huntsville, Ala. **(1903–1968)**
Banks, Tyra (model); Los Angeles, 12/4/73

Banting, Fredrick Grant (physiologist); Alliston, Ont., Canada **(1891–1941)**

Bara, Theda (Theodosia Goodman) (actress); Cincinnati **(1890–1955)**

Barak, Ehud (Israeli prime minister); Kibbutz Mishmar Hasharon, Israel, 2/12/42

Barbera, Joseph (animator, producer); New York City, 1911

Baraka, Imamu Amiri (LeRoi Jones) (playwright); Newark, N.J., 10/7/34

Baranski, Christine (actress); Buffalo, N.Y., 5/2/52

Barber, Red (Walter Lanier) (sportscaster); Columbus, Miss. **(1908–1992)**

Barber, Samuel (composer); West Chester, Pa. **(1910–1981)**

Barbie, Klaus (Nazi, "The Butcher of Lyon"); Bad Godesberg, Germany **(1913–1991)**

Bardem, Javier (actor); Gran Canaria, Spain, 5/1/69

Bardot, Brigitte (Camille Javal) (actress); Paris, 9/28/34

Barenboim, Daniel (concert pianist, conductor); Buenos Aires, 11/15/42

Barker, Bob (game-show host); Darrington, Wash., 12/12/23

Barkin, Ellen (actress); Bronx, N.Y., 4/16/54

Barnard, Christiaan N. (heart surgeon); Beauford West, South Africa **(1922–2001)**

Barnum, Phineas Taylor (showman); Bethel, Conn. **(1810–1891)**

Barrie, Sir James Matthew (author); Kirriemuir, Scotland **(1860–1937)**

Barry, John (naval officer); County Wexford, Ireland **(1745–1803)**

Barrymore, Diana (actress); New York City **(1921–1960)**

Barrymore, Drew (actress); Los Angeles, 2/22/75

Barrymore, Ethel (Ethel Blythe) (actress); Philadelphia **(1879–1959)**

Barrymore, Georgiana Drew (actress); Philadelphia **(1856–1893)**

Barrymore, John (John Blythe) (actor); Philadelphia **(1882–1942)**

Barrymore, Lionel (Lionel Blythe) (actor); Philadelphia **(1878–1954)**

Barrymore, Maurice (Herbert Blythe) (actor, playwright); Agra, India **(1847–1905)**

Barth, John (novelist); Cambridge, Md., 5/27/30

Barthelme, Donald (novelist); Philadelphia **(1931 –1989)**

Bartók, Béla (composer); Nagyszentmiklo, Hungary **(1881–1945)**

Barton, Clara (founder of American Red Cross); Oxford, Mass. **(1821–1912)**

Baruch, Bernard Mannes (statesman); Camden, S.C. **(1870–1965)**

Baryshnikov, Mikhail Nikolayevich (ballet dancer, artistic director); Riga, Latvia, 1/27/48

Basie, Count (William Basie) (band leader); Red Bank, N.J. **(1904–1984)**

Basinger, Kim (actress); Athens, Ga., 12/8/53

Bassett, Angela (actress); New York City, 8/16/58

Bassey, Shirley (singer); Cardiff, Wales, 1/8/37

Batchelor, Clarence Daniel (political cartoonist); Osage City, Kans. **(1888–1977)**

Bateman, Jason (actor); Rye, N.Y., 1/14/69

Bateman, Justine (actress); Rye, N.Y., 2/19/66

Bates, Alan (actor); Allestree, England, 2/17/34

Bates, Kathy (Kathleen Doyle Bates) (actress); Memphis, Tenn., 6/28/48

Battle, Kathleen (soprano); Portsmouth, Ohio, 8/13/48

Baudelaire, Charles Pierre (poet); Paris **(1821–1867)**

Baxter, Anne (actress); Michigan City, Ind. **(1923–1985)**

Baxter, Meredith (actress); Los Angeles, 6/21/47

Beardsley, Aubrey Vincent (illustrator); Brighton, England **(1872–1898)**

Beaton, Cecil (photographer, designer); London **(1904–1980)**

Beatty, Clyde (animal trainer); Bainbridge, Ohio **(1903–1965)**

Beatty, Warren (Henry Warren Beaty) (actor, producer); Richmond, Va., 3/30/37

Beaumont, Francis (dramatist); Grace-Dieu, England **(1584–1616)**

Becket, Thomas à (archbishop of Canterbury); London **(1118?–1170)**

Beckett, Samuel (playwright); Dublin **(1906–1989)**

Beckmann, Max (painter); Leipzig, Germany **(1884–1950)**

Bede, Saint ("The Venerable Bede") (scholar); Monkwearmouth, England **(673–735)**

Beecham, Sir Thomas (conductor); St. Helens, England **(1879–1961)**

Beecher, Henry Ward (clergyman); Litchfield, Conn. **(1813–1887)**

Beerbohm, Sir Max (author); London **(1872–1956)**

Beery, Noah (actor); Kansas City, Mo. **(1884–1946)**

Beery, Noah, Jr. (actor); New York City **(1913–1994)**

Beery, Wallace (actor); Kansas City, Mo. **(1886–1949)**

Beethoven, Ludwig van (composer); Bonn, Germany **(1770–1827)**

Begin, Menachem (Israeli prime minister); Brest-Litovsk, Belarus **(1913–1992)**

Begley, Ed (actor); Hartford, Conn. **(1901–1970)**

Beiderbecke, Bix (jazz musician); Davenport, Iowa **(1903–1931)**

Beineix, Jean-Jacques (director, producer, screenwriter) 1946

Belafonte, Harry (singer, actor); New York City, 3/1/27

Belafonte-Harper, Shari (actress); New York City, 9/22/54

Belasco, David (dramatist, producer); San Francisco **(1854–1931)**

Bel Geddes, Barbara (actress); New York City, 10/31/22

Bell, Alexander Graham (inventor); Edinburgh, Scotland **(1847–1922)**

Bell, Quentin (author, artist); England **(1910–1996)**

Bellamy, Edward (author); Chicopee Falls, Mass. **(1850–1898)**

Bellamy, Ralph (actor); Chicago **(1904–1991)**

Bellini, Giovanni (painter); Venice **(c. 1430–1516)**

Bellow, Saul (novelist); Lachine, Que., Canada, 6/10/15

Bellows, George Wesley (painter, lithographer); Columbus, Ohio **(1882–1925)**

Belushi, Jim (actor); Chicago, 6/15/54

Belushi, John (comedian, actor); Chicago **(1949–1982)**

Benchley, Peter Bradford (novelist); New York City, 5/8/40

Benchley, Robert Charles (humorist); Worcester, Mass. **(1889–1945)**

Bendix, William (actor); New York City **(1906–1964)**

Benedict, Ruth Fulton (anthropologist); New York City **(1887–1948)**

Benes, Eduard (statesman); Kozlany, former Czechoslovakia **(1884–1948)**

Benét, Stephen Vincent (poet, story writer); Bethlehem, Pa. **(1898–1943)**

Benét, William Rose (poet, novelist); Ft. Hamilton, Brooklyn, N.Y. **(1886–1950)**

Ben-Gurion, David (David Green) (statesman); Plónsk, Poland **(1886–1973)**

Benigni, Roberto (actor, director, screenwriter); Misericordia, Arezzo, Italy, 10/27/52

Bening, Annette (actress); Topeka, Kans., 5/29/58

Bennett, Enoch Arnold (novelist, dramatist); Hanley, England **(1867–1931)**

Bennett, James Gordon (editor); Keith, Scotland **(1795–1872)**

Bennett, Joan (actress); Palisades, N.J. **(1910–1990)**

Bennett, Robert Russell (composer); Kansas City, Mo. **(1894–1981)**

Bennett, Tony (Anthony Benedetto) (singer); Astoria, Queens, N.Y., 8/3/26

Benny, Jack (Benjamin Kubelsky) (comedian); Chicago **(1894–1974)**

Benson, Robby (Robert Segal) (actor); Dallas, 1/21/56

Bentham, Jeremy Heinrich (economist); London **(1748–1832)**

Benton, Thomas Hart (painter); Neosho, Mo. **(1889–1975)**

Berendt, John (writer); Syracuse, N.Y., 12/5/39

Berenger, Tom (actor); Chicago, 5/31/50

Berg, Alban (composer); Vienna **(1885–1935)**

Berg, Gertrude (writer, actress); New York City **(1899–1966)**

Bergen, Candice (actress); Beverly Hills, Calif., 5/9/46

Bergen, Edgar (ventriloquist); Chicago **(1903–1978)**

Bergen, Polly (Nellie Paulina Burgin) (actress, singer); Knoxville, Tenn., 7/14/30

Bergerac, Cyrano de (poet); Paris **(1619–1655)**

Bergman, Ingmar (film director); Uppsala, Sweden, 7/14/18

Bergman, Ingrid (actress); Stockholm **(1918–1982)**

Bergson, Henri (philosopher); Paris **(1859–1941)**

Berkeley, Busby (William Berkeley Enos) (choreographer, director); Los Angeles **(1895–1976)**

Berle, Milton (Milton Berlinger) (comedian); New York City, 7/12/08

Berlin, Irving (Israel Baline) (songwriter); Temum, Russia **(1888–1989)**

Berlioz, Louis Hector (composer); La Côte-Saint-André, France **(1803–1869)**

Berman, Lazar (concert pianist); Leningrad (St. Petersburg), Russia, 2/26/30

Bernardin, Joseph Cardinal (prelate); Columbia, S.C. **(1928–1996)**

Bernhard, Sandra (actress, comedian); Flint, Mich., 6/6/55

Bernhardt, Sarah (Rosine Bernard) (actress); Paris **(1844–1923)**

Bernini, Gian Lorenzo (sculptor, painter); Naples, Italy **(1598–1680)**

Bernoulli, Jacques (scientist); Basel, Switzerland **(1654–1705)**

Bernsen, Corbin (actor); North Hollywood, Calif., 7/7/54

Bernstein, Leonard (conductor); Lawrence, Mass. **(1918–1990)**

Berry, Chuck (Charles Edward Berry) (singer, guitarist); St. Louis, Mo., 10/19/26

Berry, Halle (actress, model); Cleveland, Ohio, 8/14/68

Berry, Ken (actor); Moline, Ill., 11/3/30

Berry, Richard (songwriter); Extension, S.C. **(1935–1997)**

Berryman, John (poet); McAlester, Okla. **(1914–1972)**

Bertinelli, Valerie (actress); Wilmington, Del., 4/23/60

Bertolucci, Bernardo (actor); Parma, Italy, 3/16/40

Bethune, Mary McLeod (educator); Mayesville, S.C. **(1875–1955)**

Betjeman, Sir John (poet laureate); London **(1906–1984)**

Bettelheim, Bruno (psychoanalyst); Vienna **(1903–1990)**

Bierce, Ambrose Gwinnett (journalist); Meigs County, Ohio **(1842–1914?)**

Bikel, Theodore (actor, folk singer); Vienna, 5/2/24

Bing, Sir Rudolf (opera manager); Vienna **(1902–1997)**

Bingham, George Caleb (painter); Augusta Co., Va. **(1811–1879)**

Binoche, Juliette (actress); Paris, 3/9/64

Bishop, Joey (Joseph Gottlieb) (comedian); New York City, 2/3/19

Bismarck-Schönhausen, Prince Otto Eduard Leopold von (statesman); Schönhausen, Germany **(1815–1898)**

Bisset, Jacqueline (actress); Weybridge, England, 9/13/44

Bixby, Bill (actor); San Francisco **(1934–1993)**

Bizet, Georges (Alexandre César Léopold Bizet) (composer); Paris **(1838–1875)**

Bjoerling, Jussi (tenor); Stora Tuna, Sweden **(1911–1960)**

Björk (Björk Gudmundsdottir) (pop musician, singer); Reykjavik, Iceland, 11/21/65

Black, Clint (singer, songwriter); Long Branch, N.J., 2/4/62

Black, Karen (Karen Ziegler) (actress); Park Ridge, Ill., 7/1/42

Black, Shirley Temple (child actress, former ambassador); Santa Monica, Calif., 4/23/28

Blackstone, Sir William (jurist); London **(1723–1780)**

Blackwell, Elizabeth (physician, educator); England **(1821–1910)**

Blades, Ruben (actor, musician, composer); Panama City, Panama, 7/16/48

Blair, Tony (British prime minister); Edinburgh, Scotland, 5/6/53

Blake, Amanda (Beverly Louise Neill) (actress); Buffalo, N.Y. **(1929–1989)**

Blake, Eubie (James Hubert) (pianist); Baltimore **(1883–1983)**

Blake, Robert (Michael Gubitosi) (actor); Nutley, N.J., 9/18/33

Blake, William (poet, artist); London **(1757–1827)**

Blanc, Mel (Melvin Jerome) (actor, voice specialist); San Francisco **(1908–1989)**

Blass, Bill (fashion designer); Fort Wayne, Ind., 6/22/22

Bleeth, Yasmine (model, actress); New York City, 6/14/68

Blige, Mary J. (hip-hop singer); Bronx, N.Y., 1/11/71

Bloch, Ernest (composer); Geneva **(1880–1959)**

Bloom, Claire (actress); London, 2/15/31

Bloomgarden, Kermit (producer); Brooklyn, N.Y. **(1904–1976)**

Blume, Judy (Judy Sussman) (young adult novelist); Elizabeth, N.J., 2/12/38

Bly, Nellie (pseud. for Elizabeth Seaman) (journalist); Cochrane Mills, Pa. **(1867–1922)**

Bly, Robert (poet, critic); Madison, Minn., 12/23/26

Boccaccio, Giovanni (author); Paris **(1313–1375)**

Boccherini, Luigi (Rodolfo) (composer); Lucca, Italy **(1743–1805)**

Boccioni, Umberto (painter, sculptor); Reggio di Calabria, Italy **(1882–1916)**

Bochco, Steven (TV producer, writer); New York City, 12/16/43

Bock, Jerry (composer); New Haven, Conn., 11/23/28

Bogarde, Dirk (Derek Van den Bogaerde) (film actor, director); London **(1921–1999)**

Bogart, Humphrey DeForest (actor); New York City **(1899–1957)**

Bogdanovich, Peter (producer, director); Kingston, N.Y., 7/30/39

Bogosian, Eric (playwright, screenwriter, actor, monologuist); Woburn, Mass., 4/24/53

Bohlen, Charles E. (diplomat); Clayton, N.Y. **(1904–1974)**

Bohr, Niels (atomic physicist); Copenhagen **(1885–1962)**

Bok, Sissela (Sissela Ann Myrdal) (scholar); Stockholm, 12/2/34

Bolger, Ray (dancer, actor); Dorchester, Mass **(1904–1987)**

Bolivar, Simón (South American liberator); Caracas, Venezuela **(1783–1830)**

Bologna, Giovanni da (sculptor); Douai, France **(1529–1608)**

Bombeck, Erma (author, columnist); Dayton, Ohio **(1927–1996)**

Bonaparte, Napoléon (Emperor of the French); Ajaccio, Corsica, France **(1769–1821)**

Bond, Julian (Georgia legislator); Nashville, Tenn., 1/14/40

Bonet, Lisa (actress); San Francisco, 11/16/67

Bonham Carter, Helena (actress); London, 5/23/66

Bon Jovi, Jon (musician, songwriter); Sayreville, N.J., 3/2/62

Bonnard, Pierre (painter); Fontenayaux-Roses, France **(1867–1947)**

Bono (Paul Hewson) (singer, songwriter); Dublin, Ireland, 5/10/60

Bono, Sonny (Salvatore Bono) (singer, politician); Detroit **(1935–1998)**

Boone, Daniel (frontiersman); nr. Reading, Pa. **(1734–1820)**

Boone, Pat (Charles Boone) (singer); Jacksonville, Fla., 6/1/34

Boone, Richard (actor); Los Angeles **(1917–1981)**

Boorstin, Daniel (historian); Atlanta, 10/1/14

Booth, Edwin Thomas (actor); Bel Air, Md. **(1833–1893)**

Booth, Evangeline Cory (religious leader); London **(1865–1950)**

Booth, John Wilkes (actor; assassin of Lincoln); Harford County, Md. **(1838–1865)**

Booth, Shirley (Thelma Booth Ford) (actress); New York City **(1907–1992)**

Borden, Lizzie (Elizabeth Andrew Borden) (accused murderer); Fall River, Mass. **(1860–1927)**

Borge, Victor (pianist, comedian); Copenhagen **(1909–2000)**

Borgia, Cesare (nobleman, soldier); Rome **(1476–1507)**

Borgia, Lucrezia (Duchess of Ferrara); Rome **(1480–1519)**

Borgnine, Ernest (actor); Hamden, Conn., 1/24/17

Borromini, Francesco (architect); Bissone, Italy **(1599–1667)**

Bosch, Hieronymus (Hieronymus van Aeken) (painter); Hertogenbosch, Netherlands **(c. 1450–1516)**

Bosley, Tom (actor); Chicago, 10/1/27

Bostwick, Barry (actor); San Mateo, Calif., 2/24/45

Boswell, James (diarist, biographer); Edinburgh, Scotland **(1740–1795)**

Botticelli, Sandro (Alessandro di Mariano dei Filipepi) (painter); Florence, Italy **(1444–1510)**

Bottoms, Timothy (actor); Santa Barbara, Calif., 8/30/50

Boulez, Pierre (conductor); Montbrison, France, 3/26/25

Bourke-White, Margaret (photographer); New York City **(1906–1971)**

Boutros-Ghali, Boutros (ex-secretary general of the UN); Cairo, Egypt, 11/14/22

Bow, Clara (actress); Brooklyn, N.Y. **(1905–1965)**

Bowen, Catherine Drinker (biographer); Haverford, Pa. **(1897–1973)**

Bowie, David (David Robert Jones) (actor, musician); London, 1/8/47

Bowie, James (soldier); Burke County, Ga. **(1799–1836)**

Bowles, Chester (diplomat); Springfield, Mass. **(1901–1986)**

Boxleitner, Bruce (actor); Elgin, Ill., 5/12/50

Boyce, William (composer); London? **(1710–1779)**

Boyd, Bill ("Hopalong Cassidy") (actor); Cambridge, Ohio **(1895–1972)**

Boyd, Stephen (Stephen Millar) (actor); Belfast, Northern Ireland **(1928–1977)**

Boyer, Charles (actor); Figeac, France **(1897–1978)**

Boy George (George Alan O'Dowd) (singer); London, 6/14/61

Boyle, Peter (actor); Philadelphia, 10/18/33

Boyle, Robert (scientist); Lismore Castle, Munster, Ireland **(1627–1691)**

Bradbury, Ray Douglas (science-fiction writer); Waukegan, Ill., 8/22/20

Bradlee, Benjamin C. (editor); Boston, 8/26/21

Bradley, Ed (broadcast journalist); Philadelphia, 6/22/41

Bradley, Omar N. (5-star general); Clark, Mo. **(1893–1981)**

Bradley, Thomas (mayor of Los Angeles); Calvert, Tex. **(1917–1998)**

Brady, Mathew (early photographer); Warren Co., N.Y. **(c. 1823–1896)**

Brahe, Tycho (astronomer); Knudstrup, Denmark **(1546–1601)**

Bragg, Billy (singer, songwriter); Barking, England, 12/20/57

Brahms, Johannes (composer); Hamburg, Germany **(1833–1897)**

Braille, Louis (teacher of blind); Coupvray, France **(1809–1862)**

Brailowsky, Alexander (pianist); Kiev, Ukraine **(1896–1976)**

Bramante, Donato D'Agnolo (architect); Monte Asdrualdo (now Fermignano), Italy **(1444–1514)**

Branagh, Kenneth (actor, director, writer, producer); Belfast, Northern Ireland, 12/10/60

Brancusi, Constantin (sculptor); Pestisansi, Romania **(1876–1957)**

Brandauer, Klaus Maria (Klaus Maria Steng) (actor); Bad Aussee, Steiermark, Austria , 6/22/44

Brando, Marlon (actor); Omaha, Neb., 4/3/24

Brandt, Willy (Herbert Frahm) (ex-chancellor); Lübeck, Germany **(1913– 1992)**

Brandy (Brandy Norwood) (actress, singer); McComb, Miss., 2/11/79

Braque, Georges (painter); Argenteuil, France **(1882–1963)**

Bratt, Benjamin (actor); San Francisco, 12/16/63

Braugher, André (actor); Chicago, 7/1/62

Braxton, Toni (R&B singer); Severn, Maryland, 10/7/67

Brazelton, T(homas) Berry II (pediatrician, writer); Waco, Tex., 5/10/18

Brecht, Bertolt (dramatist, poet); Augsburg, Bavaria **(1898–1956)**

Brel, Jacques (singer, composer); Brussels **(1929–1978)**

Brennan, Walter (actor); Lynn, Mass. **(1894–1974)**

Brennan, William J., Jr. (Supreme Court justice); Newark, N.J. **(1906–1997)**

Breslin, Jimmy (journalist); Jamaica, Queens, N.Y., 10/17/30

Breton, André (writer); Tinchebray, France **(1896–1966)**

Breuer, Marcel (architect, designer); Pécs, Hungary **(1902–1981)**

Brewster, Kingman, Jr. (ex-president of Yale); Longmeadow, Mass. **(1919–1988)**

Brezhnev, Leonid I. (Communist Party secretary); Dneprodzerzhinsk, Ukraine **(1906–1982)**

Brice, Fanny (Fannie Borach) (comedienne); New York City **(1892–1951)**

Bridges, Beau (actor); Los Angeles, 12/9/41

Bridges, Jeff (actor); Los Angeles, 12/4/49

Bridges, Lloyd (actor); San Leandro, Calif. **(1913–1998)**

Brinkley, Christie (model, actress); Malibu, Calif., 2/2/54

Brinkley, David (TV newscaster); Wilmington, N.C., 7/10/20

Britten, Benjamin (composer); Lowestoft, England **(1913–1976)**

Broderick, Matthew (actor); New York City, 3/21/62

Brodsky, Joseph Alexandrovitch (poet); St. Petersburg, Russia **(1940–1996)**

Brody, Jane (journalist); Brooklyn, N.Y., 5/19/41

Brokaw, Tom (TV newscaster); Webster, S.D., 2/6/40

Brolin, James (actor); Los Angeles, 7/18/40

Bromfield, Louis (novelist); Mansfield, Ohio **(1896–1956)**

Bronson, Charles (Charles Buchinsky) (actor); Ehrenfield, Pa., 11/3/21

Brontë, Charlotte (novelist); Thornton, England **(1816–1855)**

Brontë, Emily Jane (novelist); Thornton, England **(1818–1848)**

Bronzino, Agnolo (painter); Monticelli, Italy **(1503–1572)**

Brook, Peter (director); London, 3/21/25

Brooke, Rupert (poet); Rugby, England **(1887–1915)**

Brooks, Albert (Albert Einstein) (actor, writer, director); Beverly Hills, Calif., 7/22/47

Brooks, Avery (actor) 4/18/49

Brooks, Gwendolyn (poet); Topeka, Kans. **(1917–2000)**

Brooks, James L. (film and television producer); New York City, 5/9/40

Brooks, Mel (Melvin Kaminsky) (writer, film director); Brooklyn, N.Y., 6/28/26

Brosnan, Pierce (actor); County Meath, Ireland, 5/16/52

Brothers, Joyce (Bauer) (psychologist, author, radio-TV personality); New York City, 9/20/28

Broun, Matthew Heywood Campbell (journalist); Brooklyn, N.Y. **(1888–1939)**

Brown, Charles Brockden (novelist); Philadelphia **(1771–1810)**

Brown, Helen Gurley (editor, author); Green Forest, Ark., 2/18/22

Brown, James (singer); Augusta, Ga., 5/3/34

Brown, Joe E. (comedian); Holgate, Ohio **(1892–1973)**

Brown, John (abolitionist); Torrington, Conn. **(1800–1859)**

Brown, Les (band leader); Reinerton, Pa., 3/14/12

Brown, Margaret Wise (children's author); Brooklyn, N.Y. **(1910–1962)**

Brown, Trisha (choreographer); Aberdeen, Wash., 11/25/36

Browne, Jackson (singer, guitarist); Heidelberg, Germany, 10/9/48

Browning, Elizabeth Barrett (poet); Durham, England **(1806–1861)**

Browning, Robert (poet); London **(1812–1889)**

Brubeck, Dave (musician); Concord, Calif., 12/6/20

Bruce, Lenny (comedian); Long Island, N.Y. **(1926–1966)**

Bruce, Nigel (actor); Ensenada, Mexico **(1895–1953)**

Brueghel, Pieter (painter); nr. Breda, Flanders, Netherlands **(c. 1520–1569)**

Bruhn, Erik (Belton Evers) (ballet dancer); Copenhagen **(1928–1986)**

Brunelleschi, Filippo (architect); Florence, Italy **(1377–1446)**

Bruno, Giordano (philosopher); Nola, Italy **(1548–1600)**

Brutus, Marcus Junius (Roman politician) **(85–42 B.C.)**

Bryan, William Jennings (orator, politician); Salem, Ill. **(1860–1925)**

Bryant, Anita (singer); Barnsdall, Okla., 3/25/40

Bryant, William Cullen (poet, editor); Cummington, Mass. **(1794–1878)**

Brynner, Yul (Taidje Khan) (actor); Sakhalin Island, Russia **(1920–1985)**

Brzezinski, Zbigniew (ex-presidential adviser); Warsaw, 3/28/28

Buber, Martin (philosopher, theologian); Vienna **(1878–1965)**

Buchanan, James (15th U.S. president); near Mercersburg, Pa. **(1791–1868)**

Buchanan, Pat (politician); Washington, D.C., 11/2/38

Buchholz, Horst (actor); Berlin, 12/4/33

Büchner, Georg (dramatist); Goddelau, Germany **(1813–1837)**

Buchwald, Art (Arthur Buchwald) (columnist); Mount Vernon, N.Y., 10/20/25

Buck, Pearl S(ydenstricker) (author); Hillsboro, W. Va. **(1892–1973)**

Buckley, Christopher (writer); New York City, 1952

Buckley, Jeff (singer, songwriter); Orange County, Calif. **(1966–1997)**

Buckley, William F., Jr. (journalist); New York City, 11/24/25

Buffalo Bill (William Frederick Cody) (scout); Scott County, Iowa **(1846–1917)**

Buffett, Jimmy (singer, writer); Pascogoula, Miss., 12/25/46

Buffett, Warren (investment expert); Omaha, Neb., 8/30/30

Bujold, Genevieve (actress); Montreal, 7/1/42

Bujones, Fernando (ballet dancer); Miami, Fla., 3/9/55

Bulgakov, Mikhail (novelist); Kiev, Ukraine **(1891–1940)**

Bullins, Ed (playwright); Philadelphia, 7/2/35

Bullock, Sandra (actress); Washington D.C., 7/26/65

Bunche, Ralph J. (statesman); Detroit **(1904–1971)**

Bundy, McGeorge (educator); Boston **(1919–1996)**

Bundy, William Putnam (editor); Washington, D.C. **(1917–2000)**

Buñuel, Luis (film director); Calanda, Spain **(1900–1983)**

Bunyan, John (preacher, author); Elstow, England **(1628–1688)**

Burbank, Luther (horticulturist); Lancaster, Mass. **(1849–1926)**

Burke, Adm. Arleigh A. (ex-chief of Naval Operations); Boulder, Colo. **(1901–1996)**

Burke, Billie (Mary William Ethelbert Appleton Burke) (comedienne); Washington, D.C. **(1885–1970)**

Burke, Delta (actress); Orlando, Fla., 7/30/56

Burke, Edmund (statesman); Dublin **(1729–1797)**

Burne-Jones, Edward Coley (painter); Birmingham, England **(1833–1898)**

Burnett, Carol (comedienne); San Antonio, 4/26/33

Burney, Fanny (Frances) (writer); King's Lynn, England **(1752–1840)**

Burns, Edward (actor, film director, screenwriter, producer); Long Island, N.Y., 1/29/68

Burns, George (Nathan Birnbaum) (comedian); New York City **(1896–1996)**

Burns, Ken (documentary filmmaker); Brooklyn, N.Y., 7/29/53

Burns, Robert (poet); Alloway, Scotland **(1759–1796)**

Burr, Aaron (political leader); Newark, N.J. **(1756–1836)**

Burr, Raymond (William Stacey Burr) (actor); New Westminster, B.C., Canada **(1917–1993)**

Burroughs, Edgar Rice (novelist); Chicago **(1875–1950)**

Burroughs, William S. (writer); St. Louis **(1914–1997)**

Burrows, Abe (playwright, director); New York City **(1910–1985)**

Burstyn, Ellen (Edna Rae Gillooly) (actress); Detroit, 12/7/32

Burton, LeVar (actor); Landsthul, Germany, 2/16/57

Burton, Richard (Richard Jenkins) (actor); Pontrhyfden, Wales **(1925–1984)**

Burton, Tim (filmmaker); Burbank, Calif., 8/25/58

Buscemi, Steve (actor); Brooklyn, N.Y., 12/13/57

Bush, George Herbert Walker (41st U.S. president); Milton, Mass., 6/12/24

Butkus, Dick (NFL linebacker, actor); Chicago, 12/9/42

Butler, Samuel (author); Langar, England **(1835–1902)**

Butterworth, Charles (actor); South Bend, Ind. **(1896–1946)**

Buttons, Red (Aaron Chwatt) (actor); New York City, 2/5/19

Buzzi, Ruth (comedienne); Westerly, R.I., 7/24/36

Byrd, Richard Evelyn (polar explorer); Winchester, Va. **(1888–1957)**

Byrne, David (composer, musician, director, actor); Dumbarton, Scotland, 5/14/52

Byrne, Gabriel (actor); Dublin, 5/12/50

Byron, George Gordon (6th Baron Byron) (poet); London **(1788–1824)**

C

Caan, James (actor); Queens, N.Y., 3/26/39

Caballé, Montserrat (soprano); Barcelona, Spain, 4/12/33

Cabot, John (Giovanni Caboto) (navigator); Genoa **(1450–1498)**

Cabot, Sebastian (navigator); Venice **(c. 1476–1557)**

Cadmus, Paul (painter, etcher); New York City **(1904–1999)**

Caesar, Irving (lyricist); New York City **(1895–1996)**

Caesar, Gaius Julius (statesman); Rome **(100–44 B.C.)**

Caesar, Sid (comedian); Yonkers, N.Y., 9/8/22

Cage, Nicolas (Nicolas Coppola) (actor); Long Beach, Calif., 1/7/64

Cagney, James (actor); New York City **(1899–1986)**

Cahn, Sammy (songwriter); New York City **(1913–1993)**

Caine, Michael (Maurice J. Micklewhite) (actor); London, 3/14/33

Calder, Alexander (sculptor); Lawnton, Pa. **(1898–1976)**

Calderón de al Barca, Pedro (dramatist); Madrid **(1600–1681)**

Caldwell, Erskine (novelist); White Oak, Ga. **(1903–1987)**

Caldwell, Sarah (opera director, conductor); Maryville, Mo., 3/6/24

Caldwell, Taylor (novelist); Manchester, England **(1900–1985)**

Caldwell, Zoe (actress); Hawthorn, Australia, 9/14/33

Calhoun, John Caldwell (statesman); nr. Calhoun Mills, S.C. **(1782–1850)**

Caligula Gaius Caesar (Roman emperor); Antium, Latium **(12–41)**

Calisher, Hortense (novelist); New York City, 12/20/11

Callas, Maria (Maria Calogeropoulos) (operatic soprano); New York City **(1923–1977)**

Calloway, Cab (Cabell Calloway) (band leader); Rochester, N.Y. **(1907–1994)**

Calvin, John (Jean Chauvin) (religious reformer); Noyon, Picardy **(1509–1564)**

Calvin, Melvin (chemist, Nobel laureate); St. Paul, Minn. **(1911–1997)**

Cambridge, Godfrey (comedian); New York City **(1933–1976)**

Cameron, James (director); Kapuskasing, Ont., Canada, 8/16/54

Cameron, Rod (Rod Cox) (actor); Calgary, Alba., Canada **(1912–1983)**

Campbell, Glen (singer); nr. Delight, Ark., 4/22/38

Campbell, Naomi (model); London, England, 5/22/70

Campbell, Neve (actress); Guelph, Ont., Canada, 10/3/73

Campion, Jane (director, screenwriter); Waikanae, New Zealand, 1954

Camus, Albert (author); Mondovi, Algeria **(1913–1960)**

Canaletto (Giovanni Antonio Canale) (painter); Venice **(1697–1768)**

Candy, John (actor, comedian); Toronto **(1950–1994)**

Caniff, Milton (cartoonist); Hillsboro, Ohio **(1907–1988)**

Cannon, Dyan (Samille Diane Friesen) (actress); Tacoma, Wash., 1/4/37

Cantinflas (Mario Moreno-Reyes) (comedian); Mexico City **(1911–1993)**

Cantor, Eddie (Edward Iskowitz) (actor); New York City **(1892–1964)**

Capone, Al(fonse) (gangster); Brooklyn, N.Y. **(1899–1947)**

Capote, Truman (Truman Streckfus Persons) (novelist); New Orleans **(1924–1984)**

Capp, Al (Alfred Gerald Caplin) (cartoonist); New Haven, Conn. **(1909–1979)**

Capra, Frank (film producer, director); Palermo, Italy **(1897–1991)**

Caputo, Phil (Philip Joseph Caputo) (author, journalist); Chicago, 6/10/41

Caravaggio, Michelangelo Merisi da (painter); Caravaggio, Italy **(1573–1610)**

Cardin, Pierre (fashion designer); nr. Venice, 7/7/22

Cardinale, Claudia (actress); Tunis, Tunisia, 4/15/39

Carey, Drew (actor, producer); Cleveland, 5/23/58

Carey, Harry (actor); New York City **(1878–1947)**

Carey, Macdonald (actor); Sioux City, Iowa **(1913–1994)**

Carlin, George (comedian); Bronx, N.Y., 5/12/37

Carlisle, Kitty (singer, actress); New Orleans, 9/3/15

Carlyle, Robert (actor); Glasgow, Scotland, 4/14/61

Carlyle, Thomas (essayist, historian); Ecclefechan, Scotland **(1795–1881)**

Carmichael, Hoagy (Hoagland Howard) (songwriter); Bloomington, Ind. **(1899–1981)**

Carne, Judy (Joyce Botterill) (singer, actress); Northampton, England, 4/27/39

Carnegie, Andrew (industrialist); Dunfermline, Scotland **(1835–1919)**

Carney, Art (actor); Mt. Vernon, N.Y., 11/4/18

Caron, Leslie (actress); Paris, 7/1/31

Carpenter, Mary Chapin (singer, songwriter); Princeton, N.J., 2/21/58

Carr, Vikki (Florencia Bisenta de Casillas Martinez Cardona) (singer); El Paso, Tex., 7/19/42

Carracci, Annibale (painter); Bologna, Italy **(1560–1609)**

Carracci, Lodovico (painter); Bologna, Italy **(1555–1619)**

Carradine, David (actor); Hollywood, Calif., 12/8/36

Carradine, John (actor); New York City **(1906–1988)**

Carradine, Keith (actor); San Mateo, Calif., 8/8/49

Carreras, José (tenor); Barcelona, Spain, 12/5/46

Carroll, Diahann (Carol Diahann Johnson) (singer, actress); Bronx, N.Y., 7/17/35

Carroll, Leo G. (actor); Weedon, England **(1892–1972)**

Carroll, Lewis (Charles Lutwidge Dodgson) (author, mathematician); Daresbury, England **(1832–1898)**

Carson, Johnny (TV entertainer); Corning, Iowa, 10/23/25

Carson, Kit (Christopher Carson) (scout); Madison County, Ky. **(1809–1868)**

Carson, Rachel (biologist, author); Springdale, Pa. **(1907–1964)**

Carter, Betty (jazz singer, composer); Flint, Mich. **(1930–1998)**

Carter, Chris (television and film writer, director, producer); Bellflower, Calif., 10/13/57

Carter, Dixie (actress); McLemoresville, Tenn., 5/25/39

Carter, Jack (comedian); New York City, 6/24/23

Carter, James Earl, Jr. (39th U.S. president); Plains, Ga., 10/1/24

Carter, Lynda (actress); Phoenix, Ariz., 7/24/51

Cartier, Jacques (explorer); Saint-Malo, Brittany, France **(1491–1557)**

Cartier-Bresson, Henri (photographer); Chanteloup, France, 8/22/08

Cartland, Barbara (author); England **(1901–2000)**

Caruso, Enrico (Errico Caruso) (tenor); Naples, Italy **(1873–1921)**

Carver, George Washington (botanist); Diamond Grove, Mo. **(1864–1943)**

Cary, Arthur Joyce Lunel (novelist); Londonderry, Ireland **(1888–1957)**

Casals, Pablo (cellist); Vendrell, Spain **(1876–1973)**

Casanova de Seingalt, Giovanni Jacopo (adventurer); Venice **(1725–1798)**

Case, Steve (business executive); Honolulu, 8/21/58

Cash, Johnny (singer); nr. Kingsland, Ark., 2/26/32

Cass, Peggy (Mary Margaret Cass) (comedienne); Boston **(1924–1999)**

Cassatt, Mary (painter); Allegheny, Pa. **(1844–1926)**

Cassavetes, John (director); New York City **(1929–1989)**

Cassidy, David (singer); New York City, 4/12/50

Cassidy, Jack (actor); Richmond Hill, Queens, N.Y. **(1927–1976)**

Cassidy, Shaun (actor, television producer, singer); Los Angeles, 9/27/58

Cassini, Oleg (Oleg Lolewski-Cassini) (fashion designer); Paris, 4/11/13

Castagno, Andrea del (painter); San Martino a Corella, Italy **(c. 1421–1457)**

Castaneda, Carlos (cultural anthropologist, author); São Paulo, Brazil **(1931–1998)**

Castle, Irene (Irene Foote) (actress, dancer); New Rochelle, N.Y. **(1893–1969)**

Castle, Vernon Blythe (dancer, aviator); Norwich, England **(1887–1918)**

Castro Ruz, Fidel (premier); Mayari, Oriente, Cuba, 8/13/26

Cather, Willa Sibert (novelist); Winchester, Va. **(1876–1947)**

Cato, Marcus Porcius (called Cato the Elder) (statesman); Tusculum, Italy **(234–149 B.C.)**

Catt, Carrie Lane Chapman (woman suffragist); Ripon, Wis. **(1859–1947)**

Catton, Bruce (historian); Petoskey, Mich. **(1899–1978)**

Catullus, Gaius Valerius (poet); Verona **(c. 84–c. 54 B.C.)**

Cavallaro, Carmen (band leader); New York City **(1913–1989)**

Cavett, Dick (Richard Cavett) (TV entertainer); Gibbon, Neb., 11/19/36

Ceausescu, Nicolae (head of state); Scorniscesti, Romania **(1918–1989)**

Céline, Louis Ferdinand (pseud. of Louis Fuch Destouches) (novelist); Paris **(1894–1961)**

Cellini, Benvenuto (goldsmith, sculptor); Florence, Italy **(1500–1571)**

Cervantes Saavedra, Miguel de (novelist); Alcalá de Henares, Spain **(1547–1616)**

Cézanne, Paul (painter); Aix-en-Provence, France **(1839–1906)**

Chagall, Marc (painter); Vitebsk, Russia **(1887–1985)**

Chaliapin, Feodor Ivanovitch (operatic basso); Kazan, Russia **(1873–1938)**

Chamberlain, Arthur Neville (statesman); Edgbaston, England **(1869–1940)**

Chamberlain, Richard (actor, producer); Los Angeles, 3/31/35

Champion, Gower (choreographer); Geneva, Ill. **(1921–1980)**

Champion, Marge (Marjorie Celeste Belcher) (actress, dancer); Los Angeles, 9/2/23

Champlain, Samuel de (explorer); nr. Rochefort, France **(1567–1635)**

Chan, Jackie (Chan Kwong Sang) (actor); Hong Kong, 4/7/54

Chancellor, John (TV commentator); Chicago **(1927–1996)**

Chandler, Jeff (Ira Grossel) (actor); Brooklyn, N.Y. **(1918–1961)**

Chandler, Raymond (writer); Chicago **(1883–1959)**

Chanel, "Coco" (Gabriel Bonheur) (fashion designer); Issoire, France **(1883–1971)**

Chaney, Lon (actor); Colorado Springs, Colo. **(1883–1930)**

Channing, Carol (actress); Seattle, 1/31/23

Channing, Stockard (Susan Stockard) (actress); New York City, 2/13/44

Chaplin, Geraldine (actress); Santa Monica, Calif., 7/31/44

Chaplin, Sir Charles (actor); London **(1889–1977)**

Charisse, Cyd (Tula Finklea) (dancer, actress); Amarillo, Tex., 3/8/21

Charlemagne (Holy Roman Emperor); birthplace unknown **(742–814)**

Charles, Ray (Ray Charles Robinson) (pianist, singer, songwriter); Albany, Ga., 9/23/30

Charo (Maria Rosario Pilar Martinez) (actress); Murcia, Spain, 1/15/51

Chase, Chevy (Cornelius Crane Chase) (comedian); New York City, 10/8/43

Chase, Lucia (founder Ballet Theatre [now American Ballet Theatre]); Waterbury, Conn. **(1907–1986)**

Chateaubriand, François René de (writer, statesman); St. Malo, France **(1768–1848)**

Chaucer, Geoffrey (poet); London **(c. 1340–1400)**

Chuan, Leekpai (prime minister of Thailand); Muang District, Thailand, 7/28/38

Chávez, Carlos (composer); nr. Mexico City **(1899–1978)**

Chavez, Cesar (labor leader); nr. Yuma, Ariz. **(1927–1993)**

Chayefsky, Paddy (Sidney Chayefsky) (playwright); New York City **(1923–1981)**

Checker, Chubby (Ernest Evans) (performer); Philadelphia, 10/3/41

Cheever, John (novelist); Quincy, Mass. **(1912–1982)**

Chekhov, Anton Pavlovich (dramatist, short-story writer); Taganrog, Russia **(1860–1904)**

Chen Shui-bian (president of Taiwan); Taiwan, 2/18/51

Cher (Cherilyn Sarkisian La Piere) (actress, singer); El Centro, Calif., 5/20/46

Cherubini, Luigi (composer); Florence **(1760–1842)**

Chesterton, Gilbert Keith (author); Kensington, England **(1874–1936)**

Chesnutt, Charles Waddell (author); Cleveland **(1858–1932)**

Chevalier, Maurice (entertainer); Paris **(1888–1972)**

Chiang Kai-shek (chief of state); Feng-hwa, China **(1887–1975)**

Child, Julia (food expert); Pasadena, Calif., 8/15/12

Chippendale, Thomas (cabinet-maker); Otley, England **(1718–1779)**

Chirac, Jacques (president of France); Paris, 11/29/32

Chirico, Giorgio de (painter); Vólos, Greece **(1888–1978)**

Chisholm, Shirley Anita St. Hill (U.S. representative); Brooklyn, N.Y., 11/30/24

Chlumsky, Anna (actress); Chicago, 12/3/80

Chomsky, (Avram) Noam (linguist, educator, activist); Philadelphia, 12/7/28

Chopin, Frédéric François (composer); nr. Warsaw **(1810–1849)**

Chopin, Kate O'Flaherty (author); St. Louis **(1851–1904)**

Chow, Yun-Fat (actor); Hong Kong, 5/18/55

Chrétien, Jean Joseph-Jacques (prime minister of Canada); Shawinigan, Que., Canada, 1/11/34

Christie, Agatha (mystery writer); Torquay, England **(1890–1976)**

Christie, Julie (actress); Chukua, India, 4/14/41

Chung, Connie (broadcast journalist); Washington, D.C., 8/20/46

Churchill, Sir Winston Leonard Spencer (statesman); Blenheim Palace, Oxfordshire, England **(1874–1965)**

Cicero, Marcus Tullius (orator, statesman); Arpinum, Italy **(106–43 B.C.)**

Cid, El (Rodrigo [or Ruy] Díez de Bivar) (Spanish national hero); nr. Burgos, Spain **(c. 1043–1099)**

Cilento, Diane (actress); Queensland, Australia, 10/5/33

Cimabue, Giovanni (painter); Florence, Italy **(c. 1240–c. 1302)**

Cimino, Michael (director, writer, producer); New York City, 11/16/43

Claire, Ina (Ina Fagan) (actress); Washington, D.C. **(1895–1985)**

Clancy, Tom (novelist); Baltimore, 4/12/47

Clapton, Eric (singer, guitarist); Ripley, England, 3/30/45

Clark, Dick (TV personality); Mt. Vernon, N.Y., 11/30/29

Clark, Mary Higgins (author); New York City, 12/24/31

Clark, Petula (singer); Epsom, England, 11/15/34

Clark, Roy (country music artist); Meherrin, Va., 4/15/33

Clark, William (explorer); Caroline County, Va. **(1770–1838)**

Clarke, Arthur C. (science fiction writer); Minehead, England, 12/16/17

Claude Lorrain (Claude Gellée) (painter); Champagne, France **(1600–1682)**

Clausewitz, Karl von (military strategist); Burg, Germany **(1780–1831)**

Clay, Henry (statesman); Hanover County, Va. **(1777–1852)**

Clay, Lucius D. (banker, ex-general); Marietta, Ga. **(1897–1978)**

Clayburgh, Jill (actress); New York City, 4/30/44

Cleary, Beverly (Beverly Atlee Bunn) (children's author); McMinnville, Ore., 1916

Cleaver, Eldridge (Leroy) (author, activist); Wabbaseka, Ark. **(1935–1998)**

Cleese, John (writer, actor); Weston-super-Mare, England, 10/27/39

Clemenceau, Georges (statesman); Mouilleron-en-Pareds, Vondée, France **(1841–1929)**

Cleopatra (Queen of Egypt); Alexandria, Egypt **(69–30 B.C.)**

Cleveland, Stephen Grover (22nd & 24th U.S. president); Caldwell, N.J. **(1837–1908)**

Cliburn, Van (Harvey Lavan Cliburn, Jr.) (concert pianist); Shreveport, La., 7/12/34

Clift, Montgomery (actor); Omaha, Neb. **(1920–1966)**

Cline, Patsy (singer); Winchester, Va. **(1933–1963)**

Clinton, Hillary Rodham (First Lady); Park Ridge, Ill., 10/26/47

Clinton, William Jefferson (42nd U.S. president); Hope, Ark., 8/19/46

Clooney, George (actor); Lexington, Ky., 5/6/61

Clooney, Rosemary (singer); Maysville, Ky., 5/23/28

Close, Glenn (actress); Greenwich, Conn., 3/19/47

Cobain, Kurt (musician); Hoquiam, Wash. **(1967–1994)**

Cobb, Irvin Shrewsbury (humorist); Paducah, Ky. **(1876–1944)**

Cobb, Lee J. (Leo Jacob Cobb) (actor); New York City **(1911–1976)**

Coburn, Charles Douville (actor); Savannah, Ga. **(1877–1961)**

Coburn, James (actor); Laurel, Neb., 8/31/28

Coca, Imogene (comedienne); Philadelphia **(1908–2001)**

Cocker, Jarvis (singer, songwriter); Sheffield, England, 9/19/63

Cocker, Joe (John Robert Cocker) (singer); Sheffield, England, 5/20/44

Coco, James (actor); New York City **(1929–1987)**

Cocteau, Jean (author); Maison-Lafitte, France **(1889–1963)**

Cohan, George Michael (actor, dramatist); Providence, R.I. **(1878–1942)**

Cohen, Leonard (composer); Montreal, Que., Canada, 9/21/34

Colbert, Claudette (Lily Chauchoin) (actress); Paris **(1903–1996)**

Cole, Nat "King" (singer); Montgomery, Ala. **(1919–1965)**

Cole, Natalie (singer); Los Angeles, 2/6/50

Cole, Paula (singer, songwriter); Rockport, Mass., 4/15/68

Cole, Thomas (painter); Lancashire, England **(1801–1848)**

Coleman, Dabney (actor); Austin, Tex., 1/3/32

Coleridge, Samuel Taylor (poet); Ottery St. Mary, England **(1772–1834)**

Colette (Sidonie-Gabrielle Colette) (novelist); St.-Sauveur, France **(1873–1954)**

Collingwood, Charles (TV commentator); Three Rivers, Mich. **(1917–1985)**

Collins, Joan (actress); London, 5/23/33

Collins, Judy (singer); Seattle, 5/1/39

Colman, Ronald (actor); Richmond, England **(1891–1958)**

Colonna, Jerry (comedian); Boston **(1905–1986)**

Coltrane, John (jazz musician); Hamlet, N.C. **(1926–1967)**

Columbus, Chris (director, screenwriter); Spangler, Pa., 9/10/58

Columbus, Christopher (Cristoforo Colombo) (explorer); Genoa, Italy **(1451–1506)**

Colvin, Shawn (folk singer); Vermillion, S.D., 1/10/58

Combs, Sean "Puffy" (singer, record producer); New York City, 11/9/69

Comden, Betty (writer); New York City, 5/3/19

Comenius, Johann Amos (educational reformer); Nivnice, Moravia, Czech Republic **(1592–1670)**

Commager, Henry Steele (historian); Pittsburgh **(1902–1998)**

Como, Perry (Pierino Como) (singer); Canonsburg, Pa. **(1912–2001)**

Compton, Karl Taylor (physicist); Wooster, Ohio **(1887–1954)**

Comte, Auguste (philosopher); Montpellier, France **(1798–1857)**

Conant, James B. (educator, statesman); Dorchester, Mass. **(1893–1978)**

Condon, Eddie (jazz musician); Goodland, Ind. **(1905–1973)**

Confucius (K'ung Fu-tzu) (philosopher); Shantung province, China **(c. 551– 479 B.C.)**

Congreve, William (dramatist); nr. Leeds, England **(1670–1729)**

Connelly, Marc (playwright); McKeesport, Pa. **(1890–1980)**

Connery, Sean (actor); Edinburgh, Scotland, 8/25/30

Connick, Jr., Harry (musician, actor); New Orleans, La., 9/11/67

Conniff, Ray (band leader); Attleboro, Mass., 11/6/16

Connors, Chuck (actor); Brooklyn, N.Y. **(1921–1992)**

Connors, Mike (Krekor Ohanian) (actor); Fresno, Calif., 8/15/25

Conrad, Joseph (Teodor Jozef Konrad Korzeniowski) (novelist); Berdichev, Ukraine **(1857–1924)**

Conrad, Robert (Conrad Robert Falk) (actor); Chicago, 3/1/35

Conrad, William (actor); Louisville, Ky. **(1920–1994)**

Conried, Hans (Frank Foster) (actor); Baltimore **(1915–1982)**

Conroy, Pat (author); Atlanta, 10/26/45

Constable, John (painter); East Bergholt, Suffolk, England **(1776–1837)**

Constantine II (ex-king of Greece); Athens, 6/2/40

Constantine, Michael (actor); Reading, Pa., 5/22/27

Conte, Richard (actor); New York City **(1916–1975)**

Conti, Tom (actor); Paisley, Scotland, 11/22/41

Convy, Bert (actor, host); St. Louis **(1933–1991)**

Conway, Tim (comedian); Chagrin Falls, Ohio, 12/15/33

Coogan, Jackie (actor); Los Angeles **(1914–1984)**

Cook, Peter (actor, writer); Torquay, England **(1937–1995)**

Cooke, Alistair (Alfred Alistair) (TV narrator, journalist); Manchester, England, 11/20/08

Cooke, Jack Kent (business executive); Hamilton, Ont., Canada **(1912–1997)**

Cooley, Denton A(rthur) (heart surgeon); Houston, 8/22/20
Coolidge, (John) Calvin (30th U.S. president); Plymouth, Vt. **(1872–1933)**
Coolidge, Rita (singer); Nashville, Tenn., 5/1/45
Coolio (Artis Ivey, Jr.) (rap artist); Los Angeles, Calif., 8/1/63
Cooper, Alice (Vincent Furnier) (rock musician); Detroit, 2/4/48
Cooper, Gary (Frank James Cooper) (actor); Helena, Mont. **(1901–1961)**
Cooper, Dame Gladys (actress); Lewisham, England **(1888–1971)**
Cooper, Jackie (actor, director); Los Angeles, 9/15/22
Cooper, James Fenimore (novelist); Burlington, N.J. **(1789–1851)**
Cooper, Peter (industrialist, philanthropist); New York City **(1791–1883)**
Copernicus, Nicolaus (Mikolaj Kopernik) (astronomer); Thorn, Poland **(1473–1543)**
Copland, Aaron (composer); Brooklyn, N.Y. **(1900–1990)**
Copley, John Singleton (painter); Boston **(1738–1815)**
Copperfield, David (David Kotkin) (illusionist); Metuchen, N.J., 9/16/56
Coppola, Francis Ford (film director); Detroit, 4/7/39
Corelli, Arcangelo (composer); Fusignano, Italy **(1653–1713)**
Corelli, Franco (operatic tenor); Ancona, Italy, 4/8/23
Corgan, Billy (musician); Elk Grove, Ill., 3/17/67
Corneille, Pierre (dramatist); Rouen, France **(1606–1684)**
Cornell, Katharine (actress); Berlin **(1893–1974)**
Corot, Jean Baptiste Camille (painter); Paris **(1796–1875)**
Corella, Angel (ballet dancer); Madrid, Spain, 11/8/75
Correggio, Antonio Allegri da (painter); Correggio, Italy **(1494–1534)**
Corsaro, Frank (opera director); New York harbor, 12/22/24
Cortés (or Cortez), Hernando (explorer); Medellin, Spain **(1485–1547)**
Cosby, Bill (actor); Philadelphia, 7/12/37
Cosell, Howard (Howard Cohen) (sportscaster); Winston-Salem, N.C. **(1918–1995)**
Costello, Elvis (Declan Patrick McManus) (singer, musician, songwriter); London, 1954
Costello, Lou (Louis Cristillo) (comedian); Paterson, N.J. **(1908–1959)**
Costner, Kevin (actor); Los Angeles, 1/18/55
Cotten, Joseph (actor); Petersburg, Va. **(1905–1994)**
Couperin, François (composer); Paris **(1668–1733)**
Courbet, Gustave (painter); Ornans, France **(1819–1877)**
Couric, Katie (TV host); Arlington, Va., 1/7/57
Courtenay, Tom (actor); Hull, England, 2/25/37
Cousins, Norman (publisher); Union Hill, N.J. **(1915–1990)**
Cousteau, Jacques-Yves (marine explorer); St. André-de-Cubzac, France **(1910–1997)**
Covey, Stephen R. (author); Salt Lake City, 10/24/32
Coward, Sir Noel (playwright, actor); Teddington, England **(1899–1973)**
Cowles, Gardner, Jr. (newspaper publisher); Algona, Iowa **(1903–1985)**
Cowper, William (poet); Great Berkhamstead, England **(1731–1800)**
Cox, Archibald (Watergate prosecutor); Plainfield, N.J., 5/17/12
Cox, Courteney (actress); Birmingham, Ala., 6/15/64
Coyote, Peter (actor); New York City, 10/10/41
Cozzens, James Gould (novelist); Chicago **(1903–1978)**
Crabbe, Buster (Clarence Crabbe) (actor); Oakland, Calif. **(1908–1983)**
Cranach, Lucas, the elder (painter); Kronach, Germany **(1472–1553)**
Crane, Hart (poet); Garrettsville, Ohio **(1899–1932)**
Crane, Stephen (novelist, poet); Newark, N.J. **(1871–1900)**
Cranmer, Thomas (churchman); Aslacton, England **(1489–1556)**
Craven, Wes (director, producer, screenwriter); Cleveland, 8/2/39
Crawford, Broderick (actor); Philadelphia **(1911–1986)**
Crawford, Cheryl (stage producer); Akron, Ohio **(1902–1986)**
Crawford, Cindy (model, actress); De Kalb, Illinois, 2/20/66
Crawford, Joan (Lucille LeSueur) (actress, business executive); San Antonio **(1908–1977)**
Crazy Horse (Lakota Indian leader); nr. Bear Butte, S.D. **(1840?–1877)**
Crenna, Richard (actor); Los Angeles, 11/30/27
Crespin, Régine (operatic soprano); Marseilles, France, 2/23/29
Crichton, (John) Michael (novelist, film producer); Chicago, 10/23/42
Crick, Francis Harry Compton (scientist, Nobel laureate); Northampton, England, 6/8/16
Crisp, Donald (actor); London **(1880–1974)**
Croce, Benedetto (philosopher); Peseasseroli, Aquila, Italy **(1866–1952)**

Croce, Jim (singer); Philadelphia **(1942–1973)**
Crockett, Davy (David) (frontiersman); Greene County, Tenn. **(1786–1836)**
Cromwell, Oliver (statesman); Huntingdon, England **(1599–1658)**
Cronenberg, David (film director); Toronto, Canada, 3/15/43
Cronin, A. J. (Archibald J. Cronin) (novelist); Cardross, Scotland **(1896–1981)**
Cronkite, Walter (TV newscaster); St. Joseph, Mo., 11/4/16
Cronyn, Hume (actor); London, Ont., Canada, 7/18/11
Crosby, Bing (Harry Lillis) (singer, actor); Tacoma, Wash. **(1904–1977)**
Crosby, Bob (musician); Spokane, Wash. **(1913–1993)**
Crosby, Cathy Lee (actress); Los Angeles, 12/2/48
Crosby, Norm (comedian); Boston, 9/15/27
Cross, Ben (Bernard) (actor); Paddington, England, 12/16/47
Cross, Milton (opera commentator); New York City **(1897–1975)**
Crouse, Russell (playwright); Findlay, Ohio **(1893–1966)**
Crow, Sheryl (musician, record producer); Kennett, Mo., 2/11/62
Crowe, Russell (actor, musician); Auckland, New Zealand, 4/7/64
Crudup, Billy (actor); Manhasset, N.Y., 7/8/68
Cruise, Tom (Thomas Mapother IV) (actor, producer); Syracuse, N.Y., 7/3/62
Crystal, Billy (comedian, actor); Long Beach, N.Y., 3/14/47
Cugat, Xavier (band leader); Barcelona, Spain **(1900–1990)**
Cukor, George (film director); New York City **(1899–1983)**
Culkin, Macaulay (actor); New York City, 8/26/80
Cullen, Bill (William Lawrence Cullen) (radio and TV entertainer); Pittsburgh **(1920–1990)**
Cullen, Countee (poet); New York City **(1903–1946)**
Culp, Robert (actor); Berkeley, Calif., 8/16/30
cummings, e. e. (Edward Estlin Cummings) (poet); Cambridge, Mass. **(1894–1962)**
Cummings, Robert (actor); Joplin, Mo. **(1908–1990)**
Cunningham, Merce (choreographer); Centralia, Wash., 4/16/19
Curie, Marie (Marja Sklodowska) (physical chemist, Nobel laureate); Warsaw **(1867–1934)**
Curie, Pierre (physicist); Paris **(1859–1906)**
Curtin, Jane (actress); Cambridge, Mass., 9/6/47
Curtin, Phyllis (soprano); Clarksburg, W. Va., 12/3/27
Curtis, Jamie Lee (actress); Los Angeles, 11/22/58
Curtis, Tony (Bernard Schwartz) (actor); Bronx, N.Y., 6/3/25
Curzon, Clifford (concert pianist); London **(1907–1982)**
Cusack, Joan (actress); New York City, 10/11/62
Cusack, John (actor); Chicago, 6/28/66
Custer, George Armstrong (army officer); New Rumley, Ohio **(1839–1876)**

D

Dafoe, Willem (William Dafoe, Jr.) (actor); Appleton, Wis., 7/22/55
da Gama, Vasco (explorer); Sines, Portugal **(1460–1524)**
Daguerre, Louis (photographic pioneer); nr. Paris **(1787–1851)**
Dahl, Arlene (actress); Minneapolis, 8/11/28
Dalai Lama (Tenzin Gyatso) (spiritual and temporal head of Tibet); Taktser, China, 1935
Daley, Richard J. (mayor of Chicago); Chicago **(1902–1976)**
Dali, Salvador (painter); Figueras, Spain **(1904–1989)**
Dalton, John (chemist); nr. Cockermouth, England **(1766–1844)**
Dalton, Timothy (actor); Colwyn Bay, Wales, U.K., 3/21/46
Daly, Tyne (actress); Madison, Wis., 2/21/46
d'Amboise, Jacques (ballet dancer); Dedham, Mass., 7/28/34
Damone, Vic (Vito Farinola) (singer); Brooklyn, N.Y., 6/12/28
Damrosch, Walter Johannes (orchestra conductor); Breslau, Poland **(1862–1950)**
Dana, Charles Anderson (editor); Hinsdale, N.H. **(1819–1897)**
Dandridge, Dorothy (actress); Cleveland **(1923–1965)**
Danes, Claire (actress); New York City, 4/12/79
Dangerfield, Rodney (Jacob Cohen) (actor, comedian); Babylon, N.Y., 11/22/22
Daniels, Jeff (actor); Chelsea, Mich., 2/19/55
Daniels, William (actor); Brooklyn, N.Y., 3/31/27
Danilova, Alexandra (ballet dancer); Peterhof, Russia **(1904–1997)**
Dannay, Frederic (novelist, pseudonym Ellery Queen); Brooklyn, N.Y. **(1905–1982)**
Danner, Blythe (actress); Philadelphia, 2/3/43
D'Annunzio, Gabriele (soldier, author); Francaville at Mare, Pescara, Italy **(1863–1938)**
Danson, Ted (actor); San Diego, Calif., 12/29/47
Dante (or Durante) Alighieri (poet); Florence, Italy **(1265–1321)**
Danton, Georges Jacques (French Revolutionary leader); Arcis-sur-Aube, France **(1759–1794)**
Danza, Tony (actor); Brooklyn, N.Y., 4/21/51
Darren, James (actor); Philadelphia, 6/8/36

Darrow, Clarence Seward (lawyer); Kinsman, Ohio **(1857–1938)**

Darwin, Charles Robert (naturalist); Shrewsbury, England **(1809–1882)**

Dassin, Jules (film director); Middletown, Conn., 12/18/11

Daumier, Honoré (caricaturist); Marseilles, France **(1808–1879)**

David, Jacques-Louis (painter); Paris **(1748–1825)**

David (king of Israel and Judah); died c. 973 B.C.

Davidson, John (singer, actor); Pittsburgh, 12/13/41

Davies, Marion (Marion Douras) (actress); New York City **(1897–1961)**

Davies, (William) Robertson (writer); Thamesville, Ont., Canada **(1913–1996)**

Davis, Angela (social activist); Birmingham, Ala., 1/26/44

Davis, Ann B. (actress); Schenectady, N.Y., 5/5/26

Davis, Lt. Gen. Benjamin O., Jr. (Air Force general); Washington, D.C., 12/18/12

Davis, Brig. Gen. Benjamin O., Sr. (U.S. Army general); Washington, D.C. **(1877–1970)**

Davis, Bette (actress); Lowell, Mass. **(1908–1989)**

Davis, Geena (Virginia Davis) (actress); Wareham, Mass., 1/21/57

Davis, Jefferson (president of the Confederacy); Christian (now Todd) County, Ky. **(1808–1889)**

Davis, Judy (actress); Perth, Australia, 1955

Davis, Mac (singer); Lubbock, Tex., 1/21/42

Davis, Miles (jazz trumpeter); Alton, Ill. **(1926–1991)**

Davis, Ossie (actor, writer); Cogdell, Ga., 12/18/17

Davis, Sammy, Jr. (actor, singer); New York City **(1925–1990)**

Davis, Stuart (painter); Philadelphia **(1894–1964)**

Dawson, Richard (actor, host); Gosport, Hampshire, England, 11/20/32

Day, Doris (Doris von Kappelhoff) (singer, actress); Cincinnati, 4/3/24

Dayan, Moshe (ex-defense minister of Israel); Dagania, Palestine **(1915–1981)**

Day-Lewis, Daniel (actor); London, 4/29/58

Dean, James (actor); Marion, Ind. **(1931–1955)**

Dean, Jimmy (singer); Seth Ward, nr. Plainview, Tex., 8/10/28

De Bakey, Michael E. (heart surgeon); Lake Charles, La., 9/7/08

de Beauvoir, Simone (novelist, philosopher); Paris **(1908–1986)**

Debs, Eugene Victor (Socialist leader); Terre Haute, Ind. **(1855–1926)**

Debussy, Claude Achille (composer); St. Germain-en-Laye, France **(1862–1918)**

De Carlo, Yvonne (Peggy Yvonne Middleton) (actress); Vancouver, B.C., Canada, 9/1/24

Dee, Ruby (Ruby Ann Wallace) (actress); Cleveland, 10/27/24

Dee, Sandra (Alexandra Zuck) (actress); Bayonne, N.J., 4/23/42

Degas, Hilaire Germain Edgar (painter); Paris **(1834–1917)**

de Gaulle, Charles André Joseph Marie (soldier, statesman); Lille, France **(1890–1970)**

de Havilland, Olivia (actress); Tokyo, 7/1/16

de Kooning, Willem (artist); Rotterdam **(1904–1997)**

Delacroix, Eugène (painter); Charenton-St. Maurice, France **(1798–1863)**

Delany, Dana (actress); New York City, 3/15/56

de la Renta, Oscar (fashion designer); Santo Domingo, Dominican Republic, 7/22/32

Delaunay, Robert (painter); Paris **(1885–1941)**

De Laurentiis, Dino (film producer); Torre Annunziata, Bay of Naples, Italy, 8/8/18

Delon, Alain (actor); Sceaux, France, 11/8/35

Del Toro, Benicio (actor); Santurce, Puerto Rico, 2/19/67

DeLuise, Dom (actor, comedian); Brooklyn, N.Y., 8/1/33

Demarest, William (actor); St. Paul, Minn. **(1892–1983)**

de Mille, Agnes (choreographer); New York City **(1905–1993)**

De Mille, Cecil Blount (film director); Ashfield, Mass. **(1881–1959)**

Demme, Jonathan (director, producer, screenwriter); Baldwin, N.Y., 2/22/44

Demosthenes (orator); Athens **(384?–322 B.C.)**

Dench, Dame Judi (film and stage actress); York, England, 12/9/34

Deneuve, Catherine (actress); Paris, 10/22/43

Deng Xiaoping (Chinese leader); Sichuan province, China **(1904–1997)**

De Niro, Robert (actor, director); New York City, 8/17/43

Dennehy, Brian (actor); Bridgeport, Conn., 7/9/39

Dennis, Sandy (actress); Hastings, Neb. **(1937–1992)**

Denny, Reginald (actor); Richmond, England **(1891–1967)**

Denver, John (Henry John Deutschendorf, Jr.) (singer, actor); Roswell, N.M. **(1943–1997)**

De Palma, Brian (film director); Newark, N.J., 9/11/40

Depp, Johnny (actor); Owensboro, Ky., 6/9/63

Derain, André (painter); Chatou, Seine-et-Oise, France **(1880–1954)**

Derek, John (Derek Harris) (actor, director); Los Angeles **(1926–1998)**

Dern, Bruce (actor); Winnetka, Ill., 6/4/36

Dern, Laura (actress); Los Angeles, 2/10/67

Dershowitz, Alan (lawyer); Brooklyn, N.Y., 9/1/38

Derrida, Jacques (philosopher); El-Biar, Algeria, 7/15/30

Descartes, René (philosopher, mathematician); La Haye, France **(1596–1650)**

De Seversky, Alexander P. (aviator); Tiflis (Tbilisi), Georgia **(1894–1974)**

De Sica, Vittorio (film director); Sora, Italy **(1901–1974)**

Desmond, Johnny (singer, composer); Detroit **(1921–1985)**

De Soto, Hernando (explorer); Barcarrota, Spain **(c. 1500–1542)**

De Valera, Eamon (ex-president of Ireland); New York City **(1882–1975)**

Devane, William (actor); Albany, N.Y., 9/5/39

Devine, Andy (actor); Flagstaff, Ariz. **(1905–1977)**

DeVito, Danny (Daniel Michael DeVito) (actor, director, producer); Neptune, N.J., 11/17/44

De Vries, Peter (novelist); Chicago **(1910–1993)**

de Waart, Edo (conductor); Amsterdam, the Netherlands, 6/1/41

Dewey, George (admiral); Montpelier, Vt. **(1837–1917)**

Dewey, John (philosopher, educator); Burlington, Vt. **(1859–1952)**

Dewey, Thomas E. (political figure); Owosso, Mich. **(1902–1971)**

Dewhurst, Colleen (actress); Montreal **(1926–1991)**

Dey, Susan (actress); Pekin, Ill., 12/10/52

Diaghilev, Sergei (ballet impressario); Novgorod, Russia **(1872–1929)**

Diamond, Neil (singer); Brooklyn, N.Y., 1/24/41

Diaz, Cameron (actress, model); San Diego, Calif., 8/30/72

DiCaprio, Leonardo (actor); Los Angeles, 11/11/74

Dichter, Misha (pianist); Shanghai, 9/27/45

Dickens, Charles John Huffam (novelist); Portsea, England **(1812–1870)**

Dickey, James (writer); Atlanta **(1923–1997)**

Dickinson, Angie (Angeline Brown) (actress); Kulm, N.D., 9/30/31

Dickinson, Emily Elizabeth (poet); Amherst, Mass. **(1830–1886)**

Diddley, Bo (Elias McDaniel) (guitarist); McComb, Miss., 12/30/28

Diderot, Denis (encyclopedist); Langres, France **(1713–1784)**

Dietrich, Marlene (Maria Magdalena von Losch) (actress); Berlin **(1901–1992)**

DiFranco, Ani (singer, songwriter); Buffalo, N.Y., 9/23/70

Diller, Phyllis (Phyllis Driver) (comedienne); Lima, Ohio, 7/17/17

Dillon, Matt (actor); New Rochelle, N.Y., 2/18/64

Dine, Jim (painter); Cincinnati, 6/16/35

Dinesen, Isak (Karen Blixen) (author); Rungsted, Denmark **(1885–1962)**

Dinkins, David (ex-mayor of New York City); Trenton, N.J., 7/10/27

Diogenes (philosopher); Sinope, Turkey **(c. 412–323 B.C.)**

Dion (Dion DiMucci) (singer); Bronx, N.Y., 7/18/39

Dion, Celine (musician); Charlemagne, Que., Canada, 3/30/68

Dior, Christian (fashion designer); Granville, France **(1905–1957)**

Disney, Walt(er) Elias (film animator, producer); Chicago **(1901–1966)**

Disraeli, Benjamin (Earl of Beaconsfield) (statesman); London **(1804–1881)**

Dix, Dorothea (civil rights reformer); Hampden, Maine **(1802–1887)**

Dixon, Jeane (Jeane Pinckert) (seer); Medford, Wis. **(1918–1997)**

Dobbs, Mattiwilda (soprano); Atlanta, 7/11/25

Doctorow, E(dgar) L(aurence) (novelist); New York City, 1/6/31

Dogg, Snoop Doggy (Calvin Broadus) (musician); Long Beach, Calif., 10/20/72

Doherty, Shannen (actress); Memphis, Tenn., 4/21/71

Dole, Elizabeth Hanford (public official); Salisbury, N.C., 7/29/36

Dole, Robert (political figure); Russell, Kans., 7/22/23

Dolin, Anton (dancer); Slinfold, England **(1904–1983)**

Domingo, Placido (tenor); Madrid, 1/21/41

Domino, Fats (Antoine) (musician); New Orleans, 2/26/28

Donahue, Phil (TV host); Cleveland, 12/21/35

Donahue, Troy (Merle Johnson) (actor); New York City **(1936–2001)**

Donaldson, Sam (broadcast journalist); El Paso, Tex., 3/11/34

Donat, Robert (actor); Withington, England **(1905–1958)**

Donatello (Donato Niccolò di Betto Bardi) (sculptor); Florence **(c. 1386–1466)**

Donlevy, Brian (actor); Portadown, Ireland **(1899–1972)**

Donne, John (poet); London **(1573–1631)**

Donner, Richard (director, producer); New York City, 1939

D'Onofrio, Vincent (actor); Brooklyn, N.Y., 6/30/59

Donovan (Donovan Leitch) (singer, songwriter); Glasgow, Scotland, 2/10/46

Doolittle, James H. (ex-Air Force general); Alameda, Calif. **(1896–1993)**

Doohan, James (actor); Vancouver, B.C., 3/20/20

Dorati, Antal (orchestra conductor); Budapest **(1906–1988)**

Dorn, Michael (actor); Luling, Tex., 12/9/52

Dorris, Michael (anthropologist, writer); Louisville, Ky. **(1945–1997)**

Dorsey, Jimmy (band leader); Shenandoah, Pa. **(1904–1957)**

Dorsey, Thomas Andrew (father of gospel music); Villa Rice, Ga. **(1899–1993)**

Dorsey, Tommy (band leader); Mahanoy Plane, Pa. **(1905–1956)**

Dos Passos, John (author); Chicago **(1896–1970)**

Dostoevski, Fyodor Mikhailovich (novelist); Moscow **(1821–1881)**

Dotrice, Roy (actor); Guernsey, Channel Islands, England, 5/26/23

Douglas, Aaron (painter); Topeka, Kans. **(1900–1979)**

Douglas, Helen Gahagan (ex-representative); Boonton, N.J. **(1900–1980)**

Douglas, Kirk (Issur Danielovitch) (actor); Amsterdam, N.Y., 12/9/16

Douglas, Melvyn (Melvyn Hesselberg) (actor); Macon, Ga. **(1901–1981)**

Douglas, Michael (actor, producer); New Brunswick, N.J., 9/25/44

Douglas, Mike (Michael D. Dowd, Jr.) (TV host); Chicago, 8/11/25

Douglas, Stephen Arnold (politician); Brandon, Vt. **(1813–1861)**

Douglass, Frederick (abolitionist, author, orator); Tuckahoe, Md. **(1817–1895)**

Dow, Charles (financier); Sterling, Conn. **(1851–1902)**

Down, Lesley-Ann (actress); London, 3/17/54

Downey, Robert, Jr. (actor, director); New York City, 4/4/65

Downs, Hugh (broadcast journalist); Akron, Ohio, 2/14/21

Doyle, Sir Arthur Conan (novelist, spiritualist); Edinburgh, Scotland **(1859–1930)**

Doyle, David (actor); Lincoln, Neb. **(1929–1997)**

Drake, Sir Francis (navigator); Tavistock, England **(1545–1596)**

Dr. Dre (Andre Young) (rap singer); Los Angeles, 2/18/66

Dreiser, Theodore (writer); Terre Haute, Ind. **(1871–1945)**

Drescher, Fran (television and film actress); New York City, 9/30/57

Dreyfus, Alfred (French army officer); Mulhouse, France **(1859–1935)**

Dreyfuss, Richard (actor); Brooklyn, N.Y., 10/29/47

Drury, Allen (novelist); Houston **(1918–1998)**

Dryden, John (poet); Northamptonshire, England **(1631–1700)**

Dryer, Fred (ex-NFL player, actor); Hawthorne, Calif., 7/6/46

Dubček, Alexander (ex-president of Czechoslovakia); Uhrovek, Slovakia **(1921–1992)**

Dubinsky, David (David Dobnievski) (labor leader); Brest-Litovsk, Belarus **(1892–1982)**

Du Bois, W(illiam) E(dward) B(urghardt) (scholar, civil rights activist); Great Barrington, Mass. **(1868–1963)**

Duchamp, Marcel (painter); Blainville, France **(1887–1968)**

Duchin, Eddy (pianist, bandleader); Cambridge, Mass. **(1909–1951)**

Duchin, Peter (pianist, band leader); New York City, 7/28/37

Duchovny, David (actor); New York City, 8/7/60

Dufay, Guillaume (composer); Cambrai, France **(c. 1400–1474)**

Duffy, Julia (actress); Minneapolis, Minn., 6/27/50

Dufy, Raoul (painter); Le Havre, France **(1877–1953)**

Dukakis, Olympia (actress); Lowell, Mass., 6/20/31

Duke, James B. (industrialist); nr. Durham, N.C. **(1856–1925)**

Duke, Patty (Anna Marie Duke) (actress); New York City, 12/14/46

Dulles, Allen Welsh (ex-director of CIA); Watertown, N.Y. **(1893–1969)**

Dulles, John Foster (political figure); Washington, D.C. **(1888–1959)**

Dumas, Alexandre (called Dumas fils) (novelist); Paris **(1824–1895)**

Dumas, Alexandre (called Dumas père) (novelist); Villers-Cotterets, France **(1802–1870)**

du Maurier, Daphne (novelist); London **(1907–1989)**

du Maurier, George Louis Palmella Busson (novelist); Paris **(1834–1896)**

Dumont, Margaret (actress); Brooklyn, N.Y. **(1889–1965)**

Dunaway, Faye (actress); Bascom, Fla., 1/14/41

Dunbar, Paul Laurence (poet, novelist); Dayton, Ohio **(1872–1906)**

Duncan, Isadora (dancer); San Francisco **(1878–1927)**

Duncan, Michael Clarke (actor); Chicago, 12/10/57

Duncan, Sandy (actress); Henderson, Tex., 2/20/46

Dunham, Katherine (dancer, choreographer); Chicago, 6/22/09

Dunne, Irene (actress); Louisville, Ky. **(1898–1990)**

Duns Scotus, John (theologian); Duns, Scotland **(1265–1303)**

Du Pont, Pierre S. (economist); Paris **(1739–1817)**

Durante, Jimmy (comedian); New York City **(1893–1980)**

Duras, Marguerite (Donnadieu) (novelist, dramatist); Gia Dinh, Vietnam **(1914–1996)**

Durbin, Deanna (Edna Mae) (actress); Winnipeg, Canada, 12/4/21

Dürer, Albrecht (painter, engraver); Nürnberg, Germany **(1471–1528)**

Durning, Charles (actor); Highland Falls, N.Y., 2/28/23

Durrell, Lawrence George (novelist); Julundur, India **(1912–1990)**

Duse, Eleonora (actress); Chioggia, Italy **(1859–1924)**

Dussault, Nancy (actress); Pensacola, Fla., 6/30/36

Duvall, Robert (actor, director, producer); San Diego, Calif., 1/5/31

Duvall, Shelley (actress); Houston, 7/7/49

Dvořák, Antonin (composer); Nelahozeves, Czechoslovakia **(1841–1904)**

Dylan, Bob (Robert Zimmerman) (singer, songwriter, guitarist); Duluth, Minn., 5/24/41

Dysart, Richard (actor); Brighton, Mass., 3/30/29

E

Eakins, Thomas (painter, sculptor); Philadelphia **(1844–1916)**

Earhart, Amelia (aviator); Atchison, Kans. **(1897–1937)**

Earp, Wyatt (Berry Stapp) (sheriff, gunfighter); Monmouth, Ill. **(1848–1929)**

Eastman, George (camera inventor); Waterville, N.Y. **(1854–1932)**

Eastwood, Clint (actor, director, producer); San Francisco, 5/31/30

Ebert, Roger (film critic); Urbana, Ill., 6/18/42

Ebsen, Buddy (Christian Ebsen, Jr.) (actor); Belleville, Ill., 4/2/08

Eckstine, Billy (singer); Pittsburgh **(1914–1993)**

Eddy, Mary Baker (founder of Christian Science Church); Bow, N.H. **(1821–1910)**

Eddy, Nelson (baritone, actor); Providence, R.I. **(1901–1967)**

Edel, Leon (author); Pittsburgh **(1907–1997)**

Edelman, Marian Wright (social activist); Bennettsville, S.C., 6/6/39

Eden, Sir Anthony (Earl of Avon) (ex-prime minister); Durham, England **(1897–1977)**

Eden, Barbara (Barbara Huffman) (actress); Tucson, Ariz., 8/23/34

Edison, Thomas Alva (inventor); Milan, Ohio **(1847–1931)**

Edwards, Anthony (actor); Santa Barbara, Calif., 7/19/62

Edwards, Blake (film writer, producer); Tulsa, Okla., 7/26/22

Edwards, Jonathan (theologian); East Windsor, Conn. **(1703–1758)**

Edwards, Ralph (TV and radio producer); Merino, Colo., 6/13/13

Edwards, Vincent (Vincent Edward Zoino) (actor); Brooklyn, N.Y. **(1928–1996)**

Eglevsky, André (ballet dancer); Moscow **(1917–1977)**

Egoyan, Atom (film director, writer, editor); Cairo, 7/19/60

Ehrlich, Paul (bacteriologist); Strzelin, Poland **(1854–1915)**

Eichmann, (Karl) Adolf (Nazi, mass murderer); Solingen, Germany **(1906–1962)**

Eikenberry, Jill (actress); New Haven, Conn., 1/21/47

Einstein, Albert (physicist); Ulm, Germany **(1879–1955)**

Eisner, Michael (entertainment executive); Mt. Kisco, N.Y., 3/7/42

Eisenhower, Dwight David (34th U.S. president); Denison, Tex. **(1890–1969)**

Eisenhower, Milton S. (educator); Abilene, Kans. **(1899–1985)**

Eisenstaedt, Alfred (photographer, photojournalist); Dirschau (Prussia, now Tczew), Poland **(1898–1995)**

Ekland, Britt (Britt-Marie) (actress); Stockholm, 10/6/42

Electra, Carmen (Tara Patrick) (model, actress); Cincinnati, Ohio, 4/20/73

Elfman, Jenna (Jennifer Mary Butala) (actress); Los Angeles, 9/30/71

Elgar, Sir Edward (composer); Worcester, England **(1857–1934)**

Elgart, Larry (band leader); New York, Conn., 3/20/22

El Greco (Domenicos Theotocopoulos) (painter); Candia, Crete, Greece **(c. 1541–1614)**

Elion, Gertrude B. (chemist, Nobel laureate); New York City **(1918–1999)**

Eliot, George (Mary Ann Evans) (novelist); Chilvers Coton, England **(1819–1880)**

Eliot, Thomas Stearns (poet); St. Louis **(1888–1965)**

Elizabeth I (queen of England); Greenwich, England **(1533–1603)**

Elizabeth II (queen of England); London, 4/21/26

Elizondo, Hector (actor); New York City, 12/22/36

Ellington, Duke (Edward Kennedy) (jazz musician); Washington, D.C. **(1899–1974)**

Elliot, "Mama" Cass (Ellen Naomi Cohen) (singer); Baltimore **(1941–1974)**

Elliott, Sam (actor); Sacramento, Calif., 8/9/44

Ellison, Lawrence J. (computer industry executive); New York City, 1944

Ellison, Ralph (novelist); Oklahoma City, Okla. **(1914–1994)**

Ellsberg, Daniel (activist); Chicago, 4/7/31

Elman, Mischa (violinist); Stalnoye, Ukraine **(1891–1967)**

Emerson, Ralph Waldo (philosopher, poet); Boston **(1803–1882)**

Enesco, Georges (composer); Dorohoi, Romania **(1881–1955)**

Engels, Friedrich (Socialist writer); Barmen, Germany **(1820–1895)**

Englund, Robert (actor); Glendale, Calif., 6/6/49
Entremont, Philippe (concert pianist); Rheims, France, 6/7/34
Ephron, Nora (writer, director); New York City, 5/19/41
Epicurus (philosopher); Samos, Greece **(341–270 B.C.)**
Epstein, Sir Jacob (sculptor); New York City **(1880–1959)**
Erasmus, Desiderius (Gerhard Gerhards) (scholar); Rotterdam **(1469–1536)**
Erdrich, (Karen) Louise (writer); Little Falls, Minn., 7/6/54
Erickson, Leif (actor); Alameda, Calif. **(1911–1986)**
Ericsson, Leif (navigator) c. 10th century A.D.
Erikson, Erik H. (psychoanalyst); Frankfurt, Germany **(1902–1994)**
Ernst, Max (painter); Bruhl, Germany **(1891–1976)**
Erté (Romain de Tirtoff) (artist, designer); St. Petersburg, Russia **(1892–1990)**
Estevez, Emilio (actor, director, screenwriter); New York City, 5/12/62
Eszterhas, Joe (screenwriter); Csakanydoroslo, Hungary, 11/23/44
Euclid (mathematician); Megara, Greece, fl. 300 B.C.
Euler, Leonhard (mathematician); Basel, Switzerland **(1707–1783)**
Euripides (dramatist); Salamis, Greece **(c. 484–407 B.C.)**
Evangelista, Linda (model); St. Catharines, Ont., Canada, 5/10/65
Evans, Dale (born Lucille Wood Smith but raised as Frances Octavia Smith) (actress, singer); Uvalde, Tex. **(1912–2001)**
Evans, Dame Edith (actress); London **(1888–1976)**
Evans, Linda (actress); Hartford, Conn., 11/18/42
Evans, Maurice (actor); Dorchester, England **(1901–1989)**
Everett, Chad (Raymond Lee Cramton) (actor); South Bend, Ind., 6/11/36
Everett, Rupert (actor, model, musician); Norfolk, England, 5/29/59
Everhart, Angie (model, actress); Akron, Ohio, 9/6/69
Evers, Charles (civil rights leader); Decatur, Miss., 9/14/22
Evers, Medgar (civil rights leader); Decatur, Miss. **(1925–1963)**
Evers-Williams, Myrlie (civil rights leader); Vicksburg, Miss., 3/17/33

F

Fabares, Shelley (actress); Santa Monica, Calif., 1/19/44
Fabian (Fabian Anthony Forte) (singer); Philadelphia, 2/6/43
Fabray, Nanette (Nanette Fabarés) (actress); San Diego, Calif., 10/27/22
Fahrenheit, Gabriel (German physicist); Danzig, Poland **(1686–1736)**
Fairbanks, Douglas (Douglas Ulman) (actor); Denver **(1883–1939)**
Fairbanks, Douglas, Jr. (actor); New York City **(1909–2000)**
Fairchild, Morgan (Patsy Ann McClenny) (actress); Dallas, 2/3/50
Faith, Percy (conductor); Toronto **(1908–1976)**
Falk, Peter (actor); New York City, 9/16/27
Falla, Manuel de (composer); Cadiz, Spain **(1876–1946)**
Faludi, Susan (journalist, writer); New York City, 4/18/59
Falwell, Jerry (fundamentalist preacher); Lynchburg, Va., 8/11/33
Faraday, Michael (physicist); Newington, England **(1791–1867)**
Farentino, James (actor); Brooklyn, N.Y., 2/24/38
Farley, Chris (actor, comedian); Madison, Wis. **(1964–1997)**
Farmer, James (civil rights leader); Marshall, Tex. **(1920–1999)**
Farnsworth, Richard (actor); Los Angeles, 9/1/20
Farr, Jamie (Jameel Joseph Farah) (actor); Toledo, Ohio, 7/1/34
Farrar, Geraldine (soprano, actress); Melrose, Mass. **(1882–1967)**
Farrell, Eileen (operatic soprano); Willimantic, Conn., 2/13/20
Farrell, James T. (novelist); Chicago **(1904–1979)**
Farrell, Mike (actor); St. Paul, Minn., 2/6/39
Farrell, Perry (Perry Bernstein) (lead singer); Queens, N.Y., 3/29/59
Farrell, Suzanne (Roberta Sue Ficker) (ballet dancer); Cincinnati, 8/16/45
Farrow, Mia (actress); Los Angeles, 2/9/46
Fasanella, Ralph (painter); New York City **(1914–1997)**
Fassbinder, Rainer Werner (film, stage director); Bad Wörishofen, Germany **(1946–1982)**
Fast, Howard (novelist); New York City, 11/11/14
Faubus, Orval E(ugene) (governor of Arkansas); Combs, Ark. **(1910–1994)**
Faulkner, William (novelist); New Albany, Miss. **(1897–1962)**
Fauré, Gabriel Urbain (composer); Pamiers, France **(1845–1924)**
Fawcett, Farrah (Mary Farrah Leni Fawcett) (actress); Corpus Christi, Tex., 2/2/47
Faye, Alice (Ann Leppert) (actress); New York City **(1912–1998)**
Feiffer, Jules (cartoonist); New York City, 1/26/29
Feininger, Lyonel (painter); New York City **(1871–1956)**
Feldman, Marty (actor, screenwriter, director); London **(1938–1982)**
Feldon, Barbara (actress); Pittsburgh, 3/12/41
Feliciano, José (singer); Larez, Puerto Rico, 9/10/45
Felker, Clay S. (editor, publisher); St. Louis, 10/2/25

Fell, Norman (actor); Philadelphia **(1923–1998)**
Fellini, Federico (film director); Rimini, Italy **(1920–1993)**
Fender, Freddie (Baldemar Huerta) (singer); San Benito, Tex., 6/4/37
Ferber, Edna (novelist); Kalamazoo, Mich. **(1885–1968)**
Ferguson, Maynard (jazz trumpeter); Verdun, Que., Canada, 5/4/28
Ferlinghetti, Lawrence (poet, writer, translator); Yonkers, N.Y., 3/24/19
Fermi, Enrico (atomic physicist); Rome **(1901–1954)**
Fernandel (Fernand Joseph Desire Contandin) (actor); Marseilles, France **(1903–1971)**
Ferraro, Geraldine Anne (political figure); New York City, 8/26/35
Ferrer, José (actor, director); Santurce, Puerto Rico **(1912–1992)**
Ferrer, Mel (actor); Elberon, N.J., 8/25/17
Fiedler, Arthur (conductor); Boston **(1894–1979)**
Field, Eugene (poet); St. Louis **(1850–1895)**
Field, Marshall (merchant; nr. Conway, Mass. **(1834–1906)**
Field, Sally (actress); Pasadena, Calif., 11/6/46
Fielding, Henry (novelist); nr. Glastonbury, England **(1707–1754)**
Fields, W. C. (William Claude Dukenfield) (comedian); Philadelphia **(1880–1946)**
Fiennes, Joseph (actor); Salisbury, England, 5/27/70
Fiennes, Ralph (actor); Suffolk, England, 12/22/62
Fierstein, Harvey (Forbes) (playwright, actor); Brooklyn, 6/6/54
Figgis, Mike (director, screenwriter, composer, actor); Carlisle, England, 2/28/48
Filene, Edward A. (merchant) **(1860–1937)**
Fillmore, Millard (13th U.S. president); Locke, Cayuga County, N.Y. **(1800–1874)**
Finch, Peter (actor); Kensington, England **(1916–1977)**
Finney, Albert (actor); Salford, England, 5/9/36
Fiorentino, Linda (Clorinda Fiorentino) (actress); Philadelphia, 3/9/60
Firkusny, Rudolf (pianist); Napajedia, former Czechoslovakia **(1912–1994)**
Firth, Colin (actor); Grayshot, England, 9/10/60
Fischer-Dieskau, Dietrich (baritone); Berlin, 5/28/25
Fishburne, Laurence (actor); Augusta, Ga., 7/30/61
Fisher, Carrie (actress); Los Angeles, 10/21/56
Fisher, Eddie (Edwin) (singer); Philadelphia, 8/10/28
Fitzgerald, Barry (William Joseph Shields) (actor); Dublin **(1888–1961)**
Fitzgerald, Ella (singer); Newport News, Va. **(1918–1996)**
Fitzgerald, F. Scott (Francis Scott Key Fitzgerald) (novelist); St. Paul, Minn. **(1896–1940)**
Fitzgerald, Geraldine (actress); Dublin, 11/24/14
Fitzgerald, Pegeen (radio broadcaster); Norcatur, Kans. **(1910–1989)**
Flack, Roberta (singer); Black Mountain, N.C., 2/10/40
Flagstad, Kirsten (Wagnerian soprano); Hamar, Norway **(1895–1962)**
Flatt, Lester Raymond (bluegrass musician); Overton County, Tenn. **(1914–1979)**
Flaubert, Gustave (novelist); Rouen, France **(1821–1880)**
Fleming, Sir Alexander (bacteriologist); Lochfield, Scotland **(1881–1955)**
Fletcher, John (dramatist); Rye, Sussex, England **(1579–1625)**
Flockhart, Calista (actress); Freeport, Ill., 11/11/64
Flynn, Errol (actor); Hobart, Tasmania **(1909–1959)**
Fodor, Eugene (violinist); Turkey Creek, Colo., 3/5/50
Fokine, Michel (dancer, choreographer); St. Petersburg, Russia **(1880–1942)**
Fonda, Bridget (actress); Los Angeles, 1/27/64
Fonda, Henry (actor); Grand Island, Neb. **(1905–1982)**
Fonda, Jane (actress); New York City, 12/21/37
Fonda, Peter (actor); New York City, 2/23/39
Fontaine, Frank (singer, comedian); Cambridge, Mass. **(1920–1979)**
Fontaine, Joan (Joan de Havilland) (actress); Tokyo, 10/22/17
Fontanne, Lynn (actress); London **(1887–1983)**
Fonteyn, Dame Margot (Margaret Hookham) (ballet dancer); Reigate, England **(1919–1991)**
Foote, Shelby (historian); Greenville, Miss., 11/17/16
Forbes, Malcolm S(tevenson) (publisher, sportsman); Brooklyn, N.Y. **(1919–1990)**
Ford, Gerald Rudolph (38th U.S. president); Omaha, Neb., 7/14/13
Ford, Glenn (Gwyllyn Ford) (actor); Ste.-Christine, Que., Canada, 5/1/16
Ford, Harrison (actor); Chicago, 7/13/42
Ford, Henry (industrialist); Greenfield, Mich. **(1863–1947)**
Ford, John (film director); Cape Elizabeth, Maine **(1895–1973)**

Ford, Tennessee Ernie (Ernie Jennings Ford) (singer); Bristol, Tenn. (1919–1991)

Foreman, George (boxer, actor); Marshall, Tex., 1/10/49

Forrester, Maureen (contralto); Montreal, 7/25/30

Forsythe, John (John Lincoln Freund) (actor); Penn's Grove, N.J., 1/29/18

Fosdick, Harry Emerson (clergyman); Buffalo, N.Y. (1878–1968)

Fosse, Bob (Robert Louis Fosse) (choreographer, director); Chicago (1927–1987)

Foster, Jodie (Alicia Christian Foster) (actress, director, producer); Los Angeles, 11/19/62

Foster, Stephen Collins (composer); nr. Pittsburgh (1826–1864)

Fountain, Pete (jazz musician); New Orleans, 7/3/30

Fox, Matthew (actor); Crowheart, Wyo., 7/14/66

Fox, Michael J. (actor, producer); Edmonton, Alta., Canada, 6/9/61

Foxx, Redd (John Elroy Sanford) (actor, comedian); St. Louis (1922–1991)

Foy, Eddie, Jr. (dancer, actor); New Rochelle, N.Y. (1905–1983)

Fracci, Carla (ballet dancer); Milan, Italy, 8/20/36

Fragonard, Jean Honoré (painter); Grasse, France (1732–1806)

Frakes, Jonathan (actor); Bethlehem, Pa., 8/19/52

Frampton, Peter (rock musician); Beckenham, England, 4/20/50

France, Anatole (Jacques Anatole François Thibault) (author); Paris (1844–1924)

Francescatti, Zino (violinist); Marseilles, France (1902–1991)

Franciosa, Anthony (Anthony Papaleo) (actor); New York City, 10/25/28

Francis, Anne (actress); Ossining, N.Y., 7/16/30

Francis, Connie (Concetta Franconero) (singer); Newark, N.J., 12/12/38

Francis, Genie (actress); Englewood, N.J., 5/26/62

Francis of Assisi, Saint (Giovanni Francesco Barnardone) (founder of Franciscans); Assisi, Italy (1182–1226)

Franck, César Auguste (composer); Liège, Belgium (1822–1890)

Franco Bahamonde, Francisco (chief of state); El Ferrol, Spain (1892–1975)

Frankenheimer, John (movie director, producer); New York City, 2/19/30

Frankenthaler, Helen (artist); New York City, 12/12/28

Frankl, Victor E. (psychiatrist); Vienna (1905–1997)

Franklin, Aretha (singer); Memphis, Tenn., 3/25/42

Franklin, Benjamin (statesman, scientist); Boston (1706–1790)

Franklin, Bonnie (actress); Santa Monica, Calif., 1/6/44

Franklin, John Hope (historian); Rentiesville, Okla., 1/2/15

Frann, Mary (actress); St. Louis (1943–1998)

Franz, Dennis (Dennis Schlachta) (actor); Chicago, 10/28/44

Fraser, Brendan (actor); Indianapolis, Indiana, 12/3/67

Frazer, Sir James George (anthropologist); Glasgow, Scotland (1854–1941)

Freeman, Morgan (actor); Memphis, Tenn., 6/1/37

Freud, Sigmund (psychoanalyst); Moravia, Czech Repubic (1856–1939)

Frey, Glenn (musician); Detroit, 11/6/48

Frick, Henry Clay (industrialist); Westmoreland Co., Pa. (1849–1919)

Friedan, Betty (Betty Naomi Goldstein) (feminist, writer); Peoria, Ill., 2/4/21

Fromm, Erich (psychoanalyst); Frankfurt-am-Main, Germany (1900–1980)

Frost, David (TV entertainer); Tenterden, England, 4/7/39

Frost, Robert Lee (poet); San Francisco (1874–1963)

Fry, Christopher (playwright); Bristol, England, 12/18/07

Fugard, Athol (playwright); Middleburg, South Africa, 6/11/32

Fulbright, J. William (politician); Sumner, Mo. (1905–1995)

Fuller, Charles (playwright); Philadelphia, 3/5/39

Fuller, R(ichard) Buckminster (Jr.) (architect, educator); Milton, Mass. (1895–1983)

Fulton, Robert (inventor); Lancaster County, Pa. (1765–1815)

Funicello, Annette (actress); Utica, N.Y., 10/22/42

Funt, Allen (TV producer); Brooklyn, N.Y. (1914–1999)

G

Gabin, Jean (actor); Paris (1904–1976)

Gable, (William) Clark (actor); Cadiz, Ohio (1901–1960)

Gabo, Naum (sculptor); Briansk, Russia (1890–1977)

Gabor, Eva (actress); Budapest (1920–1995)

Gabor, Zsa Zsa (Sari) (actress); Budapest, 2/6/17

Gabriel, Peter (musician); Cobham, England, 2/13/50

Gabrieli, Giovanni (composer); Venice (c. 1557–1612)

Gaddis, William (novelist); New York City (1922–1998)

Gainsborough, Thomas (painter); Sudbury, Suffolk, England (1727–1788)

Galbraith, John Kenneth (economist); Iona Station, Ont., Canada, 10/15/08

Galilei, Galileo (astronomer, physicist); Pisa, Italy (1564–1642)

Gallico, Paul (novelist); New York City (1897–1976)

Gallup, George H. (poll taker); Jefferson, Iowa (1901–1984)

Galsworthy, John (novelist, dramatist); Coombe, England (1867–1933)

Galway, James (flutist); Belfast, Northern Ireland, 12/8/39

Gambling, John A. (radio broadcaster); New York City, 1930

Gandhi, Indira (Indira Nehru) (former prime minister); Allahabad, India (1917– 1984)

Gandhi, Mohandas Karamchand (called Mahatma Gandhi) (Hindu leader); Porbandar, India (1869–1948)

Gannett, Frank E. (editor, publisher) (1876–1957)

Garagiola, Joe (Joseph Henry Garagiola) (sportscaster); St. Louis, 2/12/26

Garbo, Greta (Greta Gustafsson) (actress); Stockholm (1905–1990)

Garcia, Andy (Andres Arturo Garcia-Menendez) (actor); Havana, Cuba, 4/12/56

Garcia, Jerry (rock musician); San Francisco (1942–1995)

Garcia Lorca, Frederico (poet, dramatist); Fuente Vaqueros, Spain (1898–1936)

Garden, Mary (soprano); Aberdeen, Scotland (1874–1967)

Gardenia, Vincent (Vincente Scognamiglio) (actor); Naples, Italy (1922–1992)

Gardner, Ava (actress); Smithfield, N.C. (1922–1990)

Gardner, Erle Stanley (novelist); Malden, Mass. (1889–1970)

Garfield, James Abram (20th U.S. president); Cuyahoga County, Ohio (1831–1881)

Garfunkel, Art (Arthur) (singer); Newark, N.J., 11/5/41

Garibaldi, Giuseppe (Italian nationalist leader); Nice, France (1807–1882)

Garland, Judy (Frances Gumm) (actress, singer); Grand Rapids, Minn. (1922–1969)

Garner, Erroll (jazz pianist); Pittsburgh (1921–1977)

Garner, James (James Bumgarner) (actor); Norman, Okla., 4/7/28

Garofalo, Janeane (actress, comedienne); Newton, N.J., 9/28/64

Garr, Teri (actress); Lakewood, Ohio, 12/11/49

Garrison, William Lloyd (abolitionist); Newburyport, Mass. (1805–1879)

Garroway, Dave (TV host); Schenectady, N.Y. (1913–1982)

Garson, Greer (actress); County Down, Northern Ireland (1903–1996)

Garth, Jennie (actress); Urbana, Ill., 4/3/72

Garvey, Marcus Moziah (black nationalist leader); Jamaica (1887–1940)

Gassman, Vittorio (film actor, director); Genoa, Italy (1922–2000)

Gates, Bill (William Henry Gates III) (software pioneer); Seattle, 10/28/55

Gates, Henry Louis, Jr. (scholar); Keyser, W. Va., 9/16/50

Gaudí, Antonio (architect); Reus, Spain (1852–1926)

Gauguin, (Eugène Henri) Paul (painter); Paris (1848–1903)

Gautama Buddha (Prince Siddhartha) (philosopher); Kapilavastu, India (c. 563–c. 483 B.C.)

Gavin, John (actor, diplomat); Los Angeles, 4/8/35

Gavras, Konstantinos (Costa-Gavras) (film director); Loutra-Iraias, Greece, 2/13/33

Gaye, Marvin (singer); Washington, D.C. (1939–1984)

Gayle, Crystal (Brenda Gayle Webb) (singer); Paintsville, Ky., 1/9/51

Gaynor, Janet (actress); Philadelphia (1906–1984)

Gaynor, Mitzi (Francesca Mitzi Marlene de Czanyi von Gerber) (actress); Chicago, 9/4/31

Gazzara, Ben (Biagio Anthony Gazzara) (actor); New York City, 8/28/30

Gedda, Nicolai (tenor); Stockholm, 7/11/25

Gellar, Sarah Michelle (actress); New York City, 4/14/77

Genet, Jean (playwright); Paris (1910–1986)

Genghis Khan (Temujin) (conqueror); nr. Lake Baikal, Russia (1162–1227)

Gentry, Bobbie (Roberta Streeter) (singer); Chickasaw Co., Miss., 7/27/44

George, David Lloyd (statesman); Manchester, England (1863–1945)

George, Henry (economist, reformer); Philadelphia (1839–1897)

Gere, Richard (actor); Philadelphia, 8/29/49

Géricault, Jean Louis (painter); Rouen, France (1791–1824)

Geronimo (Goyathlay) (Apache chieftain); Arizona (1829–1909)

Gershwin, George (composer); Brooklyn, N.Y. (1898–1937)

Gershwin, Ira (lyricist); New York City (1896–1983)

Getty, J. Paul (oil executive); Minneapolis (1892–1976)

Getz, Stan (saxophonist); Philadelphia (1927–1991)

Ghiberti, Lorenzo (goldsmith, sculptor); Florence **(1378–1455)**
Ghostley, Alice (actress); Eve, Mo., 8/14/26
Giacometti, Alberto (sculptor); Switzerland **(1901–1966)**
Giannini, Giancarlo (actor); La Spezia, Italy, 8/1/42
Gibbon, Edward (historian); Putney, England **(1737–1794)**
Gibson, Charles Dana (illustrator); Roxbury, Mass. **(1867–1944)**
Gibson, Henry (actor, comedian); Germantown, Pa., 9/21/35
Gibson, Mel (actor, director, producer); Peekskill, N.Y., 1/3/56
Gide, André (author); Paris **(1869–1951)**
Gielgud, Sir John (actor); London **(1904–2000)**
Gifford, Kathie Lee (Kathie Lee Epstein) (talk show host); Paris, 8/16/53
Gilbert, Melissa (actress); Los Angeles, 5/8/64
Gilbert, Walter (chemist, Nobel laureate); Boston, 3/21/32
Gilbert, Sir William Schwenck (librettist); London **(1836–1911)**
Gilels, Emil (concert pianist); Odessa, Ukraine **(1916–1985)**
Gillespie, Dizzy (John Birks Gillespie) (jazz trumpeter); Cheraw, S.C. **(1917–1993)**
Gilligan, Carol (Friedman) (psychologist); New York City, 11/28/36
Gilpin, Peri (actress); Waco, Tex., 5/27/61
Gimbel, Bernard F. (merchant); Vincennes, Ind. **(1885–1966)**
Gingrich, Newt (politician); Harrisburg, Pa., 6/17/43
Ginsberg, Allen (poet); Newark, N.J. **(1926–1997)**
Giordano, Luca (painter); Naples, Italy **(1632–1705)**
Giorgione (painter); Castelfranco, Italy **(c. 1477–1510)**
Giotto di Bondone (painter); Vespignano, Italy **(c. 1266–1337)**
Giovanni, Nikki (poet); Knoxville, Tenn., 6/7/43
Giroud, Françoise (French government official); Geneva, 9/21/16
Gish, Dorothy (actress); Massillon, Ohio **(1898–1968)**
Gish, Lillian (Lillian de Guiche) (actress); Springfield, Ohio **(1893–1993)**
Givenchy, Hubert (fashion designer); Beauvais, France, 2/21/27
Gladstone, William Ewart (statesman); Liverpool, England **(1809–1898)**
Glaser, Paul Michael (actor, director); Cambridge, Mass., 3/25/43
Glass, Philip (composer); Baltimore, 1/31/37
Gleason, Jackie (comedian); Brooklyn, N.Y. **(1916–1987)**
Glenn, John (legislator, astronaut); Cambridge, Ohio, 7/18/21
Gless, Sharon (actress); Los Angeles, 5/31/43
Glover, Danny (actor); San Francisco, 7/22/47
Gluck, Christoph Willibald (composer); Erasbach, Germany **(1714–1787)**
Gobel, George (comedian); Chicago **(1920–1991)**
Godard, Jean Luc (film director); Paris, 12/3/30
Goddard, Paulette (Marion Levy) (actress); Great Neck, N.Y. **(1911–1990)**
Goddard, Robert Hutchings (father of modern rocketry); Worcester, Mass. **(1882–1945)**
Godfrey, Arthur (entertainer); New York City **(1903–1983)**
Goebbels, Joseph Paul (Nazi leader); Rheydt, Germany **(1897–1945)**
Goering, Hermann (Nazi leader); Rosenheim, Germany **(1893–1946)**
Goethals, George Washington (engineer); Brooklyn, N.Y. **(1858–1928)**
Goethe, Johann Wolfgang von (poet, playwright, novelist); Frankfurt-am-Main, Germany **(1749–1832)**
Gogol, Nikolai Vasilievich (novelist); nr. Mirgorod, Ukraine **(1809–1852)**
Goldberg, Rube (cartoonist); San Francisco **(1883–1970)**
Goldberg, Whoopi (Caryn Johnson) (actress); New York City, 11/13/49
Goldblum, Jeff (actor); Pittsburgh, 10/22/52
Golden, Harry (Harry Goldhurst) (author); New York City **(1902–1981)**
Goldman, Emma (anarchist); Kovno, Lithuania **(1869–1940)**
Goldsmith, Oliver (dramatist, poet); County Longford, Ireland **(1728–1774)**
Goldwyn, Samuel (Schmuel Gelbfisz) (film producer); Warsaw **(1879–1974)**
Gompers, Samuel (labor leader); London **(1850–1924)**
Goodall, Jane (Baroness van Lawick-Goodall) (ethologist); London, 4/3/34
Gooding, Jr., Cuba (actor); Bronx, New York, 1/2/68
Goodman, Benny (clarinetist); Chicago **(1909–1986)**
Goodman, John (actor); St. Louis, 6/20/52
Goodwin, Doris (Helen) Kearns (historian); Rockville Center, N.Y., 1/4/43
Goodyear, Charles (inventor); New Haven, Conn. **(1800–1860)**
Gorbachev, Mikhail Sergeyevich (Soviet leader); Privolnoye, Russia, 3/2/31

Gordimer, Nadine (novelist, short-story writer); Springs, South Africa, 12/20/23
Gordon, Dexter (jazz musician); Los Angeles **(1923–1990)**
Gordon, Ruth (actress); Wollaston, Mass. **(1896–1985)**
Gore, Albert, Jr. (ex-vice president of the U.S.); Washington, D.C., 3/31/48
Gordy, Berry, Jr. (record company executive); Detroit, 11/28/29
Gorey, Edward (St. John) (illustrator, author); Chicago, 2/22/25
Gorki, Maxim (Alexei Maximovich Peshkov) (author); Nizhni Novgorod, Russia **(1868–1936)**
Gorky, Arshile (painter); Armenia **(1904–1948)**
Gormé, Eydie (singer); Bronx, N.Y., 8/16/32
Gorshin, Frank (actor); Pittsburgh, 4/5/34
Gossett, Louis, Jr. (actor); Brooklyn, N.Y., 5/27/36
Gottschalk, Louis Moreau (pianist, composer); New Orleans **(1829–1869)**
Gould, Chester (cartoonist); Pawnee, Okla. **(1900–1985)**
Gould, Elliott (Elliott Goldstein) (actor); Brooklyn, N.Y., 8/29/38
Gould, Glenn (concert pianist); Toronto **(1932–1982)**
Gould, Morton (composer); Richmond Hill, Queens, N.Y. **(1913–1996)**
Gould, Stephen Jay (paleontologist, science writer); New York City, 9/10/41
Goulet, Robert (singer); Lawrence, Mass., 11/26/33
Gounod, Charles François (composer); Paris **(1818–1893)**
Goya y Lucientes, Francisco José de (painter); Fuendetodos, Spain **(1746–1828)**
Grable, Betty (actress); St. Louis **(1916–1973)**
Grace, Princess of Monaco (Grace Kelly) (ex-actress); Philadelphia **(1929–1982)**
Graham, Bill (Wolfgang Grajonca) (rock impresario); Berlin **(1930–1991)**
Graham, Billy (William F. Graham) (evangelist); Charlotte, N.C., 11/7/18
Graham, Katharine Meyer (newspaper publisher); New York City **(1917–2001)**
Graham, Martha (choreographer); Pittsburgh **(1894–1991)**
Grainger, Percy Aldridge (pianist, composer); Melbourne, Australia **(1882–1961)**
Gramm, Donald (Grambach) (bass-baritone); Milwaukee **(1927–1983)**
Grammer, Kelsey (actor); St. Thomas, V.I., 2/21/55
Granger, Stewart (James Stewart) (actor); London **(1913–1993)**
Grant, Cary (Alexander Archibald Leach) (actor); Bristol, England **(1904–1986)**
Grant, Hugh (actor); London, England, 9/9/60
Grant, Lee (Lyova Haskell Rosenthal) (actress); New York City, 10/31/30
Grant, Ulysses Simpson (18th U.S. president); Point Pleasant, Ohio **(1822–1885)**
Grass, Günter (novelist); Danzig, Poland, 10/16/27
Graves, Nancy (Stevenson) (artist); Pittsfield, Mass. **(1940–1996)**
Graves, Peter (Peter Aurness) (actor); Minneapolis, 3/18/26
Graves, Robert (writer); London **(1895–1985)**
Gray, Linda (actress); Santa Monica, Calif., 9/12/40
Gray, Thomas (poet); London **(1716–1771)**
Greco, José (dancer); Montorio nei Frentani, Italy **(1918–2000)**
Greeley, Horace (journalist, politician); Amherst, N.H. **(1811–1872)**
Green, Adolph (actor, lyricist); New York City, 12/2/15
Green, Al (singer); Forrest City, Ark., 4/13/46
Greene, Graham (novelist); Berkhamsted, England **(1904–1991)**
Greene, Lorne (actor); Ottawa, Ont., Canada **(1915–1987)**
Greene, Shecky (comedian, actor); Chicago, 4/8/25
Greenstreet, Sydney (actor); Sandwich, England **(1879–1954)**
Greenspan, Alan (chairman of the Federal Reserve); New York City, 3/6/26
Greer, Germaine (feminist, writer); Melbourne, Australia, 1/29/39
Gregory, Cynthia (ballet dancer); Los Angeles, 7/8/46
Gregory, Dick (comedian); St. Louis, 10/12/32
Gregory, Lady (Isabella) Augusta (playwright); Roxborough, Ireland **(1852–1932)**
Greuze, Jean-Baptiste (painter); Tournus, France **(1725–1805)**
Grey, Joel (Joel Katz) (actor, dancer); Cleveland, 4/11/32
Grey, Zane (author); Zanesville, Ohio **(1875–1939)**
Grieg, Edvard Hagerup (composer); Bergen, Norway **(1843–1907)**
Grier, Pam (actress); Winston-Salem, N.C., 5/26/49
Griffin, Merv (TV host, producer); San Mateo, Calif., 7/6/25
Griffith, Andy (actor); Mount Airy, N.C., 6/1/26
Griffith, David Lewelyn Wark (film producer); La Grange, Ky. **(1875–1948)**
Griffith, Melanie (actress); New York City, 8/9/57

Grigorovich, Yuri (choreographer); Leningrad (St. Petersburg), Russia, 1/1/27

Grimes, Tammy (actress); Lynn, Mass., 1/30/34

Grimm, Jacob (author of fairy tales); Hanau, Germany **(1785–1863)**

Grimm, Wilhelm (author of fairy tales); Hanau, Germany **(1786–1859)**

Gris, Juan (José Victoriano González) (painter); Madrid **(1887–1927)**

Grisham, John (attorney, author); Jonesboro, Ark., 2/8/55

Grodin, Charles (actor); Pittsburgh, 4/21/35

Groening, Matt (animator, producer); Portland, Ore., 2/14/54

Gromyko, Andrei A. (diplomat); Starye Gromyki, Russia **(1909–1989)**

Gropius, Walter (architect); Berlin **(1883–1969)**

Gropper, William (painter, illustrator); New York City **(1897–1977)**

Gross, Michael (actor); Chicago, 6/21/47

Grosz, George (painter); Germany **(1893–1959)**

Grove, Andrew (Andras Grof) (computer industry executive); Budapest, Hungary, 9/2/36

Grünewald, Matthias (Mathis Gothart Neithart) (painter); Würzburg, Germany **(c. 1470–1528)**

Guest, Christopher (Christopher Haden-Guest) (actor, writer, director); New York City, 2/5/48

Guggenheim, Meyer (capitalist); Langnau, Switzerland **(1828–1905)**

Guillaume, Robert (Robert Williams) (actor); St. Louis, 11/30/27

Guinness, Sir Alec (actor); London, 4/2/14

Guitry, Sacha (Alexandre Guitry) (actor, film director); St. Petersburg, Russia **(1885–1957)**

Gumbel, Bryant Charles (TV newscaster); New Orleans, 9/29/48

Gunther, John (author); Chicago **(1901–1970)**

Gutenberg, Johann (printer); Mainz, Germany **(c. 1397–1468)**

Guthrie, Arlo (singer); New York City, 7/10/47

Guthrie, Woody (folk singer, composer); Okemah, Okla. **(1912–1967)**

Gwenn, Edmund (actor); London **(1875–1959)**

Gwynne, Fred (actor); New York City **(1926–1993)**

H

Habibie, Bacharuddin, Jusuf (president of Indonesia); Pare-Pare, Indonesia, 6/25/36

Hackett, Bobby (trumpeter); Providence, R.I. **(1915–1976)**

Hackett, Buddy (Leonard Hacker) (comedian, actor); Brooklyn, N.Y., 8/31/24

Hackman, Gene (actor); San Bernardino, Calif., 1/30/31

Hagen, Uta (actress); Göttingen, Germany, 6/12/19

Haggard, Merle (songwriter, singer); Bakersfield, Calif., 4/6/37

Hagman, Larry (Larry Hageman) (actor); Weatherford, Tex., 9/21/31

Haig, Alexander Meigs, Jr. (ex-secretary of state, ex-general); Bala-Cynwyd, Pa., 12/2/24

Haile Selassie (Ras Tafari Makonnen) (ex-emperor); Ethiopia **(1892–1975)**

Hailey, Arthur (novelist); Luton, England, 4/5/20

Halberstam, David (journalist); New York City, 4/10/34

Hale, Alan (actor, director); Washington, D.C. **(1892–1950)**

Hale, Barbara (actress); DeKalb, Ill., 4/18/21

Hale, Edward Everett (clergyman, author); Boston **(1822–1909)**

Hale, Nathan (American Revolutionary officer); Coventry, Conn. **(1755–1776)**

Halevi, Judah (Jewish poet); Toledo, Spain **(1085–1140)**

Haley, Alex (writer); Ithaca, N.Y. **(1921–1992)**

Haley, Jack (actor); Boston **(1899–1979)**

Hall, Anthony Michael (Michael Anthony Thomas Charles Hall) (actor, singer); Boston, 4/14/68

Hall, Arsenio (comedian, talk-show host); Cleveland, 2/12/58

Hall, Donald (Andrew, Jr.) (poet); New Haven, Conn., 9/20/28

Hall, Huntz (actor); New York City **(1919–1999)**

Hall, Jerry (model, actress); Mesquite, Texas, 7/2/56

Hall, Monty (TV personality); Winnipeg, Canada, 8/25/23

Halley, Edmund (astronomer); London **(1656–1742)**

Hals, Frans (painter); Antwerp, Netherlands (c. **1580–1666)**

Halsey, William Frederick, Jr. (naval officer); Elizabeth, N.J. **(1882–1959)**

Hamel, Veronica (actress); Philadelphia, 11/20/43

Hamill, Mark (actor); Oakland, 9/25/52

Hamilton, Alexander (statesman); Nevis, British West Indies **(1755–1804)**

Hamilton, Alice (physician, reformer); New York City **(1869–1970)**

Hamilton, Edith (scholar); Dresden, Germany **(1867–1963)**

Hamilton, George (actor); Memphis, Tenn., 8/12/39

Hamlin, Harry (actor); Pasadena, Calif., 10/30/51

Hamlisch, Marvin (composer, pianist); New York City, 6/2/44

Hammarskjöld, Dag (UN secretary-general); Jönköping, Sweden **(1905–1961)**

Hammerstein, Oscar, II (librettist, stage producer); New York City **(1895–1960)**

Hampton, Lionel (vibraharpist, band leader); Birmingham, Ala., 4/12/13

Hamsun, Knut (Knut Pedersen) (novelist); Lom, Norway **(1859–1952)**

Hancock, Herbie (jazz musician); Chicago, 4/12/40

Hancock, John (statesman); Braintree, Mass. **(1737–1793)**

Hand, Learned (jurist); Albany, N.Y. **(1872–1961)**

Handel, George Frideric (Georg Friedrich Händel) (composer); Halle, Germany **(1685–1759)**

Handy, William Christopher (blues composer); Florence, Ala. **(1873–1958)**

Hanks, Tom (actor, director, writer); Concord, Calif., 7/9/56

Hannah, Daryl (actress); Chicago, 12/19/60

Hannibal (Carthaginian general); North Africa **(247–182 B.C.)**

Hansberry, Lorraine (playwright); Chicago **(1930–1965)**

Hanson, Howard (conductor); Wahoo, Neb. **(1896–1981)**

Harburg, E. Y. "Yip" (songwriter); New York City **(1896–1981)**

Harden, Marcia Gay (actress); La Jolla, Calif., 8/14/59

Harding, Warren Gamaliel (29th U.S. president); Morrow County, Ohio **(1865–1923)**

Hardwicke, Sir Cedric (actor); Stourbridge, England **(1893–1964)**

Hardy, Oliver (comedian); Atlanta **(1892–1957)**

Hardy, Thomas (novelist); Dorsetshire, England **(1840–1928)**

Harkness, Edward S. (business executive); Cleveland **(1874–1940)**

Harlow, Jean (Harlean Carpentier) (actress); Kansas City, Mo. **(1911–1937)**

Harlow, Shalom (model, TV personality); Oshawa, Ontario, Canada, 12/5/73

Harmon, Mark (actor); Burbank, Calif., 9/2/51

Harnick, Sheldon (lyricist); Chicago, 4/30/24

Harper, Valerie (actress); Suffern, N.Y., 8/22/40

Harrell, Lynn (cellist); New York City, 1/30/44

Harrelson, Woody (actor); Midland, Tex., 7/23/61

Harriman, Pamela (ambassador); Farnborough, England **(1920–1997)**

Harriman, W. (William) Averell (ex-governor of New York); New York City **(1891–1986)**

Harrington, Pat, Jr. (actor, comedian); New York City, 8/13/29

Harris, Barbara (Sandra Markowitz) (actress); Evanston, Ill., 7/25/35

Harris, Ed (actor); Englewood, N.J., 11/28/50

Harris, Emmylou (singer); Birmingham, Ala., 4/2/47

Harris, Julie (actress); Grosse Pointe Park, Mich., 12/2/25

Harris, Phil (actor, band leader); Linton, Ind. **(1906–1995)**

Harris, Richard (actor); Limerick, Ireland, 10/1/33

Harris, Rosemary (actress); Ashby, England, 9/19/30

Harris, Roy (composer); Lincoln County, Okla. **(1898–1979)**

Harrison, Benjamin (23rd U.S. president); North Bend, Ohio **(1833–1901)**

Harrison, George (singer, songwriter); Liverpool, England, 2/25/43

Harrison, Gregory (actor); Avalon, Catalina Island, Calif., 5/31/50

Harrison, Sir Rex (Reginald Carey) (actor); Huyton, England **(1908–1990)**

Harrison, William Henry (9th U.S. president); Charles City County, Va. **(1773–1841)**

Harry, Deborah (Blondie) (musician); Miami, Fla., 7/1/45

Hart, Lorenz (lyricist); New York City **(1895–1943)**

Hart, Mary (Mary Johanna Harum) (host); Sioux Falls, S.D., 11/8/50

Hart, Melissa Joan (actress); Sayville, N.Y., 4/18/76

Hart, Moss (playwright); New York City **(1904–1961)**

Harte, Bret (Francis Brett Harte) (author); Albany, N.Y. **(1836–1902)**

Hartford, Huntington (George Huntington Hartford II) (A.&P. heir); New York City, 4/18/11

Hartford, John (singer, banjoist); New York City **(1937–2001)**

Hartley, Mariette (actress); New York City, 6/21/40

Hartman, David Downs (TV newscaster); Pawtucket, R.I., 5/19/35

Hartman, Phil (actor, comedian); Brantford, Ont., Canada **(1948–1998)**

Hartman Black, Lisa (actress); Houston, 6/1/56

Harvey, Laurence (Larushka Skikne) (actor); Joniskis, Lithuania **(1928–1973)**

Harvey, Polly Jean (PJ Harvey) (singer, songwriter); Yeovil, England, 10/9/69

Harvey, William (physician); Folkestone, England **(1578–1657)**

Hasselhoff, David (actor, producer); Baltimore, 7/17/52

Hatcher, Teri (actress); Sunnyvale, Calif., 12/8/64

Havel, Vaclav (political leader, dramatist, poet); Prague, 10/5/36

Havens, Richie (musician); Brooklyn, N.Y., 1/21/41

Hawke, Ethan (actor); Austin, Tex., 11/6/70

Hawking, Stephen (physicist, astronomer); Oxford, England, 1/8/42

Hawkins, Coleman (jazz musician); St. Joseph, Mo. **(1904–1969)**

Hawkins, Jack (actor); London **(1910–1973)**

Hawn, Goldie (actress, producer); Washington, D.C., 11/21/45

Haworth, Jill (actress); Sussex, England, 8/15/45

Hawthorne, Nathaniel (novelist); Salem, Mass. **(1804–1864)**

Hay, John Milton (statesman); Salem, Ind. **(1838–1905)**

Hayakawa, Sessue (actor); Honshu, Japan **(1890–1973)**

Hayden, Melissa (ballet dancer); Toronto, 4/25/23

Hayden, Sterling (Sterling Relyea Walter) (actor, writer); Montclair, N.J. **(1916–1986)**

Haydn, Franz Joseph (composer); Rohrau, Austria **(1732–1809)**

Hayek, Salma (actress); Coatzacoalcos, Mexico, 9/2/68

Hayes, Helen (Helen Hayes Brown) (actress); Washington, D.C. **(1900–1993)**

Hayes, Isaac (composer); Covington, Tenn., 8/20/42

Hayes, Peter Lind (comedian, singer); San Francisco **(1915–1998)**

Hayes, Rutherford Birchard (19th U.S. president); Delaware, Ohio **(1822–1893)**

Hayward, Leland (producer); Nebraska City, Neb. **(1902–1971)**

Hayward, Susan (Edythe Marrener) (actress); Brooklyn, N.Y. **(1918–1975)**

Hayworth, Rita (Margarita Cansino) (actress); New York City **(1918–1987)**

Head, Edith (costume designer); Los Angeles **(1907–1981)**

Heaney, Seamus (poet); Londonderry, Northern Ireland, 4/13/39

Hearst, Patricia (Campbell) (heiress); San Francisco, 2/20/54

Hearst, William Randolph (publisher); San Francisco **(1863–1951)**

Hearst, William Randolph, Jr. (publisher); New York City **(1908–1993)**

Heatherton, Joey (actress); Rockville Centre, N.Y., 9/14/44

Heche, Anne (actress); Aurora, Ohio, 5/25/69

Hecht, Ben (author); New York City **(1894–1964)**

Heckart, Eileen (actress); Columbus, Ohio, 3/29/19

Heflin, Van (Emmet Evan Heflin) (actor); Walters, Okla. **(1910–1971)**

Hefner, Hugh (publisher); Chicago, 4/9/26

Hegel, Georg Wilhelm Friedrich (philosopher); Stuttgart, Germany **(1770–1831)**

Heidegger, Martin (existentialist philosopher); Messkirch, Germany **(1889–1976)**

Heifetz, Jascha (concert violinist); Vilna, Russia **(1901–1987)**

Heine, Heinrich (Harry) (poet); Düsseldorf, Germany **(1797–1856)**

Heinemann, Gustav (ex-president of Germany); Schweim, Germany **(1899–1976)**

Heisenberg, Werner Karl (physicist); Würzburg, Germany **(1901–1976)**

Heller, Joseph (novelist); Brooklyn, N.Y. **(1923–1999)**

Hellman, Lillian (playwright); New Orleans **(1905–1984)**

Helmond, Katherine (actress); Galveston, Tex., 7/5/34

Helms, Jesse (politician); Monroe, N.C., 10/18/21

Helmsley, Harry Brakmann (business executive); New York City **(1909–1997)**

Hemingway, Ernest Miller (novelist); Oak Park, Ill. **(1899–1961)**

Hemingway, Margaux (actress); Portland, Ore. **(1955–1996)**

Hemmings, David (actor); Guilford, England, 11/2/41

Henderson, Florence (actress); Dale, Ind., 2/14/34

Henderson, Skitch (Lyle Russell Cedric) (conductor, pianist); Birmingham, England?, 1/27/18

Hendrix, Jimi (James Marshall Hendrix) (guitarist); Seattle **(1942–1970)**

Henley, Beth (playwright-actress); Jackson, Miss., 5/8/52

Henley, Don (musician); Linden, Tex., 7/22/47

Henner, Marilu (actress); Chicago, 4/6/52

Henning, Doug (magician, actor); Winnipeg, Canada **(1947–2000)**

Henri, Robert (painter); Cincinnati **(1865–1926)**

Henriksen, Lance (actor, screenwriter); New York City, 5/4/40

Henry VIII (king of England); Greenwich, England **(1491–1547)**

Henry, O. (William Sydney Porter) (story writer); Greensboro, N.C. **(1862–1910)**

Henry, Patrick (statesman); Hanover County, Va. **(1736–1799)**

Henson, Jim (puppeteer); Greenville, Miss. **(1936–1990)**

Hepburn, Audrey (actress); Brussels **(1929–1993)**

Hepburn, Katharine (actress); Hartford, Conn., 5/12/07

Hepplewhite, George (furniture designer); England **(?–1786)**

Hepworth, Barbara (sculptor); Wakefield, England **(1903–1975)**

Herbert, George (poet); Montgomery Castle, Wales **(1593–1633)**

Herbert, Victor (composer); Dublin **(1859–1924)**

Herblock (Herbert L. Block) (political cartoonist); Chicago **(1909–2001)**

Herman, Pee-wee (Paul Rubenfeld) (comedian); Peekskill, N.Y., 8/27/52

Herman, Woody (Woodrow Charles Herman) (band leader); Milwaukee **(1913–1987)**

Herod (called Herod the Great) (king of Judea) **(73–4 B.C.)**

Herodotus (historian); Halicarnassus, Asia Minor (Turkey) **(c. 484–425 B.C.)**

Herrick, Robert (poet); London **(1591–1674)**

Herschbach, Dudley Robert (chemist, Nobel laureate); San Jose, Calif., 6/18/32

Herschel, William (Frederick Wilhelm Herschel) (astronomer); Hannover, Germany **(1738–1822)**

Hershey, Barbara (Barbara Herzstein) (actress); Hollywood, Calif., 2/5/48

Herzog, Chaim (Israeli statesman); Belfast, Northern Ireland **(1918–1997)**

Hesburgh, Theodore M. (educator); Syracuse, N.Y., 5/2/17

Hesseman, Howard (actor); Salem, Ore., 2/27/40

Heston, Charlton (actor); Evanston, Ill., 10/4/24

Heyerdahl, Thor (ethnologist, explorer); Larvik, Norway, 10/6/14

Hill, Anita (lawyer, professor); Lone Tree, Okla., 7/30/56

Hill, Benny (comedian); Southampton, England **(1925–1992)**

Hill, Lauryn (actress, musician); South Orange, N.J., 5/25/75

Hillary, Sir Edmund (mountain climber); New Zealand, 7/20/19

Hillerman, John (actor); Denison, Tex., 12/20/32

Hilton, Conrad (hotelier); San Antonio, N.M. **(1887–1979)**

Hindemith, Paul (composer); Hanau, Germany **(1895–1963)**

Hindenburg, Paul von (Paul Ludwig Hans Anton von Hindenburg und Beneckendorff) (German field marshal, president); Poznan, Poland **(1847– 1934)**

Hines, Earl "Fatha" (jazz pianist); Duquesne, Pa. **(1905–1983)**

Hines, Gregory (dancer, actor); New York City, 2/14/46

Hines, Jerome (Jerome Heinz) (basso); Los Angeles, 11/8/21

Hippocrates (physician); Cos, Greece **(c. 460–c. 377 B.C.)**

Hirohito (Emperor of Japan); Tokyo **(1901–1989)**

Hiroshige, Ando (painter); Edo, Tokyo **(1797–1858)**

Hirsch, Judd (actor); New York City, 3/15/35

Hirschfeld, Al (Albert) (cartoonist); St. Louis, 6/21/03

Hirschhorn, Joseph Herman (financier, speculator, art collector); Mitau, Latvia **(1899–1981)**

Hirt, Al (trumpeter); New Orleans **(1922–1999)**

Hiss, Alger (public official); Baltimore **(1904–1996)**

Hitchcock, Alfred J. (film director); London **(1899–1980)**

Hitler, Adolf (German dictator); Braunau, Austria **(1889–1945)**

Hobbes, Thomas (philosopher); Westport, England **(1588–1679)**

Hobson, Laura Z. (Laura K. Zametkin) (novelist); New York City **(1900–1986)**

Ho Chi Minh (Nguyen That Tranh) (Vietnamese nationalist leader); Kim Lien, Vietnam **(1890–1969)**

Hockney, David (artist); Bradford, England, 7/9/37

Hodgkin, Dorothy Mary Crowfoot (chemist, Nobel laureate); Cairo, Egypt **(1910–1994)**

Hoffa, "Jimmy" James R(iddle) (labor leader); Brazil, Ind. **(1913–1975?; presumed murdered.)**

Hoffman, Dustin (actor, director); Los Angeles, 8/8/37

Hoffman, Phillip Seymour (actor); Fairport, N.Y., 1968

Hofmann, Hans (painter); Germany **(1880–1966)**

Hoffmann, Roald (chemist, Nobel laureate); Zloczow, Poland, 7/18/37

Hofstadter, Richard (historian); Buffalo, N.Y. **(1916–1970)**

Hogan, Paul (actor); Lightning Ridge, N.S.W., Australia, 10/8/39

Hogarth, William (painter, engraver); London **(1697–1764)**

Hokusai, Katsushika (artist); Yedo, Japan **(1760–1849)**

Holbein, Hans (the Elder) (painter); Augsburg, Germany **(c. 1465–1524)**

Holbein, Hans (the Younger) (painter); Augsburg, Germany **(c. 1497–1543)**

Holbrook, Hal (actor); Cleveland, 2/17/25

Holden, William (William Franklin Beedle, Jr.) (actor); O'Fallon, Ill. **(1918–1981)**

Holder, Geoffrey (dancer); Port-of-Spain, Trinidad, 8/1/30

Holiday, Billie (Eleanora Fagan) (jazz-blues singer); Baltimore **(1915–1959)**

Holliman, Earl (Anthony Numkena) (actor); Delhi, La., 9/11/28

Holly, Buddy (singer); Lubbock, Tex. **(1936–1959)**

Holly, Lauren (actress); Geneva, N.Y., 10/28/63

Holm, Celeste (actress); New York City, 4/29/19

Holmes, Katie (actress); Toledo, Ohio, 12/18/78

Holmes, Oliver Wendell (jurist); Boston **(1841–1935)**

Home, Lord (Alexander Frederick Douglas-Home) (diplomat); London, 7/2/03

Homer, Winslow (painter); Boston **(1836–1910)**

Homer (Greek poet) fl. 850 B.C.

Honegger, Arthur (composer); Le Havre, France **(1892–1955)**

Hook, Sidney (philosopher); New York City **(1902–1989)**

Hooker, John Lee (blues guitarist, singer, songwriter); Clarksdale, Miss. **(1920–2001)**

Hoover, Herbert Clark (31st U.S. president); West Branch, Iowa **(1874–1964)**
Hoover, J. Edgar (FBI director); Washington, D.C. **(1895–1972)**
Hope, Bob (Leslie Townes Hope) (comedian); London, 5/29/03
Hopkins, Sir Anthony (actor); Port Talbot, Wales, 12/31/37
Hopkins, Gerald Manley (poet); Stratford, England **(1844–1899)**
Hopkins, Johns (financier); Anne Arundel County, Md. **(1795–1873)**
Hopper, Dennis (actor); Dodge City, Kans., 5/17/36
Hopper, Edward (painter); Nyack, N.Y. **(1882–1967)**
Horace (Quintus Horatius Flaccus) (poet); Venosa, Italy **(65–8 B.C.)**
Horne, Lena (singer); Brooklyn, N.Y., 6/30/17
Horne, Marilyn (mezzo-soprano); Bradford, Pa., 1/16/34
Horowitz, Vladimir (pianist); Kiev, Ukraine **(1903–1989)** .
Horsley, Lee (actor); Muleshoe, Tex., 5/15/55
Horton, Edward Everett (comedian); Brooklyn, N.Y. **(1887–1970)**
Hoskins, Bob (actor); Bury St. Edmunds, England, 10/26/42
Houdini, Harry (Ehrich Weiss) (magician); Budapest, Hungary **(1874–1926)**
Houseman, John (Jacques Haussmann) (producer, director, actor); Bucharest **(1902–1988)**
Housman, A(lfred) E(dward) (poet); Fockburg, England **(1859–1936)**
Houston, Charles Hamilton (civil rights lawyer); Washington, D.C. **(1895–1950)**
Houston, Samuel (political leader); Rockbridge County, Va. **(1793–1863)**
Houston, Whitney (singer); Newark, N.J., 8/9/63
Howard, Ken (actor); El Centro, Calif., 3/28/44
Howard, Leslie (Leslie Stainer) (actor); London **(1893–1943)**
Howard, Ron (actor, producer, director); Duncan, Okla., 3/1/54
Howard, Trevor (actor); Kent, England **(1916–1988)**
Howe, Elias (inventor); Spencer, Mass. **(1819–1867)**
Howe, Irving (literary critic); New York City **(1920–1993)**
Howe, Julia Ward (poet, reformer); New York City **(1819–1910)**
Hudson, Henry (English navigator) **(fl. 1607–1611)**
Hudson, Rock (born Roy Scherer, Jr.; took Roy Fitzgerald as legal name) (actor); Winnetka, Ill. **(1925–1985)**
Huggins, Nathan Irvin (historian); Chicago **(1927–1989)**
Hughes, Charles Evans (jurist); Glens Falls, N.Y. **(1862–1948)**
Hughes, Howard (industrialist, film producer); Houston **(1905–1976)**
Hughes, Langston (poet); Joplin, Mo. **(1902–1967)**
Hughes, Ted (poet); Mytholmroyd, England **(1930–1998)**
Hugo, Victor Marie (author); Besançon, France **(1802–1885)**
Hulce, Tom (actor); Detroit, 12/6/53
Hume, David (philosopher); Edinburgh, Scotland **(1711–1776)**
Hume, Kirsty (model); Glasgow, Scotland, 9/4/76
Humperdinck, Engelbert (composer); Siegburg, Germany **(1854–1921)**
Humperdinck, Engelbert (Arnold Dorsey) (singer); Madras, India, 5/2/36
Hunt, Helen (actress); Los Angeles, 6/15/63
Hunt, Linda (actress); Morristown, N.J., 4/2/45
Hunter, Holly (actress); Atlanta, 3/20/58
Hunter, Kim (Janet Cole) (actress); Detroit, 11/12/22
Hunter, Tab (Arthur Andrew Gelien) (actor); New York City, 7/11/31
Hunter-Gault, Charlayne (activist, broadcast journalist); Due West, S.C., 2/27/42
Huntley, Chet (TV newscaster); Cardwell, Mont. **(1911–1974)**
Hurley, Elizabeth (actress, model); Backingstoke, England, 6/10/65
Hurok, Sol (Solomon Hurok) (impresario); Pogar, Russia **(1884–1974)**
Hurst, Fannie (novelist); Hamilton, Ohio **(1889–1968)**
Hurston, Zora Neale (author); Eatonville, Fla. **(1901–1960)**
Hurt, John (actor); Shirebrook, England, 1/22/40
Hurt, William (actor); Washington, D.C., 3/20/50
Hus, Jan (Bohemian religious reformer); Husinetz, nr. Budweis, Czech Republic **(c. 1369–1415)**
Husing, Ted (sportscaster); New York City **(1901–1962)**
Hussein I (king); Jordan **(1935–1999)**
Hussein, Saddam (al-Tikriti) (Iraqi president); Tikrit, Iraq, 4/28/37
Huston, Anjelica (actress); Los Angeles, 7/8/51
Huston, John (actor, director, writer); Nevada, Mo. **(1906–1987)**
Huston, Walter (Walter Houghston) (actor); Toronto **(1884–1950)**
Hutchins, Robert M. (educator); Brooklyn, N.Y. **(1899–1977)**
Hutton, Betty (Betty Thornburg) (actress); Battle Creek, Mich., 2/26/21
Hutton, Lauren (actress, model); Charleston, S.C., 11/17/43
Hutton, Timothy (actor); Los Angeles, 8/16/60
Huxley, Aldous (author); Godalming, England **(1894–1963)**
Huxley, Sir Julian S. (biologist, author); London **(1887–1975)**
Huxley, Thomas Henry (biologist); Ealing, England **(1825–1895)**
Hynde, Chrissie (singer); Akron, Ohio, 9/7/51

I

Iacocca, Lee (Lido Anthony) (business executive); Allentown, Pa., 10/15/24
Ian, Janis (singer); New York City, 5/7/51
Ibsen, Henrik (dramatist); Skien, Norway **(1828–1906)**
Ice Cube (O'Shea Jackson) (musician, actor); Los Angeles, 6/15/69
Ice-T (Tracy Morrow) (rap musician, actor); Newark, N.J., 2/16/68
Inge, William (playwright); Independence, Kans. **(1913–1973)**
Ingres, Jean Auguste Dominique (painter); Montauban, France **(1780–1867)**
Inness, George (painter); nr. Newburgh, N.Y. **(1825–1894)**
Ionesco, Eugene (playwright); Slatina, Romania **(1912–1994)**
Ireland, Jill (actress); London **(1936–1990)**
Ireland, Kathy (model, actress); Glendale, Calif., 3/8/63
Ireland, Patricia (feminist, social activist); Oak Park, Ill., 10/19/45
Irons, Jeremy (actor); Cowes, Isle of Wight, England, 9/19/48
Irving, Amy (actress); Palo Alto, Calif., 9/10/53
Irving, John (Winslow) (writer); Exeter, N.H., 3/2/42
Irving, Washington (author); New York City **(1783–1859)**
Isaak, Chris (musician, actor); Stockton, Calif., 6/26/56
Isherwood, Christopher (novelist, playwright); nr. Dilsey and High Lane, England **(1904–1986)**
Iturbi, José (concert pianist); Valencia, Spain **(1895–1980)**
Ives, Burl (Icle Ivanhoe) (singer); Hunt, Ill. **(1909–1995)**
Ives, Charles E(dward) (composer); Danbury, Conn. **(1874–1954)**
Ivins, Molly (journalist); Monterey, Calif., 8/30/44
Ivory, James (director, producer); Berkeley, Calif., 6/7/28

J

Jackson, Andrew (7th U.S. president); Waxhaw, S.C. **(1767–1845)**
Jackson, Anne (actress); Millvale, Pa., 9/3/26
Jackson, Glenda (actress); Cheshire, England, 5/9/36
Jackson, Janet (singer); Gary, Ind., 5/16/66
Jackson, Rev. Jesse (civil rights leader); Greenville, S.C., 10/8/41
Jackson, Kate (actress); Birmingham, Ala., 10/29/49
Jackson, Mahalia (gospel singer); New Orleans **(1911–1972)**
Jackson, Maynard (mayor of Atlanta); Dallas, 3/23/38
Jackson, Michael (singer); Gary, Ind., 8/29/58
Jackson, Samuel L. (actor); Washington, D.C., 12/21/48
Jackson, Thomas Jonathan "Stonewall" (general); Clarksburg, Va. (now W. Va.) **(1824–1863)**
Jacobi, Derek (actor); Leytonstone, England, 10/22/38
Jacobs, Jane (urbanologist); Scranton, Pa., 5/1/16
Jagger, Mick (Michael Phillip Jagger) (singer); Dartford, England, 7/26/43
James, Harry (trumpeter); Albany, Ga. **(1916–1983)**
James, Henry (novelist); New York City **(1843–1916)**
James, Jesse Woodson (outlaw); Clay County, Mo. **(1847–1882)**
James, William (psychologist); New York City **(1842–1910)**
Jameson, (Margaret) Storm (novelist); Whitby, England **(1897–1986)**
Janis, Byron (pianist); McKeesport, Pa., 3/24/28
Janis, Conrad (actor, musician); New York City, 2/11/28
Janssen, David (David Meyer) (actor); Naponee, Neb. **(1930–1980)**
Jaworkski, Leon (Watergate special prosecutor); Waco, Tex. **(1905–1982)**
Jay, John (statesman, jurist); New York City **(1745–1829)**
Jeanmaire, Renée (dancer); Paris, 4/29/24
Jefferson, Thomas (3rd U.S. president); Shadwell, Va. **(1743–1826)**
Jemison, Mae C. (astronaut, physician); Decatur, Ala., 10/17/56
Jenner, Edward (physician); Berkeley, England **(1749–1823)**
Jennings, Peter (news anchor); Toronto, 7/29/38
Jennings, Waylon (singer); Littlefield, Tex., 6/15/37
Jessel, George (entertainer); New York City **(1898–1981)**
Jessup, Philip C. (diplomat); New York City **(1897–1986)**
Jillian, Ann (Ann Jura Nauseda) (actress); Cambridge, Mass., 1/29/51
Joan of Arc (Jeanne d'Arc) (saint, patriot); Domremy-la-Pucelle, France **(1412–1431)**
Jobs, Steven Paul (computer industry pioneer); San Francisco, 1955
Joel, Billy (singer); New York City, 5/9/49
Joffrey, Robert (Abdullah Jaffa Bey Khan) (choreographer); Seattle **(1930–1988)**
John, Elton (Reginald Kenneth Dwight) (singer, pianist); Pinner, England, 3/25/47
Johns, Jasper (painter, sculptor); Augusta, Ga., 5/15/30
Johnson, Andrew (17th U.S. president); Raleigh, N.C. **(1808–1875)**
Johnson, Don (actor); Flatt Creek, Mo., 12/15/49

Johnson, James Weldon (author, educator); Jacksonville, Fla. **(1871–1938)**
Johnson, Lyndon Baines (36th U.S. president); Stonewall, Tex. **(1908–1973)**
Johnson, Philip Cortelyou (architect); Cleveland, 7/8/06
Johnson, Samuel (lexicographer, author); Lichfield, England **(1709–1784)**
Johnson, Van (actor); Newport, R.I., 8/20/16
Johnson, Virginia (human sexuality expert); Springfield, Mo., 2/11/25
Joliot-Curie, Frédéric (chemist, Nobel laureate); Paris **(1900–1958)**
Joliot-Curie, Irène (Irène Curie) (chemist, Nobel laureate); France **(1897–1956)**
Jolliet, Louis (Louis Joliet) (explorer); Beaupré, Canada **(1645–1700)**
Jolson, Al (Asa Yoelson) (actor, singer); St. Petersburg, Russia **(1886–1950)**
Jones, Dean (actor); Morgan County, Ala., 1/25/35
Jones, George (singer); Saratoga, Tex., 9/12/31
Jones, Inigo (architect); London **(1573–1652)**
Jones, James (novelist); Robinson, Ill. **(1921–1977)**
Jones, James Earl (actor); Arkabutla, Miss., 1/17/31
Jones, Jennifer (Phylis Isley) (actress); Tulsa, Okla., 3/2/19
Jones, John Paul (John Paul) (naval officer); Scotland **(1747–1792)**
Jones, Quincy (composer); Chicago, 3/14/33
Jones, Shirley (singer, actress); Smithtown, Pa., 3/31/34
Jones, Spike (host, orchestra leader); Long Beach, Calif. **(1911–1965)**
Jones, Tom (Thomas Jones Woodward) (singer); Pontypridd, Wales, 6/7/40
Jones, Tommy Lee (actor); San Saba, Tex., 9/15/46
Jong, Erica (writer); New York City, 3/26/42
Jonson, Ben (Benjamin Jonson) (poet, dramatist); Westminster, England **(1572–1637)**
Joplin, Janis (singer); Port Arthur, Tex. **(1943–1970)**
Joplin, Scott (ragtime pianist, composer); Texarkansas, Tex. **(1868–1917)**
Jordan, Barbara (U.S. representative); Houston **(1936–1996)**
Jordan, Neil (film director, screenwriter); Sligo, Ireland, 2/25/50
Joseph (Chief Joseph) (Nez Perce Indian leader); eastern Ore. **(1841–1904)**
Josquin des Prés (usually known as Josquin) (composer); Conde-sur-L'Escaut?, Hainaut, Belgium **(c. 1445–1521)**
Jourdan, Louis (Louis Gendre) (actor); Marseilles, France, 6/19/19
Jovovich, Milla (actress, model, singer); Kiev, Ukraine, 12/19/75
Joyce, James (novelist); Dublin **(1882–1941)**
Juárez, Benito Pablo (statesman); Guelatao, Mexico **(1806–1872)**
Judd, Ashley (actress); Los Angeles, 4/19/68
Julia, Raul (Raúl Rafael Carlos Julia y Arcelay) (actor); San Juan, P.R. **(1940–1994)**
Jung, Carl Gustav (psychoanalyst); Basel, Switzerland **(1875–1961)**

K

Kabalevsky, Dmitri (composer); St. Petersburg, Russia **(1904–1987)**
Kafka, Franz (author); Prague **(1883–1924)**
Kádár, János (Communist Party leader); Hungary **(1912–1989)**
Kahn, Gus (songwriter); Coblenz, Germany **(1886–1941)**
Kahn, Louis I. (architect); Oesel Island, Estonia **(1901–1974)**
Kahn, Madeline (actress); Boston **(1942–1999)**
Kandinsky, Wassily (painter); Moscow **(1866–1944)**
Kanin, Garson (playwright); Rochester, N.Y. **(1912–1999)**
Kant, Immanuel (philosopher); Königsberg (Kaliningrad), Russia **(1724–1804)**
Kantor, MacKinlay (novelist); Webster City, Iowa **(1904–1977)**
Kaplan, Justin (writer, editor); New York City, 9/5/25
Karan, Donna (fashion designer); Forest Hills, N.Y., 10/2/48
Karloff, Boris (William Henry Pratt) (actor); London **(1887–1969)**
Kasdan, Lawrence (film director, writer, actor, producer); Miami, 1/14/49
Kasem, Casey (disc jockey); Detroit, 4/27/32
Kaufman, Andy (actor, comedian); New York City **(1949–1984)**
Kaufman, George S. (playwright); Pittsburgh **(1889–1961)**
Kavner, Julie (actress); Los Angeles, 9/7/51
Kaye, Danny (David Daniel Kominski) (comedian); Brooklyn, N.Y. **(1913–1987)**
Kaye, Sammy (band leader); Cleveland **(1910–1987)**
Kazan, Elia (director); Constantinople, Turkey, 9/7/09
Kazan, Lainie (Levine) (singer); New York City, 5/15/40
Kazantzakis, Nikos (writer); Herakleion, Crete **(1883–1957)**
Keach, Stacy (actor); Savannah, Ga., 6/2/41

Keaton, Buster (Joseph Frank Keaton) (comedian); Piqua, Kans. **(1896–1966)**
Keaton, Diane (actress); Los Angeles, 1/5/46
Keaton, Michael (Michael Douglas) (actor); Robinson Township, Pa., 9/9/51
Keats, John (poet); London **(1795–1821)**
Keel, Howard (Harold Clifford Leek) (singer, actor); Gillespie, Ill., 4/13/19
Keeler, Ruby (Ethel Hilde Keeler) (actress, dancer); Halifax, N.S., Canada **(1910–1993)**
Keener, Catherine (actress); Miami, Fla., 1959(?)
Kefauver, Estes (legislator); Madisonville, Tenn **(1903–1963)**
Keitel, Harvey (actor); Brooklyn, N.Y., 5/13/39
Keith, Brian (Robert Brian Keith, Jr.) (actor); Bayonne, N.J. **(1921–1997)**
Keller, Helen Adams (author, educator); Tuscumbia, Ala. **(1880–1968)**
Kelley, DeForest (actor); Atlanta **(1920–1999)**
Kelly, Emmett (clown); Sedan, Kans. **(1898–1979)**
Kelly, Gene (dancer, actor); Pittsburgh **(1912–1996)**
Kelly, R. (Robert Kelly) (singer, record producer, actor); Chicago, 1969
Kempis, Thomas à (mystic); Kempis, Prussia (Germany) **(1380–1471)**
Kendall, Henry W. (physicist, Nobel laureate); Boston **(1926–1999)**
Kennan, George F. (diplomat); Milwaukee, 2/16/04
Kennedy, Arthur (actor); Worcester, Mass. **(1914–1990)**
Kennedy, Caroline Bessette (socialite); White Plains, N.Y. **(1966–1999)**
Kennedy, George (actor); New York City, 2/18/25
Kennedy, John Fitzgerald (35th U.S. president); Brookline, Mass. **(1917–1963)**
Kennedy, John F., Jr. (publisher); Washington, D.C. **(1960–1999)**
Kennedy, Joseph P. (financier); Boston **(1888–1969)**
Kennedy, Robert Francis (legislator); Brookline, Mass. **(1925–1968)**
Kennedy, Rose Fitzgerald (president's mother); Boston **(1890–1995)**
Kent, Allegra (ballet dancer); Santa Monica, Calif., 8/11/38
Kent, Rockwell (painter); Tarrytown Heights, N.Y. **(1882–1971)**
Kenton, Stan (Stanley Newcomb) (jazz musician); Wichita, Kans. **(1912–1979)**
Kepler, Johannes (astronomer); Weil, Germany **(1571–1630)**
Kercheval, Ken (actor); Wolcottville, Ind., 7/15/35
Kerensky, Alexander Fedorovich (statesman); Simbirsk, Russia **(1881–1970)**
Kern, Jerome David (composer); New York City **(1885–1945)**
Kerns, Joanna (actress); San Francisco, 2/12/53
Kerouac, Jack (Jean-Louis Kerouac) (writer); Lowell, Mass. **(1922–1969)**
Kerr, Deborah (actress); Helensburgh, Scotland, 9/30/21
Kettering, Charles F. (engineer, inventor); nr. Loudonville, Ohio **(1876–1958)**
Kevorkian, Jack (medical pathologist); Pontiac, Mich., 3/26/28
Key, Francis Scott (lawyer, author of national anthem); Frederick (Carroll) County, Md. **(1779–1843)**
Keyes, Frances Parkinson (novelist); Charlottesville, Va. **(1885–1970)**
Keynes, John Maynard (1st Baron of Tilton) (economist); Cambridge, England **(1883–1946)**
Khachaturian, Aram (composer); Tiflis, Russia **(1903–1978)**
Khomeini, Ayatollah Ruhollah (Islamic religious leader); Iran **(1900–1989)**
Khrushchev, Nikita S. (Soviet leader); Kalinovka, nr. Kursk, Ukraine **(1894–1971)**
Kidd, Michael (Milton Greenwald) (choreographer); Brooklyn, N.Y., 8/12/19
Kidd, William (called Captain Kidd) (pirate); Greenock, Scotland **(c. 1645–1701)**
Kidder, Margot (actress); Yellowknife, N.W.T., Canada, 10/17/48
Kidman, Nicole (actress); Honolulu, 6/20/67
Kiepura, Jan (tenor); Sosnowiec, Poland **(1902–1966)**
Kieran, John (writer); New York City **(1892–1981)**
Kierkegaard, Sören Aalys (philosopher); Copenhagen **(1813–1855)**
Kiesinger, Kurt Georg (diplomat); Ebingen, Germany **(1904–1988)**
Kiley, Richard (actor, singer); Chicago **(1922–1999)**
Kilmer, Alfred Joyce (poet); New Brunswick, N.J. **(1886–1918)**
Kilmer, Val (actor); Los Angeles,, 12/31/59
King, Alan (Irwin Alan Kniberg) (entertainer); Brooklyn, N.Y., 12/26/27
King, B.B. (Riley King) (guitarist); Itta Bena, Miss., 9/16/25
King, Carole (singer, songwriter); Brooklyn, N.Y., 2/9/41
King, Coretta Scott (civil rights leader); Marion, Ala., 4/27/27
King, Larry (Lawrence Harvey Zeigler) (TV host); New York City, 11/19/33

King, Martin Luther, Jr. (civil rights leader); Atlanta **(1929–1968)**

King, Stephen (writer); Portland, Maine, 9/21/47

Kingsley, Ben (Krishna Bhanji) (actor); Snainton, England, 12/31/43

Kingsley, Sidney (Sidney Kirschner) (playwright); New York City **(1906–1995)**

Kingsolver, Barbara (writer); Annapolis, Md., 4/8/55

Kingston, Maxine Hong (novelist); Stockton, Calif., 10/27/40

Kinsey, Alfred Charles (human sexuality expert); Hoboken, N.J. **(1894–1956)**

Kinski, Nastassja (Nastassja Nakszynski) (actress); West Berlin, 1/24/61

Kipling, Rudyard (author); Bombay (Mumbai) **(1865–1936)**

Kipnis, Alexander (basso); Ukraine **(1891–1978)**

Kirby, George (comedian); Chicago **(1923–1995)**

Kirchner, Ernst Ludwig (painter); Aschaffenburg, Germany **(1880–1938)**

Kirk, Grayson (educator); Jeffersonville, Ohio **(1903–1997)**

Kirkland, Gelsey (ballet dancer); Bethlehem, Pa., 12/29/52

Kirkpatrick, Jeane Jordan (educator-public affairs); Duncan, Okla., 11/19/26

Kirkpatrick, Ralph (harpsichordist); Leominster, Mass. **(1911–1984)**

Kirstein, Lincoln (dance, theater executive); Rochester, N.Y. **(1907–1996)**

Kirsten, Dorothy (soprano); Montclair, N.J. **(1910–1992)**

Kissinger, Henry (Heinz Alfred Kissinger) (ex-U.S. secretary of state); Furth, Germany, 5/27/23

Kitt, Eartha (singer); North, S.C., 1/26/28

Klee, Paul (painter); Münchenbuchsee, nr. Bern, Switzerland **(1879–1940)**

Klein, Calvin (fashion designer); Bronx, N.Y., 11/19/42

Klein, Robert (comedian); New York City, 2/8/42

Kleist, Henrich von (poet); Frankfurt an der Oder, Germany **(1777–1811)**

Klemperer, Otto (conductor); Breslau, Poland **(1885–1973)**

Klemperer, Werner (actor); Cologne, Germany **(1920–2000)**

Klimt, Gustav (painter); Vienna **(1862–1918)**

Kline, Kevin (actor); St. Louis, 10/24/47

Klugman, Jack (actor); Philadelphia, 4/27/22

Knight, Gladys (singer); Atlanta, 5/28/44

Knight, John S. (publisher); Bluefield, W. Va. **(1894–1981)**

Knight, Ted (Tadeus Wladyslaw Konopka) (actor); Terryville, Conn. **(1923–1986)**

Knight, Wayne (actor); Cartersville, Ga., 8/7/55

Knopf, Alfred A. (publisher); New York City **(1892–1984)**

Knopfler, Mark (musician); Glasgow, Scotland, 8/12/49

Knotts, Don (actor); Morgantown, W. Va., 7/21/24

Knox, John (religious reformer); Haddington, East Lothian, Scotland **(1505–1572)**

Koch, Robert (physician); Klausthal, Germany **(1843–1910)**

Koenig, Walter (actor); Chicago, 9/14/36

Koestler, Arthur (novelist); Budapest **(1905–1983)**

Kokoschka, Oskar (painter); Póchlarn, Austria **(1886–1980)**

Kollwitz, Käthe (graphic artist, sculptor); Königsberg, Russia **(1867–1945)**

Koop, C. Everett (ex-surgeon general); Brooklyn, N.Y., 10/14/16

Kooper, Al (singer, pianist); Brooklyn, N.Y., 2/5/44

Kopell, Bernie (actor); New York City, 6/21/33

Koppel, Ted (broadcast journalist); Lancashire, England, 2/8/40

Korman, Harvey (actor); Chicago, 2/15/27

Kosciusko, Thaddeus (Tadeusz Andrzej Bonawentura Kosciuszko) (military officer and statesman) **(1746–1817)**

Kossuth, Lajos (patriot); Monok, Hungary **(1802–1894)**

Kostelanetz, André (orchestra conductor); St. Petersburg, Russia **(1901–1980)**

Kostunica, Vojislav (president of Yugoslavia); Belgrade, 3/24/44

Kosygin, Aleksei N. (premier); St. Petersburg, Russia **(1904–1980)**

Kotto, Yaphet (actor); New York City, 11/15/37

Koussevitzky, Serge (Sergei) Alexandrovitch (orchestra conductor); Vishni Volochek, Tver, Russia **(1874–1951)**

Kramer, Stanley E. (film producer, director); New York City **(1913–2001)**

Kràus, Lili (pianist); Budapest **(1905–1986)**

Kravitz, Lenny (musician); New York City, 5/26/64

Kreisler, Fritz (violinist, composer); Vienna **(1875–1962)**

Kresge, S. S. (merchant); Bald Mount, Pa. **(1867–1966)**

Krips, Josef (orchestra conductor); Vienna **(1902–1974)**

Kristofferson, Kris (singer); Brownsville, Tex., 6/22/36

Krupa, Gene (drummer); Chicago **(1909–1973)**

Krupp, Alfred (munitions magnate); Essen, Germany **(1812–1887)**

Kubelik, Rafael (conductor); Bychory, former Czechoslovakia **(1914–1996)**

Kublai Khan (Mongol conqueror) **(1216–1294)**

Kubrick, Stanley (film director, producer); New York City **(1928–1999)**

Kudrow, Lisa (actress); Encino, Calif., 7/30/63

Kuralt, Charles (TV journalist); Wilmington, N.C. **(1934–1997)**

Kurosawa, Akira (film director); Tokyo **(1910–1998)**

Kurtz, Efrem (conductor); St. Petersburg, Russia **(1900–1995)**

Kurtz, Swoosie (actress); Omaha, Neb., 9/6/44

L

LaBelle, Patti (singer, actress); Philadelphia, 5/24/44

Ladd, Cheryl (Cheryl Stoppelmoor) (actress); Huron, S.D., 7/12/51

Ladd, Diane (actress); Meridian, Miss., 11/29/32

Lafayette, Marquis de (Marie Joseph Paul Yves Roch Gilbert du Motier) (military officer); Auvergne, France **(1757–1834)**

Lafitte, Jean (pirate); Bayonne?, France **(1780–1826)**

La Follette, Robert Marin (politician); Primrose, Wis. **(1855–1925)**

La Fontaine, Jean de (poet); Château-Thierry, France **(1621–1695)**

La Guardia, Fiorello Henry (mayor of New York); New York City **(1882–1947)**

Lahti, Christine (actress, director); Birmingham, Mich., 4/4/50

Laine, Frankie (Frank Paul LoVecchio) (singer); Chicago, 3/30/13

Laird, Melvin (ex-secretary of defense); Omaha, Neb., 9/1/22

Lamarck, Chevalier de (Jean Baptiste Pierre Antoine de Monet) (naturalist); Bazantin, France **(1744–1829)**

Lamas, Lorenzo (actor); Los Angeles, 1/20/58

Lamb, Charles (Elia) (essayist); London **(1775–1834)**

L'Amour, Louis (author); Jamestown, N.D. **(1908–1988)**

Lancaster, Burt (actor); New York City **(1913–1994)**

Landau, Martin (actor); Brooklyn, N.Y., 6/20/31

Landers, Ann (Esther Pauline Friedman) (columnist); Sioux City, Iowa, 7/4/18

Landon, Michael (Eugene Maurice Orowitz) (actor, director, producer); Forest Hills, Queens, N.Y. **(1936–1991)**

Lane, Abbe (Abigail Francine Lassman) (singer); New York City, 1933

Lane, Burton (songwriter); New York City **(1912–1997)**

Lane, Nathan (Joseph Lane) (actor, singer); Jersey City, N.J., 2/3/56

Lang, Fritz (film director); Vienna **(1890–1976)**

Lange, Hope (actress); Redding Ridge, Conn., 11/28/33

Lange, Jessica (actress); Cloquet, Minn., 4/20/49

Langella, Frank (actor); Bayonne, N.J., 1/1/40

Langmuir, Irving (chemist); Brooklyn, N.Y. **(1881–1957)**

Langtry, Lillie (Emily Le Breton) (actress); Island of Jersey **(1852–1929)**

Lansbury, Angela (actress, producer); London, 10/16/25

Lansing, Robert (Robert Howell Brown) (actor); San Diego, Calif. **(1928–1994)**

Lanza, Mario (Alfred Arnold Cocozza) (singer, actor); Philadelphia **(1921–1959)**

Lao-tse (Li Erh) (philosopher); Honan Province, China **(c. 604–531 B.C.)**

Lardner, Ring (Ringgold Wilmar Lardner) (story writer); Niles, Mich. **(1885–1933)**

La Rouchefoucauld, Francois duc de (author); Paris **(1613–1680)**

Larroquette, John (actor); New Orleans, 11/25/47

Larson, Gary (cartoonist); Tacoma, Wash., 8/14/50

La Salle, Eriq (actor); Hartford, Conn., 7/23/62

La Salle, Sieur de (Robert Cavelier) (explorer); Rouen, France **(1643–1687)**

Lasch, Christopher (historian, social critic); Omaha, Neb. **(1932–1994)**

La Tour, Georges de (painter); Vic-sur-Seille, France **(1593–1652)**

Lauer, Matt (TV host); New York City, 12/20/57

Laughton, Charles (actor); Scarborough, England **(1899–1962)**

Lauper, Cyndi (singer); New York City, 6/20/53

Laurel, Stan (Arthur Jefferson) (comedian); Ulverston, England **(1890–1965)**

Laurents, Arthur (playwright); New York City, 7/14/18

Laurie, Piper (Rosetta Jacobs) (actress); Detroit, 1/22/32

Lavin, Linda (actress); Portland, Maine, 10/15/37

Lavoisier, Antoine-Laurent (chemist); Paris **(1743–1794)**

Lawford, Peter (actor); London **(1923–1984)**

Lawless, Lucy (Lucy Ryan) (actress); Auckland, New Zealand, 3/29/68

Lawrence, David Herbert (novelist); Nottingham, England **(1885–1930)**

Lawrence, Jacob (painter); Atantic City, N.J. **(1917–2000)**

Lawrence, Martin (actor); Frankfurt, Germany, 4/16/65

Lawrence, Sharon (actress); Charlotte, N.C., 6/29/62

Lawrence, Steve (Sidney Leibowitz) (singer); Brooklyn, N.Y., 7/8/35

Lawrence of Arabia (Thomas Edward Lawrence, later changed to Shaw) (author, soldier); Tremadoc, Wales **(1888–1935)**

Lawrence, Vicki (actress); Inglewood, Calif., 3/26/49

Leach, Penelope (Balchin) (child psychologist, writer); London, 11/19/37

Leach, Robin (host, producer); London, 8/29/41

Leachman, Cloris (actress); Des Moines, Iowa, 4/30/26

Leadbelly, (Huddie Ledbetter) (blues singer, guitarist); Mooringsport, La. **(1885–1949)**

Leakey, Louis Seymour Bazett (anthropologist); Kabete, Kenya **(1903–1972)**

Leakey, Mary (anthropologist); London **(1913–1996)**

Leakey, Richard (paleoanthropologist, wildlife conservationist); Kenya, 12/19/44

Lean, David (film director); Croydon, England **(1908–1991)**

Lear, Edward (nonsense poet); London **(1812–1888)**

Lear, Evelyn (Shulman) (soprano); Brooklyn, N.Y., 1/8/26

Lear, Norman (TV producer); New Haven, Conn., 7/27/22

Learned, Michael (actress); Washington, D.C., 4/9/39

Leary, Denis (actor, screenwriter, film director); Worcester, Mass., 8/18/57

Leary, Timothy (psychologist, LSD advocate); Springfield, Mass. **(1920–1996)**

Le Blanc, Matt (actor); Newton, Mass., 7/25/67

le Carré, John (David John Moore Cornwell) (novelist); Poole, England, 10/19/31

Le Corbusier (Charles Edouard Jeanneret) (architect); La Chaux-de-Fonds, Switzerland **(1887–1965)**

Lee, Ang (film director); Pingtung, Taiwan, 10/23/54

Lee, Christopher (actor); London, 5/27/22

Lee, Manfred B. (pseudonym Ellery Queen) (novelist); Brooklyn, N.Y. **(1905–1971)**

Lee, Peggy (Norma Engstrom) (singer); Jamestown, N.D., 5/26/20

Lee, Robert E(dward) (Confederate general); Stratford Estate, Va. **(1807–1870)**

Lee, Spike (Shelton Jackson Lee) (actor, director, writer, producer); Atlanta, 3/20/57

Leeuwenhoek, Anton van (zoologist); Delft, Netherlands **(1632–1723)**

Lehár, Franz (composer); Komárom, Hungary **(1870–1948)**

Lehman, Herbert H. (governor, senator); New York City **(1878–1963)**

Lehmann, Lotte (soprano); Perleberg, Germany **(1888–1976)**

Lehrer, Jim (TV newscaster); Wichita, Kans., 5/19/34

Leibniz, Gottfried W. von (scientist); Leipzig, Germany **(1646–1716)**

Leibovitz, Annie (photographer); Westbury, Conn., 10/2/49

Leigh, Janet (Jeanette Helen Morrison) (actress); Merced, Calif., 7/6/27

Leigh, Jennifer Jason (Jennifer Morrow) (actress); Los Angeles, 2/5/62

Leigh, Mike (film director, screenwriter); Manchester, England, 2/20/43

Leigh, Vivien (Vivian Mary Hartley) (actress); Darjeeling, India **(1913–1967)**

Leinsdorf, Erich (conductor); Vienna **(1912–1993)**

Lemmon, Jack (actor); Boston **(1925–2001)**

Lenin, Vladimir (Vladimir Ilich Ulyanov) (Soviet leader); Simbirsk, Russia **(1870–1924)**

Lennon, John (singer, songwriter); Liverpool, England **(1940–1980)**

Leno, Jay (comedian, TV host); New Rochelle, N.Y., 4/28/50

Leonard, Sheldon (Sheldon Leonard Bershad) (actor, producer); New York City **(1907–1997)**

Leonardo da Vinci, (painter, scientist); Vinci, Tuscany, Italy **(1452–1519)**

Leoni, Téa (actress); New York City, 2/25/66

Lerner, Alan Jay (lyricist); New York City **(1918–1986)**

Lerner, Max (columnist); Minsk, Russia **(1902–1992)**

Lessing, Doris (novelist); Kermanshah, Iran, 10/22/19

Leto, Jared (actor); Bossier City, La., 12/26/71

Letterman, David (TV host, producer); Indianapolis, 4/12/47

Levant, Oscar (pianist); Pittsburgh **(1906–1972)**

Levenson, Sam (humorist); New York City **(1911–1980)**

Levi, Carlo (novelist); Turin, Italy **(1902–1975)**

Levine, James (artistic director, Metropolitan Opera); Cincinnati, 6/23/43

Levine, Joseph E. (film producer); Boston **(1905–1987)**

Levinson, Barry (screenwriter, director, producer, actor); Baltimore, 4/6/42

Lewis, C(live) S(taples) (author); Belfast, Northern Ireland **(1898–1963)**

Lewis, Gilbert Newton (chemist, Nobel laureate); Weymouth, Mass. **(1875–1946)**

Lewis, Jerry (Joseph Levitch) (comedian, film director); Newark, N.J., 3/16/26

Lewis, Jerry Lee (singer); Ferriday, La., 9/29/35

Lewis, John Llewellyn (labor leader); Lucas, Iowa **(1880–1969)**

Lewis, Juliette (actress); Los Angeles, 12/21/73

Lewis, Meriwether (explorer); Albemarle Co., Va. **(1774–1809)**

Lewis, (Percy) Wyndham (artist, writer); Bay of Fundy, Maine (at sea) **(1884–1957)**

Lewis, Shari (Shari Hurwitz) (puppeteer); New York City **(1934–1998)**

Lewis, Sinclair (novelist); Sauk Centre, Minn. **(1885–1951)**

Ley, Willy (science writer); Berlin **(1906–1969)**

Liberace (Wladziu Liberace) (pianist); West Allis, Wis. **(1919–1987)**

Lichtenstein, Roy (painter); New York City **(1923–1997)**

Lie, Trygve Halvdan (first U.N. secretary-general); Oslo **(1896–1968)**

Light, Judith (actress); Trenton, N.J., 2/9/49

Lightfoot, Gordon (singer, songwriter); Orillia, Ont., Canada, 11/17/38

Limbaugh, Rush (political commentator); Cape Girardeau, Mo., 1/12/51

Lin, Maya (architect, sculptor); Athens, Ohio, 10/5/59

Lin Yutang (author); Changchow, China **(1895–1976)**

Lincoln, Abraham (16th U.S. president); Hardin (Larue) County, Ky. **(1809–1865)**

Lind, Jenny (Johanna Maria Lind) (soprano); Stockholm **(1820–1887)**

Lindbergh, Anne Morrow (author); Englewood, N.J. **(1906–2001)**

Lindbergh, Charles A. (aviator); Detroit **(1902–1974)**

Linden, Hal (Harold Lipshitz) (actor); New York City, 3/20/31

Lindsay, Howard (playwright); Waterford, N.Y. **(1889–1968)**

Linkletter, Art (radio-TV personality); Moose Jaw, Sask., Canada, 7/17/12

Linnaeus, Carolus (Carl von Linné) (botanist); Råshult, Sweden **(1707–1778)**

Linney, Laura (actress); New York City, 2/5/64

Liotta, Ray (actor); Union, N.J., 12/18/55

Lipchitz, Jacques (sculptor); Druskieniki, Latvia **(1891–1973)**

Lippi, Fra Filippo (painter); Florence **(1406–1469)**

Lippmann, Walter (columnist, author, political analyst); New York City **(1889–1974)**

Lister, Joseph (1st Baron of Lyme Regis) (surgeon); Upton, England **(1827–1912)**

Liszt, Franz (composer, pianist); Raiding, Hungary **(1811–1886)**

Lithgow, John (actor); Rochester, N.Y., 6/6/45

Little, Rich (impressionist); Ottawa, Ont., Canada, 11/26/38

Livingstone, David (missionary, explorer); Lanarkshire, Scotland **(1813–1873)**

L. L. Cool J (James Todd Smith) (rap artist); New York City, 1/14/68

Llewellyn, Richard (novelist); St. David's, Wales **(1906–1983)**

Lloyd Webber, Andrew (composer); London, 3/22/48

Lloyd George, David (Earl of Dwyfor) (statesman); Manchester, England **(1863–1945)**

Lloyd, Jake (actor); Fort Collins, Colo., 3/5/89

Locke, Alain L. (philosopher); Philadelphia **(1886–1954)**

Locke, John (philosopher); Somersetshire, England **(1632–1704)**

Lockhart, June (actress); New York City, 6/25/25

Locklear, Heather (actress); Los Angeles, 9/25/61

Lodge, Henry Cabot (legislator); Boston **(1850–1924)**

Lodge, Henry Cabot, Jr. (diplomat); Nahant, Mass. **(1902–1985)**

Loesser, Frank (composer); New York City **(1910–1969)**

Loewe, Frederick (composer); Vienna **(1901–1988)**

Logan, Joshua (director, producer); Texarkana, Tex. **(1908–1988)**

Lollobrigida, Gina (Luigina Lollobrigida) (actress); Subiaco, Italy, 7/4/27

Lombard, Carole (Jane Alice Peters) (actress); Ft. Wayne, Ind. **(1908–1942)**

Lombardo, Guy (band leader); London, Ont., Canada **(1902–1977)**

London, George (baritone); Montreal **(1920–1985)**

London, Jack (John Griffith London) (novelist); San Francisco **(1876–1916)**

Long, Huey Pierce (politician); Winnfield, La. **(1893–1935)**

Long, Shelley (actress); Fort Wayne, Ind., 8/23/49

Longfellow, Henry Wadsworth (poet); Portland, Maine **(1807–1882)**

Longworth, Alice Roosevelt (social figure); New York City **(1884–1980)**

Loos, Anita (writer); Sissons, Calif. **(1888–1981)**

Lopez, Jennifer (actress, singer); Bronx, N.Y., 12/24/70

Lopez, Trini (singer); Dallas, 5/15/37

Lopez, Vincent (band leader); Brooklyn, N.Y. **(1895–1975)**

Lord, Jack (John Joseph Ryan) (actor); New York City **(1920–1998)**

Loren, Sophia (Sofia Scicolone) (actress); Rome, 9/20/34

Lorenz, Konrad (ethologist); Vienna **(1903–1989)**

Lorre, Peter (Laszlo Löewenstein) (actor); Rosenberg, former Czechoslovakia **(1904–1964)**

Loudon, Dorothy (actress, singer); Boston, 9/17/33

Louis-Dreyfus, Julia (actress); New York City, 1/13/61

Louis XIV (King of France); St.-Germain-en-Laye, France **(1638–1715)**

Louise, Tina (actress); New York City, 2/11/37

Love, Susan (surgeon, oncologist, activist); Long Branch, N.J., 2/9/48

Lovecraft, Howard Phillips (author); Providence, R.I. **(1890–1937)**

Lovett, Lyle (country singer, songwriter); Klein, Tex., 11/1/56

Lowe, Rob (actor); Charlottesville, Va., 3/17/64

Lowell, Amy (poet); Brookline, Mass. **(1874–1925)**

Lowell, James Russell (poet); Cambridge, Mass. **(1819–1891)**

Lowell, Robert (poet); Boston **(1917–1977)**

Loy, Myrna (Myrna Williams) (actress); nr. Helena, Mont. **(1905–1993)**

Loyola, St. Ignatius of (Iñigo de Oñez y Loyola) (founder of Jesuits); Gúipuzcoa Province, Spain **(1491– 1556)**

Lubitsch, Ernst (film director); Berlin **(1892–1947)**

Lucas, George (film director); Modesto, Calif., 5/14/44

Lucci, Susan (actress); Scarsdale, N.Y., 12/23/46

Luce, Clare Boothe (playwright, former ambassador); New York City **(1903–1987)**

Luce, Henry Robinson (editor, publisher); Tengchow, China **(1898–1967)**

Ludlum, Robert (author); New York City **(1927–2001)**

Lugosi, Béla (Béla Blasko) (actor); Lugos, Hungary **(1888–1956)**

Lukas, J. Anthony (author); New York City **(1933–1997)**

Lukas, Paul (actor); Budapest **(1895–1971)**

Lully, Jean Baptiste (French composer); Florence **(1639–1687)**

Lumet, Sidney (director); Philadelphia, 6/25/24

Lunden, Joan (TV host); Fair Oaks, Calif., 9/19/50

Lunt, Alfred (actor); Milwaukee **(1892–1977)**

Lupino, Ida (actress, director); London **(1918–1995)**

LuPone, Patti (actress, singer); Northport, N.Y., 4/21/49

Luther, Martin (religious reformer); Eisleben, East Germany **(1483–1546)**

Lynch, David (film director); Missoula, Mont., 1/20/46

Lynn, Loretta (singer); Butcher's Hollow, Ky., 4/14/35

M

Ma, Yo-Yo (cellist); Paris, 10/7/55

Maazel, Lorin (conductor); Neuilly, France, 3/5/30

MacArthur, Charles (playwright); Scranton, Pa. **(1895–1956)**

MacArthur, Douglas (five-star general); Little Rock Barracks, Ark. **(1880–1964)**

MacArthur, James (actor); Los Angeles, 12/8/37

Macaulay, Thomas Babington (author); Rothley Temple, England **(1800–1859)**

MacDermot, Galt (composer); Montreal, 12/19/28

MacDonald, James Ramsay (statesman); Lossiemouth, Scotland **(1866–1937)**

MacDonald, Jeanette (actress, soprano); Philadelphia **(1907–1965)**

Macdonald, Ross (Kenneth Millar) (mystery writer); Los Gatos, Calif. **(1915–1983)**

MacDowell, Edward Alexander (composer); New York City **(1861–1908)**

MacDowell, Andie (Rosalie Anderson MacDowell) (actress); Gaffney, S.C., 4/21/58

MacFadden, Bernarr (physical culturist); nr. Mill Spring, Mo. **(1868–1955)**

Machaut, Guillaume de (composer); Marchault, France **(1300–1377)**

Machiavelli, Niccolò (political philosopher); Florence, Italy **(1469–1527)**

Mackie, Bob (designer); Monterey Park, Calif., 3/24/40

MacLaine, Shirley (Shirley MacLean Beaty) (actress); Richmond, Va., 4/24/34

MacLeish, Archibald (poet); Glencoe, Ill. **(1892–1982)**

Macmillan, Harold (ex-prime minister); London **(1894–1986)**

MacMurray, Fred (actor); Kankakee, Ill. **(1908–1991)**

MacNeil, Cornell (baritone); Minneapolis, 9/24/22

MacNeil, Robert (TV newscaster); Montreal, 1/19/31

MacNicol, Peter (actor); Dallas, 4/10/54

Macpherson, Elle (Eleanor Gow) (model, actress); Sydney, Australia, 3/29/64

MacRae, Gordon (singer, actor); East Orange, N.J. **(1921–1986)**

MacRae, Sheila (comedienne); London, 9/24/24

Madison, James (4th U.S. president); Port Conway, Va. **(1751–1836)**

Madonna (Madonna Louise Ciccone) (singer, actress); Bay City, Mich., 8/16/58

Maeterlinck, Count Maurice (author); Ghent, Belgium **(1862–1949)**

Magellan, Ferdinand (Fernando de Magalhaes) (navigator); Sabrosa, Portugal (c. 1480–1521)

Magliozzi, Ray ("Car Talk" host); Cambridge, Mass., 3/30/49

Magliozzi, Tom ("Car Talk" host); Cambridge, Mass., 6/28/37

Magritte, René (painter); Belgium **(1898–1967)**

Magsaysay, Ramón (statesman); Iba, Luzon, Philippines **(1907–1957)**

Mahan, Alfred Thayer (naval historian); West Point, N.Y. **(1840–1914)**

Mahler, Gustav (composer, conductor); Kalischt, Czechoslovakia **(1860–1911)**

Mahoney, John (actor); Manchester, England, 6/20/40

Mailer, Norman (novelist); Long Branch, N.J., 1/31/23

Maillol, Aristide (sculptor); Banyuls-sur-Mer, Rousillion, France **(1861–1944)**

Maimonides, Moses (Jewish philosopher); Cordoba, Spain **(1135–1204)**

Mainbocher (Main Rousseau Bocher) (fashion designer); Chicago **(1891–1976)**

Majors, Lee (Harvey Lee Yeary) (actor); Wyandotte, Mich., 4/23/40

Makarova, Natalia (ballet dancer); Leningrad (St. Petersburg), Russia, 11/21/40

Makeba, Miriam (singer); Johannesburg, South Africa, 3/4/32

Malamud, Bernard (novelist); Brooklyn, N.Y. **(1914–1986)** ·

Malcolm X (Malcolm Little; el Hajj Malik el-Shabazz) (Black nationalist, religious leader); Omaha, Neb. **(1925–1965)**

Malden, Karl (Karl Mladen Sekulovich) (actor); Chicago, 3/22/13

Malkovich, John (actor); Christopher, Ill., 12/9/53

Mallarmé, Stephane (poet, essayist); Paris **(1842–1898)**

Malle, Louis (director); Thumeries, France **(1932–1995)**

Malraux, André (author); Paris **(1901–1976)**

Malthus, Thomas Robert (economist); nr. Dorking, England **(1766–1834)**

Maltin, Leonard (film critic and historian); New York City, 12/18/50

Mamet, David (playwright); Chicago, 11/30/47

Manchester, Melissa (singer); Bronx, N.Y., 2/15/51

Manchester, William (writer); Attleboro, Mass., 4/1/22

Mancini, Henry (composer, conductor); Cleveland **(1924–1994)**

Mandela, Nelson (Rolihlahla) (former president of South Africa); Umtata, Transkei, 7/18/18

Mandela, Winnie (Nomzamo) (South African political activist); Pondoland district of the Transkei, 1936?

Mandrell, Barbara (singer); Houston, 12/25/48

Manet, Edouard (painter); Paris **(1832–1883)**

Mangione, Chuck (hornist, pianist, composer); Rochester, N.Y., 11/29/40

Manheim, Camryn (actress); New York City, 3/8/61

Manilow, Barry (singer); Brooklyn, N.Y., 6/17/46

Mankiewicz, Frank F. (columnist); New York City, 5/16/24

Mankiewicz, Joseph L. (film writer, director); Wilkes-Barre, Pa. **(1909–1993)**

Mann, Horace (educator); Franklin, Mass. **(1796–1859)**

Mann, Thomas (novelist); Lübeck, Germany **(1875–1955)**

Mannes, Marya (writer); New York City **(1904–1990)**

Mansfield, Jayne (Jayne Palmer) (actress); Bryn Mawr, Pa. **(1932–1967)**

Mansfield, Katherine (story writer); Wellington, New Zealand **(1888–1923)**

Manson, Marilyn (Brian Warner) (rock musician); Canton, Ohio, 1/5/69

Mantegna, Andrea (painter); Isola di Carturo, Italy **(1431–1506)**

Mantegna, Joe (actor); Chicago, 11/13/47

Mantovani, Annunzio (conductor); Venice **(1905–1980)**

Mao Zedong (Tse-tung) (Chinese leader); Shao Shan, China **(1893– 1976)**

Mapplethorpe, Robert (photographer); Floral Park, Queens, N.Y. **(1946–1989)**

Marat, Jean Paul (French revolutionist); Boudry, Neuchâtel, Switzerland **(1743–1793)**

Marceau, Marcel (mime); Strasbourg, France, 3/22/23

Marceau, Sophie (actress); Paris, 11/17/66

March, Fredric (Frederick Bickel) (actor); Racine, Wis. **(1897–1975)**

Marchand, Nancy (actress); Buffalo, N.Y. **(1928–2000)**

Marconi, Guglielmo (inventor); Bologna, Italy **(1874–1937)**

Marcus Aurelius (Marcus Annius Verus) (Roman emperor); Rome **(121–180)**

Marcus, Rudolph Arthur (chemist, Nobel laureate); Montreal, 7/21/23

Marcuse, Herbert (philosopher); Berlin **(1898–1979)**

Margaret Rose (princess of England); Glamis Castle, Angus, Scotland, 8/21/30

Margrethe II (queen of Denmark); Copenhagen, 4/16/40

Margulies, Julianna (actress); Spring Valley, N.Y., 6/8/65

Marie Antoinette (Josephe Jeanne Marie Antoinette) (queen of France); Vienna (**1755 –1793**)

Marisol (Escobar) (Venezuelan-American sculptor); Paris, 1930

Markham, Edwin (poet); Oregon City, Ore. (**1852–1940**)

Markova, Dame Alicia (Lilian Alice Marks) (ballet dancer); London, 12/1/10

Marley, Bob (singer, songwriter); Kingston, Jamaica (**1945–1981**)

Marlowe, Christopher (dramatist); Canterbury, England (**1564–1593**)

Marquand, J(ohn) P(hillips) (novelist); Wilmington, Del. (**1893–1960**)

Marquette, Jacques (missionary, explorer); Laon, France (**1637–1675**)

Marriner, Neville (conductor); Lincoln, England, 4/15/24

Marsalis, Wynton (musician); New Orleans, 10/18/61

Marshall, E.G. (actor); Owatonna, Minn. (**1910–1998**)

Marshall, Garry (director, producer, screenwriter, actor); New York City, 11/13/34

Marshall, George Catlett (general); Uniontown, Pa. (**1880–1959**)

Marshall, Herbert (actor); London (**1890–1968**)

Marshall, John (jurist); nr. Germantown, Va. (**1755–1835**)

Marshall, Penny (Penny Marscharelli) (actress, director, producer); Bronx, N.Y., 10/15/42

Marshall, Thurgood (U.S. Supreme Court justice); Baltimore (**1908–1993**)

Martin, Dean (Dino Crocetti) (singer, actor); Steubenville, Ohio (**1917–1995**)

Martin, Mary (singer, actress); Weatherford, Tex. (**1913–1990**)

Martin, Steve (actor, writer, producer); Waco, Tex., 8/14/45

Martin, Tony (Alvin Morris) (singer); San Francisco, 12/25/12

Martinelli, Giovanni (tenor); Montagnana, Italy (**1885–1969**)

Martins, Peter (dancer, choreographer); Copenhagen, 10/27/45

Marvell, Andrew (poet); Winestead, England (**1621–1678**)

Marvin, Lee (actor); New York City (**1924–1987**)

Marx, Chico (Leonard) (comedian); New York City (**1891–1961**)

Marx, Groucho (Julius) (comedian); New York City (**1890–1977**)

Marx, Harpo (Arthur) (comedian); New York City (**1893–1964**)

Marx, Karl (Socialist writer); Treves, Germany (**1818–1883**)

Marx, Zeppo (Herbert) (comedian); New York City (**1901–1979**)

Mary Stuart (Mary, Queen of Scots) (queen of Scotland); Linlithgow, Scotland (**1542–1587**)

Masaccio, (Tommaso di Giovanni di Simone Cassai) (painter); San Giovanni Valdarno, Tuscany (**1401–c. 1428**)

Masaryk, Jan Garrigue (statesman); Prague (**1886–1948**)

Masaryk, Thomas Garrigue (statesman); Hodonin, Czech Republic (**1850–1937**)

Masefield, John (poet); Ledbury, England (**1878–1967**)

Masekela, Hugh (trumpeter); Wilbank, South Africa, 4/4/39

Mason, Jackie (Jacob Moshe Maza) (comedian); Sheboygan, Wis., 6/9/31

Mason, James (actor); Huddersfield, England (**1909–1984**)

Mason, Marsha (actress); St. Louis, 4/3/42

Massenet, Jules Emile Frédéric (composer); Montaud, France (**1842–1912**)

Massine, Léonide (choreographer); Moscow (**1895–1979**)

Masters, Edgar Lee (poet); Garnett, Kans. (**1869–1950**)

Masters, William (human sexuality expert); Cleveland (**1915–2001**)

Masterson, Mary Stuart (actress, writer, director); New York City, 6/28/66

Mastroianni, Marcello (actor); Fontana Liri, Italy (**1924–1996**)

Mather, Cotton (clergyman); Boston (**1663–1728**)

Mathis, Johnny (singer); Gilmer, Texas, 9/30/35

Matisse, Henri (painter); Le Cateau, France (**1869–1954**)

Matthau, Walter (Walter Matuschanskayasky) (actor); New York City (**1920–2000**)

Mature, Victor (actor); Louisville, Ky. (**1915–1999**)

Maugham, W(illiam) Somerset (author); Paris (**1874–1965**)

Mauldin, Bill (political cartoonist); Mountain Park, N.M., 10/29/21

Maupassant, Henri René Albert Guy de (story writer); Normandy, France (**1850–1893**)

Maurois, André (Emile Herzog) (author); Elbauf, France (**1885–1967**)

Maximilian (Ferdinand Maximilian Joseph) (emperor of Mexico); Vienna (**1832–1867**)

Maxwell, James Clerk (physicist); Edinburgh, Scotland (**1831–1879**)

Maxwell, (Ian) Robert (publisher); Selo Slatina, Czechoslavakia (**1923–1991**)

May, Elaine (Elaine Berlin) (entertainer, writer); Philadelphia, 4/21/32

May, Rollo (psychologist); Ada, Ohio (**1909–1994**)

Mayer, Louis B. (movie executive); Minsk, Russia (**1885–1957**)

Mayo, Charles H. (surgeon); Rochester, Minn. (**1865–1939**)

Mayo, Charles W. (surgeon); Rochester, Minn. (**1898–1968**)

Mayo, Virginia (Jones) (actress); St. Louis, 11/30/20

Mayo, William J. (surgeon); Le Sueur, Minn. (**1861–1939**)

Mayron, Melanie (actress); Philadelphia, 10/20/52

Mazzini, Giuseppe (patriot); Genoa (**1805–1872**)

McBride, Patricia (ballet dancer); Teaneck, N.J., 8/23/42

McCallum, David (actor); Glasgow, Scotland, 9/19/33

McCambridge, Mercedes (actress); Joliet, Ill., 3/17/18

McCarthy, Eugene J. (ex-senator); Watkins, Minn., 3/29/16

McCarthy, Joseph Raymond (senator); Grand Chute, Wis. (**1908–1957**)

McCarthy, Mary (novelist); Seattle (**1912–1989**)

McCartney, Linda (photographer, singer); New York City (**1941–1998**)

McCartney, Paul (singer, songwriter); Liverpool, England, 6/18/42

McClanahan, Rue (actress); Healdton, Okla., 2/21/35

McClellan, George Brinton (general); Philadelphia (**1826–1885**)

McClintock, Barbara (geneticist, Nobel laureate) (**1902–1992**)

McCloy, John J. (lawyer, banker); Philadelphia (**1895–1989**)

McCormack, John (tenor); Athlone, Ireland (**1884–1945**)

McCormack, John W. (ex-Speaker of House); Boston (**1891–1980**)

McCormick, Cyrus Hall (inventor); Rockbridge County, Va. (**1809–1884**)

McCourt, Frank (writer); Brooklyn, N.Y., 8/19/30

McCracken, James (dramatic tenor); Gary, Ind. (**1926–1988**)

McCrea, Joel (actor); Los Angeles (**1905–1990**)

McCullers, Carson (novelist); Columbus, Ga. (**1917–1967**)

McDermott, Dylan (actor); Waterbury, Conn., 10/26/62

McDormand, Frances (actress); Illinois, 6/23/57

McDowall, Roddy (actor); London (**1928–1998**)

McDowell, Malcolm (actor); Leeds, England, 6/15/43

McFadden, Gates (actress); Cuyahoga Falls, Ohio, 3/2/49

McGavin, Darren (actor); San Joaquin, Calif., 5/7/22

McGillis, Kelly (actress); Newport Beach, Calif., 7/9/57

McGinley, Phyllis (poet, writer); Ontario, Ore. (**1905–1978**)

McGoohan, Patrick (actor); Astoria, Queens, N.Y., 3/19/28

McGovern, Elizabeth (actress); Evanston, Ill., 7/18/61

McGovern, Maureen (singer); Youngstown, Ohio, 7/27/49

McGregor, Ewan (actor); Crieff, Scotland, 3/31/71

McKellen, Ian (actor); Burnley, England, 5/25/39

McKinley, William (25th U.S. president); Niles, Ohio (**1843–1901**)

McKuen, Rod (singer, composer); Oakland, Calif., 4/29/33

McLachlan, Sarah (singer, songwriter); Halifax, N.S., 1/28/68

McLaughlin, John (guitarist); Yorkshire, England, 1/4/42

McLean, Don (singer, songwriter); New Rochelle, N.Y., 10/2/45

McLuhan, Marshall (Herbert Marshall) (communications writer); Edmonton, Alta., Canada (**1911–1980**)

McMahon, Ed (TV personality); Detroit, 3/6/23

McMurtry, Larry (novelist); Wichita Falls, Tex., 6/3/36

McQueen, Butterfly (Thelma) (actress); Tampa, Fla. (**1911–1995**)

McQueen, Steve (Terence Stephen McQueen) (actor); Beech Grove, Indiana (**1930–1980**)

McRaney, Gerald (actor); Collins, Miss., 8/19/47

McTeer, Janet (actress); York, England, 1962

Mead, Margaret (anthropologist); Philadelphia (**1901–1978**)

Meadows, Audrey (actress); Wu Chang, China (**1924–1996**)

Meadows, Jayne (actress); Wu Chang, China, 9/27/26

Meaney, Colm (actor); Dublin, 5/30/53

Meany, George (labor leader); New York City (**1894–1980**)

Meara, Anne (actress); New York City, 9/20/29

Medici, Lorenzo de' (called Lorenzo the Magnificent) (Florentine ruler); Florence, Italy (**1449–1492**)

Mehta, Zubin (conductor); Bombay (Mumbai), 4/29/36

Meir, Golda (Golda Myerson, nee Mabovitz) (ex-premier of Israel); Kiev, Ukraine (**1898–1978**)

Melba, Dame Nellie (Helen Porter Mitchell) (soprano); nr. Melbourne, Australia (**1861–1931**)

Melchior, Lauritz (Lebrecht Hommel) (heroic tenor); Copenhagen (**1890–1973**)

Mellon, Andrew William (financier); Pittsburgh (**1855–1937**)

Melville, Herman (novelist); New York City (**1819–1891**)

Mencken, Henry Louis (writer); Baltimore (**1880–1956**)

Mendel, Gregor Johann (geneticist); Heinzendorf, Austrian Silesia (**1822–1884**)

Mendeleyev, Dmitri Ivanovich (chemist); Tobolsk, Russia (**1834–1907**)

Mendelssohn-Bartholdy, Jakob Ludwig Felix (composer); Hamburg (1809–1847)

Mendès-France, Pierre (ex-Premier); Paris (1905–1982)

Mengele, Josef (Nazi, "Angel of Death"); Günzberg, Germany (1911–1979)

Mennin, Peter (Peter Mennini) (composer); Erie, Pa. (1923–1983)

Menninger, William C. (psychiatrist); Topeka, Kans. (1899–1966)

Menotti, Gian Carlo (composer); Cadegliano, Italy, 7/7/11

Menuhin, Yehudi (violinist, conductor); New York City (1916–1999)

Menzies, Robert Gordon (ex-prime minister); Jeparit, Australia (1894–1978)

Mercer, Johnny (songwriter); Savannah, Ga. (1909–1976)

Mercer, Mabel (singer); Burton-on-Trent, England (1900–1984)

Merchant, Ismail (Ismail Noormohamed Abdul Rehman) (film producer); Bombay (Mumbai), 12/25/36

Merchant, Natalie (singer, songwriter); Jamestown, N.Y., 10/26/63

Mercury, Freddie (Farookh Bulsara) (musician, singer); Zanzibar (1946–1991)

Meredith, Burgess (actor); Cleveland (1908–1997)

Meredith, James (author, civil-rights leader); Kosciusko, Miss., 6/26/23

Merman, Ethel (Ethel Zimmerman) (singer, actress); Astoria, Queens, N.Y. (1909–1984)

Merrick, David (David Margulois) (stage producer); St. Louis (1912–2000)

Merton, Thomas (clergyman, writer); France (1915–1968)

Mesmer, Franz Anton (physician); Itzmang, nr. Constance, Germany (1733–1815)

Mesta, Perle (social figure); Sturgis, Mich. (1889–1975)

Metacom, (King Philip) (Wampanoag Indian sachem); southeastern Mass. (1640–1676)

Metternich, Prince Klemens Wenzel Nepomuk Lothar von (statesman); Coblenz, Germany (1773–1859)

Mfume, Kweisi (Frizzell Gray) (politician, NAACP leader); Baltimore, 10/24/48

Michaels, Lorne (producer); Toronto, 11/17/44

Michelangelo Buonarroti (painter, sculptor, architect); Caprese, Italy (1475–1564)

Michener, James A. (novelist); New York City (1907–1997)

Mickiewicz, Adam (Polish poet); Zozie, Belorussia (Belarus) (1798–1855)

Midler, Bette (singer, actress, producer); Honolulu, 12/1/45

Mielziner, Jo (stage designer); Paris (1901–1976)

Mifune, Toshiro (actor, film producer); Tsingtao, China (1920–1997)

Mies van der Rohe, Ludwig (architect, designer); Aachen, Germany (1886–1969)

Mikoyan, Anastas I. (diplomat); Sanain, Armenia (1895–1978)

Milano, Alyssa (actress); Brooklyn, New York, 12/19/72

Milhaud, Darius (composer); Aix-en-Provence, France (1892–1974)

Mill, John Stuart (philosopher); London (1806–1873)

Milland, Ray (Reginald Truscott-Jones) (actor); Neath, Wales (1907–1986)

Millay, Edna St. Vincent (poet); Rockland, Maine (1892–1950)

Miller, Ann (Lucille Ann Collier) (dancer, actress); Cherino, Tex., 4/12/23

Miller, Arthur (playwright); New York City, 10/17/15

Miller, Glenn (band leader); Clarinda, Iowa (1904–1944)

Miller, Henry (novelist); New York City (1891–1980)

Miller, Jason (John Miller) (playwright, actor); New York City (1939–2001)

Miller, Mitch (Mitchell) (musician); Rochester, N.Y., 7/4/11

Miller, Roger (singer); Fort Worth (1936–1992)

Millet, Jean François (painter); Gruchy, France (1814–1875)

Millett, Kate (feminist, writer); St. Paul, Minn., 9/14/34

Millikan, Robert A. (physicist); Morrison, Ill. (1869–1953)

Mills, Donna (actress); Chicago, 12/11/41

Mills, Hayley (actress); London, 4/18/46

Mills, Juliet (actress); London, 11/21/41

Milne, A(lan) A(lexander) (author); London (1882–1956)

Milner, Martin (actor); Detroit, 12/28/31

Milnes, Sherrill (baritone); Downers Grove, Ill., 1/10/35

Milosevic, Slobodan (Yugoslav President); Pozarevac, Serbia, 8/29/41

Milstein, Nathan (concert violinist); Odessa, Ukraine (1904–1992)

Milton, John (poet); London (1608–1674)

Mingus, Charles (jazz composer); Nogales, Ariz. (1922–1979)

Minnelli, Liza (singer, actress); Hollywood, Calif., 3/12/46

Minnelli, Vincente (film director); Chicago (1913–1986)

Minuit, Peter (Governor of New Amsterdam); Wesel, Germany (1580–1638)

Miranda, Carmen (Maria do Carmo da Cunha) (singer, dancer); Lisbon (1909–1955)

Miró, Joan (painter); Barcelona (1893–1983)

Mirren, Helen (Ilynea Lydia Mironoff) (actress); London, 7/26/45

Mitchell, John N. (former Attorney General); Detroit (1913–1988)

Mitchell, Joni (Roberta Joan Anderson) (singer, songwriter); Ft. Macleod, Alb., Canada, 11/7/43

Mitchell, Margaret (novelist); Atlanta (1900–1949)

Mitchell, Maria (astronomer); Nantucket, Mass. (1818–1889)

Mitchum, Robert (actor); Bridgeport, Conn. (1917–1997)

Mitropoulos, Dimitri (orchestra conductor); Athens (1896–1960)

Mitterrand, François (Maurice) (ex-prime minister of France); Jarnac, France (1916–1996)

Mix, Tom (actor); Mix Run, Pa. (1880–1940)

Mobutu Sese Seko (Zairean dictator); Lisala, Congo (1930–1997)

Modigliani, Amedeo (painter); Leghorn, Italy (1884–1920)

Moffo, Anna (soprano); Wayne, Pa., 6/27/34

Mohammed (prophet); Mecca, Saudi Arabia (570–632)

Molière (Jean Baptiste Poquelin) (dramatist); Paris (1622–1673)

Molina, Mario (chemist, Nobel laureate); Mexico City, 3/19/43

Moll, Richard (actor); Pasadena, Calif., 1/13/43?

Molnar, Ferenc (dramatist); Budapest (1878–1952)

Molotov, Vyacheslav M. (V. M. Skryabin) (diplomat); Kukarka, Russia (1890–1986)

Mondrian, Piet (painter); Amersfoort, Netherlands (1872–1944)

Monet, Claude (painter); Paris (1840–1926)

Monica Monica Arnold (singer); Atlanta, Ga., 10/24/80

Monk, Meredith (choreographer, composer, performing artist); Lima, Peru, 11/20/42

Monk, Thelonious (pianist); Rocky Mount, N.C. (1918–1982)

Monroe, James (5th U.S. president); Westmoreland County, Va. (1758–1831)

Monroe, Marilyn (Norma Jean Mortenson or Baker) (actress); Los Angeles (1926–1962)

Monsarrat, Nicholas (novelist); Liverpool, England (1910–1979)

Montaigne, Michel Eyquem de (essayist); nr. Bordeaux, France (1533–1592)

Montalban, Ricardo (actor); Mexico City, 11/25/20

Montand, Yves (Ivo Livi) (actor, singer); Florence, Italy (1921–1991)

Montesquieu, Charles-Louis de Secondat, baron de La Brède and de (philosopher); nr. Bordeaux, France (1689–1755)

Montessori, Maria (physician, educator); Chiaravalle, Italy (1870–1952)

Monteux, Pierre (conductor); Paris (1875–1964)

Monteverdi, Claudio (composer); Cremona Italy (1567–1643)

Montezuma II (Aztec emperor); Mexico (1466–1520)

Montgomery, Elizabeth (actress); Hollywood, Calif. (1933–1995)

Montgomery, Robert (Henry, Jr.) (actor); Beacon, N.Y. (1904–1981)

Montgomery of Alamein, 1st Viscount of Hindhead (Sir Bernard Law Montgomery) (military leader); London (1887–1976)

Montoya, Carlos (guitarist); Madrid (1903–1993)

Moore, Clayton (Jack Moore) (actor); Chicago (1914–1999)

Moore, Clement Clarke (author); New York City (1779–1863)

Moore, Demi (Demi Guynes) (actress); Roswell, N.M., 11/11/62

Moore, Dudley (actor, writer, musician); Dagenham, England, 4/19/35

Moore, Grace (soprano); Jellico, Tenn. (1901–1947)

Moore, Henry (sculptor); Castleford, England (1898–1986)

Moore, Julianne (actress); Boston, 12/3/60

Moore, Marianne (poet); Kirkwood, Mo. (1887–1972)

Moore, Mary Tyler (actress); Brooklyn, N.Y., 12/29/36

Moore, Melba (Beatrice) (singer, actress); New York City, 10/27/45

Moore, Roger (actor); London, 10/14/27

Moore, Thomas (poet); Dublin (1779–1852)

Moorehead, Agnes (actress); Clinton, Mass. (1906–1974)

Moranis, Rick (actor); Toronto, 4/18/53

More, Henry (philosopher); Grantham, England (1614–1687)

More, Sir Thomas (statesman, author); London (1478–1535)

Moreno, Rita (Rosita Dolores Alverio) (actress); Humacao, P.R., 12/11/31

Morgan, Harry (Harry Bratsburg) (actor); Detroit, 4/10/15

Morgan, John Pierpont (financier); Hartford, Conn. (1837–1913)

Moriarty, Michael (actor); Detroit, 4/5/41

Morini, Erica (concert violinist); Vienna (1904–1995)

Morison, Samuel Eliot (historian); Boston (1887–1976)

Morita, Pat (Noriyuki Morita) (actor); Berkeley, Calif., 8/28/32

Morley, Christopher Darlington (novelist); Haverford, Pa. (1890–1957)

Morris, Mark (choreographer); Seattle, 8/29/56

Morris, William (poet, craftsman); Walthamstow, England (1834–1896)

Morrison, Jim (James Douglas Morrison) (singer, songwriter); Melbourne, Fla. (1943–1971)

Morrison, Toni (Chloe Anthony Wofford) (novelist); Lorain, Ohio, 2/18/31

Morrison, Van (singer); Belfast, Northern Ireland, 8/31/45

Morse, Marston (mathematician); Waterville, Maine **(1892–1977)**

Morse, Samuel Finley Breese (painter, inventor); Charlestown, Mass. **(1791–1872)**

Morton, Jelly Roll (Ferdinand Joseph La Menthe) (jazz composer); New Orleans **(1890–1941)**

Moseley-Braun, Carol (U.S. Senator); Chicago, 8/16/47

Moses, Grandma (Mrs. Anna Mary Robertson Moses) (painter); Greenwich, N.Y. **(1860–1961)**

Moses, Robert (urban planner); New Haven, Conn. **(1888–1981)**

Moss, Kate (model); London, England, 1/16/74

Mostel, Zero (Samuel Joel Mostel) (actor); Brooklyn, N.Y. **(1915–1977)**

Mother Teresa (Agnes Gonxha Bojaxhiu) (nun); Skopje, Macedonia **(1910–1997)**

Motherwell, Robert (artist, "action" painter); Aberdeen, Wash. **(1915–1991)**

Mott, Lucretia (Coffin) (feminist, reformer, abolitionist); Nantucket, Mass. **(1793–1880)**

Moussorgsky, Modest Petrovich (composer); Karev, Russia **(1839–1881)**

Moyers, Bill D. (Billy Don) (journalist); Hugo, Okla., 6/5/34

Moynihan, Daniel Patrick (New York senator); Tulsa, Okla., 3/16/27

Mozart, Wolfgang Amadeus (Johannes Chrysostomus Wolfgangus Theophilus Mozart) (composer); Salzburg, Austria **(1756–1791)**

Mudd, Roger (TV newscaster); Washington, D.C., 2/9/28

Muggeridge, Malcolm (Thomas) (writer); Croydon, England **(1903–1990)**

Muhammad (founder of Islam); Mecca, Saudi Arabia **(c. 570–632)**

Muhammad, Elijah (Elijah Poole) (religious leader); Sandersville, Ga. **(1897–1975)**

Mulgrew, Kate (actress); Dubuque, Iowa, 4/29/55

Mulhare, Edward (actor); Ireland **(1923–1997)**

Mulliken, Robert Sanderson (chemist, Nobel laureate); Newburyport, Mass. **(1896–1986)**

Mulroney, Dermot (actor, musician, producer); Alexandria, Va., 10/31/63

Mumford, Lewis (cultural historian, city planner); Flushing, Queens, N.Y. **(1895–1990)**

Munch, Edvard (painter); Löten, Norway **(1863–1944)**

Munchhausen, Karl Friedrick Hieronymus, baron von (anecdotist); Hannover, Germany **(1720–1797)**

Muni, Paul (Muni Weisenfreund) (actor); Lemburg, Ukraine **(1895–1967)**

Muñoz Marin, Luis (ex-governor of Puerto Rico); San Juan, P.R. **(1898–1980)**

Munsel, Patrice (soprano); Spokane, Wash., 5/14/25

Murdoch, Iris (novelist); Dublin **(1919–1999)**

Murdoch, Rupert (publisher); Melbourne, Australia, 3/11/31

Murillo, Bartolomé Esteban (painter); Seville, Spain **(1617–1682)**

Murphy, Audie (actor, war hero); Kingston, Tex. **(1924–1971)**

Murphy, Eddie (actor, comedian); Brooklyn, N.Y., 4/3/61

Murphy, George (actor, dancer, ex-senator); New Haven, Conn. **(1902–1992)**

Murray, Arthur (dance teacher); New York City **(1895–1991)**

Murray, Bill (actor, comedian); Wilmette, Ill., 9/21/50

Murray, Kathryn (dance teacher); Jersey City, N.J. **(1906–1999)**

Murrow, Edward R. (commentator, government official); Greensboro, N.C. **(1908–1965)**

Musil, Robert (novelist); Klagenfurt, Austria **(1880–1942)**

Muskie, Edmund (political figure); Rumford, Maine **(1914–1996)**

Mussolini, Benito (Italian dictator); Dovia, Forli, Italy **(1883–1945)**

Muti, Riccardo (orchestra conductor); Naples, Italy, 7/28/41

Mutter, Anne-Sophie (violinist); Rheinfelden, Germany, 6/29/63

Myers, Mike (actor, writer, comedian); Scarborough, Ont., Canada, 5/25/63

Myerson, Bess (consumer advocate); Bronx, N.Y., 7/16/24

Myrdal, Gunnar (sociologist, economist); Gustaf Parish, Sweden **(1898–1987)**

N

Nabokov, Vladimir (novelist); St. Petersburg, Russia **(1899–1977)**

Nabors, Jim (actor, singer); Sylacauga, Ala., 6/12/32

Nader, Ralph (consumer advocate); Winsted, Conn., 2/27/34

Nair, Mira (director, screenwriter); Bhubaneswar, India, 10/15/57

Nash, Graham (singer); Blackpool, England, 1942

Nash, Ogden (poet); Rye, N.Y. **(1902–1971)**

Nasser, Gamal Abdel (statesman); Beni Mor, Egypt **(1918–1970)**

Nast, Thomas (cartoonist); Landau, Germany **(1840–1902)**

Nation, Carry Amelia (temperance leader); Garrard County, Ky. **(1846–1911)**

Natta, Giulio (chemist, Nobel laureate); Imperia, Italy **(1903–1979)**

Natwick, Mildred (actress); Baltimore **(1905–1994)**

Neagle, Anna (Marjorie Robertson) (actress); London **(1908–1986)**

Neal, Patricia (actress); Packard, Ky., 1/20/26

Neeson, Liam (William John) (actor); Ballymena, Northern Ireland, 6/7/52

Negri, Pola (Apolnia Mathias-Chalupec) (actress); Bromberg, Poland **(1899–1987)**

Nehru, Jawaharlal (first prime minister of India); Allahabad, India **(1889–1964)**

Neill, Sam (Nigel Neill) (actor); Omagh, Northern Ireland, 9/14/47

Nelligan, Kate (actress); London, Ont., Canada, 3/16/51

Nelson, Barry (Robert Haakon Nielsen) (actor); San Francisco, 4/16/20

Nelson, David (actor); New York City, 10/24/36

Nelson, Harriet Hilliard (Peggy Lou Snyder) (actress); Des Moines, Iowa **(1909–1994)**

Nelson, Ozzie (Oswald) (actor); Jersey City, N.J. **(1907–1975)**

Nelson, Ricky (Eric) (singer, actor); Teaneck, N.J. **(1940–1985)**

Nelson, Viscount Horatio (naval officer); Burnham Thorpe, England **(1758–1805)**

Nelson, Willie (singer); Waco, Tex., 4/30/33

Nenni, Pietro (Socialist leader); Faenza, Italy **(1891–1980)**

Nero (Nero Claudius Caesar Drusus Germanicus) (Roman emperor); Antium, Italy **(37–68)**

Nero, Peter (pianist); New York City, 5/22/34

Netanyahu, Benjamin (Binyamin) (former Israeli prime minister); Tel Aviv, Israel, 10/21/49

Neuwirth, Bebe (Beatrice Neuwirth) (actress); Newark, N.J., 12/31/58

Nevelson, Louise (sculptor); Kiev, Russia **(1899–1988)**

Neville, Aaron (singer); New Orleans, 1/24/41

Newhart, Bob (actor); Chicago, 9/5/29

Newhouse, Samuel I. (publisher); New York City **(1895–1979)**

Newley, Anthony (actor, songwriter); London **(1931–1999)**

Newman, Edwin (news commentator); New York City, 1/25/19

Newman, John Henry (prelate); London **(1801–1890)**

Newman, Paul (actor, director); Cleveland, 1/26/25

Newman, Randy (singer); Los Angeles, 11/28/43

Newton, Huey (black activist); New Orleans **(1942–1989)**

Newton, Sir Isaac (mathematician, scientist); nr. Grantham, England **(1642–1727)**

Newton, Wayne (singer); Norfolk, Va., 4/3/42

Newton-John, Olivia (singer); Cambridge, England, 9/26/48

Nichols, Nichelle (actress); Robbins, Ill., 12/28/33

Nichols, Mike (Michael Peschkowsky) (stage and film director); Berlin, 11/6/31

Nicholson, Jack (actor, director, writer); Neptune, N.J., 4/22/37

Nicks, Stevie (Stephanie Lynn Nicks) (singer, songwriter); Phoenix, Ariz., 5/26/48

Nielsen, Leslie (actor); Regina, Sask., Canada, 2/11/26

Nietzsche, Friedrich Wilhelm (philosopher); nr. Lützen, Saxony, Germany **(1844–1900)**

Nightingale, Florence (nurse); Florence, Italy **(1820–1910)**

Nijinsky, Vaslav (ballet dancer); Warsaw **(1890–1950)**

Nilsson, Birgit (soprano); West Karup, Sweden, 5/17/23

Nilsson, Harry (singer, songwriter); Brooklyn, N.Y. **(1941–1994)**

Nimitz, Chester W. (naval officer); Fredericksburg, Tex. **(1885–1966)**

Nimoy, Leonard (actor, director, writer, producer); Boston, 3/26/31

Nin, Anais (author, diarist); Neuilly, France **(1903–1977)**

Niven, David (actor); Kirriemuir, Scotland **(1910–1983)**

Nixon, Richard Milhous (37th U.S. president); Yorba Linda, Calif. **(1913–1994)**

Nizer, Louis (lawyer, author); London **(1902–1994)**

Nobel, Alfred Bernhard (industrialist); Stockholm **(1833–1896)**

Noguchi, Isamu (sculptor); Los Angeles **(1904–1988)**

Nolan, Lloyd (actor); San Francisco **(1902–1985)**

Nolte, Nick (actor); Omaha, Neb., 2/8/40

Norell, Norman (Norman Levinson) (fashion designer); Noblesville, Ind. **(1900–1972)**

Norman, Jessye (soprano); Augusta, Ga., 9/15/45

Norman, Marsha (Marsha Williams) (playwright); Louisville, Ky., 9/21/47

Normand, Mabel (actress); Boston **(1894–1930)**

Norris, Chuck (Carlos Ray Norris) (actor, athlete); Ryan, Oklahoma, 3/10/40

Norstad, Gen. Lauris (ex-commander of NATO forces); Minneapolis **(1907–1988)**

North, John Ringling (circus director); Baraboo, Wis. **(1903–1985)**

North, Oliver (ex-military officer); San Antonio, 10/7/43

North, Sheree (actress); Los Angeles, 1/17/33

Norton, Edward (actor); Columbia, Md., 8/18/69

Norton, Eleanor Holmes (New York City government official, lawyer); Washington, D.C., 6/13/37

Nostradamus (Michel de Notredame) (astrologer); St. Rémy, France **(1503–1566)**

Novaes, Guiomar (pianist); São João de Boa Vista, Brazil **(1895–1979)**

Novak, Kim (Marilyn Novak) (actress); Chicago, 2/13/33

Novarro, Ramon (Ramon Samaniegoes) (actor); Durango, Mexico **(1899–1968)**

Novello, Ivor (actor, playwright, composer); Cardiff, Wales **(1893–1951)**

Nugent, Elliott (actor, director); Dover, Ohio **(1899–1980)**

Nureyev, Rudolf (ballet dancer); Siberia **(1938–1993)**

Nyro, Laura (singer, songwriter); Bronx, N.Y. **(1947–1997)**

O

Oakie, Jack (actor); Sedalia, Mo. **(1903–1978)**

Oakley, Annie (Phoebe Anne Oakley Mozee) (markswoman); Darke County, Ohio **(1860–1926)**

Oates, Joyce Carol (novelist); Lockport, N.Y., 6/16/38

Oberon, Merle (Estelle Merle O'Brien Thompson) (actress); Tasmania, Australia **(1911–1979)**

Oberth, Hermann (rocketry and space flight pioneer); Nagyszeben, Austria-Hungary (Sibiu, Romania) **(1894–1989)**

O'Brian, Hugh (Hugh J. Krampe) (actor); Rochester, N.Y., 4/19/25

O'Brien, Conan (TV personality); Brookline, Mass., 4/18/63

O'Brien, Edmond (actor); New York City **(1915–1985)**

O'Brien, Margaret (Angela Maxine O'Brien) (actress); San Diego, Calif., 1/15/37

O'Brien, Pat (William Joseph O'Brien, Jr.) (actor); Milwaukee **(1899–1983)**

O'Brien, Tim (novelist); Austin, Minn., 10/1/46

Obuchi, Keizo (former prime minister of Japan); Nakanojo, Japan **(1937–2000)**

O'Casey, Sean (playwright); Dublin **(1881–1964)**

Ochs, Adolph Simon (publisher); Cincinnati **(1858–1935)**

O'Connor, Carroll (actor); New York City **(1924–2001)**

Odets, Clifford (playwright); Philadelphia **(1906–1963)**

Odetta (Odetta Holmes) (folk singer, actress); Birmingham, Ala., 12/31/30

O'Donnell, Chris (actor); Winnetka, Ill., 6/26/70

O'Donnell, Rosie (actress, talk show host); Commack, N.Y., 3/21/62

Offenbach, Jacques (composer); Cologne, Germany **(1819–1880)**

O'Hara, John (novelist); Pottsville, Pa. **(1905–1970)**

O'Hara, Maureen (Maureen FitzSimons) (actress); Dublin, 8/17/20

Ohlsson, Garrick (pianist); Bronxville, N.Y., 4/3/48

Oistrakh, David (concert violinist); Odessa, Russia **(1908–1974)**

O'Keeffe, Georgia (painter); Sun Prairie, Wis. **(1887–1986)**

Oland, Warner (actor); Umea, Sweden **(1880–1938)**

Oldenburg, Claes (painter); Stockholm, 1/28/29

Oldman, Gary (actor, director); London, 3/21/58

Olin, Lena (actress); Stockholm, 3/22/55

Oliphant, Patrick B. (editorial cartoonist); Adelaide, Australia, 7/24/35

Olivier, Sir Laurence (actor); Dorking, England **(1907–1989)**

Olmos, Edward James (actor); East Los Angeles, 2/24/47

Olmsted, Frederick Law (landscape architect); Hartford, Conn. **(1822–1903)**

Olsen, Ole (John Sigvard Olsen) (comedian); Peru, Ind. **(1892–1963)**

Omar Khayyam (poet, astronomer); Nishapur, Iran (died c. 1123)

Onassis, Aristotle (shipping executive); Smyrna, Turkey **(1906–1975)**

Onassis, Christina (shipping executive); New York City **(1950–1988)**

Onassis, Jacqueline Kennedy (Jacqueline Bouvier) (first lady); Southampton, N.Y. **(1929–1994)**

O'Neal, Ryan (Patrick) (actor); Los Angeles, 4/20/41

O'Neal, Tatum (actress); Los Angeles, 11/5/63

O'Neill, Eugene Gladstone (playwright); New York City **(1888–1953)**

O'Neill, Jennifer (actress); Rio de Janeiro, 2/20/49

Oppenheimer, J. Robert (nuclear physicist); New York City **(1904–1967)**

Orbach, Jerry (actor); New York City, 10/20/35

Orff, Carl (composer); Munich, Germany **(1895–1982)**

Orlando, Tony (Michael Anthony Orlando Cassavitis) (singer); New York City, 4/3/44

Ormandy, Eugene (conductor); Budapest **(1899–1985)**

Ormond, Julia (actress); Epsom, Surrey, England, 1/4/65

Orozco, José Clemente (painter); Zapotlán, Jalisco, Mexico **(1883–1949)**

Orwell, George (Eric Arthur Blair) (British author); Motihari, India **(1903–1950)**

Osborn, Paul (playwright); Evansville, Ind. **(1901–1988)**

Osborne, John (playwright); London **(1929–1994)**

Osbourne, Ozzy (John Osbourne) (singer); Birmingham, England, 12/3/48

Osler, Sir William (physician); Bondhead, Ont., Canada **(1849–1919)**

Osmond, Donny (singer, actor); Ogden, Utah, 12/9/57

Osmond, Marie (Olive Marie) (singer, actress); Ogden, Utah, 10/13/59

O'Sullivan, Maureen (actress); County Roscommon, Ireland **(1911–1998)**

Oswald, Lee Harvey (presumed assassin); New Orleans **(1939–1963)**

Otis, Elisha (inventor); Halifax, Vt. **(1811–1861)**

O'Toole, Peter (actor); Connemara, Ireland, 8/2/32

Ovid (Publius Ovidius Naso) (poet); Sulmona, Italy **(43 B.C.–A.D. 17)**

Ovitz, Michael (entertainment executive); Chicago, 12/14/46

Owens, Buck (Alvis Edgar Owens) (singer); Sherman, Tex., 8/12/29

Ozawa, Seiji (orchestra conductor); Fentian (Shenyan), Manchuria, 7/1/35

P

Paar, Jack (TV personality); Canton, Ohio, 5/1/18

Pacino, Al (Alfred) (actor); New York City, 4/25/40

Packard, Vance (author); Granville Summit, Pa. **(1914–1996)**

Paderewski, Ignace Jan (pianist, statesman); Kurylowka, Russian Podolia **(1860–1941)**

Paganini, Nicolò (violinist); Genoa, Italy **(1782–1840)**

Page, Geraldine (actress); Kirksville, Mo. **(1924–1987)**

Page, Jimmy (musician); Heston, Ireland, 1/9/44

Page, Patti (Clara Ann Fowler) (singer, entertainer); Claremore, Okla., 11/8/27

Pagels, Elaine Hiesey (religious scholar); Palo Alto, Calif., 2/13/43

Paglia, Camille (writer, social critic); Endicott, N.Y., 4/2/47

Paine, Thomas (political philosopher); Thetford, England **(1737–1809)**

Pakula, Alan J. (film director); New York City **(1928–1998)**

Palance, Jack (Walter Palanuik) (actor); Lattimer, Pa., 2/18/19

Palestrina, Giovanni Pierluigi da (composer); Palestrina, Italy **(1526–1594)**

Paley, William S. (broadcasting executive); Chicago **(1901–1990)**

Palladio, Andrea (architect); Padua or Vicenza, Italy **(1508–1580)**

Palmer, Robert (rock musician); Batley, England, 1/19/49

Palmerston, Henry John Templeton (3rd Viscount) (statesman); Broadlands, England **(1784–1865)**

Palminteri, Chazz (Calogero Lorenzo Palminteri) (actor, writer); Bronx, New York, 5/15/51

Paltrow, Gwyneth (actress); Los Angeles, 9/27/72

Papanicolaou, George N. (physician); Coumi, Greece **(1883–1962)**

Papas, Irene (Lelekou) (actress); Chiliomodian, Greece, 3/9/26

Papp, Joseph (Joseph Papirofsky) (stage producer, director); Brooklyn, N.Y. **(1921–1991)**

Paracelsus, Philippus (Aureolus Theophrastus Bombastus von Hohenheim) (physican); Einsiedeln, Switzerland **(1493–1541)**

Park, Chung Hee (ex-president of South Korea); Sangmo-ri, Korea **(1917–1979)**

Parker, Alan (director); London, 2/14/44

Parker, Charlie "Bird" (jazz musician); Kansas City, Kans. **(1920–1955)**

Parker, Dorothy (Dorothy Rothschild) (author); West End, N.J. **(1893–1967)**

Parker, Fess (actor); Fort Worth, Tex., 8/16/25

Parker, Sarah Jessica (actress); Nelsonville, Ohio, 3/25/65

Parker, Suzy (model, actress); San Antonio, 10/28/33

Parkinson, C(yril) Northcote (historian); Durham, England **(1909–1993)**

Parkman, Francis (historian); Boston **(1823–1893)**

Parks, Bert (Bert Jacobson) (entertainer); Atlanta **(1914–1992)**

Parks, Gordon (film director); Ft. Scott, Kans., 11/30/12

Parks, Rosa (civil rights activist); Tuskegee, Ala., 2/4/13

Parnell, Charles Stewart (statesman); Avondale, Ireland **(1846–1891)**

Parnis, Mollie (Mollie Parnis Livingston) (fashion designer); New York City **(1905?–1992)**

Parsons, Estelle (actress); Marblehead, Mass., 11/20/27

Parton, Dolly (singer); Locust Ridge, Tenn., 1/19/46

Pascal, Blaise (philosopher); Clermont, France **(1623–1662)**

Pasternak, Boris Leonidovich (author); Moscow **(1890–1960)**

Pasternak, Joseph (film producer); Silagy-Somlyo, Romania (1901–1991)

Pasteur, Louis (chemist); Dôle, France (1822–1895)

Pastor, Tony (Antonio) (actor, theater manager); New York City (1837–1908)

Pater, Walter (Horatio) (writer); London (1839–1894)

Patinkin, Mandy (Mandel) (actor, singer); Chicago, 11/30/52

Paton, Alan (author); Pietermaritzburg, South Africa (1903–1988)

Patric, Jason (actor); Queens, N.Y., 6/17/66

Patti, Adelina (soprano); Madrid (1843–1919)

Patton, George Smith, Jr. (general); San Gabriel, Calif. (1885–1945)

Paul, Alice (feminist, woman suffragist); Moorestown, N.J. (1885–1977)

Paul, Les (Lester William Polfus) (guitarist); Waukesha, Wis., 6/9/15

Paul VI (Giovanni Battista Montini) (Pope); Concesio, nr. Brescia, Italy (1897–1978)

Pauley, Jane (Margaret Jane Pauley) (TV newscaster); Indianapolis, 10/31/50

Pauling, Linus Carl (chemist, Nobel laureate); Portland, Ore. (1901–1994)

Pavarotti, Luciano (tenor); Modena, Italy, 10/12/35

Pavlov, Ivan Petrovich (physiologist); Ryazan district, Russia (1849–1936)

Pavlova, Anna (ballet dancer); St. Petersburg, Russia (1885–1931)

Paxton, Bill (actor); Fort Worth, Texas, 5/17/55

Peale, Norman Vincent (clergyman); Bowersville, Ohio (1898–1993)

Pearl, Minnie (Sarah Ophelia Colley Cannon) (comedienne, singer); Centerville, Tenn. (1912–1996)

Pears, Peter (tenor); Farnham, England (1910–1986)

Pearson, Drew (Andrew Russel Pearson) (columnist); Evanston, Ill. (1897–1969)

Pearson, Lester B. (statesman); Toronto (1897–1972)

Peary, Robert Edwin (explorer); Cresson, Pa. (1856–1920)

Peck, Gregory (Eldred Gregory Peck) (actor); La Jolla, Calif., 4/5/16

Peckinpah, Sam (film director); Fresno, Calif. (1925–1984)

Peerce, Jan (tenor); New York City (1904–1984)

Pegler, (James) Westbrook (columnist); Minneapolis (1894–1969)

Pei, I(eoh) M(ing) (architect); Canton, China, 4/26/17

Penn, Arthur (director); Philadelphia, 9/27/22

Penn, Sean (actor, filmmaker); Los Angeles, 8/17/60

Penn, William (American colonist); London (1644–1718)

Penney, James C. (merchant); Hamilton, Mo. (1875–1971)

Peppard, George (actor); Detroit (1928–1994)

Pepys, Samuel (diarist); Bampton, England (1633–1703)

Perelman, S(idney) J(oseph) (writer); Brooklyn, N.Y. (1904–1979)

Perez, Rosie (actress, dancer, choreographer); Brooklyn, New York, 5/16/63

Pergolesi, Giovanni Battista (composer); Jesi, Italy (1710–1736)

Pericles (statesman); Athens died 429 B.C.

Perkins, Anthony (actor); New York City (1932–1992)

Perkins, Frances (social reformer); Boston (1882–1965)

Perlman, Itzhak (violinist); Tel Aviv, Israel, 8/31/45

Perlman, Rhea (actress); Brooklyn, N.Y., 3/31/48

Perón, Isabel (María Estela Martínez Cartas) (former chief of state); La Rioja, Argentina, 2/4/31

Perón, Juan D. (statesman); nr. Lobos, Argentina (1895–1974)

Perón, Maria Eva Duarte de (political leader); Los Toldos, Argentina (1919–1952)

Perot, H. Ross (business executive); Texarkana, Tex., 6/27/30

Perrine, Valerie (actress, dancer); Galveston, Tex., 9/3/43

Perry, Luke (Coy Luther Perry III) (actor); Fredericktown, Ohio, 10/11/66

Perry, Matthew (actor); Williamstown, Mass., 8/19/69

Pershing, John Joseph (general); Linn County, Mo. (1860–1948)

Pestalozzi, Johann (educator); Zurich, Switzerland (1746–1827)

Peters, Bernadette (Bernadette Lazzara) (actress); New York City, 2/28/48

Peters, Brock (actor, singer); New York City, 7/2/27

Peters, Jean (actress); Canton, Ohio, 10/15/26

Peters, Roberta (Roberta Peterman) (soprano); New York City, 5/4/30

Petit, Roland (choreographer, dancer); Villemombe, France, 1924

Petrarch (Francesco Petrarca) (poet); Arezzo, Italy (1304–1374)

Petty, Tom (folk/rock musician); Gainesville, Fla., 10/20/50

Pfeiffer, Michelle (actress); Santa Ana, Calif., 4/29/58

Philbin, Regis (talk show host); New York City, 8/25/33

Philip (Philip Mountbatten) (Duke of Edinburgh); Corfu, Greece, 6/10/21

Phillippe, Ryan (actor); New Castle, Del., 9/10/75

Phoenix, Joaquin (actor); San Juan, Puerto Rico, 10/28/74

Phoenix, River (actor); Madras, Ore. (1970–1993)

Piaf, Edith (Edith Gassion) (singer); Paris (1916–1963)

Piatigorsky, Gregor (cellist); Ekaterinoslav, Russia (1903–1976)

Piazza, Marguerite (soprano); New Orleans, 5/6/26

Picasso, Pablo (painter, sculptor); Málaga, Spain (1881–1973)

Pickett, Wilson (singer); Prattville, Ala., 3/18/41

Pickford, Mary (Gladys Mary Smith) (actress); Toronto (1893–1979)

Picon, Molly (actress); New York City (1898–1992)

Pidgeon, Walter (actor); East St. John, N.B., Canada (1898–1984)

Pierce, David Hyde (actor); Saratoga Springs, N.Y., 4/3/59

Pierce, Franklin (14th U.S. president); Hillsboro, N.H. (1804–1869)

Pileggi, Mitch (actor); Portland, Ore., 4/5/52

Pinkett-Smith, Jada (actress); Baltimore, 9/18/71

Pinsky, Robert (ex-poet laureate of the U.S.); Long Branch, N.J., 10/20/40

Pinochet (Ugarte), Augusto (former leader of Chile's military government); Valparaiso, Chile, 11/25/15

Pinter, Harold (playwright); London, 10/10/30

Pinza, Ezio (basso); Rome (1892–1957)

Pirandello, Luigi (dramatist, novelist); nr. Girgenti, Italy (1867–1936)

Piranesi, Giambattista (artist); Mestre, Italy (1720–1778)

Pissaro, Camille Jacob (painter); St. Thomas, U.S. Virgin Islands (1830–1903)

Piston, Walter (composer); Rockland, Maine (1894–1976)

Pitman, Sir [Isaac] James (educator, publisher); Bath, England (1901–1985)

Pitt, Brad (actor); Shawnee, Okla., 12/18/63

Pitt, William ("Younger Pitt") (statesman); nr. Bromley, England (1759–1806)

Pitts, ZaSu (actress); Parsons, Kans. (1898–1963)

Pius XII (Eugenio Pacelli) (Pope); Rome (1876–1958)

Pizarro, Francisco (explorer); Trujillo, Spain (c. 1476–1541)

Planck, Max (physicist); Kiel, Germany (1858–1947)

Plant, Robert (musician, singer, song writer); West Bromwich, Staffordshire, England , 8/20/48

Plath, Sylvia (poet); Boston (1932–1963)

Plato (Aristocles) (philosopher); Athens (c. 427–347 B.C.)

Pleasence, Donald (actor); Worksop, England (1919–1995)

Pleshette, Suzanne (actress); New York City, 1/31/37

Plimpton, George (author); New York City, 3/18/27

Plimpton, Martha (actress); New York City, 11/16/70

Plisetskaya, Maya (ballet dancer); Moscow, 11/20/25

Plowright, Joan (actress); Brigg, England, 10/28/29

Plummer, Christopher (actor); Toronto, 12/13/29

Plutarch (biographer); Chaeronea, Greece (c. 46–c. 120)

Pocahontas (Matoaka) (American Indian princess); Virginia (c. 1595–1617)

Podhoretz, Norman (author); Brooklyn, N.Y., 1/16/30

Poe, Edgar Allan (poet, story writer); Boston (1809–1849)

Poitier, Sidney (actor, director); Miami, Fla., 2/20/24

Polanski, Roman (director); Paris, 8/18/33

Polk, James Knox (11th U.S. president); Mecklenburg County, N.C. (1795–1849)

Pollack, Sydney (film director, producer, actor); Lafayette, Ind., 7/1/34

Pollard, Michael J. (actor); Passaic, N.J., 5/30/39

Pollock, Jackson (painter); Cody, Wyo. (1912–1956)

Polo, Marco (traveler); Venice (c. 1254–1324)

Pol Pot (Cambodian dictator); Kompong Thom, Cambodia (1925–1998)

Pompadour, Mme. de (Jeanne Antoinette Poisson) (courtesan); Versailles (1721–1764)

Pompey (Gnaeus Pompeius Magnus) (general); Rome (106–48 B.C.)

Ponce de León, Juan (explorer); Servas, Spain (c. 1460–1521)

Pons, Lily (coloratura soprano); Cannes, France (1904–1976)

Ponselle, Rosa (soprano); Meriden, Conn. (1897–1981)

Ponti, Carlo (director); Milan, Italy, 12/11/13

Pontormo, Jacopo da (painter); Pontormo, Italy (1492–1557)

Pope, Alexander (poet); London (1688–1744)

Porter, Cole (songwriter); Peru, Ind. (1891–1964)

Porter, Katherine Anne (novelist); Indian Creek, Tex. (1891–1980)

Portman, Natalie (actress); Jerusalem, 6/9/81

Posey, Parker (actress); Baltimore, 11/8/68

Post, Wiley (aviator); Grand Plain, Tex. (1900–1935)

Poston, Tom (actor); Columbus, Ohio, 10/17/27

Potëmkin, Grigori Aleksandrovich, Prince (statesman); Khizovo (Khizov), Belarus (1739–1791)

Potok, Chaim (author); New York City, 2/17/29

Potter, (Helen) Beatrix (author, illustrator); South Kensington, Middlesex, England (1866–1943)

Potts, Annie (actress); Nashville, Tenn., 10/28/52

Poulenc, Francis (composer); Paris (1899–1963)

Pound, Ezra (poet); Hailey, Idaho (1885–1972)

Poussin, Nicolas (painter); Villers, France **(1594–1665)**
Powell, Adam Clayton, Jr. (congressman); New Haven, Conn. **(1908–1972)**
Powell, Colin L. (secretary of state); New York City, 4/5/37
Powell, Dick (actor); Mt. View, Ark. **(1904–1963)**
Powell, Eleanor (actress, tap dancer); Springfield, Mass. **(1912–1982)**
Powell, Jane (Suzanne Burce) (actress, singer); Portland, Ore., 4/1/29
Powell, William (actor); Pittsburgh **(1892–1984)**
Power, Tyrone (actor); Cincinnati, Ohio **(1914–1958)**
Powers, Stefanie (Stefania Zofia Federkiewicz) (actress); Hollywood, Calif., 11/12/42
Praxiteles (sculptor); Athens **(c. 370–c. 330 B.C.)**
Preminger, Otto (director, producer); Vienna **(1906–1986)**
Prentiss, Paula (Paula Ragusa) (actress); San Antonio, 3/4/39
Presley, Elvis (singer, actor); Tupelo, Miss. **(1935–1977)**
Presley, Priscilla (actress); Brooklyn, N.Y., 5/24/45
Preston, Robert (Robert Preston Meservey) (actor); Newton Highlands, Mass. **(1918–1987)**
Previn, André (conductor); Berlin, 4/6/29
Price, Leontyne (Mary) (soprano); Laurel, Miss., 2/10/27
Price, Ray (country music artist); Perryville, Tex., 1/12/26
Price, Vincent (actor); St. Louis **(1911–1993)**
Pride, Charley (singer); Sledge, Miss., 3/18/38?
Priestley, Jason (actor, producer); Vancouver, B.C., Canada, 8/28/69
Priestley, J. B. (John B.) (author); Bradford, England **(1894–1984)**
Priestley, Joseph (chemist); nr. Leeds, England **(1733–1804)**
Primakov, Yevgeny (Russian political leader); Kiev, Ukraine, 10/29/29
Primrose, William (violist); Glasgow, Scotland **(1904–1982)**
Prince (Prince Rogers Nelson) (singer); Minneapolis, 6/7/58
Prince, Harold (stage producer); New York City, 1/30/28
Principal, Victoria (actress); Fukuoka, Japan, 1/3/45
Prinze, Freddie (actor); New York City **(1954–1977)**
Pritchett, V(ictor) S(awdon) (literary critic); Ipswich, England **(1900–1997)**
Procter, William (scientist); Cincinnati **(1872–1951)**
Prokofiev, Sergei Sergeevich (composer); St. Petersburg, Russia **(1891–1953)**
Proulx, E. Annie (novelist); Norwich, Conn., 8/22/35
Proust, Marcel (novelist); Paris **(1871–1922)**
Provine, Dorothy (actress); Deadwood, S.D., 1/20/37
Prowse, Juliet (actress, dancer); Bombay (Mumbai) **(1936–1996)**
Pryce, Jonathan (actor); Holywell, Wales, 6/1/47
Pryor, Richard (comedian); Peoria, Ill., 12/1/40
Ptolemy (Claudius Ptolemaeus) (astronomer, geographer); Ptolemais Hermii, Egypt, fl. 2nd cent.
Pucci, Emilio (Marchese di Barsento) (fashion designer); Naples, Italy **(1914–1992)**
Puccini, Giacomo (composer); Lucca, Italy **(1858–1924)**
Puente, Tito (band leader); New York City **(1923–2000)**
Pulaski, Casimir (military officer); Podolia, Poland **(1748–1779)**
Pulitzer, Joseph (publisher); Makó, Hungary **(1847–1911)**
Pullman, Bill (actor); Delphi, N.Y., 12/17/53
Pullman, George (inventor); Brockton, N.Y. **(1831–1897)**
Purcell, Henry (composer); London **(1658–1695)**
Pusey, Nathan M. (educator); Council Bluffs, Iowa, 4/4/07
Pushkin, Alexander Sergeevich (poet, dramatist); Moscow **(1799–1837)**
Putin, Vladimir (president of Russia); Leningrad, 1952
Puzo, Mario (novelist); New York City **(1921–1999)**
Pyle, Ernest Taylor (journalist); Dana, Ind. **(1900–1945)**
Pythagoras (mathematician, philosopher); Samos, Greece **(c. 582–c. 507A.D.)**

Q

Qaddafi, Muammar al- (Libyan leader); Libya, 1942
Quaid, Dennis (actor); Houston, 4/9/54
Quaid, Randy, (actor); Houston, 10/1/50
Quayle, Anthony (actor); Ainsdale, England **(1913–1989)**
Queen, Ellery: pen name of Frederic Dannay and Manfred B. Lee
Queen Latifah (Dana Owens) (rap musician, actress); Newark, New Jersey, 3/18/70
Queler, Eve (conductor); New York City, 1/1/36
Quennell, Sir Peter Courtney (biographer); Bromley, England **(1905–1993)**
Quindlen, Anna (writer); Philadelphia, 7/8/53
Quinn, Aidan (actor); Chicago, 3/8/59
Quinn, Anthony (Antonio Quiñones) (actor); Chihuahua, Mexico **(1916–2001)**

R

Rabe, David (playwright); Dubuque, Iowa, 3/10/40
Rabelais, François (satirist); nr. Chinon, France **(c. 1490–1553)**
Rabi, I(sidor) I(saac) (physicist); Rymanow, Poland **(1898–1988)**
Rabin, Yitzhak (former Israeli prime minister); Jerusalem **(1922–1995)**
Rachmaninoff, Sergei Wassilievitch (pianist, composer); Oneg Estate, Novgorod, Russia **(1873–1943)**
Racine, Jean Baptiste (dramatist); La Ferté-Milon, France **(1639–1699)**
Radner, Gilda (comedienne); Detroit **(1946–1989)**
Raft, George (actor); New York City **(1895–1980)**
Rainier III (Prince); Monaco, 5/31/23
Rains, Claude (actor); London **(1889–1967)**
Raitt, Bonnie (singer); Burbank, Calif., 11/8/49
Raitt, John (actor, singer); Santa Ana, Calif., 1/19/17
Raleigh, Sir Walter (courtier, navigator); London **(1552?–1618)**
Rambeau, Marjorie (actress); San Francisco **(1889–1970)**
Rameau, Jean-Philippe (composer); Dijon, France **(1683–1764)**
Rampal, Jean-Pierre (Louis) (flutist); Marseilles, France, 7/1/22
Rand, Ayn (novelist, philosopher); St. Petersburg, Russia **(1905–1982)**
Randall, Tony (Leonard Rosenberg) (actor); Tulsa, Okla., 2/26/20
Randolph, A(sa) Philip (labor leader); Crescent City, Fla. **(1889–1979)**
Rankin, Jeannette (politician, pacifist); Missoula, Mont. **(1880–1973)**
Raphael (Raffaello Santi) (painter, architect); Urbino, Italy **(1483–1520)**
Rasputin, Grigori Efimovich (monk); Tobolsk Province, Russia **(1872–1916)**
Rathbone, Basil (Philip St. John Basil Rathbone) (actor); Johannesburg, South Africa **(1892–1967)**
Rather, Dan (TV newscaster); Wharton, Tex., 10/31/31
Rattigan, Terence (playwright); London **(1911–1977)**
Ratzenberger, John (actor); Bridgeport, Conn., 4/6/47
Rauschenberg, Robert (painter); Port Arthur, Tex., 10/22/25
Ravel, Maurice Joseph (composer); Ciboure, France **(1875–1937)**
Ray, Aldo (DaRe) (actor); Pen Argyl, Pa. **(1926–1991)**
Ray, Gene Anthony (actor, dancer); Harlem, N.Y., 5/24/63
Ray, Man (painter); Philadelphia **(1890–1976)**
Ray, Satyajit (film director); Calcutta **(1921–1992)**
Raye, Martha (Margie Yvonne Reed) (comedienne, actress); Butte, Mont. **(1916–1994)**
Rea, Stephen (actor); Belfast, Ireland, 10/31/43
Reagan, Ronald Wilson (40th U.S. president, actor); Tampico, Ill., 2/6/11
Reasoner, Harry (TV commentator); Dakota City, Iowa **(1923–1991)**
Redding, Otis (singer); Dawson, Ga. **(1941–1967)**
Reddy, Helen (singer); Melbourne, Australia, 10/25/41
Redford, Robert (Charles Robert Redford, Jr.) (actor); Santa Monica, Calif., 8/18/37
Redgrave, Lynn (actress); London, 3/8/43
Redgrave, Sir Michael (actor); Bristol, England **(1908–1985)**
Redgrave, Vanessa (actress); London, 1/30/37
Redon, Odilon (artist); Bordeaux, France **(1840–1916)**
Reed, Donna (Donna Belle Mullenger) (actress); Denison, Iowa **(1921–1986)**
Reed, Lou (Lewis Allen Reed) (musician, guitarist, singer, song writer); Freeport, N.Y., 3/ 2/42
Reed, Rex (critic); Ft. Worth, 10/2/40
Reed, Walter (army surgeon); Belroi, Va. **(1851–1902)**
Reese, Della (Deloreese Patricia Early) (singer, actress); Detroit, 7/6/32
Reeve, Christopher (actor, activist); New York City, 9/25/52
Reeves, Jim (singer); Panola County, Tex. **(1923–1964)**
Reeves, Keanu (actor, musician); Beirut, Lebanon, 9/2/64
Reich, Robert (Clinton Cabinet Member); Scranton, Pa., 6/24/46
Reich, Steve (composer); New York City, 10/3/36
Reid, Wallace (actor); St. Louis **(1891–1923)**
Reiner, Carl (actor); New York City, 3/20/22
Reiner, Fritz (conductor); Budapest **(1888–1963)**
Reiner, Robert (actor, director, writer, producer); Bronx, N.Y., 3/6/45
Reinhardt, Max (Max Goldmann) (theater producer); nr. Vienna **(1873–1943)**
Reiser, Paul (actor, producer); New York City, 3/30/57
Remarque, Erich Maria (novelist); Osnabrük, Germany **(1898–1970)**
Rembrandt (Rembrandt Harmensz van Rijn) (painter); Leyden, Netherlands **(1605–1669)**
Remick, Lee (Ann) (actress); Boston **(1935–1991)**

Remnick, David (writer, editor); Hackensack, N.J., 10/29/58
Renfro, Brad (actor); Knoxville, Tenn., 7/25/82
Rennert, Günther (opera director, producer); Essen, Germany, 4/1/11
Rennie, Michael (actor); Bradford, England **(1909–1971)**
Reno, Janet (U.S. attorney general); Miami, Fla., 7/21/38
Renoir, Jean (film director, writer); Paris **(1894–1979)**
Renoir, Pierre Auguste (painter); Limoges, France **(1841–1919)**
Resnais, Alain (film director); Vannes, France, 6/3/22
Resnik, Regina (mezzo-soprano); New York City, 8/30/22
Respighi, Ottorino (composer); Bologna, Italy **(1879–1936)**
Reston, James (journalist); Clydebank, Scotland **(1909–1995)**
Reuther, Walter (labor leader); Wheeling, W. Va. **(1907–1970)**
Revere, Paul (silversmith, hero of famous ride); Boston **(1735–1818)**
Revson, Charles (business executive); Boston **(1906–1975)**
Reynolds, Burt (actor, director, producer); Waycross, Ga., 2/11/36
Reynolds, Debbie (Marie Frances Reynolds) (actress); El Paso, Tex., 4/1/32
Reynolds, Sir Joshua (painter); nr. Plymouth, England **(1723–1792)**
Reynolds, Marjorie (Marjorie Goodspeed) (actress); Buhl, Idaho **(1921–1997)**
Reznor, Trent (musician); Mercer, Pa., 5/17/65
Rhodes, Cecil John (South African statesman); Bishop Stortford, England **(1853–1902)**
Ricci, Christina (actress); Santa Monica, Calif., 2/12/80
Rice, Anne (novelist); New Orleans, 10/14/41
Rice, Elmer (Elmer Leopold Reizenstein) (playwright); New York City **(1892–1967)**
Rice, Grantland (sports writer); Murfreesboro, Tenn. **(1880–1954)**
Rich, Buddy (Bernard) (drummer); Brooklyn, N.Y. **(1917–1987)**
Rich, Charlie (singer); Colt, Ark. **(1932–1995)**
Richard I the Lion-hearted (King of England); Oxford, England **(1157–1199)**
Richards, Ann (Dorothy Ann Willis) (ex-governor of Texas); Lakeview, Tex., 9/1/33
Richards, Keith (rock singer); Dartford, England, 12/18/43
Richards, Michael (actor); California, 7/21/48
Richardson, Elliot L. (ex-cabinet member); Boston **(1920–1999)**
Richardson, Sir Ralph (actor); Cheltenham, England **(1902–1983)**
Richardson, Tony (director); Shipley, England **(1928–1991)**
Richelieu, Duc de (Armand Jean du Plessis) (cardinal); Paris **(1585–1642)**
Richie, Lionel (singer, songwriter); Tuskegee, Ala., 6/20/49
Richter, Charles Francis (seismologist); Hamilton, Ohio **(1900–1985)**
Richter, Sviatoslav (pianist); Zhitomir, Ukraine **(1914–1997)**
Rickenbacker, Eddie (Edward V.) (aviator); Columbus, Ohio **(1890–1973)**
Rickles, Don (comedian); New York City, 5/8/26
Rickover, Vice Admiral Hyman G. (atomic energy expert); Russia **(1900–1986)**
Riddle, Nelson (composer); Hackensack, N.J. **(1921–1985)**
Ride, Sally K(risten) (astronaut, astrophysicist); Encino, Calif., 5/26/51
Ridgway, General Matthew B. (ex-Army Chief of Staff); Ft. Monroe, Va. **(1895–1993)**
Riemenschneider, Tilman (sculptor); Osterode, Germany **(c. 1460–1531)**
Rigg, Diana (actress); Doncaster, England, 7/20/38
Riley, James Whitcomb (poet); Greenfield, Ind. **(1849–1916)**
Rilke, Rainer Maria (poet); Prague **(1875–1926)**
Rimbaud, (Jean Nicolas) Arthur (poet); Charleville, France **(1854–1891)**
Rimes, LeAnn (singer); Jackson, Miss., 8/28/82
Rimsky-Korsakov, Nikolai Andreevich (composer); Tikhvin, Russia **(1844–1908)**
Rinehart, Mary (née Roberts) (novelist); Pittsburgh **(1876–1958)**
Ringwald, Molly (actress); Sacramento, Calif., 2/18/68
Ritchard, Cyril (actor, director); Sydney, Australia **(1898–1977)**
Ritter, John (Jonathan) (actor); Burbank, Calif., 9/17/48
Ritter, Tex (Woodward Maurice Ritter) (singer); Panola County, Tex. **(1905–1973)**
Ritter, Thelma (actress); Brooklyn, N.Y. **(1905–1969)**
Rivera, Chita (Dolores Conchita Figuero del Rivero) (dancer, actress, singer); Washington, D.C., 1/23/33
Rivera, Diego (painter); Guanajuato, Mexico **(1886–1957)**
Rivera, Geraldo (Miguel Rivera) (TV host); New York City, 7/4/43
Rivers, Joan (comedienne); Brooklyn, N.Y., 6/8/33
Rivers, Larry (Yitzroch Loiza Grossberg) (painter); New York City, 8/17/23
Roach, Hal (film producer); Elmira, N.Y. **(1892–1992)**
Robards, Jason, Jr. (actor); Chicago **(1922–2000)**
Robards, Jason, Sr. (actor); Hillsdale, Mich. **(1892–1963)**

Robbins, Harold (Harold Rubin) (novelist); New York City **(1916–1997)**
Robbins, Jerome (Jerome Rabinowitz) (choreographer); New York City **(1918–1998)**
Robbins, Marty (singer); Glendale, Ariz. **(1925–1982)**
Robbins, Tim (Timothy Francis) (actor, director); West Covina, Calif., 10/16/58
Roberts, Cokie (Mary Martha Corinne Morrison Claiborne Boggs) (broadcast journalist); New Orleans, 12/27/43
Roberts, Eric (actor); Biloxi, Miss., 4/18/56
Roberts, Julia (actress); Smyrna, Ga., 10/28/67
Roberts, Oral (Granville) (evangelist, publisher); nr. Ada, Okla., 1/24/18
Robertson, Cliff (Clifford Parker Robertson III) (actor); La Jolla, Calif., 9/9/25
Robertson, Dale (Dayle) (actor); Oklahoma City, 7/14/23
Robeson, Paul (singer, actor); Princeton, N.J. **(1898–1976)**
Robespierre, Maximilien François Marie Isidore de (French Revolutionist); Arras, France **(1758–1794)**
Robinson, Bill "Bojangles" (Luther) (dancer); Richmond, Va. **(1878–1949)**
Robinson, Edward G. (Emanuel Goldenberg) (actor); Bucharest **(1893–1973)**
Robinson, Edwin Arlington (poet); Head Tide, Maine **(1869–1935)**
Robinson Peete, Holly (Holly Robinson) (actress); Philadelphia, 9/18/64
Robinson, Robert (chemist, Nobel laureate); Chesterfield, Derbyshire, England **(1885–1975)**
Robinson, Smokey (singer, songwriter); Detroit, 2/19/40
Rock, Chris (comedian, actor); Brooklyn, New York, 2/7/66
Rockefeller, David (banker); New York City, 6/12/15
Rockefeller, John Davison (business executive); Richford, N.Y. **(1839–1937)**
Rockefeller, John Davison, Jr. (industrialist); Cleveland **(1874–1960)**
Rockefeller, John D., 3rd (philanthropist); New York City **(1906–1978)**
Rockefeller, Laurance S. (conservationist); New York City, 5/26/10
Rockwell, Norman (painter, illustrator); New York City **(1894–1978)**
Roddenberry, Gene (creator of *Star Trek*); El Paso, Tex. **(1921–1991)**
Rodgers, Jimmie (singer); Meridian, Miss. **(1897–1933)**
Rodgers, Richard (composer); New York City **(1902–1979)**
Rodin, François Auguste René (sculptor); Paris **(1840–1917)**
Rodzinski, Artur (conductor); Spalato, Dalmatia **(1894–1958)**
Roeg, Nicolas (film director); London, 8/15/28
Roentgen, Wilhelm Konrad (physicist); Lennep, Prussia **(1845–1923)**
Roethke, Theodore (poet); Saginaw, Mich. **(1908–1963)**
Rogers, Buddy (Charles Rogers) (actor); Olathe, Kans. **(1904–1999)**
Rogers, Carl (psychologist); Oak Park, Ill. **(1902–1987)**
Rogers, Fred (TV producer, host); Latrobe, Pa., 3/20/28
Rogers, Ginger (Virginia McMath) (dancer, actress); Independence, Mo. **(1911–1995)**
Rogers, Kenny (singer); Houston, 8/21/38
Rogers, Mimi (actress); Coral Gables, Fla., 1/27/56
Rogers, Roy (Leonard Frank Slye) (actor, singer); Cincinnati **(1911–1998)**
Rogers, Wayne (actor); Birmingham, Ala., 4/7/33
Rogers, Will (William Penn Adair Rogers) (humorist); Oologah, Okla. **(1879–1935)**
Rogers, William P. (ex-secretary of state); Norfolk, N.Y. **(1913–2001)**
Roland, Gilbert (Luis Antonio Damaso de Alonso) (actor); Juarez, Mexico **(1905–1994)**
Rolland, Romain (author); Clamecy, France **(1866–1944)**
Rollins, Sonny (saxophonist); New York City, 9/7/30
Romberg, Sigmund (composer); Szeged, Hungary **(1887–1951)**
Rome, Harold (composer); Hartford, Conn. **(1908–1993)**
Romero, Cesar (actor); New York City **(1907–1994)**
Romney, George W. (automobile executive, governor); Chihuahua, Mexico **(1907–1995)**
Romulo, Carlos P. (diplomat, educator); Manila **(1899–1985)**
Ronsard, Pierre de (poet); La Possonnière nr. Couture, France **(1524–1585)**
Ronstadt, Linda (singer); Tucson, Ariz., 7/30/46
Rooney, Andy (TV personality); Albany, N.Y., 1/14/19
Rooney, Mickey (Joe Yule, Jr.) (actor); Brooklyn, N.Y., 9/23/20
Roosevelt, (Anna) Eleanor (reformer, humanitarian); New York City **(1884–1962)**
Roosevelt, Franklin Delano (32nd U.S. president); Hyde Park, N.Y. **(1882–1945)**
Roosevelt, Theodore (26th U.S. president); New York City **(1858–1919)**

Rorem, Ned (composer); Richmond, Ind., 10/23/23
Rose, Billy (showman); New York City **(1899–1966)**
Rose, Leonard (concert cellist); Washington, D.C. **(1918–1984)**
Roseanne (Roseanne Barr) (actress); Salt Lake City, 11/3/52
Rosenberg, Ethel (spy); New York City **(1915–1953)**
Rosenberg, Julius (spy); New York City **(1918–1953)**
Ross, Betsy (Betsey Griscom) (flagmaker); Philadelphia **(1752–1836)**
Ross, Diana (singer); Detroit, 3/26/44
Ross, Katharine (actress); Hollywood, Calif., 1/29/42
Rossellini, Isabella (model, actress); Rome, Italy, 6/18/52
Rossellini, Roberto (film director); Rome **(1906–1977)**
Rossetti, Christina Georgina (poet); London **(1830–1894)**
Rossetti, Dante Gabriel (painter, poet); London **(1828–1882)**
Rossini, Gioacchino Antonio (composer); Pesaro, Italy **(1792–1868)**
Rosten, Leo (writer); Lódz, Poland **(1908–1997)**
Rostand, Edmond (dramatist); Marseilles, France **(1868–1918)**
Rostow, Walt Whitman (economist); New York City, 10/7/16
Rostropovich, Mstislav (cellist, conductor); Baku, Azerbaijan, 3/27/27
Roth, Henry (writer); Tysmenica, Ukraine **(1906–1995)**
Roth, Philip (novelist); Newark, N.J., 3/19/33
Roth, Tim (actor); London, 5/14/64
Rothko, Mark (Marcus Rothkovich) (painter); Russia **(1903–1970)**
Rouault, Georges (painter); Paris **(1871–1958)**
Roundtree, Richard (actor); New Rochelle, N.Y., 9/7/42
Rousseau, Henri (painter); Laval, France **(1844–1910)**
Rousseau, Jean Jacques (philosopher); Geneva **(1712–1778)**
Rovere, Richard H. (journalist); Jersey City, N.J., 5/5/15
Rowan, Carl Thomas (journalist); Ravenscroft, Tenn. **(1925–2000)**
Rowan, Dan (comedian); Beggs, Okla. **(1922–1987)**
Rowlands, Gena (actress); Cambria, Wis., 6/19/30
Royko, Mike (columnist); Chicago **(1932–1997)**
Rubens, Sir Peter Paul (painter); Siegen, Germany **(1577–1640)**
Rubinstein, Arthur (concert pianist); Lódz, Poland **(1887–1982)**
Rubinstein, Helena (cosmetics executive); Kraków, Poland **(1870–1965)**
Rubinstein, John (actor, composer); Los Angeles, 12/8/46
Rucker, Darius (musician, singer, songwriter); Charleston, S.C., 5/13/66
Rudel, Julius (conductor); Vienna, 3/6/21
Ruffo, Titta (baritone); Italy **(1878–1953)**
Runyon, (Alfred) Damon (journalist); Manhattan, Kans. **(1884–1945)**
Rush, Geoffrey (actor); Toowoomba, Australia, 7/6/51
Rushdie, (Ahmed) Salman (novelist); Bombay (Mumbai), 6/19/47
Rusk, Dean (ex-sec. of state); Cherokee County, Ga. **(1909–1994)**
Ruskin, John (art critic); London **(1819–1900)**
Russell, Keri (actress); Fountain Valley, Calif., 3/23/76
Russell, Lord Bertrand (Arthur William) (mathematician, philosopher); Trelleck, Wales **(1872–1970)**
Russell, Jane (actress); Bemidji, Minn., 6/21/21
Russell, Ken (film director); Southhampton, England, 4/3/27
Russell, Kurt (actor); Springfield, Mass., 3/17/51
Russell, Leon (pianist, singer); Lawton, Okla., 4/2/41
Russell, Lillian (Helen Louise Leonard) (soprano); Clinton, Iowa **(1861–1922)**
Russell, Mark (satirist); Buffalo, N.Y., 8/23/32
Russell, Nipsy (comedian); Atlanta, 10/13/24
Russell, Rosalind (actress); Waterbury, Conn. **(1912–1976)**
Russell, Theresa (Theresa Paup) (actress); San Diego, Calif., 3/20/57
Russo, Rene (actress); Burbank, Calif., 2/17/54
Rustin, Bayard (civil rights leader); West Chester, Pa. **(1910–1987)**
Rutherford, Dame Margaret (actress); London **(1892–1972)**
Ryan, Jeri (actress); Munich, Germany, 2/22/68
Ryan, Meg (Margaret Mary Emily Anne Hyra) (actress); Fairfield, Conn., 11/19/61
Ryan, Robert (actor); Chicago **(1909–1973)**
Rydell, Bobby (Robert Ridarelli) (singer); Philadelphia, 4/26/42
Ryder, Winona (Winona Laura Horowitz) (actress); Winona, Minn., 10/29/71
Rysanek, Leonie (dramatic soprano); Vienna **(1928–1998)**

S

Saarinen, Eero (architect); Finland **(1910–1961)**
Sabin, Albert B. (polio researcher); Bialystok, Poland **(1906–1993)**
Sabu (Dastagir) (actor); Karapur, India **(1924–1963)**
Sacagawea (Shoshone Indian guide); Lemhi River valley (Idaho) **(c. 1786–1812)**
Sachs, Jeffrey D. (economist, educator); Michigan, 1954

Sadat, Anwar (former president); Egypt **(1918–1981)**
Sade, Marquis de (Donatien Alphonse François, Comte de Sade) (libertine, writer); Paris **(1740–1814)**
Safer, Morley (TV newscaster); Toronto, 11/8/31
Sagan, Carl (Edward) (astronomer, science writer); New York City **(1934–1996)**
Sagan, Françoise (novelist); Cajarc, France, 6/21/35
Sahl, Mort (Morton Lyon Sahl) (comedian); Montreal, 5/11/27
Saint, Eva Marie (actress); Newark, N.J., 7/4/24
St. Denis, Ruth (dancer, choreographer); Newark, N.J. **(1878–1968)**
St. James, Susan (Susan Miller) (actress); Los Angeles, 8/14/46
St. John, Jill (actress); Los Angeles, 8/19/40
St. Johns, Adela Rogers (journalist, author); Los Angeles **(1894–1988)**
Sainte-Marie, Buffy (Beverly) (folk singer); Craven, Sask., Canada, 2/20/41
Saint-Gaudens, Augustus (sculptor); Dublin **(1848–1907)**
Saint-Laurent, Yves (Henri Donat Mathieu) (fashion designer); Oran, Algeria, 8/1/36
Saint-Saens, Charles Camille (composer); Paris **(1835–1921)**
Sakharov, Andrei Dmitriyevich (nuclear physicist, peace activist); Russia **(1921–1989)**
Sales, Soupy (Milton Hines) (television entertainer); Franklinton, N.C., 1/6/26
Salinger, J(erome) D(avid) (novelist); New York City, 1/1/19
Salisbury, Harrison E. (journalist); Minneapolis **(1908–1993)**
Salk, Jonas (polio researcher); New York City **(1914–1995)**
Salk, Lee (psychologist); New York City **(1926–1992)**
Salomon, Haym (American Revolution financier); Leszno, Poland **(1740–1785)**
Sand, George (Amandine Lucille Aurore Dudevant, née Dupin) (novelist); Paris **(1804–1876)**
Sandburg, Carl (poet, biographer); Galesburg, Ill. **(1878–1967)**
Sanders, George (actor); St. Petersburg, Russia **(1906–1972)**
Sandler, Adam (comedian, musician, actor, screenwriter, singer); Brooklyn, N.Y., 9/9/66
Sands, Tommy (singer); Chicago, 8/27/37
Sanger, Margaret (birth-control advocate); Corning, N.Y. **(1879–1966)**
San Giacomo, Laura (actress); Hoboken, N.J., 11/14/62
Santayana, George (philosopher); Madrid **(1863–1952)**
Sappho (poet); Lesbos, Greece **(610 b.c.–580 b.c.)**
Sarandon, Susan (Susan Tomalin) (actress); New York City, 10/4/46
Sargent, John Singer (painter); Florence, Italy **(1856–1925)**
Sarnoff, David (radio executive); Minsk, Belarus **(1891–1971)**
Saroyan, William (novelist); Fresno, Calif. **(1908–1981)**
Sarto, Andrea del (Andrea Domenico d'Agnolo di Francesco) (painter); Florence, Italy **(1486–1531)**
Sartre, Jean-Paul (existentialist writer); Paris **(1905–1980)**
Sassoon, Vidal (hair stylist); London, 1/17/28
Satie, Erik (Alfred Leslie) (composer); Paris **(1866–1925)**
Saul (King of Israel) fl. 11th cent. b.c.
Savage, Fred (actor); Highland Park, Ill., 7/9/76
Savalas, Telly (Aristoteles) (actor); Garden City, N.Y. **(1924–1994)**
Savonarola, Girolamo (religious reformer); Ferrara, Italy **(1452–1498)**
Sawyer, Diane (broadcast journalist); Glasgow, Ky., 12/22/45
Sayão, Bidú (soprano); Rio de Janeiro **(1904–1999)**
Sayles, John (director, screenwriter, actor); Schenectady, N.Y., 9/28/50
Scarlatti, Alessandro (composer); Palermo, Italy **(1659–1725)**
Scarlatti, Domenico (composer); Naples, Italy **(1685–1757)**
Scavullo, Francesco (photographer); Staten Island, N.Y., 1/16/29
Schama, Simon (historian); London, 2/13/45
Schapiro, Meyer (Meir) (art historian); Siauliai, Lithuania **(1904–1906)**
Schary, Dore (producer, writer); Newark, N.J. **(1905–1980)**
Schell, Maximilian (actor); Vienna, 12/8/30
Schiaparelli, Elsa (fashion designer); Rome **(1890–1973)**
Schiff, Dorothy (newspaper publisher); New York City **(1903–1989)**
Schiffer, Claudia (model, actress); Rheinberg/Dusseldorf, Germany, 8/25/70
Schiller, Johann Christoph Friedrich von (dramatist, poet); Marbach, Germany **(1759–1805)**
Schipa, Tito (tenor); Lecce, Italy **(1890–1965)**
Schippers, Thomas (conductor); Kalamazoo, Mich. **(1930–1977)**
Schlegel, Friedrich von (philosopher); Hanover, Germany **(1772–1829)**
Schlesinger, Arthur M., Jr. (historian); Columbus, Ohio, 10/15/17
Schnabel, Artur (pianist, composer); Lipnik, Austria **(1882–1951)**

Schneider, Romy (Rose-Marie Albach-Retty) (actress); Vienna **(1938–1982)**

Schoenberg, Arnold (composer); Vienna **(1874–1951)**

Schomberg, Arthur (bibliophile, antiquarian); San Juan, P.R. **(1874–1938)**

Schopenhauer, Arthur (philosopher); Danzig, Poland **(1788–1860)**

Schröder, Gerhard (Chancellor of Germany); Mossenberg, Germany, 4/7/44

Schubert, Franz Peter (composer); Vienna **(1797–1828)**

Schulberg, Budd (novelist); New York City, 3/27/14

Schulz, Charles M. (cartoonist); Minneapolis **(1922–2000)**

Schumacher, Joel (film director, producer, screenwriter); New York City, 8/29/39

Schuman, Robert (statesman); Luxembourg **(1886–1963)**

Schuman, William (composer); New York City **(1910–1992)**

Schumann, Robert Alexander (composer); Zwickau, Germany **(1810–1856)**

Schwartz, Arthur (songwriter); Brooklyn, N.Y. **(1900–1984)**

Schwarzenegger, Arnold (bodybuilder, actor); Graz, Austria, 7/30/47

Schwarzkopf, Elisabeth (soprano); Poznán, Poland, 12/9/15

Schwarzkopf, H. Norman (retired general); Trenton, N.J., 8/22/34

Schweitzer, Albert (humanitarian, Nobel laureate); Kaysersburg, Upper Alsace **(1875–1965)**

Schwimmer, David (actor); New York City, 11/12/66

Scofield, Paul (actor); Hurstpierpoint, England, 1/21/22

Scorsese, Martin (actor, writer, director, producer); Flushing, N.Y., 11/17/42

Scott, George C. (actor); Wise, Va. **(1927–1999)**

Scott, Hazel (singer, pianist); Port of Spain, Trinidad **(1920–1981)**

Scott, Lizabeth (Emma Matzo) (actress); Scranton, Pa., 9/29/23

Scott, Randolph (Randolph Crane) (actor); Orange County, Va. **(1898–1987)**

Scott, Robert Falcon (explorer); Devonport, England **(1868–1912)**

Scott, Sir Walter (novelist); Edinburgh, Scotland **(1771–1832)**

Scott, Zachary (actor); Austin, Tex. **(1914–1965)**

Scotto, Renata (operatic soprano); Savona, Italy, 2/24/36

Scruggs, Earl Eugene (bluegrass musician); Cleveland County, N.C., 1/6/24

Seaborg, Glenn Theodore (chemist, Nobel laureate); Ishpeming, Mich. **(1912–1999)**

Seagal, Steven (actor); Lansing, Mich., 4/10/52

Seal (Sealhenry Olumide Samuel) (singer, songwriter); London, England, 2/19/63

Seattle (Chief Seattle) (Suquamish Indian leader); Blake Island (Wash.) **(c. 1786–1866)**

Sebastian, John (composer, singer); New York City, 3/17/44

Seberg, Jean (actress); Marshalltown, Iowa **(1938–1979)**

Sedaka, Neil (singer); Brooklyn, N.Y., 3/13/39

Sedgwick, Kyra (actress); New York City, 8/19/65

Seeger, Pete (folk singer); New York City, 5/3/19

Segal, Erich (novelist); Brooklyn, N.Y., 6/16/37

Segal, George (actor); New York City, 2/13/36

Segovia, Andrés (guitarist); Linares, Spain **(1893–1987)**

Seinfeld, Jerry (comedian); Brooklyn, N.Y., 4/29/54

Selena (Selena Quintanilla Perez) (singer); Lake Jackson, Tex. **(1971–1995)**

Selleck, Tom (actor); Detroit, 1/29/45

Sellars, Peter (theater director); Pittsburgh, 1958?

Sellers, Peter (actor); Southsea, England **(1925–1980)**

Selznick, David O. (producer); Pittsburgh **(1902–1965)**

Sendak, Maurice (Bernard) (children's book author, illustrator); Brooklyn, N.Y., 6/10/28

Sennett, Mack (Michael Sinnott) (film producer); Richmond, Que., Canada **(1880–1960)**

Sequoyah (Cherokee linguist); Taskigi, Tenn. **(c. 1770–1843)**

Serkin, Peter (pianist); New York City, 7/24/47

Serkin, Rudolf (pianist); Eger, Czech Republic **(1903–1991)**

Serling, Rod (writer, TV host); Syracuse, N.Y. **(1924–1975)**

Sessions, Roger (composer); Brooklyn, N.Y. **(1896–1985)**

Seurat, Georges (painter); Paris **(1859–1891)**

Seuss, Dr. (Theodor Seuss Geisel) (author, illustrator); Springfield, Mass. **(1904–1991)**

Sevareid, Eric (TV commentator); Velva, N.D. **(1912–1991)**

Severinsen, Doc (Carl) (band leader); Arlington, Ore., 7/7/27

Sevigny, Chlöe (actress); Darien, Conn., 1975

Sewell, Rufus (actor, musician); London, 10/29/67

Sexton, Anne (poet); Newton, Mass. **(1928–1974)**

Seymour, Jane (Joyce Penelope Wilhelmina Frankenburg) (actress); Wimbledon, England, 2/15/51

Shabazz, Betty (Betty Sanders) (civil rights activist); Detroit **(1936–1997)**

Shaffer, Peter (playwright); Liverpool, England, 5/15/26

Shaham, Gil (violinist); Urbana, Ill., 1971

Shahn, Ben(jamin) (painter); Kaunas, Lithuania **(1898–1969)**

Shakespeare, William (dramatist); Stratford on Avon, England **(1564–1616)**

Shakur, Tupac (Amaru Shakur) (singer, actor); Brooklyn, N.Y. **(1971–1996)**

Shandling, Garry (comedian, actor, producer); Chicago, 11/29/49

Shange, Ntozake (Paulette Williams) (poet, playwright); Trenton, N.J., 10/18/48

Shankar, Ravi (sitar player); Benares, India, 4/7/20

Sharif, Omar (Michael Shalhoub) (actor); Alexandria, Egypt, 4/10/32

Shatner, William (actor); Montreal, 3/22/31

Shaw, Artie (Arthur Arshawsky) (band leader); New York City, 5/23/10

Shaw, George Bernard (dramatist); Dublin **(1856–1950)**

Shaw, Irwin (novelist); Brooklyn, N.Y. **(1913–1984)**

Shaw, Robert (actor); Lancashire, England **(1927–1978)**

Shaw, Robert (chorale conductor); Red Bluff, Calif. **(1916–1999)**

Shawn, Ted (Edwin Myers Shawn) (dancer, choreographer); Kansas City, Mo. **(1891–1972)**

Shawn, Wallace (actor); New York City, 11/12/43

Shearer, Moira (ballet dancer); Dunfermline, Scotland, 1/17/26

Shearer, Norma (actress); Montreal **(1900–1983)**

Shearing, George (pianist); London, 8/13/20

Sheedy, Ally (Alexandra Sheedy) (actress, writer); New York City, 6/12/62

Sheen, Charlie (actor); Los Angeles, 9/3/65

Sheen, Fulton J. (Peter Sheen) (Roman Catholic bishop); El Paso, Ill. **(1895–1979)**

Sheen, Martin (Ramon Estevez) (actor); Dayton, Ohio, 8/3/40

Shelley, Mary Wollstonecraft Godwin (writer); London **(1797–1851)**

Shelley, Percy Bysshe (poet); nr. Horsham, England **(1792–1822)**

Shelton, Henry (chairman of the Joint Chiefs of Staff); Tarboro, N.C., 1/2/42

Shepard, Sam (Samuel Shepard Rogers) (playwright); Ft. Sheridan, Ill., 11/5/43

Shepherd, Cybill (actress); Memphis, Tenn., 2/18/50

Sheraton, Thomas (furniture designer); Stockton-on-Tees, England **(1751–1806)**

Sheridan, Ann (Clara Lou Sheridan) (actress); Denton, Tex. **(1915–1967)**

Sheridan, Philip (army officer); Albany, N.Y. **(1831–1888)**

Sheridan, Richard Brinsley (dramatist); Dublin **(1751–1816)**

Sherman, William Tecumseh (army officer); Lancaster, Ohio **(1820–1891)**

Sherwood, Robert Emmet (playwright); New Rochelle, N.Y. **(1896–1955)**

Shevardnadze, Eduard Amvrosiyevich (State Council chairman, Georgia); Mamati, Georgia, 1/25/28

Shields, Brooke (actress); New York City, 5/31/65

Shire, Talia (Coppola) (actress); Lake Success, N.Y., 4/25/46

Shirer, William L. (journalist, historian); Chicago **(1904–1993)**

Sholokhov, Mikhail (novelist); Veshenskaya, Russia **(1905–1984)**

Shore, Dinah (Frances Rose Shore) (singer); Winchester,Tenn. **(1917–1994)**

Short, Bobby (Robert Waltrip Short) (singer, pianist); Danville, Ill., 9/15/24

Short, Martin (actor); Hamilton, Ont., Canada, 3/26/50

Shostakovich, Dmitri (composer); St. Petersburg, Russia **(1906–1975)**

Shriner, Herb (humorist, host); Toledo, Ohio **(1918–1970)**

Shriver, Maria (TV co-host); Chicago, 11/6/55

Shriver, Sargent (Robert Sargent Shriver, Jr.) (business executive); Westminster, Md., 11/9/15

Shue, Andrew (actor, soccer player); South Orange, N.J., 2/20/67

Shue, Elisabeth (actress); Wilmington, Del., 6/10/63

Shulman, Max (novelist); St. Paul, Minn. **(1919–1988)**

Sibelius, Jean (Johann Julius Christian Sibelius) (composer); Tavastehus, Finland **(1865–1957)**

Sidney, Sir Philip (poet); Penshurst, England **(1554–1586)**

Sidney, Sylvia (Sophia Kosow) (actress); New York City **(1910–1999)**

Siegfried and Roy (illusionists) **Siegfried Fischbacher;** Rosenheim, Bavaria, Germany, 1939 **Roy Uwe Ludwig Horn;** Nordenham, nr. Bremen, Germany, 1944

Siepi, Cesare (basso); Milan, Italy, 2/10/23

Signoret, Simone (Simone Kaminker) (actress); Wiesbaden, Germany **(1921–1985)**

Sihanouk, Norodom (king of Cambodia); Cambodia, 10/31/22

Sikorsky, Igor I. (inventor); Kiev, Ukraine **(1889–1972)**

Sills, Beverly (Belle Silverman) (soprano, opera director); Brooklyn, N.Y., 5/25/29

Sills, Milton (actor); Chicago **(1882–1930)**

Silone, Ignazio (Secondo Tranquilli) (novelist); Pescina del Marsi, Italy **(1900–1978)**

Silver, Ron (Ron Zimelman) (actor); New York City, 7/2/46

Silverheels, Jay (Harold J. Smith) (actor); Brantford, Ont., Canada **(1919–1980)**

Silverman, Fred (broadcasting executive); New York City, 9/13/37

Silvers, Phil (Philip Silversmith) (comedian); Brooklyn, N.Y. **(1912–1985)**

Silverstein, Shel (writer, poet); Chicago **(1932–1999)**

Silverstone, Alicia (actress); San Francisco, 10/4/76

Simenon, Georges (Georges Sim) (mystery writer); Liège, Belgium **(1903–1989)**

Simmons, Jean (actress); Crouch Hill, London, 1/31/29

Simon, Carly (singer, songwriter); New York City, 6/25/45

Simon, Neil (playwright); Bronx, N.Y., 7/4/27

Simon, Norton (business executive); Portland, Ore. **(1907–1993)**

Simon, Paul (singer, songwriter); Newark, N.J., 11/5/42

Simone, Nina (Eunice Kathleen Waymoa) (singer, pianist); Tryon, N.C., 2/21/33

Sinatra, Frank (Francis Albert Sinatra) (singer, actor); Hoboken, N.J. **(1915–1998)**

Sinbad (David Adkins) (actor, comedian); Benton Harbor, Mich., 11/10/56

Sinclair, Upton Beall (novelist); Baltimore **(1878–1968)**

Singer, Isaac Bashevis (novelist); Radzymin, Poland **(1904–1991)**

Singleton, John (writer, director); Los Angeles, 1/6/68

Sinise, Gary (actor, director); Chicago, 3/17/55

Siqueiros, David (painter); Chihuahua, Mexico **(1896–1974)**

Sirtis, Marina (actress); London, 3/29/59

Siskel, Gene (film critic); Chicago **(1946–1999)**

Sisley, Alfred (painter); Paris **(1839–1899)**

Sitting Bull (Prairie Sioux Indian Chief); on Grand River, S.D. **(c. 1835–1890)**

Skelton, Red (Richard) (comedian); Vincennes, Ind. **(1913–1997)**

Skerritt, Tom (actor); Detroit, 8/25/43

Skinner, B(urrhus) F(rederic) (psychologist); Susquehanna, Pa. **(1904–1990)**

Skinner, Otis (actor); Cambridge, Mass. **(1858–1942)**

Slater, Christian (Christopher Hawkins) (actor); New York City, 8/18/69

Slatkin, Leonard (conductor); Los Angeles, 9/1/44

Sloan, Alfred P., Jr. (industrialist); New Haven, Conn. **(1875–1965)**

Sloan, John (painter); Lock Haven, Pa. **(1871–1951)**

Smalley, Richard E. (chemist, Nobel laureate); Akron, Ohio, 6/6/43

Smetana, Bedrich (composer); Litomysl, Czech Republic **(1824–1884)**

Smith, Adam (economist); Kirkaldy, Scotland **(1723–1790)**

Smith, Alexis (actress); Penticon, Canada **(1921–1993)**

Smith, Alfred Emanuel (politician); New York City **(1873–1944)**

Smith, Bessie (blues singer); Chattanooga, Tenn. **(1894–1937)**

Smith, Sir C. Aubrey (actor); London **(1863–1948)**

Smith, David (sculptor); Decatur, Ind. **(1906–1965)**

Smith, Harry (TV co-anchor); Hammond, Ind., 8/21/51

Smith, Howard K. (TV commentator); Ferriday, La., 5/12/14

Smith, Jaclyn (actress); Houston, 10/26/47

Smith, John (American colonist); Willoughby, Lincolnshire, England **(1580–1631)**

Smith, Joseph (religious leader); Sharon, Vt. **(1805–1844)**

Smith, Kate (Kathryn) (singer); Greenville, Va. **(1909–1986)**

Smith, Kevin (director, screenwriter); Red Bank, N.J., 8/2/70

Smith, Dame Maggie (actress); Ilford, England, 12/28/34

Smith, Patti Lee (singer, songwriter); Chicago, 12/30/46

Smith, Red (Walter) (sports columnist); Green Bay, Wis. **(1905–1982)**

Smith, Will (actor, rap singer); Philadelphia, 9/25/68

Smits, Jimmy (actor); New York City, 7/9/55

Smollett, Tobias (novelist); Dalquhurn, Scotland **(1721–1771)**

Smothers, Dick (Richard) (comedian); New York City, 11/20/39

Smothers, Tom (Thomas) (comedian); New York City, 2/2/37

Snipes, Wesley (actor); Orlando, Fla., 7/31/62

Snow, Lord (Charles Percy) (author); Leicester, England **(1905–1980)**

Snowdon, Earl of (Anthony Armstrong-Jones) (photographer); London, 3/7/30

Snyder, Tom (TV personality); Milwaukee, 5/12/36

Socrates (philosopher); Athens **(469–399 B.C.)**

Soderbergh, Steven (film director, screenwriter); Atlanta, Ga., 1/14/63

Solomon (King of Israel); Jerusalem, fl. 950 B.C.

Solon (lawgiver); Salamis, Greece **(c. 630–559 B.C.)**

Solti, Sir Georg (conductor); Budapest **(1912–1997)**

Solzhenitsyn, Aleksandr (novelist); Kislovodsk, Russia, 12/11/18

Somers, Suzanne (Suzanne Mahoney) (actress); San Bruno, Calif., 10/16/46

Somes, Michael (ballet dancer); Horsley, England **(1917–1994)**

Sommer, Elke (Elke Schletz) (actress); Berlin, 11/5/42

Sondheim, Stephen (composer); New York City, 3/22/30

Sonnenfeld, Barry (cinematographer, film director); New York City, 4/1/53

Sontag, Susan (author, film director); New York City, 1/28/33

Sophocles (dramatist); nr. Athens **(c. 496–406 B.C.)**

Sorbo, Kevin (actor); Mound. Minn., 9/24/58

Sorvino, Mira (actress); Tenafly, N.J., 9/28/67

Sorvino, Paul (actor); Brooklyn, N.Y., 4/13/39

Sothern, Ann (Harriette Lake) (actress); Valley City, N.D. **(1909–2001)**

Soul, David (David Solberg) (actor); Chicago, 8/28/43

Sousa, John Philip (composer); Washington, D.C. **(1854–1932)**

Soyer, Raphael (painter); Borisoglebsk, Russia **(1899–1987)**

Spaak, Paul-Henri (statesman); Brussels **(1899–1972)**

Spacek, Sissy (Mary Elizabeth Spacek) (actress); Quitman, Tex., 12/25/49

Spacey, Kevin (actor); South Orange, N.J., 7/28/59

Spade, David (actor; comedian); Birmingham, Mich., 7/22/65

Spader, James (actor); Boston, 2/7/60

Spark, Muriel (novelist); Edinburgh, Scotland, 2/1/18

Spector, Phil (rock producer); Bronx, N.Y., 12/25/40

Spelling, Aaron (producer); Dallas, 4/22/28

Spelling, Tori (Victoria) (actress); Los Angeles, 5/16/73

Spencer, Herbert (philosopher); Derby, England **(1820–1903)**

Spender, Stephen (poet); nr. London **(1909–1995)**

Spengler, Oswald (philosopher); Blankenburg, Germany **(1880–1936)**

Spenser, Edmund (poet); London **(1552?–1599)**

Spewack, Bella (playwright); Hungary **(1899–1990)**

Spiegel, Sam (producer); Jaroslaw, Poland **(1901–1985)**

Spielberg, Steven (director, producer, writer, actor); Cincinnati, 12/18/47

Spillane, Mickey (Frank Spillane) (mystery writer); Brooklyn, N.Y., 3/9/18

Spiner, Brent (actor); Houston, 2/2/49

Spinoza, Baruch (philosopher); Amsterdam, Netherlands **(1632–1677)**

Spitalny, Phil (orchestra leader) **(1890–1970)**

Spivak, Lawrence (TV producer); Brooklyn, N.Y. **(1900–1994)**

Spock, Benjamin (pediatrician, writer); New Haven, Conn. **(1903–1998)**

Springsteen, Bruce (singer, songwriter); Freehold, N.J., 9/23/49

Sproul, Robert G. (educator); San Francisco **(1891–1975)**

Squanto (Wampanoag Indian emissary); Patuxet (Plymouth Bay, Mass.) **(c. 1590–1622)**

Stack, Robert (Robert Modini) (actor); Los Angeles, 1/13/19

Stafford, Jo (singer); Coalinga, Calif., 11/12/18

Stahl, Lesley (broadcast journalist); Lynn, Mass., 12/16/41

Stalin, Joseph Vissarionovich (Iosif V. Dzhugashvili) (Soviet leader); nr. Tiflis (Tbilisi), Georgia **(1879–1953)**

Stallone, Sylvester (actor, writer, director); New York City, 7/6/46

Stamp, Terence (actor); London, 1938

Stander, Lionel (actor); New York City **(1908–1994)**

Stanislavski (Konstantin Sergeevich Alekseev) (stage producer); Moscow **(1863–1938)**

Stanley, Sir Henry Morton (John Rowlands) (explorer); Denbigh, Wales **(1841–1904)**

Stanley, Kim (Patricia Reid) (actress); Tularosa, N.M., 2/11/25

Stans, Maurice H. (ex-secretary of commerce); Shakope, Minn. **(1908–1998)**

Stanton, Elizabeth Cady (woman suffragist); Johnstown, N.Y. **(1815–1902)**

Stanton, Frank (broadcasting executive); Muskegon, Mich., 3/20/08

Stanwyck, Barbara (Ruby Stevens) (actress); Brooklyn, N.Y. **(1907–1990)**

Stapleton, Jean (Jeanne Murray) (actress); New York City, 1/19/23

Stapleton, Maureen (actress); Troy, N.Y., 6/21/25

Starker, Janós (cellist); Budapest, 7/5/26

Starr, Kay (Starks) (singer); Dougherty, Okla., 7/21/22

Starr, Kenneth (independent counsel for Whitewater investigation); Vernon, Tex., 7/21/46

Starr, Ringo (Richard Starkey) (singer, songwriter); Liverpool, England, 7/7/40

Stassen, Harold E. (ex-government official); West St. Paul, Minn. **(1907–2001)**

Staudinger, Hermann (chemist, Nobel laureate); Worms, Germany **(1881–1965)**

Steber, Eleanor (soprano); Wheeling, W. Va. **(1916–1990)**

Steegmuller, Francis (biographer); New Haven, Conn. **(1906–1994)**

Steel, Danielle (Danielle Fernande Schuelein-Steel) (novelist); New York City, 8/14/47

Steele, Tommy (singer); London, 12/17/36

Stefani, Gwen (singer); Orange County, Calif., 10/3/69

Stegner, Wallace (Earle) (novelist, critic); Lake Mills, Iowa **(1909–1993)**

Steichen, Edward Jean (photographer, artist); Luxembourg **(1879–1973)**

Steiger, Rod (Rodney) (actor); Westhampton, N.Y., 4/14/25

Stein, Gertrude (author); Allegheny, Pa. **(1874–1946)**

Steinbeck, John Ernst (novelist); Salinas, Calif. **(1902–1968)**

Steinberg, David (comedian); Winnipeg, Man., Canada, 8/19/42

Steinberg, William (conductor); Cologne, Germany **(1899–1978)**

Steinem, Gloria (feminist, publisher); Toledo, Ohio, 3/25/34

Steinmetz, Charles (electrical engineer); Breslau, Poland **(1865–1923)**

Steenburgen, Mary (actress); Newport, Ark., 2/8/53

Stendhal (Marie Henri Beyle) (novelist); Grenoble, France **(1783–1842)**

Stern, Howard (radio personality); New York City, 1/2/54

Stern, Isaac (concert violinist); Kreminlecz, Russia **(1920–2001)**

Sterne, Laurence (novelist); Clonmel, Ireland **(1713–1768)**

Stevens, Cat (Steven Georgiou) (singer, songwriter); London, 7/21/47

Stevens, Connie (Concetta Ingolia) (singer); Brooklyn, N.Y., 8/8/38

Stevens, George (film director); Oakland, Calif. **(1905–1975)**

Stevens, Risë (mezzo-soprano); New York City, 6/11/13

Stevens, Wallace (poet); Reading, Pa. **(1879–1955)**

Stevenson, Adlai Ewing (statesman); Los Angeles **(1900–1965)**

Stevenson, McLean (actor); Bloomington, Ill. **(1929–1996)**

Stevenson, Parker (actor); Philadelphia, 6/4/52

Stevenson, Robert Louis Balfour (novelist, poet); Edinburgh, Scotland **(1850–1894)**

Stewart, James (actor); Indiana, Pa. **(1908–1997)**

Stewart, Jon (Jonathan Stewart Leibowitz) (comedian, actor); Trenton, N.J., 11/28/62

Stewart, Martha (entrepreneurial home stylist); Nutley, N.J., 8/3/41

Stewart, Patrick (actor); Mirfield, England, 7/13/40

Stewart, Rod (Roderick David) (singer); London, 1/10/45

Stieglitz, Alfred (photographer); Hoboken, N.J. **(1864–1946)**

Stiers, David Ogden (actor); Peoria, Ill., 10/31/42

Stiller, Ben (actor, director, comic); New York City, 11/30/65

Stiller, Jerry (actor); Brooklyn, N.Y., 6/8/29

Stills, Stephen (singer, songwriter); Dallas, 1/3/45

Stine, R.L. (Robert Lawrence Stine) (writer); Columbus, Ohio, 10/8/43

Sting (Gordon Matthew Sumner) (singer, composer); Wallsend, England, 10/2/51

Stipe, Michael (singer); Decatur, Ga., 1/4/60

Stockwell, Dean (actor); North Hollywood, Calif., 3/5/36

Stoker, Bram (novelist); Dublin **(1847–1912)**

Stokes, Carl (TV newscaster); Cleveland **(1927–1996)**

Stokowski, Leopold (conductor); London **(1882–1977)**

Stoltz, Eric (actor); Whittier, Calif., 9/30/61

Stone, Edward Durell (architect); Fayetteville, Ark. **(1902–1978)**

Stone, I(sidor) F(einstein) (journalist); Philadelphia **(1907–1989)**

Stone, Irving (Irving Tennenbaum) (novelist); San Francisco **(1903–1989)**

Stone, Lucy (woman suffragist); nr. West Brookfield, Mass. **(1818–1893)**

Stone, Oliver (director, writer, producer); New York City, 9/15/46

Stone, Robert (novelist); Brooklyn, N.Y., 8/21/37

Stone, Sharon (actress); Meadville, Pa., 3/10/58

Stone, Sly (Sylvester Stone) (rock musician) 1944

Stooges, The Three (comedy team) **Moe Howard** (Moses Horwitz); Brooklyn, N.Y. **(1897–1975);** **Shemp Howard** (Samuel Horwitz); Brooklyn, N.Y. **(1900–1955;)** **Larry Fine** (Laurence Feinburg); Philadelphia **(1911–1974;)** **Curly Howard** (Jerome Horwitz); Brooklyn, N.Y. **(1906 –1952)**

Stoppard, Tom (Thomas Straussler) (playwright); Zlin, Slovakia, 7/3/37

Stout, Rex (mystery writer); Noblesville, Ind. **(1886–1975)**

Stowe, Harriet Elizabeth Beecher (novelist); Litchfield, Conn. **(1811–1896)**

Stowe, Madeleine (actress); Eagle Rock, Calif., 8/18/58

Strachey, (Giles) Lytton (biographer); London **(1880–1932)**

Stradivari, Antonio (violinmaker); Cremona, Italy **(1644–1737)**

Straight, Beatrice (actress); Old Westbury, N.Y. **(1918–2001)**

Strasberg, Lee (stage director); Budanov, Austria **(1901–1982)**

Strasberg, Susan (actress); New York City **(1938–1999)**

Stratas, Teresa (soprano); Toronto, 5/26/38

Straus, Oskar (composer); Vienna **(1870–1954)**

Strauss, Johann (composer); Vienna **(1825–1899)**

Strauss, Lewis L. (naval officer, scientist); Charleston, W. Va. **(1896–1974)**

Strauss, Peter (actor); New York City, 2/20/47

Strauss, Richard (composer); Munich, Germany **(1864–1949)**

Stravinsky, Igor (composer); Orlenbaum, Russia **(1882–1971)**

Streep, Meryl (Mary Louise) (actress); Summit, N.J., 6/22/49

Streisand, Barbra (singer, actress, director, producer, writer); Brooklyn, N.Y., 4/24/42

Strindberg, (Johan) August (dramatist); Stockholm **(1849–1912)**

Stritch, Elaine (actress); Detroit, 2/2/25

Struthers, Sally Ann (actress); Portland, Ore., 7/28/48

Stuart, Gilbert Charles (painter); Rhode Island **(1755–1828)**

Stuart, Gloria (film actress); Santa Monica, Calif., 7/4/10

Stuart, James Ewell Brown (known as Jeb) (Confederate army officer); Patrick County, Va. **(1833–1864)**

Sturges, Preston (Edmond P. Biden) (director, screenwriter, playwright); Chicago **(1898–1959)**

Stuyvesant, Peter (Governor of New Amsterdam); West Friesland, Netherlands **(1592–1672)**

Styne, Jule (Julius Kerwin Stein) (songwriter); London **(1905–1994)**

Styron, William (William Clark Styron, Jr.) (novelist); Newport News, Va., 6/11/25

Suharto (President of Indonesia); Sedaju-Godean, Java, 2/20/21

Sukarno (Indonesian leader); Surabaja, Java **(1901–1970)**

Sullavan, Margaret Brooke (actress); Norfolk, Va. **(1911–1960)**

Sullivan, Sir Arthur Seymour (composer); London **(1842–1900)**

Sullivan, Barry (Patrick Barry) (actor); New York City **(1912–1994)**

Sullivan, Ed (columnist, TV personality); New York City **(1901–1974)**

Sullivan, Frank (Francis John) (humorist); Saratoga Springs, N.Y. **(1892–1976)**

Sullivan, Louis Henry (architect); Boston **(1856–1924)**

Sulzberger, Arthur Ochs (newspaper publisher); New York City, 2/5/26

Sumac, Yma (singer); Ichocan, Peru, 9/10/27

Summer, Donna (La Donna Andrea Gaines) (singer); Boston, 12/31/48

Sun Ra (Herman "Sunny" Blount) (jazz composer); Birmingham, Ala. **(1914?–1993)**

Sun Tzu (writer, military strategist); China **(fl. c. 500–320 B.C.)**

Sun Yat-sen (statesman); nr. Macao **(1866–1925)**

Susann, Jacqueline (novelist); Philadelphia **(1918–1974)**

Susskind, David (TV producer); New York City **(1920–1987)**

Sutherland, Donald (actor); St. John, N.B., Canada, 7/17/34

Sutherland, Joan (soprano); Sydney, Australia, 11/7/26

Sutherland, Kiefer (actor); London, 12/18/66

Suzuki, Pat (actress); Cressey, Calif., 1931

Swados, Elizabeth (composer, playwright); Buffalo, N.Y., 2/5/51

Swank, Hilary (actress); Bellingham, Wash., 7/30/74

Swanson, Gloria (Gloria May Josephine Svensson) (actress); Chicago **(1899–1983)**

Swarthout, Gladys (soprano); Deepwater, Mo. **(1904–1969)**

Swayze, John Cameron (news commentator); Wichita, Kans. **(1906–1995)**

Swayze, Patrick (actor, dancer); Houston, 8/18/54

Swedenborg, Emanuel (scientist, philosopher, mystic); Stockholm **(1688–1772)**

Swift, Jonathan (satirist); Dublin **(1667–1745)**

Swinburne, Algernon Charles (poet); London **(1837–1909)**

Swit, Loretta (actress); Passaic, N.J., 11/4/37

Swope, Herbert Bayard (journalist); St. Louis **(1882–1958)**

Sydow, Max von (Carl Adolf von Sydow) (actor); Lund, Sweden, 4/10/29

Symons, Arthur (poet, critic); Milford Haven, Wales **(1865–1945)**

Synge, John Millington (dramatist); nr. Dublin **(1871–1909)**

Szilard, Leo (physicist); Budapest **(1898–1964)**

T

Taft, Robert Alphonso (legislator); Cincinnati **(1889–1953)**

Taft, William Howard (27th U.S. president); Cincinnati **(1857–1930)**

Tagore, Sir Rabindranath (poet); Calcutta **(1861–1941)**

Tallchief, Maria (ballet dancer); Fairfax, Okla., 1/24/25

Talleyrand-Périgord, Charles Maurice de (statesman); Paris **(1754–1838)**

Talmadge, Norma (actress); Niagara Falls, N.Y. **(1897–1957)**

Talvela, Martti (basso); Hiitola, Finalnd **(1935–1989)**

Tamerlane (Timur) (Mongol conqueror); nr. Samarkand, Turkestan **(c. 1336–1405)**

Tamiroff, Akim (actor); Baku, Azerbaijan **(1899–1972)**

Tan, Amy (novelist); Oakland, Calif., 2/19/52

Tanaka, Tomoyuki (film producer); Osaka, Japan **(1910–1997)**

Tandy, Jessica (actress); London **(1909–1994)**

Tarbell, Ida Minerva (author, muckraker); Erie Co., Pa. **(1857–1944)**

Tarkington, (Newton) Booth (novelist); Indianapolis **(1869–1946)**

Tartikoff, Brandon (television executive); Freeport, N.Y. **(1949–1997)**

Tate, Allen (John Orley) (poet, critic); Winchester, Ky. **(1899–1979)**

Tate, Sharon (actress); Dallas **(1943–1969)**

Taylor, Deems (composer); New York City **(1885–1966)**

Taylor, Elizabeth (actress); London, 2/27/32

Taylor, Harold (educator); Toronto, 9/28/14

Taylor, James (singer, songwriter); Boston, 3/12/48

Taylor, Laurette (Laurette Cooney) (actress); New York City **(1884–1946)**

Taylor, Lili (actress); Glenco, Ill., 2/20/67

Taylor, Gen. Maxwell D. (former Army chief of staff); Keytesville, Mo. **(1901–1987)**

Taylor, Niki (model); Pembroke Pines, Fla., 3/5/75

Taylor, Paul (choreographer); Wilkinsburg, Pa., 7/29/30

Taylor, Rod (actor); Sydney, Australia, 1/11/30

Taylor, Zachary (12th U.S. president); Montebello, Orange County, Va. **(1784–1850)**

Tchaikovsky, Peter (Pëtr) Ilich (composer); Votkinsk, Russia **(1840–1893)**

Teasdale, Sara (poet); St. Louis **(1884–1933)**

Tebaldi, Renata (lyric soprano); Pesaro, Italy, 1/2/22

Tecumseh (Shawnee Indian chief); nr. Springfield, Ohio **(1768–1813)**

Te Kanawa, Kiri (soprano); Gisborne, New Zealand, 3/6/44

Telemann, Georg Philipp (composer); Magdeburg, Germany **(1681–1767)**

Teller, Edward (atomic physicist); Budapest, 1/15/08

Templeton, Alec Andrew (pianist, composer); Cardiff, Wales **(1910–1963)**

Tennille, Toni (singer); Montgomery, Ala., 5/8/43

Tennyson, Alfred (1st Baron Tennyson) (poet); Somersby, England **(1809–1892)**

Tenskwatawa (Shawnee prophet); Old Piqua, Ohio **(c. 1770–c. 1835)**

Terhune, Albert Payson (novelist, journalist); Newark, N.J. **(1872–1942)**

Terkel, Studs (writer, interviewer); New York City, 5/16/12

Terry, Ellen Alicia (actress); Coventry, England **(1848–1928)**

Terry-Thomas (Thomas Terry Hoar Stevens) (actor); London **(1911–1990)**

Tesla, Nikola (electrical engineer, inventor); Smiljan, Lika, Croatia **(1856–1943)**

Thackeray, William Makepeace (novelist); Calcutta **(1811–1863)**

Thalberg, Irving G. (producer); Brooklyn, N.Y. **(1899–1936)**

Thant, U (U.N. statesman); Pantanaw, Burma **(1909–1974)**

Tharp, Twyla (dancer, choreographer); Portland, Ind., 7/1/42

Thatcher, Margaret (former prime minister); Grantham, England, 10/13/25

Thebom, Blanche (mezzo-soprano); Monessen, Pa., 9/19/19

Theodorakis, Mikis (composer); Chios, Greece, 7/29/25

Thicke, Alan (actor, composer); Kirland Lake, Ont., Canada, 3/1/47

Thieu, Nguyen Van (ex-president of South Vietnam); Trithuy, Vietnam, 4/5/23

Thomas, Danny (Amos Jacobs) (entertainer, TV producer); Deerfield, Mich. **(1912–1991)**

Thomas, Dylan Marlais (poet); Carmarthenshire, Wales **(1914–1953)**

Thomas, Jonathan Taylor (actor); Bethlehem, Pa., 9/8/81

Thomas, Kristen Scott (actress); Redruth, Cornwall, England, 1960

Thomas, Lowell (explorer, commentator); Woodington, Ohio **(1892–1981)**

Thomas, Marlo (actress); Detroit, 11/21/43

Thomas, Michael Tilson (conductor); Hollywood, Calif., 12/21/44

Thomas, Norman Mattoon (Socialist leader); Marion, Ohio **(1884–1968)**

Thomas, Philip Michael (actor); Columbus, Ohio, 5/26/49

Thomas, Richard (actor); New York City, 6/13/51

Thompson, Dorothy (writer); Lancaster, N.Y. **(1894–1961)**

Thompson, Emma (actress); London, 4/15/59

Thompson, Hunter (Stockton) (writer); Louisville, Ky., 7/18/39

Thompson, Lea (actress); Rochester, Minn., 5/31/61

Thompson, Sada (actress); Des Moines, Iowa, 9/27/29

Thomson, Virgil (Garnett) (composer); Kansas City, Mo. **(1896–1989)**

Thoreau, Henry David (naturalist, author); Concord, Mass. **(1817–1862)**

Thorndike, Dame Sybil (actress); Gainsborough, England **(1882–1976)**

Thorne-Smith, Courtney (actress); San Francisco, 11/8/67

Thornton, Billy Bob (actor, screenwriter); Hot Springs, Ark., 8/4/55

Thurber, James Grover (author, cartoonist); Columbus, Ohio **(1894–1961)**

Thurman, Robert A. F. (scholar, Indo-Tibetan Buddhist studies); New York City, 8/6/40

Thurman, Uma (actress); Boston, 4/29/70

Thurmond, (James) Strom (U.S. senator); Edgefield, S.C., 12/5/02

Tibbett, Lawrence (baritone); Bakersfield, Calif. **(1896–1960)**

Tiberius Caesar Augustus (Roman emperor); Capri **(42 B.C.–A.D. 37)**

Tiegs, Cheryl (model, actress); Minnesota, 9/25/47

Tierney, Gene (actress); Brooklyn, N.Y. **(1920–1991)**

Tillich, Paul (philosopher, theologian); Starzeddel, Germany **(1886–1965)**

Tilly, Meg (Margaret Tilly) (actress); Texada Island, B.C., Canada, 2/14/60

Tintoretto, Il (Jacopo Robusti) (painter); Venice **(1518–1594)**

Tiny Tim (Herbert Khaury) (entertainer); New York City **(1932–1996)**

Tiomkin, Dmitri (composer); St. Petersburg, Russia **(1894–1979)**

Titian (Tiziano Vecelli) (painter); Pieve di Cadore, Italy **(1477–1576)**

Tito (Josip Broz or Brozovich) (president of Yugoslavia); Croatia (former Yugoslavia) **(1892–1980)**

Tocqueville, Alexis de (writer); Verneuil, France **(1805–1859)**

Todd, Michael (producer); Minneapolis **(1907–1958)**

Todd, Thelma (actress); Lawrence, Mass. **(1905–1935)**

Tolkien, J(ohn) R(onald) R(euel) (fantasy writer); Bloemfontein, South Africa **(1892–1973)**

Tolstoy, Count Leo (Lev) Nikolaevich (novelist); Tula Province, Russia **(1828–1910)**

Tomei, Marisa (actress); Brooklyn, N.Y., 12/4/64

Tomlin, Lily (actress, comedienne); Detroit, 9/1/36

Tone, Franchot (actor); Niagara Falls, N.Y. **(1905–1968)**

Tormé, Mel (Melvin) (singer); Chicago **(1925–1999)**

Torn, Rip (Elmore Torn, Jr.) (actor, director); Temple, Tex., 2/6/31

Torquamada, Tomásde (Spanish Inquisitor); Valladolid, Spain **(1420–1498)**

Toscanini, Arturo (orchestra conductor); Parma, Italy **(1867–1957)**

Totenberg, Nina (broadcast journalist); New York City, 1/14/44

Toulouse-Lautrec (Henri Marie Raymond de Toulouse-Lautrec Monfa) (painter); Albi, France **(1864–1901)**

Toynbee, Arnold J. (historian); London **(1889–1975)**

Tracy, Spencer (actor); Milwaukee **(1900–1967)**

Traubel, Helen (Wagnerian soprano); St. Louis **(1903–1972)**

Travanti, Daniel J. (actor); Kenosha, Wis., 3/7/40

Travolta, John (actor); Englewood, N.J., 2/18/54

Treacher, Arthur (actor); Brighton, England **(1894–1975)**

Tree, Sir Herbert Beerbohm (actor, manager); London **(1853–1917)**

Trevor, Claire (Wemlinger) (actress); New York City **(1909–2000)**

Trigère, Pauline (fashion designer); Paris, 11/4/12

Trilling, Diana (writer); New York City **(1905–1996)**

Trilling, Lionel (author, educator); New York City **(1905–1975)**

Trollope, Anthony (novelist); London **(1815–1882)**

Trotsky, Leon (Lev Davidovich Bronstein) (statesman); Elisavetgrad, Russia **(1879–1940)**

Troyanos, Tatiana (mezzo-soprano); New York City **(1938–1993)**

Trudeau, Garry (cartoonist); New York City, 1948

Trudeau, Pierre Elliott (former prime minister); Montreal **(1919–2000)**

Truffaut, François (film director); Paris **(1932–1984)**

Trujillo y Molina, Rafael Leonidas (dictator); San Cristóbal, Dominican Republic **(1891–1961)**

Truman, Harry S. (33rd U.S. president); near Lamar, Mo. **(1884–1972)**

Truman, Margaret (author); Independence, Mo., 2/17/24

Trump, Donald (business executive); New York City, 6/14/46

Truth, Sojourner (Isabella) (preacher, abolitionist); Ulster Co., N.Y. **(c. 1797–1883)**

Tryon, Thomas (actor, novelist); Hartford, Conn. **(1926–1991)**

Tsiolkovsky, Konstantin E. (father of cosmonautics); Izhevskoye, Russia **(1857–1935)**

Tsongas, Paul E. (politician); Lowell, Mass. **(1941–1997)**

Tubman, Harriet (Araminta) (abolitionist); Dorchester Co., Md. **(c. 1820–1913)**

Tuchman, Barbara (Wertheim) (historian, author); New York City **(1912–1989)**

Tucker, Forrest (actor); Plainfield, Ind. **(1919–1986)**

Tucker, Richard (tenor); New York City **(1914–1975)**

Tucker, Sophie (Sophia Kalish) (singer); Russia **(1884–1966)**

Tudor, Antony (choreographer); London **(1909–1987)**

Tune, Tommy (dancer, choreographer); Wichita Falls, Tex., 2/28/39

Turgenev, Ivan Sergeevich (novelist); Orel, Russia **(1818–1883)**

Turlington, Christy (model); San Francisco, 1/2/69

Turner, Frederick J. (historian); Portage, Wis. **(1861–1932)**

Turner, Ike (singer); Clarksdale, Miss., 11/5/31

Turner, Janine (actress); Lincoln, Neb., 12/6/62

Turner, Joseph M.W. (painter); London **(1775–1851)**

Turner, Kathleen (actress); Springfield, Mo., 6/19/54
Turner, Lana (Julia Jean Mildred Frances Turner) (actress); Wallace, Idaho **(1920–1995)**
Turner, Nat (civil rights leader); Southampton County, Va. **(1800–1831)**
Turner, Ted (business executive); Cincinnati, 11/19/38
Turner, Tina (Annie Mae Bullock) (singer); Nut Bush, Tenn., 11/26/39
Turpin, Ben (comedian); New Orleans **(1874–1940)**
Turturro, John (actor); Brooklyn, N.Y., 2/28/57
Twain, Mark (Samuel Langhorne Clemens) (author); Florida, Mo. **(1835–1910)**
Twain, Shania (Eileen Regina Twain) (country singer); Windsor, Ont., Canada, 8/28/65
Tweed, William Marcy (politician); New York City **(1823–1878)**
Twiggy (Leslie Hornby) (model); London, 9/19/49
Twining, Gen. Nathan F. (former Air Force chief of staff); Monroe, Wis. **(1897–1982)**
Twitty, Conway (Harold Lloyd Jenkins) (singer, guitarist); Friars Point, Miss. **(1933–1993)**
Tyler, John (10th U.S. president); Charles City County, Va. **(1790–1862)**
Tyler, Liv (actress, model); Portland, Maine, 7/1/77
Tyler, Steven (singer); New York City, 3/26/48
Tyson, Cicely (actress); New York City, 12/19/33

U

Uccello, Paolo (painter); Florence **(1397–1475)**
Udall, Stewart L. (ex-secretary of the interior); St. Johns, Ariz., 1/31/20
Uggams, Leslie (singer, actress); New York City, 5/25/43
Ulanova, Galina (ballet dancer); St. Petersburg, Russia **(1910–1998)**
Ullman, Tracey (actress, singer); Slough, England, 12/30/59
Ullmann, Liv (actress); Tokyo, 12/16/39
Ulrich, Skeet (actor, model); North Carolina, 1/20/70
Untermeyer, Louis (anthologist, poet); New York City **(1885–1977)**
Updike, John (novelist); Shillington, Pa., 3/18/32
Urey, Harold C. (chemist, Nobel laureate); Walkerton, Ind. **(1893–1981)**
Uris, Leon (novelist); Baltimore, 8/3/24
Ustinov, Peter (actor, producer); London, 4/16/21
Utrillo, Maurice (painter); Paris **(1883–1955)**

V

Vaccaro, Brenda (actress); Brooklyn, N.Y., 11/18/39
Vadim, Roger (Roger Vadim Plemiannikov) (film director); Paris **(1928–2000)**
Valentine, Karen (actress); Santa Rosa, Calif., 5/25/47
Valentino, Rudolph (Rodolpho d'Antonguolla) (actor); Castellaneta, Italy **(1895–1926)**
Valentino (Valentino Garavani) (fashion designer); nr. Milan, Italy, 5/11/32
Valéry, Paul (Ambroise Toussaint Jules) (poet, critic); Sète, France **(1871–1945)**
Vallee, Rudy (Hubert Prior Rudy Vallée) (band leader, singer); Island Pond, Va. **(1901–1986)**
Valli, Frankie (Frank Castellaccio) (singer); Newark, N.J., 5/3/37
Van Allen, James Alfred (space physicist); Mt. Pleasant, Iowa, 9/7/14
Van Buren, Abigail (Pauline Esther Friedman) (columnist); Sioux City, Iowa, 7/4/18
Van Buren, Martin (8th U.S. president); Kinderhook, N.Y. **(1782–1862)**
Vance, Vivian (Vivian Jones) (actress); Cherryvale, Kans. **(1912–1979)**
Van Der Beek, James (actor); Cheshire, Conn., 3/8/77
Vanderbilt, Alfred G. (sportsman); London **(1912–1999)**
Vanderbilt, Cornelius (financier); Port Richmond, N.Y. **(1794–1877)**
Vanderbilt, Gloria (fashion designer); New York City, 2/20/24
Van Doren, Carl (writer, educator); Hope, Ill. **(1885–1950)**
Van Doren, Mamie (actress); Rowena, S.D., 2/6/33
Vandross, Luther (R&B singer); New York City, 4/20/51
Van Dyke, Dick (actor); West Plains, Mo., 12/13/25
Vandyke (or Van Dyck), Sir Anthony (painter); Antwerp, Belgium **(1599–1641)**
Van Eyck, Jan (painter); Maeseyck, Belgium **(c. 1390–1441)**
Van Fleet, Jo (actress); Oakland, Calif. **(1915–1996)**
van Gogh, Vincent (painter); Groot Zundert, Brabant, Belgium **(1853–1890)**
van Hamel, Martine (ballet dancer); Brussels, 11/16/45

Van Heusen, Jimmy (Edward Chester Babcock) (songwriter); Syracuse, N.Y. **(1913–1990)**
Van Patten, Dick (actor); Richmond Hill, N.Y., 12/9/28
Van Peebles, Melvin (playwright); Chicago, 9/21/32
Vasari, Giorgio (art historian); Arezzo, Italy **(1511–1574)**
Vaughan, Sarah (singer); Newark, N.J. **(1924–1990)**
Vaughan Williams, Ralph (composer); Down Ampney, England **(1872–1958)**
Vaughn, Robert (actor); New York City, 11/22/32
Vaughn, Vince (actor); Minneapolis, 3/28/70
Veblen, Thorstein (economist, social critic); Cato Township, Wis. **(1857–1929)**
Veidt, Conrad (actor); Potsdam, Germany **(1893–1943)**
Velázquez, Diego Rodriguez de Silva y (painter); Seville, Spain **(1599–1660)**
Venturi, Robert (Charles) (architect); Philadelphia, 6/25/25
Verdi, Giuseppe (composer); Roncole, Italy **(1813–1901)**
Verdon, Gwen (actress); Culver City, Calif. **(1925–2000)**
Vereen, Ben (actor, singer); Miami, Fla., 10/10/46
Verlaine, Paul (poet); Metz, France **(1844–1896)**
Vermeer, Jan (or Jan van der Meer van Delft) (painter); Delft, Netherlands **(1632–1675)**
Verne, Jules (author); Nantes, France **(1828–1905)**
Veronese, Paolo (Paolo Cagliari) (painter); Verona, Italy **(1528–1588)**
Verrazano, Giovanni da (navigator); Florence, Italy **(c. 1485–1528)**
Verrett, Shirley (mezzo-soprano); New Orleans, 5/31/33
Versace, Gianni (fashion designer); Reggio di Calabria, Italy **(1946–1997)**
Vesalius, Andreas (anatomist); Brussels **(1515–1564)**
Vespucci, Amerigo (navigator); Florence, Italy **(1454–1512)**
Vico, Giovanni Battista (philosopher); Naples, Italy **(1668–1744)**
Victoria (queen of England); London **(1819–1901)**
Vidal, Gore (novelist); West Point, N.Y., 10/3/25
Vidor, King (film director, producer); Galveston, Tex. **(1895–1982)**
Vigoda, Abe (actor); New York City, 2/24/21
Villa, Pancho (Doroteo Arango) (revolutionary); Hacienda de Rio Grande, San Juan del Rio, Mexico **(1877–1923)**
Villella, Edward (ballet dancer); Bayside, Queens, N.Y., 10/1/36
Villon, François (François de Montcorbier) (poet); Paris **(1431–1463)**
Vinton, Bobby (singer); Canonsburg, Pa., 4/16/35
Virgil (or Vergil) (Publius Vergilius Maro) (poet); nr. Mantua, Italy **(70–19 b.c.)**
Vishnevskaya, Galina (soprano); St. Petersburg, Russia, 10/25/26
Vivaldi, Antonio (composer); Venice **(1678–1741)**
Vlaminck, Maurice de (painter); Paris **(1876–1958)**
Voight, Jon (actor); Yonkers, N.Y., 12/29/38
Volta, Alessandro (scientist); Como, Italy **(1745–1827)**
Voltaire (François Marie Arouet) (author); Paris **(1694–1778)**
von Braun, Wernher (rocket scientist); Wirsitz, Germany **(1912–1977)**
von Furstenberg, Betsy (Elizabeth Caroline Maria Agatha Felicitas Therese von Furstenberg-Hedringen) (actress); Nelheim-Heusen, Germany, 8/16/35
von Fürstenberg, Diane (Diane Simone Michelle Halfin) (fashion designer); Brussels, 12/31/46
von Hindenburg, Paul (statesman); Posen, Poland **(1847–1934)**
von Karajan, Herbert (conductor); Salzburg, Austria **(1908–1989)**
Vonnegut, Kurt, Jr. (novelist); Indianapolis, 11/11/22
Von Stade, Frederica (mezzo-soprano); Somerville, N.J., 6/1/45
Von Stroheim, Erich Oswald Hans Carl Maria von Nordenwall (actor, director); Vienna **(1885–1957)**
Von Zell, Harry (announcer); Indianapolis **(1906–1981)**
Vreeland, Diana (Diana Da Iziel) (fashion journalist, museum consultant); Paris **(1903?–1989)**

W

Wagner, Lindsay (actress); Los Angeles, 6/22/49
Wagner, Robert (actor); Detroit, 2/10/30
Wagner, Robert F. (ex-mayor of New York City); New York City **(1910–1991)**
Wagner, Wilhelm Richard (composer); Leipzig, Germany **(1813–1883)**
Wahlberg, Mark (actor, model, musician); Dorchester, Mass., 6/5/71
Waits, Tom (blues singer); Pomona, Calif., 12/7/49
Waldheim, Kurt (ex-UN secretary-general); St. Andrae-Wörden, Austria, 12/21/18
Walesa, Lech (Polish labor leader and ex-president); Popowo, Poland, 9/29/43
Walken, Christopher (actor); Queens, N.Y., 3/31/43
Walker, Alice (novelist, poet); Eatonon, Ga., 2/9/44

Walker, Nancy (Ann Myrtle Swoyer) (actress, comedienne); Philadelphia (1922–1992)
Walker, Robert (actor); Salt Lake City (1918–1951)
Walker, T-Bone (blues singer); Linden, Tex. (1910–1975)
Wallace, DeWitt (publisher); St. Paul, Minn. (1889–1981)
Wallace, George C. (ex-governor); Clio, Ala. (1919–1998)
Wallace, Irving (novelist); Chicago (1916–1990)
Wallace, Mike (Myron Wallace) (TV interviewer, commentator); Brookline, Mass., 5/9/18
Wallach, Eli (actor); Brooklyn, N.Y., 12/7/15
Wallenberg, Raoul (diplomat, humanitarian); Stockholm (1912–1947)
Wallenstein, Alfred (conductor); Chicago (1898–1983)
Waller, Thomas "Fats" (pianist); New York City (1904–1943)
Wallis, Hal (film producer); Chicago (1899–1986)
Walpole, Horace (statesman, novelist); London (1717–1797)
Walsh, J. T. (actor); San Francisco, Calif. (1944–1998)
Waltari, Mika (novelist); Helsinki (1903–1979)
Walter, Bruno (Bruno Walter Schlesinger) (orchestra conductor); Berlin (1876–1962)
Walters, Barbara (TV commentator); Boston, 9/25/31
Walton, Izaak (author); Stafford, England (1593–1683)
Wambaugh, Joseph (author, screenwriter); East Pittsburgh, 1/22/37
Wanamaker, John (merchant); Philadelphia (1838–1922)
Wanamaker, Sam (actor, director); Chicago (1919–1993)
Ward, Barbara (economist); York, England (1914–1981)
Ward, Rachel (actress); Cornwell Manor, England, 9/12/57
Warhol, Andy (Warhola) (artist); McKeesport, Pa. (1928–1987)
Waring, Fred (band leader); Tyrone, Pa. (1900–1984)
Warner, H. B. (Henry Bryan Warner Lickford) (actor); London (1876–1958)
Warren, Lesley Ann (actress); New York City, 8/16/46
Warren, Robert Penn (novelist); Guthrie, Ky. (1905–1989)
Warrick, Ruth (actress); St. Joseph, Mo., 6/29/15
Warwick, Dionne (singer); East Orange, N.J., 12/12/41
Washington, Booker T(aliaferro) (educator); Franklin County, Va. (1856–1915)
Washington, Denzel (actor); Mt. Vernon, N.Y., 12/28/54
Washington, George (1st U.S. president); Westmoreland County, Va. (1732–1799)
Washington, Harold (ex-mayor of Chicago); Chicago (1922–1987)
Waters, Ethel (actress, singer); Chester, Pa. (1896–1977)
Waters, Muddy (McKinley Morganfield) (singer, guitarist); Rolling Fork, Miss. (1915–1983)
Waterston, Sam (actor); Cambridge, Mass., 11/15/40
Watson, James Dewey (scientist, Nobel laureate); Chicago, 4/6/28
Watson, Thomas John (industrialist); Campbell, N.Y. (1874–1956)
Watt, James (inventor); Greenock, Scotland (1736–1819)
Watteau, Jean-Antoine (painter); Valanciennes, France (1684–1721)
Wattleton, Faye (family planning advocate); St. Louis, 7/8/43
Watts, André (concert pianist); Nuremberg, Germany, 6/20/46
Waugh, Alec (Alexander Raban Waugh) (novelist); London (1898–1981)
Waugh, Evelyn (novelist); London (1903–1966)
Wayans, Damon (actor, comedian, writer, producer); New York City, 9/4/60
Wayans, Keenan Ivory (actor, comedian, writer, director); New York City, 6/8/58
Wayne, Anthony (military officer); Waynesboro (family farm), nr. Paoli, Pa. (1745–1796)
Wayne, David (David McMeekan) (actor); Traverse City, Mich. (1914–1995)
Wayne, John (Marion Michael Morrison) (actor); Winterset, Iowa (1907–1979)
Weaver, Dennis (actor); Joplin, Mo., 6/4/25
Weaver, Fritz (actor); Pittsburgh, 1/19/26
Weaver, Sigourney (actress); New York City, 10/8/49
Webb, Clifton (Webb Parmelee Hollenbeck) (actor); Indianapolis (1893–1966)
Webb, Jack (actor, producer); Santa Monica, Calif. (1920–1982)
Weber, Karl Maria Friedrich Ernst von (composer); nr. Lübeck, Germany (1786–1826)
Webster, Daniel (statesman); Salisbury, N.H. (1782–1852)
Webster, Margaret (producer, director, actress); New York City (1905–1972)
Webster, Noah (lexicographer); West Hartford, Conn. (1758–1843)
Weill, Kurt (composer); Dessau, Germany (1900–1950)
Weir, Peter (director); Sydney, Australia, 8/21/44
Weissmuller, Johnny (Peter John Weissmuller) (actor, swimmer); Freidorf, Romania (1904–1984)
Weizmann, Chaim (statesman); Grodno Province, Russia (1874–1952)
Welch, Raquel (Raquel Tejada) (actress); Chicago, 9/5/40
Weld, Tuesday (Susan Ker Weld) (actress); New York City, 8/27/43

Welk, Lawrence (band leader); Strasburg, N.D. (1903–1992)
Welles, Orson (actor, director, producer); Kenosha, Wis. (1915–1985)
Wellington, Duke of (Arthur Wellesley) (statesman); Ireland (1769–1852)
Wells, H(erbert) G(eorge) (author); Bromley, England (1866–1946)
Wells, Ida Bell (Barnett) (journalist); Holly Springs, Miss. (1862–1931)
Welty, Eudora (novelist); Jackson, Miss. (1909–2001)
Wenner, Jann (publisher); New York City, 1/7/46
Werfel, Franz (novelist); Prague (1890–1945)
Werner, Oskar (Josef Schliessmayer) (actor, director); Vienna (1922–1984)
Wertheimer, Linda (radio journalist); Carlsbad, N.M., 3/19/43
Wertmueller, Lina (Arcanguela Felice Assunta W. von Elgg) (director); Rome, 8/14/28
Wesley, John (religious leader); Epworth Rectory, Lincolnshire, England (1703–1791)
West, Benjamin (painter); Springfield, Pa. (1738–1820)
West, Dame Rebecca (Cicily Fairfield) (novelist); County Kerry, Ireland (1892–1983)
West, Jessamyn (novelist); nr. North Vernon, Ind. (1902–1984)
West, Mae (actress); Brooklyn, N.Y. (1893–1980)
West, Nathanael (Nathan Weinstein) (novelist); New York City (1902–1940)
Westheimer, Dr. Ruth (Karola Ruth Siegel) (human sexuality expert); Frankfurt, Germany, 1928
Westinghouse, George (inventor); Central Bridge, N.Y. (1846–1914)
Westmoreland, William Childs (ex-Army chief of staff); Saxon, S.C., 3/26/14
Weyden, Roger van der (painter); Tournai, Belgium (c. 1400–1464)
Wharton, Edith Newbold (née Jones) (novelist); New York City (1862–1937)
Wheatley, Phillis (poet); Senegal (c. 1753–1784)
Wheeler, Bert (Albert Jerome Wheeler) (comedian); Paterson, N.J. (1895–1968)
Whistler, James Abbott McNeill (painter, etcher); Lowell, Mass. (1834–1903)
Whitaker, Forest (actor); Longview, Tex., 7/15/61
White, Betty (actress); Oak Park, Ill., 1/17/22
White, Edmund (writer); Cincinnati, Ohio, 1/13/40
White, E(lwyn) B(rooks) (author); Mt. Vernon, N.Y. (1899–1985)
White, Pearl (actress); Green Ridge, Mo. (1889–1938)
White, Stanford (architect); New York City (1853–1906)
White, Theodore H. (historian); Boston (1915–1986)
White, Vanna (TV personality); Conway, S.C., 2/18/57
White, William Allen (journalist); Emporia, Kans. (1868–1944)
Whitehead, Alfred North (mathematician, philosopher); Isle of Thanet, England (1861–1947)
Whiteman, Paul (band leader); Denver (1891–1967)
Whiting, Margaret (singer, actress); Detroit, 7/22/24
Whitman, Walt (Walter) (poet); West Hills, N.Y. (1819–1892)
Whitmore, James (actor); White Plains, N.Y., 10/1/21
Whitney, Cornelius Vanderbilt (sportsman); New York City (1899–1992)
Whitney, Eli (inventor); Westboro, Mass. (1765–1825)
Whitney, John Hay (publisher); Ellsworth, Maine (1904–1982)
Whittier, John Greenleaf (poet); Haverhill, Mass. (1807–1892)
Wideman, John Edgar (writer); Washington, D.C., 6/14/41
Widmark, Richard (actor); Sunrise, Minn., 12/26/14
Wiesel, Elie (Eliezer) (author); Signet, Romania, 9/30/28
Wiesenthal, Simon (Nazi hunter); Buchach, Ukraine, 12/31/08
Wilde, Cornel (film actor, producer); New York City (1915–1989)
Wilde, Oscar Fingal O'Flahertie Wills (author); Dublin (1854–1900)
Wilder, Billy (Samuel Wilder) (film producer, director); Vienna, 6/22/06
Wilder, Gene (Jerome Silberman) (actor, writer, director, producer); Milwaukee, 6/11/35
Wilder, Thornton (author); Madison, Wis. (1897–1975)
Wilkins, Roy (civil rights leader); St. Louis (1901–1981)
William, Prince (heir to British throne); London, 6/21/82
Williams, Andy (singer); Wall Lake, Iowa, 12/3/30
Williams, Anson (actor, director); Los Angeles, 9/25/49
Williams, Billy Dee (actor); New York City, 4/6/37
Williams, Cindy (actress); Van Nuys, Calif., 8/22/47
Williams, Edward Bennett (lawyer); Hartford, Conn. (1920–1988)
Williams, Emlyn (actor, playwright); Mostyn, Wales (1905–1987)
Williams, Esther (actress, swimmer); Los Angeles, 8/8/23
Williams, Gluyas (cartoonist); San Francisco (1888–1982)
Williams, Hank, Sr. (Hiram King Williams) (singer); Georgiana, Ala. (1923–1953)
Williams, Joe (singer); Cordele, Ga. (1918–1999)
Williams, John T. (composer, conductor); Queens, N.Y., 2/8/32
Williams, Lucinda (singer, songwriter); Lake Charles, La., 1/26/53

Williams, Paul (singer, composer, actor); Omaha, Neb., 9/19/40
Williams, Robin (actor, producer); Chicago, 7/21/52
Williams, Roger (clergyman); London (1603?–1683)
Williams, Tennessee (Thomas L. Williams) (playwright); Columbus, Miss. (1911–1983)
Williams, Treat (Richard Williams) (actor); Rowayton, Conn., 12/1/51
Williams, Vanessa (actress, singer); Milwood, N.Y., 3/18/63
Williams, William Carlos (physician, poet); Rutherford, N.J. (1883–1963)
Williamson, Nicol (actor); Hamilton, Scotland, 9/14/38
Willkie, Wendell Lewis (lawyer); Elwood, Ind. (1892–1944)
Willis, Bruce (actor); Germany, 3/19/55
Willson, Meredith (composer); Mason City, Iowa (1902–1984)
Wilson, August (poet, writer, playwright); Pittsburgh, 4/27/45
Wilson, Brian (musician); Inglewood, Calif., 6/20/42
Wilson, Don (radio and TV announcer); Lincoln, Neb. (1900–1982)
Wilson, Dooley (actor, musician); Tyler, Tex. (1894–1953)
Wilson, Edmund (literary critic, author); Red Bank, N.J. (1895–1972)
Wilson, Flip (Clerow Wilson) (comedian); Jersey City, N.J. (1933–1998)
Wilson, Harold (ex-prime minister); Huddersfield, England (1916–1995)
Wilson, Nancy (singer); Chillicothe, Ohio, 2/20/37
Wilson, Sloan (novelist); Norwalk, Conn., 5/8/20
Wilson, (Thomas) Woodrow (28th U.S. president); Staunton, Va. (1856–1924)
Winchell, Walter (columnist); New York City (1897–1972)
Windsor, Duchess of (Bessie Wallis Warfield) Blue Ridge Summit, Pa. (1896–1986)
Windsor, Duke of (formerly King Edward VIII of England); Richmond Park, England (1894–1972)
Winfrey, Oprah (TV host, actress, producer); Kosciusko, Miss., 1/29/54
Winger, Debra (Mary Debra) (actress); Cleveland, 5/17/55
Winkler, Henry (actor, director, producer); New York City, 10/30/45
Winningham, Mare (actress); Phoenix, Ariz., 5/16/59
Winter, Johnny (guitarist); Leland, Miss., 2/23/44
Winters, Jonathan (comedian); Dayton, Ohio, 11/11/25
Winters, Shelley (Shirley Schrift) (actress); East St. Louis, Ill., 8/18/22
Winthrop, John (first governor, Massachusetts Bay Colony); Suffolk, England (1588–1649)
Wise, Stephen Samuel (rabbi); Budapest (1874–1949)
Withers, Jane (actress); Atlanta, 4/12/26
Witherspoon, Reese (actress); Nashville, 3/22/76
Wittig, Georg F. K. (chemist, Nobel laureate); Berlin, Germany (1897–1987)
Wittgenstein, Ludwig (Josef Johann) (philosopher); Vienna (1889–1951)
Wodehouse, P(elham) G(renville) (novelist); Guildford, England (1881–1975)
Wolf, Scott (actor); Boston, 6/4/68
Wolfe, Thomas Clayton (novelist); Asheville, N.C. (1900–1938)
Wolfe, Tom (journalist); Richmond, Va., 3/2/31
Wolff, Tobias (author); Birmingham, Ala., 6/19/45
Wolsey, Thomas (prelate, statesman); Ipswich, England (c. 1475–1530)
Wonder, Stevie (Steveland Judkins, later Steveland Morris) (singer, songwriter); Saginaw, Mich., 5/13/50
Wong, Anna May (Lu Tsong Wong) (actress); Los Angeles (1907–1961)
Woo, John (actor, film director, screenwriter); Guangzhou, Canton, China, 5/1/46
Wood, Elijah (actor); Cedar Rapids, Iowa, 1/28/81
Wood, Grant (painter); Anamosa, Iowa (1892–1942)
Wood, Natalie (Natasha Viparaeff) (actress); San Francisco (1938–1981)
Woods, James (actor); Vernal, Utah, 4/18/47
Woodhouse, Barbara (Blackburn) (dog trainer, author, TV personality); Rathfarnham, Ireland (1910–1988)
Woodruff, Judy (broadcast journalist); Tulsa, Okla., 11/20/46
Woodson, Carter G. (historian); New Canton, Va. (1875–1950)
Woodward, Edward (actor); Croydon, England, 6/1/30
Woodward, Joanne (actress); Thomasville, Ga., 2/27/30
Woodward, Robert Burns (chemist, Nobel laureate); Boston (1917–1979)
Woolf, (Adeline) Virginia (née Stephens) (novelist); London (1882–1941)
Woollcott, Alexander (author, critic); Phalanx, N.J. (1887–1943)
Woolley, Monty (Edgar Montillion Woolley) (actor); New York City (1888–1963)

Woolworth, Frank (merchant); Rodman, N.Y. (1852–1919)
Wopat, Tom (actor); Lodi, Wis., 9/9/50
Wordsworth, William (poet); Cockermouth, England (1770–1850)
Wouk, Herman (novelist); New York City, 5/27/15
Wovoka (Jack Wilson) (Paiute Indian religious leader); (western Nev.) (c. 1858–1932)
Wray, Fay (actress); nr. Cardston, Alb., Canada, 9/14/07
Wren, Sir Christopher (architect); East Knoyle, England (1632–1723)
Wright, Frank Lloyd (architect); Richland Center, Wis. (1869–1959)
Wright, Martha (singer); Seattle, 3/23/26
Wright, Orville (inventor); Dayton, Ohio (1871–1948)
Wright, Richard (novelist); nr. Natchez, Miss. (1908–1960)
Wright, Wilbur (inventor); Millville, Ind. (1867–1912)
Wyatt, Jane (actress); Campgaw, N.J., 8/12/12
Wycliffe, John (church reformer); Hipswell, England (1320–1384)
Wyeth, Andrew (painter); Chadds Ford, Pa., 7/12/17
Wyle, Noah (actor); Hollywood, Calif., 6/4/71
Wyler, William (director); Mulhouse, France (1902–1981)
Wyman, Jane (Sarah Jane Fulks) (actress); St. Joseph, Mo., 1/4/14
Wynette, Tammy (Virginia Wynette Pugh) (singer); Tupelo, Miss. (1942–1998)
Wynn, Ed (Isaiah Edwin Leopold) (comedian); Philadelphia (1886–1966)
Wynn, Keenan (actor); New York City (1916–1986)

X

Xavier, St. Francis (Jesuit missionary); Pamplona, Navarre, Spain (1506–1552)
Xenophon (soldier, historian, essayist); Athens (c. 435–c. 355 B.C.)
Xerxes, the Great (king); Persian Empire (c. 519–465 B.C.)

Y

Yeats, William Butler (poet); nr. Dublin (1865–1939)
Yeltsin, Boris (Russian president); Yekaterinburg (then Sverdlovsk), Russia, 2/1/31
Yevtushenko, Yevgeny (poet); Zima, Russia, 7/18/33
York, Michael (actor); Fulmer, England, 3/27/42
York, Susannah (Fletcher) (actress); London, 1/9/42
Yorty, Samuel W. (ex-mayor of Los Angeles); Lincoln, Neb. (1909–1998)
Yothers, Tina (actress); Whittier, Calif., 5/5/73
Young, Alan (actor); North Shield, England, 11/19/19
Young, Andrew (civil rights leader); New Orleans, 3/12/32
Young, Brigham (religious leader); Whitingham, Vt. (1801–1877)
Young, Gig (Byron Barr) (actor); St. Cloud, Minn. (1917–1978)
Young, Loretta (Gretchen Young) (actress); Salt Lake City (1913–2000)
Young, Neil (singer, songwriter); Toronto, 11/12/45
Young, Robert (actor); Chicago (1907–1998)
Youngman, Henny (comedian); Whitechapel, London (1906–1998)

Z

Zane, Billy (William George Zane, Jr.) (actor); Chicago, 2/24/66
Zanuck, Darryl F. (producer); Wahoo, Neb. (1902–1979)
Zappa, Frank (Francis Vincent Zappa, Jr.) (singer, songwriter); Baltimore (1940–1993)
Zeffirelli, Franco (director); Florence, Italy, 2/12/23
Zellweger, Renee (actress); Katy, Texas, 4/25/69
Zemeckis, Robert (filmmaker); Chicago, 1952
Zhou Enlai (premier); Hualyin, China (1898–1976)
Ziegfeld, Florenz (theatrical producer); Chicago (1869–1932)
Ziegler, Karl (chemist, Nobel laureate); Helsa, Germany (1898–1973)
Zimbalist, Efrem (concert violinist); Rostov-on-Don, Russia (1889–1985)
Zimbalist, Efrem, Jr. (actor); New York City, 11/30/23
Zimbalist, Stephanie (actress); New York City, 10/8/56
Zinnemann, Fred (director); Vienna (1907–1997)
Zola, Emile (novelist); Paris (1840–1902)
Zoroaster (religious leader); Persian Empire (c. 628–c. 551 B.C.)
Zucker, Jerry (film producer, director, screenwriter); Milwaukee, 3/11/50
Zukerman, Pinchas (violinist); Tel Aviv, Israel, 7/16/48
Zukor, Adolph (movie executive); Risce, Hungary (1873–1976)
Zurbarán, Francisco de (painter); Fuentes de Cantos, Spain (1598–1664)
Zweig, Stefan (author); Vienna (1881–1942)
Zwingli, Huldrych (humanist); Wildaus, Switzerland (1484–1531)

Nobel Prizes

(For years not listed, no award was made. *See* p. 42 for 2001 winners.)

PEACE

1901	Henri Dunant (Switzerland); Frederick Passy (France)
1902	Elie Ducommun and Albert Gobat (Switzerland)
1903	Sir William R. Cremer (UK)
1904	Institut de Droit International (Belgium)
1905	Bertha von Suttner (Austria)
1906	Theodore Roosevelt (U.S.)
1907	Ernesto T. Moneta (Italy) and Louis Renault (France)
1908	Klas P. Arnoldson (Sweden) and Frederik Bajer (Denmark)
1909	Auguste M. F. Beernaert (Belgium) and Baron Paul H. B. B. d'Estournelles de Constant de Rebecque (France)
1910	Bureau International Permanent de la Paix (Switzerland)
1911	Tobias M. C. Asser (Holland) and Alfred H. Fried (Austria)
1912	Elihu Root (U.S.)
1913	Henri La Fontaine (Belgium)
1917	International Red Cross
1919	Woodrow Wilson (U.S.)
1920	Léon Bourgeois (France)
1921	Karl H. Branting (Sweden) and Christian L. Lange (Norway)
1922	Fridtjof Nansen (Norway)
1925	Sir Austen Chamberlain (UK) and Charles G. Dawes (U.S.)
1926	Aristide Briand (France) and Gustav Stresemann (Germany)
1927	Ferdinand Buisson (France) and Ludwig Quidde (Germany)
1929	Frank B. Kellogg (U.S.)
1930	Lars O. J. Söderblom (Sweden)
1931	Jane Addams and Nicholas M. Butler (U.S.)
1933	Sir Norman Angell (UK)
1934	Arthur Henderson (UK)
1935	Karl von Ossietzky (Germany)
1936	Carlos de S. Lamas (Argentina)
1937	Lord Cecil of Chelwood (UK)
1938	Office International Nansen pour les Réfugiés (Switzerland)
1944	International Red Cross
1945	Cordell Hull (U.S.)
1946	Emily G. Balch and John R. Mott (U.S.)
1947	American Friends Service Committee (U.S.) and British Society of Friends' Service Council (UK)
1949	Lord John Boyd Orr (Scotland)
1950	Ralph J. Bunche (U.S.)
1951	Léon Jouhaux (France)
1952	Albert Schweitzer (French Equatorial Africa)
1953	George C. Marshall (U.S.)
1954	Office of U.N. High Commissioner for Refugees
1957	Lester B. Pearson (Canada)
1958	Rev. Dominique Georges Henri Pire (Belgium)
1959	Philip John Noel-Baker (UK)
1960	Albert John Luthuli (South Africa)
1961	Dag Hammarskjöld (Sweden)
1962	Linus Pauling (U.S.)
1963	Intl. Comm. of Red Cross; League of Red Cross Societies (both Geneva)
1964	Rev. Dr. Martin Luther King, Jr. (U.S.)
1965	UNICEF (United Nations Children's Fund)
1968	René Cassin (France)
1969	International Labour Organization
1970	Norman E. Borlaug (U.S.)
1971	Willy Brandt (West Germany)
1973	Henry A. Kissinger (U.S.); Le Duc Tho (North Vietnam)[1]
1974	Eisaku Sato (Japan); Sean MacBride (Ireland)
1975	Andrei D. Sakharov (USSR)
1976	Mairead Corrigan and Betty Williams (both Northern Ireland)
1977	Amnesty International
1978	Menachem Begin (Israel) and Anwar el-Sadat (Egypt)
1979	Mother Teresa of Calcutta (India)
1980	Adolfo Pérez Esquivel (Argentina)
1981	Office of the United Nations High Commissioner for Refugees
1982	Alva Myrdal (Sweden) and Alfonso García Robles (Mexico)
1983	Lech Walesa (Poland)
1984	Bishop Desmond Tutu (South Africa)
1985	International Physicians for the Prevention of Nuclear War
1986	Elie Wiesel (U.S.)
1987	Oscar Arias Sánchez (Costa Rica)
1988	UN Peacekeeping Forces
1989	Dalai Lama (Tibet)
1990	Mikhail S. Gorbachev (USSR)
1991	Daw Aung San Suu Kyi (Burma)
1992	Rigoberta Menchú (Guatemala)
1993	F. W. de Klerk and Nelson Mandela (both South Africa)
1994	Yasir Arafat (Palestine), Shimon Peres, and Yitzhak Rabin (both Israel)
1995	Joseph Rotblat and Pugwash Conference on Science and World Affairs (UK)
1996	Carlos Filipe Ximenes Belo and José Ramos-Horta (East Timor)
1997	International Campaign to Ban Landmines and Jody Williams (U.S.)
1998	John Hume and David Trimble (Northern Ireland)
1999	Doctors without Borders (France)
2000	Kim Dae Jung (South Korea)

1. Le Duc Tho refused prize, charging that peace had not yet really been established in South Vietnam.

LITERATURE

1901	René F. A. Sully Prudhomme (France)
1902	Theodor Mommsen (Germany)
1903	Björnstjerne Björnson (Norway)
1904	Frédéric Mistral (France) and José Echegaray (Spain)

1905	Henryk Sienkiewicz (Poland)
1906	Giosuè Carducci (Italy)
1907	Rudyard Kipling (UK)
1908	Rudolf Eucken (Germany)
1909	Selma Lagerlöf (Sweden)
1910	Paul von Heyse (Germany)
1911	Maurice Maeterlinck (Belgium)
1912	Gerhart Hauptmann (Germany)
1913	Rabindranath Tagore (India)
1915	Romain Rolland (France)
1916	Verner von Heidenstam (Sweden)
1917	Karl Gjellerup (Denmark) and Henrik Pontoppidan (Denmark)
1919	Carl Spitteler (Switzerland)
1920	Knut Hamsun (Norway)
1921	Anatole France (France)
1922	Jacinto Benavente (Spain)
1923	William B. Yeats (Ireland)
1924	Wladyslaw Reymont (Poland)
1925	George Bernard Shaw (Ireland)
1926	Grazia Deledda (Italy)
1927	Henri Bergson (France)
1928	Sigrid Undset (Norway)
1929	Thomas Mann (Germany)
1930	Sinclair Lewis (U.S.)
1931	Erik A. Karlfeldt (Sweden)
1932	John Galsworthy (UK)
1933	Ivan G. Bunin (Russia)
1934	Luigi Pirandello (Italy)
1936	Eugene O'Neill (U.S.)
1937	Roger Martin du Gard (France)
1938	Pearl S. Buck (U.S.)
1939	Frans Eemil Sillanpää (Finland)
1944	Johannes V. Jensen (Denmark)
1945	Gabriela Mistral (Chile)
1946	Hermann Hesse (Switzerland)
1947	André Gide (France)
1948	Thomas Stearns Eliot (UK)
1949	William Faulkner (U.S.)
1950	Bertrand Russell (UK)
1951	Pär Lagerkvist (Sweden)
1952	François Mauriac (France)
1953	Sir Winston Churchill (UK)
1954	Ernest Hemingway (U.S.)
1955	Halldór Kiljan Laxness (Iceland)
1956	Juan Ramón Jiménez (Spain)
1957	Albert Camus (France)
1958	Boris Pasternak (USSR) (declined)
1959	Salvatore Quasimodo (Italy)
1960	St. John Perse (Alexis Léger) (France)
1961	Ivo Andric (Yugoslavia)
1962	John Steinbeck (U.S.)
1963	Giorgios Seferis (Seferiades) (Greece)
1964	Jean-Paul Sartre (France) (declined)
1965	Mikhail Sholokhov (USSR)
1966	Shmuel Yosef Agnon (Israel) and Nelly Sachs (Sweden)
1967	Miguel Angel Asturias (Guatemala)
1968	Yasunari Kawabata (Japan)
1969	Samuel Beckett (Ireland)
1970	Aleksandr Solzhenitsyn (USSR)
1971	Pablo Neruda (Chile)
1972	Heinrich Böll (Germany)
1973	Patrick White (Australia)
1974	Eyvind Johnson and Harry Martinson (both Sweden)
1975	Eugenio Montale (Italy)
1976	Saul Bellow (U.S.)
1977	Vicente Aleixandre (Spain)
1978	Isaac Bashevis Singer (U.S.)

1979	Odysseus Elytis (Greece)
1980	Czeslaw Milosz (U.S.)
1981	Elias Canetti (Bulgaria)
1982	Gabriel García Márquez (Colombia)
1983	William Golding (UK)
1984	Jaroslav Seifert (Czechoslovakia)
1985	Claude Simon (France)
1986	Wole Soyinka (Nigeria)
1987	Joseph Brodsky (U.S.)
1988	Naguib Mahfouz (Egypt)
1989	Camilo José Cela (Spain)
1990	Octavio Paz (Mexico)
1991	Nadine Gordimer (South Africa)
1992	Derek Walcott (Trinidad)
1993	Toni Morrison (U.S.)
1994	Kenzaburo Oe (Japan)
1995	Seamus Heaney (Ireland)
1996	Wislawa Szymborska (Poland)
1997	Dario Fo (Italy)
1998	José Saramago (Portugal)
1999	Günter Grass (Germany)
2000	Gao Xingjian (China)

PHYSICS

1901	Wilhelm K. Roentgen (Germany), for discovery of Roentgen rays
1902	Hendrik A. Lorentz and Pieter Zeeman (Netherlands), for work on influence of magnetism upon radiation
1903	A. Henri Becquerel (France), for work on spontaneous radioactivity; and Pierre and Marie Curie (France), for study of radiation
1904	John Strutt (Lord Rayleigh) (UK), for discovery of argon in investigating gas density
1905	Philipp Lenard (Germany), for work with cathode rays
1906	Sir Joseph Thomson (UK), for investigations on passage of electricity through gases
1907	Albert A. Michelson (U.S.), for spectroscopic and metrologic investigations
1908	Gabriel Lippmann (France), for method of reproducing colors by photography
1909	Guglielmo Marconi (Italy) and Ferdinand Braun (Germany), for development of wireless
1910	Johannes D. van der Waals (Netherlands), for work with the equation of state for gases and liquids
1911	Wilhelm Wien (Germany), for his laws governing the radiation of heat
1912	Gustaf Dalén (Sweden), for discovery of automatic regulators used in lighting lighthouses and light buoys
1913	Heike Kamerlingh-Onnes (Netherlands), for work leading to production of liquid helium
1914	Max von Laue (Germany), for discovery of diffraction of Roentgen rays passing through crystals
1915	Sir William Bragg and William L. Bragg (UK), for analysis of crystal structure by X rays
1917	Charles G. Barkla (UK), for discovery of Roentgen radiation of the elements
1918	Max Planck (Germany), discoveries in connection with quantum theory
1919	Johannes Stark (Germany), discovery of Doppler effect in Canal rays and decomposition of spectrum lines by electric fields

1920 Charles E. Guillaume (Switzerland), for discoveries of anomalies in nickel-steel-alloys

1921 Albert Einstein (Germany), for discovery of the law of the photoelectric effect

1922 Niels Bohr (Denmark), for investigation of structure of atoms and radiations emanating from them

1923 Robert A. Millikan (U.S.), for work on elementary charge of electricity and photoelectric phenomena

1924 Karl M. G. Siegbahn (Sweden), for investigations in X ray spectroscopy

1925 James Franck and Gustav Hertz (Germany), for discovery of laws governing impact of electrons upon atoms

1926 Jean B. Perrin (France), for work on discontinuous structure of matter and discovery of the equilibrium of sedimentation

1927 Arthur H. Compton (U.S.), for discovery of Compton phenomenon; and Charles T. R. Wilson (UK), for method of perceiving paths taken by electrically charged particles

1928 In 1929, the 1928 prize was awarded to Sir Owen Richardson (UK), for work on the phenomenon of thermionics and discovery of the Richardson Law

1929 Prince Louis Victor de Broglie (France), for discovery of the wave character of electrons

1930 Sir Chandrasekhara Raman (India), for work on diffusion of light and discovery of the Raman effect

1932 In 1933, the prize for 1932 was awarded to Werner Heisenberg (Germany), for creation of quantum mechanics

1933 Erwin Schrödinger (Austria) and Paul A. M. Dirac (UK), for discovery of new fertile forms of the atomic theory

1935 James Chadwick (UK), for discovery of the neutron

1936 Victor F. Hess (Austria), for discovery of cosmic radiation; and Carl D. Anderson (U.S.), for discovery of the positron

1937 Clinton J. Davisson (U.S.) and George P. Thomson (UK), for discovery of diffraction of electrons by crystals

1938 Enrico Fermi (Italy), for identification of new radioactivity elements and discovery of nuclear reactions effected by slow neutrons

1939 Ernest Orlando Lawrence (U.S.), for development of the cyclotron

1943 Otto Stern (U.S.), for detection of magnetic momentum of protons

1944 Isidor Isaac Rabi (U.S.), for work on magnetic movements of atomic particles

1945 Wolfgang Pauli (Austria), for work on atomic fissions

1946 Percy Williams Bridgman (U.S.), for studies and inventions in high-pressure physics

1947 Sir Edward Appleton (UK), for discovery of layer that reflects radio short waves in the ionosphere

1948 Patrick M. S. Blackett (UK), for improvement on Wilson chamber and discoveries in cosmic radiation

1949 Hideki Yukawa (Japan), for mathematical prediction, in 1935, of the meson

1950 Cecil Frank Powell (UK), for method of photographic study of atom nucleus, and for discoveries about mesons

1951 Sir John Douglas Cockcroft (UK) and Ernest T. S. Walton (Ireland), for work in 1932 on transmutation of atomic nuclei

1952 Edward Mills Purcell and Felix Bloch (U.S.), for work in measurement of magnetic fields in atomic nuclei

1953 Fritz Zernike (Netherlands), for development of "phase contrast" microscope

1954 Max Born (UK), for work in quantum mechanics; and Walther Bothe (Germany), for work in cosmic radiation

1955 Polykarp Kusch and Willis E. Lamb, Jr. (U.S.), for atomic measurements

1956 William Shockley, Walter H. Brattain, and John Bardeen (all U.S.), for developing electronic transistor

1957 Tsung Dao Lee and Chen Ning Yang (China), for disproving principle of conservation of parity

1958 Pavel A. Cherenkov, Ilya M. Frank, and Igor E. Tamm (all USSR), for work resulting in development of cosmic-ray counter

1959 Emilio Segre and Owen Chamberlain (both U.S.), for demonstrating the existence of the anti-proton

1960 Donald A. Glaser (U.S.), for invention of "bubble chamber" to study subatomic particles

1961 Robert Hofstadter (U.S.), for determination of shape and size of atomic nucleus; Rudolf Mössbauer (Germany), for method of producing and measuring recoil-free gamma rays

1962 Lev D. Landau (USSR), for his theories about condensed matter

1963 Eugene Paul Wigner, Maria Goeppert Mayer (both U.S.), and J. Hans D. Jensen (Germany), for research on structure of atom and its nucleus

1964 Charles Hard Townes (U.S.), Nikolai G. Basov, and Aleksandr M. Prochorov (both USSR), for developing maser and laser principle of producing high-intensity radiation

1965 Richard P. Feynman, Julian S. Schwinger (both U.S.), and Shinichiro Tomonaga (Japan), for research in quantum electrodynamics

1966 Alfred Kastler (France), for work on energy levels inside atom

1967 Hans A. Bethe (U.S.), for work on energy production of stars

1968 Luis Walter Alvarez (U.S.), for study of subatomic particles

1969 Murray Gell-Mann (U.S.), for study of subatomic particles

1970 Hannes Alfvén (Sweden), for theories in plasma physics; and Louis Néel (France), for discoveries in antiferromagnetism and ferromagnetism

1971 Dennis Gabor (UK), for invention of holographic method of three-dimensional imagery

1972 John Bardeen, Leon N. Cooper, and John Robert Schrieffer (all U.S.), for theory of superconductivity, where electrical resistance in certain metals vanishes above absolute zero temperature

1973 Ivar Giaever (U.S.), Leo Esaki (Japan), and Brian D. Josephson (UK), for theories that have advanced and expanded the field of miniature electronics

1974 Antony Hewish (UK), for discovery of pulsars; Martin Ryle (UK), for using radiotelescopes to probe outer space with high degree of precision

1975 James Rainwater (U.S.), Ben Mottelson, and Aage N. Bohr (both Denmark), for showing that the atomic nucleus is asymmetrical

1976 Burton Richter and Samuel C. C. Ting (both U.S.), for discovery of subatomic particles known as J and psi

1977 Philip W. Anderson, John H. Van Vleck (both U.S.), and Nevill F. Mott (UK), for work underlying computer memories and electronic devices

1978 Arno A. Penzias and Robert W. Wilson (both U.S.), for work in cosmic microwave radiation; Piotr L. Kapitsa (USSR), for basic inventions and discoveries in low-temperature physics

1979 Steven Weinberg, Sheldon L. Glashow (both U.S.), and Abdus Salam (Pakistan), for developing theory that electromagnetism and the "weak" force, which causes radioactive decay in some atomic nuclei, are facets of the same phenomenon

1980 James W. Cronin and Val L. Fitch (both U.S.), for work concerning the asymmetry of subatomic particles

1981 Nicolaas Bloembergen, Arthur L. Schawlow (both U.S.), and Kai M. Siegbahn (Sweden), for developing technologies with lasers and other devices to probe the secrets of complex forms of matter

1982 Kenneth G. Wilson (U.S.), for analysis of changes in matter under pressure and temperature

1983 Subrahmanyam Chandrasekhar and William A. Fowler (both U.S.), for complementary research on processes involved in the evolution of stars

1984 Carlo Rubbia (Italy) and Simon van der Meer (Netherlands), for their role in discovering three subatomic particles, a step toward developing a single theory to account for all natural forces

1985 Klaus von Klitzing (Germany), for developing an exact way of measuring electrical conductivity

1986 Ernst Ruska, Gerd Binnig (both Germany), and Heinrich Rohrer (Switzerland), for work on microscopes

1987 K. Alex Müller (Switzerland) and J. Georg Bednorz (Germany), for their discovery of high-temperature superconductors

1988 Leon M. Lederman, Melvin Schwartz, and Jack Steinberger (all U.S.), for research that improved the understanding of elementary particles and forces

1989 Norman F. Ramsey (U.S.), for work leading to development of the atomic clock, and Hans G. Dehmelt (U.S.) and Wolfgang Paul (Germany), for developing methods to isolate atoms and subatomic particles

1990 Richard E. Taylor (Canada), Jerome I. Friedman, and Dr. Henry W. Kendall (both U.S.), for their "breakthrough in our understanding of matter" that confirmed the reality of quarks

1991 Pierre-Gilles de Gennes (France), for his discoveries about the ordering of molecules in substances ranging from "super" glue to an exotic form of liquid helium

1992 George Charpak (France), for his inventions of particle detectors

1993 Joseph H. Taylor and Russell A. Hulse (both U.S.), for their discovery of a binary pulsar

1994 Clifford G. Shull (U.S.) and Bertram N. Brockhouse (Canada), for adapting beams of neutrons as probes to explore the atomic structure of matter

1995 Martin L. Perl and Frederick Reines (both U.S.), for their discoveries of "two of nature's most remarkable subatomic particles"—the tau and the neutrino

1996 David M. Lee, Robert C. Richardson, and Douglas D. Osheroff (all U.S.), for their discovery of superfluity in helium-3

1997 Steven Chu, William D. Phillips (both U.S.), and Claude Cohen-Tannoudji (France), for developing a method to cool and trap atoms using light from lasers

1998 Robert B. Laughlin (U.S.), Horst L. Störmer (Germany), and Daniel C. Tsui (U.S.), for their discovery of a new form of quantum fluid with fractionally charged excitations

1999 Gerardus 't Hooft (Netherlands) and Martinus J. G. Veltman (Netherlands), for their theory concerning the production of the Sun's energy

2000 Zhores I. Alferov (Russia), Herbert Kroemer, and Jack S. Kilby (both U.S.), for work in the development of transistors and microchip technology

CHEMISTRY

1901 Jacobus H. van't Hoff (Netherlands), for laws of chemical dynamics and osmotic pressure in solutions

1902 Emil Fischer (Germany), for experiments in sugar and purin groups of substances

1903 Svante A. Arrhenius (Sweden), for his electrolytic theory of dissociation

1904 Sir William Ramsay (UK), for discovery and determination of place of inert gaseous elements in air

1905 Adolf von Baeyer (Germany), for work on organic dyes and hydroaromatic combinations

1906 Henri Moissan (France), for isolation of fluorine, and introduction of electric furnace

1907 Eduard Buchner (Germany), discovery of cell-less fermentation and investigations in biological chemistry

1908 Sir Ernest Rutherford (UK), for investigations into disintegration of elements

1909 Wilhelm Ostwald (Germany), for work on catalysis and investigations into chemical equilibrium and reaction rates

1910 Otto Wallach (Germany), for work in the field of alicyclic compounds

1911 Marie Curie (France), for discovery of elements radium and polonium

1912 Victor Grignard (France), for reagent discovered by him; and Paul Sabatier (France), for methods of hydrogenating organic compounds

1913 Alfred Werner (Switzerland), for linking up atoms within the molecule

1914 Theodore W. Richards (U.S.), for determining atomic weight of many chemical elements

1915 Richard Willstätter (Germany), for research into coloring matter of plants, especially chlorophyll

1918 Fritz Haber (Germany), for synthetic production of ammonia

1920 Walther Nernst (Germany), for work in thermochemistry

1921 Frederick Soddy (UK), for investigations into origin and nature of isotopes

1922 Francis W. Aston (UK), for discovery of isotopes in nonradioactive elements and for discovery of the whole number rule

1923 Fritz Pregl (Austria), for method of microanalysis of organic substances discovered by him

1925 In 1926, the 1925 prize was awarded to Richard Zsigmondy (Germany), for work on the heterogeneous nature of colloid solutions

1926 Theodor Svedberg (Sweden), for work on disperse systems

1927 In 1928, the 1927 prize was awarded to Heinrich Wieland (Germany), for investigations of bile acids and kindred substances

1928 Adolf Windaus (Germany), for investigations on constitution of the sterols and their connection with vitamins

1929 Sir Arthur Harden (UK) and Hans K. A. S. von Euler-Chelpin (Sweden), for research on fermentation of sugars

1930 Hans Fischer (Germany), for work on coloring matter of blood and leaves and for his synthesis of hemin

1931 Karl Bosch and Friedrich Bergius (both Germany), for invention and development of chemical high-pressure methods

1932 Irving Langmuir (U.S.), for work in realm of surface chemistry

1934 Harold C. Urey (U.S.), for discovery of heavy hydrogen

1935 Frédéric and Irène Joliot-Curie (both France), for synthesis of new radioactive elements

1936 Peter J. W. Debye (Netherlands), for investigations on dipole moments and diffraction of X rays and electrons in gases

1937 Walter N. Haworth (UK), for research on carbohydrates and vitamin C; and Paul Karrer (Switzerland), for work on carotenoids, flavins, and vitamins A and B

1938 Richard Kuhn (Germany), for carotenoid study and vitamin research (declined)

1939 Adolf Butenandt (Germany), for work on sexual hormones (declined the prize); and Leopold Ruzicka (Switzerland), for work with polymethylenes

1943 Georg Hevesy De Heves (Hungary), for work on use of isotopes as indicators

1944 Otto Hahn (Germany), for work on atomic fission

1945 Artturi Illmari Virtanen (Finland), for research in the field of conservation of fodder

1946 James B. Sumner (U.S.), for crystallizing enzymes; John H. Northrop and Wendell M. Stanley (both U.S.), for preparing enzymes and virus proteins in pure form

1947 Sir Robert Robinson (UK), for research in plant substances

1948 Arne Tiselius (Sweden), for biochemical discoveries and isolation of mouse paralysis virus

1949 William Francis Giauque (U.S.), for research in thermodynamics, especially effects of low temperature

1950 Otto Diels and Kurt Alder (both Germany), for discovery of diene synthesis enabling scientists to study structure of organic matter

1951 Glenn T. Seaborg and Edwin H. McMillan (both U.S.), for discovery of plutonium

1952 Archer John Porter Martin and Richard Laurence Millington Synge (both UK), for development of partition chromatography

1953 Hermann Staudinger (Germany), for research in giant molecules

1954 Linus C. Pauling (U.S.), for study of forces holding together protein and other molecules

1955 Vincent du Vigneaud (U.S.), for work on pituitary hormones

1956 Sir Cyril Hinshelwood (UK) and Nikolai N. Semenov (USSR), for parallel research on chemical reaction kinetics

1957 Sir Alexander Todd (UK), for research with chemical compounds that are factors in heredity

1958 Frederick Sanger (UK), for determining molecular structure of insulin

1959 Jaroslav Heyrovsky (Czechoslovakia), for development of polarography, an electrochemical method of analysis

1960 Willard F. Libby (U.S.), for "atomic time clock" to measure age of objects by measuring their radioactivity

1961 Melvin Calvin (U.S.), for establishing chemical steps during photosynthesis

1962 Max F. Perutz and John C. Kendrew (UK), for mapping protein molecules with X rays

1963 Karl Ziegler (Germany) and Giulio Natta (Italy), for work in uniting simple hydrocarbons into large molecular substances

1964 Dorothy Mary Crowfoot Hodgkin (UK), for determining structure of compounds needed in combatting pernicious anemia

1965 Robert B. Woodward (U.S.), for work in synthesizing complicated organic compounds

1966 Robert Sanderson Mulliken (U.S.), for research on bond holding atoms together in molecule

1967 Manfred Eigen (Germany), Ronald G. W. Norrish, and George Porter (both UK), for work in high-speed chemical reactions

1968 Lars Onsager (U.S.), for development of system of equations in thermodynamics

1969 Derek H. R. Barton (UK) and Odd Hassel (Norway), for study of organic molecules

1970 Luis F. Leloir (Argentina), for discovery of sugar nucleotides and their role in biosynthesis of carbohydrates

1971 Gerhard Herzberg (Canada), for contributions to knowledge of electronic structure and geometry of molecules, particularly free radicals

1972 Christian Boehmer Anfinsen, Stanford Moore, and William Howard Stein (all U.S.), for pioneering studies in enzymes

1973 Ernst Otto Fischer (W. Germany) and Geoffrey Wilkinson (UK), for work that could solve problem of automobile exhaust pollution

1974 Paul J. Flory (U.S.), for developing analytic methods to study properties and molecular structure of long-chain molecules

1975 John W. Cornforth (Australia) and Vladimir Prelog (Switzerland), for research on structure of biological molecules such as antibiotics and cholesterol

1976 William N. Lipscomb, Jr. (U.S.), for work on the structure and bonding mechanisms of boranes

1977 Ilya Prigogine (Belgium), for contributions to nonequilibrium thermodynamics, particularly the theory of dissipative structures

1978 Peter Mitchell (UK), for contributions to the understanding of biological energy transfer

1979 Herbert C. Brown (U.S.) and Georg Wittig (West Germany), for developing a group of substances that facilitate very difficult chemical reactions

1980 Paul Berg, Walter Gilbert (both U.S.), and Frederick Sanger (UK), for developing methods to map the structure and function of DNA, the substance that controls the activity of the cell

1981 Roald Hoffmann (U.S.) and Kenichi Fukui (Japan), for applying quantum-mechanics theories to predict the course of chemical reactions

1982 Aaron Klug (UK), for research in the detailed structures of viruses and components of life

1983 Henry Taube (U.S.), for research on how electrons transfer between molecules in chemical reactions

1984 R. Bruce Merrifield (U.S.), for research that revolutionized the study of proteins

1985 Herbert A. Hauptman and Jerome Karle (both U.S.), for their outstanding achievements in the development of direct methods for the determination of crystal structures

1986 Dudley R. Herschback, Yuan T. Lee (both U.S.), and John C. Polanyi (Canada), for their work on "reaction dynamics"

1987 Donald J. Cram, Charles J. Pedersen (both U.S.), and Jean-Marie Lehn (France), for wide-ranging research that has included the creation of artificial molecules that can mimic vital chemical reactions of the processes of life

1988 Johann Deisenhofer, Robert Huber, and Hartmut Michel (all West Germany), for unraveling the structure of proteins that play a crucial role in photosynthesis

1989 Thomas R. Cech and Sidney Altman (both U.S.), for their discovery, independently, that RNA could actively aid chemical reactions in the cells

1990 Elias James Corey (U.S.), for developing new ways to synthesize complex molecules ordinarily found in nature

1991 Richard R. Ernst (Switzerland), for refinements he developed in nuclear magnetic-resonance spectroscopy

1992 Rudolph A. Marcus (U.S.), for his mathematical analysis of how the overall energy in a system of interacting molecules changes and induces an electron to jump from one molecule to another

1993 Kary B. Mullis (U.S.) and Michael Smith (Canada), for their contributions to the science of genetics

1994 George A. Olah (U.S.), University of Southern California in Los Angeles, for research that opened new ways to break apart and rebuild compounds of carbon and hydrogen

1995 F. Sherwood Rowland, Mario Molina (both U.S.), and Paul Crutzen (Netherlands), for their pioneering work in explaining the chemical processes that deplete the earth's ozone shield

1996 Richard E. Smalley, Robert F. Curl, Jr. (both U.S.), and Harold W. Kroto (UK), for discovery of a new class of carbon molecule

1997 Paul D. Boyer (U.S.), Jens C. Skou (Denmark), and John E. Walker (UK), for discoveries about a molecule that allows the human body to store and transfer energy between cells

1998 Walter Kohn (U.S.) and John A. Pople (UK), for their developments in the study of the properties of molecules and the chemical processes in which they are involved

1999 Ahmed H. Zewail (Egypt and U.S.), for creating the world's fastest camera, which captures atoms in motion

2000 Alan J. Heeger, Alan G. MacDiarmid (both U.S.), and Hideki Shirakawa (Japan), for the discovery and development of conductive polymers

PHYSIOLOGY OR MEDICINE

1901 Emil A. von Behring (Germany), for work on serum therapy against diphtheria

1902 Sir Ronald Ross (UK), for work on malaria

1903 Niels R. Finsen (Denmark), for his treatment of lupus vulgaris with concentrated light rays

1904 Ivan P. Pavlov (USSR), for work on the physiology of digestion

1905 Robert Koch (Germany), for work on tuberculosis

1906 Camillo Golgi (Italy) and Santiago Ramón y Cajal (Spain), for work on structure of the nervous system

1907 Charles L. A. Laveran (France), for work with protozoa in the generation of disease

1908 Paul Ehrlich (Germany) and Elie Metchnikoff (USSR), for work on immunity

1909 Theodor Kocher (Switzerland), for work on the thyroid gland

1910 Albrecht Kossel (Germany), for achievements in the chemistry of the cell

1911 Allvar Gullstrand (Sweden), for work on the dioptrics of the eye

1912 Alexis Carrel (France), for work on vascular ligature and grafting of blood vessels and organs

1913 Charles Richet (France), for work on anaphylaxy

1914 Robert Bárány (Austria), for work on physiology and pathology of the vestibular system

1919 Jules Bordet (Belgium), for discoveries in connection with immunity

1920 August Krogh (Denmark), for discovery of regulation of capillaries' motor mechanism

1922 In 1923, the 1922 prize was shared by Archibald V. Hill (UK), for discovery relating to heat-production in muscles; and Otto Meyerhof (Germany), for correlation between consumption of oxygen and production of lactic acid in muscles

1923 Sir Frederick Banting (Canada) and John J. R. Macleod (Scotland), for discovery of insulin

1924 Willem Einthoven (Netherlands), for discovery of the mechanism of the electrocardiogram

1926 Johannes Fibiger (Denmark), for discovery of the Spiroptera carcinoma

1927 Julius Wagner-Jauregg (Austria), for use of malaria inoculation in treatment of dementia paralytica

1928 Charles Nicolle (France), for work on typhus exanthematicus

1929 Christiaan Eijkman (Netherlands), for discovery of the antineuritic vitamins; and Sir Frederick Hopkins (UK), for discovery of growth-promoting vitamins

1930 Karl Landsteiner (U.S.), for discovery of human blood groups

1931 Otto H. Warburg (Germany), for discovery of the character and mode of action of the respiratory ferment

1932 Sir Charles Sherrington (UK) and Edgar D. Adrian (U.S.), for discoveries of the function of the neuron

1933 Thomas H. Morgan (U.S.), for discoveries on hereditary function of the chromosomes

1934 George H. Whipple, George R. Minot, and William P. Murphy (U.S.), for discovery of liver therapy against anemias

1935 Hans Spemann (Germany), for discovery of the organizer effect in embryonic development

1936 Sir Henry Dale (UK) and Otto Loewi (Germany), for discoveries on chemical transmission of nerve impulses

1937 Albert Szent-Györgyi von Nagyrapolt (Hungary), for discoveries on biological combustion

1938 Corneille Heymans (Belgium), for determining importance of sinus and aorta mechanisms in the regulation of respiration

1939 Gerhard Domagk (Germany), for antibacterial effect of prontocilate

1943 Henrik Dam (Denmark) and Edward A. Doisy (U.S.), for analysis of vitamin K

1944 Joseph Erlanger and Herbert Spencer Gasser (both U.S.), for work on functions of the nerve threads

1945 Sir Alexander Fleming, Ernst Boris Chain, and Sir Howard Florey (all UK), for discovery of penicillin

1946 Herman J. Muller (U.S.), for hereditary effects of X rays on genes

1947 Carl F. and Gerty T. Cori (U.S.), for work on animal starch metabolism; Bernardo A. Houssay (Argentina), for study of pituitary

1948 Paul Mueller (Switzerland), for discovery of insect-killing properties of DDT

1949 Walter Rudolf Hess (Switzerland), for research on brain control of body; and Antonio Caetano de Abreu Freire Egas Moniz (Portugal), for development of brain operation

1950 Philip S. Hench, Edward C. Kendall (both U.S.), and Tadeus Reichstein (Switzerland), for discoveries about hormones of adrenal cortex

1951 Max Theiler (South Africa), for development of anti-yellow-fever vaccine

1952 Selman A. Waksman (U.S.), for discovery of streptomycin

1953 Fritz A. Lipmann (Germany-U.S.) and Hans Adolph Krebs (Germany-UK), for studies of living cells

1954 John F. Enders, Thomas H. Weller, and Frederick C. Robbins (all U.S.), for work with cultivation of polio virus

1955 Hugo Theorell (Sweden), for work on oxidation enzymes

1956 Dickinson W. Richards, Jr., André F. Cournand (both U.S.), and Werner Forssmann (Germany), for new techniques in treating heart disease

1957 Daniel Bovet (Italy), for development of drugs to relieve allergies and relax muscles during surgery

1958 Joshua Lederberg (U.S.), for work with genetic mechanisms; George W. Beadie and Edward L. Tatum (both U.S.), for discovering how genes transmit hereditary characteristics

1959 Severo Ochoa and Arthur Kornberg (both U.S.), for discoveries related to compounds within chromosomes that play a vital role in heredity

1960 Sir Macfarlane Burnet (Australia) and Peter Brian Medawar (UK), for discovery of acquired immunological tolerance

1961 Georg von Bekesy (U.S.), for discoveries about physical mechanisms of stimulation within cochlea

1962 James D. Watson (U.S.), Maurice H. F. Wilkins, and Francis H. C. Crick (both UK), for determining structure of deoxyribonucleic acid (DNA)

1963 Alan Lloyd Hodgkin, Andrew Fielding Huxley (both UK), and Sir John Carew Eccles (Australia), for research on nerve cells

1964 Konrad E. Bloch (U.S.) and Feodor Lynen (Germany), for research on mechanism and regulation of cholesterol and fatty-acid metabolism

1965 François Jacob, André Lwolff, and Jacques Monod (all France), for study of regulatory activities in body cells

1966 Charles Brenton Huggins (U.S.), for studies in hormone treatment of cancer of prostate; Francis Peyton Rous (U.S.), for discovery of tumor-producing viruses

1967 Haldan K. Hartline, George Wald, and Ragnar Granit (all U.S.), for work on human eye

1968 Robert W. Holley, Har Gobind Khorana, and Marshall W. Nirenberg (all U.S.), for studies of genetic code

1969 Max Delbruck, Alfred D. Hershey, and Salvador E. Luria (all U.S.), for study of mechanism of virus infection in living cells

1970 Julius Axelrod (U.S.), Ulf S. von Euler (Sweden), and Sir Bernard Katz (UK), for studies of how nerve impulses are transmitted within the body

1971 Earl W. Sutherland, Jr. (U.S.), for research on how hormones work

1972 Gerald M. Edelman (U.S.), and Rodney R. Porter (UK), for research on the chemical structure and nature of antibodies

1973 Karl von Frisch, Konrad Lorenz (both Austria), and Nikolaas Tinbergen

(Netherlands), for their studies of individual and social behavior patterns

1974 George E. Palade, Christian de Duve (both U.S.), and Albert Claude (Belgium), for contributions to understanding inner workings of living cells

1975 David Baltimore, Howard M. Temin, and Renato Dulbecco (all U.S.), for work in interaction between tumor viruses and genetic material of the cell

1976 Baruch S. Blumberg and D. Carleton Gajdusek (both U.S.), for discoveries concerning new mechanisms for the origin and dissemination of infectious diseases

1977 Rosalyn S. Yalow, Roger C. L. Guillemin, and Andrew V. Schally (all U.S.), for research in role of hormones in chemistry of the body

1978 Daniel Nathans, Hamilton Smith (both U.S.), and Werner Arber (Switzerland), for discovery of restriction enzymes and their application to problems of molecular genetics

1979 Allan McLeod Cormack (U.S.) and Godfrey Newbold Hounsfield (UK), for developing computed axial tomography (CAT scan) X ray technique

1980 Baruj Benacerraf, George D. Snell (both U.S.), and Jean Dausset (France), for discoveries that explain how the structure of cells relates to organ transplants and diseases

1981 Roger W. Sperry, David H. Hubel (both U.S.), and Torsten N. Wiesel (Sweden), for studies vital to understanding the organization and functioning of the brain

1982 Sune Bergstrom, Bengt Samuelsson (both Sweden), and John R. Vane (UK), for research in prostaglandins, hormonelike substances involved in a wide range of illnesses

1983 Barbara McClintock (U.S.), for her discovery of mobile genes in the chromosomes of a plant that change the future generations of plants they produce

1984 Cesar Milstein (UK/Argentina), Georges J. F. Kohler (West Germany), and Niels K. Jerne (UK/Denmark), for their work in immunology

1985 Michael S. Brown and Joseph L. Goldstein (both U.S.), for their work, which has drastically widened our understanding of the cholesterol metabolism and increased our possibilities to prevent and treat atherosclerosis and heart attacks

1986 Rita Levi-Montalcini (dual U.S./Italy) and Stanley Cohen (U.S.), for their contributions to the understanding of substances that influence cell growth

1987 Susumu Tonegawa (Japan), for his discoveries of how the body can suddenly marshal its immunological defenses against millions of different disease agents that it has never encountered before

1988 Gertrude B. Elion, George H. Hitchings (both U.S.), and Sir James Black (UK), for their discoveries of important principles for drug treatment

1989 J. Michael Bishop and Harold E. Varmus (both U.S.), for their unifying theory of cancer development

1990 Joseph E. Murray and E. Donnall Thomas (both U.S.), for their pioneering work in transplants

1991 Erwin Neher and Bert Sakmann (both Germany), for their research, particularly for the development of a technique called patch clamp

1992 Edmond H. Fischer and Edwin G. Krebs (both U.S.), for their discovery of a regulatory mechanism affecting almost all cells

1993 Phillip A. Sharp (U.S.) and Richard J. Roberts (UK), for their independent discovery in 1977 of "split genes"

1994 Alfred G. Gilman and Martin Rodbell (both U.S.), for discovery of G-proteins that help cells respond to outside signals

1995 Edward B. Lewis, Eric F. Wieschaus (both U.S.), and Christiane Nüsslein-Volhard (Germany), for studies of the fruit fly that will help explain congenital malformations in humans

1996 Peter C. Doherty (Australia) and Rolf M. Zinkernagel (Switzerland), for discoveries about how the immune system recognizes virus-infected cells

1997 Stanley B. Prusiner (U.S.), for discovery of a new type of germ, called prions, that causes degenerative brain disorders

1998 Robert F. Furchgott, Louis J. Ignarro, and Ferid Murad (all U.S.), for discovering that nitric oxide acts as a signal in the cardiovascular system

1999 Günter Blobel (U.S.), for discovering that proteins have intrinsic signals that govern their transport and localization in the cell

2000 Arvid Carlsson (Sweden), Paul Greengard, and Eric R. Kandel (both U.S.), for discoveries concerning signal transduction in the nervous system

ECONOMIC SCIENCE

1969 Ragnar Frisch (Norway) and Jan Tinbergen (Netherlands), for work in econometrics (application of mathematics and statistical methods to economic theories and problems)

1970 Paul A. Samuelson (U.S.), for efforts to raise the level of scientific analysis in economic theory

1971 Simon Kuznets (U.S.), for developing concept of using a country's gross national product to determine its economic growth

1972 Kenneth J. Arrow (U.S.) and Sir John R. Hicks (UK), for theories that help to assess business risk and government economic and welfare policies

1973 Wassily Leontief (U.S.), for devising the input-output technique to determine how different sectors of an economy interact

1974 Gunnar Myrdal (Sweden) and Friedrich A. von Hayek (UK), for pioneering analysis of the interdependence of economic, social, and institutional phenomena

1975 Leonid V. Kantorovich (USSR) and Tjalling C. Koopmans (U.S.), for work on the theory of optimum allocation of resources

1976 Milton Friedman (U.S.), for work in consumption analysis and monetary history and theory, and for demonstration of complexity of stabilization policy

1977 Bertil Ohlin (Sweden) and James E. Meade (UK), for contributions to theory of international trade and international capital movements

1978 Herbert A. Simon (U.S.), for research into the decision-making process within economic organizations

1979 Sir Arthur Lewis (UK) and Theodore Schultz (U.S.), for work on economic problems of developing nations

1980 Lawrence R. Klein (U.S.), for developing models for forecasting economic trends and shaping policies to deal with them

1981 James Tobin (U.S.), for analyses of financial markets and their influence on spending and saving by families and businesses

1982 George J. Stigler (U.S.), for work on government regulation in the economy and the functioning of industry

1983 Gerard Debreu (U.S.), in recognition of his work on the basic economic problem of how prices operate to balance what producers supply with what buyers want

1984 Sir Richard Stone (UK) for his work to develop the systems widely used to measure the performance of national economics

1985 Franco Modigliani (U.S.), for his pioneering work in analyzing the behavior of household savers and the functioning of financial markets

1986 James M. Buchanan (U.S.), for his development of new methods for analyzing economic and political decision-making

1987 Robert M. Solow (U.S.), for seminal contributions to the theory of economic growth

1988 Maurice Allais (France), for his pioneering development of theories to better understand market behavior and the efficient use of resources

1989 Trygve Haavelmo (Norway), for his pioneering work in methods for testing economic theories

1990 Harry M. Markowitz, William F. Sharpe, and Merton H. Miller (all U.S.), whose work provided new tools for weighing the risks and rewards of different investments and for valuing corporate stocks and bonds

1991 Ronald Coase (U.S.), for his pioneering work in how property rights and the cost of doing business affect the economy

1992 Gary S. Becker (U.S.), for "having extended the domain of economic theory to aspects of human behavior which had previously been dealt with—if at all—by other social science disciplines"

1993 Robert W. Fogel and Douglass C. North (both U.S.), for their work in economic history

1994 John F. Nash, John C. Harsanyi (both U.S.), and Reinhard Selten (Germany), for their pioneering work in game theory

1995 Robert E. Lucas, Jr. (U.S.), for having had the greatest influence on macroeconomic research since 1970

1996 James A. Mirrlees (UK) and William Vickrey (U.S.), for "their fundamental contributions to the economic theory of incentives"

1997 Robert C. Merton and Myron S. Scholes (both U.S.), for developing a formula that determines the value of stock options and other derivatives

1998 Amartya Sen (India), for his contributions to welfare economics

1999 Robert A. Mundell (Canada), for his work on monetary dynamics and optimum currency areas

2000 James J. Heckman and Daniel L. McFadden (both U.S.), for developing methods used in statistical analysis of individual and household behavior

Pulitzer Prizes

For years not listed, no award was made.

PULITZER PRIZES IN JOURNALISM

Meritorious Public Service

1918 *New York Times;* also special award to Minna Lewinson and Henry Beetle Hough

1919 *Milwaukee Journal*
1921 *Boston Post*
1922 *New York World*
1923 *Memphis Commercial Appeal*
1924 *New York World*
1926 *Columbus* (Ga.) *Enquirer Sun*
1927 *Canton* (Ohio) *Daily News*
1928 *Indianapolis Times*
1929 *New York Evening World*
1931 *Atlanta Constitution*
1932 *Indianapolis News*
1933 *New York World-Telegram*
1934 *Medford* (Ore.) *Mail Tribune*
1935 *Sacramento Bee*
1936 *Cedar Rapids* (Iowa) *Gazette*

1937 *St. Louis Post-Dispatch*
1938 *Bismarck* (N.D.) *Tribune*
1939 *Miami Daily News*
1940 *Waterbury* (Conn.) *Republican* and *American*
1941 *St. Louis Post-Dispatch*
1942 *Los Angeles Times*
1943 *Omaha World-Herald*
1944 *New York Times*
1945 *Detroit Free Press*
1946 *Scranton* (Pa.) *Times*
1947 *Baltimore Sun*
1948 *St. Louis Post-Dispatch*
1949 *(Lincoln) Nebraska State Journal*
1950 *Chicago Daily News;* and *St. Louis Post-Dispatch*
1951 *Miami Herald;* and *Brooklyn Eagle*
1952 *St. Louis Post-Dispatch*
1953 *Whiteville* (N.C.) *News Reporter;* and *Tabor City* (N.C.) *Tribune*
1954 *Newsday* (Garden City, N.Y.)

1955	*Columbus* (Ga.) *Ledger* and *Sunday Ledger-Enquirer*
1956	*Watsonville* (Calif.) *Register-Pajaronian*
1957	*Chicago Daily News*
1958	(Little Rock) *Arkansas Gazette*
1959	*Utica* (N.Y.) *Observer Dispatch* and *Utica Daily Press*
1960	*Los Angeles Times*
1961	*Amarillo* (Tex.) *Globe-Times*
1962	*Panama City* (Fla.) *News-Herald*
1963	*Chicago Daily News*
1964	*St. Petersburg* (Fla.) *Times*
1965	*Hutchinson* (Kans.) *News*
1966	*Boston Globe*
1967	*Louisville Courier-Journal* and *Milwaukee Journal*
1968	*Riverside* (Calif.) *Press-Enterprise*
1969	*Los Angeles Times*
1970	*Newsday* (Garden City, N.Y.)
1971	*Winston–Salem* (N.C.) *Journal and Sentinel*
1972	*New York Times*
1973	*Washington Post*
1974	*Newsday* (Garden City, N.Y.)
1975	*Boston Globe*
1976	*Anchorage* (Alaska) *Daily News*
1977	*Lufkin* (Tex.) *News*
1978	*Philadelphia Inquirer*
1979	*Point Reyes* (Calif.) *Light*
1980	Gannett News Service
1981	*Charlotte* (N.C.) *Observer*
1982	*Detroit News*
1983	*Jackson* (Miss.) *Clarion-Ledger*
1984	*Los Angeles Times*
1985	*Fort Worth Star-Telegram*
1986	*Denver Post*
1987	*Pittsburgh Press,* reporting by Andrew Schneider and Matthew Brelis
1988	*Charlotte* (N.C.) *Observer*
1989	*Anchorage Daily News*
1990	*Philadelphia Inquirer* and *Washington* (N.C.) *Daily News*
1991	*Des Moines Register,* reporting by Jane Schorer
1992	*Sacramento Bee* for "The Sierra in Peril" series by Tom Knudson
1993	*Miami Herald*
1994	*Akron* (Ohio) *Beacon Journal*
1995	*Virgin Islands Daily News*
1996	*News and Observer* (Raleigh, N.C.)
1997	*Times-Picayune* (New Orleans, La.)
1998	*Grand Forks* (N.D.) *Herald*
1999	*Washington Post*
2000	*Washington Post*
2001	*Oregonian*

Editorial

1917	*New York Tribune*
1918	*Louisville Courier-Journal*
1920	Harvey E. Newbranch *(Omaha Evening World-Herald)*
1922	Frank M. O'Brien *(New York Herald)*
1923	William Allen White *(Emporia* [Kan.] *Gazette)*
1924	*Boston Herald;* special prize: Frank I. Cobb *(New York World)*
1925	*Charleston* (S.C.) *News and Courier*
1926	Edward M. Kingsbury *(New York Times)*
1927	F. Lauriston Bullard *(Boston Herald)*
1928	Grover Cleveland Hall *(Montgomery* [Ala.] *Advertiser)*
1929	Louis Isaac Jaffe *(Norfolk Virginian-Pilot)*
1931	Charles S. Ryckman *(Fremont* [Neb.] *Tribune)*

1933	*Kansas City* (Mo.) *Star*
1934	E. P. Chase *(Atlantic* [Iowa] *News Telegraph)*
1936	Felix Morley *(Washington Post);* George B. Parker (Scripps–Howard Newspapers)
1937	John W. Owens *(Baltimore Sun)*
1938	W. W. Waymack *(Des Moines Register and Tribune)*
1939	Ronald G. Callvert *(Portland Oregonian)*
1940	Bart Howard *(St. Louis Post-Dispatch)*
1941	Reuben Maury *(New York Daily News)*
1942	Geoffrey Parsons *(New York Herald Tribune)*
1943	Forrest W. Seymour *(Des Moines Register and Tribune)*
1944	Henry J. Haskell *(Kansas City* [Mo.] *Star)*
1945	George W. Potter *(Providence* [R.I.] *Journal-Bulletin)*
1946	Hodding Carter ([Greenville, Miss.] *Delta Democrat-Times)*
1947	William H. Grimes *(Wall Street Journal)*
1948	Virginius Dabney *(Richmond Times-Dispatch)*
1949	John H. Crider *(Boston Herald);* Herbert Elliston *(Washington Post)*
1950	Carl M. Saunders *(Jackson* [Mich.] *Citizen Patriot)*
1951	William H. Fitzpatrick *(New Orleans States)*
1952	Louis LaCoss *(St. Louis Globe-Democrat)*
1953	Vermont C. Royster *(Wall Street Journal)*
1954	Don Murray *(Boston Herald)*
1955	Royce Howes *(Detroit Free Press)*
1956	Lauren K. Soth *(Des Moines Register and Tribune)*
1957	Buford Boone *(Tuscaloosa* [Ala.] *News)*
1958	Harry S. Ashmore *(Arkansas Gazette)*
1959	Ralph McGill *(Atlanta Constitution)*
1960	Lenoir Chambers *(Virginian-Pilot)*
1961	William J. Dorvillier *(San Juan* [P.R.] *Star)*
1962	Thomas M. Storke *(Santa Barbara* [Calif.] *News-Press)*
1963	Ira B. Harkey, Jr. *(Pascagoula* [Miss.] *Chronicle)*
1964	Hazel Brannon Smith *(Lexington* [Miss.] *Advertiser)*
1965	John R. Harrison *(Gainesville* [Fla.] *Daily Sun)*
1966	Robert Lasch *(St. Louis Post-Dispatch)*
1967	Eugene Patterson *(Atlanta Constitution)*
1968	John S. Knight *(Knight Newspapers)*
1969	Paul Greenberg *(Pine Bluff* [Ark.] *Commercial)*
1970	Phillip L. Geyelin *(Washington Post)*
1971	Horance G. Davis, Jr. *(Gainesville* [Fla.] *Sun)*
1972	John Strohmeyer *(Bethlehem* [Pa.] *Globe Times)*
1973	Roger Bourne Linscott *(Berkshire Eagle* [Pittsfield, Mass.])
1974	F. Gilman Spencer *(Trenton* [N.J.] *Trentonian)*
1975	John Daniell Maurice *(Charleston* [W. Va.] *Daily Mail)*
1976	Philip P. Kerby *(Los Angeles Times)*
1977	Warren L. Lerude, Foster Church, and Norman F. Cardoza *(Reno* [Nev.] *Gazette and Nevada State Journal)*
1978	Meg Greenfield *(Washington Post)*
1979	Edwin M. Yoder, Jr. *(Washington Star)*
1980	Robert L. Bartley *(Wall Street Journal)*
1982	Jack Rosenthal *(New York Times)*
1983	*Miami Herald*
1984	Albert Scardino *(Georgia Gazette)*
1985	Richard Aregood *(Philadelphia Daily News)*
1986	Jack Fuller *(Chicago Tribune)*

1987 Jonathan Freedman (San Diego Tribune)
1988 Jane E. Healy (Orlando Sentinel)
1989 Lois Wille (Chicago Tribune)
1990 Thomas J. Hylton (Pottstown [Pa.] Mercury)
1991 Ron Casey, Harold Jackson, and Joey Kennedy (Birmingham [Ala.] News)
1992 Maria Henson (Lexington [Ky.] Herald-Leader)
1994 R. Bruce Dold (Chicago Tribune)
1995 Jeffrey Good (St. Petersburg [Fla.] Times)
1996 Robert B. Semple, Jr. (New York Times)
1997 Michael Gartner (Daily Tribune [Ames, Iowa])
1998 Bernard L. Stein (The Riverdale Press [Bronx, N.Y.])
1999 Editorial Board (Daily News [New York, N.Y.])
2000 John C. Bersia (The Orlando Sentinel [Orlando, Fla.])
2001 David Moats (Rutland Herald [Rutland, Vt.])

Correspondence

1929 Paul Scott Mowrer (Chicago Daily News)
1930 Leland Stowe (New York Herald Tribune)
1931 H. R. Knickerbocker (Philadelphia Public Ledger and New York Evening Post)
1932 Walter Duranty (New York Times); Charles G. Ross (St. Louis Post-Dispatch)
1933 Edgar Ansel Mowrer (Chicago Daily News)
1934 Frederick T. Birchall (New York Times)
1935 Arthur Krock (New York Times)
1936 Wilfred C. Barber (Chicago Tribune)
1937 Anne O'Hare McCormick (New York Times)
1938 Arthur Krock (New York Times)
1939 Louis P. Lochner (Associated Press)
1940 Otto D. Tolischus (New York Times)
1941 Group award[1]
1942 Carlos P. Romulo (Philippines Herald)
1943 Hanson W. Baldwin (New York Times)
1944 Ernie Pyle (Scripps–Howard Newspaper Alliance)
1945 Harold V. (Hal) Boyle (Associated Press)
1946 Arnaldo Cortesi (New York Times)
1947 Brooks Atkinson (New York Times)

1. For the public services and the individual achievements of American news reporters in the war zones.

Editorial Cartooning

1922 Rollin Kirby (New York World)
1924 Jay Norwood Darling (New York Tribune)
1925 Rollin Kirby (New York World)
1926 D. R. Fitzpatrick (St. Louis Post-Dispatch)
1927 Nelson Harding (Brooklyn Eagle)
1928 Nelson Harding (Brooklyn Eagle)
1929 Rollin Kirby (New York World)
1930 Charles R. Macauley (Brooklyn Eagle)
1931 Edmund Duffy (Baltimore Sun)
1932 John T. McCutcheon (Chicago Tribune)
1933 H. M. Talburt (Washington Daily News)
1934 Edmund Duffy (Baltimore Sun)
1935 Ross A. Lewis (Milwaukee Journal)
1937 C. D. Batchelor (New York Daily News)
1938 Vaughn Shoemaker (Chicago Daily News)
1939 Charles G. Werner (Daily Oklahoman [Oklahoma City])
1940 Edmund Duffy (Baltimore Sun)
1941 Jacob Burck (Chicago Times)
1942 Herbert L. Block (NEA Service)
1943 Jay Norwood Darling (New York Herald Tribune)
1944 Clifford K. Berryman (Washington Evening Star)
1945 Bill Mauldin (United Features Syndicate)
1946 Bruce Alexander Russell (Los Angeles Times)

1947 Vaughn Shoemaker (Chicago Daily News)
1948 Reuben L. Goldberg (New York Sun)
1949 Lute Pease (Newark Evening News)
1950 James T. Berryman (Washington Evening Star)
1951 Reg (Reginald W.) Manning (Arizona Republic [Phoenix])
1952 Fred L. Packer (New York Mirror)
1953 Edward D. Kuekes (Cleveland Plain Dealer)
1954 Herbert L. Block (Washington Post and Times-Herald)
1955 Daniel R. Fitzpatrick (St. Louis Post-Dispatch)
1956 Robert York (Louisville Times)
1957 Tom Little (Nashville Tennessean)
1958 Bruce M. Shanks (Buffalo Evening News)
1959 Bill Mauldin (St. Louis Post-Dispatch)
1961 Carey Orr (Chicago Tribune)
1962 Edmund S. Valtman (Hartford Times)
1963 Frank Miller (Des Moines Register)
1964 Paul Conrad (formerly of Denver Post, later of Los Angeles Times)
1966 Don Wright (Miami News)
1967 Patrick B. Oliphant (Denver Post)
1968 Eugene Gray Payne (Charlotte [N.C.] Observer)
1969 John Fischetti (Chicago Daily News)
1970 Thomas F. Darcy (Newsday [Garden City, N.Y.])
1971 Paul Conrad (Los Angeles Times)
1972 Jeffrey K. MacNelly (Richmond [Va.] News Leader)
1974 Paul Szep (Boston Globe)
1975 Garry Trudeau (Universal Press Syndicate)
1976 Tony Auth (Philadelphia Inquirer)
1977 Paul Szep (Boston Globe)
1978 Jeffrey K. MacNelly (Richmond [Va.] News Leader)
1979 Herbert L. Block (Washington Post)
1980 Don Wright (Miami News)
1981 Mike Peters (Dayton [Ohio] Daily News)
1982 Ben Sargent (Austin [Tex.] American-Statesman)
1983 Richard Locher (Chicago Tribune)
1984 Paul Conrad (Los Angeles Times)
1985 Jeff MacNelly (Chicago Tribune)
1986 Jules Feiffer (Village Voice)
1987 Berke Breathed (Washington Post Writers Group)
1988 Doug Marlette (Atlanta Constitution and Charlotte [N.C.] Observer)
1989 Jack Higgins (Chicago Sun-Times)
1990 Tom Toles (Buffalo News)
1991 Jim Borgman (Cincinnati Inquirer)
1992 Signe Wilkinson (Philadelphia Daily News)
1993 Stephen R. Benson (Arizona Republic)
1994 Michael P. Ramirez (Commercial Appeal, Memphis)
1995 Mike Luckovich (Atlanta Constitution)
1996 Jim Morin (Miami Herald)
1997 Walt Handelsman (Times-Picayune)
1998 Stephen P. Breen (Asbury Park [N.J.] Press)
1999 David Horsey (Seattle Post-Intelligencer)
2000 Joel Pett (Lexington [Ky.] Herald-Leader)
2001 Ann Telnaes (Los Angeles Times Syndicate)

News Photography

1942 Milton Brooks (Detroit News)
1943 Frank Noel (Associated Press)
1944 Frank Filan (Associated Press); Earle L. Bunker (Omaha World-Herald)
1945 Joe Rosenthal (Associated Press)

1947 Arnold Hardy
1948 Frank Cushing *(Boston Traveler)*
1949 Nat Fein *(New York Herald Tribune)*
1950 Bill Crouch *(Oakland Tribune)*
1951 Max Desfor (Associated Press)
1952 John Robinson and Don Ultang *(Des Moines Register & Tribune)*
1953 William M. Gallagher *(Flint* [Mich.] *Journal)*
1954 Mrs. Walter M. Schau
1955 John L. Gaunt, Jr. *(Los Angeles Times)*
1956 *New York Daily News*
1957 Harry A. Trask *(Boston Traveler)*
1958 William C. Beall *(Washington Daily News)*
1959 William Seaman *(Minneapolis Star)*
1960 Andrew Lopez (United Press International)
1961 Yasushi Nagao (Mainichi Newspapers, Tokyo)
1962 Paul Vathis (Harrisburg [Pa.] bureau of Associated Press)
1963 Hector Rondon *(La Republica,* Caracas, Venezuela)
1964 Robert H. Jackson *(Dallas Times Herald)*
1965 Horst Faas (Associated Press)
1966 Kyoichi Sawada (United Press International)
1967 Jack R. Thornell (Associated Press)
1968 News: Rocco Morabito *(Jacksonville* [Fla.] *Journal);* features: Toshio Sakai (United Press International)
1969 Spot news: Edward T. Adams (Associated Press); features: Moneta Sleet, Jr.
1970 Spot news: Steve Starr (Associated Press); features: Dallas Kinney *(Palm Beach Post)*
1971 Spot news: John Paul Filo *(Valley Daily News* and *Daily Dispatch* [Tarentum and New Kensington, Pa.]); features: Jack Dykinga *(Chicago Sun-Times)*
1972 Spot news: Horst Faas and Michel Laurent (Associated Press); features: Dave Kennerly (United Press International)
1973 Spot news: Huynh Cong Ut *(Associated Press);* features: Brian Lanker *(Topeka Capital-Journal)*
1974 Spot news: Anthony K. Roberts (Associated Press); features: Slava Veder (Associated Press)
1975 Spot news: Gerald H. Gay *(Seattle Times);* features: Matthew Lewis *(Washington Post)*
1976 Spot news: Stanley J. Forman *(Boston Herald-American);* features: photographic staff of *Louisville Courier-Journal* and *Times*
1977 Spot news: Neal Ulevich (Associated Press) and Stanley J. Forman *(Boston Herald-American);* features: Robin Hood *(Chattanooga News-Free Press)*
1978 Spot news: John Blair, freelance, Evansville, Ind.; features: J. Ross Baughman (Associated Press)
1979 Spot news: Thomas J. Kelly, 3rd *(Pottstown* [Pa.] *Mercury);* features: photographic staff of *Boston Herald-American*
1980 Features: Erwin H. Hagler *(Dallas Times Herald)*
1981 Spot news: Larry C. Price *(Fort Worth Star-Telegram);* features: Taro M. Yamasaki *(Detroit Free Press)*
1982 Spot news: Ron Edmonds (Associated Press); features: John H. White *(Chicago Sun-Times)*
1983 Spot news: Bill Foley (Associated Press); features: James B. Dickman *(Dallas Times Herald)*

1984 Spot news: Stan Grossfeld *(Boston Globe);* features: Anthony Suau *(Denver Post)*
1985 Spot news: photographic staff of *Register,* Santa Ana, Calif.; features: Stan Grossfeld *(Boston Globe)*
1986 Spot news: Michel duCille and Carol Guzy *(Miami Herald);* features: Tom Gralish *(Philadelphia Inquirer)*
1987 Spot news: Kim Komenich *(San Francisco Examiner);* features: David Peterson *(Des Moines Register)*
1988 Spot news: Scott Shaw *(Odessa* [Texas] *American);* features: Michel duCille *(Miami Herald)*
1989 Spot news: Ron Olshwanger *(St. Louis Post-Dispatch);* features: Manny Crisostomo *(Detroit Free Press)*
1990 Spot news: *Oakland Tribune;* features: David C. Turnley *(Detroit Free Press)*
1991 Spot news: Greg Marinovich (Associated Press); features: William Snyder *(Dallas Morning News)*
1992 Spot news: Associated Press staff; features: John Kaplan *(Herald* [Monterey, Calif.] and *Pittsburgh Post–Gazette)*
1993 Spot news: William Snyder and Ken Geiger *(Dallas Morning News);* features: Associated Press
1994 Spot news: Paul Watson *(Toronto Star);* features: Kevin Carter, freelancer for *New York Times*
1995 Spot news: Carol Guzy *(Washington Post);* features: Associated Press Staff
1996 Spot news: Charles Porter IV, freelance photographer for Associated Press; features: Stephanie Walsh, freelance photographer for Newhouse News Service
1997 Spot news: Annie Wells *(Press Democrat* [Santa Rosa, Calif.]); features: Alexander Zemlianichenko (Associated Press)
1998 Spot news: Martha Rial *(Pittsburgh Post–Gazette);* features: Clarence Williams *(Los Angeles Times)*
1999 Spot news: Associated Press photo staff; features: Associated Press photo staff
2000 Breaking news: photographic staff of *Denver Rocky Mountain News;* features: Carol Guzy, Michael Williamson, and Lucian Perkins *(Washington Post)*
2001 Breaking news: Alan Diaz (Associated Press); features: Matt Rainey *(Star-Ledger* [Newark, N.J.])

National Telegraphic Reporting
1942 Louis Stark *(New York Times)*
1944 Dewey L. Fleming *(Baltimore Sun)*
1945 James Reston *(New York Times)*
1946 Edward A. Harris *(St. Louis Post-Dispatch)*
1947 Edward T. Folliard *(Washington Post)*

National Reporting
1948 Bert Andrews *(New York Herald Tribune);* Nat S. Finney *(Minneapolis Tribune)*
1949 C. P. Trussell *(New York Times)*
1950 Edwin O. Guthman *(Seattle Times)*
1952 Anthony Leviero *(New York Times)*
1953 Don Whitehead (Associated Press)
1954 Richard Wilson (Cowles Newspapers)
1955 Anthony Lewis *(Washington Daily News)*
1956 Charles L. Bartlett *(Chattanooga Times)*
1957 James Reston *(New York Times)*

1958 Relman Morin (Associated Press) and Clark Mollenhoff *(Des Moines Register & Tribune)*
1959 Howard Van Smith *(Miami News)*
1960 Vance Trimble (Scripps-Howard Newspaper Alliance)
1961 Edward R. Cony *(Wall Street Journal)*
1962 Nathan G. Caldwell and Gene S. Graham *(Nashville Tennessean)*
1963 Anthony Lewis *(New York Times)*
1964 Merriman Smith (United Press International)
1965 Louis M. Kohlmeier *(Wall Street Journal)*
1966 Haynes Johnson *(Washington Evening Star)*
1967 Stanley Penn and Monroe Karmin *(Wall Street Journal)*
1968 Howard James *(Christian Science Monitor);* Nathan K. (Nick) Kotz *(Des Moines Register and Minneapolis Tribune)*
1969 Robert Cahn *(Christian Science Monitor)*
1970 William J. Eaton *(Chicago Daily News)*
1971 Lucinda Franks and Thomas Powers (United Press International)
1972 Jack Anderson *(United Feature Syndicate)*
1973 Robert Boyd and Clark Hoyt *(Knight Newspapers)*
1974 Jack White *(Providence* [R.I.] *Journal-Bulletin);* James R. Polk *(Washington Star-News)*
1975 Donald L. Barlett and James B. Steele *(Philadelphia Inquirer)*
1976 James Risser *(Des Moines Register)*
1977 Walter Mears (Associated Press)
1978 Gaylord D. Shaw *(Los Angeles Times)*
1979 James Risser *(Des Moines Register)*
1980 Bette Swenson Orsini and Charles Stafford *(St. Petersburg Times)*
1981 John M. Crewdson *(New York Times)*
1982 Rick Atkinson *(Kansas City* [Mo.] *Times)*
1983 *Boston Globe*
1984 John N. Wilford *(New York Times)*
1985 Thomas J. Knudson *(Des Moines Register)*
1986 Craig Flournoy and George Rodrigue *(Dallas Morning News)* and Arthur Howe *(Philadelphia Inquirer)*
1987 *Miami Herald,* staff; *New York Times,* staff
1988 Tim Weiner *(Philadelphia Inquirer)*
1989 Donald L. Barlett and James B. Steele *(Philadelphia Inquirer)*
1990 Ross Anderson, Bill Dietrich, Mary Ann Gwinn, and Eric Nalder *(Seattle Times)*
1991 Marjie Lundstrom and Rochelle Sharpe (Gannett News Service)
1992 Jeff Taylor and Mike McGraw *(Kansas City Star)*
1993 David Maraniss *(Washington Post)*
1994 Eileen Welsome *(Albuquerque* [N.M.] *Tribune)*
1995 Tony Horwitz *(Wall Street Journal)*
1996 Alix M. Freedman *(Wall Street Journal)*
1997 *Wall Street Journal* staff
1998 Russell Carollo and Jeff Nesmith *(Dayton* [Ohio] *Daily News)*
1999 *New York Times* staff
2000 *Wall Street Journal* staff
2001 *New York Times* staff

International Telegraphic Reporting

1942 Laurence Edmund Allen (Associated Press)
1943 Ira Wolfert (North American Newspaper Alliance, Inc.)
1944 Daniel De Luce (Associated Press)
1945 Mark S. Watson *(Baltimore Sun)*
1946 Homer W. Bigart *(New York Herald Tribune)*
1947 Eddy Gilmore (Associated Press)

International Reporting

1948 Paul W. Ward *(Baltimore Sun)*
1949 Price Day *(Baltimore Sun)*
1950 Edmund Stevens *(Christian Science Monitor)*
1951 Keyes Beech and Fred Sparks *(Chicago Daily News);* Homer Bigart and Marguerite Higgins *(New York Herald Tribune);* Relman Morin and Don Whitehead (Associated Press)
1952 John M. Hightower (Associated Press)
1953 Austin C. Wehrwein *(Milwaukee Journal)*
1954 Jim G. Lucas (Scripps-Howard Newspapers)
1955 Harrison E. Salisbury *(New York Times)*
1956 William Randolph Hearst, Jr., and Frank Conniff (Hearst Newspapers); Kingsbury Smith (INS)
1957 Russell Jones (United Press)
1958 *New York Times*
1959 Joseph Martin and Philip Santora *(New York Daily News)*
1960 A. M. Rosenthal *(New York Times)*
1961 Lynn Heinzerling (Associated Press)
1962 Walter Lippmann (New York Herald Tribune Syndicate)
1963 Hal Hendrix *(Miami News)*
1964 Malcolm W. Browne (Associated Press); David Halberstam *(New York Times)*
1965 J. A. Livingston *(Philadelphia Bulletin)*
1966 Peter Arnett (Associated Press)
1967 R. John Hughes *(Christian Science Monitor)*
1968 Alfred Friendly *(Washington Post)*
1969 William Tuohy *(Los Angeles Times)*
1970 Seymour M. Hersh (Dispatch News Service)
1971 Jimmie Lee Hoagland *(Washington Post)*
1972 Peter R. Kann *(Wall Street Journal)*
1973 Max Frankel *(New York Times)*
1974 Hedrick Smith *(New York Times)*
1975 William Mullen and Ovie Carter *(Chicago Tribune)*
1976 Sydney H. Schanberg *(New York Times)*
1978 Henry Kamm *(New York Times)*
1979 Richard Ben Cramer *(Philadelphia Inquirer)*
1980 Joel Brinkley and Jay Mather *(Louisville Courier-Journal)*
1981 Shirley Christian *(Miami Herald)*
1982 John Darnton *(New York Times)*
1983 Thomas L. Friedman *(New York Times)*
1984 Karen E. House *(Wall Street Journal)*
1985 Josh Friedman, Dennis Bell, and Ozier Muhammad *(Newsday)*
1986 Lewis M. Simons, Pete Carey, and Katherine Ellison *(San Jose Mercury News)*
1987 Michael Parks *(Los Angeles Times)*
1988 Thomas L. Friedman *(New York Times)*
1989 Bill Keller *(New York Times);* Glenn Frankel *(Washington Post)*
1990 Nicholas D. Kristof and Sheryl WuDunn *(New York Times)*
1991 Caryle Murphy *(Washington Post);* Serge Schmemann *(New York Times)*
1992 Patrick J. Sloyan *(Newsday)*
1993 John F. Burns *(New York Times);* Roy Gutman *(Newsday)*
1994 *Dallas Morning News* team
1995 Mark Fritz (Associated Press)
1996 David Rohde *(Christian Science Monitor)*
1997 John F. Burns *(New York Times)*
1998 *New York Times* staff
1999 *Wall Street Journal* staff
2000 Mark Schoofs *(Village Voice* [New York, N.Y.])

2001 Ian Johnson *(Wall Street Journal)* and Paul Salopek *(Chicago Tribune)*

Reporting
1917 Herbert B. Swope *(New York World)*
1918 Harold A. Littledale *(New York Evening Post)*
1920 John J. Leary, Jr. *(New York World)*
1921 Louis Seibold *(New York World)*
1922 Kirke L. Simpson (Associated Press)
1923 Alva Johnston *(New York Times)*
1924 Magner White *(San Diego Sun)*
1925 James W. Mulroy and Alvin H. Goldstein *(Chicago Daily News)*
1926 William Burke Miller *(Louisville Courier-Journal)*
1927 John T. Rogers *(St. Louis Post-Dispatch)*
1929 Paul Y. Anderson *(St. Louis Post-Dispatch)*
1930 Russell D. Owen *(New York Times)*; special award: W. O. Dapping *(Auburn* [N.Y.] *Citizen)*
1931 A. B. MacDonald *(Kansas City* [Mo.] *Star)*
1932 W. C. Richards, D. D. Martin, J. S. Pooler, F. D. Webb, and J. N. W. Sloan *(Detroit Free Press)*
1933 Francis A. Jamieson (Associated Press)
1934 Royce Brier *(San Francisco Chronicle)*
1935 William H. Taylor *(New York Herald Tribune)*
1936 Lauren D. Lyman *(New York Times)*
1937 John J. O'Neill *(New York Herald Tribune)*; William Leonard Laurence *(New York Times)*; Howard W. Blakeslee (Associated Press); Gobind Behari Lal (Universal Service); David Dietz (Scripps–Howard Newspapers)
1938 Raymond Sprigle *(Pittsburg Post-Gazette)*
1939 Thomas L. Stokes *(New York World-Telegram)*
1940 S. Burton Heath *(New York World-Telegram)*
1941 Westbrook Pegler *(New York World-Telegram)*
1942 Stanton Delaplane *(San Francisco Chronicle)*
1943 George Weller *(Chicago Daily News)*
1944 Paul Schoenstein and associates *(New York Journal-American)*
1945 Jack S. McDowell *(San Francisco Call-Bulletin)*
1946 William Leonard Laurence *(New York Times)*
1947 Frederick Woltman *(New York World-Telegram)*
1948 George E. Goodwin *(Atlanta Journal)*
1949 Malcolm Johnson *(New York Sun)*
1950 Meyer Berger *(New York Times)*
1951 Edward S. Montgomery *(San Francisco Examiner)*
1952 George de Carvalho *(San Francisco Chronicle)*
1953 Editorial staff *(Providence Journal and Evening Bulletin)*;[1] Edward J. Mowery *(New York World-Telegram and Sun)*[2]
1954 *Vicksburg* (Miss.) *Sunday Post-Herald*;[1] Alvin Scott McCoy *(Kansas City* [Mo.] *Star)*[2]
1955 Mrs. Caro Brown *(Alice* [Tex.] *Daily Echo)*;[1] Roland Kenneth Towery *(Cuero* [Tex.] *Record)*[2]
1956 Lee Hills *(Detroit Free Press)*;[1] Arthur Daley *(New York Times)*[2]
1957 *Salt Lake Tribune*;[1] Wallace Turner and William Lambert *(Portland Oregonian)*[2]
1958 *Fargo* [N.D.] *Forum*;[1] George Beveridge *(Washington* [D.C.] *Evening Star)*[2]
1959 Mary Lou Werner *(Washington* [D.C.] *Evening Star)*;[1] John Harold Brislin *(Scranton* [Pa.] *Tribune & Scrantonian)*[2]

1960 Jack Nelson *(Atlanta Constitution)*;[1] Miriam Ottenberg *(Washington Evening Star)*[2]
1961 Sanche de Gramont *(New York Herald Tribune)*;[1] Edgar May *(Buffalo Evening News)*[2]
1962 Robert D. Mullins *(Deseret News,* Salt Lake City);[1] George Bliss *(Chicago Tribune)*[2]
1963 Sylvan Fox, Anthony Shannon, and William Longgood *(New York World-Telegram and Sun)*;[1] Oscar Griffin, Jr. (former editor of *Pecos* [Tex.] *Independent and Enterprise,* now on staff of *Houston Chronicle)*[2]

1. Reporting under pressure of edition deadlines.
2. Reporting not under pressure of edition deadlines.

General Local Reporting
1964 Norman C. Miller *(Wall Street Journal)*
1965 Melvin H. Ruder *(Hungry Horse News,* Columbia Falls, Mont.)
1966 *Los Angeles Times* staff
1967 Robert V. Cox *(Chambersburg* [Pa.] *Public Opinion)*
1968 *Detroit Free Press* staff
1969 John Fetterman *(Louisville Times and Courier-Journal)*
1970 Thomas Fitzpatrick *(Chicago Sun-Times)*
1971 Akron (Ohio) *Beacon* staff
1972 Richard Cooper and John Machacek *(Rochester* [N.Y.] *Times-Union)*
1973 *Chicago Tribune*
1974 Arthur M. Petacque and Hugh F. Hough *(Chicago Sun-Times)*
1975 Xenia (Ohio) *Daily Gazette*
1976 Gene Miller *(Miami Herald)*
1977 Margo Huston *(Milwaukee Journal)*
1978 Richard Whitt *(Louisville Courier-Journal)*
1979 Staff of San Diego (Calif.) *Evening Tribune*
1980 Staff of *Philadelphia Inquirer*
1981 *Longview* (Wash.) *Daily News*
1982 *Kansas City* (Mo.) *Star* and *Kansas City* (Mo.) *Times*
1983 *Fort Wayne* (Ind.) *News-Sentinel*
1984 *Newsday*

General News Reporting
1985 Thomas Turcol *(Virginian-Pilot and Ledger-Star)*
1986 Edna Buchanan *(Miami Herald)*
1987 *Akron Beacon Journal* staff
1988 *Alabama Journal* (Montgomery) staff; *Lawrence* (Mass.) *Eagle-Tribune* staff
1989 *Louisville Courier-Journal* staff
1990 San Jose (Calif.) *Mercury News*

Spot News Reporting
1991 *Miami Herald* staff
1992 *New York Newsday* staff
1993 *Los Angeles Times* staff
1994 *New York Times* staff
1995 *Los Angeles Times* staff
1996 Robert D. McFadden *(New York Times)*
1997 *Newsday* staff (Long Island, N.Y.)

Breaking News Reporting
1998 *Los Angeles Times* staff
1999 *Hartford Courant* staff
2000 *Denver Post* staff
2001 *The Miami Herald* staff

Special Local Reporting

1964 James V. Magee, Albert V. Gaudiosi, and Frederick A. Meyer *(Philadelphia Bulletin)*
1965 Gene Goltz *(Houston Post)*
1966 John A. Frasca *(Tampa Tribune)*
1967 Gene Miller *(Miami Herald)*
1968 J. Anthony Lukas *(New York Times)*
1969 Albert L. Delugach and Denny Walsh *(St. Louis Globe-Democrat)*
1970 Harold Eugene Martin *(Montgomery Advertiser)*
1971 William Hugh Jones *(Chicago Tribune)*
1972 Timothy Leland, Gerard N. O'Neill, Stephen A. Kurkjian, and Ann DeSantis *(Boston Globe)*
1973 Sun Newspapers of Omaha, Neb.
1974 William Sherman *(New York Daily News)*
1975 *Indianapolis Star*
1976 *Chicago Tribune*
1977 Acel Moore and Wendell Rawls, Jr. *(Philadelphia Inquirer)*
1978 Anthony R. Dolan *(Stamford [Conn.] Advocate)*
1979 Gilbert M. Gaul and Elliot G. Jaspin *(Pottsville [Pa.] Republican)*
1980 Nils J. Bruzelius, Alexander B. Hawes, Jr., Stephen A. Kurkjian, Robert M. Porterfield, and Joan Vennochi *(Boston Globe)*
1981 Clark Hallas and Robert B. Lowe *(Arizona Daily Star, Tucson)*
1982 Paul Henderson *(Seattle Times)*
1983 Loretta Tofani *(Washington Post)*
1984 Kenneth Cooper, Joan FitzGerald, Jonathan Kaufman, Norman Lockman, Gary McMillan, Kirk Scharfenberg, and David Wessel *(Boston Globe)*

Investigative Reporting

1985 Lucy Morgan, Jack Reed *(St. Petersburg [Fla.] Times),* and William K. Marimow *(Philadelphia Inquirer)*
1986 Jeffrey A. Marx and Michael M. York *(Lexington [Ky.] Herald Leader)*
1987 Daniel R. Biddle, H. G. Bissinger, and Fredric N. Tulsky *(Philadelphia Inquirer)*
1988 Dean Baquet, William C. Gaines, and Ann Marie Lipinski *(Chicago Tribune)*
1989 Bill Dedman *(Atlanta Journal and Constitution)*
1990 Lou Kilzer and Chris Ison *(Minneapolis-St. Paul Star Tribune)*
1991 Joseph T. Hallinan and Susan M. Headden *(Indianapolis Star)*
1992 Lorraine Adams and Dan Malone *(Dallas Morning News)*
1993 Jeff Brazil and Steve Berry *(Orlando [Fla.] Sentinel)*
1994 *Providence (R.I.) Journal-Bulletin* staff
1995 Stephanie Saul and Brian Donovan *(Newsday)*
1996 *Orange County Register* staff (Santa Ana, Calif.)
1997 Eric Nalder, Deborah Nelson, and Alex Tizon *(Seattle Times)*
1998 Gary Cohn and Will Englund *(Baltimore Sun)*
1999 *The Miami Herald* staff
2000 Sang-Hun Choe, Charles J. Hanley, and Martha Mendoza (Associated Press)
2001 David Willman *(Los Angeles Times)*

Feature Writing

1979 Jon D. Franklin *(Baltimore Evening Sun)*
1980 Madeleine Blais *(Miami Herald)*
1981 Teresa Carpenter *(Village Voice,* New York)
1982 Saul Pett (Associated Press)
1983 Nan Robertson *(New York Times)*
1984 Peter M. Rinearson *(Seattle Times)*
1985 Alice Steinbach *(Baltimore Sun)*
1986 John Camp *(St. Paul Pioneer Press and Dispatch)*
1987 Steve Twomey *(Philadelphia Inquirer)*
1988 Jacqui Banaszynski *(St. Paul Pioneer Press Dispatch)*
1989 David Zucchino *(Philadelphia Inquirer)*
1990 Dave Curtin *(Colorado Springs Gazette Telegraph)*
1991 Sheryl James *(St. Petersburg [Fla.] Times)*
1992 Howell Raines *(New York Times)*
1993 George Lardner, Jr. *(Washington Post)*
1994 Isabel Wilkerson *(New York Times)*
1995 Ron Suskind *(Wall Street Journal)*
1996 Rick Bragg *(New York Times)*
1997 Lisa Pollak *(Baltimore Sun)*
1998 Thomas French *(St. Petersburg [Fla.] Times)*
1999 Angelo B. Henderson *(Wall Street Journal)*
2000 J. R. Moehringer *(Los Angeles Times)*
2001 Tom Hallman, Jr. *(Oregonian)*

Commentary

1970 Marquis W. Childs *(St. Louis Post-Dispatch)*
1971 William A. Caldwell *(Record [Hackensack, N.J.])*
1972 Mike Royko *(Chicago Daily News)*
1973 David S. Broder *(Washington Post)*
1974 Edwin A. Roberts, Jr. *(National Observer)*
1975 Mary McGrory *(Washington Star)*
1976 Walter W. (Red) Smith *(New York Times)*
1977 George F. Will *(Washington Post* Writers Group)
1978 William Safire *(New York Times)*
1979 Russell Baker *(New York Times)*
1980 Ellen H. Goodman *(Boston Globe)*
1981 Dave Anderson *(New York Times)*
1982 Art Buchwald *(Los Angeles Times* Syndicate)
1983 Claude Sitton *(Raleigh [N.C.] News & Observer)*
1984 Vermont Royster *(Wall Street Journal)*
1985 Murray Kempton *(Newsday)*
1986 Jimmy Breslin *(New York Daily News)*
1987 Charles Krauthammer *(Washington Post* Writers Group)
1988 Dave Barry *(Miami Herald)*
1989 Clarence Page *(Chicago Tribune)*
1990 Jim Murray *(Los Angeles Times)*
1991 Jim Hoagland *(Washington Post)*
1992 Anna Quindlen *(New York Times)*
1993 Liz Balmaseda *(Miami Herald)*
1994 William Raspberry *(Washington Post)*
1995 Jim Dwyer *(New York Newsday)*
1996 E. R. Shipp *(New York Daily News)*
1997 Eileen McNamara *(Boston Globe)*
1998 Mike McAlary *(New York Daily News)*
1999 Maureen Dowd *(New York Times)*
2000 Paul A. Gigot *(Wall Street Journal)*
2001 Dorothy Rabinowitz *(Wall Street Journal)*

Criticism

1970 Ada Louise Huxtable *(New York Times)*
1971 Harold C. Schonberg *(New York Times)*
1972 Frank Peters, Jr. *(St. Louis Post-Dispatch)*
1973 Ronald Powers *(Chicago Sun-Times)*
1974 Emily Genauer (Newsday Syndicate)

1975	Roger Ebert (Chicago Sun-Times)
1976	Alan M. Kriegsman (Washington Post)
1977	William McPherson (Washington Post)
1978	Walter Kerr (New York Times)
1979	Paul Gapp (Chicago Tribune)
1980	William A. Henry, 3rd (Boston Globe)
1981	Jonathan Yardley (Washington Star)
1982	Martin Bernheimer (Los Angeles Times)
1983	Manuela Hoelterhoff (Wall Street Journal)
1984	Paul Goldberger (New York Times)
1985	Howard Rosenberg (Los Angeles Times)
1986	Donal Henahan (New York Times)
1987	Richard Eder (Los Angeles Times)
1988	Tom Shales (Washington Post)
1989	Michael Skube (News and Observer [Raleigh, N.C.])
1990	Allan Temko (San Francisco Chronicle)
1991	David Shaw (Los Angeles Times)
1993	Michael Dirda (Washington Post)
1994	Lloyd Schwartz (Boston Phoenix)
1995	Margo Jefferson (New York Times)
1996	Robert Campbell (Boston Globe)
1997	Tim Page (Washington Post)
1998	Michiko Kakutani (New York Times)
1999	Blair Kamin (Chicago Tribune)
2000	Henry Allen (Washington Post)
2001	Gail Caldwell (Boston Globe)

Explanatory Journalism

1985	Jon Franklin (Baltimore Evening Sun)
1986	New York Times
1987	Jeff Lyon and Peter Gorner (Chicago Tribune)
1988	Daniel Hertzberg and James B. Stewart (Wall Street Journal)
1989	David Hanners, William Snyder, and Karen Blessen (Dallas Morning News)
1990	David A. Vise and Steve Coll (Washington Post)
1991	Susan C. Faludi (Wall Street Journal)
1992	Robert S. Capers and Eric Lipton (Hartford Courant)
1993	Mike Toner (Atlanta Journal–Constitution)
1994	Ronald Kotulak (Chicago Tribune)
1995	Leon Dash and Lucian Perkins (Washington Post)
1996	Laurie Garrett (Newsday [Long Island, N.Y.])
1997	Michael Vitez, Ron Cortes, and April Saul (Philadelphia Inquirer)
1998	Paul Salopek (Chicago Tribune)
1999	Richard Read (Oregonian [Portland, Ore.])
2000	Eric Newhouse (Great Falls [Mont.] Tribune)
2001	Chicago Tribune staff

Specialized Reporting

1985	Randall Savage and Jackie Crosby (Macon [Ga.] Telegraph and News)
1986	Andrew Schneider and Mary Pat Flaherty (Pittsburgh Press)
1987	Alex S. Jones (New York Times)
1988	Walt Bogdanich (Wall Street Journal)
1989	Edward Humes (Orange County Register)
1990	Tamar Stieber (Albuquerque (N.M.) Journal)

Beat Reporting

1991	Natalie Angier (New York Times)
1992	Deborah Blum (Sacramento Bee)
1993	Paul Ingrassia and Joseph B. White (Wall Street Journal)
1994	Eric Freedman and Jim Mitzelfeld (Detroit News)
1995	David M. Shribman (Boston Globe)

1996	Bob Keeler (Newsday [Long Island, N.Y.])
1997	Byron Acohido (Seattle Times)
1998	Linda Greenhouse (New York Times)
1999	Chuck Philips and Michael A. Hiltzik (Los Angeles Times)
2000	George Dohrmann (St. Paul Pioneer Press)
2001	David Cay Johnston (New York Times)

PULITZER PRIZES IN LETTERS

Fiction[1]

1918	His Family, Ernest Poole
1919	The Magnificent Ambersons, Booth Tarkington
1921	The Age of Innocence, Edith Wharton
1922	Alice Adams, Booth Tarkington
1923	One of Ours, Willa Cather
1924	The Able McLaughlins, Margaret Wilson
1925	So Big, Edna Ferber
1926	Arrowsmith, Sinclair Lewis
1927	Early Autumn, Louis Bromfield
1928	The Bridge of San Luis Rey, Thornton Wilder
1929	Scarlet Sister Mary, Julia Peterkin
1930	Laughing Boy, Oliver La Farge
1931	Years of Grace, Margaret Ayer Barnes
1932	The Good Earth, Pearl S. Buck
1933	The Store, T. S. Stribling
1934	Lamb in His Bosom, Caroline Miller
1935	Now in November, Josephine Winslow Johnson
1936	Honey in the Horn, Harold L. Davis
1937	Gone With the Wind, Margaret Mitchell
1938	The Late George Apley, John Phillips Marquand
1939	The Yearling, Marjorie Kinnan Rawlings
1940	The Grapes of Wrath, John Steinbeck
1942	In This Our Life, Ellen Glasgow
1943	Dragon's Teeth, Upton Sinclair
1944	Journey in the Dark, Martin Flavin
1945	A Bell for Adano, John Hersey
1947	All the King's Men, Robert Penn Warren
1948	Tales of the South Pacific, James A. Michener
1949	Guard of Honor, James Gould Cozzens
1950	The Way West, A. B. Guthrie, Jr.
1951	The Town, Conrad Richter
1952	The Caine Mutiny, Herman Wouk
1953	The Old Man and the Sea, Ernest Hemingway
1955	A Fable, William Faulkner
1956	Andersonville, MacKinlay Kantor
1958	A Death in the Family, James Agee
1959	The Travels of Jaimie McPheeters, Robert Lewis Taylor
1960	Advise and Consent, Allen Drury
1961	To Kill a Mockingbird, Harper Lee
1962	The Edge of Sadness, Edwin O'Connor
1963	The Reivers, William Faulkner
1965	The Keepers of the House, Shirley Ann Grau
1966	Collected Stories of Katherine Anne Porter, Katherine Anne Porter
1967	The Fixer, Bernard Malamud
1968	The Confessions of Nat Turner, William Styron
1969	House Made of Dawn, N. Scott Momaday
1970	Collected Stories, Jean Stafford
1972	Angle of Repose, Wallace Stegner
1973	The Optimist's Daughter, Eudora Welty
1975	The Killer Angels, Michael Shaara
1976	Humboldt's Gift, Saul Bellow
1978	Elbow Room, James Alan McPherson
1979	The Stories of John Cheever, John Cheever
1980	The Executioner's Song, Norman Mailer
1981	A Confederacy of Dunces, John Kennedy Toole

1982	*Rabbit Is Rich*, John Updike
1983	*The Color Purple*, Alice Walker
1984	*Ironweed*, William Kennedy
1985	*Foreign Affairs*, Alison Lurie
1986	*Lonesome Dove*, Larry McMurtry
1987	*A Summons to Memphis*, Peter Taylor
1988	*Beloved*, Toni Morrison
1989	*Breathing Lessons*, Anne Tyler
1990	*The Mambo Kings Play Songs of Love*, Oscar Hijuelos
1991	*Rabbit at Rest*, John Updike
1992	*A Thousand Acres*, Jane Smiley
1993	*A Good Scent From a Strange Mountain*, Robert Olen Butler
1994	*The Shipping News*, E. Annie Proulx
1995	*The Stone Diaries*, Carol Shields
1996	*Independence Day*, Richard Ford
1997	*Martin Dressler: The Tale of an American Dreamer*, Steven Millhauser
1998	*American Pastoral*, Philip Roth
1999	*The Hours*, Michael Cunningham
2000	*Interpreter of Maladies*, Jhumpa Lahiri
2001	*The Amazing Adventures of Kavalier & Clay*, Michael Chabon

1. Before 1948, award was for novels only.

History of United States

1917	*With Americans of Past and Present Days*, J. J. Jusserand, Ambassador of France to United States
1918	*A History of the Civil War, 1861–1865*, James Ford Rhodes
1920	*The War With Mexico*, Justin H. Smith
1921	*The Victory at Sea*, William Sowden Sims, in collaboration with Burton J. Hendrick
1922	*The Founding of New England*, James Truslow Adams
1923	*The Supreme Court in United States History*, Charles Warren
1924	*The American Revolution—A Constitutional Interpretation*, Charles Howard McIlwain
1925	*A History of the American Frontier*, Frederic L. Paxson
1926	*The History of the United States*, Edward Channing
1927	*Pinckney's Treaty*, Samuel Flagg Bemis
1928	*Main Currents in American Thought*, Vernon Louis Parrington
1929	*The Organization and Administration of the Union Army, 1861–1865*, Fred Albert Shannon
1930	*The War of Independence*, Claude H. Van Tyne
1931	*The Coming of the War: 1914*, Bernadotte E. Schmitt
1932	*My Experiences in the World War*, John J. Pershing
1933	*The Significance of Sections in American History*, Frederick J. Turner
1934	*The People's Choice*, Herbert Agar
1935	*The Colonial Period of American History*, Charles McLean Andrews
1936	*The Constitutional History of the United States*, Andrew C. McLaughlin
1937	*The Flowering of New England*, Van Wyck Brooks
1938	*The Road to Reunion, 1865–1900*, Paul Herman Buck
1939	*A History of American Magazines*, Frank Luther Mott

1940	*Abraham Lincoln: The War Years*, Carl Sandburg
1941	*The Atlantic Migration, 1607–1860*, Marcus Lee Hansen
1942	*Reveille in Washington*, Margaret Leech
1943	*Paul Revere and the World He Lived In*, Esther Forbes
1944	*The Growth of American Thought*, Merle Curti
1945	*Unfinished Business*, Stephen Bonsal
1946	*The Age of Jackson*, Arthur M. Schlesinger, Jr.
1947	*Scientists Against Time*, James Phinney Baxter III
1948	*Across the Wide Missouri*, Bernard DeVoto
1949	*The Disruption of American Democracy*, Roy Franklin Nichols
1950	*Art and Life in America*, Oliver W. Larkin
1951	*The Old Northwest, Pioneer Period 1815–1840*, R. Carlyle Buley
1952	*The Uprooted*, Oscar Handlin
1953	*The Era of Good Feelings*, George Dangerfield
1954	*A Stillness at Appomattox*, Bruce Catton
1955	*Great River: The Rio Grande in North American History*, Paul Horgan
1956	*The Age of Reform*, Richard Hofstadter
1957	*Russia Leaves the War: Soviet–American Relations, 1917–1920*, George F. Kennan
1958	*Banks and Politics in America: From the Revolution to the Civil War*, Bray Hammond
1959	*The Republican Era: 1869–1901*, Leonard D. White, assisted by Jean Schneider
1960	*In the Days of McKinley*, Margaret Leech
1961	*Between War and Peace: The Potsdam Conference*, Herbert Feis
1962	*The Triumphant Empire: Thunder-Clouds Gather in the West*, Lawrence H. Gipson
1963	*Washington, Village and Capital, 1800–1878*, Constance McLaughlin Green
1964	*Puritan Village: The Formation of a New England Town*, Sumner Chilton Powell
1965	*The Greenback Era*, Irwin Unger
1966	*Life of the Mind in America*, Perry Miller
1967	*Exploration and Empire: The Explorer and Scientist in the Winning of the American West*, William H. Goetzmann
1968	*The Ideological Origins of the American Revolution*, Bernard Bailyn
1969	*Origins of the Fifth Amendment*, Leonard W. Levy
1970	*Present at the Creation: My Years in the State Department*, Dean Acheson
1971	*Roosevelt: The Soldier of Freedom*, James McGregor Burns
1972	*Neither Black Nor White: Slavery and Race Relations in Brazil and the United States*, Carl N. Degler
1973	*People of Paradox: An Inquiry Concerning the Origin of American Civilization*, Michael Kammen
1974	*The Americans: The Democratic Experience*, Vol. 3, Daniel J. Boorstin
1975	*Jefferson and His Time*, Dumas Malone
1976	*Lamy of Santa Fe*, Paul Horgan
1977	*The Impending Crisis: 1841–1861*, David M. Potter
1978	*The Invisible Hand: The Managerial Revolution in American Business*, Alfred D. Chandler, Jr.
1979	*The Dred Scott Case: Its Significance in Law and Politics*, Don E. Fehrenbacher

1980   *Been in the Storm So Long*, Leon F. Litwack

1981   *American Education: The National Experience; 1783–1876*, Lawrence A. Cremin

1982   *Mary Chesnut's Civil War*, C. Vann Woodward, editor

1983   *The Transformation of Virginia, 1740–1790*, Rhys L. Isaac

1985   *The Prophets of Regulation*, Thomas K. McCraw

1986   *The Heavens and the Earth: A Political History of the Space Age*, Walter A. McDougall

1987   *Voyagers to the West: A Passage in the Peopling of America on the Eve of the Revolution*, Bernard Bailyn

1988   *The Launching of Modern American Science 1846–1876*, Robert V. Bruce

1989   *Parting the Waters*, Taylor Branch; *Battle Cry of Freedom*, James M. McPherson

1990   *In Our Image: America's Empire in the Philippines*, Stanley Karnow

1991   *A Midwife's Tale: The Life of Martha Ballard, Based on Her Diary 1785–1812*, Laurel Thatcher Ulrich

1992   *The Fate of Liberty: Abraham Lincoln and Civil Liberties*, Mark E. Neely, Jr.

1993   *The Radicalism of the American Revolution*, Gordon S. Wood

1995   *No Ordinary Time: Franklin and Eleanor Roosevelt: The Home Front in World War II*, Doris Kearns Goodwin

1996   *William Cooper's Town: Power and Persuasion on the Frontier of the Early American Republic*, Alan Taylor

1997   *Original Meanings: Politics and Ideas in the Making of the Constitution*, Jack N. Rakove

1998   *Summer for the Gods: The Scopes Trial and America's Continuing Debate Over Science and Religion*, Edward J. Larson

1999   *Gotham: A History of New York City to 1898*, Edwin G. Burrows and Mike Wallace

2000   *Freedom from Fear: The American People in Depression and War, 1929–1945*, David M. Kennedy

2001   *Founding Brothers: The Revolutionary Generation*, Joseph J. Ellis

Biography or Autobiography

1917   *Julia Ward Howe*, Laura E. Richards and Maude Howe Elliott, assisted by Florence Howe Hall

1918   *Benjamin Franklin, Self-Revealed*, William Cabell Bruce

1919   *The Education of Henry Adams*, Henry Adams

1920   *The Life of John Marshall*, Albert J. Beveridge

1921   *The Americanization of Edward Bok*, Edward Bok

1922   *A Daughter of the Middle Border*, Hamlin Garland

1923   *The Life and Letters of Walter H. Page*, Burton J. Hendrick

1924   *From Immigrant to Inventor*, Michael Idvorsky Pupin

1925   *Barrett Wendell and His Letters*, M. A. DeWolfe Howe

1926   *The Life of Sir William Osler*, Harvey Cushing

1927   *Whitman*, Emory Holloway

1928   *The American Orchestra and Theodore Thomas*, Charles Edward Russell

1929   *The Training of an American: The Earlier Life and Letters of Walter H. Page*, Burton J. Hendrick

1930   *The Raven*, Marquis James

1931   *Charles W. Eliot*, Henry James

1932   *Theodore Roosevelt*, Henry F. Pringle

1933   *Grover Cleveland*, Allan Nevins

1934   *John Hay*, Tyler Dennett

1935   *R. E. Lee*, Douglas S. Freeman

1936   *The Thought and Character of William James*, Ralph Barton Perry

1937   *Hamilton Fish*, Allan Nevins

1938   *Pedlar's Progress*, Odell Shepard; *Andrew Jackson*, Marquis James

1939   *Benjamin Franklin*, Carl Van Doren

1940   *Woodrow Wilson: Life and Letters*, Vols. VII and VIII, Ray Stannard Baker

1941   *Jonathan Edwards*, Ola E. Winslow

1942   *Crusader in Crinoline*, Forrest Wilson

1943   *Admiral of the Ocean Sea*, Samuel Eliot Morison

1944   *The American Leonardo: The Life of Samuel F. B. Morse*, Carleton Mabee

1945   *George Bancroft: Brahmin Rebel*, Russel Blaine Nye

1946   *Son of the Wilderness*, Linnie Marsh Wolfe

1947   *The Autobiography of William Allen White*

1948   *Forgotten First Citizen: John Bigelow*, Margaret Clapp

1949   *Roosevelt and Hopkins*, Robert E. Sherwood

1950   *John Quincy Adams and the Foundations of American Foreign Policy*, Samuel Flagg Bemis

1951   *John C. Calhoun: American Portrait*, Margaret Louise Coit

1952   *Charles Evans Hughes*, Merlo J. Pusey

1953   *Edmund Pendleton, 1721–1803*, David J. Mays

1954   *The Spirit of St. Louis*, Charles A. Lindbergh

1955   *The Taft Story*, William S. White

1956   *Benjamin Henry Latrobe*, Talbot F. Hamlin

1957   *Profiles in Courage*, John F. Kennedy

1958   *George Washington* (Vols. 1–6), Douglas Southall Freeman (Vols. 1–6) and John Alexander Carroll and Mary Wells Ashworth (Vol. 7)

1959   *Woodrow Wilson, American Prophet*, Arthur Walworth

1960   *John Paul Jones*, Samuel Eliot Morison

1961   *Charles Sumner and the Coming of the Civil War*, David Donald

1963   *Henry James: Vol. II, The Conquest of London, 1870–1881; Vol. III, The Middle Years, 1881–1895*, Leon Edel

1964   *John Keats*, Walter Jackson Bate

1965   *Henry Adams* (3 Vols.), Ernest Samuels

1966   *A Thousand Days*, Arthur M. Schlesinger, Jr.

1967   *Mr. Clemens and Mark Twain*, Justin Kaplan

1968   *Memoirs, 1925–1950*, George F. Kennan

1969   *The Man From New York*, B. L. Reid

1970   *Huey Long*, T. Harry Williams

1971   *Robert Frost: The Years of Triumph, 1915–1938*, Lawrence Thompson

1972   *Eleanor and Franklin: The Story of Their Relationship Based on Eleanor Roosevelt's Private Papers*, Joseph P. Lash

1973   *Luce and His Empire*, W. A. Swanberg

1974   *O'Neill, Son and Artist*, Louis Sheaffer

1975   *The Power Broker: Robert Moses and the Fall of New York*, Robert A. Caro

1976 *Edith Wharton: A Biography*, Richard W. B. Lewis
1977 *A Prince of Our Disorder*, John E. Mack
1978 *Samuel Johnson*, Walter Jackson Bate
1979 *Days of Sorrow and Pain: Leo Baeck and the Berlin Jews*, Leonard Baker
1980 *The Rise of Theodore Roosevelt*, Edmund Morris
1981 *Peter the Great*, Robert K. Massie
1982 *Grant: A Biography*, William S. McFeely
1983 *Growing Up*, Russell Baker
1984 *Booker T. Washington*, Louis R. Harlan
1985 *The Life and Times of Cotton Mather*, Kenneth Silverman
1986 *Louise Bogan: A Portrait*, Elizabeth Frank
1987 *Bearing the Cross: Martin Luther King, Jr., and the Southern Christian Leadership Conference*, David J. Garrow
1988 *Look Homeward: A Life of Thomas Wolfe*, David Herbert Donald
1989 *Oscar Wilde*, Richard Ellmann
1990 *Machiavelli in Hell*, Sebastian de Grazia
1991 *Jackson Pollock: An American Saga*, Steven Naifeh and Gregory White Smith
1992 *Fortunate Son: The Healing of a Vietnam Vet*, Lewis B. Puller, Jr.
1993 *Truman*, David McCullough
1994 *W. E. B. Du Bois: Biography of a Race, 1868–1919*, David Levering Lewis
1995 *Harriet Beecher Stowe: A Life*, Joan D. Hedrick
1996 *God: A Biography*, Jack Miles
1997 *Angela's Ashes: A Memoir*, Frank McCourt
1998 *Personal History*, Katharine Graham
1999 *Lindbergh*, A. Scott Berg
2000 *Vera (Mrs. Vladimir Nabokov)*, Stacy Schiff
2001 *W. E. B. DuBois: The Fight for Equality and the American Century, 1919–1963*, David Levering Lewis

Poetry[1]
1918 *Love Songs*, Sara Teasdale
1919 *Old Road to Paradise*, Margaret Widdemer; *Corn Huskers*, Carl Sandburg
1922 *Collected Poems*, Edwin Arlington Robinson
1923 *The Ballad of the Harp-Weaver; A Few Figs from Thistles; eight sonnets in American Poetry, 1922, A Miscellany*, Edna St. Vincent Millay
1924 *New Hampshire: A Poem With Notes and Grace Notes*, Robert Frost
1925 *The Man Who Died Twice*, Edwin Arlington Robinson
1926 *What's O'Clock*, Amy Lowell
1927 *Fiddler's Farewell*, Leonora Speyer
1928 *Tristram*, Edwin Arlington Robinson
1929 *John Brown's Body*, Stephen Vincent Benét
1930 *Selected Poems*, Conrad Aiken
1931 *Collected Poems*, Robert Frost
1932 *The Flowering Stone*, George Dillon
1933 *Conquistador*, Archibald MacLeish
1934 *Collected Verse*, Robert Hillyer
1935 *Bright Ambush*, Audrey Wurdemann
1936 *Strange Holiness*, Robert P. T. Coffin
1937 *A Further Range*, Robert Frost
1938 *Cold Morning Sky*, Marya Zaturenska
1939 *Selected Poems*, John Gould Fletcher
1940 *Collected Poems*, Mark Van Doren
1941 *Sunderland Capture*, Leonard Bacon
1942 *The Dust Which Is God*, William Rose Benét
1943 *A Witness Tree*, Robert Frost
1944 *Western Star*, Stephen Vincent Benét
1945 *V-Letter and Other Poems*, Karl Shapiro
1947 *Lord Weary's Castle*, Robert Lowell
1948 *The Age of Anxiety*, W. H. Auden
1949 *Terror and Decorum*, Peter Viereck
1950 *Annie Allen*, Gwendolyn Brooks
1951 *Complete Poems*, Carl Sandburg
1952 *Collected Poems*, Marianne Moore
1953 *Collected Poems, 1917–1952*, Archibald MacLeish
1954 *The Waking*, Theodore Roethke
1955 *Collected Poems*, Wallace Stevens
1956 *Poems—North & South*, Elizabeth Bishop
1957 *Things of This World*, Richard Wilbur
1958 *Promises: Poems, 1954–1956*, Robert Penn Warren
1959 *Selected Poems, 1928–1958*, Stanley Kunitz
1960 *Heart's Needle*, William Snodgrass
1961 *Times Three: Selected Verse From Three Decades*, Phyllis McGinley
1962 *Poems*, Alan Dugan
1963 *Pictures From Breughel*, William Carlos Williams
1964 *At the End of the Open Road*, Louis Simpson
1965 *77 Dream Songs*, John Berryman
1966 *Selected Poems*, Richard Eberhart
1967 *Live or Die*, Anne Sexton
1968 *The Hard Hours*, Anthony Hecht
1969 *Of Being Numerous*, George Oppen
1970 *Untitled Subjects*, Richard Howard
1971 *The Carrier of Ladders*, William S. Merwin
1972 *Collected Poems*, James Wright
1973 *Up Country*, Maxine Winokur Kumin
1974 *The Dolphin*, Robert Lowell
1975 *Turtle Island*, Gary Snyder
1976 *Self-Portrait in a Convex Mirror*, John Ashbery
1977 *Divine Comedies*, James Merrill
1978 *Collected Poems*, Howard Nemerov
1979 *Now and Then: Poems, 1976–1978*, Robert Penn Warren
1980 *Selected Poems*, Donald Rodney Justice
1981 *The Morning of the Poem*, James Schuyler
1982 *The Collected Poems*, Sylvia Plath
1983 *Selected Poems*, Galway Kinnell
1984 *American Primitive*, Mary Oliver
1985 *Yin*, Carolyn Kizer
1986 *The Flying Change*, Henry Taylor
1987 *Thomas and Beulah*, Rita Dove
1988 *Partial Accounts: New and Selected Poems*, William Meredith
1989 *New and Collected Poems*, Richard Wilbur
1990 *The World Doesn't End*, Charles Simic
1991 *Near Changes*, Mona Van Duyn
1992 *Selected Poems*, James Tate
1993 *The Wild Iris*, Louise Gluck
1994 *Neon Vernacular*, Yusef Komunyakaa
1995 *Simple Truth*, Philip Levine
1996 *The Dream of the Unified Field*, Jorie Graham
1997 *Alive Together: New and Selected Poems*, Lisel Mueller
1998 *Black Zodiac*, Charles Wright
1999 *Blizzard of One*, Mark Strand
2000 *Repair*, C. K. Williams
2001 *Different Hours*, Stephen Dunn

1. The poetry prize was established in 1922. The 1918 and 1919 awards were made from gifts provided by the Poetry Society.

General Nonfiction

1962 *The Making of the President, 1960*, Theodore H. White
1963 *The Guns of August*, Barbara W. Tuchman
1964 *Anti-Intellectualism in American Life*, Richard Hofstadter
1965 *O Strange New World*, Howard Mumford Jones
1966 *Wandering Through Winter*, Edwin Way Teale
1967 *The Problem of Slavery in Western Culture*, David Brion Davis
1968 *Rousseau and Revolution*, Will and Ariel Durant
1969 *So Human an Animal*, Rene Jules Dubos; *The Armies of the Night*, Norman Mailer
1970 *Gandhi's Truth*, Erik H. Erikson
1971 *The Rising Sun*, John Toland
1972 *Stilwell and the American Experience in China, 1911–1945*, Barbara W. Tuchman
1973 *Fire in the Lake: The Vietnamese and the Americans in Vietnam*, Frances FitzGerald; *Children of Crisis* (Vols. 1 and 2), Robert M. Coles
1974 *The Denial of Death*, Ernest Becker
1975 *Pilgrim at Tinker Creek*, Annie Dillard
1976 *Why Survive? Being Old in America*, Robert N. Butler
1977 *Beautiful Swimmers: Watermen, Crabs and the Chesapeake Bay*, William W. Warner
1978 *The Dragons of Eden*, Carl Sagan
1979 *On Human Nature*, Edward O. Wilson
1980 *Gödel, Escher, Bach: An Eternal Golden Braid*, Douglas R. Hofstadter
1981 *Fin-de-Siecle Vienna: Politics and Culture*, Carl E. Schorske
1982 *The Soul of a New Machine*, Tracy Kidder
1983 *Is There No Place on Earth for Me?*, Susan Sheehan
1984 *Social Transformation of American Medicine*, Paul Starr
1985 *The Good War: An Oral History of World War II*, Studs Terkel
1986 *Move Your Shadow: South Africa, Black and White*, Joseph Lelyveld; *Common Ground: A Turbulent Decade in the Lives of Three American Families*, J. Anthony Lukas
1987 *Arab and Jew: Wounded Spirits in a Promised Land*, David K. Shipler
1988 *The Making of the Atomic Bomb*, Richard Rhodes
1989 *A Bright Shining Lie*, Neil Sheehan
1990 *And Their Children After Them*, Dale Maharidge and Michael Williamson
1991 *The Ants*, Bert Holldobler and Edward O. Wilson
1992 *The Prize: The Epic Quest for Oil, Money and Power*, Daniel Yergin
1993 *Lincoln at Gettysburg: The Words That Remade America*, Garry Wills
1994 *Lenin's Tomb: The Last Days of the Soviet Empire*, David Remick
1995 *The Beak of the Finch: A Story of Evolution in Our Time*, Jonathan Weiner
1996 *The Haunted Land: Facing Europe's Ghosts After Communism*, Tina Rosenberg
1997 *Ashes to Ashes: America's Hundred-Year Cigarette War, the Public Health, and the Unabashed Triumph of Philip Morris*, Richard Kluger
1998 *Guns, Germs, and Steel: The Fates of Human Societies*, Jared Diamond
1999 *Annals of the Former World*, John McPhee
2000 *Embracing Defeat: Japan in the Wake of World War II*, John W. Dower
2001 *Hirohito and the Making of Modern Japan*, Herbert P. Bix

PULITZER PRIZES IN MUSIC

1943 *Secular Cantata No. 2, A Free Song*, William Schuman
1944 *Symphony No. 4* (Op. 34), Howard Hanson
1945 *Appalachian Spring*, Aaron Copland
1946 *The Canticle of the Sun*, Leo Sowerby
1947 *Symphony No. 3*, Charles Ives
1948 *Symphony No. 3*, Walter Piston
1949 *Louisiana Story* music, Virgil Thomson
1950 *The Consul*, Gian Carlo Menotti
1951 Music for opera *Giants in the Earth*, Douglas Stuart Moore
1952 *Symphony Concertante*, Gail Kubik
1954 *Concerto for Two Pianos and Orchestra*, Quincy Porter
1955 *The Saint of Bleecker Street*, Gian Carlo Menotti
1956 *Symphony No. 3*, Ernst Toch
1957 *Meditations on Ecclesiastes*, Norman Dello Joio
1958 *Vanessa*, Samuel Barber
1959 *Concerto for Piano and Orchestra*, John La Montaine
1960 *Second String Quartet*, Elliott Carter
1961 *Symphony No. 7*, Walter Piston
1962 *The Crucible*, Robert Ward
1963 *Piano Concerto No. 1*, Samuel Barber
1966 *Variations for Orchestra*, Leslie Bassett
1967 *Quartet No. 3*, Leon Kirchner
1968 *Echoes of Time and the River*, George Crumb
1969 *String Quartet No. 3*, Karel Husa
1970 *Time's Encomium*, Charles Wuorinen
1971 *Synchronisms No. 6 for Piano and Electronic Sound*, Mario Davidovsky
1972 *Windows*, Jacob Druckman
1973 *String Quartet No. 3*, Elliott Carter
1974 *Notturno*, Donald Martino
1975 *From the Diary of Virginia Woolf*, Dominick Argento
1976 *Air Music*, Ned Rorem
1977 *Visions of Terror and Wonder*, Richard Wernick
1978 *Déjà Vu for Percussion Quartet and Orchestra*, Michael Colgrass
1979 *Aftertones of Infinity*, Joseph Schwantner
1980 *In Memory of a Summer Day*, David Del Tredici
1982 *Concerto for Orchestra*, Roger Sessions
1983 *Three Movements for Orchestra*, Ellen T. Zwilich
1984 *Canti del Sole*, Bernard Rands
1985 *Symphony RiverRun*, Stephen Albert
1986 *Wind Quintet IV*, George Perle
1987 *The Flight Into Egypt*, John Harbison
1988 *12 New Etudes for Piano*, William Bolcom
1989 *Whispers Out of Time*, Roger Reynolds
1990 *Duplicates: A Concerto for Two Pianos and Orchestra*, Mel Powell
1991 *Symphony*, Shulamit Ran
1992 *The Face of the Night, The Heart of the Dark*, Wayne Peterson

1993	*Trombone Concerto,* Christopher Rouse
1994	*Of Reminiscences and Reflections,* Gunther Schuller
1995	*Stringmusic,* Morton Gould
1996	*Lilacs,* George Walker
1997	*Blood on the Field,* Wynton Marsalis
1998	*String Quartet No. 2, Musica Instrumentalis,* Aaron Jay Kernis
1999	*Concerto for Flute, Strings and Percussion,* Melinda Wagner
2000	*Life Is a Dream, Opera in Three Acts: Act II, Concert Version,* Lewis Spratlan
2001	*Symphony No. 2 for String Orchestra,* John Corigliano

PULITZER PRIZES IN DRAMA

1918	*Why Marry?,* Jesse Lynch Williams
1920	*Beyond the Horizon,* Eugene O'Neill
1921	*Miss Lulu Bett,* Zona Gale
1922	*Anna Christie,* Eugene O'Neill
1923	*Icebound,* Owen Davis
1924	*Hell-Bent Fer Heaven,* Hatcher Hughes
1925	*They Knew What They Wanted,* Sidney Howard
1926	*Craig's Wife,* George Kelly
1927	*In Abraham's Bosom,* Paul Green
1928	*Strange Interlude,* Eugene O'Neill
1929	*Street Scene,* Elmer L. Rice
1930	*The Green Pastures,* Marc Connelly
1931	*Alison's House,* Susan Glaspell
1932	*Of Thee I Sing,* George S. Kaufman, Morrie Ryskind, and Ira Gershwin
1933	*Both Your Houses,* Maxwell Anderson
1934	*Men in White,* Sidney Kingsley
1935	*The Old Maid,* Zöe Akins
1936	*Idiot's Delight,* Robert E. Sherwood
1937	*You Can't Take It with You,* Moss Hart and George S. Kaufman
1938	*Our Town,* Thornton Wilder
1939	*Abe Lincoln in Illinois,* Robert E. Sherwood
1940	*The Time of Your Life,* William Saroyan
1941	*There Shall Be No Night,* Robert E. Sherwood
1943	*The Skin of Our Teeth,* Thornton Wilder
1945	*Harvey,* Mary Chase
1946	*State of the Union,* Russel Crouse and Howard Lindsay
1948	*A Streetcar Named Desire,* Tennessee Williams
1949	*Death of a Salesman,* Arthur Miller
1950	*South Pacific,* Richard Rodgers, Oscar Hammerstein II, and Joshua Logan
1952	*The Shrike,* Joseph Kramm
1953	*Picnic,* William Inge
1954	*The Teahouse of the August Moon,* John Patrick
1955	*Cat on a Hot Tin Roof,* Tennessee Williams
1956	*The Diary of Anne Frank,* Frances Goodrich and Albert Hackett
1957	*Long Day's Journey into Night,* Eugene O'Neill
1958	*Look Homeward, Angel,* Ketti Frings
1959	*J. B.,* Archibald MacLeish
1960	*Fiorello!,* George Abbott, Jerome Weidman, Jerry Bock, and Sheldon Harnick
1961	*All the Way Home,* Tad Mosel
1962	*How to Succeed in Business without Really Trying,* Frank Loesser and Abe Burrows
1965	*The Subject Was Roses,* Frank D. Gilroy
1967	*A Delicate Balance,* Edward Albee
1969	*The Great White Hope,* Howard Sackler
1970	*No Place to Be Somebody,* Charles Gordone

1971	*The Effect of Gamma Rays on Man-in-the-Moon Marigolds,* Paul Zindel
1973	*That Championship Season,* Jason Miller
1975	*Seascape,* Edward Albee
1976	*A Chorus Line,* conceived by Michael Bennett
1977	*The Shadow Box,* Michael Cristofer
1978	*The Gin Game,* Donald L. Coburn
1979	*Buried Child,* Sam Shepard
1980	*Talley's Folly,* Lanford Wilson
1981	*Crimes of the Heart,* Beth Henley
1982	*A Soldier's Play,* Charles Fuller
1983	*'Night, Mother,* Marsha Norman
1984	*Glengarry Glen Ross,* David Mamet
1985	*Sunday in the Park with George,* Stephen Sondheim and James Lapine
1987	*Fences,* August Wilson
1988	*Driving Miss Daisy,* Alfred Uhry
1989	*The Heidi Chronicles,* Wendy Wasserstein
1990	*The Piano Lesson,* August Wilson
1991	*Lost in Yonkers,* Neil Simon
1992	*The Kentucky Cycle,* Robert Schenkkan
1993	*Angels in America: Millennium Approaches,* Tony Kushner
1994	*Three Tall Women,* Edward Albee
1995	*The Young Man from Atlanta,* Horton Foote
1996	*Rent,* Jonathan Larson
1998	*How I Learned to Drive,* Paula Vogel
1999	*Wit,* Margaret Edson
2000	*Dinner with Friends,* Donald Margulies
2001	*Proof,* David Auburn

SPECIAL CITATIONS

1938	*Edmonton* [Alberta] *Journal,* special bronze plaque for editorial leadership in defense of freedom of the press in province of Alberta
1941	*New York Times,* for the public educational value of its foreign news report
1944	Byron Price, director of the Office of Censorship, for the creation and administration of the newspaper and radio codes; Mrs. William Allen White, for her husband's interest and services during the past seven years as a member of the Advisory Board of the Graduate School of Journalism, Columbia University; Richard Rodgers and Oscar Hammerstein II, for their musical *Oklahoma!*
1945	The cartographers of the American press, for their war maps
1947	(Pulitzer centennial year.) Columbia University and the Graduate School of Journalism, for their efforts to maintain and advance the high standards governing the Pulitzer Prize awards; the *St. Louis Post-Dispatch,* for its unswerving adherence to the public and professional ideals of its founder and its leadership in American journalism
1948	Dr. Frank D. Fackenthal, for his interest and service
1951	Cyrus L. Sulzberger *(New York Times),* for his exclusive interview with Archbishop Stepinac in a Yugoslav prison
1952	*Kansas City Star,* for coverage of 1951 floods; Max Kase *(New York Journal–American),* for exposures of bribery in basketball
1953	*New York Times,* for its 17-year publication of "Review of the Week," and Lester Markel, its founder

1957   Kenneth Roberts, for his historical novels
1958   Walter Lippmann *(New York Herald Tribune)*, for his "wisdom, perception and high sense of responsibility" in his commentary on national and international affairs
1960   Garrett Mattingly, for *The Armada*
1961   *American Heritage Picture History of the Civil War*, as a distinguished example of American book publishing
1964   Gannett Newspapers, Rochester, N.Y.
1973   James Thomas Flexner, for his biography *George Washington*
1974   Roger Sessions, for his "life's work in music"
1976   John Hohenberg, for "services for 22 years as Administrator of the Pulitzer Prizes"; Scott Joplin, for his contributions to American music
1977   Alex Haley, for his novel, *Roots*
1978   E. B. White of *New Yorker* magazine and Richard L. Strout of *The Christian Science Monitor*
1982   Milton Babbitt, "for his life's work as a distinguished and seminal American composer"

1984   Theodor Seuss Geisel (Dr. Seuss), for "books full of playful rhymes, nonsense words and strange illustrations"
1985   William Schuman, for "more than half a century of contribution to American music as a composer and educational leader"
1987   Joseph Pulitzer, Jr., "for extraordinary services to American journalism and letters during his 31 years as chairman of the Pulitzer Prize Board and for his accomplishments as an editor and publisher"
1992   *Maus*, Art Spiegelman
1996   Herb Caen *(San Francisco Chronicle)*, "for his extraordinary and continuing contribution as a voice and conscience of his city"
1998   George Gershwin
1999   Edward Kennedy "Duke" Ellington, who "made an indelible contribution to art and culture"

Academy Awards (Oscars)

1928
Picture: *Wings*, Paramount
Director: Frank Borzage, *Seventh Heaven;* Lewis Milestone, *Two Arabian Nights*
Actress: Janet Gaynor, *Seventh Heaven, Street Angel, Sunrise*
Actor: Emil Jannings, *The Way of All Flesh, The Last Command*

1929
Picture: *The Broadway Melody*, MGM
Director: Frank Lloyd, *The Divine Lady*
Actress: Mary Pickford, *Coquette*
Actor: Warner Baxter, *In Old Arizona*

1930
Picture: *All Quiet on the Western Front*, Universal
Director: Lewis Milestone, *All Quiet on the Western Front*
Actress: Norma Shearer, *The Divorcee*
Actor: George Arliss, *Disraeli*

1931
Picture: *Cimarron*, RKO Radio
Director: Norman Taurog, *Skippy*
Actress: Marie Dressler, *Min and Bill*
Actor: Lionel Barrymore, *A Free Soul*

1932
Picture: *Grand Hotel*, MGM
Director: Frank Borzage, *Bad Girl*
Actress: Helen Hayes, *The Sin of Madelon Claudet*
Actor: Fredric March, *Dr. Jekyll and Mr. Hyde*, and Wallace Beery, *The Champ*

1933
Picture: *Cavalcade*, Fox
Director: Frank Lloyd, *Cavalcade*
Actress: Katharine Hepburn, *Morning Glory*
Actor: Charles Laughton, *The Private Life of Henry VIII*

1934
Picture: *It Happened One Night*, Columbia
Director: Frank Capra, *It Happened One Night*
Actress: Claudette Colbert, *It Happened One Night*
Actor: Clark Gable, *It Happened One Night*

1935
Picture: *Mutiny on the Bounty*, MGM
Director: John Ford, *The Informer*
Actress: Bette Davis, *Dangerous*
Actor: Victor McLaglen, *The Informer*

1936
Picture: *The Great Ziegfeld*, MGM
Director: Frank Capra, *Mr. Deeds Goes to Town*
Actress: Luise Rainer, *The Great Ziegfeld*
Actor: Paul Muni, *The Story of Louis Pasteur*
Supporting Actress: Gale Sondergaard, *Anthony Adverse*
Supporting Actor: Walter Brennan, *Come and Get It*

1937
Picture: *The Life of Emile Zola*, Warner Bros.
Director: Leo McCarey, *The Awful Truth*
Actress: Luise Rainer, *The Good Earth*
Actor: Spencer Tracy, *Captains Courageous*
Supporting Actress: Alice Brady, *In Old Chicago*
Supporting Actor: Joseph Schildkraut, *The Life of Emile Zola*

1938
Picture: *You Can't Take It with You*, Columbia
Director: Frank Capra, *You Can't Take It with You*
Actress: Bette Davis, *Jezebel*
Actor: Spencer Tracy, *Boys Town*
Supporting Actress: Fay Bainter, *Jezebel*
Supporting Actor: Walter Brennan, *Kentucky*

1939
Picture: *Gone with the Wind*, Selznick MGM
Director: Victor Fleming, *Gone with the Wind*
Actress: Vivien Leigh, *Gone with the Wind*
Actor: Robert Donat, *Goodbye, Mr. Chips*
Supporting Actress: Hattie McDaniel, *Gone with the Wind*
Supporting Actor: Thomas Mitchell, *Stagecoach*

1940
Picture: *Rebecca*, Selznick-United Artists
Director: John Ford, *The Grapes of Wrath*
Actress: Ginger Rogers, *Kitty Foyle*
Actor: James Stewart, *The Philadelphia Story*
Supporting Actress: Jane Darwell, *The Grapes of Wrath*
Supporting Actor: Walter Brennan, *The Westerner*

1941
Picture: *How Green Was My Valley*, 20th Century–Fox
Director: John Ford, *How Green Was My Valley*
Actress: Joan Fontaine, *Suspicion*
Actor: Gary Cooper, *Sergeant York*
Supporting Actress: Mary Astor, *The Great Lie*
Supporting Actor: Donald Crisp, *How Green Was My Valley*

1942

Picture: *Mrs. Miniver,* MGM
Director: William Wyler, *Mrs. Miniver*
Actress: Greer Garson, *Mrs. Miniver*
Actor: James Cagney, *Yankee Doodle Dandy*
Supporting Actress: Teresa Wright, *Mrs. Miniver*
Supporting Actor: Van Heflin, *Johnny Eager*

1943

Picture: *Casablanca,* Warner Bros.
Director: Michael Curtiz, *Casablanca*
Actress: Jennifer Jones, *The Song of Bernadette*
Actor: Paul Lukas, *Watch on the Rhine*
Supporting Actress: Katina Paxinou, *For Whom the Bell Tolls*
Supporting Actor: Charles Coburn, *The More the Merrier*

1944

Picture: *Going My Way,* Paramount
Director: Leo McCarey, *Going My Way*
Actress: Ingrid Bergman, *Gaslight*
Actor: Bing Crosby, *Going My Way*
Supporting Actress: Ethel Barrymore, *None but the Lonely Heart*
Supporting Actor: Barry Fitzgerald, *Going My Way*

1945

Picture: *The Lost Weekend,* Paramount
Director: Billy Wilder, *The Lost Weekend*
Actress: Joan Crawford, *Mildred Pierce*
Actor: Ray Milland, *The Lost Weekend*
Supporting Actress: Anne Revere, *National Velvet*
Supporting Actor: James Dunn, *A Tree Grows in Brooklyn*

1946

Picture: *The Best Years of Our Lives,* Goldwyn-RKO Radio
Director: William Wyler, *The Best Years of Our Lives*
Actress: Olivia de Havilland, *To Each His Own*
Actor: Fredric March, *The Best Years of Our Lives*
Supporting Actress: Anne Baxter, *The Razor's Edge*
Supporting Actor: Harold Russell, *The Best Years of Our Lives*

1947

Picture: *Gentleman's Agreement,* 20th Century–Fox
Director: Elia Kazan, *Gentleman's Agreement*
Actress: Loretta Young, *The Farmer's Daughter*
Actor: Ronald Colman, *A Double Life*
Supporting Actress: Celeste Holm, *Gentleman's Agreement*
Supporting Actor: Edmund Gwenn, *Miracle on 34th Street*

1948

Picture: *Hamlet,* Rank-Two Cities-UI
Director: John Huston, *Treasure of Sierra Madre*
Actress: Jane Wyman, *Johnny Belinda*
Actor: Laurence Olivier, *Hamlet*
Supporting Actress: Claire Trevor, *Key Largo*
Supporting Actor: Walter Huston, *Treasure of Sierra Madre*

1949

Picture: *All the King's Men,* Rossen-Columbia
Director: Joseph L. Mankiewicz, *A Letter to Three Wives*
Actress: Olivia de Havilland, *The Heiress*
Actor: Broderick Crawford, *All the King's Men*
Supporting Actress: Mercedes McCambridge, *All the King's Men*
Supporting Actor: Dean Jagger, *Twelve O'Clock High*

1950

Picture: *All About Eve,* 20th Century–Fox
Director: Joseph L. Mankiewicz, *All About Eve*
Actress: Judy Holliday, *Born Yesterday*
Actor: José Ferrer, *Cyrano de Bergerac*
Supporting Actress: Josephine Hull, *Harvey*
Supporting Actor: George Sanders, *All About Eve*

1951

Picture: *An American in Paris,* MGM
Director: George Stevens, *A Place in the Sun*
Actress: Vivien Leigh, *A Streetcar Named Desire*
Actor: Humphrey Bogart, *The African Queen*
Supporting Actress: Kim Hunter, *A Streetcar Named Desire*
Supporting Actor: Karl Malden, *A Streetcar Named Desire*

1952

Picture: *The Greatest Show on Earth,* DeMille-Paramount
Director: John Ford, *The Quiet Man*
Actress: Shirley Booth, *Come Back, Little Sheba*
Actor: Gary Cooper, *High Noon*
Supporting Actress: Gloria Grahame, *The Bad and the Beautiful*
Supporting Actor: Anthony Quinn, *Viva Zapata!*

1953

Picture: *From Here to Eternity,* Columbia
Director: Fred Zinnemann, *From Here to Eternity*
Actress: Audrey Hepburn, *Roman Holiday*
Actor: William Holden, *Stalag 17*
Supporting Actress: Donna Reed, *From Here to Eternity*
Supporting Actor: Frank Sinatra, *From Here to Eternity*

1954

Picture: *On the Waterfront,* Horizon-American Corp., Columbia
Director: Elia Kazan, *On the Waterfront*
Actress: Grace Kelly, *The Country Girl*
Actor: Marlon Brando, *On the Waterfront*
Supporting Actress: Eva Marie Saint, *On the Waterfront*
Supporting Actor: Edmond O'Brien, *The Barefoot Contessa*

1955

Picture: *Marty,* Hecht and Lancaster, United Artists
Director: Delbert Mann, *Marty*
Actress: Anna Magnani, *The Rose Tattoo*
Actor: Ernest Borgnine, *Marty*
Supporting Actress: Jo Van Fleet, *East of Eden*
Supporting Actor: Jack Lemmon, *Mister Roberts*

1956

Picture: *Around the World in 80 Days,* Michael Todd Co., Inc.-United Artists
Director: George Stevens, *Giant*
Actress: Ingrid Bergman, *Anastasia*
Actor: Yul Brynner, *The King and I*
Supporting Actress: Dorothy Malone, *Written on the Wind*
Supporting Actor: Anthony Quinn, *Lust for Life*

1957

Picture: *The Bridge on the River Kwai,* Horizon Films, Columbia
Director: David Lean, *The Bridge on the River Kwai*
Actress: Joanne Woodward, *The Three Faces of Eve*
Actor: Alec Guinness, *The Bridge on the River Kwai*
Supporting Actress: Miyoshi Umeki, *Sayonara*
Supporting Actor: Red Buttons, *Sayonara*

1958

Picture: *Gigi,* Arthur Freed Productions, Inc., MGM
Director: Vincente Minnelli, *Gigi*
Actress: Susan Hayward, *I Want to Live!*
Actor: David Niven, *Separate Tables*
Supporting Actress: Wendy Hiller, *Separate Tables*
Supporting Actor: Burl Ives, *The Big Country*

1959

Picture: *Ben-Hur,* MGM
Director: William Wyler, *Ben-Hur*
Actress: Simone Signoret, *Room at the Top*
Actor: Charlton Heston, *Ben-Hur*
Supporting Actress: Shelley Winters, *The Diary of Anne Frank*
Supporting Actor: Hugh Griffith, *Ben-Hur*

1960

Picture: *The Apartment,* Mirisch Co., Inc., United Artists
Director: Billy Wilder, *The Apartment*
Actress: Elizabeth Taylor, *Butterfield 8*
Actor: Burt Lancaster, *Elmer Gantry*
Supporting Actress: Shirley Jones, *Elmer Gantry*
Supporting Actor: Peter Ustinov, *Spartacus*

1961
Picture: *West Side Story,* Mirisch Pictures, Inc., and B and P Enterprises, Inc., United Artists
Director: Robert Wise and Jerome Robbins, *West Side Story*
Actress: Sophia Loren, *Two Women*
Actor: Maximillian Schell, *Judgment at Nuremberg*
Supporting Actress: Rita Moreno, *West Side Story*
Supporting Actor: George Chakiris, *West Side Story*

1962
Picture: *Lawrence of Arabia,* Horizon Pictures, Ltd.-Columbia
Director: David Lean, *Lawrence of Arabia*
Actress: Anne Bancroft, *The Miracle Worker*
Actor: Gregory Peck, *To Kill a Mockingbird*
Supporting Actress: Patty Duke, *The Miracle Worker*
Supporting Actor: Ed Begley, *Sweet Bird of Youth*

1963
Picture: *Tom Jones,* A Woodfall Production, United Artists-Lopert Pictures
Director: Tony Richardson, *Tom Jones*
Actress: Patricia Neal, *Hud*
Actor: Sidney Poitier, *Lilies of the Field*
Supporting Actress: Margaret Rutherford, *The V.I.P.s*
Supporting Actor: Melvyn Douglas, *Hud*

1964
Picture: *My Fair Lady,* Warner Bros.
Director: George Cukor, *My Fair Lady*
Actress: Julie Andrews, *Mary Poppins*
Actor: Rex Harrison, *My Fair Lady*
Supporting Actress: Lila Kedrova, *Zorba the Greek*
Supporting Actor: Peter Ustinov, *Topkapi*

1965
Picture: *The Sound of Music,* Argyle Enterprises Production, 20th Century–Fox
Director: Robert Wise, *The Sound of Music*
Actress: Julie Christie, *Darling*
Actor: Lee Marvin, *Cat Ballou*
Supporting Actress: Shelley Winters, *A Patch of Blue*
Supporting Actor: Martin Balsam, *A Thousand Clowns*

1966
Picture: *A Man for All Seasons,* Highland Films, Ltd., Production, Columbia
Director: Fred Zinnemann, *A Man for All Seasons*
Actress: Elizabeth Taylor, *Who's Afraid of Virginia Woolf?*
Actor: Paul Scofield, *A Man for All Seasons*
Supporting Actress: Sandy Dennis, *Who's Afraid of Virginia Woolf?*
Supporting Actor: Walter Matthau, *The Fortune Cookie*

1967
Picture: *In the Heat of the Night,* Mirisch Corp. Productions, United Artists
Director: Mike Nichols, *The Graduate*
Actress: Katharine Hepburn, *Guess Who's Coming to Dinner*
Actor: Rod Steiger, *In the Heat of the Night*
Supporting Actress: Estelle Parsons, *Bonnie and Clyde*
Supporting Actor: George Kennedy, *Cool Hand Luke*

1968
Picture: *Oliver!,* Columbia Pictures
Director: Sir Carol Reed, *Oliver!*
Actress: Katharine Hepburn, *The Lion in Winter* and Barbra Streisand, *Funny Girl*
Actor: Cliff Robertson, *Charly*
Supporting Actress: Ruth Gordon, *Rosemary's Baby*
Supporting Actor: Jack Albertson, *The Subject Was Roses*

1969
Picture: *Midnight Cowboy,* Jerome Hellman-John Schlesinger Production, United Artists
Director: John Schlesinger, *Midnight Cowboy*
Actress: Maggie Smith, *The Prime of Miss Jean Brodie*
Actor: John Wayne, *True Grit*

Supporting Actress: Goldie Hawn, *Cactus Flower*
Supporting Actor: Gig Young, *They Shoot Horses, Don't They?*

1970
Picture: *Patton,* Frank McCarthy-Franklin J. Schaffner Production, 20th Century–Fox
Director: Franklin J. Schaffner, *Patton*
Actress: Glenda Jackson, *Women in Love*
Actor: George C. Scott, *Patton*
Supporting Actress: Helen Hayes, *Airport*
Supporting Actor: John Mills, *Ryan's Daughter*

1971
Picture: *The French Connection,* D'Antoni Productions, 20th Century–Fox
Director: William Friedkin, *The French Connection*
Actress: Jane Fonda, *Klute*
Actor: Gene Hackman, *The French Connection*
Supporting Actress: Cloris Leachman, *The Last Picture Show*
Supporting Actor: Ben Johnson, *The Last Picture Show*

1972
Picture: *The Godfather,* Albert S. Ruddy Production, Paramount
Director: Bob Fosse, *Cabaret*
Actress: Liza Minnelli, *Cabaret*
Actor: Marlon Brando, *The Godfather*
Supporting Actress: Eileen Heckart, *Butterflies Are Free*
Supporting Actor: Joel Gray, *Cabaret*

1973
Picture: *The Sting,* Universal-Bill/Phillips-George Roy Hill Production, Universal
Director: George Roy Hill, *The Sting*
Actress: Glenda Jackson, *A Touch of Class*
Actor: Jack Lemmon, *Save the Tiger*
Supporting Actress: Tatum O'Neal, *Paper Moon*
Supporting Actor: John Houseman, *The Paper Chase*

1974
Picture: *The Godfather, Part II,* Coppola Co. Production, Paramount
Director: Francis Ford Coppola, *The Godfather, Part II*
Actress: Ellen Burstyn, *Alice Doesn't Live Here Anymore*
Actor: Art Carney, *Harry and Tonto*
Supporting Actress: Ingrid Bergman, *Murder on the Orient Express*
Supporting Actor: Robert De Niro, *The Godfather, Part II*

1975
Picture: *One Flew Over the Cuckoo's Nest,* Fantasy Films Production, United Artists
Director: Milos Forman, *One Flew Over the Cuckoo's Nest*
Actress: Louise Fletcher, *One Flew Over the Cuckoo's Nest*
Actor: Jack Nicholson, *One Flew Over the Cuckoo's Nest*
Supporting Actress: Lee Grant, *Shampoo*
Supporting Actor: George Burns, *The Sunshine Boys*

1976
Picture: *Rocky,* Robert Chartoff-Irwin Winkler Production, United Artists
Director: John G. Avildsen, *Rocky*
Actress: Faye Dunaway, *Network*
Actor: Peter Finch, *Network*
Supporting Actress: Beatrice Straight, *Network*
Supporting Actor: Jason Robards, *All the President's Men*

1977
Picture: *Annie Hall,* Jack Rollins-Charles H. Joffe Production, United Artists
Director: Woody Allen, *Annie Hall*
Actress: Diane Keaton, *Annie Hall*
Actor: Richard Dreyfuss, *The Goodbye Girl*
Supporting Actress: Vanessa Redgrave, *Julia*
Supporting Actor: Jason Robards, *Julia*

1978
Picture: *The Deer Hunter,* Michael Cimino Film Production, Universal
Director: Michael Cimino, *The Deer Hunter*

Actress: Jane Fonda, *Coming Home*
Actor: Jon Voight, *Coming Home*
Supporting Actress: Maggie Smith, *California Suite*
Supporting Actor: Christopher Walken, *The Deer Hunter*

1979

Picture: *Kramer vs. Kramer,* Stanley Jaffe Production, Columbia Pictures
Director: Robert Benton, *Kramer vs. Kramer*
Actress: Sally Field, *Norma Rae*
Actor: Dustin Hoffman, *Kramer vs. Kramer*
Supporting Actress: Meryl Streep, *Kramer vs. Kramer*
Supporting Actor: Melvyn Douglas, *Being There*

1980

Picture: *Ordinary People,* Wildwood Enterprises Production, Paramount
Director: Robert Redford, *Ordinary People*
Actress: Sissy Spacek, *Coal Miner's Daughter*
Actor: Robert De Niro, *Raging Bull*
Supporting Actress: Mary Steenburgen, *Melvin and Howard*
Supporting Actor: Timothy Hutton, *Ordinary People*

1981

Picture: *Chariots of Fire,* Enigma Productions, Ladd Company/Warner Bros.
Director: Warren Beatty, *Reds*
Actress: Katharine Hepburn, *On Golden Pond*
Actor: Henry Fonda, *On Golden Pond*
Supporting Actress: Maureen Stapleton, *Reds*
Supporting Actor: John Gielgud, *Arthur*

1982

Picture: *Gandhi,* Indo-British Films Production/Columbia
Director: Richard Attenborough, *Gandhi*
Actress: Meryl Streep, *Sophie's Choice*
Actor: Ben Kingsley, *Gandhi*
Supporting Actress: Jessica Lange, *Tootsie*
Supporting Actor: Louis Gossett, Jr., *An Officer and a Gentleman*

1983

Picture: *Terms of Endearment,* Paramount
Director: James L. Brooks, *Terms of Endearment*
Actress: Shirley MacLaine, *Terms of Endearment*
Actor: Robert Duvall, *Tender Mercies*
Supporting Actress: Linda Hunt, *The Year of Living Dangerously*
Supporting Actor: Jack Nicholson, *Terms of Endearment*

1984

Picture: *Amadeus,* Orion
Director: Milos Forman, *Amadeus*
Actress: Sally Field, *Places in the Heart*
Actor: F. Murray Abraham, *Amadeus*
Supporting Actress: Dame Peggy Ashcroft, *A Passage to India*
Supporting Actor: Haing S. Ngor, *The Killing Fields*

1985

Picture: *Out of Africa,* Universal
Director: Sydney Pollack, *Out of Africa*
Actress: Geraldine Page, *The Trip to Bountiful*
Actor: William Hurt, *Kiss of the Spider Woman*
Supporting Actress: Anjelica Huston, *Prizzi's Honor*
Supporting Actor: Don Ameche, *Cocoon*

1986

Picture: *Platoon,* Orion
Director: Oliver Stone, *Platoon*
Actress: Marlee Matlin, *Children of a Lesser God*
Actor: Paul Newman, *The Color of Money*
Supporting Actress: Dianne Wiest, *Hannah and Her Sisters*
Supporting Actor: Michael Caine, *Hannah and Her Sisters*

1987

Picture: *The Last Emperor,* Columbia Pictures
Director: Bernardo Bertolucci, *The Last Emperor*
Actress: Cher, *Moonstruck*
Actor: Michael Douglas, *Wall Street*
Supporting Actress: Olympia Dukakis, *Moonstruck*
Supporting Actor: Sean Connery, *The Untouchables*

1988

Picture: *Rain Man,* United Artists
Director: Barry Levinson, *Rain Man*
Actress: Jodie Foster, *The Accused*
Actor: Dustin Hoffman, *Rain Man*
Supporting Actress: Geena Davis, *The Accidental Tourist*
Supporting Actor: Kevin Kline, *A Fish Called Wanda*

1989

Picture: *Driving Miss Daisy,* Warner Bros.
Director: Oliver Stone, *Born on the Fourth of July*
Actress: Jessica Tandy, *Driving Miss Daisy*
Actor: Daniel Day-Lewis, *My Left Foot*
Supporting Actress: Brenda Fricker, *My Left Foot*
Supporting Actor: Denzel Washington, *Glory*

1990

Picture: *Dances With Wolves,* Orion
Director: Kevin Costner, *Dances With Wolves*
Actress: Kathy Bates, *Misery*
Actor: Jeremy Irons, *Reversal of Fortune*
Supporting Actress: Whoopi Goldberg, *Ghost*
Supporting Actor: Joe Pesci, *Goodfellas*

1991

Picture: *The Silence of the Lambs,* Orion
Director: Jonathan Demme, *The Silence of the Lambs*
Actress: Jodie Foster, *The Silence of the Lambs*
Actor: Anthony Hopkins, *The Silence of the Lambs*
Supporting Actress: Mercedes Ruehl, *The Fisher King*
Supporting Actor: Jack Palance, *City Slickers*

1992

Picture: *Unforgiven,* Warner Bros.
Director: Clint Eastwood, *Unforgiven*
Actress: Emma Thompson, *Howards End*
Actor: Al Pacino, *Scent of a Woman*
Supporting Actress: Marisa Tomei, *My Cousin Vinny*
Supporting Actor: Gene Hackman, *Unforgiven*

1993

Picture: *Schindler's List,* Universal
Director: Steven Spielberg, *Schindler's List*
Actress: Holly Hunter, *The Piano*
Actor: Tom Hanks, *Philadelphia*
Supporting Actress: Anna Paquin, *The Piano*
Supporting Actor: Tommy Lee Jones, *The Fugitive*

1994

Picture: *Forrest Gump,* Paramount
Director: Robert Zemeckis, *Forrest Gump*
Actress: Jessica Lange, *Blue Sky*
Actor: Tom Hanks, *Forrest Gump*
Supporting Actress: Dianne Wiest, *Bullets Over Broadway*
Supporting Actor: Martin Landau, *Ed Wood*

1995

Picture: *Braveheart,* Paramount
Director: Mel Gibson, *Braveheart*
Actress: Susan Sarandon, *Dead Man Walking*
Actor: Nicolas Cage, *Leaving Las Vegas*
Supporting Actress: Mira Sorvino, *Mighty Aphrodite*
Supporting Actor: Kevin Spacey, *The Usual Suspects*

1996

Picture: *The English Patient,* Miramax
Director: Anthony Minghella, *The English Patient*
Actress: Frances McDormand, *Fargo*
Actor: Geoffrey Rush, *Shine*
Supporting Actress: Juliette Binoche, *The English Patient*
Supporting Actor: Cuba Gooding, Jr., *Jerry Maguire*

1997

Picture: *Titanic,* 20th Century–Fox and Paramount
Director: James Cameron, *Titanic*
Actress: Helen Hunt, *As Good As It Gets*
Actor: Jack Nicholson, *As Good As It Gets*
Supporting Actress: Kim Basinger, *L.A. Confidential*
Supporting Actor: Robin Williams, *Good Will Hunting*

1998

Picture: *Shakespeare in Love*, Miramax
Director: Steven Spielberg, *Saving Private Ryan*
Actress: Gwyneth Paltrow, *Shakespeare in Love*
Actor: Roberto Benigni, *Life Is Beautiful*
Supporting Actress: Judi Dench, *Shakespeare in Love*
Supporting Actor: James Coburn, *Affliction*

1999

Picture: *American Beauty*, DreamWorks SKG
Director: Sam Mendes, *American Beauty*
Actress: Hilary Swank, *Boys Don't Cry*

Actor: Kevin Spacey, *American Beauty*
Supporting Actress: Angelina Jolie, *Girl, Interrupted*
Supporting Actor: Michael Caine, *The Cider House Rules*

2000

Picture: *Gladiator*, DreamWorks and Universal
Director: Steven Soderbergh, *Traffic*
Actress: Julia Roberts, *Erin Brockovich*
Actor: Russell Crowe, *Gladiator*
Supporting Actress: Marcia Gay Harden, *Pollock*
Supporting Actor: Benicio Del Toro, *Traffic*

Other Academy Awards for 2000

Art Direction: Tim Yip, *Crouching Tiger, Hidden Dragon*
Cinematography: Peter Pau, *Crouching Tiger, Hidden Dragon*
Costume Design: Janty Yates, *Gladiator*
Documentary (feature): *Into the Arms of Strangers: Stories of the Kindertransport* (Mark Jonathan Harris and Deborah Oppenheimer)
Editing: Stephen Mirrione, *Traffic*
Foreign-Language Film: *Crouching Tiger, Hidden Dragon*, Taiwan
Makeup: Rick Baker and Gail Ryan, *Dr. Seuss' How the Grinch Stole Christmas*
Music (original score): Tan Dun, *Crouching Tiger, Hidden Dragon*
Best Original Song: Bob Dylan, "Things Have Changed," *Wonder Boys*

Adapted Screenplay: Stephen Gaghan, *Traffic*
Original Screenplay: Cameron Crowe, *Almost Famous*
Short Subject (live action): *Quiero Ser (I Want to Be)* (Florian Gallenberger)
Sound: Scott Millan, Bob Beemer, and Ken Weston, *Gladiator*
Sound Effects Editing: Jon Johnson, *U-571*
Visual Effects: John Nelson, Neil Corbould, Tim Burke, and Rob Harvey, *Gladiator*
Honorary Awards: Jack Cardiff, cinematographer; Ernest Lehman, screenwriter, producer, director
Irving G. Thalberg Memorial Award: Dino De Laurentiis, producer
Gordon E. Sawyer Award (technological contribution): Irwin W. Young

2000 National Society of Film Critics Awards

Best Picture: *Yi Yi (A One and a Two)*
Best Actor: Javier Bardem, *Before Night Falls*
Best Actress: Laura Linney, *You Can Count on Me*
Best Supporting Actor: Benicio Del Toro, *Traffic*
Best Supporting Actress: Elaine May, *Small Time Crooks*
Best Director: Steven Soderbergh, *Traffic* and *Erin Brockovich*
Best Screenplay: Kenneth Lonergan, *You Can Count on Me*

Best Cinematography: Agnès Godard, *Beau travail*
Best Foreign Film: Not awarded
Best Documentary: *The Life and Times of Hank Greenberg*, Aviva Kempner
Best Experimental Film: *The Heart of the World*, Guy Maddin
Special Citation: Michelangelo Antonioni, for the exemplary intelligence, creativity, and integrity of his half-century-long career.
Special Award: National Film Preservation Foundation

2000 Broadcast Film Critics Association Awards

Best Picture: *Gladiator*
Best Actor: Russell Crowe, *Gladiator*
Best Actress: Julia Roberts, *Erin Brockovich*
Best Supporting Actor: Joaquin Phoenix, *Quills, The Yards,* and *Gladiator*
Best Supporting Actress: Frances McDormand, *Wonder Boys* and *Almost Famous*
Best Director: Steven Soderbergh, *Erin Brockovich* and *Traffic*
Best Original Screenplay: Cameron Crowe, *Almost Famous*
Best Song: "My Funny Friend and Me," Sting, *The Emperor's New Groove*

Best Score: Hans Zimmer, *Gladiator, Mission Impossible: 2,* and *The Road to El Dorado*
Best Foreign Language Film: *Crouching Tiger, Hidden Dragon*, Ang Lee (Taiwan)
Best Documentary: *The Life and Times of Hank Greenberg*
Best Animated Feature: *Chicken Run*
Best Family Film: *My Dog Skip*
Best Child Performance: Jamie Bell, *Billy Elliot*
Breakthrough Performer: Kate Hudson, *Almost Famous*

2000 National Board of Review Awards

Best Picture: *Quills*
Best Actor: Javier Bardem, *Before Night Falls*
Best Actress: Julia Roberts, *Erin Brockovich*
Best Supporting Actor: Joaquin Phoenix, *Gladiator, Quills,* and *The Yards*
Best Supporting Actress: Lupe Ontiveros, *Chuck & Buck*
Best Director: Steven Soderbergh, *Erin Brockovich* and *Traffic*
Best Foreign Film: *Crouching Tiger, Hidden Dragon* (Taiwan)
Outstanding Achievement in Foreign Film: Krzysztof Kieslowski, *Decalogue* series

Best Documentary: *The Life and Times of Hank Greenberg*
Best Screenplay: Ted Tally, *All the Pretty Horses*
Best Ensemble: *State and Main*
Best Animated Feature: *Chicken Run*
Production Design and Art Direction: *Gladiator*
Breakthrough Performance: Michelle Rodriguez, *Girlfight*
Outstanding Young Actor: Jamie Bell, *Billy Elliot*
Outstanding Dramatic Musical Performance: Björk, *Dancing in the Dark*
Career Achievement Award: Ellen Burstyn
Special Achievement in Filmmaking: Kenneth Lonergan

2000 Golden Globe Awards

Film Awards

Best Motion Picture—Drama: *Gladiator*
Best Actor in a Drama: Tom Hanks, *Cast Away*
Best Actress in a Drama: Julia Roberts, *Erin Brockovich*
Best Motion Picture—Musical or Comedy: *Almost Famous*
Best Actor in a Musical or Comedy: George Clooney, *O Brother, Where Art Thou?*
Best Actress in a Musical or Comedy: Renée Zellweger, *Nurse Betty*
Best Supporting Actor: Benicio Del Toro, *Traffic*
Best Supporting Actress: Kate Hudson, *Almost Famous*
Best Director: Ang Lee, *Crouching Tiger, Hidden Dragon*
Best Screenplay: Stephen Gaghan, *Traffic*
Best Original Score: Hans Zimmer and Lisa Gerrard, *Gladiator*
Best Original Song: Bob Dylan, "Things Have Changed," *Wonder Boys*
Best Foreign Film: *Crouching Tiger, Hidden Dragon* (Taiwan)

Television Awards

Best Series—Drama: *The West Wing* (ABC)
Best Actor in a Drama: Martin Sheen, *The West Wing*
Best Actress in a Drama: Sela Ward, *Once and Again*
Best Series—Musical or Comedy: *Sex and the City* (HBO)
Best Actor in a Musical or Comedy Series: Kelsey Grammer, *Frasier*
Best Actress in a Musical or Comedy Series: Sarah Jessica Parker, *Sex and the City*
Best Miniseries or Movie Made for Television: *Dirty Pictures* (Showtime)
Best Actor in a Miniseries or Movie Made for Television: Brian Dennehy, *Arthur Miller's Death of a Salesman*
Best Actress in a Miniseries or Movie Made for Television: Judi Dench, *Last of the Blond Bombshells*
Best Supporting Actor in a Series, Miniseries, or Movie Made for Television: Robert Downey Jr., *Ally McBeal*
Best Supporting Actress in a Series, Miniseries, or Movie Made for Television: Vanessa Redgrave, *If These Walls Could Talk 2*

2001 Tony (Antoinette Perry) Awards

Play: *Proof*
Musical: *The Producers*
Revival—Play: *One Flew Over the Cuckoo's Nest*
Revival—Musical: *42nd Street*
Actor—Play: Richard Easton, *The Invention of Love*
Actress—Play: Mary-Louise Parker, *Proof*
Actor—Musical: Nathan Lane, *The Producers*
Actress—Musical: Christine Ebersol, *42nd Street*
Featured Actor—Play: Robert Sean Leonard, *The Invention of Love*
Featured Actress—Play: Viola Davis, *King Hedley II*
Featured Actor—Musical: Gary Beach, *The Producers*
Featured Actress—Musical: Cady Huffman, *The Producers*
Director—Play: Daniel Sullivan, *Proof*
Director—Musical: Susan Stroman, *The Producers*
Book—Musical: Mel Brooks and Thomas Meehan, *The Producers*

Score—Musical: Mel Brooks, *The Producers*
Orchestration: Douglas Besterman, *The Producers*
Scenic Designer: Robin Wagner, *The Producers*
Costume Designer: William Ivey Long, *The Producers*
Choreographer: Susan Stroman, *The Producers*
Lighting Designer: Peter Kaczorowski, *The Producers*
Regional Theater: Victory Gardens Theater, Chicago, Illinois
Special Awards: Musical director Paul Gemignani, for lifetime achievement;
Blast!, special Tony Award for a special theatrical event
Excellence in Theatre: Betty Corwin and the Theatre on Film and Tape Archive at the New York Public Library for the Performing Arts at Lincoln Center;
the playwright workshop New Dramatists;
Theatre World, the annual statistics and photography book

2001 Drama Desk Awards

Outstanding Play: *Proof*
Outstanding Musical: *The Producers*
Outstanding Musical Revival: *42nd Street*
Outstanding Musical Revue: *Forbidden Broadway 2001: A Spoof Odyssey*
Outstanding Play Revival: *Gore Vidal's The Best Man*
Outstanding Solo Performance: Pamela Gien, *The Syringa Tree*
Unique Theatrical Experience: *Mnemonic*
Best Actor in a Play: Richard Easton, *The Invention of Love*
Best Actress in a Play: Mary-Louise Parker, *Proof*
Best Featured Actor in a Play: Charles Brown, *King Hedley II*
Best Featured Actress in a Play: Viola Davis, *King Hedley II*
Best Actor in a Musical: Nathan Lane, *The Producers*
Best Actress in a Musical: Marla Schaffel, *Jane Eyre*
Best Featured Actor in a Musical: Gary Beach, *The Producers*
Best Featured Actress in a Musical: Cady Huffman, *The Producers*
Best Director of a Play: Jack O'Brien, *The Invention of Love*

Best Director of a Musical: Susan Stroman, *The Producers*
Best Choreography: Susan Stroman, *The Producers*
Best Music: David Yazbek, *The Full Monty*
Best Lyrics: Mel Brooks, *The Producers*
Outstanding Orchestrations: Doug Besterman, *The Producers*
Outstanding Sound Design: Christopher Shutt, *Mnemonic*
Outstanding Set Design of a Play: Bob Crowley, *The Invention of Love*
Outstanding Set Design of a Musical: Robin Wagner, *The Producers*
Outstanding Costume Design: William Ivey Long, *The Producers*
Outstanding Lighting Design: Paul Anderson, *Mnemonic*
Outstanding Ensemble Performance: the casts of *Cobb* and *Tabletop*
Special Awards: Sean Campion and Conleth Hill, for their performances in *Stones in His Pockets*;
Reba McEntire for her performance in *Annie Get Your Gun*

2000–2001 Obie Awards

The Obie Awards, presented by *The Village Voice*, honor superior off-Broadway theater.

Best Play: Pamela Gien, *The Syringa Tree*
Playwriting: José Rivera, *References to Salvador Dalí Make Me Hot*
Direction: Michael Greif, *Dogeaters*; Craig Lucas, *Saved or Destroyed*
Performance: George Bartenieff, *I Will Bear Witness*; Stephanie Berry, *The Shaneequa Chronicles*; Ronnell Bey, Mandy Gonzalez, Judy Kuhn, and Anika Noni Rose, *Eli's Comin'*; Bette Bourne, *Resident Alien*; Brian d'Arcy James, *The Good Thief*; Janie Dee, *Comic Potential*; Jackie Hoffman, *The Book of Liz*; Pamela Isaacs, *Newyorkers*; Brian Murray, *The Play About the Baby*; John Ortiz, *References to Salvador Dalí Make Me Hot*; Mary-Louise Parker, *Proof*
Set Design: Neil Patel, *I Will Bear Witness, Race, Resident Alien*, and *War of the Worlds*; Douglas Stein, *Saved* and *Texts for Nothing*
Music: Diedre Murray, vocal and instrumental arrangements, *Eli's Comin'*; Bill Sims, Jr., *Lackawanna Blues*

Choreography: John Carrafa, *Urinetown*
Special Citations: Justin Bond and Kenny Mellman, *Kiki and Herb: Jesus Wept*; Kirsten Childs, music and lyrics, *The Bubbly Black Girl Sheds Her Chameleon Skin*; Rinde Eckert, *And God Created Great Whales*; Mark Hollmann and Greg Kotis, book and lyrics, *Urinetown*; Ed Kleban, music and lyrics, *A Class Act*; Bob McGrath, director; Cynthia Hopkins, Pilar Limosner, Bill Morrison, Laurie Olinder, Ruth Pongstaphone, Tim Schellenbaum, Howard S. Thies, Matthew Tierney, Fred Tietz, and Julia Wolfe, designers, *Jennie Richee*; Ruben Santiago-Hudson; *Lackawanna Blues*
Sustained Achievement: Marian Seldes
Ross Wetzsteon Grant: Classical Theater of Harlem; Clubbed Thumb; Mint Theater Company; Soho Rep; Theatre for a New Audience

Major Grammy Awards for Recording in 2000

Record: "Beautiful Day," U2
Album: *Two Against Nature*, Steely Dan
Song: "Beautiful Day," U2, songwriters
New Artist: Shelby Lynne
Female Pop Vocal: "I Try," Macy Gray
Male Pop Vocal: "She Walks This Earth (Soberana Rosa)," Sting
Pop Duo or Group with Vocals: "Cousin Dupree," Steely Dan
Pop Collaboration with Vocals: "Is You Is, or Is You Ain't (My Baby)," B. B. King and Dr. John
Pop Instrumental: "Caravan," The Brian Setzer Orchestra
Dance Recording: "Who Let the Dogs Out," Baha Men
Pop Instrumental Album: *Symphony No. 1*, Joe Jackson
Pop Vocal Album: *Two Against Nature*, Steely Dan
Traditional Pop Vocal Album: *Both Sides Now*, Joni Mitchell
Female Rock Vocal: "There Goes the Neighborhood," Sheryl Crow
Male Rock Vocal: "Again," Lenny Kravitz
Rock Duo or Group with Vocals: "Beautiful Day," U2
Hard Rock: "Guerrilla Radio," Rage Against the Machine
Metal: "Elite," Deftones
Rock Instrumental: "The Call of Ktulu," Metallica with Michael Kamen conducting the San Francisco Symphony Orchestra
Rock Song: "With Arms Wide Open," Scott Stapp and Mark Tremonti, songwriters (Creed)
Rock Album: *There Is Nothing Left to Lose*, Foo Fighters
Alternative Music Album: *Kid A*, Radiohead
Female R&B Vocal: "He Wasn't Man Enough," Toni Braxton
Male R&B Vocal: "Untitled (How Does It Feel)," D'Angelo
R&B Duo or Group with Vocals: "Say My Name," Destiny's Child
R&B Song: "Say My Name," LaShawn Daniels, Fred Jerkins III, Rodney Jerkins, Beyoncé Knowles, LeToya Luckett, LaTavia Roberson, and Kelendria Rowland, songwriters (Destiny's Child)
R&B Album: *Voodoo*, D'Angelo
Traditional R&B Vocal Performance: *Ear-Resistible*, The Temptations
Rap Solo: "The Real Slim Shady," Eminem
Rap Duo or Group: "Forgot About Dre," Dr. Dre featuring Eminem
Rap Album: *The Marshall Mathers LP*, Eminem
Female Country Vocal: "Breathe," Faith Hill
Male Country Vocal: "Solitary Man," Johnny Cash
Country Duo or Group with Vocals: "Cherokee Maiden,"

Asleep at the Wheel
Country Collaboration with Vocals: "Let's Make Love," Faith Hill and Tim McGraw
Country Instrumental: "Leaving Cottondale," Alison Brown with Béla Fleck
Country Song: "I Hope You Dance," Mark D. Sanders and Tia Sillers, songwriters (Lee Ann Womack)
Country Album: *Breathe*, Faith Hill
Bluegrass Album: *The Grass Is Blue*, Dolly Parton
New Age Album: *Thinking of You*, Kitaro
Contemporary Jazz: *Outbound*, Béla Fleck and the Flecktones
Jazz Vocal: *In the Moment—Live in Concert*, Dianne Reeves
Jazz Instrumental, Solo: "(Go) Get It," Pat Metheny
Jazz Instrumental, Individual or Group: *Contemporary Jazz*, Branford Marsalis Quartet
Large Jazz Ensemble: *52nd Street Themes*, Joe Lovano
Latin Jazz: *Live at the Village Vanguard*, Chucho Valdés
Rock Gospel Album: *Double Take*, Petra
Pop/Contemporary Gospel Album: *If I Left the Zoo*, Jars of Clay
Southern Gospel, Country Gospel, or Bluegrass Gospel Album: *Soldier of the Cross*, Ricky Skaggs and Kentucky Thunder
Traditional Soul Gospel Album: *You Can Make It*, Shirley Caesar
Contemporary Soul Gospel Album: *Thankful*, Mary Mary
Gospel Album by a Choir or Chorus: *Live—God Is Working*, Brooklyn Tabernacle Choir; Carol Cymbala, choir director
Latin Pop Album: *Shakira—MTV Unplugged*, Shakira
Latin Rock/Alternative Album: *Uno*, La Ley
Tropical Latin Album: *Alma Caribeña*, Gloria Estefan
Salsa Album: *Masterpiece/Obra Maestra*, Tito Puente and Eddie Palmieri
Mexican Merengue Album: *Olga Viva, Viva Olga*, Olga Tañón
Mexican-American Album: *Por Una Mujer Bonita*, Pepe Aguilar
Tejano Album: *¿Qué Es Música Tejana?*, The Legends
Traditional Blues Album: *Riding with the King*, B. B. King and Eric Clapton
Contemporary Blues Album: *Shoutin' in Key*, Taj Mahal and the Phantom Blues Band
Traditional Folk Album: *Public Domain—Songs from the Wild Land*, Dave Alvin
Contemporary Folk Album: *Red Dirt Girl*, Emmylou Harris
Native American Music Album: *Gathering of Nations*

Pow Wow, Various Artists
Reggae Album: *Art and Life*, Beenie Man
World Music Album: *João Voz e Violão*, João Gilberto
Polka Album: *Touched by a Polka*, Jimmy Sturr
Musical Album for Children: *Woody's Roundup Featuring Riders in the Sky*, Riders in the Sky
Spoken Word Album for Children: *Harry Potter and the Goblet of Fire* (J. K. Rowling), Jim Dale
Spoken Word or Non-Musical Album: *The Measure of a Man* (Sidney Poitier), Sidney Poitier
Spoken Comedy Album: *Braindroppings*, George Carlin
Musical Show Album: *Elton John and Tim Rice's Aida*
Best Score Soundtrack Album for a Motion Picture or for Television: *American Beauty*, Thomas Newman, composer
Song Written for a Motion Picture or for Television: "When She Loved Me" (from *Toy Story 2*), Randy Newman, songwriter
Instrumental Composition: "Theme from *Angela's Ashes*," John Williams, composer
Instrumental Arrangement: "Spain for Sextet and Orchestra," Chick Corea, arranger
Instrumental Arrangement with Accompanying Vocals: "Both Sides Now," Vince Mendoza, arranger
Classical Album: *Shostakovich: The String Quartets*,

Emerson String Quartet
Orchestral Performance: *Mahler: Sym. No. 10*, Sir Simon Rattle (Berliner Philharmonic)
Opera Recording: *Busoni: Doktor Faust*, Kent Nagano, conductor
Choral Performance: *Penderecki: Credo*, Helmuth Rilling, conductor
Instrumental Soloist with Orchestra: *Maw: Violin Concerto*, Joshua Bell, violin; Sir Roger Norrington, conductor
Instrumental Soloist Without Orchestra: *Dreams of a World* (Works of Lauro, Ruiz-Pipo, Duarte, etc.), Sharon Isbin, guitar
Chamber Music: *Shostakovich: The String Quartets*, Emerson String Quartet
Small Ensemble Performance (with or Without Conductor): "Shadow Dances (Stravinsky Miniatures—Tango; Suite No. 1; Octet, etc.)," Orpheus Chamber Orchestra
Classical Vocal: *The Vivaldi Album (Dell'aura al sussurrar; Alma oppressa, etc.)*, Cecilia Bartoli, mezzo soprano
Classical Contemporary Composition: *Crumb: Star-Child*, George Crumb, composer

2000 Country Music Association Awards

Entertainer of the Year: Dixie Chicks
Single of the Year: "I Hope You Dance," Lee Ann Womack
Album of the Year: *Fly*, Dixie Chicks
Song of the Year: "I Hope You Dance," Mark D. Sanders and Tia Sillers (Lee Ann Womack)
Male Vocalist of the Year: Tim McGraw
Female Vocalist of the Year: Faith Hill

Vocal Group of the Year: Dixie Chicks
Vocal Duo of the Year: Montgomery Gentry
Vocal Event of the Year: "Murder on Music Row," George Strait with Alan Jackson
Horizon Award: Brad Paisley
Musician of the Year: Hargus "Pig" Robbins
Music Video of the Year: "Goodbye Earl," Dixie Chicks

2000 National Book Awards

Fiction: *In America*, Susan Sontag (Farrar, Straus and Giroux)
Nonfiction: *In the Heart of the Sea: The Tragedy of the Whaleship Essex*, Nathaniel Philbrick (Viking Penguin)
Poetry: *Blessing the Boats: New and Selected Poems 1988–2000*, Lucille Clifton (BOA Editions, Ltd.)

Young People's Literature: *Homeless Bird*, Gloria Whelan (HarperCollins Children's Books)
Medal for Distinguished Contribution to American Literature: Ray Bradbury

2000 National Book Critics Circle Awards

Fiction: *Being Dead*, Jim Crace (Farrar, Straus & Giroux)
General Nonfiction: *Newjack: Guarding Sing Sing*, Ted Conover (Random House)
Biography or Autobiography: *Hirohito and the Making of Modern Japan*, Herbert P. Bix (HarperCollins)

Poetry: *Carolina Ghost Woods*, Judy Jordan (Louisiana State Univ. Press)
Criticism: *Quarrel & Quandary*, Cynthia Ozick (Knopf)

PEN/Faulkner Award

The PEN/Faulkner award is the largest annual juried prize for fiction in the United States. The winner receives $15,000.

1981 Walter Abish, *How German Is It?*
1982 David Bradley, *The Chaneysville Incident*
1983 Toby Olson, *Seaview*
1984 John Edgar Wideman, *Sent for You Yesterday*
1985 Tobias Wolff, *The Barracks Thief*
1986 Peter Taylor, *The Old Forest*
1987 Richard Wiley, *Soldiers in Hiding*
1988 T. Coraghessan Boyle, *World's End*
1989 James Salter, *Dusk*
1990 E. L. Doctorow, *Billy Bathgate*

1991 John Edgar Wideman, *Philadelphia Fire*
1992 Don Delillo, *Mao II*
1993 E. Annie Proulx, *Postcards*
1994 Philip Roth, *Operation Shylock*
1995 David Guterson, *Snow Falling on Cedars*
1996 Richard Ford, *Independence Day*
1997 Gina Berriault, *Women in Their Beds*
1998 Rafi Zabor, *The Bear Comes Home*
1999 Michael Cunningham, *The Hours*
2000 Ha Jin, *Waiting*
2001 Philip Roth, *The Human Stain*

Booker Prize

Britain's most prestigious literary award, officially the "Booker McConnell Prize," honors the best full-length novel written in English by a citizen of a current or former British Commonwealth country.

1969 *Something to Answer For*, P. H. Newby
1970 *The Elected Member*, Bernice Rubens
1971 *In a Free State*, V. S. Naipaul
1972 *G.: A Novel*, John Berger
1973 *The Siege of Krishnapur*, J. G. Farrell
1974 (tie) *The Conservationist*, Nadine Gordimer
    Holiday, Stanley Middleton
1975 *Heat and Dust*, Ruth Prawer Jhabvala
1976 *Saville*, David Storey
1977 *Staying On*, Paul Scott
1978 *The Sea, The Sea*, Iris Murdoch
1979 *Offshore*, Penelope Fitzgerald
1980 *Rites of Passage*, William Golding
1981 *Midnight's Children*, Salman Rushdie
1982 *Schindler's List*, Thomas Keneally
1983 *Life & Times of Michael K*, J. M. Coetzee
1984 *Hotel du Lac*, Anita Brookner

1985 *The Bone People*, Keri Hulme
1986 *The Old Devils*, Kingsley Amis
1987 *Moon Tiger*, Penelope Lively
1988 *Oscar and Lucinda*, Peter Carey
1989 *The Remains of the Day*, Kazuo Ishiguro
1990 *Possession: A Romance*, A. S. Byatt
1991 *The Famished Road*, Ben Okri
1992 (tie) *The English Patient*, Michael Ondaatje
    Sacred Hunger, Barry Unsworth
1993 *Paddy Clarke, Ha Ha Ha*, Roddy Doyle
1994 *How Late It Was, How Late*, James Kelman
1995 *The Ghost Road*, Pat Barker
1996 *Last Orders*, Graham Swift
1997 *The God of Small Things*, Arundhati Roy
1998 *Amsterdam*, Ian McEwan
1999 *Disgrace*, J. M. Coetzee
2000 *The Blind Assassin*, Margaret Atwood

Newbery Medal

The Newbery Medal is awarded annually by the American Library Association for the most distinguished contribution to American literature for children.

2001 Newbery Medal and Honor Books
Newbery Medal for Best Book: *A Year Down Yonder*, Richard Peck (Dial Books for Young Readers)
Newbery Honor Books: *Because of Winn Dixie*, Kate Di Camillo (Candlewick Press); *Hope Was Here*, Joan Bauer (G. P. Putnam's Sons); *The Wanderer*, Sharon Creech (Joanna Cotler/HarperCollins); *Joey Pigza Loses Control*, Jack Gantos (Farrar, Straus & Giroux)

1922–2000
1922 *The Story of Mankind*, Hendrick Willem Van Loon
1923 *The Voyages of Dr. Doolittle*, Hugh A. Lofting
1924 *The Dark Frigate*, Charles Boardman Hawes
1925 *Tales from Silver Lands*, Charles Joseph Finger
1926 *Shen of the Sea*, Arthur Bowie Chrisman
1927 *Smoky, the Cow Horse*, Will James
1928 *Gay-Neck, the Story of a Pigeon*, Dhan Gopal Mukerji
1929 *The Trumpeter of Krakow*, Eric P. Kelly
1930 *Hitty, Her First Hundred Years*, Rachel Field
1931 *The Cat Who Went to Heaven*, Elizabeth Jane Coatsworth
1932 *Waterless Mountain*, Laura Adams Armer
1933 *Young Fu of the Upper Yangtze*, Elizabeth Foreman Lewis
1934 *Invincible Louisa*, Cornelia Meigs
1935 *Dobry*, Monica Shannon
1936 *Caddie Woodlawn*, Carol Ryrie Brink
1937 *Roller Skates*, Ruth Sawyer
1938 *The White Stag*, Kate Seredy
1939 *Thimble Summer*, Elizabeth Enright
1940 *Daniel Boone*, James Henry Daugherty
1941 *Call It Courage*, Armstrong Sperry
1942 *The Matchlock Gun*, Walter Dumax Edmonds
1943 *Adam of the Road*, Elizabeth Janet Gray
1944 *Johnny Tremain*, Esther Forbes
1945 *Rabbit Hill*, Robert Lawson
1946 *Strawberry Girl*, Lois Lenski
1947 *Miss Hickory*, Carolyn Sherwin Bailey
1948 *The Twenty-One Balloons*, William Pène du Bois
1949 *King of the Wind*, Marguerite Henry
1950 *The Door in the Wall*, Marguerite de Angeli

1951 *Amos Fortune, Free Man*, Elizabeth Yates
1952 *Ginger Pye*, Eleanor Estes
1953 *Secret of the Andes*, Ann Nolan Clark
1954 *. . . And Now Miguel*, Joseph Krumgold
1955 *The Wheel on the School*, Meindert DeJong
1956 *Carry On, Mr. Bowditch*, Jean Lee Latham
1957 *Miracles on Maple Hill*, Virginia Eggertsen Sorensen
1958 *Rifles for Watie*, Harold Keith
1959 *The Witch of Blackbird Pond*, Elizabeth George Speare
1960 *Onion John*, Joseph Krumgold
1961 *Island of the Blue Dolphins*, Scott O'Dell
1962 *The Bronze Bow*, Elizabeth George Speare
1963 *A Wrinkle in Time*, Madeleine L'Engle
1964 *It's Like This, Cat*, Emily Cheney Neville
1965 *Shadow of a Bull*, Maia Wojciechowska
1966 *I, Juan de Pareja*, Elizabeth Borton de Treviño
1967 *Up a Road Slowly*, Irene Hunt
1968 *From the Mixed-Up Files of Mrs. Basil E. Frankweiler*, E. L. Konigsburg
1969 *The High King*, Lloyd Alexander
1970 *Sounder*, William H. Armstrong
1971 *Summer of the Swans*, Betsy Byars
1972 *Mrs. Frisby and the Rats of NIMH*, Robert C. O'Brien
1973 *Julie of the Wolves*, Jean Craighead George
1974 *The Slave Dancer*, Paula Fox
1975 *M. C. Higgins, the Great*, Virginia Hamilton
1976 *The Grey King*, Susan Cooper
1977 *Roll of Thunder, Hear My Cry*, Mildred D. Taylor
1978 *Bridge to Terabithia*, Katherine Paterson
1979 *The Westing Game*, Ellen Raskin
1980 *A Gathering of Days: A New England Girl's Journal, 1830–32*, Joan W. Blos
1981 *Jacob Have I Loved*, Katherine Paterson
1982 *A Visit to William Blake's Inn: Poems for Innocent and Experienced Travelers*, Nancy Willard
1983 *Dicey's Song*, Cynthia Voigt
1984 *Dear Mr. Henshaw*, Beverly Cleary
1985 *The Hero and the Crown*, Robin McKinley

1986 *Sarah, Plain and Tall*, Patricia MacLachlan
1987 *The Whipping Boy*, Sid Fleischman
1988 *Lincoln: A Photobiography*, Russell Freedman
1989 *Joyful Noise: Poems for Two Voices*, Paul Fleischman
1990 *Number the Stars*, Lois Lowry
1991 *Maniac Magee: a Novel*, Jerry Spinelli
1992 *Shiloh*, Phyllis Reynolds Naylor

1993 *Missing May*, Cynthia Rylant
1994 *The Giver*, Lois Lowry
1995 *Walk Two Moons*, Sharon Creech
1996 *The Midwife's Apprentice*, Karen Cushman
1997 *The View from Saturday*, E. L. Konigsburg
1998 *Out of the Dust*, Karen Hesse
1999 *Holes*, Louis Sachar
2000 *Bud, Not Buddy*, by Christopher Paul Curtis

Caldecott Medal

The Caldecott Medal is awarded annually by the American Library Association for the most distinguished American picture book for children.

2001 Caldecott Medal and Honor Books

Caldecott Medal for Best Picture Book: *So You Want to Be President?*, illustrated by David Small, written by Judith St. George (Philomel Books)

Caldecott Honor Books: *Olivia*, written and illustrated by Ian Falconer (Atheneum); *Casey at the Bat: A Ballad of the Republic Sung in the Year 1888*, illustrated by Christopher Bin, written by Ernest Lawrence Thayer (Handprint Books); *Click, Clack, Moo: Cows That Type*, illustrated by Betsy Lewin, written by Doreen Cronin (Simon & Schuster)

1938–2000

1938 *Animals of the Bible, a Picture Book*, text selected by Helen Dean Fish, illustrated by Dorothy P. Lathrop
1939 *Mei Li*, written and illustrated by Thomas Handforth
1940 *Abraham Lincoln*, written and illustrated by Ingri and Edgar Parin D'Aulaire
1941 *They Were Strong and Good*, written and illustrated by Robert Lawson
1942 *Make Way for Ducklings*, written and illustrated by Robert McCloskey
1943 *The Little House*, written and illustrated by Virginia Lee Burton
1944 *Many Moons*, written by James Thurber, illustrated by Louis Slobodkin
1945 *Prayer for a Child*, written by Elizabeth Orton Jones
1946 *The Rooster Crows*, written and illustrated by Maud and Miska Petersham
1947 *The Little Island*, written by Golden MacDonald, illustrated by Leonard Weisgard
1948 *White Snow, Bright Snow*, written by Alvin Tresselt, illustrated by Roger Duvoisin
1949 *The Big Snow*, written and illustrated by Berta and Elmer Hader
1950 *Song of the Swallows*, written and illustrated by Leo Politi
1951 *The Egg Tree*, written and illustrated by Katherine Milhous
1952 *Finders Keepers*, written by William Lipkind, illustrated by Nicolas Mordvinoff
1953 *The Biggest Bear*, written and illustrated by Lynd Ward
1954 *Madeline's Rescue*, written and illustrated by Ludwig Bemelmans
1955 *Cinderella, or, The Little Glass Slipper*, translated and illustrated by Marcia Brown
1956 *Frog Went A-Courtin'*, retold by John Langstaff, illustrated by Feodor Rojankovsky
1957 *A Tree Is Nice*, written by Janice May Udry, illustrated by Marc Simont
1958 *Time of Wonder*, written and illustrated by Robert McCloskey
1959 *Chanticleer and the Fox*, adapted and illustrated by Barbara Cooney

1960 *Nine Days to Christmas*, written by Marie Hall Ets and Aurora Labastida, illustrated by Marie Hall Ets
1961 *Baboushka and the Three Kings*, written by Ruth Robbins, illustrated by Nicolas Sidjakov
1962 *Once a Mouse*, retold and illustrated by Marcia Brown
1963 *The Snowy Day*, written and illustrated by Ezra Jack Keats
1964 *Where the Wild Things Are*, written and illustrated by Maurice Sendak
1965 *May I Bring a Friend?*, written by Beatrice Schenk de Regniers, illustrated by Beni Montresor
1966 *Always Room for One More*, written by Sorche Nic Leodhas, illustrated by Nonny Hogrogian
1967 *Sam, Bangs and Moonshine*, written and illustrated by Evaline Ness
1968 *Drummer Hoff*, written by Barbara Emberley, illustrated by Ed Emberley
1969 *The Fool of the World and the Flying Ship*, retold by Arthur Ransome, illustrated by Uri Shulevitz
1970 *Sylvester and the Magic Pebble*, written and illustrated by William Steig
1971 *A Story, A Story: An African Tale*, retold and illustrated by Gail E. Haley
1972 *One Fine Day*, written and illustrated by Nonny Hogrogian
1973 *The Funny Little Woman*, retold by Arlene Mosel, illustrated by Blair Lent
1974 *Duffy and the Devil*, retold by Harve Zemach, illustrated by Margot Zemach
1975 *Arrow to the Sun: A Pueblo Indian Tale*, adapted and illustrated by Gerald H. McDermott
1976 *Why Mosquitos Buzz in People's Ears (An African Tale)*, retold by Verna Aardema, illustrated by Leo and Diane Dillon
1977 *Ashanti to Zulu: African Traditions*, written by Margaret Musgrove, illustrated by Leo and Diane Dillon
1978 *Noah's Ark*, written by Jacob Revius, illustrated by Peter Spier
1979 *The Girl Who Loved Wild Horses*, written and illustrated by Paul Goble
1980 *Ox-Cart Man*, written by Donald Hall, illustrated by Barbara Cooney
1981 *Fables*, written and illustrated by Arnold Lobel
1982 *Jumanji*, written and illustrated by Chris Van Allsburg
1983 *Shadow*, translated and illustrated by Marcia Brown
1984 *The Glorious Flight: Across the Channel with Louis Blériot*, written and illustrated by Alice and Martin Provensen

1985 *St. George and the Dragon,* retold by Margaret Hodges, illustrated by Trina Schart Hyman

1986 *The Polar Express,* written and illustrated by Chris Van Allsburg

1987 *Hey, Al,* written by Arthur Yorinks, illustrated by Richard Egielski

1988 *Owl Moon,* written by Jane Yolen, illustrated by John Schoenherr

1989 *Song and Dance Man,* written by Karen Ackerman, illustrated by Stephen Gammell

1990 *Lon Po Po: A Red-Riding Hood Story from China,* by Ed Young

1991 *Black & White,* written and illustrated by David Macaulay

1992 *Tuesday,* written and illustrated by David Wiesner

1993 *Mirette on the High Wire,* written and illustrated by Emily Arnold McCully

1994 *Grandfather's Journey,* written and illustrated by Allen Say

1995 *Smoky Night,* written by Eve Bunting, illustrated by David Diaz

1996 *Officer Buckle and Gloria,* written and illustrated by Peggy Rathmann

1997 *Golem,* written and illustrated by David Wisniewski

1998 *Rapunzel,* illustrated and retold by Paul O. Zelinsky

1999 *Snowflake Bentley,* written by Jacqueline Briggs Martin, illustrated by Mary Azarian

2000 *Joseph Had a Little Overcoat,* illustrated by Simms Taback

Other American Library Association Awards for Children's Books, 2001

Coretta Scott King Award, honoring black authors and illustrators: (author): *Miracle's Boys,* Jacqueline Woodson (Putnam) **(illustrator):** *Uptown,* Bryan Collier (Henry Holt); *The Black Cat,* Christopher Myers (Scholastic)
Michael L. Printz Award for excellence in young adult literature: *Kit's Wilderness,* David Almond (Delacorte Press)
Margaret A. Edwards Award for lifetime contribution in writing for young adults: Robert Lipsyte
Robert F. Sibert Award for informational book: *Sir Walter*

Ralegh and the Quest for El Dorado, Marc Aronson (Clarion)
Mildred L. Batchelder Award, for best book originally published in a foreign language in a foreign country: *Samir and Yonatan,* written by Daniella Carmi in Hebrew and translated by John Yael Lotan (Arthur A. Levine/ Scholastic Press)
Laura Ingalls Wilder Award for lasting contributions to children's literature: Milton Meltzer

2001 National Magazine Awards

General Excellence:
The American Scholar (circulation less than 100,000)
Mother Jones (circulation 100,000 to 400,000)
The New Yorker (circulation 400,000 to 1,000,000)
Teen People (circulation more than 1,000,000)
Personal Service: *National Geographic Adventure*
Special Interests: *The New Yorker*
Reporting: *Esquire*
Essays: *The New Yorker*

Reviews and Criticism: *The New Yorker*
Profiles: *The New Yorker*
Feature Writing: *Rolling Stone*
Public Interest: *Time*
Design: *Nest*
Fiction: *Zoetrope: All-Story*
Photography: *National Geographic*
General Excellence Online: *U.S. News Online*
Best Interactive Design: *SmartMoney.com*

Bollingen Prize in Poetry

The Bollingen Prize in Poetry is administered by the Yale University Library.

1949 Ezra Pound
1950 Wallace Stevens
1951 John Crowe Ransom
1952 Marianne Moore
1953 Archibald MacLeish and William Carlos Williams
1954 W. H. Auden
1955 Léonie Adams and Louise Bogan
1956 Conrad Aiken
1957 Allen Tate
1958 e. e. cummings
1959 Theodore Roethke
1960 Delmore Schwartz
1961 Yvor Winters
1962 John Hall Wheelock and Richard Eberhart
1963 Robert Frost
1965 Horace Gregory
1967 Robert Penn Warren

1969 John Berryman and Karl Shapiro
1971 Richard Wilbur and Mona Van Duyn
1973 James Merrill
1975 Archie Randolph Ammons
1977 David Ignatow
1979 W. S. Merwin
1981 Howard Nemerov and May Swenson
1983 Anthony Hecht and John Hollander
1985 John Ashbery and Fred Chappell
1987 Stanley Kunitz
1989 Edgar Bowers
1991 Laura Riding Jackson and Donald Justice
1993 Mark Strand
1995 Kenneth Koch
1997 Gary Snyder
1999 Robert Creeley
2001 Louise Glück

Kingsley Tufts Poetry Prize

1993 Susan Mitchell, *Rapture*
1994 Yusef Komunyakaa, *Neon Vernacular*
1995 Thomas Lux, *Split Horizon*
1996 Deborah Digges, *Rough Music*
1997 Campbell McGrath, *Spring Comes to Chicago*

1998 John Koethe, *Falling Water*
1999 B. H. Fairchild, *The Art of the Lathe*
2000 Robert Wrigley, *Reign of Snakes: Poems*
2001 Alan Shapiro, *The Dead Alive and Busy*

2000 George Foster Peabody Awards for Broadcasting

60 Minutes II: "Death by Denial," CBS News
Dateline NBC: "The Paper Chase," NBC
48 Hours: "Heroes Under Fire," CBS News
Treading on Danger?: KHOU-TV, Houston
An 84-Year-Old Youngful Man Lives in the Cabin: KBS, Seoul, South Korea
Behind Closed Doors: WJXT-TV, Jacksonville, Fla.
P.O.V.: "Regret to Inform," presented on PBS
King Gimp: HBO, Whiteford-Hadary, the University of Maryland and Tapestry International
1900 House: Wall to Wall Production for Channel 4 in association with WNET, New York, presented on PBS
Cancer: Evolution to Revolution: HBO and Lovett Productions
Drug Wars: Frontline, WGBH, Boston, presented on PBS
Ali-Frazier 1: One Nation . . . Divisible: HBO Sports
Cry Freetown: CNN Perspectives, CNN Productions, Insight News Television and Channel 4 International
Napoleon: David Grubin Productions, New York, and Devillier Doregan Enterprises, presented on PBS
Walking with Dinosaurs: BBC Discovery Channel and TV Asahi in association with ProSieben and France 3
Marketplace: Minnesota Public Radio, presented on Public Radio International
Witness to an Execution: Sound Portraits Productions, presented on National Public Radio
The NPR 100: National Public Radio
Slavery: True Vision Productions for Channel 4, London
Katie Couric: Confronting Colon Cancer: NBC News
School Sleuth: The Case of an Excellent School: produced by Learning Matters and *The Merrow Report,* presented on PBS

Arthur: WGBH, Boston, and Cinar Films, presented on PBS
Hearts and Minds: Teens and Mental Illness: Idaho Public Television, Boise, and the Idaho Department of Health and Welfare
Building Big: WGBH, Boston, and Production Group, presented on PBS
H. Martin Haag: television news director, for establishing high ethical standards and promoting quality in local and national television news
The West Wing: NBC, John Wells Productions in association with Warner Bros.
The Sopranos: HBO, Chase Films and Brad Grey Television
Sharing the Secret: Robert Greenwald Productions and Pearson Television International, presented on CBS
Howard Goodall's Big Bangs: Tiger Aspect Production for Channel 4, London
Exxon/Mobil Masterpiece Theatre: David Copperfield, co-produced by BBC America and WGBH, Boston, presented on PBS
The Crossing: A&E Network and Columbia TriStar Television Productions in association with Chris/Rose Productions
The Corner: HBO
Malcolm in the Middle: Fox and Regency Television
The Daily Show with Jon Stewart: "Indecision 2000," Mad Cow Productions in association with Comedy Central

2001 Alfred I. du Pont–Columbia University Awards in Television and Radio

GOLD BATON
American RadioWorks for *Massacre at Cuska* on National Public Radio
SILVER BATONS
Television Awards:
KHOU-TV, Houston, Texas, and Anna Werner, for *Deadly Tires?*
Sorious Samura, Insight News TV, London, and CNN Productions for *Cry Freetown*
NBC News *Dateline* for *Paper Chase*
Frontline and WGBH-TV, Boston, for *John Paul II: The Millennial Pope* on PBS
ABC News *Nightline* for *AIDS in Africa*

KXLY-TV, Spokane, Washington, and Tom Grant for *Public Funds, Private Profit*
WCPO-TV, Cincinnati, Ohio, and Laure Quinlivan for the *I-Team Stadium Investigation*
Steeplechase Films for *New York: A Documentary Film* on PBS
Crowing Rooster Arts, New York, for *Abandoned: The Betrayal of America's Immigrants* on WGBH-TV, Boston
CBS News for *Armed America*
Radio Award:
National Public Radio for *Radio Expeditions*

2000 Major Emmy Awards

The 2001 Emmy Awards, originally set for September 16, were postponed after the terrorist attacks on the U.S. and indefinitely after the U.S. launched air strikes on Afghanistan.

Drama Series: *The West Wing* (NBC)
Actress: Sela Ward, *Once and Again*
Actor: James Gandolfini, *The Sopranos*
Supporting Actress: Allison Janney, *The West Wing*
Supporting Actor: Richard Schiff, *The West Wing*
Guest Actor: James Whitmore, *The Practice*
Guest Actress: Beah Richards, *The Practice*
Comedy Series: *Will & Grace* (NBC)
Actress: Patricia Heaton, *Everybody Loves Raymond*
Actor: Michael J. Fox, *Spin City*
Supporting Actress: Megan Mullally, *Will & Grace*
Supporting Actor: Sean Hayes, *Will & Grace*
Guest Actress: Jean Smart, *Frasier*
Guest Actor: Bruce Willis, *Friends*
Variety, Music, or Comedy Series: *Late Show with David Letterman* (CBS)
Variety, Music, or Comedy Special: *Saturday Night Live: The 25th Anniversary Special* (NBC)
Miniseries or Special: *The Corner* (HBO)
Actress: Halle Berry, *Introducing Dorothy Dandridge*

Actor: Jack Lemmon, *Oprah Winfrey Presents: Tuesdays with Morrie*
Supporting Actress: Vanessa Redgrave, *If These Walls Could Talk 2*
Supporting Actor: Hank Azaria, *Oprah Winfrey Presents: Tuesdays with Morrie*
Made-for-TV Movie: *Oprah Winfrey Presents: Tuesdays with Morrie* (ABC)
Individual Performance, Variety or Music Program: Eddie Izzard, *Eddie Izzard: Dress to Kill*
Outstanding Nonfiction Series (possibility of one or more than one award): *American Masters:* "Hitchcock, Selznick, and the End of Hollywood" (PBS)
Outstanding Nonfiction Special: *Children in War* (HBO)
Outstanding Children's Program (possibility of one or more than one award): *The Color of Friendship* (Disney) and *Goodnight Moon and Other Sleepytime Tales* (HBO)
Outstanding Animated Program (one hour or less): *The Simpsons:* "Behind the Laughter" (Fox)

2000–2001 Daytime Emmy Awards

Outstanding Drama Series: *As the World Turns* (CBS)
Lead Actor in a Drama Series: David Canary, *All My Children* (ABC)
Lead Actress in a Drama Series: Martha Byrne, *As the World Turns* (CBS)
Supporting Actor in a Drama Series: Michael E. Knight, *All My Children* (ABC)
Supporting Actress in a Drama Series: Lesli Kay, *As the World Turns* (CBS)
Younger Actor in a Drama Series: Justin Torkildsen, *The Bold and the Beautiful* (CBS)
Younger Actress in a Drama Series: Adrienne Frantz, *The Bold and the Beautiful* (CBS)
Drama Series Writing Team: *As the World Turns* (CBS)
Outstanding Children's Series: *Reading Rainbow* (PBS)
Outstanding Children's Special (tie): *Run the Wild Fields* (Showtime) and *A Storm in Summer* (Showtime)
Outstanding Children's Animated Program: *Arthur* (PBS)
Outstanding Children's Animated Program (special class): *Batman Beyond* (WB)
Performer in a Children's Series: Levar Burton, *Reading Rainbow* (PBS)

Performer in a Children's Special: Ossie Davis, *Finding Buck McHenry* (Showtime)
Performer in an Animated Program: Nathan Lane, *Disney's Teacher's Pet* (ABC)
Outstanding Preschool Children's Series: *Sesame Street* (PBS)
Outstanding Special Class Series: *AMC's Behind the Screen with John Burke* (AMC)
Outstanding Special Class Special: *Barbra Streisand and AMC Present Reel Models: The First Women of Film* (AMC)
Outstanding Game and Audience Participation Show: *Who Wants to Be a Millionaire* (ABC)
Outstanding Game-Show Host: Regis Philbin, *Who Wants to Be a Millionaire* (ABC)
Outstanding Talk Show: *The Rosie O'Donnell Show* (syndicated)
Outstanding Talk-Show Host (tie): Rosie O'Donnell, *The Rosie O'Donnell Show* and Regis Philbin, *Live with Regis*
Outstanding Service Show: *Martha Stewart Living* (syndicated)
Outstanding Service-Show Host: Julia Child & Jacques Pepin, *Julia and Jacques Cooking at Home* (PBS)

2001 NAACP Image Awards

MOTION PICTURE
Outstanding Motion Picture: *Remember the Titans*
Outstanding Actress in a Motion Picture: Sanaa Lathan, *Love and Basketball*
Outstanding Actor in a Motion Picture: Denzel Washington, *Remember the Titans*
Outstanding Supporting Actress in a Motion Picture: Alfre Woodard, *Love and Basketball*
Outstanding Supporting Actor in a Motion Picture: Blair Underwood, *Rules of Engagement*

TELEVISION
Outstanding Comedy Series: *The Steve Harvey Show* (WB)
Outstanding Actress in a Comedy Series: Mo'nique, *The Parkers*
Outstanding Actor in a Comedy Series: Steve Harvey, *The Steve Harvey Show*
Outstanding Supporting Actress in a Comedy Series: Terri J. Vaughn, *The Steve Harvey Show*
Outstanding Supporting Actor in a Comedy Series: Cedric "The Entertainer," *The Steve Harvey Show*
Outstanding Drama Series: *City of Angels* (CBS)
Outstanding Actress in a Drama Series: Della Reese, *Touched by an Angel*
Outstanding Actor in a Drama Series: Blair Underwood, *City of Angels*
Outstanding Supporting Actress in a Drama Series: Loretta Devine, *Boston Public*

Outstanding Supporting Actor in a Drama Series: Ossie Davis, *City of Angels*
Outstanding Television Movie/Miniseries/Dramatic Special: *Sally Hemings: An American Scandal* (CBS)
Outstanding Actress in a Television Movie/Miniseries/ Dramatic Special: Natalie Cole, *Livin' for Love: The Natalie Cole Story*
Outstanding Actor in a Television Movie/Miniseries/ Dramatic Special: Danny Glover, *Freedom Song*
Outstanding Performance in a Variety Series/Special: Yolanda Adams, *Soul Train Lady of Soul Awards*

RECORDING
Outstanding Song: Yolanda Adams, "Open My Heart"
Outstanding Album: Stevie Wonder, *At the Close of the Century*
Outstanding New Artist: Carl Thomas, *Emotional*
Outstanding Female Artist: Yolanda Adams, "Open My Heart"
Outstanding Male Artist: R. Kelly, "I Wish"
Outstanding Duo or Group: Destiny's Child, "Say My Name"
Outstanding Rap Artist: LL Cool J, "G.O.A.T."
Outstanding Jazz Artist: Grover Washington, Jr., *The Best of Grover Washington, Jr.*
Outstanding Gospel Artist—Traditional: Aaron Neville, "Mary Don't You Weep"
Outstanding Gospel Artist—Contemporary: Yolanda Adams, "Open My Heart"
Outstanding Music Video: R. Kelly, "I Wish"

Webby Awards

Activism: VolunteerMatch: www.volunteermatch.org
Arts: Young-Hae Chang Heavy Industries: www.yhchang.com
Broadband: Heavy: www.heavy.com
Commerce: Travelocity: www.travelocity.com
Community: craigslist: www.craigslist.org
Education: NationalGeographic.com: www.nationalgeographic.com
Fashion: Hint Fashion Magazine: www.hintmag.com
Film: Requiem for a Dream: www.requiemforadream.com
Finance: Yahoo! Finance: finance.yahoo.com
Games: 3D Groove: www.3dgroove.com
Government and Law: Nolo Self-Help Law Center: www.nolo.com
Health: Planned Parenthood Golden Gate: www.ppgg.org
Humor: The Onion: www.theonion.com
Kids: Fact Monster: www.factmonster.com
Living: Campaign for Our Children: www.cfoc.org

Music: sputnik7: www.sputnik7.com
News: [Inside]: www.inside.com
Personal Website: Dancing Paul: www.dancingpaul.com
Politics: OpenSecrets.org: www.opensecrets.org
Print and 'Zines: Plastic: www.plastic.com
Radio: BBC World Service: www.bbc.co.uk/worldservice
Science: Plus Magazine: plus.maths.org
Services: VolunteerMatch: www.volunteermatch.org
Spirituality: Zen: www.do-not-zzz.com
Sports: Swell: www.swell.com
Technical Achievement: Microsoft Windows Update: windowsupdate.microsoft.com
Travel: Expedia: www.expedia.com
TV: PBS Online: www.pbs.org
Weird: Peter Pan's Home Page: www.pixyland.org/peterpan
Best Practices: Google: www.google.com

The Spingarn Medal

The Spingarn Medal is awarded annually by the National Association for the Advancement of Colored People for outstanding achievement by a black American.

1915	Ernest E. Just	1944	Charles Drew	1973	Wilson C. Riles
1916	Charles Young	1945	Paul Robeson	1974	Damon Keith
1917	Harry T. Burleigh	1946	Thurgood Marshall	1975	Hank Aaron
1918	William Stanley	1947	Percy Julian	1976	Alvin Ailey
	Braithwaite	1948	Channing H. Tobias	1977	Alex Haley
1919	Archibald H. Grimke	1949	Ralph J. Bunche	1978	Andrew Young
1920	W. E. B. Du Bois	1950	Charles Hamilton Houston	1979	Rosa L. Parks
1921	Charles S. Gilpin	1951	Mabel Keaton Staupers	1980	Rayford W. Logan
1922	Mary B. Talbert	1952	Harry T. Moore	1981	Coleman Young
1923	George Washington	1953	Paul R. Williams	1982	Benjamin E. Mays
	Carver	1954	Theodore K. Lawless	1983	Lena Horne
1924	Roland Hayes	1955	Carl Murphy	1984	Tom Bradley
1925	James Weldon Johnson	1956	Jackie Robinson	1985	Bill Cosby
1926	Carter G. Woodson	1957	Martin Luther King, Jr.	1986	Benjamin L. Hooks
1927	Anthony Overton	1958	Daisy Bates and the	1987	Percy Ellis Sutton
1928	Charles W. Chesnutt		Little Rock Nine	1988	Frederick Douglass
1929	Mordecai Wyatt Johnson	1959	Edward Kennedy		Patterson
1930	Henry A. Hunt		(Duke) Ellington	1989	Jesse Jackson
1931	Richard Berry Harrison	1960	Langston Hughes	1990	L. Douglas Wilder
1932	Robert Russa Moton	1961	Kenneth B. Clark	1991	Colin T. Powell
1933	Max Yergan	1962	Robert C. Weaver	1992	Barbara Jordan
1934	William T. B. Williams	1963	Medgar Evers	1993	Dorothy Irene Height
1935	Mary McLeod Bethune	1964	Roy Wilkins	1994	Maya Angelou
1936	John Hope	1965	Leontyne Price	1995	John Hope Franklin
1937	Walter White	1966	John H. Johnson	1996	A. Leon Higginbotham, Jr.
1938	No award	1967	Edward W. Brooke III	1997	Carl Rowan
1939	Marian Anderson	1968	Sammy Davis, Jr.	1998	Myrlie Evers-Williams
1940	Louis T. Wright	1969	Clarence M. Mitchell, Jr.	1999	Earl G. Graves, Sr.
1941	Richard Wright	1970	Jacob Lawrence	2000	Oprah Winfrey
1942	A. Philip Randolph	1971	Leon Howard Sullivan	2001	Vernon E. Jordan, Jr.
1943	William H. Hastie	1972	Gordon Parks		

Fields Medal Winners

The Fields Medal has been awarded quadrennially since 1936 by the International Congress of Mathematicians in Toronto to recognize outstanding mathematics achievement.

1936 Lars Valerian Ahlfors (Harvard University) and Jesse Douglas (Massachusetts Institute of Technology)

(Fields Medals were not awarded during World War II)

1950 Laurent Schwarts (University of Nancy) and Alte Selberg (Institute for Advanced Study, Princeton)

1954 Kunihiko Kodaira (Princeton University) and Jean-Pierre Serre (University of Paris)

1958 Klaus Friedrich Roth (University of London) and René Thom (University of Strasbourgh)

1962 Lars V. Hörmander (University of Stockholm) and John Willard Milnor (Princeton University)

1966 Michael Francis Atiyah (Oxford University), Paul Joseph Cohen (Stanford University), Alexander Grothendieck (University of Paris), and Stephen Smale (University of California, Berkeley)

1970 Alan Baker (Cambridge University), Heisuke Hironaka (Harvard University), Serge P. Novikov (Moscow University), and John Griggs Thompson (Cambridge University)

1974 Enrico Bombieri (University of Pisa) and David Bryant Mumford (Harvard University)

1978 Pierre René Deligne (Institut des Hautes Études Scientifiques), Charles Louis Fefferman (Princeton University), Gregori Alexandrovitch Margulis (Moscow University), and Daniel G. Quillen (Massachusetts Institute of Technology)

1982 Alain Connes (Institut des Hautes Études Scientifiques), William P. Thurston (Princeton University), and Shing-Tung Yau (Institute for Advanced Study, Princeton)

1986 Simon Donaldson (Oxford University), Gerd Faltings (Princeton University), and Michael Freedman (University of California, San Diego)

1990 Vladimir Drinfeld (Phys. Inst. Kharkov), Vaughan Jones (University of California, Berkeley), Shigefumi Mori (University of Kyoto), and Edward Witten (Institute for Advanced Study, Princeton)

1994 Pierre-Louis Lions (Université de Paris–Dauphine), Jean-Christophe Yoccoz (Université de Paris–Sud), Jean Bourgain (Institute for Advanced Study, Princeton), and Efim Zelmanov (University of Wisconsin)

1998 Richard E. Borcherds (Cambridge University), William T. Gowers (Cambridge University), Maxim Kontsevich (Institut des Hautes Etudes Scientifiques and Rutgers University), and Curtis T. McMullen (Harvard University)

Enrico Fermi Award

The $100,000 award is given in recognition of scientific and technical achievement in atomic energy. Awarded by the president, it is the U.S. government's oldest science and technology award.

1954	Enrico Fermi	1983	Alexander Hollaender and John Lawrence
1956	John von Neumann	1984	Robert R. Wilson and Georges Vendryès
1957	Ernest O. Lawrence	1985	Norman C. Rasmussen and Marshall N.
1958	Eugene P. Wigner		Rosenblath
1959	Glenn T. Seaborg	1986	Ernest D. Courant and M. Stanley Livingston
1961	Hans A. Bethe	1987	Luis W. Alvarez and Gerald F. Tape
1962	Edward Teller	1988	Richard B. Setlow and Victor F. Weisskopf
1963	J. Robert Oppenheimer	1989	Award not given
1964	Hyman G. Rickover	1990	George A. Cowan and Robley D. Evans
1966	Otto Hahn, Lise Meitner, and Fritz Strassman	1991	Award not given
1968	John A. Wheeler	1992	Leon M. Lederman, Harold Brown, and John
1969	Walter H. Zinn		S. Foster, Jr.
1970	Norris E. Bradbury	1993	Freeman J. Dyson and Liane B. Russell
1971	Shields Warren and Stafford L. Warren	1994	Award not given
1972	Manson Benedict	1995	Ugo Fano and Martin Kamen
1976	William L. Russell	1996	Richard Garwin, Mortimer Elkind, and
1978	Harold M. Agnew and Wolfgang K. H. Panof-		H. Rodney Withers
	sky	1997	Award not given
1980	Alvin M. Weinberg and Rudolf E. Peirls	1998	Maurice Goldhaber and Michael E. Phelps
1981	W. Bennett Lewis	2000	Sidney Drell, Sheldon Datz, and Herbert York
1982	Herbert Anderson and Seth Neddermeyer		

2000 MacArthur Foundation Awards

The MacArthur Foundation awards $500,000 over five years to each innovator. The announcement of the 2001 awards, originally scheduled for mid-September, was postponed in light of the terrorist attacks on the World Trade Center Towers and the Pentagon.

Susan Alcock, 39, associate professor of classical archaeology and classics; Ann Arbor, Mich.

K. Christopher Beard, 38, associate curator, vertebrate paleontology; Mars, Pa.

Lucy Blake, 40, president, Sierra Business Council; Sierraville, Calif.

Anne Carson, 49, history professor, poet, and essayist; Berkeley, Calif., and Montreal

Peter Hayes, 47, executive director, Nautilus Institute for Security and Sustainable Development; Berkeley, Calif.

David Isay, 34, radio producer; New York

Alfredo Jaar, 44, artist; New York

Ben Katchor, 48, cartoonist; New York

Hideo Mabuchi, 28, assistant professor of physics; Pasadena, Calif.

Susan Marshall, 41, artistic director and choreographer; New York

Samuel Mockbee, 55, professor of architecture; Canton, Miss.

Cecilia Muñoz, 37, vice president, Office of Research, Advocacy, and Legislation, National Council of La Raza; Silver Springs, Md.

Margaret Murnane, 41, professor of physics; Boulder, Colo.

Laura Otis, 38, associate professor of English; Port Washington, N.Y.

Lucia Perillo, 41, associate professor of creative writing; Carbondale, Ill.

Matthew Rabin, 36, professor of economics; San Francisco

Carl Safina, 45, vice president, marine conservation at the National Audubon Society; Islip, N.Y.

Daniel Schrag, 34, professor of geochemistry; Cambridge, Mass.

Susan Sygall, 47, executive director, Mobility International USA; Eugene, Ore.

Gina Turrigiano, 37, assistant professor of biology; Acton, Mass.

Gary Urton, 53, professor of anthropology; Earlville, N.Y.

Patricia J. Williams, 48, law professor; New York

Deborah Willis, 52, curator of exhibitions, Center for African-American History and Culture and the Anacostia Museum at the Smithsonian Institution; Washington, D.C.

Erik Winfree, 30, assistant professor of computer science and computation and neural systems; Pasadena, Calif.

Horng-Tzer Yau, 40, professor of mathematics; New York

Presidential Medal of Freedom

The Presidential Medal of Freedom, the nation's highest civilian award, recognizes exceptional meritorious service. The medal was established by President Truman in 1945 to recognize notable service in the war. In 1963, President Kennedy reintroduced it as an honor for distinguished civilian service in peacetime. Shown below are only those medals awarded during President Clinton's administration. As of Sept. 2001, President Bush has not named any recipients.

1993[*]	Arthur Ashe, Jr. (tennis professional)	1993	John Minor Wisdom (public servant)
1993	William J. Brennan, Jr. (jurist)	1994	Herbert Block (cartoonist)
1993	Marjory Stoneman Douglas (conservationist)	1994[*]	Cesar Chavez (labor leader)
1993	J. William Fulbright (public servant)	1994	Arthur Flemming (government servant)
1993[*]	Thurgood Marshall (jurist)	1994	James Grant (executive director, UNICEF)
1993	General Colin L. Powell[1] (soldier)	1994	Dorothy Height (civil-rights leader)
1993[*]	Joseph L. Raugh, Jr. (civil-rights and labor activist)	1994	Barbara Jordan (public servant)
1993	Martha Raye (entertainer)	1994	Lane Kirkland (labor leader)

1994	Robert H. Michel (public servant)
1994	R. Sargent Shriver (government servant)
1995	Peggy Charren (children's television advocate)
1995	William Thaddeus Coleman, Jr. (public servant and civil-rights advocate)
1995	Joan Ganz Cooney (children's television advocate)
1995	John Hope Franklin (historian)
1995	A. Leon Higginbotham, Jr. (jurist and civil-rights advocate)
1995	Frank M. Johnson, Jr. (jurist)
1995	C. Everett Koop (public-health worker)
1995	Gaylord A. Nelson (public servant and conservationist)
1995	Walter P. Reuther (labor leader)
1995	James W. Rouse (urban planner)
1995*	William C. Velasquez (voting rights advocate)
1995	Lew R. Wasserman (media executive)
1996	James Scott Brady (gun-control advocate)
1996	Cardinal Joseph Bernadin (Catholic leader)
1996	Millard D. Fuller (founder, Habitat for Humanity)
1996	David Alan Hamburg (physician and children's advocate)
1996	John H. Johnson (founder, *Ebony* and *Jet*)
1996	Eugene M. Lang (founder, "I Have a Dream" Foundation)
1996	Jan Nowak-Jezioranski (WWII Polish resistance fighter)
1996	Antonia Pantoja (Puerto Rican educational and economic advocate)
1996	Rosa Parks (civil-rights leader)
1996	Ginetta Sagan (advocate for political prisoners)
1996	Morris Udall (public servant)
1997	Robert Dole (public servant)
1997	William J. Perry (soldier)
1998	Arnold Aronson (civil-rights advocate)
1998	Brooke Astor (philanthropist)
1998	Robert Coles (psychiatrist and author)
1998	Justin Dart, Jr. (founder of Americans with Disabilities Act)
1998	James Farmer (civil-rights leader)
1998	Dante B. Fascell (public servant)
1998	Zachary Fisher (philanthropist)

1998	Frances Hesselbein (former leader of the Girl Scouts of America)
1998	Fred Korematsu (activist redressing Japanese-American internment in WWII)
1998	Sol M. Linowitz (jurist)
1998	Wilma Mankiller (former Cherokee Nation leader)
1998	Margaret Murie (environmentalist)
1998	Mario G. Obledo (activist for Mexican-American civil rights)
1998	Elliot L. Richardson (public servant)
1998	David Rockefeller (philanthropist)
1998*	Albert Shanker (educator)
1998	Adm. Elmo R. Zumwalt, Jr. (soldier)
1999	Lloyd M. Bentsen (public servant)
1999	Edgar M. Bronfman, Sr. (president of World Jewish Congress)
1999	President Jimmy Carter (public servant, activist)
1999	Rosalynn Carter (human-rights activist)
1999	Evelyn Dubrow (lobbyist)
1999	Sister Isolina Ferré (advocate for the poor)
1999	President Gerald Ford (public servant)
1999	Oliver White Hill (civil-rights lawyer)
1999	Max Kampelman (arms-control expert)
1999	Helmut Kohl (former German chancellor)
1999	Edgar Wayburn (Sierra Club leader)
2000	Aung San Suu Kyi (human rights activist)
2000	James Edward Burke (businessman, antidrug activist)
2000*	John Chafee (public servant)
2000	Gen. Wesley Clark (soldier)
2000	Adm. William Crowe (soldier)
2000	Marian Wright Edelman (lawyer, president of Children's Defense Fund)
2000	John Kenneth Galbraith (economist)
2000	Monsignor George Higgins (labor movement advocate)
2000	Rev. Jesse Jackson (civil-rights activist)
2000	Mildred Jeffrey (women's labor activist)
2000	Mathilde Krim (AIDS researcher)
2000	George McGovern (public servant)
2000	Cruz Reynoso (lawyer, civil-rights advocate)
2000	Rev. Gardner Taylor (author, civil-rights advocate)
2000	Simon Wiesenthal (concentration camp survivor, Nazi hunter)
2000	Daniel Patrick Moynihan (public servant)

1. With Distinction. NOTE: An asterisk following a year denotes a posthumous award.

Recipients of Kennedy Center Honors

The Kennedy Center Honors recognize the lifetime achievements of selected American performing artists.

1978	Marian Anderson (contralto), Fred Astaire (dancer-actor), Richard Rodgers (Broadway composer), Arthur Rubinstein (pianist), George Balanchine (choreographer)
1979	Ella Fitzgerald (jazz singer), Henry Fonda (actor), Martha Graham (choreographer), Tennessee Williams (playwright), Aaron Copland (composer)
1980	James Cagney (actor), Leonard Bernstein (composer-conductor), Agnes de Mille (choreographer), Lynn Fontanne (actress), Leontyne Price (soprano)
1981	Count Basie (jazz composer-pianist), Cary Grant (actor), Helen Hayes (actress), Jerome Robbins (choreographer), Rudolf Serkin (pianist)
1982	George Abbott (Broadway producer), Lillian Gish (actress), Benny Goodman (jazz clarinetist), Gene Kelly (dancer-actor), Eugene Ormandy (conductor)

1983	Katherine Dunham (dancer-choreographer), Elia Kazan (director-author), James Stewart (actor), Virgil Thomson (music critic-composer), Frank Sinatra (singer)
1984	Lena Horne (singer), Danny Kaye (comedian-actor), Gian Carlo Menotti (composer), Arthur Miller (playwright), Isaac Stern (violinist)
1985	Merce Cunningham (dancer-choreographer), Irene Dunne (actress), Bob Hope (comedian), Alan Jay Lerner (lyricist-playwright), Frederick Loewe (composer), Beverly Sills (soprano)
1986	Lucille Ball (comedienne), Ray Charles (musician), Yehudi Menuhin (violinist), Antony Tudor (choreographer), Hume Cronyn and Jessica Tandy (husband-and-wife acting team)
1987	Perry Como (singer), Bette Davis (actress), Sammy Davis, Jr., (entertainer), Nathan Milstein (violinist), Alwin Nikolais (choreographer)

1988 Alvin Ailey (choreographer), George Burns (comedian-actor), Myrna Loy (actress), Alexander Schneider (violinist), Roger L. Stevens (theatrical producer and the Kennedy Center's founding chairman)

1989 Harry Belafonte (singer-actor), Claudette Colbert (actress), Alexandra Danilova (ballerina), Mary Martin (actress), William Schuman (composer)

1990 Dizzy Gillespie (jazz trumpeter), Katharine Hepburn (actress), Risë Stevens (mezzo-soprano), Jule Styne (composer), Billy Wilder (director)

1991 Roy Acuff (country songwriter and singer), Betty Comden and Adolph Green (co-authors of books and lyrics of musicals), the brothers Fayard and Harold Nicholas (dancers), Gregory Peck (actor), Robert Shaw (choral director)

1992 Lionel Hampton (jazz musician), Paul Newman (actor), Joanne Woodward (actress), Ginger Rogers (dancer-actress), Mstislav Rostropovich (cellist-conductor), Paul Taylor (choreographer)

1993 Johnny Carson (talk-show host), Arthur Mitchell (dancer and choreographer), Georg Solti (conductor), Stephen Sondheim (composer and lyricist), Marion Williams (gospel singer)

1994 Kirk Douglas (actor), Aretha Franklin (singer), Morton Gould (composer), Harold Prince (producer and director), Pete Seeger (folk singer)

1995 Jacques d'Amboise (choreographer), Marilyn Horne (mezzo soprano), B. B. King (blues singer), Sidney Poitier (actor), Neil Simon (playwright)

1996 Edward Albee (playwright), Benny Carter (jazz musician), Johnny Cash (musician), Jack Lemmon (actor), Maria Tallchief (ballerina)

1997 Lauren Bacall (actress), Bob Dylan (songwriter and singer), Charlton Heston (actor), Jessye Norman (soprano), Edward Villella (ballet dancer and director)

1998 Bill Cosby (actor and comedian), John Kander and Fred Ebb (Broadway composer and lyricist team), Willie Nelson (singer and songwriter), André Previn (composer and conductor), Shirley Temple Black (actress)

1999 Victor Borge (comedian and pianist), Sean Connery (actor), Judith Jamison (dancer and teacher), Jason Robards (actor), Stevie Wonder (singer and songwriter)

2000 Mikhail Baryshnikov (dancer), Plácido Domingo (tenor), Angela Lansbury (actress), Chuck Berry (rock 'n' roll musician), Clint Eastwood (actor, director, producer)

2001 Julie Andrews (actress), Van Cliburn (pianist), Quincy Jones (music producer and composer), Jack Nicholson (actor), Luciano Pavarotti (singer)

Templeton Foundation Prize for Progress in Religion

The Templeton Prize, an award to encourage progress in religion, was established in 1972 by Sir John Templeton, a Tennessee-born financial analyst and Presbyterian layman, and first presented in 1973. Its value has increased over the years to nearly $1 million, depending on exchange rates.

1973 Mother Teresa of Calcutta, founder, the Missionaries of Charity

1974 Brother Roger, founder and prior, the Taize Community in France

1975 Dr. Sarvepalli Radhakrishnan, former president of India and Oxford Professor of Eastern Religions and Ethics

1976 H. E. Leon Joseph Cardinal Suenens, Archbishop of Malines-Brussels

1977 Chiara Lubich, founder of the Focolare Movement, Italy

1978 Prof. Thomas F. Torrance, president of International Academy of Religion and Sciences, Scotland

1979 Nikkyo Niwano, founder of Rissho Kosel Kai and World Conferences on Religion and Peace, Japan

1980 Prof. Ralph Wendell Burhoe, founder and editor of *Zygon,* Chicago

1981 Dame Cicely Saunders, originator of Modern Hospice Movement, England

1982 The Rev. Dr. Billy Graham, founder, The Billy Graham Evangelistic Association

1983 Aleksandr Solzhenitsyn, U.S.

1984 The Rev. Michael Bourdeaux, founder, Keston College, England

1985 Sir Alister Hardy, Oxford, England

1986 Rev. Dr. James McCord, Princeton, N.J.

1987 Rev. Professor Stanley L. Jaki, Princeton, N.J.

1988 Dr. Inamullah Khan, secretary-general, World Muslim Congress

1989 The Very Reverend Lord MacLeod of the Iona Community, Scotland, and Professor Carl Friedrich von Weizsäcker, Starnberg, West Germany

1990 Baba Amte, India, and Professor Charles Birch, Sydney, Australia

1991 The Rt. Hon. Lord Jakobovits, chief rabbi of Great Britain and the Commonwealth

1992 Dr. Kyung-Chik Han, founder, Seoul's Young Nak Presbyterian Church

1993 Charles W. Colson, founder, Prison Fellowship, Virginia

1994 Michael Novak, scholar at the American Enterprise Institute, Washington, D.C.

1995 Dr. Paul Davies, professor, University of Adelaide, Australia

1996 William R. "Bill" Bright, president and founder, Campus Crusade for Christ International, California

1997 Pandurang Shastri Athavale, founder and leader of Swadhyaya, a spiritual movement credited with improving the lives of 20 million people

1998 Sir Sigmund Sternberg, founder and chairman, Sternberg Centre for Judaism, London

1999 Ian Barbour, professor emeritus, Carleton College, Minnesota

2000 Freeman J. Dyson, professor emeritus, Institute for Advanced Study, Princeton, N.J.

2001 Arthur Peacocke, physical biochemist and Anglican priest, Oxford, England

U.S. Symphony Orchestras and Their Music Directors

(with expenses over $1,050,000)

Akron Symphony Orchestra: Jeffrey K. Sperry[1]
Alabama Symphony Orchestra: Richard Westerfield
American Composers Orchestra: Dennis Russell Davies
American Symphony Orchestra: Leon Botstein[3]
Arkansas Symphony Orchestra: David Itkin
Aspen Chamber Symphony: David Zinman
Atlanta Symphony: Robert Spano
Austin Symphony: Peter Bay[3]
Baltimore Symphony: Yuri Temirkanov
Baton Rouge Symphony: Timothy Muffitt
Boca Pops (Florida Symphonic Pops): Crafton Beck[2, 3]
Boston Symphony Orchestra: Seiji Ozawa
Boston Symphony Chamber Players: Malcolm Lowe
Boulder Philharmonic Orchestra: Theodore Kuchar
Brooklyn Philharmonic: Robert Spano
Buffalo Philharmonic Orchestra: JoAnn Falletta
Cedar Rapids Symphony: Christian Tiemeyer[2]
Charleston Symphony: David Stahl
Charlotte Symphony: Janita Hauk[6]
Chattanooga Symphony & Opera Association:
  Robert Bernhardt
Chicago Sinfonietta: Paul Freeman
Chicago Symphony: Daniel Barenboim
Cincinnati Symphony: Jesus Lopez-Cobos
Cleveland Orchestra: Christoph von Dohnanyi
Colorado Springs Symphony: Yaacov Bergman
Dallas Symphony: Andrew Litton
Dayton Philharmonic: Neal Gittleman
Delaware Symphony: Stephen Gunzenhauser
Des Moines Symphony: Joseph Giunta
Detroit Symphony: Neeme Järvi
Elgin Symphony Orchestra: Robert L. Hanson[2]
El Paso Symphony Orchestra: Gurer Aykal[2]
Erie Philharmonic: Peter Bay
Evansville Philharmonic Orchestra: Alfred Savia
Florida Orchestra: Jahja Ling
Florida Philharmonic Orchestra: James Judd
Florida West Coast Symphony Orchestra:
  Leif Bjaland[2, 3]
Fort Wayne Philharmonic: Edvard Tchivzhel
Fort Worth Symphony: John Giordano
Fresno Philharmonic Orchestra: Raymond Harvey
Grand Rapids Symphony: Catherine Comet
Grant Park Symphony Orchestra & Chorus (Chicago):
  Hugh Wolff[4]
Greensboro Symphony Orchestra: Stuart Malina
Greenville Symphony Orchestra: Edvard Tchivzhel
Handel & Haydn Society: Christopher Hogwood[3]
Harrisburg Symphony Orchestra: Richard Westerfield
Hartford Symphony: Shirley A. Furry[1]
Honolulu Symphony Orchestra: Samuel Wong
Houston Symphony: Hans Graf
Indianapolis Symphony: Raymond Leppard[6]
Jacksonville Symphony: Roger Nierenberg[6]
Kalamazoo Symphony Orchestra: Yoshimi Takeda[6]
Kansas City Symphony: Anne Manson
Kennedy Center Opera House Orchestra: Heinze Fricke
Knoxville Symphony: Kirk Trevor
Little Orchestra Society of New York: Dino Anagnost[2]
Long Beach Symphony: JoAnn Falletta
Long Island Philharmonic: Karen L. Barnes[1]
Los Angeles Chamber Orchestra: Jeffrey Kahane

Los Angeles Philharmonic: Esa-Pekka Salonen
Louisiana Philharmonic Orchestra: Klauspeter Seibel
Louisville Orchestra: Robert Franz
Madison Symphony Orchestra: John De Main
Memphis Symphony: David Loebel
Milwaukee Symphony Orchestra: Andreas Delfs
Minnesota Orchestra: Eiji Oue
Mississippi Symphony: Colman Pearce[2]
Monterey Symphony: Kate Tamarkin
Music Academy of the West Summer Festival
  Orchestra: Carleen Landes[3]
Music of the Baroque Chorus & Orchestra: Thomas S.
  Wikman
Naples Philharmonic: Christopher Seaman
Nashville Symphony: Kenneth D. Schermerhorn
National Sinfonietta: Burton A. Zipser[3]
National Symphony (D.C.): Leonard Slatkin
New Haven Symphony: Michael Palmer[6]
New Jersey Symphony: Zdenek Macal[2, 3]
New Mexico Symphony: Roger Melone[2]
New West Symphony: Boris Brott[6]
New World Symphony (Fla.): Michael Tilson Thomas[3]
New York Chamber Symphony: Gerard Schwarz
New York Philharmonic: Kurt Masur
New York Pops: Skitch Henderson
North Carolina Symphony: Gerhardt Zimmermann
Northeastern Pennsylvania Philharmonic: Hugh Keelan
Ohio Chamber Orchestra: David Lockington[1]
Oklahoma City Philharmonic: Joel A. Levine
Omaha Symphony: Victor Yampoisky
Omaha Symphony Chamber Orchestra: Victor
  Yampoisky
Oregon Symphony: James DePreist
Pacific Symphony Orchestra (Calif.): Carl St. Clair
Palm Beach Pops: Bob Lappin
Philadelphia Orchestra: Wolfgang Sawallisch
Philharmonia Baroque Orchestra: Nicholas McGegan
Phoenix Symphony: Hermann Michael
Pittsburgh Symphony Orchestra: Mariss Jansons
Portland Symphony: Toshiyuki Shimada
Quad City Symphony Orchestra:
  Donald Schleicher[6]
Rhode Island Philharmonic: Larry Rachleff
Richmond Symphony: Mark Russell Smith
River City Brass Band: Denis Colwell
Rochester Philharmonic: Christopher Seaman
St. Louis Symphony: Hans Vonk
St. Paul Chamber Orchestra: Hugh Wolff
San Antonio Symphony: Christopher Wilkins
San Francisco Symphony: Michael Tilson Thomas
San Jose Symphony: Leonid Grin
Santa Barbara Symphony Orchestra: Gisele Ben-Dor
Santa Rosa Symphony: Jeffrey Kahane[6]
Savannah Symphony: Philip Greenberg[6]
Seattle Symphony: Gerard Schwarz
Shreveport Symphony: Dennis Simons
Spokane Symphony: Fabio Mechetti
Springfield Symphony (Mass.): Mark Russell Smith
Stamford Symphony Orchestra: Roger Nierenberg[2]
Symphony of United Nations: Joseph Eger
Syracuse Symphony Orchestra: Fabio Mechetti
Toledo Symphony: Andrew Massey[6]

Tucson Symphony: George Hanson[6]
Tulsa Philharmonic: Bernard Rubenstein
Utah Symphony: Keith Lockhart
Virginia Symphony: JoAnn Falletta
Westchester Philharmonic: Paul Lustig Dunkel[2]

West Virginia Symphony: Thomas B. Conlin[3]
Wichita Symphony: Zuohuan Chen[6]
Winston-Salem Piedmont Triad Symphony: Peter J. Perret
Youngstown Symphony Orchestra: Isaiah Jackson

1. Executive Director. 2. Conductor. 3. Artistic Director. 4. Principal Conductor. 5. Music Conductor. 6. Music Director and Conductor.

U.S. Opera Companies

(budgets $2,000,000 and over)

American Musical Theatre of San Jose (Calif.), Dianna Shuster, Art. Dir.
Arizona Opera Company (Tucson, Phoenix), David Speers, Gen. Dir.
Aspen Opera Theater Center (Colo.), Robert Harth, Pres. and CEO
Atlanta Opera, The (Ga.), William Fred Scott, Art. Dir.
Austin Lyric Opera (Tex.), Joseph McClain, Gen. Dir.
Baltimore Opera Company (Md.), Michael Harrison, Gen. Dir.
Boston Lyric Opera Company (Mass.), Janice Mancini Del Sesto, Gen. Dir.
Central City Opera House Association (Colo.), Pelham G. Pearce, Jr., Gen. Dir.
Cincinnati Opera Association (Ohio), Nicholas Muni, Art. Dir.
Civic Light Opera (Pittsburgh), Charles Gray, Exec. Dir.
Cleveland Opera (Ohio), David Bamberger, Gen. Dir.
Dallas Opera, The (Tex.), Plato S. Karayanis, Gen. Dir.
Florentine Opera Company (Milwaukee), Dennis W. Hanthorn, Gen. Dir.
Florida Grand Opera (Miami), Robert M. Heuer, Gen. Mgr. and CEO
Glimmerglass Opera (Cooperstown, N.Y.), Paul Kellogg, Art. Dir.
Goodspeed Opera House (East Haddam, Conn.), Michael Price, Exec. Dir.
Hawaii Opera Theatre (Honolulu), Henry G. Akina, Gen. Dir. and Art. Dir.
Houston Grand Opera Association (Tex.), R. David Gockley, Gen. Dir.
Kentucky Opera (Louisville), Thomson Smillie, Gen. Dir.
Long Beach Civic Light Opera (Calif.), J. Phillip Keene, Exec. Dir.
Los Angeles Music Center Opera (Calif.), Peter Hemmings, Gen. Dir.
Lyric Opera of Chicago (Ill.), William Mason, Gen. Dir.
Lyric Opera of Kansas City (Mo.), Ardis Krainik, Gen. Dir.
Metro Lyric Opera (Allenhurst, N.J.), Era M. Tognoli, Gen. Dir. and Art. Dir.

Metropolitan Opera Association (N.Y.), James Levine, Art. Dir.
Michigan Opera Theatre (Detroit), David DiChiera, Gen. Dir.
Minnesota Opera, The (Minneapolis), Kevin Smith, Pres. and Gen. Dir.
New York City Opera (N.Y.), Paul Kellogg, Gen. Dir. and Art. Dir.
New York City Opera National Company (N.Y.), Julie Samuels, Bus. Mgr.
Ohio Light Opera (Wooster), Steven Daigle, Art. Dir.
Opera Colorado (Denver), Stephen W. Seifert, Exec. Dir.
Opera Company of Philadelphia (Pa.), Robert B. Driver, Gen. Dir.
Opera Pacific (Irvine, Calif.), David DiChiera, Art. Dir.
Opera Theatre of St. Louis (Mo.), Charles MacKay, Gen. Dir.
Orlando Opera Company (Fla.), Robert Swedberg, Gen. Dir. and Art. Dir.
Palm Beach Opera (Fla.), Anton Guadagno, Art. Dir.
Pittsburgh Opera (Pa.), Tito Capobianco, Art. Dir.
Portland Opera Association (Ore.), Robert Bailey, Gen. Dir.
San Diego Civic Light Opera Association (Calif.), Cinda Lucas, Pres.
San Diego Opera (Calif.), Ian D. Campbell, Gen. Dir.
San Francisco Opera (Calif.), Lotfi Mansouri, Gen. Dir.
San Francisco Opera Center (Calif.), Richard Harrell, Dir.
Santa Barbara Civic Light Opera (Calif.), Paul Iannacone, Exec. Dir.
Santa Fe Opera (N.M.), John Crosby, Gen. Dir.
Sarasota Opera Association (Fla.), Deane C. Allyn, Exec. Dir.
Seattle Opera Association (Wash.), Speight Jenkins, Gen. Dir.
Utah Opera Company (Salt Lake City), Anne Ewers, Gen. Dir.
Virginia Opera (Norfolk), Peter Mark, Gen. Dir.
Washington Opera, The (D.C.), Plácido Domingo, Art. Dir. Designate

Most Frequently Produced Operas in the U.S.

(through 2000–2001)

Top 5 works[1]	Composer/Librettist	Number of productions[2]
1. *Carmen*	Bizet/Meilhac and Halévy	19
2. *The Barber of Seville*	Rossini/Sterbini	17
3. *La Traviata*	Verdi/Piave	17
4. *The Marriage of Figaro*	Mozart/Da Ponte	16
5. *Madama Butterfly*	Puccini/Giacosa and Illica	15
Top 5 works by American artists[3]		
1. *Porgy and Bess*	Gershwin/Heyward	31 (Oct. 10, 1935)
1. *Susannah*	Floyd/Floyd	24 (Feb. 24, 1955)
2. *Candide*	Bernstein/Hellman and Wilbur	20 (Oct. 29, 1956)
2. *Ballad of Baby Doe*	Moore/Latouche	17 (July 7, 1956)
2. *The Rake's Progress*	Stravinsky/Auden and Kallman	14 (Sept. 11, 1951)

1. For 2000–2001 season 2. Represents the number of productions by professional member companies of Opera America, not the number of performances. 3. Through 2000–2001 season. Date in parentheses is date of first performance. *Source:* Opera America's Annual Season Schedule of Performances; Web: www.operaamerica.org.

U.S. Dance Companies
(budgets $2,500,000 and over)

Alvin Ailey American Dance Theatre (1958): Judith Jamison, Art. Dir.
American Ballet Theatre (1940): Kevin McKenzie, Art. Dir.
Atlanta Ballet Company (1929): John McFall, Art. Dir. and CEO
Ballet Florida (1986): Marie Hale, Art. Dir.
Ballet San Jose of Silicon Valley (1976): Dennis Nahat, Art. Dir.
BalletMet Columbus (1978): David Nixon, Art. Dir.
Ballet West (1968[1]): Jonas Kåge, Exec. Dir.
Boston Ballet (1964): Mikko Nissinen, Art. Dir.
Cincinnati Ballet (1955): Victoria Morgan, Art. Dir.
Colorado Ballet (1961): Martin Fredmann, Art. Dir.
Merce Cunningham Dance Company (1952): Merce Cunningham, Art. Dir.
Dance Theater of Harlem (1968): Arthur Mitchell, Art. Dir.
Feld Ballet New York (1974): Eliot Feld, Dir.
Fort Worth Dallas Ballet (1993): David Mallette, Exec. Dir.
Martha Graham Dance Company (1926)*

Houston Ballet (1968): Ben Stevenson, Art. Dir.
Joffrey Ballet of Chicago (1954): Gerald Arpino, Art. Dir.
Bill T. Jones/Arnie Zane Dance Company (1982): Bill T. Jones, Art. Dir.
José Limón Dance Company (1946): Carla Maxwell, Art. Dir.
Miami City Ballet (1986): Edward Villella, Art. Dir.
Milwaukee Ballet (1970): Simon Dow, Art. Dir.
Mark Morris Dance Group (1980): Mark Morris, Art. Dir.
New York City Ballet (1948): Peter Martins, Ballet-Master-in-Chief
Ocheami-Afrikan Dance Company (1978): Kofe Anang, Art. Dir.
Pacific Northwest Ballet (1972): Kent Stowell and Francia Russell, Art. Dirs.
Pittsburgh Ballet Theater (1970): Terrence S. Orr, Art. Dir.
San Francisco Ballet (1933): Helgi Tomasson, Art. Dir.
Paul Taylor Dance Company (1954): Paul Taylor, Dir.
Washington Ballet (1976): Septime Webre, Art. Dir.

*The Martha Graham Dance Company suspended operations and canceled performances in May 2000 amid financial disaster and a vitriolic internal battle. Ron Protas, the company's artistic director, was fired by the board, yet has retained the rights to Graham's works. The future of the company remains uncertain. NOTE: Year founded appears in parentheses after name. 1. Prior company founded 1963, name changed to Ballet West in 1968.

Best-Selling Books, 2000
Source: Publishers Weekly

Hardcover Fiction

1. *The Brethren,* John Grisham
2. *The Mark: The Beast Rules the World,* Jerry B. Jenkins and Tim LaHaye
3. *The Bear and the Dragon,* Tom Clancy
4. *The Indwelling: The Beast Takes Possession,* Jerry B. Jenkins and Tim LaHaye
5. *The Last Precinct,* Patricia Cornwell
6. *Journey,* Danielle Steel
7. *The Rescue,* Nicholas Sparks
8. *Roses Are Red,* James Patterson
9. *Cradle and All,* James Patterson
10. *The House on Hope Street,* Danielle Steel

Hardcover Nonfiction

1. *Who Moved My Cheese?,* Spencer Johnson
2. *Guinness World Records 2001,* Guinness World Records Ltd.
3. *Body for Life,* Bill Phillips
4. *Tuesdays with Morrie,* Mitch Albom
5. *The Beatles Anthology,* The Beatles
6. *The O'Reilly Factor,* Bill O'Reilly
7. *Relationship Rescue,* Philip C. McGraw, Ph.D.
8. *The Millionaire Mind,* Thomas J. Stanley
9. *Ten Things I Wish I'd Known—Before I Went Out into the Real World,* Maria Shriver
10. *Eating Well for Optimum Health,* Andrew Weil, M.D.

Trade Paperbacks

1. *A Child Called "It,"* Dave Pelzer
2. *Left Behind,* Jerry B. Jenkins and Tim LaHaye
3. *The Poisonwood Bible,* Barbara Kingsolver
4. *Chicken Soup for the Couple's Soul,* Jack Canfield, Mark Victor Hansen, Mark and Chrissy Donnelly, and Barbara De Angelis
5. *Apollyon,* Jerry B. Jenkins and Tim LaHaye
6. *Tribulation Force,* Jerry B. Jenkins and Tim LaHaye
7. *Chicken Soup for the Teenage Soul III,* Jack Canfield, Mark Victor Hansen, and Kimberly Kirberger
8. *While I Was Gone,* Sue Miller
9. *House of Sand and Fog,* Andre Dubus III
10. *Talking Dirty with the Queen of Clean,* Linda Cobb

Mass Market Paperbacks

1. *The Testament,* John Grisham
2. *The Brethren,* John Grisham
3. *Hannibal,* Thomas Harris
4. *The Green Mile,* Stephen King
5. *Heart of the Sea,* Nora Roberts
6. *Tears of the Moon,* Nora Roberts
7. *Black Notice,* Patricia Cornwell
8. *Irresistible Forces,* Danielle Steel
9. *Timeline,* Michael Crichton
10. *The Girl Who Loved Tom Gordon,* Stephen King

Best-Selling Children's Books, 2000
Source: Publishers Weekly

Hardcover

1. *Harry Potter and the Goblet of Fire,* J. K. Rowling
2. *If You Take a Mouse to the Movies,* Laura Numeroff, illustrated by Felicia Bond
3. *The Haunted Carnival,* Ronald Kidd
4. *Dinosaur: A Read Aloud Storybook,* Mouseworks
5. *Big, Terrible Trouble?,* Craig McCracken, illustrated by Craig McCracken and Lou Romano
6. *Disney's Animal Stories,* Sarah Heller
7. *Backstreet Boys: The Official Book,* Andre Csillag
8. *Where Do Balloons Go?,* Jamie Lee Curtis, illustrated by Laura Cornell
9. *Dream Snow,* Eric Carle
10. *I Spy Extreme Challenger!,* Jean Marzollo, illustrated by Walter Wick

Paperback

1. *Harry Potter and the Chamber of Secrets*, J. K. Rowling
2. *Chicken Soup for the Teenage Soul III*, Jack Canfield, Mark Victor Hansen, Kimberly Kirberger
3. *Holes*, Louis Sachar
4. *Chicken Soup for the Preteen Soul*, Jack Canfield, Mark Victor Hansen, Patty Hansen, Iren Dunlap, Kenan Thompson
5. *Captain Underpants and the Perilous Plot of Professor Poopypants*, Dav Pilkey
6. *Left Behind: The Kids #7 Busted*, Jerry B. Jenkins and Tim LaHaye
7. *Left Behind: The Kids #8 Death Strike*, Jerry B. Jenkins and Tim LaHaye
8. *A Little Monstrous Problem*, Amy Rogers, illustrated by Dave Walston
9. *Left Behind: The Kids #10 On the Run*, Jerry B. Jenkins and Tim LaHaye
10. *Left Behind: The Kids #9 The Search*, Jerry B. Jenkins and Tim LaHaye

All-Time Best-Selling Children's Books
From the date of publication (in parentheses) through the end of 1995.
Source: Publishers Weekly

Hardcovers

1. *The Poky Little Puppy*, Janette Sebring Lowrey (1942)
2. *The Tale of Peter Rabbit*, Beatrix Potter (1902)
3. *Tootle*, Gertrude Crampton (1945)
4. *Saggy Baggy Elephant*, Kathryn and Byron Jackson (1955)
5. *Scuffy the Tugboat*, Gertrude Crampton (1955)
6. *Pat the Bunny*, Dorothy Kunhardt (1940)
7. *Green Eggs and Ham*, Dr. Seuss (1960)
8. *The Cat in the Hat*, Dr. Seuss (1957)
9. *The Littlest Angel*, Charles Tazewell (1946)
10. *One Fish, Two Fish, Red Fish, Blue Fish*, Dr. Seuss (1960)

Paperbacks

1. *Charlotte's Web*, E. B. White, illustrated by Garth Williams (1974)
2. *The Outsiders*, S. E. Hinton (1968)
3. *Tales of a Fourth Grade Nothing*, Judy Blume (1976)
4. *Shane*, Jack Schaeffer (1983)
5. *Are You There, God? It's Me, Margaret*, Judy Blume (1972)
6. *Where the Red Fern Grows*, Wilson Rawls (1974)
7. *A Wrinkle in Time*, Madeleine L'Engle (1973)
8. *Island of the Blue Dolphins*, Scott O'Dell (1971)
9. *Little House on the Prairie*, Laura Ingalls Wilder, illustrated by Garth Williams (1971)
10. *Little House in the Big Woods*, Laura Ingalls Wilder, illustrated by Garth Williams (1971)

The 100 Best Novels of the 20th Century
The Board of the Modern Library, a division of Random House, published its selections in July 1998.

1. *Ulysses*, James Joyce (1922)
2. *The Great Gatsby*, F. Scott Fitzgerald (1925)
3. *A Portrait of the Artist as a Young Man*, James Joyce (1916)
4. *Lolita*, Vladimir Nabokov (1958)
5. *Brave New World*, Aldous Huxley (1932)
6. *The Sound and the Fury*, William Faulkner (1929)
7. *Catch-22*, Joseph Heller (1961)
8. *Darkness at Noon*, Arthur Koestler (1941)
9. *Sons and Lovers*, D. H. Lawrence (1913)
10. *The Grapes of Wrath*, John Steinbeck (1939)
11. *Under the Volcano*, Malcolm Lowry (1947)
12. *The Way of All Flesh*, Samuel Butler (1903)
13. *1984*, George Orwell (1949)
14. *I, Claudius*, Robert Graves (1934)
15. *To the Lighthouse*, Virginia Woolf (1927)
16. *An American Tragedy*, Theodore Dreiser (1925)
17. *The Heart Is a Lonely Hunter*, Carson McCullers (1940)
18. *Slaughterhouse-Five*, Kurt Vonnegut (1969)
19. *Invisible Man*, Ralph Ellison (1952)
20. *Native Son*, Richard Wright (1940)
21. *Henderson the Rain King*, Saul Bellow (1959)
22. *Appointment in Samarra*, John O'Hara (1934)
23. *U.S.A.* (trilogy), John Dos Passos (1937—trilogy completed)
24. *Winesburg, Ohio*, Sherwood Anderson (1919)
25. *A Passage to India*, E. M. Forster (1924)
26. *The Wings of the Dove*, Henry James (1902)
27. *The Ambassadors*, Henry James (1903)
28. *Tender Is the Night*, F. Scott Fitzgerald (1934)
29. *The Studs Lonigan Trilogy*, James T. Farrell (1935)
30. *The Good Soldier*, Ford Madox Ford (1915)
31. *Animal Farm*, George Orwell (1946)
32. *The Golden Bowl*, Henry James (1904)
33. *Sister Carrie*, Theodore Dreiser (1900)
34. *A Handful of Dust*, Evelyn Waugh (1934)
35. *As I Lay Dying*, William Faulkner (1930)
36. *All the King's Men*, Robert Penn Warren (1946)
37. *The Bridge of San Luis Rey*, Thornton Wilder (1927)
38. *Howards End*, E. M. Forster (1910)
39. *Go Tell It on the Mountain*, James Baldwin (1953)
40. *The Heart of the Matter*, Graham Greene (1948)
41. *Lord of the Flies*, William Golding (1954)
42. *Deliverance*, James Dickey (1969)
43. *A Dance to the Music of Time* (series), Anthony Powell (1975—series completed)
44. *Point Counter Point*, Aldous Huxley (1928)
45. *The Sun Also Rises*, Ernest Hemingway (1926)
46. *The Secret Agent*, Joseph Conrad (1907)
47. *Nostromo*, Joseph Conrad (1904)
48. *The Rainbow*, D. H. Lawrence (1915)
49. *Women in Love*, D. H. Lawrence (1921)
50. *Tropic of Cancer*, Henry Miller (1934)
51. *The Naked and the Dead*, Norman Mailer (1948)
52. *Portnoy's Complaint*, Philip Roth (1969)
53. *Pale Fire*, Vladimir Nabokov (1962)
54. *Light in August*, William Faulkner (1932)
55. *On the Road*, Jack Kerouac (1957)

56. *The Maltese Falcon*, Dashiell Hammett (1930)
57. *Parade's End*, Ford Madox Ford (1950)
58. *The Age of Innocence*, Edith Wharton (1920)
59. *Zuleika Dobson*, Max Beerbohm (1911)
60. *The Moviegoer*, Walker Percy (1961)
61. *Death Comes for the Archbishop*, Willa Cather (1927)
62. *From Here to Eternity*, James Jones (1951)
63. *The Wapshot Chronicles*, John Cheever (1957)
64. *The Catcher in the Rye*, J. D. Salinger (1951)
65. *A Clockwork Orange*, Anthony Burgess (1962)
66. *Of Human Bondage*, W. Somerset Maugham (1915)
67. *Heart of Darkness*, Joseph Conrad (1902)
68. *Main Street*, Sinclair Lewis (1920)
69. *The House of Mirth*, Edith Wharton (1905)
70. *The Alexandria Quartet*, Lawrence Durrell (1960—series completed)
71. *A High Wind in Jamaica*, Richard Hughes (1929)
72. *A House for Mr. Biswas*, V. S. Naipaul (1961)
73. *The Day of the Locust*, Nathanael West (1939)
74. *A Farewell to Arms*, Ernest Hemingway (1929)
75. *Scoop*, Evelyn Waugh (1938)
76. *The Prime of Miss Jean Brodie*, Muriel Spark (1961)
77. *Finnegans Wake*, James Joyce (1939)
78. *Kim*, Rudyard Kipling (1901)
79. *A Room with a View*, E. M. Forster (1908)
80. *Brideshead Revisited*, Evelyn Waugh (1945)
81. *The Adventures of Augie March*, Saul Bellow (1953)
82. *Angle of Repose*, Wallace Stegner (1971)
83. *A Bend in the River*, V. S. Naipaul (1979)
84. *The Death of the Heart*, Elizabeth Bowen (1938)
85. *Lord Jim*, Joseph Conrad (1900)
86. *Ragtime*, E. L. Doctorow (1975)
87. *The Old Wives' Tale*, Arnold Bennett (1908)
88. *The Call of the Wild*, Jack London (1903)
89. *Loving*, Henry Green (1945)
90. *Midnight's Children*, Salman Rushdie (1981)
91. *Tobacco Road*, Erskine Caldwell (1933)
92. *Ironweed*, William Kennedy (1983)
93. *The Magus*, John Fowles (1966)
94. *Wide Sargasso Sea*, Jean Rhys (1966)
95. *Under the Net*, Iris Murdoch (1954)
96. *Sophie's Choice*, William Styron (1979)
97. *The Sheltering Sky*, Paul Bowles (1949)
98. *The Postman Always Rings Twice*, James M. Cain (1934)
99. *The Ginger Man*, J. P. Donleavy (1955)
100. *The Magnificent Ambersons*, Booth Tarkington (1918)

The 100 Best Nonfiction Books of the 20th Century

The Board of the Modern Library, a division of Random House, published its selections in April 1999.

1. *The Education of Henry Adams*, Henry Adams (1906)
2. *The Varieties of Religious Experience*, William James (1902)
3. *Up from Slavery*, Booker T. Washington (1901)
4. *A Room of One's Own*, Virginia Woolf (1929)
5. *Silent Spring*, Rachel Carson (1962)
6. *Selected Essays, 1917–1932*, T. S. Eliot (1932)
7. *The Double Helix*, James D. Watson (1968)
8. *Speak, Memory*, Vladimir Nabokov (1967)
9. *The American Language*, H. L. Mencken (1919)
10. *The General Theory of Employment, Interest, and Money*, John Maynard Keynes (1935–1936)
11. *The Lives of a Cell*, Lewis Thomas (1974)
12. *The Frontier in American History*, Frederick Jackson Turner (1920)
13. *Black Boy*, Richard Wright (1945)
14. *Aspects of the Novel*, E. M. Forster (1927)
15. *The Civil War*, Shelby Foote (1958–1974)
16. *The Guns of August*, Barbara Tuchman (1962)
17. *The Proper Study of Mankind*, Isaiah Berlin (1997)
18. *The Nature and Destiny of Man*, Reinhold Niebuhr (1941–1943)
19. *Notes of a Native Son*, James Baldwin (1955)
20. *The Autobiography of Alice B. Toklas*, Gertrude Stein (1933)
21. *The Elements of Style*, William Strunk and E. B. White (1959)
22. *An American Dilemma*, Gunnar Myrdal (1944)
23. *Principia Mathematica*, Alfred North Whitehead and Bertrand Russell (1910–1913)
24. *The Mismeasure of Man*, Stephen Jay Gould (1981)
25. *The Mirror and the Lamp*, Meyer Howard Abrams (1953)
26. *The Art of the Soluble*, Peter B. Medawar (1967)
27. *The Ants*, Bert Hoelldobler and Edward O. Wilson (1990)
28. *A Theory of Justice*, John Rawls (1971)
29. *Art and Illusion*, Ernest H. Gombrich (1961)
30. *The Making of the English Working Class*, E. P. Thompson (1963)
31. *The Souls of Black Folk*, W. E. B. Du Bois (1903)
32. *Principia Ethica*, G. E. Moore (1903)
33. *Philosophy and Civilization*, John Dewey (1927)
34. *On Growth and Form*, D'Arcy Thompson (1917)
35. *Ideas and Opinions*, Albert Einstein (1954)
36. *The Age of Jackson*, Arthur Schlesinger, Jr. (1945)
37. *The Making of the Atomic Bomb*, Richard Rhodes (1986)
38. *Black Lamb and Grey Falcon*, Rebecca West (1942)
39. *Autobiographies*, W. B. Yeats (1926)
40. *Science and Civilization in China*, Joseph Needham (1954–)
41. *Goodbye to All That*, Robert Graves (1929)
42. *Homage to Catalonia*, George Orwell (1938)
43. *The Autobiography of Mark Twain*, Mark Twain (1924)
44. *Children of Crisis*, Robert Coles (1967)
45. *A Study of History*, Arnold J. Toynbee (1934–1961)
46. *The Affluent Society*, John Kenneth Galbraith (1958)
47. *Present at the Creation*, Dean Acheson (1969)
48. *The Great Bridge*, David McCullough (1972)
49. *Patriotic Gore*, Edmund Wilson (1962)
50. *Samuel Johnson*, Walter Jackson Bate (1977)
51. *The Autobiography of Malcolm X*, Alex Haley and Malcolm X (1965)
52. *The Right Stuff*, Tom Wolfe (1979)
53. *Eminent Victorians*, Lytton Strachey (1918)
54. *Working*, Studs Terkel (1974)
55. *Darkness Visible*, William Styron (1990)
56. *The Liberal Imagination*, Lionel Trilling (1950)
57. *The Second World War*, Winston Churchill (1948–1953)
58. *Out of Africa*, Isak Dinesen (1937)

59. *Jefferson and His Time*, Dumas Malone (1948–1981)
60. *In the American Grain*, William Carlos Williams (1925)
61. *Cadillac Desert*, Marc Reisner (1986)
62. *The House of Morgan*, Ron Chernow (1990)
63. *The Sweet Science*, A. J. Liebling (1956)
64. *The Open Society and Its Enemies*, Karl Popper (1945)
65. *The Art of Memory*, Frances A. Yates (1966)
66. *Religion and the Rise of Capitalism*, R. H. Tawney (1926)
67. *A Preface to Morals*, Walter Lippmann (1929)
68. *The Gate of Heavenly Peace*, Jonathan D. Spence (1981)
69. *The Structure of Scientific Revolutions*, Thomas S. Kuhn (1962)
70. *The Strange Career of Jim Crow*, C. Vann Woodward (1955)
71. *The Rise of the West*, William H. McNeill (1963)
72. *The Gnostic Gospels*, Elaine Pagels (1979)
73. *James Joyce*, Richard Ellmann (1959)
74. *Florence Nightingale*, Cecil Woodham-Smith (1950)
75. *The Great War and Modern Memory*, Paul Fussell (1975)
76. *The City in History*, Lewis Mumford (1961)
77. *Battle Cry of Freedom*, James M. McPherson (1988)
78. *Why We Can't Wait*, Martin Luther King, Jr. (1964)
79. *The Rise of Theodore Roosevelt*, Edmund Morris (1979)
80. *Studies in Iconology*, Erwin Panofsky (1939)
81. *The Face of Battle*, John Keegan (1976)
82. *The Strange Death of Liberal England*, George Dangerfield (1935)
83. *Vermeer*, Lawrence Gowing (1952)
84. *A Bright Shining Lie*, Neil Sheehan (1988)
85. *West with the Night*, Beryl Markham (1942)
86. *This Boy's Life*, Tobias Wolff (1989)
87. *A Mathematician's Apology*, G. H. Hardy (1940)
88. *Six Easy Pieces*, Richard P. Feynman (1963)
89. *Pilgrim at Tinker Creek*, Annie Dillard (1974)
90. *The Golden Bough*, James George Frazer (1922) (1 vol. ed.)
91. *Shadow and Act*, Ralph Ellison (1964)
92. *The Power Broker*, Robert A. Caro (1974)
93. *The American Political Tradition*, Richard Hofstadter (1948)
94. *The Contours of American History*, William Appleman Williams (1966)
95. *The Promise of American Life*, Herbert Croly (1909)
96. *In Cold Blood*, Truman Capote (1965)
97. *The Journalist and the Murderer*, Janet Malcolm (1990)
98. *The Taming of Chance*, Ian Hacking (1990)
99. *Operating Instructions*, Anne Lamott (1994)
100. *Melbourne*, Lord David Cecil (1939 & 1954)

Best American Journalism of the 20th Century

The following works were chosen as the 20th century's best American journalism by a panel of experts assembled by the New York University school of journalism.

1. **John Hersey:** "Hiroshima," *The New Yorker*, 1946
2. **Rachel Carson:** *Silent Spring*, book, 1962
3. **Bob Woodward and Carl Bernstein:** Investigation of the Watergate break-in, *The Washington Post*, 1972
4. **Edward R. Murrow:** *Battle of Britain*, CBS radio, 1940
5. **Ida Tarbell:** "The History of the Standard Oil Company," *McClure's*, 1902–1904
6. **Lincoln Steffens:** "The Shame of the Cities," *McClure's*, 1902–1904
7. **John Reed:** *Ten Days That Shook the World*, book, 1919
8. **H. L. Mencken:** Scopes "Monkey" trial, *The Sun* of Baltimore, 1925
9. **Ernie Pyle:** Reports from Europe and the Pacific during World War II, Scripps-Howard newspapers, 1940–45
10. **Edward R. Murrow and Fred Friendly:** Investigation of Sen. Joseph McCarthy, CBS, 1954
11. **Edward R. Murrow, David Lowe, and Fred Friendly:** documentary "Harvest of Shame," CBS television, 1960
12. **Seymour Hersh:** Investigation of massacre by American soldiers at My Lai in Vietnam, Dispatch News Service, 1969
13. **The New York Times:** Publication of the Pentagon Papers, 1971
14. **James Agee and Walker Evans:** *Let Us Now Praise Famous Men*, book, 1941
15. **W. E. B. Du Bois:** *The Souls of Black Folk*, collected articles, 1903
16. **I. F. Stone:** *I. F. Stone's Weekly*, 1953–67
17. **Henry Hampton:** "Eyes on the Prize," documentary, 1987
18. **Tom Wolfe:** *The Electric Kool-Aid Acid Test*, book, 1968
19. **Norman Mailer:** *The Armies of the Night*, book, 1968
20. **Hannah Arendt:** *Eichmann in Jerusalem: A Report on the Banality of Evil*, collected articles, 1963
21. **William Shirer:** *Berlin Diary: The Journal of a Foreign Correspondent, 1939–1941*, collected articles, 1941
22. **Truman Capote:** *In Cold Blood: A True Account of a Multiple Murder and Its Consequences*, book, 1965
23. **Joan Didion:** *Slouching Towards Bethlehem*, collected articles, 1968
24. **Tom Wolfe:** *The Kandy-Kolored Tangerine-Flake Streamline Baby*, collected articles, 1965
25. **Michael Herr:** *Dispatches*, book, 1977
26. **Theodore White:** *The Making of the President: 1960*, book, 1961
27. **Robert Capa:** Ten photographs from D-Day, 1944
28. **J. Anthony Lukas:** *Common Ground: A Turbulent Decade in the Lives of Three American Families*, book, 1985
29. **Richard Harding Davis:** Coverage of German march into Belgium, Wheeler Syndicate and magazines, 1914
30. **Dorothy Thompson:** Reports on the rise of Hitler, *Cosmopolitan* and *Saturday Evening Post*, 1931–1934
31. **John Steinbeck:** Reports on Okie migrant camp life, *The San Francisco News*, 1936
32. **A. J. Liebling:** *The Road Back to Paris*, collected articles, 1944

33. **Ernest Hemingway:** Reports on the Spanish Civil War, *The New Republic,* 1937–1938
34. **Martha Gellhorn:** *The Face of War,* collected articles, 1959
35. **James Baldwin:** *The Fire Next Time,* book, 1963
36. **Joseph Mitchell:** *Up in the Old Hotel and Other Stories,* collection of much older articles, 1992
37. **Betty Friedan:** *The Feminine Mystique,* book, 1963
38. **Ralph Nader:** *Unsafe at Any Speed: The Designed-In Dangers of the American Automobile,* book, 1965
39. **Herblock (Herbert Block):** Cartoons on McCarthyism, *The Washington Post,* 1950
40. **James Baldwin:** "Letter from the South: Nobody Knows My Name," *The Partisan Review,* 1959
41. **Nick Ut:** Photograph of a burning girl running from a napalm attack, The Associated Press, 1972
42. **Pauline Kael:** "Trash, Art, and the Movies," *Harper's,* 1969
43. **Gay Talese:** *Fame and Obscurity: Portraits by Gay Talese,* collected articles, 1970
44. **Randy Shilts:** Reports on AIDS, *The San Francisco Chronicle,* 1981–1985
45. **Janet Flanner (Genet):** *Paris Journals* chronicling Paris' emergence from the Occupation, *The New Yorker,* 1944–1945
46. **Neil Sheehan:** *A Bright Shining Lie: John Paul Vann and America in Vietnam,* book, 1988
47. **A. J. Liebling:** *The Wayward Pressman,* collected articles, 1947
48. **Tom Wolfe:** *The Right Stuff,* book, 1979
49. **Murray Kempton:** *America Comes of Middle Age: Columns 1950–1962,* collected articles, 1963
50. **Murray Kempton:** *Part of Our Time: Some Ruins and Monuments of the Thirties,* book, 1955
51. **Donald L. Barlett and James B. Steele:** "America: What Went Wrong?," *The Philadelphia Inquirer,* 1991
52. **Taylor Branch:** *Parting the Waters: America in the King Years, 1954–63,* book, 1988
53. **Harrison Salisbury:** Reporting from the Soviet Union, *The New York Times,* 1949–1954
54. **John McPhee:** *The John McPhee Reader,* collected articles, 1976
55. **ABC:** Live television broadcast of Army-McCarthy hearings, 1954
56. **Frederick Wiseman:** *Titicut Follies,* documentary, 1967
57. **David Remnick:** *Lenin's Tomb: The Last Days of the Soviet Empire,* book, 1993
58. **Richard Ben Cramer:** *What It Takes: The Way to the White House,* book, 1992
59. **Jonathan Schell:** *The Fate of the Earth,* book, 1982
60. **Russell Baker:** "Francs and Beans," *The New York Times,* 1975
61. **Homer Bigart:** Account of being over Japan in a bomber when World War II came to an end, *The New York Herald-Tribune,* 1945
62. **Ben Hecht:** *1,001 Afternoons in Chicago,* collected articles, 1922
63. **Walter Cronkite:** Documentary on Vietnam, CBS television, 1968
64. **Walter Lippmann:** Early essays, *The New Republic,* 1914
65. **Margaret Bourke-White:** Photographs following the defeat of Germany, *Life* magazine, 1945
66. **Lillian Ross:** *Reporting,* collected articles, 1964

67. **Nicholas Lemann:** *The Promised Land: The Great Black Migration and How It Changed America,* book, 1991
68. **Joe Rosenthal:** Photograph of Marines raising an American flag on Mount Suribachi on the island of Iwo Jima, The Associated Press, 1945
69. **Hodding Carter Jr.:** "Go for Broke," editorial, Carter's *Delta Democrat-Times* (Greenville, Miss.), 1945
70. **The New Yorker:** *The New Yorker Book of War Pieces,* collected articles, 1947
71. **Meyer Berger:** Report on the murderer Howard Unruh, *The New York Times,* 1949
72. **Norman Mailer:** *The Executioner's Song,* book, 1979
73. **Robert Capa:** Spanish Civil War photos, *Life* magazine, 1936
74. **Susan Sontag:** "Notes on 'Camp'," *The Partisan Review,* 1964
75. **Bob Woodward and Carl Bernstein:** *All the President's Men,* book, 1974
76. **John Hersey:** *Here to Stay,* collected articles, 1963
77. **A. J. Liebling:** *The Earl of Louisiana,* book, 1961
78. **Mike Davis:** *City of Quartz: Excavating the Future in Los Angeles,* book, 1990
79. **Melissa Fay Greene:** *Praying for Sheetrock,* book, 1991
80. **J. Anthony Lukas:** "The Two Worlds of Linda Fitzpatrick," *The New York Times,* 1967
81. **Herbert Bayard Swope:** "Klan Exposed," *The New York World,* 1921
82. **William Allen White:** "To an Anxious Friend," *The Emporia* (Kan.) *Gazette,* 1922
83. **Edward R. Murrow:** Report of the liberation of Buchenwald, CBS radio, 1945
84. **Joseph Mitchell:** *McSorley's Wonderful Saloon,* collected articles, 1943
85. **Lillian Ross:** *Picture,* book, 1952
86. **Earl Brown:** Series of articles on race, *Harper's* and *Life* magazines, 1942–1944
87. **Greil Marcus:** *Mystery Train: Images of America in Rock 'n' Roll Music,* book, 1975
88. **Morley Safer:** Atrocities committed by American soldiers on the hamlet of Cam Ne in Vietnam, CBS television, 1965
89. **Ted Poston:** Coverage of the "Little Scottsboro" trial, *The New York Post,* 1949
90. **Leon Dash:** "Rosa Lee's Story," *The Washington Post,* 1994
91. **Jane Kramer:** *Europeans,* collected articles, 1988
92. **Eddie Adams and Vo Suu:** Associated Press photograph and NBC television footage of a Saigon execution, 1968
93. **Grantland Rice:** "Notre Dame's 'Four Horsemen'," The New York *Herald-Tribune,* 1924
94. **Jane Kramer:** *The Politics of Memory: Looking for Germany in the New Germany,* collected articles, 1996
95. **Frank McCourt:** *Angela's Ashes,* book, 1996
96. **Vincent Sheean:** *Personal History,* book, 1935
97. **W. E. B. Du Bois:** Columns on race during his tenure as editor of *The Crisis,* 1910–1934
98. **Damon Runyon:** Crime reporting, *The New York American,* 1926
99. **Joe McGinniss:** *The Selling of the President 1968,* book, 1969
100. **Hunter S. Thompson:** *Fear and Loathing on the Campaign Trail,* book, 1973

Poets Laureate of the United States

Robert Penn Warren	1986–1987	Rita Dove	1993–1995
Richard Wilbur	1987–1988	Robert Hass	1995–1997
Howard Nemerov	1988–1990	Robert Pinsky	1997–2000
Mark Strand	1990–1991	Stanley Kunitz	2000–2001
Joseph Brodsky	1991–1992	Billy Collins	2001–
Mona Van Duyn	1992–1993		

NOTE: The post was established in 1985. Appointment is for a one-year term, but is renewable.

Poets Laureate of England

Edmund Spenser	1591–1599	Laurence Eusden	1718–1730	Alfred Austin	1896–1913
Samuel Daniel	1599–1619	Colley Cibber	1730–1757	Robert Bridges	1913–1930
Ben Jonson	1619–1637	William Whitehead	1757–1785	John Masefield	1930–1967
William Davenant	1638–1668	Thomas Warton	1785–1790	Cecil Day-Lewis	1967–1972
John Dryden[1]	1670–1689	Henry James Pye	1790–1813	Sir John Betjeman	1972–1984
Thomas Shadwell	1689–1692	Robert Southey	1813–1843	Ted Hughes	1984–1998
Nahum Tate	1692–1715	William Wordsworth	1843–1850	Andrew Motion	1999–
Nicholas Rowe	1715–1718	Alfred Lord Tennyson	1850–1892		

1. First to bear the title officially.

Longest Broadway Runs

Show	Dates	Performances[1]	Show	Dates	Performances[1]
1. Cats	10/82–9/2000	7,485	13. Hello, Dolly!	1/64–12/70	2,844
2. A Chorus Line	10/75–4/90	6,137	14. My Fair Lady	3/56–9/62	2,717
3. Oh! Calcutta (revival)	9/76–8/89	5,959	15. Annie	4/77–1/83	2,377
4. Les Misérables	3/87–present	5,855	16. Man of La Mancha	11/65–6/71	2,329
5. The Phantom of the Opera	1/88–present	5,566	17. Abie's Irish Rose	5/22–10/27	2,327
6. Miss Saigon	4/91–1/2001	4,092	18. Oklahoma!	3/43–5/48	2,212
7. 42nd Street	8/80–1/89	3,486	19. Rent	4/96–present	2,120
8. Grease	2/72–4/80	3,388	20. Smokey Joe's Cafe	3/95–1/2000	2,037
9. Fiddler on the Roof	9/64–7/72	3,242	21. Pippin	10/72–6/77	1,944
10. Life with Father	11/39–7/47	3,224	22. South Pacific	4/49–1/54	1,925
11. Tobacco Road	12/33–5/41	3,182	23. The Magic Show	5/74–12/78	1,920
12. Beauty and the Beast	4/94–present	2,887	24. Chicago (revival)	11/96–present	1,891
			25. Gemini	6/77–9/81	1,819

1. As of 5/27/01. Source: League of American Theatres and Producers, Inc.

Top 15 Concert Grosses of 2000

Amusement Business annually ranks domestic and international concert grosses and touring acts. (Headliner, supporting act, dates; gross ticket sales in U.S. dollars; total attendance; venue)

1. **Barbra Streisand (12/31/99–1/1/00),** $18,231,213; 15,842; MGM Grand Garden, Las Vegas, Nev.
2. **Barbra Streisand (9/27–9/28),** $14,393,750; 25,994; Madison Square Garden, New York, N.Y.
3. **Barbra Streisand (9/20–9/21),** $12,600,000; 31,284; Staples Center, Los Angeles, Calif.
4. **Bruce Springsteen (6/12–7/1),** $12,217,343; 190,530; Madison Square Garden, New York, N.Y.
5. **Phish (12/30–12/31),** $11,639,550; 75,000; Big Cypress Seminole Indian Reservation, Big Cypress Swamp, Fla.
6. **Luis Miguel (2/24–3/20),** $8,220,194; 183,688; Auditorio Nacional, Mexico City
7. **Tina Turner (7/15–7/16),** $6,468,990; 123,222; Wembley Stadium, London, England
8. **Eagles, Jackson Browne, Linda Ronstadt (12/31),** $6,257,013; 16,632; Staples Center, Los Angeles, Calif.
9. **Dave Matthews Band, Ben Harper & The Innocent Criminals, Ozomatli (7/11–7/13),** $6,145,912; 136,695; Giants Stadium, East Rutherford, N.J.
10. **Dave Matthews Band, Ben Harper & The Innocent Criminals, Ozomatli (6/29–6/30),** $5,175,270; 115,006; Soldier Field, Chicago, Ill.
11. **Billy Joel (12/31)** $4,476,252; 18,865; Madison Square Garden, New York, N.Y.
12. **Dave Matthews Band, Ben Harper, Ozomatli (7/8–7/9),** $4,433,201; 97,433; Foxboro (Mass.) Stadium
13. **Summer Sanitarium Tour: Metallica, Korn, Kid Rock, Powerman 5000, System of a Down (7/15)**, $4,334,590; 73,458; Los Angeles Memorial Coliseum
14. **The Who, The Wallflowers (10/3–10/7),** $4,080,814; 56,443; Madison Square Garden, New York, N.Y.
15. **'N Sync, Pink, Sisqo, Innosense (7/22–7/23),** $3,991,913; 91,380; Foxboro (Mass.) Stadium

Source: © 2001 BPI Communications Inc. Used with permission from *Amusement Business* ®.

Top 10 Classical Albums, 2000

1. *Sacred Arias*, Andrea Bocelli (Philips/Universal Classics Group)
2. *Verdi*, Andrea Bocelli (Philips/Universal Classics Group)
3. *Aria—The Opera Album*, Andrea Bocelli (Philips/Universal Classics Group)
4. *Fantasia 2000*, Chicago Symphony Orchestra (Levine) (Walt Disney/Universal Classics Group)
5. *Appalachian Journey*, Yo-Yo Ma/Edgar Meyer/Mark O'Connor (Sony Classical)
6. *The Most Relaxing Classical Album in the World . . . Ever!*, Various Artists (Circa/Virgin/Angel Records)
7. *Simply Baroque*, Yo-Yo Ma (Sony Classical)
8. *The Best Opera Album in the World . . . Ever!*, Various Artists (Circa/Virgin/Angel Records)
9. *Simply Baroque II*, Yo-Yo Ma (Sony Classical)
10. *100 Years of Strauss*, Andre Rieu (Philips/Universal Classics Group)

Source: © 2001 BPI Communications Inc. Used with permission from *Billboard* ® magazine.

Top 10 Country Singles, 2000

1. "Breathe," Faith Hill (Warner Bros./WRN)
2. "Amazed," Lonestar (BNA/RLG)
3. "Goodbye Earl," Dixie Chicks (Monument/Sony)
4. "One Voice," Billy Gilman (Epic/Sony)
5. "I Need You," LeAnn Rimes (Sparrow/Capitol/Curb)
6. "Big Deal," LeAnn Rimes (Curb)
7. "Can't Fight the Moonlight," LeAnn Rimes (Curb)
8. "The Way You Love Me," Faith Hill (Warner Bros./WRN)
9. "That's the Way," Jo Dee Messina (Curb)
10. "A Country Boy Can Survive (Y2K Version)," Chad Brock with Hank Williams, Jr. and George Jones (Warner Bros/WRN)

Source: © 2001 BPI Communications Inc. Used with permission from *Billboard* ® magazine.

Top 10 Country Albums, 2000

1. *Fly*, Dixie Chicks (Monument/Sony)
2. *Breathe*, Faith Hill (Warner Bros./WRN)
3. *Come On Over*, Shania Twain (Mercury)
4. *A Place in the Sun*, Tim McGraw (Curb)
5. *Lonely Grill*, Lonestar (BNA/RLG)
6. *Wide Open Spaces*, Dixie Chicks (Monument/Sony)
7. *Latest Greatest Straitest Hits*, George Strait (MCA/Nashville)
8. *Under the Influence*, Alan Jackson (Arista Nashville/RLG)
9. *The Magic of Christmas*, Garth Brooks (Capitol)
10. *LeAnn Rimes*, LeAnn Rimes (Curb)

Source: © 2001 BPI Communications Inc. Used with permission from *Billboard* ® magazine.

Top 10 Pop Singles, 2000

1. "Maria Maria," Santana featuring The Product G&B (Arista)
2. "Hot Boyz, " Missy "Misdemeanor" Elliott featuring Nas, Eve and Q-Tip (The Gold Mind/EastWest/EEG)
3. "Incomplete," Sisqo (Dragon/Def Soul/IDJMG)
4. "Music," Madonna (Maverick/Warner Bros.)

5. "Breathe," Faith Hill (Warner Bros./WRN)
6. "Get It On Tonite," Montell Jordan (Def Soul/IDJMG)
7. "From the Bottom of My Broken Heart," Britney Spears (Jive)
8. "I Like It," Sammie (Freeworld/Capitol)
9. "I Wanna Love You Forever," Jessica Simpson (Columbia)
10. "Thank God I Found You," Mariah Carey featuring Joe and 98 Degrees (Columbia)

Source: © 2001 BPI Communications Inc. Used with permission from *Billboard* ® magazine.

Top 10 Pop Albums, 2000

1. *No Strings Attached*, 'N Sync (Jive)
2. *Supernatural*, Santana (Arista)
3. *The Marshall Mathers LP*, Eminem (Web/Aftermath/Interscope)
4. *Oops! . . . I Did It Again*, Britney Spears (Jive)
5. *Dr. Dre—2001*, Dr. Dre (Aftermath/Interscope)
6. *Human Clay*, Creed (Wind-up)
7. *All the Way . . . A Decade of Song*, Celine Dion (550 Music/Epic)
8. *Christina Aguilera*, Christina Aguilera (RCA)
9. *Millennium*, Backstreet Boys (Jive)
10. *. . . And Then There Was X*, DMX (Ruff Ryders/Def Jam/IDJMG)

Source: © 2001 BPI Communications Inc. Used with permission from *Billboard* ® magazine.

Top 10 R&B/Hip-Hop Singles, 2000

1. "Hot Boyz," Missy "Misdemeanor" Elliott featuring Nas, Eve and Q-Tip (The Gold Mind/EastWest/EEG)
2. "Maria Maria," Santana featuring The Product G&B (Arista)
3. "I Like It," Sammie (Freeworld/Capitol)
4. "One Night Stand," J-Shin featuring LaTocha Scott (Slip-N-Slide/Atlantic)
5. "He Can't Love U," Jagged Edge (So So Def/Columbia)
6. "Get It On Tonite," Montell Jordan (Def Soul/IDJMG)
7. "Thank God I Found You," Mariah Carey featuring Joe and 98 Degrees (Columbia)
8. "Incomplete," Sisqo (Dragon/Def Soul/IDJMG)
9. "24/7," Kevon Edmonds (RCA)
10. "No More," Ruff Endz (Epic)

Source: © 2001 BPI Communications Inc. Used with permission from *Billboard* ® magazine.

Top R&B/Hip-Hop Albums, 2000

1. *Dr. Dre—2001*, Dr. Dre (Aftermath/Interscope)
2. *The Marshall Mathers LP*, Eminem (Web/Aftermath/Interscope)
3. *. . . And Then There Was X*, DMX (Ruff Ryders/Def Jam/IDJMG)
4. *Unleash the Dragon*, Sisqo (Dragon/Def Soul/IDJMG)
5. *Vol. 3 . . . Life and Times of S. Carter*, Jay-Z (Roc-A-Fella/Def Jam/IDJMG)
6. *Country Grammar*, Nelly (Fo' Reel/Universal)
7. *Voodoo*, D'Angelo (Cheeba Sound/Virgin)
8. *My Name Is Joe*, Joe (Jive)
9. *Born Again*, The Notorious B.I.G. (Bad Boy/Arista)
10. *J. E. Heartbreak*, Jagged Edge (So So Def/Columbia/CRG)

Source: © 2001 BPI Communications Inc. Used with permission from *Billboard* ® magazine.

Top 10 Rap Singles, 2000

1. "Hot Boyz," Missy "Misdemeanor" Elliott featuring Nas, Eve and Q-Tip (The Gold Mind/EastWest/EEG)
2. "4, 5, 6," Sole featuring JT Money and Kandi (DreamWorks/Interscope)
3. "Wobble Wobble," 504 Boyz (No Limit/Priority)
4. "Whistle While You Twurk," Ying Yang Twins (ColliPark)
5. "(Hot S**t) Country Grammar," Nelly (Fo' Reel/Universal)
6. "Callin' Me," Lil' Zane featuring 112 (Worldwide/Priority)
7. "You Can Do It," Ice Cube featuring Mack 10 and Ms. Toi (Lench Mob/Best Side/Priority)
8. "Bounce with Me," Lil Bow Wow featuring Xscape (So So Def/Columbia/CRG)
9. "Left, Right, Left," Drama (Tight 2 Def)
10. "G'd Up," Snoop Dogg presents Tha Eastsidaz (Dogg House/TVT)

Source: © 2001 BPI Communications Inc. Used with permission from *Billboard* ® magazine.

The Recording Industry Association of America's Diamond Awards

Top-Selling Certified Albums of All Time*

The RIAA certifies recordings that sell 10,000,000 or more copies as diamond.

27 Million
Their Greatest Hits 1971–1975, Eagles (Elektra)

26 Million
Thriller, Michael Jackson (Epic)

23 Million
The Wall, Pink Floyd (Columbia)

22 Million
Led Zeppelin IV, Led Zeppelin (Swan Song)

21 Million
Greatest Hits Volumes I & II, Billy Joel (Columbia)

18 Million
Come On Over, Shania Twain (Mercury Nashville)
Rumours, Fleetwood Mac (Warner Bros.)
The Beatles, The Beatles (Capitol)

17 Million
The Bodyguard (Soundtrack), Whitney Houston (Arista)

16 Million
Back in Black, AC/DC (ATCO)
Boston, Boston (Epic)
Cracked Rear View, Hootie & the Blowfish (Atlantic)
Jagged Little Pill, Alanis Morissette (Maverick)
No Fences, Garth Brooks (Capitol Nashville)

15 Million
Appetite for Destruction, Guns 'N Roses (Geffen)
Born in the U.S.A., Bruce Springsteen (Columbia)
Dark Side of the Moon, Pink Floyd (Capitol)
Greatest Hits, Elton John (Rocket)
Hotel California, Eagles (Elektra)
Physical Graffiti, Led Zeppelin (Swan Song)
Saturday Night Fever (Soundtrack), Bee Gees (Polydor/Atlas)
The Beatles 1967–1970, The Beatles (Capitol)

14 Million
Ropin' the Wind, Garth Brooks (Capitol Nashville)
The Beatles 1962–1966, The Beatles (Capitol)

13 Million
. . . Baby One More Time, Britney Spears (Jive)
Backstreet Boys, Backstreet Boys (Jive)
Bat Out of Hell, Meat Loaf (Epic)
Bruce Springsteen & the E Street Band Live 1975–1985 (Box set), Bruce Springsteen & the E Street Band (Columbia)
Double Live, Garth Brooks (Capitol Nashville)
Purple Rain (Soundtrack), Prince and the Revolution (Warner Bros.)
Supernatural, Santana (Arista)
Whitney Houston, Whitney Houston (Arista)

12 Million
Breathless, Kenny G (Arista)
Forrest Gump (Soundtrack) (Epic)
Hysteria, Def Leppard (Mercury)
II, Boyz II Men (Motown)
Kenny Rogers' Greatest Hits, Kenny Rogers (Capitol Nashville)
Led Zeppelin II, Led Zeppelin (Atlantic)
Metallica, Metallica (Elektra)
Millennium, Backstreet Boys (Jive)
Slippery When Wet, Bon Jovi (Mercury)
The Woman in Me, Shania Twain (Mercury Nashville)

11 Million
Abbey Road, The Beatles (Capitol)
Candle in the Wind 1997/Something About the Way You Look Tonight (Single), Elton John (Rocket)
CrazySexyCool, TLC (LaFace)
Dirty Dancing (Soundtrack) (RCA)
Houses of the Holy, Led Zeppelin (Atlantic)
Greatest Hits, James Taylor (Warner Bros.)
Pieces of You, Jewel (Atlantic)
Sgt. Pepper's Lonely Hearts Club Band, The Beatles (Capitol)
Ten, Pearl Jam (Epic)
Titanic (Soundtrack) (Sony Classical)
Yourself or Someone Like You, Matchbox 20 (Atlantic)

10 Million
1984 (MCMLXXXIV), Van Halen (Warner Bros.)
Best of the Doobies, Doobie Brothers (Warner Bros.)
Can't Slow Down, Lionel Richie (Motown)
Daydream, Mariah Carey (Columbia)
Dookie, Green Day (Reprise)
Eliminator, ZZ Top (Warner Bros.)
Faith, George Michael (Columbia)
Falling into You, Celine Dion (550 Music)
Legend, Bob Marley & the Wailers (Island)
Let's Talk about Love, Celine Dion (550 Music/Epic)
Life after Death, Notorious B.I.G. (Bad Boy/Arista)
Like a Virgin, Madonna (Sire)
Music Box, Mariah Carey (Columbia)
'N Sync, 'N Sync (RCA)
Nevermind, Nirvana (DGC)
No Jacket Required, Phil Collins (Atlantic)
No Strings Attached, 'N Sync (Jive)
Please Hammer Don't Hurt 'Em, Hammer (Capitol)
Simon & Garfunkel's Greatest Hits, Simon & Garfunkel (Columbia)
Tapestry, Carole King (Ode)
The Hits, Garth Brooks (Capitol Nashville)
The Joshua Tree, U2 (Island)
The Lion King (Soundtrack) (Walt Disney)
Tragic Kingdom, No Doubt (Trauma/Interscope)
Unplugged, Eric Clapton (Reprise)
Van Halen, Van Halen (Warner Bros.)
Wide Open Spaces, Dixie Chicks (Monument)

*Through January 2001.

The Country Music Hall of Fame

1961
Jimmie Rodgers
Fred Rose
Hank Williams

1962
Roy Acuff

1963
No candidate received
enough votes to qualify for
induction.

1964
Tex Ritter

1965
Ernest Tubb

1966
Eddy Arnold
James R. Denny
George D. Hay
Uncle Dave Macon

1967
Red Foley
J. L. Frank
Jim Reeves
Stephen H. Sholes

1968
Bob Wills

1969
Gene Autry
Bill Monroe

1970
Original Carter Family

1971
Arthur Edward Satherley

1972
Jimmie H. Davis

1973
Chet Atkins
Patsy Cline

1974
Owen Bradley
Frank "Pee Wee" King

1975
Minnie Pearl

1976
Paul Cohen
Kitty Wells

1977
Merle Travis

1978
Grandpa Jones

1979
Hubert Long
Hank Snow

1980
Johnny Cash
Connie B. Gay
Original Sons of the Pioneers

1981
Vernon Dalhart
Grant Turner

1982
Lefty Frizzell
Ray Horton
Marty Robbins

1983
Little Jimmy Dickens

1984
Ralph Sylvester Peer
Floyd Tillman

1985
Lester Flatt and Earl Scruggs

1986
Whitey Ford
Wesley H. Rose

1987
Rod Brasfield

1988
Loretta Lynn
Roy Rogers

1989
Jack Stapp
Cliffie Stone
Hank Thompson

1990
Tennessee Ernie Ford

1991
Boudleaux and Felice Bryant

1992
George Jones
Frances Williams Preston

1993
Willie Nelson

1994
Merle Haggard

1995
Roger Miller
Jo Walker-Meador

1996
Patsy Montana
Buck Owens
Ray Price

1997
Cindy Walker
Harlan Howard
Brenda Lee

1998
Tammy Wynette
Elvis Presley
George Morgan

1999
Dolly Parton
Conway Twitty
Johnny Bond

2000
Faron Young
Charley Pride

Top 10 Video Sales, 2000

1. *The Matrix* (Warner Home Video)
2. *Buena Vista Social Club* (Artisan Home Entertainment)
3. *Austin Powers: The Spy Who Shagged Me* (New Line Home Video/Warner Home Video)
4. *American Pie* (Universal Studios Home Video)
5. *Slipknot: Welcome to Our Neighborhood* (Roadrunner Video)
6. *Tarzan* (Walt Disney Home Video/Buena Vista Home Entertainment)
7. *South Park: Bigger, Longer & Uncut* (Paramount Home Video) (tie)
7. *Star Wars: Episode 1—The Phantom Menace* (FoxVideo) (tie)
9. *Sex and the City* (HBO Home Video/Warner Home Video)
10. *Big Daddy* (Columbia TriStar Home Video)

Source: © 2001 BPI Communications Inc. Used with permission from *Billboard* ® magazine.

Top 10 Video Rentals, 2000

1. *American Pie* (Universal Studios Home Video)
2. *The Matrix* (Warner Home Video)
3. *American Beauty* (DreamWorks Home Entertainment)
4. *Fight Club* (FoxVideo) (tie)
4. *Magnolia* (New Line Home Video/Warner Home Video) (tie)
6. *Girl, Interrupted* (Columbia TriStar Home Video)
7. *Notting Hill* (Universal Studios Home Video)
8. *Erin Brockovich* (Universal Studios Home Video)
9. *Austin Powers: The Spy Who Shagged Me* (New Line Home Video/Warner Home Video)
10. *Double Jeopardy* (Paramount Home Video)

Source: © 2001 BPI Communications Inc. Used with permission from *Billboard* ® magazine.

Top 10 DVD Sales, 2000

1. *The Matrix* (Warner Home Video)
2. *The Sixth Sense* (Hollywood Pictures Home Video/Buena Vista Home Entertainment)
3. *The Green Mile* (Warner Home Video)
4. *American Pie* (Universal Studios Home Video)
5. *Austin Powers: The Spy Who Shagged Me* (New Line Home Video/Warner Home Video)
6. *Toy Story/Toy Story 2: 2-Pack* (Walt Disney Home Video/Buena Vista Home Entertainment)
7. *Braveheart* (Paramount Home Video)
8. *The Patriot* (Columbia TriStar Home Video)
9. *Independence Day* (FoxVideo)
10. *Saving Private Ryan* (DreamWorks Home Entertainment)

Source: © 2001 BPI Communications Inc. Used with permission from *Billboard* ® magazine.

The Rock and Roll Hall of Fame

1986
Chuck Berry
James Brown
Ray Charles
Sam Cooke
Fats Domino
The Everly Brothers
Buddy Holly
Jerry Lee Lewis
Elvis Presley
Little Richard
Nonperformers
Alan Freed
Sam Phillips
Early Influences
Robert Johnson
Jimmie Rodgers
Jimmy Yancey
Lifetime Achievement
John Hammond

1987
The Coasters
Eddie Cochran
Bo Diddley
Aretha Franklin
Marvin Gaye
Bill Haley
B.B. King
Clyde McPhatter
Ricky Nelson
Roy Orbison
Carl Perkins
Smokey Robinson
Joe Turner
Muddy Waters
Jackie Wilson
Nonperformers
Leonard Chess
Ahmet Ertegun
Jerry Leiber and Mike Stoller
Jerry Wexler
Early Influences
Louis Jordan
T-Bone Walker
Hank Williams

1988
The Beach Boys
The Beatles
The Drifters
Bob Dylan
The Supremes
Nonperformer
Berry Gordy, Jr.
Early Influences
Woody Guthrie
Leadbelly
Les Paul

1989
Dion
Otis Redding

The Rolling Stones
The Temptations
Stevie Wonder
Nonperformer
Phil Spector
Early Influences
The Ink Spots
Bessie Smith
The Soul Stirrers

1990
Hank Ballard
Bobby Darin
The Four Seasons
The Four Tops
The Kinks
The Platters
Simon and Garfunkel
The Who
Nonperformers
Gerry Goffin and Carole King
Brian Holland, Eddie Holland,
 and Lamont Dozier
Early Influences
Louis Armstrong
Charlie Christian
Ma Rainey

1991
LaVern Baker
The Byrds
John Lee Hooker
The Impressions
Wilson Pickett
Jimmy Reed
Ike and Tina Turner
Nonperformers
Dave Bartholomew
Ralph Bass
Early Influence
Howlin' Wolf
Lifetime Achievement
Nesuhi Ertegun

1992
Bobby "Blue" Bland
Booker T. and the MG's
Johnny Cash
Jimi Hendrix Experience
Isley Brothers
Sam and Dave
The Yardbirds
Nonperformers
Leo Fender
Bill Graham
Doc Pomus
Early Influences
Elmore James
Professor Longhair

1993
Ruth Brown
Cream

Creedence Clearwater
 Revival
The Doors
Etta James
Frankie Lymon and
 the Teenagers
Van Morrison
Sly and the Family Stone
Nonperformers
Dick Clark
Milt Gabler
Early Influence
Dinah Washington

1994
The Animals
The Band
Duane Eddy
The Grateful Dead
Elton John
John Lennon
Bob Marley
Rod Stewart
Nonperformer
Johnny Otis
Early Influence
Willie Dixon

1995
The Allman Brothers Band
Al Green
Janis Joplin
Led Zeppelin
Martha and the Vandellas
Neil Young
Frank Zappa
Nonperformer
Paul Ackerman
Early Influence
The Orioles

1996
David Bowie
Jefferson Airplane
Little Willie John
Gladys Knight and the Pips
Pink Floyd
The Shirelles
The Velvet Underground
Nonperformer
Tom Donahue
Early Influence
Pete Seeger

1997
The Bee Gees
Buffalo Springfield
Crosby, Stills and Nash
The Jackson Five
Joni Mitchell
Parliament-Funkadelic
The (Young) Rascals
Nonperformer
Syd Nathan

Early Influences
Mahalia Jackson
Bill Monroe

1998
The Eagles
Fleetwood Mac
Mamas and Papas
Lloyd Price
Santana
Gene Vincent
Nonperformer
Allen Toussaint
Early Influence
"Jelly Roll" Morton

1999
Billy Joel
Curtis Mayfield
Paul McCartney
Del Shannon
Dusty Springfield
Bruce Springsteen
The Staple Singers
Nonperformer
George Martin
Early Influences
Charles Brown
Bob Wills and His Texas
 Playboys

2000
Eric Clapton
Earth, Wind, and Fire
Lovin' Spoonful
The Moonglows
Bonnie Raitt
James Taylor
Nonperformer
Clive Davis
Early Influences
Nat King Cole
Billie Holiday
Side-Men
Hal Blaine
King Curtis
James Jamerson
Scotty Moore
Earl Palmer

2001
Aerosmith
Solomon Burke
The Flamingos
Michael Jackson
Queen
Paul Simon
Steely Dan
Ritchie Valens
Nonperformer
Chris Blackwell
Side-Men
James Burton
Johnnie Johnson

Top Television Specials, 2000–2001[1]

Rank	Program name (network) [first telecast]	Rating (% of TV households)	Rank	Program name (network) [first telecast]	Rating (% of TV households)
1.	*Academy Awards* (ABC) [3/25/01]	26.2%	4.	*Friends Special* (NBC) [10/12/00]	18.0%
2.	*Survivor II Premiere* (CBS) [1/28/01]	24.5	5.	*Grammy Awards* (CBS) [2/21/01]	16.7
3.	*Countdown to Oscar 2001* (ABC) [3/25/01]	18.6	6.	*Survivor II—Weds.* (CBS) [3/14/01]	16.6
			7.	*Survivor II: The Reunion* (CBS) [5/3/01]	16.0

NOTES: Each rating point represents 1,022,000 households using television. Does not include sports telecasts. 1. Through May 23, 2001. *Source:* Nielsen Media Research. © 2001, Nielsen Media Research.

Top Syndicated TV Programs, 2000–2001 Season[1]

Rank	Program name[2]	Rating (% of TV households)	Rank	Program name[2]	Rating (% of TV households)
1.	Wheel of Fortune	10.1%	14.	WCW Wrestling	4.3%
2.	Jeopardy	8.3	15.	Warner Bros. Volume 32	4.0
3.	World Wrestling Federation	7.3	16.	Live! With Regis	3.9
4.	MMN Home Team Baseball	6.8	17.	Seinfeld (Weekend)	3.8
5.	Judge Judy (AT)	6.3	18.	Buena Vista III	3.7
6.	ESPN NFL Regular Season	6.1	18.	Entertainment Tonight (Weekend)	3.7
6.	Oprah Winfrey Show (AT)	6.1			
8.	Entertainment Tonight	6.0	18.	Judge Joe Brown (AT)	3.7
9.	Friends (AT)	5.7	21.	Hollywood Squares	3.6
10.	ESPN NFL Regular Season 2	5.4	21.	Jerry Springer (AT)	3.6
11.	Frasier (AT)	4.9	21.	Warner Bros. Volume 31	3.6
11.	Seinfeld	4.9	21.	The X-Files (AT)	3.6
13.	Wheel of Fortune (Weekend)	4.7	25.	Drew Carey (AT)	3.4

NOTES: Each rating point represents 1,022,000 households using television. (AT) = Additional Telecasts. 1. Sept. 4, 2000–June 22, 2001. 2. Programs airing three or less weeks have been excluded from this ranking. *Source:* Nielsen Media Research. © 2001, Nielsen Media Research.

Top Regularly Scheduled Network Programs, 2000–2001[1]

Rank	Program name (network)	Rating (% of TV households)	Rank	Program name (network)	Rating (% of TV households)
1.	Survivor II (CBS)	17.4%	12.	West Wing (NBC)	11.6%
2.	ER (NBC)	15.2	14.	Will & Grace (NBC)	11.4
3.	Who Wants to Be a Millionaire–Weds. (ABC)	13.7	15.	60 Minutes (CBS)	11.1
			16.	Cursed (NBC)	10.9
4.	Who Wants to Be a Millionaire–Tues. (ABC)	13.0	16.	Becker (CBS)	10.9
			18.	Temptation Island (Fox)	10.7
5.	Friends (NBC)	12.9	18.	Frasier (NBC)	10.7
6.	NFL Monday Night Football (ABC)	12.7	20.	Just Shoot Me (NBC)	10.5
7.	Who Wants to Be a Millionaire–Sun. (ABC)	12.6	20.	Who Wants to Be a Millionaire–Fri. (ABC)	10.5
7.	Everybody Loves Raymond (CBS)	12.6	22.	NFL Monday Showcase (ABC)	10.2
9.	Law & Order (NBC)	12.3	23.	Judging Amy (CBS)	9.9
10.	The Practice (ABC)	12.0	24.	Touched by an Angel (CBS)	9.8
11.	CSI (CBS)	11.7	25.	NYPD Blue (ABC)	9.7
12.	Who Wants to Be a Millionaire–Thur. (ABC)	11.6			

NOTE: Each rating point represents 1,022,000 households using television. 1. 2000–2001 season through May 23, 2001. *Source:* Nielsen Media Research. © 2001, Nielsen Media Research.

Top 10 Sports Telecasts, 2000–2001[1]

Rank	Program name (network)	Description	Rating (% of TV households)
1.	Super Bowl XXXV (CBS)	N.Y. Giants vs. Baltimore	40.4%
2.	AFC Championship on CBS (CBS)	Baltimore at Oakland	22.6
3.	Fox NFC Championship (Fox)	Minnesota at N.Y. Giants	20.6
4.	AFC Divisional Playoff (CBS)	Baltimore at Tennessee	19.0
5.	Fox NFC Playoff (Fox)	Philadelphia at N.Y. Giants	18.6
6.	Orange Bowl (ABC)	Oklahoma vs. Florida State	17.8
7.	Fox NFC Wildcard Game (Fox)	Tampa Bay at Philadelphia	17.3
8.	Fox NFC Championship (Fox)	Minnesota at N.Y. Giants	17.0
9.	AFC/NFC Playoff Game 2 (ABC)	St. Louis at New Orleans	16.6
10.	Fox NFL Sunday National	Various teams and times	16.2

NOTE: Each rating point represents 1,022,000 households using television. 1. Through May 23, 2001. *Source:* Nielsen Media Research. © 2001, Nielsen Media Research.

Top-Rated TV Movies, 2000–2001[1]

Rank	Episode title (network)	Rating (% of TV households)	Rank	Episode title (network)	Rating (% of TV households)
1.	Life with Judy Garland—Me and My Shadows, Part 1 (ABC)	13.8%	9.	Personally Yours (CBS)	10.4%
2.	Amy and Isabelle (ABC)	13.4	10.	Follow the Stars Home (CBS)	9.9
3.	These Old Broads (ABC)	11.3	10.	The Last Dance (CBS)	9.9
3.	Like Mother, Like Son (CBS)	11.3	10.	The Miracle Worker (ABC)	9.9
5.	The Lost Child (ABC)	11.2	13.	Life with Judy Garland—Me and My Shadows, Part 2 (ABC)	9.6
5.	South Pacific (ABC)	11.2	13.	Papa's Angels (CBS)	9.6
7.	The Runaway (CBS)	10.9	15.	The Christmas Secret (CBS)	9.5
8.	Titanic (NBC)	10.7	15.	Second Honeymoon (CBS)	9.5

NOTE: Each rating point represents 1,022,000 households using television. 1. Through May 25, 2001. *Source:* Nielsen Media Research. © 2001, Nielsen Media Research.

Weekly TV Viewing by Age
(in hours and minutes)

	Time per week				Time per week		
	Oct. 2000	Oct. 1999	Nov. 1998		Oct. 2000	Oct. 1999	Nov. 1998
Women 18–24	21 hr 50 min	21 hr 30 min	22 hr 11 min	**Female teens 12–17**	18 hr 19 min	18 hr 49 min	19 hr 40 min
Women 25–54	31 hr 35 min	30 hr 35 min	30 hr 35 min	**Male teens 12–17**	20 hr 50 min	20 hr 28 min	20 hr 16 min
Women 55+	41 hr 10min	41 hr 20 min	42 hr 00 min	**Children 2–5**	22 hr 31 min	21 hr 50 min	23 hr 01 min
Men 18–24	21 hr 10 min	20 hr 10 min	19 hr 29 min	**Children 6–11**	19 hr 09 min	18 hr 18 min	18 hr 59 min
Men 25–54	29 hr 04 min	27 hr 33 min	27 hr 53 min				
Men 55+	37 hr 28 min	36 hr 28 min	36 hr 47 min				

Source: Nielsen Media Research. © 2001, Nielsen Media Research.

Television Set Ownership
Estimated total number of TV households: 100,800,000

	1950	1955	1960	1965	1970	1975	1980	1985	1990	1995	2000
% of total households:											
TV households	10%	67%	87%	94%	96%	97%	98%	98%	98%	98%	98%
% of TV households:											
Multi-set	—	4	12	22	35	43	50	57	65	71	76
Color	—	—	—	7	41	74	83	91	98	99	99
VCR	—	—	—	—	—	—	—	14	66	79	86
Remote control	—	—	—	—	—	—	—	29	77	91	95
Wired pay cable	—	—	—	—	—	—	—	26	29	28	32
Wired cable	—	—	—	—	7	12	20	43	56	63	68

Source: Nielsen Media Research. © 2000, Nielsen Media Research.

Top 100 Daily Newspapers in the United States
By circulation, as of Sept. 30, 2000

Rank	Newspaper	Circulation	Rank	Newspaper	Circulation
1.	*Wall Street Journal* (New York, N.Y.)	1,762,751	35.	*Star* (Kansas City, Mo.)	267,664
2.	*USA Today* (Arlington, Va.)	1,692,666	36.	*Times-Picayune* (New Orleans)	264,001
3.	*Times* (New York, N.Y.)	1,097,180	37.	*Sentinel* (Orlando, Fla.)	260,802
4.	*Times* (Los Angeles)	1,033,399	38.	*Herald* (Boston)	257,761
5.	*Post* (Washington, D.C.)	762,009	39.	*Sun-Sentinel* (Fort Lauderdale, Fla.)	256,690
6.	*Daily News* (New York, N.Y.)	704,463	40.	*Star* (Indianapolis)	248,144
7.	*Tribune* (Chicago)	661,699	41.	*Dispatch* (Columbus, Ohio)	244,177
8.	*Newsday* (Long Island, N.Y.)	576,345	42.	*Observer* (Charlotte, N.C.)	240,594
9.	*Chronicle* (Houston)	546,799	43.	*Post-Gazette* (Pittsburgh, Pa.)	240,245
10.	*Morning News* (Dallas)	495,597	44.	*News* (Detroit)	237,518
11.	*Sun-Times* (Chicago)	471,031	45.	*Courier-Journal* (Louisville, Ky.)	231,630
12.	*Globe* (Boston)	464,472	46.	*News* (Buffalo, N.Y.)	226,342
13.	*Chronicle* (San Francisco)	457,028	47.	*Times* (Seattle)	225,687
14.	*Arizona Republic* (Phoenix)	445,322	48.	*Express-News* (San Antonio, Tex.)	221,246
15.	*Post* (New York, N.Y.)	443,951	49.	*Star-Telegram* (Fort Worth, Tex.)	220,096
16.	*Rocky Mountain News* (Denver)	426,465	50.	*World-Herald* (Omaha, Neb.)	214,651
17.	*Post* (Denver)	420,033	51.	*Tribune* (Tampa, Fla.)	213,032
18.	*Star-Ledger* (Newark, N.J.)	407,537	52.	*Pioneer Press* (St. Paul, Minn.)	205,798
19.	*Inquirer* (Philadelphia)	400,385	53.	*Courant* (Hartford, Conn.)	202,509
20.	*Union-Tribune* (San Diego)	370,395	54.	*Daily News* (Los Angeles)	200,387
21.	*Free Press* (Detroit)	365,579	55.	*Daily Oklahoman* (Oklahoma City)	198,576
22.	*Plain Dealer* (Cleveland)	364,708	56.	*Virginian-Pilot* (Norfolk, Va.)	197,574
23.	*Register* (Orange County, Calif.)	358,654	57.	*Times-Dispatch* (Richmond, Va.)	196,432
24.	*Oregonian* (Portland)	348,468	58.	*Enquirer* (Cincinnati)	195,360
25.	*Herald* (Miami)	343,877	59.	*American-Statesman* (Austin, Tex.)	187,789
26.	*Star Tribune* (Minneapolis)	336,476	60.	*Tennessean* (Nashville)	186,793
27.	*Times* (St. Petersburg, Fla.)	325,633	61.	*Contra Costa Times* (Walnut Creek, Calif.)	182,682
28.	*Sun* (Baltimore)	315,306	62.	*Post-Intelligencer* (Seattle)	175,794
29.	*Constitution* (Atlanta)	311,342	63.	*Democrat and Chronicle* (Rochester, N.Y.)	173,398
30.	*Investor's Business Daily* (Los Angeles)	303,596	64.	*Times-Union* (Jacksonville, Fla.)	172,734
31.	*Post-Dispatch* (St. Louis)	294,434	65.	*Palm Beach Post* (W. Palm Beach, Fla.)	172,523
32.	*Bee* (Sacramento, Calif.)	289,751	66.	*Democrat-Gazette* (Little Rock, Ark.)	172,214
33.	*Mercury News* (San Jose, Calif.)	286,679	67.	*Press-Enterprise* (Riverside, Calif.)	166,935
34.	*Journal Sentinel* (Milwaukee)	278,377	68.	*Journal* (Providence, R.I.)	162,358

Rank	Newspaper	Circulation	Rank	Newspaper	Circulation
69.	Commercial Appeal (Memphis)	161,274	85.	Daily News (Dayton, Ohio)	134,393
70.	News & Observer (Raleigh, N.C.)	161,175	86.	News Tribune (Tacoma, Wash.)	127,629
71.	Asbury Park Press (Neptune, N.J.)	160,069	87.	Morning Call (Allentown, Pa.)	127,175
72.	Review-Journal (Las Vegas)	158,970	88.	State (Columbia, S.C.)	118,783
73.	Bee (Fresno, Calif.)	156,915	89.	La Opinion (Los Angeles, Calif.)	117,558
74.	Register (Des Moines, Iowa)	155,698	90.	News-Sentinel (Knoxville, Tenn.)	116,564
75.	Daily News (Philadelphia)	154,145	91.	Journal (Albuquerque)	108,931
76.	News (Birmingham, Ala.)	148,851	92.	Herald-Leader (Lexington, Ky.)	108,550
77.	Daily Herald (Arlington Heights, Ill.)	145,902	93.	Advertiser (Honolulu)	106,590
78.	World (Tulsa, Okla.)	145,697	94.	Post & Courier (Charleston, S.C.)	105,868
79.	Record (Bergen County, N.J.)	145,595	95.	Herald-Tribune (Sarasota, Fla.)	105,672
80.	Journal News (White Plains, N.Y.)	143,685	96.	Spokesman-Review (Spokane, Wash.)	105,550
81.	Press (Grand Rapids, Mich.)	141,303	97.	Telegram & Gazette (Worcester, Mass.)	103,565
82.	Beacon Journal (Akron, Ohio)	140,137	98.	Times (Washington, D.C.)	102,957
83.	Blade (Toledo, Ohio)	137,972	99.	Clarion-Ledger (Jackson, Miss)	101,886
84.	Tribune (Salt Lake City)	134,542	100.	News-Journal (Daytona Beach, Fla.)	100,356

Source: Editor & Publisher International Year Book 2001. Web:www.editorandpublisher.com.

Top 100 Consumer Magazines, 2000

2000		Avg. Circulation[1]	2000		Avg. Circulation[1]
1.	NRTA/AARP Bulletin	20,936,279	48.	In Style	1,578,062
2.	Modern Maturity	20,894,343	49.	Golf Digest	1,567,604
3.	Reader's Digest	12,589,919	50.	Popular Science	1,560,758
4.	TV Guide	10,388,083	51.	Entertainment Weekly	1,518,689
5.	National Geographic Magazine	7,892,852	52.	First for Women	1,511,395
6.	Better Homes and Gardens	7,622,981	53.	Parenting Magazine	1,459,669
7.	Family Circle	5,002,223	54.	Cooking Light	1,452,765
8.	Good Housekeeping	4,532,915	55.	American Rifleman	1,450,818
9.	Woman's Day	4,195,200	56.	Sunset, the Magazine of Western Living	1,445,881
10.	Ladies' Home Journal	4,137,423			
11.	McCall's	4,104,990	57.	Golf Magazine	1,403,074
12.	Time—The Weekly Newsmagazine	4,064,815	58.	Car and Driver	1,392,283
13.	People Weekly	3,539,034	59.	Health	1,382,005
14.	Home & Away	3,250,983	60.	Outdoor Life	1,361,049
15.	Sports Illustrated	3,208,918	61.	Boys' Life	1,299,944
16.	Newsweek	3,141,578	62.	Motor Trend	1,274,452
17.	Playboy	3,113,103	63.	PC World	1,266,730
18.	Prevention	3,011,498	64.	Bon Appetit	1,255,366
19.	Westways	2,676,605	65.	Rolling Stone	1,252,887
20.	Cosmopolitan	2,651,192	66.	Self	1,242,399
21.	Via Magazine	2,612,806	67.	FamilyFun	1,232,979
22.	The American Legion Magazine	2,612,135	68.	Popular Mechanics	1,231,821
23.	Guideposts	2,546,565	69.	PC Magazine	1,227,460
24.	Southern Living	2,539,153	70.	Scholastic Parent & Child	1,215,073
25.	Martha Stewart Living	2,373,557	71.	Endless Vacation	1,207,106
26.	Seventeen	2,372,269	72.	The Family Handyman	1,153,056
27.	Maxim	2,307,737	73.	Vogue	1,143,550
28.	Redbook	2,304,273	74.	ESPN the Magazine	1,123,041
29.	YM	2,202,797	75.	Life	1,120,338
30.	Glamour	2,177,589	76.	The American Hunter	1,117,186
31.	U.S. News & World Report	2,100,014	77.	Sesame Street Magazine	1,115,526
32.	National Enquirer	2,081,623	78.	The Elks Magazine	1,114,703
33.	Teen	2,077,150	79.	Soap Opera Digest	1,110,527
34.	O, the Oprah Magazine	2,066,440	80.	Mademoiselle	1,106,794
35.	AAA Going Places	2,065,799	81.	Fitness	1,091,313
36.	Smithsonian	2,053,466	82.	Vanity Fair	1,060,167
37.	Parents	1,998,647	83.	Country Home	1,056,262
38.	Money	1,907,377	84.	Kiplinger's Personal Finance Magazine	1,032,782
39.	V.F.W. Magazine	1,766,113			
40.	Ebony	1,757,066	85.	Michigan Living	1,028,858
41.	Field & Stream	1,754,163	86.	Ziff Davis Smart Business for the New Economy	1,028,061
42.	Star	1,669,923			
43.	Country Living	1,662,499	87.	Discover	1,018,412
44.	Men's Health	1,639,362	88.	Home	1,013,273
45.	Teen People	1,635,921	89.	Essence	1,006,858
46.	Woman's World	1,604,035	90.	Vim & Vigor	1,004,165
47.	Shape	1,578,161	91.	American Homestyle & Gardening	1,002,022
			92.	Sport	1,000,830

2000		Avg. Circulation[1]	2000		Avg. Circulation[1]
93.	Consumers Digest	1,000,033	97.	Jet	955,074
94.	Scouting	979,356	98.	Today's Homeowner	953,065
95.	Victoria	967,410	99.	Business Week	949,159
96.	Travel + Leisure	960,848	100.	Yahoo! Internet Life	944,366

1. Figure includes subscriptions and single-copy sales. *Source:* Audit Bureau of Circulations, tabulated by Magazine Publishers of America.

American Film Institute's 50 Greatest Screen Legends

Men

1. Humphrey Bogart
2. Cary Grant
3. James Stewart
4. Marlon Brando
5. Fred Astaire
6. Henry Fonda
7. Clark Gable
8. James Cagney
9. Spencer Tracy
10. Charlie Chaplin
11. Gary Cooper
12. Gregory Peck
13. John Wayne
14. Laurence Olivier
15. Gene Kelly
16. Orson Welles
17. Kirk Douglas
18. James Dean
19. Burt Lancaster
20. The Marx Brothers
21. Buster Keaton
22. Sidney Poitier
23. Robert Mitchum
24. Edward G. Robinson
25. William Holden

Women

1. Katharine Hepburn
2. Bette Davis
3. Audrey Hepburn
4. Ingrid Bergman
5. Greta Garbo
6. Marilyn Monroe
7. Elizabeth Taylor
8. Judy Garland
9. Marlene Dietrich
10. Joan Crawford
11. Barbara Stanwyck
12. Claudette Colbert
13. Grace Kelly
14. Ginger Rogers
15. Mae West
16. Vivien Leigh
17. Lillian Gish
18. Shirley Temple
19. Rita Hayworth
20. Lauren Bacall
21. Sophia Loren
22. Jean Harlow
23. Carole Lombard
24. Mary Pickford
25. Ava Gardner

American Film Institute's Greatest 100 Movies of All Time

1. Citizen Kane (1941)
2. Casablanca (1942)
3. The Godfather (1972)
4. Gone with the Wind (1939)
5. Lawrence of Arabia (1962)
6. The Wizard of Oz (1939)
7. The Graduate (1967)
8. On the Waterfront (1954)
9. Schindler's List (1993)
10. Singin' in the Rain (1952)
11. It's a Wonderful Life (1946)
12. Sunset Boulevard (1950)
13. The Bridge on the River Kwai (1957)
14. Some Like It Hot (1959)
15. Star Wars (1977)
16. All About Eve (1950)
17. The African Queen (1951)
18. Psycho (1960)
19. Chinatown (1974)
20. One Flew Over the Cuckoo's Nest (1975)
21. The Grapes of Wrath (1940)
22. 2001: A Space Odyssey (1968)
23. The Maltese Falcon (1941)
24. Raging Bull (1980)
25. E.T.—the Extra-Terrestrial (1982)
26. Dr. Strangelove (1964)
27. Bonnie and Clyde (1967)
28. Apocalypse Now (1979)
29. Mr. Smith Goes to Washington (1939)
30. The Treasure of the Sierra Madre (1948)
31. Annie Hall (1977)
32. The Godfather Part II (1974)
33. High Noon (1952)
34. To Kill a Mockingbird (1962)
35. It Happened One Night (1934)
36. Midnight Cowboy (1969)
37. The Best Years of Our Lives (1946)
38. Double Indemnity (1944)
39. Doctor Zhivago (1965)
40. North by Northwest (1959)
41. West Side Story (1961)
42. Rear Window (1954)
43. King Kong (1933)
44. The Birth of a Nation (1915)
45. A Streetcar Named Desire (1951)
46. A Clockwork Orange (1971)
47. Taxi Driver (1976)
48. Jaws (1975)
49. Snow White and the Seven Dwarfs (1937)
50. Butch Cassidy and the Sundance Kid (1969)
51. The Philadelphia Story (1940)
52. From Here to Eternity (1953)
53. Amadeus (1984)
54. All Quiet on the Western Front (1930)
55. The Sound of Music (1965)
56. M*A*S*H (1970)
57. The Third Man (1949)
58. Fantasia (1940)
59. Rebel without a Cause (1955)
60. Raiders of the Lost Ark (1981)
61. Vertigo (1958)
62. Tootsie (1982)
63. Stagecoach (1939)
64. Close Encounters of the Third Kind (1977)
65. The Silence of the Lambs (1991)
66. Network (1976)
67. The Manchurian Candidate (1962)
68. An American in Paris (1951)
69. Shane (1953)
70. The French Connection (1971)
71. Forrest Gump (1994)
72. Ben-Hur (1959)
73. Wuthering Heights (1939)
74. The Gold Rush (1925)
75. Dances with Wolves (1990)
76. City Lights (1931)
77. American Graffiti (1973)
78. Rocky (1976)
79. The Deer Hunter (1978)
80. The Wild Bunch (1969)
81. Modern Times (1936)
82. Giant (1956)
83. Platoon (1986)
84. Fargo (1996)
85. Duck Soup (1933)
86. Mutiny on the Bounty (1935)
87. Frankenstein (1931)
88. Easy Rider (1969)
89. Patton (1970)
90. The Jazz Singer (1927)
91. My Fair Lady (1964)
92. A Place in the Sun (1951)
93. The Apartment (1960)
94. GoodFellas (1990)
95. Pulp Fiction (1994)
96. The Searchers (1956)
97. Bringing Up Baby (1938)
98. Unforgiven (1992)
99. Guess Who's Coming to Dinner (1967)
100. Yankee Doodle Dandy (1942)

Movie Revenues

All-Time Box Office Grosses[1]		Top 25 Movies of 2000[4]	
1. Titanic (1997)	$600,788,188	1. Dr. Seuss' How the Grinch Stole Christmas (Universal)	$253,367,455
2. Star Wars (1977)[2]	460,998,007		
3. Star Wars: Episode One—The Phantom Menace (1999)	431,088,295	2. Mission: Impossible 2 (Paramount)	215,409,889
		3. Gladiator (DreamWorks)	186,610,052
4. E.T.—the Extra-Terrestrial (1982)[2]	399,804,539	4. The Perfect Storm (Warner Bros.)	182,618,434
5. Jurassic Park (1993)	357,067,947	5. Meet the Parents (Universal)	161,325,490
6. Forrest Gump (1994)[2]	329,694,499	6. X-Men (Fox)	157,299,717
7. The Lion King (1994)[2]	312,855,561	7. Scary Movie (Miramax/Dimension)	156,997,084
8. Return of the Jedi (1983)[2]	309,153,948	8. What Lies Beneath (DreamWorks)	155,370,362
9. Independence Day (1996)	306,169,255	9. Dinosaur (Buena Vista)	137,748,063
10. The Sixth Sense (1999)	293,506,292	10. Erin Brockovich (Universal)	125,548,685
11. The Empire Strikes Back (1980)[2]	290,266,497	11. Nutty Professor II: The Klumps (Universal)	123,307,945
12. Home Alone (1990)	285,761,243		
13. Dr. Seuss' How the Grinch Stole Christmas (2000)	260,031,035	12. Charlie's Angels (Sony)	122,802,761
		13. Big Momma's House (Fox)	117,559,438
14. Jaws (1975)[2]	260,000,000	14. What Women Want (Paramount)	115,761,883
15. Batman (1989)	251,188,924	15. Remember the Titans (Buena Vista)	113,746,040
16. Men in Black (1997)	250,690,539	16. The Patriot (Sony)	113,330,342
17. Toy Story 2 (1999)	245,852,179	17. Cast Away (Fox)	109,689,440
18. Raiders of the Lost Ark (1981)[2]	245,034,358	18. Chicken Run (DreamWorks)	106,793,915
19. Twister (1996)	241,708,908	19. Gone in Sixty Seconds (Buena Vista)	101,643,008
20. Ghostbusters (1984)[2]	238,600,000	20. Me, Myself & Irene (Fox)	90,570,999
21. Beverly Hills Cop (1984)	234,760,478	21. Space Cowboys (Warner Bros.)	90,179,885
22. Cast Away (2000)	233,604,271[3]	22. Unbreakable (Buena Vista)	90,033,796
23. The Lost World: Jurassic Park (1997)	229,086,679	23. Scream 3 (Miramax/Dimension)	89,143,175
24. Shrek (2001)	228,142,129[3]	24. U-571 (Universal)	77,086,030
25. Mrs. Doubtfire (1993)	219,195,243	25. Hollow Man (Sony)	73,209,340

1. As of July 1, 2001. 2. Including reissues. 3. Still tracking. 4. As of Jan. 1, 2001. *Source:* Exhibitor Relations Co. Inc.

Miss America Winners

1921	Marga2ret Gorman, Washington, D.C.	1967	Jane Anne Jayroe, Laverne, Okla.
1922–23	Mary Campbell, Columbus, Ohio	1968	Debra Dene Barnes, Moran, Kan.
1924	Ruth Malcolmson, Philadelphia, Pa.	1969	Judith Anne Ford, Belvidere, Ill.
1925	Fay Lamphier, Oakland, Calif.	1970	Pamela Anne Eldred, Birmingham, Mich.
1926	Norma Smallwood, Tulsa, Okla.	1971	Phyllis Ann George, Denton, Texas
1927	Lois Delaner, Joliet, Ill.	1972	Laurie Lea Schaefer, Columbus, Ohio
1933	Marion Bergeron, West Haven, Conn.	1973	Terry Anne Meeuwsen, DePere, Wis.
1935	Henrietta Leaver, Pittsburgh, Pa.	1974	Rebecca Ann King, Denver, Colo.
1936	Rose Coyle, Philadelphia, Pa.	1975	Shirley Cothran, Fort Worth, Texas
1937	Bette Cooper, Bertrand Island, N.J.	1976	Tawney Elaine Godin, Yonkers, N.Y.
1938	Marilyn Meseke, Marion, Ohio	1977	Dorothy Kathleen Benham, Edina, Minn.
1939	Patricia Donnelly, Detroit, Mich.	1978	Susan Perkins, Columbus, Ohio
1940	Frances Marie Burke, Philadelphia, Pa.	1979	Kylene Baker, Galax, Va.
1941	Rosemary LaPlanche, Los Angeles, Calif.	1980	Cheryl Prewitt, Ackerman, Miss.
1942	JoCaroll Dennison, Tyler, Texas	1981	Susan Powell, Elk City, Okla.
1943	Jean Bartel, Los Angeles, Calif.	1982	Elizabeth Ward, Russellville, Ark.
1944	Venus Ramey, Washington, D.C.	1983	Debra Maffett, Anaheim, Calif.
1945	Bess Myerson, New York, N.Y.	1984	Vanessa Williams, Milwood, N.Y.[1]
1946	Marilyn Buferd, Los Angeles, Calif.	1984	Suzette Charles, Mays Landing, N.J.
1947	Barbara Walker, Memphis, Tenn.	1985	Sharlene Wells, Salt Lake City, Utah
1948	BeBe Shopp, Hopkins, Minn.	1986	Susan Akin, Meridian, Miss.
1949	Jacque Mercer, Litchfield, Ariz.	1987	Kellye Cash, Memphis, Tenn.
1951	Yolande Betbeze, Mobile, Ala.	1988	Kaye Lani Rae Rafko, Monroe, Mich.
1952	Coleen Kay Hutchins, Salt Lake City, Utah	1989	Gretchen Elizabeth Carlson, Anoka, Minn.
1953	Neva Jane Langley, Macon, Ga.	1990	Debbye Turner, Mexico, Mo.
1954	Evelyn Margaret Ay, Ephrata, Pa.	1991	Marjorie Judith Vincent, Oak Park, Ill.
1955	Lee Meriwether, San Francisco, Calif.	1992	Carolyn Suzanne Sapp, Honolulu, Hawaii
1956	Sharon Ritchie, Denver, Colo.	1993	Leanza Cornett, Jacksonville, Fla.
1957	Marian McKnight, Manning, S.C.	1994	Kimberly Clarice Aiken, Columbia, S.C.
1958	Marilyn Van Derbur, Denver, Colo.	1995	Heather Whitestone, Birmingham, Ala.
1959	Mary Ann Mobley, Brandon, Miss.	1996	Shawntel Smith, Muldrow, Okla.
1960	Lynda Lee Mead, Natchez, Miss.	1997	Tara Dawn Holland, Overland Park, Kan.
1961	Nancy Fleming, Montague, Mich.	1998	Katherine Shindle, Evanston, Ill.
1962	Maria Fletcher, Asheville, N.C.	1999	Heather French, Maysville, Ken.
1963	Jacquelyn Mayer, Sandusky, Ohio	2000	Angela Perez Baraquio, Honolulu, Hawaii
1964	Donna Axum, El Dorado, Ark.	2001	Katie Harman, Gresham, Ore.
1965	Vonda Kay Van Dyke, Phoenix, Ariz.		
1966	Deborah Irene Bryant, Overland Park, Kan.	1. Resigned July 23, 1984.	

Inside College Admissions

An exclusive look at the admissions process of three top schools exposes the myths that keep students from getting into the college of their choice

By **JODIE MORSE** TIME

For high school seniors beginning the college-application process in earnest, competition has never been fiercer. Nor have students been better prepared. These days, kids in junior high take high school academic classes to make room for more demanding courses in the later grades. And in just the past decade, there's been an 83% increase in the number of ninth-graders who take the SAT—just for practice.

But even if you didn't take calculus in the ninth grade, there are steps you can take at application time to better your odds. Last year three of the country's most selective schools—Rice University, Bowdoin College, and Cornell University—allowed TIME behind the closed doors of their admissions deliberations. The insights we gleaned won't substitute for top scores and grades. But they did puncture some of the myths that often prevent an applicant from winning admission to his or her favorite college.

Myth 1: Make yourself look as well rounded as possible

You would think that a flutist-cum-poet with a 1,520 SAT, an unblemished transcript, and a passion for philosophy would find a warm welcome at Houston's Rice University. The applicant was involved in so many extracurricular activities—band, the literary magazine, the astronomy, philosophy, and poetry clubs—that it took minute handwriting to squeeze them onto the application. Yet she never made it off the waiting list.

In the parlance of Rice's admissions committee, Renaissance Girl (a pseudonym) was a "clubber," a serial joiner of school organizations who never rises to a leadership position. One Cornell applicant submitted a one-page, single-spaced addendum to his application that cataloged, as an admissions officer exasperatedly termed it, "every activity he's ever participated in." With the "spread too thin" designation on his voting sheet, even his perfect 800 score on the verbal half of the SAT wasn't enough to stave off rejection.

Says Don Saleh, Cornell's dean of admissions and financial aid: "Students should occupy leadership roles and show years of commitment. That's one way we know kids aren't doing activities just to put them on their applications." Another is to ask how many hours students spend on each activity. And in an instance where the numbers seemed high? A gimlet-eyed Cornell officer whipped out a calculator to reveal that the (unsuccessful) applicant claimed to spend 50 hours a week on after-school pursuits.

Myth 2: The essay counts only in close calls

Before even glancing at grades or test scores, admissions officers at Bowdoin College in Brunswick, Maine, rate a student's personal statement. That first impression can color the whole discussion. The committee, for example, issued a swift rejection to a student whose essay was riddled with typos. After reading a moving tale of how one student bonded with a Chilean immigrant struggling to educate his children, Assistant Dean Debbie DeVeaux went to bat for the applicant: "I love this guy. I hope you love him as much as I do."

A little warmth and humor never hurt either. Bowdoin requires a second, shorter essay on an influential teacher. Most students opt for a boiler-plate hymn to the hardest teacher in school. But a rare description of a teacher who "was big, but not overweight . . . like you could trust her to provide you with bread and beef through the winter" got the committee laughing. And the essay's touching conclusion—"she taught me how to improve from a mistake and still like myself"—sent them straight for the admit stamp. Otherwise, the student's B record would not have got him in.

Admissions officers say the most successful essays show curiosity and self-awareness. Says Cornell's Saleh: "It's the only thing that really lets us see inside your soul." While there's no one right formula for soul baring, there are many wrong ones. It's disastrous to write, as one Rice applicant did, of what he could "bring to the University of California." A self-absorbed or arrogant tone is also a guaranteed turnoff. Exhibit A: a Rice essay beginning, "I have accumulated a fair amount of wisdom in a relatively limited time of life." Exhibit B: A Cornell applicant who set out to "describe the indescribable essence of myself."

The officers accept that student essays are often heavily edited and adapted for multiple applications. But if an essay seems too polished, they'll often compare the writing with that in other parts of the application, and even to a student's verbal SAT score.

Myth 3: Send your "award-winning" art portfolio

Each spring admissions officers amass boxes full of discarded watercolors and videotaped productions of the *Music Man*—and the occasional batch of brownies—all sent by students hoping such extras will increase their prospects. More often they distract readers from the real meat of the application.

One Cornell applicant, Budding Author, directed readers to her "countless short stories and novellas." Though the admissions officers were impressed with the other parts of Budding Author's application, they didn't quite know what to make of her creative writing. "Well, it's not quite soft porn," said a confused Walbridge. Instead of receiving a fat acceptance packet, Budding Author was wait-listed.

At Cornell and Bowdoin, admissions readers typically send art slides and music tapes out to department heads to get an expert appraisal. Those rare applicants who get a ringing endorsement are usually instant hits back in the committee room. That was the case for one student's trumpet performance, which received the top rating from Cornell's music department. But, noted reader Ken Gabard, "it's only 1 in 100 who gets this kind of reception."

Myth 4: Don't spill your guts

Admissions officers love a good against-all-odds story. Provided the adversity is authentic—like a death in the family—it can make a much more gripping essay topic than a summer jaunt through Europe. And if applicants have suffered any dip in academic performance, they need to account for it, either in an essay or a counselor's letter.

With scattered Cs in the ninth and 10th grades and football and guitar as his only extracurriculars, Comeback Kid would normally have missed Bowdoin's first cut of applications. But in his essay he wrote of how he'd spent those first two years of high school: "slowly poisoning myself in a pool of malted hops." Then a close relative who was an alcoholic died of a stroke. After that, he cut out the beer, got A-pluses in his senior year, and won a national writing award. He also won a unanimous thumbs-up for admission.

Schools are also taken with good students from families with little education or money. At Bowdoin, this is known as an "NC/BC" case, for no college/ blue collar; at Rice, it's an application with "overcome" factors. At Cornell, admissions readers were initially not too impressed by a student with good test scores but whose grades were all over the map. Then one reader noticed that she came from a family with no higher education and worked up to 40 hours a week as a cashier. But it was her essay that really swayed the committee, as she described being derisively called "white girl" by some other blacks and related how one classmate told her that he "looked forward to seeing me 'flipping burgers'" after graduation."

Before you go crafting your sob story, it bears noting that college admissions officers are among the world's finest b.s. detectors. A case in point: one student's Cornell essay about a relative's homosexuality struck an admissions reader as gratuitous: "This has got shock value written all over it."

Myth 5: If a teacher says he'll write a rec, it will be a good one

For admissions officers, there's a distinct hierarchy to recommendation letters. "'Brilliant' means more than bright," says Bowdoin's senior associate dean of admissions Linda Kreamer. "'Hardworking and motivated' probably means the student isn't too smart." Cornell readers bristled at a recommendation hailing a student who "cares more about what he learns than what grades he gets." Translation: If admitted, he'd wind up on academic probation.

The best recommendations describe a student's accomplishments with specific and knowing details. Bowdoin's admissions committee was on the fence about one applicant who had good grades but below-average test scores. Then it scanned his two recommendations. "A rare gem," said one letter; the other called him a "mature humanitarian." Most compelling, though, was a tidbit missing from the rest of the application. The student had come up with a unique scheme for supporting world-famine relief: he pledged his weekly allowance and persuaded his parents to give matching grants. Cornell readers were similarly impressed with a letter that touted an applicant's papers on Billie Holiday and Vietnam veterans.

To improve his accolades, a student shouldn't necessarily ask the best teacher in school, who's probably swamped with other requests, but should instead seek out someone who really knows him and his work. A student should also jog the memory of his recommender with a cheat sheet of his accomplishments.

Myth 6: Don't be too eager

Colleges want students who want them. That's one reason why kids who apply for early decision have a leg up. But for all applicants, it's unwise to skip a college's visit to your high school or, as one Rice applicant did, to ask an alumni interviewer if Rice was just a "second-tier" institution. This was duly noted. The interviewer wrote, "I don't think Rice should accept him."

There are also less obvious faux pas. Students are sometimes asked the number of schools to which they're applying, and some colleges take offense at being one of many under consideration. Rice was weighing one superbly qualified applicant when a reader mentioned that the school was just one of 15 on his list. The student wound up on the wait list.

But such close calls can just as easily swing the other way. Bowdoin's committee was ambivalent about one applicant until it read a last-minute addition to his file, a note saying, "Bowdoin College is at the top of my list." He was admitted. □

Average SAT Scores[1]

School year	Verbal score					Mathematical score				
	Total	Male	Female	White	Black	Total	Male	Female	White	Black
1999–2000	505	507	504	528	434	514	533	498	530	426

1. Scholastic Assessment Test, formerly known as the Scholastic Aptitude Test. Minimum score 200; maximum score 800.
Source: U.S. Dept. of Education, National Center for Education Statistics, *Digest of Education Statistics 2000.*

Educational Attainment by Race and Hispanic Origin, 1960–1999
(percent of population age 25 and older)

Year	Total[1]	White	Black	Asian and Pacific Islander	Hispanic[2] Total[3]	Mexican	Puerto Rican	Cuban
Completed 4 years of high school or more								
1960	41.1%	43.2%	20.1%	—	—	—	—	—
1965	49.0	51.3	27.2	—	—	—	—	—
1970	52.3	54.5	31.4	—	32.1%	24.2%	23.4%	43.9%
1975	62.5	64.5	42.5	—	37.9	31.0	28.7	51.7
1980	66.5	68.8	51.2	—	44.0	37.6	40.1	55.3
1985	73.9	75.5	59.8	—	47.9	41.9	46.3	51.1
1990	77.6	79.1	66.2	80.4%	50.8	44.1	55.5	63.5
1994	80.9	82.0	72.9	84.8	53.3	46.7	59.4	64.1
1995[4]	81.7	83.0	73.8	—	53.4	46.5	61.3	64.7
1996[4]	81.7	82.8	74.3	83.2	53.1	46.9	60.4	63.8
1997[4]	82.1	83.0	74.9	84.9	54.7	48.6	61.1	65.2
1998[4]	82.8	83.7	76.0	84.7	55.5	48.3	63.8	67.8
1999[4]	83.4	84.3	77.0	84.7	56.1	49.7	63.9	70.3
Completed 4 years of college or more								
1960	7.7%	8.1%	3.1%	—	—	—	—	—
1965	9.4	9.9	4.7	—	—	—	—	—
1970	10.7	11.3	4.4	—	4.5%	2.5%	2.2%	11.1%
1975	13.9	14.5	6.4	—	—	—	—	—
1980	16.2	17.1	8.4	—	7.6	4.9	5.6	16.2
1985	19.4	20.0	11.1	—	8.5	5.5	7.0	13.7
1990	21.3	22.0	11.3	39.9%	9.2	5.4	9.7	20.2
1994	22.2	22.9	12.9	41.2	9.1	6.3	9.7	16.2
1995[4]	23.0	24.0	13.2	—	9.3	6.5	10.7	19.4
1996[4]	23.6	24.3	13.6	41.7	9.3	6.5	11.0	18.8
1997[4]	23.9	24.6	13.3	42.2	10.3	7.5	10.7	19.7
1998[4]	24.4	25.0	14.7	—	11.0	7.5	11.9	22.2
1999[4]	25.2	25.9	15.4	42.4	10.9	7.1	11.1	24.8

NOTES: (—) = not available. 1960, 1970, and 1980 as of April 1 and based on sample data from the censuses of population. Other years as of March and based on the Current Population Survey. 1. Includes other races, not shown separately. 2. Persons of Hispanic origin may be of any race. 3. Includes persons of other Hispanic origin, not shown separately. 4. Beginning 1995, persons who are high school graduates and those with a BA degree or higher. *Source:* U.S. Bureau of the Census, *U.S. Census of Population, U.S. Summary, Current Population Reports,* and unpublished data. From *Statistical Abstract of the United States, 2000.*

Educational Attainment by Sex, 1910–1999
(percent of population ages 25 and older)

Year	Both Sexes Less than 5 years of elementary school	Both Sexes High school completion or higher[1]	Both Sexes 4 or more years of college[2]	Male Less than 5 years of elementary school	Male High school completion or higher	Male 4 or more years of college	Female Less than 5 years of elementary school	Female High school completion or higher	Female 4 or more years of college
1910[3]	23.8%	13.5%	2.7%	—	—	—	—	—	—
1920[3]	22.0	16.4	3.3	—	—	—	—	—	—
1930[3]	17.5	19.1	3.9	—	—	—	—	—	—
April 1940	13.7	24.5	4.6	15.1%	22.7%	5.5%	12.4%	26.3%	3.8%
April 1950	11.1	34.3	6.2	12.2	32.6	7.3	10.0	36.0	5.2
April 1960	8.3	41.1	7.7	9.4	39.5	9.7	7.4	42.5	5.8
March 1970	5.3	55.2	11.0	5.9	55.0	14.1	4.7	55.4	8.2
March 1980	3.4	68.6	17.0	3.6	69.2	20.9	3.2	68.1	13.6
March 1985	2.7	73.9	19.4	—	—	—	—	—	—
March 1990	2.5	77.6	21.3	2.7	77.7	24.4	2.2	77.5	18.4
March 1994	1.9	80.9	22.2	2.1	81.1	25.1	1.7	80.8	19.6
March 1995	1.9	81.7	23.0	2.0	81.7	26.0	1.7	81.6	20.2
March 1996	1.8	81.7	23.6	1.9	81.9	26.0	1.7	81.6	21.4
March 1997	1.7	82.1	23.9	1.8	82.0	26.2	1.6	82.2	21.7
March 1998	1.7	82.8	24.4	1.7	82.8	26.5	1.6	82.9	22.4
March 1999	1.6	83.4	25.2	1.6	83.5	27.5	1.6	83.4	23.1

NOTES: (—) = not available. Data for 1980 and subsequent years are for the noninstitutional population. 1. Data for years prior to 1993 include all persons with at least 4 years of high school. 2. Data for 1993 and later years are for persons with a bachelor's degree or higher. 3. Estimates based on Bureau of the Census retrojection of 1940 Census data on education by age. *Source:* Based on data from the U.S. Department of Commerce, Bureau of the Census, *U.S. Census of Population, 1960,* Vol. 1, part 1; *Current Population Reports,* Series P-20 and unpublished data; and *1960 Census Monograph,* "Education of the American Population," by John K. Folger and Charles B. Nam. From U.S. Dept. of Education, *Digest of Education Statistics 2000.*

Enrollment in Educational Institutions, 1970–1999
(in thousands)

Year	Public elementary and secondary schools			Private elementary and secondary schools[1]			Institutions of higher education[2]		
	Total	Pre-K through grade 8	Grades 9 through 12	Total	K through grade 8	Grades 9 through 12	Total	Public	Private
Fall 1970	45,984	32,558	13,336	5,363	4,052	1,311	8,581	6,428	2,153
Fall 1980	40,877	27,647	13,231	5,331	3,992	1,339	12,097	9,457	2,640
Fall 1990	41,217	29,878	11,338	5,232	4,095	1,137	13,819	10,845	2,974
Fall 1995	44,840	32,341	12,500	5,662	4,465	1,197	14,262	11,092	3,169
Fall 1998	46,535	33,344	13,191	5,924	4,597	1,327	14,549	11,176	3,373
Fall 1999[3]	46,812	33,437	13,375	5,938	4,599	1,339	14,861	11,579	3,282

NOTE: Elementary and secondary enrollment excludes home-schooled children. Based on U.S. Department of Education estimates, the home-schooled children numbered approximately 800,000 to 1,000,000 in 1997–1998. Higher education enrollment includes students in colleges, universities, professional schools, and 2-year colleges. 1. Beginning in fall 1980, data include estimates for an expanded universe of private schools. Therefore, direct comparisons with earlier years should be avoided. 2. Enrollment for 1998 is for degree-granting institutions. 3. Projected. *Source:* U.S. Department of Education, National Center for Education Statistics, *Digest of Education Statistics 2000.*

High School Dropout Rates by Sex, 1960–1999

Year	Total	Male	Female
1960	27.2%	27.8%	26.7%
1970	15.0	14.2	15.7
1980	14.1	15.1	13.1
1985	12.6	13.4	11.8
1990	12.1	12.3	11.8
1992	11.0	11.3	10.7
1993	11.0	11.2	10.9
1994	11.4	12.3	10.6
1995	12.0	12.2	11.7
1996	11.1	11.4	10.9
1997	11.0	11.9	10.1
1998	11.8	13.3	10.3
1999	11.2	11.9	10.5

High School Dropout Rates by Race/Ethnicity, 1960–1999

Year	White	Black	Hispanic
1960	—	—	—
1970	13.2%	27.9%	—
1980	11.4	19.1	35.2%
1985	10.4	15.2	27.6
1990	9.0	13.2	32.4
1992	7.7	13.7	29.4
1993	7.9	13.6	27.5
1994	7.7	12.6	30.0
1995	8.6	12.1	30.0
1996	7.3	13.0	29.4
1997	7.6	13.4	25.3
1998	7.7	13.8	29.5
1999	7.3	12.6	28.6

NOTE: (—) = not available. Data apply to persons ages 16–24. Because of changes in data collection procedures, data for 1992–1999 may not be comparable with figures for earlier years. *Source:* U.S. Dept. of Education, National Center for Education Statistics, *Digest of Education Statistics 2000.*

Students with Disabilities

Type of disability	Percent of All Students Served by Federally Supported Programs for Students with Disabilities[1]					
	1976–1977	1980–1981	1990–1991	1995–1996	1997–1998	1998–1999
All disabilities	**8.33%**	**10.13%**	**11.55%**	**12.43%**	**12.80%**	**13.01%**
Specific learning disabilities	1.80	3.58	5.17	5.75	5.91	5.99
Speech or language impairments	2.94	2.86	2.39	2.28	2.30	2.30
Mental retardation	2.16	2.03	1.30	1.27	1.28	1.28
Serious emotional disturbance	0.64	0.85	0.95	0.98	0.98	0.99
Hearing impairments	0.20	0.19	0.14	0.15	0.15	0.15
Orthopedic impairments	0.20	0.14	0.12	0.14	0.15	0.15
Other health impairments	0.32	0.24	0.13	0.30	0.41	0.47
Visual impairments	0.09	0.08	0.06	0.06	0.05	0.06
Multiple disabilities	—	0.17	0.23	0.21	0.23	0.23
Deaf–blindness	—	0.01	(2)	(2)	(2)	(2)
Developmental delay	—	—	—	—	0.01	0.03
Autism and traumatic brain injury	—	—	—	0.09	0.12	0.14
Preschool disabled[3]	(4)	(4)	1.07	1.21	1.22	1.22

NOTES: Counts are based on reports from the 50 states and District of Columbia. Increases since 1987–1988 are due in part to legislation enacted in fall 1986, which mandates public school special education services of all handicapped children ages 3 through 5. Because of rounding, details may not add to totals. 1. Based on the enrollment in public schools, kindergarten through 12th grade, including a relatively small number of prekindergarten students. Includes students ages 0 to 21. 2. Less than .005%. 3. Includes preschool children 3–5 years and 0–5 years served under Chapter I of the Elementary and Secondary Education Act and the Individuals with Disabilities Education Act (IDEA). 4. Prior to 1987–1988, these students were included in the counts by handicapping condition. Beginning in 1987–1988, states were no longer required to report preschool handicapped students (0–5 years) by handicapping condition. *Source:* U.S. Department of Education, National Center for Education Statistics, *Digest of Education Statistics 2000.*

Cost of Higher Education, 1986–2000[1]

Year	All institutions	4-year institutions	2-year institutions	Year	All institutions	4-year institutions	2-year institutions
Public Institutions				**Private Institutions**			
1986–1987	$3,805	$4,138	$2,989	1986–1987	$ 9,676	$10,039	$ 6,384
1991–1992	5,138	5,693	3,623	1991–1992	13,892	14,258	9,632
1995–1996	6,256	7,014	4,217	1995–1996	17,208	17,612	11,563
1996–1997	6,530	7,334	4,404	1996–1997	18,039	18,442	11,954
1997–1998	6,813	7,673	4,509	1997–1998	18,516	19,070	12,921
1998–1999	7,101	8,024	4,601	1998–1999	19,306	19,866	13,317
1999–2000[2]	7,302	8,265	4,722	1999–2000[2]	20,277	20,805	13,768

1. Average undergraduate tuition fees and room and board. 2. Preliminary data based on fall 1998 enrollment weights. *Source:* U.S. Department of Education, National Center for Education Statistics, *Digest of Education Statistics 2000.*

Mean Annual Earnings by Level of Education, 1999

		Level of highest degree							
Characteristic	Total persons	Not a high school graduate	High school graduate only	Some college, no degree	Associate's	Bachelor's	Master's	Professional	Doctorate
All persons[1]	**$30,928**	**$16,053**	**$23,594**	**$25,686**	**$32,468**	**$43,782**	**$52,794**	**$ 95,488**	**$74,712**
Age:									
25 to 34	33,084	19,760	26,878	30,515	32,332	42,420	45,930	63,005	65,493
35 to 44	35,823	18,982	26,228	32,100	35,072	48,842	59,892	105,700	70,673
45 to 54	39,285	20,734	27,538	34,775	36,635	53,462	56,651	96,479	86,681
55 to 64	36,410	20,400	26,670	31,998	38,545	47,182	56,078	134,814	85,297
65 and over	23,245	12,481	17,160	23,010	28,449	32,974	21,646	82,060	48,205
Sex:									
Male	38,134	19,155	28,742	32,005	40,082	55,057	64,533	108,926	82,619
Female	22,818	11,353	17,898	19,327	25,390	31,452	40,429	65,351	54,552
White	32,057	16,474	24,409	26,357	33,212	44,852	53,497	99,858	77,970
Male	39,638	19,632	29,782	33,041	41,111	56,620	65,637	112,944	85,837
Female	23,213	11,255	18,327	19,390	25,679	31,406	40,679	67,998	55,793
Black	22,829	13,672	19,236	22,148	26,424	36,373	43,054	53,969	46,848
Male	26,090	16,013	22,698	25,807	29,532	42,539	47,951	68,693	46,743
Female	20,026	11,372	15,892	19,269	24,187	31,952	39,760	39,109	46,914
Hispanic[2]	22,117	15,832	20,978	22,151	29,933	35,014	55,581	78,353	69,942
Male	25,534	17,756	24,739	27,145	38,555	40,889	73,362	109,071	90,474
Female	17,461	12,273	15,952	16,941	22,222	29,317	36,589	45,829	33,407

1. Includes other races, not shown separately. 2. Persons of Hispanic origin may be of any race. *Source:* U.S. Census Bureau, *Current Population Reports*, P20–528. From *Statistical Abstract of the United States, 2000.*

College and University Endowments, 1999–2000

(Top 50, in millions of dollars)

Institution	Endowment[1]	Institution	Endowment[1]	Institution	Endowment[1]
Harvard Univ.	$19,148.3	Univ. of Calif., Berkeley	$2,168.7	Purdue Univ.	$1,222.0
Yale Univ.	10,092.3	Univ. of Southern		Georgia Inst. of Tech.	1,180.5
Stanford Univ.	8,886.0	California	2,152.6	Univ. of N. Carolina at	
Princeton Univ.	8,398.1	Univ. of Virginia	1,814.5	Chapel Hill	1,138.4
Mass. Inst. of Tech.	6,475.5	Univ. of Minnesota	1,806.1	New York Univ.	1,117.7
Emory Univ.	5,774.8	Johns Hopkins Univ.	1,787.8	Pomona Coll.	1,109.4
Washington Univ.	4,314.3	Univ. of Tex. at Austin	1,611.1	Univ. of Wis.-Madison	1,080.4
Columbia Univ.	4,264.0	Calif. Inst. of Tech.	1,571.6	Boston Coll.	1,070.2
Univ. of Chicago	3,826.9	Case Western Reserve		Univ. of Richmond	1,069.0
Northwestern Univ.	3,734.2	Univ.	1,551.0	Amherst Coll.	1,043.8
Univ. of Michigan	3,549.1	Williams Coll.	1,490.4	Syracuse Univ.	1,033.4
Texas A&M Univ.	3,508.4	Univ. of California, Los		Univ. of Pittsburgh	1,010.1
Cornell Univ.	3,436.9	Angeles	1,447.4	Penn. State Univ.	1,003.0
Rice Univ.	3,372.0	Brown Univ.	1,438.4	Univ. of California (state	
Univ. of Pennsylvania	3,200.9	Rockefeller Univ.	1,418.5	system)	988.0
Univ. of Notre Dame	3,143.0	Ohio State Univ.	1,294.9	Texas Christian Univ.	980.3
Duke Univ.	2,754.3	Baylor Coll. of Medicine	1,290.5	Wake Forest Univ.	969.6
Dartmouth Coll.	2,490.4	Univ. of Washington	1,278.7		
Vanderbilt Univ.	2,314.9	Wellesley Coll.	1,253.0		

NOTES: List includes only institutions that participated in the 1998–1999 Voluntary Support of Education Survey. State systems that submitted combined endowments above the current cut-off are not included. 1. Endowment is market value at fiscal year-end 1999. *Source:* 1999–2000 Voluntary Support of Education Survey. Council for Aid to Education, a subsidiary of RAND.

Accredited U.S. Senior Colleges and Universities

Source: The Princeton Review: www.review.com.

Schools are listed alphabetically within each state and are accredited four-year institutions offering at least a bachelor's degree. Tuition and room and board listed are average annual figures (including fees) subject to fluctuation, usually covering two semesters, two out of three trimesters, or three out of four quarters, depending on the school calendar.

Note that some schools include room and board expenses within the tuition figures rather than reporting them separately. List includes only schools for which data were provided. For further information, write to the registrar of the school concerned.

(Pr) = private; (Pu) = public; (Prp) = proprietary.

Institution name; city, state (type)	Students	Percent Accepted	Percent Women	Tuition In-state	Tuition Out-of-state	Room and board
ALABAMA						
Alabama A&M University; Normal, Ala. (Pu)	4,303	66%	47%	$ 1,932	$ 3,864	$3,914
Alabama State University; Montgomery, Ala. (Pu)	4,348	12	58	2,520	5,040	3,700
Auburn University; Auburn, Ala. (Pu)	18,326	85	48	3,050	9,150	5,789
Auburn University-Montgomery; Montgomery, Ala. (Pu)	4,098	99	63	3,000	9,000	5,084
Birmingham-Southern College; Birmingham, Ala. (Pr)	1,453	95	60	15,170	15,170	5,460
Faulkner University; Montgomery, Ala. (Pr)	2,379	81	59	7,800	7,800	3,950
Huntingdon College; Montgomery, Ala. (Pr)	705	73	62	11,500	11,500	5,750
Jacksonville State University; Jacksonville, Ala. (Pu)	6,640	89	57	2,440	4,880	3,100
Judson College; Marion, Ala. (Pr)	321	81	98	7,400	7,400	4,600
Miles College; Birmingham, Ala. (Pr)	1,453		57	4,280	4,280	2,950
Oakwood College; Huntsville, Ala. (Pr)	1,666			10,638	10,638	3,999
Samford University; Birmingham, Ala. (Pr)	2,870	88	62	10,738	10,738	4,720
Spring Hill College; Mobile, Ala. (Pr)	1,227	89	62	16,170	16,170	6,020
Stillman College; Tuscaloosa, Ala. (Pr)	913			8,300	8,300	3,100
Talladega College; Talladega, Ala. (Pr)	455	22	61	5,666	5,666	2,964
Troy State University at Troy; Troy, Ala. (Pu)	4,602	64	60			
Troy State University Dothan; Dothan, Ala. (Pu)	1,552		63	2,760	5,520	
Troy State University Montgomery; Montgomery, Ala. (Pu)	2,643		64	3,300	6,600	
Tuskegee University; Tuskegee, Ala. (Pr)	2,467	71	58	9,928	9,928	5,328
University of Alabama-Birmingham; Birmingham, Ala. (Pu)	10,420	89	58	2,730	5,460	6,471
University of Alabama-Huntsville; Huntsville, Ala. (Pu)	5,220	87	51	3,284	6,890	4,300
University of Alabama-Tuscaloosa; Tuscaloosa, Ala. (Pu)	15,318	86	52	3,014	8,162	3,800
University of Mobile; Mobile, Ala. (Pr)	1,724	98	68	8,160	8,160	4,460
University of Montevallo; Montevallo, Ala. (Pu)	2,678	83	68	3,040	6,080	3,212
University of North Alabama; Florence, Ala. (Pu)	4,944		59	2,328	5,054	3,506
University of South Alabama; Mobile, Ala. (Pu)	9,360	94	57	2,475	4,950	2,883
University of West Alabama; Livingston, Ala. (Pu)	1,595	66	55	2,504	5,008	2,822
ALASKA						
Alaska Pacific University; Anchorage, Alaska (Pr)	385	80	61	13,200	13,200	5,000
Sheldon Jackson College; Sitka, Alaska (Pr)	235	50	56	7,250	7,250	5,150
University of Alaska-Anchorage; Anchorage, Alaska (Pu)	14,167	96	61	2,559	7,329	5,200
University of Alaska-Fairbanks; Fairbanks, Alaska (Pu)	6,358	86	60	2,550	7,620	4,610
University of Alaska-Southeast; Juneau, Alaska (Pu)	2,782			2,168	6,428	7,650
ARIZONA						
Al Collins Graphic Design School; Tempe, Ariz. (Pr)						
Arizona State University; Tempe, Ariz. (Pu)	33,985	77	52	2,272	9,728	5,240
Arizona State University West; Phoenix, Ariz. (Pu)	3,785	100	71	2,272	9,728	0
DeVry Institute of Technology; Phoenix, Ariz. (Pr)	3,705		25	8,740	8,740	4,750
Embry Riddle Aeronautical University; Prescott, Ariz. (Pr)	1,689	73	15	11,360	11,360	4,320
Grand Canyon University; Phoenix, Ariz. (Pr)	1,594	76	66	8,960	8,960	4,246
Northern Arizona University; Flagstaff, Ariz. (Pu)	13,947	82	58	2,188	8,304	3,802
Prescott College; Prescott, Ariz. (Pr)	757		59	12,844	12,844	
University of Arizona; Tucson, Ariz. (Pu)	26,404	84	53	2,272	9,728	5,888
Western International University; Phoenix, Ariz. (Pr)	820			3,960	3,960	
ARKANSAS						
Arkansas Baptist College; Little Rock, Ark. (Pr)	157	100	60	2,200	2,200	3,000
Arkansas State University; Jonesboro, Ark. (Pu)	9,289	65	58	2,520	6,456	3,071
Arkansas Tech University; Russellville, Ark. (Pu)	4,576	59	52	2,352	4,704	3,222
Harding University; Searcy, Ark. (Pr)	3,982	81	55	8,175	8,175	4,336
Henderson State University; Arkadelphia, Ark. (Pu)	3,078	67	55	2,280	4,560	2,976
Hendrix College; Conway, Ark. (Pr)	1,130	87	54	12,340	12,340	4,625
John Brown University; Siloam Springs, Ark. (Pr)	1,393	54	54	9,482	9,482	4,478
Lyon College; Batesville, Ark. (Pr)	471	85	56	11,000	11,000	5,125
Ouachita Baptist University; Arkadelphia, Ark. (Pr)	1,536	80	54	8,410	8,410	3,100
Philander Smith College; Little Rock, Ark. (Pr)	918	55	64	3,360	3,360	2,746
Southern Arkansas University-Magnolia; Magnolia, Ark. (Pu)	2,781	92	57	2,112	3,240	2,800
University of Arkansas; Fayetteville, Ark. (Pu)	12,240	90	49	2,968	8,260	4,358
University of Arkansas-Little Rock; Little Rock, Ark. (Pu)	8,559			1,131	2,916	2,435
University of Arkansas-Monticello; Monticello, Ark. (Pu)	2,200			2,040	4,248	2,930
University of Arkansas-Pine Bluff; Pine Bluff, Ark. (Pu)	3,425			1,680	3,888	3,470
University of Central Arkansas; Conway, Ark. (Pu)	7,914	75	61	1,494	2,742	2,920

Institution name; city, state (type)	Students	Percent Accepted	Women	Tuition In-state	Out-of-state	Room and board
University of the Ozarks; Clarksville, Ark. (Pr)	573			$ 8,830	$ 8,830	$4,080
Williams Baptist College; Walnut Ridge, Ark. (Pr)	686	78%	54%	6,000	6,000	3,200
CALIFORNIA						
Academy of Art College; San Francisco, Calif. (Pr)	5,008	100	42	12,000	12,000	8,958
American Academy for Dramatic Arts-West; Hollywood, Calif. (Pr)	104	79		11,700	11,700	
Armstrong University; Oakland, Calif. (Pr)				5,940	5,940	5,940
Art Center College of Design; Pasadena, Calif. (Pr)	2,716	63	7	19,900	19,900	
Art Institute of Southern California; Laguna Beach, Calif. (Pr)	268			14,285	14,285	3,600
Art Institutes International at San Francisco; San Francisco, Calif. (Prp)	79	100	51	32,000	32,000	5,060
Azusa Pacific University; Azusa, Calif. (Pr)	3,092	80	63	14,630	14,630	4,880
Biola University; La Mirada, Calif. (Pr)	2,564	82	63	17,410	17,410	5,445
Brooks Institute of Photography; Santa Barbara, Calif. (Pr)	302		32	15,000	15,000	
California Baptist University; Riverside, Calif. (Pr)	1,524	80	63	10,920	10,920	4,966
California College of Arts and Crafts; San Francisco, Calif. (Pr)	1,116	72	59	19,280	19,280	6,576
California Institute of Technology; Pasadena, Calif. (Pr)	929	13	8	20,904	20,904	6,543
California Institute of the Arts; Valencia, Calif. (Pr)	804	40	44	19,750	19,750	5,500
California Lutheran University; Thousand Oaks, Calif. (Pr)	1,816	79	56	16,800	16,800	6,460
California Maritime Academy of California State University; Vallejo, Calif. (Pu)	583	76	3	1,428	7,380	5,750
California Polytechnic State University-San Luis Obispo; San Luis Obispo, Calif. (Pu)	15,867	45	44	0	164	6,246
California State Polytechnic University-Pomona; Pomona, Calif. (Pu)	16,450	70	44		5,904	6,113
California State University-Bakersfield; Bakersfield, Calif. (Pu)	4,309	62	62	1,506	7,380	5,801
California State University-Chico; Chico, Calif. (Pu)	13,397	80	54	1,428	8,808	5,860
California State University-Dominguez Hills; Carson, Calif. (Pu)	4,809	74	67	1,506	7,380	5,801
California State University-Fresno; Fresno, Calif. (Pu)	14,767	67	56	1,746	9,126	5,816
California State University-Fullerton; Fullerton, Calif. (Pu)	21,279	73	57		7,380	3,747
California State University-Hayward; Hayward, Calif. (Pu)	9,337	62	64	1,428	8,808	6,910
California State University-Long Beach; Long Beach, Calif. (Pu)	24,109	81	58		7,380	5,400
California State University-Los Angeles; Los Angeles, Calif. (Pu)	13,476	50	61	1,506	7,380	5,801
California State University-Northridge; Northridge, Calif. (Pu)	20,955	78	57	1,506	7,874	5,801
California State University-Sacramento; Sacramento, Calif. (Pu)	19,343	41	56	1,428	8,808	5,656
California State University-San Bernardino; San Bernardino, Calif. (Pu)	11,007			1,506	7,380	5,801
California State University-San Marcos; San Marcos, Calif. (Pu)	4,103	65	65		7,616	
California State University-Stanislaus; Turlock, Calif. (Pu)	5,353	73	65	1,828	9,208	6,480
Chapman University; Orange, Calif. (Pr)	2,956	63	55	20,724	20,724	7,928
Christian Heritage College; El Cajon, Calif. (Pr)	617		60	10,240	10,240	4,500
Claremont McKenna College; Claremont, Calif. (Pr)	2,005	28	71	20,390	20,390	7,272
Cogswell Polytechnical College; Sunnyvale, Calif. (Pr)	500	85	13	7,800	7,800	
College of Notre Dame; Belmont, Calif. (Pr)	813		65	14,976	14,976	6,400
Columbia College-Hollywood; Tarzana, Calif. (Pr)	144	88	2	10,500	10,500	5,904
Concordia University Irvine; Irvine, Calif. (Pr)	1,192	69	69	16,480	16,480	5,810
DeVry Institute of Technology-Long Beach; Long Beach, Calif. (Pr)	2,877		29	9,140	9,140	4,750
DeVry Institute of Technology-Pomona; Pomona, Calif. (Pr)	3,674		27	9,140	9,140	4,750
DeVry Institute of Technology-West Hills; West Hills, Calif. (Pr)	886		23	8,740	8,740	4,750
Dominican University of California; San Rafael, Calif. (Pr)	984	88	81	17,256	17,256	8,440
Don Bosco College; Rosemead, Calif. (Pr)						
Fresno Pacific University; Fresno, Calif. (Pr)	884	81	67	13,950	13,950	4,530
Golden Gate University; San Fransisco, Calif. (Pr)	1,302		58	8,592	8,592	
Harvey Mudd College; Claremont, Calif. (Pr)	703	33	27	22,663	22,663	8,418
Hebrew Union College-Jewish Institute of Religion; Los Angeles, Calif. (Pr)	0			0	0	
Holy Names College; Oakland, Calif. (Pr)	596	75	82	14,950	14,950	6,400
Hope International University; Fullerton, Calif. (Pr)	822			11,784	11,784	3,584
Humboldt State University; Arcata, Calif. (Pu)	6,570	80	54	0	5,904	5,845
John F. Kennedy University; Orinda, Calif. (Pr)	196		81	8,568	8,568	0
LaSierra University; Riverside, Calif. (Pr)	1,169		54	14,580	14,580	2,496
LIFE Bible College; San Dimas, Calif. (Pr)	488	94	48	6,450	6,450	3,600
Loma Linda University; Loma Linda, Calif. (Pr)	1,255			13,650	13,650	1,890
Loyola Marymount University; Los Angeles, Calif. (Pr)	4,727	63	57	19,100	19,100	7,608
Master's College; Santa Clarita, Calif. (Pr)	1,037	82	52	14,100	14,100	5,800
Menlo College; Atherton, Calif. (Pr)	626	79	45	16,800	16,800	6,800
Mills College; Oakland, Calif. (Pr)	727	78	100	17,250	17,250	7,296
Monterey Institute of International Studies; Monterey, Calif. (Pr)	20			19,500	19,500	
Mount Saint Mary's College; Los Angeles, Calif. (Pr)	1,753	54	94	16,776	16,776	6,634
National University; La Jolla, Calif. (Pr)	4,481		54	7,830	7,830	
New College of California; San Francisco, Calif. (Pr)	1,402		57	8,200	8,200	
Northrop University; Los Angeles, Calif. (Pr)						3,150
Occidental College; Los Angeles, Calif. (Pr)	1,570	60	56	23,532	23,532	6,880
Otis College of Art & Design; Los Angeles, Calif. (Pr)	811	68	60	18,894	18,894	5,500

Institution name; city, state (type)	Students	Percent Accepted	Percent Women	Tuition In-state	Tuition Out-of-state	Room and board
Pacific Oaks College; Pasadena, Calif. (Pr)	265			$12,600	$12,600	$9,000
Pacific Union College; Angwin, Calif. (Pr)	1,453		56%	15,585	15,585	4,665
Patten College; Oakland, Calif. (Pr)	636			8,972	8,972	2,300
Pepperdine University; Malibu, Calif. (Pr)	2,849	35%	59	23,980	23,980	7,290
Pitzer College; Claremont, Calif. (Pr)	924	56	62	24,260	24,260	6,900
Point Loma Nazarene University; San Diego, Calif. (Pr)	2,304	75	59	13,900	13,900	5,990
Pomona College; Claremont, Calif. (Pr)	1,565	30	49	23,910	23,910	8,170
Saint John's Seminary College; Camarillo, Calif. (Pr)				8,920	8,920	2,500
Saint Mary's College; Moraga, Calif. (Pr)	3,038	76	61	19,390	19,390	8,050
Samuel Merritt College; Oakland, Calif. (Pr)	286	63	88	14,560	14,560	3,330
San Diego State University; San Diego, Calif. (Pu)	25,658	65	57	1,506	7,410	7,586
San Francisco Art Institute; San Francisco, Calif. (Pr)	500	61	51	20,200	20,200	0
San Francisco Conservatory of Music; San Francisco, Calif. (Pr)	136	64	55	20,500	20,500	7,800
San Francisco State University; San Francisco, Calif. (Pu)	21,044	69	59	1,904	7,802	6,720
Santa Clara University; Santa Clara, Calif. (Pr)	4,308	62	54	19,776	19,776	8,034
Scripps College; Claremont, Calif. (Pr)	787	68	25	22,470	22,470	7,800
Simpson College and Graduate School; Redding, Calif. (Pr)	971	55	64	8,200	8,200	4,100
Sonoma State University; Rohnert Park, Calif. (Pu)	6,211	92	65	0	7,380	6,471
Southern California College of Optometry; Fullerton, Calif. (Pr)				16,200	16,200	
Stanford University; Stanford, Calif. (Pr)	7,886	13	52	24,441	24,441	8,030
Thomas Aquinas College; Santa Paula, Calif. (Pr)	277	77	15	15,400	15,400	4,400
United States International University; San Diego, Calif. (Pr)	401	59	54	12,015	12,015	5,040
University of California-Berkeley; Berkeley, Calif. (Pu)	22,261	28	50		9,384	8,122
University of California-Davis; Davis, Calif. (Pu)	20,388	63	56	0	10,245	6,693
University of California-Irvine; Irvine, Calif. (Pu)	14,336	63	53	4,057	10,244	6,724
University of California-Los Angeles; Los Angeles, Calif. (Pu)	25,011	29	55	0	10,244	8,565
University of California-Riverside; Riverside, Calif. (Pu)	11,436	85	54	10,248	10,248	7,200
University of California-San Diego; La Jolla, Calif. (Pu)	15,840	41	51	3,848	13,652	7,134
University of California-San Francisco; San Francisco, Calif. (Pu)	3,729			4,212	13,596	5,946
University of California-Santa Barbara; Santa Barbara, Calif. (Pu)	17,699	53	54	0	10,174	7,156
University of California-Santa Cruz; Santa Cruz, Calif. (Pu)	10,269	77	57	4,235	10,244	7,608
University of Judaism; Bel Air, Calif. (Pr)	209	100	31	15,000	15,000	8,325
University of La Verne; La Verne, Calif. (Pr)	1,349	74	58	18,000	18,000	6,280
University of Redlands; Redlands, Calif. (Pr)	1,734	78	56	21,180	21,180	7,840
University of San Diego; San Diego, Calif. (Pr)	4,793	50	59	19,020	19,020	8,440
University of San Francisco; San Francisco, Calif. (Pr)	4,572	80	62	18,860	18,860	8,242
University of Southern California; Los Angeles, Calif. (Pr)	15,705	34	50	23,644	23,644	7,610
University of the Pacific; Stockton, Calif. (Pr)	3,093	76	58	20,350	20,350	6,378
University of West Los Angeles; Inglewood, Calif. (Pr)	71		76	210	210	
Vanguard University of Southern California; Costa Mesa, Calif. (Pr)	1,289	90	62	13,310	13,310	5,120
Western State University College of Law; Fullerton, Calif. (Pr)	227					
Westmont College; Santa Barbara, Calif. (Pr)	1,269	70	20	20,378	20,378	7,068
Whittier College; Whittier, Calif. (Pr)	1,297	89	55	19,828	19,828	6,736
Woodbury University; Burbank, Calif. (Pr)	1,035	85	54	17,540	17,540	5,790
COLORADO						
Adams State College; Alamosa, Colo. (Pu)	2,198	85	57	1,532	5,748	5,320
Colorado Christian University; Lakewood, Colo. (Pu)	1,926	75	54	11,400	11,400	7,600
Colorado College; Colorado Springs, Colo. (Pr)	1,919	62	54	24,528	24,528	6,064
Colorado Mountain College-Alpine Campus; Steamboat Springs, Colo. (Pu)	1,293	100	50	1,584	5,160	5,000
Colorado Mountain College-Spring Valley; Glenwood Springs, Colo. (Pu)	827	100	60	1,584	5,160	5,000
Colorado Mountain College-Timberline Campus; Leadville, Colo. (Pu)	1,090	100	52	1,584	5,160	5,000
Colorado School of Mines; Golden, Colo. (Pu)	2,463	81	24	4,750	15,304	4,900
Colorado State University; Fort Collins, Colo. (Pu)	19,075	78	52	2,408	10,428	5,500
Colorado Technical University; Colorado Springs, Colo. (Pr)	1,232	83	8	6,075	6,075	6,075
Fort Lewis College; Durango, Colo. (Pu)	4,287	88	47	1,724	8,452	5,172
Johnson & Wales University at Denver; Denver, Colo. (Pr)	0			13,275	13,275	7,290
Mesa State College; Grand Junction, Colo. (Pu)	4,926	94	56	1,576	5,966	5,048
Metropolitan State College of Denver; Denver, Colo. (Pu)	17,916	86	57	1,976	7,062	7,320
Regis University; Denver, Colo. (Pr)	1,022	84	18	15,600	15,600	6,200
Teikyo Loretto Heights University; Denver, Colo. (Pr)	200			13,600	13,600	5,400
United States Air Force Academy; Colorado Springs, Colo. (Pu)	4,325	18	5	0	0	
University of Colorado-Boulder; Boulder, Colo. (Pu)	23,342	86	48	2,514	15,832	5,538
University of Colorado-Colorado Springs; Colorado Springs, Colo. (Pu)	5,054		61	2,298	10,102	5,893
University of Colorado-Denver; Denver, Colo. (Pu)	8,478	73	56	2,298	11,642	6,716
University of Denver; Denver, Colo. (Pr)	3,809	84	58	18,936	18,936	6,165
University of Northern Colorado; Greeley, Colo. (Pu)	10,134	79	60	2,072	9,357	4,996
University of Southern Colorado; Pueblo, Colo. (Pu)	5,082	84	57	1,808	8,448	4,768
Western State College of Colorado; Gunnison, Colo. (Pu)	2,323	84	42	1,560	7,309	5,228

Institution name; city, state (type)	Students	Percent Accepted	Percent Women	Tuition In-state	Tuition Out-of-state	Room and board
CONNECTICUT						
Albertus Magnus College; New Haven, Conn. (Pr)	1,720	93%	66%	$13,908	$13,908	$ 6,512
Bridgeport Engineering Institute; Fairfield, Conn. (Pr)						
Central Connecticut State University; New Britain, Conn. (Pu)	9,443	67	51	2,142	6,934	5,824
Charter Oak State College; New Britain, Conn. (Pu)	1,429			430	628	
Connecticut College; New London, Conn. (Pr)	1,814	32	57	31,985	31,985	31,985
Eastern Connecticut State University; Willimantic, Conn. (Pu)	4,821	64	57	2,142	6,934	5,850
Fairfield University; Fairfield, Conn. (Pr)	4,173	63	55	20,540	20,540	7,630
Lyme Academy of Fine Arts; Old Lyme, Conn. (Pr)	171	97	64	12,200	12,200	7,470
Mitchell College; New London, Conn. (Pr)	621	76	52	14,800	14,800	7,100
Quinnipiac University; Hamden, Conn. (Pr)	4,843	75	64	18,840	18,840	8,530
Sacred Heart University; Fairfield, Conn. (Pr)	4,029	74	62	15,404	15,404	7,614
Saint Joseph College; West Hartford, Conn. (Pr)	1,227	83	15	16,930	16,930	7,140
Southern Connecticut State University; New Haven, Conn. (Pu)	7,624	70	59	2,124	6,874	5,934
Teikyo Post University; Waterbury, Conn. (Pr)	1,356	71	64	13,850	13,850	6,300
Trinity College; Hartford, Conn. (Pr)	2,100	30	50	24,660	24,660	7,160
United States Coast Guard Academy; New London, Conn. (Pu)	838	9	10	0	0	0
University of Bridgeport; Bridgeport, Conn. (Pr)	1,212	78	53	14,150	14,150	7,070
University of Connecticut; Storrs, Conn. (Pu)	13,251	67	52	4,282	13,056	6,062
University of Connecticut at Avery Point, Conn. (Pu)				4,158	12,676	5,554
University of Connecticut at Hartford; Hartford, Conn. (Pu)				4,158	12,676	5,554
University of Connecticut at Stamford; Stamford, Conn. (Pu)				4,158	12,676	5,554
University of Connecticut at Waterbury; Waterbury, Conn. (Pu)				4,158	12,676	5,554
University of Hartford; West Hartford, Conn. (Pr)	5,367	71	52	19,450	19,450	8,074
University of New Haven; West Haven, Conn. (Pr)	2,537	82	40	15,210	15,210	6,960
Wesleyan University; Middletown, Conn. (Pr)	2,722	27	52	25,380	25,380	6,630
Western Connecticut State University; Danbury, Conn. (Pu)	4,881	69	55	2,142	6,934	5,668
Yale University; New Haven, Conn. (Pr)	5,351	16	50	25,220	25,220	7,440
DELAWARE						
Delaware State University; Dover, Del. (Pu)	2,910		59	3,096	7,088	4,990
Goldey-Beacom College; Wilmington, Del. (Pr)	894	77	48	7,200	7,200	3,290
University of Delaware; Newark, Del. (Pu)	17,314	49	59	4,511	13,260	5,312
Wesley College; Dover, Del. (Pr)	1,613	69	52	11,314	11,314	5,266
Wilmington College; New Castle, Del. (Pr)	4,965		74	6,060	6,060	
DISTRICT OF COLUMBIA						
American University; Washington, D.C. (Pr)	5,705	72	61	21,144	21,144	8,372
Catholic University of America; Washington, D.C. (Pr)	2,609	89	54	20,050	20,050	8,382
Corcoran College of Art and Design; Washington, D.C. (Pr)	425	58	69	14,100	14,100	7,300
Gallaudet University; Washington, D.C. (Pr)	1,258	67	53	7,870	7,870	7,570
George Washington University; Washington, D.C. (Pr)	8,837	49	57	23,396	23,396	8,538
Georgetown University; Washington, D.C. (Pr)	6,418	22	54	23,952	23,952	9,103
Howard University; Washington, D.C. (Pr)	6,099	56	63	8,750	8,750	5,250
Mount Vernon College; Washington, D.C. (Pr)	341					7,730
Southeastern University; Washington, D.C. (Pr)	508	100	64	7,200	7,200	9,714
Strayer University; Washington, D.C. (Prp)	9,111		56			
Trinity College; Washington, D.C. (Pr)	1,035	95	18	13,875	13,875	6,500
University of the District of Columbia; Washington, D.C. (Pu)	10,004			2,360	5,660	
FLORIDA						
Baptist College of Florida; Graceville, Fla. (Pr)	581	96	35	4,960	4,960	3,150
Barry University; Miami Shores, Fla. (Pr)	5,777	72	65	15,530	15,530	6,220
Bethune-Cookman College; Daytona Beach, Fla. (Pr)	2,745	74	57	9,432	9,432	6,080
Clearwater Christian College; Clearwater, Fla. (Pr)	641	67	56	8,100	8,100	3,850
Eckerd College; St. Petersburg, Fla. (Pr)	1,572	73	55	18,565	18,565	5,110
Edward Waters College; Jacksonville, Fla. (Pr)				8,370	8,370	4,800
Embry Riddle Aeronautical University; Daytona Beach, Fla. (Pr)	4,525	74	15	11,360	11,360	5,390
Flagler College; St. Augustine, Fla. (Pr)	1,830	41	63	6,320	6,320	3,910
Florida A&M University; Tallahassee, Fla. (Pu)	10,691	70	58	1,777	7,368	3,896
Florida Atlantic University; Boca Raton, Fla. (Pu)	17,016	72	61	2,396	9,734	4,993
Florida Institute of Technology; Melbourne, Fla. (Pr)	2,033	82	30	17,300	17,300	5,590
Florida International University; Miami, Fla. (Pu)	26,222	54	56	2,242	9,580	3,822
Florida Memorial College; Miami, Fla. (Pr)	1,488			5,420	5,420	2,428
Florida Southern College; Lakeland, Fla. (Pr)	1,755	80	61	12,750	12,750	5,550
Florida State University; Tallahassee, Fla. (Pu)	27,014	54	56	1,554	8,542	5,610
International Academy of Design & Technology; Tampa, Fla. (Prp)	1,359	62	59	10,260	10,260	
Jacksonville University; Jacksonville, Fla. (Pr)	1,832	72	52	15,750	15,750	5,680
Johnson & Wales University at North Miami; North Miami, Fla. (Pr)	1,156	77	41	12,885	12,885	
Lynn University; Boca Raton, Fla. (Pr)	1,633	80	54	17,300	17,300	6,550
New College of the University of South Florida; Sarasota, Fla. (Pu)	649	70	18	2,663	11,464	4,877
New World School of the Arts; Miami, Fla. (Pu)	339	81	26	1,200	4,200	0
Nova Southeastern University; Ft. Lauderdale, Fla. (Pr)	4,110	74	74	13,220	13,220	6,800
Palm Beach Atlantic College; West Palm Beach, Fla. (Pr)	2,058	63	63	11,540	11,540	4,950
Ringling School of Art & Design; Sarasota, Fla. (Pr)	958	43	45	16,230	16,230	7,844

Institution name; city, state (type)	Students	Percent Accepted	Percent Women	Tuition In-state	Tuition Out-of-state	Room and board
Rollins College; Winter Park, Fla. (Pr)	1,598	68%	60%	$21,250	$21,250	$6,700
Saint John Vianney College Seminary; Miami, Fla. (Pr)				10,400	10,400	4,000
Saint Leo University; Saint Leo, Fla. (Pr)	1,467	71	58	11,990	11,990	6,300
St. Thomas University; Miami, Fla. (Pr)	1,221	77	58	13,350	13,350	4,400
Southeastern College of Assemblies of God; Lakeland, Fla. (Pr)	1,078	83	49	4,650	4,650	3,382
Stetson University; De Land, Fla. (Pr)	2,155	75	57	18,350	18,350	6,170
University of Central Florida; Orlando, Fla. (Pu)	28,252	63	55	2,279	9,617	5,436
University of Florida; Gainesville, Fla. (Pu)	32,680	63	53	2,256	9,594	5,440
University of Miami; Coral Gables, Fla. (Pr)	8,955	53	55	22,124	22,124	7,934
University of North Florida; Jacksonville, Fla. (Pu)	10,267	72	58	1,554	8,891	4,990
University of South Florida; Tampa, Fla. (Pu)	28,916	58	59	2,388	9,725	4,994
University of Tampa; Tampa, Fla. (Pr)	2,999	76	61	15,190	15,190	5,418
University of West Florida; Pensacola, Fla. (Pu)	6,414	83	58	2,294	9,282	4,532
Warner Southern College; Lake Wales, Fla. (Pr)	781	54	59	9,856	9,856	4,870
Webber College; Babson Park, Fla. (Pr)	421	48	47	9,900	9,900	3,570
GEORGIA						
Agnes Scott College; Atlanta, Ga. (Pr)	892	72		16,600	16,600	6,900
Albany State University; Albany, Ga. (Pu)	2,935	90	67	1,808	7,232	3,106
American InterContinental University; Atlanta, Ga. (Prp)	981		73		10,868	
Armstrong Atlantic State University; Savannah, Ga. (Pu)	4,988	72	69	1,876	5,630	4,582
Art Institute of Atlanta; Atlanta, Ga. (Pr)	2,237		45	14,016	14,016	4,992
Atlanta College of Art; Atlanta, Ga. (Pr)	429	77	38	13,180	13,180	5,675
Augusta State University; Augusta, Ga. (Pu)	4,440	72	63	1,808	7,232	6,350
Berry College; Mount Berry, Ga. (Pr)	1,933	65	62	11,550	11,550	5,700
Brenau Women's College; Gainesville, Ga. (Pr)	613	85	100	0	0	4,870
Brewton-Parker College; Mt. Vernon, Ga. (Pr)	1,063	63	64	5,560	5,560	3,700
Clark Atlanta University; Atlanta, Ga. (Pr)	3,740	67	56	10,250	10,250	7,142
Columbus State University; Columbus, Ga. (Pu)	4,584		62	2,202	6,660	4,130
Covenant College; Lookout Mtn., Ga. (Pr)	1,083	98	58	16,500	16,500	5,000
DeVry Institute of Technology-Alpharetta; Alpharetta, Ga. (Pr)	1,514		32	8,740	8,740	4,750
DeVry Institute of Technology-Decatur; Decatur, Ga. (Pr)	2,916		42	8,740	8,740	4,750
Emory University; Atlanta, Ga. (Pr)	6,316	45	54	24,240	24,240	7,868
Fort Valley State College; Fort Valley, Ga. (Pu)	2,124			2,468	4,132	3,075
Georgia College & State University; Milledgeville, Ga. (Pu)	3,980	74	62	1,808	7,232	4,170
Georgia Institute of Technology; Atlanta, Ga. (Pu)	10,256	69	29	2,506	10,024	5,234
Georgia Southern University; Statesboro, Ga. (Pu)	12,909	88	54	1,876	7,504	4,154
Georgia Southwestern College; Americus, Ga. (Pu)	2,071			5,100	5,100	3,130
Georgia State University; Atlanta, Ga. (Pu)	16,309	54	61	2,322	9,288	7,948
Griffin Technical College; Griffin, Ga. (Pu)				4,800	4,800	
Kennesaw State College; Kennesaw, Ga. (Pu)	10,994	42	7	1,730	6,950	0
LaGrange College; LaGrange, Ga. (Pr)	876	83	64	11,660	11,660	4,846
Mercer University-Atlanta; Atlanta, Ga. (Pr)	235			14,706	14,706	
Mercer University-Macon; Macon, Ga. (Pr)	4,305	73	64	17,028	17,028	5,378
Morehouse College; Atlanta, Ga. (Pr)	2,970	75	0	9,510	9,510	7,382
Morris Brown College; Atlanta, Ga. (Pr)	2,785	58	59	8,368	8,368	5,262
North Georgia College and State University; Dahlonega, Ga. (Pu)	3,005	80	66	2,192	7,686	3,542
Oglethorpe University; Atlanta, Ga. (Pr)	1,178	74	66	17,500	17,500	5,300
Paine College; Augusta, Ga. (Pr)	863		68	9,240	9,240	3,020
Piedmont College; Demorest, Ga. (Pr)	1,042	69	61	9,500	9,500	6,550
Savannah College of Art and Design; Savannah, Ga. (Pr)	4,249	84	43	17,325	17,325	7,100
Savannah State University; Savannah, Ga. (Pu)	2,822			5,100	5,100	3,495
Shorter College; Rome, Ga. (Pr)	1,889	81	65	9,350	9,350	4,900
Southern Polytechnic State University; Marietta, Ga. (Pu)	3,008	64	17	1,808	7,506	4,308
Spelman College; Atlanta, Ga. (Pr)	1,899			9,250	9,250	6,560
State University of West Georgia; Carrollton, Ga. (Pu)	7,109	73	61	1,876	7,674	3,854
Toccoa Falls College; Toccoa Falls, Ga. (Pr)	926	64	56	9,600	9,600	4,170
University of Georgia; Athens, Ga. (Pu)	24,213	62	56	2,506	10,024	5,080
Valdosta State University; Valdosta, Ga. (Pu)	7,635	61	60	2,290	7,714	3,954
Wesleyan College; Macon, Ga. (Pr)	585	76	23	8,950	8,950	7,150
West Georgia College; Carrollton, Ga. (Pu)	6,189					3,471
HAWAII						
Brigham Young University; Laie, Hawaii (Pr)	2,353	55	60	3,113	3,113	5,500
Chaminade University of Honolulu; Honolulu, Hawaii (Pr)	2,029	76	57	11,600	11,600	6,640
Hawaii Pacific University; Honolulu, Hawaii (Pr)	5,886	84	44	9,360	9,360	8,430
University of Hawaii-Hilo; Hilo, Hawaii (Pu)	2,723			1,344	6,960	3,400
University of Hawaii-Manoa; Honolulu, Hawaii (Pu)	11,721	71	55	3,024	9,504	4,933
University of Hawaii-West Oahu; Pearl City, Hawaii (Pu)	648					
IDAHO						
Albertson College; Caldwell, Idaho (Pr)	812	97	53	16,000	16,000	4,300
Boise State University; Boise, Idaho (Pu)	14,750	87	55	2,294	8,174	3,370
Idaho State University; Pocatello, Idaho (Pu)	10,230	88	55		6,240	3,730
Lewis-Clark State College; Lewiston, Idaho (Pu)	2,702	62	62	2,360	7,798	3,050
Northwest Nazarene University; Nampa, Idaho (Pr)	1,114	46	57	12,990	12,990	4,020
University of Idaho; Moscow, Idaho (Pu)	8,759	83	46	0	6,000	4,064

Institution name; city, state (type)	Students	Percent Accepted	Percent Women	Tuition In-state	Tuition Out-of-state	Room and board
ILLINOIS						
American Conservatory of Music; Chicago, Ill.						
Augustana College; Rock Island, Ill. (Pr)	2,209	80%	59%	$16,866	$16,866	$5,037
Aurora University; Aurora, Ill. (Pr)	1,270			11,700	11,700	4,491
Barat College; Lake Forest, Ill. (Pr)	813	57	74	13,590	13,590	5,500
Benedictine University; Lisle, Ill. (Pr)	2,007	81	59	14,500	14,500	5,500
Blackburn College; Carlinville, Ill. (Pr)	448	72		7,795	7,795	3,240
Blessing-Rieman College of Nursing; Quincy, Ill. (Pr)	126	97	12	10,650	10,650	4,570
Bradley University; Peoria, Ill. (Pr)	5,116	79	54	14,500	14,500	5,460
Chicago State University; Chicago, Ill. (Pu)	5,585	53	73	2,957	7,253	5,825
Columbia College Chicago; Chicago, Ill. (Pr)	8,577	90	50	11,600	11,600	5,525
Concordia University, River Forest; River Forest, Ill. (Pr)	1,280	82	67	12,800	12,800	5,266
DePaul University; Chicago, Ill. (Pr)	12,436	73	59	15,390	15,390	6,675
DeVry Institute of Technology-DuPage; Addison, Ill. (Pr)	4,006		23	8,740	8,740	4,750
DeVry Institute of Technology-Chicago; Chicago, Ill. (Pr)	4,095		36	8,740	8,740	4,750
Dominican University; River Forest, Ill. (Pr)	1,147	78	69	14,720	14,720	5,030
Eastern Illinois University; Charleston, Ill. (Pu)	9,346	73	58	2,391	7,174	4,800
East-West University; Chicago, Ill. (Pr)	730	81	58	6,450	6,450	
Elmhurst College; Elmhurst, Ill. (Pr)	2,678	74	64	13,900	13,900	5,266
Eureka College; Eureka, Ill. (Pr)	498	74	58	15,850	15,850	5,100
Greenville College; Greenville, Ill. (Pr)	1,134	97	51	12,954	12,954	4,994
Harrington Institute of Interior Design; Chicago, Ill. (Pr)	512	90	87	5,738	5,738	
Illinois College; Jacksonville, Ill. (Pr)	937	74	55	10,735	10,735	4,725
Illinois Institute of Art; Chicago, Ill.						
Illinois Institute of Technology; Chicago, Ill. (Pr)	1,736	65	25	18,600	18,600	5,592
Illinois State University; Normal, Ill. (Pu)	18,025	76	58	3,332	7,275	4,544
Illinois Wesleyan University; Bloomington, Ill. (Pr)	2,027	61	57	21,504	21,504	5,330
International Academy of Merchandising & Design, Ltd.; Chicago, Ill.						
Judson College; Elgin, Ill. (Pr)	975	76	57	12,580	12,580	5,060
Kendall College; Evanston, Ill. (Pr)	545	83	49	12,000	12,000	5,008
Knox College; Galesburg, Ill. (Pr)	1,199	72	57	22,380	22,380	5,610
Lake Forest College; Lake Forest, Ill. (Pr)	1,251	71	60	21,896	21,896	5,254
Lewis University; Romeoville, Ill. (Pr)	3,327	70	56	13,320	13,320	6,000
Loyola University of Chicago; Chicago, Ill. (Pr)	7,141	80	64	18,814	18,814	7,266
MacMurray College; Jacksonville, Ill. (Pr)	3,739	69	10	13,140	13,140	4,650
Malinckrodt College; Wilmette, Ill. (Pr)						
McKendree College; Lebanon, Ill. (Pr)	2,061	69	63	13,350	13,350	4,935
Mennonite College of Nursing; Bloomington, Ill. (Pr)	175			9,364	9,364	2,556
Millikin University; Decatur, Ill. (Pr)	2,307	76	58	17,084	17,084	5,594
Monmouth College; Monmouth, Ill. (Pr)	1,069	78	57	17,000	17,000	4,550
National College of Chiropractic; Lombard, Ill. (Pr)	850		5			
National-Louis University; Evanston, Ill. (Pr)	3,586	100	72	13,095	13,095	6,336
North Central College; Naperville, Ill. (Pr)	2,117	76	58	15,975	15,975	5,472
North Park University; Chicago, Ill. (Pr)	1,655	70	62	17,790	17,790	5,830
Northeastern Illinois University; Chicago, Ill. (Pu)	8,324	70	62	2,340	7,020	6,480
Northern Illinois University; De Kalb, Ill. (Pu)	16,893	73	54	4,347		5,010
Northwestern University; Evanston, Ill. (Pr)	7,724	33	52	25,839	25,839	7,776
Olivet Nazarene University; Bourbonnais, Ill. (Pr)	1,700			11,178	11,178	4,696
Parks College of Saint Louis University; Cahokia, Ill. (Pr)	803			19,010	19,010	5,110
Principia College; Elsah, Ill. (Pr)	560	86	54	16,570	16,570	5,790
Quincy University; Quincy, Ill. (Pr)	1,041	98	56	15,010	15,010	5,020
Rockford College; Rockford, Ill. (Pr)	1,019	74	69	16,800	16,800	5,430
Roosevelt University; Chicago, Ill. (Pr)	4,180		61	10,930	10,930	6,100
Saint Xavier University; Chicago, Ill. (Pr)	2,611	73	73	14,400	14,400	5,744
School of the Art Institute of Chicago; Chicago, Ill. (Pr)	1,819	73	61	19,140	19,140	9,000
Shimer College; Waukegan, Ill. (Pr)	110	80	61	14,370	14,370	2,000
Southern Illinois University-Carbondale; Carbondale, Ill. (Pu)	17,829	71	43	3,011	6,021	4,104
Southern Illinois University-Edwardsville; Edwardsville, Ill. (Pu)	9,576	86	58	2,574	5,148	4,870
Trinity Christian College; Palos Heights, Ill. (Pr)	854	99	63	13,240	13,240	5,090
Trinity International University; Deerfield, Ill. (Pr)	1,136	86	57	15,100	15,100	5,290
University of Chicago; Chicago, Ill. (Pr)	4,008	44	49	23,820	23,820	7,835
University of Illinois at Chicago; Chicago, Ill. (Pu)	16,160	61	54	3,232	9,696	5,856
University of Illinois at Urbana-Champaign; Urbana, Ill. (Pu)	27,908	64	49	3,724	11,172	5,844
Vandercook College of Music; Chicago, Ill. (Pr)	80		43	10,000	10,000	5,100
West Suburban College of Nursing; Oak Park, Ill. (Pr)	141			15,823	15,823	4,623
Western Illinois University; Macomb, Ill. (Pu)	10,652	65	51	2,982	5,964	5,022
Wheaton College; Wheaton, Ill. (Pr)	2,418	58	53	16,390	16,390	5,544
INDIANA						
Anderson University; Anderson, Ind. (Pr)	1,977	82	60	13,740	13,740	4,540
Ball State University; Muncie, Ind. (Pu)	16,350	79	53	3,720	10,180	4,830
Bethel College; Mishawaka, Ind. (Pr)	1,534	68	65	12,550	12,550	4,150
Butler University; Indianapolis, Ind. (Pr)	3,315	84	63	18,040	18,040	6,140
Calumet College of Saint Joseph; Whiting, Ind. (Pr)	1,004	54	62			
DePauw University; Greencastle, Ind. (Pr)	2,223	61	56	19,275	19,275	6,324

Institution name; city, state (type)	Students	Percent Accepted	Percent Women	Tuition In-state	Tuition Out-of-state	Room and board
Earlham College; Richmond, Ind. (Pr)	1,104	85%	56%	$20,480	$20,480	$4,936
Franklin College of Indiana; Franklin, Ind. (Pr)	1,020	77	51	14,110	14,110	4,330
Goshen College; Goshen, Ind. (Pr)	1,041	68	58	13,600	13,600	5,060
Grace College and Seminary; Winona Lake, Ind. (Pr)	923	88	58	10,700	10,700	4,685
Hanover College; Hanover, Ind. (Pr)	1,142	83	55	11,425	11,425	4,930
Huntington College; Huntington, Ind. (Pr)	855	89	60	12,250	12,250	4,770
Indiana Institute of Technology; Fort Wayne, Ind. (Pr)	1,951	12	51	12,916	12,916	4,996
Indiana State University; Terre Haute, Ind. (Pu)	9,537	83	52	3,564	8,898	4,604
Indiana University-Bloomington; Bloomington, Ind. (Pu)	29,383	82	53	3,902	12,958	5,608
Indiana University East; Richmond, Ind. (Pu)	2,262	64	69	3,024	8,000	
Indiana University Northwest; Gary, Ind. (Pu)	4,101	75	70	3,024	8,000	
Indiana University-Purdue University Fort Wayne; Fort Wayne, Ind. (Pu)	9,815	98	56	3,213	7,361	4,900
Indiana Wesleyan University; Marion, Ind. (Pr)	1,947	74	32	12,740	12,740	4,940
Manchester College; North Manchester, Ind. (Pr)	1,091	81	55	15,230	15,230	5,610
Marian College; Indianapolis, Ind. (Pr)	1,352			12,458	12,458	4,422
Oakland City University; Oakland City, Ind. (Pr)	1,258	95	50	10,410	10,410	3,146
Purdue University-Calumet; Hammond, Ind. (Pu)	8,350		55	2,262	5,688	
Purdue University-West Lafayette; West Lafayette, Ind. (Pu)	30,899	78	43	3,872	12,904	5,800
Rose-Hulman Institute of Technology; Terre Haute, Ind. (Pr)	1,581	77	17	21,086	21,086	6,039
Saint Joseph's College; Rensselaer, Ind. (Pr)	935	74	56	14,920	14,920	5,380
Saint Mary-of-the-Woods College; Saint Mary-of-the-Woods, Ind. (Pr)	1,270	75	8	13,750	13,750	5,340
Saint Mary's College; Notre Dame, Ind. (Pr)	1,409	83	30	16,994	16,994	5,962
Taylor University; Upland, Ind. (Pr)	1,880	78	53	14,900	14,900	4,630
Tri-State University; Angola, Ind. (Pr)	1,267	81	31	15,950	15,950	5,250
University of Evansville; Evansville, Ind. (Pr)	2,624	91	60	16,100	16,100	5,220
University of Indianapolis; Indianapolis, Ind. (Pr)	2,856	82	66	14,630	14,630	5,225
University of Notre Dame; Notre Dame, Ind. (Pr)	8,038	34	46	23,180	23,180	5,920
University of Saint Francis; Fort Wayne, Ind. (Pr)	794	82	65	10,310	10,310	4,270
University of Southern Indiana; Evansville, Ind. (Pu)	8,539	94	60	2,918	7,148	5,182
Valparaiso University; Valparaiso, Ind. (Pr)	2,979	81	54	17,100	17,100	4,660
Wabash College; Crawfordsville, Ind. (Pr)	861	65	0	17,994	17,994	5,761
IOWA						
Briar Cliff College; Sioux City, Iowa (Pr)	1,001	82	65	12,690	12,690	4,071
Buena Vista University; Storm Lake, Iowa (Pr)	1,278	86	51	17,176	17,176	4,795
Central College; Pella, Iowa (Pr)	1,301	85	56	14,070	14,070	4,944
Clarke College; Dubuque, Iowa (Pr)	1,120	78	66	13,725	13,725	5,290
Coe College; Cedar Rapids, Iowa (Pr)	1,256	81	55	17,390	17,390	5,020
Cornell College; Mount Vernon, Iowa (Pr)	987	74	59	19,410	19,410	5,410
Divine Word College; Epworth, Iowa (Pr)	80			8,700	8,700	1,200
Dordt College; Sioux Center, Iowa (Pr)	1,420	95	56	13,200	13,200	3,800
Drake University; Des Moines, Iowa (Pr)	3,544	87	61	17,580	17,580	5,040
Grand View College; Des Moines, Iowa (Pr)	1,419	85	63	12,430	12,430	3,832
Grinnell College; Grinnell, Iowa (Pr)	1,344	64	56	19,982	19,982	5,820
Iowa State University; Ames, Iowa (Pu)	21,503	88	45	2,906	9,748	4,171
Iowa Wesleyan College; Mt. Pleasant, Iowa (Pr)	785	85	61	13,200	13,200	4,250
Loras College; Dubuque, Iowa (Pr)	1,626	79	53	15,190	15,190	5,804
Luther College; Decorah, Iowa (Pr)	2,621	84	60	18,080	18,080	3,914
Maharishi International University; Fairfield, Iowa (Pr)	977	89	48	15,200	15,200	5,200
Marycrest International University; Davenport, Iowa (Pr)	357	60	56	12,400	12,400	4,840
Morningside College; Sioux City, Iowa (Pr)	968	78	64	13,606	13,606	4,794
Mount Mercy College; Cedar Rapids, Iowa (Pr)	1,363	90	68	13,850	13,850	4,600
Mount Saint Clare College; Clinton, Iowa (Pr)	560	78	55	13,420	13,420	4,630
Northwestern College; Orange City, Iowa (Pr)	1,243	88	61	13,000	13,000	3,650
Saint Ambrose University; Davenport, Iowa (Pr)	2,022	88	60	13,890	13,890	5,160
Simpson College; Indianola, Iowa (Pr)	1,912	86	57	15,015	15,015	5,040
University of Dubuque; Dubuque, Iowa (Pr)	680	91	42	12,640	12,640	4,340
University of Iowa; Iowa City, Iowa (Pu)	19,284	83	54	3,116	11,544	4,870
University of Northern Iowa; Cedar Falls, Iowa (Pu)	12,100	82	57	2,786	7,546	3,926
Upper Iowa University; Fayette, Iowa (Pr)	697	75	41	11,290	11,290	4,364
Wartburg College; Waverly, Iowa (Pr)	1,600	89	57	15,510	15,510	4,400
William Penn College; Oskaloosa, Iowa (Pr)	1,096	88	50	11,924	11,924	4,140
KANSAS						
Baker University; Baldwin City, Kans. (Pr)	923	81	58	12,900	12,900	4,880
Barclay College; Haviland, Kans. (Pr)	203	73	53	6,240	6,240	3,300
Benedictine College; Atchison, Kans. (Pr)	1,323	91	56	12,390	12,390	4,790
Bethany College; Lindsborg, Kans. (Pr)	587	73	45	12,154	12,154	3,660
Bethel College; North Newton, Kans. (Pr)	477	79	51	12,200	12,200	5,150
Emporia State University; Emporia, Kans. (Pu)	4,158	100	60	2,086	6,552	3,656
Fort Hays State University; Hays, Kans. (Pu)	4,412		55	2,182	6,904	3,770
Friends University; Wichita, Kans. (Pr)	2,614	93	50	11,050	11,050	3,420
Kansas State University; Manhattan, Kans. (Pu)	18,252	61	47	2,333	9,260	4,240
Kansas Wesleyan University; Salina, Kans. (Pr)	684	70	60	11,000	11,000	4,000
McPherson College; McPherson, Kans. (Pr)	463	69	51	12,500	12,500	4,990

Institution name; city, state (type)	Students	Percent Accepted	Women	Tuition In-state	Out-of-state	Room and board
Mid America Nazarene University; Olathe, Kans. (Pr)	1,302	99%	52%	$10,650	$10,650	$5,322
Newman University; Wichita, Kans. (Pr)	1,524	84	66	10,148	10,148	3,950
Ottawa University; Ottawa, Kans. (Pr)	521	68	43	10,750	10,750	4,640
Pittsburg State University; Pittsburg, Kans. (Pu)	5,222	60	48	2,260	6,982	3,990
Saint Mary College; Leavenworth, Kans. (Pr)	506	83	65	12,070	12,070	4,880
Southwestern College; Winfield, Kans. (Pr)	1,114	96	51	12,090	12,090	4,580
Sterling College; Sterling, Kans. (Pr)	424	70	54	11,030	11,030	4,586
Tabor College; Hillsboro, Kans. (Pr)	510	68	46	11,000	11,000	4,180
University of Kansas; Lawrence, Kans. (Pu)	20,157	76	53	2,333	9,260	4,348
University of Kansas, Medical Center; Kansas City, Kans. (Pu)						
Washburn University; Topeka, Kans. (Pr)	4,888	100	62	3,210	7,230	4,300
Wichita State University; Wichita, Kans. (Pu)	11,377	75	56	2,150	8,765	4,120
KENTUCKY						
Alice Lloyd College; Pippa Passes, Ky. (Pr)	557	51	55	0	0	2,680
Asbury College; Wilmore, Ky. (Pr)	1,338	83	59	13,744	13,744	3,566
Bellarmine College; Louisville, Ky. (Pr)	2,373	87	64	13,590	13,590	4,160
Berea College; Berea, Ky. (Pr)	1,590	34	58	0	0	4,099
Brescia University; Owensboro, Ky. (Pr)	688	81	61	9,390	9,390	4,240
Campbellsville University; Campbellsville, Ky. (Pr)	1,502	84	60	8,790	8,790	4,230
Centre College; Danville, Ky. (Pr)	1,055	88	53	16,900	16,900	5,550
Cumberland College; Williamsburg, Ky. (Pr)	1,554		53	10,098	10,098	4,476
Eastern Kentucky University; Richmond, Ky. (Pu)	12,676	70	58	2,542	6,884	3,796
Georgetown College; Georgetown, Ky. (Pr)	1,365	97	58	13,200	13,200	4,820
Kentucky Christian College; Grayson, Ky. (Pr)	569	90	55	7,360	7,360	4,070
Kentucky State University; Frankfort, Ky. (Pu)	2,129		56	2,100	6,302	− 3,740
Kentucky Wesleyan College; Owensboro, Ky. (Pr)	681	79	54	10,070	10,070	4,830
Lindsey Wilson College; Columbia, Ky. (Pr)	1,006			9,144	9,144	4,230
Morehead State University; Morehead, Ky. (Pu)	6,750	74	60	2,710	7,204	3,800
Murray State University; Murray, Ky. (Pu)	7,288	78	56	2,256	6,600	3,570
Northern Kentucky University; Highland Heig, Ky. (Pu)	10,674	97	59	2,100	6,140	3,866
Pikeville College; Pikeville, Ky. (Pr)	917	100	59	7,800	7,800	3,340
Spalding University; Louisville, Ky. (Pr)	1,128	85	81	10,300	10,300	2,790
Thomas More College; Crestiew Hill, Ky. (Pr)	1,273	79	55	11,578	11,578	4,500
Transylvania University; Lexington, Ky. (Pr)	1,070	89	59	14,700	14,700	5,530
Union College; Barbourville, Ky. (Pr)	652	75	48	11,070	11,070	3,650
University of Kentucky; Lexington, Ky. (Pu)	16,897	61	52	3,270	9,810	3,980
University of Louisville; Louisville, Ky. (Pu)	14,694	80	54	3,149	9,448	3,500
Western Kentucky University; Bowling Green, Ky. (Pu)	13,235	87	58	2,150	6,450	3,813
LOUISIANA						
Centenary College of Louisiana; Shreveport, La. (Pr)	858	89	61	15,400	15,400	4,800
Dillard University; New Orleans, La. (Pr)	1,584	72	30	8,500	8,500	4,464
Grambling State University; Grambling, La. (Pu)	4,260	53	56	2,208	7,358	2,636
Louisiana College; Pineville, La. (Pr)	1,003			6,210	6,210	3,112
Louisiana State University and A&M College; Baton Rouge, La. (Pu)	26,121	78	53	2,551	7,851	4,270
Louisiana State University-Shreveport; Shreveport, La. (Pu)	3,422	100	61	2,050	5,982	0
Louisiana Tech University; Ruston, La. (Pu)	8,921	93	48	2,748	6,423	3,195
Loyola University; New Orleans, La. (Pr)	3,688	74	64	16,188	16,188	6,806
McNeese State University; Lake Charles, La. (Pu)	7,045	99	58	2,006	6,446	2,310
Nicholls State University; Thibodaux, La. (Pu)	6,556	93	62	2,368	7,504	3,002
Northwestern State University of Louisiana; Natchitoches, La. (Pu)	7,640	95	66	2,147	6,437	2,416
Our Lady of Holy Cross College; New Orleans, La. (Pr)	1,192		77	4,810	4,810	
Saint Joseph Seminary College; St. Benedict, La. (Pr)	180	100	0	6,450	6,450	4,750
Southeastern Louisiana University; Hammond, La. (Pu)	12,916	77	63	2,490	7,818	3,006
Southern University and Agricultural and Mechanical College; Shreveport, La. (Pu)	1,345	100	69	1,104	2,394	
Southern University of New Orleans; New Orleans, La. (Pr)	4,500			1,662	1,662	
Southern University-Baton Rouge; Baton Rouge, La. (Pu)	7,976			2,065	5,852	3,228
Tulane University; New Orleans, La. (Pr)	7,163	78	53	23,500	23,500	6,908
University of Louisiana at Lafayette; Lafayette, La. (Pu)	14,091	80	56	2,275	9,225	2,726
University of Louisiana at Monroe; Monroe, La. (Pu)	8,669	92	61	1,644	2,400	3,380
University of New Orleans; New Orleans, La. (Pu)	11,872	83	57	2,362	7,888	3,150
Xavier University of Louisiana; New Orleans, La. (Pr)	3,036	84	73	9,300	9,300	6,000
MAINE						
Bates College; Lewiston, Maine (Pr)	1,706	33	14	31,400	31,400	0
Bowdoin College; Brunswick, Maine (Pr)	1,609	28	14	25,345	25,345	6,760
Colby College; Waterville, Maine (Pr)	1,814	37	15	32,750	32,750	6,460
College of the Atlantic; Bar Harbor, Maine (Pr)	278	73	64	20,124	20,124	5,610
Husson College; Bangor, Maine (Pr)	1,626	97	66	9,480	9,480	5,150
Maine College of Art; Portland, Maine (Pr)	315	73	59	16,530	16,530	7,042
Maine Maritime Academy; Castine, Maine (Pu)	635	81	5	4,374	8,029	5,022
Saint Joseph's College; Standish, Maine (Pr)	832	84	67	15,260	15,260	6,650
Thomas College; Waterville, Maine (Pr)	759	96	58	12,480	12,480	5,700
Unity College; Unity, Maine (Pr)	512	92	31	12,330	12,330	5,300

Institution name; city, state (type)	Students	Percent Accepted	Percent Women	Tuition In-state	Tuition Out-of-state	Room and board
University of Maine; Orono, Maine (Pu)	8,229	81%	52%	$ 4,200	$11,940	$5,628
University of Maine-Augusta; Augusta, Maine (Pu)	5,611	67	74	3,090	7,590	0
University of Maine-Farmington; Farmington, Maine (Pu)	2,413	66	68	3,540	8,640	4,730
University of Maine-Fort Kent; Fort Kent, Maine (Pu)	926	93	64	3,120	7,590	4,000
University of Maine-Machias; Machias, Maine (Pu)	927	89	67	3,150	7,860	4,490
University of Maine-Presque Isle; Presque Isle, Maine (Pu)	1,378	88	62	3,150	7,710	4,140
University of New England; Biddeford, Maine (Pr)	1,869	72	81	15,740	15,740	6,420
University of Southern Maine; Gorham, Maine (Pu)	8,726	78	60	3,720	10,410	5,050
Westbrook College; Portland, Maine (Pr)	458			14,320	14,320	5,820
MARYLAND						
Baltimore Hebrew University; Baltimore, Md. (Pr)	204	100	68	5,035	5,035	2,000
Bowie State University; Bowie, Md. (Pu)	2,960	60		3,357	7,792	4,427
Capitol College; Laurel, Md. (Pr)	684	80	27	14,742	14,742	3,340
College of Notre Dame of Maryland; Baltimore, Md. (Pr)	2,037	74	94	15,600	15,600	6,800
Columbia Union College; Tacoma Park, Md. (Pr)	1,030	54	59	12,810	12,810	4,619
Coppin State College; Baltimore, Md. (Pu)	3,213	50	73	3,272	8,104	5,274
Frostburg State University; Frostburg, Md. (Pu)	4,313	73	54	3,444	8,942	5,266
Goucher College; Baltimore, Md. (Pr)	1,195	82	73	22,000	22,000	7,800
Hood College; Fredrick, Md. (Pr)	861	78	88	18,295	18,295	6,900
Johns Hopkins University; Baltimore, Md. (Pr)	3,910	32	42	26,220	26,220	8,580
Loyola College in Maryland; Baltimore, Md. (Pr)	3,476	61	56	22,960	22,960	6,500
Maryland Institute, College of Art; Baltimore, Md. (Pr)	1,154	46	58	19,800	19,800	6,540
Morgan State University; Baltimore, Md. (Pu)	5,356			1,853	4,405	5,296
Mount Saint Mary's College; Emmitsburg, Md. (Pr)	1,500	87	59	16,520	16,520	6,650
Peabody Conservatory of Music-Johns Hopkins University; Baltimore, Md. (Pr)				24,640	24,640	6,940
St. John's College; Annapolis, Md. (Pr)	452	79	15	25,790	25,790	6,770
St. Mary's College of Maryland; St. Mary's City, Md. (Pu)	1,547	77	59	6,474	11,459	6,555
Salisbury State University; Salisbury, Md. (Pu)	5,883	21	57	3,092	7,828	5,990
Sojourner Douglass College; Baltimore, Md. (Pr)	262					
Towson University; Towson, Md. (Pu)	13,905	62	60	3,605	10,491	6,104
United States Naval Academy; Annapolis, Md. (Pu)	4,172	15	5			
University of Baltimore; Baltimore, Md. (Pu)	1,925		53	1,771	5,442	0
University of Maryland-Baltimore County; Baltimore, Md. (Pu)	9,101	65	50	4,206	8,974	5,850
University of Maryland-College Park; College Park, Md. (Pu)	24,638	51	49	4,334	12,406	6,076
University of Maryland-Eastern Shore; Princess Anne, Md. (Pu)	2,704	51	57	3,994	8,497	4,930
University of Maryland University College; Adelphi, Md. (Pu)	13,226	100	58	4,728	8,736	0
Villa Julie College; Stevenson, Md. (Pr)	2,091	75	72	10,250	10,250	3,650
Washington College; Chestertown, Md. (Pr)	1,117	85	60	19,750	19,750	5,740
Western Maryland College; Westminster, Md. (Pr)	1,610	77	56	20,550	20,550	5,450
MASSACHUSETTS						
American International College; Springfield, Mass. (Pr)	1,426	67		11,800	11,800	5,692
Amherst College; Amherst, Mass. (Pr)	1,682	19	13	25,600	25,600	6,800
Anna Maria College; Paxton, Mass. (Pr)	719	85	64	13,495	13,495	6,200
Art Institute of Boston at Lesley; Boston, Mass. (Pr)	534	35	50	13,250	13,250	7,950
Assumption College; Worcester, Mass. (Pr)	2,455	71	64	18,800	18,800	6,980
Atlantic Union College; South Lancaster, Mass. (Pr)	1,193			12,125	12,125	3,900
Babson College; Babson Park, Mass. (Pr)	1,701	45	10	21,952	21,952	8,746
Bay Path College; Longmeadow, Mass. (Pr)	764	67	19	13,660	13,660	6,945
Becker College; Worcester, Mass. (Pr)	1,166	87	77	12,300	12,300	6,420
Bentley College; Waltham, Mass. (Pr)	4,316	49	44	18,795	18,795	8,600
Berklee College of Music; Boston, Mass. (Pr)	2,953	78		16,590	16,590	8,890
Boston College; Chestnut Hill, Mass. (Pr)	9,190	35	13	21,700	21,700	8,250
Boston Conservatory; Boston, Mass. (Pr)	350	74	71	17,300	17,300	8,200
Boston University; Boston, Mass. (Pr)	17,819	49	59	25,872	25,872	8,750
Brandeis University; Waltham, Mass. (Pr)	3,169	48	57	25,392	25,392	7,189
Bridgewater State College; Bridgewater, Mass. (Pu)	7,030	81	61	970	7,050	4,797
Clark University; Worcester, Mass. (Pr)	2,124	70	59	23,300	23,300	4,350
College of the Holy Cross; Worcester, Mass. (Pr)	2,826	41	53	26,400	26,400	7,760
Curry College; Milton, Mass. (Pr)	2,082	82	53	17,160	17,160	6,870
Eastern Nazarene College; Quincy, Mass. (Pr)	1,508			13,860	13,860	3,976
Elms College; Chicopee, Mass. (Pr)	740	85	88	14,144	14,144	5,566
Emerson College; Boston, Mass. (Pr)	3,168	52	58	19,520	19,520	9,020
Emmanuel College; Boston, Mass. (Pr)	1,360	84	89	16,112	16,112	7,390
Endicott College; Beverly, Mass. (Pr)	1,553	70	67	14,550	14,550	7,698
Fitchburg State College; Fitchburg, Mass. (Pu)	3,238	66	58	1,030	7,050	4,680
Framingham State College; Framingham, Mass. (Pu)	4,165	62	65	1,030	7,050	4,154
Gordon College; Wenham, Mass. (Pr)	1,492	80	64	17,378	17,378	5,200
Hampshire College; Amherst, Mass. (Pr)	1,172	62	17	25,709	25,709	6,814
Harvard College; Cambridge, Mass. (Pr)	6,684	11	46	22,694	22,694	7,982
Hellenic College; Brookline, Mass. (Pr)	64	63	36	7,600	7,600	5,900
Lasell College; Newton, Mass. (Pr)	841	79	76	14,700	14,700	7,700
Lesley College; Cambridge, Mass. (Pr)	564	79	23	16,300	16,300	7,520
Massachusetts College of Art; Boston, Mass. (Pu)	2,214	48	65	1,060	9,000	7,192
Massachusetts College of Liberal Arts; North Adams, Mass. (Pu)	1,392	70	61	1,090	7,050	4,290

Institution name; city, state (type)	Students	Percent Accepted	Percent Women	Tuition In-state	Tuition Out-of-state	Room and board
Massachusetts College of Pharmacy & Health Science; Boston, Mass. (Pr)	720	79%	63%	$16,900	$16,900	$7,900
Massachusetts Institute of Technology; Cambridge, Mass. (Pr)	4,300	19	41	26,050	26,050	7,175
Massachusetts Maritime Academy; Buzzards Bay, Mass. (Pu)	831	81	13	1,090	9,170	4,560
Merrimack College; North Andover, Mass. (Pr)	2,568	70	52			7,300
Montserrat College of Art; Beverly, Mass. (Pr)	402	84	57	14,980	14,980	4,258
Mount Holyoke College; South Hadley, Mass. (Pr)	2,065	55	100	25,220	25,220	7,410
Mount Ida College; Newton, Mass. (Pr)	2,009			19,720	19,720	8,460
New England College of Optometry; Boston, Mass. (Pr)				22,449	22,449	3,600
New England Conservatory of Music; Boston, Mass. (Pr)	387	45	50	18,750	18,750	8,600
Nichols College; Dudley, Mass. (Pr)	1,159	85	47	16,300	16,300	7,810
Northeastern University; Boston, Mass. (Pr)	12,300	62	14	15,560	15,560	9,135
Pine Manor College; Chestnut Hill, Mass. (Pr)	306	82	100	11,440	11,440	7,245
Regis College; Weston, Mass. (Pr)	889	89	20	17,500	17,500	8,100
Richmond, The American International University in London; Boston, Mass. (Pr)	929	83	10	14,230	14,230	8,457
Salem State College; Salem, Mass. (Pu)	7,336	69	62	1,150	6,450	4,086
School of the Museum of Fine Arts; Boston, Mass. (Pr)	522			17,000	17,000	
Simmons College; Boston, Mass. (Pr)	1,224	65	21	20,260	20,260	8,410
Simon's Rock College of Bard; Great Barrington, Mass. (Pr)	387	70	24	21,740	21,740	6,700
Smith College; Northampton, Mass. (Pr)	5,260	53	50	23,400	23,400	8,160
Springfield College; Springfield, Mass. (Pr)	2,046	59	11	16,696	16,696	5,856
Stonehill College; Easton, Mass. (Pr)	2,637	44	59	17,680	17,680	8,492
Suffolk University; Boston, Mass. (Pr)	3,305	79	57	15,538	15,538	9,660
Tufts University; Medford, Mass. (Pr)	4,869	26	53	24,126	24,126	7,375
University of Massachusetts-Amherst; Amherst, Mass. (Pu)	19,061	67	51	1,714	9,856	4,895
University of Massachusetts-Boston; Boston, Mass. (Pu)	10,442	59	57	1,714	9,758	7,110
University of Massachusetts-Dartmouth; Dartmouth, Mass. (Pu)	6,423	73	53	1,417	7,995	5,477
University of Massachusetts-Lowell; Lowell, Mass. (Pu)	9,354	67	39	1,454	8,271	4,994
Wellesley College; Wellesley, Mass. (Pr)	2,287	43	100	23,718	23,718	7,480
Wentworth Institute of Technology; Boston, Mass. (Pr)	4,073	64	33	13,000	13,000	6,800
Western New England College; Springfield, Mass. (Pr)	3,344	77	35	13,000	13,000	7,050
Westfield State College; Westfield, Mass. (Pu)	4,282	65	54	1,090	7,050	4,174
Wheaton College; Norton, Mass. (Pr)	1,474	65	64	24,225	24,225	6,920
Wheelock College; Boston, Mass. (Pr)	632	86	96	16,740	16,740	6,615
Williams College; Williamstown, Mass. (Pr)	2,020	24	48	24,619	24,619	6,730
Worcester Polytechnic Institute; Worcester, Mass. (Pr)	2,817	71	23	24,278	24,278	8,012
Worcester State College; Worcester, Mass. (Pu)	4,465	52	63	1,090	7,050	4,484
MICHIGAN						
Adrian College; Adrian, Mich. (Pr)	1,049			13,150	13,150	4,320
Albion College; Albion, Mich. (Pr)	1,521	85	58	19,390	19,390	5,604
Alma College; Alma, Mich. (Pr)	1,409	82	59	15,734	15,734	5,726
Andrews University; Berrien Sprin, Mich. (Pr)	1,847	66	57	11,685	11,685	3,630
Aquinas College; Grand Rapids, Mich. (Pr)	1,983	84	66	14,034	14,034	4,884
Baker College; Flint, Mich. (Pr)						1,725
Calvin College; Grand Rapids, Mich. (Pr)	4,263	99	55	14,040	14,040	4,890
Center for Creative Studies; Detroit, Mich. (Pr)	1,086	82	41	16,560	16,560	5,600
Central Michigan University; Mount Pleasant, Mich. (Pu)	18,620	83	59	3,245	8,421	4,828
Cleary College; Howell, Mich. (Pr)	642		66	7,605	7,605	0
Davenport University; Dearborn, Mich. (Pr)	5,382	100	75	6,984	6,984	0
Davenport University-Western Region; Grand Rapids, Mich. (Pr)						2,025
Eastern Michigan University; Ypsilanti, Mich. (Pu)	18,131	73	61	0	0	5,016
Ferris State University; Big Rapids, Mich. (Pu)	9,191	92	44	4,238	8,851	5,264
Grand Rapids Baptist Seminary; Grand Rapids, Mich. (Pr)	1,120			6,648	6,648	7,020
Grand Valley State University; Allendale, Mich. (Pu)	15,221	77	60	4,272	9,244	5,030
Hillsdale College; Hillsdale, Mich. (Pr)	1,167	84	52	13,600	13,600	5,700
Hope College; Holland, Mich. (Pr)	3,015	89	60	17,348	17,348	5,474
Kalamazoo College; Kalamazoo, Mich. (Pr)	1,322	70	14	19,188	19,188	5,787
Kendall College of Art and Design; Grand Rapids, Mich. (Pr)	527			10,500	10,500	
Kettering University; Flint, Mich. (Pr)	2,632	72	4	15,232	15,232	3,880
Lake Superior State University; Sault Ste. Ma, Mich. (Pu)	3,117	75	53	3,838	7,542	4,930
Lawrence Technological University; Southfield, Mich. (Pr)	3,073			11,436	11,436	4,200
Madonna University; Livonia, Mich. (Pr)	3,307	78	78	6,610	6,610	4,676
Marygrove College; Detroit, Mich. (Pr)	991	31	80	10,140	10,140	5,200
Michigan State University; East Lansing, Mich. (Pu)	33,966	69	53	5,093	12,675	4,472
Michigan Technological University; Houghton, Mich. (Pu)	5,666	94	26	4,530	11,086	4,917
Northern Michigan University; Marquette, Mich. (Pu)	8,366	89	54	7,786	10,222	4,640
Northwood University; Midland, Mich. (Pr)	3,190	93	47	11,325	11,325	5,208
Oakland University; Rochester, Mich. (Pu)	12,002	78	64	3,849	11,113	4,833
Olivet College; Olivet, Mich. (Pr)	889	79	48	13,382	13,382	4,452
Rochester College; Rochester Hills, Mich. (Pr)	830		54	8,448	8,448	4,768
Sacred Heart Major Seminary; Detroit, Mich. (Pr)	179					4,220
Saginaw Valley State University; University Ce, Mich. (Pu)	6,658		60	3,257	6,681	4,690
Saint Mary's College; Orchard Lake, Mich. (Pr)	381	80	40	7,380	7,380	4,900
Siena Heights College; Adrian, Mich. (Pr)	993			14,190	14,190	4,630

Institution name; city, state (type)	Students	Percent Accepted	Women	Tuition In-state	Out-of-state	Room and board
Spring Arbor University; Spring Arbor, Mich. (Pr)	2,125	90%	69%	$12,200	$12,200	$4,580
University of Detroit Mercy; Detroit, Mich. (Pr)	4,275		66	13,350	13,350	5,380
University of Michigan-Ann Arbor; Ann Arbor, Mich. (Pu)	24,412	55	50	6,328	20,138	5,780
University of Michigan-Dearborn; Dearborn, Mich. (Pu)	6,521	76	53	4,274	11,615	
University of Michigan-Flint; Flint, Mich. (Pu)	5,786	82	65	3,835	11,058	
Wayne State University; Detroit, Mich. (Pu)	18,093	78	60	3,567	8,175	6,350
Western Michigan University; Kalamazoo, Mich. (Pu)	22,756	85	53	3,492	8,730	5,073
William Tyndale College; Farmington Hills, Mich. (Pr)	625	82	52	7,050	7,050	2,800
Yeshiva Geddolah of Greater Detroit Rabbinical College; Oak Park, Mich.						
MINNESOTA						
Art Institutes International Minnesota; Minneapolis, Minn. (Prp)	728	99	45			0
Augsburg College; Minneapolis, Minn. (Pr)	2,913	75	60	17,070	17,070	5,540
Bemidji State University; Bemidji, Minn. (Pu)	4,368	77	57	2,954	6,266	4,054
Bethel College; St. Paul, Minn. (Pr)	2,721	81	63	15,300	15,300	5,410
Carleton College; Northfield, Minn. (Pr)	1,936	44	52	24,420	24,420	4,950
College of Saint Benedict; St. Joseph, Minn. (Pr)	1,977	91	100	16,195	16,195	5,025
College of Saint Catherine; St. Paul, Minn. (Pr)	2,545	87	100	15,456	15,456	4,550
College of Saint Scholastica; Duluth, Minn. (Pr)	1,429	93	74	15,420	15,420	4,760
Concordia College-Moorhead; Moorhead, Minn. (Pr)	2,969	90	63	13,904	13,904	3,900
Concordia College-St. Paul; St. Paul, Minn. (Pr)	1,027			12,658	12,658	4,726
Crown College; St. Bonifacius, Minn. (Pr)	794	93	61	9,450	9,450	4,316
Gustavus Adolphus College; Saint Peter, Minn. (Pr)	2,560	76	57	18,940	18,940	4,900
Hamline University; St. Paul, Minn. (Pr)	1,851	81	65	16,050	16,050	5,304
Macalester College; St. Paul, Minn. (Pr)	1,794	53	60	21,486	21,486	5,932
Martin Luther College; New Ulm, Minn. (Pr)	811	89	48	4,130	4,130	2,285
Minneapolis College of Art and Design; Minneapolis, Minn. (Pr)	577	73	42	17,910	17,910	4,375
Minnesota State University-Moorhead; Moorhead, Minn. (Pu)	6,729	80	63	2,728	6,118	3,264
Minnesota State University-Mankato; Mankato, Minn. (Pu)	10,350	85	53	2,582	5,769	2,965
North Central University; Minneapolis, Minn. (Pr)	1,172	62	57	12,000	12,000	3,550
Northwestern College; St. Paul, Minn. (Pr)	1,744	71	61	14,982	14,982	4,448
Saint Cloud State University; St. Cloud, Minn. (Pu)	13,949	83	55	3,135	6,470	3,468
Saint John's University/College of Saint Benedict; Collegeville, Minn. (Pr)	3,904	82	52	16,995	16,995	5,272
Saint Mary's University of Minnesota; Winona, Minn. (Pr)	1,693	91	52	13,990	13,990	4,620
Saint Olaf College; Northfield, Minn. (Pr)	3,014	74	57	19,400	19,400	4,500
Southwest State University; Marshall, Minn. (Pu)	2,900			2,648	5,965	3,000
University of Minnesota-Crookston; Crookston, Minn. (Pu)	2,464	95	55	3,780	3,780	4,046
University of Minnesota-Duluth; Duluth, Minn. (Pu)	8,605	78	51	4,230	12,660	4,338
University of Minnesota-Morris; Morris, Minn. (Pu)	1,867	87	59	4,778	9,480	3,910
University of Minnesota-Twin Cities; Minneapolis, Minn. (Pu)	31,824	75	53	4,401	12,312	4,914
University of Saint Thomas; St. Paul, Minn. (Pr)	5,469	82	53	17,088	17,088	5,407
Winona State University; Winona, Minn. (Pu)	6,772	65	63	2,800	6,200	3,500
MISSISSIPPI						
Alcorn State University; Lorman, Miss. (Pu)	2,555			2,685	5,546	2,427
Belhaven College; Jackson, Miss. (Pr)	1,467	64	64	10,450	10,450	4,280
Blue Mountain College; Blue Mountain, Miss. (Pr)	417					2,240
Delta State University; Cleveland, Miss. (Pu)	3,469	84	60	2,596	5,546	2,600
Jackson State University; Jackson, Miss. (Pu)	5,471	46	61	2,788	6,414	3,698
Millsaps College; Jackson, Miss. (Pr)	1,194	88	54	15,586	15,586	6,580
Mississippi College; Clinton, Miss. (Pr)	2,440	98	58	9,600	9,600	4,424
Mississippi State University; Mississippi State, Miss. (Pu)	13,307	71	46	3,117	7,065	3,990
Mississippi University for Women; Columbus, Miss. (Pu)	3,314	78	81	2,556	5,546	2,557
Mississippi Valley State University; Itta Bena, Miss. (Pu)	2,358	45	64	2,646	5,546	2,825
Rust College; Holly Springs, Miss. (Pr)	843	47	60	5,200	5,200	2,400
Tougaloo College; Tougaloo, Miss. (Pr)	967	99	72	6,400	6,400	3,060
University of Mississippi; University, Miss. (Pu)	9,608	82	52	3,153	7,106	5,060
University of Southern Mississippi; Hattiesburg, Miss. (Pu)	12,049	63	60	2,970	6,898	4,212
Wesley College; Florence, Miss. (Pr)	81		41	3,500	3,500	2,150
William Carey College; Hattiesburg, Miss. (Pr)	1,524	94	66	6,880	6,880	3,060
MISSOURI						
Avila College; Kansas City, Mo. (Pr)	1,061	96	71	12,720	12,720	5,000
Central Methodist College; Fayette, Mo. (Pr)	1,258	88	60	10,350	10,350	4,110
Central Missouri State University; Warrensburg, Mo. (Pu)	9,150	82	53	3,210	6,360	4,230
College of the Ozarks; Point Lookout, Mo. (Pr)	1,388	17	56			2,500
Columbia College; Columbia, Mo. (Pr)	782	97	59	10,506	10,506	4,576
Culver-Stockton College; Canton, Mo. (Pr)	821	77	55	11,200	11,200	4,975
Deaconess College of Nursing; St. Louis, Mo. (Prp)	305		93			3,200
DeVry Institute of Technology; Kansas City, Mo. (Pr)	2,708		23	8,740	8,740	4,750
Drury University; Springfield, Mo. (Pr)	1,443		56	10,950	10,950	4,046
Evangel College; Springfield, Mo. (Pr)	1,616	88	56	8,390	8,390	3,440
Fontbonne College; St. Louis, Mo. (Pr)	1,377	87	70	12,596	12,596	5,800
Hannibal-LaGrange College; Hannibal, Mo. (Pr)	1,104	96	67	8,807	8,807	3,226
Harris-Stowe State College; St. Louis, Mo. (Pu)	1,723			1,992	3,924	
Kansas City Art Institute; Kansas City, Mo. (Pr)	527	78	51	17,974	17,974	6,000

Institution name; city, state (type)	Students	Percent Accepted	Women	Tuition In-state	Out-of-state	Room and board
Lincoln University; Jefferson City, Mo. (Pu)	3,128	100%	58%	$ 2,424	$ 4,848	$3,790
Lindenwood College; St. Charles, Mo. (Pr)	2,891			14,700	14,700	5,000
Maryville University of Saint Louis; St. Louis, Mo. (Pr)	2,530	80	71	12,880	12,880	5,600
Missouri Baptist College; St. Louis, Mo. (Pr)	2,714	66	65	9,090	9,090	4,480
Missouri Southern State College; Joplin, Mo. (Pu)	5,785	91	57	2,370	4,740	3,610
Missouri Valley College; Marshall, Mo. (Pr)	1,192	81	11	12,000	12,000	5,000
Missouri Western State College; St. Joseph, Mo. (Pu)	5,089	100	61	2,754	5,070	3,942
Northwest Missouri State University; Maryville, Mo. (Pu)	5,568	90	56	2,723	4,733	3,890
Park University; Parkville, Mo. (Pr)	1,242	77	61	4,950	4,950	4,850
Rockhurst University; Kansas City, Mo. (Pr)	2,034	88	58	13,500	13,500	4,850
St. Louis College of Pharmacy; St. Louis, Mo. (Pr)	809	84	65	13,000	13,000	5,220
Saint Louis University; St. Louis, Mo. (Pr)	9,847	67	56	18,400	18,400	6,140
Southeast Missouri State University; Cape Girardeau, Mo. (Pu)	7,443	94	58	2,979	5,559	4,080
Southwest Baptist University; Bolivar, Mo. (Pr)	2,498			10,331	10,331	2,623
Southwest Missouri State University; Springfield, Mo. (Pu)	14,515	80	55	3,180	6,360	3,846
Stephens College; Columbia, Mo. (Pr)	734	84	93	15,770	15,770	5,870
Truman State University; Kirksville, Mo. (Pu)	5,809	79	58	6,664	6,664	4,452
University of Missouri-Columbia; Columbia, Mo. (Pu)	17,346	80	53	0	0	0
University of Missouri-Kansas City; Kansas City, Mo. (Pu)	8,091	71	58	4,012	10,710	4,950
University of Missouri-Rolla; Rolla, Mo. (Pu)	3,698	92	23	4,245	12,690	5,060
University of Missouri-St. Louis; St. Louis, Mo. (Pu)	9,612		58	4,940	13,109	4,850
Washington University in St. Louis; St. Louis, Mo. (Pr)	6,695	30	51	25,700	25,700	8,216
Webster University; St. Louis, Mo. (Pr)	3,489	62	63	12,150	12,150	5,440
Westminster College; Fulton, Mo. (Pr)	686	86	43	14,060	14,060	5,020
William Jewell College; Liberty, Mo. (Pr)	1,153	87	59	13,500	13,500	4,250
William Woods University; Fulton, Mo. (Pr)	697	83	76	12,900	12,900	5,400
MONTANA						
Blackfeet Community College; Browning, Mont. (Pu)						
Carroll College; Helena, Mont. (Pr)	1,251	89	60	12,716	12,716	5,168
Dawson Community College; Glendive, Mont. (Pu)	509	100	52	1,442	4,816	
Dull Knife Memorial College; Lame Deer, Mont. (Pu)						
Flathead Valley Community College; Libby, Mont. (Pu)						
Fort Peck Community College; Poplar, Mont. (Pu)						
Helena College of Technology of UM; Helena, Mont. (Pu)						
Little Big Horn College; Crow Agency, Mont. (Pu)						
Miles Community College; Miles City, Mont. (Pu)	568	100	62	1,440	4,200	3,500
Montana State University-Billings; Billings, Mont. (Pu)	3,826	100	64	3,052	8,227	4,500
Montana State University-Billings College of Technology; Billings, Mont. (Pu)						
Montana State University-Bozeman; Bozeman, Mont. (Pu)	10,458	84	45	3,079	9,075	4,650
Montana State University-Great Falls College of Technology; Great Falls, Mont. (Pu)						
Montana State University-Northern; Havre, Mont. (Pu)	1,367	100	52	2,692	8,078	3,800
Montana Tech of the University of Montana; Butte, Mont. (Pu)	1,978	97	45	3,006	8,530	4,278
Rocky Mountain College; Billings, Mont. (Pr)	801	99	53	12,088	12,088	4,147
Salish-Kootenai College; Pablo, Mont. (Pr)	1,075	63	60	1,620	1,620	
Stone Child Community College; Box Elder, Mont.						
University of Great Falls; Great Falls, Mont. (Pr)	970	100	70	10,000	10,000	2,750
University of Montana College of Technology; Missoula, Mont. (Pu)	10,501	85	53	2,365	5,085	4,000
University of Montana-Missoula; Missoula, Mont. (Pu)	10,666	86	53	3,064	8,311	4,800
Western Montana College; Dillon, Mont. (Pu)	1,160	79	59	2,795	7,885	3,800
NEBRASKA						
Chadron State College; Chadron, Nebr. (Pu)	2,331	100	58	1,973	3,945	3,300
Clarkson College; Omaha, Nebr. (Pr)	380		89	6,528	6,528	5,540
College of Saint Mary; Omaha, Nebr. (Pr)	947	99	100	13,350	13,350	4,784
Concordia College; Seward, Nebr. (Pr)	1,087			11,310	11,310	3,786
Creighton University; Omaha, Nebr. (Pr)	3,765	89	59	14,312	14,312	6,030
Dana College; Blair, Nebr. (Pr)	583	97	47	12,150	12,150	3,880
Doane College; Crete, Nebr. (Pr)	1,517	89	53	12,500	12,500	3,900
Hastings College; Hastings, Nebr. (Pr)	1,090	87	51	11,916	11,916	3,986
Midland Lutheran College; Fremont, Nebr. (Pr)	1,033	93	58	12,800	12,800	3,450
Nebraska Methodist College; Omaha, Nebr. (Pr)	387	100	93	8,550	8,550	1,500
Nebraska Wesleyan University; Lincoln, Nebr. (Pr)	1,675	94	57	14,380	14,380	4,120
Peru State College; Peru, Nebr. (Pu)	1,454	88	55	1,865	3,750	3,192
University of Nebraska-Kearney; Kearney, Nebr. (Pu)	5,886		56	2,101	3,765	3,150
University of Nebraska-Lincoln; Lincoln, Nebr. (Pu)	17,968	92	47	2,760	7,515	4,310
University of Nebraska-Omaha; Omaha, Nebr. (Pu)	10,694	87	53	2,528	6,810	2,619
Wayne State College; Wayne, Nebr. (Pu)	2,982	100	58	1,875	3,750	3,300
NEVADA						
Deep Springs College; Dyer, Nev. (Pr)	26	14	0	0	0	0
Sierra Nevada College; Incline Villa, Nev. (Pr)	540			10,800	10,800	5,600
University of Nevada-Las Vegas; Las Vegas, Nev. (Pu)	17,327	84	55	2,340	9,320	5,800
University of Nevada-Reno; Reno, Nev. (Pu)	9,402		55	2,340	9,320	5,295

Institution name; city, state (type)	Students	Percent Accepted	Percent Women	Tuition In-state	Tuition Out-of-state	Room and board
NEW HAMPSHIRE						
Colby-Sawyer College; New London, N.H. (Pr)	808	84%	65%	$18,960	$18,960	$7,240
Daniel Webster College; Nashua, N.H. (Pr)	1,099	84	31	16,250	16,250	6,340
Dartmouth College; Hanover, N.H. (Pr)	4,057	21	48	25,497	25,497	7,557
Franklin Pierce College; Rindge, N.H. (Pr)	1,489	75	49	18,900	18,900	6,600
Keene State College; Keene, N.H. (Pu)	4,297	77	58	4,060	9,370	5,086
New England College; Henniker, N.H. (Pr)	724	92	51	18,382	18,382	6,538
New Hampshire College; Manchester, N.H. (Pr)	4,058	80	52	15,598	15,598	6,790
Notre Dame College; Manchester, N.H. (Pr)	685	85	76	15,367	15,367	6,213
Plymouth State College; Plymouth, N.H. (Pu)	3,417	77	48	3,830	9,140	5,030
Rivier College; Nashua, N.H. (Pr)	1,546	78	81	15,210	15,210	6,100
Saint Anselm College; Manchester, N.H. (Pr)	2,003	73	56	19,450	19,450	7,350
Thomas More College of Liberal Arts; Merrimack, N.H. (Pr)	71	100	56	10,000	10,000	7,700
University of New Hampshire; Durham, N.H. (Pu)	10,927	76	58	6,000	15,420	5,514
University of New Hampshire at Manchester; Manchester, N.H. (Pu)	1,123	74	61	4,630	12,190	4,807
NEW JERSEY						
Berkeley College; West Paterson, N.J. (Prp)	1,960	93	81	13,185	13,185	8,100
Bloomfield College; Bloomfield, N.J. (Pr)	1,771	55	69	10,800	10,800	5,350
Caldwell College; Caldwell, N.J. (Pr)	1,844	74	69	13,100	13,100	6,250
Centenary College; Hackettstown, N.J. (Pr)	1,202	77	81	15,100	15,100	6,400
College of New Jersey; Ewing, N.J. (Pu)	6,008	50	59	4,654	8,127	6,504
College of Saint Elizabeth; Morristown, N.J. (Pr)	1,337	79	91			
DeVry College of Technology; North Brunswick, N.J. (Pr)	3,779		23	8,740	8,740	4,750
Drew University; Madison, N.J. (Pr)	1,537	71	60	24,576	24,576	7,030
Fairleigh Dickinson University, Florham-Madison Campus; Teaneck, N.J. (Pr)	2,433	73	55	14,732	14,732	6,536
Fairleigh Dickinson University, Teaneck Campus; Teaneck, N.J. (Pr)	2,077	64	55	13,996	13,996	6,040
Felician College; Lodi, N.J. (Pr)	1,324	74	80	11,010	11,010	5,960
Georgian Court College; Lakewood, N.J. (Pr)	1,582	91	90	12,134	12,134	4,000
Kean University; Union, N.J. (Pu)	9,227	57	65	3,373	5,070	5,530
Monmouth University; West Long Branch, N.J. (Pr)	4,193	84	57	15,758	15,758	6,900
Montclair State University; Upper Montclair, N.J. (Pu)	8,706	40	55	3,204	4,946	5,802
New Jersey City University; Jersey City, N.J. (Pu)	6,412	49	61	2,880	4,898	5,000
New Jersey Institute of Technology; Newark, N.J. (Pu)	5,639	62	23	5,758	10,102	7,076
Princeton University; Princeton, N.J. (Pr)	4,663	12	47	26,160	26,160	7,453
Ramapo College of New Jersey; Mahwah, N.J. (Pu)	4,655	48	57	4,166	7,291	7,044
Richard Stockton College of New Jersey; Pomona, N.J. (Pu)	5,975	47	57	3,600	5,840	6,017
Rider University; Lawrenceville, N.J. (Pr)	4,205	81	58	17,990	17,990	7,380
Rowan University; Glassboro, N.J. (Pu)	8,051	99	58	4,140	8,280	5,776
Rutgers University-Camden College of Arts & Sciences; Camden, N.J. (Pu)	3,716	59	59	4,762	9,692	5,322
Rutgers University-College of Nursing; Newark, N.J. (Pu)	466	26	92	4,762	9,692	6,090
Rutgers University-College of Pharmacy; New Brunswick, N.J. (Pu)	825	45	64	5,286	10,754	6,098
Rutgers University-Cook College; Piscataway, N.J. (Pu)	3,231	64	50	5,286	10,754	6,098
Rutgers University-Douglass College; Piscataway, N.J. (Pu)	3,099	68	21	4,762	9,692	6,098
Rutgers University-Livingston College; Piscataway, N.J. (Pu)	3,536	60	52	4,762	9,692	6,098
Rutgers University-Mason Gross School of the Arts; Piscataway, N.J. (Pu)	617	22	58	4,762	9,692	6,098
Rutgers University-Newark College of Arts & Sciences; Newark, N.J. (Pu)	5,873	52	58	4,762	9,692	6,110
Rutgers University-Rutgers College; Piscataway, N.J. (Pu)	10,993	48	51	4,762	9,692	6,098
Rutgers University-School of Engineering; Piscataway, N.J. (Pu)	2,190	68	22	5,286	10,754	6,098
Rutgers University, University College-Camden; Camden, N.J. (Pu)	3,716	59	59	5,602	10,326	5,322
Rutgers University, University College-Newark; Newark, N.J. (Pu)	5,873	52	58	4,262	8,676	5,314
Rutgers University, University College-New Brunswick; Piscataway, N.J. (Pu)	27,939	58	53	4,732	9,626	5,314
Saint Peter's College; Jersey City, N.J. (Pr)	3,211	79	57	15,240	15,240	6,586
Seton Hall University; South Orange, N.J. (Pr)	5,465	76	51	15,960	15,960	7,722
Stevens Institute of Technology; Hoboken, N.J. (Pr)	1,564	54	23	22,980	22,980	7,730
Thomas Edison State College; Trenton, N.J. (Pu)	8,414			2,200	3,150	
University of Medicine & Dentistry/Kean College of N.J./Seto; Union, N.J. (Pu)	527					
Westminster Choir College of Rider University; Princeton, N.J. (Pr)	280			20,744	20,744	6,610
William Paterson University; Wayne, N.J. (Pu)	8,454	72	59	5,150	8,010	6,350
NEW MEXICO						
College of Santa Fe; Santa Fe, N.M. (Pr)	1,316	84	63	15,000	15,000	4,892
College of the Southwest; Hobbs, N.M. (Pr)	568	55	69	4,800	4,800	3,492
Eastern New Mexico University; Portales, N.M. (Pu)	2,942		60	1,752	6,510	3,104
New Mexico Highlands University; Las Vegas, N.M. (Pu)	2,054			1,782	7,122	2,171
New Mexico Institute of Mining & Technology; Socorro, N.M. (Pu)	1,236	68	36	1,704	7,030	3,704

Institution name; city, state (type)	Students	Percent Accepted	Percent Women	Tuition In-state	Tuition Out-of-state	Room and board
New Mexico State University; Las Cruces, N.M. (Pu)	12,831	68%	53%	$ 2,502	$ 8,166	$ 3,726
St. John's College; Santa Fe, N.M. (Pr)	431	84	11	22,000	22,000	6,386
University of New Mexico; Albuquerque, N.M. (Pu)	16,874	85	57	2,430	9,172	4,800
Western New Mexico University; Silver City, N.M. (Pu)	1,758			3,654	3,654	2,260
NEW YORK						
Adelphi University; Garden City, N.Y. (Pr)	2,878	68	70	14,750	14,750	7,180
Albany College of Pharmacy; Albany, N.Y. (Pr)	581	85	63	12,650	12,650	5,100
Albert A. List College of Jewish Studies at JTS; New York, N.Y. (Pr)	435		55	8,320	8,320	6,450
Alfred University; Alfred, N.Y. (Pr)	2,085	81	52	19,918	19,918	3,300
American Academy for Dramatic Arts-East; New York, N.Y. (Pr)	221	33	43	12,200	12,200	0
Arnold & Marie Schwartz College of Pharmacy & Health Science; Brooklyn, N.Y. (Pr)	660			7,900	7,900	7,900
Audrey Cohen College; New York, N.Y. (Pr)	1,093	78	14	14,160	14,160	
Bard College; Annandale-on-Hudson, N.Y. (Pr)	1,208	48	54	24,400	24,400	7,440
Barnard College; New York, N.Y. (Pr)	2,290	37	100	22,060	22,060	9,358
Binghamton University, State University of New York; Binghamton, N.Y. (Pu)	9,858	42	54	3,400	8,300	5,772
Boricua College; New York, N.Y. (Pr)	1,072					
Broome Community College; Binghamton, N.Y. (Pu)	5,555	82	56	2,338	4,676	4,680
Canisius College; Buffalo, N.Y. (Pr)	3,349	83	53	15,990	15,990	6,730
Cazenovia College; Cazenovia, N.Y. (Pr)	956	90	70	11,230	11,230	5,744
City University of New York-Baruch College; New York, N.Y. (Pu)	12,598	21	57	3,200	6,800	0
City University of New York-Brooklyn College; Brooklyn, N.Y. (Pu)	10,094	70	61	3,200	6,800	0
City University of New York-City College; New York, N.Y. (Pu)	8,232	74	52	3,200	6,800	0
City University of New York-College of Staten Island; Staten Island, N.Y. (Pu)	10,130	74	58	3,200	6,800	0
City University of New York-Hunter College; New York, N.Y. (Pu)	15,422	53	70	3,200	6,800	1,890
City University of New York-John Jay College of Criminal Justice; New York, N.Y. (Pu)	9,772			2,450	5,050	
City University of New York-Lehman College; Bronx, N.Y. (Pu)	7,698			3,200	6,800	0
City University of New York-Medgar Evers College; Brooklyn, N.Y. (Pu)	5,401			3,200	6,800	
City University of New York-Queens College; Flushing, N.Y. (Pu)	10,964	56	63	3,200	6,800	5,800
City University of New York-York College; Jamaica, N.Y. (Pu)	5,389	71	70	3,200	6,800	0
Clarkson University; Potsdam, N.Y. (Pr)	2,581	83	27	20,600	20,600	7,781
Clinton Community College; Plattsburgh, N.Y. (Pu)						
Colgate University; Hamilton, N.Y. (Pr)	2,773	38	51	25,565	25,565	6,330
College of Aeronautics; Flushing, N.Y. (Pr)	1,305	49	7	8,550	8,550	4,280
College of Insurance; New York, N.Y. (Pr)	338	60	52	14,252	14,252	9,140
College of Mount Saint Vincent; Riverdale, N.Y. (Pr)	1,202	73	79	16,030	16,030	7,300
College of New Rochelle; New Rochelle, N.Y. (Pr)	4,705	74	87	11,600	11,600	6,000
College of Saint Rose; Albany, N.Y. (Pr)	2,726	75	73	12,870	12,870	6,550
Columbia University; New York, N.Y. (Pr)	7,763	14	50	24,150	24,150	7,732
Columbia-Greene Community College; Hudson, N.Y. (Pu)						
Concordia College; Bronxville, N.Y. (Pr)	599	82	60	12,590	12,590	5,750
Cooper Union; New York, N.Y. (Pr)	870	13	34	8,300	8,300	10,000
Cornell University; Ithaca, N.Y. (Pr)	13,590	31	11	24,760	24,760	8,086
Daemen College; Amherst, N.Y. (Pr)	1,704	74	77	12,500	12,500	6,100
DeVry Institute of Technology; Long Island City, N.Y. (Pr)	1,652		20	9,800	9,800	3,400
Dominican College of Blauvelt; Orangeburg, N.Y. (Pr)	1,645	73	75	12,000	12,000	7,000
Dowling College; Oakdale, N.Y. (Pr)	2,922	88	59	11,940	11,940	2,650
D'Youville College; Buffalo, N.Y. (Pr)	976	78	75	11,580	11,580	5,720
Eastman School of Music, University of Rochester; Rochester, N.Y. (Pr)	503	29	55	20,320	20,320	7,512
Elmira College; Elmira, N.Y. (Pr)	1,440	78	70	22,960	22,960	7,530
Erie Community College, City Campus; Buffalo, N.Y. (Pu)	2,155		63	4,950	4,950	2,410
Erie Community College, North Campus; Williamsville, N.Y. (Pu)	4,877		51	4,950	4,950	2,410
Erie Community College, South Campus; Orchard Park, N.Y. (Pu)	3,167		45	4,950	4,950	2,410
Eugene Lang College; New York, N.Y. (Pr)	520	54	68	19,620	19,620	8,857
Fashion Institute of Technology; New York, N.Y. (Pu)				2,500	5,950	5,600
Finger Lakes Community College; Canadaigua, N.Y. (Pu)						
Five Towns College; Dix Hills, N.Y. (Pr)	724		25	9,300	9,300	6,500
Fordham University; New York, N.Y. (Pr)	6,989	63	59	20,200	20,200	8,310
Fulton-Montgomery Community College; Johnston, N.Y.						
Hamilton College; Clinton, N.Y. (Pr)	1,765	39	52	26,000	26,000	6,440
Hartwick College; Oneonta, N.Y. (Pr)	1,419	83	55	24,760	24,760	6,530
Herkimer County Community College; Herkimer, N.Y. (Pu)	2,448	100	54			
Hobart and William Smith Colleges; Geneva, N.Y. (Pr)	1,854	72	53	24,700	24,700	6,808
Hofstra University; Hempstead, N.Y. (Pr)	9,346	80	54	14,280	14,280	7,240
Houghton College; Houghton, N.Y. (Pr)	1,380	88	63	15,180	15,180	5,400
Iona College; New Rochelle, N.Y. (Pr)	3,422	78	52	15,500	15,500	8,835
Ithaca College; Ithaca, N.Y. (Pr)	5,906	70	56	19,142	19,142	8,284

Institution name; city, state (type)	Students	Percent Accepted	Women	Tuition In-state	Out-of-state	Room and board
Juilliard School; New York, N.Y. (Pr)	494	8%	51%	$17,400	$17,400	$ 7,000
Keuka College; Keuka Park, N.Y. (Pr)	952	86	72	13,490	13,490	6,750
Laboratory Institute of Merchandising; New York, N.Y. (Pr)	285	74	98	13,400	13,400	0
Le Moyne College; Syracuse, N.Y. (Pr)	2,399	84	59	15,370	15,370	6,760
Long Island University-Brooklyn; Brooklyn, N.Y. (Pr)	4,193			17,480	17,480	7,620
Long Island University-C.W. Post; Brookville, N.Y. (Pr)	5,748	85	57			
Manhattan College; Riverdale, N.Y. (Pr)	2,703	70	46	15,500	15,500	7,450
Manhattan School of Music; New York, N.Y. (Pr)	400	40	47	18,200	18,200	10,000
Manhattanville College; Purchase, N.Y. (Pr)	1,581	62	69	19,620	19,620	8,320
Mannes College of Music; New York, N.Y. (Pr)	160	31	14	18,000	18,000	6,875
Marist College; Poughkeepsie, N.Y. (Pr)	4,713	53	58	15,366	15,366	7,828
Marymount College; Tarrytown, N.Y. (Pr)	938	81	96	14,700	14,700	7,800
Marymount Manhattan College; New York, N.Y. (Pr)	2,497	65	79	13,050	13,050	8,500
Medaille College; Buffalo, N.Y. (Pr)	1,444	71	70	11,700	11,700	5,500
Mercy College; Dobbs Ferry, N.Y. (Pr)	9,500			7,800	7,800	6,500
Mohawk Valley Community College; Utica, N.Y. (Pu)	5,225	91	55	2,500	3,750	3,700
Molloy College; Rockville Centre, N.Y. (Pr)	1,920		79	11,900	11,900	4,696
Mount Saint Mary College; Newburgh, N.Y. (Pr)	1,808	84	71	0	0	0
Nazareth College of Rochester; Rochester, N.Y. (Pr)	1,910	78	75	14,230	14,230	6,470
New York Institute of Technology; Old Westbury, N.Y. (Pr)	5,290	75	39	13,700	13,700	7,310
New York School of Interior Design; New York, N.Y. (Pr)	692	64	91	15,200	15,200	11,000
New York University; New York, N.Y. (Pr)	18,628	29	60	24,336	24,336	9,226
Niagara County Community College; Sanborn, N.Y. (Pu)	4,828	100	58	1,250	1,875	3,700
Niagara University; Niagara Falls, N.Y. (Pr)	2,357	84	61	13,400	13,400	6,330
Nyack College; Nyack, N.Y. (Pr)	1,724	65	59	12,480	12,480	6,200
Onondaga Community College; Syracuse, N.Y. (Pu)	7,363	79	53			
Pace University-New York; New York, N.Y. (Pr)	5,755	75	62	15,870	15,870	6,500
Pace University-Pleasantville/Briarcliff; Pleasantville, N.Y. (Pr)	3,332	82	57	15,870	15,870	6,500
Pace University-White Plains; White Plains, N.Y. (Pr)	0					
Parsons School of Design, New School University; New York, N.Y. (Pr)	2,433	39	73	21,550	21,550	9,083
Polytechnic University-Brooklyn; Brooklyn, N.Y. (Pr)	1,775	66	19	21,120	21,120	4,830
Polytechnic University-Farmingdale; Brooklyn, N.Y. (Pr)						
Pratt Institute; Brooklyn, N.Y. (Pr)	2,922	43	51	20,744	20,744	7,940
Rensselaer Polytechnic Institute; Troy, N.Y. (Pr)	5,167	73	24	22,300	22,300	7,692
Roberts Wesleyan College; Rochester, N.Y. (Pr)	1,149	93	66	13,690	13,690	4,758
Rochester Institute of Technology; Rochester, N.Y. (Pr)	11,100	74	33	18,633	18,633	7,242
Russell Sage College; Troy, N.Y. (Pr)	819	76	16	17,200	17,200	6,164
Saint Bonaventure University; St. Bonaventure, N.Y. (Pr)	2,202	89	54	13,888	13,888	5,800
Saint Francis College; Brooklyn Heights, N.Y. (Pr)	2,336	75	60	8,830	8,830	
Saint John Fisher College; Rochester, N.Y. (Pr)	2,118	80	61	13,990	13,990	6,000
St. John's University; Jamaica, N.Y. (Pr)	14,229	80	57	15,500	15,500	8,950
St. Joseph's College-Brooklyn; Brooklyn, N.Y. (Pr)	1,256	49	78	9,030	9,030	4,410
St. Joseph's College-Patchogue; Patchogue, N.Y. (Pr)	3,115	78	78	9,290	9,290	0
St. Lawrence University; Canton, N.Y. (Pr)	1,969	69	53	23,795	23,795	7,475
Saint Thomas Aquinas College; Sparkill, N.Y. (Pr)	2,038		58	11,100	11,100	6,910
Sarah Lawrence College; Bronxville, N.Y. (Pr)	1,139	38	75	26,040	26,040	8,460
Schenectady County Community College; Schenectady, N.Y. (Pu)	3,334		55	2,340	4,680	
School of Visual Arts; New York, N.Y. (Prp)	4,996	60	53			8,200
Siena College; Loudonville, N.Y. (Pr)	3,310	73	52	15,330	15,330	7,430
Skidmore College; Saratoga Spgs., N.Y. (Pr)	2,451	43	61	25,190	25,190	7,260
Southampton College of Long Island University; Southampton, N.Y. (Pr)	2,649	67	60	15,340	15,340	7,390
State University of New York at Albany; Albany, N.Y. (Pu)	11,780	58	49	3,400	8,300	5,550
State University of New York at Buffalo; Buffalo, N.Y. (Pu)	16,683	68	46	3,400	8,300	6,054
State University of New York at New Paltz; New Paltz, N.Y. (Pu)	6,050	55	63	3,400	8,300	5,246
State University of New York at Plattsburgh; Plattsburgh, N.Y. (Pu)	5,377	63	57	3,400	8,300	4,850
State University of New York at Stony Brook; Stony Brook, N.Y. (Pu)	13,257	56	49	3,400	8,300	6,524
State University of New York College at Brockport; Brockport, N.Y. (Pu)	6,751	54	58	3,400	8,300	5,800
State University of New York College at Buffalo; Buffalo, N.Y. (Pu)	16,683	68	46	3,400	8,300	6,054
State University of New York College at Cortland; Cortland, N.Y. (Pu)	5,660	64	57	3,400	8,300	5,560
State University of New York College at Fredonia; Fredonia, N.Y. (Pu)	4,727	62	59	3,400	8,300	5,400
State University of New York College at Geneseo; Geneseo, N.Y. (Pu)	5,197	50	66	3,400	8,300	4,890
State University of New York College at Old Westbury; Old Westbury, N.Y. (Pu)	2,992	56	60	3,400	8,300	5,286
State University of New York College at Oneonta; Oneonta, N.Y. (Pu)	5,341	71	60	3,400	8,300	5,626

Institution name; city, state (type)	Students	Percent Accepted	Percent Women	Tuition In-state	Tuition Out-of-state	Room and board
State University of New York College at Oswego; Oswego, N.Y. (Pu)	6,849	59%	54%	$ 3,400	$ 8,300	$6,160
State University of New York College at Potsdam; Potsdam, N.Y. (Pu)	3,580	69	60	3,400	8,300	6,100
State University of New York College at Purchase; Purchase, N.Y. (Pu)	3,837	33	56	3,400	8,300	5,654
State University of New York College of A&T at Cobleskill; Cobleskill, N.Y. (Pu)	2,325	79	45	3,200	5,000	5,620
State University of New York College of A&T at Morrisville; Morrisville, N.Y. (Pu)	2,899	77	48	3,200	5,200	6,100
State University of New York College of Technology at Alfred; Alfred, N.Y. (Pu)	2,733	72	31	3,400	8,300	5,668
State University of New York College of Technology at Canton; Canton, N.Y. (Pu)	2,260	88	48	3,200	5,000	5,510
State University of New York College of Technology at Delhi; Delhi, N.Y. (Pu)	1,893		45	3,200	5,000	5,420
State University of New York Empire State College; Saratoga, N.Y. (Pu)	7,672		54	3,400	8,300	0
State University of New York Maritime College; Throg's Neck, N.Y. (Pu)	646			3,400	8,300	5,420
Sullivan County Community College; Loch Sheldrake, N.Y. (Pu)	1,552	95	61	2,500	5,000	3,200
SUNY College of Environmental Science and Forestry; Syracuse, N.Y. (Pu)	1,171	50	37	3,400	8,300	8,310
SUNY College of Technology at Farmingdale; Farmingdale, N.Y. (Pu)	902	68	42	3,200	5,000	5,230
SUNY Health Science Center at Brooklyn; Brooklyn, N.Y. (Pu)				3,400	8,300	5,420
SUNY Health Science Center at Buffalo; Buffalo, N.Y. (Pu)						
SUNY Health Science Center at Syracuse; Syracuse, N.Y. (Pu)	303		74		8,300	5,680
SUNY Institute of Technology at Utica/Rome; Utica, N.Y. (Pu)	2,190		50	3,400	8,300	6,030
Syracuse University; Syracuse, N.Y. (Pr)	10,740	58	54	21,500	21,500	9,130
Tompkins Cortland Community College; Dryden, N.Y. (Pu)						
Touro College; Brooklyn, N.Y. (Pr)	6,661	74	68	9,250	9,250	4,500
Ulster Community College; Stone Ridge, N.Y. (Pu)	2,884		59			
Union College; Schenectady, N.Y. (Pr)	2,124	47	48	23,892	23,892	6,474
United States Merchant Marine Academy; Kings Point, N.Y. (Pu)	940	48	3	1,000	1,000	
United States Military Academy; West Point, N.Y. (Pu)	4,154	13	4			
University of Rochester; Rochester, N.Y. (Pr)	4,529	66	48	23,150	23,150	7,740
Utica College of Syracuse University; Utica, N.Y. (Pr)	2,104	82	62	16,844	16,844	6,660
Vassar College; Poughkeepsie, N.Y. (Pr)	2,400	35	61	24,600	24,600	6,940
Wadhams Hall Seminary College; Ogdensburg, N.Y. (Pr)	21	100	0	5,300	5,300	4,970
Wagner College; Staten Island, N.Y. (Pr)	1,616	70	60	18,000	18,000	6,500
Webb Institute; Glen Cove, N.Y. (Pr)	74	43	7	0	0	6,250
Wells College; Aurora, N.Y. (Pr)	462	89	27	12,200	12,200	6,200
Yeshiva University; New York, N.Y. (Pr)	1,990			14,920	14,920	4,750
NORTH CAROLINA						
Appalachian State University; Boone, N.C. (Pu)	11,694	72	50	962	8,232	3,340
Barber Scotia College; Concord, N.C. (Pr)	488	64	45	7,400	7,400	3,500
Barton College; Wilson, N.C. (Pr)	1,233	87	68	10,812	10,812	4,270
Belmont Abbey College; Belmont, N.C. (Pr)	918	31	12	12,722	12,722	6,856
Bennett College; Greensboro, N.C. (Pr)	664	72	33	6,400	6,400	3,525
Brevard College; Brevard, N.C. (Pr)	710	89	46	11,280	11,280	5,060
Campbell University; Buies Creek, N.C. (Pr)	3,260	75	38	11,700	11,700	4,290
Catawba College; Salisbury, N.C. (Pr)	1,195	78	50	13,330	13,330	4,980
Chowan College; Murfreesboro, N.C. (Pr)	726	90	43	11,820	11,820	4,780
Davidson College; Davidson, N.C. (Pr)	1,679	36	14	22,873	22,873	6,572
Duke University; Durham, N.C. (Pr)	6,325	26	48	26,000	26,000	7,628
East Carolina University; Greenville, N.C. (Pu)	15,018	74	58	1,195	9,058	4,220
Elizabeth City State College; Elizabeth City, N.C. (Pu)	1,937	72	63	1,552	7,816	4,952
Elon University; Elon, N.C. (Pr)	3,900	61	61	13,556	13,556	4,652
Fayetteville State University; Fayetteville, N.C. (Pu)	3,249	87		900	8,028	3,400
Gardner-Webb University; Boiling Springs, N.C. (Pr)	2,474	81	64	11,660	11,660	4,760
Greensboro College; Greensboro, N.C. (Pr)	973	75	52	12,500	12,500	5,100
Guilford College; Greensboro, N.C. (Pr)	1,246	78	53	16,400	16,400	5,610
High Point University; High Point, N.C. (Pr)	2,658	91	59	11,120	11,120	5,300
Johnson C. Smith University; Charlotte, N.C. (Pr)	1,283			8,126	8,126	3,846
Lees-McRae College; Banner Elk, N.C. (Pr)	713	92	54	12,292	12,292	4,664
Lenoir-Rhyne College; Hickory, N.C. (Pr)	1,353	85	64	12,870	12,870	4,920
Livingstone College/Hood Theological Seminary; Salisbury, N.C. (Pr)				9,540	9,540	3,450
Mars Hill College; Mars Hill, N.C. (Pr)	1,224	90	57	12,000	12,000	4,500
Meredith College; Raleigh, N.C. (Pr)	2,432	80		12,300	12,300	4,400
Methodist College; Fayetteville, N.C. (Pr)	1,851	94	44	12,600	12,600	4,830
Montreat College; Montreat, N.C. (Pr)	1,116	80	58			4,614
Mount Olive College; Mount Olive, N.C. (Pr)	1,822	91	53	9,100	9,100	4,000
North Carolina A&T State University; Greensboro, N.C. (Pu)	6,850	72	53	982	8,252	4,250

Institution name; city, state (type)	Students	Percent Accepted	Women	Tuition In-state	Out-of-state	Room and board
North Carolina Central University; Durham, N.C. (Pu)	4,057	74%	64%	$ 962	$ 8,232	$3,904
North Carolina School of the Arts; Winston-Salem, N.C. (Pu)	692	42	41	1,587	10,215	4,920
North Carolina State University; Raleigh, N.C. (Pu)	21,990	65	42	1,860	11,026	5,274
North Carolina Wesleyan College; Rocky Mount, N.C. (Pr)	2,421		62	11,100	11,100	4,830
Pfeiffer University; Misenheimer, N.C. (Pr)	847			10,230	10,230	1,860
Queens College; Charlotte, N.C. (Pr)	1,156	77	76	11,360	11,360	5,890
Saint Andrews Presbyterian College; Laurinburg, N.C. (Pr)	638	81	60	13,515	13,515	5,300
Saint Augustine's College; Raleigh, N.C. (Pr)	1,492	45	58	5,132	5,132	4,508
Salem College; Winston-Salem, N.C. (Pr)	923	88	98	13,200	13,200	7,920
Shaw University; Raleigh, N.C. (Pr)	2,394	67	66	6,712	6,712	4,648
University of North Carolina-Asheville; Asheville, N.C. (Pu)	3,187	64	57	822	7,668	4,300
University of North Carolina-Chapel Hill; Chapel Hill, N.C. (Pu)	15,608	37	61	1,860	11,026	5,630
University of North Carolina-Charlotte; Charlotte, N.C. (Pu)	14,388	71	54	1,132	8,402	4,354
University of North Carolina-Greensboro; Greensboro, N.C. (Pu)	10,021	74	67	1,126	9,580	4,742
University of North Carolina-Pembroke; Pembroke, N.C. (Pu)	3,076	86	63	982	8,252	3,680
University of North Carolina-Wilmington; Wilmington, N.C. (Pu)	9,138	61	60	1,102	8,452	4,862
Wake Forest University; Winston-Salem, N.C. (Pr)	4,086	49	52	22,410	22,410	6,430
Warren Wilson College; Asheville, N.C. (Pr)	762	81	61	15,094	15,094	4,874
Western Carolina University; Cullowhee, N.C. (Pu)	5,611	74	52	1,022	8,292	3,424
Wingate University; Wingate, N.C. (Pr)	1,115	91	50	12,300	12,300	5,200
Winston-Salem State University; Winston-Salem, N.C. (Pu)	2,865	80	67	1,575	7,868	3,403
NORTH DAKOTA						
Bismarck State College; Bismarck, N.D. (Pu)	2,594		51	1,888		3,200
Dickinson State University; Dickinson, N.D. (Pu)	1,800	100	59	2,096	5,256	2,670
Jamestown College; Jamestown, N.D. (Pr)	1,161	99	57	7,550	7,550	3,300
Mayville State University; Mayville, N.D. (Pu)	776	96	55	1,982	5,292	3,026
Minot State University; Minot, N.D. (Pu)	2,907	97	63	2,144	5,724	3,080
Minot State University-Bottineau Campus; Bottineau, N.D. (Pu)	450	100	52	1,632	4,357	2,816
North Dakota State College of Science; Wahpeton, N.D. (Pu)	2,345		34			
North Dakota State University; Fargo, N.D. (Pu)	8,965	78	43	2,604	6,953	3,592
University of Mary; Bismarck, N.D. (Pr)	1,934	95	63	7,900	7,900	3,150
University of North Dakota; Grand Forks, N.D. (Pu)	9,122	59	48	3,088	7,438	3,614
University of North Dakota-Lake Region; Lake Region, N.D.						
Valley City State University; Valley City, N.D. (Pu)	1,081	95	55	3,176	6,483	2,892
Williston State College; Williston, N.D. (Pu)	714		57			
OHIO						
Antioch College; Yellow Spring, Ohio (Pr)	595	85	66	21,628	21,628	4,176
Art Academy of Cincinnati; Cincinnati, Ohio (Pr)	187			9,990	9,990	9,990
Ashland University; Ashland, Ohio (Pr)	2,850	81	64	15,134	15,134	5,610
Baldwin-Wallace College; Berea, Ohio (Pr)	4,043	82	62	15,340	15,340	5,460
Bluffton College; Bluffton, Ohio (Pr)	999	86	54	15,046	15,046	5,268
Bowling Green State University; Bowling Green, Ohio (Pu)	15,494	88	57	4,330	10,228	5,768
Capital University; Columbus, Ohio (Pr)	2,738	81	63	16,880	16,880	5,170
Case Western Reserve University; Cleveland, Ohio (Pr)	3,434	71	39	21,000	21,000	6,250
Cedarville University; Cedarville, Ohio (Pr)	2,847	74	54	11,424	11,424	4,929
Central State University; Wilberforce, Ohio (Pu)	1,101	34	54	1,992	6,249	5,031
Cleveland Institute of Art; Cleveland, Ohio (Pr)	525	74	48	14,175	14,175	5,076
Cleveland Institute of Music; Cleveland, Ohio (Pr)	222	29	11	17,875	17,875	5,590
Cleveland State University; Cleveland, Ohio (Pu)	16,326	79	54	1,872	3,744	4,848
College of Mount Saint Joseph; Cincinnati, Ohio (Pr)	2,061	85	71	13,500	13,500	5,100
College of Wooster; Wooster, Ohio (Pr)	1,837	74	53	21,520	21,520	5,680
Columbus College of Art & Design; Columbus, Ohio (Pr)	1,629	76	49	14,520	14,520	6,100
Defiance College; Defiance, Ohio (Pr)	833	72	53	14,850	14,850	4,480
Denison University; Granville, Ohio (Pr)	2,108	68	57	21,710	21,710	6,300
DeVry Institute of Technology; Columbus, Ohio (Pr)	3,571		25	8,740	8,740	4,750
Franciscan University of Steubenville; Steubenville, Ohio (Pr)	1,701	90	60	13,520	13,520	5,200
Franklin University; Columbus, Ohio (Pr)	3,812	100	59	5,642	5,642	
Heidelberg College; Tiffin, Ohio (Pr)	1,360	86	51	16,998	16,998	5,474
Hiram College; Hiram, Ohio (Pr)	1,204	80	55	1	1	6,514
John Carroll University; University Heights, Ohio (Pr)	3,527	88	53	16,334	16,334	6,128
Kent State University; Kent, Ohio (Pu)	17,580	92	60	4,234	9,410	4,764
Kenyon College; Gambier, Ohio (Pr)	1,599	65	55	30,450	30,450	4,370
Lake Erie College; Painesville, Ohio (Pr)	509	87	74	15,140	15,140	5,420
Lourdes College; Sylvania, Ohio (Pr)	1,303	66	79	12,200	12,200	4,950
Malone College; Canton, Ohio (Pr)	1,945	84	62	13,310	13,310	5,640
Marietta College; Marietta, Ohio (Pr)	1,206	94	51	18,838	18,838	5,504
Miami University; Oxford, Ohio (Pu)	14,914	69	55	5,358	12,398	5,830
Mount Union College; Alliance, Ohio (Pr)	1,407			16,890	16,890	3,870
Mount Vernon Nazarene College; Mount Vernon, Ohio (Pr)	1,843	88	58	12,122	12,122	4,329
Muskingum College; New Concord, Ohio (Pr)	1,564	85	52	12,250	12,250	5,100
Notre Dame College of Ohio; South Euclid, Ohio (Pr)	639	55	50	13,418	13,418	5,248
Oberlin College; Oberlin, Ohio (Pr)	2,951	50	59	24,096	24,096	6,178
Ohio Dominican College; Columbus, Ohio (Pr)	2,085	67	69	10,710	10,710	5,220
Ohio Northern University; Ada, Ohio (Pr)	2,668	95	50	22,275	22,275	5,490
Ohio State University-Columbus; Columbus, Ohio (Pu)	35,749	72	49	4,383	12,732	5,807

Institution name; city, state (type)	Students	Percent Accepted	Women	Tuition In-state	Out-of-state	Room and board
Ohio State University-Lima; Lima, Ohio (Pu)	1,166	86%	58%	$ 3,528	$11,097	$4,278
Ohio State University-Mansfield; Mansfield, Ohio (Pu)	1,225			3,906	11,088	5,800
Ohio State University-Marion; Marion, Ohio (Pu)	1,060			3,906	11,088	5,800
Ohio State University-Newark; Newark, Ohio (Pu)	1,522			3,906	11,088	5,800
Ohio University-Athens; Athens, Ohio (Pu)	16,511	77	55	5,085	10,704	5,922
Ohio University-Chillecothe; Chillicothe, Ohio (Pu)	1,565		37	3,102	7,581	5,800
Ohio University-Eastern; West Saint Cl, Ohio (Pu)	1,000		40		7,383	
Ohio University-Lancaster; Lancaster, Ohio (Pu)	1,500		41		7,383	
Ohio University-Southern; Ironton, Ohio (Pu)	1,963		63	3,087	3,219	0
Ohio University-Zanesville; Zanesville, Ohio (Pu)	1,347	100	68	3,033	7,803	
Ohio Wesleyan University; Delaware, Ohio (Pr)	1,880	81	52	21,880	21,880	6,610
Otterbein College; Westerville, Ohio (Pr)	2,587	86	64	16,911	16,911	5,289
Pontifical College Josephinum; Columbus, Ohio (Pr)	42					2,320
Shawnee State University; Portsmouth, Ohio (Pu)	3,280	100	63		5,004	4,588
Tiffin University; Tiffin, Ohio (Pr)	1,150	87	12	11,130	11,130	5,050
Union Institute; Cincinnati, Ohio (Pr)	681	62	63			
University of Akron; Akron, Ohio (Pu)	18,905	90	55	3,980	10,182	5,350
University of Cincinnati; Cincinnati, Ohio (Pu)	20,656	92	48	4,467	12,744	6,375
University of Dayton; Dayton, Ohio (Pr)	7,132	79	51	16,320	16,320	5,280
University of Findlay; Findlay, Ohio (Pr)	3,459	81	57	17,088	17,088	6,434
University of Rio Grande; Rio Grande, Ohio (Pr)	1,851		60	7,593	7,593	4,612
University of Toledo; Toledo, Ohio (Pu)	16,729	95	55	4,416	10,783	4,798
Urbana University; Urbana, Ohio (Pr)	1,113	79	49	11,862	11,862	4,350
Ursuline College; Pepper Pike, Ohio (Pr)	1,016	94	93	13,500	13,500	4,560
Walsh University; North Canton, Ohio (Pr)	1,261	82	19	10,900	10,900	5,110
Wilberforce University; Wilberforce, Ohio (Pr)	775			7,760	7,760	4,260
Wilmington College; Wilmington, Ohio (Pr)	1,262	82	54	15,360	15,360	6,080
Wittenberg University; Springfield, Ohio (Pr)	2,274	87	57	22,680	22,680	5,776
Wright State University; Dayton, Ohio (Pu)	10,904	92	56	4,128	8,256	5,053
Xavier University; Cincinnati, Ohio (Pr)	4,019	88	59	16,540	16,540	6,960
Youngstown State University; Youngstown, Ohio (Pu)	10,619	62	53			
OKLAHOMA						
Bartlesville Wesleyan College; Bartlesville, Okla. (Pr)	571	60	64	8,200	8,200	3,800
Cameron University; Lawton, Okla. (Pu)	4,493	91	54	2,000	4,800	2,830
East Central University; Ada, Okla. (Pu)	3,786			1,106	3,323	2,200
Langston University; Langston, Okla. (Pu)	3,864			4,700	7,000	2,944
Mid-America Bible College; Oklahoma City, Okla. (Pr)	512					2,896
Northeastern State University; Tahlequah, Okla. (Pu)	7,187		60	1,800	4,200	3,260
Northwestern Oklahoma State University; Alva, Okla. (Pu)	1,648	100	55	1,830	4,340	2,316
Oklahoma Baptist University; Shawnee, Okla. (Pr)	1,993	86	56	9,500	9,500	3,470
Oklahoma Christian University; Oklahoma City, Okla. (Pr)	1,593	90	47	9,700	9,700	4,200
Oklahoma City University; Oklahoma City, Okla. (Pr)	2,100	63	57	9,320	9,320	4,400
Oklahoma Panhandle State University; Goodwell, Okla. (Pu)	1,589			3,160	3,160	2,330
Oklahoma State University; Stillwater, Okla. (Pu)	16,203	92	47	1,890	6,225	4,716
Oral Roberts University; Tulsa, Okla. (Pr)	3,064	81	58	11,900	11,900	5,228
Phillips University; Enid, Okla. (Pr)	525			6,685	6,685	3,900
Southeastern Oklahoma State University; Durant, Okla. (Pu)	3,384	93	54	1,470	3,900	2,689
Southern Nazarene University; Bethany, Okla. (Pr)	1,536			11,134	11,134	4,028
Southwestern College of Christian Ministries; Bethany, Okla. (Pr)	122		42	6,000	6,000	3,000
Southwestern Oklahoma State University; Weatherford, Okla. (Pu)	3,853	93	54	1,485	4,140	2,440
University of Central Oklahoma; Edmond, Okla. (Pu)	11,752	95	56	1,470	3,990	2,905
University of Oklahoma; Norman, Okla. (Pu)	18,308	86	50	1,890	6,225	4,610
University of Science and Arts of Oklahoma; Chickasha, Okla. (Pu)	1,409	83	64	1,470	3,990	2,390
OREGON						
Art Institutes International at Portland; Portland, Ore. (Prp)	214	96	73			
Eastern Oregon University; LaGrande, Ore. (Pu)	2,549	92	58	2,316	2,316	4,830
George Fox University; Newberg, Ore. (Pr)	1,709	90	59	17,300	17,300	5,550
Lewis & Clark College; Portland, Ore. (Pr)	1,709	68	60	22,410	22,410	6,400
Linfield College; McMinnville, Ore. (Pr)	1,534	93	56	18,450	18,450	5,350
Marylhurst University; Marylhurst, Ore. (Pr)	832	77	78	10,575	10,575	5,928
Mount Angel Seminary; St. Benedict, Ore. (Pr)						3,300
Northwest Christian College; Eugene, Ore. (Pr)	384			14,300	14,300	4,310
Oregon College of Art and Craft; Portland, Ore.						
Oregon Health Sciences University; Portland, Ore. (Pu)	243			4,939	12,272	0
Oregon Institute of Technology; Klamath Falls, Ore. (Pu)	2,831	77	43	2,592	11,211	4,898
Oregon State University; Corvallis, Ore. (Pu)	13,776	87	46	2,694	12,144	5,508
Pacific Northwest College of Art; Portland, Ore. (Pr)	317	99	61	11,500	11,500	5,170
Pacific University; Forest Grove, Ore. (Pr)	1,082	86	61	17,300	17,300	5,295
Portland State University; Portland, Ore. (Pu)	13,625	86	56	2,694	11,460	6,150
Reed College; Portland, Ore. (Pr)	1,366	74	53	26,060	26,060	7,090
Southern Oregon University; Ashland, Ore. (Pu)	4,879	96	57	2,520	9,666	5,649
University of Oregon; Eugene, Ore. (Pu)	14,076	90	53	2,694	12,714	5,564
University of Portland; Portland, Ore. (Pr)	2,392	89	56	16,930	16,930	5,190

Institution name; city, state (type)	Students	Percent Accepted	Women	Tuition In-state	Out-of-state	Room and board
Warner Pacific College; Portland, Ore. (Pr)	645	79%	66%	$14,410	$14,410	$4,600
Western Baptist College; Salem, Ore. (Pr)	696	72	58	14,160	14,160	5,340
Western Oregon University; Monmouth, Ore. (Pu)	4,201	93	60	2,520	10,038	5,245
Willamette University; Salem, Ore. (Pr)	1,749	87	55	22,420	22,420	5,930
PENNSYLVANIA						
Albright College; Reading, Pa. (Pr)	1,728	76	57	19,760	19,760	6,040
Allegheny College; Meadville, Pa. (Pr)	1,904	76	52	22,210	22,210	5,290
Alvernia College; Reading, Pa. (Pr)	1,506	76	66	12,950	12,950	5,840
Arcadia University (formerly Beaver College); Glenside, Pa. (Pr)	1,628	76	74	17,550	17,550	7,740
Baptist Bible College and Seminary of Pennsylvania; Clarks Summit, Pa. (Pr)	636	76	56	7,620	7,620	4,714
Bloomsburg University of Pennsylvania; Bloomsburg, Pa. (Pu)	6,878	61	62	3,792	9,480	4,032
Bryn Athyn College of the New Church; Bryn Athyn, Pa. (Pr)	129	100	58			4,404
Bryn Mawr College; Bryn Mawr, Pa. (Pr)	1,358	59	99	22,730	22,730	8,100
Bucknell University; Lewisburg, Pa. (Pr)	3,426	42	48	23,698	23,698	5,596
Cabrini College; Radnor, Pa. (Pr)	1,654	87	66	16,150	16,150	7,560
California University of Pennsylvania; California, Pa. (Pu)	5,041	81	54	9,164	14,500	4,526
Carlow College; Pittsburgh, Pa. (Pr)	1,631	70	93	12,950	12,950	5,280
Carnegie Mellon University; Pittsburgh, Pa. (Pr)	5,224	36	37	23,820	23,820	7,264
Cedar Crest College; Allentown, Pa. (Pr)	1,554	73	95	18,680	18,680	6,725
Chatham College; Pittsburgh, Pa. (Pr)	585	87	99	18,803	18,803	6,496
Chestnut Hill College; Philadelphia, Pa. (Pr)	936	75	85	16,900	16,900	7,170
Cheyney University of Pennsylvania; Cheyney, Pa. (Pu)	1,132	82	56	3,792	9,480	4,983
Clarion University of Pennsylvania; Clarion, Pa. (Pu)	5,687	86	61	3,792	5,688	3,862
College Misericordia; Dallas, Pa. (Pr)	1,153	84	37	15,800	15,800	6,600
Combs College of Music; Philadelphia, Pa. (Pr)						3,800
Delaware Valley College; Doylestown, Pa. (Pr)	1,838	82	51	16,148	16,148	6,340
DeSales University; Center Valley, Pa. (Pr)	1,743	72	55	16,000	16,000	6,270
Dickinson College; Carlisle, Pa. (Pr)	2,115	64	61	25,250	25,250	6,725
Drexel University; Philadelphia, Pa. (Pr)	10,582	78	38	16,644	16,644	8,705
Duquesne University; Pittsburgh, Pa. (Pr)	5,499	84	58	15,169	15,169	6,504
East Stroudsburg University of Pennsylvania; E Stroudsburg, Pa. (Pu)	4,782	67	58	3,618	9,046	3,938
Eastern College; St. Davids, Pa. (Pr)	1,902	52	66	13,200	13,200	5,654
Edinboro University of Pennsylvania; Edinboro, Pa. (Pu)	6,486	80	57	3,792	5,688	4,104
Elizabethtown College; Elizabethtown, Pa. (Pr)	1,825	77	65	19,100	19,100	5,600
Franklin & Marshall College; Lancaster, Pa. (Pr)	1,891	56	50	24,816	24,816	5,994
Gannon University; Erie, Pa. (Pr)	2,470	90	59	14,490	14,490	5,850
Geneva College; Beaver Falls, Pa. (Pr)	2,047	78	56	13,000	13,000	5,690
Gettysburg College; Gettysburg, Pa. (Pr)	2,218	68	52	24,761	24,761	5,956
Gratz College; Melrose Park, Pa. (Pr)	24	50	71	7,560	7,560	9,180
Grove City College; Grove City, Pa. (Pr)	2,323	51	50	7,220	7,220	4,206
Gwynedd-Mercy College; Gwynedd Valle, Pa. (Pr)	1,395	36	77	13,500	13,500	6,500
Haverford College; Haverford, Pa. (Pr)	1,135	32	16	25,826	25,826	8,230
Holy Family College; Philadelphia, Pa. (Pr)	1,882	89	77	12,300	12,300	0
Immaculata College; Immaculata, Pa. (Pr)	2,360	83	82	13,950	13,950	6,800
Indiana University of Pennsylvania; Indiana, Pa. (Pu)	11,735	58	56	3,792	9,480	3,966
Juniata College; Huntingdon, Pa. (Pr)	1,291	81	57	20,170	20,170	5,490
King's College; Wilkes-Barre, Pa. (Pr)	2,090	86	52	16,000	16,000	6,890
Kutztown University of Pennsylvania; Kutztown, Pa. (Pu)	7,033	73	60	3,792	9,480	4,342
Lafayette College; Easton, Pa. (Pr)	2,279	40	49	24,828	24,828	7,734
Lancaster Bible College; Lancaster, Pa. (Pr)	686	82	54	9,600	9,600	4,500
LaRoche College; Pittsburgh, Pa. (Pr)	1,627	86	63	11,600	11,600	6,474
LaSalle University; Philadelphia, Pa. (Pr)	3,961	72	57	18,020	18,020	7,000
Lebanon Valley College; Annville, Pa. (Pr)	1,773	73	59	17,870	17,870	5,680
Lehigh University; Bethlehem, Pa. (Pr)	4,722	46	41	24,000	24,000	6,860
Lincoln University; Lincoln University, Pa. (Pu)	1,576	28	57	3,570	5,820	4,720
Lock Haven University of Pennsylvania; Lock Haven, Pa. (Pu)	3,740	83	56	3,468	6,824	3,676
Lycoming College; Williamsport, Pa. (Pr)	1,402	79	56	18,240	18,240	5,145
Mansfield University of Pennsylvania; Mansfield, Pa. (Pu)	2,892	80	59	3,618	9,046	3,852
Marywood University; Scranton, Pa. (Pr)	1,609	81	73	15,840	15,840	6,900
Medical College of PA/Hahnemann University; Philadelphia, Pa. (Pr)				15,000	15,000	5,000
Mercyhurst College; Erie, Pa. (Pr)	2,832	79	57	13,190	13,190	5,364
Messiah College; Grantham, Pa. (Pr)	2,797	78	61	15,830	15,830	5,770
Millersville University of Pennsylvania; Millersville, Pa. (Pu)	6,497	71	58	3,792	9,480	4,900
Moore College of Art & Design; Philadelphia, Pa. (Pr)	495	59	18	15,475	15,475	6,100
Moravian College; Bethlehem, Pa. (Pr)	1,703	73	58	18,245	18,245	5,920
Mount Aloysius College; Cresson, Pa. (Pr)	1,221	53	73	9,800	9,800	4,640
Muhlenberg College; Allentown, Pa. (Pr)	2,470	44	58	20,865	20,865	5,650
Neumann College; Aston, Pa. (Pr)	1,445	98	67	14,320	14,320	6,760
Penn State Abington; Abington, Pa. (Pu)	3,048	81	50	6,436	9,998	4,932
Penn State Altoona; Altoona, Pa. (Pu)	3,749	84	50	6,436	9,998	4,910
Penn State Beaver; Monaca, Pa. (Pu)	759	88	35	6,340	8,912	4,910
Penn State Berks; Reading, Pa. (Pu)	2,186	85	39	6,436	9,998	4,910

Institution name; city, state (type)	Students	Percent Accepted	Percent Women	Tuition In-state	Tuition Out-of-state	Room and board
Penn State Delaware County; Media, Pa. (Pu)	1,678	79%	48%	$ 6,340	$ 9,812	$4,932
Penn State DuBois; Dubois, Pa. (Pu)	1,005	93	50	6,340	6,340	4,716
Penn State Erie, The Behrend College; Erie, Pa. (Pu)	3,606	73	38	6,546	12,560	4,910
Penn State Fayette; Uniontown, Pa. (Pu)	1,127	87	53	6,340	9,812	4,932
Penn State Harrisburg; Middletown, Pa. (Pu)	1,865	100	52	6,546	12,560	4,910
Penn State Hazleton; Hazleton, Pa. (Pu)	1,372	91	45	6,340	9,812	4,910
Penn State McKeesport; McKeesport, Pa. (Pu)	901	88	36	6,340	9,812	4,910
Penn State Mont Alto; Mont Alto, Pa. (Pu)	1,176	89	56	6,340	9,812	4,910
Penn State New Kensington; New Kensington, Pa. (Pu)	871	88	39	6,340	9,812	4,932
Penn State Schuylkill; Schuylkill Haven, Pa. (Pu)	1,096	89	54	6,340	9,812	4,910
Penn State Shenango; Sharon, Pa. (Pu)	1,032	93	65	6,340	9,812	4,932
Pennsylvania State University-University Park; State College, Pa. (Pu)	34,406	48	47	6,546	14,088	4,910
Penn State Wilkes-Barre; Lehman, Pa. (Pu)	831	88	36	6,340	9,812	4,932
Penn State Worthington Scranton; Dunmore, Pa. (Pu)	1,539	79	51	6,340	9,812	4,932
Penn State York; York, Pa. (Pu)	1,689	83	46	6,340	9,812	4,932
Philadelphia Biblical University; Langhorne, Pa. (Pr)	1,069	67	53	10,815	10,815	5,195
Philadelphia University; Philadelphia, Pa. (Pr)	2,809	79	65	15,412	15,412	6,882
Point Park College; Pittsburgh, Pa. (Pr)	2,417	81	54	12,054	12,054	5,334
Robert Morris College; Moon Township, Pa. (Pr)	3,833	91	50	8,460	8,460	6,062
Rosemont College; Rosemont, Pa. (Pr)	892	97	12	14,580	14,580	7,030
Saint Francis College; Loretto, Pa. (Pr)	1,486	89	63	15,040	15,040	6,480
Saint Joseph's University; Philedelphia, Pa. (Pr)	4,517	59	56	19,680	19,680	7,856
Saint Vincent College; Latrobe, Pa. (Pr)	1,746	84	65	15,531	15,531	5,268
Seton Hill College; Greensburg, Pa. (Pr)	1,141	79	83	15,225	15,225	5,200
Shippensburg University of Pennsylvania; Shippensburg, Pa. (Pu)	5,990	65	54	3,792	9,480	4,274
Slippery Rock University of Pennsylvania; Slippery Rock, Pa. (Pu)	6,130	91	57	3,618	9,046	3,810
Susquehanna University; Selinsgrove, Pa. (Pr)	1,829	75	58	20,140	20,140	5,770
Swarthmore College; Swarthmore, Pa. (Pr)	1,428	24	53	24,950	24,950	7,804
Temple University; Philadelphia, Pa. (Pu)	18,394	71	58	6,322	11,450	6,302
Thiel College; Greenville, Pa. (Pr)	1,039	78	53	10,732	10,732	5,674
Thomas Jefferson University; Philadelphia, Pa. (Pr)	838	57	83	17,500	17,500	5,443
University of Pennsylvania; Philadelphia, Pa. (Pr)	9,687	23	48	22,682	22,682	7,826
University of Pittsburgh-Bradford; Bradford, Pa. (Pu)	1,204	82	59	6,422	14,104	5,150
University of Pittsburgh-Johnstown; Johnstown, Pa. (Pu)	3,031	83	55	5,884	12,918	5,700
University of Pittsburgh-Greensburg; Greensburg, Pa. (Pu)	1,548	78	55	6,118	13,434	4,820
University of Pittsburgh-Pittsburgh Campus; Pittsburgh, Pa. (Pu)	17,424	62	53	6,422	14,104	5,936
University of Scranton; Scranton, Pa. (Pr)	3,964	84	58	18,460	18,460	8,112
University of the Arts; Philadelphia, Pa. (Pr)	1,919	54	53	17,250	17,250	4,800
University of the Sciences in Philadelphia; Philadelphia, Pa. (Pr)	2,041	82	67	16,500	16,500	7,000
Ursinus College; Collegeville, Pa. (Pr)	1,241	72	53	22,420	22,420	6,500
Villa Maria College; Erie, Pa. (Pr)				11,890	11,890	3,890
Villanova University; Villanova, Pa. (Pr)	7,023	52	50	20,555	20,555	3,040
Washington & Jefferson College; Washington, Pa. (Pr)	1,241	89	49	19,275	19,275	5,160
Waynesburg College; Waynesburg, Pa. (Pr)	1,379	91	54	12,250	12,250	5,050
West Chester University of Pennsylvania; West Chester, Pa. (Pu)	10,326	57	60	3,792	9,480	4,768
Westminster College; New Wilmington, Pa. (Pr)	1,451	89	62	16,180	16,180	4,980
Widener University; Chester, Pa. (Pr)	2,235	76	45	15,750	15,750	3,400
Wilkes University; Wilkes-Barre, Pa. (Pr)	1,762	84	48	16,388	16,388	7,438
Wilson College; Chambersburgh, Pa. (Pr)	764	90	86	14,020	14,020	6,478
York College of Pennsylvania; York, Pa. (Pr)	5,073	67	59	6,600	6,600	4,860
RHODE ISLAND						
Brown University; Providence, R.I. (Pr)	6,029	16	53	25,600	25,600	7,346
Bryant College; Smithfield, R.I. (Pr)	2,901	73	41	18,480	18,480	7,500
Johnson & Wales University; Providence, R.I. (Pr)	8,533	82	48	13,740	13,740	6,150
Providence College; Providence, R.I. (Pr)	4,405	57	58	18,440	18,440	7,625
Rhode Island College; Providence, R.I. (Pu)	6,917	72	68	2,860	8,250	5,946
Rhode Island School of Design; Providence, R.I. (Pr)	1,829	35	19	21,020	21,020	6,490
Roger Williams University; Bristol, R.I. (Pr)	3,676	86	51	18,270	18,270	8,500
Salve Regina University; Newport, R.I. (Pr)	1,835	67	69	17,950	17,950	8,100
University of Rhode Island; Kingston, R.I. (Pu)	10,647	75	56	3,464	11,906	6,688
SOUTH CAROLINA						
Anderson College; Anderson, S.C. (Pr)	1,398	80	62	9,810	9,810	4,705
Benedict College; Columbia, S.C. (Pr)	2,208	79	53	7,284	7,284	4,182
Charleston Southern University; Charleston, S.C. (Pr)	2,226		59	9,820	9,820	3,776
Citadel, The Military College of S.C.; Charleston, S.C. (Pu)	1,995	81	7			
Claflin College; Orangeburg, S.C. (Pr)	1,161	54	60	6,068	6,068	3,314
Clemson University; Clemson, S.C. (Pu)	14,066	64	45	3,280	9,266	4,122
Coastal Carolina University; Conway, S.C. (Pu)	4,405	72	56	3,500	9,810	5,240
Coker College; Hartsville, S.C. (Pr)	445	89	64	15,072	15,072	4,820
College of Charleston; Charleston, S.C. (Pu)	9,750	67	63	3,630	7,910	4,260
Columbia College; Columbia, S.C. (Pr)	1,242	77	100	13,200	13,200	4,500

Institution name; city, state (type)	Students	Percent		Tuition		Room and board
		Accepted	Women	In-state	Out-of-state	
Columbia International University; Columbia, S.C. (Pr)	580	56%	54%	$ 8,980	$ 8,980	$4,520
Converse College; Spartanburg, S.C. (Pr)	730	81	26	16,850	16,850	5,140
Erskine College; Due West, S.C. (Pr)	469	91	58	14,265	14,265	4,921
Francis Marion University; Florence, S.C. (Pu)	2,923	80	59	3,470	6,850	3,550
Furman University; Greenville, S.C. (Pr)	2,789	60	56	19,680	19,680	5,416
Johnson & Wales University; Charleston, S.C. (Pr)	1,442	85	35	11,820	11,820	4,200
Lander University; Greenwood, S.C. (Pu)	2,436	81	63	3,888	7,776	3,732
Limestone College; Gaffey, S.C. (Pr)	1,784	80	58	9,500	9,500	4,400
Medical University of South Carolina; Charleston, S.C. (Pu)	405		83	5,000	13,000	
Morris College; Sumter, S.C. (Pr)	940	50	66	5,894	5,894	3,051
Newberry College; Newberry, S.C. (Pr)	750	86	46	13,602	13,602	3,960
Presbyterian College; Clinton, S.C. (Pr)	1,119	81	52	15,870	15,870	4,900
South Carolina State University; Orangeburg, S.C. (Pu)	4,911			5,256	5,256	4,100
Southern Wesleyan University; Central, S.C. (Pr)	1,472	34	62			
University of South Carolina-Aiken; Aiken, S.C. (Pu)	3,148		66		7,544	3,890
University of South Carolina-Columbia; Columbia, S.C. (Pu)	15,266	69	55	3,768	10,054	4,588
University of South Carolina-Spartanburg; Spartanburg, S.C. (Pu)	3,585	62	65	3,494	8,386	4,040
Voorhees College; Denmark, S.C. (Pr)	677	100	67	6,152	6,152	3,350
Winthrop University; Rock Hill, S.C. (Pu)	4,650	72	69	4,262	7,680	4,156
Wofford College; Spartanburg, S.C. (Pr)	1,087	83	47	17,030	17,030	5,235
SOUTH DAKOTA						
Augustana College; Sioux Falls, S.D. (Pr)	1,728	83	65	15,280	15,280	4,478
Black Hills State University; Spearfish, S.D. (Pu)	3,469	73	60	1,867	5,941	2,785
Dakota State University; Madison, S.D. (Pu)	1,632	91	49			
Dakota Wesleyan University; Mitchell, S.D. (Pr)	676	87	61	11,354	11,354	3,838
Huron University; Huron, S.D. (Prp)	544	94	50	11,500	11,500	2,850
Mount Marty College; Yankton, S.D. (Pr)	949	99	71	9,248	9,248	4,020
Northern State University; Aberdeen, S.D. (Pu)	2,861	97	60	1,868	5,940	2,663
Oglala Lakota College; Kyle, S.D. (Pr)				1,200	1,200	
Presentation College; Aberdeen, S.D. (Pr)	461		78	6,820	6,820	3,100
Sinte Gleska University; Rosebud, S.D. (Pr)	642			1,660	1,660	
South Dakota School of Mines & Technology; Rapid City, S.D. (Pu)	2,020	97	31	1,867	5,940	3,122
South Dakota State University; Brookings, S.D. (Pu)	7,382	94	50	1,868	5,940	2,864
University of Sioux Falls; Sioux Falls, S.D. (Pr)	1,070	94	56	12,600	12,600	4,000
University of South Dakota; Vermillion, S.D. (Pu)	5,147	97	57	1,867	5,941	2,946
TENNESSEE						
Austin Peay State University; Clarksville, Tenn. (Pu)	6,658	48	59	2,222	7,850	3,350
Belmont University; Nashville, Tenn. (Pr)	2,507	74	62	11,990	11,990	7,379
Bethel College; McKenzie, Tenn. (Pr)	726	65	49	7,550	7,550	4,380
Bryan College; Dayton, Tenn. (Pr)						3,950
Carson-Newman College; Jefferson City, Tenn. (Pr)	1,946	88	58	11,000	11,000	3,940
Christian Brothers University; Memphis, Tenn. (Pr)	1,724	82	55	13,930	13,930	5,370
Cumberland University; Lebanon, Tenn. (Pr)	966	72	52	8,000	8,000	5,200
East Tennessee State University; Johnson City, Tenn. (Pu)	9,125	79	57	2,222	7,850	3,818
Fisk University; Nashville, Tenn. (Pr)	812	97	72	8,480	8,480	4,930
Freed-Hardeman University; Henderson, Tenn. (Pr)	1,438	71	54	7,696	7,696	4,620
Johnson Bible College; Knoxville, Tenn. (Pr)	388			7,500	7,500	3,200
King College; Bristol, Tenn. (Pr)	602	64	55	11,800	11,800	4,250
Knoxville College; Knoxville, Tenn. (Pr)	1,177			5,400	5,400	3,450
Lambuth University; Jackson, Tenn. (Pr)	979	72	57	9,398	9,398	4,500
Lane College; Jackson, Tenn. (Pr)	661	65	50	5,600	5,600	3,800
Lee University; Cleveland, Tenn. (Pr)	3,155	90	56	10,970	10,970	4,020
LeMoyne-Owen College; Memphis, Tenn. (Pr)	1,121			7,000	7,000	3,916
Lincoln Memorial University; Harrogate, Tenn. (Pr)	875	84	67	9,600	9,600	3,900
Lipscomb University; Nashville, Tenn. (Pr)	2,317	93	56	8,470	8,470	3,910
Maryville College; Maryville, Tenn. (Pr)	982	81	56	16,985	16,985	5,650
Memphis College of Art; Memphis, Tenn. (Pr)	225		48	11,450	11,450	4,500
Middle Tennessee State University; Murfreesboro, Tenn. (Pu)	15,890			1,906	6,732	3,030
Milligan College; Milligan Coll, Tenn. (Pr)	796	69	59	11,900	11,900	4,200
Rhodes College; Memphis, Tenn. (Pr)	1,546	70	57	19,303	19,303	5,790
Southern Adventist University; Collegedale, Tenn. (Pr)	1,939	72	54	11,250	11,250	3,990
Tennessee State University; Nashville, Tenn. (Pu)	7,277	68	63	2,442	7,558	3,060
Tennessee Technological University; Cookeville, Tenn. (Pu)	7,043	89	47	2,390	5,116	3,484
Tennessee Temple University; Chattanooga, Tenn. (Pr)	0			5,000	5,000	4,000
Tennessee Wesleyan College; Athens, Tenn. (Pr)	795	82	63	7,900	7,900	4,150
Trevecca Nazarene University; Nashville, Tenn. (Pr)	1,021	82	59	10,848	10,848	4,904
Tusculum College; Greenville, Tenn. (Pr)	1,137		54	11,800	11,800	3,900
Union University; Jackson, Tenn. (Pr)	1,961	83	61	12,300	12,300	4,110
University of Memphis; Memphis, Tenn. (Pu)	15,485			4,582	4,582	3,995
University of Tennessee; Knoxville, Tenn. (Pu)	20,009	62	51	2,812	9,616	4,490
University of Tennessee at Martin; Martin, Tenn. (Pu)	5,478	61	43	2,172	7,432	3,606
University of Tennessee at Chattanooga; Chattanooga, Tenn. (Pu)	6,993	56	57	2,834	8,514	4,548

Institution name; city, state (type)	Students	Percent Accepted	Percent Women	Tuition In-state	Tuition Out-of-state	Room and board
University of the South; Sewanee, Tenn. (Pr)	1,385	68%	53%	$18,900	$18,900	$5,230
Vanderbilt University; Nashville, Tenn. (Pr)	5,935	55	53	24,080	24,080	8,324
TEXAS						
Abilene Christian University; Abilene, Tex. (Pr)	4,231	91	55	10,410	10,410	4,420
Angelo State University; San Angelo, Tex. (Pu)	5,859	71	56	2,000	6,096	4,066
Austin College; Sherman, Tex. (Pr)	1,196	84	55	15,838	15,838	6,187
Baylor University; Waco, Tex. (Pr)	11,806	84	58	11,370	11,370	5,481
College of Saint Thomas More; Fort Worth, Tex. (Pr)	60	100	50	5,200	5,200	
Concordia University at Austin; Austin, Tex. (Pu)	785	52	55	12,300	12,300	5,000
Criswell College; Dallas, Tex. (Pr)	575			2,490	2,490	
Dallas Baptist University; Dallas, Tex. (Pr)	3,190	43	62	9,150	9,150	3,774
DeVry Institute of Technology; Irving, Tex. (Pr)	3,462		29	8,740	8,740	4,750
East Texas Baptist University; Marshall, Tex. (Pr)	1,402	92	55	8,250	8,250	3,298
East Texas State University; Commerce, Tex. (Pu)	5,347			5,985	6,330	3,600
Hardin-Simmons University; Abilene, Tex. (Pr)	1,910	45	54	9,900	9,900	3,663
Houston Baptist University; Houston, Tex. (Pr)	1,730	54	68	4,608	4,608	2,300
Howard Payne University; Brownwood, Tex. (Pr)	1,488		50	8,400	8,400	3,710
Huston-Tillotson College; Austin, Tex. (Pr)	701			9,413	9,413	4,253
Jarvis Christian College; Hawkins, Tex. (Pr)	519	67	57	8,685	8,685	3,485
Lamar University; Beaumont, Tex. (Pu)	9,551		55	864	5,976	3,040
LeTourneau University; Longview, Tex. (Pr)	2,728	86	47	12,670	12,670	5,420
Lubbock Christian University; Lubbock, Tex. (Pr)	1,278	91	59	8,760	8,760	3,700
McMurry University; Abilene, Tex. (Pr)	1,339	68	49	8,100	8,100	4,244
Midwestern State University; Wichita Falls, Tex. (Pu)	5,093		57	0	6,804	3,534
Our Lady of the Lake University (OLLU); San Antonio, Tex. (Pr)	2,233	14	77	11,708	11,708	5,040
Paul Quinn College; Dallas, Tex. (Pr)	517			7,350	7,350	3,450
Prairie View A&M University; Prairie View, Tex. (Pu)	5,285	97	56	0	0	0
Rice University; Houston, Tex. (Pr)	2,769	28	47	14,300	14,300	6,600
St. Edward's University; Austin, Tex. (Pr)	3,105	78	55	11,896	11,896	5,000
St. Mary's University of San Antonio; San Antonio, Tex. (Pr)	2,642	86	59	11,500	11,500	4,908
Sam Houston State University; Huntsville, Tex. (Pu)	10,855	81	57	1,536	6,696	3,672
Schreiner College; Kerrville, Tex. (Pr)	762	72	60	10,990	10,990	6,480
Southern Methodist University; Dallas, Tex. (Pr)	5,662	82	55	17,406	17,406	7,177
Southwest Texas State University; San Marcos, Tex. (Pu)	18,856	65	55	1,200	7,680	4,349
Southwestern Adventist University; Keene, Tex. (Pr)	1,065			11,918	11,918	4,084
Southwestern Christian College; Terrell, Tex. (Pr)				5,926	5,926	2,208
Southwestern University; Georgetown, Tex. (Pr)	1,309	59	58	15,750	15,750	5,560
Stephen F. Austin State University; Nacogdoches, Tex. (Pu)	10,246	71	58	960	6,120	4,370
Sul Ross State University; Alpine, Tex. (Pu)	2,270		53	1,080	7,470	3,480
Tarleton State University; Stephenville, Tex. (Pu)	6,102	74	54	1,608	6,768	3,636
Texas Christian University; Fort Worth, Tex. (Pr)	6,675	76	59	11,700	11,700	4,240
Texas A&M University-Galveston; Galveston, Tex. (Pu)	1,291	89	49	1,140	7,112	3,976
Texas A&M University-College Station; College Station, Tex. (Pu)	36,229	66	49	2,400	8,850	5,164
Texas A&M University-Corpus Christi; Corpus Christi, Tex. (Pu)	4,690	88	60	864	5,976	5,259
Texas College; Tyler, Tex. (Pu)						2,630
Texas Lutheran University; Seguin, Tex. (Pr)	1,547	83	52	13,440	13,440	4,120
Texas Southern University; Houston, Tex. (Pu)	8,832			2,058	7,180	4,000
Texas Tech University; Lubbock, Tex. (Pu)	20,518	70	46			5,349
Texas Wesleyan University; Fort Worth, Tex. (Pr)	2,015	79	65	9,260	9,260	3,964
Texas Woman's University; Denton, Tex. (Pu)	5,752			2,084	7,196	3,578
Trinity University; San Antonio, Tex. (Pr)	2,356	65	52	16,410	16,410	6,560
University of Central Texas; Killeen, Tex. (Pr)	1,117		57	3,144	3,144	3,449
University of Dallas; Irving, Tex. (Pr)	1,184	76	59	14,928	14,928	5,416
University of Houston-Clear Lake; Houston, Tex. (Pu)	3,946		63	2,250	8,700	0
University of Houston-Downtown; Houston, Tex. (Pu)	8,000	100	6	2,006	7,166	5,600
University of Houston-Victoria Campus; Victoria, Tex. (Pu)	832		73	912	6,096	
University of Mary Hardin-Baylor; Belton, Tex. (Pr)	2,010			6,500	6,500	4,000
University of North Texas; Denton, Tex. (Pu)	20,449	74	54	2,070	8,550	8,192
University of Saint Thomas; Houston, Tex. (Pu)	1,904	78	65	12,300	12,300	5,550
University of Texas at Arlington; Arlington, Tex. (Pu)	15,266	97	53	1,824	7,008	1,686
University of Texas at Austin; Austin, Tex. (Pu)	37,159	63	50	2,400	8,850	5,113
University of Texas at Brownsville; Brownsville, Tex. (Pu)						
University of Texas at Dallas; Richardson,, Tex. (Pu)	6,560	49	47	960	6,120	5,799
University of Texas at El Paso; El Paso, Tex. (Pu)	12,955	93	54	1,776	7,152	5,165
University of Texas at San Antonio; San Antonio, Tex. (Pu)	16,026	99	55	2,580	8,880	5,994
University of Texas at Tyler; Tyler, Tex. (Pu)						
University of Texas-Houston Health Science Center; Houston, Tex. (Pu)	262		93	2,880	12,510	5,400
University of Texas Medical Branch at Galveston; Galveston, Tex. (Pu)	653		85	1,971	10,827	6,612
University of Texas-Pan American; Edinburg, Tex. (Pu)	1,465	76	53	1,860	8,210	5,531
University of Texas-Permian Basin; Odessa, Tex. (Pu)	1,219			1,776	8,166	3,934
University of the Incarnate Word; San Antonio, Tex. (Pr)	2,905	97	70	11,850	11,850	4,870
Wayland Baptist University; Plainview, Tex. (Pr)	4,637	99	42	7,500	7,500	3,121
West Texas A&M University; Canyon, Tex. (Pu)	5,623	72	55	1,500	6,660	3,474

Institution name; city, state (type)	Students	Percent Accepted	Women	Tuition In-state	Out-of-state	Room and board
Wiley College; Marshall, Tex. (Pr)	463			$ 4,080	$ 4,080	$3,230
UTAH						
Brigham Young University; Provo, Utah (Pr)	30,037	64%	53%	2,830	2,830	4,454
Southern Utah University; Cedar City, Utah (Pu)	0	84	65	1,570	5,927	2,790
University of Utah; Salt Lake City, Utah (Pu)	20,963	94	46	3,013	9,181	4,700
Utah State University; Logan, Utah (Pu)	17,903	98	52	1,947	6,816	4,040
Weber State University; Ogden, Utah (Pu)	15,854	100	52	1,654	5,790	3,196
Westminster College of Salt Lake City; Salt Lake City, Utah (Pr)	1,878	72	63	13,450	13,450	4,750
VERMONT						
Bennington College; Bennington, Vt. (Pr)	545	70	21	23,250	23,250	6,150
Burlington College; Burlington, Vt. (Pr)	160	91	3	8,420	8,420	
Castleton State College; Castleton, Vt. (Pu)	1,480	85	58	4,236	9,924	5,346
Champlain College; Burlington, Vt. (Pr)	2,530	77	55	10,905	10,905	7,975
College of St. Joseph in Vermont; Rutland, Vt. (Pr)	393	97	64	11,500	11,500	6,200
Goddard College; Plainfield, Vt. (Pr)	349	93	70	15,218	15,218	5,288
Green Mountain College; Poultney, Vt. (Pr)	668	65	49	17,000	17,000	5,300
Johnson State College; Johnson, Vt. (Pu)	1,361	78	57	4,236	9,924	5,346
Lyndon State College; Lyndonville, Vt. (Pu)	1,153	93	45	4,236	9,924	5,346
Marlboro College; Marlboro, Vt. (Pr)	290	80	59	18,800	18,800	6,750
Middlebury College; Middlebury, Vt. (Pr)	2,292	25	51	32,765	32,765	0
Norwich University; Northfield, Vt. (Pr)	2,214	94	40	14,926	14,926	5,718
Saint Michael's College; Colchester, Vt. (Pr)	2,073	71	55	19,500	19,500	7,255
Southern Vermont College; Bennington, Vt. (Pr)	515	82	64	10,990	10,990	5,450
Trinity College of Vermont; Burlington, Vt. (Pr)	600	99	92	13,620	13,620	6,700
University of Vermont; Burlington, Vt. (Pu)	8,618	80	56	7,692	19,236	5,806
VIRGINIA						
Averett College; Danville, Va. (Pr)	1,589	76	61	12,585	12,585	4,385
Bluefield College; Bluefield, Va. (Pr)	827	100	52	6,900	6,900	4,890
Bridgewater College; Bridgewater, Va. (Pr)	1,223	92	57	15,490	15,490	7,460
Christendom College; Front Royal, Va. (Pr)	257	82	53	11,750	11,750	4,700
Christopher Newport University; Newport News, Va. (Pu)	5,101	59	61	1,888	7,910	5,350
College of William and Mary; Williamsburg, Va. (Pu)	5,585	42	57			
Eastern Mennonite University; Harrisonburg, Va. (Pr)	1,086	83	58	14,150	14,150	5,120
Emory and Henry College; Emory, Va. (Pr)	956	80	50	12,950	12,950	5,322
Ferrum College; Ferrum, Va. (Pr)	913	81	41	11,900	11,900	5,950
George Mason University; Fairfax, Va. (Pu)	15,185	61	56	2,376	11,220	5,400
Hampden-Sydney College; Hampden-Sydney, Va. (Pr)	997	72	0	16,690	16,690	6,110
Hampton University; Hampton, Va. (Pr)	4,891	48	61	9,966	9,966	5,090
Hollins University; Roanoke, Va. (Pr)	806	81	100	16,960	16,960	6,415
James Madison University; Harrisonburg, Va. (Pu)	14,156	65	57	3,926	9,532	5,182
Johnson & Wales University at Norfolk; Norfolk, Va. (Pr)	583	80	37	13,650	13,650	5,760
Liberty University; Lynchburg, Va. (Pr)	5,942	100	49	9,000	9,000	5,000
Longwood College; Farmville, Va. (Pu)	3,387	77	65	8,823	14,294	4,820
Lynchburg College; Lynchburg, Va. (Pr)	1,652	76	64	17,120	17,120	4,400
Mary Baldwin College; Staunton, Va. (Pr)	1,388	93	95	15,815	15,815	7,450
Mary Washington College; Fredericksburg, Va. (Pu)	3,965		69	1,550	7,980	5,298
Marymount University; Arlington, Va. (Pr)	2,004	78	72	13,750	13,750	6,160
Norfolk State University; Norfolk, Va. (Pu)	5,890	82	64	1,326	6,526	5,267
Old Dominion University; Norfolk, Va. (Pu)	13,065	71	56	2,184	9,774	5,114
Radford University; Radford, Va. (Pu)	7,622	76	60	1,629	7,542	4,938
Randolph-Macon College; Ashland, Va. (Pr)	1,145	74	53	17,160	17,160	4,520
Randolph-Macon Woman's College; Lynchburg, Va. (Pr)	748	82	100	18,090	18,090	7,350
Roanoke College; Salem, Va. (Pr)	1,677	81	61	17,320	17,320	5,722
Saint Paul's College; Lawrenceville, Va. (Pr)				9,090	9,090	3,834
Shenandoah University; Winchester, Va. (Pr)	1,339	97	57	15,080	15,080	5,150
Sweet Briar College; Sweet Briar, Va. (Pr)	749	89	95	17,860	17,860	7,300
University of Richmond; Richmond, Va. (Pr)	2,910	42	13	22,570	22,570	4,730
University of Virginia; Charlottesville, Va. (Pu)	13,712	39	54	3,046	16,295	4,767
University of Virginia's College at Wise; Wise, Va. (Pu)	1,447	73	56	1,885	8,379	4,696
Virginia Commonwealth University; Richmond, Va. (Pu)	15,824	74	59	2,492	11,946	4,839
Virginia Intermont College; Bristol, Va. (Pr)	835	69	75	11,890	11,890	5,300
Virginia Military Institute; Lexington, Va. (Pr)	1,300	66	2	2,924	13,210	4,564
Virginia State University; Petersburg, Va. (Pu)	3,499	87	57	3,228	9,200	5,310
Virginia Tech; Blacksburg, Va. (Pu)	21,419	63	41	2,792	11,280	4,776
Virginia Union University; Richmond, Va. (Pr)	1,307					3,950
Virginia Wesleyan College; Norfolk/Virginia Beach, Va. (Pr)	1,421	95	68	16,035	16,035	5,750
Washington and Lee University; Lexington, Va. (Pr)	1,740	35	45	19,170	19,170	5,750
WASHINGTON						
Central Washington University; Ellensburg, Wash. (Pu)	7,604	85	54	2,838	10,089	4,821
Cornish College of the Arts; Seattle, Wash. (Pr)	649	79	61	14,900	14,900	5,400
Eastern Washington University; Cheney, Wash. (Pu)	7,149	89	58	2,790	9,594	4,558
Evergreen State College; Olympia, Wash. (Pu)	3,901	87	57	2,856	10,110	5,244
Gonzaga University; Spokane, Wash. (Pr)	2,852	82	55	18,300	18,300	5,680
Heritage College; Toppenish, Wash. (Pr)	664			6,450	6,450	
Lutheran Bible Institute of Seattle; Issaquah, Wash. (Pr)	132		62	5,750	5,750	4,525

Institution name; city, state (type)	Students	Percent Accepted	Women	Tuition In-state	Out-of-state	Room and board
Northwest College; Kirkland, Wash. (Pr)	848	99%	57%	$ 9,672	$ 9,672	$5,030
Pacific Lutheran University; Tacoma, Wash. (Pr)	3,246	82	61	17,728	17,728	5,590
Saint Martin's College; Lacey, Wash. (Pr)	1,224	92	50	15,560	15,560	4,926
Seattle Pacific University; Seattle, Wash. (Pr)	2,692	91	66	16,335	16,335	6,249
Seattle University; Seattle, Wash. (Pr)	3,302	80	60	17,865	17,865	6,318
Trinity Western University; Blaine, Wash. (Pr)	2,379	78	56	10,350	10,350	5,990
University of Puget Sound; Tacoma, Wash. (Pr)	2,619	72	61	22,350	22,350	5,780
University of Washington; Seattle, Wash. (Pu)	25,638	77	52	3,638	12,029	5,844
Walla Walla College; College Place, Wash. (Pr)	1,580	83	49	18,744	18,744	4,176
Washington State University; Pullman, Wash. (Pu)	16,839	84	52	3,351	10,267	4,826
Western Washington University; Bellingham, Wash. (Pu)	10,914	86	56	2,832	10,086	5,100
Whitman College; Walla Walla, Wash. (Pr)	1,424	50	58	22,600	22,600	6,290
Whitworth College; Spokane, Wash. (Pr)	1,771	88	59	15,970	15,970	5,400
WEST VIRGINIA						
Alderson-Broaddus College; Philippi, W.Va. (Pr)	679	70	60	13,740	13,740	5,100
Bethany College; Bethany, W.Va. (Pr)	718	71	46	19,141	19,141	6,909
Bluefield State College; Bluefield, W.Va. (Pu)	2,648	99	60	2,288	5,554	4,120
College of West Virginia; Beckley, W.Va. (Pr)	1,948	100	68			4,748
Concord College; Athens, W.Va. (Pu)	2,955	98	57	2,620	5,762	4,150
Davis & Elkins College; Elkins, W.Va. (Pr)	658	94	56	12,080	12,080	5,330
Fairmont State College; Fairmont, W.Va. (Pu)	6,496	100	56	2,316	5,396	4,084
Glenville State College; Glenville, W.Va. (Pu)	2,198	100	59	4,810	4,810	3,480
Marshall University; Huntington, W.Va. (Pu)	9,621	90	55	2,160	6,364	4,850
Ohio Valley College; Vienna, W.Va. (Pr)	417	45	53	8,380	8,380	4,430
Salem-Teikyo University; Salem, W.Va. (Pr)	659	70	45	12,800	12,800	4,408
Shepherd College; Shepherdstown, W.Va. (Pu)	4,597	94	58	2,430	5,754	4,112
University of Charleston; Charleston, W.Va. (Pr)	1,037	75	67	14,900	14,900	5,930
West Liberty State College; West Liberty, W.Va. (Pu)	2,606	96	55	2,420	5,860	3,340
West Virginia State College; Institute, W.Va. (Pu)	4,530			2,116	5,150	3,550
West Virginia University; Morgantown, W.Va. (Pu)	15,463	94	46	1,994	7,520	5,152
West Virginia University Institute of Technology; Montgomery, W.Va. (Pu)	2,587	100	39	2,646	6,458	4,048
West Virginia Wesleyan College; Buckhannon, W.Va. (Pr)	1,601	84	57	16,800	16,800	4,350
Wheeling Jesuit University; Wheeling, W.Va. (Pr)	1,530			15,000	15,000	5,200
WISCONSIN						
Alverno College; Milwaukee, Wis. (Pr)	1,982	90	100	10,800	10,800	4,250
Beloit College; Beloit, Wis. (Pr)	1,254	67	58	22,184	22,184	5,078
Cardinal Stritch College; Milwaukee, Wis. (Pr)	2,955	70	66	11,000	11,000	4,410
Carroll College; Waukesha, Wis. (Pr)	2,444		66	14,740	14,740	4,600
Carthage College; Kenosha, Wis. (Pr)	2,101	91	58	21,500	21,500	4,810
Concordia University Wisconsin; Mequon, Wis. (Pr)	3,852	82	64	13,610	13,610	5,070
Edgewood College; Madison, Wis. (Pr)	1,520	48	72	12,250	12,250	4,516
Lakeland College; Sheboygan, Wis. (Pr)	3,328	74	61	11,980	11,980	4,860
Lawrence University; Appleton, Wis. (Pr)	1,285	73	54	22,584	22,584	4,983
Marian College of Fond du Lac; Fond du Lac, Wis. (Pr)	1,571	81	67	11,966	11,966	4,364
Marquette University; Milwaukee, Wis. (Pr)	7,496	84	55	18,180	18,180	6,362
Milwaukee Institute of Art and Design; Milwaukee, Wis. (Pr)	646	86	50	16,800	16,800	6,458
Milwaukee School of Engineering; Milwaukee, Wis. (Pr)	2,279	82	18	20,835	20,835	4,845
Mount Mary College; Milwaukee, Wis. (Pr)	1,174	83	99	11,380	11,380	3,970
Mount Senario College; Ladysmith, Wis. (Pr)	829	64	36	12,800	12,800	4,950
Northland College; Ashland, Wis. (Pr)	821	87	59	15,500	15,500	4,610
Ripon College; Ripon, Wis. (Pr)	862	83	53	18,000	18,000	4,400
St. Norbert College; De Pere, Wis. (Pr)	2,033	88	59	16,570	16,570	5,162
Silver Lake College; Manitowoc, Wis. (Pr)	700	48	69	11,150	11,150	4,365
University of Wisconsin-Eau Claire; Eau Claire, Wis. (Pu)	10,101	74	60	3,252	10,780	3,435
University of Wisconsin-Green Bay; Green Bay, Wis. (Pu)	5,334	81	65	2,594	10,122	3,706
University of Wisconsin-La Crosse; La Crosse, Wis. (Pu)	8,487	65	58	2,697	10,122	3,450
University of Wisconsin-Madison; Madison, Wis. (Pu)	29,336	72	53	3,650	12,400	5,250
University of Wisconsin-Milwaukee; Milwaukee, Wis. (Pu)	17,032	82	54	3,741	3,741	3,594
University of Wisconsin-Oshkosh; Oshkosh, Wis. (Pu)	9,295	89	58	2,950	9,606	3,130
University of Wisconsin-Parkside; Kenosha, Wis. (Pu)	4,486		60	2,838	9,120	3,730
University of Wisconsin-Platteville; Platteville, Wis. (Pu)	4,665			2,806	9,068	3,254
University of Wisconsin-River Falls; River Falls, Wis. (Pu)	5,399	74	62	3,137	10,665	3,512
University of Wisconsin-Stevens Point; Stevens Point, Wis. (Pu)	8,400	58	56	3,165	10,693	3,616
University of Wisconsin-Stout; Menomonie, Wis. (Pu)	6,931	81	49	2,724	10,260	3,530
University of Wisconsin-Superior; Superior, Wis. (Pu)	2,314	80	11	2,768	9,050	3,296
University of Wisconsin-Whitewater; Whitewater, Wis. (Pu)	9,537	84	53	3,000	9,113	2,800
Viterbo University; La Crosse, Wis. (Pr)	1,734	89	76	13,350	13,350	4,710
Wisconsin Lutheran College; Milwaukee, Wis. (Pr)	440	93	60	11,960	11,960	4,500
WYOMING						
University of Wyoming; Laramie, Wyo. (Pu)	8,490	97	53	2,166	7,284	4,568

Births to Unmarried Women Level Off During the 1990s

After rising dramatically during the half century from 1940 to 1990, out-of-wedlock childbearing leveled off, or slowed its rate of increase during the 1990s. Between 1940 and 1990, the number of births to unmarried women rose 13-fold, from 89,500 to 1.17 million, with the increase over this period averaging more than 5% per year. During the 1990s, this rate of increase slowed, to about 1% per year.

The birth rate for unmarried women increased more than six times between 1940 and 1990, from 7.1 births per 1,000 unmarried women to 43.8 births. The rise in the birth rate was most rapid during the late 1970s through the 1980s, when the rate increased about 4% per year. Between 1994 and 1999 the rate declined about 6% overall.

Another measure looked at by researchers is the percent of all births to unmarried women, which rose steadily from 1940 (3.8%) to 1994 (32.6%). From 1994 to 1999 there was little change—it was 33% in 1999.

A key factor contributing to the rising numbers of out-of-wedlock births through 1990 was the steep increase in the number of unmarried women of child-bearing age. This was due in part to a change in the overall size of the population, which swelled during the postwar baby boom, and the fact that women and men began postponing marriage from the mid-1960s, a trend that shows no sign of abating.

Source: National Center for Health Statistics, *National Vital Statistics Reports*, vol. 48, no. 16, Oct. 18, 2000.

Births to Unmarried Women, 1940–1999

Year	Number of births to unmarried women	Percent of all births to unmarried women	Birth rate per 1,000 unmarried women 15–44	Birth rate per 1,000 married women 15–44
1999[1]	1,304,594	33.0	43.9	87.3
1998	1,293,567	32.8	44.3	85.7
1997	1,257,444	32.4	44.0	84.3
1996	1,260,306	32.4	44.8	83.7
1995	1,253,976	32.2	45.1	83.7
1990	1,165,384	28.0	43.8	93.2
1980	665,747	18.4	29.4	97.0
1970	398,700	10.7	26.4	121.1
1960	224,300	5.3	21.6	156.6
1950	141,600	4.0	14.1	141.0
1940	89,500	3.8	7.1	—

(—) = not available. 1. Data are preliminary. Figures are based on weighted data rounded to the nearest individual. *Source:* National Center for Health Statistics, *National Vital Statistics Reports*, vol. 48, no. 16, Oct. 18, 2000.

Distribution of Nonmarital Births by Age, 1970 and 1999

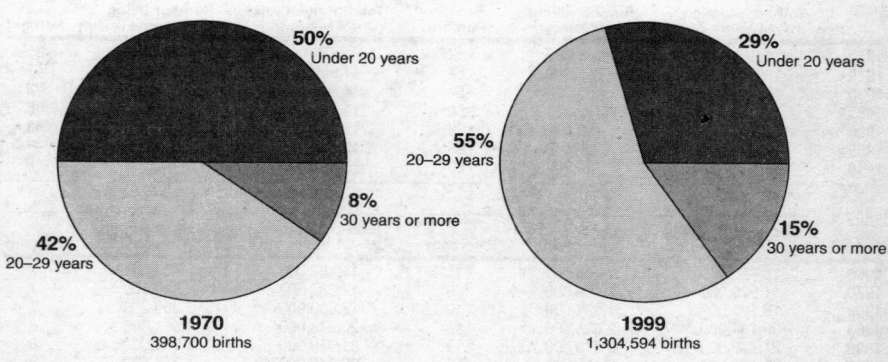

1970
398,700 births

50%
Under 20 years

55%
20–29 years

8%
30 years or more

42%
20–29 years

1999
1,304,594 births

29%
Under 20 years

15%
30 years or more

Source: National Center for Health Statistics, *National Vital Statistics Reports*, vol. 48, no. 16, Oct. 18, 2000.

Teen Birth Rates Continue to Decline

Source: Centers for Disease Control and Prevention, National Center for Health Statistics

The birth rate for U.S. teenagers in 1998 was 51.1 live births per 1,000 women aged 15–19 years, 2% lower than in 1997 and 18% lower than in 1991, when it reached its recent peak. The 1998 rate is close to the 1986 record low of 50.2.

Several factors likely account for the falling teenage birth (and pregnancy) rates. One is changing attitudes toward premarital sex, possibly reflecting the influence of widespread public and private efforts focusing teenagers' attention on the importance of pregnancy prevention through abstinence and responsible behavior. Teenage sexual activity has leveled off according to several national surveys. Also important are increases in condom use and the adoption of the effective injectable and implant contraceptives. Another factor is the long economic expansion in the 1990s, increasing economic opportunity for teenagers (as well as older women). Economic opportunity may have given teenagers a reason to value education and work more highly and to postpone early pregnancy and parenthood. □

Teen Birth Rates in the U.S., Selected Years
(rates per 1,000 females in specified group)

Age	1980	1985	1990	1991	1993	1995	1997	1998
All races								
10–14 years	1.1	1.2	1.4	1.4	1.4	1.3	1.1	1.0
15–19 years	53.0	51.0	59.9	62.1	59.6	56.8	52.3	51.1
White, total								
10–14 years	—	—	0.7	0.8	0.8	0.8	0.7	0.6
15–19 years	—	—	50.8	52.8	51.1	50.1	46.3	45.4
White, non-Hispanic								
10–14 years	0.4	—	0.5	0.5	0.5	0.4	0.4	0.3
15–19 years	41.2	—	42.5	43.4	40.7	39.3	36.0	35.2
Black								
10–14 years	4.3	4.5	4.9	4.8	4.6	4.2	3.3	2.9
15–19 years	97.8	95.4	112.8	115.5	108.6	96.1	88.2	85.4
American Indian[1]								
10–14 years	1.9	1.7	1.6	1.6	1.4	1.8	1.7	1.6
15–19 years	82.2	79.2	81.1	85.0	83.1	78.0	71.8	72.1
Asian/Pacific Islander								
10–14 years	0.3	0.4	0.7	0.8	0.6	0.7	0.5	0.4
15–19 years	26.2	23.8	26.4	27.4	27.0	26.1	23.7	23.1
Hispanic[2]								
10–14 years	1.7	—	2.4	2.4	2.7	2.7	2.3	2.1
15–19 years	82.2	—	100.3	106.7	106.8	106.7	97.4	93.6

1. Includes births to Aleuts and Eskimos. 2. Persons of Hispanic origin may be of any race. *Source:* Centers for Disease Control and Prevention, National Center for Health Statistics. *National Vital Statistics Reports,* vol. 48, no. 6. April 24, 2000.

Young Adults Living at Home, 1960–1998

	Male			Female		
	Total population, 18–24 years old	Number living at home	Percent	Total population, 18–24 years old	Number living at home	Percent
1960	6,842,000	3,583,000	52%	7,876,000	2,750,000	35%
1970	10,398,000	5,641,000	54	11,959,000	4,941,000	41
1980	14,278,000	7,755,000	54	14,844,000	6,336,000	43
1985	13,695,000	8,172,000	60	14,149,000	6,758,000	48
1990	12,450,000	7,232,000	58	12,860,000	6,135,000	48
1995	12,545,000	7,328,000	58	12,613,000	5,896,000	47
1998	12,633,000	7,399,000	59	12,568,000	5,974,000	48

	Male			Female		
	Total population, 25–34 years old	Number living at home	Percent	Total population, 25–34 years old	Number living at home	Percent
1960	10,896,000	1,185,000	11%	11,587,000	853,000	7%
1970	11,929,000	1,129,000	9	12,637,000	829,000	7
1980	18,107,000	1,894,000	10	18,689,000	1,300,000	7
1985	20,184,000	2,685,000	13	20,673,000	1,661,000	8
1990	21,462,000	3,213,000	15	21,779,000	1,774,000	8
1995	20,589,000	3,166,000	15	20,800,000	1,759,000	8
1998	19,526,000	2,845,000	15	19,828,000	1,680,000	8

NOTE: Unmarried college students living in dorms are counted as living at home. *Source:* U.S. Bureau of the Census, *Current Population Reports,* March 1998.

Households,[1] Families, and Married Couples, 1890–1999

	All households		Families		Married couples
Date	Number	Average population per household	Number	Average population per family	Number
June 1890	12,690,000	4.93	—	—	—
April 1930	29,905,000	4.11	—	—	25,174,000
April 1940	34,949,000	3.67	32,166,000	3.76	26,571,000
March 1950	43,554,000	3.37	39,303,000	3.54	34,075,000
March 1960[2]	52,799,000	3.35	45,111,000	3.67	39,254,000
March 1970	63,401,000	3.14	51,586,000	3.58	44,728,000
March 1980	80,776,000	2.76	59,550,000	3.29	49,112,000
March 1990	93,347,000	2.63	66,090,000	3.17	52,317,000
March 1999	103,874,000	2.61	71,535,000	3.18	55,849,000

1. A person or group of persons that live in a housing unit. 2. First year in which figures for Alaska and Hawaii were included. *Source:* U.S. Census Bureau, *Current Population Reports.* From *Statistical Abstract of the United States, 2000.*

Households, 1980–1999

	Households				
	Number			Percent distribution	
Type of household	1980	1990	1999	1990	1999
Total households	80,776,000	93,347,000	103,874,000	100%	100%
Family households	59,550,000	66,090,000	71,535,000	71	69
Married couple family	49,112,000	52,317,000	54,770,000	56	53
Male householder, no spouse present	1,733,000	2,884,000	3,976,000	3	4
Female householder, no spouse present	8,705,000	10,890,000	12,789,000	12	12
Nonfamily households	21,226,000	27,257,000	32,339,000	29	31
Living alone	18,296,000	22,999,000	26,606,000	25	26
Male householder	8,807,000	11,606,000	14,368,000	12	14
Living alone	6,966,000	9,049,000	10,966,000	10	11
Female householder	12,419,000	15,651,000	17,971,000	17	17
Living alone	11,330,000	13,950,000	15,640,000	15	15

Source: U.S. Census Bureau, *Current Population Reports.* From *Statistical Abstract of the United States, 2000.*

Families by Type, Race, and Hispanic Origin, 1999

(In thousands, except as indicated)

		Married couple families				Female family householder[3]				Male family householder,[3] all races
Characteristic	All families	All races[1]	White	Black	His-panic[2]	All races[1]	White	Black	His-panic[2]	
All families	71,535	54,770	48,456	3,975	4,945	12,789	8,526	3,809	1,725	3,976
Without own children under 18	36,922	29,703	26,697	2,005	1,727	4,948	3,416	1,332	551	2,270
With own children under 18	34,613	25,066	21,759	1,971	3,218	7,841	5,110	2,477	1,174	1,706
Average per family with own children under 18	1.86	1.91	1.90	1.93	2.17	1.78	1.70	1.91	2.09	1.54
Marital status of householder:										
Married, spouse present	54,770	54,770	48,456	3,975	4,945	—	—	—	—	—
Married, spouse absent	2,521	—	—	—	—	1,966	1,276	609	409	555
Widowed	2,648	—	—	—	—	2,209	1,657	480	205	439
Divorced	6,008	—	—	—	—	4,620	3,602	874	469	1,387
Never married	5,589	—	—	—	—	3,994	1,991	1,846	643	1,595

(—) = not applicable. 1. Includes other races not shown separately. 2. Persons of Hispanic origin may be of any race. 3. No spouse present. *Source:* U.S. Census Bureau, unpublished data. From *Statistical Abstract of the United States, 2000.*

Unmarried Couples, 1980–1999

Presence of children and age of householder	1980	1985	1990	1995	1999
Unmarried couples, total	1,589,000	1,983,000	2,856,000	3,668,000	4,486,000
No children under 15 years old	1,159,000	1,380,000	1,966,000	2,349,000	2,981,000
Some children under 15 years old	431,000	603,000	891,000	1,319,000	1,505,000
Under 25 years old	411,000	425,000	596,000	742,000	824,000
25 to 44 years old	837,000	1,203,000	1,775,000	2,188,000	2,554,000
45 to 64 years old	221,000	239,000	358,000	558,000	888,000
65 years and over	119,000	116,000	127,000	180,000	220,000

Source: U.S. Census Bureau, *Current Population Reports.* From *Statistical Abstract of the United States, 2000.*

Coresident Grandparents and Grandchildren

Source: U.S. Census Bureau, *Current Population Reports*, P23-198, May 1999

Web: www.census.gov/population/www/socdemo/grandparents.html

Researchers first began to notice an increase in the number of grandchildren living in grandparent-maintained households in the early 1990s. The U.S. Census Bureau's Current Population Report *Marital Status and Living Arrangements: March 1992* noted that the number of children under 18 living in grandparent-maintained households had increased from 2.2 million in 1970, to 2.3 million in 1980, to 3.3 million in 1992. In 1970, a little over 3 percent of all children under age 18 were living in a home maintained by their grandparents. By 1992, this percentage had increased to nearly 5 percent. More recent data show that this trend has continued. In 1997, 3.9 million children were living in homes maintained by their grandparents—5.5 percent of all children under 18.

In most cases (51%), these households have both a grandmother and a grandfather present living with the children. In most other cases (43% of the total), the household is maintained by a grandmother only, with no spouse present. Only 6% of such families are maintained by a grandfather alone. Thus coresident grandmothers outnumber coresident grandfathers five to three. The reasons for this discrepancy may have to do with the fact that women in general are longer lived than men, and they are also more likely than men to assume a caregiving role.

Other data show that substantial increases in the number of children living in households maintained by grandparents appear to have occurred regardless of the presence or absence of the grandchildren's parents. Between 1970 and 1992, these increases were greatest among children with only one parent in the household. Between 1992 and 1997, the greatest growth occurred among grandchildren living with grandparents with no parent present.[1] The increase in grandchildren in these "skipped generation" living arrangements has been attributed to a variety of factors, including the growth in drug use among parents, teen pregnancy, divorce, the rapid rise of single-parent households, child abuse and neglect, and incarceration of parents.[2]

---

1. Fuller-Thomson, Minkler, and Driver refer to skipped-generation households as those composed of grandparents and their grandchildren with neither of the child's parents present. Fuller-Thomson, Esme, Meredith Minkler, and Diane Driver. 1997. "A Profile of Grandparents Raising Grandchildren in the United States." *The Gerontologist* 37: 406–411. 2. For a more thorough discussion of these causes see Minkler, M. 1998. "Intergenerational Households Headed by Grandparents: Demographic and Sociological Contexts." In Generations United (eds.) *Grandparents and Other Relatives Raising Children: Background Papers from Generations United's Expert Symposiums.* Washington, D.C.: Generations United.

Grandchildren Living with Their Grandparents

Percent of children under 18

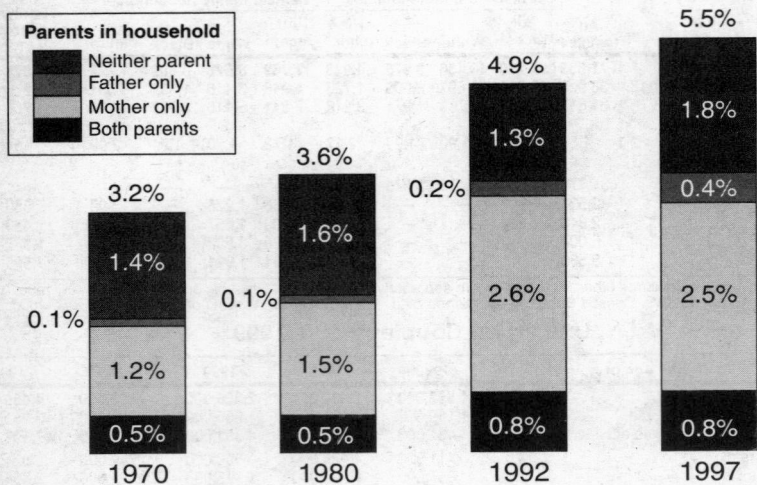

Source: U.S. Bureau of the Census, 1970 and 1980 censuses and 1992 and 1997 Current Population Surveys as reported in *Marital Status and Living Arrangements: March 1992* and *Marital Status and Living Arrangements: March 1997*.

Adoption Trends

Background

Although adoption is mentioned in the legal codes and writings of many ancient peoples, including the Romans and Hebrews, no such laws existed in England or her colonies prior to the middle of the 19th century. Instead, indigent children were generally sent to public institutions known as almshouses until the age of 6 or 7, when they could be "put out" as indentured servants or apprentices. Families also sometimes took in children informally, especially in rural areas to help on the farm.

In the United States, these practices worked well enough until the early 19th century, when changes in economic conditions and the size of the population produced numbers of children the system couldn't cope with. At the same time, largely through the efforts of certain social reformers, society's attitude toward adoption began to change. Private agencies were established to place children in homes where they would be treated as members of the family rather than servants. And families who took in children increasingly petitioned state legislatures for private adoption acts to ensure the legal status and inheritance rights of adopted children.

Finally, as a result of pressure from individual families and to provide better care for destitute children, the state legislatures were prompted to take action. Between 1851 and 1873, 17 states enacted adoption legislation, and by 1929 all states had such laws. (England did not enact general adoption laws until 1926.) Under these new statutes, adoptions had to be approved by a judge, after which the adopted child assumed the same rights accorded any natural, legitimate child of the petitioners.

Adoption in the 20th Century

Despite the legislation, foundling homes continued to exist, and legal adoption was still relatively infrequent until about the 1920s. Many people feared that poor, abandoned, or illegitimate children were doomed to grow into troubled adults. Infants in particular were undesirable because of high mortality rates and the lack of readily available breast milk.

Following World War I, however, the demand for babies began to grow. This was partly a response to the sharp drop in population caused by the war and the influenza epidemic of 1918, and partly also due to the development of a successful feeding formula. The number of adoptions exploded, and "closed" adoptions became the norm. In closed adoptions, the identities of the birth parents and adoptive parents were kept a secret because, it was thought, this helped the child bond to its new family and avoid the stigma of illegitimacy.

By the mid-1950s the demand for healthy infants began to exceed the number available. Agencies began screening prospective parents more selectively, and by 1975 many had stopped accepting applications for nondisabled white children altogether. Other agencies were obliged to put prospective parents on waiting lists, usually for an average of three to five years. Factors contributing to the decline in available infants included the increased availability of effective contraception, a rise in the abortion rate following *Roe* v. *Wade* in 1973, and an increase in the numbers of unmarried women keeping their babies rather than giving them up for adoption.

It was also during the 1970s that "open" adoption, in which adoptive and birth parents were known to each other, became more accepted. A growing number of prospective parents adopted through private placement, contacting a birth mother directly through an advertisement or through the services of a lawyer or other professional specializing in adoption.

More Recent Trends

At the end of the 20th century, infertile couples and single people have increasingly turned to transracial and international adoptions, as well as new advanced medical techniques for treating infertility and providing alternative methods of reproduction. Meanwhile, the number of older special needs children waiting adoption has skyrocketed. These children often come from backgrounds of abuse and neglect, and finding appropriate placements for them is one of the most pressing concerns in child welfare today.

Source: Columbia Encyclopedia, 6th Edition. Web: www.infoplease.com. Sokoloff, Burton Z., "Antecedents of American Adoption" in *The Future of Children: Adoption*, vol. 3, no. 1. (David and Lucile Packard Foundation: Los Altos, Calif.) Spring 1993. Web: www.futureofchildren.org/adp/ADP_02.PDF.

Some Adoption Statistics:

- In 1992, the last year for which total adoption statistics were available, 127,441 children of all races and nationalities were adopted in the United States.
- Of the adoptions that occurred in 1992, 42% were by a stepparent or relative; 15.5% were adopted from foster care; 5% were adopted from other countries by U.S. families.
- States with the highest number of adoptions are the states with larger populations. In 1992, there were 14,722 adoptions in California, 9,570 in New York, 8,235 in Texas, and 6,839 in Florida.
- According to the most recent estimates, which include international adoptions, 8% of adoptions were transracial.
- International adoptions have increased dramatically over the last decade. According to the U.S. State Department, in 1992, 6,472 children were adopted from abroad. In 1999, the number had increased to 16,396.
- According to the U.S. Department of Health and Human Services, in 1999, 33% of children adopted from foster care were adopted by a single parent, the overwhelming majority of which were single women (31%).
- It is estimated that about 1 million children in the United States live with adoptive parents, and that between 2% and 4% of U.S. families include an adopted child.

Source: National Adoption Information Clearinghouse. Web: www.calib.com/naic/. U.S. State Department. Web: http://travel.state.gov/children's_issues.html. U.S. Dept. of Health and Human Services. Web: http://www.acf.dhhs.gov/programs/cb/.

Historical Living Arrangements of Children

(in thousands)

Living arrangements	Year										
	1880[1]	1900[1]	1910[1]	1920[1]	1940[1]	1950[1]	1960[1]	1970[2]	1980[2]	1990[2]	1996[3]
Children	22,027	30,784	34,997	39,535	40,435	46,506	64,586	69,162	63,427	64,137	71,494
Living with:											
Two parents	18,359	25,916	29,880	34,122	34,404	40,365	55,885	58,939	48,624	46,503	50,685
One parent	2,332	3,172	3,389	3,742	4,178	4,144	6,644	8,200	12,466	15,867	18,165
Mother only	1,770	2,310	2,470	2,588	3,186	3,452	5,820	7,452	11,406	13,874	16,340
Father only	562	862	919	1,154	992	692	824	748	1,060	1,993	1,825
Neither parent	1,337	1,695	1,729	1,672	1,852	1,998	2,057	2,023	2,337	1,767	2,644
Percent living with:											
Two parents	83.3	84.2	85.4	86.3	85.1	86.8	86.5	85.2	76.7	72.5	70.9
One parent	10.6	10.3	9.7	9.5	10.3	8.9	10.3	11.9	19.7	24.7	25.4
Mother only	8.0	7.5	7.1	6.5	7.9	7.4	9.0	10.8	18.0	21.6	22.9
Father only	2.6	2.8	2.6	2.9	2.5	1.5	1.3	1.1	1.7	3.1	2.6
Neither parent	6.1	5.5	4.9	4.2	4.6	4.3	3.2	2.9	3.7	2.8	3.7

1. *Source:* Data for these years come from the Public Use Micro Samples collected and made available by IPUMS, Historical Census Projects. 2. *Source:* U.S. Census Bureau, Current Population Survey, Historical Table CH-1. 3. *Source:* U.S. Census Bureau, 1996 Survey of Income and Program Participation, Wave 2.

Children in Foster Care

	Percent	Number		Percent	Number
Total		**568,000**	**Race/ethnicity**		
			White	36%	203,001
Ages			Black	42	239,516
Under 1 year	4%	20,180	Hispanic[1]	15	84,924
1–5 years	25	140,013	American Indian/Alaskan Native	2	8,910
6–10 years	26	149,595	Asian/Pacific Islander	1	6,304
11–15 years	28	159,912	Unknown/unable to determine	4	25,346
16–18 years	16	88,374	**Gender**		
19 years and over	2	9,926	Male	52	295,547
			Female	48	272,453

NOTE: Data as of Oct. 2000. Percentages may not add up to 100% and numbers may not add up to totals due to rounding. 1. Hispanic can be of any race. *Source:* U.S. Dept. of Health and Human Services, Admin. for Children and Families, Adoption and Foster Care Analysis and Reporting System (AFCARS) Report #4. Web: www.acf.dhhs.gov/programs/cb.

Child Abuse and Neglect

Based on reports alleging child abuse and neglect that were referred for investigation by the respective child-protective services agency in each state. The reporting period may be either calendar year or fiscal year.

Item	1990		1995		1997		1998	
	Number	Percent	Number	Percent	Number	Percent	Number	Percent
Types of substantiated maltreatment								
Victims, total[1, 2]	690,658	—	970,285	—	798,358	—	861,602	—
Neglect	338,770	49.1%	507,015	52.3%	436,630	54.7%	461,274	53.5%
Physical abuse	186,801	27.0	237,840	24.5	195,517	24.5	195,891	22.7
Sexual abuse	119,506	17.3	122,964	12.7	97,425	12.2	99,278	11.5
Emotional maltreatment	45,621	6.6	42,051	4.3	49,146	6.2	51,618	6.0
Medical neglect	n.a.	n.a.	28,541	2.9	18,866	2.4	20,338	2.4
Sex of victim								
Victims, total[2]	794,101	100.0	809,634	100.0	669,057	100.0	760,438	100.0
Male	357,367	45.0	381,075	47.1	316,842	47.4	359,568	47.3
Female	405,409	51.1	425,193	52.5	349,606	52.3	388,187	51.0
Age of victim								
Victims, total[2]	807,965	100.0	808,575	100.0	668,059	100.0	767,749	100.0
1 year and younger	106,507	13.2	103,335	12.8	83,921	12.6	105,097	13.7
2 to 5 years old	192,018	23.8	215,303	26.6	167,658	25.1	187,522	24.4
6 to 9 years old	175,609	21.7	195,400	24.2	166,718	25.0	193,316	25.2
10 to 13 years old	150,507	18.6	154,682	19.1	130,840	19.6	151,126	19.7
14 to 17 years old	116,015	14.4	121,548	15.0	97,348	14.6	111,894	14.6
18 years and over	5,464	0.7	7,506	0.9	3,063	0.5	4,210	0.5

NOTE: n.a. = not available. (—) = not applicable. 1. More than one type of maltreatment may be substantiated per child. Therefore, totals for this category will add up to more than 100 percent. Victim totals and maltreatment types are based on subset of states that reported both the number of child victims and maltreatment incidences by type for that year. 2. Includes other and unknown not shown separately. *Source: Statistical Abstract of the United States, 2000.*

Child Care for Children Under Six Years Old, 1995

	Children		Type of nonparental arrangement				
Characteristic	Number (1,000s)	Percent distribution	Total[1]	Relative care	Nonrelative care	Center-based program[2]	No nonparental arrangement
Total	21,421	100%	60%	21%	18%	31%	40%
Race/ethnicity							
White, non-Hispanic	13,996	65	62	18	21	33	38
Black, non-Hispanic	3,344	6	66	31	12	33	34
Hispanic	2,838	13	46	23	12	17	54
Other	1,243	6	58	25	13	28	42
Mother's employment status[3]							
35 or more hours per week	7,101	34	88	33	32	39	12
Less than 35 hours per week	4,034	19	75	30	26	35	25
Looking for work	1,635	8	42	16	4	25	58
Not in labor force	8,354	40	32	7	6	22	68
Household income							
Less than $10,001	4,502	21	50	22	10	25	50
$10,001 to $20,000	2,909	14	54	27	12	24	46
$20,001 to $30,000	3,385	16	53	22	14	25	47
$30,001 to $40,000	3,047	14	60	23	20	27	40
$40,001 to $50,000	2,304	11	63	19	22	32	37
$50,001 to $75,000	3,063	14	74	20	26	40	26
$75,001 or more	2,211	10	77	14	30	49	23

NOTES: Estimates are based on children under 6 years old who have yet to enter kindergarten. Based on 14,064 interviews from a sample survey of the civilian, noninstitutional population in households with telephones; see source for details. 1. Columns do not add to total because some children participated in more than one type of nonparental arrangement. 2. Center-based programs include day-care centers, head-start programs, preschool, prekindergartens, and other early childhood programs. 3. Children without mothers are not included. *Source:* U.S. Dept. of Education, National Center for Education Statistics, *Statistics in Brief,* Oct. 1995 (NCES 95-824).

Breast-Feeding by Selected Characteristics of Mother, 1972–1994

Breast-feeding, which has gone in and out of fashion over the decades, nearly doubled between 1972 and 1994 and continues to be on the rise. Breast milk contains antibodies that help protect babies against illnesses and allergies, and is considered by doctors to be more beneficial than formula.

Selected characteristics of mother	Percent of babies breast-fed							
	1972–74	1975–77	1978–80	1981–83	1984–86	1987–89	1990–92	1993–94
Total	30.1%	36.7%	47.5%	58.1%	54.5%	52.3%	54.2%	58.1%
Race								
White, non-Hispanic	32.5	38.9	53.2	64.3	59.7	58.3	59.1	61.2
Black, non-Hispanic	12.5	16.8	19.6	26.0	22.9	21.0	22.9	27.5
Hispanic[1]	33.1	42.9	46.3	52.8	58.9	51.3	58.8	67.4
Education[2]								
No high school diploma or GED[3]	14.0	19.4	27.6	31.4	36.8	30.0	38.6	43.0
High school diploma or GED[3]	25.0	33.6	40.2	54.3	46.7	46.6	46.0	51.2
Some college, no bachelor's degree	35.2	43.5	63.2	66.7	66.1	57.8	60.7	65.9
Bachelor's degree or higher	65.5	66.9	71.3	83.2	75.3	79.2	80.8	80.6
Geographic region								
Northeast	29.9	34.7	49.3	68.2	55.3	49.9	54.0	56.7
Midwest	22.3	30.9	34.4	46.0	50.9	50.4	51.6	49.7
South	30.6	33.1	49.5	57.9	45.3	42.5	43.6	49.7
West	47.1	54.5	66.6	69.9	70.9	69.1	70.5	79.3
Age at baby's birth								
Under 20 years	17.0	22.1	31.4	31.0	30.6	26.2	35.2	45.3
20–24 years	28.7	33.5	44.7	50.8	50.2	46.7	44.7	50.9
25–29 years	38.7	45.9	53.6	62.2	59.8	57.1	56.5	55.9
30–44 years	43.1	47.5	55.2	73.1	65.9	65.3	67.5	71.1

NOTE: Years indicate babies' birth year. Based on household interviews of samples of women ages 15–44. 1. Hispanic may be of any race. 2. For women 22–44 years of age. Education is as of year of interview. 3. General equivalency diploma. *Source:* Centers for Disease Control and Prevention, National Center for Health Statistics, National Survey of Family Growth. From *Health, United States, 2000.*

The Marrying Kind

Vermont's year-old civil-union law is making the state the prime gay and lesbian honeymoon spot

By TAMMERLIN DRUMMOND TIME

Karen Kunz and Angela French had both been married once before, to men. In April 2001, after running the Boston Marathon, Kunz, 45, a nurse from Chandler, Ariz., and French, 42, a graduate student, made a symbolic pilgrimage to Vermont to wed each other. Tears streaming down their faces, the women, who have known each other for 18 years, exchanged rings; the Rev. Peter Denny proclaimed their union "the equivalent of marriage." That may be true in Vermont, but Arizona, where Kunz and French live with their nine-year-old daughter, doesn't recognize same-sex unions. They made the trip, says French, "because we wanted people to know how much it means for gay couples to get this kind of support."

Vermont in the Vanguard

In July 2000, Vermont became the first state in the nation to recognize civil unions between two people of the same sex: marriages in virtually every legal respect but name. Kunz and French are among the 3,000 gays and lesbians who have come to Vermont to tie the knot in the first year since the law went into effect. When the law was adopted, Vermont became the focus of a national debate over gay marriage. Opponents warned that it would become "a gay state," and that same-sex marriage would sweep the country as homosexuals in other states demanded the same rights.

None of that has happened. Instead, Vermont is enjoying a modest boomlet in gay tourism: 80% of the 2,000 gay civil-union licenses granted between July 2001 and May 2001, have been issued to out-of-state residents. (In that time, about 5,000 traditional marriage licenses have been granted.) Inns and B and Bs advertise civil-union packages on gay and lesbian websites. K. C. David, CEO of an online concierge called gayweddings.com, has booked travel arrangements for couples from Russia, Indonesia, and Australia who are planning civil unions in Vermont. "It's snowballing," he says.

In economic terms, it's barely a snowflake. The gay and lesbian couples coming to Vermont to wed are but a tiny fraction of the 4 million visitors the state attracts each year. What's significant is that in some Vermont towns, civil unions have become a part of the fabric of everyday life. In Brattleboro, a bucolic community of 12,000 residents in liberal southern Vermont, there were 292 civil unions from July to December 2000—the same number as there were straight marriages for the whole year.

Brattleboro is one of Vermont's more liberal enclaves. Conservative farming communities, by contrast, saw a ferocious backlash shortly after the law's passage. Thousands of "Take Back Vermont" signs sprouted on lawns. Half a dozen town clerks quit rather than grant licenses to gay couples. Five state legislators who supported civil unions were defeated at the polls. But other civil-union proponents, such as Governor Howard Dean, survived, and the Take Back Vermont campaign eventually fizzled. Efforts by opponents to overturn the law have failed.

"Defense-of-Marriage" Laws

The national "Defense of Marriage Act" (Public Law 104-199, Sept. 21, 1996) prohibits federal benefits for spouses in same-sex marriages and guarantees that no state shall be required to legally recognize same-sex unions. Thirty-two states specifically prohibit same-sex unions.

Alabama	Indiana	North Carolina
Alaska	Iowa	North Dakota
Arizona	Kansas	Oklahoma
Arkansas	Kentucky	Pennsylvania
California	Louisiana	South Carolina
Delaware	Maine	South Dakota
Florida	Michigan	Tennessee
Georgia	Minnesota	Utah
Hawaii	Mississippi	Virginia
Idaho	Missouri	Washington
Illinois	Montana	

Source: Wisconsin Policy Library, La Follette Institute for Public Affairs. Web: portal.lafollette.wisc.edu.

The National Debate Continues

Nationally, the battle over gay marriage continues. In May 2001 seven gay and lesbian couples in Massachusetts filed a lawsuit for the right to marry. So far, 32 states have passed "defense-of-marriage laws," which state that same-sex marriages sanctioned elsewhere are null and void. Yet even though the licenses are worthless in their home states, for many gay couples making it legal in Vermont is better than nothing at all. "You wait all your life for something like that," says Vivienne Armstrong, a nurse from Dallas who has been with her partner Louise Young for 30 years. "We would have crawled to Vermont."

For some, marital bliss may be short-lived. No one in Vermont has yet filed for dissolution, but town clerks and local attorneys are already getting calls asking how to terminate a civil union. As it turns out, that's harder than getting hitched. Though residency isn't required for a civil union, it is to get out of one. That's a six months' stay in Vermont for at least one partner. But couples in the throes of marital bliss rarely bother to read the fine print. □

Gender of Sexual Partners in the United States

(sexually active only)

	Same gender		Both genders		Opposite genders	
	Men	Women	Men	Women	Men	Women
1988	2.3%	0.2%	0.3%	0.0%	97.4%	99.8%
1989	1.4	1.2	0.3	0.4	98.3	98.4
1990	1.1	0.5	0.9	0.0	98.0	99.5
1991	2.0	0.3	0.7	0.1	97.3	99.6
1993	1.8	1.8	0.3	0.4	97.9	97.8
1994	2.1	2.1	0.5	0.4	97.5	97.5
1996	3.5	2.1	0.6	0.9	96.0	97.0

Source: General Social Survey (GSS), National Opinion Research Center, University of Chicago, 1996.

Key Events in the Women's Rights Movement

1848 The first women's rights convention is held in Seneca Falls, New York. A Declaration of Sentiments, which outlines grievances and sets the agenda for the women's rights movement, is signed by 68 women and 32 men.

1850 The first National Women's Rights Convention takes place in Worcester, Mass., attracting more than 1,000 participants. National conventions are held yearly (except for 1857) through 1860.

1869 In May, Susan B. Anthony and Elizabeth Cady Stanton form the National Woman Suffrage Association. Its primary goal is to achieve voting rights for women by means of a congressional amendment to the Constitution.

In November Lucy Stone, Henry Blackwell, and others form the American Woman Suffrage Association, which focuses exclusively on gaining voting rights for women through amendments to individual state constitutions. In December the territory of Wyoming passes the first women's suffrage law. The following year, women begin serving on juries in the territory.

1890 The National Woman Suffrage Association and the American Woman Suffrage Association merge to form the National American Woman Suffrage Association (NAWSA). As the movement's mainstream organization, NAWSA wages state-by-state campaigns to obtain voting rights for women.

1893 Colorado is the first state to adopt an amendment granting women the right to vote. Utah and Idaho follow suit in 1896, Washington State in 1910, California in 1911, Oregon, Kansas, and Arizona in 1912, Alaska and Illinois in 1913, Montana and Nevada in 1914, New York in 1917, Michigan, South Dakota, and Oklahoma in 1918.

1896 The National Association of Colored Women is formed, bringing together more than 100 black women's clubs. Leaders in the black women's club movement include Josephine St. Pierre Ruffin, Mary Church Terrell, and Anna Julia Cooper.

1913 Alice Paul and Lucy Burns form the Congressional Union to work toward the passage of a federal amendment to give women the vote. The group is later renamed the National Women's Party. Members picket the White House and practice other forms of civil disobedience.

1919 The federal woman suffrage amendment, originally written by Susan B. Anthony and introduced in Congress in 1878, is passed by the House of Representatives and the Senate. It is then sent to the states for ratification.

1920 On Aug. 26, the 19th Amendment to the Constitution, granting women the right to vote, is signed into law.

1921 Margaret Sanger founds the American Birth Control League, which evolves into the Planned Parenthood Federation of America in 1942.

1936 The federal law prohibiting the dissemination of contraceptive information through the mail is modified, and birth control information is no longer classified as obscene. Throughout the 1940s and 1950s, birth control advocates are engaged in numerous legal suits.

1961 President John F. Kennedy establishes the President's Commission on the Status of Women and appoints Eleanor Roosevelt as chairwoman. The report issued by the commission in 1963 documents substantial discrimination against women in the workplace and urges reform, including fair hiring practices, paid maternity leave, and affordable child care.

1963 Betty Friedan publishes her highly influential book *The Feminine Mystique,* which becomes a best-seller and galvanizes the modern women's rights movement.

In June Congress passes the Equal Pay Act, making it illegal for employers to pay a woman less than what a man would receive for the same job.

1964 Title VII of the Civil Rights Act bars discrimination in employment on the basis of race and sex. At the same time it establishes the Equal Employment Opportunity Commission (EEOC) to investigate complaints and impose penalties.

1965 In *Griswold* v. *Connecticut,* the Supreme Court strikes down the one remaining state law prohibiting the use of contraceptives by married couples.

1966 The National Organization for Women (NOW) is founded. The largest women's rights group in the United States, NOW seeks to end sexual discrimination by means of legislative lobbying, litigation, and public demonstrations.

1967 Executive Order 11375 expands President Lyndon Johnson's affirmative action policy of 1965 to cover discrimination based on gender. As a result, federal agencies and contractors must take active measures to ensure that women as well as minorities enjoy the same educational and employment opportunities as white males.

1968 The EEOC rules that sex-segregated help wanted ads in newspapers are illegal. This ruling is upheld in 1973 by the Supreme Court, opening the way for women to apply for higher-paying jobs hitherto open only to men.

1969 California becomes the first state to adopt a "no fault" divorce law, which allows couples to divorce by mutual consent. By 1985 every state has adopted a similar law. Laws are also passed regarding the equal division of common property.

1971 *Ms.* magazine is first published as a sample insert in *New York* magazine; 300,000 copies are sold out in 8 days. The first regular issue is published in July 1972. The magazine becomes the major forum for feminist voices and turns cofounder and editor Gloria Steinem into an icon of the modern feminist movement.

In *Eisenstadt* v. *Baird* the Supreme Court rules that the right to privacy includes an unmarried person's right to use contraceptives.

1972 The Equal Rights Amendment (ERA) is passed by Congress and sent to the states for ratification. Originally drafted by Alice Paul in 1923, the amendment reads: "Equality of rights under the law shall not be denied or abridged by the United States or by any State on account of sex." The amendment died in 1982 when it failed to achieve ratification by a minimum of 38 states.

Title IX of the Education Amendments bans sex discrimination in schools. As a result, the enrollment of women in athletics programs and professional schools increases dramatically.

1973 As a result of *Roe* v. *Wade*, the Supreme Court establishes a woman's legal right to abortion, overriding the antiabortion laws of many states.

1974 The Equal Credit Opportunity Act prohibits discrimination in consumer credit practices on the basis of sex, race, marital status, religion, national origin, age, or receipt of public assistance.

1978 The Pregnancy Discrimination Act bans employment discrimination against pregnant women.

1984 EMILY's List (Early Money Is Like Yeast) is established as a financial network for pro-choice Democratic women running for national political office. The organization makes a significant impact on the increasing numbers of women elected to Congress.

1986 In *Meritor Savings Bank* v. *Vinson*, the Supreme Court finds that sexual harassment is a form of illegal job discrimination.

1994 The Violence against Women Act tightens federal penalties for sex offenders, funds services for victims of rape and domestic violence, and provides for special training of police officers.

Domestic Violence

Type of victimization over lifetime	Percent		Number	
	Women	Men	Women	Men
Rape	7.7%	0.3%	7,753,669	278,244
Physical assault	22.1	7.4	22,254,037	6,863,352
Rape and/or physical assault	24.8	7.6	24,972,856	7,048,848
Stalking	4.8	0.6	4,833,456	556,488
Total victimized	25.5	7.9	25,677,735	7,327,092

Survey consisted of telephone interviews with a nationally representative sample of 8,000 U.S. women and 8,000 men. **Definitions:** Rape includes completed or attempted forced vaginal, oral, or anal sex. Physical assault includes a range of behaviors from slapping and hitting to using a gun. Stalking involves repeated acts of harassment and intimidation with the victim reporting a high level of fear. *Source:* National Violence Against Women Survey, National Institute of Justice and Centers for Disease Control, July 2000.

The Wage Gap

Source: National Women's Law Center

The wage gap is a statistical indicator often used as an index of the status of women's earnings relative to men's. It is also used to compare the earnings of other races and ethnicities to those of white males, a group generally not subject to race- or sex-based discrimination. The wage gap is expressed as a percentage (e.g., in 1999, women earned 72% as much as men) and is calculated by dividing the median annual earnings for women by the median annual earnings for men.

The Equal Pay Act was signed in 1963, making it illegal for employers to pay unequal wages to men and women who hold the same job and do the same work. At the time of the EPA's passage, women earned just 58 cents for every dollar earned by men.

By 1999, nearly 40 years later, that rate has only increased to 72 cents, an improvement of less than half a penny a year. Minority women fare the worst. African-American women earn just 65 cents to every dollar earned by white men, and for Hispanic women that figure drops to merely 52 cents per dollar.

The wage gap between women and men cuts across a wide spectrum of occupations. The Bureau of Labor Statistics reported in 1999 that women physicians earned 62.5% of the median weekly wages of male physicians, and women in sales occupations earned just 59.9% of the wages of men in equivalent positions. And women in the construction industry earned only 74.1% of what their male counterparts earned.

Women's Earnings as a Percentage of Men's, 1951–1999

(for year-round full-time work)

Year	Percent	Year	Percent	Year	Percent	Year	Percent	Year	Percent
1951	63.9%	1961	59.2%	1971	59.5%	1981	59.2%	1991	69.9%
1952	63.9	1962	59.3	1972	57.9	1982	61.7	1992	70.8
1953	63.9	1963	58.9	1973	56.6	1983	63.6	1993	71.5
1954	63.9	1964	59.1	1974	58.8	1984	63.7	1994	72.0
1955	63.9	1965	59.9	1975	58.8	1985	64.6	1995	71.4
1956	63.3	1966	57.6	1976	60.2	1986	64.3	1996	73.8
1957	63.8	1967	57.8	1977	58.9	1987	65.2	1997	74.2
1958	63.0	1968	58.2	1978	59.4	1988	66.0	1998	73.2
1959	61.3	1969	58.9	1979	59.7	1989	68.7	1999	72.2
1960	60.7	1970	59.4	1980	60.2	1990	71.6		

Source: U.S. Women's Bureau.

The Wage Gap, by Gender and Race

(median annual earnings of black men and women, Hispanic men and women, and white women as a percentage of white men's median annual earnings)

Year	White men	Black men	Hispanic men	White women	Black women	Hispanic women
1970	100%	69.0%	n.a.	58.7%	48.2%	n.a.
1975	100	74.3	72.1%	57.5	55.4	49.3%
1980	100	70.7	70.8	58.9	55.7	50.5
1985	100	69.7	68.0	63.0	57.1	52.1
1990	100	73.1	66.3	69.4	62.5	54.3
1992	100	72.6	63.3	70.0	64.0	55.4
1994	100	75.1	64.3	71.6	63.0	55.6
1995	100	75.9	63.3	71.2	64.2	53.4
1996	100	80.0	63.9	73.3	65.1	56.6
1997	100	75.1	61.4	71.9	62.6	53.9
1998	100	74.9	61.6	72.6	62.6	53.1
1999	100	80.6	61.6	71.6	65.0	52.1

Source: National Committee on Pay Equity.

20 Leading Occupations of Employed Women

(2000 annual averages)

Occupations	(in thousands) Total employed (women)	(in thousands) Total employed (men and women)	Percent women	Women's median usual weekly earnings[1]	Ratio of women's earnings to men's earnings
Total, 16 years and over	**62,915**	**135,208**	**46.5%**	**$491**	**76.0%**
Sales workers, retail, and personal services	4,306	6,782	63.5	301	55.8
Secretaries	2,594	2,623	98.9	450	n.a.
Managers and administrators, n.e.c.[2]	2,418	7,797	31.0	733	66.3
Cashiers	2,277	2,939	77.5	276	88.2
Sales supervisors and proprietors	1,989	4,937	40.3	485	69.8
Registered nurses	1,959	2,111	97.8	782	87.9
Elementary school teachers	1,814	2,177	83.3	701	81.5
Nursing aides, orderlies, and attendants	1,784	1,983	90.0	333	88.1
Bookkeepers, accounting, and auditing clerks	1,584	1,719	92.1	478	88.7
Receptionists	984	1,017	96.8	388	n.a.
Sales workers, other commodities[3, 4]	949	1,428	66.5	319	69.3
Accountants and auditors	903	1,592	56.7	690	72.4
Cooks	899	2,076	43.3	290	89.5
Investigators and adjusters, excluding insurance	833	1,097	75.9	459	82.6
Janitors and cleaners	811	2,233	36.3	309	83.1
Secondary school teachers	764	1,319	57.9	741	88.6
Hairdressers and cosmetologists	748	820	91.2	339	n.a.
General office clerks	722	864	83.6	430	91.3
Managers, food serving and lodging establishments	677	1,446	46.8	475	73.0
Teachers' aides	646	710	91.0	338	n.a.

NOTE: n.a. = not available. Median not available where base is less than 50,000 male workers. 1. Wage and salary for full-time workers. 2. Not elsewhere classified. 3. Included in sales workers, personal, and retail services. 4. Includes foods, drugs, health, and other commodities. Source: U.S. Dept. of Labor, Bureau of Labor Statistics.

Courting a Sleeping Giant

Hispanics have yet to flex their political muscle

By KAREN TUMULTY TIME

The spirit of Cinco de Mayo wasn't the only thing that inspired George W. Bush to deliver his weekly radio address in Spanish on May 5, 2001. His strategists have been doing the math, and it goes like this: unless Bush raises his marks with minorities—particularly Hispanics—he could lose the 2004 election by 3.5 million votes. By next year, Hispanics will be the dominant ethnic group in at least 15 additional House districts; and every state slated for a new seat in Congress has a growing Hispanic population to thank for it.

The biggest political news of the 2000 Census was that Hispanics—more than half of them tracing their roots to Mexico—have become the largest minority group in the United States, surpassing African Americans at least six years sooner than expected. Where that's happening is turning out to be as surprising as how fast. Of the congressional districts that saw the biggest increases in their Latino populations over the past decade, not a single one is in a state along the Mexican border. Rural areas saw huge growth in Hispanic populations, but so did cities and suburbs. By the end of this year, four of the eight largest U.S. cities may have Hispanic mayors.

Strength in Numbers?

But while that means that politicians in places as diverse as Las Vegas and Jasper County, S.C., are courting these constituents as never before, Hispanic political clout still lags far behind the numbers—and will for perhaps a generation to come, Latino leaders fear. Even in parts of the country where Latinos have long been the largest ethnic group, they only "help shape things," says University of Texas political scientist Rodolfo de la Garza. "They don't lead things. They don't define things."

Where Hispanics have just arrived, they've only just begun to crack the city councils, the school boards, and the county commissions. Though Hispanics account for one-fifth of Nevada's population, there are only two Latinos in the 63-member state legislature, and virtually none hold local office in the cities and counties where they are the most highly concentrated.

The once-a-decade exercise of redistricting will help mobilize Latino voters and encourage them to seek elected office. But no one expects Latinos to show the kind of huge gains that the Congressional Black Caucus made after the 1992 election. Indeed, the boom in the Hispanic population has fostered political tension between the two minority groups.

TIME/CNN POLL: EVOLVING PERCEPTIONS

The Canadian border separates the U.S. from 31 million people; the Mexican border divides us from 97 million—or 440 million if you count all the way to Chile. So which is more important—and which has more impact?

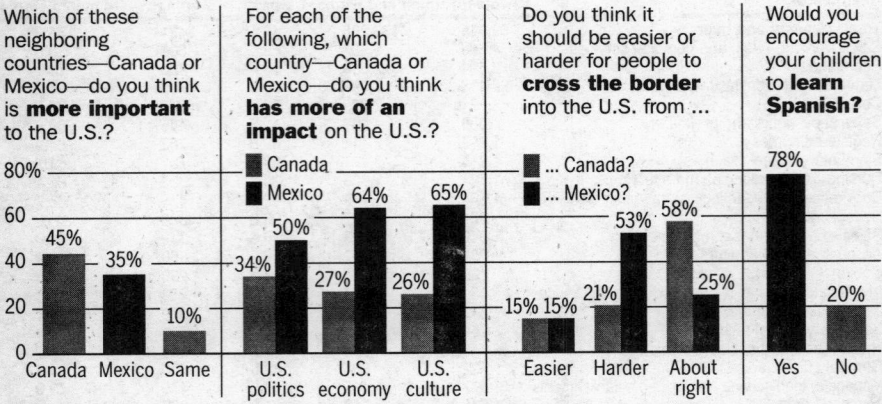

Which of these neighboring countries—Canada or Mexico—do you think is **more important** to the U.S.?

- Canada 45%
- Mexico 35%
- Same 10%

For each of the following, which country—Canada or Mexico—do you think **has more of an impact** on the U.S.?

■ Canada
■ Mexico

- U.S. politics: Canada 34%, Mexico 50%
- U.S. economy: Canada 27%, Mexico 64%
- U.S. culture: Canada 26%, Mexico 65%

Do you think it should be easier or harder for people to **cross the border** into the U.S. from ...

■ ... Canada?
■ ... Mexico?

- Easier: Canada 15%, Mexico 15%
- Harder: Canada 21%, Mexico 53%
- About right: Canada 58%, Mexico 25%

Would you encourage your children to **learn Spanish?**

- Yes 78%
- No 20%

About the poll: From a telephone poll of 1,031 adult Americans taken for TIME/CNN on May 23–24, 2001 by Harris Interactive. Sampling error plus or minus 3.1%. "Not sures" omitted.

Black legislators in Georgia, a state that saw a quadrupling of its Hispanic population over the past decade, opposed a bill that would expand a minority-business tax break to include brown-owned firms.

Little Political Clout

There are many reasons that Latino political influence has not kept pace with the Census, the most obvious being that many of those counted are neither citizens nor even legal residents of the United States. Hispanics are more dispersed than, say, African Americans, which means legislators have to work harder to draw districts to maximize their voting power. More than a third of Latinos are under the voting age; and those who are eligible to vote often don't. Though the Latino and African-American populations in the United States are roughly the same size, 6 million more blacks are registered to vote.

Turnout rates are lower than average even among more educated and affluent Hispanics.

But what really worries Hispanic leaders is that many newcomers don't seem to want to participate. For whatever reason—longer waits, higher application fees, cultural factors that work against assimilation—a smaller and smaller portion of new immigrants are even trying to become citizens. Some Latino politicians blame bilingualism, the cause for which they fought in the 1970s and 1980s, for discouraging assimilation. "Latinos can exist in their own community and never have to learn English to survive," says Texas congressman Charles Gonzalez. "My fear is that we have not only isolated ourselves, but we have handicapped ourselves."

George W. Bush, for his part, intends to stay ahead of the curve. The day before Cinco de Mayo 2001, he invited 200 guests to the South Lawn for mariachi music and Mexican food. "Mi Casa Blanca," he declared, "es su Casa Blanca." □

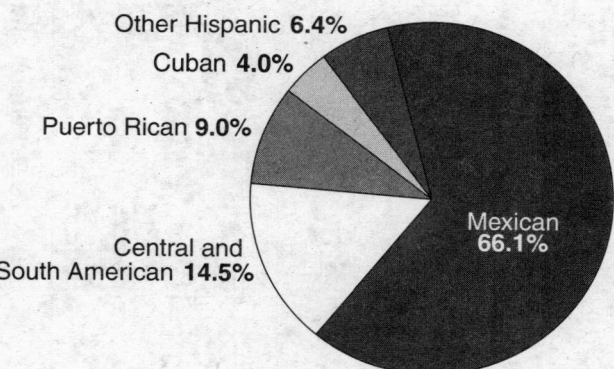

U.S. Hispanics by Origin: 2000 (in percent)

- Other Hispanic **6.4%**
- Cuban **4.0%**
- Puerto Rican **9.0%**
- Central and South American **14.5%**
- Mexican **66.1%**

Source: U.S. Census Bureau, *Current Population Survey*, March 2000.

Persons Speaking a Language Other than English at Home

Language	Persons five years old and over who speak language	Language	Persons five years old and over who speak language	Language	Persons five years old and over who speak language
Speak only English	198,601,000	Portuguese	430,000	Armenian	150,000
Spanish	17,339,000	Japanese	428,000	Navajo	149,000
French	1,702,000	Greek	388,000	Hungarian	148,000
German	1,547,000	Arabic	355,000	Hebrew	144,000
Italian	1,309,000	Hindi (Urdu)	331,000	Dutch	143,000
Chinese	1,249,000	Russian	242,000	Mon-Khmer (Cambodian)	127,000
Tagalog	843,000	Yiddish	213,000		
Polish	723,000	Thai (Laotian)	206,000	Gujarathi (Indian)	102,000
Korean	626,000	Persian	202,000		
Vietnamese	507,000	French Creole	188,000		

NOTE: 2000 Census data were not available at press time. *Source:* U.S. Census Bureau, 1990 Census of Population and Housing Data Paper Listing (CPH-L-133).

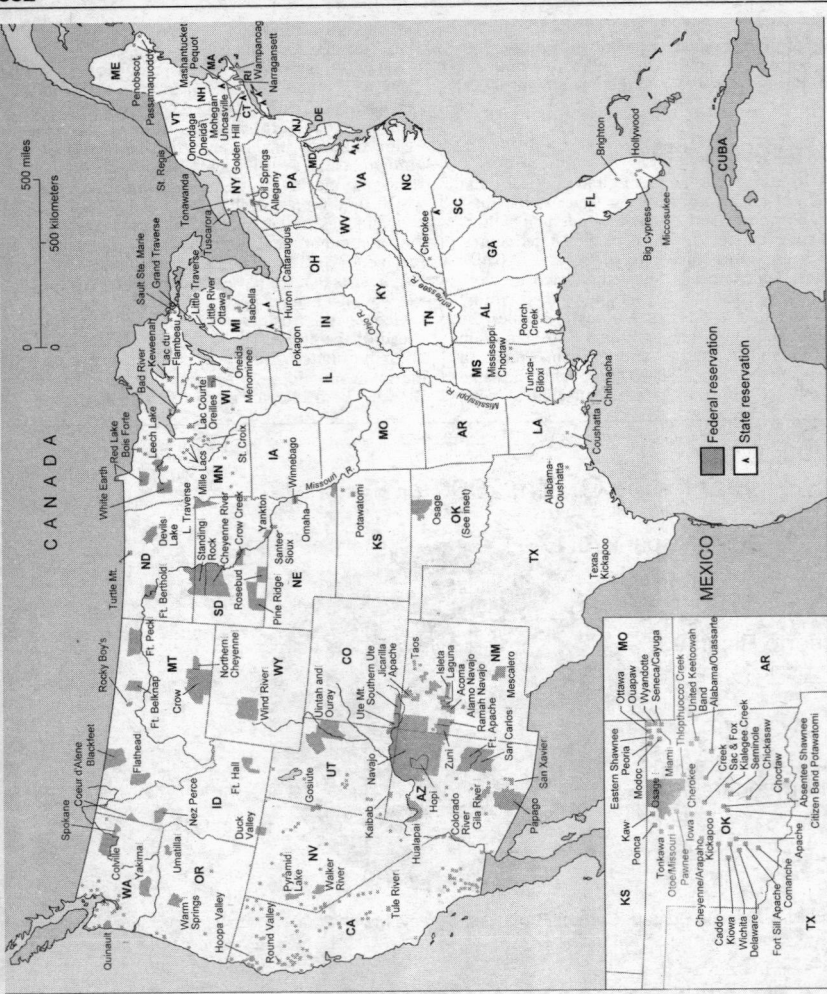

U.S. Federal and State Reservations

Federal reservation

▲ State reservation

Populations of the Ten Largest Reservations
(1990 Census figures)

Name	Population
Navajo (Ariz., N.M., Utah)	143,405
Pine Ridge (Neb., S.D.)	11,182
Fort Apache (Ariz.)	9,825
Gila River (Ariz.)	9,116
Papago (Ariz.)	8,480
Rosebud (S.D.)	8,043
San Carlos (Ariz.)	7,110
Zuni Pueblo (Ariz., N.M.)	7,073
Hopi (Ariz.)	7,061
Blackfeet (Mont.)	7,025

The 218,320 American Indians living on these 10 reservations account for about half of all American Indians living on reservations and trust lands. *Source:* 1990 Census Bureau. *Map source:* Frederick E. Hoxie, ed., *Encyclopedia of North American Indians* (Boston: Houghton Mifflin, 1996). Reprinted with permission.

Population of the United States by Race and Hispanic Origin: 2000 Census Results

	Total population	% of population		Total population	% of population
Total population	281,421,906	100.0%	Native Hawaiian and other		
White	211,460,626	75.1	Pacific Islander	398,835	0.1%
Black or African American	34,658,190	12.3	Some other race	15,359,073	5.5
American Indian and Alaska			Two or more races	6,826,228	2.4
Native	2,475,956	0.9	Hispanic or Latino	35,305,818	12.5
Asian	10,242,998	3.6			

NOTE: Percentages add up to more than 100% because Hispanics may be of any race and are therefore counted under more than one category. *Source:* U.S. Census 2000.

Black or African American Population for the U.S. by Region: 2000

	Black or African American	
Area	Number	Percent of total population
United States	**34,658,190**	**12.3%**
Region		
Northeast	6,099,881	11.4
Midwest	6,499,733	10.1
South	18,981,692	18.9
West	3,076,884	4.9

Source: U.S. Census Burea, Census 2000.

Ten Cities of 100,000 or More with Highest Percentage of Blacks or African Americans: 2000

City	Percent
Gary, Ind.	84.0%
Detroit, Mich.	81.6
Birmingham, Ala.	73.5
Jackson, Miss.	70.6
New Orleans, La.	67.3
Baltimore, Md.	64.3
Atlanta, Ga.	61.4
Memphis, Tenn.	61.4
Washington, DC	60.0
Richmond, Va.	57.2

Source: U.S. Census Bureau, Census 2000.

American Indian Tribes with Populations Greater than 10,000

(1990 U.S. Census figures)

American Indian tribe	Number	Percent distribution	American Indian tribe	Number	Percent distribution
American Indian population, total[1]	**1,878,285**	**100.0%**	Canadian and Latin American tribes	22,379	1.2%
Cherokee	308,132	16.4	Chickasaw	20,631	1.1
Navajo	219,198	11.7	Potawatomi	16,763	0.9
Chippewa	103,826	5.5	Tohono O'Odham	16,041	0.9
Sioux	103,255	5.5	Pima	14,431	0.8
Choctaw	82,299	4.4	Tlingit	13,925	0.7
Pueblo	52,939	2.8	Seminole	13,797	0.7
Apache	50,051	2.7	Alaskan Athabaskans	13,738	0.7
Iroquois	49,038	2.6	Cheyenne	11,456	0.6
Lumbee	48,444	2.6	Comanche	11,322	0.6
Creek	43,550	2.3	Paiute	11,142	0.6
Blackfoot	32,234	1.7	Puget Sound Salish	10,246	0.5

NOTE: 2000 Census data were not available at press time. 1. Includes other American Indian tribes not shown separately. *Source:* U.S. Census Bureau, *1990 Census of Population, General Population Characteristics, American Indian and Alaska Native Areas* (CP-1-1A); and press releases CB91-232 and CB92-244.

Preference for Racial or Ethnic Terminology

Preferred term[1]	Percent	Preferred term[1]	Percent
Hispanic		**Black**	
Hispanic	57.88%	Black	44.15%
Of Spanish origin	12.34	African American	28.07
Latino	11.74	Afro-American	12.12
Some other term	7.85	Negro	3.28
No preference	10.18	Some other term	2.19
White		Colored	1.09
White	61.66%	No preference	9.11
Caucasian	16.53	**American Indian**	
European American	2.35	American Indian	49.76%
Some other term	1.97	Native American	37.35
Anglo	.96	Some other term	3.66
No preference	16.53	Alaska Native	3.51
		No preference	5.72

NOTE: 2000 census data were not available at press time. 1. Preferred term by group of people the term is meant to represent. *Source:* U.S. Census Bureau Survey, May 1995.

The Foreign-Born Population in the United States

(25 most common places of birth; 1990 Census)

1990 rank	Place of birth	Number	Percent	1990 rank	Place of birth	Number	Percent
1	Mexico	4,298,014	21.7%	14	Dominican Republic	347,858	1.8%
2	Philippines	912,674	4.6	15	Jamaica	334,140	1.7
3	Canada	744,830	3.8	16	Soviet Union	333,725	1.7
4	Cuba	736,971	3.7	17	Japan	290,128	1.5
5	Germany	711,929	3.6	18	Colombia	286,124	1.4
6	United Kingdom	640,145	3.2	19	Taiwan	244,102	1.2
7	Italy	580,592	2.9	20	Guatemala	225,739	1.1
8	Korea	568,397	2.9	21	Haiti	225,393	1.1
9	Vietnam	543,262	2.7	22	Iran	210,941	1.1
10	China	529,837	2.7	23	Portugal	210,122	1.1
11	El Salvador	465,433	2.4	24	Greece	177,398	0.9
12	India	450,406	2.3	25	Laos	171,577	0.9
13	Poland	388,328	2.0				

NOTE: 2000 Census data were not available at press time. *Source:* U.S. Census Bureau.

Percent of U.S. Foreign Born: 1900 and 1990

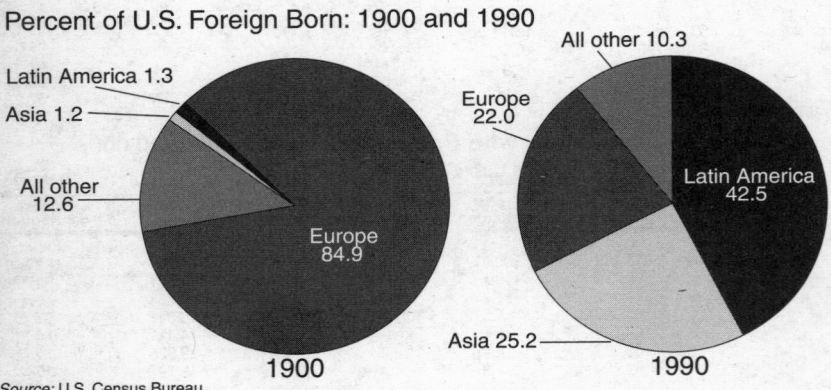

Latin America 1.3
Asia 1.2
All other 12.6
Europe 84.9
1900

All other 10.3
Europe 22.0
Latin America 42.5
Asia 25.2
1990

Source: U.S. Census Bureau

Immigration to U.S.: 1850–1930, 1960–1990

Year	Total[1]	Region of birth reported					
		Europe	Asia	Africa	Oceania	Latin America	North America
1990	19,767,316	4,350,403	4,979,037	363,819	104,145	8,407,837	753,917
1980	14,079,906	5,149,572	2,539,777	199,723	77,577	4,372,487	853,427
1970	9,619,302	5,740,891	824,887	80,143	41,258	1,803,970	812,421
1960	9,738,091	7,256,311	490,996	35,355	34,730	908,309	952,500
1930	14,204,149	11,784,010	275,665	18,326	17,343	791,840	1,310,369
1920	13,920,692	11,916,048	237,950	16,126	14,626	588,843	1,138,174
1910	13,515,886	11,810,115	191,484	3,992	11,450	279,514	1,209,717
1900	10,341,276	8,881,548	120,248	2,538	8,820	137,458	1,179,922
1890	9,249,547	8,030,347	113,383	2,207	9,353	107,307	980,938
1880	6,679,943	5,751,823	107,630	2,204	6,859	90,073	717,286
1870	5,567,229	4,941,049	64,565	2,657	4,028	57,871	493,467
1860	4,138,697	3,807,062	36,796	526	2,140	38,315	249,970
1850	2,244,602	2,031,867	1,135	551	588	20,773	147,711

NOTE: 2000 Census data were not available at press time. 1. The sum of the regions for a particular year will not equal the total. Totals include significant numbers of immigrants for whom no region of birth was reported. *Source:* U.S. Census Bureau, March 9, 1999.

Ancestry of U.S. Population by Rank

(1990 U.S. Census figures; groups with populations exceeding one million)

1990 Rank	Ancestry group	Number	Percent	1990 Rank	Ancestry group	Number	Percent
1	German	57,947,873	23.2%	18	Welsh	2,033,893	0.8%
2	Irish	38,735,539	15.6	19	Spanish	2,024,004	0.8
3	English	32,651,788	13.1	20	Puerto Rican	1,955,323	0.8
4	African	23,777,098	9.6	21	Slovak	1,882,897	0.8
5	Italian	14,664,550	5.9	22	White	1,799,711	0.7
6	American	12,395,999	5.0	23	Danish	1,634,669	0.7
7	Mexican	11,586,983	4.7	24	Hungarian	1,582,302	0.6
8	French	10,320,935	4.1	25	Chinese	1,505,245	0.6
9	Polish	9,366,106	3.8	26	Filipino	1,450,512	0.6
10	American Indian	8,708,220	3.5	27	Czech	1,296,411	0.5
11	Dutch	6,227,089	2.5	28	Portuguese	1,153,351	0.5
12	Scotch-Irish	5,617,773	2.3	29	British	1,119,154	0.4
13	Scottish	5,393,581	2.2	30	Hispanic	1,113,259	0.4
14	Swedish	4,680,863	1.9	31	Greek	1,110,373	0.4
15	Norwegian	3,869,395	1.6	32	Swiss	1,045,495	0.4
16	Russian	2,952,987	1.2	33	Japanese	1,004,645	0.4
17	French Canadian	2,167,127	0.9				

NOTE: 2000 Census data were not available at press time. Data are based on a sample and subject to sampling variability. Since persons who reported multiple ancestries were included in more than one group, the sum of the persons reporting the ancestry is greater than the total; for example, a person reporting "English-French" was tabulated in both the "English" and "French" categories. *Source:* U.S. Census Bureau.

Immigrants Admitted as Permanent Residents Under Refugee Acts, by Country of Birth, 1971–1998

Covers immigrants who were allowed to enter the United States under 1953 Refugee Relief Act and later acts; Hungarian parolees under July 1958 act; refugee-escapee parolees under July 1960 act; conditional entries by refugees under Oct. 1965 act; Cuban parolees under Nov. 1966 act; beginning 1978, Indochina refugees under Oct. 1977 act; beginning 1980, refugee-parolees under the Oct. 1978 act, and asylees under the March 1980 act; and beginning 1981, refugees under the March 1980 act.

Country of birth	1971–80, total	1981–90, total	1991–96, total	1998
Total	**539,447**	**1,013,620**	**748,122**	**54,645**
Europe[1]	**71,858**	**155,512**	**312,815**	**19,048**
Czecho-slovakia, former	3,646	8,204	1,201	15
Hungary	4,358	4,942	1,231	14
Poland	5,882	33,889	7,210	54
Romania	6,812	29,798	15,139	116
Soviet Union, former[2]	31,309	72,306	264,187	13,200
Armenia	n.a.	n.a.	1,546[4]	158
Azerbaijan	n.a.	n.a.	10,049[4]	196
Belarus	n.a.	n.a.	19,545[4]	557
Georgia	n.a.	n.a.	1,834[4]	100
Kazakhstan	n.a.	n.a.	2,823[4]	152
Moldova	n.a.	n.a.	9,300[4]	272
Russia	n.a.	n.a.	44,367[4]	2,225
Tajikistan	n.a.	n.a.	2,191[4]	24
Ukraine	n.a.	n.a.	81,263[4]	3,641
Uzbekistan	n.a.	n.a.	14,638[4]	292
Yugoslavia	11,297	324	13,271[4]	5,312

Country of birth	1971–80, total	1981–90, total	1991–96, total	1998
Asia[1]	**210,683**	**712,092**	**286,125**	**11,743**
Afghanistan	542	22,946	9,065	137
Cambodia	7,739	114,064	6,088	62
China[3]	13,760	7,928	5,079	898
India	n.a.	n.a.	1,125	373
Iran	364	46,773	20,126	754
Iraq	6,851	7,540	14,464	999
Laos	21,690	142,964	33,701	1,110
Thailand	1,241	30,259	19,323	1,134
Vietnam	150,266	324,453	169,560	4,921
North America[1]	**252,633**	**121,840**	**111,744**	**16,372**
Cuba	251,514	113,367	76,370	14,915
El Salvador	45	1,383	3,623	129
Haiti	n.a.	n.a.	7,309	537
Nicaragua	36	5,590	21,252	316
South America[1]	**1,244**	**1,976**	**3,025**	**712**
Peru	n.a.	n.a.	1,285	338
Africa[1]	**2,991**	**22,149**	**34,224**	**4,225**
Ethiopia	1,307	18,542	15,849	507
Liberia	n.a.	n.a.	2,712	225
Somalia	n.a.	n.a.	7,864	2,270
Sudan	n.a.	n.a.	3,422	287
Other	38	51	189	2,545

n.a. = not available. 1. Includes other countries, not shown separately. 2. Includes other republics and unknown republics, not shown separately. 3. Includes Taiwan. 4. Covers the years 1992–1996. *Source:* U.S. Immigration and Naturalization Service, *Statistical Yearbook,* annual, and releases.

Affirmative Action Timeline

In its tumultuous 30-year history, affirmative action has been both praised and pilloried as an answer to racial inequality. The policy was introduced in 1965 by President Johnson as a method of redressing discrimination that had persisted in spite of civil rights laws and constitutional guarantees. Focusing in particular on education and jobs, affirmative action policies required active measures to ensure that blacks and other minorities enjoyed the same opportunities for promotions, salary increases, career advancement, school admissions, scholarships, and financial aid that had been the nearly exclusive province of whites. From the outset, affirmative action was envisioned as a temporary remedy that would end once there was a "level playing field" for all Americans.

By the late '70s, however, flaws in the policy began to show up amid its good intentions. Reverse discrimination became a passionate issue, epitomized by the famous *Bakke* case in 1978. A backlash against affirmative action mounted, and in the last decade the tide has turned against it in both the courts and on a state level—California and Washington have gone as far as abolishing the policy.

Yet the questions of fairness and racial equality remain troubling for most of those not positioned at the ideological poles of the issue. Even a once-adamant opponent of affirmative action like John Bunzel, president of San Jose State University, has acknowledged that "perhaps the most important lesson I've learned is that there are no airtight, completely coherent, unassailable, and holistic answers on the question of affirmative action. . . . Any intelligent person who wrestles with it is going to be vulnerable and subject to the twists and turns of unintended consequences." Serious advocates both for and against affirmative action could easily share such an estimation.

March 6, 1961: Executive Order 10925 makes the first reference to "affirmative action." President John F. Kennedy issues Executive Order 10925, which creates the Committee on Equal Employment Opportunity and mandates that projects financed with federal funds "take affirmative action" to ensure that hiring and employment practices are free of racial bias.

July 2, 1964: Civil Rights Act signed by President Lyndon Johnson. The most sweeping civil rights legislation since Reconstruction, the Civil Rights Act prohibits discrimination of all kinds based on race, color, religion, or national origin.

June 4, 1965: Speech defining concept of affirmative action. In a speech to the graduating class at Howard University, President Johnson frames the concept underlying affirmative action, asserting that civil rights laws alone are not enough to remedy discrimination: "You do not wipe away the scars of centuries by saying: 'now, you are free to go where you want, do as you desire, and choose the leaders you please.' You do not take a man who for years has been hobbled by chains, liberate him, bring him to the starting line of a race, saying, 'you are free to compete with all the others,' and still justly believe you have been completely fair. . . . This is the next and more profound stage of the battle for civil rights. We seek not just freedom but opportunity—not just legal equity but human ability—not just equality as a right and a theory, but equality as a fact and as a result."

Sept. 24, 1965: Executive Order 11246 enforces affirmative action for the first time. Issued by President Johnson, the executive order requires government contractors to "take affirmative action" toward prospective minority employees in all aspects of hiring and employment. Contractors must take specific measures to ensure equality in hiring and must document these efforts. On Oct. 13, 1967, the order was amended to cover discrimination on the basis of gender.

1969: The Philadelphia Order. Initiated by President Richard Nixon, the "Philadelphia Order" was the most forceful plan thus far to guarantee fair hiring practices in construction jobs. Philadelphia was selected as the test case because, as Assistant Secretary of Labor Arthur Fletcher explained,

"The craft unions and the construction industry are among the most egregious offenders against equal opportunity laws . . . openly hostile toward letting blacks into their closed circle." The order included definite "goals and timetables." As President Nixon asserted, "We would not impose quotas, but would require federal contractors to show 'affirmative action' to meet the goals of increasing minority employment."

June 28, 1978: *Regents of the University of California* v. *Bakke*. This landmark Supreme Court case imposed limitations on affirmative action to ensure that providing greater opportunities for minorities did not come at the expense of the rights of the majority—affirmative action was unfair if it led to reverse discrimination. The case involved the University of California at Davis Medical School, which had two separate admissions pools, one for standard applicants, and another for minority and economically disadvantaged students. The school reserved 16 of its 100 places for this latter group. Allan Bakke, a white applicant, was rejected twice even though there were minority applicants admitted with significantly lower scores than his. Bakke maintained that judging him on the basis of his race was a violation of the Equal Protection Clause of the Fourteenth Amendment. The Supreme Court ruled that while race was a legitimate factor in school admissions, the use of such inflexible quotas as the medical school had set aside was not. The Supreme Court, however, was split 5–4 in its decision on the Bakke case and addressed only a minimal number of the many complex issues that had sprung up about affirmative action.

July 2, 1980: *Fullilove* v. *Klutznick*. While Bakke struck down strict quotas, in Fullilove the Supreme Court ruled that some modest quotas were perfectly constitutional. The Court upheld a federal law requiring that 15% of funds for public works be set aside for qualified minority contractors. The "narrowed focus and limited extent" of the affirmative action program did not violate the equal rights of nonminority contractors, according to the Court—there was no "allocation of federal funds according to inflexible percentages solely based on race or ethnicity."

May 19, 1986: *Wygant* v. *Jackson Board of Education.* This case challenged a school board's policy of protecting minority employees by laying off nonminority teachers first, even though the nonminority employees had seniority. The Supreme Court ruled against the school board, maintaining that the injury suffered by nonminorities affected could not justify the benefits to minorities.

Feb. 25, 1987: *United States* v. *Paradise.* In July 1970, a federal court found that the State of Alabama Department of Public Safety systematically discriminated against blacks in hiring: "in the thirty-seven-year history of the patrol there has never been a black trooper." The court ordered that the state reform its hiring practices to end "pervasive, systematic, and obstinate discriminatory exclusion of blacks." A full 12 years and several lawsuits later, the department still had not promoted any blacks above entry level. In response, the court ordered specific racial quotas to correct the situation. For every white hired or promoted, one black would also be hired or promoted until at least 25% of the upper ranks of the department were composed of blacks. The case challenged this use of numerical quotas. The Supreme Court, however, upheld the use of strict quotas in this case as one of the only means of combating the department's overt and defiant racism.

Jan. 23, 1989: *City of Richmond* v. *Croson.* Affirmative action on the state and local level was challenged in this case involving a Richmond, Va., program setting aside 30% of city construction funds for black-owned firms. For the first time, affirmative action was judged as a "highly suspect tool." The Supreme Court ruled that an "amorphous claim that there has been past discrimination in a particular industry cannot justify the use of an unyielding racial quota." It maintained that affirmative action must be subject to "strict scrutiny" and is unconstitutional unless racial discrimination can be proven to be "widespread throughout a particular industry."

June 12, 1995: *Adarand Constructors, Inc.* v. *Peña.* What Croson was to state- and local-run affirmative action programs, Adarand was to federal programs. The Court again called for "strict scrutiny" in determining whether discrimination existed before implementing a federal affirmative action program. "Strict scrutiny" meant that affirmative action programs fulfilled a "compelling governmental interest," and were "narrowly tailored" to fit the particular situation. Although two of the judges (Scalia and Thomas) felt that there should be a complete ban on affirmative action, the majority of judges asserted that "the unhappy persistence of both the practice and the lingering effects of racial discrimination against minority groups in this country" justified the use of race-based remedial measures in certain circumstances.

July 19, 1995: White House guidelines on affirmative action. President Clinton asserted in a speech that while Adarand set "stricter standards to mandate reform of affirmative action, it actually reaffirmed the need for affirmative action and reaffirmed the continuing existence of systematic discrimination in the United States." In a White House memorandum on the same day, he called for the elimination of any program that "(a) creates a quota; (b) creates preferences for unqualified individuals; (c) creates reverse discrimination; or (d) continues even after its equal opportunity purposes have been achieved."

March 18, 1996: *Hopwood* v. *University of Texas Law School.* Four white law-school applicants at the University of Texas challenged the school's affirmative action program, asserting that they were rejected because of unfair preferences toward less qualified minority applicants. As a result, the 5th U.S. Court of Appeals suspended the university's affirmative action admissions program and ruled that the 1978 Bakke decision was invalid—while Bakke rejected racial quotas, it maintained that race could serve as a factor in admissions. In addition to remedying past discrimination, Bakke maintained that the inclusion of minority students would create a diverse student body, and that was beneficial to the educational environment as a whole. Hopwood, however, rejected the legitimacy of diversity as a goal, asserting that "educational diversity is not recognized as a compelling state interest." The Supreme Court allowed the ruling to stand. In 1997, the Texas attorney general announced that all "Texas public universities [should] employ race-neutral criteria."

Nov. 3, 1997: Proposition 209 enacted in California. A state ban on all forms of affirmative action was passed in California: "The state shall not discriminate against, or grant preferential treatment to, any individual or group on the basis of race, sex, color, ethnicity, or national origin in the operation of public employment, public education, or public contracting." Proposed in 1996, the controversial ban had been delayed in the courts for almost a year before it went into effect.

Dec. 3, 1998: Initiative 200 enacted in Washington State. Washington becomes the second state to abolish state affirmative action measures when it passed "I 200," which is similar to California's Proposition 209.

Feb. 22, 2000: Florida bans race as factor in college admissions. Florida legislature approves education component of Gov. Jeb Bush's "One Florida" initiative, aimed at ending affirmative action in the state.

Dec. 13, 2000: Univ. of Michigan's undergraduate affirmative action policy. In *Gratz* v. *Bollinger,* a federal judge ruled that the use of race as a factor in admissions at the university was constitutional. The gist of the university's argument was as follows: just as preference is granted to children of alumni, scholarship athletes, and other groups for reasons deemed beneficial to the university, so too does the affirmative action program serve "a compelling interest" by providing educational benefits derived from a diverse student body.

March 27, 2001: Univ. of Michigan Law School's affirmative action policy. In a case similar to the University of Michigan undergraduate lawsuit, a different judge drew an opposite conclusion, invalidating the law school's policy and ruling that "intellectual diversity bears no obvious or necessary relationship to racial diversity."

After the Exoneration

DNA evidence is freeing more innocent people, but few are compensated for those years in prison

By **AMANDA RIPLEY** TIME

One unlucky evening in 1984, Ricky Daye was riding in a Buick with a broken taillight in San Diego. The police pulled the car over and thought they recognized Daye's face from a WANTED sketch. He was arrested and five months later convicted of the brutal rape and kidnapping of a young San Diego mother. Daye spent ten years in California prisons, insisting all the time that he was innocent. Finally, in 1994, a DNA test showed he could not have been the culprit, and he was freed.

A happy ending? Not entirely. For months afterward, strangers who recognized Daye from TV talk shows would corner him in Kmarts and gas stations and ask, "You got paid at least, right?" Yet six years later, Daye, 42, has not received a cent. He sued the city of San Diego, its police, and its prosecutors for millions of dollars. But a jury declined to award any damages.

DNA Hasn't Solved Everything

Despite the wonderful clarity of DNA evidence, which has exonerated more than 80 Americans of crimes for which they had been imprisoned, two-thirds have never been given any compensation for their lost years. In a country in which some slip-and-fall claims win millions of dollars, it is startling to realize that decades wrongly spent in maximum-security prisons are typically worth nothing. "In America, when someone is wronged, we pay them," says Adele Bernhard, a Pace University law professor. "It may not be a perfect system, but that's what we do. Why don't we do that here?"

In 36 states, according to Bernhard, no laws explicitly provide for compensating the wrongly imprisoned, while other laws protect police and prosecutors from lawsuits. The reasoning is that public servants could not do their job if they constantly had to fear being sued. As long as officials do not jail the wrong person intentionally (and they almost never do), they are not to blame—and in our justice system, someone has to be blamed before anyone pays. Even in the 14 states that do have laws to compensate victims of courtroom mistakes, the caps on awards are often miserly. For those coming out of federal prisons, damages cannot exceed a laughable $5,000.

There have been exceptions in cases involving blatant police or prosecutorial misconduct. Last year four men who collectively spent 65 years in prison settled with Illinois officials for $36 million. In New York State, even in the absence of police misconduct, victims can sue under a no-fault compensation law. And some people have managed to get paid by persuading state legislatures to pass special bills awarding them damages.

Obsolete Laws

By and large, though, the law is messy and outdated. In September 1999, California governor Gray Davis signed a law to pay innocent men and women $100 for every day spent in prison. But it won't affect Ricky Daye—the law doesn't apply to older cases.

Not everyone feels sorry for Daye. Despite the evidence, the rape victim has said she still believes Daye is the one who attacked her. And like many of those exonerated by DNA tests, Daye has been convicted of other, less serious crimes, both before and after his release. Contends San Diego city attorney William Donnell, who defended the police against Daye's civil suit: "Those ten years [in prison] kept him alive."

Daye disagrees. "There were six thousand guys at Folsom prison," he says, "and I was the only one from Iowa." He learned to make a knife out of a sardine can and sew a steel tray into his coat as body armor. "They put my life in far more peril than I was ever in on the street." Daye, who makes $7 an hour as a cook in Raleigh, N.C., still hopes that his lawsuit, now under appeal, will help set things right. □

State Prison Inmates, by Most Serious Offense, 1997

Most serious offense	Percent	Most serious offense	Percent	Most serious offense	Percent	Most serious offense	Percent
Total	100.0%	Other sexual		**Property**		Fraud	2.7%
Violent offenses	47.2	assault	6.0%	**offenses**	22.0%	Other property[3]	2.6
Murder[1]	11.7	Robbery	14.1	Burglary	10.7	**Drug offenses**	20.7%
Manslaughter	1.6	Assault	9.4	Larceny	4.2	**Public-order**	
Rape	2.6	Other violent[2]	1.9	Motor vehicle		**offenses**[4]	9.9%
				theft	1.8	**Unspecified**[5]	0.2%

NOTE: Latest statistics available. Data may not sum to total due to rounding. 1. Includes nonnegligent manslaughter. 2. Includes extortion, intimidation, criminal endangerment, and other violent offenses. 3. Includes possession and selling of stolen property, destruction of property, trespassing, vandalism, criminal tampering, and other property offenses. 4. Includes weapons, drunk driving, escape, court offenses, obstruction, commercialized vice, morals and decency charges, liquor law violations, and other public-order offenses. 5. Includes juvenile offenses and unspecified felonies. *Source: Correctional Populations in the United States, 1997,* U.S. Bureau of Justice Statistics.

Federal Prison Inmates, by Most Serious Offense, 1997

Most serious offense	Percent	Most serious offense	Percent	Most serious offense	Percent	Most serious offense	Percent
Total	100.0%	Other violent[3]	1.5%	Larceny/theft/ other property[5]	1.9%	Immigration	5.6%
Violent offenses	11.9	Property offenses	8.4	Drug offenses	60.0	Weapons	8.3
Homicide[1]	1.0	Burglary	0.2	Public-order		Escape/court[6]	0.4
Assault[2]	0.7	Fraud[4]	6.3	offenses	19.7	Other public-order[7]	5.4
Robbery	8.7						

NOTE: Latest statistics available. 1. Includes murder, nonnegligent manslaughter, and negligent manslaughter. 2. Beginning in 1996 assaults with intent to commit robbery were coded as robbery. 3. Includes kidnapping, rape, other sexual assault, threats against the president, and other offenses. 4. Includes embezzlement, counterfeiting, forgery, bankruptcy, and fraud (excluding tax fraud but including securities fraud). 5. Includes motor vehicle theft, trespassing, destruction of property, and transport of stolen property. 6. Includes flight to avoid prosecution, escape, parole and probation violation, and other court offenses. 7. Includes liquor laws, national security laws, income tax, selective service acts, bribery, gambling, traffic offenses, and other public-order offenses. *Source: Correctional Populations in the United States, 1997, U.S. Bureau of Justice Statistics.*

Selected Characteristics of State and Federal Prison Inmates, 1997

Characteristic	State inmates 1997	Federal inmates 1997	Characteristic	State inmates 1997	Federal inmates 1997
Gender			**Marital status**		
Male	93.7%	92.8%	Married	16.6%	30.4%
Female	6.3	7.2	Widowed	1.9	1.7
Race/Hispanic origin			Separated	5.8	5.8
White non-Hispanic	33.3%	29.9%	Divorced	18.6	20.5
Black non-Hispanic	46.5	37.8	Never married	57.1	41.6
Hispanic	17.0	27.3	**Educational attainment**		
Other[1]	3.2	5.0	8th grade or less	14.2%	12.0%
Age			Some high school	28.9	17.4
17 or younger	0.5%	0.0%	GED	25.1	19.8
18–24	19.3	8.9	High school graduate	18.5	24.3
25–34	38.1	36.6	Some college	10.7	17.5
35–44	29.4	30.6	College graduate or more	2.7	9.1
45–54	9.8	16.3	Median education	12 yrs	12 yrs
55–64	2.2	6.2			
65 or older	0.7	1.4			
Median age	32 yrs	36 yrs			

NOTE: Latest statistics available. 1. Includes Asians, Pacific Islanders, American Indians, Alaska Natives, and other racial groups. *Source: Correctional Populations in the United States, 1997, U.S. Bureau of Justice Statistics.*

Murder Victims: by Race and Sex, 1999

Race and sex	Total no. victims	% distribution[1]	Race and sex	Total no. victims	% distribution[1]
Race			**Sex**		
White	6,310	49.8%	Male	9,558	75.5%
Black	5,855	46.3	Female	3,085	24.4
Other	369	2.9	Unknown	15	.1
Unknown	124	1.0	**Total**	**12,658**	**100.0**

1. Because of rounding, percentages may not add up to 100. *Source: Crime in the United States, 1999, FBI, Uniform Crime Reports.*

Murder Victims: Types of Weapon Used, 1999

Type of weapon	Total no. victims	% distribution[1]	Type of weapon	Total no. victims	% distribution[1]
Firearms	8,259	65.2%	Explosives	—	—
Knives or cutting instruments	1,667	13.2	Fire	125	1.0%
Blunt objects (clubs, hammers, etc.)	736	5.8	Narcotics	23	0.2
			Strangulation	190	1.5
Personal weapons (hands, fists, feet, etc.)[2]	855	6.8	Asphyxiation	103	0.8
			Other weapon or not stated[3]	689	5.4
Poison	11	.1	Total	12,658	100.0

1. Because of rounding, percentages may not add up to 100. 2. Pushed is included in personal weapons. 3. Includes drowning. *Source: Crime in the United States, 1999, FBI, Uniform Crime Reports.*

Homicide Rate (per 100,000), 1950–1999

Year	Homicide rate	Year	Homicide rate	Year	Homicide rate	Year	Homicide rate	Year	Homicide rate
1950	4.6	1960	5.1	1970	7.9	1980	10.2	1990	9.4
1951	4.4	1961	4.8	1971	8.6	1981	9.8	1991	9.8
1952	4.6	1962	4.6	1972	9.0	1982	9.1	1992	9.3
1953	4.5	1963	4.6	1973	9.4	1983	8.3	1993	9.5
1954	4.2	1964	4.9	1974	9.8	1984	7.9	1994	9.0
1955	4.1	1965	5.1	1975	9.6	1985	7.9	1995	8.2
1956	4.1	1966	5.6	1976	8.8	1986	8.6	1996	7.4
1957	4.0	1967	6.2	1977	8.8	1987	8.3	1997	6.8
1958	4.8	1968	6.9	1978	9.0	1988	8.4	1998	6.3
1959	4.9	1969	7.3	1979	9.7	1989	8.7	1999	5.7

Source: Crime in the United States, 1999, FBI, Uniform Crime Reports.

Number of Persons Executed,[1] by Jurisdiction, 1930–1999

State	Number executed since 1930	1977[2]	State	Number executed since 1930	1977[2]	State	Number executed since 1930	1977[2]
Texas	496	199	Missouri	103	41	Delaware	22	10
Georgia	389	23	Illinois	102	12	Oregon	21	2
New York	329	—	Tennessee	93	—	Connecticut	21	—
California	299	7	Oklahoma	79	19	Utah	19	6
North Carolina	278	15	New Jersey	74	—	Iowa	18	—
Florida	214	44	Maryland	71	3	Kansas	15	—
South Carolina	186	24	Arizona	57	19	Montana	8	2
Ohio	173	1	Washington	50	3	Wyoming	8	1
Virginia	165	73	Indiana	48	7	New Mexico	8	—
Louisiana	158	25	Colorado	48	1	Nebraska	7	3
Mississippi	158	4	District of Columbia	40	—	Idaho	4	1
Pennsylvania	155	3	West Virginia	40	—	Vermont	4	—
Alabama	154	19	Nevada	37	8	New Hampshire	1	—
Arkansas	139	21	Federal system	33	—	South Dakota	1	—
Kentucky	105	2	Massachusetts	27	—	**U.S. total**	**4,457**	**598**

1. Executed under civil authority; military authorities carried out an additional 160 executions, 1930–97. 2. In 1972 the Supreme Court ruled that capital punishment, as it was then administered, was "cruel and unusual" and therefore unconstitutional. On July 1, 1976, however, the Court overturned the ruling by a 7–2 decision, and capital punishment was reinstated. *Source: Capital Punishment, 1999, U.S. Bureau of Justice Statistics.*

Characteristics of Prisoners under Sentence of Death

Characteristic	1980	1990	1997	1998	Characteristic	1980	1990	1997	1998
Race and age					**Marital status**				
White	418	1,368	1,876	1,906	Never married	268	998	1,561	1,641
Black and other	270	978	1,459	1,546	Married	229	632	744	749
Under 20 years	11	8	14	15	Divorced[1]	217	726	1,030	1,062
20 to 24 years	173	168	275	267	**Time elapsed since sentencing**				
25 to 34 years	334	1,110	1,075	1,101	Less than 12 months	185	231	242	275
35 to 54 years	186	1,006	1,818	1,899	12 to 47 months	389	753	849	813
55 years and over	10	64	153	170	48 to 71 months	102	438	462	482
Years of schooling completed					72 months and over	38	934	1,782	1,882
7 years or less	68	178	199	206	**Legal status at arrest**				
8 years	74	186	204	217	Not under sentence	384	1,345	1,946	2,029
9 to 11 years	204	775	1,065	1,111	Parole or probation[2]	115	578	909	877
12 years	162	729	1,077	1,120	Prison or escaped	45	128	114	127
More than 12 years	43	209	286	297	Unknown	170	305	366	419
Unknown	163	279	504	501	**Total**	**688**	**2,346**	**3,335**	**3,452**

1. Includes widows, widowers, and unknown. 2. Includes persons on mandatory conditional release, work release, leave, AWOL, or bail. Excludes prisoners under sentence of death confined in local correctional systems pending appeal or who have not been committed to prison. *Source: U.S. Bureau of Justice Statistics, Capital Punishment, annual, from Statistical Abstract of the United States, 2000.*

Methods of Execution

State	Minimum age	Method	State	Minimum age	Method
Alabama	16	Electrocution	Nevada	16	Lethal injection
Alaska	—	No death penalty	New Hampshire[7]	17	Lethal injection or hanging
Arizona[1]	none	Lethal injection or gas	New Jersey	18	Lethal injection
Arkansas[2]	14	Lethal injection or electrocution	New Mexico	18	Lethal injection
			New York	18	Lethal injection
California	18	Lethal gas or injection	North Carolina[8]	17	Lethal gas or injection
Colorado	18	Lethal injection	North Dakota	—	No death penalty
Connecticut	18	Lethal injection	Ohio	18	Electrocution or lethal injection
Delaware[3]	16	Lethal injection or hanging	Oklahoma[9]	16	Lethal injection, electrocution, or firing squad
DC	—	No death penalty			
Florida	16	Electrocution	Oregon	18	Lethal injection
Georgia	17	Electrocution	Pennsylvania	none	Lethal injection
Hawaii	—	No death penalty	Rhode Island	—	No death penalty
Idaho	none	Lethal injection or firing squad	South Carolina	none	Electrocution or lethal injection
Illinois	18	Lethal injection	South Dakota[10]	none	Lethal injection
Indiana	16	Lethal injection	Tennessee[11]	18	Electrocution
Iowa	—	No death penalty	Texas	17	Lethal injection
Kansas	18	Lethal injection	Utah	14	Firing squad or lethal injection
Kentucky[4]	16	Electrocution	Vermont	—	No death penalty
Louisiana	none	Lethal injection	Virginia[12]	14	Electrocution or lethal injection
Maine	—	No death penalty	Washington	18	Hanging or lethal injection
Maryland	18	Lethal injection	West Virginia	—	No death penalty
Massachusetts	—	No death penalty	Wisconsin	—	No death penalty
Michigan	—	No death penalty	Wyoming[13]	16	Lethal injection or gas
Minnesota	—	No death penalty	Federal system[14]	18	Lethal injection
Mississippi[5]	16	Lethal injection or gas	American Samoa	—	No death penalty
Missouri	16	Lethal injection or gas	Guam	—	No death penalty
Montana[6]	none	Lethal injection	Puerto Rico	—	No death penalty
Nebraska	18	Electrocution	Virgin Islands	—	No death penalty

1. Ariz. authorizes lethal injection for persons sentenced after 11/15/92; before that date methods are lethal injection or lethal gas. 2. Ark. authorizes lethal injection for those sentenced on or after 7/4/83; before that date, methods available are lethal injection or electrocution. 3. Del. also authorizes lethal injection for those sentenced after 6/13/86; before that date, methods available are lethal injection or hanging. 4. Ky. authorizes lethal injection for persons sentenced on or after 3/31/98; before that date methods available are lethal injection or electrocution. 5. Miss. minimum age defined by statute is 13. 6. Montana law specifies that offenders tried under the capital sexual statute be 18 or older. 7. N.H. authorizes hanging only if lethal injection cannot be given. 8. N.C.'s minimum age is 17, unless the person was already incarcerated for murder when the subsequent murder occurred; then the minimum age is 14. 9. Okla. authorizes electrocution if lethal injection is ever held to be unconstitutional and firing squad if both lethal injection and electrocution are held unconstitutional. 10. S.D. authorizes juveniles to possibly be transferred to adult court; age can be a mitigating factor. 11. Tenn. also authorizes lethal injection for those whose capital offense occurred after 12/31/98; before that date methods available are lethal injection or electrocution. 12. Va.'s minimum age for transfer to adult court by statute is 14. 13. Wyo. authorizes lethal gas if lethal injection is ever held to be unconstitutional. 14. The method of execution of federal prisoners is lethal injection. For offenses under the Violent Crime Control and Law Enforcement Act of 1994, the method is that of the state in which the conviction took place. *Source: Capital Punishment, 1999, U.S. Bureau of Justice Statistics.*

Federal Prosecutions of Public Corruption

Prosecution status	1998	1997	1996	1995	1994	1993	1992	1990	1985	1980
Total: Indicted	1,174	1,057	952	1,051	1,165	1,371	1,189	1,176	1,157	727
Convicted	1,014	853	878	878	969	1,362	1,081	1,084	997	602
Federal officials: Indicted	442	459	440	527	571	627	624	615	563	123
Convicted	414	392	450	438	488	595	532	583	470	131
State officials: Indicted	91	51	66	61	99	113	84	96	79	72
Convicted	58	49	55	61	97	133	92	79	66	51
Local officials: Indicted	277	255	232	236	248	309	232	257	248	247
Convicted	264	169	190	191	202	272	211	225	221	168

NOTE: Figures are latest available. *Source:* U.S. Department of Justice, *Report to Congress on the Activities and Operations of the Public Integrity Section,* annual, from *Statistical Abstract of the United States, 2000.*

Law Enforcement Officers Killed or Assaulted[1]

	1998	1997	1996	1995	1994	1993	1992	1991	1990	1989	1980
Total officers killed	142	132	100	130	133	129	129	122	132	144	164
Officers assaulted											
Firearm	2,073	1,844	1,887	2,277	3,168	4,002	4,455	3,532	3,662	3,154	3,295
Knife or cutting instrument	1,077	895	871	1,325	1,513	1,574	2,095	1,493	1,641	1,379	1,653
Other dangerous weapon	7,266	5,389	5,084	6,299	7,210	7,551	8,604	7,014	7,390	5,778	5,415
Hands, fists, feet, etc.	49,129	41,023	38,853	46,634	53,021	53,848	66,098	50,813	59,101	51,861	47,484
Total assaulted	59,545	49,151	46,695	56,535	64,912	66,975	81,252	62,852	71,794	62,172	57,847

1. Covers officers killed feloniously and accidentally in line of duty; includes federal officers. NOTE: Data are latest available. *Source: Statistical Abstract of the United States, 2000.*

A Time Line of Recent School Shootings

Feb. 2, 1996 **Moses Lake, Wash.**	2 students and 1 teacher killed, 1 other wounded when 14-year-old Barry Loukaitis opened fire on his algebra class.
Feb. 19, 1997 **Bethel, Alaska**	Principal and 1 student killed, 2 others wounded by Evan Ramsey, 16.
Oct. 1, 1997 **Pearl, Miss.**	2 students killed and 7 wounded by Luke Woodham, 16, who was also accused of killing his mother. He and his friends were said to be outcasts who worshiped Satan.
Dec. 1, 1997 **West Paducah, Ky.**	3 students killed, 5 wounded by Michael Carneal, 14, as they participated in a prayer circle at Heath High School.
Dec. 15, 1997 **Stamps, Ark.**	2 students wounded. Colt Todd, 14, was hiding in the woods when he shot the students as they stood in the parking lot.
March 24, 1998 **Jonesboro, Ark.**	4 students and 1 teacher killed, 10 others wounded outside as Westside Middle School emptied during a false fire alarm. Mitchell Johnson, 13, and Andrew Golden, 11, shot at their classmates and teachers from the woods.
April 24, 1998 **Edinboro, Pa.**	1 teacher, John Gillette, killed, 2 students wounded at a dance at James W. Parker Middle School. Andrew Wurst, 14, was charged.
May 19, 1998 **Fayetteville, Tenn.**	1 student killed in the parking lot at Lincoln County High School 3 days before he was to graduate. The victim was dating the ex-girlfriend of his killer, 18-year-old honor student Jacob Davis.
May 21, 1998 **Springfield, Ore.**	2 students killed, 22 others wounded in the cafeteria at Thurston High School by 15-year-old Kip Kinkel. Kinkel had been arrested and released a day earlier for bringing a gun to school. His parents were later found dead at home.
June 15, 1998 **Richmond, Va.**	1 teacher and 1 guidance counselor wounded by a 14-year-old boy in the school hallway.
April 20, 1999 **Littleton, Colo.**	14 students (including killers) and 1 teacher killed, 23 others wounded at Columbine High School in the nation's deadliest school shooting. Eric Harris, 18, and Dylan Klebold, 17, had plotted for a year to kill at least 500 and blow up their school. At the end of their hour-long rampage, they turned their guns on themselves.
April 28, 1999 **Taber, Alberta, Canada**	1 student killed, 1 wounded at W. R. Myers High School in first fatal high school shooting in Canada in 20 years. The suspect, a 14-year-old boy, had dropped out of school after he was severely ostracized by his classmates.
May 20, 1999 **Conyers, Ga.**	6 students injured at Heritage High School by Thomas Solomon, 15, who was reportedly depressed after breaking up with his girlfriend.
Nov. 19, 1999 **Deming, N.M.**	Victor Cordova Jr., 12, shoots and kills Araceli Tena, 13, in the lobby of Deming Middle School.
Dec. 6, 1999 **Fort Gibson, Okla.**	4 students wounded as Seth Trickey, 13, opened fire with a 9mm semiautomatic handgun at Fort Gibson Middle School.
February 29, 2000 **Mount Morris Township, Mich.**	6-year-old Kayla Rolland shot dead at Buell Elementary School near Flint, Mich. The assailant is identified as a 6-year-old boy with a .32-caliber handgun.
May 26, 2000 **Lake Worth, Fla.**	1 teacher, Barry Grunow, shot and killed at Lake Worth Middle School by Nate Brazill, 13, with a .25-caliber semiautomatic pistol on the last day of classes.
March 5, 2001 **Santee, Calif.**	Charles Andrew Williams, 15, kills 2 and wounds 13, after firing from a bathroom at Santana High School.
March 7, 2001 **Williamsport, Pa.**	Elizabeth Catherine Bush, 14, wounded student Kimberly Marchese in the cafeteria of Bishop Neumann High School; she was depressed and frequently teased.

Total Arrests by Age, 1999

	Number of arrests	Percent distribution		Number of arrests	Percent distribution
Total, all ages	9,141,201	100.0%	16	372,066	4.1%
Total, under 18	1,588,839	17.4	15	298,239	3.3
Total, under 15	506,817	5.5	13–14	364,608	4.0
18	460,578	5.0	10–12	117,679	1.3
17	411,717	4.5	Under 10	24,530	0.3

NOTE: Because of rounding, the percentages may not add up to total. *Source: Crime in the United States, 1999*, FBI, Uniform Crime Reports.

Summary of Hate Crime Statistics, 1999

	Number of incidents	Number of offenses	Number of victims	Number of known offenders
Race	4,295	5,240	5,485	4,362
Anti-white	781	970	996	1,011
Anti-black	2,958	3,542	3,679	2,861
Anti-American Indian/Alaskan Native	47	49	50	40
Anti-Asian/Pacific Islander	298	363	379	288
Anti-multi-racial group	211	316	381	162
Ethnicity/national origin	829	1,011	1,040	904
Anti-Hispanic	466	576	588	562
Anti-other ethnicity/national origin	363	435	452	342
Religion	1,411	1,532	1,686	602
Anti-Jewish	1,109	1,198	1,289	429
Anti-Catholic	36	41	41	18
Anti-Protestant	48	49	50	19
Anti-Islamic	32	34	34	14
Anti-other religious group	151	170	221	98
Anti-multi-religious group	31	35	46	21
Anti-atheism/agnosticism/etc.	4	5	5	3
Sexual orientation	1,317	1,487	1,558	1,376
Anti-male homosexual	915	1,025	1,070	1,043
Anti-female homosexual	187	216	231	150
Anti-homosexual	178	205	216	154
Anti-heterosexual	14	16	16	15
Anti-bisexual	23	25	25	14
Disability	19	21	23	21
Anti-physical	10	11	13	9
Anti-mental	9	10	10	12
Multiple-bias incidents[1]	5	10	10	6
Total	7,876	9,301	9,802	7,271

1. There were 5 multiple-bias incidents. Within these incidents, there were 10 offenses, 10 victims, and 6 known offenders.
Source: Crime in the United States, 1999, FBI, Uniform Crime Reports.

Index of Crime, United States, 1979–1999

(rate per 100,000 inhabitants)

Year	Crime index total	Violent crime[1]	Property crime[2]	Murder and non-negligent man-slaughter	Forcible rape	Robbery	Aggra-vated assault	Burglary	Larceny-theft	Motor vehicle theft
1979	5,565.5	548.9	5,016.6	9.7	34.7	218.4	286.0	1,511.9	2,999.1	505.6
1980	5,950.0	596.6	5,353.3	10.2	36.8	251.1	298.5	1,684.1	3,167.0	502.2
1981	5,858.2	594.3	5,263.9	9.8	36.0	258.7	289.7	1,649.5	3,139.7	474.7
1982	5,603.6	571.1	5,032.5	9.1	34.0	238.9	289.2	1,488.8	3,084.8	458.8
1983	5,175.0	537.7	4,637.4	8.3	33.7	216.5	279.2	1,337.7	2,868.9	430.8
1984	5,031.3	539.2	4,492.1	7.9	35.7	205.4	290.2	1,263.7	2,791.3	437.1
1985	5,207.1	556.6	4,650.5	8.0	37.1	208.5	302.9	1,287.3	2,901.2	462.0
1986	5,480.4	617.7	4,862.6	8.6	37.9	225.1	346.1	1,344.6	3,010.3	507.8
1987	5,550.0	609.7	4,940.3	8.3	37.4	212.7	351.3	1,329.6	3,081.3	529.4
1988	5,664.2	637.2	5,027.1	8.4	37.6	220.9	370.2	1,309.2	3,134.9	582.9
1989	5,741.0	663.1	5,077.9	8.7	38.1	233.0	383.4	1,276.3	3,171.3	630.4
1990	5,820.3	731.8	5,088.5	9.4	41.2	257.0	424.1	1,235.9	3,194.8	657.8
1991	5,897.8	758.1	5,139.7	9.8	42.3	272.7	433.3	1,252.0	3,228.8	659.0
1992	5,660.2	757.5	4,902.7	9.3	42.8	263.6	441.8	1,168.2	3,103.0	631.5
1993	5,484.4	746.8	4,737.6	9.5	41.1	255.9	440.3	1,099.2	3,032.4	606.1
1994	5,373.5	713.6	4,660.0	9.0	39.3	237.7	427.6	1,042.0	3,026.7	591.3
1995	5,275.9	684.6	4,591.3	8.2	37.1	220.9	418.3	987.1	3,043.8	560.4
1996	5,086.6	636.5	4,450.1	7.4	36.3	201.9	390.9	944.8	2,797.7	525.6
1997	4,930.0	611.3	4,318.7	6.8	35.9	186.3	382.3	919.4	2,893.4	506.0
1998	4,619.3	567.5	4,051.8	6.3	34.5	165.4	361.3	863.0	2,729.0	459.8
1999	4,266.8	524.7	3,742.1	5.7	32.7	150.2	336.1	770.0	2,551.4	420.7

1. Violent crimes are offenses of murder, forcible rape, robbery, and aggravated assault. 2. Property crimes are offenses of burglary, larceny-theft, and motor vehicle theft. Data are not included for the property crime of arson. *Source: Crime in the United States*, 1999, FBI, Uniform Crime Reports.

Arrests by Race, 1999

Offense charged	Percent distribution[1]				Offense charged	Percent distribution[1]			
	White	Black	American Indian or Alaskan Native	Asian or Pacific Islander		White	Black	American Indian or Alaskan Native	Asian or Pacific Islander
Total	69.0%	28.6%	1.2%	1.1%	Sex offenses, except forcible rape and prostitution	76.5	21.1	1.2	1.2
Murder[2]	45.9	51.8	1.1	1.3	Drug abuse violation	63.6	35.2	.5	.7
Forcible rape	61.5	36.2	1.1	1.2	Gambling	30.9	63.7	.1	5.3
Robbery	43.9	54.4	.6	1.1	Offenses against family and children	66.4	30.8	1.0	1.8
Aggravated assault	63.0	34.8	1.0	1.2	Driving under the influence	87.4	10.2	1.4	1.1
Burglary	68.6	29.2	.9	1.3	Liquor laws	85.5	10.6	3.1	.9
Larceny-theft	66.1	30.8	1.3	1.7	Drunkenness	83.5	14.9	1.2	.4
Motor vehicle theft	54.9	42.2	1.1	1.8	Disorderly conduct	65.8	32.0	1.5	.7
Arson	74.4	23.7	1.0	.9	Vagrancy	56.1	40.3	3.0	.6
Other assaults	64.9	32.7	1.4	1.1	All other offenses except traffic	64.8	32.6	1.3	1.2
Forgery and counterfeiting	66.1	32.1	.5	1.3	Suspicion	68.9	29.8	.7	.6
Fraud	65.7	33.2	.4	.7	Curfew and loitering law violations	72.5	25.2	1.1	1.2
Embezzlement	64.4	33.9	.3	1.4	Runaways	77.3	17.9	1.1	3.8
Stolen property—buying, receiving, possessing	55.4	42.8	.8	1.1					
Vandalism	75.2	22.2	1.5	1.1					
Weapons—carrying, possessing, etc.	60.3	37.9	.7	1.1					
Prostitution and commercialized vice	59.3	38.4	.7	1.6					

1. Because of rounding, the percentages may not add up to total. 2. Includes nonnegligent manslaughter. *Source: Crime in the United States, 1999,* FBI, Uniform Crime Reports.

Crime Index by State, 1999

State	Crime index total		Violent crime	Property crime	Murder[1]	State	Crime index total		Violent crime	Property crime	Murder[1]
	Number	Rate per 100,000					Number	Rate per 100,000			
Ala.	192,819	4,412.3	21,421	171,398	345	Nebr.	68,444	4,108.3	7,167	61,277	60
Alaska	27,008	4,363.2	3,909	23,099	53	Nev.	84,185	4,653.7	10,311	73,874	165
Ariz.	281,735	5,896.5	26,334	255,401	384	N.H.[2]	27,406	2,281.9	1,159	26,247	18
Ark.	103,131	4,042.8	10,848	92,283	143	N.J.	276,873	3,400.1	33,540	243,333	287
Calif.	1,261,164	3,805.0	207,879	1,053,285	2,005	N.M.	103,740	5,962.1	14,520	89,220	170
Colo.	164,813	4,063.4	13,811	151,002	185	N.Y.	596,743	3,279.3	107,147	489,596	903
Conn.	111,236	3,389.3	11,342	99,894	107	N.C.	395,971	5,175.4	41,474	354,497	552
Del.	36,456	4,835.0	5,534	30,922	24	N.D.	15,172	2,393.1	424	14,748	10
DC	41,868	8,067.1	8,448	33,420	241	Ohio	449,880	3,996.4	35,616	414,264	397
Fla.	937,718	6,205.5	129,044	808,674	859	Okla.	157,286	4,683.9	17,066	140,220	231
Ga.	400,968	5,148.5	41,585	359,383	583	Ore.	165,866	5,022.0	12,432	153,434	88
Hawaii	57,324	4,837.5	2,785	54,539	44	Pa.	373,452	3,113.7	50,431	323,021	592
Idaho	39,429	3,149.3	3,066	36,363	25	P.R.	81,854	2,105.3	14,180	67,674	567
Ill.[2]	546,561	4,506.6	88,838	457,723	937	R.I.	35,497	3,581.9	2,840	32,657	36
Ind.	223,808	3,765.9	22,261	201,547	391	S.C.	206,907	5,324.4	32,920	173,987	258
Iowa	92,497	3,224.0	8,034	84,463	43	S.D.	19,386	2,644.7	1,227	18,159	18
Kans.[2]	117,803	4,438.7	10,159	107,644	160	Tenn.	257,413	4,693.9	38,111	219,302	391
Ky.[2]	114,003	2,878.1	11,908	102,095	212	Tex.	1,008,567	5,031.8	112,306	896,261	1,217
La.	251,252	5,746.8	32,033	219,219	468	Utah	105,999	4,976.5	5,869	100,130	44
Maine[2]	36,024	2,875.0	1,406	34,618	27	Vt.	16,735	2,817.3	676	16,059	17
Md.	254,420	4,919.2	38,447	215,973	465	Va.	231,886	3,373.9	21,626	210,260	392
Mass.	201,460	3,262.5	34,023	167,437	122	Wash.	302,509	5,255.5	21,716	280,793	171
Mich.	426,596	4,324.8	56,709	369,887	695	W.Va.	49,161	2,720.6	6,336	42,825	79
Minn.	171,802	3,597.2	13,085	158,717	134	Wisc.	173,062	3,296.4	12,908	160,154	179
Miss.	118,231	4,269.8	9,671	108,560	213	Wyo.	16,583	3,454.8	1,115	15,468	11
Mo.	250,363	4,578.7	27,353	223,010	359	**U.S. total**	11,635,149	4,266.8	1,430,693	10,204,456	15,533
Mont.[2]	35,937	4,069.9	1,823	34,114	23						

NOTE: The Crime Index is composed of the violent and property crime categories. Violent crimes are murder, forcible rape, robbery, and aggravated assault. Property crimes are burglary, larceny-theft, and auto-theft. Data are not included for the property crime of arson. 1. Includes nonnegligent manslaughter. 2. Limited data for 1999 were available for the states of Illinois, Kansas, Kentucky, Maine, Montana, and New Hampshire; therefore, it was necessary that their crime counts be estimated. *Source: Crime in the United States, 1999,* FBI Uniform Crime Reports.

Crime Rates for Selected Large Cities, 1998
(offenses known to the police per 100,000 population)

City ranked by population size, 1998[1]	Crime index, total		Violent crime				Property crime	
		Murder	Forcible rape	Robbery	Aggravated assault	Burglary	Larceny-theft	Motor vehicle theft
New York, N.Y.	4,392	8.6	27.8	535	596	628	1,998	599
Los Angeles, Calif.	5,072	11.8	38.5	437	871	720	2,209	785
Chicago, Ill.	(²)	25.6	(²)	840	1,336	1,309	4,418	1,157
Houston, Tex.	7,112	14.1	36.4	429	643	1,283	3,565	1,141
Philadelphia, Pa.	7,319	23.3	51.9	789	600	1,065	3,442	1,347
Phoenix, Ariz.	8,545	15.1	28.2	307	482	1,528	4,729	1,456
San Diego, Calif.	4,514	3.5	30.8	176	515	610	2,354	824
San Antonio, Tex.	7,032	8.1	66.7	162	215	1,089	4,842	650
Dallas, Tex.	9,236	23.1	66.5	540	833	1,722	4,525	1,526
Detroit, Mich.	11,791	43.0	85.8	856	1,458	2,152	4,332	2,865
Las Vegas, Nev.	5,846	12.8	55.1	362	346	1,258	2,685	1,127
Honolulu, Hawaii	5,425	1.9	27.7	120	118	879	3,735	543
San Jose, Calif.	3,532	3.4	41.5	105	450	480	2,084	369
Indianapolis, Ind.	6,257	18.8	77.1	381	658	1,482	2,876	764
San Francisco, Calif.	6,224	7.8	32.9	530	419	905	3,419	910
Jacksonville, Fla.	7,782	10.5	74.1	292	777	1,543	4,333	752
Baltimore, Md.	10,947	47.1	70.8	1,161	1,141	1,990	5,427	1,111
Columbus, Ohio	9,468	11.8	101.0	395	309	2,046	5,496	1,111
El Paso, Tex.	5,730	2.7	38.6	132	527	421	4,183	425
Memphis, Tenn.	8,807	19.0	119.5	690	670	2,469	3,459	1,380
Charlotte-Mecklenburg, N.C.	8,852	11.0	56.1	405	983	1,804	4,933	661
Milwaukee, Wisc.	7,843	18.9	48.6	505	430	1,199	4,393	1,249
Austin, Tex.	7,002	5.5	39.1	196	300	1,242	4,669	551
Boston, Mass.	6,251	6.1	63.6	417	840	645	3,141	1,138
Seattle, Wash.	9,825	9.1	45.0	321	456	1,293	6,193	1,507
Nashville, Tenn.	10,160	18.5	92.2	424	1,096	1,431	5,874	1,224
Washington, DC	8,828	49.7	36.3	689	943	1,216	4,650	1,243
Denver, Colo.	5,306	10.0	62.8	209	291	1,158	2,531	1,045
Fort Worth, Tex.	7,129	12.9	58.9	273	525	1,491	3,942	826
Cleveland, Ohio	6,981	16.3	116.2	679	496	1,382	2,837	1,454
Portland, Ore.	9,424	5.3	73.9	335	958	1,373	5,443	1,236
New Orleans, La.	8,662	48.8	63.5	629	720	1,487	3,957	1,755
Tucson, Ariz.	9,685	9.6	77.8	318	629	1,440	5,992	1,220
Oklahoma City, Okla.	10,077	12.1	90.8	274	618	1,999	6,224	859
Kansas City, Mo.	12,000	29.0	85.3	594	1,159	2,346	6,136	1,650
Virginia Beach, Va.	4,050	3.2	19.3	112	92	624	2,987	212
Long Beach, Calif.	4,437	8.8	25.8	410	415	909	1,842	826
Albuquerque, N.M.	10,806	8.8	51.8	401	856	1,903	6,086	1,501
Atlanta, Ga.	14,032	36.0	92.9	1,124	1,794	2,195	6,883	1,907
Fresno, Calif.	7,934	8.9	43.3	345	655	1,287	4,192	1,403
Tulsa, Okla.	7,326	9.8	69.1	220	833	1,681	3,623	891
Sacramento, Calif.	8,219	8.1	36.7	439	394	1,691	4,090	1,561
Oakland, Calif.	9,794	19.1	90.3	704	1,048	1,626	4,930	1,377
Miami, Fla.	12,045	23.1	37.5	1,018	1,470	2,100	5,605	1,791
Omaha, Neb.	7,171	7.6	47.0	257	1,003	881	3,954	1,022
Mesa, Ariz.	6,945	3.0	32.9	.137	488	1,082	4,364	838
Minneapolis, Minn.	9,561	16.0	126.5	655	728	1,795	5,002	1,239
Pittsburgh, Pa.	5,964	10.0	53.8	438	374	1,054	3,249	784
Colorado Springs, Colo.	5,848	2.2	74.6	143	320	974	3,972	363
Cincinnati, Ohio	7,350	5.8	117.2	391	359	1,504	4,345	628
St. Louis, Mo.	14,952	32.8	48.8	1,017	1,472	2,627	7,814	1,940
Wichita, Kans.	7,079	9.4	56.8	242	358	1,433	4,376	605
Toledo, Ohio	8,046	6.9	56.9	281	560	1,630	4,437	1,073
Santa Ana, Calif.	3,687	6.7	21.8	270	255	482	1,866	786
Buffalo, N.Y.	7,232	12.6	63.8	562	490	1,670	3,471	962
Arlington, Tex.	6,380	4.2	45.1	165	393	972	4,152	648
Anaheim, Calif.	3,495	6.0	24.4	184	294	698	1,744	545
Tampa, Fla.	12,189	13.6	90.2	835	1,618	1,939	5,973	1,720
Corpus Christi, Tex.	7,833	5.9	49.8	122	551	1,343	5,299	463
Newark, N.J.	8,560	22.3	60.2	1,057	954	1,270	3,339	1,858
Riverside, Calif.	4,682	6.4	32.9	264	546	888	2,236	708
St. Paul, Minn.	7,720	8.4	92.6	320	488	1,502	4,414	895
Aurora, Colo.	5,536	10.7	72.0	182	306	885	3,381	700
Louisville, Ky.	6,820	14.9	35.4	484	409	1,750	3,198	929
Birmingham, Ala.	8,685	32.8	79.4	373	727	1,592	4,861	1,019

1. Resident population estimated by the F.B.I. 2. The rates for forcible rape, violent crime, and crime index are not shown because the forcible rape figures were not in accordance with national Uniform Crime Reporting guidelines. *Source: Statistical Abstract of the United States, 2000.*

Battle Over a U.S. Missile Shield

Essential Deterrent or Expensive Folly?

By the TIME staff

As national defense officials working under a new president eyed the future of America's military needs, the notion of creating a protective umbrella to shield the United States from assault by foreign missiles—an idea first seriously proposed by President Ronald Reagan—moved to center stage. Controversial and costly, the proposed program roiled diplomatic waters around the world, even though it was years away from deployment and technologically unproven.

Advocates of the shield touted it as a purely defensive umbrella that would threaten no one, even as it sheltered America from long-range missiles fired by rogue states like North Korea and Iran that are acquiring increasingly sophisticated missile technology. Critics, who included some of America's firmest allies abroad, argued that the program, whose deployment would require the United States to negate the Anti-Ballistic Missile Treaty of 1972, would destabilize the world's nuclear balance—and would not protect America against equally destructive threats from its enemies.

Under President Bill Clinton, Pentagon officials proceeded with the development and testing of a limited ground-based missile-defense system, but Clinton left office without endorsing deployment of the shield. New president George W. Bush and Secretary of Defense Donald Rumsfeld, a longtime advocate of the program, came into office determined to make the development of a much more elaborate missile shield system a cornerstone of U.S. defense policy. But their vision of the shield has to overcome three major hurdles before it can become a reality: physics, fiscal reality, and foreign policy.

First Hurdle: Physics

According to the Pentagon, Clinton's ground-based system is the nearest to being fielded—a handful of missiles to be deployed as early as 2005, followed by more research into ship- and plane-based interceptors. The program flunked two of its three tests during the Clinton administration, but an anti-missile rocket successfully intercepted and destroyed a missile in July 2001, though Pentagon officials acknowledged the test was simplified.

Ultimately, the most vocal missile-defense advocates want a space-based laser system, ready to destroy missiles fired from anywhere at any time, bound for any place. But even if approved, this system would not be ready until at least 2020. So the Pentagon is scurrying to modify two systems now in development. The Navy's ship-based missile system and the Air Force's plane-based laser system were originally designed to take out shorter-range missiles. But the military is grooming them to play major roles in a national missile-defense system aimed at ocean-crossing ICBMs.

Second Hurdle: Fiscal Reality

The second concern involves the enormous cost of this big-ticket item. Building it is a challenge on a par with building the atom bomb and putting a man on the moon. But those challenges were forged amid World War II and the cold war, when the White House, Congress, and the public saw their achievement as high national priorities. There is no such consensus on missile defense. Most Democrats were balking. Even CIA analysts say the most likely threats to U.S. security are not incoming missiles but rather such portable weapons of mass destruction as truck and suitcase bombs.

Contrary to public perception, even the U.S. military is not uniformly gung-ho on the missile shield. Budget plans now floating inside the Pentagon call for boosting missile-defense spending about $1 billion, or 20%, a year, to more than $5 billion annually. But that's not nearly enough to build Bush's expanded version of the system, which could top $200 billion. Many military leaders believe their planes, tanks, and ships would provide greater utility against future threats than a missile shield.

Third Hurdle: World Reaction

While the Pentagon faces the challenge of building the shield, it is the nation's diplomats spreading out over the world who face the equally arduous task of selling it overseas. It won't be easy. Washington's allies and its foes have grown accustomed to dealing with a world larded with nuclear weapons. During the cold war, the Anti-Ballistic Missile Treaty of 1972 ensured that the United States and the Soviet Union would remain naked to the other's atomic wrath. While the logic of such mutual assured destruction was ghoulish, it did have one thing going for it: it worked.

In Europe, the British gave the strongest support to the Bush plan, and the French were the most opposed. The Bush team responded by repackaging the missile-defense concept as a collaborative venture, inviting Russia and European Union members to be founding partners. At his first meeting with Russian president Vladimir Putin (June 2001), President Bush tried to convince a doubtful Putin that the plan was not directed against Russia.

Not surprisingly, China reacted most vehemently to the plan, saying the United States "has violated the ABM Treaty, will destroy the balance of international security forces, and could cause a new arms race." Indeed, the Bush administration plainly views the ABM treaty as a relic. Bush said he was willing to reduce the United States' 7,200 nuclear weapons quickly and unilaterally to entice both allies and such potential foes as China and Russia into embracing a more defensive strategic balance. □

STAR WARS II

By 2005 the U.S. wants to build a national missile-defense system to protect against potential attacks on U.S. territory from North Korea and other "rogue" states

Source: Department of Defense
TIME Graphic by Lon Tweeten

NORTH KOREA

CHINA

JAPAN

RUSSIA

Alaska

U.S. spy satellite

Warhead

Tracking satellite

Thruster

Fuel tank

Sensor

Kill vehicle

Interceptor

1 In this scenario, U.S. spy satellites in orbit detect an enemy missile launch.

2 An X-band radar in the Aleutian Islands tracks the path of the incoming missile, distinguishing a real warhead from its decoys.

3 The Battle Management Center in Colorado hands off the radar's data to the fleet of Interceptor missiles in Alaska.

4 The Exoatmospheric Kill Vehicle separates and, using infrared sensors, guides itself into the enemy missile destroying it 140 miles (225 km) above the earth.

Highest-Ranking Officers in U.S. History

General and Commander-in-Chief[1]

George Washington (1732–1799), b. Westmoreland County, Va., unanimously voted by Congress on June 15, 1775, to the rank of general and commander-in-chief (of the Continental army).

General of the Armies[2]

John Joseph Pershing (1860–1948), b. Linn County, Mo., made permanent general of the armies, 1919.

General of the Army, General of the Air Force, Admiral of the Navy (Five-Stars)

George Catlett Marshall (1880–1959), b. Uniontown, Pa., promoted Dec. 1944.

Douglas MacArthur (1880–1964), b. Little Rock, Ark., promoted Dec. 1944.

Dwight David Eisenhower (1890–1969), b. Denison, Tex., promoted Dec. 1944.

Henry Harley Arnold (1866–1950), b. Gladwyne, Pa. Arnold had the unique distinction of being a five-star general twice—in 1944 as general of the army, and in June, 1949 as general of the air force. He is the only air force general to have held the five-star rank.

Omar Nelson Bradley (1893–1981), b. Clark, Mo., promoted Sept. 1950.

Fleet Admiral (Five-Star)

William Daniel Leahy (1875–1959), b. Hampton, Iowa, promoted Dec. 1944.

Ernest Joseph King (1878–1956), b. Lorain, Ohio, promoted Dec. 1944.

Chester William Nimitz (1885–1966), b. Fredericksburg, Tex., promoted Dec. 1944.

William Frederick Halsey (1882–1959), b. Elizabeth, N.J., promoted Dec. 1945.

1. On March 15, 1978, George Washington was promoted posthumously to the newly created rank of General of the Armies of the United States. Congress authorized this title to make it clear that Washington was the army's senior general. 2. General Pershing was given the option of five stars but he declined. *Source:* Department of Defense and U.S. Army Historian, Research and Analysis Center.

The Joint Chiefs of Staff (JCS)

The Joint Chiefs of Staff consist of the chairman, the vice chairman, the chief of staff of the army, the chief of naval operations, the chief of staff of the air force, and the commandant of the Marine Corps.

The collective body of the JCS is headed by the chairman (or vice chairman in the chairman's absence), who sets the agenda and presides over JCS meetings. Their responsibilities take precedence over their duties as the Chiefs of Military Services. The chairman is the principal military adviser to the president, the secretary of defense, and the National Security Council (NSC); however, all JCS members are by law military advisers, and they may respond to a request or voluntarily submit, through the chairman, advice or opinions to the president, the secretary of state, or the NSC. The Joint Chiefs of Staff have no executive authority to commit combatant forces.

In addition to their responsibilities on the JCS, the military service chiefs are responsible to the secretaries of their military departments for management of the services. The service chiefs serve for four years. By custom the vice chiefs of the services act for their chiefs in most matters having to do with day-to-day operation of the services.

Joint Chiefs of Staff, 2001

Chairman of the Joint Chiefs of Staff, General Richard B. Myers, U.S. Air Force; vice chairman of the Joint Chiefs of Staff, General Peter Pace, Marine Corps; General Eric K. Shinseki, chief of staff of the U.S. Army; Admiral Vern Clark, chief of naval operations; General Michael E. Ryan, chief of staff of the U.S. Air Force; and General James L. Jones, commandant of the Marine Corps.

Past Chairmen of the JCS

General of the Army, Omar N. Bradley, 1949–1953
Adm. Arthur W. Radford, U.S. Navy, 1953–1957
Gen. Nathan F. Twining, U.S. Air Force, 1957–1960
Gen. Lyman L. Lemnitzer, U.S. Army, 1960–1962
Gen. Maxwell D. Taylor, U.S. Army, 1962–1964
Gen. Earle G. Wheeler, U.S. Army, 1964–1970
Adm. Thomas H. Moorer, U.S. Navy, 1970–1974
Gen. George S. Brown, U.S. Air Force, 1974–1978
Gen. David C. Jones, U.S. Air Force, 1978–1982
Gen. John W. Vessey, Jr., U.S. Army, 1982–1985
Adm. William J. Crowe, U.S. Navy, 1985–1989
Gen. Colin L. Powell, U.S. Army, 1989–1993
Gen. John M. Shalikashvili, U.S. Army, 1993–1997
Gen. Henry H. Shelton, U.S. Army, 1997–2001

Federal Budget Outlays for Defense Functions: 1980 to 2000

(in billions of dollars [$134.0 represents $134,000,000,000])

Defense function	1980	1990	1992	1993	1994	1995	1996	1997	1998	1999	2000, est.
Total	134.0	299.3	298.4	291.1	281.6	272.1	265.8	270.5	268.5	274.9	290.6
Percent change[1]	15.2	–1.4	9.2	–2.4	–3.3	–3.4	–2.3	1.8	–0.7	3.1	5.7
Defense Dept., military	130.9	289.8	286.9	278.6	268.6	259.4	253.2	258.3	256.1	261.4	277.5
Military personnel	40.9	75.6	81.2	75.9	73.1	70.8	66.7	69.7	69.0	69.5	73.5
Operation, maintenance	44.8	88.3	92.0	94.1	87.9	91.1	88.8	92.5	93.5	96.4	103.8
Procurement	29.0	81.0	74.9	69.9	61.8	55.0	48.9	47.7	48.2	48.8	48.0
Research and development	13.1	37.5	34.6	37.0	34.8	34.6	36.5	37.0	37.4	37.4	37.4
Military construction	2.5	5.1	4.3	4.8	5.0	6.8	6.7	6.2	6.0	5.5	4.8
Family housing	1.7	3.5	3.3	3.3	3.3	3.6	3.8	4.0	3.9	3.7	3.8
Other[2]	–1.1	–1.2	–3.3	–6.4	2.7	–2.4	1.8	1.2	–1.9	0.1	6.3

1. Change from immediate year. 2. Revolving and management funds, trust funds, special foreign currency program allowances, and offsetting receipts. *Source:* U.S. Office of Management and Budget, *Historical Tables,* annual.

Service Academies

U.S. Military Academy

Established in 1802 by an act of Congress, the U.S. Military Academy is located in West Point, N.Y. To gain admission a candidate must first secure a nomination from a member of Congress or the Department of the Army.

Cadets are members of the U.S. Army. Upon successful completion of the four-year course, the graduate receives the degree of bachelor of science and is commissioned a second lieutenant in the U.S. Army with a requirement to serve as an officer on active duty for a minimum of five years.

U.S. Naval Academy

The Naval School, established in 1845 at Fort Severn, Annapolis, Md., was renamed the U.S. Naval Academy in 1850. A four-year course was adopted a year later. The "Yard," as the campus is referred to, blends French Renaissance and modern architecture with many new academic, athletic, and laboratory facilities.

Upon being commissioned as an ensign in the navy or a second lieutenant in the Marine Corps, the commitment is at least five years' active duty. Aviation service commitment depends upon type of aircraft and whether you are a pilot or naval flight officer. Most aviators serve seven years after they complete their initial flight training.

U.S. Air Force Academy

The bill establishing the U.S. Air Force Academy was signed by President Eisenhower on April 1, 1954. The first class of 306 cadets was sworn in on July 11, 1955, at Lowry Air Force Base, Denver, Colo., the academy's temporary location. The Cadet Wing moved into the academy's permanent home north of Colorado Springs, Colo., in 1958.

Upon completion of the four-year program, leading to a bachelor of science degree, a cadet who meets the qualifications is commissioned a second lieutenant in the U.S. Air Force.

Military & Veterans Websites

U.S. Air Force: www.af.mil
U.S. Army: www.army.mil
U.S. Navy: www.navy.mil
MarineLINK: www.usmc.mil
U.S. Coast Guard: www.uscg.mil
DefenseLink (DOD): www.defenselink.mil
Military Woman: www.militarywoman.org
   (not a DOD or armed forces site)
Selective Service System: www.sss.gov
Department of Veterans Affairs (VA): www.va.gov
BosniaLINK: www.dtic.mil/bosnia/index.html
Gulf War Veterans: www.gulfweb.org
Vietnam Veterans: www.vva.org
WWII U.S. Veterans: ww2.vet.org
Korean War Veterans Association: www.kwva.org
Kosovo Peacekeeping Force: http://kforonline.com
American Legion: www.legion.org
Air America: www.air-america.org
North Atlantic Treaty Organization (NATO):
   www.nato.int

U.S. Coast Guard Academy

The U.S. Coast Guard Academy in New London, Conn., was founded in 1876. It is the only one of the four armed forces service academies that offers appointments based solely on the basis of an annual nationwide competition, with no congressional appointments or geographical quotas.

Upon graduation, there is a five-year commitment to serve as a commissioned Coast Guard officer, the first two years of which are on a Coast Guard cutter.

U.S. Merchant Marine Academy

The U.S. Merchant Marine Academy, situated at Kings Point, N.Y., was dedicated Sept. 30, 1943. It is maintained by the Department of Transportation under direction of the Maritime Administration.

Upon completion of the course of study, a graduate receives a bachelor of science degree, a license as a merchant marine officer (issued by the U.S. Coast Guard), and a commission as an ensign in the Naval Reserve.

Women Graduates of U.S. Service Academies

The first women to attend the service academies graduated in 1980. Since that time, the percentage of each graduating class who are women has gradually increased. The most dramatic increase is in women graduates of the Coast Guard Academy—where, in the class of 1999, they represented almost a third of the graduates.

Service academy	Women as a percentage of graduates			Number of women in class of 1999
	Class of 1980	Class of 1990	Class of 1999	
Air Force	10.9%	10.4%	14.7%	140
Coast Guard	9.2	12.6	31.5	42
Military (West Point)	6.8	9.8	13.4	125
Naval Academy	5.8	9.7	15.2	132

Source: Department of Defense, unpublished data provided by each service academy, June 1993 and July 1999; and Department of Transportation, unpublished data provided by the Coast Guard Academy, June 1993 and July 1999.

U.S. Military Ranks

Source: U.S. Department of Defense

Pay Grade	Army	Navy	Marines	Air Force
Commissioned Officers				
O-1	Second Lieutenant	Ensign	Second Lieutenant	Second Lieutenant
O-2	First Lieutenant	Lieutenant Junior Grade	First Lieutenant	First Lieutenant
O-3	Captain	Lieutenant	Captain	Captain
O-4	Major	Lieutenant Commander	Major	Major
O-5	Lieutenant Colonel	Commander	Lieutenant Colonel	Lieutenant Colonel
O-6	Colonel	Captain	Colonel	Colonel
O-7	Brigadier General	Rear Admiral (L)	Brigadier General	Brigadier General
O-8	Major General	Rear Admiral	Major General	Major General
O-9	Lieutenant General	Vice Admiral	Lieutenant General	Lieutenant General
O-10	General	Admiral	General	General
Special Grades[1]				
(5 stars)	General of the Army	Fleet Admiral	(none)	General of the Air Force
Warrant Officers				
W-1	Warrant Officer. Grades W-2 to W-5 Chief Warrant Officer			
Enlisted Personnel				
E-1	Private	Seaman Recruit	Private	Airman Basic
E-2	Private	Seaman Apprentice	Private First Class	Airman
E-3	Private First Class	Seaman	Lance Corporal	Airman First Class
E-4	Corporal / Specialist 4	Petty Officer, Third Class	Corporal	Sergeant / Senior Airman
E-5	Sergeant / Specialist 5	Petty Officer, Second Class	Sergeant	Staff Sergeant
E-6	Staff Sergeant / Specialist 6	Petty Officer, First Class	Staff Sergeant	Technical Sergeant
E-7	Sergeant First Class / Specialist 7	Chief Petty Officer	Gunnery Sergeant	Master Sergeant
E-8	First Sergeant / Master Sergeant	Senior Chief Petty Officer	First Sergeant / Master Sergeant	Senior Master Sergeant
E-9	Command Sergeant Major / Sergeant Major	Master Chief Petty Officer	Sergeant Major / Master Gunnery Sergeant	Chief Master Sergeant
Special Grades[2]				
	Sergeant Major of the Army	Master Chief Petty Officer of the Navy	Sergeant Major of the Marine Corps	Chief Master Sergeant of the Air Force

1. There are no living five-star commissioned officers. 2. Senior enlisted advisers. There is only one for each branch of service.

U.S. Military Personnel on Active Duty in Selected Foreign Countries, 1998

Country	1998	Country	1998	Country	1998
In foreign countries[1]	**259,871**	Egypt	5,846	New Zealand	25
Ashore	218,957	El Salvador	28	Norway	107
Afloat	40,914	France	74	Oman	28
Antarctica	22	Germany	60,053	Pakistan	29
Argentina	27	Greece	498	Panama	5,400
Australia	333	Greenland	131	Peru	29
Austria	34	Haiti	239	Philippines	35
Bahamas, The	24	Honduras	427	Portugal	1,066
Bahrain	748	Hungary	4,220	Qatar	26
Belgium	1,679	Iceland	1,960	Russia	68
Bolivia	26	India	25	Saudi Arabia	1,722
Bosnia and Herzegovina	8,170	Indonesia	48	Singapore	168
Brazil	45	Israel	40	South Africa	25
Canada	179	Italy	11,677	Spain	3,575
Chile	25	Jamaica	11	Switzerland	22
China	58	Japan	41,257	Thailand	126
Colombia	32	Jordan	30	Tunisia	193
Croatia	866	Kenya	31	Turkey	2,864
Cuba	1,527	Korea, Rep. of	35,663	Ukraine	10
Cyprus	25	Kuwait	1,640	United Arab Emirates	22
Denmark	39	Macedonia	518	United Kingdom	11,379
Diego Garcia	705	Mexico	27	Venezuela	35
Ecuador	164	Netherlands	703	Zimbabwe	11

1. Includes areas not listed below. *Source:* U.S. Department of Defense, *Selected Manpower Statistics, annual.*

Active Military Duty Personnel, 1940–2000[1]

Year	Army[2]	Air Force[2, 3]	Navy	Marine Corps	Total
1940	269,023		160,997	28,345	458,365
1945	8,266,373		3,319,586	469,925	12,055,884
1950	593,167	411,277	380,739	74,279	1,459,462
1955	1,109,296	959,946	660,695	205,170	2,935,107
1960	873,078	814,752	616,987	170,621	2,475,438
1965	969,066	824,662	669,985	190,213	2,653,926
1970	1,322,548	791,349	691,126	259,737	3,064,760
1975	784,333	612,751	535,085	195,951	2,128,120
1980	777,036	557,969	527,153	188,469	2,050,627
1985	780,787	601,515	570,705	198,025	2,151,032
1990	732,403	535,233	579,417	196,652	2,043,705
1991	710,821	510,432	570,262	194,040	1,985,555
1992	610,450	470,315	541,883	184,529	1,807,177
1993	572,423	444,351	509,950	178,379	1,705,103
1994	541,343	426,327	468,662	174,158	1,610,490
1995	508,559	400,409	434,617	174,639	1,518,224
1996	491,103	389,001	416,735	174,883	1,471,722
1997	491,707	377,385	395,564	173,906	1,438,562
1998	483,880	367,470	382,338	173,142	1,406,830
1999[4]	473,595	363,449	370,343	172,369	1,379,756
2000[4]	474,205	355,891	368,440	171,701	1,370,237

1. Military personnel on extended or continuous active duty. Excludes reserves on active duty for training. Prior year totals have been corrected. 2. Represents "Command Strength" prior to June 30, 1956. 3. Army Air Forces and its predecessors for period prior to Sept. 18, 1947. 4. Totals as of Sept. 30, except 1999 and 2000 totals are for Jan. 31. Figures for 1998 through 2000 include cadets-midshipmen. *Source:* Department of Defense.

The Medal of Honor

Often called the Congressional Medal of Honor, it is the nation's highest military award for "uncommon valor" by men and women in the armed forces. It is given for actions that are above and beyond the call of duty in combat against an armed enemy. The medal was first awarded by the army on March 25, 1863. More than 3,400 men have been awarded the medal, as well as one woman, Dr. Mary Walker, a surgeon in the Civil War.

Recipients of the medal are awarded $400 per month for life, a right to burial at Arlington National Cemetery, admission for them or their children to a service academy (if they qualify and quotas permit), and free travel on government aircraft to almost anywhere in the world, on a space-available basis.

Medal of Honor Recipients

	Total[1]	Army	Navy	Marines	Coast Guard	Air Force	Civilian
Civil War	1,522	1,196	305	17	—	—	4
Noncombat, 1865–1870	13	1	12	—	—	—	—
Indian Wars (1861–1898)	426	422	—	—	—	—	4
Korea (1871)	15	—	9	6	—	—	—
Noncombat, 1871–1899	106	—	104	2	—	—	—
Spanish-American War	110	31	64	15	—	—	—
Samoa	4	—	1	3	—	—	—
Philippines	80	69	5	6	—	—	—
China	59	4	22	33	—	—	—
Noncombat, 1901–1910	49	1	46	2	—	—	—
Philippines (1911)	6	1	5	—	—	—	—
Mexican Campaign (1914)	56	1	46	9	—	—	—
Haiti (1915)	6	—	—	6	—	—	—
Noncombat, 1915–1916	8	—	8	—	—	—	—
Dominican Republic	3	—	—	3	—	—	—
World War I	119	90	21	8	—	—	—
Haiti (1919–1920)	2	—	—	2	—	—	—
Nicaragua (1927–1933)	2	—	—	2	—	—	—
Noncombat, 1920–1940	17	1	15	1	—	—	—
World War II	463	323	57	82	1	—	—
Korean War	131	82	7	42	—	—	—
Vietnam War	242	156	16	57	—	13	—
Somalia (1993)	2	2	—	—	—	—	—
Unknown Soldiers	9	9	—	—	—	—	—
Total	3,450	2,389	743	296	1	13	8

1. These totals reflect the total number of Medals of Honor awarded. Nineteen (19) men received a second award. In Feb. 2000, the medal was awarded to an army Vietnam War medic. In May 2000, the medal was awarded to 21 Asian-American army veterans for their heroism in World War II. *Source:* The Congressional Medal of Honor Society, Mt. Pleasant, S.C.

Veterans of U.S. Wars and Their Dependents
(on the VA Compensation and Pension Rolls as of May 2001)

Veterans' benefits have existed since the origins of the nation. As of May 2001, 3,247,975 veterans, their dependents, and survivors of deceased veterans are receiving VA benefits and services.

The last dependent of a Revolutionary War veteran died in 1911; the War of 1812's last dependent

died in 1946; and the last dependent of the Mexican War died in 1962. Some 631 children and widows of Spanish-American War veterans are receiving VA benefits today. There is in fact still a surviving widow and 12 children of Civil War veterans who still draw VA benefits.

	Veterans	Children[1]	Parents	Surviving spouses
Civil War	—	12	—	1
Indian Wars	—	1	—	—
Spanish-American War	—	245	—	386
Mexican Border	9	25	—	181
World War I	144	5,810	1	25,573
World War II	647,205	18,707	1,388	272,793
Korean Conflict	249,515	4,110	1,496	63,579
Vietnam Era	851,143	13,465	6,118	114,514
Gulf War[2]	344,174	344,174	338	6,261
Total wartime	**2,092,190**	**50,883**	**9,341**	**483,288**
Nonservice-connected	352,761	27,221	—	230,194
Service-connected	2,306,731	30,757	11,650	288,661
Total	**2,659,492**	**57,978**	**11,650**	**518,855**

1. Children connotes a minor or a helpless adult. 2. For VA benefits purposes, the Gulf War period of service remains open-ended and also includes those discharged from 1991 to date. *Source:* Department of Veterans Affairs.

Last Living Veterans of America's Wars

American Revolution (1775–1783)
• Last veteran, Daniel F. Bakeman, died 4/5/1869, age 109
• Last widow, Catherine S. Damon, died 11/11/06, age 92
• Last dependent, Phoebe M. Palmeter, died 4/25/11, age 90

War of 1812 (1812–1815)
• Last veteran, Hiram Cronk, died 5/13/05, age 105
• Last widow, Carolina King, died 6/28/36, age unknown
• Last dependent, Esther A. H. Morgan, died 3/12/46, age 89

Indian Wars (c. 1861–1898)
• Last veteran, Fredrak Fraske, died 6/18/73, age 101

Mexican War (1846–1848)
• Last veteran, Owen Thomas Edgar, died 9/3/29, age 98
• Last widow, Lena James Theobald, died 6/20/63, age 89
• Last dependent, Jesse G. Bivens, died 11/1/62, age 94

Civil War (1861–1865)
• Last Union veteran, Albert Woolson, died 8/2/56, age 109
• Last Confederate veteran, John Salling, died 3/16/58, age 112

Spanish-American War (1898)
• Last veteran, Nathan E. Cook, died 9/10/92, age 106

Active Duty Servicewomen by Branch of Service and Rank, 1999

As of May 31, 1999, women in the military (including the Coast Guard) numbered 194,219—14% of the total active force. The Air Force has the highest percentage of women and the Marine Corps the lowest. The Army has the highest percentage of African-American women; the Marine Corps has the highest percentage of women of Hispanic origin. The Navy is the only service with a higher percentage of women serving in its officer ranks than in its enlisted ones.

Service and rank[1]	Number of women	Women as a percentage of total personnel	Service and rank[1]	Number of women	Women as a percentage of total personnel
Total DOD forces[2]			**Marine Corps**		
Enlisted	160,383	14.1%	Enlisted	9,060	5.9%
Officers	30,425	13.9	Officers	866	4.8
Army			**Air Force**		
Enlisted	58,119	15.0	Enlisted	53,632	18.7
Officers	10,219	13.2	Officers	11,629	16.7
Navy			**Coast Guard**		
Enlisted	39,572	12.8	Enlisted	2,726	10.0
Officers	7,711	14.3	Officers	685	9.8

1. Officers include warrant officers. 2. Defense Department (DOD) forces do not include Coast Guard. *Source:* U.S. Department of Defense, Defense Manpower Data Center, unpublished data, May 31, 1999.

America's Wars: Casualties and Veterans

American Revolution (1775–1783)
Total servicemembers	217,000
Battle deaths	4,435
Nonmortal woundings	6,188

War of 1812 (1812–1815)
Total servicemembers	286,730
Battle deaths	2,260
Nonmortal woundings	4,505

Indian Wars (approx. 1817–1898)
Total servicemembers	106,000[1]
Battle deaths	1,000[1]

Mexican War (1846–1848)
Total servicemembers	78,718
Battle deaths	1,733
Other deaths in service (nontheater)	11,550
Nonmortal woundings	4,152

Civil War (1861–1865)
Total servicemembers (Union)	2,213,363
Battle deaths (Union)	140,414
Other deaths in service (nontheater) (Union)	224,097
Nonmortal woundings (Union)	281,881
Total servicemembers (Conf.)	1,050,000
Battle deaths (Conf.)	74,524
Other deaths in service (nontheater) (Conf.)	59,297[2]
Nonmortal woundings (Conf.)	unknown

Spanish-American War (1898–1902)
Total servicemembers	306,760
Battle deaths	385
Other deaths in service (nontheater)	2,061
Nonmortal woundings	1,662

World War I (1917–1918)
Total servicemembers	4,734,991
Battle deaths	53,402
Other deaths in service (nontheater)	63,114
Nonmortal woundings	204,002
Living veterans	2,503[1]

World War II (1940–1945)
Total servicemembers	16,112,566
Battle deaths	291,557
Other deaths in service (nontheater)	113,842
Nonmortal woundings	671,846
Living veterans	5,451,378[1]

Korean War (1950–1953)
Total servicemembers	5,720,000
Battle deaths	33,686
Other deaths in service (theater)	2,830
Other deaths in service (nontheater)	17,730
Nonmortal woundings	103,284
Living veterans	3,913,749[1]

Vietnam War (1964–1975)
Total servicemembers	9,200,000
Deployed to Southeast Asia	3,100,000
Battle deaths	47,410
Other deaths in service (theater)	10,788
Other deaths in service (nontheater)	32,000
Nonmortal woundings	153,303
Living veterans	8,300,106[1]

Gulf War (1990–1991)
Total servicemembers	2,322,332
Deployed to Gulf	1,136,658
Battle deaths	148
Other deaths in service (theater)	235
Other deaths in service (nontheater)	914
Nonmortal woundings	467
Living veterans	1,753,530[1]

America's Wars Total
Military service during war	42,348,460
Battle deaths	650,954
Other deaths in service (theater)	13,853
Other deaths in service (nontheater)	229,661
Nonmortal woundings	1,431,290
Living war veterans	19,421,266[1]
Living veterans	25,497,691[1]

1. Veterans Administration estimate. 2. Estimated figure. Does not include 26,000–31,000 who died in Union prisons. *Source:* Department of Defense and Veterans Administration, May 2001.

Post-Vietnam Combat Casualties[1]

Place	Dates	Casualties
Lebanon	Aug. 1982–Feb. 1984	254
Grenada	Oct.–Nov. 1983	18
Libya	April 10–16, 1986	2
Panama	Dec. 1989–Jan. 1990	23

Place	Dates	Casualties
Persian Gulf	Aug. 1990–March 1998, Dec. 1998–present	148
Somalia	Dec. 1992–May 1993	29
Haiti	Sept. 1994–April 1996	0
Yugoslavia	March–June 1999	0

1. Does not include deaths from accidents. *Source:* U.S. Department of Defense.

American Prisoners of War

Congress defines a former prisoner of war as a person who, while serving on active military, naval, or air service, was forcibly detained or interned in the line of duty by an enemy government or a hostile force, during a period of war or in situations comparable to war. Less than half (40%) of the Americans held prisoner in the last six conflicts are now living.

	Total	WWI	WWII	Korea	Vietnam	Persian Gulf	Somalia
Captured and interned	142,257	4,120	130,201	7,140	772	23	1
Returned to U.S. military control	125,202	3,973	116,129	4,418	658	23	1
Refused repatriation	21	0	0	21	0	0	0
Died while POW	17,034	147	14,072	2,701	144	0	0
Alive, Jan. 1998	55,999	5	52,531	2,814	625	23	1

Source: U.S. Department of Veterans Affairs.

For international military affairs, *see* p. 715.

Einstein's Repulsive Idea

He invented antigravity and then abandoned it first chance he got—but it may be the most powerful force in the universe

By **MICHAEL D. LEMONICK** TIME

Albert Einstein never did like the idea of antigravity. It wasn't that he had a problem with far-fetched notions. After all, his special and general relativity theories made the astonishing assertion that time, space, and matter could be squeezed and stretched like so much India rubber. The trouble was that some sort of antigravity force—Einstein called it the "cosmological term"—was required to make the predictions of general relativity match what astronomers believed the actual universe looked like. And that extra term marred the mathematical elegance of his beloved equations. The great physicist was hugely relieved when the discovery of the expanding universe in the 1920s let him cross out what he declared was "my greatest blunder."

But he might have been a bit too hasty. In the spring of 2001 scientists made a powerful case that Einstein's blunder may actually have been another Nobel-worthy prediction. Using the Hubble Space Telescope to find and study a distant supernova—an exploding star—astronomers from two rival research teams have jointly gathered the strongest evidence yet that the expansion of the universe is actually speeding up. And that means something is pushing it.

A Mysterious Force

What that something might be is, at this point, anybody's guess. "Shake a tree full of theorists," says Adam Riess of the Space Telescope Science Institute in Baltimore, Md., leader of the collaboration, "and 20 ideas will fall out." For now, the unknown force is simply being called "dark energy."

But its existence is becoming hard to dispute. The first hint came a couple of years ago, when two independent teams of astronomers tried to calibrate the cosmic expansion using Type Ia supernovas, a kind of exploding star whose intrinsic brightness is highly consistent. Comparing the known brightness of such a supernova with how bright it appears in the sky gives a good measure of how far away it is—and thus how long ago in cosmic history its light was emitted. Then, by measuring how fast each supernova is moving away from Earth in the overall ballooning of the universe, it can be determined what the expansion rate was at different times in the past.

To everyone's astonishment, both groups found that instead of the gradual, gravity-driven slowdown they expected, the rate was getting faster. Says Saul Perlmutter of Lawrence Berkeley National Laboratory in California, who heads one of the groups: "We spent at least a year struggling to understand what we were seeing." In the end, both groups decided that dark energy, functioning as a kind of antigravity, was their best guess.

Other Explanations?

Critics argued that there might be a more conventional explanation, such as intergalactic dust, which could contaminate the brightness measurements. But the new observations seem to have closed that loophole. The newly identified supernova went off about 11 billion years ago—about 50% further back in time than the previous record holder. "If the dust were there," says Lawrence Berkeley astrophysicist Peter Nugent, a member of Perlmutter's team and Riess's collaborator on the new research, "the supernova would have been much dimmer than it was."

The new supernova's remoteness was even more important for another reason. "If dark energy is really the explanation for what we see," says Riess, "then its effect should have been weaker in the early universe." That's because while the force of gravity between galaxies falls as they move farther apart, dark energy gets stronger as the universe expands. Shortly after the Big Bang, when the universe took up relatively little space, there wasn't much dark energy. Now much bigger, the modern universe has more space and thus more energy to shove galaxies apart. This distant supernova shows that the expansion was slower long ago.

Wanted: More Evidence

While the new observations go a long way toward confirming that dark energy is real, astronomers would love to see a few more distant supernovas, just to be sure. Unfortunately, that won't be happening soon. The Hubble pictures that Riess and Nugent analyzed were all taken purely by chance, while the telescope was looking for other things. Aiming at distant galaxies in hopes a supernova will go off is an inefficient use of the telescope's valuable time. The best bet would be a satellite devoted to such a project—and indeed, Perlmutter and others are working on that idea, although it will take years to get off the ground.

If space really does seethe with dark energy, the fate of the universe, a matter of longstanding debate, will be clear. With more dark energy today than yesterday, and more of the stuff tomorrow than today, the cosmos should fly apart faster and faster as time goes by. There will be no Big Crunch, as some have predicted, with billions of galaxies falling in on one another in a fiery apocalypse. Tens of billions of years from now, our Milky Way galaxy will find itself alone in empty space, with its nearest neighbors too far away to see. In the end, the stars will simply wink out—and the universe will end not with a bang but with the meekest of whimpers. □

GRAVITY AND ANTIGRAVITY

Size of visible universe today

Galaxies

Size of universe 6 billion years ago

① GRAVITY

Supernova 11 billion years ago, observed by Hubble telescope over past few years

Size of universe 2 billion years after the Big Bang

First galaxies form

Size of universe at az

EXPANSION SLOWING DOWN

EXPANSION SPEEDING UP

Big Bang 14 billion years ago begins universe

② ANTIGRAVITY

① GRAVITY

● **WHAT IT IS:** An attractive force that pulls matter together like a rubber band

● **HOW IT OPERATES:** Gravity weakens over distance; when the distance between two galaxies doubles, the force between them is one-fourth as strong

● **WHAT THAT MEANS:** As the universe expands, gravity is less and less effective at slowing the expansion

TIME Diagram by Joe Lertola

② ANTIGRAVITY (Dark Energy)

● **WHAT IT IS:** A property of empty space that exerts an outward force like a compressed spring at every point in space

● **HOW IT OPERATES:** A given volume of space always has the same amount of dark energy, so when the distance between two galaxies doubles, the force pushing them away from each other is twice as strong

● **WHAT THAT MEANS:** As the universe expands the volume of space increases, which means more dark energy. By now, 14 billion years after the Big Bang, antigravity has overwhelmed gravity, so the expansion will get faster and faster

New Moons Found Orbiting Saturn and Jupiter

In recent months astronomers searching the skies for new moons have hit the jackpot. A total of 22 natural satellites—twelve orbiting Saturn and ten orbiting Jupiter—were discovered between Aug. and Dec. 2000. Saturn, the second-largest planet in our solar system, now tops them all with 30 moons; Jupiter, the largest planet, is in second place with 28 moons; Uranus is in third with 21.

All of the newly discovered moons are considered irregular by astronomers because they have weak, elliptical orbits and are probably asteroids or small, icy bodies that were "captured" after the planet formed. Regular moons, on the other hand, orbit relatively close to their planet in nearly circular paths and are thought to form from the same gas and dust that formed their planets.

Recent Discoveries Result of International Efforts

Saturn's new moons were found by an international team of astronomers headed by Brett Gladman of France's Observatoire de la Côte d'Azur and J. J. Kavelaars of McMaster University in Canada. Gladman made the initial discovery in Aug. 2000, when he spotted two new satellites of Saturn using a telescope at the European Southern Observatory (ESO) in Chile. Subsequent observations from tele-

scopes in Hawaii and California confirmed the new moons' existence and led to the discovery of the rest. The new moons—whose orbits are being closely monitored—have been temporarily designated S/2000 S1 through S12.

Meanwhile, in late Nov. and early Dec. 2000, a group of astronomers at the University of Hawaii observed a total of ten new moons circling the planet Jupiter. The team, led by graduate student Sam S. Sheppard and professor David Jewitt, used a telescope located atop Mauna Kea. Like the Saturn discoveries, the Jovian moons have been given temporary designations, S/2000 J2 through J11.

(An additional moon, initially designated S/2000 J1, was later determined to be a moon first seen in 1975 but lost soon after.)

Technology a Factor

These latest findings come on the heels of the discovery of a new Jupiter moon in 1999 and six new moons around Uranus between 1997 and 1999. Astronomers attribute the boom in new findings in part to improved technology, which allows them to scan larger areas of the sky. More observations and measurements need to be taken in the coming months to pin down precisely the orbits of the new moons.

Astronomical Terms

Aphelion: see **Orbit.**

Apogee: see **Orbit.**

Black hole: the theoretical end-product of the total gravitational collapse of a massive star or group of stars. Crushed even smaller than the incredibly dense neutron star, the black hole may become so dense that not even light can escape its gravitational field. It has been suggested that black holes may be detectable in proximity to normal stars when they pull matter away from their visible neighbors. Strong sources of X rays in our galaxy and beyond may also indicate the presence of black holes. In 1996, astronomers found strong evidence for a massive black hole at the center of the Milky Way. Recent evidence suggests that black holes are so common that they probably exist at the core of nearly all galaxies.

Conjunction: the alignment of two celestial bodies at the same celestial longitude. Conjunction of the Moon and planets is often determined with reference to the Sun. For example, Saturn is said to be in conjunction with the Sun when Saturn and the Earth are aligned on opposite sides of the Sun.

Mercury and Venus, the two planets with orbits within Earth's orbit, have two positions of conjunction. Mercury (or Venus) is said to be in *inferior conjunction* when the Sun and the Earth are aligned on opposite sides of Mercury (or Venus). Mercury is in *superior conjunction* when Mercury and the Earth are aligned on opposite sides of the Sun.

Elongation: the angular distance between two points in the sky as measured from a third point. The elongation of Mercury, for example, is the angular distance between Mercury and the Sun as measured from Earth. Planets whose orbits are out-

side the Earth's can have elongations between 0° and 180°. (When a planet's elongation is 0° it is at conjunction; when it is 180°, it is at opposition.) Because Mercury and Venus are within the Earth's orbit, their greatest elongations measured from the Earth are 28° and 47°, respectively.

Galaxy: gas and millions of stars held together by gravity. All that you can see in the sky (with a very few exceptions) belongs to our galaxy—a system of roughly 200 billion stars. The exceptions you can see are other galaxies. Our own galaxy, the rim of which we see as the "Milky Way," is about 100,000 light-years in diameter and about 10,000 light-years in thickness. Its shape is roughly that of a thick lens; more precisely, it is a *spiral nebula,* a term first used for other galaxies when they were discovered and before it was realized that these were separate and distinct galaxies. The spiral galaxy nearest to ours is in the constellation *Andromeda.* It is somewhat larger than our own galaxy and is visible to the naked eye. Astronomers have estimated that the universe could contain 40 to 50 billion galaxies.

Neutron star: the extremely dense spinning star that is one of the possible results when a massive star's core has imploded on itself in a supernova. Some neutron stars pulse radio waves into space as they spin; these are known as pulsars.

Occultation: the eclipse of one celestial body by another. For example, a star is occulted when the Moon passes between it and the Earth.

Opposition: the alignment of two celestial bodies when their longitude differs by 180°. Opposition of the Moon and planets is often determined with reference to the Sun. For example, Saturn is said to be at opposition when Saturn and the Sun are aligned on opposite sides of the Earth. Only the planets whose orbits lie outside the Earth's can be in opposition to the Sun.

Orbit: the path traveled by a body in space. The term comes from the Latin *orbis,* which means circle or circuit, and *orbita,* which means a rut or a wheel track. Theoretically, there are four mathematical figures, or models, of possible orbits: two are open (hyperbola and parabola) and two are closed (ellipse and circle), but in reality all closed orbits are ellipses. Ellipses can be nearly circular, as are the orbits of most planets, or very elongated, as are the orbits of most comets, but the orbit revolves around a fixed, or *focal,* point. In our solar system, the Sun's gravitational pull keeps the planets in their elliptical orbits; the planets hold their moons in place similarly. For planets, the point of the orbit closest to the Sun is the *perihelion,* and the point farthest from the Sun is the *aphelion.* For orbits around the Earth, the point of closest proximity is the *perigee;* the farthest point is the *apogee.* See also **Retrograde.**

Perigee: see **Orbit.**

Perihelion: see **Orbit.**

Planet: a celestial body in orbit around a star. Even in ancient times, it was known that a number of "stars" did not stay in the same position relative to the others. There were five such restless "stars" known—Mercury, Venus, Mars, Jupiter, and Saturn—and the Greeks referred to them as *planetes,* a word which means "wanderers." That Earth is one of the planets was realized later. The additional planets were discovered after the invention of the telescope.

In 1994, Dr. Alexander Wolszcan, an astronomer at Pennsylvania State University, presented convincing evidence of the first known planets to exist outside our solar system. They circle a pulsar, or exploded star, in the constellation *Virgo.*

In 1995, several of these *extrasolar planets* were discovered orbiting stars similar to our Sun. Swiss astronomers found a planet orbiting star 51 in the constellation *Pegasus,* about 40 light-years away. It is the first planet ever discovered to circle a normal Sun-like star. As of Sept. 2001, more than 60 planets have been discovered. The nearest star to Earth known to have a planet is Epsilon Eridani, which is bright enough to be seen with the naked eye.

Pulsar: a source of radio waves, emitted in bursts at regular intervals. Pulsars are believed to be rapidly spinning neutron stars, so crushed by their own gravity that a million tons of their matter would hardly fill a thimble.

Quasar: "quasi-stellar" object. Originally thought to be peculiar stars in our own galaxy, quasars are now believed to be the most remote objects in the universe. Quasars emit tremendous amounts of light and microwave radiation. Recent Hubble Space Telescope images suggest that there may be a variety of mechanisms for "turning on" quasars. Although a number of images show collisions between pairs of galaxies, which could trigger the birth of quasars, some pictures reveal apparently normal, undisturbed galaxies possessing quasars.

Quasars are among the most baffling objects in the universe because of their small size and enormous energy output. Quasars are not much bigger than Earth's solar system, but pour out 100 to 1,000 times as much light as an entire galaxy containing a hundred billion stars. A quasar detected in March 2000 with a redshift of 5.8 is 12 billion light-years from Earth and is the most distant object ever observed to date.[1]

A super massive black hole, gobbling up stars, gas, and dust, is theorized to be the "engine" powering a quasar. Most astronomers agree that an active black hole is the only credible possibility that explains how quasars can be so compact, variable, and powerful. However, no conclusive evidence supports this assumption.

Retrograde: describes the clockwise orbit or rotation of a planet or other celestial body, which is in the direction opposite to the Earth and most celestial bodies. As viewed from a position in space north of the solar system (from some great distance above the Earth's North Pole), all the planets revolve counterclockwise around the Sun, and all but Venus, Uranus, and Pluto rotate counterclockwise on their own axes. These three planets, therefore, have retrograde motion.

Sometimes *retrograde* is also used to describe apparent backward motion as viewed from Earth. This motion happens when two bodies rotate at different speeds around another fixed body. For example, the planet Mars appears to be retrograde when the Earth overtakes and passes by it as they both move around the Sun.

Satellite (or **moon**): a body in orbit around a planet. Until the discovery of Jupiter's four main moons by Galileo Galilei, bodies in orbit around a planet were called *moons.* However, upon Galilei's discovery, Johannes Kepler (in a letter to Galileo) suggested *satellite* (from the Latin *satelles,* which means "attendant") as a general term for such bodies. The word *satellite* is used interchangeably with *moon,* and astronomers speak and write about the moons of Neptune, Saturn, etc. The term *satellite* is also used to describe man-made devices of any size that are launched into orbit.

Star: a celestial body consisting of intensely hot gases held together by its own gravity. Stars derive their energy from nuclear reactions going on in their interiors, generating their own heat and light. Stars are very large. Our Sun, which is the nearest star, has a diameter of 865,400 mi—a comparatively small star.

A dwarf star is a small star that is of relatively low mass and average or below average luminosity. The Sun is a *yellow dwarf,* which is in its main sequence, or prime of life. This means that nuclear

---

1. Redshift is the amount by which light from a distant object is shifted toward the red end of the spectrum by the expansion of the universe. The higher the redshift, the greater the distance and the younger the universe when the light was emitted.

The Milky Way, the galaxy containing our solar system, is about 100,000 light-years in diameter and about 10,000 light-years thick.

reactions of hydrogen maintain its size and temperature. By contrast, a *white dwarf* is near death in the life cycle of a star. White dwarfs come into being in one of two ways: either as the result of the implosion, or supernova, of a massive star, or after the collapse of a red giant.

A *red giant* is a star nearing the end of its life. When a star begins to lose hydrogen and burn helium instead, it gradually collapses, and its outer region begins to expand and cool. The light we see from these stars is red because of their cooler temperature. There are also red super giants, which are even more massive.

A *brown dwarf* lacks the mass to generate nuclear fission like a true star, but it is also too massive and hot to be a planet. A brown dwarf usually cools into a dark, practically invisible object. The existence of brown dwarfs, also called *failed stars*, was confirmed in Nov. 1995 when astronomers at Palomar Observatory in California took the first photograph of this mysterious object.

Supernova: a celestial event involving the explosion of a star. There are two common types of supernova. Type Ia is the brighter of the two and happens when a white dwarf star draws large amounts of matter from a nearby star into itself, creating a superpowered fusion process ending in the star's collapse.

The second, more well-known type, IIa, is the result of the collapse of a massive star. (Massive is a classification for a star that is at least eight times the size of our Sun.) Massive stars are born and develop through the process of atomic fusion of hydrogen into helium, which uses and releases an immense amount of energy. The massive star's heat causes the creation of the star's dense center, made of heavier and heavier elements (even iron) as the process continues. This core of heavy elements causes there to be a gravitational force inside the star. When there isn't enough hydrogen to power the fusion any longer, the star's core collapses inward on itself, releasing a huge amount of energy (the supernova), which may be brighter than the massive star's host galaxy.

Origin of the Universe

Before the universe as we now know it existed, there was no space or time. The Big Bang and its associated theories try to explain or describe the moment of change from nothingness and no time to the existence of the universe filled with space and marked by time. Many physicists describe this event as an explosion, or flash, hence the name *Big Bang*. The big bang is a process of expansion in our universe that is still active today.

The universe flashed into existence (according to the Big Bang theory) from a very small agglomeration of matter of extremely high density and temperatures. As a dense, hot globule of gas, containing nothing but hydrogen and a small amount of helium, it began expanding rapidly outward. There were no stars or planets. The first stars probably began to condense out of the primordial hydrogen when the universe was about 100 million years old and continued to form as the universe aged. The Sun was formed in this way 4.6 billion years ago. Many stars came into being before the Sun was formed; many others formed after the Sun appeared. This process continues, and through telescopes we can now see stars forming out of compressed pockets of hydrogen in outer space.

In 1992 instruments aboard the Cosmic Background Explorer (COBE) satellite, launched in 1989, showed that 99.97% of the radiant energy of the universe was released within the first year of the Big Bang event. This evidence seems to confirm the Big Bang theory. In March 1995 astronomers found more supporting evidence for the big bang when they concluded that data obtained from the space shuttle's *Astro 2* observatory showed that helium was widespread in the early universe. The Big Bang theory holds that hydrogen and helium were the first elements created when the universe was formed. Astronomers also theorize that 99% of the matter in the universe is invisible, or *dark matter,* composed of some kind of matter that they cannot yet detect.

In 1999 the age of the cosmos was determined by NASA's Hubble Space Telescope Key Project Team to be about 12 billion years old (plus or minus 10%), with a maximum age of 18 billion years, depending on a number of variables.

Birth and Death of a Star

Astronomers think that a star begins to form as a dense cloud of gas in the arms of spiral galaxies. Individual hydrogen atoms fall with increasing speed and energy toward the center of the cloud under the force of the star's gravity. The increase in energy heats the gas. When this process has continued for some millions of years, the temperature reaches about 20 million degrees Fahrenheit. At this temperature, the hydrogen within the star ignites and burns in a continuing series of nuclear reactions. The onset of these reactions marks the birth of a star. When a star begins to exhaust its hydrogen supply, its life nears an end. The first sign of a star's old age is a swelling and reddening of its outer regions. Such an aging, swollen star is called a *red giant*. The Sun, a middle-aged star, will probably swell to a red giant in 5 billion years, vaporizing Earth and any creatures that may be on its surface. When all its fuel has been exhausted, a star cannot generate sufficient pressure at its center to balance the crushing force of gravity. The star collapses under the force of its own weight; if it is a small star, it collapses gently and remains collapsed. Such a collapsed star, at its life's end, is called a *white dwarf.* The Sun will probably end its life in this way. A different fate awaits a large star. Its

Astronomical Constants

Light-year (distance traveled by light in one year)	5,880,000,000,000 mi
Parsec (parallax of one second, or stellar distances)	3.259 light-years
Velocity of light	c. 186,282.4 mi/sec
Astronomical unit (A.U.), or mean distance Earth to Sun	ca. 93,000,000 mi[1]
Mean distance, Earth to Moon	238,860 mi
General precession	50′,.26
Obliquity of the ecliptic	23° 27′8′.26-0′.4684(t-1900)[2]
Equatorial radius of Earth	3963.34 statute mi
Polar radius of Earth	3949.99 statute mi
Earth's mean radius	3958.89 statute mi
Oblateness of Earth	1/297
Equatorial horizontal parallax of the moon	57′2′.70
Earth's mean velocity in orbit	18.5 mi/sec
Sidereal year	365d.2564
Tropical year	365d.2422
Sidereal month	27d.3217
Synodic month	29d.5306
Mean sidereal day	23h56m4s.091 of mean solar time
Mean solar day	24h3m56s.555 of sidereal time

1. Actual mean distance derived from radar bounces: 92,935,700 mi. The value of 92,897,400 mi (based on parallax of 8″.80) is used in calculations. 2. *t* refers to the year in question, for example, 2001.

final collapse generates a violent explosion, blowing the innards of the star out into space. There, the materials of the exploded star mix with the primeval hydrogen of the universe. Later in the history of the galaxy, other stars are formed out of this mixture. The Sun is one of these stars. It contains the debris of countless other stars that exploded before the Sun was born.

Formation of the Solar System

The Sun's age was calculated in 1989 to be 4.49 billion years old, less than the 4.7 billion years previously believed. It was formed from a cloud of hydrogen mixed with small amounts of other substances that had been produced in the bodies of other stars before the Sun was born. This was the parent cloud of the solar system. The dense, hot gas at the center of the cloud gave rise to the Sun; the outer regions of the cloud—cooler and less dense— gave birth to the planets.

Our solar system consists of one star (the Sun), nine planets and all their moons, several thousand minor planets called asteroids or planetoids, and an equally large number of comets.

The Sun

All the stars, including our Sun, are gigantic balls of superheated gas, kept hot by atomic reactions in their centers. In our Sun, this atomic reaction is hydrogen fusion: four hydrogen atoms are combined to form one helium atom. The temperature at the core of our Sun is thought to be 20 million degrees Celsius, and the surface temperature averages 6,000°C, or about 11,000°F. The diameter of the Sun is 865,400 mi, and its surface area is approximately 12,000 times that of Earth. Compared with other stars, our Sun is just a bit below average in size and temperature, and is a yellow dwarf star. Its fuel supply (hydrogen) is estimated to be sufficient for another 5 billion years.

Our Sun is not motionless in space; in fact, it has two kinds of motion. One is a seemingly straight-line motion in the direction of the constellation Hercules at the rate of about 12 miles per second. But since the Sun is a part of the Milky Way system and since the whole system rotates slowly around its own center, the Sun also moves at the rate of 175 miles per second as part of the rotating Milky Way system.

In addition to this motion, the Sun rotates on its axis. Observations of the motion of sunspots (darkish areas that look like enormous whirling storms) and solar flares, which are usually associated with sunspots, have shown that the rotational period of the Sun is just short of 25 days. But this figure is valid for the Sun's equator only; the sections near the Sun's poles seem to have a rotational period of 34 days. Since the Sun generates its own heat and light, there is no temperature difference between poles and equator.

What we call the Sun's "surface" is scientifically known as the *photosphere*. Since the whole Sun is a ball of expanding hot gas, there is really no such thing as a surface; it is a question of visual impression. The layer outside the photosphere is known as the *chromosphere*, which extends several thousand miles beyond the photosphere. It is in steady motion, and often enormous prominences can be seen to burst from it, extending as much as 100,000 mi into space. Outside the chromosphere is the *corona*. The corona consists of very tenuous gases (essentially hydrogen) and makes a magnificent sight when the Sun is eclipsed.

Solar flares and related outbursts called coronal mass ejections are immensely powerful, capable of hurling streams of plasma into space with the energy of a billion megatons of TNT. These solar belches occur when coiled magnetic fields on the Sun's surface release massive amounts of energy. Following such outbursts, scientists theorize, those magnetic fields still anchored on the Sun arch backward, forming new connections to the Sun, and then snap back into place like stretched rubber bands.

As the Sun ages, it gradually expands and heats. In 1994, American astrophysicists studying the eventual fate of the Sun estimated that its brilliancy will increase by 10% over the next 1.1 billion years or more and, in about 6.5 billion years hence, our aging star will have doubled its present luminosity. The extreme heat generated will cause a catastrophic

A Star's Magnitude

Magnitude is the degree of brightness of a star. In 1856, British astronomer Norman Pogson proposed a quantitative scale of stellar magnitudes, which was adopted by the astronomical community. He noted that we receive 100 times more light from a first magnitude star as from a sixth; thus with a difference of five magnitudes, there is a 100:1 ratio of incoming light energy, which is called *luminous flux.*

Because of the nature of human perception, equal intervals of brightness are actually equal ratios of luminous flux. Pogson's proposal was that one increment in magnitude be the fifth root of 100. This means that each increment in magnitude corresponds to an increase in the amount of energy by 2.512, approximately. A fifth magnitude star is 2.512 times as bright as a sixth, and a fourth magnitude star is 6.310 times as bright as a sixth, and so on. The naked eye, upon optimum conditions, can see down to around the sixth magnitude, that is +6. Under Pogson's system, a few of the brighter stars now have negative magnitudes. For example, Sirius is –1.5. The lower the magnitude number, the brighter the object. The full moon has a magnitude of about –12.5, and the sun is a bright –26.51!

The Brightest Stars

Star	Constellation	Mag.	Dist (l.-y.)	Star	Constellation	Mag.	Dist (l.-y.)
Sirius	Canis Major	-1.6	8	Antares	Scorpius	1.2	170
Canopus	Carina	-0.9	650	Fomalhaut	Piscis Austrinus	1.3	27
Alpha Centauri	Centaurus	+0.1	4	Deneb	Cygnus	1.3	465
Vega	Lyra	0.1	23	Regulus	Leo	1.3	70
Capella	Auriga	0.2	42	Beta Crucis	Crux	1.5	465
Arcturus	Boötes	0.2	32	Eta Carinae	Carina	1-7	—
Rigel	Orion	0.3	545	Alpha-one Crucis	Crux	1.6	150
Procyon	Canis Minor	0.5	10	Castor	Gemini	1.6	44
Achernar	Eridanus	0.6	70	Gamma Crucis	Crux	1.6	—
Beta Centauri	Centaurus	0.9	130	Epsilon Canis Majoris	Canis Major	1.6	325
Altair	Aquila	0.9	18	Epsilon Ursae Majoris	Ursa Major	1.7	50
Betelgeuse	Orion	0.9	600	Bellatrix	Orion	1.7	215
Aldebaran	Taurus	1.1	54	Lambda Scorpii	Scorpius	1.7	205
Spica	Virgo	1.2	190	Epsilon Carinae	Carina	1.7	325
Pollux	Gemini	1.2	31	Mira	Cetus	2-10	250

greenhouse effect on Earth and our oceans will boil away, and life on Earth as we know it will end.

The Sun will eventually expand enormously to 166 times its present size and become over 2,000 times as bright. Eight billion years from now, the Sun's radius will engulf the planet Mercury and extend beyond the present orbit of Venus, causing the total destruction of Earth.

The Moon

Mercury and Venus do not have any moons. The planet that comes after the Earth, Mars, has two very small moons. Jupiter has four major moons and at least 24 minor ones. Saturn, the ringed planet, has 30 known moons, of which one (Titan) is larger than the planet Mercury. Uranus has at least 21 moons (four of them large) as well as rings, while Neptune has one large and seven small moons. Pluto has one moon, discovered in 1978. Some astronomers still consider Pluto to be a "runaway moon" of Neptune.

Our Moon, with a diameter of 2,160 mi, is one of the larger moons in our solar system and is especially large when compared with the planet that it orbits. In fact, the common center of gravity of the Earth–Moon system is only about 1,000 mi below Earth's surface. The closest the Moon can come to us (its perigee) is 221,463 mi; the farthest it can go away (its apogee) is 252,710 mi. The period of rotation of the Moon is equal to its period of revolution around Earth, so from Earth we can see only one hemisphere of the Moon. Both periods are 27

days, 7 hours, 43 minutes, and 11.47 seconds. But while the rotation of the Moon is constant, its velocity in its orbit is not, since it moves more slowly in apogee than in perigee. Consequently, some portions near the rim of the Moon that are not normally visible will appear briefly. This phenomenon is called *libration,* and by taking advantage of the librations, astronomers have succeeded in mapping approximately 59% of the lunar surface. The other 41% can never be seen from Earth but has been mapped by American and Russian Moon-orbiting spacecraft.

Though the Moon goes around Earth in the time mentioned, the interval from new moon to new moon is 29 days, 12 hours, 44 minutes, and 2.78 seconds. This delay of nearly two days is due to the fact that Earth is moving around the Sun, so that the Moon needs two extra days to reach a spot in its orbit where no part is illuminated by the Sun, as seen from Earth.

If the plane of Earth's orbit around the Sun (the ecliptic) and the plane of the Moon's orbit around Earth were the same, the Moon would be eclipsed by Earth every time it is full, and the Sun would be eclipsed by the Moon every time the Moon is "new" (it would be better to call it the "black moon" when it is in this position). But because the two orbits do not coincide, the Moon's shadow normally misses Earth and Earth's shadow misses the Moon. The inclination of the two orbital planes to each other is 5°.

The tides are caused by the Moon with the help of the Sun, but in the open ocean they are surprisingly low, amounting to about one yard. The very high tides that can be observed near the shore in some places are due to funneling effects of the shorelines. At new moon and at full moon the tides raised by the Moon are reinforced by the Sun; these are the *spring tides.* If the Sun's tidal power acts at right angles to that of the Moon (quarter moons) we get the low *neap tides.*

The *Lunar Prospector* spacecraft, launched in Jan. 1998, found that as much as three billion metric tons of water ice is hidden in the permanently shaded craters at the poles. The water probably came from interstellar comets that crashed into the Moon. *Lunar Prospector* also confirmed that the Moon has a small core, supporting the theory that the Moon was ripped away from the early Earth when an object the size of Mars collided with the Earth.

At the end of its mission, on July 31, 1999, the spacecraft was intentionally crashed into a permanently shadowed crater at the Moon's south pole in the hope of detecting a rising plume of water ice, but no cloud of water vapor molecules was observed by powerful Earth telescopes.

Earth

Earth, circling the Sun at an average distance of 93 million miles, is the fifth-largest planet and the third from the Sun. It orbits the Sun at a speed of 67,000 mph, making one revolution in 365 days, 5 hours, 48 minutes, and 45.51 seconds. Earth completes one rotation on its axis every 23 hours, 56 minutes, and 4.09 seconds. Actually a bit pear-shaped rather than a true sphere, Earth has a diameter of 7,927 mi at the equator and a few miles less at the poles. It has an estimated mass of about 6.6 sextillion tons, with an average density of 5.52 grams per cubic centimeter. Earth's surface area encompasses 196,949,970 mi of which about three-fourths is water.

Origin of Earth

Earth, along with the other planets, is believed to have been born 4.5 billion years ago as a solidified cloud of dust and gases left over from the creation of the Sun. For perhaps 500 million years, the interior of Earth stayed solid and relatively cool, perhaps 2000°F. The main ingredients, according to the best available evidence, were iron and silicates, with small amounts of other elements, some of them radioactive. As millions of years passed, energy released by radioactive decay—mostly of uranium, thorium, and potassium—gradually heated Earth, melting some of its constituents. The iron melted before the silicates and, being heavier, sank toward the center. This forced up the silicates that it found there. After many years, the iron reached the center, almost 4,000 mi deep, and began to accumulate. No eyes were around at that time to view the turmoil that must have taken place on the face of Earth— gigantic heaves and bubblings on the surface, exploding volcanoes, and flowing lava covering everything in sight. Finally, the iron in the center accumulated as the core. Around it, a thin but fairly stable crust of solid rock formed as Earth cooled. Depressions in the crust were natural basins in which water, rising from the interior of the planet through volcanoes and fissures, collected to form the oceans. Slowly, Earth acquired its present appearance.

Earth Today

As a result of radioactive heating over millions of years, Earth's molten *core* is probably fairly hot today, around 11,000°F. By comparison, lead melts at around 800°F. Most of Earth's 2,100-mile-thick core is liquid, but there is evidence that the center of the core is solid. The liquid outer portion, about 95% of the core, is constantly in motion, causing Earth to have a magnetic field that makes compass needles point north and south. The details are not known, but the latest evidence suggests that planets that have a magnetic field probably have a solid core or a partially liquid one.

Outside the core is Earth's *mantle,* 1,800 mi thick and extending nearly to the surface. The mantle is composed of heavy silicate rock, similar to that brought up by volcanic eruptions. It is somewhere between liquid and solid, slightly yielding, and therefore contributing to an active, moving Earth. Most of Earth's radioactive material is in the thin *crust* that covers the mantle, but some is in the mantle and continues to give off heat. The crust's thickness ranges from 5 to 25 mi.

Scientists recently discovered that Earth's core is not a perfect sphere. X ray–like images of inside Earth show that there are vast mountains six to seven miles high and deep valleys on the core. These features are in an upside-down relationship to Earth's surface.

In 1996, geophysicists discovered that Earth's solid-iron inner core rotates slightly faster than the rest of the planet and gains a quarter-turn every century. The finding may help explain how Earth's magnetic field periodically reverses its polarity.

Continental Drift

A great deal of recent evidence confirms the theory that the continents of Earth, made mostly of relatively light granite, float in the slightly yielding mantle, like logs in a pond. For many years it had been noticed that if North and South America could be pushed toward western and southern Europe and western Africa, they would fit like pieces in a jigsaw puzzle. Today, there is little question—the continents have drifted widely and continue to do so.

In 10 million years, the world as we know it may be unrecognizable, with California drifting out to sea, Florida joining South America, and Africa moving farther away from Europe and Asia.

Earth's Atmosphere

The thin blanket of atmosphere that envelops Earth extends several hundred miles into space. From sea level—the very bottom of the ocean of air—to a height of about 60 mi, the air in the atmosphere is made up of the same gases in the same ratio: about 78% nitrogen, 21% oxygen, and the remaining 1% being a mixture of argon, carbon dioxide, and tiny amounts of neon, helium, krypton, xenon, and other gases. The atmosphere becomes less dense with increasing altitude: more than three-fourths of Earth's huge envelope is concentrated in the first 5 to 10 mi above the surface. At sea level, a cubic foot of atmosphere weighs about an ounce and a quarter. The entire atmosphere weighs 5,700 trillion tons, and the force with which gravity holds it in place causes it to exert a pressure of nearly 15 psi. Going out from Earth's surface, the atmosphere is divided into five regions. The regions, and the heights to which they extend, are: *troposphere,* 0 to 7 mi (at middle latitudes); *stratosphere,* 7 to 30 mi; *mesosphere,* 30 to 50 mi; *thermosphere,* 50 to 400 mi; and *exosphere,* above 400 mi. The boundaries between each of the regions are known respectively as the *tropopause, stratopause, mesopause,* and *thermopause.* Alternative terms often used for the layers above the troposphere are *ozonosphere* (for stratosphere) and *ionosphere* for the remaining upper layers.

The Seasons

Seasons are caused by the 23.4° tilt of Earth's axis, which alternately turns the North and South Poles toward the Sun. Times when the Sun's apparent path crosses the equator are known as *equinoxes.* Times when the Sun's apparent path is at the greatest distance from the equator are known as *solstices.* The lengths of the days are most extreme at each solstice. If Earth's axis were perpendicular to the plane of Earth's orbit around the Sun, there would be no seasons, and the days always would be equal in length. Since Earth's axis is at an angle, the Sun strikes Earth directly at the equator only twice a year: in March (vernal equinox) and September (autumnal equinox). In the Northern Hemisphere, spring begins at the vernal equinox, summer at the summer solstice, fall at the autumnal equinox, and winter at the winter solstice. The situation is reversed in the Southern Hemisphere.

Mercury

Mercury is the planet nearest the Sun. Appropriately named for the wing-footed Roman messenger of the gods, Mercury whizzes around the Sun at a speed of 30 miles per second, completing one circuit in 88 days. The days and nights are long on Mercury. It takes 59 Earth days for Mercury to make a single rotation. It spins at a rate of about 6 mph (about 10 km/h), measured at the equator, as compared to Earth's spin of about 1,000 mph (about 1,600 km/h) at the equator.

The photographs *Mariner 10* (1974–1975) radioed back to Earth revealed an ancient, heavily cratered surface on Mercury, closely resembling our own Moon. The pictures showed huge cliffs, or scarps, crisscrossing the planet. These apparently were created when Mercury's interior cooled and shrank, compressing the planet's crust. The cliffs are as high as 1.2 mi (2 km) and as long as 932 mi (1,500 km). Another unique feature is the Caloris Basin, a large impact crater about 808 mi (1,300 km) in diameter.

Mercury, like Earth, appears to have a crust of light silicate rock. Scientists believe it has a heavy iron-rich core that makes up about half of its volume.

Instruments onboard *Mariner 10* discovered that the planet has a weak magnetic field and a trace of atmosphere—a trillionth the density of Earth's and composed chiefly of argon, neon, and helium. The spacecraft reported temperatures ranging from 950°F (510°C) on Mercury's sunlit side to –346°F (–210°C) on the dark side. Mercury literally bakes in daylight and freezes at night.

Until the *Mariner 10* probe, little was known about the planet. Even the best telescopic views from Earth showed Mercury as an indistinct object lacking any surface detail. The planet is so close to the Sun that it is usually lost in the Sun's glare.

Radar images taken by astronomers at Jet Propulsion Laboratories and California Institute of Technology during the summer of 1991 suggest that the polar regions of Mercury may be covered with patches of water ice. Although this seems impossible due to the planet's sizzling heat, the polar regions receive very little sunlight and may get as cold as –235°F (–148°C). The radar images showed bright patterns at the poles that are characteristic of ice reflecting radar signals. Other explanations may be offered for this unexpected discovery.

In March or April 2004, NASA plans to launch a spacecraft, *Messenger,* that will orbit Mercury in April 2009. It will map the planet for one Earth year and search for water, a magnetic field, and other phenomena.

Mercury is visible to the naked eye at morning or evening twilight when it is at greatest elongation.

Venus

Although Venus is Earth's closest neighbor, very little is known about the planet because it is permanently covered by thick clouds. In 1962, Soviet and American space probes, coupled with Earth-based radar and infrared spectroscopy, began slowly unraveling some of the mystery surrounding Venus. Twenty-eight years later, the *Magellan* spacecraft, sent by the United States, arrived at Venus in Aug. 1990 and began radar-mapping the planet's surface in greater detail.

According to the latest results, Venus's atmosphere exerts a pressure at the surface 94.5 times greater than Earth's. Walking on Venus would be as difficult as walking a half-mile beneath the ocean. Because of a thick blanket of carbon dioxide, a "greenhouse effect" exists on Venus. Venus intercepts twice as much of the Sun's light as does Earth. The light enters freely through the carbon dioxide gas and is changed to heat radiation in molecular collisions. But carbon dioxide prevents the heat from escaping. Consequently, the temperature of the surface of Venus is over 800°F (427°C), hot enough to melt lead.

The atmospheric composition of Venus is about 96% carbon dioxide, 4% nitrogen, and minor amounts of water, oxygen, and sulfur compounds. There are at least four distinct cloud and haze layers that exist at different altitudes above the planet's surface. The haze layers contain small aerosol particles, possibly droplets of sulfuric acid. A concentration of sulfur dioxide above the cloud tops has been observed to be decreasing since 1978. The source of sulfur dioxide at this altitude is unknown; it may be injected by volcanic explosions or atmospheric overturning.

Measurements of the Venusian atmosphere and its cloud patterns reveal nearly constant high-speed zonal winds, about 220 mph (100 meters per second) at the equator. The winds decrease toward the poles so that the atmosphere at cloud-top level rotates almost like a solid body. The wind speeds at the equator correspond to Venus's rotation period of four to five days at most latitudes. The circulation is always in the same direction—east to west—as Venus's slow retrograde motion. Earth's winds blow from west to east, the same direction as its rotation.

Venus is round, very different from the other planets and from the Moon. Venus has neither polar flattening nor an equatorial bulge. The diameter of

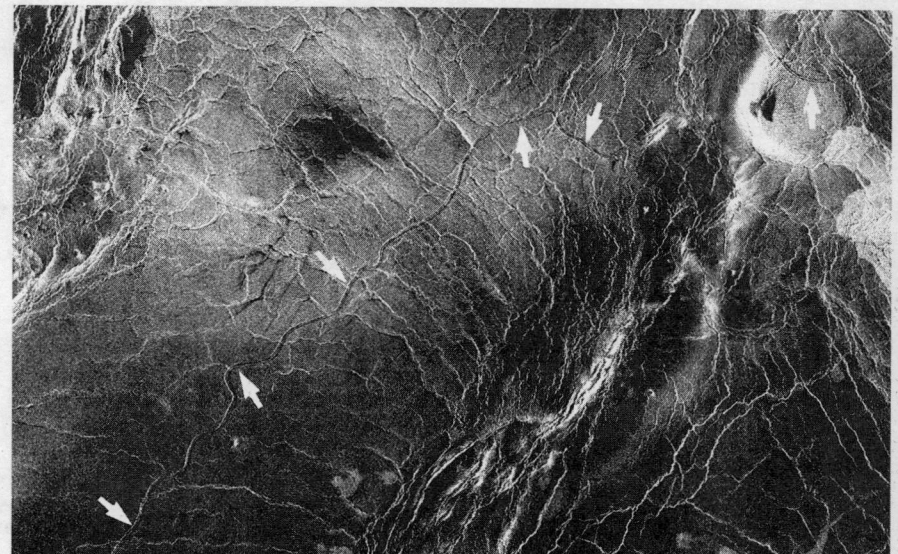

Largest Channel in Solar System. *Magellan* took the above image of the largest known channel on Venus. At 4,200 mi (6,800 km) long and an average of 1.1 mi (1.8 km) wide, it is longer than the Nile River, Earth's longest river, making it the longest known channel in the solar system. The channel was originally discovered by the Soviet *Venery 15* and *16* spacecraft orbiters. *Source:* NASA.

Venus is 7,519 mi (12,100 km). Venus has a retrograde axial rotation period of 243.1 Earth days. The surface atmospheric pressure is 1,396 psi (95 Earth atmospheres). The planet's mean distance from the Sun is 67.2 million miles (108.2 million kilometers). The period of its revolution around the Sun is 224.7 days.

The highest point on Venus is the summit of Maxwell Montes, 6.71 mi (10.8 km) above the mean level, more than a mile higher than Mount Everest. There is some evidence that this huge mountain is an active volcano. The lowest point is in the rift valley, Diana Chasma, 1.8 mi (2.9 km) below the mean level. This point is about one-fifth the greatest depth on Earth in the Marianas Trench.

Venus has an extreme lowland basin, Atalanta Planitia, which is about the size of Earth's North Atlantic Ocean basin. The smooth surface of the Atalanta Planitia resembles the mare basins of the Moon.

There are only two highland or continental masses on Venus: Ishtar Terra and Aphrodite Terra. Ishtar Terra is 6.8 mi (11 km) at its highest points (the highest peaks on Venus) and those of Aphrodite Terra rise to about 3.10 mi (5 km) above the planet. Ishtar Terra is about the size of the continental United States and Aphrodite Terra is about the size of Africa.

The unmanned NASA spacecraft *Magellan* was launched on May 4, 1989, from the shuttle *Atlantis* and arrived at Venus Aug. 10, 1990, to map most of the planet. Despite some problems with its radio transmissions, the results of the radar mapping delighted scientists and provided them with the sharpest images ever taken of the planet's surface.

Images taken from *Magellan* show ten times more detail than ever seen before.

The radar images provided scientists with compelling evidence that the planet has been dominated by volcanism on a global scale. The photos also showed that the planet's second-highest mountain, Maat Mons, rising 5 mi (8 km) above the Venusian plains, appears to be covered with fresh lava and is possibly an active volcano.

Magellan discovered the longest known channel in the solar system on Venus. It is 4,200 mi (6,800 km) long and averages slightly over a mile (1.8 km) wide. Its origin is puzzling to scientists because high-temperature lava is unlikely to have caused such a long-distance flow on the surface, and there are no known substances that could remain liquid long enough under the planet's atmospheric pressure and temperature to have carved out this snakelike feature. The channel is slightly longer than the Nile River, the longest river on Earth. *Magellan* ended its radar and emissions mapping in Sept. 1992 after covering 98% of the planet's surface.

Venus is the brightest of all the planets and is often visible in the morning or evening, when it is frequently referred to as the Morning Star or Evening Star. At its brightest, it can sometimes be seen in full daylight with the naked eye, if one knows where to look.

Mars

Mars, on the other side of Earth from Venus, is Venus's direct opposite in terms of physical properties. Its atmosphere is cold, thin, and transparent, and readily permits observation of the planet's features. We know more about Mars than any other planet except Earth. Mars is a forbidding, rugged planet with huge volcanoes and deep chasms. The largest volcano, Olympus Mons (Olympic Mountain) rises 78,000 ft above the surface, higher than Mount Everest. The plains of Mars are pockmarked by the hits of thousands of meteors over the years.

Until the arrival of *Mars Pathfinder* and *Mars Global Surveyor* in 1997, most of our information about Mars came from the *Mariner* and *Viking* spacecrafts. *Mariner 9* orbited the planet in 1971 and photographed 100% of the planet, uncovering spectacular geological formations, including a Martian "Grand Canyon" that dwarfs the one on Earth. Called Valles Marineris (Mariner Valley), it stretches more than 3,000 mi along the equatorial region of Mars and is over 2.5 mi (4 km) deep in places and 50–62 mi (80 to 100 km) wide. The spacecraft's cameras also recorded what appeared to be dried riverbeds, suggesting the one-time presence of water on the planet. The latter idea gave encouragement to scientists looking for life on Mars, for where there is water, there may be life. However, to date, no evidence of life has been found. Temperatures range from 80°F at the equator during the day to –199°F at the poles at night.

Mars rotates upon its axis in nearly the same period as Earth—24 hours, 37 minutes—so that a Mars day is almost identical to an Earth day. Mars takes 687 days to make one trip around the Sun. Because of its eccentric orbit, Mars's distance from the Sun can vary by about 36 million miles. Its distance from Earth can vary by as much as 200 million miles. The atmosphere of Mars is much thinner than Earth's; atmospheric pressure is about 1% that of our planet. Its gravity is one-third of Earth's. Major constituents are carbon dioxide and nitrogen. Water vapor and oxygen are minor constituents. Mars's polar caps, composed mostly of frozen carbon dioxide (dry ice), recede and advance according to the Martian seasons.

Mars has four seasons like Earth, but they are much longer. For example, in the northern hemisphere, the Martian spring is 198 days, and the winter season lasts 158 days.

The *Mars Pathfinder* lander and its rover, *Sojourner*, set down on the edge of a boulder-strewn outflow channel known as *Ares Vallis* on July 4, 1997, and provided scientists with a wealth of information on the rocks, soils, and atmosphere of Mars. The lander sent back the first live pictures of the planet's topography, and its tiny rover explored a variety of rocks and analyzed their mineral composition with its cameras and on-board X-ray spectrometer.

Analysis of the reddish surface soil pointed to the presence of oxidized iron, indicating that the planet's surface is rusting. *Sojourner* samples of soil taken from several sites found their composition similar to those analyzed by the two *Viking* landers in 1976, indicating that the Martian winds have distributed the soil evenly over the planet.

Scientists were surprised to learn how rapidly the Martian temperature fluctuates due to atmospheric turbulence. It can change by as much as 30°–40°F (17°–22°C) in a matter of minutes, possibly due to strong, gusty winds bringing warm air from one region or cold air from another.

Pictures and subsequent data from *Pathfinder* give the strongest evidence that Mars had an abundance of water millions of years ago. Scientists have inferred from the variety of rocks and sediments found in the *Ares* basin that the spacecraft landed in a channel that was once awash with torrential floods greater than any known on Earth. The diversity of rocks deposited there suggests their different origins, and it appears that they were washed down from the highlands at a time when great floods moved over the surface of Mars.

Before *Pathfinder*, knowledge of the kinds of rocks present on Mars was based mostly on the Martian meteorites found on Earth. Chemical analysis of the Martian rocks and soil found at *Ares Vallis* confirmed that these rocks have compositions distinct from those of the Martian meteorites found on Earth.

In its three months of operation, the mission returned more than 16,000 images of the Martian landscape from the lander's camera and 550 images from the rover.

The *Sojourner* rover traveled a total of about 328 ft (100 m), performed more than 16 chemical analyses of rocks and soil, and explored 820 sq ft (250 sq m) of the planet's surface. Communications were lost with the lander on Sept. 27, 1997, after 83 days of relaying data.

NASA launched the *Mars Global Surveyor* spacecraft on Nov. 7, 1996, to provide detailed maps of the planet's surface, its distribution of minerals, and to monitor its weather. The spacecraft entered Mars's orbit on Sept. 11, 1997, and began mapping operations in mid-March 1999.

Surveyor discovered the first clear evidence of an ancient hydrothermal system near the equator. This implies that water was stable at or near the surface and that a thicker atmosphere existed in Mars's early history.

Most surprising to mission scientists was finding that the planet's northern hemisphere was exceptionally flat, with slopes and surface roughness increasing towards the equator.

Surveyor's three-dimensional views of the planet's northern polar ice cap showed often striking canyons and spiral troughs in the water and carbon dioxide ice that can reach depths as great as 3,600 ft below the surface. Its data also showed that large areas of the ice cap were extremely smooth, with elevations varying only a few feet over many miles.

In 1999, the *Mars Global Surveyor* discovered magnetic stripes about 100 mi (160 km) wide, the remnants of the planet's ancient magnetism, running east and west on the surface of Mars. At their longest, the band-patterns of magnetic fields extend as far as 1,240 mi (1,996 km) along the surface.

NASA's recent Mars exploration program suffered a setback with the loss of the *Climate Orbiter* as it entered the Martian atmosphere in Sept. 1999. The following December scientists also failed to establish contact with the *Polar Lander* after it reached Mars.

In June 2000, NASA announced that the *Mars Global Surveyor* had observed features that looked like gullies carved out by flowing water and deposits of soil and rocks that were transported by the flow. Because gullies had never been seen before on Mars, the *Surveyor* images suggest that there may be current sources of liquid water at or near the surface.

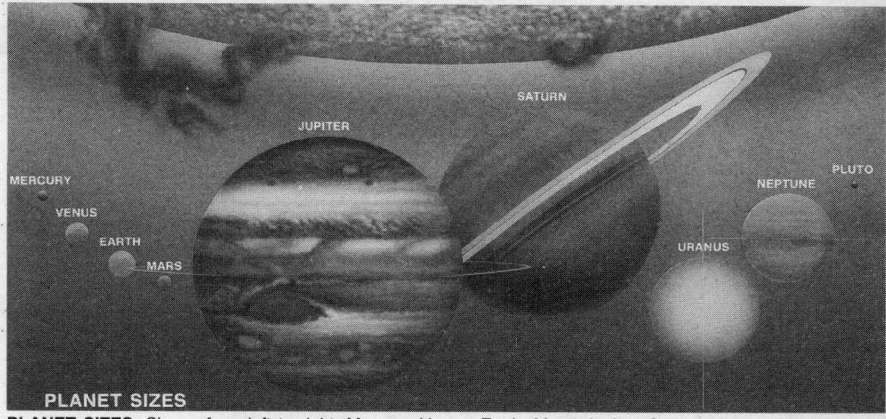

PLANET SIZES. Shown from left to right: Mercury, Venus, Earth, Mars, Jupiter, Saturn, Uranus, Neptune, and Pluto. *Copyright 1990 Hansen Planetarium, Salt Lake City, Utah. Reproduced with permission.*

Mars was named for the Roman god of war, because when seen from Earth its distinct red color reminded the ancient people of blood. We know now that the reddish hue reflects the oxidized (rusted) iron in the surface material.

The Martian Moons

Mars has two very small elliptical-shaped moons, Deimos and Phobos—the Greek names for the companions of the god Mars: Deimos (Terror) and Phobos (Fear). They were discovered in Aug. 1877 by the American astronomer Asaph Hall (1829–1907) of the U.S. Naval Observatory in Washington, DC.

The inner satellite, Phobos, is 16.78 mi (27 km) long, and it revolves around the planet in 7.6 hours. The outer moon, Deimos, is 9.32 mi (15 km) long, and it circles the planet in 30.35 hours. The short orbital period of Phobos means that the satellite travels around Mars three times in a Martian day.

Recent studies of Phobos indicate that its orbit is slowly decreasing downward; in about 40 million years, it will crash into the planet's surface.

Meteorites from Mars

Eighteen meteorites, almost certainly from Mars, have been discovered as of May 2001. They are known as SNCs[1] (named for the towns where they were found: Shergotty, India, in 1865; Nakhla, Egypt, in 1911; and Chassigny, France, in 1815). This hypothesis was based largely on the composition of noble gases (particularly argon and xenon) trapped in the meteorites, and the shergottites in particular, which resemble measurements of the Martian atmosphere made by the *Viking* spacecraft. Major element compositions of the SNCs are also similar to Martian soil analyses made by *Viking*.

The relatively young isotopic ages of the SNC meteorites (1.3 billion years or less) suggest that Mars has been volcanically active during its recent past.

In 1991, a ninth meteorite, LEW 88516, was identified as having reached Earth from Mars some 180 million years ago. It was discovered in Dec. 1988 near Lewis Cliff in Antarctica. The meteorite is very

small with a dark pitted surface and weighs less than half an ounce (13.2 g).

A 4-pound, 7-ounce (1.9-kilogram) meteorite, ALH 84001, found in the Allen Hills of Antarctica in 1984, was reclassified in 1993 as coming from the Red Planet, making it the tenth meteorite known to have originated from Mars. In 1996, NASA announced that meteorite ALH 84001 contained fossils of ancient Martian life forms.

A 40-pound meteorite that crashed to Earth in Nigeria in 1962 has been classified as coming from Mars. It was named Zagami for the region in which it was found.

A 0.38-ounce (12-gram) meteorite (QUE 94201) found in Antarctica in 1995 became the 12th meteorite identified as having a Martian origin.

In 1997, the thirteenth known Martian meteorite, Dar al Gani 476, a 4.8-pound (2.2-kilogram) meteorite, was found in the Sahara Desert.

Two rock specimens weighing 8.6 oz (245.4 g) and 16 oz (452.6 g) that were found in the Mojave Desert about 20 years ago were classified in Feb. 2000 as the fourteenth Mars meteorite. The rocks are known as the Los Angeles meteorites.

Jupiter

Jupiter is the largest planet in the solar system—a gaseous world as large as 1,300 Earths. Its equatorial diameter is 88,736 mi (142,800 km), while from pole to pole, Jupiter measures only 84,201 mi (133,500 km). For comparison, the diameter of Earth is 7,926.2 mi (12,756 km). The massive planet rotates at a dizzying speed—once every 9 hours and 55 minutes. It takes Jupiter almost 12 Earth years to complete a journey around the Sun.

The giant planet appears as a banded disk of turbulent clouds with all of its stripes running parallel to its bulging equator. Large dusky gray regions surround each pole. Darker gray or brown stripes called belts intermingle with lighter, yellow-white stripes called zones. The belts are regions of descending air masses and the zones are rising cloudy air masses. The strongest winds—up to 250 mph (400 km)—are found at boundaries between the belts and zones.

---

1. Pronounced "snick."

Basic Planetary Data

	Mercury	Venus	Earth	Mars	Jupiter
Mean distance from Sun (millions of kilometers)	57.9	108.2	149.6	227.9	778.3
Mean distance from Sun (millions of miles)	36.0	67.24	92.9	141.71	483.88
Period of revolution	88 days	224.7 days	365.2 days	687 days	11.86 yrs
Rotation period	59 days	243 days retrograde	23 hr 56 min 4 sec	24 hr 37 min	9 hr 55 min 30 sec
Inclination of axis	Near 0°	3°	23°27′	25° 12′	3° 5′
Inclination of orbit to ecliptic	7°	3.4°	0°	1.9°	1.3°
Eccentricity of orbit	.206	.007	.017	.093	.048
Equatorial diameter (kilometers)	4,880	12,100	12,756	6,794	142,800
(miles)	3,032.4	7,519	7,926.2	4,194	88,736
Atmosphere (main components)	Virtually none	Carbon dioxide	Nitrogen oxygen	Carbon dioxide	Hydrogen helium
Satellites	0	0	1	2	28[1]
Rings	0	0	0	0	1

	Saturn	Uranus	Neptune	Pluto
Mean distance from Sun (millions of kilometers)	1,427	2,870	4,497	5,900
Mean distance from Sun (millions of miles)	887.14	1,783.98	2,796.46	3,666
Period of revolution	29.46 yrs	84 yrs	165 yrs	248 yrs
Rotation period	10 hr 40 min 24 sec	16.8 hr (?) retrograde	16 hr 11 min (?)	6 days 9 hr 18 mins retrograde
Inclination of axis	26°44′	97°55′	28°48′	60° (?)
Inclination of orbit to ecliptic	2.5°	0.8°	1.8°	17.2°
Eccentricity of orbit	.056	.047	.009	.254
Equatorial diameter (kilometers)	120,660	51,810	49,528	2,290 (?)
(miles)	74,978	32,193	30,775	1,423 (?)
Atmosphere (main components)	Hydrogen helium	Helium hydrogen methane	Hydrogen helium methane	None detected
Satellites	30[2]	21	8	1
Rings	1,000 (?)	11	4	?

1. Ten of these moons, designated S/2000 J2 through J11, were discovered only recently in late 2000. Their orbits have not yet been confirmed. 2. Twelve of these moons, designated S/2000 S1 through S12, were discovered in late 2000. Their orbits have not yet been confirmed. *Source:* Basic NASA data and other sources.

This uniquely colorful atmosphere is mainly 89% molecular hydrogen and 11% helium. It contains small amounts of methane, ammonia, ethane, and water.

Cloud-type lightning bolts similar to those on Earth have been found in the Jovian atmosphere. At the polar regions, auroras have been observed. A very thin ring of material less than 0.6 mi (1 km) in thickness and about 4,000 mi (6,000 km) in radial extent has been observed circling the planet about 35,000 mi (55,000 km) above the cloud tops.

The most prominent feature on Jupiter is its "Great Red Spot," an oval larger than the planet Earth. It is a tremendous atmospheric storm that rotates counterclockwise with one revolution every six days at the outer edge, while at the center almost no motion can be seen. The spot is about 16,000 mi (25,000 km) on its long axis, and would cover three Earths. Along the outer rim the winds blow at speeds reaching 225 mph (360 km/h).

Jupiter is circled by faint rings. They are very tenuous and contain many microscopic-sized particles. The rings are formed by dust kicked up as interplanetary meteoroids smash into the planet's four small inner moons.

Jupiter emits 67% more heat than it absorbs from the Sun. This heat is thought to have been accumulated during the planet's formation several billion years ago.

Twenty-one fragments of comet Shoemaker-Levy 9 bombarded the cloud-covered surface of Jupiter, July 16–22, 1994. It was the most violent event in the recorded history of our solar system. The impact of the comet fragments caused towering plumes of debris and hot gas to rise from the planet's surface.

On Dec. 7, 1995, the *Galileo* spacecraft released a probe into Jupiter's atmosphere to study the planet's physical and chemical properties. The probe lasted 57 minutes and early results indicated a lower abundance of water than was expected.

Galileo data has shown that Jupiter has both wet and dry regions, just as Earth has tropics and deserts. This could explain why the probe found less water than anticipated. These dry spots cover less than 1% of the Jovian atmosphere.

Jovian Moons

Jupiter has a total of 28 known satellites. The four great moons of Jupiter were discovered by Galileo

Galilei (1564–1642) in Jan. 1610, and are called the Galilean satellites after their discoverer. Their names are Io, Europa, Ganymede, and Callisto. Like our Moon, the satellites always keep the same face turned toward the planet they circle. Jupiter's four largest moons all have thin atmospheres. A carbon dioxide atmosphere envelops Callisto; Europa and Ganymede each have thin oxygen atmospheres; and Io's contains sulfur dioxide.

Ganymede

Ganymede, 3,275 mi (5,270 km) in diameter, is Jupiter's largest moon, and it is also the largest satellite in the solar system. Ganymede is about one and one-half times the size of our Moon. It is heavily cratered and probably has the greatest variety of geologic process recorded on its surface. Ganymede is half water and half rock, resulting in a density about two-thirds that of Europa, an ice-coated satellite.

The first close-up photos of Ganymede, taken by the *Galileo* spacecraft during its June 1996 flyby, revealed a surface pockmarked with ancient craters and a landscape wrinkled and torn by the same forces that make mountains and move continents on Earth. *Galileo*'s findings also indicated that Ganymede is enveloped in its own magnetic field, possibly created by a molten iron core or even a thin layer of electricity-conducting salty water underneath its icy crust.

Ganymede is the first known moon with its own magnetosphere.

Europa

Europa, the brightest of Jupiter's satellites, is about 1,950 mi (3,160 km) in diameter or about the size of Earth's Moon. Its density is about three times that of water. The moon is covered with a thin ice crust and is crisscrossed with an amazingly complex network of ridges. Some of the fractures on its crust are more than 1,850 mi (3,000 km) long. Very few impact craters are visible on the surface.

Europa is the smoothest object in the solar system. Its mostly flat surface doesn't exceed 0.62 mi (1 km) in height.

Galileo spacecraft photos taken at its closest flyby on Feb. 20, 1997, at a distance of 363 mi (586 km), showed the existence of ice flows on the surface that strongly suggest that the moon has a hidden subsurface ocean of water or ice-slush. The photos revealed chunky ice rafts that appear to be floating, comparable to icebergs on Earth. The presence of water and enough heat to keep water in a liquid state on Europa enhances the possibility that it could provide an environment for some form of extraterrestrial ocean life.

New evidence that a liquid ocean lies beneath Europa's crust was found when *Galileo* visited the moon in Jan. 2000. The spacecraft detected changes in Europa's magnetic field that are best explained by an electrically conducting (salty) body of water.

Definitive answers may not be possible for another decade, however. NASA scientists had proposed sending a spacecraft called the *Europa Ice Clipper* to the moon in 2001, but the mission was scrapped due to lack of funding. The *Europa Orbiter* mission, scheduled for launch in 2008, is currently under consideration. This spacecraft would include instruments such as an ice-penetrating radar that could see through the ice to any ocean below.

Callisto

Callisto, 2,400 mi (4,800 km) in diameter, is the outermost and, apparently, the least geologically active of Jupiter's four major satellites. Its density is less than twice that of water. Callisto has the oldest body and most cratered face of any body yet observed in the solar system. Like Ganymede, it seems to have a rocky core surrounded by ice. Unlike Ganymede, the surface of Callisto is completely covered with scars left by tens of thousands of meteoric impacts. Scientists estimate that it would take several billion years to accumulate the number of craters found there. So Callisto is believed to be inactive for at least that long. Although it is the darkest of the Galilean satellites, it is twice as bright as Earth's Moon.

Data from the *Galileo* spacecraft in 1998 suggest that Callisto has a salty ocean beneath its crust, similar to Europa's.

Io

Io, 2,262 mi (3,640 km) in diameter, is the most spectacular of the Galilean moons. Its brilliant colors of red, orange, and yellow set it apart from any other moon or planet. Active volcanoes have been detected on Io, with some plumes extending up to 200 mi (320 km) above the surface. The relative smoothness of Io's surface and its volcanic activity suggest that it has the youngest surface of Jupiter's moons. Its surface is composed of large amounts of sulfur and sulfur-dioxide frost, which account for the primarily yellow-orange surface color.

The volcanoes seem to eject a sufficient amount of sulfur dioxide to form a doughnut-shaped ring (torus) of ionized sulfur and oxygen atoms around Jupiter near Io's orbit. Close-up views taken in 1999 and 2000 showed that Io had more than 100 erupting volcanoes, gigantic lava flows and lava lakes, and towering, collapsing mountains. The eruptions of Loki, the most powerful volcano in the solar system, can be seen by Earth telescopes.

Observations by *Galileo* during 1998 revealed dozens of volcanic vents on Io where lava is hotter than any surface temperatures recorded on any planetary body in our solar system. At one such volcanic vent, known as Pillan Patera, two of the spacecraft's instruments indicated that the lava temperature may have been 3,140°F.

In 1996, the *Galileo* spacecraft detected a huge iron core within Io that occupies half the moon's diameter. *Galileo* also discovered evidence that Io has its own magnetic field.

Amalthea

Amalthea, Jupiter's innermost satellite, was discovered in 1892. It is so small—165 mi (265 km) long and 90 mi (150 km) wide—that it is extremely difficult to observe from Earth. Amalthea is an elongated, irregularly shaped satellite of reddish color. It orbits the planet every 12 hours and is in synchronous rotation, with its long axis always oriented toward Jupiter.

Amalthea is heavily cratered, with two that are especially large. The largest crater, Pan, is 56 mi (90 km) long and the other large crater, Gaea, is 47 mi (75 km) in length.

Galileo images of the tiny moon taken at the end of 1999 showed that a bright surface feature, previously named Ida, is a linear streak of bright material

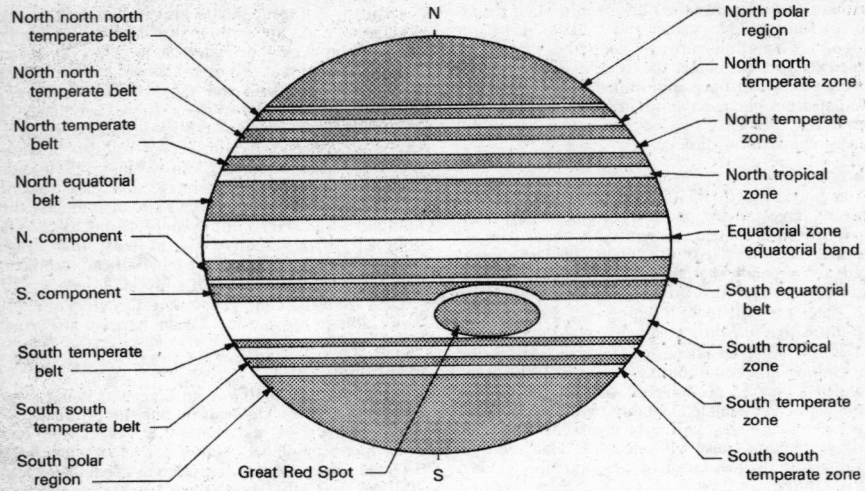

North north north temperate belt

North north temperate belt

North temperate belt

North equatorial belt

N. component

S. component

South temperate belt

South south temperate belt

South polar region

Great Red Spot

N

S

North polar region

North north temperate zone

North temperate zone

North tropical zone

Equatorial zone equatorial band

South equatorial belt

South tropical zone

South temperate zone

South south temperate zone

Schematic diagram of Jupiter's major features. *Source:* NASA.

about 31 mi (50 km) long. The images also revealed a large meteoroid impact crater about 25 mi (40 km) across.

Jupiter's other named moons are Adrasta, Metis, Thebe, Leda, Himalia, Lysithea, Elara, Ananke, Carne, Pasiphae, and Sinope. *Galileo* images of Thebe taken in Jan. 2000 found a prominent impact crater that is about 25 mi (40 km) across and provisionally named Zethus.

The rest of Jupiter's moons have not been named and carry the temporary designations S/1975 J1 (also S/2000 J1), S/1999 J1, and S/2000 J2 through J11. The ten most recently discovered moons (S/2000 J2 through J11, announced in Jan. 2001) are thought to be very small—no more than 3 mi (5 km) across. Nine of the moons move in retrograde orbits, and all move in distant, moderately elliptical orbits.

The Magnetosphere of Jupiter

Perhaps the largest structure in the solar system is the magnetosphere of Jupiter. This is the region of space that is filled with Jupiter's magnetic field and is bounded by the interaction of that magnetic field with the solar wind, which is the Sun's outward flow of charged particles. The plasma of electrically charged particles that exists in the magnetosphere is flattened into a large disk more than 3 million miles (4.8 million kilometers) in diameter, is coupled to the magnetic field, and rotates around Jupiter. The Galilean satellites are located in the inner regions of the magnetosphere and are subjected to intense radiation bombardment.

The intense radiation field that surrounds Jupiter is fatal to humans. If astronauts were one day able to approach the planet as close as the *Voyager 1* spacecraft did, they would receive a dose of 400,000 rads, or roughly 1,000 times the lethal dose for humans.

Even when nearest Earth, Jupiter is still almost 400 million miles away. However, because of its

size, it may rival Venus in brilliance when near. Jupiter's four large moons may be seen through field glasses moving rapidly around Jupiter and changing their positions from night to night.

Saturn

Saturn, the second-largest planet in the solar system, is the least dense. Its mass is 95 times the mass of Earth and its density is 0.70 gram per cubic centimeter, so that it would float in an ocean if there were one big enough to hold it.

Saturn radiates about 80% more energy than it receives from the Sun. However, the excess thermal energy cannot be primarily attributed to Saturn's primordial heat loss, as is speculated for Jupiter.

Saturn's diameter is 74,978 mi (120,660 km) but 10% less at the poles, a consequence of its rapid rotation. Its axis of rotation is tilted by 27° and the length of its day is 10 hours, 39 minutes, and 24 seconds.

Saturn is composed primarily of liquid metallic hydrogen (about 80%) and the second most common element is believed to be helium.

Saturn's atmospheric appearance is very similar to Jupiter's with dark and light cloud markings and swirls, eddies, and curling ribbons; the belts and zones are more numerous and a thick haze mutes the markings. Temperatures recorded by *Voyager II* ranged from 82°K (–312°F) to 143°K (–202°F).

Winds blow at extremely high speeds on Saturn. Near the equator, the *Voyagers* measured winds of about 1,100 mph (500 meters per second). The winds blow primarily in an eastward direction.

Saturn's Rings

Saturn's spectacular ring system is unique in the solar system, with uncountable billions of tiny particles of water ice (with traces of other material) in orbit around the planet. The ring particles range in size from smaller than grains of sugar to as large as

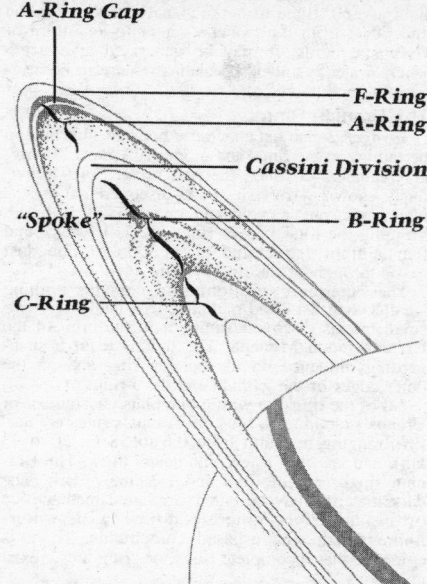

A-Ring Gap

F-Ring

A-Ring

Cassini Division

"Spoke"

B-Ring

C-Ring

NASA illustration of the divisions in Saturn's ring system.

a house. The main rings stretch out from about 4,350 mi (7,000 km) to above the atmosphere of the planet out to the F ring, a total span of 45,984 mi (74,000 km). Saturn's rings can be likened to a phonograph, rings within rings numbering in the hundreds, and spokes in the B rings, and shepherding satellites controlling the F ring.

The main rings are called the A, B, and C rings moving from outside to inside. The gap between the A and B rings is called Cassini's Division and is named for the Italian-French astronomer Gian Domenico Cassini, who discovered four of Saturn's major moons and the dark, narrow gap, Cassini's Division, splitting the planet's rings.

Saturn's magnetic field has well-defined north and south magnetic poles, and is aligned with Saturn's axis of rotation to within one degree.

Saturn's Moons

Saturn has 30 known moons, 12 of which were discovered in late 2000, but their orbits haven't been confirmed. The five largest moons—Tethys, Dione, Rhea, Titan, and Iapetus—range from 650 to 3,200 mi (1,060 to 5,150 km) in diameter. The planet's outstanding satellite is Titan, first discovered by the Dutch astronomer Christiaan Huygens in 1656.

Titan

Titan is remarkable because it is the only known moon in the solar system that has a substantial atmosphere—largely nitrogen with a minor amount of methane and a rich variety of other hydrocarbons. Its surface is completely hidden from view (except at infrared and radio wavelengths) by a dense, hazy atmosphere.

The diameter of Titan is 3,200 mi (5,150 km), and it is the second-largest satellite in the solar system after Jupiter's Ganymede. Titan is larger than the planet Mercury.

Titan's surface temperature is about −175°C (−280°F), and its surface pressure is about 50% greater than the surface pressure of Earth. In 1990, radio telescope data showed that Titan reflects and scatters radio waves, suggesting that the satellite has a solid surface, possibly with small hydrocarbon lakes or ponds.

Infrared images of Titan taken in late 1999 by the W. M. Keck II telescope in Hawaii also revealed features that could be frozen land masses separated by frigid hydrocarbon seas and lakes. Other features might be highlands, and one dark area appeared to be a large impact crater or basin.

NASA plans to send a scientific probe to the surface of Titan in 2004 as part of its *Cassini* mission. The probe will be provided by the European Space Agency (ESA).

Other Notable Saturnian Moons

The other four largest moons of Saturn are Tethys, Dione, Rhea, and Iapetus.

Tethys is 650 mi (1,060 km) in diameter. Its surface is heavily cratered, and it has a huge, globe-girdling canyon, Ithaca Chasma. Part of the canyon stretches over three-quarters of the satellite's surface. Ithaca Chasma is about 1,550 mi (2,500 km) long. It has an average width of about 62 mi (100 km) and a depth of 1.8 to 3.1 mi (3 to 5 km).

Tethys also has a huge impact crater named Odysseus that is 244 mi (4,400 km) in diameter, or more than one-third of the moon's diameter.

Dione is slightly larger than Tethys, 696 mi (1,120 km) in diameter, and is more than half composed of water ice. It has bright wispy markings resembling thin veils covering its features.

Rhea, the largest of the inner satellites, is 951 mi (1,530 km) in diameter. It is composed mainly of water ice, causing its reflective surface to present an almost uniform white appearance.

Iapetus is the outermost of Saturn's icy satellites. Its appearance is unique because it has one dark and one bright hemisphere. The origin of the black coating of its dark face is unknown. Iapetus has a diameter of 907 mi (1,460 km).

Other notable moons of Saturn are Mimas, Enceladus, Hyperion, Phoebe, and Pan.

Mimas is small, only 244 mi (329 km) in diameter. It has a huge impact crater, Herschel, nearly one-third of its diameter. The crater is about 81 mi (130 km) wide and its icy peak rises almost 6.2 mi (10 km) above the floor.

Mimas is believed to be composed mainly of water and ice and to contain between 20% and 50% rock.

Enceladus is remarkable in that its surface shows signs of extensive and recent geological activity. There may be active water volcanism. The surface is extremely bright, reflecting more than 90% of incident sunlight. This suggests that its surface is composed of extremely pure ice without dust or rocks to contaminate it. Enceladus has a diameter of 310 mi (500 km).

Hyperion orbits between Iapetus and Titan. It is irregular in shape, measuring about 248 by 155 by

124 mi (400 by 250 by 200 km). It may be a remnant of a much larger object that was shattered by impact with another space body. It appears that Hyperion is composed primarily of water ice.

Hyperion orbits Saturn with an irregular motion ("chaotic tumbling").

Phoebe travels in a retrograde orbit at a distance of over 6.2 million miles (10 million kilometers) away from the planet. It is the darkest moon of Saturn and is the planet's only known satellite that does not keep the same face always turned to Saturn. It has been speculated that it is an asteroid that was captured by the planet. Phoebe rotates in about nine hours and orbits Saturn in 406 days. It has a diameter of 124 mi (200 km).

Pan was discovered in 1990 from *Voyager 2* photos taken in 1981. The satellite is estimated to be about 12.43 mi (20 km) in diameter, which makes it the planet's smallest known moon. It orbits within the Encke Gap, a 202-mile (325-kilometer) division in Saturn's A ring. It was identified by Johann Franz Encke (1791–1865) in 1837.

Saturn's other named moons are Atlas, Prometheus, Pandora, Epimetheus, Janus, Telesto, Calypso, and Helene. They are all nonspherical in shape and range from 15 to 120 mi (25 to 190 km) in diameter. In addition, 12 new moons were discovered in late 2000. Designated S/2000 S1 through S12, these new moons are quite small—only about 5 to 30 mi (10 to 50 km) in diameter—and have weak elliptical orbits.

NASA's *Cassini* mission to Saturn, launched in Oct. 1997, will shed more light on the planet's mysteries when it arrives there in 2004.

Saturn is the last of the planets visible to the naked eye. Saturn is never an object of overwhelming brilliance, but it looks like a bright star. The rings can be seen with a small telescope.

Uranus

Uranus, the first planet discovered in modern times by Sir William Herschel in 1781, is the seventh planet from the Sun, twice as far out as Saturn. Its mean distance from the Sun is 1,783 million miles (2,869 million km). Uranus's equatorial diameter is 32,200 mi (51,810 km). The axis of Uranus is tilted at 97°, so it goes around the Sun nearly lying on its side.

Due to Uranus's unusual inclination, the polar regions receive more sunlight during a Uranus year of 84 Earth years. Scientists had thought that the temperature of its poles would be warmer than that at its equator, but *Voyager 2* discovered that the equatorial temperatures were similar to the temperatures at the poles, –209°C (–344°F), implying that some redistribution of heat toward the equatorial region must occur within the atmosphere. The wind patterns are much like Saturn's, flowing parallel to the equator in the direction of the planet's rotation.

Ninety-eight percent of the upper atmosphere is composed of hydrogen and helium; the remaining 2% is methane. Scientists speculate that the bulk of the lower atmosphere is composed of water (perhaps as much as 50%), methane, and ammonia. Methane is responsible for Uranus's blue-green color because it selectively absorbs red sunlight and condenses to form clouds of ice crystals in the cooler, higher regions of Uranus's atmosphere.

It was also discovered that the planet's magnetic field was 60° tilted from the planet's axis of rotation and offset from the planet's center by one-third of Uranus's radius. It may be generated at a depth where water is under sufficient pressure to be electrically conductive.

The Uranian Rings

Voyager 2 also expanded the body of information pertaining to the rings and moons of Uranus. *Voyager*'s cameras obtained the first images of 9 previously known narrow rings and discovered at least 2 new rings, one narrow and one broadly diffused, bringing the total known rings to 11. It was found that a highly structured distribution of fine dust exists throughout the ring system.

The outermost (epsilon) ring contains nothing smaller than fist-sized particles. It is flanked by two small moons discovered interior to the orbit of the Uranian moon Miranda. The moons exert a shepherding influence on the epsilon ring and on the outer edges of the gamma and delta rings.

All of the rings lie within one planetary radius[1] of Uranus's cloud tops. Most of Uranus's rings are narrow, ranging in width from 0.6 to 58 mi (1 to 93 km), and are only a few kilometers thick. The Uranian rings are colorless and extremely dark. The dark material may be either irradiated methane ice or organic-rich minerals mixed with water-impregnated, silicon-based compounds. There is evidence that incomplete rings, or "ring arcs," exist at Uranus.

The Uranian Moons

There are 21 known moons of Uranus. In order of decreasing distance from the planet, the moons are Prospero (1999 U3), Stephano (1999 U2), Sycorax, Setebos (1999 U1), Caliban, Oberon, Titania, Umbriel, Ariel, Miranda, Puck, 1986 U10, Belinda, Cressida, Portia, Rosalind, Desdemona, Juliet, Bianca, Ophelia, and Cordelia. Ten of the moons range in size from 16 to 67 mi (26 to 108 km) in diameter and, being closer to the planet, have faster periods of revolution (8–15 hours) than their more distant relatives.

Oberon and Titania

The two largest moons, Oberon, 942 mi (1,516 km) in diameter, and Titania, 982 mi (1,580 km) in diameter, are less than half the diameter of Earth's Moon. Titania, the reddest of Uranus's moons, may have endured global tectonics as evidenced by complex valleys and fault lines etched into its surface. Smooth sections indicate that volcanic resurfacing has taken place.

Umbriel and Ariel

Umbriel and Ariel are roughly three-fourths the size of Oberon and Titania. Umbriel is the darkest of the large moons, with huge craters peppering its surface. Umbriel has a paucity of what are known as bright ray craters, which are formed on an older darker surface when bright submerged ice is excavated and sprayed by meteoroid impacts.

In contrast, the surface of Ariel, the brightest of the Uranian moons, is relatively free of pockmarks due to volcanism that periodically erases the damage done by foreign projectiles. However, there are several extremely deep cuts on Ariel's surface.

---

1. The equatorial radius of Uranus is 15,880 mi (25,560 km) at a pressure of 1 bar.

Miranda

The smallest of Uranus's large moons, Miranda, 293 mi (472 km) in diameter, has been described as "the most bizarre body in the solar system," with the most geologically complex surface. Miranda's remarkable terrain consists of rolling, heavily cratered plains (the oldest known in the Uranian system) adjoined by three huge, 120- to 180-mile (200- to 300-kilometer) oval-to-trapezoidal regions known as coronae, which are characterized by networks of concentric canyons.

Puck

Puck was the first new moon discovered by *Voyager.* It is 96 mi (154 km) in diameter and makes a trip around Uranus every 18 hours. Puck is shaped somewhat like a potato, with a huge impact crater marring roughly one-fourth of its surface.

Caliban and Sycorax

In 1997, two new moons, the first with irregular, noncircular orbits, were discovered around Uranus. These far distant satellites were temporarily designated S/1997 U1 and S/1997 U2 and later named Caliban and Sycorax, respectively. Caliban has a diameter of 37 mi (60 km) and orbits Uranus at an average distance of 4.5 million miles (7.2 million kilometers). Sycorax has a diameter of 74.5 mi (120 km) and a much more elliptical orbit than Caliban, bringing it as close as 3.7 million miles (6 million km) to the planet.

New Uranian Moons Discovered

On May 18, 1999, the International Astronomical Union announced that Erich Karkoschka, a researcher at the Lunar and Planetary Lab of the University of Arizona in Tucson, had discovered the 18th moon orbiting Uranus.

Although the moon was found in 1999, it is designated as satellite S/1986 U10. According to its discoverer, the satellite is approximately 25 mi (40 km) in diameter, about the size of comet Hale-Bopp, and it may have a similar composition to the comet. It orbits 35,000 mi (51,000 km) from Uranus, circling the planet every 15 hours and 18 minutes, similar to the planet's rotational period of about 16.8 hours.

In Sept. 1999, Cornell University astronomers announced the discovery of three more satellites, bringing the total up to 21. The moons, designated 1999 U1, 1999 U2, and 1999 U3, have been provisionally named Setebos, Stephano, and Prospero. The new satellites are about 12 mi (20 km) in diameter and orbit 6 to 12 mi (10 to 20 km) from the planet.

Uranus can—on rare occasions—become bright enough to be seen with the naked eye, if one knows exactly where to look; normally, a good set of field glasses or a small portable telescope is required.

Neptune

Little was known about Neptune until Aug. 1989, when NASA's *Voyager 2* became the first spacecraft to observe the planet. Passing about 3,000 mi (4,950 km) above Neptune's north pole, *Voyager 2* made its closest approach to any planet since leaving Earth 12 years prior. The spacecraft passed about 25,000 mi (40,000 km) from Neptune's largest moon, Triton, the last solid body that *Voyager 2* will have studied.

Nearly 3 billion miles (4.5 billion kilometers) from the Sun, Neptune orbits the Sun once in 165 years, and therefore has made not quite a full circle around the Sun since it was discovered.[1]

With an equatorial diameter of 30,775 mi (49,528 km), Neptune is the smallest of our solar system's four gas giants, which also include Jupiter, Saturn, and Uranus.[2] Even so, its volume could hold nearly 60 Earths. Neptune is also denser than the other gas giants and about 64% heavier than if it were composed entirely of water.

Neptune has a blue color as a result of methane in its atmosphere. Methane preferentially absorbs the longer wavelengths of sunlight (those near the red end of the spectrum). What are left to be reflected are colors at the blue end of the spectrum. The atmosphere of Neptune is mainly composed of hydrogen, with helium and traces of methane and ammonia.

Neptune is a dynamic planet even though it receives only 3% as much sunlight as Jupiter does. *Voyager 2* discovered several large, dark spots that were prominent features on the planet. The largest spot was about the size of Earth and was designated the "Great Dark Spot" by its discoverers. It appeared to be an anticyclone similar to Jupiter's Great Red Spot. While Neptune's Great Dark Spot is comparable in size, relative to the planet, and at the same latitude (22°S latitude) as Jupiter's Great Red Spot, it was far more variable in size and shape than its Jovian counterpart. Bright, wispy "cirrus-type" clouds overlaid the Great Dark Spot at its southern and northeast boundaries.

At about 42°S latitude, a bright, irregularly shaped eastward-moving cloud circles much faster than did the Great Dark Spot, "scooting" around Neptune in about 16 hours. This "scooter" may have been a cloud plume rising between cloud decks.

Another spot, designated "D2," was located far to the south of the Great Dark Spot, at 55°S latitude. It is almond-shaped, with a bright central core, and moves eastward around the planet in about 16 hours.

In 1995, images taken by the Hubble Space Telescope showed that the Great Dark Spot has vanished. The great storm center has either dissipated or is obscured by other atmospheric conditions.

The atmosphere above Neptune's clouds is hotter near the equator, cooler in the mid-latitudes, and warm again at the south pole. Temperatures in the stratosphere were measured to be 750°K (900°F), while at the 100-millibar pressure level they were measured to be 55°K (−360°F).

Long, bright clouds, reminiscent of cirrus clouds on Earth, were seen high in Neptune's atmosphere. They appear to form above most of the methane, and consequently are not blue.

At northern low latitudes (27°N), *Voyager* captured images of cloud streaks casting their shadows

---

1. Astronomers have studied Neptune since Sept. 23, 1846, when Johann Gottfried Galle, of the Berlin Observatory, and Louis d'Arrest, an astronomy student, discovered the eighth planet on the basis of mathematical predictions by Urbain Jean Joseph Le Verrier. Similar predictions were made independently by John Couch Adams. Galileo Galilei had seen Neptune during several nights of observing Jupiter, in Jan. 1613, but didn't realize he was seeing a new planet.
2. These four planets are about 4 to 12 times greater in diameter than Earth. They have no solid surfaces, but possess massive atmospheres that contain substantial amounts of hydrogen and helium with traces of other gases.

on cloud decks estimated to be about 30 to 60 mi (50 to 100 km) below. The widths of these cloud streaks range from 30 to 125 mi (50 to 200 km). Cloud streaks were also seen in the southern polar regions (71°S) where the cloud heights were about 30 mi (50 km).

Most of the winds on Neptune blow in a westward direction, which is retrograde, or opposite to the rotation of the planet.

In Jan. 2000, astronomers announced taking the best Earth-based infrared images of Neptune, captured by the W. M. Keck II telescope in Hawaii. They revealed giant 600-mph (966-km/hr) storms born of heat generated from the planet's still-contracting core. Storm features are pulled across the face of Neptune as it whirls through its 16-hour day.

The Magnetic Field of Neptune

Neptune's magnetic field is tilted 47° from the planet's rotation axis and is offset at least 0.55 radii, about 8,500 mi (13,500 km) from the physical center. The dynamo electric currents produced within the planet, therefore, must be relatively closer to the surface than for Earth, Jupiter, or Saturn. Because of its unusual orientation, and the tilt of the planet's rotation axis, Neptune's magnetic field goes through dramatic changes as the planet rotates in the solar wind.

Voyager's planetary radio astronomy instrument measured the periodic radio waves generated by the magnetic field and determined that the rotation rate of the interior of Neptune is 16 hours and 7 minutes.

Voyager also detected auroras, similar to the northern and southern lights on Earth, in Neptune's atmosphere. Unlike those on Earth, due to Neptune's complex magnetic field, the auroras are extremely complicated processes that occur over wide regions of the planet, not just near the planet's magnetic poles.

Neptune's Moons

Triton

The largest of Neptune's eight known satellites, Triton is different from all other icy moons that *Voyager* has studied. Triton circles Neptune in a tilted, circular, retrograde orbit, completing an orbit in 5.875 days at an average distance of 205,000 mi (330,000 km) above the planet's cloud tops.

Triton shows evidence of a remarkable geologic history, and *Voyager 2* images show active geyser-like eruptions spewing invisible nitrogen gas and dark dust particles 1 to 5 mi (2 to 8 km) into space.

Triton is about three-quarters the size of Earth's Moon and has a diameter of about 1,680 mi (2,705 km) and a mean density of about 2.066 grams per cubic centimeter. (The density of water is 1.0 grams per cubic centimeter.) This means that Triton contains more rock in its interior than the icy satellites of Saturn and Uranus.

The relatively high density and the retrograde orbit offer strong evidence that Triton did not originate near Neptune, but is a captured object.

An extremely thin atmosphere extends as much as 500 mi (800 km) above the satellite's surface. Tiny nitrogen ice particles may form thin clouds a few kilometers above the surface. Triton is very bright, reflecting 60% to 95% of the sunlight that strikes it. (By comparison, Earth's Moon reflects only 11%.)

The atmospheric pressure at Triton's surface is about 14 microbars, a mere 1/70,000th the surface pressure on Earth. Temperature at the surface is about 38°K (–391°F), making it the coldest surface of any body yet visited in the solar system.

Nereid

Nereid was discovered in 1948 through Earth-based telescopes. Little is known about Nereid, which is slightly smaller than Proteus, having a diameter of 211 mi (340 km). The satellite's surface reflects about 14% of the sunlight that strikes it. Nereid's orbit is the most eccentric in the solar system, ranging from about 841,100 mi (1,353,600 km) to 5,980,200 mi (9,623,700 km).

The Smaller Satellites

In addition to the previously known moons, Triton and Nereid, *Voyager 2* found six more satellites, making the total eight.

Proteus

Like all six of Neptune's recently discovered small satellites, it is one of the darkest objects in the solar system—"as dark as soot" is a good description. It reflects only 6% of the sunlight that strikes it. Proteus is an ellipsoid about 258 mi (416 km) in diameter, larger than Nereid. It circles Neptune at a distance of about 57,700 mi (92,800 km) above the cloud tops, and completes one orbit in 26 hours and 54 minutes. Scientists say that it is about as large as a satellite can be without being pulled into a spherical shape by its own gravity.

Proteus and its tiny companions are cratered and irregularly shaped—they are not round—and show no signs of any geologic modifications. All circle the planet in the same direction as Neptune rotates and remain close to Neptune's equatorial plane.

Larissa

This object is only about 30,300 mi (48,800 km) from Neptune and circles the planet in 13 hours and 18 minutes. Its diameter is 120 mi (190 km).

Despina

The satellite is 17,200 mi (27,700 km) from Neptune's clouds and makes one orbit every 8 hours. Its diameter is about 90 mi (150 km).

Galatea

It lies 23,100 mi (37,200 km) from Neptune. Its diameter is 110 mi (180 km), and it completes an orbit in 10 hours and 18 minutes.

Thalassa

The satellite appears to be about 50 mi (80 km) in diameter. It orbits Neptune in 7 hours and 30 minutes some 15,700 mi (25,200 km) above the cloud tops.

Naiad

The last satellite discovered, it is about 37 mi (60 km) in diameter and orbits Neptune about 14,400 mi (23,200 km) above the clouds in 7 hours and 6 minutes.

Neptune's Rings

Voyager found four rings and evidence of ring *arcs* or incomplete rings. The "Main Ring" orbits Neptune at about 23,812.5 mi (38,100 km) above the cloud tops. The "Inner Ring" is about 17,750 mi (28,400 km) from Neptune's cloud tops. An "Inside

The First Ten Minor Planets (Asteroids)

Name	Year of discovery	Mean distance from Sun (millions of mi)	Orbital period (years)	Diameter (mi)	Magnitude
1. Ceres	1801	257.0	4.60	485	7.4
2. Pallas	1802	257.4	4.61	304	8.0
3. Juno	1804	247.8	4.36	118	8.7
4. Vesta	1807	219.3	3.63	243	6.5
5. Astraea	1845	239.3	4.14	50	9.9
6. Hebe	1847	225.2	3.78	121	8.5
7. Iris	1847	221.4	3.68	121	8.4
8. Flora	1847	204.4	3.27	56	8.9
9. Metis	1848	221.7	3.69	78	8.9
10. Hygeia	1849	222.6	5.59	40(?)	9.5

Diffuse Ring"—a complete ring—is located about 10,687.5 mi (17,100 km) from the planet's cloud tops. Some scientists suspect that this ring may extend all the way down to Neptune's cloud tops. An area called "the Plateau" is a broad, diffuse sheet of fine material just outside the so-called Inner Ring. The fine material is approximately the size of smoke particles. All other rings contain a greater proportion of larger material.

Pluto

Pluto, the outermost and smallest planet in the solar system, is the only planet not visited by an exploring spacecraft. So little is known about it that it is difficult to classify. Its distance is so great that the Hubble Space Telescope cannot reveal its surface features. Appropriately named for the Roman god of the underworld, it must be frozen, dark, and dead. Pluto's mean distance from the Sun is 3,687.5 million miles (5,900 million kilometers).

In 1978, light-curve studies gave evidence of a moon revolving around Pluto within the same period as Pluto's rotation. Therefore, it stays over the same point on Pluto's surface. In addition, it keeps the same face toward the planet. The satellite was later named Charon and is estimated to be about 789 mi (1,262.4 km) in diameter. Recent estimates indicate Pluto's diameter is about 1,441.6 mi (2,306.56 km), making the pair more like a double planet than any other in the solar system. Previously, the Earth–Moon system held this distinction. The density of Pluto is slightly greater than that of water.

There is evidence that Pluto has an atmosphere containing methane and polar ice caps that increase and decrease in size with the planet's seasons. It is not known to have water. The Hubble Space Telescope's faint-object camera revealed light and dark regions on Pluto indicating an ice cap at the planet's north pole. It is not known if there is an ice cap at Pluto's south pole.

Pluto was predicted by calculation when Percival Lowell (1855–1916) noticed irregularities in the orbits of Uranus and Neptune. Clyde Tombaugh (1906–1997) discovered the planet in 1930, precisely where Lowell predicted it would be. The name Pluto was chosen because the first two letters represent the initials of Percival Lowell.

Pluto has the most eccentric orbit in the solar system, bringing it at times closer to the Sun than Neptune. Pluto approached the perihelion of its orbit on Sept. 5, 1989, and until Feb. 1999 was closer to the Sun than Neptune. Even then, it could be seen only with a large telescope.

The Asteroids

Between the orbits of Mars and Jupiter are an estimated 30,000 pieces of rocky debris, known collectively as the asteroids, or planetoids. The first and, incidentally, the largest (Ceres), was discovered during the New Year's night of 1801 by the Italian astronomer Father Piazzi (1746–1826), and its orbit was calculated by the German mathematician Karl Friedrich Gauss (1777–1855). Gauss invented a new method of calculating orbits on that occasion. A few asteroids do not move in orbits beyond the orbit of Mars, but in orbits that cross the orbit of Mars. The first of them was named Eros because of this peculiar orbit. It had become the rule to bestow female names on the asteroids, but when it was found that Eros crossed the orbit of a major planet, it received a male name. These orbit-crossing asteroids are often referred to as the "male asteroids." A few of them—Albert, Adonis, Apollo, Amor, and Icarus—cross the orbit of Earth, and two of them may come closer than our Moon; but the crossing is like a bridge crossing a highway, not like two highways intersecting. Hence there is very little danger of collision from these bodies. They are all small, 3 to 5 mi (4.8 to 8.0 km) in diameter, and therefore very difficult objects to identify, even when quite close. Some scientists believe the asteroids represent the remains of an exploded planet.

On Oct. 29, 1991, the Galileo spacecraft took a historic photograph of asteroid 951 Gaspra from a distance of 10,000 mi (16,000 km) away. It was the first close-up photo ever taken of an asteroid in space.

Gaspra is an irregular, potato-shaped object about 12.5 mi (20 km) by 7.5 mi (12 km) by 7 mi (11.2 km) in size. Its surface is covered with a layer of loose rubble and its terrain is covered with several dozen small craters.

Close-up photos of asteroid 243 Ida taken by the Galileo spacecraft on Aug. 28, 1993, revealed that Ida had a tiny egg-shaped moon measuring 0.9 by 0.7 mi (1.44 by 1.12 km). The moon has been named Dactyl.

NASA's Near-Earth Asteroid Rendezvous spacecraft was launched on Feb. 17, 1996. (Near-Earth asteroids come within 121 million miles [195 million kilometers] of the Sun. Their orbits come close enough that one could eventually hit Earth.) It flew within 750 mi (1,200 km) of minor planet 253

Mathilde on June 27, 1997, and took spectacular images of the dark, crater-battered world. The asteroid's mean diameter was found to be 33 mi (52.8 km). The *NEAR* spacecraft discovered that the carbon-rich Mathilde is one of the darkest objects in the solar system, only reflecting about 3% of the Sun's light, making it twice as dark as a chunk of charcoal. The asteroid is almost completely cratered, and at least five of its craters just on the lighted side are larger than 12 mi (19.2 km).

The spacecraft reached asteroid 433 Eros in Dec. 1998, but because of engine problems its original mission to enter into the asteroid's orbit was aborted, and NEAR flew past Eros instead. However, the spacecraft was reset, and on Feb. 14, 2000, NEAR successfully entered into orbit around Eros. NEAR remained in orbit for one year, taking photographs of the asteroid and gathering information about its composition, structure, size, and shape. The spacecraft landed safely on the surface of Eros in a controlled crash on Feb. 12, 2001. Against tremendous odds, it continued to relay information for another two weeks before being shut down.

NEAR measured Eros to be 21 mi (33.6 km) long by 8 mi (12.8 km) wide and 8 mi (12.8 km) deep. It rotates once every 5.27 hours and has no visible moons. NEAR data also showed that the asteroid's ancient surface is covered with craters, ridges, boulders, and other complex features.

NEAR was the first spacecraft to orbit an asteroid and the first craft to operate on solar power so far from the Sun. NEAR gathered about 160,000 images of Eros, about 10 times more than was planned. The spacecraft was renamed *NEAR-Shoemaker* in honor of geologist Dr. Eugene M. Shoemaker (1928–1997), who researched the influence of asteroids and comets in shaping planets.

Comets

Comets, according to the noted astronomer Fred L. Whipple (1906–), are enormous "snowballs" of frozen gases (mostly carbon dioxide, methane, and water vapor) and contain very little solid material. The whole behavior of comets can then be explained as the behavior of frozen gas being heated by the Sun. When the comet Kohoutek made its first appearance to human observers in 1973, its behavior seemed to confirm this theory, and later the international study by five spacecraft that encountered Halley's comet in March 1986 confirmed Whipple's idea of the make-up of comets.

Since comets appear in the sky without any warning, people in classical times and especially during the Middle Ages believed that they had a special meaning, which, of course, was bad. Since a natural catastrophe of some sort or a military conflict occurs every year, it was quite simple to blame the comet that happened to be visible. But even in the past, there were some people who used logical reasoning. When, in Roman times, a comet was blamed for the loss of a battle and hence was called a "bad omen," a Roman writer observed that the victors in the battle probably did not think so.

Up until the middle of the 16th century, comets were believed to be phenomena of the upper atmosphere; they were usually explained as "burning vapors" which had risen from "distant swamps." That nobody had ever actually seen burning vapors rise from a swamp did not matter.

But a large comet which appeared in 1577 was carefully observed by Tycho Brahe (1546–1601), a Danish astronomer who is often, and with the best of reasons, called eccentric, but who insisted on precise measurements for everything. It was Tycho Brahe's accumulation of literally thousands of precise measurements that later enabled his younger collaborator, Johannes Kepler (1571–1630), to discover the laws of planetary motion. Measuring the motion of the comet of 1577, Brahe could show that it had been far beyond the atmosphere, even though he could not give figures for the distance. Brahe's work proved that comets were astronomical and not meteorological phenomena.

In 1682, the second Astronomer Royal of Great Britain, Dr. Edmond Halley (1656–1742), checked the orbit of a bright comet that was in the sky and then compared it with earlier comet orbits that were known in part. Halley found that the comet of 1682 was the third to move through what appeared to be the same orbit, and that the three appearances were roughly 76 years apart. Halley concluded that this was the same comet, moving around the Sun in a closed orbit, like the planets. He predicted that it would reappear in 1758 or 1759. Halley himself died in 1742, but a large comet appeared 16 years after his death as predicted and was immediately referred to as "Halley's comet."

Halley's comet appeared again in 1986, sparking a worldwide effort to study it up close. Five satellites in all took readings from the comet at various distances. Two Soviet craft, *Vega 1* and *Vega 2,* went in close to provide detailed pictures of the comet, including the first of the comet's core. The European Space Agency's craft, *Giotto,* entered the comet itself, coming to within 450 mi of the comet's center and successfully passing through its tail. In addition, two Japanese craft, the *Suisei* and the *Sakigake,* passed at a farther distance and analyzed the cloud and tail of the comet and the effect of solar radiation upon it.

Astronomers refer to comets as *periodic* or *nonperiodic,* but the latter term does not mean that these comets have no period; it merely means that their period is not known. The actual periods of comets run from 3.3 years (the shortest known) to many thousands of years. Their orbits are elliptical, like those of the planets, but they are very eccentric, long, and narrow ellipses. Only comet Schwassmann-Wachmann has an orbit that has such a low eccentricity (for a cometary orbit) that it could be the orbit of a minor planet.

When a comet coming from deep space approaches the Sun, it is at first indistinguishable from a minor planet. Somewhere between the orbits of Mars and Jupiter, its outline becomes fuzzy; it is said to develop a *coma* (the word used here is the Latin word *coma,* which means "hair," not the phonetically identical Greek word that means "deep sleep"). Then, near the orbit of Mars, the comet develops its tail, which at first trails behind. This grows steadily as the comet comes closer and closer to the Sun. As it rounds the Sun (as first noticed by Girolamo Fracastoro, 1483–1553), the tail always points away from the Sun so that the comet, when moving away from the Sun, points its tail ahead like the landing lights of an airplane.

The reason for this behavior is that the tail is pushed in these directions by the radiation pressure of the Sun. It sometimes happens that a comet loses its tail at perihelion; it then grows another one. Although the tail is clearly visible against the black of the sky, it is very tenuous. It has been said that if the tail of Halley's comet could be compressed to the density of iron, it would fit into a small suitcase.

Although very low in mass, comets are among the largest members of the solar system. The nucleus of a comet may be up to 10,000 mi in diameter; its coma between 10,000 and 50,000 mi in diameter; and its tail as long as 28 million miles.

Comet Shoemaker-Levy 9 broke up into 21 fragments in July 1992 and crashed into the surface of Jupiter, July 16–22, 1994, in the most violent event in the recorded history of the solar system.

In 1951, Dutch astronomer Gerard Kuiper first suggested the existence of a disk-shaped swarm of short-period comets that begin beyond the orbit of Neptune and extend past Pluto. In 1995, the Hubble Space Telescope detected the long-sought Kuiper Belt and an estimated 200 million comets were discovered orbiting it.

Meteors and Meteorites

The term *meteor* for what is usually called a *shooting star* bears an unfortunate resemblance to the term *meteorology*, the science of weather and weather forecasting. This resemblance is due to an ancient misunderstanding that wrongly considered meteors an atmospheric phenomenon. Actually, the streak of light in the sky that scientists call a meteor is essentially an astronomical phenomenon: the entry of a small piece of cosmic matter into our atmosphere.

The distinction between *meteors* and *fireballs* (formerly also called *bolides*) is merely one of convenience; a fireball is an unusually bright meteor. Incidentally, it also means that a fireball is larger than a faint meteor.

Bodies that enter our atmosphere become visible when they are about 60 mi above the ground. The fact that they grow hot enough to emit light is not due to the "friction" of the atmosphere, as one often reads. The phenomenon responsible for the heating is one of compression. Unconfined air cannot move faster than the speed of sound. Since the entering meteorite moves with 30 to 60 times the speed of sound, the air simply cannot get out of the way. Therefore, it is compressed like the air in the cylinder of a diesel engine and is heated by compression. This heat—or part of it—is transferred to the moving body. The details of this process are now fairly well understood as a result of reentry tests with ballistic-missile nose cones.

The average weight of a body producing a faint *shooting star* is only a small fraction of an ounce. Even a bright fireball may not weigh more than 2 or 3 lb. Naturally, the smaller bodies are worn to dust by the passage through the atmosphere; only rather large ones reach the ground. Those that are found are called meteorites. (The *meteor,* to repeat, is the term for the light streak in the sky.) About 1,000 meteorites fall to Earth each year.

The largest meteorite known is still embedded in the ground near Grootfontein in southwest Africa and is estimated to weigh 70 tons. The second-largest known is the 34-ton Anighito (on exhibit in the Hayden Planetarium, New York), which was found by Admiral Peary in 1892 at Cape York in Greenland. The largest meteorite found in the United States is the Willamette meteorite (found in Oregon, weight ca. 15 tons), but large portions of this meteorite weathered away before it was found. Its weight as it struck the ground may have been 20 tons.

All these are iron meteorites (an iron meteorite normally contains about 7% nickel), which form one class of meteorites. The other class consists of the stony meteorites, and between them there are the so-called stony irons. Tektites consist of silica-rich glass similar to our volcanic glass obsidian, and because of the similarity, there is doubt in a number of cases whether the glass is of terrestrial or of extraterrestrial origin.

Though no meteorite larger than the Grootfontein is actually known, we do know that Earth has, on occasion, been struck by much larger bodies. Evidence for such hits are the meteorite craters, of which an especially good example is located near the Cañon Diablo in Arizona. Another meteor crater in the United States is a rather old crater near Odessa, Tex. A large number of others are known, especially in eastern Canada; and for many "probables," meteoric origin has now been proved.

The 13th known lunar meteorite was found in Dec. 1993 by a team from the Antarctic Search for Meteorites project. It is approximately 2 in. long and weighs 0.75 oz.

Some scientists theorize that the mass extermination of dinosaurs from the face of Earth 65 million years ago was due to a large meteor that struck our planet at that time.

Meteor showers are caused by multitudes of very small bodies traveling in swarms. Earth travels in its orbit through these swarms like a car driving through falling snow. The point from which the meteors seem to emanate is called the *radiant* and is named for the constellation in that area. The Perseid meteor shower in August is the most spectacular of the year, boasting, at peak, roughly 60 meteors per hour under good atmospheric conditions. The presence of a bright moon diminishes the number of visible meteors.

The Constellations

Constellations are groupings of stars that form easily recognized and remembered patterns, such as Orion and the Big Dipper. The Big Dipper is actually an asterism, not a constellation, because it is only part of the constellation Ursa Major (the Big Bear). Actually, the stars in the majority of all constellations do not "belong together." Usually they are at greatly varying distances from Earth and just happen to lie more or less in the same line of sight as seen from our solar system. But in a few cases, the stars of a constellation are actually associated; most of the bright stars of the Big Dipper travel together and form what astronomers call an *open cluster*.

If you observe a planet, say Mars, for one complete revolution, you will see that it passes successively through 12 constellations. All planets (except Pluto at certain times) can be observed only in these 12 constellations, which form the so-called zodiac, and the Sun also moves through the zodiacal signs, though the Sun's apparent movement is actually caused by the movement of Earth.

Although the constellations are due mainly to the optical accident of line of sight and have no real significance, astronomers have retained them as reference areas. It is much easier to speak of a star in

The 88 Recognized Constellations

In astronomical works, the Latin names of the constellations are used. The letter N or S following the Latin name indicates whether the constellation is located to the north or south of the Zodiac. The letter Z indicates that the constellation is within the Zodiac.

Latin name	Letter	English version	Latin name	Letter	English version	Latin name	Letter	English version
Andromeda	N	Andromeda	Delphinus	N	Dolphin	Pegasus	N	Pegasus
Antlia	S	Airpump	Dorado	S	Swordfish (Gold-fish)	Perseus	N	Perseus
Apus	S	Bird of Paradise	Draco	N	Dragon	Phoenix	S	Phoenix
Aquarius	Z	Water Bearer	Equuleus	N	Filly	Pictor	S	Painter (or his Easel)
Aquila	N	Eagle	Eridanus	S	Eridanus (river)	Pisces	Z	Fishes
Ara	S	Altar	Fornax	S	Furnace	Piscis Austrinus	S	Southern Fish
Aries	Z	Ram	Gemini	Z	Twins	Puppis	S	Poop (of Argo)[1]
Auriga	N	Charioteer	Grus	S	Crane	Pyxis	S	Mariner's Compass
Boötes	N	Herdsmen	Hercules	N	Hercules	Reticulum	S	Net
Caelum	S	Sculptor's Tool	Horologium	S	Clock	Sagitta	N	Arrow
Camelopardalis	N	Giraffe	Hydra	N	Sea Serpent	Sagittarius	Z	Archer
Cancer	Z	Crab	Hydrus	S	Water Snake	Scorpius	Z	Scorpion
Canes Venatici	N	Hunting Dogs	Indus	S	Indian	Sculptor	S	Sculptor
Canis Major	S	Great Dog	Lacerta	N	Lizard	Scutum	N	Shield
Canis Minor	S	Little Dog	Leo	Z	Lion	Serpens	N	Serpent
Capricornus	Z	Goat (or Sea-Goat)	Leo Minor	N	Little Lion	Sextans	S	Sextant
Carina	S	Keel (of Argo)[1]	Lepus	S	Hare	Taurus	Z	Bull
Cassiopeia	N	Cassiopeia	Libra	Z	Scales	Telescopium	S	Telescope
Centaurus	S	Centaur	Lupus	S	Wolf	Triangulum	N	Triangle
Cepheus	N	Cepheus	Lynx	N	Lynx	Triangulum Australe	S	Southern Triangle
Cetus	S	Whale	Lyra	N	Lyre (Harp)	Tucana	S	Toucan
Chameleon	S	Chameleon	Mensa	S	Table (mountain)	Ursa Major	N	Big Dipper[2]
Circinus	S	Compasses	Microscopium	S	Microscope	Ursa Minor	N	Little Dipper[3]
Columba	S	Dove	Monoceros	S	Unicorn	Vela	S	Sail (of Argo)[1]
Coma Berenices	N	Berenice's Hair	Musca	S	Southern Fly	Virgo	Z	Virgin
Corona Australis	S	Southern Crown	Norma	S	Rule (straight-edge)	Volans	S	Flying Fish
Corona Borealis	N	Northern Crown	Octans	S	Octant	Vulpecula	N	Fox
Corvus	S	Crow (Raven)	Ophiuchus	N	Serpent-Bearer			
Crater	S	Cup	Orion	N	Orion			
Crux	S	Southern Cross	Pavo	S	Peacock			
Cygnus	N	Swan						

1. The original constellation Argo Navis (the Ship Argo) has been divided into Carina, Puppis, and Vela. Normally the brightest star in each constellation is designated by alpha, the first letter of the Greek alphabet, the second brightest by beta, the second letter of the Greek alphabet, and so forth. But the Greek letters run through Carina, Puppis, and Vela as if it were still one constellation. 2. The Big Dipper is only a part of the constellation Ursa Major (Great Bear) and is not a constellation by itself. 3. The Little Dipper is called Ursa Minor (Little Bear).

Orion than to give its geometrical position in the sky. During the Astronomical Congress of 1928, it was decided to recognize 88 constellations. A description of their agreed-upon boundaries was published at Cambridge, England, in 1930, under the title *Atlas Céleste*.

The Auroras

The "northern lights" (*Aurora borealis*) as well as the "southern lights" (*Aurora australis*) are upper-atmosphere phenomena of astronomical origin. The auroras center around the magnetic (not the geographical) poles of Earth, which explains why, in the Western Hemisphere, they have been seen as far to the south as New Orleans and Florida, while the equivalent latitude in the Eastern Hemisphere never sees an aurora. The northern magnetic pole happens to be in the Western Hemisphere.

The lower limit of an aurora is at about 50 mi (80 km). Upper limits have been estimated to be as high as 400 mi (640 km). Since about 1880, a connection between the auroras on Earth and sunspots has been suspected and has gradually come to be accepted. It was said that the sunspots probably eject "particles" (later the word *electrons* was substituted), which on striking Earth's atmosphere cause the auroras. But this explanation suffered from certain difficulties. Sometimes a very large sunspot group on the Sun,

with individual spots bigger than Earth itself, would not cause an aurora. Moreover, even if a sunspot caused an aurora, the time that passed between the appearance of the one and the occurrence of the other was highly unpredictable.

This problem of the time lag is, in all probability, solved by the discovery of the Van Allen layer by artificial satellite *Explorer I*. The Van Allen layer[1] is a double layer of charged subatomic particles around Earth. The inner layer, with its center some 1,500 mi (2,400 km) from the ground, reaches from about 40°N to about 40°S and does not touch the atmosphere. The outer layer, much larger and with its center several thousand miles from the ground, does touch the atmosphere in the vicinity of the magnetic poles.

It seems probable that the "leakage" of electrons from the outer Van Allen layer causes the auroras. A new burst of electrons from the Sun seems to be caught in the outer layer first. Under the assumption that all electrons are first caught in the outer layer, the time lag can be understood. There has to be an "overflow" from the outer layer to produce an aurora.

1. Named after the American physicist, James Alfred Van Allen (1914–), who discovered the broad bands of intense radiation surrounding Earth in 1958.

The Atmosphere

Though reasonably transparent to visible light, the atmosphere may absorb as much as 60% of the visible and near-visible light. It is opaque to most other wavelengths, except certain fairly short radio waves. In addition to absorbing much light, our atmosphere bends light rays entering at a slant (for a given observer) so that the true position of a star close to the horizon is not what it seems to be. One effect is that we see the Sun above the horizon before it actually is. And the unsteady movement of the atmosphere causes the "twinkling" of the stars, which may be romantic, but is a nuisance when it comes to observing.

The composition of our atmosphere near the ground is 78% nitrogen and 21% oxygen, the remaining 1% consisting of other gases, most of it argon. The composition stays the same to an altitude of at least 70 mi (112 km) (except that higher up two impurities, carbon dioxide and water vapor, are missing), but the pressure drops very fast. At 18,000 ft, half of the total mass of the atmosphere is below, and at 100,000 ft, 99% of the mass of the atmosphere is below. The upper limit of the atmosphere is usually given as 120 mi (192 km); no definitive figure is possible, since there is no boundary line between the incredibly attenuated gases 120 mi (192 km) up and space.

Phenomena, 2002

Configurations of Sun, Moon, and Planets

NOTE: The hour listings are in Universal Time. For conversion to U.S. time zones, *see* Conversion of Universal Time to Civil Time, p. 400. Terms in boldface can be found on pp. 376–378.

JANUARY

day	phenomenon	hour
1	Jupiter is at **opposition**.	0600
2	The Moon is at **perigee**.	0700
2	Earth is at **perihelion**.	1400
6	LAST QUARTER	0400
8	Pallas, the second-largest asteroid, is in **conjunction** with the Sun.	2200
9	Mercury is 1° 3′ south of Neptune.	0500
11	Mercury is at its greatest **elongation**, at 19° east of the Sun.	2300
13	NEW MOON	1300
14	Venus is in superior **conjunction**.	1200
15	Mercury is 4° north of the Moon.	0200
15	Uranus is 4° north of the Moon.	2200
16	Vesta, the third-largest asteroid, appears to be motionless in the sky as it goes from **retrograde** to direct motion.	1700
18	Mercury appears to be motionless in the sky as it goes from direct motion to **retrograde** motion.	0900
18	The Moon is at its **apogee**.	0900
18	Mars is 5° north of the Moon.	2200
21	FIRST QUARTER	1800
24	Saturn is 0° 8′ south of the Moon. **Occultation** of Saturn by the Moon.	1600
26	Jupiter is 0° 9′ south of the Moon. **Occultation** of Jupiter by the Moon.	1900
27	Mercury is in inferior **conjunction**.	1900
28	Neptune is in **conjunction** with the Sun.	1400
28	FULL MOON	2300
30	The Moon is at **perigee**.	0900

FEBRUARY

day	phenomenon	hour
4	LAST QUARTER	1400
8	Mercury appears to be motionless in the sky as it goes from **retrograde** to direct motion.	1000
8	Saturn appears to be motionless in the sky as it goes from **retrograde** to direct motion.	1000
10	Mercury is 5° north of the Moon.	0500
11	The asteroid Juno is at **opposition**.	0100
12	NEW MOON	0800
13	Uranus is in **conjunction** with the Sun.	1700
14	The Moon is at **apogee**.	2200
16	Ceres, the largest asteroid, is in **conjunction** with the Sun.	1300

day	phenomenon	hour
17	Mars is 5° north of the Moon.	0000
20	FIRST QUARTER	1200
20	Vesta, the third-largest asteroid, is 0° 6′ south of the Moon. **Occultation** of Vesta by the Moon.	1300
21	Saturn is 0° 2′ south of the Moon. **Occultation** of Saturn by the Moon.	0000
21	Mercury is at its greatest **elongation**, at 27° west of the Sun.	1600
23	Jupiter is 0° 9′ south of the Moon. **Occultation** of Jupiter by the Moon.	0200
24	Mercury is 0° 5′ south of Neptune.	1300
27	FULL MOON	0900
27	The Moon is at **perigee**.	2000

MARCH

day	phenomenon	hour
1	Jupiter appears to be motionless in the sky as it goes from **retrograde** to direct motion.	1500
6	LAST QUARTER	0100
9	Mercury is 1° 2′ south of Uranus.	0300
10	Neptune is 4° north of the Moon.	0900
11	Uranus is 4° north of the Moon.	1700
12	Mercury is 3° north of the Moon.	0100
14	The Moon is at **apogee**.	0100
14	NEW MOON	0200
18	Mars is 4° north of the Moon.	0100
20	Saturn is 0° 5′ south of the Moon. **Occultation** of Saturn by the Moon.	1000
20	Vesta, the third-largest asteroid, is 0° 5′ south of the Moon. **Occultation** of Vesta by the Moon.	1000
20	Equinox	1900
21	Pluto appears to be motionless in the sky as it goes from direct motion to **retrograde** motion.	0600
22	FIRST QUARTER	0200
22	Jupiter is 1° 1′ south of the Moon.	1200
23	The asteroid Juno appears to be motionless in the sky as it goes from **retrograde** to direct motion.	1200
28	The Moon is at **perigee**.	0800
28	FULL MOON	1800
31	Saturn is 4° north of Aldebaran, the brightest star in the constellation Taurus.	1600

APRIL

day	phenomenon	hour
4	LAST QUARTER	1500
6	Neptune is 4° north of the Moon.	1600
7	Mercury is in superior **conjunction**.	0900
8	Uranus is 4° north of the Moon.	0100
10	The Moon is at **apogee**.	0500
12	NEW MOON	1900
14	Venus is 3° north of the Moon.	1700
15	Mars is 2° north of the Moon.	2300
16	Saturn is 0° 8′ south of the Moon. **Occultation** of Saturn by the Moon.	2000
17	Vesta, the third-largest asteroid, is 0° 7′ south of the Moon. **Occultation** of Vesta by the Moon.	1000
18	Jupiter is 1° 6′ south of the Moon.	2300
20	FIRST QUARTER	1300
25	The Moon is at **perigee**.	1600
27	FULL MOON	0300
29	Mars is 6° north of Aldebaran, the brightest star in the constellation Taurus.	1300

MAY

day	phenomenon	hour
4	Neptune is 4° north of the Moon.	0000
4	Mercury is at its greatest **elongation**, at 21° east of the Sun.	0400
4	LAST QUARTER	0700
4	Venus is 6° north of Aldebaran, the brightest star in the constellation Taurus.	1400
4	Mars is 2° north of Saturn.	1700
5	Uranus is 4° north of the Moon.	1000
7	Venus is 2° north of Saturn.	1800
7	The Moon is at **apogee**.	1900
10	Venus is 0° 3′ north of Mars.	2100
12	NEW MOON	1100
13	Neptune appears to be motionless in the sky as it goes from direct motion to **retrograde** motion.	1400
13	Mercury is 3° north of the Moon.	2100
14	Saturn is 1° 1′ south of the Moon. **Occultation** of Saturn by the Moon.	0800
14	Mars is 0° 6′ north of the Moon. **Occultation** of Mars by the Moon.	1900
14	Venus is 0° 8′ north of the Moon. **Occultation** of Venus by the Moon.	2300
15	Vesta, the third-largest asteroid, is 1° 1′ south of the Moon. **Occultation** of Vesta by the Moon.	1200
16	Mercury appears to be motionless in the sky as it goes from direct motion to **retrograde** motion.	0500
16	Jupiter is 2° south of the Moon.	1200
19	FIRST QUARTER	2000
23	The Moon is at **perigee**.	1600
26	FULL MOON Partial eclipse.	1200
27	Mercury is in inferior **conjunction**.	0700
31	Neptune is 4° north of the Moon.	0800

JUNE

day	phenomenon	hour
1	Uranus is 4° north of the Moon.	1800
3	LAST QUARTER	0000
3	Uranus appears to be motionless in the sky as it goes from direct motion to **retrograde** motion.	0700
3	Venus is 1° 6′ north of Jupiter.	1800
4	The Moon is at **apogee**.	1300
7	Pluto is at **opposition**.	0500

day	phenomenon	hour
8	Mercury appears to be motionless in the sky as it goes from **retrograde** to direct motion.	1100
8	Pallas, the second-largest asteroid, appears to be motionless in the sky as it goes from direct motion to **retrograde** motion.	2300
9	Saturn is in **conjunction** with the Sun.	1100
9	Mercury is 3° south of the Moon.	1400
9	Venus is 5° south of Pollux, the brightest star in the constellation Gemini.	2000
11	NEW MOON Annular eclipse of the Sun.	0000
12	Mars is 0° 9′ south of the Moon. **Occultation** of Mars by the Moon.	1200
13	Jupiter is 2° south of the Moon.	0400
13	Venus is 1° 5′ south of the Moon.	2100
18	FIRST QUARTER	0000
19	The Moon is at **perigee**.	0700
21	Solstice	1300
21	Mercury is at its greatest **elongation**, at 23° west of the Sun.	1500
24	Mercury is 2° north of Aldebaran, the brightest star in the constellation Taurus.	0400
24	FULL MOON Partial eclipse.	2200
27	Neptune is 4° north of the Moon.	1600
29	Uranus is 4° north of the Moon.	0200

JULY

day	phenomenon	hour
2	The Moon is at **apogee**.	0800
2	Mercury is 0° 2′ south of Saturn.	1100
2	LAST QUARTER	1700
3	Mars is 0° 8′ north of Jupiter.	0600
4	Mars is 6° south of Pollux, the brightest star in the constellation Gemini.	1700
6	Earth is at **aphelion**.	0400
8	Saturn is 1° 7′ south of the Moon.	1300
10	NEW MOON	1000
10	Venus is 1° 1′ north of Regulus, the brightest star in the constellation Leo.	1000
13	Venus is 4° south of the Moon.	1200
14	The Moon is at **perigee**.	1300
17	FIRST QUARTER	0500
20	Jupiter is in **conjunction** with the Sun.	0100
21	Mercury is in superior **conjunction**.	0200
23	Vesta, the third-largest asteroid, is in **conjunction** with the Sun.	0800
24	FULL MOON	0900
24	Neptune is 4° north of the Moon.	2300
26	Uranus is 4° north of the Moon.	0900
30	The Moon is at **apogee**.	0200

AUGUST

day	phenomenon	hour
1	LAST QUARTER	1000
2	Neptune is at **opposition**.	0100
5	Saturn is 2° south of the Moon.	0400
6	Mercury is 0° 9′ north of Regulus, the brightest star in the constellation Leo.	0400
8	NEW MOON	1900
10	Mercury is 4° south of the Moon.	0100
10	Mars is in **conjunction** with the Sun.	2200
10	The Moon is at **perigee**.	2300
11	Venus is 6° south of the Moon.	2200
12	Pallas, the second-largest asteroid, is at **opposition**.	1200
15	FIRST QUARTER	1000
17	Ceres, the largest asteroid, appears to be motionless in the sky as it goes from direct motion to **retrograde** motion.	1500

day	phenomenon	hour
20	Uranus is at **opposition**.	0100
21	Neptune is 4° north of the Moon.	0400
22	Venus is at its greatest **elongation**, at 46° east of the Sun.	1300
22	Uranus is 4° north of the Moon.	1400
22	FULL MOON	2200
26	The Moon is at **apogee**.	1800
27	Pluto appears to be motionless in the sky as it goes from **retrograde** to direct motion.	2000
31	LAST QUARTER	0300

SEPTEMBER

day	phenomenon	hour
1	Venus is 0° 9′ south of Spica, the brightest star in the constellation Virgo.	0600
1	Mercury is at its greatest **elongation**, at 27° east of the Sun.	1000
1	Saturn is 2° south of the Moon.	1700
4	Jupiter is 4° south of the Moon.	1300
7	NEW MOON	0300
8	The Moon is at **perigee**.	0300
8	Mercury is 9° south of the Moon.	1700
10	Venus is 8° south of the Moon.	0200
13	FIRST QUARTER	1800
14	Mercury appears to be motionless in the sky as it goes from direct motion to **retrograde** motion.	1400
17	Neptune is 4° north of the Moon.	0900
18	Uranus is 4° north of the Moon.	1800
21	FULL MOON	1400
23	The Moon is at **apogee**.	0300
23	Equinox	0500
26	Venus is at its greatest brilliancy.	1100
27	Mercury is in inferior **conjunction**.	1900
29	Saturn is 3° south of the Moon.	0300
29	LAST QUARTER	1700
30	Pallas, the second-largest asteroid, appears to be motionless in the sky as it goes from **retrograde** to direct motion.	0000

OCTOBER

day	phenomenon	hour
2	Jupiter is 4° south of the Moon.	0700
3	The asteroid Juno is in **conjunction** with the Sun.	2200
4	Ceres, the largest asteroid, is at **opposition**.	0800
5	Mars is 4° south of the Moon.	0100
6	Mercury appears to be motionless in the sky as it goes from **retrograde** to direct motion.	0200
6	NEW MOON	1100
6	The Moon is at **perigee**.	1300
8	Venus is 10° south of the Moon.	1000
10	Venus appears to be motionless in the sky as it goes from direct motion to **retrograde** motion.	0900
11	Saturn appears to be motionless in the sky as it goes from direct motion to **retrograde** motion.	1300
13	FIRST QUARTER	0600
13	Mercury is at its greatest **elongation**, at 18° west of the Sun.	0800
14	Neptune is 5° north of the Moon.	1400
15	Uranus is 4° north of the Moon.	2200
20	The Moon is at **apogee**.	0500
20	Neptune appears to be motionless in the sky as it goes from **retrograde** to direct motion.	1100

day	phenomenon	hour
21	FULL MOON	0700
26	Saturn is 3° south of the Moon.	0900
27	Mercury is 4° north of Spica, the brightest star in the constellation Virgo.	0900
29	LAST QUARTER	0500
29	Jupiter is 4° south of the Moon.	2200
31	Venus is in inferior **conjunction**.	1200

NOVEMBER

day	phenomenon	hour
1	Vesta, the third-largest asteroid, is 1° 3′ south of the Moon. **Occultation** of Vesta by the Moon.	0000
2	Mars is 4° south of the Moon.	1800
3	The asteroid Juno is 0° 6′ north of the Moon. **Occultation** of Juno by the Moon.	1200
4	The Moon is at **perigee**.	0100
4	Uranus appears to be motionless in the sky as it goes from **retrograde** to direct motion.	1200
4	NEW MOON	2100
10	Neptune is 5° north of the Moon.	2200
11	FIRST QUARTER	2100
12	Uranus is 5° north of the Moon.	0500
14	Mercury is in superior **conjunction**.	0500
16	The Moon is at **apogee**.	1100
19	Venus appears to be motionless in the sky as it goes from **retrograde** to direct motion.	0400
20	FULL MOON Partial eclipse.	0200
20	Mars is 3° north of Spica, the brightest star in the constellation Virgo.	0500
22	Saturn is 3° south of the Moon.	1200
26	Jupiter is 4° south of the Moon.	0700
27	LAST QUARTER	1600
29	Vesta, the third-largest asteroid, is 0° 4′ north of the Moon. **Occultation** of Vesta by the Moon.	0300
29	Ceres, the largest asteroid, appears to be motionless in the sky as it goes from **retrograde** to direct motion.	1800

DECEMBER

day	phenomenon	hour
1	Mars is 3° south of the Moon.	1000
1	Venus is 2° south of the Moon.	1300
2	The Moon is at **perigee**.	0900
4	NEW MOON Total eclipse of the Sun.	0800
4	Jupiter appears to be motionless in the sky as it goes from direct motion to **retrograde** motion.	2100
7	Venus is at its greatest brilliancy.	0100
8	Neptune is 5° north of the Moon.	0800
9	Uranus is 5° north of the Moon.	1400
9	Pluto is in **conjunction** with the Sun.	1700
11	FIRST QUARTER	1600
14	The Moon is at **apogee**.	0400
17	Saturn is at **opposition**.	1700
19	Saturn is 3° south of the Moon.	1500
19	FULL MOON	1900
22	Solstice	0100
23	Jupiter is 4° south of the Moon.	1200
26	Mercury is at its greatest **elongation**, at 20° east of the Sun.	0500
27	LAST QUARTER	0100
30	Mars is 1° 2′ south of the Moon. **Occultation** of Mars by the Moon.	0100
30	The Moon is at **perigee**.	0100
30	Venus is 2° north of the Moon.	0900

Conversion of Universal Time (U.T.) to Civil Time

U.T.	E.D.T.[1]	E.S.T.[2]	C.S.T.[3]	M.S.T.[4]	P.S.T.[5]
00	*8P	*7P	*6P	*5P	*4P
01	*9P	*8P	*7P	*6P	*5P
02	*10P	*9P	*8P	*7P	*6P
03	*11P	*10P	*9P	*8P	*7P
04	M	*11P	*10P	*9P	*8P
05	1A	M	*11P	*10P	*9P
06	2A	1A	M	*11P	*10P
07	3A	2A	1A	M	*11P
08	4A	3A	2A	1A	M
09	5A	4A	3A	2A	1A
10	6A	5A	4A	3A	2A
11	7A	6A	5A	4A	3A
12	8A	7A	6A	5A	4A
13	9A	8A	7A	6A	5A
14	10A	9A	8A	7A	6A
15	11A	10A	9A	8A	7A
16	N	11A	10A	9A	8A
17	1P	N	11A	10A	9A
18	2P	1P	N	11A	10A
19	3P	2P	1P	N	11A
20	4P	3P	2P	1P	N
21	5P	4P	3P	2P	1P
22	6P	5P	4P	3P	2P
23	7P	6P	5P	4P	3P

NOTES: * denotes previous day. N = noon. M = midnight. 1. Eastern Daylight Time. 2. Eastern Standard Time, same as Central Daylight Time. 3. Central Standard Time, same as Mountain Daylight Time. 4. Mountain Standard Time, same as Pacific Daylight Time. 5. Pacific Standard Time.

Eclipses of the Sun and Moon, 2002

Note: The day of an eclipse is given in Universal Time (U.T.) and may start a day earlier or later depending on your time zone. (*See* Phenomena, 2002 table, pp. 397–399, to find time of eclipse.)

May 26. Partial eclipse of the Moon. The beginning of the penumbral phase visible in most of North America except the northeast, Central America, western South America, extreme northeast Russia, eastern Asia, Australia, most of Antarctica, the Pacific Ocean, and the southeast Indian Ocean; the end visible in southwest Alaska, Asia except the extreme north, Australia, the eastern Indian Ocean, and most of the Pacific Ocean except the extreme eastern part.

June 10–11. Annular eclipse of the Sun. Visible in eastern Asia, Japan, Indonesia, northern Australia, Pacific Ocean, northern Mexico, the United States, and Canada except the extreme northeast part.

June 24. Partial eclipse of the Moon. The beginning of the penumbral phase visible in Australia, Indonesia, southern and western Asia, Europe except the extreme north, Africa, extreme eastern South America, Antarctica, the Indian Ocean, the eastern North Atlantic Ocean, the South Atlantic Ocean, and the southwest Pacific Ocean; the end

visible in Africa, Europe except the extreme north, most of South America except the northwest, Antarctica, western Australia, southwest Asia, the Indian Ocean, the eastern North Atlantic Ocean, the South Atlantic Ocean, and the southeast South Pacific Ocean.

November 19–20. Partial eclipse of the Moon. The beginning of the penumbral phase visible in Africa, Europe, Greenland, North America except the western part, the Arctic region, Central America, South America except the southern tip, extreme western Asia, the Atlantic Ocean, and the western Indian Ocean; the end visible in North America, the Arctic region, Central America, South America, Greenland, Europe, northern and western Russia, the western Middle East, western Africa, the Antarctic Peninsula, the Atlantic Ocean, and the eastern Pacific Ocean.

December 4. Total eclipse of the Sun. Visible in Africa except the north, southeast Atlantic Ocean, central Indian Ocean, part of Antarctica, Indonesia, Australia, South Island of New Zealand.

Visibility of Planets in Morning and Evening Twilight, 2002

	Morning		Evening
Venus	November 7–December 31	Venus	February 25–October 26
Mars	September 25–December 31	Mars	January 1–June 24
Jupiter	January 1	Jupiter	January 1–July 6
	August 3–December 31	Saturn	January 1–May 22
Saturn	June 28–December 17		December 17–December 31

Beyond Hubble

A new crop of bigger, sharper, smarter telescopes is revolutionizing the way astronomers search the skies

By MICHAEL D. LEMONICK TIME

For nearly a half-century, starting in 1949, the world's most powerful research-quality telescope was the Hale, on Palomar Mountain, in California. Its mirror, 5 m (17 ft) in diameter, focused more faint starlight than anything else on the planet. But in the past few years, the Hale has been humbled. On the summit of the long-dormant volcano of Mauna Kea, Hawaii, sit the Subaru telescope (no relation to the car), with a mirror more than 8 m (27 ft) across; the Gemini North telescope, also topping 8 m; and the kings of the mountain, the twin Keck telescopes, whose light-gathering surfaces are an astonishing 10 m—33 ft—in diameter.

The story is the same all over the world. In the high Andes of northern Chile, five more 8-m-class telescopes are either finished or nearing completion, while peaks in Arizona, Texas, and South Africa too boast scopes more powerful than anything known to science just a decade ago.

That's not all. While each of these instruments trumps the Hale in light-gathering power, many are poised to outshine even the Hubble Space Telescope, which has been delivering astonishing snapshots of deepest space since it was refurbished in 1993. The orbiting observatory's nearly 2.5-m (8-ft) mirror isn't all that powerful, but since it floats above Earth's constantly roiling atmosphere, the Hubble has been unrivaled in the sharpness of its images. No more. Using an ingenious technological trick to eliminate atmospheric blur, most of the new telescopes will soon achieve Hubble-quality focus—and even beat it under the right conditions.

This is a breakthrough of astronomical proportions. Whereas for years scientists have had only one Hubble-quality telescope, they will soon have access to more than a dozen.

The Leap Forward

It has been a long time coming. Impressive as the Hale telescope was for its day, it represented a technological dead end. The Hale, like its smaller predecessors, was powered by a mirror that's essentially a huge hockey puck of glass ground into a concave light-focusing curve on one face and coated with reflective metal. To keep from sagging under its own weight and distorting the curve, the mirror had to be a bulky 26 in. thick, and it weighed 20 tons. That enormous heft called for an even more massive support structure to hold the whole thing up while at the same time adjusting constantly to counteract the effect of Earth's rotation. Everyone agreed that telescopes needed some sort of radical new design. Unfortunately, says Matt Mountain, director of the Gemini Observatory, "nobody knew how to make the conceptual leap."

By the early '80s, though, telescope designers were leaping all over the place. University of Arizona astronomer Roger Angel's solution to the sagging-glass problem was to cast huge mirrors that are mostly hollow, with a honeycomb-like structure inside to guarantee stiffness. University of California at Santa Cruz astronomer Jerry Nelson opted instead to create a mirror not from a single huge slab of glass but from 36 smaller sheets that would, under a computer's control, act as one. And in Europe, design teams came up with yet another idea, the exact opposite of Angel's: instead of making the mirror hollow to save weight, let it be thin—about 8 in. thick for an 8-m mirror, in contrast to the 5-m Hale's 26 in.—and counteract the resulting floppiness with computer-controlled supports that continually readjust its shape.

"People argued at the time that it would be crazy to rely on computers because they might fail," recalls Mountain, whose Gemini telescopes in Hawaii and Chile were built on the European model. "But when you think about it, planes are controlled by onboard computers, and those computers essentially never fail."

Neither do the ones that run the telescopes. The European Southern Observatory's New Technology Telescope, built in the 1980s as a 3.5-m precursor to the Very Large Telescope (VLT), worked beautifully. So did Keck 1 when it went into operation in 1992. And so, in turn, have the other big telescopes as they've come online over the past two years. With both enormous size and smooth performance, these giant telescopes are doing science on a heroic scale—especially the Keck, which has had more than a half-decade head start on its rivals.

Keck vs. Hubble

The Hubble's forte is taking brilliantly sharp pictures. But the real meat of astronomical discovery comes not so much in pretty photos of celestial objects but in the detailed analysis of their light. By smearing that light into a spectrum—the rainbow of its component colors—scientists can identify the chemical makeup of a star or galaxy, how far away it is, and how fast it's rotating, among other data. If the image of a star is going to be smeared anyway, sharp pictures don't matter much, so ground-based telescopes are at no disadvantage.

And in many cases the ground-based giants can find their own way through the universe. Geoff Marcy, for example, leader of the world's most prolific planet-hunting team, began his research at the relatively modest 3.5-m telescope at Lick Observatory in California. Then, in 1996, he moved most of his project to the Keck, with dramatic results. "We've discovered 35 planets orbiting sunlike stars so far," says Marcy, who holds joint appointments at the University of California, Berkeley, and San Francisco State University. "And the majority of them have been with the Keck."

Europeans Catching Up?

With their six-year head start, the Kecks have done more science than the newer telescopes, but the newcomers haven't wasted any time catching up. The European Southern Observatory's VLT, for example, built and operated by a consortium of eight countries, got the first of its four 8.2-m telescopes up and running in 1998 and achieved "first light" with the fourth in 2000.

But it's already doing first-rate science. Earlier this year, for example, astronomers from Sweden, Italy, Denmark, and Germany used one of the scopes to help solve astronomy's so-called age paradox. In the mid-1990s, astronomers used the Hubble to measure the age of the universe at between 8 billion and 12 billion years. But other experts insisted they knew of stars that were at least 14 billion years old—obviously a problem, since stars can't be older than the cosmos. Using the VLT, though, observers have measured minute traces of radioactive uranium and thorium in the oldest stars—a technique akin to radiocarbon dating—and proved that they're more like 12 billion years old (the age of the universe, meanwhile, is now estimated at 14 billion years).

Technology Keeps U.S. Ahead

Still, U.S.-based telescopes remain ahead on several fronts, including the detwinkling of starlight. The technology that does this is called adaptive optics, and it was originally developed in secrecy by the Department of Defense to help military snoops take sharp pictures of Soviet spy satellites. Largely declassified in the 1980s, it's now being adapted for major telescopes everywhere. The idea is straightforward: stars and galaxies twinkle and shimmer because turbulent pockets of air act as weak light-distorting lenses (heat rising from a car's hood or an asphalt parking lot causes a similar effect). With adaptive optics, though, a computer can measure the shimmer and cancel it out.

Will adaptive optics make space telescopes like the Hubble obsolete? Not entirely. Space is still the best place to take supersharp pictures in ordinary light. And some radiation—ultraviolet, for example, and some wavelengths of infrared—can't penetrate the atmosphere at all. Moreover, telescopes radiate infrared light of their own, which contaminates celestial images. That's why NASA's plan to launch a Next Generation Space Telescope by 2009 still makes sense. With an 8-m mirror of its own, NGST will be able to see distant galaxies, for example, that no earthly telescope could ever see through the glare of its own heat.

A New Trick

Adaptive-optics systems may sound complicated, but they pale beside another technological trick that will ultimately boost telescopes' power even more. Called interferometry, it achieves the precise focus of a truly huge telescope without actually having the thing built. Instead, light is combined from widely separated telescopes—the two Kecks, say, whose observatory building was designed with a basement-level chamber for that purpose, or two or more of the four VLT telescopes in Chile. The system is complex, but its astonishing precision will let astronomers tease out the details of galactic structures and distant solar systems as never before.

Yet even this remarkable technology could become obsolete. Telescope designers are already thinking about the next generation of ground-based supergiant telescopes, devices that will range in size from 30 m (100 ft) across to a staggering 100 m, or 330 ft—a telescope mirror wider than the length of a football field. Armed with a new generation of adaptive-optics systems now under development, these futuristic scopes will once again revolutionize astronomy. □

Hubble Space Telescope

The $2 billion Edwin P. Hubble Space Telescope (HST) is the most complex and sensitive space observatory ever constructed. It is 43.3 ft (13 m) long and 14 ft (4 m) wide, about the size of a school bus. Hubble weighs 25,500 lb (11,000 kg) and orbits 335 nautical miles (536 km) above Earth.

HST was placed into orbit by the space shuttle *Discovery* on April 25, 1990, and every few years astronauts conduct a servicing mission to install new components and make general repairs. Hubble will be decommissioned in 2010 and replaced by the Next Generation Space Telescope (NGST). □

Some Giant Telescopes

Radio (dish-antenna) telescopes:
• The fixed-dish telescope (1963) near Arecibo, Puerto Rico: 1,000 ft (305 m) in diameter, covering 25 acres.
• Very Large Array (VLA) radio telescope (1980) near Socorro, N.M. It has 27 mobile dishes, each 82 ft in diameter.
• The fully steerable radio telescope (1972) at Effelsberg, Germany: 328 ft (100 m) in diameter.

• The fully steerable radio telescope (2000) at Green Bank, W. Va.: 328 by 360.89 ft (100 by 110 m) in diameter.

Optical (mirror) telescopes:
• Hale telescope (1948) at Mt. Palomar, Calif. The reflector is 200 in. (5 m) in diameter.
• The Special Astrophysical Observatory 236-inch (6-meter) reflector telescope (1976) at Zelenchukskaya, Russia.
• W. M. Keck telescope (1991) at Mauna Kea, Hawaii. Its primary mirror is composed of 36 hexagonal segments, each 5.9 ft (1.8 m) across.
• The European Southern Observatory (ESO) Very Large Telescope (VLT) at Cerro Paranal, Chile. It consists of four 27-foot (8.2-meter) telescopes that can work independently or in combined mode. In the combined mode, the VLT has the total light-collecting power of a 52.5-foot (16-meter) single telescope.
• The Yerkes Observatory 40-inch (1.01-meter) refractor telescope (1897) at Williams Bay, Wis.
• The National Astronomical Observatory of Japan (NAOJ) Subaru telescope (1999) at Mauna Kea, Hawaii. Its single mirror is 27 ft (8.2 m) in diameter.

Major Space Explorations

Ongoing Missions

Galileo (U.S.)

Destination: Jupiter. **Launched:** Oct. 18, 1989. **Achieved Orbit:** Dec. 7, 1995. **Mission:** To study the chemical composition and physical state of the largest planet in the solar system, its atmosphere, and four of its moons, for almost two years. The spacecraft encountered the asteroid 951 Gaspra on Oct. 29, 1991, and took the first close-up photographs ever of an asteroid in space. On Aug. 28, 1993, it passed by asteroid 243 Ida and took close-up photographs, which revealed that Ida has a tiny moon. Upon arrival at Jupiter, *Galileo* released a probe into the planet's atmosphere that descended for 57 minutes before it was destroyed by the planet's extreme temperature and pressure. In 1996, *Galileo* visited and photographed Jupiter's large moons Io, Callisto, and Europa and made flybys of Io, Ganymede, Europa, and Callisto in 1997. *Galileo* was named for the Italian astronomer Galileo Galilei, who discovered the four great moons of Jupiter that were the major targets of this mission.

Galileo Europa Mission (GEM):

A two-year continuation of the original *Galileo* mission, which was completed in Dec. 1997. GEM included eight flybys of Europa, four flybys of Callisto, and two flybys of Io by the end of 1999. The spacecraft also observed the smaller moons Amalthea, Thebe, and Metis on Jan. 3, 2000. GEM mission has been extended indefinitely.

Galileo Millennium Mission:

An extended mission to explore Jupiter and its moons through the end of 2000. On Feb. 22, 2000, *Galileo* made the closest pass ever of Io at 124 mi (200 km). Two flybys of Ganymede were conducted May 20 and Dec. 28, 2000. *Galileo* embarked on a joint scientific expedition with the Saturn-bound *Cassini* spacecraft in Dec. 2000 to make simultaneous observations of the Jupiter system from two vantage points.

Ulysses (U.S. and European Space Agency)

Destination: The Sun. **Launched:** Oct. 6, 1990. **Flew by Jupiter:** Feb. 8, 1992. **Achieved Highest Southern Latitude:** Sept. 13, 1994 (−80.2 degrees). **Achieved Highest Northern Latitude:** July 31, 1995 (+80.2 degrees). **Mission:** An international project to study the Sun and interstellar space above and below its poles. The spacecraft was put into orbit at right angles to the solar system's ecliptic plane. This special orbit enabled *Ulysses* to examine for the first time the Sun's north and south polar regions. Besides investigating the Sun, the spacecraft is also studying phenomena from the Milky Way and beyond. The spacecraft completed its first full orbit around the Sun on April 17, 1998. *Ulysses* continues to orbit the Sun, and has passed over the north and south poles in 2000 and 2001.

Mars Global Surveyor (U.S.)

Destination: Mars. **Launched:** Nov. 7, 1996. **Arrival:** Sept. 11, 1997. **Mission:** An orbiting spacecraft designed to provide detailed maps of the planet's surface and distribution of minerals, and to monitor the Martian weather. Six instruments are studying Martian surface, atmosphere, and gravitational and magnetic fields. *Surveyor*'s cameras are able to distinguish features as small as 10 ft across.

The primary mapping mission was delayed until March 1999, due to problems with the craft's solar panels. The spacecraft orbited Mars for 687 days, or the length of one Martian year, and completed its mapping in Feb. 2001. *Mars Global Surveyor* will continue to provide data through April 2002.

Cassini (U.S., the European Space Agency, and the Italian Space Agency)

Destination: Saturn. **Launched:** Oct. 15, 1997. **Arrival:** July 1, 2004. **Mission:** Will orbit Saturn for four years. While orbiting Saturn, *Cassini* will send a small probe named *Huygens* (after the Dutch astronomer Christiaan Huygens, who discovered Titan) to the surface of Saturn's largest moon, Titan, to learn more about its dense atmosphere and its surface state and composition. After relaying data to Earth from Titan, *Cassini* will continue with orbits of Saturn and flybys of the planet's moons. The spacecraft will also examine Saturn's equatorial zone and study the planet's polar regions. *Cassini* encountered Jupiter on Dec. 30, 2000, and flew down the giant planet's magnetotail, performing studies complementing the *Galileo* mission. The spacecraft flew by asteroid 2685 Masursky on Jan. 23, 2000. The *Cassini* mission is named for the Italian-French astronomer Gian Domenico Cassini, who discovered four of Saturn's major moons.

Nozomi ("Hope") (Japan)

Destination: Mars. **Launched:** July 4, 1998, from Kagoshima Space Center. **Arrival:** Dec. 2003. Engine problems delayed its scheduled 1999 arrival at Mars until 2003. **Mission:** To send an orbiter around Mars to study the effect of the solar wind on the planet's atmosphere for one Martian year (687 days). Its cameras will provide photographic data on cloud distribution, polar haze, dust storms, polar ice, and the planet's surface. After its successful launch, the Planet-B spacecraft was renamed *Nozomi* (hope). Japan's new effort made it the third nation after the United States and Russia to conduct a mission to another planet.

Deep Space 1 (U.S.)

Launched: Oct. 24, 1998. **Mission:** First launch of NASA's New Millennium program, a series of missions to test new technologies. *Deep Space 1* is the first craft to employ an ion-propulsion system. It flew past near-Earth asteroid Braille on July 28, 1999, took photos, and collected scientific data. The primary mission ended Sept. 18, 1999, and its mission was extended to fly past comet Borrelly, Sept. 2001.

Stardust (U.S.)

Destination: Comet Wild 2. **Launched:** Feb. 7, 1999. **Mission:** To fly through coma of Comet Wild 2 in 2004, capture particles spewing out of comet, and return comet dust samples to Earth in 2006. *Stardust* will be the first mission to return with comet samples. En route to Wild 2, the spacecraft collected particles from the interstellar dust stream between Feb. 22 and May 1, 2000.

2001 Mars Odyssey (U.S.)

Destination: Mars. **Launch:** April 7, 2001. **Arrival:** Oct. 24, 2001. **Mission:** To conduct mineralogical mapping of the planet and study the radiation risk to humans over the course of three years. A goal of the program is to determine if Mars's atmosphere could support life.

This mission was originally part of the Mars Surveyor 2001 Project, which consisted of two separately launched missions, the *Mars Surveyor 2001 Orbiter* and the *Mars Surveyor 2001 Lander*. The lander spacecraft was cancelled as part of the reorganization of the Mars Exploration Program at NASA. The orbiter was renamed the *2001 Mars Odyssey*.

Genesis (U.S.)

Destination: The Sun. **Launch:** Aug. 8, 2001. **Mission:** Gather samples of charged particles of the solar wind and return them to Earth in April 2004 for detailed analysis. The reentry vehicle will separate from the spacecraft and parachute its sample return capsule to a location in the Utah desert. The data to be obtained are crucial for improving theories about the origin of the Sun and planets that formed from the same primordial dust cloud.

Future Missions
(Note: Dates are tentative.)

Contour (U.S.)

Destination: Comet Nucleus Tour. **Launch:** Aug. 2002. **Mission:** To fly by Comet Encke at 60 mi (100 km) in Nov. 2003, followed by encounters with Comet Schwassmann-Wachmann-3 in June 2006, and Comet d'Arrest in Aug. 2008. The spacecraft will take images and spectral maps of nuclei and analyze dust flowing from them. The mission will help scientists to learn more about the composition and structure of comets, which are believed to be quite individual in their properties.

Mars Exploration Rovers (MER) 2003 (U.S.)

Destination: Mars. **First launch:** June 4, 2003. **Arrival:** Jan. 2004. **Second launch:** 2003. **Arrival:** 2004. **Mission:** To deploy two identical large long-range rovers (larger than *Pathfinder's Sojourner*) in two different locations that can trek up to 300 yards (100 m) across the surface in a Martian day. The rovers' sophisticated instruments will enable them to act as mobile field geologists, taking color pictures, analyzing soil and rocks, and searching for past and present evidence of water. The rovers are designed to operate for 90 days but could continue longer.

Selene SELenological and Engineering Explorer (Japan)

Destination: The Moon. **Launch:** 2003. **Mission:** An orbiting spacecraft to study the origin and evolution of the Moon for one year. It will map the entire surface and gather data on chemical and mineralogical composition, magnetic fields, and interior structure. After a year, the propulsion module of the orbiter will separate from the spacecraft and soft-land on the lunar surface to continue the mission for two more months.

Space Technology 5 (U.S.)

Destination: Earth's magnetosphere. **Launch:** 2003. **Mission:** Fourth deep-space mission of NASA's New Millennium program. The Nanosat Constellation Trailblazer, known as Space Technology 5 or ST5, will test methods for operating three miniature spacecraft as a single system. Each of the spacecraft is about the size of a birthday cake, 17 in. (42 cm) across by 8 in. (20 cm) high and weighing about 47 lb.

Herschel Space Observatory (European Space Agency)

Destination: Earth's magnetosphere. **Launch:** 2007. **Mission:** To study how the first stars and galaxies were formed and to search for water in space. Formerly called the Far Infrared and Submillimetre Telescope (FIRST), Herschel will be equipped with an infrared telescope, a high-resolution spectrograph, and two infrared cameras. Construction of the observatory will begin in the spring of 2002.

U.S. Unstaffed Planetary and Lunar Programs

Lunar Orbiter. Series of spacecraft designed to orbit the Moon, taking pictures and obtaining data in support of the subsequent staffed *Apollo* landings. The U.S. launched five *Lunar Orbiter*s between Aug. 10, 1966 and Aug. 2, 1967.

Mariner. Designation for a series of spacecraft designed to fly past or orbit the planets, particularly Mercury, Venus, and Mars. *Mariner*s provided the early information on Venus and Mars. *Mariner 9,* orbiting Mars in 1971, returned the most revealing photographs of that planet and helped pave the way for a *Viking* landing in 1976. *Mariner 10* explored Venus and Mercury in 1973 and was the first probe to use a planet's gravity to propel it toward another.

Pioneer. Designation for the United States' first series of sophisticated interplanetary spacecraft. *Pioneer*s *10* and *11* reached Jupiter in 1973 and 1974 and continued on to explore Saturn and the other outer planets. *Pioneer 11,* renamed *Pioneer Saturn,* examined the Saturn system in Sept. 1979. Significant discoveries were the finding of a small new moon and a narrow new ring. In 1986, *Pioneer 10* was the first man-made object to escape the solar system. *Pioneer Venus 1* and *2* reached Venus in 1978 and provided detailed information about that planet's surface and atmosphere.

Ranger. NASA's earliest Moon-exploration program. Spacecraft were designed for a crash landing on the Moon, taking pictures and returning scientific data up to the moment of impact. Provided the first close-up views of the lunar surface. The *Ranger*s provided more than 17,000 close-up pictures, giving us more information about the Moon in a few years than in all the time that had gone before.

Surveyor. Series of unstaffed spacecraft designed to land gently on the Moon and provide information on the surface in preparation for the staffed lunar landings. *Surveyor's* legs were instrumented to return data on the surface hardness of the Moon. *Surveyor* dispelled the fear that *Apollo* spacecraft might sink several feet or more into the lunar dust.

Viking. Designation for two spacecraft designed to conduct detailed scientific examination of the planet Mars, including a search for life. *Viking 1* landed on July 20, 1976; *Viking 2,* Sept. 3, 1976. More was learned about the red planet in a few short months than in all previous missions, but the question of whether there is life on Mars remains unresolved.

Voyager. Designation for two spacecraft designed to explore Jupiter and the other outer planets. *Voyager 1* and *Voyager 2* passed Jupiter in 1979 and sent back surprising color TV images of that planet and its moons. They took a total of about 33,000 pictures. *Voyager 1* passed Saturn in Nov. 1980. *Voyager 2* passed Saturn in Aug. 1981 and Uranus in Jan. 1986.

Voyager 2 encountered Neptune on Aug. 29, 1989, and made many discoveries. It found four rings around the planet, six new moons, a giant spot, and evidence of volcanic-like activity on its largest moon, Triton. The spacecraft sent back over 9,000 pictures of the planet and its system.

On Feb. 13, 1990, at a distance of 3.7 billion miles, *Voyager 1* took its final pictures—the Sun and six of its planets as seen from deep space. NASA released the extraordinary images to the public on June 6, 1990. Only Mercury, Mars, and Pluto were not seen.

Notable Unstaffed Lunar and Interplanetary Probes

Spacecraft	Launch date	Destination	Remarks
Pioneer 3 (U.S.)	Dec. 6, 1958	Moon	Max. alt.: 66,654 mi. Discovered outer Van Allen layer.
Luna 2 (USSR)	Sept. 12, 1959	Moon	Impacted on Sept. 14. First space vehicle to reach Moon.
Luna 3 (USSR)	Oct. 4, 1959	Moon	Flew around Moon and transmitted first pictures of lunar far side, Oct. 7.
Mariner 2 (U.S.)	Aug. 27, 1962	Venus	Venus probe. Successful mid-course correction. Passed 21,648 mi from Venus Dec. 14, 1962. Reported 800°F surface temp. Contact lost Jan. 3, 1963, at 54 million mi.
Ranger 7 (U.S.)	July 28, 1964	Moon	Impacted near Crater Guericke 68.5 hr after launch. Sent 4,316 pictures during last 15 min. of flight as close as 1,000 ft above lunar surface.
Mariner 4 (U.S.)	Nov. 28, 1964	Mars	Transmitted first close-up pictures on June 14, 1965, from altitude of 6,000 mi.
Luna 9 (USSR)	Jan. 31, 1966	Moon	3,428 lb instrument capsule of 220 lb soft-landed Feb. 3, 1966. Sent back about 30 pictures.
Surveyor 1 (U.S.)	May 30, 1966	Moon	Landed June 2, 1966. Sent almost 10,400 pictures, a number after surviving the 14-day lunar night.
Lunar Orbiter 1 (U.S.)	Aug. 10, 1966	Moon	Orbited Moon Aug. 14. 21 pictures sent.
Surveyor 3 (U.S.)	April 17, 1967	Moon	Soft-landed on Oceanus Procellarum 65 hr after launch. Scooped and tested lunar soil.
Venera 4 (USSR)	June 12, 1967	Venus	Arrived Oct. 17. Instrument capsule sent temperature and chemical data.
Surveyor 5 (U.S.)	Sept. 8, 1967	Moon	Landed near lunar equator Sept. 10. Radiological analysis of lunar soil. Mechanical claw for digging soil.
Surveyor 7 (U.S.)	Jan. 6, 1968	Moon	Landed near Crater Tycho Jan. 10. Soil analysis. Sent 3,343 pictures.
Pioneer 9 (U.S.)	Nov. 8, 1968	Sun	Achieved orbit. Six experiments returned solar radiation data.
Venera 5 (USSR)	Jan. 5, 1969	Venus	Landed May 16, 1969. Returned atmospheric data.
Mariner 6 (U.S.)	Feb. 24, 1969	Mars	Came within 2000 mi of Mars July 31, 1969. Sent back data and TV pictures.
Luna 16 (USSR)	Sept. 12, 1970	Moon	Soft-landed Sept. 20, scooped up rock, returned to Earth Sept. 24.
Luna 17 (USSR)	Nov. 10, 1970	Moon	Soft-landed on Sea of Rains Nov. 17. *Lunokhod 1*, self-propelled vehicle, used for first time. Sent TV photos, made soil analysis, etc.
Mariner 9 (U.S.)	May 30, 1971	Mars	First craft to orbit Mars, Nov. 13. 7,300 pictures, 1st close-ups of one of Mars's moons. Transmission ended Oct. 27, 1972.
Luna 20 (USSR)	Feb. 14, 1972	Moon	Soft-landed Feb. 21 in Sea of Fertility. Returned Feb. 25 with rock samples.
Pioneer 10 (U.S.)	March 3, 1972	Jupiter	620-million-mi flight path through asteroid belt past Jupiter Dec. 3, 1973, to give man first close-up of planet. In 1986, it became first man-made object to escape solar system.
Luna 21 (USSR)	Jan. 8, 1973	Moon	Soft-landed Jan. 16. *Lunokhod 2* (moon-car) scooped up soil samples, returned them to Earth Jan. 27.
Mariner 10 (U.S.)	Nov. 3, 1973	Venus, Mercury	Passed Venus Feb. 5, 1974. Arrived Mercury March 29, 1974, for man's first close-up look at planet. First time gravity of one planet (Venus) used to propel spacecraft toward another (Mercury).
Viking 1 (U.S.)	Aug. 20, 1975	Mars	Carrying life-detection labs. Landed July 20, 1976, for detailed scientific research, including pictures. Designed to work for only 90 days, it operated for almost 6½ years before it went silent in Nov. 1982.

Spacecraft	Launch date	Destination	Remarks
Viking 2 (U.S.)	Sept. 9, 1975	Mars	Like Viking 1. Landed Sept. 3, 1976. Functioned 3½ years.
Luna 24 (USSR)	Aug. 9, 1976	Moon	Soft-landed Aug. 18, 1976. Returned soil samples Aug. 22, 1976.
Voyager 2 (U.S.)	Aug. 20, 1977	Jupiter, Saturn, Uranus	Launched before *Voyager 1*. Encountered Jupiter in July 1979; flew by Saturn Aug. 1981; passed Uranus Jan. 1986; and passed Neptune in Aug. 1989.
Voyager 1 (U.S.)	Sept. 5, 1977	Jupiter, Saturn	Flyby mission. Reached Jupiter in March 1979; passed Saturn Nov. 1980; passed Uranus 1986.
Pioneer Venus 1 (U.S.)	May 20, 1978	Venus	Arrived Dec. 4 and orbited Venus, photographing surface and atmosphere. Crashed into planet's surface mid-Oct. 1992 after circling Venus for 14 years.
Pioneer Venus 2 (U.S.)	Aug. 8, 1978	Venus	Four-part multiprobe, landed Dec. 9.
Venera 13 (USSR)	Oct. 30, 1981	Venus	Landed March 1, 1982. Took first X-ray fluorescence analysis of the planet's surface. Transmitted data 2 hours, 7 minutes.
VEGA 1 (USSR)	Deployed on Venus, June 10, 1985	Halley's Comet	In flyby over Venus while en route to encounter Halley's Comet, *VEGA 1* and *2* dropped scientific capsules onto Venus to study atmosphere and surface material. Encountered Halley's Comet on March 6 and March 9, 1986. Took TV pictures and studied comet's dust particles.
VEGA 2 (USSR)	Deployed on Venus, June 14, 1985	Halley's Comet	See *VEGA 1* above.
Suisei (Japan)	Encountered Halley's Comet March 8, 1986	Halley's Comet	Spacecraft made flyby of comet and studied atmosphere with ultraviolet camera. Observed rotation nucleus.
Sakigake (Japan)	Encountered Halley's Comet March 10, 1986	Halley's Comet	Spacecraft made flyby to study solar wind and magnetic fields. Detected plasma waves.
Giotto (E.S.A.)	Encountered Halley's Comet March 13, 1986	Halley's Comet	European Space Agency spacecraft made closest approach to comet. Studied atmosphere and magnetic fields. Sent back best pictures of nucleus. Flew by comet Grigg-Skjellerup July 10, 1992. Unable to send pictures.
Phobos Mission (USSR)	July 7 and July 12, 1988	Mars and Phobos	Two spacecraft to probe Martian moon Phobos starting April 1989. Were to study orbit and soil chemistry, and send TV pictures and data of planet. Contact was lost with *Phobos 1* in Aug. 1988 and with *Phobos 2* in March 1989 after it reached the Martian moon.
Magellan (U.S.)	May 4, 1989	Venus	Arrived at Venus on Aug. 10, 1990, and made a geologic map of planet with a powerful radar. Crashed into Venus Oct. 12, 1994.
Galileo (U.S.)	Oct. 18, 1989	Jupiter	To study Jupiter's atmosphere and its moons during 22-month mission.
Ulysses (U.S., E.S.A.)	Oct. 6, 1990	Sun	To study the poles of the Sun and interstellar space above and below the poles. First solar encounter was in 1994, second encounter in 1995.
Gamma-Ray Observatory (U.S.)	April 7, 1991	Earth orbit	To make first survey of gamma-ray sources across the whole sky, studying explosive energy sources such as supernovae, quasars, neutron stars, pulsars, and black holes. Mission ended, it was deorbited and crashed into Pacific Ocean, June 4, 2000.
Clementine (U.S.)	Jan. 25, 1994	Moon and asteroid 1620 Geographos	Entered lunar orbit Feb. 21 and took close-up photos of lunar surface for two months. Computer malfunction prevented planned rendezvous with *Geographos*.
Near-Earth Asteroid Rendezvous (NEAR) (U.S.)	Feb. 17, 1996	asteroid 433 Eros	Photographed asteroid 253 Mathilde June 27, 1997. Entered into orbit around Eros Feb. 14, 2000, and landed on surface in controlled crash Feb. 12, 2001. Took detailed measurements and generated about 160,000 images of Eros. Renamed NEAR-Shoemaker in honor of geologist Eugene M. Shoemaker. First craft to orbit an asteroid.

Spacecraft	Launch date	Destination	Remarks
Mars Pathfinder (U.S.)	Dec. 5, 1996	Ares Vallis, Mars	Landed July 4, 1997. The spacecraft lander and its rover, *Sojourner,* provided a wealth of information on the Martian rocks, soil, and atmosphere. Sent back the first live pictures. All *Pathfinder's* objectives were fulfilled and communications failed on Sept. 27, 1997.
Lunar Prospector (U.S.)	Jan. 6, 1998	Moon	Orbited Moon for one year, mapped chemical composition of lunar surface. Found frozen water at north and south poles. At end of its mission on July 31, 1999, it was intentionally crashed into south polar crater in hope of detecting plume of water ice, but no cloud of molecular water vapor was observed by powerful Earth telescopes.

U.S. Staffed Space Flight Programs

Mercury. *Project Mercury,* initiated in 1958 and completed in 1963, was the United States' first human-in-space program. It was designed to further knowledge about humanity's capabilities in space.

In April 1959, seven military-jet test pilots were introduced to the public as America's first astronauts. They were: Lt. M. Scott Carpenter, USN; Capt. L. Gordon Cooper, Jr., USAF; Lt. Col. John H. Glenn, Jr., USMC; Cap. Virgil I. Grissom, USAF; Lt. Cdr. Walter M. Schirra, Jr., USN; Lt. Cdr. Alan B. Shepard, Jr., USN; and Capt. Donald K. Slayton, USAF. Six of the original seven would make a Mercury flight. Slayton was grounded for medical reasons but remained a director of NASA's astronaut office. He returned to flight status in 1975 as Docking Module Pilot on the *Apollo-Soyuz* flight.

Flight Summary

Each astronaut named his capsule and added the numeral 7 to denote the teamwork of the original astronauts.

May 5, 1961. Alan B. Shepard, Jr., made a suborbital flight in *Freedom 7* and became the first American in space. Time: 15 minutes, 22 seconds.

July 21, 1961. Virgil I. Grissom made the second successful suborbital flight in *Liberty Bell 7,* but spacecraft sank shortly after splashdown. Time: 15 minutes, 37 seconds. Grissom was later killed in *Apollo 1* fire, Jan. 27, 1967.

Feb. 20, 1962. John H. Glenn, Jr., made a three-orbit flight and became the first American in orbit. Time: 4 hours, 55 minutes.

May 24, 1962. M. Scott Carpenter duplicated Glenn's flight in *Aurora 7.* Time: 4 hours, 56 minutes.

Oct. 3, 1962. Walter M. Schirra, Jr., made a six-orbit engineering test flight in *Sigma 7.* Time: 9 hours, 13 minutes.

May 15–16, 1963. L. Gordon Cooper, Jr., performed the last *Mercury* mission and completed 22 orbits in *Faith 7* to evaluate effects of one day in space. Time: 34 hours, 19 minutes.

The Women in Space Program

In 1960, NASA also tested the first female trainees for astronaut duty in the *Mercury* program. Thirteen out of America's 25 top female civilian pilots (women weren't allowed to be military pilots then) passed the same rigorous testing that male candidates underwent in the *Mercury* space program. Although all the pilots proved fit to become *Mercury* astronauts, NASA suddenly canceled its testing of qualified women in July 1961, claiming that they required jet test-pilot training at Edwards Air Force Base. Unfortunately, instruction at Edwards was closed to women. This new requirement ended America's chance to put the first women in space.

It is ironic that unlike her skilled American counterparts, Valentina Tereshkova, the first woman to fly in space, was a textile factory worker when she entered the Soviet space program. She had no experience as a pilot and her only qualification was that of an amateur parachute jumper before being trained as a cosmonaut in 1962.

These outstanding "Mercury 13" candidates deserve much credit for preparing the way for American women in space. They were: Jerrie Cobb, Rhea Allison, Jane Hart, Mary Wallace Funk, Jean Hixson, Myrtle Cagle, Irene Leverton, Sarah Gorelick, twins Jan and Marion Dietrich, Gene Stumbough, Bernice Steadman, and Gerry Sloan Truhill.

Gemini. *Gemini* was an extension of *Project Mercury,* to determine the effects of prolonged space flight on humans for two weeks or longer—the time it would take to reach the Moon and return. "Walks in space" provided invaluable information for astronauts' later walks on the Moon. The *Gemini* spacecraft, twice as large as the *Mercury* capsule, accommodated two astronauts. Its crew named the project *Gemini* for the third constellation of the Zodiac and its twin stars, Castor and Pollux. The capsule differed from the *Mercury* spacecrafts in that it had hatches above the capsules so that the astronauts could leave the spacecraft and perform spacewalks or extra-vehicular activities (EVAs).

There were 10 staffed flights in the *Gemini* program, starting with *Gemini 3* on March 23, 1965, and ending with the *Gemini 12* mission on Nov. 15, 1966. *Gemini 1* and *2* were unstaffed test flights of the equipment.

Apollo. *Apollo* was the designation for the United States' effort to land a person on the Moon and return him safely to Earth. The goal was successfully accomplished with *Apollo 11* on July 20, 1969, culminating eight years of rehearsal and centuries of dreaming. Astronauts Neil A. Armstrong and Col. Edwin E. Aldrin, Jr., scooped up and brought back the first lunar rocks ever seen on Earth—about 47 pounds.

Tragedy struck Jan. 27, 1967, on the launch pad during a preflight test of what would have become *Apollo 1,* the first staffed mission. Astronauts Lt. Col. Virgil "Gus" Grissom, Lt. Col. Edward H. White, and Lt. Cdr. Roger Chafee lost their lives when a fire swept through the command module.

Six *Apollo* flights followed, ending with *Apollo 17* in December 1972. The last three *Apollos* carried mechanized vehicles called lunar rovers for wide-ranging surface exploration of the Moon by astronauts. The rendezvous and docking of an *Apollo* spacecraft with a Russian *Soyuz* craft in Earth orbit on July 18, 1975, closed out the *Apollo* program.

During the Apollo project, the following 12 astronauts explored the lunar terrain: Col. Edwin E. "Buzz" Aldrin, Jr., and Neil A. Armstrong, *Apollo 11;* Cdr. Alan L. Bean and Cdr. Charles "Pete" Conrad, Jr., *Apollo 12;* Edgar D. Mitchell and Alan B. Shepard, *Apollo 14;* Lt. Col. James B. Irwin and Col. David R. Scott, *Apollo 15;* Col. Charles M. Duke, Jr., and Capt. John W. Young, *Apollo 16;* and Capt. Eugene A. Cernan and Dr. Harrison H. Schmitt, *Apollo 17.*

Apollo was a three-part spacecraft: the command module (CM), the crew's quarters and flight control section; the service modules (SM) for the propulsion and spacecraft support systems (when together, the two modules were called CSM); and the lunar module (LM) that took two of the crew to the lunar surface, supported them on the Moon, and returned them to the CSM in orbit.

The third lunar attempt, *Apollo 13,* April 11–17, 1970, 5 days, 22.9 hours, was aborted after the service module oxygen tank ruptured. The *Apollo 13* crew members were James A. Lovell, Jr., John L. Swigert, Jr., and Fred W. Haise, Jr. The mission was classified as a "successful failure" because the crew was rescued.

Skylab. America's first Earth-orbiting space station. *Project Skylab* was designed to demonstrate that men can work and live in space for prolonged periods without ill effects. Originally the spent third stage of a *Saturn 5* Moon rocket, *Skylab* measured 118 ft from stem to stern, and carried the most varied assortment of experimental equipment ever assembled in a single spacecraft. Three three-man crews visited the space stations, spending more than 740 hours observing the Sun and bringing home more than 175,000 solar pictures. These were the first recordings of solar activity above Earth's obscuring atmosphere. *Skylab* also evaluated systems designed to gather information on Earth's resources and environmental conditions. *Skylab*'s biomedical findings indicated that humans adapt well to space for at least a period of three months, provided they have a proper diet and adequately programmed exercise, sleep, work, and recreation periods. *Skylab* orbited Earth at a distance of about 300 mi. Five years after the last *Skylab* mission, the 77-ton space station's orbit began to deteriorate faster than expected, owing to unexpectedly high sunspot activity. On July 11, 1979, the parts of *Skylab* that did not burn up in the atmosphere came crashing down on parts of Australia and the Indian Ocean. No one was hurt.

Space Shuttle. The space shuttle *Columbia* was successfully launched on April 12, 1981. It made five flights (the first four were test runs), the last completed on Nov. 16, 1982. The second shuttle, *Challenger,* made its maiden flight on April 4, 1983. The third shuttle, *Discovery,* made its first flight on Aug. 30, 1984. The fourth space shuttle, *Atlantis,* made its maiden flight on Oct. 3, 1985.

A tragedy occurred on Jan. 28, 1986, when the shuttle *Challenger* exploded, killing the crew of

seven 73 seconds after takeoff. It was the world's worst space flight disaster.

The crew members who were killed were: Francis R. Scobee, shuttle commander; Cdr. Michael J. Smith, pilot; mission specialists Judith A. Resnik, Lt. Col. Ellison S. Onizuka, and Ronald E. McNair; and payload specialists Gregory B. Jarvis and Christa McAuliffe (who was to be the first civilian schoolteacher in space).

The cause of the explosion was a rupture in a seal on one of the booster rockets that let a jet of flame escape, igniting the fuel. The weakness in the seal was caused by the cold air temperature when the shuttle was launched.

The first U.S. space mission since the *Challenger* disaster was launched 32 months later, on Sept. 29, 1988, with the flight of *Discovery.* It had a crew of five and deployed a communications satellite.

The fifth and last orbiter, *Endeavour,* was built as a replacement for *Challenger.* It was named after the 16th-century British explorer James Cook's first ship. *Endeavour* was launched on its maiden voyage on May 7, 1992, with a crew of seven astronauts. They made four spacewalks and retrieved a disabled *Intelsat-6* communications satellite. During the mission, Dr. Kathryn Thornton became the second American woman to walk in space.

The shuttle *Columbia* spent a record 17 days, 15 hours in space, Nov. 19–Dec. 7, 1996.

The crew of the 50th mission aboard the *Endeavour,* launched Sept. 12, 1992, included the first black woman astronaut, Dr. Mae C. Jemison, and the first married couple to fly together in space, Air Force Lt. Col. Mark C. Lee and Dr. N. Jan Davis.

Lt. Col. Eileen M. Collins became the first woman to pilot a shuttle, *Discovery,* during the spacecraft's historic rendezvous with the Russian space station *Mir* on Feb. 6, 1995. The shuttle *Atlantis* made the first link-up with the *Mir* on June 29, 1995.

Lt. Col. Collins became the first woman to command a space shuttle when *Columbia* was launched in July 1999 on a mission to deploy the Chandra X-ray Observatory (formerly called AXAF).

Senator John Glenn, 76, the first American to orbit the Earth, flew as a payload specialist on the Oct. 1998 *Discovery* mission. He studied the effects of aging and microgravity on the human body.

Space Web Sites

Soviet Staffed Space Flight Programs

Vostok. The Soviets' first staffed capsule, roughly spherical, used to place the first six cosmonauts in Earth orbit (1961–1965).

Voskhod. Adaptation of the *Vostok* capsule to accommodate two and three cosmonauts. *Voskhod 1* orbited three persons, and *Voskhod 2* orbited two persons, performing the world's first staffed extra-vehicular activity.

Soyuz. Late-model staffed spacecraft with provisions for three cosmonauts and a "working compartment" accessible through a hatch. Soyuz is the Russian word for "union." The *Soyuz* spacecraft can carry three cosmonauts, and routinely brought cosmonauts and their foreign "guests" to the *Mir* space station. *Soyuz 19*, launched July 15, 1975, docked with the American *Apollo* spacecraft.

Salyut. Earth-orbiting space station intended for prolonged occupancy and revisitation by cosmonauts. They were usually launched by Soviet Proton rockets. *Salyut 1* was launched April 19, 1971. *Salyut 2*, launched April 3, 1973, malfunctioned in orbit and was never occupied. *Salyut 3* was launched June 25, 1974. *Salyut 4* was launched Dec. 26, 1974. *Salyut 5* was launched June 22, 1976. *Salyut 6* was launched on Sept. 29, 1977. *Salyut 7* was launched on April 19, 1982. A record-breaking Russian endurance flight was set (Feb. 8, 1984–Oct. 2, 1985) when Soviet astronauts spent 237 days in orbit aboard *Salyut 7*. *Salyut 7* reentered the atmosphere and crashed into the Atlantic Ocean on Feb. 6, 1991.

Mir. Soviet space station, launched into orbit on Feb. 20, 1986. The Russian government had planned to deorbit the abandoned *Mir* in early 2000 due to lack of funds, but the space station got a new lease on life when private investors provided the cash to keep the craft in orbit. The new Russian partners, MirCorp, a Netherlands-based company, funded cosmonauts Sergei Zaloytin and Alexander Kaleri's return mission to reopen and repair the *Mir*, April 4 to June 15, 2000. However, *Mir* was deorbited on March 23, 2001. ◻

China's Unstaffed Spacecraft

China launched its first unstaffed spacecraft from the Jiuquan Space Center in Gansu province on Nov. 19, 1999. The space capsule, named "Shenzhou" (God Vessel, or Divine Ship), made 14 orbits of Earth in 21 hours before landing in Inner Mongolia. *Shenzhou 2*, China's second test flight of its unmanned spacecraft, was launched on Jan. 9, 2001, and completed 108 orbits of Earth before landing in Inner Mongolia nearly seven days later.

The *Shenzhou* spacecraft are prototypes for future manned Chinese spacecraft. Chinese officials have stated publicly that they plan to put a taikonaut (Chinese astronaut) into orbit by 2005. ◻

Notable Staffed Space Flights

Designation and country	Date	Astronauts	Flight time (hr./min)	Remarks
Vostok 1 (USSR)	April 12, 1961	Yuri A. Gagarin	1/48	First person in space.
MR III (U.S.)	May 5, 1961	Alan B. Shepard, Jr.	0/15	Range 486 km (302 mi), peak 187 km (116.5 mi); capsule recovered. First American in space.
Vostok 2 (USSR)	Aug. 6–7, 1961	Gherman S. Titov	25/18	First long-duration flight.
MA VI (U.S.)	Feb. 20, 1962	John H. Glenn, Jr.	4/55	First American in orbit.
MA IX (U.S.)	May 15–16, 1963	L. Gordon Cooper, Jr.	34/20	Longest *Mercury* flight.
Vostok 6 (USSR)	June 16–19, 1963	Valentina V. Tereshkova	70/50	First woman in space.
Voskhod 1 (USSR)	Oct. 12, 1964	Vladimir M. Komarov, Konstantin P. Feoktistov, Boris G. Yegorov	24/17	First 3-person orbital flight; also first flight without space suits.
Voskhod 2 (USSR)	March 18, 1965	Alexei A. Leonov, Pavel I. Belyayev	26/2	First "space walk" (by Leonov), 10 min.
GT III (U.S.)	March 23, 1965	Virgil I. Grissom, John W. Young	4/53	First American 2-person crew.
GT IV (U.S.)	June 3–7, 1965	James A. McDivitt, Edward H. White, II	97/48	First American "space walk" (by White), lasting slightly over 20 min.
GT VIII (U.S.)	March 16–17, 1966	Neil A. Armstrong, David R. Scott	10/42	First docking between staffed spacecraft and an unstaffed space vehicle (an orbiting *Agena* rocket).
Apollo 7 (U.S.)	Oct. 11–22, 1968	Walter M. Schirra, Jr., Donn F. Eisele, R. Walter Cunningham	260/9	First staffed test of *Apollo* command module; first live TV transmissions from orbit.
Soyuz 3 (USSR)	Oct. 26–30, 1968	Georgi T. Bergeovoi	94/51	First staffed rendezvous and possible docking by Soviet cosmonaut.
Apollo 8 (U.S.)	Dec. 21–27, 1968	Frank Borman, James A. Lovell, Jr., William A. Anders	147/01	First spacecraft in circumlunar orbit; TV transmissions from this orbit. The three astronauts were also the first astronauts to view the whole Earth.
Apollo 9 (U.S.)	Mar. 3–13, 1969	James A. McDivitt, David R. Scott, Russell L. Schweikart	241/1	First staffed flight of Lunar Module.
Apollo 10 (U.S.)	May 18–26, 1969	Thomas P. Stafford, Eugene A. Cernan, John W. Young	192/3	First descent to within nine miles of Moon's surface by staffed craft.

Designation and country	Date	Astronauts	Flight time (hr./min)	Remarks
Apollo 11 (U.S.)	July 16–24, 1969	Neil A. Armstrong, Edwin E. Aldrin, Jr., Michael Collins	195/18	First staffed landing and EVA on Moon; soil and rock samples collected; experiments left on lunar surface.
Soyuz 6 (USSR)	Oct. 11–16, 1969	Gorgiy Shonin, Valriy Kabasov	118/42	Three spacecraft and seven men put into Earth orbit simultaneously for first time.
Apollo 12 (U.S.)	Nov. 14–24, 1969	Charles Conrad, Jr., Richard F. Gordon, Jr., Alan Bean	244/36	Staffed lunar landing mission; investigated *Surveyor 3* spacecraft; collected lunar samples. EVA time: 15 hr., 30 min.
Apollo 13 (U.S.)	April 11–17, 1970	James A. Lovell, Jr., Fred W. Haise, Jr., John L. Swigert, Jr.	142/54	Third staffed lunar landing attempt; aborted due to pressure loss in liquid oxygen in service module and failure of fuel cells.
Apollo 14 (U.S.)	Jan. 31–Feb. 9, 1971	Alan B. Shepard, Stuart A. Roosa, Edgar D. Mitchell	216/42	Third staffed lunar landing: returned largest amount of lunar material.
Soyuz 11 (USSR)	June 6–30, 1971	Georgiy Tomofeyevich Dobrovolskiy, Vladislav Nikolayevich Volkov, Viktor Ivanovich Patsyev	569/40	Longest stay in space. Linked up with first space station, *Salyut 1.* Astronauts died just before reentry due to loss of pressurization in spacecraft.
Apollo 15 (U.S.)	July 26–Aug. 7, 1971	David R. Scott, James B. Irwin, Alfred M. Worden	295/12	Fourth staffed lunar landing; first use of lunar rover propelled by Scott and Irwin; first live pictures of LM lift-off from Moon; exploration time: 18 hr.
Apollo 16 (U.S.)	April 16–27, 1972	John W. Young, Thomas K. Mattingly, Charles M. Duke, Jr.	265/51	Fifth staffed lunar landing; second use of lunar rover vehicle, propelled by Young and Duke. Total exploration time on the Moon was 20 hr., 14 min., setting new record. Mattingly's in-flight "walk in space" was 1 hr., 23 min. Approximately 213 lb of lunar rock returned.
Apollo 17 (U.S.)	Dec. 7–19, 1972	Eugene A. Cernan, Ronald E. Evans, Harrison H. Schmitt	301/51	Sixth and last staffed lunar landing; third to carry lunar rover. Cernan and Schmitt, during three EVAs, completed total of 22 hr., 05 min., 3 sec. USS *Ticonderoga* recovered crew and about 250 lbs of lunar samples.
Skylab SL-2 (U.S.)	May 25–June 22, 1973	Charles Conrad, Jr., Joseph P. Kerwin, Paul J. Weitz	672/50	First staffed *Skylab* launch. Established Skylab Orbital Assembly and conducted scientific and medical experiments.
Skylab SL-3 (U.S.)	July 28–Sept. 25, 1973	Alan L. Bean, Jr., Jack R. Lousma, Owen K. Garriott	1427/9	Second staffed *Skylab* launch. New crew remained in space for 59 days, continuing scientific and medical experiments and Earth observations from orbit.
Skylab SL-4 (U.S.)	Nov. 16, 1973– Feb. 8, 1974	Gerald Carr, Edward Gibson, William Pogue	2017/16	Third staffed *Skylab* launch; obtained medical data on crew for use in extending the duration of staffed space flight; crews "walked in space" 4 times, totaling 44 hr., 40 min. Longest space mission yet: 84 d, 1 hr., 16 min. Splashdown in Pacific, Feb. 9, 1974.
Apollo/Soyuz Test Project (U.S. and U.S.S.R.)	July 15–24, 1975 (U.S.)	U.S.: Brig. Gen. Thomas P. Stafford, Vance D. Brand, Donald K. Slayton	216/05	World's first international staffed rendezvous and docking in space; aimed at developing a space rescue capability.
Apollo/Soyuz Test Project (U.S. and U.S.S.R.)	July 15–21, 1975 (USSR)	U.S.S.R.: Col. A. A. Leonov, V. N. Kubasov	223/35	*Apollo* and *Soyuz* docked and crewmen exchanged visits on July 17, 1975. Mission duration for *Soyuz:* 142 hr., 31 min. For *Apollo:* 217 hr., 28 min.
Columbia (U.S.)	April 12–14, 1981	Capt. Robert L. Crippen, John W. Young	54/20	Maiden voyage of space shuttle.
Mir (USSR)	Dec. 21, 1987– Dec. 21, 1988	Col. Vladimir Titov, Musa Manarov	366 days	Set current record for Soviet team endurance flight in orbiting space station.
Endeavour (U.S.)	May 7–16, 1992	Richard J. Hieb, Maj. Thomas D. Akers, Cdr. Pierre J. Thugt	8 days, 23 hr., 17 min.	The three mission specialists remained free of the *Endeavour* for 8 hr., 20 min. on May 13 during the repair of communications satellite, setting an absolute record for extravehicular duration in space. First capture of a satellite using hands only.

Designation and country	Date	Astronauts	Flight time (hr./min)	Remarks
Endeavour (U.S.)	Dec. 2–13, 1993	Col. Richard O. Covey, Cdr. Kenneth D. Bowersox, Lt. Col. Tom Akers,* Dr. Jeffrey A. Hoffman,** Dr. Story Musgrave,** Claude Nicollier, Dr. Kathryn C. Thornton* (*two space walks; **three space walks)	10 days, 19 hr., 59 min.	Repaired Hubble Space Telescope. Replaced gyroscopes, solar arrays, camera, electronics, and hardware. Installed COSTAR corrective optics to compensate for flaw in Hubble's primary mirror. Record five space walks in a single mission.
Mir-17 (Russia)	Jan. 8, 1994– Mar. 22, 1995	Dr. Valery Polyakov	439[1] days	Record single endurance flight in orbiting space station. Returned to Earth with crewmates cosmonaut Helena Kondakova and commander Alexander Viktorenko, who spent 169 days each in *Mir*.
Discovery (U.S.)	Feb. 3–11, 1995	Cdr. James D. Wetherbee, Lt. Col. Eileen M. Collins, Dr. Janice Voss, Dr. Bernard A. Harris, Jr.,* Dr. C. Michael Foale,* Russian cosmonaut Co. Vladimir G. Titov *performed spacewalks.	8 days, 6 hr., 29 min.	First rendezvous of U.S. spacecraft with a Russian space station *(Mir)*, Feb. 6. Lt. Col. Collins was first female shuttle pilot. Deployed and retrieved solar observatory satellite. Extravehicular activity to test new space suit modifications and practice space station assembly techniques. EVA time: 4 hr., 35 min.
Soyuz TM-21 (Russia)	March 14–22, 1995	Russian cosmonauts Lieut. Col. Vladimir N. Dezhurov and Gennady M. Strekalov, and U.S. astronaut Dr. Norman E. Thagard		Dr. Thagard became the first American astronaut to fly aboard a *Soyuz* spacecraft with a Russian crew launched from Baikonur Space Center in Kazakhstan. He also became the first American to enter the *Mir* space station on March 16.
Atlantis (U.S.)	June 27–July 7, 1995	Lt. Col. Charles J. Prescourt, Capt. Robert L. (Hoot) Gibson, Dr. Eileen M. Baker, Gregory J. Harbaugh, Dr. Bonnie Dunbar, Russian cosmonauts: *Mir-19* commander Anatoly Y. Solovyev, Nikolai M. Budarin	10 days	Marked 100th human mission in U.S. space program and first shuttle link-up with *Mir*: docked June 29, undocked July 4. Joined spacecraft held a record 10 people: 6 Americans and 4 Russians. Three *Mir* crew (*Mir-18* commander Lieut. Col. Vladimir N. Dezhurov, cosmonaut Grennady M. Strekalov, and U.S. astronaut Dr. Norman E. Thagard) returned to Earth aboard the *Atlantis*. Dr. Thagard set a U.S. space record of 112 days in space aboard *Mir.*. Cosmonauts Solovyev and Budarin remained aboard *Mir*.
Atlantis (U.S.)	Nov. 12–20, 1995	Col. Kenneth D. Cameron, Lieut. Col. James D. Halsell, Jr., Col. Jerry L. Ross, Lieut. Col. William S. McArthur, Jr., Canadian Major Chris A. Hadfield, who operated the robot arm	8 days, 4 hr., 31 min.	Second docking with *Mir*. Carried 15-foot-long Russian-made docking module and attached it to *Mir*. Brought 2 new solar-powered panels for *Mir* and also supplies and scientific equipment. U.S. and Russian astronauts spent 3 days together on *Mir* conducting experiments.
Endeavour (U.S.)	Jan. 11–20, 1996	Col. Brian Duffy, Brent Jett, Dr. Leroy Chiao,** Capt. Winston E. Scott,* Dr. Daniel T. Berry,* and Japanese astronaut Koichi Wakata, who operated robot arm (*one spacewalk; **two spacewalks)	8 days, 22 hr., 1 min.	Deployed and retrieved NASA satellite, retrieved Japanese satellite. Two spacewalks performed to test spacesuit components and practice space station construction, tools, and techniques. Total EVA time: 13 hr.
Atlantis (U.S.)	March 22–31, 1996	Col. Kevin P. Chilton, Lieut. Col. Richard A. Searfoss, Dr. Ronald M. Sega, Dr. Linda M. Goodwin, Lieut. Col. Michael R. Clifford, Shannon W. Lucid	9 days, 5 hr., 15 min.	Third link-up with *Mir* (March 22–27). Clifford and Goodwin conducted 6-hour spacewalk in shuttle cargo bay while docked with *Mir*. Lucid remained on board *Mir* for scheduled 140-day tour to conduct biomedical and material science experiments. Booster problems delayed her return until mid-September. Lucid is first American woman to live on *Mir*. On July 15, 1996, she broke the previous record for the longest U.S. manned space flight.
Endeavour (U.S.)	May 19–29, 1996	Col. John H. Casper, Lieut. Col. Curtis L. Brown, Jr., Cdr. Daniel W. Bursch, Mario Runco, Jr., Dr. Andrew S.W. Thomas, Canadian astronaut Dr. Marc Garneau	10 days, 0 hr., 40 min.	Made record of four satellite rendezvous, including three with small PAMS satellite to test the concept of a self-stabilizing satellite in orbit. Deployed and retrieved a Spartan satellite that carried an experimental inflatable antenna.

Designation and country	Date	Astronauts	Flight time (hr./min)	Remarks
Columbia (U.S.)	June 20–July 7, 1996	Col. Terence T. Henricks, Kevin R. Kregel, Lieut. Col. Susan J. Helms, Richard M. Linnehan, Cdr. Charles E. Brady, Jr., Dr. Jean-Jacques Favier (France), Dr. Robert Brent Thirsk (Canada)	16 days, 21 hr., 48 min.	Second-longest mission to date. Studied the effects of weightlessness on people, plants, and animals, and material manufacturing in near-zero gravity.
Atlantis (U.S.)	Sept. 16–26, 1996	William F. Readdy, Terrence W. Wilcutt, Thomas D. Akers, John E. Blaha, Jerome Apt, Carl E. Waltz. Download: Shannon W. Lucid	10 days, 3 hr., 19 min.	Fourth *Mir* docking. Carried a Spacelab module. Transferred supplies and equipment to *Mir*. After breaking all American and women's space endurance records (188 days, 5 hr., 0 min.), Lucid returned with *Atlantis* crew. John E. Blaha remained on *Mir* for a four-month stay.
Columbia (U.S.)	Nov. 19–Dec. 7, 1996	Kenneth D. Cockrell, Cdr. Kent V. Romingel, Tamara E. Jernigan, Thomas D. Jones, Dr. F. Story Musgrave	17 days, 15 hr., 53 min.	Deployed and recovered two free-flying satellites during mission: an ultraviolet telescope and Wake Shield (semiconductor processing) Facility. A jammed airlock hatch canceled two scheduled spacewalks. Is longest mission to date. Dr. Musgrave, 61, became first person to fly on all five space shuttles.
Atlantis (U.S.)	Jan. 12–22, 1997	Capt. Michael A. Baker, Cdr. Brent W. Jett, Jr., John M. Grunsfeld, Marsha S. Ivins, Peter J.K. Wiscoff, Dr. Jerry L. Linenger. Download: John E. Blaha	10 days, 4 hr., 6 min.	Fifth *Mir* docking (Jan.14–19). Carried Spacehab double module. Transferred supplies to *Mir*. Conducted experiments in Spacehab and *Mir*. John E. Blaha returned with *Atlantis* crew after 128 days in space, 118 aboard *Mir*. Jerry Linenger remained aboard *Mir* for 4.5-month stay.
Discovery (U.S.)	Feb. 11–21, 1997	Cdr. Kenneth Bowersox, Lt. Col. Scott J. Harowitz, Col. Mark C. Lee,* Steven A. Hawley, Gregory J. Harbaugh,* Steven L. Smith,* Joseph R. Tanner* (*spacewalks)	9 days, 23 hr., 38 min.	Second space telescope servicing mission. Installed new imaging spectrograph and infrared camera. Also patched torn telescope insulating cover. Deployed telescope at higher altitude: 335 x 321 nautical mile orbit. Mission required five spacewalks totaling 33 hr., 11 min.
Atlantis (U.S.)	May 15–24,1997	Col. Charles J. Precourt, Lt. Col. Eileen M. Collins, Edward T. Lu, Maj. Carlos I. Noriega, Jean-François Clervoy (France), Elena V. Kondakova (Russia), C. Michael Foale. Download: Dr. Jerry M. Linenger	9 days, 5 hr., 20 min.	Sixth *Mir* docking (May 16–21). Carried a Spacehab double module. Transferred supplies and equipment. Jerry M. Linenger returned with *Atlantis* after 132 days in space. Michael Foale remained on *Mir* for a 4.5-month stay.
Atlantis (U.S.)	Sept. 25–Oct. 6, 1997	James T. Wetherbee, Michael J. Boomfield, Col. Vladimir G Titov,* Scott E. Parazynski,* Jean-Loup J.M. Chretien (France), Wendy B. Lawrence. Up: Dr. David Wolf. Down: C. Michael Foale after 145 days in space, 134 days on *Mir* (*spacewalks)	10 days, 19 hr., 22 min.	7th Mir docking (Sept. 27–Oct. 3). 5-hr. spacewalks (Oct.1) retrieved U.S. experimental packages from *Mir* for return to Earth. Transferred supplies. Tested emergency jet packs for space station workers. Dr. David Wolf replaced Michael Foale on *Mir* for 4-month stay.
Endeavour (U.S.)	Jan. 22–31, 1998	Lt. Col. Terrence W. Wilcutt, Joe F. Edwards, Bonnie J. Dunbar, Maj. Michael P. Anderson, James F. Reilly, II, Salizhan S. Sharipov (Kirghizia), Andrew S.W. Thomas. Down: Dr. David Wol	8 days, 19 hr., 48 min.	8th *Mir* docking (Jan. 24–29). Thomas replaced David Wolf after 128 days in orbit. Thomas is the seventh and last American to live aboard *Mir*.
Discovery (U.S.)	June 2–12, 1998	Col. Charles J. Precourt, Cmdr. Dominic L. Gorie, Cmdr. Wendy B. Lawrence, Franklin R. Chang-Diaz, Janet Kavandi, Valeriy Ruymin (Russia) Down: Andrew S.W. Thomas	9 days, 19 hr., 54 min.	Ninth and final *Mir* docking mission concluded the joint U.S.–Russian program as a precursor to the International Space Station partnership. Thomas returned to Earth after a 4.5-month stay.

Designation and country	Date	Astronauts	Flight time (hr./min)	Remarks
Discovery (U.S.)	Oct. 29–Nov.7, 1998	Lt. Col. Curtis L. Brown, Maj. Steven W. Lindsey, Stephen K. Robinson, Dr. Scott E. Parazynski, Pedro Duque (Spain), Dr. Chiaki Mukai (Japan), Senator John H. Glenn, Jr.	8 days, 21 hr., 56 min.	Deployed and retrieved Spartan solar observing satellite. Did research with Hubble Telescope Optical Systems Test Platform (HOST). Studied the effects of aging and microgravity in space.
Endeavour (U.S.)	Dec. 4–15, 1998	Capt. Robert D. Cabana, Capt. Frederick W. Sturckow, Lt. Col. Nancy Currie, Col. Jerry L. Ross, Jim H. Newman, Sergei K. Krikalev (Russia)	11 days, 19 hr., 18 min.	International Space Station assembly mission. Connected Node 1, "Unity," to Functional Cargo Block, "Zarya." Ross and Newman made three spacewalks, total EVA: 21 hr., 22 min.
Discovery (U.S.)	May 27–June 6, 1999	Cmdr. Ken V. Rominger, Rick D. Husband, Ellen Ochoa, Tamara E. Jernigan, Daniel T. Barry, Julie Payette (Canada), Valery Tokarev (Russia)	9 days, 19 hr., 13 min.	Docked 5 days, 18 hr. with uninhabited International Space Station. Readied it for arrival of first resident crew. Jernigan and Barry conducted space walks (7 hr., 55 min.) for assembly work.
Columbia (U.S.)	July 23–27, 1999	Lt. Col. Eileen M. Collins, Capt. Jeffrey S. Ashby, Steven A. Hawley, Lt. Col. Catherine G. Coleman, Col. Michel Tognini (France)	4 days, 22 hr., 50 min.	Deployed Chandra X-ray Observatory (formerly AXAF). Eileen Collins became the first female shuttle commander.
Discovery (U.S.)	Dec. 19–27, 1999	Col. Curtis L. Brown Jr., Lt. Cmdr. Scott J. Kelly, Steven L. Smith, C. Michael Foale, John M. Grunsfeld, Claude Nicollier (Switzerland), Jean-François Clervoy (France)	7 days, 23 hr., 10 min.	Third Hubble Space Telescope servicing mission. Three EVAs totaled 24 hr., 33 min.: Dec. 22, Smith and Grunsfeld, 8 hr., 15 min.; Dec. 23, Foale and Nicollier, 8 hr., 10 min.; Dec. 24, Smith and Grunsfeld, 8 hr., 8 min.
Endeavour (U.S.)	Feb.11–22, 2000	Cmdr. Dominic L. Pudwill Gorie, Janet Lynn Kavandi, Janet Voss, Kevin R. Kregel, Mamoru Mohri (Japan), Gerhard P. J. Thiele (Germany)	11 days, 5 hr., 38 min.	Radar mapping obtained most detailed topographical map of Earth to date.
Atlantis (U.S.)	May 19–29, 2000	Col. James D. Halsell, Jr., Lt. Col. Scott J. Horowitz, Mary Ellen Weber, Lt. Col. (Ret.) Jeffrey N. Williams, Col. James S. Voss, Lt. Col. Susan J. Helms, Yuri V. Usachev (Russia)	9 days, 20 hr., 9 min.	Docked with International Space Station May 20–26. Prepared station for arrival of *Zvezda (Star)* service module. EVAs by Voss and Williams May 21–22 totaled 6 hr., 44 min.
Atlantis (U.S.)	Sept. 8–18, 2000	Lt. Col. Terance Wilcutt, Lt. Cmdr. Scott Altman, Edward Tsang Lu, Richard Mastracchio, Lt. Cmdr. Dan Burbank, Col. Yuri I. Malenchenko (Russia), Boris Morukov (Russia)	10 days, 18 hr., 41 min.	Prepare International Space Station for arrival of first resident crew. Outfit *Zvezda* module.
Discovery (U.S.)	Oct. 11–22, 2000	Col. Brian Duffy, Lt. Col. Pamela A. Melroy, Koichi Wakata (Japan), Peter J. K. Wisoff, Cmdr. Michael E. Lopez-Alegria, Col. William S. McArthur, Jr.	10 days, 19 hr., 28 min.	Assemble Integrated Truss Structure on space station to allow U.S. solar arrays to be installed on *Unity* for early power.
Endeavour (U.S.)	April 19–May 1, 2001	Capt. Kent Rominger, Capt. Jeffrey Ashby, Col. Chris Hadfield (Canada), Dr. John Phillips, Dr. Scott Parazynski, Dr. Umberto Guidoni (Italy), Lt. Col. Yuri Lonchakov (Russia)	11 days, 21 hr., 30 min.	Most international crew members to date. Delivered and installed Canadarm2. First use of the Raffaello Multi-Purpose Logistics Module. Two space walks.

1. From launch to landing. NOTES: EVA = Extravehicular Activity. The letters MR stand for Mercury (capsule) and Redstone (rocket); MA, for Mercury and Atlas (rocket); GT, for Gemini (capsule) and Titan-II (rocket). The first astronaut listed in the Gemini and Apollo flights is the command pilot. The Mercury capsules had names: MR-III was *Freedom 7*, MR-IV was *Liberty Bell 7*, MA-VI was *Friendship 7*, MA-VII was *Aurora 7*, MA-VIII was *Sigma 7*, and MA-IX was *Faith 7*. The figure 7 referred to the fact that the first group of U.S. astronauts numbered seven men. Only one Gemini capsule had a name: GT-III was called *Molly Brown* (after the Broadway musical *The Unsinkable Molly Brown*); thereafter the practice of naming the capsules was discontinued.

Kitty Hawk to World War II

Early 20th-century developments in human flight

Although there is some debate about who was the first to fly an airplane, credit for this feat is usually given to **Wilbur** (1867–1912) and **Orville Wright** (1871–1948), who made four controlled, sustained flights in a powered heavier-than-air vehicle on Dec. 17, 1903, near Kitty Hawk, N.C. Interestingly, the Wrights never claimed to be the first to fly. The main claim of the Wright brothers, and their supporters, was that they were first to design and build a flying craft that gave the pilot adequate control while in the air. The unique feature of the Wright brothers' aircraft, beginning with their 1902 glider, was the ability to roll the wings right or left, to pitch the nose up or down, and to yaw the nose from side to side. A pilot must have control of all three dimensions—roll, pitch, and yaw—to navigate a plane. This development was perhaps the Wrights' greatest contribution to aviation.

Over and on the Sea

One of the next major advancements in human flight came in response to a contest sponsored by *The Daily Mail* of London, which offered a prize to the first aviator to fly across the English Channel. **Louis Blériot** (1872–1936) won the contest, flying from Calais, France, to Dover, England, on July 25, 1909, in a monoplane of his own design with a 25-horsepower engine. His flight caused concern among the British that the airplane could eventually be used for military aggression, and the world came to see the airplane as a future weapon.

The pioneers of the seaplane were **Henri Fabre** (1882–1984) and **Glenn H. Curtiss** (1878–1930). Fabre is generally credited with making the first seaplane flight, on March 28, 1910, at Martigues, France. His seaplane, or *hydravion*, had a 50-horsepower Gnome rotary engine and was mounted on lightweight hollow wooden floats. The apparatus flew only short distances, however, and just two months later it was wrecked when it took a sudden nosedive into the Mediterranean. The first practical seaplane was constructed and flown by Curtiss in 1911, and in 1919 one of Curtiss's "flying boats" made the first transatlantic crossing (with stops). He became one of the most successful American aircraft builders in the decades following the invention of the airplane.

Aerobatics

The American public may have known airplanes best for their acrobatic flying, or aerobatics, in the years immediately following the Wright brothers' flights because of large cash prizes offered by newspapers. Dubbed the "glorious year of flying," 1913 was marked by races, competitions, and demonstrations. By flying upside-down and doing loops and other stunts, daredevil pilots proved the maneuverability of airplanes. Pilots also tested the mettle of airplanes in long-distance flights in 1913, including a 4,000-kilometer (2,500-mile) flight from France to Egypt (with stops) and the first nonstop flight from France to Tunisia across the Mediterranean Sea. The end of World War I left a large number of cheap airplanes available for barnstorming and stunt-flying and also for airmail, which was initiated in the mid-1920s. Famous pilots **Charles Lindbergh** (1902–1974) and **Antoine de Saint Exupéry** (1900–1944) were among the early airmail fliers.

Early Military Developments

Before 1914 militaries used airplanes mostly for surveying of enemy territory. (In 1913, the U.S. Army had only six active pilots and the fledgling U.S. aeronautical industry had fewer than 170 employees.) As World War I progressed, manufacturers began designing aircraft to carry guns, bombs, and torpedoes. Glenn H. Curtiss, the pioneer of the seaplane, established his own airplane company in 1916 and was a major supplier of aircraft equipment to the U.S. and Allied navies during World War I.

On the other side of the Atlantic, Dutch-born aeronaut **Anthony Herman Fokker** (1890–1939) produced numerous planes for Germany, including the Fokker Eindecker (monoplane) fighter, which featured a machine gun that could fire through a moving propeller without hitting the blades. In the 1920s, Fokker established an aircraft company in New Jersey and set about designing aircraft for the fledgling U.S. commercial aviation industry. The first nonstop flight across the United States was made in a Fokker T-2 in 1923.

Another important development during World War I was the family of engines known as Liberty engines, which featured interchangeable parts and went on to be used in civilian as well as military applications through World War II and beyond.

Commercial Aviation

Commercial air passenger service began in the United States (and in the world) in 1914, with a regularly scheduled flight that carried passengers between St. Petersburg and Tampa, Fla. However, there was little demand for commercial aviation and it developed slowly until after World War II. Most of the development in the aeronautical industry prior to World War II happened in the military sphere and was overseen by the National Advisory Committee on Aeronautics (NACA), which was established by Congress in 1915. The period between the two World Wars was a time for improvements in airfoils, propellers, engines, and instruments and innovations in construction techniques and materials.

To regulate the aeronautic industry, the U.S. Congress passed the Air Commerce Act of 1926, which created a Bureau of Aeronautics within the Commerce Department. The bureau moderated commercial airlines, licensed pilots, and certified aircraft. Further regulation of passenger safety, route markings, and air traffic control was provided by the

Civil Aeronautics Act of 1938 and the Civil Aeronautics Board and Civil Aeronautics Administration Act (1940).

Technological Advancements

Certain advancements during the 1920s in the design and technology of aircraft gave the United States a new role in the international sphere of aviation. Improvements in wind-tunnel testing, engine and airframe design, and maintenance equipment made for better-performing airplanes. As a result, private planes became less expensive and, in turn, grew in number and popularity.

The development of the autopilot can be traced back to 1908, when **Elmer Sperry** (1860–1930) introduced a type of gyrocompass that was later used in ship piloting systems (magnetic compasses were unreliable in steel-hulled ships). In 1929, Sperry's company tested a similar device for aircraft, as well as another device, the artificial horizon. These instruments, which enabled the pilot to fly without seeing the ground below, were rapidly installed aboard mail and commercial airplanes.

Important planes of the interwar period were Boeing's 247, introduced in 1933 and considered to be the first modern airliner. In order to compete, the Douglas Aircraft Company created its DC line: DC-1, DC-2, and DC-3. Boeing countered with its Model 307 Stratoliner. However, the DC-3, which went into service in 1936, is generally considered the first commercially popular (and profitable) plane. It had a number of innovative design features, including a retractable landing gear, and with twin 1,200-horsepower engines it could reach a maximum speed of 230 mph. A variant of the DC-3, the C-47, became the mainstay of the military's transport fleet in World War II.

Growing demand for passenger airline service soon pushed the aviation industry to even further advancements in passenger capacity and comfort, new elevation capabilities, and speed. ☐

Famous Firsts in Aviation

1783 **First balloon flight.** Jacques and Joseph Montgolfier of Annonay, France, sent up a small smoke-filled balloon about mid-November.

First hydrogen-filled balloon flight. Jacques A. C. Charles, Paris physicist, supervised construction by A. J. and M. N. Robert of a 13-foot-in-diameter balloon that was filled with hydrogen. It got up to about 3,000 ft and traveled about 16 mi in a 45-min. flight (Aug. 27).

First human balloon flights. A Frenchman, Jean Pilâtre de Rozier, made the first captive-balloon ascension (Oct. 15). With the Marquis d'Arlandes, Pilâtre de Rozier made the first free flight, reaching a peak altitude of about 500 f., and traveling about 5½ mi in 20 min. (Nov. 21).

1784 **First powered balloon.** Gen. Jean Baptiste Marie Meusnier developed the first propeller-driven and elliptically shaped balloon—the crew cranking three propellers on a common shaft to give the craft a speed of about 3 mph.

First balloon flight by a woman. Mme. Thible, a French opera singer (June 4).

1793 **First balloon flight in America.** Jean Pierre Blanchard, a French pilot, made it from Philadelphia to near Woodbury, N.J., in just over 45 min. (Jan. 9).

1794 **First military use of the balloon.** Jean Marie Coutelle, using a balloon built for the French Army, made two 4-hour observation ascents. The military purpose of the ascents seems to have been to damage the enemy's morale.

1797 **First parachute jump.** André-Jacques Garnerin dropped from about 6,500 ft over Monceau Park in Paris in a 23-foot-diameter parachute made of white canvas with a basket attached (Oct. 22).

1843 **First air transport company.** In London, William S. Henson and John Stringfellow filed articles of incorporation for the Aerial Transit Company (March 24). It failed.

1852 **First dirigible.** Henri Giffard, a French engineer, flew in a controllable (more or less) steam-engine-powered balloon, 144 ft long and 39 ft in diameter, inflated with 88,000 cu. ft. of coal gas. It reached 6.7 mph on a flight from Paris to Trappe (Sept. 24).

1860 **First aerial photographers.** Samuel Archer King and William Black made two photos of Boston, which are still in existence.

1872 **First gas-engine-powered dirigible.** Paul Haenlein, a German engineer, flew in a semi-rigid-frame dirigible, powered by a 4-cylinder internal-combustion engine running on coal gas drawn from the supporting bag.

1873 **First transatlantic attempt.** *The New York Daily Graphic* sponsored the attempt with a 400,000-cubic-foot balloon carrying a lifeboat. A rip in the bag during inflation brought collapse of the balloon and the project.

1897 **First successful metal dirigible.** An all-metal dirigible, designed by David Schwarz, a Hungarian, took off from Berlin's Tempelhof Field and, powered by a 16-hp Daimler engine, got several miles before leaking gas caused it to crash (Nov. 13).

1900 **First zeppelin flight.** Germany's Count Ferdinand von Zeppelin flew the first of his long series of rigid-frame airships. It attained a speed of 18 mph and got 3½ mi before its steering gear failed (July 2).

1903 **First successful heavier-than-air machine flight.** Aviation was really born on the sand dunes at Kitty Hawk, N.C., when Orville Wright crawled to his prone position between the wings of the biplane he and his brother Wilbur had built, opened the throttle of their home-made 12-hp engine, and took to the air. He covered 120 ft in 12 sec. Later that day, in one of four flights, Wilbur stayed up 59 sec. and covered 852 ft (Dec. 17).

1904 **First airplane maneuvers.** Orville Wright made the first turn with an airplane (Sept. 15); five days later his brother Wilbur made the first complete circle.

1905 **First airplane flight over half an hour.** Orville Wright kept his craft up 33 min., 17 sec. (Oct. 4).

1906 **First European airplane flight.** Alberto Santos-Dumont, a Brazilian, flew a heavier-than-air machine at Bagatelle Field, Paris (Sept. 13).

1908 **First airplane fatality.** Lt. Thomas E. Selfridge, U.S. Army Signal Corps, was in a group evaluating the Wright plane at Fort Myer, Va. He was up 75 ft with Orville Wright when the propeller hit a bracing wire and was broken, throwing the plane out of control, killing Selfridge and seriously injuring Wright (Sept. 17).

1909 **First cross-Channel flight.** Louis Blériot flew in a 25-hp Blériot VI monoplane from Les Baraques near Calais, France, and landed near Dover Castle, England, in a 26.61-mile (38-kilometer) 37-minute flight across the English Channel (July 25).

First International Aviation Competition Meeting. American Glenn Curtiss narrowly beat France's Louis Blériot in the main event and won the Gordon Bennett Cup. Meet held at Rheims, France (Aug. 22–28).

1910 **First licensed woman pilot.** Baroness Raymonde de la Roche of France, who learned to fly in 1909, received ticket No. 36 on March 8.

First flight from shipboard. Lt. Eugene Ely, USN, took a Curtiss plane off from the deck of the cruiser *Birmingham* at Hampton Roads, Va., and flew to Norfolk (Nov. 14). The following January he reversed the process, flying from Camp Selfridge to the deck of the armored cruiser *Pennsylvania* in San Francisco Bay (Jan. 18).

First aircraft to take off from water. Henri Fabre in a Gnome-powered floatplane, at Martigues, France (March 28).

1911 **First U.S. woman pilot.** Harriet Quimby, a magazine writer, got ticket No. 37, making her the second licensed female pilot in the world.

1912 **First woman's cross-Channel flight.** Harriet Quimby flew from Dover, England, across the English Channel and landed at Hardelot, France, in a Blériot monoplane loaned to her by Louis Blériot (April 16). She was later killed in a flying accident over Dorchester Bay during a Harvard-Boston aviation meet on July 1, 1912.

First parachute jump from a powered airplane. Albert Berry jumped in a test over Jefferson Barracks military post, St. Louis (March 1). Some sources credit Grant Morton as making first jump in 1911.

1913 **First multi-engined aircraft.** Built and flown by Igor Ivan Sikorsky while still in his native Russia.

1914 **First aerial combat.** In Aug., Allied and German pilots and observers started shooting at each other with pistols and rifles—with negligible results.

1915 **First air raids on England.** German zeppelins started dropping bombs on four English communities (Jan. 19).

1918 **First U.S. air squadron.** The U.S. Army Air Corps made its first independent raids over enemy lines, in DH-4 planes (British-designed) powered with 400-hp American-designed Liberty engines (April 8).

First regular airmail service. Operated for the Post Office Department by the Army, the first regular service was inaugurated with one round trip a day (except Sunday) between Washington, DC, and New York City (May 15).

1919 **First transatlantic flight.** The NC-4, one of four Curtiss flying boats commanded by Lt. Comdr. Albert C. Read, reached Lisbon, Portugal (May 27), after hops from Trepassy Bay, Newfoundland, to Horta, Azores (May 16–17), to Ponta Delgada (May 20). The Liberty-powered craft was piloted by Walter Hinton.

First nonstop transatlantic flight. Capt. John Alcock and Lt. Arthur Whitten Brown, British World War I flyers, made the 1,900-mile trip from St. John's, Newfoundland, to Clifden, Ireland, in 16 hr., 12 min. in a Vickers-Vimy bomber with two 350-hp Rolls-Royce engines (June 15–16).

First lighter-than-air transatlantic flight. The British dirigible R-34, commanded by Maj. George H. Scott, left Firth of Forth, Scotland (July 2), and touched down at Mineola, L.I., 108 hr. later. The eastbound trip was made in 75 hr. (completed July 13).

First scheduled London–Paris passenger service (using airplanes). Aircraft Travel and Transport inaugurated London–Paris service (Aug. 25). Later the company started the first trans-Channel mail service on the same route (Nov. 10).

First free-fall parachute jump. Leslie Irvin jumped over McCook Field, Dayton, Ohio, to prove that one won't lose consciousness during a delayed free-fall using a manually operated parachute (April 28).

1921 **First U.S. black female pilot.** Bessie Coleman received license June 15. Was killed April 30, 1926, in flying accident.

First naval vessel sunk by aircraft. Two battleships being scrapped by treaty were sunk by bombs dropped from Army planes in demonstration put on by Brig. Gen. William S. Mitchell (July 21).

First helium balloon. The C-7, nonrigid Navy dirigible was first to use noninflammable helium as lifting gas, making a flight from Hampton Roads, Va., to Washington, D.C. (Dec. 1).

1922 **First member of Caterpillar Club.** Lt. (later Maj. Gen.) Harold Harris bailed out of a crippled plane he was testing at McCook Field, Dayton, Ohio (Oct. 20), and became the first man to join the Caterpillar Club—those whose lives have been saved by parachutes.

1923 **First nonstop transcontinental flight.** Lts. John A. Macready and Oakley Kelly flew a single-engine Fokker T-2 nonstop from New York to San Diego, a distance of just over 2,500 mi in 26 hr., 50 min. (May 2–3).

First autogyro flight. Juan de la Cierva, a brilliant Spanish mathematician, made the first successful flight in a rotary wing aircraft in Madrid (June 9).

1924 **First round-the-world flight.** Four Douglas Cruiser biplanes of the U.S. Army Air Corps took off from Seattle under command of Maj. Frederick Martin (April 6). 175 days later, two of the planes (Lt. Lowell Smith's and Lt. Erik Nelson's) landed in Seattle after a circuitous route—one source saying 26,345 mi, another saying 27,553 mi.

1926 First polar flight. Then–Lt. Cmdr. Richard E. Byrd, acting as navigator, and Floyd Bennett as pilot, flew a trimotor Fokker from Kings Bay, Spitsbergen, over the North Pole and back in 15½ hr. (May 8–9).

1927 First solo nonstop transatlantic flight. Charles Augustus Lindbergh lifted his Wright-powered Ryan monoplane, *Spirit of St. Louis,* from Roosevelt Field, N.Y., to stay aloft 33 hr. 39 min. and travel 3,600 mi to Le Bourget Field outside Paris (May 20–21). Although 91 persons in 13 separate flights crossed the Atlantic before him, he flew directly between two great world cities and did it alone.

First transatlantic passenger. Charles A. Levine was piloted by Clarence D. Chamberlin from Roosevelt Field, N.Y., to Eisleben, Germany, in a Wright-powered Bellanca (June 4–5).

1928 First east–west transatlantic crossing. Baron Guenther von Huenefeld, piloted by German Capt. Hermann Koehl and Irish Capt. James Fitzmaurice, left Dublin for New York City (April 12) in a single-engine all-metal Junkers-monoplane. Some 37 hr. later, they crashed on Greely Island, Labrador. Rescued.

First U.S.–Australia flight. Sir Charles Kingsford-Smith and Capt. Charles T. P. Ulm, Australians, and two American navigators, Harry W. Lyon and James Warner, crossed the Pacific from Oakland to Brisbane. They went via Hawaii and the Fiji Islands in a trimotor Fokker (May 31–June 8).

First transarctic flight. Sir Hubert Wilkins, an Australian explorer, and Carl Ben Eielson, who served as pilot, flew from Point Barrow, Alaska, to Spitsbergen (mid-April).

1929 First of the endurance records. With Air Corps Maj. Carl Spaatz in command and Capt. Ira Eaker as chief pilot, an Army Fokker, aided by refueling in the air, remained aloft 150 hr. 40 min. at Los Angeles (Jan. 1–7).

First round-the-world airship flight. The LZ-127, known as the *Graf Zeppelin,* flew 21,300 mi in 20 days and 4 hr. Also set distance record (Aug.).

First blind flight. James H. Doolittle proved the feasibility of instrument-guided flying when he took off and landed entirely on instruments (Sept. 24).

First rocket-engine flight. Fritz von Opel, a German auto maker, stayed aloft in his small rocket-powered craft for 75 sec., covering nearly 2 mi (Sept. 30).

First South Pole flight. Comdr. Richard E. Byrd, with Bernt Balchen as pilot, Harold I. June, radio operator, and Capt. A. C. McKinley, photographer, flew a trimotor Fokker from the Bay of Whales, Little America, over the South Pole and back (Nov. 28–29).

1930 First Paris–New York nonstop flight. Dieudonné Coste and Maurice Bellonte, French pilots, flew a Hispano-powered Breguet biplane from Le Bourget Field to Valley Stream, L.I., in 37 hr., 18 min. (Sept. 2–3).

1931 First flight into the stratosphere. Auguste Piccard, a Swiss physicist, and Charles Knipfer ascended in a balloon from Augsburg, Germany, and reached a height of 51,793 ft in a 17-hr. flight that terminated on a glacier near Innsbruck, Austria (May 27).

First nonstop transpacific flight. Hugh Herndon and Clyde Pangborn took off from Sabishiro Beach, Japan, dropped their landing gear, and flew 4,860 mi to near Wenatchee, Wash., in 41 hr. 13 min. (Oct. 4–5).

1932 First woman's transatlantic solo. Amelia Earhart, flying a Pratt & Whitney Wasp-powered Lockheed Vega, flew alone from Harbor Grace, Newfoundland, to Ireland in approximately 15 hr. (May 20–21).

First westbound transatlantic solo. James A. Mollison, a British pilot, took a de Havilland Puss Moth from Portmarnock, Ireland, to Pennfield, New Brunswick (Aug. 18).

First woman airline pilot. Ruth Rowland Nichols, first woman to hold three international records at the same time—speed, distance, and altitude—was employed by N.Y.–New England Airways.

1933 First round-the-world solo. Wiley Post took a Lockheed Vega, *Winnie Mae,* 15,596 mi around the world in 7 days, 18 hr., 49½ min. (July 15–22).

1937 First successful helicopter flight. Hanna Reitsch, a German pilot, flew Dr. Heinrich Focke's FW-61 in free, fully controlled flight at Bremen (July 4). Ms. Reitsch was also the first woman civil and military aviation test pilot.

First woman known to fly combat. Sabiha Gokcen, Turkish female army pilot, bombed and strafed Kurdish tribesmen during a rebellion.

1939 First turbojet flight. Just before their invasion of Poland, the Germans flew a Heinkel He-178 plane powered by a Heinkel S3B turbojet (Aug. 27).

1940 First wartime use of military gliders. German commandos made a successful glider assault on Belgium's Fort Eben-Emael during WWII (May 10).

1941–1945 Most combat missions flown by a pilot in any war. Captain Hans-Ulrich Rudel of Germany flew 2,530 combat missions during WWII while flying a JU-87 Stuka dive bomber. He survived the war.

1942–1945 Top-scoring fighter pilot of any war. German Luftwaffe ace Maj. Erich Hartmann scored 352 victories all while flying a Messerschmitt BF 109 during WWII. He was involved in 800 dogfights, and flew 1,425 missions. Maj. Hartmann survived the war.

1942 First and only enemy bombing of U.S. mainland. During WWII, a floatplane launched from a Japanese submarine off Cape Blanco, Ore., dropped incendiary bombs on the Oregon forest in two attempts to start forest fires and terrorize American civilians, but the bombs did little damage (Sept. 9 and 29).

First American jet plane flight. Robert Stanley, chief pilot for Bell Aircraft Corp., flew the Bell XP-59 *Airacomet* at Muroc Army Base, Calif. (Oct. 1).

First woman fighter pilot to shoot down an enemy aircraft. Soviet Lieutenant Lilya Litvyak, flying a Yak-1 fighter of the women's 586th Fighter Aviation Regiment, shot down two German planes over Stalingrad on Sept. 13, 1942.

1944 First production stage rocket-engine fighter plane. The German Messerschmitt Me 163B *Komet* (test flown 1941) became operational in June 1944. Some 350 of these delta-wing fighters were built before WWII in Europe ended.

1947 First piloted supersonic flight in an airplane. Capt. Charles E. Yeager, U.S. Air Force, flew the X-1 rocket-powered research plane built by Bell Aircraft Corp., faster than the speed of sound at Muroc Air Force Base, Calif. (Oct. 14).

1949   **First round-the-world nonstop flight.** Capt. James Gallagher and USAF crew of 13 flew a Boeing B-50A Superfortress around the world nonstop from Ft. Worth, returning to same point: 23,452 mi in 94 hr., 1 min., with four aerial refuelings en route (Feb. 27–March 2).

1950   **First nonstop transatlantic jet flight.** Col. David C. Schilling (USAF) flew 3,300 mi from England to Limestone, Maine, in 10 hr., 1 min. (Sept. 22).

1951   **First solo across North Pole.** Charles F. Blair, Jr., flew a converted P-51 (May 29).

1952   **First jetliner service.** The De Havilland Comet flight was inaugurated by BOAC between London and Johannesburg, South Africa (May 2). Flight, including stops, took 23 hr., 38 min.

     First transatlantic helicopter flight. Capt. Vincent H. McGovern and 1st Lt. Harold W. Moore piloted two Sikorsky H-19s from Westover, Mass., to Prestwick, Scotland (3,410 mi). Trip was made in five stops, with a flying time of 42 hr., 25 min. (July 15–31).

     First transatlantic round trip in same day. A British Canberra twin-jet bomber flew from Aldergrove, Northern Ireland, to Gander, Newfoundland, and back in 7 hr., 59 min. flying time (Aug. 26).

1955   **First transcontinental round trip in same day.** Lt. John M. Conroy piloted an F-86 Sabrejet across U.S. (Los Angeles–New York) and back—5,085 mi—in 11 hr., 33 min., 27 sec. (May 21).

1957   **First round-the-world nonstop jet plane flight.** Maj. Gen. Archie J. Old, Jr., USAF, led a flight of three Boeing B-52 bombers, powered with eight 10,000-pound-thrust Pratt & Whitney Aircraft J57 engines around the world in 45 hr., 19 min; distance 24,325 mi; average speed 525 mph (completed Jan. 18).

1958   **First transatlantic jet passenger service.** BOAC, New York to London (Oct. 4). Pan American started daily service, New York to Paris (Oct. 26).

     First domestic jet passenger service. National Airlines inaugurated service between New York and Miami (Dec. 10).

1968   **Prototype of world's first supersonic airliner.** The Soviet-designed Tupolev Tu-144 made its first flight, Dec. 31. It first achieved supersonic speed on June 5, 1969.

1973   **First female pilot of a major U.S. scheduled airline.** Emily H. Warner became employed by Frontier Airlines on Jan. 29 as second officer on a Boeing 737.

1976   **First regularly scheduled commercial supersonic transport (SST) flights begin.** Air France and British Airways inaugurated service (Jan. 21). Air France flew the Paris–Rio de Janeiro route; B.A., the London–Bahrain. Both airlines began SST service to Washington, D.C. (May 24).

1977   **First successful human-powered aircraft.** Paul MacCready, an aeronautical engineer from Pasadena, Calif., was awarded the Kremer Prize for creating the world's first successful human-powered aircraft. The *Gossamer Condor* was flown by Bryan Allen over the required 3-mile course on Aug. 23.

1978   **First successful transatlantic balloon flight.** Three Albuquerque, N.M., men, Ben Abruzzo, Larry Newman, and Maxie Anderson, completed the crossing (Aug. 16.; landed, Aug. 17) in their helium-filled balloon, *Double Eagle II*.

1979   **First man-powered aircraft to fly across the English Channel.** The Kremer Prize for the

Active Pilot Certificates Held

Year	Total	Airline transport	Commercial	Private
1970	720,028	31,442	176,585	299,491
1980	814,667	63,652	182,097	343,276
1985	722,376	79,192	155,929	320,086
1990	702,659	107,732	149,666	299,111
1995	639,184	123,877	133,980	261,399
1996	622,261	127,486	129,187	254,002
1997	616,342	130,858	125,300	247,604
1998	618,298	134,612	122,053	247,226
1999	635,472	137,642	124,261	258,749
2000	625,581	141,596	121,858	251,561

NOTE: Includes student (97,359), glider (9,390), recreational (343), and other pilot categories. Also nonpilot, i.e., mechanic, parachute rigger, etc. Data as of Dec. 31, 1999. *Source:* April 2001 FAA Fact Book.

Channel crossing was won by Bryan Allen, who flew the *Gossamer Albatross* from Folkestone, England, to Cap Gris-Nez, France, in 2 hr., 55 min. (June 12).

1980   **First successful balloon flight over the North Pole.** Sidney Conn and his wife, Eleanor, in hot-air balloon *Joy of Sound* (April 11).

     First nonstop transcontinental balloon flight, and also record for longest overland voyage in a balloon. Maxie Anderson and his son, Kris, completed four-day flight from Fort Baker, Calif., to successful landing outside Matane, Quebec, on May 12 in their helium-filled balloon, *Kitty Hawk*.

     First long-distance solar-powered flight. Janice Brown, a 98-pound former teacher, flew a tiny experimental solar-powered aircraft, *Solar Challenger*, 6 mi in 22 min. near Marana, Ariz. (Dec. 3). The craft was powered by a 2.75-hp engine.

     First solar-powered aircraft to fly across the English Channel. Stephen R. Ptacek flew the 210-pound *Solar Challenger* at an average speed of 30 mph from Cormeilles-en-Vexin near Paris to the Royal Manston Air Force Base on England's southeast coast in 5 hr., 30 min. (July 7).

1984   **First solo transatlantic balloon flight.** Joe W. Kittinger landed Sept. 18 near Savona, Italy, in his helium-filled balloon *Rosie O'Grady's Balloon of Peace* after a flight of 3,535 mi from Caribou, Maine.

1986   **First nonstop flight around the world without refueling.** From Edwards AFB, Calif., Dick Rutan and Jeana Yeager flew in *Voyager* around the world (24,986.727 mi), returning to Edwards in 216 hr., 3 min., 44 sec. (Dec. 14–23).

1987   **First transatlantic hot-air balloon flight.** Richard Branson and Per Lindstrand flew 2,789.6 mi from Sugarloaf Mt., Maine, to Ireland in the hot-air balloon *Virgin Atlantic Flyer* (July 2–4).

1991   **First transpacific hot-air balloon flight.** Richard Branson and Per Lindstrand flew about 6,700 mi from Miyakonyo, Japan, to 150 mi west of Yellowknife, Northwest Territories, Canada (Jan. 15–17).

1993   **First woman to copilot a commercial supersonic plane.** Barbara Harmer, British Airways, flew as first officer on the Concorde from London to New York City (March 25).

1995   **First solo transpacific balloon flight.** Steve Fossett made a flight of more than 5,430 mi from Seoul, South Korea, to Leader, Saskatchewan, Canada, in a helium-filled balloon. Also set record for distance (Feb. 18–21, 1995).

1999 First nonstop round-the-world balloon flight. Bertrand Piccard (Switzerland) and Brian Jones (UK) flew 28,431 mi (45,755 km) from Chateaux d'Oex, Switzerland, to Dakhla, Egypt, in 19 days, 21 hr., and 55 min. (March 1–21).

2001 First solar-powered flight to shatter altitude records. NASA's solar-powered propeller-driven plane Helios reached an altitude of 96,500 ft during a flight over Hawaii, breaking not only the 80,200-foot record for propeller-driven aircraft, but the 85,068-foot mark for all nonrocket aircraft as well (Aug. 13–14).

Absolute World Records

(maximum performance in any class)

Source: National Aeronautic Association

Speed around the World, Nonstop, Nonrefueled

Speed (mph)	Date	Plane	Pilots	Place
115.65	Dec. 14–23, 1986	*Voyager*	Dick Rutan & Jeana Yeager (U.S.)	Edwards AFB, Calif.—Edwards AFB, Calif.

Distance, Great Circle without Landing, also Distance, Closed Circuit without Landing

Distance (mi.)	Date	Plane	Pilots	Place
24,986.727	Dec. 14–23, 1986	*Voyager*	Dick Rutan & Jeana Yeager (U.S.)	Edwards AFB, Calif.—Edwards AFB, Calif.

Speed over a Straight Course

Speed (mph)	Date	Plane type	Pilot	Place
2,193.16	July 28, 1976	Lockheed SR-71A	Capt. Eldon W. Joersz (USAF)	Beale AFB, Calif.

Speed over a Closed Circuit

Speed (mph)	Date	Plane type	Pilot	Place
2,092.294	July 27, 1976	Lockheed SR-71A	Maj. Adolphus H. Bledsoe, Jr. (USAF)	Beale AFB, Calif.

Altitude

Height (ft.)	Date	Plane type	Pilot	Place
123,523.58	Aug. 31, 1977	MIG-25, E-266M	Alexander Fedotov (U.S.S.R.)	U.S.S.R.

Altitude in Horizontal Flight

Height (ft.)	Date	Pilot	Place
85,068.997	July 28, 1976	Capt. Robert C. Helt (USAF)	Beale AFB, Calif.

Altitude, Aircraft Launched from a Carrier Airplane

Height (ft.)	Date	Plane type	Pilot	Place
314,750.00	July 17, 1962	N. American X-15-1	Maj. Robert White (USAF)	Edwards AFB, Calif.

World-Class Helicopter Records

Selected records. *Source:* National Aeronautic Association
Great Circle Distance without Landing
International: 2,213.04 mi; 3,561.55 km.
Robert G. Ferry (U.S.) in Hughes YOH-6A helicopter powered by Allison T-63-A-5 engine; from Culver City, Calif., to Ormond Beach, Fla., April 6–7, 1966.
Distance, Closed Circuit without Landing
International: 1,739.96 mi; 2,800.20 km.
Jack Schweibold (U.S.) in Hughes YOH-6A helicopter powered by Allison T-63-A-5 engine; Edwards Air Force Base, Calif., March 26, 1966.
Altitude without Payload
International: 40,820 ft; 12,442 m.
Jean Boulet (France) in Alouette SA 315-001 *Lama* powered by Artouste IIIB 735 KW engine; Istres, France, June 21, 1972.
Speed around the World, Eastbound
40.99 mph; 65.97 kph.
Joe Ronald Bower (U.S.) pilot, in Bell JetRanger III, powered by one Allison 250-C20J (317 shp), covered 23,800 mi in 24 days, 4 hr., 36 min. June 28–July 22, 1994.
Speed around the World, Westbound
57.01 mph; 91.75 kph.

Joe Ronald Bower (U.S.) pilot, John W. Williams (U.S.), co-pilot in Bell 430 powered by 2 Allison 250–C40, (811 shp), Aug. 17–Sept. 3, 1996.

Absolute World Records, Balloons

Selected records. *Source:* National Aeronautic Association
Altitude
113,739.9 ft; 34,668 m.
Cmdr. M.D. Ross (U.S.) and Lt. Cmdr. V.A. Prather, *Lee Lewis Memorial,* Gulf of Mexico, May 4, 1961.
Distance
25,360 mi; 40,814 km.
Bertrand Piccard (Switzerland) and Brian Jones (UK), *Cameron Balloons R-650,* Château d'Oex, Switzerland, to Dakhla, Egypt, March 1–21, 1999.
Duration
477 hr., 47 min.
Bertrand Piccard (Switzerland) and Brian Jones (UK), *Cameron Balloons R-650,* Château d'Oex, Switzerland, to Dakhla, Egypt, March 1–21, 1999.
Shortest time around the world
370 hr., 24 min.
Bertrand Piccard (Switzerland) and Brian Jones (UK), *Cameron Balloons R-650,* Château d'Oex, Switzerland, to Dakhla, Egypt, March 1–21, 1999.

2002

January

S	M	T	W	T	F	S
		1	2	3	4	5
6	7	8	9	10	11	12
13	14	15	16	17	18	19
20	21	22	23	24	25	26
27	28	29	30	31		

February

S	M	T	W	T	F	S
					1	2
3	4	5	6	7	8	9
10	11	12	13	14	15	16
17	18	19	20	21	22	23
24	25	26	27	28		

March

S	M	T	W	T	F	S
					1	2
3	4	5	6	7	8	9
10	11	12	13	14	15	16
17	18	19	20	21	22	23
24	25	26	27	28	29	30
31						

April

S	M	T	W	T	F	S
	1	2	3	4	5	6
7	8	9	10	11	12	13
14	15	16	17	18	19	20
21	22	23	24	25	26	27
28	29	30				

1—New Year's Day
6—Epiphany
21—Martin Luther King, Jr.'s Birthday observed

2—Groundhog Day
12—Lincoln's Birthday
13—Ash Wednesday
14—Valentine's Day
18—Washington's Birthday observed
22—Washington's Birthday
26—Purim*

17—St. Patrick's Day
24—Palm Sunday
28—1st Day of Passover*
29—Good Friday
31—Easter Sunday

7—Daylight Saving Time begins

May

S	M	T	W	T	F	S
			1	2	3	4
5	6	7	8	9	10	11
12	13	14	15	16	17	18
19	20	21	22	23	24	25
26	27	28	29	30	31	

June

S	M	T	W	T	F	S
						1
2	3	4	5	6	7	8
9	10	11	12	13	14	15
16	17	18	19	20	21	22
23	24	25	26	27	28	29
30						

July

S	M	T	W	T	F	S
	1	2	3	4	5	6
7	8	9	10	11	12	13
14	15	16	17	18	19	20
21	22	23	24	25	26	27
28	29	30	31			

August

S	M	T	W	T	F	S
				1	2	3
4	5	6	7	8	9	10
11	12	13	14	15	16	17
18	19	20	21	22	23	24
25	26	27	28	29	30	31

5—Orthodox Easter
12—Mother's Day
17—1st Day of Shavuot*
19—Pentecost
27—Memorial Day observed

14—Flag Day
16—Father's Day
23—Orthodox Pentecost

1—Canada Day
4—Independence Day

September

S	M	T	W	T	F	S
1	2	3	4	5	6	7
8	9	10	11	12	13	14
15	16	17	18	19	20	21
22	23	24	25	26	27	28
29	30					

October

S	M	T	W	T	F	S
		1	2	3	4	5
6	7	8	9	10	11	12
13	14	15	16	17	18	19
20	21	22	23	24	25	26
27	28	29	30	31		

November

S	M	T	W	T	F	S
					1	2
3	4	5	6	7	8	9
10	11	12	13	14	15	16
17	18	19	20	21	22	23
24	25	26	27	28	29	30

December

S	M	T	W	T	F	S
1	2	3	4	5	6	7
8	9	10	11	12	13	14
15	16	17	18	19	20	21
22	23	24	25	26	27	28
29	30	31				

2—Labor Day
7—Rosh Hashanah*
16—Yom Kippur*

14—Columbus Day observed
14—Thanksgiving Day (Canada)
27—Daylight Saving Time ends
31—Halloween

1—All Saints' Day
5—Election Day
6—Ramadan begins*
11—Veterans Day
28—Thanksgiving Day
30—1st Day of Hanukkah*

1—1st Sunday of Advent
6—Ramadan ends (Eid al-Fitr)*
25—Christmas Day

*All Jewish and Islamic holidays begin at sundown the day before they are listed here.

Seasons for the Northern Hemisphere, 2002

Mar. 20, 2:16 P.M. EST (19:16 UT[1]), Sun enters sign of Aries; spring begins

June 21, 9:24 A.M. EDT (13:24 UT[1]), Sun enters sign of Cancer; summer begins

Sept. 23, 12:55 A.M. EDT (04:55 UT[1]), Sun enters sign of Libra; fall begins

Dec. 21, 8:14 P.M. EST (Dec. 22, 01:14 UT[1]), Sun enters sign of Capricorn; winter begins

1. Universal Time (UT), also known as Greenwich Mean Time (GMT). *See* p. 400 for a conversion table of Universal Time.

2001

January
S	M	T	W	T	F	S
	1	2	3	4	5	6
7	8	9	10	11	12	13
14	15	16	17	18	19	20
21	22	23	24	25	26	27
28	29	30	31			

February
S	M	T	W	T	F	S
				1	2	3
4	5	6	7	8	9	10
11	12	13	14	15	16	17
18	19	20	21	22	23	24
25	26	27	28			

March
S	M	T	W	T	F	S
				1	2	3
4	5	6	7	8	9	10
11	12	13	14	15	16	17
18	19	20	21	22	23	24
25	26	27	28	29	30	31

April
S	M	T	W	T	F	S
1	2	3	4	5	6	7
8	9	10	11	12	13	14
15	16	17	18	19	20	21
22	23	24	25	26	27	28
29	30					

May
S	M	T	W	T	F	S
		1	2	3	4	5
6	7	8	9	10	11	12
13	14	15	16	17	18	19
20	21	22	23	24	25	26
27	28	29	30	31		

June
S	M	T	W	T	F	S
					1	2
3	4	5	6	7	8	9
10	11	12	13	14	15	16
17	18	19	20	21	22	23
24	25	26	27	28	29	30

July
S	M	T	W	T	F	S
1	2	3	4	5	6	7
8	9	10	11	12	13	14
15	16	17	18	19	20	21
22	23	24	25	26	27	28
29	30	31				

August
S	M	T	W	T	F	S
			1	2	3	4
5	6	7	8	9	10	11
12	13	14	15	16	17	18
19	20	21	22	23	24	25
26	27	28	29	30	31	

September
S	M	T	W	T	F	S
						1
2	3	4	5	6	7	8
9	10	11	12	13	14	15
16	17	18	19	20	21	22
23	24	25	26	27	28	29
30						

October
S	M	T	W	T	F	S
	1	2	3	4	5	6
7	8	9	10	11	12	13
14	15	16	17	18	19	20
21	22	23	24	25	26	27
28	29	30	31			

November
S	M	T	W	T	F	S
				1	2	3
4	5	6	7	8	9	10
11	12	13	14	15	16	17
18	19	20	21	22	23	24
25	26	27	28	29	30	

December
S	M	T	W	T	F	S
						1
2	3	4	5	6	7	8
9	10	11	12	13	14	15
16	17	18	19	20	21	22
23	24	25	26	27	28	29
30	31					

2003

January
S	M	T	W	T	F	S
			1	2	3	4
5	6	7	8	9	10	11
12	13	14	15	16	17	18
19	20	21	22	23	24	25
26	27	28	29	30	31	

February
S	M	T	W	T	F	S
						1
2	3	4	5	6	7	8
9	10	11	12	13	14	15
16	17	18	19	20	21	22
23	24	25	26	27	28	

March
S	M	T	W	T	F	S
						1
2	3	4	5	6	7	8
9	10	11	12	13	14	15
16	17	18	19	20	21	22
23	24	25	26	27	28	29
30	31					

April
S	M	T	W	T	F	S
		1	2	3	4	5
6	7	8	9	10	11	12
13	14	15	16	17	18	19
20	21	22	23	24	25	26
27	28	29	30			

May
S	M	T	W	T	F	S
				1	2	3
4	5	6	7	8	9	10
11	12	13	14	15	16	17
18	19	20	21	22	23	24
25	26	27	28	29	30	31

June
S	M	T	W	T	F	S
1	2	3	4	5	6	7
8	9	10	11	12	13	14
15	16	17	18	19	20	21
22	23	24	25	26	27	28
29	30					

July
S	M	T	W	T	F	S
		1	2	3	4	5
6	7	8	9	10	11	12
13	14	15	16	17	18	19
20	21	22	23	24	25	26
27	28	29	30	31		

August
S	M	T	W	T	F	S
					1	2
3	4	5	6	7	8	9
10	11	12	13	14	15	16
17	18	19	20	21	22	23
24	25	26	27	28	29	30
31						

September
S	M	T	W	T	F	S
	1	2	3	4	5	6
7	8	9	10	11	12	13
14	15	16	17	18	19	20
21	22	23	24	25	26	27
28	29	30				

October
S	M	T	W	T	F	S
			1	2	3	4
5	6	7	8	9	10	11
12	13	14	15	16	17	18
19	20	21	22	23	24	25
26	27	28	29	30	31	

November
S	M	T	W	T	F	S
						1
2	3	4	5	6	7	8
9	10	11	12	13	14	15
16	17	18	19	20	21	22
23	24	25	26	27	28	29
30						

December
S	M	T	W	T	F	S
	1	2	3	4	5	6
7	8	9	10	11	12	13
14	15	16	17	18	19	20
21	22	23	24	25	26	27
28	29	30	31			

Astrological Signs

♈ **Aries (Ram):** March 21–April 19

♉ **Taurus (Bull):** April 20–May 20

♊ **Gemini (Twins):** May 21–June 20

♋ **Cancer (Crab):** June 21–July 22

♌ **Leo (Lion):** July 23–Aug. 22

♍ **Virgo (Virgin):** Aug. 23–Sept. 22

♎ **Libra (Scales):** Sept. 23–Oct. 22

♏ **Scorpio (Scorpion):** Oct. 23–Nov. 21

♐ **Sagittarius (Archer):** Nov. 22–Dec. 21

♑ **Capricorn (Goat):** Dec. 22–Jan. 19

♒ **Aquarius (Water Bearer):** Jan. 20–Feb. 18

♓ **Pisces (Fish):** Feb. 19–March 20

PERPETUAL CALENDAR

1800...4	1844...9	1888...8	1932.13	1976.12
1801...5	1845...4	1889...3	1933...1	1977...7
1802...6	1846...5	1890...4	1934...2	1978...1
1803...7	1847...6	1891...5	1935...3	1979...2
1804...8	1848.14	1892.13	1936.11	1980.10
1805...3	1849...2	1893...1	1937...6	1981...5
1806...4	1850...3	1894...2	1938...7	1982...6
1807...5	1851...4	1895...3	1939...1	1983...7
1808.13	1852.12	1896.11	1940...9	1984...8
1809...1	1853...7	1897...6	1941...4	1985...3
1810...2	1854...1	1898...7	1942...5	1986...4
1811...3	1855...2	1899...1	1943...6	1987...5
1812.11	1856.10	1900...2	1944.14	1988.13
1813...6	1857...5	1901...3	1945...2	1989...1
1814...7	1858...6	1902...4	1946...3	1990...2
1815...1	1859...7	1903...5	1947...4	1991...3
1816...9	1860...8	1904.13	1948.12	1992.11
1817...4	1861...3	1905...1	1949...7	1993...6
1818...5	1862...4	1906...2	1950...1	1994...7
1819...6	1863...5	1907...3	1951...2	1995...1
1820.14	1864.13	1908.11	1952.10	1996...9
1821...2	1865...1	1909...6	1953...5	1997...4
1822...3	1866...2	1910...7	1954...6	1998...5
1823...4	1867...3	1911...1	1955...7	1999...6
1824.12	1868.11	1912...9	1956...8	2000.14
1825...7	1869...6	1913...4	1957...3	2001...2
1826...1	1870...7	1914...5	1958...4	2002...3
1827...2	1871...1	1915...6	1959...5	2003...4
1828.10	1872...9	1916.14	1960.13	2004.12
1829...5	1873...4	1917...2	1961...1	2005...7
1830...6	1874...5	1918...3	1962...2	2006...1
1831...7	1875...6	1919...4	1963...3	2007...2
1832...8	1876.14	1920.12	1964.11	2008.10
1833...3	1877...2	1921...7	1965...6	2009...5
1834...4	1878...3	1922...1	1966...7	2010...6
1835...5	1879...4	1923...2	1967...1	2011...7
1836.13	1880.12	1924.10	1968...9	2012...8
1837...1	1881...7	1925...5	1969...4	2013...3
1838...2	1882...1	1926...6	1970...5	2014...4
1839...3	1883...2	1927...7	1971...6	2015...5
1840.11	1884.10	1928...8	1972.14	2016.13
1841...6	1885...5	1929...3	1973...2	2017...1
1842...7	1886...6	1930...4	1974...3	2018...2
1843...1	1887...6	1931...5	1975...4	2019...3
				2020.11
				2021...6
				2022...7
				2023...1
				2024...9
				2025...4
				2026...5
				2027...6
				2028.14
				2029...2
				2030...3
				2031...4
				2032.12
				2033...7
				2034...1
				2035...2
				2036.10
				2037...5
				2038...6
				2039...7
				2040...8
				2041...3
				2042...4
				2043...5
				2044.13
				2045...1
				2046...2
				2047...3
				2048.11
				2049...6
				2050...7
				2051...1
				2052...9
				2053...4
				2054...5
				2055...6
				2056.14
				2057...2
				2058...3
				2059...4
				2060.12
				2061...7
				2062...1
				2063...2

DIRECTIONS: The number given with each year in the key above is the number of the calendar to use for that year.

Calendar 1

```
JANUARY               FEBRUARY              MARCH                 APRIL
S  M  T  W  T  F  S    S  M  T  W  T  F  S    S  M  T  W  T  F  S    S  M  T  W  T  F  S
   1  2  3  4  5  6  7             1  2  3  4             1  2  3  4                      1
 8  9 10 11 12 13 14    5  6  7  8  9 10 11    5  6  7  8  9 10 11    2  3  4  5  6  7  8
15 16 17 18 19 20 21   12 13 14 15 16 17 18   12 13 14 15 16 17 18    9 10 11 12 13 14 15
22 23 24 25 26 27 28   19 20 21 22 23 24 25   19 20 21 22 23 24 25   16 17 18 19 20 21 22
29 30 31               26 27 28               26 27 28 29 30 31      23 24 25 26 27 28 29
                                                                     30

MAY                   JUNE                  JULY                  AUGUST
S  M  T  W  T  F  S    S  M  T  W  T  F  S    S  M  T  W  T  F  S    S  M  T  W  T  F  S
       1  2  3  4  5  6             1  2  3                      1          1  2  3  4  5
 7  8  9 10 11 12 13    4  5  6  7  8  9 10    2  3  4  5  6  7  8    6  7  8  9 10 11 12
14 15 16 17 18 19 20   11 12 13 14 15 16 17    9 10 11 12 13 14 15   13 14 15 16 17 18 19
21 22 23 24 25 26 27   18 19 20 21 22 23 24   16 17 18 19 20 21 22   20 21 22 23 24 25 26
28 29 30 31           25 26 27 28 29 30       23 24 25 26 27 28 29   27 28 29 30 31
                                              30 31

SEPTEMBER             OCTOBER               NOVEMBER              DECEMBER
S  M  T  W  T  F  S    S  M  T  W  T  F  S    S  M  T  W  T  F  S    S  M  T  W  T  F  S
                1  2    1  2  3  4  5  6  7             1  2  3  4                1  2
 3  4  5  6  7  8  9    8  9 10 11 12 13 14    5  6  7  8  9 10 11    3  4  5  6  7  8  9
10 11 12 13 14 15 16   15 16 17 18 19 20 21   12 13 14 15 16 17 18   10 11 12 13 14 15 16
17 18 19 20 21 22 23   22 23 24 25 26 27 28   19 20 21 22 23 24 25   17 18 19 20 21 22 23
24 25 26 27 28 29 30   29 30 31               26 27 28 29 30         24 25 26 27 28 29 30
                                                                     31
```

Calendar 2

```
JANUARY               FEBRUARY              MARCH                 APRIL
S  M  T  W  T  F  S    S  M  T  W  T  F  S    S  M  T  W  T  F  S    S  M  T  W  T  F  S
   1  2  3  4  5  6             1  2  3             1  2  3          1  2  3  4  5  6  7
 7  8  9 10 11 12 13    4  5  6  7  8  9 10    4  5  6  7  8  9 10    8  9 10 11 12 13 14
14 15 16 17 18 19 20   11 12 13 14 15 16 17   11 12 13 14 15 16 17   15 16 17 18 19 20 21
21 22 23 24 25 26 27   18 19 20 21 22 23 24   18 19 20 21 22 23 24   22 23 24 25 26 27 28
28 29 30 31           25 26 27 28             25 26 27 28 29 30 31   29 30

MAY                   JUNE                  JULY                  AUGUST
S  M  T  W  T  F  S    S  M  T  W  T  F  S    S  M  T  W  T  F  S    S  M  T  W  T  F  S
      1  2  3  4  5                1  2    1  2  3  4  5  6  7             1  2  3  4
 6  7  8  9 10 11 12    3  4  5  6  7  8  9    8  9 10 11 12 13 14    5  6  7  8  9 10 11
13 14 15 16 17 18 19   10 11 12 13 14 15 16   15 16 17 18 19 20 21   12 13 14 15 16 17 18
20 21 22 23 24 25 26   17 18 19 20 21 22 23   22 23 24 25 26 27 28   19 20 21 22 23 24 25
27 28 29 30 31        24 25 26 27 28 29 30    29 30 31               26 27 28 29 30 31

SEPTEMBER             OCTOBER               NOVEMBER              DECEMBER
S  M  T  W  T  F  S    S  M  T  W  T  F  S    S  M  T  W  T  F  S    S  M  T  W  T  F  S
                   1    1  2  3  4  5  6             1  2  3                      1
 2  3  4  5  6  7  8    7  8  9 10 11 12 13    4  5  6  7  8  9 10    2  3  4  5  6  7  8
 9 10 11 12 13 14 15   14 15 16 17 18 19 20   11 12 13 14 15 16 17    9 10 11 12 13 14 15
16 17 18 19 20 21 22   21 22 23 24 25 26 27   18 19 20 21 22 23 24   16 17 18 19 20 21 22
23 24 25 26 27 28 29   28 29 30 31           25 26 27 28 29 30       23 24 25 26 27 28 29
30                                                                   30 31
```

Calendar 3

```
JANUARY               FEBRUARY              MARCH                 APRIL
S  M  T  W  T  F  S    S  M  T  W  T  F  S    S  M  T  W  T  F  S    S  M  T  W  T  F  S
      1  2  3  4  5                1  2                1  2             1  2  3  4  5  6
 6  7  8  9 10 11 12    3  4  5  6  7  8  9    3  4  5  6  7  8  9    7  8  9 10 11 12 13
13 14 15 16 17 18 19   10 11 12 13 14 15 16   10 11 12 13 14 15 16   14 15 16 17 18 19 20
20 21 22 23 24 25 26   17 18 19 20 21 22 23   17 18 19 20 21 22 23   21 22 23 24 25 26 27
27 28 29 30 31        24 25 26 27 28         24 25 26 27 28 29 30    28 29 30
                                             31

MAY                   JUNE                  JULY                  AUGUST
S  M  T  W  T  F  S    S  M  T  W  T  F  S    S  M  T  W  T  F  S    S  M  T  W  T  F  S
         1  2  3  4                      1    1  2  3  4  5  6             1  2  3
 5  6  7  8  9 10 11    2  3  4  5  6  7  8    7  8  9 10 11 12 13    4  5  6  7  8  9 10
12 13 14 15 16 17 18    9 10 11 12 13 14 15   14 15 16 17 18 19 20   11 12 13 14 15 16 17
19 20 21 22 23 24 25   16 17 18 19 20 21 22   21 22 23 24 25 26 27   18 19 20 21 22 23 24
26 27 28 29 30 31      23 24 25 26 27 28 29   28 29 30 31           25 26 27 28 29 30 31
                       30

SEPTEMBER             OCTOBER               NOVEMBER              DECEMBER
S  M  T  W  T  F  S    S  M  T  W  T  F  S    S  M  T  W  T  F  S    S  M  T  W  T  F  S
 1  2  3  4  5  6  7             1  2  3  4  5                1  2    1  2  3  4  5  6  7
 8  9 10 11 12 13 14    6  7  8  9 10 11 12    3  4  5  6  7  8  9    8  9 10 11 12 13 14
15 16 17 18 19 20 21   13 14 15 16 17 18 19   10 11 12 13 14 15 16   15 16 17 18 19 20 21
22 23 24 25 26 27 28   20 21 22 23 24 25 26   17 18 19 20 21 22 23   22 23 24 25 26 27 28
29 30                 27 28 29 30 31         24 25 26 27 28 29 30    29 30 31
```

Calendar 4

```
JANUARY               FEBRUARY              MARCH                 APRIL
S  M  T  W  T  F  S    S  M  T  W  T  F  S    S  M  T  W  T  F  S    S  M  T  W  T  F  S
         1  2  3  4                      1                      1          1  2  3  4  5
 5  6  7  8  9 10 11    2  3  4  5  6  7  8    2  3  4  5  6  7  8    6  7  8  9 10 11 12
12 13 14 15 16 17 18    9 10 11 12 13 14 15    9 10 11 12 13 14 15   13 14 15 16 17 18 19
19 20 21 22 23 24 25   16 17 18 19 20 21 22   16 17 18 19 20 21 22   20 21 22 23 24 25 26
26 27 28 29 30 31      23 24 25 26 27 28      23 24 25 26 27 28 29   27 28 29 30
                                             30 31

MAY                   JUNE                  JULY                  AUGUST
S  M  T  W  T  F  S    S  M  T  W  T  F  S    S  M  T  W  T  F  S    S  M  T  W  T  F  S
            1  2  3    1  2  3  4  5  6  7          1  2  3  4  5                1  2
 4  5  6  7  8  9 10    8  9 10 11 12 13 14    6  7  8  9 10 11 12    3  4  5  6  7  8  9
11 12 13 14 15 16 17   15 16 17 18 19 20 21   13 14 15 16 17 18 19   10 11 12 13 14 15 16
18 19 20 21 22 23 24   22 23 24 25 26 27 28   20 21 22 23 24 25 26   17 18 19 20 21 22 23
25 26 27 28 29 30 31   29 30                 27 28 29 30 31         24 25 26 27 28 29 30
                                                                     31

SEPTEMBER             OCTOBER               NOVEMBER              DECEMBER
S  M  T  W  T  F  S    S  M  T  W  T  F  S    S  M  T  W  T  F  S    S  M  T  W  T  F  S
   1  2  3  4  5  6             1  2  3  4                      1          1  2  3  4  5  6
 7  8  9 10 11 12 13    5  6  7  8  9 10 11    2  3  4  5  6  7  8    7  8  9 10 11 12 13
14 15 16 17 18 19 20   12 13 14 15 16 17 18    9 10 11 12 13 14 15   14 15 16 17 18 19 20
21 22 23 24 25 26 27   19 20 21 22 23 24 25   16 17 18 19 20 21 22   21 22 23 24 25 26 27
28 29 30              26 27 28 29 30 31       23 24 25 26 27 28 29   28 29 30 31
                                             30
```

Calendar 5

```
JANUARY               FEBRUARY              MARCH                 APRIL
S  M  T  W  T  F  S    S  M  T  W  T  F  S    S  M  T  W  T  F  S    S  M  T  W  T  F  S
            1  2  3    1  2  3  4  5  6  7    1  2  3  4  5  6  7                1  2  3  4
 4  5  6  7  8  9 10    8  9 10 11 12 13 14    8  9 10 11 12 13 14    5  6  7  8  9 10 11
11 12 13 14 15 16 17   15 16 17 18 19 20 21   15 16 17 18 19 20 21   12 13 14 15 16 17 18
18 19 20 21 22 23 24   22 23 24 25 26 27 28   22 23 24 25 26 27 28   19 20 21 22 23 24 25
25 26 27 28 29 30 31                          29 30 31               26 27 28 29 30

MAY                   JUNE                  JULY                  AUGUST
S  M  T  W  T  F  S    S  M  T  W  T  F  S    S  M  T  W  T  F  S    S  M  T  W  T  F  S
               1  2       1  2  3  4  5  6             1  2  3  4                      1
 3  4  5  6  7  8  9    7  8  9 10 11 12 13    5  6  7  8  9 10 11    2  3  4  5  6  7  8
10 11 12 13 14 15 16   14 15 16 17 18 19 20   12 13 14 15 16 17 18    9 10 11 12 13 14 15
17 18 19 20 21 22 23   21 22 23 24 25 26 27   19 20 21 22 23 24 25   16 17 18 19 20 21 22
24 25 26 27 28 29 30   28 29 30              26 27 28 29 30 31       23 24 25 26 27 28 29
31                                                                   30 31

SEPTEMBER             OCTOBER               NOVEMBER              DECEMBER
S  M  T  W  T  F  S    S  M  T  W  T  F  S    S  M  T  W  T  F  S    S  M  T  W  T  F  S
      1  2  3  4  5                1  2  3    1  2  3  4  5  6  7             1  2  3  4  5
 6  7  8  9 10 11 12    4  5  6  7  8  9 10    8  9 10 11 12 13 14    6  7  8  9 10 11 12
13 14 15 16 17 18 19   11 12 13 14 15 16 17   15 16 17 18 19 20 21   13 14 15 16 17 18 19
20 21 22 23 24 25 26   18 19 20 21 22 23 24   22 23 24 25 26 27 28   20 21 22 23 24 25 26
27 28 29 30           25 26 27 28 29 30 31   29 30                  27 28 29 30 31
```

Calendar 6

```
JANUARY               FEBRUARY              MARCH                 APRIL
S  M  T  W  T  F  S    S  M  T  W  T  F  S    S  M  T  W  T  F  S    S  M  T  W  T  F  S
                  1  2    1  2  3  4  5  6       1  2  3  4  5  6                1  2  3
 3  4  5  6  7  8  9    7  8  9 10 11 12 13    7  8  9 10 11 12 13    4  5  6  7  8  9 10
10 11 12 13 14 15 16   14 15 16 17 18 19 20   14 15 16 17 18 19 20   11 12 13 14 15 16 17
17 18 19 20 21 22 23   21 22 23 24 25 26 27   21 22 23 24 25 26 27   18 19 20 21 22 23 24
24 25 26 27 28 29 30   28                     28 29 30 31           25 26 27 28 29 30
31

MAY                   JUNE                  JULY                  AUGUST
S  M  T  W  T  F  S    S  M  T  W  T  F  S    S  M  T  W  T  F  S    S  M  T  W  T  F  S
                   1       1  2  3  4  5             1  2  3    1  2  3  4  5  6  7
 2  3  4  5  6  7  8    6  7  8  9 10 11 12    4  5  6  7  8  9 10    8  9 10 11 12 13 14
 9 10 11 12 13 14 15   13 14 15 16 17 18 19   11 12 13 14 15 16 17   15 16 17 18 19 20 21
16 17 18 19 20 21 22   20 21 22 23 24 25 26   18 19 20 21 22 23 24   22 23 24 25 26 27 28
23 24 25 26 27 28 29   27 28 29 30           25 26 27 28 29 30 31   29 30 31
30 31

SEPTEMBER             OCTOBER               NOVEMBER              DECEMBER
S  M  T  W  T  F  S    S  M  T  W  T  F  S    S  M  T  W  T  F  S    S  M  T  W  T  F  S
         1  2  3  4                1  2       1  2  3  4  5  6             1  2  3  4
 5  6  7  8  9 10 11    3  4  5  6  7  8  9    7  8  9 10 11 12 13    5  6  7  8  9 10 11
12 13 14 15 16 17 18   10 11 12 13 14 15 16   14 15 16 17 18 19 20   12 13 14 15 16 17 18
19 20 21 22 23 24 25   17 18 19 20 21 22 23   21 22 23 24 25 26 27   19 20 21 22 23 24 25
26 27 28 29 30        24 25 26 27 28 29 30   28 29 30              26 27 28 29 30 31
                       31
```

7

JANUARY

S	M	T	W	T	F	S
						1
2	3	4	5	6	7	8
9	10	11	12	13	14	15
16	17	18	19	20	21	22
23	24	25	26	27	28	29
30	31					

FEBRUARY

S	M	T	W	T	F	S
		1	2	3	4	5
6	7	8	9	10	11	12
13	14	15	16	17	18	19
20	21	22	23	24	25	26
27	28					

MARCH

S	M	T	W	T	F	S
		1	2	3	4	5
6	7	8	9	10	11	12
13	14	15	16	17	18	19
20	21	22	23	24	25	26
27	28	29	30	31		

APRIL

S	M	T	W	T	F	S
					1	2
3	4	5	6	7	8	9
10	11	12	13	14	15	16
17	18	19	20	21	22	23
24	25	26	27	28	29	30

MAY

S	M	T	W	T	F	S
1	2	3	4	5	6	7
8	9	10	11	12	13	14
15	16	17	18	19	20	21
22	23	24	25	26	27	28
29	30	31				

JUNE

S	M	T	W	T	F	S
			1	2	3	4
5	6	7	8	9	10	11
12	13	14	15	16	17	18
19	20	21	22	23	24	25
26	27	28	29	30		

JULY

S	M	T	W	T	F	S
					1	2
3	4	5	6	7	8	9
10	11	12	13	14	15	16
17	18	19	20	21	22	23
24	25	26	27	28	29	30
31						

AUGUST

S	M	T	W	T	F	S
	1	2	3	4	5	6
7	8	9	10	11	12	13
14	15	16	17	18	19	20
21	22	23	24	25	26	27
28	29	30	31			

SEPTEMBER

S	M	T	W	T	F	S
				1	2	3
4	5	6	7	8	9	10
11	12	13	14	15	16	17
18	19	20	21	22	23	24
25	26	27	28	29	30	

OCTOBER

S	M	T	W	T	F	S
						1
2	3	4	5	6	7	8
9	10	11	12	13	14	15
16	17	18	19	20	21	22
23	24	25	26	27	28	29
30	31					

NOVEMBER

S	M	T	W	T	F	S
		1	2	3	4	5
6	7	8	9	10	11	12
13	14	15	16	17	18	19
20	21	22	23	24	25	26
27	28	29	30			

DECEMBER

S	M	T	W	T	F	S
				1	2	3
4	5	6	7	8	9	10
11	12	13	14	15	16	17
18	19	20	21	22	23	24
25	26	27	28	29	30	31

8

JANUARY

S	M	T	W	T	F	S
1	2	3	4	5	6	7
8	9	10	11	12	13	14
15	16	17	18	19	20	21
22	23	24	25	26	27	28
29	30	31				

FEBRUARY

S	M	T	W	T	F	S
			1	2	3	4
5	6	7	8	9	10	11
12	13	14	15	16	17	18
19	20	21	22	23	24	25
26	27	28	29			

MARCH

S	M	T	W	T	F	S
				1	2	3
4	5	6	7	8	9	10
11	12	13	14	15	16	17
18	19	20	21	22	23	24
25	26	27	28	29	30	31

APRIL

S	M	T	W	T	F	S
1	2	3	4	5	6	7
8	9	10	11	12	13	14
15	16	17	18	19	20	21
22	23	24	25	26	27	28
29	30					

MAY

S	M	T	W	T	F	S
		1	2	3	4	5
6	7	8	9	10	11	12
13	14	15	16	17	18	19
20	21	22	23	24	25	26
27	28	29	30	31		

JUNE

S	M	T	W	T	F	S
					1	2
3	4	5	6	7	8	9
10	11	12	13	14	15	16
17	18	19	20	21	22	23
24	25	26	27	28	29	30

JULY

S	M	T	W	T	F	S
1	2	3	4	5	6	7
8	9	10	11	12	13	14
15	16	17	18	19	20	21
22	23	24	25	26	27	28
29	30	31				

AUGUST

S	M	T	W	T	F	S
			1	2	3	4
5	6	7	8	9	10	11
12	13	14	15	16	17	18
19	20	21	22	23	24	25
26	27	28	29	30	31	

SEPTEMBER

S	M	T	W	T	F	S
						1
2	3	4	5	6	7	8
9	10	11	12	13	14	15
16	17	18	19	20	21	22
23	24	25	26	27	28	29
30						

OCTOBER

S	M	T	W	T	F	S
	1	2	3	4	5	6
7	8	9	10	11	12	13
14	15	16	17	18	19	20
21	22	23	24	25	26	27
28	29	30	31			

NOVEMBER

S	M	T	W	T	F	S
				1	2	3
4	5	6	7	8	9	10
11	12	13	14	15	16	17
18	19	20	21	22	23	24
25	26	27	28	29	30	

DECEMBER

S	M	T	W	T	F	S
						1
2	3	4	5	6	7	8
9	10	11	12	13	14	15
16	17	18	19	20	21	22
23	24	25	26	27	28	29
30	31					

9

JANUARY

S	M	T	W	T	F	S
	1	2	3	4	5	6
7	8	9	10	11	12	13
14	15	16	17	18	19	20
21	22	23	24	25	26	27
28	29	30	31			

FEBRUARY

S	M	T	W	T	F	S
				1	2	3
4	5	6	7	8	9	10
11	12	13	14	15	16	17
18	19	20	21	22	23	24
25	26	27	28	29		

MARCH

S	M	T	W	T	F	S
					1	2
3	4	5	6	7	8	9
10	11	12	13	14	15	16
17	18	19	20	21	22	23
24	25	26	27	28	29	30
31						

APRIL

S	M	T	W	T	F	S
	1	2	3	4	5	6
7	8	9	10	11	12	13
14	15	16	17	18	19	20
21	22	23	24	25	26	27
28	29	30				

MAY

S	M	T	W	T	F	S
			1	2	3	4
5	6	7	8	9	10	11
12	13	14	15	16	17	18
19	20	21	22	23	24	25
26	27	28	29	30	31	

JUNE

S	M	T	W	T	F	S
						1
2	3	4	5	6	7	8
9	10	11	12	13	14	15
16	17	18	19	20	21	22
23	24	25	26	27	28	29
30						

JULY

S	M	T	W	T	F	S
	1	2	3	4	5	6
7	8	9	10	11	12	13
14	15	16	17	18	19	20
21	22	23	24	25	26	27
28	29	30	31			

AUGUST

S	M	T	W	T	F	S
				1	2	3
4	5	6	7	8	9	10
11	12	13	14	15	16	17
18	19	20	21	22	23	24
25	26	27	28	29	30	31

SEPTEMBER

S	M	T	W	T	F	S
1	2	3	4	5	6	7
8	9	10	11	12	13	14
15	16	17	18	19	20	21
22	23	24	25	26	27	28
29	30					

OCTOBER

S	M	T	W	T	F	S
		1	2	3	4	5
6	7	8	9	10	11	12
13	14	15	16	17	18	19
20	21	22	23	24	25	26
27	28	29	30	31		

NOVEMBER

S	M	T	W	T	F	S
					1	2
3	4	5	6	7	8	9
10	11	12	13	14	15	16
17	18	19	20	21	22	23
24	25	26	27	28	29	30

DECEMBER

S	M	T	W	T	F	S
1	2	3	4	5	6	7
8	9	10	11	12	13	14
15	16	17	18	19	20	21
22	23	24	25	26	27	28
29	30	31				

10

JANUARY

S	M	T	W	T	F	S
		1	2	3	4	5
6	7	8	9	10	11	12
13	14	15	16	17	18	19
20	21	22	23	24	25	26
27	28	29	30	31		

FEBRUARY

S	M	T	W	T	F	S
					1	2
3	4	5	6	7	8	9
10	11	12	13	14	15	16
17	18	19	20	21	22	23
24	25	26	27	28	29	

MARCH

S	M	T	W	T	F	S
						1
2	3	4	5	6	7	8
9	10	11	12	13	14	15
16	17	18	19	20	21	22
23	24	25	26	27	28	29
30	31					

APRIL

S	M	T	W	T	F	S
		1	2	3	4	5
6	7	8	9	10	11	12
13	14	15	16	17	18	19
20	21	22	23	24	25	26
27	28	29	30			

MAY

S	M	T	W	T	F	S
				1	2	3
4	5	6	7	8	9	10
11	12	13	14	15	16	17
18	19	20	21	22	23	24
25	26	27	28	29	30	31

JUNE

S	M	T	W	T	F	S
1	2	3	4	5	6	7
8	9	10	11	12	13	14
15	16	17	18	19	20	21
22	23	24	25	26	27	28
29	30					

JULY

S	M	T	W	T	F	S
		1	2	3	4	5
6	7	8	9	10	11	12
13	14	15	16	17	18	19
20	21	22	23	24	25	26
27	28	29	30	31		

AUGUST

S	M	T	W	T	F	S
					1	2
3	4	5	6	7	8	9
10	11	12	13	14	15	16
17	18	19	20	21	22	23
24	25	26	27	28	29	30
31						

SEPTEMBER

S	M	T	W	T	F	S
	1	2	3	4	5	6
7	8	9	10	11	12	13
14	15	16	17	18	19	20
21	22	23	24	25	26	27
28	29	30				

OCTOBER

S	M	T	W	T	F	S
			1	2	3	4
5	6	7	8	9	10	11
12	13	14	15	16	17	18
19	20	21	22	23	24	25
26	27	28	29	30	31	

NOVEMBER

S	M	T	W	T	F	S
						1
2	3	4	5	6	7	8
9	10	11	12	13	14	15
16	17	18	19	20	21	22
23	24	25	26	27	28	29
30						

DECEMBER

S	M	T	W	T	F	S
	1	2	3	4	5	6
7	8	9	10	11	12	13
14	15	16	17	18	19	20
21	22	23	24	25	26	27
28	29	30	31			

11

JANUARY

S	M	T	W	T	F	S
			1	2	3	4
5	6	7	8	9	10	11
12	13	14	15	16	17	18
19	20	21	22	23	24	25
26	27	28	29	30	31	

FEBRUARY

S	M	T	W	T	F	S
						1
2	3	4	5	6	7	8
9	10	11	12	13	14	15
16	17	18	19	20	21	22
23	24	25	26	27	28	29

MARCH

S	M	T	W	T	F	S
1	2	3	4	5	6	7
8	9	10	11	12	13	14
15	16	17	18	19	20	21
22	23	24	25	26	27	28
29	30	31				

APRIL

S	M	T	W	T	F	S
			1	2	3	4
5	6	7	8	9	10	11
12	13	14	15	16	17	18
19	20	21	22	23	24	25
26	27	28	29	30		

MAY

S	M	T	W	T	F	S
					1	2
3	4	5	6	7	8	9
10	11	12	13	14	15	16
17	18	19	20	21	22	23
24	25	26	27	28	29	30
31						

JUNE

S	M	T	W	T	F	S
	1	2	3	4	5	6
7	8	9	10	11	12	13
14	15	16	17	18	19	20
21	22	23	24	25	26	27
28	29	30				

JULY

S	M	T	W	T	F	S
			1	2	3	4
5	6	7	8	9	10	11
12	13	14	15	16	17	18
19	20	21	22	23	24	25
26	27	28	29	30	31	

AUGUST

S	M	T	W	T	F	S
						1
2	3	4	5	6	7	8
9	10	11	12	13	14	15
16	17	18	19	20	21	22
23	24	25	26	27	28	29
30	31					

SEPTEMBER

S	M	T	W	T	F	S
		1	2	3	4	5
6	7	8	9	10	11	12
13	14	15	16	17	18	19
20	21	22	23	24	25	26
27	28	29	30			

OCTOBER

S	M	T	W	T	F	S
				1	2	3
4	5	6	7	8	9	10
11	12	13	14	15	16	17
18	19	20	21	22	23	24
25	26	27	28	29	30	31

NOVEMBER

S	M	T	W	T	F	S
1	2	3	4	5	6	7
8	9	10	11	12	13	14
15	16	17	18	19	20	21
22	23	24	25	26	27	28
29	30					

DECEMBER

S	M	T	W	T	F	S
		1	2	3	4	5
6	7	8	9	10	11	12
13	14	15	16	17	18	19
20	21	22	23	24	25	26
27	28	29	30	31		

12

JANUARY

S	M	T	W	T	F	S
				1	2	3
4	5	6	7	8	9	10
11	12	13	14	15	16	17
18	19	20	21	22	23	24
25	26	27	28	29	30	31

FEBRUARY

S	M	T	W	T	F	S
1	2	3	4	5	6	7
8	9	10	11	12	13	14
15	16	17	18	19	20	21
22	23	24	25	26	27	28
29						

MARCH

S	M	T	W	T	F	S
	1	2	3	4	5	6
7	8	9	10	11	12	13
14	15	16	17	18	19	20
21	22	23	24	25	26	27
28	29	30	31			

APRIL

S	M	T	W	T	F	S
				1	2	3
4	5	6	7	8	9	10
11	12	13	14	15	16	17
18	19	20	21	22	23	24
25	26	27	28	29	30	

MAY

S	M	T	W	T	F	S
						1
2	3	4	5	6	7	8
9	10	11	12	13	14	15
16	17	18	19	20	21	22
23	24	25	26	27	28	29
30	31					

JUNE

S	M	T	W	T	F	S
		1	2	3	4	5
6	7	8	9	10	11	12
13	14	15	16	17	18	19
20	21	22	23	24	25	26
27	28	29	30			

JULY

S	M	T	W	T	F	S
				1	2	3
4	5	6	7	8	9	10
11	12	13	14	15	16	17
18	19	20	21	22	23	24
25	26	27	28	29	30	31

AUGUST

S	M	T	W	T	F	S
1	2	3	4	5	6	7
8	9	10	11	12	13	14
15	16	17	18	19	20	21
22	23	24	25	26	27	28
29	30	31				

SEPTEMBER

S	M	T	W	T	F	S
			1	2	3	4
5	6	7	8	9	10	11
12	13	14	15	16	17	18
19	20	21	22	23	24	25
26	27	28	29	30		

OCTOBER

S	M	T	W	T	F	S
					1	2
3	4	5	6	7	8	9
10	11	12	13	14	15	16
17	18	19	20	21	22	23
24	25	26	27	28	29	30
31						

NOVEMBER

S	M	T	W	T	F	S
	1	2	3	4	5	6
7	8	9	10	11	12	13
14	15	16	17	18	19	20
21	22	23	24	25	26	27
28	29	30				

DECEMBER

S	M	T	W	T	F	S
			1	2	3	4
5	6	7	8	9	10	11
12	13	14	15	16	17	18
19	20	21	22	23	24	25
26	27	28	29	30	31	

13

JANUARY

S	M	T	W	T	F	S
					1	2
3	4	5	6	7	8	9
10	11	12	13	14	15	16
17	18	19	20	21	22	23
24	25	26	27	28	29	30
31						

FEBRUARY

S	M	T	W	T	F	S
	1	2	3	4	5	6
7	8	9	10	11	12	13
14	15	16	17	18	19	20
21	22	23	24	25	26	27
28	29					

MARCH

S	M	T	W	T	F	S
		1	2	3	4	5
6	7	8	9	10	11	12
13	14	15	16	17	18	19
20	21	22	23	24	25	26
27	28	29	30	31		

APRIL

S	M	T	W	T	F	S
					1	2
3	4	5	6	7	8	9
10	11	12	13	14	15	16
17	18	19	20	21	22	23
24	25	26	27	28	29	30

MAY

S	M	T	W	T	F	S
1	2	3	4	5	6	7
8	9	10	11	12	13	14
15	16	17	18	19	20	21
22	23	24	25	26	27	28
29	30	31				

JUNE

S	M	T	W	T	F	S
			1	2	3	4
5	6	7	8	9	10	11
12	13	14	15	16	17	18
19	20	21	22	23	24	25
26	27	28	29	30		

JULY

S	M	T	W	T	F	S
					1	2
3	4	5	6	7	8	9
10	11	12	13	14	15	16
17	18	19	20	21	22	23
24	25	26	27	28	29	30
31						

AUGUST

S	M	T	W	T	F	S
	1	2	3	4	5	6
7	8	9	10	11	12	13
14	15	16	17	18	19	20
21	22	23	24	25	26	27
28	29	30	31			

SEPTEMBER

S	M	T	W	T	F	S
				1	2	3
4	5	6	7	8	9	10
11	12	13	14	15	16	17
18	19	20	21	22	23	24
25	26	27	28	29	30	

OCTOBER

S	M	T	W	T	F	S
						1
2	3	4	5	6	7	8
9	10	11	12	13	14	15
16	17	18	19	20	21	22
23	24	25	26	27	28	29
30	31					

NOVEMBER

S	M	T	W	T	F	S
		1	2	3	4	5
6	7	8	9	10	11	12
13	14	15	16	17	18	19
20	21	22	23	24	25	26
27	28	29	30			

DECEMBER

S	M	T	W	T	F	S
				1	2	3
4	5	6	7	8	9	10
11	12	13	14	15	16	17
18	19	20	21	22	23	24
25	26	27	28	29	30	31

14

JANUARY

S	M	T	W	T	F	S
						1
2	3	4	5	6	7	8
9	10	11	12	13	14	15
16	17	18	19	20	21	22
23	24	25	26	27	28	29
30	31					

FEBRUARY

S	M	T	W	T	F	S
		1	2	3	4	5
6	7	8	9	10	11	12
13	14	15	16	17	18	19
20	21	22	23	24	25	26
27	28	29				

MARCH

S	M	T	W	T	F	S
			1	2	3	4
5	6	7	8	9	10	11
12	13	14	15	16	17	18
19	20	21	22	23	24	25
26	27	28	29	30	31	

APRIL

S	M	T	W	T	F	S
						1
2	3	4	5	6	7	8
9	10	11	12	13	14	15
16	17	18	19	20	21	22
23	24	25	26	27	28	29
30						

MAY

S	M	T	W	T	F	S
	1	2	3	4	5	6
7	8	9	10	11	12	13
14	15	16	17	18	19	20
21	22	23	24	25	26	27
28	29	30	31			

JUNE

S	M	T	W	T	F	S
				1	2	3
4	5	6	7	8	9	10
11	12	13	14	15	16	17
18	19	20	21	22	23	24
25	26	27	28	29	30	

JULY

S	M	T	W	T	F	S
						1
2	3	4	5	6	7	8
9	10	11	12	13	14	15
16	17	18	19	20	21	22
23	24	25	26	27	28	29
30	31					

AUGUST

S	M	T	W	T	F	S
		1	2	3	4	5
6	7	8	9	10	11	12
13	14	15	16	17	18	19
20	21	22	23	24	25	26
27	28	29	30	31		

SEPTEMBER

S	M	T	W	T	F	S
					1	2
3	4	5	6	7	8	9
10	11	12	13	14	15	16
17	18	19	20	21	22	23
24	25	26	27	28	29	30

OCTOBER

S	M	T	W	T	F	S
1	2	3	4	5	6	7
8	9	10	11	12	13	14
15	16	17	18	19	20	21
22	23	24	25	26	27	28
29	30	31				

NOVEMBER

S	M	T	W	T	F	S
			1	2	3	4
5	6	7	8	9	10	11
12	13	14	15	16	17	18
19	20	21	22	23	24	25
26	27	28	29	30		

DECEMBER

S	M	T	W	T	F	S
					1	2
3	4	5	6	7	8	9
10	11	12	13	14	15	16
17	18	19	20	21	22	23
24	25	26	27	28	29	30
31						

History of the Calendar

The purpose of the calendar is to reckon past or future time, to show how many days until a certain event takes place—the harvest or a religious festival—or how long since something important happened.

The earliest calendars must have been strongly influenced by the geographical location of the people who made them. In colder countries, the concept of the year was determined by the seasons, specifically by the end of winter. But in warmer countries, where the seasons are less pronounced, the Moon became the basic unit for time reckoning; an old Jewish book says that "the Moon was created for the counting of the days."

Most of the oldest calendars for which we have reliable information were lunar calendars, based on the time interval from one new moon to the next—a so-called lunation. But even in a warm climate there are annual events that pay no attention to the phases of the Moon. In some areas it was a rainy season; in Egypt it was the annual flooding of the Nile River. The calendar had to account for these yearly events as well.

The Egyptian Calendar

The ancient Egyptians used a calendar with 12 months of 30 days each, for a total of 360 days per year. About 4000 B.C. they added five extra days at the end of every year to bring it more into line with the solar year.[1] These five days became a festival because it was thought to be unlucky to work during that time.

The Egyptians had calculated that the solar year was actually closer to 365¼ days, but instead of having a single leap day every four years to account for the fractional day (the way we do now), they let the one-quarter day accumulate. After 1,460 years, or four periods of 365 years, they added an entire leap year of 365 days. This means that as the years passed, the Egyptian months fell out of sync with the seasons, so that the summer months eventually fell during winter. Only once every 1,460 years did their calendar year coincide precisely with the solar year.

In addition to the civic calendar, the Egyptians also had a religious calendar that was based on the 29½-day lunar cycle and was more closely linked with agricultural cycles and the movements of the stars.

Lunar Calendars

During antiquity the lunar calendar that best approximated a solar-year calendar was based on a 19-year period, with 7 of these 19 years having 13 months. In all, the period contained 235 months. Still using the lunation value of 29½ days, this made a total of 6,932½ days, while 19 solar years added up to 6,939.7 days, a difference of just one week per period and about five weeks per century.

Even the 19-year period required adjustment, but it became the basis of the calendars of the ancient Chinese, Babylonians, Greeks, and Jews. This same calendar was also used by the Arabs, but Muhammad later forbade shifting from 12 months to 13 months, so that the Islamic calendar, even today, has a lunar year of 354 days. As a result, the months of the Islamic calendar, as well as the Islamic religious festivals, migrate through all the seasons of the year.

The Roman Calendar

When Rome emerged as a world power, the difficulties of making a calendar were well known, but the Romans complicated their lives because of their superstition that even numbers were unlucky. Hence their months were 29 or 31 days long, with the exception of February, which had 28 days. However, four months of 31 days, seven months of 29 days, and one month of 28 days added up to only 355 days. Therefore the Romans invented an extra month called Mercedonius of 22 or 23 days. It was added every second year.

Even with Mercedonius, the Roman calendar eventually became so far off that **Julius Caesar,** advised by the astronomer Sosigenes, ordered a sweeping reform in 45 B.C. One year, made 445 days long by imperial decree, brought the calendar back in step with the seasons. Then the solar year (with the value of 365 days and 6 hours) was made the basis of the calendar. The months were 30 or 31 days in length, and to take care of the 6 hours, every fourth year was made a 366-day year. Moreover, Caesar decreed the year began with the first of January, not with the vernal equinox in late March.

This calendar was named the **Julian calendar,** after Julius Caesar, and it continues to be the calendar of the Eastern Orthodox churches to this day. However, despite the correction, the Julian calendar is still 11½ minutes longer than the actual solar year, and after a number of centuries, even 11½ minutes adds up.

The Gregorian Reform

By the 15th century the Julian calendar had drifted behind the solar calendar by about a week, so that the vernal equinox was falling around March 12 instead of around March 20. Pope Sixtus IV (who reigned from 1471 to 1484) decided that another reform was needed and called the German astronomer Regiomontanus to Rome to advise him. Regiomontanus arrived in 1475, but unfortunately he died shortly afterward, and the pope's plans for reform died with him.

Then in 1545, the Council of Trent authorized Pope Paul III to reform the calendar once more. Most of the mathematical and astronomical work was done by Father Christopher Clavius, S.J. The immediate correction, advised by Father Clavius and ordered by Pope Gregory XIII, was that Thursday, Oct. 4, 1582, was to be the last day of the Julian calendar. The next day would be Friday, Oct. 15. For long-range accuracy, a formula suggested by the Vatican librarian Aloysius Giglio was adopted: every fourth year is a leap year *unless* it is a century year like 1700 or 1800. Century years can be leap years *only* when they are divisible by 400 (e.g., 1600 and 2000). This rule eliminates three leap years in four centuries, making the calendar sufficiently accurate.

For in spite of the revised leap year rule, an average calendar year is still about 26 seconds longer

---

1. The correct figures are lunation: 29 d, 12 h, 44 min, 2.8 sec (29.530585 d); solar year: 365 d, 5 h, 48 min, 46 sec (365.242216 d); 12 lunations: 354 d, 8 h, 48 min, 34 sec (354.3671 d).

Drift of the Vernal Equinox in the Julian Calendar

Date of equinox	Julian year	Date of equinox	Julian year	Date of equinox	Julian year	Date of equinox	Julian year
March 21	A.D. 325	March 18	A.D. 709	March 15	A.D. 1093	March 12	A.D. 1477
March 20	A.D. 453	March 17	A.D. 837	March 14	A.D. 1221	March 11	A.D. 1605
March 19	A.D. 581	March 16	A.D. 965	March 13	A.D. 1349		

than the Earth's orbital period. But this discrepancy will need 3,323 years to build up to a single day.

Reform Adopted Gradually

The Gregorian reform was not adopted throughout the West immediately. All the Protestant princes in 1582 chose to ignore the papal bull; they continued with the Julian calendar. It was not until 1698 that the German professor Erhard Weigel persuaded the Protestant rulers of Germany and the Netherlands to change to the new calendar. In England the shift took place in 1752, and in Russia it needed the revolution to introduce the Gregorian calendar in 1918. Greece switched over in 1923.

A Better Calendar?

Despite its widespread use, the Gregorian calendar has a number of weaknesses. It cannot be divided into equal halves or quarters; the number of days per month is haphazard; and month and years may begin on any day of the week. Holidays pegged to specific dates may also fall on any day of the week, and few Americans can predict when Thanksgiving will occur next year.

Since Gregory XIII, many other proposals for calendar reform have been made, but none has been permanently adopted. In the meantime, the Gregorian calendar keeps the calendar dates in reasonable unison with astronomical events. □

Time and Calendar

The two natural cycles on which time measurements are based are the year and the day. The year is defined as the time required for Earth to complete one revolution around the Sun, while the day is the time required for Earth to complete one turn upon its axis. Unfortunately Earth needs 365 days plus about six hours to go around the Sun once, so that the year does not consist of so and so many days; the fractional day has to be taken care of by an extra day every fourth year.

But because Earth, while turning upon its axis, also moves around the Sun, there are two kinds of days. A day may be defined as the interval between the highest point of the Sun in the sky on two successive days. This, averaged out over the year, produces the customary 24-hour day. But one might also define a day as the time interval between the moments when a certain point in the sky, say a conveniently located star, is directly overhead. This is called:

Sidereal time. A sidereal day is the time that it takes the Earth to complete one rotation on its axis so that a particular star can be observed twice at the meridian that runs directly overhead. Because the Earth is moving around the Sun as it rotates on its axis, the sidereal day is about four minutes shorter than the solar day, being equivalent to 23 hours, 56 minutes, and 4 seconds in mean solar time. As a result, a star will appear to rise about four minutes

earlier every night, and different stars will be visible at different times of the year. Astronomers use a point that they call the "vernal equinox" to determine local sidereal time.

Apparent solar time is the time based directly on the Sun's position in the sky. In ordinary life the day runs from midnight to midnight. It begins when the Sun is invisible by being 12 hours from its zenith.

Mean solar time, rather than apparent solar time, is the basis for local civil and standard time. The mean solar time is based on the position of a fictitious "mean sun." The reason why this fictitious sun has to be introduced is the following: Earth turns on its axis regularly; it needs the same number of seconds regardless of the season. But the movement of Earth around the Sun is not regular because Earth's orbit is an ellipse. This has the result (as explained in the section on the seasons below) that Earth moves faster in January and slower in July. Though it is Earth that changes velocity, it looks to us as if the Sun does. In January, when Earth moves faster, the *apparent* movement of the Sun looks faster. The mean sun of time measurements, then, is a sun that moves regularly all year round; the real Sun will be either ahead of or behind the mean sun. The difference between the real Sun and the fictitious mean sun is called the *equation of time.*

Time zones. But if all clocks were actually set by mean solar time we would be plagued by a welter of time differences that would be "correct" but a major nuisance. A clock on Long Island, correctly showing mean solar time for its location (this would be *local civil time*), would be slightly ahead of a clock in Newark, N.J. The Newark clock would be slightly ahead of a clock in Trenton, N.J., which, in turn, would be ahead of a clock in Philadelphia. This condition prevailed until 1884, when a system of standard time was adopted by the International Meridian Conference. Earth's surface was divided into 24 zones. The standard time of each zone is the mean astronomical time of one of 24 meridians, 15 degrees apart, beginning at the Greenwich, England, meridian and extending east and west around the globe to the International Date Line. (This system was actually put into use a year earlier by the railroad companies of the U.S. and Canada who, until then, had to contend with some 100 conflicting local sun times observed in terminals across the land.)

For practical purposes, this convention is sometimes altered. For example, Alaska, for a time, consisted of four of the eight U.S. time zones: the Pacific standard time zone (east of Juneau) and the 6th (Juneau), 7th (Anchorage), and 8th (Nome) zones, encompassing the 135°, 150°, and 165° meridians, respectively. In 1983, by act of Congress, the entire state (except the westernmost Aleutians) was united into the 6th zone, Alaska standard time.

The Names of the Months

January: named after Janus, the god of doors and gates

February: named after Februalia, a time period when sacrifices were made to atone for sins

March: named after Mars, the god of war

April: from *aperire*, Latin for "to open" (buds)

May: named after Maia, the goddess of growth of plants

June: from *junius*, Latin for the goddess Juno

July: named after Julius Caesar in 44 B.C.

August: named after Augustus Caesar in 8 B.C.

September: from *septem*, Latin for "seven"

October: from *octo*, Latin for "eight"

November: from *novem*, Latin for "nine"

December: from *decem*, Latin for "ten"

NOTE: The earliest Latin calendar was a 10-month one, beginning with March; thus, September was the seventh month, October, the eighth, etc. July was originally called Quintilis, meaning fifth; August was originally called Sextilis, meaning sixth.

The Names of the Days of the Week

Latin	Old English	English	German	French	Italian	Spanish
Dies Solis	Sunnandaeg	Sunday	Sonntag	dimanche	domenica	domingo
Dies Lunae	Monandaeg	Monday	Montag	lundi	lunedì	lunes
Dies Martis	Tiwesdaeg	Tuesday	Dienstag	mardi	martedì	martes
Dies Mercurii	Wodnesdaeg	Wednesday	Mittwoch	mercredi	mercoledì	miércoles
Dies Jovis	Thunresdaeg	Thursday	Donnerstag	jeudi	giovedì	jueves
Dies Veneris	Frigedaeg	Friday	Freitag	vendredi	venerdì	viernes
Dies Saturni	Saeternesdaeg	Saturday	Samstag	samedi	sabato	sábado

NOTE: The seven-day week originated in ancient Mesopotamia and became part of the Roman calendar in A.D. 321. The names of the days are based on the seven celestial bodies (the Sun, the Moon, Mars, Mercury, Jupiter, Venus, and Saturn), believed at that time to revolve around Earth and influence its events. Most of Western Europe adopted the Roman nomenclature. The Germanic languages substituted Germanic equivalents for the names of four of the Roman gods: Tiw, the god of war, replaced Mars; Woden, the god of wisdom, replaced Mercury; Thor, the god of thunder, replaced Jupiter; and Frigg, the goddess of love, replaced Venus.

The eight U.S. standard time zones are: Atlantic (includes Puerto Rico and the Virgin Islands), eastern, central, mountain, Pacific, Alaska, Hawaii-Aleutian (includes all of Hawaii and those Aleutians west of the Fox Islands), and Samoa standard time.

The Date Line. While the time zones are based on the natural event of the Sun crossing a meridian, the date must be an arbitrary decision. The meridians are traditionally counted from the meridian of the observatory of Greenwich, in England, which is called the zero meridian. The logical place for changing the date is 12 hours, or 180°, from Greenwich. Fortunately, the 180th meridian runs mostly through the open Pacific. The Date Line makes a zigzag in the north to incorporate the eastern tip of Siberia into the Siberian time system and then another one to incorporate a number of islands into the Hawaii-Aleutian time zone. In the south there is a similar zigzag for the purpose of tying a number of British-owned islands to the New Zealand time system. Otherwise, the Date Line is the same as 180° from Greenwich. At points to the east of the Date Line the calendar is one day earlier than at points to the west of it. A traveler going eastward across the Date Line from one island to another would not have to reset his watch because he would stay inside the time zone (provided he does so where the Date Line does *not* coincide with the 180° meridian), but it would be the same time of the *previous* day.

The Seasons

The seasons are caused by the tilt of Earth's axis (23.4°) and not by the fact that Earth's orbit around the Sun is an ellipse. The average distance of Earth from the Sun is 93 million miles; the difference between aphelion (farthest away from the Sun) and perihelion (closest to the Sun) is 3 million miles, so that perihelion is about 91.4 million miles from the Sun. Earth goes through the perihelion point a few days after New Year's Day, just when the Northern Hemisphere has winter. Aphelion is passed during the first days of July. This by itself shows that the distance from the Sun is not important within these limits. What is important is that when Earth passes through perihelion, the northern end of Earth's axis happens to tilt away from the Sun, so that the areas beyond the Tropic of Cancer receive only slanting rays from a Sun low in the sky.

The tilt of Earth's axis is responsible for four lines you find on every globe. When, say, the North Pole is tilted away from the Sun as much as possible, the farthest points in the North which can still be reached by the Sun's rays are 23.5° from the pole. This is the Arctic Circle. The Antarctic Circle is the corresponding limit 23.4° from the South Pole; the Sun's rays cannot reach beyond this point when we have midsummer in the North.

When the Sun is vertically above the equator, the day is of equal length all over Earth. This happens twice a year, and these are the "equinoxes" in March and in September. After having been over the equator in March, the Sun will seem to move northward. The northernmost point where the Sun can be straight overhead is 23.4° north of the equator. This is the Tropic of Cancer; the Sun can never be vertically overhead to the north of this line. Similarly the Sun cannot be vertically overhead to the south of a line 23.4° south of the equator—the Tropic of Capricorn.

This explains the climatic zones. In the belt (the Greek word *zone* means "belt") between the Tropic of Cancer and the Tropic of Capricorn, the Sun can be straight overhead; this is the tropical zone. The two zones where the Sun cannot be overhead but will be above the horizon every day of the year are the two temperate zones; the two areas where the Sun will not rise at all for varying lengths of time are the two polar areas, Arctic and Antarctic. □

The Islamic (Hijri) Calendar

The Islamic calendar is based on the lunar year of 354 days. The number of days each month is adjusted according to the lunar cycle, beginning about two days after the new moon. The months drift backward over the seasons, beginning again on the same day every 32½ years. The Islamic year begins on the first day of Muharram, and is counted from the year of the Hegira (*anno Hegirae*)—the year in which Muhammad emigrated from Mecca to Medina (A.D. 622). The year 2002 translates to A.H. 1422–1423.

Months	Number of days	Months	Number of days	Months	Number of days	Months	Number of days
Muharram	29 or 30	Rabi II	29 or 30	Rajab	29 or 30	Shawwal	29 or 30
Safar	29 or 30	Jumada I	29 or 30	Sha'ban	29 or 30	Dhu'l-Qa'dah	29 or 30
Rabi I	29 or 30	Jumada II	29 or 30	Ramadan	29 or 30	Dhu'l-Hijjah	29 or 30

The Jewish Calendar

The Jewish calendar is based on both solar and lunar years. The average lunar year of 354 days is adjusted to the solar year by the addition of a leap year and an intercalary month. Nisan is considered the first month, although the new year begins with Rosh Hashanah, on the first of Tishri, which is in fact the seventh month—the calendar has different starting points for different purposes. The year 2002 translates to the Jewish year 5762–5763.

Months	Number of days	Months	Number of days	Months	Number of days
Nisan (March–April)*	30	Tishri (Sept.–Oct.)	30	Shevat (Jan.–Feb.)	30
Iyar (April–May)	29	Heshvan (Oct.–Nov.)	29	Adar (Feb.–March)	29
Sivan (May–June)	30	in some years	30	in some years	30
Tammuz (June–July)	29	Kislev (Nov.–Dec.)	29	Adar Sheni	29
Av (July–Aug.)	30	in some years	30	(intercalary month	
Elul (Aug.–Sept.)	29	Tevet (Dec.–Jan.)	29	in leap year only)	

*The months correspond approximately to those of the Gregorian calendar.

The Hindu (Indian National) Calendar

The Indian National Calendar, often called the "Hindu Calendar," is based on both lunar and solar years. This calendar was introduced in 1957 in a government push for all of India to use the same calendar, but various traditional calendars are also used. The start of the Indian National Calendar year coincides with March 22, except in a leap year, when it coincides with March 21. The year is counted from the first year of the Saka era, in A.D. 78. The year 2002 translates to Saka era 1923–1924.

Month	Number of Days	Month	Number of Days	Month	Number of Days	Month	Number of Days
Caitra	30*	Asadha	31	Asvina	30	Pausa	30
Vaisakha	31	Sravana	31	Kartika	30	Magha	30
Jyaistha	31	Bhadra	31	Agrahayana	30	Phalguna	30

* In a leap year Caitra has 31 days.

The Chinese Calendar

The Chinese lunar year is divided into 12 months of 29 or 30 days. The calendar is adjusted to the length of the solar year by the addition of extra months at regular intervals. The years are arranged in major cycles of 60 years. Each successive year is named after one of 12 animals. These 12-year cycles are continuously repeated. The Chinese New Year is celebrated at the second new moon after the winter solstice and falls between January 21 and February 19 on the Gregorian calendar. The year 2002 translates to the Chinese year 4699–4700.

Rat	Ox	Tiger	Cat (Rabbit)	Dragon	Snake	Horse	Sheep (Goat)	Monkey	Rooster	Dog	Pig
1900	1901	1902	1903	1904	1905	1906	1907	1908	1909	1910	1911
1912	1913	1914	1915	1916	1917	1918	1919	1920	1921	1922	1923
1924	1925	1926	1927	1928	1929	1930	1931	1932	1933	1934	1935
1936	1937	1938	1939	1940	1941	1942	1943	1944	1945	1946	1947
1948	1949	1950	1951	1952	1953	1954	1955	1956	1957	1958	1959
1960	1961	1962	1963	1964	1965	1966	1967	1968	1969	1970	1971
1972	1973	1974	1975	1976	1977	1978	1979	1980	1981	1982	1983
1984	1985	1986	1987	1988	1989	1990	1991	1992	1993	1994	1995
1996	1997	1998	1999	2000	2001	2002	2003	2004	2005	2006	2007

Holidays

Religious and Secular, 2002

In the United States, there are 10 federal holidays set by law. Four are set by date (New Year's Day, Independence Day, Veterans Day, and Christmas Day). The other six are set by a day of the week and month: Martin Luther King, Jr.'s Birthday, Washington's Birthday, Memorial Day, Labor Day, Columbus Day, and Thanksgiving. All but the last are celebrated on Mondays to create three-day weekends for federal employees. All Jewish and Islamic holidays begin at sundown the day before they are listed here.

New Year's Day, Tues., Jan. 1. A federal holiday in the United States, New Year's Day has its origin in Roman times, when sacrifices were offered to Janus, the two-faced Roman deity who looked back on the past and forward to the future.

Epiphany (from Greek *epiphaneia,* "manifestation"), Sun., Jan. 6. Falls on the 12th day after Christmas and commemorates the manifestation of Jesus Christ to the Gentiles, as represented by the Magi, the baptism of Jesus, and the miracle of the wine at the marriage feast at Cana. One of the three major Christian festivals, along with Christmas and Easter. Epiphany originally marked the beginning of the carnival season preceding Lent, and the evening preceding it is known as Twelfth Night.

Martin Luther King, Jr.'s Birthday, Mon., Jan. 21. (The actual date of his birthday is Jan. 15.) A federal holiday observed on the third Monday in January that honors the late civil rights leader. It became a federal holiday in 1986. In 1999, New Hampshire became the last state to officially honor the holiday.

Groundhog Day, Sat., Feb. 2. Legend has it that if the groundhog sees his shadow, he'll return to his hole, and winter will last another six weeks.

Lincoln's Birthday, Tues., Feb. 12. A holiday in many states, this day was first formally observed in Washington, DC, in 1866, when both houses of Congress gathered for a memorial address in tribute to the assassinated president.

Shrove Tuesday, Feb. 12. Falls the day before Ash Wednesday and marks the end of the carnival season, which once began on Epiphany but is now usually celebrated the last three days before Lent. In France, the day is known as Mardi Gras (Fat Tuesday), and Mardi Gras celebrations are also held in several American cities, particularly in New Orleans. The day is sometimes called Pancake Tuesday by the English because fats, which were prohibited during Lent, had to be used up.

Ash Wednesday, Feb. 13. The seventh Wednesday before Easter and the first day of Lent, which lasts 40 days. Having its origin sometime before A.D. 1000, it is a day of public penance and is marked in the Roman Catholic Church by the burning of the palms blessed on the previous year's Palm Sunday. With the ashes from the palms the priest then marks a cross with his thumb upon the forehead of each worshipper. The Anglican Church and a few Protestant groups in the United States also observe the day, but generally without the use of ashes.

St. Valentine's Day, Thurs., Feb. 14. This day is the festival of two third-century martyrs, both named St. Valentine. It is not known why this day is associated with lovers. It may derive from an old pagan festival, or it may have been inspired by the belief that birds mate on this day.

Washington's Birthday, Mon., Feb. 18. (The actual date of his birthday is Feb. 22.) A federal holiday observed the third Monday in February. It is a common misperception that the federal holiday was changed to "Presidents' Day" and now celebrates both Washington and Lincoln. Only Washington is commemorated by the federal holiday; 12 states, however, officially celebrate "Presidents' Day."

Eid al-Adha, Sat., Feb. 23. Eid al-Adha, or the Feast of Sacrifice, commemorates Abraham's willingness to obey God by sacrificing his son. Lasting for three days, it concludes the annual Hajj, or pilgrimage to Mecca. Muslims worldwide sacrifice a lamb or other animal and distribute the meat to relatives or the needy.

Purim (Feast of Lots), Tues., Feb. 26. A day of joy and feasting celebrating the deliverance of the Jews from a massacre planned by the Persian minister Haman. According to the Book of Esther, the Jewish queen Esther interceded with her husband, King Ahasuerus, to spare the life of her uncle, Mordecai, and Haman was hanged on the same gallows he had built for Mordecai. The holiday is marked by the reading of the Book of Esther (The Megillah), and by the exchange of gifts, donations to the poor, and the presentation of Purim plays.

First Day of Muharram, Fri., March 15. The month of Muharram marks the beginning of the Islamic liturgical year. On the tenth day of the month, many Muslims may observe a day of fasting, known as Ashurah.

St. Patrick's Day, Sun., March 17. St. Patrick, patron saint of Ireland, has been honored in America since the first days of the nation. Perhaps the most notable part of the observance is the annual St. Patrick's Day parade in New York City.

Palm Sunday, March 24. Observed the Sunday before Easter to commemorate the entry of Jesus into Jerusalem. The procession and the ceremonies introducing the benediction of palms probably had their origins in Jerusalem.

First Day of Passover (Pesach), Thurs., March 28. The Feast of the Passover, also called the Feast of Unleavened Bread, commemorates the escape of the Jews from Egypt. As the Jews fled, they ate unleavened bread, and from that time the Jews have allowed no leavening in their houses during Passover, bread being replaced by matzoh.

Good Friday, March 29. The Friday before Easter, it commemorates the Crucifixion, which is retold during services from the Gospel according to St. John. A feature in Roman Catholic churches is the Liturgy of the Passion; there is no Consecration, the Host having been consecrated the previous day. The eating of hot-cross buns on this day is said to have started in England.

Easter Sunday, March 31. Observed in all Western Christian churches, Easter commemorates the Resurrection of Jesus. It is celebrated on the first Sunday after the full moon that occurs on or next after the vernal equinox (fixed at March 21) and is therefore celebrated between March 22 and April 25 inclusive. This date was fixed by the Council of Nicaea in A.D. 325.

Orthodox Easter (Pascha), Sun., May 5. The Orthodox church uses the same formula to calculate Easter as the Western church, but bases it on the traditional Julian calendar instead of the more contemporary Gregorian calendar. For this reason Orthodox Easter generally falls on a different date than the Western Christian Easter.

Ascension Day, Thurs., May 9. The Ascension of Jesus took place in the presence of His apostles 40 days after the Resurrection. It is traditionally thought to have occurred on Mount Olivet in Bethany.

Mother's Day, Sun., May 12. Observed the second Sunday in May, as proposed by Anna Jarvis of Philadelphia in 1907. West Virginia was the first state to recognize the holiday in 1910, and President Woodrow Wilson officially proclaimed Mother's Day a national holiday in 1914.

First Day of Shavuot (Hebrew Pentecost), Fri., May 17. This festival, sometimes called the Feast of Weeks, or of Harvest, or of the First Fruits, falls 50 days after Passover and originally celebrated the end of the seven-week grain-harvesting season. In later tradition, it also celebrated the giving of the Law to Moses on Mount Sinai.

Pentecost (Whitsunday), May 19. This day commemorates the descent of the Holy Ghost upon the apostles 50 days after the Resurrection. The sermon by the apostle Peter, which led to the baptism of 3,000 who professed belief, originated the ceremonies that have since been followed. "Whitsunday" is believed to have come from "white Sunday" when, among the English, white robes were worn by those baptized on the day.

Mawlid an-Nabi, Fri., May 24. This holiday celebrates the birthday of Muhammad, the founder of Islam. It is fixed as the 12th day of the month of Rabi I in the Islamic calendar.

Memorial Day, Mon., May 27. Memorial Day became a federal holiday in 1971 that is observed on the last Monday in May. It originated in 1868, when Union general John A. Logan designated a day in which the graves of Civil War soldiers would be decorated. Originally known as Decoration Day, the holiday was changed to Memorial Day within twenty years, becoming a holiday dedicated to the memory of all war dead.

Flag Day, Fri., June 14. This day commemorates the adoption by the Continental Congress on June 14, 1777, of the Stars and Stripes as the U.S. flag. Although it is a legal holiday only in Pennsylvania, President Truman, on Aug. 3, 1949, signed a bill requesting the president to call for its observance each year by proclamation.

Father's Day, Sun., June 16. Observed the third Sunday in June. The exact origin of the holiday is not clear, but it was first celebrated June 19, 1910, in Spokane, Wash. In 1966 President Lyndon Johnson signed a proclamation making Father's Day official.

Independence Day, Thurs., July 4. The day of the adoption of the Declaration of Independence in 1776, celebrated in all states and territories. The observance began the next year in Philadelphia.

Labor Day, Mon., Sept. 2. A federal holiday observed the first Monday in September. Labor Day was first celebrated in New York in 1882 under the sponsorship of the Central Labor Union, following the suggestion of Peter J. McGuire, of the Knights of Labor, that the day be set aside in honor of labor.

First Day of Rosh Hashanah (Jewish New Year), Sat., Sept. 7. This day marks the beginning of the Jewish year 5763 and opens the Ten Days of Penitence, which close with Yom Kippur.

Yom Kippur (Day of Atonement), Mon., Sept. 16. This day marks the end of the Ten Days of Penitence that began with Rosh Hashanah. It is described in Leviticus as a "Sabbath of rest," and synagogue services begin the preceding sundown, resume the following morning, and continue to sundown.

First Day of Sukkot (Feast of Tabernacles), Sat., Sept. 21. This festival, also known as the Feast of the Ingathering, originally celebrated the harvest. The name of the festival comes from the booths or tabernacles in which the Jews lived during the harvest, although one tradition traces it to the shelters used by the Jews in their wandering through the wilderness. During the festival many Jews build small huts in their backyards or on the roofs of their houses.

Simchat Torah (Rejoicing of the Law), Sun., Sept. 29. This joyous holiday falls on the eighth day of Sukkot. It marks the end of the year's reading of the Torah (Five Books of Moses) in the synagogue every Saturday and the beginning of the new cycle of reading.

Columbus Day, Mon., Oct. 14. A federal holiday, observed the second Monday in October, it commemorates Christopher Columbus's landing in the New World in 1492. Quite likely the first celebration of Columbus Day was that organized in 1792 by the Society of St. Tammany, or the Columbian Order, widely known as Tammany Hall.

Halloween, Thurs., Oct. 31. Eve of All Saints' Day, formerly called All Hallows and Hallowmass. Halloween is traditionally associated in some countries with customs such as bonfires, masquerading, and the telling of ghost stories. These are old Celtic practices marking the beginning of winter.

All Saints' Day, Fri., Nov. 1. A Roman Catholic and Anglican holiday celebrating all saints, known and unknown.

Election Day (legal holiday in certain states), Tues., Nov. 5. Since 1845, by act of Congress, the first Tuesday after the first Monday in November is the date for choosing presidential electors. State elections are also generally held on this day.

First Day of Ramadan, Wed., Nov. 6. This day marks the beginning of a monthlong fast that all Muslims must keep during the daylight hours. It commemorates the first revelation of the Qur'an. Following the last day of Ramadan, **Eid al-Fitr** is celebrated on Fri., Dec. 6.

Veterans Day, Mon., Nov. 11. Armistice Day, a federal holiday, was established in 1926 to commemorate the signing in 1918 of the armistice ending World War I. On June 1, 1954, the name was changed to Veterans Day to honor all men and women who have served America in its armed forces.

Thanksgiving, Thurs., Nov. 28. A federal holiday observed the fourth Thursday in November by act of Congress (1941), it was the first such national proclamation, issued by President Lincoln in 1863 on the urging of Mrs. Sarah J. Hale, editor of *Godey's Lady's Book.* Most Americans believe that the holiday dates back to the day of thanks ordered by Governor Bradford of Plymouth Colony in New England in 1621, but scholars point out that days of thanks stem from ancient times.

First Day of Hanukkah (Festival of Lights), Sat., Nov. 30. This festival was instituted by Judas Maccabaeus in 165 B.C. to celebrate the purification of the Temple of Jerusalem, which had been desecrated three years earlier by Antiochus Epiphanes, who set up a pagan altar and offered sacrifices to Zeus Olympius. In Jewish homes, a light is lighted on each night of the eight-day festival.

First Sunday of Advent, Dec. 1. Advent is the season in which the faithful must prepare themselves for the coming, or advent, of the Savior on Christmas. The four Sundays before Christmas are marked by special church services.

Christmas (Feast of the Nativity), Wed., Dec. 25. The most widely celebrated holiday of the Christian year, Christmas is observed as the anniversary of the birth of Jesus. Christmas customs are centuries old. The mistletoe, for example, comes from the Druids, who, in hanging the mistletoe, hoped for peace and good fortune. Comparatively recent is the Christmas tree, first set up in Germany in the 17th century. Colonial Manhattan Islanders introduced the name Santa Claus, a corruption of the Dutch name St. Nicholas, who lived in fourth-century Asia Minor.

Christian and Secular Holidays, 2001–2003

Year	Ash Wednesday	Easter	Pentecost	Labor Day	Election Day	Thanksgiving	1st Sun. Advent
2001	Feb. 28	April 15	June 3	Sept. 3	Nov. 6	Nov. 22	Dec. 2
2002	Feb. 13	March 31	May 19	Sept. 2	Nov. 5	Nov. 28	Dec. 1
2003	March 5	April 20	June 8	Sept. 1	Nov. 4	Nov. 27	Nov. 30

Shrove Tuesday: 1 day before Ash Wednesday. Palm Sunday: 7 days before Easter. Maundy Thursday: 3 days before Easter. Good Friday: 2 days before Easter. Holy Saturday: 1 day before Easter. Ascension Day: 10 days before Pentecost. Trinity Sunday: 7 days after Pentecost. Corpus Christi: 11 days after Pentecost.

Orthodox Holidays, 2001–2004

Year	Great Lent Begins	Pascha (Easter)	Ascension	Pentecost	Year	Great Lent Begins	Pascha (Easter)	Ascension	Pentecost
2001	Feb. 26	April 15	May 24	June 3	2003	March 10	April 27	June 5	June 15
2002	March 18	May 5	June 13	June 23	2004	Feb. 23	April 11	May 20	May 30

Jewish Holidays, 2001–2003

Year	Purim[1]	1st day Passover[2]	1st day Shavuot[3]	1st day Rosh Hashanah[4]	Yom Kippur[5]	1st day Sukkot[6]	Simchat Torah[7]	1st day Hanukkah[8]
2001	March 9	April 8	May 28	Sept. 18	Sept. 27	Oct. 2	Oct. 10	Dec. 10
2002	Feb. 26	March 28	May 17	Sept. 7	Sept. 16	Sept. 21	Sept. 29	Nov. 30
2003	March 18	April 17	June 6	Sept. 27	Oct. 6	Oct. 11	Oct. 19	Dec. 20

1. Feast of Lots. 2. Feast of Unleavened Bread. 3. Hebrew Pentecost; or Feast of Weeks, or of Harvest, or of First Fruits. 4. Jewish New Year. 5. Day of Atonement. 6. Feast of Tabernacles, or of the Ingathering. 7. Rejoicing of the Law. In Israel, Simchat Torah is celebrated on the day before the date given. 8. Festival of Lights.

Length of Jewish holidays (O=Orthodox, C=Conservative, R=Reform): Passover: O & C, 8 days (holy days: first 2 and last 2); R, 7 days (holy days: first and last). Shavuot: O & C, 2 days; R, 1 day. Rosh Hashanah: O & C, 2 days; R, 1 day. Yom Kippur: All groups, 1 day. Sukkot: All groups, 7 days (holy days: O & C, first 2; R, first only); O & C observe 2 additional days: Shemini Atseret (Eighth Day of the Feast) and Simchat Torah; R observes Shemini Atseret but not Simchat Torah. Hanukkah: All groups, 8 days. NOTE: All holidays begin at sundown on the evening before the date given.

Islamic Holidays, 2000–2004 (A.H. 1421–1424)

In the Year of the Hegira	Muharram (Islamic New Year)	Mawlid al-Nabi (Muhammad's Birthday)	Ramadan begins	Eid al-Fitr (Ramadan ends)	Eid al-Adha (Festival of Sacrifice)
A.H. 1421	April 6, 2000	June 15, 2000	Nov. 28, 2000	Dec. 27, 2000	March 6, 2001
A.H. 1422	March 26, 2001	June 4, 2001	Nov. 17, 2001	Dec. 17, 2001	Feb. 23, 2002
A.H. 1423	March 15, 2002	May 24, 2002	Nov. 6, 2002	Dec. 6, 2002	Feb. 12, 2003
A.H. 1424	March 5, 2003	May 14, 2003	Oct. 27, 2003	Nov. 26, 2003	Feb. 2, 2004

NOTE: All holidays begin at sundown on the evening before the date given. Islamic holidays are based on the lunar calendar and thus may vary by one or two days. Dates apply to North America.

Hindu Festival Dates, 2002

Source: Indian Calendars for the 21st Century, by Pal Singh Purewall

Jan. 14	Makar Sankranti	Aug. 22	Raksha Bandhan
Feb. 17	Vasant Panchami	Aug. 30	Sri Krishna Jayanti
March 12	Maha Shivaratri Vrat (fast)	Sept. 9	Ganesh Chaturathi
March 28	Holi (last day)	Sept. 21	Saradhas begin
April 13	Bikrami Samvat (2059 begins)	Oct. 7	Asuj Navratras begin
April 13	Chetra Navratras begin	Oct. 15	Dassehra
April 13	Vaisakhi (solar new year)	Oct. 25	Karva Chauth Vrat (fast)
April 21	Rama Navmi	Nov. 4	Diwali (Festival of Lights)

Sikh Festival Dates, 2002*

Source: Indian Calendars for the 21st Century, by Pal Singh Purewall

Festival	Nanakshahi (Sikh)	Bikrami (Hindu)	Festival	Nanakshahi (Sikh)	Bikrami (Hindu)
Birthday of Guru Gobind Singh Sahib	Jan. 5	Jan. 21	Installation of Holy Scriptures as Guru Granth Sahib	Oct. 20	Nov. 6
Maghi	Jan. 13	Jan. 14	Bandi Chhor Divas (Diwali)	Nov. 4	Nov. 4
Hola Mohalla	March 29	March 29	Birthday of Guru Nanak Dev Sahib	Nov. 19	Nov. 19
Nanakshahi Era 534 begins	March 14	—			
Vaisakhi	April 14	April 13	Martyrdom of Guru Tegh Bahadur Sahib	Nov. 24	Dec. 8
Martyrdom of Guru Arjan Dev Sahib	June 16	June 14			
First Parkash Guru Granth Sahib	Sept. 1	Sept. 7			

*The dates for the Sikh festivals are given according to both the Bikrami (Hindu) calendar, which is based on the sidereal year, and the reformed Nanakshahi (Sikh) calendar, which is based on the tropical year. All Bikrami dates are moveable.
NOTE: Dates for Sikh and Hindu holidays are determined according to the date of their observance in India.

Chinese New Year

2000	Feb. 5	**2003**	Feb. 1	**2006**	Jan. 29	**2009**	Jan. 26
2001	Jan. 24	**2004**	Jan. 22	**2007**	Feb. 18	**2010**	Feb. 14
2002	Feb. 12	**2005**	Feb. 9	**2008**	Feb. 7	**2011**	Feb. 3

State Holidays

Jan. 6, Three Kings' Day: P.R.
Jan. 8, Battle of New Orleans Day: La.
Jan. 11, De Hostos's Birthday: P.R.
Jan. 19, Robert E. Lee's Birthday: Ark., Fla., Ky., La., S.C.; **(third Mon.):** Ala., Miss.
Jan. 19, Confederate Heroes Day: Tex.
Jan. (third Mon.), Lee-Jackson-King Day: Va.
Jan. 30, F. D. Roosevelt's Birthday: Ky.
Feb. 15, Susan B. Anthony's Birthday: Fla., Minn.
March (first Tues.), Town Meeting Day: Vt.
March 2, Texas Independence Day: Tex.
March (first Mon.), Casimir Pulaski's Birthday: Ill.
March 17, Evacuation Day: Mass. (in Suffolk County)
March 20 (first day of spring), Youth Day: Okla.
March 22, Abolition Day: P.R.
March 25, Maryland Day: Md.
March 26, Prince Jonah Kuhio Kalanianaole Day: Hawaii
March (last Mon.), Seward's Day: Alaska
April 2, Pascua Florida Day: Fla.
April 13, Thomas Jefferson's Birthday: Ala., Okla.
April 16, De Diego's Birthday: P.R.
April (third Mon.), Patriots' Day: Maine, Mass.
April 21, San Jacinto Day: Tex.
April 22, Arbor Day: Nebr.
April 22, Oklahoma Day: Okla.
April 26, Confederate Memorial Day: Fla., Ga.
April (fourth Mon.), Fast Day: N.H.
April (last Mon.), Confederate Memorial Day: Ala., Miss.
May 1, Bird Day: Okla.
May 8, Truman Day: Mo.
May 11, Minnesota Day: Minn.
May 20, Mecklenburg Independence Day: N.C.

June (first Mon.), Jefferson Davis's Birthday: Ala., Miss.
June 3, Jefferson Davis's Birthday: Fla., S.C.
June 3, Confederate Memorial Day: Ky., La.
June 9, Senior Citizens Day: Okla.
June 11, King Kamehameha I Day: Hawaii
June 15, Separation Day: Del.
June 17, Bunker Hill Day: Mass. (in Suffolk County)
June 19, Emancipation Day: Tex.
June 20, West Virginia Day: W.Va.
July 17, Muñoz Rivera's Birthday: P.R.
July 24, Pioneer Day: Utah
July 25, Constitution Day: P.R.
July 27, Barbosa's Birthday: P.R.
Aug. (first Sun.), American Family Day: Ariz.
Aug. (first Mon.), Colorado Day: Colo.
Aug. (second Mon.), Victory Day: R.I.
Aug. 16, Bennington Battle Day: Vt.
Aug. (third Friday), Admission Day: Hawaii
Aug. 27, Lyndon B. Johnson's Birthday: Tex.
Aug. 30, Huey P. Long Day: La.
Sept. 9, Admission Day: Calif.
Sept. 12, Defenders' Day: Md.
Sept. 16, Cherokee Strip Day: Okla.
Sept. (first Sat. after full moon), Indian Day: Okla.
Oct. 10, Leif Eriksson Day: Minn.
Oct. 10, Oklahoma Historical Day: Okla.
Oct. 18, Alaska Day: Ala.
Oct. 31, Nevada Day: Nev.
Nov. 4, Will Rogers Day: Okla.
Nov. (week of the 16th), Oklahoma Heritage Week: Okla.
Nov. 19, Discovery Day: P.R.
Dec. 7, Delaware Day: Del.

Birthstones

Month	Stone	Month	Stone	Month	Stone
January	Garnet	June	Pearl, Alexandrite, or	October	Opal or Tourmaline
February	Amethyst		Moonstone	November	Topaz or Citrine
March	Aquamarine or Bloodstone	July	Ruby or Star Ruby	December	Turquoise, Lapis Lazuli,
April	Diamond	August	Peridot or Sardonyx		Blue Zircon, or Blue
May	Emerald	September	Sapphire or Star Sapphire		Topaz

Source: Jewelry Industry Council.

Traditional Wedding Anniversary Gift List

Anniv.	Gift	Anniv.	Gift	Anniv.	Gift	Anniv.	Gift
1st	Paper	7th	Copper, wool	13th	Lace	35th	Coral
2nd	Cotton	8th	Bronze, pottery	14th	Ivory	40th	Ruby
3rd	Leather	9th	Pottery, willow	15th	Crystal	45th	Sapphire
4th	Fruit, flowers	10th	Tin	20th	China	50th	Gold
5th	Wood	11th	Steel	25th	Silver	55th	Emerald
6th	Sugar	12th	Silk, linen	30th	Pearl	60th	Diamond

Modern Wedding Anniversary Gift List

Anniv.	Gift	Anniv.	Gift	Anniv.	Gift	Anniv.	Gift
1st	Gold jewelry	8th	Tourmaline	15th	Ruby	30th	Pearl jubilee
2nd	Garnet	9th	Lapis	16th	Peridot	35th	Emerald
3rd	Pearls	10th	Diamond jewelry	17th	Watch	40th	Ruby
4th	Blue topaz	11th	Turquoise	18th	Cat's-eye	45th	Sapphire
5th	Sapphire	12th	Jade	19th	Aquamarine	50th	Golden jubilee
6th	Amethyst	13th	Citrine	20th	Emerald	60th	Diamond jubilee
7th	Onyx	14th	Opal	25th	Silver jubilee		

Source: Jewelry Industry Council.

Selected National Holidays Around the World, 2002

Country	Date	Country	Date	Country	Date
Afghanistan	Aug. 19	Haiti	Jan. 1	Pakistan	March 23
Albania	Nov. 28	Hungary	Aug. 20	Panama	Nov. 3
Argentina	May 25	Iceland	June 17	Papua New Guinea	Sept. 16
Armenia	Sept. 21	India	Jan. 26	Paraguay	May 15
Australia	Jan. 26	Indonesia	Aug. 17	Peru	July 28
Austria	Oct. 26	Iran	Feb. 11	Philippines	June 12
Bahamas	July 10	Iraq	July 17	Poland	May 3
Bangladesh	March 26	Ireland	March 17	Portugal	June 10
Barbados	Nov. 30	Israel	May 12[1]	Romania	Dec. 1
Belgium	July 21	Italy	June 2	Samoa	June 1
Belize	Sept. 21	Jamaica	Aug. 6[2]	Saudi Arabia	Sept. 23
Bolivia	Aug. 6	Japan	Dec. 23	Senegal	April 4
Brazil	Sept. 7	Jordan	May 25	Singapore	Aug. 9
Bulgaria	March 3	Kenya	Dec. 12	Slovakia	Sept. 1
Canada	July 1	North Korea	Sept. 9	Slovenia	June 25
Chile	Sept. 18	South Korea	Aug. 15	Somalia	Oct. 21
China	Oct. 1	Kuwait	Feb. 25	South Africa	April 27
Colombia	July 20	Lebanon	Nov. 22	Spain	Oct. 12
Congo, Republic of	Aug. 15	Liberia	July 26	Sri Lanka	Feb. 4
Croatia	May 30	Lithuania	Feb. 16	Swaziland	Sept. 6
Cuba	Jan. 1	Luxembourg	June 23	Sweden	June 6
Czech Republic	Oct. 28	Macedonia	Aug. 2	Switzerland	Aug. 1
Denmark	April 16	Malaysia	Aug. 31	Tanzania	April 26
Dominican Republic	Feb. 27	Malta	Sept. 21	Thailand	Dec. 5
Ecuador	Aug. 10	Mexico	Sept. 16	Tunisia	March 20
Egypt	July 23	Monaco	Nov. 19	Turkey	Oct. 29
El Salvador	Sept. 15	Mongolia	July 11	Uganda	Oct. 9
Ethiopia	May 28	Morocco	March 3	United Arab Emirates	Dec. 2
Finland	Dec. 6	Mozambique	June 25	United States	July 4
France	July 14	Nepal	Dec. 28	Uruguay	Aug. 25
Gabon	Aug. 17	Netherlands	April 30	Venezuela	July 5
Georgia	May 26	New Zealand	Feb. 6	Vietnam	Sept. 2
Germany	Oct. 3	Nicaragua	Sept. 15	Yemen, Republic of	May 22
Greece	March 25	Nigeria	Oct. 1	Zambia	Oct. 24
Guatemala	Sept. 15	Norway	May 17	Zimbabwe	April 18

1. Changes yearly according to Hebrew calendar. 2. Celebrated on first Monday in August.

Major Religions of the World

Judaism

Judaism is the oldest of the monotheistic faiths. It affirms the existence of one God, Yahweh, who entered into covenant with the descendants of Abraham, God's chosen people. Judaism's holy writings reveal how God has been present with them throughout their history. These writings are known as the Torah, specifically the five books of Moses, but most broadly conceived as the Hebrew Scriptures (traditionally called the Old Testament by Christians) and the compilation of oral tradition known as the Talmud (which includes the Mishnah, the oral law).

According to Scripture, the Hebrew patriarch Abraham (20th century? B.C.) founded the faith that would become known as Judaism. He obeyed the call of God to depart northern Mesopotamia and travel to Canaan. God promised to bless his descendants if they remained faithful in worship. Abraham's line descended through Isaac, then Jacob

(also called Israel; his descendants came to be called Israelites). According to Scripture, 12 families that descended from Jacob migrated to Egypt, where they were enslaved. They were led out of bondage (13th century? B.C.) by Moses, who united them in the worship of Yahweh. The Hebrews returned to Canaan after a 40-year sojourn in the desert, conquering from the local peoples the "promised land" that God had provided for them.

The 12 tribes of Israel lived in a covenant association during the period of the judges (1200?–1000? B.C.), leaders known for wisdom and heroism. Saul first established a monarchy (r. 1025?–1005? B.C.); his successor, David (r. 1005?–965? B.C.), unified the land of Israel and made Jerusalem its religious and political center. Under his son, Solomon (r. 968?–928? B.C.), a golden era culminated in the building of a temple, replacing the portable sanctuary in use until that time. Following Solomon's death, the kingdom was split into Israel in the north

Religious Population of the World, 1998*
(in thousands)

Statistics of the world's religions are only very rough approximations. Aside from Christianity, few religions, if any, attempt to keep statistical records; and even Protestants and Catholics employ different methods of counting members.

Religion	Total	Percent distribution	Africa	Asia	Latin America	North America	Europe[1]	Oceania
Total population	5,929,839	100.0%	778,484	3,588,877	499,534	304,078	729,406	29,460
Christians	1,943,038	32.8%	356,277	283,734	462,965	256,882	558,729	24,451
Affiliated Christians	1,835,352	31.0%	323,782	275,836	456,919	222,678	536,092	20,045
Roman Catholics	1,026,501	17.3%	114,316	106,399	442,808	69,536	286,124	7,318
Protestants	316,445	5.3%	74,436	43,998	45,295	69,437	76,776	6,503
Orthodox	213,743	3.6%	33,660	15,232	549	4,852	158,775	675
Anglicans	63,748	1.1%	27,957	856	853	3,260	25,632	5,190
Other Christians	373,832	6.3%	74,853	143,080	44,331	83,519	25,551	2,498
Unaffiliated Christians	107,686	1.8%	32,495	7,898	6,046	34,204	22,637	4,406
Atheists	149,913	2.5%	420	121,451	2,673	1,569	23,444	356
Baha'is	6,764	0.1%	1,695	3,260	825	753	126	105
Buddhists	353,794	6.0%	138	348,806	622	2,445	1,517	266
Chinese folk religionists[2]	379,162	6.4%	33	377,795	184	839	250	61
Confucians	6,241	0.1%	—	6,207	—	—	11	23
Ethnic Religionists	248,565	4.2%	97,200	148,189	1,231	424	1,262	259
Hindus	761,689	12.8%	2,411	755,500	785	1,266	1,382	345
Jains	3,922	0.1%	65	3,850	—	7	—	—
Jews	14,111	0.2%	230	4,139	1,121	5,996	2,530	95
Mandeans	38	—	—	38	—	—	—	—
Muslims	1,164,622	19.6%	315,000	812,000	1,624	4,349	31,401	248
New Religionists[3]	100,144	1.7%	27	98,548	604	759	155	51
Nonreligious[4]	759,655	12.8%	4,863	600,822	15,300	27,500	108,000	3,170
Other religionists	1,001	0.0%	68	11	95	585	233	9
Shintoists	2,789	0.0%	—	2,727	—	7	55	—
Sikhs	22,332	0.4%	53	21,531	—	498	236	14
Spiritists	11,785	0.2%	3	—	11,498	148	129	7
Zoroastrians	274	—	—	269	—	—	3	1

NOTES: — Represents or rounds to zero. *Latest data available. 1. Includes Russia. 2. Followers of traditional Chinese religion. 3. Followers of Asiatic 20th-century New Religions, New Religious movements, radical new crisis religions, and non-Christian syncretistic mass religions. 4. Persons professing no religion, nonbelievers, agnostics, freethinkers, and dereligionized secularists indifferent to all religions. *Source:* Encyclopædia Britannica, Inc., Chicago, Ill., *Britannica Book of the Year.* Reprinted with permission from *Britannica Book of the Year,* 1999 © 1999 Encyclopædia Britannica, Inc.

and Judah in the south. Political conflicts resulted in the conquest of Israel by Assyria (721 B.C.) and the defeat of Judah by Babylon (586 B.C.). Jerusalem and its temple were destroyed, and many Judeans were exiled to Babylon.

During the era of the kings, the prophets were active in Israel and Judah. Their writings emphasize faith in Yahweh as God of Israel and of the entire universe, and they warn of the dangers of worshiping other gods. They also cry out for social justice.

The Judeans were permitted to return in 539 B.C. to Judea, where they were ruled as a Persian province. Though temple and cult were restored in Jerusalem, during the exile a new class of religious leaders had emerged—the scribes. They became rivals to the temple hierarchy and would eventually evolve into the party known as the Pharisees.

Persian rule ended when Alexander the Great conquered Palestine in 332 B.C. After his death, rule of Judea alternated between Egypt and Syria. When the Syrian ruler Antiochus IV Epiphanes tried to prevent the practice of Judaism, a revolt was led by the Maccabees (a Jewish family), winning Jewish independence in 128 B.C. The Romans conquered Jerusalem in 63 B.C.

During this period the Sadducees (temple priests) and the Pharisees (teachers of the law in the synagogues) offered different interpretations of Judaism. Smaller groups that emerged were the Essenes, a religious order; the Apocalyptists, who expected divine deliverance led by the Messiah; and the Zealots, who were prepared to fight for national independence. Hellenism also influenced Judaism at this time.

When the Zealots revolted, the Roman armies destroyed Jerusalem and its temple (A.D. 70). The Jews were scattered in the Diaspora (dispersion) and experienced much persecution. Rabbinic Judaism, developed according to Pharisaic practice and centered on Torah and synagogue, became the primary expression of faith. The Scriptures became codified, and the Talmud took shape. In the 12th century Maimonides formulated the influential 13 Articles of Faith, including belief in God, God's oneness and lack of physical or other form, the changelessness of Torah, restoration of the monarchy under the Messiah, and resurrection of the dead.

Two branches of European Judaism developed during the Middle Ages: the Sephardic, based in Spain and with an affinity to Babylonian Jews; and the Ashkenazic, based in Franco-German lands and affiliated with Rome and Palestine. Two forms of Jewish mysticism also arose at this time: medieval Hasidism and attention to the Kabbalah (a mystical interpretation of Scripture).

After a respite during the 18th-century Enlightenment, anti-Semitism again plagued European Jews in the 19th century, sparking the Zionist movement that culminated in the founding of the state of Israel in 1948. The Holocaust of World War II took the lives of more than 6 million Jews.

Jews today continue synagogue worship, which includes readings from the Law and the Prophets and prayers, such as the Shema (Hear, O Israel) and the Amidah (the 18 Benedictions). Religious life is guided by the commandments of the Torah, which include the practice of circumcision and Sabbath observance.

Present-day Judaism has three main expressions: Orthodox, Conservative, and Reform. Reform movements, resulting from the Haskala (Jewish Enlightenment) of the 18th century, began in western Europe but took root in North America. Reform Jews do not hold the oral law (Talmud) to be a divine revelation, and they emphasize ethical and moral teachings. Orthodox Jews follow the traditional faith and practice with great seriousness. They follow a strict kosher diet and keep the Sabbath with care. Conservative Judaism, which developed in the mid-18th century, holds the Talmud to be authoritative and follows most traditional practices, yet tries to make Judaism relevant for each generation, believing that change and tradition can complement each other. Because the Torah assumes belief in God but does not require it, a strong secular movement also exists within Judaism, including atheist and agnostic elements.

In general, Jews do not proselytize, but they do welcome newcomers to their faith.

Christianity

Christianity is a monotheistic religion founded by the followers of Jesus of Nazareth. Jesus, a Jew, was born in about 7 B.C. and assumed his public life, probably after his 30th year, in Galilee. The New Testament Gospels describe Jesus as a teacher and miracle worker. He proclaimed the kingdom of God, a future reality that is at the same time already present. Jesus set the requirements for participation in the kingdom of God as a change of heart and repentance for sins, love of God and neighbor, and concern for justice. Circa A.D. 30 he was executed on a cross in Jerusalem, a brutal form of punishment for those considered a political threat to the Roman Empire.

After his death his followers came to believe in him as the Christ, the Messiah. The Gospels report his resurrection and how the risen Jesus was witnessed by many of his followers. The apostle Paul helped spread the new faith in his missionary travels. Historically, Christianity arose out of Judaism and claims that Jesus fulfilled many of the promises of the Hebrew Scripture (often referred to as the Old Testament).

The new religion spread rapidly throughout the Roman Empire. In its first two centuries, Christianity began to take shape as an organization, developing distinctive doctrine, liturgy, and ministry. By the fourth century the Christian church had taken root in countries stretching from Spain in the West to Persia and India in the East. Christians had been subject to persecution by the Roman state, but gained tolerance under Constantine the Great (A.D. 313). The church became favored under his successors, and in 380 the emperor Theodosius proclaimed Christianity the state religion. Other religions were suppressed.

Because differences in doctrine threatened to divide the church, a standard Christian creed was formulated by bishops at successive ecumenical councils, the first of which was held in A.D. 325 (Nicaea). Important doctrines were defined concerning the Trinity—in other words, that there is one God in three persons: Father, Son, and Holy Spirit (Constantinople, A.D. 381), and the nature of Christ as both divine and human (Chalcedon, A.D. 541). Christians came to accept both Hebrew Scripture and the New Testament as authoritative. The New

Testament comprises four Gospels (narratives of Jesus' life), 21 Epistles, The Acts of the Apostles, and Revelation.

Because of differences between Christians of the East and West, the unity of the church was broken in 1054. The religious center for the Eastern Orthodox Church was Constantinople, and the Roman Catholic Church defined doctrine and practice for Christians in the West. In 1517 began the Reformation, which ultimately caused a schism in the Western church. Reformers wished to correct certain practices within the Roman church, but they also came to view the Christian faith in a distinctly new way. The major Protestant denominations (Lutheran, Presbyterian, Reformed, and Anglican [Episcopalian]) thus came into being. Over the centuries, numerous denominations have broken with these major traditions, resulting in a spectrum of Christian expression.

In the 21st century, many Christians hope to regain a sense of unity through dialogue and cooperation among different traditions. The ecumenical movement led to the formation of the World Council of Churches in 1948 (Amsterdam), which has since been joined by many denominations.

Through its missionary activity Christianity has spread to most parts of the globe.

Eastern Orthodoxy

Eastern Orthodoxy comprises the faith and practices stemming from ancient churches in the eastern part of the Roman Empire. It encompasses Orthodox churches in communion with the see of Constantinople.

The Orthodox, Catholic, Apostolic Church is the direct descendant of the Byzantine state church and consists of independent national churches that are united by doctrine, liturgy, and hierarchical organization (church leaders include deacons and priests, who may either be married or be monks before ordination, and bishops, who must be celibates). The heads of these churches are called patriarchs or metropolitans. Rivalry between the pope of Rome and the patriarch of Constantinople, as well as differences that existed for centuries between the eastern and western parts of the empire, led to a schism in 1054. The mutual excommunication pronounced in that year was lifted in 1965, however, and a climate of better understanding has ensued. Orthodox churches belong to the World Council of Churches.

The Eastern Orthodox churches recognize only the canons of the seven ecumenical councils (325–787) as binding for faith, and they reject doctrines that have been added in the West.

The central worship service is called the Liturgy, which is understood as representing God's acts of salvation. Its center is the celebration of the Eucharist, or Lord's Supper. Icons (sacred pictures) have a special place in Orthodox worship. The Mother of Christ, angels, and saints are venerated. The Orthodox Church and the Western Catholic Church recognize the same number of sacraments.

Orthodox Churches are found in Greece, Turkey, Russia, the Balkans, and other parts of the former Soviet Union. In this century Orthodox faith has spread to western Europe and other parts of the world, particularly America.

Eastern Rite Churches

These include the Uniate Churches that recognize the authority of the pope but keep their own traditional liturgies and those churches dating back to the fifth century that emancipated themselves from the Byzantine state church. They include the Melchites, Syrian Catholics, Maronites (Arab Christians in Lebanon), Catholic Copts and Ethiopians, the autonomous Nestorian Church, and others.

Roman Catholicism

Roman Catholicism comprises the belief and practice of the Roman Catholic Church. It stands under the authority of the bishop of Rome, the pope, and is led by him and bishops who are held to be, through ordination, successors of Peter and the apostles. Doctrine and sacraments are administered by the hierarchy of archbishops, bishops, priests, and deacons. As successor to Peter, the pope is considered the Vicar of Christ. Roman Catholics believe their church to be the one, holy, catholic, and apostolic church, possessing all the properties of the one, true church of Christ.

The faith of the church is understood to be identical with that taught by Christ and his apostles

U.S. Religious Bodies with More Than 500,000 Members

Religious body (year reporting)	Members
Roman Catholic Church (1998)	62,018,436
Southern Baptist Convention (1998)	15,729,356
United Methodist Church (1998)	8,400,000
National Baptist Convention, U.S.A., Inc. (1997)	8,200,000
Church of God in Christ (1991)	5,499,875
Evangelical Lutheran Church in America (1998)	5,178,225
Church of Jesus Christ of Latter-day Saints (1997)	4,923,100
Presbyterian Church (U.S.A.) (1998)	3,574,959
National Baptist Convention of America, Inc. (1987)	3,500,000
Lutheran Church—Missouri Synod (1998)	2,594,404
Assemblies of God (1998)	2,525,812
African Methodist Episcopal Church (1999)	2,500,000
National Missionary Baptist Convention of America (1992)	2,500,000
Progressive National Baptist Convention, Inc. (1995)	2,500,000
Episcopal Church (1996)	2,364,559
Greek Orthodox Archdiocese of America (1998)	1,954,500
American Baptist Churches in the U.S.A. (1998)	1,507,400
Churches of Christ (1999)	1,500,000
Pentecostal Assemblies of the World (1998)	1,500,000
United Church of Christ (1998)	1,421,088
African Methodist Episcopal Zion Church (1998)	1,252,369
Baptist Bible Fellowship International (1997)	1,200,000
Christian Churches and Churches of Christ (1988)	1,071,616
Jehovah's Witnesses (1999)	1,040,283
Orthodox Church in America (1998)	1,000,000
Christian Church (Disciples of Christ) (1997)	879,436
Seventh-Day Adventist Church (1998)	839,915
Church of God (Cleveland, Tenn.) (1995)	753,230
Christian Methodist Episcopal Church (1983)	718,922
Church of the Nazarene (1998)	627,054

Source: Yearbook of American & Canadian Churches, 2000.

and contained in the Bible and tradition. New definitions of doctrines, such as the Immaculate Conception of Mary (1854) and the bodily Assumption of Mary (1950), have been declared by popes, however. At Vatican Council I (1870) the pope was proclaimed "endowed with infallibility, *ex cathedra,* in other words, when exercising the office of pastor and teacher of all Christians."

The center of Roman Catholic worship is the celebration of the Mass, the Eucharist, which is the commemoration of Christ's sacrificial death and resurrection. Other sacraments are baptism, confirmation, penance, matrimony, anointing of the sick (formerly known as extreme unction), and holy orders. The Virgin Mary and the other saints, and their relics, are venerated, and prayers are made to them to intercede with God, in whose presence they are believed to dwell.

The Roman Catholic Church is the largest Christian organization in the world, found in most countries.

Vatican Council II (1962–1965) sought to "update" the church, bringing about changes in practice and more deeply involving the laity. The immensely popular Pope John Paul II (1978–) has taken a more conservative course and has reached out to Catholics worldwide through his extensive travels.

Protestantism

Protestantism encompasses the Christian churches that separated from Rome during the Reformation in the 16th century. This movement was initiated by an Augustinian monk, Martin Luther. The term *Protestant* was originally applied to followers of Luther, who protested at the Diet of Spires (1529) against the decree that prohibited all further ecclesiastical reforms. Other influential reformers included John Calvin, Ulrich Zwingli, and John Knox. Protestantism rejected attempts to tie God's revelation to earthly institutions and strictly adhered to the Word of God as sole authority in matters of faith and practice *(sola scriptura)*. Central in the reformers' understanding of the biblical message is the justification of the sinner by faith alone. The church is understood as a fellowship, and the priesthood of all believers is stressed.

The Augsburg Confession (1530) was the principal statement of Lutheran faith and practice. It became a model for other Protestant confessions of faith. Major Protestant denominations include the

---

U.S. Protestant Groups

According to the Hartford Institute for Religious Research, U.S. Protestant groups are commonly divided into four broad categories:
Liberal Protestant: Episcopal, Presbyterian, Unitarian-Universalist, United Church of Christ
Moderate Protestant: American Baptist, Disciples of Christ, Evangelical Lutheran, Mennonite, Reformed Church in America, United Methodist
Evangelical Protestant: Assemblies of God, Christian Reformed, Nazarene, Churches of Christ, Independent Christian Churches (Instrumental), Mega-churches, Nondenominational Protestant, Seventh-day Adventist, Southern Baptist
Historically Black Protestant denominations

Lutheran, Reformed (Calvinist), Presbyterian, and Anglican (Episcopalian). Innumerable sects and denominations sprang from these roots, including Quakers, Baptists, Pentecostals, Congregationalists, Methodists, and nondenominational assemblies. Sects that base their faith on additional revelations or insights gained in the modern period include Mormons, Christian Scientists, and Jehovah's Witnesses.

Since the latter part of the 19th century, national councils of churches have been established in many countries, for example, the Federal Council of Churches of Christ in America in 1908. Churches of a particular denomination have joined in federations and world alliances, beginning with the Anglican Lambeth Conference in 1867.

Protestant missionary activity, particularly strong in the 19th century, resulted in the founding of many churches in Asia and Africa. The ecumenical movement, which originated with Protestant missions, aims at unity among Christians and churches.

Islam

Islam, one of the three major monotheistic faiths, was founded in Arabia by Muhammad between 610 and 632. There are an estimated 5.5 million Muslims in North America and 1 billion Muslims worldwide.

Muhammad was born in A.D. 570 at Mecca and belonged to the Quraysh tribe, which was active in the caravan trade. At the age of 25 he joined the trade from Mecca to Syria in the employment of a rich widow, Khadija, whom he later married. Critical of the lax moral standards and polytheistic practices of the inhabitants of Mecca, he began to lead a contemplative life in the desert. In a dramatic religious vision, the angel Gabriel announced to Muhammad that he was to be a prophet. Encouraged by Khadija, he devoted himself to the reform of religion and society. Polytheism was to be abandoned. But leaders of the Quraysh generally rejected his teaching, and Muhammad gained only a small following and suffered persecution. He eventually fled Mecca.

The Hegira (*Hijra,* meaning "emigration") of Muhammad from Mecca, where he was not honored, to Medina, where he was well received, occurred in 622 and marks the beginning of the Muslim era. After a number of military conflicts with Mecca, in 630 he marched on Mecca and conquered it. Muhammad died at Medina in 632. His grave there has since been a place of pilgrimage.

Muhammad's followers, called Muslims, revered him as the prophet of Allah (God), the only God. Muslims consider Muhammad to be the last in the line of prophets that included Abraham and Jesus. Islam spread quickly, stretching from Spain in the west to India in the east within a century after the prophet's death. Sources of the Islamic faith are the Qur'an (Koran), regarded as the uncreated, eternal Word of God, and tradition *(hadith)* regarding sayings and deeds of the prophet.

Islam means "surrender to the will of Allah," the all-powerful, who determines humanity's fate. Good deeds will be rewarded at the Last Judgment in paradise, and evil deeds will be punished in hell.

The Five Pillars, or primary duties, of Islam are profession of faith; prayer, to be performed five times a day; almsgiving to the poor and the mosque (house of worship); fasting during daylight hours in the month of Ramadan; and pilgrimage to Mecca at least once in a Muslim's lifetime, if it is physically and financially possible. The pilgrimage includes homage to the ancient shrine of the Ka'aba, the most sacred site in Islam.

Muslims gather for corporate worship on Fridays. Prayers and a sermon take place at the mosque, which is also a center for teaching of the Qur'an. The community leader, the *imam*, is considered a teacher and prayer leader.

Islam succeeded in uniting an Arab world of separate tribes and castes, but disagreements concerning the succession of the prophet caused a division in Islam between two groups, Sunnis and Shi'ites. The Shi'ites rejected the first three successors to Muhammad as usurpers, claiming the fourth, Muhammad's son-in-law Ali, as the rightful leader. The Sunnis (from the word *tradition*), the largest division of Islam (today more than 80%), believe in the legitimacy of the first three successors. Among these, other sects arose (such as the conservative Wahhabi of Saudi Arabia), as well as different schools of theology. Another development within Islam, beginning in the eighth and ninth centuries, was Sufism, a form of mysticism. This movement was influential for many centuries and was instrumental in the spread of Islam in Asia and Africa.

Islam has expanded greatly under Muhammad's successors. It is the principal religion of the Middle East, Asia, and the northern half of Africa.

Hinduism

Hinduism is the major religion of India, practiced by more than 80% of the population. In contrast to other religions, it has no founder. Considered the oldest religion in the world, it dates back, perhaps, to prehistoric times.

No single creed or doctrine binds Hindus together. Intellectually there is complete freedom of belief, and one can be monotheist, polytheist, or atheist. Hinduism is a syncretic religion, welcoming and incorporating a variety of outside influences.

The most ancient sacred texts of the Hindu religion are written in Sanskrit and called the *Vedas* (*vedah* means "knowledge"). There are four Vedic books, of which the Rig-Veda is the oldest. It discusses multiple gods, the universe, and creation. The dates of these works are unknown (1000 B.C.?). Present-day Hindus rarely refer to these texts but do venerate them.

The Upanishads (dated 1000–300 B.C.), commentaries on the Vedic texts, speculate on the origin of the universe and the nature of deity, and *atman* (the individual soul) and its relationship to *Brahman* (the universal soul). They introduce the doctrine of *karma* and recommend meditation and the practice of yoga.

Further important sacred writings include the Epics, which contain legendary stories about gods and humans. They are the Mahabharata (composed between 200 B.C. and A.D. 200) and the Ramayana. The former includes the Bhagavad-Gita (Song of the Lord), an influential text that describes the three paths to salvation. The Puranas (stories in verse, probably written between the 6th and 13th centuries) detail myths of Hindu gods and heroes and also comment on religious practice and cosmology.

According to Hindu beliefs, Brahman is the principle and source of the universe. This divine intelligence pervades all beings, including the individual soul. Thus the many Hindu deities are manifestations of the one Brahman. Hinduism is based on the concept of reincarnation, in which all living beings, from plants on earth to gods above, are caught in a cosmic cycle of becoming and perishing.

Life is determined by the law of karma—one is reborn to a higher level of existence based on moral behavior in a previous phase of existence. Life on earth is regarded as transient and a burden. The goal of existence is liberation from the cycle of rebirth and death and entrance into the indescribable state of *moksha* (liberation).

The practice of Hinduism consists of rites and ceremonies centering on birth, marriage, and death. There are many Hindu temples, which are considered to be dwelling places of the deities and to which people bring offerings. Places of pilgrimage include Benares on the Ganges, the most sacred river in India. Of the many Hindu deities, the most popular are the cults of Vishnu, Shiva, and Shakti, and their various incarnations. Also important is Brahma, the creator god. Hindus also venerate human saints.

Orthodox Hindu society in India was divided into four major hereditary classes: (1) the Brahmin (priestly and learned class); (2) the Kshatriya (military, professional, ruling, and governing occupations); (3) the Vaishya (landowners, merchants, and business occupations); and (4) the Sudra (artisans, laborers, and peasants). Below the Sudra was a fifth group, the Untouchables (lowest menial occupations and no social standing). The Indian government banned discrimination against the Untouchables in the constitution of India in 1950. Observance of class and caste distinctions varies throughout India.

In modern times work has been done to reform and revive Hinduism. One of the outstanding reformers was Ramakrishna (1836–1886), who inspired many followers, one of whom founded the Ramakrishna mission. The mission is active both in India and in other countries and is known for its scholarly and humanitarian works.

Buddhism

Buddhism was founded in the fourth or fifth century B.C. in northern India by a man known traditionally as Siddhartha (meaning "he who has reached the goal") Gautama, the son of a warrior prince. Some scholars believe that he lived from 563 to 483 B.C., though his exact life span is uncertain. Troubled by the inevitability of suffering in human life, he left home and a pampered life at the age of 29 to wander as an ascetic, seeking religious insight and a solution to the struggles of human existence. He passed through many trials and practiced extreme self-denial. Finally, while meditating under the bodhi tree ("tree of perfect knowledge"), he reached enlightenment and taught his followers about his new spiritual understanding.

Gautama's teachings differed from the Hindu faith prevalent in India at the time. Whereas in Hinduism the Brahmin caste alone performed religious functions and attained the highest spiritual understanding, Gautama's beliefs were more egalitarian, accessible to all who wished to be enlightened. At the core of his understanding were the Four Noble

Truths: (1) all living beings suffer; (2) the origin of this suffering is desire—for material possessions, power, and so on; (3) desire can be overcome; and (4) there is a path that leads to release from desire. This way is called the Noble Eightfold Path: right views, right intention, right speech, right action, right livelihood, right effort, right concentration, and right ecstasy.

Gautama promoted the concept of *anatman* (that a person has no actual self) and the idea that existence is characterized by impermanence. This realization helps one let go of desire for transient things. Still, Gautama did not recommend extreme self-denial but rather a disciplined life called the Middle Way. Like the Hindus, he believed that existence consisted of reincarnation, a cycle of birth and death. He held that it could be broken only by reaching complete detachment from worldly cares. Then the soul could be released into *nirvana* (literally "blowing out")—an indescribable state of total transcendence. Gautama traveled to preach the *dharma* (sacred truth) and was recognized as the Buddha (enlightened one). After his death his followers continued to develop doctrine and practice, which came to center on the Three Jewels: the *dharma* (the sacred teachings of Buddhism), the *sangha* (the community of followers, which now includes nuns, monks, and laity), and the Buddha. Under the patronage of the Mauryan emperor Ashoka (third century B.C.), Buddhism spread throughout India and to other parts of Asia. Monasteries were established, as well as temples dedicated to Buddha; at shrines his relics were venerated. Though by the fourth century A.D. Buddhist presence in India had dwindled, it flourished in other parts of Asia.

Numerous Buddhist sects have emerged. The oldest, called the Theravada (Way of the Elders) tradition, interprets Buddha as a great sage but not a deity. It emphasizes meditation and ritual practices that help the individual become an *arhat*, an enlightened being. Its followers emphasize the authority of the earliest Buddhist scriptures, the Tripitaka (Three Baskets), a compilation of sermons, rules for celibates, and doctrine. This sect is prevalent in Southeast Asia and Sri Lanka. It is sometimes called the Hinayana (Lesser Vehicle) tradition (once considered a pejorative term).

Between the second century B.C. and the second century A.D., the Mahayana (Greater Vehicle) tradition refocused Buddhism to concentrate less on individual attainment of enlightenment and more on concern for humanity. It promotes the ideal of the *bodhisattva* (enlightened being), who shuns entering nirvana until all sentient beings can do so as well, willingly remaining in the painful cycle of birth and death to perform works of compassion. Members of this tradition conceive of Buddha as an eternal being to whom prayers can be made; other Buddhas are revered as well, adding a polytheistic dimension to the religion. Numerous sects have developed from the Mahayana tradition, which has been influential in China, Korea, and Japan.

A third broad tradition, variously called Vajrayana (Diamond Vehicle), Mantrayana (Vehicle of the Mantra), or Tantric Buddhism, offers a quicker, more demanding way to achieve nirvana. Because of its level of challenge—enabling one to reach enlightenment in one lifetime—it requires the guidance of a spiritual leader. It is most prominent in Tibet and Mongolia.

Zen Buddhism encourages individuals to seek the Buddha nature within themselves and to practice a disciplined form of sitting meditation in order to reach *satori*—spiritual enlightenment.

Sikhism

A major religion of India and the fifth-largest faith in the world, Sikhism emerged in the Punjab under the guidance of the guru Nanak (1469–1539?). This region had been influenced by the Hindu *bhakti* movement, which promoted both the idea that God comprises one reality alone as well as the practice of devotional singing and prayer. The Muslim mystical tradition of Sufism, with its emphasis on meditation, also had some prominence there. Drawing on these resources, Nanak forged a new spiritual path.

In his youth, Nanak began to compose hymns. At the age of 29, he had a mystical experience that led him to proclaim "There is no Hindu; there is no Muslim." A strict monotheist, he rejected Hindu polytheism but accepted the Hindu concept of life as a cycle of birth, death, and rebirth; *moksha,* release from this cycle into unity with God, could be achieved only with the help of a guru, or spiritual teacher. Nanak believed that communion with God could be gained through devotional repetition of the divine name, singing of hymns and praises, and adherence to a demanding ethical code. He rejected idols and the Hindu caste system; it became a custom for Sikhs of all social ranks to take meals together. These beliefs are still central to modern Sikhism.

Nanak was first in a line of ten gurus who shaped and inspired Sikhism. The fifth, Arjun (1563–1606), compiled hymns and other writings by earlier Sikh gurus, as well as medieval Hindu and Muslim saints, in the *Adi Granth* (First Book), or *Guru Granth Sahib* (the Granth Personified). This book became the sacred scripture of Sikhism. In addition to his spiritual leadership, Arjun wielded considerable secular power as he grappled with leaders of the Mughal Empire.

The tenth guru, Gobind Singh (1666–1708), was both a scholar and a military hero. He established the Khalsa (community of pure ones), an order that combined spiritual devotion, personal discipline, and ideals of military valor. Baptism initiates new members into the Khalsa. The *Adi Granth* took its final form under the supervision of Gobind Singh, as did the *Dasam Granth* (Tenth Book), a collection of prayers, poetry, and narrative. After the deaths of his four sons, Gobind Singh declared the line of gurus at an end. The *Adi Granth* would instead be reverenced in houses of worship, taking the place of a living guru.

Today, Sikhs worship at *gurdwaras* (temples), where the *Adi Granth* is the object of devotion. This book is consulted regarding questions of faith and practice. On certain occasions, it is recited in its entirety (requiring more than a day) or carried in procession; offerings may be placed before it. Worshipful singing, meditation, and focus on the divine name remain essential to spiritual life. Some Sikhs undertake pilgrimages to historical *gurdwaras,* such as the Golden Temple of Amritsar, that are associated with the gurus. Some become disciples of living saints. There is no established Sikh priesthood.

Confucianism

Confucius (K'ung Fu-tzu), born in the state of Lu (northern China), lived from 551 to 479 B.C. He was a brilliant teacher, viewing education not merely as the accumulation of knowledge but as a means of self-transformation. His legacy was a system of thought emphasizing education, proper behavior, and loyalty. His effect on Chinese culture was immense.

The teachings of Confucius are contained in the *Analects*, a collection of his sayings as remembered by his students. They were further developed by philosophers such as Mencius (Meng Tse, fl. 400 B.C.). Confucianism is little concerned with metaphysical discussion of religion or with spiritual attainments. It instead emphasizes moral conduct and right relationships in the human sphere.

Cultivation of virtue is a central tenet of Confucianism. Two important virtues are *jen*, a benevolent and humanitarian attitude, and *li*, maintaining proper relationships and rituals that enhance the life of the individual, the family, and the state. The "five relations," between king and subject, father and son, man and wife, older and younger brother, and friend and friend, are of utmost importance. These relationships are reinforced by participation in rituals, including the formal procedures of court life and religious rituals such as ancestor worship.

Confucius revolutionized educational thought in China. He believed that learning was not to be focused only on attaining the skills for a particular profession, but for growth in moral judgment and self-realization. Confucius's standards for the proper conduct of government shaped the statecraft of China for centuries. Hundreds of temples in honor of Confucius testify to his stature as sage and teacher.

Confucianism was far less dominant in 20th-century China, at least on an official level. The state cult of Confucius was ended in 1911. Still, Confucian traditions and moral standards are part of the cultural essence of China and other East Asian countries.

Shinto

Shinto comprises the religious ideas and practices indigenous to Japan. Ancient Shinto focused on the worship of the *kami*, a host of supernatural beings that could be known through forms (objects of nature, remarkable people, abstract concepts such as justice) but were ultimately mysterious. Shinto has no formal dogma and no holy writ, though early collections of Japanese religious thought and practice (*Kojiki*, "Records of Ancient Matters," A.D. 712, and *Nihon shoki*, "Chronicles of Japan," A.D. 720) are highly regarded.

Shinto has been influenced by Confucianism and by Buddhism, which was introduced in Japan in the 6th century. Syncretic schools (such as Ryobu Shinto) emerged, as did other sects that rejected Buddhism (such as Ise Shinto).

Under the reign of the emperor Meiji (1868–1912), Shinto became the official state religion. State Shinto, the national cult, emphasized the divinity of the emperor, whose succession was traced back to the first emperor, Jimmu (660 B.C.), and beyond him to the sun goddess Amaterasu-o-mi-kami. State Shinto was disestablished after World War II.

Sect Shinto, deriving from sects that developed during the 19th and 20th centuries, continues to thrive in Japan. Shrines dedicated to particular *kami* are visited by parishioners for prayer and traditional ceremonies, such as presenting a newborn child to the *kami*. Traditional festivals celebrated at the shrines include purification rites, presentation of food offerings, prayer, sacred music and dance, and a feast.

No particular day of the week is set aside for prayer. A person may visit a shrine at will, entering through the *torii* (gateway). It is believed that the *kami* can respond to prayer and can offer protection and guidance.

A variety of Shinto sects and practices exist today. Ten-rikyo emphasizes faith healing. Folk Shinto is characterized by veneration of roadside shrines and rites related to agriculture. Buddhist priests serve at many Shinto shrines, and many families keep a small shrine, or god-shelf, at home. Veneration of ancestors and pilgrimage are also common practices.

Taoism

Taoism, one of the major religions of China, is based on ancient philosophical works, primarily the Tao Te Ching, "Classic of Tao and Its Virtue." Traditionally, this book was thought to be the work of Lao-tzu, a quasi-historical philosopher of the 6th century B.C.; scholars now believe that the book dates from about the 3rd century B.C. The philosopher Chuang Tzu (4th–3rd centuries B.C.) also contributed to the seminal ideas of Taoism.

Tao, "the Way," is the ultimate reality of the universe, according to Taoism. It is a creative process, and humans can live in harmony with it by clearing the self of obstacles. By cultivating *wu-wei*, a type of inaction characterized by humility and prudence, a person can participate in the simplicity and spontaneity of Tao. Striving to attain virtue or achievement is counterproductive and unnecessary. Taoism values mystical contemplation and balance. The human being is viewed as a microcosm of the universe, and the Chinese principle of *yin-yang*, complementary duality, is a model of harmony.

The religious practices of Taoism emerged from these ancient philosophies and from Chinese shamanistic tradition; by the 2nd century A.D., it constituted an organized religion. Longevity and immortality were sought through regulating the energies of the body through breathing exercises, meditation, and use of medicinal plants, talismans, and magical formulas. A cult of immortals, including the divinized Lao-tzu, also developed. Influenced by Buddhism, Taoists organized monastic orders. Temple worship and forms of divination, including the *I ching*, were practiced.

Since its beginnings, many sects have arisen within Taoism. All subscribe to the philosophical origins of the religion; some have emphasized faith healing, exorcism, the worship of the immortals, meditation, or alchemy. Buddhism and Confucianism influenced some sects; some operated as secret societies.

Though the present Chinese government has tried to suppress it, Taoism is still practiced in mainland China, Taiwan, and Hong Kong. It profoundly influenced Chinese art and literature, and Taoist ideas have become popular in the West.

U.S. Religious Sects Originating in the 19th Century

The United States was the setting for new developments in religion in the 19th century. Sects and movements of many types arose, inspired variously by new interpretations of the Bible, the teachings of new prophets and thinkers, the expectation of Christ's second coming, and the social, scientific, and philosophical questions of the time. Sects that have thrived for over 100 years include the Christian Scientists, the Mormons, the Seventh-day Adventists, and the Jehovah's Witnesses.

Christian Scientists

Founded by Mary Baker Eddy (1821–1910) in the 1860s and 1870s, Christian Science views creation as entirely spiritual. The church holds the Bible as authoritative yet interprets it in a distinct way, focusing on the life of Jesus as a model of healing by prayer, a necessary element of spiritual growth. According to the Christian Science concept of Mind-healing, physical illness and injury result from error or wrong belief and can be healed through one's own prayer or the ministrations of a Christian Science practitioner. Worship services focus on readings from the Bible and *Science and Health with Key to the Scriptures,* Eddy's definitive textbook. Christian Science is based at the Mother Church in Boston, Massachusetts. *The Christian Science Monitor,* established under the direction of Eddy, has long been recognized for excellence in journalism.

Mormons

The Church of Jesus Christ of Latter-day Saints was established by Joseph Smith Jr. (1805–1844) of New York. He described an encounter with an angel who gave him the text that would become the *Book of Mormon,* which, together with the Bible and other texts, forms the Mormon scriptures (Mormon is an ancient American prophet found in the book). Smith organized a church in 1830; due to persecution, church members searched for a place to practice their faith, finally settling in Utah. Salt Lake City, Utah, is home to institutions such as the Family History Library, the world's largest collection of genealogical information. Mormons believe that the Godhead consists of three separate personages (Father, Son, Holy Spirit), that souls preexist this life, and that the faithful will gain eternal life as gods. These rites can be undertaken by proxy for one's dead forebears. In the Mormon view, the second coming of Christ will lead to a chain of events culminating in a final resurrection, after which earth will become a celestial home for all people.

Seventh-day Adventists

Seventh-day Adventists trace their beginnings to the preacher William Miller (1782–1849), who expounded the idea that the second coming of Christ would occur between March 21, 1844, and March 21, 1843. His followers, called Adventists, had to rethink their convictions when that event did not occur. Some believed that Miller's dates designated the beginning of God's examination of the Book of Life, which would soon culminate in the final judgment and Christ's reign on earth. In 1863 they established the Seventh-day Adventist denomination, appointing Saturday (the seventh day) for worship and rest. Seventh-day Adventists practice vegetarianism and avoid alcohol and caffeine. They accept the Bible as the word of God and await the second coming. Among their leaders, Ellen Harmon White (1827–1915) was particularly influential; some consider her writings prophetic. Other Adventist groups hold to somewhat different views.

Jehovah's Witnesses

This sect grew out of the International Bible Students Association, founded in 1872 in Pittsburgh, Pennsylvania, by Charles Taze Russell (1852–1916). After intensive study of the Bible, he concluded that the invisible return of Christ had occurred in 1874, that the Gentile period would cease in 1914, and that, following a war, the kingdom of God would be established on earth. Jehovah's Witnesses no longer set such specific dates but believe that God's kingdom, the Theocracy, will follow Armageddon, the great war described in prophetic books of the Bible. They believe that biblical prophecies are being fulfilled in world events and that Jesus was created by God and acts as his agent. Jehovah's Witnesses worship at meeting places called Kingdom Halls. Because they believe that secular governments are unknowingly entangled with Satan, they do not salute flags or join the military. Jehovah's Witnesses actively seek converts; members are expected to spread the message. Their publishing efforts include the magazines *Watchtower* and *Awake!*

Roman Catholic Pontiffs

Name	Birthplace	Reigned		Name	Birthplace	Reigned	
		From	To			From	To
St. Peter	Bethsaida	42?	67?	St. Victor I	Africa	-189	199
St. Linus	Tuscia	c. 67	76	St. Zephyrinus	Rome	199	217
St. Anacletus (Cletus)	Rome	76	88	St. Callistus I	Rome	217	222
				St. Urban I	Rome	222	230
St. Clement	Rome	88	97	St. Pontian	Rome	230	235
St. Evaristus	Greece	97	105	St. Anterus	Greece	235	236
St. Alexander I	Rome	105	115	St. Fabian	Rome	236	250
St. Sixtus I	Rome	115	125	St. Cornelius	Rome	251	253
St. Telesphorus	Greece	125	136	St. Lucius I	Rome	253	254
St. Hyginus	Greece	136	140	St. Stephen I	Rome	254	257
St. Pius I	Aquileia	140	155	St. Sixtus II	Greece	257	258
St. Anicetus	Syria	155	166	St. Dionysius	Unknown	259	268
St. Soter	Campania	166	175	St. Felix I	Rome	269	274
St. Eleutherius	Epirus	175	189	St. Eutychian	Luni	275	283

Name	Birthplace	Reigned From	Reigned To	Name	Birthplace	Reigned From	Reigned To
St. Caius	Dalmatia	283	296	St. Paul I	Rome	757	767
St. Marcellinus	Rome	296	304	Stephen III (IV)	Sicily	768	772
St. Marcellus I	Rome	308	309	Adrian I	Rome	772	795
St. Eusebius	Greece	309[1]	309[1]	St. Leo III	Rome	795	816
St. Meltiades	Africa	311	314	Stephen IV (V)	Rome	816	817
St. Sylvester I	Rome	314	335	St. Paschal I	Rome	817	824
St. Marcus	Rome	336	336	Eugene II	Rome	824	827
St. Julius I	Rome	337	352	Valentine	Rome	827	827
Liberius	Rome	352	366	Gregory IV	Rome	827	844
St. Damasus I	Spain	366	384	Sergius II	Rome	844	847
St. Siricius	Rome	384	399	St. Leo IV	Rome	847	855
St. Anastasius I	Rome	399	401	Benedict III	Rome	855	858
St. Innocent I	Albano	401	417	St. Nicholas I	Rome	858	867
St. Zozimus	Greece	417	418	(the Great)			
St. Boniface I	Rome	418	422	Adrian II	Rome	867	872
St. Celestine I	Campania	422	432	John VIII	Rome	872	882
St. Sixtus III	Rome	432	440	Marinus I	Gallese	882	884
St. Leo I	Tuscany	440	461	St. Adrian III	Rome	884	885
(the Great)				Stephen V (VI)	Rome	885	891
St. Hilary	Sardinia	461	468	Formosus	Portus	891	896
St. Simplicius	Tivoli	468	483	Boniface VI	Rome	896	896
St. Felix III (II)[2]	Rome	483	492	Stephen VI (VII)	Rome	896	897
St. Gelasius I	Africa	492	496	Romanus	Gallese	897	897
Anastasius II	Rome	496	498	Theodore II	Rome	897	897
St. Symmachus	Sardinia	498	514	John IX	Tivoli	898	900
St. Hormisdas	Frosinone	514	523	Benedict IV	Rome	900	903
St. John I	Tuscany	523	526	Leo V	Ardea	903	903
St. Felix IV (III)	Samnium	526	530	Sergius III	Rome	904	911
Boniface II	Rome	530	532	Anastasius III	Rome	911	913
John II	Rome	533	535	Landus	Sabina	913	914
St. Agapitus I	Rome	535	536	John X	Tossignano	914	928
St. Silverius	Campania	536	537	Leo VI	Rome	928	928
Vigilius	Rome	537	555	Stephen VII (VIII)	Rome	928	931
Pelagius I	Rome	556	561	John XI	Rome	931	935
John III	Rome	561	574	Leo VII	Rome	936	939
Benedict I	Rome	575	579	Stephen VIII (IX)	Rome	939	942
Pelagius II	Rome	579	590	Marinus II	Rome	942	946
St. Gregory I	Rome	590	604	Agapitus II	Rome	946	955
(the Great)				John XII	Tusculum	955	964
Sabinianus	Tuscany	604	606	Leo VIII[5]	Rome	963	965
Boniface III	Rome	607	607	Benedict V[5]	Rome	964	966
St. Boniface IV	Marsi	608	615	John XIII	Rome	965	972
St. Deusdedit	Rome	615	618	Benedict VI	Rome	973	974
(Adeodatus I)				Benedict VII	Rome	974	983
Boniface V	Naples	619	625	John XIV	Pavia	983	984
Honorius I	Campania	625	638	John XV	Rome	985	996
Severinus	Rome	640	640	Gregory V	Saxony	996	999
John IV	Dalmatia	640	642	Sylvester II	Auvergne	999	1003
Theodore I	Greece	642	649	John XVII	Rome	1003	1003
St. Martin I	Todi	649	655	John XVIII	Rome	1004	1009
St. Eugene I[3]	Rome	654	657	Sergius IV	Rome	1009	1012
St. Vitalian	Segni	657	672	Benedict VIII	Tusculum	1012	1024
Adeodatus II	Rome	672	676	John XIX	Tusculum	1024	1032
Donus	Rome	676	678	Benedict IX[6]	Tusculum	1032	1044
St. Agatho	Sicily	678	681	Sylvester III	Rome	1045	1045
St. Leo II	Sicily	682	683	Benedict IX	Tusculum	1045	1045
St. Benedict II	Rome	684	685	(2nd time)			
John V	Syria	685	686	Gregory VI	Rome	1045	1046
Conon	Unknown	686	687	Clement II	Saxony	1046	1047
St. Sergius I	Syria	687	701	Benedict IX	Tusculum	1047	1048
John VI	Greece	701	705	(3rd time)			
John VII	Greece	705	707	Damasus II	Bavaria	1048	1048
Sisinnius	Syria	708	708	St. Leo IX	Alsace	1049	1054
Constantine	Syria	708	715	Victor II	Germany	1055	1057
St. Gregory II	Rome	715	731	Stephen IX (X)	Lorraine	1057	1058
St. Gregory III	Syria	731	741	Nicholas II	Burgundy	1059	1061
St. Zachary	Greece	741	752	Alexander II	Milan	1061	1073
Stephen II (III)[4]	Rome	752	757	St. Gregory VII	Tuscany	1073	1085

Name	Birthplace	Reigned From	To	Name	Birthplace	Reigned From	To
Bl. Victor III	Benevento	1086	1087	Sixtus IV	Savona	1471	1484
Bl. Urban II	France	1088	1099	Innocent VIII	Genoa	1484	1492
Paschal II	Ravenna	1099	1118	Alexander VI	Jativa	1492	1503
Gelasius II	Gaeta	1118	1119	Pius III	Siena	1503	1503
Callistus II	Burgundy	1119	1124	Julius II	Savona	1503	1513
Honorius II	Flagnano	1124	1130	Leo X	Florence	1513	1521
Innocent II	Rome	1130	1143	Adrian VI	Utrecht	1522	1523
Celestine II	Città di Castello	1143	1144	Clement VII	Florence	1523	1534
Lucius II	Bologna	1144	1145	Paul III	Rome	1534	1549
Bl. Eugene III	Pisa	1145	1153	Julius III	Rome	1550	1555
Anastasius IV	Rome	1153	1154	Marcellus II	Montepulciano	1555	1555
Adrian IV	England	1154	1159	Paul IV	Naples	1555	1559
Alexander III	Siena	1159	1181	Pius IV	Milan	1559	1565
Lucius III	Lucca	1181	1185	St. Pius V	Bosco	1566	1572
Urban III	Milan	1185	1187	Gregory XIII	Bologna	1572	1585
Gregory VIII	Benevento	1187	1187	Sixtus V	Grottammare	1585	1590
Clement III	Rome	1187	1191	Urban VII	Rome	1590	1590
Celestine III	Rome	1191	1198	Gregory XIV	Cremona	1590	1591
Innocent III	Anagni	1198	1216	Innocent IX	Bologna	1591	1591
Honorius III	Rome	1216	1227	Clement VIII	Florence	1592	1605
Gregory IX	Anagni	1227	1241	Leo XI	Florence	1605	1605
Celestine IV	Milan	1241	1241	Paul V	Rome	1605	1621
Innocent IV	Genoa	1243	1254	Gregory XV	Bologna	1621	1623
Alexander IV	Anagni	1254	1261	Urban VIII	Florence	1623	1644
Urban IV	Troyes	1261	1264	Innocent X	Rome	1644	1655
Clement IV	France	1265	1268	Alexander VII	Siena	1655	1667
Bl. Gregory X	Piacenza	1271	1276	Clement IX	Pistoia	1667	1669
Bl. Innocent V	Savoy	1276	1276	Clement X	Rome	1670	1676
Adrian V	Genoa	1276	1276	Bl. Innocent XI	Como	1676	1689
John XXI[7]	Portugal	1276	1277	Alexander VIII	Venice	1689	1691
Nicholas III	Rome	1277	1280	Innocent XII	Spinazzola	1691	1700
Martin IV[8]	France	1281	1285	Clement XI	Urbino	1700	1721
Honorius IV	Rome	1285	1287	Innocent XIII	Rome	1721	1724
Nicholas IV	Ascoli	1288	1292	Benedict XIII	Gravina	1724	1730
St. Celestine V	Isernia	1294	1294	Clement XII	Florence	1730	1740
Boniface VIII	Anagni	1294	1303	Benedict XIV	Bologna	1740	1758
Bl. Benedict XI	Treviso	1303	1304	Clement XIII	Venice	1758	1769
Clement V	France	1305	1314	Clement XIV	Rimini	1769	1774
John XXII	Cahors	1316	1334	Pius VI	Cesena	1775	1799
Benedict XII	France	1334	1342	Pius VII	Cesena	1800	1823
Clement VI	France	1342	1352	Leo XII	Genga	1823	1829
Innocent VI	France	1352	1362	Pius VIII	Cingoli	1829	1830
Bl. Urban V	France	1362	1370	Gregory XVI	Belluno	1831	1846
Gregory XI	France	1370	1378	Pius IX	Senegallia	1846	1878
Urban VI	Naples	1378	1389	Leo XIII	Carpineto	1878	1903
Boniface IX	Naples	1389	1404	St. Pius X	Riese	1903	1914
Innocent VII	Sul mona	1404	1406	Benedict XV	Genoa	1914	1922
Gregory XII	Venice	1406	1415	Pius XI	Desio	1922	1939
Martin V	Rome	1417	1431	Pius XII	Rome	1939	1958
Eugene IV	Venice	1431	1447	John XXIII	Sotto il Monte	1958	1963
Nicholas V	Sarzana	1447	1455	Paul VI	Concesio	1963	1978
Callistus III	Jativa	1455	1458	John Paul I	Forno di Canale	1978	1978
Pius II	Siena	1458	1464	John Paul II	Wadowice, Poland	1978	
Paul II	Venice	1464	1471				

1. Or 310. 2. He should be called Felix II, and his successors of the same name should be numbered accordingly. The discrepancy was caused by the erroneous insertion in some lists of the name of St. Felix of Rome, Martyr. 3. He was elected during the exile of St. Martin I, who endorsed him as pope. 4. After St. Zachary died, a Roman priest named Stephen was elected but died before his consecration as bishop of Rome. His name is not included in all lists for this reason. In view of this historical confusion, the *National Catholic Almanac* lists the true Stephen II as Stephen II (III), the true Stephen III as Stephen III (IV), etc. 5. Confusion exists concerning the legitimacy of claims. If the deposition of John was invalid, Leo was an antipope until after the end of Benedict's reign. If the deposition of John was valid, Leo was the legitimate pope and Benedict an antipope. 6. If the triple removal of Benedict IX was not valid, Sylvester III, Gregory VI, and Clement II were antipopes. 7. Elimination was made of the name of John XX in an effort to rectify the numerical designation of popes named John. The error dates back to the time of John XV. 8. The names of Marinus I and Marinus II were construed as Martin. In view of these two pontificates and the earlier reign of St. Martin I, this pontiff was called Martin IV. *Source: National Catholic Almanac,* from *Annuarto Pontificio.*

The Books of the Bible

Below is the Protestant canon of the Bible (New Revised Standard Version). The Roman Catholic canon also includes the Deuterocanonical books as part of the Old Testament (these are considered apocryphal by most Protestants). The Hebrew Bible recognizes the books referred to as the Old Testament in the Protestant Bible, but not the Apocryphal/Deuterocanonical books or the New Testament.

**The Old Testament
with the Apocryphal/
Deuterocanonical
Books**
*The Hebrew
Scriptures*
  Genesis
  Exodus
  Leviticus
  Numbers
  Deuteronomy
  Joshua
  Judges
  Ruth
  1 Samuel
  2 Samuel
  1 Kings
  2 Kings
  1 Chronicles
  2 Chronicles
  Ezra
  Nehemiah
  Esther
  Job
  Psalms

Proverbs
Ecclesiastes
Song of Solomon
Isaiah
Jeremiah
Lamentations
Ezekiel
Daniel
Hosea
Joel
Amos
Obadiah
Jonah
Micah
Nahum
Habakkuk
Zephaniah
Haggai
Zechariah
Malachi
*The Apocryphal/
Deuterocanonical
Books*
  Tobit
  Judith

Additions to the Book
  of Esther
Wisdom of Solomon
Ecclesiasticus, or the
  Wisdom of Jesus
  Son of Sirach
Baruch
The Letter of Jeremiah
The Prayer of Azariah
  and the Song of the
  Three Jews
Susanna
Bel and the Dragon
1 Maccabees
2 Maccabees
1 Esdras
Prayer of Manasseh
Psalm 151
3 Maccabees
2 Esdras
4 Maccabees
The New Testament
  Matthew
  Mark
  Luke

John
Acts of the Apostles
Romans
1 Corinthians
2 Corinthians
Galatians
Ephesians
Philippians
Colossians
1 Thessalonians
2 Thessalonians
1 Timothy
2 Timothy
Titus
Philemon
Hebrews
James
1 Peter
2 Peter
1 John
2 John
3 John
Jude
Revelation

The Ten Commandments

The Ten Commandments, also called the Decalogue (Greek, "ten words"), were divine laws revealed to Moses by God on Mt. Sinai. Appearing in both Exodus (Ex. 20: 2–17) and Deuteronomy (Deut. 5:6–21), the commandments are numbered differently depending on whether they appear in a Catholic, Protestant, or Hebrew Bible. The following is the version given in the Revised Standard Version of the Bible.

You shall have no other gods before me.

You shall not make for yourself a graven image, or any likeness of anything that is in heaven above, or that is in the earth beneath, or that is in the water under the earth; you shall not bow down to them or serve them; for I the Lord your God am a jealous God, visiting the iniquity of the fathers upon the children to the third and the fourth generation of those who hate me, but showing steadfast love to thousands of those who love me and keep my commandments.

You shall not take the name of the Lord your God in vain; for the Lord will not hold him guiltless who takes his name in vain.

Remember the Sabbath day, to keep it holy. Six days you shall labor, and do all your work; but the seventh day is a Sabbath to the Lord your God; in it you shall not do any work, you, or your son, or your daughter, your manservant, or your maidservant, or

your cattle, or the sojourner who is within your gates; for in six days the Lord made heaven and earth, the sea, and all that is in them, and rested the seventh day; therefore the Lord blessed the Sabbath day and hallowed it.

Honor your father and your mother, that your days may be long in the land which the Lord your God gives you.

You shall not kill.

You shall not commit adultery.

You shall not steal.

You shall not bear false witness against your neighbor.

You shall not covet your neighbor's wife, or his manservant, or his maidservant, or his ox, or his ass, or anything that is your neighbor's.

Source: Revised Standard Version of the Bible
(Ex.20: 2–17)

The Seven Deadly Sins

In Christianity, the seven deadly sins are considered "deadly" because it is believed they can do terrible damage to the soul. The now-famous list does not appear in the Bible and may have been formulated by Gregory the Great (540–604). The deadly sins are sometimes known as "capital" or "cardinal" sins: pride, greed, lust, envy, gluttony, anger, and sloth.

See Calendar and Holidays for listings of religious holidays.

The Seven Wonders of the World

Since ancient times, people have put together many "seven wonders" lists; examples include the Seven Wonders of the Natural World, the Seven Wonders of the Modern World, and the Seven Natural Wonders of the U.S. The content of these lists tends to vary, and none is definitive. The original list of seven wonders is the Seven Wonders of the Ancient World, which is made up of a selection of ancient architectural and sculptural accomplishments. The seven wonders that are most widely agreed upon as being in the original list are outlined below. (* indicates photo can be found in the Headline History section.)

Pyramids of Egypt.* A group of three pyramids, *Khufu, Khafra,* and *Menkaura* at Giza, outside modern Cairo, is often called the first wonder of the world. The largest pyramid, built by Khufu (Cheops), a king of the fourth dynasty, had an original estimated height of 482 ft (now approximately 450 ft). The base has sides 755 ft long. It contains 2,300,000 blocks; the average weight of each is 2.5 tons. Estimated date of completion is 2680 B.C. Of all the Ancient Wonders, the pyramids alone survive.

Hanging Gardens of Babylon. Often listed as the second wonder, these gardens were supposedly built by Nebuchadnezzar around 600 B.C. to please his queen, Amuhia. They are also associated with the mythical Assyrian queen, Semiramis. Archeologists surmise that the gardens were laid out atop a vaulted building, with provisions for raising water. The terraces were said to rise from 75 to 300 ft.

The Walls of Babylon, also built by Nebuchadnezzar, are sometimes referred to as the second (or the seventh) wonder instead of the Hanging Gardens.

Statue of Zeus (Jupiter) at Olympia. The work of Phidias (5th century B.C.), this colossal figure in gold and ivory was reputedly 40 ft high. All trace of it is lost, except for reproductions on coins.

Temple of Artemis (Diana) at Ephesus. A beautiful structure, begun about 350 B.C., in honor of a non-Hellenic goddess who later became identified with the Greek goddess of the same name. The temple, with Ionic columns 60 ft high, was destroyed by invading Goths in A.D. 262.

Mausoleum at Halicarnassus. This famous monument was erected by Queen Artemisia in memory of her husband, King Mausolus of Caria in Asia Minor, who died in 353 B.C. Some remains of the structure are in the British Museum. This shrine is the source of the modern word "mausoleum."

Colossus at Rhodes. This bronze statue of Helios (Apollo), about 105 ft high, was the work of the sculptor Chares, who reputedly labored for 12 years before completing it in 280 B.C. It was destroyed during an earthquake in 224 B.C.

Pharos of Alexandria. The seventh wonder was the Pharos (lighthouse) of Alexandria, built by Sostratus of Cnidus during the 3rd century B.C. on the island of Pharos off the coast of Egypt. It was destroyed by an earthquake in the 13th century.

Famous Structures

Ancient

The **Great Sphinx** of Egypt, one of the wonders of ancient Egyptian architecture, adjoins the pyramids of Giza and has a length of 240 ft. Built in the fourth dynasty, it is approximately 4,500 years old. A 10-year $2.5 million restoration project was completed in 1998. Other Egyptian buildings of note include the *Temples of Karnak, Edfu,* and *Abu Simbel,* and the *Tombs at Beni Hassan.*

The **Parthenon*** of Greece, built on the Acropolis in Athens, was the chief temple to the goddess Athena. It was believed to have been completed by 438 B.C. The present temple remained intact until the 5th century A.D. Today, though the Parthenon is in ruins, its majestic proportions are still discernible.

Other great structures of ancient Greece were the *Temples at Paestum* (c. 540 and 420 B.C.); the famous *Erechtheum* (c. 421–405 B.C.), the *Temple of Athena Niké* (c. 426 B.C.), and the *Olympieum* (174 B.C.–A.D. 131) atop the Acropolis; the *Athenian Treasury* at Delphi (c. 515 B.C.); and the *Theater* at Epidaurus (c. 325 B.C.).

The **Colosseum** (Flavian Amphitheater) of Rome, the largest and most famous of the Roman amphitheaters, was opened for use A.D. 80. Elliptical in shape, it consisted of three stories and an upper gallery,

rebuilt in stone in its present form in the third century A.D. It was principally used for gladiatorial combat and could seat between 40,000 and 50,000 spectators.

The **Pantheon** at Rome, begun by Agrippa in 27 B.C. as a temple, was rebuilt in its present circular form by Hadrian (A.D. 118–128). Literally the Pantheon was intended as a temple of "all the gods." It is remarkable for its perfect preservation today, and it has served continuously for 20 centuries as a place of worship.

Famous Roman triumphal arches, built to commemorate major military victories, include the **Arch of Titus** (c. A.D. 80) and the **Arch of Constantine** (c. A.D. 315).

Teotihuacán, located in central Mexico, was the largest city in the Americas at its height between A.D. 300 and 900. Built on a grid plan with a central avenue known as the Street of the Dead, it is the site of two enormous pyramid temples and the temple of the plumed serpent god Quetzalcoatl.

Machu Picchu is an ancient Inca fortress in the Andes Mountains of Peru. Thought to have been built and occupied from the mid-15th century, it is surrounded on three sides by stepped agricultural terraces, which are connected to the main plazas and buildings by thousands of stone steps.

Later European

St. Mark's Cathedral in Venice (1063–1071), one of the great examples of Byzantine architecture, was begun in the 9th century. Partly destroyed by fire in 976, it was later rebuilt as a Byzantine edifice.

Other famous examples of Byzantine architecture are *St. Sophia* in Istanbul (532–537); *San Vitale* in Ravenna (542); and *Assumption Cathedral* in the Kremlin, Moscow (begun in 1475).

The cathedral group at Pisa (1067–1173), one of the most celebrated groups of structures built in Romanesque style, consists of the cathedral, the cathedral's baptistery, and the campanile (**Leaning Tower***). The campanile, a form of bell tower, is 180 ft high and now leans 13.5 ft out of the perpendicular.

Other examples of Romanesque architecture include the *Vézelay Abbey* in France (1130) and *Durham Cathedral* in England.

The **Alhambra** (1248–1354), located in Granada, Spain, is universally esteemed as one of the greatest masterpieces of Muslim architecture. Designed as a palace and fortress for the Moorish monarchs of Granada, it is surrounded by a heavily fortified wall more than a mile in perimeter. The location of the Alhambra in the Sierra Nevada provides a magnificent setting for this jewel of Moorish Spain.

The **Tower of London** is a group of buildings and towers covering 13 acres along the north bank of the Thames. The central *White Tower,* begun in 1078 during the reign of William the Conqueror, was originally a fortress and royal residence, but was later used as a prison. The *Bloody Tower* is associated with Anne Boleyn and other notables.

Westminster Abbey, in London, was begun in 1050 and completed in 1065. It was rebuilt and enlarged in several phases, beginning in 1245. With only two exceptions (Edward V and Edward VIII), every British monarch since William the Conqueror has been crowned in the Abbey.

Notre-Dame de Paris (begun in 1163), one of the great examples of Gothic architecture, is a twin-towered church with a steeple over the crossing and immense flying buttresses supporting the masonry at the rear of the church.

Other famous Gothic structures are *Chartres Cathedral** (France; 12th century); *Sainte Chapelle* (Paris, France; 1246–1248); *Reims Cathedral* (France; 13th–14th centuries; rebuilt after its almost complete destruction in World War I); *Rouen Cathedral* (France; 13th–16th centuries); *Salisbury Cathedral* (England; 1220–1260); *York Minster* or the *Cathedral of St. Peter* (England; 1220–1472); *Milan Cathedral* (Italy; begun 1386); and *Cologne Cathedral* (Germany; 13th–19th centuries; badly damaged in World War II).

The **Duomo*** (cathedral) in Florence was founded in 1296, completed by Brunelleschi, and consecrated in 1436. The oval-shaped dome dominates the entire structure.

The **Vatican** is a group of buildings in Rome comprising the official residence of the pope. The *Basilica of St. Peter,* the largest church in the Christian world, was begun in 1452, and it was rebuilt between 1506 and 1626. The *Sistine Chapel,* begun in 1473, is noted for the art masterpieces of Michelangelo, Botticelli, and others. To the southeast of Vatican City is the *Basilica of the Savior* (known as

St. John Lateran). As the cathedral of the pope, it is the first-ranking Catholic Church in the world.

Other examples of Renaissance architecture are the *Palazzo Riccardi,* the *Palazzo Pitti,* and the *Palazzo Strozzi* in Florence; the *Farnese Palace* in Rome; *Palazzo Grimani* (completed about 1550) in Venice; the *Escorial* (1563–93) near Madrid; the *Town Hall* of Seville (1527–32); the *Louvre,* Paris; the *Château* at Blois, France; *St. Paul's Cathedral,* London (1675–1710; badly damaged in World War II); the *École Militaire,* Paris (1752); the *Pazzi Chapel,* Florence, designed by Brunelleschi (1429); and the *Palace of Fontainebleau* and the *Château de Chambord* in France.

The **Palace of Versailles** in France, containing the famous Hall of Mirrors, was built during the reign of Louis XIV in the 17th century and served as the royal palace until 1793.

Outstanding European buildings of the 18th and 19th centuries are the *Superga* at Turin (Italy); the *Hôtel-Dieu* in Lyons; the *Belvedere Palace* at Vienna; the *Royal Palace* of Stockholm; the *Bank of England,* the *British Museum,* the *University of London,* and the *Houses of Parliament,* all in London; and the *Panthéon,* the *Church of the Madeleine,* the *Bourse,* the *Palais de Justice,* and the *Opera House,* all in Paris.

The **Eiffel Tower,** in Paris, was built for the Exposition of 1889 by Alexandre Gustave Eiffel. It is 984 ft high (1,056 ft including the television tower).

Asian and African

The **Taj Mahal*** (1632–1650), at Agra, India, built by Shah Jahan as a tomb for his wife, is considered by some as the most perfect example of the Mogul style and by others as the most beautiful building in the world. Four slim white minarets flank the building, which is topped by a white dome; the entire structure is made of marble. Other examples of Indian architecture are the temples at Benares and Tanjore.

Among famed Muslim edifices are the *Dome of the Rock* or *Mosque of Omar,* Jerusalem (A.D. 691); the *Citadel* (1166) and the *Tombs of the Mamelukes* (15th century) in Cairo; the *Tomb of Humayun* in Delhi; the *Blue Mosque* (1468) at Tabriz; and the *Tamerlane Mausoleum* at Samarkand.

Angkor Wat, outside the city of Angkor Thom, Cambodia, is one of the most beautiful examples of Cambodian or Khmer architecture. The sanctuary was built during the 12th century.

The **Great Wall of China** (begun c. 214 B.C.), designed specifically as a defense against nomadic tribes, has large watch towers that could be called buildings. It was erected by Emperor Ch'in Shih Huang Ti and is 1,400 mi long. Built mainly of earth and stone, it varies in height between 18 and 30 ft.

Typical of Chinese architecture are the pagodas or temple towers. Among some of the better-known pagodas are the *Great Pagoda of the Wild Geese* at Sian (founded in 652) and *Nan t'a* (11th century) at Fang Shan.

Other well-known Chinese buildings are the *Drum Tower* (1273), the *Three Great Halls* in the Forbidden City (1627), *Buddha's Perfume Tower* (19th century), the *Porcelain Pagoda,* and the *Summer Palace,* all at Beijing.

The painted wooden **Torii,** or Gateway, at Miyajima Island, Japan, stands in the tidal flats opposite the historic Itsukushima Shrine. Built in the traditional Shinto style, with two columns supporting a concave crosspiece on top, the gate serves to welcome the spirits of the dead as they come from across the Inland Sea.

Other famous Japanese buildings include *Himeji Castle* (17th century) and the Buddhist temples of *Horyuji* (7th century) and *Todaiji* (8th century) at Nara, and *Phoenix Hall* (11th century) at Uji near Kyoto.

United States

The **Chrysler Building** in New York City is one of the finest examples of Art Deco style high-rise architecture. Built for the automotive magnate Walter P. Chrysler between 1928 and 1930, the building makes use of decorative elements borrowed from automobiles. At 1,046 ft it was briefly the tallest building in the world before the Empire State Building was completed the following year.

The **Empire State Building,** one of the most popular tourist attractions in the heart of Manhattan, was constructed between 1930 and 1931. Features include a tiered structure that recalls ancient Egyptian and Aztec pyramids and a mast at the top for mooring dirigibles. Rising to 1,250 ft (not including the mast), it remained the tallest building in the world until the 1970s.

Rockefeller Center, in New York City, extends from 5th Ave. to the Avenue of the Americas between 48th and 52nd Sts. (and halfway to 7th Ave. between 47th and 51st Sts.). It occupies more than 22 acres and has 19 buildings.

The **Cathedral of St. John the Divine,** at 112th St. and Amsterdam Ave. in New York City, was begun in 1892 and is now in the final stages of completion. When completed, it will be the largest cathedral in the world: 601 ft long, 146 ft wide at the nave, 320 ft wide at the transept. The east end is designed in Romanesque-Byzantine style, and the nave and west end are Gothic.

The **World Trade Center,** in New York City, was dedicated in 1973. Its twin towers are 110 stories high (about 1,365 ft), and the complex contains over 9 million sq ft of office space. A restaurant is on the 107th floor of the North Tower.[1]

The **Statue of Liberty*** was designed by Frédéric Auguste Bartholdi of Alsace as a gift to Americans from the people of France. The statue of a female figure holding a torch in her raised hand was accepted on Oct. 28, 1886, by President Grover Cleveland. The 225-ton steel-reinforced copper structure stands on Liberty Island in New York Harbor. It is 152 ft tall and stands on a 150-foot pedestal.

The **Sears Tower** in Chicago is, at 1,450 ft, the tallest building in the United States. Constructed between 1974 and 1976 for Sears, Roebuck and Company, the structure is composed of 75-foot square tubes that rise to varying levels.

The **Gateway Arch,** located on the riverfront in St. Louis, Mo., is a tapered curve of stainless steel rising to 630 ft. The tallest manmade memorial in the United States, the Arch was designed by Finnish-born U.S. architect Eero Saarinen and built between 1963 and 1966. Visitors can ride to the top in specially devised capsule-like tram cars.

Mount Rushmore (6,000 ft), in South Dakota, became a celebrated American landmark after sculptor Gutzon Borglum took on the project of carving into the side of it the heads of four great presidents. From 1927 until his death in 1941, Borglum worked on chiseling the 60-foot likenesses of Washington, Jefferson, Lincoln, and Theodore Roosevelt. His son, Lincoln, finished the sculpture later that year.

San Francisco's **Golden Gate Bridge,** completed in 1937, is one of the most recognizable structures in the United States. Designed by Joseph B. Strauss, this elegant suspension bridge has a main span of 4,200 ft.

The Seattle **Space Needle** was planned as the central structure and symbol of the 1962 Seattle World's Fair, the theme of which was "Century 21." The Needle, which is 605 ft tall, is topped by an observation deck and a revolving restaurant.

* Photos of these structures can be found in the Headline History section. 1. Both towers were destroyed in a terrorist attack on Sept. 11, 2001.

Famous Ship Canals

Name	Location	Length (miles)[1]	Width (feet)	Depth (feet)	Locks	Year opened
Albert	Belgium	80.0	53.0	16.5	6	1939
Amsterdam-Rhine	Netherlands	45.0	164.0	41.0	3	1952
Beaumont-Port Arthur	United States	40.0	200.0	34.0	—	1916
Canal du Midi	France	149.0	n.a.	n.a.	100	1692
Chesapeake and Delaware	United States	14.0	450.0	35.0	—	1829
Erie Canal	United States	363.0	70	7	82	1825
Grand Canal	China	1,085.0	n.a.	n.a.	n.a.	7th cent.
Göta Canal	Sweden	240.0	n.a.	n.a.	58	1832
Houston	United States	50.0	(2)	40.0	—	1914
Kiel (Nord-Ostsee Kanal)	Germany	61.3	144.0	36.0	4	1895
Panama	Panama	50.7	110.0	41.0	12	1914
St. Lawrence Seaway	U.S. and Canada	2,400.0[3]	(4)	—	—	1959
Montreal to Prescott	U.S. and Canada	11.5	80.0	30.0	7	1959
Welland	Canada	27.5	80.0	27.0	8	1931
Sault Ste. Marie	Canada	1.2	60.0	16.8	1	1895
Sault Ste. Marie	United States	1.6	80.0	25.0	4	1915
Suez	Egypt	119.9[5]	1197.5	68.9	—	1869

1. Statute miles. 2. 300–400 ft. 3. From Montreal to Duluth. 4. 442–550 ft; there are 11.5 mi of locks, 80 ft wide and 30 ft deep. 5. From Port Said lighthouse to entrance channel in Suez roads. *Source:* American Society of Civil Engineers.

Notable Modern Bridges

Name	Location	Length of main span		Year completed
		feet	meters	
Suspension	**United States**			
Verrazano-Narrows	Lower New York Bay	4,260	1,298	1964
Golden Gate	San Francisco Bay	4,200	1,280	1937
Mackinac	Mackinac Straits, Mich.	3,800	1,158	1957
George Washington	Hudson River at New York City	3,500	1,067	1931
Tacoma Narrows II	Puget Sound at Tacoma, Wash.	2,800	853	1950
San Francisco–Oakland Bay[1]	San Francisco Bay	2,310	704	1936
Bronx-Whitestone	East River, New York City	2,300	701	1939
Delaware Memorial[1]	Delaware River near Wilmington, Del.	2,150	655	1951, 1968
Seaway Skyway	St. Lawrence River at Ogdensburg, N.Y.	2,150	655	1960
Walt Whitman	Delaware River at Philadelphia	2,000	610	1957
Ambassador International	Detroit River at Detroit	1,850	564	1929
Throgs Neck	East River, New York City	1,800	549	1961
Benjamin Franklin	Delaware River at Philadelphia	1,750	533	1926
William Preston Lane, Jr.[1]	Chesapeake Bay, Md.	1,600	488	1952, 1973
Brooklyn Bridge	East River, New York City	1,596	486	1883
Royal Gorge	Arkansas River, Colo.	1,053	321	1929
Wheeling Bridge	Ohio River, Wheeling, W.Va.	1,010	308	1847
	International			
Akashi Kaikyo	Hyogo, Japan	6,529	1,990	1998
Izmit Bay	Marmara Sea, Turkey	5,472	1,668	UC
Storebælt	Denmark	5,328	1,624	1998
Humber	Humberside, England	4,626	1,410	1981
Jiangyin	Yangtze River, China	4,543	1,385	1999
Tsing Ma	Hong Kong	4,518	1,377	1997
Höga Kusten (High Coast)	Västernorrland, Sweden	3,969	1,210	1997
Minami Bisan-Seto	Japan	3,609	1,100	1988
Second Bosporus	Istanbul, Turkey	3,576	1,090	1988
First Bosporus	Istanbul, Turkey	3,524	1,074	1973
Third Kurushima	Japan	3,379	1,030	1999
Second Kurushima	Japan	3,346	1,020	1999
Ponte 25 de Abril	Tagus River at Lisbon, Portugal	3,323	1,013	1966
Forth Road	Queensferry, Scotland	3,300	1,006	1964
Kita Bisan-Seto	Japan	3,248	990	1988
Severn	Severn River at Beachley, England	3,240	988	1966
Yicang	Yangtze River, Hubei Province, China	3,150	960	UC
Shimotsui Straits	Japan	3,084	940	1988
Xiling Yangtze	Three Gorges Dam, China	2,952	900	1996
Tigergate (Humen)	Pearl River, Guangdong Province, China	2,913	888	1997
Ohnaruto	Japan	2,874	876	1988
Pierre Laporte	Quebec, Canada	2,190	668	1970
Cantilever	**United States**			
Commodore John Barry	Chester, Pa.	1,644	501	1974
Crescent City Connection[1]	Mississippi River, New Orleans, La.	1,576	480	1958, 1985
Transbay Bridge	San Francisco Bay	1,400	427	1936
	International			
Quebec Railway	Quebec, Canada	1,800	549	1917
Forth Railway[1]	Queensferry, Scotland	1,710	521	1890
Minato Ohashi	Osaka, Japan	1,673	510	1974
Howrah	Hooghly River at Calcutta, India	1,500	457	1943
Steel Arch	**United States**			
New River Gorge	Fayetteville, W. Va.	1,700	518	1977
Bayonne	Kill Van Kull at Bayonne, N.J.	1,675	510	1931
Fremont	Portland, Ore.	1,255	383	1973
Hell Gate	East River (Hell Gate), New York City	978	298	1916
	International			
Sydney Harbor	Sydney, Australia	1,670	509	1932
Zdákov	Vltava River, Czech Republic	1,244	380	1967
Port Mann	Fraser River at Vancouver, British Columbia	1,200	366	1964
Cable-Stayed	**United States**			
Dames Point	Jacksonville, Fla.	1,300	396	1988
Houston Ship Channel	Baytown, Tex.	1,250	381	1995

Name	Location	Length of main span		Year completed
		feet	meters	
Sidney Lanier	Brunswick River, Ga.	1,250	381	UC
Hale Boggs Memorial	Luling, La.	1,222	373	1983
Sunshine Skyway	Tampa, Fla.	1,200	366	1987
	International			
Tatara	Honshu–Shikoku, Japan	2,920	890	1999
Ponte de Normandie	Le Havre, France	2,808	856	1995
Second Nanjing	Yangtze River, Nanjing, China	2,060	628	UC
Wuhan Third Yangtze	Wuhan, Hubei Province, China	2,028	618	UC
Qingzhou Minjiang	Fuzhou, China	1,985	605	1996
Yang Pu	Shanghai, China	1,975	602	1993
Xupu	Shanghai, China	1,936	590	1997
Meiko Chuo	Aichi, Japan	1,936	590	1997
Patras	Greece	1,837	560	UC
Skarnsundet	near Trondheim, Norway	1,739	530	1991
Quishi	Guangdong Province, China	1,700	518	UC
Tsurumi Tsubasa	Kanagawa, Japan	1,673	510	1995
Jingsha	Yangtze River, Hubei Province, China	1,640	500	UC
Oresund	Denmark/Sweden	1,614	492	2000
Ikuchi	Honshu-Shikoku, Japan	1,608	490	1991
Higashi Kobe	Hyogo, Japan	1,591	485	1994
Zhanjiang Bay	Guangdong Province, China	1,575	480	1998
Ting Kau	Hong Kong	1,558	475	1997
Seohae Grand	South Korea	1,542	470	1999
Alex Fraser	Vancouver, B.C., Canada	1,525	465	1986
Yokohama-ko-odan	Kanagawa, Japan	1,509	460	1989
Second Hooghly	Calcutta, India	1,500	457	1992
Second Severn Crossing	Severn River, England	1,496	456	1996
Dartford	Thames River, Dartford, England	1,476	450	1992
Dao Kanong	Chao Phraya River, Bangkok, Thailand	1,476	450	1987
Queen Elizabeth II	Thames River, Dartford, England	1,476	450	1991
Chongqing 2nd	Sichuan Province, China	1,457	444	1996
Continuous Truss	**United States**			
Astoria	Columbia River, Ore.	1,232	376	1966
Croton Reservoir	Croton, N.Y.	1,052	321	1970
Ravenswood	Ohio River, Ravenswood, W. Va.	902	275	1981
Central	Ohio River, Newport, Ky.	850	259	1995
Dubuque	Mississippi River at Dubuque, Iowa	845	258	1943
	International			
Oshima	Oshima Island, Japan	1,066	325	1976
Tenmon	Kumamoto, Japan	984	300	1966
Kuronoseto	Nagashima-Kyushu, Japan	984	300	1974
Graf Spee	Germany	839	256	1936
Concrete Arch	**United States**			
Natchez Trace Pkwy.	Franklin, Tenn.	582	177	1994
Westinghouse	Pittsburgh, Pa.	460	140	1931
Jack's Run	Pittsburgh, Pa.	400	120	1930
Cappelen	Minneapolis, Minn.	400	120	1923
	International			
Wanxian	Wanxian, Sichuan Province, China	1,378	420	1997
Krk (I)	Krk, Croatia	1,280	390	1980
Gladesville	Parramatta River at Sydney, Australia	1,000	305	1964
Amizade	Paraná River at Foz do Iguassu, Brazil	951	290	1964
Arrábida	Porto, Portugal	886	270	1963
Sandö	Angerman River at Kramfors, Sweden	866	264	1943
Confederation	Northumberland Strait, Canada	820	250	1997
Sibenik	Sibenik, Yugoslavia	808	246	1966
Krk (II)	Krk, Croatia	800	244	1979
Fiumarella	Catanzaro, Italy	758	231	1961
Zaporozhe	Old Dnepr River, Ukraine	748	228	1952
Esla	Esla River at Zamora, Spain	645	197	1940
Segmental Construction	**United States**			
Jesse H. Jones Memorial	Houston Ship Channel, Tex.	750	228	1982

NOTES: UC = under construction in 2001. 1. Twin span. *Source:* Federal Highway Administration.

World's Tallest Buildings

Building, city	Year	Stories	Height m	Height ft	Building, city	Year	Stories	Height m	Height ft
Petronas Tower 1, Kuala Lumpur, Malaysia	1998	88	452	1,483	311 South Wacker Drive, Chicago	1990	65	293	961
Petronas Tower 2, Kuala Lumpur, Malaysia	1998	88	452	1,483	American International Building, New York	1932	67	290	952
Sears Tower, Chicago	1974	110	442	1,450	Cheung Kong Center, Hong Kong	1999	70	290	951
Jin Mao Building, Shanghai	1999	88	421	1,381	First Canadian Place, Toronto	1975	72	290	951
World Trade Center One, New York[1]	1972	110	417	1,368	Key Tower, Cleveland	1991	57	290	950
World Trade Center Two, New York[1]	1973	110	415	1,362	One Liberty Place, Philadelphia	1987	61	288	945
Citic Plaza, Guangzhou, China	1996	80	391	1,283	Plaza66, Shanghai	UC00	66	288	945
Shun Hing Square, Shenzhen, China	1996	69	384	1,260	Columbia Seafirst Center, Seattle	1984	76	287	943
Empire State Building, New York	1931	102	381	1,250	Sunjoy Tomorrow Square, Shanghai	1999	59	285	934
Central Plaza, Hong Kong	1992	78	374	1,227	40 Wall Street, New York	1930	72	283	927
Bank of China Tower, Hong Kong	1989	70	369	1,209	NationsBank Plaza, Dallas	1985	72	281	921
Emirates Tower One, Dubai	UC00	55	355	1,165	Overseas Union Bank Centre, Singapore	1986	66	280	919
The Center, Hong Kong	1998	79	350	1,148	United Overseas Bank Plaza, Singapore	1992	66	280	919
T & C Tower, Kaohsiung, Taiwan	1997	85	348	1,140	Republic Plaza, Singapore	1995	66	280	919
Amoco Building, Chicago	1973	80	346	1,136	Citicorp Center, New York	1977	59	279	915
Kingdom Centre, Riyadh	UC00	30	345	1,132	Scotia Plaza, Toronto	1989	68	275	902
John Hancock Center, Chicago	1969	100	344	1,127	Williams Tower, Houston	1983	64	275	901
Burj al Arab Hotel, Dubai	1998	60	321	1,053	Faisaliah Complex, Riyadh	UC00	30	274	899
Baiyoke Tower II, Bangkok	1997	90	320	1,050	Renaissance Tower, Dallas	1975	56	270	886
Chrysler Building, New York	1930	77	319	1,046	900 North Michigan Ave., Chicago	1989	66	265	871
Bank of America Plaza, Atlanta	1993	55	312	1,023	NationsBank Corporate Center, Charlotte	1992	60	265	871
Library Tower, Los Angeles	1990	75	310	1,018	SunTrust Plaza, Atlanta	1992	60	265	871
Telekom Malaysia Headquarters, Kuala Lumpur	1999	55	310	1,017	BCE Place–Canada Trust Tower, Toronto	1990	51	263	863
Emirates Tower Two, Dubai	UC00	54	309	1,014	Water Tower Place, Chicago	1976	74	262	859
AT&T Corporate Center, Chicago	1989	60	307	1,007	First Interstate Tower, Los Angeles	1974	62	262	858
Chase Tower, Houston	1982	75	305	1,000	Transamerica Pyramid, San Francisco	1972	48	260	853
Two Prudential Plaza, Chicago	1990	64	303	995	G.E. Building, New York	1933	70	259	850
Ryugyong Hotel, Pyongyang, N. Korea	1995	105	300	984	One First National Plaza, Chicago	1969	60	259	850
Commerzbank Tower, Frankfurt	1997	63	299	981	Two Liberty Place, Philadelphia	1990	58	258	848
Wells Fargo Plaza, Houston	1983	71	296	972	Messeturm, Frankfurt	1990	63	257	843
Landmark Tower, Yokohama, Japan	1993	70	296	971					

NOTE: Height is measured from sidewalk level of main entrance to structural top of building. Antennas and flag poles are not included. UC00 = Under construction, scheduled for completion in 2000. 1. Destroyed in a terrorist attack on Sept. 11, 2001. *Source:* Council on Tall Buildings and Urban Habitat, Lehigh University.

Pritzker Architecture Prize

The Pritzker Architecture Prize, sponsored by the Hyatt Foundation of Los Angeles, is considered to be the highest accolade in the profession.

Year	Architect(s), country	Year	Architect(s), country
1979	Philip Johnson, United States	1991	Robert Venturi, United States
1980	Luis Barragán, Mexico	1992	Alvaro Siza, Portugal
1981	James Stirling, Great Britain	1993	Fumihiko Maki, Japan
1982	Kevin Roche, United States	1994	Christian de Portzamparc, France
1983	Ieoh Ming Pei, United States	1995	Tadao Ando, Japan
1984	Richard Meier, United States	1996	Rafael Moneo, Spain
1985	Hans Hollein, Austria	1997	Sverre Fehn, Norway
1986	Gottfried Boehm, Germany	1998	Renzo Piano, Italy
1987	Kenzo Tange, Japan	1999	Sir Norman Foster, United Kingdom
1988	Gordon Bunshaft, United States, and Oscar Niemeyer, Brazil	2000	Rem Koolhaas, the Netherlands
1989	Frank O. Gehry, United States	2001	Jacques Herzog and Pierre de Meuron, Switzerland
1990	Aldo Rossi, Italy		

World's Highest Dams

Name	River, state, and country	Structural height feet	Structural height meters	Gross reservoir capacity thousands of acre feet	Gross reservoir capacity millions of cubic meters	Year completed
Rogun	Vakhsh, Tajikistan	1099	335	9,404	11,600	1985
Nurek	Vakhsh, Tajikistan	984	300	8,512	10,500	1980
Grande Dixence	Dixence, Switzerland	935	285	324	400	1962
Inguri	Inguri, Georgia	892	272	801	1,100	1984
Vaiont	Vaiont, Italy	859	262	137	169	1961
Manuel M. Torres	Grijalva, Mexico	856	261	1,346	1,660	1981
Tehri	Bhagirathi, India	856	261	2,869	3,540	UC
Alvaro Obregon	Mextiquic, Mexico	853	260	n.a.	n.a.	1926
Mauvoisin	Drance de Bagnes, Switzerland	820	250	146	180	1957
Alberto Lleras	Orinoco, Colombia	797	243	811	1,000	1989
Mica	Columbia, Canada	797	243	20,000	24,670	1972
Sayano-Shushensk	Yenisei, Russia	794	242	25,353	31,300	1980
Ertan	Yangtze/Yalong, China	787	240	4,702	5,800	1999
La Esmeralda	Batá, Colombia	778	237	661	815	1975
Kishau	Tons, India	774	236	1,946	2,400	1985
Oroville	Feather, Calif., U.S.	770	235	3,538	4,299	1968
El Cajón	Humuya, Honduras	768	234	4,580	5,650	1984
Chirkey	Sulak, Russia	764	233	2,252	2,780	1977
Bhakra	Sutlej, India	741	226	8,002	9,870	1963
Luzzone	Brenno di Luzzone, Switzerland	738	225	71	87	1963
Hoover	Colorado, Ariz./Nev., U.S.	732	223	28,500	35,154	1936
Contra	Verzasca, Switzerland	722	220	70	86	1965
Mratinje	Piva, Herzegovina	722	220	713	880	1973
Dworshak	N. Fk. Clearwater, Idaho, U.S.	717	219	3,453	4,259	1974
Glen Canyon	Colorado, Ariz., U.S.	710	216	27,000	33,304	1964

NOTES: UC = under construction in 2001. n.a. = not available. *Source:* International Commission on Large Dams, *World Register of Dams 1998.*

World's Largest Dams

Dam	Location	Volume (thousands) Cubic meters	Volume (thousands) Cubic yards	Year completed
Syncrude Tailings	Canada	540,000	706,320	UC
Chapetón	Argentina	296,200	311,539	UC
Pati	Argentina	238,180	274,026	UC
New Cornelia Tailings	United States	209,500	274,026	1973
Tarbela	Pakistan	121,720	159,210	1976
Kambaratinsk	Kyrgyzstan	112,200	146,758	UC
Fort Peck	Montana	96,049	125,628	1940
Lower Usuma	Nigeria	93,000	121,644	1990
Cipasang	Indonesia	90,000	117,720	UC
Atatürk	Turkey	84,500	110,522	1990
Yacyretá-Apipe	Paraguay/Argentina	81,000	105,944	UC
Guri (Raul Leoni)	Venezuela	78,000	102,014	1986
Rogun	Tajikistan	75,500	98,750	1985
Oahe	South Dakota	70,339	92,000	1963
Mangla	Pakistan	65,651	85,872	1967
Gardiner	Canada	65,440	85,592	1968
Afsluitdijk	Netherlands	63,400	82,927	1932
Oroville	California	59,639	78,008	1968
San Luis	California	59,405	77,700	1967
Nurek	Tajikistan	58,000	75,861	1980
Garrison	North Dakota	50,843	66,500	1956
Cochiti	New Mexico	48,052	62,850	1975
Tabka (Thawra)	Syria	46,000	60,168	1976
Bennett W.A.C.	Canada	43,733	57,201	1967
Tucuruí	Brazil	43,000	56,242	1984

NOTE: UC = under construction in 1999. *Source:* Department of the Interior, Bureau of Reclamation and *International Water Power and Dam Construction.*

World's Largest Hydroelectric Plants
(over 4,000 MW capacity)

Name of dam	Location	Rated capacity (MW)		Year of initial operation
		Present	Ultimate	
Itaipu	Brazil/Paraguay	12,600	14,000	1983
Guri	Venezuela	10,000	10,000	1986
Grand Coulee	Washington	6,494	6,494	1942
Sayano-Shushensk	Russia	6,400	6,400	1989
Krasnoyarsk	Russia	6,000	6,000	1968
Churchill Falls	Canada	5,428	5,428	1971
La Grande 2	Canada	5,328	5,328	1979
Bratsk	Russia	4,500	4,500	1961
Moxoto	Brazil	4,328	4,328	n.a.
Ust-Ilim	Russia	4,320	4,320	1977
Tucurui	Brazil	4,245	8,370	1984

NOTES: MW = megawatts. n.a. = not available. *Source:* International Hydropower Association, Sutton, England.

Notable Tunnels

Name	Location	Length		Year completed
		mi.	km	
Railroad, excluding subways				
Seikan	Tsugaru Strait, Japan	33.5	53.9	1988
Channel Tunnel[1]	English Channel, England–France	31.1	50.0	1994
Simplon (I and II)	Alps, Switzerland–Italy	12.3	19.8	1906 & 1922
Apennine	Bologna–Florence, Italy	11.5	18.5	1934
St. Gotthard	Swiss Alps	9.3	15.0	1880
Lötschberg	Swiss Alps	9.1	14.6	1911
Mont Cénis	French Alps	8.5[2]	13.7	1871
New Cascade	Cascade Mountains, Washington	7.8	12.6	1929
Vosges	Vosges, France	7.0	11.3	1940
Flathead	Rocky Mountains, Montana	7.0	11.3	1970
Arlberg	Austrian Alps	6.3	10.1	1884
Moffat	Rocky Mountains, Colorado	6.2	9.9	1928
Shimizu	Shimizu, Japan	6.1	9.8	1931
Rimutaka	Wairarapa, New Zealand	5.5	8.9	1955
Storebaelt	Great Belt, Denmark	5.0	8.0	1995
Vehicular				
Laerdal	Laerdal–Aurland, Norway	15.2	24.5	2000
St. Gotthard	Alps, Switzerland	10.2	16.4	1980
Mt. Blanc	Alps, France–Italy	7.0	11.3	1965
Aqualine Expressway	Tokyo Bay, Japan	5.9	9.5	1997
Mt. Ena	Japan Alps, Japan	5.3	8.5	1976[3]
Great St. Bernard	Alps, Switzerland–Italy	3.4	5.5	1964
Mount Royal	Montreal, Canada	3.2	5.1	1918
Queensway	Mersey River, Liverpool, England	2.2	3.5	1934
Brooklyn-Battery	East River, New York City	1.7	2.7	1950
Fort McHenry	Baltimore, Maryland	1.7	2.7	1985
Holland	Hudson River, New York–New Jersey	1.6	2.6	1927
Lincoln	Hudson River, New York–New Jersey	1.6	2.6	1937
Hampton Roads[4]	Norfolk, Virginia	1.4	2.3	1957
Queens-Midtown	East River, New York City	1.3	2.1	1940
Liberty Tubes	Pittsburgh, Pennsylvania	1.2	1.9	1923
Baltimore Harbor	Baltimore, Maryland	1.2	1.9	1957
Allegheny Tunnels	Pennsylvania Turnpike	1.2	1.9	1940[5]
Yerba	Yerba Buena Island, Calif.	0.5	0.8	1936

1. Three-tunnel system including two rail tunnels (one carries passengers from England to France, the other from France to England) and a central service tunnel. 2. Lengthened to its present 8.5 miles in 1881. 3. Parallel tunnel begun in 1976. 4. Parallel bridge-tunnel opened in 1976. 5. Parallel tunnel built in 1965, twin tunnel in 1966. *Source:* American Society of Civil Engineers and International Bridge, Tunnel & Turnpike Association, Wittiker's.

First Aid for Crossword Puzzlers

We cannot begin to list all the odd words you might encounter in your daily and Sunday crossword puzzles, for such words run into the thousands. But we have tried to include those that turn up most frequently, as well as many others that should be of help to you when you are unable to go any further.

We do not guarantee that the definitions in your puzzle will be exactly the same as ours, although we have checked every word with a standard dictionary and have followed its definition.

In nearly every case, we have used as the key word the principal noun of the definition, rather than any adjective, adjective phrase, or noun used as an adjective. And, to simplify your searching, we have grouped the words according to the number of spaces you have to fill.

Words of Two Letters

Ambary, DA
And (French, Latin), ET
Article (Arabic), AL
  (French), LA, LE, UN
  (Spanish), EL, LA, UN
At the (French), AU
  (Spanish), AL
Behold, LO
Bird: Hawaiian, OO
Birthplace: Abraham's, UR
Bone, OS
Buddha, FO
Butterfly: Peacock, IO
Champagne, AY
Chaos, NU
Chief: Burmese, BO
Coin: Roman, AS
  Siamese, AT
Concerning, RE
Dialect: Chinese, WU
Double (Egy. relig.), KA
Drama: Japanese, NO
Egg (comb. form), OO
Esker, OS

Eye (Scottish), EE
Factor: Amplification, MU
Fifty (Greek), NU
Fish: Carplike, ID
Force, OD
Forty (Greek), MU
From (French, Latin, Spanish), DE
  (Latin prefix), AB
From the (French), DU
God: Babylonian, EA, ZU
  Egyptian sun, RA
  Hindu unknown, KA
  Semitic, EL
Goddess: Babylonian, AI
  Greek Earth, GE
Gold (heraldry), OR
Gulf: Arctic, OB
Heart (Egy. relig.), AB
Indian: South American, GE
King: Of Bashan, OG
Language: Artificial, RO
  Assamese, AO
Lava: Hawaiian, AA

Letter: Greek, MU, NU, PI, XI
  Hebrew, HE, PE
Lily: Palm, TI
Measure: Chinese, HO, HU, KO, LI, MU, PU, TO, TU
  Japanese, GO, JO, MO, RI, SE, TO
  Netherlands, EL
  Portuguese, PE
  Siamese, WA
  Swedish, AM
  Type, EM, EN
  Vietnamese, LY
Monk: Buddhist, BO
Month: Jewish, AB
Mouth, OS
Mulberry: Indian, AL
Native: Burmese, WA
Note: Of scale, DO, FA, MI, LA, RE, TI
Of (French, Latin, Spanish), DE
Of the (French), DU

One (Scottish), AE
Pagoda: Chinese, TA
Plant: East Indian fiber, DA
Ridge: Sandy, AS, OS
River: Russian, OB
Sloth: Three-toed, AI
Soul (Egy. relig.), BA
Sound: Hindu mystic, OM
Suffix: Comparative, ER
To the: French, AU
  Spanish, AL
Tree: Buddhist sacred, BO
Tribe: Assamese, AO
Type: Jumbled, PI
Weight: Chinese, LI
  Danish, ES
  Japanese, MO
  Roman, AS
  Vietnamese, TA
Whirlwind: Faeroe Is., OE
Yes (German), JA
  (Italian, Spanish), SI
  (Russian), DA

Words of Three Letters

Adherent, IST
Again, BIS
Age, ERA
Antelope: African, GNU, KOB
Apricot: Japanese, UME
Article (German), DAS, DEM, DEN, DER, DES, DIE, EIN
  (French), LES, UNE
  (Spanish), LAS, LOS, UNA
Banana: Polynesian, FEI
Barge, HOY
Bass: African, IYO
Beak, NEB, NIB
Beard: Grain, AWN
Beetle: June, DOR
Being, ENS
Berry: Hawthorn, HAW
Beverage: Hawaiian, AVA
Bird: Australian, EMU
  Crowlike, JAY
  Extinct, MOA
  Fabulous, ROC
  Frigate, IWA
  Parson, POE, TUE, TUI
  Sea, AUK
Blackbird, ANI, ANO
Born, NEE
Bronze: Roman, AES
Bugle: Yellow, IVA
By way of, VIA
Canton: Swiss, URI
Cap: Turkish, FEZ
Catnip, NEP
Character: In "Faerie Queene," UNA
Coin (Money of account):
  Afghan, PUL
  Albanian, LEK
  Bulgarian, LEV, LEW

French, ECU, SOU
Guyanese, BIT
Indian, PIE
Japanese, SEN, YEN
Korean, WON
Lithuanian, LIT
Macao, Timor, AVO
Palestinian, MIL
Persian, PUL
Peruvian, SOL
Rumanian, BAN, LEU, LEY
Scandinavian, ORE
Siamese, ATT
Collection: Facts, ANA
Commune: Belgian, ANS, ATH
  Netherlands, EDE, EPE
Community: Russian, MIR
Constellation: Southern, ARA
Contraction: Poetic, EEN, EER, OER
Covering: Apex of roof, EPI
Crab: Fiddler, UCA
Crag: Rocky, TOR
Cry: Crow, rook, raven, CAW
Cup: Wine, AMA
Cymbal, Oriental, TAL, ZEL
Disease: Silkworm, UJI
Division: Danish territorial, AMT
  Geologic, EON
Doctrine, ISM
Dowry, DOT
Dry (French), SEC
Dynasty: Chinese, CHI, HAN, SUI, WEI, YIN
Eagle: Sea, ERN
Earth (comb. form), GEO
Egg: Louse, NIT
Eggs: Fish, ROE
Emmet, ANT

Enzyme, ASE
Equal (comb. form), ISO
Extension: building, ELL
Far (comb. form), TEL
Farewell, AVE
Fiber: Palm, TAL
Finial, EPI
Fish: Carplike, IDE
  Pikelike, DAB
Flatfish, DAB
Fleur-de-lis, LIS, LYS
Food: Hawaiian, POI
Formerly, NEE
Friend (French), AMI
Game: Card, LOO
Garment: Camel-hair, ABA
Gateway, DAR
Gazelle: Tibetan, GOA
Genus: Ducks, AIX
  Grasses, POA
  Grasses (maize), ZEA
  Herbs or shrubs, IVA
  Lizards, UTA
  Rodents (incl. house mice), MUS
  Ruminants (incl. cattle), BOS
  Swine, SUS
Gibbon: Malay, LAR
God: Assyrian, SIN
  Babylonian, ABU, ANU, BEL, HEA, SIN, UTU
  Irish sea, LER
  Phrygian, MEN
  Polynesian, ORO
Goddess: Babylonian, AYA
  Etruscan, UNI
  Hindu, SRI, UMA, VAC
  Teutonic, RAN

Governor: Algerian, DEY
  Turkish, BEY
Grampus, ORC
Grape, UVA
Grass: Meadow, POA
Gypsy, ROM
Hail, AVE
Hare: Female, DOE
Hawthorn, HAW
Hay: Spread for drying, TED
Herb: Japanese, UDO
  Perennial, PIA
  Used for blue dye, WAD
Herd: Whales, GAM, POD
Hero: Spanish, CID
High (music), ALT
Honey (pharm.), MEL
Humorist: American, ADE
I (Latin), EGO
I love (Latin), AMO
Indian: Algonquin, FOX, SAC, WEA
  Chimakuan, HOH
  Keresan, SIA
  Mayan, MAM
  Shoshonean, UTE
  Siouan, KAW, OTO
  South American, ITE, ONA, URO, URU, YAO
  Tierra del Fuego, ONA
  Wakashan, AHT
Ingot, PIG
Inlet: Narrow, RIA
Island: Cyclades, IOS
  Dodecanese, COS, KOS
  (French), ILE
  River, AIT
Jackdaw, DAW

John (Gaelic), IAN
Keelbill: ANI, ANO
Kiln, OST
King: British legendary, LUD
Kobold, NIS
Lace: To make, TAT
Lamprey, EEL
Language: Artificial, IDO
  Bantu, ILA
  Siamese, LAO, TAI
Leaf: Palm, OLA, OLE
Leaving, ORT
Left: Cause to turn, HAW
Letter: Greek, CHI, ETA, PHI,
  PSI, RHO, TAU
  Hebrew, MEM, NUN, SIN,
  TAV, VAU
Lettuce, COS
Life (comb. form), BIO
Lily: Palm, TOI
Lizard, EFT
Louse: Young, NIT
Love (Anglo-Irish), GRA
Lute: Oriental, TAR
Macaw: Brazilian, ARA
Marble, TAW
Match: Shooting (French), TIR
Meadow, LEA
Measure: Abyssinian, TAT
  Algerian, PIK
  Arabian, DEN, SAA
  Belgian, VAT
  Bulgarian, OKA, OKE
  Chinese, FEN, TOU, YIN
  Cloth, ELL
  Cyprus, OKA, OKE, PIK
  Czech, LAN, SAH
  Danish, FOD, MIL, POT
  Dominican Republic, ONA
  Dutch, old, AAM
  East Indian, KIT
  Egyptian, APT, HEN, PIK,
  ROB
  Electric, MHO, OHM
  Energy, ERG
  English, PIN
  Estonian, TUN
  French, POT
  German, AAM
  Greek, PIK
  Hebrew, CAB, HIN, KOR,
  LOG
  Hungarian, AKO
  Icelandic, FET
  Indian, GAZ, GUZ, JOW,
  KOS
  Japanese, BOO, CHO, KEN,
  RIN, SHO, SUN, TAN
  Malabar, ADY
  Metric (land), ARE
  Netherlands, KAN, KOP,
  MUD, VAT, ZAK
  Norwegian, FOT, POT
  Persian, GAZ, GUZ, MOU,
  ZAR, ZER
  Polish, CAL
  Rangoon, PES, URN
  Roman, PES, URN
  Russian, FUT, LOF
  Scottish, COP

  Siamese, KEN, NIU, RAI,
  SAT, SEN, SOK, WAH, YOT
  Somaliland, TOP
  Spanish, PIE
  Straits Settlements, PAU,
  TUN
  Swedish, ALN, FOT, MIL,
  REF, TUM
  Swiss, POT
  Tunisian, SAA
  Turkish, OKA, OKE, PIK
  Vietnamese, GON, MAU,
  NGU, VUO, SAO, TAO, TAT
  Wire, MIL
  Württemberg, IMI
  Yarn, LEA
  Yugoslav, OKA, RIF
Milk, LAC
Milkfish, AWA
Moccasin, PAC
Money: Yap stone, FEI
Money of Account (also Coin):
  Anglo-Saxon, ORA, ORE
  French, SOU
  Indian, LAC
  Japanese, RIN
  Oman, GAJ
  Virgin Islands, BIT
Monkey: Capuchin, SAI
Morsel, ORT
Mother: Peer Gynt's, ASE
Mountain: Asia Minor, IDA
Mulberry: Indian, AAL, ACH,
  AWL
Muttonbird: New Zealand, OII
Nahoor, SNA
Native: Mindanao, ATA
Neckpiece, BOA
Newt, EFT
No (Scottish), NAE
Note: Guido's highest, ELA
  Of scale, SOL
Nursemaid: Oriental, AMA, IYA
Ocher: Yellow, SIL
One (Scottish), YIN
Ornament: Pagoda, TEE
Oven: Polynesian, UMU
Ox: Tibetan, YAK
Pagoda: Chinese, TAA
Parrot: Hawk, HIA
  New Zealand, KEA
Part: Footlike, PES
Particle: Electrified, ION
Pasha, DEY
Pass: Mountain, COL
Paste: Rice, AME
Pea: Indian split, DAL
Peasant: Philippine, TAO
Penpoint, NEB, NIB
Piece out, EKE
Pigeon, NUN
Pine: Textile screw, ARA
Pistol (slang), GAT
Pit: Baking, IMU
Plant: Pepper, AVA
Play: By Capek, RUR
Poem: Old French, DIT
Porgy: Japanese, TAI
Priest: Biblical high, ELI
Prince: Ethiopian, RAS

Pseudonym: Dickens', BOZ
Queen: Fairy, MAB
Quince: Bengal, BEL
Record: Ship's, LOG
Refuse: Flax (Scottish), PAB,
  POB
Resin, LAC
Resort, SPA
Revolver (slang), GAT
Right: Cause to turn, GEE
River: Scottish or English, DEE
  (Spanish), RIO
  Swiss, AAR
Room: Harem, ODA
Rootstock: Fern, ROI
Rose (Persian), GUL
Ruff: Female, REE
Rule: Indian, RAJ
Sailor, GOB, TAR
Saint: Female (abbr.), STE
  Islamic, PIR
Salt, SAL
Sash: Japanese, OBI
Scrap, ORT
Seed: Poppy, MAW
Self, EGO
Serpent: Vedic sky, AHI
Sesame, TIL
Sheep: Female, EWE
  Indian, SHA
  Male, RAM
Sheepfold (Scottish), REE
Shelter, LEE
Shield, ECU
Shooting match (French), TIR
Shrew: European, ERD
Shrub: Evergreen, YEW
Silkworm, ERI
Snake, ASP, BOA
Soak, RET
Son-in-law: Mohammed's, ALI
Sorrel: Wood, OCA
Spade: Long, narrow, LOY
Spirit: Malignant, KER
Spot: Playing-card, PIP
Spread for drying, TED
Spring: Mineral, SPA
Sprite: Water, NIX
Statesman: Japanese, ITO
Stern: Toward, AFT
Stomach: Bird's, MAW
Street (French), RUE
Summer (French), ETE
Sun, SOL
Swamp, BOG, FEN
Swan: Male, COB
Tea: Chinese, CHA
Temple: Shinto, SHA
Thing (law), RES
Title: Etruscan, LAR
  Monk's, FRA
  Portuguese, DOM
  Spanish, DON
  Turkish, AGA, BEY
Tool: Cutting, ADZ, AXE
  Mining, GAD
  Piercing, AWL
Tree: Candlenut, AMA
  Central American, EBO

East Indian, SAJ, SAL
Evergreen, YEW
Hawaiian, KOA, KOU
Indian, BEL, DAR
Linden, LIN
New Zealand, AKE
Philippine, DAO, OKE, TUA, TUI
Rubber, ULE
South American, APA
Tribe: New Zealand, ATI
Turmeric, REA
Twice, BIS
Twin: Siamese, ENG
Uncle (dialect), EAM, EME
Veil: Chalice, AER, AIR
Vessel: Wine, AMA
Vestment: Ecclesiastical, ALB
Vetch: Bitter, ERS
Victorfish, AKU
Vine: New Zealand, AKA
  Philippine, IYO
Wallaba, APA
Wapiti, ELK
Water (French), EAU
Waterfall, LIN
Watering place: Prussian, EMS
Weave: Designating plain,
  UNI
Weight: Bulgarian, OKA, OKE
  Burmese, MOO, VIS
  Chinese, FEN, HAO, KIN,
  SSU, TAN, YIN
  Cyprus, OKA, OKE
  Danish, LOD, ORT, VOG
  East Indian, TJI
  Egyptian, KAT, OKA, OKE
  English, for wool, TOD
  German, LOT
  Greek, MNA, OKA, OKE
  Indian, SER
  Japanese, FUN, KIN, RIN,
  SHI
  Korean, KON
  Malacca, KIP
  Mongolian, LAN
  Netherlands, ONS
  Norwegian, LOD
  Polish, LUT
  Rangoon, PAI
  Roman, BES
  Russian, LOT
  Siamese, BAT, HAP, PAI
  Swedish, ASS, ORT
  Turkish, OKA, OKE
  Vietnamese, CAN
  Yugoslav, OKA, OKE
Whales: Herd, GAM, POD
Wildebeest, GNU
Wing, ALA
Witticism, MOT
Wolframite, CAL
Worm: African, LOA
Wreath: Hawaiian, LEI
Yale, ELI
Yam: Hawaiian, HOI
Yes (French), OUI
Young: Bring forth, EAN
Z (letter), ZED

Words of Four Letters

Aborigine: Borneo, DYAK
Agave, ALOE
Animal: Footless, APOD
Ant: White, ANAI, ANAY
Antelope: African, ASSE, BISA, GUIB,
  KOBA, KUDU, ORYX, POKU, PUKU,
  TOPI, TORA
Apoplexy: Plant, ESCA
Apple, POME
Apricot, ANSU
Ardor, ELAN
Armadillo, APAR, PEBA, PEVA, TATU
Ascetic: Islamic, SUFI
Association: Chinese, TONG

Astronomer: Persian, OMAR
Avatar: Of Vishnu, RAMA
Axillary, ALAR
Band: Horizontal (heraldry), FESS
Barracuda, SPET
Bark: Mulberry, TAPA
Base: Column, DADO
Bearing (heraldry), ORLE
Beer: Russian, KVAS
Beige, ECRU
Being, ESSE
Beverage: Japanese rice, SAKE
Bird: Asian, MINA, MYNA
  Egyptian sacred, IBIS

Extinct, DODO, MAMO
Flightless, KIWI
Gull-like, TERN
Hawaiian, IIWI, MAMO
Parson, KOKO
Unfledged, EYAS
Birds: As class, AVES
Black, EBON
  (French), NOIR
Blackbird: European, MERL
Boat: Flat-bottomed, DORY
Bone: Forearm, ULNA
Bones, OSSA
Box, Japanese, INRO

Bravo (rare), EUGE
Buffalo: Indian wild, ARNA
Bull (Spanish), TORO
Burden, ONUS
Cabbage: Sliced, SLAW
Caliph: Islamic, OMAR
Canoe: Malay, PRAU, PROA
Cap: Military, KEPI
Cape, NESS
Capital: Ancient Irish, TARA
Case: Article, ETUI
Cat: Wild, BALU, EYRA
Chalcedony, SARD
Chamber: Indian ceremonial, KIVA
Channel: Brain, ITER
Cheese: Dutch, EDAM
Chest: Sepulchral stone, CIST
Chieftain: Arab, EMIR
Church: Part of, APSE, NAVE
  (Scottish), KIRK
Claim (law), LIEN
Cluster: Flower, CYME
Coin: Chinese, TAEL, YUAN
  German, MARK
  Indian, ANNA
  Iranian, RIAL
  Italian, LIRA
  Moroccan, OKIA
  Siamese, BAHT
  South American, PESO
  Spanish, DURO, PESO
  Turkish, PARA
Commune: Belgian, AATH
Composition: Musical, OPUS
Compound: Chemical, DIOL
Constellation: Southern, PAVO
Council: Russian, DUMA
Counsel, REDE
Covering: Seed, ARIL
Cross: Egyptian, ANKH
Cry: Bacchanalian, EVOE
Cup (Scottish), TASS
Cupbearer, SAKI
Dagger, DIRK
  Malay, KRIS
Dam: River, WEIR
Dash, ELAN
Date: Roman, IDES
Dawn: Pertaining to, EOAN
Dean: English, INGE
Decay: In fruit, BLET
Deer: Sambar, MAHA
Disease: Skin, ACNE
Disk: Solar, ATEN
Dog: Hunting, ALAN
Drink: Hindu intoxicating, SOMA
Duck, SMEE, SMEW, TEAL
Dynasty: Chinese, CHEN, CHIN, CHOU,
  CHOW, HSIA, MING, SUNG, TANG,
  TSIN
  Mongol, YUAN
Eagle: Biblical, GIER
  Sea, ERNE
Ear: Pertaining to, OTIC
Egyptian: Christian, COPT
Entrance: Mine, ADIT
Esau, EDOM
Escutcheon: Voided, ORLE
Eskers, OSAR
Evergreen: New Zealand, TAWA
Fairy: Persian, PERI
Family: Italian, ESTE
Far (comb. form), TELE
Farewell, VALE
Father (French), PERE
Fennel: Philippine, ANIS
Fever: Malarial, AGUE
Fiber: East Indian, JUTE
Firn, NEVE
Fish: Carplike, DACE
  Hawaiian, ULUA
  Herringlike, SHAD
  Mackerellike, CERO
  Marine, HAKE
  Sea, LING, MERO, OPAH
  Spiny-finned, GOBY

Food: Tropical, TARO
Foot: Metric, IAMB
Formerly, ERST
Founder: Of Carthage, DIDO
France: Southern, MIDI
Furze, ULEX
Gaelic, ERSE
Gaiter, SPAT
Game: Card, FARO, SKAT
Garlic: European wild, MOLY
Garment: Hindu, SARI
  Roman, TOGA
Gazelle, CORA
Gem: JADE, ONYX, OPAL, RUBY
Genus: Amphibians (incl. frogs), RANA
  Amphibians (incl. tree toads), HYLA
  Antelopes, ORYX
  Auks, ALCA, URIA
  Bees, APIS
  Birds (American ostriches), RHEA
  Birds (cranes), CRUS
  Birds (magpies), PICA
  Birds (peacocks), PAVO
  Cetaceans, INIA
  Ducks (incl. mallards), ANAS
  Fishes (burbots), LOTA
  Fishes (incl. bowfins), AMIA
  Geese (snow geese), CHEN
  Gulls, XEMA
  Herbs, ARUM, GEUM
  Insects (water scorpions), NEPA
  Lilies, ALOE
  Mammals (humans), HOMO
  Orchids, DISA
  Owls, ASIO, BUBO, OTUS
  Palms, NIPA
  Sea birds, SULA
  Sheep, OVIS
  Shrubs, Eurasian, ULEX
  Shrubs (hollies), ILEX
  Shrubs (incl. Virginia Willow), ITEA
  Shrubs, tropical, EVEA
  Snakes (sand snakes), ERYX
  Swans, OLOR
  Trees, chocolate, COLA
  Trees (ebony family), MABA
  Trees (incl. maples), ACER
  Trees (olives), OLEA
  Trees, tropical, EVEA
  Turtles, EMYS
Goat: Wild, IBEX, KRAS, TAHR, TAIR,
  THAR
God: Assyrian, ASUR
  Babylonian, ADAD, ADDU, ENKI,
  ENZU, IRRA, NABU, NEBO, UTUG
  Celtic, LLEU, LLEW
  Hindu, AGNI, CIVA, DEVA, DEWA,
  KAMA, RAMA, SIVA, VAYU
  Phrygian, ATYS
  Semitic, BAAL
  Teutonic, HLER
Goddess: Babylonian, ERUA, GULA
  Hawaiian, PELE
  Hindu, DEVI, KALI, SHRI, VACH
Gooseberry: Hawaiian, POHA
Gourd, PEPO
Grafted (heraldry), ENTE
Grandfather (obsolete), AIEL
Grandparents: Pertaining to, AVAL
Grass: Hawaiian, HILO
Gray (French), GRIS
Green (heraldry), VERT
Groom: Indian, SYCE
Half (prefix), DEMI, HEMI, SEMI
Hamlet, DORP
Hammerhead: Part of, PEEN
Handle, ANSA
Harp: Japanese, KOTO
Hartebeest, ASSE, TORA
Hautboy, OBOE
Hawk: Taken from nest (falconry), EYAS
Hearing (law), OYER
Heater: For liquids, ETNA
Herb: Aromatic, ANET, DILL
  Fabulous, MOLY
  Perennial, GEUM, SEGO

Pot, WORT
  Used for blue dye, WADE, WOAD
Hill: Flat-topped, MESA
  Sand, DENE, DUNE
Hoarfrost, RIME
Hog: Immature female, GILT
Holly, ILEX
House: Cow, BYRE
  (Spanish), CASA
Ice: Floating, FLOE
Image, ICON, IKON
Incarnation: Of Vishnu, RAMA
Indian: Algonquin, CREE, SAUK
  Central American, MAYA
  Iroquoian, ERIE
  Mexican, CORA
  Peruvian, CANA, INCA, MORO
  Shoshonean, HOPI
  Siouan, OTOE
  Southwestern, HOPI, PIMA, YUMA,
  ZUNI
Insect: Immature, PUPA
Instrument: Stringed, LUTE, LYRE
Ireland, EIRE, ERIN
Jacket: English, ETON
Jail (British), GAOL
Jar, OLLA
Judge: Islamic, CADI
Juniper: European, CADE
Kiln, OAST, OVEN
King: British legendary, LUDD, NUDD
Kiss, BUSS
Knife: Philippine, BOLO
Koran: Section of, SURA
Laborer: Spanish American, PEON
Lake: Mountain, TARN
  (Scottish), LOCH
Lamp: Miner's, DAVY
Landing place: Indian, GHAT
Language: Buddhist, PALI
  Japanese, AINU
Latvian, LETT
Layer: Of iris, UVEA
Leaf: Palm, OLAY, OLLA
Legislature: Ukrainian, RADA
Lemur, LORI
Leopard, PARD
Let it stand, STET
Letter: Greek, BETA, IOTA, ZETA
  Hebrew, AYIN, BETH, CAPH, KOPH,
  RESH, SHIN, TETH, YODH
  Papal, BULL
Lily, ALOE
Literature: Hindu sacred, VEDA
Lizard, GILA
  Monitor, URAN
Loquat, BIWA
Magistrate: Genoese or Venetian, DOGE
Man (Latin), HOMO
Mark: Omission, DELE
Marmoset: South American, MICO
Meadow: Fertile, VEGA
Measure: Electric, VOLT, WATT
  Force, DYNE
  Hebrew, OMER
  Printing, PICA
  Spanish or Portuguese, VARA
  Swiss land, IMMI
Medley, OLIO
Merganser, SMEW
Milk (French), LAIT
Molding, GULA
  Curved, OGEE
Mongoose: Crab-eating, URVA
Monk: Tibetan, LAMA
Monkey: African, MONA, WAAG
  Ceylonese, MAHA
  Cochin-China, DOUC
  South American, SAKI, TITI
Monkshood, ATIS
Month: Jewish, ADAR, ELUL, IYAR
Mother (French), MERE
Mountain: Thessaly, OSSA
Mouse: Meadow, VOLE
Mythology: Norse, EDDA
Nail (French), CLOU

Native: Philippine, MORO
Nest: Of pheasants, NIDE
Network, RETE
No (German), NEIN
Noble: Islamic, AMIR
Notice: Death, OBIT
Novel: By Zola, NANA
Nursemaid: Oriental AMAH, AYAH, EYAH
Nut: Philippine, PILI
Oak: Holm, ILEX
Oil (comb. form), OLEO
Ostrich: American, RHEA
Oven, KILN, OAST
Owl: Barn, LULU
Ox: Celebes wild, ANOE
  Extinct wild, URUS
Palm, ATAP, NIPA, SAGO
Parliament, DIET
Parrot: New Zealand, KAKA
Pass: Indian mountain, GHAT
Passage: Closing (music), CODA
Peach: Clingstone, PAVY
Peasant: Indian, RYOT
  Old English, CARL
Pepper: Australasian, KAVA
Perfume, ATAR
Persia, IRAN
Person: Extraordinary, ONER
Pickerel or pike, ESOX
Pitcher, EWER
Plant: Aromatic, NARD
  Century, ALOE
  Indigo, ANIL
  Pepper, KAVA
Platform: Raised, DAIS
Plum: Wild, SLOE
Pods: Vegetable, OKRA, OKRO
Poem: Epic, EPOS
Poet: Persian, OMAR
  Roman, OVID
Poison, BANE
  Arrow, INEE
Porkfish, SISI
Portico: Greek, STOA
Premium, AGIO
Priest: Islamic, IMAM
Prima donna, DIVA
Prong: Fork, TINE
Pseudonym: Lamb's, ELIA
Queen: Carthaginian, DIDO
  Hindu, RANI
Rabbit, CONY
Race: Of Japan, AINU
Rail: Ducklike, COOT
  North American, SORA
Redshank, CLEE
Refuse: After pressing, MARC
Regiment: Turkish, ALAI
Reliquary, ARCA
Resort: Italian, LIDO
Ridges: Sandy, ASAR, OSAR
River: German, ELBE, ODER
  Italian, ADDA
  Siberian, LENA
Road: Roman, ITER

Rockfish: California, RENA
Rodent: Mouselike, VOLE
  South American, PACA
Rootstock, TARO
Salamander, NEWT
Salmon: Silver, COHO
  Young, PARR
Same (Greek), HOMO
  (Latin), IDEM
Sauce: Fish, ALEC
School: English, ETON
Seaweed, AGAR, ALGA, KELP
Secular, LAIC
Sediment, SILT
Seed: Dill, ANET
  Of vetch, TARE
Serf, ILOT
Sesame, TEEL
Settlement: Eskimo, ETAH
Shark: Atlantic, GATA
  European, TOPE
Sheep: Wild, UDAD
Sheltered, ALEE
Shield, EGIS
Ship: Jason's, ARGO
  Left side of, PORT
  Two-masted, BRIG
Shrine: Buddhist, TOPE
Shrub: New Zealand, TUTU
Sign: Magic, RUNE
Silkworm, ERIA
Skin: Beaver, PLEW
Skink: Egyptian, ADDA
Slave, ESNE
Sloth: Two-toed, UNAU
Smooth, LENE
Snow: Glacial, NEVE
Soapstone, TALC
Society: African secret, EGBO, PORO
Son: Of Seth, ENOS
Song (German), LIED
  Unaccompanied, GLEE
Sound: Lung, RALE
Sour, ACID
Sow: Young, GILT
Spike: Brad-shaped, BROB
Spirit: Buddhist evil, MARA
Stake: Poker, ANTE
Star: Temporary, NOVA
Starch: East Indian, SAGO
Stone: Precious, OPAL
Strap: Bridle, REIN
Strewn (heraldry), SEME
Sweetsop, ATES, ATTA
Sword: Fencing, EPEE, FOIL
Tambourine: African, TAAR
Tapir: Brazilian, ANTA
Tax, CESS
Tea: South American, MATE
Therefore (Latin), ERGO
Thing: Extraordinary, ONER
Three (dice, cards, etc.), TREY
Thrush: Hawaiian, OMAO
Tide, NEAP

Tipster: Racing, TOUT
Tissue, TELA
Title: Etruscan, LARS
  Hindu, BABU
  Indian, RAJA
  Islamic, EMIR, IMAM
  Persian, BABA
  Spanish, DONA
  Turkish, AGHA, BABA
Toad: Largest-known, AGUA
  Tree, HYLA
Tool: Cutting, ADZE
Track: Deer, SLOT
Tract: Sandy, DENE
Tree: Apple, SORB
  Central American, EBOE
  East Indian, TEAK
  Eucalyptus, YATE
  Guyanese and Trinidadian, MORA
  Javanese, UPAS
  Linden, LIME, LINN, TEIL, TILL
  Sandarac, ARAR
  Sassafras, AGUE
  Tamarisk salt, ATLE
Tribe: Moro, SULU
Trout, CHAR
Vessel: Arab, DHOW
Vestment: Ecclesiastical, COPE
Vetch, TARE
Vine: East Indian, SOMA
Violinist: Famous, AUER
Vortex, EDDY
Wampum, PEAG
Wapiti, STAG
Waste: Allowance for, TRET
Watchman: Indian, MINA
Water (Spanish), AGUA
Waterfall, LINN
Wavy (heraldry), ONDE, UNDE
Wax, CERE
  Chinese, PELA
Weed: Biblical, TARE
Weight: Ancient, MINA
  Danish (pl.), ESER
  East Asian, TAEL
  Greek, MINA
  Siamese, BAHT
Well done (rare), EUGE
Whale, CETE
  Killer, ORCA
  White, HUSE, HUSO
Whirlpool, EDDY
Wife: Of Geraint, ENID
Willow: Virginia, ITEA
Wine, PORT
Winged, ALAR
  (Heraldry), AILE
Wings, ALAE
Withered, SERE
Without (French), SANS
Wool: To comb, CARD
Work, OPUS
Wrong: Civil, TORT
Young: Bring forth, YEAN

Words of Five Letters

Automaton, GOLEM, ROBOT
Award: Motion-picture, OSCAR
Basket: Fishing, CREEL
Beer: Russian, KVASS
Bible: Islamic, KORAN, QUR'AN
Bird: Asian, MINAH, MYNAH
  Indian, SHAMA
  Larklike, PIPIT
  Loonlike, GREBE
  Oscine, VIREO
  South American, AGAMI
  Swimming, GREBE
Black: (French), NOIRE
  (Heraldry), SABLE
Blackbird: European, MERLE, OUSEL,
  OUZEL
Block: Glacial, SERAC
Blue (heraldry), AZURE
Boat: Eskimo, BIDAR, UMIAK

Bobwhite, COLIN, QUAIL
Bone (comb. form), OSTEO
  Leg, TIBIA
  Thigh, FEMUR
Broom: Twig, BESOM
Brother (French), FRERE
  Moses, AARON
Canoe: Eskimo, BIDAR, KAYAK
Cape: Papal, FANON, ORALE
Caravansary, SERAI
Card: Old playing, TAROT
Caterpillar: New Zealand, AWETO
Catkin, AMENT
Cavity: Stone, GEODE
Cephalopod, SQUID
Cetacean, WHALE
Chariot, ESSED
Cheek: Pertaining to, MALAR
Chieftain: Arab, EMEER

Abode of dead: Babylonian, ARALU
Aborigine: Borneo, DAYAK
Aftersong, EPODE
Aloe, AGAVE
Animal: Footless, APODE
Ant, EMMET
Antelope: African, ADDAX, BEISA,
  CAAMA, ELAND, GUIBA, ORIBI,
  TIANG
  Goat, GORAL, SEROW
  Indian, SASIN
  Siberian, SAIGA
Arch: Pointed, OGIVE
Armadillo, APARA, POYOU, TATOU
Arrowroot, ARARU
Artery: Trunk, AORTA
Association: Russian, ARTEL
  Secret, CABAL
Author: English, READE

Child (Scottish), BAIRN
Cigar, CLARO
Coating: Seed, TESTA
Cockatoo: Palm, ARARA
Coin: Costa Rican, COLON
　Danish, KRONE
　Ecuadorian, SUCRE
　English, GROAT, PENCE
　French, FRANC
　German, KRONE, TALER
　Hungarian, PENGO
　Icelandic, KRONA
　Indian, RUPEE
　Iraqi, DINAR
　Norwegian, KRONE
　Polish, ZLOTY
　Russian, COPEC, KOPEK, RUBLE
　Swedish, KRONA
　Turkish, ASPER
　Yugoslav, DINAR
Collar: Papal, FANON, ORALE
　Roman, RABAT
Commune: Italian, TREIA
Composition: Choral, MOTET
Compound: Chemical, ESTER
Conceal (law), ELOIN
Council: Ecclesiastical, SYNOD
Court: Anglo-Saxon, GEMOT
　Inner, PATIO
Crest: Mountain, ARETE
Crown: Papal, TIARA
Cuttlefish, SEPIA
Date: Roman, NONES
Decree: Islamic, IRADE
　Russian, UKASE
Deposit: Loam, LOESS
Desert: Gobi, SHAMO
Devilfish, MANTA
Disease: Cereals, ERGOT
Disk, PATEN
Dog: Wild, DHOLE, DINGO
Dormouse, LEROT
Drum, TABOR
Duck: Sea, EIDER
Dynasty: Chinese, CHING, LIANG,
　SHANG
Earthquake, SEISM
Eel, ELVER, MORAY
Ermine: European, STOAT
Ether: Crystalline, APIOL
Fabric: Velvetlike, PANNE
Fabulist, AESOP
Family: Italian, CENCI
Fiber: West Indian, SISAL
Fig: Smyrna, ELEME, ELEMI
Figure: Of speech, TROPE
Finch: European, SERIN
Fish: American small, KILLY
Flower: Garden, ASTER
Friend (Spanish), AMIGO
Fruit: Tropical, MANGO
Fungus: Rye, ERGOT
Furze, GORSE
Gateway, TORAN, TORII
Gem, AGATE, BERYL, PEARL, TOPAZ
Genus: Barnacles, LEPAS
　Bears, URSUS
　Birds (loons), GAVIA
　Birds (nuthatches), SITTA
　Cats, FELIS
　Dogs, CANIS
　Fishes (chiros), ELOPS
　Fishes (perch), PERCA
　Geese, ANSER
　Grasses, STIPA
　Grasses (incl. oats), AVENA
　Gulls, LARUS
　Hares, rabbits, LEPUS
　Hawks, BUTEO
　Herbs, old world, INULA
　Herbs, trailing or climbing, APIOS
　Herbs, tropical, TACCA, URENA
　Horses, EQUUS
　Insects (olive flies), DACUS
　Lice, plant, APHIS
　Lichens, USNEA

Lizards, AGAMA
Moles, TALPA
Mollusks, OLIVA
Monkeys, CEBUS
Palms, ARECA
Pigeons, GOURA
Plants (amaryllis family), AGAVE
Ruminants (goats), CAPRA
Shrubs, Asiatic, SABIA
Shrubs (heath), ERICA
Shrubs (incl. raspberry), RUBUS
Shrubs, tropical, IXORA, TREMA,
　URENA
Ticks, ARGAS
Trees (of elm family), TREMA, ULMUS
Trees, tropical, IXORA, TREMA
Goat: Bezoar, PASAN
God: Assyrian, ASHIR, ASHUR, ASSUR
　Babylonian, DAGAN, SIRIS
　Gaelic, DAGDA
　Hindu, BHAGA, INDRA, SHIVA
　Japanese, EBISU
　Philistine, DAGON
　Phrygian, ATTIS
　Teutonic, AEGIR, GYMIR
　Welsh, DYLAN
Goddess: Babylonian, ISTAR, NANAI
　Hindu, DURGA, GAURI, SHREE
Group: Of six, HEXAD
Grove: Sacred to Diana, NEMUS
Growing out, ENATE
Guitar: Hindu, SITAR
Gull: PEWEE, PEWIT
Hartebeest, CAAMA
Headdress: Jewish or Persian, TIARA
　Liturgical, MITER, MITRE
Heath, ERICA
Herb: Grasslike marsh, SEDGE
Heron, EGRET
Hog: Young, SHOAT, SHOTE
Image, EIKON
Indian: Cariban, ARARA
　Iroquoian, HURON
　Mexican, AZTEC, OPATA, OTOMI
　Muskhogean, CREEK
　Siouan, OSAGE, TETON
　Spanish American, ARARA, CARIB
Inflorescence: Racemose, AMENT
Insect: Immature, LARVA
Intrigue, CABAL
Iris: Yellow, SEDGE
Juniper, GORSE, RETEM
Kidneys: Pertaining to, RENAL
King: British legendary, LLUDD
Kite: European, GLEDE
Kobold, NISSE
Land: Cultivated, ARADA, ARADO
Landholder (Scottish), LAIRD, THANE
Language: Dravidian, TAMIL
Lariat, LASSO, REATA
Laughing, RIANT
Lawgiver: Athenian, DRACO, SOLON
Leaf: Calyx, SEPAL
　Fern, FROND
Lemur, LORIS
Letter: English, AITCH
　Greek, ALPHA, DELTA, GAMMA,
　KAPPA, OMEGA, SIGMA, THETA
　Hebrew, ALEPH, CHETH, GIMEL,
　SADHE, ZAYIN
Lichen, USNEA
Lighthouse, PHARE
Lizard: Old World, AGAMA
Loincloth, DHOTI
Louse: Plant, APHID
Macaw: Brazilian, ARARA
Mahogany: Philippine, ALMON
Mammal: Badgerlike, RATEL
　Civetlike, GENET
　Giraffelike, OKAPI
　Raccoonlike, COATI
Man (French), HOMME
Marble, AGATE
Mark: Insertion, CARET
Market place: Greek, AGORA
Marsupial: Australian, KOALA

Measure: Electric, FARAD, HENRY
　Energy, JOULE
　Metric, LITER, STERE
　Printing, AGATE
　Russian, VERST
Mixture: Smelting, MATTE
Mohicans: Last of, UNCAS
Molding: Convex, OVOLO, TORUS
Mole, TALPA
Monkey: African, PATAS
　Capuchin, SAJOU
　Howling, ARABA
Monkshood, ATEES
Month: Jewish, NISAN, SIVAN, TEBET
Museum (French), MUSEE
Musketeer, ATHOS
Native: Aleutian, ALEUT
　New Zealand, MAORI
Neckpiece: Ecclesiastical, AMICE
Nerve (comb. form), NEURO
Nest: Eagle's or hawk's, AERIE
　Insect's, NIDUS
Net: Fishing, SEINE
Newsstand, KIOSK
Nitrogen, AZOTE
Noble: Islamic, AMEER
Nodule: Stone, GEODE
Nostrils, NARES
Notched irregularly, EROSE
Nymph: Islamic, HOURI
Official: Roman, EDILE
Oleoresin, ELEMI
Opening: Mouthlike, STOMA
Oration: Funeral, ELOGE
Ostiole, STOMA
Page: Left-hand, VERSO
　Right-hand, RECTO
Palm, ARECA, BETEL
Park: Colorado, ESTES
Perfume, ATTAR
Philosopher: Greek, PLATO
Pillar: Stone, STELA, STELE
Pinnacle: Glacial, SERAC
Plain, LLANO
Plant: Century, AGAVE
　Climbing, LIANA
　Dwarf, CUMIN
　East Asian perennial, RAMIE
　Medicinal, SENNA
　Mustard family, CRESS
Plate: Communion, PATEN
Poem: Lyric, EPODE
Point: Lowest, NADIR
Poplar, ABELE, ALAMO, ASPEN
Porridge: Spanish American, ATOLE
Post: Stair, NEWEL
Priest: Islamic, IMAUM
Protozoan, AMEBA
Queen: (French), REINE
　Hindu, RANEE
Rabbit, CONEY
Rail, CRAKE
Red (heraldry), GULES
Religion: Moslem, Muslim, ISLAM
Resin, ELEMI
Revoke (law), ADEEM
Rich man, MIDAS, NABOB
Ridge: Sandy, ESKAR, ESKER
River: French, LOIRE, SEINE
Rockfish: California, REINA
Rootstock: Fragrant, ORRIS
Ruff: Female, REEVE
Sack: Pack, KYACK
Salt: Ethereal, ESTER
Saltpeter, NITER, NITRE
Salutation: Eastern, SALAM
Sandpiper: Old World, TEREK
Scented, OLENT
School: Fish, SHOAL
　French public, LYCEE
Scriptures: Islamic, KORAN
Seaweeds, ALGAE
Seed: Aromatic, ANISE
Seraglio, HAREM, SERAI
Serf, HELOT
Sheep: Wild, AUDAD

Sheeplike, OVINE
Shield, AEGIS
Shoe: Wooden, SABOT
Shoots: Pickled bamboo, ACHAR
Shot: Billiard, CAROM, MASSE
Shrine: Buddhist, STUPA
Shrub: Burning bush, WAHOO
  Ornamental evergreen, TOYON
  Used in tanning, SUMAC
Silk: Watered, MOIRE
Sister (French), SOEUR
  (Latin), SOROR
Six: Group of, HEXAD
Skeleton: Marine, CORAL
Slave, HELOT
Snake, ABOMA, ADDER, COBRA,
  RACER
Soldier: French, POILU
  Indian, SEPOY
Sour, ACERB
Spirit: Air, ARIEL
Staff: Shepherd's, CROOK
Starwort, ASTER
Steel (German), STAHL
Stockade: Russian, ETAPE

Stop (nautical), AVAST
Storehouse, ETAPE
Subway: Parisian, METRO
Tapestry, ARRAS
Tea: Paraguayan, YERBA
Temple: Hawaiian, HEIAU
Terminal: Positive, ANODE
Theater: Greek, ODEON, ODEUM
Then (French), ALORS
Thread: Surgical, SETON
Thrush: Wilson's, VEERY
Title: Hindu, BABOO
  Indian, RAJAH, SAHEB, SAHIB
  Islamic, EMEER, IMAUM
Tree: Buddhist sacred, PIPAL
  East Indian cotton, SIMAL
  Hickory, PECAN
  Light-wooded, BALSA
  Malayan, TERAP
  Mediterranean, CAROB
  Mexican, ABETO
  Mexican pine, OCOTE
  New Zealand, MAIRE
  Philippine, ALMON
  Rain, SAMAN

South American, UMBRA
Tamarack, LARCH
Tamarisk salt, ATLEE
West Indian, ACANA
Trout, CHARR
Troy, ILION, ILIUM
Twin: Siamese, CHANG
Vestment: Ecclesiastical, STOLE
Violin: Famous, AMATI, STRAD
Volcano: Mud, SALSE
Wampum, PEAGE
War cry: Greek, ALALA
Wavy (heraldry), UNDEE
Weight: Jewish, GERAH
Wen, TALPA
Wheat, SPELT
Wheel: Persian water, NORIA
Whitefish, CISCO
Willow, OSIER
Window: Bay, ORIEL
Wine, MEDOC, RHINE, TINTA, TOKAY
Winged, ALATE
Woman (French), FEMME
Year: Excess of solar over lunar, EPACT
Zoroastrian, PARSI

Words of Six or More Letters

Agave, MAGUEY
Alkaloid: Crystalline, ESERIN, ESERINE
Alligator, CAYMAN
Amphibole, EDENITE, URALITE
Ant: White, TERMITE
Antelope: African, DIKDIK, DUIKER,
  GEMSBOK, IMPALA, KOODOO
  European, CHAMOIS
  Indian, NILGAI, NILGAU, NILGHAI,
  NILGHAU
Ape: Asian or East Indian, GIBBON
Appendage: Leaf, STIPEL, STIPULE
Armadillo, PELUDO, TATOUAY
Arrowroot, ARARAO
Ascetic: Jewish, ESSENE
Ass: Asian wild, ONAGER
Avatar: Of Vishnu, KRISHNA
Babylonian, ELAMITE
Badge: Shoulder, EPAULET
Baldness, ALOPECIA
Barracuda, SENNET
Bark: Aromatic, SINTOC
Bearlike, URSINE
Beetle, ELATER
Bible: Zoroastrian, AVESTA
Bird: Sea, PETREL
  South American, SERIEMA
  Wading, AVOCET, AVOSET
Bone: Leg, FIBULA
Branched, RAMATE
Brother (Latin), FRATER
Bunting: European, ORTOLAN
Call: Trumpet, SENNET
Canoe: Eskimo, BAIDAR, OOMIAK
Caravansary, IMARET
Cat: Asian or African, CHEETAH
  Leopardlike, OCELOT
Cenobite: Jewish, ESSENE
Centerpiece: Table, EPERGNE
Cetacean, DOLPHIN, PORPOISE
Chariot, ESSEDA, ESSEDE
Chief: Seminole, OSCEOLA
Claim: Release as (law), REMISE
Clock: Water, CLEPSYDRA
Cloud, CUMULUS, NIMBUS
Coach: French hackney, FIACRE
Coin: Czech, KORUNA
  Dutch, GUILDER
  Ethiopian, TALARI
  Finnish, MARKKA
  German, THALER
  Greek, DRACHMA
  Haitian, GOURDE
  Honduran, LEMPIRA
  Hungarian, FORINT
  Indo-Chinese, PIASTER
  Panamanian, BALBOA
  Paraguayan, GUARANI
  Portuguese, ESCUDO

  Russian, COPECK, KOPECK,
  ROUBLE
  Spanish, PESETA
  Venezuelan, BOLIVAR
Communion: Last holy, VIATICUM
Conceal (law), ELOIGN
Confection, PRALINE
Construction: Sentence, SYNTAX
Convexity: Shaft of column, ENTASIS
Court: Anglo-Saxon, GEMOTE
Cow: Sea, DUGONG, MANATEE
Cylindrical, TERETE
Dagger, STILETTO
  Malay, CREESE, KREESE
Date: Roman, CALENDS, KALENDS
Deer, CARIBOU, WAPITI
Disease: Plant, ERINOSE
Doorkeeper, OSTIARY
Dragonflies: Order of, ODANATA
Drink: Of gods, NECTAR
Drum: TABOUR
  Moorish, ATABAL, ATTABAL
Duck: Fish-eating, MERGANSER
  Sea, SCOTER
Dynasty: Chinese, MANCHU
Eel, CONGER
Edit, REDACT
Envelope: Flower, PERIANTH
Eskimo, AMERIND
Ether: Crystalline, APIOLE
Excuse (law), ESSOIN
Eyespots, OCELLI
Fabric, ESTAMENE, ESTAMIN,
  ETAMINE
Falcon: European, KESTREL
Figure: Used as column, CARYATID,
  TELAMON
Fine: For punishment, AMERCE
Fish: Asian fresh-water, GOURAMI
  Pikelike, BARRACUDA
Five: Group of, PENTAD
Fly: African, TSETSE
Foot: Metric, ANAPEST, IAMBUS
Foxlike, VULPINE
Frying pan, SPIDER
Fur, KARAKUL
Galley: Greek or Roman, BIREME,
  TRIREME
Game: Card, ECARTE
Garment: Greek, CHLAMYS
Gateway, GOPURA, TORANA
Genus: Birds (ravens, crows), CORVUS
  Eels, CONGER
  Fishes, ANABAS
  Foxes, VULPES
  Herbs, ANEMONE
  Insects, CICADA
  Lemurs, GALAGO
  Mints (incl. catnip), NEPETA

  Mollusks, ANOMIA, ASTARTE,
  TEREDO
  Mollusks (incl. oysters), OSTREA
  Monkeys (spider monkeys), ATELES
  Thrushes (incl. robins), TURDUS
  Trees (of elm family), CELTIS
  Trees (inc. dogwood), CORNUS
  Trees, tropical American, SAPOTA
  Wrens, NANNUS
Gibbon, SIAMANG, WOUWOU
Gland: Salivary, RACEMOSE
Goat: Bezoar, PASANG
Goatlike, CAPRINE
God: Assyrian, ASHSHUR, ASSHUR
  Babylonian, BABBAR, MARDUK,
  MERODACH, NANNAR, NERGAL,
  SHAMASH
  Hindu, BRAHMA, KRISHNA, VISHNU
  Tahitian, TAAROA
Goddess: Babylonian, ISHTAR
  Hindu, CHANDI, HAIMAVATI,
  LAKSHMI, PARVATI, SARASVATI,
  SARASWATI
Government, POLITY
Governor: Persian, SATRAP
Grandson (Scottish), NEPOTE
Group: Of five, PENTAD
  Of nine, ENNEAD
  Of seven, HEPTAD
Hare: in first year, LEVERET
Harpsichord, SPINET
Herb: Alpine, EDELWEISS
  Chinese, GINSENG
  South African, FREESIA
Hermit, EREMITE
Hero: Legendary, PALADIN
Heron, BITTERN
Horselike, EQUINE
Hound: Short-legged, BEAGLE
House (French), MAISON
Idiot, CRETIN
Implement: Stone, NEOLITH
Incarnation: Hindu, AVATAR
Indian, APACHE, COMANCHE, PAIUTE,
  SENECA
Inn: Turkish, IMARET
Insects: Order of, DIPTERA
Instrument: Japanese banjolike,
  SAMISEN
  Musical, CLAVIER, SPINET
Interstice, AREOLA
Ironwood, COLIMA
Juniper: Old Testament, RAETAM
Kettledrum, ATABAL
King: Fairy, OBERON
Kneecap, PATELLA
Knife, MACHETE
Langur: Sumatran, SIMPAI
Legislature: Spanish, CORTES

Lemur: African, GALAGO
  Madagascar, AYEAYE
Letter: Greek, EPSILON, LAMBDA,
  OMICRON, UPSILON
  Hebrew, DALETH, LAMEDH, SAMEKH
Lighthouse, PHAROS
Lizard, IGUANA
Llama, ALPACA
Lockjaw, TETANUS
Locust, CICADA, CICALA
Macaw: Brazilian, MARACAN
Maid: Of Astolat, ELAINE
Mammal: Madagascar, TENDRAC,
  TENREC
Man (Spanish), HOMBRE
Marmoset: South American, TAMARIN
Marsupial, BANDICOOT, WOMBAT
Massacre, POGROM
Mayor: Spanish, ALCALDE
Measure: Electric, AMPERE, COULOMB,
  KILOWATT
Medicine: Quack, NOSTRUM
Member: Religious order, CENOBITE
Molasses, TREACLE
Monkey: African, GRIVET, NISNAS
  Asian, LANGUR
  Philippine, MACHIN
  South American, PINCHE, SAIMIRI,
  SAMIRI, SAPAJOU
Monster, CHIMERA, GORGON
  (Comb. form), TERATO
  Cretan, MINOTAUR
Month: Jewish, HESHVAN, KISLEV,
  SHEBAT, TAMMUZ, TISHRI, VEADAR
Mountain: Asia Minor, ARARAT
Mulct, AMERCE
Musketeer, ARAMIS, PORTHOS
Nearsighted, MYOPIC
Net, TRAMMEL
New York City, GOTHAM
Nine: Group of, ENNEAD
Nobleman: Spanish, GRANDEE
Official: Roman, AEDILE
Onyx: Mexican, TECALI
Order: Dragonflies, ODANATA
  Insects, DIPTERA
Organ: Plant, PISTIL

Ornament: Shoulder, EPAULET
Overcoat: Military, CAPOTE
Ox: Wild, BANTENG
Oxidation: Bronze or copper, PATINA
Paralysis: Incomplete, PARESIS
Pear: Alligator, AVOCADO
Persimmon: Mexican, CHAPOTE
Pipe: Peace, CALUMET
Plaid (Scottish), TARTAN
Plain, PAMPAS, STEPPE, TUNDRA
Plant: Buttercup family, ANEMONE
  Century, MAGUEY
  On rocks, LICHEN
Plowing: Fit for, ARABLE
Poem: Heroic, EPOPEE
  Six-lined, SESTET
Point: Highest, ZENITH
Potion: Love, PHILTER, PHILTRE
Protozoan, AMOEBA
Punish, AMERCE
Purple (heraldry), PURPURE
Queen: Fairy, TITANIA
Race: Skiing, SLALOM
Rat, BANDICOOT, LEMMING
Retort, RIPOST, RIPOSTE
Ring: Harness, TERRET
  Little, ANNULET
Rodent: Jumping, JERBOA
  Spanish American, AGOUTI, AGOUTY
Sailor: East Indian, LASCAR
Salmon: Young, GRILSE
Salutation: Eastern, SALAAM
Sandpiper, PLOVER
Sandy, ARENOSE
Sapodilla, SAPOTA, SAPOTE
Saw: Surgical, TREPAN
Seven: Group of, HEPTAD
Sexes: Common to both, EPICENE
Shawl: Mexican, SERAPE
Sheathing: Flower, SPATHE
Sheep: Wild, AOUDAD, ARGALI
Shipworm, TEREDO
Shoes: Mercury's winged, TALARIA
Shortening: Syllable, SYSTOLE
Shrub, SPIRAEA
Sickle-shaped, FALCATE

Silver (heraldry), ARGENT
Snake, ANACONDA
Speech: Loss of, APHASIA
Spiral, HELICAL
Staff: Bishop's, CROSIER, CROZIER
Stalk: Plant, PETIOLE
State: Swiss, CANTON
Studio, ATELIER
Swan: Young, CYGNET
Swimming, NATANT
Sword-shaped, ENSATE
Terminal: Negative, CATHODE
Third (music), TIERCE
Thrust: Fencing, RIPOST, RIPOSTE
Tile: Pertaining to, TEGULAR
Tomb: Empty, CENOTAPH
Tooth (comb. form), ODONTO
Tower: Islamic, MINARET
Tree: African timber, BAOBAB
  Black gum, TUPELO
  East Indian, MARGOSA
  Locust, ACACIA
  Malayan, SINTOC
  Marmalade, SAPOTE
Urn: Tea, SAMOVAR
Vehicle, LANDAU, TROIKA
Verbose, PROLIX
Viceroy: Egyptian, KHEDIVE
Vulture: American, CONDOR
Warehouse (French), ENTREPOT
Whale: White, BELUGA
Whirlpool, VORTEX
Will: Addition to, CODICIL
  Having left, TESTATE
Wind, CHINOOK, MONSOON, SIMOOM,
  SIMOON, SIROCCO
Window: In roof, DORMER
Wine, BARBERA, BURGUNDY,
  CABERNET, CHABLIS, CHIANTI,
  CLARET, MUSCATEL, RIESLING,
  SAUTERNE, SHERRY, ZINFANDEL
Wolfish, LUPINE
Woman: Boisterous, TERMAGANT
Woolly, LANATE
Workshop, ATELIER
Zoroastrian, PARSEE

Old Testament Names

We do not pretend that this list is all-inclusive. We list only those names that occur most often in crossword puzzles.

Aaron: First high priest of Jews; son of Amram; brother of Miriam and Moses; father of Abihu, Eleazer, Ithamar, and Nadab.
Abel: Son of Adam and Eve; slain by Cain.
Abigail: Wife of Nabal; later, wife of David.
Abihu: Son of Aaron.
Abimelech: King of Gerar.
Abner: Commander of army of Saul and Ishbosheth; slain by Joab.
Abraham (or Abram): Patriarch; forefather of the Jews; son of Terah; husband of Sarah; father of Isaac and Ishmael.
Absalom: Son of David and Maacah; revolted against David; slain by Joab.
Achish: King of Gath; gave refuge to David.
Achsa (or Achsah): Daughter of Caleb; wife of Othniel.
Adah: Wife of Lamech.
Adam: First man; husband of Eve; father of Cain, Abel, and Seth.
Adonijah: Son of David and Haggith.
Agag: King of Amalek; spared by Saul; slain by Samuel.
Ahasuerus: King of Persia; husband of Vashti and, later, Esther; sometimes identified with Xerxes the Great.
Ahijah: Prophet; foretold accession of Jeroboam.
Ahinoam: Wife of David.
Amasa: Commander of army of David; slain by Joab.
Amnon: Son of David and Ahinoam; raped Tamar; slain by Absalom.
Amram: Husband of Jochebed; father of Aaron, Miriam and Moses.
Asenath: Wife of Joseph.
Asher: Son of Jacob and Zilpah.

Balaam: Prophet; rebuked by his donkey for cursing God.
Barak: Jewish captain; associated with Deborah.
Baruch: Secretary to Jeremiah.
Bathsheba: Wife of Uriah; later, wife of David.
Belshazzar: Crown prince of Babylon.
Benaiah: Warrior of David; proclaimed Solomon King.
Ben-Hadad: Name of several kings of Damascus.
Benjamin: Son of Jacob and Rachel.
Bezaleel: Chief architect of Tabernacle.
Bilhah: Servant of Rachel; mistress of Jacob.
Bildad: Comforter of Job.
Boaz: Husband of Ruth; father of Obed.
Cain: Son of Adam and Eve; slayer of Abel; father of Enoch.
Cainan: Son of Enos.
Caleb: Spy sent out by Moses to visit Canaan; father of Achsa.
Canaan: Son of Ham.
Chilion: Son of Elimelech; husband of Orpah.
Cush: Son of Ham; father of Nimrod.
Dan: Son of Jacob and Bilhah.
Daniel: Prophet; saved from lions by God.
Deborah: Hebrew prophetess and judge; helped Israelites conquer Canaanites.
Delilah: Mistress and betrayer of Samson.
Elam: Son of Shem.
Eleazar: Son of Aaron; succeeded him as high priest.
Eli: High priest and judge; teacher of Samuel; father of Hophni and Phinehas.
Eliakim: Chief minister of Hezekiah.
Eliezer: Servant of Abraham.
Elihu: Comforter of Job.
Elijah (or Elias): Prophet; went to heaven in chariot of fire.

Elimelech: Husband of Naomi; father of Chilion and Mahlon.
Eliphaz: Comforter of Job.
Elisha (or Eliseus): Prophet; successor of Elijah.
Elkanah: Husband of Hannah; father of Samuel.
Enoch: Son of Cain.
Enoch: Father of Methuselah.
Enos: Son of Seth; father of Cainan.
Ephraim: Son of Joseph.
Esau: Son of Isaac and Rebecca; sold his birthright to his twin brother Jacob.
Esther: Jewish wife of Ahasuerus; saved Jews from Haman's plotting.
Eve: First woman; wife of Adam.
Ezra (or Esdras): Hebrew scribe and priest.
Gad: Son of Jacob and Zilpah.
Gehazi: Servant of Elisha.
Gideon: Israelite hero; defeated Midianites.
Goliath: Philistine giant; slain by David.
Hagar: Handmaid of Sarah; concubine of Abraham; mother of Ishmael.
Haggith: Mother of Adonijah.
Ham: Son of Noah; father of Cush, Mizraim, Phut, and Canaan.
Haman: Chief minister of Ahasuerus; hanged on gallows prepared for Mordecai.
Hannah: Wife of Elkanah; mother of Samuel.
Hanun: King of Ammonites.
Haran: Brother of Abraham; father of Lot.
Hazael: King of Damascus.
Hephzi-Bah: Wife of Hezekiah; mother of Mannaseh.
Hiram: King of Tyre.
Holofernes: General of Nebuchadnezzar; slain by Judith.
Hophni: Son of Eli.
Isaac: Hebrew patriarch; son of Abraham and Sarah; half brother of Ishmael; husband of Rebecca; father of Esau and Jacob.
Ishmael: Son of Abraham and Hagar; half brother of Isaac.
Issachar: Son of Jacob and Leah.
Ithamar: Son of Aaron.
Jabal: Son of Lamech and Adah.
Jabin: King of Hazor.
Jacob: Hebrew patriarch; founder of Israel; son of Isaac and Rebecca; husband of Leah and Rachel; father of sons Asher, Benjamin, Dan, Gad, Issachar, Joseph, Judah, Levi, Naphtali, Reuben, Simeon, and Zebulun, and daughter Dinah.
Jael: Slayer of Sisera.
Japheth: Son of Noah.
Jehoiada: High priest; husband of Jehoshabeath; revolted against Athaliah and made Joash King of Judah.
Jehoshabeath (or Jehosheba): Daughter of Jehoram of Judah; wife of Jehoiada.
Jephthah: Judge in Israel; sacrificed his only daughter because of vow.
Jesse: Son of Obed; father of David.
Jethro: Midianite priest; father of Zipporah.
Jezebel: Phoenician princess; wife of Ahab; mother of Ahaziah, Athaliah, and Jehoram.
Joab: Commander in chief under David; slayer of Abner, Absalom, and Amasa.
Job: Patriarch; underwent many afflictions; comforted by Bildad, Elihu, Eliphaz and Zophar.
Jochebed: Wife of Amram.
Jonah: Prophet; cast into sea and swallowed by great fish.
Jonathan: Son of Saul; friend of David.
Joseph: Son of Jacob and Rachel; sold into slavery by his brothers; husband of Asenath; father of Ephraim and Manassah.
Joshua: Successor of Moses; son of Nun.
Jubal: Son of Lamech and Adah.
Judah: Son of Jacob and Leah.
Judith: Slayer of Holofernes.
Kish: Father of Saul.

Laban: Father of Leah and Rachel.
Lamech: Son of Methuselah; father of Noah.
Lamech: Husband of Adah and Zillah; father of Jabal, Jubal, and Tubal-Cain.
Leah: Daughter of Laban; wife of Jacob; sister of Rachel.
Levi: Son of Jacob and Leah.
Lot: Son of Haran; escaped destruction of Sodom.
Maacah: Mother of Absalom and Tamar.
Mahlon: Son of Elimelech; first husband of Ruth.
Manasseh: Son of Joseph.
Melchizedek: King of Salem.
Methuselah: Patriarch; son of Enoch; father of Lamech.
Michal: Daughter of Saul; wife of David.
Miriam: Prophetess; daughter of Amram; sister of Aaron and Moses.
Mizraim: Son of Ham.
Mordecai: Uncle of Esther; with her aid, saved Jews from Haman's plotting.
Moses: Prophet and lawgiver; son of Amram; brother of Aaron and Miriam; husband of Zipporah.
Naaman: Syrian captain; cured of leprosy by Elisha.
Nabal: Husband of Abigail.
Naboth: Owner of vineyard; stoned to death because he would not sell it to Ahab.
Nadab: Son of Aaron.
Nahor: Father of Terah.
Naomi: Wife of Elimelech; mother-in-law of Ruth.
Naphtali: Son of Jacob and Bilhah.
Nathan: Prophet; reproved David for causing Uriah's death.
Nebuchadnezzar (or Nebuchadrezzar): King of Babylon; destroyer of Jerusalem.
Nehemiah: Jewish leader; empowered by Artaxerxes to rebuild Jerusalem.
Nimrod: Mighty hunter; son of Cush.
Noah: Patriarch; son of Lamech; escaped Deluge by building Ark; father of Ham, Japheth and Shem.
Nun (or Non): Father of Joshua.
Obed: Son of Boaz; father of Jesse.
Og: King of Bashan.
Orpah: Wife of Chilion.
Othniel: Kenezite; judge of Israel; husband of Achsa.
Phinehas: Son of Eleazer.
Phinehas: Son of Eli.
Phut (or Put): Son of Ham.
Potiphar: Egyptian official; bought Joseph.
Rachel: Wife of Jacob; mother of Joseph; sister of Leah.
Rebecca (or Rebekah): Wife of Isaac; mother of Esau and Jacob.
Reuben: Son of Jacob and Leah.
Ruth: Wife of Mahlon, later of Boaz; daughter-in-law of Naomi.
Samson: Judge of Israel; famed for strength; betrayed by Delilah.
Samuel: Hebrew judge and prophet; son of Elkanah.
Sarah (or Sara, Sarai): Wife of Abraham; mother of Isaac.
Sennacherib: King of Assyria.
Seth: Son of Adam; father of Enos.
Shem: Son of Noah; father of Elam.
Simeon: Son of Jacob and Leah.
Sisera: Canaanite captain; slain by Jael.
Tamar: Daughter of David and Maachah; raped by Amnon.
Terah: Son of Nahor; father of Abraham.
Tubal-Cain: Son of Lamech and Zillah.
Uriah: Husband of Bathsheba; sent to death in battle by David.
Vashti: Wife of Ahasuerus; set aside by him.
Zadok: High priest during David's reign.
Zebulun (or Zabulon): Son of Jacob and Leah.
Zillah: Wife of Lamech.
Zilpah: Servant of Leah; mistress of Jacob.
Zipporah: Daughter of Jethro; wife of Moses.
Zophar: Comforter of Job.

Kings of Judah and Israel

Kings Before Division of Kingdom

Saul: First King of Israel; son of Kish; father of Ish-Bosheth, Jonathan and Michal.
Ish-Bosheth (or Eshbaal): King of Israel; son of Saul.
David: King of Judah; later of Israel; son of Jesse; husband of Abigail, Ahinoam, Bathsheba, Michal, etc.; father of Absalom, Adonijah, Amnon, Solomon, Tamar, etc.
Solomon: King of Israel and Judah; son of David; father of Rehoboam.
Rehoboam: Son of Solomon; during his reign the kingdom was divided into Judah and Israel.

Kings of Judah (Southern Kingdom)

Rehoboam: First King.
Abijam (or Abijam or Abia): Son of Rehoboam.
Asa: Probably son of Abijah.
Jehoshaphat: Son of Asa.
Jehoram (or Joram): Son of Jehoshaphat; husband of Athaliah.
Ahaziah: Son of Jehoram and Athaliah.
Athaliah: Daughter of King Ahab of Israel and Jezebel; wife of Jehoram; only queen to occupy the throne of Judah.
Joash (or Jehoash): Son of Ahaziah.

Amaziah: Son of Joash.
Uzziah (or Azariah): Son of Amaziah.
Jotham: Regent, later King; son of Uzziah.
Ahaz: Son of Jotham.
Hezekiah: Son of Ahaz; husband of Hephzi-Bah.
Manasseh: Son of Hezekiah and Hephzi-Bah.
Amon: Son of Manasseh.
Josiah (or Josias): Son of Amon.
Jehoahaz (or Joahaz): Son of Josiah.
Jehoiakim: Son of Josiah.
Jehoiachin: Son of Jehoiakim.
Zedekiah: Son of Josiah; kingdom overthrown by Babylonians under Nebuchadnezzar.

Kings of Israel (Northern Kingdom)

Jeroboam I: Led secession of Israel.
Nadab: Son of Jeroboam I.
Baasha: Overthrew Nadab.
Elah: Son of Baasha.
Zimri: Overthrew Elah.
Omri: Overthrew Zimri.

Ahab: Son of Omri; husband of Jezebel.
Ahaziah: Son of Ahab.
Jehoram (or Joram): Son of Ahab.
Jehu: Overthrew Jehoram.
Jehoahaz (or Joahaz): Son of Jehu.
Jehoash (or Joash): Son of Jehoahaz.
Jeroboam II: Son of Jehoash.
Zechariah: Son of Jeroboam II.
Shallum: Overthrew Zechariah.
Menahem: Overthrew Shallum.
Pekahiah: Son of Menahem.
Pekah: Overthrew Pekahiah.
Hoshea: Overthrew Pekah; kingdom overthrown by Assyrians under Sargon II.

Prophets

Major. Isaiah, Jeremiah, Ezekiel, Daniel.
Minor. Hosea, Obadiah, Nahum, Haggai, Joel, Jonah, Habakkuk, Zechariah, Amos, Micah, Zephaniah, Malachi.

Greek and Roman Mythology

Most of the Greek deities were adopted by the Romans, although in many cases there was a change of name. In the list below, information is given under the Greek name; the name in parentheses is the Roman equivalent. However, all Latin names are listed with cross-references to the Greek ones. In addition, there are several deities that are exclusively Roman. **Bold** words within entries indicate cross references.

Acheron: One of several **Rivers of Underworld.**
Achilles: Greek warrior; slew Hector at Troy; slain by Paris, who wounded him in his vulnerable heel.
Actaeon: Hunter; surprised Artemis bathing; changed by her to stag; and killed by his dogs.
Admetus: King of Thessaly; his wife, Alcestis, offered to die in his place.
Adonis: Beautiful youth loved by Aphrodite.
Aeacus: One of three judges of dead in Hades; son of Zeus.
Aeëtes: King of Colchis; father of Medea; keeper of Golden Fleece.
Aegeus: Father of Theseus; believing Theseus killed in Crete, he drowned himself; Aegean Sea named for him.
Aegisthus: Son of Thyestes; slew Atreus; with Clytemnestra, his paramour, slew Agamemnon; slain by Orestes.
Aegyptus: Brother of Danaus; his sons, except Lynceus, slain by Danaides.
Aeneas: Trojan; son of Anchises and Aphrodite; after fall of Troy, led his followers eventually to Italy; loved and deserted Dido.
Aeolus: One of several **Winds.**
Aesculapius: See Asclepius.
Aeson: King of Iolcus; father of Jason; overthrown by his brother Pelias; restored to youth by Medea.
Aether: Personification of sky.
Aethra: Mother of Theseus.
Agamemnon: King of Mycenae; son of Atreus; brother of Menelaus; leader of Greeks against Troy; slain on his return home by Clytemnestra and Aegisthus.
Aglaia: One of several **Graces.**
Ajax: Greek warrior; killed himself at Troy because Achilles's armor was awarded to Odysseus.
Alcestis: Wife of Admetus; offered to die in his place but saved from death by Hercules.
Alcmene: Wife of Amphitryon; mother by Zeus of Hercules.
Alcyone: One of several **Pleiades.**
Alecto: One of several **Furies.**
Alectryon: Youth changed by Ares into cock.
Althaea: Wife of Oeneus; mother of Meleager.
Amazons: Female warriors in Asia Minor; supported Troy against Greeks.
Amor: See Eros.
Amphion: Musician; husband of Niobe; charmed stones to build fortifications for Thebes.
Amphitrite: Sea goddess; wife of Poseidon.
Amphitryon: Husband of Alcmene.
Anchises: Father of Aeneas.
Ancile: Sacred shield that fell from heavens; palladium of Rome.
Andraemon: Husband of Dryope.
Andromache: Wife of Hector.
Andromeda: Daughter of Cepheus; chained to cliff for monster to devour; rescued by Perseus.
Anteia: Wife of Proetus; tried to induce Bellerophon to elope with her.
Anteros: God who avenged unrequited love.

Antigone: Daughter of Oedipus; accompanied him to Colonus; performed burial rite for Polynices and hanged herself.
Antinoüs: Leader of suitors of Penelope; slain by Odysseus.
Aphrodite (Venus): Goddess of love and beauty; daughter of Zeus and Dione; mother of Eros.
Apollo: God of beauty, poetry, music; later identified with Helios as Phoebus Apollo; son of Zeus and Leto.
Aquilo: One of several **Winds.**
Arachne: Maiden who challenged Athena to weaving contest; changed to spider.
Ares (Mars): God of war; son of Zeus and Hera.
Argo: Ship in which Jason and followers sailed to Colchis for Golden Fleece.
Argus: Monster with hundred eyes; slain by Hermes; his eyes placed by Hera into peacock's tail.
Ariadne: Daughter of Minos; aided Theseus in slaying Minotaur; deserted by him on island of Naxos and married to Dionysus.
Arion: Musician; thrown overboard by pirates but saved by dolphin.
Artemis (Diana): Goddess of moon; huntress; twin sister of Apollo.
Asclepius (Aesculapius): Mortal son of Apollo; slain by Zeus for raising dead; later deified as god of medicine. Also known as Asklepios.
Astarte: Phoenician goddess of love; variously identified with Aphrodite, Selene, and Artemis.
Asterope: See Sterope.
Astraea: Goddess of Justice; daughter of Zeus and Themis.
Atalanta: Princess who challenged her suitors to a foot race; Hippomenes won race and married her.
Athena (Minerva): Goddess of wisdom; known poetically as Pallas Athene; sprang fully armed from head of Zeus.
Atlas: Titan; held world on his shoulders as punishment for warring against Zeus; son of Iapetus.
Atreus: King of Mycenae; father of Menelaus and Agamemnon; brother of Thyestes, three of whose sons he slew and served to him at banquet; slain by Aegisthus.
Atropos: One of several **Fates.**
Aurora: See Eos.
Auster: One of several **Winds.**
Avernus: Infernal regions; name derived from small vaporous lake near Vesuvius which was fabled to kill birds and vegetation.
Bacchus: See Dionysus.
Bellerophon: Corinthian hero; killed Chimera with aid of Pegasus; tried to reach Olympus on Pegasus and was thrown to his death.
Bellona: Roman goddess of war.
Boreas: One of several **Winds.**
Briareus: Monster with hundred hands; son of Uranus and Gaea.
Briseis: Captive maiden given to Achilles; taken by Agamemnon in exchange for loss of Chryseis, which caused Achilles to cease fighting, until death of Patroclus.
Cadmus: Brother of Europa; planter of dragon seeds from which first Thebans sprang.

Calliope: One of several **Muses.**

Calypso: Sea nymph; kept Odysseus on her island Ogygia for seven years.

Cassandra: Daughter of Priam; prophetess who was never believed; slain with Agamemnon.

Castor: One of **Dioscuri.**

Celaeno: One of several **Pleiades.**

Centaurs: Beings half man and half horse; lived in mountains of Thessaly.

Cephalus: Hunter; accidentally killed his wife Procris with his spear.

Cepheus: King of Ethiopia; father of Andromeda.

Cerberus: Three-headed dog guarding entrance to Hades.

Ceres: See Demeter.

Chaos: Formless void; personified as first of gods.

Charon: Boatman on Styx who carried souls of dead to Hades; son of Erebus.

Charybdis: Female monster; personification of whirlpool.

Chimera: Female monster with head of lion, body of goat, tail of serpent; killed by Bellerophon.

Chiron: Most famous of centaurs.

Chronos: Personification of time.

Chryseis: Captive maiden given to Agamemnon; his refusal to accept ransom from her father Chryses caused Apollo to send plague on Greeks besieging Troy.

Circe: Sorceress; daughter of Helios; changed Odysseus's men into swine.

Clio: One of several **Muses.**

Clotho: One of several **Fates.**

Clytemnestra: Wife of Agamemnon, whom she slew with aid of her paramour, Aegisthus; slain by her son Orestes.

Cocytus: One of several **Rivers of Underworld.**

Creon: Father of Jocasta; forbade burial of Polynices; ordered burial alive of Antigone.

Creüsa: Princess of Corinth, for whom Jason deserted Medea; slain by Medea, who sent her poisoned robe; also known as Glaüke.

Creusa: Wife of Aeneas; died fleeing Troy.

Cronus (Saturn): Titan; god of harvests; son of Uranus and Gaea; dethroned by his son Zeus.

Cupid: See Eros.

Cybele: Anatolian nature goddess; adopted by Greeks and identified with Rhea.

Cyclopes: Race of one-eyed giants (singular: Cyclops).

Daedalus: Athenian artificer; father of Icarus; builder of Labyrinth in Crete; devised wings attached with wax for him and Icarus to escape Crete.

Danae: Princess of Argos; mother of Perseus by Zeus, who appeared to her in form of golden shower.

Danaïdes: Daughters of Danaüs; at his command, all except Hypermnestra slew their husbands, the sons of Aegyptus.

Danaüs: Brother of Aegyptus; father of Danaïdes; slain by Lynceus.

Daphne: Nymph; pursued by Apollo; changed to laurel tree.

Decuma: One of several **Fates.**

Deino: One of several **Graeae.**

Demeter (Ceres): Goddess of agriculture; mother of Persephone.

Diana: See Artemis.

Dido: Founder and queen of Carthage; stabbed herself when deserted by Aeneas.

Diomedes: Greek hero; with Odysseus, entered Troy and carried off Palladium, sacred statue of Athena.

Diomedes: Owner of man-eating horses, which Hercules, as ninth labor, carried off.

Dione: Titan goddess; mother by Zeus of Aphrodite.

Dionysus (Bacchus): God of wine; son of Zeus and Semele.

Dioscuri: Twins Castor and Pollux; sons of Leda by Zeus.

Dis: See Pluto, Hades.

Dryads: Wood nymphs.

Dryope: Maiden changed to Hamadryad.

Echo: Nymph who fell hopelessly in love with Narcissus; faded away except for her voice.

Electra: Daughter of Agamemnon and Clytemnestra; sister of Orestes; urged Orestes to slay Clytemnestra and Aegisthus.

Electra: One of several **Pleiades.**

Elysium: Abode of blessed dead.

Endymion: Mortal loved by Selene.

Enyo: One of several **Graeae.**

Eos (Aurora): Goddess of dawn.

Epimetheus: Brother of Prometheus; husband of Pandora.

Erato: One of several **Muses.**

Erebus: Spirit of darkness; son of Chaos.

Erinyes: One of several **Furies.**

Eris: Goddess of discord.

Eros (Amor or Cupid): God of love; son of Aphrodite.

Eteocles: Son of Oedipus, whom he succeeded to rule alternately with Polynices; refused to give up throne at end of year; he and Polynices slew each other.

Eumenides: One of several **Furies.**

Euphrosyne: One of several **Graces.**

Europa: Mortal loved by Zeus, who, in form of white bull, carried her off to Crete.

Eurus: One of several **Winds.**

Euryale: One of several **Gorgons.**

Eurydice: Nymph; wife of Orpheus.

Eurystheus: King of Argos; imposed twelve labors on Hercules.

Euterpe: One of several **Muses.**

Fates: Goddesses of destiny; Clotho (Spinner of thread of life), Lachesis (Determiner of length), and Atropos (Cutter of thread); also called Moirae. Identified by Romans with their goddesses of fate; Nona, Decuma, and Morta; called Parcae.

Fauns: Roman deities of woods and groves.

Faunus: See Pan.

Favonius: One of several **Winds.**

Flora: Roman goddess of flowers.

Fortuna: Roman goddess of fortune.

Furies: Avenging spirits; Alecto, Megaera, and Tisiphone; known also as Erinyes or Eumenides.

Gaea: Goddess of earth; daughter of Chaos; mother of Titans; known also as Ge, Gea, Gaia, etc.

Galatea: Statue of maiden carved from ivory by Pygmalion; given life by Aphrodite.

Galatea: Sea nymph; loved by Polyphemus.

Ganymede: Beautiful boy; successor to Hebe as cupbearer of gods.

Glaucus: Mortal who became sea divinity by eating magic grass.

Golden Fleece: Fleece from ram that flew Phrixos to Colchis; Aeëtes placed it under guard of dragon; carried off by Jason.

Gorgons: Female monsters; Euryale, Medusa, and Stheno; had snakes for hair; their glances turned mortals to stone.

Graces: Beautiful goddesses: Aglaia (Brilliance), Euphrosyne (Joy), and Thalia (Bloom); daughters of Zeus.

Graeae: Sentinels for Gorgons; Deino, Enyo, and Pephredo; had one eye among them, which passed from one to another.

Hades (Dis): Name sometimes given Pluto; also, abode of dead, ruled by Pluto.

Haemon: Son of Creon; promised husband of Antigone; killed himself in her tomb.

Hamadryads: Tree nymphs.

Harpies: Monsters with heads of women and bodies of birds.

Hebe (Juventas): Goddess of youth; cupbearer of gods before Ganymede; daughter of Zeus and Hera.

Hecate: Goddess of sorcery and witchcraft.

Hector: Son of Priam; slayer of Patroclus; slain by Achilles.

Hecuba: Wife of Priam.

Helen: Fairest woman in world; daughter of Zeus and Leda; wife of Menelaus; carried to Troy by Paris, causing Trojan War.

Heliades: Daughters of Helios; mourned for Phaëthon and were changed to poplar trees.

Helios (Sol): God of sun; later identified with Apollo.

Helle: Sister of Phrixos; fell from ram of Golden Fleece; water where she fell named Hellespont.

Hephaestus (Vulcan): God of fire; celestial blacksmith; son of Zeus and Hera; husband of Aphrodite.

Hera (Juno): Queen of heaven; wife of Zeus.

Hercules: Hero and strong man; son of Zeus and Alcmene; performed twelve labors or deeds to be free from bondage under Eurystheus; after death, his mortal share was destroyed, and he became immortal. Also known as Herakles or Heracles. Labors: (1) killing Nemean lion; (2) killing Lernaean Hydra; (3) capturing Erymanthian boar; (4) capturing Ceryneian hind; (5) killing man-eating Stymphalian birds; (6) procuring girdle of Hippolyte; (7) cleaning Augean stables; (8) capturing Cretan bull; (9) capturing man-eating horses of Diomedes; (10) capturing cattle of Geryon; (11) procuring golden apples of Hesperides; (12) bringing Cerberus up from Hades.

Hermes (Mercury): God of physicians and thieves; messenger of gods; son of Zeus and Maia.

Hero: Priestess of Aphrodite; Leander swam Hellespont nightly to see her; drowned herself at his death.

Hesperus: Evening star.

Hestia (Vesta): Goddess of hearth; sister of Zeus.

Hippolyte: Queen of Amazons; wife of Theseus.

Hippolytus: Son of Theseus and Hippolyte; falsely accused by Phaedra of trying to kidnap her; slain by Poseidon at request of Theseus.

Hippomenes: Husband of Atalanta, whom he beat in race by dropping golden apples, which she stopped to pick up.

Hyacinthus: Beautiful youth accidentally killed by Apollo, who caused flower to spring up from his blood.

Hydra: Nine-headed monster in marsh of Lerna; slain by Hercules.

Hygeia: Personification of health.

Hyman: God of marriage.

Hyperion: Titan; early sun god; father of Helios.

Hypermnestra: Daughter of Danaüs; refused to kill her husband Lynceus.

Hypnos (Somnus): God of sleep.

Iapetus: Titan; father of Atlas, Epimetheus, and Prometheus.

Icarus: Son of Daedalus; flew too near sun with wax-attached wings and fell into sea and was drowned.

Io: Mortal maiden loved by Zeus; changed by Hera into heifer.

Iobates: King of Lycia; sent Bellerophon to slay Chimera.

Iphigenia: Daughter of Agamemnon; offered as sacrifice to Artemis at Aulis; carried by Artemis to Tauris where she became priestess; escaped from there with Orestes.

Iris: Goddess of rainbow; messenger of Zeus and Hera.

Ismene: Daughter of Oedipus; sister of Antigone.

Iulus: Son of Aeneas.

Ixion: King of Lapithae; for making love to Hera he was bound to endlessly revolving wheel in Tartarus.

Janus: Roman god of gates and doors; represented with two opposite faces.

Jason: Son of Aeson; to gain throne of Ioclus from Pelias, went to Colchis and brought back Golden Fleece; married Medea; deserted her for Creüsa.

Jocasta: Wife of Laius; mother of Oedipus; unwittingly became wife of Oedipus; hanged herself when relationship was discovered.

Juno: See Hera.

Jupiter: See Zeus.

Juventas: See Hebe.

Lachesis: One of several **Fates.**

Laius: Father of Oedipus, by whom he was slain.

Laocoön: Priest of Apollo at Troy; warned against bringing wooden horse into Troy; destroyed with his two sons by serpents sent by Athena.

Lares: Roman ancestral spirits protecting descendants and homes.

Latona: See Leto.

Lavinia: Wife of Aeneas after defeat of Turnus.

Leander: Swam Hellespont nightly to see Hero; drowned in storm.

Leda: Mortal loved by Zeus in form of swan; mother of Helen, Clytemnestra, Dioscuri.

Lethe: One of several **Rivers of Underworld.**

Leto (Latona): Mother by Zeus of Artemis and Apollo.

Lucina: Roman goddess of childbirth; identified with Juno.

Lynceus: Son of Aegyptus; husband of Hypermnestra; slew Danaüs.

Maia: Daughter of Atlas; mother of Hermes.

Maia: One of several **Pleiades.**

Manes: Souls of dead Romans, particularly of ancestors.

Mars: See Ares.

Marsyas: Shepherd; challenged Apollo to music contest and lost; flayed alive by Apollo.

Medea: Sorceress; daughter of Aeëtes; helped Jason obtain Golden Fleece; when deserted by him for Creüsa, killed her children and Creüsa.

Medusa: One of several **Gorgons;** slain by Perseus, who cut off her head.

Megaera: One of several **Furies.**

Meleager: Son of Althaea; his life would last as long as brand burning at his birth; Althaea quenched and saved it but destroyed it when Meleager slew his uncles.

Melpomene: One of several **Muses.**

Memnon: Ethiopian king; made immortal by Zeus; son of Tithonus and Eos.

Menelaus: King of Sparta; son of Atreus; brother of Agamemnon; husband of Helen.

Mercury: See Hermes.

Merope: One of several **Pleiades.** Merope is said to have hidden in shame for loving a mortal.

Mezentius: Cruel Etruscan king; ally of Turnus against Aeneas; slain by Aeneas.

Midas: King of Phrygia; given gift of turning to gold all he touched.

Minerva: See Athena.

Minos: King of Crete; after death, one of three judges of dead in Hades; son of Zeus and Europa.

Minotaur: Monster, half man and half beast, kept in Labyrinth in Crete; slain by Theseus.

Mnemosyne: Goddess of memory; mother by Zeus of Muses.

Moirae: One of several **Fates.**

Momus: God of ridicule.

Morpheus: God of dreams.

Mors: See Thanatos.

Morta: One of several **Fates.**

Muses: Goddesses presiding over arts and sciences: Calliope (epic poetry), Clio (history), Erato (lyric and love poetry), Euterpe (music), Melpomene (tragedy), Polymnia or Polyhymnia (sacred poetry), Terpsichore (choral dance and song), Thalia (comedy and bucolic poetry), Urania (astronomy); daughters of Zeus and Mnemosyne.

Naiads: Nymphs of waters, streams, and fountains.

Napaeae: Wood nymphs.

Narcissus: Beautiful youth loved by Echo; in punishment for not returning her love, he was made to fall in love with his image reflected in pool; pined away and became flower.

Nemesis: Goddess of retribution.

Neoptolemus: Son of Achilles; slew Priam; also known as Pyrrhus.

Neptune: See Poseidon.

Nereids: Sea nymphs; attendants on Poseidon.

Nestor: King of Pylos; noted for wise counsel in expedition against Troy.

Nike: Goddess of victory.

Niobe: Daughter of Tantalus; wife of Amphion; her children slain by Apollo and Artemis; changed to stone but continued to weep her loss.

Nona: One of several **Fates.**

Notus: One of several **Winds.**

Nox: See Nyx.

Nymphs: Beautiful maidens; minor deities of nature.

Nyx (Nox): Goddess of night.

Oceanids: Ocean nymphs; daughters of Oceanus.

Oceanus: Eldest of Titans; god of waters.

Odysseus (Ulysses): King of Ithaca; husband of Penelope; wandered ten years after fall of Troy before arriving home.

Oedipus: King of Thebes; son of Laius and Jocasta; unwittingly murdered Laius and married Jocasta; tore his eyes out when relationship was discovered.

Oenone: Nymph of Mount Ida; wife of Paris, who abandoned her; refused to cure him when he was poisoned by arrow of Philoctetes at Troy.

Ops: See Rhea.

Oreads: Mountain nymphs.

Orestes: Son of Agamemnon and Clytemnestra; brother of Electra; slew Clytemnestra and Aegisthus; pursued by Furies until his purification by Apollo.

Orion: Hunter; slain by Artemis and made heavenly constellation.

Orpheus: Famed musician; son of Apollo and Muse Calliope; husband of Eurydice.

Pales: Roman goddess of shepherds and herdsmen.

Palinurus: Aeneas' pilot; fell overboard in his sleep and was drowned.

Pan (Faunus): God of woods and fields; part goat; son of Hermes.

Pandora: Opener of box containing human ills; mortal wife of Epimetheus.

Parcae: One of several **Fates.**

Paris: Son of Priam; gave apple of discord to Aphrodite, for which she enabled him to carry off Helen; slew Achilles at Troy; slain by Philoctetes.

Patroclus: Great friend of Achilles; wore Achilles' armor and was slain by Hector.

Pegasus: Winged horse that sprang from Medusa's body at her death; ridden by Bellerophon when he slew Chimera.

Pelias: King of Ioclus; seized throne from his brother Aeson; sent Jason for Golden Fleece; slain unwittingly by his daughters at instigation of Medea.

Pelops: Son of Tantalus; his father cooked and served him to gods; restored to life; Peloponnesus named for him.

Penates: Roman household gods.

Penelope: Wife of Odysseus; waited faithfully for him for many years while putting off numerous suitors.

Pephredo: One of several **Graeae.**

Periphetes: Giant; son of Hephaestus; slain by Theseus.

Persephone (Proserpine): Queen of infernal regions; daughter of Zeus and Demeter; wife of Pluto.

Perseus: Son of Zeus and Danaë; slew Medusa; rescued Andromeda from monster and married her.

Phaedra: Daughter of Minos; wife of Theseus; caused the death of her stepson, Hippolytus.

Phaethon: Son of Helios; drove his father's sun chariot and was struck down by Zeus before he set world on fire.

Philoctetes: Greek warrior who possessed Hercules' bow and arrows; slew Paris at Troy with poisoned arrow.

Phineus: Betrothed of Andromeda; tried to slay Perseus but turned to stone by Medusa's head.

Phlegethon: One of several **Rivers of Underworld.**

Phosphor: Morning star.

Phrixos: Brother of Helle; carried by ram of Golden Fleece to Colchis.

Pirithous: Son of Ixion; friend of Theseus; tried to carry off Persephone from Hades; bound to enchanted rock by Pluto.

Pleiades: Alcyone, Celaeno, Electra, Maia, Merope, Sterope or Asterope, Taygeta; seven daughters of Atlas; transformed into heavenly constellation, of which six stars are visible (Merope is said to have hidden in shame for loving a mortal).

Pluto (Dis): God of Hades; brother of Zeus.

Plutus: God of wealth.

Pollux: One of **Dioscuri.**

Polyhymnia: *See* Polymnia.

Polymnia (Polyhymnia): One of several **Muses.**

Polynices: Son of Oedipus; he and his brother Eteocles killed each other; burial rite, forbidden by Creon, performed by his sister Antigone.

Polyphemus: Cyclops; devoured six of Odysseus's men; blinded by Odysseus.

Polyxena: Daughter of Priam; betrothed to Achilles, whom Paris slew at their betrothal; sacrificed to shade of Achilles.

Pomona: Roman goddess of fruits.

Pontus: Sea god; son of Gaea.

Poseidon (Neptune): God of sea; brother of Zeus.

Priam: King of Troy; husband of Hecuba; ransomed Hector's body from Achilles; slain by Neoptolemus.

Priapus: God of regeneration.

Procris: Wife of Cephalus, who accidentally slew her.

Procrustes: Giant; stretched or cut off legs of victims to make them fit iron bed; slain by Theseus.

Proetus: Husband of Anteia; sent Bellerophon to Iobates to be put to death.

Prometheus: Titan; stole fire from heaven for man. Zeus punished him by chaining him to rock in Caucasus where vultures devoured his liver daily.

Proserpine: *See* Persephone.

Proteus: Sea god; assumed various shapes when called on to prophesy.

Psyche: Beloved of Eros; punished by jealous Aphrodite; made immortal and united with Eros.

Pygmalion: King of Cyprus; carved ivory statue of maiden which Aphrodite gave life as Galatea.

Pyramus: Babylonian youth; made love to Thisbe through hole in wall; thinking Thisbe slain by lion, killed himself.

Python: Serpent born from slime left by Deluge; slain by Apollo.

Quirinus: Roman war god.

Remus: Brother of Romulus; slain by him.

Rhadamanthus: One of three judges of dead in Hades; son of Zeus and Europa.

Rhea (Ops): Daughter of Uranus and Gaea; wife of Cronus; mother of Zeus; identified with Cybele.

Rivers of Underworld: Acheron (woe), Cocytus (wailing), Lethe (forgetfulness), Phlegethon (fire), Styx (across which souls of dead were ferried by Charon).

Romulus: Founder of Rome; he and Remus suckled in infancy by she-wolf; slew Remus; deified by Romans.

Sarpedon: King of Lycia; son of Zeus and Europa; slain by Patroclus at Troy.

Saturn: *See* Cronus.

Satyrs: Hoofed demigods of woods and fields; companions of Dionysus.

Sciron: Robber; forced strangers to wash his feet, then hurled them into sea where tortoise devoured them; slain by Theseus.

Scylla: Female monster inhabiting rock opposite Charybdis; menaced passing sailors.

Selene: Goddess of moon.

Semele: Daughter of Cadmus; mother by Zeus of Dionysus; demanded Zeus appear before her in all his splendor and was destroyed by his lightning bolts.

Sibyis: Various prophetesses; most famous, Cumaean sibyl, accompanied Aeneas into Hades.

Sileni: Minor woodland deities similar to satyrs (singular: silenus). Sometimes Silenus refers to eldest of satyrs, son of Hermes or of Pan.

Silvanus: Roman god of woods and fields.

Sinis: Giant; bent pines, with which he hurled victims against side of mountain; slain by Theseus.

Sirens: Minor deities who lured sailors to destruction with their singing.

Sisyphus: King of Corinth; condemned in Tartarus to roll huge stone to top of hill; it always rolled back down again.

Sol: *See* Helios.

Somnus: *See* Hypnos.

Sphinx: Monster of Thebes; killed those who could not answer her riddle; slain by Oedipus. Name also refers to other monsters having body of lion, wings, and head and bust of woman.

Sterope (Asterope): One of several **Pleiades.**

Stheno: One of several **Gorgons.**

Styx: One of several **Rivers of Underworld.** The souls of the dead were ferried across the Styx by Charon.

Symplegades: Clashing rocks at entrance to Black Sea; Argo passed through, causing them to become forever fixed.

Syrinx: Nymph pursued by Pan; changed to reeds, from which he made his pipes.

Tantalus: Cruel king; father of Pelops and Niobe; condemned in Tartarus to stand chin-deep in lake surrounded by fruit branches; as he tried to eat or drink, water or fruit always receded.

Tartarus: Underworld below Hades; often refers to Hades.

Taygeta: One of several **Pleiades.**

Telemachus: Son of Odysseus; made unsuccessful journey to find his father.

Tellus: Roman goddess of earth.

Terminus: Roman god of boundaries and landmarks.

Terpsichore: One of several **Muses.**

Terra: Roman earth goddess.

Thalia: One of several **Graces.** Also one of several **Muses.**

Thanatos (Mors): God of death.

Themis: Titan goddess of laws of physical phenomena; daughter of Uranus; mother of Prometheus.

Theseus: Son of Aegeus; slew Minotaur; married and deserted Ariadne; later married Phaedra.

Thisbe: Beloved of Pyramus; killed herself at his death.

Thyestes: Brother of Atreus; Atreus killed three of his sons and served them to him at banquet.

Tiresias: Blind soothsayer of Thebes.

Tisiphone: One of several **Furies.**

Titans: Early gods from which Olympian gods were derived; children of Uranus and Gaea.

Tithonus: Mortal loved by Eos; changed into grasshopper.

Triton: Demigod of sea; son of Poseidon.

Turnus: King of Rutuli in Italy; betrothed to Lavinia; slain by Aeneas.

Ulysses: *See* Odysseus.

Urania: One of several **Muses.**

Uranus: Personification of Heaven; husband of Gaea; father of Titans; dethroned by his son Cronus.

Venus: *See* Aphrodite.

Vertumnus: Roman god of fruits and vegetables; husband of Pomona.

Vesta: *See* Hestia.

Vulcan: *See* Hephaestus.

Winds: Aeolus (keeper of winds), Boreas (Aquilo) (north wind), Eurus (east wind), Notus (Auster) (south wind), Zephyrus (Favonius) (west wind).

Zephyrus: One of several **Winds.**

Zeus (Jupiter): Chief of Olympian gods; son of Cronus and Rhea; husband of Hera.

Norse Mythology

Aesir: Chief gods of Asgard.

Andvari: Dwarf; robbed of gold and magic ring by Loki.

Angerbotha (Angrbotha): Giantess; mother by Loki of Fenrir, Hel, and Midgard serpent.

Asgard (Asgarth): Abode of gods.

Ask (Aske, Askr): First man; created by Odin, Hoenir, and Lothur.

Asynjur: Goddesses of Asgard.

Atli: Second husband of Gudrun; invited Gunnar and Hogni to his court, where they were slain; slain by Gudrun.

Audhumia (Audhumbla): Cow that nourished Ymir; created Buri by licking ice cliff.

Balder (Baldr, Baldur): God of light, spring, peace, joy; son of Odin; slain by Hoth at instigation of Loki.

Bifrost: Rainbow bridge connecting Midgard and Asgard.

Bragi (Brage): God of poetry; husband of Ithunn.

Branstock: Great oak in hall of Volsungs; into it, Odin thrust Gram, which only Sigmund could draw forth.

Brynhild: Valkyrie; wakened from magic sleep by Sigurd; married Gunnar; instigated death of Sigurd; killed herself and was burned on pyre beside Sigmund.

Bur (Bor): Son of Buri; father of Odin, Hoenir, and Lothur.

Buri (Bori): Progenitor of gods; father of Bur; created by Audhumla.

Embla: First woman; created by Odin, Hoenir, and Lothur.

Fafnir: Son of Rodmar, whom he slew for gold in Otter's skin; in form of dragon, guarded gold; slain by Sigurd.

Fenrir: Wolf; offspring of Loki; swallows Odin at Ragnarok and is slain by Vitharr.

Forseti: Son of Balder.

Frey (Freyr): God of fertility and crops; son of Njorth; originally one of **Vanir.**

Freya (Freyja): Goddess of love and beauty; sister of Frey; originally one of **Vanir.**

Frigg (Frigga): Goddess of sky; wife of Odin.

Garm: Watchdog of Hel; slays, and is slain by, Tyr at Ragnarok.

Gimle: Home of blessed after Ragnarok.

Giuki: King of Nibelungs; father of Gunnar, Hogni, Guttorm, and Gudrun.

Glathsehim (Gladsheim): Hall of gods in Asgard.

Gram (meaning "Angry"): Sigmund's sword; rewelded by Regin; used by Sigurd to slay Fafnir.

Greyfell: Sigmund's horse; descended from Sleipnir.

Grimhild: Mother of Gudrun; administered magic potion to Sigurd which made him forget Brynhild.

Gudrun: Daughter of Giuki; wife of Sigurd; later wife of Atli and Jonakr.

Gunnar: Son of Giuki; in his semblance Sigurd won Brynhild for him; slain at hall of Atli.

Guttorm: Son of Giuki; slew Sigurd at Brynhild's request.

Heimdall (Heimdallr): Guardian of Asgard.

Hel: Goddess of dead and queen of underworld; daughter of Loki.

Hiordis: Wife of Sigmund; mother of Sigurd.

Hoenir: One of creators of Ask and Embla; son of Bur.

Hogni: Son of Giuki; slain at hall of Atli.

Hoth (Hoder, Hodur): Blind god of night and darkness; slayer of Balder at instigation of Loki.

Ithunn (Ithun, Iduna): Keeper of golden apples of youth; wife of Bragi.

Jonakr: Third husband of Gudrun.

Jormunrek: Slayer of Swanhild; slain by sons of Gudrun.

Jotunnheim (Jotunheim): Abode of giants.

Lif and Lifthrasir: First man and woman after Ragnarok.

Loki: God of evil and mischief; instigator of Balder's death.

Lothur (Lodur): One of creators of Ask and Embla.

Midgard (Midgarth): Abode of mankind; the earth.

Midgard Serpent: Sea monster; offspring of Loki; slays, and is slain by, Thor at Ragnarok.

Mimir: Giant; guardian of well in Jotunnheim at root of Yggdrasill; knower of past and future.

Mjolnir: Magic hammer of Thor.

Nagifar: Ship to be used by giants in attacking Asgard at Ragnarok; built from nails of dead men.

Nanna: Wife of Balder.

Nibelungs: Dwellers in northern kingdom ruled by Giuki.

Niflheim (Nifelheim): Outer region of cold and darkness; abode of Hel.

Njorth: Father of Frey and Freya; originally one of **Vanir.**

Norns: Demigoddesses of fate: Urth (Urdur) (past), Verthandi (Verdandi) (present), Skuld (future).

Odin (Othin): Head of **Aesir;** creator of world with Vili and Ve; equivalent to Woden (Wodan, Wotan) in Teutonic mythology.

Otter: Son of Rodmar; slain by Loki; his skin filled with gold hoard of Andvari to appease Rodmar.

Ragnarok: Final destruction of present world in battle between gods and giants; some minor gods will survive, and Lif and Lifthrasir will repeople world.

Regin: Blacksmith; son of Rodmar; foster-father of Sigurd.

Rerir: King of Huns; son of Sigi.

Rodmar: Father of Regin, Otter, and Fafnir; demanded Otter's skin be filled with gold; slain by Fafnir, who stole gold.

Sif: Wife of Thor.

Siggeir: King of Goths; husband of Signy; he and his sons slew Volsung and his sons, except Sigmund; slain by Sigmund and Sinflotli.

Sigi: King of Huns; son of Odin.

Sigmund: Son of Volsung; brother of Signy, who bore him Sinflotli; husband of Hiordis, who bore him Sigurd.

Signy: Daughter of Volsung; sister of Sigmund; wife of Siggeir; mother by Sigmund of Sinflotli.

Sigurd: Son of Sigmund and Hiordis; wakened Brynhild from magic sleep; married Gudrun; slain by Guttorm at instigation of Brynhild.

Sigyn: Wife of Loki.

Sinflotli: Son of Sigmund and Signy.

Skuld: One of several **Norns.**

Sleipnir (Sleipner): Eight-legged horse of Odin.

Surt (Surtr): Fire demon; slays Frey at Ragnarok.

Svartalfaheim: Abode of dwarfs.

Swanhild: Daughter of Sigurd and Gudrun; slain by Jormunrek.

Thor: God of thunder; oldest son of Odin; equivalent to Germanic deity Donar.

Tyr: God of war; son of Odin; equivalent to Tiu in Teutonic mythology.

Ull (Ullr): Son of Sif; stepson of Thor.

Urth: One of several **Norns.**

Valhalla (Valhall): Great hall in Asgard where Odin received souls of heroes killed in battle.

Vali: Odin's son; Ragnarok survivor.

Valkyries: Virgins, messengers of Odin, who selected heroes to die in battle and took them to Valhalla; generally considered as nine in number.

Vanir: Early race of gods; three survivors, Njorth, Frey, and Freya, are associated with **Aesir.**

Ve: Brother of Odin; one of creators of world.

Verthandi: One of several **Norns.**

Vili: Brother of Odin; one of creators of world.

Vingolf: Abode of goddesses in Asgard.

Vitharr (Vithar): Son of Odin; survivor of Ragnarok.

Volsung: Descendant of Odin, and father of Signy, Sigmund; his descendants were called Volsungs.

Yggdrasill: Giant ash tree springing from body of Ymir and supporting universe; its roots extended to Asgard, Jotunnheim, and Niffheim.

Ymir (Ymer): Primeval frost giant killed by Odin, Vili, and Ve; world created from his body; also, from his body sprang Yggdrasill.

Egyptian Mythology

Aaru: Abode of the blessed dead.

Amen (Amon, Ammdn): One of chief Theban deities; united with sun god under form of Amen-Ra; husband of Mut.

Amenti: Region of dead where souls were judged by Osiris.

Anubis: Guide of souls to Amenti; son of Osiris; jackal-headed.

Apis: Sacred bull, an embodiment of Ptah; identified with Osiris as Osiris-Apis or Serapis.

Geb (Keb, Seb): Earth god; father of Osiris; represented with goose on head.

Hathor (Athor): Goddess of love and mirth; cow-headed.

Horus: God of day; son of Osiris and Isis; hawk-headed.

Isis: Goddess of motherhood and fertility; sister and wife of Osiris.

Khepera: God of morning sun.

Khnemu (Khnum, Chnuphis, Chnemu, Chnum): Ram-headed god.

Khonsu (Khensu, Khuns): Son of Amen and Mut.

Mentu (Ment): Solar deity, sometimes considered god of war; falcon-headed.

Min (Khem, Chem): Principle of physical life.

Mut (Maut): Wife of Amen.

Nephthys: Goddess of the dead; sister and wife of Set.

Nu: Chaos from which world was created, personified as a god.

Nut: Goddess of heavens; consort of Geb.

Osiris: God of underworld and judge of dead; son of Geb and Nut; brother and husband of Isis.

Ptah (Phtha): Chief deity of Memphis.

Ra: God of the Sun, the supreme god; son of Nut; Pharaohs claimed descent from him; represented as lion, cat, or falcon.

Serapis: God uniting attributes of Osiris and Apis.

Set (Seth): God of darkness or evil; brother and enemy of Osiris; brother and husband of Nephthys.

Shu: Solar deity; son of Ra and Hathor.

Tem (Atmu, Atum, Tum): Solar deity.

Thoth (Dhouti): God of wisdom and magic; scribe of gods; ibis-headed.

A Concise Guide to Style

This section discusses and illustrates the basic conventions of American capitalization, italicization, and punctuation.

Capitalization

Capitalize the following:

- **Proper nouns and adjectives derived from proper nouns:**

  Marie Curie   China, Chinese
  Smokey Robinson   Darwin, Darwinian

  But vocabulary words derived from proper nouns are generally lowercase:

  china cups   plaster of paris
  french fries   vienna sausage

- **The names of geographic divisions, regions, and localities and topographical features such as rivers, lakes, and mountains:**

  North Pole   Gulf States
  Middle East   Atlantic Ocean
  Southern Hemisphere Rocky Mountains
  the North   Lake Tahoe
  Lower East Side   Erie Canal

  Do not capitalize directions: She lives 10 miles north of Boston.

- **The names of nationalities, ethnic groups, tribes, and languages:**

  Spanish   Bantu
  Asian-American   Creole

- **Titles when preceding a name:**

  President Lincoln   Aunt Mary
  Queen Victoria   Doctor Johnson
  Senator Kennedy   Professor Davies

  Do not capitalize such terms elsewhere: a biography of the queen; the senator's speech; my aunt, Mary Wilson; the president's fundraising efforts; the residence of the vice president.

- **Epithets:** Ivan the Terrible; Lincoln is known as The Great Emancipator.

- **The names of political and judicial bodies, social organizations, councils, and departments:**

  U.S. Senate   Rotary Club
  Democratic Party   United Negro College Fund
  State Department   U.S. Supreme Court

- **The names for periods, events, and documents of historical importance:**

  Middle Ages   Constitution
  Renaissance   Treaty of Versailles
  Battle of Waterloo   Magna Carta

- **The names for streets, buildings, and monuments:**

  Fifth Avenue   World Trade Center
  Broadway   Statue of Liberty

- **The names for the supreme deity and sacred works:**

  God, the Father Almighty   Bible
  Yahweh   Talmud
  Allah   Qu'ran

- **The names for religious denominations and their members:**

  Buddhism, Buddhists
  Catholicism, Catholics
  Judaism, Jews
  Methodist Church, Methodists
  Society of Friends, Quakers

- **The days of the weeks, months of the year, holidays, and holy days:**

  Thursday   Labor Day
  December   Passover

- **The pronoun I:**

  I told her I didn't want to go.

- **The first word in the salutation and complimentary close of a letter:**

  My dear Carol . . .
  Very truly yours . . .

- **The first word of a sentence:**

  Are you hungry? Lunch will be served soon.

- **The first word of a direct quotation, except when the quotation is split:**

  I asked, "Do you really like bats?"
  "Yes," said Holly, "they're so cute."

- **The first word and all the key words in the title of a literary or other artistic work:**

  The Bluest Eye (novel)
  A Streetcar Named Desire (play)
  "The Road Not Taken" (poem)
  Starry Night (painting)
  "Only the Lonely" (song)

- **The names of ships, aircraft, and space vehicles:**

  USS *Maine*
  The Spirit of St. Louis
  space shuttle *Challenger*

- **The names of constellations, planets, and stars:**

  Milky Way   Saturn
  the asteroid Juno   Little Dipper

- **The names of geologic eras, periods, epochs, and names of prehistoric divisions:**

  Paleozoic Era   *Pleistocene*
  Quaternary Period *Stone Age*

- **The genus but not the species name in binomial nomenclature:**

  Canis familiaris (dog)
  Malus pumila (apple tree)

Italicization

Italicize the following:

- **The titles of books, plays, book-length poems, magazines, and newspapers:**

  War and Peace   *TIME magazine*
  Twelfth Night   *National Geographic*
  Beowulf   *Miami Herald*

- **The titles of movies and radio and television programs:**

  Toy Story   *The X-Files*
  Car Talk   *Masterpiece Theater*

- **The titles of works of art, including paintings, sculptures, and major musical compositions:**

  Mona Lisa (painting)
  The Thinker (sculpture)
  Swan Lake (ballet)
  Porgy and Bess (opera)

  Do not italicize musical compositions named by number or key: Symphony No. 4; Quartet in E minor.

- **Words, letters, and numbers used as such:**

  How do you spell *ache*?
  Does your name end with a *c* or a *k*?
  The *6* looked like a *0*.

- **Foreign words and phrases that have not been assimilated into English:**

  Alex's *Weltanschauung* was gloomy.
  Ed made a *tarte au citron* for dessert.

- **Words and phrases that are being emphasized:**

  Paris was *the* place to be in the '20s.

- **The names of the plaintiff and defendant in legal citations:** *Johnson* v. *Smith.*

- **The names of ships, aircraft, and space vehicles:**

  USS *Maine*
  The Spirit of St. Louis
  space shuttle *Challenger*

- **The New Latin names of genera, species, subspecies, and varieties in botanical and zoological nomenclature:** *Quercus alba; Homo sapiens.*

Punctuation

End Marks

- **Use a period after a declarative or imperative statement:**

  I went to the library.
  Sign your name here.

- **Use a question mark after a direct question or to indicate uncertainty:**

  What is your name?
  Chaucer's dates are 1340?–1400.

  Do not use a question mark after an indirect question: I asked them what time they were leaving.

- **Use an exclamation point after an exclamatory or emphatic sentence or an interjection:**

  Give me a break!
  Hey! Ouch! Wow!

Comma

Use a comma:

- **To separate words in a list or series:**

  The baby likes grapes, bananas, and cantaloupe.

- **To separate two or more adjectives that come before a noun when *and* can be substituted without changing the meaning:**

  He had a kind, generous nature.
  The dog had thick, soft, shiny fur.

  Do not use the comma if the adjectives together express a single idea or the noun is a compound made up of an adjective and a noun:

  The kitchen had bright yellow curtains.
  A majestic bald eagle soared overhead.

- **To set off words or phrases in apposition to a noun:**

  George Eliot, the great 19th-century novelist, was born in 1819.

  Do not use commas when the appositive word or phrase is essential to the meaning of the sentence:
  The novelist George Eliot was born in 1819.

- **To set off nonessential phrases and clauses:**

  My French professor, who has an odd sense of humor, has been teaching for some 30 years.

  Do not use commas when the phrase or clause is essential to the meaning of the sentence:

  The professor who teaches my French class has an odd sense of humor.

- **To separate the independent clauses joined by a coordinating conjunction in a compound sentence:**

  He lives in New York, and she lives in London.
  Some people like golf, but others prefer tennis.

- **To set off interrupters such as *of course, however, I think,* and *by the way* from the rest of the sentence:**

  She knew, of course, that he was lying.
  By the way, I'll be away next week.

- **To set off an introductory word, phrase, or clause at the beginning of a sentence:**

  Yes, I'd like to go with you.
  After some years, we met again.
  Being tall, she often gets teased.

- **To set off a word in direct address:**

  Thanks, guys, for all your help.
  How was your trip, Kathy?

- **To set off a tag question:**

  You won't do that again, will you?

- **To introduce a short quotation:**

  The queen said, "Let them eat cake!"

- **To close the salutation in a personal letter and the complimentary close in a business or personal letter:**

  Dear Mary, . . .   Sincerely, Fred

- **To set off titles and degrees:**

  Sarah Little, Ph.D.   Robert Johnson, Jr.

- **To separate sentence elements that might be read incorrectly without the comma:**

  As they entered, in the shadows you could see a figure lurking.

- **To set off the month and day from the year in full dates:**

  The conference will be held on August 6, 2001.

  Do not use a comma when only the month and year appear:

  The conference will be held in August 2001.

- **To set off the city and state in an address:**

  Sam Green
  10 Joy Street
  Boston, MA 02116

  If the address is inserted into text, add a second comma after the state:

  Cincinnati, Ohio, is their home.

Colon

Use a colon:

- **To introduce a list, or words, phrases, and clauses that explain, enlarge upon, or summarize what has gone before:**

  Please provide the following: your name, address, and phone number.

  "No honest poet can ever feel quite sure of the permanent value of what he has written: He may have wasted his time and messed up his life for nothing."—T. S. Eliot

- **To introduce a long quotation:**

  In 1780 John Adams wrote: "English is destined to be in the next and succeeding centuries more generally the language of the world than Latin was in the last or French is in the present age . . . "

- **To separate hour and minute(s) in standard time notation:**

  The train arrives at 9:30.

- **To close the salutation in a business letter:**

  Dear Sir or Madam:

Semicolon

Use a semicolon:

- **To separate the independent clauses in a compound sentence not joined by a conjunction:**

  Only two seats were left; we needed three.

  The situation is hopeful; the storm may lift soon.

- **To separate two independent clauses, the second of which begins with an adverb such as *however, consequently, moreover,* and *therefore*:**

  We waited an hour; however, we couldn't hang around indefinitely.

- **To separate elements already punctuated with commas:**

  Invitations were mailed to the various professors, associate professors, and assistant professors; the secretary of the department; and some of the grad students.

Dashes & Hyphens

- **Use a dash to indicate a sudden break in continuity or to set off an explanatory, a defining, or an emphatic phrase:**

  The sky grew dark—where were the kids?

  Dairy foods—milk, cheese, yogurt—are a good source of calcium.

- **Use a hyphen to join the elements of a compound word or to join the elements of a compound modifier before a noun:**

  well-wisher   ice-skating rink
  fifty-three   college-age students

- **Use a hyphen to divide a word at the end of a line:**

  Rasputin is one of history's most enigmatic and intriguing figures.

Brackets & Parentheses

- **Use brackets to set off words or letters in quoted matter that have been added by someone other than the author:**

  "She [Willa Cather] is certainly one of the great American writers of the 20th century."

- **Use parentheses to set off nonessential information:**

  We spent an hour (more or less) cleaning up.

Apostrophe

Use an apostrophe to indicate:

- **The possessive case of singular and plural nouns, indefinite pronouns, and proper nouns:**

  my sister's son   somebody's lunch
  my two sisters' sons Charles's house
  the children's toys   the Rosses' friends

- **The plural of letters, numbers, symbols, and words used as such:**

  too many *thus*'s   ten *5*'s in a row
  spelled with two *e*'s delete some *&*'s

- **Missing letters in contractions and missing numbers in dates:**

  I'm (I am)   class of '95
  ma'am (madam)   winter of '97–'98

Quotation Marks

Use quotation marks:

- **To set off direct quotations:**

  "Let's go to the beach," she suggested.

- **To set off titles of short stories, articles, chapters, essays, songs, poems, and individual radio and television programs:**

  Chapter 9, "The New Englishes"
  sang the "Star-Spangled Banner"
  "The Apparent Trap" episode of *Frasier*

- **To set off words and phrases that are being used in an unusual or questionable way or might be preceded by *so-called*:**

  Mari's "fine" was a day's volunteer work.

  According to the article, bees appear to "remember" landmarks.

Forms of Address

Addressee	Address	Salutation
Clerical and religious orders		
Archbishop, Eastern Orthodox	The Most Reverend *First name*, Archbishop of *Place name*	Your Eminence
Archbishop, Roman Catholic	The Most Reverend *First name*, Archbishop of *Place name*	Your Excellency
Archdeacon, Episcopal	The Venerable *Full name*, Archdeacon of *Place name*	Dear Archdeacon *Last name*
Bishop, Episcopal	The Right Reverend *Full name*, Bishop of *Place name*	Right Reverend Sir *or* Dear Bishop *Last name*
Bishop, other Protestant	The Reverend *Full name*	Dear Bishop *Last name*
Bishop, Roman Catholic	The Most Reverend *Full name*, Bishop of *Place name*	Your Excellency *or* Dear Bishop *Last name*
Cardinal	His Eminence *First name* Cardinal *Last name*	Your Eminence
Clergyman/woman, Protestant	The Reverend *Full name or* The Reverend *Full name*, D.D.	Dear Mr./Ms. *Last name or* Dear Dr. *Last name*
Dean of a Cathedral, Episcopal	The Very Reverend *Full name*, Dean of *Place name*	Dear Dean *Last name*
Monsignor	The Right Reverend Monsignor *Full name*	Dear Monsignor
Patriarch, Greek Orthodox	His All Holiness the Patriarch of *Place name*	Your All Holiness
Patriarch, Russian Orthodox	His Holiness the Patriarch of *Place name*	Your Holiness
Pope	His Holiness The Pope	Your Holiness *or* Most Holy Father
Priest, Roman Catholic	The Reverend *Full name or* The Reverend *Full name*, S.J. (or other order)	Dear Reverend Father *or* Dear Father
Rabbi, man or woman	Rabbi *Full name or Full name*, D.D.	Dear Rabbi *Last name or* Dear Dr. *Last name*
Government officials		
Assemblyman/woman	The Honorable *Full name*	Dear Mr./Ms. *Last name*
Associate Justice, U.S. Supreme Court	The Honorable Justice *Full name*	Dear Sir/Madam *or* Justice *Last name*
Cabinet member	The Honorable *Full name*, Secretary of *Department name*	Sir/Madam *or* Dear Mr./Madam Secretary
Chief Justice, U.S. Supreme Court	The Honorable *Full name*, Chief Justice of the United States	Dear Mr./Madame Chief Justice
Commissioner	The Honorable *Full name*	Dear Mr./Mrs. *Last name*
Governor	The Honorable *Full name*, Governor of *State name*	Dear Governor *Last name*
Judge, federal	The Honorable *Full name*, Judge, United States District Court	Dear Sir/Madam *or* Judge *Last name*
Judge, state or local	The Honorable *Full name*, Judge of the Court of *Place name*	Dear Judge *Last name*
Mayor	The Honorable *Full name*, Mayor of *Place name*	Dear Mayor *Last name*
President, U.S.	The President	Dear Mr./Madam President
President, U.S., former	The Honorable *Full name*	Dear Mr./Madam *Last name*
Representative, state	The Honorable *Full name*, *State name* House of Representatives	Dear Mr./Ms. *Last name*
Representative, U.S.	The Honorable *Full name*, United States House of Representatives	Dear Mr./Mrs. *Last name*
Senator, state	The Honorable *Full name*, The State Senate, *State Capital*	Dear Senator *Last name*
Senator, U.S.	The Honorable *Full name*, United States Senate	Dear Senator *Last name*
Speaker, U.S. House of Representatives	The Honorable *Full name*, Speaker of the House of Representatives	Dear Mr./Madam Speaker
Vice President, U.S.	The Vice President of the United States	Sir/Madam *or* Dear Mr./Madam Vice President
Military and naval officers		
All ranks	*Rank Full name*, USA/USN/USCG/ USAF/USMC	Dear *Rank Last name*

Easily Confused Words

affect / effect *Effect* is usually a noun that means a result or the power to produce a result: "The sound of the falling rain had a calming effect, nearly putting me to sleep." *Affect* is usually a verb that means to have an influence on: "His loud humming was affecting my ability to concentrate." Note that *effect* can also be a verb meaning to bring about or execute: "The speaker's somber tone effected a dampening in the general mood of the audience."

all together / altogether *All together* is applied to people or things that are being treated as a group. "We put the pots and pans all together on the shelf." *All together* is the form that must be used if the sentence can be reworded so that *all* and *together* are separated by other words: "We put all the pots and pans together on the shelf." *Altogether* is used to mean entirely: "I am altogether pleased to be receiving this award."

allusion / illusion *Allusion* is a noun that means an indirect reference: "The speech made allusions to the final report." *Illusion* is a noun that means a misconception: "The policy is designed to give an illusion of reform."

alternately / alternatively *Alternately* is an adverb that means in turn; one after the other: "We alternately spun the wheel in the game." *Alternatively* is an adverb that means on the other hand; one or the other: "You can choose a large bookcase or, alternatively, you can buy two small ones."

a.m. / p.m. The abbreviation *a.m.* (from Latin *ante meridiem,* before noon) is used to refer to any hour between midnight and noon. Similarly, *p.m.* (from Latin *post meridiem,* after noon) is used to refer to any hour between noon and midnight. Midnight is 12 a.m. and noon is 12 p.m.

beside / besides *Beside* is a preposition that means next to: "Stand here beside me." *Besides* is an adverb that means also: "Besides, I need to tell you about the new products my company offers."

bimonthly / semimonthly *Bimonthly* is an adjective that means every two months: "I brought the cake for the bimonthly office party." *Bimonthly* is also a noun that means a publication issued every two months: "The company publishes several popular bimonthlies." *Semimonthly* is an adjective that means happening twice a month: "We have semimonthly meetings on the 1st and the 15th."

capital / capitol The city or town that is the seat of government is called the *capital*; the building in which the legislative assembly meets is the *capitol*. The term *capital* can also refer to an accumulation of wealth or to a capital letter.

cite / site *Cite* is a verb that means to quote as an authority or example: "I cited several eminent scholars in my study of water resources." It also means to recognize formally: "The public official was cited for service to the city." It can also mean to summon before a court of law: "Last year the company was cited for pollution violations." *Site* is a noun meaning location: "They chose a new site for the factory just outside town."

complement / compliment *Complement* is a noun or verb that means something that completes or makes up a whole: "The red sweater is a perfect complement to the outfit." *Compliment* is a noun or

verb that means an expression of praise or admiration: "I received many compliments about my new outfit."

comprise / compose According to the traditional rule, the whole comprises the parts, and the parts compose the whole. Thus, the board comprises five members, whereas five members compose (or make up) the board. It is also correct to say that the board is composed (not comprised) of five members.

concurrent / consecutive *Concurrent* is an adjective that means simultaneous or happening at the same time as something else: "The concurrent strikes of several unions crippled the economy." *Consecutive* means successive or following one after the other: "The union called three consecutive strikes in one year."

connote / denote *Connote* is a verb that means to imply or suggest: "The word 'espionage' connotes mystery and intrigue." *Denote* is a verb that means to indicate or refer to specifically: "The symbol for 'pi' denotes the number 3.14159."

convince / persuade Strictly speaking, one convinces a person that something is true but persuades a person to do something. "Pointing out that I was overworked, my friends persuaded [not convinced] me to take a vacation. Now that I'm relaxing on the beach with my book, I am convinced [not persuaded] that they were right." Following this rule, *convince* should not be used with an infinitive.

council / councilor / counsel / counselor A *councilor* is a member of a *council,* which is an assembly called together for discussion or deliberation. A *counselor* is one who gives *counsel,* which is advice or guidance. More specifically, a *counselor* can be an attorney or a supervisor at camp.

discreet / discrete *Discreet* is an adjective that means prudent, circumspect, or modest: "Their discreet comments about the negotiations led the reporters to expect an early settlement." *Discrete* is an adjective that means separate or individually distinct: "Each company in the conglomerate operates as a discrete entity."

disinterested / uninterested *Disinterested* is an adjective that means unbiased or impartial: "We appealed to the disinterested mediator to facilitate the negotiations." *Uninterested* is an adjective that means not interested or indifferent: "They seemed uninterested in our offer."

emigrant / immigrant *Emigrant* is a noun that means one who leaves one's native country to settle in another: "The emigrants spent four weeks aboard ship before landing in Los Angeles." *Immigrant* is a noun that means one who enters and settles in a new country: "Most of the immigrants easily found jobs."

farther / further *Farther* is an adjective and adverb that means to or at a more distant point: "We drove 50 miles today; tomorrow, we will travel 100 miles farther." *Further* is an adjective and adverb that means to or at a greater extent or degree: "We won't be able to suggest a solution until we are further along in our evaluation of the problem." It can also mean in addition or moreover: "They stated further that they would not change the policy."

few / less *Few* is an adjective that means small in number. It is used with countable objects: "This department has few employees." *Less* is an adjective that means small in amount or degree. It is used with objects of indivisible mass: "Which jar holds less water?"

figuratively / literally *Figuratively* is an adverb that means metaphorically or symbolically: "Happening upon the shadowy figure, they figuratively jumped out of their shoes." *Literally* is an adverb that means word for word or according to the exact meaning of the words: "I translated the Latin passage literally."

flammable / inflammable These two words are actually synonyms, both meaning easily set on fire. "The highly flammable (inflammable) fuel was stored safely in a specially built tank."

flaunt / flout To *flaunt* means to show off shamelessly: "Eager to flaunt her knowledge of a wide range of topics, Helene dreamed of appearing on a TV trivia show." To *flout* means to show scorn or contempt for: "Lewis disliked boarding school and took every opportunity to flout the house rules."

foreword / forward *Foreword* is a noun that means an introductory note or preface: "In my foreword I explained my reasons for writing the book." *Forward* is an adjective or adverb that means toward the front: "I sat in the forward section of the bus. Please step forward when your name is called." *Forward* is also a verb that means to send on: "Forward the letter to the customer's new address."

founder / flounder In its primary sense *founder* means to sink below the surface of the water: "The ship foundered after colliding with an iceberg." By extension, *founder* means to fail utterly. *Flounder* means to move about clumsily, or to act or proceed with confusion. A good synonym for *flounder* is blunder: "After floundering through the first half of the course, Amy finally passed with the help of a tutor."

hanged / hung *Hanged* is the past tense and past participle of hang when the meaning is to execute by suspending by the neck: "They hanged the prisoner

for treason." "The convicted killer was hanged at dawn." *Hung* is the past tense and participle of hang when the meaning is to suspend from above with no support from below: "I hung the painting on the wall." "The painting was hung at a crooked angle."

historic / historical In general usage, *historic* refers to what is important in history, while *historical* applies more broadly to whatever existed in the past whether it was important or not: "A historic summit meeting between the prime ministers; historical buildings torn down in the redevelopment."

it's / its *It's* is a contraction for it is, whereas *its* is the possessive form of it: "It's a shame that we cannot talk about its size."

laid / lain / lay *Laid* is the past tense and the past participle of the verb lay and not the past tense of lie. *Lay* is the past tense of the verb lie and *lain* is the past participle: "He laid his books down and lay down on the couch, where he has lain for an hour."

lend / loan Although some people feel *loan* should only be used as a noun, *lend* and *loan* are both acceptable as verbs in standard English: "Can you lend (loan) me a dollar?" However, only *lend* should be used in figurative senses: "Will you lend me a hand?"

principal / principle *Principal* is a noun that means a person who holds a high position or plays an important role: "The school principal has 20 years of teaching experience. The principals in the negotiations will meet tomorrow at 10 o'clock." It also means a sum of money on which interest accrues: "The depositors were guaranteed they would not lose their principal." *Principal* is also an adjective that means chief or leading: "The necessity of moving to another city was the principal reason I turned down the job offer." *Principle* is a noun that means a rule or standard: "They refused to compromise their principles."

stationary / stationery *Stationary* is an adjective that means fixed or unmoving: "They maneuvered around the stationary barrier in the road." *Stationery* is a noun that means writing materials: "We printed the letters on company stationery."

Foreign Words and Phrases

The English meanings given below are not necessarily literal translations. Foreign words and phrases should be set in italics (or underlined if written in longhand) if their meanings are likely to be unknown to the reader. Whether the expression is familiar or unfamiliar, however, is a matter of judgment. Below, all foreign words have been italicized for the sake of emphasis.

ad absurdum (ad ab-sir'dum) [Lat.]: to the point of absurdity. "He tediously repeated his argument *ad absurdum.*"

ad infinitum (ad in-fun-eye'tum) [Lat.]: to infinity. "The lecture seemed to drone on *ad infinitum.*"

ad nauseam (ad noz'ee-um) [Lat.]: to a sickening degree. "The politician uttered one platitude after another *ad nauseam.*"

aficionado (uh-fish'ya-nah'doh) [Span.]: an ardent devotee. "I was surprised at what a baseball *aficionado* she had become."

annus mirabilis (an'us muh-ra'buh-lis) [Lat.]: wonderful year. "Last year was the *annus mirabilis* for my company."

a priori (ah pree or'ee) [Lat.]: based on theory rather than observation. "The fact that their house is

in such disrepair suggests *a priori* that they are having financial difficulties."

au courant (oh' koo-rahn') [Fr.]: up-to-date. "The shoes, the hair, the clothes—every last detail of her dress, in fact—was utterly *au courant.*"

beau geste (boh zhest') [Fr.]: a fine or noble gesture, often futile. "My fellow writers supported me by writing letters of protest to the publisher, but their *beau geste* could not prevent the inevitable."

beau monde (boh' mond') [Fr.]: high society. "Such elegant decor would impress even the *beau monde.*"

bête noire (bet nwahr') [Fr.]: something or someone particularly disliked. "Talk of the good old college days way back when had become his *bête noire,* and he began to avoid his school friends."

bona fide (boh′na fide) [Lat.]: in good faith; genuine. "For all her reticence and modesty, it was clear that she was a *bona fide* expert in her field."

bon mot (bon moe′) [Fr.]: a witty remark or comment. "One *bon mot* after another flew out of his mouth, charming the audience."

bon vivant (bon vee-vahnt′) [Fr.]: a person who lives luxuriously and enjoys good food and drink. "It's true he's quite the *bon vivant,* but when he gets down to business he conducts himself like a Spartan."

carpe diem (kar′pay dee′um) [Lat.]: seize the day. "So what if you have an 8:00 a.m. meeting tomorrow and a full day of appointments? *Carpe diem!*"

carte blanche (kart blonsh′) [Fr.]: unrestricted power to act on one's own. "I may have *carte blanche* around the office, but at home I'm a slave to my family's demands."

cause célèbre (koz suh-leb′ruh) [Fr.]: a widely known controversial case or issue. "The Sacco and Vanzetti trial became an international *cause célèbre* during the 1920s."

caveat emptor (kav′ee-ot emp′tor) [Lat.]: let the buyer beware. "Before you leap at that real estate deal, *caveat emptor!*"

comme ci comme ça (kom see′ kom sah′) [Fr.]: so-so. "The plans for the party strike me as *comme ci comme ça.*"

comme il faut (kom eel foe′) [Fr.]: as it should be; fitting. "His end was truly *comme il faut.*"

coup de grâce (koo de grahss′) [Fr.]: finishing blow. "After an already wildly successful day, the *coup de grâce* came when she won best all-around athlete."

cri de coeur (kree′ de kur′) [Fr.]: heartfelt appeal. "About to leave the podium, he made a final *cri de coeur* to his people to end the bloodshed."

de rigueur (duh ree-gur′) [Fr.]: strictly required, as by etiquette, usage, or fashion. "Loudly proclaiming one's support for radical causes had become *de rigueur* among her crowd."

deus ex machina (day′us ex mahk′uh-nuh) [Lat.]: a contrived device to resolve a situation. "Stretching plausibility, the movie concluded with a *deus ex machina* ending in which everyone was rescued at the last minute."

dolce vita (dole′chay vee′tuh) [Ital.]: sweet life; the good life perceived as one of physical pleasure and self-indulgence. "My vacation this year is going to be two uninterrupted weeks of *dolce vita.*"

Doppelgänger* (dop′pul-gang-ur) [Ger.]: a ghostly double or counterpart of a living person. "I could not shake the sense that some shadowy *Doppelgänger* echoed my every move."

ecce homo (ek′ay ho′mo) [Lat.]: behold the man. "The painting depicted the common Renaissance theme, *ecce homo*—Christ wearing the crown of thorns."

enfant terrible (ahn-fahn′ tay-reeb′luh) [Fr.]: an incorrigible child; an outrageously outspoken or bold person. "He played the role of *enfant terrible,* jolting us with his blunt assessment."

entre nous (ahn′truh noo′) [Fr.]: between ourselves; confidentially. "*Entre nous,* their marriage is on the rocks."

ex cathedra (ex kuh-thee′druh) [Lat.]: with authority; used especially of those pronouncements of the pope that are considered infallible. "I resigned myself to obeying; my father's opinions were *ex cathedra* in our household."

ex post facto (ex′ post fak′toh) [Lat.]: retroactively. "I certainly hope that the change in policy will be honored *ex post facto.*"

fait accompli (fate ah-kom-plee′) [Fr.]: an accomplished fact, presumably irreversible. "There's no use protesting—it's a *fait accompli.*"

faux pas (foh pah′) [Fr.]: a social blunder. "Suddenly, she realized she had unwittingly committed yet another *faux pas.*"

flagrante delicto (fla-grahn′tee di-lik′toh) [Lat.]: in the act. "The detective realized that without hard evidence he had no case; he would have to catch the culprit *flagrante delicto.*"

glasnost (glaz′nohst) [Rus.]: open and frank discussion: initiated by Mikhail Gorbachev in 1985 in the Soviet Union. "Once the old chairman retired, the spirit of *glasnost* pervaded the department."

hoi polloi (hoy′ puh-loy′) [Gk.]: the common people. "Marie Antoinette recommended cake to the *hoi polloi.*"

in loco parentis (in loh′koh pa-ren′tiss) [Lat.]: in the place of a parent. "The court appointed a guardian for the children, to serve *in loco parentis.*"

in situ (in sit′too) [Lat.]: situated in the original or natural position. "I prefer seeing statues *in situ* rather than in the confines of a museum."

in vino veritas (in vee′no vare′i-toss) [Lat.]: in wine there is truth. "By the end of the drunken banquet, several of the guests had made a good deal of their private lives public, prompting the host to murmur to his wife, '*in vino veritas.*'"

ipso facto (ip′soh fak′toh) [Lat.]: by the fact itself. "An extremist, *ipso facto,* cannot become part of a coalition."

je ne sais quoi (zhun say kwah′) [Fr.]: I know not what; an elusive quality. "She couldn't explain it, but there was something *je ne sais quoi* about him that she found devastatingly attractive."

mano a mano (mah′no ah mah′no) [Span.]: a direct confrontation or conflict. "'Stay out of it,' he admonished his friends, 'I want to handle this guy *mano a mano.*'"

mea culpa (may′uh kul′puh) [Lat.]: I am to blame. "His *mea culpa* was so offhand that I hardly think he meant it."

memento mori (muh-men′toh more′ee) [Lat.]: a reminder that you must die. "The skull rested on the mantlepiece as a *memento mori.*"

modus operandi (moh′dus op-er-an′dee) [Lat.]: a method of operating. "Her *modus operandi* is to sugarcoat the truth so thoroughly that the news almost seems welcome."

mot juste (moh zhoost′) [Fr.]: the exact, appropriate word. "'Rats!' screamed the defiant three-year-old, immensely proud of his *mot juste.*"

ne plus ultra (nee′ plus ul′truh) [Lat.]: the most intense degree of a quality or state. "Pulling it from the box, he realized he was face to face with the *ne plus ultra* of computers."

nom de guerre (nom duh gair') [Fr.]: pseudonym. "He went by his *nom de guerre* when frequenting trendy nightclubs."

nom de plume (nom duh ploom') [Fr.]: pen name. "Deciding it was time to sit down and begin a novel, the would-be writer spent the first several hours deciding upon a suitably dashing *nom de plume*."

nota bene (noh'tuh ben'nee) [Ital.]: note well; take notice. "She appended her suggestions to the manuscript, underlining the words *nota bene* for added emphasis."

persona non grata (per-soh'nuh non grah'tuh) [Lat.]: unacceptable or unwelcome person. "Once I was cut out of the will, I became *persona non grata* among my relatives."

pro bono (pro boh'noh) [Lat.]: done or donated without charge; free. "The lawyer's *pro bono* work gave him a sense of value that his work on behalf of the corporation could not."

quid pro quo (kwid' pro kwoh') [Lat.]: something for something; an equal exchange. "She vowed that when she had the means, she would return his favors *quid pro quo*."

sans souci (sahn soo-see') [Fr.]: carefree. "Their mood was definitely *sans souci*."

savoir-faire (sav'wahr fair') [Fr.]: the ability to say and do the correct thing. "She presided over the gathering with impressive *savoir-faire*."

sine qua non (sin'ay kwah nohn') [Lat.]: indispensable. "Lemon is the *sine qua non* of this recipe."

terra incognita (tare'uh in-kog-nee'tuh) [Lat.]: unknown territory. "When the conversation suddenly switched from contemporary fiction to medieval Albanian playwrights, he felt himself entering *terra incognita*."

tout le monde (too luh mond') [Fr.]: everybody; everyone of importance. "Don't miss the event; it's bound to be attended by *tout le monde*."

veni, vidi, vici (ven'ee vee'dee vee'chee) [Lat.]: I came, I saw, I conquered. "After the takeover the business mogul gloated, '*veni, vidi, vici.*'"

verboten (fer-boh'ten) [Ger.]: forbidden, as by law; prohibited. "That topic, I am afraid, is *verboten* in this household."

vox populi (voks pop'yoo-lie) [Lat.]: the voice of the people. "My sentiments echo those of the *vox populi*."

Wanderjahr* (vahn'der-yahr) [Ger.]: a year or period of travel, especially following one's schooling. "The trio took off on their *Wanderjahr* soon after they graduated, planning to circle the globe by bicycle."

Weltanschauung* (velt'an-shou'ung) [Ger.]: a comprehensive conception or image of the universe and of humanity's relation to it. "His *Weltanschauung* gradually metamorphized from a grim and pessimistic one to a sunny, but no less complex, view."

Weltschmerz* (velt'shmerts) [Ger.]: sorrow over the evils of the world. "His poetry expressed a certain *Weltschmerz*, or world-weariness."

Zeitgeist* (zite'guyst) [Ger.]: the spirit of the time; general trend of thought or feeling characteristic of a particular period of time. "She blamed it on the *Zeitgeist*, which encouraged hedonistic excess."

---

*German nouns are capitalized. A familiar German expression that is not italicized, however, should be lowercased, following the English conventions of not capitalizing common nouns. "His proclivities leaned more to the occult than to the philosophical: a poltergeist he could understand; the *Zeitgeist* he could not."

National Spelling Bee

The National Spelling Bee was launched by the Louisville, Kentucky, *Courier-Journal* in 1925. With competitions, cash prizes, and a trip to the nation's capital, it was hoped the Bee would stimulate "general interest among pupils in a dull subject."

The Scripps Howard News Service took over the Bee in 1941. Over the years the national finals have grown from a mere 9 contestants to about 250, and competition week is marked by ice-cream socials, talent shows, and other events. At the end of the 2001 activities, 13-year-old champion Sean Conley took home $10,000 cash, among other prizes, for correctly spelling *succedaneum*. Here are the winning words that made past spellers into national champions.

1925	gladiolus	1944	NO BEE	1964	sycophant	1983	Purim
1926	abrogate	1945	NO BEE	1965	eczema	1984	luge
1927	luxuriance	1946	semaphore	1966	ratoon	1985	milieu
1928	albumen	1947	chlorophyll	1967	chihuahua	1986	odontalgia
1929	asceticism	1948	psychiatry	1968	abalone	1987	staphylococci
1930	fracas	1949	dulcimer	1969	interlocutory	1988	elegiacal
1931	foulard	1950	haruspex	1970	croissant	1989	spoliator
1932	knack	1951	insouciant	1971	shalloon	1990	fibranne
1933	propitiatory	1952	vignette	1972	macerate	1991	antipyretic
1934	deteriorating	1953	soubrette	1973	vouchsafe	1992	lyceum
1935	intelligible	1954	transept	1974	hydrophyte	1993	kamikaze
1936	interning	1955	custaceology	1975	incisor	1994	antediluvian
1937	promiscuous	1956	condominium	1976	narcolepsy	1995	xanthosis
1938	sanitarium	1957	schappe	1977	cambist	1996	vivisepulture
1939	canonical	1958	syllepsis	1978	deification	1997	euonym
1940	therapy	1959	cacolet	1979	maculature	1998	chiaroscurist
1941	initials	1960	troche	1980	elucubrate	1999	logorrhea
1942	sacrilegious	1961	smaragdine	1981	sarcophagus	2000	demarche
1943	NO BEE	1962	esquamulose	1982	psoriasis	2001	succedaneum
		1963	equipage				

Frequently Misspelled Words

absence	decease	guarantee	miniature	pumpkin
address	deceive	harass	miscellaneous	raspberry
advice	definite	height	mischievous	receive
all right	descent	humorous	misspell	rhythm
arctic	desperate	independent	mysterious	sacrilegious
beginning	device	jealous	necessary	science
believe	disastrous	jewelry	neighbor	scissors
bicycle	ecstasy	judgment	nuclear	separate
broccoli	embarrass	ketchup	occasion	sincerely
bureau	exercise	knowledge	occurrence	special
calendar	fascinate	leisure	odyssey	thorough
camaraderie	February	library	piece	through
ceiling	fiery	license	pigeon	truly
cemetery	fluorescent	maintenance	playwright	until
changeable	foreign	mathematics	precede	Wednesday
conscientious	government	mediocre	prejudice	weird
conscious	grateful	millennium	privilege	you're

American Sign Language

Sign language for the deaf was first systematized in France during the 18th century by Abbot Charles-Michel l'Epée. French Sign Language (FSL) was brought to the United States in 1816 by Thomas Gallaudet, founder of the American School for the Deaf in Hartford, Conn. He developed American Sign Language (ASL), a language of gestures and hand symbols that express words and concepts. It is the fourth most used language in the United States today.

In most respects, sign language is just like any spoken language, with a rich vocabulary and a highly organized, rule-governed grammar. The only difference is that in sign language, information is processed through the eyes rather than the ears. Thus, facial expression and body movement play an important part in conveying information.

In spoken language, the relationship between most words and the objects and concepts they represent is arbitrary—there is nothing about the word "tree" that actually suggests a tree, either in the way it is spelled or pronounced. In the same way, in sign language most signs do not suggest, or imitate, the thing or idea they represent, and must be learned. Sign language may be acquired naturally as a child's first language, or it may be learned through study and practice.

Sign language shares other similarities with spoken languages. Like any living language, ASL grows and changes over time to accommodate native users' needs. ASL also has regional varieties, equivalent to spoken accents, with different signs being used in different parts of the country.

Along with sign language and lip reading, many deaf people also communicate with the manual alphabet, which uses finger positions that correspond to the letters of the alphabet to spell out words and names.

American Manual Alphabet

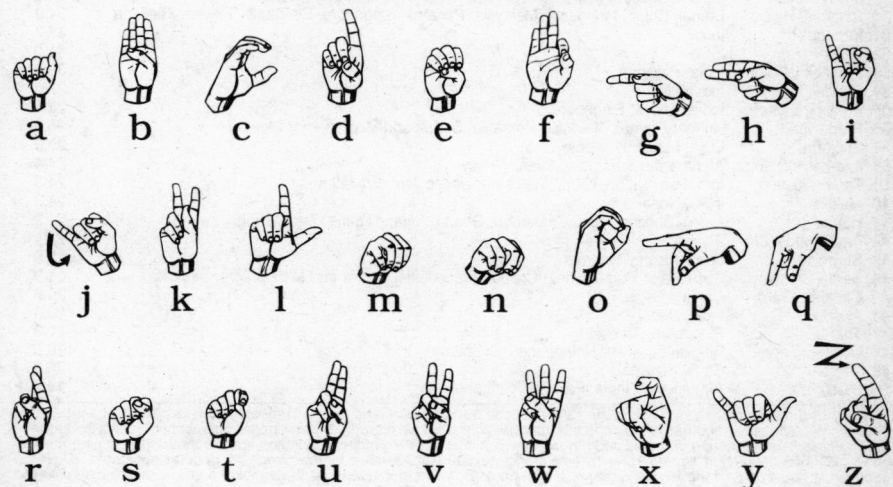

The 50 Most Widely Spoken Languages[1] in the World

Rank, language	Countries[2]	Population[3] (in millions)
1. Chinese, Mandarin	Brunei, Cambodia, China, Indonesia, Malaysia, Mongolia, Philippines, Singapore, S. Africa, Taiwan, Thailand	885.0
2. Spanish	Andorra, Argentina, Belize, Bolivia, Chile, Colombia, Costa Rica, Cuba, Dominican Rep., Ecuador, El Salvador, Eq. Guinea, Guatemala, Honduras, Mexico, Nicaragua, Panama, Paraguay, Peru, Spain, Uruguay, U.S., Venezuela	332.0
3. English	Australia, Botswana, Brunei, Cameroon, Canada, Eritrea, Ethiopia, Fiji, The Gambia, Guyana, India, Ireland, Israel, Lesotho, Liberia, Malaysia, Micronesia, Namibia, Nauru, New Zealand, Palau, Papua New Guinea, Samoa, Seychelles, Sierra Leone, Singapore, Solomon Islands, Somalia, S. Africa, Suriname, Swaziland, Tonga, U.K., U.S., Vanuatu, Zimbabwe, many Caribbean states	322.0
4. Bengali	Bangladesh, India, Singapore	189.0
5. Hindi	India, Nepal, Singapore, S. Africa, Uganda	182.0
6. Portuguese	Angola, Brazil, Cape Verde, France, Guinea-Bissau, Mozambique, Portugal, São Tomé and Príncipe	170.0
7. Russian	China, Israel, Mongolia, Russia, U.S.	170.0
8. Japanese	Japan, Singapore, Taiwan	125.0
9. German, Standard	Austria, Belgium, Bolivia, Czech Rep., Denmark, Germany, Hungary, Italy, Kazakhstan, Liechtenstein, Luxembourg, Paraguay, Poland, Romania, Slovakia, Switzerland	98.0
10. Chinese, Wu	China	77.2
11. Javanese	Indonesia, Malaysia, Singapore	75.5
12. Korean	China, Japan, N. Korea, S. Korea, Singapore, Thailand	75.0
13. French	Andorra, Belgium, Burkina Faso, Burundi, Cameroon, Canada, Comoros, Congo, Congo (Dem. Rep. of), Djibouti, France, Gabon, Guinea, Haiti, Luxembourg, Mauritania, Monaco, Rwanda, Senegal, Seychelles, Switzerland, Vanuatu	72.0
14. Vietnamese	China, Vietnam	67.7
15. Telugu	India, Singapore	66.4
16. Chinese, Yue (Cantonese)	Brunei, China, Costa Rica, Indonesia, Malaysia, Panama, Philippines, Singapore, Thailand, Vietnam	66.0
17. Marathi	India	64.8
18. Tamil	India, Malaysia, Mauritius, Singapore, S. Africa, Sri Lanka	63.1
19. Turkish	Bulgaria, Cyprus, Greece, Macedonia, Romania, Turkey, Uzbekistan	59.0
20. Urdu	Afghanistan, India, Mauritius, Pakistan, S. Africa, Thailand	58.0
21. Chinese, Min Nan	Brunei, China, Indonesia, Malaysia, Philippines, Singapore, Taiwan, Thailand	49.0
22. Chinese, Jinyu	China	45.0
23. Gujarati	India, Kenya, Pakistan, Singapore, S. Africa, Tanzania, Uganda, Zambia, Zimbabwe	44.0
24. Polish	Czech Rep., Germany, Israel, Poland, Romania, Slovakia	44.0
25. Arabic, Egyptian	Egypt	42.5
26. Ukrainian	Poland, Slovakia, Ukraine	41.0
27. Italian	Croatia, Eritrea, France, Italy, San Marino, Slovenia, Switzerland	37.0
28. Chinese, Xiang	China	36.0
29. Malayalam	India, Singapore	34.0
30. Chinese, Hakka	Brunei, China, Indonesia, Malaysia, Panama, Singapore, Suriname, Taiwan, Thailand	34.0
31. Kannada	India	33.7
32. Oriya	India	31.0
33. Panjabi, Western	India, Pakistan	30.0
34. Sunda	Indonesia	27.0
35. Panjabi, Eastern	India, Kenya, Singapore	26.0
36. Romanian	Hungary, Israel, Moldova, Romania, Serbia and Montenegro, Ukraine	26.0
37. Bhojpuri	India, Mauritius, Nepal	25.0
38. Azerbaijani, South	Afghanistan, Iran, Iraq, Syria, Turkey	24.4
39. Farsi, Western	Iran, Iraq, Oman, Qatar, Tajikistan, United Arab Emirates	24.3
40. Maithili	India, Nepal	24.3
41. Hausa	Benin, Burkina Faso, Cameroon, Ghana, Niger, Nigeria, Sudan, Togo	24.2
42. Arabic, Algerian	Algeria	22.4
43. Burmese	Bangladesh, Myanmar	22.0
44. Serbo-Croatian[4]	Bosnia and Herzegovina, Croatia, Macedonia, Serbia and Montenegro, Slovenia	21.0
45. Chinese, Gan	China	20.6
46. Awadhi	India, Nepal	20.5
47. Thai	Singapore, Thailand	20.0
48. Dutch	Belgium, France, Netherlands, Suriname	20.0
49. Yoruba	Benin, Nigeria	20.0
50. Sindhi	Afghanistan, India, Pakistan, Singapore	19.7

1. Many of the languages listed are technically dialects, not separate languages. They are listed separately because they differ from each other enough to be mutually unintelligible. 2. The countries listed under Spanish, English, Portuguese, French, and Serbo-Croatian do not include those in which less than 1% of the population speaks the language as a first language. 3. The population figures refer to first language speakers in all countries and are general estimates. 4. Serbo-Croatian is now known variously as Serbian, Croatian, or Bosnian, depending on the speaker's ethnic or political affiliation. *Source: Ethnologue*, 13th Edition, Barbara F. Grimes, Editor. © 1996, Summer Institute of Linguistics, Inc.

U.S. Societies and Associations

Names are listed alphabetically according to key word in title; figure in parentheses is year of founding; other figure is membership.

The following is a partial list selected for general readership interest. A comprehensive listing of approximately 23,000 national and international organizations can be found in the *Encyclopedia of Associations*, 34th ed., 2000, published by Gale Research Company, 835 Penobscot Building, 645 Griswold St., Detroit, Mich. 48226-4049, available in most public libraries.

AARP (American Association of Retired Persons) (1958): 601 E. St. N.W., Washington, D.C. 20049. 33,000,000. Phone: (800) 424-3410. www.aarp.org.

Abortion Federation, National (1977): 1755 Mass. Ave., Ste. 600, Washington, D.C. 20036. Phone: (202) 667-5881 (Communications Director) or (800) 772-9100. www.prochoice.org.

Accountants, American Institute of Certified Public (1887): 1211 Avenue of the Americas, New York, N.Y. 10036-8775. 330,000. Phone: (212) 596-6200. www.aicpa.org.

ACSM: American Congress on Surveying and Mapping (1941): 6 Montgomery Village Ave., Ste. 403, Gaithersburg, Md. 20879. 8,000. Phone: (240) 632-9716. www.survmap.org.

Actors' Equity Association (1913): 165 W. 46th St., New York, N.Y. 10036. 40,000. Phone: (212) 869-8530. www.actorsequity.org.

Actuaries, Society of (1949): 475 N. Martingale Rd., Ste. 800, Schaumburg, Ill. 60173-2226. 16,500. Phone: (847) 706-3500. www.soa.org.

Aeronautic Association, National (1905): 1815 N. Fort Myer Dr., Ste. 500, Arlington, Va. 22209. 300,000. Phone: (703) 527-0226. www.naa-usa.org.

African-American Institute, The (1953): 380 Lexington Ave., New York, N.Y. 10168-4298. Phone: (212) 949-5666.

AFS Intercultural Programs—USA (American Field Service) (1947): 198 Madison Avenue, 8th Flr., New York, N.Y. 10016. 100,000. Phone: (212) 299-9000 or (800) AFS-INFO. www.afs.org.

Agricultural History Society (1919): Univ. of Arkansas, 2801 University Ave., Little Rock, Ark. 72204. 1,400. Phone: (501) 569–3235. www.iastate.edu/~history_info/aghissoc.htm.

Agronomy, American Society of (1907): 677 S. Segoe Rd., Madison, Wis. 53711-1086. 11,400. Phone: (608) 273-8080; fax: (608) 273-2021. www.agronomy.org.

Air & Waste Management Association (1907): One Gateway Center, 3rd Flr., Pittsburgh, Pa. 15222. 14,000. Phone: (412) 232-3444. www.awma.org.

Aircraft Association, Experimental (1953): EAA Aviation Center, 3000 Poberezny Rd., Oshkosh, Wis. 54903-3086. 170,000. Phone: (920) 426-4800. www.eaa.org.

Aircraft Owners and Pilots Association (1939): 421 Aviation Way, Frederick, Md. 21701-4798. 350,000. Phone: (301) 695-2000; fax: (301) 695-2375. www.aopa.org.

Air Force Association (1946): 1501 Lee Highway, Arlington, Va. 22209-1198. 150,000. Phone: (703) 247-5800. www.afa.org.

Air Line Pilots Association (1931): 1625 Massachusetts Ave. N.W., Washington, D.C. 20036 and 535 Herndon Pkwy., Herndon, Va. 20170. 50,000. Phone: (703) 689-2270. www.alpa.org.

Al-Anon Family Group Headquarters, Inc. For families and friends of alcoholics. (1951): 1600 Corporate Landing Pkwy., Virginia Beach, Va. 23454-5617. 33,000 groups worldwide. Phone: (757) 563-1600. www.al-anon.org.

Alcoholics Anonymous (1935): A.A. World Services, Inc., P.O. Box 459, New York, N.Y. 10163. 2,000,000. Phone: (212) 870-3400. www.aa.org.

Alexander Graham Bell Association for the Deaf (1890): 3417 Volta Place N.W., Washington, D.C. 20007-2778. 6,200. Phone: (202) 337-5220 V, 337-5221 TTY; fax: (202) 337-8314. www.agbell.org.

Alzheimer's Association (1980): 919 N. Michigan Ave., Ste. 1100, Chicago, Ill. 60611-1676. 200 chapters. Phone: (312) 335-8700; (800) 272-3900. www.alz.org.

American Academy of Allergy, Asthma and Immunology (1943): 611 E. Wells St., Milwaukee, Wis. 53202. 5,000. Phone: (414) 272-6071. www.aaaai.org.

American Alliance for Health, Physical Education, Recreation and Dance (1885): 1900 Association Dr., Reston, Va. 20191. 26,000. Phone: (703) 476-3400. www.aahperd.org.

American Automobile Association (1902): 1000 AAA Dr., Heathrow, Fla. 32746-5063. Phone: (407) 444-7000. www.aaa.com.

American Civil Liberties Union (1920): 125 Broad St., 18th Flr., New York, N.Y. 10004-2400. 275,000. Phone: (212) 549-2500. www.aclu.org.

American Contract Bridge League (1927): 2990 Airways Blvd., Memphis, Tenn. 38116-3847. Phone: (800) 467-1623; fax: (901) 398-7754. www.acbl.org.

American Federation of Labor and Congress of Industrial Organizations (AFL-CIO) (1955): 815 16th St. N.W., Washington, D.C. 20006. 13,000,000. Phone: (202) 637-5000. www.aflcio.org.

American Federation of Musicians of the United States and Canada (1896): 1501 Broadway, Ste. 600, Paramount Bldg., New York, N.Y. 10036. Phone: (212) 869-1330. www.afm.org.

American Forests (1875): P.O. Box 2000, Washington, D.C. 20013. 115,000. Phone: (202) 955-4500. www.americanforests.org.

American Foundrymen's Society, Inc. (1896): 505 State St., Des Plaines, Ill. 60016-8399. 13,000. Phone: (847) 824-0181; (800) 537-4237. www.afsinc.org.

American Friends Service Committee (1917): 1501 Cherry St., Philadelphia, Pa. 19102-1479. Phone: (215) 241-7000. www.afsc.org.

American Geographical Society, The (1851): 120 Wall St., Ste. 100, New York, N.Y. 10005-3904. 1,500. Phone: (212) 422-5456; fax: (212) 422-5480. email: amgeosoc@earthlink.net. www.amergeog.org.

American Geriatrics Society (1942): 350 Fifth Ave., Ste. 801, New York, N.Y. 10118. 6,000. Phone: (212) 308-1414; fax: (212) 832-8646. www.americangeriatrics.org.

American Heart Association (1924): 7272 Greenville Ave., Dallas, Tex. 75231-4596. 4,200,000 volunteers. Phone: (800) AHA-USA1. www.americanheart.org.

American Historical Association (1884): 400 A St. S.E., Washington, D.C. 20003-3889. 15,000. Phone: (202) 544-2422. email: aha@theaha.org. www.theaha.org.

American Indian Affairs, Association on (1923): Tekakwitha Complex, Agency Road #7, Box 268, Sisseton, S.D. 57262. 40,000. Phone: (605) 698-3998. www.indian-affairs.org.

American Jewish Committee (1906): Jacob Blaustein Building, 165 East 56th Street, New York, N.Y. 10022. 100,000. Phone: (212) 751-4000; fax: (212) 838-2120. www.ajc.org.

American Kennel Club (1884): 260 Madison Ave., New York, N.Y. 10016. 505 member clubs. Phone: (212) 696-8200; (919) 233-9767 (customer service). www.akc.org.

American Legion, The (1919): 700 N. Pennsylvania St., Indianapolis, Ind. 46206. 3,000,000. Phone: (317) 630-1200. www.legion.org.

American Legion Auxiliary (1919): 777 N. Meridian St., 3rd Flr., Indianapolis, Ind. 46204. 1,000,000. Phone: (317) 955-3845. www.legion-aux.org.

American Mensa, Ltd. (1960): 1229 Corporate Drive West, Arlington, Texas 76006–6103. 50,000. Phone: (817) 607-0060. www.us.mensa.org.

American Montessori Society (1960): 281 Park Avenue South, 6th Flr., New York, N.Y. 10010-6102. Phone: (212) 358-1250; fax: (212) 358-1256. www.amshq.org.

American Museum of Natural History (1869): Central Park West at 79th St., New York, N.Y. 10024-5192. 500,000. Phone: (212) 769-5606. www.amnh.org.

American Planning Association (1917) and American Institute of Certified Planners: Administrative Offices: 122 S. Michigan Ave., Chicago, Ill. 60603. 30,000. Phone: (312) 431-9100. Headquarters: 1776 Massachusetts Ave. N.W., Washington, D.C. 20036. Phone: (202) 872-0611. www.planning.org.

Americans for Democratic Action, Inc. (1947): 1625 K St. N.W., Ste. 210, Washington, D.C. 20006. 70,000. Phone: (202) 785-5980. www.adaction.org.

American Society for Nutritional Sciences (1928): 9650 Rockville Pike, Bethesda, Md. 20814-3990. 3,600. Phone: (301) 530-7050. www.faseb.org/asns.

American Society for Public Administration (ASPA) (1939): 1120 G St. N.W., Ste. 700, Washington, D.C. 20005. 12,000. Phone: (202) 393-7878. www.aspanet.org.

American Universities, Association of (1900): 1200 New York Avenue NW, Ste. 550, Washington, D.C. 20005. Phone: (202) 408-7500. www.aau.edu.

American Water Resources Association (1964): 4 W. Federal St., P.O. Box 1626, Middleburg, Va. 20118-1626. Phone: (540) 687-8390. www.awra.org.

Amnesty International USA (1961): 322 Eighth Ave., New York, N.Y. 10001. 300,000. Phone: (212) 807-8400. www.amnesty-usa.org.

AMVETS (American Veterans of World War II, Korea, and Vietnam) (1943): 4647 Forbes Blvd., Lanham, Md. 20706-4380. 250,000. Phone: (301) 459-9600. www.amvets.org.

Animals, The American Society for the Prevention of Cruelty to (ASPCA) (1866): 424 E. 92nd St., New York, N.Y. 10128-6804. 400,000+. Phone: (212) 876-7700. www.aspca.org.

Animals, The Fund For, Inc. (1967): 200 W. 57th St., New York, N.Y. 10019. 175,000. Phone: (212) 246-2096. www.fund.org.

Anthropological Association, American (1902): 4350 N. Fairfax Dr., Ste. 640, Arlington, Va. 22203-1620. 11,500. Phone: (703) 528-1902. www.aaanet.org.

Anti-Defamation League (1913): 823 United Nations Plaza, New York, N.Y. 10017-3560. Phone: (212) 885-7700. www.adl.org.

Anti-Vivisection Society, The American (1883): 801 Old York Rd., #204, Jenkintown, Pa. 19046-1685. 15,000. Phone: (215) 887-0816; fax: (215) 887-2088. www.aavs.org.

Appraisers, American Society of (1936): 555 Herndon Parkway, Ste. 125, Herndon, VA 20170. 6,500. Phone: (800) ASA-VALU or (703) 478-2228. www.appraisers.org.

Arboriculture, International Society of (1924): P.O. Box 3129, Champaign, Ill. 61826-3129. 8,000. Phone: (217) 355-9411; fax (217) 355-9516. email: isa@isa-arbor.com. www2.champaign.isa-arbor.com.

Archaeological Institute of America (1879): 656 Beacon St., Boston, Mass. 02215-2006. 11,000. Phone: (617) 353-9361. email: aia@bu.edu. www.archaeological.org.

Architects, The American Institute of (1857): 1735 New York Ave. N.W., Washington, D.C. 20006-5292. 59,000. Phone: (202) 626-7300. www.aiaonline.org.

Architectural Historians, Society of (1940): 1365 N. Astor St., Chicago, Ill. 60610-2144. 4,000. Phone: (312) 573-1365; fax: (312) 573-1141. www.sah.org.

Army, Association of the United States (1950): 2425 Wilson Blvd., Arlington, Va. 22201-3385. 100,000+. Phone: (703) 841-4300. www.ausa.org.

Arthritis Foundation (1948): 1330 West Peachtree St., Atlanta, Ga. 30309. Over 150 local offices. Phone: (404) 872-7100; (800) 283-7800. www.arthritis.org.

Arts, National Endowment for the (1965): 1100 Pennsylvania Ave. N.W., Washington, D.C. 20506. Phone: (202) 682-5400. arts.endow.gov.

ASM International ® (formerly the American Society for Metals) (1913): 9639 Kinsman Rd., Materials Park, Ohio 44073-0002. 44,000. Phone: (440) 338-5151; fax: (440) 338-4634. www.asm-intl.org.

Association for Investment Management and Research (1990): 560 Ray C. Hunt Dr., Charlottesville, Va. 22903-0668. 36,000. Phone: (800) 247-8132. www.aimr.com.

Astronomical Society, American (1899): 2000 Florida Ave. ,Ste. 400, Washington, D.C. 20009. 6,300. Phone: (202) 328-2010. www.aas.org.

Atheists, American (1963): P.O. Box 5733, Parsippany, N.J. 07054-6733. 40,000 families. Phone: (908) 276-7300. www.atheists.org.

Audubon Society, National (1905): 700 Broadway, New York, N.Y. 10003-9562. 550,000. Phone: (212) 979-3000. www.audubon.org.

Authors League of America (1912): 330 W. 42nd St., 29th Flr., New York, N.Y. 10036-6902. 14,000. Phone: (212) 268-1208.

Autism Society of America (1965): 7910 Woodmont Ave., Ste. 300, Bethesda, Md. 20814-3015. 18,000+. Phone: (301) 657-0881; (800) 3AUTISM. www.autism-society.org.

Automobile Club, National (1924): 1151 East Hillsdale Blvd., Foster City, Calif. 94404. 200,000. Phone: (650) 294-7000. www.nationalautoclub.com.

Bar Association, American (1878): 541 N. Fairbanks Court, Chicago, Ill. 60611. 371,000. Phone: (312) 988-5522. www.abanet.org.

Barber Shop Quartet Singing in America, Society for the Preservation and Encouragement of (SPEBSQSA, Inc.) (1938): 6315 Third Ave., Kenosha, Wis. 53143. 34,000. Phone: (800) 876-SING. www.spebsqsa.org.

Better Business Bureaus, Council of (1912): 4200 Wilson Blvd., Ste. 800, Arlington, Va. 22203-1804. Phone: (703) 276-0100; fax: (703) 525-8277. www.bbb.org.

Bible Society, American (1816): 1865 Broadway, New York, N.Y. 10023-7505. Phone: (800) 32-BIBLE; (212) 408-1200. www.americanbible.org.

Biblical Literature, Society of (1880): 825 Houston Mill Road, Ste. 350, Atlanta, Ga. 30329. 7,000 members, 1,200 subscribers. Phone: (404) 727-3100; fax: (404) 727-3101. www.sbl-site.org.

Big Brothers Big Sisters of America (1977): 230 N. 13th St., Philadelphia, Pa. 19107. Phone: (215) 567-7000. www.bbbsa.org.

Biochemistry and Molecular Biology, American Society for (1906): 9650 Rockville Pike, Bethesda, Md. 20814. 10,000. Phone: (301) 530-7145. www.faseb.org/asbmb.

Biological Sciences, American Institute of (1947): 1444 I St. N.W., Ste. 200, Washington, D.C. 20005. 6,000. Phone: (202) 628-1500. www.aibs.org.

Blind, American Council of the (1961): 1155 15th St. N.W., Ste. 1004, Washington, D.C. 20005. 40,000. Phone: (202) 467-5081. www.acb.org.

Blind, National Federation of the (1940): 1800 Johnson St., Baltimore, Md. 21230. 50,000. Phone: (410) 659-9314. www.nfb.org.

B'nai B'rith International (1843): 1640 Rhode Island Ave. N.W., Washington, D.C. 20036-3278. 500,000. Phone: (202) 857-6589. www.bnaibrith.org.

Booksellers Association, American (1900): 828 So. Broadway, Tarrytown, N.Y. 10591. 4,500. Phone: (914) 591-2665, (800) 637-0037. www.bookweb.org.

Boys & Girls Clubs of America (1906): 1230 West Peachtree St. N.W., Atlanta, Ga., 30309. 2,800,000 youth served. Phone: (404) 815-5700; fax: (404) 815-5757. www.bgca.org.

Boy Scouts of America (1910): 1325 W. Walnut Hill Lane, P.O. Box 152079, Irving, Tex. 75015-2079. 4.8 mil. www.bsa.scouting.org.

Brady Campaign, The (1974) (formerly Handgun Control, Inc.): 1225 Eye St. N.W., Ste. 1100, Washington, D.C. 20005. 380,000. Phone: (202) 898-0792. www.bradycampaign.org.

Broadcasters, National Association of (1922): 1771 N St. N.W., Washington, D.C. 20036-2891. Phone: (202) 429-5300. www.nab.org.

Brookings Institution, The (1916): 1775 Massachusetts Ave. N.W., Washington, D.C. 20036-2188. Phone: (202) 797-6000. www.brookings.org.

Business Education Association, National (1946): 1914 Association Dr., Reston, Va. 20191-1596. 16,000. Phone: (703) 860-8300; fax: (703) 620-4483. email: nbea@nbea.org; www.nbea.org.

Business Women's Association, American (1949): 9100 Ward Parkway, P.O. Box 8728, Kansas City, Mo. 64114-0728. 80,000. Phone: (800) 228-0007. fax: (816) 361-4991. email: abwa@abwahq.org. www.abwahq.org.

Camp Fire Boys and Girls (1910): 4601 Madison Ave., Kansas City, Mo. 64112-1278. 629,000. Phone: (816) 756-1950. www.campfire.org.

Camping Association, The American (1910): 5000 State Rd. 67 N., Martinsville, Ind. 46151-7902. 5,500, 2,000+ camps. Phone: (765) 342-8456. www.acacamps.org.

Cancer Society, American (1913): 1599 Clifton Rd. N.E., Atlanta, Ga. 30329. Over 2 million volunteers. Phone: (800) ACS-2345 or check local listings. www.cancer.org.

CARE, Inc. (1945): 151 Ellis St. NE, Atlanta, Ga. 30303-2439. Programs in 62 developing countries. Phone: (800) 521-CARE. www.care.org.

Carnegie Endowment for International Peace (1910): 1779 Massachusetts Ave., N.W., Washington, D.C. 20036–2103. Phone: (202) 483-7600; fax: (202) 483-1840. www.ceip.org.

Catholic Charities USA (1910): 1731 King St., Ste. 200, Alexandria, Va. 22314. 1,400 agencies and institutions. Phone: (703) 549-1390. www.catholiccharitiesusa.org.

Catholic Daughters of the Americas (1903): 10 W. 71st St., New York, N.Y. 10023. 115,000. Phone: (212) 877-3041. www.catholicdaughters.org.

Catholic War Veterans of the U.S.A. Inc. (1935): 441 N. Lee St., Alexandria, Va. 22314. 35,000. Phone: (703) 549-3622. www.va.gov/vso/.

Cerebral Palsy Associations, Inc., United (1949): 1660 L St. N.W., Ste. 700, Washington, D.C. 20036. 153 affiliates. Phone: (800) USA-5-UCP, (202) 776-0406, TTY (202) 973-7197. www.ucpa.org.

Chamber of Commerce of the U.S. (1912): 1615 H St. N.W., Washington, D.C. 20062. 220,000. Phone: (202) 659-6000. www.uschamber.org.

Chemical Engineers, American Institute of (1908): 3 Park Ave., New York, N.Y. 10016-5991. 52,000. Phone: (212) 591-8100; (800) 242-4363. www.aiche.org.

Chemical Society, American (1876): 1155 16th St. N.W., Washington, D.C. 20036. 151,024. Phone: (800) 227-5558. www.acs.org.

Chess Federation, United States (1939): 3054 NYS Rte. 9W, New Windsor, N.Y. 12553. 50,000+. Phone: (914) 562-8350; (800) 388-KING. www.uschess.org.

Child Labor Committee, National (1904): 1501 Broadway, Ste. 403, New York, N.Y. 10036. Phone: (212) 840-1801. www.kapow.org.

Children's Book Council (1945): 12 W. 37th St., 2nd Fl., New York, N.Y. 10018-7480. Phone: (212) 966-1990; fax: (212) 966-2073. email: staff@cbcbooks.org. www.cbcbooks.org.

Child Welfare League of America (1920): 440 First St. N.W., Ste. 310, Washington, D.C. 20001-2085. 1,000 agencies. Phone: (202) 638-2952. www.cwla.org.

Chiropractic Association, American (1963): 1701 Clarendon Blvd., Arlington, Va. 22209. 22,000. Phone: (703) 276-8800, (800) 986-4636; fax: (703) 243-2593. www.amerchiro.org.

Cities, National League of (1924): 1301 Pennsylvania Ave. N.W., Washington, D.C. 20004-1763. 18,000 cities and towns. Phone: (202) 626-3000. www.nlc.org.

Civil Air Patrol, National Headquarters (1941): 105 S. Hansell St., Bldg. 714, Maxwell AFB, Ala. 36112-6332. 53,000. Phone: (334) 953-4287. www.capnhq.gov.

Civil Engineers, American Society of (1852): 1801 Alexander Bell Dr., Reston, Va. 20191-4400. 123,000. Phone: (800) 548-ASCE (2723); (703) 295-6300. www.asce.org.

Clinical Pathologists, American Society of (1922): 2100 W. Harrison St., Chicago, Ill. 60612. 77,200. Phone: (312) 738-1336; fax: (312) 738-9798. www.ascp.org.

The College Fund/UNCF (1944): 8260 Willow Oaks Corporate Dr., P.O. Box 10444, Fairfax, Va. 22031. 39 member institutions. Phone: (703) 205-3400, (800) 331-2244; fax: (703) 205-3576. www.uncf.org.

Colleges and Employers, National Association of (formerly College Placement Council) (1956): 62 E. Highland Ave., Bethlehem, Pa. 18017. 3,200. Phone: (800) 544-5272. www.jobweb.org.

Common Cause (1970): 1250 Connecticut Ave. N.W., Washington, D.C. 20036. 250,000. Phone: (800) 926-1064; fax: (202) 659-3716. www.commoncause.org.

Community Cultural Center Association, American (1978): 149 Cannongate 3, Nashua, N.H. 03063. Phone: (603) 886-2748; fax: (603) 886-7944.

Composers/USA, National Association of (1933): P.O. Box 49256, Barrington Station, Los Angeles, Calif. 90049. 600. Phone: (310) 541-8213. www.music-usa.org/nacusa/.

Congress of Racial Equality (CORE) (1942): 817 Broadway, 3rd Flr., New York, N.Y. 10003. Nationwide network of chapters. Phone: (212) 598-4000; fax: (212) 598-4000. www.core-online.org.

Conscientious Objectors, Central Committee for (1948): 1515 Cherry St., Philadelphia, Pa. 19102. Phone: (215) 563-8787.   630 20th St., Oakland, Calif. 94612. Phone: (510) 465-1617. www.objector.org.

Conservation Engineers, Association of (1961): Attn: Greg Mihalevich, Missouri Dept. of Conservation. Phone: (573) 522-2323 x2236; fax: (573) 522-2324. www.conservation.state.mo.us/engineering/ace.

Consumer Federation of America (1968): 1424 16th St. N.W., Ste. 604, Washington, D.C. 20036. 260 member organizations. Phone: (202) 387-6121. www.consumerfed.org.

Consumers League, National (1899): 1701 K St. N.W., Ste. 1200, Washington, D.C. 20006. Phone: (202) 835-3323. www.natlconsumersleague.org.

Consumers Union (1936): 101 Truman Ave., Yonkers, N.Y. 10703-1057. 4.6 million subscribers to *Consumer Reports Magazine.* Phone: (914) 378-2000. www.consumersunion.org.

Country Music Association (1958): One Music Circle South, Nashville, Tenn. 37203. 7,000+. Phone: (615) 244-2840. www.cmaworld.com.

Credit Management, National Association of (1896): 8840 Columbia 100 Parkway, Columbia, Md. 21045-2158. 30,000+ members. Phone: (410) 740-5560. www.nacm.org.

Credit Union National Association (1934): P.O. Box 431, Madison, Wis. 53701-0431. 51 state leagues representing 12,400 credit unions. Phone: (800) 356-9655. www.cuna.org.

Crime and Delinquency, National Council on (1907): 685 Market St., #620, San Francisco, Calif. 94105. Criminal justice research, nationwide membership. Phone: (415) 896-6223.

CSA/USA, Celiac Sprue Association/United States of America, Inc., (1978): P.O. Box 31700, Omaha, Neb. 68131-0700. 6 regions in U.S., 74 chapters, 36 active resource units. Phone: (402) 558-0600; fax: (402) 558-1347. www.csaceliacs.org.

Dairy Council, National (1915): 3030 Airport Rd., LaCross, Wis. 54603. Phone: (800) 426-8271. www.nationaldairycouncil.org.

Daughters of the American Revolution, National Society (1896): 1776 D St N.W., Washington, D.C. 20006-5392. 172,000. Phone: (202) 628-1776. www.dar.org.

Deaf, National Association of the (1880): 814 Thayer Ave., Silver Spring, Md. 20910-4500. 51 state association affiliates. Phone: (301) 587-1788 V; (301) 587-1789 TTY. www.nad.org.

Defenders of Wildlife (1947): 1101 14th St. N.W., #1400, Washington, D.C. 20005. 200,000 members and supporters. Phone: (202) 682-9400. www.defenders.org.

Dental Association, American (1859): 211 E. Chicago Ave., Chicago, Ill. 60611. 141,000. Phone: (312) 440-2500. www.ada.org.

Diabetes Association, American (1940): 1701 N. Beauregard St., Alexandria, Va. 22311. Phone: (703) 549-1500; (800) 342-2383. www.diabetes.org/default.asp.

Dignity (1969): 1500 Massachusetts Ave. N.W., Ste. 11, Washington, D.C. 20005. 5,000. Phone: (202) 861-0017 and (800) 877-8797. www.dignityusa.org.

Disabled American Veterans (1920): 807 Maine Ave. S.W., Washington, D.C. 20024. 1,400,000. Phone: (202) 554-3501. www.dav.org.

Dowsers, Inc., The American Society of (1961): P.O. Box 24, Danville, Vt. 05828. 5,000. Phone: (800) 711-9530; fax: (802) 748-8565. email: ASD@dowsers.org. www.dowsers.org.

Ducks Unlimited, Inc. (1937): One Waterfowl Way, Memphis, Tenn. 38120. 600,000. Phone: (800) 45DUCKS. www.ducks.org.

Earthwatch (1971): 3 Clock Tower Place, Ste. 100, Box 75, Maynard, Mass. 01754. 75,000. Phone: (800) 776-0188. www.earthwatch.org.

Eastern Star, Order of, General Grand Chapter (1876): 1618 New Hampshire Ave. N.W., Washington, D.C. 20009-2549. 1,207,301. Phone: (202) 667-4737. www.easternstar.org.

Easter Seal Society, The National (1919): 230 W. Monroe, Ste. 1800, Chicago, Ill. 60606. 109 state and local affiliate societies operating 500 service sites. Phone: (312) 726-6200; (312) 726-4258 TTY. www.easter-seals.org.

Economic Association, American (1885): 2014 Broadway, Ste. 305, Nashville, Tenn. 37203. 22,000. 5,500 inst. subscribers. Phone: (615) 322-2595. www.vanderbilt.edu/AEA.

Edison Electric Institute (1933): 701 Pennsylvania Ave. N.W., Washington, D.C. 20004-2696. Phone: (202) 508-5000. www.eei.org.

Education, American Council on (ACE), (1918): One Dupont Circle N.W., Washington, D.C. 20036-1193. 1,600+ colleges and universities and 200+ higher education associations. Phone: (202) 939-9300. www.acenet.edu.

Educational Exchange, Council on International (1947): 633 Third Ave., 2nd Fl., New York, N.Y. 10017. www.ciee.org.

Educational Research Association, American (1916): 1230 17th St. N.W., Washington, D.C. 20036-3078. 22,000. Phone: (202) 223-9485. www.aera.net.

Education Association, National (1857): 1201 16th St. N.W., Washington, D.C. 20036-3290. 2.3 million. Phone: (202) 833-4000. www.nea.org.

Electrochemical Society, The (1902): 65 S. Main St., Pennington, N.J. 08534-2839. 7,000. Phone: (609) 737-1902; fax: (609) 737-2743. email: ecs@electrochem.org. www.electrochem.org.

Elks of the U.S.A., Benevolent and Protective Order of the (1868): 2750 N. Lakeview Ave., Chicago, Ill. 60614-1889. 1,300,000. Phone: (773) 755-4700. www.elks.org/default.cfm.

Energy Engineers, Association of (1977): 4025 Pleasantdale Rd., Ste. 420, Atlanta, Ga. 30340. 8,500. Phone: (770) 447-5083; fax: (770) 446-3969. email: info@aeecenter.org. www.aeecenter.org.

English-Speaking Union of the United States (1920): 25 W. 45th St., Ste. 1303, New York, N.Y. 10021. 18,000. Phone: (917) 777-0460. www.english-speakingunion.org.

Entomological Society of America (1889): 9301 Annapolis Rd., Lanham, Md. 20706-3115. 7,400+. Phone: (301) 731-4535; fax: (301) 731-4538. email: esa@entsoc.org. www.entsoc.org.

Esperanto League for North America, The (1952): P.O. Box 1129, El Cerrito, Calif. 94530. Over 1,000. Phone: (800) 377-3726. www.esperanto-usa.org.

Exceptional Children, The Council for (1922): 1110 N. Glebe Rd., Ste. 300, Arlington, Va. 22201-5704. 54,000. Phone: (888) 232-7733 V; (703) 264-9446 TTY; fax: (703) 264-9494. email: cec@cec.sped.org. www.cec.sped.org.

Exploration Geophysicists, Society of (1930): 8801 South Yale, Tulsa, Okla. 74137-3575. 16,536. Phone: (918) 497-5500. www.seg.org.

Family and Consumer Sciences, American Association of (1909): 1555 King St., Alexandria, Va. 22314. 14,500. Phone: (703) 706-4600. www.aafcs.org.

Family Campers & RVers (1949): 4804 Transit Rd., Bldg. 2, Depew, N.Y. 14043. 42,000 families. Phone: (800) 245-9755; fax: (716) 668-6242. www.fcrv.org.

Family, Career, and Community Leaders of America [evolved from Future Homemakers of America, Inc. (1945)]: 1910 Association Dr., Reston, Va. 20191-1584. 230,000. Phone: (703) 476-4900. www.fcclainc.org.

Family Physicians, American Academy of (1947): 11400 Tomahawk Creek Pkwy., Leawood, Kans. 66211-2672. 88,000. Phone: (913) 906-6000. www.aafp.org.

Family Relations, National Council on (1938): 3989 Central Ave. N.E., #550, Minneapolis, Minn. 55421. 42,000 families. Phone: (888) 781-9331. www.ncfr.com.

Farm Bureau Federation, American (1919): 225 Touhy Ave., Park Ridge, Ill. 60068. 4.7 million member families. Phone: (847) 685-8600. www.fb.com.

Federal Bar Association (1920): 2215 M St. N.W., Washington, D.C. 20037. 15,000. Phone: (202) 785-1614; fax: (202) 785-1568. www.fedbar.org.

Federal Employees, National Federation of (1917): 1016 16th St. N.W., Washington, D.C. 20036. 150,000. Phone: (202) 862-4400. www.nffe.org.

Fellowship of Reconciliation (1915): Box 271, Nyack, N.Y. 10960. 20,000. Phone: (845) 358-4601. www.forusa.org.

Female Executives, National Association for (1972): P.O. Box 469031, Escondido, Calif. 92046-9925. 150,000+. Phone: (800) 634-6233. www.nafe.com.

FFA Organization, National (1928): P.O. Box 68960, 6060 FFA Dr., Indianapolis, Ind. 46268. 451,997. Phone: (317) 802-6060. www.ffa.org.

Fire Protection Association, National (1896): One Batterymarch Park, P.O. Box 9101, Quincy, Mass. 02269-9101. 65,000+. Phone: (617) 770-3000. www.nfpa.org.

Flag Foundation, National (1968): Flag Plaza, Pittsburgh, Pa. 15219-3630. 3,000+. Phone: (800) 615-1776. www.icss.com/usflag/nff.html.

Fleet Reserve Association (1924): 125 N. West St., Alexandria, Va. 22314-2754. 162,000. Phone: (703) 683-1400; (800) 372-1924. email: news-fra@fra.org. www.fra.org.

Foreign Policy Association (1918): 470 Park Ave. So., New York, N.Y. 10016-6819. Phone: (212) 481-8100. www.fpa.org.

Foreign Relations, Council on (1921): 58 E. 68th St., New York, N.Y. 10021. 3,400. Phone: (212) 434-9400. www.foreignrelations.org.

Foreign Study, American Institute for (1964): River Plaza, 9 W. Broad St., Stamford, Conn. 06902-3788. Phone: (800) 727-2437. www.aifs.org.

Forensic Sciences, American Academy of (1948): 410 N. 21st St., Ste. 203., P.O. Box 669, Colorado Springs, Colo. 80901-0669. 4,315. Phone: (719) 636-1100; fax: (719) 636-1993. www.aafs.org.

Foresters, Society of American (1900): 5400 Grosvenor Lane, Bethesda, Md. 20814. 18,000. Phone: (301) 897-8720. www.safnet.org.

4-H Program (early 1900s): 1400 Independence Ave., S.W., Washington, D.C. 20250. 5.6 million. Phone: (202) 720-2908. www.4h-usa.org.

Freedom of Information Center (1958): 127 Neff Annex, Univ. of Missouri, Columbia, Mo. 65211. Phone: (573) 882-4856. www.missouri.edu/~foiwww/

French Institute/Alliance Française (1898): 22 E. 60th St., New York, N.Y. 10022. 9,000. Phone: (212) 355-6100. www.fiaf.org.

Friends of Animals Inc. (1957): 777 Post Rd., Darien, Conn. 06820. 120,000. Phone: (203) 656-1522. www.friendsofanimals.org/.

Friends of the Earth (1969): 1025 Vermont Ave. N.W., 3rd Flr., Washington, D.C. 20005. 35,000. Phone: (877) 843-8687. www.foe.org.

Gamblers Anonymous: Box 17173, Los Angeles, Calif. 90017. Phone: (213) 386-8789. www.gamblersanonymous.org.

Gay and Lesbian Task Force, National (1973): 1700 Kalorama Rd. N.W., Washington, D.C. 20009-2624. 35,000 members. Phone: (202) 332-6483. www.ngltf.org.

Genealogical Society, National (1903): 4527 17th St. N., Arlington, Va. 22207-2399. 17,000+. Phone: (703) 525-0050; fax: (703) 525-0052. www.ngsgenealogy.org.

Geographers, Association of American (1904): 1710 16th St. N.W., Washington, D.C. 20009-3198. 7,000. Phone: (202) 234-1450; fax: (202) 234-2744. email: gaia@aag.org. www.aag.org.

Geographic Education, National Council for (1915): 16A Leonard Hall, Indiana University of Pennsylvania, Indiana, Pa. 15705. 3,700. Phone: (724) 357-6290. www.ncge.org.

Geographic Society, National (1888): 1145 17th St. N.W., Washington, D.C. 20036-4688. 9,200,000. Phone: (800) 647-5463. www.nationalgeographic.com.

Geological Institute, American (1948): 4220 King St., Alexandria, Va. 22302-1502. 34 geoscience societies representing 100,000 geoscientists. Phone: (703) 379-2480. www.agiweb.org/.

Geological Society of America, Inc. (1888): P.O. Box 9140, Boulder, Colo. 80301-9140. 15,000. Phone: (303) 447-2020. www.geosociety.org.

German American National Congress, The (Deutsch-Amerikanischer National Kongress—D.A.N.K.) (1958): 4740 N. Western Ave., Executive Office, Chicago, Ill. 60625-2097. Phone: (773) 275-1100. www.dank.org.

Gideons International, The (1889): P.O. Box 140800, Nashville, Tenn. 37214-0800. 130,000. Phone: (615) 883-8533. www.gideons.org.

Gifted, The Association for the (1958): The Council for Exceptional Children, 1920 Association Dr., Reston, Va. 20191-1589. 2,200. Phone: (703) 620-3660. education.idbsu.edu/tag

Girl Scouts of the U.S.A. (1912): 420 Fifth Ave., New York, N.Y. 10018-2798. 2,500,000. Phone: (212) 852-6559. www.gsusa.org.

Girls Incorporated (1945): 120 Wall St., 3rd. Flr., New York, N.Y. 10005. 350,000. Phone: (800) 374-4475. www.girlsinc.org.

Graphoanalysis Society, International (1929): 111 N. Canal St., Ste. 955, Chicago, Ill. 60606. 10,000. Phone: (312) 930-9446; www.igas.com.

Gray Panthers (1970): 733 15th St. N.W., Ste. 437, Washington, D.C. 20005. Over 50 chapters (networks). Phone: (202) 737-1160. www.graypanthers.org.

Greenpeace (1971): 702 H St. N.W., Washington, D.C. 20001. 2.5 million. Phone: (800) 326-0959. www.greenpeaceusa.org.

Guide Dog Foundation for the Blind, Inc.® (1946): 371 E. Jericho Turnpike, Smithtown, N.Y. 11787-2976. 100,000. Phone: (631) 265-2121; (800) 548-4337; fax: (631) 361-5192. www.guidedog.org.

Hadassah, The Women's Zionist Organization of America (1912): 50 W. 58th St., New York, N.Y. 10019. 385,000. Phone: (212) 355-7900. www.hadassah.org.

Heating, Refrigerating and Air-Conditioning Engineers, Inc., American Society of (1959): 1791 Tullie Circle N.E., Atlanta, Ga. 30329. 50,000. Phone: (404) 636-8400. www.ashrae.org.

Helicopter Association International (1948): 1635 Prince St., Alexandria, Va. 22314. Phone: (703) 683-4646; fax: (703) 683-4745. www.rotor.com.

Historians, The Organization of American (1907): Indiana Univ., 112 N. Bryan St., Bloomington, Ind. 47408-4199. 12,000. Phone: (812) 855-7311. www.oah.org.

Historic Preservation, National Trust for (1949): 1785 Massachusetts Ave. N.W., Washington, D.C. 20036. 275,000. Phone: (800) 944-6847. www.nationaltrust.org.

Horse Council, Inc., American (1969): 1700 K St. N.W., #300, Washington, D.C. 20006. More than 190 organizations and 2,400 individuals. Phone: (202) 296-1970. www.horsecouncil.org.

Horse Shows Association, Inc., American (1917): 4047 Iron Works Parkway, Lexington, Ky. 40511. 70,000+. Phone: (859) 258-2472. www.ahsa.org.

Horticultural Association, National Junior (1935): 15 Railroad Ave., Homer City, Pa. 15748. Phone: (724) 479-3254. www.njha.org.

Horticultural Society, American (1922): 7931 East Boulevard Dr., Alexandria, Va. 22308. 22,000. Phone: (703) 768-5700 or (800) 777-7931; fax: (703) 768-8700. www.ahs.org.

Hostelling International—American Youth Hostels (1934): 733 15th St. N.W., Ste. 840, Washington, D.C. 20005. 120,000. Phone: (202) 783-6161 for membership and reservations. www.hiayh.org.

Humane Association, American (1877): 63 Inverness Drive East, Englewood, Colo. 80112-5117. Phone: (800) 227-4645. www.americanhumane.org.

Humane Society of the United States (1954): 2100 L St. N.W., Washington, D.C. 20037. 5,000,000. Phone: (202) 452-1100. www.hsus.org.

Humanities, National Endowment for the (1965): 1100 Pennsylvania Ave. N.W., Washington, D.C. 20506. Phone: (202) 606-8400. www.neh.fed.us.

Hydrogen Energy, International Association for (1975): P.O. Box 248266, Coral Gables, Fla. 33124. 2,500. Phone: (305) 284-4666. www.iahe.org.

Industrial Engineers, Institute of (1948): 25 Technology Park/Atlanta, Norcross, Ga. 30092. 17,000+. Phone: (800) 494-0460. www.iienet.org.

Izaak Walton League of America (1922): 707 Conservation Lane, Gaithersburg, Md. 20878-2983. 50,000+. Phone: (800) 453-5463. www.iwla.org.

Jewish Community Centers Association (JCC) of North America (1917): 15 E. 26th St., New York, N.Y. 10010-1579. 275+ affiliated Jewish Community Centers, YM-YWHAs, and camps serving 1 million+ members. Phone: (212) 532-4958; fax: (212) 481-4174. email: info@jcca.org. www.jcca.org.

Jewish Congress, American (1918): 15 E. 84th St., New York, N.Y. 10028. 50,000. Phone: (212) 879-4500. www.ajcongress.org.

Jewish Historical Society, American (1892): 2 Thornton Rd., Waltham, Mass. 02453. 3,500. Phone: (781) 891-8110; fax: (781) 899-9208. email: ajhs@ajhs.org. www.ajhs.org.

Jewish War Veterans of the U.S.A. (1896): 1811 R St. N.W., Washington, D.C. 20009-1659. Phone: (202) 265-6280. www.nichecom.com/~vfw/jwv.html.

Jewish Women, National Council of (1893): 820 2nd Ave., New York, N.Y. 10017-4504. 90,000. Phone: (212) 687-5030. www.ncjw.org.

John Birch Society (1958): P.O. Box 8040, Appleton, Wis. 54912. Under 100,000. Phone: (920) 749-3780; fax: (920) 749-5062. www.jbs.org.

Journalists, Society of Professional (1909): 3909 N. Meridian St., Indianapolis, Ind. 46208. 13,500. Phone: (317) 927-8000. www.spj.org.

Judaism, American Council for (1943): P.O. Box 9009, Alexandria, Va. 22304. Phone: (703) 836-2546. www.acjna.org.

Junior Achievement Inc. (1919): One Education Way, Colorado Springs, Colo. 80906. 5.2 million. Phone: (719) 540-8000; fax: (719) 540-6299. www.ja.org.

Junior Chamber of Commerce, The United States, Jaycees (1920): 4 West 21 Street, Tulsa, Okla. 74114-1116. 113,000. Phone: (918) 584-2481; fax: (918) 584-4422. www.usjaycees.org.

Junior Leagues International, Inc., Association of (1921): 132 W. 31st St., 11th flr.; New York, N.Y. 10001-3406. 295 Leagues, 193,000+ members. Phone: (212) 683-1515. www.ajli.org.

Junior State of America (1934): 60 E. Third Ave., Ste. 320, San Mateo, Calif. 94401-4302. 15,000. Phone: (650) 347-1600 or (800) 334-5353. www.jsa.org.

Kiwanis International (1915): 3636 Woodview Trace, Indianapolis, Ind. 46268. 316,000. Phone: (317) 875-8755. email: kiwanismail@kiwanis.org. www.kiwanis.org.

Knights of Columbus (1852): One Columbus Plaza, New Haven, Conn. 06510. 1,600,000. Phone: (203) 772-2130. www.kofc.org.

Knights Templar, Grand Encampment of (1816): 5097 N. Elston Ave., Ste. 101, Chicago, Ill. 60630-2460. 220,000. Phone: (773) 777-3300. www.knightstemplar.org.

La Leche League International (1956): 1400 N. Meacham Rd., Schaumburg, Ill. 60168-4079. 50,000. Phone: (847) 519-7730. www.lalecheleague.org.

Law, American Society of International (1906): 2223 Massachusetts Ave. N.W., Washington, D.C. 20008. 4,300. Phone: (202) 939-6000. www.asil.org.

League of Women Voters of the U.S. (1920): 1730 M St. N.W., Washington, D.C. 20036-4508. Phone: (202) 429-1965; fax: (202) 429-0854. www.lwv.org.

Legal Aid and Defender Association, National (1911): 1625 K St. N.W., Ste. 800, Washington, D.C. 20006-1604. 2,400. Phone: (202) 452-0620. www.nlada.org.

Legal Professionals, National Association of (1949): 314 East 3rd St., Ste. 210, Tulsa, Okla. 74120-2409. 6,000. Phone: (918) 582-5188. www.nals.org.

Leukemia & Lymphoma Society (1949): 1311 Mamaroneck Ave., White Plains, NY 10605. Phone: (914) 949-5213. www.leukemia-lymphoma.org.

Library Association, American (1876): 50 E. Huron St., Chicago, Il. 60611. 57,000. Phone: (312) 280-3215. www.ala.org.

Lions Clubs International (1917): 300 22nd St., Oak Brook, Ill. 60521-8842. 1,419,408. Phone: (708) 571-5466. www.lionsclubs.org.

Lung Association, American (1904): 1740 Broadway, New York, N.Y. 10019-4374. 99 constituent and affiliate associations. Phone: (212) 315-8700. www.lungusa.org.

Magazine Editors, American Society of (1963): 919 Third Ave., 22nd Flr., New York, N.Y. 10022. 900. Phone: (212) 872-3700. www.asme.magazine.org

Management Accountants, Institute of (1919): 10 Paragon Dr., Montvale, N.J. 07645-1759. 80,000. Phone: (800) 638-4427 x 265. www.imanet.org.

Management Association, American (1923): 1601 Broadway, New York, N.Y. 10019-7420. 700,000. Phone: (212) 586-8100. www.amanet.org.

Management Consultants, Institute of (1968): 2025 M St. N.W., Ste. 800, Washington, D.C. 20036–2422. 25 chapters. Phone: (202) 367-1134. www.imcusa.org/imc.html.

Manufacturers, National Association of (1895): 1331 Pennsylvania Ave. N.W., Washington, D.C. 20004-1790. Approx. 14,000. Phone: (202) 637-3000. www.nam.org.

March of Dimes Birth Defects Foundation (1938): 1275 Mamaroneck Ave., White Plains, N.Y. 10605. 104 chapters. Phone: (914) 428-7100, (888) 663-4637; tty: (914) 997-4764; fax: (914) 997-4763. email: resourcecenter@modimes.org. www.modimes.org.

Marine Conservation, Center for (1972): 1725 De Sales St. N.W., Ste. 600, Washington, D.C. 20036. 120,000. Phone: (202) 429-5609. www.cmc-ocean.org.

Marine Corps Association (1913): 715 Broadway, Quantico, Va. 22134. 100,723. Phone: (703) 640-6161; (800) 336-0291. www.mca-marines.org.

Marine Technology Society (1963): 1828 L St. N.W., Ste. 906, Washington, D.C. 20036. 2,000+. Phone: (202) 775-5966; fax: (202) 429-9417. www.mtsociety.org.

Masons, Royal Arch, General Grand Chapter International (1797): P.O. Box 489, Danville, Ky. 40423-0489. 230,000. Phone: (606) 236-0757. members.aol.com/GGCHAPTER/HomePage.html.

Mathematical Association of America (1915): P.O. Box 91112, Washington, D.C. 20090-1112. Phone: (800) 331-1622. www.maa.org.

Mathematical Society, American (1888): 201 Charles St., Providence, R.I. 02940-6248. Phone: (401) 455-4000. email: ams@ams.org. www.ams.org.

Mayflower Descendants, General Society of (1897): 4 Winslow St., P.O. Box 3297, Plymouth, Mass. 02361. 24,500+. Phone: (508) 746-3188. www.mayflower.org.

Mechanical Engineers, American Society of (1880): 3 Park Ave., New York, N.Y. 10016-5990. 125,000. Phone: (800) THE-ASME. www.asme.org.

Medical Association, American (1847): 515 N. State St., Chicago, Ill. 60610. 300,000 physicians. Phone: (312) 464-5000. www.ama-assn.org.

Mental Health Association, National (1909): 1021 Prince St., Alexandria, Va., 22314-2971. 340 affiliates. Phone: (703) 684-7722; (800) 969-NMHA; TTY (800) 433-5959; fax: (703) 684-5968. email: nmhainfo@aol.com. www.nmha.org

Meteorological Society, American (1919): 45 Beacon St., Boston, Mass. 02108-3693. 11,000+. Phone: (617) 227-2425. www.ametsoc.org/ams.

Military Chaplains Association of the U.S.A. (1925): P.O. Box 42660, Washington, D.C. 20015-0660. 1,500. Phone: (202) 574-2423.

Mining, Metallurgical, and Petroleum Engineers, The American Institute of (1871): 3 Park Ave., New York, N.Y. 10016-5998. 4 Member Societies: Society for Mining, Metallurgy and Exploration; The Minerals, Metals & Materials Society; Iron & Steel Society; Society of Petroleum Engineers. Phone: (212) 419-7679; fax: (212) 419-7671. email: AIMENY@aol.com. www.idis.com/aime.

Model Aeronautics, Academy of (1936): 5151 East Memorial Dr., Muncie, Ind. 47302. 150,000. Phone: (765) 287-1256. www.modelaircraft.org.

Modern Language Association of America (1883): 26 Broadway, 3rd Fl., New York, N.Y. 10004-1789. 30,000+. Phone: (646) 576-5000. www.mla.org.

Moose International, Inc. (1888): Mooseheart, Ill. 60539. 1,600,000+. Phone: (630) 859-2000. www.mooseintl.org.

Mothers Against Drunk Driving (MADD) (1980): P.O. Box 541688, Dallas, Tex. 75354-1688. 3 million members and supporters. Victim hotline: (800) GET-MADD. www.madd.org.

Motion Picture Arts & Sciences, Academy of (1927): 8949 Wilshire Blvd., Beverly Hills, Calif. 90211-1972. Phone: (310) 247-3000. www.oscars.org.

Multiple Sclerosis Society, National (1946): 733 Third Ave., New York, N.Y. 10017. 350,000. Phone: (800) FIGHT-MS (344-4867). www.nmss.org.

Muscular Dystrophy Association (1950): 3300 East Sunrise Dr., Tucson, Ariz. 85718. 2,300,000 volunteers. Phone: (800) 572-1717. www.mdausa.org.

Museums, American Association of (1906): 1575 Eye St. N.W., Ste. 400, Washington, D.C. 20005. 16,000+. Phone: (202) 289-1818; fax: (202) 289-6578, TTY (202) 289-8439. www.aam-us.org.

Muzzle Loading Rifle Association, National (1933): P.O. Box 67, Friendship, Ind. 47021-0067. 25,000. Phone: (812) 667-5131. www.nmlra.org.

NAFSA: Association of International Educators (1948): 1307 New York Ave. N.W., 8th Flr., Washington, D.C. 20005-4701. 8,000+. Phone: (202) 737-3699. www.nafsa.org.

National Abortion and Reproductive Rights Action League (NARAL) (1969): 1156 15th St. N.W., Washington, D.C. 20005. 500,000. Phone: (202) 973-3000. www.naral.org.

National Association for the Advancement of Colored People (1909): 4805 Mt. Hope Dr., Baltimore, Md. 21215. 500,000+. Phone: (410) 358-8900. www.naacp.org.

National Association of Insurance and Financial Advisors (1890): 2901 Telestar Court, Falls Church, Va. 22042-1205. 80,000. Phone: (703) 770-8100. www.naifa.org/index.html.

National Conference for Community and Justice, The (founded as The Natl. Conf. of Christians & Jews) (1927): 475 Park Avenue South, 19th Flr., New York, N.Y. 10016-6901. Phone: (212) 545-1300. www.nccj.org.

National Cooperative Business Association (formerly Cooperative League of the U.S.A.) (1916): 1401 New York Ave. N.W., Ste. 1100, Washington, D.C. 20005. Phone: (202) 638-6222. www.cooperative.org.

National Council of La Raza (1968): 1111 19th St. N.W., Ste. 1000, Washington, D.C. 20036. 20,000+. Phone: (202) 785-1670. www.nclr.org.

National Council of the Churches of Christ in the USA (1950): 475 Riverside Drive, Rm. 850, New York, N.Y. 10115. 35 Protestant and Orthodox communions. Phone: (212) 870-2227. www.ncccusa.org.

National Grange of the Order of Patrons of Husbandry (1867): 1616 H St. N.W., Washington, D.C. 20006-4999. 300,000. Phone: (202) 628-3507; fax: (202) 347-1091. www.nationalgrange.org.

National Press Club (1908): National Press Bldg., 529 14th St. N.W., 13th Flr., Washington, D.C. 20045. 4,500+. Phone: (202) 662-7500. npc.press.org.

National PTA (National Congress of Parents and Teachers) (1897): 330 N. Wabash Ave., Ste. 2100, Chicago, Ill. 60611. 6.5 million. Phone: (800) 307-4782. email: info@pta.org. www.pta.org.

National Rifle Association of America (1871): 11250 Waples Mill Rd., Fairfax, Va. 22030. 3,300,000. Phone: (703) 267-1000. www.nra.org.

National Urban League, Inc. (1910): 120 Wall St., New York, N.Y. 10005. 115 affiliates in 34 states and D.C. Phone: (212) 558-5300. www.nul.org.

National Wildlife Federation (1936): 11100 Wildlife Center Dr., Reston, Va. 20190. 4,000,000+. Phone: (703) 438-6000. www.nwf.org.

Nature Conservancy, The (1951): 4245 N. Fairfax Dr., Ste. 100, Arlington, Va. 22203-1606. 900,000. Phone: (703) 841-5300. www.tnc.org.

Naturopathic Physicians, American Association of (1986): 8201 Greensboro Dr., Ste. 300, McLean, Va. 22102. 1,700. Phone: (703) 610-9037. http://naturopathic.org.

Naval Architects and Marine Engineers, The Society of (1893): 601 Pavonia Ave., Jersey City, N.J. 07306. 10,000+. Phone: (800) 798-2188; fax: (201) 798-4975. www.sname.org.

Naval Engineers, American Society of (1888): 1452 Duke St., Alexandria, Va. 22314. 6,800. Phone: (703) 836-6727; fax: (703) 836-7491. www.navalengineers.org.

Naval Institute, United States (1873): 291 Wood Rd., Annapolis, Md. 21402. 80,000+. Phone: (410) 268-6110. www.usni.org.

Navigation, The Institute of (1945): 1800 Diagonal Rd., Ste. 480, Alexandria, Va. 22314. 3,800. Phone: (703) 683-7101; fax: (703) 683-7105. email: membership@ion.org. www.ion.org.

Navy League of the United States (1902): 2300 Wilson Blvd., Arlington, Va. 22201-3308. 71,500. Phone: (703) 528-1775. www.navyleague.org.

NDIA (National Defense Industrial Association) (1997): 2111 Wilson Blvd., Ste. 400, Arlington, Va. 22201. 28,000 individual, 900 companies. Phone: (703) 522-1820. www.ndia.org.

Neurofibromatosis Foundation, Inc., The National (1978): 95 Pine St., 16th Flr., New York, N.Y. 10005. 38,000. Phone: (800) 323-7938; in N.Y. State (212) 344-NNFF; fax: (212) 747-0004. email: nnff@aol.com. www.nf.org.

Newspaper Association of America (1992): 1921 Gallows Rd., Ste. 600, Vienna, Va. 22182. 70,000+ newspaper executives. Phone (703) 902-1600. www.naa.org.

Nondestructive Testing, Inc., The American Society for (1941): 1711 Arlingate Lane, P.O. Box 28518, Columbus, Ohio 43228-0518. 10,240. Phone: (800) 222-ASNT. www.asnt.org.

Nuclear Society, American (1954): 555 N. Kensington Ave., La Grange Park, Ill. 60526. 13,000. Phone: (708) 352-6611. www.ans.org.

Numismatic Association, American (1891): 818 N. Cascade Ave., Colorado Springs, Colo. 80903-3279. 28,000. Phone: (719) 632-2646. email: ana@money.org. www.money.org.

Nurses Association, American (1897): 600 Maryland Ave. S.W., Ste. 100, Washington, D.C. 20024. 180,000. Phone: (800) 274-4ANA. www.ana.org.

Odd Fellows, Sovereign Grand Lodge, Independent Order of (1819): 422 North Trade St., Winston-Salem, N.C. 27101. 460,000. Phone: (336) 725-5955. http://128.125.109.137/IOOF.shtml

Olympic Committee, United States (1921): One Olympic Plaza, Colorado Springs, Colo. 80909-5760. Phone: (719) 632-5551. www.olympic-usa.org.

Optimist International (1919): 4494 Lindell Blvd., St. Louis, Mo. 63108. 130,000+. Phone: (314) 371-6000. www.optimist.org.

Optometric Association, American (1898): 243 N. Lindbergh Blvd., St. Louis, Mo. 63141. 32,000. Phone: (314) 991-4100. www.aoanet.org.

Ornithologists' Union, American (1883): c/o Division of Birds, National Museum of Natural History, MRC-116, Washington, D.C. 20560. 4,000. Phone: (202) 357-2051. pica.wru.umt.edu/aou/aou.html.

Overeaters Anonymous, Inc. (1960): 6075 Zenith Court N.E., Rio Rancho, N.M. 87124. 150,000. Phone: (505) 891-2664. www.overeatersanonymous.org.

Parents, Families and Friends of Lesbians and Gays (1981): 1726 M St. N.W., Ste. 400, Washington, D.C. 20036. 77,000 households. Phone: (202) 467-8180. www.pflag.org.

Parents Without Partners (1957): 1650 South Dixie Hwy., Ste. 510, Boca Raton, Fla. 33432. 50,000+. Phone: (561) 391-8833. www.parentswithoutpartners.org.

Peace Action (a merger of SANE and the Nuclear Weapons Freeze Campaign) (1957): 1819 H St. N.W., Ste. 420, Washington D.C. 20006. 55,000. Phone: (202) 862-9740. www.webcom.com/peaceact.

People For the American Way (1980): 2000 M St. N.W., Ste. 400, Washington, D.C. 20036. 300,000. Phone: (202) 467-4999. www.pfaw.org.

Petroleum Geologists, American Association of (1917): P.O. Box 979, Tulsa, Okla. 74101-0979. 31,500. Phone: (918) 584-2555. www.aapg.org.

Pharmaceutical Association, American (1852): 2215 Constitution Ave. N.W., Washington, D.C. 20037-2985. 50,000+. Phone: (202) 628-4410. www.aphanet.org.

Philatelic Society, American (1886): P.O. Box 8000, State College, Pa. 16803. 55,000+. Phone: (814) 237-3803. www.stamps.org.

Photogrammetry and Remote Sensing, American Society for (1934): 5410 Grosvenor Lane, Ste. 210, Bethesda, Md. 20814-2160. 7,000+. Phone: (301) 493-0290; fax: (301) 493-0208. email: asprs@asprs.org. www.asprs.org.

Photographic Society of America (1934): 3000 United Founders Blvd., Ste. 103, Oklahoma City, Okla. 73112-3940. Phone: (405) 843-1437. www.psa-photo.org.

Physical Society, The American (1899): One Physics Ellipse, College Park, Md. 20740-3200. 41,000. Phone: (301) 209-3200. www.aps.org.

Physical Therapy Association, American (APTA) (1921): 1111 N. Fairfax St., Alexandria, Va. 22314-1488. 66,000+. Phone: (703) 684-2782. www.apta.org.

Physics, American Institute of (1931): One Physics Ellipse, College Park, Md. 20740-3843. 125,000. Phone: (301) 209-3100. www.aip.org.

Pilot International (1921): Pilot International Headquarters, 244 College St., P.O. Box 4844, Macon, Ga. 31208-4844. 25,000. Phone: (912) 743-7403. www.pilotinternational.org.

Planetary Society, The (1980): 65 N. Catalina Ave., Pasadena, Calif. 91106-2301. 100,000. Phone: (626) 793-5100. www.planetary.org.

Planned Parenthood® Federation of America, Inc., (1916): 810 Seventh Ave., New York, N.Y. 10019. 150 affiliates. Phone: (212) 541-7800; fax: (212) 261-4560. www.plannedparenthood.org.

Plastics Engineers, Society of (1942): P.O. Box 403, 14 Fairfield Dr., Brookfield, Conn. 06804-0403. 32,000+. Phone: (203) 775-0471. www.4spe.org.

Police and Concerned Citizens, American Federation of (1966): Records Center, 3801 Biscayne Blvd., Miami, Fla. 33137. 100,000. Phone: (305) 573-0070. www.aphf.org.

Police, International Association of Chiefs of (1893): 515 N. Washington St., Alexandria, Va. 22314-2357. 19,000+. Phone: (703) 836-6767. www.theiacp.org.

Political and Social Science, American Academy of (1889): 3937 Chestnut St., Philadelphia, Pa. 19104. Phone: (215) 386-4630. www.asc.upenn.edu/aapss.

Political Science, Academy of (1880): 475 Riverside Dr., Ste. 1274, New York, N.Y. 10115-1274. 8,500. Phone: (212) 870-2500. www.psqonline.org.

Prevent Blindness America (1908): 500 E. Remington Rd., Schaumburg, Ill. 60173. 21 affiliates and divisions. Phone: (847) 843-2020; (800) 331-2020. www.preventblindness.org.

Professional Engineers, National Society of (1934): 1420 King St., Alexandria, Va. 22314-2794. 60,000. Phone: (703) 684-2800; fax: (703) 836-4875. www.nspe.org.

Professional Photographers of America, Inc. (1880): 299 Peachtree St. N.W., #2200, Atlanta, Ga. 30303-2206. 14,000. Phone: (404) 522-8600. www.ppa.com.

Psychiatric Association, American (1844): 1400 K St. N.W., Washington, D.C. 20005. 40,537. Phone: (202) 682-6000. www.psych.org.

Psychoanalytic Association, The American (1911): 309 E. 49th St., New York, N.Y. 10017. 3,000+ psychoanalysts. Phone: (212) 752-0450; fax: (212) 593-0571. www.apsa.org.

Psychological Association, American (1892): 750 First St. N.E., Washington, D.C. 20002. 159,000. Phone: (202) 336-5500; (202) 336-5662 TTY. www.apa.org.

Public Health Association, American (1872): 800 I St. N.W., Washington, D.C. 20001-3710. 50,000+. Phone: (202) 777-2742. www.apha.org.

Puppeteers of America (1937): P.O. Box 29417, Parma, Ohio 44129-0417. Phone: (888) 568-6235. www.puppeteers.org

Quality, The American Society for (1946): 600 N. Plankinton Ave., P.O. Box 3005, Milwaukee, Wis. 53201-3005. 135,000+. Phone: (414) 272-8575. www.asq.org.

Railroads, Association of American (1934): 50 F St. N.W., Washington, D.C. 20001-1564. Phone: (202) 639-2100. www.aar.org.

Recording Arts & Sciences, Inc., National Academy of (1957): 3402 Pico Blvd., Santa Monica, Calif. 90405. 13,000. Phone: (310) 392-3777. www.grammy.com.

Red Cross, American (1881): 431 18th St. N.W., Washington, D.C. 20006. Approx. 1,650 chapters. Phone: (202) 639-3520. www.redcross.org.

Rehabilitation Association, National (1925): 633 S. Washington St., Alexandria, Va. 22314. 12,000. Phone: (703) 836-0850; TDD: (703) 836-0849. www.nationalrehab.org.

Reserve Officers Association of the United States (1922): 1 Constitution Ave. N.E., Washington, D.C. 20002-5655. 93,000. Phone: (202) 479-2200. www.roa.org.

Retired Federal Employees, National Association (1921): 606 N. Washington St., Alexandria, Va. 22314. 422,000+. Phone: (703) 838-7760. www.narfe.org.

Reye's Syndrome Foundation, National (1974): P.O. Box 829, Bryan, Ohio 43506-0829. Phone: (800) 233-7393; fax: (419) 636-3366. email: reyessyn@mail.bright.net. www.reyessyndrome.org.

RID-USA (Remove Intoxicated Drivers) (1978): Box 520, Schenectady, N.Y. 12301. Phone: (518) 372-0034/(518) 393-HELP; fax: (518) 370-4917. www.crisny.org/not-for-profit/ridusa/.

Right to Life, Committee, Inc., National (1973): 419 7th St. N.W., Ste. 500, Washington, D.C. 20004. Phone: (202) 626-8800. www.nrlc.org

Rotary International (1905): One Rotary Center, 1560 Sherman Ave., Evanston, Ill. 60201. 1.2 million in 161 countries and 35 geographical regions. Phone: (847) 866-3000. www.rotary.org.

SAE (Society of Automotive Engineers) (1905): 400 Commonwealth Dr., Warrendale, Pa. 15096-0001. 80,000. Phone: (724) 776-5760. www.sae.org.

Safety Council, National (1913): 1121 Spring Lake Dr., Itasca, Ill. 60143-3201. Phone: (630) 285-1121. www.nsc.org.

Salvation Army, The (1865): National Headquarters, 615 Slaters Lane, P.O. Box 269, Alexandria, Va. 22313. 453,150. Phone: (703) 684-5500. www.salvationarmy.org.

Save-the-Redwoods League (1918): 114 Sansome St., Ste. 605, San Francisco, Calif. 94104-3814. 45,000. Phone: (415) 362-2352. www.savetheredwoods.org.

Science, American Association for the Advancement of (1848): 1200 New York Ave. N.W., Washington, D.C. 20005. 143,000. Phone: (202) 326-6400. www.aaas.org.

Science and Health, American Council on (1978): 1995 Broadway, 2nd Flr., New York, N.Y. 10023-5860. Phone: (212) 362-7044; fax: (212) 362-4919. email: acsh@acsh.org. www.acsh.org.

Science Fiction Society, World (1939): P.O. Box 426159, Kendall Square Station, Cambridge, Mass. 02142. email: mpc@wsfs.org www.wsfs.org.

Scientists, Federation of American (FAS) (1945): 1717 K St. N.W., Ste. 209, Washington, D.C. 20036. 4,000. Phone: (202) 546-3300. www.fas.org.

SCRABBLE® Association, National (1978): P.O. Box 700, 120 Front Street Garden, Greenport, N.Y. 11944. 10,000. Phone: (516) 477-0033. www.scrabble-assoc.com

Screen Actors Guild (1933): 5757 Wilshire Blvd., Los Angeles, Calif. 90036-3600. 96,000. Phone: (323) 954-1600. www.sag.com.

Sculpture Society, National (1893): 1177 Ave. of the Americas, New York, N.Y. 10036. 4,000. Phone: (212) 764-5645. www.nationalsculpture.org

Seeing Eye Inc., The (1929): P.O. Box 375, Morristown, N.J. 07963-0375. Phone: (973) 539-4425. www.seeingeye.org.

Senior Citizens, National Alliance of (1974): 2525 Wilson Blvd., Arlington, Va. 22201. 117,000. Fax: (703) 528-4380.

Shriners of North America and Shriners Hospitals for Children, The (1872 and 1922): 2900 Rocky Point Drive, Tampa, Fla. 33607-1408. 525,000. Phone: (813) 281-0300. www.shrinershq.org.

Sierra Club (1892): 85 2nd Street, San Francisco, Calif. 94105-3441. 700,000+. Phone: (415) 977-5500. www.sierraclub.org.

SIETAR INTERNATIONAL (The International Society for Intercultural Education, Training and Research) (1974): c/o ICHEC, Blvd. Brand Whitlock 2, 1150 Brussels, Belgium. 1,500. Phone: (+32-2) 739 3743. www.sietarinternational.org.

Simon Wiesenthal Center (1977): 9786 W. Pico Blvd., Los Angeles, Calif. 90035. 400,000 member families. Phone: (800) 900-9036. www.wiesenthal.org.

Small Business United, National (1937): 1156 15th St. N.W., Washington, D.C. 20005. 65,000+. Phone:

(202) 293-8830; fax: (202) 872-8543. email: nsbu@nsbu.org. www.nsbu.org.

Social Work Education, Council on (1952): 1725 Duke St., Ste. 500, Alexandria, Va. 22314. Phone: (703) 683-8080; fax: (703) 683-8099. www.cswe.org.

Social Workers, National Association of (1955): 750 First St. N.E., Ste. 700, Washington, D.C. 20002-4241. Phone: (202) 408-8600. www.naswdc.org.

Society for Integrative and Comparative Biology (formerly the American Society of Zoologists) (1890): 1313 Dolley Madison Blvd. #402, McLean, Va. 22101-3926. 2,100. Phone: (703) 790-1745; (800) 955-1236. email: SICB@BurkInc.com www.sicb.org.

Soil and Water Conservation Society (1945): 7515 N.E. Ankeny Rd., Ankeny, Iowa 50021. 10,000. Phone: (515) 289-2331; fax: (515) 289-1227. email: swcs@swcs.org. www.swcs.org.

Songwriters Guild of America, The (1931): 1500 Harbor Blvd., Weehawken, N.J. 07087-6732. Phone: (201) 867-7603. www.songwriters.org.

Sons of Italy in America, Order (1905): 219 E St. N.E., Washington, D.C. 20002. 500,000. Phone: (202) 547-2900. www.osia.org.

Sons of the American Revolution, National Society of the (1889): 1000 S. 4th St., Louisville, Ky. 40203. 26,000. Phone: (502) 589-1776. www.sar.org.

Soroptimist International of the Americas (1921): Two Penn Center Plaza, Ste. 1000, Philadelphia, Pa. 19102-1883. 100,000. Phone: (215) 557-9300. www.siahq.com.

Southern Early Childhood Association (formerly SACUS) (1948): P.O. Box 55930, Little Rock, Ark. 72215-5930. 21,000. Phone: (800) 305-7322; fax: (501) 663-2114. email: seca@aristotle.net. www.seca50.org.

Space Education Association, U.S. (1973): 231 School Lane, P.O. Box 249, Rheems, Pa. 17570. Phone: (717) 367–5196.

Space Society, National (1974): 600 Pennsylvania Ave. S.E., Ste. 201, Washington, D.C. 20003. Phone: (202) 543-1900; fax: (202) 546-4189. www.nss.org/.

Special Olympics International, Inc. (1968): 1325 G St. N.W., Ste. 500, Washington, D.C., 20005. 1,000,000. Phone: (202) 628-3630. www.specialolympics.org.

Speech-Language-Hearing Association, American (1925): 10801 Rockville Pike, Rockville, Md. 20852. 99,000+. Phone & TTY: (800) 638-8255. www.asha.org.

Sports Car Club of America Inc. (1944): 9033 E. Easter Place, Englewood, Colo. 80112. 55,000. Phone: (303) 694-7222. www.scca.org/index.html.

Statistical Association, American (1839): 1429 Duke St., Alexandria, Va. 22314-3402. 19,000. Phone: (888) 231-3473. www.amstat.org.

Student Association, United States (1947): 1413 K Street N.W., 9th Flr., Washington, D.C. 20005. 350 schools (3.5 million students). Phone: (202) 347-8772. www.usstudents.org.

Surgeons, American College of (1913): 633 North Saint Clair, Chicago, Ill. 60611-3211. 56,000+. Phone: (312) 202-5000. www.facs.org.

Symphony Orchestra League, American (1942): 33 W. 60th St., 5th Fl., New York, N.Y. 10023. 5,500. Phone: (212) 262-5161. www.symphony.org.

TASH: The Association for Persons with Severe Handicaps (1974): 29 W. Susquehanna Ave., Ste. 210, Baltimore, Md. 21204. 8,500. Phone: (410) 828-TASH. www.tash.org.

Teachers, American Federation of (1916): 555 New Jersey Ave. N.W., Washington, D.C., 20001. 900,000+. Phone: (202) 879-4400. www.aft.org.

Testing & Materials, American Society for (1898): 100 Barr Harbor Dr., W. Conshohocken, Pa. 19428-2959. 35,000. Phone: (610) 832-9585. www.astm.org.

The Arc (1950): 1010 Wayne Ave., Ste. 650, Silver Spring, Md. 20910. A national organization on mental retardation. 140,000 members, 1,200 state and local chapters. Phone: (301) 565-3842. www.thearc.org.

Theosophical Society in America, The (1875): P.O. Box 270, Wheaton, Ill. 60189-0270. 4,400. Phone: (630) 668-1571. www.theosophical.org.

Tin Can Sailors, Inc. (1976): P.O. Box 100, Somerset, Mass. 02726. 20,900. Phone: (800) 223-5535. www.destroyers.org.

Toastmasters International (1924): P.O. Box 9052, Mission Viejo, Calif. 92690-7052. 170,000. Phone: (949) 858-8255; fax: (949) 858-1207. email: tminfo@toastmasters.org. www.toastmasters.org.

TOUGHLOVE International (1977): P.O. Box 1069, Doylestown, Pa. 18901. 500 registered groups. Phone: (215) 348-7090. www.toughlove.org.

TransAfrica Forum (1981): 1744 R. St. N.W., Washington, D.C. 20009. Phone: (202) 797-2301; fax: (202) 797-2382. email: transforum@igc.org. www.transafricaforum.org.

Travel Agents, American Society of (ASTA) (1931): 1101 King St., Alexandria, Va. 22314. 26,000. Phone: (703) 739-2782. www.astanet.com.

Travelers Aid International (1851): 1612 K St. N.W., Ste. 506, Washington, D.C. 20006. 45 agencies, 500+ corporate representatives. Phone: (202) 546-1127; fax: (202) 546-1127. www.travelersaid.org.

Tuberous Sclerosis Association, Inc., National (1974): 8181 Professional Place, Ste. 110, Landover, Md. 20785-2226. 5,000. Phone: (301) 459-9888; (800) 225-6872; fax: (301) 459-0394. email: ntsa@ntsa.org. www.tsalliance.org.

UFOs, National Investigations Committee on (1967): 14617 Victory Blvd., Ste. 4, Van Nuys, Calif. 91411. Phone: (818) 989-5942. www.nicufo.com.

UNICEF, U.S. Committee for (1947): 333 E. 38th St., New York, N.Y. 10016. 20,000 volunteers. Phone: (800) FOR-KIDS. www.unicefusa.org.

Union of Concerned Scientists (1969): 2 Brattle Square, Cambridge, Mass. 02238. 70,000. Phone: (617) 547-5552. www.ucsusa.org.

United Daughters of the Confederacy® (1894): 328 N. Boulevard, Richmond, Va. 23220-4057. 24,000. Phone: (804) 355-1636. www.hqudc.org.

United Jewish Communities (formerly United Jewish Appeal) (1939): Ste. 11E, 111 Eighth Ave., New York, N.Y. 10011. Phone: (212) 284-6500. www.ujc.org.

United Way of America (1918): 701 N. Fairfax St., Alexandria, Va. 22314-2045. 1,400 local United Ways. Phone: (703) 836-7100; fax: (703) 683-7840. www.unitedway.org.

University Women, American Association of (1881): 1111 16th St. N.W., Washington, D.C. 20036. 150,000. Phone: (800) 326-AAUW (2289); TDD: (202) 785-7777. www.aauw.org.

USO (United Service Organizations) (1941): World Headquarters, Washington Navy Yard, 1008 Eberle Place SE, Ste. 301, Washington, D.C. 20374-5096. 120 centers worldwide. Phone: (800) 876-7469. www.uso.org.

Veterans Committee, American (AVC) (1944): Bethesda, Md. 20817. 15,000. Phone & fax: (301) 320-6490. www.va.gov/vso/avc.htm.

Veterans of Foreign Wars of the U.S. (1899): 406 W. 34th St., Kansas City, Mo. 64111. VFW and Auxiliary, 2.1 million. Phone: (816) 756-3390. www.vfw.org.

Veterinary Medical Association, American (1863): 1931 N. Meacham Rd., Ste. 100, Schaumburg, Ill. 60173. 62,000. Phone: (847) 925-8070. www.avma.org.

Volunteers of America (1896): 1660 Duke St., Alexandria, Va. 22314-3421. 40,000+ volunteers. Phone: (703) 341-5000; (800) 899-0089. www.voa.org.

War Resisters League (1923): 339 Lafayette St., New York, N.Y. 10012. 12,000. Phone: (212) 228-0450; fax: (212) 228-6193. www.warresisters.org.

Washington Legal Foundation (1977): 2009 Massachusetts Ave. N.W., Washington, D.C. 20036. 100,000. Phone: (202) 588-0302. www.wlf.org.

Water Quality Association (1974): 4151 Naperville Rd., Lisle, Ill. 60532. 2,200. Phone: (630) 505-0160; fax: (630) 505-9637. www.wqa.org.

Welding Society, American (1919): 550 N.W. LeJeune Rd., Miami, Fla. 33126. 50,000. Phone: (305) 443-9353; (800) 443-9353. www.aws.org.

Wildlife Fund (U.S.), World (1961): 1250 24th St. N.W., Washington, D.C. 20037. 1.2 million. Phone: (800) 225-5993. www.wwf.org.

Woman's Christian Temperance Union, National (1874): 1730 Chicago Ave., Evanston, Ill. 60201-4585. Under 20,000. Phone: (847) 864-1397. www.wctu.org.

Women, National Organization for (NOW) (1966): 733 15th St. N.W., 2nd fl., Washington, D.C. 20005. 500,000. Phone: (202) 628-8669. www.now.org.

Women Police, The International Association of (1915): Box 149, Deer Isle, Me. 04627-9700. 3,000. Phone: (207) 348-6976; fax: (207) 348-6171. www.iawp.org.

Women's American ORT (1927): 315 Park Ave. South, New York, N.Y. 10010. Chapters throughout the U.S. Phone: (212) 505-7700. www.waort.org.

Women's Educational and Industrial Union (1877): 356 Boylston St., Boston, Mass. 02116. 1,500. Phone: (617) 536-5651; fax: (617) 247-8826. www.weiu.org.

Women's International League for Peace and Freedom (1915): 1213 Race St., Philadelphia, Pa. 19107. 10,000. Phone: (215) 563-7110. www.wilpf.org.

World Future Society (1966): 7910 Woodmont Ave., Ste. 450, Bethesda, Md. 20814. 30,000. Phone: (301) 656-8274; fax: (301) 951-0394. www.wfs.org.

World Health, American Association for (1953): 1825 K St. N.W., Washington, D.C. 20006. Phone: (202) 466-5883, fax: (202) 466-5896. email: AAWHstaff@aol.com. www.aawhworldhealth.org.

World Peace, International Association of Educators for (1967): 2267 Sacramento St. #2, San Francisco, Calif. 94115. 102 countries. Phone: (415) 567-9143. www.homeplanet.org/iaewp.

World Peace Foundation (1910): 79 John F. Kennedy St., Cambridge, Mass. 02138. Phone: (617) 496-2258; fax: (617) 491-8588. www.worldpeacefoundation.org

Worldwatch Institute (1974): 1776 Massachusetts Ave. N.W., Washington, D.C. 20036-1904. Global environmental research organization. Phone: (202) 452-1999; fax: (202) 296-7365. email: worldwatch@worldwatch.org. www.worldwatch.org.

Writers Union, National (1981): 113 University Place, 6th Flr., New York, N.Y. 10003. 6,500. Phone: (212) 254-0279. www.nwu.org.

YMCA of the USA (1844): 101 N. Wacker Dr., Chicago, Ill. 60606. 16.9 million. Phone: (312) 977-0031. www.ymca.net.

Young Women's Christian Association of the U.S.A. (1858 in U.S.A., 1855 in England): Empire State Building, 350 Fifth Ave., Ste. 301, New York, N.Y. 10118. 2,000,000. Phone: (212) 273-7800. www.ywca.org.

Zero Population Growth (1968): 1400 Sixteenth St. N.W., Ste. 320, Washington, D.C. 20036. 55,000. Phone: (202) 332-2200. www.zpg.org.

Zionist Organization of America (1897): 4 E. 34th St., New York, N.Y. 10016. 50,000. Phone: (212) 481-1500; fax: (212) 481-1515. www.zoa.org.

Explorations

Country or place	Event	Explorer	Date
AFRICA			
Sierra Leone	Explored	Hanno, Carthaginian seaman	c. 520 B.C.
Zaire River (Congo)	Mouth visited[1]	Diogo Cão, Portuguese explorer	c. 1484
Cape of Good Hope	Rounded	Bartolomeu Diaz, Portuguese explorer	1488
Gambia River	Explored	Mungo Park, Scottish explorer	1795
Sahara	Crossed	Dixon Denham and Hugh Clapperton, English explorers	1822–1823
Zambezi River	Explored[1]	David Livingstone, Scottish explorer	1851
Sudan	Explored	Heinrich Barth, German explorer	1852–1855
Victoria Falls	Explored[1]	David Livingstone, Scottish explorer	1855
Lake Tanganyika	Explored[1]	Richard Burton and John Speke, British explorers	1858
Lake Victoria, identified as the source of the Nile	Explored	John Speke, British explorer	1858
Zaire River (Congo)	Traced	Sir Henry M. Stanley, British explorer	1877
ASIA			
Punjab (India)	Invaded	Alexander the Great, king of Macedonia	327 B.C.
China	Explored	Marco Polo, Italian traveler	c. 1272
Tibet	Visited	Odoric of Pordenone, Italian monk	c. 1325
Southern China	Explored	Niccolò dei Conti, Venetian traveler	c. 1440
India	Explored (Cape route)	Vasco da Gama, Portuguese navigator	1498
Japan	Visited	St. Francis Xavier of Spain, missionary	1549
Arabia	Explored	Carsten Niebuhr, German explorer	1762
China	Explored	Ferdinand Richthofen, German scientist	1868
Mongolia	Explored	Nikolai M. Przhevalsky, Russian explorer	1870–1873
Central Asia	Explored	Sven Hedin, Swedish scientist	1890–1908
EUROPE			
Shetland Islands	Visited	Pytheas of Massilia (Marseille), Greek navigator and geographer	c. 325 B.C.
North Cape	Rounded	Ottar, Norwegian explorer	c. 870
Iceland	Colonized	Norwegian noblemen	c. 890–900
NORTH AMERICA			
Greenland	Colonized	Eric the Red, Norwegian	c. 985
Labrador, Newfoundland, Nova Scotia (?)	Explored[1]	Leif Ericsson, Norse explorer	1000
West Indies	Explored[1]	Christopher Columbus, Italian	1492
North America	Coast explored[1]	Giovanni Caboto (John Cabot), for British	1497
Pacific Ocean	Sighted[1]	Vasco Núñez de Balboa, Spanish explorer	1513
Florida	Explored	Ponce de León, Spanish explorer	1513
Mexico	Conquered	Hernando Cortés, Spanish adventurer	1519–1521
St. Lawrence River	Explored[1]	Jacques Cartier, French navigator	1534
Southwest United States	Explored	Francisco Coronado, Spanish explorer	1540–1542
Colorado River	Explored[1]	Hernando de Alarcón, Spanish explorer	1540
Mississippi River	Explored[1]	Hernando de Soto, Spanish explorer	1541
Frobisher Bay	Explored[1]	Martin Frobisher, English seaman	1576
Maine Coast	Explored	Samuel de Champlain, French explorer	1604
Jamestown, Va.	Settled	John Smith, English colonist	1607
Hudson River	Explored	Henry Hudson, English navigator	1609
Hudson Bay (Canada)	Explored	Henry Hudson	1610
Baffin Bay	Explored[1]	William Baffin, English navigator	1616
Lake Michigan	Navigated	Jean Nicolet, French explorer	1634
Arkansas River	Explored[1]	Jacques Marquette and Louis Jolliet, French explorers	1673
Mississippi River	Explored	Sieur de La Salle, French explorer	1682
Bering Strait	Explored[1]	Vitus Bering, Danish explorer	1728
Alaska	Explored[1]	Vitus Bering	1741
Mackenzie River (Canada)	Explored[1]	Sir Alexander Mackenzie, Scottish-Canadian explorer	1789
Northwest United States	Explored	Meriwether Lewis and William Clark, American explorers	1804–1806
Northeast Passage (Arctic Ocean)	Navigated	Nils Nordenskjöld, Swedish explorer	1879
Greenland	Explored	Robert E. Peary, American explorer	1892
Northwest Passage	Navigated	Roald Amundsen, Norwegian explorer	1906

Country or place	Event	Explorer	Date
SOUTH AMERICA			
Continent	Explored	Christopher Columbus, Italian	1498
Brazil	Explored[1]	Pedro Alvarez Cabral, Portuguese	1500
Peru	Conquered	Francisco Pizarro, Spanish explorer	1532–1533
Amazon River	Explored	Francisco Orellana, Spanish explorer	1541
Cape Horn	Explored[1]	Willem C. Schouten, Dutch navigator	1615
OCEANIA			
Papua New Guinea	Explored	Jorge de Menezes, Portuguese explorer	1526
Australia	Explored	Abel Janszoon Tasman, Dutch navigator	1642
Tasmania	Explored[1]	Abel Janszoon Tasman	1642
Australia	Crossed	John McDouall Stuart, English explorer	1862
Australia	Explored	Robert Burke and William Wills, Australian explorers	1861
New Zealand	Sighted (and named)	Abel Janszoon Tasman, Dutch navigator	1642
New Zealand	Explored	James Cook, English navigator	1769
ARCTIC, ANTARCTIC, AND MISCELLANEOUS			
Africa, Middle East, Asia, and Europe	Explored	Ibn Batuta, greatest Arab traveler	1325–1349
Ocean exploration	Expedition	Ferdinand Magellan's ships circled globe for Spain	1519–1522
Galápagos Islands	Explored	Diego de Rivadeneira, Spanish captain	1535
Spitsbergen	Explored	Willem Barents, Dutch navigator	1596
Antarctic Circle	Crossed	James Cook, English navigator	1773
Antarctica	Explored[1]	Nathaniel Palmer, American whaler (archipelago), and Fabian Gottlieb von Bellingshausen, Russian admiral (mainland)	1820–1821
Antarctica	Explored	Charles Wilkes, American explorer	1840
North Pole	Reached[2]	Robert E. Peary, American explorer	1909
South Pole	Reached	Roald Amundsen, Norwegian explorer	1911

1. First European to reach the area. 2. Admiral Peary's claim to have reached the Pole has been disputed from the beginning—as was the claim made by his former colleague, Dr. Frederick Cook, who has been generally dismissed as a charlatan. The credit ultimately went to Peary, a claim officially backed by the U.S. Congress. But recent scholarship, including evidence culled from the journals and diaries of both Cook and Peary, has cast doubt on both explorers' veracity. If it is the case that neither reached the Pole, then the credit goes to Joseph Fletcher, who landed a U.S. Air Force C-47 plane there in 1952.

The Continents

A continent is defined as a large unbroken land mass completely surrounded by water, although in some cases continents are (or were in part) connected by land bridges. The seven continents are North America, South America, Europe, Asia, Africa, Australia, and Antarctica. The island groups in the Pacific are often called Oceania but this name does *not* imply that scientists consider them the remains of a continent.

Political considerations have often overridden geographical facts when it came to naming continents. Geographically, Europe, including the British Isles, is a large western peninsula of the continent of Asia; and many geographers, when referring to Europe and Asia, speak of the Eurasian continent. But traditionally, Europe is counted as a separate continent, with the Ural and the Caucasus mountains forming the line of demarcation between Europe and Asia. To the south of Europe, Asia has an odd-shaped peninsula jutting westward, which has a large number of political subdivisions. The northern section is taken up by Turkey; to the south of Turkey are Syria, Iraq, Israel, Jordan, Saudi Arabia, and a number of smaller Arab countries. All these are part of Asia. Traditionally, the island of Cyprus in the Mediterranean is also considered to be part of Asia.

Continental Drift and Plate-Tectonics Theory

Source: U.S. Dept. of the Interior, Geological Survey

According to the theory of continental drift, the world was made up of a single continent through most of geologic time. That continent eventually separated and drifted apart, forming into the seven continents we have today. The first comprehensive theory of continental drift was suggested by the German meteorologist Alfred Wegener in 1912. The hypothesis asserts that the continents consist of lighter rocks that rest on heavier crustal material—similar to the manner in which icebergs float on water. Wegener contended that the relative positions of the continents are not rigidly fixed but are slowly moving—at a rate of about one yard per century.

According to the generally accepted plate-tectonics theory, scientists believe that Earth's surface is broken into a number of shifting slabs or plates, which average about 50 miles in thickness. These plates move relative to one another above a hotter, deeper, more mobile zone at average rates as great as a few inches per year. Most of the world's active volcanoes are located along or near the boundaries between shifting plates and are called plate-boundary volcanoes.

The peripheral areas of the Pacific Ocean Basin, containing the boundaries of several plates, are dotted with many active volcanoes that form the so-called Ring of Fire.

World Land Areas and Elevations

Area	Approximate land area sq. km	Approximate land area sq. mi.	Percentage of total land area	Elevation, feet and meters	
				Highest	Lowest
WORLD	148,429,000	57,308,738	100.0%	Mt. Everest, Tibet-Nepal, 29,035 ft. (8,850 m)[1]	Dead Sea, Israel-Jordan, 1,349 ft. below sea level (−411 m)
ASIA (includes the Middle East)	44,579,000	17,212,041	30.0	Mt. Everest, Tibet-Nepal, 29,035 ft. (8,850 m)	Dead Sea, Israel-Jordan, 1,349 ft. below sea level (−411 m)
AFRICA	30,065,000	11,608,156	20.3	Mt. Kilimanjaro, Tanzania, 19,340 ft. (5,895 m)	Lake Assal, Djibouti, 512 ft. below sea level (−156 m)
NORTH AMERICA	24,256,000	9,365,290	16.3	Mt. McKinley, Alaska, 20,320 ft. (6,194 m)	Death Valley, Calif., 282 ft. below sea level (−86 m)
SOUTH AMERICA (includes Central America and the Caribbean)	17,819,000	6,879,952	12.0	Mt. Aconcagua, Argentina, 22,834 ft. (6,960 m)	Valdes Peninsula, Argentina 131 ft. below sea level (−40 m)
ANTARCTICA	13,209,000	5,100,021	8.9	Vinson Massif, Ellsworth Mts., 16,066 ft. (4,897 m)	Bentley Subglacial Trench, 8,327 ft. below sea level (−2,538 m)
EUROPE (includes the recently independent states of the former Soviet Union)	9,938,000	3,837,082	6.7	Mt. Elbrus, Russia/Georgia, 18,510 ft. (5,642 m)	Caspian Sea, Russia/Kazakhstan 92 ft. below sea level (−28 m)
AUSTRALIA (includes Oceania)	7,687,000	2,967,966	5.2	Mt. Kosciusko, Australia, 7,310 ft. (2,228 m)	Lake Eyre, Australia, 52 ft. below sea level (−12 m)

1. The 1954 elevation of Everest, 29,028 ft. (8,848 m) was revised on Nov. 11, 1999, and now stands at 29,035 ft. (8,850 m). *Source:* National Geographic Society.

Volcanoes of the World

Source: U.S. Dept. of the Interior, Geological Survey

About 550 volcanoes have erupted on Earth's surface since recorded history; about 60 are active each year. Far more have erupted unobserved on the ocean floor. Most volcanoes exist at the boundaries of Earth's crustal plates, such as the famous Ring of Fire that surrounds the Pacific Ocean plate. Fifty volcanoes have erupted in the United States since recorded history, and the United States ranks third, behind Indonesia and Japan, in the number of historically active volcanoes.

The Nature of Volcanoes

Volcanoes are built by the accumulation of their own eruptive products—lava, bombs (crusted over ash flows), and tephra (airborne ash and dust). A volcano is most commonly a conical hill or mountain built around a vent that connects with reservoirs of molten rock below the surface of Earth. The term *volcano* also refers to the opening or vent through which molten rock and gases are expelled.

Driven by buoyancy and gas pressure, the molten rock, which is lighter than the surrounding solid rock, forces its way upward and may ultimately break though zones of weaknesses in Earth's crust. If so, an eruption begins, and the molten rock may pour from the vent as nonexplosive lava flows, or it may shoot violently into the air as dense clouds of lava fragments. Larger fragments fall back around the vent, and accumulations of fall-back fragments may move downslope as ash flows under the force of gravity. Some of the finer ejected materials may be carried by the wind and fall to the ground many miles away. The finest ash particles may be injected miles into the atmosphere and carried many times around the world by stratospheric winds before settling out.

Magma, Lava, and Pumice

Molten rock below the surface of Earth that rises in volcanic vents is known as magma, but after it erupts from a volcano it is called lava. Originating many tens of miles beneath the ground, the ascending magma commonly contains some crystals, fragments of surrounding (unmelted) rocks, and dissolved gases, but it is primarily a liquid composed of oxygen, silicon, aluminum, iron, magnesium, calcium, sodium, potassium, titanium, and manganese. Magmas also contain many other chemical elements in trace quantities. Upon cooling, the liquid magma may precipitate crystals of various minerals until solidification is complete to form an igneous or magmatic rock.

Lava is red-hot when it pours or blasts out of a vent but soon changes to dark red, gray, black, or some other color as it cools and solidifies. Very hot, gas-rich lava containing abundant iron and magnesium is fluid and flows like hot tar, whereas cooler, gas-poor lava high in silicon, sodium, and potassium flows sluggishly, like thick honey, or in other cases, like pasty, blocky masses.

All magmas contain dissolved gases, and as they rise to the surface to erupt, the confining pressures are reduced and the dissolved gases are liberated either quietly or explosively. If the lava is a thin fluid (not viscous), the gases may escape easily. But if the lava is thick and pasty (highly viscous), the gases will not move freely but will build up tremendous pressure and ultimately escape with explosive violence, throwing out great masses of solid rock as well as lava, dust, and ashes.

The violent separation of gas from lava may produce rock froth called pumice. Some of this froth is so light—because of the many gas bubbles—that it floats on water. In many eruptions the froth is shattered explosively into small fragments that are hurled high into the air in the form of volcanic cinders (red or black), volcanic ash (commonly tan or gray), and volcanic dust. ☐

Recent Volcanic Activity
(**Bold** indicates activity in 2001)

Volcano	Date of last eruption or activity	Volcano	Date of last eruption or activity
Adatara, Honshu, Japan	Sept. 7, 1997	**Maroa, New Zealand**	**March 30, 2001**
Akutan, Alaska	March 10, 1996	**Masaya, Nicaragua**	**April 23, 2001**
Amukta, Alaska	Sept. 17, 1996	**Mayon, Philippines**	**July 26, 2001**
Arenal, Costa Rica	**April 4, 2001**	McDonald Island, Australia	Dec. 1996
Axial Seamount	Jan. 25–28, 1998	**Merapi, Indonesia**	**March 21, 2001**
Bandai, Honshu, Japan	Aug. 16, 2000	Metis Shoal, Tonga	June 6, 1995
Barren Island, Indian Ocean	Dec. 20, 1994	Momotombo, Nicaragua	April 4, 1996
Bezymianny, Kamchatka, Russia	March 15, 2000	Monowai Seamount, Kermadec Islands	Dec. 5, 1997
Bromo, Java, Indonesia	Dec. 19, 2000		
Mount Cameroon, Cameroon	June 7, 2000	Montserrat, West Indies	Sept. 11–15, 2000
Canlaon, Philippines	**Jan. 2001**	Northern Gorda Ridge	Feb. 28, 1996
Cerro Negro, Nicaragua	Aug. 6, 1999	**Nyamuragira, Congo, Africa**	**Feb. 6, 2001**
Mt. Cleveland, Chuginadak, Alaska	**March 20, 2001**	Okmok, Alaska	May. 2, 1997
		Mount Oyama, Miyakejima, Japan	**May 24, 2001**
Colima, Mexico	**May 26, 2001**		
Copahue, Argentina & Chile	July 16, 2000	**Pacaya, Guatemala**	**Feb. 21, 2001**
Eastern Gemini Seamount, Vanuatu	Feb. 23, 1996	Papandayan, Java, Indonesia	July 1, 1998
		Pavlof, Alaska	June 3, 1997
Etna, Sicily, Italy	**July 13, 2001**	Peuet Sague, Indonesia	April 27, 1998
Fernandina, Galápagos	Jan. 25, 1995	Piparo, Trinidad	Feb. 22, 1997
Fogo, Cape Verde	April 2, 1995	**Piton de la Fournaise, Réunion, Indian Ocean**	**March 27, 2001**
Fuego, Guatemala	Dec. 9, 2000		
Grimsvotn Volcano, Iceland	Dec. 18–28, 1998	**Popocatepetl, Mexico**	**May 31, 2001**
Guagua Pichincha, Ecuador	July 12, 2000	Rabaul, Papua New Guinea	May 28, 1997
Hakkoda, Japan	July 12, 1997	Rincon de la Vieja, Costa Rica	Feb. 16, 1998
Hekla, Iceland	Feb. 26, 2000	**Rotorua, New Zealand**	**Jan. 26, 2001**
Mount Hili Aludo, Indonesia	May 13, 1997	Ruapehu, New Zealand	Sept. 13, 1999
Hosho, Kyushu, Japan	Oct. 12, 1995	Ruby Seamount, Mariana Islands	Oct. 25, 1995
Ijen, Java, Indonesia	**Feb. 5, 2001**	Sakura-Jima, Japan	Oct. 9, 2000
Iwate-san, Honshu, Japan	July 10, 1998	**San Cristobal, Nicaragua**	**May 10, 2001**
Jackson Segment, N. Gorda Ridge (nr. Oregon)	**April 3, 2001**	Semeru, Java, Indonesia	1967–continuing
		Sheveluch, Kamchatka, Russia	**July 2, 2001**
Kaba, Sumatra, Indonesia	Aug. 17, 2000	Shin-dake, Kuchinoerabujima Island, Japan	Aug. 26, 1999
Mount Karangetang, Indonesia	**Jan. 25, 2001**		
Karymsky, Kamchatka, Russia	Feb. 12, 2000	Shishaldin, Unimak Island, Alaska	May 15, 2000
Kavachi Seamount, Solomon Islands	May 14, 2000	Mount St. Helens, Washington	July 1, 1998
		South Sister, Oregon	**May 8, 2001**
Kelut, Java, Indonesia	**Jan. 29, 2001**	Stromboli, Italy	Aug. 23, 1998
Kilauea, Hawaii	**1983–continuing**	Tavurvur, Papua New Guinea	Sept. 6, 2000
Kliuchevskoi, Kamchatka, Russia	**March 4, 2001**	Taal, Philippines	Sept. 30, 1999
		Telica, Nicaragua	Aug. 11, 1999
Komagatake, Hokkaido, Japan	Nov. 8, 2000	Terceira, Azores	Jan. 8, 1999
Korovin, Alaska	June 30, 1998	Tonga (unnamed volcano)	Jan. 18, 1999
Krakatau, Indonesia	**March 27, 2001**	**Tungurahua, Ecuador**	**June 17, 2001**
Lascar, Chile	July 20, 2000	**Ulawun, New Britain, Papua New Guinea**	**April 30, 2001**
Mount Lewotobi, Indonesia	July 1, 1999		
Loihi Seamount, Hawaii	July 26, 1996	Usu, Japan	April 20, 2000
Lokon, Sulawesi, Indonesia	**May 20, 2001**	Villarica, Chile	Jan. 20–May 30, 2000
Long Valley caldera, California	April 2, 1996		
Lopevi, Central Islands, Vanuatu	**June 8, 2001**	**White Island, New Zealand**	**July 27, 2000–continuing**
Maderas, Nicaragua	Sept. 27, 1996	Yellowstone, Wyoming	Jan. 9, 1998
Manam, Papua New Guinea	May 28, 1997	Zacatecas, Mexico	June 1997

Source: Volcano World, University of North Dakota (http://volcano.und.nodak.edu).

The Deadliest Volcanic Eruptions

Volcano	Year	Deaths	Major cause of deaths
Tambora, Indonesia	1815	92,000	Starvation
Krakatau, Indonesia	1883	36,417	Tsunami
Mount Pelee, Martinique	1902	29,025	Ash flows
Ruiz, Colombia	1985	25,000	Mudflows
Unzen, Japan	1792	14,300	Volcano collapse, tsunami
Laki, Iceland	1783	9,350	Starvation
Kelut, Indonesia	1919	5,110	Mudflows
Galunggung, Indonesia	1882	4,011	Mudflows
Vesuvius, Italy	1631	3,500	Mudflows, lava flows
Vesuvius, Italy	79	3,360	Ash flows and falls
Papandayan, Indonesia	1772	2,957	Ash flows
Lamington, Papua New Guinea	1951	2,942	Ash flows
El Chichon, Mexico	1982	2,000	Ash flows
Soufriere, St. Vincent	1902	1,680	Ash flows
Oshima, Japan	1741	1,475	Tsunami
Asama, Japan	1783	1,377	Ash flows, mudflows
Taal, Philippines	1911	1,335	Ash flows
Mayon, Philippines	1814	1,200	Mudflows
Agung, Indonesia	1963	1,184	Ash flows
Cotopaxi, Ecuador	1877	1,000	Mudflows
Pinatubo, Philippines	1991	800	Disease
Komagatake, Japan	1640	700	Tsunami
Ruiz, Colombia	1845	700	Mudflows
Hibok-Hibok, Philippines	1951	500	Ash flows

NOTE: All eruptions with more than 500 known human fatalities. Based on data in *Volcanic Hazards: A Sourcebook on the Effects of Eruptions* by Russell J. Blong (Academic Press, 1984). *Source:* Volcano World, University of North Dakota (http://volcano.und.nodak.edu).

Principal Types of Volcanoes

Source: U.S. Dept. of the Interior, Geological Survey

Geologists generally group volcanoes into four main kinds—cinder cones, composite volcanoes, shield volcanoes, and lava domes.

Cinder Cones

Cinder cones are the simplest type of volcano. They are built from particles and blobs of congealed lava ejected from a single vent. As the gas-charged lava is blown violently into the air, it breaks into small fragments that solidify and fall as cinders around the vent to form a circular or oval cone. Most cinder cones have a bowl-shaped crater at the summit and rarely rise more than a thousand feet or so above their surroundings. Cinder cones are numerous in western North America as well as throughout other volcanic terrains of the world.

Composite Volcanoes

Composite volcanoes, sometimes called *stratovolcanoes,* are typically deep-sided, symmetrical cones of large dimension built of alternating layers of lava flows, volcanic ash, cinders, blocks, and bombs and may rise as much as 8,000 feet above their bases. Some of the most beautiful mountains in the world are composite volcanoes, including Mount Fuji in Japan, Mount Cotopaxi in Ecuador, Mount Shasta in California, Mount Hood in Oregon, and Mount St. Helens and Mount Rainier in Washington.

Most composite volcanoes have a crater at the summit that contains a central vent or a clustered group of vents. Lavas either flow through breaks in the crater wall or issue from fissures on the flanks of the cone. Lava, solidified within the fissures, forms *dikes* that act as ribs which greatly strengthen the cone.

The essential feature of a composite volcano is a conduit system through which magma from a reservoir deep in Earth's crust rises to the surface. The volcano is built up by the accumulation of material erupted through the conduit and increases in size as lava, cinders, and ash are added to its slopes.

Shield Volcanoes

Shield volcanoes are built almost entirely of fluid lava flows. Flow after flow pours out in all directions from a central summit vent, or group of vents, building a broad, gently sloping cone of flat, domical shape, with a profile much like that of a warrior's shield. They are built up slowly by the accretion of thousands of flows of highly fluid basaltic (from *basalt,* a hard, dense dark volcanic rock) lava that spread widely over great distances, and then cool as thin, gently dipping sheets. Lavas also commonly erupt from vents along fractures (rift zones) that develop on the flanks of the cone. Some of the largest volcanoes in the world are shield volcanoes. In northern California and Oregon, many shield volcanoes have diameters of 3 or 4 miles and heights of 1,500 to 2,000 feet. The Hawaiian Islands are composed of linear chains of these volcanoes, including Kilauea and Mauna Loa on the island of Hawaii.

In some shield volcano eruptions, basaltic lava pours out quietly from long fissures instead of central vents and floods the surrounding countryside, forming broad plateaus. Lava plateaus of this type can be seen in Iceland, southeastern Washington, eastern Oregon, and southern Idaho.

Lava Domes

Volcanic or lava domes are formed by relatively small, bulbous masses of lava too viscous to flow any great distance; consequently, on extrusion, the lava piles over and around its vent. A dome grows largely by expansion from within. As it grows, its outer surface cools and hardens, then shatters, spilling loose fragments down its sides. Some domes form craggy knobs or spines over the volcanic vent, whereas others form short, steep-sided lava flows known as *coulees*. Volcanic domes commonly occur within the craters or on the flanks of large composite volcanoes. The nearly circular Novarupta Dome that formed during the 1912 eruption of Katmai Volcano, Alaska, measures 800 feet across and 200 feet high. The internal structure of this dome—defined by layering of lava fanning upward and outward from the center—indicates that it grew largely by expansion from within. Mount Pelée in Martinique, West Indies, and Lassen Peak and Mono domes in California are examples of lava domes.

Submarine Volcanoes

Submarine volcanoes and volcanic vents are common features on certain zones of the ocean floor. Some are active at the present time and, in shallow water, disclose their presence by blasting steam and rock-debris high above the surface of the sea.

Many others lie at such great depths that the tremendous weight of the water above them results in high, confining pressure and prevents the formation and release of steam and gases. Even very large, deepwater eruptions may not disturb the ocean floor.

The famous black sand beaches of Hawaii were created virtually instantaneously by the violent interaction between hot lava and seawater.

Earthquakes

The Severity of an Earthquake

Source: National Earthquake Information Center, U.S. Geological Survey

Earthquakes are the result of forces deep within Earth's interior that continuously affect its surface. The energy from these forces is stored in a variety of ways within the rocks. When this energy is released suddenly—by shearing movements along faults in the crust of Earth, for example—an earthquake results. The area of the fault where the sudden rupture takes place is called the focus or hypocenter of the earthquake. The point on Earth's surface directly above the focus is called the epicenter of the earthquake.

The severity of an earthquake can be expressed in terms of both intensity and magnitude. The two terms are quite different, however, and they are often confused. Intensity is based on the observed effects of ground shaking on people, buildings, and natural features. It varies from place to place within the disturbed region depending on the location of the observer with respect to the earthquake epicenter. Magnitude is related to the amount of seismic energy released at the hypocenter of the earthquake. It is based on the amplitude of the earthquake waves recorded on instruments, which have a common calibration. Magnitude is thus represented by a single, instrumentally determined value.

The Richter Magnitude Scale

Seismic waves are the vibrations from earthquakes that travel through Earth; they are recorded on instruments called seismographs. Seismographs record a zigzag trace that shows the varying amplitude of ground oscillations beneath the instrument. Sensitive seismographs, which greatly magnify these ground motions, can detect strong earthquakes from sources anywhere in the world. The time, location, and magnitude of an earthquake can be determined from the data recorded by seismograph stations.

The Richter magnitude scale was developed in 1935 by Charles F. Richter of the California Institute of Technology as a mathematical device to compare the size of earthquakes. The magnitude of an earthquake is determined from the logarithm of the amplitude of waves recorded by seismographs. Adjustments are included in the magnitude formula to compensate for the variation in the distance between the various seismographs and the epicenter

of the earthquakes. On the Richter Scale, magnitude is expressed in whole numbers and decimal fractions. For example, a magnitude of 5.3 might be computed for a moderate earthquake, and a strong earthquake might be rated as magnitude 6.3. Because of the logarithmic basis of the scale, each whole number increase in magnitude represents a tenfold increase in measured amplitude; as an estimate of energy, each whole number step in the magnitude scale corresponds to the release of about 31 times more energy than the amount associated with the preceding whole number value. Although the Richter Scale has no upper limit, the largest known shocks have had magnitudes in the 8.8 to 8.9 range.

Why Are There So Many Earthquake Magnitude Scales?

Earthquake size, as measured by the Richter Scale, is a well-known, but not well understood, concept. What is even less well understood is the proliferation of magnitude scales and their relation to Richter's original magnitude scale. Richter's magnitude scale was first created for measuring the size of earthquakes occurring in southern California, using relatively high-frequency data from nearby seismograph stations. This magnitude scale was referred to as ML, with the L standing for local.

As more seismograph stations were installed around the world, it became apparent that the method developed by Richter was strictly valid only for certain frequency and distance ranges. In order to take advantage of the growing number of globally distributed seismograph stations, new magnitude scales that are an extension of Richter's original idea were developed. These include body-wave magnitude, "mb," and surface-wave magnitude, "MS." Each is valid for a particular frequency range and type of seismic signal. In its range of validity each is equivalent to the Richter magnitude.

Because of the limitations of all three magnitude scales—ML, mb, and MS—a new, more uniformly applicable extension of the magnitude scale, known as moment magnitude, or "MW," was developed. In particular, for very large earthquakes moment magnitude gives the most reliable estimate of earthquake size. New techniques that take advantage of modern telecommunications have recently been implemented, allowing reporting agencies to obtain rapid estimates of moment magnitude for significant earthquakes. So nowadays, when most seismologists announce a magnitude number, they are rarely referring to the Richter Scale.

The Modified Mercalli Intensity Scale

The effect of an earthquake on Earth's surface is called the intensity. The intensity scale consists of a series of certain key responses, such as people awakening, movement of furniture, damage to chimneys, and finally—total destruction. Although numerous intensity scales have been developed over the past several hundred years to evaluate the effects of earthquakes, the one currently used in the United

States is the Modified Mercalli (MM) Intensity Scale. It was developed in 1931 by the American seismologists Harry Wood and Frank Neumann. This scale, composed of 12 increasing levels of intensity that range from imperceptible shaking to catastrophic destruction, is designated by Roman numerals. It does not have a mathematical basis; instead it is an arbitrary ranking based on observed effects. The Modified Mercalli Intensity value assigned to a specific site after an earthquake has a more meaningful measure of severity to the nonscientist than the magnitude because intensity refers to the effects actually experienced at that place.

Frequency of Earthquakes Worldwide[1]

Descriptor	Magnitude	Annual average	Descriptor	Magnitude	Annual average
Great	8 or higher	1	Light	4–4.9	c. 6,200
Major	7–7.9	18	Minor	3–3.9	c. 49,000
Strong	6–6.9	120	Very minor	2–3	c. 1,000[2]
Moderate	5–5.9	800	Very minor	1–2	c. 8,000[2]

1. Since 1900. 2. Per day. *Source:* National Earthquake Information Center, U.S. Geological Survey.

Number of Earthquakes Worldwide, 1990–2001, and Mortality Figures

Magnitude	1990	1992	1993	1994	1995	1996	1997	1998	1999	2000	2001
8.0–9.9	0	0	1	2	3	1	0	2	0	4	1
7.0–7.9	12	23	15	13	22	21	20	14	23	14	6
6.0–6.9	115	104	141	161	185	160	125	113	123	157	45
5.0–5.9	1,635	1,541	1,449	1,542	1,327	1,223	1,118	979	1,106	1,318	382
4.0–4.9	4,493	5,196	5,034	4,544	8,140	8,794	7,938	7,303	7,042	8,114	2,127
3.0–3.9	2,457	4,643	4,263	5,000	5,002	4,869	4,467	5,945	5,521	4,741	1,624
2.0–2.9	2,364	3,068	5,390	5,369	3,838	2,388	2,397	4,091	4,201	3,728	1,319
1.0–1.9	474	887	1,177	779	645	295	388	805	715	1,028	225
0.1–0.9	0	2	9	17	19	1	4	10	5	6	0
No magnitude	5,062	4,084	3,997	1,944	1,826	2,186	3,415	2,426	2,096	3,199	749
Total	16,612	19,548	21,476	19,371	21,007	19,938	19,872	21,688	20,832	22,309[1]	6,478[1]
Estimated deaths	51,916	3,814	10,036	1,038	7,949	419	2,907	8,928	22,711	231	14,923

1. As of May 5, 2001. *Source:* National Earthquake Information Center, U.S. Geological Survey.

Major Earthquakes around the World, 2001

Date	Location	Magnitude[1]	Date	Location	Magnitude[1]
Jan. 1	Mindanao, Philippines	7.5	Feb. 13	Southern Sumatera, Indonesia	7.4
Jan. 9	Vanuatu Islands	7.0	Feb. 24	Northern Molucca Sea	7.1
Jan. 10	Kodiak Island region, Alaska, U.S.A.	7.1	June 3	Kermadec Islands, New Zealand	7.2
			June 23	Near coast of Peru	8.4
Jan. 13	Off coast of Central America	7.7	July 7	Near coast of Peru	7.6
Jan. 26	Gujarat, India	7.7	Aug. 21	East of North Island, N.Z.	7.0

NOTE: A major earthquake is defined here as having a magnitude of 7.0 or more. 1. Unless otherwise indicated, magnitudes listed are moment magnitudes, the newest, most uniformly applicable magnitude scale. *Source:* National Earthquake Information Center, U.S. Geological Survey.

Estimated Deaths from Earthquakes in 2001

Date	Region	Magnitude	Number killed[1]	Date	Region	Magnitude	Number killed[1]
Jan. 13	El Salvador	7.7	852	June 1	Hindu Kush Region, Afghanistan	5.0	4
Jan. 26	Gujarat, India	7.7	20,103				
Feb. 13	El Salvador	6.6	315	June 21	Germany	4.2	1
Feb. 17	El Salvador	4.1	1	June 23	Near coast of Peru	8.4	139
Feb. 23	Sichuan, China	5.6	3	July 7	Near coast of Peru	7.6	1
March 24	W. Honshu, Japan	6.8	2	July 7	Northern Italy	4.7	4
April 19	Yunnan, China	5.6	2	July 24	Northern Chile	6.3	1
May 8	El Salvador	5.4	1	Aug. 9	Central Peru	5.5	19
May 23	Sichuan, China	5.3	2	**Total**			**21,450**

NOTE: Through June 1, 2001. 1. Includes "missing and presumed dead." *Source:* National Earthquake Information Center, U.S. Geological Survey.

The Ten Largest[1] Earthquakes of the 20th Century

Location	Date	Magnitude[2]	Location	Date	Magnitude[2]
1. Chile	May 22, 1960	9.5	6. Rat Islands, Aleutian Islands	Feb. 4, 1965	8.7
2. Prince William Sound, Alaska	March 28, 1964	9.2	7. India-China border	Aug. 15, 1950	8.6
3. Andreanof Islands, Aleutian Islands	March 9, 1957	9.1	8. Kamchatka	Feb. 3, 1923	8.5
4. Kamchatka	Nov. 4, 1952	9.0	9. Banda Sea, Indonesia	Feb. 1, 1938	8.5
5. Off the coast of Ecuador	Jan. 31, 1906	8.8	10. Kuril Islands	Oct. 13, 1963	8.5

1. In terms of magnitude. 2. Moment magnitude. *Source:* National Earthquake Information Center, U.S. Geological Survey.

Deadliest Earthquakes on Record

(50,000 deaths or more)

Date	Location	Deaths	Magnitude	Date	Location	Deaths	Magnitude
Jan. 23, 1556	Shansi, China	830,000	n.a.	Sept. 1290	Chihli, China	100,000	n.a.
July 27, 1976	Tangshan China	255,000[1]	8.0	Nov. 1667	Shemakha, Caucasia	80,000	n.a.
Aug. 9, 1138	Aleppo, Syria	230,000	n.a.	Nov. 18, 1727	Tabriz, Iran	77,000	n.a.
May 22, 1927	near Xining, China	200,000	8.3	Nov. 1, 1755	Lisbon, Portugal	70,000	8.7
Dec. 22, 856[2]	Damghan, Iran	200,000	n.a.	Dec. 25, 1932	Gansu, China	70,000	7.6
Dec. 16, 1920	Gansu, China	200,000	8.6	May 31, 1970	Peru	66,000	7.8
March 23, 893[2]	Ardabil, Iran	150,000	n.a.	1268[4]	Silicia, Asia Minor	60,000	n.a.
Sept. 1, 1923	Kwanto, Japan	143,000	8.3	Jan. 11, 1693	Sicily, Italy	60,000	n.a.
Oct. 5, 1948	Ashgabat, Turkmenistan, USSR	110,000	7.3	May 30, 1935	Quetta, Pakistan	30,000–60,000	7.5
Dec. 28, 1908	Messina, Italy	70,000–100,000[3]	7.5	Feb. 4, 1783	Calabria, Italy	50,000	n.a.
				June 20, 1990	Iran	50,000	7.7

1. Official. Estimated death toll as high as 655,000. 2. Note that these dates are prior to A.D. 1000. No digit is missing. 3. Estimated. 4. No date available. *Source:* National Earthquake Information Center, U.S. Geological Survey. Data compiled from several sources.

The World's 14 Highest Mountain Peaks (above 8,000 meters)

All 14 of the world's 8,000-meter peaks are located in the Himalaya or the Karakoram ranges in Asia. Thus far, only six climbers have reached the summits of all 14: Reinhold Messner (Italy) was first, followed by Jerzy Kukuczka (Poland), Ehardt Loretan. (Switzerland), Carlos Carsolio (Mexico), Krzysztof Wielicki (Poland), Juan Oiarzabal (Spain). and Sergio Martini (Italy).

Mountain	Height Meters	Feet	First to summit	Date	Nationality
1. Everest[1]	8,850	29,035	Edmund Hillary, Tenzing Norgay	May 29, 1953	New Zealander (U.K.) and Nepalese
2. K2 (Godwin Austen)	8,611	28,250	A. Compagnoni, L. Lacedelli	July 31, 1954	Italian
3. Kangchenjunga	8,586	28,169	G. Band, J. Brown, N. Hardie, S. Streather	May 25, 1955	U.K.
4. Lhotse	8,516	27,940	F. Luchsinger, E. Reiss	May 18, 1956	Swiss
5. Makalu	8,463	27,766	J. Couzy, L. Terray, J. Franco, G. Magnone-Gialtsen, J. Bouier, S. Coupé, P. Leroux, A. Vialatte	May 15, 1955	French
6. Cho Oyu	8,201	26,906	H. Tichy, S. Jöchler, Pasang Dawa Lama	Oct. 19, 1954	Austrian
7. Dhaulagiri	8,167	26,795	A. Schelbert, E. Forrer, K. Diemberger, P. Diener, Nyima Dorji, Nawang Dorji	May 13, 1960	Swiss and Nepalese
8. Manaslu	8,163	26,781	T. Iminaschi, G. Norbu, K. Kato, M. Higeta	May 9, 1956	Japanese and Nepalese
9. Nanga Parbat	8,125	26,660	Hermann Buhl	July 3, 1953	Austrian
10. Annapurna	8,091	26,545	M. Herzog, L. Lachenal	June 3, 1950	French
11. Gasherbrum I	8,068	26,470	P. K. Schoeing, A. J. Kauffman	July 4, 1958	U.S.
12. Broad Peak	8,047	26,400	M. Schmuck, F. Wintersteller, K. Diemberger, H. Buhl	June 9, 1957	Austrian
13. Gasherbrum II	8,035	26,360	F. Moravec, S. Larch, H. Willenpart	July 7, 1956	Austrian
14. Shisha Pangma	8,013	26,289	Hsu Ching and team of 9	May 2, 1964	Chinese

1. The 1955 elevation of Everest, 29,028 ft. (8,848 m), was revised on Nov. 11, 1999, and now stands at 29,035 ft. (8,850 m).

Highest Mountain Peaks of the World (continued from p. 492)

(*See* p. 502 for U.S. peaks.)

Mountain peak	Range	Location	Height ft.	m
Annapurna II	Himalayas	Nepal	26,041	7,937
Gyachung Kang	Himalayas	Nepal	25,910	7,897
Disteghil Sar	Karakoram	Pakistan	25,858	7,882
Himalchuli	Himalayas	Nepal	25,801	7,864
Nuptse	Himalayas	Nepal	25,726	7,841
Nanda Devi	Himalayas	India	25,663	7,824
Masherbrum	Karakoram	Kashmir[1]	25,660	7,821
Rakaposhi	Karakoram	Pakistan	25,551	7,788
Kanjut Sar	Karakoram	Pakistan	25,461	7,761
Kamet	Himalayas	India/Tibet	25,446	7,756
Namcha Barwa	Himalayas	Tibet	25,445	7,756
Gurla Mandhata	Himalayas	Tibet	25,355	7,728
Ulugh Muztagh	Kunlun	Tibet	25,340	7,723
Kungur	Muztagh Ata	China	25,325	7,719
Tirich Mir	Hindu Kush	Pakistan	25,230	7,690
Saser Kangri	Karakoram	India	25,172	7,672
Makalu II	Himalayas	Nepal	25,120	7,657
Minya Konka (Gongga Shan)	Daxue Shan	China	24,900	7,590
Kula Kangri	Himalayas	Bhutan	24,783	7,554
Chang-tzu	Himalayas	Tibet	24,780	7,553
Muztagh Ata	Muztagh Ata	China	24,757	7,546
Skyang Kangri	Himalayas	Kashmir	24,750	7,544
Ismail Samani Peak (formerly Communism Peak)	Pamirs	Tajikistan	24,590	7,495
Jongsong Peak	Himalayas	Nepal	24,472	7,459
Pobeda Peak	Tien Shan	Kyrgyzstan	24,406	7,439
Sia Kangri	Himalayas	Kashmir	24,350	7,422
Haramosh Peak	Karakoram	Pakistan	24,270	7,397
Istoro Nal	Hindu Kush	Pakistan	24,240	7,388
Tent Peak	Himalayas	Nepal	24,165	7,365
Chomo Lhari	Himalayas	Tibet/Bhutan	24,040	7,327
Chamlang	Himalayas	Nepal	24,012	7,319
Kabru	Himalayas	Nepal	24,002	7,316
Alung Gangri	Himalayas	Tibet	24,000	7,315
Baltoro Kangri	Himalayas	Kashmir	23,990	7,312
Muztagh Ata (K-5)	Kunlun	China	23,890	7,282
Mana	Himalayas	India	23,860	7,273
Baruntse	Himalayas	Nepal	23,688	7,220
Nepal Peak	Himalayas	Nepal	23,500	7,163
Amne Machin	Kunlun	China	23,490	7,160
Gauri Sankar	Himalayas	Nepal/Tibet	23,440	7,145
Badrinath	Himalayas	India	23,420	7,138
Nunkun	Himalayas	Kashmir	23,410	7,135
Lenin Peak	Pamirs	Tajikistan/Kyrgyzstan	23,405	7,134
Pyramid	Himalayas	Nepal	23,400	7,132
Api	Himalayas	Nepal	23,399	7,132
Pauhunri	Himalayas	India/China	23,385	7,128
Trisul	Himalayas	India	23,360	7,120
Korzhenevski Peak	Pamirs	Tajikistan	23,310	7,105
Kangto	Himalayas	Tibet	23,260	7,090
Nyainqentanglha	Nyainqentanglha Shan	China	23,255	7,088
Trisuli	Himalayas	India	23,210	7,074
Dunagiri	Himalayas	India	23,184	7,066
Revolution Peak	Pamirs	Tajikistan	22,880	6,974
Aconcagua	Andes	Argentina	22,834	6,960
Ojos del Salado	Andes	Argentina/Chile	22,664	6,908
Bonete	Andes	Argentina/Chile	22,546	6,872
Ama Dablam	Himalayas	Nepal	22,494	6,856
Tupungato	Andes	Argentina/Chile	22,310	6,800
Moscow Peak	Pamirs	Tajikistan	22,260	6,785
Pissis	Andes	Argentina	22,241	6,779
Mercedario	Andes	Argentina/Chile	22,211	6,770
Huascarán	Andes	Peru	22,205	6,768
Llullaillaco	Andes	Argentina/Chile	22,057	6,723
El Libertador	Andes	Argentina	22,047	6,720
Cachi	Andes	Argentina	22,047	6,720
Kailas	Himalayas	Tibet	22,027	6,714
Incahuasi	Andes	Argentina/Chile	21,720	6,620
Yerupaja	Andes	Peru	21,709	6,617
Kurumda	Pamirs	Tajikistan	21,686	6,610
Galan	Andes	Argentina	21,654	6,600
El Muerto	Andes	Argentina/Chile	21,463	6,542
Sajama	Andes	Bolivia	21,391	6,520
Nacimiento	Andes	Argentina	21,302	6,493
Illampu	Andes	Bolivia	21,276	6,485
Illimani	Andes	Bolivia	21,201	6,462
Coropuna	Andes	Peru	21,083	6,426
Laudo	Andes	Argentina	20,997	6,400
Ancohuma	Andes	Bolivia	20,958	6,388
Cuzco (Ausangate)	Andes	Peru	20,945	6,384

1. Kashmir is divided between India, Pakistan, and China, and the three countries dispute the boundaries. *Source:* National Geographic Society.

Climbing the Seven Summits

Fewer than fifty mountaineers have climbed all "Seven Summits"—the highest peak on each of the seven continents. The first was Dick Bass, an American businessman, on April 30, 1985. The seven summits are Mt. Everest (Asia) 29,035 ft., Mt. Aconcagua (South America) 22,834 ft., Mt. McKinley (North America) 20,320 ft., Mt. Kilimanjaro (Africa) 19,340 ft., Mt. Elbrus (Europe) 18,510 ft., Vinson Massif (Antarctica) 16,066 ft., and Kosciusko (Australia) 7,310 ft.

Oceans and Seas

Name	Area		Average depth		Greatest known depth		Place of greatest known depth
	sq. mi.	sq. km	ft.	m	ft.	m	
Pacific Ocean	64,000,000	165,760,000	13,215	4,028	36,198	11,033	Mariana Trench
Atlantic Ocean	31,815,000	82,400,000	12,880	3,926	30,246	9,219	Puerto Rico Trench
Indian Ocean	25,300,000	65,526,700	13,002	3,963	24,460	7,455	Sunda Trench
Arctic Ocean	5,440,200	14,090,000	3,953	1,205	18,456	5,625	77°45′N; 175°W
Mediterranean Sea[1]	1,145,100	2,965,800	4,688	1,429	15,197	4,632	Off Cape Matapan, Greece
Caribbean Sea	1,049,500	2,718,200	8,685	2,647	22,788	6,946	Off Cayman Islands
South China Sea	895,400	2,319,000	5,419	1,652	16,456	5,016	West of Luzon
Bering Sea	884,900	2,291,900	5,075	1,547	15,659	4,773	Off Buldir Island
Gulf of Mexico	615,000	1,592,800	4,874	1,486	12,425	3,787	Sigsbee Deep
Okhotsk Sea	613,800	1,589,700	2,749	838	12,001	3,658	146°10′E; 46°50′N
East China Sea	482,300	1,249,200	617	188	9,126	2,782	25°16′N; 125°E
Hudson Bay	475,800	1,232,300	420	128	600	183	Near entrance
Japan Sea	389,100	1,007,800	4,429	1,350	12,276	3,742	Central Basin
Andaman Sea	308,100	797,700	2,854	870	12,392	3,777	Off Car Nicobar Island
North Sea	222,100	575,200	308	94	2,165	660	Skagerrak
Red Sea	169,100	438,000	1,611	491	7,254	2,211	Off Port Sudan
Baltic Sea	163,000	422,200	180	55	1,380	421	Off Gotland

1. Includes Black Sea and Sea of Azov. NOTE: For Caspian Sea, *see* Large Lakes of the World.

Large Lakes of the World

(area more than 1,600 sq. miles)

Name and location	Area		Length		Maximum depth	
	sq. mi.	km	mi.	km	ft.	m
Caspian Sea, Azerbaijan-Russia- Kazakhstan-Turkmenistan-Iran[1]	152,239	394,299	745	1,199	3,104	946
Superior, U.S.-Canada	31,820	82,414	383	616	1,333	406
Victoria, Tanzania-Uganda	26,828	69,485	200	322	270	82
Huron, U.S.-Canada	23,010	59,596	247	397	750	229
Michigan, U.S.	22,400	58,016	321	517	923	281
Aral, Kazakhstan-Uzbekistan	13,000	33,800	266	428	223	68
Tanganyika, Tanzania-Congo	12,700	32,893	420	676	4,708	1,435
Baikal, Russia	12,162	31,500	395	636	5,712	1,741
Great Bear, Canada	12,000	31,080	232	373	270	82
Nyasa, Malawi-Mozambique-Tanzania	11,600	30,044	360	579	2,316	706
Great Slave, Canada	11,170	28,930	298	480	2,015	614
Chad,[2] Chad-Niger-Nigeria	9,946	25,760	—	—	23	7
Erie, U.S.-Canada	9,930	25,719	241	388	210	64
Winnipeg, Canada	9,094	23,553	264	425	204	62
Ontario, U.S.-Canada	7,520	19,477	193	311	778	237
Balkhash, Kazakhstan	7,115	18,428	376	605	87	27
Ladoga, Russia	7,000	18,130	124	200	738	225
Onega, Russia	3,819	9,891	154	248	361	110
Titicaca, Bolivia-Peru	3,141	8,135	110	177	1,214	370
Nicaragua, Nicaragua	3,089	8,001	110	177	230	70
Athabaska, Canada	3,058	7,920	208	335	407	124
Rudolf, Kenya	2,473	6,405	154	248	—	—
Reindeer, Canada	2,444	6,330	152	245	—	—
Eyre, South Australia	2,400[3]	6,216	130	209	varies	varies
Issyk-Kul, Kyrgyzstan	2,394	6,200	113	182	2,297	700
Urmia,[2] Iran	2,317	6,001	81	130	49	15
Torrens, South Australia	2,200	5,698	130	209	—	—
Vänern, Sweden	2,141	5,545	87	140	322	98
Winnipegosis, Canada	2,086	5,403	152	245	59	18
Mobutu Sese Seko, Uganda	2,046	5,299	100	161	180	55
Nettilling, Baffin Island, Canada	1,950	5,051	70	113	—	—
Nipigon, Canada	1,870	4,843	72	116	—	—
Manitoba, Canada	1,817	4,706	140	225	22	7
Great Salt, U.S.	1,800	4,662	75	121	15–25	5–8
Kioga, Uganda	1,700	4,403	50	80	about 30	9
Koko-Nor, China	1,630	4,222	66	106		

1. The Caspian Sea is called "sea" because the Romans, finding it salty, named it *Mare Caspium*. Many geographers, however, consider it a lake because it is land-locked. 2. Figures represent high-water data. 3. Varies with the rainfall of the wet season. It has been reported to dry up almost completely on occasion.

Principal Rivers of the World

(See pp. 500–501 for other U.S. rivers.)

River	Source	Outflow	Approx. length mi.	km
Nile	Tributaries of Lake Victoria, Africa	Mediterranean Sea	4,180	6,690
Amazon	Glacier-fed lakes, Peru	Atlantic Ocean	3,912	6,296
Mississippi-Missouri-Red Rock	Source of Red Rock, Montana	Gulf of Mexico	3,710	5,970
Chang Jiang (Yangtze)	Tibetan plateau, China	China Sea	3,602	5,797
Ob	Altai Mts., Russia	Gulf of Ob	3,459	5,567
Huang Ho (Yellow)	Eastern part of Kunlan Mts., West China	Gulf of Chihli	2,900	4,667
Yenisei	Tannu-Ola Mts., western Tuva, Russia	Arctic Ocean	2,800	4,506
Paraná	Confluence of Paranaiba and Grande rivers	Río de la Plata	2,795	4,498
Irtish	Altai Mts., Russia	Ob River	2,758	4,438
Zaire (Congo)	Confluence of Lualab and Luapula rivers, Congo	Atlantic Ocean	2,716	4,371
Heilong (Amur)	Confluence of Shilka (Russia) and Argun (Manchuria) rivers	Tatar Strait	2,704	4,352
Lena	Baikal Mts., Russia	Arctic Ocean	2,652	4,268
Mackenzie	Head of Finlay River, British Columbia, Canada	Beaufort Sea (Arctic Ocean)	2,635	4,241
Niger	Guinea	Gulf of Guinea	2,600	4,184
Mekong	Tibetan highlands	South China Sea	2,500	4,023
Mississippi	Lake Itasca, Minnesota	Gulf of Mexico	2,348	3,779
Missouri	Confluence of Jefferson, Gallatin, and Madison rivers, Montana	Mississippi River	2,315	3,726
Volga	Valdai plateau, Russia	Caspian Sea	2,291	3,687
Madeira	Confluence of Beni and Maumoré rivers, Bolivia–Brazil boundary	Amazon River	2,012	3,238
Purus	Peruvian Andes	Amazon River	1,993	3,207
São Francisco	Southwest Minas Gerais, Brazil	Atlantic Ocean	1,987	3,198
Yukon	Junction of Lewes and Pelly rivers, Yukon Territory, Canada	Bering Sea	1,979	3,185
St. Lawrence	Lake Ontario	Gulf of St. Lawrence	1,900	3,058
Rio Grande	San Juan Mts., Colorado	Gulf of Mexico	1,885	3,034
Brahmaputra	Himalayas	Ganges River	1,800	2,897
Indus	Himalayas	Arabian Sea	1,800	2,897
Danube	Black Forest, Germany	Black Sea	1,766	2,842
Euphrates	Confluence of Murat Nehri and Kara Su rivers, Turkey	Shatt-al-Arab	1,739	2,799
Darling	Central part of Eastern Highlands, Australia	Murray River	1,702	2,739
Zambezi	11°21′S, 24°22′E, Zambia	Mozambique Channel	1,700	2,736
Tocantins	Goiás, Brazil	Pará River	1,677	2,699
Murray	Australian Alps, New South Wales	Indian Ocean	1,609	2,589
Nelson	Head of Bow River, western Alberta, Canada	Hudson Bay	1,600	2,575
Paraguay	Mato Grosso, Brazil	Paraná River	1,584	2,549
Ural	Southern Ural Mts., Russia	Caspian Sea	1,574	2,533
Ganges	Himalayas	Bay of Bengal	1,557	2,506
Amu Darya (Oxus)	Nicholas Range, Pamir Mts., Turkmenistan	Aral Sea	1,500	2,414
Japurá	Andes, Colombia	Amazon River	1,500	2,414
Salween	Tibet, south of Kunlun Mts.	Gulf of Martaban	1,500	2,414
Arkansas	Central Colorado	Mississippi River	1,459	2,348
Colorado	Grand County, Colorado	Gulf of California	1,450	2,333
Dnieper	Valdai Hills, Russia	Black Sea	1,419	2,284
Ohio-Allegheny	Potter County, Pennsylvania	Mississippi River	1,306	2,102
Irrawaddy	Confluence of Nmai and Mali rivers, northeast Burma	Bay of Bengal	1,300	2,092
Orange	Lesotho	Atlantic Ocean	1,300	2,092
Orinoco	Serra Parima Mts., Venezuela	Atlantic Ocean	1,281	2,062
Pilcomayo	Andes Mts., Bolivia	Paraguay River	1,242	1,999
Xi Jiang (Si Kiang)	Eastern Yunnan Province, China	China Sea	1,236	1,989
Columbia	Columbia Lake, British Columbia, Canada	Pacific Ocean	1,232	1,983
Don	Tula, Russia	Sea of Azov	1,223	1,968
Sungari	China–North Korea boundary	Amur River	1,215	1,955
Saskatchewan	Canadian Rocky Mts.	Lake Winnipeg	1,205	1,939
Peace	Stikine Mts., British Columbia, Canada	Great Slave River	1,195	1,923
Tigris	Taurus Mts., Turkey	Shatt-al-Arab	1,180	1,899

Large Islands of the World

Island	Location and political affiliation	Area sq. mi.	Area sq. km
Greenland	North Atlantic (Danish)	839,999	2,175,597
New Guinea	Southwest Pacific (West Papua [Irian Jaya], Indonesia, western part; Papua New Guinea, eastern part)	316,615	820,033
Borneo	West mid-Pacific (Indonesian, south part; Brunei and Malaysian, north part)	286,914	743,107
Madagascar	Indian Ocean (Malagasy Republic)	226,657	587,042
Baffin	North Atlantic (Canadian)	183,810	476,068
Sumatra	Northeast Indian Ocean (Indonesian)	182,859	473,605
Honshu	Sea of Japan–Pacific (Japanese)	88,925	230,316
Great Britain	Off coast of NW Europe (England, Scotland, and Wales)	88,758	229,883
Ellesmere	Arctic Ocean (Canadian)	82,119	212,688
Victoria	Arctic Ocean (Canadian)	81,930	212,199
Sulawesi (Celebes)	West mid-Pacific (Indonesian)	72,986	189,034
South Island	South Pacific (New Zealand)	58,093	150,461
Java	Indian Ocean (Indonesian)	48,990	126,884
North Island	South Pacific (New Zealand)	44,281	114,688
Cuba	Caribbean Sea (republic)	44,218	114,525
Newfoundland	North Atlantic (Canadian)	42,734	110,681
Luzon	West mid-Pacific (Philippines)	40,420	104,688
Iceland	North Atlantic (republic)	39,768	102,999
Mindanao	West mid-Pacific (Philippines)	36,537	94,631
Ireland	West of Great Britain (republic, south part; United Kingdom, north part)	32,597	84,426
Hokkaido	Sea of Japan–Pacific (Japanese)	30,372	78,663
Hispaniola	Caribbean Sea (Dominican Republic, east part; Haiti, west part)	29,355	76,029
Tasmania	South of Australia (Australian)	26,215	67,897
Sri Lanka (Ceylon)	Indian Ocean (republic)	25,332	65,610
Sakhalin (Karafuto)	North of Japan (Russian)	24,560	63,610
Banks	Arctic Ocean (Canadian)	23,230	60,166
Devon	Arctic Ocean (Canadian)	20,861	54,030

NOTE: Australia is not included in this list because it is defined as a continent rather than an island.

Highest Waterfalls of the World

Name(s) (foreign)	Location	Height Feet	Height Meters
Angel (Salto Angel)	Canaima Nat'l Park, Venezuela	3,212	979
Tugela	Natal Nat'l Park, South Africa	2,800	850
Utigord (Utigordsfoss)	Norway	2,625	800
Monge (Mongefoss)	Marstein, Norway	2,540	774
Mutarazi (Mtarazi)	Nyanga Nat'l Park, Zimbabwe	2,499	762
Yosemite	Yosemite Nat'l Park, California, U.S.	2,425	739
Espelands (Espelandsfoss)	Hardanger Fjord, Norway	2,307	703[1]
Lower Mar Valley (Østra Mardolafoss)	Eikesdal, Norway	2,151	655[2]
Tyssestrengene	Odda, Norway	2,123	647[2]
Cuquenan (Salto Kukenan)	Kukenan Tepuy, Venezuela	2,000	610
Sutherland	Milford Sound, New Zealand	1,904	580
Kjell (Kjellfossen)	Gudvanger, Norway	1,841	561
Takkakaw	Yoho Nat'l Park, B.C., Canada	1,650	503
Ribbon	Yosemite Nat'l Park, California, U.S.	1,612	491
Upper Mar Valley (Mardalsfossen)	nr. Eikesdal, Norway	1,536	468
Gavarnie	nr. Lourdes, France	1,388	423
Vettis (Vettisfoss)	Jotunheimen, Norway	1,215	370
Hunlen	British Columbia, Canada	1,198	365
Tin Mine	Kosciusko Nat'l Park, Australia	1,182	360[1]
Silver Strand (Widows' Tears)	Yosemite Nat'l Park, California, U.S.	1,170	357
Basaseachic (Salto Basaseachic)	Barance del Cobre, Mexico	1,120	311
Spray Stream (Staubbachfalle)	Lauterburnnental, Switzerland	985	300
Fachoda (Cascade de Fachoda)	Tahiti, Fr. Polynesia	985	300[1]
King Edward VIII	Guyana	850	259
Wallaman	nr. Ingham, Australia	844	257[3]
Gersoppa (Jog)	Western Ghats, India	829	253
Kaieteur	Guyana	822	251
Montezuma	nr. Rosebery, Tasmania, Australia	800	240[1]
Wollomombi	nr. Armidale, Australia	722	220[3]

1. Unofficial (estimated) height. Subject to revision. 2. Incorporated in hydroelectric scheme. Greatly diminished flow. 3. Official heights established in April 2000. *Source:* Fifth Continent Australia Pty Limited.

Polar Regions

Antarctica

The second smallest continent, mostly south of the Antarctic Circle.

Area: 14.2 million sq. km (5.5 million sq. mi.).

Geographic South Pole: Earth's southernmost point, at latitude 90°S, where all lines of longitude meet.

Magnetic South Pole: The magnetic South Pole shifts about 5 miles (km) a year and is now located at about 66°S and 139°E on the Adélie Coast of Antarctica.

Terrain: About 98% thick ice sheet and 2% barren rock; glaciers form ice shelves along about half of the coastline, and floating ice shelves constitute 11% of the area of the continent. **Ice sheet:** The continental ice sheet contains approximately 7 million cubic miles (30 million cu km) of ice, representing about 90% of the world's total. **Major ice shelves:** Amery, Filchner, Larsen, Ronne, Ross. Ice shelves make up about 10% of Antarctica's ice, and are floating sheets of ice attached to land that project out into coastal waters.

Climate: The coldest, windiest, driest continent.

Regions: East Antarctica (c. 3,000,000 sq. mi./ 7,770,000 sq. km), the largest portion of the continent, is a high, ice-covered plateau. West Antarctica (c. 2,500,000 sq. mi./6,475,000 sq. km), is an archipelago of mountainous islands connected by ice. A mountain range divides them.

Elevation extremes: *Lowest point:* Bentley Subglacial Trench –8,327 ft. below sea level (–2,538 m). *Highest point:* Vinson Massif 16,066 ft. (4,897 m), Ellsworth Mountains.

The Arctic

Region, primarily made up of the frozen Arctic Ocean, that surrounds the North Pole. Land masses include islands and the northern parts of the European, Asian, and North American continents.

Area: 14.056 million sq. km (5.4 million sq. mi.), largely frozen ocean.

Geographic North Pole: Northern end of Earth's axis, located at about latitude 90°N.

Magnetic North Pole: Continues to shift and is located at about 78°N and 104°W in the Queen Elizabeth Islands of northern Canada.

Terrain: Central surface covered by a perennial drifting polar icepack that averages about 3 meters in thickness; the icepack is surrounded by open seas during the summer, but more than doubles in size during the winter and extends to the encircling landmasses.

Climate: Polar climate characterized by persistent cold and relatively narrow annual temperature ranges; winters characterized by continuous darkness, cold and stable weather conditions, and clear skies; summers characterized by continuous daylight, damp and foggy weather, and weak cyclones with rain or snow.

Regions: The Arctic is divided by the summer isotherm, a climatic boundary between regions with summer temperatures averaging 50°F (or 10°C)—the subarctic—and colder regions (the true Arctic).

Elevation extremes: *Lowest point:* Fram Basin –4,665 m. *Highest point:* sea level 0 m.

Interesting Caves and Caverns of the World

Aggtelek. In village of same name, northern Hungary. Large stalactitic cavern about 5 mi. long.

Altamira Cave. Near Santander, Spain. Contains Stone Age animal paintings on roof and walls.

Antiparos. On island of same name in the Grecian Archipelago. Some stalactites are 20 ft. long. Brilliant colors and fantastic shapes.

Blue Grotto. On island of Capri, Italy. Sea cavern hollowed out in limestone by constant wave action. Now half filled with water because of sinking coast. Name derived from unusual blue light permeating the cave. Source of light is a submerged opening allowing light to pass through the water.

Carlsbad Caverns. Southeast New Mexico. Contains some of the largest and most impressive stalactites and stalagmites, particularly in the Lechuguilla Cave.

Fingal's Cave. On island of Staffa off coast of western Scotland. Penetrates about 200 ft. inland. Contains basaltic columns almost 40 ft. high.

Jenolan Caves. In Blue Mountain plateau, New South Wales, Australia. Beautiful stalactitic formations.

Kent's Cavern. Near Torquay, England. Source of much information on Paleolithic humans.

Lascaux Cave. Southwestern France. Features prehistoric cave paintings estimated to be tens of thousands of years old. Closed to the public.

Lubang Nasib Bagus. Sarawak, Malaysia. World's largest cave chamber: 2,300 ft. long, 1,480 ft. wide, and everywhere at least 230 ft. high.

Luray Caverns. Near Luray, Va. Has large stalactitic and stalagmitic columns of many colors.

Mogao Caves. Located along the old Silk Route in China, Mogao is composed of 492 cells and cave sanctuaries that are famous for their statues and wall paintings, spanning a thousand years of Buddhist art.

Mammoth Cave. This limestone cavern in central Kentucky is the longest cave system in the world. Cave area is about 10 mi. in diameter but has 345 mi. of irregular subterranean passageways at various levels, plus underground lakes and rivers.

Peak Cavern or Devil's Hole. Derbyshire, England. About 2,250 ft. into a mountain. Lowest part is about 600 ft. below the surface.

Postojna Grotto. Postojna, Slovenia. Largest cavern in Europe; numerous beautiful stalactites. Famous example of a karst cave—grooved and irregularly eroded limestone formations carved out by underground streams. Pivka River flows through part of it.

Singing Cave. Iceland. A lava cave; name derived from echoes of people singing in it.

Waitomo Cave. North Island, New Zealand. Glowworms on cave ceiling look like thousands of stars in the night sky.

Wind Cave. In Black Hills of South Dakota. Limestone caverns with stalactites and stalagmites almost entirely missing. Variety of crystal formations called "boxwork."

Wyandotte Cave. In Crawford County, southern Indiana. A limestone cavern with five levels of passages; one of the largest in North America. "Monumental Mountain," approximately 135 ft. high, is believed to be one of the world's largest underground "mountains."

Principal Deserts of the World

Deserts are arid regions, generally receiving less than ten inches of precipitation a year, or regions where the potential evaporation rate is twice as great as the precipitation.

The world's deserts are divided into four categories. **Subtropical deserts** are the hottest, with parched terrain and rapid evaporation. Although **cool coastal deserts** are located within the same latitudes as subtropical deserts, the average temperature is much cooler because of frigid offshore ocean currents. **Cold winter deserts** are marked by stark temperature differences from season to season, ranging from 100° F (38° C) in the summer to 10° F (−12° C) in the winter. **Polar regions** are also considered to be deserts because nearly all moisture in these areas is locked up in the form of ice.

Desert	Location	Size	Topography
SUBTROPICAL DESERTS			
Sahara	Morocco, Western Sahara, Algeria, Tunisia, Libya, Egypt, Mauritania, Mali, Niger, Chad, Ethiopia, Eritrea, Somalia	3.5 million sq. mi.	70% gravel plains, sand, and dunes. Contrary to popular belief, the desert is only 30% sand. The world's largest nonpolar desert gets its name from the Arabic word *Sahra'*, meaning desert
Arabian	Saudi Arabia, Kuwait, Qatar, United Arab Emirates, Oman, Yemen	1 million sq. mi.	Gravel plains, rocky highlands; one-fourth is the Rub al-Khali ("Empty Quarter"), the world's largest expanse of unbroken sand
Kalahari	Botswana, South Africa, Namibia	220,000 sq. mi.	Sand sheets, longitudinal dunes
Australian Desert			
Gibson	Australia (southern portion of the Western Desert)	120,000 sq. mi.	Sandhills, gravel, grass. These three regions of desert are collectively referred to as the Great Western Desert— otherwise known as "the Outback." Contains Ayers Rock, or Uluru, one of the world's largest monoliths
Great Sandy	Australia (northern portion of the Western Desert)	150,000 sq. mi.	
Great Victoria	Australia (southernmost portion of the Western Desert)	250,000 sq. mi.	
Simpson and Sturt Stony	Australia (eastern half of the continent)	56,000 sq. mi.	Simpson's straight, parallel sand dunes are the longest in the world—up to 125 mi. Encompasses the Stewart Stony Desert, named for the Australian explorer
Mojave	U.S.: Arizona, Colorado, Nevada, Utah, California	54,000 sq. mi.	Mountain chains, dry alkaline lake beds, calcium carbonate dunes
Sonoran	U.S.: Arizona, California; Mexico	120,000 sq. mi.	Basins and plains bordered by mountain ridges; home to the Saguaro cactus
Chihuahuan	Mexico; southwestern U.S.	175,000 sq. mi.	Shrub desert; largest in North America
Thar	India, Pakistan	175,000 sq. mi.	Rocky sand and sand dunes
COOL COASTAL DESERTS			
Namib	Angola, Namibia, South Africa	13,000 sq. mi.	Gravel plains
Atacama	Chile	54,000 sq. mi.	Salt basins, sand, lava; world's driest desert
COLD WINTER DESERTS			
Great Basin	U.S.: Nevada, Oregon, Utah	190,000 sq. mi.	Mountain ridges, valleys, 1% sand dunes
Colorado Plateau	U.S.: Arizona, Colorado, New Mexico, Utah, Wyoming	130,000 sq. mi.	Sedimentary rock, mesas, and plateaus— includes the Grand Canyon and is also called the "Painted Desert" because of the spectacular colors in its rocks and canyons
Patagonian	Argentina	260,000 sq. mi.	Gravel plains, plateaus, basalt sheets
Kara-Kum	Uzbekistan, Turkmenistan	135,000 sq. mi.	90% gray layered sand—name means "black sand"
Kyzyl-Kum	Uzbekistan, Turkmenistan, Kazakhstan	115,000 sq. mi.	Sands, rock—name means "red sand"
Iranian	Iran	100,000 sq. mi.	Salt, gravel, rock
Taklamakan	China	105,000 sq. mi.	Sand, dunes, gravel
Gobi	China, Mongolia	500,000 sq. mi.	Stony, sandy soil, steppes (dry grasslands)
POLAR			
Arctic	U.S., Canada, Greenland, Iceland, Norway, Sweden, Finland, Russia		Snow, glaciers, tundra
Antarctic	Antarctica	5.4 million sq. mi.	Ice, snow, bedrock

Latitude and Longitude of World Cities
(and time corresponding to 12:00 noon, Eastern Standard Time)

City	Latitude °	′	Longitude °	′	Time
Aberdeen, Scotland	57	9 N	2	9 W	5:00 p.m.
Adelaide, Australia	34	55 S	138	36 E	2:30 a.m.[1]
Algiers, Algeria	36	50 N	3	0 E	6:00 p.m.
Amsterdam, Netherlands	52	22 N	4	53 E	6:00 p.m.
Ankara, Turkey	39	55 N	32	55 E	7:00 p.m.
Asunción, Paraguay	25	15 S	57	40 W	1:00 p.m.
Athens, Greece	37	58 N	23	43 E	7:00 p.m.
Auckland, New Zealand	36	52 S	174	45 E	5:00 a.m.[1]
Bangkok, Thailand	13	45 N	100	30 E	midnight
Barcelona, Spain	41	23 N	2	9 E	6:00 p.m.
Beijing, China	39	55 N	116	25 E	1:00 a.m.[1]
Belém, Brazil	1	28 S	48	29 W	2:00 p.m.
Belfast, Northern Ireland	54	37 N	5	56 W	5:00 p.m.
Belgrade, Yugoslavia	44	52 N	20	32 E	6:00 p.m.
Berlin, Germany	52	30 N	13	25 E	6:00 p.m.
Birmingham, England	52	25 N	1	55 W	5:00 p.m.
Bogotá, Colombia	4	32 N	74	15 W	12:00 noon
Bombay, India	19	0 N	72	48 E	10:30 p.m.
Bordeaux, France	44	50 N	0	31 W	6:00 p.m.
Bremen, Germany	53	5 N	8	49 E	6:00 p.m.
Brisbane, Australia	27	29 S	153	8 E	3:00 a.m.[1]
Bristol, England	51	28 N	2	35 W	5:00 p.m.
Brussels, Belgium	50	52 N	4	22 E	6:00 p.m.
Bucharest, Romania	44	25 N	26	7 E	7:00 p.m.
Budapest, Hungary	47	30 N	19	5 E	6:00 p.m.
Buenos Aires, Argentina	34	35 S	58	22 W	2:00 p.m.
Cairo, Egypt	30	2 N	31	21 E	7:00 p.m.
Calcutta, India	22	34 N	88	24 E	10:30 p.m.
Canton, China	23	7 N	113	15 E	1:00 a.m.[1]
Cape Town, South Africa	33	55 S	18	22 E	7:00 p.m.
Caracas, Venezuela	10	28 N	67	2 W	1:00 p.m.
Cayenne, French Guiana	4	49 N	52	18 W	1:00 p.m.
Chihuahua, Mexico	28	37 N	106	5 W	11:00 a.m.
Chongqing, China	29	46 N	106	34 E	1:00 a.m.[1]
Copenhagen, Denmark	55	40 N	12	34 E	6:00 p.m.
Córdoba, Argentina	31	28 S	64	10 W	2:00 p.m.
Dakar, Senegal	14	40 N	17	28 W	5:00 p.m.
Darwin, Australia	12	28 S	130	51 E	2:30 a.m.[1]
Djibouti, Djibouti	11	30 N	43	3 E	8:00 p.m.
Dublin, Ireland	53	20 N	6	15 W	5:00 p.m.
Durban, South Africa	29	53 S	30	53 E	7:00 p.m.
Edinburgh, Scotland	55	55 N	3	10 W	5:00 p.m.
Frankfurt, Germany	50	7 N	8	41 E	6:00 p.m.
Georgetown, Guyana	6	45 N	58	15 W	1:15 p.m.
Glasgow, Scotland	55	50 N	4	15 W	5:00 p.m.
Guatemala City, Guatemala	14	37 N	90	31 W	11:00 a.m.
Guayaquil, Ecuador	2	10 S	79	56 W	12:00 noon
Hamburg, Germany	53	33 N	10	2 E	6:00 p.m.
Hammerfest, Norway	70	38 N	23	38 E	6:00 p.m.
Havana, Cuba	23	8 N	82	23 W	12:00 noon
Helsinki, Finland	60	10 N	25	0 E	7:00 p.m.
Hobart, Tasmania	42	52 S	147	19 E	3:00 a.m.[1]
Iquique, Chile	20	10 S	70	7 W	1:00 p.m.
Irkutsk, Russia	52	30 N	104	20 E	1:00 a.m.
Jakarta, Indonesia	6	16 S	106	48 E	0:30 a.m.[1]
Johannesburg, South Africa	26	12 S	28	4 E	7:00 p.m.
Kingston, Jamaica	17	59 N	76	49 W	12:00 noon
Kinshasa, Congo	4	18 S	15	17 E	6:00 p.m.
La Paz, Bolivia	16	27 S	68	22 W	1:00 p.m.
Leeds, England	53	45 N	1	30 W	5:00 p.m.
Lima, Peru	12	0 S	77	2 W	12:00 noon
Lisbon, Portugal	38	44 N	9	9 W	5:00 p.m.
Liverpool, England	53	25 N	3	0 W	5:00 p.m.
London, England	51	32 N	0	5 W	5:00 p.m.
Lyons, France	45	45 N	4	50 E	6:00 p.m.
Madrid, Spain	40	26 N	3	42 W	6:00 p.m.
Manchester, England	53	30 N	2	15 W	5:00 p.m.
Manila, Philippines	14	35 N	120	57 E	1:00 a.m.[1]
Marseilles, France	43	20 N	5	20 E	6:00 p.m.
Mazatlán, Mexico	23	12 N	106	25 W	10:00 a.m.
Mecca, Saudi Arabia	21	29 N	39	45 E	8:00 p.m.
Melbourne, Australia	37	47 S	144	58 E	3:00 a.m.[1]
Mexico City, Mexico	19	26 N	99	7 W	11:00 a.m.
Milan, Italy	45	27 N	9	10 E	6:00 p.m.
Montevideo, Uruguay	34	53 S	56	10 W	2:00 p.m.
Moscow, Russia	55	45 N	37	36 E	8:00 p.m.
Munich, Germany	48	8 N	11	35 E	6:00 p.m.
Nagasaki, Japan	32	48 N	129	57 E	2:00 a.m.[1]
Nagoya, Japan	35	7 N	136	56 E	2:00 a.m.[1]
Nairobi, Kenya	1	25 S	36	55 E	8:00 p.m.
Nanjing (Nanking), China	32	3 N	118	53 E	1:00 a.m.[1]
Naples, Italy	40	50 N	14	15 E	6:00 p.m.
Newcastle-on-Tyne, England	54	58 N	1	37 W	5:00 p.m.
Odessa, Ukraine	46	27 N	30	48 E	8:00 p.m.
Osaka, Japan	34	32 N	135	30 E	2:00 a.m.[1]
Oslo, Norway	59	57 N	10	42 E	6:00 p.m.
Panama City, Panama	8	58 N	79	32 W	12:00 noon
Paramaribo, Suriname	5	45 N	55	15 W	1:30 p.m.
Paris, France	48	48 N	2	20 E	6:00 p.m.
Perth, Australia	31	57 S	115	52 E	1:00 a.m.[1]
Plymouth, England	50	25 N	4	5 W	5:00 p.m.
Port Moresby, Papua New Guinea	9	25 S	147	8 E	3:00 a.m.[1]
Prague, Czech Republic	50	5 N	14	26 E	6:00 p.m.
Rangoon, Myanmar	16	50 N	96	0 E	11:30 p.m.
Reykjavík, Iceland	64	4 N	21	58 W	4:00 p.m.
Rio de Janeiro, Brazil	22	57 S	43	12 W	2:00 p.m.
Rome, Italy	41	54 N	12	27 E	6:00 p.m.
Salvador, Brazil	12	56 S	38	27 W	2:00 p.m.
Santiago, Chile	33	28 S	70	45 W	1:00 p.m.
St. Petersburg, Russia	59	56 N	30	18 E	8:00 p.m.
São Paulo, Brazil	23	31 S	46	31 W	2:00 p.m.
Shanghai, China	31	10 N	121	28 E	1:00 a.m.[1]
Singapore, Singapore	1	14 N	103	55 E	0:30 a.m.[1]
Sofia, Bulgaria	42	40 N	23	20 E	7:00 p.m.
Stockholm, Sweden	59	17 N	18	3 E	6:00 p.m.
Sydney, Australia	34	0 S	151	0 E	3:00 a.m.[1]
Tananarive, Madagascar	18	50 S	47	33 E	8:00 p.m.
Teheran, Iran	35	45 N	51	45 E	8:30 p.m.
Tokyo, Japan	35	40 N	139	45 E	2:00 a.m.[1]
Tripoli, Libya	32	57 N	13	12 E	7:00 p.m.
Venice, Italy	45	26 N	12	20 E	6:00 p.m.
Veracruz, Mexico	19	10 N	96	10 W	11:00 a.m.
Vienna, Austria	48	14 N	16	20 E	6:00 p.m.
Vladivostok, Russia	43	10 N	132	0 E	3:00 a.m.[1]
Warsaw, Poland	52	14 N	21	0 E	6:00 p.m.
Wellington, New Zealand	41	17 S	174	47 E	5:00 a.m.[1]
Zürich, Switzerland	47	21 N	8	31 E	6:00 p.m.

1. On the following day.

Miscellaneous Data for the United States

Highest point: Mount McKinley, Alaska	20,320 ft. (6,198 m)
Lowest point: Death Valley, Calif.	282 ft. (86 m) below sea level
Approximate mean elevation	2,500 ft. (763 m)
Points farthest apart (50 states): Log Point, Elliot Key, Fla., and Kure Island, Hawaii	5,859 mi. (9,429 km)
Geographic center (50 states): in Butte County, S.D. (west of Castle Rock)	44°58′N lat.103°46′W long.
Geographic center (48 conterminous states): in Smith County, Kan. (near Lebanon)	39°50′N lat. 98°35′W long.
Boundaries:	
Between Alaska and Canada	1,538 mi. (2,475 km)
Between the 48 conterminous states and Canada (incl. the Great Lakes)	3,987 mi. (6,416 km)
Between the United States and Mexico	1,933 mi. (3,111 km)

Source: U.S. Geological Survey.

Extreme Points of the United States (50 States)

Extreme point	Latitude	Longitude	Distance[1] mi.	km
Northernmost point: Point Barrow, Alaska	71°23′ N	156°29′ W	2,507	4,034
Easternmost point: West Quoddy Head, Maine	44°49′ N	66°57′ W	1,788	2,997
Southernmost point: Ka Lae (South Cape), Hawaii	18°55′ N	155°41′ W	3,463	5,573
Westernmost point: Cape Wrangell, Alaska (Attu Island)	52°55′ N	172°27′ E	3,625	5,833

1. From geographic center of United States (incl. Alaska and Hawaii), west of Castle Rock, S.D., 44°58′ lat., 103°46′ W long. If measured from the prime meridian in Greenwich, England, Cape Wrangell, Attu Island, Alaska, would be the easternmost point.

The Continental Divide

The Continental Divide is a ridge of high ground that runs irregularly north and south through the Rocky Mountains and separates eastward-flowing from westward-flowing streams. The waters that flow eastward empty into the Atlantic Ocean, chiefly by way of the Gulf of Mexico; those that flow westward empty into the Pacific. Every continent with the exception of Antarctica has a continental divide.

Rivers of the United States
(350 or more miles long)

Alabama-Coosa (600 mi.; 966 km): From junction of Oostanula and Etowah R. in Georgia to Mobile R.

Altamaha-Ocmulgee (392 mi.; 631 km): From junction of Yellow R. and South R., Newton Co. in Georgia to Atlantic Ocean.

Apalachicola-Chattahoochee (524 mi.; 843 km): From Towns Co. in Georgia to Gulf of Mexico in Florida.

Arkansas (1,459 mi.; 2,348 km): From Lake Co. in Colorado to Mississippi R. in Arkansas.

Brazos (923 mi.; 1,490 km): From junction of Salt Fork and Double Mountain Fork in Texas to Gulf of Mexico.

Canadian (906 mi.; 1,458 km): From Las Animas Co. in Colorado to Arkansas R. in Oklahoma.

Cimarron (600 mi.; 966 km): From Colfax Co. in New Mexico to Arkansas R. in Oklahoma.

Colorado (1,450 mi.; 2,333 km): From Rocky Mountain National Park in Colorado to Gulf of California in Mexico.

Colorado (862 mi.; 1,387 km): From Dawson Co. in Texas to Matagorda Bay.

Columbia (1,243 mi.; 2,000 km): From Columbia Lake in British Columbia to Pacific Ocean (entering between Oregon and Washington).

Colville (350 mi.; 563 km): From Brooks Range in Alaska to Beaufort Sea.

Connecticut (407 mi.; 655 km): From Third Connecticut Lake in New Hampshire to Long Island Sound in Connecticut.

Cumberland (720 mi.; 1,159 km): From junction of Poor and Clover Forks in Harlan Co. in Kentucky to Ohio R.

Delaware (390 mi.; 628 km): From Schoharie Co. in New York to Liston Point, Delaware Bay.

Gila (649 mi.; 1,044 km): From Catron Co. in New Mexico to Colorado R. in Arizona.

Green (360 mi.; 579 km): From Lincoln Co. in Kentucky to Ohio R. in Kentucky.

Green (730 mi.; 1,175 km): From Sublette Co. in Wyoming to Colorado R. in Utah.

Illinois (420 mi.; 676 km): From St. Joseph Co. in Indiana to Mississippi R. at Grafton in Illinois.

James (sometimes called *Dakota*) (710 mi.; 1,143 km): From Wells Co. in North Dakota to Missouri R. in South Dakota.

Kanawha-New (352 mi.; 566 km): From junction of North and South Forks of New R. in North Carolina, through Virginia and West Virginia (New R. becoming Kanawha R.), to Ohio R.

Kansas (743 mi.; 1,196 km): From source of Arikaree R. in Elbert Co., Colorado, to Missouri R. at Kansas City, Kansas.

Koyukuk (470 mi.; 756 km): From Brooks Range in Alaska to Yukon R.

Kuskokwim (724 mi.; 1,165 km): From Alaska Range in Alaska to Kuskokwim Bay.

Licking (350 mi.; 563 km): From Magoffin Co. in Kentucky to Ohio R. at Cincinnati in Ohio.

Little Missouri (560 mi.; 901 km): From Crook Co. in Wyoming to Missouri R. in North Dakota.

Milk (625 mi.; 1,006 km): From junction of forks in Alberta Province to Missouri R.

Mississippi (2,348 mi.; 3,779 km): From Lake Itasca in Minnesota to mouth of Southwest Pass in Louisiana.

Mississippi-Missouri-Red Rock (3,710 mi.; 5,970 km): From source of Red Rock R. in Montana to mouth of Southwest Pass in Louisiana.

Missouri (2,315 mi.; 3,726 km): From junction of Jefferson R., Gallatin R., and Madison R. in Montana to Mississippi R. near St. Louis.

Missouri-Red Rock (2,540 mi.; 4,090 km): From source of Red Rock R. in Montana to Mississippi R. near St. Louis.

Mobile-Alabama-Coosa (645 mi.; 1,040 km): From junction of Etowah R. and Oostanula R. in Georgia to Mobile Bay.

Neosho (460 mi.; 740 km): From Morris Co. in Kansas to Arkansas R. in Oklahoma.

Niobrara (431 mi.; 694 km): From Niobrara Co. in Wyoming to Missouri R. in Nebraska.

Noatak (350 mi.; 563 km): From Brooks Range in Alaska to Kotzebue Sound.

North Canadian (800 mi.; 1,290 km): From Union Co. in New Mexico to Canadian R. in Oklahoma.

North Platte (618 mi.; 995 km): From Jackson Co. in Colorado to junction with South Platte R. in Nebraska to form Platte R.

Ohio (981 mi.; 1,579 km): From junction of Allegheny R. and Monongahela R. at Pittsburgh to Mississippi R. between Illinois and Kentucky.

Ohio-Allegheny (1,306 mi.; 2,102 km): From Potter Co. in Pennsylvania to Mississippi R. at Cairo in Illinois.

Osage (500 mi.; 805 km): From east-central Kansas to Missouri R. near Jefferson City in Missouri.

Ouachita (605 mi.; 974 km): From Polk Co. in Arkansas to Red R. in Louisiana.

Pearl (411 mi.; 661 km): From Neshoba County in Mississippi to Gulf of Mexico (Mississippi-Louisiana).

Pecos (926 mi.; 1,490 km): From Mora Co. in New Mexico to Rio Grande in Texas.

Pee Dee-Yadkin (435 mi.; 700 km): From Watauga Co. in North Carolina to Winyah Bay in South Carolina.

Pend Oreille–Clark Fork (531 mi.; 855 km): Near Butte in Montana to Columbia R. on Washington-Canada border.

Platte (990 mi.; 1593 km): From source of Grizzly Creek in Jackson Co., Colorado, to Missouri R. south of Omaha, Nebraska.

Porcupine (569 mi.; 916 km): From Yukon Territory, Canada, to Yukon R. in Alaska.

Potomac (383 mi.; 616 km): From Garrett Co. in Maryland to Chesapeake Bay at Point Lookout in Maryland.

Powder (375 mi.; 603 km): From junction of forks in Johnson Co. in Wyoming to Yellowstone R. in Montana.

Red (1,290 mi.; 2,080 km): From source of Tierra Blanca Creek in Curry County, New Mexico, to Mississippi R. in Louisiana.

Red (also called *Red River of the North*) (545 mi.; 877 km): From junction of Otter Tail R. and Bois de Sioux R. in Minnesota to Lake Winnipeg in Manitoba, Canada.

Republican (445 mi.; 716 km): From junction of North Fork and Arikaree R. in Nebraska to junction with Smoky Hill R. in Kansas to form the Kansas R.

Rio Grande (1,900 mi.; 3,060 km): From San Juan Co. in Colorado to Gulf of Mexico.

Roanoke (380 mi.; 612 km): From junction of forks in Montgomery Co. in Virginia to Albemarle Sound in North Carolina.

Sabine (380 mi.; 612 km): From junction of forks in Hunt Co. in Texas to Sabine Lake between Texas and Louisiana.

Sacramento (377 mi.; 607 km): From Siskiyou Co. in California to Suisun Bay.

Saint Francis (425 mi.; 684 km): From Iron Co. in Missouri to Mississippi R. in Arkansas.

Salmon (420 mi.; 676 km): From Custer Co. in Idaho to Snake R.

San Joaquin (350 mi.; 563 km): From junction of forks in Madera Co. in California to Suisun Bay.

San Juan (360 mi.; 579 km): From Archuleta Co. in Colorado to Colorado R. in Utah.

Santee-Wateree-Catawba (538 mi.; 866 km): From McDowell Co. in North Carolina to Atlantic Ocean in South Carolina.

Smoky Hill (540 mi.; 869 km): From Cheyenne Co. in Colorado to junction with Republican R. in Kansas to form Kansas R.

Snake (1,038 mi.; 1,670 km): From Ocean Plateau in Wyoming to Columbia R. in Washington.

South Platte (424 mi.; 682 km): From Park Co. in Colorado to junction with North Platte R. in Nebraska to form Platte R.

Stikine (379 mi.; 610 km): From British Columbia in Canada to Stikine Strait near Wrangell, Alaska.

Susquehanna (444 mi.; 715 km): From Otsego Lake in New York to Chesapeake Bay in Maryland.

Tanana (659 mi.; 1,060 km): From Wrangell Mts. in Yukon Territory, Canada, to Yukon R. in Alaska.

Tennessee (652 mi.; 1,049 km): From junction of Holston R. and French Broad R. in Tennessee to Ohio R. in Kentucky.

Tennessee–French Broad (886 mi.; 1,417 km): From Transylvania Co. in North Carolina to Ohio R. at Paducah in Kentucky.

Tombigbee (525 mi.; 845 km): From junction of forks in Itawamba Co. in Mississippi to Mobile R. in Alabama.

Trinity (360 mi.; 579 km): From junction of forks in Dallas Co. in Texas to Galveston Bay.

Wabash (512 mi.; 824 km): From Darke Co. in Ohio to Ohio R. between Illinois and Indiana.

Washita (500 mi.; 805 km): From Hemphill Co. in Texas to Red R. in Oklahoma.

White (722 mi.; 1,160 km): From Madison Co. in Arkansas to Mississippi R.

Wisconsin (430 mi.; 692 km): From Vilas Co. in Wisconsin to Mississippi R.

Yellowstone (692 mi.; 1,110 km): From Park Co. in Wyoming to Missouri R. in North Dakota.

Yukon (1,979 mi.; 3,185 km): From source of McNeil R. in Yukon Territory, Canada, to Bering Sea in Alaska.

Coastline of the United States

State	Lengths, statute miles		State	Lengths, statute miles	
	General coastline[1]	Tidal shoreline[2]		General coastline[1]	Tidal shoreline[2]
Atlantic Coast:			**Gulf Coast:**		
Maine	228	3,478	Florida (Gulf)	770	5,095
New Hampshire	13	131	Alabama	53	607
Massachusetts	192	1,519	Mississippi	44	359
Rhode Island	40	384	Louisiana	397	7,721
Connecticut	—	618	Texas	367	3,359
New York	127	1,850	Total Gulf Coast	1,631	17,141
New Jersey	130	1,792	**Pacific Coast:**		
Pennsylvania	—	89	California	840	3,427
Delaware	28	381	Oregon	296	1,410
Maryland	31	3,190	Washington	157	3,026
Virginia	112	3,315	Hawaii	750	1,052
North Carolina	301	3,375	Alaska (Pacific)	5,580	31,383
South Carolina	187	2,876	Total Pacific Coast	7,623	40,298
Georgia	100	2,344	**Arctic Coast:**		
Florida (Atlantic)	580	3,331	Alaska (Arctic)	1,060	2,521
Total Atlantic Coast	2,069	28,673	Total Arctic Coast	1,060	2,521
			States Total	**12,383**	**88,633**

1. Figures are lengths of general outline of seacoast. Measurements are made with unit measure of 30 minutes of latitude on charts as near scale of 1:1,200,000 as possible. Coastline of bays and sounds is included to point where they narrow to width of unit measure, and distance across at such point is included. 2. Figures were obtained in 1939–1940 with recording instrument on the largest-scale maps and charts then available. Shoreline of outer coast, offshore islands, sounds, bays, rivers, and creeks is included to head of tidewater, or to point where tidal waters narrow to width of 100 feet. *Source:* Department of Commerce, National Oceanic and Atmospheric Administration, National Ocean Service.

Mountain Peaks in the United States Higher Than 14,000 Feet

Name	State	Height (ft.)	Name	State	Height (ft.)	Name	State	Height (ft.)
Mt. McKinley	Alaska	20,320	Castle Peak	Colo.	14,265	Mt. Eolus	Colo.	14,083
Mt. St. Elias	Alaska	18,008	Quandary Peak	Colo.	14,265	Windom Peak	Colo.	14,082
Mt. Foraker	Alaska	17,400	Mt. Evans	Colo.	14,264	Mt. Columbia	Colo.	14,073
Mt. Bona	Alaska	16,500	Longs Peak	Colo.	14,255	Mt. Augusta	Alaska	14,070
Mt. Blackburn	Alaska	16,390	Mt. Wilson	Colo.	14,246	Missouri Mtn.	Colo.	14,067
Mt. Sanford	Alaska	16,237	White Mtn.	Calif.	14,246	Humboldt Peak	Colo.	14,064
Mt. Vancouver	Alaska	15,979	North Palisade	Calif.	14,242	Mt. Bierstadt	Colo.	14,060
South Buttress	Alaska	15,885	Mt. Cameron	Colo.	14,238	Sunlight Peak	Colo.	14,059
Mt. Churchill	Alaska	15,638	Mt. Shavano	Colo.	14,229	Split Mtn.	Calif.	14,058
Mt. Fairweather	Alaska	15,300	Crestone Needle	Colo.	14,197	Handies Peak	Colo.	14,048
Mt. Hubbard	Alaska	14,950	Mt. Belford	Colo.	14,197	Culebra Peak	Colo.	14,047
Mt. Bear	Alaska	14,831	Mt. Princeton	Colo.	14,197	Mt. Lindsey	Colo.	14,042
East Buttress	Alaska	14,730	Mt. Yale	Colo.	14,196	Ellingwood Point	Colo.	14,042
Mt. Hunter	Alaska	14,573	Mt. Bross	Colo.	14,172	Middle Palisade	Calif.	14,040
Browne Tower	Alaska	14,530	Kit Carson Mtn.	Colo.	14,165	Little Bear Peak	Colo.	14,037
Mt. Alverstone	Alaska	14,500	Mt. Wrangell	Alaska	14,163	Mt. Sherman	Colo.	14,036
Mt. Whitney	Calif.	14,494[1]	Mt. Sill	Calif.	14,163	Redcloud Peak	Colo.	14,034
University Peak	Alaska	14,470	Mt. Shasta	Calif.	14,162	Mt. Langley	Calif.	14,027
Mt. Elbert	Colo.	14,433	El Diente Peak	Colo.	14,159	Conundrum Peak	Colo.	14,022
Mt. Massive	Colo.	14,421	Point Success	Wash.	14,158	Mt. Tyndall	Calif.	14,019
Mt. Harvard	Colo.	14,420	Maroon Peak	Colo.	14,156	Pyramid Peak	Colo.	14,018
Mt. Rainier	Wash.	14,410	Tabeguache Mtn.	Colo.	14,155	Wilson Peak	Colo.	14,017
Mt. Williamson	Calif.	14,370	Mt. Oxford	Colo.	14,153	Wetterhorn Peak	Colo.	14,015
La Plata Peak	Colo.	14,361	Mt. Sill	Calif.	14,153	North Maroon Peak	Colo.	14,014
Blanca Peak	Colo.	14,345	Mt. Sneffels	Colo.	14,150	San Luis Peak	Colo.	14,014
Uncompahgre Peak	Colo.	14,309	Mt. Democrat	Colo.	14,148	Middle Palisade	Calif.	14,012
Crestone Peak	Colo.	14,294	Capitol Peak	Colo.	14,130	Mt. Muir	Calif.	14,012
Mt. Lincoln	Colo.	14,286	Liberty Cap	Wash.	14,112	Mt. of the Holy Cross	Colo.	14,005
Grays Peak	Colo.	14,270	Pikes Peak	Colo.	14,110	Huron Peak	Colo.	14,003
Mt. Antero	Colo.	14,269	Snowmass Mtn.	Colo.	14,092	Thunderbolt Peak	Calif.	14,003
Torreys Peak	Colo.	14,267	Mt. Russell	Calif.	14,088	Sunshine Peak	Colo.	14,001

1. National Geodetic Survey. *Source:* U.S. Dept. of the Interior, Geological Survey.

Highest, Lowest, and Mean Elevations in the United States

State	Elevation (ft.)[1]	Highest point	Elevation (ft.)	Lowest point	Elevation (ft.)
Alabama	500	Cheaha Mountain	2,405	Gulf of Mexico	Sea level
Alaska	1,900	Mt. McKinley	20,320	Pacific Ocean	Sea level
Arizona	4,100	Humphreys Peak	12,633	Colorado River	70
Arkansas	650	Magazine Mountain	2,753	Ouachita River	55
California	2,900	Mt. Whitney	14,494	Death Valley	−282[2]
Colorado	6,800	Mt. Elbert	14,433	Arkansas River	3,350
Connecticut	500	Mt. Frissell, on south slope	2,380	Long Island Sound	Sea level
Delaware	60	Ebright Road, Del.–Pa. state line	448	Atlantic Ocean	Sea level
D.C.	150	Tenleytown, at Reno Reservoir	410	Potomac River	1
Florida	100	Sec. 30, T6N, R20W, Walton County	345	Atlantic Ocean	Sea level
Georgia	600	Brasstown Bald	4,784	Atlantic Ocean	Sea level
Hawaii	3,030	Puu Wekiu, Mauna Kea	13,796	Pacific Ocean	Sea level
Idaho	5,000	Borah Peak	12,662	Snake River	710
Illinois	600	Charles Mound	1,235	Mississippi River	279
Indiana	700	Franklin Township, Wayne County	1,257	Ohio River	320
Iowa	1,100	Sec. 29, T100N, R41W, Osceola County	1,670	Mississippi River	480
Kansas	2,000	Mt. Sunflower	4,039	Verdigris River	679
Kentucky	750	Black Mountain	4,139	Mississippi River	257
Louisiana	100	Driskill Mountain	535	New Orleans	−8[2]
Maine	600	Mt. Katahdin	5,267	Atlantic Ocean	Sea level
Maryland	350	Backbone Mountain	3,360	Atlantic Ocean	Sea level
Massachusetts	500	Mt. Greylock	3,487	Atlantic Ocean	Sea level
Michigan	900	Mt. Arvon	1,979	Lake Erie	572
Minnesota	1,200	Eagle Mountain	2,301	Lake Superior	600
Mississippi	300	Woodall Mountain	806	Gulf of Mexico	Sea level
Missouri	800	Taum Sauk Mountain	1,772	St. Francis River	230
Montana	3,400	Granite Peak	12,799	Kootenai River	1,800
Nebraska	2,600	Johnson Township, Kimball County	5,424	Missouri River	840
Nevada	5,500	Boundary Peak	13,140	Colorado River	479
New Hampshire	1,000	Mt. Washington	6,288	Atlantic Ocean	Sea level
New Jersey	250	High Point	1,803	Atlantic Ocean	Sea level
New Mexico	5,700	Wheeler Peak	13,161	Red Bluff Reservoir	2,842
New York	1,000	Mt. Marcy	5,344	Atlantic Ocean	Sea level
North Carolina	700	Mt. Mitchell	6,684	Atlantic Ocean	Sea level
North Dakota	1,900	White Butte	3,506	Red River	750
Ohio	850	Campbell Hill	1,549	Ohio River	455
Oklahoma	1,300	Black Mesa	4,973	Little River	289
Oregon	3,300	Mt. Hood	11,239	Pacific Ocean	Sea level
Pennsylvania	1,100	Mt. Davis	3,213	Delaware River	Sea level
Rhode Island	200	Jerimoth Hill	812	Atlantic Ocean	Sea level
South Carolina	350	Sassafras Mountain	3,560	Atlantic Ocean	Sea level
South Dakota	2,200	Harney Peak	7,242	Big Stone Lake	966
Tennessee	900	Clingmans Dome	6,643	Mississippi River	178
Texas	1,700	Guadalupe Peak	8,749	Gulf of Mexico	Sea level
Utah	6,100	Kings Peak	13,528	Beaverdam Wash	2,000
Vermont	1,000	Mt. Mansfield	4,393	Lake Champlain	95
Virginia	950	Mt. Rogers	5,729	Atlantic Ocean	Sea level
Washington	1,700	Mt. Rainier	14,410	Pacific Ocean	Sea level
West Virginia	1,500	Spruce Knob	4,861	Potomac River	240
Wisconsin	1,050	Timms Hill	1,951	Lake Michigan	579
Wyoming	6,700	Gannett Peak	13,804	Belle Fourche River	3,099
United States	**2,500**	**Mt. McKinley (Alaska)**	**20,320**	**Death Valley (California)**	**−282[2]**

1. Approximate mean elevation. 2. Below sea level. *Source:* U.S. Geological Survey.

Latitude and Longitude of U.S. and Canadian Cities
(and time corresponding to 12:00 noon, Eastern Standard Time)

City	Lat. °	Lat. ′	Long. °	Long. ′	Time
Albany, N.Y.	42	40	73	45	12:00 noon
Albuquerque, N.M.	35	05	106	39	10:00 a.m.
Amarillo, Tex.	35	11	101	50	11:00 a.m.
Anchorage, Alaska	61	13	149	54	8:00 a.m.
Atlanta, Ga.	33	45	84	23	12:00 noon
Austin, Tex.	30	16	97	44	11:00 a.m.
Baker, Ore.	44	47	117	50	9:00 a.m.
Baltimore, Md.	39	18	76	38	12:00 noon
Bangor, Maine	44	48	68	47	12:00 noon
Birmingham, Ala.	33	30	86	50	11:00 a.m.
Bismarck, N.D.	46	48	100	47	11:00 a.m.
Boise, Idaho	43	36	116	13	10:00 a.m.
Boston, Mass.	42	21	71	5	12:00 noon
Buffalo, N.Y.	42	55	78	50	12:00 noon
Calgary, Alba., Can.	51	1	114	1	10:00 a.m.
Carlsbad, N.M.	32	26	104	15	10:00 a.m.
Charleston, S.C.	32	47	79	56	12:00 noon
Charleston, W. Va.	38	21	81	38	12:00 noon
Charlotte, N.C.	35	14	80	50	12:00 noon
Cheyenne, Wyo.	41	9	104	52	10:00 a.m.
Chicago, Ill.	41	50	87	37	11:00 a.m.
Cincinnati, Ohio	39	8	84	30	12:00 noon
Cleveland, Ohio	41	28	81	37	12:00 noon
Columbia, S.C.	34	0	81	2	12:00 noon
Columbus, Ohio	40	0	83	1	12:00 noon
Dallas, Tex.	32	46	96	46	11:00 a.m.
Denver, Colo.	39	45	105	0	10:00 a.m.
Des Moines, Iowa	41	35	93	37	11:00 a.m.
Detroit, Mich.	42	20	83	3	12:00 noon
Dubuque, Iowa	42	31	90	40	11:00 a.m.
Duluth, Minn.	46	49	92	5	11:00 a.m.
Eastport, Maine	44	54	67	0	12:00 noon
El Centro, Calif.	32	38	115	33	9:00 a.m.
El Paso, Tex.	31	46	106	29	10:00 a.m.
Eugene, Ore.	44	3	123	5	9:00 a.m.
Fargo, N.D.	46	52	96	48	11:00 a.m.
Flagstaff, Ariz.	35	13	111	41	10:00 a.m.
Fort Worth, Tex.	32	43	97	19	11:00 a.m.
Fresno, Calif.	36	44	119	48	9:00 a.m.
Grand Junction, Colo.	39	5	108	33	10:00 a.m.
Grand Rapids, Mich.	42	58	85	40	12:00 noon
Havre, Mont.	48	33	109	43	10:00 a.m.
Helena, Mont.	46	35	112	2	10:00 a.m.
Honolulu, Hawaii	21	18	157	50	7:00 a.m.
Hot Springs, Ark.	34	31	93	3	11:00 a.m.
Houston, Tex.	29	45	95	21	11:00 a.m.
Idaho Falls, Idaho	43	30	112	1	10:00 a.m.
Indianapolis, Ind.	39	46	86	10	12:00 noon
Jackson, Miss.	32	20	90	12	11:00 a.m.
Jacksonville, Fla.	30	22	81	40	12:00 noon
Juneau, Alaska	58	18	134	24	8:00 a.m.
Kansas City, Mo.	39	6	94	35	11:00 a.m.
Key West, Fla.	24	33	81	48	12:00 noon
Kingston, Ont., Can.	44	15	76	30	12:00 noon
Klamath Falls, Ore.	42	10	121	44	9:00 a.m.
Knoxville, Tenn.	35	57	83	56	12:00 noon
Las Vegas, Nev.	36	10	115	12	9:00 a.m.
Lewiston, Idaho	46	24	117	2	9:00 a.m.
Lincoln, Neb.	40	50	96	40	11:00 a.m.
London, Ont., Can.	43	2	81	34	12:00 noon
Long Beach, Calif.	33	46	118	11	9:00 a.m.
Los Angeles, Calif.	34	3	118	15	9:00 a.m.
Louisville, Ky.	38	15	85	46	12:00 noon
Manchester, N.H.	43	0	71	30	12:00 noon
Memphis, Tenn.	35	9	90	3	11:00 a.m.
Miami, Fla.	25	46	80	12	12:00 noon
Milwaukee, Wis.	43	2	87	55	11:00 a.m.
Minneapolis, Minn.	44	59	93	14	11:00 a.m.
Mobile, Ala.	30	42	88	3	11:00 a.m.
Montgomery, Ala.	32	21	86	18	11:00 a.m.
Montpelier, Vt.	44	15	72	32	12:00 noon
Montreal, Que., Can.	45	30	73	35	12:00 noon
Moose Jaw, Sask., Can.	50	37	105	31	10:00 a.m.
Nashville, Tenn.	36	10	86	47	11:00 a.m.
Nelson, B.C., Can.	49	30	117	17	9:00 a.m.
Newark, N.J.	40	44	74	10	12:00 noon
New Haven, Conn.	41	19	72	55	12:00 noon
New Orleans, La.	29	57	90	4	11:00 a.m.
New York, N.Y.	40	47	73	58	12:00 noon
Nome, Alaska	64	25	165	30	8:00 a.m.
Oakland, Calif.	37	48	122	16	9:00 a.m.
Oklahoma City, Okla.	35	26	97	28	11:00 a.m.
Omaha, Neb.	41	15	95	56	11:00 a.m.
Ottawa, Ont., Can.	45	24	75	43	12:00 noon
Philadelphia, Pa.	39	57	75	10	12:00 noon
Phoenix, Ariz.	33	29	112	4	10:00 a.m.
Pierre, S.D.	44	22	100	21	11:00 a.m.
Pittsburgh, Pa.	40	27	79	57	12:00 noon
Port Arthur, Ont., Can.	48	30	89	17	12:00 noon
Portland, Maine	43	40	70	15	12:00 noon
Portland, Ore.	45	31	122	41	9:00 a.m.
Providence, R.I.	41	50	71	24	12:00 noon
Quebec, Que., Can.	46	49	71	11	12:00 noon
Raleigh, N.C.	35	46	78	39	12:00 noon
Reno, Nev.	39	30	119	49	9:00 a.m.
Richfield, Utah	38	46	112	5	10:00 a.m.
Richmond, Va.	37	33	77	29	12:00 noon
Roanoke, Va.	37	17	79	57	12:00 noon
Sacramento, Calif.	38	35	121	30	9:00 a.m.
St. John, N.B., Can.	45	18	66	10	1:00 p.m.
St. Louis, Mo.	38	35	90	12	11:00 a.m.
Salt Lake City, Utah	40	46	111	54	10:00 a.m.
San Antonio, Tex.	29	23	98	33	11:00 a.m.
San Diego, Calif.	32	42	117	10	9:00 a.m.
San Francisco, Calif.	37	47	122	26	9:00 a.m.
San Jose, Calif.	37	20	121	53	9:00 a.m.
San Juan, P.R.	18	30	66	10	1:00 p.m.
Santa Fe, N.M.	35	41	105	57	10:00 a.m.
Savannah, Ga.	32	5	81	5	12:00 noon
Seattle, Wash.	47	37	122	20	9:00 a.m.
Shreveport, La.	32	28	93	42	11:00 a.m.
Sioux Falls, S.D.	43	33	96	44	11:00 a.m.
Sitka, Alaska	57	10	135	15	8:00 a.m.
Spokane, Wash.	47	40	117	26	9:00 a.m.
Springfield, Ill.	39	48	89	38	11:00 a.m.
Springfield, Mass.	42	6	72	34	12:00 noon
Springfield, Mo.	37	13	93	17	11:00 a.m.
Syracuse, N.Y.	43	2	76	8	12:00 noon
Tampa, Fla.	27	57	82	27	12:00 noon
Toledo, Ohio	41	39	83	33	12:00 noon
Toronto, Ont., Can.	43	40	79	24	12:00 noon
Tulsa, Okla.	36	09	95	59	11:00 a.m.
Victoria, B.C., Can.	48	25	123	21	9:00 a.m.
Virginia Beach, Va.	36	51	75	58	12:00 noon
Washington, D.C.	38	53	77	02	12:00 noon
Wichita, Kan.	37	43	97	17	11:00 a.m.
Wilmington, N.C.	34	14	77	57	12:00 noon
Winnipeg, Man., Can.	49	54	97	7	11:00 a.m.

For more on U.S. geography, *see* National Parks, pp. 599–603.

TERROR FROM THE SKY: On Sept. 11, 2001, a day of horror that many Americans compared with the attack on Pearl Harbor 60 years before, 19 terrorists hijacked four U.S. airplanes and used them as guided missiles. Two planes crashed into the towers of New York City's World Trade Center, above, collapsing them; a third hit the Pentagon near Washington; and a fourth crashed in rural Pennsylvania. More than 5,000 lives were lost.

SECOND ATTACK: As the north tower of the World Trade Center burns, a hijacked United Airlines jet aims for the south tower.

PANIC: New Yorkers flee a fast-moving cloud of dust, smoke, and debris as the south tower of the Trade Center collapses.

AMID THE RUINS: New York City fire fighters work in the debris of the Trade Center after the dual collapse; more than 300 of their colleagues were victims of the terrorist attack.

ATTACK ON THE PENTAGON: Shortly after two jets struck New York City, an American Airlines flight smashed into the Pentagon, killing 125, as well as 64 aboard the plane, including the hijackers. In all, 266 passengers and crew died in the four plane crashes.

STANDING TALL: Three days after the New York City attack, President George Bush toured the site to support rescue workers.

PRIME SUSPECT: Veteran terrorist Osama bin Laden, a dissident Saudi millionaire, was suspected of coordinating the attack.

HAIL TO THE CHIEF: As wife Laura and daughters Jenna and Barbara look on, George W. Bush is sworn in as the 43rd President of the United States by Chief Justice of the Supreme Court William Rehnquist. In December, with the election undecided, the Court had voted 5-4 to stop the ballot recount in Florida, thus handing Bush the presidency.

EXECUTED: Admitted Oklahoma City bomber Timothy McVeigh was put to death by lethal injection in June; his execution had been delayed by a procedural error.

FBI SPY: Agent Robert Hanssen, a 25-year veteran, was arrested in February and charged with having passed secrets to the Soviet Union and Russia for some 15 years.

ENERGY CRISIS: Early in the year, Californians faced soaring utility bills and endured rolling blackouts as the Golden State fought a crippling power shortage. Above, Governor Gray Davis, attending the dedication of the Calpine gas-powered energy unit near Yuba City in February, announces a plan to speed up power-plant construction in the state.

TRAGEDY AT SEA: U.S. Navy commander Scott Waddle, above with wife Jill, was in command of the nuclear submarine USS *Greeneville* when it abruptly surfaced during a training cruise off Hawaii and collided with the fishing boat *Ehime Maru* on Feb. 9, killing nine Japanese civilians. Waddle was forced to retire but received an honorable discharge.

VICTORS: Voters overwhelmingly returned moderate cleric Mohammad Khatami to the presidency of Iran in June. Britons endorsed Tony Blair's Labour government the same month, handing him a strong majority in the House of Commons. In Israel, Ariel Sharon of the Likud Party defeated incumbent Ehud Barak to become prime minister in February.

SPY-PLANE CRASH: The U.S. and China weathered a major crisis in April, when a U.S. EP-3E reconnaissance plane monitoring China collided with a Chinese fighter jet while flying just outside that nation's airspace. The Chinese pilot died, while the damaged American plane landed on Chinese soil on the island of Hainan and its crew of 24 was taken into custody. In a victory for diplomacy, the U.S. crew was returned 11 days later.

TERROR IN ISRAEL: Police search for clues and medics tend to the injured following the terrorist bombing of a pizzeria in Jerusalem on Aug. 9, killing 15 people and wounding 70. As tensions in the Middle East continued to escalate, Israel was struck by a number of deadly bombings and retaliated strongly against Palestinian insurgents.

ROYAL MURDERS IN NEPAL: Nine members of Nepal's ruling family, including King Birendra and Queen Aiswarya, were slain in a horrendous bloodbath in the royal palace. Crown Prince Dipendra, believed to be romantically involved with a woman his parents did not approve of, was charged with the crimes. He shot himself after the murder spree and died days later. Below, the royal funeral pyres illuminate Kathmandu.

EARTHQUAKE IN INDIA: The small town of Rapar was reduced to rubble when a massive quake, measuring 7.7 in magnitude, struck India's western state of Gujarat on Feb. 1. Some 20,000 people were killed; tens of thousands more were left injured or homeless.

ON TRIAL: On June 28 Yugoslav authorities released former Serbian strongman Slobodan Milosevic into the custody of United Nations officials, who took him to stand trial before the UN war-crimes tribunal in The Hague. The unrepentant former president refused to enter a plea to the charges against him, branding the tribunal illegal and declaring himself a political prisoner. UN prosecutors said they would try Milosevic for the atrocities committed in Kosovo in 1999, and perhaps for the 1995 massacre of more than 7,000 Muslims in Srebrenica.

BALKAN BATTLES: Macedonia erupted in violence as government troops fought ethnic Albanian rebels. Above, shells from an army tank hit a house in March. After a peace agreement was signed in August, a NATO force entered the country to disarm the rebels.

THE NEW VANDALS: A soldier of the Taliban stands guard over the ruins of a 2,000-year-old statue of Buddha in Bamyan, 150 miles west of Kabul. The iconoclastic Muslim clerics of the nation's ruling party ordered all statues in the country destroyed. Inset: an earlier view of the 175-foot-tall statue, partially defaced.

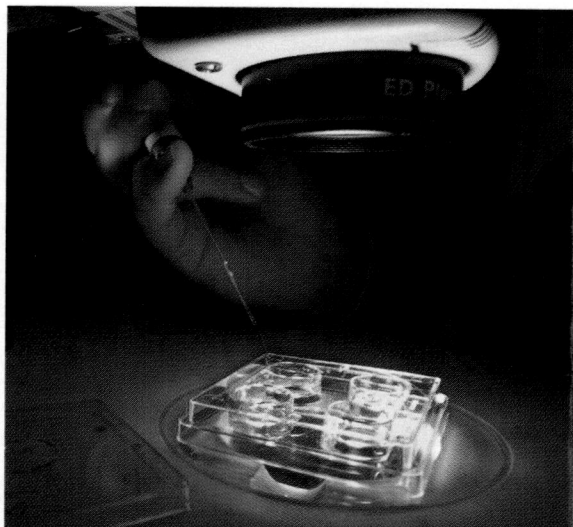

STEM-CELL DEBATE: A researcher works with human stem cells, which are extracted from embryos created for fertility treatments but not used to produce children. Scientists say the stem cells can potentially be made to grow into any cell in the human body, making them a potent resource in the fight against Alzheimer's, Parkinson's, diabetes, and other diseases. Pro-life advocates, including the Pope, branded the research a form of abortion and called for a halt to it. President George Bush strove for the middle ground in a major address, calling for limited research with a small number of stem-cell lines already in existence.

JUST VISITING: California millionaire Dennis Tito, 60, became the first tourist in space when he journeyed to the International Space Station in April. The reported cost for his ride aboard a Russian rocket: $20 million. NASA fought the trip, then reluctantly agreed to it.

CHINA'S GOT GAME: Sparking controversy, the International Olympic Committee awarded the Summer Games of 2008 to Beijing.

STRONG RETURN: Jennifer Capriati, 24, the one-time teen sensation of tennis, won both the Australian and French Opens.

SMACK! San Francisco's Barry Bonds hit 73 home runs to break the single-season record for homers held by Mark McGwire.

THIRD-TIME CHARMER: U.S. cycling hero Lance Armstrong won his sport's prestigious Tour de France for the third year in a row.

SHE'S BACK: Now 43, Madonna married British film director Guy Ritchie, had a second child, and mounted a world tour.

WISEGUY: HBO's portrait of a Mafia family, *The Sopranos,* won three Emmys, including one for James Gandolfini as Best Actor.

THAT'S SHOW BIZ: Nathan Lane, left, and Matthew Broderick starred in Broadway's biggest musical hit in years, funnyman Mel Brooks's adaptation of his 1968 movie *The Producers.* Brooks also wrote the score of the show, which garnered 12 Tony Awards.

JACK LEMMON: The popular actor, 76, whose career spanned five decades, died a year after his screen pal, Walter Matthau.

DALE EARNHARDT: The NASCAR racing circuit's legendary "Intimidator," 49, was killed in February when his car hit a wall.

KATHARINE GRAHAM: The publisher of the *Washington Post,* 84, led her paper to journalistic glory in the Watergate crisis.

CARROLL O'CONNOR: The veteran actor, 76, is indelibly linked with his portrayal of Archie Bunker on TV's *All in the Family.*

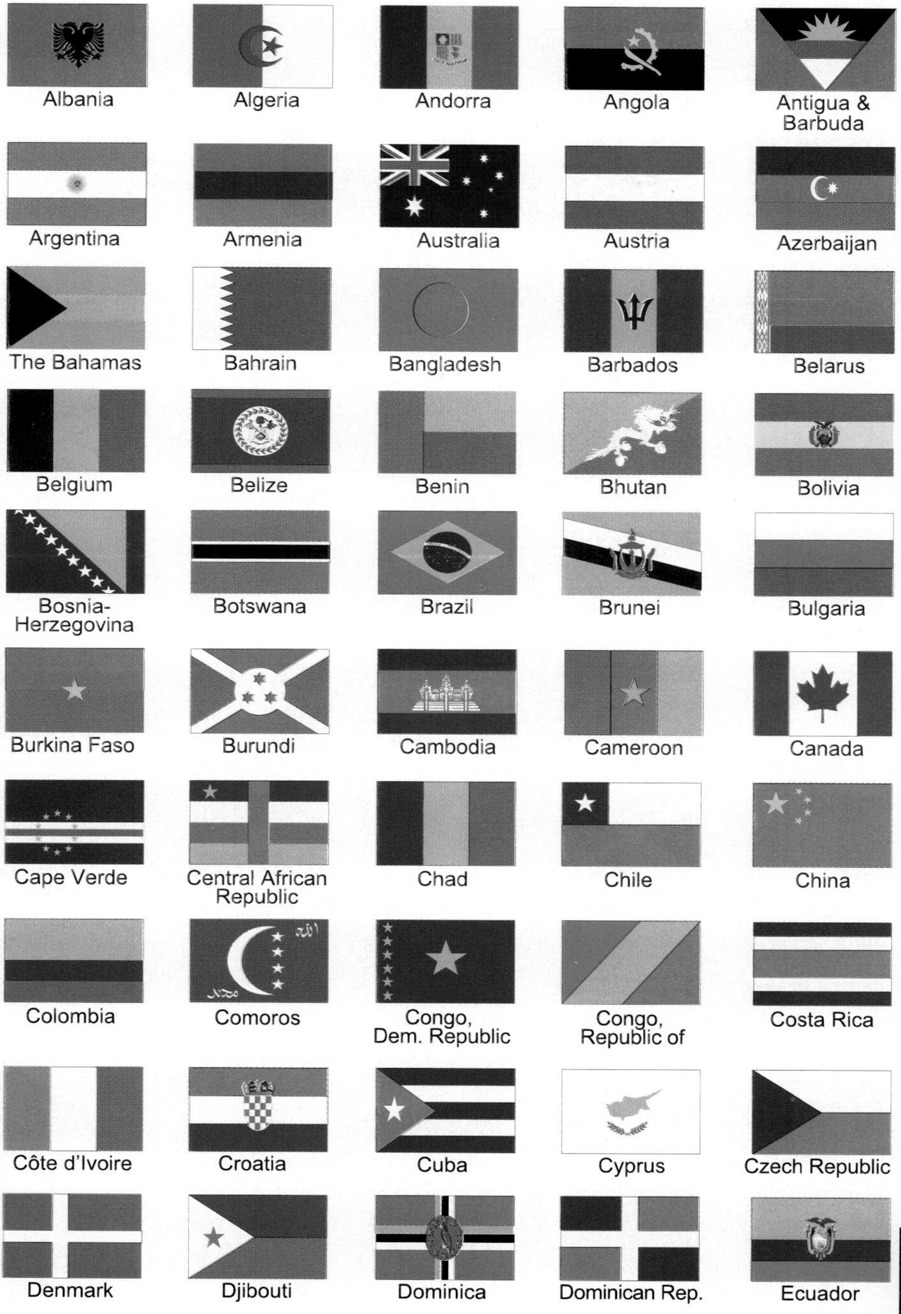

Albania	Algeria	Andorra	Angola	Antigua & Barbuda
Argentina	Armenia	Australia	Austria	Azerbaijan
The Bahamas	Bahrain	Bangladesh	Barbados	Belarus
Belgium	Belize	Benin	Bhutan	Bolivia
Bosnia-Herzegovina	Botswana	Brazil	Brunei	Bulgaria
Burkina Faso	Burundi	Cambodia	Cameroon	Canada
Cape Verde	Central African Republic	Chad	Chile	China
Colombia	Comoros	Congo, Dem. Republic	Congo, Republic of	Costa Rica
Côte d'Ivoire	Croatia	Cuba	Cyprus	Czech Republic
Denmark	Djibouti	Dominica	Dominican Rep.	Ecuador

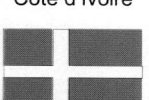

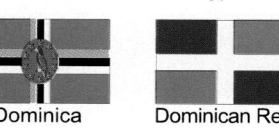

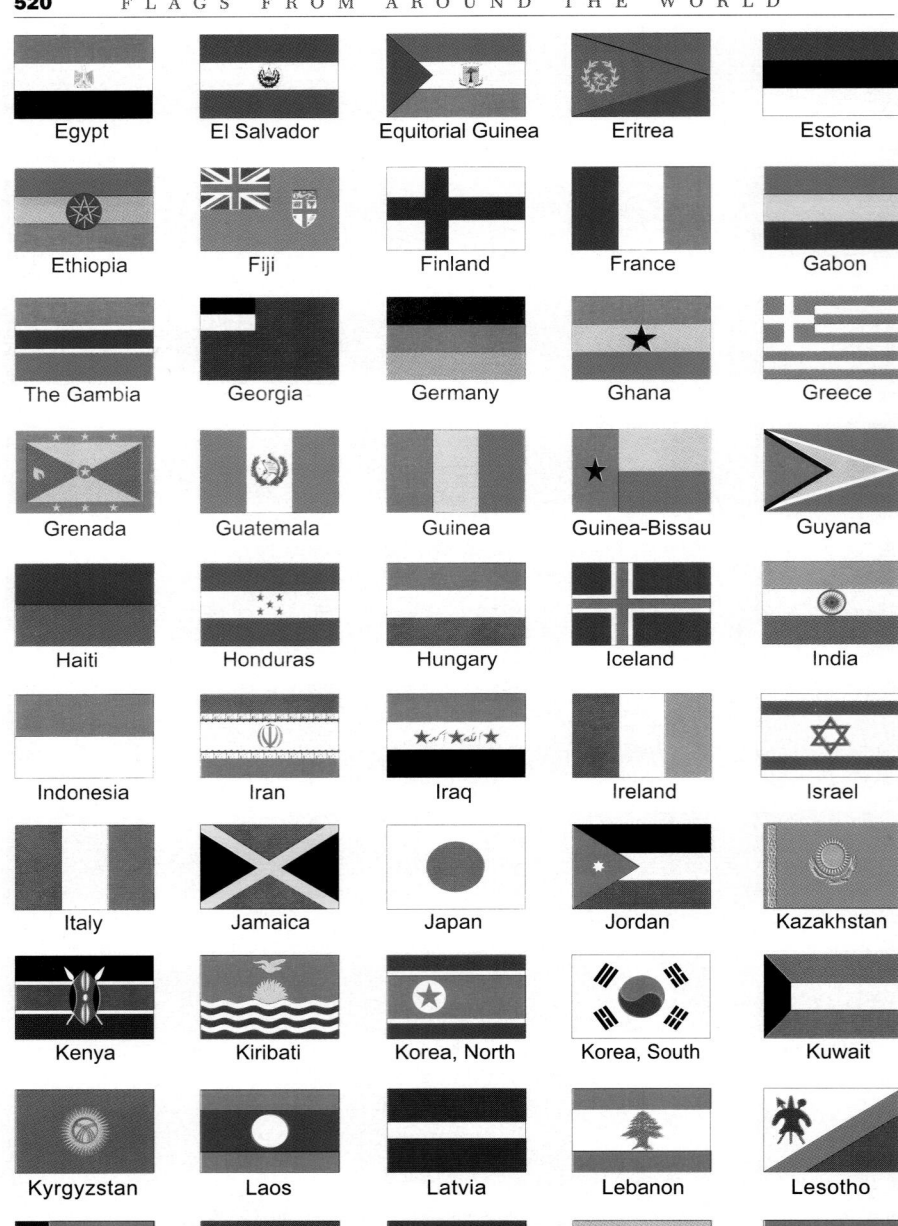

Egypt

El Salvador

Equitorial Guinea

Eritrea

Estonia

Ethiopia

Fiji

Finland

France

Gabon

The Gambia

Georgia

Germany

Ghana

Greece

Grenada

Guatemala

Guinea

Guinea-Bissau

Guyana

Haiti

Honduras

Hungary

Iceland

India

Indonesia

Iran

Iraq

Ireland

Israel

Italy

Jamaica

Japan

Jordan

Kazakhstan

Kenya

Kiribati

Korea, North

Korea, South

Kuwait

Kyrgyzstan

Laos

Latvia

Lebanon

Lesotho

Liberia

Libya

Liechtenstein

Lithuania

Luxembourg

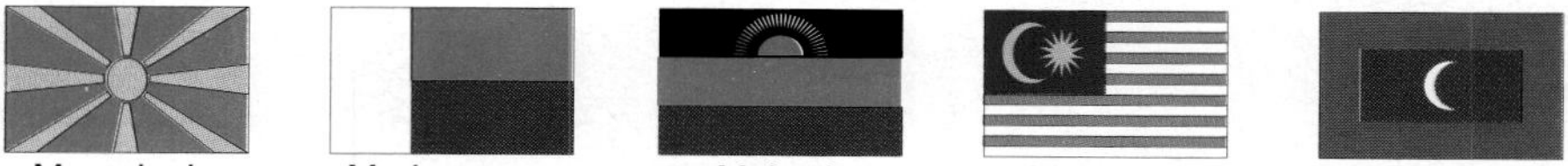

Macedonia

Madagascar

Malawi

Malaysia

Maldives

Mali

Malta

Marshall Is.

Mauritania

Mauritius

Mexico

Micronesia

Moldova

Monaco

Mongolia

Morocco

Mozambique

Myanmar

Namibia

Nauru

Nepal

The Netherlands

New Zealand

Nicaragua

Niger

Nigeria

Norway

Oman

Pakistan

Palau

Panama

Papua New Guinea

Paraguay

Peru

The Philippines

Poland

Portugal

Qatar

Romania

Russia

Rwanda

St. Kitts & Nevis

St. Lucia

St. Vincent &
The Grenadines

Samoa

San Marino

São Tomé &
Príncipe

Saudi Arabia

Senegal

Seychelles

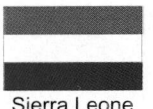
Sierra Leone

Singapore

Slovakia

Slovenia

Solomon Is.

Somalia

South Africa

Spain

Sri Lanka

The Sudan

Suriname

Swaziland

Sweden

Switzerland

Syria

Taiwan

Tajikistan

Tanzania

Thailand

Togo

Tonga

Trinidad & Tobago

Tunisia

Turkey

Turkmenistan

Tuvalu

Uganda

Ukraine

United Arab Emirates

United Kingdom

United States

Uruguay

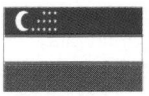
Uzbekistan

Vanuatu

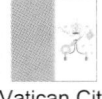
Vatican City

Venezuela

Vietnam

Yemen

Yugoslavia

Zambia

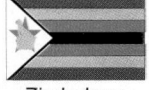
Zimbabwe

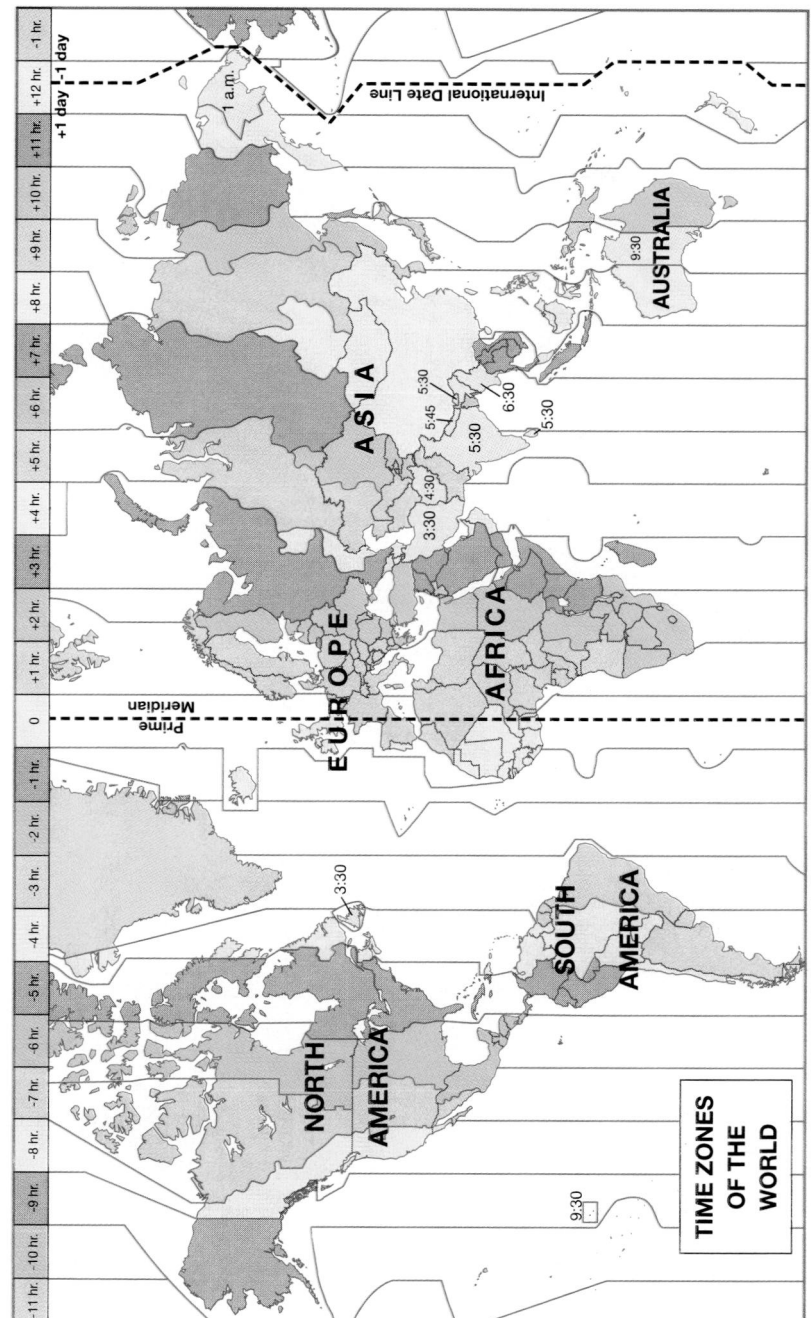

TIME ZONES
OF THE
WORLD

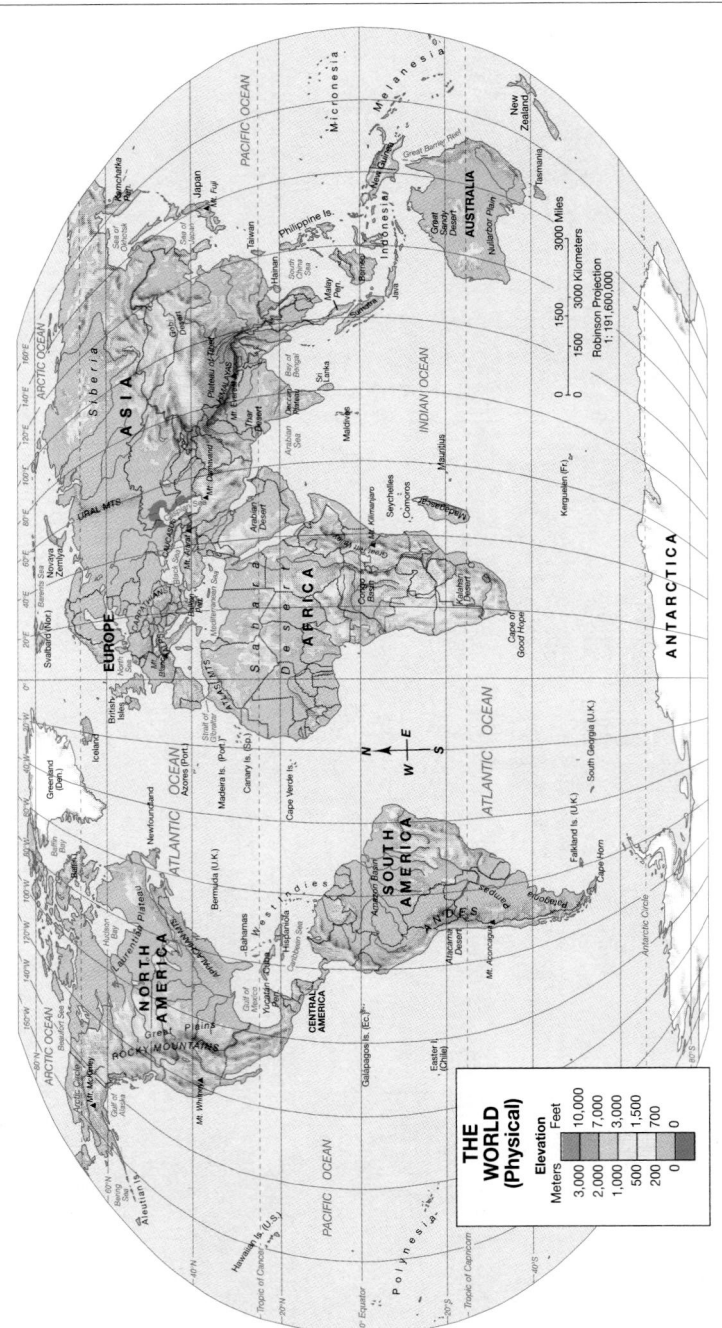

THE
WORLD
(Physical)

Elevation

Meters	Feet
3,000	10,000
2,000	7,000
1,000	3,000
500	1,500
200	700
0	0

Robinson Projection
1: 191,600,000

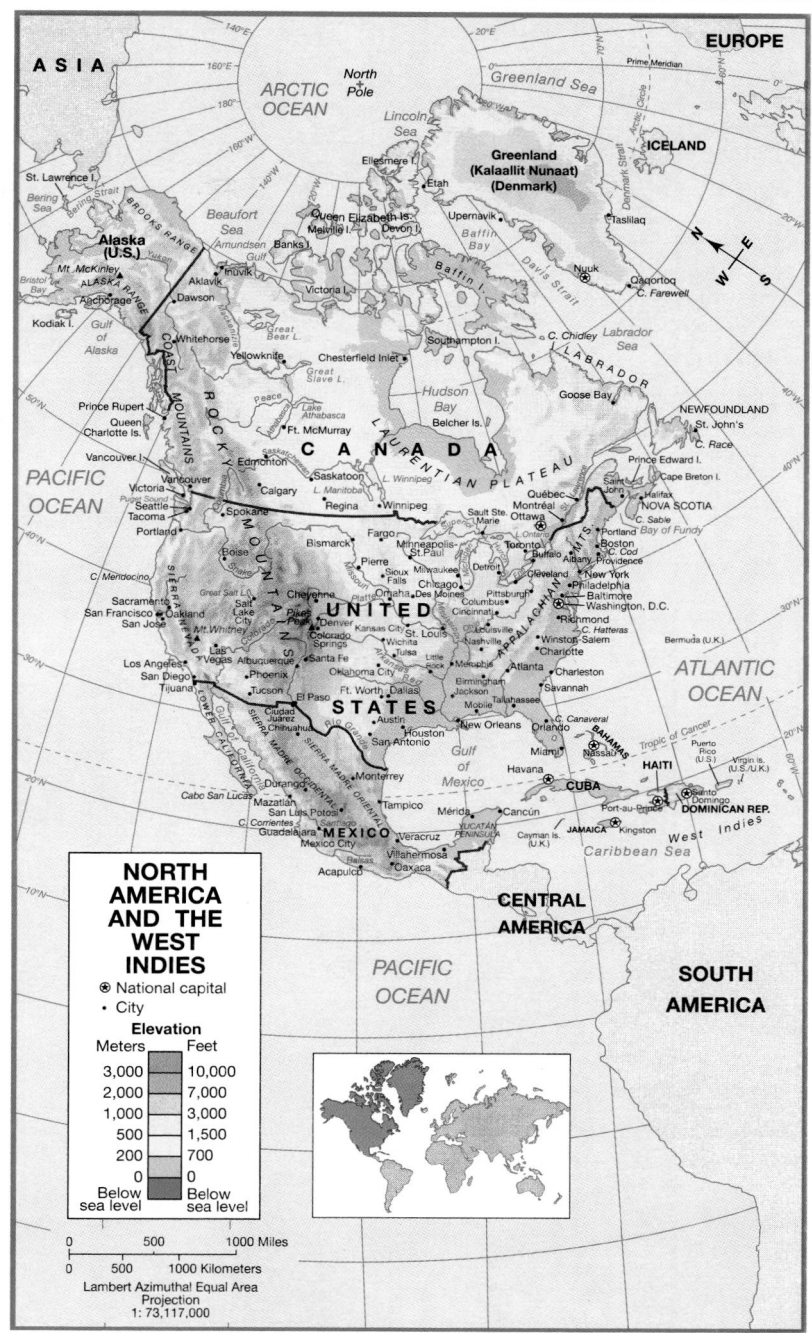

NORTH AMERICA AND THE WEST INDIES

⊛ National capital
• City

Elevation

Meters	Feet
3,000	10,000
2,000	7,000
1,000	3,000
500	1,500
200	700
0	0
Below sea level	Below sea level

| 0 | 500 | 1000 Miles |
| 0 | 500 | 1000 Kilometers |

Lambert Azimuthal Equal Area Projection
1: 73,117,000

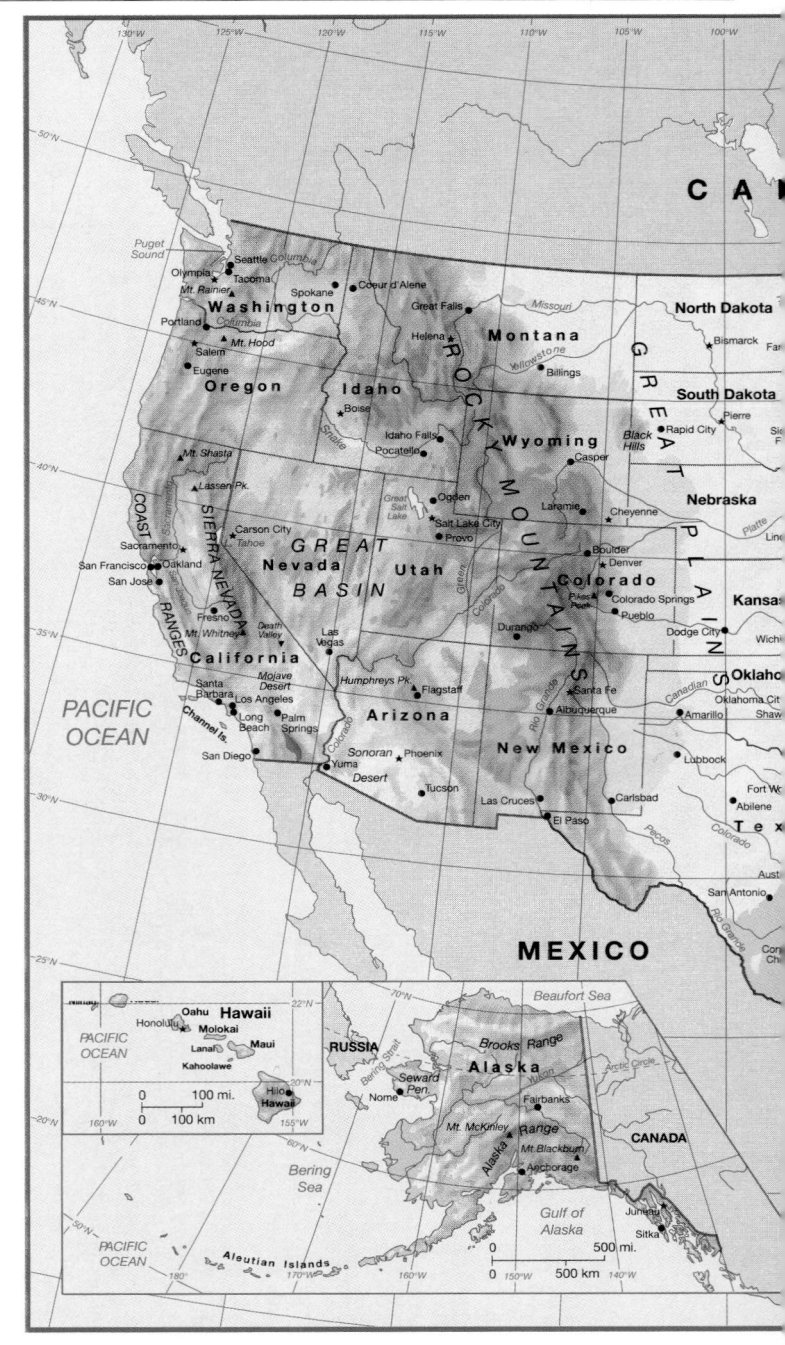

A D A

Maine

L. Champlain

Augusta *Gulf of Maine*

nesota
Duluth
Superior

Lake Superior

Sault Ste. Marie

Montpelier
Mt. Washington
Portland

Vt. N.H.
Portsmouth
Concord

Manchester

St. Paul
Green Bay
Eau Claire

Lake Huron

L. Ontario
New York
Albany
Boston *Cape Cod*

inneapolis

Rochester

Wisconsin
Madison

Grand Rapids
Flint

Rochester
Syracuse
Hartford
Worcester

Buffalo
Mass.
Conn.

ux City

Milwaukee
Lansing
Ann Arbor
Detroit
Providence
R.I.

Iowa
Cedar Rapids
Rockford

Kenosha
Chicago
Gary

Erie
Cleveland
Akron

Pennsylvania
Reading
New Haven
Long Island
New York

Newark
New Jersey
Trenton

Rock Island

Fort Wayne
Toledo

Harrisburg

Philadelphia

omaha
Des Moines

Illinois

Ohio

Pittsburgh
Baltimore
Md.
Atlantic City

Champaign

Muncie
Springfield
Columbus
Clarksburg

Dover
Delaware

Springfield

Indianapolis
Indiana

Dayton
Cincinnati

W. Va.
Virginia

Annapolis
Washington, D.C.

aka
Missouri

Louisville
Frankfort

Charleston

Richmond
Chesapeake Bay

Kansas City
St. Louis

Ohio

Lexington

Lynchburg
Williamsburg

Jefferson City

Missouri
Springfield

Kentucky

Winston-Salem
Durham

Norfolk
Virginia Beach

Bowling Green

Knoxville
Raleigh

Cape Hatteras

Nashville

North Carolina

Tulsa

Tennessee
Chattanooga

Charlotte

ATLANTIC OCEAN

Arkansas
Fort Smith

Memphis

Columbia

Wilmington

N

Little Rock

Tennessee

Athens
South Carolina

W   E

Birmingham
Atlanta
Augusta
Charleston

S

las

Alabama
Georgia
Macon

Savannah

Mississippi
Jackson

Montgomery

Shreveport

Albany

Louisiana

Mobile
Pensacola
Tallahassee

Jacksonville
St. Augustine

BAHAMAS

Baton Rouge

Daytona Beach

Port Arthur
ston

New Orleans

Florida
Orlando
Cape Canaveral

Galveston

Tampa

St. Petersburg
L. Okeechobee

Gulf of Mexico

Fort Lauderdale

Miami

Straits of Florida

Florida Keys

CUBA

0	200	400 Miles
0	200	400 Kilometers

Albers Equal-Area Projection
1: 26,044,000

UNITED STATES

⊛ National capital
★ State capital
● City

Elevation

Meters	Feet
3,000	10,000
2,000	7,000
1,000	3,000
500	1,500
200	700
0	0

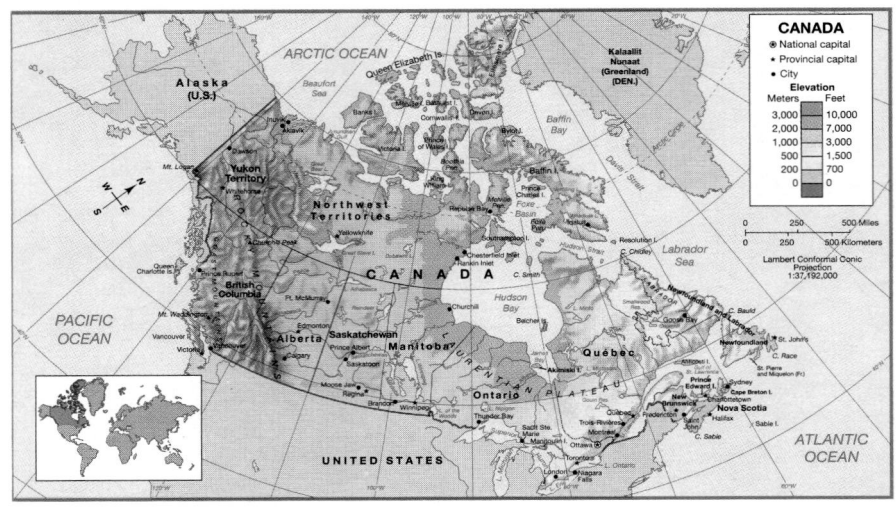

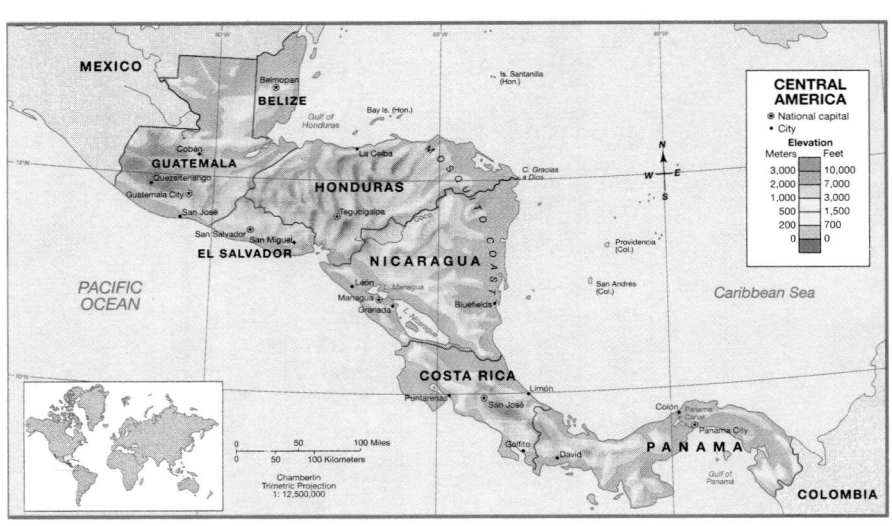

Galápagos Is. (Ecuador)
I. Marchena
I. San Salvador
I. Santa Cruz
I. Fernandina
I. Sta.Maria
I. San Cristóbal
I. Española

WEST INDIES

Caribbean Sea

CENTRAL AMERICA

Neth. Antilles (Neth.)
I. de Margarita
Curaçao
Gulf of Venezuela
Gulf of Paria

Barranquilla
Cartagena
Maracaibo
Caracas
Montería
Cúcuta
Medellín
San Cristóbal
Manizales
Bucaramanga
Bogotá
C. Corrientes
Buenaventura
Cali
Mt. Huila

VENEZUELA
Ciudad Bolívar
Morawhanna
Georgetown
New Amsterdam
Paramaribo

GUYANA
SURINAME
Devil's I.
Cayenne
French Guiana (Fr.)

ATLANTIC OCEAN

I. de Maracá
I. Caviana

ECUADOR
Mt. Cotopaxi
Mt. Chimborazo
Quito
Ambato
Guayaquil
Cuenca
Gulf of Guayaquil
Iquitos

Equator

I. Malpelo (Colombia)

COLOMBIA

PERU
Piura
Trujillo
Mt. Huascarán
Callao
Lima

Manaus

BRAZIL

Belém
I. São Luis
Fortaleza
C. São Roque
Recife
São Francisco
Salvador

A N D E S

Cuzco
El Misti
La Paz
Arequipa
Cochabamba
Potosí
Sucre
Poopó
Iquique

BOLIVIA
Trinidad
Santa Cruz

Brasília
Belo Horizonte

PACIFIC OCEAN

Antofagasta

San Felix (Chile)
San Ambrosio (Chile)

PARAGUAY
Asunción

San Miguel de Tucumán

Mt. Ojos del Salado

CHILE

Córdoba

São Paulo
Santos
Rio de Janeiro
C. São Tomé

Curitiba
I. de Santa Catarina
Porto Alegre
Tropic of Capricorn

Mt. Aconcagua
Viña del Mar
Valparaíso
Santiago
Juan Fernández Is. (Chile)
I. Robinson Crusoe
I. Alejandro Selkirk
Concepción

Mendoza
Rosario
Vol. Maipo
Buenos Aires
La Plata

Salto
Rivera
Paysandú
URUGUAY
Montevideo

L. dos Patos
L. Mirí

Río de la Plata
C. San Antonio
Mar del Plata

ARGENTINA

Negro
Bahía Blanca
Gulf of San Matías
Pen. Valdés

ATLANTIC OCEAN

I. de Chiloé
Gulf of Corcovado
Archipiélago de los Chonos
Pen. Taitao
C. Tres Montes
Gulf of Penas

Gulf of San Jorge

SOUTH AMERICA

⊛ National capital
• City

Elevation

Meters		Feet
3,000		10,000
2,000		7,000
1,000		3,000
500		1,500
200		700
0		0

Falkland Islands (U.K.; claimed by Arg.)
Stanley

Strait of Magellan
Tierra del Fuego
I. Sta. Inés
Cape Horn
I. de los Estados

South Georgia (U.K.)

Antarctic Circle

0	300	600 Miles
0	300	600 Kilometers

Lambert Azimuthal Equal-Area Projection
1: 43,697,000

N
W — E
S

WESTERN EUROPE

⊛ National capital
• City

Elevation

Meters	Feet
3,000	10,000
2,000	7,000
1,000	3,000
500	1,500
200	700
0	0

0   200   400 Miles

0   200   400 Kilometers

Azimuthal Equal-Area Projection
1: 31,019,000

EASTERN EUROPE

⊛ National capital
• City

Elevation

Meters	Feet
3,000	10,000
2,000	7,000
1,000	3,000
500	1,500
200	700
0	0

0   200   400 Miles

0   200   400 Kilometers

Azimuthal Equal-Area Projection
1: 31,019,000

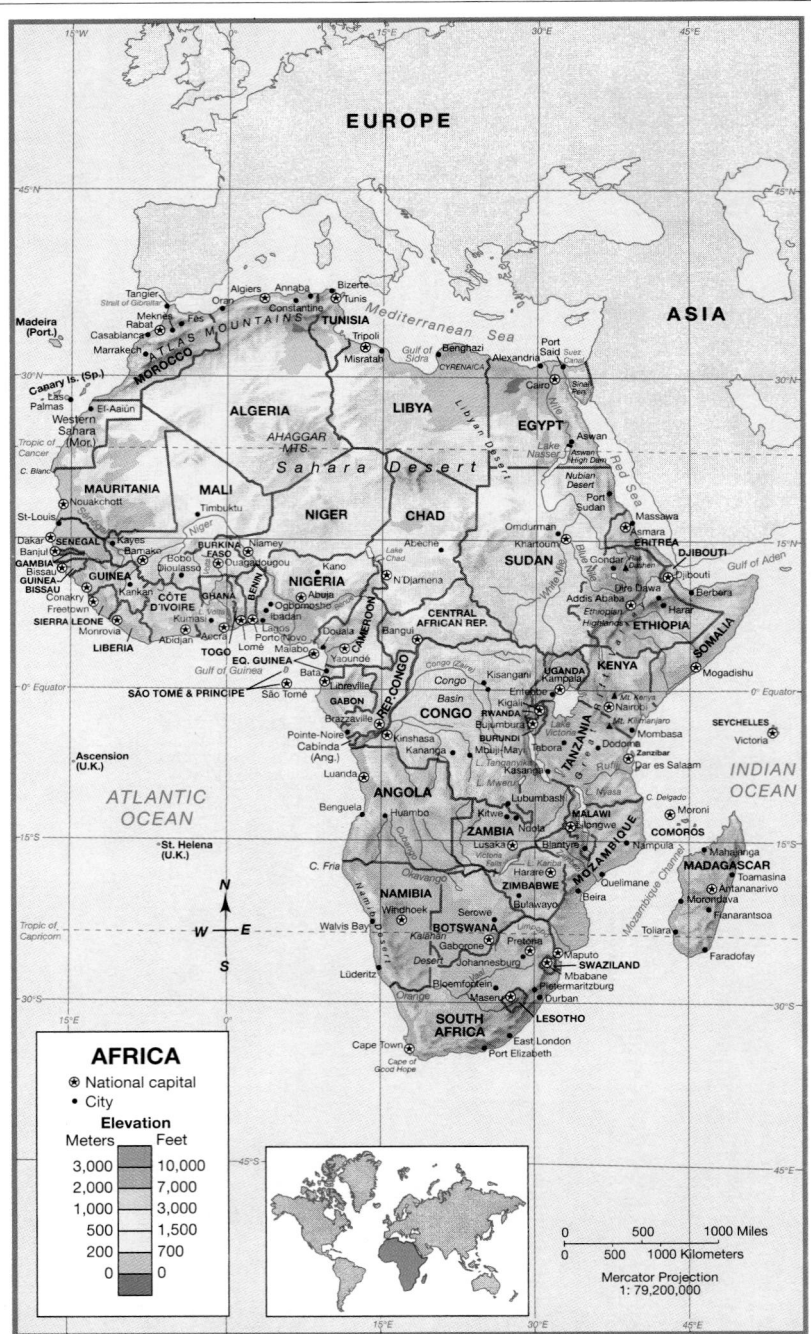

AFRICA

⊛ National capital
• City

Elevation

Meters		Feet
3,000		10,000
2,000		7,000
1,000		3,000
500		1,500
200		700
0		0

0   500   1000 Miles

0   500   1000 Kilometers

Mercator Projection
1: 79,200,000

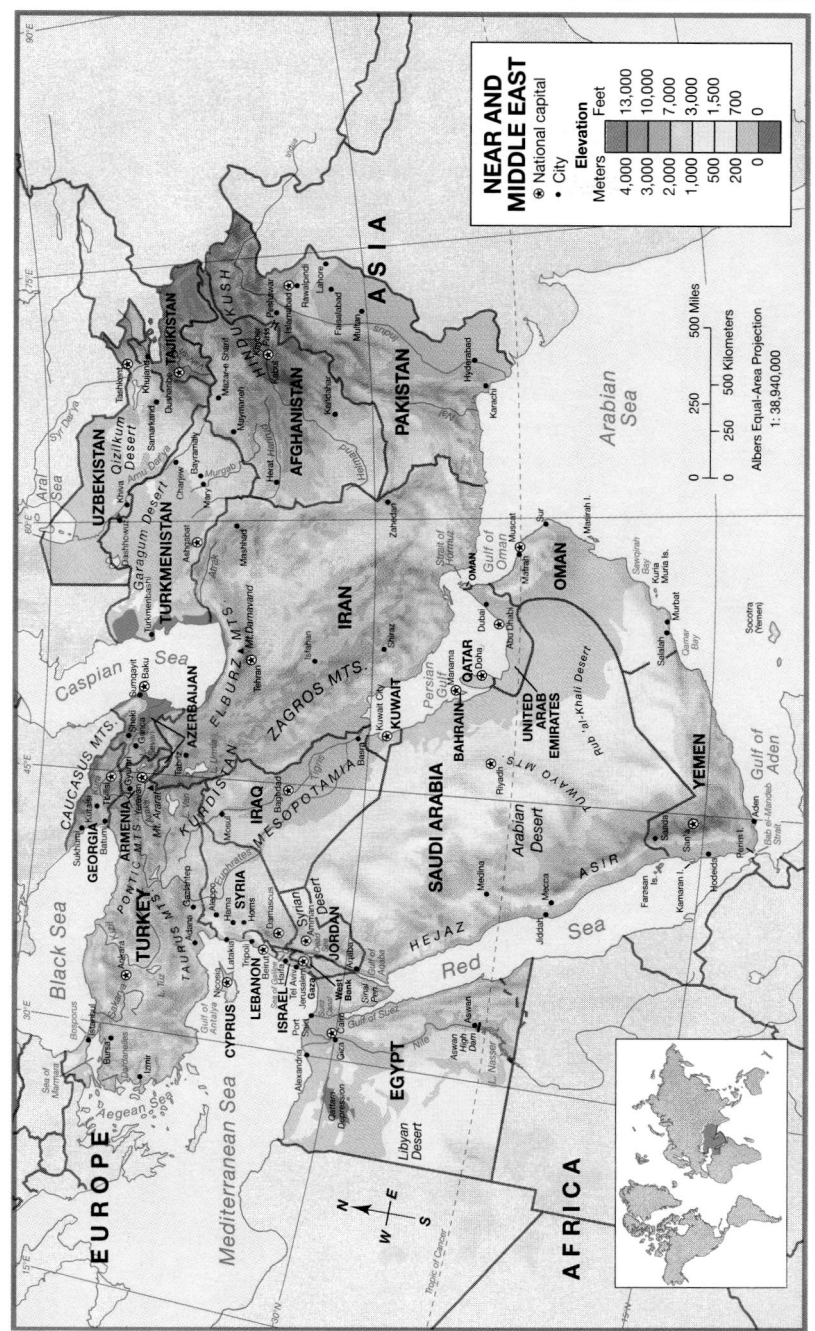

NEAR AND MIDDLE EAST

⊛ National capital
● City

Elevation

Meters	Feet
4,000	13,000
3,000	10,000
2,000	7,000
1,000	3,000
500	1,500
200	700
0	0

Albers Equal-Area Projection
1: 38,940,000

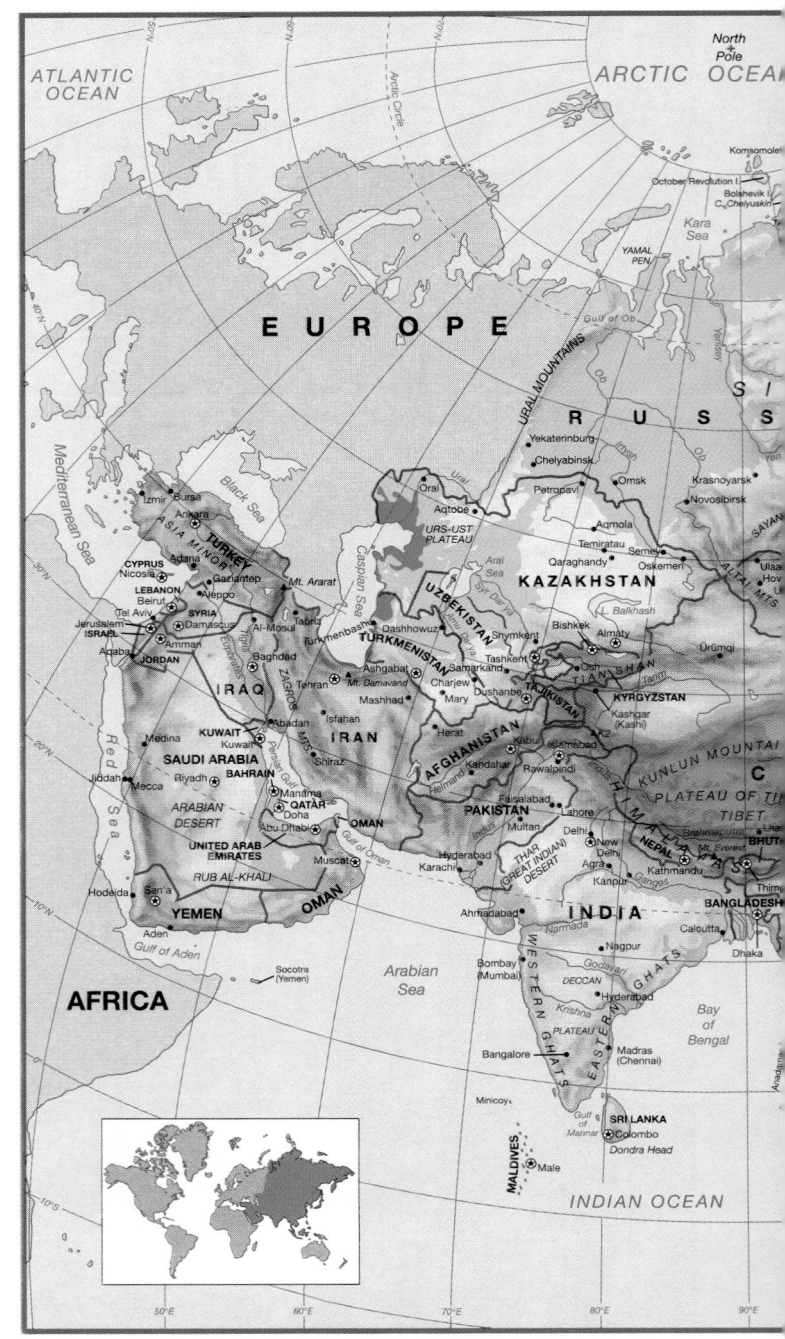

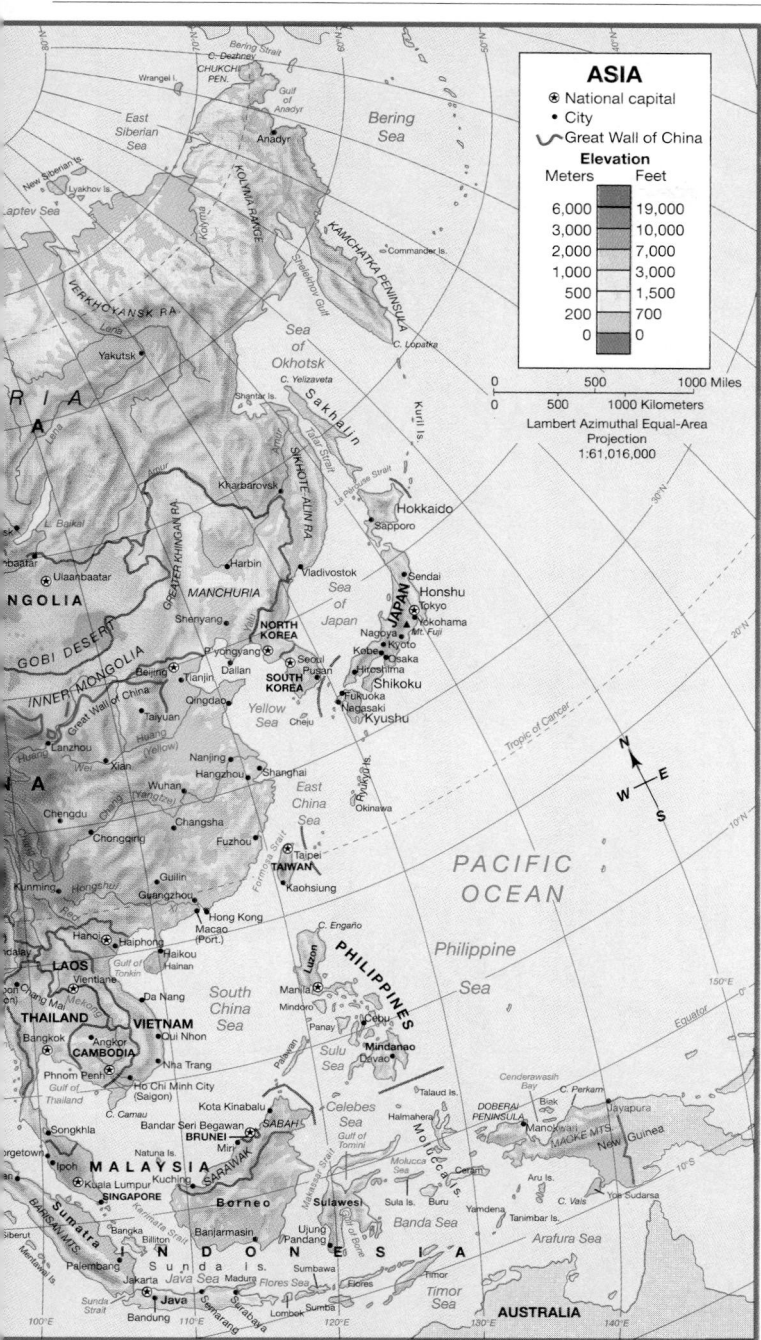

ASIA

⊕ National capital
• City
〜 Great Wall of China

Elevation

Meters	Feet
6,000	19,000
3,000	10,000
2,000	7,000
1,000	3,000
500	1,500
200	700
0	0

0   500   1000 Miles
0   500   1000 Kilometers

Lambert Azimuthal Equal-Area
Projection
1:61,016,000

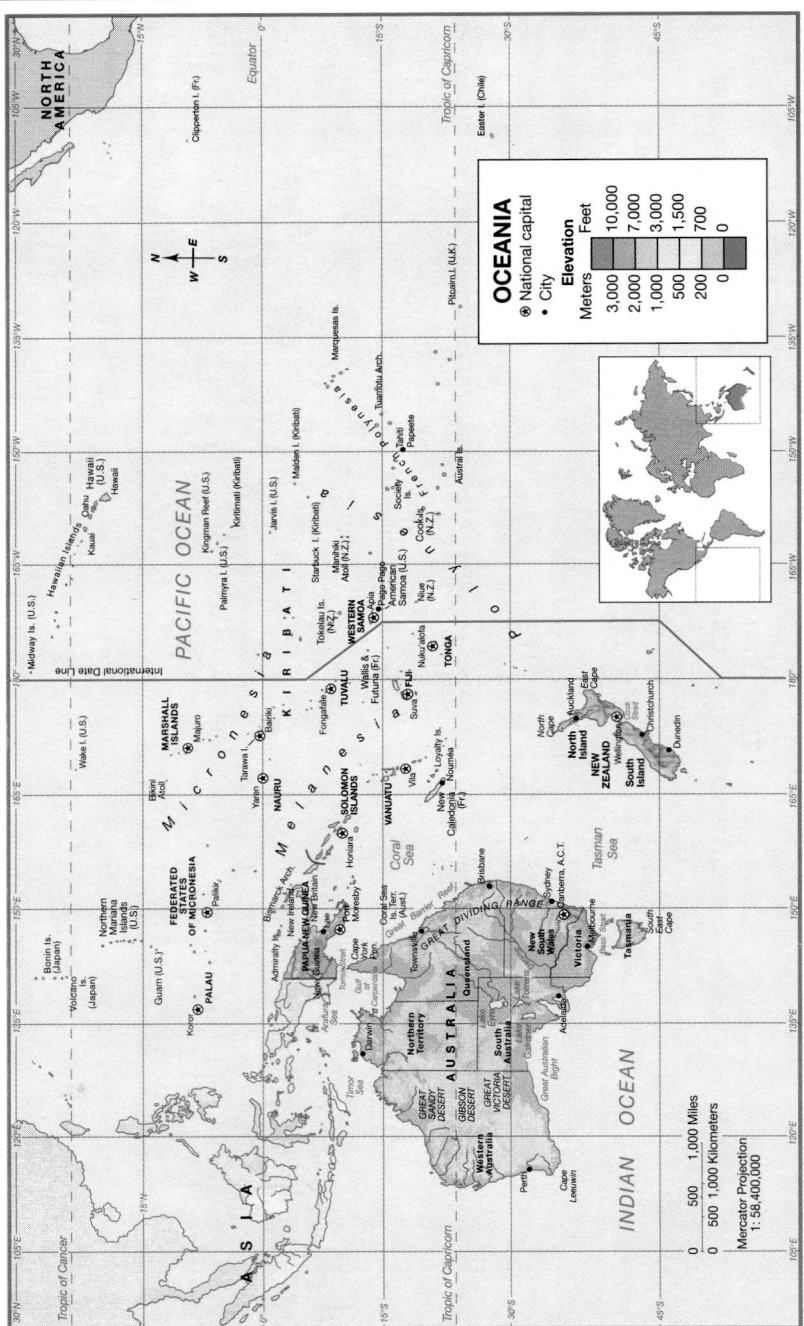

OCEANIA

⊛ National capital
• City

Elevation

Meters	Feet
3,000	10,000
2,000	7,000
1,000	3,000
500	1,500
200	700
0	0

PACIFIC OCEAN

INDIAN OCEAN

NORTH AMERICA

A S I A

AUSTRALIA

NEW ZEALAND

Equator

Tropic of Cancer

Tropic of Capricorn

International Date Line

Mercator Projection
1: 58,400,000

0   500   1,000 Miles
0   500   1,000 Kilometers

Conversion Factors

To change	To	Multiply by	To change	To	Multiply by
acres	square feet	43,560	liters	quarts (liquid)	1.0567
acres	square miles	.001562	meters	feet	3.2808
atmospheres	cms. of mercury	76	meters	miles	.0006214
Btu	kilowatt-hour	.0002931	meters	yards	1.0936
Btu/hour	watts	.2931	metric tons	tons (long)	.9842
bushels	cubic inches	2150.4	metric tons	tons (short)	1.1023
centimeters	inches	.3937	miles	kilometers	1.6093
centimeters	feet	.03281	miles	feet	5280
cubic feet	cubic meters	.0283	miles (nautical)	miles (statute)	1.1516
cubic meters	cubic feet	35.3145	miles (statute)	miles (nautical)	.8684
cubic meters	cubic yards	1.3079	miles/hour	feet/minute	88
cubic yards	cubic meters	.7646	millimeters	inches	.0394
fathoms	feet	6.0	ounces (avdp)	grams	28.3495
feet	meters	.3048	ounces	pounds	.0625
feet	miles (nautical)	.0001645	ounces (troy)	ounces (avdp)	1.09714
feet	miles (statute)	.0001894	pecks	liters	8.8096
feet/second	miles/hour	.6818	pints (dry)	liters	.5506
furlongs	feet	660.0	pints (liquid)	liters	.4732
furlongs	miles	.125	pounds (ap or troy)	kilograms	.3782
gallons (U.S.)	liters	3.7853	pounds (avdp)	kilograms	.4536
grains	grams	.0648	pounds	ounces	16
grams	ounces (avdp)	.0353	quarts (dry)	liters	1.1012
grams	pounds	.002205	quarts (liquid)	liters	.9463
hectares	acres	2.4710	radians	degrees	57.30
hectoliters	bushels (U.S.)	2.8378	rods	meters	5.029
horsepower	watts	745.7	rods	feet	16.5
horsepower	Btu/hour	.001341	square feet	square meters	.0929
hours	days	.04167	square kilometers	square miles	.3861
inches	millimeters	25.4000	square meters	square feet	10.7639
inches	centimeters	2.5400	square miles	square kilometers	2.5900
kilograms	pounds (avdp or troy)	2.2046	square yards	square meters	.8361
kilometers	miles	.6214	tons (long)	metric tons	1.016
kilowatt-hour	Btu	3412	tons (short)	metric tons	.9072
knots	nautical miles/hour	1.0	tons (long)	pounds	2240
knots	statute miles/hour	1.151	tons (short)	pounds	2000
liters	gallons (U.S.)	.2642	watts	Btu/hour	3.4121
liters	pints (dry)	1.8162	watts	horsepower	.001341
liters	pints (liquid)	2.1134	yards	meters	.9144
liters	quarts (dry)	.9081	yards	miles	.0005682

NOTE: avdp = avoirdupois weight, ap = apothecaries' weight. *See also* p.539.

Fahrenheit and Celsius (Centigrade) Scales

°Celsius	°Fahrenheit	°Celsius	°Fahrenheit
−273.15	−459.67	30	86
−250	−418	35	95
−200	−328	40	104
−150	−238	45	113
−100	−148	50	122
−50	−58	55	131
−40	−40	60	140
−30	−22	65	149
−20	−4	70	158
−10	14	75	167
0	32	80	176
5	41	85	185
10	50	90	194
15	59	95	203
20	68	100	212
25	77		

Zero on the Fahrenheit scale represents the temperature produced by the mixing of equal weights of snow and common salt.

	°Fahrenheit	°Celsius
Boiling point of water	212°	100°
Freezing point of water	32°	0°
Absolute zero	−459.6°	−273.1°

Absolute zero is theoretically the lowest possible temperature, the point at which all molecular motion would cease.

To convert Fahrenheit to Celsius (Centigrade), subtract 32 and divide by 1.8.

To convert Celsius (Centigrade) to Fahrenheit, multiply by 1.8 and add 32.

Kelvin Scale

Absolute zero, −273.15° on the Celsius (Centigrade) scale, is 0 Kelvin. Thus, Kelvin is equivalent to Celsius plus 273.15. The freezing point of water, 0°C and 32°F, is 273.15K. The conversion formula is K = C° + 273.15.

Cardinal, Ordinal, and Nominal Numbers

Cardinal numbers, known as the "counting numbers," indicate quantity. **Ordinal numbers** indicate the order or rank of things in a set (e.g., sixth in line; fourth place). **Nominal numbers** name or identify something (e.g., a zip code or a player on a team.) They do not show quantity or rank.

Roman Numerals

Roman numerals are expressed by letters of the alphabet and are rarely used today except for formality or variety. There are four basic principles for reading Roman numerals:

1. A letter repeated once or twice repeats its value that many times (XXX = 30, CC = 200, etc.).
2. One or more letters placed after another letter of greater value increases the greater value by the amount of the smaller (VI = 6, LXX = 70, MCC = 1200, etc.).
3. A letter placed before another letter of greater value decreases the greater value by the amount of the smaller (IV = 4, XC = 90, CM = 900, etc.).
4. A bar placed on top of a letter or string of letters increases the numeral's value by 1,000 times (XV = 15, $\overline{XV}$ = 15,000).

Letter	Value	Letter	Value	Letter	Value	Letter	Value	Letter	Value
I	1	VII	7	XL	40	C	100	$\overline{C}$	100,000
II	2	VIII	8	L	50	D	500	$\overline{D}$	500,000
III	3	IX	9	LX	60	M	1,000	$\overline{M}$	1,000,000
IV	4	X	10	LXX	70	$\overline{V}$	5,000		
V	5	XX	20	LXXX	80	$\overline{X}$	10,000		
VI	6	XXX	30	XC	90	$\overline{L}$	50,000		

Mean and Median

The arithmetic mean, also called the average, of a series of quantities is obtained by finding the sum of the quantities and dividing it by the number of quantities. In the series 1, 3, 5, 18, 19, 20, 25, the mean or average is 13—in other words, 91 divided by 7.

The median of a series is that point which so divides it that half the quantities are on one side, half on the other. In the above series, the median is 18.

The median often better expresses the common-run, since it is not, as is the mean, affected by an excessively high or low figure. In the series 1, 3, 4, 7, 55, the median of 4 is a truer expression of the common-run than is the mean of 14.

Prime Numbers between 1 and 1,000

	2	3	5	7	11	13	17	19	23
29	31	37	41	43	47	53	59	61	67
71	73	79	83	89	97	101	103	107	109
113	127	131	137	139	149	151	157	163	167
173	179	181	191	193	197	199	211	223	227
229	233	239	241	251	257	263	269	271	277
281	283	293	307	311	313	317	331	337	347
349	353	359	367	373	379	383	389	397	401
409	419	421	431	433	439	443	449	457	461
463	467	479	487	491	499	503	509	521	523
541	547	557	563	569	571	577	587	593	599
601	607	613	617	619	631	641	643	647	653
659	661	673	677	683	691	701	709	719	727
733	739	743	751	757	761	769	773	787	797
809	811	821	823	827	829	839	853	857	859
863	877	881	883	887	907	911	919	929	937
941	947	953	967	971	977	983	991	997	(1009)

Portraits and Designs of U.S. Paper Currency

Currency[1]	Portrait	Design on back	Currency[1]	Portrait	Design on back
$1	Washington	ONE between obverse and reverse of Great Seal of U.S.	$50[5]	Grant	U.S. Capitol
			$100[6]	Franklin	Independence Hall
$2[2]	Jefferson	Monticello	$500	McKinley	Ornate FIVE HUNDRED
$2[3]	Jefferson	"The Signing of the Declaration of Independence"	$1,000	Cleveland	Ornate ONE THOUSAND
			$5,000	Madison	Ornate FIVE THOUSAND
$5	Lincoln	Lincoln Memorial	$10,000	Chase	Ornate TEN THOUSAND
$10	Hamilton	U.S. Treasury Building	$100,000[7]	Wilson	Ornate ONE HUNDRED THOUSAND
$20[4]	Jackson	White House			

1. Denominations of $500 and higher were discontinued in 1969. 2. Discontinued in 1966. 3. New issue, April 1976. 4. New issue, Sept. 1998. 5. New issue, Fall 1997. 6. New issue, March 1996. 7. For use only in transactions between Federal Reserve System and Treasury Department.

New Quarters and Dollar Coin

The 50 State Quarters Program Act began in 1999 and is expected to run until 2008, with five new quarters released every year over ten years. The quarters are being released in the order that the states joined the union. 700 million copies of each quarter will be produced. Each quarter will feature a different state design on the back

In 2000, a new dollar coin, featuring the Shoshone guide Sacagawea, replaced the Susan B. Anthony coin, whose reserves are running low.

State	Date of Statehood	Year of Issue	Design
Delaware	Dec. 7, 1787	1999	Caesar Rodney's horseback ride
Pennsylvania	Dec. 12, 1787	1999	Commonwealth statue, keystone, and outline of state
New Jersey	Dec. 18, 1787	1999	Washington crossing the Delaware River
Georgia	Jan. 2, 1788	1999	Peach, Live Oak, and outline of state
Connecticut	Jan. 9, 1788	1999	The Charter Oak
Massachusetts	Feb. 6, 1788	2000	Minuteman statue and outline of state
Maryland	April 28, 1788	2000	Maryland Statehouse and White Oak
South Carolina	May 23, 1788	2000	Palmetto tree, Carolina wren, and Yellow Jessamine
New Hampshire	June 21, 1788	2000	Old Man of the Mountain rock formation
Virginia	June 25, 1788	2000	First three ships to Jamestown
New York	July 26, 1788	2001	Statue of Liberty, state outline, the words, "Gateway to Freedom," 11 stars
North Carolina	November 21, 1789	2001	First flight at Kitty Hawk
Rhode Island	May 29, 1790	2001	A sailboat on the open sea, commemorating the "Ocean State"
Vermont	March 4, 1791	2001	Camel's Hump Mountain, maple trees with sap buckets
Kentucky	June 1, 1792	2001	Federal Hill, or "My Old Kentucky Home," race horse behind a fence

Customary U.S. Weights and Measures

Linear Measure

12 inches (in.) = 1 foot (ft.)
3 feet = 1 yard (yd)
5½ yards = 1 rod (rd), pole, or perch (16½ ft.)
40 rods = 1 furlong (fur) = 220 yds = 660 ft.
8 furlongs = 1 statute mile (mi.) = 1,760 yds
= 5,280 ft.
3 land miles = 1 league
5,280 feet = 1 statute or land mile
6,076.11549 feet = 1 international nautical mile

Area Measure

144 square inches = 1 sq ft.
9 square feet = 1 sq yd = 1,296 sq in.
30¼ square yards = 1 sq rd = 272¼ sq ft.
160 square rods = 1 acre = 4,840 sq yds
= 43,560 sq ft.
640 acres = 1 sq mi.
1 mile square = 1 section (of land)
6 miles square = 1 township = 36 sections
= 36 sq mi.

Cubic Measure

1,728 cubic inches = 1 cu ft.
27 cubic feet = 1 cu yd

Liquid Measure

When necessary to distinguish the liquid pint or quart from the dry pint or quart, the word "liquid" or the abbreviation "liq" should be used in combination with the name or abbreviation of the liquid unit.

4 gills (gi) = 1 pint (pt) (= 28.875 cu in.)
2 pints = 1 quart (qt) (= 57.75 cu in.)
4 quarts = 1 gallon (gal) (= 231 cu in.)
= 8 pts = 32 gills

Apothecaries' Fluid Measure

60 minims (min.) = 1 fluid dram (fl dr) (= 0.2256 cu in.)
8 fluid drams = 1 fluid ounce (fl oz) (= 1.8047 cu in.)
16 fluid ounces = 1 pt (= 28.875 cu in.) = 128 fl drs
2 pints = 1 qt (= 57.75 cu in.) = 32 fl oz
= 256 fl drs
4 quarts = 1 gal (= 231 cu in.) = 128 fl oz
= 1,024 fl drs

Dry Measure

When necessary to distinguish the dry pint or quart from the liquid pint or quart, the word "dry" should be used in combination with the name or abbreviation of the dry unit.

2 pints = 1 qt (= 67.2006 cu in.)
8 quarts = 1 peck (pk) (= 537.605 cu in.) = 16 pts
4 pecks = 1 bushel (bu) (= 2,150.42 cu in.) = 32 qts

Avoirdupois Weight

When necessary to distinguish the avoirdupois dram from the apothecaries' dram, or to distinguish the avoirdupois dram or ounce from the fluid dram or ounce, or to distinguish the avoirdupois ounce or pound from the troy or apothecaries' ounce or pound, the word "avoirdupois" or the abbreviation "avdp" should be used in combination with the name or abbreviation of the avoirdupois unit. (The "grain" is the same in avoirdupois, troy, and apothecaries' weights.)

27^{11}⁄$_{32}$ grains = 1 dram (dr)
16 drams = 1 oz = 437½ grains
16 ounces = 1 lb = 256 drams = 7,000 grains
100 pounds = 1 hundredweight (cwt)[1]
20 hundredweights = 1 ton (tn) = 2,000 lbs[1]

In "gross" or "long" measure, the following values are recognized:

112 pounds = 1 gross or long cwt[1]
20 gross or long hundredweights = 1 gross or long ton
= 2,240 lbs[1]

1. When the terms "hundredweight" and "ton" are used unmodified, they are commonly understood to mean the 100-pound hundredweight and the 2,000-pound ton, respectively; these units may be designated "net" or "short" when necessary to distinguish them from the corresponding units in gross or long measure.

Units of Circular Measure

Second (″) = —
Minute (′) = 60 seconds
Degree (°) = 60 minutes
Right angle = 90 degrees
Straight angle = 180 degrees
Circle = 360 degrees

Troy Weight

24 grains = 1 pennyweight (dwt)
20 pennyweights = 1 ounce troy (oz t) = 480 grains
12 ounces troy = 1 pound troy (lb t)
= 240 pennyweights
= 5,760 grains

Gunter's or Surveyor's Chain Measure

7.92 inches = 1 link (li)
100 links = 1 chain (ch) = 4 rods = 66 ft.
80 chains = 1 statute mile = 320 rods = 5,280 ft.

Apothecaries' Weight

20 grains = 1 scruple (s ap)
3 scruples = 1 dram apothecaries' (dr ap)
= 60 grains
8 drams apothecaries' = 1 ounce apothecaries' (oz ap)
= 24 scruples = 480 grains
12 ounces apothecaries' = 1 pound apothecaries' (lb ap)
= 96 drams apothecaries'
= 288 scruples
= 5,760 grains

The International System (Metric)

Source: Department of Commerce, National Bureau of Standards.

The International System of Units is a modernized version of the metric system, established by international agreement, that provides a logical and interconnected framework for all measurements in science, industry, and commerce. The system is built on a foundation of seven basic units, and all other units are derived from them. (Use of metric weights and measures was legalized in the United States in 1866, and our customary units of weights and measures are defined in terms of the meter and kilogram.)

Length. Meter. Up until 1983, the meter was defined as 1,650,763.73 wavelengths in a vacuum of the orange-red line of the spectrum of krypton-86. Since then, it is equal to the distance traveled by light in a vacuum in 1/299,792,45 of a second.

Time. Second. The second is defined as the duration of 9,192,631,770 cycles of the radiation associated with a specified transition of the cesium-133 atom.

Mass. Kilogram. The standard for the kilogram is a cylinder of platinum-iridium alloy kept by the International Bureau of Weights and Measures at Paris. A duplicate at the National Bureau of Standards serves as the mass standard for the United States. The kilogram is the only base unit still defined by a physical object.

Temperature. Kelvin. The Kelvin is defined as the fraction 1/273.16 of the thermodynamic temperature of the triple point of water; that is, the point at which water forms an interface of solid, liquid, and vapor. This is defined as 0.01°C on the Centigrade or Celsius scale and 32.02°F on the Fahrenheit scale. The temperature 0°K is called "absolute zero."

Electric Current. Ampere. The ampere is defined as that current that, if maintained in each of two long parallel wires separated by one meter in free space, would produce a force between the two wires (due to their magnetic fields) of 2×10^{-7} newton for each meter of length. (A newton is the unit of force that when applied to one kilogram mass would experience an acceleration of one meter per second per second.)

Luminous Intensity. Candela. The candela is defined as the luminous intensity of 1/600,000 of a square meter of a cavity at the temperature of freezing platinum (2,042°K).

Amount of Substance. Mole. The mole is the amount of substance of a system that contains as many elementary entities as there are atoms in 0.012 kilogram of carbon-12.

Tables of Metric Weights and Measures

Linear Measure

10 millimeters (mm) = 1 centimeter (cm)
10 centimeters = 1 decimeter (dm) = 100 millimeters
10 decimeters = 1 meter (m) = 1,000 millimeters
10 meters = 1 dekameter (dam)
10 dekameters = 1 hectometer (hm) = 100 meters
10 hectometers = 1 kilometer (km) = 1,000 meters

Volume Measure

10 milliliters (ml) = 1 centiliter (cl)
10 centiliters = 1 deciliter (dl) = 100 milliliters
10 deciliters = 1 liter (l) = 1,000 milliliters
10 liters = 1 dekaliter (dal)
10 dekaliters = 1 hectoliter (hl) = 100 liters
10 hectoliters = 1 kiloliter (kl) = 1,000 liters

Area Measure

100 square millimeters (mm^2) = 1 sq centimeter (cm^2)
10,000 square centimeters = 1 sq meter (m^2) =
1,000,000 sq millimeters
100 square meters = 1 are (a)
100 ares = 1 hectare (ha) =
10,000 sq meters
100 hectares = 1 sq kilometer (km^2) =
1,000,000 sq meters

Cubic Measure

1,000 cubic millimeters (mm^3) = 1 cu centimeter (cm^3)
1,000 cubic centimeters = 1 cu decimeter (dm^3) =
1,000,000 cu millimeters
1,000 cubic decimeters = 1 cu meter (m^3) =
1 stere = 1,000,000 cu
centimeters =
1,000,000,000 cu
millimeters

Weight

10 milligrams (mg) = 1 centigram (cg)
10 centigrams = 1 decigram (dg) = 100 milligrams
10 decigrams = 1 gram (g) = 1,000 milligrams
10 grams = 1 dekagram (dag)

10 dekagrams = 1 hectogram (hg) = 100 grams
10 hectograms = 1 kilogram (kg) = 1,000 grams
1,000 kilograms = 1 metric ton (t)

Metric and U.S. Equivalents

1 angstrom[1] (light wave measurement)	0.1 millimicron 0.000 1 micron 0.000 000 1 millimeter 0.000 000 004 inch	1 meter	39.37 inches 1.094 yards
1 cable's length	120 fathoms 720 feet 219.456 meters	1 micron	0.001 millimeter 0.000 039 37 inch
1 centimeter	0.3937 inch	1 mil	0.001 inch 0.025 4 millimeter
1 decimeter	3.937 inches	1 mile (statute or land)	5,280 feet 1.609 kilometers
1 dekameter	32.808 feet	1 mile (nautical international)	1.852 kilometers 1.151 statute miles 0.999 U.S. nautical miles
1 fathom	6 feet 1.8288 meters	1 millimeter	0.03937 inch
1 foot	0.3048 meter	1 millimicron (m+GRKm)	0.001 micron 0.000 000 039 37 inch
1 furlong	10 chains (surveyor's) 660 feet 220 yards ⅛ statute mile 201.168 meters	1 nanometer	0.001 micrometer or 0.000 000 039 37 inch
		1 point (typography)	0.013 837 inch 1/72 inch (approximately) 0.351 millimeter
1 inch	2.54 centimeters		
1 kilometer	0.621 mile	1 rod, pole, or perch	16½ feet 5.0292 meters
1 league (land)	3 statute miles 4.828 kilometers	1 yard	0.9144 meter

Areas or Surfaces

1 acre	43,560 square feet 4,840 square yards 0.405 hectare	1 square kilometer	0.386 square mile 247.105 acres
1 are	119.599 square yards 0.025 acre	1 square meter	1.196 square yards 10.764 square feet
1 hectare	2.471 acres	1 square mile	258.999 hectares
1 square centimeter	0.155 square inch	1 square millimeter	0.002 square inch
1 square decimeter	15.5 square inches	1 square rod, square pole or square perch	25.293 square meters
1 square foot	929.030 square centimeters	1 square yard	0.836 square meters
1 square inch	6.4516 square centimeters		

Capacities or Volumes

1 barrel, liquid	31 to 42 gallons[2]	1 cord (firewood)	128 cubic feet
1 bushel (U.S.) struck measure[3]	2,150.42 cubic inches 35.238 liters	1 cubic centimeter	0.061 cubic inch
1 bushel, heaped (U.S.)	2,747.715 cubic inches 1.278 bushels, struck measure[4]	1 cubic decimeter	61.024 cubic inches

1 cubic foot	7.481 gallons
	28.316 cubic decimeters
1 cubic inch	0.554 fluid ounce
	4.433 fluid drams
	16.387 cubic centimeters
1 cubic meter	1.308 cubic yards
1 cubic yard	0.765 cubic meter
1 cup, measuring	8 fluid ounces
	½ liquid pint
1 dram, fluid or liquid (U.S.)	⅛ fluid ounces
	0.226 cubic inch
	3.697 milliliters
	1.041 British fluid drachms
1 dekaliter	2.642 gallons
	1.135 pecks
1 gallon (U.S.)	231 cubic inches
	3.785 liters
	0.833 British gallon
	128 U.S. fluid ounces
1 gallon (British Imperial)	277.42 cubic inches
	1.201 U.S. gallons
	4.546 liters
	160 British fluid ounces
1 hectoliter	26.418 gallons
	2.838 bushels
1 liter	1.057 liquid quarts
	0.908 dry quart
	61.024 cubic inches
1 milliliter	0.271 fluid dram
	16.231 minims
	0.061 cubic inch
1 ounce, fluid or liquid (U.S.)	1.805 cubic inch
	29.574 milliliters
	1.041 British fluid ounces
1 peck	8.810 liters
1 pint, dry	33.600 cubic inches
	0.551 liter
1 pint, liquid	28.875 cubic inches
	0.473 liter
1 quart, dry (U.S.)	67.201 cubic inches
	1.101 liters
	0.969 British quart
1 quart, liquid (U.S.)	57.75 cubic inches
	0.946 liter
	0.833 British quart
1 quart (British)	69.354 cubic inches
	1.032 U.S. dry quarts
	1.201 U.S. liquid quarts
1 tablespoon, measuring	3 teaspoons
	4 fluid drams
	½ fluid ounce
1 teaspoon, measuring	⅓ tablespoon
	1⅓ fluid drams
1 carat	200 milligrams
	3.086 grains
1 dram, apothecaries'	60 grains
	3.888 grams
1 dram, avoirdupois	27 1/32 (=27.344) grains
	1.772 grams
1 grain	64.798 91 milligrams
1 gram	15.432 grains
	0.035 avoirdupois ounce
1 kilogram	2.205 pounds
1 microgram (µg— the Greek letter mu in combination with the letter g)	0.000 001 gram
1 milligram	0.015 grain
1 ounce, avoirdupois	437.5 grains
	0.911 troy or apothecaries' ounce
	28.350 grams
1 ounce, troy or apothecaries'	480 grains
	1.097 avoirdupois ounces
	31.103 grams
1 pennyweight	1.555 grams
1 point	0.01 carat
	2 milligrams
1 pound, avoirdupois	7,000 grains
	1.215 troy or apothecaries' pounds
	453.592 37 grams
1 pound, troy or apothecaries'	5,760 grains
	0.823 avoirdupois pound
	373.242 grams
1 ton, gross or long[5]	2,240 pounds
	1.12 net tons
	1.016 metric tons
1 ton, metric	2,204.623 pounds
	0.984 gross ton
	1.102 net tons
1 ton, net or short	2,000 pounds
	0.893 gross ton
	0.907 metric ton

1. The angstrom is basically defined as 10^{-10} meter. 2. There is a variety of "barrels" established by law or usage. For example, federal taxes on fermented liquors are based on a barrel of 31 gallons; many state laws fix the "barrel for liquids" at 31½ gallons; one state fixes a 36-gallon barrel for cistern measurement; federal law recognizes a 40-gallon barrel for "proof spirits"; by custom, 42 gallons compose a barrel of crude oil or petroleum products for statistical purposes, and this equivalent is recognized "for liquids" by four states. 3. "Struck measure" refers to a struck, or level, bushel. It is the only official bushel measure in the UK. 4. Frequently recognized as 1¼ bushels, struck measure. 5. The gross or long ton is used commercially in the United States to only a limited extent, usually in restricted industrial fields. These units are the same as the British "ton."

Definitions of Gold Terminology

The term "fineness" defines a gold content in parts per thousand. For example, a gold nugget containing 885 parts of pure gold, 100 parts of silver, and 15 parts of copper would be considered 885-fine.

The word "karat" indicates the proportion of solid gold in an alloy based on a total of 24 parts. Thus, 14-karat (14K) gold indicates a composition of 14 parts of gold and 10 parts of other metals.

The term "gold-filled" is used to describe articles of jewelry made of base metal that are covered on one or more surfaces with a layer of gold alloy. No article having a gold alloy portion of less than one twentieth by weight may be marked "gold-filled." Articles may be marked "rolled gold plate" provided the proportional fraction and fineness designations are also shown.

Electroplated jewelry items carrying at least 7 millionths of an inch of gold on significant surfaces may be labeled "electroplate." Plate thicknesses less than this may be marked "gold-flashed" or "gold-washed."

Bolts and Screws: Conversion from Fractions of an Inch to Millimeters

Inch	mm	Inch	mm	Inch	mm	Inch	mm
1/64	0.40	17/64	6.75	33/64	13.10	49/64	19.45
1/32	0.79	9/32	7.14	17/32	13.50	25/32	19.84
3/64	1.19	19/64	7.54	35/64	13.90	51/64	20.24
1/16	1.59	5/16	7.94	9/16	14.29	13/16	20.64
5/64	1.98	21/64	8.33	37/64	14.69	53/64	21.03
3/32	2.38	11/32	8.73	19/32	15.08	27/32	21.43
7/64	2.78	23/64	9.13	39/64	15.48	55/64	21.83
1/8	3.18	3/8	9.53	5/8	15.88	7/8	22.23
9/64	3.57	25/64	9.92	41/64	16.27	57/64	22.62
5/32	3.97	13/32	10.32	21/32	16.67	29/32	23.02
11/64	4.37	27/64	10.72	43/64	17.06	59/64	23.42
3/16	4.76	7/16	11.11	11/16	17.46	15/16	23.81
13/64	5.16	29/64	11.51	45/64	17.86	61/64	24.21
7/32	5.56	15/32	11.91	23/32	18.26	31/32	24.61
15/64	5.95	31/64	12.30	47/64	18.65	63/64	25.00
1/4	6.35	1/2	12.70	3/4	19.05	1	25.40

Cooking Measurement Equivalents

16 tablespoons = 1 cup

12 tablespoons = 3/4 cup

10 tablespoons + 2 teaspoons = 2/3 cup

8 tablespoons = 1/2 cup

6 tablespoons = 3/8 cup

5 tablespoons + 1 teaspoon = 1/3 cup

4 tablespoons = 1/4 cup

2 tablespoons = 1/8 cup

2 tablespoons + 2 teaspoons = 1/6 cup

1 tablespoon = 1/16 cup

2 cups = 1 pint

2 pints = 1 quart

3 teaspoons = 1 tablespoon

48 teaspoons = 1 cup

U.S.–Metric Cooking Conversions

U.S. to Metric

Capacity		Weight	
1/5 teaspoon	1 milliliter	1 oz	28 grams
1 teaspoon	5 ml	1 pound	454 grams
1 tablespoon	15 ml		
1 fluid oz	30 ml		
1/5 cup	47 ml		
1 cup	237 ml		
2 cups (1 pint)	473 ml		
4 cups (1 quart)	.95 liter		
4 quarts (1 gal.)	3.8 liters		

Metric to U.S.

Capacity		Weight	
1 milliliter	1/5 teaspoon	1 gram	.035 ounce
5 ml	1 teaspoon	100 grams	3.5 ounces
15 ml	1 tablespoon	500 grams	1.10 pounds
100 ml	3.4 fluid oz	1 kilogram	2.205 pounds
240 ml	1 cup		35 oz
1 liter	34 fluid oz		
	4.2 cups		
	2.1 pints		
	1.06 quarts		
	0.26 gallon		

Prefixes and Multiples

Prefix	Suffix	Equivalent	Multiple/submultiple	Prefix	Suffix	Equivalent	Multiple/submultiple
atto	a	quintillionth part	10^{-18}	deci	d	tenth part	10^{-1}
femto	f	quadrillionth part	10^{-15}	deka	da	tenfold	10
pico	p	trillionth part	10^{-12}	hecto	h	hundredfold	10^2
nano	n	billionth part	10^{-9}	kilo	k	thousandfold	10^3
micro	μ	millionth part	10^{-6}	mega	M	millionfold	10^6
milli	m	thousandth part	10^{-3}	giga	G	billionfold	10^9
centi	c	hundredth part	10^{-2}	tera	T	trillionfold	10^{12}

Common Formulas

CIRCUMFERENCE

Circle: $C = \pi d$, in which π is 3.1416 and d the diameter.

AREA

Triangle: $A = \dfrac{ab}{2}$, in which a is the base and b the height.

Square: $A = a^2$, in which a is one of the sides.

Rectangle: $A = ab$, in which a is the base and b the height.

Trapezoid: $A = \dfrac{h(a+b)}{2}$, in which h is the height, a the longer parallel side, and b the shorter.

Regular pentagon: $A = 1.720a^2$, in which a is one of the sides.

Regular hexagon: $A = 2.598a^2$, in which a is one of the sides.

Regular octagon: $A = 4.828a^2$, in which a is one of the sides.

Circle: $A = \pi r^2$, in which π is 3.1416 and r the radius.

VOLUME

Cube: $V = a^3$, in which a is one of the edges.

Rectangular prism: $V = abc$, in which a is the length, b is the width, and c the depth.

Pyramid: $V = \dfrac{Ah}{3}$, in which A is the area of the base and h the height.

Cylinder: $V = \pi r^2 h$, in which π is 3.1416, r the radius of the base, and h the height.

Cone: $V = \dfrac{\pi r^2 h}{3}$, in which π is 3.1416, r the radius of the base, and h the height.

Sphere: $V = \dfrac{4 \pi r^3}{3}$, in which π is 3.1416 and r the radius.

TEMPERATURE SCALES

Degrees Fahrenheit to Degrees Celsius:

$$T_C = \frac{5}{9}(T_F - 32)$$

Degrees Celsius to Degrees Fahrenheit:

$$T_F = \frac{9}{5}T_C + 32$$

Degrees Celsius to Kelvin:

$$T_K = T_C + 273.15$$

MISCELLANEOUS

Distance in feet traveled by falling body:
$d = 16t^2$, in which t is the time in seconds.

Speed of sound in feet per second through any given temperature of air:

$$V = \frac{1087 \sqrt{273 + t}}{16.52}$$, in which t is the temperature Celsius.

Cost in cents of operation of electrical device:

$$C = \frac{Wtc}{1000}$$, in which W is the number of watts, t the time in hours, and c the cost in cents per kilowatt-hour.

Conversion of matter into energy (Einstein's Theorem): $E = mc^2$, in which E is the energy in ergs, m the mass of the matter in grams, and c the speed of light in centimeters per second:

$$(c^2 = 9 \times 10^{20})$$

Decimal Equivalents of Common Fractions

1/2	.5000	1/10	.1000	2/7	.2857	3/11	.2727	5/9	.5556	7/11	.6364
1/3	.3333	1/11	.0909	2/9	.2222	4/5	.8000	5/11	.4545	7/12	.5833
1/4	.2500	1/12	.0833	2/11	.1818	4/7	.5714	5/12	.4167	8/9	.8889
1/5	.2000	1/16	.0625	3/4	.7500	4/9	.4444	6/7	.8571	8/11	.7273
1/6	.1667	1/32	.0313	3/5	.6000	4/11	.3636	6/11	.5455	9/10	.9000
1/7	.1429	1/64	.0156	3/7	.4286	5/6	.8333	7/8	.8750	9/11	.8182
1/8	.1250	2/3	.6667	3/8	.3750	5/7	.7143	7/9	.7778	10/11	.9091
1/9	.1111	2/5	.4000	3/10	.3000	5/8	.6250	7/10	.7000	11/12	.9167

U.S. Postal Rates and Fees

Domestic Rates, last revised by the U.S. Postal Service on July 1, 2001

First-Class Mail

First-Class Mail includes all personal correspondence, all bills and statements of accounts, all matter sealed or otherwise closed against inspection, and matter wholly or partly in writing or typewriting. Any mailable items may be sent as First-Class Mail. Each piece must weigh 13 oz or less. Pieces over 13 oz can be sent as Priority Mail.

Single-Piece Letter/Flat Rates

1st oz	$0.34
Each additional oz	0.23

Weight not over (oz)	Rate	Weight not over (oz)	Rate
1*	$0.34	9	$2.18
2	0.57	10	2.41
3	0.80	11	2.64
4	1.03	12	2.87
5	1.26	13	3.10
6	1.49	Over 13 oz, see	
7	1.72	Priority Mail.	
8	1.95		

*Nonstandard surcharge may apply to pieces weighing 1 oz or less based on size.

Card Rates

Single postcard (commercial)	$0.21
Single postal card sold by United States Postal Service	0.23

Postcard Dimensions: Not larger than 4¼ by 6 in. by 0.016 in. thick. Not smaller than 3½ by 5 in. by 0.007 in. thick.

Express Mail

Express Mail is the fastest service, with next day delivery by 12 noon to most destinations. Express Mail is delivered 365 days a year—with no extra charge for Saturday, Sunday, or holiday delivery. Items must weigh 70 lbs or less and measure 108 in. or less in combined length and girth.

Customer Service—1-800-222-1811. Order Express Mail supplies and labels, arrange pickup service, obtain delivery information between ZIP Codes, and determine delivery status.

Post Office to Addressee Service

Up to 8 oz	$12.45
Up to 2 lbs	16.25
Up to 3 lbs	19.15
Up to 4 lbs	22.05
Up to 5 lbs	24.85
Up to 6 lbs	27.70
Up to 7 lbs	30.45
Over 7 lbs, see postmaster.	

Express Mail Flat-Rate Envelope

$16.25, regardless of weight or destination, for matter sent in a flat-rate envelope provided by the Postal Service.

Priority Mail

Priority Mail offers 2-day service to most domestic destinations. Items must weigh 70 lbs or less and measure 108 in. or less in combined length and girth.

Single-Piece Rates

Up to 1 lb	$3.50
Up to 2 lbs	3.95
Up to 3 lbs	5.20
Up to 4 lbs	6.45
Up to 5 lbs	7.70
Over 5 pounds, see postmaster.	

Priority Mail Flat-Rate Envelope

$3.95, regardless of weight or destination, for matter sent in a flat-rate envelope provided by the Postal Service.

Media Mail (Book Rate)

Generally used for books (at least eight pages), film (16 mm or narrower), printed music, printed test materials, sound recordings, play scripts, printed educational charts, loose-leaf pages and binders consisting of medical information, and computer-readable media. Advertising restrictions apply. Packages must measure 108 in. or less in combined length and girth.

Weight not over (lbs)	Rate	Weight not over (lbs)	Rate
1	$1.33	9	$4.63
2	1.78	10	4.93
3	2.23	11	5.23
4	2.68	12	5.53
5	3.13	13	5.83
6	3.58	14	6.13
7	4.03	15	6.43
8	4.33	16	6.73

Special Services (Domestic Mail)

Certificate of Mailing

Provides evidence of mailing only. Certificate of mailing does not provide a record of delivery. Must be purchased at time of mailing. Available for First-Class Mail, Priority Mail, Parcel Post, Bound Printed Matter, and Media Mail.
Fee, in addition to postage—$0.75

Certified Mail

Provides the sender with a mailing receipt. A delivery record is maintained by the USPS. No insurance provided. Available with First-Class Mail and Priority Mail. For an additional fee, certified mail may be combined with restricted delivery or return receipt.
Fee, in addition to postage—2.10

Insurance

Provides coverage against loss or damage. Coverage up to $5,000 for Parcel Post, Bound Printed Matter, and Media Mail matter as well as merchandise mailed at Priority Mail or First-Class Mail rates. Items must not be insured for more than their value. Insured mail must be presented to a retail employee at a post office or a rural carrier.

Liability	Fee, in addition to postage
$.01 to $50.00	$1.10
$50.01 to $100.00	2.00
$100.01 to $200.00	3.00
$200.01 to $300.00	4.00
$300.01 to $400.00	5.00
$400.01 to $500.00	6.00
$500.01 to $600.00	7.00
$600.01 to $5,000*	

*$7.00 plus $1.00 for each $100 or fraction over $600 in declared value.

Money Orders

Provides safe transmission of money. Available in amounts up to $700.
Fee, in addition to postage—$0.90

Registered Mail

Provides maximum protection and security for valuables. Provides sender with mailing receipt and a delivery record is maintained by the USPS. A record of mailing is maintained at the mailing post office. Available only for items paid at Priority Mail and First-Class Mail rates.

	Declared Value	Fee, in addition to postage
Without Insurance	$0.00	$7.25
With Insurance	$0.01 to $100	7.50
	$100.01 to $500.00	8.25
	$500.01 to $1,000.00	9.00
	$1,000.01 to $2,000.00	9.75

For higher values, consult your postmaster.

Restricted Delivery

Permits a mailer to direct delivery only to the addressee or addressee's authorized agent. The addressee must be an individual specified by name. Available for First-Class Mail, Priority Mail, Parcel Post, Bound Printed Matter, and Media Mail that is sent certified mail, COD, mail insured for more than $50, or registered mail.
Fee, in addition to postage—$3.20

Return Receipt

Available only for Express Mail, Certified Mail, COD, Insured Mail for more than $50.00, or Registered Mail.
Requested at time of mailing:
Showing to whom (signature), date, and addressee's address (in conjunction with another service) $1.50
Requested after mailing: 3.50
Showing to whom (signature) and date delivered

Special Handling

Provides preferential handling, but not preferential delivery, to extent practicable in dispatch and transportation. Available for First-Class Mail, Priority Mail, Parcel Post, Bound Printed Matter, and Media Mail.
Fee, in addition to postage:
Pieces weighing not more than 10 pounds—$5.40
Pieces weighing more than 10 pounds—$7.50

Collect on Delivery (COD)

Allows mailers to collect the price of goods and/or postage on merchandise ordered by addressee when it is delivered. Fees include insurance. Maximum amount $1,000; see postmaster for details.

Sizes for Domestic Mail

Mail must meet these standards:
• Thickness—No less than 0.007 in. thick. Pieces that are ¼ in. thick or less must be at least 3½ in. high, 5 in. long, and rectangular in shape.
• Combined length and girth—No more than 108 in.
• Weight—No more than 70 lbs.
Postcards must be:
• Minimum 3½ in. high, 5 in. long by .007 in. thick.
• Maximum 4¼ in. high, 6 in. long by .016 in. thick.

The Mail-Order Merchandise Rule

The mail-order rule adopted by the Federal Trade Commission in October 1975 provides that when you order by mail:
• You must receive the merchandise when the seller says you will.
• If you are not promised delivery within a certain time period, the seller must ship the merchandise to you no later than 30 days after your order comes in.
• If you don't receive it shortly after that 30-day period, you can cancel your order and get your money back.

ZIP Codes

The ZIP Code was instituted in 1963 and allows for electronic processing and delivery of mail. An envelope that does not include a ZIP Code in the delivery address must be manually sorted, which increases the cost of sorting the mail and causes mail to be delayed en route to the delivery address. ZIP Code directories are available for use or sale at your local post office, or you can look up ZIP Codes on-line: www.usps.gov/ncsc/.

In 1983, the Postal Service began to use an expanded ZIP Code called ZIP+4. It is composed of the original five-digit code plus a four-digit add-on. The four-digit add-on number identifies a geographic segment within the five-digit delivery area such as a city block, an office building, an individual high-volume receiver of mail, or any other unit that would aid efficient mail sorting and delivery.

Postal Information Web Sites

United States Postal Service: http://www.usps.gov/
ZIP Code Look Up: http://www.usps.gov/ncsc/
U.S. Postal Service Rate Calculators:
   domestic: http://postcalc.usps.gov/
   international: http://ircalc.usps.gov/
   business: http://dbcalc.usps.gov/nsw.htm

International Postal Rates
Last revised by the U.S. Postal Service on Jan. 7, 2001

Single Piece Letter-Post

Weight not over (oz)	Canada	Mexico	Western Europe	Australia, Japan, New Zealand	Other countries
1	$ 0.60	$ 0.60	$ 0.80	$ 0.80	$ 0.80
2	0.85	0.85	1.60	1.70	1.55
3	1.10	1.25	2.40	2.60	2.30
4	1.35	1.65	3.20	3.50	3.05
5	1.60	2.05	4.00	4.40	3.80
6	1.85	2.45	4.80	5.30	4.55
7	2.19	2.85	5.60	6.20	5.30
8	2.35	3.25	6.40	7.10	6.05
12	3.10	4.00	7.55	8.40	7.65
16	3.75	5.15	8.70	9.70	9.25
20	4.40	6.30	9.85	11.00	10.85
24	5.05	7.45	11.00	12.30	12.45
28	5.70	8.60	12.15	13.60	14.05
32	6.35	9.75	13.30	14.90	15.65
36	7.00	10.95	14.50	16.25	17.35
40	7.65	12.15	15.70	17.60	19.05
44	7.39	13.35	16.90	18.95	20.75
48	8.95	14.55	18.10	20.30	22.45
52	9.65	15.80	19.35	21.70	24.20
56	10.35	17.05	20.60	23.10	25.95
60	11.05	18.30	21.85	24.50	27.70
64	11.75	19.55	23.10	25.90	29.45

Maximum weight: 64 oz. **Postcards and Postal Rates:** Canada and Mexico—$0.50; all others—$0.70

All-Time Top 10 Most Popular Commemorative Stamps

Issue	No. saved (millions)
Elvis '93	124.0
Wildflowers '92	76.2
Rock and Roll '93	75.8
Civil War '95	46.6
Legends of the West '94	46.5
Marilyn Monroe '95	46.3
Bugs Bunny '97	45.3
Summer Olympics '92	39.6
The World of Dinosaurs	38.5
Centennial Olympic Games '96	38.1

Source: U.S.P.S., 1998; latest data available. Popularity of stamps is measured by number saved, not used.

Postal Workers Bitten by Dogs, by City

City	Dog bites
1. Houston	58
2. Los Angeles	38
3. Chicago	31
4. Cleveland, Miami[1]	27
5. Dallas	26
6. Boston, Detroit[1]	21
7. Denver	20
8. San Diego	19
9. Fort Lauderdale, San Antonio[1]	18
10. Indianapolis	17

1. ties. *Source:* U.S.P.S., 2000. A total of 2,725 postal workers were bitten by dogs in FY1999.

State Abbreviations and State Postal Codes

State	Abbreviation	Postal code	State	Abbreviation	Postal code	State	Abbreviation	Postal code
Alabama	Ala.	AL	Kentucky	Ky.	KY	Ohio	Ohio	OH
Alaska	Alaska	AK	Louisiana	La.	LA	Oklahoma	Okla.	OK
Arizona	Ariz.	AZ	Maine	Maine	ME	Oregon	Ore.	OR
Arkansas	Ark.	AR	Maryland	Md.	MD	Pennsylvania	Pa.	PA
California	Calif.	CA	Massachusetts	Mass.	MA	Puerto Rico	P.R.	PR
Colorado	Colo.	CO	Michigan	Mich.	MI	Rhode Island	R.I.	RI
Connecticut	Conn.	CT	Minnesota	Minn.	MN	South Carolina	S.C.	SC
Delaware	Del.	DE	Mississippi	Miss.	MS	South Dakota	S.D.	SD
Dist. of Columbia	D.C.	DC	Missouri	Mo.	MO	Tennessee	Tenn.	TN
Florida	Fla.	FL	Montana	Mont.	MT	Texas	Tex.	TX
Georgia	Ga.	GA	Nebraska	Nebr.	NE	Utah	Utah	UT
Guam	Guam	GU	Nevada	Nev.	NV	Vermont	Vt.	VT
Hawaii	Hawaii	HI	New Hampshire	N.H.	NH	Virginia	Va.	VA
Idaho	Idaho	ID	New Jersey	N.J.	NJ	Virgin Islands	V.I.	VI
Illinois	Ill.	IL	New Mexico	N.M.	NM	Washington	Wash.	WA
Indiana	Ind.	IN	New York	N.Y.	NY	West Virginia	W.Va.	WV
Iowa	Iowa	IA	North Carolina	N.C.	NC	Wisconsin	Wis.	WI
Kansas	Kans.	KS	North Dakota	N.D.	ND	Wyoming	Wyo.	WY

Life-Saving Skills Summary

Skill	Adult (9 years and older)	Child (1 to 8 years)	Infant (birth to 1 year)
Rescue breathing (used when victim is not breathing)	Give 1 slow breath about every 5 seconds; about 1½ seconds per breath; 1 minute = about 10 to 12 breaths	Give 1 slow breath about every 3 seconds; about 1½ seconds per breath; 1 minute = about 20 breaths	Give 1 slow breath about every 3 seconds; about 1½ seconds per breath; 1 minute = about 20 breaths
CPR (used if victim is not breathing *and* does not have a heart-beat)	Depth of compression is about 2 inches; compressions are performed with both hands; complete 15 compressions in about 10 seconds; do cycles of 15 compressions and 2 breaths	Depth of compression is about 1½ inches; compressions are performed with 1 hand; complete 5 compressions in about 3 seconds; do cycles of 5 compressions and 1 breath	Depth of compression is about 1 inch; compressions are performed with 2 fingers; complete 5 compressions in about 3 seconds; do cycles of 5 compressions and 1 breath
Choking (conscious)	Determine if person is choking; stand behind person and deliver abdominal thrusts; repeat until object is expelled or victim loses consciousness	Determine if child is choking; stand or kneel behind child and deliver abdominal thrusts; repeat until object is expelled or child loses consciousness	Determine if infant is choking; give 5 back blows; give 5 chest thrusts; repeat until object is expelled or infant loses consciousness
Choking (unconscious)	Give 2 slow breaths; retilt head and give 2 slow breaths; give up to 5 abdominal thrusts; do finger sweep; give 2 slow breaths; repeat abdominal thrusts, finger sweep, and 2 slow breaths	Give 2 slow breaths; retilt head and give 2 slow breaths; give up to 5 abdominal thrusts; check for object in throat; do finger sweep if object is visible; give 2 slow breaths; repeat abdominal thrusts, foreign-body check/finger sweep, and 2 slow breaths	Give 2 slow breaths; retilt head and give 2 slow breaths; give 5 back blows; give 5 chest thrusts; check for object in throat; do finger sweep if object is visible; repeat back blows, chest thrusts, foreign-body check/finger sweep, and 2 slow breaths

Rescue Breathing

1. With head tilted back, pinch nose shut.

2. ADULT: Give 1 slow breath about every 5 seconds.

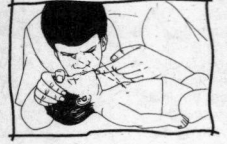

CHILD/INFANT: Give 1 slow breath about every 3 seconds.

CPR (Adult)

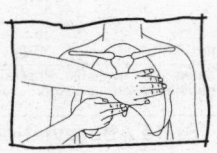

1. Find hand position.

2. Position shoulders over hands. Compress chest 15 times.

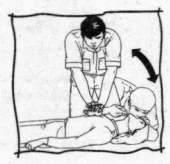

3. Give 2 slow breaths. Recheck pulse and breathing. If no pulse, continue sets of 15 compressions and 2 breaths.

Choking

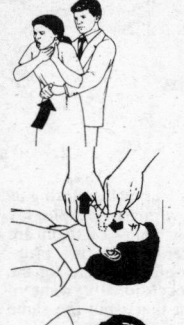

If conscious but choking, give abdominal thrusts until object comes out.

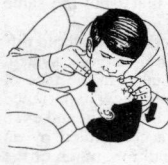

If a person becomes unconscious:

Step 1. Clear any object from mouth.

Step 2. Give 2 slow breaths.

If air won't go in, give up to 5 abdominal thrusts.

Other Emergencies

Burns

First Degree: Signs/Symptoms—reddened skin. **Treatment**—Immerse quickly in cold water or apply ice until pain stops.

Second Degree: Signs/Symptoms—reddened skin, blisters. **Treatment**—(1) Cut away loose clothing. (2) Cover with several layers of cold moist dressings or, if limb is involved, immerse in cold water for relief of pain. (3) Treat for shock.

Third Degree: Signs/Symptoms—skin destroyed, tissues damaged, charring. **Treatment**—(1) Cut away loose clothing (do not remove clothing adhered to skin). (2) Cover with several layers of sterile, cold, moist dressings for relief of pain and to stop burning action. (3) Treat for shock.

Poisons

Treatment—(1) Dilute by drinking large quantities of water. (2) Induce vomiting except when poison is corrosive or a petroleum product. (3) Call the poison-control center or a doctor.

Shock

Shock may accompany any serious injury: blood loss, breathing impairment, heart failure, burns. Shock can kill—treat as soon as possible and continue until medical aid is available.

Signs/Symptoms—(1) Shallow breathing. (2) Rapid and weak pulse. (3) Nausea, collapse, vomiting. (4) Shivering. (5) Pale, moist skin. (6) Mental confusion. (7) Drooping eyelids, dilated pupils.

Treatment—(1) Establish and maintain an open airway. (2) Control bleeding. (3) Keep victim lying down. Exception: Head and chest injuries, heart attack, stroke, sun stroke. If no spine injury, victim may be more comfortable and breathe better in a semi-reclining position. If in doubt, keep the victim flat. Elevate the feet unless injury would be aggravated. Maintain normal body temperature. Place blankets under and over victim.

Frostbite

Most frequently frostbitten: toes, fingers, nose, and ears. It is caused by exposure to cold.

Signs/Symptoms—(1) Skin becomes pale or a grayish-yellow color. (2) Parts feel cold and numb. (3) Frozen parts feel doughy.

Treatment—(1) Victim should be wrapped in woolen cloth and kept dry. (2) Do not rub, chafe, or manipulate frostbitten parts. (3) Bring victim indoors. (4) Place affected parts in warm water (102° to 105°) and make sure water remains warm. Never thaw if the victim has to go back out into the cold, which may cause the affected area to be refrozen. (5) Do not use hot water bottles or a heat lamp, and do not place victim near a hot stove. (6) For serious frostbite, seek medical aid for thawing because pain will be intense and tissue damage extensive.

Heat Cramps

Affects people who work or do strenuous exercises in a hot environment. To prevent it, such people should drink large amounts of cool water and add a pinch of salt to each glass of water.

Signs/Symptoms—(1) Painful muscle cramps in legs and abdomen. (2) Faintness. (3) Profuse perspiration.

Treatment—(1) Move victim to a cool place. (2) Give victim sips of salted drinking water (one teaspoon of salt to one quart of water). (3) Apply manual pressure to the cramped muscle.

Heat Exhaustion

Signs/Symptoms—(1) Pale and clammy skin. (2) Profuse perspiration. (3) Rapid and shallow breathing. (4) Weakness, dizziness, and headache.

Treatment—(1) Care for victim as if he or she were in shock. (2) Remove victim to a cool area, do not allow chilling. (3) If body gets too cold, cover victim.

Heat Stroke

Signs/Symptoms—(1) Face is red and flushed. (2) Victim becomes rapidly unconscious. (3) Skin is hot and dry with no perspiration.

Treatment—(1) Lay victim down with head and shoulders raised. (2) Reduce the high body temperature as quickly as possible. (3) Apply cold applications to the body and head. (4) Use ice and fan if available. (5) Watch for signs of shock and treat accordingly. (6) Get medical aid as soon as possible.

Fear Not!

For millions of sufferers of phobias, science is offering new treatments—and new hope

By JEFFREY KLUGER TIME

For every phobia the infinitely inventive—and infinitely fearful—human mind can create, there is a word that has been coined to describe it. There's *nephophobia*, or fear of clouds, and *coulrophobia*, the fear of clowns. There's *kathisophobia*, fear of sitting, and *kyphophobia*, fear of stooping. There are *xanthophobia, leukophobia*, and *chromophobia*, fear of yellow, white, and colors in general. There are *alektorophobia* and *apiphobia*, fear of chickens and bees. And deep in the list, lost in the *L*s, there's *lutraphobia*, or fear of otters—a fear that's useful, it would seem, only if you happen to be a mollusk.

101 Forms of Fear

The list of identified phobias is expanding every day and is now, of course, also collected online (*www.phobialist.com*), where more than 500 increasingly quirky human fears are labeled, sometimes tongue-in-cheek, and cataloged alphabetically. Some have more to do with neology than psychology. (It's one thing to invent a word like *arachibutyrophobia*, another thing to find someone who's really afraid of peanut butter sticking to the roof of the mouth.) Other phobias, however—like *acrophobia* (fear of heights), *claustrophobia* (fear of enclosed spaces), and *agoraphobia* (a crushing, paralyzing terror of anything outside the safety of the home)—can be deadly serious business.

If the names of phobias can be found online, the people who actually suffer from at least one of them at some point in their life—about 50 million in the U.S. by some estimates—are everywhere. For most people, the treatment of phobias has been a cope-as-you-go business: preflight cocktails for the fearful flyer, stairways instead of elevators for the claustrophobe. But such home-brew tactics are usually only stopgaps at best. Happily, safe and lasting phobia treatments are now at hand. In an era in which more and more emotional disorders are falling before the scythe of science, phobias are among the disorders falling fastest.

Researchers are making enormous progress in determining what phobias are, what kinds of neurochemical storms they trigger in the brain, and for what evolutionary purpose the potential for such psychic squalls was encoded into us in the first place. With this understanding has come a magic bag of treatments: exposure therapy that can stomp out a lifetime phobia in a single six-hour session; virtual-reality programs that can safely simulate the thing the phobic most fears, slowly stripping it of its power to terrorize; new medications that can snuff the brain's phobic spark before it can catch.

Bona Fide Phobias

For something that can cause as much suffering as a phobia, it's remarkable how many people lay claim to having one—and how many of them are wrong. Self-described computer phobics are probably nothing of the kind. They may not care for the infernal machines and may occasionally want to throw one out the window, but that's not the same as a full-fledged phobia.

Experts say a true phobic reaction is a whole different category of terror, a central nervous system wildfire that's impossible to mistake. In the face of the thing that triggers fear, phobics experience sweating, racing heart, difficulty breathing, and even a fear of imminent death—all accompanied by an overwhelming need to flee. In addition, much of the time that they are away from the feared object or situation is spent dreading the next encounter and developing elaborate strategies to avoid it.

Most psychologists now assign phobias to one of three broad categories: social phobias, in which the sufferer feels paralyzing fear at the prospect of social or professional encounters; panic disorders, in which the person is periodically blindsided by overwhelming fear for no apparent reason; and specific phobias—fear of snakes and enclosed spaces and heights and the like. Of the three, the specific phobias are the easiest to treat, partly because they are the easiest to understand.

An Ancient Alarm System

The human brain may be a sophisticated thing, but there is an awful lot of ancient programming still etched into it. One of the things that helped early humans survive was a robust fear-and-flight response: an innate sense of the places and things that represent danger and a reflexive impulse to hightail it when one of them is encountered. When the species became top predator a few million years later, those early lessons were not easy to unlearn.

Contemporary researchers believe it's no coincidence that specific phobias usually fall into one of four subcategories, all of which would have had meaning for our ancient ancestors: fear of insects or animals; fear of natural environments, like heights and the dark; fear of blood or injury; and fear of dangerous situations, like being trapped in a tight space.

It turns out that we process the fear of these modern menaces in the same area of the brain our ancient ancestors did—the paralimbic region, which mediates a whole range of primal responses, including anger and sexual arousal. Not all of us, however, parlay that ancient history into a modern-day phobia. It may be our distant ancestors who predispose us to phobias, but it's our immediate ancestors—specifically our parents—who seal the deal. As many as 40% of all people suffering from a specific phobia have at least one phobic parent, seemingly a clue that phobias could be genetically influenced. But genetics doesn't even have to be involved as long as learning is. A childhood trauma—a house fire, say, or a dog bite—may be more than enough to seize the brain's attention and serve as a repository for incipient fears.

What turns up the wattage of a phobia the most is the strategy the phobics rely on to ease their discomfort: avoidance. The harder phobics work to avoid the things they fear, the more the brain grows convinced that the threat is real. "The things you do to reduce anxiety just make it worse," says Barlow. "We have to strip those things away."

The Only Thing to Fear . . .

And that's what doctors do. A patient visiting Barlow's Boston clinic is first assessed for the presence of a specific phobia and then guided through an intensive day or two of graduated exposure. People who are afraid of syringes and blood, for example, may first be shown a magazine photo with a trace of blood depicted in it. Innocuous photos give way to graphic ones, and graphic ones to a display of a real, empty syringe. Over time, the syringe is brought closer, and the patient learns to hold it and even tolerate having blood drawn.

With that habituation comes profound recovery. In studies recently conducted by Lars Goran Ost, a psychology professor at Stockholm University and one of the pioneers of one-day phobia treatments, a staggering 80% to 95% of patients get their phobias under control after just one session. And when symptoms disappear, they usually stay gone. Patients, he says, rarely experience a significant phobic relapse, and almost never replace the thing they no longer fear with a fresher phobia object.

Given the apparent simplicity of exposure therapy, phobics may be tempted to try it themselves. That can be a mistake. It is important that exposure take place under the care of a professional, since it takes a trained person to know when patients are being pushed too far and when it's safe to go further. For some situations impossible to re-create in a doctor's office—like heights and flying in airplanes—virtual-reality programs are available to provide simulated exposure under professional supervision. If specific phobias were the only type of phobias around, things would be decidedly easier for doctors and patients. But the two other members of the phobia troika—social phobias and panic disorders—can be a little trickier.

Social Phobias

Of the 50 million Americans who have experienced or will someday suffer from a phobia (and many will have more than one), 35 million will suffer from social phobia, and the battle they fight is a harrowing one. To a social phobic, the mere prospect of a social encounter is frightening enough to cause sweating, trembling, light-headedness, and nausea, accompanied by an overwhelming feeling of inadequacy. As sufferers grow increasingly isolated, they grow increasingly hopeless and risk developing such conditions as depression and alcoholism.

But things don't have to be so bleak. While social phobias do not respond to a single intensive exposure session as specific phobias do, therapy can still be relatively straightforward. A successful treatment regimen may involve no more than a dozen sessions of cognitive-behavioral therapy, in which patients slowly expose themselves to the places and circumstances that frighten them and reframe the catastrophic thinking that torments them. Often group therapy works better than one-on-one therapy. It provides more than a supportive circle of fellow sufferers: the very act of gathering with other people can serve as a first, critical rebellion against the disorder.

If such therapy doesn't help social phobics, drugs can. Ever since the popularization of Prozac in the early 1990s, the family of modern psychopharmacological drugs has grown steadily. Most of these medications are selective serotonin reuptake inhibitors—or SSRIs—which, as the name implies, selectively block the brain's reabsorption of the neurotransmitter serotonin, helping produce feelings of satisfaction, and kickstart recovery. Last year the drug manufacturer Smith-Kline Beecham asked the Food and Drug Administration to take a second look at the popular SSRI Paxil and consider approving it specifically for the treatment of social-anxiety disorder. The FDA agreed, making Paxil the first drug ever to be formally endorsed for such use. While the flood of marketing tends to overstate the case, the fact is, Paxil works—not by eliminating anxiety entirely but by controlling it enough for traditional therapy to take hold.

Panic Disorder

Progress in treating social-anxiety disorder is also providing hope for the last—and most disabling—of the family of phobias: panic disorder. Panic disorder is to anxiety conditions what a tornado is to weather conditions: a devastating sneak attack that appears from nowhere, wreaks havoc, and then simply vanishes. Unlike the specific phobic and the social phobic who know what will trigger their fear, the victim of panic attacks never knows where or when one will hit. Someone who experiences an attack in, say, a supermarket will often not return there, associating the once neutral place with the traumatic event. But the perceived circle of safety can quickly shrink, until sufferers may be confined entirely to their homes. When this begins to happen, panic disorder mutates into full-blown agoraphobia. The treatment for agoraphobia is much the same as it is for social phobia: cognitive-behavioral therapy and drugs. In many cases, recovery takes longer than it does for social phobias because agoraphobic behavior can become so entrenched.

If science has so many phobias on the run, does that mean that the problem as a whole can soon be considered solved? Hardly. Like all other emotional disorders, phobias cause a double dip of psychic pain: from the condition and from the shame of having the problem in the first place. Over the years, researchers have made much of the fact that the large majority of phobia sufferers are women—from 55% for social phobias and up to 90% for specific phobias and extreme cases of agoraphobia. Hormones, genes, and culture have all been explored as explanations. But the simplest answer may be that women own up to the condition more readily than men do. If you don't come forward with your problem, you can't be included in the epidemiologists' count. Worse, you can never avail yourself of the therapists' cure. □

Overview of Mental Illness

Source: Mental Health: A Report of the Surgeon General, 1999

Mental illness is a term rooted in history that refers collectively to all of the diagnosable mental disorders. Mental disorders are characterized by abnormalities in cognition, emotion or mood, or the highest integrative aspects of behavior, such as social interactions or planning of future activities.

This overview of mental illness focuses on the most common of these disorders.

Anxiety

Anxiety is one of the most readily accessible and easily understood of the major symptoms of mental disorders. Each of us encounters anxiety in many forms throughout the course of our routine activities. Anxiety has evolved as a vitally important physiological response to dangerous situations that prepares one to evade or confront a threat in the environment. However, the mechanisms that regulate anxiety may break down in a wide variety of circumstances, leading to excessive or inappropriate expression of anxiety. Specific examples include phobias, panic attacks, and generalized anxiety. In phobias, high-level anxiety is aroused by specific situations or objects that may range from concrete entities such as snakes, to complex circumstances such as social interactions or public speaking. Panic attacks are brief and very intense episodes of anxiety that often occur without a precipitating event or stimulus. Generalized anxiety represents a more diffuse and nonspecific kind of anxiety that is most often experienced as excessive worrying, restlessness, and tension occurring with a chronic and sustained pattern. In each case, an anxiety disorder may be said to exist if the anxiety experienced is disproportionate to the circumstance, is difficult for the individual to control, or interferes with normal functioning.

In addition to these common manifestations of anxiety, obsessive-compulsive disorder and post-traumatic stress disorder are generally believed to be related to the anxiety disorders. In the case of obsessive-compulsive disorder, individuals experience a high level of anxiety that drives their obsessional thinking or compulsive behaviors. When such an individual fails to carry out a repetitive behavior such as hand washing or checking, there is an experience of severe anxiety. Post-traumatic stress disorder is produced by an intense and overwhelmingly fearful event that is often life-threatening in nature. The characteristic symptoms that result from such a traumatic event include the persistent reexperience of the event in dreams and memories, persistent avoidance of stimuli associated with the event, and increased arousal.

Psychosis

Disturbances of perception and thought process fall into a broad category of symptoms referred to as psychosis. The threshold for determining whether thought is impaired varies somewhat with the cultural context. Like anxiety, psychotic symptoms may occur in a wide variety of mental disorders. They are most characteristically associated with schizophrenia, but psychotic symptoms can also occur in severe mood disorders.

One of the most common groups of symptoms that result from disordered processing and interpretation of sensory information are hallucinations. Hallucinations are said to occur when an individual experiences a sensory impression that has no basis in reality. Hallucinations may be auditory, olfactory, gustatory, kinesthetic, tactile, or visual. For example, auditory hallucinations frequently involve the impression that one is hearing a voice. In each case, the sensory impression is falsely experienced as real.

A more complex group of symptoms resulting from disordered interpretation of information consists of delusions. A delusion is a false belief that an individual holds despite evidence to the contrary. A common example is paranoia, in which a person has delusional beliefs that others are trying to harm him or her. Attempts to convince the person that these beliefs are unfounded typically fail and may even result in the further entrenchment of the beliefs.

Hallucinations and delusions are among the most commonly observed psychotic symptoms. Symptoms of schizophrenia are divided into two broad classes: positive symptoms and negative symptoms. Positive symptoms generally involve the experience of something in consciousness that should not normally be present. For example, hallucinations and delusions represent perceptions or beliefs that should not normally be experienced. In addition to hallucinations and delusions, patients with psychotic disorders such as schizophrenia frequently have marked disturbances in the logical process of their thoughts. Specifically, psychotic thought processes are characteristically loose, disorganized, illogical, or bizarre. The severe disturbances of thought content and process that comprise the positive symptoms often are the most recognizable and striking features of psychotic disorders such as schizophrenia or manic depressive illness.

Common signs of acute anxiety
- Feelings of fear or dread
- Trembling, restlessness, and muscle tension
- Rapid heart rate
- Lightheadedness or dizziness
- Perspiration
- Cold hands/feet
- Shortness of breath

Common manifestations of schizophrenia

Positive symptoms
- Hallucinations
- Delusions
- Disorganized thoughts and behaviors
- Loose or illogical thoughts
- Agitation

Negative symptoms
- Flat or blunted affect
- Concrete thoughts
- Anhedonia (inability to experience pleasure)
- Poor motivation, spontaneity, and initiative

However, in addition to positive symptoms, patients with schizophrenia and other psychoses have been noted to exhibit major deficits in motivation and spontaneity that are referred to as negative symptoms. While positive symptoms represent the presence of something not normally experienced, negative symptoms reflect the absence of thoughts and behaviors that would otherwise be expected. Concreteness of thought represents impairment in the ability to think abstractly. Blunting of affect refers to a general reduction in the ability to express emotion. Motivational failure and inability to initiate activities represent a major source of long-term disability in schizophrenia. Anhedonia reflects a deficit in the ability to experience pleasure and to react appropriately to pleasurable situations. Positive symptoms such as hallucinations are responsible for much of the acute distress associated with schizophrenia, but negative symptoms appear to be responsible for much of the chronic and long-term disability associated with the disorder.

Disturbances of Mood

Most of us have an immediate and intuitive understanding of the notion of mood. We readily comprehend what it means to feel sad or happy. These concepts are nonetheless very difficult to formulate in a scientifically precise and quantifiable way; the challenge is greater given the cultural differences that are associated with the expression of mood. Nevertheless, dysregulation of mood and the expression of mood, or affect, represent a major category among mental disorders.

Disturbances of mood characteristically manifest themselves as a sustained feeling of sadness or sustained elevation of mood. As with anxiety and psychosis, disturbances of mood may occur in a variety of patterns associated with different mental disorders. The disorder most closely associated with persistent sadness is major depression, while that associated with sustained elevation or fluctuation of mood is bipolar disorder. Along with the prevailing feelings of sadness or elation, disorders of mood are associated with a host of related symptoms that include disturbances in appetite, sleep patterns, energy level, concentration, and memory.

Disturbances of Cognition

Cognitive function refers to the general ability to organize, process, and recall information. Progressive deterioration of cognitive function is referred to as dementia. Dementia may be caused by a number of specific conditions including Alzheimer's disease. It is not uncommon to find profound disturbances of

---

Common signs of mood disorders

Symptoms commonly associated with depression

- Persistent sadness or despair
- Insomnia (sometimes hypersomnia)
- Decreased appetite
- Psychomotor retardation
- Anhedonia (inability to experience pleasure)
- Irritability
- Apathy, poor motivation, social withdrawal
- Hopelessness
- Poor self-esteem, feelings of helplessness
- Suicidal ideation

Symptoms commonly associated with mania

- Persistently elevated or euphoric mood
- Grandiosity (inappropriately high self-esteem)
- Psychomotor agitation
- Decreased sleep
- Racing thoughts and distractibility
- Poor judgment and impaired impulse control
- Rapid or pressured speech

---

cognition in patients suffering from severe mood disturbances. More recently, cognitive deficits have been reported in schizophrenia and now have become a major new topic of research. Last, cognitive impairment frequently occurs in a host of chemical, metabolic, and infectious diseases that exert an impact on the brain.

Other Symptoms

Anxiety, psychosis, mood disturbances, and cognitive impairments are among the most common and disabling manifestations of mental disorders. It is important, however, to appreciate that mental disorders leave no aspect of human experience untouched. Other common manifestations include, for example, somatic or other physical symptoms and impairment of impulse control.

Diagnosis of Mental Illness

The standard manual used for diagnosis of mental disorders in the United States is the *Diagnostic and Statistical Manual of Mental Disorders*. Most recently revised in 1994, this manual, first published in 1952, is now in its fourth edition. *DSM-IV* organizes mental disorders into 16 major diagnostic classes. *DSM-IV* is descriptive in its listing of symptoms and does not take a position about underlying causation.

Major diagnostic classes of mental disorders *(DSM-IV)*

- Delirium, dementia, and amnestic and other cognitive disorders
- Mental disorders due to a general medical condition
- Substance-related disorders
- Schizophrenia and other psychotic disorders
- Mood disorders
- Anxiety disorders
- Somatoform disorders

- Factitious disorders
- Dissociative disorders
- Sexual and gender identity disorders
- Eating disorders
- Sleep disorders
- Impulse-control disorders
- Adjustment disorders
- Personality disorders

Measuring Body Mass

The new body mass index (BMI) applies to both men and women. To determine BMI, weight in kilograms is divided by height in meters, squared. To calculate your body mass index from the table below, locate your height in inches in the left-hand column, then follow it across until you locate your weight; the number at the very top is your body mass index. A BMI of less than 18.5 is considered underweight, 18.5 to 24.9 is considered normal weight, 25 to 29.9 is considered overweight, and one of 30 or above is considered obese.

Body Mass Index Chart

Height (inches)	19	20	21	22	23	24	25	26	27	28	29	30	31	32	33	34	35
								Body Weight (pounds)									
58	91	96	100	105	110	115	119	124	129	134	138	143	148	153	158	162	167
59	94	99	104	109	114	119	124	128	133	138	143	148	153	158	163	168	173
60	97	102	107	112	118	123	128	133	138	143	148	153	158	163	168	174	179
61	100	106	111	116	122	127	132	137	143	148	153	158	164	169	174	180	185
62	104	109	115	120	126	131	136	142	147	153	158	164	169	175	180	186	191
63	107	113	118	124	130	135	141	146	152	158	163	169	175	180	186	191	197
64	110	116	122	128	134	140	145	151	157	163	169	174	180	186	192	197	204
65	114	120	126	132	138	144	150	156	162	168	174	180	186	192	198	204	210
66	118	124	130	136	142	148	155	161	167	173	179	186	192	198	204	210	216
67	121	127	134	140	146	153	159	166	172	178	185	191	198	204	211	217	223
68	125	131	138	144	151	158	164	171	177	184	190	197	203	210	216	223	230
69	128	135	142	149	155	162	169	176	182	189	196	203	209	216	223	230	236
70	132	139	146	153	160	167	174	181	188	195	202	209	216	222	229	236	243
71	136	143	150	157	165	172	179	186	193	200	208	215	222	229	236	243	250
72	140	147	154	162	169	177	184	191	199	206	213	221	228	235	242	250	258
73	144	151	159	166	174	182	189	197	204	212	219	227	235	242	250	257	265
74	148	155	163	171	179	186	194	202	210	218	225	233	241	249	256	264	272
75	152	160	168	176	184	192	200	208	216	224	232	240	248	256	264	272	279
76	156	164	172	180	189	197	205	213	221	230	238	246	254	263	271	279	287

Source: National Heart, Lung, and Blood Institute.

First Federal Obesity Guidelines: More Than Half of All Americans Are Too Fat

Source: National Heart, Lung, and Blood Institute

Overweight and obesity continue to be an alarming public-health problem in the United States, affecting 97 million American adults—an astonishing 55% of the population. Between 1960 and 1994, the prevalence of obesity in adults increased from nearly 13% to 22.5% of the U.S. population, with most of the increase occurring in the 1990s. These findings are recorded in the first federal guidelines on the identification, evaluation, and treatment of overweight and obesity in adults, which was released by the National Heart, Lung, and Blood Institute (NHLBI) in June 1998.

"There are several possible reasons for the increase," asserted Karen Donato, coordinator of the Obesity Education Initiative. "When people read labels, they're more likely to notice what's 'low-fat and healthy' but may not be looking at calories. Also, more people are eating out and portion sizes have increased. Another issue is decreased physical activity. So people are consuming more calories and are less active. It doesn't take much to tip the energy balance," she said.

According to the guidelines, assessment of overweight involves evaluation of three key measures—body mass index (BMI), waist circumference, and a patient's risk factors for diseases and conditions associated with obesity. Overweight is defined as having a BMI of 25 to 29.9 and obesity as a BMI of 30 and above, which is consistent with the definitions used in many other countries. BMI describes body weight relative to height and is strongly correlated with total body-fat content in adults. According to the guidelines, a BMI of 30 is about 30 pounds overweight and is equivalent to 221 pounds in a 6′ person and to 186 pounds in someone who is 5′6″. The BMI numbers apply to both men and women. Some very muscular people may have a high BMI without health risks.

Waist circumference, which is strongly associated with abdominal fat, is another measure of overweight—excess abdominal fat is an independent predictor of disease risk. A waist circumference of over 40 inches in men and over 35 inches in women signifies increased risk in those who have a BMI of 25 to 34.9.

According to the guidelines, the most successful strategies for weight loss include calorie reduction, increased physical activity, and behavior therapy designed to improve eating and physical activity habits.

The guidelines have been reviewed by 115 health experts at major medical and professional societies, and have been endorsed by 54 professional societies, government agencies, and consumer organizations. The published report is available on the NHLBI Web site: http://www.nhlbi.nih.gov/guidelines/obesity/ob_home.htm. Single free copies of the consumer tips referred to above are available by writing to the NHLBI Information Center, P.O. Box 30105, Bethesda, Md. 20824-0105.

Healthy Weight, Overweight, and Obesity in the United States

	Healthy weight[1]		Overweight[2]		Obesity[3]	
	1960–1962	1988–1994	1960–1962	1988–1994	1960–1962	1988–1994
Male						
20–34 years	54.2%	50.3%	42.7%	47.5%	9.2%	14.1%
35–44 years	44.1	33.3	53.5	65.5	12.1	21.5
45–54 years	43.9	33.5	53.9	66.1	12.5	23.2
55–64 years	43.5	28.1	52.2	70.5	9.2	27.2
65–74 years	44.0	29.8	47.8	68.5	10.4	24.1
75 years and over	—	40.6	—	56.5	—	13.2
Female[4]						
20–34 years	62.6	54.3	21.2	37.0	7.2	18.5
35–44 years	56.2	45.5	37.2	49.6	14.7	25.5
45–54 years	46.1	35.6	49.3	60.3	20.3	32.4
55–64 years	37.2	31.2	59.9	66.3	24.4	33.7
65–74 years	35.5	36.0	60.9	60.3	23.2	26.9
75 years and over	—	41.0	—	52.3	—	19.2

NOTE: (—) = Data not available. 1. Body mass index (BMI) of 19 to less than 25 kilograms/meter (*see* table "Measuring Body Mass," p. 554). 2. BMI greater than or equal to 25. 3. BMI greater than or equal to 30. 4. Excludes pregnant women. *Source: Health, United States, 2000,* Centers for Disease Control and Prevention.

How Many Servings Do You Need?

Food group	Children ages 2 to 6 years, women, some older adults (about 1,600 calories)	Older children, teen girls, active women, most men (about 2,200 calories)	Teen boys, active men (about 2,800 calories)
Bread, cereal, rice, and pasta group (grains group)—especially whole grain	6	9	11
Vegetable group	3	4	5
Fruit group	2	3	4
Milk, yogurt, and cheese group (milk group)—preferably fat free or low fat	2 or 3[1]	2 or 3[1]	2 or 3[1]
Meat, poultry, fish, dry beans, eggs, and nuts group (meat and beans group)—preferably lean or low fat	2, for a total of 5 ounces	2, for a total of 6 ounces	3, for a total of 7 ounces

1. The number of servings depends on your age. Older children and teenagers (ages 9 to 18 years) and adults over the age of 50 need 3 servings daily. Others need 2 servings daily. During pregnancy and lactation, the recommended number of milk group servings is the same as for nonpregnant women. *Source: Dietary Guidelines for Americans, 2000,* U.S. Department of Agriculture, Center for Nutrition Policy and Promotion.

Which Fruits and Vegetables Provide the Most Nutrients?

Source: Dietary Guidelines for Americans, 2000, United States Department of Agriculture

The lists below show which fruits and vegetables are the best sources of vitamin A (carotenoids), vitamin C, folate, and potassium. Eat at least 2 servings of fruits and at least 3 servings of vegetables each day.

Sources of vitamin A (carotenoids)
• Orange vegetables like carrots, sweet potatoes, pumpkin
• Dark-green leafy vegetables such as spinach, collards, turnip greens
• Orange fruits like mango, cantaloupe, apricots
• Tomatoes

Sources of vitamin C
• Citrus fruits and juices, kiwi fruit, strawberries, cantaloupe
• Broccoli, peppers, tomatoes, cabbage, potatoes
• Leafy greens such as romaine lettuce, turnip greens, spinach

Sources of folate
• Cooked dry beans and peas, peanuts
• Oranges, orange juice
• Dark-green leafy vegetables like spinach and mustard greens, romaine lettuce
• Green peas

Sources of potassium
• Baked white or sweet potato, cooked greens (such as spinach), winter (orange) squash
• Bananas, plantains, dried fruits such as apricots and prunes, orange juice
• Cooked dry beans (such as baked beans) and lentils

Percentage of Adults Engaging in Leisure Time Physical Activity, 1998

Characteristic	No participation in physical activity	Participates in regular, sustained activity[1]	Participates in regular, vigorous activity[2]	Characteristic	No participation in physical activity	Participates in regular, sustained activity[1]	Participates in regular, vigorous activity[2]
Total	**28.7%**	**20.8%**	**13.6%**	30 to 44 years old	28.2%	19.9%	14.8%
Male	26.2	21.9	13.3	45 to 64 years old	31.5	19.8	13.2
Female	31.0	19.7	13.8	65 to 74 years old	35.9	20.3	13.0
White, non-Hispanic	26.7	21.6	14.0	75 years old and over	47.1	14.9	12.3
Black, non-Hispanic	33.8	17.8	12.3	**School years completed**			
Hispanic	38.4	17.4	11.4	Less than 12 years	49.7	14.3	8.2
Other	28.8	21.8	14.3	12 years	33.9	18.2	10.7
Males				Some college	23.9	22.3	13.9
18 to 29 years old	17.6	26.5	12.2	College	16.3	25.7	19.7
30 to 44 years old	24.9	19.0	11.8	**Household income**			
45 to 64 years old	30.6	20.5	14.1	Less than $10,000	42.4	17.8	10.7
65 to 74 years old	31.1	24.8	14.2	$10,000 to $19,999	39.8	16.9	10.5
75 years old and over	39.1	22.2	22.0	$20,000 to $34,999	31.3	19.4	12.1
Females				$35,000 to $49,999	24.4	21.4	14.0
18 to 29 years old	25.1	20.9	14.2	$50,000 and over	16.9	25.5	17.6

NOTE: Covers persons 18 years old and over. 1. Any type or intensity of activity that occurs 5 times or more per week and 30 minutes or more per occasion. 2. Rhythmic contraction of large muscle groups performed at 50% or more of estimated age- and sex-specific maximum cardio-respiratory capacity, 3 times per week or more for at least 20 minutes per occasion. *Source:* U.S. National Center for Chronic Disease Prevention and Health Promotion, unpublished data; *Statistical Abstract of the United States, 2000.*

Caffeine Content of Selected Foods and Drugs

Product	Serving size[1]	Caffeine (mg)	Product	Serving size[1]	Caffeine (mg)
Over-the-counter			**Soft drinks**		
Excedrin	2 tablets	130	Mountain Dew	12 ounces	55
Anacin	2 tablets	64	Diet Coke	12 ounces	47
Coffees			Coca-Cola	12 ounces	45
Coffee, brewed	8 ounces	135	Dr. Pepper	12 ounces	41
Coffee, instant	8 ounces	95	Sunkist Orange		
Coffee, decaffeinated	8 ounces	5	Soda	12 ounces	40
Teas			Pepsi-Cola	12 ounces	37
Tea, leaf or bag	8 ounces	50	**Chocolates or candies**		
Snapple Iced Tea	16-ounce bottle	48	Hershey Bar, 1 bar	1.5 ounces	10
Tea, green	8 ounces	30	Cocoa or hot		
Tea, instant	8 ounces	15	chocolate	8 ounces	5

1. Serving sizes are based on commonly eaten portions, pharmaceutical instructions, or the amount of the leading-selling container size. *Source:* Center for Science in the Public Interest. Reprinted/Adapted from *Nutrition Action Healthletter* (1875 Connecticut Ave., NW., Suite 300, Washington, DC 20009–5728. $24.00 for 10 issues.)

Blood Types

Human blood is grouped into four types: A, B, AB, and O. Each letter refers to a kind of antigen, or protein, on the surface of red blood cells. For example, the surface of red blood cells in Type A blood has antigens known as A-antigens.

Each blood type is also grouped by its Rhesus factor, or Rh factor. Blood is either Rh positive (Rh+) or Rh negative (Rh-). About 85% of Americans have Rh+ blood.

Rhesus refers to another type of antigen, or protein, on the surface of red blood cells. The name Rhesus comes from Rhesus monkeys, in which the protein was discovered.

Blood types become very important when a blood transfusion is necessary. In a blood transfusion, a patient must receive a blood type that is compatible with his or her own blood type—that is, the donated blood must be accepted by the patient's own blood. If the blood types are not compatible, red blood cells will clump together, making clots that can block blood vessels and cause death.

Type O- blood is considered the "universal donor" because it can be donated to people of any blood type. Type AB+ blood is considered the "universal recipient" because people with this type can receive any blood type.

Blood Type	Percent of Americans with this type	Who can receive this type
O+	37%	O+, A+, B+, AB+
O-	6%	All blood types
A+	34%	A+, AB+
A-	6%	A+, A-, AB+, AB-
B+	10%	B+, AB+
B-	2%	B+, B-, AB+, AB-
AB+	4%	AB+
AB-	1%	AB+, AB-

Leading Causes of Mortality throughout the World

Deaths	All countries rank	All countries % of total	Africa rank	Africa % of total	The Americas rank	The Americas % of total	Eastern Mediterranean rank	Eastern Mediterranean % of total	Europe rank	Europe % of total	Southeast Asia rank	Southeast Asia % of total	Western Pacific rank	Western Pacific % of total
Ischemic heart disease	1	13.7%	9	2.9%	1	17.9%	1	13.6%	1	25.5%	1	13.8%	3	11.1%
Cerebrovascular disease	2	9.5	7	4.7	2	10.3	5	5.3	2	13.7	4	6.5	1	14.3
Acute lower respiratory infections	3	6.4	3	8.2	3	4.2	2	9.1	4	3.6	2	9.3	4	4.0
HIV/AIDS	4	4.2	1	19.0	13	1.8	27	0.4	42	0.2	8	2.2	42	0.2
Chronic obstructive pulmonary disease	5	4.2	14	1.1	6	2.8	10	1.7	5	2.7	11	1.6	2	12.0
Diarrheal diseases	6	4.1	4	7.6	10	2.0	3	7.4	22	0.7	3	6.6	17	1.2
Perinatal conditions	7	4.0	5	5.5	7	2.6	4	7.3	13	1.2	5	6.0	10	2.2
Tuberculosis	8	2.8	11	2.2	19	1.0	7	3.7	23	0.6	6	5.1	9	2.9
Cancer of trachea/bronchus/lung	9	2.3	38	0.3	4	3.2	20	1.0	3	4.2	15	1.2	6	3.6
Road traffic accidents	10	2.2	12	1.8	5	3.1	9	1.9	8	1.9	7	2.5	12	2.0

Source: The World Health Report, 1999.

Global Estimates[1] of the HIV/AIDS Epidemic as of End 2000

Western Europe 540,000

Eastern Europe & Central Asia 700,000

North America 920,000

East Asia & Pacific 640,000

Caribbean 390,000

North Africa & Middle East 400,000

South & Southeast Asia 5.8 million

Latin America 1.4 million

Sub-Saharan Africa 25.3 million

Australia & New Zealand 15,000

Global Total 36.1 million

1. Number of people currently infected with HIV/AIDS.
Source: World Health Organization, UNAIDS.

Understanding AIDS

Acquired Immune Deficiency Syndrome, or AIDS, was first reported in mid-1981 in the United States; it is believed to have originated in Sub-Saharan Africa. The human immunodeficiency virus (HIV) that causes AIDS was identified in 1983, and by 1985 tests to detect the virus were available. The credit for discovering the AIDS virus is jointly shared by Dr. Robert Gallo, a researcher at the National Cancer Institute, and Luc Montagnier of the Pasteur Institute, France.

Destruction of Immune System

A fatal and incurable disease caused by the human immunodeficiency virus (HIV), AIDS attacks and destroys the immune system, gradually leaving the individual defenseless against illnesses that lead to death. These illnesses are referred to as "opportunistic" infections or diseases: in AIDS patients the most common are Pneumocystis carinii pneumonia (PCP), a parasitic infection of the lungs; and a type of cancer known as Kaposi's sarcoma (KS). Other opportunistic infections include unusually severe infections with yeast, cytomegalovirus, herpes virus, and parasites such as Toxoplasma or Cryptosporidia. Milder infections with these organisms do not suggest immune deficiencies. Symptoms of full-blown AIDS include a persistent cough, fever, and difficulty in breathing. Multiple purplish blotches and bumps on the skin may indicate Kaposi's sarcoma. The virus can also cause brain damage.

People infected with the virus can have a wide range of symptoms—from none to mild to severe. At least a fourth to a half of those infected will develop AIDS within four to ten years. Many experts think the percentage will be much higher.

Transmission

Although the first reported cases involved homosexual men in Los Angeles who were infected through sexual contact, the principal mode of transmission throughout the world is through the exchange of bodily fluids during heterosexual intercourse. According to the World Health Organization, extensive spread of HIV appears to have begun in the late 1970s and early 1980s. It spread in men and women with multiple sexual partners in East and Central Africa and among homosexual and bisexual men in certain urban areas of the Americas, Australasia, and Western Europe.

In addition to sexual contact, AIDS has been spread by intravenous drug users sharing infected hypodermic needles. The virus can also be passed on through transfused blood or its components. It may also be transmitted from infected mother to infant before, during, or shortly after birth.

Two major types of HIV have been recognized, HIV-l and HIV-2. HIV-l is the dominant type worldwide. HIV-2 is found principally in West Africa but cases have been reported in East Africa, Europe, Asia, and Latin America. There are at least ten different genetic subtypes of HIV-l, but their biological and epidemiological significance is unclear at present. Both HIV-l and HIV-2 are transmitted in the same ways.

Pandemic

With no cure at present, prudence could save thousands of people who have yet to be exposed to the virus. Use of condoms lessens the possibility of transmission as does the elimination of sharing hypodermic needles. The fate of many will depend less on science than on the ability of large numbers of human beings to change their behavior in the face of growing danger.

New drugs, such as AZT, have given researchers renewed optimism in treating AIDS. Powerful drug combinations, called "cocktails," are able to decrease the amount of HIV in the blood to undetectable levels. However, not everyone can tolerate the potent medications, which can have devastating side effects—including diabetes, anemia, and high cholesterol. In addition, doctors are reporting a significant increase of patients with drug-resistant HIV strains, prompting research to produce different drugs. As of June 2001, some 100 separate drugs were either in use or being tested for use against AIDS. Meanwhile, HIV has been spreading, with rising rates of infection in Eastern Europe, Russia, China, and Southeast Asia, prompting some scientists to grimly warn that the epidemic has only just begun.

Status of the World AIDS Epidemic, End of 2000

	Total	Adults	Women	Children under 15 years
People newly infected with HIV in 2000	5.3 million	4.7 million	2.2 million	600,000
Number of people living with HIV/AIDS	36.1 million	34.7 million	16.4 million	1.4 million
AIDS deaths in 2000	3 million	2.5 million	1.3 million	500,000
Total number of AIDS deaths since beginning of epidemic	21.8 million	17.5 million	9 million	4.3 million

Source: World Health Organization; UNAIDS. Web: www.unaids.org.

HIV/AIDS Statistics and Features by World Region

(as of Dec. 2000)

World region	Epidemic started	Adults & children living with HIV/AIDS	Adults & children newly infected with HIV	Adult prevalence rate[1]	Percent of HIV-positive adults who are women	Main mode(s) of transmission for adults[2]
Sub-Saharan Africa	late '70s–early '80s	25.3 million	3.8 million	8.8%	55%	Hetero
North Africa & Middle East	late '80s	400,000	80,000	0.2%	40%	Hetero, IDU
South & Southeast Asia	late '80s	5.8 million	780,000	0.56%	35%	Hetero, IDU
East Asia & Pacific	late '80s	640,000	130,000	0.07%	13%	IDU, Hetero, MSM
Latin America	late '70s–early '80s	1.4 milion	150,000	0.5%	25%	MSM, IDU, Hetero
Caribbean	late '70s–early '80s	390,000	60,000	2.3%	35%	Hetero, MSM
Eastern Europe & Central Asia	early '90s	700,000	250,000	0.35%	25%	IDU
Western Europe	late '70s–early '80s	540,000	30,000	0.24%	25%	MSM, IDU
North America	late '70s–early '80s	920,000	45,000	0.6%	20%	MSM, IDU, Hetero
Australia & New Zealand	late '70s–early '80s	15,000	500	0.13%	10%	MSM
Total		36.1 million	5.3 million	1.1%	47%	

1. The proportion of adults (15 to 49 years of age) living with HIV/AIDS in 2000, using 2000 population numbers. 2. Hetero (heterosexual transmission), IDU (transmission through injecting drug use), MSM (sexual transmission among men who have sex with men). 3. "'70s–'80s" refers to late '70s–early '80s. *Source:* World Health Organization, UNAID. Web: www.unaids.org.

Human Carcinogens

The *Ninth Report on Carcinogens,* published May 15, 2000, lists 218 substances known or suspected to cause cancer. The *Ninth Report* added (or upgraded) 14 substances, including secondhand smoke, alcoholic beverages, excessive sun, sun lamps, and tanning beds. Saccharin, the artificial sweetener, was removed from the list of suspected carcinogens; it had been listed since 1981.

Substances Known to Be Human Carcinogens

Aflatoxins
Alcoholic Beverage Consumption
4-Aminobiphenyl (4-Aminodiphenyl)
Analgesic Mixtures Containing Phenacetin
Arsenic and Certain Arsenic Compounds
Asbestos
Azathioprine
Benzene
Benzidine
bis(Chloromethyl) Ether
1,3-Butadiene
1,4-Butanediol Dimethylsulfonate
Cadmium and Cadmium Compounds
Chlorambucil
1-(2-Chloroethyl)-3-(4-methylcyclohexyl)-1-nitrosourea (MeCCNU)

Chromium Hexavalent Compounds
Coke Oven Emissions
Conjugated Estrogens
Cyclophosphamide
Cyclosporin A
Diethylstilbestrol
Dyes that Metabolize to Benzidine
  Direct Black 38
  Direct Blue 6
Environmental Tobacco Smoke
Erionite
Ethylene Oxide
Melphalan
Methoxsalen with Ultraviolet A Therapy (PUVA)
Mustard Gas
2-Naphthylamine
Radon

Silica, Crystalline (Respirable Size)
  Quartz
  Cristobalite
  Tridymite
Smokeless Tobacco
Solar Radiation and Exposure to Sun Lamps or Sunbeds
Soots
Strong Inorganic Acid Mists Containing Sulfuric Acid
Tamoxifen
Tars and Mineral Oils
Thiotepa
Thorium Dioxide
Tobacco Smoking
Vinyl Chloride

Source: *Ninth Report on Carcinogens,* The National Institute for Environmental Health Sciences.

Cancer Incidence Rates in the United States, 1987–1992

	Incidence rates per 100,000			Incidence rates per 100,000	
Cancer site	**Blacks**	**Whites**	**Cancer site**	**Blacks**	**Whites**
All sites	436.5	402.9	Kidney and renal pelvis	9.6	9.0
Males	584.5	484.2	Breast (females)	96.9	113.2
Females	337.3	351.4	<50 years	33.8	32.9
Esophagus	9.8	3.4	>50 years	291.4	360.6
Multiple myeloma	9.2	4.1	Leukemias	8.8	10.5
Liver	4.8	2.5	Hodgkin's disease	2.3	3.1
Stomach	12.3	6.6	Non-Hodgkin's lymphomas	10.8	15.5
Cervix uterine	13.4	8.0	Corpus and uterus	14.8	22.3
Larynx	7.2	4.4	Ovary	10.4	15.9
Pancreas	13.5	8.8	Thyroid	2.7	4.7
Lung and bronchus	79.2	58.4	Brain	3.8	6.8
Males	124.3	80.2	Urinary bladder	9.5	18.2
Females	46.8	42.5	Testis	0.7	5.2
Prostate	187.6	139.4	Melanomas of skin	0.8	13.1
Oral cavity and pharynx	13.9	10.4	All sites except lung and		
Colon and rectum	52.5	47.4	bronchus	357.3	344.5
Colon	40.6	33.9	Males	460.2	403.9
Rectum	12.0	13.6	Females	290.6	308.9

America's Best Hospitals, 2001

The annual *U.S. News & World Report* list of the United States' best hospitals is prepared by the National Opinion Research Center at the University of Chicago. The list recognizes hospitals that excel in many areas.

1. Johns Hopkins Hospital, Baltimore, Md.
2. Mayo Clinic, Rochester, Minn.
3. Massachusetts General Hospital, Boston
4. Cleveland Clinic, Ohio
5. University of California, Los Angeles Medical Center
6. Duke University Medical Center, Durham, N.C.
7. Barnes-Jewish Hospital, St. Louis, Mo.
7. University of Michigan Medical Center, Ann Arbor
9. University of California, San Francisco Medical Center
10. Stanford University Hospital, Calif.
11. Brigham and Women's Hospital, Boston, Mass.
12. University of Washington Medical Center, Seattle
13. New York Presbyterian Hospital, NYC
14. Hospital of the University of Pennsylvania, Philadelphia
15. University of Chicago Hospitals, Ill.
16. University of Pittsburgh Medical Center, Pa.

People Without Health Insurance[1] by Characteristic, 1999

Characteristic	Percent	Characteristic	Percent
Total	**15.5%**	**Nativity**	
Total poor	**32.4**	Native	13.5%
Race and ethnicity		Foreign born	33.4
White non-Hispanic	11.0	**Household income**	
Black	21.2	Less than $25,000	24.1
Asian and Pacific Islander	20.8	$25,000 to $49,999	18.2
Hispanic[2]	33.4	$50,000 to $74.999	11.8
Age		$75,000 or more	8.3
Under 18 years	13.9	**Work experience (18 to 64 years)**	
18 to 24 years	29.0	Worked during year	17.4
65 years and over	1.3	Did not work	26.5

1. For the entire year. 2. Hispanics may be of any race. *Source:* U.S. Census Bureau, *Current Population Survey, March 2000.*

Percent of People Without Health Insurance, by State, 1999

State	Percent	State	Percent	State	Percent
Alabama	14.3%	Louisiana	22.5%	Oklahoma	17.5%
Alaska	19.1	Maine	11.9	Oregon	14.6
Arizona	21.2	Maryland	11.8	Pennsylvania	9.4
Arkansas	14.7	Massachusetts	10.5	Rhode Island	6.9
California	20.3	Michigan	11.2	South Carolina	17.6
Colorado	16.8	Minnesota	8.0	South Dakota	11.8
Connecticut	9.8	Mississippi	16.6	Tennessee	11.5
Delaware	11.4	Missouri	8.6	Texas	23.3
D.C.	15.4	Montana	18.6	Utah	14.2
Florida	19.2	Nebraska	10.8	Vermont	12.3
Georgia	16.1	Nevada	20.7	Virginia	14.1
Hawaii	11.1	New Hampshire	10.2	Washington	15.8
Idaho	19.1	New Jersey	13.4	West Virginia	17.1
Illinois	14.1	New Mexico	25.8	Wisconsin	11.0
Indiana	10.8	New York	16.4	Wyoming	16.1
Iowa	8.3	North Carolina	15.4	**Total U.S.**	**15.5**
Kansas	12.1	North Dakota	11.8		
Kentucky	14.5	Ohio	11.0		

NOTE: These estimates should not be used to rank the states. Results from different samplings could easily show different estimates and rankings because of small sampling sizes. For example, the high noncoverage for Texas is not statistically different from that of New Mexico. *Source:* U.S. Census Bureau, *March 2000 Current Population Survey.*

Legal Abortion Ratios in the United States, 1973–1997

	Abortions per 100 live births[1]											
Characteristic	1973	1975	1980	1985	1990	1991	1992	1993	1994	1995	1996	1997
Total	**19.6**	**27.2**	**35.9**	**35.4**	**34.5**	**33.9**	**33.5**	**33.4**	**32.1**	**31.1**	**31.4**	**30.5**
Age												
Under 15 years	123.7	119.3	139.7	137.6	84.4	76.7	79.0	74.4	70.4	66.7	72.3	72.9
15–19 years	53.9	54.2	71.4	68.8	51.5	46.2	44.0	44.0	41.5	39.9	41.5	40.7
20–24 years	29.4	28.9	39.5	38.6	37.7	37.8	37.6	38.4	36.4	34.9	35.5	34.4
25–29 years	20.7	19.2	23.7	21.7	22.0	22.1	22.2	22.7	22.2	22.1	22.7	22.3
30–34 years	28.0	25.0	23.7	19.9	19.1	18.7	18.3	18.0	17.2	16.5	16.5	16.0
35–39 years	45.1	42.2	41.0	33.6	27.3	26.2	25.6	24.8	23.4	22.4	22.0	20.8
40 years and over	68.4	66.8	80.7	62.3	50.1	46.9	45.4	43.0	41.2	38.7	37.6	35.0
Race												
White[2]	32.6	27.7	33.2	27.7	25.8	24.6	23.6	23.1	21.7	20.4	20.2	19.3
Black[3]	42.0	47.6	54.3	47.2	52.1	50.2	51.8	55.2	53.8	53.4	55.5	54.3
Marital status												
Married	7.6	9.6	10.5	8.0	8.9	8.9	8.4	8.4	7.9	7.6	7.8	7.3
Unmarried	139.8	161.0	147.6	117.4	87.9	81.5	79.0	78.9	68.9	65.0	65.5	65.7

NOTE: Data are based on reporting by state health departments and by hospitals and other medical facilities. 1. For calculation of ratios according to each characteristic, abortions with the characteristic unknown have been distributed in proportion to abortions with the characteristic known. 2. For 1989 and later years, white race includes women of Hispanic ethnicity. 3. Before 1989 black race includes races other than white. *Source: Health, United States, 2000,* Centers for Disease Control and Prevention.

Overview of Drug Use in the United States

Source: U.S. Department of Justice, Drug Enforcement Administration

The *National Household Survey on Drug Abuse,* an annual survey conducted by the Substance Abuse and Mental Health Services Administration, estimates the prevalence of illicit drug use in the United States and monitors the trends in use over time. It is based on a representative sample of 25,500 persons from the U.S. population aged 12 and older. Some of the more notable statistics from the 2000 study follow.

• An estimated 14.8 million Americans were current users of illicit drugs in 1999, meaning they used an illicit drug at least once during the 30 days prior to being interviewed. By comparison, the number of current illicit drug users was at its highest level in 1979 when the estimate was 25.4 million.

• More than 1 in 10 (10.9%) youths aged 12–17 were current users of illicit drugs in 1999. The rate was highest in 1979 (16.3%), declined to 5.3% in 1992, then increased to 10.9 in 1995. The percentage of youths reporting current use of illicit drugs has fluctuated since 1995 (9% in 1996; 11.4% in 1997).

• The survey found that 17.1% of young adults aged 18–25 were current users of illicit drugs in 1999. This rate rose from 13.3% in 1994.

• In 1999, an estimated 208,000 Americans were current users of heroin, more than tripling the number in 1993 (68,000). The average age of heroin users is rapidly dropping. In 1998, the typical heroin user was 21.3 years old the first time he or she tried the drug, down from 25 years old in 1990.

• There were an estimated 991,000 new inhalant users in 1998. This number is up 154% from 1990, when it was 390,000. Of first-time inhalant users in 1998, 62% were between the ages of 12 and 17.

• Numerous states have experienced an increase in drug-related deaths. Heroin-related deaths, in particular, are rising as a result of the increasing purity and decreasing price of that drug.

New Mexico: The Office of the Medical Investigator reported that drug-related deaths increased by nearly 100% over the past nine years. Viewed in 3-year increments, deaths rose from 205 during 1989–91, to 317 during 1992–94, to 401 during 1995–97.

Florida: The Medical Examiner's Commission reported that heroin-related deaths skyrocketed from 28 in 1993 to 206 in 1998, an increase of more than 600%.

California: The Department of Alcohol & Drug Programs reported an increase in drug-related deaths for the two-year period 1996–97 (5,407 deaths) compared to the previous period, 1994–95 (5,335 deaths).

Drug Use by Americans, 12 Years and Older

Type of drug	Ever used			Current user		
	1979	1990	1998	1979	1990	1998
Marijuana and hashish	27.9%	30.5%	33.0%	13.2%	5.4%	5.0%
Cocaine	8.6	11.2	10.6	2.6	0.9	0.8
Inhalants	n.a.	5.7	5.8	n.a.	0.4	0.3
Hallucinogens	8.9	7.9	9.9	1.9	0.4	0.7
Heroin	1.3	0.8	1.1	0.1	—	0.1
Stimulants[1]	n.a.	5.5	4.4	n.a.	0.6	0.3
Sedatives[1]	n.a.	2.8	2.1	n.a.	0.2	0.1
Tranquilizers[1]	n.a.	4.0	3.5	n.a.	0.6	0.3
Analgesics[1]	n.a.	6.3	5.3	n.a.	0.9	0.8
Alcohol	88.5	82.2	81.3	63.2	52.6	51.7
Cigarettes	n.a.	75.4	69.7	n.a.	32.6	27.7

NOTE: Current users are those who used drugs at least once within month prior to this study. 1. Nonmedical use; does not include over-the-counter drugs. *Source:* U.S. Substance Abuse and Mental Health Services Administration (SAMHSA), Office of Applied Studies, *National Household Survey on Drug Abuse.*

Marijuana Use
(over a lifetime)

Characteristic	1979	1982	1985	1988	1991	1992	1993	1994	1995	1996	1997	1998
Total	28.0%	28.6%	29.4%	30.6%	30.5%	30.2%	31.0%	31.1%	31.0%	32.0%	32.9%	33.0%
Age												
12–17 years	27.0	23.2	20.1	15.0	11.1	9.1	9.9	13.6	16.2	16.8	18.9	17.0
18–25 years	66.0	61.3	57.6	54.6	48.8	46.6	45.7	41.9	44.0	41.5	44.6	
26–34 years	45.0	51.5	54.1	57.6	55.2	54.3	54.9	52.7	51.8	50.5	47.9	47.9
35 years or more	9.0	10.4	13.9	17.6	21.1	22.2	23.8	25.4	25.3	27.0	29.4	29.4
Race												
White	28.0	29.3	31.1	32.0	32.0	32.4	33.6	33.5	33.5	34.4	35.6	35.5
Black	28.0	28.2	26.6	26.8	28.7	25.0	24.6	27.5	28.2	29.6	28.5	30.2
Hispanic	21.0	23.7	18.4	21.7	21.0	20.0	21.8	21.6	20.2	22.0	22.3	23.2
Other	29.5	*	12.8	30.8	24.0	21.6	18.5	18.0	16.1	19.7	22.4	20.1
Sex												
Male	34.0	34.0	34.7	33.9	34.6	34.8	35.9	35.9	35.6	37.0	37.8	38.5
Female	22.0	23.6	24.5	27.6	26.8	25.9	26.4	26.8	26.8	27.5	28.3	27.9

Source: Substance Abuse and Mental Health Services Administration (SAMHSA).

Smoking Prevalence Among U.S. Adults, 1965–1998
(as a percent of population, 18 years of age and older)

Year	Overall population	Males	Females	White male	Black male	White female	Black female
1965	41.9%	51.2%	33.7%	50.4%	58.8%	33.9%	31.8%
1974	37.0	42.8	32.2	41.7	53.6	32.0	35.6
1983	31.9	34.8	29.4	34.2	41.7	29.6	31.3
1985	29.9	32.2	27.9	31.3	40.2	27.9	30.9
1990	25.3	28.0	22.9	27.6	32.8	23.5	20.8
1992	26.3	28.1	24.6	27.7	33.3	25.3	24.5
1993	24.8	27.3	22.6	26.6	33.7	23.4	20.6
1994	25.3	27.6	23.1	27.1	34.3	24.0	21.6
1995	24.6	26.5	22.7	26.2	29.4	23.4	23.5
1997	24.6	27.1	22.2	26.8	32.4	22.8	22.5
1998	24.0	25.9	22.1	26.0	29.0	23.0	21.1

Source: Health, United States, 2000, Centers for Disease Control and Prevention.

Alcohol Consumption, 1998
(persons 18 years of age and over)

	Both sexes	Male	Female		Both sexes	Male	Female
Drinking status[1]				**Level of alcohol consumption in past year for current drinkers**[2]			
All	100.0%	100.0%	100.0%	All drinking levels	100.0%	100.0%	100.0%
Lifetime abstainer	21.8	14.5	28.5	Light	69.8	59.5	81.4
Former drinker	15.9	16.2	15.7	Moderate	22.8	32.4	12.0
Infrequent	9.0	7.4	10.5	Heavier	7.4	8.1	6.6
Regular	6.9	8.8	5.1	**Number of days in the past year with 5 or more drinks**			
Current drinker	62.3	69.3	55.8	All current drinkers	100.0%	100.0%	100.0%
Infrequent	14.6	11.0	17.8	No days	67.2	56.3	79.3
Regular	47.7	58.3	38.0	At least 1 day	32.8	43.7	20.7
				1–11 days	18.5	22.3	14.2
				12 or more days	14.3	21.4	6.4

1. Lifetime abstainers had fewer than 12 drinks in their lifetime. Former drinkers had at least 12 drinks in their lifetime and none in the past year. Former infrequent drinkers are former drinkers who had fewer than 12 drinks in any one year. Former regular drinkers are former drinkers who had at least 12 drinks in any one year. Current drinkers had 12 drinks in their lifetime and at least one drink in the past year. Current infrequent drinkers are current drinkers who had fewer than 12 drinks in the past year. Current regular drinkers are current drinkers who had at least 12 drinks in the past year. 2. Level of alcohol consumption categories are defined as follows: light drinkers, up to 3 drinks per week; moderate drinkers, 4–14 drinks per week for men and 4–7 drinks per week for women; heavier drinkers, more than 14 drinks per week for men and more than 7 drinks per week for women. Source: Centers for Disease Control and Prevention, National Center for Health Statistics, National Health Interview Survey, sample adult questionnaire.

National Transplant Data

Registered U.S. Patients Waiting for Transplants
(as of July 27, 2001)

Kidney	49,546	Lung	3,776	Pancreas Islet Cell	248
Liver	18,137	Kidney-Pancreas	2,532	Heart-Lung	219
Heart	4,233	Pancreas	1,129	Intestine	177
				Total patients	**77,589[1]**

NOTE: Patients can be listed with more than one transplant center, thus the number of registrations is greater than the actual number of patients. 1. Some patients are waiting for more than one organ; therefore the total number of patients is less than the sum of patients waiting for each organ. Source: National Organ Procurement & Transplantation Network.

Number of U.S. Transplants Per Year, 1988–2000

	1988	1990	1993	1996	2000		1988	1990	1993	1996	2000
Heart	1,676	2,107	2,297	2,345	2,197	Liver	1,713	2,690	3,441	4,063	4,934
Heart-Lung	74	52	60	39	48	Lung	33	203	668	810	956
Intestine	—	5	34	45	79	Pancreas	79	69	113	165	436
Kidney	8,873	9,416	10,359	11,317	13,290						
Kidney-Pancreas	170	459	661	859	914	**Total**	**12,618**	**15,001**	**17,633**	**19,643**	**22,854**

NOTE: Kidney-pancreas transplants are counted apart from kidney transplants and pancreas transplants and do not show up in the totals for the individual organs. Double kidney, double lung, and heart-lung transplants are each counted as one transplant. All other multi-organ transplants are included in the total for each individual organ. Source: National Organ Procurement & Transplantation Network.

The Common Cold

Source: National Institute of Allergy and Infectious Diseases, National Institutes of Health

The problem. Adults average about two to four colds a year, although the range varies widely. Women, especially those aged 20–30 years, have more colds than men, possibly because of their closer contact with children. On average, individuals older than 60 have fewer than one cold a year. Colds are most prevalent among children, and seem to be related to youngsters' relative lack of resistance to infection and to contacts with other children in day-care centers and schools. Children have about 6–10 colds a year.

The causes: viruses. More than 200 different viruses are known to cause the symptoms of the common cold. **Rhinoviruses** (from the Greek *rhin,* meaning nose) cause an estimated 30 to 35 percent of all adult colds, and are most active in early fall, spring, and summer. **Coronaviruses** are believed to cause a large percentage of all adult colds. They induce colds primarily in the winter and early spring. Of the more than 30 isolated strains, three or four infect humans.

Does cold weather cause a cold? Although many people are convinced that a cold results from exposure to cold weather, or from getting chilled or overheated, these conditions in fact have little or no effect on the development or severity of a cold.

How cold viruses cause disease. Viruses cause infection by overcoming the body's complex defense system. The body's first line of defense is mucus, produced by the membranes in the nose and throat. Mucus traps the material we inhale: pollen, dust, bacteria, and viruses. When a virus penetrates the mucus and enters a cell, it commandeers the protein-making machinery to manufacture new viruses, which, in turn, attack surrounding cells.

Cold symptoms: the body fights back. Cold symptoms are probably the result of the body's immune response to the viral invasion. Virus-infected cells in the nose send out signals that recruit specialized white blood cells to the site of the infection. In turn, these cells emit a range of immune system chemicals such as kinins. These chemicals probably lead to the symptoms of the common cold by causing swelling and inflammation

of the nasal membranes, leakage of proteins and fluid from capillaries and lymph vessels, and the increased production of mucus.

How colds are spread. Depending on the virus type, any or all of the following routes of transmission may be common:

• Touching infectious respiratory secretions on the skin and on environmental surfaces and then touching the eyes or nose.

• Inhaling relatively large particles of respiratory secretions transported briefly in the air.

• Inhaling droplet nuclei, smaller infectious particles suspended in the air for long periods of time.

Prevention. Handwashing is the simplest and most effective way to keep from getting rhinovirus colds. Not touching the nose or eyes is another. Individuals with colds should always sneeze or cough into a facial tissue, and promptly throw it away. Rhinoviruses can survive up to three hours outside the nasal passages on inanimate objects and skin.

Treatment. Only symptomatic treatment is available for uncomplicated cases of the common cold: bed rest, plenty of fluids, gargling with warm salt water, applying petroleum jelly to a raw nose, and taking aspirin or acetaminophen to relieve headache or fever. Nonprescription cold remedies, including decongestants and cough suppressants, may relieve some cold symptoms but will not prevent, cure, or even shorten the duration of illness.

Antibiotics do not kill viruses. These prescription drugs should be used only for rare bacterial complications, such as sinusitis or ear infections, that can develop as secondary infections. (The flu, also caused by a virus, should also not be treated by antibiotics.)

Does vitamin C have a role? Many people are convinced that taking large quantities of vitamin C will prevent colds or relieve symptoms. To test this theory, several large-scale, controlled studies involving children and adults have been conducted. To date, no conclusive data have shown that large doses of vitamin C prevent colds. The vitamin may reduce the severity or duration of symptoms, but there is no definitive evidence.

Is It a Cold or the Flu?

Symptoms	Cold	Flu
fever	rare	characteristic, high (102–104° F); lasts 3–4 days
headache	rare	prominent
general aches, pains	slight	usual; often severe
fatigue, weakness	quite mild	can last up to 2–3 weeks
extreme exhaustion	never	early and prominent
stuffy nose, sore throat	common	sometimes
Complications	sinus congestion or earache	bronchitis, pneumonia; can be life-threatening
Prevention	none	annual vaccination; antiviral medicines—see your doctor
Treatment	only temporary relief of symptoms	antiviral medicines—see your doctor

Source: National Institute of Allergy and Infectious Diseases.

Down-Covered Dinosaur

A fabulously preserved fossil from China all but proves that dinos and birds are the closest of kin

By **MICHAEL D. LEMONICK** TIME

The once radical notion that birds descended from dinosaurs—or may even *be* dinosaurs, the only living branch of the family that ruled the earth eons ago—has got stronger and stronger since paleontologists first started taking it seriously a couple of decades ago. Remarkable similarities in bone structure between dinos and birds were the first clue. Then came evidence, thanks to a series of astonishing discoveries in China's Liaoning province over the past five years, that some dinosaurs may have borne feathers. But a few scientists still argued that the link was weak; the bone similarities could be a coincidence, they said. And maybe those primitive structures visible in some fossils were feathers—but maybe not. You had to use your imagination to see them.

Not anymore. A spectacularly preserved fossil of a juvenile dinosaur, announced by a team of paleontologists from the Chinese Academy of Geological Sciences and New York City's American Museum of Natural History in the spring 2001 issue of *Nature*, is about as good a missing link as anyone could want. "It has things that are undeniably feathers," exults Richard Prum, of the University of Kansas Natural History Museum, an expert on the evolution of feathers. "But it is clearly a small, vicious theropod similar to the velociraptors that chased the kids around the kitchen in *Jurassic Park*."

A Cat with Feathers

In fact, this duck-size relative of *Tyrannosaurus rex*, dating from 124 million to 147 million years ago, has no fewer than three different types of feathers. The head sports a thick, fuzzy mat of short, hollow fibers ("like a butch cut," says Prum), while the shoulders and torso have plumelike "sprays" of extremely thin fibers up to 2 in. long. The backs of its arms and legs, meanwhile, are draped in multiple filaments arranged in a classic herringbone pattern around a central stem. Even the tail is covered with feathers, with a fan, or tuft, at the end. "It doesn't look anything like what most people think dinosaurs look like," explains the American Museum's Mark Norell, one of the team's co-leaders. "When this thing was alive, it looked like a Persian cat with feathers."

For Flight . . .

The find helps cement the dinosaur-bird connection, but it also casts new light on the mystery of why nature invented feathers in the first place. For the better part of a century, biologists have assumed that these specialized structures evolved for flight, but that's clearly not true. "The feathers on these dinosaurs aren't flight-worthy, and the animals couldn't fly," says paleontologist Kevin Padian, of the University of California, Berkeley. "They're too big, and they don't have wings." So what was the original purpose of feathers? Nobody knows for sure; they might have been useful for keeping dinos dry, distracting predators, or attracting mates, as peacocks do today.

. . . Or Warmth?

But many biologists suspect that feathers originally arose to keep dinosaurs warm. The bone structure of dinosaurs shows that, unlike modern reptiles, they grew as fast as birds and mammals—which dovetails with a growing body of evidence that dinos were, in fact, warm-blooded. Says Padian: "They must have had a high basal metabolic rate to grow that fast. And I wouldn't be surprised if they had some sort of skin covering for insulation when they were small." Says Norell: "Even baby tyrannosaurs probably looked like this one."

At the rate feathered dinosaurs are turning up, it shouldn't take long to solidify scientists' understanding of precisely how and why feathers first arose and when the first birdlike creature realized they were useful for flight. Meanwhile, kids had better get used to the idea that *T. rex* may have started life looking an awful lot like Tweety Bird. □

When Did Dinosaurs Live?

Dinosaurs lived throughout the Mesozoic Era, which began 245 million years ago and lasted for 180 million years. It is sometimes called the "Age of Reptiles." The era is divided into three periods.

TRIASSIC	JURASSIC	CRETACEOUS
245 to 208 million years ago	208 to 146 million years ago	146 to 65 million years ago

Classification of the Dinosaurs

Dinosaurs ("terrible lizards") belong to a large group of reptiles called Archosauria ("ruling reptiles"). They are classified into two distinct orders, which are distinguished by their pelvic differences.

Saurischia

All Saurischian ("lizard-hipped") dinosaurs had modern lizardlike pelvises and clawed feet. Saurischians roamed Earth from the Middle Triassic to the end of the Cretaceous period. They included carnivores and herbivores. Members of the order included Allosaurus ("different lizard"), Apatosaurus ("deceptive lizard"), which was formerly called Brontosaurus, and Tyrannosaurus ("tyrant lizard"). The group is divided into two suborders: **Theropoda** ("beast footed") and **Sauropodomor-** pha ("lizard-footed forms"). The Velociraptor ("swift robber") was a theropod.

Ornithischia

All Ornithischian ("bird-hipped") dinosaurs had pelvises similar to those of modern birds, and hoofed toes. All were herbivores. These dinosaurs lived throughout the world from the Middle Triassic to the end of the Cretaceous period. Members of the order included Iguanodon ("iguana tooth"), Stegosaurus ("plated lizard"), and Triceratops ("three-horned face"). The order is divided into four suborders: **Ornithopoda** ("bird footed"), **Stegosauria** ("plated lizards"), **Ankylosauria** ("armored lizards"), and **Certopsia** ("horned faces").

Tyrannosaurus Sue
The prehistoric giant stands again

Sue is a sensation. It's not just that she's 42 ft long and 65 million years old. She's the world's most complete, best preserved, and largest *Tyrannosaurus rex* skeleton, on permanent view at Chicago's Field Museum of Natural History.

Rest in Pieces

Amazingly, more than 200 of Sue's bones were preserved. The skeleton includes the most complete *T. rex* tail ever found, as well as one of only two *T. rex* arms ever found. Sue's skull contains the longest (and scariest) *T. rex* tooth yet known—it's a foot long.

One amazing discovery in Sue's skeleton is that she has a wishbone, or furcula, such as you would find in most bird skeletons. This is the first wishbone found on a *T. rex*. It supports the theory that birds evolved from dinosaurs, either directly or from a common ancestor.

Even though Sue's bones are more than 65 million years old, they are so well preserved that you can see marks where muscles and tendons once lay.

Slow, But Deadly

Studies of Sue's foot bones have indicated that *T. rex* probably walked at about 6 mph and ran at not more than 15 mph, much slower than previously thought.

The lead researcher on Sue says that the way the *T. rex* moved in the movie *Jurassic Park* was probably very accurate. Most likely *T. rex* bent over so that its huge tail did not touch the ground, and walked on its toes—*T. rex* is *digitigrade*, meaning it walks on its toes like a cat. (People are *plantigrade*, meaning we walk flat-footed.)

But the movie was wrong in suggesting that *T. rex* would have to see its prey move in order to find it—from studying Sue, researchers have determined that *T. rex* had an excellent sense of smell. Sue's skull reveals that in a *T. rex* brain the olfactory nodes were much larger than the cerebrum.

Sue or Sir?

Tyrannosaurus Sue was named for Sue Hendrickson, the fossil hunter who found the skeleton in 1990. But although the skeleton is generally referred to as a "she," no one really knows whether Tyrannosaurus Sue was male or female. The skeleton's very large size could suggest that the dinosaur was female, because among birds of prey—*T. rex*'s closest ancestors—females are generally larger than males.

Senior Sue

Throughout her life Sue suffered some hard knocks, including broken ribs and an injured arm. Although scientists do not know exactly what illnesses dinosaurs had, it looks as though Sue was affected by an age-related disease much like arthritis. "Here is a very, very old dinosaur that just got sick and died after a long, active life," says John Flynn, a Field Museum paleontologist.

Just how old was she? Scientists don't know for sure how long a *T. rex* might have lived. Says Flynn, "We know turtles and crocodiles can live to 150 years, and they are cold-blooded. We know some birds, which are warm-blooded, can live for many decades. My guess is that dinosaurs could live for decades, some 100 years or more."

Queen of the Dinosaurs

For many of the researchers who have gotten to know Sue, the discovery of the massive *T. rex* was the event of a lifetime. "It's truly a dream fossil," says Tony Wentz, who worked to dig Sue out of the ground and helped prepare her skeleton for the exhibit. "It's the best of the best, the biggest, the most well preserved. Everything you could ever want in digging a dinosaur was in Sue."

Tyrannosaurus rex Classification		
Kingdom	Animalia	animal
Phylum	Chordata	has a nerve cord ending at a brain
Class	Archosauria	has hollow teeth, special ankles, pointy head
Order	Saurischia	"lizard-hipped"
Suborder	Theropoda	walks on two feet, eats meat
Family	Tyrannosauroidea	a predator with tiny forelimbs ("arms")
Genus	Tyrannosaurus	"tyrant lizard"
Species	rex	"king"

Major Discoveries about Human Ancestors

Living and extinct human beings and their near human ancestors are called "hominids" and belong to the *Hominidae* family of primates. They should not be confused with "hominoids," which belong to the *Hominoidea* family of primates and include apes and humans. Scientists theorize that the human and ape lines branched off from a common ancestor 8 million to 6 million years ago.

Years ago	Species	Discovered	Remarks
5.8–5.2 million	*Ardipithecus ramidus kadabba*	1997–1998 in Alayla, Ethiopia	Oldest known human ancestor. About the size of modern chimpanzees, or 4 ft tall standing. Walked upright
c. 4.4 million	*Ardipithecus ramidus ramidus*	1994 in Aramis, Ethiopia	Similar to *A. ramidus kadabba*
c. 4.2 million	*Australopithecus anamensis*	1995, two sites at Lake Turkana in Kenya: Kanapoi and Allia Bay	Possible ancestor of *A. afarensis* (Lucy). Walked upright
c. 3.2 million	*Australopithecus afarensis*	1974 at Hadar in the Afar triangle of eastern Ethiopia; Laetoli, Tanzania	Nicknamed "Lucy." Her skeleton was 3.5 ft (100 cm) tall. Had apelike skull. Walked fully upright. Lived in family groups throughout eastern Africa
c. 2.5 million	*Australopithecus africanus*	1924 at Taung, northern Cape Province, South Africa	Descendant of "Lucy." Lived in social groups
c. 2 million	*Australopithecus robustus*	1938 in Kromdraai, South Africa	Was related to *A. africanus*
c. 2 million	*Homo habilis* ("skillful" or "handy man")	1960 in Olduvai Gorge, Tanzania	First brain enlargement; is believed to have used stone tools
c. 1.8 million	*Homo erectus* ("upright man")	1891 at Trinil, Java, Indonesia	Brain size twice that of *australopithecine* species. "Java Man" may have been a direct ancestor of *Homo sapiens* or instead developed on a separate evolutionary track. He is the first hominid to use fire and the hand ax, and to live in caves
c. 100,000(?)	*Homo sapiens* ("knowing or wise man")	1868, Cro-Magnon, France	Anatomically modern humans

Scientific Classification

Classification, or taxonomy, is a system of categorizing living things. There are seven divisions in the system: (1) Kingdom; (2) Phylum or Division; (3) Class; (4) Order; (5) Family; (6) Genus; (7) Species.

Kingdom is the broadest division. There is no consensus about the number of kingdoms, though most scientists support a four-kingdom (Animalia, Plantae, Protista, and Monera) or five-kingdom (Animalia, Plantae, Protista, Monera, and Fungi) system. The lowest, most basic division is species, which consists of organisms that resemble each other and are capable of interbreeding to produce fertile offspring. Species are identified by two names (binomial nomenclature). The first name is the genus, the second is the species.

For example, a lion is *Panthera leo*, a tiger is *Panthera tigris*. The first word is always capitalized, the second is not, and both should be italicized. Humans, of course, are *Homo sapiens*. The full classification for a lion would be: Kingdom, Animalia (animals); Phylum, Chordata (vertebrate animals); Class, Mammalia (mammals); Order, Carnivora (meat eaters); Family, Felidae (all cats); Genus, Panthera (great cats); Species, leo (lions).

Table of Geological Periods

It is generally assumed that planets are formed by the accretion of gas and dust in a cosmic cloud, but there is no way of estimating the length of this process. Our Earth acquired its present size, more or less, between 4 billion and 5 billion years ago. Life on Earth originated about 2 billion years ago, but there are no good fossil remains from periods earlier than the Cambrian, which began about 550 million years ago. The largely unknown past before the Cambrian Period is referred to as the Pre-Cambrian and is subdivided into the Lower (or older) and Upper (or younger) Pre-Cambrian—also called the Archaeozoic and Proterozoic Eras.

The known geological history of Earth since the beginning of the Cambrian Period is subdivided into three eras, each of which includes a number of periods. They, in turn, are subdivided into subperiods. In a subperiod, a certain section may be especially well known because of rich fossil finds. Such a section is called a formation, and it is usually identified by a place name.

Paleozoic Era

This era began 570 million years ago and lasted for 325 million years. The name was compounded from Greek *palaios* (old) and *zoön* (animal).

Period	Duration[1]	Subperiods	Events
Cambrian (from *Cambria,* Latin name for Wales)	60	Lower Cambrian Middle Cambrian Upper Cambrian	Invertebrate sea life of many types, proliferating during this and the following period
Ordovician (from Latin *Ordovices,* people of early Britain)	70	Lower Ordovician Upper Ordovician	First known fishes
Silurian (from Latin *Silures,* people of early Wales)	30	Lower Silurian Upper Silurian	Gigantic sea scorpions
Devonian (from Devonshire in England)	50	Lower Devonian Upper Devonian	Proliferation of fishes and other forms of sea life; land still largely lifeless
Carboniferous (from Latin *carbo* = coal + *fero* = to bear)	70	Lower or Mississippian Upper or Pennsylvanian	Period of maximum coal formation in swampy forests; early insects and first known amphibians
Permian (from district of Perm in Russia)	45	Lower Permian Upper Permian	Early reptiles and mammals; earliest form of turtles

1. In millions of years.

Mesozoic Era

This era began 245 million years ago and lasted for 180 million years. The name was compounded from Greek *mesos* (middle) and *zoön* (animal). Popular name: Age of Reptiles.

Period	Duration[1]	Subperiods	Events
Triassic (from *trias* = triad)	37	Lower or Buntsandstein (from German *bunt* = colorful + *sandstein* = sandstone). Middle or Muschelkalk (from German *muschel* = shell + *kalk* = limestone). Upper or Keuper (old miner's term)	Early saurians (reptiles that resemble lizards)
Jurassic (from Jura Mountains)	62	Lower or Black Jurassic, or Lias (from French *liais* = hard stone) Middle or Brown Jurassic, or Dogger (old provincial English for ironstone) Upper or White Jurassic, or Malm (Middle English for sand)	Many seagoing reptiles; early large dinosaurs; somewhat later, flying reptiles (pterosaurs), earliest known birds
Cretaceous (from Latin *creta* = chalk)	81	Lower Cretaceous Upper Cretaceous	Maximum development of dinosaurs; birds proliferating; opossumlike mammals

1. In millions of years.

Cenozoic Era

This era began 65 million years ago and includes the geological present. The name was compounded from Greek *kainos* (new) and *zoön* (animal). Popular name: Age of Mammals.

Period	Duration[1]	Subperiods	Events
Tertiary (originally thought to be the third of only three periods)	c. 65	Paleocene (from Greek *palaios* = old + *kainos* = new). Eocene (from Greek *eos* = dawn + *kainos* = new). Oligocene (from Greek *oligos* = few + *kainos* = new). Miocene (from Greek *meios* = less + *kainos* = new). Pliocene (from Greek *pleios* = more + *kainos* = new)	First mammals other than marsupials. Formation of amber, rich insect fauna, early bats, steady increase of large mammals. Mammals closely resembling present types; protohumans
Pleistocene (from Greek *pleistos* = most + *kainos* = new) (popular name: Ice Age)	2.0	Four major glaciations, named Günz, Mindel, Riss, and Würm, originally the names of rivers. Last glaciation ended 10,000 to 15,000 years ago	Various forms of early humans
Holocene (from Greek *holos* = entire + *kainos* = new)	0.01	The last 10,000 years to the present	Earliest written documents c. 3200 B.C., Sumer

1. In millions of years.

The Nation's Highest Science and Technology Honors

The National Medal of Science

The National Medal of Science, established by Congress in 1959, is administered by the National Science Foundation. The medal honors the contributions made by outstanding individuals who have significantly advanced knowledge in the following fields: physics, biology, chemistry, mathematics, engineering, and sociology and other behavioral sciences.

The 2000 National Medal of Science recipients were awarded their medals by Dr. Neal Lane, Assistant to the President for Science and Technology, on Dec. 1, 2000.

2000 National Medal of Science Recipients

Nancy C. Andreasen, Andrew H. Woods Chair of Psychiatry, University of Iowa College of Medicine, for her pivotal contributions to the social and behavioral sciences, through the integrative study of mind, brain, and behavior, by joining behavioral science with the technologies of neuroscience and neuroimaging in order to understand mental processes such as memory and creativity, and mental illnesses such as schizophrenia.

Peter H. Raven, Director of Missouri Botanical Garden and Engelmann Professor of Botany, Washington University, for his contributions to the dynamics of plant systematics and evolution, the introduction of the concept of coevolution, and his major contribution to the international efforts to preserve biodiversity.

Carl R. Woese, Stanley O. Ikenberry Professor of Microbiology, University of Illinois, for his brilliant and original insights, through molecular studies of RNA sequences, into the history of life on Earth.

John D. Baldeschwieler, J. Stanley Johnson Professor and Professor of Chemistry, California Institute of Technology, for his imaginative development of new methods for determining the properties, structures, motions, and interactions of molecules and molecular assemblies, the translation of these advances into practical pharmaceutical and instrumentation products for the public benefit, and extensive service to his government and the scientific community.

Ralph F. Hirschmann, Rao Makineni Professor of Bio-organic Chemistry, University of Pennsylvania, for his seminal contributions to organic and to medicinal chemistry including the synthesis in solution of an enzyme (ribonuclease), his stimulation of peptide research in the pharmaceutical industry, and for his leadership role in fostering interdisciplinary research in academia and in industry, which led to the discovery of several widely prescribed medications for human and animal health.

Gary S. Becker, Professor of Economics and Sociology, University of Chicago, for his pioneering work in the economic analysis of racial discrimination, inventing the economics of human resources, producing major modern innovations in economic demography and in economic criminology, and leading recent developments in how social forces shape individual economic behavior.

Yuan-Cheng B. Fung, Professor Emeritus and Research Bioengineer, University of California at San Diego, for his pioneering research and leadership in the fields of bioengineering and aeroelasticity. He also founded the study of biomechanics, especially of the lungs and arteries.

Willis E. Lamb, Jr., Regents Professor, University of Arizona, Optical Sciences Center, for his towering contributions to classical and quantum theories of laser radiation and quantum optics, and to the proper interpretation of quantum mechanics.

Jeremiah P. Ostriker, Provost and Charles A. Young Professor of Astronomy, Princeton University, for his bold astrophysical insights, which have revolutionized concepts of the nature of pulsars, the ecosystem of stars and gas in our galaxy, the sizes and masses of galaxies, the nature and distribution of dark matter and ordinary matter in the universe, and the formation of galaxies and other cosmological structures.

Gilbert F. White, Gustavson Distinguished Professor Emeritus of Geography, University of Colorado, Institute of Behavioral Science, for outstanding leadership and scientific contributions to geography and other earth and environmental sciences, and for helping shape cooperative efforts to assess the nation's floodplain, water use, and natural disaster policies for more than five decades.

John Griggs Thompson, Graduate Research Professor of Mathematics, University of Florida, for his profound and lasting contributions to the mathematical sciences, providing fundamental advances for the study of finite simple groups, the inverse Galois problem, and connections between group theory and number theory.

Karen K. Uhlenbeck, Sid W. Richardson Foundation Regents Chair in Mathematics, University of Texas at Austin, for her many pioneering contributions to global geometry that resulted in advances in mathematical physics and the theory of partial differential equations.

The National Medal of Technology

The National Medal of Technology, established by Congress in 1980, is administered by the U.S. Department of Commerce. The medal is awarded for technological innovation and the advancement of U.S. global competitiveness. The medal also recognizes groundbreaking contributions that commercialize a technology, create jobs, improve productivity, or stimulate the nation's growth and development in other ways.

The 2000 National Medal of Technology recipients were awarded their medals by President Clinton on Dec. 1, 2000.

2000 National Medal of Technology Recipients

Douglas C. Engelbart, Director, Bootstrap Institute, for developing the technology behind personal computing, including continuous, real-time interaction based on cathode-ray tube displays and the mouse, hypertext linking, text editing, online journals, shared-screen teleconferencing, and remote collaborative work.

Dean Kamen, Medical Entrepreneur at the DEKA Research and Development Corporation, for leadership in founding three medical device companies and for inventions related to medical devices that have advanced medical care worldwide, and for innovative and imaginative guidance in awakening America to the excitement of science and technology. He has earned more than 100 patents, both U.S. and foreign, as well as directed a national youth organization and a robotics competition for young people.

The Corning Team of Corning, Inc.: Donald B. Keck, Division Vice President and Technology Director, Optical Physics Technology Group; Robert D. Maurer, Corning Research Fellow (Retired); Peter C. Schultz, President, Heraeus Amersil, Inc. This group assembled in 1970 at the Corning Glass Corporation and invented the low-loss fiber-optic cable. Their invention has galvanized the telecommunications revolution, rapidly transformed our society, the way we work, learn, and live—and our expectations for the future.

It is the basis for one of the largest, most dynamic industries in the world today.

The IBM Corporation. IBM holds more than 2,000 U.S. patents and has contributed its innovations in the technology of hard disk drives and information storage products for the past 40 years. The corporation is a top innovator of component technologies, such as flying magnetic heads (thin film heads and magnetoresistive heads), film disks, head accessing systems, digital signal processing and coding, as well as innovative hard disk drive systems. Some specific IBM inventions are used in every modern hard drive today: thin film inductive heads, MR and GMR heads, rotary actuators, sector servos, and advanced disk designs. These advances outran foreign hard disk technology and enabled the U.S. industry to maintain the lead it holds today.

Branches of Science

Science describes an area of knowledge, typically something in the physical universe, that is explained in terms of scientific observation or by the scientific method and is further defined by reproducible experiments. This means that what is considered science, also called natural science, must be describable in terms of the scientific method:

- a phenomenon in the physical world is observed
- an explanation, or hypothesis, for the phenomenon is formed
- an objective and physical experiment is designed to test the hypothesis

The physical universe and the natural sciences associated with it are categorized in many ways. The largest distinction in science is whether a science is pure, or theoretical, or if it is applied, or practical. Pure science explains a phenomenon, while applied science determines the applications of the explanation to particular questions brought about by the phenomena. In general, pure science is divided into:

- Physical sciences: These sciences allow us to describe our physical universe. Physical sciences give us measurements, such as weight, mass, volume, and explain concepts associated with motion and energy. Chemistry is usually included in this group.
- Earth sciences: These sciences explain the phenomena of the Earth, its atmosphere, and the solar system, to which it belongs.
- Life sciences: These sciences describe the processes associated with living beings and the characteristics that all living beings share.

However, these three categories of pure science have shared points, where the explanations of one affect the explanations of another, for example, light being the energy behind the process of photosynthesis, or food production in plants, which provide food or energy for almost all living beings. For this reason, the distinctions between pure sciences, and even between pure and applied sciences, can blur, and a new, compound science can be developed; for example, organic chemistry, in which the chemical, or physical, processes of living things are observed and explained.

Physical Science	Life Science	Earth Science
Physics 　Kinetics 　Mechanics 　Electromagnetism 　Thermodynamics	Biology Botany Zoology	Geology Meteorology Astronomy
Chemistry 　Inorganic 　　Electrochemistry 　Analytical		
Examples of Overlapping Sciences		
Physics + Chemistry = 　Physical Chemistry	Biology + Chemistry = Biochemistry Organic chemistry	Geology + Chemistry = Geochemistry
Astronomy + Physics = 　Astrophysics	Biology + Geology = Paleontology	Geology + Astronomy = Astrogeology
	Biology + Astronomy + Physics = Astronautics	

The Elements

Elements are the building blocks of nature. Water, for example, is a compound consisting of the elements hydrogen and oxygen. Each element is a pure substance that cannot be split up into any simpler pure substance.

The smallest particle of an element that can exist is an atom. An atom consists of subatomic particles. The most important of these are protons, which have positive electrical charges; electrons, which have negative electrical charges; and neutrons, which are electrically neutral.

The atomic number of an element is the number of protons in one atom of the element. Each element has a different atomic number. For example, the atomic numbers of hydrogen and oxygen are 1 and 8, respectively.

Elements with atomic numbers 1 (hydrogen) to 94 (plutonium) occur naturally on Earth. The remaining artificial elements have been created since 1940 by using nuclear reactors and particle accelerators. Element 100 is named fermium. Elements with atomic numbers 101 onward are known as the transfermium elements. They are also known as heavy elements because their atoms have very large masses compared with atoms of hydrogen, the lightest of all elements.

Chemical Elements

Element	Symbol	Atomic no.	Atomic wt.	Specific gravity	Melting point °C	Boiling point °C	No. of isotopes[1]	Discoverer	Year
Actinium	Ac	89	227[2]	10.07[2]	1051	3198	11	Debierne/Giesel	1899/1902
Aluminum	Al	13	26.9815	2.6989	660.32	2519	8	Wöhler	1827
Americium	Am	95	243[5]	13.67	1176	2011	13[3]	Seaborg et al.	1944
Antimony	Sb	51	121.75	6.61	630.63	1587	29	Early historic times	—
Argon	Ar	18	39.948	1.7837[4]	−189.35	−185.85	8	Rayleigh and Ramsay	1894
Arsenic (gray)	As	33	74.9216	5.73	817	603	14	Albertus Magnus	1250
Astatine	At	85	210	—	302	—	21	Corson et al.	1940
Barium	Ba	56	137.34	3.5	727	1897	25	Davy	1808
Berkelium	Bk	97	247[5]	14.00[6]	1050 (α form)	—	8[3]	Seaborg et al.	1949
Beryllium	Be	4	9.01218	1.848	1287	2471	6	Vauquelin	1798
Bismuth	Bi	83	208.9806	9.747	271.40	1564	19	Geoffroy the Younger	1753
Bohrium	Bh	107	262	—	—	—	—	Armbruster and Münzenberg	1981
Boron	B	5	10.81	2.37[7]	2075	4000	6	Gay-Lussac and Thénard; Davy	1808
Bromine	Br	35	79.904	3.12[4]	−7.2	58.8	19	Balard	1826
Cadmium	Cd	48	112.40	8.65	321.07	767	22	Stromeyer	1817
Calcium	Ca	20	40.08	1.55	842	1484	14	Davy	1808
Californium	Cf	98	251[5]	—	900	—	12[3]	Seaborg et al.	1950
Carbon	C	6	12.011	1.8–3.5[8]	4492 (graphite)	3825	7	Prehistoric	—
Cerium	Ce	58	140.12	6.771	798	3443	19	Berzelius and Hisinger; Klaproth	1803
Cesium	Cs	55	132.9055	1.873	28.5	671	22	Bunsen and Kirchoff	1860
Chlorine	Cl	17	35.453	1.56[4]	−101.5	−34.04	11	Scheele	1774
Chromium	Cr	24	51.996	7.18-7.20	1907	2671	9	Vauquelin	1797
Cobalt	Co	27	58.9332	8.9	1495	2927	14	Brandt	c.1735
Copper	Cu	29	63.546	8.96	1084.62	2562	11	Prehistoric	—
Curium	Cm	96	247[5]	13.51[2]	1345	3100	13[3]	Seaborg et al.	1944
Dubnium	Db	105	262	—	—	—	—	Ghiorso et al.	1970
Dysprosium	Dy	66	162.50	8.540	1412	2567	21	de Boisbaudran	1886
Einsteinium	Es	99	254[5]	—	860	—	12[3]	Ghiorso et al.	1952
Erbium	Er	68	167.26	9.045	1529	2868	16	Mosander	1843
Europium	Eu	63	151.96	5.283	822	1529	21	Demarcay	1901
Fermium	Fm	100	257[5]	—	1527	—	10[3]	Ghiorso et al.	1953
Fluorine	F	9	18.9984	1.108[4]	−219.67	−188.12	6	Moissan	1886
Francium	Fr	87	223[5]	—	27	—	21	Perey	1939
Gadolinium	Gd	64	157.25	7.898	1313	3273	17	de Marignac	1880
Gallium	Ga	31	69.72	5.904	29.76	2204	14	de Boisbaudran	1875
Germanium	Ge	32	72.59	5.323	938.25	2833	17	Winkler	1886
Gold	Au	79	196.9665	19.32	1064.18	2856	21	Prehistoric	—
Hafnium	Hf	72	178.49	13.31	2233	4603	17	Coster and von Hevesy	1923
Hassium	Hs	108	265	—	—	—	—	Armbruster and Münzenberg	1983
Helium	He	2	4.00260	0.1785[4]	−272.2	−268.934	5	Janssen	1868
Holmium	Ho	67	164.9303	8.781	1474	2700	29	Delafontaine and Soret	1878
Hydrogen	H	1	1.0080	0.070[4]	−259.34	−252.87	3	Cavendish	1766
Indium	In	49	114.82	7.31	156.60	2072	34	Reich and Richter	1863
Iodine	I	53	126.9045	4.93	113.7	184.4	24	Courtois	1811
Iridium	Ir	77	192.22	22.42	2446	4428	25	Tennant	1804
Iron	Fe	26	55.847	7.894	1538	2861	10	Prehistoric	—
Krypton	Kr	36	83.80	3.733[4]	−157.38	−153.22	23	Ramsay and Travers	1898
Lanthanum	La	57	138.9055	6.166	918	3464	19	Mosander	1839
Lawrencium	Lr	103	257[5]	—	1627	—	20[3]	Ghiorso et al.	1961
Lead	Pb	82	207.2	11.35	327.46	1749	29	Prehistoric	—

Element	Symbol	Atomic no.	Atomic wt.	Specific gravity	Melting point °C	Boiling point °C	No. of isotopes[1]	Discoverer	Year
Lithium	Li	3	6.941	0.534	180.50	1342	5	Arfvedson	1817
Lutetium	Lu	71	174.97	9.835	1663	3402	22	Urbain/ von Welsbach	1907
Magnesium	Mg	12	24.305	1.738	650	1090	8	Black	1755
Manganese	Mn	25	54.9380	7.21–7.44[9]	1246	2061	11	Gahn, Scheele, and Bergman	1774
Meitnerium	Mt	109	266	—	—	—	—	GSI, Darmstadt, West Germany	1982
Mendelevium	Md	101	256[5]	—	827	—	3[3]	Ghiorso et al.	1955
Mercury	Hg	80	200.59	13.546	–38.83	356.73	26	Prehistoric	
Molybdenum	Mo	42	95.94	10.22	2623	4639	20	Scheele	1778
Neodymium	Nd	60	144.24	6.80 & 7.004[9]	1021	3074	16	von Welsbach	1885
Neon	Ne	10	20.179	0.89990 (g/10°C/1 atm)	–248.59	–246.08	8	Ramsay and Travers	1898
Neptunium	Np	93	237.0482	20.25	644		15[3]	McMillan and Abelson	1940
Nickel	Ni	28	58.71	8.902	1455	2913	11	Cronstedt	1751
Niobium (Columbium)	Nb	41	92.9064	8.57	2477	4744	24	Hatchett	1801
Nitrogen	N	7	14.0067	0.808[4]	–210.00	–195.79	8	Rutherford	1772
Nobelium	No	102	254[5]		827	—	7[3]	Ghiorso et al.	1958
Osmium	Os	76	190.2	22.57	3033	5012	19	Tennant	1803
Oxygen	O	8	15.9994	1.14[4]	–218.79	–182.95	8	Priestley/Scheele	1774
Palladium	Pd	46	106.4	12.02	1554.9	2963	21	Wollaston	1803
Phosphorous (white)	P	15	30.9738	1.82	44.15	280.5	7	Brand	1669
Platinum	Pt	78	195.09	21.45	1768.4	3825	32	Ulloa/Wood	1735/1741
Plutonium	Pu	94	244[5]	19.84	640	3228	16[3]	Seaborg et al.	1940
Polonium	Po	84	210[5]	9.32	254	962	34	Curie	1898
Potassium	K	19	39.102	0.862	63.5	759	10	Davy	1807
Praseodymium	Pr	59	140.9077	6.772	931	3520	15	von Welsbach	1885
Promethium	Pm	61	145[5]		1042	3000	14	Marinsky et al.	1945
Protactinium	Pa	91	231.0359	15.37[2]	1572	—	14	Hahn and Meitner	1917
Radium	Ra	88	226.0254	5.0?	700	—	15	Pierre and Marie Curie	1898
Radon	Rn	86	222[5]	4.44	–71	–61.7	20	Dorn	1900
Rhenium	Re	75	186.2	21.02	3186	5596	21	Noddack, Berg, and Tacke	1925
Rhodium	Rh	45	102.9055	12.41	1964	3695	20	Wollaston	1803
Rubidium	Rb	37	85.4678	1.532	39.30	688	20	Bunsen and Kirchoff	1861
Ruthenium	Ru	44	101.07	12.44	2334	4150	16	Klaus	1844
Rutherfordium	Rf	104	261	—	—	—	—	Ghiorso et al.	1969
Samarium	Sm	62	150.4	7.536	1074	1794	17	Boisbaudran	1879
Scandium	Sc	21	44.9559	2.989	1541	2836	15	Nilson	1878
Seaborgium	Sg	106	263	—	—	—	—	Ghiorso et al.	1974
Selenium (gray)	Se	34	78.96	4.79	220.5	685	20	Berzelius	1817
Silicon	Si	14	28.086	2.33	1414	3265	8	Berzelius	1824
Silver	Ag	47	107.868	10.5	961.78	2162	27	Prehistoric	—
Sodium	Na	11	22.9898	0.971	97.80	883	7	Davy	1807
Strontium	Sr	38	87.62	2.54	777	1382	18	Davy	1808
Sulfur	S	16	32.06	2.07[9]	95.3 (rhombic)	444.60	10	Prehistoric	—
Tantalum	Ta	73	180.9479	16.654	3017	5458	19	Ekeberg	1801
Technetium	Tc	43	98.062	11.50[2]	2157	4265	23	Perrier and Segré	1937
Tellurium	Te	52	127.60	6.24	449.51	988	29	von Reichenstein	1782
Terbium	Tb	65	158.9254	8.234	1356	3230	24	Mosander	1843
Thallium	Tl	81	204.37	11.85	304	1473	28	Crookes	1861
Thorium	Th	90	232.0381	11.72	1750	4788	12	Berzelius	1828
Thulium	Tm	69	168.9342	9.314	1545	1950	18	Cleve	1879
Tin (white)	Sn	50	118.69	7.31	231.93	2602	28	Prehistoric	—
Titanium	Ti	22	47.90	4.55	1668	3287	9	Gregor	1791
Tungsten	W	74	183.85	19.3	3422	5555	22	J. and F. d'Elhuyar	1783
Uranium	U	92	238.029	19.05	1135	4131	15	Peligot	1841
Vanadium	V	23	50.9414	6.11	1910	3407	9	del Rio	1801
Xenon	Xe	54	131.30	3.52[4]	–111.79	–108.12	31	Ramsay and Travers	1898
Ytterbium	Yb	70	173.04	6.972	819	1196	16	Marignac	1878
Yttrium	Y	39	88.9059	4.457	1522	3345	21	Gadolin	1794
Zinc	Zn	30	65.38	7.133	419.5	907	15	Prehistoric	—
Zirconium	Zr	40	91.22	6.506[2]	1855	4409	20	Klaproth	1789

NOTES: Elements 110, 111, 112, 114, 116, and 118 have not yet been named and are thus not included. ≈ means "approximately." < means "less than." 1. Isotopes are different forms of the same element having the same atomic number but different atomic weights. 2. Calculated figure. 3. Artificially produced. 4. Liquid. 5. Mass number of the isotope of longest known life. 6. Estimated. 7. Amorphous. 8. Depending on whether amorphous, graphite, or diamond. 9. Depending on allotropic form.

Roundup of Recent Discoveries

The Fog at the Beginning of the Universe

A team of astronomers from the California Institute of Technology, led by S. George Djorgovski, may have glimpsed the dawn of our universe. In Aug. 2001, this team reported that it had spotted the "cosmic renaissance," the era when the first starlight shone through the cosmos. Just days earlier a team from the Sloan Digital Sky Survey had announced finding evidence of the cosmic "dark ages"—the period of about half a billion years after the Big Bang when dark fog filled the newly created space of our universe. The cosmic renaissance brought an end to the dark ages, as the first galaxies and quasars burned through the murky cosmos, making it transparent.

The teams used data collected with powerful telescopes to observe the light emissions of quasars, the most distant known objects in the universe. Quasars, which are amazingly bright, can essentially offer snapshots of the universe from hundreds of millions of years ago. The Sloan team observed fog around a quasar that they believe began shining just as the dark ages were drawing to a close. The quasar studied by the Djorgovski team was slightly closer and glowed more brilliantly; it had probably sent forth its light after the fog began to dissipate, some 100 million years later.

Astronomers estimate that the cosmic fog started to burn away about 900 million years ago. For decades they had been searching for proof, but until this time had not been able to collect data from distant enough objects.

The Titanosaur from Madagascar

The skeleton of a new species of titanosaur, a common type of plant-eating sauropod, was found in Madagascar in July 2001 by American scientists Catherine Forster and Kristina Curry Rogers. The titanosaur is one of the least understood dinosaurs, though its fossils have been found on nearly every continent. The Madagascar find is significant because the titanosaur's skull and skeleton were both well preserved, offering scientists their first head-to-tail look at this type of dinosaur. Until now, only partial skeletons had been found in Madagascar and Patagonia, and no complete skull has ever been discovered. Although more than 30 types of titanosaur have been recognized, poor fossil records have left scientists unable to adequately compare these species.

The titanosaur's skeleton was relatively flexible and light, which permitted the long-necked 50-foot quadruped to manage its enormous size. As a result, its fossil bones broke easily and disintegrated, making it a poor candidate for preservation.

As Plain as the Nose on Its . . . *Face?*

Paleontologists from the "DinoNose Project" have confounded a couple of centuries' worth of thinking about the location of dinosaurs' noses. Since the 19th century, artists' renderings—based on paleontologists' conceptions—have shown the nostrils drawn on the top of some dinosaurs' heads. This position was thought to be accurate for semi-aquatic dinosaurs such as Diplodocus, but recent findings maintain that the nostrils for both aquatic and land-locked lizards are in fact right above the mouth. The size of the nasal cavity is also believed to be far larger—up to half the volume of the dinosaur's skull. Ohio University's Dr. Lawrence Witmer, paleontologist and the study's author, researched the skulls of more than 60 distant dinosaur relatives living today and found that all shared common nostril placement and function. The soft-tissue markings on these skulls compared favorably with the soft-tissue markings on dinosaur skulls. "We looked at as many modern-day animals as we could get a hold of," Witmer said, "and found an extraordinary amount of evidence to suggest the nostrils of dinosaurs actually were parked out front."

This isn't the first time that Witmer's research could change how we imagine dinosaurs. In 1998, he ripped the lips from Tyrannosaurus rex by reporting that the movie snarler did not in reality have the correct facial bone structure for lips.

Cell Controversy

One of the most politicized science issues of 2001 was the federal funding of stem-cell research to find treatments for human diseases. Originally isolated in 1998, stem cells are undifferentiated cells that can develop indefinitely into more specialized body cells, including neural, muscle, blood, and organ cells. These cells show promise in being able to regenerate human tissue of various kinds, with notable success in treating neurological diseases and conditions, such as Parkinson's disease and spinal cord damage.

The use of these stem cells is controversial because the best source for the cells is human fetal tissue from the earliest stages of embryonic development. Scientists typically use unwanted fertilized eggs from frozen in-vitro fertilization to harvest the stem cells, which form 4–5 days after fertilization. These embryos must be destroyed to harvest the cells, and those opposing the research consider this tantamount to the taking of human life.

In Aug. 2001, President Bush announced that he would permit federal funding of research on stem cells from human embryos, but only those cells that had already been extracted. This effort toward compromise seemed to satisfy neither side of the debate. Many scientists advocating stem-cell research responded that the number of existing lines of stem cells (according to the Bush administration about 60 lines exist) may not be enough to adequately complete research because existing cell lines can be easily contaminated or die out. Other advocates felt that limiting research would limit the potential of stem cells to cure diseases and help the millions living with Alzheimer's, diabetes, Parkinson's, and other medical conditions. Academic biologists were also concerned about whether the private companies and foundations holding the cell lines would be willing to allow their use in public research, and at what cost and with what restrictions. Meanwhile, those opposed to stem-cell research claimed that Bush had broken his promises not to federally fund research that destroyed human life.

Faster than a Speeding Bullet

In June 2001, Intel Corporation researchers, led by Dr. Robert Chau, announced that they had created the technology needed to produce the world's smallest and fastest silicon transistor on a mass scale. With these diminutive gatekeepers of electronic current, switching on and off 1.5 trillion times a second, microprocessors could complete a billion calculations in the time it takes a person to blink. And these transistors run at speeds of nearly 20 gigahertz—just a year ago the top speed of a transistor was one gigahertz, which was considered absolutely breathtaking.

These tiny transistors, elements of which are just 20 nanometers long (a nanometer is one-billionth of a meter, or about 1/50,000 of a human hair) and 80 atoms wide, are created using electron-beam lithography. In this process, a thin stream of electrons etches features onto a film-covered slice of silicon.

Currently, computer-chip producers use photolithography to shine ultraviolet light through a stencil punched with millions of miniscule patterns. The UV light that penetrates the stencil is then absorbed by tiny plastic-coated silicon slices. The finished product of photolithography is about 125 nanometers wide—a behemoth compared to the results of electron-beam lithography. Electron-beam lithography is part of nanotechnology, a new science that builds microscopic structures molecule by molecule. Intel Corporation plans to produce computers using the tiny transistors by 2007.

Tomato Triumph

Plant biologists Eduardo Blumwald of the University of California at Davis and Hong-Xia Zhang of the University of Toronto have developed a tomato plant with a salt-tolerant gene. This new plant is important because it can grow successfully in soil irrigated, and often ruined, by salty water. Some 24.7 million acres of the planet's farmable land are poisoned every year by such irrigation when there is not enough seasonal rainfall to wash away the accumulation of salt—areas of the U.S., China, India, and Pakistan are significantly affected. Salty irrigation water spoils plants and leaves deposits of minerals that weaken future crops by damaging their ability to take in water through their roots. High salt concentrations in soil also draw water out of these crops, dehydrating and eventually killing the plants. Not only does the new tomato manage to grow in salt-affected areas, but it also promises to act as a sponge, soaking up the salinity in the soil and helping to restore it to an arable state.

Mr. Mom

An ongoing study of Canadian fathers-to-be at the Mayo Clinic revealed changes in the men's hormone levels as they approached fatherhood for the first time. The authors of the study, Sandra J. Berg and Katherine E. Wynne-Edwards of Queen's University in Kingston, Ont., tested saliva samples for levels of testosterone, cortisol, and estradiol. Results of the study show decreased levels of testosterone, the principal male hormone, and cortisol, a stress hormone, and increased levels of estradiol, a female hormone associated with maternal behavior. Wynne-Edwards speculates that the study points to evidence of "subtle modulations that occur at this absolutely critically biological time in a man's life that make it—we would guess, and it is just a guess at this point—easier for him to make the transformation into committed fatherhood."

A Body in Motion

Results published in the Aug. 2001 *Journal of Experimental Psychology: Human Perception and Performance* show that doing several tasks at once—multitasking—may diminish the productivity with which any of the tasks is performed. Researchers Joshua Rubenstein from the Federal Aviation Administration and David Meyer and Jeffrey Evans from the University of Michigan studied the performance of subjects as they switched between tasks including math problems and sorting geometrical objects.

The study's results support the idea that executive control is composed of two stages: goal shifting ("I choose to do X and not Y now") and rule activation ("I am working according to the rules of X now and not the rules of Y"). Moving between these stages, people unconsciously evaluate the familiarity and complexity of tasks and then assign their cognitive resources to executing the task.

Rubenstein, Meyer, and Evans determined that switching tasks caused the subjects to lose time, and that time losses increased significantly as the tasks became more complex or unfamiliar. The study also showed that the phase of rule activation could take several tenths of a second, a considerable length of time if the person switched tasks often. Meyer offers the example of a driver using a cellular phone: a half second lost to task-switching can mean the difference between life and death, because during the time that the car is not totally under control, it can travel far enough to crash.

To Clone or Not to Clone

In March 2001, fertility doctors Severino Antinori of Italy and Panayiotis Zavos of the U.S. announced to a symposium of international fertility experts in Rome that they planned to begin reproducing human beings through cloning in Oct. 2001. The doctors stated that "they were motivated solely by the desire to help infertile couples have children" and claimed that 200 couples are ready to have children through cloning. In response to this announcement, the Italian government threatened to revoke Antinori's medical license if he went through with these plans. In Aug. 2001, the U.S. House of Representatives voted to ban human cloning completely and threatened arrest and prison sentences for offenders.

Scientists opposed to human cloning have cited instances of early death, unpredictable genetic deformities, and genetically triggered diseases such as cancer in animal clones. Dr. Harry Griffin of the Scottish Roslin Institute, which produced the cloned sheep Dolly, said, "Many of the animal clones die late in pregnancy or soon after birth and show developmental abnormalities . . . [T]he efficiency . . . in published work is very low—around 2% of the embryos that are created by cloning make it to term."

Countering these concerns, Duke University Medical Center researchers have found that humans can be cloned with fewer complications than animals because of a gene protein known as insulin-like growth factor 2 receptor (IGF2R). This gene protein functions in the normal growth and development of the embryo, keeping in check any developmental abnormalities. In human sexual reproduction, an active copy of IGF2R is passed to the offspring from each parent. In animal sexual reproduction one copy of the gene is "turned off," increasing the chances of abnormal embryonic development.

You Gotta Have Heart!

Fifty-nine-year-old Robert Tools hasn't heard his own heartbeat since July 2, 2001. That was the day surgeons Laman Gray and Robert Dowling at Jewish Hospital in Louisville, Ky., replaced Tool's heart with a battery-powered mechanical version called AbioCor, which makes a whirring sound. The 10-hour operation made Tools the first person equipped with a self-contained autonomous artificial heart. Earlier artificial hearts were bulky and had to be connected to an external power source, which meant that the recipient had wires and tubes sticking out of his chest. The titanium-and-plastic AbioCor is the size of a small grapefruit, weighs just 2 lbs, runs on a battery imbedded in the ribcage, and can be charged by an external battery pack. Two months after Tools' success, four more patients had been approved to receive the AbioCor.

A Pill with a Purpose

Following lightning-fast FDA approval in May 2001, a new form of targeted cancer therapy known as Gleevec (formerly ST1-571) may become available by the end of 2001. During a three-year study, Gleevec was used successfully to treat chronic myelogenous leukemia (CML), an adult cancer of the white blood cells. Gleevec, which is taken in pill form, targets an abnormal cancer-causing protein called BCR-ABL. Doctors conducting Gleevec research at the Oregon Health Sciences University reported that during the study Gleevec brought white blood cell counts to normal levels in all but one of 85 subjects. In June 2001, it was reported that some of the subjects had become resistant to Gleevec; developing another drug to be used along with Gleevec may yield a solution.

Gleevec is currently being tested on other cancers that are motivated by proteins similar to BCR-ABL. Clinical trials have shown that it is useful in treating gastrointestinal stromal tumors (GIST), and research is underway to test Gleevec's effectiveness against gliobastoma (a deadly brain tumor) and forms of prostate cancer and lung cancer.

Inventions & Discoveries

See also Famous Firsts in Aviation, Nobel Prizes.

Adrenaline: (isolation of) John Jacob Abel, U.S., 1897.

Aerosol can: Erik Rotheim, Norway, 1926.

Air brake: George Westinghouse, U.S., 1868.

Air conditioning: Willis Carrier, U.S., 1911.

Airship: (non-rigid) Henri Giffard, France, 1852; (rigid) Ferdinand von Zeppelin, Germany, 1900.

Aluminum manufacture: (by electrolytic action) Charles M. Hall, U.S., 1866.

Anatomy, human: (*De fabrica corporis humani,* an illustrated systematic study of the human body) Andreas Vesalius, Belgium, 1543; (comparative: parts of an organism are correlated to the functioning whole) Georges Cuvier, France, 1799–1805.

Anesthetic: (first use of anesthetic—ether—on humans) Crawford W. Long, U.S., 1842.

Antibiotics: (first demonstration of antibiotic effect) Louis Pasteur, Jules-François Joubert, France, 1887; (discovery of penicillin, first modern antibiotic) Alexander Fleming, Scotland, 1928; (penicillin's infection-fighting properties) Howard Florey, Ernst Chain, England, 1940.

Antiseptic: (surgery) Joseph Lister, England, 1867.

Antitoxin, diphtheria: Emil von Behring, Germany, 1890.

Appliances, electric: (fan) Schuyler Wheeler, U.S., 1882; (flatiron) Henry W. Seely, U.S., 1882; (stove) Hadaway, U.S., 1896; (washing machine) Alva Fisher, U.S., 1906.

Aqualung: Jacques-Yves Cousteau, Emile Gagnan, France, 1943.

Aspirin: Dr. Felix Hoffman, Germany, 1899.

Astronomical calculator: The Antikythera device, first century B.C., Greece. Found off island of Antikythera in 1900.

Atom: (nuclear model of) Ernest Rutherford, England, 1911.

Atomic theory: (ancient) Leucippus, Democritus, Greece, c. 500 B.C.; Lucretius, Rome c.100 B.C.; (modern) John Dalton, England, 1808.

Atomic structure: (formulated nuclear model of atom, Rutherford model) Ernest Rutherford, England, 1911; (proposed current concept of atomic structure, the Bohr model) Niels Bohr, Denmark, 1913.

Automobile: (first with internal combustion engine, 250 rpm) Karl Benz, Germany, 1885; (first with practical high-speed internal combustion engine, 900 rpm) Gottlieb Daimler, Germany, 1885; (first true automobile, not carriage with motor) René Panhard, Emile Lavassor, France, 1891; (carburetor, spray) Charles E. Duryea, U.S., 1892.

Autopilot: (for aircraft) Elmer A. Sperry, U.S., c.1910, first successful test, 1912, in a Curtiss flying boat.

Avogadro's law: (equal volumes of all gases at the same temperature and pressure contain equal number of molecules) Amedeo Avogadro, Italy, 1811.

Bacteria: Anton van Leeuwenhoek, The Netherlands, 1683.

Balloon, hot-air: Joseph and Jacques Montgolfier, France, 1783.

Barbed wire: (most popular) Joseph E. Glidden, U.S., 1873.

Bar codes (computer-scanned binary signal code): (retail trade use) Monarch Marking, U.S. 1970; (industrial use) Plessey Telecommunications, England, 1970.

Science Websites

National Science Foundation: www.nsf.gov
National Academy of Sciences: www.nas.edu
American Association for the Advancement of Science: www.aaas.org/
Federation of American Scientists: www.fas.org
The Franklin Institute: www.fi.edu/tfi/welcome.html
Science News Online: www.sciencenews.org
Popular Science: www.popsci.com
Periodic Table of Elements: WebElements Periodic Table: www.webelements.com
Dinosauria Online: www.dinosauria.com/
Discovery Channel Online: www.discovery.com
Fermi National Accelerator Lab: www.fnal.gov/
Argonne National Laboratory: www.anl.gov/
American Geophysical Union: http://earth.agu.org/homepage.html
American Museum of Natural History: www.amnh.org
Newton (for K–12 teachers and students): www.newton.dep.anl.gov
Field Museum (Chicago): www.fmnh.org
Santa Barbara Museum of Natural History: www.sbnature.org
Inventors Hall of Fame: www.invent.org/
The Smithsonian Web: www.si.edu

Barometer: Evangelista Torricelli, Italy, 1643.
Bicycle: Karl D. von Sauerbronn, Germany, 1816; (first modern model) James Starley, England, 1884.
Big Bang theory: (the universe originated with a huge explosion) George LeMaitre, Belgium, 1927; (modified LeMaitre theory labeled "Big Bang") George A. Gamow, U.S., 1948; (cosmic microwave background radiation discovered, confirms theory) Arno A. Penzias and Robert W. Wilson, U.S., 1965.
Blood, circulation of: William Harvey, England, 1628.
Boyle's law: (relation between pressure and volume in gases) Robert Boyle, Ireland, 1662.
Braille: Louis Braille, France, 1829.
Bridges: (suspension, iron chains) James Finley, Pa., 1800; (wire suspension) Marc Seguin, Lyons, 1825; (truss) Ithiel Town, U.S., 1820.
Bullet: (conical) Claude Minié, France, 1849.
Calculating machine: (logarithms: made multiplying easier and thus calculators practical) John Napier, Scotland, 1614; (slide rule) William Oughtred, England, 1632; (digital calculator) Blaise Pascal, 1642; (multiplication machine) Gottfried Leibniz, Germany, 1671; (important 19th-century contributors to modern machine) Frank S. Baldwin, Jay R. Monroe, Dorr E. Felt, W. T. Ohdner, William Burroughs, all U.S.; ("analytical engine" design, included concepts of programming, taping) Charles Babbage, England, 1835.
Calculus: Isaac Newton, England, 1669; (differential calculus) Gottfried Leibniz, Germany, 1684.
Camera: (hand-held) George Eastman, U.S., 1888; (Polaroid Land) Edwin Land, U.S., 1948.
"Canals" of Mars: Giovanni Schiaparelli, Italy, 1877.
Carpet sweeper: Melville R. Bissell, U.S., 1876.
Car radio: William Lear, Elmer Wavering, U.S., 1929, manufactured by Galvin Manufacturing Co., "Motorola."
Cells: (word used to describe microscopic examination of cork) Robert Hooke, England, 1665; (theory: cells are common structural and functional unit of all living organisms) Theodor Schwann, Matthias Schleiden, 1838–1839.
Cement, Portland: Joseph Aspdin, England, 1824.
Chewing gum: (spruce-based) John Curtis, U.S., 1848; (chicle-based) Thomas Adams, U.S., 1870.
Cholera bacterium: Robert Koch, Germany, 1883.

Circuit, integrated: (theoretical) G.W.A. Dummer, England, 1952; (phase-shift oscillator) Jack S. Kilby, Texas Instruments, U.S., 1959.
Classification of plants: (first modern, based on comparative study of forms) Andrea Cesalpino, Italy, 1583; (classification of plants and animals by genera and species) Carolus Linnaeus, Sweden, 1737–1753.
Clock, pendulum: Christian Huygens, The Netherlands, 1656.
Coca-Cola: John Pemberton, U.S., 1886.
Combustion: (nature of) Antoine Lavoisier, France, 1777.
Compact disk: RCA, U.S., 1972.
Computers: (first design of analytical engine) Charles Babbage, 1830s; (ENIAC, Electronic Numerical Integrator and Calculator, first all-electronic, completed) 1945; (dedicated at University of Pennsylvania) 1946; (UNIVAC, Universal Automatic Computer, handled both numeric and alphabetic data) 1951; (personal computer) Steve Wozniak, U.S., 1976.
Concrete: (reinforced) Joseph Monier, France, 1877.
Condensed milk: Gail Borden, U.S., 1853.
Conditioned reflex: Ivan Pavlov, Russia, c.1910.
Conservation of electric charge: (the total electric charge of the universe or any closed system is constant) Benjamin Franklin, U.S., 1751–1754.
Contagion theory: (infectious diseases caused by living agent transmitted from person to person) Girolamo Fracastoro, Italy, 1546.
Continental drift theory: (geographer who pieced together continents into a single landmass on maps) Antonio Snider-Pellegrini, France, 1858; (first proposed in lecture) Frank Taylor, U.S.; (first comprehensive detailed theory) Alfred Wegener, Germany, 1912.
Contraceptive, oral: Gregory Pincus, Min Chuch Chang, John Rock, Carl Djerassi, U.S., 1951.
Converter, Bessemer: William Kelly, U.S., 1851.
Cosmetics: Egypt, c. 4000 B.C.
Cosmic string theory: (first postulated) Thomas Kibble, 1976.
Cotton gin: Eli Whitney, U.S., 1793.
Crossbow: China, c. 300 B.C.
Cyclotron: Ernest O. Lawrence, U.S., 1931.
Deuterium: (heavy hydrogen) Harold Urey, U.S., 1931.
Disease: (chemicals in treatment of) crusaded by Philippus Paracelsus, 1527–1541; (germ theory) Louis Pasteur, France, 1862–1877.
DNA: (deoxyribonucleic acid) Friedrich Meischer, Germany, 1869; (determination of double-helical structure) Rosalind Elsie Franklin, F. H. Crick, England, James D. Watson, U.S., 1953.
Dye: (aniline, start of synthetic dye industry) William H. Perkin, England, 1856.
Dynamite: Alfred Nobel, Sweden, 1867.
Electric cooking utensil: (first) patented by St. George Lane-Fox, England, 1874.
Electric generator (dynamo): (laboratory model) Michael Faraday, England, 1832; Joseph Henry, U.S., c.1832; (hand-driven model) Hippolyte Pixii, France, 1833; (alternating-current generator) Nikola Tesla, U.S., 1892.
Electric lamp: (arc lamp) Sir Humphrey Davy, England, 1801; (fluorescent lamp) A.E. Becquerel, France, 1867; (incandescent lamp) Sir Joseph Swann, England, Thomas A. Edison, U.S., contemporaneously, 1870s; (carbon arc street lamp) Charles F. Brush, U.S., 1879; (first widely marketed incandescent lamp) Thomas A. Edison, U.S., 1879; (mercury vapor lamp) Peter Cooper Hewitt, U.S., 1903; (neon lamp) Georges Claude, France, 1911; (tungsten filament) Irving Langmuir, U.S., 1915.
Electrocardiography: Demonstrated by Augustus Waller, 1887; (first practical device for recording activity of heart) Willem Einthoven, 1903, Dutch physiologist.

Thomas Alva Edison
(1847–1931) *Library of Congress*

Electromagnet: William Sturgeon, England, 1823.

Electron: Sir Joseph J. Thompson, England, 1897.

Elevator, passenger: (safety device permitting use by passengers) Elisha G. Otis, U.S., 1852; (elevator utilizing safety device) 1857.

E = mc²: (equivalence of mass and energy) Albert Einstein, Switzerland, 1907.

Engine, internal combustion: No single inventor. Fundamental theory established by Sadi Carnot, France, 1824; (two-stroke) Etienne Lenoir, France, 1860; (ideal operating cycle for four-stroke) Alphonse Beau de Roche, France, 1862; (operating four-stroke) Nikolaus Otto, Germany, 1876; (diesel) Rudolf Diesel, Germany, 1892; (rotary) Felix Wankel, Germany, 1956.

Evolution: (organic) Jean-Baptiste Lamarck, France, 1809; (by natural selection) Charles Darwin, England, 1859.

Exclusion principle: (no two electrons in an atom can occupy the same energy level) Wolfgang Pauli, Germany, 1925.

Expanding universe theory: (first proposed) George LeMaitre, Belgium, 1927; (discovered first direct evidence that the universe is expanding) Edwin P. Hubble, U.S., 1929; (Hubble constant: a measure of the rate at which the universe is expanding) Edwin P. Hubble, U.S., 1929.

Falling bodies, law of: Galileo Galilei, Italy, 1590.

Fermentation: (microorganisms as cause of) Louis Pasteur, France, c.1860.

Fiber optics: Narinder Kapany, England, 1955.

Fibers, man-made: (nitrocellulose fibers treated to change flammable nitrocellulose to harmless cellulose, precursor of rayon) Sir Joseph Swann, England, 1883; (rayon) Count Hilaire de Chardonnet, France, 1889; (Celanese) Henry and Camille Dreyfuss, U.S., England, 1921; (research on polyesters and polyamides, basis for modern man-made fibers) U.S., England, Germany, 1930s; (nylon) Wallace H. Carothers, U.S., 1935.

Frozen food: Clarence Birdseye, U.S., 1924.

Gene transfer: (recombinant DNA organism) Herbert Boyer, Stanley Cohen, U.S., 1973; (human) Steven Rosenberg, R. Michael Blaese, W. French Anderson, U.S., 1989.

Geometry, elements of: Euclid, Alexandria, Egypt, c. 300 B.C.; (analytic) René Descartes, France; and Pierre de Fermat, Switzerland, 1637.

Gravitation, law of: Sir Isaac Newton, England, c.1665 (published 1687).

Gunpowder: China, c.700.

Gyrocompass: Elmer A. Sperry, U.S., 1905.

Gyroscope: Jean Léon Foucault, France, 1852.

Halley's Comet: Edmund Halley, England, 1705.

Heart implanted in human, permanent artificial: Dr. Robert Jarvik, U.S., 1982.

Heart, temporary artificial: Willem Kolff, 1957.

Helicopter: (double rotor) Heinrich Focke, Germany, 1936; (single rotor) Igor Sikorsky, U.S., 1939.

Helium first observed on sun: Sir Joseph Lockyer, England, 1868.

Heredity, laws of: Gregor Mendel, Austria, 1865.

Holograph: Dennis Gabor, England, 1947.

Home videotape systems (VCR): (Betamax) Sony, Japan, 1975; (VHS) Matsushita, Japan, 1975.

Ice age theory: Louis Agassiz, Swiss-American, 1840.

Induction, electric: Joseph Henry, U.S., 1828.

Insulin: (first isolated) Sir Frederick G. Banting and Charles H. Best, Canada, 1921; (discovery first published) Banting and Best, 1922; (Nobel Prize awarded for purification for use in humans) John Macleod and Banting, 1923; (first synthesized) China, 1966.

Intelligence testing: Alfred Binet, Theodore Simon, France, 1905.

Interferon: Alick Isaacs, Jean Lindemann, England, Switzerland, 1957.

Isotopes: (concept of) Frederick Soddy, England, 1912; (stable isotopes) J. J. Thompson, England, 1913; (existence demonstrated by mass spectrography) Francis W. Ashton, 1919.

Jet propulsion: (engine) Sir Frank Whittle, England, Hans von Ohain, Germany, 1936; (aircraft) *Heinkel He 178,* 1939.

Kinetic theory of gases: (molecules of a gas are in a state of rapid motion) Daniel Bernoulli, Switzerland, 1738.

Laser: (theoretical work on) Charles H. Townes, Arthur L. Schawlow, U.S., N. Basov, A. Prokhorov, U.S.S.R., 1958; (first working model) T. H. Maiman, U.S., 1960.

Lawn mower: Edwin Budding, John Ferrabee, England, 1830–1831.

LCD (liquid crystal display): Hoffmann-La Roche, Switzerland, 1970.

Lens, bifocal: Benjamin Franklin, U.S., c.1760.

Leyden jar: (prototype electrical condenser) Canon E. G. von Kleist of Kamin, Pomerania, 1745; independently evolved by Cunaeus and P. van Musschenbroek, University of Leyden, Holland, 1746, from where name originated.

Light, nature of: (wave theory) Christian Huygens, The Netherlands, 1678; (electromagnetic theory) James Clerk Maxwell, England, 1873.

Light, speed of: (theory that light has finite velocity) Olaus Roemer, Denmark, 1675.

Lightning rod: Benjamin Franklin, U.S., 1752.

Locomotive: (steam powered) Richard Trevithick, England, 1804; (first practical, due to multiple-fire-tube boiler) George Stephenson, England, 1829; (largest steam-powered) Union Pacific's "Big Boy," U.S., 1941.

Lock, cylinder: Linus Yale, U.S., 1851.

Loom: (horizontal, two-beamed) Egypt, c. 4400 B.C.; (Jacquard drawloom, pattern controlled by punch cards) Jacques de Vaucanson, France, 1745, Joseph-Marie Jacquard, 1801; (flying shuttle) John Kay, England, 1733; (power-driven loom) Edmund Cartwright, England, 1785.

Machine gun: (hand-cranked multibarrel) Richard J. Gatling, U.S., 1862; (practical single barrel, belt-fed) Hiram S. Maxim, Anglo-American, 1884.

Magnet, Earth is: William Gilbert, England, 1600.

Match: (phosphorus) François Derosne, France, 1816; (friction) Charles Sauria, France, 1831; (safety) J. E. Lundstrom, Sweden, 1855.

Measles vaccine: John F. Enders, Thomas Peebles, U.S., 1953.

Metric system: revolutionary government of France, 1790–1801.

Microphone: Charles Wheatstone, England, 1827.

Microscope: (compound) Zacharias Janssen, The Netherlands, 1590; (electron) Vladimir Zworykin et al., U.S., Canada, Germany, 1932–1939.

Microwave oven: Percy Spencer, U.S., 1947.

Motion, laws of: Isaac Newton, England, 1687.

Motion pictures: Thomas A. Edison, U.S., 1893.

Motion pictures, sound: Product of various inventions. First picture with synchronized musical score: *Don Juan*, 1926; with spoken dialogue: *The Jazz Singer*, 1927; both Warner Bros.

Motor, electric: Michael Faraday, England, 1822; (alternating-current) Nikola Tesla, U.S., 1892.

Motorcycle: (motor tricycle) Edward Butler, England, 1884; (gasoline-engine motorcycle) Gottlieb Daimler, Germany, 1885.

Moving assembly line: Henry Ford, U.S., 1913.

Neptune: (discovery of) Johann Galle, Germany, 1846.

Neptunium: (first transuranic element, synthesis of) Edward M. McMillan, Philip H. Abelson, U.S., 1940.

Neutron: James Chadwick, England, 1932.

Neutron-induced radiation: Enrico Fermi et al., Italy, 1934.

Nitroglycerin: Ascanio Sobrero, Italy, 1846.

Nuclear fission: Otto Hahn, Fritz Strassmann, Germany, 1938.

Nuclear reactor: Enrico Fermi, Italy, et al., 1942.

Ohm's law: (relationship between strength of electric current, electromotive force, and circuit resistance) Georg S. Ohm, Germany, 1827.

Oil well: Edwin L. Drake, U.S., 1859.

Oxygen: (isolation of) Joseph Priestley, 1774; Karl Scheele, 1773.

Ozone: Christian Schönbein, Germany, 1839.

Pacemaker: (internal) Clarence W. Lillehie, Earl Bakk, U.S., 1957.

Paper China, c.100 A.D.

Parachute: Louis S. Lenormand, France, 1783.

Pen: (fountain) Lewis E. Waterman, U.S., 1884; (ball-point, for marking on rough surfaces) John H. Loud, U.S., 1888; (ball-point, for handwriting) Lazlo Biro, Argentina, 1944.

Periodic law: (that properties of elements are functions of their atomic weights) Dmitri Mendeleev, Russia, 1869.

Periodic table: (arrangement of chemical elements based on periodic law) Dmitri Mendeleev, Russia, 1869.

Phonograph: Thomas A. Edison, U.S., 1877.

Photography: (first paper negative, first photograph, on metal) Joseph Nicéphore Niepce, France, 1816–1827; (discovery of fixative powers of hyposulfite of soda) Sir John Herschel, England, 1819; (first direct positive image on silver plate, the daguerreotype) Louis Daguerre, based on work with Niepce, France, 1839; (first paper negative from which a number of positive prints could be made) William Talbot, England, 1841. Work of these four men, taken together, forms basis for all modern photography. (First color images) Alexandre Becquerel, Claude Niepce de Saint-Victor, France, 1848–1860; (commercial color film with three emulsion layers, Kodachrome) U.S., 1935.

Photovoltaic effect: (light falling on certain materials can produce electricity) Edmund Becquerel, France, 1839.

Piano: (Hammerklavier) Bartolommeo Cristofori, Italy, 1709; (pianoforte with sustaining and damper pedals) John Broadwood, England, 1873.

Planetary motion, laws of: Johannes Kepler, Germany, 1609, 1619.

Plant respiration and photosynthesis: Jan Ingenhousz, Holland, 1779.

Plastics: (first material, nitrocellulose softened by vegetable oil, camphor, precursor to Celluloid) Alexander Parkes, England, 1855; (Celluloid, involving recognition of vital effect of camphor) John W. Hyatt, U.S., 1869; (Bakelite, first completely synthetic plastic) Leo H. Baekeland, U.S., 1910; (theoretical background of macromolecules and process of polymerization on which modern plastics industry rests) Hermann Staudinger, Germany, 1922; (polypropylene and low-pressure method for producing high-density polyethylene) Robert Banks, Paul Hogan, U.S., 1958.

Plate tectonics: Alfred Wegener, Germany, 1912–1915.

Plow, forked: Mesopotamia, before 3000 B.C.

Plutonium, synthesis of: Glenn T. Seaborg, Edwin M. McMillan, Arthur C. Wahl, Joseph W. Kennedy, U.S., 1941.

Polio, vaccine: (experimentally safe dead-virus vaccine) Jonas E. Salk, U.S., 1952; (effective large-scale field trials) 1954; (officially approved) 1955; (safe oral live-virus vaccine developed) Albert B. Sabin, U.S., 1954; (available in the U.S.) 1960.

Positron: Carl D. Anderson, U.S., 1932.

Pressure cooker: (early version) Denis Papin, France, 1679.

Printing: (block) Japan, c.700; (movable type) Korea, c.1400; Johann Gutenberg, Germany, c.1450 (lithography, offset) Aloys Senefelder, Germany, 1796; (rotary press) Richard Hoe, U.S., 1844; (linotype) Ottmar Mergenthaler, U.S., 1884.

Probability theory: René Descartes, France; and Pierre de Fermat, Switzerland, 1654.

Johann Gutenberg
(c. 1400–1468)

Proton: Ernest Rutherford, England, 1919.

Prozac: (antidepressant fluoxetine) Bryan B. Malloy, Scotland, and Klaus K. Schmiegel, U.S., 1972; (released for use in U.S.) Eli Lilly & Company, 1987.

Psychoanalysis: Sigmund Freud, Austria, c.1904.

Pulsars: Antony Hewish and Jocelyn Bell Burnel, England, 1967.

Quantum theory: (general) Max Planck, Germany, 1900; (sub-atomic) Niels Bohr, Denmark, 1913; (quantum mechanics) Werner Heisenberg, Erwin Schrödinger, Germany, 1925.

Quarks: Jerome Friedman, Henry Kendall, Richard Taylor, U.S., 1967.

Quasars: Marten Schmidt, U.S., 1963.

Rabies immunization: Louis Pasteur, France, 1885.

Radar: (limited to one-mile range) Christian Hulsmeyer, Germany, 1904; (pulse modulation, used for measuring height of ionosphere) Gregory Breit, Merle Tuve, U.S., 1925; (first practical radar—radio detection and ranging) Sir Robert Watson-Watt, England, 1934–1935.

Radio: (electromagnetism, theory of) James Clerk Maxwell, England, 1873; (spark coil, generator of electromagnetic waves) Heinrich Hertz, Germany, 1886; (first practical system of wireless telegraphy) Guglielmo Marconi, Italy, 1895; (first long-distance telegraphic radio signal sent across the Atlantic) Marconi, 1901; (vacuum electron tube, basis for radio telephony) Sir John Fleming, England, 1904; (triode amplifying tube) Lee de Forest, U.S., 1906; (regenerative circuit, allowing long-distance sound reception) Edwin H. Armstrong, U.S., 1912; (frequency modulation—FM) Edwin H. Armstrong, U.S., 1933.

Radioactivity: (X-rays) Wilhelm K. Roentgen, Germany, 1895; (radioactivity of uranium) Henri Becquerel, France, 1896; (radioactive elements, radium and polonium in uranium ore) Marie Sklodowska-Curie, Pierre Curie, France, 1898; (classification of alpha and beta particle radiation)

Pierre Curie, France, 1900; (gamma radiation) Paul-Ulrich Villard, France, 1900.

Radiocarbon dating, carbon-14 method: (discovered) 1947, Willard F. Libby, U.S.; (first demonstrated) U.S., 1950.

Radio signals, extraterrestrial: first known radio noise signals were received by U.S. engineer, Karl Jansky, originating from the Galactic Center, 1931.

Radio waves: (cosmic sources, led to radio astronomy) Karl Jansky, U.S., 1932.

Razor: (safety, successfully marketed) King Gillette, U.S., 1901; (electric) Jacob Schick, U.S., 1928, 1931.

Reaper: Cyrus McCormick, U.S., 1834.

Refrigerator: Alexander Twining, U.S., James Harrison, Australia, 1850; (first with a compressor device) the Domelse, Chicago, U.S., 1913.

Refrigerator ship: (first) the *Frigorifique,* cooling unit designed by Charles Teller, France, 1877.

Relativity: (special and general theories of) Albert Einstein, Switzerland, Germany, U.S., 1905–1953.

Revolver: Samuel Colt, U.S., 1835.

Richter scale: Charles F. Richter, U.S., 1935.

Rifle: (muzzle-loaded) Italy, Germany, c.1475; (breech-loaded) England, France, Germany, U.S., c.1866; (bolt-action) Paul von Mauser, Germany, 1889; (automatic) John Browning, U.S., 1918.

Rocket: (liquid-fueled) Robert Goddard, U.S., 1926.

Roller bearing: (wooden for cartwheel) Germany or France, c.100 B.C.

Rotation of Earth: Jean Bernard Foucault, France, 1851.

Royal Observatory, Greenwich: established in 1675 by Charles II of England; John Flamsteed first Astronomer Royal.

Rubber: (vulcanization process) Charles Goodyear, U.S., 1839.

Saccharin: Constantine Fuhlberg, Ira Remsen, U.S., 1879.

Safety pin: Walter Hunt, U.S., 1849.

Saturn, ring around: Christian Huygens, The Netherlands, 1659.

"Scotch" tape: Richard Drew, U.S., 1929.

Screw propeller: Sir Francis P. Smith, England, 1836; John Ericsson, England, worked independently of and simultaneously with Smith, 1837.

Seismograph: (first accurate) John Milne, England, 1880.

Sewing machine: Elias Howe, U.S., 1846; (continuous stitch) Isaac Singer, U.S., 1851.

Solar energy: First realistic application of solar energy using parabolic solar reflector to drive caloric engine on steam boiler, John Ericsson, U.S., 1860s.

Solar system, universe: (Sun-centered universe) Nicolaus Copernicus, Warsaw, 1543; (establishment of planetary orbits as elliptical) Johannes Kepler, Germany, 1609; (infinity of universe) Giordano Bruno, Italian monk, 1584.

Spectrum: (heterogeneity of light) Sir Isaac Newton, England, 1665–1666.

Spectrum analysis: Gustav Kirchhoff, Robert Bunsen, Germany, 1859.

Spermatozoa: Anton van Leeuwenhoek, The Netherlands, 1683.

Spinning: (spinning wheel) India, introduced to Europe in Middle Ages; (Saxony wheel, continuous spinning of wool or cotton yarn) England, c.1500–1600; (spinning jenny) James Hargreaves, England, 1764; (spinning frame) Sir Richard Arkwright, England, 1769; (spinning mule, completed mechanization of spinning, permitting production of yarn to keep up with demands of modern looms) Samuel Crompton, England, 1779.

Star catalog: (first modern) Tycho Brahe, Denmark, 1572.

Steam engine: (first commercial version based on principles of French physicist Denis Papin) Thomas Savery, England, 1639; (atmospheric steam engine) Thomas

Newcomen, England, 1705; (steam engine for pumping water from collieries) Savery, Newcomen, 1725; (modern condensing, double acting) James Watt, England, 1782; (high-pressure) Oliver Evans, U.S., 1804.

Steamship: Claude de Jouffroy d'Abbans, France, 1783; James Rumsey, U.S., 1787; John Fitch, U.S., 1790; (high-pressure) Oliver Evans, U.S., 1804. All preceded Robert Fulton, U.S., 1807, credited with launching first commercially successful steamship.

Stethoscope: René Laënnec, France, 1819.

Sulfa drugs: (parent compound, para-aminobenzenesulfanomide) Paul Gelmo, Austria, 1908; (antibacterial activity) Gerhard Domagk, Germany, 1935.

Superconductivity: (theory) John Bardeen, Leon Cooper, John Scheiffer, U.S., 1957.

Symbolic logic: George Boule, 1854; (modern) Bertrand Russell, Alfred North Whitehead, England, 1910–1913.

Tank, military: Sir Ernest Swinton, England, 1914.

Tape recorder: (magnetic steel tape) Valdemar Poulsen, Denmark, 1899.

Teflon: DuPont, U.S., 1943.

Telegraph: Samuel F. B. Morse, U.S., 1837.

Telephone: Alexander Graham Bell, U.S., 1876.

Telescope: Hans Lippershey, The Netherlands, 1608; (astronomical) Galileo Galilei, Italy, 1609; (reflecting) Isaac Newton, England, 1668.

Samuel F. B. Morse (1791–1872)
Library of Congress

Television: (Iconoscope–T.V. camera table) Vladimir Zworkin, U.S., 1923, and also kinescope (cathode ray tube) 1928; (mechanical disk-scanning method) successfully demonstrated by J.L. Baird, Scotland, C.F. Jenkins, U.S., 1926; (first all-electric television image) 1927, Philo T. Farnsworth, U.S; (color, mechanical disk) Baird, 1928; (color, compatible with black and white) George Valensi, France, 1938; (color, sequential rotating filter) Peter Goldmark, U.S., first introduced, 1951; (color, compatible with black and white) commercially introduced in U.S., National Television Systems Committee, 1953.

Thermodynamics: (first law: energy cannot be created or destroyed, only converted from one form to another) Julius von Mayer, Germany, 1842; James Joule, England, 1843; (second law: heat cannot of itself pass from a colder to a warmer body) Rudolph Clausius, Germany, 1850; (third law: the entropy of ordered solids reaches zero at the absolute zero of temperature) Walter Nernst, Germany, 1918.

Thermometer: (open-column) Galileo Galilei, c.1593; (clinical) Santorio Santorio, Padua, c.1615; (mercury, also Fahrenheit scale) Gabriel D. Fahrenheit, Germany, 1714; (centigrade scale) Anders Celsius, Sweden, 1742; (absolute-temperature, or Kelvin, scale) William Thompson, Lord Kelvin, England, 1848.

Tire, pneumatic: Robert W. Thompson, England, 1845; (bicycle tire) John B. Dunlop, Northern Ireland, 1888.

Toilet, flush: Product of Minoan civilization, Crete, c. 2000 B.C. Alleged invention by "Thomas Crapper" is untrue.

Tractor: Benjamin Holt, U.S., 1900.

Transformer, electric: William Stanley, U.S., 1885.

Transistor: John Bardeen, Walter H. Brattain, William B. Shockley, U.S., 1947.

Tuberculosis bacterium: Robert Koch, Germany, 1882.

Typewriter: Christopher Sholes, Carlos Glidden, U.S., 1867.

Uncertainty principle: (that position and velocity of an object cannot both be measured exactly, at the same time) Werner Heisenberg, Germany, 1927.

Uranus: (first planet discovered in recorded history) William Herschel, England, 1781.

Vaccination: Edward Jenner, England, 1796.

Vacuum cleaner: (manually operated) Ives W. McGaffey, 1869; (electric) Hubert C. Booth, England, 1901; (upright) J. Murray Spangler, U.S., 1907.

Van Allen (radiation) Belt: (around Earth) James Van Allen, U.S., 1958.

Video disk: Philips Co., The Netherlands, 1972.

Vitamins: (hypothesis of disease deficiency) Sir F. G. Hopkins, Casimir Funk, England, 1912; (vitamin A) Elmer V. McCollum, M. Davis, U.S., 1912–1914; (vitamin B) McCollum, U.S., 1915–1916; (thiamin, B_1) Casimir Funk,

England, 1912; (riboflavin, B_2) D. T. Smith, E. G. Hendrick, U.S., 1926; (niacin) Conrad Elvehjem, U.S., 1937; (B_6) Paul Gyorgy, U.S., 1934; (vitamin C) C. A. Hoist, T. Froelich, Norway, 1912; (vitamin D) McCollum, U.S., 1922; (folic acid) Lucy Wills, England, 1933.

Voltaic pile: (forerunner of modern battery, first source of continuous electric current) Alessandro Volta, Italy, 1800.

Wallpaper: Europe, 16th and 17th century.

Wassermann test: (for syphilis) August von Wassermann, Germany, 1906.

Wheel: (cart, solid wood) Mesopotamia, c.3800–3600 B.C.

Windmill: Persia, c.600.

World Wide Web: (developed while working at CERN) Tim Berners-Lee, England, 1989; (development of Mosaic browser makes WWW available for general use) Marc Andreeson, U.S., 1993.

Xerography: Chester Carlson, U.S., 1938.

Zero: India, c.600; (absolute zero temperature, cessation of all molecular energy) William Thompson, Lord Kelvin, England, 1848.

Zipper: W. L. Judson, U.S., 1891.

The National Inventors Hall of Fame

The Inventors Hall of Fame, located in Akron, Ohio, was established in 1973 by the National Council of Patent Law Associations, now the National Council of Intellectual Property Law Associations, and the Patent and Trademark Office of the U.S. Department of Commerce.

The 2001 Class of Inductees

Robert L. Banks, 1921–1989, and **John Paul Hogan,** 1919– , POLYPROPYLENE AND HIGH-DENSITY POLYETHYLENE (HDPE). While working for the Phillips Petroleum Company, Banks and Hogan developed two of the world's most commonly used plastics, polypropylene and high-density polyethylene (HDPE). The plastics are used separately and in compounds to create everything from garbage bags and grocery sacks to wire insulation and automotive parts.

Stanley N. Cohen, 1935–, and **Herbert W. Boyer,** 1936– , RECOMBINANT DNA TECHNOLOGY. Biochemists Boyer and Cohen combined their expertise in 1973 to create the first genetically engineered organism. They did this by splicing together DNA fragments from several different species of an organism, mixing the traits of each to create a previously unknown variation. Their accomplishment is the basis for modern biotechnology. In 1978 Boyer and Cohen's company, Gerentech, was successful in synthesizing human insulin.

Oliver Evans, 1755–1819, HIGH PRESSURE STEAM ENGINE. Evans was one of the first Americans to recognize and explore the potential of cogeneration, the process of using waste energy to produce heat, which had been patented by Sutton Thomas Wood in 1784. He invented a small, high-pressure engine that used exhaust steam to heat water for the boiler. His steam engine contributed greatly to the industrialization of the United States.

Thomas J. Fogarty, 1934– , EMBOLECTOMY BALLOON CATHETER. Dr. Fogarty's embolectomy catheter, which is used to remove blood clots, consists of a small hollow tube (catheter) with a balloon attached to the tip. The tube is inserted into the blood vessel and through the blood clot (embo-

lus). The balloon is then inflated, so that when the tube is pulled out, the balloon drags the clot out with it. Because it is less invasive than regular surgery, this technique reduces the health risks and trauma to the patient. A modified version of the embolectomy catheter is also used in angioplasty to clear plaque from clogged arteries.

Elijah J. McCoy, 1844–1929, IMPROVEMENT IN LUBRICATORS FOR STEAM ENGINES. McCoy, a mechanical engineer from Detroit, Mich., developed an automatic lubricator that provided a constant flow of oil onto machine parts as the machine was working. McCoy's invention, later known as "the real McCoy," increased the life span and productivity of machines. In all, McCoy received more than 50 patents.

Patsy O. Sherman, 1930– , and **Samuel Smith,** 1927– , STAIN BLOCKER FOR FABRIC (Scotchgard™). Chemist Patsy Sherman discovered an oil- and water-resistant fabric treatment quite by accident while working for 3M on a new kind of rubber. One day in the lab, an assistant spilled some of a test material on her (the assistant's) canvas shoes and wasn't able to wash it off. Intrigued, Sherman teamed up with colleague Sam Smith to develop what came to be known as Scotchgard™.

Christopher L. Sholes, 1819–1890, TYPEWRITING MACHINE. Publisher and politician Sholes invented the first practical typewriting machine (the name was coined by the *Scientific American* journal). His chief innovation was the development of the QWERTY keyboard, which is still the one most commonly used today. In this arrangement, the most common letters of the alphabet were placed far apart so that the machine's type bars had time to fall back into place before the next one came up. As a result, Sholes's machine was less subject to jamming and made for more efficient typing.

The Digital Divide—So Close And Yet So Far

It's in everyone's interest to pull the stragglers aboard the high-tech express, but only education will keep them there

By CHRIS TAYLOR TIME

Although hundreds of programs exist across the country to narrow the digital divide—the gulf between people with access to computers and the Internet and those without—the gap remains unfathomably deep. The phrase "digital divide" has become mired in the blurry realm of cliché, applied variously to women, the disabled, seniors, ethnic minorities, rural, and inner-city populations. But the underlying threat is real. Technology has moved so fast that a new upper class—composed largely of the same white, affluent, college-educated males that made up the old upper class—has spurted ahead of the rest of society, mostly because they have the time and money necessary to acquire and understand the tools of the digital revolution.

This is not merely an apocalyptic vision. Members of this digital class are already banking and trading stocks over high-speed Internet connections and whipping out wireless Palm Pilots while others wait in sluggish teller lines with pockets full of Post-it notes. Buy online, and you generally avoid sales tax; if shopping in the real world is your only option, you pay full whack. By 2004, there will also be a digital divide between 29 million households with superfast broadband Internet access and the online equivalent of the middle class—those who still lumber along on 56K modems. Taken all together, these tiny, day-to-day advantages potentially add up to a class gap of Dickensian proportions.

It's not as if the dangers are unrecognized. Congress will likely play host to a paper storm of some 50 bills and provisions supposedly designed to close the gap. But most deal in the abstract world of FCC regulation and tax relief for telecommunications companies. Programs with practical ends—like a successful night school run by San Jose, California's Emergency Housing Consortium that turns the homeless into network technicians—exist largely in the private sector. Maybe Washington is better at the high-concept stuff, but politicians run the risk of paying mere lip service to the main issues.

Digital Disenfranchisement

Leah Garland, a second-grade teacher who transferred from an inner-city school in Macon, Ga., to one in the middle-class suburb of McDonough, south of Atlanta, has seen the digital divide firsthand. Her Macon pupils were just as eager as her McDonough counterparts to get their hands on computers. But in Macon, Garland had to battle both short attention spans and the kids' belief that the Internet had nothing to do with their future. "There's little to no parental support for the kids who don't have technology in their homes," says Garland.

Which is why the $1.6 billion spent during the past seven years by the state of Georgia to get computer equipment into schools doesn't count for much by itself. Well aware of that, town leaders in LaGrange, Ga., are going the extra distance to build an entire Internet-friendly community. Mayor Jeff Lukken negotiated a deal with cable provider Charter Communications, based in St. Louis, Mo., in which all 11,000 LaGrange households would have the option of free high-speed cable-modem access. Charter provides the cable box and basic service (cost: $9 a month), and if you can't afford even that, the city will pay for it. "People resist technology because it's irrelevant to their lives, because they

Percent of Households with a Computer

	Dec. 1998	Aug. 2000	Point change	Expan-sion rate		Dec. 1998	Aug. 2000	Point change	Expan-sion rate
All	42.1%	51.0%	8.9	21.1%	**Education**				
Ethnicity					Less than high school	12.5%	18.2%	5.7	**45.6%**
White non-Hispanic	46.6	55.7	**9.1**	19.5	High school graduate	31.2	39.6	8.4	**26.9**
Black non-Hispanic	23.2	32.6	**9.4**	**40.5**	Some college	49.3	60.3	**11.0**	**22.3**
Asian Amer. & Pac. Isl.	55.0	65.6	**10.6**	19.3	College graduate	66.9	74.0	7.1	10.6
Hispanic	25.5	33.7	8.2	**32.2**	Post graduate	72.2	79.0	6.8	9.4
Income					**Location**				
Less than $15,000	14.5	19.2	4.7	**32.4**	Rural	39.9	50.4	**10.5**	**26.3**
$15,000–24,999	23.7	30.1	6.4	**27.0**	Urban	42.9	51.5	8.6	20.0
$25,000–34,999	35.8	44.6	8.8	**24.6**	Central city	38.5	53.7	**15.2**	**39.5**
$35,000–49,999	50.2	58.6	8.4	16.7					
$50,000–74,999	66.3	73.2	6.9	10.4					
$75,000 and above	79.9	86.3	6.4	8.0					

NOTE: Bold figure indicates above the national average—an 8.9 point change and 21.1% expansion rate. *Source:* U.S. Dept. of Commerce, National Telecommunications and Information Administration. *Falling Through the Net: Defining the Digital Divide.* Web: www.ntia.doc.gov/ntiahome/digitaldivide/index.html.

fear it, distrust it, or can't afford it," says Lukken. "We want to take away every barrier to entry." The result is a town of Capra-esque perfection, where the senior center and public housing have superfast hookups to the largest repository of knowledge and commerce ever created.

High Tech Versus Home Ec.

But is LaGrange's perfection replicable? Will other broadband companies—especially those serving poor or isolated rural districts—be willing to repeat the experiment? Right now 18 million urban and suburban homes and only 1 million rural homes have broadband Internet access. The most popular digital-divide bill before Congress offers tax relief to Baby Bells that make rural phone lines DSL-ready. Trouble is, DSL is the kind of broadband service that requires you to be within a certain distance of your local switching station. Upgrading rural lines across the country would cost a staggering $11 billion. It's hard to imagine a tax break that could compensate.

Corporations do occasionally dole out digital freebies—especially to their own employees. Delta Airlines, for one, has started offering dirt-cheap laptops and desktops to its 74,000 staff members. Americans who don't enjoy the shelter of corporate wings often have to rely on charity to join the 21st century—or, in some cases, to get a recycled piece of the 20th. Computers to Help People, a nonprofit based in Madison, Wis., turns donated computer parts into systems for people who can't afford new ones. It's a wonderfully well-intentioned enterprise but one more doomed than most others by blitzkrieg advances in computing. Admits Carl Durocher, the agency's assistant technology manager: "We're not closing the digital divide a whole lot like this."

So who is? More and more, it's those with enough determination and luck to scrape together the necessary equipment and learning. Take Withrow High School in Cincinnati, Ohio, an inner-city, 85% African-American school where students were being taught on typewriters a few years ago. Now all its classrooms have Internet access of some kind, on whatever computers the school could beg, borrow, or recycle. It took all the state grants, vocational funds,

and educational charities principal Paul Ramstetter could muster. He had to eliminate the home-economics class in order to buy a couple of $2,500 laptops. "We decided to go for technology," says Ramstetter. "We thought it was more important."

Contentedly Offline

Yet it appears there is a large and stubborn minority of the population who do not share Ramstetter's priorities. Professors at UCLA conducted the first of what is to be an annual, large-scale study of patterns of Internet usage. The first survey, while offering good news on the gender and race front, uncovered a whole new group of disaffected—those who are Luddites and proud of it. Half of those with no Internet access, around 20%, were simply not interested in getting online. "That will take a generation or two to straighten out," predicts Professor Jeffrey Cole, author of the study. "The U.S. may well end up being the last industrialized nation to achieve 90% Internet penetration."

Bridging the Gap

What, then, does it take to get everyone on the right side of the digital divide? The answer is simple, if expensive—college. Degree-bearing graduates are eight times as likely to have a computer at home and 16 times as likely to access the Internet from home as those with lower levels of education, according to a recent Commerce Department study.

That's what motivated Carlos Watson to found the successful college-prep program Achiever.com. With the help of school districts around the country, he recruits at-risk students—most of whom hadn't thought of college—for an intensive online course that covers nailing the SATs, college applications, and scholarships. Result: 85% of Achiever.com students go on to one of the four-year schools of their choice.

Self-interest, when it comes down to it, is the strongest reason for any of us to join the digital era. There are still a lot of disaffected people with a lot to prove to the world. Given means, motive and opportunity, anyone can breach the digital divide. □

Percent of Households with Internet Access

	Dec. 1998	Aug. 2000	Point change	Expansion rate		Dec. 1998	Aug. 2000	Point change	Expansion rate
All	26.2%	41.5%	**15.3**	58.4%	**Education**				
Ethnicity					Less than high school	5.0%	11.7%	**6.7**	**134.0%**
White non-Hispanic	29.8	46.1	**16.3**	54.7	High school graduate	16.3	29.9	**13.6**	83.4
Black non-Hispanic	11.2	23.5	**12.3**	**109.8**	Some college	30.2	49.0	**18.8**	62.3
Asian Amer. & Pac. Isl.	36.0	56.8	**20.8**	57.8	College graduate	46.8	64.0	**17.2**	36.8
Hispanic	12.6	23.6	**11.0**	**87.3**	Post graduate	53.0	69.9	**16.9**	31.9
Income					**Location**				
Less than $15,000	7.1	12.7	**5.6**	**78.9**	Rural	22.2	38.9	**16.7**	75.2
$15,000–24,999	11.0	21.3	**10.3**	**93.6**	Urban	27.5	42.3	**14.8**	53.8
$25,000–34,999	19.1	34.0	**14.9**	**78.0**	Central city	24.5	37.7	**13.2**	53.9
$35,000–49,999	29.5	46.1	**16.6**	56.3					
$50,000–74,999	43.9	60.9	**17.0**	38.7					
$75,000 and above	60.3	77.7	**17.4**	28.9					

NOTE: Bold figure indicates above the national average—national average is a 15.3 point change and 58.4% expansion rate. *Source:* U.S. Dept. of Commerce, National Telecommunications and Information Administration. *Falling Through the Net: Defining the Digital Divide.* Web: www.ntia.doc.gov/ntiahome/digitaldivide/index.html.

Internet Use: Individuals Age 3 and Older

	Dec. 1998 (in thousands)		Aug. 2000 (in thousands)		Internet use		Percentage point difference	Growth in use rate
	Internet users	Total	Internet users	Total	Dec. 1998	Aug. 2000		
Total population	84,587	258,453	116,480	262,620	32.7%	44.4%	11.7	36%
Sex								
Male	43,033	125,932	56,962	127,844	34.2	44.6	10.4	30
Female	41,555	132,521	59,518	134,776	31.4	44.2	12.8	41
Ethnicity								
White non-Hispanic	69,470	184,980	93,714	186,439	37.6	50.3	12.7	34
Black non-Hispanic	6,111	32,123	9,624	32,850	19.0	29.3	10.3	54
Asian/Pacific Islanders	3,467	9,688	5,095	10,324	35.8	49.4	13.6	38
Hispanic	4,887	29,452	7,325	30,918	16.6	23.7	7.1	43
Employment status								
Employed[1]	56,790	133,516	77,507	136,756	42.5	56.7	14.2	33
Not employed[1]	1,647	5,726	2,698	5,961	28.8	45.3	16.5	58
Not in the labor force	14,411	70,924	20,661	71,232	20.3	29.0	8.7	43
Income								
Less than $15,000	5,170	37,864	6,057	32,096	13.7	18.9	5.2	38
$15,000–24,999	5,623	30,581	7,063	27,727	18.4	25.5	7.1	38
$25,000–34,999	8,050	31,836	11,054	31,001	25.3	35.7	10.4	41
$35,000–49,999	13,528	39,026	16,690	35,867	34.7	46.5	11.9	34
$50,000–74,999	19,902	43,776	25,059	43,451	45.5	57.7	12.2	27
$75,000 and above	24,861	42,221	36,564	52,189	58.9	70.1	11.2	19
Education								
Elementary[2]	206	12,529	452	12,253	1.6	3.7	2.1	131
Not a high school graduate[2]	1,022	16,510	2,030	16,002	6.2	12.7	6.5	105
High school graduate[2]	10,961	57,103	17,425	56,889	19.2	30.6	11.4	59
Some college[2]	16,603	43,038	24,201	44,628	38.6	54.2	15.6	40
Bachelors degree or higher[2]	26,571	43,509	34,083	45,755	61.1	74.5	13.4	22
Age								
3 to 8	2,680	24,282	3,671	23,962	11.0	15.3	4.3	39
9 to 17	15,396	35,821	19,579	36,673	43.0	53.4	10.4	24
18 to 24	11,356	25,662	15,039	26,458	44.3	56.8	12.6	28
25 to 49	41,694	101,836	56,433	101,946	40.9	55.4	14.4	35
50+	13,669	70,852	21,758	73,580	19.3	29.6	10.3	53

1. Age 16 and older. 2. Age 25 and older. *Source:* U.S. Dept. of Commerce, National Telecommunications and Information Administration. *Falling Through the Net: Defining the Digital Divide.* Web: www.ntia.doc.gov/ntiahome/digitaldivide/index.html.

Internet Users in the U.S.

(number of persons 2+ in the U.S. having access to/using the Internet at home)

Date	User access (millions)	Active users (millions)	Female/male ratio among active users
April 2001	167	103	51.1/48.9
Jan. 2001	163	101	51.0/49.0
Oct. 2000	150	91	51.1/48.9
July 2000	144	88	50.5/49.5
April 2000	130	80	50.3/49.7

Source: Nielsen Media Research.

How Many Online Worldwide?

(as of Nov. 2000)

World total	**407.10 million**
Africa	3.11 million
Asia/Pacific	104.88 million
Europe	113.14 million
Middle East	2.40 million
Canada & U.S.	167.12 million
Latin America	16.45 million

NOTE: These are estimated figures based on several surveys. *Source:* Nua Internet Surveys.

Top 15 Countries in Internet Users at Year-End 2000

Rank	Country	Weekly Internet users (millions)	All Internet users (millions)	Rank	Country	Weekly Internet users (millions)	All Internet users (millions)
1.	U.S.	114.4	134.6	9.	France	6.3	9.0
2.	Japan	25.4	33.9	10.	Australia	5.3	7.6
3.	Germany	14.9	19.9	11.	Taiwan	4.5	7.0
4.	Canada	13.1	15.4	12.	Netherlands	4.1	5.5
5.	U.K.	12.6	16.8	13.	Sweden	3.8	4.4
6.	South Korea	12.4	19.0	14.	Spain	3.6	5.6
7.	China	11.3	22.5	15.	Russia	3.0	7.5
8.	Italy	9.3	12.5		**Top 15 countries**	**244.0**	**321.2**

Reprinted with permission from Computer Industry Almanac Inc. Web: www.c-i-a.com.

Top Online Activities by Age

Online activities	Kids 5–12	Online activities	Kids 5–12	Online activities	Teens 13–17	Online activities	Teens 13–17
Email	61%	Played board/card games	23%	Email	95%	Downloaded music files	62%
Homework/research for school	55	Instant messaging	21	Used search engine	86	E-greeting/post cards	61
Played fantasy/ action games	51	Downloaded free software	19	Instant messaging	82	Downloaded free software	61
E-greeting/post cards	43	Movie sites	17	Music sites	73	Watched video online	60
Used search engine	40	Contests/ sweepstakes	16	Contests/ sweepstakes	73	Played fantasy/ action games	52
TV program sites	38	Created or viewed personal Web pages	14	Chat	68	Local content	48
Watched video online	30	Chat	12	Homework/research for school	68	Message boards	46
Music sites	24			Created or viewed personal Web pages	64		

Online activities	Young adults 19–35	Online activities	Adults 35–49	Online Activities	Older adults 50+
Email	92%	Email	92%	Email	95%
Used search engine	83	Used search engine	79	Used search engine	73
Researched products and services	81	Researched products and services	78	Researched products and services	72
Local content	62	Local content	61	E-greeting/post cards	59
Contests/sweepstakes	62	E-greeting/post cards	58	Health sites	51
Instant messaging	60	Contests/sweepstakes	56	Researched travel	48
E-greeting/post cards	56	Daily news	53	Local content	48
Downloaded free software	54	Online directory	49	Daily news	48
Online directory	50	Health sites	49	Online directory	47
Daily news	47	Downloaded free software	46	Contests/sweepstakes	46
Health sites	45	Instant messaging	45	Checked stocks and quotes	46
Chat	43	Researched travel	45	Downloaded free software	45
Music sites	41	Newspaper sites	37	Instant messaging	40
Researched travel	37	Checked stocks and quotes	35	Newspaper sites	28
Listened to audio online	37	Work research	35	Chat	27

Source: Jupiter Media Metrix, Jupiter Consumer Survey, July 2000. Web: www.mediametrix.com.

Online Shopping Survey, November 2000–January 2001

	Purchased in Last 3 Months			Ever Researched		
	Percent of total surveyed	Male	Female	Percent of total surveyed	Male	Female
Books	17.4%	17.2%	17.5%	29.2%	29.9%	28.5%
Music	12.1	13.1	11.2	23.4	25.5	21.4
General apparel	11.8	10.3	13.2	18.2	16.9	19.5
Airline tickets	11.1	12.6	9.7	34.8	36.9	32.8
Software	10.1	12.8	7.5	24.9	29.9	20.1
Toys	9.9	9.0	10.7	17.4	16.8	17.8
Hotel reservations	7.7	9.4	6.0	29.8	32.2	27.5
Videos	7.4	8.5	6.4	15.7	18.1	13.4
Event tickets	5.4	6.0	4.9	21.3	22.4	20.2
Office supplies	5.3	5.5	5.0	14.0	15.3	12.7
Car rentals	5.1	6.5	3.7	21.0	23.7	18.4
Clothing accessories	4.8	4.4	5.2	11.1	10.2	12.0
Computer hardware	4.7	6.5	3.0	22.0	27.8	16.6
Health and beauty, nonprescription	4.4	3.8	5.1	10.2	8.3	11.9
Food and beverages	4.3	4.1	4.5	10.3	10.3	10.2
Pet supplies	3.9	3.5	4.3	10.9	10.1	11.6
Flowers	3.9	4.3	3.6	11.0	11.0	10.9
Footwear	3.7	3.4	4.0	11.3	11.0	11.6
Consumer electronics	3.6	5.0	2.3	18.2	23.6	13.0
Linens/home décor	3.2	2.4	4.0	9.2	7.3	11.1
Video games	3.2	3.4	2.9	10.8	12.7	8.9
Cosmetics/fragrances	3.1	2.3	3.8	8.1	5.9	10.3
Sporting goods	3.1	3.8	2.4	10.8	14.1	7.8
Jewelry	2.8	2.2	3.5	9.9	8.9	11.0
Prescription medicines	2.7	3.0	2.4	9.0	8.9	9.1

NOTE: Data based on a survey of 100,954 adults in the U.S. and Canada. *Source:* Forrester Research, Inc.

Hours per Week Spent on Various Media Among Online Users, 2000

	Hours per week		Hours per week
TV	15.7	Newspapers	4.0
Radio	11.7	Magazines	3.3
Online	8.0		

Source: Jupiter Media Metrix, Jupiter Consumer Survey, July 2000. Web: www.mediametrix.com.

Reasons for U.S. Households with a Computer (or WebTV) Never Accessing the Internet, Percent Distribution, 2000

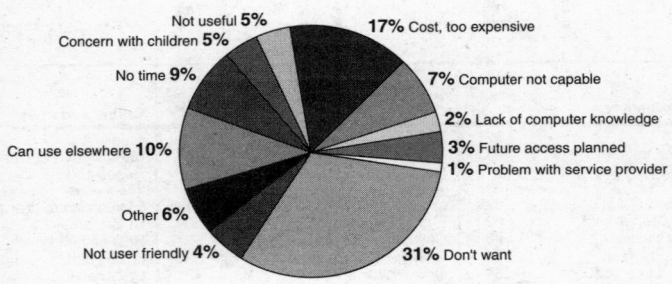

Not useful **5%**
Concern with children **5%**
No time **9%**
Can use elsewhere **10%**
Other **6%**
Not user friendly **4%**

17% Cost, too expensive
7% Computer not capable
2% Lack of computer knowledge
3% Future access planned
1% Problem with service provider
31% Don't want

Source: U.S. Dept. of Commerce, National Telecommunications and Information Administration.
Falling Through the Net: Defining the Digital Divide. Web: www.ntia.doc.gov/ntiahome/digitaldivide/index.html.

Top Domains/Websites, May 2001

Rank	website	Unique visitors (thousands)	Rank	website	Unique visitors (thousands)
1.	Yahoo.com*	55,062	14.	BlueMountainArts.com	12,868
2.	MSN.com	50,672	15.	NBCi*	12,583
3.	AOL.com	36,202	16.	Google.com	12,574
4.	Microsoft.com	33,323	17.	Tripod.com	12,061
5.	Passport.com	29,780	18.	About.com	12,028
6.	X10.com	28,603	19.	Real.com	11,402
7.	Hotmail.com	26,935	20.	Zdnet.com	11,080
8.	Lycos.com*	25,795	21.	AskJeeves.com	11,078
9.	Go.com	19,455	22.	Angelfire.com	11,021
10.	Amazon.com	18,928	23.	Cnet*	11,020
11.	Netscape.com	18,161	24.	Flowgo.com	10,841
12.	Ebay.com	16,610	25.	Goto.com	10,539
13.	Excite*	13,469			

NOTES: "Unique visitors" refers to the estimated number of total users who visited the website once in the given month. All unique visitors are unduplicated (only counted once). *Represents an aggregation of commonly owned/branded domain names. *Source:* Jupiter Media Metrix. Web: www.mediametrix.com.

Top Entertainment Sites, May 2001

Rank	Website	Unique visitors (thousands)	Rank	Website	Unique visitors (thousands)
1.	About.com	12,028	6.	WindowsMedia.com	6,864
2.	Real.com	11,402	7.	BMGMusicService.com	5,956
3.	Flowgo.com	10,841	8.	Sony Online*	5,948
4.	Disney Online*	8,204	9.	CitySearch*	5,224
5.	iwin.com	7,742	10.	TwistedHumor.com	5,065

NOTES: "Unique visitors" refers to the estimated number of total users who visited the website once in the given month. All unique visitors are unduplicated (only counted once). *Represents an aggregation of commonly owned/branded domain names. *Source:* Jupiter Media Metrix. Web: www.mediametrix.com.

Top General News Sites, May 2001

Rank	Website	Unique visitors (thousands)	Rank	Website	Unique visitors (thousands)
1.	MSNBC.com	9,589	6.	USAToday.com	3,068
2.	CNN.com	9,080	7.	TIME.com	2,344
3.	NYTimes.com	5,107	8.	LA Times*	2,147
4.	ABC News*	3,695	9.	Slate.com	1,886
5.	WashingtonPost.com	3,229	10.	WSJ.com	1,324

NOTES: "Unique visitors" refers to the estimated number of total users who visited the website once in the given month. All unique visitors are unduplicated (only counted once). *Represents an aggregation of commonly owned/branded domain names. *Source:* Jupiter Media Metrix. Web: www.mediametrix.com.

Top Education Sites, May 2001

Rank	Website	Unique visitors (thousands)	Rank	Website	Unique visitors (thousands)
1.	FastWeb.com	1,916	6.	UPenn.edu	1,464
2.	Berkeley.edu	1,904	7.	MIT.edu	1,427
3.	UTexas.edu	1,684	8.	Cornell.edu	1,381
4.	UIUC.edu	1,595	9.	Wisc.edu	1,344
5.	UMich.edu	1,495	10.	Stanford.edu	1,302

NOTES: "Unique visitors" refers to the estimated number of total users who visited the website once in the given month. All unique visitors are unduplicated (only counted once). *Source:* Jupiter Media Metrix. Web: www.mediametrix.com.

Top Travel Sites, May 2001

Rank	Website	Unique visitors (thousands)	Rank	Website	Unique visitors (thousands)
1.	MapQuest.com	9,853	6.	AA.com	2,788
2.	Expedia Travel*	7,808	7.	Cheaptickets.com	2,647
3.	Travelocity.com	7,423	8.	Priceline.com	2,587
4.	AmericanExpress.com	6,474	9.	Delta.com	2,560
5.	Southwest.com	2,814	10.	United.com	2,383

NOTES: "Unique visitors" refers to the estimated number of total users who visited the website once in the given month. All unique visitors are unduplicated (only counted once). *Represents an aggregation of commonly owned/branded domain names. *Source:* Jupiter Media Metrix. Web: www.mediametrix.com.

Top Government Sites, May 2001

Rank	Website	Unique visitors (thousands)	Rank	Website	Unique visitors (thousands)
1.	NASA.gov	2,596	6.	Army.mil	1,394
2.	NIH.gov	2,564	7.	NPS.gov	1,326
3.	CA.gov	2,422	8.	State.tx.us	1,305
4.	ED.gov	1,933	9.	IRS.gov	1,216
5.	NOAA.gov	1,783	10.	LOC.gov	1,209

NOTES: "Unique visitors" refers to the estimated number of total users who visited the website once in the given month. All unique visitors are unduplicated (only counted once). *Source:* Jupiter Media Metrix. Web: www.mediametrix.com.

Internet Timeline

1969 ARPA (Advanced Research Projects Agency) goes online in December, connecting four major U.S. universities. Designed for research, education, and government organizations, it provides a communications network linking the country in the event that a military attack destroys conventional communications systems.

1972 Electronic mail is introduced. Queen Elizabeth sends her first email in 1976.

1973 Transmission Control Protocol/Internet Protocol (TCP/IP) is designed and in 1983 it becomes the standard for communicating between computers over the Internet. One of these protocols, FTP (File Transfer Protocol), allows users to log onto a remote computer, list the files on that computer, and download files from that computer.

1989 The first effort to index the Internet is created by Peter Deutsch at McGill University in Montreal, who devises Archie, an archive of FTP sites. Another indexing system, WAIS (Wide Area Information Server), is developed by Brewster Kahle of Thinking Machines Corp. Tim Berners-Lee of CERN (European Laboratory for Particle Physics) develops a new technique for distributing information on the Internet, which eventually is called the World Wide Web. The Web is based on hypertext, which permits the user to connect from one document to another at different sites on the Internet via hyperlinks (specially programmed words, phrases, buttons, or graphics). Unlike other Internet protocols, such as FTP and email, the Web is accessible through a graphical user interface.

1991 Gopher, the first user-friendly interface, is created at the University of Minnesota and named after the school mascot. Gopher becomes the most popular interface for several years.

1993 Mosaic is developed by Marc Andreeson at the National Center for Supercomputing Applications (NCSA). It becomes the dominant navigating system for the World Wide Web, which at this time accounts for merely 1% of all Internet traffic.

1994 The White House launches its website, www-.whitehouse.gov. Initial commerce sites are established and mass marketing campaigns are launched via email, introducing the term "spamming" to the Internet vocabulary.

1996 Approximately 45 million people are using the Internet, with roughly 30 million of those in North America (United States and Canada), 9 million in Europe, and 6 million in Asia/Pacific (Australia, Japan, etc.). 43.2 million (44%) of U.S. households own a personal computer, and 14 million of them are online.

1997 On July 8, 1997, Internet traffic records are broken as the NASA website broadcasts images taken by *Pathfinder* on Mars. The broadcast generates 46 million hits in one day.

1999 The number of Internet users worldwide reaches 150 million by the beginning of 1999. More than 50% are from the United States. "E-commerce" becomes the new buzzword as Internet shopping rapidly spreads.

2000 To the chagrin of the Internet population, deviant computer programmers begin designing and circulating viruses with greater frequency. "Love Bug" and "Stages" are two examples of self-replicating viruses that send themselves to people listed in a computer user's email address book. The heavy volume of email messages being sent and received forces many infected companies to temporarily shut down their clogged networks.

The Internet bubble bursts, as the fountain of investment capital dries up and the Nasdaq stock index plunges, causing the initial public offering (IPO) window to slam shut and many dotcoms to shutter their doors.

2001 Napster is dealt a potentially fatal blow when the 9th U.S. Circuit Court of Appeals in San Francisco rules that the company is violating copyright laws and orders it to stop distributing copyrighted music. The company, which runs a computer application that allows users who are logged on to one of its servers to download an MP3 recording directly from another user logged onto the same server, is developing a subscription-based service. Many labels—both independent and major—have said they will make their songs available for download once the new system is in place.

Sources for this timeline include International Data Corporation, the W3C Consortium, and the Internet Society.

Internet Resource Guide

The Internet has become a convenient tool for finding information on just about anything. These days it's hard to find a company or organization that doesn't have its own homepage. Because sifting through search engine returns can be more time-consuming than a trek to the library, we've compiled a list of websites that we've found to be especially useful and informative.

Arts and Literature
Library of Congress: www.loc.gov
The Louvre: www.louvre.fr/louvrea.htm
National Endowment for the Arts: www.arts.endow.gov
Smithsonian American Art Museum: www.nmaa.si.edu
World Wide Arts Resources: www.wwar.com

Business and Investing
Better Business Bureau: www.bbb.org
Commodity Futures Trading Commission: www.cftc.gov
E*TRADE: www.etrade.com
Nasdaq: www.nasdaq.com
New York Stock Exchange: www.nyse.com
Securities and Exchange Commission (SEC): www.sec.gov
Small Business Administration (SBA): www.sba.gov
Standard & Poor's: www.standardpoor.com

Computers and the Internet
CNET: www.cnet.com
CNET Shareware.com: shareware.cnet.com/
WIRED News: www.wired.com
World Wide Web Consortium: www.w3.org
ZDNet: www.zdnet.com

Education
College Board Online: www.collegeboard.com
FamilyEducation.com: www.familyeducation.com
FinAid: www.finaid.org
Learning Network: www.learningnetwork.com
Peterson's: www.petersons.com
Princeton Review: www.review.com
TeacherVision: www.teachervision.com
U.S. News Online Education Page:
    www.usnews.com/usnews/edu

Entertainment
All Music Guide: www.allmusic.com
Entertainment Weekly Online: www.ew.com/ew/
IndieWIRE: www.indiewire.com
[Inside]: www.inside.com
Internet Movie Database: www.imdb.com
Moviefone: www.moviefone.com
Mr. Showbiz: www.mrshowbiz.com
MTV: www.mtv.com
NetRadio: www.netradio.com
SonicNet: www.sonicnet.com

Government
White House: www.whitehouse.gov
Senate: www.senate.gov
House of Representatives: www.house.gov
Supreme Court Collection: supct.law.cornell.edu/supct
Department of Agriculture: www.usda.gov
Department of Commerce: www.doc.gov
Department of Defense: www.defenselink.mil
Department of Education: www.ed.gov
Department of Energy: www.energy.gov
Department of Health and Human Services: www.dhhs.gov
Department of Housing and Urban Development:
    www.hud.gov
Department of the Interior: www.doi.gov
Department of Justice: www.usdoj.gov
Department of Labor: www.dol.gov
Department of State: www.state.gov
Department of Transportation: www.dot.gov
Department of the Treasury: www.ustreas.gov
Department of Veterans' Affairs: www.va.gov
Search gov: www.searchgov.com

Other Government Resources

Census Bureau: www.census.gov
Central Intelligence Agency (CIA): www.cia.gov
Consumer Product Safety Commission: www.cpsc.gov
Environmental Protection Agency (EPA): www.epa.gov
Equal Employment Opportunity Commission (EEOC):
   www.eeoc.gov
Federal Bureau of Investigation: www.fbi.gov
Federal Communications Commission: www.fcc.gov
Federal Deposit Insurance Corporation (FDIC):
   www.fdic.gov
Federal Election Commission (FEC): www.fec.gov
Federal Emergency Management Agency: www.fema.gov
Federal Housing Finance Board: www.fhfb.gov
Federal Reserve System (FRS), Board of Governors of
   (the Federal Reserve Board): www.federalreserve.gov
Federal Trade Commission (FTC): www.ftc.gov
Internal Revenue Service: www.IRS.gov
National Transportation Safety Board: www.ntsb.gov
Postal Rate Commission: www.prc.gov
Social Security Administration: www.ssa.gov
U.S. Commission on Civil Rights: www.usccr.gov
U.S. International Trade Commission: www.usitc.gov
U.S. Postal Service: www.usps.gov

Health and Fitness

American Academy of Pediatrics: www.aap.org
Centers for Disease Control and Prevention: www.cdc.gov
Fitness Online: www.fitnessonline.com
MedExplorer: www.medexplorer.com
National Institutes of Health: www.nih.gov
New England Journal of Medicine: www.nejm.org
President's Council on Physical Fitness and Sports:
   www.fitness.gov
ReutersHealth: www.reutershealth.com
World Health Organization: www.who.int/

Jobs

careerbuilder.com: www.carrerbuilder.com
Headhunter.net: www.headhunter.net
Hot Jobs: www.hotjobs.com
Monster Board: www.monster.com

Kids

Fact Monster: www.factmonster.com
Funbrain: www.funbrain.com
Kids' Learning Network: www.klnlive.com
Lycos Zone: www.lycoszone.lycos.com
Scholastic: www.scholastic.com
Sports Illustrated Kids: www.sikids.com
Teenwire: www.teenwire.com
TIME for Kids: www.timeforkids.com/TFK
Yahooligans!: www.yahooligans.com

Labor

Federal Labor Relations Authority: www.flra.gov
National Labor Relations Board (NLRB): www.nlrb.gov
Occupational Safety and Health Review Commission:
   www.oshrc.gov
President's Task Force on Employment of Adults with Dis-
   abilities: www.dol.gov/_sec/programs/ptfead/main.htm

Magazines

Consumer Reports Online: www.consumerreports.org
Fortune: www.fortune.com/fortune
People: people.aol.com/people/index.html
Rolling Stone: www.rollingstone.com
Salon: www.salon.com
TIME: www.time.com/time
U.S. News & World Report:
   www.usnews.com/usnews/home.htm

Military

U.S. Marine Corps: www.usmc.mil
Selective Service System: www.sss.gov
U.S. Air Force: www.af.mil
U.S. Army: www.army.mil
U.S. Coast Guard: www.uscg.mil
U.S. Navy: www.navy.mil

News/Media

Associated Press: wire.ap.org
BBC Online: www.bbc.co.uk
CNN Interactive: www.cnn.com
Los Angeles Times: www.latimes.com
MSNBC: www.msnbc.com
National Public Radio Online: www.npr.org
Newspapers Online: www.newspapers.com
New York Times: www.nytimes.com
Reuters: www.reuters.com
USA Today: www.usatoday.com
Wall Street Journal: www.wsj.com
Washington Post: www.washingtonpost.com

Public Service

Corporation for National Service: www.cns.gov
Habitat for Humanity: www.habitat.org
Peace Corps: www.peacecorps.gov

Reference

Ask Jeeves: www.askjeeves.com
CIA World Factbook:
   www.odci.gov/cia/publications/factbook
eHow: www.ehow.com
FedStats (gov't. statistics): www.fedstats.gov
Information Please: www.infoplease.com
Internet Public Library: www.ipl.org
MapQuest: www.mapquest.com
Refdesk: www.refdesk.com

Science

National Aeronautics and Space Administration (NASA):
   www.nasa.gov
National Science Foundation (NSF): www.nsf.gov
Science Magazine: www.sciencemag.org
Scientific American Magazine: www.scientificamerican.com

Search Engines

AltaVista: www.altavista.com
Excite: www.excite.com
Google: www.google.com
Go To: www.goto.com
Lycos: www.lycos.com
Metacrawler: www.metacrawler.com
Yahoo!: www.yahoo.com

Sports

CNN Sports Illustrated: www.CNNSI.com
ESPN: espn.go.com
Major League Baseball: www.majorleaguebaseball.com
Major League Soccer: www.majorleaguesoccer.com
National Basketball Association: www.nba.com
National Football League: www.nfl.com
National Hockey League: www.nhl.com
Women's National Basketball Association: www.wnba.com

Travel

Centers for Disease Control Home Travel Information
   Page: www.cdc.gov/travel/
Expedia: www.expedia.com
Flight Tracker:
   www.trip.com/trs/trip/flighttracker/flight_tracker_home.xsl
Fodor's: www.fodors.com
Frommer's BudgetTravel Online: www.frommers.com
Hostelling International: www.iyhf.org
Lonely Planet Online: www.lonelyplanet.com
National Park Service: www.nps.gov
Priceline.com: www.priceline.com
Rough Guides to Travel: In.travel.roughguides.com/
Travelocity.com: www.travelocity.com

Weather

AccuWeather: www.accuweather.com
Environment Canada: www.weather.ec.gc.ca
Farmer's Almanac: www.almanac.com
IntelliCast: www.intellicast.com
National Weather Service: www.nws.noaa.gov
The Weather Channel: www.weather.com

Top-Selling Software, 2000

Rank	Title	Publisher	Average price	Rank	Title	Publisher	Average price
1.	TurboTax Deluxe	Intuit	$29	7.	Who Wants to Be a Millionaire	Disney	$17
2.	The Sims	Electronic Arts	41				
3.	TurboTax	Intuit	19	8.	MS Windows 98 2nd Ed. Upgrade	Microsoft	89
4.	MP Roller Coaster Tycoon	Infogrames Entertainment	26	9.	Who Wants to Be a Millionaire, 2nd Ed.	Disney	18
5.	Norton Antivirus 2000 6.0	Symantec	29				
6.	Diablo 2	Vivendi Universal Publishing	50	10.	MS Expedia Streets/Trip Planner	Microsoft	28

Source: NPD INTELECT Market Tracking. Web: www.npd.com.

Top-Selling Education Software, 2000

Rank	Title	Publisher	Average price	Rank	Title	Publisher	Average price
1.	Winnie the Pooh Preschool	Disney	$19	6.	Jumpstart Third Grade	Vivendi Universal Publishing	$18
2.	Winnie the Pooh Toddler	Disney	19	7.	Jumpstart Second Grade	Vivendi Universal Publishing	18
3.	Winnie the Pooh Kindergarten	Disney	19	8.	Pokemon Studio Blue	The Learning Company	18
4.	Jumpstart First Grade	Vivendi Universal Publishing	18	9.	Jumpstart Phonics Learning	Vivendi Universal Publishing	19
5.	Jumpstart Kindergarten II	Vivendi Universal Publishing	18	10.	Jumpstart Preschool	Vivendi Universal Publishing	18

Source: NPD INTELECT Market Tracking. Web: www.npd.com.

Top-Selling Business Software, 2000

Rank	Title	Publisher	Average price	Rank	Title	Publisher	Average price
1.	Norton Antivirus 2000 6.0	Symantec	$29	7.	Norton System Works 2001 4.0	Symantec	$55
2.	MS Windows 98 2nd Ed. Upgrade	Microsoft	89	8.	MS Exchange Clnt Acc OPEN Lic	Microsoft	53
3.	MS Windows ME Step Up Promo	Microsoft	49	9.	Norton Antivirus Entpr Sol 4.0 Mnt PVP Lic	Symantec	15
4.	VirusScan 5.0	Network Associates	26				
5.	Norton System Works 2000 3.0	Symantec	54	10.	MS Windows NT Clnt Acc OPEN Lic	Microsoft	29
6.	Norton Antivirus 7.0	Symantec	33				

Source: NPD INTELECT Market Tracking. Web: www.npd.com.

Top-Selling Games Software, 2000

Rank	Title	Publisher	Average price	Rank	Title	Publisher	Average price
1.	The Sims	Electronic Arts	$41	6.	The Sims Livin' Large Expansion Pack	Electronic Arts	$27
2.	MP Roller Coaster Tycoon	Infogrames Entertainment	26				
3.	Who Wants to Be a Millionaire	Disney	17	7.	MS Age of Empires II: Age of Kings	Microsoft	44
4.	Diablo 2	Vivendi Universal Publishing	50	8.	Sim Theme Park	Electronic Arts	23
5.	Who Wants to Be a Millionaire, 2nd Ed.	Disney	18	9.	MS Age of Empires II: Conquerors Expansion Add-on	Microsoft	28
				10.	Sim City 3000	Electronic Arts	27

Source: NPD INTELECT Market Tracking. Web: www.npd.com.

Life in the Greenhouse

Making the case that our climate is changing

By MICHAEL D. LEMONICK TIME

A decade ago, the idea that the planet was warming up as a result of human activity was largely theoretical. We knew that since the industrial revolution began in the eighteenth century, factories and power plants and automobiles and farms have been loading the atmosphere with heat-trapping gases, including carbon dioxide and methane. But evidence that the climate was actually getting hotter was still murky.

Not anymore. As an authoritative report issued in April 2001 by the UN-sponsored Intergovernmental Panel on Climate Change made plain, the trend toward a warmer world has unquestionably begun. Worldwide temperatures have climbed more than 1°F over the past century, and the 1990s was the hottest decade on record. After analyzing data going back at least two decades on everything from air and ocean temperatures to the spread and retreat of wildlife, the IPCC asserts that this slow but steady warming has had an impact on no fewer than 420 physical processes and animal and plant species on all continents.

Snows of Kilimanjaro Melting

Glaciers, including the legendary snows of Kilimanjaro, are disappearing from mountaintops around the globe. Coral reefs are dying off as the seas get too warm for comfort. Drought is the norm in parts of Asia and Africa. El Niño events, which trigger devastating weather in the eastern Pacific, are more frequent. The Arctic permafrost is starting to melt. Lakes and rivers in colder climates are freezing later and thawing earlier each year. Plants and animals are shifting their ranges poleward and to higher altitudes, and migration patterns for animals as diverse as polar bears, butterflies, and beluga whales are being disrupted.

Faced with these hard facts, scientists no longer doubt that global warming is happening, and almost nobody questions the fact that humans are at least partly responsible. Nor are the changes over. Already, humans have increased the concentration of carbon dioxide, the most abundant heat-trapping gas in the atmosphere, to 30% above preindustrial levels—and each year the rate of increase gets faster. The obvious conclusion: temperatures will keep going up.

Unfortunately, they may be rising faster and heading higher than anyone expected. By 2100, says the IPCC, average temperatures will increase between 2.5°F and 10.4°F—more than 50% higher than predictions of just a half decade ago. That may not seem like much, but consider that it took only a 9°F shift to end the last Ice Age. Even at the low end, the changes could be problematic enough, with storms getting more frequent and intense, droughts more pronounced, coastal areas ever more severely eroded by rising seas, rainfall scarcer on agricultural land and ecosystems thrown out of balance.

But if the rise is significantly larger, the result could be disastrous. With seas rising as much as 3 ft,

---

America's Attitudes Toward Global Warming: A TIME/CNN Poll

■ Is global warming a very serious problem, a fairly serious problem, or not at all serious?

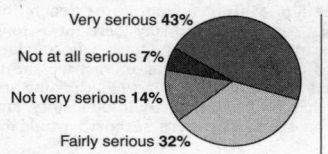

Very serious 43%

Not at all serious 7%

Not very serious 14%

Fairly serious 32%

■ Would you be willing to pay an extra 25¢ per gal. of gas to reduce pollution and global warming?

Nov. 1990	Mar. 2001
Yes 59%	Yes 48%
No 36%	No 49%

■ Would you personally be willing to support tough government actions to help reduce global warming even if each of the following happened as a result?

	Yes	No
Your utility bills went up	47%	49%
Unemployment increased	38%	55%
A mild increase in inflation	54%	39%

■ Are the emissions of gases like carbon dioxide causing global temperature increases?

Yes	64%
No	23%

■ When it comes to protecting the environment, does the government give in to business interests too often?

Yes	69%
No	26%

■ Should the government require improvements in fuel efficiency for cars and trucks even if this means higher prices and smaller vehicles?

Yes	55%
No	40%

■ Should President Bush develop a plan to reduce the emission of gases that may contribute to global warming?

Yes	67%
No	26%

Source: From a telephone poll of 1,025 adult Americans taken for TIME/CNN on March 21–22, 2001, by Yankelovich Partners Inc./Harris. Sampling error is ±3.1%. "Not sures" omitted.

---

enormous areas of densely populated land—coastal Florida, much of Louisiana, the Nile Delta, the Maldives, Bangladesh—would become uninhabitable. Entire climatic zones might shift dramatically, making central Canada look more like central Illinois, Georgia more like Guatemala. Agriculture would be thrown into turmoil. Hundreds of millions of people would have to migrate out of unlivable regions.

Public Health Hazards

Public health could suffer. Rising seas would contaminate water supplies with salt. Higher levels of urban ozone, the result of stronger sunlight and warmer temperatures, could worsen respiratory illnesses. More frequent hot spells could lead to a rise in heat-related deaths. Warmer temperatures could widen the range of disease-carrying rodents and bugs, such as mosquitoes and ticks, increasing the incidence of dengue fever, malaria, encephalitis, Lyme disease, and other afflictions. Worst of all, this increase in temperatures is happening at a pace that outstrips anything the earth has seen in the past 100 million years. Humans may have a hard enough time adjusting, especially in poorer countries, but for wildlife, the changes could be devastating.

Like any other area of science, the case for human-induced global warming has uncertainties—and like many pro-business lobbyists, President Bush has proclaimed those uncertainties a reason to study the problem further rather than act. But while the evidence is circumstantial, it is powerful, thanks to the IPCC's painstaking research. The UN-sponsored group was organized in the late 1980s. Its mission: to sift through climate-related studies from a dozen different fields and integrate them into a coherent picture. "It isn't just the work of a few green people," says Sir John Houghton, one of the early leaders who at the time ran the British Meteorological Office. "The IPCC scientists come from a wide range of backgrounds and countries."

Computer Models

Measuring the warming that has already taken place is relatively simple; the trick is unraveling the causes and projecting what will happen over the next century. To do that, IPCC scientists fed a wide range of scenarios involving varying estimates of population and economic growth, changes in technology, and other factors into computers. That process gave them about 35 estimates, ranging from 6 billion to 35 billion tons, of how much excess carbon dioxide will enter the atmosphere.

Then they loaded those estimates into the even larger, more powerful computer programs that attempt to model the planet's climate. Because no one climate model is considered definitive, they used seven different versions, which yielded 235 independent predictions of global temperature increase. That's where the range of 2.5°F to 10.4°F (1.4°C to 5.8°C) comes from.

The computer models were criticized in the past largely because the climate is so complex that the limited hardware and software of even a half decade ago couldn't do an adequate simulation. Today's climate models, however, still aren't perfect.

A number of the IPCC scientists are distressed that only the most extreme scenarios, based on huge population growth and the maximum use of dirty fuels like coal, have made headlines. It won't take the greatest extremes of warming to make life uncomfortable for large numbers of people. Even slightly higher temperatures in regions that are already drought- or flood-prone would exacerbate those conditions. In temperate zones, warmth and increased CO_2 would make some crops flourish—at first. But beyond 3°F of warming, says Bill Easterling, a professor of geography and agronomy at Penn State and a lead author of the IPCC report, "there would be a dramatic turning point. U.S. crop yields would start to decline rapidly." In the tropics, where crops are already at the limit of their temperature range, the decrease would start right away.

The Tipping Point

Even if temperatures rise only moderately, some scientists fear, the climate would reach a "tipping point"—a point at which even a tiny additional increase would throw the system into violent change. If peat bogs and Arctic permafrost warm enough to start releasing the methane stored within them, for example, that potent greenhouse gas would suddenly accelerate the heat-trapping process.

By contrast, if melting ice caps dilute the salt content of the sea, major ocean currents like the Gulf Stream could slow or even stop, and so would their warming effects on northern regions. More snowfall reflecting more sunlight back into space could actually cause a net cooling. Global warming could, paradoxically, throw the planet into another ice age.

Even if such a tipping point doesn't materialize, the more drastic effects of global warming might be only postponed rather than avoided. The IPCC's calculations end with the year 2100, but the warming won't. World Bank chief scientist, Robert Watson, currently serving as IPCC chair, points out that the CO_2 entering the atmosphere today will be there for a century. Says Watson: "If we stabilize [CO_2 emissions] now, the concentration will continue to go up for hundreds of years. Temperatures will rise over that time."

That could be truly catastrophic. The ongoing disruption of ecosystems and weather patterns would be bad enough. But if temperatures reach the IPCC's worst-case levels and stay there for as long as 1,000 years, says Michael Oppenheimer, chief scientist at Environmental Defense, vast ice sheets in Greenland and Antarctica could melt, raising sea level more than 30 ft. Florida would be history, and every city on the U.S. eastern seaboard would be inundated.

In the short run, there's not much chance of halting global warming, not even if every nation in the world ratifies the Kyoto Protocol tomorrow. The treaty doesn't require reductions in carbon dioxide emissions until 2008. By that time, a great deal of damage will already have been done. But we can slow things down. If action today can keep the climate from eventually reaching an unstable tipping point or can finally begin to reverse the warming trend a century from now, the effort would hardly be futile. Humanity embarked unknowingly on the dangerous experiment of tinkering with the climate of our planet. Now that we know what we're doing, it would be utterly foolish to continue. □

International Energy Annual 1999

Source: Energy Information Administration, Dept. of Energy. Web: www.eia.doe.gov/emeu/iea/overview.html.

World Primary Energy Production Trends

Between 1990 and 1999, the world's total output of primary energy—petroleum, natural gas, coal, and electric power (hydro, nuclear, geothermal, solar, wind, and wood and waste)—increased at an average annual rate of 0.9%. World production increased from 351 quadrillion Btu (British thermal units) in 1990 to 380 quadrillion Btu in 1999.

In 1999, petroleum (crude oil and natural gas plant liquids) continued to be the world's most important primary energy source, accounting for 39.4%, or 150 quadrillion Btu, of world primary energy production. Between 1990 and 1999, petroleum production increased 10.2%, from 65.2 to 71.9 million barrels per day. The Middle East had the largest production gain, followed by Western Europe, and Central and South America. Their combined gains were 8.6 million barrels per day. In Eastern Europe and the former Soviet Union, average daily production fell 3.8 million barrels per day.

Dry natural gas ranked second, accounting for 23% of world primary energy production in 1999. Production of dry natural gas was 84.7 trillion cubic feet, or 87 quadrillion Btu, a 15% increase since 1990.

Coal ranked third in 1999, accounting for 22.3% of world primary energy production, totaling 4.7 billion short tons—85 quadrillion Btu—in 1999, down 12.1% from 1990.

Between 1990 and 1999, nuclear electric power generation rose from 1.9 trillion kilowatt-hours to 2.4 trillion kilowatt-hours, a 25.8% increase. Geothermal, solar, wind, and wood and waste electric power generation increased from 129 billion kilowatt-hours to 227 billion kilowatt-hours, a 76.3% increase. Hydroelectric power continued to represent the largest share of primary electric power generation, 2.6 trillion kilowatt-hours in 1999, up 20.3% from 2.2 trillion kilowatt-hours in 1990.

Major Energy Producers and Consumers

In 1999, the United States, Russia, and China were the leading producers and consumers of energy, producing 38%, and consuming 41%, of the world's energy.

The United States, Russia, China, Saudi Arabia, and Canada were the five largest producers of energy in 1999, supplying 47.9% of the world's total. The United States supplied 72.3 quadrillion Btu of primary energy; Russia, 41.5 quadrillion Btu; and China, 30.9 quadrillion Btu. The next leading producers—the United Kingdom, Iran, Norway, India, and Mexico—together supplied 13.1% of the world's energy.

The United States, China, Russia, Japan, and Germany were the largest consumers in 1999, using 49.9% of world energy. Canada, India, France, the United Kingdom, and Brazil together used an additional 14%. The United States consumed 97.0 quadrillion Btu; China, 31.9 quadrillion Btu; and Russia, 26.0 quadrillion Btu.

Regional Energy Production and Consumption

Between 1990 and 1999, energy production and consumption increased in every region of the world except in Eastern Europe and the former Soviet bloc. East Asia and Oceania saw a production increase of 13.6 quadrillion Btu, and a consumption increase of 24.9 quadrillion Btu. Energy production in the Middle East increased by 12.1 quadrillion Btu, the second-largest increase for any region, while consumption increased 5.3 quadrillion Btu. Energy production in Central and South America increased by 8.2 quadrillion Btu, while consumption rose by 6.2 quadrillion Btu.

In North America, energy production rose by 7.1 quadrillion Btu, and consumption increased 15.6 quadrillion Btu. Energy production in Western Europe rose by 5.8 quadrillion Btu, and consumption increased by 6.6 quadrillion Btu. Energy production in Africa increased by 5.2 quadrillion Btu, while consumption rose 2.4 quadrillion Btu. In Eastern Europe and the former USSR production declined 22.9 quadrillion Btu and consumption dropped 25.3 quadrillion Btu.

Petroleum

Global production of petroleum (crude oil and natural gas plant liquids) increased by 6.7 million barrels per day between 1990 and 1999, an average annual growth rate of 1.1%. Saudi Arabia, the United States, and Russia were the largest producers of petroleum in 1999, together producing 31.4% of the world's petroleum. Iran and Mexico together accounted for an additional 9.7%.

In 1999, the United States consumed 19.5 million barrels per day of petroleum—26% of world consumption. Japan used 5.6 million barrels per day, followed by China, Germany, and Russia.

Natural Gas

World production of dry natural gas increased by 11.1 trillion cubic feet, an average annual rate of 1.6%, from 1990 to 1999. Russia and the United States produced 47% of the world total, followed by Canada, the United Kingdom, and Algeria. The United States and Russia accounted for 42% of world consumption, followed by the United Kingdom, Canada, and Germany.

Coal

Coal production declined by 650 million short tons from 1990 to 1999. Five countries—China, the United States, India, Australia, and Russia—accounted for 66% of world coal production in 1999.

Hydroelectric Power

The generation of hydroelectric power increased by 440 billion kilowatt-hours between 1990 and 1999, an average annual rate of 2.1%. Canada, Brazil, the United States, China, and Russia, were the largest producers of hydroelectric power in 1999, generating 51% of the world total.

Nuclear Electric Power

The generation of nuclear electric power increased by 491 billion kilowatt-hours between 1990 and 1999, an average annual rate of 2.6%. The United States led the world in nuclear electric power generation in 1999, followed by France and Japan. Together, the three countries generated 59% of the world's nuclear electric power.

Geothermal, Solar, Wind, and Wood and Waste Electric Power

The generation of geothermal, solar, wind, and wood and waste electric power increased by 98 billion kilowatt-hours between 1990 and 1999, an average annual rate of 6.5%. The United States, Japan, Germany, Brazil, and Finland accounted for 62% of the total.

World Energy Consumption and Carbon Emissions, 1990–2020

Region	Energy consumption (quadrillion btu)				Carbon emissions (million metric tons)			
	1990	1999	2010	2020	1990	1999	2010	2020
Industrialized nations[1]	182.4	209.6	243.4	270.4	2,842	3,122	3,619	4,043
Eastern Europe/Former Soviet Union	76.3	50.5	60.3	72.3	1,337	810	940	1,094
Developing nations								
Asia[2]	52.0	70.9	113.4	162.2	1,053	1,361	2,137	3,013
Middle East[3]	13.1	19.3	26.9	37.2	231	330	451	627
Africa	9.3	11.8	16.1	20.8	179	218	294	373
Central and South America[4]	13.7	19.8	29.6	44.1	178	249	394	611
Total developing	87.2	121.8	186.1	264.4	1,641	2,158	3,276	4,624
Total world	346.0	381.8	489.7	607.1	5,821	6,091	7,835	9,762

1. Includes the U.S., Canada, Mexico, Japan, France, Germany, Italy, the Netherlands, and the United Kingdom. 2. China, India, and South Korea are represented in developing Asia. 3. Turkey is represented in the Middle East. 4. Brazil is represented in Central and South America. *Source:* U.S. Energy Information Administration, *International Energy Annual 1999* (Jan. 2001). Projections: EIA, World Energy Projection System. Web: www.eia.doe.gov/oiaf/ieo/tbl_1.html

Renewable Energy Consumption in the U.S. by Source, 1989–1999
(quadrillion btu)

Year	Wood and waste[1]	Geothermal[2]	Conventional hydroelectric power[3, 4]	Solar[5]	Wind[6]	Total
1989	3.050	0.338	2.999	0.059	0.024	6.470
1990	2.665	0.359	3.140	0.063	0.032	6.260
1991	2.679	0.368	3.222	0.066	0.032	6.367
1992	2.826	0.379	2.863	0.068	0.030	6.167
1993	2.782	0.393	3.147	0.071	0.031	6.424
1994	2.914	0.395	2.971	0.072	0.036	6.387
1995	3.044	0.339	3.474	0.073	0.033	6.963
1996	3.104	0.352	3.915	0.075	0.035	7.482
1997	2.982	0.328	3.940	0.074	0.034	7.358
1998	2.991	0.335	3.552	0.074	0.031	6.984
1999e	3.514	0.327	3.417	0.076	0.038	7.373

NOTES: Totals may not equal sum of components due to independent rounding. 1. Wood, wood waste, black liquor, red liquor, spent sulfite liquor, pitch, wood sludge, peat, railroad ties, utility poles, municipal solid waste, landfill gas, methane, digester gas, liquid acetonitrile waste, tall oil, waste alcohol, medical waste, paper pellets, sludge waste, solid byproducts, tires, agricultural byproducts, closed looped biomass, fish oil, and straw. 2. Includes electricity imports from Mexico that are derived from geothermal energy. Includes grid-connected electricity, and geothermal heat pump and direct use energy. Excludes shaft power and remote electrical power. 3. Hydroelectricity generated by pumped storage is not included in renewable energy. 4. Includes electricity net imports from Canada that are derived from hydroelectric power. 5. Includes solar thermal and photovoltaic energy. 6. Includes only grid-connected electricity. e = estimated. *Source:* Energy Information Administration (EIA). Web: www.eia.doe.gov.

U.S. Emissions of Greenhouse Gases, 1990–1999
(million metric tons of gas)

Gas	1990	1992	1993	1994	1995	1996	1997	1998	1999[1]
Carbon dioxide	4,951.9	5,005.3	5,121.6	5,215.7	5,260.6	5,441.6	5,519.0	5,527.1	5,598.2
Methane	31.7	32.0	31.1	31.2	31.2	30.2	30.1	29.3	28.8
Nitrous oxide	1.2	1.2	1.2	1.3	1.3	1.2	1.2	1.2	1.2
HFCs, PFCs, and SF$_6$	—	—	—	—	—	—	—	—	—
Carbon monoxide	88.7	87.9	88.4	92.4	84.0	85.9	85.0	80.4	n.a.
Nitrogen oxides	21.7	22.1	22.5	22.8	22.4	22.2	22.3	22.0	n.a.
Nonmethane VOCs	19.0	18.7	18.9	19.5	18.9	16.9	17.1	16.2	n.a.

NOTES: (—) Less than 0.05 million metric tons of gas. n.a. = not available. 1. Preliminary data. *Source:* Compiled by the U.S. Energy Information Administration. Web: www.eia.doe.gov/oiaf/1605/ggrpt/tbld3.html.

Air Quality in Selected U.S. Cities, 1990–1999
(number of days with AQI values greater than 100)[1]

Metropolitan statistical area	1990	1991	1992	1993	1994	1995	1996	1997	1998	1999
Atlanta, Ga.	42	23	20	36	15	35	25	31	50	61
Baltimore, Md.	29	50	23	48	41	36	28	30	51	40
Boston, Mass.-N.H.	7	13	9	6	10	8	2	8	7	5
Chicago, Ill.	4	22	4	3	8	21	6	9	7	12
Cleveland/Lorain/Elyria, Ohio	10	23	11	13	23	24	18	11	20	18
Dallas, Tex.	24	2	12	14	27	36	12	20	28	23
Denver, Colo.	9	6	11	3	1	2	0	0	5	1
Detroit, Mich.	11	28	8	5	11	14	13	12	17	15
El Paso, Tex.	19	7	10	7	11	8	7	4	6	6
Houston, Tex.	51	36	32	28	38	66	26	47	38	50
Kansas City, Mo.-Kans.	2	11	1	4	10	22	10	18	15	5
Los Angeles/Long Beach, Calif.	173	168	175	134	139	113	94	60	56	27
Miami, Fla.	1	1	3	6	1	2	1	3	8	5
Minneapolis/St. Paul, Minn.-Wis.	4	2	1	0	2	5	0	0	1	0
New York, N.Y.	36	49	10	19	21	19	15	23	17	24
Philadelphia, Pa.-N.J.	39	49	24	51	26	30	22	32	37	32
Phoenix/Mesa, Ariz.	12	11	13	16	10	22	17	12	17	12
Pittsburgh, Pa.	19	21	9	13	19	25	11	21	39	23
St. Louis, Mo.-Ill.	23	32	15	9	32	34	20	15	23	29
San Diego, Calif.	96	67	66	58	46	48	31	14	33	16
San Francisco, Calif.	0	0	0	0	0	2	0	0	0	0
Seattle/Bellevue/Everett, Wash.	9	4	3	0	3	0	6	1	3	1
Washington, D.C.-Md.-Va.-W.Va.	25	48	14	52	20	29	18	29	47	39

1. AQI—Air Quality Index. AQI measures how polluted air is by measuring five major pollutants: ground-level ozone, particulate matter, carbon monoxide, sulfur dioxide, and nitrogen oxide. Based on the amount of each pollutant in the air, the AQI assigns a numerical value to air quality as follows: 0 to 50 (good); 51 to 100 (moderate); 101 to 150 (unhealthy for sensitive groups); 151 to 200 (unhealthy); 201 to 300 (very unhealthy); 301 to 500 (hazardous). *Source:* U.S. Environmental Protection Agency, Office of Air Quality Planning & Standards. www. epa.gov/oar/aqtrnd99/aqiall.pdf.

World Net Electricity Consumption by Region, 1990–2020

(billion kilowatt-hours)

Region	History		Projections				Average annual percent change, 1999–2020
	1990	1999	2005	2010	2015	2020	
Industrialized countries	6,385	7,517	8,580	9,352	10,112	10,888	1.8%
United States	2,817	3,236	3,761	4,147	4,484	4,804	1.9
Eastern Europe/ Former Soviet Union	1,906	1,452	1,622	1,760	1,972	2,138	1.9
Developing countries	2,258	3,863	4,988	6,191	7,615	9,203	4.2
Developing Asia	1,259	2,319	3,088	3,883	4,815	5,856	4.5
China	551	1,084	1,533	2,035	2,635	3,331	5.5
India	257	424	545	656	798	949	3.9
South Korea	93	233	294	333	386	437	3.0
Other	357	578	716	858	996	1,139	3.3
Central and South America	449	684	844	1,035	1,268	1,552	4.0
Total world	10,549	12,833	15,190	17,303	19,699	22,230	2.7

Sources: Energy Information Administration (EIA): *International Energy Annual 1999,* DOE/EIA-0219(99), and World Energy Projection System (2001). Web: www.eia.doe.gov/oiaf/ieo/tbl_20.html.

Greatest Oil Reserves by Country, 2001

2001 rank	Country	2001 proved reserves (1,000 bbl)	2001 rank	Country	2001 proved reserves (1,000 bbl)
1.	Saudi Arabia	259,200,000	6.	Venezuela	76,862,000
2.	Iraq	112,500,000	7.	Russia	48,573,000
3.	United Arab Emirates	97,800,000	8.	Libya	29,500,000
4.	Kuwait	94,000,000	9.	Mexico	28,260,000
5.	Iran	89,700,000	10.	China	24,000,000

NOTES: Figures for Russia are "explored reserves," which are understood to be proved plus some probable. All other figures are proved reserves recoverable with present technology and prices. bbl = barrels. *Source:* "Worldwide Look at Reserves and Production," *Oil & Gas Journal,* Dec. 18, 2000. Web: http://ogj.pennnet.com.

Greatest Gas Reserves by Country, 2001

2001 rank	Country	2001 proved reserves (billion cu. ft.)	2001 rank	Country	2001 proved reserves (billion cu. ft.)
1.	Russia	1,700,000	6.	United States	167,400
2.	Iran	812,300	7.	Algeria	159,700
3.	Qatar	393,800	8.	Venezuela	146,800
4.	Saudi Arabia	213,300	9.	Nigeria	124,000
5.	United Arab Emirates	212,100	10.	Iraq	109,800

NOTES: Figures for Russia are "explored reserves," which are understood to be proved plus some probable. All other figures are proved reserves recoverable with present technology and prices. *Source:* "Worldwide Look at Reserves and Production," *Oil & Gas Journal,* Dec. 18, 2000. Web: http://ogj.pennnet.com.

Motor Vehicle Fuel Consumption and Travel in the U.S., 1960–1999

	1960	1970	1980	1990	1995	1996	1997	1998	1999
Number registered (thousands)									
Passenger car	61,671	89,244	121,601	133,700	128,387	129,728	129,749	n.a.	n.a.
Total[1]	73,858	111,242	161,490	193,057	205,427	210,441	211,580	215,496	n.a.
Vehicle-miles traveled (millions)									
Passenger car	587,000	917,000	1,112,000	1,408,000	1,438,000	1,470,000	1,502,000	n.a.	n.a.
Total[1]	719,000	1,110,000	1,527,000	2,144,000	2,423,000	2,486,000	2,560,000	2,625,000	n.a.
Fuel consumed (million gallons)									
Passenger car	41,171	67,819	69,982	69,568	68,072	69,221	69,867	n.a.	n.a.
Total[1]	57,880	92,329	114,960	130,755	143,834	147,365	150,386	154,884	n.a.
Average miles traveled per vehicle (thousands)									
Passenger car	9.5	10.3	9.1	10.5	11.2	11.3	11.6	11.7	11.8
Total[1]	9.7	10.0	9.5	11.1	11.8	11.8	12.1	12.2	n.a.
Average miles traveled per gallon									
Passenger car	14.3	13.5	15.9	20.2	21.1	21.2	21.5	n.a.	n.a.
Total[1]	12.4	12.0	13.3	16.4	16.8	16.9	17.0	17.0	n.a.
Average fuel consumed per vehicle (gallons)									
Passenger car	668	760	576	520	530	534	538	544	552
Total[1]	784	830	712	677	700	700	711	719	n.a.

1. Includes personal passenger vehicles, buses, and trucks. *Source:* U.S. Department of Transportation. Web: www.dot.gov.

Major Air Pollutants

Pollutant	Sources	Effects
Ozone. A gas that can be found in two places. Near the ground (the troposphere), it is a major part of smog. Higher in the air (the stratosphere), it helps block radiation from the sun.	Ozone is not created directly, but is formed when nitrogen oxides and volatile organic compounds mix in sunlight. That is why ozone is mostly found in the summer. Nitrogen oxides come from burning gasoline, coal, or other fossil fuels. There are many types of volatile organic compounds, and they come from sources ranging from factories to trees.	Ozone near the ground can cause a number of health problems. Ozone can lead to more frequent asthma attacks in people who have asthma and can cause sore throats, coughs, and breathing difficulty. It may even lead to premature death. Ozone can also hurt plants and crops.
Carbon monoxide. A gas that comes from the burning of fossil fuels, mostly in cars. It cannot be seen or smelled.	Carbon monoxide is released when engines burn fossil fuels. Emissions are higher when engines are not tuned properly, and when fuel is not completely burned. Cars emit a lot of the carbon monoxide found outdoors. Furnaces and heaters in the home can emit high concentrations of carbon monoxide, too, if they are not properly maintained.	Carbon monoxide makes it hard for body parts to get the oxygen they need to run correctly. Exposure to carbon monoxide makes people feel dizzy and tired, and gives them headaches. Elderly people with heart disease are hospitalized more often when they are exposed to higher amounts of carbon monoxide.

Pollutant	Sources	Effects
Nitrogen dioxide. A reddish-brown gas that comes from the burning of fossil fuels. It has a strong smell at high levels.	Nitrogen dioxide mostly comes from power plants and cars. Nitrogen dioxide is formed in two ways—when nitrogen in the fuel is burned, or when nitrogen in the air reacts with oxygen at very high temperatures. Nitrogen dioxide can also react in the atmosphere to form ozone, acid rain, and particles.	High levels of nitrogen dioxide exposure can give people coughs and can make them feel short of breath. People who are exposed to nitrogen dioxide for a long time have a higher chance of getting respiratory infections. Acid rain can hurt plants and animals and can make lakes dangerous to swim or fish in.
Particulate matter. Solid or liquid matter that is suspended in the air. To remain in the air, particles are usually less than 0.1 mm wide and can be as small as 0.00005 mm.	Particulate matter can be divided into two types—coarse particles and fine particles. Coarse particles are bigger than 0.002 mm and are formed from sources like road dust, sea spray, and construction. Fine particles are smaller than 0.002 mm and are formed when fuel is burned in automobiles and power plants.	Particulate matter that is small enough can enter the lungs and cause health problems. Some of these problems include: more frequent asthma attacks, respiratory problems, and premature death. Particulate matter can also make clothes and other materials dirty.
Sulfur dioxide. A corrosive gas that cannot be seen or smelled at low levels but can have a "rotten egg" smell at high levels.	Sulfur dioxide mostly comes from the burning of coal or oil in power plants. It also comes from factories that make chemicals, paper, or fuel. Like nitrogen dioxide, sulfur dioxide also reacts in the atmosphere to form acid rain and particles.	Sulfur dioxide exposure can affect people who have asthma or emphysema by making it more difficult for them to breathe. It can also irritate people's eyes, noses, and throats. Sulfur dioxide can harm trees and crops, damage buildings, and make it harder for people to see long distances.
Lead. A blue-gray metal that is very toxic and is found in a number of forms and locations.	Outside, lead comes from cars in areas where unleaded gasoline is not used. Lead can also come from power plants and other industrial sources. Inside, lead paint is an important source of lead, especially in houses where paint is peeling. Lead in old pipes can also be a source of lead in drinking water.	High amounts of lead can be dangerous for small children and can lead to lower IQs and kidney problems. For adults, exposure to lead can increase the chance of having heart attacks or strokes.
Toxic air pollutants. A large number of chemicals that are known or suspected to cause cancer. Some important pollutants in this category include arsenic, asbestos, benzene, and dioxin.	Each toxic air pollutant comes from a slightly different source, but many are created in chemical plants or are emitted when fossil fuels are burned. Some toxic air pollutants, like asbestos and formaldehyde, can be found in building materials and can lead to indoor air problems. Many toxic air pollutants can also enter the food and water supply, and people can be exposed when they eat or drink.	Toxic air pollutants can cause cancer. Some toxic air pollutants can also cause birth defects. Other effects depend on the pollutant, but can include skin and eye irritation and breathing problems.
Stratospheric ozone depleters. Chemicals that can destroy the ozone in the stratosphere. These chemicals include chlorofluorocarbons (CFCs), halons, and other compounds that include chlorine or bromine.	CFCs are used in air conditioners and refrigerators, since they work well as coolants. They can also be found in aerosol cans and fire extinguishers. Other stratospheric ozone depleters are used as solvents in industry.	If the ozone in the stratosphere is destroyed, people are exposed to more radiation from the sun (ultraviolet radiation). This can lead to skin cancer and eye problems. Higher ultraviolet radiation can also harm plants and animals.
Greenhouse gases. Gases that stay in the air for a long time and warm up the planet by trapping sunlight. This is called the "greenhouse effect" because the gases act like the glass in a greenhouse. Some of the important greenhouse gases are carbon dioxide, methane, and nitrous oxide.	Carbon dioxide is the most important greenhouse gas, and it comes from the burning of fossil fuels in cars, power plants, houses, and industry. Methane is released during the processing of fossil fuels, and also comes from natural sources like cows and rice paddies. Nitrous oxide comes from industrial sources and decaying plants.	The greenhouse effect can lead to changes in the climate of the planet. Some of these changes might include more temperature extremes, higher sea levels, changes in forest composition, and damage to land near the coast. Human health might be affected by diseases that are related to temperature or by damage to land and water.

Source: Jonathan Levy, Harvard School of Public Health. Based on information provided by the Environmental Protection Agency.

Largest Nuclear Power Plants in the U.S.

Plant	Operating utility	Capacity (net MWe)	Year operative
Palo Verde 3, Ariz.	Arizona Public Service	1262	1987
Palo Verde 1, Ariz.	Arizona Public Service	1258	1985
Palo Verde 2, Ariz.	Arizona Public Service	1258	1986
South Texas 1, Tex.	Houston Lighting & Power	1250	1988
South Texas 2, Tex.	Houston Lighting & Power	1250	1989
Grand Gulf 1, Miss.	System Energy Resources	1200	1984
Washington Nuclear 2, Wash.	Washington Public Power Supply System	1170	1984
Perry 1, Ohio	Cleveland Electric Illuminating	1169	1986
Vogtle 2, Ga.	Georgia Power	1169	1989
Vogtle 1, Ga.	Georgia Power	1164	1987
Wolf Creek, Kans.	Wolf Creek Nuclear Operating	1163	1985
Seabrook 1, N.H.	Public Service Co. of N.H.	1162	1990
Millstone 3, Conn.	Northeast Nuclear Energy	1155	1986
Comanche Peak 1, Tex.	Texas Utilities Electric Co.	1150	1990
Comanche Peak 2, Tex.	Texas Utilities Electric Co.	1150	1993
Limerick 2, Pa.	Philadelphia Electric Co.	1150	1989
Callaway 1, Mo.	Union Electric	1143	1984
Nine Mile Point 2, N.Y.	Niagara Mohawk Power Corp.	1136	1987
Limerick 1, Pa.	Philadelphia Electric Co.	1134	1985
Catawba 1, S.C.	Duke Power Co.	1129	1985
Catawba 2, S.C.	Duke Power Co.	1129	1986
McGuire 1, N.C.	Duke Power Co.	1129	1981
McGuire 2, N.C.	Duke Power Co.	1129	1983
Byron 1, Ill.	Commonwealth Edison	1120	1985
Byron 2, Ill.	Commonwealth Edison	1120	1987
Sequoyah 1, Tenn.	Tennessee Valley Authority	1119	1980
Sequoyah 2, Tenn.	Tennessee Valley Authority	1119	1981
Watts Bar 1, Tenn.	Tennessee Valley Authority	1119	1996

Source: Department of Energy, Energy Information Administration.

Animals and Nature

Animal Names: Male, Female, and Young

Animal	Male	Female	Young	Animal	Male	Female	Young	Animal	Male	Female	Young
Ass	Jack	Jenny	Foal	Duck	Drake	Duck	Duckling	Sheep	Ram	Ewe	Lamb
Bear	Boar	Sow	Cub	Elephant	Bull	Cow	Calf	Swan	Cob	Pen	Cygnet
Cat	Tom	Queen	Kitten	Fox	Dog	Vixen	Cub	Swine	Boar	Sow	Piglet
Cattle	Bull	Cow	Calf	Goose	Gander	Goose	Gosling	Tiger	Tiger	Tigress	Cub
Chicken	Rooster	Hen	Chick	Horse	Stallion	Mare	Foal	Whale	Bull	Cow	Calf
Deer	Buck	Doe	Fawn	Lion	Lion	Lioness	Cub	Wolf	Dog	Bitch	Pup
Dog	Dog	Bitch	Pup	Rabbit	Buck	Doe	Bunny				

Source: James G. Doherty, General Curator, The Wildlife Conservation Society.

Gestation, Incubation, and Longevity of Certain Animals

Animal	Gestation or incubation, in days (average)	Longevity, in years (record exceptions)	Animal	Gestation or incubation, in days (average)	Longevity, in years (record exceptions)
Ass	365	18–20 (63)	Horse	329–345 (336)	20–25 (50+)
Bear	180–240[1]	15–30 (47)	Human	253–303	[2]
Cat	52–69 (63)	10–12 (26+)	Kangaroo	32–39[1]	4–6 (23)
Chicken	22	7–8 (14)	Lion	105–113 (108)	10 (29)
Cow	280	9–12 (39)	Monkey	139–270[1]	12–15[1] (29)
Deer	197–300[1]	10–15 (26)	Mouse	19–31[1]	1–3 (4)
Dog	53–71 (63)	10–12 (24)	Parakeet (Budgerigar)	17–20 (18)	8 (12+)
Duck	21–35[1] (28)	10 (15)	Pig	101–130 (115)	10 (22)
Elephant	510–730[1] (624)	30–40 (71)	Pigeon	11–19	10–12 (39)
Fox	51–63[1]	8–10 (14)	Rabbit	30–35 (31)	6–8 (15)
Goat	136–160 (151)	12 (17)	Rat	21	3 (5)
Groundhog	31–32	4–9	Sheep	144–152[1] (151)	12 (16)
Guinea pig	58–75 (68)	3 (6)	Squirrel	44	8–9 (15)
Hamster, golden	15–17	2 (8)	Whale	365–547[1]	—
Hippopotamus	220–255 (240)	30 (49+)	Wolf	60–63	10–12 (16)

1. Depending on kind. 2. For life expectancy charts, *see* Life Expectancy at Birth by Race and Sex, p. 132. *Source:* James G. Doherty, General Curator, The Wildlife Conservation Society.

Animal Group Terminology

Source: James G. Doherty, General Curator, The Wildlife Conservation Society

ants: colony
bears: sleuth, sloth
bees: grist, hive, swarm
birds: flight, volery
cattle: drove
cats: clutter, clowder
chicks: brood, clutch
clams: bed
cranes: sedge, seige
crows: murder
doves: dule
ducks: brace, team
elephants: herd
elks: gang
finches: charm

fish: school, shoal, draught
foxes: leash, skulk
geese: flock, gaggle, skein
gnats: cloud, horde
goats: trip
gorillas: band
hares: down, husk
hawks: cast
hens: brood
hogs: drift
horses: pair, team
hounds: cry, mute, pack
kangaroos: troop
kittens: kindle, litter
larks: exaltation

lions: pride
locusts: plague
magpies: tidings
mules: span
nightingales: watch
oxen: yoke
oysters: bed
parrots: company
partridges: covey
peacocks: muster,
 ostentation
pheasants: nest, bouquet
pigs: litter
ponies: string
quail: bevy, covey

rabbits: nest
seals: pod
sheep: drove, flock
sparrows: host
storks: mustering
swans: bevy, wedge
swine: sounder
toads: knot
turkeys: rafter
turtles: bale
vipers: nest
whales: gam, pod
wolves: pack, route
woodcocks: fall

Speed of Animals

Most of the following measurements are for maximum speeds over approximate quarter-mile distances. Exceptions—which are included to give a wide range of animals—are the lion and elephant, whose speeds were clocked in the act of charging; the whippet, which was timed over a 200-yard course; the cheetah over a 100-yard distance; humans for a 15-yard segment of a 100-yard run; and the black mamba snake, six-lined race runner, spider, giant tortoise, three-toed sloth, and garden snail, which were measured over various small distances.

Animal	Speed (mph)	Animal	Speed (mph)	Animal	Speed (mph)
Peregrine falcon	200.00+	Zebra	40.00	Cat (domestic)	30.00
Cheetah	70.00	Mongolian wild ass	40.00	Human	27.89
Pronghorn antelope	61.00	Greyhound	39.35	Elephant	25.00
Wildebeest	50.00	Whippet	35.50	Black mamba snake	20.00
Lion	50.00	Rabbit (domestic)	35.00	Six-lined race runner	18.00
Thomson's gazelle	50.00	Mule deer	35.00	Squirrel	12.00
Quarter horse	47.50	Jackal	35.00	Pig (domestic)	11.00
Elk	45.00	Reindeer	32.00	Chicken	9.00
Cape hunting dog	45.00	Giraffe	32.00	House mouse	8.00
Coyote	43.00	Kangaroo	30.00	Spider (Tegenearia atrica)	1.17
Gray fox	42.00	White-tailed deer	30.00	Giant tortoise	0.17
Ostrich	40.00	Wart hog	30.00	Three-toed sloth	0.15
Hyena	40.00	Grizzly bear	30.00	Garden snail	0.03

Source: Natural History Magazine, March 1974, copyright 1974. The American Museum of Natural History; and James G. Doherty, General Curator, The Wildlife Conservation Society.

Threatened and Endangered Species

Group	Endangered[1] U.S.	Endangered[1] Foreign	Threatened[2] U.S.	Threatened[2] Foreign	Total species	Species with recovery plans
Mammals	63	251	9	17	340	48
Birds	78	175	14	6	273	75
Reptiles	14	64	22	15	115	30
Amphibians	10	8	8	1	27	12
Fishes	70	11	44	0	125	94
Clams	61	2	8	0	71	56
Snails	20	1	11	0	32	27
Insects	33	4	9	0	46	28
Arachnids	12	0	0	0	12	5
Crustaceans	18	0	3	0	21	12
Animal subtotal	379	516	128	39	1,062	387
Flowering plants	564	1	141	0	706	555
Conifers and cycads	2	0	1	2	5	2
Ferns and allies	24	0	2	0	26	26
Lichens	2	0	0	0	2	2
Plant subtotal	592	1	144	2	739	585
Total	971	517	272[3]	41	1,801[3]	972

NOTE: As of April 30, 2001. 1. *Endangered species* are those in danger of extinction. 2. *Threatened species* are those likely to become an endangered species within the foreseeable future. 3. Nine U.S. species have dual status. *Source:* U.S. Fish and Wildlife Service. Web: http://ecos.fws.gov/tess/html/boxscore.html.

America's 13 Most Endangered Rivers (2001)

Each year American Rivers analyzes the condition of the nation's rivers to determine which are the most "endangered." Threats to these rivers include dams and channelizations that are harmful to fish or wildlife populations; depletion due to the rivers' use as a water supply for human populations; and coal mining operations that fill streams with coal and dirt. For more information, refer to the American Rivers web site: http://www.amrivers.org/mer00rivers.html.

Rank	River	State(s)	Threat(s)
1.	Missouri River	Mont., N.D., S.D., Neb., Kans., Iowa, Mo.	Six federal dams
2.	Canning River	Alaska	Oil, gas drilling
3.	Eel River	Calif.	Two dams
4.	Hudson River	N.Y.	PCB pollution
5.	Powder River	Wyo., Mont.	Water pollution from planned natural gas extraction
6.	Mississippi River	Minn., Wis., Iowa, Ill., Mo., Ky., Tenn., Ark., Miss., La.	Two flood control projects
7.	Big Sandy River	W.Va., Ky.	Water pollution from coal mining accident
8.	Snoqualmie River	Wash.	Residential, business development in watershed
9.	Animas River	Colo., N.M.	Water diversion project
10.	East Fork, Lewis River	Wash.	Gravel mine expansion
11.	Paine Run	Va.	Acid rain from coal-fired power plants
12.	Hackensack River	N.Y., N.J.	Residential, business development
13.	Catawba River	N.C., S.C.	Development along banks

Water Supply of the World

The Antarctic Icecap is the largest supply of fresh water, nearly 2% of the world's total of fresh and salt water. As can be seen from the table below, the amount of water in our atmosphere is over ten times as much as the water in all the rivers taken together. The fresh water actually available for human use in lakes and rivers and the accessible ground water amounts to only about one-third of 1% of the world's total water supply.

	Surface area (square miles)	Volume (cubic miles)	Percentage of total[1]
Salt Water			
The oceans	139,500,000	317,000,000	97.2
Inland seas and saline lakes	270,000	25,000	0.008
Fresh Water			
Freshwater lakes	330,000	30,000	0.009
All rivers (average level)	—	300	0.0001
Antarctic Icecap	6,000,000	6,300,000	1.9
Arctic Icecap and glaciers	900,000	680,000	0.21
Water in the atmosphere	197,000,000	3,100	0.001
Ground water within half a mile from surface	—	1,000,000	0.31
Deep-lying ground water	—	1,000,000	0.31
Total (rounded)	—	**326,000,000**	**100.00**

1. All figures are estimated. *Source:* Department of the Interior, Geological Survey.

National Forest System, 1900–2000

Year	Number of forests	Area (million acres)	Year	Number of forests	Area (million acres)
1900	38	46.52	1970	154	182.57
1905	83	75.35	1975	155	183.28
1910	149	168.03	1980	155	183.06
1915	162	162.77	1985	156	186.32
1920	152	156.03	1992	156	187.11
1925	159	158.40	1993	155	187.23
1930	149	160.09	1994	155	187.27
1935	142	163.31	1995	155	187.24
1940	160	174.77	1996	155	187.28
1945	155	177.64	1997	155	187.42
1950	151	179.69	1998	155	187.49
1955	149	180.30	1999	155	187.67
1960	151	180.84	2000	155	187.74
1965	154	182.14			

Source: U.S. Dept. of Agriculture, Forest Service. *Land Areas of the National Forest System.* Web: www.fs.fed.us.

The National Park System

Source: Department of the Interior, National Park Service

The National Park System of the United States is administered by the National Park Service, a bureau of the Department of the Interior. Started with the establishment of Yellowstone National Park on March 1, 1872, the system includes not only the most extraordinary and spectacular scenic exhibits in the United States, but also a large number of sites distinguished either for their historic or prehistoric importance or scientific interest, or for their superior recreational assets. The National Park System is made up of 375 areas covering more than 83 million acres in every state except Delaware. It also includes areas in the District of Columbia, American Samoa, Guam, Puerto Rico, and the Virgin Islands. A list of the areas follows. Note that the National Park System does not include the Affiliated Areas, National Heritage Areas, Wild and Scenic Rivers System, and the National Trails System. See also the excellent website of the Park Service: www.nps.gov.

NATIONAL PARKS

Name, location, and year authorized	Acreage	Outstanding characteristics
Acadia (Maine), 1919	47,656.84	Rugged seashore on Mt. Desert Island and adjacent mainland
Arches (Utah), 1971	76,518.98	Unusual stone arches, windows, pedestals caused by erosion (park was a National Monument 1929–1971)
Badlands (S.D.), 1978	242,755.94	Arid land of fossils, prairie, bison, deer, bighorn sheep, ante-lope (park was a National Monument 1929–1978)
Big Bend (Tex.), 1935	801,163.21	Mountains and desert bordering the Rio Grande
Biscayne (Fla.), 1980	172,924.07	Aquatic, coral reef park south of Miami (park was a National Monument, 1968–1980)
Bryce Canyon (Utah), 1924	35,835.08	Area of grotesque eroded rocks brilliantly colored
Canyonlands (Utah), 1964	337,597.83	Colorful wilderness with impressive red-rock canyons, spires, arches
Capitol Reef (Utah), 1971	241,904.26	Highly colored sedimentary rock formations in high, narrow gorges (park was a National Monument 1937–1971)
Carlsbad Caverns (N.M.), 1930	46,766.45	One of the world's largest known caves
Channel Islands (Calif.), 1980	249,561.00	Area is rich in marine mammals, sea birds, endangered spe-cies, and archeology (park was a National Monument 1938–1980)
Crater Lake (Ore.), 1902	183,224.05	Deep blue lake in heart of inactive volcano
Cuyahoga Valley (Ohio)	32,863.95	Wilderness area offering recreational, historic, and cultural attractions, including scenic rail journeys (park was a National Recreation Area 1974–2000)
Death Valley (Calif.-Nev.), 1994	3,286,241.46	Largest desert, surrounded by high mountains, containing the lowest point in the Western Hemisphere (park was a National Monument 1933–1994)
Denali (Alaska), 1917	4,740,911.72	Contains Mt. McKinley, N. America's highest mountain (20,320 ft) (formerly Mt. McKinley National Park, 1917–1980)
Dry Tortugas (Fla.), 1992	64,701.22	Located 70 mi off Key West. Features an underwater nature trail (formerly Ft. Jefferson National Monument 1935–1992)
Everglades (Fla.), 1934	1,508,571.36	Subtropical area with abundant bird and animal life
Gates of the Arctic (Alaska), 1980	7,523,897.77	Diverse north central wilderness contains part of Brooks Range
Glacier (Mont.), 1910	1,013,572.42	Rocky Mountain scenery with many glaciers and lakes
Glacier Bay (Alaska), 1980	3,224,840.31	Popular for wildlife, whale-watching, glacier-calving, and scen-ery (park was a National Monument 1925–1980)
Grand Canyon (Ariz.), 1919	1,217,403.32	Mile-deep gorge, 4 to 18 mi wide, 217 mi long
Grand Teton (Wyo.), 1929	309,994.02	Picturesque range of high mountain peaks
Great Basin (Nev.), 1986	77,180.00	Exceptional scenic, biologic, and geologic attractions (formerly Lehman Caves National Monument 1922–1986)
Great Sand Dunes (Colo.)	38,662.18	Includes spectacular sand dunes, alpine lakes, tundra, ancient forests, grass and wetlands in the Sangre de Cristo Moun-tains (park was a National Monument 1932–2000)
Great Smoky Mts. (N.C.-Tenn.), 1926	521,490.18	Highest mountain range east of Black Hills; luxuriant plant life
Guadalupe Mountains (Tex.), 1966	86,415.97	Contains highest point in Texas: Guadalupe Peak (8,751 ft)
Haleakala (Hawaii), 1916	29,830.15	World-famous 10,023-foot Haleakala volcano (dormant) (for-merly part of Hawaii National Park. Renamed in 1960)
Hawaii Volcanoes (Hawaii), 1916	209,695.38	Spectacular volcanic area; luxuriant vegetation at lower levels (formerly Hawaii National Park. Renamed in 1961)
Hot Springs (Ark.), 1921	5,549.46	47 mineral hot springs said to have therapeutic value
Isle Royale (Mich.), 1931	571,790.11	Largest wilderness island in Lake Superior; moose, wolves, lakes
Joshua Tree (Calif.), 1994	1,018,198.01	Desert region featuring Joshua trees and a great variety of plants and animals (park was a National Monument 1936–1994)
Katmai (Alaska), 1980	3,674,529.68	Expansion may assure brown bear's preservation. Park is known for fishing, 1912 eruption of Novarupta, bears (park was a National Monument 1918–1980)
Kenai Fjords (Alaska), 1980	669,982.99	Mountain goats, marine mammals, birdlife are features at this seacoast park near Seward (park was a National Monu-ment 1978–1980)

Name, location, and year authorized	Acreage	Outstanding characteristics
Kings Canyon (Calif.), 1890	461,901.20	Huge canyons; high mountains; giant sequoias (formerly General Grant National Park 1890–1940)
Kobuk Valley (Alaska), 1980	1,750,736.86	Native culture and anthropology center around the broad Kobuk River in northwest Alaska (park was a National Monument 1978–1980)
Lake Clark (Alaska), 1980	2,619,733.22	Park provides scenic and wilderness recreation across Cook Inlet from Anchorage (park was a National Monument 1978–1980)
Lassen Volcanic (Calif.), 1916	106,372.36	Exhibits of impressive volcanic phenomena
Mammoth Cave (Ky.), 1926	52,830.19	Vast limestone labyrinth with underground river
Mesa Verde (Colo.), 1906	52,121.93	Best-preserved prehistoric cliff dwellings in United States
Mount Rainier (Wash.), 1899	235,625.00	Single-peak glacial system; dense forests, flowered meadows
National Park of American Samoa, 1988	9,000.00	Samoa National Park, American Samoa: two rain forest preserves and a coral reef on the island of Ofu are home to unique tropical animals. The park also includes several thousand acres on the islands of Tutuila and Ta'u
North Cascades (Wash.), 1968	504,780.94	Roadless Alpine landscape; jagged peaks; mountain lakes; glaciers
Olympic (Wash.), 1938	922,650.94	Finest Pacific Northwest rain forest; scenic mountain park
Petrified Forest (Ariz.), 1962	93,532.57	Extensive natural exhibit of petrified wood (park was a National Monument 1906–1962)
Redwood (Calif.), 1968	112,612.58	Coastal redwood forests; contains world's tallest known tree (369.2 ft)
Rocky Mountain (Colo.), 1915	265,769.14	Section of the Rocky Mountains; 107 named peaks over 10,000 ft
Saguaro (Ariz.), 1994	91,445.96	Giant saguaro cacti, unique to the Sonoran Desert, sometimes reach a height of 50 ft in this cactus forest (park was a National Monument 1933–1994)
Sequoia (Calif.), 1890	402,510.05	Giant sequoias; magnificent High Sierra scenery, including Mt. Whitney
Shenandoah (Va.), 1926	198,979.33	Tree-covered mountains; scenic Skyline Drive
Theodore Roosevelt (N.D.), 1978	70,446.89	Scenic valley of Little Missouri River; T.R. Ranch; wildlife (Theodore Roosevelt National Memorial Park 1947–1978)
Virgin Islands (U.S. V.I.), 1956	14,688.87	Beaches; lush hills; prehistoric Carib Indian relics
Voyageurs (Minn.), 1971	218,200.17	Wildlife, canoeing, fishing, and hiking
Wind Cave (S.D.), 1903	28,295.03	Limestone caverns in Black Hills; buffalo herd
Wrangell-St. Elias (Alaska), 1980	8,323,617.68	Largest Park System area has abundant wildlife, second highest peak in U.S. (Mt. St. Elias); adjoins Canadian park (park was a National Monument 1978–1980)
Yellowstone (Wyo.-Mont.-Idaho), 1872	2,219,790.71	World's greatest geyser area; abundant falls, wildlife, and canyons
Yosemite (Calif.), 1890	761,266.28	Mountains; inspiring gorges and waterfalls; giant sequoias
Zion (Utah), 1919	146,592.31	Multicolored gorge in heart of southern Utah desert

Name and location	Total acreage
National Historical Parks	
Appomattox Court House (Va.)	1,774.56
Boston (Mass.)	43.32
Cane River Creole (La.)	207.38
Chaco Culture (N.M.)	33,974.29
Chesapeake and Ohio Canal (Md.-W.Va.-D.C.)	19,592.98
Colonial (Va.)	9,349.44
Cumberland Gap (Ky.-Tenn.-Va.)	20,454.02
Dayton Aviation Heritage (Ohio)	86.46
George Rogers Clark (Ind.)	26.17
Harpers Ferry (W.Va.-Md.)	2,343.48
Hopewell Culture (Ohio)	1,169.96
Independence (Pa.)	44.88
Jean Lafitte (La.)	20,020.00
Kalaupapa (Hawaii)	10,778.88
Kaloko-Honokohau (Hawaii)	1,160.91
Keweenaw (Mich.)	1,936.81
Klondike Goldrush (Alaska-Wash.)	13,191.35
Lowell (Mass.)	141.24
Lyndon B. Johnson (Tex.)	1,570.15
Marsh-Billings-Rockefeller (Vt.)	643.07

Name and location	Total acreage
Minuteman (Mass.)	965.03
Morristown (N.J.)	1,702.80
Natchez (Miss.)	108.39
New Bedford Whaling (Mass.)	34.00
New Orleans Jazz (La.)	5.13
Nez Perce (Idaho)	2,133.65
Pecos (N.M.)	6,666.79
Pu'uhonua o Honaunau (Hawaii)	181.80
Rosie the Riveter/WW II Home Front (Calif.)	145.19
Salt River Bay and Ecological Preserve (U.S. V.I.)	947.75
San Antonio Missions (Tex.)	816.39
San Francisco Maritime (Calif.)	49.86
San Juan Island (Wash.)	1,751.99
Saratoga (N.Y.)	3,392.42
Sitka (Alaska)	106.83
Tumacacori (Ariz.)	46.28
Valley Forge (Pa.)	3,466.47
War in the Pacific (Guam)	2,030.65
Women's Rights (N.Y.)	7.44

Name and location	Total acreage
National Monuments	
Agate Fossil Beds (Neb.)	3,055.22
Alibates Flint Quarries (Tex.)	1,370.97
Aniakchak (Alaska)	137,176.00
Aztec Ruins (N.M.)	317.71
Bandelier (N.M.)	33,676.67
Black Canyon of the Gunnison (Colo.)	27,705.14
Booker T. Washington (Va.)	223.92
Buck Island Reef (U.S. V.I.)	880.00
Cabrillo (Calif.)	159.94
Canyon de Chelly (Ariz.)	83,840.00
Cape Krusenstern (Alaska)	649,182.18
Capulin Volcano (N.M.)	792.84
Casa Grande Ruins (Ariz.)	472.50
Castillo de San Marcos (Fla.)	20.21
Castle Clinton (N.Y.)	1.00
Cedar Breaks (Utah)	6,154.60
Chiricahua (Ariz.)	11,984.73
Colorado (Colo.)	20,533.93
Congaree Swamp (S.C.)	21,887.53
Craters of the Moon (Idaho)	714,440.05
Devils Postpile (Calif.)	798.46
Devils Tower (Wyo.)	1,346.91
Dinosaur (Utah-Colo.)	210,277.55
Effigy Mounds (Iowa)	2,526.39
El Malpais (N.M.)	114,276.95
El Morro (N.M.)	1,278.72
Florissant Fossil Beds (Colo.)	5,998.09
Fort Frederica (Ga.)	241.42
Fort Matanzas (Fla.)	300.11
Fort McHenry (Md.)	43.26
Fort Pulaski (Ga.)	5,623.10
Fort Stanwix (N.Y.)	15.52
Fort Sumter (S.C.)	199.57
Fort Union (N.M.)	720.60
Fossil Butte (Wyo.)	8,198.00
George Washington Birthplace (Va.)	550.23
George Washington Carver (Mo.)	210.00
Gila Cliff Dwellings (N.M.)	533.13
Governor's Island (N.Y.)	20.00
Grand Canyon–Parashant (Ariz.)	1,217,403.32
Grand Portage (Minn.)	709.97
Hagerman Fossil Beds (Idaho)	4,351.15
Hohokam Pima (Ariz.)	1,690.00
Homestead (Neb.)	195.11
Hovenweep (Utah-Colo.)	784.93
Jewel Cave (S.D.)	1,273.51
John Day Fossil Beds (Ore.)	14,056.73
Lava Beds (Calif.)	46,559.87
Little Big Horn Battlefield (Mont.)	765.34
Montezuma Castle (Ariz.)	857.69
Muir Woods (Calif.)	553.55
Natural Bridges (Utah)	7,636.49
Navajo (Ariz.)	360.00
Ocmulgee (Ga.)	701.54
Oregon Caves (Ore.)	487.98
Organ Pipe Cactus (Ariz.)	330,688.50
Petroglyph (N.M.)	7,231.63
Pinnacles (Calif.)	16,265.44
Pipe Spring (Ariz.)	40.00
Pipestone (Minn.)	281.78
Poverty Point (La.)	910.85
Rainbow Bridge (Utah)	160.00
Russell Cave (Ala.)	310.45
Salinas Pueblo Missions (N.M.)	1,071.42
Scotts Bluff (Neb.)	3,003.30

Name and location	Total acreage
Statue of Liberty (N.Y.-N.J.)	58.38
Sunset Crater Volcano (Ariz.)	3,040.00
Timpanogos Cave (Utah)	250.00
Tonto (Ariz.)	1,120.00
Tuzigoot (Ariz.)	800.62
U.S. Virgin Islands Coral Reef (V.I.)	12,700.00
Walnut Canyon (Ariz.)	3,579.46
White Sands (N.M.)	143,732.92
Wupatki (Ariz.)	35,422.13
Yucca House (Colo.)	33.97
National Preserves	
Aniakchak (Alaska)	465,603.00
Bering Land Bridge (Alaska)	2,697,405.72
Big Cypress (Fla.)	720,570.67
Big Thicket (Tex.)	97,191.01
Denali (Alaska)	1,334,117.99
Gates of the Arctic (Alaska)	948,628.90
Glacier Bay (Alaska)	58,406.00
Great Sand Dunes (Colo.)	41,686.00
Katmai (Alaska)	418,699.22
Lake Clark (Alaska)	1,410,291.92
Little River Canyon (Ala.)	13,632.96
Mojave (Calif.)	1,497,437.54
Noatak (Alaska)	6,569,904.43
Tallgrass Prairie (Kans.)	10,894.00
Timucuan Ecological and Historic Preserve (Fla.)	46,019.00
Wrangell-St. Elias (Alaska)	4,852,753.24
Yukon-Charley (Alaska)	2,526,512.31
National Reserves	
City of Rocks (Idaho)	14,107.19
Ebey's Landing (Wash.)	19,018.64
National Military Parks	
Chickamauga and Chattanooga (Ga.-Tenn.)	8,190.04
Fredericksburg and Spotsylvania (Va.)	8,382.60
Gettysburg Nat. Mil. Park (Pa.)	5,992.09
Guilford Courthouse (N.C.)	220.69
Horseshoe Bend (Ala.)	2,040.00
Kings Mountain (S.C.)	3,945.29
Pea Ridge (Ark.)	4,300.35
Shiloh Nat. Park (Tenn.)	3,989.46
Vicksburg Nat. Mil. Park (Miss.)	1,737.65
National Battlefields	
Antietam (Md.)	3,364.93
Big Hole (Mont.)	655.61
Cowpens (S.C.)	841.56
Fort Donelson (Tenn.)	551.69
Fort Necessity (Pa.)	902.80
Monocacy (Md.)	1,647.01
Moores Creek (N.C.)	87.75
Petersburg (Va.)	2,659.19
Stones River (Tenn.)	713.63
Tupelo (Miss.)	1.00
Wilson's Creek (Mo.)	1,749.91
National Battlefield Parks	
Kennesaw Mountain (Ga.)	2,884.14
Manassas (Va.)	5,071.62
Richmond (Va.)	1,718.15
National Battlefield Site	
Brices Cross Roads (Miss.)	1.00

Name and location	Total acreage
National Historic Sites	
Abraham Lincoln Birthplace (Ky.)	116.50
Adams (Mass.)	13.82
Allegheny Portage Railroad (Pa.)	1,249.20
Andersonville (Ga.)	494.61
Andrew Johnson (Tenn.)	16.68
Bent's Old Fort (Colo.)	798.80
Boston African-American (Mass.)	0.59
Brown v. Board of Education (Kans.)	1.85
Carl Sandburg Home (N.C.)	263.65
Charles Pinckney (S.C.)	28.45
Christiansted (U.S. V.I.)	27.15
Clara Barton (Md.)	8.59
Edgar Allan Poe (Pa.)	0.52
Edison (N.J.)	21.25
Eisenhower (Pa.)	690.46
Eleanor Roosevelt (N.Y.)	180.50
Eugene O'Neill (Calif.)	13.19
First Ladies (Ohio)	0.33
Ford's Theatre (Lincoln Museum) (D.C.)	0.29
Fort Bowie (Ariz.)	999.45
Fort Davis (Tex.)	473.87
Fort Laramie (Wyo.)	832.85
Fort Larned (Kan.)	718.39
Fort Point (Calif.)	29.00
Fort Raleigh (N.C.)	512.93
Fort Scott (Kan.)	16.69
Fort Smith (Ark.-Okla.)	75.05
Fort Union Trading Post (N.D.-Mont.)	443.81
Fort Vancouver (Wash.)	208.89
Frederick Douglass Home (D.C.)	8.53
Frederick Law Olmsted (Mass.)	7.21
Friendship Hill (Pa.)	674.56
Golden Spike (Utah)	2,735.28
Grant-Kohrs Ranch (Mont.)	1,618.38
Hampton (Md.)	62.04
Harry S. Truman (Mo.)	6.67
Herbert Hoover (Iowa)	186.80
Home of F. D. Roosevelt (N.Y.)	799.97
Hopewell Furnace (Pa.)	848.06
Hubbell Trading Post (Ariz.)	160.09
James A. Garfield (Ohio)	7.82
Jimmy Carter (Ga.)	70.86
John F. Kennedy (Mass.)	0.09
John Muir (Calif.)	344.73
Knife River Indian Villages (N.D.)	1,758.35
Lincoln Home (Ill.)	12.24
Little Rock Central High School (Ark.)	17.95
Longfellow (Mass.)	1.98
Maggie L. Walker (Va.)	1.29
Manzanar (Calif.)	813.81
Martin Luther King, Jr. (Ga.)	38.70
Martin Van Buren (N.Y.)	39.55
Mary McLeod Bethune Council House (D.C.)	0.07
Minuteman Missile (S.D.)	15.00
Nicodemus (Kans.)	161.35
Ninety Six (S.C.)	989.14
Palo Alto Battlefield (Tex.)	3,357.42
Pennsylvania Avenue (D.C.)	0.00
Puukohola Heiau (Hawaii)	86.24
Sagamore Hill (N.Y.)	83.02
Saint-Gaudens (N.H.)	148.15
Saint Paul's Church (N.Y.)	6.13
Salem Maritime (Mass.)	9.02
San Juan (P.R.)	75.13

Name and location	Total acreage
Saugus Iron Works (Mass.)	8.51
Springfield Armory (Mass.)	54.93
Steamtown (Pa.)	62.48
Theodore Roosevelt Birthplace (N.Y.)	0.11
Theodore Roosevelt Inaugural (N.Y.)	1.03
Thomas Stone (Md.)	328.25
Tuskegee Airmen (Ala.)	86.69
Tuskegee Institute (Ala.)	57.92
Ulysses S. Grant (Mo.)	9.60
Vanderbilt Mansion (N.Y.)	211.65
Washita Battlefield (Okla.)	315.20
Weir Farms (Conn.)	74.30
Whitman Mission (Wash.)	98.15
William Howard Taft (Ohio)	3.10
National Memorials	
Arkansas Post (Ark.)	746.88
Arlington House, the Robert E. Lee Memorial (Va.)	27.91
Chamizal (Tex.)	54.90
Coronado (Ariz.)	4,750.22
De Soto (Fla.)	26.84
Federal Hall (N.Y.)	0.45
Fort Caroline (Fla.)	138.39
Fort Clatsop (Ore.)	125.20
Franklin Delano Roosevelt Memorial (D.C.)	7.50
General Grant (N.Y.)	0.76
Hamilton Grange (N.Y.)	1.04
Jefferson National Expansion Memorial (Mo.)	192.83
Johnstown Flood (Pa.)	164.12
Korean War Veterans (D.C.)	2.20
Lincoln Boyhood (Ind.)	199.65
Lincoln Memorial (D.C.)	107.43
Lyndon Baines Johnson Memorial Grove on the Potomac (D.C.)	17.00
Mount Rushmore (S.D.)	1,278.45
Oklahoma City (Okla.)	6.24
Perry's Victory and International Peace Memorial (Ohio)	25.38
Roger Williams (R.I.)	4.56
Thaddeus Kosciuszko (Pa.)	0.02
Theodore Roosevelt Island (D.C.)	88.50
Thomas Jefferson Memorial (D.C.)	18.36
USS *Arizona* Memorial (Hawaii)	10.50
Vietnam Veterans Memorial (D.C.)	2.00
Washington Monument (D.C.)	106.01
Wright Brothers (N.C.)	428.44
National Seashores	
Assateague Island (Md.-Va.)	39,732.86
Canaveral (Fla.)	57,661.69
Cape Cod (Mass.)	43,604.38
Cape Hatteras (N.C.)	30,321.46
Cape Lookout (N.C.)	28,243.36
Cumberland Island (Ga.)	36,415.13
Fire Island (N.Y.)	19,579.59
Gulf Islands (Fla.-Miss.)	137,457.89
Padre Island (Tex.)	130,434.27
Point Reyes (Calif.)	71,067.54
National Parkways	
Blue Ridge (Va.-N.C.)	90,860.28
George Washington Memorial (Va.-Md.)	7,247.63
John D. Rockefeller, Jr., Memorial (Wyo.)	23,777.22

Name and location	Total acreage
Natchez Trace (Miss.-Tenn.-Ala.)	51,980.15

National Lakeshores
Apostle Islands (Wis.)	69,371.89
Indiana Dunes (Ind.)	15,062.46
Pictured Rocks (Mich.)	73,228.37
Sleeping Bear Dunes (Mich.)	71,194.57

National Park System Rivers
Alagnak Wild River (Alaska)	30,665.45
Big South Fork National River and Recreation Area (Ky.-Tenn.)	125,310.34
Bluestone National Scenic River (W. Va.)	4,309.51
Buffalo National River (Ark.)	94,294.06
Delaware National Scenic River (Pa.)	1,973.33
Great Egg Harbor Scenic and Recreational River (N.J.-Pa.)	43,311.42
Mississippi National River and Recreation Area (Minn.)	53,775.00
Missouri National Recreational River (Neb.)	45,350.00
New River Gorge National River (W.Va.)	69,832.19
Niobrara National Scenic Riverway (Neb.)	5,962.00
Obed Wild and Scenic River (Tenn.)	5,173.69
Ozark National Scenic Riverways (Mo.)	80,785.04
Rio Grande Wild and Scenic River (Tex.)	9,600.00
St. Croix National Scenic River (Minn.-Wis.)	92,735.00
Upper Delaware Scenic and Recreational River (Pa.)	75,004.80

National Recreation Areas
Amistad (Tex.)	58,500.00
Bighorn Canyon (Wyo.-Mont.)	120,296.22
Boston Harbor Islands (Mass.)	1,482.25
Chattahoochee River (Ga.)	9,329.95
Chickasaw (Okla.)	9,888.83
Curecanti (Colo.)	41,972.42
Delaware Water Gap (Pa.-N.J.)	66,749.32
Gateway (N.Y.-N.J.)	26,610.38
Gauley River (W. Va.)	11,505.55
Glen Canyon (Ariz.-Utah)	1,254,306.19
Golden Gate (Calif.)	74,825.14
Lake Chelan (Wash.)	61,957.92
Lake Mead (Ariz.-Nev.)	1,495,665.69
Lake Meredith (Tex.)	44,977.63
Lake Roosevelt (Wash.)	100,390.31
Ross Lake (Wash.)	117,574.59

Name and location	Total acreage
Santa Monica Mountains (Calif.)	153,686.66
Whiskeytown-Shasta-Trinity (Calif.)	42,503.46

National Scenic Trails
Appalachian (Maine-N.H.-Vt.-Mass.-Conn.-N.Y.-N.J.-Pa.-Md.-W.Va.-Va.-N.C.-Tenn., Ga.)	214,361.57
Natchez Trace (Ala.-Miss.-Tenn.)	10,995.00
Potomac Heritage (D.C.-Md.-Va.-Pa.)	n.a.

International Historic Site
Saint Croix Island (Maine)	44.90

National Cemeteries[1]
Andersonville (Ga.)	494.61
Andrew Johnson (Tenn.)	16.68
Antietam (Md.)	11.36
Battleground (D.C.)	1.03
Chalmette Cemetery (La.)	17.5
Fort Donelson (Tenn.)	15.30
Fredericksburg (Va.)	12.00
Gettysburg (Pa.)	20.58
Little Big Horn (Mont.)	765.34
Poplar Grove (Va.)	8.72
Shiloh (Tenn.)	10.05
Stones River (Tenn.)	719.81
Vicksburg (Miss.)	116.28
Yorktown (Va.)	2.91

1. The National Cemeteries are not independent areas of the National Park System; each is part of a military park, battlefield, etc., except Battleground. Their acreage is kept separately. Arlington National Cemetery is under the Department of the Army.

Other Parks
Catoctin Mountain (Md.)	5,809.86
Constitution Gardens (D.C.)	52.00
Fort Washington Park (Md.)	341.00
Greenbelt (Md.)	1,175.99
National Capital Parks (D.C.)	6,605.44
National Mall (D.C.)	146.35
Piscataway (Md.)	4,626.52
Prince William Forest (Va.)	18,714.12
Rock Creek Park (D.C.)	1,754.70
White House (D.C.)	18.07
Wolf Trap Farm Park for the Performing Arts (Va.)	130.28

Ten Most Visited National Park Sites, 2000

Rank	Name and location	Number of visitors
1.	Blue Ridge Parkway, Va.-N.C.	19,153,081
2.	Golden Gate Nat'l. Recreation Area, Calif.	14,486,065
3.	Great Smoky Mountains Nat'l. Park, Tenn.	10,175,812
4.	Lake Mead Nat'l. Recreation Area, Nev.-Ariz.	8,755,005
5.	Gateway Nat'l. Recreation Area, N.Y.-N.J.	7,927,567
6.	George Washington Memorial Parkway, Va.-Md.-D.C.	7,897,161
7.	Natchez Trace Parkway, Miss.-Ala.-Tenn.	5,737,183
8.	Statue of Liberty Nat'l. Monument, N.Y.-N.J.	5,509,706
9.	Delaware Water Gap Nat'l. Recreation Area, Pa.-N.J.	4,900,745
10.	Gulf Islands Nat'l. Seashore, Fla.-Miss.	4,590,595

Source: Based on data from the National Park Service. Web: www.nps.gov.

Billion Dollar U.S. Weather Disasters, 1980–2001

Source: National Climatic Data Center

The U.S. has sustained 49 weather-related disasters over the past 22 years in which overall damages and costs reached or exceeded $1 billion. Seven occurred during 1998 alone—the most for any year on record, though other years have recorded higher damage totals. All figures below reflect direct and indirect damages, costs, and deaths.

Two damage figures are given for events prior to 1996: the first represents actual dollar costs and is not adjusted for inflation. The second (in parentheses) is the dollar cost normalized to 1998 dollars using a GNP inflation/wealth index. The total normalized losses for the 49 events are over $280 billion.

2001
Tropical Storm Allison (June); preliminary estimate of approximately $5.0 billion; 41 deaths.
2000
Drought/Heat Wave (Spring–Summer); preliminary estimate more than $4.0 billion; estimated 140 deaths nationwide.
Western Fire Season (Spring–Summer); more than $2.0 billion; no deaths reported.
1999
Hurricane Floyd (Sept.); at least $6.0 billion; 77 deaths.
Eastern Drought/Heat Wave (Summer); more than $1.0 billion; estimated 502 deaths.
Oklahoma-Kansas Tornadoes (May); at least $1.1 billion; 55 deaths.
Arkansas-Tennessee Tornadoes (Jan.); approximately $1.3 billion; 17 deaths.
1998
Texas Flooding (Oct.–Nov.); approximately $1.0 billion; 31 deaths.
Hurricane Georges (Sept.); estimated $5.9 billion; 16 deaths.
Hurricane Bonnie (Aug.); approximately $1.0 billion; 3 deaths.
Southern Drought/Heat Wave (Summer); $6.0–$9.0 billion; at least 200 deaths.
Minnesota Severe Storms/Hail (May); more than $1.5 billion; 1 death.
Southeast Tornadoes and Flooding (Winter–Spring); more than $1.0 billion; at least 132 deaths.
Northeast Ice Storm (Jan.); more than $1.4 billion; 16 deaths.
1997
Northern Plains Flooding (April–May); approximately $3.7 billion; 11 deaths.
Mississippi and Ohio Valleys Flooding and Tornadoes (March); estimated $1.0 billion; 67 deaths.
West Coast Flooding (Dec. 1996–Jan. 1997); approximately $3.0 billion; 36 deaths.
1996
Hurricane Fran (Sept.); more than $5.0 billion; 37 deaths.
Southern Plains Severe Drought (Fall 1995–Summer 1996); approximately $5.0 billion; no deaths.
Pacific Northwest Severe Flooding (Feb.); approximately $1.0 billion; 9 deaths.
Blizzard of '96 and Flooding (Jan.); approximately $3.0 billion; 187 deaths.
1995
Hurricane Opal (Oct.); more than $3.0 billion (3.3); 27 deaths.
Hurricane Marilyn (Sept.); estimated $2.1 (2.3) billion; 13 deaths.
Southern Severe Weather and Flooding (May); $5.0–$6.0 (5.5–6.6) billion; 32 deaths.
California Flooding (Jan.–March); more than $3.0 (3.3) billion; 27 deaths.

1994
Western Fire Season (Summer–Fall); approximately $1.0 (1.1) billion; death toll undetermined.
Texas Flooding (Oct.); approximately $1.0 (1.1) billion; 19 deaths.
Tropical Storm Alberto (July); approximately $1.0 (1.1) billion; 32 deaths.
Southeast Ice Storm (Feb.); approximately $3.0 (3.3) billion; 9 deaths.
1993
California Wildfires (Fall); approximately $1.0 (1.1) billion; 4 deaths.
Midwest Flooding (Summer); approximately $21.0 (23.1) billion; 48 deaths.
Drought/Heat Wave (Summer); about $1.0 (1.1) billion; at least 16 deaths.
"Storm of the Century" Blizzard (March); $3.0–$6.0 (3.3–6.6) billion; approximately 270 deaths.
1992
Nor'easter of 1992 (Dec.); $1.0–$2.0 (1.2–2.4) billion; 19 deaths.
Hurricane Iniki (Sept.); about $1.8 (2.2) billion; 7 deaths.
Hurricane Andrew (Aug.); approximately $27.0 (32.4) billion; 61 deaths.
1991
Oakland Firestorm (Oct.): approximately $2.5 (3.3) billion; 25 deaths.
Hurricane Bob (Aug.); $1.5 (2.0) billion; 18 deaths.
1990
Texas/Oklahoma/Louisiana/Arkansas Flooding (May); more than $1.0 (1.3) billion; 13 deaths.
1989
Hurricane Hugo (Sept.); more than $9.0 (12.6) billion; 86 deaths.
Northern Plains Drought (Summer); at least $1.0 (1.4) billion; no deaths reported.
1988
Drought/Heat Wave (Summer); estimated $40.0 (56.0) billion; estimated 5,000 to 10,000 deaths.
1986
Southeast Drought/Heat Wave (Summer); $1.0–$1.5 (1.6–2.4) billion; estimated 100 deaths.
1985
Hurricane Juan (Oct.–Nov.); $1.5 (2.6) billion; 63 deaths.
Hurricane Elena (Aug.–Sept.); $1.3 (2.2) billion; 4 deaths.
Florida Freeze (Jan.); about $1.2 (2.0) billion; no deaths.
1983
Florida Freeze (Dec.); about $2.0 (3.6) billion; no deaths.
Hurricane Alicia (Aug.); $3.0 (5.4) billion; 21 deaths.
1980
Drought/Heat Wave (June–Sept.); estimated $20.0 (44.0) billion; estimated 10,000 deaths.

Retired Hurricane Names

Because hurricanes often occur at the same time, officials assign short, distinctive names to the storms to avoid confusion among weather stations, coastal bases, and ships at sea. Prior to 1979, only female names were used to name hurricanes. That year, the United States began alternating between male and female names in the Atlantic Ocean and Gulf of Mexico. When hurricanes are particularly destructive, their names are retired from the list of usable titles. Below is a list of infamous hurricanes which have settled into retirement.

Name	Year	Location(s) affected	Name	Year	Location(s) affected
Agnes	1972	Florida, Northeast U.S.	Elena	1985	Mississippi, Alabama, Western Florida
Alicia	1983	North Texas	Ekiuse	1975	Antilles, Northwest Florida, Alabama
Allen	1980	Antilles, Mexico, South Texas	Flora	1963	Haiti, Cuba
Andrew	1992	Bahamas, South Florida, and Louisiana	Frederic	1979	Alabama and Mississippi
Anita	1977	Mexico	Gilbert	1988	Lesser Antilles, Jamaica, Yucatan
Audrey	1957	Louisiana, North Texas			Peninsula, Mexico
Betsy	1965	Bahamas, Southeast Florida, Southeast Louisiana	Gloria	1985	North Carolina, Northeast U.S.
			Hattie	1961	Belize, Guatemala
Beulah	1967	Antilles, Mexico, South Texas	Hazel	1954	Antilles, North and South Carolina
Bob	1991	North Carolina, Northeast U.S.	Hilda	1964	Louisiana
Camille	1969	Louisiana, Mississippi, and Alabama	Hugo	1989	Antilles, South Carolina
Carla	1961	Texas	Ione	1955	North Carolina
Carmen	1974	Mexico	Inez	1966	Lesser Antilles, Hispanola, Cuba,
Carol	1954	Northeast U.S.			Florida Keys, Mexico
Celia	1970	South Texas	Janet	1955	Lesser Antilles, Belize, Mexico
Cleo	1964	Lesser Antilles, Haiti, Cuba, Southeast Florida	Joan	1988	Curacao, Venezuela, Colombia, Nicaragua (crossed Pacific and became
Connie	1955	North Carolina			Miriam)
David	1979	Lesser Antilles, Hispanola, Florida, and Eastern U.S.	Klaus	1990	Martinique
			Luis	1995	Lesser Antilles
Diana	1990	Mexico	Marilyn	1995	Lesser Antilles, Puerto Rico
Diane	1955	Mid-Atlantic U.S. and Northeast U.S.	Mitch	1998	Central America, Nicaragua, Honduras
Donna	1960	Bahamas, Florida, and Eastern U.S.	Opal	1995	Central America, Mexico, Florida
Dora	1964	Northeast Florida	Roxanne	1995	Mexico

Source: U.S. Department of Commerce, NOAA, National Weather Service.

Costliest Hurricanes in the United States[1]
(U.S. Mainland)

Rank	Hurricane	Location	Year	Category[2]	Damage (in billions)	Rank	Hurricane	Location	Year	Category[2]	Damage (in billions)
1.	Andrew	Fla./La.	1992	4	$26.5	6.	Agnes	NE U.S.	1972	1	2.1
2.	Hugo	S.C.	1989	4	7.0	7.	Alicia	Tex.	1983	3	2.0
3.	Fran	N.C.	1996	3	3.2	8.	Bob	N.C./NE U.S.	1991	2	1.5
4.	Opal	Fla./Ala.	1995	3	3.0	9.	Juan	La.	1985	1	1.5
5.	Frederic	Ala./Miss.	1979	3	2.3	10.	Camille	Miss./Ala.	1969	5	1.4

1. 1900–1996. 2. Saffir-Simpson Hurricane scale: Cat. 1 = weak; Cat. 5 = devastating. *Source:* National Oceanic and Atmospheric Administration.

Deadliest Hurricanes in the United States[1]
(U.S. Mainland)

Rank	Hurricane	Year	Category[2]	Deaths	Rank	Hurricane	Year	Category[2]	Deaths
1.	Galveston, Tex.	1900	4	8,000[3]	6.	Audrey (SW La./N. Tex.)	1957	4	390
2.	Lake Okeechobee, Fla.	1928	4	1,836	7.	NE U.S.	1944	3[5]	390[6]
3.	Florida Keys/S. Tex.	1919	4	600[4]	8.	Grand Isle, La.	1909	4	350
4.	New England	1938	3[5]	600	9.	New Orleans, La.	1915	4	275
5.	Florida Keys	1935	5	408	10.	Galveston, Tex.	1915	4	275

1. 1900–1996. 2. Saffir-Simpson Hurricane scale: Cat. 1 = weak; Cat. 5 = devastating. 3. May actually been as high as 10,000 to 12,000. 4. Over 500 of these lost on ships at sea; 600–900 estimated deaths. 5. Moving more than 30 mph. 6. Some 344 of these lost on ships at sea. *Source:* National Oceanic and Atmospheric Administration.

Most Intense[1] Hurricanes in the United States[2]
(U.S. Mainland)

Rank	Hurricane	Year	Category[3]	Rank	Hurricane	Year	Category[3]
1.	Florida Keys	1935	5	6.	Donna (Fla./Eastern U.S.)	1960	4
2.	Camille (Miss./La./Va.)	1969	5	7.	Galveston, Tex.	1900	4
3.	Andrew (Fla./La.)	1992	4	7.	Grand Isle, La.	1909	4
4.	Florida Keys/Tex.	1919	4	7.	New Orleans, La.	1915	4
5.	Lake Okeechobee, Fla.	1928	4	7.	Carla (Tex.)	1961	4

1. Intensity is for time of landfall. May have been stronger at other times. 2. 1900–1996. 3. Saffir-Simpson Hurricane scale: Cat. 1 = weak; Cat. 5 = devastating. *Source:* National Oceanic and Atmospheric Administration.

Climate of 100 Selected U.S. Cities

City	Average monthly temperature (°F)[1]				Precipitation		Snowfall	
					Average annual		Average annual	
	Jan.	April	July	Oct.	(in.)[1]	(days)[2]	(in.)[2]	Years[2]
Albany, N.Y.	21.1	46.6	71.4	50.5	35.74	134	65.5	38
Albuquerque, N.M.	34.8	55.1	78.8	57.4	8.12	59	10.6	45
Anchorage, Alaska	13.0	35.4	58.1	34.6	15.20	115	69.2	41[3]
Asheville, N.C.	36.8	55.7	73.2	56.0	47.71	124	17.5	20
Atlanta, Ga.	41.9	61.8	78.6	62.2	48.61	115	1.9	50
Atlantic City, N.J.	31.8	51.0	74.4	55.5	41.93	112	16.4	40[3]
Austin, Texas	49.1	68.7	84.7	69.8	31.50	83	0.9	43
Baltimore, Md.	32.7	54.0	76.8	56.9	41.84	113	21.8	34
Baton Rouge, La.	50.8	68.4	82.1	68.2	55.77	108	0.1	34[3]
Billings, Mont.	20.9	44.6	72.3	49.3	15.09	96	57.2	50
Birmingham, Ala.	42.9	62.8	80.1	62.6	54.52	117	1.3	41
Bismarck, N.D.	6.7	42.5	70.4	46.1	15.36	96	40.3	45
Boise, Idaho	29.9	48.6	74.6	51.9	11.71	92	21.4	45
Boston, Mass.	29.6	48.7	73.5	54.8	43.81	127	41.8	49[3]
Bridgeport, Conn.	29.5	48.6	74.0	56.0	41.56	117	26.0	36
Buffalo, N.Y.	23.5	45.4	70.7	51.5	37.52	169	92.2	41
Burlington, Vt.	16.6	42.7	69.6	47.9	33.69	153	78.2	41
Caribou, Maine	10.7	37.3	65.1	43.1	36.59	160	113.3	45
Casper, Wyo.	22.2	42.1	70.9	47.1	11.43	95	80.5	34
Charleston, S.C.	47.9	64.3	80.5	65.8	51.59	113	0.6	42
Charleston, W.Va.	32.9	55.3	74.5	55.9	42.43	151	31.5	37
Charlotte, N.C.	40.5	60.3	78.5	60.7	43.16	111	6.1	45
Cheyenne, Wyo.	26.1	41.8	68.9	47.5	13.31	98	54.1	49
Chicago, Ill.	21.4	48.8	73.0	53.5	33.34	127	40.3	26
Cleveland, Ohio	25.5	48.1	71.6	53.2	35.40	156	53.6	43
Columbia, S.C.	44.7	63.8	81.0	63.4	49.12	109	1.9	37
Columbus, Ohio	27.1	51.4	73.8	53.9	36.97	137	28.3	37[3]
Concord, N.H.	19.9	44.1	69.5	48.3	36.53	125	64.5	43
Dallas-Ft. Worth, Texas	44.0	65.9	86.3	67.9	29.46	78	3.1	31
Denver, Colo.	29.5	47.4	73.4	51.9	15.31	88	59.8	50
Des Moines, Iowa	18.6	50.5	76.3	54.2	30.83	107	34.7	45
Detroit, Mich.	23.4	47.3	71.9	51.9	30.97	133	40.4	26
Dodge City, Kan.	29.5	54.3	80.0	57.7	20.66	78	19.5	42
Duluth, Minn.	6.3	38.3	65.4	44.2	29.68	135	77.4	41[3]
El Paso, Texas	44.2	63.6	82.5	63.6	7.82	47	5.2	45
Fairbanks, Alaska	−12.7	30.2	61.5	25.1	10.37	106	67.5	33
Fargo, N.D.	4.3	42.1	70.6	46.3	19.59	100	35.9	42
Grand Junction, Colo.	25.5	51.7	78.9	54.9	8.00	72	26.1	38
Grand Rapids, Mich.	22.0	46.3	71.4	50.9	34.35	143	72.4	21
Hartford, Conn.	25.2	48.8	73.4	52.4	44.39	127	50.0	30
Helena, Mont.	18.1	42.3	67.9	45.1	11.37	96	47.9	44
Honolulu, Hawaii	72.6	75.7	80.1	79.5	23.47	100	0.0	38[3]
Houston, Texas	51.4	68.7	83.1	69.7	44.76	105	0.4	50
Indianapolis, Ind.	26.0	52.4	75.1	54.8	39.12	125	23.1	53[3]
Jackson, Miss.	45.7	65.1	81.9	65.0	52.82	109	1.2	21
Jacksonville, Fla.	53.2	67.7	81.3	69.5	52.76	116	T	43
Juneau, Alaska	21.8	39.1	55.7	41.8	53.15	220	102.8	41
Kansas City, Mo.	28.4	56.9	80.9	59.6	29.27	98	20.0	43
Knoxville, Tenn.	38.2	59.6	77.6	59.5	47.29	127	12.3	42
Las Vegas, Nev.	44.5	63.5	90.2	67.5	4.19	26	1.4	36
Lexington, Ky.	31.5	55.1	75.9	56.8	45.68	131	16.3	40
Little Rock, Ark.	39.9	62.4	82.1	63.1	49.20	104	5.4	42
Long Beach, Calif.	55.2	60.9	72.8	67.5	11.54	32	T	41[3]
Los Angeles, Calif.	56.0	59.5	69.0	66.3	12.08	36	T	49
Louisville, Ky.	32.5	56.6	77.6	57.7	43.56	125	17.5	37
Madison, Wisc.	15.6	45.8	70.6	49.5	30.84	118	40.8	36
Memphis, Tenn.	39.6	62.6	82.1	62.9	51.57	107	5.5	34
Miami, Fla.	67.1	75.3	82.5	77.9	57.55	129	0.0	42
Milwaukee, Wisc.	18.7	44.6	70.5	50.9	30.94	125	47.0	44
Minneapolis–St. Paul, Minn.	11.2	46.0	73.1	49.6	26.36	115	48.9	46
Mobile, Ala.	50.8	68.0	82.2	68.5	64.64	123	0.3	43
Montgomery, Ala.	46.7	65.2	81.7	65.3	49.16	108	0.3	40
Mt. Washington, N.H.	5.1	22.4	48.7	30.5	89.92	209	246.8	52
Nashville, Tenn.	37.1	59.7	79.4	60.2	48.49	119	11.1	43
Newark, N.J.	31.2	52.1	76.8	57.2	42.34	122	28.2	43
New Orleans, La.	52.4	68.7	82.1	69.2	59.74	114	0.2	38[3]
New York, N.Y.	31.8	51.9	76.4	57.5	42.82	119	26.1	40[3]

City	Average monthly temperature (°F)[1]				Precipitation		Snowfall	
						Average annual	Average annual	
	Jan.	April	July	Oct.	(in.)[1]	(days)[2]	(in.)[2]	Years[2]
Norfolk, Va.	39.9	58.2	78.4	61.3	45.22	115	7.9	36
Oklahoma City, Okla.	35.9	60.2	82.1	62.3	30.89	82	9.0	45
Olympia, Wash.	37.2	47.3	63.0	50.1	50.96	164	18.0	43
Omaha, Neb.	20.2	52.2	77.7	54.5	30.34	98	31.1	49[3]
Philadelphia, Pa.	31.2	52.9	76.5	56.5	41.42	117	21.9	42[3]
Phoenix, Ariz.	52.3	68.1	92.3	73.4	7.11	36	T	47[3]
Pittsburgh, Pa.	26.7	50.1	72.0	52.5	36.30	154	44.6	32
Portland, Maine	21.5	42.8	68.1	48.5	43.52	128	72.4	44
Portland, Ore.	38.9	50.4	67.7	54.3	37.39	154	6.8	44
Providence, R.I.	28.2	47.9	72.5	53.2	45.32	124	37.1	31
Raleigh, N.C.	39.6	59.4	77.7	59.7	41.76	112	7.7	40
Reno, Nev.	32.2	46.4	69.5	50.3	7.49	51	25.3	42
Richmond, Va.	36.6	57.9	77.8	58.6	44.07	113	14.6	47
Roswell, N.M.	41.4	61.9	81.4	61.7	9.70	52	11.4	37[3]
Sacramento, Calif.	45.3	58.2	75.6	63.9	17.10	58	0.1	36[3]
Salt Lake City, Utah	28.6	49.2	77.5	53.0	15.31	90	59.1	56
San Antonio, Texas	50.4	69.6	84.6	70.2	29.13	81	0.4	42
San Diego, Calif.	56.8	61.2	70.3	67.5	9.32	43	T	44
San Francisco, Calif.	48.5	54.8	62.2	60.6	19.71	63	T	57
Savannah, Ga.	49.1	66.0	81.2	66.9	49.70	111	0.3	34
Seattle-Tacoma, Wash.	39.1	48.7	64.8	52.4	38.60	158	12.8	40
Sioux Falls, S.D.	12.4	46.4	74.0	49.4	24.12	96	39.9	39
Spokane, Wash.	25.7	45.8	69.7	47.5	16.71	114	51.5	37
Springfield, Ill.	24.6	53.3	76.5	56.0	33.78	114	24.5	37
St. Louis, Mo.	28.8	56.1	78.9	57.9	33.91	111	19.8	48[3]
Tampa, Fla.	59.8	71.5	82.1	74.4	46.73	107	T	38
Toledo, Ohio	23.1	47.8	71.8	51.7	31.78	137	38.3	29
Tucson, Ariz.	51.1	64.9	86.2	70.4	11.14	52	1.2	44
Tulsa, Okla.	35.2	61.0	83.2	62.6	38.77	89	9.0	46
Vero Beach, Fla.	61.9	71.7	81.1	75.2	51.41	n.a.	n.a.	0
Washington, D.C.	35.2	56.7	78.9	59.3	39.00	112	17.0	41[3]
Wichita, Kan.	29.6	56.3	81.4	59.1	28.61	85	16.4	31
Wilmington, Del.	31.2	52.4	76.0	56.3	41.38	117	20.9	37

1. Based on 30-year period 1951–80. Data latest available. 2. Data through 1984 based on number of years as indicated in Years column. 3. For snowfall data where number of years differs from that for precipitation data. T = trace. n.a. = not available. *Source:* National Oceanic and Atmospheric Administration.

Greatest Snowfalls

	Place	Date	Inches	Centimeters
1 month (U.S.)	Tamarack, Calif.	Jan. 1911	390	991
24 hours (N. America)	Silver Lake, Colo.	April 14–15, 1921	76	195.6
24 hours (Alaska)	Thompson Pass	Dec. 29, 1955	62	157.5
19 hours (France)	Bessans	April 5–6, 1969	68	173
1 storm (N. America)	Mt. Shasta Ski Bowl, Calif.	Feb. 13–19, 1959	189	480
1 storm (Alaska)	Thompson Pass	Dec. 26–31, 1955	175	445.5
1 season (N. America)	Mount Baker, Wash.	1998–1999	1,140	2,895.6
1 season (Alaska)	Thompson Pass	1952–1953	974.5	2,475
1 season (Canada)	Revelstoke Mt. Copeland, British Columbia	1971–1972	964	2,446.5

Source: U.S. Army Corps of Engineers, Engineer Topographic Laboratories.

Recorded Weather Extremes

Highest average annual mean temperature (world): Dallol, Ethiopia (Oct. 1960–Dec. 1966), 94° F (34.4° C). **(U.S.):** Key West, Fla. (30-year normal), 78.2° F (25.7° C).

Lowest average annual mean temperature (world): Plateau Station, Antarctica, –70° F (–56.7° C). **(U.S.):** Barrow, Alaska (30-year normal), 9.3° F (–12.6° C).

Greatest average yearly rainfall (world): Cherrapunji, India (74-year avg), 450 in. (1,143 cm). **(U.S.):** Mt. Waialeale, Kauai, Hawaii (32-year avg), 460 in. (1,168 cm).

Minimum average yearly rainfall (world): Arica, Chile (59-year avg), 0.03 in. (0.08 cm) (no rainfall for 14 consecutive

years). **(U.S.):** Death Valley, Calif. (42-year avg), 1.63 in. (4.14 cm). Bagdad, Calif., holds the U.S. record for the longest period with no measurable rain, 767 days, from Oct. 3, 1912 to Nov. 8, 1914.

Hottest summer average in Western Hemisphere (U.S.): Death Valley, Calif., 98° F (36.7° C).

Longest hot spell (world): Marble Bar, W. Australia, 100° F (37.8° C) (or above) for 162 consecutive days, Oct. 30, 1923 to Apr. 7, 1924.

Largest hailstone (U.S.): Coffeyville, Kans., 17.5 in. (44.5 cm), Sept. 3, 1970.

World and U.S. Extremes of Climate

Highest Recorded Temperatures

	Place	Date	Degrees Fahrenheit	Degrees Celsius
World (Africa)	El Azizia, Libya	Sept. 13, 1922	136	58
North America (U.S.)	Death Valley, Calif.	July 10, 1913	134	57
Asia	Tirat Tsvi, Israel	June 21, 1942	129	54
Australia	Cloncurry, Queensland	Jan. 16, 1889	128	53
Europe	Seville, Spain	Aug. 4, 1881	122	50
South America	Rivadavia, Argentina	Dec. 11, 1905	120	49
Canada	Midale and Yellow Grass, Saskatchewan, Canada	July 5, 1937	113	45
Oceania	Tuguegarao, Philippines	April 29, 1912	108	45.6
Persian Gulf (sea-surface)		Aug. 5, 1924	96	36
Antarctica	Vanda Station, Scott Coast	Jan. 5, 1974	59	15
South Pole		Dec. 27, 1978	7.5	−14

Lowest Recorded Temperatures

	Place	Date	Degrees Fahrenheit	Degrees Celsius
World (Antarctica)	Vostok	July 21, 1983	−129	−89
Asia	Oimekon, Russia	Feb. 6, 1933	−90	−68
	Verkhoyansk, Russia	Feb. 7, 1892	−90	−68
Greenland	Northice	Jan. 9, 1954	−87	−66
North America (excl. Greenland)	Snag, Yukon, Canada	Feb. 3, 1947	−81	−63
United States	Prospect Creek, Alaska	Jan. 23, 1971	−80	−62
U.S. (excl. Alaska)	Rogers Pass, Mont.	Jan. 20, 1954	−70	−56.5
Europe	Ust 'Shchugor, Russia	Jan.	−67	−55
South America	Sarmiento, Argentina	June 1, 1907	−27	−33
Africa	Ifrane, Morocco	Feb. 11, 1935	−11	−24
Australia	Charlotte Pass, N.S.W.	June 29, 1994	−9	−22
Oceania	Haleakala Summit, Maui, Hawaii	Jan. 2, 1961	14	−10.8

Greatest Rainfalls

	Place	Date	Inches	Centimeters
1 minute (World)	Unionville, Md.	July 4, 1956	1.23	3.1
20 minutes (World)	Curtea-de-Arges, Romania	July 7, 1889	8.1	20.5
42 minutes (World)	Holt, Mo.	June 22, 1947	12	30.5
12 hours (World)	Grand Ilet, La Réunion	Jan. 26, 1980	46	114
24 hours (World)	Foc-Foc, La Réunion	Jan. 7–8, 1966	72	182.5
24 hours (N. Hemisphere)	Paishih, Taiwan	Sept. 10–11, 1963	49	125
24 hours (Australia)	Bellenden Ker, Queensland	Jan. 4, 1979	44	114
24 hours (U.S.)	Alvin, Tex.	July 25–26, 1979	43	109
24 hours (Canada)	Ucluelet Brynnor Mines, British Columbia	Oct. 6, 1967	19	49
5 days (World)	Commerson, La Réunion	Jan. 23–28, 1980	156	395
1 month (World)	Cherrapunji, India	July 1861	366	930
12 months (World)	Cherrapunji, India	Aug. 1860–Aug. 1861	1,042	2,647
12 months (U.S.)	Kukui, Maui, Hawaii	Dec. 1981–Dec. 1982	739	1878

Lowest Average Annual Precipitation Extremes

Continent	Place	Lowest avg. (inches)	Elevation (ft)	Years of record
World (South America)	Arica, Chile	0.03	95	59
Africa	Wadi Halfa, Sudan	<0.10	410	39
Antarctica	Amundsen-Scott South Pole Station	0.80[1]	9,186	10
North America	Batagues, Mexico	1.20	16	14
Asia	Aden, Yemen	1.80	22	50
Australia	Mulka (Troudaninna), South Australia	4.05	160*	42
Europe	Astrakhan, Russia	6.40	45	25
Oceania	Puako, Hawaii, Hawaii	8.93	5	13

1. The value given is the average amount of solid snow accumulating in one year as indicated by snow markers. The liquid content of the snow is undetermined. *Approximate elevation. *Source:* U.S. Army Corps of Engineers, Engineer Topographic Laboratories.

Temperature Extremes in the United States

Source: National Oceanic and Atmospheric Administration, Environmental Data and Information Service, and National Climatic Center

The Highest Temperature Extremes

Greenland Ranch, Calif., with 134°F on July 10, 1913, holds the record for the highest temperature ever officially observed in the United States. This station was located in barren Death Valley, 178 ft below sea level. Death Valley is about 140 mi long, 4 to 6 mi wide, and oriented north to south in southwest California. Much of the valley is below sea level and is flanked by towering mountain ranges with Mt. Whitney, the highest landmark in the 48 conterminous states, rising to 14,495 ft above sea level, less than 100 mi to the west. Death Valley has the hottest summers in the Western Hemisphere, and is the only known place in the United States where nighttime temperatures sometimes remain above 100°F.

The highest annual normal (1941–1970 mean) temperature in the United States, 78.2°F, and the highest summer (June–August) normal temperature, 92.8°F, are for Death Valley, Calif. The highest winter (December–February) normal temperature is 72.8°F for Honolulu, Hawaii.

Amazing temperature rises of 40° to 50°F in a few minutes occasionally may be brought about by chinook winds.[1]

1. A warm, dry wind that descends from the eastern slopes of the Rocky Mountains, causing a rapid rise in temperature.

Some Outstanding Temperature Rises

In 12 hours: 83°F, Granville, N.D., Feb. 21, 1918, from −33°F to 50°F from early morning to late afternoon.

In 15 minutes: 42°F, Fort Assiniboine, Mont., Jan. 19, 1892, from −5°F to 37°F.

In seven minutes: 34°F, Kipp, Mont., Dec. 1, 1896. The observer also reported that a total rise of 80°F occurred in a few hours and that 30 in. of snow disappeared in half a day.

In two minutes: 49°F, Spearfish, S.D., Jan. 22, 1943, from −4°F at 7:30 A.M. to 45°F at 7:32 A.M.

The Lowest Temperature Extremes

The lowest temperature on record in the United States, −79.8°F, was observed at Prospect Creek Camp in the Endicott Mountains of northern Alaska (latitude 66°48′N, longitude 150°40′W) on Jan. 23, 1971. The lowest ever recorded in the conterminous 48 states, −69.7°F, occurred at Rogers Pass, in Lewis and Clark County, Mont., on Jan. 20, 1954. Rogers Pass is in mountainous and heavily forested terrain about one half of a mile east of and 140 ft below the summit of the Continental Divide.

The lowest annual normal (1941–1970 mean) temperature in the United States is 9.3°F for Barrow, Alaska, which lies on the Arctic coast. Barrow also has the coolest summers (June–August) with a normal temperature of 36.4°F. The lowest winter (December–February) normal temperature, is −15.7°F for Barter Island on the Arctic coast of northeast Alaska.

In the 48 conterminous states, Mt. Washington, N.H. (elevation 6,262 ft), has the lowest annual normal temperature, 26.9°F, and the lowest normal summer temperature, 46.8°F. A few stations in the northeast United States and in the upper Rocky Mountains have normal annual temperatures in the 30s; summer normal temperatures at these stations are in the low 50s. Winter normal temperatures are lowest in northeast North Dakota, 5.6°F for Langdon Experiment Farm, and in northwest Minnesota, 5.3°F for Hallock.

Some Outstanding Temperature Falls

In 24 hours: 100°F, Browing, Mont., Jan. 23–24, 1916, from 44°F to −56°F.

In 12 hours: 84°F, Fairfield, Mont., Dec. 24, 1924, from 63°F at noon to −21°F at midnight.

In 2 hours: 62°F, Rapid City, S.D., Jan. 12, 1911, from 49°F at 6:00 A.M. to −13°F at 8:00 A.M.

In 27 minutes: 58°F, Spearfish, S.D., Jan. 22, 1943, from 54°F at 9:00 A.M. to −4°F at 9:27 A.M.

In 15 minutes: 47°F, Rapid City, S.D., Jan. 10, 1911, from 55°F at 7:00 A.M. to 8°F at 7:15 A.M.

Lightning Dangers

Chances are slim that you'll meet your end from a bolt of lightning. According to the National Climatic Data Center, the average annual number of deaths by lightning in the United States is 89. But just to make sure, avoid open spaces, trees, telephone booths, and ball parks.

The safest place to be during a thunderstorm is in a building, preferably with a lightning rod. The rod offers protection by intercepting lightning—an electrical charge—and transmitting its current into the ground. Made out of metal so that it conducts the charge, the lightning rod is usually located as high as possible because of lightning's tendency to strike the nearest object to it. The other safe place is a car with the windows rolled up, as long as you don't touch any of the metal parts. If lightning strikes, the car's metal body will conduct the charge down to the ground—contrary to popular belief, the rubber of the wheels offers no protection.

Ten States with Most Lightning Deaths, 1959–1994

Rank	State	Number of deaths	Number of injuries
1.	Florida	345	1,178
2.	North Carolina	165	464
3.	Texas	164	334
4.	New York	128	449
5.	Tennessee	124	349
6.	Louisiana	116	231
7.	Maryland	116	134
8.	Ohio	115	430
9.	Arkansas	110	245
10.	Pennsylvania	109	535

Source: National Severe Storms Laboratory, National Oceanic and Atmospheric Administration.

Facts and Figures About Twisters

Although tornadoes can happen at any time of year, they are especially common during the spring and early summer. May and June are the peak months in terms of numbers of tornadoes, but April appears to be the deadliest month—an average of 27 tornado deaths occurred during this month between 1950 and 1999.

What Is a Tornado?

A tornado is a dark funnel-shaped cloud made up of violently rotating winds that can reach speeds of up to 300 mph. The diameter of a tornado can vary between a few feet and a mile, and its track can extend from less than a mile to several hundred miles. Tornadoes generally travel in a northeast direction (depending on the prevailing winds) at speeds ranging from 20–60 mph.

What Causes a Tornado?

Tornadoes are most often spawned by giant thunderstorms known as "supercells." These powerful, highly organized storms form when warm, moist air along the ground rushes upward, meeting cooler, drier air. As the rising warm air cools, the moisture it carries condenses, forming a massive thundercloud, sometimes growing to as much as 50,000 ft in height. Variable winds at different levels of the atmosphere feed the updraft and cause the formation of the tornado's characteristic funnel shape.

Where Do Tornadoes Occur?

The conditions that lead to the formation of tornadoes are most often met in the central and southern United States, where warm, humid air from the Gulf of Mexico collides with cool, dry air from the Rock-

ies and Canada. This area, dubbed "tornado alley," extends roughly from the Rocky Mountains to the Appalachians, and from Iowa and Nebraska to the Gulf of Mexico. Tornadoes can also occur elsewhere, though, including all U.S. states, Europe, Asia, and Australia.

What Kinds of Destruction?

The Fujita scale classifies tornadoes according to the damage they cause. Almost half of all tornadoes fall into the F1 or "moderate damage" category. These tornadoes reach speeds of 73–112 mph and can overturn automobiles and mobile homes, rip off the roofs of houses, and uproot trees. Only about one percent of tornadoes are classified as F5, causing "incredible damage." With wind speeds in excess of 261 mph, these tornadoes are capable of lifting houses off their foundations and hurling them considerable distances.

Tornado Index

- Average number of tornadoes per year (1950–1998): **816**
- State with highest number of tornadoes per year (1950–1994): **Texas (avg. 125)**
- Top 5 tornado states (based on average number of tornadoes per year 1950–1994): **Texas (125), Oklahoma (52), Kansas (48), Florida (46), Nebraska (38)**
- States with lowest incidence of tornadoes (1950–1994): **Alaska (1), Rhode Island (8), Hawaii (28), Vermont (32), Oregon (44)**
- Most tornado deaths in one year: **519 (1953)**
- Fewest tornado deaths in one year: **15 (1986)**

Average No. of Tornado Deaths, 1950–1999

Jan.	Feb.	Mar.	Apr.	May	June	July	Aug.	Sept.	Oct.	Nov.	Dec.
3	6	13	27	19	11	1	2	2	2	3	3

Average No. of Tornadoes, 1950–1999

Jan.	Feb.	Mar.	Apr.	May	June	July	Aug.	Sept.	Oct.	Nov.	Dec.
20	22	54	109	180	171	96	60	41	29	30	17

The 25 Deadliest Tornadoes

Date	Location(s)	Deaths	Date	Location(s)	Deaths
1. March 18, 1925	Tri-State (Mo., Ill., Ind.)	689	14. June 23, 1944	Shinnston, W. Va.	100
2. May 6, 1840	Natchez, Miss.	317	15. April 18, 1880	Marshfield, Mo.	99
3. May 27, 1896	St. Louis, Mo.	255	16. June 1, 1903	Gainesville, Holland, Ga.	98
4. April 5, 1936	Tupelo, Miss.	216	17. May 9, 1927	Poplar Bluff, Mo.	98
5. April 6, 1936	Gainesville, Ga.	203	18. May 10, 1905	Snyder, Okla.	97
6. April 9, 1947	Woodward, Okla.	181	19. April 24, 1908	Natchez, Miss.	91
7. April 24, 1908	Amite La.; Purvis, Miss.	143	20. June 9, 1953	Worcester, Mass.	90
8. June 12, 1899	New Richmond, Wis.	117	21. April 20, 1920	Starkville, Miss.; Waco, Ala.	88
9. June 8, 1953	Flint, Mich.	115	22. June 28, 1924	Lorain, Sandusky, Ohio	85
10. May 11, 1953	Waco, Tex.	114	23. May 25, 1955	Udall, Kans.	80
10. May 18, 1902	Goliad, Tex.	114	24. Sept. 29, 1927	St. Louis, Mo.	79
12. March 23, 1913	Omaha, Neb.	103	25. March 27, 1890	Louisville, Ky.	76
13. May 26, 1917	Mattoon, Ill.	101			

Source: Storm Prediction Center at the National Weather Service, National Oceanographic and Atmospheric Administration. Web: www.spc.noaa.gov/.

Record Highest Temperatures by State

State	Temp. °F	Temp. °C	Date	Station	Elevation in feet
Alabama	112	44	Sept. 5, 1925	Centerville	345
Alaska	100	38	June 27, 1915	Fort Yukon	est. 420
Arizona	128	53	June 29, 1994	Lake Havasu City	505
Arkansas	120	49	Aug. 10, 1936	Ozark	396
California	134	57	July 10, 1913	Greenland Ranch	-178
Colorado	118	48	July 11, 1888	Bennett	5,484
Connecticut	106	41	July 15, 1995	Danbury	450
Delaware	110	43	July 21, 1930	Millsboro	20
D.C.	106	41	July 20, 1930	Washington	410
Florida	109	43	June 29, 1931	Monticello	207
Georgia	112	44	Aug. 20, 1983	Greenville	860
Hawaii	100	38	Apr. 27, 1931	Pahala	850
Idaho	118	48	July 28, 1934	Orofino	1,027
Illinois	117	47	July 14, 1954	E. St. Louis	410
Indiana	116	47	July 14, 1936	Collegeville	672
Iowa	118	48	July 20, 1934	Keokuk	614
Kansas	121	49	July 24, 1936*	Alton (near)	1,651
Kentucky	114	46	July 28, 1930	Greensburg	581
Louisiana	114	46	Aug. 10, 1936	Plain Dealing	268
Maine	105	41	July 10, 1911*	North Bridgton	450
Maryland	109	43	July 10, 1936*	Cumberland & Frederick	623; 325
Massachusetts	107	42	Aug. 2, 1975	New Bedford & Chester	120; 640
Michigan	112	44	July 13, 1936	Mio	963
Minnesota	114	46	July 6, 1936*	Moorhead	904
Mississippi	115	46	July 29, 1930	Holly Springs	600
Missouri	118	48	July 14, 1954*	Warsaw & Union	705; 560
Montana	117	47	July 5, 1937	Medicine Lake	1,950
Nebraska	118	48	July 24, 1936*	Minden	2,169
Nevada	125	52	June 29, 1994	Laughlin	605
New Hampshire	106	41	July 4, 1911	Nashua	125
New Jersey	110	43	July 10, 1936	Runyon	18
New Mexico	122	50	June 27, 1994	Waste Isolat. Pilot Pit	3,418
New York	108	42	July 22, 1926	Troy	35
North Carolina	110	43	Aug. 21, 1983	Fayetteville	213
North Dakota	121	49	July 6, 1936	Steele	1,857
Ohio	113	45	July 21, 1934*	Gallipolis (near)	673
Oklahoma	120	49	June 27, 1994*	Tipton	1,350
Oregon	119	48	Aug. 10, 1898	Pendleton	1,074
Pennsylvania	111	44	July 10, 1936*	Phoenixville	100
Rhode Island	104	40	Aug. 2, 1975	Providence	51
South Carolina	111	44	June 28, 1954*	Camden	170
South Dakota	120	49	July 5, 1936	Gannvalley	1,750
Tennessee	113	45	Aug. 9, 1930*	Perryville	377
Texas	120	49	Aug. 12, 1936	Seymour	1,291
Utah	117	47	July 5, 1895	Saint George	2,880
Vermont	105	41	July 4, 1911	Vernon	310
Virginia	110	43	July 15, 1954	Balcony Falls	725
Washington	118	48	Aug. 5, 1961*	Ice Harbor Dam	475
West Virginia	112	44	July 10, 1936*	Martinsburg	435
Wisconsin	114	46	July 13, 1936	Wisconsin Dells	900
Wyoming	114	46	July 12, 1900	Basin	3,500

* Also on earlier dates at the same or other places. *Source:* National Climatic Data Center, Asheville, N.C., and Storm Phillips, STORMFAX, INC.

Record Lowest Temperatures by State

State	Temp. °F	Temp. °C	Date	Station	Elevation in feet
Alabama	-27	-33	Jan. 30, 1966	New Market	760
Alaska	-80	-62	Jan. 23, 1971	Prospect Creek Camp	1,100
Arizona	-40	-40	Jan. 7, 1971	Hawley Lake	8,180
Arkansas	-29	-34	Feb. 13, 1905	Pond	1,250
California	-45	-43	Jan. 20, 1937	Boca	5,532
Colorado	-61	-52	Feb. 1, 1985	Maybell	5,920
Connecticut	-32	-36	Feb. 16, 1943	Falls Village	585
Delaware	-17	-27	Jan. 17, 1893	Millsboro	20
D.C.	-15	-26	Feb. 11, 1899	Washington	410
Florida	-2	-19	Feb. 13, 1899	Tallahassee	193
Georgia	-17	-27	Jan. 27, 1940	CCC Camp F-16	est. 1,000
Hawaii	12	-11	May 17, 1979	Mauna Kea	13,770
Idaho	-60	-51	Jan. 18, 1943	Island Park Dam	6,285
Illinois	-36	-38	Jan. 5, 1999	Congerville	635
Indiana	-36	-38	Jan. 19, 1994	New Whiteland	785
Iowa	-47	-44	Feb. 3, 1996	Elkader	770
Kansas	-40	-40	Feb. 13, 1905	Lebanon	1,812
Kentucky	-37	-38	Jan. 19, 1994	Shelbyville	730
Louisiana	-16	-27	Feb. 13, 1899	Minden	194
Maine	-48	-44	Jan. 19, 1925	Van Buren	510
Maryland	-40	-40	Jan. 13, 1912	Oakland	2,461
Massachusetts	-35	-37	Jan. 12, 1981	Chester	640
Michigan	-51	-46	Feb. 9, 1934	Vanderbilt	785
Minnesota	-60	-51	Feb. 2, 1996	Tower	1,460
Mississippi	-19	-28	Jan. 30, 1966	Corinth	420
Missouri	-40	-40	Feb. 13, 1905	Warsaw	700
Montana	-70	-57	Jan. 20, 1954	Rogers Pass	5,470
Nebraska	-47	-44	Feb. 12, 1899	Camp Clarke	3,700
Nevada	-50	-46	Jan. 8, 1937	San Jacinto	5,200
New Hampshire	-47	-44	Jan. 29, 1934	Mt. Washington	6,262
New Jersey	-34	-37	Jan. 5, 1904	River Vale	70
New Mexico	-50	-46	Feb. 1, 1951	Gavilan	7,350
New York	-52	-47	Feb. 18, 1979*	Old Forge	1,720
North Carolina	-34	-37	Jan. 21, 1985	Mt. Mitchell	6,525
North Dakota	-60	-51	Feb. 15, 1936	Parshall	1,929
Ohio	-39	-39	Feb. 10, 1899	Milligan	800
Oklahoma	-27	-33	Jan. 18, 1930	Watts	958
Oregon	-54	-48	Feb. 10, 1933*	Seneca	4,700
Pennsylvania	-42	-41	Jan. 5, 1904	Smethport	est. 1,500
Rhode Island	-23	-31	Jan. 11, 1942	Kingston	100
South Carolina	-19	-28	Jan. 21, 1985	Caesars Head	3,115
South Dakota	-58	-50	Feb. 17, 1936	McIntosh	2,277
Tennessee	-32	-36	Dec. 30, 1917	Mountain City	2,471
Texas	-23	-31	Feb. 8, 1933*	Seminole	3,275
Utah	-69	-56	Feb. 1, 1985	Peter's Sink	8,092
Vermont	-50	-46	Dec. 30, 1933	Bloomfield	915
Virginia	-30	-34	Jan. 22, 1985	Mountain Lake	3,870
Washington	-48	-44	Dec. 30, 1968	Mazama & Winthrop	2,120; 1,765
West Virginia	-37	-38	Dec. 30, 1917	Lewisburg	2,200
Wisconsin	-55	-48	Feb. 4, 1996	Couderay	1,300
Wyoming	-66	-54	Feb. 9, 1933	Riverside R.S.	6,500

* Also on earlier dates at the same or other places. *Source:* National Climatic Data Center, Asheville, N.C., and Storm Phillips, STORMFAX, INC.

Record Monthly High and Low Temperatures in the United States

Source: National Climatic Data Center, Asheville, N.C., and Storm Phillips, STORMFAX, Inc.

January

The highest temperature ever recorded for the month of January occurred on January 17, 1936, and again in 1954, in Laredo, Tex. (elevation 421 ft), where the temperature reached 98°F.

The lowest temperature ever recorded for the month of January occurred on January 20, 1954, in Rogers Pass, Mont. (elevation 5,470 ft), where the temperature fell to –70°F.

February

The highest temperature ever recorded for the month of February occurred on February 3, 1963, in Montezuma, Ariz. (elevation 735 ft), where the temperature reached 105°F.

The lowest temperature ever recorded for the month of February occurred on February 1, 1985, at the Peters Sink station in Utah (elevation 8,095 ft), where the temperature fell to –69°F.

March

The highest temperature ever recorded for the month of March occurred on March 31, 1954, in Rio Grande City, Tex. (elevation 168 ft), where the temperature reached 108°F.

The lowest temperature ever recorded for the month of March occurred on March 17, 1906, in Snake River, Wyo. (elevation 6,862 ft), where the temperature dropped to –50°F.

April

The highest temperature ever recorded for the month of April occurred on April 25, 1898, at Volcano Springs, Calif. (elevation –220 ft), where the temperature reached 118°F.

The lowest temperature ever recorded for the month of April occurred on April 5, 1945, in Eagle Nest, N.M. (elevation 8,250 ft), where the temperature dropped to –36°F.

May

The highest temperature ever recorded for the month of May occurred on May 27, 1896, in Salton, Calif. (elevation –263 ft), where the temperature reached 124°F.

The lowest temperature ever recorded for the month of May occurred on May 7, 1964, in White Mountain 2, Calif. (elevation 12,470 ft), where the temperature dropped to –15°F.

June

The highest temperature ever recorded for the month of June occurred on June 23, 1902, at Volcano Springs, Calif. (elevation –220 ft), where temperature reached 129°F.

The lowest temperature ever recorded for the month of June occurred on June 13, 1907, in Tamarack, Calif. (elevation 8,000 ft), where the temperature dropped to 2°F.

July

The highest temperature ever recorded for the month of July occurred on July 10, 1913, at Greenland Ranch, Calif. (elevation –178 ft), where the temperature reached 134°F.

The lowest temperature ever recorded for the month of July occurred on July 21, 1911, at Painter, Wyo. (elevation 6,800 ft), where the temperature fell to 10°F.

August

The highest temperature ever recorded for the month of August occurred on August 12, 1933, at Greenland Ranch, Calif. (elevation –178 ft), where the temperature reached 127°F.

The lowest temperature ever recorded for the month of August occurred on August 25, 1910, in Bowen, Mont. (elevation 6,080 ft), where the temperature fell to 5°F.

September

The highest temperature ever recorded for the month of September occurred on September 2, 1950, in Mecca, Calif. (elevation –175 ft), where temperature reached 126°F.

The lowest temperature ever recorded for the month of September occurred on September 24, 1926, at Riverside Ranger Station, Mont. (elevation 6,700 ft), where the temperature fell to –9°F.

October

The highest temperature ever recorded for the month of October occurred on October 5, 1917, in Sentinel, Ariz. (elevation 685 ft), where the temperature reached 116°F.

The lowest temperature ever recorded for the month of October occurred on October 29, 1917, in Soda Butte, Wyo. (elevation 6,600 ft), where the temperature fell to –33°F.

November

The highest temperature ever recorded for the month of November occurred on November 12, 1906, in Craftonville, Calif. (elevation 1,759 ft), where the temperature reached 105°F.

The lowest temperature ever recorded for the month of November occurred on November 16, 1959, at Lincoln, Mont. (elevation 5,130 ft), where the temperature fell to –53°F.

December

The highest temperature ever recorded for the month of December occurred on December 8, 1938, in La Mesa, Calif. (elevation 539 ft), where the temperature reached 100°F.

The lowest temperature ever recorded for the month of December occurred on December 19, 1924, at Riverside Ranger Station, Mont. (elevation 6,700 ft), where the temperature fell to –59°F.

GREAT DISASTERS

The following lists are not all-inclusive due to space limitations. Only disasters involving great loss of life and/or property, historical interest, or unusual circumstances are listed. Data as of mid–September 2001. For other disasters *see* Current Events: What Happened in 2001.

WORST UNITED STATES DISASTERS

AIRCRAFT

1979 **May 25, Chicago:** American Airlines DC-10 crashed seconds after takeoff killing all 272 persons aboard and three on the ground.

AVALANCHE

1910 **March 1, Wellington, Wash.:** two trains snowbound in Stevens Pass in Cascade Range swept off tracks into canyon 150 ft below, killing 96.

DROUGHT

1930s **Many states:** longest drought of 20th century. Peak periods were 1930, 1934, 1936, 1939, and 1940. During 1934, dry regions stretched solidly from N.Y. and Pa. across the Great Plains to the Calif. coast. A great "dust bowl" covered 50 million acres in south-central plains during winter of 1935–1936.

EARTHQUAKE

1906 **April 18, San Francisco:** earthquake accompanied by fire razed more than 4 sq mi; more than 500 dead or missing.

EPIDEMIC

1918 **Nationwide:** Spanish influenza killed over 500,000 Americans.

EXPLOSION

1947 **April 16–18, Texas City, Tex.:** a fire and subsequent explosion on the French freighter *Grandcamp* destroyed most of the city; 516 killed.

FIRE

1871 **Oct. 8, Peshtigo, Wis.:** over 1,200 lives lost and 2 billion trees burned in forest fire.

FLOOD

1889 **May 31, Johnstown, Pa.:** collapse of South Fork Dam left more than 2,200 dead.

HURRICANE

1900 **Sept. 8, Galveston, Tex.:** an estimated 6,000–8,000 dead, mostly from devastation due to tidal surge.

MARINE

1865 **April 27, Mississippi River, nr. Memphis, Tenn.:** explosion on steamboat *Sultana* killed 1,547.

MINE

1907 **Dec. 6, Monongha, W. Va.:** coal mine explosion killed 361.

OIL SPILL

1989 **Mar. 24, Prince William Sound, Alaska:** tanker *Exxon Valdez* hit an undersea reef and released 10 million plus gallons of oil into the waters.

RAILROAD

1918 **July 9, Nashville, Tenn.:** 101 killed in a two-train collision near Nashville.

SUBMARINE

1963 **April 10, North Atlantic:** atomic-powered submarine *Thresher* sank; 129 dead.

TERRORIST ATTACK

2001 **Sept. 11, New York City and Arlington, Va.:** hijackers crashed two commercial jets from Boston into the north and south towers of the World Trade Center in New York City, causing the collapse of both towers and another nearby building. A short time later, two more hijacked U.S. planes crashed, one into the Pentagon and one into a field near Shanksville, Pa. All 266 passengers and crew aboard the planes were killed; total dead and missing numbered more than 5,000. Persons responsible were unknown, but the names of 19 suspects, all connected with terrorist Osama bin Laden, were released in mid-September.

TORNADO

1925 **March 18, Mo., Ill., and Ind.:** great "Tri-State Tornado"; 689 dead; over 2,000 injured. Property damage estimated at $16.5 million.

WINTER STORM

1888 **March 11–14, East Coast:** the "Blizzard of 1888." 400 people died; as much as 5 ft of snow. Damage was estimated at $20 million.

EARTHQUAKES AND VOLCANIC ERUPTIONS

A.D. **79 Aug. 24, Italy:** eruption of Mt. Vesuvius buried cities of Pompeii and Herculaneum, killing thousands.

856 Dec. 22, Damghan, Iran: 200,000 were killed in one of the deadliest earthquakes on record.

893 March 23, Ardabil, Iran: earthquake killed about 150,000 people.

1138 Aug. 9, Aleppo, Syria: deadly earthquake claimed lives of 230,000 people.

1290 Sept., Chihli, China: earthquake killed about 100,000 people.

1556 Jan. 23, Shaanxi (Shensi) province, China: most deadly earthquake in history; 830,000 killed.

1667 Nov., Shemakha, Caucasia: earthquake killed about 80,000 people.

1727 Nov. 18, Tabriz, Iran: about 77,000 victims killed in deadly earthquake.

1755 Nov. 1, Portugal: earthquake leveled Lisbon and was felt as far away as southern France and North Africa; 70,000 killed.

1811 Dec. 16, Mississippi Valley nr. New Madrid, Mo.: earthquake reversed the course of the Mississippi River. Fatalities unknown due to sparse population in area. Aftershocks and tremors continued into 1812. It has been estimated that three of the series of earthquakes had surface-wave magnitudes of 8.6, 8.4, and 8.8 on the Richter scale. It is the largest series of earthquakes known to have occurred in North America.

1883 Aug. 26–28, Netherlands Indies: eruption of Krakatau; violent explosions destroyed two-thirds of island, leaving an estimated 36,000 dead. Sea waves occurred as far away as Cape Horn and possibly England.

1902 May 8, Martinique, West Indies: Mt. Pelée erupted and wiped out city of St. Pierre; 40,000 dead.

1908 **Dec. 28, Messina, Sicily:** city totally destroyed by earthquake. Death toll 70,000–100,000 in Sicily and southern Italy.

1915 **Jan. 13, Avezzano, Italy:** earthquake left 29,980 dead.

1920 **Dec. 16, Gansu province, China:** magnitude 8.6 earthquake killed 100,000 in northwest China.

1923 **Sept. 1, Japan:** magnitude 8.3 earthquake destroyed one third of Tokyo and most of Yokohama. More than 140,000 killed.

1927 **May 22, nr. Xining, China:** magnitude 8.3 earthquake claimed approximately 200,000 victims.

1932 **Dec. 25, Gansu, China:** magnitude 7.6 earthquake rattled China, killing approximately 70,000.

1935 **May 30, Pakistan:** earthquake at Quetta killed 30,000–60,000.

1939 **Jan. 24, Chile:** earthquake razed 50,000 sq mi; about 30,000 killed.

Dec. 27, northern Turkey: severe quakes destroyed city of Erzingan; about 100,000 casualties.

1950 **Aug. 15, India:** earthquake affected 30,000 sq mi in Assam; 20,000–30,000 believed killed.

1960 **Agadir, Morocco:** 10,000–12,000 dead as earthquake set off tidal wave and fire, destroying most of city.

1964 **March 28, Alaska:** strongest earthquake ever to strike North America hit 80 mi east of Anchorage; followed by seismic wave 50 ft high that traveled 8,445 mi at 450 mph; 117 killed.

1970 **May 31, Peru:** earthquake left more than 50,000 dead, 17,000 missing.

1972 **Dec. 22, Managua, Nicaragua:** earthquake devastated city, leaving up to 6,000 dead.

1976 **Feb. 4, Guatemala:** quake left over 23,000 dead.

July 28, Tangshan, China: worst earthquake to hit China in 20th century; devastated 20 sq mi of city, leaving 242,000 confirmed dead.

Aug. 17, Mindanao, Philippines: earthquake and tidal wave left up to 8,000 dead or missing.

1978 **Sept. 16, Tabas, Iran:** earthquake destroyed city in eastern Iran, leaving 25,000 dead.

1985 **Sept. 19–20, Mexico:** earthquake registering 8.1 on Richter scale struck central and southwest regions, devastating part of Mexico City and three coastal states; estimated 25,000 killed.

Nov. 14–16, Colombia: eruption of Nevada del Ruiz, 85 mi northwest of Bogotá. Mudslides buried most of the town of Armero and devastated Chinchiná; estimated 25,000 killed.

1988 **Dec. 7, Armenia:** earthquake measuring 6.9 on the Richter scale killed nearly 25,000, injured 15,000, and left at least 400,000 homeless.

1989 **Oct. 17, San Francisco Bay area:** earthquake measuring 7.1 on Richter scale killed 67 and injured over 3,000. Over 100,000 buildings damaged or destroyed. Damage cost city billions of dollars.

1990 **June 21, northwest Iran:** earthquake measuring 7.7 on Richter scale destroyed cities and villages in Caspian Sea area. At least 50,000 dead, over 60,000 injured, and 400,000 homeless.

1994 **Jan. 17, San Fernando Valley, Calif.:** earthquake measuring 6.6 on Richter scale killed 61 and injured over 8,000. Damage estimated at $13–20 billion.

1995 **Jan.17, Osaka, Kyoto, and Kobe, Japan:** 5,100 killed and 26,800 injured; estimated damage $100 billion. Magnitude: 7.2.

1997 **May 12, northeast Iran:** severe earthquake measuring 7.1 on Richter scale left more than 1,500 people dead and at least 4,460 injured.

June–Sept., southern Montserrat: ongoing eruption of Soufriere Hills volcano since July 1995; killed 20 persons in major eruption on June 25, 1997, rendered southern two-thirds of Montserrat uninhabitable, and forced some 8,000 of the island's 12,000 residents to abandon the island.

1998 **May 30, northern Afghanistan:** magnitude 7.1 earthquake and aftershocks killed an estimated 5,000 and injured at least 1,500. A quake on Feb. 4 in same area had killed about 2,300.

1999 **Jan. 25, Armenia, Colombia:** 1,124 dead and 4,000 injured in magnitude 6 earthquake. More than 200,000 left homeless.

Aug. 17, northwest Turkey: magnitude 7.4 quake centered near Izmit killed over 17,000 and injured about 44,000. Damage estimated at $8.5 billion.

Sept. 21, central Taiwan: severe 7.6 earthquake and aftershocks killed 2,295 and injured 8,729.

Nov. 12, northwest Turkey: another severe 7.2 temblor killed more than 700 in Ducze and surrounding towns.

2001 **Jan. 13, El Salvador:** magnitude 7.7 earthquake set off some 185 landslides across El Salvador; at least 844 died and nearly 100,000 houses were destroyed.

Jan. 26, Bhuj, India: magnitude 7.7 earthquake rocked western Indian state of Gujarat, killing more than 20,000 people and leaving 600,000 homeless. Total cost was estimated at $1.3 billion.

MAJOR U.S. EPIDEMICS

1793 **Philadelphia:** more than 4,000 residents died from yellow fever.

1832 **July–Aug., New York City:** over 3,000 people killed in a cholera epidemic.

Oct., New Orleans: cholera took the lives of 4,340 people.

1848 **New York City:** more than 5,000 deaths caused by cholera.

1853 **New Orleans:** yellow fever killed 7,790.

1867 **New Orleans:** 3,093 perished from yellow fever.

1878 **Southern states:** over 13,000 people died from yellow fever in lower Mississippi Valley.

1916 **Nationwide:** over 7,000 deaths occurred and 27,363 cases were reported of polio (infantile paralysis) in America's worst polio epidemic.

1918 **March–Nov., nationwide:** outbreak of Spanish influenza killed over 500,000 people in the worst single U.S. epidemic.

1949 **Nationwide:** 2,720 deaths occurred from polio, and 42,173 cases were reported.

1952 **Nationwide:** polio killed 3,300; 57,628 cases reported; worst epidemic since 1916.

1981 **1981 to June 2000:** total U.S. AIDS cases reported to Centers for Disease Control: 753,907; total AIDS deaths reported: 438,795.

FLOODS, AVALANCHES, AND TIDAL WAVES

1228 **Holland:** 100,000 people reputedly drowned by sea flood in Friesland.

1642 **China:** rebels destroyed Kaifeng seawall; 300,000 drowned.

1889 **May 31, Johnstown, Pa.:** more than 2,200 died in flood after South Fork Dam collapsed.

1896 **June 15, Sanriku, Japan:** earthquake and tidal wave killed 27,000.

1910 **March 1, Wellington, Wash.:** avalanche in Cascade Range swept two trains into canyon, killing 96. Worst U.S. avalanche.

1928 **March 12, Santa Paula, Calif.:** collapse of St. Francis Dam left 450 dead.

1954 **Jan. 31–Feb. 5, northwest Europe:** storm followed by floods devastated North Sea coastal areas. Netherlands was hardest hit with 1,794 dead.

1959 **Dec. 2, Fréjus, France:** flood caused by collapse of Malpasset Dam left 412 dead.

1962 **Jan. 10, Peru:** avalanche down extinct Huascaran volcano killed more than 3,000.

1963 **Oct. 9, Italy:** landslide into the Vaiont Dam; flood killed about 2,000.

1966 **Oct. 21, Aberfan, Wales:** avalanche of coal, waste, mud, and rocks killed 144 people, including 116 children in school.

1969 **Jan. 18–26, southern Calif.:** floods and mudslides from heavy rains caused widespread property damage; at least 100 dead. Another downpour (Feb. 23–26) caused further floods and mudslides; at least 18 dead.

1970 **Nov. 13, East Pakistan:** 200,000 killed by cyclone-driven tidal wave from Bay of Bengal. Over 100,000 missing.

1972 **Feb. 26, Man, W. Va.:** more than 118 died when slag-pile dam collapsed under pressure of torrential rains and flooded 17-mile valley.

June 9–10, Rapid City, S.D.: flash flood caused 237 deaths and $160 million in damage.

June 20, Eastern Seaboard: tropical storm Agnes, in ten-day rampage, caused widespread flash floods. Death toll 129; 115,000 left homeless; damage estimated at $3.5 billion.

1976 **Aug. 1, Loveland, Colo.:** flash flood along Route 34 in Big Thompson Canyon left 139 dead.

1988 **Aug.–Sept., Bangladesh:** heaviest monsoon in 70 years inundated three-fourths of country, killing more than 1,300 and leaving 30 million homeless. Damage estimated at over $1 billion.

1993 **June–Aug., Ill., Iowa, Kan., Ky., Minn., Mo., Neb., N.D., S.D., Wis.:** two months of heavy rain caused Mississippi River and tributaries to flood; almost 50 deaths and about $12 billion in damage. Almost 70,000 left homeless.

1997 **Dec. 1996–Jan. 1997, U.S. West Coast:** torrential rains and snowmelt produced severe floods in parts of Calif., Ore., Wash., Idaho, Nev., and Mont., causing 36 deaths and about $2–3 billion in damage.

March, Ohio and Mississippi Valleys: flooding and tornadoes plagued Ark., Mo., Miss., Tenn., Ill., Ind., Ky., Ohio, and W.Va. 67 were killed and damage totaled approximately $1 billion.

April, N.D., S.D., and Minn.: Grand Forks, N.D., and surrounding area devastated as the Red River swelled 13 ft above flood level.

1998 **July 17, Papua New Guinea:** spurred by undersea earthquake, three tsunamis wiped out entire villages in the northwest province of Sepik. One tidal wave reported by survivor to be 30 ft high. At least 2,000 found or presumed dead. Many who were injured by the tsunamis were later killed by deadly gangrene infections.

Summer, central and northeast China: heaviest flooding of Yangtze and other rivers since 1954. More than 3,000 killed and 14 million homeless. Estimated damages exceeded $20 billion.

1999 **Summer, Asia:** flooding plagued Asia again after weeks of torrential downpours. More than 950 killed and millions left homeless in S. Korea, China, Japan, the Philippines, and Thailand.

Oct., southwest Mexico: over a week of heavy rains killed at least 360 people in mudslides and flood waters.

Nov. and Dec., Vietnam: devastating floods caused $285 million in damage and killed more than 700 people.

Dec. 15–16, northern Venezuela: heavy rains caused catastrophic flooding and mudslides, killing an estimated 5,000 to 20,000 people. Is country's worst modern-day natural disaster.

2000 **Feb., southeast Africa:** weeks of rain resulted in deadly floods in Mozambique and Zimbabwe. About 700 people were killed and more than 280,000 were left homeless.

TROPICAL STORMS

Cyclones, hurricanes, and typhoons are the same kind of tropical storm but are called by different names in different areas of the world.

CYCLONES

1864 **Oct. 5, Calcutta, India:** 70,000 killed.

1942 **Oct. 16, Bengal, India:** about 40,000 lives lost.

1960 **Oct. 10, East Pakistan:** cyclone and tidal wave killed about 6,000.

1963 **May 28–29, East Pakistan:** cyclone killed about 22,000 along coast.

1965 **May 11–12 and June 1–2, East Pakistan:** cyclones killed about 47,000.

Dec. 15, Karachi, Pakistan: cyclone killed about 10,000.

1970 **Nov. 12–13, East Pakistan:** cyclone and tidal waves killed 200,000 and another 100,000 were reported missing.

1971 **Sept. 29, Orissa state, India:** cyclone and tidal wave off the Bay of Bengal killed as many as 10,000.

1974 **Dec. 25, Darwin, Australia:** cyclone destroyed nearly the entire city; 50 reported dead.

1977 **Nov. 19, Andhra Pradesh, India:** cyclone and tidal wave claimed lives of 20,000.

1991 **April 30, southeast Bangladesh:** cyclone killed over 131,000 and left as many as 9 million homeless. Thousands of survivors died from hunger and water-borne disease.

1999 **Oct. 29, Orissa state, India:** supercyclone swept in from Bay of Bengal, killing at least 9,573 and leaving over 10 million homeless.

U.S. HURRICANES

(U.S. deaths only, except where noted)

1776 **Sept. 2–Sept. 9, N.C. to Nova Scotia:** called the "Hurricane of Independence," it is believed that 4,170 in the U.S. and Canada died in the storm.

1856 **Aug. 11, Last Island, La.:** 400 died.

1893 **Aug. 28, Savannah, Ga., Charleston, S.C., Sea Islands, S.C.:** at least 1,000 died.

1900 **Sept. 8, Galveston, Tex.:** an estimated 6,000–8,000 died in hurricane and tidal surge. The "Galveston Hurricane" is considered the deadliest in U.S. history.

1909 **Sept. 10–21, La. and Miss.:** 350 deaths.

1915 **Aug. 5–23, East Tex. and La.:** 275 killed.

1919 **Sept. 2–15, Fla., La., and Tex.:** 287 deaths, and 488 deaths at sea.

1926 **Sept. 11–22, Fla. and Ala.:** 243 deaths.

1928 **Sept. 6–20, southern Fla.:** 1,836 died and 1,870 injured.

1935 **Aug. 29–Sept. 10, southern Fla.:** 408 killed.

1938 **Sept. 10–22, Long Island and southern New England:** 600 deaths; 1,764 injured.

1944 **Sept. 9–16, N.C. to New England:** 46 deaths, and 344 deaths at sea.

1947 **Sept. 4–21, Fla. and mid-Gulf Coast:** 51 killed.

1954 **Aug. 25–31, N.C. to New England:** "Carol" killed 60 and injured 1,000 in Long Island–New England area.

Oct. 5–18, S.C. to N.Y.: "Hazel" killed 95 in U.S.; about 400–1,000 in Haiti; 78 in Canada.

1955 **Aug. 7–21, N.C. to New England:** "Diane" took 184 lives.

1957 **June 25–28. Tex. to Ala.:** "Audrey" wiped out Cameron, La., causing 390 deaths.

1960 **Aug. 29–Sept. 13, Fla. to New England:** "Donna" killed 50 in the U.S. 115 deaths in Antilles—mostly from flash floods in Puerto Rico.

1961 **Sept. 3–15, Tex. coast:** "Carla" devastated Tex. gulf cities, taking 46 lives.

1965 **Aug. 27–Sept. 12, southern Fla. and La.:** "Betsy" killed 75 people.

1969 **Aug. 14–22, Miss., La., Ala., Va., and W. Va.:** 256 killed and 68 persons missing as a result of "Camille."

1972 **June 14–23, Fla. to N.Y.:** "Agnes" caused 117 deaths (50 in Pa.).

1979 **Aug. 25–Sept. 7, Caribbean islands to New England:** "David" caused five U.S. deaths; 1,200 in the Dominican Republic.

1980 **Aug. 3–10, Caribbean islands to Tex. Gulf:** "Allen" killed 28 in U.S.; over 200 in Caribbean.

1985 **Oct.–Nov.:** "Juan" struck La. and the Southeast. Though only a category 1 hurricane, it caused severe flooding and $1.5 billion in damages; 63 lives were lost.

1989 **Sept. 10–22, Caribbean Sea, S.C., and N.C.:** "Hugo" claimed 49 U.S. lives (71 killed overall); $4.2 billion paid in insurance claims.

1992 **Aug. 22–26, Bahamas, southern Fla., and La.:** Hurricane "Andrew" left 26 dead and more than 100,000 homes destroyed or damaged. With total U.S. damages estimated at $25 billion, it is most costly hurricane in U.S. history.

1994 **Nov. 8–21, Caribbean and southern Fla.:** flooding and mudslides caused by "Gordon" led to an estimated 1,122 deaths in Haiti. There were eight deaths in Fla.; total estimated U.S. damage nearly $400 million.

1995 **Nov. 29, Fla. panhandle and Ala.:** storm surge during "Opal" caused extensive damage to coastal areas. In U.S. death toll reached nine and damages $3 billion.

1996 **Sept. 5, N.C. and Va.:** "Fran," a category 3 hurricane, took 37 lives and caused $5.0 billion in damage.

1999 **Sept. 14–18, Bahamas to New England:** "Floyd" and associated flooding caused at least 75 deaths including one in the Bahamas. Hardest-hit N.C. suffered 49 "Floyd" related deaths. Damage estimated to be over $6 billion.

OTHER HURRICANES

1780 **Oct. 10–16, Barbados, West Indies:** "The Great Hurricane of 1780" killed 20,000–22,000 persons and completely flattened the islands of Barbados, Martinique, and St. Eustatius; is the deadliest western hemisphere hurricane on record.

1926 **Oct. 20, Cuba:** powerful hurricane killed 650.

1930 **Sept. 3, Santo Domingo:** hurricane killed about 8,000 people.

1955 **Sept. 19, Mexico:** "Hilda" took 200 lives.

Sept. 22–28, Caribbean: "Janet" killed 200 in Honduras and 300 in Mexico.

1961 **Oct. 31, British Honduras:** "Hattie" devastated capital Belize, killed at least 400.

1963 **Oct. 2–7, Caribbean:** "Flora" killed about 7,200 in Haiti and Cuba.

1966 **Sept. 24–30, Caribbean area:** "Inez" killed 293.

1974 **Sept. 14–19, Honduras:** "Fifi" struck northern part of country, leaving 8,000 dead and 100,000 homeless.

1988 **Sept. 12–17, Caribbean Sea and Gulf of Mexico:** "Gilbert" took at least 260 lives and caused some 39 tornadoes in Tex.

1997 **Oct. 8–10, southern Mexico:** "Pauline" devastated resort city of Acapulco and villages along the coast in states of Oaxaca and Guerrero, leaving 217 dead and 20,000 homeless.

1998 **Sept. 20–29, Caribbean, Fla. Keys, and Gulf Coast:** "Georges" killed about 600 people, mostly in Dominican Republic. Damage estimated to be $5 billion, including $2 billion in Puerto Rico.

Oct. 26–Nov. 4, Central America (notably Honduras and Nicaragua): "Mitch" killed more than 11,000 people, becoming the deadliest Atlantic storm in 200 years. Two to three million people were left homeless; damages were more than $5 billion in Honduras, Nicaragua, and Guatemala.

TYPHOONS

1906 **Sept. 18, Hong Kong:** typhoon with tsunami killed an estimated 10,000 persons.

1934 **Sept. 21, Japan:** typhoon killed more than 4,000 on Honshu.

1949 **Dec. 5, off Korea:** typhoon struck fishing fleet; several thousand men reported dead.

1959 **Aug. 20, Fukien province, China:** "Iris" killed 2,334.

Sept. 27, Honshu, Japan: "Vera" killed an estimated 4,464.

1960 **June 9, Fukien province, China:** "Mary" caused at least 1,600 deaths.

1984 **Sept. 2–3, Philippines:** "Ike" hit seven major islands, leaving 1,300 dead.

1991 **Nov. 5, central Philippines:** flash floods triggered by tropical storm "Thelma" killed about 3,000 people. City of Ormoc on Leyte was worst hit.

RECENT HURRICANE-LIKE STORMS

1999 **Dec. 26, northern Europe:** sweeping killer storm with winds gusting up to 124 mph caused the deaths of more than 60 people, including 15 in Germany and 11 in Switzerland.

U.S. TORNADOES

1840 **May 6, Natchez, Miss.:** tornado struck heart of the city, killing 317 and injuring over 1,000.

1880 **April 18, Marshfield, Mo.:** series of 24 tornadoes demolished city, killing 99 people.

1884 **Feb. 19, Miss., Ala., N.C., S.C., Tenn., Ky., Ind.:** tornadoes caused estimated 800 deaths.

1896 **May 27, St. Louis, Mo.:** tornado destroyed large section of the city, killing 255.

1899 **June 12, New Richmond, Wis.:** tornado struck while circus was in town, causing 117 deaths.

1902 **May 18, Goliad, Tex.:** tornado killed 114.

1903 **June 1, Gainesville, Holland, Ga.:** twister caused 98 deaths.

1905 **May 10, Snyder, Okla.:** tornado killed 97.

1908 **April 24, Amite, La.; Purvis, Miss.:** tornado killed 143.
      April 24, Natchez, Miss.: twister struck, causing 91 deaths.

1913 **March 23, Omaha, Neb.:** tornado devastated city Easter Sunday evening, killing 103.

1917 **May 26, Mattoon, Ill.:** tornado smashed area, causing 101 deaths.

1924 **June 28, Lorain, Sandusky, Ohio:** tornado swept through cities, causing 85 deaths.

1925 **March 18, Mo., Ill., Ind.:** the "Tri-State Tornado" was the most violent single twister in U.S. history. It caused the deaths of 689 people and injured over 2,000. Property damage was estimated at $16.5 million.

1927 **May 9, Poplar Bluff, Mo.:** twister killed 98.
      Sept. 29, St. Louis, Mo.: a five-minute tornado ripped through the city and caused 79 deaths.

1932 **March 21, Ala., Miss., Ga., Tenn.:** outbreak of tornadoes killed 268.

1936 **April 5, Tupelo, Miss.:** tornado ripped through the town, killing 216.
      April 6, Gainesville, Ga.: twister obliterated the small mill town, causing 203 deaths.

1944 **June 23, Shinnston, W.Va.:** tornadoes caused 100 deaths.

1947 **April 9, Woodward, Okla.:** tornado demolished town, killing 181.

1952 **March 21–22, Ark., Tenn., Mo., Miss., Ala., Ky.:** tornadoes caused 343 deaths.

1953 **May 11, Waco, Tex.:** a single tornado struck, killing 114.
      June 8, Flint, Mich.: tornado killed 116.
      June 9, Worcester, Mass.: tornado hit town, causing 90 deaths.

1955 **May 25, Udall, Kans.:** tornado killed 80.

1965 **April 11, Iowa, Ind., Ohio, Mich:** tornadoes in Iowa, Ill., Ind., Ohio, Mich., and Wis. caused 256 deaths.

1974 **April 3–4:** a series of 148 twisters comprised the deadly "Super Tornado Outbreak" that struck 13 states in the East, South, and Midwest. Before it was over, 330 died and 5,484 were injured in a damage path covering more than 2,500 mi. It was the worst tornado outbreak in U.S. history.

1999 **May 3, Okla. and Kans.:** unusually large twister, thought to have been a mile wide at times, killed 41 people and injured at least 748 others in Okla. A separate tornado killed another 5 and injured about 150 in Kans. Damages totaled at least $1 billion.

NUCLEAR POWER PLANT ACCIDENTS

1952 **Dec. 12, Chalk River, nr. Ottawa, Canada:** a partial meltdown of the reactor's uranium fuel core resulted after the accidental removal of four control rods. Although millions of gallons of radioactive water accumulated inside the reactor, there were no injuries.

1957 **Oct. 7, Windscale Pile No. 1, north of Liverpool, England:** fire in a graphite-cooled reactor spewed radiation over the countryside, contaminating a 200-square-mile area.
      South Ural Mountains: explosion of radioactive wastes at Soviet nuclear weapons factory 12 mi from city of Kyshtym forced the evacuation of over 10,000 people from a contaminated area. No casualties were reported by Soviet officials.

1976 **nr. Greifswald, East Germany:** radioactive core of reactor in the Lubmin nuclear power plant nearly melted down due to the failure of safety systems during a fire.

1979 **March 28, Three Mile Island, nr. Harrisburg, Pa.:** one of two reactors lost its coolant, which caused overheating and partial meltdown of its uranium core. Some radioactive water and gases were released.

1986 **April 26, Chernobyl, nr. Kiev, Ukraine:** explosion and fire in the graphite core of one of four reactors released radioactive material that spread over part of the Soviet Union, eastern Europe, Scandinavia, and later western Europe. 31 claimed dead. Total casualties are unknown and estimates run into the thousands. Worst such accident to date.

1999 **Sept. 30, Tokaimura, Japan:** uncontrolled chain reaction in a uranium-processing nuclear fuel plant spewed high levels of radioactive gas into the air, exposing 69 people, killing one worker, and seriously injuring two others. Japan's worst nuclear accident.

FIRES AND EXPLOSIONS

1666 **Sept. 2, England:** "Great Fire of London" destroyed St. Paul's Cathedral, etc. Damage £10 million.

1835 **Dec. 16, New York City:** 530 buildings destroyed by fire.

1871 **Oct. 8, Chicago:** the "Chicago Fire" burned 17,450 buildings and killed 250 persons; $196 million in damage.

1872 **Nov. 9, Boston:** fire destroyed 800 buildings; $75 million in damage.

1876 **Dec. 5, New York City:** fire in Brooklyn Theater killed more than 300.

1881 **Dec. 8, Vienna:** at least 620 died in fire at Ring Theatre.

1900 **June 30, Hoboken, N.J.:** piers of North German Lloyd Steamship line burned; 326 dead.

1903 **Dec. 30, Chicago:** Iroquois Theatre fire killed 602.

1906 **March 10, France:** explosion in coal mine in Courrières killed 1,060.

1907　**Dec. 6, Monongha, W. Va.:** coal mine explosion killed 361.

Dec. 19, Jacobs Creek, Pa.: explosion in coal mine left 239 dead.

1909　**Nov. 13, Cherry, Ill.:** explosion in coal mine killed 259.

1911　**March 25, New York City:** fire in Triangle Shirtwaist Factory fatal to 145.

1913　**Oct. 22, Dawson, N.M.:** coal mine explosion left 263 dead.

1917　**Dec. 6, Halifax Harbor, Nova Scotia:** Belgian steamer collided with ammunition ship *Mont Blanc*, which was carrying over 2,500 tons of explosives. Explosion leveled part of Halifax and left about 1,600 people dead.

1930　**April 21, Columbus, Ohio:** fire in Ohio State Penitentiary killed 320 convicts.

1937　**March 18, New London, Tex.:** explosion destroyed schoolhouse; 294 killed.

1942　**April 26, Manchuria:** explosion in Honkeiko Colliery killed 1,549.

Nov. 28, Boston, Mass.: Coconut Grove nightclub fire killed 491.

1944　**July 6, Hartford, Conn.:** fire and ensuing stampede in main tent of Ringling Brothers Circus killed 168, injured 487.

July 17, Port Chicago, Calif.: 322 killed when ammunition ships exploded.

1946　**Dec. 7, Atlanta:** fire in Winecoff Hotel killed 119.

1947　**April 16–18, Texas City, Tex.:** most of the city destroyed by a fire and subsequent explosion on the French freighter *Grandcamp*, which was carrying a cargo of ammonium nitrate. At least 516 were killed and over 3,000 injured.

1949　**Sept. 2, China:** fire on Chongqing (Chungking) waterfront killed 1,700.

1954　**May 26, off Quonset Point, R.I.:** explosion and fire aboard aircraft carrier *Bennington* killed 103 crewmen.

1956　**Aug. 7, Colombia:** about 1,100 reported killed when seven army ammunition trucks exploded at Cali.

Aug. 8, Belgium: 262 died in coal mine fire at Marcinelle.

1960　**Jan. 21, Coalbrook, South Africa:** coal mine explosion killed 437.

Nov. 13, Syria: 152 children killed in moviehouse fire.

1961　**Dec. 17, Niteroi, Brazil:** circus fire fatal to 323.

1962　**Feb. 7, Saarland, West Germany:** coal mine gas explosion killed 298.

1963　**Nov. 9, Japan:** explosion in coal mine at Omuta killed 447.

1965　**May 28, India:** coal mine fire in state of Bihar killed 375.

June 1, nr. Fukuoka, Japan: coal mine explosion killed 236.

1967　**May 22, Brussels, Belgium:** fire in L'Innovation department store, left 322 dead.

July 29, off North Vietnam: fire on U.S. carrier *Forrestal* killed 134.

1972　**June 6, Wankie, Rhodesia:** explosion in coal mine killed 427.

1973　**Nov. 29, Kumamoto, Japan:** fire in Taiyo department store killed 101.

1974　**Feb. 1, São Paulo, Brazil:** fire in upper stories of bank building killed 189 persons, many of whom leaped to their deaths.

1975　**Dec. 27, Dhanbad, India:** explosion in coal mine followed by flooding from nearby reservoir left 372 dead.

1977　**May 28, Southgate, Ky.:** fire in Beverly Hills Supper Club; 167 dead.

1978　**Aug. 20, Abadan, Iran:** nearly 400 killed when arsonists set fire to crowded theater.

1986　**Dec. 31, San Juan, P.R.:** fire in Dupont Plaza Hotel set by three employees, killing 96 people.

1989　**June 3, Ural Mountains:** liquefied petroleum gas leaking from a pipeline running alongside the Trans-Siberian railway near Uta, 72 mi east of Moscow, exploded and destroyed two passing passenger trains. About 500 travelers were killed and 723 injured of an estimated 1,200 passengers on both trains.

1990　**March 25, New York City:** arson fire in the illegal Happy Land Social Club, in the Bronx, killed 87 people.

1993　**May 10, nr. Bangkok, Thailand:** fire in doll factory killed at least 187 persons and injured 500 others. World's deadliest factory fire.

1999　**March 24, Chamonix, France:** Belgian truck carrying margarine and flour broke out in flames in the Mont Blanc tunnel, trapping dozens of cars. Death toll was at least 42.

2000　**Nov. 11, nr. Kaprun, Austria:** cable car transporting skiers to the Kitzsteinhorn glacier broke into flames while moving through mountain tunnel. Final death toll reached 156 in what was termed Austria's worst Alpine disaster.

Dec. 25, Luoyang, China: at least 309 people were killed in fire at shopping center. Most of the victims had been attending Christmas party at unlicensed disco in building.

WORST U.S. FOREST FIRES

1871　**Oct. 8–14, Peshtigo, Wis:** over 1,200 lives lost and 4 million acres burned in nation's worst forest fire.

1889　**June 6, Seattle, Wash.:** fire destroyed 64 acres of the city and killed 2 persons. Damage was estimated at $15 million.

1894　**Sept. 1, Minn.:** forest fires ravaged over 160,000 acres and destroyed six towns, killing 600, including 413 in town of Hinckley.

1910　**Aug. 10, Idaho:** fires burned 2 million acres of woods and killed over 70 people.

1918　**Oct. 13–15, Minn. and Wis.:** forest fire struck towns in both states; 1,000 died, including 400 in town of Cloquet, Minn. About $1 million in losses.

1947　**Oct. 25–27, Maine:** forest fire destroyed part of Bar Harbor and damaged Acadia National Park.

1956　**Nov. 25, Calif.:** fire destroyed 40,000 acres in Cleveland National Forest and caused 11 deaths.

1988　**Aug.–Sept., western U.S.:** fires destroyed over 1.2 million acres in Yellowstone National Park and thousand Alaska woodlands.

1991　**Oct. 20–23, Oakland–Berkeley, Calif.:** brush fire in drought-stricken area destroyed over 3,000 homes and apartments. At least 24 persons died; damage estimated at $1.5 billion.

2000　**April–May, northern N.M.:** fire started by National Park Service to clear brush from Bandelier National Monument raged out of control, destroying at least 250 homes and forcing evacuation of more than 20,000 people. Blaze consumed an estimated 47,000 acres and threatened Los Alamos National Laboratory.

Summer, western U.S.: as of Aug. 31 nearly 6.5 million acres had burned nationwide, more than double the ten-year average. States hardest hit included Alaska, Calif., Colo., Idaho, Mont., N.M., Nev., Ore., Tex., Utah, Wash., and Wyo.

SHIPWRECKS

(*see also* Wartime Disasters, p. 624)

1833 **May 11,** *Lady of the Lake:* bound from England to Quebec, struck iceberg; 215 perished.

1853 **Sept. 29,** *Annie Jane:* emigrant vessel off coast of Scotland; 348 died.

1865 **April 27,** *Sultana:* boiler explosion on Mississippi River steamboat, near Memphis; 1,547 killed. Most of the dead were Union POWs finally heading home at the end of the Civil War.

1898 **Feb. 15,** *Maine:* U.S. battleship destroyed in Havana harbor by an explosion that killed 260 men. The incident led to the outbreak of the Spanish-American War in April 1898.

Nov. 26, *City of Portland:* 157 died nr. Cape Cod.

1904 **June 15,** *General Slocum:* excursion steamer burned in East River, N.Y.; 1,021 perished.

1912 **March 5,** *Principe de Asturias:* Spanish steamer struck rock off Sebastien Point; 500 drowned.

April 15, *Titanic:* supposedly unsinkable British ocean liner went down on maiden voyage after colliding with an iceberg. More than 1,500 people died.

1914 **May 29,** *Empress of Ireland:* sank after collision in St. Lawrence River; 1,024 perished.

1915 **July 24,** *Eastland:* Great Lakes excursion steamer overturned in Chicago River; 812 died.

1934 **Sept. 8,** *Morro Castle:* 134 killed in fire off Asbury Park, N.J.

1949 **Sept. 17,** *Noronic:* Canadian Great Lakes cruise ship burned at Toronto dock; about 130 died.

1952 **April 26,** *Hobson:* minesweeper collided with aircraft carrier *Wasp* and sank during night maneuvers in mid-Atlantic; 176 persons lost.

1953 **Jan. 9,** *Chang Tyong-Ho:* South Korean ferry foundered off Pusan; 249 reported dead.

1954 **Sept. 26,** *Toya Maru:* more than 1,000 killed when commercial ferry sank in Tsugaru Strait, Japan.

1956 **July 25,** *Andrea Doria:* Italian liner collided with Swedish liner *Stockholm* off Nantucket Island, Mass., and sank next day. At least 52 died or were unaccounted for.

1962 **April 8,** *Dara:* British liner exploded and sank in Persian Gulf; 236 dead. Caused by time bomb.

1963 **April 10,** *Thresher:* atomic-powered U.S. submarine sank in North Atlantic; 129 dead.

1968 **Late May,** *Scorpion:* U.S. nuclear submarine sank in Atlantic 400 mi southwest of Azores; 99 dead.

1983 **May 25,** *10th of Ramadan:* Nile steamer caught fire and sank in Lake Nasser, near Aswan, Egypt; 272 dead and 75 missing.

1987 **March 9:** British ferry capsized after leaving Belgian port of Zeebrugge with 500 aboard; 134 drowned.

Dec. 20: over 4,000 killed when passenger ferry *Dona Paz* collided with oil tanker *Victor* off Mindoro Is., 110 mi south of Manila.

1990 **April 7,** *Scandinavian Star:* suspected arson fire aboard Danish-owned North Sea ferry killed at least 110 passengers in Skagerrak Strait off Norway.

1991 **Dec. 14:** ferry carrying 569 passengers sank in Red Sea off coast of Safaga, Egypt, after hitting a coral reef. Over 460 people believed drowned.

1993 **Feb. 17,** *Neptune:* triple-deck ferry capsized off southern peninsula of Haiti during a squall. Over 1,000 passengers believed drowned. About 300 survived the sinking.

1994 **Sept. 28,** *Estonia:* passenger ferry capsized off coast of southwest Finland and sank in a stormy Baltic Sea. Only about 140 of the estimated 1,040 passengers aboard survived.

1996 **Jan. 21,** *Gurita:* overloaded ferry sank off the coast of northern Sumatra, killing 340.

1999 **Feb.,** *Harta Rimba:* ship sank in the South China Sea, killing about 325 people. The ship had not been licensed for passenger use.

2000 **June 29,** *Cahaya Bahari:* ferry carrying mostly Christian refugees from the island of Halmahera sank approximately 40 mi off the coast of Sulawesi. None of the 492 persons on board survived.

Aug. 12, *Kursk:* Russian nuclear submarine sank to bottom of Barents Sea following an explosion; 118 dead.

2001 **Feb. 9,** *Ehime Maru:* U.S. submarine *Greeneville* collided with Japanese fishing boat near Pearl Harbor, Hawaii. Twenty-six people aboard the *Ehime Maru* were rescued; nine others, including four students, were presumed dead.

MYSTERIOUS DISAPPEARANCES

1872 *Mary Celeste:* the brigantine set sail from New York harbor for Genoa, Italy, on Nov. 5. A British brigantine, the *DeGratia*, discovered the ship derelict on Dec. 5 and boarded her. Everyone aboard the *Mary Celeste* had vanished—her captain, his family, and its 14-man crew. The ship was in perfect order with ample supplies and there was no sign of violence or trouble. The fate of the crew remains unknown.

1928 **Dec. 22,** *Köbenhavn:* the five-masted Danish steel barque, a sail-training ship with a crew of 75 including 45 boy cadets, sailed from the River Plate for Melbourne, Australia, on Dec. 14. The last radio contact with the ship was made on Dec. 22 and all was well. The *Köbenhavn* and its crew disappeared without a trace and no one knows what happened to it.

AIRCRAFT CRASHES

(150 deaths or more, with exceptions)

1921 **Aug. 24, England:** British dirigible *AR-2* broke in two on trial trip near Hull; 62 died.

1925 **Sept. 3, Caldwell, Ohio:** U.S. dirigible *Shenandoah* broke apart; 14 dead.

1930 **Oct. 5, Beauvais, France:** British dirigible *R 101* crashed, killing 47.

1933 **April 4, N.J.:** U.S. dirigible *Akron* crashed; 73 died.

1937 **May 6, Lakehurst, N.J.:** German zeppelin *Hindenburg* destroyed by fire at tower mooring; 36 killed.

1945 **July 28, New York City:** U.S. Army bomber B-25 crashed into Empire State Building; 13 dead.

1960 **Dec. 16, New York City:** United DC-8 and Trans World Super Constellation collided then crashed in two boroughs, killing 134 in air and on ground.

1961 **Feb. 15, nr. Brussels, Belgium:** 72 on board and farmer on ground killed in crash of Sabena plane; U.S. figure skating team wiped out.

1966 Dec. 24, Binh Thai, South Vietnam: crash of military-chartered CL-44 into village killed 129.

1971 July 30, Morioka, Japan: Japanese Boeing 727 and F-86 fighter collided in midair; 162 died.

1973 Jan. 22, Kano, Nigeria: 171 Nigerian Muslims returning from Mecca and five crewmen died in crash.

Feb. 21, Sinai: civilian Libyan Arab Airlines Boeing 727 shot down by Israeli fighters after it had strayed off course; 108 died, five survived. Officials claimed that the pilot had ignored fighters' warnings to land.

1974 March 3, Paris: Turkish DC-10 jumbo jet crashed in forest shortly after takeoff; all 346 passengers and crew killed.

Dec. 4, Colombo, Sri Lanka: Dutch DC-8 carrying Muslims to Mecca crashed on landing approach, killing all 191 persons aboard.

1975 April 4, nr. Saigon, Vietnam: Air Force Galaxy C-5A crashed after takeoff, killing 172, mostly Vietnamese children.

Aug. 3, Agadir, Morocco: chartered Boeing 707, returning Moroccan workers home after vacation in France, plunged into mountainside; all 188 aboard killed.

1976 Sept. 10, Zagreb, Yugoslavia: midair collision between British Airways Trident and Yugoslav charter DC-9 fatal to all 176 persons aboard.

1977 March 27, Santa Cruz de Tenerife, Canary Islands: Pan American and KLM Boeing 747s collided on runway. All 249 on KLM plane and 333 of 394 aboard Pan Am jet killed. Total of 582 is highest for any type of aviation disaster.

1978 Jan. 1, Bombay: Air India 747 with 213 aboard exploded and plunged into sea minutes after takeoff.

Nov. 15, Colombo, Sri Lanka: chartered Icelandic Airlines DC-8, carrying 249 Muslim pilgrims from Mecca, crashed in thunderstorm during landing approach; 183 killed.

1979 May 25, Chicago: American Airlines DC-10 lost left engine upon takeoff and crashed seconds later, killing all 272 persons aboard and three on the ground in worst U.S. air disaster.

Nov. 26, Jidda, Saudi Arabia: Pakistan International Airlines 707 carrying pilgrims returning from Mecca crashed on takeoff; all 156 aboard killed.

Nov. 28, Mt. Erebus, Antarctica: Air New Zealand DC-10 crashed on sightseeing flight; 257 killed.

1980 Aug. 19, Riyadh, Saudi Arabia: all 301 aboard Saudi Arabian jet killed when burning plane made safe landing but passengers were unable to escape.

1981 Dec. 1, Ajaccio, Corsica: Yugoslav DC-9 Super 80 carrying tourists crashed into mountain on landing approach, killing all 178 aboard.

1983 Aug. 30, nr. island of Sakhalin off Siberia: South Korean civilian jetliner Boeing 747, flight KAL-007, shot down by Soviet fighter after it strayed off course into Soviet airspace. All 269 aboard killed. Secret Soviet documents released in Oct. 1992 reveal that the plane was flying a straight course for two hours with its navigational lights on and did not take evasive action. The Soviet fighter did not give a warning by firing tracer bullets as originally claimed. Recorded conversations indicated that the crew members did not know what hit them.

1985 June 23, off coast of Ireland: Air-India Boeing 747 exploded over Atlantic; all 329 aboard were killed.

Aug. 12, Japan: Japan Air Lines Boeing 747 crashed into a mountain, killing 520 of the 524 aboard.

Dec. 12, Gander, Newfoundland: a chartered Arrow Air DC-8 bringing American soldiers home for Christmas crashed on takeoff. All 256 aboard died.

1987 Aug. 16, Romulus, Mich.: Northwest Airlines McDonnell Douglas MD-80 crashed into a highway shortly after takeoff from Detroit Metropolitan Airport, killing 156 (including 2 on the ground). Girl, 4, only survivor.

Nov. 29, Burma: Korean Air Boeing 747 jetliner exploded from bomb planted by North Korean agents and crashed into sea, killing all 115 aboard.

1988 July 3, Persian Gulf: U.S. Navy cruiser *Vincennes* shot down Iran Air A300 Airbus, killing 290 persons, after mistaking it for an attacking jet fighter.

Aug. 28, Ramstein Air Force Base, West Germany: three jets from Italian Air Force acrobatic team- collided in midair during air show and crashed, killing 70 persons, including the pilots and spectators on the ground. It is worst air-show disaster in history.

Dec. 21, Lockerbie, Scotland: N.Y.-bound Pan-Am Boeing 747 exploded in flight from a terrorist bomb and crashed into Scottish village, killing all 259 aboard and 11 on the ground. Passengers included 35 Syracuse University students and many U.S. military personnel.

1989 June 7, Paramaribo, Suriname: a Surinam Airways DC-8 carrying 174 passengers and 9 crew members crashed into the jungle while making a third attempt to land in a thick fog, killing 168 aboard.

1991 July 11, Jedda, Saudi Arabia: Canadian-chartered DC-8 carrying pilgrims returning to Nigeria crashed after takeoff, killing 261 persons.

1994 April 14, northern Iraq: two American F-15C fighter aircraft mistook two U.S. Army blackhawk helicopters for Russian-made Iraqi MI-24 helicopters and shot them down over no-fly zone, killing all 26 on board.

April 26, Nagoya, Japan: China Airlines A-300 Airbus from Taiwan crash-landed and exploded on the tarmac. Only 7 of the 271 passengers aboard survived.

1995 Dec. 20, nr. Cali, Colombia: 160 people killed when American Airlines Boeing 757 crashed in Andean Mountains.

1996 Jan. 8, Kinshasa, Zaire: Russian-built Antonov-32 cargo plane crashed after takeoff from Kinshasa into the center of the city, killing over 350 people and injuring at least 470.

Feb. 5, off coast of Puerto Plata, Dominican Republic: a Boeing 737 crashed into Atlantic Ocean after takeoff, killing 189.

May 11, Everglades, Fla.: ValuJet flight went down in swamp, killing 110. Cargo fire caused by oxygen generators missing safety caps.

July 17, off coast of Long Island, N.Y.: TWA Boeing 747-100 bound for Paris from New York exploded over waters of eastern L.I. and crashed into Atlantic Ocean, killing all 230 aboard.

Nov. 12, nr. New Delhi, India: shortly after takeoff, Saudi Arabian Airlines Boeing 747 collided in midair with Kazak Airlines Ilyushin 76 plane approaching the New Delhi airport. All 349 passengers and crew were killed; the world's worst midair collision.

1997 Aug. 6, Guam: South Korean Air Boeing 747-300 from Seoul crashed into jungle near Agana International Airport killing 227 persons; 27 survived.

Sept. 26, nr. northern Indonesia: Indonesian Garuda Airlines A-300 Airbus jetliner crashed while approaching Medan Airport, Sumatra, killing all 234 persons aboard.

1998 **Feb. 3, Mt. Cermis, Italy:** low-flying U.S. Marine surveillance jet on training flight accidentally cut ski-lift cable-car line, causing all 20 people aboard to fall some 260 ft to their deaths.

Feb. 16, Taipei, Taiwan: China Airlines Airbus 300 jumbo jet crashed while trying to land in fog at Chiang Ki-Shek International Airport, killing all 196 passengers and crew and at least 6 persons on the ground.

Sept. 2, Nova Scotia, Canada: Swissair flight from New York to Geneva crashed off Canadian coast, killing all 229 aboard. 136 Americans were on the McDonnell Douglas MD-11.

1999 **Oct. 31, southeast of Nantucket Island:** Egypt Air Boeing 767-300 on flight from N.Y. to Cairo crashed into the Atlantic Ocean, killing all 217 aboard.

2000 **Jan. 30, off the Ivory Coast:** Kenya Airways Airbus 310, carrying 179 passengers and crew, crashed after takeoff from Abidjan into the Atlantic Ocean. Ten persons survived.

July 25, Gonesse, France: Air France Concorde jet en route to New York crashed into a hotel just after taking off from Charles de Gaulle airport near Paris; all 109 aboard and 4 on the ground were killed; first Concorde jet to crash since the plane went into commercial service in 1976.

Aug. 23, off Bahrain: Gulf Air jet crashed into the Persian Gulf, killing all 143 aboard.

SPACE ACCIDENTS

1967 **Jan. 27, *Apollo 1*:** a fire aboard the space capsule on the ground at Cape Kennedy, Fla., killed astronauts Virgil I. Grissom, Edward H. White, and Roger Chaffee.

April 23–24, *Soyuz 1*: Vladimir M. Komarov was killed when his craft crashed after its parachute lines, released at 23,000 ft for reentry, became snarled.

1971 **June 6–30, *Soyuz 11*:** three cosmonauts, Georgi T. Dolrovolsky, Vladislav N. Volkov, and Viktor I. Patsayev, found dead in the craft after its automatic landing. Apparent cause of death was loss

of pressurization in the space craft during reentry into the earth's atmosphere.

1980 **March 18, USSR:** a Vostok rocket exploded on its launch pad while being refueled, killing 50 at the Plesetsk Space Center.

1986 **Jan. 28, *Challenger* Space Shuttle:** exploded 73 seconds after liftoff, killing all seven crew members. They were: Francis R. Scobee, Michael J. Smith, Judith A. Resnick, Ronald E. McNair, Ellison S. Onizuka, Gregory B. Jarvis, and schoolteacher Christa McAuliffe. A booster leak ignited the fuel, causing the explosion.

RAILROAD ACCIDENTS

NOTE: Very few passengers were killed in a single U.S. train wreck up until 1853. These early trains ran slowly and made short trips, night travel was rare, and there were not many of them in operation.

1831 **June 17:** boiler exploded on America's first passenger locomotive, *The Best Friend of Charleston,* killing the fireman. He was the first person in America to be killed in a railroad accident.

1833 **Nov. 8, nr. Heightstown, N.J.:** world's first train wreck and first passenger fatalities recorded. A 24-passenger Camden & Amboy train derailed due to a broken axle, killing two passengers and injuring all others. Former President John Quincy Adams and Cornelius Vanderbilt, who later made a fortune in railroads, were aboard the train.

1853 **May 6, Norwalk, Conn.:** New Haven Railroad train ran through an open drawbridge and plunged into the Norwalk River. Forty-six passengers were crushed to death or drowned. This was the first major drawbridge accident.

1856 **July 17, Camp Hill, Pa.:** two Northern Penn trains crashed head-on. Sixty-six church-school children bound for a picnic died in the flaming wreckage.

1876 **Dec. 29, Ashtabula, Ohio:** Lake Shore train fell into the Ashtabula River when the bridge it was crossing collapsed; 92 people were killed.

1887 **Aug. 10, nr. Chatsworth, Ill.:** a burning railroad trestle collapsed while a Toledo, Peoria & Western train was crossing, killing 81 and injuring 372.

1910 **March 1, Wellington, Wash.:** two trains swept into canyon by avalanche; 96 dead.

1915 **May 22, Gretna, Scotland:** two passenger trains and troop train collided; 227 killed.

1917 **Dec. 12, Modane, France:** nearly 550 killed in derailment of troop train near mouth of Mt. Cenis tunnel.

1918 **July 9, Nashville, Tenn.:** 101 killed in a two-train collision near Nashville.

Nov. 1, New York City: derailment of subway train in Malbone St. tunnel in Brooklyn left 92 dead.

1926 **March 14, Virilla River Canyon, Costa Rica:** an overcrowded train carrying pilgrims derailed while crossing the Colima Bridge, killing over 300 people and injuring hundreds more.

1943 **Dec. 16, nr. Rennert, N.C.:** 72 killed in derailment and collision of two Atlantic Coast Line trains.

1944 **March 2, nr. Salerno, Italy:** 521 suffocated when Italian train stalled in tunnel.

1949 **Oct. 22, nr. Nowy Dwor, Poland:** more than 200 reported killed in derailment of Danzig-Warsaw express.

1950 **Nov. 22, Richmond Hill, N.Y.:** 79 died when one Long Island Railroad commuter train crashed into rear of another.

1951 **Feb. 6, Woodbridge, N.J.:** 85 died when Pennsylvania Railroad commuter train plunged through temporary overpass.

1952 **Oct. 8, Harrow-Wealdstone, England:** two express trains crashed into commuter train; 112 dead.

1957 **Sept. 1, nr. Kendal, Jamaica:** about 175 killed when train plunged into ravine.

Sept. 29, nr. Montgomery, West Pakistan: express train crashed into standing oil train; nearly 300 killed.

Dec. 4, St. John's, England: 92 killed and 187 injured as one commuter train crashed into another in fog.

1962 **May 3, nr. Tokyo:** 163 killed and 400 injured when train crashed into wreckage of collision between inbound freight train and outbound commuter train.

1963 **Nov. 9, nr. Yokohama, Japan:** two passenger trains crashed into derailed freight train, killing 162.

1970 **Feb. 4, nr. Buenos Aires:** 236 killed when express train crashed into standing commuter train.

1972 **Oct. 6, nr. Saltillo, Mexico:** train carrying religious pilgrims derailed and caught fire, killing 204 and injuring over 1,000.

Oct. 30, Chicago: two Illinois Central commuter trains collided during morning rush hour; 45 dead and over 200 injured.

1974 **Aug. 30, Zagreb, Yugoslavia:** train entering station derailed, killing 153 and injuring over 60.

1981 **June 6, nr. Mansi, India:** driver of train carrying over 500 passengers braked to avoid hitting a cow, causing train to plunge off a bridge into the Baghmati River; 268 passengers were reported killed, but at least 300 more were missing.

1982 **July 11, Tepic, Mexico:** Nogales-Guadalajara train plunged down mountain gorge, killing 120.

1989 **Jan. 15, Maizdi Khan, Bangladesh:** train carrying Muslim pilgrims crashed head-on with a mail train, killing at least 110 persons and injuring as many as 1,000.

1990 **Jan. 4, Sangi village, Sindh province, Pakistan:** overcrowded 16-car passenger train rammed into a standing freight train. At least 210 persons were killed and 700 were believed injured in what is said to be Pakistan's worst train disaster.

1993 **Sept. 22, nr. Mobile, Ala.:** Amtrak's *Sunset Limited,* en route to Miami, jumped rails on weakened bridge and plunged in Big Bayou Canot, killing 47 persons.

1995 **Aug. 20, Firozabad, northern India:** a speeding passenger train rammed another train that was stalled after hitting a cow. About 300 persons were killed and over 400 injured.

1997 **March 3, Punjab province, Pakistan:** passenger train crashed due to failed brakes, killing 119 and injuring at least 80 persons.

1998 **June 3, nr. Eschede, Germany:** Inter City Express passenger train traveling at 125 mph crashed into support pier of overpass, killing 98. Is nation's worst postwar train accident.

OIL SPILLS

1978 **March 16, off Portsall, France:** wrecked supertanker *Amoco Cadiz* spilled 68 million gallons, causing widespread environmental damage over 100 mi of Brittany coast—world's largest tanker disaster.

1979 **June 3, Gulf of Mexico:** exploratory oil well Ixtoc I blew out, spilling an estimated 140 million gallons of crude oil into the open sea. Although it is the largest known oil spill, it had a low environmental impact.

1989 **Mar. 24, Prince William Sound, Alaska:** tanker *Exxon Valdez* hit an undersea reef and spilled 10 million plus gallons of oil into the waters, causing the worst oil spill in U.S. history.

Dec. 19, off Las Palmas, the Canary Islands: explosion in Iranian supertanker, the *Kharg-5,* caused 19 million gallons of crude oil to spill into Atlantic Ocean about 400 mi north of Las Palmas, forming a 100-square-mile oil slick.

1991 **Jan. 25, southern Kuwait:** during the Persian Gulf War, Iraq deliberately released an estimated 460 million gallons of crude oil into the Persian Gulf from tankers 10 mi off Kuwait. Spill had little military significance. On Jan. 27, U.S. warplanes bombed pipe systems to stop the flow of oil.

1994 **Sept. 8, Russia:** dam built to contain oil burst and spilled oil into Kolva River tributary. U.S. Energy Department estimated spill at 2 million barrels. Russian state-owned oil company claimed spill was only 102,000 barrels.

1996 **Feb. 15, off Welsh coast:** supertanker *Sea Empress* ran aground at port of Milford Haven, Wales, spewed out 70,000 tons of crude oil, and created a 25-mile slick.

SPORTS DISASTERS

1955 **June 11, Le Mans, France:** racing car in Grand Prix hurtled into grandstand, killing 82 spectators.

1964 **May 24, Lima, Peru:** more than 300 soccer fans killed and over 500 injured during riot and panic following unpopular ruling by referee in Peru vs. Argentina soccer game. It is worst soccer disaster on record.

1971 **Jan. 2, Glasgow, Scotland:** 66 killed in crush at Glasgow Rangers home stadium when soccer fans trying to leave encountered fans trying to return to stadium after hearing that a late goal had been scored.

1982 **Oct. 20, Moscow:** according to *Sovietsky Sport,* as many as 340 died at Lenin Stadium when exiting soccer fans collided with returning fans after final goal was scored. All the fans had been crowded into one section of stadium by police.

1985 **May 11, Bradford, England:** 56 burned to death and over 200 injured when fire engulfed main grandstand at Bradford's soccer stadium.

May 29, Brussels, Belgium: group of drunken British soccer fans supporting Liverpool club stormed stand filled with Italian supporters of Juventus team before European Champion's Cup final. While British fans attacked rival spectators at the Heysel Stadium, concrete retaining wall collapsed and 39 persons were crushed or trampled to death, 32 of them Italians. More than 400 persons were injured.

1988 **March 12, Katmandu, Nepal:** some 80 soccer fans seeking cover during a violent hail storm at the national stadium were trampled to death in a stampede because the stadium doors were locked.

1989 **April 15, Sheffield, England:** 96 people were killed at Hillsborough stadium during a semifinal match between Liverpool and Nottingham Forest. Most of the victims, who were Liverpool fans, were crushed when a barrier collapsed on an overcrowded pen behind one of the goals. It is Britain's worst soccer disaster.

1996 **Oct. 16, Guatemala City:** at least 84 killed and 147 injured by stampeding soccer fans before a 1998 World Cup qualifying match between Guatemala and Peru held at Mateo Flores National Stadium.

2001 **May 9, Accra, Ghana:** at least 120 people were killed in a stampede at a soccer match. It was Africa's worst soccer-related disaster ever.

TERRORIST ATTACKS IN U.S.

1920 **Sept. 16, New York City:** TNT bomb planted in unattended horse-drawn wagon exploded on Wall Street opposite House of Morgan, killing 35 persons and injuring hundreds more: Bolshevist or anarchist terrorists believed responsible, but crime never solved.

1975 **Jan. 24, New York City:** bomb set off in historical Fraunces Tavern killed four and injured more than 50 persons. Puerto Rican nationalist group (FALN) claimed responsibility and police tied 13 other bombings to it.

1993 **Feb. 26, New York City:** bomb exploded in basement garage of World Trade Center; killed six and injured at least 1,040 others. Six Middle Eastern men were later convicted in this act of vengeance for the Palestinian people. They claimed to be retaliating against U.S. support for the Israeli government.

1995 **April 19, Oklahoma City:** car bomb exploded outside federal office building, collapsing wall and floors. 168 persons were killed, including 19 children and one person who died in rescue effort. Over 220 buildings sustained damage.

Timothy McVeigh and Terry Nichols later convicted in the antigovernment plot to avenge the Branch Davidian standoff in Waco, Tex., exactly two years earlier. (*See* Miscellaneous Disasters.)

2001 **Sept. 11, New York City and Arlington, Va.:** American Airlines Boeing 767 and United Airlines Boeing 767, both en route from Boston to Los Angeles, were hijacked and flown only minutes apart into the north and south towers of the World Trade Center in New York City. Shortly afterwards, American Airlines Boeing 757, en route from Washington, DC, to Los Angeles, crashed into the Pentagon. A fourth hijacked plane, operated by United and headed from Newark to San Francisco, crashed in a field near Shanksville, Pa. Both World Trade Center towers collapsed, and a section of the Pentagon was destroyed. All 266 passengers and crew aboard the planes were killed; total dead and missing numbered more than 5,000. Persons responsible were unknown, but the names of 19 suspects, all connected with terrorist Osama bin Laden, were released in mid-September.

WARTIME DISASTERS

1915 **May 6, off the coast of Ireland:** Cunard Liner *Lusitania,* sailing from N.Y. for Liverpool, England, was sunk by a German submarine. 1,198 passengers and crew, 128 of them Americans, died. Unknown to the passengers, the ship was carrying a cargo of small arms. Disaster contributed to entry of the U.S. into World War I.

1916 **Feb. 26, Mediterranean:** 3,100 people died when the French cruiser *Provence* was sunk by a German submarine.

1917 **Dec. 6, *Mont Blanc:*** French ammunition ship collided with Belgian steamer in Halifax Harbor, Canada; 1,600 people died.

1940 **Sept. 13, Atlantic Ocean:** luxury liner SS *City of Benares,* sailing from Liverpool with over 90 British children who were being evacuated to Canada during World War II, was torpedoed by a German submarine during the night. Only 13 children survived the disaster.[1]

1941 **Dec. 7, Pearl Harbor, Hawaii:** 1,177 crewmen killed when U.S. battleship *Arizona* was sunk during a surprise attack on the American naval base by Japanese warplanes. The devastating air strike, which damaged or destroyed every battleship in the U.S. Pacific Fleet, is the worst naval catastrophe in U.S. history.

1942 **Feb. 24, *Struma:*** steamer sunk by Soviet submarine in the Black Sea near the Bosporus. Of the 778 people aboard, mostly Romanian Jews fleeing the Holocaust, only one person survived.

Oct. 2, *Queen Mary:* rammed and sank a British cruiser; 338 aboard the cruiser died.

1943 **Nov. 26, Mediterranean Sea:** 1,105 U.S. soldiers died when the British troopship HMT *Rohna* was sunk by a German air-to-surface guided missile. It is the worst U.S. troopship disaster.

Dec., Bari Harbor, Italy: U.S. ship, damaged during German bombing attack, leaked mustard gas into harbor, killing 83 U.S. servicemen and nearly 1,000 civilians.

1944 **June 29, off the coast of Japan:** Japanese troop ship carrying about 6,000 troops and crew was torpedoed by American submarine USS *Sturgeon.* Only 400–600 survived.

July 17, Port Chicago, Calif.: explosion at naval ammunition base killed 320 people, including 202 African-American enlisted men.

Sept. 12, South China Sea: U.S. submarines torpedoed and sank two Japanese troopships, the *Kachidoki Maru* and the *Rakuyo Maru.* Unknown to the submarines, the Japanese, in disregard for the rules of treatment of prisoners of war, had forced 2,000 British, Australian, and American POWs into the holds of the ships, which were designed to hold only 300 troops. Later, when the subs discovered the tragedy, they sought to rescue as many survivors as possible. Japanese vessels picked up 656 of *Kachidoki Maru's* prisoners. Of the 1,318 POWs aboard the *Rakuyo Maru,* only 136 were rescued by the Japanese and 159 by American submarines.

Oct. 24, South China Sea: the *Arisan Maru* carrying 1,800 American prisoners was torpedoed by a U.S. submarine and sunk. The Japanese destroyer escort rescued Japanese military and civilian personnel and left the POWs to their fate. It is estimated that only ten prisoners survived the disaster.

Dec. 17–18, Philippine Sea: a typhoon struck U.S. Third Fleet's Task Force 38, sank three destroyers, damaged seven other ships, destroyed 186 aircraft, and killed 800 officers and men.

1945 **Jan. 30, Baltic Sea:** Nazi passenger ship *Wilhelm Gustloff,* carrying German refugees and soldiers, was torpedoed by a Soviet submarine. As many as 9,000–10,000 may have died. World's largest marine disaster.

April 9: U.S. ship, loaded with aerial bombs, exploded at Bari, Italy; at least 360 killed.

May 3: several days before World War II ended in Europe, the German passenger ship *Cap Arcona,* carrying about 6,000, of which an estimated 5,000 were concentration camp prisoners,

---

1. During the war (1939–1945), some 10,000 children were evacuated to stay with foster parents in the United States and Canada. The sinking of the *City of Benares* ended the British government's evacuation program.

was sunk by British aircraft. An estimated 5,000 persons were killed.

May 4, Gearhart Mountain, south-central Ore.: six people on a picnic, including a mother and her unborn child, were the only persons ever killed by a balloon-carried bomb launched from Japan. During the war, Japan launched some 6,000 FUGO ("windship weapon") balloons to drift across the Pacific to the U.S. and Canada, each carrying bombs and incendiaries for starting forest fires and creating death and havoc. Although over 200 of the deadly balloons floated to the U.S. before the war ended, the government kept it a secret from the American people.

July 29, nr. Leyte Gulf, Philippines: heavy cruiser *Indianapolis* torpedoed and sunk by a Japanese submarine. Of the crew of 1,199 men, only 316 survived. Due to Navy blundering, the warship was not reported missing when it did not arrive at Leyte on July 31 as scheduled, and therefore no search was ever made for crew. The survivors were discovered by a Navy patrol plane 82 hours after the ship had gone down.

1948 Nov.: unidentified Chinese troopship evacuating Nationalist troops from Manchuria sank nr. Yingkow, killing an estimated 6,000 persons.

Dec. 3, *Kiangya*: Chinese passenger ship carrying refugees fleeing Communist troops sank off Shanghai; over 3,000 believed to have been killed.

1991 Feb., Kuwait: during Persian Gulf War, Iraqi troops systematically dynamited and set fire to 650 of Kuwait's 950 oil wells, causing world's worst man-made environmental disaster. Total of 749 wells damaged. Last of oil fires extinguished on Nov. 6, 1991.

MISCELLANEOUS DISASTERS

1888 March 11–14, East Coast: the "Blizzard of 1888." 400 people died; as much as 5 ft of snow. Damage was estimated at $20 million.

1928 March 12, Santa Paula, Calif.: collapse of St. Francis Dam left 450 dead.

1930s Many states: longest drought of the 20th century. Peak periods were 1930, 1934, 1936, 1939, and 1940. During 1934, dry regions stretched solidly from N.Y. and Pa. across the Great Plains to the Calif. coast. A great "dust bowl" covered some 50 million acres in the south-central plains during the winter of 1935–1936.

1980 June–Sept., central and eastern U.S.: an estimated 10,000 people were killed during the summer in a long heat wave and drought. Damages totaled about $20 billion.

1981 July 18, Kansas City, Mo.: suspended walkway in Hyatt Regency Hotel collapsed; 113 dead, 186 injured.

1984 Dec. 3, Bhopal, India: toxic gas, methyl isocyanate, seeped from Union Carbide insecticide plant, killed more than 2,000, injured about 150,000.

1987 Sept. 18. Goiânia, Brazil: 244 people contaminated with cesium-137 that was removed from a steel cylinder taken from a cancer-therapy machine in an abandoned clinic and sold as scrap. Four people died in worst radiation disaster in Western Hemisphere.

1988 Summer, central and eastern U.S.: a severe drought and heat wave killed an estimated 5,000–10,000 people, including heat stress-related deaths. Damages reached $40 billion.

July 6, North Sea off Scotland: 166 workers killed in explosion and fire on Occidental Petroleum's *Piper Alpha* rig in North Sea; 64 survivors. It is the world's worst offshore oil disaster.

1993 March 12–14, eastern U.S.: "storm of the century" struck the eastern seaboard, killing approximately 270. Record snowfalls (with rates of 2–3 inches per hour) and high winds caused $3–6 billion in damage.

April 19, Waco, Tex.: 51-day stalemate between federal agents and members of Christian Branch Davidian cult ended in a fiery tragedy after federal agents botched their assault on the sect's compound. About 80 Branch Davidians, including at least 17 children, died when the compound burned to the ground in a suspicious blaze. Earlier, on Feb. 28, four agents were shot to death in failed attack on heavily armed compound. Jurors in the criminal trial of surviving cult members were unable to determine who fired the first shot. The incident was reopened for investigation in Aug. 1999.

1995 July 12–17, U.S. Midwest and Northeast: over 800 persons, including 560 in Chicago, died in record heat wave.

1996 Jan. 6–8, eastern U.S.: heavy snow paralyzed the Appalachians, the mid-Atlantic, and the Northeast. 187 were killed in the blizzard and in the floods that resulted after a sudden warm-up. Damages reached $3 billion.

May 10–11, Mt. Everest, Nepal: eight climbers died near summit during storm on mountain. Is worst single loss of lives to occur in a season on Mt. Everest. Another four died over the remaining course of the month.

1998 Summer, southern U.S.: severe heat and drought spread across Tex. and Okla., all the way to North and South Carolina. At least 200 were left dead and $6–9 billion of damage was estimated.

1999 Summer, eastern U.S.: rainfall shortages resulted in what was the worst drought on record for Md., Del., N.J., and R.I. The state of W.Va. was declared a disaster area. 3.81 million acres were consumed by fire as of mid-Aug. Crops were severely damaged in many states, putting losses in the mid-Atlantic region at at least $800 million.

Summer, continental U.S.: record heat continued throughout the country, resulting in drought, crop damage, and 282 deaths nationwide.

Nov. 17, College Station, Tex.: twelve Texas A&M students were killed when the 40-foot log-pile they were constructing collapsed. They were preparing a bonfire for an annual celebration.

Dec. 26–28, western Europe: fierce wind and rain storms swept through Europe, killing 30 in Britain, Spain, Italy, and Switzerland, and 83 in France, which bore the brunt of the storms. 3.4 million homes were left without electricity as winds reached 124 mph.

2000 June 18, Dover, England: British customs officials discovered the bodies of 58 illegal immigrants in the back of a tomato truck. The victims, all from China, suffocated to death in an airless compartment.

Oct. 12, Aden, Yemen: U.S. Navy destroyer USS *Cole* was heavily damaged when a small boat loaded with explosives blew up alongside it. Seventeen sailors were killed in what was apparently a deliberate terrorist attack.

Selling the Sun . . . and the Wind

Renewable energy has come of age—but it's mostly foreign companies that are making money on it

By EUGENE LINDEN   TIME

There's an old joke in Brazil that it is the nation of the future—and always will be. For decades the same has been said of the renewable-energy industry. Someday soon, its promoters kept promising, solar cells and wind turbines would produce electricity more cheaply than would traditional plants burning coal and oil and natural gas. There have been many false dawns, as fossil-fuel prices soared and then swooned. But the promised day appears finally to have arrived at, among other places, a windswept hilltop in Texas. On King Mountain, near McCamey, Tex., Renewable Energy Systems has teamed with Cielo Wind Power to build one of the world's largest wind-powered generating facilities, with a capacity to light as many as 139,000 homes. This was no feel-good exercise. Wind power was chosen according to the cold calculus of business. It will produce electricity over the 20-year life of the facility for an estimated 3¢ to 6¢ a kilowatt-hour (kWh). That compares with a recent average of 7.6¢ a kWh charged by Texas utilities.

The Future Is Now

Since 1998, wind power has been the fastest-growing new source of electricity in the world, expanding an average of 30% a year. Sales of photovoltaic panels (also known as solar cells), which convert the sun's energy directly into electricity, grew by 37% last year. At high-tech companies and hospitals, executives with a special concern about power disruptions are looking at fuel cells to supply clean and reliable power on site (albeit at prices that currently remain higher on average than those charged by the big utilities). The value of the world's electrical power generated from renewable sources such as wind and solar is about $7 billion—up from less than $1 billion a decade ago, but still a tiny fraction of the total electricity market, according to a study by green-technology consultants Clean Edge, of Oakland, Calif. That study projects the renewable market to reach $82 billion by 2010, as technological advances lower the price and make renewables easier to use. And governments around the world are pushing power producers to reduce emissions that contribute to air pollution and global warming. Joel Makower, cofounder of Clean Edge, calls this moment "a unique historical opportunity" for companies that produce renewable energy.

As the global market for renewable energy expands, however, it is European and Japanese companies—not American ones—that are winning most of the new business. As recently as 1996, manufacturers in the United States accounted for more than 40% of the world's photovoltaic shipments. But two years ago, Japan emerged as the world's leading manufacturer of these solar devices. The 214 giant wind turbines going to King Mountain in Texas at an estimated cost of $250 million come from Bonus, based in Brande, Denmark. Danish firms are supplying 60% of the wind turbines being installed in the fast-growing U.S. market, which this year alone will nearly double the total installed base of wind power. The only American wind firm with the heft to compete with the large European companies is an arm of the energy giant Enron, based in Houston.

Government Incentives

European and Japanese firms have also established solid footholds in the enormous potential power markets in developing countries such as China and India, where solar and wind power offer the cheapest way to bring electricity to some of the 2 billion people just now getting their first lights and refrigeration. India is turning to renewables to bring electricity to some of the roughly 300 million of its people who lack power. The nation now has the fifth-largest installed base of wind generators in the world and plans to use renewables as much as 15% of its new power over the next decade. So far, most of India's estimated $100 million annual spending on renewable-energy plants is going to Indian companies or firms such as Denmark's NEG Micon, which in 2000 had 9.1% of India's wind market—more than four times the share of the U.S. firm Enron.

To be sure, Enron has opened a new wind turbine plant south of Madrid. And Cannon, a U.S. wind-energy developer, has launched big projects in Turkey. But the wind turbines Cannon is installing are made by Danish firms. Most galling for some is that the United States pioneered many of the key wind and solar technologies finding commercial success today. Notes Hal Harvey, president of the Energy Foundation, based in San Francisco, in frustration: "We paid to create wind and solar power, and we have been giving it away." Some of it, though, is coming back. Big Danish firms such as Vestas are building turbine factories in the United States. The two largest solar-device manufacturers on American soil are British-owned BP Solar and German-owned Siemens. Ownership may be foreign, but American workers benefit.

European and Japanese renewable-energy firms have prospered in part thanks to citizen commitment and government subsidies far more generous than those available to U.S. firms. A greater advantage for the foreign firms, however, is the higher price charged in their home countries for electricity generated by fossil fuels. Governments in Europe and Japan heavily tax oil, gas, and coal to capture some of the hidden costs—from pollution and global warming to vehicular traffic—of consuming it. In the United States, solar and wind energy have looked less attractive—at least until recently when fuel-generated electricity prices spiked for some customers in California to more than 25¢ a kWh.

In Britain, the fuel tax–driven rise in electricity costs helped encourage Sainsbury's in March 2001 to refrigerate part of a food-storage depot in East Kilbride, Scotland, with electricity generated by a towering, 213-foot-tall wind turbine. Denmark's government used to subsidize the installation of wind turbines but abolished the program in 1989, when wind power was regarded as fully competitive with electricity produced from heavily taxed fossil fuels.

The global situation today in some ways compares to the decade after the 1973 oil embargo, when fuel prices soared. Americans suddenly wanted smaller and more fuel-efficient vehicles. The Japanese, who had been building such cars for years, won lucrative market share and customer loyalty that U.S. producers have never entirely regained. Now as then, the affected U.S. companies are debating not only corporate strategy but also the appropriate role for government.

Priming the Pump

While the Bush administration's energy policy tilts toward traditional oil and coal interests, many renewable-energy entrepreneurs believe that global political and market forces are now on their side—and that their technologies have developed to the point where they can win, even on a playing field that is canted against them. Such assistance has proved invaluable to some renewable-energy technologies. Allen Barnett, founder and president of Astropower, America's largest independent producer of photovoltaics, developed his design at the University of Delaware with the assistance of U.S. Department of Energy funding. The U.S. government, he argues, could make American renewable-energy companies more competitive globally simply by treating them fairly in government-purchasing decisions. "The U.S. government is the biggest buyer of electricity in the world," he says, "and often at prices above what we can deliver with solar. All we are asking is that the government look at what it's paying, and anyplace where solar or other renewables are cost effective, use them."

Such pioneering purchases are a traditional way by which governments encourage new technologies. The now ubiquitous microchip is perhaps the best example. At first the U.S. military was the only market for the early integrated circuits, but by selling to it in bulk, companies learned how to make chips better and cheaper. Between 1962 and 1968, says Dennis Hayes, president of Seattle's Bullitt Foundation, the price of these components dropped 95% as their capabilities expanded, eventually making integrated circuits viable for commercial applications such as personal computers. Mahler of FuelCell Energy says such economies of scale would make fuel cells even more competitive with fossil fuels. He estimates that with its current production at 50 megawatts a year, his company's cells can deliver power at 7¢ or 8¢ a kWh. But when FuelCell increases production by 2004 to 400 megawatts a year, as it plans, the attendant savings could drop the price to 5¢ or 6¢ per kWh, all else being equal.

This is the path by which Japanese companies were able to win the lead in solar exports from U.S. competitors. As Astropower vice president Howard Wenger notes, the Japanese government's approach has been to "massively build up the domestic market through incentives to encourage industry to scale up and then, in phase two, take the show on the road and dominate the world." Japan is currently the largest market for solar in the world, and 75% of the 4 million devices sold so far are on rooftops, partly because of government incentives.

Now Japan is applying the same approach as it seeks to develop ultra-efficient green cars. The government instituted a goal to make 100% of its fleet of 7,000 official cars "green," meaning they get ultrahigh mileage running, at least in part, on some ultra-clean fuel such as hydrogen. Denmark, Italy, Spain, Portugal, Greece, Austria, and Sweden also use government purchases to stimulate production of renewables. By contrast, the United States has no comparable federal policies to stimulate the market for green cars. A number of states, however, have set ambitious targets for using renewables.

Good Business Sense

What U.S. renewable-energy execs are asking is that government provide a regulatory environment that, at minimum, doesn't discriminate against them. Amory Lovins, cofounder of the Rocky Mountain Institute and a longtime cheerleader for clean energy, points out that in 1996 the California legislature discontinued a policy that encouraged alternatives and efficiency by allowing utilities to make money even if they sold less power (a policy that was reinstituted in April 2001). Policies that allow solar and wind power to be sold to the grid during peak production periods—now in place in more than 30 states—also are encouraging use of renewables.

Some green-energy advocates argue that U.S. tax policy discriminates against renewable-energy companies by taxing them at virtually the same rate as fossil-fuel competitors who impose big costs on society through pollution and greenhouse gases. Almost everywhere else in the world, fossil fuels bear cumbersome taxes. Japan has a "green tax" and the UK a "Climate Change Levy," as well as other taxes on fossil fuels.

As the Bush administration resists international action on climate change, governments and companies in Europe and Asia are positioning themselves to deal with the threat posed by emissions of greenhouse gases. British Petroleum, for example, is investing large sums in solar and other renewables and experimenting with carbon-trading schemes that offset emissions in one place with protection of forests that capture carbon. While such U.S.-based companies as General Motors and American Electric Power are also experimenting with carbon trading and clean fuels, they seem at the moment to be motivated more by the threat of boycotts by international environmental groups than by market economics. The interest in renewables on the part of such big oil companies as BP and Shell, on the other hand, "has gone beyond window dressing," says Vince, the British wind-power executive. "They can see the future of energy. For them, it's business." And that may be the best evidence that renewable energy's future has finally come. ☐

Economic Outlook Through 2008

Source: Bureau of Labor Statistics, *Monthly Labor Review,* Nov. 1999

Every two years, the Bureau of Labor Statistics (BLS) publishes its latest projections on the structure of the economy, labor force demographics, and future job growth. The following is a summary of the most recent BLS projections that were released at the end of 1999. They focused on occupational changes over the period 1998–2008. The full report is located on the BLS website: http://stats.bls.gov/opub/mls/1999/11/contents.htm.

Moderate Economic Growth Projected

Bureau of Labor Statistics (BLS) projections envision a moderately growing economy over the 1998–2008 decade, with gross domestic product (GDP) reaching $9.5 trillion in chained 1992 dollars by the end of the decade, an increase of almost $2 trillion over the period. Rising by an average annual rate of 2.4%, GDP growth is projected to be somewhat slower than the 2.6% annual rate of growth over the preceding ten-year period, from 1988 to 1998.

Slower growth of civilian household employment, from 1.3% a year during the 1988–1998 period to 1.1% from 1998 to 2008, accompanies the slowdown in GDP growth. Civilian household employment is projected to increase by almost 16 million employees over the 1998–2008 period, slightly less than the increase of 16.5 million persons experienced between 1988 and 1998. The employment projection is accompanied by an assumed unemployment rate of 4.7%, only marginally higher than the 1998 annual average of 4.5%.

Consumer Spending to Decline

Consumer demand is projected to slow over the projection period, growing at an average annual rate of 2.4% from 1998 to 2008, matching the 2.4% growth rate of GDP. As a result, consumption

expenditures will amount to 68.3% of GDP in 2008, virtually the same as in 1998. The projection for real disposable income is that it will grow at a 2.5% annual rate between 1998 and 2008, 0.4 percentage point higher than the rate during 1988–1998.

Consumer durables—items with an expected life in excess of three years, such as motor vehicles, personal computers, and household furnishings—have a higher income elasticity than does personal consumption spending on nondurables and services. Over the next decade, with a projected rise in family income, the fastest growth sector still is expected to be durable goods, and the continued demand for computers will lead the way.

During the past three decades, expenditures for nondurable goods, such as food, clothing, and gasoline, have increased at a significantly slower pace than has spending on durable goods and consumer services. As family income rises, spending on these short-term consumable necessities also rises, up to a point. After that point is reached, spending on such items tends to increase much more slowly than rises in income, although increases in income enhance the demand for higher quality products.

Continued Trade Deficit

As the world is assumed to become more open to trade, the share of GDP of both exports and imports is expected to grow apace. With these conditions in place, the dollar is expected to remain moderately strong throughout the projection period, but not so strong as to significantly weaken anticipated export growth.

Exports are expected to grow faster than imports between 1998 and 2008. Exports are projected to grow at a 6.9% annual rate over the period, with exports of goods leading the way with a 7.4% annual rate of growth. Exports of services are expected to grow at a rate of 5.9%.

Characteristics of the Civilian Labor Force, 1988–2008
(numbers in thousands)

Group	Level			Percent change		Percent distribution		
	1988	1998	2008	1988–1998	1998–2008	1988	1998	2008
Total	121,669	137,673	154,576	13.2%	12.3%	100.0%	100.0%	100.0%
Sex								
Men	66,927	73,959	81,132	10.5	9.7	55.0	53.7	52.5
Women	54,742	63,714	73,444	16.4	15.3	45.0	46.3	47.5
Age								
16 to 24	22,536	21,894	25,210	-2.8	15.1	18.5	15.9	16.3
25 to 54	84,041	98,718	104,133	17.5	5.5	69.1	71.7	67.4
55 and older	15,092	17,062	25,233	13.1	47.9	12.4	12.4	16.3
Race								
White	104,756	115,415	126,665	10.2	9.7	86.1	83.8	81.9
Black	13,205	15,982	19,101	21.0	19.5	10.9	11.6	12.4
Asian and other[1]	3,708	6,278	8,809	69.3	40.3	3.0	4.6	5.7
Hispanic origin	8,982	14,317	19,585	59.4	36.8	7.4	10.4	12.7
Other than Hispanic origin	112,687	123,356	134,991	9.5	9.4	92.6	89.6	87.3
White non-Hispanic	96,141	101,767	109,216	5.9	7.3	79.0	73.9	70.7

NOTE: Data apply to workers aged 16 and older. 1. Includes Asians, Pacific Islanders, American Indians, and Alaska Natives. *Source:* Bureau of Labor Statistics, *Monthly Labor Review,* Nov. 1999. Web: stats.bls.gov.

Imports, on the other hand, are projected to grow at a relatively slower rate of 6.4% annually during 1998–2008, compared with the 7.7% annual rate of growth over the 1988–1998 ten-year span. Imports of goods are expected to grow at 7.0% annually, and a 3.0% annual rate of growth is projected for imports of services during the 1998–2008 period.

These projections result in a trade deficit of $347.5 billion in real terms by 2008, with both exports and imports increasing their share of GDP, the former from 13.0% in 1998 to 20.2% in 2008 and the latter from 16.2% to 23.8%.

Disposable Income on the Rise

On a per capita basis, nominal disposable income is anticipated to increase at an average annual rate of 3.8% from 1998 to 2008, reaching a level of $32,400 in 2008, a gain of more than $10,000 over the projection span.

In real terms—that is, chained 1992 dollars—per capita income is projected to grow 1.6% per year from 1998 to 2008, up from a 1.2% rate of growth between 1988 and 1998. Thus, the bureau expects its projections to be characterized by a long-term improvement in the real standard of living—at least, measured on the basis of growth in disposable personal income.

Employment Outlook

Total employment is projected to increase by 20.3 million jobs over the 1998–2008 period, rising from 140.5 million to 160.8 million, according to the latest projections of the Bureau of Labor Statistics. The projected 14.4% change in employment is less than the 17.1% increase attained during the previous ten-year period, 1988–1998, when the economy added 20.5 million jobs.

The economy will continue generating jobs for workers at all levels of education and training, although growth rates are projected to be faster, on average, for occupations requiring at least an associate's degree than for occupations requiring less training. However, most job growth will be in occupations requiring less formal education or training, even though many of these occupations are projected to have below-average growth rates. There also will be numerous job openings resulting from the need to replace workers who leave the labor force or move to other occupations.

Persons in the Labor Force, 1840–1990

Year	Labor force[1] Number (thousands)	Percent of working-age population	Percent in labor force in[2] Farm occupation	Nonfarm occupation	Year	Labor force[1] Number (thousands)	Percent of working-age population	Percent in labor force in[2] Farm occupation	Nonfarm occupation
1840	5,420	46.6%	68.6%	31.4%	1920	42,434	51.3%	27.0%	73.0%
1850	7,697	46.8	63.7	36.3	1930	48,830	49.5	21.4	78.6
1860	10,533	47.0	58.9	41.1	1940	52,789	52.2	17.4	82.6
1870	12,925	45.8	53.0	47.0	1950	60,054	53.5	11.6	88.4
1880	17,392	47.3	49.4	50.6	1960	69,877	55.3	6.0	94.0
1890	23,318	49.2	42.6	57.4	1970	82,049	58.2	3.1	96.9
1900	29,073	50.2	37.5	62.5	1980	106,085	62.0	2.2	97.8
1910	37,371	52.2	31.0	69.0	1990	125,182	65.3	1.6	98.4

1. For 1830 to 1930, the data relate to the population and gainful workers at age 10 and over. For 1940 to 1960, the data relate to the population and labor force at age 14 and over; for 1970 and 1980, the data relate to the population and labor force at age 16 and over. For 1940 to 1980, the data include the Armed Forces. 2. The farm and nonfarm percentages relate only to the experienced civilian labor force. *Source:* U.S. Bureau of the Census. Web: www.census.gov.

Fastest-Growing Occupations, 1998–2008

(numbers in thousands of jobs)

Occupation	Employment 1998	2008	Change Number	Percent	Occupation	Employment 1998	2008	Change Number	Percent
Computer engineers	299	622	323	108%	Paralegals and legal assistants	136	220	84	62%
Computer support specialists	429	869	439	102	Personal care and home health aides	746	1,179	433	58
Systems analysts	617	1,194	577	94	Medical assistants	252	398	146	58
Database administrators	87	155	67	77	Social and human service assistants	268	410	141	53
Desktop publishing specialists	26	44	19	73	Physician assistants	66	98	32	48

Source: U.S. Department of Labor, Bureau of Labor Statistics, *Monthly Labor Review*, Nov. 1999. Web: stats.bls.gov.

Percent Distribution of Employed Persons by Occupation and Sex

Occupation	Total		Men		Women	
	1998	1999	1998	1999	1998	1999
Total, 16 years and over (thousands)	131,463	133,488	70,693	71,446	60,771	62,042
Percent	100.0%	100.0%	100.0%	100.0%	100.0%	100.0%
Managerial and professional specialty	29.6	30.3	28.1	28.6	31.4	32.3
Executive, administrative, and managerial	14.5	14.7	15.0	15.0	13.9	14.2
Professional specialty	15.1	15.6	13.1	13.6	17.4	18.0
Technical, sales, and administrative support	29.3	29.2	19.5	19.7	40.7	40.0
Technicians and related support	3.2	3.3	2.8	2.9	3.8	3.6
Sales occupations	12.1	12.1	11.1	11.3	13.1	13.0
Administrative support, including clerical	14.0	13.8	5.6	5.5	23.8	23.4
Service occupations	13.6	13.4	10.2	9.9	17.5	17.4
Private household	.6	.6	.1	.1	1.3	1.3
Protective service	1.8	1.8	2.8	2.8	.7	.7
Service, except private household and protective	11.1	11.0	7.3	7.1	15.4	15.4
Precision production, craft, and repair	11.0	10.9	18.7	18.6	2.0	2.1
Operators, fabricators, and laborers	13.9	13.6	19.5	19.3	7.4	7.0
Machine operators, assemblers, and inspectors	5.9	5.5	6.9	6.5	4.8	4.4
Transportation and material moving occupations	4.1	4.1	6.8	7.0	.9	.9
Handlers, equipment cleaners, helpers, and laborers	3.9	3.9	5.8	5.9	1.7	1.7
Farming, forestry, and fishing	2.7	2.6	4.0	3.8	1.1	1.1

NOTE: Beginning in Jan. 1999, data reflect revised population controls used in the household survey. *Source:* U.S. Department of Labor, Bureau of Labor Statistics. Web: stats.bls.gov.

Number of Employed and Unemployed Workers by Sex and Age, 1970–2000

(in thousands)

	2000[1]	1999[1]	1998[1]	1997[1]	1995[1]	1990[2]	1985	1980	1970
Men, 20 years and over									
Employed	68,580	67,761	67,134	66,524	64,085	61,678	56,562	53,101	45,581
Unemployed	2,350	2,433	2,580	2,826	3,239	3,239	3,715	3,353	1,638
Women, 20 years and over									
Employed	59,352	58,655	57,278	57,647	54,396	50,535	44,154	38,492	26,952
Unemployed	2,212	2,285	2,424	2,187	2,819	2,596	3,129	2,615	1,349
Total, 16 years and over									
Employed	135,208	133,488	131,463	130,785	124,900	118,793	107,150	99,303	78,678
Unemployed	5,655	5,880	6,209	5,957	7,404	7,047	8,312	7,637	4,093
Total, 16–19 years									
Employed	7,276	7,172	7,051	6,614	6,419	6,581	6,434	7,710	6,144
Unemployed	1,093	1,162	1,205	944	1,346	1,212	1,468	1,669	1,106

1. Data beginning in 1994 are not directly comparable with earlier years due to the introduction of a major redesign of the Current Population Survey. 2. Revised; data beginning in 1990 are not directly comparable with earlier years due to the introduction of 1990 census-based population controls, adjusted for the estimated undercount. *Source:* U.S. Department of Labor, Bureau of Labor Statistics. Current Population Survey. Web: stats.bls.gov.

Overall Unemployment Rate in the Civilian Labor Force, 1920–2001

Year	Rate	Year	Rate	Year	Rate	Year	Rate	Year	Rate	Year	Rate
1920	5.2%	1944	1.2%	1962	5.5%	1980	7.1%	1992	7.5%	2001	
1928	4.2	1946	3.9	1964	5.2	1982	9.7	1993	6.9	Jan.	4.2%
1930	8.7	1948	3.8	1966	3.8	1984	7.5	1994	6.1	Feb.	4.2
1932	23.6	1950	5.3	1968	3.6	1986	7.0	1995	5.6	March	4.3
1934	21.7	1952	3.0	1970	4.9	1987	6.2	1996	5.4	April	4.5
1936	16.9	1954	5.5	1972	5.6	1988	5.5	1997	4.9	May	4.4
1938	19.0	1956	4.1	1974	5.6	1989	5.3	1998	4.5	June	4.5
1940	14.6	1958	6.8	1976	7.7	1990	5.6	1999	4.2		
1942	4.7	1960	5.5	1978	6.1	1991	6.8	2000	4.0		

NOTES: Estimates prior to 1940 are based on sources other than direct enumeration. Data prior to 1948 are for persons age 14 and over. Data beginning in 1948 are for persons age 16 and over. *Source:* U.S. Department of Labor, Bureau of Labor Statistics. Web: stats.bls.gov.

Unemployment Rate by Race, Age, and Sex, 1998–2000

Age and sex	Total			White			Black			Hispanic		
	1998	1999	2000	1998	1999	2000	1998	1999	2000	1998	1999	2000
Men, 16 years and over	4.4%	4.1%	3.9%	3.9%	3.6%	3.4%	8.9%	8.2%	8.1%	6.4%	5.6%	4.9%
Men, 20 years and over	3.7	3.5	3.3	3.2	3.0	2.8	7.4	6.7	7.0	5.4	4.7	4.2
Women, 16 years and over	4.6	4.3	4.1	3.9	3.8	3.6	9.0	7.8	7.2	8.2	7.6	6.7
Women, 20 years and over	4.1	3.8	3.6	3.4	3.3	3.1	7.9	6.8	6.3	7.1	6.6	5.9
Both sexes, 16 years and over	4.5	4.2	4.0	3.9	3.7	3.5	8.9	8.0	7.6	7.2	6.4	5.7

NOTE: Detail for race and Hispanic-origin groups will not sum to totals because data for the "other races" group are not presented and Hispanics are included in both the white and black population groups. *Source:* U.S. Department of Labor, Bureau of Labor Statistics. Web: stats.bls.gov.

Youth Employment Trends, 1996–1998

Source: U.S. Department of Labor. *Report on the Youth Labor Force,* June 2000. Based on Current Population Survey data. Web: stats.bls.gov/opub/rylf/rylfhome.htm.

How Many Youths Work?

During the 1996–1998 period, 2.9 million youths age 15 to 17 worked during school months, and 4.0 million worked during the summer months.

Among youths, employment increased markedly with age. During the school months of 1996–1998, only 9% of 15-year-olds were employed in an average month, compared with 26% of those a year older and 39% of 17-year-olds. Youths in each age group were more likely to work in the summer, during which employment rates increased to 18%, 36%, and 48% at each age, respectively.

Despite popular perceptions that youths work more than they did in the past, the proportion of 15- to 17-year-olds who work has declined over time. Employment-population ratios declined with economic downturns in the early 1980s and 1990s. After the decline in the early 1990s, however, the rates did not return to earlier levels. During the 1996–1998 period, a quarter of youths worked during the school months, down from 30% in 1977–1979. Just over a third worked during the summer, down from 43% during the late 1970s.

How Much Do Youths Earn?

The minimum wage often is associated with young workers first entering the labor force. CPS data indicate that earnings were at or below the minimum wage for most youths, but a large proportion of youths actually earned more than minimum wage, which was $5.15 in 1998.

In 1998, median earnings of 15- to 17-year-olds combined were $5.57 per hour. In 1998, the earnings increased with age: 15-year-olds earned a median of $5.38 per hour, 16-year-olds earned $5.52, and 17-year-olds earned $5.65 per hour. Earnings varied slightly across sex and race groups. Hispanic and white males had the highest median hourly earnings; Hispanic and black females had the lowest.

Where Do Youths Work?

About 62% of youths aged 15 to 17 employed during the school months of the 1996–1998 period worked in retail trade, more than in any other major industry. Within retail trade, eating and drinking places accounted for the greatest share of employed youths, about one-third of all employed 15- to 17-year-olds. Another 1 in 4 youths was employed in service industries. In the summer, youth employment was less concentrated in retail trade and youths were employed in a wider variety of industries than during the school months. Retail trade still accounted for about half, services increased to 30%, and employment in agriculture and goods-producing industries (mining, construction, and manufacturing) increased. This seasonal pattern of employment also was present in earlier periods.

Most Popular Occupations Among Youths Aged 15–17

Industry	Percent of total employed youths	Industry	Percent of total employed youths
Male		**Female**	
Stock handlers and baggers	13.4%	Cashiers	24.3%
Cooks	12.0	Food counter, fountain, and related occupations	6.5
Cashiers	9.6	Waiters and waitresses	6.4
Waiters' and waitresses' assistants	5.2	Sales workers, other commodities	5.1
Miscellaneous food preparation occupations	5.1	Child care workers, private household	4.9
Farm workers	4.7	Cooks	4.4
Janitors and cleaners	4.2	Stock handlers and baggers	3.3
Food counter, fountain, and related occupations	3.5	Sales workers, apparel	3.2
Groundskeepers and gardeners, except farm	3.3	Supervisors, food preparation and service occupations	3.1
Sales workers, other commodities	2.3	Waiters' and waitresses' assistants	2.9

NOTE: School months are January to May and September to December. *Source:* U.S. Department of Labor. *Report on the Youth Labor Force,* June 2000. Web: stats.bls.gov/opub/rylf/rylfhome.htm.

Mothers Participating in Labor Force, 1955–2000

	Percentage of mothers with children		
Year	Under 18 years	6 to 17 years	Under 6 years[1]
1955	27.0%	38.4%	18.2%
1965	35.0	45.7	25.3
1975	47.3	54.8	38.8
1980	56.6	64.3	46.8
1985	62.1	69.9	53.5
1986	62.8	70.4	54.4
1987	64.7	72.0	56.7
1988	65.1	73.3	56.1
1989	65.7	74.2	56.7
1990	66.7	74.7	58.2
1991	66.6	74.4	58.4
1992	67.2	75.9	58.0
1993	67.0	75.4	57.9
1994	68.4	76.0	60.3
1995	69.7	76.4	62.3
1996	70.2	77.2	62.3
1997	72.1	78.1	65.0
1998	71.8	77.6	64.9
1999	72.2	78.2	64.8
2000	72.3	78.7	64.6

1. May also have older children. NOTE: 1955 data are for April; 1965 and 1975–94 data are for March. Data for 1994 and subsequent years are not directly comparable to previous years because of major revisions to the survey questionnaire and the data collection methodology, and the introduction of 1990 census-based population controls into the estimation process. *Source:* U.S. Department of Labor, Bureau of Labor Statistics. Web: stats.bls.gov.

Women in the Civilian Labor Force, 1900–2000

Year	Number[1] (thousands)	% female population aged 16 and over[1]	% of labor force population aged 16 and over[1]
1900	5,319	18.8%	18.3%
1910	7,445	21.5	19.9
1920	8,637	21.4	20.4
1930	10,752	22.0	22.0
1940	12,845	25.4	24.3
1950	18,389	33.9	29.6
1960	23,240	37.7	33.4
1970	31,543	43.3	38.1
1980	45,487	51.5	42.5
1990[2]	56,829	57.5	45.2
1993	58,795	57.9	45.5
1994[3]	60,239	58.8	46.0
1996	61,857	59.3	46.2
1997	63,036	59.8	46.2
1998	63,714	59.8	46.3
1999	64,855	60.0	46.5
2000	65,616	60.2	46.6

1. For 1900–1930, data relate to population and labor force aged 10 and over; for 1940, to population and labor force aged 14 and over; beginning 1950, to civilian population and labor force aged 16 and over. 2. Data beginning in 1990 are not strictly comparable with data for prior years because population controls were adjusted. 3. Data beginning 1994 are not strictly comparable with data for prior years because of a major redesign of the Current Population Survey (household survey) questionnaire and collection methodology. *Source:* U.S. Department of Labor, Women's Bureau.

Work Stoppages (Strikes) Involving 1,000 Workers or More

Year	Work stoppages	Workers involved (thousands)	Days idle (thousands)	Year	Work stoppages	Workers involved (thousands)	Days idle (thousands)
1950	424	1,698	30,390	1990	44	185	5,926
1960	222	896	13,260	1991	40	392	4,584
1970	381	2,468	52,761	1992	35	364	3,989
1975	235	965	17,563	1993	35	184	3,981
1980	187	795	20,844	1994	45	322	5,020
1983	81	909	17,461	1995	28	176	5,736
1984	68	391	8,499	1996	37	273	4,887
1985	61	584	7,079	1997	29	339	4,497
1986	72	900	11,861	1998	34	387	5,116
1987	46	174	4,456	1999	17	73	1,996
1988	40	118	4,381	2000	39	394	20,419
1989	51	452	16,996				

NOTE: Refers to stoppages that began in the year. Days idle is total for all stoppages in effect. Workers are counted more than once if they were involved in more than one stoppage during the year. *Source:* U.S. Department of Labor, Bureau of Labor Statistics, *Monthly Labor Review,* March 2001. Web: stats.bls.gov.

Union Membership by Occupation, 2000

Occupation	Percent of workers	Occupation	Percent of workers
Protective service[1]	39.4%	Technicians	10.1%
Precision production, craft, repair	21.9	Service (nonprotective)	8.9
Operators, fabricators, laborers	19.8	Executive, managerial	5.3
Professional specialty	19.3	Sales	3.5
Administrative, clerical	12.1		

1. Protective service: police, prison guards, firefighters. *Source:* Bureau of Labor Statistics.

Federal Minimum Wage Rates, 1955–2000

Year	Value of the minimum wage		Year	Value of the minimum wage		Year	Value of the minimum wage		Year	Value of the minimum wage	
	Current dollars	Constant (1996) dollars[1]		Current dollars	Constant (1996) dollars[1]		Current dollars	Constant (1996) dollars[1]		Current dollars	Constant (1996) dollars[1]
1955	$0.75	$4.39	1967	$1.40	$6.58	1979	$2.90	$6.27	1991	$4.25	$4.90
1956	1.00	5.77	1968	1.60	7.21	1980	3.10	5.90	1992	4.25	4.75
1957	1.00	5.58	1969	1.60	6.84	1981	3.35	5.78	1993	4.25	4.61
1958	1.00	5.43	1970	1.60	6.47	1982	3.35	5.45	1994	4.25	4.50
1959	1.00	5.39	1971	1.60	6.20	1983	3.35	5.28	1995	4.25	4.38
1960	1.00	5.30	1972	1.60	6.01	1984	3.35	5.06	1996	4.75	4.75
1961	1.15	6.03	1973	1.60	5.65	1985	3.35	4.88	1997	5.15	5.03
1962	1.15	5.97	1974	2.00	6.37	1986	3.35	4.80	1998	5.15	4.96
1963	1.25	6.41	1975	2.10	6.12	1987	3.35	4.63	1999	5.15	4.85
1964	1.25	6.33	1976	2.30	6.34	1988	3.35	4.44	2000	5.15	4.72
1965	1.25	6.23	1977	2.30	5.95	1989	3.35	4.24	2001	5.15	n.a.
1966	1.25	6.05	1978	2.65	6.38	1990	3.80	4.56			

NOTE: n.a. = not available. 1. Adjusted for inflation using the CPI-U. *Source:* Web: www.dol.gov/esa/public/minwage.

Union Membership, by States

Source: Monthly Labor Review Online, Bureau of Labor Statistics, http://www.bls.gov.

Roughly 14% of nonagricultural wage-and-salary workers are union members. Union membership among wage and salary workers shows a distinct geographic pattern, according to the Current Population Survey. Union membership is highest in the Northeast, Midwest, and Pacific regions, and lowest in the South.

New York, Hawaii, and Michigan have the highest rates of union membership, all more than 21.0% of workers. These states, along with Alaska and New Jersey, have been among the most unionized since at least 1995. North Carolina and South Carolina have the lowest rates, 3.2% and 3.5%, respectively. New York has a union membership rate eight times that of North Carolina (25.3% vs. 3.2% of workers).

California (2.3 million), New York (1.9 million), and Illinois and Michigan (both 1 million) have the greatest number of union members. More than half (53%) of the 16.5 million union members in the United States live in seven states, although these states accounted for only 38% of wage and salary employment nationally. Interestingly, Washington has slightly more union members than Texas, despite having less than one-third as much employment.

Union Membership Rates by State, 1999 Annual Average
(U.S. Rate = 13.9%)

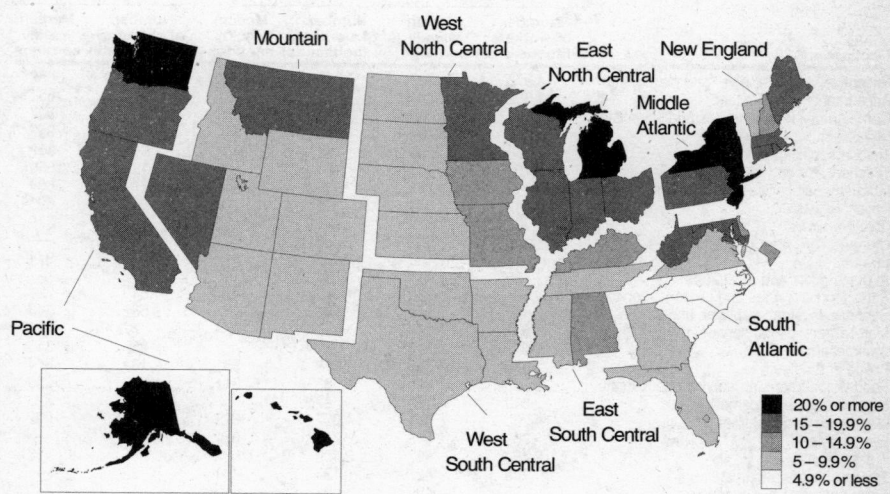

Source: Current Population Survey, Bureau of Labor Statistics; Web: www.bls.gov.

National Labor Organizations with Membership over 100,000

Members	Union[1]	Members	Union[1]
760,000	United International Union of Automobile, Aerospace, and Agricultural Implement Workers of America[2]	110,000	American Federation of Musicians of the United States and Canada
120,000	Bakery, Confectionery, and Tobacco Workers International Union	215,000	Union of Needletrades, Industrial, and Textile Employees[3]
100,000	International Union of Bricklayers and Allied Craftworkers	180,000	American Nurses Association (Ind.)
125,000	International Association of Bridge, Structural, Ornamental, and Reinforcing Iron Workers	118,000	Office and Professional Employees International Union
		370,000	International Union of Operating Engineers
515,000	United Brotherhood of Carpenters and Joiners of America	114,000	International Brotherhood of Painters and Allied Trades
490,000	Communications Workers of America	290,000	Paper, Allied-Industrial, Chemical, and Energy Workers International Union[4]
110,000	Transportation Communications Workers Union of America	300,000	United Association of Journeymen and Apprentices of the Plumbing and Pipe Fitting Industry of the U.S. and Canada
2,500,000	National Education Association (Ind.)		
720,000	International Brotherhood of Electrical Workers	300,000	National Fraternal Order of Police
		420,000	National Postal Mail Handlers Union
113,000	International Union of Electronic, Electrical, Salaried, Machine, and Furniture Workers	315,000	American Postal Workers Union
		100,000	Retail, Wholesale, and Department Store Union
235,000	International Association of Fire Fighters		
1,400,000	United Food and Commercial Workers International Union	165,000	American Association of Classified School Employees
191,000	American Federation of Government Employees	1,300,000	Service Employees International Union
		143,000	Sheet Metal Workers' International
142,000	Graphic Communications International	1,300,000	American Federation of State, County, and Municipal Employees
245,000	Hotel Employees and Restaurant Employees International Union	635,000	United Steelworkers of America[2]
		685,000	American Federation of Teachers
775,000	Laborers' International Union of N.A.	1,500,000	International Brotherhood of Teamsters
308,000	National Association of Letter Carriers	100,000	Theatrical Stage Employees
740,000	International Association of Machinists and Aerospace Workers[2]	165,000	Amalgamated Transit Union
130,000	United Mine Workers of America	110,000	Transport Workers Union of America

NOTE: List is arranged alphabetically by keyword. 1. Unless otherwise noted, unions are AFL-CIO affiliated. 2. These three unions will merge over 5 years. 3. Merger of the International Ladies Garment Workers' Union and the Amalgamated Clothing and Textile Workers Union. 4. The United Paperworkers International Union merged with the Oil, Chemical, and Atomic Workers International Union on Jan. 4, 1999. *Source:* U.S. Department of Labor. From *Directory of U.S. Labor Organizations, 2000.*

Median Weekly Earnings of Selected Occupations, 1999

	Both sexes		Men		Women	
Occupation	Number of workers (in thousands)	Median weekly earnings	Number of workers (in thousands)	Median weekly earnings	Number of workers (in thousands)	Median weekly earnings
Executive, administrative, and managerial	14,973	$ 792	7,981	$ 967	6,992	$652
Accountants and auditors	1,362	723	549	891	813	651
Computer systems analysts and scientists	1,348	1,008	959	1,079	390	907
Physicians	460	1,266	335	1,364	125	852
Teachers, college and university	638	953	397	1,038	241	859
Teachers, except college and university	4,259	688	1,130	768	3,129	659
Librarians, archivists, and curators	210	701	39	—	171	684
Psychologists	141	673	55	760	86	623
Social workers	705	601	220	661	485	579
Clergy	295	657	256	676	38	—
Lawyers	577	1,168	386	1,340	191	974
Airplane pilots and navigators	99	1,048	97	1,050	3	—
Sales workers, retail and personal services	3,324	329	1,475	423	1,849	296
Secretaries, stenographers, and typists	2,629	446	47	—	2,582	446
Mail carriers, postal service	301	697	218	714	82	646
Bank tellers	288	346	21	—	267	343
Police and detectives	1,079	657	898	681	181	574
Food preparation and service occupations	3,189	298	1,583	311	1,607	286
Hairdressers and cosmetologists	310	322	47	—	263	323
Mechanics and repairers	4,263	621	4,057	622	206	592
Electricians	739	645	723	651	17	—
Truck drivers	2,493	527	2,409	532	85	412
Taxicab drivers and chauffeurs	149	427	127	441	22	—
Farm operators and managers	72	499	61	525	11	—
Forestry and logging occupations	58	503	55	508	2	—

NOTES: Dash indicates base is less than 50,000 workers, so no data are provided. *Source:* U.S. Department of Labor, Bureau of Labor Statistics. Web: stats.bls.gov.

Median Income of Households with Selected Characteristics, 1999

Characteristic	White Number (thousands)	White Median income	Black Number (thousands)	Black Median income	Hispanic origin[1] Number (thousands)	Hispanic origin[1] Median income	All races Number (thousands)	All races Median income
All households	87,671	$42,504	12,849	$27,910	9,319	$30,735	104,705	$40,816
Region								
Northeast	17,110	44,211	2,316	27,181	1,469	27,997	20,087	41,984
Midwest	21,534	44,971	2,446	26,876	704	38,377	24,508	42,679
South	29,494	40,425	7,001	27,548	3,286	29,981	37,303	37,442
West	19,533	42,527	1,086	36,100	3,860	31,089	22,808	42,720
Type of household								
Family households	60,251	51,912	8,664	33,805	7,561	33,077	72,025	49,940
Married-couple families	48,790	57,242	4,144	50,758	5,133	37,583	55,311	56,827
Single-father household	3,081	42,401	706	37,825	658	34,320	4,028	41,838
Single-mother household	8,380	29,629	3,814	19,133	1,769	20,765	12,687	26,164
Nonfamily households	27,420	25,161	4,185	19,860	1,758	20,462	32,680	24,566
Male householder	12,204	31,619	1,876	24,235	974	24,387	14,641	30,753
Living alone	9,198	27,375	1,580	22,022	666	19,637	11,181	26,852
Female householder	15,215	20,311	2,309	15,886	783	14,682	18,039	19,917
Living alone	13,109	17,720	2,025	14,036	630	10,787	15,543	17,347
Size of household								
One person	22,307	21,460	3,605	17,062	1,296	15,162	26,724	21,083
Two persons	30,142	45,091	3,436	28,952	1,945	26,864	34,666	43,342
Three persons	13,837	54,052	2,525	33,347	1,787	31,832	17,152	51,190
Four persons	12,798	61,983	1,739	40,816	1,939	36,267	15,309	59,768
Five persons	5,682	57,392	898	40,510	1,265	36,292	6,981	54,440
Six persons	1,837	53,798	418	40,508	558	35,708	2,445	51,887
Seven persons or more	1,066	54,353	229	32,583	529	44,003	1,428	52,146
Number of earners								
No earners	17,500	16,699	2,492	8,776	1,168	9,278	20,521	15,405
One	29,544	33,984	5,593	23,097	3,321	21,708	36,689	31,948
Two	31,761	60,864	3,770	49,320	3,354	40,396	37,070	59,699
Three	6,526	74,577	780	64,465	974	51,934	7,687	74,074
Four or more	2,340	89,308	214	77,230	502	71,784	2,738	89,420

1. Persons of Hispanic origin may be of any race. *Source:* U.S. Bureau of the Census, *Money Income in the United States: 2000.* Web: www.census.gov.

Median Four-Person Family Income
(in current dollars)

Year	Income	Percent change	Year	Income	Percent change	Year	Income	Percent change
1999	$59,981	4.70%	1990	$41,151	1.7%	1981	$26,274	8.0%
1998	56,061	3.5	1989	40,763	4.4	1980	24,332	8.6
1997	53,350	3.6	1988	39,051	6.1	1979	22,395	9.6
1996	51,518	3.7	1987	36,812	6.0	1978	20,428	9.1
1995	49,687	5.7	1986	34,716	5.9	1977	18,723	8.1
1994	47,012	4.1	1985	32,777	5.4	1976	17,315	9.3
1993	45,161	2.1	1984	31,097	6.6	1975	15,848	7.5
1992	44,251	2.8	1983	29,184	5.7			
1991	43,056	3.9	1982	27,619	5.1			

Source: Income Statistics Branch/HHES Division, U.S. Bureau of the Census. Web: www.census.gov.

Per Capita Personal Income

Year	Amount	Year	Amount	Year	Amount	Year	Amount	Year	Amount	Year	Amount
1935	$ 474	1965	$2,773	1981	$10,949	1986	$15,122	1991	$19,652	1996	$24,651
1945	1,223	1970	3,893	1982	11,731	1987	15,968	1992	20,576	1997	25,924
1950	1,501	1975	5,851	1983	12,352	1988	17,052	1993	21,231	1998	27,203
1955	1,881	1979	8,638	1984	13,585	1989	18,176	1994	22,086	1999	28,546
1960	2,219	1980	9,910	1985	14,427	1990	19,188	1995	23,562	2000	29,676

Source: U.S. Department of Commerce, Bureau of Economic Analysis, *Survey of Current Business.* Web: www.bea.doc.gov/bea/regional/spi/.

Distribution of Household Income by Race

Income range	White 1972	White 1985	White 1998	Black 1972	Black 1985	Black 1998	Hispanic origin[1] 1972	Hispanic origin[1] 1985	Hispanic origin[1] 1998
Number of households (thousands)	60,618	76,576	87,212	6,809	9,797	12,579	2,655	5,213	9,060
Percent distribution									
Under $5,000	3.4%	3.0%	2.6%	8.0%	8.0%	7.3%	3.7%	5.0%	4.9%
$5,000 to $9,999	7.7	7.5	6.1	15.0	17.0	14.1	8.0	12.0	10.1
$10,000 to $14,999	7.3	7.4	7.4	12.7	11.2	10.6	11.7	11.5	10.9
$15,000 to $24,999	13.9	14.9	13.7	20.1	19.0	17.4	20.7	19.0	17.9
$25,000 to $34,999	14.7	14.0	13.2	15.6	13.6	13.5	20.1	15.4	16.3
$35,000 to $49,999	20.9	18.2	16.3	13.9	14.0	14.3	19.9	16.6	15.8
$50,000 to $74,999	20.0	18.9	19.3	11.4	11.3	13.2	11.4	13.0	14.0
$75,000 to $99,999	7.1	9.0	10.0	2.1	4.1	5.6	2.9	5.2	5.6
$100,000 and over	5.0	7.1	11.3	1.3	1.8	4.0	1.5	2.3	4.6
Median income	$37,347	$37,732	$40,912	$21,799	$22,449	$25,351	$28,184	$26,457	$28,330

1. Persons of Hispanic origin may be of any race. *Source:* U.S. Bureau of the Census. *Current Population Reports*, P60-206. Sept. 1999. Web: www.census.gov/hhes/www/income.html.

Per Capita Income and Personal Consumption Expenditures
(in current dollars)

Year	Gross national product	Personal income	Disposable personal income	Personal consumption expenditures Durable goods	Personal consumption expenditures Nondurable goods	Personal consumption expenditures Services	Personal consumption expenditures Total
1950	$ 1,950	$ 1,516	$ 1,388	$ 203	$ 648	$ 420	$ 1,270
1960	2,935	2,283	2,026	240	846	753	1,838
1970	5,101	4,101	3,591	414	1,326	1,424	3,164
1980	12,431	10,205	8,869	940	3,057	3,744	7,741
1990	23,331	19,614	17,176	1,871	4,985	8,472	15,327
1998	32,444	27,447	23,491	2,562	6,315	12,767	21,644
1999	33,927	28,489	24,242	2,787	6,708	13,399	22,895
2000	35,802	30,205	25,528	2,976	7,224	14,230	24,429

Source: U.S. Department of Commerce, Bureau of Economic Analysis, July 2001. Web: www.bea.doc.gov.

Per Capita Personal Income by State

State	1980	1990	1995	2000	State	1980	1990	1995	2000
Alabama	$ 7,465	$14,899	$19,683	$23,471	Montana	$ 8,342	$14,743	$18,764	$22,569
Alaska	13,007	20,887	25,798	30,064	Nebraska	8,895	17,379	22,196	27,829
Arizona	8,854	16,262	20,634	25,578	Nevada	10,848	20,248	25,808	30,529
Arkansas	7,113	13,779	18,546	22,257	New Hampshire	9,150	20,231	25,008	33,332
California	11,021	20,656	24,496	32,275	New Jersey	10,966	24,182	29,277	36,983
Colorado	10,143	18,818	24,865	32,949	New Mexico	7,940	14,213	18,852	22,203
Connecticut	11,532	25,426	31,947	40,640	New York	10,179	22,322	27,721	34,547
Delaware	10,059	19,719	25,391	31,255	North Carolina	7,780	16,284	21,938	27,194
DC	12,251	24,643	33,045	37,383	North Dakota	8,642	15,320	19,084	25,068
Florida	9,246	18,785	23,512	28,145	Ohio	9,399	17,547	22,887	28,400
Georgia	8,021	17,121	22,230	27,940	Oklahoma	9,018	15,117	19,394	23,517
Hawaii	10,129	20,905	25,584	28,221	Oregon	9,309	17,201	22,668	28,350
Idaho	8,105	15,304	19,630	24,180	Pennsylvania	9,353	18,884	23,738	29,539
Illinois	10,454	20,159	25,643	32,259	Rhode Island	9,227	19,035	24,046	29,685
Indiana	8,914	16,815	21,845	27,011	South Carolina	7,392	15,101	19,473	24,321
Iowa	9,226	16,683	21,181	26,723	South Dakota	7,800	15,628	19,848	26,115
Kansas	9,880	17,639	21,889	27,816	Tennessee	7,711	15,903	21,800	26,239
Kentucky	7,679	14,751	19,215	24,294	Texas	9,439	16,747	21,526	27,871
Louisiana	8,412	14,279	19,541	23,334	Utah	7,671	14,063	18,858	23,907
Maine	7,760	17,041	20,240	25,623	Vermont	7,957	17,444	21,359	26,901
Maryland	10,394	22,088	26,896	33,872	Virginia	9,413	19,543	24,456	31,162
Massachusetts	10,103	22,248	28,051	37,992	Washington	10,256	19,268	23,878	31,528
Michigan	9,801	18,239	23,975	29,612	West Virginia	7,764	13,964	17,913	21,915
Minnesota	9,673	18,784	24,583	32,101	Wisconsin	9,364	17,399	22,573	28,232
Mississippi	6,573	12,578	17,185	20,993	Wyoming	11,018	16,905	21,514	27,230
Missouri	8,812	17,407	22,094	27,445	**United States**	**9,494**	**18,667**	**23,562**	**29,676**

NOTE: Per capita personal income was computed using midyear population estimates of the Bureau of the Census. *Source:* U.S. Department of Commerce, Bureau of Economic Analysis, *Survey of Current Business.* Web: www.bea.doc.gov/bea/regional/spi/.

Consumer Credit Outstanding[1]
(in billions of dollars; not seasonally adjusted)

	Total	Commercial banks	Finance companies	Credit unions	Savings institutions	Nonfinancial business	Pools of securitized assets[2]
1975	$ 168.7	$ 82.9	$ 32.7	$ 25.7	n.a.	n.a.	n.a.
1980	302.1	147.0	62.3	44.0	n.a.	n.a.	n.a.
1985	526.3	245.1	111.7	72.7	n.a.	n.a.	n.a.
1990	751.9	347.1	133.3	93.1	n.a.	n.a.	n.a.
1995	1,122.8	502.0	152.1	131.9	$40.1	$85.1	$211.6
1999	1,426.2	499.8	181.6	167.9	61.5	80.3	435.1
2000	1,566.5	541.5	193.2	184.4	64.6	82.7	500.1

1. Covers most short- and intermediate-term credit extended to individuals, excluding loans secured by real estate. 2. Outstanding balances of pools upon which securities have been issued; these balances are no longer carried on the balance sheets of the loan originators. *Source:* Federal Reserve Board. Web http://www.bog.frb.fed.us.

Financial Debt Held by Families, 1998

Family characteristic	Any debt	Home-secured	Other residential property	Installment loans	Other lines of credit	Credit card balances	Other
Percent of families holding debt							
Total	74.1%	43.1%	5.1%	43.7%	2.3%	44.1%	8.8%
By age of head of family							
Under 35 years old	81.2	33.2	2.0	60.0	2.4	50.7	9.6
35 to 44 years old	87.6	58.7	6.7	53.3	3.6	51.3	11.4
45 to 54 years old	87.0	58.8	6.7	51.2	3.6	52.5	11.1
55 to 64 years old	76.4	49.4	7.8	37.9	1.6	45.7	8.3
65 to 74 years old	51.4	26.0	5.1	20.2	(1)	29.2	4.1
75 years old and over	24.6	11.5	1.8	4.2	(1)	11.2	2.0
By family income							
Less than $10,000	41.7	8.3	(1)	25.7	(1)	20.6	3.6
$10,000 to $24,999	63.7	21.3	1.8	34.4	1.2	37.9	7.0
$25,000 to $49,999	79.6	43.7	4.1	50.0	2.9	49.9	7.7
$50,000 to $99,999	89.4	71.0	7.7	55.0	3.3	56.7	12.2
$100,000 or more	87.8	73.4	16.4	43.2	2.6	40.4	14.8

NOTE: Percentages may not add up to 100 due to rounding. 1. Ten or fewer instances. *Source:* Board of Governors of the Federal Reserve System. *Federal Reserve Bulletin,* vol. 86 (Jan. 2000), pp. 1–29. Web: www.bog.frb.fed.us/pubs/bulletin.

Financial and Nonfinancial Assets of Families, 1989–1998

Type of financial asset	Percent distribution				Type of nonfinancial asset	Percent distribution			
	1989	1992	1995	1998		1989	1992	1995	1998
Total financial assets	100.0%	100.0%	100.0%	100.0%	**Total nonfinancial assets**	100.0%	100.0%	100.0%	100.0%
Transaction accounts	19.1	17.5	14.0	11.4	Vehicles	5.6	5.7	7.1	6.5
Certificates of deposit	10.2	8.1	5.7	4.3	Primary residence	45.9	47.0	47.4	47.1
Savings bonds	1.5	1.1	1.3	0.7	Other residential property	8.1	8.5	8.0	8.5
Bonds	10.2	8.4	6.3	4.3	Equity in nonresidential property	11.0	10.9	7.9	7.7
Stocks	15.0	16.5	15.7	22.7	Business equity	26.9	26.3	27.3	28.5
Mutual funds (excluding money market funds)	5.3	7.7	12.7	12.5	Other	2.5	1.6	2.3	1.7
Retirement accounts	21.5	25.5	27.9	27.5	**Nonfinancial assets as a share of total assets**	69.6%	68.5%	63.4%	59.4%
Cash value of life insurance	6.0	6.0	7.2	6.4					
Other managed assets	6.6	5.4	5.9	8.6					
Other	4.8	3.8	3.4	1.7					
Financial assets as a percentage of total assets	30.4%	31.5%	36.6%	40.6%					

NOTE: Percentages may not add up to 100 due to rounding. *Source:* Board of Governors of the Federal Reserve System. *Federal Reserve Bulletin,* vol. 86 (Jan. 2000), pp. 1–29. Web: www.bog.frb.fed.us/pubs/bulletin.

Poverty in the United States

Source: U.S. Bureau of the Census, *Poverty in the United States, 1999.* Web: www.census.gov.

The poverty rate dropped from 12.7% in 1998 to 11.8% in 1999—the lowest rate since 1979. In 1999, 32.3 million people were poor, down from 34.5 million in 1998. (Poverty is measured according to income thresholds that vary by family size.)

The poverty rate for people under age 18 dropped from 18.9% in 1998 to 16.9% in 1999—the lowest child poverty rate since 1979.

The poverty rate declined for people 65 years and over, from 10.5% in 1998 to a record-low 9.7% in 1999. Poverty rates and the number of poor declined for every racial and ethnic group.

Poverty rates have fallen below or equaled the lowest rate ever recorded for each group except whites:

• The poverty rate for blacks fell to a record low of 23.6% in 1999, down from the previous low of 26.1% in 1998. However, the poverty rate for blacks in 1999 was still about three times the poverty rate for white non-Hispanics (7.7%).
• The white non-Hispanic poverty rate fell to 7.7%, the lowest rate for this group since 1979 and not significantly different from the low rates during 1973–1974 and 1976–1979.
• The poverty rate for Hispanics (who may be of any race) declined from 25.6% in 1998 to 22.8% in 1999—not statistically different from the lowest rates recorded for this group (1972–1974 and 1976–1979).
• The poverty rate for Asians and Pacific Islanders declined from 12.5% in 1998 to 10.7% in 1999, equaling its record low since 1987, when poverty data for this group first became available.

The 1997–1999 average poverty rate for American Indians and Alaska Natives was 25.9%, higher than for white non-Hispanics and Asians and Pacific Islanders, but not statistically different from blacks and Hispanics.

Poverty rates declined in the Northeast and West in 1999, to 10.9% and 12.6%, down from 12.3% and 14%, respectively, in 1998. The poverty rate did not change significantly in the South or Midwest.

Four-fifths (81%) of the net decline in the number of poor occurred in central cities within metropolitan areas, where only 29% of all people and 41% of the poor lived.

In seven states and in the District of Columbia, the poverty rate decreased significantly, based on comparing two-year moving averages of 1998–1999 with those for 1997–1998, and no state showed an increase. Poverty rates dropped in Arizona, Arkansas, California, the District of Columbia, New York, South Dakota, Utah, and Virginia.

The average income deficit for poor families (the average dollar amount needed to raise a poor family out of poverty) was $6,687 in 1999, statistically unchanged from 1998.

Age

The number of poor and the poverty rate decreased significantly for people under age 18, people age 65 and over, and people aged 25 to 44. For children (people under age 18), the poverty rate declined to 12.1 million in 1999, down from 18.9% and 13.5 million in 1998. The 1999 child poverty rate of 16.9% was not statistically different from the child poverty rate in 1979 (16.4%), but was lower than the rate for every year since.

Despite this decline, children were more likely to be poor than most of the other age groups. The 1999 child poverty rate of 16.9% was not significantly different from the poverty rate for 18–24-year-olds (17.3%) but was higher than the poverty rates for the other age groups. Related children under age 6 remained particularly vulnerable—with a 1999 poverty rate of 18%, although that was significantly lower than the 20.6% reported for 1998. Related children under age 6 living in families with a female householder, no husband present, had a poverty rate (50.3% in 1999) that was more than five times the rate for their counterparts in married-couple families (9%).

Weighted Average Poverty Thresholds[1] for Families of Specified Size, 1960–2000

Calendar year	Individual	Families of 2 persons or more						
		2 persons	3 persons	4 persons	5 persons	6 persons	7 persons
1960	$1,490	$ 1,924	$ 2,359	$ 3,022	$ 3,560	$ 4,002	$ 4,921[2]
1965	1,582	2,048	2,514	3,223	3,797	4,264	5,248[2]
1970	1,954	2,525	3,099	3,968	4,680	5,260	6,468[2]
1975	2,724	3,506	4,293	5,500	6,499	7,316	9,022[2]
1980	4,190	5,363	6,565	8,414	9,966	11,269	12,761
1985	5,469	6,998	8,573	10,989	13,007	14,696	16,656
1990	6,652	8,509	10,419	13,359	15,792	17,839	20,241
1995	7,763	9,933	12,158	15,569	18,408	20,804	23,552
1996	7,995	10,223	12,516	16,036	18,952	21,389	24,268
1997	8,183	10,473	12,802	16,400	19,380	21,886	24,802
1998	8,316	10,634	13,003	16,660	19,680	22,228	25,257
1999	8,501	10,869	13,290	17,029	20,127	22,727	25,912
2000	8,959	11,531	13,470	17,761	21,419	24,636	28,347

1. Annual income. 2. For years before 1980, data are for families with seven persons or more. *Source:* U.S. Bureau of the Census. Web: www.census.gov.

Persons Below Poverty Level, 1975–1999
(in thousands)

Year	All persons	White	Black	Hispanic origin[1]	Year	All persons	White	Black	Hispanic origin[1]
1975	25,877	17,770	7,545	2,991	1988	31,745	20,715	9,356	5,357
1976	24,975	16,713	7,595	2,783	1989	32,415	21,294	9,525	6,086
1977	24,720	16,416	7,726	2,700	1990	33,585	22,326	9,837	6,006
1978	24,497	16,259	7,625	2,607	1991	35,708	23,747	10,242	6,339
1979	26,072	17,214	8,050	2,921	1992	38,014	25,259	10,827	7,592
1980	29,272	19,699	8,579	3,491	1993	39,265	26,226	10,877	8,126
1981	31,822	21,553	9,173	3,713	1994	38,059	25,379	10,196	8,416
1982	34,398	23,517	9,697	4,301	1995	36,425	24,423	9,872	8,574
1983	35,303	23,984	9,882	4,633	1996	36,529	24,650	9,694	8,697
1984	33,700	22,955	9,490	4,806	1997	35,574	24,396	9,116	8,308
1985	33,064	22,860	8,926	5,236	1998	34,476	23,454	9,091	8,070
1986	32,370	22,183	8,983	5,117	1999	32,258	21,922	8,360	7,439
1987	32,221	21,195	9,520	5,422					

1. Persons of Hispanic origin may be of any race. *Source:* U.S. Bureau of the Census. Web: www.census.gov.

Characteristics of Persons Below Poverty Level in 1989 and 1999
(in thousands)

	1999 Number	1999 Percent	1989 Number	1989 Percent		1999 Number	1999 Percent	1989 Number	1989 Percent
Total[1]	**32,258**	**11.8%**	**32,415**	**13.1%**	35 to 44 years	3,733	8.3%	3,115	8.3%
Race					45 to 54 years	2,466	6.7	1,873	7.5
White	21,922	9.8	21,294	10.2	55 to 59 years	1,179	9.2	971	9.5
Black	8,360	23.6	9,525	30.8	60 to 64 years	1,033	9.8	986	9.4
Asian and Pacific					65 years and				
Islander	1,118	10.4	1,032	14.2	over	3,167	9.7	3,312	11.4
Hispanic origin[2]	7,439	22.8	6,086	26.3	**Region**				
Age					Northeast	5,678	10.9	5,213	10.2
Under 18 years	12,109	16.9	13,154	20.1	Midwest	6,210	9.8	7,088	12.0
18 to 24 years	4,603	17.3	4,132	15.4	South	12,538	13.1	13,277	15.6
25 to 34 years	3,968	10.5	4,873	11.2	West	7,833	12.6	6,838	12.8

1. Includes races not shown separately. 2. Persons of Hispanic origin may be of any race. *Source:* U.S. Census Bureau, *Poverty in the United States, 1999,* Sept. 2000. Web: www.census.gov.

Percent of People in Poverty by State, 1997–1999

State	3-year average 1997–1999	Average 1998–1999	Average 1997–1998	State	3-year average 1997–1999	Average 1998–1999	Average 1997–1998
United States	12.6%	12.3%	13.0%	Missouri	11.1%	10.7%	10.8%
Alabama	15.1	14.8	15.1	Montana	15.9	16.1	16.1
Alaska	8.6	8.5	9.1	Nebraska	11.0	11.6	11.1
Arizona	15.2	14.3	16.9	Nevada	11.0	10.9	10.8
Arkansas	16.4	14.7	17.2	New Hampshire	8.9	8.8	9.4
California	15.3	14.6	16.0	New Jersey	8.5	8.2	8.9
Colorado	8.6	8.7	8.7	New Mexico	20.8	20.5	20.8
Connecticut	8.4	8.3	9.0	New York	15.7	15.4	16.6
Delaware	10.1	10.3	10.0	North Carolina	13.0	13.8	12.7
DC	19.7	18.6	22.0	North Dakota	13.9	14.1	14.4
Florida	13.3	12.8	13.7	Ohio	11.4	11.6	11.1
Georgia	13.7	13.2	14.0	Oklahoma	13.5	13.4	13.9
Hawaii	11.9	10.9	12.4	Oregon	13.1	13.8	13.3
Idaho	13.9	13.5	13.8	Pennsylvania	10.6	10.3	11.2
Illinois	10.4	10.0	10.6	Rhode Island	11.4	10.7	12.2
Indiana	8.3	8.0	9.1	South Carolina	12.8	12.7	13.4
Iowa	8.7	8.3	9.3	South Dakota	11.7	9.3	13.7
Kansas	10.5	10.9	9.6	Tennessee	13.2	12.7	13.9
Kentucky	13.8	12.8	14.7	Texas	15.6	15.0	15.9
Louisiana	18.2	19.1	17.7	Utah	7.9	7.3	8.9
Maine	10.4	10.5	10.2	Vermont	9.6	9.8	9.6
Maryland	7.6	7.2	7.8	Virginia	9.8	8.4	10.8
Massachusetts	10.9	10.3	10.4	Washington	9.2	9.2	9.1
Michigan	10.3	10.3	10.6	West Virginia	16.7	16.8	17.1
Minnesota	9.1	8.8	10.0	Wisconsin	8.5	8.7	8.5
Mississippi	16.8	16.9	17.1	Wyoming	11.9	11.1	12.1

Source: U.S. Census Bureau, *Poverty in the United States, 1999,* published Sept. 2000. Web: www.census.gov.

Social Welfare Expenditures Under Public Programs
(in millions of dollars)

Item	1965	1970	1975	1980	1985	1990	1995
Amount							
Gross domestic product	$701,000	$1,023,100	$1,590,800	$2,718,900	$4,108,000	$5,682,900	$7,186,900
Total social welfare expenditures[1]	77,084	145,979	288,967	492,213	731,840	1,048,951	1,505,136
Social insurance	28,123	54,691	123,013	229,754	369,595	513,822	705,483
Public aid	6,283	16,488	41,447	72,703	98,362	146,811	253,530
Health and medical programs	6,155	10,030	16,535	26,762	38,643	61,684	85,507
Veterans' programs	6,031	9,078	17,019	21,466	27,042	30,916	39,072
Education	28,108	50,846	80,834	121,050	172,048	258,332	365,625
Housing	318	701	3,172	6,879	12,598	19,468	29,361
Other social welfare	2,066	4,145	6,947	13,599	13,552	17,918	26,558
All health and medical care[2]	9,302	24,801	51,022	99,145	170,665	274,472	435,075
As percent of gross domestic product							
Gross domestic product	100.0%	100.0%	100.0%	100.0%	100.0%	100.0%	100.0%
Total social welfare expenditures	11.0	14.3	18.2	18.1	17.8	18.5	20.9
Social insurance	4.0	5.3	7.7	8.5	9.0	9.0	9.8
Public aid	.9	1.6	2.6	2.7	2.4	2.6	3.5
Health and medical programs	.9	1.0	1.0	1.0	.9	1.1	1.2
Veterans' programs	.9	.9	1.1	.8	.7	.5	.5
Education	4.0	5.0	5.1	4.5	4.2	4.5	5.1
Housing	(3)	.1	.2	.3	.3	.3	.4
Other social welfare	.3	.4	.4	.5	.3	.3	.4
All health and medical care	1.3	2.4	3.2	3.6	4.2	4.8	6.1

NOTES: Through 1976, fiscal year ended June 30 for federal government, most states, and some localities. Beginning in 1977, federal fiscal year ended Sept. 30. 1. Represents program and administrative expenditures from federal, state, and local public revenues and trust funds under public law. Includes workers' compensation and temporary disability insurance payments made through private carriers and self-insurers. Includes capital outlay and some expenditures abroad. 2. Combines "health and medical programs" with medical services provided in connection with social insurance, public aid, veterans', and "other social welfare" categories. 3. Less than 0.05%. *Source:* Social Security Administration. Web: www.ssa.gov/statistics/Supplement/1999/tables/index.html.

Drop in Welfare Rolls, 1993–2000

	Number of families on welfare Jan. 1993	Number of families on welfare June 2000	Percent reduction 1993–2000		Number of families on welfare Jan. 1993	Number of families on welfare June 2000	Percent reduction 1993–2000
Alabama	51,910	18,677	−64%	Nebraska	16,637	10,088	−39%
Alaska	11,626	7,542	−35	Nevada	12,892	6,916	−46
Arizona	68,982	31,897	−54	New Hampshire	10,805	5,791	−46
Arkansas	26,897	12,046	−55	New Jersey	126,179	50,126	−60
California	844,494	489,054	−42	New Mexico	31,103	22,701	−27
Colorado	42,445	10,772	−75	New York	428,191	248,148	−42
Connecticut	56,759	27,149	−52	North Carolina	128,946	44,731	−65
Delaware	11,315	5,819	−49	North Dakota	6,577	2,887	−56
DC	24,628	22,397	−09	Ohio	257,665	95,835	−63
Florida	256,145	62,805	−75	Oklahoma	50,955	7,251	−86
Georgia	142,040	51,215	−64	Oregon	42,409	17,121	−60
Guam	1,406	2,760	96	Pennsylvania	204,216	87,972	−57
Hawaii	17,869	14,942	−16	Puerto Rico	60,950	31,273	−49
Idaho	7,838	1,382	−82	Rhode Island	21,900	16,324	−25
Illinois	229,308	85,807	−63	South Carolina	54,599	15,496	−72
Indiana	73,115	35,068	−52	South Dakota	7,262	2,789	−62
Iowa	36,515	20,082	−45	Tennessee	112,159	55,491	−51
Kansas	29,818	12,404	−58	Texas	279,002	128,289	−54
Kentucky	83,320	37,471	−55	Utah	18,606	8,157	−56
Louisiana	89,931	25,521	−72	Vermont	10,081	5,858	−42
Maine	23,903	10,654	−55	Virgin Islands	1,073	778	−27
Maryland	80,256	28,895	−64	Virginia	73,446	30,078	−59
Massachusetts	113,571	41,682	−63	Washington	100,568	54,768	−46
Michigan	228,237	70,897	−69	West Virginia	41,525	10,661	−74
Minnesota	63,995	39,295	−39	Wisconsin	81,291	16,410	−80
Mississippi	60,520	14,979	−75	Wyoming	6,493	565	−91
Missouri	88,744	45,912	−48	**U.S. total**	**4,963,050**	**2,208,095**	**−56**
Montana	11,793	4,467	−62				

Source: U.S. Dept. of Health and Human Services, Administration for Children and Families. Web: www.acf.dhhs.gov.

Social Security

Source: Social Security Administration

The original Social Security Act was passed in 1935 and is administered by the Social Security Administration and other agencies within the Department of Health and Human Services.

What Does Social Security Offer?

The Social Security contribution you pay gives you four different kinds of protection: (1) retirement benefits, (2) survivors' benefits, (3) disability benefits, and (4) Medicare hospital insurance benefits.

Retirement Benefits

Currently, as a worker you become eligible for the full amount of your retirement benefits at age 65. You may retire at age 62 and get 80% of your full benefit. The closer you are to age 65 when you start collecting your benefit, the larger the fraction of your full benefit you will get.

The amount of the retirement benefit you are entitled to at age 65 is the key to all other benefits under the program. The retirement benefit is based on covered earnings, which will be updated (indexed) to reflect the increases in average wages that have occurred since the earnings were paid. Your largest 35 years of adjusted earnings are averaged together and a formula is applied to the adjusted average to figure the benefit rate.

In general, the highest retirement check that can be paid to a worker who retired at 65 in January 1997 is about $1,327.60 a month. Maximum payment to the family of this retired worker is about $2,324.40 as of January 1997.

Survivor Benefits

This feature of the Social Security program gives your family valuable life-insurance protection. The amount of protection is again geared to what the worker would be entitled to if he had been age 65 when he died. Total family survivor benefits were estimated to be as high as $2,534.00 a month if the worker died in 1995. Your survivors could get:

1. A one-time cash payment of $255 for your spouse or minor children if you have enough work credits.
2. A benefit for each child until he or she reaches 18 (or 19, if the child is in full-time attendance at an elementary or secondary school), or at any age if disabled before 22. "Child" includes biological or legally adopted children, or dependent stepchildren or grandchildren.
3. A benefit for your widow(er), at any age, if she/he has your entitled children under 16 or disabled in care.
4. Your spouse or divorced spouse can get a widow's, widower's, or surviving divorced spouse's benefit starting at age 60. A widow, or widower, who first becomes entitled at 65 or later will get 100% of his or her deceased spouse's basic amount (or the amount of the deceased spouse's reduced benefits).
5. Dependent parents can sometimes collect survivors' benefits. They are usually eligible if: (a) they were getting at least half their support from the deceased worker; (b) they have reached 62; (c) they are not eligible for a greater retirement benefit based on their own earnings; and (d) they have not married since the worker's death.

Disability Benefits

Disability benefits can be paid to several groups of people:

• Disabled workers under age 65 and their families.

• Persons disabled before age 22 who continue to be disabled. These benefits are payable as early as age 18 when a parent (or step-parent or grandparent under certain circumstances) receives Social Security retirement or disability benefits or when an insured parent dies.

• Disabled widows and widowers and (under certain conditions) disabled, surviving, and divorced spouses of workers who were insured at death. These benefits are payable as early as 50. Consult your local Social Security office for the latest disability information.

The SSA determines whether or not you qualify for disability benefits based on criteria including the severity of your condition and the earnings you continue to receive after you become disabled. To be considered for disability benefits, you should file a claim with a Social Security office as soon as you become disabled. However, even if you are approved, benefits will not begin until after a waiting period of six months after the beginning of your disability.

Medicare Program

Medicare is the nation's largest health insurance program. Generally, you are eligible for Medicare if you or your spouse worked for at least ten years in Medicare-covered employment and you are 65 years old and a citizen or permanent resident of the United States. You might also qualify for coverage if you are a younger person with a disability or with chronic kidney disease.

Medicare-covered services include:

• **Hospital insurance.** Financial assistance is available for necessary medical care and services furnished by Medicare-certified hospitals, skilled nursing facilities, home health agencies, and hospices.

• **Inpatient hospital care.** Medicare helps pay for up to 90 days of inpatient hospital care in each benefit period. Covered services include your semi-private room and meals, general nursing services, operating and recovery room costs, intensive care, drugs, laboratory tests, X rays, and all other necessary medical services and supplies.

• **Skilled nursing facility care.** You may need inpatient skilled nursing or rehabilitation services after a hospital stay. If you meet certain conditions, Medicare will help pay for up to 100 days in a participating skilled nursing facility in each benefit period.

• **Home health care.** If you meet certain conditions, Medicare pays the full approved cost of covered home health care services. This includes part-time or intermittent skilled nursing services prescribed by a physician for treatment or rehabilitation of homebound patients.

• **Hospice care.** Medicare helps pay for hospice care for terminally ill beneficiaries who select the hospice care benefit.

• **Medical insurance (Part B).** Medicare Part B helps pay for doctor's services, outpatient hospital services (including emergency room visits), ambulance transportation, diagnostic tests, laboratory services, some preventive care like mammography and Pap smear screening, outpatient therapy services, durable medical equipment and supplies, and a variety of other health services.

Additional benefits are available through the Medicare program. For further information contact the Social Security Administration at 1-800-772-1213.

Average Monthly Social Security Benefits, 1940–1999

Year	Retired workers			Disabled workers			Non-disabled widows
	Total	Men	Women	Total	Men	Women	
1940	$ 22.71	$ 23.26	$ 18.38	—	—	—	$ 20.36
1945	25.11	25.71	19.99	—	—	—	20.17
1950[1]	29.03	30.16	22.98	—	—	—	21.65
1955	69.74	75.86	56.05	—	—	—	49.68
1960	81.73	92.03	63.26	$ 91.16	$ 94.02	$ 78.91	62.12
1965[1]	82.69	90.89	68.78	93.26	97.89	80.27	73.81
1970	123.82	136.80	103.67	139.79	148.39	115.74	106.95
1975[2]	196.42	220.35	160.50	220.60	241.48	175.27	185.34
1980[2]	321.10	374.00	244.90	352.10	388.80	269.70	277.50
1985[3]	432.00	509.60	322.20	459.20	514.00	345.00	431.10
1990[3]	550.50	654.60	403.30	566.90	637.80	438.90	541.10
1995[3]	671.70	794.30	505.80	675.70	767.30	546.00	662.50
1998[3]	744.70	882.10	577.10	737.00	841.50	610.60	716.70
1999	757.71	904.62	697.50	754.12	846.48	629.63	776.07

1. Jan.–Aug. 2. Jan.–May. 3. Jan.–Nov. *Source:* Social Security Administration, *Social Security Bulletin: Annual Statistical Supplement, 2000.*

The Federal Budget, 1995–2002

(in millions of dollars)

Description	Actual			Estimates	
	1995	1999	2000	2001	2002
Receipts by source					
Individual income taxes	$590,244	$879,480	$1,004,462	$1,072,927	$1,078,789
Corporate income taxes	157,004	184,680	207,289	213,069	218,786
Social insurance and retirement receipts	484,473	611,833	652,852	689,656	725,798
Excise taxes	57,484	70,414	68,865	71,148	74,020
Estate and gift taxes	14,763	27,782	29,010	31,072	28,699
Customs duties and fees	19,301	18,336	19,914	21,442	22,537
Miscellaneous receipts:					
Deposits of earnings by Federal Reserve System	23,378	25,917	32,293	26,599	31,893
All other[1]	5,183	9,012	10,533	11,033	11,212
Total receipts	1,351,830	1,827,454	2,025,218	2,136,946	2,191,734
Outlays by function					
National defense	272,066	274,873	294,494	299,136	319,193
International affairs	16,434	15,243	17,216	17,461	21,000
General science, space, and technology	16,724	18,125	18,637	19,726	20,798
Energy	4,936	912	−1,060	−655	−322
Natural resources and environment	21,915	23,968	25,031	27,370	27,494
Agriculture	9,778	23,011	36,641	25,922	18,622
Commerce and housing credit	−17,808	2,647	3,211	−768	6,946
Transportation	39,350	42,533	46,854	51,079	55,038
Community and regional development	10,749	11,870	10,629	10,572	11,743
Education, training, employment, and social services	54,263	56,241	59,201	65,251	76,602
Health	115,418	141,074	154,534	175,306	201,501
Medicare	159,855	190,447	197,113	219,258	229,903
Income security	220,493	237,707	247,895	262,617	275,675
Social security	335,846	390,041	409,436	433,623	455,119
Veterans benefits and services	37,890	43,212	47,083	45,363	51,582
Administration of justice	16,216	25,924	27,820	29,430	32,283
General government	13,998	15,757	13,454	16,834	16,308
Net interest	232,169	229,735	223,218	206,369	188,131
Total outlays	1,515,837	1,702,875	1,788,826	1,856,238	1,960,564
Total surplus or deficit (−)	−164,007	124,579	236,392	280,708	231,170

1. Beginning 1984, includes universal service fund receipts. *Source:* Department of the Treasury and Office of Management and Budget.

Receipts and Outlays of the Federal Government, 1789–2005
(in millions of dollars)

From 1789 to 1842, the federal fiscal year ended on December 31; from 1844 to 1976, on June 30; and beginning in 1977, on September 30.

Year	Total			On-budget[1]		
	Receipts	Outlays	Surplus or deficit (–)	Receipts	Outlays	Surplus or deficit (–)
1789–1849	$ 1,160	$ 1,090	$ 70	$ 1,160	$ 1,090	$ 70
1850–1900	14,462	15,453	–991	14,462	15,453	–991
1905	544	567	–23	544	567	–23
1910	676	694	–18	676	694	–18
1915	683	746	–63	683	746	–63
1920	6,649	6,358	291	6,649	6,358	291
1925	3,641	2,924	717	3,641	2,924	717
1930	4,058	3,320	738	4,058	3,320	738
1935	3,609	6,412	–2,803	3,609	6,412	–2,803
1940	6,548	9,468	–2,920	5,998	9,482	–3,484
1945	45,159	92,712	–47,553	43,849	92,569	–48,720
1950	39,443	42,562	–3,119	37,336	42,038	–4,702
1955	65,451	68,444	–2,933	60,370	64,461	–4,091
1960	92,492	92,191	301	81,851	81,341	510
1965	116,817	118,228	–1,411	100,094	101,699	–1,605
1970	192,807	195,649	–2,842	159,348	168,042	–8,694
1975	279,090	332,332	–53,242	216,633	271,892	–55,260
1980	517,112	590,947	–73,835	403,903	476,618	–72,715
1985	734,088	946,423	–212,334	547,918	769,615	–221,698
1990	1,031,969	1,253,198	–221,229	750,314	1,028,133	–277,819
1995	1,351,830	1,515,837	–164,007	1,000,751	1,227,173	–226,422
2000[2]	2,025,218	1,788,826	236,392	1,544,634	1,458,061	86,573
2005[2]	2,437,783	2,168,745	269,038	1,808,786	1,776,379	32,407

1. Excludes the Social Security surplus. For years prior to 1933, on-budget surplus was not calculated separately. 2. Estimated. *Source:* The Budget for Fiscal Year 2001.

Gross Domestic Product or Expenditure, 1930–2000
(in billions of dollars)

Item	1930	1940	1950	1960	1970	1980	1990	1999	2000[1]
Gross domestic product	$91.3	$101.3	$294.3	$527.4	$1,039.7	$2,795.6	$5,803.2	$9,268.6	$9,872.9
Personal consumption expenditures	70.2	71.2	192.7	332.2	648.9	1,762.9	3,831.5	6,250.2	6,728.4
Gross private domestic investment	10.8	13.6	54.1	75.7	150.4	484.2	847.2	1,636.7	1,767.5
Exports of goods and services	4.4	4.8	12.3	25.3	57.0	278.9	557.2	989.8	1,102.9
Imports of goods and services	4.1	3.4	11.6	22.8	55.8	293.8	628.6	1,240.6	1,466.9
Government	10.0	15.1	46.9	113.8	237.1	569.7	1,181.4	1,632.5	1,741.0

NOTE: Government consumption expenditures and gross investment. 1. Preliminary data. *Source:* U.S. Bureau of Economic Analysis. Web: www.bea.doc.gov.

The Public Debt

Year	Gross debt amount	Year	Gross debt amount	Year	Gross debt amount	Year	Gross debt amount
1800	$82,976,294	1855	$ 35,586,957	1910	$ 2,652,665,838	1965	$ 320,904,110,042
1805	82,312,151	1860	64,842,288	1915	3,058,136,873	1970	389,158,403,690
1810	53,173,218	1865	2,680,647,870	1920	25,952,456,406	1975	576,649,000,000[1]
1815	99,833,660	1870	2,480,672,428	1925	20,516,193,888	1980	930,210,000,000[1]
1820	91,015,566	1875	2,232,284,532	1930	16,185,309,831	1985	1,945,941,616,460
1825	83,788,433	1880	2,120,415,371	1935	28,700,892,625	1990	3,233,313,451,777
1830	48,565,407	1885	1,863,964,873	1940	42,967,531,038	1995	4,973,982,900,709
1835	33,733	1890	1,552,140,205	1945	258,682,187,410	1999	5,656,270,901,615
1840	3,573,344	1895	1,676,120,983	1950	257,357,352,351	2000	5,674,178,209,887
1845	15,925,303	1900	2,136,961,092	1955	280,768,553,189		
1850	63,452,774	1905	2,274,615,064	1960	290,216,815,242		

NOTE: Figures as of Jan. 1 for years 1800–1840; as of July 1 for years 1845–1920; as of June 30 for years 1925–1950; as of Dec. 31 for years 1955–1985; as of Sept. 30 for years 1990–present. 1. Rounded to millions. *Source:* U.S. Department of the Treasury, The Public Debt Online. Web: www.publicdebt.treas.gov/opd/opd.htm.

Summary of Federal Government Expenditure, by State and Territory, Fiscal Year 2000

(in millions of dollars)

State and outlying area	Total	Retirement and disability	Other direct payments	Grants	Procurement	Salaries and wages
United States total	1,637,170	555,757	365,023	308,530	223,324	184,537
Alabama	29,217	10,540	6,280	4,833	4,691	2,873
Alaska	5,953	845	477	2,174	1,108	1,349
Arizona	29,244	10,138	6,252	4,704	5,286	2,865
Arkansas	14,828	6,164	4,120	2,778	587	1,178
California	175,751	54,224	40,657	36,080	26,955	17,835
Colorado	22,918	7,280	3,911	3,591	4,349	3,787
Connecticut	19,517	6,734	4,656	4,033	2,699	1,396
Delaware	3,959	1,646	904	838	149	422
District of Columbia	28,254	1,768	2,113	4,675	7,491	12,208
Florida	92,776	39,748	24,151	12,149	8,594	8,135
Georgia	42,460	14,221	8,916	7,520	5,102	6,700
Hawaii	9,015	2,583	1,377	1,348	1,278	2,429
Idaho	7,009	2,385	1,279	1,270	1,347	728
Illinois	60,008	22,171	16,401	11,228	3,999	6,210
Indiana	28,723	11,677	7,543	5,108	2,192	2,204
Iowa	14,751	6,022	3,912	2,714	1,115	988
Kansas	14,260	5,485	3,312	2,323	1,297	1,844
Kentucky	24,444	8,915	5,371	4,687	2,747	2,724
Louisiana	25,955	8,413	6,883	5,300	3,096	2,264
Maine	7,849	2,941	1,478	1,770	881	779
Maryland	45,089	11,441	7,012	6,911	10,551	9,174
Massachusetts	40,824	12,434	10,227	9,070	6,006	3,087
Michigan	46,823	19,207	12,009	10,107	2,374	3,126
Minnesota	22,992	8,297	5,954	4,753	2,090	1,897
Mississippi	18,358	6,063	5,082	3,517	1,978	1,718
Missouri	35,687	11,805	8,455	5,939	6,053	3,437
Montana	5,917	1,982	1,484	1,474	288	689
Nebraska	9,611	3,450	2,920	1,720	486	1,035
Nevada	8,626	3,774	1,701	1,340	836	976
New Hampshire	5,802	2,446	1,124	1,238	523	471
New Jersey	43,469	16,337	11,411	7,876	4,106	3,739
New Mexico	14,470	3,740	1,872	3,032	4,134	1,692
New York	110,333	36,155	27,827	31,564	6,909	7,879
North Carolina	41,367	15,960	8,807	8,518	2,555	5,527
North Dakota	5,245	1,272	2,017	1,101	238	616
Ohio	57,355	22,751	14,445	10,665	4,867	4,627
Oklahoma	20,613	7,630	4,509	3,583	1,940	2,951
Oregon	16,553	6,893	3,598	3,684	790	1,589
Pennsylvania	73,715	28,477	19,400	13,940	6,284	5,615
Rhode Island	6,876	2,288	1,708	1,574	584	722
South Carolina	22,294	8,646	4,231	4,163	2,774	2,481
South Dakota	5,138	1,548	1,639	1,088	279	584
Tennessee	33,560	11,883	7,255	6,372	5,217	2,833
Texas	106,493	33,539	23,500	18,346	18,981	12,126
Utah	10,037	3,337	1,436	2,065	1,597	1,603
Vermont	3,362	1,175	618	929	320	320
Virginia	62,709	16,548	7,199	5,163	21,321	12,477
Washington	33,897	11,749	6,199	6,345	4,664	4,940
West Virginia	11,739	4,962	2,462	2,729	622	963
Wisconsin	24,300	10,145	5,841	5,254	1,460	1,600
Wyoming	3,220	989	468	1,022	323	417
American Samoa	112	34	1	59	15	3
Micronesia	27	—	5	22	—	—
Guam	839	161	72	138	222	247
Marshall Islands	41	1	—	10	30	—
Northern Marianas	70	14	4	47	2	2
Palau	16	—	—	5	11	—
Puerto Rico	12,103	4,604	2,423	3,842	415	819
Virgin Islands	487	118	114	195	14	45
Undistributed	20,107	3	—	10	16,501	3,593

NOTE: Detail may not add to total due to rounding. *Source: Consolidated Federal Funds Report for Fiscal Year 2000.* www.census.gov.

U.S. Direct Investment in Other Countries, 2000
(in millions of dollars)

	All industries	Petro-leum	Manu-facturing	Wholesale trade	Banking	Finance, insurance, real estate	Services	Other industries
All countries	$1,244,654	$105,486	$343,992	$88,090	$37,155	$497,267	$79,857	$92,809
Canada	126,421	18,018	50,425	9,834	1,999	29,125	8,297	8,724
Europe	648,731	32,566	177,445	50,869	23,941	272,340	49,504	42,066
Austria	3,676	(D)	1,114	592	1,601	126	164	(D)
Belgium	16,409	−164	7,346	1,828	543	4,024	2,996	−163
Denmark	5,618	1,099	2,340	619	(*)	1,278	111	171
Finland	1,279	81	672	328	20	−3	68	114
France	39,087	1,010	16,515	2,558	1,823	9,964	5,537	1,680
Germany	53,610	2,946	26,801	3,215	699	14,678	2,729	2,542
Greece	672	78	29	178	117	152	40	77
Ireland	33,369	667	9,874	620	−50	12,668	9,277	313
Italy	23,622	(D)	14,498	2,637	270	1,929	2,236	(D)
Luxembourg	19,470	49	2,297	1,111	310	15,649	35	19
Netherlands	115,506	3,149	24,228	10,486	(D)	71,373	4,602	(D)
Norway	6,303	4,192	810	325	(D)	609	253	(D)
Portugal	1,784	(D)	479	278	128	214	491	(D)
Spain	14,561	149	8,603	1,608	2,096	1,176	559	370
Sweden	11,371	93	2,860	354	(D)	6,022	1,141	(D)
Switzerland	54,873	152	4,698	15,577	2,974	28,384	1,687	1,402
Turkey	1,378	46	746	30	351	2	53	150
United Kingdom	233,384	15,749	50,994	7,953	9,930	100,273	17,258	31,227
Other	12,760	2,126	2,543	571	(D)	3,822	269	(D)
Latin America and other								
Western Hemisphere	239,388	9,084	50,696	9,076	−1,639	140,655	7,301	24,215
South America	79,354	6,317	27,245	2,063	5,871	17,993	2,768	17,096
Argentina	14,489	654	3,623	389	2,319	5,633	698	1,172
Brazil	35,560	1,102	18,940	792	2,139	6,240	925	5,424
Chile	10,846	73	1,363	374	700	3,557	210	4,569
Colombia	4,423	772	1,373	96	(D)	758	48	(D)
Ecuador	838	461	175	53	(D)	124	5	(D)
Peru	3,317	358	196	56	(D)	841	55	(D)
Venezuela	8,423	2,803	1,366	176	51	727	811	2,489
Other	1,456	93	210	129	309	112	17	587
Central America	74,754	1,264	21,874	3,112	1,238	41,506	1,393	4,366
Costa Rica	1,983	31	764	1,147	0	2	−2	41
Guatemala	904	474	230	34	(D)	123	3	(D)
Honduras	115	(D)	192	3	(D)	9	0	−119
Mexico	35,414	163	20,379	1,450	1,189	6,732	1,200	4,301
Panama	35,407	273	152	446	16	34,388	182	−50
Other	931	(D)	157	33	(D)	252	10	(D)
Other Western Hemisphere	85,280	1,502	1,577	3,901	−8,748	81,156	3,139	2,753
Bahamas	668	631	(D)	(D)	−3,783	3,507	32	55
Barbados	1,227	(D)	65	331	24	312	331	(D)
Bermuda	54,114	(D)	(D)	2,682	0	49,316	2,380	(D)
Dominican Republic	1,126	(D)	590	49	90	(*)	19	(D)
Jamaica	2,596	(D)	239	259	(D)	14	53	1,969
Netherlands Antilles	3,725	(*)	(D)	62	0	3,641	(D)	(*)
Trinidad and Tobago	1,331	1,063	62	(D)	(D)	(D)	1	118
United Kingdom Islands, Caribbean	20,165	322	146	322	−5,174	23,970	261	317
Other	329	−74	(D)	(*)	(D)	(D)	(D)	(D)
Africa	15,813	10,085	2,226	268	413	1,425	98	1,298
Egypt	2,735	2,053	581	(D)	(D)	0	−138	4
Nigeria	1,283	881	58	(D)	(D)	274	0	6
South Africa	2,826	6	947	166	(D)	(D)	118	(Other)
Other	8,969	7,145	640	(D)	140	(D)	118	(D)
Middle East	11,851	2,864	2,490	299	863	2,283	1,018	2,033
Israel	3,426	4	2,326	74	0	236	588	197
Saudi Arabia	4,784	218	132	109	(D)	1,527	297	(D)

	All industries	Petro-leum	Manu-facturing	Wholesale trade	Banking	Finance, insurance, real estate	Services	Other industries
United Arab Emirates	$573	$ 211	(D)	$ 115	(D)	$ −1	$ 71	(D)
Other	3,069	2,431	(D)	(*)	$ −1	520	62	(D)
Asia and Pacific	199,599	29,736	$60,710	17,744	11,578	51,439	13,638	$14,755
Australia	35,324	6,992	7,964	2,512	2,627	8,145	2,242	4,843
China	9,577	1,846	5,663	362	78	740	295	594
Hong Kong	23,308	202	3,283	5,617	2,405	7,828	546	3,427
India	1,258	−430	790	124	291	179	68	236
Indonesia	11,605	8,440	273	(D)	249	385	(D)	2,219
Japan	55,606	(D)	15,173	4,689	733	20,685	8,646	(D)
Korea, Republic of	9,432	(D)	3,954	858	2,104	91	510	(D)
Malaysia	5,995	1,252	3,411	271	(D)	470	150	(D)
New Zealand	5,340	63	711	232	(D)	3,291	(D)	(D)
Philippines	2,910	1	1,207	232	201	975	−15	308
Singapore	23,245	1,718	11,834	1,590	696	6,217	908	282
Taiwan	7,737	60	3,692	871	703	1,972	154	285
Thailand	7,124	2,666	2,767	318	650	421	70	232
Other	1,138	574	−12	(D)	(D)	39	28	(D)

NOTES: Only countries receiving more than ten trillion dollars in 1999 are listed separately. * Less than $500,000 (+/−). (D) Suppressed to avoid disclosure of data of individual companies. *Source:* U.S. Department of Commerce, Bureau of Economic Analysis. Web: www.bea.doc.gov/bea/di/diapos_99.htm.

U.S. Contributions to International Organizations

(in millions of dollars)

Organization	1999	2000 (est.)	2001 (est.)
UN and affiliated agencies:			
Food and Agriculture Organization	$ 81	$ 81	$ 81
International Atomic Energy Agency	49	49	55
International Civil Aviation Organization	13	12	12
International Labor Organization	61	56	59
International Telecommunications Union	7	7	7
United Nations	297	256	300
UN War Crimes Tribunals	21	36	43
World Health Organization	108	108	108
World Meteorological Organization	11	10	10
Other organizations	4	4	4
Subtotal	*652*	*619*	*679*
Inter-American organizations:			
Inter-American Institute for Cooperation on Agriculture	17	17	17
Organization of American States	55	57	54
Pan American Health Org.	50	50	51
Subtotal	*122*	*124*	*122*
Regional organizations:			
Asia Pacific Economic Coop.	1	1	1
North Atlantic Assembly	1	1	1
North Atlantic Treaty Org.	40	43	49
Org. for Economic Coop. and Development	54	57	57
South Pacific Commission	1	1	1
Subtotal	*97*	*103*	*109*
Other international organizations:			
World Trade Org./GATT	13	13	13

Organization	1999	2000 (est.)	2001 (est.)
Org. for Prohibition of Chemical Weapons	$ 12	$ 12	$ 14
Other international organizations	10	9	9
Subtotal	*35*	*34*	*36*
UN Buydown	28	—	—
Total	**934**	**880**	**946**
International peacekeeping activities:			
UN Disengagement Observer Force	7	8[1]	10
UN Interim Force in Lebanon	36	32[1]	64
UN Operations in Angola	24	2[1]	—
UN Iraq-Kuwait Observer Mission	4	4[1]	6
UN Mission for the Referendum in Western Sahara	—	—	13
War Crimes Tribunal—Rwanda	8	11[1]	12
UN Operations in the former Yugoslavia	42	16[1]	64
War Crimes Tribunal—Yugoslavia	12	12[1]	14
UN Mission in East Timor	—	145[1]	190
UN Observer Mission in Georgia	7	7[1]	9
UN Force in Cyprus	6	6[1]	6
UN Mission in Tajikistan	4	2[1]	—
UN Observer Mission in Sierra Leone	2	128[1]	180
UN Mission in Kosovo	67	95[1]	187
UN Liaison Mission in the Dem. Rep. of the Congo	—	30[1]	5
UN Mission in Ethiopia and Eritrea	—	—	84
Total	**219**	**544**	**844**

NOTE: All years are fiscal years. 1. Actual. *Source:* Budget of the United States Government Fiscal Year 2001.

National Income by Type
(in billions of dollars)

Type of income	1930	1940	1950	1960	1970	1980	1990	1995	2000
National income	$75.6	$81.1	$241.0	$427.5	$837.5	$2,243.0	$4,642.1	$5,876.7	$7,980.9
Compensation of employees	46.9	52.2	155.4	296.4	617.2	1,651.7	3,351.0	4,202.5	5,715.2
Wage and salary accruals	46.2	49.9	147.2	272.8	551.5	1,377.4	2,754.6	3,441.1	4,837.2
Supplements to wages and salaries	0.7	2.3	8.1	23.6	65.7	274.3	596.4	761.4	878.0
Proprietors' income[1,2]									
Farm	4.4	4.5	13.5	11.4	14.3	13.1	31.1	22.2	30.6
Nonfarm	7.3	8.4	25.1	40.4	65.5	164.5	349.9	475.5	684.4
Rental income[1]	4.9	3.4	8.7	16.2	20.3	31.3	49.1	117.9	141.6
Corporate profits[1,2]	7.3	9.5	35.4	52.3	81.6	198.5	408.6	668.8	876.4
Net interest	4.8	3.2	3.0	10.7	38.4	183.9	452.4	389.8	532.7
Personal income	76.5	78.6	229.9	412.7	841.1	2,323.9	4,903.2	6,200.9	8,319.2
Disposable personal income	74.6	76.7	210.6	366.2	736.5	2,019.8	4,293.6	5,422.6	7,031.0
Personal savings	3.2	4.5	15.2	26.4	69.5	205.6	334.3	302.4	67.7

1. Includes capital consumption adjustment. 2. Includes inventory valuation adjustment. *Source:* U.S. Department of Commerce, Bureau of Economic Analysis, *Survey of Current Business,* May 1999. Web: www.bea.doc.gov.

Exports and Imports of Goods and Services, 1978–2008

Category	Billions of chained 1992 dollars				Average annual rate of change		
	1978	1988	1998	2008[1]	1978–1988	1988–1998	1998–2008[1]
Exports of goods and services	$273.1	$ 465.8	$ 984.7	$ 1,925.0	5.5%	7.8%	6.9%
Goods	189.5	321.4	742.6	1,522.6	5.4	8.7	7.4
Foods, feeds, and beverages	29.2	32.4	43.1	57.2	1.0	2.9	2.9
Industrial supplies and materials	57.7	82.2	130.6	195.6	3.6	4.7	4.1
Capital goods except autos	47.3	110.3	408.4	1,224.7	8.8	14.0	11.6
Computers	.6	15.1	153.5	1,314.1	38.1	26.1	24.0
Civilian aircraft and parts	15.2	26.3	45.7	44.5	5.6	5.7	–0.3
Other	44.3	69.2	241.4	715.9	4.6	13.3	11.5
Autos and parts	31.9	36.8	68.7	106.5	1.4	6.4	4.5
Consumer goods	18.9	30.5	75.8	112.8	4.9	9.5	4.0
Other merchandise exports	11.9	29.6	39.7	61.5	9.5	3.0	4.5
Services	83.0	145.0	246.4	436.0	5.7	5.4	5.9
Residual[2]	–19.6	–1.3	–60.3	–1,118.8	—	—	—
Imports of goods and services	$338.6	$ 580.2	$1,222.9	$ 2,272.5	5.5%	7.7%	6.4%
Goods	274.8	463.2	1,054.4	2,076.2	5.4	8.6	7.0
Foods, feeds, and beverages	21.5	25.9	38.1	43.7	1.9	3.9	1.4
Industrial supplies and materials	128.0	125.3	210.4	282.6	–0.2	5.3	3.0
Petroleum and products	55.4	47.8	71.8	89.1	–1.5	4.1	2.2
Other	59.8	76.9	137.0	193.2	2.5	5.9	3.5
Capital goods, except autos	15.6	87.9	426.7	1,578.1	18.9	17.1	14.0
Computers	.2	12.4	202.5	1,672.5	51.1	32.2	23.5
Other	18.5	76.7	257.5	744.6	15.3	12.9	11.2
Autos and parts	50.5	95.6	138.0	197.3	6.6	3.7	3.6
Consumer goods	47.4	106.0	213.7	340.0	8.4	7.3	4.8
Other merchandise imports	9.1	25.7	57.3	99.6	10.9	8.3	5.7
Services	62.5	117.1	171.2	230.1	6.5	3.9	3.0
Residual[3]	13.7	–3.9	–64.1	–1,337.6	—	—	—
Trade deficit	$–65.5	$–114.4	$ –238.2	$ –347.5	5.7%	7.6%	3.8%

1. Projected. 2. The residual following the detailed categories for exports is the difference between the aggregate of "exports of goods and services" and the sum of the figures for those separate categories for exports of goods and services. 3. The residual following the detailed categories for imports is the difference between the aggregate of "imports of goods and services" and the sum of the figures for those separate categories for imports of goods and services. *Source:* Bureau of Labor Statistics, *Monthly Labor Review,* Nov. 1999.

Producer Price Indexes by Major Commodity Groups
(1982 = 100)

Commodity	2000	1999	1995	1990	1985	1980	1975	1970
All commodities	132.7	125.5	124.7	116.3	103.2	89.8	58.4	38.1
Farm products	99.5	98.4	107.4	112.2	95.1	102.9	77.0	45.8
Processed foods and feeds	133.1	131.1	127.0	121.9	103.5	95.9	72.6	44.6
Textile products and apparel	121.4	121.1	120.8	114.9	102.9	89.7	67.4	52.4
Hides, skins, and leather products	151.5	146	153.7	141.7	108.9	94.7	56.5	42.0
Fuels and related products and power	103.5	80.5	78.0	82.2	91.4	82.8	35.4	15.3
Chemicals and allied products	151.0	144.2	142.5	123.6	103.7	89.0	62.0	35.0
Rubber and plastic products	125.5	122.5	124.3	113.6	101.9	90.1	62.2	44.9
Lumber and wood products	178.2	183.6	178.1	129.7	106.6	101.5	62.1	39.9
Pulp, paper, and allied products	183.7	174.1	172.2	141.3	113.3	86.3	59.0	37.5
Metals and metal products	128.1	124.6	134.5	123.0	104.4	95.0	61.5	38.7
Machinery and equipment	124.0	124.3	126.6	120.7	107.2	86.0	57.9	40.0
Furniture and household durables	132.6	131.7	128.2	119.1	107.1	90.7	67.5	51.9
Nonmetallic mineral products	142.5	138.9	129.0	114.7	108.6	88.4	54.4	35.3
Transportation equipment	143.8	141.8	139.7	121.5	107.9	82.9	56.7	41.9

NOTE: n.a. = not available. *Source:* U.S. Department of Labor, Bureau of Labor Statistics, Division of Industrial Prices and Price Indexes. Web: stats.bls.gov.

Imports and Exports of Leading Commodities
by Principal SITC Groupings (in millions of dollars)

Item	2000 Cumulative Exports	2000 Cumulative Imports	Item	2000 Cumulative Exports	2000 Cumulative Imports
Selected commodities					
Total Balance of Payment Basis	$311,536	$481,275	Liquified propane/butane	$ 280	$ 550
Net Adjustments	–4,245	2,947	Live animals	246	734
ADP equipment; office machines	17,922	34,824	Meat and preparations	2,916	1,558
Airplane parts	6,085	2,221	Metal manufactures, n.e.s.	5,563	6,635
Airplanes	10,748	4,161	Metal ores; scrap	1,656	1,727
Alcoholic bev.,distilled	141	1,037	Metalworking machinery	2,421	3,173
Aluminum	1,606	3,020	Mineral fuels, other	1,252	835
Animal feeds	1,548	239	Natural gas	123	3,503
Artwork/antiques	702	2,809	Nickel	157	663
Basketware, etc.	1,405	1,967	Oils/fats, vegetable	371	524
Cereal flour	516	642	Optical goods	1,196	1,569
Chemicals—cosmetics	2,013	1,367	Paper and paperboard	4,563	6,054
Chemicals—dyeing	1,613	1,093	Petroleum preparations	1,907	9,712
Chemicals—fertilizers	897	772	Photographic equipment	1,863	2,670
Chemicals—inorganic	2,080	2,418	Platinum	355	1,905
Chemicals—medicinal	4,886	5,735	Power generating mach.	13,530	14,323
Chemicals—organic	7,374	10,949	Printed materials	1,934	1,400
Chemicals—plastics	7,895	4,385	Pulp and waste paper	1,803	1,361
Cigarettes	1,330	101	Records/magnetic media	2,174	2,060
Clothing	3,440	23,304	Rice	394	76
Coal	840	329	Rubber tires and tubes	1,032	2,110
Coffee	4	1,275	Scientific instruments	11,985	8,327
Copper	634	1,664	Ships, boats	502	546
Cork, wood, lumber	1,869	3,754	Silver and bullion	98	420
Corn	2,016	145	Soybeans	2,264	19
Cotton, raw and linters	972	18	Spacecraft	102	151
Crude fertilizers	705	556	Specialized ind. mach.	12,358	9,681
Crude oil	381	34,006	Sugar	2	169
Electrical machinery	34,605	41,535	Television, VCR, etc.	10,850	24,958
Fish and preparations	1,038	3,415	Textile yarn, fabric	4,293	6,287
Footwear	267	6,038	Tobacco, unmanufactured	624	214
Furniture and bedding	1,924	7,705	Toys/games/sporting goods	1,582	6,076
Gem diamonds	376	5,055	Vegetables and fruits	2,841	4,440
General industrial machinery	13,694	14,822	Vehicles	25,661	67,920
Glass	971	894	Watches/clocks/parts	138	1,257
Glassware	325	744	Wheat	1,224	95
Gold, nonmonetary	2,835	1,248	Wood manufactures	795	3,039
Hides and skins	527	48	Re-exports	26,477	n.a.
Iron and steel mill products	2,373	6,839	Agricultural commodities	819	n.a.
Jewelry	595	2,391	Manufactured goods	25,240	n.a.
Lighting, plumbing	526	1,785	Mineral fuels	115	n.a.

NOTES: SITC = Standard International Trade Classification; n.a. = not applicable. Details may not equal totals due to rounding. Data not seasonally adjusted. *Source:* U.S. Census Bureau, Foreign Trade Division. Web: http://www.census.gov/foreign-trade/Press-Release/current_press_release/exh15.txt.

Consumer Price Index for All Urban Consumers
(1982–1984 = 100)

Group	2000	1999	1995	1990	1985	1980	1975	1970	1965	1960	1950
All items	172.2	166.6	152.4	130.7	107.6	82.4	53.8	38.8	31.5	29.6	24.1
Food and beverages	168.4	164.6	148.9	132.1	105.6	86.7	60.2	40.1	n.a.	n.a.	n.a.
Housing	169.6	163.9	148.5	128.5	107.7	81.1	50.7	36.4	n.a.	n.a.	n.a.
Apparel	129.6	131.3	132.0	124.1	105.0	90.9	72.5	59.2	47.8	45.7	40.3
Transportation	153.3	144.4	139.1	120.5	106.4	83.1	50.1	37.5	31.9	29.8	22.7
Medical care	260.8	250.6	220.5	162.8	113.5	74.9	47.5	34.0	25.2	22.3	15.1

NOTE: n.a. = not available. *Source:* U.S. Department of Labor, Bureau of Labor Statistics. Web: www.bls.gov.

Retail Prices of Selected Foods in U.S. Cities, 1890–1970
(in cents per unit indicated)

Year	Flour (5 lbs)	Bread (lb)	Round steak (lb)	Bacon (lb)	Butter (lb)	Eggs (doz.)	Milk (½ gal.)	Oranges (doz.)	Potatoes (10 lbs)	Coffee (lb)	Sugar (5 lb)
1970	58.9	24.3	130.2	94.9	86.6	61.4	65.9	86.4	89.7	91.1	64.8
1965	58.1	20.9	108.4	81.3	75.4	52.7	52.6	77.8	93.7	83.3	59.0
1960	55.4	20.3	105.5	65.5	74.9	57.3	52.0	74.8	71.8	75.3	58.2
1955	53.8	17.7	90.3	65.9	70.9	60.6	46.2	52.8	56.4	93.0	52.1
1950	49.1	14.3	93.6	63.7	72.9	60.4	41.2	49.3	46.1	79.4	48.7
1945	32.1	8.8	40.6	41.1	50.7	58.1	31.2	48.5	49.3	30.5	33.4
1940	21.5	8.0	36.4	27.3	36.0	33.1	25.6	29.1	23.9	21.2	26.0
1935	25.3	8.3	36.0	41.3	37.6	37.6	23.4	22.0	19.1	25.7	28.2
1930	23.0	8.6	42.6	42.5	46.4	44.5	28.2	57.1	36.0	39.5	30.5
1925	30.5	9.3	36.2	47.1	55.2	55.4	27.8	57.1	36.0	50.4	35.0
1920	40.5	11.5	39.5	52.3	70.1	68.1	33.4	63.2	63.0	47.0	97.0
1915	21.0	7.0	23.0	26.9	35.8	34.1	17.6	n.a.	15.0	30.0	33.0
1910	18.0	n.a.	17.4	25.5	35.9	33.7	16.8	n.a.	17.0	n.a.	30.0
1905	16.0	n.a.	14.0	18.1	29.0	27.2	14.4	n.a.	17.0	n.a.	30.0
1900	12.5	n.a.	13.2	14.3	26.1	20.7	13.6	n.a.	14.0	n.a.	30.5
1895	12.0	n.a.	12.3	13.0	24.9	20.6	13.6	n.a.	14.0	n.a.	26.5
1890	14.5	n.a.	12.3	12.5	25.5	20.8	13.6	n.a.	16.0	n.a.	34.5

NOTE: n.a. = not available. *Source:* U.S. Bureau of the Census, *Historical Statistics of the United States, Colonial Times to 1970, Bicentennial Edition,* Part 2.

Output by Major Industry Division, 1998–2008

Industry	Billions of chained 1992 dollars 1998	Billions of chained 1992 dollars 2008	Percent distribution 1998	Percent distribution 2008	Average annual rate of change 1998–2008
Total	$13,509.4	$18,241.5	100.0%	100.0%	3.0%
Goods producing	4,932.2	6,609.6	36.5	36.2	3.0
Mining	174.8	197.0	1.3	1.1	1.2
Construction	696.7	791.8	5.2	4.3	1.3
Manufacturing	4,060.7	5,650.2	30.1	31.0	3.4
Durable	2,428.0	3,813.0	18.0	20.9	4.6
Nondurable	1,632.7	1,909.2	12.1	10.5	1.6
Service producing	7,700.9	10,537.1	57.0	57.8	3.2
Transportation, communications, and utilities	1,071.7	1,502.3	7.9	8.2	3.4
Wholesale trade	820.2	1,178.3	6.1	6.5	3.7
Retail trade	1,065.4	1,393.4	7.9	7.6	2.7
Finance, insurance, and real estate	1,330.0	1,787.8	9.8	9.8	3.0
Services	2,434.3	3,566.9	18.0	19.6	3.9
Government	979.3	1,109.6	7.2	6.1	1.3
Federal government	306.6	309.0	2.3	1.7	.1
State and local government	672.6	800.5	5.0	4.4	1.8
Agriculture	267.4	308.2	2.0	1.7	1.4
Private households	11.1	10.3	.1	.1	-.8
Special industries[1]	608.9	780.5	4.5	4.3	2.5
Residual[2]	-11.1	-4.2	-.1	.0	—

1. Consists of nonproducing accounting categories to reconcile input-output system with NIPA accounts. 2. Residual is shown for the first level only. Subcategories do not necessarily add to higher categories as a byproduct of chainweighting. *Source:* U.S. Department of Labor, Bureau of Labor Statistics, *Monthly Labor Review,* Nov. 1999.

Farm Income
(in millions of dollars)

Year	Crops[1]	Livestock, livestock products	Government payments	Gross cash income	Year	Crops[1]	Livestock, livestock products	Government payments	Gross cash income
	Cash receipts from marketings					Cash receipts from marketings			
1930	$ 3,868	$ 5,187	—	$ 9,055	1990	$80,131	$89,843	$ 9,298	$186,824
1935	2,977	4,143	$ 573	7,693	1991	82,060	86,735	8,214	184,858
1940	3,469	4,913	723	9,105	1992	84,853	86,350	9,169	188,160
1945	9,655	12,008	742	22,405	1993	87,500	90,200	13,402	200,100
1950	12,356	16,105	283	28,764	1994	93,100	88,200	7,900	198,300
1955	13,523	15,967	229	29,842	1995	101,000	87,100	7,300	205,900
1960	15,023	18,989	703	34,958	1996	106,200	93,000	7,300	217,400
1965	17,479	21,886	2,463	42,215	1997	111,100	96,500	7,500	227,500
1970	20,977	29,532	3,717	54,768	1998	102,200	94,500	12,200	225,000
1975	45,813	43,089	807	90,707	1999	93,100	95,500	20,600	225,000
1980	71,746	67,991	1,285	143,295	2000[2]	96,600	99,500	22,100	234,400
1985	74,293	69,822	7,705	157,854	2001[3]	100,200	99,800	14,100	230,200

1. Includes items not listed. 2. Preliminary. 3. Forecast. *Source:* U.S. Department of Agriculture, Economic Research Service. *Agricultural Income and Finance.* Web: www.usda.gov.

Per Capita Consumption of Principal Foods[1]
(in pounds)

Food	1990	1995	1997	1998	1999	Food	1990	1995	1997	1998	1999
Red meats[2,3,4]	112.3	115.1	111.0	115.6	117.7	Fats and oils	63.0	66.3	64.9	65.6	68.5
Beef	63.9	64.4	63.8	64.9	65.8	Butter and margarine (product weight)	15.3	13.7	12.8	12.8	12.9
Veal	0.9	0.8	0.9	0.7	0.6						
Lamb & mutton	1.0	0.9	0.8	0.9	0.9	Shortening	22.2	22.5	20.9	21.0	21.6
Pork	46.4	49.0	45.5	49.2	50.5	Lard	2.2	4.3	4.1	5.2	5.7
Poultry[2,3,4]	56.3	62.9	64.2	65.0	68.3	Salad and cooking oils	25.3	26.9	28.6	27.9	29.4
Chicken	42.4	48.8	50.3	50.8	54.2	Fruits and vegetables	656.0	694.3	717.9	702.4	719.0
Turkey	13.8	14.1	13.9	14.2	14.1	Fruit	272.6	284.9	296.9	284.4	297.9
Fish and shellfish[3]	15.0	14.9	14.5	14.8	15.2	Vegetables	383.5	409.4	421.0	418.0	421.2
Eggs[4]	30.2	30.2	30.7	31.8	32.8	Peanuts (shelled)	6.0	5.7	5.9	5.9	6.4
Cheese [2,5]	24.6	27.3	28.0	28.3	29.8	Tree nuts (shelled)	2.4	1.9	2.1	2.3	2.7
Cottage cheese	3.4	2.7	2.7	2.7	2.7	Flour and cereal products[8]	181.0	192.8	200.9	198.4	201.9
Beverage milks[2]	221.8	209.8	206.8	204.6	203.8	Wheat flour	136.0	141.8	149.5	146.0	148.4
Fluid cream products[5]	7.6	8.4	9.0	9.2	9.7	Rice (milled basis)	15.8	18.9	18.4	18.9	19.4
Yogurt (excluding frozen)	4.0	5.1	5.1	5.1	4.9	Caloric sweeteners[9]	136.9	149.8	154.0	155.1	158.4
Ice cream	15.8	15.7	16.4	16.6	16.8	Coffee (green bean equiv.)	10.3	8.0	9.3	9.5	10.0
Lowfat ice cream[6]	7.7	7.5	7.9	8.3	7.9						
Frozen yogurt	2.8	3.5	2.1	2.2	2.1	Cocoa (chocolate liquor equiv.)	4.3	3.6	4.1	4.4	4.6
All dairy products, milk equivalent, milkfat basis[7]	568.3	583.8	577.6	581.7	597.9						

1. In pounds, retail weight unless otherwise stated. Consumption normally represents total supply minus exports, nonfood use, and ending stocks. Calendar-year data, except fresh citrus fruits, peanuts, tree nuts, and rice, which are on crop-year basis. 2. Totals may not add due to rounding. 3. Boneless, trimmed weight. Chicken series revised to exclude amount of ready-to-cook chicken going to pet food as well as some water leakage that occurs when chicken is cut up before packaging. 4. Excludes shipments to the U.S. territories. 5. Heavy cream, light cream, half and half, eggnog, sour cream, and dip. 6. Formerly known as ice milk. 7. Includes condensed and evaporated milk and dry milk products. 8. Includes rye, corn, oats, and barley products. Excludes quantities used in alcoholic beverages, corn sweeteners, and fuel. 9. Dry weight equivalent. *Source:* U.S. Department of Agriculture, Economic Research Service. Web: www.usda.gov.

Farm Indexes
(1990–1992 = 100)

Year	Prices paid by farmers[1]	Prices rec'd by farmers[2]	Ratio[3]	Year	Prices paid by farmers[1]	Prices rec'd by farmers[2]	Ratio[3]
1975	47	73	155	1994	106	100	94
1980	75	98	137	1995	109	102	93
1985	86	91	106	1996	115	112	98
1990	99	104	105	1997	118	107	91
1991	100	100	99	1998	115	101	88
1992	101	98	97	1999	115	96	83
1993	104	101	97	2000	120	96	80

1. Commodities and services, interest, taxes, and wage rates. 2. All farm products. 3. Ratio of index of prices received by farmers to index of prices paid by farmers. May not compute directly due to rounding. *Source:* U.S. Department of Agriculture, National Agricultural Statistics Service. Web: www.usda.gov.

Agricultural Output by State, 2000 Crops

State	Corn (1,000 bu)	Wheat (1,000 bu)	Cotton, ginned (1,000 ba)	Potatoes (1,000 cwt)	Rice (1,000 cwt)	Cattle[1] (1,000 head)	Hogs and pigs[2] (1,000 head)
Alabama	10,725	4,860	543	697		1,360	165
Alaska						11	0.8
Arizona	6,468	8,775	798	2,520		850	9
Arkansas	22,750	59,400	1,425		86,112	1,810	685
California	39,950	34,200	2,556	16,355	43,521	5,150	150
Colorado	149,860	71,370		30,658		3,150	840
Connecticut						63	4
Delaware	25,272	4,158		1,128		27	29
Florida	2,100	441	106	8,423		1,800	40
Georgia	32,100	10,800	1,663			1,270	380
Hawaii						150	26
Idaho	9,120	108,450		152,320		1,970	24
Illinois	1,668,550	52,440		1,855		1,470	4,150
Indiana	815,580	35,190		784		880	3,350
Iowa	1,740,00	846				3,650	15,100
Kansas	416,000	347,800	22	986		6,700	1,520
Kentucky	159,900	23,940				2,260	430
Louisiana	42,920	9,805	911		24,402	860	29
Maine				17,920		97	7
Maryland	62,775	12,600		1,222		235	58
Massachusetts				638		50	20
Michigan	244,280	36,000		14,963		980	950
Minnesota	957,000	96,526		21,240		2,550	5,800
Mississippi	38,500	12,925	1,711		12,862	1,070	315
Missouri	396,110	49,400	540	1,678	9,633	4,250	2,900
Montana	2,520	135,210		3,503		2,550	155
Nebraska	1,014,300	59,400		10,127		6,600	3,050
Nevada		1,470		3,150		520	8
New Hampshire						42	4
New Jersey	10,050	1,995		713		48	14
New Mexico	11,680	4,200	106	3,770		1,580	3
New York	47,040	7,420		5,964		1,380	80
North Carolina	75,400	27,500	1,429	3,400		950	9,300
North Dakota	104,160	313,785		26,950		1,980	185
Ohio	485,100	79,920		1,134		1,240	1,490
Oklahoma	37,800	142,800	152			5,050	2,310
Oregon	5,220	51,010		30,683		1,360	32
Pennsylvania	137,160	10,335		3,510		1,640	1,030
Rhode Island				138		6	3
South Carolina	18,200	9,065	379			445	290
South Dakota	431,200	114,268		812		4,050	1,320
Tennessee	67,260	20,900	710			2,170	230
Texas	235,600	66,000	3,971	5,196	14,342	13,700	920
Utah	3,024	6,850		435		910	550
Vermont						295	3
Virginia	48,180	12,915	166	1,292		1,650	425
Washington	18,500	164,880		108,000		1,180	27
West Virginia	4,550	549				400	10
Wisconsin	363,000	8,730		33,800		3,350	610
Wyoming	8,184	4,312				1,550	108
Total U.S.	**9,968,358**	**2,223,440**	**17,188**	**516,083**	**190,872**	**97,309**	**59,138**

NOTE: All figures are for the year 2000, unless otherwise indicated. 1. Inventory as of Jan. 1, 2001. 2. Inventory as of Dec. 1, 2000. *Source:* U.S. Department of Agriculture, National Agricultural Statistics Service. Web: www.usda.gov.

Number of Farms, Land in Farms, and Average Size Farm: United States, 1990–2000

Year	Number of farms	Land in farms (1,000 acres)	Average farm size (acres)	Year	Number of farms	Land in farms (1,000 acres)	Average farm size (acres)
1990	2,145,820	986,850	460	1996	2,190,500	958,675	438
1991	2,116,760	981,736	464	1997	2,190,510	956,010	436
1992	2,107,840	978,503	464	1998	2,191,360	953,500	435
1993	2,201,590	968,845	440	1999	2,192,070	947,440	432
1994	2,197,690	965,935	440	2000	2,172,080	942,990	434
1995	2,196,400	962,515	438				

NOTE: A farm is any establishment from which $1,000 or more of agricultural products were sold or would normally be sold during the year. *Source:* U.S. Department of Agriculture. Web: www.usda.gov.

Number of Farms by State, 1998–2000

State	1998	1999	2000	State	1998	1999	2000
Alabama	49,000	48,000	47,000	Nebraska	55,000	55,000	54,000
Alaska	560	570	580	Nevada	3,000	3,000	3,000
Arizona	7,800	7,700	7,500	New Hampshire	3,100	3,100	3,100
Arkansas	49,500	48,500	48,000	New Jersey	9,600	9,600	9,600
California	89,000	89,000	87,500	New Mexico	16,000	15,500	15,200
Colorado	29,500	29,000	29,000	New York	38,000	39,000	38,000
Connecticut	4,100	4,000	3,900	North Carolina	58,000	58,000	57,000
Delaware	2,700	2,600	2,600	North Dakota	31,000	30,500	30,300
Florida	45,000	45,000	44,000	Ohio	80,000	80,000	80,000
Georgia	50,000	50,000	50,000	Oklahoma	83,000	84,000	85,000
Hawaii	5,500	5,500	5,700	Oregon	39,500	40,500	40,000
Idaho	24,500	24,500	24,500	Pennsylvania	60,000	59,000	59,000
Illinois	79,000	79,000	78,000	Rhode Island	700	700	700
Indiana	66,000	65,000	64,000	South Carolina	25,000	25,000	24,000
Iowa	97,000	96,000	95,000	South Dakota	32,500	32,500	32,500
Kansas	65,000	65,000	64,000	Tennessee	91,000	91,000	90,000
Kentucky	90,000	91,000	90,000	Texas	226,000	227,000	226,000
Louisiana	30,000	30,000	29,500	Utah	15,000	15,500	15,500
Maine	6,900	6,900	6,800	Vermont	6,700	6,700	6,800
Maryland	12,500	12,400	12,400	Virginia	49,000	49,000	49,000
Massachusetts	6,000	6,100	6,100	Washington	40,000	40,000	40,000
Michigan	52,000	53,000	52,000	West Virginia	21,000	20,500	20,500
Minnesota	80,000	80,000	79,000	Wisconsin	78,000	78,000	77,000
Mississippi	42,000	43,000	43,000	Wyoming	9,200	9,200	9,200
Missouri	110,000	110,000	109,000	**U.S. total**	**2,191,360**	**2,192,070**	**2,172,080**
Montana	27,500	28,000	27,600				

NOTE: A farm is any establishment from which $1,000 or more of agricultural products were sold or would normally be sold during the year. *Source:* U.S. Department of Agriculture. Web: www.usda.gov.

Top U.S.-Based Advertising Agency Networks
(ranked by revenues in thousands of dollars)

2000 Rank	1998 Rank	Agency	2000 revenues	% change	2000 billings	% change
1	1	McCann-Erickson WorldGroup (IPG)	$2,658,512	17.5%	$23,410,090	23.0%
2	2	BBDO (OMC)	2,241,966	8.9	18,820,296	12.0
3	3	DDB Worldwide Communications Group (OMC)	2,175,040	9.6	18,669,221	12.1
4	6	Euro RSCG (Havas)	1,900,000	19.7	14,000,000	19.4
5	14	The Lowe Group (IPG)	1,667,187	7.1	12,328,012	7.6
6	4	J. Walter Thompson (WPP)	1,583,400	14.6	10,874,500	14.3
7	9	Grey	1,297,800	15.0	8,656,300	14.9
8	5	Young & Rubicam (WPP)	1,274,528	5.8	14,748,390	21.1
9	11	TBWA (OMC)	1,265,412	16.9	8,647,039	16.9
10	10	Leo Burnett Co. (Bcom3)	1,109,283	13.2	8,293,501	13.6
11	7	Ogilvy & Mather (WPP)	1,075,399	16.6	10,339,189	18.7
12	13	FCB (TN)	1,060,051	4.9	9,453,259	11.3
13	12	D'Arcy Masius Benton & Bowles (Bcom3)	724,755	9.1	6,743,563	8.2
14	*	Bates (CCG)	707,000	15.1	6,147,000	9.5

*Not ranked in 1998. *Source: Adweek,* Top U.S.-Based Agency Networks, April 16, 2001, edition. © 2001 *Adweek.* Used with permission of *Adweek.*

Top Advertising Categories

Rank	Category	2000 spending (in millions)	Change vs. '99	Rank	Category	2000 spending (in millions)	Change vs. '99
1	Automotive	$1,732.6	–4.4%	11	Cigarettes, tobacco	$400.6	–17.6%
2	Computers, software, Internet	1,370.4	39.2	12	Telecommunications	333.9	40.5
3	Media and advertising	1,211.4	36.3	13	Misc. services and amusements	327.3	31.5
4	Direct response companies	1,071.3	–7.6	14	Dairy, produce, meat, bakery goods	322.0	13.9
5	Medicine and proprietary remedies	983.1	18.2	15	General necessities	292.5	7.7
6	Financial	932.0	24.6	16	Audio and video equipment	288.1	8.9
7	Retail	882.3	32.8	17	Liquor	287.6	23.9
8	Public transportation, hotels, resorts	751.4	7.5	18	Personal hygiene and health	286.2	0.1
9	Cosmetics and beauty aids	669.7	16.4	19	Jewelry and watches	282.9	36.9
10	Ready-to-wear	596.1	20.4	20	Household furnishings, accessories	275.4	–0.9

Source: © 2000/2001 ASM Communications, Inc. All rights reserved.

World Port Ranking, 1999

	Total cargo volume, metric tons (000s)				Container traffic (TEUs)		
Rank	Port	Country	Tons	Rank	Port	Country	TEUs
1	Singapore	Singapore	325,902	1	Hong Kong	China	16,211,000
2	Rotterdam	Netherlands	303,520	2	Singapore	Singapore	15,945,000
3	South Louisiana	United States	194,448	3	Kaohsiung	Taiwan	6,985,361
4	Shanghai	China	187,000	4	Rotterdam	Netherlands	6,400,000
5	Hong Kong	China	168,838	5	Busan	South Korea	6,310,664
6	Chiba	Japan	164,741	6	Long Beach	United States	4,408,480
7	Ulsan	South Korea	148,332	7	Shanghai	China	4,210,000
8	Houston	United States	144,184	8	Los Angeles	United States	3,828,851
9	Nagoya	Japan	133,038	9	Hamburg	Germany	3,738,307
10	Kwangyushu	South Korea	131,059	10	Antwerp	Belgium	3,614,246
11	New York/New Jersey	United States	121,387	11	Dubai	UAE	2,844,634
12	Antwerp	Belgium	115,654	12	New York/New Jersey	United States	2,828,878
13	Yokohama	Japan	114,538	13	Felixstowe	UK	2,610,000
14	Kaohsiung	Taiwan	110,722	14	Tokyo	Japan	2,595,000
15	Inchon	South Korea	108,227	15	Port Kelang	Malaysia	2,550,419
16	Busan	South Korea	107,757	16	Gioia Tauro	Italy	2,253,401
17	Kobe	Japan	102,527	17	Bremen Ports	Germany	2,201,220
18	Marseilles	France	90,258	18	Yokohama	Japan	2,172,919
19	Kitayushu	Japan	87,346	19	Manila	Philippines	2,147,422
20	Richards Bay	South Africa	86,120	20	San Juan	United States	2,084,711
21	Tokyo	Japan	85,415	21	Algeciras	Spain	1,832,557
22	Osaka	Japan	85,391	22	Laem Chabang	Thailand	1,828,460
23	Dampier	Australia	82,528	23	Colombo	Sri Lanka	1,704,389
24	Hamburg	Germany	81,037	24	Keelung	Taiwan	1,665,618
25	New Orleans	United States	79,443	25	Oakland	United States	1,663,756
26	Dalian	China	75,150	26	Yantian	China	1,580,000
27	Newcastle	Australia	72,711	27	Nagoya	Japan	1,566,961
28	Vancouver (BC)	Canada	71,213	28	Quindao	China	1,540,000
29	Corpus Christi	United States	70,796	29	Seattle	United States	1,490,048
30	Qindao	China	70,180	30	Charleston	United States	1,482,995
31	Tubarao	Brazil	67,069	31	LeHavre	France	1,378,379
32	Port Hedland	Australia	65,431	32	Hampton Roads	United States	1,306,537
33	LeHavre	France	63,922	33	Xingang/Tientijin	China	1,300,000
34	Beaumont	United States	63,007	34	Tacoma	United States	1,271,011
35	Port Kelang	Malaysia	60,970	35	Barcelona	Spain	1,234,987
36	Manila	Philippines	59,133	36	Genoa	Italy	1,233,817
37	Baton Rouge	United States	57,853	37	Cristobal	Panama	1,153,000
38	Plaquemines	United States	56,702	38	Valencia	Spain	1,152,780
39	Amsterdam	Netherlands	55,725	39	Melbourne	Australia	1,125,748
40	Long Beach	United States	55,269	40	Taichung	Taiwan	1,106,668

Source: American Association of Port Authorities. Web: www.aapa-ports.org.

Life Insurance in Force
(in millions of dollars)

As of Dec. 31	Ordinary	Group	Industrial	Credit	Total
1900	$ 6,124	—	$ 1,449	—	$ 7,573
1915	16,650	$ 100	4,279	—	21,029
1930	78,576	9,801	17,963	$ 73	106,413
1945	101,550	22,172	27,675	365	151,762
1950	149,116	47,793	33,415	3,844	234,168
1955	216,812	101,345	39,682	14,493	372,332
1960	341,881	175,903	39,563	29,101	586,448
1965	499,638	308,078	39,818	53,020	900,554
1970	734,730	551,357	38,644	77,392	1,402,123
1975	1,083,421	904,695	39,423	112,032	2,139,571
1980	1,760,474	1,579,355	35,994	165,215	3,541,038
1985	3,247,289	2,561,595	28,250	215,973	6,053,107
1990	5,366,982	3,753,506	24,071	248,038	9,392,597
1995	6,872,252	4,604,856	18,134	201,083	11,696,325
1998	8,505,894	5,735,273	17,365	212,917	14,471,449
1999	(1)	6,110,200	(1)	213,500	15,496,100

1. For 1999, the Ordinary and Industrial have been combined as Individual, for a total of $9,172,400. Figures for 1999 are rounded. Source: American Council of Life Insurers.

Largest U.S. Businesses

1998	1999	2000	Company	Revenues ($ millions)	1998	1999	2000	Company	Revenues ($ millions)
—	3	1	Exxon Mobil	$210,392.0	93	59	51	Cardinal Health	$29,870.6
3	2	2	Wal-Mart Stores	193,295.0	46	46	52	United Parcel Service	29,771.0
1	1	3	General Motors	184,632.0	—	—	53	Pfizer	29,574.0
2	4	4	Ford Motor	180,598.0	—	—	54	Dynegy	29,444.9
5	5	5	General Electric	129,853.0	—	—	55	Reliant Energy	29,339.0
7	7	6	Citigroup	111,826.0	16	42	56	E.I. du Pont de Nemours	29,202.0
27	18	7	Enron	100,789.0	—	—	57	Delphi Automotive Systems	29,139.0
6	6	8	Intl. Business Machines	88,396.0	51	43	57	Johnson & Johnson	29,139.0
10	8	9	AT&T	65,981.0	42	47	59	Allstate	29,134.0
—	—	10	Verizon Communications	64,707.0	—	90	60	UtiliCorp United	28,974.9
8	9	11	Philip Morris	63,276.0	70	61	61	International Paper	28,180.0
—	—	12	J.P. Morgan Chase	60,065.0	62	68	62	Wells Fargo	27,568.0
—	11	13	Bank of America Corp.	57,747.0	61	49	63	Aetna	26,818.9
35	12	14	SBC Communications	51,476.0	43	57	64	United Technologies	26,583.0
9	10	15	Boeing	51,321.0	66	88	65	Lehman Brothers Holdings	26,447.0
24	28	16	Texaco	51,130.0	52	58	66	BellSouth	26,151.0
81	69	17	Duke Energy	49,318.0	53	66	67	Walt Disney	25,402.0
36	14	18	Kroger	49,000.4	50	60	68	ConAgra	25,385.8
14	13	19	Hewlett-Packard	48,782.0	41	52	69	Lockheed Martin	25,329.0
38	35	20	Chevron	48,069.0	44	50	70	Bank One Corp.	25,168.0
12	15	21	State Farm Insurance Cos.	47,863.1	—	65	71	Honeywell International	25,023.0
22	17	22	American International Group	45,972.0	—	—	72	Tosco	24,545.0
32	21	23	Home Depot	45,738.0	56	67	73	First Union Corp.	24,246.0
29	30	24	Morgan Stanley Dean Witter	45,413.0	72	71	74	American Express	23,675.0
19	29	25	Merrill Lynch	44,872.0	88	81	75	Sprint	23,613.0
26	26	26	Fannie Mae	44,088.9	—	—	76	Southern	23,381.0
28	20	27	Compaq Computer	42,383.0	—	—	77	Alcoa	23,090.0
33	22	28	Lucent Technologies	41,420.0	75	89	78	Dow Chemical	23,008.0
15	16	29	Sears Roebuck	40,937.0	—	84	79	Microsoft	22,956.0
37	34	30	Merck	40,363.2	20	48	80	Prudential Ins. Co. of America	22,759.9
17	23	31	Procter & Gamble	39,951.0	—	80	81	FleetBoston Financial	22,608.0
—	—	32	WorldCom	39,090.0	65	73	82	PG&E Corp.	22,483.0
18	19	33	TIAA-CREF	38,063.5	—	—	83	AutoNation	22,330.8
34	37	34	Motorola	37,580.0	—	96	84	Georgia-Pacific	22,218.0
59	38	35	McKesson HBOC	37,100.5	—	—	85	TXU	22,009.0
21	27	36	Kmart	37,028.0	—	—	86	El Paso Corp.	21,950.0
—	32	37	Target	36,903.0	68	70	87	New York Life Insurance	21,450.4
92	24	38	Albertson's	36,762.0	77	78	88	Bristol-Myers Squibb	21,331.0
47	51	39	USX	35,570.0	—	—	89	Phillips Petroleum	21,227.0
—	64	40	Berkshire Hathaway	33,976.0	98	95	90	Walgreen	21,206.9
40	39	41	Intel	33,726.0	84	86	91	UnitedHealth Group	21,122.0
—	54	42	Goldman Sachs Group	33,000.0	60	72	92	Loews	20,669.9
31	36	43	J.C. Penney	32,965.0	73	83	93	Coca-Cola	20,458.0
—	74	44	Conoco	32,513.0	54	76	94	PepsiCo	20,438.0
49	44	45	Costco Wholesale	32,164.3	—	—	95	Tech Data	20,427.7
48	40	46	Safeway	31,976.9	64	79	96	Sara Lee	20,414.0
39	53	47	MetLife	31,947.0	86	99	97	Supervalu	20,339.1
—	—	48	Dell Computer	31,888.0	71	77	98	AMR	20,245.0
55	41	49	Ingram Micro	30,715.1	58	85	99	Caterpillar	20,175.0
79	62	50	Freddie Mac	30,000.0	99	93	100	CVS	20,087.5

NOTE: Dash indicates the company was not in the top 100 for the year noted. *Source:* Fortune 500, © 2001 Time, Inc. All rights reserved. For more detailed information, visit *Fortune* on the Web, www.fortune.com/fortune500.

United States' Largest Banks
(in thousands of U.S. dollars)

Rank	Name (city, state)	Total assets	Rank	Name (city, state)	Total assets
1	Bank of America, National Association (Charlotte, N.C.)	$584,284,000	16	State Street Bank and Trust Company (Boston, Mass.)	$64,643,911
2	Citibank, N.A. (New York, N.Y.)	382,106,000	17	PNC Bank, National Association (Pittsburgh, Pa.)	63,185,903
3	Chase Manhattan Bank, The (New York, N.Y.)	377,116,000	18	Wells Fargo Bank Minnesota, National Association (Minneapolis, Minn.)	53,117,860
4	First Union National Bank (Charlotte, N.C.)	231,837,000	19	Lasalle Bank, National Association (Chicago, Ill.)	48,852,837
5	Morgan Guaranty Trust Company of New York (New York, N.Y.)	185,762,000	20	Branch Banking and Trust Company (Winston-Salem, N.C.)	46,991,799
6	Fleet National Bank (Providence, R.I.)	166,281,000	21	Southtrust Bank (Birmingham, Ala.)	45,170,172
7	Wells Fargo Bank, National Association (San Francisco, Calif.)	115,539,000	22	Bankers Trust Company (New York, N.Y.)	44,324,000
8	Bank One, National Association (Chicago, Ill.)	101,228,538	23	Regions Bank (Birmingham, Ala.)	43,528,061
9	Suntrust Bank (Atlanta, Ga.)	99,528,008	24	Merrill Lynch Bank USA (Salt Lake City, Utah)	43,171,125
10	U.S. Bank National Association (Minneapolis, Minn.)	82,023,123	25	Mellon Bank, N.A. (Pittsburgh, Pa.)	41,974,315
11	HSBC Bank USA (Buffalo, N.Y.)	80,121,433	26	Chase Manhattan Bank USA, National Association (Newark, Del.)	39,792,293
12	Keybank National Association (Cleveland, Ohio)	77,760,463	27	Amsouth Bank (Birmingham, Ala.)	38,917,484
13	Bank of New York, The (New York, N.Y.)	74,266,429	28	Bank One, National Association (Columbus, Ohio)	38,716,898
14	Firstar Bank, National Association (Cincinnati, Ohio)	72,593,553	29	MBNA America Bank, National Association (Wilmington, Del.)	36,657,574
15	Wachovia Bank, National Association (Winston-Salem, N.C.)	69,187,160	30	National City Bank (Cleveland, Ohio)	35,407,656

NOTE: As of March 31, 2001. *Source:* Federal Reserve System, National Information Center.

Top 10 Selling Light Trucks in the U.S., 1998–2000

Rank	1998	Number	1999	Number	2000	Number
1	Ford F Series	787,552	Ford F Series	806,579	Ford F Series	820,248
2	Chevy C/K Pickup/Silverado	533,177	Chevy Silverado	533,177	Chevy Silverado	634,118
3	Ford Explorer	431,488	Dodge Ram Pickup	428,930	Ford Explorer	445,157
4	Dodge Ram Pickup	410,130	Ford Explorer	428,772	Dodge Ram Pickup	380,874
5	Ford Ranger	328,136	Ford Ranger	348,358	Ford Ranger	330,125
6	Dodge Caravan	293,819	Jeep Grand Cherokee	300,031	Dodge Caravan	285,739
7	Jeep Grand Cherokee	229,135	Dodge Caravan	293,100	Jeep Grand Cherokee	271,723
8	Chevrolet S10 Pickup	228,093	Chevrolet S10 Pickup	233,669	Chevrolet S Blazer	225,948
9	Ford Expedition	225,703	Ford Expedition	233,125	Ford Windstar	222,298
10	Chevrolet S Blazer	219,710	Chevrolet S Blazer	232,140	Ford Expedition	213,483

Source: Ward's AutoInfoBank. Web: www.wardsauto.com.

Top 20 Selling Passenger Cars in the U.S., 1998–2000

Rank	1998	Number	1999	Number	2000	Number
1	Toyota Camry	429,575	Toyota Camry	448,162	Toyota Camry	422,961
2	Honda Accord	401,071	Honda Accord	404,192	Honda Accord	404,515
3	Ford Taurus	371,074	Ford Taurus	368,327	Ford Taurus	382,035
4	Honda Civic	334,562	Honda Civic	318,308	Honda Civic	324,528
5	Ford Escort	291,936	Chevrolet Cavalier	272,122	Ford Focus	286,166
6	Chevrolet Cavalier	256,099	Ford Escort	260,486	Chevrolet Cavalier	236,803
7	Toyota Corolla	250,501	Toyota Corolla	249,128	Toyota Corolla	230,156
8	Saturn S	231,522	Pontiac Grand Am	234,936	Pontiac Grand Am	214,923
9	Chevrolet Malibu	223,703	Chevrolet Malibu	218,540	Chevrolet Malibu	207,376
10	Pontiac Grand Am	180,428	Saturn S	207,977	Saturn S	177,355
11	Chevrolet Lumina	177,631	Ford Mustang	166,915	Chevrolet Impala	174,358
12	Ford Mustang	144,732	Buick Century	157,035	Ford Mustang	173,676
13	Nissan Altima	144,451	Nissan Altima	153,525	Buick Lesabre	148,633
14	Ford Contour	139,838	Buick Lesabre	149,445	Pontiac Grand Prix	148,521
15	Buick Lesabre	136,551	Pontiac Grand Prix	148,197	Volkswagen Jetta	144,853
16	Buick Century	126,220	Dodge Intrepid	144,355	Dodge Intrepid	143,840
17	Pontiac Grand Prix	122,915	Ford Contour	134,487	Buick Century	143,085
18	Dodge Neon	117,964	Nissan Maxima	131,182	Nissan Altima	136,971
19	Mercury Grand Marquis	114,162	Volkswagen Jetta	130,054	Nissan Maxima	129,235
20	Nissan Maxima	113,843	Mercury Grand Marquis	122,776	Oldsmobile Alero	122,722

Source: Ward's AutoInfoBank. Web: www.wardsauto.com.

Top NYSE Stocks by Market Value

(shares and value in millions)

Rank 2000	Company (Symbol)	Listed shares[1]	Market value[1]	Rank 2000	Company (Symbol)	Listed shares[1]	Market value[1]
1	General Electric (GE)	11,145	$534,241	27	BellSouth Corporation (BLS)	2,020	$ 82,707
2	Exxon Mobil Corp. (XOM)	4,009	348,494	28	America Online (AOL)	2,329	81,065
3	Merck & Co. (MRK)	2,968	277,918	29	Texas Instruments (TXN)	1,642	77,806
4	Citigroup Inc. (C)	4,811	245,660	30	Abbott Laboratories (ABT)	1,566	75,846
5	Wal-Mart Stores (WMT)	4,615	245,157	31	Nokia Corporation (NOK)	1,739	75,634
6	American International Group (AIG)	2,486	244,979	32	Bank of America Corporation (BAC)	1,633	74,906
7	Coca-Cola Co. (KO)	3,476	211,822	33	American Express (AXP)	1,340	73,616
8	Pfizer Inc. (PFE)	4,138	190,347	34	Medtronic, Inc. (MDT)	1,200	72,439
9	Bristol-Myers Squibb (BMY)	2,194	162,210	35	BP Amoco p.l.c. (BP)	1,447	69,269
10	Johnson & Johnson (JNJ)	1,535	161,263	36	The Boeing Company (BA)	1,012	66,762
11	Int'l Business Machines (IBM)	1,892	160,832	37	Merrill Lynch & Co. (MER)	962	65,577
12	Verizon Communications (VZ)	2,799	140,297	38	Time Warner Inc. (TWX)	1,212	63,311
13	EMC Corporation (EMC)	2,046	136,075	39	Hewlett-Packard (HWP)	1,991	62,838
14	Philip Morris Cos., Inc. (MO)	2,806	123,462	40	Enron Corp. (ENE)	746	62,026
15	Schering-Plough (SGP)	2,030	115,181	41	Disney (Walt) Co. (DIS)	2,117	61,259
16	Home Depot Inc. (HD)	2,317	105,871	42	AT&T Corp. (T)	3,508	60,728
17	Lilly (Eli) Co. (LLY)	1,128	104,963	43	Chevron Corp. (CHV)	712	60,161
18	Procter & Gamble (PG)	1,326	104,045	44	Minnesota Mining and Manufacturing Co. (MMM)	472	56,878
19	Fannie Mae (FNM)	1,129	97,949	45	The Bank of New York Company (BK)	978	53,973
20	Morgan Stanley Dean Witter (MWD)	1,212	96,026	46	Schlumberger Limited (SLB)	667	53,325
21	Berkshire Hathaway Inc. (Class A) (BRKA)	1,344	95,429	47	Corning Inc. (GLW)	960	50,691
22	SBC Communications Inc. (SBC)	1,981	94,612	48	du Pont (E.I.) de Nemours (DD)	1,043	50,387
23	Wells Fargo (WFC)	1,666	92,781	49	Royal Dutch Petroleum (RD)	823	49,822
24	Tyco International Ltd. (TYC)	1,636	90,773	50	The Gillette Company (G)	1,365	49,308
25	American Home Products (AHP)	1,422	90,379				5,906,647
26	Pepsico, Inc. (PEP)	1,726	85,553		**Total**	**101,977**	

NOTE: Based on closing prices on Dec. 29, 2000. 1. Includes treasury shares. *Source:* New York Stock Exchange.

Dow 101

Five Fundamental Facts About the Dow Jones Industrial Average

The Index Is Not Truly Industrial

Though its name would lead you to believe it is composed of only industrial companies, in fact the DJIA contains stocks across many "industries," not all of which are industrial.

The industries represented include financial, food, technology, retail, heavy equipment, oil, chemical, pharmaceutical, consumer goods, and entertainment. Dow Jones also collects and reports data for two other sectors of the economy in its Transportation and Utilities indexes.

The DJIA Represents Only 30 Stocks

To be chosen for inclusion in the index, a stock must be a leader in its industry and must be widely held by both individual and institutional investors (i.e., pension plans, mutual funds, etc.). Together, the 30 stocks in the average represent about 20% of the market value of all U.S. stocks, so although the DJIA is not the whole stock market, it is certainly representative of the stock market as a whole.

The DJIA Is Not Really an "Average"

A simple average is calculated by adding up a value for a number of items, then dividing by the number of items. The Dow reflects the value of stock prices, but a simple average cannot accurately reflect the value of stock prices.

Here's why. When stocks become pricey, companies routinely announce stock splits to make their stocks more appealing to individual investors.

For example, a company may have 100 shares outstanding priced at $100 per share, for a market value of $10,000. If the firm announces a 2-for-1 split, the price is cut in half, and the number of shares is doubled, so there would be 200 shares outstanding, priced at $50 per share. The market value is still $10,000, but the price point is now more attractive to smaller investors.

To take into account the changes in price associated with stock splits, the Dow Jones Industrial "Average" is adjusted to account for any stock splits in each of the included companies.

The Following 30 Companies Currently Compose the Dow Industrials

- Alcoa Inc. (AA)
- American Express Co. (AXP)
- AT&T Corp. (T)
- Boeing Co. (BA)
- Caterpillar Inc. (CAT)
- Citigroup Inc. (C)
- Coca-Cola Co. (KO)
- DuPont Co. (DD)
- Eastman Kodak Co. (EK)
- Exxon Mobil Corp. (XOM)
- General Electric Co. (GE)
- General Motors Corp. (GM)
- Hewlett-Packard Co. (HWP)
- Home Depot Inc. (HD)
- Honeywell International Inc. (HON)
- Intel Corp. (INTC)
- International Business Machines Corp. (IBM)
- International Paper Co. (IP)
- J. P. Morgan & Co. (JPM)
- Johnson & Johnson (JNJ)
- McDonald's Corp. (MCD)
- Merck & Co., Inc. (MRK)
- Microsoft Corp. (MSFT)
- Minnesota Mining & Manufacturing Co. (MMM)
- Philip Morris Companies Inc. (MO)
- Procter & Gamble Co. (PG)
- SBC Communications Inc. (SBC)
- United Technologies Corp. (UTX)
- Wal-Mart Stores, Inc. (WMT)
- Walt Disney Co. (DIS)

Who Is Dow Jones?

Charles Dow and Edward Jones are two-thirds of the team that founded Dow Jones & Company in 1882. Charles Bergstresser was the "& Company," but by 1889 he was joined by 47 others as the company grew. They specialized in newsletters (the precursor to *The Wall Street Journal*) focusing on financial news. When Dow died in 1902, Clarence Barron, originally hired as a correspondent, purchased a controlling interest in the firm.

50 Most Active Stocks on NYSE, 2000

2000 Rank	Company name (symbol)	Share volume (in millions)	2000 Rank	Company name (symbol)	Share volume (in millions)
1	Lucent Technologies, Inc. (LU) (5)	3,972.4	27	Vodafone Group Plc (VOD)	1,135.5
2	Compaq Computer (CPQ) (2)	3,610.3	28	Time Warner Inc. (TWX) (42)	1,104.2
3	AT&T Corp. (T) (3)	3,417.6	29	Xerox Corp. (XRX) (23)	1,093.6
4	America Online (AOL) (1)	3,106.0	30	AT&T Corp. Liberty Media Group (LMGA)	1,075.6
5	Nortel Networks (NT)	2,863.0	31	Schering-Plough (SGP) (39)	1,068.7
6	Pfizer Inc. (PFE) (8)	2,457.7	32	Advanced Micro Devices (AMD)	1,066.5
7	Citigroup Inc. (C) (4)	2,366.6	33	Corning Inc. (GLW)	1,057.9
8	General Electric (GE) (13)	2,363.0	34	Coca-Cola Co. (KO) (17)	1,052.5
9	Nokia Inc. (NOK)	2,191.8	35	Hewlett-Packard (HWP) (24)	1,007.3
10	Motorola, Inc. (MOT) (31)	2,178.5	36	Proctor & Gamble (PG)	997.2
11	Philip Morris Cos., Inc. (MO) (6)	2,070.4	37	McDonald's Corp. (MCD)	980.5
12	Texas Instruments Inc. (TXN) (33)	1,719.9	38	Honeywell Int'l Inc. (HON)	967.6
13	EMC Corp. (EMC) (14)	1,683.1	39	Ford Motor Co. (F)	935.2
14	Tyco International Ltd. (TYC) (10)	1,674.4	40	Cendant Corp. (CD) (19)	921.1
15	Micron Technology, Inc. (MU) (11)	1,633.2	41	Gap Inc. (GPS)	920.8
16	Wal-Mart Stores (WMT) (12)	1,630.2	42	Sprint Corp. (PCS)	892.2
17	IBM Corporation (IBM) (7)	1,507.0	43	Wells Fargo (WFC)	891.3
18	Chase Manhattan Corp. (CMB) (22)	1,479.6	44	Pepsico, Inc. (PEP) (21)	886.7
19	SBC Communications Inc. (SBC) (29)	1,438.4	45	Morgan Stanley Dean Witter (MWD)	885.3
20	Home Depot Inc. (HD) (35)	1,363.5	46	General Motors (GM)	868.8
21	Qwest Communications Int'l (Q)	1,275.6	47	Bank One Corp. (ONE) (26)	868.5
22	Bristol-Myers Squibb (BMY) (38)	1,262.9	48	LSI Logic Corp. (LSI)	867.6
23	Bank of America Corp. (BAC) (15)	1,258.0	49	Schwab (Charles) Corp. (SCH) (30)	864.3
24	Disney (Walt) Co. (DIS) (9)	1,253.8	50	The Boeing Company (BA) (41)	853.6
25	Merck & Co. (MRK) (16)	1,249.3			
26	Exxon Mobil Corp. (XOM)	1,199.5			

NOTES: As of Dec. 29, 2000. In case of stock splits, volume in old and new issues was combined. 1999 rankings in parentheses, if among top 50. *Source:* New York Stock Exchange.

Most Active NASDAQ Stocks

Rank	Name	TSEC	Total volume (in thousands)	Rank	Name	TSEC	Total volume (in thousands)
1	Cisco Systems, Inc.	CSCO	14,122,775	26	Amazon.com, Inc.	AMZN	2,232,543
2	Intel Corporation	INTC	13,669,218	27	Commerce One, Inc.	CMRC	2,217,632
3	Oracle Corporation	ORCL	13,565,634	28	Apple Computer, Inc.	AAPL	2,180,002
4	Sun Microsystems, Inc.	SUNW	10,404,002	29	i2 Technologies, Inc.	ITWO	2,154,452
5	Microsoft Corporation	MSFT	10,324,624	30	Ariba, Inc.	ARBA	2,024,974
6	WorldCom, Inc.	WCOM	8,634,250	31	CMGI, Inc.	CMGI	2,019,586
7	3Com Corporation	COMS	8,562,819	32	BEA Systems, Inc.	BEAS	1,967,033
8	Dell Computer Corporation	DELL	8,317,578	33	Xilinx, Inc.	XLNX	1,857,448
9	JDS Uniphase Corporation	JDSU	6,320,515	34	VERITAS Software Corporation	VRTS	1,832,694
10	LM Ericsson Telephone Company	ERICY	5,359,161	35	Comcast Corporation	CMCSK	1,828,594
11	QUALCOMM Incorporated	QCOM	4,668,613	36	Network Appliance, Inc.	NTAP	1,817,371
12	Applied Materials, Inc.	AMAT	4,012,494	37	Palm, Inc.	PALM	1,815,527
13	CIENA Corporation	CIEN	3,338,285	38	Brocade Communications Systems, Inc.	BRCD	1,813,889
14	Applied Micro Circuits Corporation	AMCC	3,184,334	39	Flextronics International Ltd.	FLEX	1,757,213
15	Yahoo! Inc.	YHOO	3,098,211	40	Staples, Inc.	SPLS	1,679,534
16	Exodus Communications, Inc.	EXDS	2,999,158	41	RF Micro Devices, Inc.	RFMD	1,664,967
17	Atmel Corporation	ATML	2,983,905	42	Citrix Systems, Inc.	CTXS	1,656,704
18	BroadVision, Inc.	BVSN	2,884,618	43	InfoSpace, Inc.	INSP	1,649,564
19	ADC Telecommunications, Inc.	ADCT	2,680,622	44	Conexant Systems, Inc.	CNXT	1,626,938
20	Rambus, Inc.	RMBS	2,429,260	45	Costco Wholesale Corporation	COST	1,594,829
21	Juniper Networks, Inc.	JNPR	2,411,182	46	PMC-Sierra, Inc.	PMCS	1,589,676
22	Altera Corporation	ALTR	2,367,409	47	Immunex Corporation	IMNX	1,585,998
23	Siebel Systems, Inc.	SEBL	2,320,019	48	Broadcom Corporation	BRCM	1,581,012
24	Amgen Inc.	AMGN	2,301,536	49	Covad Communications Group, Inc.	COVD	1,577,927
25	Nextel Communications, Inc.	NXTL	2,295,959	50	At Home Corporation	ATHM	1,531,772

Source: The NASDAQ Stock Market, Inc.

Top NASDAQ Stocks by Market Value

Rank	Name	TSEC	Market value (in thousands)	Rank	Name	TSEC	Market value (in thousands)
1	Cisco Systems, Inc.	CSCO	$275,290,988	29	Northern Trust Corporation	NTRS	$18,088,983
2	Microsoft Corporation	MSFT	231,290,161	30	Nextel Communications, Inc.	NXTL	17,972,955
3	Intel Corporation	INTC	202,317,260	31	Costco Wholesale Corporation	COST	17,895,690
4	Oracle Corporation	ORCL	163,614,236	32	Comverse Technology, Inc.	CMVT	17,884,346
5	Sun Microsystems, Inc.	SUNW	88,565,900	33	Yahoo! Inc.	YHOO	16,787,312
6	Amgen Inc.	AMGN	66,045,770	34	Palm, Inc.	PALM	16,021,478
7	QUALCOMM Incorporated	QCOM	61,510,805	35	Xilinx, Inc.	XLNX	15,207,413
8	Dell Computer Corporation	DELL	45,107,880	36	Linear Technology Corporation	LLTC	14,648,300
9	WorldCom, Inc.	WCOM	40,485,904	37	VeriSign, Inc.	VRSN	14,646,220
10	Juniper Networks, Inc.	JNPR	40,031,997	38	LM Ericsson Telephone Company	ERICY	14,390,263
11	Comcast Corporation	CMCSK	36,382,829	39	ADC Telecommunications, Inc.	ADCT	14,095,378
12	VERITAS Software Corporation	VRTS	35,756,700	40	Adobe Systems Incorporated	ADBE	13,985,711
13	JDS Uniphase Corporation	JDSU	32,834,057	41	Maxim Integrated Products, Inc.	MXIM	13,588,696
14	Applied Materials, Inc.	AMAT	30,974,812	42	Ariba, Inc.	ARBA	13,285,969
15	Siebel Systems, Inc.	SEBL	29,047,778	43	Millennium Pharmaceuticals, Inc.	MLNM	13,150,479
16	Fifth Third Bancorp	FITB	27,598,406	44	SDL, Inc.	SDLI	12,954,952
17	BEA Systems, Inc.	BEAS	25,581,656	45	Broadcom Corporation	BRCM	12,840,408
18	CIENA Corporation	CIEN	23,280,644	46	PMC-Sierra, Inc.	PMCS	12,582,831
19	Tellabs, Inc.	TLAB	23,194,098	47	Level 3 Communications, Inc.	LVLT	12,047,188
20	VoiceStream Wireless Corporation	VSTR	22,933,243	48	Flextronics International Ltd.	FLEX	11,995,878
21	Applied Micro Circuits Corporation	AMCC	22,187,875	49	Sanmina Corporation	SANM	11,608,611
22	i2 Technologies, Inc.	ITWO	21,545,659	50	PeopleSoft, Inc.	PSFT	10,614,955
23	Immunex Corporation	IMNX	21,130,322				
24	Network Appliance, Inc.	NTAP	20,594,078				
25	Check Point Software Technologies Ltd.	CHKP	20,303,828				
26	Brocade Communications Systems, Inc.	BRCD	$ 19,924,673				
27	Gemstar-TV Guide International Inc	GMST	18,913,879				
28	Paychex, Inc.	PAYX	18,100,899				

Source: The NASDAQ Stock Market, Inc.

The articles and opinions in this section are for general information only and are not intended to provide specific advice or recommendations for any individual.

How to Navigate the Storm

If you own stocks, the worst is over. Now grab some bargains on cars, mortgages, and new investments

By J. DANIEL KADLEC TIME

The gyrations of the stock market have jolted many investors. The correction will take time. The more than $2.5 trillion of stock-market wealth that has vanished since March 2000 won't be easy to get back. The NASDAQ would have to rise more than 15% a year for five years to return to its high. Meanwhile, consumer debt (excluding mortgages) has doubled over the past decade and averages nearly $15,000 per household. It will take years for borrowers to pay down those debts—and for lenders to deal with defaults.

Still, it's important at times like this to step back and count your blessings. Inflation is no longer on the top of Alan Greenspan's worry list. Corporate profits, though slowing, will still be up in the coming year. Mortgage rates have declined sharply, putting a floor under home values. That's critical because despite the explosion of stock-market wealth over the past decade, the most valuable asset most Americans own is their home. The unemployment rate remains low at about 4%, and many economists believe that even in a recession it wouldn't go much higher than 4.5%, so you'll probably keep another of your major assets—your job.

Even in the stock market, if you have been investing for two years or longer, you're probably still ahead. The declines since 2000 have wrung many excesses out of the markets, and the shares of many solid companies are now available at bargain prices. So although there's danger dead ahead, there are also opportunities. Here are some ideas for dealing with both.

Investments

The most important concept to grasp at this point is how the stock market interacts with the economy. Both run in cycles. But because investors focus on the future, the stock-market cycle is usually ahead of the economic cycle by six months to a year. With an unprecedented 49% of all American households owning stocks, and so much information available immediately via the Web and financial TV channels, this linkage is tightening. But there will always be a gap between the market and the real economy. That means stocks may be at their lows just as a slow-down becomes apparent.

That doesn't necessarily mean stocks have already bottomed. If the slowdown becomes a deep recession, the stock market is likely to fall again—and soon—because such a recession isn't generally expected. But if we're through the worst of it, as many economists believe, then the stock market

could begin to recover right away as it looks ahead to the next expansion. That's how bull markets are born. Indeed, many on Wall Street predict double-digit returns from the Dow and S&P 500. The tech-laden NASDAQ they see as more problematic, but still going higher.

Not even the pros can consistently pick the market's tops and bottoms. That's why individual investors are well served by a disciplined approach: investing a certain amount each month, perhaps in a broad-based index fund like the Wilshire 5000. Such dollar-cost averaging ensures that you'll buy more shares when prices are relatively low. And there's also no better time to start a regular investing program.

Diversification

Diversification, a concept that fell out of favor in the tech boom, will be critical. If you've still got more than 20% of your money in tech stocks, consider selling the ones with no earnings or with price-earnings ratios that far exceed their projected growth. If you invest in individual stocks, the past year should have taught you to do your homework rather than rely on stock analysts from the big brokerages. Most of them were of little use in warning investors of trouble brewing in their stocks—especially the stocks of companies that do business with the brokerage.

Replace the tech stocks that you shed with a mix of steady growers like food and drug stocks; companies that benefit from falling interest rates like banks, insurers, utilities, and real estate investment trusts; and beaten-down cyclical stocks like home builders and retailers, which will rebound with a recovery. Some stocks in these groups have risen sharply in the past year, especially utilities, so pay attention to valuations. Or you can diversify easily through value-oriented mutual funds, like Clipper and Berger Small Cap Value.

Mutual Funds

Mutual funds are especially helpful in gaining exposure to stocks in other countries, and when reaching down to smaller, less understood companies. Exposure to both areas is a good way to further diversify and reduce risk. A recent study by Kirk Butler, a finance professor at Michigan State University, finds that especially in down markets, the fortunes of multinationals across the globe tend to move together. That's because they all sell their stuff everywhere. That's less true of small companies, though, which are more hinged to local economies. So for maximum diversification think small when you think international. Two top-rated funds that invest in smaller foreign companies are T. Rowe Price International Discovery and Wanger International Small Cap.

Your goal is to move toward an all-weather portfolio that seeks the higher returns that stocks historically deliver but also includes enough bonds and cash to cover any financial obligations you expect over the next few years—for example, college tuition. Part of this process is ratcheting down your investment expectations. Having come through five consecutive years of stocks gaining more than 20%, we can now expect something closer to the 11% a year that stocks have averaged since 1926. So bonds and cash won't hurt as much as you think.

Among bonds, Treasury securities that mature in five to seven years offer the best combination of safety and potential total return. For cash, six-month bank CDs probably beat money funds, where interest payments will float lower as the Fed cuts short-term interest rates.

Career

Not long ago desperate companies were wooing a broad range of new hires with signing bonuses and stock options. Suddenly blue-chip companies including GM, Whirlpool, and Gillette were letting people go—and there are no dotcoms to snap them up. So stop waiting for the next offer and make yourself useful. That means being versatile. Take full advantage of training courses—especially ones that will teach you to apply new productivity-enhancing technologies. No matter what you hear, says Jeff Joerres, CEO of the staffing firm Manpower, "most people prefer to stay where they are, and, by the same token, employers want loyal workers."

Joerres believes the biggest hurt will be on those in entry-level positions, for many of whom the minimum wage will again become the norm. But there remains a great need for mid-level and skilled employees. "Even if we move toward 5% unemployment," Joerres says, "you are still going to find companies saying they can't find the right people." The most secure jobs are in information technology, finance, engineering, nursing, and teaching, Joerres says.

The slowdown is also a reminder of the need to constantly network inside and outside your company. "Time and again people work very hard and are good at what they do, but they don't know anybody," says John Challenger, CEO of Challenger Gray & Christmas, an outplacement firm. "They put their head down and spend no time developing social capital. When they're let go, they have a hard time finding a job."

Home

If you're house hunting you may finally get a break. As the economy slows, more homes will become available at attractive prices. And mortgage rates should decline as the Fed cuts short-term rates. But don't wait too long; mortgage rates will head higher as a recovery takes shape. With the job market expected to stay fairly strong, others will be bidding against you, so don't hold out for a screaming bargain.

If you're happy where you are, look for a chance to refinance. Another opportunity may exist for those in a mortgage just over the break point between so-called conforming and jumbo loans. In 2000 the break point was a loan value of $252,700. It rose to $275,000 for 2001. You may have a chance to refinance out of the more costly jumbo into a conforming mortgage. For rates and options, check out hsh.com, eloan.com, and bankrate.com.

Car

If your auto lease is coming due, consider buying the car instead of leasing another. You may be able to keep your vehicle for less than the buyout, or residual, value stated in the lease. That's because a glut of cars coming off lease are driving prices lower amid slack demand.

Insurance

The less financial security you have, the more important it is to protect what you own. Consider taking higher deductibles to drive down premiums, and maybe you can drop comprehensive coverage on an aging vehicle. But don't skimp on homeowners' or your umbrella liability policy. Burglaries tend to pick up in tough times, and some folks look to lawsuits to make ends meet. Double-check coverage on jewelry, art, and antiques. Such items can decline in value during a slowdown, and many policies pay only what the item would cost at the time of the loss. "You want a cash-value policy that pays at least what you paid," says Mary Ann Avnet, marketing manager at Chubb's personal-insurance division.

Credit Cards

Whittling down high-cost debt is the most important thing you can do to get ready for a period of relative job insecurity and meager pay raises. Put off purchases of things like cars and appliances. They'll get cheaper as the economy slows and manufacturers try to lure back consumers. Pay off your high-rate debt first and fixed-rate debt ahead of variable-rate debt. As interest rates decline, so will variable rates. Try to build a cash cushion equal to three months' living expenses. That's less important when you are debt free and have access to borrowed money. But no one ever lost sleep because they saved too much.   □

Useful Government Websites

Financial Documents You Should Have

Financial advisers recommend that your long-term financial plan include the following:

Wills

A will states how you want your property disposed of after your death. Seventy percent of Americans don't have a will, which is odd considering that dying is the one thing we are all guaranteed to do. Having a will saves time and money for your family, since dying without one—called "intestate"—means more money from your estate will likely go to taxes and requires extra legal fees. In addition, your property will be disposed of according to state law.

Executor

The executor of your estate is the person (family member or attorney) or entity (such as a trust company) that carries out the instructions in your will. If you do not name an executor, the court will appoint one.

Letter of Instruction

Some experts recommend leaving a letter of instruction to let your family know: where documents are located, what money you are owed, what burial or funeral arrangements you wish, and who should be notified. This is not a substitute for a will.

Trusts

Trusts are not just for the very rich. You might want to discuss the creation of a trust with your lawyer or financial planner. Assets placed in trusts are automatically given to the beneficiaries, avoiding probate costs. A revocable living trust says who will control your assets while you are alive and after you have died.

Durable Power of Attorney for Health Care

Also called a living trust, this ensures that your affairs will be handled as you wish if you become incapacitated. Unless you specify otherwise, a court could be asked to name a guardian to handle your affairs if you could not do so.

As people live longer and need more health care, many financial advisers are also recommending long-term care insurance to cover nursing home costs.

Long-term disability insurance, which will provide for you if you become incapacitated and unable to work for a long period, is also frequently recommended. Remember, many employers offer this type of insurance but it often only applies to on-the-job injuries.

Life Insurance

Not everyone needs life insurance. Life insurance is intended to provide for those who would be hurt financially by your death. Single people with no dependents do not usually need life insurance.

Top 10 Ways to Prepare for Retirement

Source: Department of Labor, Web: http://www.dol.gov/dol/pwba/public/pubs/topten/top10txt.htm

1. Know your retirement needs.

Retirement is expensive. Experts estimate that you'll need about 70% of your pre-retirement income—lower earners, 90% or more—to maintain your standard of living when you stop working.

2. Find out about Social Security.

Social Security pays the average retiree about 40% of pre-retirement earnings. Call the Social Security Administration at 1-800-772-1213 for a free Personal Earnings and Benefit Estimate Statement (PEBES).

3. Learn about your employer's pension or profit sharing plan.

If your employer offers a plan, check to see what your benefit is worth. Most employers will provide an individual benefit statement. Before you change jobs, find out what will happen to your pension. Learn what benefits you may have from previous employment. Find out if you will be entitled to benefits from your spouse's plan. For a free booklet on private pensions, call the U.S. Department of Labor at 1-800-998-7542.

4. Contribute to a tax-sheltered plan.

If your employer offers a tax-sheltered savings plan, such as a 401(k), sign up and contribute all you can. Your taxes will be lower, your company may kick in more, and automatic deductions make it easy.

5. Ask your employer to start a plan.

If your employer doesn't offer a retirement plan, suggest that he/she start one. Simplified plans can be set up by certain employers. For information on simplified employee pensions, order Internal Revenue Service Publication 590 by calling 1-800-829-3676.

6. Put money into an IRA.

You can put $2,000 a year into an Individual Retirement Account (IRA) and delay paying taxes on investment earnings until retirement age. If you don't have a retirement plan (or are in a plan and earn less than a certain amount), you can also take a tax deduction for your IRA contributions. IRS Publication 590 contains information about IRAs.

7. Don't touch your savings.

Don't dip into your retirement savings. You'll lose principal and interest, and you may lose tax benefits. If you change jobs, roll over your savings directly into an IRA or your new employer's retirement plan.

8. Start now, set goals, and stick to them.

Start early. The sooner you start saving, the more time your money has to grow.

9. Consider basic investment principles.

How you save can be as important as how much you save. Inflation and the type of investments you make play important roles in how much you'll have saved at retirement. Know how your pension or savings plan is invested.

10. Ask questions.

Talk to your employer, your bank, your union, or a financial adviser.

Glossary of Financial Terms

Adjusted gross income Amount of income which is subject to federal income tax. In addition to any other tax credits, contributions to IRAs and 401(k) plans are subtracted from the total.

Aggressive Relating or referring to an investment philosophy that seeks above-average returns by accepting above-average risk.

American Stock Exchange (AMEX) Specializes in small-to-medium-size companies.

Annuity Contract issued by a life insurance company that promises to make periodic payments to the buyer over a set period of time. Payments are made to individuals, referred to as annuitants.

Appreciation An increase in value of an asset.

Balanced fund A type of mutual fund that spreads its investments among stocks and bonds. Essentially, a balanced fund is a middle-of-the-road fund that balances its portfolio to achieve both moderate income and moderate capital growth.

Bear market An extended period of general price declines in the securities market.

Bellwether A stock whose performance is indicative of the overall market direction.

Blue chip A very high-quality investment involving a lower-than-average risk of loss of principal or reduction in income.

Bond A long-term promissory note that obligates the borrower to make specified payments over a set period of time.

Bull market An extended period of general price increases in the securities market.

Capital gain The excess by which proceeds from the sale of a capital asset exceeds the cost.

Capitalization The company's stock price per share multiplied by the total number of shares outstanding. **Small-cap:** less than $1.5 billion. **Mid-cap:** between $1.5 billion and $10 billion. **Large-cap:** over $10 billion.

Certificate of deposit (CD) A receipt for a deposit of funds in a financial institution that permits the holder to receive interest plus the deposit at maturity.

Commercial paper A short-term unsecured promissory note issued by a finance company or a large industrial firm. Commonly found in money market funds.

Common stock A class of stock that has no preference as to dividends or any distribution of assets.

Compound interest Interest paid on interest from previous periods in addition to principal.

Consumer price index (CPI) A measure of the average change over time in the prices paid by urban consumers for a fixed "market basket" of day-to-day expenses.

Correction Reverse movement in the price of an individual stock, bond, commodity, or index after any long-term move. Can be a movement up or down, but usually refers to a fall in the price.

Diversification Minimizing risk by investing in a wide range of securities invested in many industries.

Dividend A share of a company's net profits distributed to a class of its stockholders.

Dollar-cost averaging Investment of an equal amount of money at regular intervals resulting in the purchase of more shares during market downturns and fewer shares during market upturns.

Dow Jones Industrial Average (DJIA) A widely quoted measure of stock market price movements of 30 large, seasoned industrial firms.

Earnings per share The amount a stock will pay in income or dividends.

Emerging growth stock The common stock of a relatively young firm operating in an industry with very good growth prospects. This kind of stock offers unusually high returns and a high risk.

Emerging market Market in a country that does not have a fully developed economy. Investments in these markets are usually characterized by a high level of risk and possibility of a high return.

Federal funds Reserve balances above those required that are maintained by commercial banks in the Federal Reserve System.

Federal Reserve Board The seven governing members of the Federal Reserve System who determine the country's monetary policy.

Fixed annuity Annuity that guarantees fixed payments to the annuitant, either for life or for a set period of time.

401(k) plan Plan in which employees elect to contribute pretax dollars to a qualified, tax-deferred investment plan.

Global fund A mutual fund that includes at least 25% foreign securities in its portfolio.

Gross national product (GNP) The dollar output of final goods and services in the economy during a period of time.

Growth stock The stock of a firm that is expected to have above-average increases in revenues and earnings. These firms normally retain most of their earnings for reinvestment and therefore pay small dividends.

Hedge fund A very specialized, volatile investment company (mutual fund) that permits the manager to use a variety of investment techniques normally prohibited in other types of funds.

Income fund An investment company (mutual fund) whose main objective is to achieve current income for its owners; typically, the fund purchases bonds, preferred stocks, and common stocks paying high dividends.

Index Statistical composite that measures changes in the economy or in financial markets and that can be expressed in percent changes from a base year or from the previous month. Most common are the S&P and the Dow Jones Industrial Average.

Index fund A mutual fund that keeps a portfolio of securities designed to match the performance of a certain market as a whole.

Individual Retirement Account (IRA) A custodial account or trust in which individuals may set aside earned income in a tax-deferred retirement plan.

Initial Public Offering (IPO) The first sale of a corporation's stock to the investing public.

International fund A mutual fund that invests only outside the country in which it is located.

Junk bonds Debt issued by a company whose credit rating is below investment grade (BBB for S&P and Baa for Moody's). Because there is a considerable risk, the company must offer a high coupon to make the bond attractive to an investor.

Keogh plan A federally approved retirement program that permits self-employed people to set aside for savings up to $30,000 or 25% of their income, whichever is lower.

Large-capitalization stock The stock of a big company that has considerable retained earnings and a large amount of common stock outstanding, typically a market capitalization of over $3 billion.

Liquid asset A security that can easily be sold for cash.

Load The sales fee that the buyer pays in order to acquire a security, typically a mutual fund.

Long-term bonds Debt securities with maturities of 10 to 30 years. The benchmark for this asset class is the Lehman Government Long Bond Index.

Money market fund A mutual fund that purchases short-term, high-quality securities such as treasury bills, negotiable CDs, and commercial paper.

Money market securities Low-risk, very liquid securities with maturities of one year or less. Other short-term debt that is scheduled to mature within one year may also be classified as money market securities.

Moody's A company rating service issuing ratings denoting the relative investment quality of corporate and municipal bonds.

Mutual fund An investment company that continually offers new shares and stands ready to redeem existing shares from the owners. Also an investment company.

NASDAQ The National Association of Securities Dealers' Automated Quotation marketplace, which trades shares electronically. Companies traded on the NASDAQ include many small-to-medium-size firms and many technology companies.

Net Asset Value (NAV) The market value of an investment company's (mutual fund) asset less any liabilities divided by the number of shares outstanding. This is the value of each share if the fund sold all of its assets at their current market value and paid off any outstanding debts.

Net income Income after all expenses and taxes have been deducted.

New York Stock Exchange The oldest stock exchange in the U.S., located at 11 Wall Street in New York City. Companies traded on the NYSE are typically the largest in the U.S.

No-load fund An open-end investment company (mutual fund), shares of which are sold without a sales charge.

Option A contract that permits the owner, depending on the contract, to purchase or sell a security at a fixed price until a specific date.

Over-the-counter stock Stock that is traded outside of an organized exchange, usually through telephone or electronic connections.

Preferred stock A security that shows ownership in a corporation and gives the holder a claim prior to the claim of common stockholders on earnings and also generally on assets in the event of liquidation.

Price/earnings ratio Price of a stock divided by its earnings per share.

Profit-sharing plan An agreement that allows employees to share in the corporation's profit.

Prospectus A formally written document containing information necessary to make an educated decision to purchase a security or not.

Sector fund An investment company that concentrates its holdings among securities or other assets sharing a common interest.

Small-cap stocks The stock of a relatively small firm with little equity and few shares of common stock outstanding. Small-capitalization stocks tend to be subject to large fluctuations; therefore, the potential for short-term gains and losses is great.

Standard & Poor's 500 (S&P 500) An inclusive index of 500 stocks, including 400 industrial stocks, 40 utilities, 20 transportation stocks, and 40 financial stocks.

Stock An ownership share(s) in a corporation; also equity, common stock. See also **Preferred stock.**

Treasuries All bonds backed by the U.S. government that are issued through the Department of the Treasury.

Yield to maturity The total return an investor will get by holding a long-term, interest-bearing instrument (usually a bond) until it matures.

How to Measure the Shrinking Value of the Dollar

The CPI inflation calculator uses the average Consumer Price Index for a given calendar year. This data represents changes in prices of all goods and services purchased for consumption by urban households. This index value has been calculated every year since 1913. For the current year, the latest monthly index value is used. In 2001, for example, it took $17.95 to buy what $1 bought in 1913. Note that in 1920, it cost $2.02, and declined in 1925 and through the 1930s, illustrating the effect of the Great Depression, when prices slumped. Prices only passed $2 again in 1950.

Year	Amount it took to equal $1 in 1913	Year	Amount it took to equal $1 in 1913	Year	Amount it took to equal $1 in 1913	Year	Amount it took to equal $1 in 1913
1913	$1.00	1940	1.41	1965	3.18	1990	13.20
1920	2.02	1945	1.82	1970	3.92	1995	15.39
1925	1.77	1950	2.43	1975	5.43	2000	17.39
1930	1.69	1955	2.71	1980	8.32	2001	17.95
1935	1.38	1960	2.99	1985	10.87		

Cracking the Credit Code

Glossary of Credit Terms

Source: The Federal Reserve Board. Web: http://www.federalreserve.gov/pubs/shop/.

Annual fee A flat yearly charge similar to a membership fee.

Annual percentage rate (APR) A measure of the cost of credit expressed as a yearly rate. Many credit card plans charge different APRs for credit used in different ways—for example, one APR for purchases, another for cash advances, and still another for balance transfers. Some plans may increase the APR if a payment is late.

Cash-advance fee A fee charged if you obtain a cash advance. This fee is in addition to the interest rate charged on the amount of the advance.

Finance charge The dollar amount you pay to use credit. Besides interest costs, the finance charge may include other charges such as cash-advance fees.

Grace period A period of time, often about 25 days, during which you can pay your credit card bill without incurring a finance charge. Under nearly all credit card plans, the grace period applies only if you pay your balance in full each month. It does not apply if you carry a balance forward. Also, the grace period usually does not apply to cash advances.

Interest rate A measure of the cost of credit, expressed as a percent. For variable-rate credit card plans, the interest rate is explicitly tied to another interest rate, such as the prime rate or the Treasury bill rate. If the other rate changes, the rate on your card will, too. The interest rate on fixed-rate credit card plans, though not explicitly tied to changes in other interest rates, can also change over time. The card issuer must notify you before the "fixed" interest rate is changed. A tiered interest rate means that different rates apply to different levels of the outstanding balance (for example, 16% on balances of $1–$500; 17% on balances over $500).

Late-payment charge A charge imposed when your payment is late. If your payment arrives after the grace period, you may be charged both a finance charge (the interest on your outstanding balance) and a late-payment charge. Some card issuers may also impose a penalty rate if you have more than one late payment within several months.

Over-the-limit fee A fee imposed when your charges exceed the credit limit set on your card.

Penalty rate The rate that applies under specific circumstances set out by the card issuer. For example, if you make 2 late payments within 6 months, a card issuer may have a policy of raising the interest rate.

Periodic rate The rate you are charged each billing period. For most credit card plans, the periodic rate is a monthly rate, calculated by dividing the APR by 12. For example, a credit card with an 18% APR has a monthly periodic rate of 1.5%.

Credit Card Use, 1989–1998

General-purpose credit cards include Mastercard, Visa, Optima, and Discover. All dollar figures are given in constant 1998 dollars based on consumer price index data as published by the U.S. Bureau of Labor Statistics.

Age of family head and family income[1]	Percent having a general-purpose credit card	Percent having a balance after last month's bills	Median balance[2]	Percent of cardholding families who:		
				Almost always pay off the balance	Sometimes pay off the balance	Hardly ever pay off the balance
1989, total	56.0%	52.1%	$1,300	52.9%	21.2%	25.8%
1992, total	62.4	52.6	1,100	53.0	19.6	27.4
1995, total	66.4	56.0	1,600	52.4	20.1	27.5
1998 total	**67.5**	**54.7**	**1,900**	**53.6**	**19.3**	**26.9**
Under 35 years old	58.3	71.6	1,500	39.0	22.5	38.5
35 to 44 years old	71.3	62.5	2,000	46.5	19.1	34.4
45 to 54 years old	75.3	59.2	2,000	48.2	22.7	29.1
55 to 64 years old	76.0	48.8	2,300	61.0	20.1	18.9
65 to 74 years old	71.2	33.9	1,000	74.0	14.9	11.1
75 years old and over	50.8	16.7	700	86.3	7.8	5.9
Less than $10,000	23.2	64.0	900	46.4	19.9	33.8
$10,000 to $24,999	50.8	56.9	1,200	52.3	19.3	28.4
$25,000 to $49,999	73.2	58.2	1,700	48.3	20.5	31.2
$50,000 to $99,999	89.6	55.9	2,400	53.9	20.2	25.9
$100,000 and more	97.9	36.4	3,100	72.0	13.8	14.1

1. Families include one-person units. 2. Among families having a balance. *Source:* Board of Governors of the Federal Reserve System, unpublished data, *Statistical Abstract of the U.S., 2000;* www.census.gov/prod/www/statistical abstract-us.html.

How to Write a Complaint Letter

- Include your name, address, and home and work phone numbers.
- Type your letter if possible. If it is handwritten, make sure it is neat and easy to read.
- Make your letter brief and to the point. Include all important facts about your purchase, including the date and place where you made the purchase and any information you can give about the product or service such as serial or model numbers or specific type of service.

- State exactly what you want done about the problem and how long you are willing to wait to get it resolved. Be reasonable.
- Include all documents regarding your problem. Be sure to send COPIES, not originals.
- Avoid writing an angry, sarcastic, or threatening letter. The person reading your letter probably was not responsible for your problem but may be very helpful in resolving it.
- Keep a copy of the letter for your records.

Name of Contact Person, if available
Title, if available
Company Name
Consumer Complaint Division, if you have no contact person
Street Address
City, State, Zip Code

Dear (Contact Person):

Re: (account number, if applicable)

On (date), I (bought, leased, rented, or had repaired) a (name of the product, with serial or model number or service performed) at (location and other important details of the transaction).

Unfortunately, your product (or service) has not performed well (or the service was inadequate) because (state the problem). I am disappointed because (explain the problem: for example, the product does not work properly, the service was not performed correctly, I was billed the wrong amount, something was not disclosed clearly or was misrepresented, etc.).

To resolve the problem, I would appreciate it if you could (state the specific action you want—money back, charge card credit, repair, exchange, etc.). Enclosed are copies of my records (include copies of receipts, guarantees, warranties, canceled checks, contracts, model and serial numbers, and any other documents).

I look forward to your reply and a resolution to my problem, and will wait until (set a time limit) before seeking help from a consumer protection agency or the Better Business Bureau. Please contact me at the above address or by phone at (home and/or office numbers with area code).

Sincerely,

Your name
Enclosure(s) cc: (reference to whom you are sending a copy of this letter, if anyone)

Source: Consumer Action Handbook 2001, Federal consumer Information Center, Pueblo, CO, 82009, www.pueblo.gsa.gov

Better Business Bureaus

Better Business Bureaus (BBBs) are nonprofit organizations supported primarily by local business members. BBBs offer a variety of consumer services including educational materials, information on charities and other organizations seeking public donations, and mediation and arbitration services. If you need help with a consumer question or complaint, call your local BBB to ask about its services, or contact the BBB online at www.bbb.org.

National Consumer Organizations

NOTE: For other organizations, *see* Societies & Associations, pp. 475–484

Alliance Against Fraud In Telemarketing & Electronic Commerce (AAFTEC), c/o National Consumers League, 1701 K St. N.W., Suite 1200, Washington, D.C. 20006; 202-835-3323; 202-835-0747 (fax); Web: www.nclnet.org.

Combats telemarketing and Internet fraud through consumer education.

American Association of Retired Persons (AARP), Consumer Affairs Section, 601 E St. N.W., Washington, D.C. 20049; 800-424-3410; Web: www.aarp.org.

Offers information on housing, insurance, funeral practices, eligibility for public benefits, financial security, transportation, and consumer protection issues on behalf of mid-life and older consumers.

American Council on Consumer Interests (ACCI), 240 Stanley Hall, University of Missouri, Columbia, Mo. 65211-0001; 573-882-3817; 573-884-6571 (fax); Web: www.consumerinterests.org.

Provides research-based information on topics of consumer interest. Provides information about consumer publications, policies, and resources.

American Council on Science and Health (ACSH), 1995 Broadway, 2nd Fl., New York, N.Y. 10023-5860; 212-362-7044; 212-362-4919 (fax); Web: www.acsh.org.

A consumer education consortium concerned with issues related to food, nutrition, chemicals, pharmaceuticals, lifestyle, the environment, and health.

American Savings Education Council, 2121 K Street N.W., Suite 600, Washington, D.C. 20037; 202-659-0670; Web: www.asec.org.

Raises public awareness about what is needed to ensure long-term personal financial independence.

Center for Auto Safety (CAS), 1825 Connecticut Ave. N.W., Suite 3301, Washington, D.C. 20009; 202-328-7700; Web: www.autosafety.org.

Founded by Consumers Union and Ralph Nader in 1970 to advocate for auto safety and quality.

Center for Science in the Public Interest (CSPI), 1875 Connecticut Ave. N.W., Suite 300, Washington, D.C. 20009; 202-332-9110; 202-265-4954 (fax); Web: www.cspinet.org.

Provides research, education, and advocacy on nutrition, health, food safety, and related issues.

Center for the Study of Services, 733 15th Street N.W., Suite 820, Washington, D.C. 20005; 202-347-7283; Web: www.checkbook.org.

Aids consumers in selecting doctors, hospitals, and health plans.

Coalition Against Insurance Fraud, 1012 14th St. N.W., Washington, D.C. 20005; 202-393-7330; Web: www.insurancefraud.org.

Organization of consumers, government agencies, and insurers dedicated to combating all forms of insurance fraud.

Community Nutrition Institute (CNI), 910 17th Street N.W., Suite 413, Washington, D.C. 20006; 202-776-0595; Web: www.unidial.com/~cni.

Advocates an adequate, safe, and healthy diet.

Congress Watch, 215 Pennsylvania Ave. S.E., Washington, D.C. 20003; 202-546-4996; Web: www.citizen.org/congress.

Champions consumer and citizen interest before the U.S. Congress.

Consumer Action (CA), 717 Market St., Suite 310, San Francisco, Calif. 94103; 415-777-9635 (consumer complaint hotline); 415-777-9456 (voice/ttd); Web: www.consumer-action.org.

Advocate for credit, finance, and telecommunications issues.

Consumer Federation of America (CFA), 1424 16th St. N.W., Suite 604, Washington, D.C. 20036; 202-387-6121; Web: www.consumerfed.org.

Composed of more than 260 organizations, CFA is a consumer advocacy and education organization. CFA focuses much of its advocacy in the areas of financial service, utilities, product safety, transportation, health care, and food safety.

The Consumer Action Handbook

Source: U.S. Office of Consumer Affairs

The *2001 Consumer Action Handbook,* published by the Federal Consumer Information Center, is 148 pages of valuable information that no consumer should be without. It provides advice on car repair, purchase and leasing, shopping from home, avoiding consumer and investment fraud, home improvement and financing, and much more. Also included is the *Consumer Assistance Directory* with thousands of useful names, addresses, phone numbers, and websites.

Single copies of the *Consumer Action Handbook* are available free by writing to: Handbook, Federal Consumer Information Center, Pueblo, Colo. 81009, or by calling 1-800-688-9889. The handbook can also be viewed and ordered on the FCIC website: www.pueblo.gsa.gov.

Consumers Union of U.S., Inc. (CU), 101 Truman Ave., Yonkers, N.Y. 10703-1057; 914-378-2000; Web: www.consumersunion.org.

Researches and tests consumer goods and services.

Families USA Foundation, 1334 G St. N.W., Washington, D.C. 20005; 202-628-3030; Web: www.familiesusa.org.

Advocates for high-quality, affordable health and long-term care.

HALT: An Organization of Americans for Legal Reform, 1612 K Street N.W., Suite 510, Washington, D.C. 20006; 202-887-8255, toll-free: 1-888-367-4258; 202-347-2417 (fax); Web: www.halt.org

Helps consumers handle their legal affairs affordably, equitably, and simply.

Health Research Group (HRG), 1600 20th St. N.W., Washington, D.C. 20009; 202-588-1000; Web: www.citizen.org/hrg.

Works for protection against unsafe foods, drugs, medical devices, and workplaces.

National Community Reinvestment Coalition (NCRC), 733 15th Street N.W., Suite 540, Washington, D.C. 20005; 202-628-8866; 202-628-9800 (fax); Web: www.ncrc.org.

Works toward ending discriminatory banking practices, and increasing the flow of private capital and credit into underserved communities.

National Consumer Law Center (NCLC), 18 Tremont Street, Boston, Mass. 02108; 617-523-8010; Web: www.consumerlaw.org.

Focuses on the interests of low-income consumers in court, before administrative agencies, and before legislatures.

National Consumers League (NCL), 1701 K St. N.W., Suite 1201, Washington, D.C. 20006; 202-835-3323; Web: nclnet.org.

Founded in 1899, NCL is America's pioneer consumer advocacy organization, and focuses on consumer health and safety protection as well as fairness in the marketplace and workplace.

National Foundation for Consumer Credit, Inc. (NFCC), 801 Roeder Rd., Suite 900, Silver Spring, Md. 20910; 301-589-5600; 301-495-5623 (fax); Web: www.nfcc.org.

Provides assistance dealing with stressful financial situations.

National Fraud Information Center/Internet Fraud Watch (NFIC/IFW), P.O. Box 65868, Washington, D.C. 20035; 800-876-7060, TDD/TTY: 202-835-0778; Web: www.fraud.org.

Help on avoiding telemarketing fraud and online and Internet fraud, and assistance in filing complaints.

National Senior Citizens Law Center, 1101 14th St. N.W., Suite 400, Washington, D.C. 20005; 202-289-6976; Web: www.nsclc.org.

Helps older Americans with legal services.

Public Citizen, Inc., 1600 20th St. N.W., Washington, D.C. 20009; 202-885-1000; Web: www.citizen.org.

Represents consumer interests in Congress, the courts, government agencies, and the media.

Public Voice for Food and Health Policy, 1012 14th St. N.W., Suite 800, Washington, D.C. 20005; 202-347-6200.

Promotes a safer, healthier, and more affordable food supply.

United Seniors Health Cooperative (USHC), 409 Third Street S.W., Suite 200, Washington, D.C. 20024; 202-479-6973; Web: www.unitedseniorshealth.org.

Helps seniors achieve good health, independence, and financial security.

U.S. Public Interest Research Group (U.S. PIRG), 218 D St. S.E., Washington, D.C. 20003; 202-546-9707; Web: www.uspirg.org.

Advocates on issues such as the environment, product safety, and financial privacy and identity theft.

Women's Bureau, Dept. of Labor, 200 Constitution Ave., N.W., Washington, D.C. 20210; 202-219-5529; 1-800-827-5335; Web: www.dol.gov/dol/wb.

Advocates for work issues such as sexual harassment, pregnancy discrimination, and child care.

Recalls

Several federal government agencies enforce product safety regulations and provide recall information. Recalls are also posted regularly on the FCIC website: www.pueblo.gsa.gov.

Cars: National Highway Traffic Safety Administration; Phone: 1-800-DASH-2-DOT; Web: www.nhtsa.dot.gov

Drugs, medical devices, food: Food and Drug Administration (FDA); Phone: 1-888-INFO-FDA; Web: fda.com

Seafood: FDA; U.S. Department of Commerce; Web: www.doc.gov

Toy, baby and play equipment, household products: U.S. Consumer Product Safety Commission; Web: www.cpsc.gov

---

Copyrights

Source: Excerpted from *Copyright Basics (Circular 1)*, U.S. Copyright Office

Copyright is a form of protection provided by the laws of the United States to the creators of "original works of authorship," including literary, dramatic, musical, artistic, and certain other intellectual works. This protection is available to both published and unpublished works. The 1976 Copyright Act generally gives the owner of copyright the exclusive right to do and to authorize others to do the following:

• to reproduce the copyrighted work in copies or phonorecords;

• to prepare derivative works based upon the copyrighted work;

• to distribute copies or phonorecords of the copyrighted work to the public by sale or other transfer of ownership, or by rental, lease, or lending;

• to perform the copyrighted work publicly;

• to display the copyrighted work publicly; and

• in the case of sound recordings, to perform the work publicly by means of a digital audio transmission.

It is illegal for anyone to violate these rights. However, these rights are not unlimited in scope. In some cases they are limited by the doctrine of "fair use," or by a "compulsory license" under which certain limited uses of copyrighted works are permitted in exchange for payment. For further information about the limitations of any of these rights, consult the Copyright Law or write to the Copyright Office.

Copyright protection exists from the time the work is created in fixed form. The copyright in the work of authorship immediately becomes the property of the author who created it. Only the property of the author, or those deriving their rights through the author, can rightfully claim copyright.

In the case of works made for hire, the employer and not the employee is considered the author.

The authors of a joint work are co-owners of the copyright in the work, unless there is an agreement to the contrary.

Copyright in each separate contribution to a periodical or other collective work is distinct from copyright in the collective work as a whole and vests initially with the author of the contribution.

Two General Principles:

• Mere ownership of a book, manuscript, painting, or any other copy or phonorecord does not give the possessor the copyright. The law provides that transfer of ownership of any material object that embodies a protected work does not of itself convey any rights in the copyright.

• Minors may claim copyright, but state laws may regulate the business dealings involving copyrights owned by minors. For information on relevant state laws, consult an attorney.

Copyright is secured automatically when the work is created, and a work is "created" when it is fixed in a copy or phonorecord for the first time. "Copies" are material objects from which a work can be read or visually perceived, such as books, manuscripts, sheet music, film, videotape, or microfilm. "Phonorecords" are material objects embodying fixations of sounds (excluding, by statutory definition, motion picture soundtracks), such as cassette tapes, CDs, or LPs. Thus, for example, a song (the "work") can be fixed in sheet music ("copies") or in phonograph disks ("phonorecords"), or both. If a work is prepared over a period of time, the part of the work that is fixed on a particular date constitutes the created work as of that date.

Copyright protection is available for all unpublished works, regardless of the nationality or domicile of the author. Published works are eligible for copyright protection in the United States if any one of the several conditions regarding the nationality of the authors or place of publication is met. Check with the Copyright Office for details.

What Works Are Protected

Copyright protects "original works of authorship" that are fixed in a tangible form of expression. The fixation need not be directly perceptible so long as it may be communicated with the aid of a machine or device. Categories include:

• literary works;
• musical works, including any accompanying words;
• dramatic works, including any accompanying music;
• pantomimes and choreographic works;
• pictorial, graphic, and sculptural works;
• motion pictures and other audiovisual works;
• sound recordings; and
• architectural works.

These categories should be viewed quite broadly. For example, computer programs and most "compilations" are registrable as "literary works." Maps and architectural plans are registrable as "pictorial, graphic, and sculptural works."

Several categories of material are generally not eligible for federal copyright protection. These include, among others:

• works that have not been fixed in a tangible form of expression. For example, choreographic works that have not been notated or recorded, or improvisational speeches or performances that have not been written or recorded;

• titles, names, short phrases, and slogans; familiar symbols or designs; mere variations of typographic ornamentation, lettering, or coloring; mere listings of ingredients or contents;

• ideas, procedures, methods, systems, processes, concepts, principles, discoveries, or devices, as distinguished from a description, explanation, or illustration;

• works consisting entirely of information that is common property and containing no original authorship. For example, standard calendars, height and weight charts, tape measures and rulers, and lists or tables taken from public documents or other common sources.

Notice of Copyright

The use of a copyright notice is no longer required under U.S. law, although it is often beneficial. Because prior law did contain such a requirement, however, the use of notice is still relevant to the copyright status of older works. Use of the notice may be important because it informs the public that the work is protected by copyright, identifies the copyright owners, and shows the year of first publication.

Furthermore, in the event that a work is infringed, if a proper notice of copyright appears on the published copy or copies to which a defendant in a copyright infringement suit had access, then no weight shall be given to such a defendant's interposition of a defense based on innocent infringement in mitigation of actual or statutory damages, except as provided in section 504(c)(2) of the Copyright Code. Innocent infringement occurs when the infringer did not realize that the work was protected.

The use of the copyright notice is the responsibility of the copyright owner and does not require advance permission from, or registration with, the Copyright Office.

Form of Notice for Visually Perceptible Copies

The notice for visually perceptible copies should contain all of the following three elements:

1. the symbol © (the letter C in a circle), or the word "Copyright," or the abbreviation "Copr.";
2. the year of first publication of the work; and
3. the name of the owner of copyright in the work, or an abbreviation by which the name can be recognized, or a generally known alternative designation of the owner.

Example: © 2001 John Doe

Form of Notice for Sound Recordings

The copyright notice for phonorecords of sound recordings should contain the following three elements:

1. the symbol Ⓟ (the letter P in a circle);
2. the year of first publication of the sound recording; and
3. the name of the owner of copyright in the sound recording, or an abbreviation by which the name can be recognized, or a generally known alternative designation of the owner. If the producer of the sound recording is named on the phonorecord labels or containers, and if no other name appears in conjunction with the notice, the producer's name shall be considered a part of the notice.

Example: Ⓟ 2001 A.B.C., Inc.

NOTE: Since questions may arise from the use of variant forms of the notice, you may wish to seek legal advice before using any form of the notice other than those given here.

Position of Notice

The notice should be positioned so as to "give reasonable notice of the claim of copyright." The Copyright Office has issued regulations concerning the form and position of the copyright notice. For more information, contact them directly.

Publications Incorporating United States Government Works

Works by the U.S. government are not eligible for copyright protection. For works published on or after March 1, 1989, the previous notice requirement for works that consist primarily of one or more works of the U.S. government has been eliminated. Copies of works published before March 1, 1989, that consist mostly of one or more works of the U.S. government should have a notice and the accompanying statement. Example:

© 2001 Jane Brown. Copyright claimed in Chapters 7–10, exclusive of U.S. government maps.

Unpublished Works

The author or other owner of copyright may wish to place a copyright notice on any unpublished copies or phonorecords that leave his or her control. An appropriate notice for an unpublished work is "Unpublished work © 2001 Jane Doe."

Copyright Protection Endurance

Works Originally Created on or after Jan. 1, 1978

A work that is created on or after Jan. 1, 1978, is automatically protected from the moment of its creation, and is ordinarily given a term of the author's life, plus an additional 70 years after the author's death. In the case of a joint work prepared by two or more authors who did not work for hire, the term lasts for 70 years after the last surviving author's death. For works made for hire, and for anonymous and pseudonymous works (unless the author's identity is revealed in Copyright Office records), the duration of copyright will be 95 years from publication or 120 years from creation, whichever is shorter.

Works Originally Created before Jan. 1, 1978

Works that were created but not published or registered for copyright before Jan. 1, 1978, have been automatically brought under the statute and are now given federal copyright protection. The duration of copyright in these works will generally be computed in the same way as for works created on or after Jan. 1, 1978: the life-plus-70 or 95/120-year terms will apply to them as well. The law provides that in no case will the term of copyright for works in this category expire before Dec. 31, 2002, and for works published on or before Dec. 31, 2002, the term of copyright will not expire before Dec. 31, 2047. Works that were created and published or registered before Jan. 1, 1978, generally enjoy a copyright term of 75 years from the date of publication or registration. Check with the Copyright Office for details.

International Copyright Protection

There is no "international copyright" that will automatically protect an author's work throughout the entire world. Protection against unauthorized use in a particular country depends basically on the national laws of that country. However, most countries do offer protection to foreign works under certain conditions, and these conditions have been greatly simplified by international copyright treaties and conventions.

For a list of countries that maintain copyright relations with the United States, request Circular 38a from the Copyright Office.

Copyright Registration

Copyright registration makes a public record of the basic facts of a particular copyright. Even though registration is not a requirement for protection, the copyright law provides several incentives to encourage copyright owners to register. They include the following:

• Registration establishes a public record of the copyright claim;
• Before an infringement suit may be filed in court, registration is necessary for works of U.S. origin;
• If made before or within five years of publication, registration will establish *prima facie* evidence in court of the validity of the copyright and of the facts stated in the certificate;
• If registration is made within three months after publication of the work or prior to an infringement of the work, statutory damages and attorney's fees will be available to the copyright owner in court actions. Otherwise, only an award of actual damages and profits is available to the copyright owner; and
• Copyright registration allows the owner of the copyright to record the registration with the U.S. Customs Service for protection against the importation of infringing copies.

Registration may be made at any time within the life of the copyright. When a work has been registered in unpublished form, it is not necessary to make another registration when the work becomes published (although the copyright owner may register the published edition, if desired).

To register a work, send the following three elements in the same envelope or package to the Registrar of Copyrights, Copyright Office, Library of Congress, 101 Independence Ave. S.E., Washington, D.C. 20559-6000:

1. a properly completed application form;

2. a nonrefundable filing fee of $30 (effective through June 30, 2002) for each application; and

3. a nonreturnable deposit of the work that is being registered. The deposit requirements vary in particular situations. Contact the Copyright Office for current information on fees and special requirements.

A copyright registration is effective on the date the Copyright Office receives all of the required elements in acceptable form, regardless of how long it takes to process the application and mail the certificate of registration. The time the Copyright Office requires to process an application varies, depending on the amount of material the office is receiving. If you apply for copyright registration, you will not receive an acknowledgment that your application has been received, but you can expect a letter or telephone call from a Copyright Office staff member if further information is needed.

For More Information

Information on registration and application forms may be obtained free of charge by writing or calling the Copyright Office. Address inquiries to the Copyright Office, Publications Section, LM-455, Library of Congress, 101 Independence Ave. S.E., Washington, D.C. 20559-6000. To speak with an information specialist, call 202-707-3000.

Copyright information, including the most frequently requested circulars, is also available on the Web at www.loc.gov/copyright.

Trademarks
Source: Department of Commerce, Patent and Trademark Office

A trademark may be defined as a word, letter, device, or symbol, as well as any combination of these, that is used in connection with merchandise and that points distinctly to the origin of the goods.

Certificates of registration of trademarks are issued under the seal of the Patent and Trademark Office and may be registered by the owner if he or she is engaged in interstate or foreign commerce. Federal jurisdiction over trademarks arises under the commerce clause of the Constitution. Effective Nov. 16, 1989, applications to register may also be based on a "bona fide intention to use the mark in commerce." Trademarks may be registered by foreign owners who comply with U.S. law, as well as by citizens of foreign countries with which the United States has treaties relating to trademarks. American citizens may register trademarks in foreign countries by complying with the laws of those countries. The right to registration and protection of trademarks in many foreign countries is guaranteed by treaties.

General jurisdiction in trademark cases involving Federal Registrations is given to federal courts. Adverse decisions of examiners on applications for registration are appealable to the Trademark Trial and Appeal Board, whose affirmances and decisions in *inter partes* proceedings are subject to court review. Before adopting a trademark, a person should make a search of prior marks to avoid unwittingly infringing upon them.

The duration of a trademark registration is ten years, but it may be renewed indefinitely for 10-year periods, provided the trademark is still in use at the time of expiration.

The application fee for registering is $325 per class.

Patents
Source: Department of Commerce, Patent and Trademark Office

A patent, in the most general sense, is a document issued by a government, conferring some special right or privilege. The term is now restricted mainly to patents for inventions, and occasionally, land patents.

The grant of a patent for an invention gives the inventor the privilege, for a limited period of time, of excluding others from making, using, or selling a certain article.

In the United States, the law provides that a patent may be granted, for a term of 20 years from the date of application, to any person who has invented or discovered any new and useful art, machine, manufacture, or composition of matter, as well as any new and useful improvements thereof. A patent may also be granted to a person who has invented or discovered and asexually reproduced a new and distinct variety of plant (other than a tuber-propagated one) or has invented a new, original, and ornamental design for an article of manufacture, for a term of 20 years and 14 years, respectively.

A patent is granted only upon receipt of a complete, regularly filed application and the appropriate fees, and upon determination that the invention is new, useful, and, in view of the prior art, unobvious to one skilled in the art. The disclosure must be of such nature as to enable others to reproduce the invention.

Patents are not granted for printed matter, for methods of doing business, or for devices for which claims contrary to natural laws are made. Applications for a perpetual-motion machine have been made from time to time, but until a working model is presented that actually fulfills the claim, no patent will be issued.

A complete application, which must be addressed to the Commissioner of Patents and Trademarks, Washington, D.C. 20231, consists of a specification with one or more claims; oath or declaration; drawing (whenever the nature of the case admits of it); and a basic filing fee of $380. The filing fee is not returned to the applicant if the patent is refused. If the patent is allowed, another fee of $660 is required before the patent is issued. The fee for design patent application is $155; the issue fee is $215. The fee for a plant patent application is $240; the issue fee is $290. Maintenance fees are required on utility patents at stipulated intervals. Phone 1-800-786-9199 for the latest fees.

In any broad overview of history, arbitrary compartmentalization of facts is self-defeating (and makes locating interrelated people, places, and things that much harder). Therefore, Headline History is designed as a "timeline"—a chronology that highlights both the march of time and interesting, sometimes surprising, juxtapositions.

See also related sections of the almanac, particularly Inventions and Discoveries, U.S. Government and History, and Countries of the World.

B.C.

Before Christ (B.C.) or Before the Common Era (B.C.E.)

4.5 billion B.C. Planet Earth formed.

3 billion B.C. First signs of primeval life (bacteria and blue-green algae) appear in oceans.

600 million B.C. Earliest date to which fossils can be traced.

4.4 million B.C. Earliest known hominid fossils (*Ardipithecus ramidus*) found in Aramis, Ethiopia, 1994.

4.2 million B.C. *Australopithecus anamensis* found in Lake Turkana, Kenya, 1995.

3.2 million B.C. *Australopithecus afarensis* (nicknamed "Lucy") found in Ethiopia, 1974.

2.5 million B.C. *Homo habilis* ("Skillful Man"). First brain expansion; is believed to have used stone tools.

1.8 million B.C. *Homo erectus* ("Upright Man"). Brain size twice that of *Australopithecine* species.

1.7 million B.C. *Homo erectus* leaves Africa.

100,000 B.C. First modern *Homo sapiens* in South Africa.

70,000 B.C. Neanderthal man (use of fire and advanced tools).

35,000 B.C. Neanderthal man replaced by later groups of *Homo sapiens* (i.e., Cro-Magnon man, etc.).

18,000 B.C. Cro-Magnons replaced by later cultures.

15,000 B.C. Migrations across Bering Straits into the Americas.

10,000 B.C. Semi-permanent agricultural settlements in Old World.

10,000–4,000 B.C. Development of settlements into cities and development of skills such as the wheel, pottery, and improved methods of cultivation in Mesopotamia and elsewhere.

5500–3000 B.C. Predynastic Egyptian cultures develop (5500–3100 B.C.); begin using agriculture (c. 5000 B.C.). Earliest known civilization arises in Sumer (4500–4000 B.C.). Earliest recorded date in Egyptian calendar (4241 B.C.). First year of Jewish calendar (3760 B.C.). First phonetic writing appears (c. 3500 B.C.). Sumerians develop a city-state civilization (c. 3000 B.C.). Copper used by Egyptians and Sumerians. Western Europe is neolithic, without metals or written records.

3000–2000 B.C. Pharaonic rule begins in Egypt. King Khufu (Cheops), 4th dynasty (2700–2675 B.C.), completes construction of the Great Pyramid at Giza (c. 2680 B.C.). The Great Sphinx of Giza (c. 2540 B.C.) is built by King Khafre. Earliest Egyptian mummies. Papyrus. Phoenician settlements on coast of what is now Syria and Lebanon. Semitic tribes settle in Assyria. Sargon, first Akkadian king, builds Mesopotamian empire. The Gilgamesh epic (c. 3000 B.C.). Abraham leaves Ur (c. 2000 B.C.). Systematic astronomy in Egypt, Babylon, India, China.

3000–1500 B.C. The most ancient civilization on the Indian subcontinent, the sophisticated and extensive Indus Valley civilization, flourishes in what is today Pakistan. In Britain, Stonehenge erected according to some unknown astronomical rationale. Its three main phases of construction are thought to span c. 3000–1500 B.C.

2000–1500 B.C. Hyksos invaders drive Egyptians from Lower Egypt (17th century B.C.). Amosis I frees Egypt from Hyksos (c. 1600 B.C.). Assyrians rise to power—cities of Ashur and Nineveh. Twenty-four-character alphabet in Egypt. Israelites enslaved in Egypt. Cuneiform inscriptions used by Hittites. Peak of Minoan culture on Isle of Crete—earliest form of written Greek. Hammurabi, king of Babylon, develops oldest existing code of laws (18th century B.C.).

**Ra, Egyptian
Sun God
(3000–2000 B.C.)**

**The Great Pyramid
at Giza
(c. 2680 B.C.)**

**Stonehenge
(c. 3000–1500 B.C.)**

Pythagoras
(c. 582–c. 507 B.C.)

Buddha
(c. 563–c. 483 B.C.)

1500–1000 B.C. Ikhnaton develops monotheistic religion in Egypt (c. 1375 B.C.). His successor, Tutankhamen, returns to earlier gods. Moses leads Israelites out of Egypt into Canaan—Ten Commandments. Greeks destroy Troy (c. 1193 B.C.). End of Greek civilization in Mycenae with invasion of Dorians. Chinese civilization develops under Shang Dynasty. Olmec civilization in Mexico—stone monuments; picture writing.

1000–900 B.C. Solomon succeeds King David, builds Jerusalem temple. After Solomon's death, kingdom divided into Israel and Judah. Hebrew elders begin to write Old Testament books of Bible. Phoenicians colonize Spain with settlement at Cadiz.

900–800 B.C. Phoenicians establish Carthage (c. 810 B.C.). The *Iliad* and the *Odyssey,* perhaps composed by Greek poet Homer.

800–700 B.C. Prophets Amos, Hosea, Isaiah. First recorded Olympic games (776 B.C.). Legendary founding of Rome by Romulus (753 B.C.). Assyrian king Sargon II conquers Hittites, Chaldeans, Samaria (end of Kingdom of Israel). Earliest written music. Chariots introduced into Italy by Etruscans.

700–600 B.C. End of Assyrian Empire (616 B.C.)—Nineveh destroyed by Chaldeans (Neo-Babylonians) and Medes (612 B.C.). Founding of Byzantium by Greeks (c. 660 B.C.). Building of the Acropolis in Athens. Solon, Greek lawgiver (640–560 B.C.). Sappho of Lesbos, Greek poet (fl. 610–c. 580 B.C.). Lao-tse, Chinese philosopher and founder of Taoism (born c. 604 B.C.).

600–500 B.C. Babylonian King Nebuchadnezzar builds empire, destroys Jerusalem (586 B.C.). Babylonian Captivity of the Jews (starting 587 B.C.). Hanging Gardens of Babylon. Cyrus the Great of Persia creates great empire, conquers Babylon (539 B.C.), frees the Jews. Athenian democracy develops. Aeschylus, Greek dramatist (525–465 B.C.). Pythagoras, Greek philosopher and mathematician (c. 582–c. 507 B.C.). Confucius (551–479 B.C.) develops ethical and social philosophy in China. The *Analects* or Lun-yü ("collected sayings") are compiled by the second generation of Confucian disciples. Buddha (c. 563–c. 483 B.C.) founds Buddhism in India.

SOME ANCIENT CIVILIZATIONS

Name	Approximate dates	Location	Major cities
Akkadian	2350–2230 B.C.	Mesopotamia, parts of Syria, Asia Minor, Iran	Akkad, Ur, Erich
Assyrian	1800–889 B.C.	Mesopotamia, Syria	Assur, Nineveh, Calah
Babylonian	1728–1686 B.C. (old) 625–539 B.C. (new)	Mesopotamia, Syria, Palestine	Babylon
Cimmerian	750–500 B.C.	Caucasus, northern Asia Minor	—
Egyptian	2850–715 B.C.	Nile valley	Thebes, Memphis, Tanis
Etruscan	900–396 B.C.	Northern Italy	—
Greek	900–200 B.C.	Greece	Athens, Sparta, Thebes, Mycenae, Corinth
Hittite	1640–1200 B.C.	Asia Minor, Syria	Hattusas, Nesa
Indus Valley	3000–1500 B.C.	Pakistan, Northwestern India	—
Lydian	700–547 B.C.	Western Asia Minor	Sardis, Miletus
Mede	835–550 B.C.	Iran	Media
Minoan	3000–1100 B.C.	Crete	Knossos
Persian	559–330 B.C.	Iran, Asia Minor, Syria	Persepolis, Pasargadae
Phoenician	1100–332 B.C.	Palestine (colonies: Gibraltar, Carthage, Sardinia)	Tyre, Sidon, Byblos
Phrygian	1000–547 B.C.	Central Asia Minor	Gordion
Roman	500 B.C.–A.D. 300	Italy, Mediterranean region, Asia Minor, western Europe	Rome, Byzantium
Scythian	800–300 B.C.	Caucasus	—
Sumerian	3200–2360 B.C.	Mesopotamia	Ur, Nippur

500–400 B.C. Greeks defeat Persians: battles of Marathon (490 B.C.), Thermopylae (480 B.C.), Salamis (480 B.C.). Peloponnesian Wars between Athens and Sparta (431–404 B.C.)—Sparta victorious. Pericles comes to power in Athens (462 B.C.). Flowering of Greek culture during the Age of Pericles (450–400 B.C.). The Parthenon is built in Athens as a temple of the goddess Athena (447–432 B.C.). Ictinus and Callicrates are the architects and Phidias is responsible for the sculpture. Sophocles, Greek dramatist (496–c.406 B.C.). Hippocrates, Greek "Father of Medicine" (born 460 B.C.). Xerxes I, king of Persia (rules 485–465 B.C.).

400–300 B.C. Pentateuch—first five books of the Old Testament evolve in final form. Philip of Macedon, who believed himself to be a descendant of the Greek people, assassinated (336 B.C.) after subduing the Greek city-states; succeeded by son, Alexander the Great (356–323 B.C.), who destroys Thebes (335 B.C.), conquers Tyre and Jerusalem (332 B.C.), occupies Babylon (330 B.C.), invades India, and dies in Babylon. His empire is divided among his generals; one of them, Seleucis I, establishes Middle East empire with capitals at Antioch (Syria) and Seleucia (in Iraq). Trial and execution of Greek philosopher Socrates (399 B.C.). Dialogues recorded by his student, Plato (c. 427–348 or 347 B.C.). Euclid's work on geometry (323 B.C.). Aristotle, Greek philosopher (384–322 B.C.). Demosthenes, Greek orator (384–322 B.C.). Praxiteles, Greek sculptor (400–330 B.C.).

300–251 B.C. First Punic War (264–241 B.C.): Rome defeats the Carthaginians and begins its domination of the Mediterranean. Temple of the Sun at Teotihuacan, Mexico (c. 300 B.C.). Invention of Mayan calendar in Yucatán—more exact than older calendars. First Roman gladiatorial games (264 B.C.). Archimedes, Greek mathematician (287–212 B.C.).

250–201 B.C. Second Punic War (219–201 B.C.): Hannibal, Carthaginian general (246–142 B.C.), crosses the Alps (218 B.C.), reaches gates of Rome (211 B.C.), retreats, and is defeated by Scipio Africanus at Zama (202 B.C.). Great Wall of China built (c. 215 B.C.).

200–151 B.C. Romans defeat Seleucid King Antiochus III at Thermopylae (191 B.C.)—beginning of Roman world domination. Maccabean revolt against Seleucids (167 B.C.).

150–101 B.C. Third Punic War (149–146 B.C.): Rome destroys Carthage, killing 450,000 and enslaving the remaining 50,000 inhabitants. Roman armies conquer Macedonia, Greece, Anatolia, Balearic Islands, and southern France. Venus de Milo (c. 140 B.C.). Cicero, Roman orator (106–43 B.C.).

100–51 B.C. Julius Caesar (100–44 B.C.) invades Britain (55 B.C.) and conquers Gaul (France) (c. 50 B.C.). Spartacus leads slave revolt against Rome (71 B.C.). Romans conquer Seleucid empire. Roman general Pompey conquers Jerusalem (63 B.C.). Cleopatra on Egyptian throne (51–31 B.C.). Chinese develop use of paper (c. 100 B.C.). Virgil, Roman poet (70–19 B.C.). Horace, Roman poet (65–8 B.C.).

50–1 B.C. Caesar crosses Rubicon to fight Pompey (50 B.C.). Herod made Roman governor of Judea (37 B.C.). Caesar murdered (44 B.C.). Caesar's nephew, Octavian, defeats Mark Antony and Cleopatra at Battle of Actium (31 B.C.), and establishes Roman empire as Emperor Augustus—rules 27 B.C.–A.D. 14. Pantheon built for the first time under Agrippa, 27 B.C. Ovid, Roman poet (43 B.C.–A.D. 18).

**Confucius
(551–479 B.C.)**

**Parthenon
(447–432 B.C.)**

**Plato
(c. 427–348 or 347 B.C.)**

A.D.

Christian Era (A.D.) or the Common Era (C.E.)

1–49 Birth of Jesus Christ (variously given from 4 B.C. to A.D. 7). After Augustus, Tiberius becomes emperor (dies, A.D. 37), succeeded by Caligula (assassinated, A.D. 41), who is followed by Claudius. Crucifixion of Jesus (probably A.D. 30). Han dynasty in China founded by Emperor Kuang Wu Ti. Buddhism introduced to China.

50–99 Claudius poisoned (A.D. 54), succeeded by Nero (commits suicide, A.D. 68). Missionary journeys of Paul the Apostle (A.D. 34–60). Jews revolt against Rome; Jerusalem destroyed (A.D. 70). Roman persecutions of Christians begin (A.D. 64). Colosseum built in Rome (A.D. 71–80). Trajan (rules A.D. 98–116); Roman empire extends to Mesopotamia, Arabia, Balkans. First Gospels of St. Mark, St. John, St. Matthew.

**Roman Aqueduct
Montpellier, France**

Mayan Pyramid at Chichén Itzá

Celtic Cross

Japanese Pagoda

Viking Ship (c. 900)

100–149 Hadrian rules Rome (A.D. 117–138); codifies Roman law, rebuilds Pantheon, establishes postal system, builds wall between England and Scotland. Jews revolt under Bar Kokhba (A.D. 122–135); final Diaspora (dispersion) of Jews begins.

150–199 Marcus Aurelius rules Rome (A.D. 161–180). Oldest Mayan temples in Central America (c. A.D. 200).

200–249 Goths invade Asia Minor (c. A.D. 220). Roman persecutions of Christians increase. Persian (Sassanid) empire re-established. End of Chinese Han dynasty.

250–299 Increasing invasions of the Roman empire by Franks and Goths. Buddhism spreads in China. Classic period of Mayan civilization (A.D. 250–900); develop hieroglyphic writing, advances in art, architecture, science.

300–349 Constantine the Great (rules A.D. 312–337) reunites eastern and western Roman empires, with new capital (Constantinople) on site of Byzantium (A.D. 330); issues Edict of Milan legalizing Christianity (A.D. 313); becomes a Christian on his deathbed (A.D. 337). Council of Nicaea (A.D. 325) defines orthodox Christian doctrine. First Gupta dynasty in India (c. A.D. 320).

350–399 Huns (Mongols) invade Europe (c. A.D. 360). Theodosius the Great (rules A.D. 392–395)—last emperor of a united Roman empire. Roman empire permanently divided in A.D. 395: western empire ruled from Rome; eastern empire ruled from Constantinople.

400–449 Western Roman empire disintegrates under weak emperors. Alaric, king of the Visigoths, sacks Rome (A.D. 410). Attila, Hun chieftain, attacks Roman provinces (A.D. 433). St. Patrick returns to Ireland (A.D. 432) and brings Christianity to the island. St. Augustine's *City of God* (A.D. 411).

450–499 Vandals destroy Rome (A.D. 455). Western Roman empire ends as Odoacer, German chieftain, overthrows last Roman emperor, Romulus Augustulus, and becomes king of Italy (A.D. 476). Ostrogothic kingdom of Italy established by Theodoric the Great (A.D. 493). Clovis, ruler of the Franks, is converted to Christianity (A.D. 496). First schism between western and eastern churches (A.D. 484).

500–549 Eastern and western churches reconciled (519). Justinian I, the Great (483–565), becomes Byzantine emperor (527), issues his first code of civil laws (529), conquers North Africa, Italy, and part of Spain. Plague spreads through Europe (542 *et seq.*). Arthur, semi-legendary king of the Britons (killed, c. 537). Boëthius, Roman scholar (executed, 524).

550–599 Beginnings of European silk industry after Justinian's missionaries smuggle silkworms out of China (553). Mohammed, founder of Islam (570–632). Buddhism in Japan (c. 560). St. Augustine of Canterbury brings Christianity to Britain (597). After killing about half the population, plague in Europe subsides (594).

600–649 Mohammed flees from Mecca to Medina (the *Hegira*); first year of the Muslim calendar (622). Muslim empire grows (634). Arabs conquer Jerusalem (637), destroy Alexandrian library (641), conquer Persians (641). Fatima, Mohammed's daughter (606–632).

650–699 Arabs attack North Africa (670), destroy Carthage (697). Venerable Bede, English monk (672–735).

700–749 Arab empire extends from Lisbon to China (by 716). Charles Martel, Frankish leader, defeats Arabs at Tours/Poitiers, halting Arab advance in Europe (732). Charlemagne (742–814). Introduction of pagodas in Japan from China.

750–799 Charlemagne becomes king of the Franks (771). Caliph Harun al-Rashid rules Arab empire (786–809): the "golden age" of Arab culture. Vikings begin attacks on Britain (790), land in Ireland (795). City of Machu Picchu flourishes in Peru.

800–849 Charlemagne crowned first Holy Roman Emperor in Rome (800). Charlemagne dies (814), succeeded by his son, Louis the Pious, who divides France among his sons (817). Arabs conquer Crete, Sicily, and Sardinia (826–827).

850–899 Norsemen attack as far south as the Mediterranean but are thwarted (859), discover Iceland (861). Alfred the Great becomes king of Britain (871), defeats Danish invaders (878). Russian nation founded by Vikings under Prince Rurik, establishing capital at Novgorod (855–879).

900–949 Beginning of Mayan Post-Classical period (900–1519). Vikings discover Greenland (c. 900). Arab Spain under Abd ar-Rahman III becomes center of learning (912–961). Otto I becomes King of Germany (936).

950–999 Mieczyslaw I becomes first ruler of Poland (960). Eric the Red establishes first Viking colony in Greenland (982). Hugh Capet elected King of France in 987; Capetian dynasty to rule until 1328. Musical notation systematized (c.

990). Vikings and Danes attack Britain (988–999). Otto I crowned Holy Roman Emperor by Pope John XII (962).

1000–1099 (A.D.)

c. 1000–1300 Classic Pueblo period of Anasazi culture; cliff dwellings.

c.1000 Hungary and Scandinavia converted to Christianity. Viking raider Leif Eriksson discovers North America, calls it Vinland. *Beowulf*, Old English epic.

c. 1008 Murasaki Shikibu finishes *The Tale of Genji*, the world's first novel.

1009 Muslims destroy Holy Sepulchre in Jerusalem.

1013 Danes control England. Canute takes throne (1016), conquers Norway (1028), dies (1035); kingdom divided among his sons: Harold Harefoot (England), Sweyn (Norway), Hardecanute (Denmark).

1040 Macbeth murders Duncan, king of Scotland.

1053 Robert Guiscard, Norman invader, establishes kingdom in Italy, conquers Sicily (1072).

1054 Final separation between Eastern (Orthodox) and Western (Roman) churches.

1055 Seljuk Turks, Asian nomads, move west, capture Baghdad, Armenia (1064), Syria, and Palestine (1075).

1066 William of Normandy invades England, defeats last Saxon king, Harold II, at Battle of Hastings, crowned William I of England ("the Conqueror").

1068 Construction on the cathedral in Pisa, Italy, begins.

1073 Emergence of strong papacy when Gregory VII is elected. Conflict with English and French kings and German emperors will continue throughout medieval period.

1095 At Council of Clermont, Pope Urban II calls for a holy war to wrest control of Jerusalem from Muslims, which launches the First Crusade (1096), one of at least 8 European military campaigns between 1095 and 1291 to regain the Holy Land.

**Mesa Verde
Cliff Dwellings
(c. 1000–1300)**

1100–1199 (A.D.)

1100–1300 Construction of Cathedral at Chartres, France.

1144 Second Crusade begins.

c. 1150 Angkor Wat is completed.

1150–1167 Universities of Paris and Oxford founded in France and England.

1162 Thomas á Becket named Archbishop of Canterbury, murdered by Henry II's men (1170). Troubadours (wandering minstrels) glorify romantic concepts of feudalism.

1169 Ibn-Rushd begins translating Aristotle's works.

1189 Richard I ("the Lionhearted") succeeds Henry II in England, killed in France (1199), succeeded by King John. Third Crusade.

**Cathedral and Tower
at Pisa**

1200–1299 (A.D.)

1200–1204 Fourth Crusade.

1211 Genghis Khan invades China, captures Peking (1214), conquers Persia (1218), invades Russia (1223), dies (1227).

1212 Children's Crusade.

1215 King John forced by barons to sign Magna Carta at Runneymede, limiting royal power.

1217 Fifth Crusade.

1228 Sixth Crusade.

Chartres Cathedral

**King John
(1167–1216)**

THE CRUSADES (1096–1291)

In 1095 at Council of Clermont, Pope Urban II calls for war to rescue Holy Land from Muslim infidels. The *First Crusade* (1096) is assembled in response to Emperor Alexius I. The Christians capture Antioch (1098) and Jerusalem (1099). They establish the Crusader States, ruled by Europeans. It is the only successful crusade. The *Second Crusade* begins after the Seljuk Turks recapture Edessa, one of the Crusader States, in 1144. It is led by King Louis VIII of France and Holy Roman Emperor Conrad III. Crusaders perish in Asia Minor (1147).

Saladin controls Egypt (1171), unites Islam in Holy War *(Jihad)* against Christians, recaptures Jerusalem (1187). *Third Crusade* (1189) under kings of France, England, and Germany fails to reduce Saladin's power. *Fourth Crusade* (1200–1204)—French knights sack Greek Christian Constantinople, establish Latin empire in Byzantium. Greeks reestablish Orthodox faith (1262).

Children's Crusade (1212)—only one of 30,000 French children and about 200 of 20,000 German children survive to return home. Other Crusades—*Fifth*, against Egypt (1217), *Sixth* (1228), *Seventh* (1248), *Eighth* (1270). Mamelukes conquer Acre; end of the Crusades (1291).

**Thomas Aquinas
(1225–1274)**

**The Duomo in
Florence**

**Joan of Arc
(1412–1431)**

**Michelangelo's David
(1504)**

**Balboa
(1475–1517)**

1231 The Inquisition begins as Pope Gregory IX assigns Dominicans responsibility for combating heresy. Torture used (1252). Ferdinand and Isabella establish Spanish Inquisition (1478). Tourquemada, Grand Inquisitor, forces conversion or expulsion of Spanish Jews (1492). Forced conversion of Moors (1499). Inquisition in Portugal (1531). First Protestants burned at the stake in Spain (1543). Spanish Inquisition abolished (1834).

1241 Mongols defeat Germans in Silesia, invade Poland and Hungary, withdraw from Europe after Ughetai, Mongol leader, dies.

1248 Seventh Crusade.

1251 Kublai Khan governs China, becomes ruler of Mongols (1259), establishes Yuan dynasty in China (1280), invades Burma (1287), dies (1294).

1260 Chartres cathedral consecrated.

1270 Eighth Crusade.

1271 Marco Polo of Venice travels to China, in court of Kublai Khan (1275–1292), returns to Genoa (1295) and writes *Travels.*

1273 Thomas Aquinas stops work on *Summa Theologica,* the basis of all Catholic theological teaching; never completes it.

1295 English King Edward I summons the Model Parliament.

1300–1399 (A.D.)

1312–1337 Mali Empire reaches its height in Africa under King Mansa Musa.

c.1325 The beginning of the Renaissance in Italy: writers Dante, Petrarch, Boccaccio; painter Giotto. Development of *Noh* drama in Japan. Aztecs establish Tenochtitlán on site of modern Mexico City. Peak of Muslim culture in Spain. Small cannon in use.

1337–1453 Hundred Years' War—English and French kings fight for control of France.

1347–1351 At least 25 million people die in Europe's "Black Death" (bubonic plague).

1368 Ming Dynasty begins in China.

1376–1382 John Wycliffe, pre-Reformation religious reformer, and followers translate Latin Bible into English.

1378 The Great Schism (to 1417)—rival popes in Rome and Avignon, France, fight for control of Roman Catholic Church.

c.1387 Chaucer's *Canterbury Tales.*

1399 Tamerlane begins last great conquest.

1400–1499 (A.D.)

1407 Casa di San Giorgio, one of the first public banks, founded in Genoa.

1415 Henry V defeats French at Agincourt. Jan Hus, Bohemian preacher and follower of Wycliffe, burned at stake in Constance as heretic.

1418–1460 Portugal's Prince Henry the Navigator sponsors exploration of Africa's coast.

1420 Brunelleschi begins work on the Duomo in Florence.

1428 Joan of Arc leads French against English, captured by Burgundians (1430) and turned over to the English, burned at the stake as a witch after ecclesiastical trial (1431).

1438 Incas rule in Peru.

1450 Florence becomes center of Renaissance arts and learning under the Medicis.

1453 Turks conquer Constantinople, end of the Byzantine empire, beginning of the Ottoman empire.

1455 The Wars of the Roses, civil wars between rival noble factions, begin in England (to 1485). Having invented printing with movable type at Mainz, Germany, Johann Gutenberg completes first Bible.

1462 Ivan the Great rules Russia until 1505 as first czar; ends payment of tribute to Mongols.

1492 Moors conquered in Spain by troops of Ferdinand and Isabella. Columbus becomes first European to encounter Caribbean islands, returns to Spain (1493). Second voyage to Dominica, Jamaica, Puerto Rico (1493–1496). Third voyage to Orinoco (1498). Fourth voyage to Honduras and Panama (1502–1504).

1497 Vasco da Gama sails around Africa and discovers sea route to India (1498). Establishes Portuguese colony in India (1502). John Cabot, employed by England, reaches and explores Canadian coast. Michelangelo's *Bacchus* sculpture.

1500–1599 (A.D.)

1501 First black slaves in America brought to Spanish colony of Santo Domingo.

c.1503 Leonardo da Vinci paints the *Mona Lisa.* Michelangelo sculpts the *David* (1504).

1506 St. Peter's Church started in Rome; designed and decorated by such artists and architects as Bramante, Michelangelo, da Vinci, Raphael, and Bernini before its completion in 1626.

1509 Henry VIII ascends English throne. Michelangelo paints the ceiling of the Sistine Chapel.

1513 Balboa becomes the first European to encounter the Pacific Ocean. Machiavelli's *The Prince.*

1517 Turks conquer Egypt, control Arabia. Martin Luther posts his 95 theses denouncing church abuses on church door in Wittenberg—start of the Reformation in Germany.

1519 Ulrich Zwingli begins Reformation in Switzerland. Hernando Cortes conquers Mexico for Spain. Charles I of Spain is chosen Holy Roman Emperor Charles V. Portuguese explorer Ferdinand Magellan sets out to circumnavigate the globe.

Martin Luther
(1483–1546)

1520 Luther excommunicated by Pope Leo X. Suleiman I ("the Magnificent") becomes Sultan of Turkey, invades Hungary (1521), Rhodes (1522), attacks Austria (1529), annexes Hungary (1541), Tripoli (1551), makes peace with Persia (1553), destroys Spanish fleet (1560), dies (1566). Magellan reaches the Pacific, is killed by Philippine natives (1521). One of his ships under Juan Sebastián del Cano continues around the world, reaches Spain (1522).

1524 Verrazano, sailing under the French flag, explores the New England coast and New York Bay.

1527 Troops of the Holy Roman Empire attack Rome, imprison Pope Clement VII—the end of the Italian Renaissance. Castiglione writes *The Courtier.* The Medici family expelled from Florence.

Henry VIII
(1491–1547)

1532 Pizarro marches from Panama to Peru, kills the Inca chieftain, Atahualpa, of Peru (1533). Machiavelli's *The Prince* published posthumously.

1535 Reformation begins as Henry VIII makes himself head of English Church after being excommunicated by Pope. Sir Thomas More executed as traitor for refusal to acknowledge king's religious authority. Jacques Cartier sails up the St. Lawrence River, basis of French claims to Canada.

1536 Henry VIII executes second wife, Anne Boleyn. John Calvin establishes Reformed and Presbyterian form of Protestantism in Switzerland, writes *Institutes of the Christian Religion.* Danish and Norwegian Reformations. Michelangelo's *Last Judgment.*

1541 John Knox leads Reformation in Scotland, establishes Presbyterian church there (1560).

Queen Elizabeth I
(1533–1603)

1543 Publication of *On the Revolution of Heavenly Bodies* by Polish scholar Nicolaus Copernicus—giving his theory that the earth revolves around the sun.

1545 Council of Trent to meet intermittently until 1563 to define Catholic dogma and doctrine, reiterate papal authority.

1547 Ivan IV ("the Terrible") crowned as czar of Russia, begins conquest of Astrakhan and Kazan (1552), battles nobles (boyars) for power (1564), kills his son (1580), dies, and is succeeded by his weak and feeble-minded son, Fyodor I.

1553 Roman Catholicism restored in England by Queen Mary I.

1556 Akbar the Great becomes Mogul emperor of India, conquers Afghanistan (1581), continues wars of conquest (until 1605).

1558 Queen Elizabeth I ascends the throne (rules to 1603). Restores Protestantism, establishes state Church of England (Anglicanism). Renaissance will reach height in England—Shakespeare, Marlowe, Spenser.

William Shakespeare
(1564–1616)

1561 Persecution of Huguenots in France stopped by Edict of Orleans. French religious wars begin again with massacre of Huguenots at Vassy. St. Bartholomew's Day Massacre—thousands of Huguenots murdered (1572). Amnesty granted (1573). Persecution continues periodically until Edict of Nantes (1598) gives Huguenots religious freedom (until 1685).

1568 Protestant Netherlands revolts against Catholic Spain; independence will be acknowledged by Spain in 1648. High point of Dutch Renaissance—painters Rubens, Van Dyck, Hals, and Rembrandt.

1570 Japan permits visits of foreign ships. Queen Elizabeth I excommunicated by Pope. Turks attack Cyprus and war on Venice. Turkish fleet defeated at Battle of Lepanto by Spanish and Italian fleets (1571). Peace of Constantinople (1572) ends Turkish attacks on Europe.

Rembrandt van Rijn
(1606–1669)

1580 Francis Drake returns to England after circumnavigating the globe; knighted by Queen Elizabeth I (1581). Montaigne's *Essays* published.

1582 Pope Gregory XIII implements the Gregorian calendar.

Catherine de Medici
(1519–1589)

Galileo
(1564–1642)

Pocahontas
(c. 1595–1617)

Taj Mahal

John Milton
(1608–1674)

1583 William of Orange rules the Netherlands; assassinated on orders of Philip II of Spain (1584).

1587 Mary, Queen of Scots, executed for treason by order of Queen Elizabeth I. Monteverdi's *First Book of Madrigals*.

1588 Defeat of the Spanish Armada by English. Henry, King of Navarre and Protestant leader, recognized as Henry IV, first Bourbon king of France. Converts to Roman Catholicism in 1593 in attempt to end religious wars.

1590 Henry IV enters Paris, wars on Spain (1595), marries Marie de Medici (1600), assassinated (1610). Spenser's *The Faerie Queen*. El Greco's *St. Jerome*. Galileo's experiments with falling objects.

1598 Boris Godunov becomes Russian czar. Tycho Brahe describes his astronomical experiments.

1600–1699 (A.D.)

1600 Giordano Bruno burned as a heretic. English East India Company established.

1603 Ieyasu rules Japan, moves capital to Edo (Tokyo). Shakespeare's *Hamlet*.

1605 Cervantes's *Don Quixote de la Mancha,* the first modern novel.

1607 Jamestown, Virginia, established—first permanent English colony on American mainland. Pocahontas, daughter of Chief Powhatan, saves life of John Smith.

1609 Samuel de Champlain establishes French colony of Quebec. The *Relation,* the first newspaper, debuts in Germany.

1610 Galileo sees the moons of Jupiter through his telescope.

1611 Gustavus Adolphus elected King of Sweden. King James Version of the Bible published in England. Rubens paints his *Descent from the Cross*.

1614 John Napier discovers logarithms.

1618 Start of the Thirty Years' War—Protestants revolt against Catholic oppression; Denmark, Sweden, and France will invade Germany in later phases of war. Kepler proposes last of three laws of planetary motion.

1619 A Dutch ship brings the first African slaves to British North America.

1620 Pilgrims, after three-month voyage in *Mayflower,* land at Plymouth Rock. Francis Bacon's *Novum Organum*.

1623 New Netherland founded by Dutch West India Company.

1630 Massachusetts Bay Colony.

1632 Maryland founded by Lord Baltimore.

1633 Inquisition forces Galileo to recant his belief in Copernican theory.

1642 English Civil War. Cavaliers, supporters of Charles I, against Roundheads, parliamentary forces. Oliver Cromwell defeats Royalists (1646). Parliament demands reforms. Charles I offers concessions, brought to trial (1648), beheaded (1649). Cromwell becomes Lord Protector (1653). Rembrandt paints his *Night Watch*.

1643 Taj Mahal completed.

1644 End of Ming Dynasty in China—Manchus come to power. Descartes's *Principles of Philosophy*.

1648 End of the Thirty Years' War. German population about half of what it was in 1618 because of war and pestilence.

1658 Cromwell dies; son Richard resigns and Puritan government collapses.

1660 English Parliament calls for the restoration of the monarchy; invites Charles II to return from France.

1661 Charles II is crowned King of England. Louis XIV begins personal rule as absolute monarch; starts to build Versailles.

1664 British take New Amsterdam from the Dutch. English limit "Nonconformity" with reestablished Anglican Church. Isaac Newton's experiments with gravity.

1665 Great Plague in London kills 75,000.

1666 Great Fire of London. Molière's *Misanthrope*.

1667 Milton's *Paradise Lost,* widely considered the greatest epic poem in English.

1682 Pennsylvania founded by William Penn.

1683 War of European powers against the Turks (to 1699). Vienna withstands three-month Turkish siege; high point of Turkish advance in Europe.

1684 Gottfried Wilhelm Leibniz's calculus published.

1685 James II succeeds Charles II in England, calls for freedom of conscience (1687). Protestants fear restoration of Catholicism and demand "Glorious Revolution." William of Orange invited to England and James II escapes to France (1688). William III and his wife, Mary, crowned. In France, Edict of Nantes of 1598, granting freedom of worship to Huguenots, is revoked by Louis XIV; thousands of Protestants flee.

1689 Peter the Great becomes Czar of Russia—attempts to westernize nation and build Russia as a military power. Defeats Charles XII of Sweden at Poltava (1709). Beginning of the French and Indian Wars (to 1763), campaigns in America linked to a series of wars between France and England for domination of Europe.

1690 William III of England defeats former king James II and Irish rebels at Battle of the Boyne in Ireland. John Locke's *Human Understanding*.

1700–1799 (A.D.)

1701 War of the Spanish Succession begins—the last of Louis XIV's wars for domination of the continent. The Peace of Utrecht (1714) will end the conflict and mark the rise of the British Empire. Called Queen Anne's War in America, it ends with the British taking New Foundland, Acadia, and Hudson's Bay Territory from France, and Gibraltar and Minorca from Spain.

1704 Deerfield (Mass.) Massacre of English colonists by French and Indians. Bach's first cantata. Jonathan Swift's *Tale of a Tub*. *Boston News Letter*—first newspaper in America.

1707 United Kingdom of Great Britain formed—England, Wales, and Scotland joined by parliamentary Act of Union.

1729 Bach's *St. Matthew Passion*. Isaac Newton's *Principia* translated from Latin into English.

1732 Benjamin Franklin begins publishing *Poor Richard's Almanack*. James Oglethorpe and others found Georgia.

1735 John Peter Zenger, New York editor, acquitted of libel in New York, establishing press freedom.

1740 Capt. Vitus Bering, Dane employed by Russia, discovers Alaska. Frederick II "the Great" crowned king of Prussia.

1746 British defeat Scots under Stuart Pretender Prince Charles at Culloden Moor. Last battle fought on British soil.

1751 Publication of the *Encyclopédie* begins in France, the "bible" of the Enlightenment.

1755 Samuel Johnson's *Dictionary* first published. Great earthquake in Lisbon, Portugal—over 60,000 die. U.S. postal service established.

1756 Seven Years' War (French and Indian Wars in America) (to 1763), in which Britain and Prussia defeat France, Spain, Austria, and Russia. France loses North American colonies; Spain cedes Florida to Britain in exchange for Cuba. In India, over 100 British prisoners die in "Black Hole of Calcutta."

1757 Beginning of British Empire in India as Robert Clive, British commander, defeats Nawab of Bengal at Plassey.

1759 British capture Quebec from French. Voltaire's *Candide*. Haydn's *Symphony No. 1*.

1762 Catherine II ("the Great") becomes czarina of Russia. Jean Jacques Rousseau's *Social Contract*. Mozart tours Europe as six-year-old prodigy.

1765 James Watt invents the steam engine. Britain imposes the Stamp Act on the American colonists.

**Sir Isaac Newton
(1642–1727)**

**Frederick the Great
(1712–1786)**

**Samuel Johnson
(1709–1784)**

THE REVOLUTIONARY WAR

Conflicts increase between colonists and Britain on western frontier because of royal edict limiting western expansion (1763) and regulation of colonial trade and increased taxation of colonies (Writs of Assistance allow search for illegal shipments, 1761; Sugar Act, 1764; Currency Act, 1764; Stamp Act, 1765; Quartering Act, 1765; Duty Act, 1767). Boston Massacre (1770). Lord North attempts conciliation (1770). Boston Tea Party (1773), followed by punitive measures passed by Parliament—the "Intolerable Acts."

First Continental Congress (1774) sends "Declaration of Rights and Grievances" to King George III, urges colonies to form Continental Association. Paul Revere's ride and Lexington and Concord battle between Massachusetts Minutemen and British (1775).

Second Continental Congress (1775), while sending "olive branch" to the king, begins to raise army, appoints Washington commander-in-chief, and seeks alliance with France. Some colonial legislatures urge their delegates to vote for independence. Declaration of Independence **(July 4, 1776)**.

Major Battles of the Revolutionary War: *Long Island:* Howe defeats Putnam's division of Washington's Army in Brooklyn Heights, but Americans escape across East River (1776). *Trenton and Princeton:* Washington defeats Hessians at Trenton, British at Princeton. Winters at Morristown (1776–1777). Howe winters in Philadelphia; Washington at Valley Forge (1777–1778). Burgoyne surrenders British army to General Gates at *Saratoga* (1777).

France recognizes American independence (1778). The War moves south: Savannah captured by British (1778); Charleston occupied (1780); Americans fight successful guerrilla actions under Marion, Pickens, and Sumter. In the West, George Rogers Clark attacks Forts Kaskaskia and Vincennes (1778–1779), defeating British in the region. Cornwallis surrenders at *Yorktown*, Virginia **(Oct. 19, 1781).** By 1782, Britain is eager for peace because of conflicts with European nations. *Peace of Paris* (1783): Britain recognizes American independence.

Benjamin Franklin
(1706–1790)

George Washington
(1732–1799)

Alexander Hamilton
(1755–1804)

Ludwig van Beethoven
(1770–1827)

1769 Sir William Arkwright patents a spinning machine—an early step in the Industrial Revolution.

1770 The Boston Massacre.

1772 Joseph Priestley and Daniel Rutherford independently discover nitrogen. Partition of Poland—in 1772, 1793, and 1795, Austria, Prussia, and Russia divide land and people of Poland, end its independence.

1773 The Boston Tea Party.

1774 First Continental Congress drafts "Declaration of Rights and Grievances."

1775 The American Revolution begins with battle of Lexington and Concord. Second Continental Congress. Priestley discovers hydrochloric and sulfuric acids.

1776 Declaration of Independence. Gen. George Washington crosses the Delaware Christmas night. Adam Smith's *Wealth of Nations.* Edward Gibbon's *Decline and Fall of the Roman Empire.* Thomas Paine's *Common Sense.* Fragonard's *Washerwoman.* Mozart's *Haffner Serenade.*

1778 Capt. James Cook discovers Hawaii. Franz Mesmer uses hypnotism.

1781 Immanuel Kant's *Critique of Pure Reason.* Herschel discovers Uranus.

1783 Revolutionary War ends with Treaty of Paris. William Blake's poems. Beethoven's first printed works.

1784 Crimea annexed by Russia. John Wesley's *Deed of Declaration,* the basic work of Methodism.

1785 Russians settle Aleutian Islands.

1787 The Constitution of the United States signed. Lavoisier's work on chemical nomenclature. Mozart's *Don Giovanni.*

1788 French *Parlement* presents grievances to Louis XVI who agrees to convening of Estates-General in 1789—not called since 1613. Goethe's *Egmont.* Laplace's *Laws of the Planetary System.*

1789 French Revolution begins with the storming of the Bastille. In U.S., Washington elected president with all 69 votes of the Electoral College, takes oath of office in New York City. Vice President: John Adams. Secretary of State: Thomas Jefferson. Secretary of Treasury: Alexander Hamilton.

1790 H.M.S. *Bounty* mutineers settle on Pitcairn Island. Aloisio Galvani experiments on electrical stimulation of the muscles. Philadelphia temporary capital of U.S. as Congress votes to establish new capital on Potomac. U.S. population about 3,929,000, including 698,000 slaves. Lavoisier formulates *Table of 31 chemical elements.*

1791 U.S. Bill of Rights ratified. Boswell's *Life of Johnson.*

1792 Mary Wollstonecraft's *Vindication of the Rights of Woman.*

1793 Louis XVI and Marie Antoinette executed. Reign of Terror begins in France. Eli Whitney invents the cotton gin, spurring the growth of the cotton industry and helping to institutionalize slavery in the U.S. South.

1794 Kosciusko's uprising in Poland quelled by the Russians. In U.S., Whiskey Rebellion in Pennsylvania as farmers object to liquor taxes. Reign of Terror ends with execution of Robespierre.

1796 Napoléon Bonaparte, French general, defeats Austrians. In the U.S., Washington's Farewell Address **(Sept. 17);** John Adams elected president; Thomas Jefferson, vice president. Edward Jenner introduces smallpox vaccination.

1798 Napoleon extends French conquests to Rome and Egypt. U.S. Navy Department established.

FRENCH REVOLUTION (1789–1799)

Revolution begins when Third Estate (Commons) delegates swear not to disband until France has a constitution. Paris mob storms Bastille, symbol of royal power **(July 14, 1789).** National Assembly votes for Constitution, Declaration of the Rights of Man, a limited monarchy, and other reforms (1789–1790). Legislative Assembly elected, Revolutionary Commune formed, and French Republic proclaimed (1792). War of the First Coalition—Austria, Prussia, Britain, Netherlands, and Spain fight to restore French nobility (1792–1797).

Start of series of wars between France and European powers that will last, almost without interruption, for 23 years. Louis XVI and Marie Antoinette executed. Committee of Public Safety begins Reign of Terror as political control measure. Interfactional rivalry leads to mass killings. Danton and Robespierre executed. Third French Constitution sets up Directory government (1795). Napoleon abolishes the Directory, establishes the Consulate, becomes the First Consul of France (1799).

1799 Rosetta Stone discovered in Egypt. Napoleon leads coup that overthrows Directory, establishes the Consulate, becomes First Consul—one of three who rule France together.

1800–1899 (A.D.)

1800 Napoleon conquers Italy, firmly establishes himself as First Consul in France. In the U.S., federal government moves to Washington, D.C. Robert Owen's social reforms in England. William Herschel discovers infrared rays. Alessandro Volta produces electricity.

1801 Austria makes temporary peace with France. United Kingdom of Great Britain and Ireland established with one monarch and one parliament; Catholics excluded from voting.

Napoléon Bonaparte (1769–1821)

1803 U.S. negotiates Louisiana Purchase from France: for $15 million, U.S. doubles its domain, increasing its territory by 827,000 sq. mi. (2,144,500 sq km), from Mississippi River to Rockies and from Gulf of Mexico to British North America.

1804 Haiti declares independence from France; first black nation to gain freedom from European colonial rule. Napoleon transforms the Consulate of France into an empire, proclaims himself emperor of France, systematizes French law under *Code Napoleon*. In the U.S., Alexander Hamilton is mortally wounded in duel with Aaron Burr. Lewis and Clark expedition begins exploration of what is now northwest U.S.

1805 Lord Nelson defeats the French-Spanish fleets in the Battle of Trafalgar. Napoleon victorious over Austrian and Russian forces at the Battle of Austerlitz.

Edgar Allan Poe (1809–1849)

1807 Robert Fulton makes first successful steamboat trip on *Clermont* between New York City and Albany.

1808 French armies occupy Rome and Spain, extending Napoleon's empire. Britain begins aiding Spanish guerrillas against Napoleon in Peninsular War. In the U.S., Congress bars importation of slaves. Beethoven's *Fifth* and *Sixth Symphonies* performed.

1812 Napoleon's Grand Army invades Russia in June. Forced to retreat in winter, most of Napoleon's 600,000 men are lost. In the U.S., war with Britain declared over freedom of the seas for U.S. vessels (War of 1812). USS *Constitution* sinks British frigate.

Richard Wagner (1813–1883)

1814 French defeated by allies (Britain, Austria, Russia, Prussia, Sweden, and Portugal) in War of Liberation. Napoleon exiled to Elba, off Italian coast. Bourbon king Louis XVIII takes French throne. George Stephenson builds first practical steam locomotive.

1815 Napoleon returns: "Hundred Days" begin. Napoleon defeated by Wellington at Waterloo, banished again to St. Helena in South Atlantic. Congress of Vienna: victorious allies change the map of Europe. War of 1812 ends with Treaty of Ghent.

1819 Simón Bolívar liberates New Granada (now Colombia, Venezuela, and Ecuador) as Spain loses hold on South American countries; named president of Colombia.

1820 Missouri Compromise—Missouri admitted as slave state but slavery barred in rest of Louisiana Purchase north of 36°30′ N.

Harriet Beecher Stowe (1811–1896)

1821 Guatemala, Panama, and Santo Domingo proclaim independence from Spain.

1822 Greeks proclaim a republic and independence from Turkey. Turks invade Greece. Russia declares war on Turkey (1828). Greece also aided by France and Britain. War ends and Turks recognize Greek independence (1829). Brazil becomes independent of Portugal. Schubert's *Eighth Symphony* ("The Unfinished").

1823 U.S. Monroe Doctrine warns European nations not to interfere in Western Hemisphere.

1824 Mexico becomes a republic, three years after declaring independence from Spain. Bolívar liberates Peru, becomes its president. Beethoven's *Ninth Symphony.*

1825 First passenger-carrying railroad in England.

1826 Joseph-Nicéphore Niepce takes the world's first photograph.

Walt Whitman (1819–1892)

WAR OF 1812

British interference with American trade, impressment of American seamen, and "War Hawks" drive for western expansion lead to war. American attacks on Canada foiled; U.S. Commodore Perry wins battle of Lake Erie (1813). British capture and burn Washington (1814) but fail to take Fort McHenry at Baltimore. Andrew Jackson repulses assault on New Orleans after Treaty of Ghent ends war (1815). War settles little but strengthens U.S. as independent nation.

**Dred Scott
(1795?–1858)**

**Charles Darwin
(1809–1882)**

**Frederick Douglass
(1817–1895)**

**Harriet Tubman
(c. 1820–1913)**

**Samuel Clemens
(Mark Twain)
(1835–1910)**

1830 French invade Algeria. Louis Philippe becomes "Citizen King" as revolution forces Charles X to abdicate. Mormon church formed in U.S. by Joseph Smith.

1831 Polish revolt against Russia fails. Belgium separates from the Netherlands. In U.S., Nat Turner leads unsuccessful slave rebellion.

1833 Slavery abolished in British Empire.

1834 Charles Babbage invents "analytical engine," precursor of computer. McCormick patents reaper.

1836 Boer farmers start "Great Trek"—Natal, Transvaal, and Orange Free State founded in South Africa. Mexican army besieges Texans in Alamo. Entire garrison, including Davy Crockett and Jim Bowie, wiped out. Texans gain independence from Mexico after winning Battle of San Jacinto. Dickens's *Pickwick Papers.*

1837 Victoria becomes queen of Great Britain. Mob kills Elijah P. Lovejoy, Illinois abolitionist publisher.

1839 First Opium War (to 1842) between Britain and China, over importation of drug into China.

1840 Lower and Upper Canada united.

1841 U.S. President Harrison dies (**April 4**) one month after inauguration; John Tyler becomes first vice president to succeed to presidency.

1842 Crawford Long uses first anesthetic (ether).

1843 Wagner's opera *The Flying Dutchman.*

1844 Democratic convention calls for annexation of Texas and acquisition of Oregon ("Fifty-four-forty-or-fight"). Five Chinese ports opened to U.S. ships. Samuel F. B. Morse patents telegraph.

1845 Congress adopts joint resolution for annexation of Texas. Edgar Allan Poe publishes *The Raven and Other Poems.*

1846 U.S. declares war on Mexico. California and New Mexico annexed by U.S. Brigham Young leads Mormons to Great Salt Lake. W. T. Morton uses ether as anesthetic. Sewing machine patented by Elias Howe. Frederick Douglass launches abolitionist newspaper *The North Star.* Failure of potato crop causes famine in Ireland.

1848 Revolt in Paris: Louis Philippe abdicates; Louis Napoleon elected president of French Republic. Revolutions in Vienna, Venice, Berlin, Milan, Rome, and Warsaw. Put down by royal troops in 1848–1849. U.S.-Mexico War ends; Mexico cedes claims to Texas, California, Arizona, New Mexico, Utah, Nevada. U.S. treaty with Britain sets Oregon Territory boundary at 49th parallel. Karl Marx and Friedrich Engels's *Communist Manifesto.* Harriet Tubman escapes from slavery and joins the Underground Railroad. Women's Rights Convention in Seneca Falls, N.Y.

1849 California gold rush begins.

1850 Henry Clay opens great debate on slavery, warns South against secession.

1851 Herman Melville's *Moby-Dick.*

1852 South African Republic established. Louis Napoleon proclaims himself Napoleon III ("Second Empire"). Harriet Beecher Stowe's *Uncle Tom's Cabin.*

1853 Crimean War begins as Turkey declares war on Russia. Commodore Perry reaches Tokyo.

1854 Britain and France join Turkey in war on Russia. In U.S., Kansas-Nebraska Act permits local option on slavery; rioting and bloodshed. Japanese allow American trade. Antislavery men in Michigan form Republican Party. Tennyson's *Charge of the Light Brigade.* Thoreau's *Walden.*

1855 Armed clashes in Kansas between pro- and anti-slavery forces. Florence Nightingale nurses wounded in Crimea. Walt Whitman's *Leaves of Grass.*

1856 Flaubert's *Madame Bovary.*

1857 Supreme Court, in Dred Scott decision, rules that a slave is not a citizen. Financial crisis in Europe and U.S. Great Mutiny (Sepoy Rebellion) begins in India. India placed under crown rule as a result.

1858 Pro-slavery constitution rejected in Kansas. Abraham Lincoln makes strong antislavery speech in Springfield, Ill.: "this Government cannot endure permanently half slave and half free." Lincoln-Douglas debates. First trans-Atlantic telegraph cable completed by Cyrus W. Field.

1859 John Brown raids Harpers Ferry; is captured and hanged. Work begins on Suez Canal. Unification of Italy starts under leadership of Count Cavour, Sardinian premier. Joined by France in war against Austria. Jean-Joseph-Étienne Lenoir builds first practical internal-combustion engine. Edward Fitzgerald's translation of *The Rubaiyat of Omar Khayyam.* Charles Darwin's *Origin of Species.* J. S. Mill's *On Liberty.*

1860 South Carolina secedes from the Union.

1861 U.S. Civil War begins as attempts at compromise fail. Mississippi, Florida, Alabama, Georgia, Louisiana, and Texas secede; with South Carolina, they form the Confederate States of America, with Jefferson Davis as president. Virginia, Arkansas, Tennessee, North Carolina secede and join Confederacy. First Battle of Bull Run (Manassas). Congress creates Colorado, Dakota, and Nevada territories; adopts income tax; Lincoln inaugurated. Serfs emancipated in Russia. Pasteur's theory of germs. Independent Kingdom of Italy proclaimed under Sardinian king Victor Emmanuel II.

1862 Several major Civil War battles: Battle of Shiloh, Second Battle of Bull Run (Manassas), Battle of Antietam. Salon des Refusés introduces impressionism.

Abraham Lincoln
(1809–1865)

1863 French capture Mexico City; proclaim Archduke Maximilian of Austria emperor. Battle of Gettysburg.

1864 Gen. Sherman's Atlanta campaign and "march to the sea."

1865 Gen. Lee surrenders to Grant at Appomattox; the Civil War is over. Lincoln fatally shot at Ford's Theater by John Wilkes Booth. Vice President Johnson sworn as successor. Booth caught and dies of gunshot wounds; four conspirators are hanged. Joseph Lister begins antiseptic surgery. Gregor Mendel's *Law of Heredity*. Lewis Carroll's *Alice's Adventures in Wonderland*.

1866 Alfred Nobel invents dynamite (patented in Britain, 1867). Seven Weeks' War: Austria defeated by Prussia and Italy.

1867 Austria-Hungary Dual Monarchy established. French leave Mexico; Maximilian executed. Dominion of Canada established. U.S. buys Alaska from Russia for $7,200,000. South African diamond field discovered. Japan ends 675–year shogun rule. Volume I of Marx's *Das Kapital*. Strauss's *Blue Danube*.

Robert E. Lee
(1807–1870)

1868 Revolution in Spain; Queen Isabella deposed, flees to France. In U.S., Fourteenth Amendment giving civil rights to blacks is ratified. Georgia under military government after legislature expels blacks.

1869 First U.S. transcontinental rail route completed. James Fisk and Jay Gould's attempt to control gold market causes Black Friday panic. Suez Canal opens. Mendeleev's periodic table of elements.

1870 Franco-Prussian War (to 1871): Napoleon III capitulates at Sedan. Revolt in Paris; Third Republic proclaimed.

William Tecumseh
Sherman
(1820–1891)

1871 France surrenders Alsace-Lorraine to Germany; war ends. German Empire proclaimed with Prussian King as Kaiser Wilhelm I. Fighting with Apaches begins in American West. Boss Tweed corruption exposed in New York. The Chicago Fire, with 250 deaths and $196-million damage. Stanley meets Livingstone in Africa.

1872 Congress gives amnesty to most Confederates. Jules Verne's *Around the World in 80 Days*.

THE CIVIL WAR

Apart from the matter of slavery, the Civil War arose out of both the economic and political rivalry between an agrarian South and an industrial North and the issue of the right of states to secede from the Union.

1861 After South Carolina secedes **(Dec. 20, 1860)**, Mississippi, Florida, Alabama, Georgia, Louisiana, and Texas follow, forming the Confederate States of America, with Jefferson Davis as president **(Jan.–March)**. War begins as Confederates fire on Fort Sumter **(April 12)**. Lincoln calls for 75,000 volunteers. Southern ports blockaded by superior Union naval forces. Virginia, Arkansas, Tennessee, and North Carolina secede to complete 11-state Confederacy. Union army advancing on Richmond repulsed at first Battle of Bull Run (Manassas) **(July)**.

1862 Edwin M. Stanton named Secretary of War **(Jan.)**. Grant wins first important Union victory in West, at Fort Donelson; Nashville falls **(Feb.)**. Ironclads, Union's *Monitor* and Confederate's *Virginia* (*Merrimac*) duel at Hampton Roads **(March)**. New Orleans falls to Union fleet under Farragut; city occupied **(April)**. Grant's army escapes defeat at Shiloh. Memphis falls as Union gunboats control upper Mississippi **(June)**. Confederate General Robert E. Lee victorious at second Battle of Bull Run (Manassas) **(Aug.)**. Union army under McClellan halts Lee's attack on Washington in the Battle of Antietam **(Sept.)**. Lincoln removes McClellan for lack of aggressiveness. Burnside's drive on Richmond fails at Fredericksburg **(Dec.)**. Union forces under Rosecrans chase Bragg through Tennessee; battle of Murfreesboro **(Oct.–Jan. 1863)**.

1863 Lee defeats Hooker at Chancellorsville; "Stonewall" Jackson, Confederate general, dies **(May)**. Confederate invasion of Pennsylvania stopped at Gettysburg by George Meade—Lee loses 20,000 men—the greatest battle of the War **(July)**. It and the Union victory at Vicksburg mark the war's turning point. Union general George H. Thomas, the "Rock of Chickamauga," holds Bragg's forces on Georgia-Tennessee border **(Sept.)**. Sherman, Hooker, and Thomas drive Bragg back to Georgia. Tennessee restored to the Union **(Nov.)**.

1864 Ulysses S. Grant named commander-in-chief of Union forces **(March)**. In the Wilderness campaign, Grant forces Lee's Army of Northern Virginia back toward Richmond **(May–June)**. Sherman's Atlanta campaign and "march to the sea" **(May–Sept.)**. Farragut's victory at Mobile Bay **(Aug.)**. Hood's Confederate army defeated at Nashville. Sherman takes Savannah **(Dec.)**.

1865 Sheridan defeats Confederates at Five Forks; Confederates evacuate Richmond **(April)**. On **April 9,** Lee surrenders to Grant at Appomattox.

Johannes Brahms
(1833–1897)

Chief Joseph
(c. 1840–1904)

Statue of Liberty

Marie Curie
(1867–1934)

1873 Economic crisis in Europe. U.S. establishes gold standard.

1875 First Kentucky Derby.

1876 Sioux kill Gen. George A. Custer and 264 troopers at Little Big Horn River. Alexander Graham Bell patents the telephone.

1877 After presidential election of 1876, Electoral Commission gives disputed Electoral College votes to Rutherford B. Hayes despite Tilden's popular majority. Russo-Turkish war (ends in 1878 with power of Turkey in Europe broken). Reconstruction ends in the American South. Thomas Edison patents phonograph. The Nez Perce leader Chief Joseph is forced to surrender. Tchaikovsky's *Swan Lake.*

1878 Congress of Berlin revises Treaty of San Stefano, ending Russo-Turkish War; makes extensive redivision of southeastern Europe. First commercial telephone exchange opened in New Haven, Conn.

1879 Thomas A. Edison invents electric light.

1880 U.S.-China treaty allows U.S. to restrict immigration of Chinese labor.

1881 President Garfield fatally shot by assassin; Vice President Arthur succeeds him. Charles J. Guiteau convicted and executed (1882).

1882 Terrorism in Ireland after land evictions. Britain invades and conquers Egypt. Germany, Austria, and Italy form Triple Alliance. In U.S., Congress adopts Chinese Exclusion Act. Rockefeller's Standard Oil Trust is first industrial monopoly. In Berlin, Robert Koch announces discovery of tuberculosis germ.

1883 Congress creates Civil Service Commission. Brooklyn Bridge and Metropolitan Opera House completed.

1884 Berlin West Africa Conference held in Berlin (lasting until **Feb. 1885**), at which the major European nations discuss expansion in Africa.

1885 British Gen. Charles G. "Chinese" Gordon killed at Khartoum in Egyptian Sudan. World's first skyscraper built in Chicago.

1886 Bombing at Haymarket Square, Chicago, kills seven policemen and injures many others. Eight alleged anarchists accused—three imprisoned, one commits suicide, four hanged. (In 1893, Illinois Governor Altgeld, critical of trial, pardons three survivors.) Statue of Liberty dedicated. Geronimo, Apache Indian chief, surrenders.

1887 Queen Victoria's Golden Jubilee. Sir Arthur Conan Doyle's first Sherlock Holmes story, *A Study in Scarlet.*

1888 Historic March blizzard in Northeast U.S.—many perish, property damage exceeds $25 million. George Eastman's box camera (the Kodak). J. B. Dunlop invents pneumatic tire. Jack the Ripper murders in London.

1889 Second (Socialist) International founded in Paris. Indian Territory in Oklahoma opened to settlement. Thousands die in Johnstown, Pa. flood. Eiffel Tower built for the Paris exposition. Mark Twain's *A Connecticut Yankee in King Arthur's Court.*

1890 Congress votes to pass Sherman Antitrust Act. Sioux Chief Sitting Bull arrested and killed by police on Pine Ridge reservation; two weeks later, U.S. troops kill over 200 Sioux at Battle of Wounded Knee.

1892 Battle between steel strikers and Pinkerton guards at Homestead, Pa.; union defeated after militia intervenes. Silver mine strikers in Idaho fight non-union workers; U.S. troops dispatched. Diesel engine patented.

1893 New Zealand becomes first country in the world to grant women the vote.

1894 Sino-Japanese War begins (ends in 1895 with China's defeat). In France, Capt. Alfred Dreyfus convicted on false treason charge (pardoned in 1906). In U.S., Jacob S. Coxey of Ohio leads "Coxey's Army" of unemployed on Washington. Eugene V. Debs calls general strike of rail workers to support Pullman Company strikers; strike broken, Debs jailed for six months. Edison's kinetoscope given first public showing in New York City.

1895 X-rays discovered by German physicist Wilhelm Roentgen. Auguste and Louis Lumière premiere motion pictures at a café in Paris.

SPANISH-AMERICAN WAR (1898–1899)

War fires stoked by "jingo journalism" as American people support Cuban rebels against Spain. American business sees economic gain in Cuban trade and resources and American power zones in Latin America. Outstanding events: Submarine mine sinks U.S. battleship *Maine* in Havana Harbor **(Feb. 15)**; 260 killed; responsibility never fixed. Congress declares independence of Cuba **(April 19)**. Spain declares war on U.S. **(April 24)**; Congress **(April 25)** formally declares nation has been at war with Spain since **April 21**. Commodore George Dewey wins seven-hour battle of Manila Bay **(May 1)**. Spanish fleet destroyed off Santiago, Cuba **(July 3)**; city surrenders **(July 17)**. Treaty of Paris (ratified by Senate 1899) ends war. U.S. given Guam and Puerto Rico and agrees to pay Spain $20 million for Philippines. Cuba independent of Spain; under U.S. military control for three years until **May 20, 1902**. Yellow fever is eradicated and political reforms achieved.

1896 Supreme Court's *Plessy v. Ferguson* decision—"separate but equal" doctrine. Alfred Nobel's will establishes prizes for peace, science, and literature. Marconi receives first wireless patent in Britain. William Jennings Bryan delivers "Cross of Gold" speech at Democratic Convention in Chicago. First modern Olympic games held in Athens, Greece.

1897 Theodor Herzl launches Zionist movement.

1898 Chinese "Boxers," anti-foreign organization, established. They stage uprisings against Europeans in 1900; U.S. and other Western troops relieve Peking legations. U.S. Battleship *Maine* is sunk in Havana Harbor. Spanish-American War begins. U.S. destroys Spanish fleet near Santiago, Cuba. Pierre and Marie Curie discover radium and polonium.

1899 Boer War (or South African War): conflict between British and Boers (descendants of Dutch settlers of South Africa). Causes rooted in long-standing territorial disputes and in friction over political rights for English and other "uitlanders" following 1886 discovery of vast gold deposits in Transvaal. (British victorious as war ends in 1902.) Casualties: 5,774 British dead, about 4,000 Boers. Union of South Africa established in 1908 as confederation of colonies; becomes British dominion in 1910.

Sigmund Freud
(1856–1939)

1900–2000 (A.D.)

1900 Hurricane ravages Galveston, Tex.; 6,000–8,000 dead. Fauvist movement in painting begins, led by Henri Matisse. Sigmund Freud's *The Interpretation of Dreams*. Carrie Chapman Catt succeeds Susan B. Anthony as president of National Woman Suffrage Association.

1901 Queen Victoria dies, and is succeeded by her son, Edward VII. As President McKinley begins second term, he is shot fatally by anarchist Leon Czolgosz. Theodore Roosevelt sworn in as successor.

1902 Enrico Caruso's first gramophone recording. Aswan Dam completed.

1903 Wright brothers, Orville and Wilbur, fly first powered, controlled, heavier-than-air plane at Kitty Hawk, N.C. Henry Ford organizes Ford Motor Company. The Boston Red Sox win the first World Series against the Pittsburgh Pirates. W. E. B. Du Bois publishes *The Souls of Black Folk.*

1904 Russo-Japanese War begins—competition for Korea and Manchuria. *Entente Cordiale:* Britain and France settle their international differences. General theory of radioactivity by Rutherford and Soddy. New York City subway opens.

1905 In Russo-Japanese War, Port Arthur surrenders to Japanese; Russia suffers other defeats. President Roosevelt mediates Treaty of Portsmouth, N.H., which recognizes Japan's control of Korea and restores southern Manchuria to China. The Russian Revolution of 1905 begins on "Bloody Sunday" when troops fire onto a defenseless group of demonstrators in St. Petersburg. Strikes and riots follow. Sailors on battleship *Potemkin* mutiny; reforms, including first Duma (parliament), established by Czar Nicholas II's "October Manifesto." Albert Einstein's special theory of relativity and other key theories in physics. Franz Lehar's *Merry Widow.*

1906 San Francisco earthquake and three-day fire; more than 500 dead. Roald Amundsen, Norwegian explorer, fixes magnetic North Pole.

1907 Second Hague Peace Conference, of 46 nations, adopts 10 conventions on rules of war. Financial panic of 1907 in U.S. Mahler begins work on "Song of the Earth." Oklahoma becomes 46th state. Picasso's *Les Demoiselles d'Avignon* introduces cubism.

1908 Earthquake kills 150,000 in southern Italy and Sicily. U.S. Supreme Court, in Danbury Hatters' case, outlaws secondary union boycotts. Model T produced by Ford Motor Company.

1909 North Pole reportedly reached by American explorers Robert E. Peary and Matthew Henson. The National Association for the Advancement of Colored People is founded in New York by prominent black and white intellectuals and led by W. E. B. Du Bois.

1910 Boy Scouts of America incorporated. Angel Island, in San Francisco Bay, becomes immigration center for Asians entering U.S.

1911 First use of aircraft as offensive weapon in Turkish-Italian War. Italy defeats Turks and annexes Tripoli and Libya. Chinese Republic proclaimed after revolution overthrows Manchu dynasty. Sun Yat-sen named president. Mexican Revolution: Porfirio Diaz, president since 1877, replaced by Francisco Madero. Triangle Shirtwaist Company fire in New York; 146 killed. Amundsen reaches South Pole. Ernest Rutherford discovers the structure of the atom. Richard Strauss's *Der Rosenkavalier.* Irving Berlin's *Alexander's Ragtime Band.*

Carrie Chapman Catt
(1859–1947)

Albert Einstein
(1879–1955)

Vladimir Lenin
(1870–1924)

Robert Peary
(1856–1920)

**W. E. B. Du Bois
(1868–1963)**

**Woodrow Wilson
(1856–1924)**

**Bessie Smith
(1894–1937)**

1912 Balkan Wars (1912–1913) resulting from territorial disputes: Turkey defeated by alliance of Bulgaria, Serbia, Greece, and Montenegro; London peace treaty (1913) partitions most of European Turkey among the victors. In second war (1913), Bulgaria attacks Serbia and Greece and is defeated after Romania intervenes and Turks recapture Adrianople. *Titanic* sinks on maiden voyage; over 1,500 drown. New Mexico and Arizona admitted as states.

1913 Suffragists demonstrate in London. Garment workers strike in New York and Boston; win pay raise and shorter hours. Henry Ford develops first moving assembly line. 16th Amendment (income tax) and 17th (popular election of U.S. senators) adopted. Bill creating U.S. Federal Reserve System becomes law. Stravinsky's *The Rite of Spring*. Woodrow Wilson becomes 28th U.S. president. Armory Show introduces modern art to U.S.; Duchamp's *Nude Descending a Staircase* shocks public.

1914 World War I begins: Austrian Archduke Francis Ferdinand and wife Sophie are assassinated; Austria declares war on Serbia, Germany on Russia and France, Britain on Germany. Panama Canal officially opened. Congress sets up Federal Trade Commission, passes Clayton Antitrust Act. U.S. Marines occupy Veracruz, Mexico, intervening in civil war to protect American interests.

1915 *Lusitania* sunk by German submarine. Second Battle of Ypres. U.S. banks lend $500 million to France and Britain. Genocide of estimated 600,000 to 1 million Armenians by Turkish soldiers. D. W. Griffith's film *Birth of a Nation*. Albert Einstein's *General Theory of Relativity*.

1916 Congress expands armed forces. Battle of Verdun. Battle of the Somme. Tom Mooney arrested for San Francisco bombing (pardoned in 1939). Pershing fails in raid into Mexico in quest of rebel Pancho Villa. U.S. buys Virgin Islands from Denmark for $25 million. President Wilson re-elected with "he kept us out of war" slogan. "Black Tom" explosion at munitions dock in Jersey City, N.J., $40,000,000 damages; traced to German saboteurs. Margaret Sanger opens first birth control clinic. Easter Rebellion in Ireland put down by British troops. Jeannette Rankin becomes first woman elected to Congress.

1917 First U.S. combat troops in France as U.S. declares war on Germany (**April 6**). Third Battle of Ypres. Russian Revolution of 1917—climax of long unrest under czars. February Revolution—Nicholas II forced to abdicate, liberal government created. Kerensky becomes prime minister and forms provisional government (**July**). In October Revolution, Bolsheviks seize power in armed coup d'état led by Lenin and Trotsky. Kerensky flees. Balfour Declaration promises Jewish homeland in Palestine. U.S. declares war on Austria-Hungary (**Dec. 7**). Armistice between

---

WORLD WAR I (1914–1918)

Imperial, territorial, and economic rivalries led to the "Great War" between the Central Powers (Austria-Hungary, Germany, Bulgaria, and Turkey) and the Allies (U.S., Britain, France, Russia, Belgium, Serbia, Greece, Romania, Montenegro, Portugal, Italy, Japan). About 10 million combatants killed, 20 million wounded.

1914 Austrian Archduke Francis Ferdinand and wife assassinated in Sarajevo by Serbian nationalist, Gavrilo Princip (**June 28**). Austria declares war on Serbia (**July 28**). Germany declares war on Russia (**Aug. 1**), on France (**Aug. 3**), invades Belgium (**Aug. 4**). Britain declares war on Germany (**Aug. 4**). Germans defeat Russians in Battle of Tannenberg on Eastern Front (**Aug.**). First Battle of the Marne (**Sept.**). German drive stopped 25 miles from Paris. By end of year, war on the Western Front is "positional" in the trenches.

1915 German submarine blockade of Great Britain begins (**Feb.**). Dardanelles Campaign—British land in Turkey (**April**), withdraw from Gallipoli (**Dec.–Jan. 1916**). Germans use gas at second Battle of Ypres (**April–May**). *Lusitania* sunk by German submarine—1,198 lost, including 128 Americans (**May 7**). On Eastern Front, German and Austrian "great offensive" conquers all of Poland and Lithuania; Russians lose 1 million men (by **Sept.** 6). "Great Fall Offensive" by Allies results in little change from 1914 (**Sept.–Oct.**). Britain and France declare war on Bulgaria (**Oct. 14**).

1916 Battle of Verdun—Germans and French each lose about 350,000 men (**Feb.**). Extended submarine

warfare begins (**March**). British-German sea battle of Jutland (**May**); British lose more ships, but German fleet never ventures forth again. On Eastern Front, the Brusilov offensive demoralizes Russians, costs them 1 million men (**June–Sept.**). Battle of the Somme—British lose over 400,000; French, 200,000; Germans, about 450,000; all with no strategic results (**July–Nov.**). Romania declares war on Austria-Hungary (**Aug. 27**). Bucharest captured (**Dec.**).

1917 U.S. declares war on Germany (**April 6**). Submarine warfare at peak (**April**). On Italian Front, Battle of Caporetto—Italians retreat, losing 600,000 prisoners and deserters (**Oct.–Dec.**). On Western Front, Battles of Arras, Champagne, Ypres (third battle), etc. First large British tank attack (**Nov.**). U.S. declares war on Austria-Hungary (**Dec. 7**). Armistice between new Russian Bolshevik government and Germans (**Dec. 15**).

1918 Great offensive by Germans (**March–June**). Americans' first important battle role at Château-Thierry—as they and French stop German advance (**June**). Second Battle of the Marne (**July–Aug.**)—start of Allied offensive at Amiens, St. Mihiel, etc. Battles of the Argonne and Ypres panic German leadership (**Sept.–Oct.**). British offensive in Palestine (**Sept.**). Germans ask for armistice (**Oct. 4**). British armistice with Turkey (**Oct.**). German Kaiser abdicates (**Nov.**). Hostilities cease on Western Front (**Nov. 11**).

new Russian Bolshevik government and Germans **(Dec. 15).** Sigmund Freud's *Introduction to Psychoanalysis.*

1918 Russian revolutionaries execute the former czar and his family. Russian Civil War between Reds (Bolsheviks) and Whites (anti-Bolsheviks); Reds win in 1920. Allied troops (U.S., British, French) intervene **(March);** leave in 1919. Second Battle of the Marne **(July–Aug.)** German Kaiser abdicates **(Nov.);** hostilities cease on the Western Front. Japanese hold Vladivostok until 1922. Worldwide influenza epidemic strikes; by 1920, nearly 20 million are dead. In U.S. alone, 500,000 perish.

1919 Third International (Comintern) establishes Soviet control over international Communist movements. Paris peace conference. Versailles Treaty, incorporating Woodrow Wilson's draft Covenant of League of Nations, signed by Allies and Germany; rejected by U.S. Senate. Congress formally ends war in 1921. 18th (Prohibition) Amendment adopted. Alcock and Brown make first trans-Atlantic nonstop flight. Mahatma Gandhi initiates satyagraha ("truth force") campaigns, beginning his nonviolent resistance movement against British rule in India.

Mahatma Gandhi
(1869–1948)

1920 League of Nations holds first meeting at Geneva, Switzerland. U.S. Dept. of Justice "red hunt" nets thousands of radicals; aliens deported. Women's suffrage (19th) amendment ratified. Treaty of Sèvres dissolves Ottoman Empire. First Agatha Christie mystery. Sinclair Lewis's *Main Street.*

1921 Reparations Commission fixes German liability at 132 billion gold marks. German inflation begins. Major treaties signed at Washington Disarmament Conference limit naval tonnage and pledge to respect territorial integrity of China. In U.S., Nicola Sacco and Bartolomeo Vanzetti, Italian-born anarchists, convicted of armed robbery murder; case stirs worldwide protests; they are executed in 1927.

William Butler Yeats
(1865–1939)

1922 Mussolini marches on Rome; forms Fascist government. Irish Free State, a self-governing dominion of British Empire, officially proclaimed. Kemal Atatürk, founder of modern Turkey, overthrows last sultan. James Joyce's *Ulysses.*

1923 Adolf Hitler's "Beer Hall Putsch" in Munich fails; in 1924 he is sentenced to five years in prison where he writes *Mein Kampf;* released after eight months. Occupation of Ruhr by French and Belgian troops to enforce reparations payments. Widespread Ku Klux Klan violence in U.S. Earthquake destroys third of Tokyo. George Gershwin's *Rhapsody in Blue.* Bessie Smith, known as "the Empress of the Blues," makes her first record. Irish poet William Butler Yeats wins Nobel Prize in Literature.

Robert Frost
(1874–1963)

1924 Death of Lenin; Stalin wins power struggle, rules as Soviet dictator until death in 1953. Italian Fascists murder Socialist leader Giacomo Matteotti. Interior Secretary Albert B. Fall and oilmen Harry Sinclair and Edward L. Doheny are charged with conspiracy and bribery in the Teapot Dome scandal, involving fraudulent leases of naval oil reserves. In 1931, Fall is sentenced to year in prison; Doheny and Sinclair acquitted of bribery. Nathan Leopold and Richard Loeb convicted in "thrill killing" of Bobby Franks in Chicago; defended by Clarence Darrow; sentenced to life imprisonment. (Loeb killed by fellow convict in 1936; Leopold paroled in 1958, dies in 1971.) Robert Frost wins first of four Pulitzers.

Pablo Picasso
(1881–1973)

1925 Nellie Tayloe Ross elected governor of Wyoming; first woman governor elected in U.S. Locarno conferences seek to secure European peace by mutual guarantees. John T. Scopes convicted and fined for teaching evolution in a public school in Tennessee "Monkey Trial"; sentence set aside. John Logie Baird, Scottish inventor, transmits human features by television. Hitler publishes Volume I of *Mein Kampf.*

1926 General strike in Britain brings nation's activities to standstill. U.S. marines dispatched to Nicaragua during revolt; they remain until 1933. Gertrude Ederle of U.S. is first woman to swim English Channel. Ernest Hemingway's *The Sun Also Rises.*

1927 German economy collapses. Socialists riot in Vienna; general strike follows acquittal of Nazis for political murder. Trotsky expelled from Russian Communist Party. Charles A. Lindbergh flies first successful solo nonstop flight from New York to Paris. Ruth Snyder and Judd Gray convicted of murder of Albert Snyder; they are executed at Sing Sing prison in 1928. Philo T. Farnsworth demonstrates working television model. Georges Lemaître proposes Big Bang Theory. Babe Ruth hits 60 home runs in the season; record stands for next 34 years. *The Jazz Singer,* with Al Jolson, first part-talking motion picture.

Babe Ruth
(George Herman Ruth)
(1895–1948)

Benito Mussolini
(1883–1945)

Joseph Stalin
(1879–1953)

Adolf Hitler
(1889–1945)

1928 Kellogg-Briand Pact, outlawing war, signed in Paris by 65 nations. Alexander Fleming discovers penicillin. Richard E. Byrd starts expedition to Antarctic; returns in 1930. Anthropologist Margaret Mead publishes *Coming of Age in Samoa. Oxford English Dictionary* published after 44 years of research.

1929 Trotsky expelled from U.S.S.R. Lateran Treaty establishes independent Vatican City. In U.S., stock market prices collapse, with U.S. securities losing $26 billion—first phase of Depression and world economic crisis. St. Valentine's Day gangland massacre in Chicago. Edwin Powell Hubble proposes theory of expanding universe.

1930 Britain, U.S., Japan, France, and Italy sign naval disarmament treaty. Nazis gain in German elections. Cyclotron developed by Ernest O. Lawrence, U.S. physicist. Pluto discovered by astronomers.

1931 Spain becomes a republic with overthrow of King Alfonso XIII. German industrialists finance 800,000-strong Nazi party. British parliament enacts statute of Westminster, legalizing dominion equality with Britain. Mukden Incident begins Japanese occupation of Manchuria. In U.S., Hoover proposes one-year moratorium of war debts. Harold C. Urey discovers heavy hydrogen. Gangster Al Capone sentenced to 11 years in prison for tax evasion (freed in 1939; dies in 1947). Notorious Scottsboro trial begins, exposing depth of Southern racism. "The Star Spangled Banner" officially becomes national anthem.

1932 Nazis lead in German elections with 230 Reichstag seats. Famine in U.S.S.R. In U.S., Congress sets up Reconstruction Finance Corporation to stimulate economy. Veterans march on Washington—most leave after Senate rejects payment of cash bonuses; others removed by troops under Douglas MacArthur. U.S. protests Japanese aggression in Manchuria. Amelia Earhart is first woman to fly Atlantic solo. Charles A. Lindbergh's baby son kidnapped, killed. (Bruno Richard Hauptmann arrested in 1934, convicted in 1935, executed in 1936.)

1933 Hitler appointed German chancellor, gets dictatorial powers. Reichstag fire in Berlin; Nazi terror begins. Germany and Japan withdraw from League of Nations. Giuseppe Zangara executed for attempted assassination of president-elect Roosevelt in which Chicago mayor Cermak is fatally shot. Roosevelt inaugurated ("the only thing we have to fear is fear itself"); launches New Deal. Prohibition repealed. U.S.S.R. recognized by U.S.

1934 Chancellor Dollfuss of Austria assassinated by Nazis. Hitler becomes führer. U.S.S.R. admitted to League of Nations. Dionne sisters, first quintuplets to survive beyond infancy, born in Canada. Mao Zedong begins the Long March north with 100,000 soldiers.

1935 Saar incorporated into Germany after plebiscite. Nazis repudiate Versailles Treaty, introduce compulsory military service. Mussolini invades Ethiopia; League of Nations invokes sanctions. Roosevelt opens second phase of

---

THE HOLOCAUST (1933–1945)

"Holocaust" is the term describing the Nazi annihilation of about 6 million Jews (two thirds of the pre-World War II European Jewish population), including 4,500,000 from Russia, Poland, and the Baltic; 750,000 from Hungary and Romania; 290,000 from Germany and Austria; 105,000 from The Netherlands; 90,000 from France; 54,000 from Greece.

The Holocaust was unique in its being *genocide*—the systematic destruction of a people solely because of religion, race, ethnicity, nationality, or sexual preference—on an unmatched scale. Along with the Jews, another 9 to 10 million people—Gypsies, Slavs (Poles, Ukrainians, and Belarussians), homosexuals, and the disabled—were exterminated.

1933 Hitler named German Chancellor **(Jan.)**. Dachau, first concentration camp, established **(March)**. Boycotts against Jews begin **(April)**.

1935 Anti-Semitic Nuremberg Laws passed by Reichstag; Jews lose citizenship and civil rights **(Sept.)**.

1937 Buchenwald concentration camp opens **(July)**.

1938 Extension of anti-Semitic laws to Austria after annexation **(March)**. *Kristallnacht* (Night of Broken Glass)—anti-Semitic riots and destruction of Jewish institutions in Germany and Austria **(Nov. 9)**. 26,000 Jews sent to concentration camps; Jewish children expelled from schools **(Nov. 9–10)**. Expropriation of Jewish property and businesses **(Dec.)**.

1940 As war continues, Einsatzgruppen (mobile killing squads) follow German army into conquered lands, rounding up and massacring Jews and other "undesirables."

1941 Goering instructs Heydrich to carry out the "final solution to the Jewish question" **(July 31)**. Deportation of German Jews begins; massacres of Jews in Odessa and Kiev **(Nov.)**; and in Riga and Vilna **(Dec.)**.

1942 Mass killings using Zyklon-B begin at Auschwitz-Birkenau **(Jan.)**. Nazi leaders attend Wannsee Conference to coordinate the "final solution" **(Jan. 20)**. 100,000 Jews from Warsaw Ghetto deported to Treblinka death camp **(July)**.

1943 Warsaw Ghetto uprisings **(Jan.** and **April)**; Ghetto exterminated **(May)**.

1944 476,000 Hungarian Jews sent to Auschwitz **(May–June)**. D-day **(June 6)**. Soviet Army liberates Maidanek death camp **(July)**. Nazis try to hide evidence of death camps **(Nov.)**.

1945 As Allies advance, Nazis force concentration camp inmates on death marches. Americans liberate Buchenwald and British liberate Bergen-Belsen camps **(April)**. Nuremberg War Crimes Trial **(Nov. 1945–Oct. 1946)**.

New Deal in U.S., calling for social security, better housing, equitable taxation, and farm assistance. Huey Long assassinated in Louisiana.

1936 Germans occupy Rhineland. Italy annexes Ethiopia. Rome-Berlin Axis proclaimed (Japan to join in 1940). Trotsky exiled to Mexico. King George V dies; succeeded by son, Edward VIII, who soon abdicates to marry an American-born divorcée, and is succeeded by brother, George VI. Spanish civil war begins. Hundreds of Americans join the "Lincoln Brigades." (Franco's fascist forces defeat Loyalist forces by 1939, when Madrid falls.) War between China and Japan begins, to continue through World War II. Japan and Germany sign anti-Comintern pact; joined by Italy in 1937.

1937 Hitler repudiates war guilt clause of Versailles Treaty; continues to build German power. Italy withdraws from League of Nations. U.S. gunboat *Panay* sunk by Japanese in Yangtze River. Japan invades China, conquers most of coastal area. Amelia Earhart lost somewhere in Pacific on round-the-world flight. Picasso's *Guernica* mural.

1938 Hitler marches into Austria; political and geographical union of Germany and Austria proclaimed. Munich Pact—Britain, France, and Italy agree to let Germany partition Czechoslovakia. Douglas "Wrong-Way" Corrigan flies from New York to Dublin. Fair Labor Standards Act establishes minimum wage. Orson Welles's radio broadcast *War of the Worlds*.

1939 Germany invades Poland; occupies Bohemia and Moravia; renounces pact with England and concludes 10-year non-aggression pact with U.S.S.R. Russo-Finnish War begins; Finns to lose one-tenth of territory in 1940 peace treaty. World War II begins. In U.S., Roosevelt submits $1,319-million defense budget, proclaims U.S. neutrality, and declares limited emergency. Einstein writes FDR about feasibility of atomic bomb. New York World's Fair opens. DAR refuses to allow Marian Anderson to perform. *Gone with the Wind* premieres.

Dorothea Lange's photo "Migrant Mother" (1936) documented the Great Depression (1929–1940)

Amelia Earhart (1897–1937)

WORLD WAR II (1939–1945)

Axis powers (Germany, Italy, Japan, Hungary, Romania, Bulgaria) *versus* Allies (U.S., Britain, France, U.S.S.R., Australia, Belgium, Brazil, Canada, China, Denmark, Greece, Netherlands, New Zealand, Norway, Poland, South Africa, Yugoslavia).

1939 Germany invades Poland and annexes Danzig; Britain and France give Hitler ultimatum **(Sept. 1)**, declare war **(Sept. 3)**. Disabled German pocket battleship *Admiral Graf Spee* blown up off Montevideo, Uruguay, on Hitler's orders **(Dec. 17)**. Limited activity ("Sitzkrieg") on Western Front.

1940 Nazis invade Netherlands, Belgium, and Luxembourg **(May 10)**. Chamberlain resigns as Britain's prime minister; Churchill takes over **(May 10)**. Germans cross French frontier **(May 12)** using air/tank/infantry "Blitzkrieg" tactics. Dunkerque evacuation—about 335,000 out of 400,000 Allied soldiers rescued from Belgium by British civilian and naval craft **(May 26–June 3)**. Italy declares war on France and Britain; invades France **(June 10)**. Germans enter Paris; city undefended **(June 14)**. France and Germany sign armistice at Compiègne **(June 22)**. Nazis bomb Coventry, England **(Nov. 14)**.

1941 Germans launch attacks in Balkans. Yugoslavia surrenders—General Mihajlovic continues guerrilla warfare; Tito leads left-wing guerrillas **(April 17)**. Nazi tanks enter Athens; remnants of British Army quit Greece **(April 27)**. Hitler attacks Russia **(June 22)**. Atlantic Charter—FDR and Churchill agree on war aims **(Aug. 14)**. Japanese attacks on Pearl Harbor, Philippines, Guam force U.S. into war; U.S. Pacific fleet crippled **(Dec. 7)**. U.S. and Britain declare war on Japan. Germany and Italy declare war on U.S.; Congress declares war on those countries **(Dec. 11)**.

1942 British surrender Singapore to Japanese **(Feb. 15)**. Roosevelt orders Japanese and Japanese Americans in western U.S. to be exiled to "relocation centers," many for the remainder of the war **(Feb. 19)**. U.S. forces on Bataan peninsula in Philippines surrender **(April 9)**. U.S. and Filipino troops on Corregidor island in Manila Bay surrender to Japanese **(May 6)**. Village of Lidice in Czechoslovakia razed by Nazis

(June 10). U.S. and Britain land in French North Africa **(Nov. 8)**.

1943 Casablanca Conference—Churchill and FDR agree on unconditional surrender goal **(Jan. 14–24)**. German 6th Army surrenders at Stalingrad—turning point of war in Russia **(Feb. 1–2)**. Remnants of Nazis trapped on Cape Bon, ending war in Africa **(May 12)**. Mussolini deposed; Badoglio named premier **(July 25)**. Allied troops land on Italian mainland after conquest of Sicily **(Sept. 3)**. Italy surrenders **(Sept. 8)**. Nazis seize Rome **(Sept. 10)**. Cairo Conference: FDR, Churchill, Chiang Kai-shek pledge defeat of Japan, free Korea **(Nov. 22–26)**. Teheran Conference: FDR, Churchill, Stalin agree on invasion plans **(Nov. 28–Dec. 1)**.

1944 U.S. and British troops land at Anzio on west Italian coast and hold beachhead **(Jan. 22)**. U.S. and British troops enter Rome **(June 4)**. D-Day—Allies launch Normandy invasion **(June 6)**. Hitler wounded in bomb plot **(July 20)**. Paris liberated **(Aug. 25)**. Athens freed by Allies **(Oct. 13)**. Americans invade Philippines **(Oct. 20)**. Germans launch counteroffensive in Belgium—Battle of the Bulge **(Dec. 16)**.

1945 Yalta Agreement signed by FDR, Churchill, Stalin—establishes basis for occupation of Germany, returns to Soviet Union lands taken by Germany and Japan; U.S.S.R. agrees to friendship pact with China **(Feb. 11)**. Mussolini killed at Lake Como **(April 28)**. Admiral Doenitz takes command in Germany; suicide of Hitler announced **(May 1)**. Berlin falls **(May 2)**. Germany signs unconditional surrender terms at Rheims **(May 7)**. Allies declare V-E Day **(May 8)**. Potsdam Conference—Truman, Churchill, Atlee (after **July 28**), Stalin establish council of foreign ministers to prepare peace treaties; plan German postwar government and reparations **(July 17–Aug. 2)**. A-bomb dropped on Hiroshima by U.S. **(Aug. 6)**. U.S.S.R. declares war on Japan **(Aug. 8)**. Nagasaki hit by A-bomb **(Aug. 9)**. Japan agrees to surrender **(Aug. 14)**. V-J Day—Japanese sign surrender terms aboard battleship *Missouri* **(Sept. 2)**.

Franklin Delano Roosevelt (1882–1945)

Winston Churchill (1874–1965)

Harry S. Truman (1884–1972)

Atomic Bomb

Anne Frank (1929–1945)

1940 Hitler invades Norway, Denmark (**April 9**), the Netherlands, Belgium, Luxembourg (**May 10**), and France (**May 12**). Churchill becomes Britain's prime minister. Trotsky assassinated in Mexico (**Aug. 20**). Estonia, Latvia, and Lithuania annexed by U.S.S.R. U.S. trades 50 destroyers for leases on British bases in Western Hemisphere. Selective Service Act signed. The first official network television broadcast is put out by NBC.

1941 Germany attacks the Balkans and Russia. Japanese surprise attack on U.S. fleet at Pearl Harbor brings U.S. into World War II; U.S. and Britain declare war on Japan. Manhattan Project (atomic bomb research) begins. Roosevelt enunciates "four freedoms," signs Lend-Lease Act, declares national emergency, promises aid to U.S.S.R. Orson Welles's *Citizen Kane.*

1942 Declaration of United Nations signed in Washington (**Jan. 1**). Nazi leaders attend Wannsee Conference to coordinate the "final solution to the Jewish question," the systematic genocide of Jews known as the Holocaust. Women's military services established. Enrico Fermi achieves nuclear chain reaction. More than 120,000 Japanese and persons of Japanese ancestry living in western U.S. moved to "relocation centers," some for the duration of the war (Executive Order 9066). Coconut Grove nightclub fire in Boston kills 492 (**Nov. 28**).

1943 Churchill and Roosevelt hold Casablanca Conference (**Jan. 14–23**). Mussolini deposed. President freezes prices, salaries, and wages to prevent inflation. Income tax withholding introduced.

1944 Allies invade Normandy on D-Day (**June 6**). G.I. Bill of Rights enacted. Bretton Woods Conference creates International Monetary Fund and World Bank (**July 1–22**). Dumbarton Oaks Conference—U.S., British Commonwealth, and U.S.S.R. propose establishment of United Nations (**Aug. 21–Oct. 7**). Battle of the Bulge (**Dec. 16**). Gunnar Myrdal's *An American Dilemma.*

1945 Yalta Conference (Roosevelt, Churchill, Stalin) plans final defeat of Germany (**Feb. 4–11**). FDR dies (**April 12**). Hitler commits suicide (**April 30**); Germany surrenders (**May 7**); May 8 is declared V-E Day. Potsdam Conference (Truman, Churchill, Stalin) establishes basis of German reconstruction (**July–Aug.**). U.S. drops atomic bombs on Japanese cities of Hiroshima (**Aug. 6**) and Nagasaki (**Aug. 9**). Japan signs official surrender on V-J Day (**Sept. 2**). United Nations established (**Oct. 24**). First electronic computer, ENIAC, built.

1946 First meeting of UN General Assembly opens in London (**Jan. 10**). Winston Churchill's "Iron Curtain" speech warns of Soviet expansion (**March 5**). League of Nations dissolved (**April**). Italy abolishes monarchy (**June**). Verdict in Nuremberg war trial: 12 Nazi leaders (including 1 tried in absentia) sentenced to hang; 7 imprisoned; 3 acquitted (**Oct. 1**). Goering commits suicide a few hours before 10 other Nazis are executed (**Oct. 15**). Juan Perón becomes president of Argentina. Benjamin Spock's childcare classic published.

1947 Britain nationalizes coal mines (**Jan. 1**). Peace treaties for Italy, Romania, Bulgaria, Hungary, Finland signed in Paris (**Feb. 10**). Soviet Union rejects U.S. plan for UN atomic-energy control (**March 4**). Truman proposes Truman Doctrine, which was to aid Greece and Turkey in resisting communist expansion (**March 12**). Marshall Plan for European recovery proposed—a coordinated program to help European nations recover from ravages of war (**June**). (By the time it ended in 1951, this "European Recovery Program" had cost $13 billion.) India and Pakistan gain independence from Britain (**Aug. 15**). U.S. Air Force pilot Chuck Yeager becomes first person to break the sound barrier (**Oct. 14**). Jackie Robinson joins the Brooklyn Dodgers. Anne Frank's *The Diary of a Young Girl* published.

1948 Gandhi assassinated in New Delhi by Hindu fanatic (**Jan. 30**). Burma (**Jan. 4**) and Ceylon (**Feb. 4**) granted independence by Britain. Communists seize power in Czechoslovakia (**Feb. 23–25**). Organization of American States (OAS) Charter signed at Bogotá, Colombia (**April 30**). Nation of Israel proclaimed; British end mandate at midnight; Arab armies attack (**May 14**). Berlin blockade begins (**June 24**), prompting Allied airlift (**June 26**). (Blockade ends May 12, 1949; airlift continues until Sept. 30, 1949.) Stalin and Tito break (**June 28**). Independent Republic of Korea is proclaimed, following election supervised by UN (**Aug. 15**). Verdict in Japanese war trial: 18 imprisoned (**Nov. 12**); Tojo and six others hanged (**Dec. 23**). United States of Indonesia established as Dutch and Indonesians settle conflict (**Dec. 27**). Alger Hiss, former

U.S. State Department official, indicted on perjury charges after denying passing secret documents to communist spy ring; convicted in second trial (1950) and sentenced to five-year prison term. Truman ends racial segregation in military. Alfred Kinsey publishes *Sexual Behavior in the American Male*. Tennessee Williams's *A Streetcar Named Desire* wins Pulitzer.

1949 Cease-fire in Palestine (**Jan. 7**). Truman proposes Point Four Program to help world's less developed areas (**Jan. 20**). Israel signs armistice with Egypt (**Feb. 24**). Start of North Atlantic Treaty Organization (NATO)—treaty signed by 12 nations (**April 4**). Federal Republic of Germany (West Germany) established (**May 23**). First successful Soviet atomic test (**July 14**). Communist People's Republic of China formally proclaimed by Chairman Mao Zedong (**Oct. 1**). German Democratic Republic (East Germany) established under Soviet rule (**Oct. 7**). South Africa institutionalizes apartheid.

1950 Brink's robbery in Boston; almost $3 million stolen (**Jan. 17**). Truman orders development of hydrogen bomb (**Jan. 31**). Robert Schuman proposes Schuman Plan to pool European coal and steel (**May 9**). Korean War begins when North Korean Communist forces invade South Korea (**June 25**). Assassination attempt on President Truman by Puerto Rican nationalists (**Nov. 1**). McCarthyism begins.

1951 Julius and Ethel Rosenberg sentenced to death for passing atomic secrets to Russians (**March**). Spurred by Schuman Plan, six nations form European Coal and Steel Community (**April**); effective 1952. Japanese peace treaty signed in San Francisco by 49 nations (**Sept. 8**). Color television introduced in U.S. Libya gains independence (**Dec. 24**).

1952 George VI dies; his daughter becomes Elizabeth II (**Feb. 6**). AEC announces "satisfactory" experiments in hydrogen-weapons research; eyewitnesses tell of blasts near Enewetak (**Nov.**). Ralph Ellison's *The Invisible Man*.

1953 Gen. Dwight D. Eisenhower inaugurated president of United States (**Jan. 20**). Stalin dies (**March 5**). Malenkov becomes Soviet premier; Beria, minister of interior; Molotov, foreign minister (**March 6**). Dag Hammarskjöld begins term as UN secretary-general (**April 10**). James Watson and Francis Crick publish their discovery of the molecular model of DNA (**April–May**). Edmund Hillary of New Zealand and Tenzing Norgay of Nepal reach top of Mt. Everest (**May 29**). East Berliners rise against Communist rule; quelled by tanks (**June 17**). Egypt becomes republic ruled by military junta (**June 18**). Julius and Ethel Rosenberg executed in Sing Sing prison (**June 19**). Korean armistice signed (**July 27**). Moscow announces explosion of hydrogen bomb (**Aug. 20**). Tito becomes president of Yugoslavia. James Watson, Francis Crick, and Rosalind Franklin discover structure of DNA. Ernest Hemingway wins Pulitzer for *The Old Man and the Sea*.

1954 First atomic submarine *Nautilus* launched (**Jan. 21**). Five U.S. congressmen shot on floor of House as Puerto Rican nationalists fire from spectators' gallery; all five recover (**March 1**). Soviet Union grants sovereignty to East Germany (**March 23**). *Army* v. *McCarthy* inquiry—Senate subcommittee report blames both sides (**April 22–June 17**). Dien Bien Phu, French military outpost in Vietnam, falls to Vietminh army (**May 7**). U.S. Supreme Court (in *Brown* v. *Board of Education of Topeka*) unanimously bans racial segregation in public schools (**May 17**). Eisenhower launches world atomic pool without Soviet Union (**Sept. 6**). Eight-nation Southeast Asia defense treaty (SEATO) signed at Manila (**Sept. 8**). Dr. Jonas Salk starts inoculating children against polio. Algerian War of Independence against France begins (**Nov.**); France struggles to maintain colonial rule until 1962 when it agrees to Algeria's independence. William Faulkner's *A Fable* wins Pulitzer.

Tennessee Williams
(1911–1983)

Woody Guthrie
(1912–1967)

Dwight D. Eisenhower
(1890–1969)

Dag Hammarskjöld
(1905–1961)

KOREAN WAR (1950–1953)

1950 North Korean Communist forces invade South Korea (**June 25**). UN calls for cease-fire and asks UN members to assist South Korea (**June 27**). Truman orders U.S. forces into Korea (**June 27**). North Koreans capture Seoul (**June 28**). Gen. Douglas MacArthur designated commander of unified forces (**July 8**). Pusan Beachhead—UN forces counterattack and capture Seoul (**Aug.–Sept.**), capture Pyongyang, North Korean capital (**Oct.**). Chinese Communists enter war

(**Oct. 26**), force UN retreat toward 39th parallel (**Dec.**).

1951 Gen. Matthew B. Ridgeway replaces MacArthur after he threatens Chinese with massive retaliation (**April 11**). Armistice negotiations (**July**) continue with interruptions until **June 1953**.

1953 Armistice signed (**July 27**). Chinese troops withdraw from North Korea (**Oct. 26, 1958**), but over 200 violations of armistice noted in **1959**.

Fidel Castro
(1926–)

John H. Glenn, Jr.
(1921–)

Martin Luther King, Jr.
(1929–1968)

John F. Kennedy
(1917–1963)

1955   Nikolai A. Bulganin becomes Soviet premier, replacing Malenkov (**Feb. 8**). Churchill resigns; Anthony Eden succeeds him (**April 6**). West Germany becomes a sovereign state (**May 5**). Western European Union (WEU) comes into being (**May 6**). Warsaw Pact, east European mutual defense agreement, signed (**May 14**). Argentina ousts Perón (**Sept. 19**). President Eisenhower suffers coronary thrombosis in Denver (**Sept. 24**). Rosa Parks refuses to sit at the back of the bus. Martin Luther King, Jr., leads black boycott of Montgomery, Ala., bus system (**Dec. 1**); desegregated service begins **Dec. 21, 1956**. AFL and CIO become one organization—AFL-CIO (**Dec. 5**). Tennessee Williams's *Cat on a Hot Tin Roof* wins Pulitzer.

1956   Nikita Khrushchev, First Secretary of U.S.S.R. Communist Party, denounces Stalin's excesses (**Feb. 24**). First aerial H-bomb tested over Namu islet, Bikini Atoll—10 million tons TNT equivalent (**May 21**). Workers' uprising against Communist rule in Poznan, Poland, is crushed (**June 28–30**); rebellion inspires Hungarian students to stage a protest against Communism in Budapest (**Oct. 23**). Egypt takes control of Suez Canal (**July 26**). Hungarian rebellion forces Soviet troops to withdraw from Budapest (**Oct.**). Israel launches attack on Egypt's Sinai peninsula and drives toward Suez Canal (**Oct. 29**). Imre Nagy announces Hungary's withdrawal from Warsaw Pact (**Nov. 1**); Soviet troops enter and reclaim Budapest (**Nov. 4**). British and French invade Port Said on the Suez Canal (**Nov. 5**). Cease-fire forced by U.S. pressure stops British, French, and Israeli advance (**Nov. 6**). Morocco gains independence. Ingmar Bergman's *The Seventh Seal*. Woody Guthrie composes "This Land is Your Land." Allen Ginsberg's *Howl*.

1957   Eisenhower Doctrine calls for aid to Mideast countries which resist armed aggression from Communist-controlled nations (**Jan. 5**). The "Little Rock Nine" integrate Arkansas high school. Eisenhower sends troops to quell mob and protect school integration (**Sept. 24**). Russians launch *Sputnik I*, first Earth-orbiting satellite—the Space Age begins (**Oct. 4**).

1958   European Economic Community (Common Market) becomes effective (**Jan. 1**). Army's Jupiter-C rocket fires first U.S. Earth satellite, *Explorer I*, into orbit (**Jan. 31**). Egypt and Syria merge into United Arab Republic (**Feb. 1**). Khrushchev becomes premier of Soviet Union as Bulganin resigns (**Mar. 27**). Gen. Charles de Gaulle becomes French premier (**June 1**), remaining in power until 1969. Eisenhower orders U.S. Marines into Lebanon at request of President Chamoun, who fears overthrow (**July 15**). New French constitution adopted (**Sept. 28**), de Gaulle elected president of 5th Republic (**Dec. 21**).

1959   Cuban President Batista resigns and flees—Castro takes over (**Jan. 1**). Tibet's Dalai Lama escapes to India (**Mar. 31**). St. Lawrence Seaway opens, allowing ocean ships to reach Midwest (**April 25**). Alaska and Hawaii become states. Leakeys discover hominid fossils.

1960   American U-2 spy plane, piloted by Francis Gary Powers, shot down over Russia (**May 1**). Khrushchev kills Paris summit conference because of U-2 (**May 16**). Top Nazi murderer of Jews, Adolf Eichmann, captured by Israelis in Argentina (**May 23**)—executed in Israel in 1962. Powers sentenced to prison for 10 years (**Aug. 19**)—freed in **February 1962** in exchange for Soviet spy. Communist China and Soviet Union split in conflict over Communist ideology. Senegal, Ghana, Nigeria, Madagascar, and Zaire (Belgian Congo) gain independence. Cuba begins confiscation of $770 million of U.S. property (**Aug. 7**). There are 900 U.S. military advisers in South Vietnam.

1961   U.S. breaks diplomatic relations with Cuba (**Jan. 3**). Robert Frost recites "The Gift Outright" at John F. Kennedy's inauguration as president of U.S. (**Jan. 20**). Moscow announces putting first man in orbit around Earth, Maj. Yuri A. Gagarin (**April 12**). Cuba invaded at Bay of Pigs by an estimated 1,200 anti-Castro exiles aided by U.S.; invasion crushed (**April 17**). First U.S. spaceman, Navy Cmdr. Alan B. Shepard, Jr., rockets 116.5 miles up in 302-mile trip (**May 5**). Virgil Grissom becomes second American astronaut, making 118-mile-high, 303-mile-long rocket flight over Atlantic (**July 21**). Gherman Stepanovich Titov is launched in Soviet spaceship *Vostok II:* makes 17½ orbits in 25 hours, covering 434,960 miles before landing safely (**Aug. 6**). East Germans erect Berlin Wall between East and West Berlin to halt flood of refugees (**Aug. 13**). U.S.S.R. fires 50-megaton hydrogen bomb, biggest explosion in history (**Oct. 29**). There are 2,000 U.S. military advisers in South Vietnam.

1962 Lt. Col. John H. Glenn, Jr., is first American to orbit Earth—three times in 4 hr 55 min **(Feb. 20).** France transfers sovereignty to new republic of Algeria **(July 3).** Cuban missile crisis—U.S.S.R. to build missile bases in Cuba; Kennedy orders Cuban blockade, lifts blockade after Russians back down **(Aug.–Nov.).** James H. Meredith, escorted by federal marshals, registers at University of Mississippi **(Oct. 1).** Pope John XXIII opens Second Vatican Council **(Oct. 11)**—Council holds four sessions, finally closing **Dec. 8, 1965.** Cuba releases 1,113 prisoners of 1961 invasion attempt **(Dec. 24).** Burundi, Jamaica, Western Samoa, Uganda, and Trinidad and Tobago become independent. William Faulkner wins Pulitzer for *The Reivers.* Rachel Carson's *Silent Spring.*

**James H. Meredith
(1933–)**

1963 France and West Germany sign treaty of cooperation ending four centuries of conflict **(Jan. 22).** Michael E. De Bakey implants artificial heart in human for first time at Houston hospital; plastic device functions and patient lives for four days **(April 21).** Pope John XXIII dies **(June 3)**—succeeded **June 21** by Cardinal Montini, who becomes Paul VI. U.S. Supreme Court rules no locality may require recitation of Lord's Prayer or Bible verses in public schools **(June 17).** U.K.'s Profumo scandal **(June).** Civil rights rally held by 200,000 blacks and whites in Washington, D.C.; Martin Luther King delivers "I have a dream" speech **(Aug. 28).** Washington-to-Moscow "hot line" communications link opens, designed to reduce risk of accidental war **(Aug. 30).** President Kennedy shot and killed by sniper in Dallas, Tex. Lyndon B. Johnson becomes president same day **(Nov. 22).** Lee Harvey Oswald, accused assassin of President Kennedy, is shot and killed by Jack Ruby, Dallas nightclub owner **(Nov. 24).** Kenya achieves independence. Betty Friedan publishes *The Feminine Mystique.* There are 15,000 U.S. military advisers in South Vietnam.

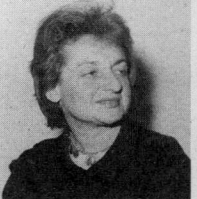

**Betty Friedan
(1921–)**

VIETNAM WAR (1950–1975)

U.S., South Vietnam, and Allies versus North Vietnam and National Liberation Front (Viet Cong).

1950 President Truman sends 35-man military advisory group to aid French fighting to maintain colonial power in Vietnam.

1954 After defeat of French at Dien Bien Phu, Geneva Agreements **(July)** provide for withdrawal of French and Vietminh to either side of demarcation zone (DMZ) pending reunification elections, which are never held. Presidents Eisenhower and Kennedy (from 1954 onward) send civilian advisers and, later, military personnel to train South Vietnamese.

1960 Communists form National Liberation Front in South.

1960–1963 U.S. military advisers in South Vietnam rise from 900 to 15,000.

1963 Ngo Dinh Diem, South Vietnam's premier, slain in coup **(Nov. 1).**

1964 North Vietnamese torpedo boats reportedly attack U.S. destroyers in Gulf of Tonkin **(Aug. 2).** President Johnson orders retaliatory air strikes. Congress approves Gulf of Tonkin resolution **(Aug. 7)** authorizing president to take "all necessary measures" to win in Vietnam, allowing for the war's expansion.

1965 U.S. planes begin combat missions over South Vietnam. In **June,** 23,000 American advisers committed to combat. By end of year over 184,000 U.S. troops in area.

1966 B-52s bomb DMZ, reportedly used by North Vietnam for entry into South **(July 31).**

1967 South Vietnam National Assembly approves election of Nguyen Van Thieu as president **(Oct. 21).**

1968 U.S. has almost 525,000 men in Vietnam. In Tet offensive **(Jan.–Feb.),** Viet Cong guerrillas attack Saigon, Hue, and some provincial capitals. In My Lai massacre, American soldiers kill 300 Vietnamese villagers **(March 16).** President Johnson orders halt to U.S. bombardment of North Vietnam **(Oct. 31).** Saigon and N.L.F. join U.S. and North Vietnam in Paris peace talks.

1969 President Nixon announces Vietnam peace offer **(May 14)**—begins troop withdrawals **(June).** Viet Cong forms Provisional Revolutionary Government. U.S. Senate calls for curb on commitments **(June 25).** Ho Chi Minh, 79, North Vietnam president, dies **(Sept. 3);** collective leadership chosen. Some 6,000 U.S. troops pulled back from Thailand and 1,000 marines from Vietnam (announced **Sept. 30).** Massive demonstrations in U.S. protest or support war policies **(Oct. 15).**

1970 U.S. troops invade Cambodia in order to destroy North Vietnamese sanctuaries **(May 1).**

1971 Congress bars use of combat troops, but not air power, in Laos and Cambodia **(Jan. 1).** South Vietnamese troops, with U.S. air cover, fail in Laos thrust. Many American ground forces withdrawn from Vietnam combat. *New York Times* publishes Pentagon papers, classified material on expansion of war **(June).**

1972 Nixon responds to North Vietnamese drive across DMZ by ordering mining of North Vietnam ports and heavy bombing of Hanoi-Haiphong area **(April 1).** Nixon orders "Christmas bombing" of North to get North Vietnamese back to conference table **(Dec.).**

1973 President orders halt to offensive operations in North Vietnam **(Jan. 15).** Representatives of North and South Vietnam, U.S., and N.L.F. sign peace pacts in Paris, ending longest war in U.S. history **(Jan. 27).** Last American troops departed in their entirety **(March 29).**

1974 Both sides accuse each other of frequent violations of cease-fire agreement.

1975 Full-scale warfare resumes. South Vietnam premier Nguyen Van Thieu resigns **(April 21).** South Vietnamese government surrenders to North Vietnam; U.S. Marine embassy guards and U.S. civilians and dependents evacuated **(April 30).** More than 140,000 Vietnamese refugees leave by air and sea, many to settle in U.S. Provisional Revolutionary Government takes control **(June 6).**

1976 Election of National Assembly paves way for reunification of North and South.

The Beatles

**Malcolm X
(1925–1965)**

**Thurgood Marshall
(1908–1993)**

**Lyndon B. Johnson
(1908–1973)**

**Richard Nixon
(1913–1994)**

1964 U.S. Supreme Court rules that congressional districts should be roughly equal in population (**Feb. 17**). Jack Ruby convicted of murder in slaying of Lee Harvey Oswald; sentenced to death by Dallas jury (**March 14**)—conviction reversed **Oct. 5, 1966;** Ruby dies **Jan. 3, 1967,** before second trial can be held. Three civil rights workers—Schwerner, Goodman, and Cheney—murdered in Mississippi (**June**). Twenty-one arrests result in trial and conviction of seven by federal jury. Nelson Mandela sentenced to life imprisonment (**June 11**). Congress approves Gulf of Tonkin resolution (**Aug. 7**). President's Commission on the Assassination of President Kennedy issues Warren Report concluding that Lee Harvey Oswald acted alone. The Beatles appear on *The Ed Sullivan Show.*

1965 Rev. Dr. Martin Luther King, Jr., and more than 2,600 other blacks arrested in Selma, Ala., during three-day demonstrations against voter-registration rules (**Feb. 1**). Malcolm X, black-nationalist leader, shot to death at Harlem rally in New York City (**Feb. 21**). U.S. Marines land in Dominican Republic as fighting persists between rebels and Dominican army (**April 28**). Medicare, senior citizens' government medical assistance program, begins (**July 1**). Blacks riot for six days in Watts section of Los Angeles: 34 dead, over 1,000 injured, nearly 4,000 arrested, fire damage put at $175 million (**Aug. 11–16**). Power failure in Ontario plant blacks out parts of eight states of northeast U.S. and two provinces of southeast Canada (**Nov. 9**). Ralph Nader's *Unsafe at Any Speed.*

1966 Black teenagers riot in Watts, Los Angeles; two men killed and at least 25 injured (**March 15**). Supreme Court decides *Miranda* v. *Arizona.*

1967 Three Apollo astronauts—Col. Virgil I. Grissom, Col. Edward White II, and Lt. Cmdr. Roger B. Chaffee—killed in spacecraft fire during simulated launch (**Jan. 27**). Biafra secedes from Nigeria (**May 30**). Israeli and Arab forces battle; six-day war ends with Israel occupying Sinai Peninsula, Golan Heights, Gaza Strip, and east bank of Suez Canal (**June 5**). Red China announces explosion of its first hydrogen bomb (**June 17**). Racial violence in Detroit; 7,000 National Guardsmen aid police after night of rioting. Similar outbreaks occur in New York City's Spanish Harlem, Rochester, N.Y., Birmingham, Ala., and New Britain, Conn. (**July 23**). Thurgood Marshall sworn in as first black U.S. Supreme Court justice (**Oct. 2**). Dr. Christiaan N. Barnard and team of South African surgeons perform world's first successful human heart transplant (**Dec. 3**)—patient dies 18 days later.

1968 North Korea seizes U.S. Navy ship *Pueblo;* holds 83 on board as spies (**Jan. 23**). Tet offensive, turning point in Vietnam war (**Jan.–Feb.**). My Lai massacre (**March 16**). President Johnson announces he will not seek or accept presidential renomination (**March 31**). Martin Luther King, Jr., civil rights leader, is slain in Memphis (**April 4**)—James Earl Ray, indicted in murder, captured in London on **June 8.** In 1969 Ray pleads guilty and is sentenced to 99 years. Sen. Robert F. Kennedy is shot and critically wounded in Los Angeles hotel after winning California primary (**June 5**)—dies **June 6.** Sirhan B. Sirhan convicted 1969. Czechoslovakia is invaded by Russians and Warsaw Pact forces to crush liberal regime (**Aug. 20**).

1969 Richard M. Nixon is inaugurated 37th president of the U.S. (**Jan. 20**). Stonewall riot in New York City marks beginning of gay rights movement (**June 28**). Apollo 11 astronauts—Neil A. Armstrong, Edwin E. Aldrin, Jr., and Michael Collins—take man's first walk on moon (**July 20**). Sen. Edward M. Kennedy pleads guilty to leaving scene of fatal accident at Chappaquiddick, Mass. (**July 18**), in which Mary Jo Kopechne was drowned—gets two-month suspended sentence (**July 25**). Woodstock Festival (**Aug. 15–17**). *Sesame Street* debuts. Internet (ARPA) goes online.

1970 Biafra surrenders after 32-month fight for independence from Nigeria (**Jan. 15**). Rhodesia severs last tie with British crown and declares itself a racially segregated republic (**March 1**). U.S. troops invade Cambodia (**May 1**). Four students at Kent State University in Ohio slain by National Guardsmen at demonstration protesting incursion into Cambodia (**May 4**). Senate repeals Gulf of Tonkin resolution (**June 24**).

1971 Supreme Court rules unanimously that busing of students may be ordered to achieve racial desegregation (**April 20**). Anti-war militants attempt to disrupt government business in Washington (**May 3**)—police and military units arrest as many as 12,000; most are later released. *Pentagon Papers* published (**June**). Twenty-sixth Amendment to U.S. Constitution lowers voting age to 18. UN seats Communist China and expels Nationalist China (**Oct. 25**).

1972 President Nixon makes unprecedented eight-day visit to Communist China and meets with Mao Zedong **(Feb. 21–27).** Britain takes over direct rule of Northern Ireland in bid for peace **(March 24).** Gov. George C. Wallace of Alabama is shot by Arthur H. Bremer at Laurel, Md., political rally **(May 15).** Five men are apprehended by police in attempt to bug Democratic National Committee headquarters in Washington, D.C.'s Watergate complex—start of the Watergate scandal **(June 17).** Supreme Court rules that death penalty is unconstitutional **(June 29).** Eleven Israeli athletes at Olympic Games in Munich are killed after eight members of an Arab terrorist group invade Olympic Village; five guerrillas and one policeman are also killed **(Sept. 5).** "Christmas bombing" of North Vietnam **(Dec. 25).**

1973 Great Britain, Ireland, and Denmark enter European Economic Community **(Jan. 1).** Supreme Court rules on *Roe* v. *Wade* **(Jan. 22).** Vietnam War ends with signing of peace pacts **(Jan. 27).** Nixon, on national TV, accepts responsibility, but not blame, for Watergate; accepts resignations of advisers H. R. Haldeman and John D. Ehrlichman, fires John W. Dean III as counsel **(April 30).** Greek military junta abolishes monarchy and proclaims republic **(June 1).** U.S. bombing of Cambodia ends, marking official halt to 12 years of combat activity in Southeast Asia **(Aug. 15).** Chile's Marxist president, Salvadore Allende, is overthrown **(Sept. 11).** Fourth and biggest Arab-Israeli conflict begins as Egyptian and Syrian forces attack Israel as Jews mark Yom Kippur, holiest day in their calendar **(Oct. 6).** Spiro T. Agnew resigns as vice president and then, in federal court in Baltimore, pleads no contest to charges of evasion of income taxes on $29,500 he received in 1967, while governor of Maryland. He is fined $10,000 and put on three years' probation **(Oct. 10).** In the "Saturday Night Massacre," Nixon fires special Watergate prosecutor Archibald Cox and Deputy Attorney General William D. Ruckelshaus; Attorney General Elliot L. Richardson resigns **(Oct. 20).** Egypt and Israel sign U.S.-sponsored cease-fire accord **(Nov. 11).** Duke Ellington's autobiography, *Music Is My Mistress,* is published.

1974 Patricia Hearst, 19-year-old daughter of publisher Randolph Hearst, kidnapped by Symbionese Liberation Army **(Feb. 5).** House Judiciary Committee adopts three articles of impeachment charging President Nixon with obstruction of justice, failure to uphold laws, and refusal to produce material subpoenaed by the committee **(July 30).** Richard M. Nixon announces he will resign the next day, the first president to do so **(Aug. 8).** Vice President Gerald R. Ford of Michigan is sworn in as 38th president of the U.S. **(Aug. 9).** Ford grants "full, free, and absolute pardon" to ex-president Nixon **(Sept. 8).**

1975 John N. Mitchell, H. R. Haldeman, John D. Ehrlichman found guilty of Watergate cover-up **(Jan. 1);** sentenced to 30 months to 8 years in jail **(Feb. 21).** Pol Pot and Khmer Rouge take over Cambodia **(April).** American merchant ship *Mayaguez,* seized by Cambodian forces, is rescued in operation by U.S. Navy and Marines, 38 of whom are killed **(May 15).** *Apollo* and *Soyuz* spacecraft take off for U.S.-Soviet link-up in space **(July 15).** President Ford escapes assassination attempt in Sacramento, Calif. **(Sept. 5).** President Ford escapes second assassination attempt in 17 days **(Sept. 22).**

1976 Supreme Court rules that blacks and other minorities are entitled to retroactive job seniority **(March 24).** Ford signs Federal Election Campaign Act **(May 11).** Supreme Court rules that death penalty is not inherently cruel or unusual and is a constitutionally acceptable form of punishment **(July 3).** Nation celebrates bicentennial **(July 4).** Israeli airborne commandos attack Uganda's Entebbe Airport and free 103 hostages held by pro-Palestinian hijackers of Air France plane; one Israeli and several Ugandan soldiers killed in raid **(July 4).** Mysterious disease that eventually claims 29 lives strikes American Legion convention in Philadelphia **(Aug. 4).** Jimmy Carter elected U.S. president **(Nov. 2).**

1977 First woman Episcopal priest ordained **(Jan. 1).** Scientists identify previously unknown bacterium as cause of mysterious "legionnaire's disease" **(Jan. 18).** Carter pardons Vietnam draft evaders **(Jan. 21).** Scientists report using bacteria in lab to make insulin **(May 23).** Supreme Court rules that states are not required to spend Medicaid funds on elective abortions **(June 20).** Deng Xiaoping, purged Chinese leader, restored to power as "Gang of Four" is expelled from Communist Party **(July 22).** South African activist Stephen Biko dies in police custody

Mao Zedong
(1893–1976)

Duke Ellington
(1899–1974)

Gerald R. Ford
(1913–)

Jimmy Carter
(1924–)

**Pope John Paul II
(1920–)**

**Anwar Sadat
(1918–1981)**

**Ayatollah Ruhollah
Khomeini
(1900–1989)**

**Ronald Reagan
(1911–)**

**Sandra Day O'Connor
(1930–)**

(**Sept. 12**). Nuclear-proliferation pact, curbing spread of nuclear weapons, signed by 15 countries, including U.S. and U.S.S.R. (**Sept. 21**).

1978 President chooses Federal Appeals Court Judge William H. Webster as F.B.I. Director (**Jan. 19**). Rhodesia's prime minister Ian D. Smith and three black leaders agree on transfer to black majority rule (**Feb. 15**). U.S. Senate approves Panama Canal neutrality treaty (**March 16**); votes treaty to turn canal over to Panama by year 2000 (**April 18**). Former Italian premier Aldo Moro kidnapped by left wing terrorists, who kill five bodyguards (**March 16**); he is found slain (**May 9**). Californians in referendum approve Proposition 13 for nearly 60% slash in property tax revenues (**June 6**). Supreme Court, in Bakke case, bars quota systems in college admissions but affirms constitutionality of programs giving advantage to minorities (**June 28**). Pope Paul VI, dead at 80, mourned (**Aug. 6**); new Pope, John Paul I, 65, dies unexpectedly after 34 days in office (**Sept. 28**); succeeded by Karol Cardinal Wojtyla of Poland as John Paul II (**Oct. 16**). "Framework for Peace" in Middle East signed by Egypt's president Anwar Sadat and Israeli premier Menachem Begin after 13-day conference at Camp David led by President Carter (**Sept. 17**). Jim Jones's followers commit mass suicide in Jonestown, Guyana (**Nov. 18**).

1979 Oil spills pollute ocean waters in Atlantic and Gulf of Mexico (**Jan. 1, June 8, July 21**). Ohio agrees to pay $675,000 to families of dead and injured in Kent State University shootings (**Jan. 4**). Vietnam and Vietnam-backed Cambodian insurgents announce fall of Phnom Penh, Cambodian capital, and collapse of Pol Pot regime (**Jan. 7**). Shah leaves Iran after year of turmoil (**Jan. 16**); revolutionary forces under Muslim leader, Ayatollah Ruhollah Khomeini, take over (**Feb. 1** *et seq.*). Conservatives win British election; Margaret Thatcher new prime minister (**March 28**). Nuclear power plant accident at Three Mile Island, Pa., releases radiation (**March 28**). Carter and Brezhnev sign SALT II agreement (**June 14**). Nicaraguan president Gen. Anastasio Somoza Debayle resigns and flees to Miami (**July 17**); Sandinistas form government (**July 19**). Earl Mountbatten of Burma, 79, British World War II hero, and three others killed by blast on fishing boat off Irish coast (**Aug. 27**); two I.R.A. members accused (**Aug. 30**). Iranian militants seize U.S. embassy in Teheran and hold hostages (**Nov. 4**). Soviet invasion of Afghanistan stirs world protests (**Dec. 27**).

1980 Six U.S. embassy aides escape from Iran with Canadian help (**Jan. 29**). F.B.I.'s undercover operation "Abscam" (for Arab scam) implicates public officials (**Feb. 2**). U.S. breaks diplomatic ties with Iran (**April 7**). Eight U.S. servicemen are killed and five are injured as helicopter and cargo plane collide in abortive desert raid to rescue American hostages in Teheran (**April 25**). Supreme Court upholds limits on federal aid for abortions (**June 30**). Shah of Iran dies at 60 (**July 27**). Anastasio Somoza Debayle, ousted Nicaragua ruler, and two aides assassinated in Asunción, Paraguay capital (**Sept. 17**). Iraq troops hold 90 square miles of Iran after invasion; 8-year Iran-Iraq war begins (**Sept. 19**). Ronald Reagan elected president in Republican sweep (**Nov. 4**). Three U.S. nuns and lay worker found shot in El Salvador (**Dec. 4**). John Lennon of the Beatles shot dead in New York City (**Dec. 8**). Smallpox eradicated.

1981 Ronald Reagan takes oath as 40th president (**Jan. 20**). U.S.-Iran agreement frees 52 hostages held in Teheran since 1979 (**Jan. 20**); hostages welcomed back in U.S. (**Jan. 25**). President Reagan wounded by gunman, with press secretary and two law-enforcement officers (**March 30**). Pope John Paul II wounded by gunman (**May 14**). Supreme Court rules, 4–4, that former president Nixon and three top aides may be required to pay monetary damages for unconstitutional wiretap of home telephone of former national security aide (**June 22**). Reagan nominates Judge Sandra Day O'Connor, 51, of Arizona, as first woman on Supreme Court (**July 7**). More than 110 die in collapse of aerial walkways in lobby of Hyatt Regency Hotel in Kansas City; 188 injured (**July 18**). Air controllers strike, disrupting flights (**Aug. 3**); government dismisses strikers (**Aug. 11**). AIDS is first identified.

1982 British overcome Argentina in Falklands war (**April 2–June 15**). Israel invades Lebanon in attack on P.L.O. (**June 4**). John W. Hinckley, Jr., found not guilty because of insanity in shooting of President Reagan (**June 21**). Alexander M. Haig, Jr., resigns as secretary of state (**June 25**). Equal Rights Amendment fails ratification (**June 30**). Princess

Grace, 52, dies of injuries when car plunges off mountain road; daughter Stephanie, 17, suffers serious injuries (**Sept. 14**). Lebanese Christian Phalangists kill hundreds of people in two Palestinian refugee camps in West Beirut (**Sept. 15**). Leonid Brezhnev, Soviet leader, dies at 75 (**Nov. 10**). Yuri V. Andropov, 68, chosen as successor (**Nov. 15**). Permanent artificial heart implanted in human for first time in Dr. Barney B. Clark, 61, at University of Utah Medical Center in Salt Lake City (**Dec. 2**).

Indira Gandhi
(1917–1984)

1983 Pope John Paul II signs new Roman Catholic code incorporating changes brought about by Second Vatican Council (**Jan. 25**). Second space shuttle, *Challenger,* makes successful maiden voyage, which includes the first U.S. space walk in nine years (**April 4**). U.S. Supreme Court declares many local abortion restrictions unconstitutional (**June 15**). Sally K. Ride, 32, first U.S. woman astronaut in space as a crew member aboard space shuttle *Challenger* (**June 18**). U.S. admits shielding former Nazi Gestapo chief Klaus Barbie, 69, the "butcher of Lyon," wanted in France for war crimes (**Aug. 15**). Benigno S. Aquino, Jr., 50, political rival of Philippines president Marcos, slain in Manila (**Aug. 21**). South Korean Boeing 747 jetliner bound for Seoul apparently strays into Soviet airspace and is shot down by a Soviet SU-15 fighter after it had tracked the airliner for two hours; all 269 aboard are killed, including 61 Americans (**Aug. 30**). Terrorist explosion kills 237 U.S. Marines in Beirut (**Oct. 23**). U.S. and Caribbean allies invade Grenada (**Oct. 25**).

1984 Bell System broken up (**Jan. 1**). France gets first deliveries of Soviet natural gas (**Jan. 1**). Syria frees captured U.S. Navy pilot, Lieut. Robert C. Goodman, Jr. (**Jan. 3**). U.S. and Vatican exchange diplomats after 116-year hiatus (**Jan. 10**). Reagan orders U.S. Marines withdrawn from Beirut international peacekeeping force (**Feb. 7**). Yuri V. Andropov dies at 69; Konstantin U. Chernenko, 72, named Soviet Union leader (**Feb. 9**). Italy and Vatican agree to end Roman Catholicism as state religion (**Feb. 18**). Reagan ends U.S. role in Beirut by relieving Sixth Fleet from peacekeeping force (**March 30**). Congress rebukes President Reagan on use of federal funds for mining Nicaraguan harbors (**April 10**). Soviet Union withdraws from summer Olympic games in U.S., and other bloc nations follow (**May 7** *et seq.*). José Napoleón Duarte, moderate, elected president of El Salvador (**May 11**). Three hundred slain as Indian Army occupies Sikh Golden Temple in Amritsar (**June 6**). Thirty-ninth Democratic National Convention, in San Francisco, nominates Walter F. Mondale and Geraldine A. Ferraro (**July 16–19**). Thirty-third Republican National Convention, at Dallas, renominates President Reagan and Vice President Bush (**Aug. 20–25**). Brian Mulroney and Conservative party win Canadian election in landslide (**Sept. 4**). Indian prime minister Indira Gandhi assassinated by two Sikh bodyguards; 1,000 killed in anti-Sikh riots; son Rajiv succeeds her (**Oct. 31**). President Reagan re-elected in landslide with 59% of vote (**Nov. 7**). Toxic gas leaks from Union Carbide plant in Bhopal, India, killing 2,000 and injuring 150,000 (**Dec. 3**).

Corazon Aquino
(1933–)

Mikhail S. Gorbachev
(1931–)

1985 Ronald Reagan, 73, takes oath for second term as 40th president (**Jan. 20**). General Westmoreland settles libel action against CBS (**Feb. 18**). Prime Minister Margaret Thatcher addresses Congress, endorsing Reagan's policies (**Feb. 20**). U.S.S.R. leader Chernenko dies at 73 and is replaced by Mikhail Gorbachev, 54 (**March 11**). Two Shi'ite Muslim gunmen capture TWA airliner with 133 aboard, 104 of them Americans (**June 14**); 39 remaining hostages freed in Beirut (**June 30**). Supreme Court, 5–4, bars public school teachers from parochial schools (**July 1**). Arthur James Walker, 50, retired naval officer, convicted by federal judge of participating in Soviet spy ring operated by his brother, John Walker (**Aug. 9**). P.L.O. terrorists hijack *Achille Lauro,* Italian cruise ship, with 80 passengers, plus crew (**Oct. 7**); American, Leon Klinghoffer, killed (**Oct. 8**); Italian government toppled by political crisis over hijacking (**Oct. 16**). John A. Walker and son, Michael I. Walker, 22, sentenced in Navy espionage case (**Oct. 28**). Reagan and Gorbachev meet at summit (**Nov. 19**); agree to step up arms control talks and renew cultural contacts (**Nov. 21**). Terrorists seize Egyptian Boeing 737 airliner after take-off from Athens (**Nov. 23**); 59 dead as Egyptian forces storm plane on Malta (**Nov. 24**). U.S. budget-balancing bill enacted (**Dec. 12**).

Margaret Thatcher
(1925–)

1986 Spain and Portugal join European Economic Community (**Jan. 1**). President freezes Libyan assets in U.S. (**Jan. 8**). Supreme Court bars racial bias in trial jury selection (**Jan. 14**). *Voyager 2* spacecraft reports secrets of Uranus (**Jan. 26**). Space shuttle *Challenger* explodes after launch at Cape Canaveral, Fla., killing all seven aboard (**Jan. 28**). Haiti president

Sally K. Ride
(1951–)

**William Rehnquist
(1924–)**

**George Bush
(1924–)**

**Benazir Bhutto
(1953–)**

Jean-Claude Duvalier flees to France **(Feb. 7)**. President Marcos flees Philippines after ruling 20 years, as newly elected Corazon Aquino succeeds him **(Feb. 26)**. Prime Minister Olof Palme of Sweden shot dead **(Feb. 28)**. Austrian president Kurt Waldheim's service as Nazi army officer revealed **(March 3)**. Union Carbide agrees to settlement with victims of Bhopal gas leak in India **(March 22)**. Halley's comet yields information on return visit **(April 10)**. U.S. planes attack Libyan "terrorist centers" **(April 14)**. Desmond Tutu elected archbishop in South Africa **(April 14)**. Major nuclear accident at Soviet Union's Chernobyl power station alarms world **(April 26** *et seq.*). Ex-Navy analyst, Jonathan Jay Pollard, 31, guilty as spy for Israel **(June 4)**. Supreme Court reaffirms abortion rights **(June 11)**. World Court rules U.S. broke international law in mining Nicaraguan waters **(June 27)**. Supreme Court voids automatic provisions of budget-balancing law **(July 7)**. Jerry A. Whitworth, ex-Navy radioman, convicted as spy **(July 24)**; he is also part of Walker family spy ring. Muslim captors release Rev. Lawrence Martin Jenco **(July 26)**. Senate Judiciary Committee approves William H. Rehnquist as chief justice of U.S. **(Aug. 14)**. House votes arms appropriations bill rejecting administration's "star wars" policy **(Aug. 15)**. Three Lutheran church groups in U.S. set to merge **(Aug. 29)**. Congress overrides Reagan veto of stiff sanctions against South Africa **(Sept. 29** and **Oct. 2)**. Congress approves immigration bill barring hiring of illegal aliens, with amnesty provision **(Oct. 17)**. Reagan signs $11.7-billion budget reduction measure **(Oct. 21)**. He approves sweeping revision of U.S. tax code **(Oct. 22)**. Democrats triumph in elections, gaining eight seats to win Senate majority **(Nov. 4)**. Secret initiative to send arms to Iran revealed **(Nov. 6** *et seq.*); Reagan denies exchanging arms for hostages and halts arms sales **(Nov. 19)**; diversion of funds from arms sales to Nicaraguan Contras revealed **(Nov. 25)**.

1987 William Buckley, U.S. hostage in Lebanon, reported slain **(Jan. 20)**. Supreme Court rules Rotary Clubs must admit women **(May 4)**. Iraqi missiles kill 37 in attack on U.S. frigate *Stark* in Persian Gulf **(May 17)**; Iraqi president apologizes **(May 18)**. Prime Minister Thatcher wins rare third term in Britain **(June 11)**. Supreme Court justice Lewis F. Powell, Jr., retires **(June 26)**. Klaus Barbie, 73, Gestapo wartime chief in Lyon, sentenced to life by French court for war crimes **(July 4)**. Oliver North, Jr., tells congressional inquiry higher officials approved his secret Iran-Contra operations **(July 7–10)**. Admiral John M. Poindexter, former National Security Adviser, testifies he authorized use of Iran arms sale profits to aid Contras **(July 15–22)**. Secretary of State George P. Shultz testifies he was deceived repeatedly on Iran-Contra affair **(July 23–24)**. Defense Secretary Caspar W. Weinberger tells inquiry of official deception and intrigue **(July 31, Aug. 3)**. Reagan says Iran arms-Contra policy went astray and accepts responsibility **(Aug. 12)**. Severe earthquake strikes Los Angeles, leaving 100 injured and six dead **(Oct. 1)**. Senate, 58–42, rejects Robert H. Bork as Supreme Court justice **(Oct. 23)**.

1988 U.S. and Canada reach free trade agreement **(Jan. 2)**. Robert C. McFarlane, former National Security Adviser, pleads guilty in Iran-Contra case **(March 11)**. U.S. Navy ship shoots down Iranian airliner in Persian Gulf, mistaking it for jet fighter; 290 killed **(July 3)**. Terrorists kill nine tourists on Aegean cruise **(July 11)**. Democratic convention nominates Gov. Michael Dukakis of Massachusetts for president and Texas senator Lloyd Bentsen for vice president **(July 17** *et seq.*). Republicans nominate George Bush for president and Indiana senator Dan Quayle for vice president **(Aug. 15** *et seq.*). Plane blast kills Pakistani president Mohammad Zia ul-Haq **(Aug. 17)**. Republicans sweep 40 states in election. Bush beats Dukakis **(Nov. 8)**. Benazir Bhutto, first Islamic woman prime minister, chosen to lead Pakistan **(Dec. 1)**. Pan-Am 747 explodes from terrorist bomb and crashes in Lockerbie, Scotland, killing all 259 aboard and 11 on ground **(Dec. 21)**.

1989 U.S. planes shoot down two Libyan fighters over international waters in Mediterranean **(Jan. 4)**. Emperor Hirohito of Japan dead at 87 **(Jan. 7)**. George Herbert Walker Bush inaugurated as 41st U.S. president **(Jan. 20)**. Iran's Ayatollah Khomeini declares author Salman Rushdie's book *The Satanic Verses* offensive and sentences him to death **(Feb. 14)**. Ruptured tanker *Exxon Valdez* sends 11 million gallons of crude oil into Alaska's Prince William Sound **(March 24)**. Tens of thousands of Chinese students take over Beijing's Tiananmen Square in rally for democracy **(April 19** *et seq.*). U.S. jury convicts Oliver North in Iran-Contra affair (**May 4**). More than one million in Beijing demonstrate for democracy; chaos spreads across nation (**mid-May** *et seq.*). Mikhail S. Gorbachev named Soviet president (**May 25**). Thousands killed in Tiananmen Square as Chinese leaders take hard line toward demonstrators (**June 4** *et seq.*). Army general Colin R. Powell is first black chairman of Joint Chiefs of Staff (**Aug. 9**). P. W. Botha quits as South Africa's president (**Aug. 14**). *Voyager 2* spacecraft speeds by Neptune after making startling discoveries about the planet and its moons (**Aug. 29**). Deng Xiaoping resigns from China's leadership (**Nov. 9**). After 28 years, Berlin Wall is open to West (**Nov. 11**). Czech Parliament ends Communists' dominant role (**Nov. 30**). Romanian uprising overthrows Communist government (**Dec. 15** *et seq.*); President Ceausescu and wife executed (**Dec. 25**). U.S. troops invade Panama, seeking capture of Gen. Manuel Noriega (**Dec. 20**); resistance to U.S. collapses (**Dec. 24**). Dalai Lama wins Nobel Peace Prize.

François Mitterrand
(1916–1996)

1990 World Wide Web debuts, popularizes Internet. Gen. Manuel Noriega surrenders in Panama (**Jan. 3**). Yugoslav Communists end 45-year monopoly of power (**Jan. 22**). Soviet Communists relinquish sole power (**Feb. 7**). South Africa frees Nelson Mandela, imprisoned 27½ years (**Feb. 11**). Violeta Barrios de Chamorro inaugurated as Nicaraguan president. Hubble Space Telescope launched (**April 25**). U.S.-Soviet summit reaches accord on armaments (**June 1**). Western Alliance ends cold war and proposes joint action with Soviet Union and Eastern Europe (**July 6**). U.S. Appeals Court overturns Oliver North's Iran-Contra conviction (**July 20**). Iraqi troops invade Kuwait and seize petroleum reserves, setting off Persian Gulf War (**Aug. 2** *et seq.*). East and West Germany reunited (**Oct. 3**). Republicans set back in midterm elections (**Nov. 8**). Gorbachev assumes emergency powers (**Nov. 17**). Leaders of 34 nations in Europe and North America proclaim a united Europe (**Nov. 21**); Margaret Thatcher resigns as British prime minister (**Nov. 22**); John Major succeeds her (**Nov. 28**). Lech Walesa wins Poland's runoff presidential election (**Dec. 9**). Haiti elects leftist priest as president in first democratic election (**Dec. 17**).

General Colin Powell
(1937–)

1991 U.S. and Allies at war with Iraq (**Jan. 15**). Warsaw Pact dissolves military alliance (**Feb. 25**). Cease-fire ends Persian Gulf War; UN forces are victorious (**April 3**). Europeans end sanctions on South Africa (**April 15**). Supreme Court limits death row appeals (**April 16**). Winnie Mandela sentenced in kidnapping (**May 13**). William H. Webster retires as director of CIA; Robert H. Gates succeeds him (**May 14**). France agrees to sign 1968 treaty banning spread of atomic weapons (**June 3**). Communist government of Albania resigns (**June 4**). Jiang Qing, widow of Mao, commits suicide (**June 4**). South African Parliament repeals apartheid laws (**June 5**). Warsaw Pact dissolved (**July 1**). Boris N. Yeltsin inaugurated as first freely elected president of Russian Republic (**July 10**). Bush-Gorbachev summit negotiates strategic arms reduction treaty (**July 31**). China accepts nuclear nonproliferation treaty (**Aug. 10**). Lithuania, Estonia, and Latvia win independence (**Aug. 25**); Bush recognizes them (**Sept. 2**). Haitian

Saddam Hussein
(1937–)

THE PERSIAN GULF WAR (Aug. 2, 1990–April 6, 1991)

1990 Iraq invades its tiny neighbor, Kuwait, after talks break down over oil production and debt repayment. Iraqi president Saddam Hussein later annexes Kuwait and declares it a 19th province of Iraq (**Aug. 2**). President Bush believes that Iraq intends to invade Saudi Arabia and take control of the region's oil supplies. He begins organizing a multinational coalition to seek Kuwait's freedom and restoration of its legitimate government. The UN Security Council authorizes economic sanctions against Iraq. Bush orders U.S. troops to protect Saudi Arabia at the Saudis' request and "Operation Desert Shield" begins (**Aug. 6**). 230,000 American troops arrive in Saudi Arabia to take defensive action, but when Iraq continues a huge military buildup in Kuwait, the President orders an additional 200,000 troops deployed to prepare for a possible offensive action by the U.S.-led coalition forces. He subsequently obtains a UN Security Council resolution setting a **Jan. 15, 1991** deadline for Iraq to withdraw unconditionally from Kuwait (**Nov. 8**).

1991 Bush wins congressional approval for his position with the most devastating air assault in history

against military targets in Iraq and Kuwait (**Jan. 16**). He rejects a Soviet-Iraq peace plan for a gradual withdrawal that does not comply with all the UN resolutions and gives Iraq an ultimatum to withdraw from Kuwait by noon **Feb. 23** (**Feb. 22**). The president orders the ground war to begin (**Feb. 24**). In a brilliant and lightning-fast campaign, U.S. and coalition forces smash through Iraq's defenses and defeat Saddam Hussein's troops in only four days of combat. Allies enter Kuwait City (**Feb. 26**). Iraqi army sets fire to over 500 of Kuwait's oil wells as final act of destruction to Kuwait's infrastructure. Bush orders a unilateral cease-fire 100 hours after the ground offensive started (**Feb. 27**). Allied and Iraqi military leaders meet on battlefield to discuss terms for a formal cease-fire to end the Gulf War. Iraq agrees to abide by all of the UN resolutions (**Mar. 3**). The first Allied prisoners of war are released (**Mar. 4**). Official cease-fire accepted and signed (**April 6**). 532,000 U.S. forces served in Operation Desert Storm. There were a total of 148 U.S. battle deaths during the Gulf War, 145 nonbattle deaths, and 467 wounded in action.

Hubble Space Telescope

Lech Walesa
(1943–)

Toni Morrison
(1931–)

Ruth Bader Ginsburg
(1933–)

troops seize president in uprising (**Sept. 30**). U.S. suspends assistance to Haiti (**Oct. 1**). Professor Anita Hill accuses Judge Clarence Thomas of sexual harassment (**Oct. 6**); Senate, 52–48, confirms Thomas for Supreme Court after stormy hearings (**Oct. 15**). Israel and Soviet Union resume relations after 24 years (**Oct. 18**). U.S. indicts two Libyans in 1988 bombing of Pan Am Flight 103 over Lockerbie, Scotland (**Nov. 15**). Anglican envoy Terry Waite and U.S. Prof. Thomas M. Sutherland freed by Lebanese (**Nov. 18**). Last three U.S. hostages freed in Lebanon (**Dec. 2–4**). Soviet Union breaks up after President Gorbachev's resignation; constituent republics form Commonwealth of Independent States (**Dec. 25**).

1992 Yugoslav Federation broken up (**Jan. 15**). Bush and Yeltsin proclaim formal end to cold war (**Feb. 1**). U.S. lifts trade sanctions against China (**Feb. 21**). U.S. recognizes three former Yugoslav republics (**April 7**). Gen. Noriega, former Panama leader, convicted in U.S. court (**April 9**). Four police officers acquitted in Los Angeles beating of Rodney King; rioting erupts in South-Central Los Angeles (**April 29** *et seq.*). Caspar W. Weinberger indicted in Iran-Contra affair (**June 16**). Last Western hostages freed in Lebanon (**June 17**). Supreme Court reaffirms right to abortion (**June 29**). Democrats nominate Bill Clinton and Al Gore (**July 1**). Gen. Noriega sentenced to 40 years on drug charges (**July 10**). Court clears *Exxon Valdez* skipper (**July 10**). Israeli Parliament approves Yitzhak Rabin's coalition government, dominated by Labor Party (**July 13**). Police officers acquitted in April on criminal charges in Rodney King beating are indicted on federal civil rights charges (**Aug. 5**). North American trade compact announced (**Aug. 12**). Republicans renominate Bush and Quayle (**Aug. 20**). UN expels Serbian-dominated Yugoslavia (**Sept. 22**). Senate ratifies second Strategic Arms Limitation Treaty (**Oct. 1**). Top Japanese leader, Shin Kanemaru, resigns in scandal (**Oct. 14**). Bill Clinton elected president, Al Gore vice president; Democrats keep control of Congress (**Nov. 3**). Russian Parliament approves START treaty (**Nov. 4**). U.S. forces leave Philippines, ending nearly a century of American military presence (**Nov. 24**). Czechoslovak Parliament approves separation into two nations (**Nov. 25**). UN approves U.S.-led force to guard food for Somalia (**Dec. 3**). Prince and Princess of Wales agree to separate (**Dec. 9**). Bush pardons former Reagan administration officials involved in Iran-Contra affair (**Dec. 24**).

1993 Vaclav Havel elected as Czech president (**Jan. 26**). Clinton agrees to compromise on military's ban on homosexuals (**Jan. 29**). U.S. begins airlift of supplies to besieged Bosnia towns (**Feb. 28**). Federal agents besiege Texas Branch Davidian religious cult after six are killed in raid (**March 1** *et seq.*). Five arrested, sixth sought in bombing of World Trade Center in New York (**March 29**). Two police officers convicted on federal civil rights charges in Rodney King beating (**April 17**); sentenced **Aug. 4**. Fire kills 72 as cult standoff in Texas ends with federal assault (**April 19**). President of Sri Lanka assassinated (**May 1**). British Commons approves European unity pact (**May 20**). Twenty-two UN troops killed in Somalia (**June 5**). Ruth Bader Ginsburg appointed to Supreme Court (**June 14**). Iraq accepts UN weapons monitoring (**July 19**). Vincent W. Foster, Jr., senior White House lawyer, commits suicide (**July 22**). Midwest flood damage expected to exceed $10 billion (**July 24**). Israeli-Palestinian accord reached (**Aug. 28**). U.S. agents blamed in Waco, Tex., siege (**Oct. 1**). Yeltsin's forces crush revolt in Russian Parliament (**Oct. 4** *et seq.*). China breaks nuclear test moratorium (**Oct. 5**). Canada's opposition Liberal Party regains power in landslide (**Oct. 25**). Europe's Maastricht Treaty takes effect, creating European Union (**Nov. 1**). Jean Chretien sworn in as Canada's 20th prime minister (**Nov. 4**). House of Representatives approves North American Free Trade Agreement (**Nov. 17**); Senate follows (**Nov. 21**). South Africa adopts majority rule constitution (**Nov. 18**). Clinton signs Brady bill regulating firearms purchases (**Nov. 30**). Toni Morrison wins Nobel prize for literature.

1994 Serbs' heavy weapons pound Sarajevo (**Jan. 5–6**). Olympic figure skater Nancy Kerrigan attacked (**Jan. 6**); three arrested in attack (**Jan. 13**). Major earthquake jolts Los Angeles; 51 dead (**Jan. 17** *et seq.*). Clinton ends trade embargo on Vietnam (**Feb. 9**). Aldrich Ames, high C.I.A. official, charged with spying for Soviets (**Feb. 22**). Four convicted in World Trade Center bombing (**March 4**). Mexican presidential candidate assassinated (**March 23**). Rwandan genocide of Tutsis by Hutus begins; estimated 800,000 slaughtered in c. 100 days (**April 6**). South Africa holds first interracial national election (**April 29**);

Nelson Mandela elected president. Israel and Palestinians sign accord **(May 4).** Clinton accused of sexual harassment while governor of Arkansas **(May 6).** Congress votes protection for women's health clinics **(May 12).** O. J. Simpson arrested in killings of wife, Nicole Brown Simpson, and friend, Ronald Goldman **(June 18).** Supreme Court approves limit on abortion protests **(June 30).** Senate confirms Stephen G. Breyer for Supreme Court **(July 29).** Women's health clinic doctor shot dead outside Florida clinic **(July 29).** Major league baseball players strike **(Aug. 13).** "Carlos the Jackal," international terrorist, captured **(Aug. 15).** IRA declares cease-fire in Northern Ireland **(Aug. 31).** Small plane crashes into White House **(Sept. 12).** Baseball owners end season and cancel World Series **(Sept. 14).** Powerful earthquake strikes Japan **(Oct. 4).** Aristide returns to joyous Haiti **(Oct. 4).** U.S. sends forces to Persian Gulf **(Oct. 7).** Ulster Protestants declare cease-fire **(Oct. 13).** Israel and Jordan sign peace treaty **(Oct. 17).** Reagan, 83, reveals he has Alzheimer's disease **(Nov. 6).** G.O.P. wins control of House and Senate **(Nov. 8).** Aristide forms Haitian government with prime minister and full cabinet **(Nov. 9).** Clinton orders Bosnian arms embargo ended **(Nov. 10).** Newt Gingrich named House Speaker **(Dec. 5).** Bentsen resigns as Treasury Secretary **(Dec. 6).** Russians attack secessionist Republic of Chechnya **(Dec. 11** *et seq.***).** John Salvi kills two at Massachusetts Planned Parenthood clinic **(Dec. 30).**

Nelson Mandela
(1918–)

1995 Republicans take control of Congress **(Jan. 4).** More than 5,000 dead in Japanese earthquake **(Jan. 17** *et seq.***).** Criminal trial of O. J. Simpson opens in California **(Jan. 24).** U.S. rescues Mexico's economy with $20-billion aid program **(Feb. 21).** Senate rejects balanced-budget amendment **(March 2).** Nerve gas attack in Tokyo subway kills eight and injures thousands. The Aum Shinrikyo ("Supreme Truth") cult is to blame **(March 20).** Major League Baseball strike ends **(April 2).** Appeals court upholds woman's plea to enter Citadel military academy **(April 13).** UN Council votes easier sanctions for Iraq **(April 14).** Scores killed as terrorist's car bomb blows up block-long Oklahoma City federal building **(April 19);** Timothy McVeigh, 27, Army veteran, arrested as suspect **(April 21);** authorities seek second suspect, link right-wing paramilitary groups to bombing **(April 22).** Death toll 2,000 in Rwanda massacre **(April 22).** Fighting escalates in Bosnia and Croatia **(May 1).** U.S. shuttle docks with Russian space station **(June 27).** F.B.I. suspends four in Idaho siege inquiry **(Aug. 11).** France explodes nuclear device in Pacific; wide protests ensue **(Sept. 5).** Senator Bob Packwood of Oregon resigns under pressure for sexual and official misconduct **(Sept. 6).** Israelis and Palestinians agree on transferring West Bank to Arabs **(Sept. 24).** Los Angeles jury finds O. J. Simpson not guilty of murder charges **(Oct. 3).** Pope John Paul II visits U.S. on whirlwind tour **(Oct. 4–8).** Warring parties agree on cease-fire in Bosnia **(Oct. 5).** Million Man March draws hundreds of thousands of black men to capital **(Oct. 16).** Quebec narrowly rejects independence from Canada **(Oct. 30).** Israeli prime minister Yitzhak Rabin slain by Jewish extremist at peace rally **(Nov. 4).** U.S. servicemen admit rape of Japanese schoolgirl in Okinawa **(Nov. 7).** Nigeria hangs writer Ken Saro-Wiwa and eight other minority rights advocates **(Nov. 10).** Irish voters approve end to constitutional ban on divorce **(Nov. 24).** Combatants sign Bosnia peace treaty **(Dec. 14).** House move stalls Congress–White House negotiations to avert government shutdown **(Dec. 20).** Seamus Heaney wins Nobel prize for literature.

Jean-Bertrand Aristide
(1953–)

Dalai Lama
(1935–)

Yitzhak Rabin
(1922–1995)

1996 U.S. budget crisis in fourth month **(Jan 3).** Clinton approves resumption of many government operations **(Jan. 6).** Senate ratifies major arms reduction treaty **(Jan. 26).** France announces end to nuclear tests **(Jan. 29).** At least 73 dead in Sri Lankan suicide bombing **(Feb. 1).** Suicide bombers kill 59 in Israel **(March 4).** Bob Dole sweeps Republican primaries **(March 5).** Britain alarmed by deadly cow disease **(March 20** *et seq.***).** UN tribunal charges war crimes by Bosnian Muslims and Croats **(March 22).** Commerce Secretary Ronald H. Brown killed in plane crash **(April 3).** FBI arrests suspected Unabomber **(April 3).** Clinton signs line-item veto bill **(April 9).** President blocks ban on late-term abortions **(April 10).** ValuJet crashes in Everglades; all 110 aboard killed **(May 11).** Chechnya peace treaty signed **(May 27).** Israel elects Benjamin Netanyahu as prime minister **(May 31).** China agrees to world ban

Seamus Heaney
(1939–)

Ella Fitzgerald
(1918–1996)

Madeleine Albright
(1937–)

Kofi Annan
(1938–)

Hale-Bopp Comet

Princess Diana
(1961–1997)

on atomic testing (**June 6**). Leaders in Balkans sign accord on arms limits (**June 14**). Jazz great Ella Fitzgerald dies (**June 15**). Truck bomb kills 19 at U.S. base in Saudi Arabia (**June 25**). Boris Yeltsin is reelected in Russian election (**July 3**). Prince Charles and Princess Diana agree on divorce (**July 12**). 747 airliner crashes in Atlantic off Long Island; all 230 aboard perish (**July 17**). Bomb mars Summer Olympic games in Atlanta (**July 25**). Clinton signs bill to raise minimum wage (**Aug. 2**). Congress passes welfare reform bill (**Aug. 2**); approved by Clinton (**Aug. 22**). Republican convention opens in San Diego (**Aug. 12**); Bob Dole and Jack Kemp nominated (**Aug. 14**). Democrats convene in Chicago (**Aug. 26**). Iraqis strike at Kurdish enclave (**Aug. 31**); after warning, U.S. attacks Iraq's southern air defenses (**Sept. 2–3**); Iraq halts attacks on U.S. planes enforcing flight exclusion zones in north and south (**Sept. 13**). Violence flares in Jerusalem over Israel opening tourist tunnel (**Sept. 24**). Taliban Muslim fundamentalists capture Afghan capital (**Sept. 27**). Ethnic violence breaks out in Zairian refugee camps (**Oct. 13**); thousands of refugees from Rwanda and Burundi abandon camps (**Oct. 21**). Clinton-Gore ticket wins national election; Republicans retain control of Congress (**Nov. 5**). Mid-air collision in India kills 342 (**Nov. 12**). Texaco settles racial bias suit (**Nov. 15**). Hundreds of thousands of Hutu refugees return to Rwanda (**Nov. 15–18**). Clinton appoints Madeleine Albright as first female U.S. secretary of state (**Dec. 5**). Kofi Annan named UN secretary-general (**Dec. 13**). FBI agent charged with spying for Moscow (**Dec. 18**). Thousands march in Belgrade in continuing protest against president's annulment of election results (**Dec. 26**).

1997 Two Hutu sentenced to death in Rwandan genocide (**Jan. 3**). Floods cause wide damage in U.S. West (**Jan. 5**). Newt Gingrich reelected as House Speaker (**Jan. 7**). Hebron agreement signed; Israel gives up large part of West Bank city of Hebron (**Jan. 16**). U.S. shuttle joins Russian space station (**Jan. 17**). Gingrich found guilty of ethics violations (**Jan. 17**). President Clinton starts second term (**Jan. 20**). U.S., U.K., and France agree to freeze Nazis' gold loot (**Feb. 3**). O. J. Simpson found liable in civil suit (**Feb. 5**). Deng Xiaoping, Chinese leader, dead at 92 (**Feb. 19**). Israeli government approves establishment of Jewish settlement in East Jerusalem, a setback in Middle East peace process (**Feb. 26**). Tornadoes wreak havoc in Arkansas, Ohio, and Kentucky (**March 3**). State of anarchy in Albania when third of population loses savings because of pyramid schemes (**March 13**). Hale-Bopp comet is the closest it will be to Earth until 4397 (**March 22**). Heaven's Gate cult members commit mass suicide in California (**March 27**). U.S. Appeals Court upholds California ban on affirmative action (**April 8**). U.S. judge upholds California marijuana law (**April 11**). Tiger Woods breaks multiple records in Masters golf tournament (**April 13**). Fire kills 300 pilgrims outside Mecca (**April 15**). Senate, 74–26, approves chemical-weapons treaty (**April 24**). Thousands flee North Dakota flood (**April 27**). Sergeant Major of the Army, Gene C. McKinney, charged in sex cases (**May 7**). Russian president Yeltsin signs Chechnya peace treaty (**May 12**). U.S.-Russian spaceship linkup in orbit ends (**May 21**). U.S. jobless rate for May reported 4.8%, lowest since 1973 (**June 6**). European Union bolsters currency merger (**June 16**). Congress votes major tax cuts (**June 26**). Hong Kong returns to Chinese rule (**June 30**). U.S. spacecraft begins exploration of Mars (**July 4**). Andrew Cunanan murders fashion designer Gianni Versace (**July 15**). Khmer Rouge hold trial of longtime leader Pol Pot (**July 25**). White House and GOP agree on measure to balance budget (**July 28**). U.S. spacecraft transmits thousands of pictures from Mars (**Aug. 8**). Clinton exercises new line-item veto (**Aug. 11**). Timothy J. McVeigh sentenced to death for Oklahoma City bombing (**Aug. 14**). Princess Diana, 36, killed with two others in Paris car crash (**Aug. 31**). Three Islamic suicide bombers kill four persons in Jerusalem (**Sept. 4**). Mother Teresa dead at 87 (**Sept. 5**). Swiss plan first payment to Holocaust victims (**Sept. 17**). Militant Taliban leaders seize Kabul (**Sept. 27**). Iraq expels all U.S. members of UN arms-inspection team (**Oct. 29**). GOP victorious in off-year elections (**Nov. 4**). Pakistani convicted in 1993 CIA killings (**Nov. 10**). Two convicted in New York World Trade Center bombing (**Nov. 12**). Egyptian Islamic militants kill 62 at Luxor tourist site (**Nov. 17**). FBI ends 16-month investigation of crash of Flight 800 off Long Island; denies sabotage (**Nov. 18**). European Union plans to admit six nations (**Dec. 13**). U.S. company launches first commercial spy satellite (**Dec. 24**). Paris court convicts "Carlos the Jackal" of murder (**Dec. 24**).

1998 Ramzi Ahmed Yousef sentenced to life for 1993 World Trade Center bombing (**Jan. 9**). Pope John Paul II visits Cuba (**Jan. 21–25**). President accused in White House sex scandal; denies allegations of affair with White House intern, Monica Lewinsky (**Jan. 21** *et seq.*). President outlines first balanced budget in 30 years (**Feb. 3**). U.S. plane cuts ski cable in Italy and sends car plunging; 20 killed (**Feb. 3**). Thousands dead in Afghanistan quake (**Feb. 4** *et seq.*). U.S. court rules line-item veto unconstitutional (**Feb. 12**). Serbs battle ethnic Albanians in Kosovo (**March 5** *et seq.*). U.S. drops condemnation of China's human rights record (**March 13**). Hindu nationalist Vajpayee becomes India's prime minister (**March 19**). FDA approves Viagra, male impotence drug (**March 27**). Federal judge in Arkansas throws out Paula Jones case (**April 1**). Landmark peace settlement, the Good Friday Accord, reached in Northern Ireland (**April 10**). U.S. trade deficit biggest in decade (**April 17**). Europeans agree on single currency, the euro (**May 3**). Unabomber, Theodore Kaczynski, sentenced to four life terms (**May 4**). India conducts three atomic tests despite worldwide disapproval (**May 11, 13**). Indonesian dictator Suharto steps down after 32 years in power (**May 21**). Pakistan stages five nuclear tests in response to India's (**May 29, 30**). Serbs renew attack on Kosovo rebels (**June 1**). Life sentence meted out to Terry Nichols, convicted in Oklahoma City bombing fatal to 168 (**June 4**). Nigerian dictator Sani Abacha dies (**June 8**). Congress votes to overhaul IRS (**July 9**). Iraq ends cooperation with UN arms inspectors (**Aug. 5**). U.S. embassies in Kenya and Tanzania bombed (**Aug. 7**). Clinton admits to affair with White House intern in televised address to nation (**Aug. 17**). Russia fights to avert financial collapse (**Aug. 17**). U.S. cruise missiles hit suspected terrorist bases in Sudan and Afghanistan (**Aug. 20**). North Korea fires missile across Japan (**Aug. 31**). Swissair jet crashes; kills 229 (**Sept. 2**). Starr Report by independent counsel outlines case for impeachment proceedings against president (**Sept. 11**). Senate sustains veto of bill to outlaw late-term abortions (**Sept. 18**). Iran lifts death threat against Salman Rushdie (**Sept. 24**). German chancellor Helmut Kohl defeated by Gerhard Schröder (**Sept. 27**). U.S. budget surplus largest in three decades (**Oct. 5**). Matthew Shepard, gay Wyoming student, fatally beaten in hate crime (**Oct. 6**). NATO, on verge of air strikes, reaches settlement with Milosevic on Kosovo (**Oct. 12**). Former Chilean dictator Pinochet arrested in London (**Oct. 16**). Wye Mills Agreement between Netanyahu and Arafat moves Middle East peace talks forward (**Oct. 23**). More than 10,000 die in Central American hurricane, Mitch (**Nov. 1**). Democrats unexpectedly gain five House seats in national election; Republicans keep control of House and Senate (**Nov. 3**). House Speaker Gingrich to step down (**Nov. 9**). House panel drafts impeachment charges; votes along party lines to approve four articles (**Dec. 11–12**). Clinton orders air strikes on Iraq (**Dec. 16–19**). House impeaches President Clinton along party lines on two charges, perjury and obstruction of justice (**Dec. 19**).

1999 U.S. agrees to ease restrictions on Cuba (**Jan. 4**). Dennis Hastert elected to replace Newt Gingrich as Speaker of the House (**Jan. 6**). NBA ends 191-day labor dispute (**Jan. 6**). Michael Jordan retires from the Chicago Bulls (**Jan. 13**). International Olympic Committee expels six members as bribery scandal widens (**Jan. 24**). King Hussein of Jordan dies (**Feb. 7**). Senate acquits President Clinton of impeachment charges (**Feb. 12**). Gen. Olusegun Obasanjo elected president of Nigeria (**Feb. 28**). First nonstop balloon flight around world completed in 20 days by Bertrand Piccard (Switzerland) and Brian Jones (UK) (**March 1–20**). Marine pilot acquitted in killing of 20 in 1998 Italian ski gondola accident; Italians outraged (**March 4**). U.S. accuses China of stealing nuclear secrets (**March 5**). Joe DiMaggio dies at age 84 (**March 8**). Czech Republic, Poland, and Hungary join NATO (**March 12**). NATO launches air strikes on Serbia to end attacks against ethnic Albanians in Kosovo (**March 24**). Dr. Jack Kevorkian convicted of second-degree murder in assisted-suicide case (**March 26**). "Melissa" computer virus spreads through the Internet (**March 27**). Libya hands over two suspects in 1988 Pan Am jet bombing (**April 5**). Two Colo. students go on shooting spree in Columbine High School, killing 15, including themselves (**April 20**). NATO bombs mistakenly hit Chinese embassy in Belgrade (**May 7**). Citadel graduates its first woman (**May 8**). Crime rate in U.S. falls for seventh consecutive year (**May 16**). Ehud Barak defeats Benjamin Netanyahu in Israeli prime minister election (**May 17**). U.S. inspects suspected nuclear weapons site in North Korea, finds nothing (**May 20–24**). Serbs sign agreement to pull

**Mother Teresa
(1910–1997)**

Euro 100

Mars Sojourner Rover

**William J. Clinton
(1946–)**

Boris Yeltsin
(1931–)

Eileen Collins
(1956–)

George W. Bush
(1946–)

troops out of Kosovo after 11 weeks of NATO air attacks **(June 9)**. Nelson Mandela retires as president of South Africa; succeeded by Thabo Mbeki **(June 16)**. Britain's Prince Edward marries Sophie Rhys-Jones **(June 19)**. Kurd leader Abdullah Ocalan sentenced to death for treason in Turkey **(June 29)**. White supremacist goes on shooting spree in Midwest, killing three including self and wounding eight **(July 2–5)**. U.S. soccer team tops China for women's World Cup **(July 10)**. Taiwanese leader Lee Teng-hui challenges "One China" policy **(July 11)**. Serial killer Rafael Reséndez-Ramirez surrenders himself to U.S. authorities **(July 13)**. John F. Kennedy, Jr., wife Carolyn Bessette Kennedy, and sister-in-law Lauren Bessette killed in plane crash off coast of Martha's Vineyard **(July 16)**. Col. Eileen Collins becomes first female to head a space shuttle mission **(July 16)**. Falun Gong meditation sect banned by Chinese government **(July 22)**. Day-trader kills 9 and wounds 13 in two Atlanta brokerage offices before committing suicide **(July 29)**. Yeltsin replaces Prime Minister Stepashin with Vladimir Putin in fourth government shakeup in 17 months **(Aug. 9)**. Islamic militants declare independence for Dagestan and announce holy war against Russia **(Aug. 10)**. White supremacist opens fire at Jewish community center in LA, wounding five and killing one as he flees **(Aug. 10)**. More than 17,000 people die in 7.4 earthquake in Turkey **(Aug. 17)**. Attorney General Janet Reno reopens investigation of 1993 Waco, Tex., stand-off **(Aug. 25)**. People of East Timor vote for independence from Indonesia **(Aug. 31)**. Israeli prime minister Ehud Barak and PLO leader Yasir Arafat announce peace accord **(Sept. 4)**. Larry Gene Ashbrook goes on rampage in Tex. church, killing seven and himself **(Sept. 15)**. NASA accidentally loses $125 million spacecraft as it orbits Mars **(Sept. 23)**. Dozens of people exposed to radiation in Japan's worst nuclear accident **(Sept. 30)**. Russia sends ground troops to Chechnya as conflict with Islamic militants intensifies **(Oct. 1)**. World population reaches six billion milestone **(Oct. 11)**. Military coup led by Gen. Pervez Musharraf overthrows Pakistani government **(Oct. 12)**. Tobacco companies admit to harm caused by cigarette smoking **(Oct. 13)**. Senate rejects 1996 nuclear test-ban treaty; international leaders upset by U.S. stand **(Oct. 13)**. Indonesia elects Muslim leader Abdurrahman Wahid president **(Oct. 20)**. Pro golfer Payne Stewart and five others killed in plane crash **(Oct. 25)**. EgyptAir flight crashes over Atlantic, killing all 217 on board **(Oct. 31)**. Judge finds Microsoft to be a monopoly **(Nov. 5)**. U.S. and China reach landmark trade agreement **(Nov. 15)**. China launches first spacecraft **(Nov. 21)**. Five-year-old Cuban refugee Elián González gets caught in politically charged custody battle **(Nov. 25)**. World Trade Organization conference disrupted by violent protests in Seattle **(Nov. 29 et seq.)**. New Northern Ireland government begins self-rule for first time in 25 years **(Dec. 2)**. Muslim terrorists hijack Indian Airlines jet with 189 on board **(Dec. 24)**.

2000 Socialist president, Ricardo Lagos, elected in Chile **(Jan. 16)**. George W. Bush and Al Gore take Iowa caucuses in U.S. presidential race **(Jan. 22)**. Austria at center of European dispute after conservative People's Party forms coalition with the far-right Freedom Party, headed by xenophobe Jörg Haider **(Feb. 3)**. First Lady Hillary Clinton officially enters N.Y. Senate race **(Feb. 6)**. Hijackers seize Afghan plane; release hostages in Stansted, England **(Feb. 6–12)**. Britain ends self-rule in Northern Ireland after Irish Republican Army misses disarmament deadline **(Feb. 11)**. NEAR spacecraft becomes first to orbit an asteroid **(Feb. 14)**. Wary investors cause stock plunge; beginning of the end of the Internet stock boom **(Feb. 25)**. Reformists win control of Iranian parliament for first time since 1979 Islamic revolution **(Feb. 26)**. Gun maker Smith & Wesson limits the manufacture and distribution of handguns in light of lawsuits **(March 17)**. Mass murder or suicide of hundreds in Ugandan doomsday cult **(March 18)**. Acting Russian president Vladimir V. Putin formally chosen for post **(March 25)**. Microsoft loses antitrust suit; appeal expected **(April 3)**. Controversial Osprey plane crash kills 19 marines **(April 8)**. Cuban boy Elián González, reunited with father after federal raid of Miami relatives' home **(April 22)**. Vermont approves same-sex unions **(April 25)**. "I love you" virus disrupts computers worldwide **(May 4)**. South Carolina removes Confederate battle flag from capitol dome **(May 18)**. Chile ends Augusto Pinochet's immunity, clearing way for trial on murder and torture during years as dictator **(May 24)**. Israeli troops withdraw from Lebanese security zone after 22 years of occupation **(May 24)**. Former Indonesian president Suharto under house arrest, charged with corruption and abuse of power (**May 29**). Britain restores parliamentary powers to Northern Ireland after Sinn Fein agrees to disarm (**June 4**). Presidents of North and South Korea sign peace accord, ending half-century of antagonism (**June 15**). British find 58 bodies of illegal Asian immigrants suffocated in Dutch truck that transported them (**June 20**). Elián González returns to Cuba with father (**June 23**). U.S. navy resumes shelling of Puerto Rico's Vieques Island, used as a training site (**June 25**). Human genome deciphered; expected to revolutionize the practice of medicine (**June 26**). Iraq believed to resume missile program (**June 30**). Mexico elects reform president, Vicente Fox Quesada (**July 1**). Vicente Fox Quesada elected president of Mexico (**July 2**). Bashar al-Assad succeeds late father, Hafez al-Assad, as Syrian president (**July 10**). Concorde crash kills 113 near Paris (**July 25**). Republican convention picks Texas governor George W. Bush as presidential candidate; Dick Cheney for vice presidential spot (**Aug. 2**). Democratic convention selects Vice President Al Gore and Sen. Joseph I. Lieberman to head ticket (**Aug. 14**). Los Alamos scientist Wen Ho Lee, accused of stealing sensitive nuclear weapons data, freed after serving nine months in prison (**Sept. 13**). Olympic Games open in Australia (**Sept. 15**). Six-year Whitewater investigation of the Clintons ends without indictments (**Sept. 20**). Yugoslav opposition claims victory; incumbent Slobodan Milosevic denies results (**Sept. 25**). Danish voters reject euro (**Sept. 26**). Abortion pill, RU-486, wins U.S. approval (**Sept. 28**). Palestinians and Israelis clash, spurred by visit of right-wing Israeli leader Ariel Sharon to a joint Jewish/Muslim holy site; "Al Aksa intifada" continues unabated (**Sept. 30** *et seq.*). Nationwide uprising overthrows Yugoslavian president Milosevic (**Oct. 5**). Vojislav Kostunica sworn in as Yugoslav president (**Oct. 7**). 17 U.S. sailors on navy destroyer *Cole* die in Yemen terrorist explosion (**Oct. 12**). U.S. presidential election closest in decades; Bush's slim lead in Florida leads to automatic recount in that state (**Nov. 7–8**). Republicans file federal suit to block manual recount of Florida presidential election ballots sought by Democrats (**Nov. 11**). Philippine president Joseph Estrada impeached after receiving gambling payoffs (**Nov. 13**). Florida Supreme Court rules hand count of presidential ballots may continue (**Nov. 21**). Global warming talks collapse at Hague conference (**Nov. 25**). Florida Secretary of State Katherine Harris certifies Bush as winner by 537 votes (**Nov. 26**). Mad Cow disease alarms Europe (**Nov. 30**). Israeli prime minister Ehud Barak resigns (**Dec. 9**). U.S. Supreme Court orders halt to manual recount of presidential votes in Florida (**Dec. 9**). Supreme Court seals Bush victory by 5–4; rules there can be no further recounting (**Dec. 12**).

Vojislav Kostunica
(1944–)

PICTURE CREDITS

The editors wish to thank the following organizations and individuals who have contributed illustrations to Headline History.

Agence France Press/Archive Photos: **Mao Zedong;** AIP Niels Bohr Library: **Marie Curie, Albert Einstein;** AMW Pressediensf/Archive Photos: **Nelson Mandela;** Archive Photos: **Richard Wagner, William Butler Yeats, Pablo Picasso, Anne Frank, Woody Guthrie, Robert Frost, William Faulkner, The Beatles, Mahatma Gandhi, Duke Ellington, Tennessee Williams, Toni Morrison, Seamus Heaney, Ella Fitzgerald, Lech Walesa, Princess Diana, Pope John Paul, Mother Teresa, Yitzhak Rabin, Malcolm X, William Rehnquist, Anwar Sadat;** Linda J. Barnes: **the Duomo in Florence;** British Information Services: **Margaret Thatcher;** Consolidated News/Archive Photos: **Jean-Bertrand Aristide;** Tina Diodati: **Aqueduct, Parthenon;** Embassy of the Philippines: **Corazon Aquino;** The French Consulate, Boston: **François Mitterrand;** Gerald R. Ford Library: **Gerald Ford;** Peter F. Harrington: **Stonehenge;** Erik Hjortshoj: **Pagoda;** Imapress/Archive Photos: **Boris Yeltsin;** INA/Reuters/Archive Photos: **Saddam Hussein;** John Fitzgerald Kennedy Library, Boston: **John F. Kennedy;** Priscilla Lee: **Dalai Lama;** Leo Baeck Inst./Archive Photos: **Sigmund Freud;** Jimmy Carter Library: **Jimmy Carter;** The Library of Congress Picture Collection: **Pocahontas, Taj Mahal, Edgar Allan Poe, Harriet Tubman, Walt Whitman, Dred Scott, Samuel Clemens (Mark Twain), Henri Matisse, W. E. B. Du Bois, Woodrow**

Wilson, Bessie Smith, Dorothea Lange photo, Amelia Earhart, Harry S. Truman, John H. Glenn, Jr., James H. Meredith, Betty Friedan, Richard Nixon, Lyndon B. Johnson; Pete Maio: **Mesa Verde;** Muzammil Paha/Reuters/Archive Photos: **Benazir Bhutto;** National Archives and Records Admin.: **Frederick Douglass, Harriet Beecher Stowe, Abraham Lincoln, Robert E. Lee, William Tecumseh Sherman, Chief Joseph, Benito Mussolini, Franklin Delano Roosevelt, Adolf Hitler, Winston Churchill, Atomic Bomb, Dwight D. Eisenhower, Rev. Martin Luther King, Jr.;** NASA: **Eileen Collins, Hubble Space Telescope;** NASA/JPL/Caltech: **Mars Sojourner Rover;** Novosti Photos: **Vladimir Lenin, Mikhail S. Gorbachev;** Elaine Ouellette: **Pantheon in Rome;** The Permanent Mission of India to the UN: **Indira Gandhi;** Permanent Mission of Islamic Republic of Iran to the UN: **Ayatollah Ruhollah Khomeini;** Renée Scott: **Celtic Cross, Mayan Pyramid;** The Republican National Committee: **Ronald Reagan, George Bush;** Kim Storm: **Egyptian Pyramid;** United Nations: **Dag Hammarskjöld, Fidel Castro, Kofi Annan;** U.S. Army Photos: **Joseph Stalin, Yalta Conference, General Colin Powell;** U.S. State Department: **Madeleine Albright;** U.S. Supreme Court: **Ruth Bader Ginsburg, Thurgood Marshall, Sandra Day O'Connor;** Tasha Vincent: **Cathedral and Tower at Pisa, Chartres Cathedral, Michelangelo's David, Statue of Liberty;** The White House: **William J. Clinton, George W. Bush;** Yugoslavia, Embassy of: **Vojislav Kostunica.**

Country Statistics at a Glance

Country rankings of the type presented below cannot pretend to be definitive; instead they aspire only to provide the reader with an approximation of the high and low ends on a particular scale. Country data vary enormously depending on the sources, and the absence of reliable data on some countries requires their omission, which further skews the results.

LARGEST COUNTRIES[1] (in sq mi)*: 2001			SMALLEST COUNTRIES[1] (in sq mi): 2001			HIGHEST POPULATION DENSITY[2] (per sq mi): 2001		
(1)	Russia	6,592,735	(1)	Vatican City	0.17	(1)	Monaco	42,293
(2)	Canada	3,851,788	(2)	Monaco	0.75	(2)	Singapore	17,188
(3)	United States	3,717,792	(3)	Nauru	8.0	(3)	Malta	3,234
(4)	China	3,705,386	(4)	Tuvalu	10.0	(4)	Bahrain	2,696
(5)	Brazil	3,286,470	(5)	San Marino	24.0	(5)	Maldives	2,683
(6)	Australia	2,967,893	(6)	Liechtenstein	62.0	(6)	Bangladesh	2,361
(7)	India	1,269,338	(7)	Marshall Islands	70.0	(7)	Barbados	1,658
(8)	Argentina	1,068,296	(8)	St. Kitts & Nevis	101.0	(8)	Mauritius	1,657
(9)	Kazakhstan	1,049,150	(9)	Maldives	116.0	(9)	Taiwan	1,610
(10)	Sudan	967,493	(10)	Malta	122.0	(10)	Nauru	1,491

LOWEST POPULATION DENSITY[2] (per sq mi): 2001			HIGHEST GDP PER CAPITA[3] (PPP in U.S. dollars): 1999			LOWEST GDP PER CAPITA[3] (PPP in U.S. dollars): 1999		
(1)	Greenland	0.1	(1)	Luxembourg	$34,200	(1)	Sierra Leone	$500
(2)	Western Sahara	2.4	(2)	United States	33,900	(2)	Tanzania	550
(3)	Mongolia	4.4	(3)	Singapore	27,800	(3)	Ethiopia	560
(4)	Namibia	5.6	(4)	Switzerland	27,100	(4)	Somalia	600
(5)	Australia	6.5	(5)	Monaco	27,000	(5)	Cambodia	710
(6)	Suriname	6.9	(6)	Norway	25,100		Congo, Dem. Rep. of	710
	Mauritania	6.9	(7)	Belgium	23,900	(7)	Rwanda	720
(8)	Iceland	7.0	(8)	Denmark	23,800	(8)	Comoros	725
(9)	Libya	7.7	(9)	Iceland	23,500	(9)	Burundi	730
(10)	Canada	8.2	(10)	Austria	23,400	(10)	Eritrea	750

HIGHEST INFLATION:[3] 1999			LOWEST INFLATION:[3] 1999			HIGHEST INFANT MORTALITY RATE:[2] 2001 (deaths per 1,000 births)		
(1)	Belarus	295.0%	(1)	Azerbaijan	−6.8%	(1)	Angola	193.72
(2)	Angola	270.0	(2)	Nauru	−3.6	(2)	Afghanistan	147.02
(3)	Suriname	170.0	(3)	Argentina	−2.0	(3)	Sierra Leone	146.52
(4)	Laos	140.0	(4)	China	−1.3	(4)	Mozambique	139.20
(5)	Iraq	135.0	(5)	Saudi Arabia	−1.2	(5)	Western Sahara	133.59
(6)	Russia	86.0	(6)	Belize	−0.9	(6)	Liberia	132.42
(7)	Cyprus (Turkish)	66.0	(7)	Japan	−0.8	(7)	Guinea	129.03
(8)	Turkey	65.0	(8)	Oman	−0.1	(8)	Somalia	123.97
(9)	Ecuador	59.9	(9)	Djibouti	0.0	(9)	Niger	123.57
(10)	Zimbabwe	59.0	(10)	Fiji	0.0	(10)	Mali	121.44

LOWEST INFANT MORTALITY RATE:[2] 2001 (deaths per 1,000 births)			HIGHEST LIFE EXPECTANCY[2] (in years): 2001			LOWEST LIFE EXPECTANCY[2] (in years): 2001		
(1)	Sweden	3.47	(1)	Andorra	83.47	(1)	Mozambique	36.45
(2)	Iceland	3.56	(2)	San Marino	81.23	(2)	Malawi	37.08
(3)	Singapore	3.62	(3)	Japan	80.80	(3)	Botswana	37.13
(4)	Finland	3.79	(4)	Singapore	80.17		Zimbabwe	37.13
(5)	Japan	3.88	(5)	Australia	79.87	(5)	Zambia	37.29
(6)	Norway	3.94	(6)	Switzerland	79.73	(6)	Angola	38.59
(7)	Andorra	4.08	(7)	Sweden	79.71	(7)	Swaziland	38.62
(8)	Netherlands	4.37	(8)	Canada	79.56	(8)	Rwanda	38.99
(9)	Austria	4.44	(9)	Ireland	79.52	(9)	Namibia	40.62
(10)	France	4.46	(10)	Italy	79.14	(10)	Niger	41.59

NOTE: Only countries for which statistics were available in sources 1, 2, or 3 figure in these lists. *Sources:* 1. Information Please Database. 2. U.S. Census Bureau, International Database. 3. *The World Factbook, 2000.* *Size refers to the total area of a country, which includes the land area plus bodies of water.

A Profile of the World

Source: The World Factbook, 2000

Geography

Total area: 510.072 million sq km (196.93 million sq mi). **Land area:** 148.94 million sq km (57.50 million sq mi). **Water area:** 361.132 million sq km (139.43 million sq mi). **Comparative area:** Land area about 16 times the size of the United States. **Note:** 70.8% of the world is water, 29.2% is land.

Terrain: Highest elevation is Mt. Everest at 8,850 m (29,035 ft) and lowest land depression is the Dead Sea at −411 m (−1,349 ft) below sea level. The greatest ocean depth is the Mariana Trench at 10,924 m in the Pacific Ocean.

Land use: *Arable land:* 10%. *Permanent crops:* 1%. *Meadows and pastures:* 26%. *Forests and woodlands:* 32%. *Other:* 31% (1993 est.). *Irrigated land:* 2,481,250 sq km.

People

Population: 6,163,890,100 (Aug. 1, 2001, est. from U.S. Census Bureau)

Growth rate: 1.3% (2000 est.)

Birth rate: 22 births/1,000 population (2000 est.)

Death rate: 9 deaths/1,000 population (2000 est.)

Sex ratio (at birth): 1.05 male(s)/female (2000 est.)

Infant mortality rate: 54 deaths/1,000 live births (2000 est.)

Life expectancy at birth: *Total population:* 64 years. *Male:* 62 years. *Female:* 65 years (2000 est.)

Total fertility rate: 2.8 children born/woman (2000 est.)

Literacy: Age 15 and over can read and write (1999 est., UN figs.) *Combined:* 79.4%. *Male:* 85.2%. *Female:* 73.6%.

Government and Economy

Political divisions: 194 sovereign nations, 61 dependent areas, and 6 disputed territories.

Economy: The GWP rose to 3% in 1999 from 2% in 1998 despite continued recession in Japan, severe financial difficulties in other East Asian countries, and widespread dislocations in several transition economies, notably Russia. The U.S. economy continued to prosper, growing at 4.1% in 1999, and accounted for 23% of GWP. Western Europe's economies grew at roughly 2%, not enough to cut deeply into the region's high unemployment; the EU economies produced 20% of GWP. China, the world's second-largest economy, continued its strong growth and accounted for 12% of GWP.

GDP: GWP (gross world product/purchasing power parity)—$40.7 trillion (1999 est.)

GDP—real growth rate: 3% (1999 est.)

GDP—per capita: $6,800 (1999)

Inflation rate (consumer price index): *All countries:* 25%. *Developed countries:* 1%–3% typically (1999 est.). *Developing countries:* 5%–60% typically (1999 est.). **Note:** *National inflation rates vary widely.*

Unemployment rate: 30% combined unemployment and underemployment in many nonindustrialized countries; developed countries, typically 4%–12% unemployment (1999 est.)

Exports: $5.6 trillion (f.o.b., 1999 est.)

Imports: $5.6 trillion (c.i.f., 1999 est.)

External debt: $2 trillion for less developed nations (1999 est.)

Military expenditures: roughly 2% of GWP (1999 est.)

Total Population of the World by Decade, 1950–2050

(historical and projected)

Year	Total world population (mid-year figures)	Ten-year growth rate (%)	Year	Total world population (mid-year figures)	Ten-year growth rate (%)
1950	2,556,000,053	18.9%	2010	6,848,932,929	10.7%
1960	3,039,451,023	22.0	2020	7,584,821,144	8.7
1970	3,706,618,163	20.2	2030	8,246,619,341	7.3
1980	4,453,831,714	18.5	2040	8,850,045,889	5.6
1990	5,278,639,789	15.2	2050	9,346,399,468	—
2000	6,082,966,429	12.6			

Source: U.S. Census Bureau, International Database.

World's 50 Most Populous Countries: 2001

Rank	Country	Population	Rank	Country	Population	Rank	Country	Population
1.	China	1,273,111,290	19.	Thailand	61,797,751	35.	Canada	31,592,805
2.	India	1,029,991,145	20.	United Kingdom	59,647,790	36.	Kenya	30,765,916
3.	United States	278,058,881	21.	France	59,551,227	37.	Morocco	30,645,305
4.	Indonesia	228,437,870	22.	Italy	57,679,825	38.	Peru	27,483,864
5.	Brazil	174,468,575	23.	Congo, Dem.		39.	Afghanistan	26,813,057
6.	Russia	145,470,197		Rep. of	53,624,718	40.	Nepal	25,284,463
7.	Pakistan	144,616,639	24.	Ukraine	48,760,474	41.	Uzbekistan	25,155,064
8.	Bangladesh	131,269,860	25.	Korea, South	47,904,370	42.	Uganda	23,985,712
9.	Japan	126,771,662	26.	South Africa	43,586,097	43.	Venezuela	23,916,810
10.	Nigeria	126,635,626	27.	Burma		44.	Iraq	23,331,985
11.	Mexico	101,879,171		(Myanmar)	41,994,678	45.	Saudi Arabia	22,757,092
12.	Germany	83,029,536	28.	Colombia	40,349,388	46.	Taiwan	22,370,461
13.	Philippines	82,841,518	29.	Spain	40,037,995	47.	Romania	22,364,022
14.	Vietnam	79,939,014	30.	Poland	38,633,912	48.	Malaysia	22,229,040
15.	Egypt	69,536,644	31.	Argentina	37,384,816	49.	Korea, North	21,968,228
16.	Turkey	66,493,970	32.	Tanzania	36,232,074	50.	Ghana	19,894,014
17.	Iran	66,128,965	33.	Sudan	36,080,373			
18.	Ethiopia	65,891,874	34.	Algeria	31,736,053			

Source: U.S. Census Bureau, International Database.

World Population Milestones

Source: United Nations Population Division

- 1 billion in 1804
- 2 billion in 1927   (123 years later)
- 3 billion in 1960   (33 years later)
- 4 billion in 1974   (14 years later)
- 5 billion in 1987   (13 years later)
- 6 billion in 1999   (12 years later)

World Vital Events per Time Unit: 2001

Time unit	Births	Deaths	Natural increase	Time unit	Births	Deaths	Natural increase
Year	131,571,719	55,001,289	76,570,430	Hour	15,020	6,279	8,741
Month	10,964,310	4,583,441	6,380,869	Minute	250	105	146
Day	360,470	150,688	209,782	Second	4.2	1.7	2.4

NOTE: Figures may not add to totals due to rounding. *Source:* U.S. Census Bureau, *International Data Base.*

Territories, Colonies, and Dependencies

Source: The World Factbook, 2000

The following is a list of dependencies—territories under the jurisdiction of another country.

Under Australian Jurisdiction (6)
Ashmore and Cartier Islands
Christmas Island
Cocos (Keeling) Islands
Coral Sea Islands
Heard Island and McDonald Islands
Norfolk Island

Under Danish Jurisdiction (2)
Faeroe Islands
Greenland

Under Dutch Jurisdiction (2)
Aruba
Netherlands Antilles

Under French Jurisdiction (16)
Bassas da India
Clipperton Island
Europa Island
French Guiana
French Polynesia
French Southern and Antarctic Lands
Glorioso Islands
Guadeloupe
Juan de Nova Island
Martinique
Mayotte
New Caledonia
Réunion
Saint Pierre and Miquelon
Tromelin Island
Wallis and Futuna

Under New Zealand Jurisdiction (3)
Cook Islands
Niue
Tokelau

Under Norwegian Jurisdiction (3)
Bouvet Island
Jan Mayen
Svalbard

Under UK Jurisdiction (15)
Anguilla
Bermuda
British Indian Ocean Territory
British Virgin Islands
Cayman Islands
Falkland Islands
Gibraltar
Guernsey
Jersey
Isle of Man
Montserrat
Pitcairn Islands
Saint Helena
South Georgia and the South Sandwich Islands
Turks and Caicos Islands

Under U.S. Jurisdiction (14)
American Samoa
Baker Island
Guam
Howland Island
Jarvis Island
Johnston Atoll
Kingman Reef
Midway Islands
Navassa Island
Northern Mariana Islands
Palmyra Atoll
Puerto Rico
Virgin Islands
Wake Island

Disputed Territories (6): Antarctica, Gaza Strip, Paracel Islands, Spratly Islands, West Bank, Western Sahara

Kingdoms and Monarchs of the World

Country	Monarch	Type of monarchy	Country	Monarch	Type of monarchy
Bahrain	Sheik Hamad bin Isa al-Khalifa	Constitutional	Monaco	Prince Rainier III	Constitutional principality
Belgium	King Albert II	Constitutional	Morocco	King Muhammad VI	Constitutional
Bhutan	King Jigme Singye Wangchuck	Constitutional	Nepal	King Gyanendra Bir Bikram Shah Deva	Constitutional
Brunei	Sultan Haji Hassanal Bolkiah	Constitutional	Netherlands	Queen Beatrix	Constitutional
			Norway	King Harald V	Constitutional
Cambodia	King Norodom Sihanouk	Constitutional	Oman	Sultan Qabus ibn Sa'id	Absolute
Denmark	Queen Margrethe II	Constitutional	Qatar	Emir Sheik Hamad ibn Khalifa al-Thani	Traditional
Japan	Emperor Akihito	Constitutional			
Jordan	King Abdullah II	Constitutional	Saudi Arabia	King Fahd bin 'Abdulaziz	Absolute
Kuwait	Sheik Jaber al-Ahmad al-Sabah	Constitutional	Spain	King Juan Carlos I	Parliamentary
			Swaziland	King Mswati III	Near-absolute
Lesotho	King Letsie III	Constitutional	Sweden	King Carl XVI Gustaf	Constitutional
Liechtenstein	Prince Hans Adam II	Constitutional	Thailand	King Bhumibol Adulyadej	Constitutional
Luxembourg	Grand Duke Henri	Constitutional	Tonga	King Taufa'ahau Tupou IV	Constitutional
Malaysia	King Salahuddin Abdul Aziz Shah	Constitutional	United Kingdom	Queen Elizabeth II[1]	Constitutional[2]

1. Queen Elizabeth II is also the Sovereign of 15 countries in the Commonwealth of Nations: Antigua and Barbuda, Australia, the Bahamas, Barbados, Belize, Canada, Grenada, Jamaica, New Zealand, Papua New Guinea, St. Kitts and Nevis, St. Lucia, St. Vincent and the Grenadines, the Solomon Islands, and Tuvalu. 2. Also parliamentary democracy.

Area and Population of Countries

(mid-2001 estimates)

Country	Area (in sq km)	Population	Country	Area (in sq km)	Population
Afghanistan	652,000	26,813,057	Grenada	340	89,227
Albania	28,748	3,510,484	Guatemala	108,890	12,974,361
Algeria	2,381,740	31,736,053	Guinea	245,857	7,613,870
Andorra	468	67,627	Guinea-Bissau	36,120	1,315,822
Angola	1,246,700	10,366,031	Guyana	214,970	697,181
Antigua and Barbuda	442	66,970	Haiti	27,750	6,964,549
Argentina	2,766,890	37,384,816	Honduras	112,090	6,406,052
Armenia	29,800	3,336,100	Hungary	93,030	10,106,017
Australia	7,686,850	19,357,594	Iceland	103,000	277,906
Austria	83,858	8,150,835	India	3,287,590	1,029,991,145
Azerbaijan	86,600	7,771,092	Indonesia	1,919,440	228,437,870
Bahamas, The	13,940	297,852	Iran	1,648,000	66,128,965
Bahrain	620	645,361	Iraq	437,072	23,331,985
Bangladesh	144,000	131,269,860	Ireland	70,280	3,840,838
Barbados	430	275,330	Israel	20,770	5,938,093
Belarus	207,600	10,350,194	Italy	301,230	57,679,825
Belgium	30,510	10,258,762	Jamaica	10,990	2,665,636
Belize	22,960	256,062	Japan	377,835	126,771,662
Benin	112,620	6,590,782	Jordan	89,213	5,153,378
Bhutan	47,000	2,049,412	Kazakhstan	2,717,300	16,731,303
Bolivia	1,098,580	8,300,463	Kenya	582,650	30,765,916
Bosnia and Herzegovina	51,129	3,922,205	Kiribati	717	94,149
Botswana	600,370	1,586,119	Korea, North	120,540	21,968,228
Brazil	8,511,965	174,468,575	Korea, South	98,480	47,904,370
Brunei	5,770	343,653	Kuwait	17,820	2,041,961
Bulgaria	110,910	7,707,495	Kyrgyzstan	198,500	4,753,003
Burkina Faso	274,200	12,272,289	Laos	236,800	5,635,967
Burma (Myanmar)	678,500	41,994,678	Latvia	64,589	2,385,231
Burundi	27,830	6,223,897	Lebanon	10,400	3,627,774
Cambodia	181,040	12,491,501	Lesotho	30,355	2,177,062
Cameroon	475,440	15,803,220	Liberia	111,370	3,225,837
Canada	9,976,140	31,592,805	Libya	1,759,540	5,240,599
Cape Verde	4,033	405,163	Liechtenstein	160	32,528
Central African Republic	622,984	3,576,884	Lithuania	65,200	3,610,535
Chad	1,284,000	8,707,078	Luxembourg	2,586	442,972
Chile	756,950	15,328,467	Macedonia	25,333	2,046,209
China	9,596,960	1,273,111,290	Madagascar	587,040	15,982,563
Colombia	1,138,910	40,349,388	Malawi	118,480	10,548,250
Comoros	2,170	596,202	Malaysia	329,750	22,229,040
Congo, Republic of the	342,000	2,894,336	Maldives	300	310,764
Congo, Democratic Republic of the (formerly Zaire)	2,345,410	53,624,718	Mali	1,240,000	11,008,518
Costa Rica	51,100	3,773,057	Malta	316	394,583
Côte d'Ivoire	322,460	16,393,221	Marshall Islands	181	70,822
Croatia	56,538	4,334,142	Mauritania	1,030,700	2,747,312
Cuba	110,860	11,184,023	Mauritius	1,860	1,189,825
Cyprus	9,250	762,887	Mexico	1,972,550	101,879,171
Czech Republic	78,866	10,264,212	Micronesia, Federated States of	702	134,597
Denmark	43,094	5,352,815	Moldova	33,843	4,431,570
Djibouti	22,000	460,700	Monaco	1.95	31,842
Dominica	754	70,786	Mongolia	1,565,000	2,654,999
Dominican Republic	48,730	8,581,477	Morocco	446,550	30,645,305
Ecuador	283,560	13,183,978	Mozambique	801,590	19,371,057
Egypt	1,001,450	69,536,644	Namibia	825,418	1,797,677
El Salvador	21,040	6,237,662	Nauru	21	12,088
Equatorial Guinea	28,051	486,060	Nepal	140,800	25,284,463
Eritrea	121,320	4,298,269	Netherlands	41,532	15,981,472
Estonia	45,226	1,423,316	New Zealand	268,680	3,864,129
Ethiopia	1,127,127	65,891,874	Nicaragua	129,494	4,918,393
Fiji	18,270	844,330	Niger	1,267,000	10,355,156
Finland	337,030	5,175,783	Nigeria	923,768	126,635,626
France	547,030	59,551,227	Norway	324,220	4,503,440
Gabon	267,667	1,221,175	Oman	212,460	2,622,198
Gambia, The	11,300	1,411,205	Pakistan	803,940	144,616,639
Georgia	69,700	4,989,285	Palau	458	19,092
Germany	357,021	83,029,536	Panama	78,200	2,845,647
Ghana	238,540	19,894,014	Papua New Guinea	462,840	5,049,055
Greece	131,940	10,623,835	Paraguay	406,750	5,734,139

Country	Area (in sq km)	Population	Country	Area (in sq km)	Population
Peru	1,285,220	27,483,864	Swaziland	17,363	1,104,343
Philippines	300,000	82,841,518	Sweden	449,964	8,875,053
Poland	312,685	38,633,912	Switzerland	41,290	7,283,274
Portugal	92,391	10,066,253	Syria	185,180	16,728,808
Qatar	11,437	769,152	Taiwan	35,980	22,370,461
Romania	237,500	22,364,022	Tajikistan	143,100	6,578,681
Russia	17,075,200	145,470,197	Tanzania	945,087	36,232,074
Rwanda	26,338	7,312,756	Thailand	514,000	61,797,751
Saint Kitts and Nevis	261	38,756	Togo	56,785	5,153,088
Saint Lucia	620	158,178	Tonga	748	104,227
Saint Vincent and the Grenadines	389	115,942	Trinidad and Tobago	5,128	1,169,682
Samoa	2,860	179,058	Tunisia	163,610	9,705,102
San Marino	61	27,336	Turkey	780,580	66,493,970
São Tomé and Príncipe	1,001	165,034	Turkmenistan	488,100	4,603,244
Saudi Arabia	1,960,582	22,757,092	Tuvalu	26	10,991
Senegal	196,190	10,284,929	Uganda	236,040	23,985,712
Serbia and Montenegro (Yugoslavia)	102,350	10,677,290	Ukraine	603,700	48,760,474
Seychelles	455	79,715	United Arab Emirates	82,880	2,407,460
Sierra Leone	71,740	5,426,618	United Kingdom	244,820	59,647,790
Singapore	648	4,300,419	United States	9,629,091	278,058,881
Slovakia	48,845	5,414,937	Uruguay	176,220	3,360,105
Slovenia	20,253	1,930,132	Uzbekistan	447,400	25,155,064
Solomon Islands	28,450	480,442	Vanuatu	14,760	192,910
Somalia	637,657	7,488,773	Vatican City	0.44	880
South Africa	1,219,912	43,586,097	Venezuela	912,050	23,916,810
Spain	504,782	40,037,995	Vietnam	329,560	79,939,014
Sri Lanka	65,610	19,408,635	Western Sahara	266,000	250,559
Sudan	2,505,810	36,080,373	Yemen	527,970	18,078,035
Suriname	163,270	433,998	Zambia	752,614	9,770,199
			Zimbabwe	390,580	11,365,366

Source: U.S. Census Bureau, International Database and *The World Factbook, 2000.*

Most Populous Cities of the World

Rank	City[1]	Population	Year[2]	Rank	City[1]	Population	Year[2]
1.	Seoul, South Korea	9,981,649	2000e	11.	New York City, U.S.	7,420,166	1998e
2.	Mumbai (Bombay), India	9,925,891	1991c	12.	Delhi, India	7,206,700	1991c
3.	Karachi, Pakistan	9,863,000	1995e	13.	London, United Kingdom	7,007,100	1995e
4.	São Paulo, Brazil	9,811,776	1996c	14.	Beijing, China	6,970,000	1995e
5.	Shanghai, China	9,220,000	1995e	15.	Cairo, Egypt	6,955,000	1995e
6.	Jakarta, Indonesia	9,122,700	1995c	16.	Teheran, Iran	6,750,000	1994e
7.	Mexico City, Mexico	8,483,600	1995e	17.	Lima, Peru	6,214,100	1996e
8.	Moscow, Russia	8,434,000	1996e	18.	Bangkok, Thailand	5,584,200	1994e
9.	Tokyo, Japan	8,130,000	2000e	19.	Rio de Janeiro, Brazil	5,533,011	1996c
10.	Istanbul, Turkey	7,774,169	1995e	20.	Bogotá, Colombia	5,237,635	1995e

1. Refers to the city proper, as opposed to an urban agglomeration, which would also count the surrounding urban areas in the total. 2. Year of population count: "e" = estimated; "c" = census figure. *Source:* © Xist.org, 2001. Reprinted with permission. Web: www.xist.org/city_nonagg.htm.

Most Populous Urban Agglomerations[1]

Name	Country	Est. population (in millions)	Name	Country	Est. population (in millions)
1. Tokyo	Japan	34.5	11. Buenos Aires	Argentina	13.4
2. New York	USA	21.4	12. Jakarta	Indonesia	13.4
3. Seoul	Korea	20.3	13. Calcutta	India	13.2
4. Mexico City	Mexico	19.3	14. Moscow	Russia	13.2
5. Bombay (Mumbai)	India	19.0	15. Delhi	India	12.3
6. São Paulo	Brazil	18.5	16. London	UK	11.8
7. Osaka	Japan	17.9	17. Shanghai	China	11.8
8. Los Angeles	USA	16.6	18. Rio de Janeiro	Brazil	11.2
9. Cairo	Egypt	14.7	19. Karachi	Pakistan	10.8
10. Manila	Philippines	13.8	20. Istanbul	Turkey	10.6

NOTE: The definitions of agglomerations vary significantly from city to city, hence the difficulty of compiling an accurate, comparative list of the world's most populous urban areas. 1. Includes metropolitan areas and surrounding urban agglomerations. Agglomerations include a central city and bordering urban areas. Some agglomerations have more than one central city (e.g., Washington, DC, includes Baltimore; Tokyo includes Yokohama and Kawasaki; New York includes Newark and Paterson, N.J.) *Source:* Thomas Brinkhoff, *Principal Agglomerations and Cities of the World.* Web: www.citypopulation.de, May 13, 2001.

Newspapers, Radio, Television, Telephones, and Computers by Country

(rates per 1,000 persons)

Country	Daily newspaper circulation,[1] 1996	Radio receivers,[2] 1997	Television receivers,[3] 1997	Telephone main lines,[4] 1999	Cellular phone subscribers,[4] 1999	Personal computers,[5] 1999
Algeria	38	242	105	52	2	6
Argentina	123	681	223	201	121	49
Australia	296	1,391	554	521	344	471
Brazil	40	434	223	149	90	36
Bulgaria	254	537	394	342	42	27
Canada	158	1,067	710	635[6]	230	361
Chile	98	354	215	207	151	67
China	n.a.	335	321	86	34	12
Cuba	118	352	239	39	1	7
Czech Republic	254	803	531	371	190	107
Egypt	38	317	119	60[6]	7	11
Finland	455	1,498	622	553	667	360
France	218	946	595	579	364	221
Germany	311	948	567	588	286	297
Ghana	14	236	93	8	4	3
Greece	n.a.	475	240	528	311	60
Hungary	186	690	435	402	160	74
India	n.a.	120	65	22[6]	1[6]	3
Indonesia	23	155	68	29	11	9
Iran	26	263	71	125	7	52
Iraq	20	229	83	31[6]	—[6]	n.a.
Israel	288	524	288	459	459	246
Italy	104	880	528	462	528	192
Japan	578	956	686	494	449	287
Korea, South	n.a.	1,039	348	441	504	183
Mexico	97	329	272	112	78	44
Pakistan	n.a.	94	22	22	2	4
Peru	84	273	126	67	39	20
Russia	105	417	410	197[6]	9	37
Saudi Arabia	59	321	262	143[6]	31[6]	57
South Africa	34	355	134	138	132	60
Spain	99	331	409	418	312	122
Syria	20	278	70	102	—	15
Taiwan	156[6]	n.a.	n.a.	544	521	181
Thailand	64	234	254	84[6]	33[6]	23
Turkey	110	178	330	265	117	32
United Kingdom	331	1,443	521	557[6]	408	306
United States	**212**	**2,116**	**806**	**661[6]**	**312**	**511**
Venezuela	206	472	180	109	143	42

1. Publications containing general news and appearing at least 4 times a week; may range in size from a single sheet to 50 or more pages. Circulation data refer to average circulation per issue or number of printed copies per issue and include copies sold outside the country. 2. Data cover estimated number of receivers in use and apply to all types of receivers for radio broadcasts to the public, including receivers connected to a radio "redistribution system" but excluding television sets. 3. Estimated number of sets in use. 4. As of Dec. 31. 5. In many countries mainframe computers are used extensively, and thousands of users can be connected to a single mainframe computer; thus the number of PCs understates the total use of computers. 6. 1998 data. *Sources:* Except as noted, newspapers, radio, and television—United Nations Educational, Scientific, and Cultural Organization, Paris, France, *Statistical Yearbook* (copyright); telephones, cellular phones, and personal computers—International Telecommunications Union, Geneva, Switzerland, *World Telecommunication Indicators* (copyright).

Crude Marriage Rates for Selected Countries

(per 1,000 population)

Country	1999	1997	1990	Country	1999	1997	1990	Country	1999	1997	1990
Australia	6.0	5.8	6.9	Hungary	4.5	4.6	6.4	Portugal	6.8	6.5	7.3
Austria	4.8	5.1	5.8	Ireland	4.9	4.3	5.0	Romania	6.5	6.5	8.3
Belgium	4.3	4.7	6.6	Israel	5.9	5.6	7.0	Russia	5.8	6.3	8.9
Bulgaria	4.2	4.1	6.7	Italy	—	4.7	5.4	Sweden	4.0	3.7	4.7
Czech Republic	5.2	5.6	8.4	Japan	6.3	6.2	5.8	Switzerland	4.9	5.3	6.9
Denmark	6.6	6.4	6.1	Luxembourg	4.9	4.8	6.2	United Kingdom	5.1	—	6.8
Finland	4.7	4.6	4.8	Netherlands	5.6	5.5	6.4	United States	8.3	8.9	9.8
France	—	4.8	5.1	New Zealand	5.3	5.3	7.0	Yugoslavia[3]	5.0	5.3	6.2
Germany[2]	5.2	5.2	6.5	Norway	5.3	—	5.2				
Greece	6.4	5.7	5.8	Poland	5.7	5.3	6.7				

1. Data prior to 1993 pertain to the former Czechoslovakia. 2. All data pertaining to Germany prior to 1990 are for West Germany. 3. Beginning Jan. 1992, data refer to the Federal Republic of Yugoslavia. Prior to that date, data refer to the Socialist Federal Republic of Yugoslavia. *Source:* United Nations, *Monthly Bulletin of Statistics*, April 2001.

Infant Mortality and Life Expectancy for Selected Countries, 2001

Country	Infant mortality[1]	Life expectancy[2]	Country	Infant mortality[1]	Life expectancy[2]	Country	Infant mortality[1]	Life expectancy[2]
Albania	39.99	71.83	Germany	4.71	77.61	Peru	39.39	70.30
Australia	4.97	79.87	Greece	6.38	78.59	Poland	9.39	73.42
Austria	4.44	77.84	Guatemala	45.79	66.51	Portugal	5.94	75.94
Bangladesh	69.85	60.54	Hungary	8.96	71.63	Russia	20.05	67.34
Belgium	4.70	77.96	India	63.19	62.86	Slovakia	8.97	73.97
Brazil	36.96	63.24	Iran	29.04	69.95	S. Africa	60.33	48.09
Canada	5.02	79.56	Ireland	5.53	76.99	Spain	4.92	78.93
Chile	9.36	75.94	Israel	7.72	78.71	Sri Lanka	16.08	72.09
China	28.08	71.62	Italy	5.84	79.14	Sweden	3.47	79.71
Costa Rica	11.18	76.02	Japan	3.88	80.80	Switzerland	4.48	79.73
Cyprus	7.89	76.89	Kenya	67.99	47.49	Syria	33.80	68.77
Czech Rep.	5.55	74.73	Korea, South	7.71	74.65	Trinidad	24.98	68.27
Denmark	5.04	76.72	Mexico	25.36	71.76	United Kingdom	5.54	77.82
Ecuador	34.08	71.33	New Zealand	6.28	77.99	United States	6.76	77.26
Egypt	60.46	63.69	Norway	3.94	78.79	Uruguay	14.70	75.44
Finland	3.79	77.58	Pakistan	80.50	61.45	Venezuela	25.37	73.31
France	4.46	78.90	Panama	20.18	75.68	Zimbabwe	62.61	37.13

1. Infant deaths per 1,000 live births. 2. Life expectancy at birth, in years. *Source:* U.S. Census Bureau, International Database.

Crude Birth and Death Rates for Selected Countries
(per 1,000 population)

Country	Birth rate						Death rate					
	2001	1998	1990	1985	1980	1975	2001	1998	1990	1985	1980	1975
Australia	12.86	13.47	15.4	15.7	15.3	16.9	7.18	6.89	7.0	7.5	7.4	7.9
Austria	9.74	9.89	11.6	11.6	12.0	12.5	9.80	10.05	10.6	11.9	12.2	12.8
Belgium	10.74	10.21	12.6	11.5	12.7	12.2	10.10	10.41	10.6	11.2	11.6	12.2
Czech Republic[1]	9.11	8.96	13.4	14.5	16.4	19.6	10.81	10.92	11.7	11.8	12.1	11.5
France	12.10	11.68	13.5	13.9	14.8	14.1	9.09	9.12	9.3	10.1	10.2	10.6
Germany[2]	9.16	8.84	11.4	9.6	10.0	9.7	10.42	10.77	11.2	11.5	11.6	12.1
Greece	9.83	9.65	10.2	11.7	15.4	15.7	9.73	9.37	9.3	9.4	9.1	8.9
Ireland	14.57	13.49	15.1	17.6	21.9	21.5	8.07	8.51	9.1	9.4	9.7	10.6
Israel	19.12	19.99	22.2	23.5	24.1	28.2	6.22	6.19	6.2	6.6	6.7	7.1
Italy	9.05	9.13	9.8	10.1	11.2	14.8	10.07	10.18	9.4	9.5	9.7	9.9
Japan	10.04	10.26	9.9	11.9	13.7	17.2	8.34	7.94	6.7	6.2	6.2	6.4
Mauritius	16.50	18.64	21.0	18.8	27.0	25.1	6.82	6.69	6.5	6.8	7.2	8.1
Netherlands	11.85	11.62	13.3	12.3	12.8	13.0	8.69	8.69	8.6	8.5	8.1	8.3
New Zealand	14.28	14.89	18.0	15.6	—	18.4	7.56	7.60	7.9	8.4	—	8.1
Norway	12.60	12.90	14.3	12.3	12.5	14.1	9.83	10.17	10.7	10.7	10.1	9.9
Panama	19.06	21.99	23.9	26.6	26.8	32.3	4.95	5.14	—	—	—	—
Poland	10.20	9.79	14.3	18.2	19.5	18.9	9.98	9.76	10.2	10.3	9.8	8.7
Portugal	11.51	10.63	11.8	12.8	16.4	19.1	10.21	10.26	10.4	9.6	9.9	10.4
Romania	10.80	9.33	13.6	15.8	—	—	12.28	11.62	10.6	10.9	—	—
Switzerland	10.12	10.81	12.5	11.6	11.3	12.3	8.77	9.03	9.5	9.2	9.2	8.7
Tunisia	17.11	20.07	25.8	31.3	35.2	36.6	4.99	5.06	—	—	—	—
United Kingdom	11.54	12.01	13.9	13.3	13.5	12.5	10.35	10.72	11.2	11.8	11.8	11.9
United States	14.20	14.40	16.7	15.7	16.2	14.0	8.70	8.80	8.6	8.7	8.9	8.9

1. Data prior to 1994 pertain to the former Czechoslovakia. 2. All data pertaining to Germany prior to 1990 are for West Germany. NOTE: (—) = not available. *Source:* United Nations, *Monthly Bulletin of Statistics, June 1997.* Data for 2001 from the U.S. Census Bureau, International Database.

Legal Abortions in Selected Countries

Country	1985	1990	1995	Country	1985	1990	1995
Bulgaria	132,041	144,644	97,023	Israel	18,406	15,509	—
Canada	60,956	71,092	70,549	Italy	210,192	161,285	134,137
Cuba	138,671	147,530	83,963	Japan	550,127	456,797	343,024
Finland	13,832	12,232	9,884	New Z.	7,130	11,173	—
France	173,335	161,129	—	Norway	14,599	15,551	13,672
Germany[1]	—	145,267	97,937	Poland	135,564	59,417	559
Greece	180	1,216	—	Russia	—	4,103,425	2,766,362
Hungary	81,970	90,394	76,957	Sweden	30,838	37,489	—
Iceland	705	714	807	UK	180,983	184,092	167,297
India	583,704	596,345	—	U.S.	1,588,600	1,429,577	1,210,883

1. Figures for Germany represent those available after the unification of the Federal Republic of Germany and the German Democratic Republic in Oct. 1990. *Source:* United Nations, *Demographic Yearbook, 1997.*

Prevalence of Contraceptive Use in Selected Countries[1]

Country	Year of data	Contra-ceptive use[2]	Country	Year of data	Contra-ceptive use[2]	Country	Year of data	Contra-ceptive use[2]
Australia	1986	76.1%	India	1992–1993	40.7%	Romania	1993	57.3%
Bangladesh	1993–1994	44.6	Indonesia	1994	54.7	Russia	1994	66.8
Brazil	1996	76.7	Iran	1992	65.0	South Africa	1988	49.7
Canada	1984	73.1	Jamaica	1993	62.0	South Korea	1991	79.0
China	1992	76.9	Japan	1992	64.0	Switzerland	1994–1995	81.9
Colombia	1995	72.2	Jordan	1990	34.9	Thailand	1987	65.5
Costa Rica	1993	75.0	Kenya	1993	33.0	Turkey	1993	62.6
Denmark	1988	78.0	Mexico	1987	52.7	United Kingdom	1989	72.0
Egypt	1995	47.9	New Zealand	1976	69.5	United States	1990	70.7
El Salvador	1993	53.3	Nigeria	1990	6.0	Uzbekistan	1996	55.6
Ethiopia	1990	4.3	Pakistan	1990–1991	11.8	Venezuela	1977	60.3
France	1994	75.1	Peru	1996	64.2			

1. Data refer to currently married women, 15–49. 2. Contraception includes use of the birth control pill, the IUD (intra-uterine device), condoms, male and female sterilization, and other modern methods, as well as traditional methods. *Source: World Population Profile: 1998*, U.S. Census Bureau.

The Death Penalty Worldwide

Death Penalty Outlawed (year)
Andorra (1990)
Angola (1992)
Australia (1985)
Austria (1968)
Azerbaijan (1998)
Belgium (1996)
Bermuda (1999)
Bulgaria (1998)
Cambodia (1989)
Canada (1998)
Cape Verde (1981)
Colombia (1910)
Costa Rica (1877)
Croatia (1990)
Czech Republic (1990)
Denmark (1978)
Dominican Republic (1966)
East Timor (1999)
Ecuador (1906)
Estonia (1998)
Finland (1972)
France (1981)
Georgia (1997)
Germany (1987)
Greece (1993)
Guinea-Bissau (1993)
Haiti (1987)
Honduras (1956)
Hungary (1990)
Iceland (1928)
Ireland (1990)
Italy (1994)
Kiribati (1979)
Liechtenstein (1987)
Lithuania (1998)
Luxembourg (1979)
Macedonia (n.a.)
Marshall Islands (1986)
Mauritius (1995)
Micronesia (1986)
Moldova (1995)

Monaco (1962)
Mozambique (1990)
Namibia (1990)
Nepal (1997)
Netherlands (1982)
New Zealand (1989)
Nicaragua (1979)
Norway (1979)
Palau (n.a.)
Panama (1903)
Paraguay (1992)
Poland (1997)
Portugal (1976)
Romania (1989)
San Marino (1865)
São Tomé and Príncipe (1990)
Seychelles (1993)
Slovak Republic (1990)
Slovenia (1989)
Solomon Islands (1966)
South Africa (1997)
Spain (1995)
Sweden (1972)
Switzerland (1992)
Turkmenistan (1999)
Tuvalu (1978)
Ukraine (1999)
United Kingdom (1998)
Uruguay (1907)
Vanuatu (1980)
Vatican City State (1969)
Venezuela (1863)

Death Penalty Permitted in Exceptional Cases[1]
Argentina
Bolivia
Bosnia-Herzegovina
Brazil
Canada

Cook Islands
Cyprus
El Salvador
Fiji
Israel
Latvia
Malta
Mexico
Peru
Seychelles

De Facto Ban on Death Penalty[2]
Albania (n.a.)
Bermuda (1977)
Bhutan (1964)[3]
Brunei Darussalam (1957)[3]
Central African Republic (1981)
Congo (Republic) (1982)
Côte d'Ivoire (n.a.)
Djibouti (1977)[3]
Gambia (1981)
Grenada (1978)
Madagascar (1958)[3]
Maldives (1952)[3]
Mali (1980)
Nauru (1968)
Niger (1976)[3]
Papua New Guinea (1950)
Samoa (1962)
Senegal (1967)
Sri Lanka (1976)
Suriname (1982)
Togo (n.a.)
Tonga (1982)
Turkey (1984)

Death Penalty Permitted
Afghanistan
Algeria
Antigua and Barbuda
Armenia

Bahamas
Bahrain
Bangladesh
Barbados
Belarus
Belize
Benin
Botswana
Burkina Faso
Burundi
Cameroon
Chad
Chile
China (People's Republic)
Comoros
Congo (Democratic Republic)
Cuba
Dominica
Egypt
Equatorial Guinea
Eritrea
Ethiopia
Gabon
Ghana
Guatemala
Guinea
Guyana
India
Indonesia
Iran
Iraq
Jamaica
Japan
Jordan
Kazakhstan
Kenya
Korea, North
Korea, South
Kuwait
Kyrgyzstan
Laos
Lebanon
Lesotho
Liberia

Libya
Malawi
Malaysia
Mauritania
Mongolia
Morocco
Myanmar
Nigeria
Oman
Pakistan
Palestinian Authority
Philippines
Qatar
Russian Federation
Rwanda
St. Kitts and Nevis
St. Lucia
St. Vincent and the Grenadines
Saudi Arabia
Sierra Leone
Singapore
Somalia
Sudan
Swaziland
Syria
Taiwan
Tajikistan
Tanzania
Thailand
Trinidad and Tobago
Tunisia
Turkmenistan
Uganda
Ukraine
United Arab Emirates
United States of America
Uzbekistan
Vietnam
Yemen
Yugoslavia
Zambia
Zimbabwe

NOTE: n.a. = date not available. 1. Exceptional crimes include some committed under military law or crimes committed in wartime. 2. Death penalty is sanctioned by law but has not been the practice for 10 or more years (year of last execution). 3. Year of last known execution. *Source:* Amnesty International, July 2001.

Most and Least Livable Countries: UN Human Development Index, 2001

The Human Development Index (HDI), published annually by the UN, ranks nations according to their citizens' quality of life rather than strictly by a nation's traditional economic figures. The criteria for calculating rankings include life expectancy, adult literacy, school enrollment, educational attainment, and per capita GDP.

Most Livable Countries, 2001		Least Livable Countries, 2001	
1. Norway	14. United Kingdom	1. Sierra Leone	14. Gambia
2. Australia	15. Denmark	2. Niger	15. Eritrea
3. Canada	16. Austria	3. Burundi	16. Benin
4. Sweden	17. Germany	4. Burkina Faso	17. Angola
5. Belgium	18. Ireland	5. Ethiopia	18. Senegal
6. United States	19. New Zealand	6. Mozambique	19. Côte d'Ivoire
7. Iceland	20. Italy	7. Guinea-Bissau	20. Zambia
8. Netherlands	21. Spain	8. Chad	21. Congo, Dem. Rep. of
9. Japan	22. Israel	9. Central African Republic	22. Uganda
10. Finland	23. Greece	10. Mali	23. Tanzania
11. Switzerland	24. Cyprus	11. Rwanda	24. Mauritania
12. Luxembourg	25. Singapore	12. Malawi	25. Sudan
13. France		13. Guinea	

Source: Human Development Report, 2001, United Nations; www.undp.org/hdr2001.

The 2001 Transparency International Corruption Perceptions Index (CPI)

According to the annual survey by the Berlin-based organization Transparency International, the world's least corrupt country is Finland and its most corrupt is Bangladesh. The CPI rates a country's propensity to accept bribes according to the perceptions of business people, risk analysts, and the general public. Because of the absence of reliable data, only 91 of the countries of the world—a little more than half—are included in the survey. The scores range from 10 (squeaky clean) to zero (highly corrupt). More than two-thirds of the countries surveyed scored less than 5.5, which is the number Transparency International considers the borderline figure distinguishing countries that do and do not have a serious corruption problem.

Country rank	Country	2001 CPI Score	Country rank	Country	2001 CPI Score	Country rank	Country	2001 CPI Score
1.	Finland	9.9		Trinidad &			Thailand	3.2
2.	Denmark	9.5		Tobago	5.3	63.	Dominican	
3.	New Zealand	9.4		Tunisia	5.3		Republic	3.1
4.	Iceland	9.2	34.	Slovenia	5.2		Moldova	3.1
	Singapore	9.2	35.	Uruguay	5.1	65.	Guatemala	2.9
6.	Sweden	9.0	36.	Malaysia	5.0		Philippines	2.9
7.	Canada	8.9	37.	Jordan	4.9		Senegal	2.9
8.	Netherlands	8.8	38.	Lithuania	4.8		Zimbabwe	2.9
9.	Luxembourg	8.7		South Africa	4.8	69.	Romania	2.8
10.	Norway	8.6	40.	Costa Rica	4.5		Venezuela	2.8
11.	Australia	8.5		Mauritius	4.5	71.	Honduras	2.7
12.	Switzerland	8.4	42.	Greece	4.2		India	2.7
13.	United Kingdom	8.3		South Korea	4.2		Kazakhstan	2.7
14.	Hong Kong	7.9	44.	Peru	4.1		Uzbekistan	2.7
15.	Austria	7.8		Poland	4.1	75.	Vietnam	2.6
16.	Israel	7.6	46.	Brazil	4.0		Zambia	2.6
	United States	7.6	47.	Bulgaria	3.9	77.	Côte d'Ivoire	2.4
18.	Chile	7.5		Croatia	3.9		Nicaragua	2.4
	Ireland	7.5		Czech Republic	3.9	79.	Ecuador	2.3
20.	Germany	7.4	50.	Colombia	3.8		Pakistan	2.3
21.	Japan	7.1	51.	Mexico	3.7		Russia	2.3
22.	Spain	7.0		Panama	3.7	82.	Tanzania	2.2
23.	France	6.7		Slovak Republic	3.7	83.	Ukraine	2.1
24.	Belgium	6.6	54.	Egypt	3.6	84.	Azerbaijan	2.0
25.	Portugal	6.3		El Salvador	3.6		Bolivia	2.0
26.	Botswana	6.0		Turkey	3.6		Cameroon	2.0
27.	Taiwan	5.9	57.	Argentina	3.5		Kenya	2.0
28.	Estonia	5.6		China	3.5	88.	Indonesia	1.9
29.	Italy	5.5	59.	Ghana	3.4		Uganda	1.9
30.	Namibia	5.4		Latvia	3.4	90.	Nigeria	1.0
31.	Hungary	5.3	61.	Malawi	3.2	91.	Bangladesh	0.4

NOTE: The Bangladesh score was based on only three available independent survey sources, which varied greatly. Transparency International stresses that these results need to be viewed with caution. *Source:* Transparency International, 2001. Web: www.transparency.de.

The 1999 Bribe Payers' Index

The Bribe Payers' Index (BPI) ranks the 19 leading exporting countries according to the degree to which their companies are perceived to be paying bribes abroad to senior public officials. According to the survey published by Transparency International in 1999, the countries most likely to offer bribes—from most to least likely—were China, South Korea, Taiwan, Italy, Malaysia, Japan, France, Spain, Singapore, United States, Germany, Belgium, United Kingdom, Netherlands, Switzerland, Austria, Canada, Australia, and Sweden.

Top 30 Countries with Highest Military Expenditures, 1997

Rank	Country	In millions of dollars	Rank	Country	In millions of dollars	Rank	Country	In millions of dollars
1.	United States	$276,300	11.	Brazil	$14,150	22.	Poland	$6,698
2.	China, People's Rep. of	74,910	12.	Taiwan	13,060	23.	Sweden	5,550
3.	Russia	41,730	13.	India	10,850	24.	Greece	5,533
4.	France	41,520	14.	Israel	9,335	25.	Indonesia	4,812
5.	Japan	40,840	15.	Australia	8,463	26.	Iran	4,726
6.	United Kingdom	35,290	16.	Canada	7,800	27.	Mexico	4,294
7.	Germany	32,870	17.	Turkey	7,792	28.	Ukraine	4,285
8.	Italy	22,720	18.	Spain	7,670	29.	Switzerland	3,859
9.	Saudi Arabia	21,150	19.	Netherlands	6,839	30.	Argentina	3,701
10.	South Korea	15,020	20.	North Korea	6,000			
			21.	Singapore	5,664			

Source: U.S. Arms Control and Disarmament Agency, World Military Expenditures and Arms Transfers, 1998.

Top 30 Countries with Highest Military Expenditures Ranked by Percent of Country's GNP, 1997

Rank	Country	Percentage	Rank	Country	Percentage	Rank	Country	Percentage
1.	Burma	n.a.	10.	Russia	30.9	20.	Qatar	n.a.
2.	Sudan	53.8%	11.	Liberia	n.a.	21.	Uganda	23.9
3.	United Arab Emirates	46.5	12.	Central African Republic	27.7	22.	Taiwan	23.8
4.	Congo, Dem. Rep. of	41.4	13.	Kuwait	26.8	23.	Rwanda	22.2
5.	Oman	36.4	14.	Burundi	25.8	24.	Sri Lanka	21.2
6.	Angola	36.3		Cambodia	25.8	25.	Israel	20.9
7.	Saudi Arabia	35.8	16.	Jordan	25.0	26.	Ecuador	20.3
8.	Sierra Leone	33.0	17.	Bahrain	24.9	27.	Croatia	20.1
9.	North Korea	n.a.	18.	Pakistan	24.2	28.	Colombia	19.9
			19.	Syria	n.a.	29.	Singapore	19.4
						30.	Eritrea	18.1

Source: U.S. Arms Control and Disarmament Agency, World Military Expenditures and Arms Transfers, 1998.

Worldwide Armed Conflicts, 2000

An armed conflict is defined as a political conflict involving armed combat by the military forces of at least one state (or one or more armed factions seeking to gain control of all or part of the state), and in which at least 1,000 people have been killed during the fighting. At the end of 2000, there were 40 armed conflicts being fought on the territories of 35 countries. The total number of armed conflicts was unchanged from 1999, although the number of countries involved was down by one. *The Armed Conflicts Report 2001* includes 3 new armed conflicts: Guinea, Nepal, and the Aceh region of Indonesia. Three conflicts ended in 2000: Cambodia, Egypt, and Tajikistan.

	No. of conflicts in region	No. of countries hosting conflicts	Percentage of world conflicts
Africa	17	18	42.5%
Asia	14	8	35.0%
Europe	2	2	5.0%
The Americas	2	2	5.0%
Middle East	5	5	12.5%
World Total	**40**	**35**	**100.0%**

Source: The Armed Conflicts 2001 Report, Project Ploughshares, Institute of Peace and Conflict Studies, Conrad Grebel College; Waterloo, Ontario, Canada. www.ploughshares.ca.

Countries with Nuclear Weapons Capability

Acknowledged Nuclear Weapons Capability

Britain	France	Pakistan	United States
China	India	Russia	

Unacknowledged Nuclear Weapons Capability
Israel

Seeking Nuclear Weapons Capability

Iran	Iraq

Abandoned Nuclear Weapons Development

North Korea—An accord was reached with the North Korean government in 1994 to freeze and dismantle nuclear weapons development.

South Africa—Constructed but then voluntarily dismantled 6 uranium bombs.

Belarus, Kazakhstan, Ukraine—When Soviet Union broke up, these former states possessed nuclear warheads that they have since given up.

Source: U.S. State Department, Time Magazine.

Worldwide Refugees and Asylum Seekers, 2000

Group or country of origin	Number	Group or country of origin	Number	Group or country of origin	Number
Palestinians	4,000,000[1]	Yugoslavia	190,000[1]	Russian Federation	38,000
Afghanistan	3,600,000[1]	China	145,000	Turkey	36,000
Sudan	460,000	Bhutan	144,000	Georgia	26,000
Iraq	450,000[1]	East Timor	120,000	Haiti	23,000
Burundi	420,000	Sri Lanka	110,000	Congo, Dem. Rep. of	20,000
Angola	400,000	Western Sahara	110,000[1]	Uganda	20,000
Sierra Leone	400,000[1]	Guatemala	100,000[2]	India	17,000[1]
Myanmar (Burma)	380,000[1]	Tajikistan	60,000[1]	Cambodia	16,000
Somalia	370,000[1]	Philippines	57,000	Nicaragua	16,000
Congo, Rep. of	350,000	Rwanda	55,000[1]	Colombia	10,000[1]
Eritrea	350,000[1]	Chad	53,000	Ghana	10,000
Croatia	315,000[1]	Iran	51,000	Senegal	10,000
Vietnam	300,000	Algeria	50,000[1]	Nigeria	7,000
Bosnia and Herzegovina	250,000[1]	Mauritania	50,000	Indonesia	6,000
El Salvador	230,000[2]	North Korea	50,000[1]		
Liberia	200,000[1]	Ethiopia	40,000[1]		

NOTE: This table shows the countries that have produced the greatest numbers of refugees and asylum seekers. Statistics on refugees and other uprooted people are often inexact and controversial. One country's refugee is another's illegal alien. Government tallies cannot always be trusted to give full and unbiased accounts of refugee movements. As of Dec. 31, 2000, the U.S. Committee for Refugees estimated that there were 14,500,000 refugees throughout the world. 1. Sources vary widely in number reported. 2. Includes asylum cases pending in the United States; USCR approximates the number of individuals represented per case. *Source:* U.S. Committee for Refugees.

Economic Statistics by Country, 1999

Country	GDP/PPP	GDP/PPP per capita	Real growth rate (%)	Inflation (%)	Country	GDP/PPP	GDP/PPP per capita	Real growth rate (%)	Inflation (%)
Afghanistan	$21 billion	$ 800	n.a.	n.a.	Congo, Rep. of	$4.15 billion	$ 1,530	5.0%	4.0%
Albania	5.6 billion	1,650	8.0%	0.5%	Congo, Dem. Rep. of	35.7 billion	710	1.0	46.0
Algeria	147.6 billion	4,700	3.9	4.2	Costa Rica	26 billion	7,100	7.0	10.8
Andorra	1.2 billion[1]	18,000	n.a.	1.6[2]	Côte d'Ivoire	25.7 billion	1,600	5.0	2.5
Angola	11.6 billion	1,030	4.0	270.0	Croatia	23.9 billion	5,100	0.0	4.4
Antigua	524 million	8,200	2.8	1.6	Cuba	18.6 billion	1,700	6.2	0.3
Argentina	367 billion	10,000	–3.0	–2.0	Cyprus*	9 billion[2]	15,400	3.0	2.3[2]
Armenia	9.9 billion	2,900	5.0	2.5		820 million	5,000	5.3	66.0
Australia	416.2 billion	22,200	4.3	1.8	Czech Rep.	120.8 billion	11,700	–0.5	2.5
Austria	190.6 billion	23,400	2.0	0.5	Denmark	127.7 billion	23,800	1.3	2.5
Azerbaijan	14 billion	1,770	7.0	–6.8	Djibouti	550 million	1,200	2.0	0.0
Bahamas	5.58 billion[2]	20,000	3.0	1.3	Dominica	225 million[2]	3,400	2.0	1.1[2]
Bahrain	8.6 billion	13,700	4.0	0.5[2]	Dominican Rep.	43.7 billion	5,400	8.3	5.1
Bangladesh	187 billion	1,470	5.2	9.0[3]	Ecuador	54.5 billion	4,300	–8.0	59.9
Barbados	2.9 billion[2]	11,200	4.4	1.7[2]	Egypt	200 billion	3,000	5.0	3.7
Belarus	55.2 billion	5,300	1.5	295.0	El Salvador	18.1 billion	3,100	2.2	1.3
Belgium	243.4 billion	23,900	1.8	1.0	Eq. Guinea	960 million	2,000	15.0	6.0
Belize	740 million	3,100	4.0	–0.9	Eritrea	2.9 billion	750	3.0	9.0[2]
Benin	8.1 billion	1,300	5.0	3.0	Estonia	7.9 billion	5,600	–0.5	3.7
Bhutan	2.1 billion	1,060	7.0	9.0[2]	Ethiopia	33.3 billion	560	0.0	4.0
Bolivia	24.2 billion	3,000	2.0	2.1	Fiji	5.9 billion	7,300	7.8	0.0
Bosnia	6.2 billion	1,770	5.0	5.0[4]	Finland	108.6 billion	21,000	3.5	1.0
Botswana	5.7 billion	3,900	6.5	7.7	France	1.373 trillion	23,300	2.7	0.5
Brazil	1.057 trillion	6,150	0.8	5.0	Gabon	7.9 billion	6,500	1.7	2.9
Brunei	5.6 billion	17,400	2.5	1.0	Gambia, The	1.4 billion	1,030	4.2	2.5
Bulgaria	34.9 billion	4,300	2.5	6.2	Georgia	11.7 billion	2,300	3.5	19.0
Burkina Faso	12.4 billion	1,100	5.5	2.5	Germany	1.864 trillion	22,700	1.5	0.8
Burundi	4.2 billion	730	–1.0	26.0	Ghana	35.5 billion	1,900	4.3	12.8
Cambodia	8.2 billion	710	4.0	4.5	Greece	149.2 billion	13,900	3.0	2.6
Cameroon	31.5 billion	2,000	5.2	2.1	Grenada	360 million	3,700	5.0	1.3[2]
Canada	722.3 billion	23,300	3.6	1.7	Guatemala	47.9 billion	3,900	3.5	6.8
Cape Verde	618 million	1,500	5.0	5.0	Guinea	9.2 billion	1,200	3.7	4.5
Central African Republic	5.8 billion	1,700	5.0	2.6	Guinea-Bis.	1.1 billion	900	9.5	5.5
Chad	7.6 billion	1,000	0.6	12.0[2]	Guyana	1.86 billion	2,500	1.8	5.5
Chile	185.1 billion	12,400	–1.0	3.4	Haiti	9.2 billion	1,340	2.4	9.0
China	4.8 trillion	3,800	7.0	–1.3	Honduras	14.1 billion	2,050	–3.0	14.0
Colombia	245.1 billion	6,200	–5.0	9.2					
Comoros	410 million[2]	725	0.0	4.0[2]					

Country	GDP/PPP	GDP/PPP per capita	Real growth rate (%)	Inflation (%)	Country	GDP/PPP	GDP/PPP per capita	Real growth rate (%)	Inflation (%)
Hungary	$79.4 billion	$ 7,800	4.0%	10.0%	Papua New Guinea	$11.6 billion	$ 2,500	3.6%	16.5%
Iceland	6.42 billion	23,500	4.5	1.9	Paraguay	19.9 billion	3,650	–1.0	5.0
India	1.805 trillion	1,800	5.5	6.7	Peru	116 billion	4,400	2.4	5.5
Indonesia	610 billion	2,800	0.0	2.0	The Philippines	282 billion	3,600	2.9	6.8
Iran	347.6 billion	5,300	1.0	30.0	Poland	276.5 billion	7,200	3.8	8.4
Iraq	59.9 billion	2,700	13.0	135.0	Portugal	151.4 billion	15,300	3.2	2.4
Ireland	73.7 billion	20,300	8.4	2.2	Qatar	12.3 billion	17,000	1.5	2.0
Israel	105.4 billion	18,300	2.1	1.3	Romania	87.4 billion	3,900	–4.8	44.0
Italy	1.212 trillion	21,400	1.3	1.7	Russia	620.3 billion	4,200	3.2	86.0
Jamaica	8.8 billion	3,350	–0.5	9.4	Rwanda	5.9 billion	720	5.3	10.0[2]
Japan	2.95 trillion	23,400	0.3	–0.8	St. Kitts	244 million[2]	6,000	1.6	1.0
Jordan	16 billion	3,500	2.0	3.0	St. Lucia	656 million[2]	4,300	2.9	3.7
Kazakhstan	54.5 billion	3,200	1.7	8.3	St. Vincent	309 million	2,600	4.0	2.0
Kenya	45.1 billion	1,600	1.5	6.0	Samoa	485 million[2]	2,100	1.8	2.2
Kiribati	74 million	860	2.5	2.0	San Marino	500 million[4]	20,000	n.a.	2.0
Korea, North	22.6 billion	1,000	1.0	n.a.	São Tomé	169 million	1,100	1.5	10.5
Korea, South	625.7 billion	13,300	10.0	0.8	Saudi Arabia	191 billion	9,000	1.6	–1.2
Kuwait	44.8 billion	22,500	1.1	2.0	Senegal	16.6 billion	1,650	5.0	2.0
Kyrgyzstan	10.3 billion	2,300	3.4	37.0	Seychelles	590 million	7,500	1.8	3.0
Laos	7 billion	1,300	5.2	140.0	Sierra Leone	2.5 billion	500	–10.0	30.0
Latvia	9.8 billion	4,200	0.0	3.2	Singapore	98 billion	27,800	5.5	0.4
Lebanon	16.2 billion	4,500	1.0	4.5	Slovakia	45.9 billion	8,500	1.9	14.0
Lesotho	4.7 billion[2]	2,240	–10.0	8.0	Slovenia	21.4 billion	10,900	3.5	6.3
Liberia	2.85 billion	1,000	0.5	3.0[2]	Solomon Is.	1.21 billion	2,650	3.5	10.0
Libya	39.3 billion	7,900	2.0	18.0	Somalia	4.3 billion	600	n.a.	n.a.
Liechtenstein	730 million[2]	23,000	n.a.	0.5[4]	South Africa	296.1 billion	6,900	0.6	5.5
Lithuania	17.3 billion	4,800	–3.0	0.3	Spain	677.5 billion	17,300	3.6	2.3
Luxembourg	14.7 billion	34,200	4.2	1.1	Sri Lanka	50.5 billion	2,600	3.7	6.0
Macedonia	7.6 billion	3,800	2.5	1.0	Sudan	32.6 billion	940	3.0	20.0
Madagascar	11.5 billion	780	4.5	9.5	Suriname	1.48 billion	3,400	–1.0	170.0
Malawi	9.4 billion	940	4.2	45.0	Swaziland	4.2 billion	4,200	3.1	n.a.
Malaysia	229.1 billion	10,700	5.0	2.8	Sweden	184 billion	20,700	3.8	0.4
Maldives	540 million	1,800	7.0	3.0	Switzerland	197 billion	27,100	1.4	1.0
Mali	8.5 billion	820	5.0	3.0	Syria	42.2 billion	2,500	0.0	2.3
Malta	5.3 billion	13,800	4.0	1.8	Taiwan	357 billion	16,100	5.5	0.4
Marshall Is.	105 million[2]	1,670	–5.0	5.0[4]	Tajikistan	6.2 billion	1,020	2.0	22.0
Mauritania	4.9 billion	1,910	3.7	9.8[2]	Tanzania	23.3 billion	550	4.0	8.8
Mauritius	12.3 billion	10,400	4.0	6.8	Thailand	388.7 billion	6,400	4.0	2.4
Mexico	865.5 billion	8,500	3.7	15.0	Togo	8.6 billion	1,700	4.0	3.0
Micronesia	240 million[4]	2,000	3.0	4.0[1]	Tonga	238 million[2]	2,200	–0.3	3.2
Moldova	9.7 billion	2,200	–4.4	38.0	Trinidad	9.41 billion	8,500	5.0	3.5
Monaco	870 million	27,000	n.a.	n.a.	Tunisia	52.6 billion	5,500	6.0	2.7
Mongolia	6.1 billion	2,320	3.5	9.5[2]	Turkey	409.4 billion	6,200	–5.0	65.0
Morocco	108 billion	3,600	0.0	1.9	Turkmenistan	7.7 billion	1,800	9.0	30.0
Mozambique	18.7 billion	1,000	10.0	4.0	Tuvalu	7.8 million[6]	800	8.7	3.9[7]
Myanmar	59.4 billion	1,200	4.6	38.0	Uganda	24.2 billion	1,060	5.5	7.0
Namibia	7.1 billion	4,300	3.0	8.5	Ukraine	109.5 billion	2,200	–0.4	20.0
Nauru	100 million[5]	10,000	n.a.	–3.6	UAE	41.5 billion	17,700	2.5	4.0
Nepal	27.4 billion	1,100	3.4	11.8[3]	UK	1.29 trillion	21,800	1.9	2.3
The Netherlands	365.1 billion	23,100	3.4	2.2	U.S.	9.255 trillion	33,900	4.1	2.2
New Zealand	63.8 billion	17,400	3.1	1.3	Uruguay	28 billion	8,500	–2.5	4.0
Nicaragua	12.5 billion	2,650	6.3	12.0	Uzbekistan	59.3 billion	2,500	–1.0	29.0
Niger	9.6 billion	1,000	2.0	4.8	Vanuatu	245 million	1,300	n.a.	3.9[2]
Nigeria	110.5 billion	970	2.7	12.5	Venezuela	182.8 billion	8,000	–7.2	20.0
Norway	111.3 billion	25,100	0.8	2.8	Vietnam	143.1 billion	1,850	4.8	4.0
Oman	19.6 billion	8,000	4.0	–0.1	Yemen	12.7 billion	750	4.0	10.0
Pakistan	282 billion	2,000	3.1	6.0	Yugoslavia	20.6 billion	1,800	–20.0	42.0
Palau	160 million[4]	8,800	10.0	n.a.	Zambia	8.5 billion	880	1.5	27.4
Palestinian State	1.17 billion	1,060	4.6	5.0	Zimbabwe	26.5 billion	2,400	0.0	59.0
Panama	21 billion	7,600	4.4	1.5					

Definitions: Gross domestic product (GDP): The value of all goods and services produced domestically. Purchasing power parity (PPP): The PPP method involves the use of standardized international dollar price weights, which are applied to the GDP produced in a given economy. The data derived from the 1998 method provide a better comparison of economic well-being between countries than conversions at official currency exchange rates. n.a. = not available. *First line of figures for Greek Cyprus, second for Turkish Cyprus. 1. 1996 est. 2. 1998 est. 3. FY98/99 est. 4. 1997 est. 5. 1993 est. 6. 1995 est. 7. average 1985–1993. Source: U.S. Census Bureau, International Database; and The World Factbook, 2000.

Major sources: Questionnaires to the individual countries; *The World Factbook 2000;* Center for International Research, U.S. Bureau of the Census; *The Columbia Encyclopedia; The World Book Encyclopedia; Encyclopædia Britannica;* U.S. State Dept., and various newspapers. (information as of Sept. 2001)

Definitions: Gross domestic product (GDP): The value of all goods and services produced domestically; purchasing power parity (PPP): The PPP method involves the use of standardized international dollar price weights, which are applied to the GDP produced in a given economy. The data derived from the PPP method provide a better comparison of economic well-being between countries than conversions at official currency exchange rates. Literacy rates and population figures are supplied by the U.S. Census Bureau.

Afghanistan

ISLAMIC EMIRATE OF AFGHANISTAN

National name: Dowlat-e Eslami-ye Afghanestan
Head of State: Mullah Mohammad Omar (1996)
Area: 251,737 sq mi (652,000 sq km)
Population (2001 est.): 26,813,057 (average annual rate of natural increase: 2.4%); birth rate: 41.4/1000; infant mortality rate: 147.0/1000; density per sq mi: 107
Capital (2000 est.): Kabul, 2,450,000. **Largest cities (2000 est.):** Mazare Sharif, 2,500,000; Kandahar, 225,500; Herat, 177,300. **Monetary unit:** Afghani.
Languages: Pushtu, Dari Persian, other Turkic and minor languages. **Ethnicity/race:** Pashtun 38%, Tajik 25%, Uzbek 6%, Hazara 19%, minor ethnic groups (Chahar Aimaks, Turkmen, Baloch, and others).
Religion: Islam (Sunni 84%, Shi'ite 15%, other 1%).
Literacy rate: 29% (1990)
Economic summary: GDP/PPP (1999 est.): $21 billion; per capita $800. **Real growth rate:** n.a. **Inflation:** n.a. **Unemployment:** 8% (1995 est.). **Arable land:** 12%. **Agriculture:** opium poppies, wheat, fruits, nuts, karakul pelts; wool, mutton. **Labor force:** 8 million (1997 est.); agriculture, 68%; industry, 16%; services, 16% (1980 est.). **Natural resources:** natural gas, petroleum, coal, copper, chromite, talc, barites, sulfur, lead, zinc, iron ore, salt, precious and semi-precious stones. **Industries:** small-scale production of textiles, soap, furniture, shoes, fertilizer, and cement; handwoven carpets; natural gas, oil, coal, copper. **Exports:** $80 million (does not include opium) (1996 est.): opium, fruits and nuts, handwoven carpets, wool, cotton, hides and pelts, precious and semi-precious gems. **Imports:** $150 million (1996 est.): capital goods, food and petroleum products; most consumer goods. **Major trading partners:** Former Soviet Union, Pakistan, Iran, Germany, India, UK, Belgium, Luxembourg, Czech Republic, Iran, Japan, Singapore, South Korea.

Geography Afghanistan, approximately the size of Texas, is bordered on the north by Turkmenistan, Uzbekistan, and Tajikistan, on the extreme northeast by China, on the east and south by Pakistan, and by Iran on the west. The country is split east to west by the Hindu Kush mountain range, rising in the east to heights of 24,000 ft (7,315 m). With the exception of the southwest, most of the country is covered by high snow-capped mountains and is traversed by deep valleys.

Government On Sept. 27, 1996, the ruling members of the Afghan government were displaced by members of the Islamic Taliban movement, who have declared themselves the legitimate government of Afghanistan. The UN has deferred a decision on the question of legitimacy. Mullah Mohammad Omar, known as the Emir al-Momineen (Leader of the Faithful), has served as the de facto leader since the Taliban came to power in 1996.

History Darius I and Alexander the Great were the first to use Afghanistan as the gateway to India. Islamic conquerors arrived in the 7th century, and Genghis Khan and Tamerlane followed in the 13th and 14th centuries.

In the 19th century, Afghanistan became a battleground in the rivalry of imperial Britain and czarist Russia for control of Central Asia. Three Anglo-Afghan Wars (1839–42, 1878–80, and 1919) ended inconclusively. In 1893 Britain established an unofficial border, the Durand Line, separating Afghanistan from British India, and London granted full independence in 1919. Emir Amanullah founded an Afghan monarchy in 1926.

During the cold war, King Mohammed Zahir Shah developed close ties with the Soviet Union, accepting extensive economic assistance from Moscow. He was overthrown in 1973 by his cousin Mohammed Daoud, who was himself ousted in a 1978 coup by Noor Taraki. Taraki and his successor, Babrak Karmal, attempted to create a Marxist state. However, the new leadership was criticized by armed insurgents who bitterly opposed communism and hoped to create an Islamic state in Afghanistan. Fearing his government was on the verge of collapse, Karmal called for Soviet troops. Moscow responded with a full-scale invasion of the country in Dec. 1979.

The Soviets were met with fierce resistance from groups already energized by opposition to the Karmal government. The guerrilla forces, calling themselves *mujahedeen,* pledged a jihad, or holy war, to expel the invaders. Initially armed with outdated weapons, the mujahedeen became a focus of U.S. cold war strategy against the Soviet Union, and with Pakistan's help, Washington began funneling sophisticated arms to the resistance. Moscow's troops were soon bogged down in a no-win conflict with determined Afghan fighters. In April 1988 the USSR, U.S., Afghanistan, and Pakistan signed accords calling for an end to outside aid to the warring factions. In return, a Soviet withdrawal took place in Feb. 1989, but the pro-Soviet government of President Najibullah was left in the capital, Kabul.

By mid-April 1992 Najibullah was ousted as Islamic rebels advanced on the capital. Almost immediately, the various rebel groups began fighting one another for control. Amid the chaos of competing factions, a group calling itself the Taliban—consisting of Islamic students—seized control of Kabul in Sept. 1996. It imposed harsh fundamentalist laws, including stoning for adultery and severing hands for theft. Women were prohibited from work and school, and they were required to cover themselves in public from head to toe. By fall 1998 the Taliban controlled about 90% of the country.

On Aug. 20, 1998, U.S. cruise missiles struck a terrorism training complex in Afghanistan believed to have been financed by Osama bin Laden, a wealthy Islamic radical sheltered by the Taliban. The U.S. asked for the deportation of bin Laden, whom they believed was involved in the bombing of the U.S. embassies in Kenya and Tanzania on Aug. 7, 1998.

In 1999, the Taliban concentrated on defeating the forces of Ahmed Shah Masoud, their last significant hurdle in gaining complete control of Afghanistan.

The Taliban's scorched-earth tactics and human rights abuses have further isolated them from the international community. The country remains in dire poverty, with some 500,000 living in refugee camps. In July 2000 Mullah Omar banned opium cultivation; Afghanistan had once been the world's largest supplier of the drug.

In March 2001, despite worldwide protests, the Taliban destroyed several enormous Buddhist statues, dating from the second and fifth centuries A.D. The Taliban said they were destroying "graven images," which were being worshiped in violation of Islam. In Sept. 2001, legendary guerrilla leader Ahmed Shah Masoud was killed by Taliban suicide bombers, a seeming death knell for the anti-Taliban forces.

The Taliban is suspected of allowing terrorist organizations to run training camps in their territory, and since 1994 has provided refuge for Osama bin Laden and his radical al-Qaeda organization. The United Nations Security Council has passed two resolutions in 1999 and 2000 demanding that the Taliban cease their support for terrorism and hand over bin Laden for trial. Bin Laden is the primary suspect in Sept. 2001's catastrophic bombing of New York's World Trade Center Towers and the Pentagon.

Albania

THE REPUBLIC OF ALBANIA

National name: Republika E Shqiperise
President: Rexhep Mejdani (1997)
Prime Minister: Ilir Meta (1999)
Area: 11,100 sq mi (28,748 sq km)
Population (2001 est.): 3,510,484 (average annual rate of natural increase: 1.3%); birth rate: 19.0/1000; infant mortality rate: 40.0/1000; density per sq mi: 316
Capital and largest city (1991 est.): Tirana, 300,000.
Monetary unit: Lek. **Languages:** Albanian (Tosk is the official dialect), Greek. **Ethnicity/race:** Albanian 95%, Greeks 3%, other 2%: Vlachs, Gypsies, Serbs, and Bulgarians (1989 est.). **Religions (1980):** Muslim 70%, Albanian Orthodox 20%, Roman Catholic 10%.
Literacy rate: 72% (1955)
Economic summary:GDP/PPP (1999 est.): $5.6 billion; per capita $1,650. **Real growth rate:** 8%. **Inflation:** 0.5%. **Unemployment:** 14% (October 1997) officially, but may be as high as 28%. **Arable land:** 21%.
Agriculture: wheat, corn, potatoes, vegetables, fruits, sugar beets, grapes; meat, dairy products. **Labor force:** 1.692 million (including 352,000 emigrant workers and 261,000 domestically unemployed) (1994 est.); agriculture, 49.5%; industry and services, 50.5%. **Industries:** food processing, textiles and clothing; lumber, oil, cement, chemicals, mining, basic metals, hydropower. **Natural resources:** petroleum, natural gas, coal, chromium, copper, timber, nickel, hydropower. **Exports:** $242 million (f.o.b., 1999 est.): textiles and footwear; asphalt, metals and metallic ores, crude oil; vegetables, fruits, tobacco. **Imports:** $925 million (f.o.b., 1999 est.): machinery and equipment, foodstuffs, textiles, chemicals. **Major trading partners:** Italy, Greece, Germany, Netherlands, Belgium, U.S., Turkey, Bulgaria, The Former Yugoslav Republic of Macedonia.

Geography Albania is situated on the eastern shore of the Adriatic Sea, with Montenegro and Serbia to the north, Macedonia to the east, and Greece to the south.

Slightly larger than Maryland, Albania may be divided into two major regions: a mountainous highland region (north, east, and south) constituting 70% of the land area, and a western coastal lowland region that contains nearly all of the country's agricultural lands and is the most densely populated part of Albania.

Government Emerging democracy.

History A part of Illyria in ancient times and later of the Roman Empire, Albania was ruled by the Byzantine Empire from 535 to 1204. An alliance (1444–66) of Albanian chiefs failed to halt the advance of the Ottoman Turks, and the country remained under at least nominal Turkish rule for more than four centuries, until it proclaimed its independence on Nov. 28, 1912.

Largely agricultural, Albania is one of the poorest countries in Europe. A battlefield in World War I, after the war it became a republic in which a conservative Muslim landlord, Ahmed Zogu, proclaimed himself president in 1925, and king (Zog I) in 1928. He ruled until Italy annexed Albania in 1939. Communist guerrillas under Enver Hoxha seized power in 1944, near the end of World War II. Hoxha was a devotee of Stalin, emulating the Soviet leader's repressive tactics, imprisoning or executing landowners and others who did not conform to the socialist ideal. Hoxha eventually broke with Soviet communism in 1961 because of differences with Khrushchev and then aligned himself with Chinese communism, which he also abandoned in 1978 after the death of Mao. From then on Albania went its own way to forge its individual version of the socialist state and became one of the most isolated countries in the world. Hoxha was succeeded by Ramiz Alia in 1982.

Elections in March 1991 gave the Communists a decisive majority. But a general strike and street demonstrations soon forced the all-Communist cabinet to resign. In June 1991 the Communist Party of Labor renamed itself the Socialist Party and renounced its past ideology. The opposition Democratic Party won a landslide victory in the 1992 elections.

But Albania's experiment with democratic reform and a free-market economy went disastrously awry in March 1997, when large numbers of its citizens invested in shady get-rich-quick pyramid schemes. When five of these schemes collapsed in the beginning of the year, robbing Albanians of an estimated $1.2 billion in savings, their rage turned against the government, which appeared to have sanctioned the nationwide swindle. Rioting broke out, the country's fragile infrastructure collapsed, and gangsters and rebels overran the country, plunging it into virtual anarchy. A multinational protection force eventually restored order and set up the elections that formally ousted President Sali Berisha.

In spring 1999, Albania was heavily involved in the affairs of its fellow ethnic Albanians to the north, in Kosovo. Albania served as an outpost for NATO troops and took in approximately 440,000 Kosovar refugees, about half the total number of ethnic Albanians who were driven from their homes in Kosovo.

Ilir Meta, elected prime minister in 1999 at age 30, rapidly moved forward in his first years, modernizing the economy, privatizing business, fighting crime, and reforming the judiciary and tax systems. In 2001, after the outbreak of an ethnic Albanian separatist movement in neighboring Macedonia, Meta supported greater rights for Macedonia's Albanian minority but condemned the rebels' violence.

Algeria

DEMOCRATIC AND POPULAR REPUBLIC OF ALGERIA

National name: Al Jumhuriyah al Jaza'iriyah ad Dimuqratiyah ash Shabiyah
President: Abdel-Aziz Bouteflika (1999)
Prime Minister: Ali Benflis (2000)
Area: 919,590 sq mi (2,381,740 sq km)
Population (2001 est.): 31,736,053 (average annual rate of natural increase: 1.8%); birth rate: 22.8/1000; infant mortality rate: 40.6/1000; density per sq mi: 35
Capital: Algiers. **Largest cities (1987):** Algiers, 1,507,241; Oran, 628,558; Constantine, 440,842; Annaba, 305,526.
Monetary unit: Dinar. **Languages:** Arabic (official), French, Berber dialects. **Ethnicity/race:** Arab-Berber 99%, European less than 1%. **Religion:** 99% Islam (Sunni). **Literacy rate:** 57% (1990)
Economic summary: GDP/PPP (1999 est.): $147.6 billion; per capita $4,700. **Real growth rate:** 3.9%. **Inflation:** 4.2% (1999 est.). **Unemployment:** 30%. **Arable land:** 3%. **Agriculture:** wheat, barley, oats, grapes, olives, citrus, fruits; sheep, cattle. **Labor force:** 9.1 million (2000 est.); government, 29.5%; agriculture, 22%; construction and public works, 16.2%; industry, 13.6%; commerce and services, 13.5%; transportation and communication, 5.2% (1989). **Industries:** petroleum, natural gas, light industries, mining, electrical, petrochemical, food processing. **Natural resources:** petroleum, natural gas, iron ore, phosphates, uranium, lead, zinc. **Exports:** $13.7 billion (f.o.b., 1999 est.): petroleum, natural gas, and petroleum products 97%. **Imports:** $9.3 billion (f.o.b., 1999 est.): capital goods, food and beverages, consumer goods. **Major trading partners:** Italy, U.S., France, Spain, Brazil, Netherlands, Germany, Canada.

Geography Nearly four times the size of Texas, Algeria is bordered on the west by Morocco and Western Sahara and on the east by Tunisia and Libya. To the south are Mauritania, Mali, and Niger. The Saharan region, which is 85% of the country, is almost completely uninhabited. The highest point is Mount Tahat in the Sahara, which rises 9,850 ft (3,000 m).

Government Parliamentary republic.

History Excavations in Algeria have indicated that *Homo erectus* resided there between 500,000 and 700,000 years ago. Phoenician traders settled on the coast in the 1st millennium B.C. As ancient Numidia, Algeria became a Roman colony, part of what was called Mauretania Caesariensis, at the close of the Punic Wars (145 B.C.). Conquered by the Vandals about A.D. 440, it fell from a high state of civilization to virtual barbarism, from which it partly recovered after an invasion by Arabs about 650. Christian during its Roman period, the indigenous Berbers were then converted to Islam. Falling under control of the Ottoman Empire by 1536, Algiers served for three centuries as the headquarters of the Barbary pirates. Ostensibly to rid the region of the pirates, the French occupied Algeria in 1830 and made it a part of France in 1848.

Algerian independence movements led to the uprisings of 1954–55, which developed into full-scale war. In 1962, French president Charles de Gaulle began the peace negotiations, and on July 5, 1962, Algeria was proclaimed independent. In Oct. 1963, Ahmed Ben Bella was elected president, and the country became socialist. He began to nationalize foreign holdings and aroused opposition. He was overthrown in a military coup on June 19, 1965, by Col. Houari Boumediène, who suspended the constitution and sought to restore economic stability.

In Dec. 1991 in the first parliamentary elections ever held in Algeria, the fundamentalist Islamic Salvation Front (Front Islamique du Salut; FIS) won the largest number of votes. To thwart the electoral results, the army cancelled the general election, which plunged the country into a bloody civil war. An estimated 100,000 people have been massacred by Islamic terrorists since war began in Jan. 1992. The undeclared civil war escalated in 1997–98 in its brutality and senselessness. Islamic extremists, who had originally focused their attacks on government officials and then shifted to intellectuals and journalists, abandoned political motivations entirely and targeted defenseless villagers. The mass slaughters were as savage as they were random, and the government was markedly ineffectual in stemming the violence. There is some evidence that the army in fact looked the other way while its civilians were slaughtered. Algeria refused international mediation and kept the outside world largely in the dark about the war within its borders.

The rise of Abdel-Aziz Bouteflika to the presidency in April 1999 was initially expected to bring peace and some economic improvement to this desperate war-torn country. Bouteflika, however, has been locked in power struggles with the military, whose support was crucial to his rise to the presidency. His plan of national reconciliation, which included an amnesty for Islamic militants not convicted of murder or rape, has done little to heal wounds. In 2001 violence by Islamic militants was again on the rise, and the long-disaffected Berber minority engaged in several large-scale protests.

Andorra

PRINCIPALITY OF ANDORRA

National name: Valls d'Andorra
Head of Government: Marc Forné Molné (1994)
Area: 181 sq mi (468 sq km)
Population (2001 est.): 67,627 (average annual growth rate: 0.5%); birth rate: 10.3/1000; infant mortality rate: 4.1/1000; density per sq mi: 374
Capital and largest city (1993 est.): Andorra la Vella, 22,390. **Monetary units:** French franc and Spanish peseta. **Languages:** Catalán (official), French, Spanish. **Ethnicity/race:** Spanish 61%, Andorran 30%, French 6%, other 3%. **Religion:** Roman Catholic. **Literacy rate:** 100%
Economic summary: GDP/PPP (1996 est.): $1.2 billion; per capita $18,000 (1999 est.). **Real growth rate:** n.a. **Inflation:** 1.62% (1998). **Unemployment:** 0%. **Arable land:** 4%. **Agriculture:** small quantities of tobacco, rye, wheat, barley, oats, vegetables; sheep. **Labor force:** 30,787 salaried employees (1998); agriculture, 1%; industry, 21%; services, 72%; other, 6% (1998). **Industries:** tourism (particularly skiing), cattle raising, timber, tobacco, banking. **Natural resources:** hydropower, mineral water, timber, iron ore, lead. **Exports:** $58 million (f.o.b., 1998): tobacco products, furniture. **Imports:** $1.077 billion (c.i.f., 1998): consumer goods, food, electricity. **Major trading partners:** France, Spain, U.S.

Geography Andorra is nestled high in the Pyrenees Mountains on the French-Spanish border.

Government A parliamentary coprincipality composed of the bishop of Urgel (Spain) and the president of France. The principality was internationally recognized as a sovereign state in 1993.

History An autonomous and semi-independent coprincipality, Andorra has been under the joint suzerainty of the French state and the Spanish bishops of Urgel since 1278. It maintains closer ties to Spain, however, and Catalán is its official language. In the late 20th century, Andorra became a popular tourist and winter sports destination and a wealthy international commercial center because of its banking facilities, low taxes, and lack of customs duties. In 1990 Andorra approved a customs union treaty with the EU permitting free movement of industrial goods between the two, but Andorra would apply the EU's external tariffs to third countries. Andorra became a member of the UN in 1993 and a member of the Council of Europe in 1994.

Angola

REPUBLIC OF ANGOLA

President: José Eduardo dos Santos (1979)
Area: 481,351 sq mi (1,246,700 sq km)
Population (2001 est.): 10,366,031 (average annual rate of natural increase: 2.2%); birth rate: 46.5/1000; infant mortality rate: 193.7/1000; density per sq mi: 22
Capital and largest city (1993): Luanda, 2,000,000. **Other large cities (1993 est.):** Huambo, 400,000; Lubango, 105,000. **Monetary unit:** Kwanza. **Languages:** Bantu, Portuguese (official). **Ethnicity/race:** Ovimbundu 37%, Kimbundu 25%, Bakongo 13%, mestico (mixed European and Native African) 2%, European 1%, other 22%. **Religions:** Roman Catholic 47%, Protestant 38%, Indigenous 15%. **Literacy rate:** 42% (1990)
Economic summary: GDP/PPP (1999 est.): $11.6 billion; per capita $1,030. **Real growth rate:** 4%. **Inflation:** 270%. **Unemployment:** extensive unemployment and underemployment affecting more than half the population. **Arable land:** 2%. **Agriculture:** bananas, sugarcane, coffee, sisal, corn, cotton, manioc (tapioca), tobacco, vegetables, plantains; livestock; forest products; fish. **Labor force:** 5 million (1997 est.); agriculture, 85%; industry and services, 15% (1997 est.). **Industries:** petroleum; diamonds, iron ore, phosphates, feldspar, bauxite, uranium, and gold; cement; basic metal products; fish processing; food processing; brewing; tobacco products; sugar; textiles. **Natural resources:** petroleum, diamonds, iron ore, phosphates, copper, feldspar, gold, bauxite, uranium. **Exports:** $5 billion (f.o.b., 1999 est.): crude oil, diamonds, refined petroleum products, gas, coffee, sisal, fish and fish products, timber, cotton. **Imports:** $3 billion (f.o.b., 1999 est.): machinery and electrical equipment, vehicles and spare parts; medicines, food, textiles, military goods. **Major trading partners:** U.S., Benelux, China, Chile, France, Portugal, South Africa, Spain, Brazil.

Geography Angola, more than three times the size of California, extends for more than 1,000 mi (1,609 km) along the South Atlantic in southwest Africa. The Democratic Republic of the Congo and the Republic of Congo are to the north and east, Zambia is to the east, and Namibia is to the south. A plateau averaging 6,000 ft (1,829 m) above sea level rises abruptly from the coastal lowlands. Nearly all the land is desert or savanna, with hardwood forests in the northeast.

Government Angola underwent a transition from a one-party socialist state to a nominally multiparty democracy in 1992.

History The original inhabitants of Angola are thought to have been Khoisan speakers. After 1000, large numbers of Bantu speakers migrated to the region and became the dominant group. Angola derives its name from the Bantu kingdom of Ndongo, whose name for its king is *ngola*.

Explored by the Portuguese navigator Diego Cão in 1482, Angola became a link in trade with India and Southeast Asia. Later it was a major source of slaves for Portugal's New World colony of Brazil. Development of the interior began after the Berlin Conference in 1885 fixed the colony's borders, and British and Portuguese investment fostered mining, railways, and agriculture.

Following World War II, independence movements began but were sternly suppressed by Portuguese military force. The major nationalist organizations were the Popular Movement for the Liberation of Angola (MPLA), a Marxist party, National Front for the Liberation of Angola (FNLA), and the National Union for the Total Independence of Angola (UNITA). After 14 years of war, Portugal finally granted independence to Angola in 1975. The MPLA, which had led the independence movement, has controlled the government ever since. But after its long war for independence, the country has yet to experience an extended period of peace. UNITA disputed the MPLA's ascendancy, and civil war broke out almost immediately. With the Soviet Union and Cuba supporting the Marxist MPLA, and the United States and South Africa supporting the anticommunist UNITA, the country became a cold war battleground.

With the waning of the cold war and the withdrawal of Cuban troops in 1989, the MPLA began to make the transition to a multiparty democracy. Despite shifting ideologies, the civil war continued for more than 30 years, with UNITA's charismatic rebel leader, Jonas Savimbi, armed and sustained by his control of approximately 80% of the country's diamond trade. Free elections took place in 1992, with incumbent president José Eduardo dos Santos and the MPLA winning the UN-certified election over Savimbi and UNITA. Savimbi then withdrew, charging election fraud, and the civil war resumed.

In 1997 Angola played a crucial role in the civil wars of both the Republic of Congo and the Democratic Republic of the Congo. By aiding in the overthrow of these countries' leaders, Pascal Lissouba and Mobutu Sese Seko, the Angolan government was also able to destroy the UNITA strongholds within their borders. Angola again came to the aid of the Democratic Republic of the Congo's new leader, Laurent Kabila, in 1998, helping to fight the rebellion against his shaky year-old administration.

Four years of relative peace took place between 1994 and 1998, when the United Nations, at a cost of $1.6 billion, oversaw the 1994 Lusaka peace accord. In 1997 it was agreed that a coalition government with UNITA would be implemented. But Savimbi violated the accord repeatedly by refusing to give up his strongholds, failing to demobilize his army, and retaking territory. As a result, the government suspended coalition rule in Sept. 1998, and the country again plunged into civil war, which, analysts say, neither side has the military power to win. Meanwhile, Angola's citizens continue to suffer. The hostilities affect an estimated four million people, about a third of the total population, and there are almost two million refugees.

Antigua and Barbuda

Sovereign: Queen Elizabeth II (1952)
Governor-General: James Beethoven Carlisle (1993)
Prime Minister: Lester Bryant Bird (1994)
Land area: 171 sq mi (442 sq km)
Population (2001 est.): 66,970 (average annual growth rate: 1.4%); birth rate: 19.5/1000; infant mortality rate: 22.3/1000; density per sq mi: 392
Capital and largest city (1991): St. John's, 21,514; Codrington (capital of Barbuda), est. pop. 1,000.
Monetary unit: East Caribbean dollar. **Language:**

English. **Ethnicity/race:** black, British, Portuguese, Lebanese, Syrian. **Religions:** Anglican and Roman Catholic. **Literacy rate:** 89% (1960)
Economic summary: GDP/PPP (1999 est.): $524 million; per capita $8,200. **Real growth rate:** 2.8%. **Inflation:** 1.6%. **Unemployment:** 7%. **Arable land:** 18%. **Agriculture:** cotton, fruits, vegetables, bananas, coconuts, cucumbers, mangoes, sugarcane; livestock. **Labor force:** 30,000; commerce and services, 82%; agriculture, 11%; industry, 7% (1983). **Industries:** tourism, construction, light manufacturing (clothing, alcohol, household appliances). **Natural resources:** negl.; pleasant climate fosters tourism. **Exports:** $38 million (1998): petroleum products, manufactures, food and live animals, machinery and transport equipment. **Imports:** $330 million (1998): food and live animals, machinery and transport equipment, manufactures, chemicals, oil. **Major trading partners:** OECS, Barbados, Guyana, Trinidad and Tobago, U.S., UK, Canada. **Member of Commonwealth of Nations**

Geography Antigua, the larger of the two main islands, is 108 sq mi (280 sq km). The island dependencies of Redonda (an uninhabited rocky islet) and Barbuda (a coral island formerly known as Dulcina) are 0.5 sq mi (1.30 sq km) and 62 sq mi (161 sq km), respectively.

Government Parliamentary democracy.

History Antigua was explored by Christopher Columbus in 1493 and named for the Church of Santa Maria de la Antigua in Seville. Antigua was colonized by Britain in 1632; Barbuda was first colonized in 1678. The country joined the West Indies Federation in 1958. With the breakup of the federation, it became one of the West Indies Associated States in 1967, self-governing its internal affairs. Full independence was granted Nov. 1, 1981.

The Bird family has controlled the islands since Vere C. Bird founded the Antigua Labor Party in the mid-1940s. While tourism and financial services have turned the country into one of the more prosperous in the Caribbean, law enforcement officials have charged that Antigua and Barbuda is a major center of money laundering, drug trafficking, and arms smuggling. Several scandals have tainted the Bird family, especially the 1995 conviction of Lester Bird's brother, Ivor, for cocaine smuggling.

Argentina

ARGENTINE REPUBLIC

National name: República Argentina.
President: Fernando de la Rúa (1999)
Area: 1,068,296 sq mi (2,766,890 sq km)
Population (2001 est.): 37,384,816 (average annual rate of natural increase: 1.1%); birth rate: 18.4/1000; infant mortality rate: 17.8/1000; density per sq mi: 35
Capital and largest city (2000 est.): Buenos Aires, 13,250,000 (metro. area). **Other large cities (1999 est.):** Córdoba, 1,200,000; Rosario, 950,000; Mar del Plata, 900,000; Mendoza, 400,000. **Monetary unit:** Peso. **Languages:** Spanish (official), English, Italian, German, French. **Ethnicity/race:** European 97% (mostly of Spanish and Italian descent), 3% other (mostly Indian or mestizo). **Religions:** Roman Catholic 92%, Protestant 2%, Jewish 2%, other 4%. **Literacy rate:** 96% (1991)
Economic summary: GDP/PPP (1999 est.): $367 billion; per capita $10,000. **Real growth rate:** –3%. **Inflation:** –2%. **Unemployment:** 14%. **Arable land:** 9%. **Agriculture:** sunflower seeds, lemons, soybeans, grapes, corn, tobacco, peanuts, tea, wheat; livestock.

Labor force: 15 million (1999); agriculture, n.a; industry, n.a.; services, n.a. **Industries:** food processing, motor vehicles, consumer durables, textiles, chemicals and petrochemicals, printing, metallurgy, steel. **Natural resources:** fertile plains of the pampas, lead, zinc, tin, copper, iron ore, manganese, petroleum, uranium. **Exports:** $23 billion (f.o.b., 1999 est.): edible oils, fuels and energy, cereals, feed, motor vehicles. **Imports:** $25 billion (c.i.f., 1999 est.): machinery and equipment, motor vehicles, chemicals, metal manufactures, plastics. **Major trading partners:** Brazil, EU, U.S.

Geography Second in South America only to Brazil in size and population, Argentina is a plain, rising from the Atlantic to the Chilean border and the towering Andes peaks. Aconcagua (23,034 ft; 7,021 m) is the highest peak in the world outside Asia. Argentina is also bordered by Bolivia and Paraguay on the north, and by Uruguay and Brazil on the east. The northern area is the swampy and partly wooded Gran Chaco, bordering on Bolivia and Paraguay. South of that are the rolling, fertile Pampas, which are rich in agriculture and sheep- and cattle-grazing and support most of the population. Next southward is Patagonia, a region of cool, arid steppes with some wooded and fertile sections.

Government Republic.

History First explored in 1516 by Juan Díaz de Solis, Argentina developed slowly under Spanish colonial rule. Buenos Aires was settled in 1580; the cattle industry was thriving as early as 1600. Invading British forces were expelled in 1806–07, and after Napoléon conquered Spain (1808), the Argentinians set up their own government in 1810. On July 9, 1816, independence was formally declared.

As it had in World War I, Argentina proclaimed neutrality at the outbreak of World War II, but in the closing phase declared war on the Axis powers on March 27, 1945. Juan D. Perón, an army colonel, emerged as the strongman of the postwar era, winning the presidential elections of 1946 and 1951. Perón's political strength was reinforced by his second wife—Eva Duarte de Perón (Evita)—and her popularity with the working classes. Although she never held a government post, Evita acted as de facto minister of health and labor, establishing a national charitable organization, and awarding generous wage increases to the unions, who responded with political support for Perón. Opposition to Perón's increasing authoritarianism led to a coup by the armed forces, which sent Perón into exile in 1955, three years after Evita's death. Argentina entered a long period of military dictatorships with brief intervals of constitutional government.

The former dictator returned to power in 1973 and his third wife, Isabel Martínez de Perón, was elected vice president. After Perón's death in 1974, she became the hemisphere's first woman chief of state, assuming control of a nation teetering on economic and political collapse. In 1975, terrorist acts by left- and right-wing groups killed some 700 people. The cost of living rose 355%, while strikes and demonstrations were constant. On March 24, 1976, a military junta led by army commander Lt. Gen. Jorge Rafael Videla seized power and imposed martial law.

The military began the "Dirty War" to restore order and eradicate its opponents. The Argentine Commission for Human Rights, in Geneva, has charged the junta with 2,300 political murders, over 10,000 political arrests, and the disappearances of 20,000 to

30,000 people. While violence declined, the economy remained in chaos. In March 1981 Field Marshal Roberto Viola deposed Videla, who in turn was succeeded by Lt. Gen. Leopoldo Galtieri.

On April 2, 1982, Galtieri invaded the British-held Falkland Islands, known as Las Islas Malvinas (Malvinas Islands) in Spanish, in what was seen as an attempt to increase his popularity. However, Great Britain decisively won, and Galtieri resigned in disgrace three days after Argentina's surrender. Maj. Gen. Reynaldo Bignone took over June 14, amid increasing pro-democratic public sentiment. As the 1983 elections approached, inflation hit 900% and Argentina's crippling foreign debt reached unprecedented levels.

In the presidential election of Oct. 1983, Raúl Alfonsín, leader of the Radical Civic Union, handed the Peronist Party its first defeat since its founding. However, growing unemployment and quadruple-digit inflation led to a Peronist victory in the elections of May 1989. Alfonsín resigned a month later in the wake of riots over high food prices, in favor of the new Peronist president, Carlos Menem.

In 1991, Menem promoted economic reforms designed to reverse decades of state intervention and protectionism. Menem had the constitution changed in 1994 to allow him to serve for a second term.

Throughout the 1990s, Argentina won international praise for continued reforms and for its conclusion of a new arrangement with the International Monetary Fund at the end of 1997. Beginning in Sept. 1998, however, Argentina faced its worst recession in a decade, and unemployment hit 15% in Aug. 1999. Exports to Brazil, which traditionally bought almost one-third of Argentina's exports, dropped 30% in 1999.

In Dec. 1999 Fernando de la Rua became president. Despite the introduction of several tough economic austerity plans, by 2001 the recession slid into its third year. In March 2001, Rua brought back former Peronist economy minister Domingo Cavallo, who had rescued the country from hyperinflation in 1991, but thus far he has not been able to perform miracles. The IMF gave Argentina $13.7 billion in emergency aid in Jan. 2001 and again in Aug. 2001 ($8 billion).

Armenia

President: Robert Kocharian (1998)
Prime Minister: Andranik Markarian (2000)
Area: 11,506 sq mi (29,800 sq km)
Population (2001 est.): 3,336,100 (average annual rate of increase: 0.2%) (Armenian, 93%; others, Kurds, Ukrainians, and Russians); birth rate: 11.5/1000; infant mortality rate: 41.3/1000, density per sq mi: 290
Capital and largest city (1998 est.): Yerevan, 1,226,000. **Other large cities (1998 est.):** Gyumri (Leninakan), 121,000; Vanadzor, 74,000; Abovian, 54,000. **Monetary unit:** Dram. **Language:** Armenian. **Ethnicity/race:** Armenian 93%, Azeri 3%, Russian 2%, other (mostly Yezidi Kurds) 2% (1989). Note: as of the end of 1993, virtually all Azeris had emigrated from Armenia. **Religion:** Armenian Orthodox 94%. **Literacy rate:** 99% (1989)
Economic summary: GDP/PPP (1999 est.): $9.9 billion; per capita $2,900. **Real growth rate:** 5%. **Inflation:** 2.5%. **Unemployment:** 20% (1998 est.). Note: official rate is 9.3% for 1998. **Arable land:** 17%. **Agriculture:** fruit (especially grapes), vegetables; livestock. **Labor force:** 1.5 million (1999); agriculture 55%, services 25%, manufacturing, mining, and construction 20% (1999 est.). **Industries:** metal-cutting machine tools, forging-pressing machines, electric motors, tires, knitted wear, hosiery, shoes, silk fabric, washing machines, chemicals, trucks, watches, instruments, microelectronics. **Natural resources:** small deposits of gold, copper, molybdenum, zinc, alumina. **Exports:** $240 million (1999 est.): diamonds, scrap metal, machinery and equipment, cognac, copper ore. **Imports:** $782 million (1999 est.): natural gas, petroleum, tobacco products, foodstuffs, diamonds. **Major trading partners:** Belgium, Russia, Iran, Turkmenistan, U.S., Georgia, UK, Turkey.

Geography Armenia is located in the southern Caucasus and is the smallest of the former Soviet republics. It is bounded by Georgia on the north, Azerbaijan on the east, Iran on the south, and Turkey on the west. Contemporary Armenia is a fraction of the size of ancient Armenia. A land of rugged mountains and extinct volcanoes, its highest point is Mount Aragats, 13,435 ft (4,095 m).

Government Republic.

History One of the world's oldest civilizations, Armenia once included Mount Ararat, which biblical tradition identifies as the mountain that Noah's ark rested on after the flood. It was the first country in the world to officially embrace Christianity as its religion (c. A.D. 300).

In the 6th century B.C., Armenians settled in the kingdom of Urartu (the Assyrian name for Ararat), which was in decline. Under Tigrane the Great (fl. 95–55 B.C.) the Armenian empire reached its height and became one of the most powerful in Asia, stretching from the Caspian to the Mediterranean Seas. Throughout most of its long history, however, Armenia has been invaded by a succession of empires. Under constant threat of domination by foreign forces, Armenians became both cosmopolitan as well as fierce protectors of their culture and tradition.

Over the centuries Armenia was conquered by Greeks, Romans, Persians, Byzantines, Mongols, Arabs, Ottoman Turks, and Russians. From the 16th century through World War I major portions of Armenia were controlled by their most brutal invader, the Ottoman Turks, under whom the Armenians experienced discrimination, religious persecution, heavy taxation, and armed attacks. In response to Armenian nationalist stirrings, the Turks massacred thousands of Armenians in 1894 and 1896. The most horrific massacre took place in April 1915 during World War I, when the Turks ordered the deportation of the Armenian population to the deserts of Syria and Mesopotamia. According to the majority of historians, between 600,000 and 1.5 million Armenians were murdered or died of starvation. The Armenian massacre is considered the first genocide in the 20th century. Turkey denies that a genocide took place, and claims that a much smaller number died in a civil war.

After the Turkish defeat in World War I, the independent Republic of Armenia was established on May 28, 1918, but survived only until Nov. 29, 1920, when it was annexed by the Soviet Army. On March 12, 1922, the Soviets joined Georgia, Armenia, and Azerbaijan to form the Transcaucasian Soviet Socialist Republic, which became part of the USSR. In 1936, after a reorganization, Armenia became a separate constituent republic of the USSR. Since 1988, Armenia has been involved in a territorial dispute with Azerbaijan over the enclave of Nagorno-Karabakh, to which both lay claim. Also in 1988, a devastating earthquake killed thousands and wreaked economic havoc.

Armenia declared its independence from the collapsing Soviet Union on Sept. 23, 1991. In the years that followed, Armenia successfully fought Azerbaijan for control of Nagorno-Karabakh. The majority population of the enclave are Armenian Christians who want to secede from Azerbaijan and either become part of Armenia or gain full independence. A cease-fire agreement was reached between the two countries in 1994, but the fate of Nagorno-Karabakh remained unresolved. Real progress finally began in April 2001, when Azerbaijani president Heidar Aliev and Armenian president Robert Kocharian met with American, French, and Russian negotiators, and began to hammer out the details regarding the future of the enclave.

An Armenian diaspora has existed throughout the nation's history, and Armenian emigration has been particularly heavy since independence from the Soviet Union. An estimated 60% of the total eight million Armenians worldwide live outside the country, with one million each in the U.S. and Russia. Significant Armenian communities are located in Georgia, France, Iran, Lebanon, Syria, Argentina, and Canada.

Prime Minister Vazgen Sarkisian and six others were assassinated Oct. 27, 1999, when gunmen broke into Parliament and began firing. The prime minister's brother, Aras Sarkisian, was appointed to succeed him, but in May 2000 President Kocharian replaced Sarkisian, a political rival, with a new prime minister, Andranik Markarian.

Australia

COMMONWEALTH OF AUSTRALIA

Sovereign: Queen Elizabeth II (1952)
Governor-General: Peter Hollingworth (2001)
Prime Minister: John Howard (1996)
Area: 2,967,893 sq mi (7,686,850 sq km)
Population (2001 est.): 19,357,594 (average annual rate of natural increase: 0.6%); birth rate: 12.9/1000; infant mortality rate: 5.0/1000; density per sq mi: 7
Capital (1996 est.): Canberra, 307,700. **Largest cities (1993 est.):** Sydney, 3,713,500; Melbourne, 3,189,200; Brisbane, 1,520,600; Perth, 1,295,100; Adelaide, 1,079,200. **Monetary unit:** Australian dollar.
Language: English. **Ethnicity/race:** Caucasian 95%, Asian 4%, aboriginal (353,000) and other 1%.
Religions: Anglican 26.1%, Roman Catholic 26.0%, other Christian 24.3%. **Literacy rate:** 100% (1980)
Economic summary: GDP/PPP (1999 est.): $416.2 billion; per capita $22,200. **Real growth rate:** 4.3%. **Inflation:** 1.8%. **Unemployment:** 7.5%. **Arable land:** 6%. **Agriculture:** wheat, barley, sugarcane, fruits; cattle, sheep, poultry. **Labor force:** 8.9 million (Dec. 1999); services 73%, industry 22%, agriculture 5% (1997 est.). **Industries:** mining, industrial and transportation equipment, food processing, chemicals, steel. **Natural resources:** bauxite, coal, iron ore, copper, tin, silver, uranium, nickel, tungsten, mineral sands, lead, zinc, diamonds, natural gas, petroleum. **Exports:** $58 billion (f.o.b., 1999 est.): coal, gold, meat, wool, alumina, iron ore, wheat, machinery and transport equipment. **Imports:** $67 billion (f.o.b., 1999 est.): machinery and transport equipment, computers and office machines, telecommunication equipment and parts; crude oil and petroleum products. **Major trading partners:** Japan, EU, ASEAN, U.S., South Korea, New Zealand, Taiwan, Hong Kong, China.
Member of Commonwealth of Nations

Geography The continent of Australia, with the island state of Tasmania, is approximately equal in area to the United States (excluding Alaska and Hawaii). Mountain ranges run from north to south along the east coast, reaching their highest point in Mount Kosciusko (7,308 ft; 2,228 m). The western half of the continent is occupied by a desert plateau that rises into barren, rolling hills near the west coast. It includes the Great Victoria Desert to the south and the Great Sandy Desert to the north. The Great Barrier Reef, extending about 1,245 mi (2,000 km), lies along the northeast coast. The island of Tasmania (26,178 sq mi; 67,800 sq km) is off the southeast coast.

Government Democracy. Symbolic executive power is vested in the British monarch, who is represented throughout Australia by the governor-general.

History The first inhabitants of Australia were the Aborigines, who migrated there at least 40,000 years ago from Southeast Asia. There may have been between a half million to a full million Aborigines at the time of European settlement; today there are about 350,000.

Dutch, Portuguese, and Spanish ships sighted Australia in the 17th century; the Dutch landed at the Gulf of Carpentaria in 1606. In 1616 the territory became known as New Holland. The British arrived in 1688, but it was not until Captain James Cook's voyage in 1770 that Great Britain claimed possession of the vast island, calling it New South Wales. A British penal colony was set up at Port Jackson (what is now Sydney) in 1788, and about 161,000 transported English convicts were settled there until the system was suspended in 1839.

Free settlers established six colonies: New South Wales (1786), Tasmania (then Van Diemen's Land) (1825), Western Australia (1829), South Australia (1834), Victoria (1851), and Queensland (1859). Various gold rushes attracted settlers, as did the mining of other minerals. Sheep farming and grain soon became important economic enterprises. The six colonies became states and in 1901 federated into the Commonwealth of Australia with a constitution that incorporated British parliamentary and U.S. federal traditions. Australia became known for its liberal legislation: free compulsory education, protected trade unionism with industrial conciliation and arbitration, the secret ballot, women's suffrage, maternity allowances, and sickness and old-age pensions.

Australia fought alongside Britain in World War I, notably with the Australia and New Zealand Army Corps (ANZAC) in the Dardanelles campaign (1915). Participation in World War II brought Australia closer to the United States. Parliamentary power in the second half of the 20th century shifted between three political parties: the Australian Labour Party, the Liberal Party, and the National Party. Australia relaxed its discriminatory immigration laws in the 1960s and 1970s, which favored Northern Europeans. Thereafter, about 40% of its immigrants came from Asia, diversifying a population that was predominantly of English and Irish heritage.

In March 1996 the opposition Liberal Party–National Party coalition easily won the national elections, removing the Labour Party after 13 years in power. Pressure from the new, conservative One Nation Party threatened to reduce the gains made by Aborigines and to limit immigration. An Aboriginal movement had grown in the 1960s that gained full citizenship and improved education for the country's poorest socioeconomic group.

In Sept. 1999, Australia led the international peacekeeping force sent to restore order in East Timor, Indonesia. Pro-Indonesian militias had begun massacring civilians following a UN-sponsored referendum that overwhelmingly called for East Timor's independence.

In Nov. 1999, Australia's 11.6 million voters rejected a referendum that would have ended Australia's formal allegiance to the British Crown. The referendum would have replaced the British governor-general with an Australian president chosen by Parliament. Although the vast majority of Australians do not consider themselves monarchists, they rejected the referendum because it did not provide for direct, popular elections but gave Parliament the power to select the president.

In 2000, Prime Minister Howard instituted a new tax system, lowering income and corporate taxes, and adding sales taxes on goods and services. Sydney hosted the 2000 Summer Olympic games from Sept. 15–Oct.1, 2000.

Australian External Territories

Norfolk Island (13.36 sq mi; 34.6 sq km) was placed under Australian administration in 1914. Population 1,892 (2000). A former penal colony, Norfolk Island became home to the entire population of Pitcairn Island in 1856. The 194 residents of tiny Pitcairn—all of whom were the descendants of the mutineers from the HMS *Bounty* and their Tahitian wives—embarked on the 3,700-mile journey to Norfolk because of overpopulation. Many Norfolk residents can trace their genealogy directly to the adventurers from *Bounty*.

The Ashmore and Cartier Islands (1.93 sq mi), situated in the Indian Ocean off the northwest coast of Australia, came under Australian administration in 1934.

The Australian Antarctic Territory (2,360,000 sq mi; 6,112,400 sq km) is made up of all the islands and territories, other than Adélie Land, situated south of lat. 60°S and lying between long. 160° and 45°E. It came under Australian administration in 1936.

Heard Island and the McDonald Islands (159 sq mi; 412 sq km), lying in the sub-Antarctic, were placed under Australian administration in 1947. The islands are uninhabited.

Christmas Island (52 sq mi; 135 sq km) is situated in the Indian Ocean. It came under Australian administration in 1958. Most of the island's residents had been phosphate miners until the 1990s, when the Australian-based Casinos Austria International Ltd. built a $45 million casino on Christmas Island. As a result, the population has more than doubled, to 2,564 (2000).

Coral Sea Islands (400,000 sq mi; 1,036,000 sq km, but only a few sq mi of land) became a territory of Australia in 1969. There is no permanent population on the islands.

Cocos (Keeling) Islands are made up of a group of 27 small coral islands in two separate atolls in the Indian Ocean, 1,721 mi (2,768 km) northwest of Perth. West Island is the largest, about 6.2 mi (10 km) long. The islands became an Australian territory in 1955. In April 1984 the residents voted to merge with Australia. The population of the Cocos is 635 (July 2000 est.).

Austria

REPUBLIC OF AUSTRIA

National name: Republik Österreich
President: Thomas Klestil (1992)
Chancellor: Wolfgang Schüssel (2000)
Area: 32,378 sq mi (83,858 sq km)
Population (2001 est.): 8,150,835 (average annual rate of natural increase: 0.0%); birth rate 9.7/1000; infant mortality rate: 4.4/1000; density per sq mi: 252
Capital and largest city (1991 est.): Vienna, 1,600,000. **Other large cities (1995 est.):** Graz, 237,150; Linz, 203,000; Salzburg, 144,000; Innsbruck, 118,000.
Monetary units: Schilling and euro. **Languages:** German 98% (small Slovene, Croatian, and Hungarian-speaking minorities). **Ethnicity/race:** German 99.4%, Croatian 0.3%, Slovene 0.2%.
Religions: Roman Catholic 85%, Protestant 6%, other 9%. **Literacy rate:** 99% (1974)
Economic summary: GDP/PPP (1999 est.): $190.6 billion; per capita $23,400. **Real growth rate:** 2%. **Inflation:** 0.5%. **Unemployment:** 4.4%. **Arable land:** 17%. **Agriculture:** grains, potatoes, sugar beets, wine, fruit; dairy products, cattle, pigs, poultry; lumber. **Labor force:** 3.7 million (1999); services 68%, industry and crafts 29%, agriculture and forestry 3% (1999 est.). **Industries:** construction, machinery, vehicles and parts, food, chemicals, lumber and wood processing, paper and paperboard, communications equipment, tourism (1997). **Natural resources:** iron ore, oil, timber, magnesite, lead, coal, lignite, copper, hydropower. **Exports:** $62.9 billion (1999 est.): machinery and equipment, paper and paperboard, metal goods, chemicals, iron and steel; textiles, foodstuffs (1998). **Imports:** $69.9 billion (1999 est.): machinery and equipment, chemicals, metal goods, oil and oil products; foodstuffs (1998). **Major trading partners:** EU, U.S.

Geography Slightly smaller than Maine, Austria includes much of the mountainous territory of the eastern Alps (about 75% of the area). The country contains many snowfields, glaciers, and snowcapped peaks, the highest being the Grossglockner (12,530 ft; 3,819 m). The Danube is the principal river. Forests and woodlands cover about 40% of the land.

Government Federal republic.

History Settled in prehistoric times, the central European land that is now Austria was overrun in pre-Roman times by various tribes, including the Celts. After the fall of the Roman Empire, of which Austria was part, the area was invaded by Bavarians and Slavic Avars. Charlemagne conquered the area in 788 and encouraged colonization and Christianity. In 1252, Ottokar, king of Bohemia, gained possession, only to lose the territories to Rudolf of Hapsburg in 1278. Thereafter, until World War I, Austria's history was largely that of its ruling house, the Hapsburgs. Austria emerged from the Congress of Vienna in 1815 as the continent's dominant power. The *Ausgleich* of 1867 provided for a dual sovereignty, the empire of Austria and the kingdom of Hungary, under Franz Joseph I, who ruled until his death on Nov. 21, 1916. The Austrian-Hungarian minority rule of this immensely diverse empire became increasingly difficult in an age of emerging nationalist movements. When Archduke Francis Ferdinand was assassinated by a Serbian nationalist in Sarajevo in 1914, World War I, as well as the destruction of the Austro-Hungarian Empire, began.

During World War I, Austria-Hungary was one of the Central powers with Germany, Bulgaria, and Turkey, and the conflict left the country in political chaos and economic ruin. Austria, shorn of Hungary, was proclaimed a republic in 1918, and the monarchy was dissolved in 1919. A parliamentary democracy was set up by the constitution of Nov. 10, 1920. To check the power of Nazis advocating union with Germany, Chancellor Engelbert Dolfuss in 1933 established a dictatorship, but was assassinated by the Nazis on July 25, 1934. Kurt von Schuschnigg, his successor, struggled to keep Austria independent, but on March 12, 1938, German troops occupied the country, and Hitler proclaimed its *Anschluss* (union) with Germany, annexing it to the Third Reich.

After World War II, the U.S. and Britain declared the Austrians a "liberated" people. But the Russians prolonged the occupation. Finally Austria concluded a state treaty with the USSR and the other occupying powers and regained its independence on May 15, 1955. The second Austrian republic, established Dec. 19, 1945, on the basis of the 1920 constitution (amended in 1929), was declared by the federal Parliament to be permanently neutral.

On June 8, 1986, former UN secretary-general Kurt Waldheim was elected to the ceremonial office of president in a campaign marked by controversy over his alleged links to Nazi war crimes in Yugoslavia. Austria became a member of the European Union in 1995, but it retained its strict constitutional neutrality and forbade the stationing of foreign troops on its soil.

In 1998, Austria discussed the return of hundreds of art objects now owned by Austria that had been confiscated by the Nazi regime from their former, primarily Jewish owners.

In Feb. 2000 the conservative People's Party formed a coalition with the far-right Freedom Party, headed by Jörg Haider. A nationalist against immigration, Haider had made several controversial remarks praising some Nazi policies, which he has since recanted. His gradual rise to power—from 5% in 1983 to 28% in the October 1999 election—was credited to voters weary of decades of stasis under the rule of the Social Democrats. The European Union condemned Austria's new coalition, froze diplomatic contacts, and imposed sanctions, accusing Haider of being a racist, xenophobe, and Nazi-sympathizer. Austria responded angrily by criticizing the EU for interfering in the affairs of a democratically elected government. Large demonstrations in Austria and throughout Europe followed. Haider did not join the government and resigned from the party in May 2000, but continued to wield influence from the sidelines. In Sept. 2000, the EU lifted sanctions against Austria. The Freedom Party's popularity began to decline markedly in 2001: in Vienna's state election in March the party pulled in just 20.3% of the vote.

Azerbaijan

REPUBLIC OF AZERBAIJAN
President: Heydar Aliyev (1993)
Prime Minister: Artur Rasizade (1996)
Area: 33,436 sq mi (86,600 sq km)
Population (2001 est.): 7,771,092 (average annual rate of natural increase: 0.9%). Birth rate: 18.4/1000; infant mortality rate: 83.1/1000; density per sq mi: 232
Capital and largest city (1991): Baku, 1,713,300, a port on the Caspian Sea. **Other large cities:** Ganja (1989), 278,000; Sumgait, 231,000. **Monetary unit:** Manat. **Languages:** Azerbaijani Turkic, 82%; Russian, 7%; Armenian, 2%. **Ethnicity/race:** Azeri 90%, Dagestani 3.2%, Russian 2.5%, Armenian 2.3%, other 2% (1995 est.). Note: almost all Armenians live in the separatist Nagorno-Karabakh region. **Religions:** Muslim 87%, Russian Orthodox 5.6%, Armenian Orthodox 2%. **Literacy rate:** 97% (1989)
Economic summary: GDP/PPP (1999 est.): $14 billion; per capita $1,770. **Real growth rate:** 7%. **Inflation:** –6.8%. **Unemployment:** 20%. **Arable land:** 18%. **Agriculture:** cotton, grain, rice, grapes, fruit, vegetables, tea, tobacco; cattle, pigs, sheep, goats. **Labor force:** 2.9 million (1997); agriculture and forestry 32%, industry and construction 15%, services 53% (1997). **Industries:** petroleum and natural gas, petroleum products, oil field equipment; steel, iron ore, cement; chemicals and petrochemicals; textiles. **Natural resources:** petroleum, natural gas, iron ore, nonferrous metals, alumina. **Exports:** $885 million (f.o.b., 1999 est.): oil and gas 70%, machinery, cotton, foodstuffs. **Imports:** $1.62 billion (c.i.f., 1999 est.): machinery and equipment, foodstuffs, metals, chemicals. **Major trading partners:** Turkey, Russia, Georgia, Italy, Iran, Ukraine, UAE, Iran.

Geography Azerbaijan is located on the western shore of the Caspian Sea at the southeast extremity of the Caucasus. The region is a mountainous country. About 7% of it is arable land. The Kura River Valley is the area's major agricultural zone.

Government Constitutional republic.

History Northern Azerbaijan was known as Caucasian Albania in ancient times. The area was the site of many conflicts involving Arabs, Kazars, and Turks. After the 11th century, the territory became dominated by Turks and eventually a stronghold of the Shi'ite Muslim religion and Islamic culture. The territory of Soviet Azerbaijan was acquired by Russia from Persia through the Treaty of Gulistan in 1813 and the Treaty of Turkamanchai in 1828.

After the Bolshevik Revolution, Azerbaijan declared its independence from Russia in May 1918. The republic was reconquered by the Red Army in 1920, and was annexed into the Transcaucasian Soviet Socialist Republic in 1922. It was later reestablished as a separate Soviet Republic on Dec. 5, 1936. Azerbaijan declared independence from the collapsing Soviet Union on Aug. 30, 1991.

Since 1988, Azerbaijan and Armenia have been feuding over the enclave of Nagorno-Karabakh. The majority of the enclave's inhabitants are Armenian Christians agitating to secede from the predominantly Muslim Azerbaijan and join with Armenia. War broke out in 1988 when Nagorno-Karabakh tried to break away and annex itself to Armenia, and 30,000 died before a cease-fire agreement was reached in 1994, with Armenia retaining its hold over the disputed enclave. Final plans on the status of Nagorno-Karabakh have yet to be determined; in April 2001, however, Azerbaijani president Heidar Aliev and Armenian president Robert Kocharian met with American, French, and Russian negotiators, and made significant progress toward a settlement.

The country's economic troubles are expected to be transformed through Western investment in Azerbaijan's oil resources, an untapped reserve whose estimated worth is trillions of dollars. Since 1994, the Azerbaijan state oil company (SOCAR) has signed several billion-dollar agreements with international oil companies. A total of 15 production-sharing agreements have been signed; only one, run by BP-led Azerbaijan International Operating Company (AIOC) is thus far producing crude oil. Azerbaijan's pro-Western stance and its careful economic management have made it the most attractive of the oil-rich Caspian countries for foreign investment. In the years since its independence, the country has undergone rapid privatization and the IMF has given it high marks as one of the most successful economic overhauls ever.

But difficult negotiations over the route of the pipeline have stalled Azerbaijan's potential oil boom. Routes through Russia, Turkey, Georgia, and Iran have been proposed, and U.S., Russian, British, Iranian, and Chinese contenders in the "pipeline war" are all vying for dominance. In the volatile Caucasus region the options are complex, since all the proposed routes must pass through an unstable field of political, ethnic, religious, and environmental land mines.

In July 2001 an Iranian warship chased two Azerbaijani oil-exploration ships out of disputed waters in the Caspian, intensifying the hostilities between the two countries over oil rights.

Bahamas

COMMONWEALTH OF THE BAHAMAS

Sovereign: Queen Elizabeth II (1952)
Governor-General: Sir Orville Alton Turnquest (1995)
Prime Minister: Hubert Ingraham (1992)
Area: 5,382 sq mi (13,940 sq km)
Population (2001 est.): 297,852 (average annual rate of natural increase: 1.2%); birth rate: 19.1/1000; infant mortality rate: 17.0/1000; density per sq mi: 55
Capital and largest city (1991 census): Nassau, 171,542. **Monetary unit:** Bahamian dollar. **Language:** English. **Ethnicity/race:** black 85%, white 15%. **Religions:** Baptist 29%, Anglican 23%, Roman Catholic 22%, others. **Literacy rate:** 90% (1963)
Economic summary: GDP/PPP (1998 est.): $5.58 billion; per capita $20,000. **Real growth rate:** 3%. **Inflation:** 1.3%. **Unemployment:** 9%. **Arable land:** 1%. **Agriculture:** citrus, vegetables; poultry. **Labor force:** 148,000 (1996); tourism, 40%; other services, 50%; industry, 5%; agriculture, 5% (1995 est.). **Industries:** tourism, banking, cement, oil refining and transshipment, salt, rum, aragonite, pharmaceuticals, spiral-welded steel pipe. **Natural resources:** salt, aragonite, timber. **Exports:** $362.8 million (1998): pharmaceuticals, cement, rum, crawfish, refined petroleum products. **Imports:** $1.74 billion (1998): foodstuffs, manufactured goods, crude oil, vehicles, electronics. **Major trading partners:** U.S., Switzerland, UK, Italy, Japan. **Member of Commonwealth of Nations**

Geography The Bahamas are an archipelago of about 700 islands and 2,400 uninhabited islets and cays lying 50 mi off the east coast of Florida. They extend for about 760 mi (1,223 km). Only about 30 of the islands are inhabited; the most important is New Providence (80 sq mi; 207 sq km), on which the capital, Nassau, is situated. Other islands include Grand Bahama, Abaco, Eleuthera, Andros, Cat Island, and San Salvador (or Watling's Island).

Government Commonwealth.

History The Arawak Indians were the first inhabitants of the Bahamas. Columbus's first encounter with the New World on Oct. 12, 1492, was the Bahamian island of San Salvador. The British first built settlements on the islands in the 17th century. In the early 18th century, the Bahamas were a favorite pirate haunt.

The Bahamas were a crown colony from 1717 until they were granted internal self-government in 1964. The islands moved toward greater autonomy in 1968 after the overwhelming victory in general elections of the Progressive Liberal Party, led by Prime Minister Lynden O. Pindling, over the predominantly white United Bahamians Party. With its new mandate from the 85% black population, Pindling's government negotiated a new constitution with Britain under which the colony became the Commonwealth of the Bahama Islands in 1969. On July 10, 1973, the Bahamas became an independent nation.

Hubert A. Ingraham, of the Free National Movement Party, was sworn in as prime minister on Aug. 20, 1992, ending 25 years of rule by the Progressive Liberal Party. Once heavily reliant on agriculture and fishing, the Bahamas has diversified its economy into tourism, financial services, and international shipping. While it enjoys a per capita income that is among the top 30 in the world, there is a big gap between the urban middle class and poor farmers. In addition, the nation is vulnerable to hurricanes, which regularly inflict serious damage.

Bahrain

STATE OF BAHRAIN

Emir: Sheik Hamad ibn Isa al-Khalifa (1999)
Prime Minister: Sheik Khalifah ibn Sulman al-Khalifa (1970)
Area: 239 sq mi (620 sq km)
Population (2001 est.): 645,361 (average annual rate of natural increase: 1.6%); birth rate: 20.1/1000; infant mortality rate: 19.8/1000; density per sq mi: 2,696
Capital (1992 est.): Al-Manámah, 140,401. **Monetary unit:** Bahrain dinar. **Languages:** Arabic (official), English, Farsi, Urdu. **Ethnicity/race:** Bahraini 63%, Asian 13%, other Arab 10%, Iranian 8%, other 6%. **Religion:** Islam. **Literacy rate:** 77% (1990)
Economic summary: GDP/PPP (1999 est): $8.6 billion; per capita $13,700. **Real growth rate:** 4%. **Inflation:** 0.5% (1998 est.). **Unemployment:** 15% (1998 est.). **Arable land:** 1%. **Agriculture:** fruit, vegetables; poultry, dairy products; shrimp, fish. **Labor force:** 295,000 (1998 est.); industry, commerce, and service, 79%; government, 20%; agriculture, 1% (1997 est.). **Industries:** petroleum processing and refining, aluminum smelting, offshore banking, ship repairing; tourism. **Natural resources:** oil, associated and nonassociated natural gas, fish. **Exports:** $3.3 billion (f.o.b., 1998): petroleum and petroleum products, aluminum. **Imports:** $3.5 billion (f.o.b., 1998): nonoil, crude oil. **Major trading partners:** India, Japan, Saudi Arabia, South Korea, UAE, U.S., UK, Germany.

Geography Bahrain is an archipelago in the Persian Gulf off the coast of Saudi Arabia. The islands for the most part are level expanses of sand and rock. A causeway connects Bahrain to Saudi Arabia.

Government Constitutional monarchy.

History Known in ancient times as Dilmun, Bahrain was an important center of trade by the 3rd millennium B.C. The islands were ruled by the Persians in the 4th century A.D., and then by Arabs until 1541, when the Portuguese invaded them. Persia again claimed Bahrain in 1602. In 1783 Ahmad ibn al-Khalifah took over, and the al-Khalifahs remain the ruling family today. Bahrain became a British protectorate in 1820. It did not gain full independence until Aug. 14, 1971.

Although oil was discovered in Bahrain in the 1930s, it was relatively little compared to other Gulf states, and the wells are expected to be the first in the region to dry up. Sheik Isa ibn-Sulman al-Khalifah, who became emir in 1961, was determined to diversify his country's economy, and set about establishing Bahrain as a major financial center. The country provides its people with free medical care, education, and old-age pensions.

Conflicts between the Shi'ites and Sunnis are a continuing problem in Bahrain. The Sunni minority, to which the ruling al-Khalifah family belongs, controls nearly all the power and wealth in the country. Shi'ite Muslims have continued to agitate for more representation in government, and minor violent clashes have led to about two dozen deaths since 1994.

Bahrain has been an important Western ally, serving as a Western air base during the Persian Gulf War in 1991, and continuing to serve as the base of the United States' Fifth Fleet, which patrols the Gulf.

Sheik Isa ibn-Sulman al-Khalifah died in 1999 after four decades of rule. He was succeeded by his son, Sheik Hamad ibn Isa al-Khalifah, who immediately began a sweeping democratization of the country: censorship has been relaxed and draconian laws repealed, exiles have been repatriated, and the stateless Bidoons have been granted citizenship. In a Feb. 2001 referendum, which permitted women to vote for the first time, Bahrainis overwhelmingly supported the transformation of the traditional monarchy into a constitutional one.

Bangladesh

PEOPLE'S REPUBLIC OF BANGLADESH

President: Shahabuddin Ahmed (1996)
Prime Minister: Latifur Rahman (2001)
Area: 55,598 sq mi (144,000 sq km)
Population (2001 est.): 131,269,860 (average annual rate of natural increase: 1.7%); birth rate: 25.3/1000; infant mortality rate: 69.9/1000; density per sq mi: 2,361
Capital and largest city (2000 est.): Dhaka, 9,600,000 (metro. area). **Other large cities (est. mid-1994):** Chittagong, 3,000,000; Khulna, 2,000,000. **Monetary unit:** Taka. **Principal languages:** Bangla (official), English. **Ethnicity/race:** Bengali 98%, Biharis 250,000, tribals less than 1 million. **Religions:** Muslim 83%, Hindu 16%, Buddhist, Christian, other. **Literacy rate:** 36% (1991)
Economic summary: GDP/PPP (1999 est.): $187 billion; per capita $1,470. **Real growth rate:** 5.2%. **Inflation:** 9% (FY98/99 est.). **Unemployment:** 35.2% (1996). **Arable land:** 73%. **Agriculture:** rice, jute, tea, wheat, sugarcane, potatoes; beef, milk, poultry, tobacco, pulses, oilseeds, spices, fruit. **Labor force:** 56 million (1995–96); note: extensive export of labor to Saudi Arabia, Kuwait, UAE, Oman, Qatar, Malaysia, and Singapore; agriculture, 63%; services, 26%; industry, 11% (FY95/96). **Industries:** cotton textiles, jute, garments, tea processing, newsprint, cement, chemical fertilizer, light engineering, sugar. **Natural resources:** natural gas, arable land, timber. **Exports:** $5.1 billion (1998): garments, jute and jute goods, leather, frozen fish and seafood. **Imports:** $8.01 billion (1998): machinery and equipment, chemicals, iron and steel, textiles, raw cotton, food, crude oil and petroleum products, cement. **Major trading partners:** U.S., Germany, UK, France, Italy, India, China, Japan, Hong Kong, South Korea. **Member of Commonwealth of Nations**

Geography Bangladesh, on the northern coast of the Bay of Bengal, is surrounded by India, with a small common border with Myanmar in the southeast. The country is low-lying riverine land traversed by the many branches and tributaries of the Ganges and Brahmaputra Rivers. Tropical monsoons and frequent floods and cyclones inflict heavy damage in the delta region.

Government Republic within the British Commonwealth.

History What is now called Bangladesh is part of the historic region of Bengal, the northeast portion of the Indian subcontinent. The earliest reference to the region was to a kingdom called Vanga, or Banga (c.1000 B.C.). Buddhists ruled for centuries, but by the 10th century Bengal was primarily Hindu. In 1576, Bengal became part of the Mogul Empire, and the majority of East Bengalis converted to Islam. Bengal was ruled by British India from 1757 until Britain withdrew in 1947, and Pakistan was founded out of the two predominantly Muslim regions of the Indian subcontinent. West Pakistan and East Pakistan were united by religion (Islam), but their peoples were separated by culture, physical features, and 1,000 miles of Indian territory. Bangladesh consists primarily of East Bengal (West Bengal is part of India and its people are primarily Hindu) plus the Sylhet district of the Indian state of Assam. For almost 25 years after independence from Britain, its history was part of Pakistan's (*see* Pakistan).

Tension between East and West Pakistan developed from the outset because of their vast geographic, economic, and cultural differences. East Pakistan's Awami League, a political party founded by the Bengali nationalist Sheik Mujibur Rahman in 1949, sought independence from West Pakistan. Although 56% of the population resided in East Pakistan, the West held the lion's share of political and economic power. In 1970 East Pakistanis secured a majority of the seats in the National Assembly. President Yahya Khan postponed the opening of the National Assembly in an attempt to circumvent East Pakistan's demand for greater autonomy. As a consequence East Pakistan seceded, and the independent state of Bangladesh, or Bengali nation, was proclaimed on March 26, 1971. Civil war broke out, and with the help of Indian troops in the last few weeks of the war, East Pakistan defeated West Pakistan on Dec. 16, 1971. An estimated one million Bengalis were killed in the fighting or later slaughtered. Ten million more took refuge in India. In Feb. 1974, Pakistan agreed to recognize the independent state of Bangladesh.

Founding president Sheikh Mujibur was assassinated in 1975, as was the next president, Zia ur-Rahman. On March 24, 1982, Gen. Hossain Mohammad Ershad, army chief of staff, took control in a bloodless coup but was forced to resign on Dec. 6, 1990, amid violent protests and numerous allegations of corruption. A succession of prime ministers governed in the 1990s, including Khaleda Zia, wife of the assassinated president Zia ur-Rahman and Sheikh Hasina Wazed, the daughter of Sheik Mujibur.

Prime Minister Sheikh Hasina completed her five-year term as prime minister in July 2000—the first leader to do so since the country gained independence from Pakistan in 1974—and handed over power to a caretaker administration, led by former chief justice Latifur Rahman, who will serve until Oct. 2001 parliamentary elections.

Barbados

Sovereign: Queen Elizabeth II (1952)
Governor-General: Sir Clifford Husbands (June 1996)
Prime Minister: Owen Arthur (1994)
Area: 166 sq mi (430 sq km)
Population (2001 est.): 275,330 (average annual rate of natural increase: 0.5%); birth rate: 13.5/1000; infant mortality rate: 12.0/1000; density per sq mi: 1,658
Capital and largest city (1990): Bridgetown, 6,700. **Monetary unit:** Barbados dollar. **Language:** English. **Ethnicity/race:** African 80%, European 4%, other 16%. **Religions:** Anglican 40%, Methodist 7%, Pentecostal 8%, Roman Catholic 4%. **Literacy rate:** 99% (1970)
Economic summary: GDP/PPP (1998 est.): $2.9 billion; per capita: $11,200. **Real growth rate:** 4.4%. **Inflation:** 1.7% (1998). **Unemployment:** 12% (1998 est.). **Arable land:** 37%. **Agriculture:** sugarcane, vegetables, cotton. **Labor force:** 136,000; services, 75%; industry, 15%; agriculture, 10% (1996 est.). **Industries:** tourism, sugar, light manufacturing, component assembly for export. **Natural resources:** petroleum, fish, natural gas. **Exports:** $211.2 million (1998): sugar and molasses, rum, other foods and beverages, chemicals, electrical components, clothing. **Imports:** $1.01 billion (1998): consumer goods, machinery, foodstuffs, construction materials, chemicals, fuel, electrical components. **Major trading partners:** UK, U.S., Trinidad and Tobago, Venezuela, Jamaica, Japan, Canada. **Member of Commonwealth of Nations**

Geography An island in the Atlantic about 300 mi (483 km) north of Venezuela, Barbados is only 21 mi long (34 km) and 14 mi across (23 km) at its widest point. It is circled by fine beaches and narrow coastal plains. The highest point is Mount Hillaby (1,105 ft; 337 m) in the north-central area.

Government Parliamentary democracy.

History Barbados is thought to have been originally inhabited by Arawak Indians. By the time Europeans explored the island, however, it was uninhabited.

Barbados was settled by the British in 1627. Slaves were brought in from Africa to work sugar plantations, and from the time of its settlement, the population was about 90% black. Slavery was abolished in the British Empire in 1834, and in 1838 slaves on the island gained their freedom.

Barbados was the administrative headquarters of the Windward Islands until it became a separate colony in 1885. Barbados was a member of the Federation of the West Indies from 1958 to 1962. Britain granted the colony independence on Nov. 30, 1966, and it became a parliamentary democracy within the Commonwealth.

Since independence, Barbados has been politically stable. However, local anger over rulings by the final appeals court, appointed by Queen Elizabeth, led to the creation in 1997 of a constitutional commission to consider abandoning all ties to Great Britain. Prime Minister Arthur, who has seen Barbados's unemployment fall from 22% to 11%, was reelected in 1999 by a landslide. With one of the highest literacy rates in the world, 98%, Barbados has expanded its financial services and tourist industries, reducing reliance on sugar cane exports.

Belarus

REPUBLIC OF BELARUS

President: Alyaksandr Lukashenka (1994)
Prime Minister: Uladzimir Yarmoshyn (2000)
Area: 80,154 sq mi (207,600 sq km)
Population (2001 est.): 10,350,194 (average annual rate of natural increase: –0.4%); birth rate: 9.6/1000; infant mortality rate: 14.4/1000; density per sq mi: 129
Capital (1992 est.): Mensk (Minsk), 1,666,000. **Other large cities (1992 est.):** Gomel, 517,300; Vitebsk, 373,000; Mogilyov, 364,000; Grodno, 291,800; Brest, 284,000; Bobruysk, 224,000. **Monetary unit:** Belorussian ruble. **Language:** Belorussian (White Russian). **Ethnicity/race:** Belorussian 77.9%, Russian 13.2%, Polish 4.1%, Ukrainian 2.9%, other 1.9%. **Religion:** Orthodoxy is predominant. **Literacy rate:** 100% (1979)
Economic summary: GDP/PPP (1999 est.): $55.2 billion; per capita $5,300. **Real growth rate:** 1.5%. **Inflation:** 295%. **Unemployment:** 2.3% officially registered unemployed (Dec. 1998); large number of underemployed workers. **Arable land:** 29%. **Agriculture:** grain, potatoes, vegetables, sugar beets, flax; beef, milk. **Labor force:** 4.3 million (1998); industry and construction, n.a.; agriculture and forestry, n.a.; services, n.a. **Industries:** metal-cutting machine tools, tractors, trucks, earth movers, motorcycles, TV sets, chemical fibers, fertilizer, textiles, radios, refrigerators. **Natural resources:** forests, peat deposits, small quantities of oil and natural gas. **Exports:** $6 billion (f.o.b., 1999): machinery and equipment, chemicals, metals, textiles, foodstuffs. **Imports:** $6.4 billion (c.i.f., 1999): mineral products, machinery and equipment, metals, chemicals, foodstuffs. **Major trading partners:** Russia, Ukraine, Poland, Germany, Lithuania.

Geography Much of Belarus (formerly the Belorussian Soviet Socialist Republic of the USSR, and then Byelorussia) is a hilly lowland with forests, swamps, and numerous rivers and lakes. There are wide rivers emptying into the Baltic and Black Seas. Its forests cover over one-third of the land and its peat marshes are a valuable natural resource. The largest lake is Narach, 31 sq mi (79.6 sq km).

Government Republic.

History In the 5th century A.D., Belarus (also known as White Russia) was colonized by east Slavic tribes. Kiev dominated it from the 9th to 12th centuries. After the destruction of Kiev by the Mongols in the 13th century, the territory was conquered by the dukes of Lithuania, although it retained a degree of autonomy. Belarus became part of the Grand Duchy of Lithuania, which merged with Poland in 1569. Following the partitions of Poland in 1772, 1793, and 1795, in which Poland was divided among Russia, Prussia, and Austria, Belarus became part of the Russian empire.

Following World War I, Belarus proclaimed itself a republic, only to find itself occupied by the Red Army soon after its March 1918 announcement. The Polish-Soviet War of 1918–21 was fought to decide the fate of Belarus. West Belarus was ceded to Poland; the larger eastern part formed the Belorussian SSR, and was then joined to the USSR in 1922. In 1939, the Soviet Union took back West Belarus from Poland under the secret protocol of the Nazi-Soviet Nonaggression Pact and incorporated it into the Belorussian Soviet Socialist Republic. Occupied by the Nazis in World War II, Belarus was one of the most devastated battlefields.

Belarus declared its sovereignty in July 1990 and its independence in Aug. 1991. The Chernobyl nuclear power plant in Ukraine exploded in 1986, and 70% of its radioactivity fell on Belarus. Cancer and other illnesses have multiplied as a result.

The Belarus president, Nikolai Dementei, a communist hard-liner, was forced to resign under pressure following the Aug. 1991 attempted coup, and Stanislav S. Shushkevich, first deputy chairman of the Parliament, assumed leadership of the country. Belarus became a cofounder of the Commonwealth of Independent States (CIS) in Dec. 1991. In Jan. 1994, the country's Parliament ousted its reform-minded leader in protest against his support for market economics. In March 1994, Parliament adopted a new constitution, creating a presidency and reconstructing the 260-seat Parliament.

With much fanfare, Belarus and Russia signed a treaty in April 1997 aimed at significantly increasing cooperation between the two states, stopping just short of union.

The Russian financial crisis that began in fall 1998 severely affected Belarus's Soviet-style planned economy. Belarus is almost completely dependent on Russia, which buys 70% of its exports.

Critics continue to denounce the increasingly oppressive political atmosphere and human rights violations in Belarus under the Soviet-style authoritarianism of President Alyaksandr Lukashenka. In 1999, the year President Lukashenko was to step down, he rigged a national referendum allowing him to cancel the elections and remain president. Lukashenko's government has been accused of running a death squad that has killed dozens, including opposition party members and underworld figures.

After harassing the opposition and curtailing their campaign activities, Lukashenka won reelection in the Sept. 9, 2001, presidential race.

Belgium

KINGDOM OF BELGIUM

National name: Royaume de Belgique—Koninkrijk België
Sovereign: King Albert II (1993)
Prime Minister: Guy Verhofstadt (1999)
Area: 11,780 sq mi (30,510 sq km)
Population (2001 est.): 10,258,762 (average annual rate of natural increase: 0.1%); birth rate: 10.7/1000; infant mortality rate: 4.7/1000; density per sq mi: 871
Capital and largest city (1994): Brussels, 949,070 (metro area). **Other large cities (1994):** Antwerp, 476,044; Ghent, 229,900; Liège, 207,496; Charleroi, 206,898; Bruges, 116,724. **Monetary units:** Belgian franc and euro. **Languages:** Dutch (Flemish), 57%; French, 32%; bilingual (Brussels), 10%; German, 0.7%. **Ethnicity/race:** Fleming 55%, Walloon 33%, mixed or other 12%. **Religion:** Roman Catholic 75%. **Literacy rate:** 99% (1980)
Economic summary: GDP/PPP (1999 est.): $243.4 billion; per capita $23,900. **Real growth rate:** 1.8%. **Inflation:** 1%. **Unemployment:** 9%. **Arable land:** 24%. **Agriculture:** sugar beets, fresh vegetables, fruits, grain, tobacco; beef, veal, pork, milk. **Labor force:** 4.341 million (1999); services, 73%; industry, 25%; agriculture, 2%. **Industries:** engineering and metal products, motor vehicle assembly, processed food and beverages, chemicals, basic metals, textiles, glass, petroleum, coal. **Natural resources:** coal, natural gas. **Exports:** $187.3 billion (f.o.b., 1999): machinery and equipment, chemicals, diamonds, metals and metal products. **Imports:** $172.8 billion (f.o.b., 1999): machinery and equipment, chemicals, metals and metal products. **Major trading partners:** EU.

Geography Located in western Europe, Belgium has about 40 mi of seacoast on the North Sea, at the Strait of Dover, and is approximately the size of Maryland. The Meuse and the Schelde, Belgium's principal rivers, are important commercial arteries.

Government Parliamentary democracy under a constitutional monarch. Under the 1994 constitution, autonomy was granted to the Walloon region (Wallonia), the Flemish region (Flanders), and the bilingual Brussels-Capital region; autonomy was also guaranteed for the Flemish-, French-, and German-speaking "communities." The central government retains responsibility for foreign policy, defense, taxation, and social security.

History Belgium occupied part of the Roman province of Belgica, named after the Belgae, a people of ancient Gaul. The area was conquered by Julius Caesar in 57–50 B.C., then was overrun by the Franks in the 5th century A.D. It was part of Charlemagne's empire in the 8th century, then in the next century was absorbed into Lotharingia and later into the duchy of Lower Lorraine. In the 12th century it was partitioned into the duchies of Brabant and Luxembourg, the bishopric of Liège, and the domain of the count of Hainaut, which included Flanders. In the 16th century, Belgium, with most of the area of the low countries, passed to the duchy of Burgundy and was inherited by Charles V, who incorporated it into his Holy Roman Empire. Then, in 1555, the low countries were united with Spain. By the Treaty of Utrecht in 1713, the country's sovereignty passed to Austria. During the wars that followed the French Revolution, Belgium was occupied and later annexed to France. But with the downfall of Napoléon, the Congress of Vienna in 1815 gave the country to the Netherlands. The Belgians revolted in 1830 and declared their independence.

Germany's invasion of Belgium in 1914 set off World War I. The Treaty of Versailles (1919) gave the areas of Eupen, Malmédy, and Moresnet to Belgium. Leopold III succeeded Albert, king during World War I, in 1934. In World War II, Belgium was overwhelmed by Nazi Germany, and Leopold III was held prisoner. When he attempted to return in 1950, socialists and liberals revolted. He abdicated July 16, 1951, and his son, Baudouin, became king. Because of growing opposition to Belgian rule in its African colonies, Belgium granted independence to the Congo (now Democratic Republic of the Congo) in 1960 and to Ruanda-Urundi (now the nations of Rwanda and Burundi) in 1962.

Divisions between Flemings and Walloons grew, and linguistic regionalization increased, culminating in the revised constitution of 1994, which granted more autonomy to Belgium's three regions and language "communities."

In the 1990s the Belgian government was involved in numerous scandals that tainted it with a reputation for incompetence and corruption. In 1991, a deputy prime minister was murdered in a contract killing that remained unsolved. In 1998, Belgian statesman and former NATO secretary-general Willy Claes was convicted of bribery. International relations fared no better. Belgian peacekeeping troops abandoned Rwanda, a former colony, at the height of the 1994 genocide against the Tutsis. The discovery of the Dutroux child-sex-and-murder ring in 1996 led to further national outrage that was compounded by disclosures that official negligence and corruption had resulted in even more children's deaths. As the scandal continued into 1997, it fueled pressure for reform of the political, judicial, and police systems.

It was evident that little had changed, however, when Belgium stumbled into its next crisis in spring 1999. Dioxin, a cancer-causing chemical, was leaked into batches of chicken feed, contaminating the country's poultry and dairy products. Government ministers admitted to keeping the public in the dark for months after they realized the public health danger. Prime Minister Jean-Luc Dehaene resigned under the weight of the scandal. Dehaene has been credited with having reduced the budget deficit from 7% in 1993 to 1% in 1999, and for reducing the public debt by 20% during the same period—it had been 135% of the GDP.

The new prime minister, Guy Verhofstadt of the Liberal Party, cobbled together a coalition of six political parties in June 1999. Verhofstadt has promised a series of reforms aimed at the legal system and the civil service.

Under "universal jurisdiction," Belgian prosecutors may try anyone accused of war crimes, whatever their nationality and wherever the crimes took place. In 2001, Belgian courts convicted four Rwandans, including two nuns, for the massacre of the Tutsi people in Rwanda.

Belize

Sovereign: Queen Elizabeth II (1952)
Governor-General: Colville Young (1993)
Prime Minister: Said Musa (1998)
Area: 8,865 sq mi (22,960 sq km)
Population (2001 est.): 256,062 (average annual rate of natural increase: 2.7%); birth rate: 31.7/1000; infant mortality rate: 25.1/1000.; density per sq mi: 29
Capital (1997 est.): Belmopan, 8,130. **Largest city (1997 est.):** Belize City, 52,500. **Monetary unit:** Belize dollar. **Languages:** English (official), Creole, Spanish, Garifuna, Mayan. **Ethnicity/race:** mestizo 44%, Creole 30%, Maya 11%, Garifuna 7%, other 8%. **Religions:** Roman Catholic 62%, Protestant 30%. **Literacy rate:** 91% (1970)
Economic summary: GDP/PPP (1999 est.): $740 million; per capita $3,100. **Real growth rate:** 4%. **Inflation:** –0.9%. **Unemployment:** 14.3% (1998). **Arable land:** 2%. **Agriculture:** bananas, coca, citrus, sugarcane; lumber; fish, cultured shrimp. **Labor force:** 71,000; note: shortage of skilled labor and all types of technical personnel (1997 est.); agriculture, 38%; industry, 32%; services, 30% (1994). **Industries:** garment production, food processing, tourism, construction. **Natural resources:** arable land potential, timber, fish, hydropower. **Exports:** $150 million (f.o.b., 1998): sugar, bananas, citrus fruits, clothing, fish products, molasses, wood. **Imports:** $320 million (c.i.f., 1998): machinery and transportation equipment, manufactured goods, food, fuels, chemicals, pharmaceuticals. **Major trading partners:** U.S., UK, EU, Caricom, Mexico, Canada. **Member of Commonwealth of Nations**

Geography Belize is situated on the Caribbean Sea south of Mexico and east and north of Guatemala in Central America. In area, it is about the size of New Hampshire. Most of the country is heavily forested with various hardwoods. Mangrove swamps and cays along the coast give way to hills and mountains in the interior. The highest point is Victoria Peak, 3,681 ft (1,122 m).

Government Parliamentary democracy within the British Commonwealth.

History The Mayan civilization spread into the area of Belize between 1500 B.C. and A.D. 300 and flourished until about 1200. Several major archeological sites—notably Caracol, Lamanai, Lubaantun, Altun Ha, and Xunantunich—reflect the advanced civilization and much denser population of that period. European contact began in 1502 when Columbus sailed along the coast. The first recorded European settlement was begun by shipwrecked English seamen in 1638. Over the next 150 years, more English settlements were established. This period was also marked by piracy, indiscriminate logging, and sporadic attacks by Indians and neighboring Spanish settlements. Great Britain first sent an official representative to the area in the late 18th century, but Belize was not formally termed the Colony of British Honduras until 1840. It became a Crown colony in 1862. Subsequently, several constitutional changes were enacted to expand representative government. Full internal self-government under a ministerial system was granted in Jan. 1964.

Guatemala had long made claims on Honduran territory. Although the dispute between Guatemala and Great Britain remained unresolved, Belize became independent on Sept. 21, 1981, after having been self-governing since 1964. Guatemala recognized Belize's sovereignty in Sept. 1991. However, Guatemala still claims more than half of Belize's territory. At talks held at the Organization of American States' conference in July 2000, Belize and Guatemala agreed to an agenda for formal negotiations to resolve the dispute.

Benin

REPUBLIC OF BENIN

National name: Republique du Benin
President: Mathieu Kérékou (1996)
Area: 43,483 sq mi (112,620 sq km)
Population (2001 est.): 6,590,782 (average annual rate of natural increase: 3.0%); birth rate: 44.2/1000; infant mortality rate: 89.7/1000; density per sq mi: 152
Capital and largest city (1996): Porto-Novo (official), 177,660; Cotonou (de facto capital) 33,212. **Other large city (1992):** Djougou, 132,192. **Monetary unit:** Franc CFA. **Languages:** French (official), African languages. **Ethnicity/race:** African 99% (42 ethnic groups, most important being Fon, Adja, Yoruba, Bariba), Europeans 5,500. **Religions:** indigenous 70%, Christian 15%, Islam 15%. **Literacy rate:** 23% (1990)
Economic summary: GDP/PPP (1999 est.): $8.1 billion; per capita $1,300. **Real growth rate:** 5%. **Inflation:** 3%. **Unemployment:** n.a. **Arable land:** 13%. **Agriculture:** corn, sorghum, cassava (tapioca), yams, beans, rice, cotton, palm oil, peanuts; poultry, livestock. **Labor force:** n.a. **Industries:** textiles, cigarettes; beverages, food; construction materials, petroleum. **Natural resources:** small offshore oil deposits, limestone, marble, timber. **Exports:** $396 million (f.o.b., 1999): cotton, crude oil, palm products, cocoa. **Imports:** $566 million (f.o.b., 1999): foodstuffs, tobacco, petroleum products, capital goods. **Major trading partners:** Brazil, Libya, Indonesia, Spain, France, China, UK, Netherlands.

Geography This West African nation on the Gulf of Guinea, between Togo on the west and Nigeria on the east, is about the size of Tennessee. It is bounded also by Burkina Faso and Niger on the north. The land consists of a narrow coastal strip that rises to a swampy, forested plateau and then to highlands in the north. A hot and humid climate blankets the entire country.

Government Republic under a multiparty democratic rule.

History The Abomey kingdom of the Dahomey, or Fon, peoples was established in 1625. A rich cultural life flourished, and Benin's wooden masks, bronze statues, tapestries, and pottery are world renowned. One of the smallest and most densely populated states in Africa, Benin was annexed by the French in 1893 and incorporated into French West Africa in 1904. It became an autonomous republic within the French Community in 1958, and on Aug. 1, 1960, Dahomey was granted its independence within the community.

Gen. Christophe Soglo deposed the first president, Hubert Maga, in an army coup in 1963. He dismissed the civilian government in 1965, proclaiming himself chief of state. A group of young army officers seized power in 1967, deposing Soglo. In Dec. 1969, Benin had its fifth coup of the decade, with the army again taking power. In May 1970, a three-man presidential commission with a six-year term was created to take over the government. In May 1972, yet another army coup ousted the triumvirate and installed Lt. Col. Mathieu Kérékou as president. Between 1974 and 1989 Dahomey embraced socialism, and changed its name to the People's Republic of Benin. The name *Benin* commemorates an African kingdom that flourished from the 15th to the 17th century in what is now southwest Nigeria. In 1990 Benin abandoned Marxist ideology, began moving toward multiparty democracy, and changed its name again, to the Republic of Benin.

By the end of the 1980s, Benin's economy was near collapse. As its oil boom ended, Nigeria expelled 100,000 Beninese migrant workers and closed the border with Benin. Kérékou's socialist collectivization of Benin's agriculture and the ballooning bureaucracy further damaged the economy. By 1988, international financial institutions feared Benin would default on its loans and pressured Kérékou to make financial reforms.

Kérékou subsequently embarked on a major privatization campaign, cut the government payroll, and reduced social services, prompting student and labor union unrest. Fearing a revolution, Kérékou agreed to a new constitution and free elections. In 1991, Nicéphore Soglo, an economist and former director of the International Bank for Reconstruction and Development, was elected president with 67% of the vote.

Although he enjoyed widespread support at first, Soglo gradually became unpopular as austerity measures reduced living standards and a 50% currency devaluation in 1994 caused inflation. Kérékou defeated Soglo in the 1996 elections, with 52.5% of the vote.

In March 2001, Kérékou was easily reelected after two of his main opponents withdrew from the race, charging fraud.

Bhutan

KINGDOM OF BHUTAN

National name: Druk-yul
Ruler: King Jigme Singye Wangchuck (1972)
Prime Minister: Lyonpo Yeshey Zimba (2000)
Area: 18,147 sq mi (47,000 sq km)
Population (2001 est.): 2,049,412 (average annual rate of natural increase: 2.2%); birth rate: 35.7/1000; infant mortality rate: 108.9/1000; density per sq mi: 113
Capital and largest city (1993): Thimphu (official), 30,340. **Monetary unit:** Ngultrum. **Language:** Dzongkha (official). **Ethnicity/race:** Bhote 50%, ethnic Nepali 35%, indigenous or migrant tribes 15%.
Religions: Buddhist 75%, Hindu 25%. **Literacy rate:** 42% (1995)
Economic summary: GDP/PPP (1999 est.): $2.1 billion; per capita $1,060. **Real growth rate:** 7%. **Inflation:**

9% (1998). **Unemployment:** n.a. Arable land: 2%.
Agriculture: rice, corn, root crops, citrus, foodgrains; dairy products, eggs. **Labor force:** n.a.; note: massive lack of skilled labor; agriculture, 93%; services, 5%; industry and commerce, 2%. **Industries:** cement, wood products, processed fruits, alcoholic beverages, calcium carbide. **Natural resources:** timber, hydropower, gypsum, calcium carbide. **Exports:** $111 million (f.o.b., 1998): cardamom, gypsum, timber, handicrafts, cement, fruit, electricity (to India), precious stones, spices. **Imports:** $136 million (c.i.f., 1998): fuel and lubricants, grain, machinery and parts, vehicles, fabrics, rice. **Major trading partners:** India, Bangladesh, Japan, UK, Germany, U.S.

Geography Mountainous Bhutan, half the size of Indiana, is situated on the southeast slope of the Himalayas, bordered on the north and east by Tibet and on the south and west and east by India. The landscape consists of a succession of lofty and rugged mountains running generally from north to south and separated by deep valleys. In the north, towering peaks reach a height of 24,000 ft (7,315 m).

Government In the 1990s, the king gradually gave up absolute rule, transforming his kingdom into a constitutional monarchy.

History Although archeological exploration of Bhutan has been limited, evidence of civilization in the region dates back to at least 2000 B.C. Aboriginal Bhutanese, known as Monpa, are believed to have migrated from Tibet. The traditional name of the country since the 17th century has been Drukyul, Land of the Drokpa (Dragon People), a reference to the dominant branch of Tibetan Buddhism that is still practiced in the Himalayan kingdom.

British troops invaded the region in 1865 and negotiated an agreement under which Britain agreed to pay an annual allowance to the Bhutanese monarchy on condition of good behavior. A treaty between India and the seat of government, Thimphu, in 1949 increased this subsidy and placed Bhutan's foreign affairs under Indian control. Until the 1960s Bhutan was largely isolated from the rest of the world, and its people carried on a tranquil, traditional way of life of farming and trading that had remained intact for centuries. After China invaded Tibet, however, Bhutan strengthened its ties and contact with India in an effort to avoid Tibet's fate. New roads and other connections to India began to end its isolation. In the 1960s Bhutan also undertook social modernization, abolishing slavery and the caste system, emancipating women, and enacting land reform. In 1985, Bhutan made its first diplomatic links with non-Asian countries.

A pro-democracy campaign emerged in 1991, which the government claimed was composed largely of Nepali immigrants. As a result of the campaign, some 100,000 Nepali civil servants were either evicted or encouraged to emigrate. Most of them crossed the border back into Nepal, where they were housed in UN-administered refugee camps.

In 1998, King Jigme Singye Wangchuck voluntarily curtailed his powerful monarchy by yielding to the formerly rubber-stamp legislature, giving it the right to remove him from leadership and appoint his cabinet. The move was the largest step to date in a gradual program to dilute the monarchy after nearly a century of absolute rule. Income tax was introduced, with tax forms due for the first time in Feb. 2000.

Nepal and Bhutan reached a significant breakthrough on the refugee issue in Dec. 2000's 10th round of bilateral talks. Both sides agreed to begin a joint verification process in the Nepali refugee camps, with repatriation to Bhutan the intended goal. The verification program began in March, though it was conducted at a snail's pace.

The United Liberation Front of Assam (ULFA), a group of separatist rebels fighting for independence from India, has maintained nine well-fortified bases in southern Bhutan since 1990. In a series of talks with Bhutanese officials, the group promised to cut the number of bases in Bhutan to five by the end of 2001.

Bolivia

REPUBLIC OF BOLIVIA

National name: República de Bolivia
President: Jorge Quiroga (2001)
Area: 424,162 sq mi (1,098,580 sq km)
Population (2001 est.): 8,300,463 (average annual rate of natural increase: 1.9%); birth rate: 27.3/1000; infant mortality rate: 59.0/1000; density per sq mi: 20
Historic and judicial capital (1997 est.): Sucre, 131,800; **Administrative capital and largest city (1997 est.):** La Paz, 713,400. **Other large cities (1997 est.):** Santa Cruz, 697,000; Cochabamba, 407,800; El Alto, 405,500; Oruro, 184,000. **Monetary unit:** Boliviano. **Languages:** Spanish (official), Quechua, Aymara, Guarani. **Ethnicity/race:** Quechua 30%, Aymara 25%, mestizo (mixed European and Indian ancestry) 25%–30%, European 5%–15%. **Religion:** Roman Catholic 85%. **Literacy rate:** 82% (1992)
Economic summary: GDP/PPP (1999 est.): $24.2 billion; per capita $3,000. **Real growth rate:** 2%. **Inflation:** 2.1%. **Unemployment:** 11.4% (1997) with widespread underemployment. **Arable land:** 2%. **Agriculture:** soybeans, coffee, coca, cotton, corn, sugarcane, rice, potatoes; timber. **Labor force:** 2.5 million; agriculture, n.a.; industry, n.a.; services, n.a. **Industries:** mining, smelting, petroleum, food and beverages, tobacco, handicrafts, clothing. **Natural resources:** tin, natural gas, petroleum, zinc, tungsten, antimony, silver, iron, lead, gold, timber, hydropower. **Exports:** $1.1 billion (f.o.b., 1999 est.): soybeans, natural gas, zinc, gold, wood. **Imports:** $1.6 billion (c.i.f., 1999 est.): capital goods, raw materials and semi-manufactures, chemicals, petroleum, food. **Major trading partners:** UK, U.S., Peru, Argentina, Colombia, Japan, Brazil, Chile, Germany.

Geography Landlocked Bolivia is equal in size to California and Texas combined. Brazil forms its eastern border; its other neighbors are Peru and Chile on the west and Argentina and Paraguay on the south. The western part, enclosed by two chains of the Andes, is a great plateau—the Altiplano, with an average altitude of 12,000 ft (3,658 m). Almost half the population lives on the plateau, which contains Oruro, Potosí, and La Paz. At an altitude of 11,910 ft (3,630 m), La Paz is the highest administrative capital city in the world. The Oriente, a lowland region ranging from rain forests to grasslands, comprises the northern and eastern two-thirds of the country. Lake Titicaca, at an altitude of 12,507 ft (3,812 m), is the highest commercially navigable body of water in the world.

Government Republic.

History Famous since Spanish colonial days for its mineral wealth, modern Bolivia was once a part of the ancient Incan empire. After the Spaniards defeated the Incas in the 16th century, Bolivia's predominantly Indian population was reduced to slavery. The remoteness of the Andes helped protect the Bolivian Indians from the European diseases that decimated other South American Indians. But the existence of a large indigenous group forced to live under the thumb of their colonizers created a stratified society of haves and have-nots that continues to this day.

By the end of the 17th century the mineral wealth had begun to dry up. The country won its independence in 1825 and was named after Simón Bolívar, the famous liberator. Hampered by internal strife, Bolivia lost great slices of territory to three neighboring nations. Several thousand square miles and its outlet to the Pacific were taken by Chile after the War of the Pacific (1879–84). In 1903, a piece of Bolivia's Acre province, rich in rubber, was ceded to Brazil. And in 1938, after losing the Chaco War of 1932–35 to Paraguay, Bolivia gave up its claim to nearly 100,000 square mi of the Gran Chaco. Political instability ensued.

In 1965, a guerrilla movement mounted from Cuba and headed by Maj. Ernesto (Ché) Guevara began a revolutionary war. With the aid of U.S. military advisers, the Bolivian army smashed the guerrilla movement, capturing and killing Guevara on Oct. 8, 1967. Faltering steps toward restoration of civilian government were halted abruptly on July 17, 1980, when Gen. Luis García Meza Tejada seized power. A series of military leaders followed before the military returned the government to civilian rule in 1982, when Hernán Siles Zuazo became president. Under Siles's left-of-center government, the country was regularly shut down by work stoppages, and the bulk of Bolivia's natural resources—natural gas, gold, lithium, potassium, and tungsten—were either sold on the black market or left in the ground. The country also had the lowest per capita income in South America, and inflation approached 3000%. In 1985, Siles decided he was unable to carry on and quit a year early.

Since 1985, Bolivia has implemented economic changes that have been phenomenally successful. Still at the bottom of the South American economic ladder, its economy has steadily improved over the past fifteen years. Political stability has helped.

In June 1993 free-market advocate Gonzalo Sánchez de Lozada was elected president. Former general Hugo Bánzer was elected president for the second time in Aug. 1997. Bánzer made significant progress in wiping out illicit coca production and drug trafficking. He has also initiated a rural literacy campaign and is implementing a plan for the poor to acquire loans.

President Hugo Bánzer, battling lung cancer, resigned as president in Aug. 2001 after serving four years out of his five-year term. Vice President Jorge Quiroga assumed the presidency. Quiroga has good relations with the U.S. and international monetary institutions, and he has pledged to improve his country's dire economic situation.

Bosnia and Herzegovina

THE FEDERATION OF BOSNIA AND HERZEGOVINA

President: Jozo Krizanovic (2001)
Prime Minister: Zlatko Lagumdzija (2001)
Area: 19,741 sq mi (51,129 sq km)
Population (2001 est.): 3,922,205 (all data dealing with population is subject to considerable error because of the dislocations caused by military action and ethnic cleansing) (average annual rate of natural increase: 0.5%); birth rate: 12.9/1000; infant mortality rate: 24.4/1000; density per sq mi: 199
Capital and largest city (1998 est.): Sarajevo, 387,876 (unofficial). **Other large cities:** Banja Luka, 220,407; Mostar, 208,904; Tuzla 118,500. **Monetary unit:** Dinar. **Language:** The language that used to be known as

Serbo-Croatian but is now known as Serbian, Croatian, or Bosnian, depending on the speaker's ethnic and political affiliation. It is written in Latin and Cyrillic.
Ethnicity/race: Serb 40%, Muslim 38%, Croat 22% (1998 est.). **Religions:** Slavic Muslim 44%, Orthodox 31%, Catholic 15%, Protestant 4%, other 6%
Economic summary: GDP/PPP (1999 est.): $6.2 billion; per capita $1,770. **Real growth rate:** 5%. **Inflation:** 5% (1997 est.). **Unemployment:** 35%-40% (1999 est.). **Arable land:** 14%. **Agriculture:** wheat, corn, fruits, vegetables; livestock. **Labor force:** 1.026 million; agriculture, n.a.; industry, n.a.; services, n.a. **Industries:** steel, coal, iron ore, lead, zinc, manganese, bauxite, vehicle assembly, textiles, tobacco products, wooden furniture, tank and aircraft assembly, domestic appliances, oil refining (much of capacity damaged or shut down) (1995). **Natural resources:** coal, iron, bauxite, manganese, forests, copper, chromium, lead, zinc, hydropower. **Exports:** $450 million (1997 est.): n.a. **Imports:** $2.95 billion (1997 est.): n.a. **Major trading partners:** n.a.

Geography Bosnia and Herzegovina make up a triangular-shaped republic, about half the size of Kentucky, on the Balkan peninsula. The Bosnian region in the north is mountainous and covered with thick forests. The Herzegovina region in the south is largely a rugged and flat farmland. It had a narrow coastline without natural harbors stretching 13 mi (20 km) along the Adriatic Sea.

Government Emerging democracy.

History Since the time of the Roman Empire, the Balkans has been a crossroads of religions and civilizations. The ethnic groups now known as Bosnians, Croats, and Serbs are largely the result of different religious and cultural identities created by contact with neighboring empires that expanded and contracted in the Balkans over centuries. With minor differences, they speak the same language, called Serbo-Croatian or sometimes Bosnian.

Called Illyricum in ancient times, the Romans conquered the area now called Bosnia and Herzegovina in the 2nd and 1st centuries B.C. and folded it into the Roman province of Dalmatia. In the 4th and 5th centuries A.D. Goths overran that portion of the declining Roman Empire and occupied the area until the 6th century, when the Byzantine Empire claimed it. Slavs began settling the region during the 7th century. Around 1200, Bosnia won independence from Hungary and endured as an independent Christian state for some 260 years.

The expansion of the Ottoman Empire into the Balkans introduced another cultural, political, and religious framework. The Turks defeated the Serbs at the famous battle of Kosovo in 1389. They conquered Bosnia in 1463. During the roughly 450 years Bosnia and Herzegovina were under Ottoman rule, many Christian Slavs became Muslim. A Bosnian Islamic elite gradually developed and ruled the country on behalf of the Turkish overlords. As the borders of the Ottoman Empire began to shrink in the 19th century, Muslims from elsewhere in the Balkans migrated to Bosnia. Bosnia also developed a sizable Jewish population, with many Jews settling in Sarajevo after their expulsion from Spain in 1492. However, through the 19th century the term *Bosnian* commonly included residents of all faiths. A relatively secular society, intermarriage among religious groups was not unknown.

Neighboring Serbia and Montenegro fought against the Ottoman Empire in 1876, and were aided by the Russians, their fellow Slavs. At the Congress of Berlin

in 1878 following the end of the Russo-Turkish War (1877–78), Austria-Hungary was given a mandate to occupy and govern Bosnia and Herzegovina, in an effort by Europe to ensure that Russia did not dominate the Balkans. Although the provinces were still officially part of the Ottoman Empire, they were annexed by the Austro-Hungarian Empire on Oct. 7, 1908. As a result, relations with Serbia, which had claims on Bosnia and Herzegovina, became embittered. The hostility between the two countries climaxed in the assassination of Austrian Archduke Franz Ferdinand in Sarajevo on June 28, 1914, by a Serbian nationalist. This event precipitated the start of World War I (1914–18). Bosnia and Herzegovina were annexed to Serbia as part of the newly formed Kingdom of Serbs, Croats, and Slovenes on Oct. 26, 1918. The name was later changed to Yugoslavia in 1929.

When Germany invaded Yugoslavia in 1941, Bosnia and Herzegovina were made part of Nazi-controlled Croatia. During the German and Italian occupation, Bosnian and Herzegovinian resistance fighters fought a fierce guerrilla war against the Ustachi, the Croatian Fascist troops. At the end of World War II, Bosnia and Herzegovina were reunited into a single state as one of the six republics of the newly reestablished Communist Yugoslavia, under Marshall Tito. His authoritarian control kept the ethnic enmities of his patchwork nation in check. Tito died in 1980, and with growing economic dissatisfaction and the fall of the iron curtain over the next decade, Yugoslavia began to splinter.

In Dec. 1991, Bosnia and Herzegovina declared independence from Yugoslavia and asked for recognition by the European Union (EU). In a March 1992 referendum, Bosnian voters chose independence, and President Izetbegovic declared the nation an independent state. Unlike the other former Yugoslav states, which were generally composed of a dominant ethnic group, Bosnia was an ethnic tangle of Muslims (44%), Serbs (31%), and Croats (17%), and this mix contributed to the duration and savagery of its fight for independence.

Both the Croatian and Serbian presidents had planned to partition Bosnia between themselves. Attempting to carve out their own enclaves, the Serbian minority, with the help of the Serbian Yugoslav army, took the offensive and laid siege, particularly on Sarajevo, and began its ruthless campaigns of ethnic cleansing, which involved the expulsion or massacre of Muslims. Croats also began carving out their own communities. By the end of Aug. 1992, rebel Bosnian Serbs had conquered over 60% of Bosnia. The war did not begin to wane until NATO stepped in, bombing Serb positions in Bosnia in Aug. and Sept. 1995. This was followed by a joint offensive by Bosnian Muslim and Croatian forces that took back a significant amount of critical Bosnian territory.

U.S.-sponsored peace talks in Dayton, Ohio, led to an agreement in 1995 that called for a Muslim-Croat federation and a Serb entity within the larger federation of Bosnia. Sixty thousand NATO troops were to supervise its implementation. Fighting abated and orderly elections were held in Sept. 1996. President Alija Izetbegovic, a Bosnian Muslim, or Bosniac, won the majority of votes to become the leader of the three-member presidency, each representing one of the three ethnic groups.

But this alliance of unreconstructed enemies had little success in creating a working government or keeping violent clashes in check. The terms of the Dec. 1995 Dayton Peace Accord were largely ignored by Bosnian Serbs, with its former president, arch-nationalist Radovan Karadzic, still in de facto control of the Serbian enclave. Many indicted war criminals, including Karadzic, remain at large. Despite NATO's pledge in Oct. 1997 to remain in Bosnia beyond the 1998 mandate, the peacekeeping force remained mired in chronic ambivalence, unable to decide whether to jump into the fray or remain passive, hoping its presence was enough to spawn peace.

The crucial priorities facing postwar Bosnian leaders were rebuilding the economy, resettling the estimated one million refugees still displaced, and establishing a working government. Progress on these goals has been minimal, and a massive corruption scandal uncovered in 1999 severely tested the goodwill of the international community. Millions of dollars from international aid projects earmarked for reconstruction and humanitarian purposes had been pilfered by Bosnian officials, according to an American-led international antifraud unit.

In 1994, the UN's Interntional Criminal Tribunal for the former Yugoslavia adjourned in The Hague, Netherlands. As of 2001, more than 100 individuals had been indicted. The first genocide conviction was handed down in Aug. 2001. Radislav Drstic, a Bosnian Serb general, was found guilty of genocide in the killing of up to 8,000 Bosnian Muslims in Srebrenica in 1995. It was the first genocide conviction in Europe since the UN genocide treaty was drawn up in 1951.

Botswana

REPUBLIC OF BOTSWANA

President: Festus Mogae (1998)
Area: 231,803 sq mi (600,370 sq km)
Population (2001 est.): 1,586,119 (average annual rate of natural increase: 0.5%); birth rate: 28.9/1000; infant mortality rate: 63.2/1000; density per sq mi: 7
Capital and largest city (1992 est.): Gaborone, 138,000. **Monetary unit:** Pula. **Languages:** English (official), Setswana. **Ethnicity/race:** Batswana 95%, Kalanga, Basarwa, and Kgalagadi 4%, white 1%. **Religions:** indigenous beliefs 50%, Christian 50%. **Literacy rate:** 69% (1993)
Economic summary: GDP/PPP (1999 est.): $5.7 billion; per capita $3,900. **Real growth rate:** 6.5%. **Inflation:** 7.7%. **Unemployment:** 20%–40%. **Arable land:** 1%. **Agriculture:** sorghum, corn, millet, pulses, groundnuts (peanuts), beans, cowpeas, sunflower seed; livestock. **Labor force:** 235,000 formal sector employees (1995); 100,000, public sector; 135,000, private sector; including 14,300 who are employed in various mines in South Africa; most others engaged in cattle raising and subsistence agriculture (1995 est.). **Industries:** diamonds, copper, nickel, coal, salt, soda ash, potash; livestock processing. **Natural resources:** diamonds, copper, nickel, salt, soda ash, potash, coal, iron ore, silver. **Exports:** $2.36 billion (f.o.b., 1999 est.): diamonds 72%, vehicles, copper, nickel, meat (1998). **Imports:** $2.05 billion (f.o.b., 1999 est.): foodstuffs, machinery and transport equipment, textiles, petroleum products. **Major trading partners:** EU, Southern African Customs Union (SACU), Zimbabwe.
Member of Commonwealth of Nations

Geography Twice the size of Arizona, Botswana is in south-central Africa, bounded by Namibia, Zambia, Zimbabwe, and South Africa. Most of the country is near-desert, with the Kalahari occupying the western part of the country. The eastern part is hilly, with salt lakes in the north.

Government Parliamentary democracy.

History The earliest inhabitants of the region were the San, who were followed by the Tswana. About half the country today is ethnic Tswana. The term for the country's people, *Batswana*, refers to national rather than ethnic origin.

Encroachment by the Zulu in the 1820s and by Boers from Transvaal in the 1870s and 1880s threatened the peace of the region. In 1885 Britain established the area as a protectorate, then known as Bechuanaland. In 1961, Britain granted a constitution to the country. Self-government began in 1965, and on Sept. 30, 1966, the country became independent. Botswana is Africa's oldest democracy.

The new country maintained good relations with its white-ruled neighbors, but gradually changed its policies, harboring rebel groups from South Rhodesia as well as some from South Africa.

Although Botswana is rich in diamonds, it has high unemployment and stratified socioeconomic classes. In 1999 it suffered its first budget deficit in 16 years because of a slump in the international diamond market. Yet it remains one of the wealthiest as well as most stable countries on the continent.

After 17 years in power, President Ketumile Masire retired in 1997, and Festus Mogae, an Oxford-educated economist, became the new president. Mogae has won high marks from the international financial community for continuing to privatize Botswana's mining and industrial operations.

Although Botswana's economic outlook remains strong, the devastation that AIDS is causing threatens to destroy the country's future. In 2001 Botswana had the highest rate of HIV infection in the world: 350,000 of its 1.6 million people were infected, and half the population between 25 and 29 are dying of the disease.

Brazil

FEDERATIVE REPUBLIC OF BRAZIL

National name: República Federativa do Brasil
President: Fernando Henrique Cardoso (1995)
Area: 3,286,470 sq mi (8,511,965 sq km)
Population (2001 est.): 174,468,575 (average annual rate of natural increase: 0.9%); birth rate: 18.5/1000; infant mortality rate: 37.0/1000; density per sq mi: 53
Capital (1997 est.): Brasília, 1,800,000. **Largest cities:** São Paulo (2000 est.), 17,900,000 (metro. area); Rio de Janeiro (2000 est.), 10,650,000 (metro. area); Porto Alegre, 3,000,000; Recife, 2,900,999; Salvador, 2,600,000; Belo Horizonte, 2,600,000. **Monetary unit:** Real. **Language:** Portuguese. **Ethnicity/race:** white (includes Portuguese, German, Italian, Spanish, Polish) 55%, mixed white and African 38%, African 6%, other (includes Japanese, Arab, Amerindian) 1%. **Religion:** Roman Catholic 90% (nominal). **Literacy rate:** 81% (1990)
Economic summary: GDP/PPP (1999 est.): $1.057 trillion; per capita $6,150. **Real growth rate:** 0.8%. **Inflation:** 5%. **Unemployment:** 7.5%. **Arable land:** 5%. **Agriculture:** coffee, soybeans, wheat, rice, corn, sugarcane, cocoa, citrus; beef. **Labor force:** 74 million (1997 est.); services, 42%; agriculture, 31%; industry, 27%. **Industries:** textiles, shoes, chemicals, cement, lumber, iron ore, tin, steel, aircraft, motor vehicles and parts, other machinery and equipment. **Exports:** $46.9 billion (f.o.b., 1999): manufactures, iron ore, soybeans, footwear, coffee. **Imports:** $48.7 billion (f.o.b., 1999): machinery and equipment, chemical products, oil, electricity. **Major trading partners:** U.S., Argentina, Germany, Netherlands, Japan, Italy.

Geography Brazil covers nearly half of South America and is the continent's largest nation. It extends 2,965 mi (4,772 km) north-south, 2,691 mi (4,331 km) east-west, and borders every nation on the continent except Chile and Ecuador. Brazil may be divided into the Brazilian Highlands, or plateau, in the south and the Amazon River Basin in the north. More than a third of Brazil is drained by the Amazon and its more than 200 tributaries. The Amazon is navigable for ocean steamers to Iquitos, Peru, 2,300 mi (3,700 km) upstream. Southern Brazil is drained by the Plata system—the Paraguay, Uruguay, and Paraná Rivers. The most important stream entirely within Brazil is the São Francisco, navigable for 1,000 mi (1,903 km), but broken near its mouth by the 275-ft (84 m) Paulo Afonso Falls.

Government Federal republic.

History Brazil is the only Latin American nation that derives its language and culture from Portugal. The native inhabitants mostly consisted of the nomadic Tupí-Guaraní Indians. Adm. Pedro Alvares Cabral claimed the territory for Portugal in 1500. The early explorers brought back a wood that produced a red dye, *pau-brasil*, from which the land received its name. Portugal began colonization in 1532 and made the area a royal colony in 1549.

During the Napoleonic Wars, King João VI, fearing the advancing French armies, fled the country in 1808 and set up his court in Rio de Janeiro. João was drawn home in 1820 by a revolution, leaving his son as regent. When Portugal tried to reimpose colonial rule, the prince declared Brazil's independence on Sept. 7, 1822, becoming Pedro I, emperor of Brazil. Harassed by his Parliament, Pedro I abdicated in 1831 in favor of his five-year-old son, who became emperor in 1840 (Pedro II). The son was a popular monarch, but discontent built up and, in 1889, following a military revolt, he abdicated. Although a republic was proclaimed, Brazil was ruled by military dictatorships until a revolt permitted a gradual return to stability under civilian presidents.

President Wenceslau Braz cooperated with the Allies and declared war on Germany during World War I. In World War II, Brazil again cooperated with the Allies, welcoming Allied air bases, patrolling the South Atlantic, and joining the invasion of Italy after declaring war on the Axis powers.

After a military coup in 1964, Brazil had a series of military governments. Gen. João Baptista de Oliveira Figueiredo became president in 1979 and pledged a return to democracy in 1985. The election of Tancredo Neves on Jan. 15, 1985, the first civilian president since 1964, brought a nationwide wave of optimism, but when Neves died several months later, Vice President José Sarney became president. Collor de Mello won the election of late 1989, pledging to lower hyperinflation with free-market economics. When Collor faced impeachment by Congress because of a corruption scandal in Dec. 1992 and resigned, Vice President Itamar Franco assumed the presidency.

A former finance minister, Fernando Cardoso, won the presidency in the Oct. 1994 election with 54% of the vote. Cardoso has sold off inefficient government-owned monopolies in the telecommunication, electrical power, port, mining, railway, and banking industries. In his short time in office Cardoso's economic acumen has made a measurable dent in Brazil's poverty level. In Jan. 1999, the Asian economic crisis spread to Brazil. Rather than prop up the currency through financial markets, Brazil opted to let the currency float, which sent the real plummeting—at one time as much as 40%. Cardoso has been highly praised by the international community for quickly turning around his country's economic crisis. He has shown strong political courage in forcing belt-tightening measures on the economy, causing short-term misery and discontent in an effort to reap long-term stability and growth. Despite Cardoso's efforts, however, the economy continued to slow throughout 2001, and the country also faced an energy crisis. The IMF offered Brazil an additional aid package in Aug. 2001.

Brunei Darussalam

STATE OF BRUNEI DARUSSALAM

Sultan: Haji Hassanal Bolkiah (1967)
Area: 2,228 sq mi (5,770 sq km)
Population (2001 est.): 343,653 (annual rate of natural increase: 1.7%); birth rate: 20.5/1000; infant mortality rate: 14.4/1000; density per sq mi: 154
Capital and largest city (1991 est.): Bandar Seri Begawan, 52,300. **Other large cities:** Seria 23,511, Kuala Belait 19,335. **Monetary unit:** Brunei dollar.
Languages: Malay (official), Chinese, English.
Ethnicity/race: Malay 64%, Chinese 20%, other 16%.
Religions: Islam (official religion) 67%, Buddhist 12%, Christian 9%, indigenous beliefs and other 12%.
Literacy rate: 80% (1981)
Economic summary: GDP/PPP (1999 est.): $5.6 billion; per capita $17,400. **Real growth rate:** 2.5%.
Inflation: 1%. **Unemployment:** 4.9% (1995 est.).
Arable land: 1%. **Agriculture:** rice, cassava (tapioca), bananas; water buffalo. **Labor force:** 144,000 (1995 est.); note: includes foreign workers and military personnel; government, 48%; production of oil, natural gas, services, and construction, 42%; agriculture, forestry, and fishing, 10%. **Industries:** petroleum, petroleum refining, liquefied natural gas, construction.
Natural resources: petroleum, natural gas, timber.
Exports: $2.04 billion (f.o.b., 1998 est.): crude oil, liquefied natural gas, petroleum products. **Imports:** $1.38 billion (c.i.f., 1998 est.): machinery and transport equipment, manufactured goods, food, chemicals.
Major trading partners: Japan, UK, U.S., Singapore, Thailand, Malaysia, France

Geography About the size of Delaware, Brunei is an independent sultanate on the northwest coast of the island of Borneo in the South China Sea, wedged between the Malaysian states of Sabah and Sarawak. Three-quarters of the thinly populated country is covered with tropical rain forest; there are rich oil and gas deposits.

Government Constitutional sultanate.

History Brunei was trading with China during the 6th century, and, through allegiance to the Javanese Majapahit kingdom (13th to 15th century), it came under Hindu influence. In the early 15th century, with the decline of the Majapahit kingdom and widespread conversion to Islam, Brunei became an independent sultanate. It was a powerful state from the 16th to the 19th century, ruling over the northern part of Borneo and adjacent island chains. But it fell into decay and lost Sarawak in 1841, becoming a British protectorate in 1888 and a British dependency in 1905. Japan occupied Brunei during World War II; it was liberated by Australia in 1945.

The sultan regained control over internal affairs in 1959, but Britain retained responsibility for the state's defense and foreign affairs until 1984, when the sultanate became fully independent. Sultan Bolkiah was crowned in 1968 at the age of 22, succeeding his father, Sir Omar Ali Saifuddin, who had abdicated. During his reign, exploitation of the rich Seria oilfield had made the sultanate wealthy. Brunei has one of the highest per capita incomes in Asia, and the sultan is believed to be one of the richest men in the world. In Aug. 1998, Oxford-educated Prince Al-Muhtadee Billah was inaugurated as heir to the 500-year-old monarchy. The sultan has had to punish his wayward younger brother, Prince Jefri, for squandering billions of dollars. In Feb. 2000, Prince Jefri was charged with misappropriation of state funds. During his tenure as finance minister and head of the Brunei Investment Agency, Jefri allegedly squandered about $15 billion on personal items and extravagant pet projects.

Bulgaria
REPUBLIC OF BULGARIA

National name: Narodna Republika Bulgariya
President: Petur Stoyanov (1997)
Prime Minister: Simeon Koburgotski (2001)
Area: 42,822 sq mi (110,910 sq km)
Population (2001 est.): 7,707,495 (average annual rate of natural increase: −0.6%); birth rate: 8.1/1000; infant mortality rate: 14.7/1000; density per sq mi: 180
Capital and largest city (1994 est.): Sofia, 1,113,674. **Largest cities (1994 est.):** Plovdiv, 345,205; Varna, 307,200; Burgas, 198,439; Ruse, 170,209. **Monetary unit:** Lev. **Language:** Bulgarian. **Ethnicity/race:** Bulgarian 85.3%, Turk 8.5%, Gypsy 2.6%, Macedonian 2.5%, Armenian 0.3%, Russian 0.2%, other 0.6%. **Religions:** Bulgarian Orthodox 85%, Muslim 13%, Jewish 0.8%, Roman Catholic 0.5%, Uniate Catholic 0.2%, Protestant, Gregorian-Armenian, and other 0.5%. **Literacy rate:** 93% (1970)
Economic summary: GDP/PPP (1999 est.): $34.9 billion; per capita $4,300. **Real growth rate:** 2.5%. **Inflation:** 6.2%. **Unemployment:** 15%. **Arable land:** 43%. **Agriculture:** vegetables, fruits, tobacco, livestock, wine, wheat, barley, sunflowers, sugar beets. **Labor force:** 3.82 million (1998 est.); agriculture, 26%; industry, 31%; services, 43% (1998 est.). **Industries:** machine building and metal working, food processing, chemicals, construction materials, ferrous and nonferrous metals, nuclear fuel. **Natural resources:** bauxite, copper, lead, zinc, coal, timber, arable land. **Exports:** $3.8 billion (f.o.b., 1999 est.): machinery and equipment; metals, minerals, and fuels; chemicals and plastics; food, tobacco, clothing (1998). **Imports:** $5.3 billion (f.o.b., 1999 est.): fuels, minerals, and raw materials; machinery and equipment; metals and ores; chemicals and plastics; food, textiles (1998). **Major trading partners:** Italy, Germany, Greece, Turkey, Russia, U.S.

Geography Two mountain ranges and two great valleys mark the topography of Bulgaria, a country the size of Tennessee and situated on the Black Sea. The Maritsa is Bulgaria's principal river, and the Danube also flows through the country.

Government Democratic republic.

History The Thracians lived in what is now known as Bulgaria from about 3500 B.C. They were incorporated into the Roman Empire by the first century A.D. At the decline of the empire, the Goths, Huns, Bulgars, and Avars invaded. The Bulgars, who crossed the Danube from the north in 679, took control of the region. Although the country bears the name of the Bulgars, the Bulgar language and culture died out, replaced by a Slavic language, writing, and religion. In 865, Boris I adopted Orthodox Christianity. The Bulgars twice conquered most of the Balkan penin-

sula between 893 and 1280. But in 1396 they were invaded by the Ottoman Empire, which made Bulgaria a Turkish province until 1878. Ottoman rule was harsh and inescapable, given Bulgaria's proximity to its oppressor. In 1878, Russia forced Turkey to give Bulgaria its independence after the Russo-Turkish War (1877–78), but the European powers, fearing Russia's and Bulgaria's dominance in the Balkans, intervened at the Congress of Berlin (1878), limited Bulgaria's territory, and fashioned it into a small principality ruled by the nephew of the Russian czar, Alexander of Battenburg.

Alexander was succeeded in 1887 by Prince Ferdinand of Saxe-Coburg-Gotha, who declared a kingdom independent of Russia on Oct. 5, 1908. In the First Balkan War (1912–13), Bulgaria and the other members of the Balkan League fought against Turkey to regain Balkan territory. Angered by the small portion of Macedonia it received after the battle—it considered Macedonia an integral part of Bulgaria—the country instigated the Second Balkan War (June–Aug. 1913) against Turkey as well as its former allies. Bulgaria lost the war and all the territory it had gained in the First Balkan War. Bulgaria joined Germany in World War I in the hope of again gaining Macedonia. After this second failure, Ferdinand abdicated in favor of his son in 1918. Boris III squandered Bulgaria's resources and assumed dictatorial powers in 1934–35. Bulgaria fought on the side of the Nazis in World War II, but after Russia declared war on Bulgaria on Sept. 5, 1944, Bulgaria switched sides. Three days later, on Sept. 9, 1944, a Communist coalition took control of the country and set up a government under Kimon Georgiev.

A Soviet-style People's Republic was established in 1947 and Bulgaria acquired the reputation of being the most slavishly loyal to Moscow of all the East European Communist countries. The general secretary of the Bulgarian Communist Party, Todor Zhikov, resigned in 1989 after 35 years in power. His successor, Peter Mladenov, purged the Politburo, ended the Communist monopoly on power, and held free elections in May 1990 that led to a surprising victory for the Communist Party, renamed the Bulgarian Socialist Party (BSP). Mladenov was forced to resign in July 1990.

In Oct. 1991, the Union of Democratic Forces won, forming Bulgaria's first non-Communist government since 1946. Power has shifted back and forth between the pro-Western Union of Democratic Forces (UDF) and the BSP during the 1990s. The economy continued to deteriorate amid growing concern over the spread of organized crime. The new UDF government, led by Prime Minister Ivan Kostov, was elected in 1997 to overhaul the economic system and institute reforms aimed at stopping the rise of public corruption. Progress on both fronts remained slow. As a result, the UDF lost the July 2001 election to the former king of Bulgaria, leader of the recently founded Simeon II National Movement (SNM). The new prime minister, Simeon Koburgotski (Simeon II), had been dethroned 55 years earlier (at age nine) during the Communist take-over of the country.

Burkina Faso

National name: Burkina Faso
President: Blaise Compaoré (1991)
Prime Minister: Paramanga Ernest Yonli (2000)
Area: 105,869 sq mi (274,200 sq km)
Population (2001 est.): 12,272,289 (average annual rate of natural increase: 2.8%); birth rate: 44.8/1000; infant

mortality rate: 106.9/1000; density per sq mi: 116
Capital and largest city (1994 est.): Ouagadougou, 500,000. **Monetary unit:** Franc CFA. **Languages:** French (official), tribal languages. **Ethnicity/race:** Mossi (about 24%), Gurunsi, Senufo, Lobi, Bobo, Mande, Fulani. **Religions:** Muslim 50%, Christian (mainly Roman Catholic) 10%, indigenous beliefs 40%. **Literacy rate:** 18% (1990)
Economic summary: GDP/PPP (1999 est.): $12.4 billion; per capita $1,100. **Real growth rate:** 5.5%. **Inflation:** 2.5%. **Unemployment:** n.a. **Arable land:** 13%. **Agriculture:** peanuts, shea nuts, sesame, cotton, sorghum, millet, corn, rice; livestock. **Labor force:** 4.679 million (persons 10 years old and over, according to a sample survey taken in 1991); note: a large part of the male labor force migrates annually to neighboring countries for seasonal employment; agriculture, n.a.; industry, n.a.; services, n.a. **Industries:** cotton lint, beverages, agricultural processing, soap, cigarettes, textiles, gold. **Natural resources:** manganese, limestone, marble; small deposits of gold, antimony, copper, nickel, bauxite, lead, phosphates, zinc, silver. **Exports:** $311 million (f.o.b., 1998 est.): cotton, animal products, gold. **Imports:** $572 million (f.o.b., 1998 est.): machinery, food products, petroleum. **Major trading partners:** Côte d'Ivoire, Taiwan, France, Colombia, Italy, Mali, Senegal, Togo, Nigeria, U.S.

Geography Slightly larger than Colorado, Burkina Faso, formerly known as Upper Volta, is a landlocked country in West Africa. Its neighbors are Côte d'Ivoire, Mali, Niger, Benin, Togo, and Ghana. The country consists of extensive plains, low hills, high savannas, and a desert area in the north.

Government Military rule since independence.

History Burkina Faso was originally inhabited by the Bobo, Lobi, and Gurunsi peoples, with the Mossi and Gurma peoples immigrating to the region in the 14th century. The lands of the Mossi empire became a French protectorate in 1897, and by 1903 France had subjugated the other ethnic groups. Called Upper Volta by the French, it became a separate colony in 1919, was partitioned among Niger, the Sudan, and Côte d'Ivoire in 1932, and was reconstituted in 1947. An autonomous republic within the French Community, Upper Volta became independent on Aug. 5, 1960.

President Maurice Yameogo was deposed on Jan. 3, 1966, by a military coup led by Col. Sangoulé Lamizana, who dissolved the National Assembly and suspended the constitution. Constitutional rule returned in 1978 with the election of an Assembly and a presidential vote in June in which Gen. Lamizana won by a narrow margin over three other candidates.

On Nov. 25, 1980, Col. Sayé Zerbo led a bloodless coup that toppled Lamizana. In turn, Maj. Jean-Baptist Ouedraogo ousted Zerbo on Nov. 7, 1982. But the real revolutionary change occurred the following year when a 33-year-old flight commander, Thomas Sankara, took control. A Marxist-Leninist, he challenged the traditional Mossi chiefs, advocated women's liberation, and allied the country with North Korea, Libya, and Cuba. To sever ties to the colonial past, Sankara changed the name of the country in 1984 to Burkina Faso, which combines two of the nation's languages and means "the land of upright men."

While Sankara's investments in schools, food production, and clinics brought some improvement in living standards, foreign investment declined, many businesses left the country, and unhappy labor unions began strikes. On Oct. 15, 1987, formerly loyal soldiers assassinated Sankara. His best friend and ally Blaise Compaoré became president. Compaoré immediately set about "rectifying" Sankara's revolution. In 1991 he agreed to economic reforms proposed by the World Bank. A new constitution paved the way for elections in 1991, which Compaoré won easily, although opposition parties boycotted.

In 2000, the UN accused Burkina Faso's president of being a chief player in Africa's illicit diamond trade. Compaoré, the reports claim, has traded weapons for diamonds with UNITA rebels in Angola, Sierra Leone's Revolutionary United Front (RUF), and Liberia, ignoring the international arms embargo and fueling the continuing violence plaguing western Africa.

Burma (Myanmar)

SEE MYANMAR.

Burundi

REPUBLIC OF BURUNDI
National name: Republika Y'Uburundi
President: Pierre Buyoya (1996)
Prime Minister: Frederic Bamvuginyumvira (1998)
Area: 10,745 sq mi (27,830 sq km)
Population (2001 est.): 6,223,897 (average annual rate of natural increase: 2.4%); birth rate: 40.1/1000; infant mortality rate: 70.7/1000; density per sq mi: 579
Capital and largest city (1994 est.): Bujumbura, 300,000. **Other large city (est. 1982):** Gitega, 101,827. **Monetary unit:** Burundi franc. **Languages:** Kirundi and French (official), Swahili. **Ethnicity/race:** Hutu (Bantu) 85%, Tutsi (Hamitic) 14%, Twa (Pygmy) 1%. **Religions:** Roman Catholic 62%, Protestant 5%, indigenous 32%. **Literacy rate:** 41% (1990)
Economic summary: GDP/PPP (1999 est.): $4.2 billion; per capita $730. **Real growth rate:** –1%. **Inflation:** 26%. **Unemployment:** n.a. **Arable land:** 44%. **Agriculture:** coffee, cotton, tea, corn, sorghum, sweet potatoes, bananas, manioc (tapioca); beef, milk, hides. **Labor force:** 1.9 million; agriculture, 93%; government, 4%; industry and commerce, 1.5%; services, 1.5% (1983 est.). **Industries:** light consumer goods such as blankets, shoes, soap; assembly of imported components; public works construction; food processing. **Natural resources:** nickel, uranium, rare earth oxides, peat, cobalt, copper, platinum (not yet exploited), vanadium, arable land, hydropower. **Exports:** $56 million (f.o.b., 1999): coffee, tea, sugar, cotton, hides. **Imports:** $108 million (f.o.b., 1999): capital goods, petroleum products, foodstuffs. **Major trading partners:** UK, Germany, Benelux, Switzerland, France, Zambia, Kenya, Japan.

Geography Wedged between Tanzania, the Democratic Republic of the Congo, and Rwanda in east-central Africa, Burundi occupies a high plateau divided by several deep valleys. It is equal in size to Maryland.

Government Republic.

History The original inhabitants of Burundi were the Twa, a Pygmy people who now make up only 1% of the population. While the Hutu and Tutsi are considered to be two separate ethnic groups, scholars point out that they speak the same language, have a history of intermarriage, and share many cultural characteristics. Traditionally, the differences between the two groups were occupational rather than ethnic. Agricultural people were considered Hutu, while the cattle-owning elite were identified as Tutsi. Supposedly Tutsi were tall and thin, while Hutu were short and square, but in fact it is often impossible to tell one from the other. The 1933 requirement by the Belgians that everyone carry an identity card indicating tribal ethnicity as Tutsi or Hutu increased the distinction. Since independence, repeated violence in both Burundi and Rwanda has increased ethnic differentiation between the groups. Since independence, the land-owning Tutsi aristocracy has dominated Burundi.

Burundi was once part of German East Africa. Belgium won a League of Nations mandate in 1923, and subsequently Burundi, with Rwanda, was transferred to the status of a United Nations trust territory. In 1962, Burundi gained independence and became a kingdom under Mwami Mwambutsa IV, a Tutsi. A Hutu rebellion took place in 1965, leading to brutal Tutsi retaliations. Mwambutsa was deposed by his son, Ntaré V, in 1966. Ntaré in turn was overthrown the same year in a military coup by Premier Michel Micombero, also a Tutsi. In 1970–71, a civil war erupted, leaving more than 100,000 Hutu dead.

On Nov. 1, 1976, Lt. Col. Jean-Baptiste Bagaza led a coup and assumed the presidency. He suspended the constitution and announced that a 30-member Supreme Revolutionary Council would be the governing body. In Sept. 1987 Bagaza was overthrown by Maj. Pierre Buyoya, who became president. Ethnic hatred again flared in Aug. 1988, and about 20,000 Hutu were slaughtered. Buyoya, however, began reforms to heal the country's ethnic rift. The Burundi Democracy Front's candidate, Melchior Ndadaye, won the country's first democratic presidential elections, held on June 2, 1993. Ndadaye, the first Hutu to assume power in Burundi, was killed within months during a coup. The second Hutu president, Cyprien Ntaryamira, was killed on April 6, 1994, when a plane carrying him and the Rwandan president was shot down. As a result, Hutu youth gangs began massacring Tutsi; the Tutsi-controlled army retaliated by killing Hutus.

The frequency of ethnic clashes increased, developing into a low-intensity civil war. A six-nation regional proposal to send troops into Burundi to maintain peace and order was devised in July 1996. Distrustful of the scheme, the Tutsi-dominated army led a coup deposing the Hutu president and installed Maj. Pierre Buyoya that month. More than 200,000 people have been killed since the conflict began, and both the Tutsi-dominated army and the Hutu rebel forces are responsible for the continuing slaughter. Nelson Mandela was appointed the new mediator for the civil war in early 2000. In July 2001 a fragile peace accord was signed by the government and 18 political groups, but Hutu rebels fighting against the government did not participate, which essentially rendered the accord meaningless.

Cambodia

King: Norodom Sihanouk (1991)
Prime Minister: Hun Sen (1993)
Area: 69,900 sq mi (181,040 sq km)
Population (2001 est.): 12,491,501 (average annual rate of natural increase: 2.3%); birth rate: 33.2/1000; infant mortality rate: 65.4/1000; density per sq mi: 179
Capital and largest city (1991 est.): Phnom Penh, 900,000. **Monetary unit:** Riel. **Languages:** Khmer (official), French, English. **Ethnicity/race:** Khmer 90%, Vietnamese 5%, Chinese 1%, other 4%. **Religions:** Theravada Buddhist 95%, others 5%. **Literacy rate:** 69% (1996)
Economic summary: GDP/PPP (1999 est.): $8.2 billion; per capita $710. **Real growth rate:** 4%. **Inflation:** 4.5%. **Unemployment:** 2.8%. **Arable land:** 13%. **Agriculture:** rice, rubber, corn, vegetables. **Labor force:** 6 million (1998 est.); agriculture, 80%. **Industries:** garments, rice milling, fishing, wood and wood products, rubber, cement, gem mining, textiles. **Natural resources:** timber, gemstones, some iron ore, manganese, phosphates, hydropower potential. **Exports:** $821 million (f.o.b., 1999 est.): timber, garments, rubber, rice, fish. **Imports:** $1.2 billion (f.o.b., 1999 est.): cigarettes, gold, construction materials, petroleum products, machinery, motor vehicles. **Major trading partners:** U.S., Singapore, Japan, Thailand, Hong Kong, Indonesia, Malaysia, Vietnam, Australia.

Geography Situated on the Indochinese peninsula, Cambodia is bordered by Thailand and Laos on the north and Vietnam on the east and south. The Gulf of Thailand is off the western coast. The country, the size of Missouri, consists chiefly of a large alluvial plain ringed by mountains and on the east by the Mekong River. The plain is centered on Lake Tonle Sap, which is a natural storage basin of the Mekong.

Government Constitutional monarchy.

History The area that is present-day Cambodia came under Khmer rule about 600, when the region was at the center of a vast empire that stretched over most of Southeast Asia. Under the Khmers, who were Hindus, a magnificent temple complex was constructed at Angkor. Buddhism was introduced in the 12th century during the rule of Jayavaram VII. However, the kingdom, then known as Kambuja, fell into decline after Jayavaram's reign and was nearly annihilated by Thai and Vietnamese invaders. Its power steadily diminished until 1863, when France colonized the region, joining Cambodia, Laos, and Vietnam into a single protectorate known as French Indochina.

The French quickly usurped all but ceremonial powers from the monarch, Norodom. When he died in 1904, the French passed over his sons and handed the throne to his brother, Sisowath. Sisowath and his son ruled until 1941, when Norodom Sihanouk was elevated to power. Sihanouk's coronation, along with the Japanese occupation during the war, worked to reinforce a sentiment among Cambodians that the region should be free from outside control. After World War II, Cambodians sought independence, but France was reluctant to part with its colony. Cambodia was granted independence within the French Union in 1949. But the French-Indochinese War provided an opportunity for Sihanouk to gain full military control of the country. He abdicated in 1955 in favor of his parents, remaining head of the government, and when his father died in 1960, became chief of state without returning to the throne. In 1963, he sought a guarantee of Cambodia's neutrality from all parties to the Vietnam War.

However, North Vietnamese and Vietcong troops had begun using eastern Cambodia as a safe haven from which to launch attacks into South Vietnam, making it increasingly difficult to stay out of the war. An indigenous Communist guerrilla movement known as the Khmer Rouge also began to put pressure on the government in Phnom Penh. On March 18, 1970, while Sihanouk was abroad, anti-Vietnamese riots broke out and Sihanouk was overthrown by Gen. Lon Nol. The Vietnam peace agreement of 1973 stipulated withdrawal of foreign forces from Cambodia, but fighting continued between Hanoi-backed insurgents and U.S.-supplied government troops.

Combat climaxed in April 1975 when the Lon Nol regime was overthrown by Pol Pot, leader of the Khmer Rouge forces. The four years of nightmarish Khmer Rouge rule led to the state-sponsored extermination of citizens by its own government. Between 1 million and 2 million people were massacred on the "killing fields" of Cambodia or worked to death through forced labor. Pol Pot's radical vision of transforming the country into a Marxist agrarian society led to the virtual extermination of the country's professional and technical class.

Pol Pot was ousted by Vietnamese forces on Jan. 8, 1979, and a new pro-Hanoi government led by Heng Samrin was installed. Pol Pot and 35,000 Khmer Rouge fighters fled into the hills of western Cambodia, where they were joined by forces loyal to the ousted Sihanouk in a guerrilla movement aimed at overthrowing the Heng Samrin government. The Vietnamese plan originally called for a withdrawal by early 1990 and a negotiated political settlement. The talks became protracted, however, and a UN agreement was not signed until 1992, when Sihanouk was appointed leader of an interim Supreme National Council to run the country until elections could be held in 1993.

Free elections in May 1993 saw the defeat of Heng Samrin's successor, Hun Sen, who refused to accept the outcome of the vote and insisted instead on a power-sharing agreement. Under the arrangement, Hun Sen and Sihanouk's son, Prince Norodom Ranariddh, would act as co–prime ministers.

The Khmer Rouge stronghold in the western jungles splintered in 1997, with factions either battling each other or defecting. Ranariddh and Hun Sen both courted Khmer Rouge factions in an effort to shore up their power. In early July, Hun Sen took advantage of the charged political atmosphere to depose Ranariddh, officially the first prime minister and the country's only popularly elected leader. Hun Sen later launched a brutal purge, executing more than 40 political opponents. Meanwhile, King Norodom Sihanouk was unable to broker peace between Hun Sen and his son, Prince Ranariddh.

Shortly after the July coup, the Khmer Rouge organized a show trial of their notorious leader, Pol Pot. Pol Pot had not been seen by the West in more than two decades, and he was sentenced to house arrest for his crimes against humanity. He died on April 15, 1998.

In the July 1998 election, Hun Sen defeated opposition leaders Sam Rainsy and Prince Ranariddh, but the opposition parties accused him of voter fraud. Although Hun Sen's CCP Party won the most seats, it needed a coalition with Ranariddh's FUNCINPEC Party to reach the two-thirds majority needed to form a government. A coalition government was formed in Nov. 1998, with Hun Sen as sole prime minister and Ranariddh accepting the lesser role of president of the National Assembly. Cambodia was able to regain its UN seat, lost nearly a year earlier following Hun Sen's coup.

In July 2001, the Cambodian senate agreed to set up an international war crimes tribunal to try senior Khmer Rouge officials. The special tribunal will be made up of Cambodians and foreign judges. King Norodom Sihanouk must also endorse the law before the United Nations can approve the tribunal. Among those expected to stand trial are Ta Mok, alias "the butcher," and Kang Kech Iev, alias Duch, who ran the notorious Tuol Sleng prison.

Cameroon

REPUBLIC OF CAMEROON

National name: République du Cameroun
President: Paul Biya (1988)
Prime Minister: Peter Musonge Mafani (1996)
Area: 183,567 sq mi (475,440 sq km)
Population (2001 est.): 15,803,220 (average annual rate of natural increase: 2.4%); birth rate: 36.1/1000; infant mortality rate: 69.8/1000; density per sq mi: 86
Capital: Yaoundé. **Largest cities (1991 est.):** Douala, 908,000; Yaoundé, 730,000. **Monetary unit:** Franc CFA. **Languages:** French and English (both official); 24 major African language groups. **Ethnicity/race:** Cameroon Highlanders 31%, Equatorial Bantu 19%, Kirdi 11%, Fulani 10%, Northwest Bantu 8%, Eastern Nigritic 7%, other African 13%, non-African less than 1%. **Religions:** 51% indigenous beliefs, 33% Christian, 16% Muslim. **Literacy rate:** 54% (1990)
Economic summary: GDP/PPP (1999 est.): $31.5 billion; per capita $2,000. **Real growth rate:** 5.2%. **Inflation:** 2.1%. **Unemployment:** 30% (1998 est.). **Arable land:** 13%. **Agriculture:** coffee, cocoa, cotton, rubber, bananas, oilseed, grains, root starches; livestock; timber. **Labor force:** n.a.; agriculture, 70%; industry and commerce, 13%; other, 17%. **Industries:** petroleum production and refining, food processing, light consumer goods, textiles, lumber. **Natural resources:** petroleum, bauxite, iron ore, timber, hydropower. **Exports:** $2 billion (f.o.b., 1999): crude oil and petroleum products, lumber, cocoa beans, aluminum, coffee, cotton. **Imports:** $1.5 billion (f.o.b., 1999): machines and electrical equipment, transport equipment, fuel, food. **Major trading partners:** Italy, Spain, France, Netherlands, Nigeria, U.S., Germany.

Geography Cameroon is a Central African nation on the Gulf of Guinea, bordered by Nigeria, Chad, the Central African Republic, the Republic of Congo, Equatorial Guinea, and Gabon. It is nearly twice the size of Oregon. Mount Cameroon (13,350 ft; 4,069 m), near the coast, is the highest elevation in the country. The main rivers are the Benue, Nyong, and Sanaga.

Government After a 1972 plebiscite, a unitary nation was formed out of East and West Cameroon to replace the former federal republic.

History Bantu speakers were among the first groups to settle Cameroon, followed by the Muslim Fulani in the 18th and 19th centuries. The land escaped colonial rule until 1884, when treaties with tribal chiefs brought the area under German domination. After World War I, the League of Nations gave the French a mandate over 80% of the area, and the British 20% adjacent to Nigeria. After World War II, when the country came under a UN trusteeship in 1946, self-government was granted, and the Cameroon People's Union emerged as the dominant party by campaigning for reunification of French and British Cameroon and for independence. Accused of being under Communist control, the party waged a campaign of revolutionary terror from 1955 to 1958, when it was crushed. In British Cameroon, unification was also promoted by the leading party, the Kamerun National Democratic Party, led by John Foncha.

France set up Cameroon as an autonomous state in 1957, and the next year its legislative assembly voted for independence by 1960. In 1959 a fully autonomous government of Cameroon was formed under Ahmadou Ahidjo. Cameroon became an independent republic on Jan. 1, 1960. In 1961 the southern part of the British territory joined the new Federal Republic of Cameroon and the northern section voted for uni-fication with Nigeria. The president of Cameroon since independence, Ahmadou Ahidjo, was replaced in 1982 by the prime minister, Paul Biya. Both administrations have been authoritarian.

With the expansion of oil, timber, and coffee exports, the economy has continued to improve, although corruption is prevalent, and environmental degradation remains a concern. In June 2000 the World Bank agreed to provide more than $200 million to build a $3.7 billion pipeline connecting the oil fields in neighboring Chad with the Cameroon coast.

Canada

Sovereign: Queen Elizabeth II (1952)
Governor-General: Adrienne Clarkson (1999)
Prime Minister: Jean Chrétien (1993)
Area: 3,851,788 sq mi (9,976,140 sq km)
Population (2001 est.): 31,592,805. Average annual rate of natural increase: 0.4%; birth rate: 11.2/1000; infant mortality rate: 5.0/1000; density per sq mi: 8
Capital: Ottawa, Ontario. **Largest cities (1996 census; metropolitan areas):** Toronto, 4,263,757; Montreal, 3,326,510; Vancouver, 1,831,665; Ottawa/Hull, 1,010,498; Edmonton, 862,597; Calgary, 821,628; Quebec, 671,889; Winnipeg, 667,209; Hamilton, 624,360; London, 398,616. **Monetary unit:** Canadian dollar. **Languages:** English, French (both official). **Ethnicity/race:** British Isles origin 40%, French origin 27%, other European 20%, indigenous Indian and Inuit 1.5%, other, mostly Asian 11.5%. **Religions:** Roman Catholic 46%, United Church 16%, Anglican 10%. **Literacy rate:** 96% (1986)
Economic summary: GDP/PPP (1999 est.): $722.3 billion; per capita $23,300. **Real growth rate:** 3.6%. **Inflation:** 1.7%. **Unemployment:** 7.6%. **Arable land:** 5%. **Agriculture:** wheat, barley, oilseed, tobacco, fruits, vegetables; dairy products; forest products; fish. **Labor force:** 15.9 million (1999); services, 75%; manufacturing, 16%; construction, 5%; agriculture, 3%; other, 1% (1997). **Industries:** processed and unprocessed minerals, food products, wood and paper products, transportation equipment, chemicals, fish products, petroleum and natural gas. **Natural resources:** iron ore, nickel, zinc, copper, gold, lead, molybdenum, potash, silver, fish, timber, wildlife, coal, petroleum, natural gas, hydropower. **Exports:** $277 billion (f.o.b., 1999 est.): motor vehicles and parts, newsprint, wood pulp, timber, crude petroleum, machinery, natural gas, aluminum, telecommunications equipment, electricity. **Imports:** $259.3 billion (f.o.b., 1999 est.): machinery and equipment, crude oil, chemicals, motor vehicles and parts, durable consumer goods, electricity. **Major trading partners:** U.S., Japan, UK, Germany, South Korea, Netherlands, China, France, Mexico, Taiwan.

Geography Covering most of the northern part of the North American continent and with an area larger than that of the United States, Canada has an extremely varied topography. In the east the mountainous maritime provinces have an irregular coastline on the Gulf of St. Lawrence and the Atlantic. The St. Lawrence plain, covering most of southern Quebec and Ontario, and the interior continental plain, covering southern Manitoba and Saskatchewan and most of Alberta, are the principal cultivable areas. They are separated by a forested plateau rising from Lakes Superior and Huron.

Westward toward the Pacific, most of British Columbia, Yukon, and part of western Alberta are covered by parallel mountain ranges, including the Rockies. The Pacific border of the coast range is ragged with fjords and channels. The highest point in Canada is Mount Logan (19,850 ft; 6,050 m), which is in the Yukon. The two principal river systems are the Mackenzie and the St. Lawrence. The St. Lawrence, with its tributaries, is navigable for over 1,900 mi (3,058 km).

Government Canada is a federation of 10 provinces (Alberta, British Columbia, Manitoba, New Brunswick, Newfoundland, Nova Scotia, Ontario, Prince Edward Island, Quebec, and Saskatchewan) and three territories (Northwest Territories, Yukon, and as of April 1, 1999, Nunavut). Formally considered a constitutional monarchy, Canada is governed by its own House of Commons. While the governor-general is officially the representative of Queen Elizabeth II, in reality the governor-general acts only upon the advice of the Canadian prime minister.

History The first inhabitants of Canada were native Indian peoples, primarily the Inuit (Eskimo). The Norse explorer Leif Eriksson probably reached the shores of Canada (Labrador or Nova Scotia) in 1000, but the history of the white man in the country actually began in 1497, when John Cabot, an Italian in the service of Henry VII of England, reached Newfoundland or Nova Scotia. Canada was taken for France in 1534 by Jacques Cartier. The actual settlement of New France, as it was then called, began in 1604 at Port Royal in what is now Nova Scotia; in 1608, Quebec was founded. France's colonization efforts were not very successful, but French explorers by the end of the 17th century had penetrated beyond the Great Lakes to the western prairies and south along the Mississippi to the Gulf of Mexico. Meanwhile, the English Hudson's Bay Company had been established in 1670. Because of the valuable fisheries and fur trade, a conflict developed between the French and English; in 1713, Newfoundland, Hudson Bay, and Nova Scotia (Acadia) were lost to England. During the Seven Years' War (1756–63), England extended its conquest, and the British Maj. Gen. James Wolfe won his famous victory over Gen. Louis Montcalm outside Quebec on Sept. 13, 1759. The Treaty of Paris in 1763 gave England control.

At that time the population of Canada was almost entirely French, but in the next few decades, thousands of British colonists emigrated to Canada from the British Isles and from the American colonies. In

Population by Provinces and Territories

Province	2000	1999
	(in thousands)	
Alberta	2,997.2	2,964.7
British Columbia	4,063.8	4,023.1
Manitoba	1,147.9	1,143.5
New Brunswick	756.6	755.0
Newfoundland	538.8	541.0
Nova Scotia	941.0	939.8
Ontario	11,669.3	11,513.8
Prince Edward Island	138.9	138.0
Quebec	7,372.4	7,345.4
Saskatchewan	1,023.6	1,027.8
Northwest Territories	42.1	41.6
Yukon Territory	30.7	30.6
Nunavut	27.7	27.0

Source: Statistics Canada.

Canadian Prime Ministers Since 1867

Term	Prime Minister	Party	Term	Prime Minister	Party
1867–1873	Sir John A. Macdonald	Conservative	1926–1930	W. L. Mackenzie King	Liberal
1873–1878	Alexander Mackenzie	Liberal	1930–1935	Richard B. Bennett	Conservative
1878–1891	Sir John A. Macdonald	Conservative	1935–1948	W. L. Mackenzie King	Liberal
1891–1892	Sir John J. C. Abbott	Conservative	1948–1957	Louis S. St. Laurent	Liberal
1892–1894	Sir John S. D. Thompson	Conservative	1957–1963	John G. Diefenbaker	Conservative
1894–1896	Sir Mackenzie Bowell	Conservative	1963–1968	Lester B. Pearson	Liberal
1896	Sir Charles Tupper	Conservative	1968–1979	Pierre Elliott Trudeau	Liberal
1896–1911	Sir Wilfrid Laurier	Liberal	1979–1980	Charles Joseph Clark	Conservative
1911–1917	Sir Robert L. Borden	Conservative	1980–1984	Pierre Elliott Trudeau	Liberal
1917–1920	Sir Robert L. Borden	Unionist	1984–1984	John Turner	Liberal
1920–1921	Arthur Meighen	Unionist	1984–1993	Brian Mulroney	Conservative
1921–1926	W. L. Mackenzie King	Liberal	1993–1993	Kim Campbell	Conservative
1926	Arthur Meighen	Conservative	1993–	Jean Chrétien	Liberal

1849, the right of Canada to self-government was recognized. By the British North America Act of 1867, the dominion of Canada was created through the confederation of Upper and Lower Canada, Nova Scotia, and New Brunswick. Prince Edward Island joined the dominion in 1873. In 1869, Canada purchased from the Hudson's Bay Company the vast middle west (Rupert's Land) from which the provinces of Manitoba (1870), Alberta (1905), and Saskatchewan (1905) were later formed. In 1871, British Columbia joined the dominion. The country was linked from coast to coast in 1885 by the Canadian Pacific Railway.

During the formative years between 1866 and 1896, the Conservative Party, led by Sir John A. Macdonald, governed the country, except during the years 1873–1878. In 1896, the Liberal Party took over and, under Sir Wilfrid Laurier, an eminent French Canadian, ruled until 1911. By the Statute of Westminster in 1931 the British dominions, including Canada, were formally declared to be partner nations with Britain, "equal in status, in no way subordinate to each other," and bound together only by allegiance to a common Crown.

Newfoundland became Canada's 10th province on March 31, 1949, following a plebiscite. Canada also includes three territories—the Yukon Territory, the Northwest Territories, and the newest territory, Nunavut. This new territory includes all of the Arctic north of the mainland, Norway having recognized Canadian sovereignty over the Sverdrup Islands in the Arctic in 1931.

The Liberal Party, led by William Lyon Mackenzie King, dominated Canadian politics from 1921 until 1957, when it was succeeded by the Progressive Conservatives. The Liberals, under the leadership of Lester B. Pearson, returned to power in 1963. Pearson remained prime minister until 1968, when he retired and was replaced by a former law professor, Pierre Elliott Trudeau. Trudeau maintained Canada's defensive alliance with the United States but began moving toward a more independent policy in world affairs.

Trudeau's election was considered in part a response to the most serious problem confronting the country, the division between French- and English-speaking Canadians, which had led to a separatist movement in the predominantly French province of Quebec. In 1974, the provincial government, the Parti Québécois (PQ) passed a law making French the official language of Quebec, but in Dec. 1979, the law was voided by the Canadian Supreme Court. In May 1980, Quebec held a referendum on whether the province should seek independence from Canada; it was defeated by 60% of the voters.

Resolving a dispute that had occupied Trudeau since the beginning of his tenure, Queen Elizabeth II signed the Constitution Act (also called the Canada Act) in Ottawa on April 17, 1982, thereby cutting the last legal tie between Canada and Britain. The constitution retains Queen Elizabeth as queen of Canada and keeps Canada's membership in the Commonwealth.

In the national election on Sept. 4, 1984, the Progressive Conservative Party scored an overwhelming victory, fundamentally changing the country's political landscape. The Conservatives, led by Brian Mulroney, won the highest political majority in Canadian history. The dominant foreign issue was a free-trade pact with the U.S., a treaty bitterly opposed by the Liberal and New Democratic Parties. The conflict led to elections in Nov. 1988 that solidly reelected Mulroney and gave him a mandate to proceed with the agreement.

The issue of separatist sentiments in French-speaking Quebec flared up again in 1990 with the failure of the Meech Lake Accord. The accord was designed to ease the Quebecers' fear of losing their identity within the English-speaking majority by giving Quebec constitutional status as a "distinct society." In an attempt to keep Canada united, the three major political parties came to an agreement in Feb. 1992 on constitutional reforms. Voters in the Northwest Territories authorized the division of their region in two, creating a homeland for Canadian Eskimos, the Inuits, which in April 1999 became the territory of Nunavut. Also in 1992, Canada announced its decision to withdraw its combat units from NATO command. The economy continued to be mired in a long recession that many blamed on the free-trade agreement. A national referendum was held in Oct. 1992 on the proposal to change the constitution to ensure greater representation in Parliament for the more populous regions and thereby the French-speaking Quebecers. The referendum, however, was defeated.

Brian Mulroney's popularity continued to decline, causing him to resign before the next election. In June 1993 the governing Progressive Conservative Party chose Defense Minister Kim Campbell as its leader, making her the first female prime minister in Canadian history. The national election in Oct. 1993 resulted in the reemergence of the Liberal Party and the installation of Jean Chrétien as prime minister.

The Quebec referendum on secession in Oct. 1995 yielded a narrow rejection of the proposal. But separatists vowed to try again. Since then, however, the Reform Party has replaced the Bloc Québécois as the official opposition.

On April 1, 1999, the Northwest Territories were officially divided to create a new territory in the east that would be governed by Canada's Inuits, who make up 85% of the area's population. Composed of 770,000 sq mi of mostly snow and ice reaching well to the north of the Arctic Circle, the 25,700 residents of Nunavut are governed from the new capital, Iqaluit.

In July 2000, Stockwell Day of the new conservative Canadian Alliance Party unexpectedly emerged as the leader of Canada's opposition. In elections held in Nov. 2000, however, Prime Minister Jean Chrétien of the Liberal Party won a landslide victory of a third five-year term. The Liberals won 173 seats in the 301-member parliament, an increase of 12. The Canadian Alliance Party captured 66 seats, an increase of 8. After the election, the conservatives rapidly lost steam.

In Aug. 2001, Canada became the first country to legalize the use of marijuana for certain medical purposes.

Cape Verde

REPUBLIC OF CAPE VERDE

National name: República de Cabo Verde
President: Pedro Pires (2001)
Prime Minister: José Maria Neves (2001)
Area: 1,557 sq mi (4,033 sq km)
Population (2001 est.): 405,163 (average annual rate of natural increase: 2.2%); birth rate: 28.7/1000; infant mortality rate: 53.2/1000; density per sq mi: 260
Capital (1990): Praia, 61,797. **Other large city (est. 1982):** Mindelo, 50,000. **Monetary unit:** Cape Verdean escudo. **Languages:** Portuguese, Criuolo. **Ethnicity/race:** Creole (mulatto) 71%, African 28%, European 1%. **Religion:** Roman Catholic fused with indigenous beliefs. **Literacy rate:** 67% (1989)
Economic summary: GDP/PPP (1999 est.): $618 million; per capita $1,500. **Real growth rate:** 5%. **Inflation:** 5% (1999). **Unemployment:** n.a. **Arable land:** 11%. **Agriculture:** bananas, corn, beans, sweet potatoes, sugarcane, coffee, peanuts; fish. **Labor force:** n.a. **Industries:** food and beverages, fish processing, shoes and garments, salt mining, ship repair. **Natural resources:** salt, basalt rock, pozzuolana (a siliceous volcanic ash used to produce hydraulic cement), limestone, kaolin, fish. **Exports:** $38 million (f.o.b., 1999 est.): fuel, shoes, garments, fish, bananas, hides. **Imports:** $225 million (f.o.b., 1999 est.): foodstuffs, industrial products, transport equipment, fuels. **Major trading partners:** Portugal, Germany, Spain, France, UK, Malaysia, Netherlands, U.S.

Geography Cape Verde, only slightly larger than Rhode Island, is an archipelago in the Atlantic 385 mi (500 km) west of Senegal.

The islands are divided into two groups: Barlavento in the north, composed of Santo Antão (291 sq mi; 754 sq km), Boa Vista (240 sq mi; 622 sq km), São Nicolau (132 sq mi; 342 sq km), São Vicente (88 sq mi; 246 sq km), Sal (83 sq mi; 298 sq km), and Santa Luzia (13 sq mi; 34 sq km); and Sotavento in the south, consisting of São Tiago (383 sq mi; 992 sq km), Fogo (184 sq mi; 477 sq km), Maio (103 sq mi; 267 sq km), and Brava (25 sq mi; 65 sq km). The islands are mostly mountainous, with the land deeply scarred by erosion. There is an active volcano on Fogo.

Government Republic.

History Uninhabited upon their discovery in 1456, the Cape Verde islands became part of the Portuguese empire in 1495. A majority of their modern inhabitants are of mixed Portuguese and African ancestry.

Positioned on the great trade routes between Africa, Europe, and the New World, the islands became a prosperous center for the slave trade but suffered economic decline after the slave trade was abolished in 1876. In the 20th century Cape Verde served as a shipping port.

In 1951 Cape Verde's status changed from a Portuguese colony to an overseas province, and in 1961 the inhabitants became full Portuguese citizens. An independence movement led by the African Party for the Independence of Guinea-Bissau (another former Portuguese colony) and Cape Verde (PAIGC) was founded in 1956. Following the 1974 coup in Portugal, after which Portugal began abandoning its colonial empire, the islands became independent (July 5, 1975).

The first multiparty elections since independence on Jan. 13, 1991, resulted in the ruling African Party for the Independence of Cape Verde (PAICV) to lose its majority to the Movement for Democracy Party (MPD). The MPD candidate, Antonio Monteiro, won the subsequent presidential election. Monteiro was easily reelected in 1996.

In an effort to take advantage of its proximity to cross-Atlantic sea and air lanes, the government has embarked on a major expansion of its port and airport capacities. It is also modernizing the fishing fleet and enhancing its fish processing industry. These projects are being partly paid for by the EU and the World Bank, making Cape Verde one of the largest per capita aid recipients in the world. Disenchantment with the government's privatization program, continued high unemployment, and widespread poverty helped defeat the MPD in elections held in Jan. 2001. The PAICV swept back into power and José Maria Neves became prime minister.

Central African Republic

National name: République Centrafricaine
Head of government: Gen. André Kolingba (1986)
President: Ange-Félix Patassé (1993)
Prime Minister: Martin Ziguélé (2001)
Area: 240,534 sq mi (622,984 sq km)
Population (2001 est.): 3,576,884 (average annual rate of natural increase: 1.9%); birth rate: 37.1/1000; infant mortality rate: 105.3/1000; density per sq mi: 15
Capital and largest city (1990 est.): Bangui, 706,000. **Monetary unit:** Franc CFA. **Languages:** French (official), Sangho, Arabic, Hansa, Swahili. **Ethnicity/race:** Baya 34%, Banda 27%, Sara 10%, Mandjia 21%, Mboum 4%, M'Baka 4%, Yakoma, Ubangi, Europeans 6,500 (including 3,600 French). **Religions:** indigenous beliefs 24%, Protestant and Roman Catholic with animist influence 50%, Muslim 15%, other 11%. **Literacy rate:** 38% (1990)
Economic summary: GDP/PPP (1999 est.): $5.8 billion. **Real growth rate:** 5%; per capita $1,700. **Inflation:** 2.6%. **Unemployment:** 6% (1993). **Arable land:** 3%. **Agriculture:** cotton, coffee, tobacco, manioc (tapioca), yams, millet, corn, bananas; timber. **Labor force:** n.a. **Industries:** diamond mining, sawmills, breweries, textiles, footwear, assembly of bicycles and motorcycles. **Natural resources:** diamonds, uranium, timber, gold, oil, hydropower. **Exports:** $195 million (f.o.b., 1999): diamonds, timber, cotton, coffee, tobacco. **Imports:** $170 million (f.o.b., 1999): food, textiles, petroleum products, machinery, electrical equipment, motor vehicles, chemicals, pharmaceuticals, consumer goods, industrial products. **Major trading partners:** Benelux, Côte d'Ivoire, Spain, Egypt, France, Cameroon, Germany, Japan.

Geography Situated about 500 mi (805 km) north of the equator, the Central African Republic is a landlocked nation bordered by Cameroon, Chad, the Sudan, the Democratic Republic of the Congo, and the Republic of Congo. The Ubangi and the Shari are the largest of many rivers.

Government Multiparty republic since 1991.

History From the 16th to 19th century, the people of this region were ravaged by slave traders. The Banda, Baya, Ngbandi, and Azande make up the largest ethnic groups.

The French occupied the region in 1894. As the colony of Ubangi-Shari, what is now the Central African Republic was united with Chad in 1905. In 1910 it was joined with Gabon and the Middle Congo to become French Equatorial Africa. After World War II a rebellion in 1946 forced the French to grant self-government. In 1958 the territory voted to become an autonomous republic within the French Community, and on Aug. 13, 1960, President David Dacko proclaimed the republic's independence from France. Dacko moved the country into Beijing's orbit, but was overthrown in a coup on Dec. 31, 1965, by Col. Jean-Bédel Bokassa, army chief of staff.

On Dec. 4, 1976, the Central African Republic became the Central African Empire. Marshal Jean-Bédel Bokassa, who had ruled the republic since he took power in 1965, was declared Emperor Bokassa I. Brutality and excess characterized his regime. He was overthrown in a coup on Sept. 20, 1979. Former president David Dacko returned to power and changed the country's name back to the Central African Republic. An army coup on Sept. 1, 1981, deposed President Dacko again.

In 1991, President André Kolingba, under pressure, announced a move toward parliamentary democracy. In elections held in Aug. 1993, Prime Minister Ange-Félix Patassé defeated Kolingba. Part of Patassé's popularity rested on his pledge to pay the back salaries of the military and civil servants.

A 1994 economic upturn was too small to effectively improve the catastrophic financial condition of the nation. Patassé was unable to pay the salaries due government workers, and the military revolted in 1996. At Patassé's request, French troops suppressed the uprising. In 1998 the United Nations sent an all-African peacekeeping force to the country. In elections held in Sept. 1999, amid widespread charges of massive fraud, Patassé easily defeated Kolingba.

President Ange-Félix Patassé survived a failed coup attempt in May 2001 with the help of Libya and Congolese rebels. Former president André Kolingba was thought to be behind it. Reprisals against Kolingba's ethnic group, the Yakomas, followed the coup attempt.

Chad

REPUBLIC OF CHAD

National name: République du Tchad
President: Lieut. Gen. Idriss Déby (1990)
Prime Minister: Nagoum Yamassoum (1999)
Area: 495,752 sq mi (1,284,000 sq km)
Population (2001 est.): 8,707,078 (average annual rate of natural increase, 3.3%); birth rate: 48.3/1000; infant mortality rate: 95.1/1000; density per sq mi: 18
Capital and largest city (1993): N'Djamena, 529,555.
Monetary unit: Franc CFA. **Languages:** French and Arabic (official), more than 100 tribal languages.
Ethnicity/race: North and center: Muslims (Arabs, Toubou, Hadjerai, Fulbe, Kotoko, Kanembou, Baguirmi, Boulala, Zaghawa, and Maba); South: non-Muslims (Sara [the largest ethnic group, 25% of the population], Ngambaye, Mbaye, Goulaye, Moundang, Moussei, Massa). **Religions:** Islam 44%, Christian 33%, traditional 23%. **Literacy rate:** 30% (1990)
Economic summary: GDP/PPP (1999 est.): $7.6 billion; per capita $1,000. **Real growth rate:** 0.6%. **Inflation:** 12% (1998 est.). **Unemployment:** n.a. **Arable land:** 3%. **Agriculture:** cotton, sorghum, millet, peanuts, rice, potatoes, manioc (tapioca); cattle, sheep, goats, camels. **Labor force:** n.a.; agriculture, 85% (subsistence farming, herding, and fishing). **Industries:** cotton textiles, meat packing, beer brewing, natron (sodium carbonate), soap, cigarettes, construction materials. **Natural resources:** petroleum (unexploited but exploration under way), uranium, natron, kaolin, fish (Lake Chad). **Exports:** $288 million (f.o.b., 1999 est.): cotton, cattle, textiles. **Imports:** $359 million (f.o.b., 1999 est.): machinery and transportation equipment, industrial goods, petroleum products, foodstuffs, textiles. **Major trading partners:** Portugal, Germany, Thailand, Costa Rica, South Africa, France, Nigeria, Cameroon, India.

Geography A landlocked country in north-central Africa, Chad is about 85% the size of Alaska. Its neighbors are Niger, Libya, the Sudan, the Central African Republic, Cameroon, and Nigeria. Lake Chad, from which the country gets its name, lies on the western border with Niger and Nigeria. In the north is a desert that runs into the Sahara.

Government Republic.

History The area around Lake Chad has been inhabited since at least 500 B.C. In the 8th century A.D. Berbers began migrating to the area. Islam arrived in 1085, and by the 16th century a trio of rival kingdoms flourished: the Kanem-Bornu, the Baguirmi, and Ouaddaï. In 1883–1893, all three kingdoms came under the rule of the Sudanese conqueror Rabih al-Zubayr. In 1900, Rabih was overthrown by the French, who absorbed these kingdoms into the colony of French Equatorial Africa, as part of Ubangi-Shari, in 1910.

France began the country's development after 1920, when it became a separate colony. In 1946, French Equatorial Africa was admitted to the French Union, and in 1958 the Chad territory became an autonomous republic within the French Union. An independence movement led by the first premier and president, François (later Ngarta) Tombalbaye, achieved complete independence on Aug. 11, 1960. Tombalbaye was killed in the 1975 coup and succeeded by Gen. Félix Malloum, who faced a Libyan-financed civil war throughout his tenure in office. In 1977 Libya seized a strip of Chadian land and launched an invasion two years later.

Nine rival groups meeting in Lagos, Nigeria, in March 1979 agreed to form a provisional government headed by Goukouni Oueddei, a former rebel leader. Fighting broke out again in Chad in March 1980, when Defense Minister Hissen Habré challenged Goukouni and seized the capital. Libyan president Muammar al-Qaddafi in Jan. 1981 proposed a merger of Chad with Libya. The Libyan proposal was rejected and Libyan troops withdrew from Chad that year, but in 1983 they poured back into the northern part of the country in support of Goukouni. France, in turn, sent troops into southern Chad in support of

Habré. Government troops then launched an offensive in early 1987 that drove the Libyans out of most of the country.

In 1990 Idriss Déby, a former defense minister and head of a rebel group, the Patriotic Salvation Movement, overthrew Habré, suspended the constitution, and dissolved the legislature. In 1994 a new constitution was drafted and an amnesty for political prisoners was declared. Déby won multiparty elections in 1996 and his party won legislative elections the following year. International observers said the elections were fair, although Déby's opponents charged voter fraud.

Chad continues to grapple with insurgencies in both the southern and northern parts of the country, as well as with massive economic and environmental problems. In June 2000 the World Bank agreed to provide more than $200 million to build a $3.7 billion pipeline connecting the oil fields of neighboring Cameroon. Oil revenues are estimated to earn $2.5 billion over the next 30 years.

Chile

REPUBLIC OF CHILE

National name: República de Chile
President: Ricardo Lagos (2000)
Area: 292,258 sq mi (756,950 sq km)
Population (2001 est.): 15,328,467 (average annual rate of natural increase: 1.1%); birth rate: 16.8/1000; infant mortality rate: 9.4/1000; density per sq mi: 52
Capital and largest city (2000 est.): Santiago, 5,400,000 (metro. area). **Other large cities (1996 est.):** Concepción, 356,371; Viña del Mar, 326,448; Valparaíso, 282,850; Talcahuano, 265,060; Temuco, 246,304. **Monetary unit:** Peso. **Language:** Spanish. **Ethnicity/race:** European and European-Indian 95%, Indian 3%, other 2%. **Religions:** Roman Catholic 89%, Protestant 11%, small Jewish and Muslim populations. **Literacy rate:** 95% (1992)
Economic summary: GDP/PPP (1999 est.): $185.1 billion; per capita $12,400. **Real growth rate:** −1%. **Inflation:** 3.4%. **Unemployment:** 9% (1999). **Arable land:** 5%. **Agriculture:** wheat, corn, grapes, beans, sugar beets, potatoes, fruit; beef, poultry, wool; fish; timber. **Labor force:** 5.8 million (1999 est.); agriculture, 14%; industry, 27%; services, 59% (1997 est.). **Industries:** copper, other minerals, foodstuffs, fish processing, iron and steel, wood and wood products, transport equipment, cement, textiles. **Natural resources:** copper, timber, iron ore, nitrates, precious metals, molybdenum, hydropower. **Exports:** $15.6 billion (f.o.b., 1999): copper, fish, fruits, paper and pulp, chemicals. **Imports:** $13.9 billion (c.i.f., 1999): consumer goods, chemicals, motor vehicles, fuels, electrical machinery, heavy industrial machinery, food. **Major trading partners:** EU, U.S., Japan, Brazil, Argentina, Mexico.

Geography Situated south of Peru and west of Bolivia and Argentina, Chile fills a narrow 1,800-mile (2,897 km) strip between the Andes and the Pacific. One-third of Chile is covered by the towering ranges of the Andes. In the north is the driest place on Earth, the Atacama Desert, and in the center is a 700-mile-long (1,127 km), thickly populated valley with most of Chile's arable land. At the southern tip of Chile's mainland is Punta Arenas, the southernmost city in the world, and beyond that lies the Strait of Magellan and Tierra del Fuego, an island divided between Chile and Argentina. The southernmost point of South America is Cape Horn, a 1,390-foot (424 m) rock on Horn Island in the Wollaston group, which belongs to

Chile. Chile also claims sovereignty over 482,628 sq mi (1,250,000 sq km) of Antarctic territory, the Juan Fernández Islands, about 400 mi (644 km) west of the mainland, and Easter Island, about 2,000 mi (3,219 km) west.

Government Republic.

History Chile was originally under the control of the Incas in the north and the nomadic Araucanos in the south. In 1541, a Spaniard, Pedro de Valdivia, founded Santiago. Chile won its independence from Spain in 1818 under Bernardo O'Higgins and an Argentinian, José de San Martin. O'Higgins, dictator until 1823, laid the foundations of the modern state with a two-party system and a centralized government.

The dictator from 1830 to 1837, Diego Portales, fought a war with Peru in 1836–39 that expanded Chilean territory. Chile fought the War of the Pacific with Peru and Bolivia from 1879 to 1883, winning Antofagasta, Bolivia's only outlet to the sea, and extensive areas from Peru. Pedro Montt led a revolt that overthrew José Balmaceda in 1891 and established a parliamentary dictatorship lasting until a new constitution was adopted in 1925. Industrialization began before World War I and led to the formation of Marxist groups. Juan Antonio Ríos, president during World War II, was originally pro-Nazi but in 1944 led his country into the war on the side of the Allies.

A small abortive army uprising in 1969 raised the fear of military intervention in preventing a Marxist, Salvador Allende Gossens, from taking office after his election to the presidency on Sept. 4, 1970. Allende was the first president in a non-Communist country freely elected on a Marxist-Leninist program. Allende quickly established relations with Cuba and the People's Republic of China and nationalized several American companies. Allende's overthrow and death in an army assault on the presidential palace in Sept. 1973 ended a 46-year era of constitutional government in Chile.

The takeover was led by a four-man junta headed by Army Chief of Staff Augusto Pinochet Ugarte, who assumed the office of president. Committed to "exterminat[ing] Marxism," the junta suspended Parliament, banned political activity, and broke relations with Cuba. It also abolished DINA, the secret police, and decreed an amnesty for political prisoners, while free-market reforms improved the economy. In 1977 Pinochet promised elections by 1985 if conditions warranted. After losing the plebiscite, Pinochet stepped down in Jan. 1990 in favor of Patricio Aylwin, who was elected in Dec. 1989 as the head of a 17-party coalition. In Dec. 1993 Eduardo Frei Ruiz-Tagle, the candidate of a center-left coalition and son of a previous president, was elected president.

In March 1998, Pinochet retired as army commander in chief. In Oct. 1998 he was arrested and detained in England on an extradition request issued by a Spanish judge who sought Pinochet in connection with the disappearance of Spanish citizens during his rule. British courts ultimately denied his extradition, and Pinochet returned to Chile in March 2000. The Chilean Supreme Court stripped Pinochet of his immunity from prosecution in June 2000, but in July 2001 Chilean courts ruled that he was mentally unfit to stand trial.

Ricardo Lagos became president in March 2000, the first socialist to run the country since Allende.

China

PEOPLE'S REPUBLIC OF CHINA

National name: Zhonghua Renmin Gongheguo
President: Jiang Zemin (1993)
Premier: Zhu Rongji (1998)
Area: 3,705,386 sq mi (9,596,960 sq km)[1]
Population (2001 est.): 1,273,111,290 (average rate of natural increase: 0.9%); birth rate: 16.0/1000; infant mortality rate: 28.1/1000; density per sq mi: 344.
Capital (2000 est.): Beijing, 8,450,000 (metro. area).
Largest cities (1990 est.): Shanghai (2000 est.), 11,800,000 (metro. area); Hong Kong (Xianggang) (2000 est.), 6,750,000 (metro. area); Tianjin (Tientsin) (2000 est.), 5,350,000 (metro. area); Shenyang (Mukden), 4,669,737; Wuhan, 4,040,113; Guangzhou, 3,935,193; Chungking (Chongqing) 3,127,178; Haerbin, 2,990,921; Chengdu, 2,954,872; Xian, 2,872,539. **Monetary unit:** Yuan. **Languages:** Chinese, Mandarin, also local dialects. **Ethnicity/race:** Han Chinese 91.9%, Zhuang, Uygur, Hui, Yi, Tibetan, Miao, Manchu, Mongol, Buyi, Korean, and other nationalities 8.1%. China has 56 ethnic groups.
Religions: Officially atheist but traditional religion contains elements of Confucianism, Taoism, Buddhism. **Literacy rate:** 84% (1995)
Economic summary: GDP/PPP (1999 est.): $4.8 trillion; per capita $3,800. **Real growth rate:** 7%. **Inflation:** –1.3%. **Unemployment:** urban unemployment roughly 10%; substantial unemployment and underemployment in rural areas. **Arable land:** 10%. **Agriculture:** rice, wheat, potatoes, sorghum, peanuts, tea, millet, barley, cotton, oilseed; pork; fish. **Labor force:** 700 million (1998 est.); agriculture, 50%; industry, 24%; services, 26% (1998). **Industries:** iron and steel, coal, machine building, armaments, textiles and apparel, petroleum, cement, chemical fertilizers, footwear, toys, food processing, automobiles, consumer electronics, telecommunications. **Natural resources:** coal, iron ore, petroleum, natural gas, mercury, tin, tungsten, antimony, manganese, molybdenum, vanadium, magnetite, aluminum, lead, zinc, uranium, hydropower potential (world's largest). **Exports:** $194.9 billion (f.o.b., 1999): machinery and equipment; textiles and clothing, footwear, toys and sporting goods; mineral fuels, chemicals. **Imports:** $165.8 billion (c.i.f., 1999): machinery and equipment, plastics, chemicals, iron and steel, mineral fuels. **Major trading partners:** U.S., Hong Kong, Japan, Germany, South Korea, Netherlands, UK, Singapore, Taiwan, Russia.

1. Including Manchuria and Tibet.

Geography China is slightly larger in area than the U.S. The greater part of the country is mountainous. Its principal ranges are the Tien Shan, the Kunlun chain, and the Trans-Himalaya. In the southwest is Tibet, which China annexed in 1950. The Gobi Desert lies to the north. China proper consists of three great river systems: the Yellow River (Huang He), 2,109 mi (5,464 km) long; the Yangtze River (Chang Jiang), the third-longest river in the world at 2,432 mi (6,300 km); and the Pearl River (Zhu Jiang), 848 mi (2,197 km) long.

Government Communist state.

History The earliest recorded human settlements in what is today called China were discovered in the Huang Ho basin and date from about 5000 B.C. During the Shang dynasty (1500–1000 B.C.), the precursor of modern China's ideographic writing system developed, allowing the emerging feudal states of the era to achieve an advanced stage of civilization,

rivaling in sophistication anything found at the time in Europe, the Middle East, or the Americas. It was following this initial flourishing of civilization, in a period known as the Chou dynasty (1122–249 B.C.), that Lao-tse, Confucius, Mo Ti, and Mencius laid the foundation of Chinese philosophical thought.

The feudal states, often at war with one another, were first united under Emperor Ch'in Shih Huang Ti, during whose reign (246–210 B.C.) work was begun on the Great Wall of China, a monumental bulwark against invasion from the West. Although the Great Wall symbolized China's desire to protect itself from the outside world, under the Han dynasty (206 B.C.–A.D. 220), the civilization opened extensive commercial trading with the West.

In the T'ang dynasty (618–907)—often called the golden age of Chinese history—painting, sculpture, and poetry flourished, and woodblock printing, which enabled the mass production of books, made its earliest known appearance. The Mings, last of the native rulers (1368–1644), overthrew the Mongol, or Yuan, dynasty (1271–1368) established by Kublai Khan. The Mings in turn were overthrown in 1644 by invaders from the north, the Manchus.

China remained largely isolated from the rest of the world's civilizations, closely restricting foreign activities. By the end of the 18th century only Canton (location of modern-day Hong Kong) and the Portuguese port of Macao were open to European merchants. But with the first Anglo-Chinese War in 1839–42, a long period of instability and concessions to Western colonial powers began. Following the war, several ports were opened up for trading, and Hong Kong was ceded to Britain. Treaties signed after further hostilities (1856–60) weakened Chinese sovereignty and gave foreigners immunity from Chinese jurisdiction. European powers took advantage of the disastrous Sino-Japanese War of 1894–95 to gain further trading concessions from China. Peking's response, the Boxer Rebellion (1900), was suppressed by an international force.

The death of Empress Dowager Tzu Hsi in 1908 and the accession of the infant emperor Hsüan T'ung (Pu-Yi) were followed by a nationwide rebellion led by Dr. Sun Yat-sen, who overthrew the Manchus and became the first president of the Provisional Chinese Republic in 1911. Dr. Sun resigned in favor of Yuan Shih-k'ai, who suppressed the Republicans in a bid to consolidate his power. Yuan's death in June 1916 was followed by years of civil war between rival militarists and Dr. Sun's Republicans. Nationalist forces, led by General Chiang Kai-shek and with the advice of Communist experts, soon occupied most of China, setting up a Kuomintang regime in 1928. Internal strife continued, however, and Chiang eventually broke with the Communists.

On Sept. 18, 1931, Japan launched an invasion of Manchuria, capturing the province. Tokyo set up a puppet state dubbed Manchukuo and installed the last Manchu emperor, Henry Pu-Yi (Hsüan T'ung), as its nominal leader. Japanese troops moved to seize China's northern provinces in July 1937 but were resisted by Chiang, who had been able to use the Japanese invasion to unite most of China behind him. Within two years, however, Japan had seized most of the nation's eastern ports and railways. The Kuomintang government retreated first to Hankow and then to Chungking, while the Japanese set up a puppet government at Nanking, headed by Wang Jingwei.

Japan's surrender in 1945 touched off civil war between the Kuomintang forces under Chiang and

Communists led by Mao Zedong, who had been battling since the 1930s for control of China. Despite U.S. aid, the Kuomintang were overcome by the Soviet-supported Communists, and Chiang and his followers were forced to flee the mainland, establishing a government-in-exile on the island of Formosa (Taiwan). The Mao regime proclaimed the People's Republic of China on Oct. 1, 1949, with Beijing as the new capital and Zhou Enlai as premier.

After the Korean War began in June 1950, China led the Communist bloc in supporting North Korea, and on Nov. 26, 1950, the Mao regime sent troops to assist the North in its efforts to capture the South.

In an attempt to restructure China's primarily agrarian economy, Mao undertook the "Great Leap Forward" campaign in 1958, a disastrous program that aimed to combine the establishment of rural communes with a crash program of village industrialization. The Great Leap forced the abandonment of farming activities, leading to widespread famine in which more than 20 million people died of malnutrition.

In 1959, a failed uprising against China's invasion and occupation of Tibet forced Tibetan Buddhism's spiritual leader, the Dalai Lama, and 100,000 of his followers to flee to India. The invasion of Tibet, as well as border disputes between China and India—with whom Moscow had warm relations—and a perceived rivalry for the leadership of the world Communist movement caused a serious souring of relations between China and the USSR, former allies.

The failure of the Great Leap Forward touched off a power struggle within the Chinese Communist Party between Mao and his supporters and a reformist faction including future premier Deng Xiaoping. Mao moved to Shanghai, and from that base he and his supporters waged what they called the Cultural Revolution. Beginning in the spring of 1966, Mao ordered the closing of schools and the formation of ideologically pure Red Guard units, dominated by youths and students. The Red Guards campaigned against "old ideas, old culture, old habits, and old customs." Millions died as a series of violent purges were carried out. By early 1967, the Cultural Revolution had succeeded in bolstering Mao's position as China's paramount leader.

Anxious to exploit the Sino-Soviet rift, the Nixon administration made a dramatic announcement in July 1971 that National Security Adviser Henry Kissinger had secretly visited Beijing and reached an agreement whereby Nixon would visit China. The movement toward reconciliation, which signaled the end of the U.S. containment policy toward China, provided momentum for China's admission to the UN. Despite U.S. opposition to expelling Taiwan (Nationalist China), the world body overwhelmingly voted to oust Taiwan in favor of Beijing's Communist government.

President Nixon went to Beijing for a week early in 1972, meeting Mao as well as Zhou. The summit ended with a historic communiqué on Feb. 28, in which both nations promised to work toward improved relations. Full diplomatic relations were barred by China as long as the U.S. continued to recognize the legitimacy of Nationalist China.

Following Zhou's death on Jan. 8, 1976, his successor, Vice Premier Deng Xiaoping, was supplanted within a month by Hua Guofeng, former minister of public security. Hua became permanent premier in April. In Oct. he was named successor to Mao as chairman of the Communist Party. But Mao's death on Sept. 10 unleashed the bitter intraparty rivalries that had been suppressed since the Cultural Revolution. Old opponents of Mao launched a campaign against his widow, Jiang Qing, and three of her "radical" colleagues. The so-called Gang of Four was denounced for having undermined the party, the government, and the economy. They were tried and convicted in 1981. Meanwhile, in 1977 Deng Xiaoping was reinstated as deputy premier, chief of staff of the army, and member of the Central Committee of the Politburo.

Beijing and Washington announced full diplomatic relations on Jan. 1, 1979, and the Carter administration abrogated the Taiwan defense treaty. Deputy Premier Deng sealed the agreement with a visit to the U.S. that coincided with the opening of embassies in both capitals on March 1. On Deng's return from the U.S., Chinese troops invaded and briefly occupied an area along Vietnam's northern border. The action was seen as a response to Vietnam's invasion of Cambodia and ouster of the Khmer Rouge government, which China had supported.

In 1981, Deng protégé Hu Yaobang replaced Hua Guofeng as party chairman. Deng became chairman of the committee's military commission, giving him control over the army. The body's 215 members concluded the session with a statement holding Mao Zedong responsible for the "grave blunder" of the Cultural Revolution.

Under Deng Xiaoping's leadership, meanwhile, China's Communist ideology went through a massive reinterpretation, and sweeping economic changes were set in motion in the early 1980s. The Chinese scrapped the personality cult that idolized Mao Zedong, muted Mao's old call for class struggle and exportation of the Communist revolution, and imported Western technology and management techniques to replace the Marxist tenets that had slowed modernization. Deng concluded an agreement for the return of Hong Kong following the expiration of Britain's 99-year lease on the territory on July 1, 1997.

The removal of Hu Yaobang as party chairman in Jan. 1987 signaled a hard-line resurgence within the party. Hu—who had become a hero to many reform-minded Chinese—was replaced by former premier Zhao Ziyang. With the death of Hu in April 1989, the ideological struggle spilled into the streets of the capital, as student demonstrators occupied Beijing's Tiananmen Square in May, calling for democratic reforms. Less than a month later, the demonstrations were crushed in a bloody crackdown as troops and tanks moved into the square and fired on protesters, killing several hundred.

In annual sessions of the rubber-stamp National People's Congress in 1992 and 1993, the government called for accelerating the drive for economic reform, but the sessions were widely seen as an effort to maintain China's moves toward a market economy while retaining political authoritarianism. At the session in 1993, Communist Party leader Jiang Zemin was elected president, while hard-liner Li Peng was reelected to another five-year term as prime minister. Since 1993, the Chinese economy has continued to grow rapidly. In Nov. 1993 the Central Committee adopted a resolution envisaging the conversion of state-owned enterprises into joint-stock companies, and the creation of a central bank and modern tax system.

Deng Xiaoping's death in Feb. 1997 left a younger generation in charge of managing the enormous country. In 1998, Prime Minister Zhu Rongji introduced a sweeping program to privatize state-run businesses and further liberalize the nation's economy, a move lauded by Western economists.

After two years of painstaking negotiation, authorities of Britain and the People's Republic of China agreed in 1984 that Hong Kong would return to Chinese sovereignty on July 1, 1997, when Britain's lease on the New Territories expired. They also agreed that the capitalist enclave would retain its status as a free port, with its laws remaining unchanged for 50 years. The chief executive under the new government, Tung Chee Hwa, formulated a policy agenda based upon the concept of "one country, two systems," thus preserving Hong Kong's economic freedom. Hong Kong will continue to have its own finances and issue its own travel documents, and Beijing will not levy taxes.

Chinese-U.S. relations in May 1999 were severely strained when Congress accused China of stealing U.S. nuclear secrets over the past two decades. Relations eroded even further when a month later the U.S. mistakenly bombed the Chinese embassy in Belgrade during Operation Allied Force, killing three Chinese journalists and wounding 20 others.

In Aug. 1999, China rounded up thousands of members of the Falun Gong sect, a highly popular religious movement that combines elements of Buddhism, Taoism, and martial arts. China, which has now outlawed the sect, was thought to consider the apolitical spiritual group threatening because its numbers exceeded the membership of the Chinese Communist Party.

In March 2000 relations with Taiwan nearly reached a boiling point when Chen Shui-bian was elected president of Taiwan. Chen and his Democratic Progressive Party had previously called for independence from mainland China, but he softened his stance days before the election. The move stabilized the growing threat of armed conflict, and China adapted a "wait and see" attitude and signaled it was open to talks with Chen.

Tensions between the U.S. and China reached crisis levels in April 2001, when a U.S. Navy EP-3 surveillance plane and a Chinese fighter F-8 jet collided near the Chinese coast. The Chinese plane went down and its pilot, Wang Wei, is presumed dead. U.S. pilot Shane Osborn made an emergency landing on China's Hainan Island without permission. The 24 crew members of the U.S. plane were detained on the island for 11 days and released after the U.S. issued a formal statement of regret. The U.S. resumed reconnaissance missions a month after the incident.

The International Olympic Committee (IOC) in July 2001 awarded Beijing the 2008 Summer Games, despite some criticism of China's human rights practices and its environmental record.

At the 30th anniversary of the Communist Party on July 1, 2001, President Jiang Zemin declared that capitalists should be allowed to join the Communist Party.

Hong Kong

Status: Special Administrative Region of China
Chief Executive: Tung Chee Hwa (1997)
Area: 422 sq mi (1,092 sq km)
Population (2001 est.): 7,210,505 (average annual rate of natural increase: 0.5%); birth rate: 11.1/1000; infant mortality rate: 5.8/1000; density per sq mi: 17,102

Hong Kong consists of the island of Hong Kong (32 sq mi; 83 sq km), Stonecutters' Island, Kowloon Peninsula, and the New Territories on the adjoining mainland. The island of Hong Kong was ceded to Britain in 1841. Stonecutters' Island and Kowloon were annexed in 1860, and the New Territories, which are mainly agricultural lands, were leased from China in 1898 for 99 years. On July 1, 1997 Hong Kong was returned to China. The vibrant capitalist enclave retains its status as a free port, with its laws remaining unchanged for 50 years. Chief Executive Tung Chee Hwa formulated a policy agenda based upon the concept of "one country, two systems," thus preserving Hong Kong's economic independence.

Macao

Status: Special Administrative Region of China
Chief Executive: Edmund Ho (1999)
Area: 8 sq mi (21 sq km)
Population (2001 est.): 453,733 (average annual growth rate: 0.9%); birth rate: 22.4/1000; infant mortality rate: 4.5/1000; density per sq mi: 55,960

Colonized by the Portuguese in 1557, Macao was the oldest European outpost in China. In 1987, Portugal and China reached an agreement to return Macao to Chinese rule on Dec. 20, 1999. They agreed upon provisions to insure the autonomy of Macao, including its right to elect local leaders, the right of its residents to travel freely, and the right to maintain its way of life for 50 years after the start of Chinese rule.

Colombia

REPUBLIC OF COLOMBIA

National name: República de Colombia
President: Andrés Pastrana Arango (1998)
Area: 439,733 sq mi (1,138,910 sq km)
Population (2001 est.): 40,349,388 (average annual rate of natural increase, 1.7%); birth rate: 22.4/1000; infant mortality rate: 24.0/1000; density per sq mi: 92
Capital and largest city (2000 est.): Santafé de Bogotá, 7,350,000 (metro. area). **Largest cities (1995 est.):** Cali, 1,718,871; Medellín, 1,621,356; Barranquilla, 1,064,255; Cartagena, 745,689.
Monetary unit: Peso. **Language:** Spanish. **Ethnicity/race:** mestizo 58%, white 20%, mulatto 14%, black 4%, mixed black-Indian 3%, Indian 1%. **Religion:** Roman Catholic 95%. **Literacy rate:** 87% (1990)
Economic summary: GDP/PPP (1999 est.): $245.1 billion; per capita $6,200. **Real growth rate:** –5%. **Inflation:** 9.2% (1999). **Unemployment:** 20% (1999 est.). **Arable land:** 4%. **Agriculture:** coffee, cut flowers, bananas, rice, tobacco, corn, sugarcane, cocoa beans, oilseed, vegetables; forest products; shrimp. **Labor force:** 16.8 million (1997 est.); services, 46%; agriculture, 30%; industry, 24% (1990). **Industries:** textiles, food processing, oil, clothing and footwear, beverages, chemicals, cement; gold, coal, emeralds. **Natural resources:** petroleum, natural gas, coal, iron ore, nickel, gold, copper, emeralds, hydropower. **Exports:** $11.5 billion (f.o.b., 1999 est.): petroleum, coffee, coal, gold, bananas, cut flowers. **Imports:** $10 billion (f.o.b., 1999 est.): industrial equipment, transportation equipment, consumer goods, chemicals, paper products, fuels, electricity. **Major trading partners:** U.S., EU, Andean Community, Japan.

Geography Colombia, in the northwest part of South America, is the only country on that continent that borders both the Atlantic and Pacific Oceans. It is nearly equal in size to the combined areas of California and Texas. Colombia is bordered by Panama on the northwest, on the east by Venezuela and Brazil, and on the southwest by Peru and Ecuador. Through the western half of the country, three Andean ranges run north and south, merging into one at the Ecuadorian border. The eastern half is a low, jungle-covered plain, drained by spurs of the Amazon and Orinoco Rivers, inhabited mostly by isolated tropical-forest Indian tribes. The fertile plateau and valley of the eastern range are the most densely populated parts of the country.

Government Republic.

History Little is known about the various Indian tribes who inhabited Colombia before the Spanish arrived. In 1510 Spaniards founded Darien, the first permanent European settlement on the American mainland. In 1538 they established the colony of New Granada, the area's name until 1861.

After a 14-year struggle, in which Simón Bolívar's Venezuelan troops won the battle of Boyacá in Colombia on Aug. 7, 1819, independence was attained in 1824. Bolívar united Colombia, Venezuela, Panama, and Ecuador in the Republic of Greater Colombia (1819–1830), but lost Venezuela and Ecuador to separatists. Two political parties dominated the region: the Conservatives believed in a strong central government and a powerful church; the Liberals believed in a decentralized government, strong regional power, and a less influential role for the church. Bolívar was himself a Conservative, while his vice president, Francisco de Paula Santander, was the founder of the Liberal Party.

Santander served as president between 1832 and 1836, a period of relative stability, but by 1840 civil war erupted. Other periods of Liberal dominance (1849–1857 and 1861–1880), which sought to disestablish the Roman Catholic Church, were marked by insurrection. Nine different governments followed, each rewriting the constitution. In 1861, the country was called the United States of New Granada; in 1863 it became the United States of Colombia; and in 1885, it became the Republic of Colombia. In 1899 a brutal civil war broke out, the War of a Thousand Days, that lasted until 1902. The following year, Colombia lost its claims to the U.S. of the Canal Zone. Panama declared its independence in 1903.

The Conservatives held power until 1930, when revolutionary pressure put the Liberals back in power. The Liberal administrations of Enrique Olaya Herrera and Alfonso López (1930–1938) were marked by social reforms that failed to solve the country's problems, and in 1946, a period of insurrection and banditry broke out, referred to as La Violencia, which claimed hundreds of thousands of lives by 1958. Laureano Gómez (1950–1953); the army chief of staff, Gen. Gustavo Rojas Pinilla (1953–1956); and a military junta (1956–1957) sought to curb disorder by repression.

Marxist guerrilla groups organized in the 1960s and 1970s, most notably the May 19th Movement (M-19) and the Revolutionary Armed Forces of Colombia (FARC), plunged the country into violence and instability. In the 1970s and 1980s Colombia became one of the international centers for illegal drug production and trafficking, and at times the drug cartels (the Medellín and Cali cartels were the most notorious) virtually controlled the country.

Belisario Betancur Cuartas, a Conservative who assumed the presidency in 1982, unsuccessfully attempted to stem the guerrilla violence. In an official war against drug trafficking, Colombia became a public battleground with bombs, killings, and kidnappings. By 1989, homicide had become the leading cause of death in the nation. Elected president in 1990, César Gaviria Trujillo proposed lenient punishment in exchange for surrender by the leading drug dealers.

Ernesto Samper of the Liberal Party became president in 1994. In 1996 he was accused of accepting campaign contributions from drug traffickers, but the House of Representatives absolved him of the charges.

Andrés Pastrana Arango was elected president in 1998, pledging to clean up corruption. In Dec. 1999 the Colombian military reported that 2,787 people were kidnapped that year—the largest number in the world—and blamed rebels. The murder rate soared in 1999, with some 23,000 people reported killed by leftist guerrillas, right-wing paramilitaries, drug traffickers, and common criminals. The violence has created more than 100,000 refugees, while 2 million Colombians have left the country in the past several years.

In Aug. 2000, the U.S. government approved "Plan Colombia," a $1.3 billion in antidrug trafficking aid that Pastrana is using to undercut drug production and to prevent guerrilla groups from benefiting from drug production. In Aug. 2001, Pastrana signed "war legislation," which expands the rights of the military in dealing with rebels.

Comoros

UNION OF COMOROS ISLANDS

President: Col. Azaly Assoumani (1999)
Area: 838 sq mi (2,170 sq km)
Population (2001 est.): 596,202 (average annual rate of natural increase: 3.0%); birth rate: 39.5/1000; infant mortality rate: 84.1/1000; density per sq mi: 712
Capital and largest city (1990 est.): Moroni (on Grande Comoro), 23,432. **Monetary unit:** Franc CFA.
Languages: French and Arab (both official), Shaafi Islam (Swahili dialect), Malagasu. **Ethnicity/race:** Antalote, Cafre, Makoa, Oimatsaha, Sakalava.
Religions: Sunni Muslim 86%, Roman Catholic 14%.
Literacy rate: 48% (1980)
Economic summary: GDP/PPP: (1998 est.) $410 million; per capita $725. **Real growth rate:** 0%. **Inflation:** 4% (1998). **Unemployment:** 20% (1996 est.). **Arable land:** 35%. **Agriculture:** vanilla, cloves, perfume essences, copra, coconuts, bananas, cassava (tapioca). **Labor force:** 144,500 (1996 est.): agriculture, 80%; government, 3%. **Industries:** tourism, perfume distillation, textiles, furniture, jewelry, construction materials, soft drinks. **Natural resources:** negl. **Exports:** $9.3 million (f.o.b., 1998 est.): vanilla, ylang-ylang, cloves, perfume oil, copra. **Imports:** $49.5 million (f.o.b., 1998 est.): rice and other foodstuffs, consumer goods; petroleum products, cement, transport equipment. **Major trading partners:** France, U.S., Germany, South Africa, Kenya.

Geography The Comoros Islands—Grande Comoro (Ngazidja), Anjouan, Mohéli, and Mayotte (which is not part of the country and retains ties to France)—are an archipelago of volcanic origin in the Indian Ocean, 190 mi off the coast of Mozambique.

Government Islamic republic run by a military junta.

History Comoros was frequented by travelers from Africa, Madagascar, Indonesia, and Arabia before the first Europeans encountered the islands. Arabic influence has been the strongest.

France colonized Mayotte in 1843 and by 1904 had annexed the remainder of the archipelago. In a 1974 referendum, 95% of the population voted for independence. The exception was Mayotte, which, with its Christian majority, voted against joining the other mainly Islamic islands in independence. Today it remains a French overseas territory. The remaining Comoros islands declared themselves independent on July 6, 1975.

A month after independence, Justice Minister Ali Soilih staged a coup with the help of a group of white mercenaries known as Les Affreux (The Terrible Ones), overthrowing the new nation's first president, Ahmed Abdallah. He was himself overthrown on May 13, 1978. In 1989 another coup took place.

A slump in world prices during the 1990s for Comoros's main exports, vanilla and ylang-ylang, exacerbated the country's poverty—the annual per capita income is $725.

The island of Anjouan declared independence on Aug. 3, 1997, after months of protests and clashes with security forces. The secessionists wanted a return to French rule, contending that independence from France has brought economic disaster and political chaos. Mohéli, the smallest island, also seceded. But France refused to support the secession of either island.

In Sept. 1997, President Mohamed Taki's forces attempted to retake Anjouan but failed. Taki then declared a state of emergency. Peace talks in spring 1999 ended inconclusively when all other Anjouan representatives failed to sign a peace agreement that the other two islands had agreed to. Anti-Anjouan riots took place on Grande Comoros, and on April 30, 1999, Col. Azaly Assoumani led a coup, overthrowing interim president Tadjidine. He promised interim military rule would end in a year. This was the first of Comoros's four coups to be carried out by the Comorian army itself rather than by mercenaries. The other three were led by the notorious French mercenary leader "Colonel" Bob Denard. The island of Anjouan continued to fight against the government on Grande Comoros throughout 1999.

In March 2000 the Organization of African Unity cut communications with Anjouan in an effort to end the rebellion. The OAU also demanded that President Assoumani return the Comoros to civilian rule and imposed a trade embargo. In Feb. 2001 the president signed an OAU-brokered reconciliation agreement with various political leaders from the three islands, including the secessionist leader of Anjouan, Col. Said Abeid. Negotiations over a new constitution proceeded at a snail's pace. But in Aug. 2001, the peace process was again disrupted when soldiers on Anjouan led a coup against its separatist leader, Abeid.

Congo

REPUBLIC OF CONGO

National name: République Populaire du Congo
President: Denis Sassou-Nguesso (1997)
Area: 132,046 sq mi (342,000 sq km)
Population (2001 est.): 2,894,336 (average annual rate of natural increase: 2.2%); birth rate: 38.2/1000; infant mortality rate: 99.7/1000; density per sq mi: 22
Capital and largest city (1992 est.): Brazzaville, 937,580. **Other large city (1992 est.):** Pointe-Noire, 576,206. **Monetary unit:** Franc CFA. **Languages:** French (official), Lingala, Kikongo, others. **Ethnicity/ race:** south: Kongo 48%; north: Sangha 20%, M'Bochi 12%; center: Teke 17%, Europeans 8,500 (mostly French). **Religions:** Christian 50%, animist 48%, Muslim 2%. **Literacy rate:** 57% (1990)
Economic summary: GDP/PPP (1999 est.): $4.15 billion; per capita $1,530. **Real growth rate:** 5%. **Inflation:** 4%. **Unemployment:** n.a. **Arable land:** 0%. **Agriculture:** cassava (tapioca), sugar, rice, corn, peanuts, vegetables, coffee, cocoa; forest products. **Labor force:** n.a. **Industries:** petroleum extraction, cement kilning, lumbering, brewing, sugar milling, palm oil, soap, cigarette making. **Natural resources:** petroleum, timber, potash, lead, zinc, uranium, copper, phosphates, natural gas, hydropower. **Exports:** $1.7 billion (f.o.b., 1999): petroleum 50%, lumber, plywood, sugar, cocoa, coffee, diamonds. **Imports:** $770 million (f.o.b., 1999): petroleum products, capital equipment, construction materials, foodstuffs. **Major trading partners:** U.S., Benelux, Germany, Italy, Taiwan, China, France, Belgium, UK

Geography The Congo is situated in west-central Africa astride the equator. It borders Gabon, Cameroon, the Central African Republic, the Democratic Republic of the Congo, and the Angola exclave of Cabinda, with a short stretch of coast on the South Atlantic. Its area is nearly three times that of Pennsylvania. Most of the inland is tropical rain forest, drained by tributaries of the Congo River, which flows south along the eastern border with the Democratic Republic of the Congo to Stanley Pool. The narrow coastal plain rises to highlands separated from the inland plateaus by the 200-mile-wide Niari River valley, which gives passage to the coast.

Government Republic.

History In precolonial times, the region now called the Republic of Congo was dominated by three kingdoms: Kongo (originating about 1000), the Loango (flourishing in the 17th century), and Tio. After the Portuguese located the Congo River in 1482, commerce was carried on with the tribes, especially the slave trade.

The Frenchman Pierre Savorgnan de Brazza signed a treaty with Makoko, ruler of the Bateke people, in 1880, thus establishing French control. It was first called French Congo, and after 1905 Middle Congo. With Gabon and Ubangi-Shari, it became the colony of French Equatorial Africa in 1910. Abuse of laborers led to public outcry against the French colonialists as well as rebellions among the Congolese, but the exploitation of the native workers continued until 1930. During World War II the colony joined Chad in supporting the Free French cause against the Vichy government. The Congo proclaimed its independence without leaving the French Community in 1960, calling itself the Republic of Congo.

Congo's second president, Alphonse Massemba-Débat, instituted a Marxist-Leninist government. In 1968, Maj. Marien Ngouabi overthrew him but kept Congo on a socialist course. He was sworn in for a second five-year term in 1975. A four-man commando squad assassinated Ngouabi on March 18, 1977. Col. Joachim Yhombi-Opango, army chief of staff, assumed the presidency on April 4. Yhombi-Opango resigned on Feb. 4, 1979, and was replaced by Col. Denis Sassou-Nguesso.

In July 1990 the leaders of the ruling party voted to end the one-party system. A national political conference, hailed as a model for sub-Saharan Africa, renounced Marxism in 1991, and scheduled the country's first free elections for 1992. The national conference ending in June 1991 rewrote the constitution.

Political and ethnic tensions intensified in 1993 after legislative elections in May and runoffs in June. The opposition's rejection of the results developed into violence. A peace agreement was achieved between the government and the opposition in Aug. 1994. A four-month civil war (June 5–Oct. 15, 1997) devastated Brazzaville, the capital. Buttressed by military aid from Angola, former Marxist dictator Denis Sassou-Nguesso overthrew President Pascal Lissouba, the country's first democratically elected president. In late 1999 a peace agreement was signed between Sassou-Nguesso, who comes from the north, and the rebels representing the populous south. The postwar period has been traumatic: a recurrence of sleeping sickness and other diseases have swept the country, yet 60% of its health centers are out of commission.

Congo, Democratic Republic of the

DEMOCRATIC REPUBLIC OF THE CONGO

President: Joseph Kabila (2001)
Area: 905,563 sq mi (2,345,410 sq km)
Population (2001 est.): 53,624,718 (average annual rate of natural increase: 3.1%); birth rate: 46.0/1000; infant mortality rate: 99.9/1000; density per sq mi: 59
Capital and largest city (2000 est.): Kinshasa, 6,050,000 (metro. area). **Other large cities:** Lubumbashi, 851,381; Mbuji-Mayi, 806,475; Kisangani, 417,517; Kolwezi, 417,810. **Monetary unit:** Congolese franc. **Languages:** French (official), Swahili, Lingala, Ishiluba, and Kikongo, others. **Ethnicity/race:** over 200 African ethnic groups, the majority are Bantu; the four largest tribes—Mongo, Luba, Kongo (all Bantu), and the Mangbetu-Azande (Hamitic)—make up about 45% of the population. **Religions:** Roman Catholic 50%, Protestant 20%, Kimbanguist 10%, Islam 10%; syncretic and traditional, 10%. **Literacy rate:** 72% (1990)
Economic summary: GDP/PPP (1999 est.): $35.7 billion; per capita $710. **Real growth rate:** 1%. **Inflation:** 46%. **Unemployment:** n.a. **Arable land:** 3%. **Agriculture:** coffee, sugar, palm oil, rubber, tea, quinine, cassava (tapioca), palm oil, bananas, root crops, corn, fruits; wood products. **Labor force:** 14.51 million (1993 est.); agriculture, 65%; industry, 16%; services,19% (1991 est.). **Industries:** mining, mineral processing, consumer products (including textiles, footwear, cigarettes, processed foods and beverages), cement, diamonds. **Natural resources:** cobalt, copper, cadmium, petroleum, industrial and gem diamonds, gold, silver, zinc, manganese, tin, germanium, uranium, radium, bauxite, iron ore, coal, hydropower, timber. **Exports:** $530 million (f.o.b., 1998 est.): diamonds, copper, coffee, cobalt, crude oil. **Imports:** $460 million (f.o.b., 1998 est.): foodstuffs, mining and other machinery, transport equipment, fuels. **Major trading partners:** Benelux, U.S., South Africa, Finland, Nigeria, Kenya, China.

Geography Congo, in west-central Africa, is bordered by the Congo Republic, the Central African Republic, the Sudan, Uganda, Rwanda, Burundi, Tanzania, Zambia, Angola, and the Atlantic Ocean. It is one-quarter the size of the U.S. The principal rivers are the Ubangi and Bomu in the north and the Congo in the west, which flows into the Atlantic. The entire length of Lake Tanganyika lies along the eastern border with Tanzania and Burundi.

Government Dictatorship.

History Formerly the Belgian Congo, this territory was inhabited by ancient Negrito peoples (Pygmies), who were pushed into the mountains by Bantu and Nilotic invaders. The American correspondent Henry M. Stanley navigated the Congo River in 1877 and opened the interior to exploration. Commissioned by King Leopold II of the Belgians, Stanley made treaties with native chiefs that enabled the king to obtain personal title to the territory at the Berlin Conference of 1885.

Leopold accumulated a vast personal fortune from ivory and rubber through Congolese slave labor; 10 million people are estimated to have died from forced labor, starvation, and outright extermination during Leopold's colonial rule. His brutal exploitation of the Congo eventually became an international cause célèbre, prompting Belgium to take over administration of the Congo, which remained a colony until agitation for independence forced Brussels to grant freedom on June 30, 1960. The Katanga Province, led by Moise Tshombe, seceded from the new republic on July 11, and another mining province, South Kasai, followed. Belgium sent paratroopers to quell the civil war, and with President Joseph Kasavubu and Prime Minister Patrice Lumumba of the national government in conflict, the United Nations flew in a peacekeeping force.

Kasavubu staged an army coup in 1960 and handed Lumumba over to the Katangan forces. A UN investigating commission found that Lumumba had been killed by a Belgian mercenary in the presence of Tshombe, who was then the president of Katanga. Dag Hammarskjold, UN secretary-general, died in a plane crash en route to a peace conference with Tshombe on Sept. 17, 1961.

Tshombe rejected a national reconciliation plan in 1962 submitted by the UN. Tshombe's troops fired on the UN force in Dec., and in the ensuing conflict he capitulated on Jan. 14, 1963. The peacekeeping force withdrew, and, in a complete about-face, Kasavubu named Tshombe premier in order to fight a spreading rebellion. Tshombe used foreign mercenaries, and with the help of Belgian paratroops airlifted by U.S. planes, defeated the most serious opposition, a Communist-backed regime in the northeast.

Kasavubu abruptly dismissed Tshombe in 1965 and was himself ousted by Gen. Joseph-Desiré Mobutu, army chief of staff. The new president nationalized the Union Minière, the Belgian copper mining enterprise that had been a dominant force in the Congo since colonial days.

Mobutu eliminated opposition to win the election in 1970. In 1975, he nationalized much of the economy, barred religious instruction in schools, and decreed the adoption of African names. On March 8, 1977, invaders from Angola calling themselves the Congolese National Liberation Front pushed into Shaba and threatened the important mining center of Kolwezi. France and Belgium responded to Mobutu's pleas for help with weapons, but the U.S. gave only nonmilitary supplies. In April, France flew 1,500 Moroccan troops to Shaba to defeat the invaders, who were, Mobutu charged, Soviet-inspired and Cuban-led. U.S. intelligence sources, however, confirmed Soviet and Cuban denials of any participation and identified the rebels as former Katanga gendarmes who had fled to Angola after their 1963 defeat.

In April 1990 Mobutu announced he intended to introduce multiparty democracy but that elections in

Jan. 1991 would reduce the number of political parties to two besides his own. Opposition leaders denounced the scheme as giving Mobutu's party an unfair advantage.

In early 1993 Mobutu rejected Western demands that he yield power and announced plans to regroup his one-party Parliament, dismissing the main opposition leader, Prime Minister Tshisekedi. In Jan. 1994 Mobutu dissolved Parliament and dismissed his prime minister, which led to a general strike in the capital.

Mobutu Sese Seko was overthrown in May 1997, ending one of the world's most corrupt and megalomaniacal regimes. The last of the CIA-nurtured cold war despots, Mobutu deftly courted France and the U.S., which used Zaire as a launching pad for covert operations against bordering countries, particularly Marxist Angola. Mobutu's disastrous policies drove his country to economic collapse while he siphoned off millions of dollars for himself.

Laurent Kabila and his long-standing but little-known guerrilla movement launched a seven-month campaign that ousted Mobutu. The country was renamed the Democratic Republic of the Congo, its name before Mobutu changed it to Zaire in 1971. Mobutu's downfall began in Oct. 1996, when he planned to banish the Zairian Tutsis who had lived for centuries in eastern Zaire. Neighboring Rwanda's Tutsi-led government came to their aid, as did other rebel groups, one of which was led by Kabila. After conquering eastern Zaire, Kabila earned the support of a host of Mobutu's enemies, including Uganda, Burundi, Tanzania, Zambia, Zimbabwe, and Angola. His troops swept through the country, encountering little resistance. Mobutu fled in exile to Morocco on May 16, where he died of cancer in Sept.

Elation over Mobutu's downfall faded as Kabila's own autocratic style emerged, and he seemed devoid of a clear plan for reconstructing the country. He stymied UN human rights investigations into the alleged massacres of Hutu refugees and continued to depend on foreign troops for border skirmishes rather than establish a strong national army. Many Congolese dismissed him as a puppet ruler who allowed his country to be overrun by outsiders, particularly the Rwandans. At the same time he alienated many of his former supporters, including Rwanda and Uganda.

In Aug. 1998, Congolese rebel forces, led by ethnic Tutsis in eastern Congo, who were backed by Rwanda and Uganda, began attacking Kabila's forces. The rebels gained control of a large portion of the country until Angolan, Namibian, and Zimbabwean troops came to Kabila's aid and pushed the rebels back. In July 1999, a cease-fire agreement was signed by all six of the countries involved, but it has not held. Further complicating the situation, the rebel force, the Congolese Rally for Democracy, RCD, split in May 1999 and have at times fought against each other.

In Jan. 2001, Kabila was assassinated, allegedly by one of his bodyguards. His young and inexperienced son Joseph became the new president, and the new president has demonstrated a willingness to engage in talks to end the civil war. In Feb. 2001, the UN Security Council approved a plan for the withdrawal of various fighting factions and to locate UN peacekeepers throughout the country. In response, both Rwanda and Uganda withdrew some of their troops. There are an estimated 50,000 foreign troops from five nations currently fighting in the Congo.

Costa Rica

REPUBLIC OF COSTA RICA

National name: República de Costa Rica
President: Miguel Angel Rodríguez (1998)
Area: 19,730 sq mi (51,100 sq km)
Population (2001 est.): 3,773,057 (average annual rate of natural increase: 1.6%); birth rate: 20.3/1000; infant mortality rate: 11.2/1000; density per sq mi: 191
Capital and largest city (1994 est.): San José, 315,909. **Monetary unit:** Colón. **Language:** Spanish. **Ethnicity/race:** white (including mestizo) 96%, black 2%, Indian 1%, Chinese 1%. **Religion:** Roman Catholic 95%. **Literacy rate:** 93% (1990)
Economic summary: GDP/PPP (1999 est.): $26 billion; per capita $7,100. **Real growth rate:** 7%. **Inflation:** 10.8%. **Unemployment:** 5.6% (1998 est.); 7.5% underemployment. **Arable land:** 6%. **Agriculture:** coffee, bananas, sugar, corn, rice, beans, potatoes; beef; timber. **Labor force:** 1.377 million (1998); agriculture, 20%; industry, 22%; services, 58%. **Industries:** microprocessors, food processing, textiles and clothing, construction materials, fertilizer, plastic products. **Natural resources:** hydropower. **Exports:** $6.4 billion (f.o.b., 1999 est.): coffee, bananas, sugar; textiles, electronic components, electricity. **Imports:** $6.5 billion (c.i.f., 1999 est.): raw materials, consumer goods, capital equipment, petroleum, electricity. **Major trading partners:** U.S., EU, Central America, Japan, Mexico, Venezuela.

Geography This Central American country lies between Nicaragua to the north and Panama to the south. Its area slightly exceeds that of Vermont and New Hampshire combined. It has a narrow Pacific coastal region. Cocos Island (10 sq mi; 26 sq km), about 300 mi (483 km) off the Pacific Coast, is under Costa Rican sovereignty.

Government Democratic republic.

History Costa Rica was inhabited by an estimated 25,000 Indians when Columbus explored it in 1502. Few of the Indians survived the Spanish conquest, which began in 1563. The region grew slowly and was administered as a Spanish province. Costa Rica achieved independence in 1821 but was absorbed for two years by Agustín de Iturbide in his Mexican empire. It became a republic in 1848. Except for the military dictatorship of Tomás Guardia from 1870 to 1882, Costa Rica has enjoyed one of the most democratic governments in Latin America.

In the 1970s rising oil prices, falling international commodity prices, and inflation hurt the economy. Efforts have since been made to reduce reliance on coffee, banana, and beef exports. Tourism is now a major business. Rodrigo Carazo Odio became president in 1978. Oscar Arias Sanchez, who became president in 1986, was awarded the Nobel Peace Prize in 1987 for his role in negotiating settlements to both the Nicaraguan and the Salvadoran civil wars.

José Maria Figueres Olsen of the National Liberation Party became president in 1994. He opposed economic suggestions made by the International Monetary Fund, instead favoring greater government intervention in the economy. The World Bank subsequently withheld $100 million of financing. In 1998, Miguel Angel Rodríguez of the Social Christian Unity Party became president. He favors economic reforms, such as privatization. In 2000 Costa Rica and Nicaragua resolved a long-standing dispute over navigation of the San Juan River, which forms their border.

Côte d'Ivoire

REPUBLIC OF CÔTE D'IVOIRE

National name: République de la Côte d'Ivoire
President: Gen. Robert Guei (1999)
Prime Minister: Seydou Elimane Diarra (2000)
Area: 124,502 sq mi (322,460 sq km)
Population (2001 est.): 16,393,221 (average annual rate of natural increase: 2.4%); birth rate: 40.4/1000; infant mortality rate: 93.7/1000; density per sq mi: 132
Capital (1984): Yamoussoukro (official), 120,000; Abidjan (administrative). **Largest city (est. 1988):** Abidjan, 2,797,000. **Monetary unit:** Franc CFA.
Languages: French (official) and African languages (Diaula esp.). **Ethnicity/race:** Baoule 23%, Bete 18%, Senoufou 15%, Malinke 11%, Agni, foreign Africans (mostly Burkinabe and Malians, about 3 million). **Religions:** indigenous 60%, Islam 23%, Christian 17%. **Literacy rate:** 54% (1990)
Economic summary:GDP/PPP (1999 est.): $25.7 billion; per capita $1,600. **Real growth rate:** 5%. **Inflation:** 2.5%. **Unemployment:** n.a. **Arable land:** 8%. **Agriculture:** coffee, cocoa beans, bananas, palm kernels, corn, rice, manioc (tapioca), sweet potatoes, sugar, cotton, rubber; timber. **Labor force:** n.a. **Industries:** foodstuffs, beverages; wood products, oil refining, automobile assembly, textiles, fertilizer, construction materials, electricity. **Natural resources:** petroleum, diamonds, manganese, iron ore, cobalt, bauxite, copper, hydropower. **Exports:** $3.9 billion (f.o.b., 1999 est.): cocoa 37%, coffee, tropical woods, petroleum, cotton, bananas, pineapples, palm oil, cotton, fish (1998). **Imports:** $2.6 billion (f.o.b., 1999 est.): food, consumer goods; capital goods, fuel, transport equipment. **Major trading partners:** France, Netherlands, U.S., Italy, Germany.

Geography Côte d'Ivoire (also known as the Ivory Coast), in western Africa on the Gulf of Guinea is a little larger than New Mexico. Its neighbors are Liberia, Guinea, Mali, Burkina Faso, and Ghana. The country consists of a coastal strip in the south, dense forests in the interior, and savannas in the north.

Government Presidential/parliamentary democracy until Dec. 1999, when a coup installed a military dictatorship.

History Côte d'Ivoire was originally made up of numerous isolated settlements; today it represents more than sixty distinct tribes, including the Baoule, Bete, Senoufou, Agni, Malinke, Dan, and Lobi. Côte d'Ivoire attracted both French and Portuguese merchants in the 15th century who were in search of ivory and slaves. French traders set up establishments early in the 19th century, and in 1842, the French obtained territorial concessions from local tribes, gradually extending their influence along the coast and inland. The area was organized as a territory in 1893, became an autonomous republic in the French Union after World War II, and achieved independence on Aug. 7, 1960. Côte d'Ivoire formed a customs union in 1959 with Dahomey (Benin), Niger, and Burkina Faso. The nation's economy is one of the most developed in sub-Saharan Africa. It is the world's largest exporter of cocoa and one of the largest exporters of coffee.

From independence until his death in 1993, Felix Houphouët-Boigny served as president. Massive protests by students, farmers, and professionals forced the president to legalize opposition parties and hold the first contested presidential election in Oct. 1990, which Houphouët-Boigny won with 81% of the vote. Beginning in Sept. 1998, thousands of demonstrators protested a constitutional revision that granted President Henri Konan Bédié greatly enhanced powers. Bédié has also promoted the concept of *ivoirité,* which, roughly translated, means "pure Ivoirian pride." Although its defenders describe *ivoirité* as a term of positive national pride, it has led to a dangerous xenophobia, with numerous ethnic Malians and Burkinans being driven out of the country in 1999.

President Bédié was overthrown in the country's first military coup in Dec. 1999, and Gen. Robert Guei assumed control of the country. As a result, the majority of foreign aid to the country has ceased.

Presidential elections were held in Oct. 2000, between the country's military ruler, Gen. Robert Guei, and a civilian opposition candidate, Laurent Gbagbo. Each declared victory in an election most believe to have been rife with fraud. Popular outcry against Guei soon turned violent, forcing him to leave the country, and Gbagbo assumed the presidency. Many observers questioned his mandate, however, since the opposition leader Alassane Ouattara had been excluded from the election on the specious grounds that he was not a pure-blooded Ivoirian. Parliamentary elections in March 2001 were considered an important indication of genuine political support because each of the three main political parties—those affiliated with Gbagbo, Ouattara, and Guei—were permitted to participate. Ouattara's party in fact trounced Gbagbo's party, weakening the president's authority.

Croatia

REPUBLIC OF CROATIA

President: Stipe Mesic (2000)
Prime Minister: Ivica Racan (2000)
Area: 21,829 sq mi (56,538 sq km)
Population (2001 est.): 4,334,142 (average annual rate of natural increase: 0.1%); birth rate: 12.8/1000; infant mortality rate: 7.2/1000; density per sq mi: 199
Capital (1991): Zagreb, 930,753. **Other large cities (1991):** Split, 189,444; Rijeka, 167,757; Osijek, 129,792. **Monetary unit:** Kuna (May 1994). **Language:** What was once known as Serbo-Croatian is now known as Serbian, Croatian, or Bosnian, depending on the speaker's political and ethnic affiliation. **Ethnicity/race:** Croat 78%, Serb 12%, Muslim 0.9%, Hungarian 0.5%, Slovenian 0.5%, others 8.1% (1991). **Religions:** Catholic 76.5%, Orthodox 11.1%, Slavic Muslim 1.2%, Protestant 0.4%, others 10.8%. **Literacy rate:** 97% (1991)
Economic summary: GDP/PPP (1999 est.): $23.9 billion; per capita $5,100. **Real growth rate:** 0%. **Inflation:** 4.4% (1999). **Unemployment:** 20%. **Arable land:** 21%. **Agriculture:** wheat, corn, sugar beets, sunflower seed, alfalfa, clover, olives, citrus, grapes, vegetables; livestock, dairy products. **Labor force:** 1.65 million (1999); agriculture, n.a.; industry, n.a.; services, n.a. **Industries:** chemicals and plastics, machine tools, fabricated metal, electronics, pig iron and rolled steel products, aluminum, paper, wood products, construction materials, textiles, shipbuilding, petroleum and petroleum refining, food and beverages; tourism. **Natural resources:** oil, some coal, bauxite, low-grade iron ore, calcium, natural asphalt, silica, mica, clays, salt, hydropower. **Exports:** $4.5 billion (f.o.b., 1998): textiles, chemicals, foodstuffs, fuels. **Imports:** $8.4 billion (c.i.f., 1998): machinery, transport and electrical equipment, chemicals, fuels and lubricants, foodstuffs. **Major trading partners:** Italy, Germany, Bosnia and Herzegovina, Slovenia, Austria.

Geography Croatia is a former Yugoslav republic on the Adriatic Sea; it is about the size of West Virginia. Part of Croatia is a barren, rocky region lying in the Dinaric Alps. The Zagorje region north of the capital, Zagreb, is a land of rolling hills, and the fertile agricultural region of the Pannonian Plain is bordered by the Drava, Danube, and Sava Rivers in the east. Over one-third of Croatia is forested.

Government Parliamentary democracy.

History Croatia, at one time the Roman province of Pannonia, was settled in the 7th century by the Croats. They converted to Christianity between the 7th and 9th centuries and adopted the Roman alphabet under the suzerainty of Charlemagne. In 925, the Croats defeated Byzantine and Frankish invaders and established their own independent kingdom, which reached its peak during the 11th century. A civil war ensued in 1089, which later led to the country being conquered by the Hungarians in 1091. The signing of the *Pacta Conventa* by Croatian tribal chiefs and the Hungarian king in 1102 united the two nations politically under the Hungarian monarch, but Croatia retained its autonomy.

When the Hungarians were defeated by the Turks in 1526, most of Croatia fell under Ottoman rule until the end of the 17th century. It maintained its Catholicism (the religion of about 80% of the country) during the centuries of Muslim rule, and its religion has always been one of Croatia's defining characteristics, distinguishing it from the other Balkan states. The rest of Croatia elected Ferdinand of Austria as its king and became associated with the Hapsburgs of Austria. After the establishment of the Austro-Hungarian kingdom in 1867, Croatia and Slovenia became part of Hungary until the collapse of Austria-Hungary in 1918 following its defeat in World War I. On Oct. 29, 1918, Croatia proclaimed its independence and joined in union with Montenegro, Serbia, and Slovenia to form the Kingdom of Serbs, Croats, and Slovenes. The name was changed to Yugoslavia in 1929.

When Germany invaded Yugoslavia in 1941, Croatia became a Nazi puppet state. Croatian Fascists, the Ustachi, slaughtered countless Serbs and Jews during the war. After Germany was defeated in 1945, Croatia was made into a republic of the newly reestablished Communist nation of Yugoslavia. In June 1991, the Croatian Parliament passed a declaration of independence from Yugoslavia. A six-month civil war followed with the Serbian-dominated Yugoslavian army. The war claimed thousands of lives and wrought mass destruction.

A UN cease-fire was arranged on Jan. 2, 1992. The Security Council in Feb. approved sending a 14,000-member peacekeeping force to monitor the cease-fire and protect the minority Serbs in Croatia. In a 1993 referendum the Serb-occupied portion of Croatia (Krajina) resoundingly voted for integration with Serbs in Bosnia and Serbia proper. Although the Zagreb government and representatives of Krajina signed a cease-fire in March 1994, further negotiations broke down. In a lightning-quick operation, the Croatian army retook western Slavonia in May 1995. Similarly, in Aug. the central Croatian region of Krajina, held by Serbs, was returned to Zagreb's control.

Announcing on television in 1999 that "national issues are more important than democracy," President Tudjman continued to alienate Croatians with his authoritarian rule, out-of-touch nationalism, and disastrous handling of the war-shattered economy. In Dec. 1999, Tudjman died and was succeeded by Stipe Mesic, a reformer. One of his first acts in office was to invite back the 300,000 ethnic Serbs who had been banished from the country under Tudjman.

Cuba

REPUBLIC OF CUBA

National name: República de Cuba
President: Fidel Castro (1976)
Area: 42,803 sq mi (110,860 sq km)
Population (2001 est.): 11,184,023 (average annual rate of natural increase: 0.5%); birth rate: 12.4/1000; infant mortality rate: 7.4/1000; density per sq mi: 261
Capital and largest city (1994 est.): Havana, 2,241,000. **Other large cities (1994 est.):** Santiago de Cuba, 440,084; Camagüey, 293,961; Holguin, 242,085; Guantánamo, 207,796; Santa Clara, 205,400. **Monetary unit:** Peso. **Language:** Spanish. **Ethnicity/race:** mulatto 51%, white 37%, black 11%, Chinese 1%. **Religion:** at least 85% nominally Roman Catholic before Castro assumed power. **Literacy rate:** 94% (1990)
Economic summary: GDP/PPP (1999 est.): $18.6 billion; per capita $1,700. **Real growth rate:** 6.2%. **Inflation:** 0.3%. **Unemployment:** 6% (December 1999 est.). **Arable land:** 24%. **Agriculture:** sugarcane, tobacco, citrus, coffee, rice, potatoes, beans; livestock. **Labor force:** 4.5 million economically active population; note: state sector, 76%; nonstate sector, 24% (1996 est.); agriculture, 23%; industry, 24%; services, 53%. **Industries:** sugar, petroleum, food, tobacco, textiles, chemicals, paper and wood products, metals (particularly nickel), cement, fertilizers, consumer goods, agricultural machinery. **Natural resources:** cobalt, nickel, iron ore, copper, manganese, salt, timber, silica, petroleum, arable land. **Exports:** $1.4 billion (f.o.b., 1999 est.): sugar, nickel, tobacco, shellfish, medical products, citrus, coffee. **Imports:** $3.2 billion (c.i.f., 1999 est.): petroleum, food, machinery, chemicals. **Major trading partners:** Russia, Netherlands, Canada, Spain, Venezuela, Mexico.

Geography The largest island of the West Indies group (equal in area to Pennsylvania), Cuba is also the westernmost—just west of Hispaniola (Haiti and the Dominican Republic), and 90 mi (145 km) south of Key West, Fla., at the entrance to the Gulf of Mexico. The island is mountainous in the southeast and south-central area (Sierra Maestra). It is flat or rolling elsewhere. Cuba also includes numerous smaller islands, islets, and cays.

Government Communist state.

History Arawak (or Taino) Indians inhabiting Cuba when Columbus landed on the island in 1492 died from diseases brought by sailors and settlers. By 1511, Spaniards under Diego Velásquez had established settlements. Havana's superb harbor made it a common transit point to and from Spain.

In the early 1800s, Cuba's sugarcane industry boomed, requiring massive numbers of black slaves. A simmering independence movement turned into open warfare from 1867 to 1878. Slavery was abolished in 1886. In 1895, the poet José Marti led the struggle that finally ended Spanish rule, thanks largely to U.S. intervention in 1898 after the sinking of the battleship *Maine* in Havana harbor.

An 1899 treaty made Cuba an independent republic under U.S. protection. The U.S. occupation, which ended in 1902, suppressed yellow fever and brought large American investments. The 1901 Platt Amendment allowed the U.S. to intervene in Cuba's affairs, which it did four times from 1906 to 1920. Cuba terminated the amendment in 1934.

In 1933 a group of army officers, including army sergeant Fulgencio Batista, overthrew President Gerado Machado. Batista became president in 1940, running a corrupt police state.

In 1956, Fidel Castro Ruz launched a revolution from his camp in the Sierra Maestra mountains. Castro's brother Raul, and Ernesto (Ché) Guevara, an Argentine physician, were his top lieutenants. Many anti-Batista landowners supported the rebels. The U.S. ended military aid to Cuba in 1958, and on New Year's Day 1959, Batista fled into exile and Castro took over the government.

The U.S. initially welcomed what looked like a democratic Cuba, but a rude awakening came within a few months when Castro established military tribunals for political opponents and jailed hundreds. Castro disavowed Cuba's 1952 military pact with the U.S., confiscated U.S. assets, and established Soviet-style collective farms. The U.S. broke relations with Cuba on Jan. 3, 1961, and Castro formalized his alliance with the Soviet Union. Thousands of Cubans fled the country.

In 1961 a U.S.-backed group of Cuban exiles invaded Cuba. Planned during the Eisenhower administration, President John Kennedy gave the go-ahead for the invasion but refused to give U.S. air support. The landing at the Bay of Pigs on April 17, 1961, was a fiasco. The invaders did not receive popular Cuban support and were easily repulsed by the Cuban military.

A Soviet attempt to install medium-range missiles in Cuba—capable of striking targets in the United States with nuclear warheads—provoked a crisis in 1962. Denouncing the Soviets for "deliberate deception," on Oct. 22 Kennedy said that the U.S. would blockade Cuba so the missiles could not be delivered. Six days later Soviet premier Nikita Khrushchev ordered the missile sites dismantled and returned to the USSR, in return for a U.S. pledge not to attack Cuba.

Cuba fomented Communist revolution around the world, especially in Angola, where thousands of Cuban troops were sent in the 1980s. The U.S. established limited diplomatic ties with Cuba on Sept. 1, 1977, making it easier for Cuban Americans to visit the island. Contact with the more affluent Cuban Americans prompted a wave of discontent in Cuba, producing a flood of asylum seekers. In response, Castro opened the port of Mariel to a "freedom flotilla" of boats from the U.S., allowing 125,000 to flee to Miami. After the refugees arrived, it was discovered their ranks were swelled with prisoners, mental patients, homosexuals, and others unwanted by the Cuban government.

Russian aid, which had long supported Cuba's failing economy, ended when communism collapsed in eastern Europe in 1990. Cuba's foreign trade also plummeted, producing a severe economic crisis. In 1993, Castro permitted limited private enterprise, allowed Cubans to possess convertible currencies, and encouraged foreign investment in its tourist industry. In March 1996, the U.S. tightened its embargo with the Helms-Burton Act.

Christmas became an official holiday in 1997, for the first time since the revolution, in response to Pope John Paul II's 1998 visit to Cuba, which raised hopes for greater religious freedom.

In June 2000 Castro won a publicity bonanza when the Clinton administration sent Elian Gonzalez, a young boy found clinging to an inner tube, back to Cuba. The U.S. Cuban community had demanded that the boy remain in Miami rather than be returned to his father in Cuba. By many accounts, the influential Cuban-Americans lost public sympathy by pitting political ideology against familial bonds. In 2001 Castro's poor appearance prompted speculation on his health and possible successor.

Cyprus

REPUBLIC OF CYPRUS

National name: Kypriaki Dimokratia—Kibris Cumhuriyeti
President: Glafcos Klerides (1993)
Area: 3,571 sq mi (9,250 sq km)
Population (1998 est.): 762,887 (average annual rate of natural increase: 0.5%; birth rate: 13.1/1000; infant mortality rate: 7.9/1000; density per sq mi: 214
Capital and largest city (1993): Lefkosia (Nicosia) (in government-controlled area), 186,400. **Monetary unit:** Cyprus pound. **Languages:** Greek, Turkish (official), English is widely spoken. **Ethnicity/race:** total: Greek 78% (99.5% of the Greeks live in the Greek area, 0.5% live in the Turkish area), Turkish 18% (1.3% live in the Greek area, 98.7% live in the Turkish area), other 4%. **Religions (1993 est.):** Greek Orthodox 78%, Sunni Muslim 18%, Maronite, Armenian, Apostolic, Latin, and others 4%. **Literacy rate:** 94% (1987)
Economic summary: GDP/PPP (1998 est.): Greek Cypriot area: $9 billion; $15,400 per capita; Turkish Cypriot area: $820 million; $5,000 per capita. **Real growth rate:** Greek Cypriot area: 3.0%; Turkish Cypriot area: 5.3%. **Inflation:** Greek Cypriot area: 2.3% (1998 est.); Turkish Cypriot area: 66% (1998 est.). **Unemployment:** Greek Cypriot area: 3.3% (1998 est.); Turkish Cypriot area: 6.4% (1997). **Arable land:** 12%. **Agriculture:** potatoes, citrus, vegetables, barley, grapes, olives, vegetables. **Labor force:** Greek Cypriot area: 289,400; Turkish Cypriot area: 80,200 (1998); Greek Cypriot area: services, 66.6%; industry, 23.2%; agriculture, 10.2% (1998); Turkish Cypriot area: services, 55.4%; industry, 21.6%; agriculture, 23% (1997). **Industries:** food, beverages, textiles, chemicals, metal products, tourism, wood products. **Natural resources:** copper, pyrites, asbestos, gypsum, timber, salt, marble, clay earth pigment. **Exports:** Greek Cypriot area: $1.1 billion (f.o.b., 1998 est.); Turkish Cypriot area: $63.9 million (f.o.b., 1998): Greek Cypriot area: citrus, potatoes, grapes, wine, cement, clothing, and shoes; Turkish Cypriot area: citrus, potatoes, textiles (1998). **Imports:** Greek Cypriot area: $3.5 billion (f.o.b., 1998 est.); Turkish Cypriot area: $374 million (f.o.b., 1997): Greek Cypriot area: consumer goods, petroleum and lubricants, food and feed grains, machinery (1998); Turkish Cypriot area: food, minerals, chemicals, machinery (1997). **Major trading partners:** Greek Cypriot area: UK, Russia, Greece, Lebanon, UAE; Turkish Cypriot area: Turkey, UK, other EU. **Member of Commonwealth of Nations**

Geography The third-largest island in the Mediterranean (one and one-half times the size of Delaware), Cyprus lies off the southern coast of Turkey and the western shore of Syria. The highest peak is Mount Olympus at 6,406 ft (1,953 m).

Government Republic. Mediation efforts by the UN seek to achieve reunification of the island under one federated system of government.

History Cyprus was the site of early Phoenician and Greek colonies. For centuries its rule passed through many hands. It fell to the Turks in 1571, and a large Turkish colony settled on the island.

In World War I, at the outbreak of hostilities with Turkey, Britain annexed the island. It was declared a Crown colony in 1925. For centuries the Greek population, regarding Greece as its mother country, has sought self-determination and reunion with Greece *(enosis)*. The resulting quarrel with Turkey threatened NATO. Cyprus became an independent nation on Aug. 16, 1960, with Britain, Greece, and Turkey as guarantor powers.

Archbishop Makarios, president since 1959, was overthrown on July 15, 1974, by a military coup led by the Cypriot National Guard. The new regime named Nikos Giorgiades Sampson as president and Bishop Gennadios as head of the Cypriot Church to replace Makarios. Diplomacy failed to resolve the crisis. Turkey invaded Cyprus by sea and air on July 20, 1974, asserting its right to protect the Turkish Cypriot minority. Geneva talks involving Greece, Turkey, Britain, and the two Cypriot factions failed in mid-Aug., and the Turks subsequently gained control of 40% of the island. Some 180,000 Greek Cypriots were uprooted by the Turkish troops. Greece made no armed response to the superior Turkish force but bitterly suspended military participation in the NATO alliance. The tension continued after Makarios returned to become president on Dec. 7, 1974. He offered self-government to the Turkish minority, but rejected any solution "involving transfer of populations and amounting to partition of Cyprus."

Turkish Cypriots proclaimed a separate state under Rauf Denktas in the northern part of the island on Nov. 15, 1983, naming it the "Turkish Republic of Northern Cyprus." The UN Security Council, in its Resolution 541 of Nov. 18, 1983, declared this action legally invalid and called for withdrawal. No country except Turkey has recognized this illegal entity.

In 1988, George Vassiliou, a conservative and critic of UN proposals to reunify Cyprus, became president. The purchase of missiles capable of reaching the Turkish coast evoked threats of retaliation from Turkey in 1997, and Cyprus's plans to deploy more missiles in Aug. 1999 again raised Turkey's ire.

Cyprus has a good chance at joining the European Union; it has in fact met all the economic standards. But the continued strife between Greek Cypriots and Turkish Cypriots threatens Cyprus's potential EU membership.

Czech Republic

President: Vaclav Havel (1993)
Prime Minister: Milos Zeman (1998)
Area: 30,450 sq mi (78,866 sq km)
Population (2001 est.): 10,264,212 (average annual rate of natural increase: −0.2%); birth rate: 9.1/1000; infant mortality rate: 5.6/1000; density per sq mi: 337
Capital and largest city (Jan. 1, 1994): Prague, 1,215,771. **Other large cities:** Brno, 389,727; Ostrava, 326,396; Plzen, 172,402; Olomouc, 106,003.
Monetary unit: Koruna. **Languages:** Czech; Slovak minority. **Ethnicity/race:** Czech 94.4%, Slovak 3%, Polish 0.6%, German 0.5%, Roma (Gypsy) 0.3%, Hungarian 0.2%, other 1%. **Religions:** atheist 39.8%, Roman Catholic 39.2%, Protestant 4.6%, Orthodox 3%, other 13.4%. **Literacy rate:** 99%
Economic summary: GDP/PPP (1999 est.): $120.8 billion; per capita $11,700. **Real growth rate:** −0.5%. **Inflation:** 2.5%. **Unemployment:** 9%. **Arable land:** 41%. **Labor force:** 5.203 million; industry, 32%; agriculture, 5.6%; construction, 8.7%; transport and communications, 6.9%; services, 46.8% (1997 est.).
Agriculture: grains, potatoes, sugar beets, hops, fruit; pigs, cattle, poultry; forest products. **Industries:** fuels, ferrous metallurgy, machinery and equipment, coal, motor vehicles, glass, armaments. **Natural resources:** hard coal, soft coal, kaolin, clay, graphite, timber. **Exports:** $26.9 billion (f.o.b., 1999): machinery and transport equipment 41%, other manufactured goods 40%, chemicals 8%, raw materials and fuel 7% (1998). **Imports:** $29 billion (f.o.b., 1999): machinery and transport equipment 39%, other manufactured goods 21%, chemicals 12%, raw materials and fuels 10%, food 5% (1998). **Major trading partners:** Germany, Slovakia, Austria, Poland, France, Russia.

Geography   The Czech Republic's central European landscape is dominated by the Bohemian Massif, which rises to heights of 3,000 ft (900 m) above sea level. This ring of mountains encircles a large elevated basin, the Bohemian Plateau. The principal rivers are the Elbe and the Vltava.

Government   Parliamentary democracy.

History   Probably about the 5th century A.D., Slavic tribes from the Vistula basin settled in the region of Bohemia, Moravia, and Silesia. The Czechs founded the kingdom of Bohemia and the Premyslide dynasty, which ruled Bohemia and Moravia from the 10th to the 16th centuries. One of the Bohemian kings, Charles IV, Holy Roman emperor, made Prague an imperial capital and a center of Latin scholarship. The Hussite movement founded by Jan Hus (1369?–1415) linked the Slavs to the Reformation and revived Czech nationalism, previously under German domination. A Hapsburg, Ferdinand I, ascended the throne in 1526. The Czechs rebelled in 1618, precipitating the Thirty Years' War (1618–1648). Defeated in 1620, they were ruled for the next 300 years as part of the Austrian empire. Full independence from the Hapsburgs was not achieved until the end of World War I, following the collapse of the Austrian-Hungarian Empire.

A union of the Czech lands and Slovakia was proclaimed in Prague on Nov. 14, 1918, and the Czech nation became one of the two component parts of the newly formed Czechoslovakian state. In March 1939, German troops occupied Czechoslovakia, and Czech Bohemia and Moravia became German protectorates for the duration of World War II. The former government returned in April 1945 when the war ended and the country's pre-1938 boundaries were restored. When elections were held in 1946, Communists became the dominant political party and gained control of the Czechoslovakian government in 1948. Thereafter, the former democracy was turned into a Soviet-style state.

Nearly 42 years of Communist rule ended when Vaclav Havel, a highly respected writer and dissident, was elected president of Czechoslovakia in 1989. The return of democratic political reform saw a strong Slovak nationalist movement emerge by the end of 1991, which sought independence for Slovakia. When the general elections of June 1992 failed to resolve the continuing coexistence of the two republics within the federation, Czech and Slovak political leaders agreed to separate their states into two fully independent nations. On Jan. 1, 1993, the Czechoslovakian federation was dissolved and two separate independent countries were established—the Czech Republic and Slovakia.

In March 1999, the Czech Republic joined NATO. The country's next goal in international relations is to gain entrance into the European Union.

Denmark

KINGDOM OF DENMARK

National name: Kongeriget Danmark
Sovereign: Queen Margrethe II (1972)
Prime Minister: Poul Nyrup Rasmussen (1993)
Area: 16,639 sq mi (43,094 sq km)[1]
Population (2001 est.): 5,352,815 (average annual rate of natural increase: 0.1%); birth rate: 12.0/1000; infant mortality rate: 5.0/1000; density per sq mi: 322
Capital and largest city (1992): Copenhagen, 1,339,395. **Other large cities (1992):** Århus, 204,139; Odense, 140,886; Ålborg, 114,970. **Monetary unit:** Krone. **Languages:** Danish, Faeroese, Greenlandic (an Inuit dialect), small German-speaking minority. **Ethnicity/race:** Scandinavian, Eskimo, Faeroese, German. **Religions:** Evangelical Lutheran 91%, other Protestant and Roman Catholic 2%, other 7%. **Literacy rate:** 99% (1980)
Economic summary: GDP/PPP (1999 est.): $127.7 billion; per capita $23,800. **Real growth rate:** 1.3%. **Inflation:** 2.5%. **Unemployment:** 5.7%. **Arable land:** 60%. **Agriculture:** grain, potatoes, rape, sugar beets; beef, dairy products; fish. **Labor:** 2.896 million; services, 71%; industry, 25%; agriculture, 4% (1997 est.). **Industries:** food processing, machinery and equipment, textiles and clothing, chemical products, electronics, construction, furniture, and other wood products, shipbuilding. **Natural resources:** petroleum, natural gas, fish, salt, limestone, stone, gravel, and sand. **Exports:** $49.5 billion (f.o.b., 1999): machinery and instruments, meat and meat products, fuels, dairy products, ships, fish, chemicals. **Imports:** $43.9 billion (f.o.b., 1999): machinery and equipment, petroleum, chemicals, grain and foodstuffs, textiles, paper. **Major trading partners:** EU, Norway, U.S.

1. Excluding Faeroe Islands and Greenland.

Geography Smallest of the Scandinavian countries (half the size of Maine), Denmark occupies the Jutland peninsula, a lowland area. The country also consists of several islands in the Baltic Sea; the two largest are Sjælland, the site of Copenhagen, and Fyn.

Government Constitutional monarchy.

History From 10,000 to 1500 B.C., the population of present-day Denmark evolved from a society of hunters and fishers into an agricultural one. Called Jutland by the end of the 8th century, its mariners were among the Vikings, or Norsemen, who raided western Europe and the British Isles from the 9th to 11th century.

The country was Christianized by Saint Ansgar and Harald Blaatand (Bluetooth)—the first Christian king—in the 10th century. Harald's son, Sweyn, conquered England in 1013. His son, Canute the Great, who reigned from 1014 to 1035, united Denmark, England, and Norway under his rule; the southern tip of Sweden was part of Denmark until the 17th century. On Canute's death, civil war tore apart the country until Waldemar I (1157–1182) reestablished Danish hegemony over the north.

In 1282, the nobles won the Great Charter, and Eric V was forced to share power with Parliament and a Council of Nobles. Waldemar IV (1340–1375) restored Danish power, checked only by the Hanseatic League of north German cities allied with ports from Holland to Poland. Denmark, Norway, and Sweden united under the rule of his daughter Margrethe in 1397. But Sweden later achieved autonomy and in 1523, under Gustavus I, independence.

Denmark supported Napoléon, for which it was punished at the Congress of Vienna in 1815 by the loss of Norway to Sweden. In 1864, the Prussians under Bismarck and the Austrians made war on Denmark as an initial step in the unification of Germany. Denmark was neutral in World War I.

In 1940, Denmark was invaded by the Nazis. King Christian X reluctantly cautioned his fellow Danes to accept the occupation, but there was widespread resistance against the Nazis. Denmark was the only occupied country in World War II to save all its Jews from extermination, by smuggling them out of the country.

Beginning in 1944, Denmark's relationship with its territories changed substantially. In that year, Iceland declared its independence from Denmark, ending a union that had existed since 1380. In 1948, the Faeroe Islands, which had also belonged to Denmark since 1380, were granted home rule, and in 1953, Greenland officially became a territory of Denmark.

A referendum on the Maastricht Accord, which paved the way for greater EU economic integration, passed in May 1993. Denmark has been a member of the EC (now the EU) since 1973. On Sept. 28, 2000, Denmark voted to reject adoption of the euro, the European common currency.

Outlying Territories of Denmark

Faeroe Islands

Status: Autonomous part of Denmark
Chief of State: Queen Margrethe II (1972)
High Commissioner: Vibeke Larsen (1995)
Prime Minister: Anfinn Kallsberg (1998)
Area: 540 sq mi (1,399 sq km)
Population (2001 est.): 45,661 (average annual growth rate: 0.5%); birth rate: 13.6/1000; infant mortality rate: 6.8/1000; density per sq mi: 85
Capital and largest city (1993 est.): Tórshavn, 16,100. **Monetary unit:** Faeroese krone. **Languages:** Faeroese, Danish (both official). **Ethnicity/race:** Scandinavian. **Literacy rate:** 99%

This group of 18 islands, of which 17 are inhabited, is located in the North Atlantic about 200 mi (322 km) northwest of the Shetland Islands. They were settled by the Vikings, the ancestors of the modern-day Faeroese, in the 8th century. The Faeroese language is derived from Old Norse. The islands joined Denmark in 1386 and have been part of the Danish kingdom ever since. The Faeroes have had home rule, under Danish authority, since 1948.

Greenland

Status: Autonomous part of Denmark
Chief of State: Queen Margrethe II (1972)
High Commissioner: Gunnar Martens (1995)
Premier: Jonathan Motzfeldt (1997)
Area: 839,999 sq mi (incl. 708,069 sq mi covered by icecap) (2,175,600 sq km)
Population (2001 est.): 56,352 (average annual growth rate: 0.9%); birth rate: 16.5/1000; infant mortality rate: 17.8/1000; density per sq mi: 0.07
Capital and largest city (1995 est.): Godthaab, 12,723. **Monetary unit:** Krone. **Ethnicity/race:** Greenlander 87% (Eskimos and Greenland-born whites), Danish and other 13%. **Literacy rate:** 99%

The Inuit are believed to have crossed from North America to northwest Greenland, the world's largest island, between 4000 B.C. and A.D. 1000. Greenland was colonized in A.D. 985–986 by Eric the Red. The Norse settlements declined in the 14th century, however, mainly as a result of a cooling in Greenland's climate, and in the 15th century they became extinct. In 1721, Greenland was recolonized by the Royal Greenland Trading Company of Denmark.

Greenland was under U.S. protection during World War II, but maintained Danish sovereignty. A definitive agreement for the joint defense of Greenland within the framework of NATO was signed in 1951. A large U.S. air base at Thule in the far north was completed in 1953.

Under 1953 amendments to the Danish constitution, Greenland became part of Denmark, with two representatives in the Danish Folketing. On May 1, 1979, Greenland gained home rule, with its own local Parliament (Landsting). In Feb. 1982, Greenlanders voted to withdraw from the European Union, which they had joined as part of Denmark in 1973.

Djibouti

REPUBLIC OF DJIBOUTI

National name: Jumhouriyya Djibouti
President: Ismail Omar Guelleh (1999)
Prime Minister: Dileita Mohamed Dileita (2001)
Area: 8,494 sq mi (22,000 sq km)
Population (2001 est.): 460,700 (average annual rate of natural increase: 2.6%); birth rate: 40.7/1000; infant mortality rate: 101.5/1000; density per sq mi: 54
Capital (1992 est.): Djibouti, 395,000. **Monetary unit:** Djibouti franc. **Languages:** Arabic and French (both official), Afar, Somali. **Ethnicity/race:** Somali 60%, Afar 35%, French, Arab, Ethiopian, and Italian 5%. **Religions:** Muslim 94%, Christian 6%. **Literacy rate:** 46% (1995)
Economic summary: GDP/PPP (1999 est.): $550 million; per capita $1,200. **Real growth rate:** 2% **Inflation:** 0%. **Unemployment:** 40%-50% (1996 est.). **Arable land:** 0%. **Agriculture:** fruits, vegetables; goats, sheep, camels. **Labor:** 282,000; agriculture, 75%; industry, 11%; services, 14% (1991 est.). **Industries:** limited to a few small-scale enterprises, such as dairy products and mineral-water bottling. **Natural resources:** geothermal areas. **Exports:** $260 million (f.o.b., 1999 est.): reexports, hides and skins, coffee (in transit). **Imports:** $440 million (f.o.b., 1999 est.): foods, beverages, transport equipment, chemicals, petroleum products. **Major trading partners:** Somalia, Yemen, Ethiopia, France, Italy, Saudi Arabia, UK

Geography Djibouti lies in northeast Africa on the Gulf of Aden at the southern entrance to the Red Sea. It borders on Ethiopia, Eritrea, and Somalia. The country, the size of Massachusetts, is mainly a stony desert, with scattered plateaus and highlands.

Government Republic with a unicameral legislature.

History Ablé immigrants from Arabia migrated to what is now Djibouti in about the 3rd century B.C. Their descendants are the Afars, one of the two main ethnic groups that make up Djibouti today. Somali Issas arrived thereafter. Islam came to the region in A.D. 825.

Djibouti was acquired by France between 1843 and 1886 by treaties with the Somali sultans. Small, arid, and sparsely populated, it is important chiefly because of the capital city's port, the terminal of the Djibouti–Addis Ababa railway that carries 60% of Ethiopia's foreign trade. Originally known as French Somaliland, the colony voted in 1958 and 1967 to remain under French rule. It was renamed the Territory of the Afars and Issas in 1967 and took the name of its capital city on June 27, 1977, when France transferred sovereignty to the new independent nation of Djibouti. On Sept. 4, 1992, voters approved in referendum a new multiparty constitution. In 1991 conflict

between the Afars and the Issa-dominated government erupted and the continued warfare has ravaged the country.

The dictatorial president, Hassan Gouled Aptidon, who had run the country since its independence, finally stepped aside in 1999, and Ismail Omar Guelleh was elected president. In March 2000, the main Afars rebel group signed a peace accord with the government.

In Dec. 2000, a coup attempt by former chief of police Gen. Yacin Yabeh Galab was foiled.

Dominica

COMMONWEALTH OF DOMINICA

President: Vernon Shaw (1998)
Prime Minister: Pierre Charles (2000)
Area: 291 sq mi (754 sq km)
Population (2001 est.): 70,786 (average annual rate of natural increase: 1.1%); birth rate: 17.8/1000; infant mortality rate: 16.5/1000; density per sq mi: 243
Capital and largest city (1991): Roseau, 15,853. **Monetary unit:** East Caribbean dollar. **Languages:** English (official) and French patois. **Ethnicity/race:** black, Carib Indians. **Religions:** Roman Catholic 77%, Protestant 15%. **Literacy rate:** 94% (1970)
Economic summary: GDP/PPP (1998 est.): $225 million; per capita $3,400. **Real growth rate:** 2%. **Inflation:** 1.1% (1998). **Labor force:** 25,000; agriculture, 40%; industry and commerce, 32%; services, 28%. **Unemployment:** 20%. **Arable land:** 9%. **Agriculture:** bananas, citrus, mangoes, root crops, coconuts, cocoa; forest and fishery potential not exploited. **Industries:** soap, coconut oil, tourism, copra, furniture, cement blocks, shoes. **Natural resources:** timber, hydropower, arable land. **Exports:** $60.8 million (1998): bananas 50%, soap, bay oil, vegetables, grapefruit, oranges. **Imports:** $120.4 million (1998): manufactured goods, machinery and equipment, food, chemicals. **Major trading partners:** Caricom countries, UK, U.S., Netherlands, Canada. **Member of Commonwealth of Nations**

Geography Dominica is a mountainous island of volcanic origin of the Lesser Antilles in the Caribbean south of Guadeloupe and north of Martinique.

Government Republic.

History Explored by Columbus in 1493, Dominica was claimed by Britain and France until 1763, when it was formally ceded to Britain. Along with other Windward Isles, it became a self-governing member of the West Indies Associated States in free association with Britain in 1967.

Dissatisfaction over the slow pace of reconstruction after Hurricane David devastated the island in Sept. 1979 brought a landslide victory to Mary Eugenia Charles of the Freedom Party in July 1980. The Freedom Party won again in 1985 and 1990, and the government sold state enterprises. The opposition United Workers' Party won in June 1995. In 1997 Dominica became the first Caribbean country to participate in the work of Green Globe, aiming to make Dominica a model ecotourism destination. Although the island is poorer than some of its Caribbean neighbors, Dominica has a relatively low crime rate and does not have the extremes of wealth and poverty evident on other islands. On Oct. 3, 2000, Pierre Charles, previously Communications and Works Minister, became the country's sixth prime minister.

Dominican Republic

National name: República Dominicana
President: Hipólito Mejía (2000)
Area: 18,815 sq mi (48,730 sq km)
Population (2001 est.): 8,581,477 (average annual rate of natural increase: 2.0%); birth rate: 24.8/1000; infant mortality rate: 34.7/1000; density per sq mi: 456
Capital and largest city (1993): Santo Domingo, 2,100,000. **Other large city (1993):** Santiago de los Caballeros, 690,000. **Monetary unit:** Peso.
Languages: Spanish, English widely spoken.
Ethnicity/race: white 16%, black 11%, mixed 73%.
Religion: Roman Catholic 90%. **Literacy rate:** 84% (1990)
Economic summary: GDP/PPP (1999 est.): $43.7 billion; per capita $5,400. **Real growth rate:** 8.3%. **Inflation:** 5.1%. **Unemployment:** 13.8%. **Arable land:** 21%. **Agriculture:** sugarcane, coffee, cotton, cocoa, tobacco, rice, beans, potatoes, corn, bananas; cattle, pigs, dairy products, beef, eggs. **Labor force:** 2.3 million to 2.6 million; services and government, 58.7%; industry, 24.3%; agriculture, 17% (1998 est.).
Industries: tourism, sugar processing, ferronickel and gold mining, textiles, cement, tobacco. **Natural resources:** nickel, bauxite, gold, silver. **Exports:** $5.1 billion (f.o.b., 1999): ferronickel, sugar, gold, silver, coffee, cocoa, tobacco, meats. **Imports:** $8.2 billion (f.o.b., 1999): foodstuffs, petroleum, cotton and fabrics, chemicals and pharmaceuticals. **Major trading partners:** U.S., Belgium, Asia, Canada, Venezuela, Mexico, Japan.

Geography The Dominican Republic in the West Indies occupies the eastern two-thirds of the island of Hispaniola, which it shares with Haiti. Its area equals that of Vermont and New Hampshire combined. Duarte Peak, at 10,417 ft (3,175 m), is the highest point in the West Indies.

Government Republic.

History The Dominican Republic was explored by Columbus on his first voyage in 1492. He named it La Española, and his son, Diego, was its first viceroy. The capital, Santo Domingo, founded in 1496, is the oldest European settlement in the Western Hemisphere.

Spain ceded the colony to France in 1795, and Haitian blacks under Toussaint L'Ouverture conquered it in 1801. In 1808 the people revolted and captured Santo Domingo the next year, setting up the first republic. Spain regained title to the colony in 1814. In 1821 Spanish rule was overthrown, but in 1822 the colony was reconquered by the Haitians. In 1844 the Haitians were thrown out, and the Dominican Republic was established, headed by Pedro Santana. Uprisings and Haitian attacks led Santana to make the country a province of Spain from 1861 to 1865.

President Buenaventura Báez, faced with an economy in shambles, attempted to have the country annexed to the U.S. in 1870, but the U.S. Senate refused to ratify a treaty of annexation. Disorder continued until the dictatorship of Ulíses Heureaux; in 1916, when chaos broke out again, the U.S. sent in a contingent of marines, who remained until 1934.

A sergeant in the Dominican army trained by the marines, Rafaél Leonides Trujillo Molina overthrew Horacio Vásquez in 1930 and established a dictatorship that lasted until his assassination 31 years later. Leftists rebelled on April 24, 1965, and U.S. president Lyndon Johnson sent in marines and troops. After a cease-fire on May 6, a compromise installed Hector Garcia-Godoy as provisional president.

Joaquin Balaguer won in free elections in 1966 against Bosch, and U.S. and other foreign troops withdrew. Balaguer restored political and economic stability.

In 1978, the army suspended the counting of ballots when Balaguer trailed in a fourth-term bid. After a warning from President Jimmy Carter, however, Balaguer accepted the victory of Antonio Guzmán of the Dominican Revolutionary Party. Salvador Jorge Blanco of the Dominican Revolutionary Party was elected president on May 16, 1982, defeating Balaguer and Bosch. Balaguer was again elected president in May 1986 and remained in office for the next ten years.

In 1996, U.S.-raised Leonel Fernandez secured more than 51% of the vote through an alliance with Balaguer. The first item on the president's agenda was the partial sale of some state-owned enterprises. Fernandez was praised for ending decades of isolationism and improving ties with other Caribbean countries, but he was criticized for not fighting corruption and alleviating the poverty that affects 60% of the population.

In Aug. 2000 the center-left Hipólito Mejía was elected president amid popular discontent over power outages in the recently privatized electric industry. In 2001, the army was deployed in major cities to fight rising crime.

Ecuador

REPUBLIC OF ECUADOR

National name: República del Ecuador
President: Gustavo Noboa (2000)
Area: 109,483 sq mi (283,560 sq km)
Population (2001 est.): 13,183,978 (average annual rate of natural increase: 2.1%); birth rate: 26.0/1000; infant mortality rate: 34.1/1000; density per sq mi: 120
Capital (1998 est.): Quito, 1,500,000. **Other large cities (1998 est.):** Guayaquil, 2,000,000 / Cuenca, 200,000.
Monetary unit: U.S. dollar. **Languages:** Spanish (official), Quechua. **Ethnicity/race:** mestizo (mixed Indian and Spanish) 65%, Indian 25%, Spanish 7%, black 3%. **Religion:** Roman Catholic 95%. **Literacy rate:** 90% (1990)
Economic summary: GDP/PPP (1999 est.): $54.5 billion; per capita $4,300. **Real growth rate:** –8%. **Inflation:** 59.9%. **Unemployment:** 12% with widespread underemployment (November 1998 est.). **Arable land:** 6%. **Agriculture:** bananas, coffee, cocoa, rice, potatoes, manioc (tapioca), plantains, sugarcane; cattle, sheep, pigs, beef, pork, dairy products; balsa wood; fish, shrimp. **Labor force:** 4.2 million; agriculture, 30%; industry, 25%; services, 45%. **Industries:** petroleum, food processing, textiles, metal work, paper products, wood products, chemicals, plastics, fishing, lumber. **Natural resources:** petroleum, fish, timber, hydropower. **Exports:** $4.1 billion (f.o.b., 1999): petroleum, bananas, shrimp, coffee, cocoa, cut flowers, fish. **Imports:** $2.8 billion (c.i.f., 1999): machinery and equipment, raw materials, fuels; consumer goods. **Major trading partners:** U.S., Colombia, Italy, Peru, Chile, Japan, Venezuela, Mexico.

Geography Ecuador, about equal in area to Nevada, is in the northwest part of South America fronting on the Pacific. To the north is Colombia and to the east and south is Peru. Two high and parallel ranges of the Andes, traversing the country from north to south, are topped by tall volcanic peaks. The highest is Chimborazo at 20,577 ft (6,272 m). The Galápagos Islands (or Colón Archipelago; 3,029 sq mi; 7,845 sq km), in the Pacific Ocean about 600 mi (966 km) west of the South American mainland, became part of Ecuador in 1832.

Government Republic.

History The tribes in the northern highlands of Ecuador formed the Kingdom of Quito around 1000. It was absorbed, by conquest and marriage, into the Inca empire. Spanish conquistador Francisco Pizarro conquered the land in 1532, and through the 17th century a Spanish colony thrived by exploitation of the Indians. The first revolt against Spain occurred in 1809. Ecuador then joined Venezuela, Colombia, and Panama in a confederacy known as Greater Colombia.

When Greater Colombia collapsed in 1830, Ecuador became independent. Revolts and dictatorships followed; it had 48 presidents during the first 131 years of the republic. Conservatives ruled until the revolution of 1895 ushered in nearly a half century of Radical Liberal rule, during which the church was disestablished and freedom of worship, speech, and press was introduced. Although it was under military rule in the 1970s, the country did not experience the violence and repression characteristic of other Latin American military regimes. Its last twenty years of democracy, however, have been largely ineffectual because of a weak executive branch and a strong, fractious Congress.

Peru invaded Ecuador in 1941 and seized a large tract of Ecuadorian territory in the disputed Amazon. In 1981 and 1995 war broke out again. In May 1999, Ecuador and Peru signed a treaty ending a nearly 60-year border dispute involving the stretch of Amazon jungle.

In 1998, Ecuador experienced one of its worst economic crises. El Niño caused $3 billion in damage, the price of its principal export, oil, plunged, and its inflation rate, 43%, was the highest in Latin America. In 1999, the government was near bankruptcy, the currency lost 40% of its value against the dollar, and the poverty rate soared to 70%, doubling in five years. The president's economic austerity plan was protested with massive strikes in March 1999.

President Jamil Mahuad was overthrown in Jan. 2000, the first military coup in Latin America in a decade—the country has had four presidents in five years. The junta gave power to the vice president, Gustavo Noboa. Noboa restructured Ecuador's foreign debt, adopted the U.S. dollar as the national currency, and continued privatization of state-owned industries, generating enormous opposition. In Feb. 2001, the government cut fuel prices after violent protests by Indians, who are among Ecuador's most disadvantaged people.

Egypt

ARAB REPUBLIC OF EGYPT

President: Hosni Mubarak (1981)
Prime Minister: Atef Ebeid (1999)
Area: 386,660 sq mi (1,001,450 sq km)
Population (2001 est.): 69,536,644 (average annual rate of natural increase: 1.7%); birth rate: 24.9/1000; infant mortality rate: 60.5/1000; density per sq mi: 180
Capital and largest city (2000 est.): Cairo, 14,350,000 (metro. area). **Other large cities (1992 est.):** Alexandria, 3,380,000; Giza, 2,144,000 (part of Cairo metro. area); Shubra el Khema, 834,000 (part of Cairo metro. area); El Mahalla el Kubra, 408,000. **Monetary unit:** Egyptian pound. **Language:** Arabic. **Ethnicity/race:** Eastern Hamitic stock (Egyptians, Bedouins, and Berbers) 99%, Greek, Nubian, Armenian, other European (primarily Italian and French) 1%. **Religions:** Islam 94%, Christian (mostly Coptic) 6%. **Literacy rate:** 48% (1990)
Economic summary: GDP/PPP (1999 est.): $200 billion; per capita $3,000. **Real growth rate:** 5%. **Inflation:** 3.7%. **Unemployment:** 11.8%. **Arable land:** 2%. **Agriculture:** cotton, rice, corn, wheat, beans, fruits, vegetables; cattle, water buffalo, sheep, goats; fish. **Labor force:** 19 million; agriculture, 40%; services, 38%; industry, 22% (1990 est.). **Industries:** textiles, food processing, tourism, chemicals, petroleum, construction, cement, metals. **Natural resources:** petroleum, natural gas, iron ore, phosphates, manganese, limestone, gypsum, talc, asbestos, lead, zinc. **Exports:** $4.6 billion (f.o.b., 1999 est.): crude oil and petroleum products, cotton, textiles, metal products, chemicals. **Imports:** $15.8 billion (f.o.b., 1999 est.): machinery and equipment, foodstuffs, chemicals, wood products, fuels. **Major trading partners:** EU, U.S., Turkey, Japan.

Geography Egypt, at the northeast corner of Africa on the Mediterranean Sea, is bordered on the west by Libya, on the south by the Sudan, and on the east by the Red Sea and Israel. It is nearly one and one-half times the size of Texas. Egypt is divided into two unequal, extremely arid regions by the landscape's dominant feature, the northward-flowing Nile River. The Nile starts 100 mi (161 km) south of the Mediterranean and fans out to a sea front of 155 mi between the cities of Alexandria and Port Said.

Government Republic.

History Egyptian history dates back to about 4000 B.C., when the kingdoms of upper and lower Egypt, already highly sophisticated, were united. Egypt's "Golden Age" coincided with the 18th and 19th dynasties (16th to 13th century B.C.), during which the empire was established. Persia conquered Egypt in 525 B.C., Alexander the Great subdued it in 332 B.C., and then the dynasty of the Ptolemies ruled the land until 30 B.C., when Cleopatra, last of the line, committed suicide and Egypt became a Roman, then Byzantine, province. Arab caliphs ruled Egypt from 641 until 1517, when the Turks took it for their Ottoman Empire.

Napoléon's armies occupied the country from 1798 to 1801. In 1805, Mohammed Ali, leader of a band of Albanian soldiers, became pasha of Egypt. After completion of the Suez Canal in 1869, the French and British took increasing interest in Egypt. British troops occupied Egypt in 1882, and British resident agents became its actual administrators, though it remained under nominal Turkish sovereignty. In 1914, this fiction was ended, and Egypt became a protectorate of Britain.

Egyptian nationalism forced Britain to declare Egypt an independent, sovereign state on Feb. 28, 1922, although the British reserved rights for the protection of the Suez Canal and the defense of Egypt. In 1936, by an Anglo-Egyptian treaty of alliance, all British troops and officials were to be withdrawn, except from the Suez Canal Zone. When World War II started, Egypt remained neutral. British imperial troops finally ended the Nazi threat to Suez in 1942 in the battle of El Alamein, west of Alexandria. In 1951, Egypt abrogated the 1936 treaty and the 1899 Anglo-Egyptian condominium of the Sudan. Rioting and attacks on British troops in the Suez Canal Zone followed, reaching a climax in Jan. 1952. The army, led by Gen. Mohammed Naguib, seized power on July 23, 1952. Three days later, King Farouk abdicated in favor of his infant son. The monarchy was abolished and a republic proclaimed on June 18, 1953, with Naguib holding the posts of provisional president and premier. He relinquished the latter in 1954 to Gamal Abdel Nasser, leader of the ruling military junta, who was confirmed as president in a referendum on June 23, 1956.

Nasser's policies embroiled his country in continual conflict. In 1956, the U.S. and Britain withdrew their pledges of financial aid for the building of the Aswan High Dam. In response, Nasser nationalized the Suez Canal and expelled British oil and embassy officials. Israel, barred from the canal and exasperated by terrorist raids, invaded the Gaza Strip and the Sinai Peninsula. Britain and France, after demanding Egyptian evacuation of the canal zone, attacked Egypt on Oct. 31, 1956. Worldwide pressure forced Britain, France, and Israel to halt the hostilities. A UN emergency force occupied the canal zone, and all troops were evacuated in the spring of 1957.

On June 5, 1967, Israel invaded the Sinai Peninsula, the East Bank of the Jordan River, and the zone around the Gulf of Aqaba. A UN cease-fire on June 10 saved the Arabs from complete rout. Nasser declared the 1967 cease-fire void along the canal in April 1969 and began a war of attrition. The U.S. peace plan of June 19, 1970, resulted in Egypt's agreement to reinstate the cease-fire for at least three months (from Aug.) and to accept Israel's existence within "recognized and secure" frontiers that might emerge from UN-mediated talks. In return, Israel accepted the principle of withdrawing from occupied territories. On Sept. 28, 1970, Nasser died of a heart attack. Anwar el-Sadat, an associate of Nasser and a former newspaper editor, became the next president.

In July 1972, Sadat ordered the expulsion of Soviet "advisers and experts" from Egypt because the Russians had not provided the sophisticated weapons he felt were needed to retake territory lost to Israel in 1967. The fourth Arab-Israeli War broke out on Oct. 6, 1973, during the Jewish holiday of Yom Kippur. Egypt swept deep into the Sinai, while Syria strove to throw Israel off the Golan Heights. A UN-sponsored truce was accepted on Oct. 22. In Jan. 1974, both sides agreed to a settlement negotiated by U.S. secretary of state Henry A. Kissinger that gave Egypt a narrow strip along the entire Sinai bank of the Suez Canal. In June, President Nixon made the first visit by a U.S. president to Egypt and full diplomatic relations were established. The Suez Canal was cleared and reopened on June 5, 1975.

In the most audacious act of his career, Sadat flew to Jerusalem at the invitation of Prime Minister Menachem Begin and pleaded before Israel's Knesset on Nov. 20, 1977, for a permanent peace settlement. The Arab world reacted with fury—only Morocco, Tunisia, Sudan, and Oman approved. Egypt and Israel signed a formal peace treaty on March 26, 1979. The pact ended 30 years of war and established diplomatic and commercial relations.

Egyptian and Israeli officials met in the Sinai desert on April 26, 1979, to implement the peace treaty calling for the phased withdrawal of occupation forces from the peninsula. By mid-1980, two-thirds of the Sinai was transferred, but progress was not matched elsewhere—the negotiation of Arab autonomy in the Gaza Strip and the West Bank remained stymied.

Sadat halted further talks in Aug. 1980 because of continued Israeli settlement of the West Bank. On Oct. 6, 1981, Sadat was assassinated by extremist Muslim soldiers at a parade in Cairo. Vice President Hosni Mubarak, a former air force chief of staff, succeeded him. Israel completed the return of the Sinai to Egyptian control on April 25, 1982. Israel's invasion of Lebanon in June brought a marked cooling in Egyptian-Israeli relations, but not a disavowal of the peace treaty.

While President Mubarak's support of the U.S. and Britain during the Persian Gulf War won wide praise in the West, domestically this position proved far less popular.

The government has concentrated much of its time and attention in recent years on combating Islamic extremism, particularly attacks against Copts (Egyptian Christians).

El Salvador

REPUBLIC OF EL SALVADOR

National name: República de El Salvador
President: Francisco Guillermo Flores Pérez (1999)
Area: 8,124 sq mi (21,040 sq km)
Population (2001 est.): 6,237,662 (average annual rate of natural increase: 2.2%); birth rate: 28.7/1000; infant mortality rate: 28.4/1000; density per sq mi: 768
Capital and largest city (1993 est.): San Salvador, 972,810. **Other large cities (1993 est.):** Santa Ana, 208,322; San Miguel, 161,156; Zacatecoluca, 81,035.
Monetary unit: Colón. **Language:** Spanish. **Ethnicity/race:** mestizo 94%, Indian 5%, white 1%. **Religion:** Roman Catholic. **Literacy rate:** 73% (1990)
Economic summary: GDP/PPP (1999 est.): $18.1 billion; per capita $3,100. **Real growth rate:** 2.2%. **Inflation:** 1.3%. **Unemployment:** 7.7% (1997 est.). **Arable land:** 27%. **Agriculture:** coffee, sugarcane, corn, rice, beans, oilseed, cotton, sorghum; beef, dairy products; shrimp. **Labor force:** 2.35 million; agriculture, 30%; industry 15%; services 55%. **Industries:** food processing, beverages, petroleum, chemicals, fertilizer, textiles, furniture, light metals. **Natural resources:** hydropower, geothermal power, petroleum, arable land. **Exports:** $2.5 billion (f.o.b., 1999): offshore assembly exports, coffee, sugar, shrimp, textiles, chemicals, electricity. **Imports:** $4.15 billion (c.i.f., 1999): raw materials, consumer goods, capital goods, fuels, foodstuffs, petroleum, electricity. **Major trading partners:** U.S., Guatemala, Germany, Costa Rica, Honduras, Mexico, Japan.

Geography Situated on the Pacific coast of Central America, El Salvador has Guatemala to the west and Honduras to the north and east. It is the smallest of the Central American countries, its area equal to that of Massachusetts, and the only one without an Atlantic coastline. Most of the country is on a fertile volcanic plateau about 2,000 ft (607 m) high.

Government Republic.

History The Pipil Indians, descendants of the Aztecs, likely migrated to the region in the 11th century. In 1525, Pedro de Alvarado, a lieutenant of Cortés, conquered El Salvador.

El Salvador, with the other countries of Central America, declared its independence from Spain on Sept. 15, 1821, and was part of a federation of Central American states until that union dissolved in 1838. For decades after its independence, El Salvador experienced numerous revolutions and wars against other Central American republics. From 1931 to 1979 El Salvador was ruled by a series of military dictatorships.

In 1969, El Salvador invaded Honduras after Honduran landowners deported several thousand Salvadorans. Five thousand people ultimately died in what became known as the "football war" because it broke out during a soccer game between the two countries.

In the 1970s discontent with societal inequalities, a poor economy, and the repressive measures of dictatorship led to civil war between the government, the right-wing ARENA party, and leftist antigovernment guerrilla units, whose leading group was the Farabundo Martí National Liberation Front (FMLN). The U.S. intervened on the side of the military, despite its scores of human rights violations. The presidency of José Napoleón Duarte, a moderate civilian, from 1984–1989, offered an alternative to the political extremes of right and left, but Duarte was unable to end the war and in 1989, Alfredo Cristiani of ARENA was elected.

On Jan. 16, 1992, the government signed a peace treaty with the guerrilla forces, formally ending the 12-year civil war that had killed 75,000. El Salvador's subsequent presidents have all belonged to ARENA, including the current president, Francisco Flores, who took office in 1999.

Along with Guatemala and Honduras, El Salvador signed a free trade agreement with Mexico in June 2000. Flores also won parliamentary approval for a U.S. military base in El Salvador over opposition by former Marxist rebels who feared U.S. intervention in the country's internal affairs. The base will fight drug trafficking and replaces facilities lost when the U.S. withdrew from the Panama Canal.

Equatorial Guinea

REPUBLIC OF EQUATORIAL GUINEA

National name: República de Guinea Ecuatorial
President: Col. Teodoro Obiang Nguema Mbasogo (1979)
Prime Minister: Cándido Muatetema Rivas (2001)
Area: 10,830 sq mi (28,051 sq km)
Population (2001 est.): 486,060 (average annual rate of natural increase: 2.5%); birth rate: 37.7/1000; infant mortality rate: 92.9/1000; density per sq mi: 45
Capital and largest city (1983): Malabo, 30,418.
  Monetary unit: CFA Franc. **Languages:** Spanish (official), French (2nd official), pidgin English, Fang, Bubi, Creole. **Ethnicity/race:** Bioko (primarily Bubi, some Fernandinos), Río Muni (primarily Fang), Europeans less than 1,000, mostly Spanish. **Religions:** Roman Catholic, Protestant, traditional. **Literacy rate:** 50% (1990)
Economic summary: GDP/PPP (1999 est.): $960 million; per capita $2,000. **Real growth rate:** 15%. **Inflation:** 6%. **Unemployment:** 30% (1998 est.). **Arable land:** 5%. **Agriculture:** coffee, cocoa, rice, yams, cassava (tapioca), bananas, palm oil, nuts; livestock; timber. **Labor force:** n.a. **Industries:** petroleum, fishing, sawmilling, natural gas. **Natural resources:** oil, petroleum, timber, small unexplored deposits of gold, manganese, uranium. **Exports:** $555 million (f.o.b., 1999): petroleum, timber, cocoa. **Imports:** $300 million (f.o.b., 1999): petroleum, manufactured goods and equipment. **Major trading partners:** U.S., Spain, China, France, Japan, Cameroon, UK

Geography Equatorial Guinea, formerly Spanish Guinea, consists of Río Muni (10,045 sq mi; 26,117 sq km), on the western coast of Africa, and several islands in the Gulf of Guinea, the largest of which is Bioko (formerly Fernando Po) (785 sq mi; 2,033 sq km). The other islands are Annobón, Corisco, Elobey Grande, and Elobey Chico. The total area is twice that of Connecticut.

Government President with a 17-member Supreme Military Council since a 1979 coup.

History The mainland was originally inhabited by Pygmies. The Fang and Bubi migrated there in the 17th century and to the main island of Fernando Po (now called Bioko) in the 19th century. In the 18th century, the Portuguese ceded the land to the Spanish that included Equatorial Guinea. From 1827 to 1844, Britain administered Fernando Po, but it was then reclaimed by Spain. Río Muni, the mainland, was not occupied by the Spanish until 1926. Spanish Guinea, as it was then called, gained independence from Spain on Oct. 12, 1968. It is Africa's only Spanish-speaking country.

From the outset, President Francisco Macías Nguema, considered the father of independence, began a brutal reign, destroying the economy of the fledgling country and abusing human rights. Calling himself the "Unique Miracle," Nguema is considered one of the worst despots in African history. In 1971, the U.S. State Department reported that his regime was "characterized by abandonment of all government functions except internal security, which was accomplished by terror; this led to the death or exile of up to one-third of the population."

On Aug. 3, 1979, Nguema was overthrown and executed by his nephew, Lieut. Col. Teodoro Obiang Nguema Mbasogo. Obiang has been gradually modernizing the country but has retained many of his uncle's dictatorial practices, including the amassing of personal wealth by siphoning it from the public coffers.

A recent off-shore oil boom has filled the country's coffers. Equatorial Guinea's economy grew by 71.2% in 1997, the first year of the petroleum bonanza, and has sustained this phenomenal rate of growth. It is unlikely, however, that the country's new wealth will benefit the average citizen—the president's family and cronies control the industry.

Eritrea

President: Isaias Afwerki (1993)
Area: 46,842 sq mi (121,320 sq km)
Population (2001 est.): 4,298,269 (of which 0.5 million are refugees awaiting repatriation) (average annual rate of natural increase: 3.0%); birth rate: 42.5/1000; infant mortality rate: 75.1/1000; density per sq mi: 92
Capital and largest city (1993): Asmara, 400,000.
  Other major cities: the ports of Massawa and Assab. **Monetary unit:** Nakfa. **Languages:** Afar, Bilen, Kunama, Nara, Arabic, Tobedawi, Saho, Tigre, Tigrinya. **Ethnicity/race:** ethnic Tigrinya 50%, Tigre and Kunama 40%, Afar 4%, Saho (Red Sea coast dwellers) 3%. **Religions:** Islam and Eritrean Orthodox Christianity. **Literacy rate:** 25%
Economic summary: GDP/PPP (1999 est.): $2.9 billion; per capita $750. **Real growth rate:** 3%. **Inflation:** 9% (1998 est). **Unemployment:** n.a. **Arable land:** 12%. **Agriculture:** sorghum, lentils, vegetables, corn, cotton, tobacco, coffee, sisal; livestock, goats; fish. **Labor force:** n.a.; agriculture, 80%; industry and commerce, 20%. **Industries:** food processing, beverages, clothing and textiles. **Natural resources:** gold, potash, zinc, copper, salt, possibly oil and natural gas, fish.

Exports: $52.9 million (f.o.b., 1997): livestock, sorghum, textiles, food, small manufactures. **Imports:** $489.4 million (c.i.f., 1997): processed goods, machinery, petroleum products. **Major trading partners:** Ethiopia, Sudan, Italy, Saudi Arabia, U.S., Yemen, UAE, Germany.

Geography Eritrea was formerly the northernmost province of Ethiopia and is about the size of Indiana. Much of the country is mountainous. Its narrow Red Sea coastal plain is one of the hottest and driest places in Africa. The cooler central highlands have fertile valleys that support agriculture. Eritrea is bordered by the Sudan on the north and west, the Red Sea on the north and east, and Ethiopia and Djibouti on the south.

Government A transitional government committed to a democratic system.

History Eritrea was part of the first Ethiopian kingdom of Aksum until its decline in the 8th century. It came under the control of the Ottoman Empire in the 16th century, and later of the Egyptians. The Italians captured the coastal areas in 1885, and the Treaty of Uccialli (May 2, 1889) gave Italy sovereignty over part of Eritrea. The Italians named their colony after the Roman name for the Red Sea—*Mare Erythraeum*—and ruled it up until World War II. The British captured Eritrea in 1941 and later administered it as a UN Trust Territory until it became federated with Ethiopia on Sept. 15, 1952. It was made an Ethiopian province on Nov. 14, 1962. A civil war broke out against the Ethiopian government led by rebel groups who opposed the union and wanted independence for Eritrea. The bitter conflict raged on for 17 years against the hard-line Communist regime of the Ethiopian dictator Mengistu Haile Mariam until he was overthrown in May 1991.

The Eritrean People's Liberation Front (EPLF) took control of Eritrea and shared power in a multi-party government in Addis Ababa with the Ethiopian People's Revolutionary Democratic Front (EPRDF). They agreed to hold a referendum on Eritrean independence within two years and on April 23–25, 1993, Eritrean voters almost unanimously opted for an independent republic. Ethiopia recognized Eritrea's sovereignty on May 3, 1993, and sought a new era of cooperation between the two countries.

While relations with Ethiopia remained good in 1995, those with the Sudan deteriorated. In Nov. 1996 Eritrea accused the Sudan of plotting to assassinate the president. The mission was thwarted by a Sudanese antigovernment group. Sudan denied the charge, although Eritrea provided specific names and dates of those allegedly involved.

Since Eritrea's independence, Eritrea and Ethiopia had disagreed about the exact demarcation of their borders, and in May 1998 border clashes broke out between them. After an eight-month lull that both sides used to reinforce their 600-mile common border, civil war broke out again in earnest. Both impoverished countries spent millions of dollars on warplanes and weapons, tens of thousands of soldiers have died, and refugees are legion.

A June 2000 cease-fire remains in effect, and a formal peace agreement was signed in Dec. 2000. The United Nations has provided several thousand troops to patrol the buffer zone between the two nations until a permanent border can be agreed upon.

Estonia
REPUBLIC OF ESTONIA

National name: Eesti
President: Arnold Ruutel (2001)
Prime Minister: Mart Laar (1999)
Area: 17,462 sq mi (45,226 sq km)
Population (2001 est.): 1,423,316 (average annual rate of natural increase: –0.5%); birth rate: 8.7/1000; infant mortality rate: 12.6/1000; density per sq mi: 82
Capital and largest city (1992 est.): Tallinn, 471,608.
Other large city (1992 est.): Tartu, 113,400.
Monetary unit: Kroon. **Languages:** Estonian (official), Russian, Finnish, English. **Ethnicity/race:** Estonian 61.5%, Russian 30.3%, Ukrainian 3.2%, Belorussian 1.8%, Finn 1.1%, other 2.1% (1989). **Religions:** Lutheran 78%, Orthodox 19%. **Literacy:** 100% (1989)
Economic summary: GDP/PPP (1999 est.): $7.9 billion; per capita $5,600. **Real growth rate:** –0.5%. **Inflation:** 3.7%. **Unemployment:** 11.7%. **Arable land:** 25%. **Agriculture:** potatoes, fruits, vegetables; livestock and dairy products; fish. **Labor force:** 785,500; industry, 20%; agriculture and forestry, 11%; services, 69%. **Industries:** oil shale, shipbuilding, phosphates, electric motors, excavators, cement, furniture, clothing, textiles, paper, shoes, apparel. **Natural resources:** shale oil (kukersite), peat, phosphorite, amber, cambrian blue clay, limestone, dolomite, arable land. **Exports:** $2.5 billion (f.o.b., 1999): machinery and appliances, wood products, textiles, food products, metals, chemical products. **Imports:** $3.4 billion (f.o.b., 1999): machinery and appliances, foodstuffs, chemical products, metal products, textiles. **Major trading partners:** Sweden, Finland, Russia, Latvia, Germany, U.S.

Geography Estonia is mainly a lowland country that borders on the Baltic Sea. It has numerous lakes and forests and many rivers, most draining northward into the Gulf of Finland or eastward into Lake Peipus. Lake Peipus is Estonia's largest lake and is important to the fishing and shipping industries.

Government Parliamentary democracy.

History Born out of World War I, this small Baltic state enjoyed a mere two short decades of independence before it was absorbed again by its powerful neighbor, the Soviet Union. Estonians were able to resist assaults by Vikings, Danes, Swedes, and Russians before the 13th century. In 1346 the Danes, who possessed northern Estonia, sold the land to the Teutonic Knights of Germany, who already possessed Livonia (southern Estonia and Latvia). The Teutonic Knights reduced the Estonians to serfdom. In 1526, the Swedes took over, and the power of the German (Balt) landowning class was reduced. But after 1721, when Russia succeeded Sweden as the ruling power under the Peace of Nystad, the Estonians were subject to a double bondage—the Balts and the czarist officials. The oppression lasted until the closing months of World War I, when Estonia finally achieved independence after a victorious war (1918–20). Shortly after the start of World War II, the nation was occupied by Russian troops and incorporated as the 16th republic of the USSR in 1940. Germany occupied the nation from 1941 to 1944, when it was retaken by the Soviets.

Estonia declared independence from the Soviet Union in March 1990. Soviet resistance ensued, but by 1991, after recognition by European and other countries, the Soviet Union acknowledged Estonian nationhood on Sept. 6, 1991. UN membership followed on Sept. 17, 1991. The newly independent nation embraced free-market reforms. Fueled by foreign investments, economic advances continued unabated in 1997. This prompted the European Commission (EC) to recommend that Estonia begin accession talks for membership in the European Union.

At the end of 1998, Estonia relaxed the strict citizenship requirements that kept the country's Russian speakers—about one-third of the population—from gaining citizenship. This reform eased the way for Estonia's bid for entry into the European Union.

In Oct. 2001, ex-communist Arnold Ruutel assumed the presidency.

Ethiopia

FEDERAL DEMOCRATIC REPUBLIC OF ETHIOPIA

President: Negasso Gidada (1995)
Prime Minister: Meles Zenawi (1995)
Area: 435,184 sq mi (1,127,127 sq km)
Population (2001 est.): 65,891,874 (average annual rate of natural increase: 2.7%); birth rate: 44.7/1000; infant mortality rate: 100.0/1000; density per sq mi: 151
Capital and largest city (1993 est.): Addis Ababa, 2,200,186. **Monetary unit:** Birr. **Languages:** Amharic (official), English, Orominga, Tigrigna, over 70 languages spoken. **Ethnicity/race:** Oromo 40%, Amhara and Tigrean 32%, Sidamo 9%, Shankella 6%, Somali 6%, Afar 4%, Gurage 2%, other 1%. **Religions:** Ethiopian Orthodox 35%–40%, Islam 40%–45%, animist 15%–20%, other 5%. **Literacy rate:** 28% (1984)
Economic summary: GDP/PPP (1999 est.): $33.3 billion; per capita $560. **Real growth rate:** 0%. **Inflation:** 4%. **Unemployment:** n.a. **Arable land:** 12%. **Agriculture:** cereals, pulses, coffee, oilseed, sugarcane, potatoes; hides, cattle, sheep, goats. **Labor force:** n.a; agriculture and animal husbandry, 80%; government and services, 12%; industry and construction, 8% (1985). **Industries:** food processing, beverages, textiles, chemicals, metals processing, cement. **Natural resources:** small reserves of gold, platinum, copper, potash, natural gas, hydropower. **Exports:** $420 million (f.o.b., 1998): coffee, gold, leather products, oilseeds. **Imports:** $1.25 billion (f.o.b., 1998 est.): food and live animals, petroleum and petroleum products, chemicals, machinery, motor vehicles. **Major trading partners:** Germany, Japan, Italy, UK, U.S., Jordan.

Geography Ethiopia is in east-central Africa, bordered on the west by the Sudan, the east by Somalia and Djibouti, the south by Kenya, and the northeast by Eritrea. It is nearly three times the size of California. Over its main plateau land, Ethiopia has several high mountains, the highest of which is Ras Dashan at 15,158 ft (4,620 m). The Blue Nile, or Abbai, rises in the northwest and flows in a great semicircle east, south, and northwest before entering the Sudan. Its chief reservoir, Lake Tana, lies in the northwest part of the plateau.

Government Federal republic.

History Archeologists have found the oldest known human ancestors in Ethiopia, including *Ardipithecus ramidus kadabba* (c. 5.8–5.2 million years old) and *Australopithecus anamensis* (c. 4.2 million years old). Originally called Abyssinia, Ethiopia is sub-Saharan Africa's oldest state, and its Solomonic dynasty claims descent from King Menelik I, traditionally believed to have been the son of the queen of Sheba and King Solomon. The current nation is a consolida-

tion of smaller kingdoms that owed feudal allegiance to the Ethiopian emperor.

Hamitic peoples migrated to Ethiopia from Asia Minor in prehistoric times. Semitic traders from Arabia penetrated the region in the 7th century B.C. Its Red Sea ports were important to the Roman and Byzantine Empires. Coptic Christianity was brought to the region in A.D. 341, and a variant of it became Ethiopia's state religion. Ancient Ethiopia reached its peak in the 5th century, then was isolated by the rise of Islam and weakened by feudal wars.

Modern Ethiopia emerged under Emperor Menelik II, who established its independence by routing an Italian invasion in 1896. He expanded Ethiopia by conquest. Disorders that followed Menelik's death brought his daughter to the throne in 1917, with his cousin, Tafari Makonnen, as regent and heir apparent. When the empress died in 1930, Tafari was crowned Emperor Haile Selassie I.

Haile Selassie, called the "Lion of Judah," outlawed slavery and tried to centralize his scattered realm, in which 70 languages were spoken. In 1931, he created a constitution, revised in 1955, that called for a Parliament with an appointed senate and an elected chamber of deputies, and a system of courts. But basic power remained with the emperor.

Fascist Italy invaded Ethiopia on Oct. 3, 1935, forcing Haile Selassie into exile in May 1936. Ethiopia was annexed to Eritrea, then an Italian colony, and to Italian Somaliland, forming Italian East Africa. In 1941, British troops routed the Italians, and Haile Selassie returned to Addis Ababa. In 1952, Eritrea was incorporated into Ethiopia.

On Sept. 12, 1974, Haile Selassie was deposed, the constitution suspended, and Ethiopia proclaimed a socialist state under a collective military dictatorship called the Provisional Military Administrative Council (PMAC), also known as the Derg. U.S. aid stopped, and Cuban and Soviet aid began. Lt. Col. Mengistu Haile Mariam became head of state in 1977. During this period Ethiopia fought against Eritrean secessionists as well as Somali rebels, and the government fought against its own people in a campaign called the "red terror." Mengistu remained leader until 1991, when his greatest supporter, the Soviet Union, dismantled itself.

A group called the Ethiopian People's Revolutionary Democratic Front seized the capital in 1991, and in May a separatist guerrilla organization, the Eritrean People's Liberation Front, took control of the province of Eritrea. The two groups agreed that Eritrea would have an internationally supervised referendum on independence. This election took place in April 1993 with almost unanimous support for Eritrean independence. Ethiopia accepted and recognized Eritrea as an independent state within a few days. Sixty-eight leaders of the former military government were put on trial in April 1996 on charges that included genocide and crimes against humanity.

Since Eritrea's independence, Eritrea and Ethiopia had disagreed about the exact demarcation of their borders, and in May 1998 Eritrea initiated border clashes that developed into a full-scale war that left tens of thousands dead and further destroyed both countries' ailing economies. After a costly and bloody two-year war, a permanent cease-fire was reached in June 2000—Ethiopia had the upper hand when the fighting ceased—and a formal peace agreement was signed in Dec. 2000. The United Nations has provided several thousand peacekeeping forces to patrol the buffer zone between the two nations until a permanent border can be agreed upon. Prime Minister Zenawi's political backing has eroded somewhat since the war—hardliners, who felt he had been too soft on Eritrea, have tried to unseat him.

Fiji

REPUBLIC OF THE FIJI ISLANDS

President: Ratu Josefa Iloilo (2000)
Prime Minister: Laisenia Qarase (2001)
Area: 7,054 sq mi (18,270 sq km)
Population (2001 est.): 844,330 (average annual rate of natural increase: 1.8%); birth rate: 23.3/1000; infant mortality rate: 14.1/1000; density per sq mi: 120
Capital (1990 est.): Suva (on Viti Levu), 200,000.
  Monetary unit: Fiji dollar. **Languages:** Fijian, Hindustani, English (official). **Ethnicity/race:** Fijian 49%, Indian 46%, European, other Pacific Islanders, overseas Chinese, and other 5%. **Religions:** Christian 52%, Hindu 38%, Islam 8%, other 2%. **Literacy rate:** 79% (1976)
Economic summary: GDP/PPP (1999 est.): $5.9 billion; per capita $7,300. **Real growth rate:** 7.8%. **Inflation:** 0%. **Unemployment:** 6% (1997 est.). **Arable land:** 10%. **Agriculture:** sugarcane, coconuts, cassava (tapioca), rice, sweet potatoes, bananas; cattle, pigs, horses, goats; fish. **Labor force:** 235,000; subsistence agriculture, 67%; wage earners, 18%; salary earners, 15% (1987). **Industries:** tourism, sugar, clothing, copra, gold, silver, lumber, small cottage industries. **Natural resources:** timber, fish, gold, copper, offshore oil potential, hydropower. **Exports:** $393 million (f.o.b., 1998): sugar, clothing, gold, processed fish, lumber. **Imports:** $612 million (f.o.b., 1998): machinery and transport equipment, petroleum products, food, chemicals. **Major trading partners:** Australia, UK, other Pacific island countries, U.S., New Zealand, Japan, Singapore.

Geography Fiji consists of 332 islands in the southwest Pacific Ocean about 1,960 mi (3,152 km) from Sydney, Australia. About 110 of these islands are inhabited. The two largest are Viti Levu (4,109 sq mi; 10,642 sq km) and Vanua Levu (2,242 sq mi; 5,807 sq km). The island of Rotuma (18 sq mi; 47 sq km), about 400 mi (644 km) to the north, is a province of Fiji. The largest islands in the group are mountainous and volcanic, with the tallest peak being Mount Victoria (4,341 ft; 1,323 m) on Viti Levu.

Government Republic until May 2000, when coup installed interim military dictatorship.

History Fiji, which had been inhabited since the second millennium B.C., was explored by the Dutch and the British in the 17th and 18th centuries. In 1874, an offer of cession by the Fijian chiefs was accepted, and Fiji was proclaimed a possession and dependency of the British Crown. In the 1880s large-scale cultivation of sugarcane began. During World War II, the archipelago was an important air and naval station on the route from the U.S. and Hawaii to Australia and New Zealand.

Fiji became independent on Oct. 10, 1970. The next year it joined the five-island South Pacific Forum, which intends to become a permanent regional group to promote collective diplomacy of the newly independent members. In Oct. 1987, Brig. Gen. Sitiveni Rabuka staged a coup, declared Fiji a republic, and removed it from the British Commonwealth. The military coup caused an exodus of thousands of Fijians of Indian origin who suffered ethnic discrimination at the hands of the government.

In July 1997, the Parliament unanimously approved a new constitution for Fiji. The new constitution, which took effect in July 1998, provided for a multiracial cabinet and raised the prospect of a coalition government. The previous constitution, from 1990, guaranteed the dominance to ethnic Fijians over ethnic Indians. Following the approval of the new constitution, Fiji was readmitted to the Commonwealth of Nations. In 1999, Fiji's first ethnic Indian prime minister, Mahendra Chaudhry, took office.

Continuing ethnic differences, partly fueled by economic problems, plunged Fiji into a national nightmare in 2000. On May 19, a group of armed soldiers entered the Parliament and took three dozen people hostage, including the country's ethnic Indian prime minister. George Speight, a part-Fijian businessman, led the insurrection, and demanded that the 1997 constitution be rewritten to allow dominance of ethnic Fijians. The standoff lasted two months. In July 2000, Speight and other coup leaders were taken into custody and charged with treason.

But when the attempted coup ended, deposed prime minister Chaudry and his democratically elected government were not restored to power. Instead, the military and the Great Council of Chiefs, a group of 50 traditional Fijian leaders, appointed an interim government dominated by ethnic Fijians. Elections were held in Aug.-Sept. 2001, but no party achieved a majority. Interim prime minister Laisenia Qarase's Fijian United Party won 31 of 71 seats, and Qarase was sworn in as prime minister on September 10. His cabinet consists entirely of ethnic Fijians.

Finland

REPUBLIC OF FINLAND

National name: Suomen Tasavalta—Republiken Finland
President: Tarja Halonen (2000)
Prime Minister: Paavo Lipponen (1995)
Area: 130,127 sq mi (337,030 sq km)
Population (2001 est.): 5,175,783 (average annual rate of natural increase: 0.1%); birth rate: 10.7/1000; infant mortality rate: 3.8/1000; density per sq mi: 40
Capital and largest city (1995 est.): Helsinki, 515,765.
  Other large cities (1995 est.): Espoo, 186,507; Tampere, 179,251; Vantaa, 164,376; Turku, 162,370.
  Monetary units: Markka and euro. **Languages:** Finnish, Swedish (both official); small Sami- (Lapp) and Russian-speaking minorities. **Ethnicity/race:** Finn 93%, Swede 6%, Sami (Lapp) 0.11%, Romany (Gypsy) 0.12%, Tatar 0.02%. **Religions:** Evangelical Lutheran 90%, Greek Orthodox 1.2%, none 9%, other 1%. **Literacy rate:** 100% (1980)
Economic summary: GDP/PPP (1999 est.): $108.6 billion; per capita $21,000. **Real growth rate:** 3.5%. **Inflation:** 1%. **Unemployment:** 10%. **Arable land:** 8%. **Agriculture:** cereals, sugar beets, potatoes; dairy cattle; fish. **Labor force:** 2.533 million; public services, 32%; industry, 22%; commerce, 14%; finance, insurance, and business services, 10%; agriculture and forestry, 8%; transport and communications, 8%; construction, 6%. **Industries:** metal products, shipbuilding, pulp and paper, copper refining, foodstuffs, chemicals, textiles, clothing. **Natural resources:** timber, copper, zinc, iron ore, silver. **Exports:** $43 billion (f.o.b., 1998): machinery and equipment, chemicals, metals; timber, paper, and pulp. **Imports:** $30.7 billion (f.o.b., 1998): foodstuffs, petroleum and petroleum products, chemicals, transport equipment, iron and steel, machinery, textile yarn and fabrics, fodder grains. **Major trading partners:** EU, U.S., Russia, Japan.

Geography Finland is three times the size of Ohio. It is heavily forested and contains thousands of lakes, numerous rivers, and extensive areas of marshland. Except for a small highland region in the extreme northwest, the country is a lowland less than 600 ft (180 m) above sea level. Off the southwest coast are the Swedish-populated Åland Islands (581 sq mi; 1,505 sq km), which have had an autonomous status since 1921.

Government Republic.

History The first inhabitants of Finland were the Sami (Lapp) people. When Finnish speakers migrated to Finland in the first millennium B.C., the Sami were forced to move northward to the arctic regions, with which they are traditionally associated. The Finns' repeated raids on the Scandinavian coast impelled Eric IX, the Swedish king, to conquer the country in 1157. It was made a part of the Swedish kingdom and converted to Christianity.

By 1809 the whole of Finland was conquered by Alexander I of Russia, who set up Finland as a grand duchy. The period of Russification (1809–1914) sapped Finnish political power and made Russian the country's official language. When Russia became engulfed by the March Revolution of 1917, Finland seized the opportunity to declare independence on Dec. 6, 1917.

The USSR attacked Finland on Nov. 30, 1939, after Finland refused to give into Soviet territorial demands. The Finns staged a strong defense for three months before capitulating. They were forced to cede the Soviets 16,000 sq mi (41,440 sq km). Under German pressure, the Finns joined the Nazis against Russia in 1941, but were defeated again and ceded the Petsamo area to the USSR. In 1948, a treaty of friendship and mutual assistance was signed by the two nations. Finland continued to pursue a foreign policy of nonalignment throughout the cold war era.

Running on a platform to revitalize the economy, Ahtisaari, a Social Democrat, won the country's first direct presidential election in a runoff in Feb. 1994. Previously, presidents had been chosen by electors. Finland became a member of the European Union in Jan. 1995. Showing concern over NATO expansion eastward, Russian president Yeltsin in March 1997 iterated his view that Finnish membership in the military alliance was unacceptable. On Jan. 1, 1999, Finland, along with ten other European countries, adopted the euro as its currency. In 2000, Tarja Halonen, who had been Finland's foreign minister, became its first woman president.

In both 2000 and 2001, Finland was judged to be the world's least corrupt country, according to the annual corruption survey by the Berlin-based organization Transparency International.

France

FRENCH REPUBLIC

National name: République Française
President: Jacques Chirac (1995)
Prime Minister: Lionel Jospin (1997)
Area: 211,208 sq mi (547,030 sq km)
Population (2001 est.): 59,551,227 (average annual rate of natural increase: 0.3%); birth rate: 12.1/1000; infant mortality rate: 4.5/1000; density per sq mi: 282
Capital and largest city (2000 est.): Paris, 10,150,000 (metro. area). **Other large cities:** Marseille, 801,000; Lyon, 415,000; Toulouse, 359,000; Nice, 342,000; Strasbourg, 252,000; Nantes, 245,000; Bordeaux,

201,000. **Monetary units:** French Franc and euro.
Languages: French, declining regional dialects (Provençal, Breton, Alsatian, Corsican). **Ethnicity/ race:** Celtic and Latin with Teutonic, Slavic, North African, Southeast Asian, and Basque minorities. **Religions:** Roman Catholic 81%, Protestant 1.7%, Muslim 6.9%, Jewish 1.3%. **Literacy rate:** 99% (1980)
Economic summary: GDP/PPP (1999 est.): $1.373 trillion; per capita $23,300. **Real growth rate:** 2.7%. **Inflation:** 0.5%. **Unemployment:** 11%. **Arable land:** 33%. **Agriculture:** wheat, cereals, sugar beets, potatoes, wine grapes; beef, dairy products; fish. **Labor force:** 25.4 million (1994); services, 69%; industry, 26%; agriculture, 5% (1995). **Industries:** steel, machinery, chemicals, automobiles, metallurgy, aircraft, electronics, mining; textiles, food processing; tourism. **Natural resources:** coal, iron ore, bauxite, fish, timber, zinc, potash. **Exports:** $304.7 billion (f.o.b., 1999): machinery and transportation equipment, chemicals, iron and steel products; agricultural products, textiles and clothing. **Imports:** $280.8 billion (f.o.b., 1999): crude oil, machinery and equipment, chemicals; agricultural products. **Major trading partners:** EU, U.S.

Geography France is about 80% the size of Texas. In the Alps near the Italian and Swiss borders is western Europe's highest point—Mont Blanc (15,781 ft; 4,810 m). The forest-covered Vosges Mountains are in the northeast, and the Pyrénées are along the Spanish border. Except for extreme northern France, the country may be described as four river basins and a plateau. Three of the streams flow west—the Seine into the English Channel, the Loire into the Atlantic, and the Garonne into the Bay of Biscay. The Rhône flows south into the Mediterranean. For about 100 mi (161 km), the Rhine is France's eastern border. In the Mediterranean, about 115 mi (185 km) east-southeast of Nice, is the island of Corsica (3,367 sq mi; 8,721 sq km).

Government Fifth republic.

History Archeological excavations indicate that France has been continuously settled since Paleolithic times. The Celts, who were later called *Gauls* by the Romans, migrated from the Rhine valley into what is now France. In about 600 B.C. Greeks and Phoenicians established settlements along the Mediterranean, most notably at Marseille. Julius Caesar conquered part of Gaul in 57–52 B.C., and it remained Roman until Franks invaded in the 5th century A.D.

The Treaty of Verdun (843) divided the territories corresponding roughly to France, Germany, and Italy among the three grandsons of Charlemagne. Charles the Bald inherited *Francia Occidentalis,* which became an increasingly feudalized kingdom. By 987, the crown passed to Hugh Capet, a princeling who controlled only the Ile-de-France, the region surrounding Paris. For 350 years, an unbroken Capetian line added to its domain and consolidated royal authority until the accession in 1328 of Philip VI, first of the Valois line. France was then the most powerful nation in Europe, with a population of 15 million.

The missing pieces in Philip Valois's domain were the French provinces still held by the Plantagenet kings of England, who also claimed the French crown. Beginning in 1338, the Hundred Years' War eventually settled the contest. After France's victory in the final battle, Castillon (1453), the Valois were the ruling family, and the English had no French possessions left except Calais. Once Burgundy and Brittany were added, the Valois dynasty's holdings resembled modern France. Protestantism spread

Rulers of France

Name	Born	Ruled[1]	Name	Born	Ruled[1]
Carolingian Dynasty			Louis XV the Well-Beloved	1710	1715–1774
Pepin the Short	c. 714	751–768	Louis XVI	1754	1774–1792[13]
Charlemagne[2]	742	768–814	Louis XVII (Louis Charles de	1785	1793–1795
Louis I the Pious[3]	778	814–840	France)[14]		
Charles I the Bald[4]	823	840–877	**First Republic**		
Louis II the Stammerer	846	877–879	National Convention	—	1792–1795
Louis III[5]	c. 863	879–882	Directory (Directoire)	—	1795–1799
Carloman[5]	?	879–884	**Consulate**		
Charles II the Fat[6]	839	884–887[7]	Napoléon Bonaparte[15]	1769	1799–1804
Eudes (Odo), count of Paris	?	888–898	**First Empire**		
Charles III the Simple[8]	879	893–923[9]	Napoléon I	1769	1804–1815[16]
Robert I[10]	c. 865	922–923	**Restoration of House of Bourbon**		
Rudolf (Raoul), duke of Burgundy	?	923–936	Louis XVIII le Désiré	1755	1814–1824
Louis IV d'Outremer	c. 921	936–954	Charles X	1757	1824–1830[17]
Lothair	941	954–986	**Bourbon-Orleans Line**		
Louis V the Sluggard	c. 967	986–987	Louis Philippe ("Citizen King")	1773	1830–1848[18]
Capetian Dynasty			**Second Republic**		
Hugh Capet	c. 940	987–996	Louis Napoléon[19]	1808	1848–1852
Robert II the Pious[11]	c. 970	996–1031	**Second Empire**		
Henry I	1008	1031–1060	Napoléon III (Louis Napoléon)	1808	1852–1870[20]
Philip I	1052	1060–1108	**Third Republic (Presidents)**		
Louis VI the Fat	1081	1108–1137	Louis Adolphe Thiers	1797	1871–1873
Louis VII the Young	c.1121	1137–1180	Marie E. P. M. de MacMahon	1808	1873–1879
Philip II (Philip Augustus)	1165	1180–1223	François P. J. Grévy	1807	1879–1887
Louis VIII the Lion	1187	1223–1226	Sadi Carnot	1837	1887–1894
Louis IX (St. Louis)	1214	1226–1270	Jean Casimir-Périer	1847	1894–1895
Philip III the Bold	1245	1270–1285	François Félix Faure	1841	1895–1899
Philip IV the Fair	1268	1285–1314	Émile Loubet	1838	1899–1906
Louis X the Quarreler	1289	1314–1316	Clement Armand Fallières	1841	1906–1913
John I[12]	1316	1316	Raymond Poincaré	1860	1913–1920
Philip V the Tall	1294	1316–1322	Paul E. L. Deschanel	1856	1920–1920
Charles IV the Fair	1294	1322–1328	Alexandre Millerand	1859	1920–1924
House of Valois			Gaston Doumergue	1863	1924–1931
Philip VI	1293	1328–1350	Paul Doumer	1857	1931–1932
John II the Good	1319	1350–1364	Albert Lebrun	1871	1932–1940
Charles V the Wise	1337	1364–1380	**Vichy Government (Chief of State)**		
Charles VI the Well-Beloved	1368	1380–1422	Henri Philippe Pétain	1856	1940–1944
Charles VII	1403	1422–1461	**Provisional Government (Presidents)**		
Louis XI	1423	1461–1483	Charles de Gaulle	1890	1944–1946
Charles VIII	1470	1483–1498	Félix Gouin	1884	1946–1946
Louis XII the Father of the People	1462	1498–1515	Georges Bidault	1899	1946–1947
Francis I	1494	1515–1547	**Fourth Republic (Presidents)**		
Henry II	1519	1547–1559	Vincent Auriol	1884	1947–1954
Francis II	1544	1559–1560	René Coty	1882	1954–1959
Charles IX	1550	1560–1574	**Fifth Republic (Presidents)**		
Henry III	1551	1574–1589	Charles de Gaulle	1890	1959–1969
House of Bourbon			Georges Pompidou	1911	1969–1974
Henry IV of Navarre	1553	1589–1610	Valéry Giscard d'Estaing	1926	1974–1981
Louis XIII	1601	1610–1643	François Mitterrand	1916	1981–1995
Louis XIV the Great	1638	1643–1715	Jacques Chirac	1932	1995–

1. For kings and emperors through the Second Empire, year of end of rule is also that of death, unless otherwise indicated. 2. Crowned Emperor of the West in 800. His brother, Carloman, ruled as king of the Eastern Franks from 768 until his death in 771. 3. Holy Roman Emperor, 814–840. 4. Holy Roman Emperor, 875–877 as Charles II. 5. Ruled jointly, 879–882. 6. Holy Roman Emperor, 881–887, as Charles III. 7. Died 888. 8. King, 893–898, in opposition to Eudes. 9. Died 929. 10. Not counted in regular line of kings of France by some authorities. Elected by nobles but killed in Battle of Soissons. 11. Sometimes called Robert I. 12. Posthumous son of Louis X; lived for only five days. 13. Executed 1793. 14. Titular king only. He died in prison according to official reports, but many pretenders appeared during the Bourbon restoration. 15. As first consul, Napoléon held the power of government. In 1804, he became emperor. 16. Abdicated first time, June 1814. Reentered Paris, March 1815, after escape from Elba; Louis XVIII fled to Ghent. Abdicated second time, June 1815. He named as his successor his son, Napoléon II, who was not acceptable to the Allies. He died 1821. 17. Died 1836. 18. Died 1850. 19. President; became emperor in 1852. 20. Died 1873.

throughout France in the 16th century and led to civil wars. Henry IV, of the Bourbon dynasty, issued the Edict of Nantes (1598), granting religious tolerance to the Huguenots (French Protestants). Absolute monarchy reached its apogee in the reign of Louis XIV (1643–1715), the Sun King, whose brilliant court was the center of the Western world.

After a series of costly foreign wars that weakened the government, the French Revolution plunged France into a bloodbath beginning in 1789 with the establishment of the First Republic and ending with a new authoritarianism under Napoléon Bonaparte, who had successfully defended the infant republic from foreign attack and then made himself first consul in

1799 and emperor in 1804. The Congress of Vienna (1815) sought to restore the pre-Napoléonic order in the person of Louis XVIII, but industrialization and the middle class, both fostered under Napoléon, built pressure for change, and a revolution in 1848 drove Louis Philippe, last of the Bourbons, into exile. Prince Louis Napoléon, a nephew of Napoléon I's, declared the Second Empire in 1852 and took the throne as Napoléon III. His opposition to the rising power of Prussia ignited the Franco-Prussian War (1870–1871), ending in his defeat, his abdication, and the creation of the Third Republic.

A new France emerged from World War I as the continent's dominant power. But four years of hostile occupation had reduced northeast France to ruins. Beginning in 1919, French foreign policy aimed at keeping Germany weak through a system of alliances, but it failed to halt the rise of Adolf Hitler and the Nazi war machine. On May 10, 1940, Nazi troops attacked, and, as they approached Paris, Italy joined with Germany. The Germans marched into an undefended Paris and Marshal Henri Philippe Pétain signed an armistice on June 22. France was split into an occupied north and an unoccupied south, Vichy France, the latter becoming a totalitarian German puppet state with Pétain as its chief. Allied armies liberated France in Aug. 1944, and a provisional government in Paris headed by Gen. Charles de Gaulle was established. The Fourth Republic was born on Dec. 24, 1946. The empire became the French Union; the National Assembly was strengthened and the presidency weakened; and France joined NATO. A war against Communist insurgents in French Indochina, now Vietnam, was abandoned after the defeat of French forces at Dien Bien Phu in 1954. A new rebellion in Algeria threatened a military coup, and on June 1, 1958, the assembly invited de Gaulle to return as premier with extraordinary powers. He drafted a new constitution for a Fifth Republic, adopted on Sept. 28, which strengthened the presidency and reduced legislative power. He was elected president on Dec. 21, 1958.

France next turned its attention to decolonization in Africa; the French protectorates of Morocco and Tunisia had received independence in 1956. French West Africa was partitioned and the new nations were granted independence in 1960. Algeria, after a long civil war, finally became independent in 1962. Relations with most of the former colonies remained amicable. De Gaulle took France out of the NATO military command in 1967 and expelled all foreign-controlled troops from the country. De Gaulle's government was weakened by massive protests in May 1968 when student rallies became violent and millions of factory workers engaged in wildcat strikes across France. After normalcy was reestablished in 1969, de Gaulle's successor, Georges Pompidou, modified Gaullist policies to include a classical laissez-faire attitude toward domestic economic affairs. The conservative, pro-business climate contributed to the election of Valéry Giscard d'Estaing as president in 1974.

Socialist François Mitterrand attained a stunning victory in the May 10, 1981, presidential election. The victors immediately moved to carry out campaign pledges to nationalize major industries, halt nuclear testing, suspend nuclear power plant construction, and impose new taxes on the rich. The Socialists' policies during Mitterrand's first two years created a 12% inflation rate, a huge trade deficit, and devaluations of the franc. In March 1986, a center-

right coalition led by Jacques Chirac won a slim majority in legislative elections. Chirac became prime minister, initiating a period of "cohabitation" between him and the Socialist president, Mitterrand. Mitterrand's decisive reelection in 1988 led to Chirac being replaced as premier by Michel Rocard, a Socialist. Relations, however, cooled with Rocard, and in May 1991 he was replaced with Edith Cresson, France's first female prime minister and, like Mitterrand, a Socialist. But Cresson's unpopularity forced Mitterrand to replace Cresson with a more well-liked Socialist, Pierre Bérégovoy, who eventually was embroiled in a scandal and committed suicide. Mitterrand did succeed in helping draft the Maastricht Treaty and, after winning a slim victory in a referendum, confirming close economic and security ties between France and the European Union (EU).

On his third try Chirac won the presidency in May 1995, campaigning vigorously on a platform to reduce unemployment. He moved quickly to cement ties with Germany and the rest of the EU. Elections for the National Assembly in 1997 gave the Socialist coalition a majority. Shortly after becoming president, Chirac resumed France's nuclear testing in the South Pacific, despite widespread international protests as well as rioting in the countries affected by it. Socialist leader Lionel Jospin became prime minister in 1997. On Jan. 1, 1999, France adopted the euro as its currency. In the spring of 1999, the country took part in the NATO airstrikes in Kosovo, despite some internal opposition.

In the fall of 1999, Britain and France argued heatedly about France's refusal to allow the importation of British beef. France remained leery of the possibility of infection from bovine spongiform encephalopathy (BSE), commonly known as mad cow disease, despite the fact that the EU had lifted the three-year ban on British beef in Aug. 1999. European protests over rising fuel prices originated in France on Sept. 4, 2000, when truckers blockaded refineries and service stations. The blockades succeeded in forcing the government to issue a tax break, which spurred on other European countries to attempt similar protests.

In 2001, Chirac was investigated on corruption charges during his tenure as mayor of Paris.

Overseas Departments

Overseas Departments elect representatives to the National Assembly, and the same administrative organization as that of continental France applies to them.

French Guiana (including Inini)
Status: Overseas Department
Prefect: Henri Masse (1999)
Area: 35,135 sq mi (91,000 sq km)
Population (2001 est.): 177,562 (average annual growth rate: 1.7%); birth rate 22.0/1000; infant mortality rate 13.6/1000; density per sq mi: 5
Capital and largest city (1995 est.): Cayenne, 41,659.
Monetary unit: Franc. **Language:** French. **Ethnicity/race:** black or mulatto 66%, white 12%, East Indian, Chinese, Amerindian 12%, other 10%. **Religion:** Roman Catholic. **Literacy rate:** 80% (1982)
Economic summary: GDP/PPP (1998 est.): $1 billion; per capita $6,000. **Real growth rate:** n.a. **Inflation:** 2.5% (1992). **Unemployment:** 21.4%. **Arable land:** 0%. **Agriculture:** rice, manioc (tapioca), sugar, cocoa, vegetables, bananas; cattle, pigs, poultry. **Labor force:** 58,800 (1997); services, government, and commerce, 60.6%; industry, 21.2%; agriculture, 18.2% (1980). **Industries:** construction, shrimp processing, forestry products, rum, gold mining. **Natural**

resources: bauxite, timber, gold (widely scattered), cinnabar, kaolin, fish. **Exports:** $155 million (f.o.b., 1997): shrimp, timber, gold, rum, rosewood essence, clothing. **Imports:** $625 million (c.i.f., 1997): food (grains, processed meat), machinery and transport equipment, fuels and chemicals. **Major trading partners:** France, Switzerland, U.S., Trinidad and Tobago.

French Guiana, lying north of Brazil and east of Suriname on the northeast coast of South America, was variously settled by the Spanish, Dutch, and French. The Treaty of Breda awarded France the territory in 1667. The French used it as a penal colony between 1852 and 1939, which included the infamous Devil's Island. In 1958 it became an Overseas Department of the French Republic, which sends two elected representatives to France's National Assembly and one to the Senate. Since then, many indigenous French Guianians have called for increased autonomy, although only around 5% favor independence from France, partly due to the vast subsidies from the French government. The European Space Center at Kourou has brought a corner of French Guiana into the modern world and attracted a sizable expatriate workforce.

Guadeloupe

Status: Overseas Department
Prefect: Jean-François Carenco (1999)
Area: 687 sq mi (1,780 sq km)
Population (2001 est.): 431,170 (average annual growth rate: 1.1%); birth rate: 16.9/1000; infant mortality rate: 9.5/1000; density per sq mi: 627
Capital (1990): Basse-Terre, 14,000. **Largest city (1990):** Pointe-à-Pitre, over 26,029. **Monetary unit:** Franc. **Languages:** French, Creole patois. **Ethnicity/race:** black or mulatto 90%, white 5%, East Indian, Lebanese, Chinese less than 5%. **Religion:** Roman Catholic. **Literacy rate:** 91% (1982)
Economic summary: GDP/PPP (1996 est.): $3.7 billion; per capita $9,000. **Real growth rate:** n.a. **Inflation:** n.a. **Unemployment:** 27.8% (1998). **Arable land:** 14%. **Agriculture:** bananas, sugarcane, tropical fruits and vegetables; cattle, pigs, goats. **Labor force:** 125,900 (1997); agriculture, 15%; industry, 17%; services, 68% (1997). Industries: construction, cement, rum, sugar, tourism. **Natural resources:** cultivable land, beaches, and climate that foster tourism. **Exports:** $140 million (f.o.b., 1997): bananas, sugar, rum. **Imports:** $1.7 billion (c.i.f., 1997): foodstuffs, fuels, vehicles, clothing and other consumer goods, construction materials. **Major trading partners:** France, Martinique, U.S., Germany, Japan, Netherlands Antilles.

Guadeloupe, in the West Indies about 300 mi (483 km) southeast of Puerto Rico, was explored by Columbus in 1493. It consists of the twin islands of Basse-Terre and Grande-Terre and five dependencies—Marie-Galante, Les Saintes, La Désirade, St. Barthélemy, and the northern three-fifths of St. Martin. The volcano Soufrière (4,813 ft; 1,467 m), also called La Grande Soufrière, is the highest point on Guadeloupe. Violent activity in 1976 and 1977 caused thousands to flee their homes.

French colonization began in 1635, and in 1674 Guadeloupe became part of the domain of France. In 1958, Guadeloupe voted in favor of the new constitution of the French Fifth Republic and remained an Overseas Department of the French Republic. It is represented in the French National Assembly by four deputies and in the French Senate by two senators.

Martinique

Status: Overseas Department
Prefect: Michel Cadot (2000)
Area: 425 sq mi (1,100 sq km)
Population (2001 est.): 418,454 (average annual growth rate: 0.9%); birth rate: 15.8/1000; infant mortality rate: 7.8/1000; density per sq mi: 985
Capital and largest city (1990): Fort-de-France, 100,072. **Other cities (1990):** Le Lamentin, 30,026; Schoelcher, 19,683; Sainte-Marie, 19,683. **Monetary unit:** Franc. **Languages:** French, Creole patois. **Ethnicity/race:** African and African-white-Indian mixture 90%, white 5%, East Indian, Lebanese, Chinese less than 5%. **Religion:** Roman Catholic. **Literacy rate:** 100% (1983)
Economic summary: GDP/PPP (1996 est.): $4.24 billion; per capita $10,700. **Real growth rate:** n.a. **Inflation:** 3.9% (1990). **Unemployment:** 24% (1997). **Arable land:** 8%. **Agriculture:** pineapples, avocados, bananas, flowers, vegetables, sugarcane. **Labor force:** 170,000 (1997); agriculture, 10%; industry, 17%; services, 73% (1997). **Industries:** construction, rum, cement, oil refining, sugar, tourism. **Natural resources:** coastal scenery and beaches, cultivable land. **Exports:** $250 million (f.o.b., 1997): refined petroleum products, bananas, rum, pineapples. **Imports:** $2 billion (c.i.f., 1997): petroleum products, crude oil, foodstuffs, construction materials, vehicles, clothing and other consumer goods. **Major trading partners:** France, Guadeloupe, Venezuela, Germany, Italy, U.S.

Martinique, a mountainous island lying in the Lesser Antilles about 300 mi (483 km) northeast of Venezuela, was probably explored by Columbus in 1502 and was taken for France in 1635. Martinique became a domain of the French crown in 1674. In 1958, Martinique voted in favor of the new constitution of the French Fifth Republic and remained an Overseas Department of the French Republic, sending four deputies to the French National Assembly and two senators to the French Senate. Martinique's young people continue to emigrate heavily, mostly to France.

Réunion

Status: Overseas Department
Prefect: Jean Doubigny (1998)
Area: 970 sq mi (2,512 sq km)
Population (2001 est.): 732,570 (average annual growth rate: 1.6%); birth rate: 21.3/1000; infant mortality rate: 8.5/1000; density per sq mi: 755
Capital and largest city (1993): Saint-Denis, 121,999. **Other cities (est. 1993):** Saint-Paul, 71,667; Saint-Pierre, 58,846; Le Tampon, 47,598. **Monetary unit:** Franc. **Languages:** French, Creole. **Ethnicity/race:** French, African, Malagasy, Chinese, Pakistani, Indian. **Religion:** Roman Catholic 70%. **Literacy rate:** 70% (1982)
Economic summary: GDP/PPP (1998 est.): $3.4 billion; per capita $4,800. **Real growth rate:** 3.8%. **Inflation:** n.a. **Unemployment:** 42.8%. **Arable land:** 17%. **Agriculture:** sugarcane, vanilla, tobacco, tropical fruits, vegetables, corn. **Labor force:** 261,000 (1995); agriculture, 8%; industry, 19%; services, 73% (1990). **Industries:** sugar, rum, cigarettes, handicraft items, flower oil extraction. **Natural resources:** fish, arable land, hydropower. **Exports:** $214.162 million (f.o.b., 1997): sugar, rum and molasses, perfume essences, lobster. **Imports:** $2.5 billion (c.i.f., 1997): manufactured goods, food, beverages, tobacco, machinery and transportation equipment, raw materials, and petroleum products. **Major trading partners:** France, Japan, Comoros, Bahrain, Germany, Italy.

Of volcanic origin, Réunion consists mostly of rugged mountains and short torrential rivers. It is located about 450 mi (724 km) east of Madagascar, in the Indian Ocean. First explored by Portuguese navigators in the 16th century, the island of Réunion, then uninhabited, was taken as a French possession in 1642. African slaves were imported first to work coffee and then sugar plantations; with the abolition of slavery in 1848, indentured laborers from Indochina, India, and East Africa were brought in. In 1958, Réunion approved the constitution of the Fifth French Republic and remained an Overseas Department of the French Republic. Réunion elects five deputies to the French National Assembly and three to the Senate. The island is administered by an appointed prefect and a general council composed of 44 elected members.

Overseas Territories

Overseas Territories are comparable to Departments except that their administrative organization includes a locally elected government.

French Polynesia

Status: Overseas Territory
High Commissioner: Jean Aribaud (1999)
Area: 1,609 sq mi (4,167 sq km)
Population (2001 est.): 253,506 (average annual growth rate: 1.4%); birth rate: 18.6/1000; infant mortality rate: 9.1/1000; density per sq mi: 158
Capital (1988): Papeete (on Tahiti), 23,555. **Monetary unit:** Pacific financial community franc. **Language:** French. **Ethnicity/race:** Polynesian 78%, Chinese 12%, local French 6%, metropolitan French 4%. **Religions:** Protestant 55%, Roman Catholic 30%, other 16%. **Literacy rate:** 98% (1977)
Economic summary: GDP/PPP (1997 est.): $2.6 billion; per capita $10,800. **Real growth rate:** n.a. **Inflation:** 1.5% (1994). **Unemployment:** 15% (1992 est.). **Arable land:** 1%. **Agriculture:** coconuts, vanilla, vegetables, fruits; poultry, beef, dairy products. **Labor force:** 118,744 (of which 70,044 are employed) (1988); agriculture, 13%; industry, 19%; services, 68% (1997). **Industries:** tourism, pearls, agricultural processing, handicrafts. **Natural resources:** timber, fish, cobalt, hydropower. **Exports:** $212 million (f.o.b., 1996): cultured pearls, coconut products, mother-of-pearl, vanilla, shark meat (1997). **Imports:** $860 million (c.i.f., 1996): fuels, foodstuffs, equipment. **Major trading partners:** U.S., France.

The term *French Polynesia* is applied to the scattered French possessions in the South Pacific—Mangareva (Gambier), Makatea, the Marquesas Islands, Rapa, Rurutu, Rimatara, the Society Islands, the Tuamotu Archipelago, Tubuai, Raivavae, and the island of Clipperton—which were organized into a single colony in 1903. There are 120 islands, of which 25 are uninhabited.

The president of the Territorial Government is assisted by a Council of Government and a popularly elected Territorial Assembly. The principal and most populous island—Tahiti, in the Society group—was claimed by the French in 1768. In 1958, French Polynesia voted in favor of the new constitution of the French Fifth Republic and remained an Overseas Territory of the French Republic. The indigenous people are mostly Maoris.

The Pacific Nuclear Test Center on the atoll of Mururoa, 744 mi (1,200 km) from Tahiti, was completed in 1966. In 1975 worldwide opposition forced the French to move the testing underground on Fangataufa. To compensate the residents for the nuclear weapons tests in 1995–96, France offered a 10-year $194-million annual compensation package. An independence movement continues to flourish in French Polynesia.

New Caledonia and Dependencies

Status: Overseas Territory
President: Pierre Frogier (2001)
High Commissioner: Thierry Lataste (1998)
Area: 7,359 sq mi (19,060 sq km)
Population (2001 est.): 204,863 (average annual growth rate: 1.5%); birth rate: 20.4/1000; infant mortality rate: 8.4/1000; density per sq mi: 28
Capital (1989): Nouméa, 65,110. **Monetary unit:** Pacific financial community franc. **Languages:** Melanesian and Polynesian dialects. **Ethnicity/race:** Kanak (Melanesian) 42.5%, European 37.1%, Wallisian 8.4%, Polynesian 3.8%, Indonesian 3.6%, Vietnamese 1.6%, other 3%. **Religions:** Roman Catholic 60%, Protestant 30%. **Literacy rate:** 91% (1976)
Economic summary: GDP/PPP (1998 est.): $3 billion; per capita $15,000. **Real growth rate:** 3.5%. **Inflation:** 1.5%. **Unemployment:** 15% (1994). **Arable land:** 0%. **Agriculture:** vegetables; beef, deer, other livestock products. **Labor force:** 79,395 (including 15,018 unemployed, 1996); agriculture, 7%; industry, 23%; services, 70% (1999 est.). **Industries:** nickel mining and smelting. **Natural resources:** nickel, chrome, iron, cobalt, manganese, silver, gold, lead, copper. **Exports:** $381 million (f.o.b., 1998): ferronickels, nickel ore, fish. **Imports:** $922 million (c.i.f., 1998): foods, machinery and equipment, fuels, minerals. **Major trading partners:** Japan, France, U.S., Taiwan, Australia, New Zealand.

New Caledonia (6,466 sq mi; 16,747 sq km), about 1,070 mi (1,722 km) northeast of Sydney, Australia, was explored by Capt. James Cook in 1774 and annexed by France in 1853. The government also administers the Isle of Pines, the Loyalty Islands (Uvéa, Lifu, and Maré), the Belep Islands, the Huon Island group, and Chesterfield Islands. The native people are Melanesians called the Kanak. In 1984, the French National Assembly passed a law that granted internal autonomy to New Caledonia. In 1998 the Nouméa Accords postponed discussions about independence for the territory until at least 2013.

Southern and Antarctic Lands

Status: Overseas Territory
Administrator: François Garde (2000)
Area: 3,004 sq mi (7,781 sq km, excluding Adélie Land)
Capital: Port-au-Français

This territory is uninhabited except for the personnel of scientific bases. It consists of Adélie Land (166,752 sq mi; 431,888 sq km) on the Antarctic mainland (which the U.S. does not recognize) and the following islands in the southern Indian Ocean: the Kerguelen and Crozet archipelagos and the islands of Saint-Paul and New Amsterdam.

Wallis and Futuna Islands

Status: Overseas Territory
Administrator: Alain Waquet (2000)
Area: 106 sq mi (274 sq km)
Population (2001 est.): 15,435 (average annual growth rate 1.7%); birth rate 21.7/1000; infant mortality rate 18.3/1000; density per sq mi: 146
Capital (1983): Mata-Utu. **Languages:** French, Wallisian. **Ethnicity/race:** Polynesian. **Religion:**

Roman Catholic. **Literacy rate:** 50% (1969)
Economic summary: GDP/PPP (1995 est.): $28.7 million; per capita $2,000. **Real growth rate:** n.a. **Inflation:** n.a. **Unemployment:** n.a. **Arable land:** 5%. **Agriculture:** breadfruit, yams, taro, bananas; pigs, goats. **Labor force:** n.a.; agriculture, livestock, and fishing, 80%; government, 4%. **Industries:** copra, handicrafts, fishing, lumber. **Natural resources:** negl. **Exports:** $370,000 (f.o.b., 1995 est.): copra, breadfruit, yams, taro roots, handicrafts. **Imports:** $13.5 million (c.i.f., 1995 est.): foodstuffs, manufactured goods, transportation equipment, fuel, clothing. **Major trading partners:** France, Australia, New Zealand.

The two island groups in the South Pacific between Fiji and Samoa were settled by French missionaries at the beginning of the 19th century. A protectorate was established in the 1880s. There is a French-appointed high administrator, a 20-member Territorial Assembly, and a deputy and a senator to the French national Parliament. The three traditional Polynesian kings also help decide internal policy matters. Following a referendum by the Polynesian inhabitants, the status was changed to that of an Overseas Territory in 1961.

Territorial Collectivities

The Territorial Collectivity status was created in 1976 for Mayotte; it was conceived as being midway between an Overseas Territory and an Overseas Department.

Saint Pierre and Miquelon

Status: Territorial Collectivity
Prefect: Jean-François Tallec (2001)
Area: 93 sq mi (242 sq km)
Population (2001 est.): 6,928 (average annual growth rate 0.9%); birth rate 15.9/1000; infant mortality rate 8.4/1000; density per sq mi: 74
Capital (1990): Saint Pierre, 5,683. **Ethnicity/race:** Basques and Bretons (French fishermen). **Literacy rate:** 99% (1982)
Economic summary: GDP/PPP (1996 est.): $74 million, supplemented by annual payments from France of about $65 million; per capita $11,000. **Real growth rate:** n.a.. **Inflation:** 2.1% (1991–96 average). **Unemployment:** 9.8% (1997). **Arable land:** 13%. **Agriculture:** vegetables; poultry, cattle, sheep, pigs; fish. **Labor force:** 3,000 (1997); fishing, 18%; industry (mainly fish processing), 41%; services, 41% (1996 est.). **Industries:** fish processing and supply base for fishing fleets; tourism. **Natural resources:** fish, deepwater ports. **Exports:** $5 million (f.o.b., 1997): fish and fish products, mollusks and crustaceans, fox and mink pelts. **Imports:** $66 million (c.i.f., 1997 est.): meat, clothing, fuel, electrical equipment, machinery, building materials. **Major trading partners:** U.S., France, UK, Canada, Portugal, Netherlands.

The sole remnant of the French colonial empire in North America, these islands were first occupied by the French in 1604. Their only importance arises from proximity to the Grand Banks, located 10 mi south of Newfoundland, making them the center of the French Atlantic cod fisheries. On July 19, 1976, the islands became an Overseas Department of the French Republic. In May 1985, the archipelago was given a new status with a new name, Territorial Collectivity, because the former departmental arrangement conflicted with the tariff structure of the European Union, to which France belongs.

Mayotte

Status: Territorial Collectivity
Prefect: Pierre Bayle (1998)
Area: 144 sq mi (374 sq km)
Population (2001 est.): 163,366 (average annual rate of natural increase 3.6%); birth rate 44.4/1000; infant mortality rate 69.5/1000; density per sq mi: 1,131
Capital and largest city (1991): Mamoudzou (Dzaoudzi), 20,450
Economic summary: GDP/PPP (1998 est.): $85 million; per capita $600. **Real growth rate:** n.a.. **Inflation:** n.a.. **Unemployment:** 45% (1997). **Arable land:** n.a.. **Agriculture:** vanilla, ylang-ylang (perfume essence), coffee, copra. **Labor force:** n.a. **Industries:** newly created lobster and shrimp industry, construction. **Natural resources:** negl. **Exports:** $3.44 million (f.o.b., 1997): ylang-ylang (perfume essence), vanilla, copra, coconuts, coffee, cinnamon. **Imports:** $141.3 million (f.o.b., 1997): food, machinery and equipment, transportation equipment, metals, chemicals. **Major trading partners:** France, Comoros, Reunion, Africa, Southeast Asia.

France gained colonial control over Mayotte in 1843. It is the most populous of the four Comoros Islands in the Indian Ocean off Mozambique in Africa. Mayotte chose to remain a French dependency rather than join the other Comoran islands in declaring independence in 1975. Comoros laid claim to Mayotte shortly after independence and continues to do so. In July 2000, 70% of voters opted to accept greater autonomy but remain a part of France.

Gabon

GABONESE REPUBLIC

National name: République Gabonaise
President: Omar Bongo (1967)
Premier: Jean-François Ntoutoume (1999)
Area: 103,346 sq mi (267,667 sq km)
Population (2001 est.): 1,221,175 (average annual rate of natural increase: 1.0%); birth rate: 27.4/1000; infant mortality rate: 94.9/1000; density per sq mi: 12
Capital and largest city (1994): Libreville, 419,596. **Other cities (1994):** Port-Gentil, 80,000; Franceville, 42,000. **Monetary unit:** Franc CFA. **Languages:** French (official), Fang, Myene, Bateke, Bapounou/Eschira, Bandjabi. **Ethnicity/race:** (1993) Bantu tribes, including six major tribal groupings: Fang 25%, Punu 23%, Nzeiby 13%, Mbede (Obamba/Bateke) 9%, Kota 7%, and Myene 5%; Pygmies 0.7%, naturalized population 0.3%, foreigners 15%. **Religions:** Catholic 75%, Protestant 20%, Animist 4%. **Literacy rate:** 61% (1990)
Economic summary: GDP/PPP (1999 est.): $7.9 billion; per capita $6,500. **Real growth rate:** 1.7%. Inflation: 2.9%. **Unemployment:** 21% (1997 est.). **Arable land:** 1%. **Agriculture:** cocoa, coffee, sugar, palm oil, rubber; cattle; okoume (a tropical softwood); fish. **Labor force:** 600,000; agriculture, 60%; services and government, 25%; industry and commerce, 15%. **Industries:** food and beverage; textile; lumbering and plywood; cement; petroleum extraction and refining; manganese, uranium, and gold mining; chemicals; ship repair. **Natural resources:** petroleum, manganese, uranium, gold, timber, iron ore, hydropower. **Exports:** $2.4 billion (f.o.b., 1999 est.): crude oil 75%, timber, manganese, uranium (1998). **Imports:** $1.2 billion (f.o.b., 1999 est.): machinery and equipment, foodstuffs, chemicals, petroleum products, construction materials. **Major trading partners:** U.S., China, France, Japan, Cameroon, Netherlands, Côte d'Ivoire. **Member of French Community**

Geography This West African country with the Atlantic as its western border is also bounded by Equatorial Guinea, Cameroon, and the Congo. Its area is slightly less than Colorado's. Most of the country is covered by a dense tropical forest.

Government Republic.

History The earliest humans in Gabon were believed to be the Babinga, or Pygmies, dating back to 7000 B.C., who were later followed by Bantu groups from southern and eastern Africa. Now there are many tribal groups in the country, the largest being the Fang peoples, who constitute 25% of the population.

Gabon was first explored by the Portuguese navigator Diego Cam in the 15th century. In 1472 the Portuguese explorers encountered the mouth of the Como River, and named it "Rio de Gabao," river of Gabon, which later became the name of the country. The Dutch began arriving in 1593, and the French in 1630. In 1839, the French founded their first settlement on the left bank of the Gabon estuary and gradually occupied the hinterland during the second half of the 19th century. The land became a French territory in 1888, an autonomous republic within the French Union after World War II, and an independent republic on Aug. 17, 1960.

After his conversion to Islam in 1973, President Bongo changed his given name, Albert Bernard, to Omar. He has been reelected every five years since 1967. Strikes and riots led to a transitional constitution in May 1990 legalizing political parties and calling for free elections. In its first multiparty election in Dec. 1993, the incumbent president received just over 51% of the vote, while the opposition candidate refused to accept defeat; he alleged fraud and tried to establish a rival government.

In Dec. 1998, President Bongo, who has ruled the country for 31 years, was elected for an additional seven. Gabon lacks roads, schools, and adequate health care, yet the oil-rich country has lined the pockets of its ruler, who, according to the French weekly *L'Autre Afrique,* is said to own more real estate in Paris than any other foreign leader. Despite his reputation for corruption and authoritarianism, however, Bongo has a strong national following.

Gambia, The

REPUBLIC OF THE GAMBIA

President: Yahya Jammeh (1997)
Area: 4,363 sq mi (11,300 sq km)
Population (2001 est.): 1,411,205 (average annual rate of natural increase: 2.9%); birth rate: 41.8/1000; infant mortality rate: 77.8/1000; density per sq mi: 323
Capital (1986): Banjul, 44,188. **Monetary unit:** Dalasi.
Languages: Native tongues, English (official).
Ethnicity/race: African 99% (Mandinka 42%, Fula 18%, Wolof 16%, Jola 10%, Serahuli 9%, other 4%), non-Gambian 1%. **Religions:** Islam 90%, Christian 9%, traditional 1%. **Literacy rate:** 27% (1990)
Economic summary: GDP/PPP (1999 est.): $1.4 billion; per capita $1,030. **Real growth rate:** 4.2%. **Inflation:** 2.5%. **Unemployment:** n.a. **Arable land:** 18%. **Agriculture:** peanuts, millet, sorghum, rice, corn, cassava (tapioca); palm kernels; cattle, sheep, goats; forest and fishery resources not fully exploited. **Labor force:** 400,000; agriculture, 75%; industry, commerce, and services, 19%; government, 6%. **Industries:** processing peanuts, fish, and hides; tourism; beverages; agricultural machinery assembly, woodworking, metalworking; clothing. **Natural resources:** fish. **Exports:** $132 million (f.o.b., 1998):

peanuts and peanut products, fish, cotton lint, palm kernels. **Imports:** $201 million (f.o.b., 1998): foodstuffs, manufactures, fuel, machinery and transport equipment. **Major trading partners:** Benelux, Japan, UK, Hong Kong, France, Spain, Netherlands, Côte d'Ivoire, Senegal. **Member of Commonwealth of Nations**

Geography Situated on the Atlantic coast in westernmost Africa and surrounded on three sides by Senegal, Gambia is twice the size of Delaware. The Gambia River flows for 200 mi (322 km) through Gambia on its way to the Atlantic. The country, the smallest on the continent, averages only 20 mi (32 km) in width.

Government Republic.

History Since the 13th century, the Wolof, Malinke, and Fulani peoples settled in what is now The Gambia. The Portuguese were the first European explorers, encountering the Gambia River in 1455, and in 1681 the French founded an enclave at Albredabut. During the 17th century, Gambia was settled by various companies of English merchants. Slavery was the chief source of revenue before it was abolished in 1807. Gambia became a Crown colony in 1843 and an independent nation within the Commonwealth of Nations on Feb. 18, 1965. Full independence was approved in a 1970 referendum, and on April 24 of that year Gambia proclaimed itself a republic.

Elections on April 29, 1992, returned President Jawara for a fifth term. His People's Progressive Party won 25 of the 36 seats in the House of Representatives. A military coup led by Capt. Yahya Jammeh deposed the president in July 1994, suspended the constitution, and banned existing political parties. Jammeh promised new elections, which were held in Sept. 1996, and he won 55% of the vote against his nearest rival, Ousseynou Darboe. In April 1997 he completed the promised return to civilian rule. Censorship of the press and other repressive measures continue to mar the country's transition to democracy.

Unrest plagued Gambia throughout much of 2000. In January Jammeh crushed a coup attempt staged by some of his own bodyguards, and in April violent student protests rocked the country. The peanut export system collapsed in the same year from mismanagement, leaving farmers unpaid and unable to sell a bumper crop of the country's main commodity. In 2001, Jammeh lifted the ban against various opposition parties he had outlawed after his 1994 coup.

Georgia

GEORGIA

National Name: Sakartvelo
President: Eduard Shevardnadze (1992)
Secretary of State: Giorgi Arsenishvili (2000)
Area: 26,911 sq mi (69,700 sq km)
Population (2001 est.): 4,989,285 (average annual rate of natural increase: –0.3%); birth rate: 11.2/1000; infant mortality rate: 52.4/1000; density per sq mi: 185
Capital and largest city (1991): Tbilisi, 1,279,000.
Other cities (1989): Kutaisi, 235,000; Batoumi, 136,000; and Sokhumi, 121,000. **Monetary unit:** Lari.
Languages: Georgian (official), 71%; Russian, 9%; Armenian, 7%; Azerbaijani, 6%. **Ethnicity/race:** Georgian 70.1%, Armenian 8.1%, Russian 6.3%, Azeri 5.7%, Ossetian 3%, Abkhaz 1.8%, other 5%.
Religions: Georgian Orthodox 65%, Russian Orthodox 10%, Armenian Orthodox 8%, Muslim 11%.
Literacy rate: 99% (1989)

Economic summary: GDP/PPP (1999 est.): $11.7 billion; per capita $2,300. **Real growth rate:** 3.5%. **Inflation:** 19%. **Unemployment:** 14.5% (1998 est.). **Arable land:** 9%. **Agriculture:** citrus, grapes, tea, vegetables, potatoes; livestock. **Labor force:** 3.08 million (1997); industry and construction, 20%; agriculture and forestry, 40%; services, 40%. **Industries:** steel, aircraft, machine tools, electric locomotives, trucks, tractors, textiles, shoes, chemicals, wood products, wine. **Natural resources:** forests, hydropower, manganese deposits, iron ore, copper, minor coal and oil deposits; coastal climate and soils allow for important tea and citrus growth. **Exports:** $330 million (1999 est.): citrus fruits, tea, wine, other agricultural products; diverse types of machinery and metals; chemicals; fuel reexports; textiles. **Imports:** $840 million (1999 est.): fuel, grain and other foods, machinery and parts, transport equipment. **Major trading partners:** Russia, Turkey, Azerbaijan, Armenia, EU, U.S.

Geography Georgia is bordered by the Black Sea in the west, by Turkey and Armenia in the south, by Azerbaijan in the east, and Russia in the north. The republic also includes the Abkhaz and Adzhar autonomous republics and the Yugo-Ossetian Autonomous Oblast. Mount Elbrus (Ialbuzi in Georgian) at 18,841 ft is the highest peak in Europe.

Government Republic.

History Georgia became a kingdom about 4 B.C. and Christianity was introduced in A.D. 337. During the reign of Queen Tamara (1184–1213), its territory included the whole of Transcaucasia. During the 13th century, Tamerlane and the Mongols decimated its population. From the 16th century on, the country was the scene of a struggle between Persia and Turkey. In the 18th century it became a vassal to Russia in exchange for protection from the Turks and Persians.

Georgia joined Azerbaijan and Armenia in 1917 to establish the anti-Bolshevik Transcaucasian Federation, and upon its dissolution, proclaimed its independence in 1918. In 1922, Georgia, Armenia, and Azerbaijan were annexed by the USSR and formed the Transcaucasian Soviet Socialist Republic. In 1936, it became a separate Soviet republic. Under Soviet rule Georgia was transformed from an agrarian country to a largely industrial, urban society.

Georgia proclaimed its independence from the USSR on April 6, 1991. In Jan. 1992, its leader Zviad Gamsakhurdia was sacked, and later accused of dictatorial policies, the jailing of opposition leaders, human rights abuses, and clamping down on the media. A ruling military council was established by the opposition until a civilian authority could be restored. In 1992, Eduard Shevardnadze, the Soviet Union's foreign minister under Gorbachev, became president.

In 1992–93, the government engaged in armed conflict with separatists in the breakaway province of Abkhazia. In 1994, Russia and Georgia signed a cooperation treaty that authorized Russia to keep three military bases in Georgia and allowed Russians to train and equip the Georgian army. In 1996, Georgia and its breakaway region of South Ossetia agreed to a cessation of hostilities in their six-year conflict. With little progress in resolving the Abkhazia situation, however, Parliament in April 1997 voted overwhelmingly to threaten Russia with loss of its military bases should it fail to extend Russian military control over the separatist region. In 1998 the U.S.

and Britain began an operation to remove nuclear material from Georgia, dangerous remains from its Soviet years. A darling of the West since his days as the Soviet Union's foreign minister, Shevardnadze is viewed less favorably by his own people, who are frustrated by unemployment, poverty, and rampant corruption. In the 2000 presidential elections, Shevardnadze was reelected with 80% of the vote, though international observers have determined the election was marred by irregularities.

Germany

FEDERAL REPUBLIC OF GERMANY

National name: Bundesrepublik Deutschland
President: Johannes Rau (1999)
Chancellor: Gerhard Schröder (1998)
Area: 137,846 sq mi (357,021 sq km)
Population (2001 est.): 83,029,536 (average annual growth rate: –0.1%); birth rate: 9.2/1000; infant mortality rate: 4.7/1000; density per sq mi: 602
Capital and largest city (1995 est.): Berlin (capital since Oct. 3, 1990), 3,471,418. **Other large cities (1997):** Hamburg, 1,703,800; Munich, 1,251,100; Cologne, 963,300; Frankfurt, 656,200; Essen, 619,600; Dortmund, 601,500; Stuttgart, 592,000; Düsseldorf, 573,100; Bremen, 551,000; Hanover, 526,400; Duisburg, 536,500. **Monetary units:** Deutsche Mark and euro. **Language:** German. **Ethnicity/race:** German 91.5%, Turkish 2.4%, Italians 0.7%, Greeks 0.4%, Poles 0.4%, other 4.6%. **Religions:** Protestant 38%, Roman Catholic 34%, Muslim 1.7%, Unaffiliated or other 26.3%. **Literacy rate:** 99% (1977)
Economic summary GDP/PPP (1999 est.): $1.864 trillion; per capita $22,700. **Real growth rate:** 1.5% **Inflation:** 0.8%. **Unemployment:** 10.5%. **Arable land:** 33%. **Agriculture:** potatoes, wheat, barley, sugar beets, fruit, cabbages; cattle, pigs, poultry. **Labor force:** 40.5 million; industry, 33.7%; agriculture, 2.7%; services, 63.6% (1998). **Industries:** among world's largest and technologically advanced producers of iron, steel, coal, cement, chemicals, machinery, vehicles, machine tools, electronics, food and beverages; shipbuilding; textiles. **Natural resources:** iron ore, coal, potash, timber, lignite, uranium, copper, natural gas, salt, nickel, arable land. **Exports:** $610 billion (f.o.b., 1999 est.): machinery, vehicles, chemicals, metals and manufactures, foodstuffs, textiles (1999). **Imports:** $587 billion (f.o.b., 1999 est.): machinery, vehicles, chemicals, foodstuffs, textiles, metals (1999). **Major trading partners:** EU, U.S., Japan.

Geography Located in central Europe, Germany is made up of the North German Plain, the Central German Uplands (Mittelgebirge), and the Southern German Highlands. The Bavarian plateau in the southwest averages 1,600 ft (488 m) above sea level, but it reaches 9,721 ft (2,962 m) in the Zugspitze Mountains, the highest point in the country. Germany's major rivers are the Danube, the Elbe, the Oder, the Weser, and the Rhine. Germany is about the size of Montana.

Government Parliamentary democracy.

History The Celts are believed to have been the first inhabitants of Germany. They were followed by German tribes at the end of the 2nd century B.C. German invasions destroyed the declining Roman Empire in the 4th and 5th centuries A.D. One of the tribes, the Franks, attained supremacy in western Europe under Charlemagne, who was crowned Holy Roman

Emperor in 800. By the Treaty of Verdun (843), Charlemagne's lands east of the Rhine were ceded to the German Prince Louis. Additional territory acquired by the Treaty of Mersen (870) gave Germany approximately the area it maintained throughout the Middle Ages. For several centuries after Otto the Great was crowned king in 936, German rulers were also usually heads of the Holy Roman Empire.

By the 14th century, the Holy Roman Empire was little more than a loose federation of the German princes who elected the Holy Roman emperor. In 1438, Albert of Hapsburg became emperor, and for the next several centuries the Hapsburg line ruled the Holy Roman Empire until its decline in 1806. Relations between state and church were changed by the Reformation, which began with Martin Luther's 95 theses, and came to a head in 1547, when Charles V scattered the forces of the Protestant League at Mühlberg. The Counter Reformation followed. A dispute over the succession to the Bohemian throne brought on the Thirty Years' War (1618–48), which devastated Germany and left the empire divided into hundreds of small principalities virtually independent of the emperor.

Meanwhile, Prussia was developing into a state of considerable strength. Frederick the Great (1740–86) reorganized the Prussian army and defeated Maria Theresa of Austria in a struggle over Silesia. After the defeat of Napoléon at Waterloo (1815), the struggle between Austria and Prussia for supremacy in Germany continued, reaching its climax in the defeat of Austria in the Seven Weeks' War (1866) and the formation of the Prussian-dominated North German Confederation (1867). The architect of this new German unity was Otto von Bismarck, a conservative, monarchist, and militaristic Prussian prime minister. He unified all of Germany in a series of three wars against Denmark (1864), Austria (1866), and France (1870–71). On Jan. 18, 1871, King Wilhelm I of Prussia was proclaimed German emperor in the Hall of Mirrors at Versailles. The North German Confederation, created in 1867, was abolished, and the Second German Reich, consisting of the North and South German states, was born. With a powerful army, an efficient bureaucracy, and a loyal bourgeoisie, Chancellor Bismarck consolidated a powerful centralized state.

Wilhelm II dismissed Bismarck in 1890 and embarked upon a "New Course," stressing an intensified colonialism and a powerful navy. His chaotic foreign policy culminated in the diplomatic isolation of Germany and the disastrous defeat in World War I (1914–18). The Second German Empire collapsed following the defeat of the German armies in 1918, the naval mutiny at Kiel, and the flight of the kaiser to the Netherlands. The Social Democrats, led by Friedrich Ebert and Philipp Scheidemann, crushed the Communists and established a moderate state, known as the Weimar Republic, with Ebert as president. President Ebert died on Feb. 28, 1925, and on April 26, Field Marshal Paul von Hindenburg was elected president. The mass of Germans regarded the Weimar Republic as a child of defeat, imposed upon a Germany whose legitimate aspirations to world leadership had been thwarted by a world conspiracy. Added to this were a crippling currency debacle, a tremendous burden of reparations, and acute economic distress.

Adolf Hitler, an Austrian war veteran and a fanatical nationalist, fanned discontent by promising a Greater Germany, abrogation of the Treaty of Versailles, restoration of Germany's lost colonies, and the destruction of the Jews, whom he scapegoated as the reason for Germany's downfall and depressed economy. When the Social Democrats and the Communists refused to combine against the Nazi threat, President von Hindenburg made Hitler the chancellor on Jan. 30, 1933. With the death of von Hindenburg on Aug. 2, 1934, Hitler repudiated the Treaty of Versailles and began full-scale rearmament. In 1935 he withdrew Germany from the League of Nations, and the next year he reoccupied the Rhineland and signed the Anti-Comintern pact with Japan, at the same time strengthening relations with Italy. Austria was annexed in March 1938. By the Munich agreement in Sept. 1938, he gained the Czech Sudetenland, and in violation of this agreement he completed the dismemberment of Czechoslovakia in March-1939. His invasion of Poland on Sept. 1, 1939, precipitated World War II.

Hitler established death camps to carry out "the final solution to the Jewish question." By the end of the war, Hitler's Holocaust had killed 6 million Jews, as well as Gypsies, homosexuals, Communists, the handicapped, and others not fitting the Aryan ideal. After some dazzling initial successes in 1939–42, Germany surrendered unconditionally to Allied and Soviet military commanders on May 8, 1945. On June 5 the four-nation Allied Control Council became the de facto government of Germany.

(For details of World War II and of the Holocaust, *see* Headline History, World War II.)

At the Berlin (or Potsdam) Conference (July 17–Aug. 2, 1945) President Truman, Premier Stalin, and Prime Minister Clement Attlee of Britain set forth the guiding principles of the Allied Control Council: Germany's complete disarmament and demilitarization, destruction of its war potential, rigid control of industry, and decentralization of the political and economic structure. Pending final determination of territorial questions at a peace conference, the three victors agreed to the ultimate transfer of the city of Königsberg (now Kaliningrad) and its adjacent area to the USSR and to the administration by Poland of former German territories lying generally east of the Oder-Neisse Line. For purposes of control, Germany was divided into four national occupation zones.

The Western powers were unable to agree with the USSR on any fundamental issues. Work of the Allied Control Council was hamstrung by repeated Soviet vetoes; and finally, on March 20, 1948, Russia walked out of the council. Meanwhile, the U.S. and Britain had taken steps to merge their zones economically (Bizone); and on May 31, 1948, the U.S., Britain, France, and the Benelux countries agreed to set up a German state comprising the three Western Zones. The USSR reacted by clamping a blockade on all ground communications between the Western Zones and West Berlin, an enclave in the Soviet Zone. The Western Allies countered by organizing a gigantic airlift to fly supplies into the beleaguered city. The USSR was finally forced to lift the blockade on May 12, 1949.

The Federal Republic of Germany was proclaimed on May 23, 1949, with its capital at Bonn. In free elections, West German voters gave a majority in the Constituent Assembly to the Christian Democrats, with the Social Democrats largely making up the opposition. Konrad Adenauer became chancellor, and Theodor Heuss of the Free Democrats was elected first president.

The East German states adopted a more centralized constitution for the Democratic Republic of Germany, put into effect on Oct. 7, 1949. The USSR thereupon dissolved its occupation zone but Soviet troops remained. The Western Allies declared that the East German Republic was a Soviet creation undertaken without self-determination and refused to recognize it. Soviet forces created a state controlled by the secret police with a single party, the Socialist Unity (Communist) Party.

Agreements in Paris in 1954 giving the Federal Republic full independence and complete sovereignty came into force on May 5, 1955. Under the agreement, West Germany and Italy became members of the Brussels treaty organization created in 1948 and renamed the Western European Union. West Germany also became a member of NATO. In 1955 the USSR recognized the Federal Republic. The Saar territory, under an agreement between France and West Germany, held a plebiscite and despite economic links to France, elected to rejoin West Germany on Jan. 1, 1957.

The division between West Germany and East Germany was intensified when the Communists erected the Berlin Wall in 1961. In 1968, the East German Communist leader, Walter Ulbricht, imposed restrictions on West German movements into West Berlin. The Soviet-bloc invasion of Czechoslovakia in Aug. 1968 added to the tension. West Germany in 1970 signed a treaty with Poland, renouncing force and setting Poland's western border as the Oder-Neisse Line. It subsequently resumed formal relations with Czechoslovakia in a pact that "voided" the Munich treaty that gave Nazi Germany the Sudetenland. By 1973, normal relations were established between East and West Germany and the two states entered the United Nations.

Willy Brandt, winner of a Nobel Peace Prize for his foreign policies, was forced to resign in 1974 when an East German spy was discovered to be one of his top staff members. Succeeding him was a moderate Social Democrat, Helmut Schmidt. Schmidt staunchly backed U.S. military strategy in Europe, staking his political fate on the strategy of placing U.S. nuclear missiles in Germany unless the Soviet Union reduced its arsenal of intermediate missiles. The chancellor also strongly opposed nuclear freeze proposals.

Helmut Kohl of the Christian Democrat Party became chancellor in 1982. An economic upswing in 1986 led to Kohl's reelection. The fall of the Communist government in East Germany left only Soviet objections to German reunification to be dealt with. This was resolved in July 1990. On Oct. 3, 1989, the German Democratic Republic acceded to the Federal Republic and Germany became a united and sovereign state for the first time since 1945.

Following unification, the Federal Republic became the second-largest country in Europe after the Soviet Union. A reunited Berlin serves as the official capital, although the government would continue to have administrative functions in Bonn during the 12-year transition period. The issue of the cost of reunification and the modernization of the former East Germany were serious considerations facing the reunified nation. Germany ratified the Maastricht Treaty in Oct. 1993, being the last of the 12 EU members to do so. Voters in the relatively new state of Brandenburg in the east rejected in May 1996 a proposal to merge with Berlin, dramatizing a lingering psychological division between eastern and western Germany.

Owing to a budget deficit that threatened the country's eligibility for introducing the future common European currency, the government in June 1997 proposed to revalue its foreign exchange holdings. Germany's other main challenge was to render the country competitively attractive as an industrial location by radically reducing taxes so as to attract investment capital, foreign and domestic, within the EU, and thus lower the high rate of unemployment.

In its most important election in decades, on Sept. 27, 1998, Germans chose Social Democrat Gerhard Schröder as chancellor over Christian Democrat incumbent Helmut Kohl, ending a 16-year-long rule that oversaw the reunification of Germany and symbolized the end of the cold war in Europe. A centrist in the style of Clinton and Blair, Schröder campaigned for "the new middle" and promised to rectify Germany's high unemployment rate of 10.6%.

Tension between the old-style left-wing and the more pro-business pragmatists within Schröder's government came to a head with the abrupt resignation of Finance Minister Oskar Lafontaine in March 1999, who was also chairman of the ruling Social Democratic Party. Lafontaine's plans to raise taxes on industry and raise German wages—already nearly the highest in the world—went against the more centrist policies of Schröder. Hans Eichel was chosen to become the next finance minister. Germany had one of the slowest rates of economic growth in western Europe—on par with Italy—and the most that was expected in 1999 was mild improvement. But in June Schröder presented an ambitious reform package that cut billions from the federal budget and offered lower corporate taxes. In Sept. 1999, the German Parliament returned to its historic seat in Berlin.

Germany joined the other NATO allies in the military conflict in Kosovo in 1999. Before the Kosovo crisis, Germans had not participated in an armed conflict since World War II. Germany agreed to take 40,000 Kosovar refugees, the most of any NATO country.

In Dec. 1999, former chancellor Helmut Kohl and other high officials in the Christian Democrat Party, including his successor, Wolfgang Schäuble, admitted accepting tens of millions of dollars in illegal donations during the 1980s and 1990s. The enormity of the scandal led to the virtual dismemberment of the CDU in early 2000, a party that had long been a stable conservative force in German politics.

In July 2000, Schröder managed to pass significant tax reforms that would lower the top income-tax rate from 51% to 42% by 2005. He also eliminated the capital gains tax on companies selling shares in other companies, a measure that was expected to spur mergers. In an effort to stem rising neo-Nazi violence, Schröder has contemplated banning the far-right National Democratic Party (NPD). In May 2001, the German Parliament authorized the payment of $4.4 billion in compensation to 1.2 million surviving Nazi-era slave laborers.

Ghana

REPUBLIC OF GHANA

President: John Agyekum Kufuor (2001)
Area: 92,100 sq mi (238,540 sq km)
Population (2001 est.): 19,894,014 (average annual rate of natural increase: 1.9%); birth rate: 29.0/1000; infant mortality rate: 56.5/1000; density per sq mi: 216
Capital: Accra. **Largest cities (est. 1988):** Accra, 949,100; Kumasi, 385,200; Tamale, 151,100.
Monetary unit: Cedi. **Languages:** English (official), Native tongues (Brong Ahafo, Twi, Fanti, Ga, Ewe, Dagbani). **Ethnicity/race:** black African 99.8% (major tribes: Akan 44%, Moshi-Dagomba 16%, Ewe 13%, Ga 8%), European and other 0.2%. **Religions:**

indigenous beliefs 38%, Islam 30%, Christian 24%. **Literacy rate:** 60% (1990) **Economic summary: GDP/PPP** (1999 est.): $35.5 billion; per capita $1,900. **Real growth rate:** 4.3%. **Inflation:** 12.8%. **Unemployment:** 20% (1997 est.). **Arable land:** 12%. **Agriculture:** cocoa, rice, coffee, cassava (tapioca), peanuts, corn, shea nuts, bananas; timber. **Labor force:** 4 million; agriculture, 60%; industry, 15%; services, 25%. **Industries:** mining, lumbering, light manufacturing, aluminum smelting, food processing. **Natural resources:** gold, timber, industrial diamonds, bauxite, manganese, fish, rubber, hydropower. **Exports:** $1.7 billion (f.o.b., 1999): gold, cocoa, timber, tuna, bauxite, aluminum, manganese ore, diamonds. **Imports:** $2.5 billion (f.o.b., 1999): capital equipment, petroleum, foodstuffs. **Major trading partners:** Togo, UK, Italy, Netherlands, Germany, U.S., France, Nigeria, Spain. **Member of Commonwealth of Nations**

Geography A West African country bordering on the Gulf of Guinea, Ghana is bounded by Côte d'Ivoire to the west, Burkina Faso to the north, Togo to the east, and the Atlantic Ocean to the south. It compares in size to Oregon, and its largest river is the Volta.

Government Republic.

History Several major civilizations flourished in the general region of what is now Ghana. The ancient empire of Ghana (located 500 mi northwest of the contemporary state) reigned until the 13th century. The Akan peoples established the next major civilization, beginning in the 13th century, and then the Ashanti empire flourished in the 18th and 19th centuries.

Called the Gold Coast, the area was first seen by Portuguese traders in 1470. They were followed by the English (1553), the Dutch (1595), and the Swedes (1640). British rule over the Gold Coast began in 1820, but it was not until after quelling the severe resistance of the Ashanti in 1901 that it was firmly established. British Togoland, formerly a colony of Germany, was incorporated into Ghana by referendum in 1956. Created as an independent country on March 6, 1957, Ghana, as the result of a plebiscite, became a republic on July 1, 1960.

Premier Kwame Nkrumah attempted to take leadership of the Pan-African Movement, holding the All-African People's Congress in his capital, Accra, in 1958 and organizing the Union of African States with Guinea and Mali in 1961. But he oriented his country toward the Soviet Union and China and built an autocratic rule over all aspects of Ghanaian life. In Feb. 1966, while Nkrumah was visiting Beijing and Hanoi, he was deposed by a military coup led by Gen. Emmanuel K. Kotoka.

A series of military coups followed and on June 4, 1979, Flight Lieutenant Jerry Rawlings overthrew Lt. Gen. Frederick Akuffo's military rule. Rawlings permitted the election of a civilian president to go ahead as scheduled the following month, and Hilla Limann, candidate of the People's National Party, took office. Charging the civilian government with corruption and repression, Rawlings staged another coup on Dec. 31, 1981. As chairman of the Provisional National Defense Council, Rawlings instituted an austerity program and reduced budget deficits. Rawlings was reelected in 1982 and again in 1996.

A major cocoa producer, Ghana has been hurt by several year-long slumps in cocoa prices. In July 2000 Ghana and neighboring countries began destroying massive amounts of cocoa to drive up the price. Together they account for 70% of the world's cocoa production. Since gold is Ghana's largest source of foreign exchange, fluctuating prices have hammered the economy, and mining companies cut 10,000 jobs in 1999. Saudi Arabian investors rescued Ashanti Goldfields, the largest company in sub-Saharan Africa, from near collapse in Feb. 2000.

In Jan. 2001, John Agyekum Kufuor took office, becoming Ghana's first democratically elected president since independence.

Greece

HELLENIC REPUBLIC

National name: Elliniki Dimokratia
President: Kostis Stephanopoulos (1995)
Prime Minister: Kostas Simitis (1996)
Area: 50,942 sq mi (131,940 sq km)
Population (2001 est.): 10,623,835 (average annual rate of natural increase: 0.0%); birth rate: 9.8/1000; infant mortality rate: 6.4/1000; density per sq mi: 209
Capital: Athens. **Largest cities (1991 est.):** Athens, 3,000,000; Thessaloníki, 720,000; Piraeus, 170,000; Patras, 155,000. **Monetary unit:** Drachma.
Language: Greek. **Ethnicity/race:** Greek 98%, other 2%; note: the Greek government states there are no ethnic divisions in Greece. **Religions:** Greek Orthodox 98%, Muslim 1.3%, other 0.7%. **Literacy rate:** 93% (1990)
Economic summary: GDP/PPP (1999 est.): $149.2 billion; per capita $13,900. **Real growth rate:** 3%. **Inflation:** 2.6%. **Unemployment:** 9.9%. **Arable land:** 19%. **Agriculture:** wheat, corn, barley, sugar beets, olives, tomatoes, wine, tobacco, potatoes; beef, dairy products. **Labor force:** 4.32 million; services, 59.2%; agriculture, 19.8%; industry, 21% (1998). **Natural resources:** bauxite, lignite, magnesite, petroleum, marble, hydropower. **Industries:** tourism; food and tobacco processing, textiles; chemicals; metal products; mining, petroleum. **Exports:** $12.4 billion (f.o.b., 1998): manufactured goods, food and beverages, fuels. **Imports:** $27.7 billion (c.i.f., 1998): manufactured goods, foodstuffs, fuels, chemicals. **Major trading partners:** EU, U.S.

Geography Located in southern Europe, Greece forms an irregular-shaped peninsula in the Mediterranean with two additional large peninsulas projecting from it: the Chalcidice and the Peloponnese. The Greek Islands are generally subdivided into two groups, according to location: the Ionian Islands (including Corfu, Cephalonia, and Leucas) west of the mainland and the Aegean Islands (including Euboea, Samos, Chios, Lesbos, and Crete) to the east and south. North-central Greece, Epirus, and western Macedonia are all mountainous. The main chain of the Pindus Mountains extends from northwest Greece to the Peloponnese. Mount Olympus, rising to 9,570 ft (2,909 m), is the highest point in the country.

Government Ceremonial executive power is held by the president; the prime minister heads the government and is responsible to a 300-member unicameral Parliament.

History Indo-European peoples, including the Mycenaeans, began entering Greece about 2000 B.C. and set up sophisticated civilizations. About 1200 B.C. the Dorians, another Indo-European people, invaded Greece, and a dark age followed, known mostly through the Homeric epics. At the end of this time, classical Greece began to emerge (c. 750 B.C.) as a loose composite of city-states with a heavy involvement in maritime trade and a devotion to art, literature, politics, and philosophy. Greece reached the peak of its glory in the 5th century B.C., but the Peloponnesian War (431–404 B.C.) weakened the nation, and it was conquered by Philip II and his son Alexander the Great of Macedonia, who considered themselves Greek. By the middle of the 2nd century B.C., Greece had declined to the status of a Roman province. It remained within the eastern Roman Empire until Constantinople fell to the Crusaders in 1204. In 1453, the Turks took Constantinople and by 1460, Greece was a Turkish province with its Orthodox Church intact. The insurrection made famous by the poet Lord Byron broke out in 1821, and in 1827 Greece won independence with sovereignty guaranteed by Britain, France, and Russia.

The protecting powers chose Prince Otto of Bavaria as the first king of modern Greece in 1832 to reign over an area only slightly larger than the Peloponnese peninsula. Chiefly under the next king, George I, chosen by the protecting powers in 1863, Greece acquired much of its present territory. During his 57-year reign, a period in which he encouraged parliamentary democracy, Thessaly, Epirus, Macedonia, Crete, and most of the Aegean islands were added from the disintegrating Turkish empire. Unfavorable economic conditions forced about one-sixth of the entire Greek population to emigrate (mostly to the U.S.) in the late 19th and early 20th centuries. An unsuccessful war against Turkey after World War I brought down the monarchy, which was replaced by a republic in 1923.

Two military dictatorships and a financial crisis brought George II back from exile, but only until 1941, when Italian and German invaders defeated tough Greek resistance. After British and Greek troops liberated the country in Oct. 1944, Communist guerrillas staged a long military campaign against the government; the Greek civil war, infamous for its brutality, began in Dec. 1944 and continued until Oct. 16, 1949, when the Communist guerrillas conceded defeat. The Greek government received U.S. aid under the Truman Doctrine, the predecessor of the Marshall Plan, to fight against the Communists.

Greece was a charter member of the UN, and became a member of the North Atlantic Treaty Organization (NATO) in 1951. A military junta seized power in April 1967, sending young King Constantine II into exile. Col. George Papadopoulos, a leader of the junta, gradually attempted to revamp his hardline, right-wing image: first, by giving up his military post for that of prime minister in 1973, and later, as president, by ending martial law. A coup ousted Papadopoulos in Nov. 1973. The seven-year regime of the "colonels," infamous for torturing and exiling opponents and scoffing at human rights, collapsed entirely a year later, after having bungled an attempt to seize Cyprus.

A referendum in Dec. 1974, five months after the demise of the military dictatorship, ended the Greek monarchy and established a republic. Former premier Karamanlis returned from exile to become premier of Greece's first civilian government since 1967. Greece has continued to be ruled by freely elected civilian governments ever since. On Jan. 1, 1981, Greece became the 10th member of the European Union. Anreas Papandreou, son of former premier George Papandeou, founded the Panhellenic Socialist Movement (PASOK) and became Greece's first socialist premier (1981–1989).

The Greeks were the most vocal dissenters within the NATO alliance regarding the 1999 intervention in Kosovo. They were both wary of the economic and political instability that would accompany a large influx of refugees and reluctant to ignore an Eastern Orthodox religious history shared with the Serbs.

Greece continued to experience tensions with Turkey over a disputed, unpopulated 10-acre island and over Cyprus, which is divided into Greek and Turkish sectors.

Prime Minister Kostis Simitis is credited with reviving the Greek economy, and the country adopted the euro in 2001. Still, *The Economist* magazine estimates it will be at least 15 years before the per capita GDP in Greece comes close to the current EU average.

Grenada

STATE OF GRENADA

Sovereign: Queen Elizabeth II (1952)
Governor-General: Daniel Williams (1996)
Prime Minister: Keith C. Mitchell (1995)
Area: 131 sq mi (340 sq km)
Population (2001 est.): 89,227 (average annual growth rate 1.5%); birth rate: 23.1/1000; infant mortality rate: 14.6/1000; density per sq mi: 680
Capital and largest city (1991): St. George's, 4,439. **Monetary unit:** East Caribbean dollar. **Language:** English. **Ethnicity/race:** black African descent 85%, mixed 11%, white, other 0.3%. **Religions:** Roman Catholic 64%, Anglican 21%. **Literacy rate:** 98% (1970)
Economic summary: GDP/PPP (1999 est.): $360 million; per capita $3,700. **Real growth rate:** 5%. **Inflation:** 1.3% (1998). **Unemployment:** 15% (1997). **Arable land:** 15%. **Agriculture:** bananas, cocoa, nutmeg, mace, citrus, avocados, root crops, sugarcane, corn, vegetables. **Labor force:** 42,300 (1996); services, 62%; agriculture, 24%; industry, 14% (1999 est.). **Industries:** food and beverages, textiles, light assembly operations, tourism, construction. **Natural resources:** timber, tropical fruit, deepwater harbors. **Exports:** $26.8 million (1998): bananas, cocoa, nutmeg, fruit and vegetables, clothing, mace. **Imports:** $200 million (1998): food, manufactured goods, machinery, chemicals, fuel (1989). **Major trading partners:** Caricom, UK, U.S., Netherlands, Japan. **Member of Commonwealth of Nations**

Geography Grenada (the first "a" is a long vowel) is the most southerly of the Windward Islands, about 100 mi (161 km) from the Venezuelan coast. It is a volcanic island traversed by a mountain range, the highest peak of which is Mount St. Catherine (2,756 ft; 840 m).

Government Parliamentary democracy. A governor-general represents the sovereign, Elizabeth II.

History The Arawak Indians were the first to inhabit Grenada, but they were all eventually massacred by the belligerent Carib Indians. When Columbus arrived in 1498 he encountered the Caribs, who continued to rule over the island for another 150 years. The French gained control of the island in 1672 and held on to it until 1762, when the British invaded. Black slaves were granted freedom in 1833. After more than 200 years of British rule, most recently as part of the West Indies Associated States, Grenada became independent on Feb. 7, 1974, with Eric M. Gairy as prime minister.

In 1979 the Marxist New Jewel Movement staged a coup, and its leader, Maurice Bishop, became prime minister. Bishop, a protégé of Cuba's President Castro, was killed in a military coup on Oct. 19, 1983.

In an effort to establish order on the island and eliminate the Cuban military presence, U.S. president Ronald Reagan ordered an invasion of Grenada on Oct. 25 involving over 1,900 U.S. troops and a small military force from Barbados, Dominica, Jamaica, St. Lucia, and St. Vincent. The troops met strong resistance from Cuban military personnel on the island but soon occupied it. After a gradual withdrawal of peacekeeping forces, a centrist coalition led by Herbert A. Blaize, won a parliamentary majority in 1984. The New National Party, led by Dr. Keith C. Mitchell, won a majority in the 1995 parliamentary elections. Mitchell improved ties with Cuba and in 1998 Castro visited Grenada. In 1999, Mitchell became the second prime minister in Grenada's history to be reelected.

Guatemala

REPUBLIC OF GUATEMALA

National name: República de Guatemala
President: Alfonso Portillo Cabrera (2000)
Area: 42,042 sq mi (108,890 sq km)
Population (2001 est.): 12,974,361 (average annual rate of natural increase: 2.8%); birth rate: 34.6/1000; infant mortality rate: 45.8/1000; density per sq mi: 309
Capital and largest city (1994 est.): Guatemala City, 1,150,452. **Other large cities (1994 est.):** Mixco, 413,002; Villa Nueva, 154,508. **Monetary unit:** Quetzal. **Languages:** Spanish, Indian languages. **Ethnicity/race:** Mestizo—mixed Amerindian-Spanish ancestry (in local Spanish called Ladino) 56%, Amerindian or predominantly Amerindian 44%. **Religions:** Roman Catholic, Protestant, Mayan. **Literacy rate:** 55% (1990)
Economic summary: GDP/PPP (1999 est.): $47.9 billion; per capita $3,900. **Real growth rate:** 3.5%. **Inflation:** 6.8%. **Unemployment:** 7.5%. **Arable land:** 12%. **Agriculture:** sugarcane, corn, bananas, coffee, beans, cardamom; cattle, sheep, pigs, chickens. **Labor force:** 3.32 million (1997 est.); agriculture, 50%; industry, 15%; services, 35%. **Industries:** sugar, textiles and clothing, furniture, chemicals, petroleum, metals, rubber, tourism. **Natural resources:** petroleum, nickel, rare woods, fish, chicle, hydropower. **Exports:** $2.4 billion (f.o.b., 1999): coffee, sugar, bananas, fruits and vegetables, meat, apparel, petroleum, electricity. **Imports:** $4.5 billion (c.i.f., 1999): fuels, machinery and transport equipment, construction materials, grain, fertilizers, electricity. **Major trading partners:** U.S., El Salvador, Honduras, Germany, Costa Rica, Mexico, Venezuela, Japan.

Geography The northernmost of the Central American nations, Guatemala is the size of Tennessee. Its neighbors are Mexico on the north and west, and Belize, Honduras, and El Salvador on the east. The country consists of three main regions—the cool highlands with the heaviest population, the tropical area along the Pacific and Caribbean coasts, and the tropical jungle in the northern lowlands (known as the Petén).

Government Republic.

History Once the site of the impressive ancient Mayan civilization, Guatemala was conquered by Spanish conquistador Pedro de Alvarado in 1524 and became a republic in 1839 after the United Provinces of Central America collapsed. From 1898 to 1920, dictator Manuel Estrada Cabrera ran the country, and from 1931 to 1944, Gen. Jorge Ubico Castaneda served as strongman.

After Ubico's overthrow in 1944, liberal-democratic coalitions led by Juan José Arévalo (1945–51) and Jacobo Arbenz Guzmán (1951–54) instituted social and political reforms that strengthened the peasantry and urban workers at the expense of the military and big landowners like the United Fruit Company. With covert U.S. backing, Col. Carlos Castillo Armas led a coup, and Arbenz took refuge in Mexico.

A 36-year civil war followed between military governments and leftist rebels. Amnesty International charged the administration of Gen. Romeo Lucas Garcia with some 5,000 political murders. The U.S. ended military aid in 1978.

After several other military governments, civilian Marco Vinicio Cerezo Arévalo took office in 1986. He was followed by Jorge Serrano Elías in 1991. In 1993, Serrano moved to dissolve Congress and the Supreme Court and suspend constitutional rights, but the military deposed Serrano and allowed the inauguration of de Leon Carpio, the former attorney general for human rights. A peace agreement was signed in Dec. 1996, ending the longest civil war in Latin American history, which had left some 150,000 dead and 50,000 missing. In June 1997, the new president Álvaro Arzú Irigoyen and the guerrilla movement leader Ricardo Ramirez received the UNESCO Houphouet-Boigny Peace Prize.

In 1999, a Guatemalan truth commission blamed the army for 93% of the atrocities and the rebels (the Guatemalan National Revolutionary Unit) for 3%. The former guerrillas apologized for their crimes, and President Clinton apologized for U.S. support of the right-wing military governments. The army has not acknowledged its guilt.

In 1998 Guatemala reestablished ties with Cuba. Alfonso Portillo Cabrera became president in Jan. 2000. Although he campaigned with former president Efrain Rios Montt, whose administration has been charged with human rights atrocities, in Aug. 2000 Portillo apologized for the government's abuses and pledged to prosecute those responsible and compensate victims.

Guinea

REPUBLIC OF GUINEA

National name: République de Guinée
President: Lansana Conté (1984)
Premier: Lamine Sidime (1999)
Area: 94,925 sq mi (245,857 sq km)
Population (2001 est.): 7,613,870 (average annual rate of natural increase: 2.2%); birth rate: 39.8/1000; infant mortality rate: 129.0/1000; density per sq mi: 80
Capital and largest city (1995 est.): Conakry, 1,508,000. **Monetary unit:** Guinean franc. **Languages:** French (official), native tongues (Malinké, Susu, Fulani). **Ethnicity/race:** Peuhl 40%, Malinke 30%, Susu 20%, smaller tribes 10%. **Religions:** Islam 85%, indigenous 7%, Christian 8%. **Literacy rate:** 24% in French; 48% in local languages (1990)
Economic summary: GDP/PPP (1999 est.): $9.2 billion; per capita $1,200. **Real growth rate:** 3.7%. **Inflation:** 4.5%. **Unemployment:** n.a. **Arable land:** 2%. **Agriculture:** rice, coffee, pineapples, palm kernels, cassava (tapioca), bananas, sweet potatoes; cattle, sheep, goats; timber. **Labor force:** 2.4 million (1983); agriculture, 80%; industry and commerce, 11%; services, 5.4%; civil service, 3.6%. **Industries:**

bauxite, gold, diamonds; alumina refining; light manufacturing and agricultural processing industries. **Natural resources:** bauxite, iron ore, diamonds, gold, uranium, hydropower, fish. **Exports:** $695 million (f.o.b., 1998 est.): bauxite, alumina, gold, diamonds, coffee, fish, agricultural products. **Imports:** $560 million (f.o.b., 1998 est.): petroleum products, metals, machinery, transport equipment, textiles, grain and other foodstuffs (1997). **Major trading partners:** Russia, U.S., Benelux, Ukraine, Ireland, Spain, France, Côte d'Ivoire, Hong Kong.

Geography Guinea, in West Africa on the Atlantic, is also bordered by Guinea-Bissau, Senegal, Mali, Côte d'Ivoire, Liberia, and Sierra Leone. Slightly smaller than Oregon, the country consists of a coastal plain, a mountainous region, a savanna interior, and a forest area in the Guinea Highlands. The highest peak is Mount Nimba at 5,748 ft (1,752 m).

Government Republic.

History Beginning in 900, the Susu migrated from the north and began settling in the area that is now Guinea. The Susu civilization reached its height in the 13th century. Today the Susu make up about 20% of Guinea's population. From the 16th to the 19th century, the Fulani empire dominated the region. In 1849, the French claimed it as a protectorate. First called Rivières du Sud, the protectorate was rechristened French Guinea, and finally, in 1895, it became part of French West Africa.

Guinea achieved independence on Oct. 2, 1958, and became an independent state with Sékou Touré as president. Under Touré, the country became the first avowedly Marxist state in Africa. Diplomatic relations with France were suspended in 1965, with the Soviet Union replacing France as the country's chief source of economic and technical assistance.

Prosperity came in 1960 after the start of exploitation of bauxite deposits. Touré was reelected to a seven-year term in 1974 and again in 1981. Touré died after 26 years as president in March 1984. A week later, a military regime headed by Col. Lansana Conté took power.

In 1989, President Conté announced that Guinea would move to a multiparty democracy, and in 1991 voters approved a new constitution. In Dec. 1993 elections, the president's Unity and Progress Party took almost 51% of the vote.

Guinea has had ongoing difficulties with its neighbor Liberia, which was embroiled in a long civil war during the 1990s. The fighting in Liberia spilled over the border into Guinea on several occasions, and border skirmishes continued after the civil war subsided. Guinea had taken sides against rebel leader Charles Taylor in Liberia's civil war and was part of the Nigerian-led ECOMOG forces that intervened in the crisis. As a consequence, President Conté's relations with Taylor remained sour after Taylor became Liberia's president in 1997.

Since Sept. 2000, fighting at the junction of Guinea's border with Sierra Leone and Liberia has increased. Guinea's army has been battling a variety of factions, including rebel Guineans and Liberians, and Sierra Leone's Revolutionary United Front (RUF). Already burdened by an inadequate infrastructure and a weak economy, nearly 300,000 refugees fleeing the civil war in Sierra Leone have overwhelmed Guinea.

Guinea-Bissau

REPUBLIC OF GUINEA-BISSAU

National name: República da Guiné-Bissau
President: Kumba Yalá (2000)
Prime Minister: Faustino Imbali (2001)
Area: 13,946 sq mi (36,120 sq km)
Population (2001 est.): 1,315,822 (average annual rate of natural increase: 2.4%); birth rate: 39.3/1000; infant mortality rate: 110.4/1000; density per sq mi: 94
Capital and largest city (1991 est.): Bissau, 200,000.
Monetary unit: Guinea-Bissau peso. **Languages:** Portuguese Criolo, African languages. **Ethnicity/race:** African 99% (Balanta 30%, Fula 20%, Manjaca 14%, Mandinga 13%, Papel 7%), European and mulatto less than 1%. **Religions:** traditional 65%, Islam 30%, Christian 5%. **Literacy rate:** 37% (1990)
Economic summary: GDP/PPP (1999 est.): $1.1 billion; per capita $900. **Real growth rate:** 9.5%. **Inflation:** 5.5% (1999). **Unemployment:** n.a. **Arable land:** 11%. **Agriculture:** rice, corn, beans, cassava (tapioca), cashew nuts, peanuts, palm kernels, cotton; timber; fish. **Labor force:** 480,000; agriculture, 78%. **Industries:** agricultural products processing, beer, soft drinks. **Natural resources:** fish, timber, phosphates, bauxite, unexploited deposits of petroleum. **Exports:** $26.8 million (f.o.b., 1998): cashew nuts, shrimp, peanuts, palm kernels, sawn lumber (1996). **Imports:** $22.9 million (f.o.b., 1998): foodstuffs, machinery and transport equipment, petroleum products (1996). **Major trading partners:** India, Singapore, Italy, Portugal, France, Senegal, Netherlands.

Geography A neighbor of Senegal and Guinea in West Africa, on the Atlantic coast, Guinea-Bissau is about half the size of South Carolina. The country is a low-lying coastal region of swamps, rain forests, and mangrove-covered wetlands, with about 25 islands off the coast. The Bijagos archipelago extends 30 mi (48 km) out to sea.

Government Republic.

History The land now known as Guinea-Bissau was once the kingdom of Gabú, which was part of the larger Mali empire. After 1546 Gabú became more autonomous, and at least portions of the kingdom existed until 1867. The first European to encounter Guinea-Bissau was the Portuguese explorer Nuño Tristão in 1446; colonists in the Cape Verde Islands obtained trading rights in the territory, and it became a center of the Portuguese slave trade. In 1879 the connection with the islands was broken.

The African Party for the Independence of Guinea-Bissau and Cape Verde (another Portuguese colony) was founded in 1956, and guerrilla warfare by nationalists grew increasingly effective. By 1974 the rebels controlled most of the countryside, where they formed a government that was soon recognized by scores of countries. The military coup in Portugal in April 1974 brightened the prospects for freedom, and in Aug. the Lisbon government signed an agreement granting independence to the province. The new republic took the name Guinea-Bissau.

In Nov. 1980, Premier João Bernardo Vieira headed a military coup that deposed Luis Cabral, president since 1974. In his 19 years of rule, Vieira was criticized for crony capitalism and corruption and for failing to alleviate the poverty of Guinea-Bissau, one of the world's poorest countries. Vieira also brought in troops from Senegal and the Republic of Guinea to help fight against an insurgency movement, a highly unpopular move. The rebels managed to gain control of most of the country and part of the capital in 1998 before a Nov. peace deal halted the fighting. But in May 1999, after the presidential guard refused to disarm, the rebels deposed Vieira.

Following a period of military rule, presidential elections were held in Jan. 2000. Kumba Yalá, a former teacher and popular leader of Guinea-Bissau's independence movement, was elected with 72% of the vote in the second round of balloting.

Guyana

COOPERATIVE REPUBLIC OF GUYANA

President: Bharrat Jagdeo (1999)
Prime Minister: Samuel Hinds (1997)
Area: 83,000 sq mi (214,970 sq km)
Population (2001 est.): 697,181 (average annual rate of natural increase: 0.9%; birth rate: 17.9/1000; infant mortality rate: 38.7/1000; density per sq mi: 8
Capital and largest city (1992 est.): Georgetown, 248,500. **Monetary unit:** Guyana dollar. **Languages:** English (official); Amerindian dialects. **Ethnicity/race:** East Indian 51%, black and mixed 43%, Amerindian 4%, European and Chinese 2%. **Religions:** Hindu 34%, Protestant 18%, Islam 9%, Roman Catholic 18%, Anglican 16%. **Literacy rate:** 96% (1990)
Economic summary: GDP/PPP (1999 est.): $1.86 billion; per capita $2,500. **Real growth rate:** 1.8%. **Inflation:** 5.5%. **Unemployment:** 12% (1992 est.). **Labor force:** 245,492 (1992); agriculture, n.a.; industry, n.a.; services, n.a. **Arable land:** 2%. **Agriculture:** sugar, rice, wheat, vegetable oils; beef, pork, poultry, dairy products; forest and fishery potential not exploited. **Industries:** bauxite, sugar, rice milling, timber, fishing (shrimp), textiles, gold mining. **Natural resources:** bauxite, gold, diamonds, hardwood timber, shrimp, fish. **Exports:** $574 million (f.o.b., 1999 est.): sugar, gold, bauxite/alumina, rice, shrimp, molasses, rum, timber. **Imports:** $620 million (c.i.f., 1999 est.): manufactures, machinery, petroleum, food. **Major trading partners:** U.S., Canada, UK, Netherlands Antilles, Jamaica, Trinidad and Tobago, Japan. **Member of Commonwealth of Nations**

Geography Guyana is the size of Idaho and is situated on the northern coast of South America east of Venezuela, west of Suriname, and north of Brazil. The country consists of a low coastal area and the Guyana Highlands, a tropical forest zone covering more than 80% of the country, in the south. There is an extensive north-south network of rivers.

Government Republic.

History The Dutch, English, and French established colonies in what is now known as Guyana, but by the early 17th century the majority of the settlements were Dutch. During the Napoleonic wars Britain took over the Dutch colonies of Berbice, Demerara, and Essequibo, which became British Guiana in 1831.

Slavery was outlawed in 1834, and the great need for plantation workers led to a large wave of immigration, primarily of East Indians. Today, about half of the population is of East Indian descent and about 43% are of African descent.

British Guiana was made a Crown colony in 1928, and in 1953 it was granted home rule. In 1950, Forbes Burnham and Cheddi Jagan, the former black and the latter East Indian, created the colony's first political party, which was dedicated to gaining the colony's independence. The two leaders split in 1955, creating separate parties. The leftist Jagan and the more moderate Burnham were to dominate Guyanan politics for decades to come. On May 26, 1966, the country gained independence, and resumed its traditional name, Guyana.

Burnham and his People's National Congress ruled Guyana for 21 years, until Burnham's death in 1985. In 1992, Jagan's People's Progressive Party won a majority in the general election. Jagan, who had served as prime minister in the 1960s while Guyana was still a colony, became president.

The current president, former finance minister Bharrat Jagdeo, assumed the presidency in Aug. 1999.

Guyana's potential economic development was hurt in 2000 as border disputes with both Venezuela to the west and Suriname to the east heated up. Suriname and Guyana have been unable to resolve the border dispute in an oil-rich coastal area. Venezuela's president Hugo Chavez has revived a 19th-century claim to more than half of Guyana's territory.

In March 2001, Bharrat Jagdeo won a second term in elections that highlighted Guyana's racial and cultural split. An ethnic East Indian, Jagdeo could not be sworn in for two weeks, until a court dismissed a challenge seeking to nullify the results. Meanwhile, many Guyanese of African ancestry claimed widespread election fraud, and sporadic violence rocked the country, marring what had been a peaceful election process.

Haiti

REPUBLIC OF HAITI

National name: République d'Haïti
President: Jean Betrand Aristide (2000)
Prime Minister: Jean-Marie Chérestal (2001)
Area: 10,714 sq mi (27,750 sq km)
Population (2001 est.): 6,964,549 (average annual rate of natural increase: 1.7%; birth rate: 31.7/1000; infant mortality rate: 95.2/1000; density per sq mi: 650
Capital and largest city (1993 est.): Port-au-Prince, 1.5 million. **Monetary unit:** Gourde. **Languages:** Creole and French (both official). **Ethnicity/race:** black 95%, mulatto and European 5%. **Religions:** Roman Catholic 80%, Protestant 16%, Vaudou 95%. **Literacy rate:** 53% (1990)
Economic summary: GDP/PPP (1999 est.): $9.2 billion; per capita $1,340. **Real growth rate:** 2.4%. **Inflation:** 9%. **Unemployment:** 70%; widespread underemployment; more than two-thirds of the labor force do not have formal jobs. **Arable land:** 20%. **Agriculture:** coffee, mangoes, sugarcane, rice, corn, sorghum; wood. **Labor force:** 3.6 million (1995); note: shortage of skilled labor, unskilled labor abundant (1998); agriculture, 66%; services, 25%; industry, 9%. **Industries:** sugar refining, flour milling, textiles, cement, tourism, light assembly industries based on imported parts. **Natural resources:** bauxite, copper, calcium carbonate, gold, marble, hydropower. **Exports:** $322 million (f.o.b., 1999): manufactures, coffee, oils, mangoes. **Imports:** $762 million (c.i.f., 1999): food, machinery and transport equipment, fuels. **Major trading partners:** U.S., EU.

Geography Haiti, in the West Indies, occupies the western third of the island of Hispaniola, which it shares with the Dominican Republic. About the size of Maryland, Haiti is two-thirds mountainous, with the rest of the country marked by great valleys, extensive plateaus, and small plains.

Government Republic.

History Visited by Columbus on Dec. 6, 1492, Haiti's native Arawaks fell victim to Spanish rule. In 1697 Haiti became the French colony of Saint-Dominique, which became a leading sugarcane producer dependent on slaves. In 1791 an insurrection erupted among the slave population of 480,000, resulting in a declaration of independence by Pierre-Dominique Toussaint l'Ouverture in 1801. Napoléon Bonaparte suppressed the independence movement, but it eventually triumphed in 1804 under Jean-Jacques Dessalines, who gave the new nation the Arawak name *Haiti*.

The revolution wrecked Haiti's economy. Years of strife between the light-skinned mulattos who dominated the economy and the majority black population, plus disputes with neighboring Santo Domingo, continued to hurt the nation's development. After a succession of dictatorships a bankrupt Haiti accepted a U.S. customs receivership from 1905 to 1941. Occupation by U.S. Marines from 1915 to 1934 brought stability. Haiti's high population growth made it the most densely populated nation in the hemisphere.

In 1949, after four years of democratic rule by President Dumarsais Estimé, dictatorship returned under Gen. Paul Magloire, who was succeeded by François Duvalier, nicknamed "Papa Doc," in 1957. Duvalier's secret police, the "Tontons Macoutes," ensured political stability with brutal efficiency. Duvalier's son, Jean-Claude, or "Baby Doc," succeeded his father in 1971 as ruler of the poorest nation in the Western Hemisphere. In the early 1980s, Haiti became one of the first countries to face an AIDS epidemic. Fear of the disease caused tourists to stay away, and the tourist industry collapsed, causing rising unemployment. Unrest generated by the economic crisis forced Duvalier to flee the country in 1986.

Throughout the 1990s the international community tried to establish democracy in Haiti. The country's first elected chief executive, Jean-Betrand Aristide, a Roman Catholic priest, took office on Feb. 7, 1991. The military, however, soon took control. A UN peacekeeping force, led by the U.S.—Operation Uphold Democracy—arrived in 1994. Aristide was restored to office and René Preval became his successor in 1996 elections.

U.S. soldiers left in 2000, but UN peacekeepers remain. Haiti's government is ineffectual and the economy is in ruins. Haiti has become a major drug shipment point. With 50% unemployment, Haiti produces a steady flow of refugees to the U.S.

In 2000, former president Aristide was reelected president in elections boycotted by the opposition and questioned by many foreign observers. The government charged opposition leaders with masterminding an attempted coup in July 2001, while opposition leaders claimed the government arranged the attack itself as an excuse to crack down on critics. The U.S. and other countries have threatened Haiti, already one of the world's poorest countries, with sanctions unless democratic procedures are strengthened.

Honduras

REPUBLIC OF HONDURAS

National name: República de Honduras
President: Carlos Roberto Flores Facusse (1998)
Area: 43,278 sq mi (112,090 sq km)
Population (2001 est.): 6,406,052 (average annual rate of natural increase: 2.6%); birth rate: 31.9/1000; infant mortality rate: 30.9/1000; density per sq mi: 148
Capital and largest city (1995): Tegucigalpa, 1,500,000.
Monetary unit: Lempira. **Languages:** Spanish (official), English widely spoken in business. **Ethnicity/ race:** mestizo (mixed Indian and European) 90%, Indian 7%, black 2%, white 1%. **Religions:** Roman Catholic 94%, Protestant minority. **Literacy rate:** 73% (1990)
Economic summary: GDP/PPP (1999 est.): $14.1 billion; per capita $2,050. **Real growth rate:** –3%. **Inflation:** 14%. **Unemployment:** 12%; underemployed, 30% (1997 est.). **Arable land:** 15%. **Agriculture:** bananas, coffee, citrus; beef; timber; shrimp. **Labor force:** 2.3 million (1997 est.); agriculture, 29%; industry, 21%; services, 60% (1998 est.). **Industries:** sugar, coffee, textiles, clothing, wood products. **Natural resources:** timber, gold, silver, copper, lead, zinc, iron ore, antimony, coal, fish, hydropower. **Exports:** $1.6 billion (f.o.b., 1999 est.): coffee, bananas, shrimp, lobster, meat; zinc, lumber. **Imports:** $2.7 billion (f.o.b., 1999 est.): machinery and transport equipment, industrial raw materials, chemical products, fuels, foodstuffs. **Major trading partners:** U.S., Japan, Germany, Belgium, Spain, Guatemala, Netherlands Antilles, Mexico, El Salvador.

Geography Honduras, in the north-central part of Central America, has a 400-mile (644-km) Caribbean coastline and a 40-mile (64-km) Pacific frontage. Its neighbors are Guatemala to the west, El Salvador to the south, and Nicaragua to the east. The second-largest country in Central America, Honduras is slightly larger than Tennessee. Generally mountainous, the country is marked by fertile plateaus, river valleys, and narrow coastal plains.

Government Republic.

History During the first millennium, Honduras was inhabited by the Maya. Columbus explored the country in 1502. Honduras, with four other Central American nations, declared its independence from Spain in 1821 to form a federation of Central American states. In 1838 Honduras left the federation and became independent. Political unrest rocked Honduras in the early 1900s, resulting in an occupation by U.S. Marines. Dictator Gen. Tiburcio Carias Andino established a strong government in 1932.

In 1969, El Salvador invaded Honduras after Honduran landowners deported several thousand Salvadorans. Five thousand people ultimately died in what is called "the football war," because it broke out during a soccer game between the two countries. By threatening economic sanctions and military intervention, the OAS induced El Salvador to withdraw. After a decade of military rule, parliamentary democracy returned with the election of Roberto Suazo Córdova as president in 1982. However, Honduras faced severe economic problems and tensions along its border with Nicaragua. "Contra" rebels, waging a guerrilla war against the Sandinista regime in Nicaragua, used Honduras as a training and staging area. The U.S. also used Honduras for military exercises and built bases to train Honduran and Salvadoran troops.

In 1997 Carlos Flores Facussé of the Liberal Party was elected president. He began to reform the economy and modernize the government. In recent years, Honduras has faced high unemployment, inflation, and dependence on coffee and bananas. In Oct. 1998, Hurricane Mitch killed some 13,000 Hondurans, left 2 million homeless, and caused more than $5 billion in damage.

In 1999, Honduras and Colombia ended a long maritime disagreement. However, Nicaragua, already at odds with Honduras over a border dispute, claimed the agreement infringed on its sovereignty. Honduras, along with Guatemala and El Salvador, signed a free trade agreement with Mexico in June 2000. The UN sent food aid to southern Honduras in the summer of 2000 because of severe drought.

Hungary

REPUBLIC OF HUNGARY

National name: Magyar Köztársaság
President: Ferenc Mádl (2000)
Premier: Viktor Orbán (1998)
Area: 35,919 sq mi (93,030 sq km)
Population (2001 est.): 10,106,017 (average annual rate of natural increase: −0.4%); birth rate: 9.3/1000; infant mortality rate: 9.0/1000; density per sq mi: 281
Capital and largest city (1995 est.): Budapest, 2,008,546. **Other large cities (1995 est.):** Debrecen, 210,000; Miskolc, 182,000; Szeged, 169,000; Pécs, 163,000. **Monetary unit:** Forint. **Languages:** Magyar (Hungarian), 98.2%; other, 1.8%. **Ethnicity/race:** Hungarian 89.9%, Gypsy 4%, German 2.6%, Serb 2%, Slovak 0.8%, Romanian 0.7%. **Religions:** Roman Catholic 67.5%, Protestant 25%, atheist and others 7.5%. **Literacy rate:** 98% (1980)
Economic summary: GDP/PPP (1999 est.): $79.4 billion; per capita $7,800. **Real growth rate:** 4%. **Inflation:** 10%. **Unemployment:** 10%. **Arable land:** 51%. **Agriculture:** wheat, corn, sunflower seed, potatoes, sugar beets; pigs, cattle, poultry, dairy products. **Labor force:** 4.2 million (1997); services, 65%; industry, 27%; agriculture, 8% (1996). **Industries:** mining, metallurgy, construction materials, processed foods, textiles, chemicals (especially pharmaceuticals), motor vehicles. **Natural resources:** bauxite, coal, natural gas, fertile soils, arable land. **Exports:** $22.6 billion (f.o.b., 1999): machinery and equipment, other manufactures, agriculture and food products, raw materials, fuels and electricity. **Imports:** $25.1 billion (f.o.b., 1999): machinery and equipment, other manufactures, fuels and electricity, agricultural and food products, raw materials. **Major trading partners:** Germany, Austria, Italy, Netherlands, Russia.

Geography   This central European country is the size of Indiana. Most of Hungary is a fertile, rolling plain lying east of the Danube River and drained by the Danube and Tisza Rivers. In the extreme northwest is the Little Hungarian Plain. South of that area is Lake Balaton (250 sq mi; 648 sq km).

Government   Republic.

History   By 14 B.C., western Hungary was part of the Roman Empire's provinces of Pannonia and Dacia. The area east of the Danube was never a part of the Roman Empire and was largely occupied by various Germanic and Asiatic peoples. In A.D. 896 all of Hungary was invaded by the Magyars, who founded a kingdom. Christianity was accepted during the reign of Stephen I (Saint Stephen), 977–1038. A devastating invasion by the Mongols killed half of Hungary's population in 1241. The peak of Hungary's great period of medieval power came during the reign of Louis I the Great (1342–82), whose dominions touched the Baltic, Black, and Mediterranean seas. War with the Turks broke out in 1389, and for more than 100 years the Turks advanced through the Balkans. When the Turks smashed a Hungarian army in 1526, western and northern Hungary accepted Hapsburg rule to escape Turkish occupation. Transylvania became independent under Hungarian princes. Intermittent war with the Turks was waged until a peace treaty was signed in 1699.

After the suppression of the 1848 revolt against Hapsburg rule, led by Louis Kossuth, the dual monarchy of Austria-Hungary was set up in 1867. The dual monarchy was defeated with the other Central Powers in World War I. After a short-lived republic in 1918,

the chaotic Communist rule of 1919 under Béla Kun ended with the Romanians occupying Budapest on Aug. 4, 1919. When the Romanians left, Adm. Nicholas Horthy entered the capital with a national army. The Treaty of Trianon of June 4, 1920, by which the Allies parceled out Hungarian territories, cost Hungary 68% of its land and 58% of its population. Meanwhile, the National Assembly had restored the legal continuity of the old monarchy and, on March 1, 1920, Horthy was elected regent.

In World War II, Hungary allied with Germany, which aided the country in recovering lost territories. Following the German invasion of Russia on June 22, 1941, Hungary joined the attack against the Soviet Union, but the war was not popular and Hungarian troops were almost entirely withdrawn from the eastern front by May 1943. Germany occupied the country for the remainder of the war. German occupation troops set up a puppet government after Horthy's appeal for an armistice with advancing Soviet troops on Oct. 15, 1944, had resulted in his overthrow. The German regime soon fled the capital, however, and on Dec. 23 a provisional government was formed in Soviet-occupied eastern Hungary. On Jan. 20, 1945, the government signed an armistice in Moscow. Early the next year, the National Assembly approved a constitutional law abolishing the thousand-year-old monarchy and establishing a republic.

By the Treaty of Paris (1947), Hungary had to give up all territory it had acquired since 1937 and to pay $300 million reparations to the USSR, Czechoslovakia, and Yugoslavia. In 1948 the Communist Party, with the support of Soviet troops, seized control. Hungary was proclaimed a People's Republic and one-party state in 1949. Industry was nationalized, the land collectivized into state farms, and the opposition terrorized by the secret police. The terror, modeled after that of the USSR, reached its height with the trial and life imprisonment of József Cardinal Mindszenty, the leader of Hungary's Roman Catholics, in 1948. On Oct. 23, 1956, an anti-Communist revolution broke out in Budapest. To cope with it, the Communists set up a coalition government and called former premier Imre Nagy back to head the government. But he and most of his ministers were swept by the logic of events into the anti-Communist opposition, and he declared Hungary a neutral power, withdrawing from the Warsaw Treaty and appealing to the United Nations for help. One of his ministers, János Kádár, established a counterregime and asked the USSR to send in military power. Soviet troops and tanks suppressed the revolution in bloody fighting after 190,000 people had fled the country. Under Kádár (1956–88), Communist Hungary henceforth maintained more liberal policies in the economic and cultural spheres, and Hungary became the most liberal of the Soviet-bloc nations of eastern Europe. Continuing his program of national reconciliation, Kádár emptied prisons, reformed the secret police, and eased travel restrictions.

Hungary's Communists abandoned their monopoly on power in 1989 voluntarily, and the constitution was amended in Oct. 1989 to allow for a multiparty state. The last Soviet troops left Hungary in June 1991, thereby ending almost 47 years of military presence. The transition to a market economy proved difficult. Hungary strengthened its ties with Poland and Czechoslovakia but grew concerned about the fate of ethnic Hungarians in neighboring countries. Hungary normalized relations with the Catholic Church in 1997 by signing an agreement concerning restitution or compensation for property seized during the Communist era.

In April 1999, Hungary became part of NATO, along with the Czech Republic and Poland. By the summer of 2001, Hungary had met 22 of the 31 terms it must complete to gain entry in the European Union. The country hopes to join the EU in 2004.

Iceland

REPUBLIC OF ICELAND

National name: Lydveldid Island
President: Ólafur Ragnar Grimsson (1996)
Prime Minister: David Oddsson (1991)
Area: 39,768 sq mi (103,000 sq km)[1]
Population (2001 est.): 277,906 (average annual rate of natural increase: 0.8%); birth rate: 14.6/1000; infant mortality rate: 3.6/1000; density per sq mi: 7
Capital and largest city (1994 est.): Reykjavik, 103,036. **Monetary unit:** Icelandic króna. **Language:** Icelandic. **Ethnicity/race:** homogeneous mixture of descendants of Norwegians and Celts. **Religions:** Church of Iceland (Evangelical Lutheran) 96%, other Protestant and Roman Catholic 3%, none 1%. **Literacy rate:** 100% (1976)
Economic summary: GDP/PPP (1999 est.): $6.42 billion; per capita $23,500. **Real growth rate:** 4.5%. **Inflation:** 1.9%. **Unemployment:** 2.4%. **Arable land:** 0%. **Agriculture:** potatoes, turnips; cattle, sheep; fish. **Labor force:** 131,000; manufacturing, 12.9%; fishing and fish processing, 11.8%; construction, 10.7%; other services, 59.5%; agriculture, 5.1%. **Industries:** fish processing; aluminum smelting, ferrosilicon production, geothermal power; tourism. **Natural resources:** fish, hydropower, geothermal power, diatomite. **Exports:** $1.9 billion (f.o.b., 1998): fish and fish products 70%, animal products, aluminum, diatomite and ferrosilicon. **Imports:** $2.4 billion (f.o.b., 1998): machinery and equipment, petroleum products; foodstuffs, textiles. **Major trading partners:** EU, U.S., Japan.

1. Including some offshore islands.

Geography Iceland, an island about the size of Kentucky, lies in the north Atlantic Ocean east of Greenland and just touches the Arctic Circle. It is one of the most volcanic regions in the world. The island is dotted with small freshwater lakes, and there are many natural phenomena, including hot springs, geysers, sulfur beds, canyons, waterfalls, and swift rivers. More than 13% of the area is covered by snowfields and glaciers, and most of the people live in the 7% of the island that is made up of fertile coastland. The Gulf Stream keeps Iceland's climate milder than one would expect from an island near the Arctic Circle.

Government Constitutional republic.

History The earliest inhabitants of Iceland were Irish hermits, who left the island upon the arrival of the pagan Norse people in the late 9th century. A constitution drawn up c. 930 created a form of democracy and provided for an *Althing*, the world's oldest practicing legislative assembly. The island's early history was preserved in the Icelandic sagas of the 13th century.

In 1262–64, Iceland came under Norwegian rule and passed to ultimate Danish control through the unification of the kingdoms of Norway, Sweden, and Denmark (the Kalmar Union) in 1397.

In 1874, Icelanders obtained their own constitution, and in 1918, Denmark recognized Iceland, via the Act of Union, as a separate state with unlimited sovereignty. It remained, however, nominally under the Danish monarchy.

During the German occupation of Denmark during World War II, British, then American, troops occupied Iceland and used it for a strategic air base. While officially neutral, Iceland cooperated with the Allies throughout the conflict. On June 17, 1944, after a popular referendum, the Althing proclaimed Iceland an independent republic.

The country joined the North Atlantic Treaty Organization in 1949, and subsequently received an American air force base in 1951. In 1970, it was admitted to the European Free Trade Association. Iceland unilaterally extended its territorial fishing limit from 3 to 200 nautical mi in 1972, precipitating a dispute with the UK known as the "cod wars," which ended in 1976, when the UK recognized the new limits. In 1980, the Icelanders elected a woman to the office of the presidency, the first elected female chief of state (i.e., president as distinct from prime minister) in the world.

After the recession of the early 1990s, Iceland began strengthening its economy. Government projections in mid-1997 showed that the country would have a large budget surplus for the year owing to fiscal management and a healthy economy. The government hoped to cut public spending further and boost the surplus.

At the International Whaling Commission meeting in July 2001, Iceland refused to agree to the moratorium on commercial whaling that has been in effect since 1986. Iceland has not resumed whaling, but it does not want to give up the possibility of commercial whaling altogether.

India

REPUBLIC OF INDIA

National name: Bharat
President: K. R. Narayanan (1997)
Prime Minister: Atal Bihari Vajpayee (1998)
Area: 1,269,338 sq mi (3,287,590 sq km)
Population (2001 est.): 1,029,991,145 (average annual rate of natural increase: 1.6%); birth rate: 24.3/1000; infant mortality rate: 63.2/1000; density per sq mi: 811
Capital (2000 est.): Delhi, 11,500,000 (metro. area). **Largest cities:** Bombay (Mumbai) (2000 est.), 17,850,000 (metro. area); Calcutta (Kolkata) (2000 est.), 12,900,000 (metro. area); Madras (Chennai) (2000 est.), 6,600,000 (metro. area); Hyderabad (2000 est.), 6,650,000 (metro. area); Bangalore (2000 est.), 5,500,000 (metro. area); Ahmedabad, 4,150,000; Kanpur, 1,874,409. **Monetary unit:** Rupee. **Principal languages:** Hindi (official), English (official), Bengali, Gujarati, Kashmiri, Malayalam, Marathi, Oriya, Punjabi, Tamil, Telugu, Urdu, Kannada, Assamese, Sanskrit, Sindhi (all recognized by the constitution). Dialects, 1,652. **Ethnicity/race:** Indo-Aryan 72%, Dravidian 25%, Mongoloid and other 3%. **Religions:** Hindu 82.6%, Islam 11.3%, Christian 2.4%, Sikh 2%, Buddhists 0.71%, Jains 0.48%. **Literacy rate:** 52% (1991)
Economic summary: GDP/PPP (1999 est.): $1.805 trillion; per capita $1,800. **Real growth rate:** 5.5%. **Inflation:** 6.7%. **Unemployment:** n.a. **Arable land:** 56%. **Agriculture:** rice, wheat, oilseed, cotton, jute, tea, sugarcane, potatoes; cattle, water buffalo, sheep, goats, poultry; fish. **Labor force:** n.a. agriculture, 67%; services, 18%; industry, 15% (1995 est.). **Industries:** textiles, chemicals, food processing, steel, transportation equipment, cement, mining, petroleum, machinery. **Natural resources:** coal (fourth-largest reserves in the world), iron ore, manganese, mica, bauxite, titanium ore, chromite, natural gas, diamonds, petroleum, limestone, arable land. **Exports:** $36.3

billion (f.o.b., 1999 est.): textile goods, gems and jewelry, engineering goods, chemicals, leather manufactures. **Imports:** $50.2 billion (f.o.b., 1999 est.): crude oil and petroleum products, machinery, gems, fertilizer, chemicals. **Major trading partners:** U.S., UK, Germany, Hong Kong, Japan, UAE, Belgium, Saudi Arabia. **Member of Commonwealth of Nations**

Geography One-third the area of the United States, the Republic of India occupies most of the subcontinent of India in south Asia. It borders on China in the northeast. Other neighbors are Pakistan on the west, Nepal and Bhutan on the north, and Burma and Bangladesh on the east.

The country can be divided into three distinct geographic regions: the Himalayan region in the north, which contains some of the highest mountains in the world, the Gangetic Plain, and the plateau region in the south and central part. Its three great river systems have extensive deltas and all rise in the Himalayas: the Ganges, 1,540 mi (2,478 km), the Indus, and the Brahmaputra.

India includes several groups of islands—the Laccadives (14 islands) in the Arabian Sea and the Andamans (204 islands) and the Nicobars (19 islands) in the Bay of Bengal.

Government Federal republic.

History One of the earliest civilizations, the Indus Valley civilization flourished on the Indian subcontinent from c. 2600 B.C. to c. 2000 B.C. The Aryans who invaded India c. 1500 B.C. from the northwest found a land that was already home to an advanced civilization. They introduced Sanskrit and the Vedic religion, a forerunner of Hinduism, to the area. Buddhism was founded in the 6th century B.C. and spread throughout northern India, most notably by one of the great ancient kings of the Mauryan dynasty, Asoka (c. 269–232 B.C.), who also unified most of the Indian subcontinent for the first time.

In 1526, Muslim invaders founded the great Mogul empire, centered on Delhi, which lasted, at least in name, until 1857. Akbar the Great (1542–1605) strengthened and consolidated this empire. The long reign of his great-grandson, Aurangzeb (1618–1707), represents both the greatest extent of the Mogul empire and the beginning of its decay.

Vasco da Gama, the Portuguese explorer, visited India first in 1498, and for the next 100 years the Portuguese had a virtual monopoly on trade with the subcontinent. Meanwhile, the English founded the East India Company, which set up its first factory at Surat in 1612 and began expanding its influence, fighting the Indian rulers and the French, Dutch, and Portuguese traders simultaneously.

Bombay, taken from the Portuguese, became the seat of English rule in 1687. The defeat of French and Mogul armies by Lord Clive in 1757 laid the foundation of the British Empire in India. The East India Company continued to suppress native uprisings and extend British rule until 1858, when the administration of India was formally transferred to the British Crown following the Sepoy Mutiny of native troops in 1857–58.

After World War I, in which the Indian states sent more than 6 million troops to fight beside the Allies, Indian nationalist unrest rose to new heights under the leadership of a Hindu lawyer, Mohandas K. Gandhi, called Mahatma Gandhi. His philosophy of civil disobedience called for nonviolent noncooperation against British authority. He soon became the leading spirit of the Indian National Congress Party, which

was the spearhead of revolt. In 1919 the British gave added responsibility to Indian officials, and in 1935 India was given a federal form of government and a measure of self-rule.

In 1942, with the Japanese pressing hard on the eastern borders of India, the British War Cabinet tried and failed to reach a political settlement with nationalist leaders. The Congress Party took the position that the British must quit India. In 1942, fearing mass civil disobedience, the government of India carried out widespread arrests of Congress leaders, including Gandhi.

Gandhi was released in 1944 and negotiations for a settlement were resumed. Finally, in Aug. 1947, India gained full independence. The victory was soured, however, by the partitioning of the predominantly Muslim regions of the north into the separate nation of Pakistan. The Muslim League, led by Mohammed Ali Jinnah, demanded a separate nation for the Muslim minority to prevent Hindu political and social domination. Indian Hindus, however, had hoped for a unified rather than balkanized Indian subcontinent. Lord Mountbatten as viceroy partitioned India along religious lines and split the provinces of Bengal and the Punjab, which both nations claimed. The partition of Pakistan and India led to the largest migration in human history, with 17 million people fleeing across the borders in both directions to escape the bloody riots occurring among sectarian groups. Armed conflict also broke out over rival claims to the princely states of Jammu and Kashmir.

Jawaharlal Nehru, nationalist leader and head of the Congress Party, was made prime minister. In 1949 a constitution, along the lines of the U.S. Constitution, was approved making India a sovereign republic. Under a federal structure the states were organized on linguistic lines. The dominance of the Congress Party contributed to stability. In 1956 the republic absorbed the former French settlements. Five years later, the republic forcibly annexed the Portuguese enclaves of Goa, Damao, and Diu.

Nehru died in 1964. His successor, Lal Bahadur Shastri, died on Jan. 10, 1966. Nehru's daughter, Indira Gandhi, became prime minister, and she continued his policy of nonalignment.

In 1971 the Pakistani army moved in to quash the independence movement in East Pakistan that was supported by India, and some 10 million Bengali refugees poured across the border into India, creating social, economic, and health problems. After numerous border incidents, India invaded East Pakistan and in two weeks forced the surrender of the Pakistani army. East Pakistan was established as an independent state and renamed Bangladesh.

In the summer of 1975, the world's largest democracy veered suddenly toward authoritarianism when a judge in Allahabad, Indira Gandhi's home constituency, found Gandhi's landslide victory in the 1971 elections invalid because civil servants had illegally aided her campaign. Amid demands for her resignation, Gandhi decreed a state of emergency on June 26 and ordered mass arrests of her critics, including all opposition party leaders except the Communists.

Despite strong opposition to her repressive measures, particularly resentment against compulsory birth control programs, Gandhi in 1977 announced parliamentary elections for March. At the same time, she freed most political prisoners. The landslide victory of Morarji R. Desai unseated Gandhi, but she staged a spectacular comeback in the elections of Jan. 1980.

In 1984, she ordered the Indian army to root out a band of Sikh holy men and gunmen who were using the most sacred shrine of the Sikh religion, the Golden Temple in Amritsar, as a base for terrorist raids in a violent campaign for greater political autonomy in the strategic Punjab border state. The perceived sacrilege to the Golden Temple kindled outrage among many of India's 14 million Sikhs and brought a spasm of mutinies and desertions by Sikh officers and soldiers in the army.

On Oct. 31, 1984, Indira Gandhi was assassinated by two men identified by police as Sikh members of her bodyguard. The ruling Congress Party chose her older son, Rajiv Gandhi, to succeed her as prime minister for four years. While running for reelection, former prime minister Rajiv Gandhi was assassinated on May 22, 1991, by Tamil militants who objected to India's mediation of the civil war in Sri Lanka. Final phases of the election were postponed for a month. When they were resumed, the Congress Party and its allies won 236 seats in the lower house, 20 short of a majority. P. V. Narasimha Rao was chosen to form a new government.

The ruling Congress Party lost the parliamentary elections of May 1996, and its waning has resulted in a period of political instability. The Hindu nationalist Bharatiya Janata Party's leader, Atal Bihari Vajpayee, became prime minister in May 1996, but his government lasted only 13 days. H. D. Deve Gowda of the United Front coalition became the next prime minister. Losing the support of the Congress Party, Prime Minister Deve Gowda lost a confidence vote in April 1997. Foreign Minister Inder Gujral was sworn in later that month, only to be replaced by Vajpayee in March 1998, his second time as prime minister.

In May 1998 India set off five nuclear tests, surprising the international community, which widely condemned India's pro-nuclear stance. Despite international urging for restraint, Pakistan responded by conducting several nuclear tests of its own two weeks later. India has resisted signing the Comprehensive Test Ban Treaty for nuclear weapons and has been slapped with sanctions by the U.S. and other countries. Less than a year later, in April 1999, both India and Pakistan tested nuclear-capable ballistic missiles. On April 17, Prime Minister Vajpayee's government lost a confidence vote, leaving India's government in disarray.

India and Pakistan have held various talks about the disputed territory of Kashmir, which is the issue at the base of their chronic antagonism as well as their displays of nuclear strength. India controls two-thirds of this Himalayan region, which is the only Indian state that is predominantly Muslim.

The Indian Air Force launched air strikes on May 26, 1999, and later sent in ground troops against Islamic guerrilla forces in Kashmir. India blamed Pakistan for orchestrating the Kashmiri attacks by sending soldiers and mercenaries across the so-called Line of Control that divides Kashmir between India and Pakistan. Pakistan countered that the guerrillas are independent Kashmiri freedom fighters struggling for India's ouster from the region. Most international sources agreed with India's assumption that Pakistan was arming the soldiers. In Aug. Pakistan was forced to withdraw, but fighting continued sporadically during the coming year.

In Jan. 2001, the state of Gujarat was rocked by a magnitude 7.7 earthquake, killing more than 20,000 people and leaving 600,000 homeless. The total cost of the disaster was set at an estimated $1.3 billion.

Prime Minister Vajpayee and Pakistan's military ruler Gen. Pervez Musharraf met in Agra in July 2001 to discuss Kashmir, terrorism, and their nuclear weapons arsenals. The talks were scuttled after two days of lengthy negotiations bore no fruit.

Native States Most of the 560-odd native states and subdivisions of pre-1947 India acceded to the new nation, and the central government pursued a vigorous policy of integration. This took three forms: merger into adjacent provinces, conversion into centrally administered areas, and grouping into unions of states. Finally, under a controversial reorganization plan effective on Nov. 1, 1956, the unions of states were abolished and India became a union of 15 states and 8 centrally administered areas. A 16th state was added in 1962, and in 1966, the Punjab was partitioned into two states. In 2000, India created three new states: Uttranchal, Chhattisgarh, and Jharkhand. Today India consists of 28 states and 7 Union Territories.

In April 1975, the Indian Parliament voted to make the 300-year-old kingdom of Sikkim a full-fledged Indian state, and the annexation took effect on May 16. Situated in the Himalayas, Sikkim was a virtual dependency of Tibet until the early 19th century. Under an 1890 treaty between China and Great Britain, it became a British protectorate, and was made an Indian protectorate after Britain quit the subcontinent.

Indonesia

REPUBLIC OF INDONESIA

National name: Republik Indonesia
President: Megawati Sukarnoputri (2001)
Area: 741,096 sq mi (1,919,440 sq km)
Population (2001 est.): 228,437,870 (average annual rate of natural increase: 1.6%); birth rate: 22.3/1000; infant mortality rate: 40.9/1000; density per sq mi: 308
Capital and largest city (2000 est.): Jakarta, 12,300,000 (metro. area). **Other large cities (1995 est.):** Surabaya, 2,701,300; Bandung, 2,368,200; Medan, 1,909,700; Semarang, 1,366,500. **Monetary unit:** Rupiah. **Languages:** Bahasa Indonesia (official), Dutch, English, and more than 583 languages and dialects. **Ethnicity/race:** Javanese 45%, Sundanese 14%, Madurese 7.5%, coastal Malays 7.5%, other 26%. **Religions:** Islam 87%, Christian 9%, Hindu 2%, other 2%. **Literacy rate:** 84% (1990)
Economic summary: GDP/PPP (1999 est.): $610 billion; per capita $2,800. **Real growth rate:** 0%. **Inflation:** 2%. **Unemployment:** 15%–20% (1998 est.). **Arable land:** 10%. **Agriculture:** rice, cassava (tapioca), peanuts, rubber, cocoa, coffee, palm oil, copra; poultry; beef, pork, eggs. **Labor force:** 88 million (1998); agriculture, 45%; trade, restaurant, and hotel, 19%; manufacturing, 11%; transport and communications, 5%; construction, 4%. **Industries:** petroleum and natural gas; textiles, apparel, and footwear; mining, cement, chemical fertilizers, plywood; rubber; food; tourism. **Natural resources:** petroleum, tin, natural gas, nickel, timber, bauxite, copper, fertile soils, coal, gold, silver. **Exports:** $48 billion (f.o.b., 1999 est.): oil and gas, plywood, textiles, rubber. **Imports:** $24 billion (c.i.f., 1999 est.): machinery and equipment; chemicals, fuels, foodstuffs. **Major trading partners:** Japan, EU, U.S., Singapore, South Korea, Hong Kong, China, Taiwan, Germany, Australia.

Geography Indonesia is an archipelago in Southeast Asia consisting of 17,000 islands (6,000 inhabited) and straddling the equator. The largest islands are Sumatra, Java (the most populous), Bali, Kalimantan (Indonesia's part of Borneo), Sulawesi (Celebes), the Nusa Tenggara islands, the Maluku Islands, and West Papua (formerly Irian Jaya), the western part of New Guinea. Its neighbor to the north is Malaysia and to the east is Papua New Guinea.

Indonesia, part of the "ring of fire," has the largest number of active volcanoes in the world. Earthquakes are frequent. The "Wallace Line," a zoological demarcation between Asian and Australian flora and fauna, divides Indonesia.

Government Republic.

History The 17,000 islands that make up Indonesia were home to a diversity of cultures and indigenous beliefs when the islands came under the influence of Hindu priests and traders in the first and second centuries A.D. Muslim invasions began in the 13th century, and most of the archipelago had converted to Islam by the 15th. Portuguese traders arrived early in the next century but were ousted by the Dutch around 1595. The Dutch United East India Company established posts on the island of Java, in an effort to control the spice trade.

After Napoléon subjugated the Netherlands in 1811, the British seized the islands but returned them to the Dutch in 1816. In 1922 Indonesia was made an integral part of the Dutch kingdom. During World War II, Japan seized the islands. Tokyo was primarily interested in Indonesia's oil, which was vital to the war effort, and tolerated fledgling nationalists such as Sukarno and Mohammed Hatta. After Japan's surrender, Sukarno and Hatta proclaimed Indonesian independence on Aug. 17, 1945. Allied troops, mostly British Indian forces, fought nationalist militia to reassert the prewar status quo until the arrival of Dutch troops.

In Nov. 1946, a draft agreement on forming a Netherlands-Indonesian Union was reached, but differences in interpretation resulted in more fighting between Dutch and nationalist forces. Following a bitter war for independence, leaders on both sides agreed to terms of a union on Nov. 2, 1949. The transfer of sovereignty took place at Amsterdam on Dec. 27, 1949. In Feb. of 1956 Indonesia abrogated the union, and began seizing Dutch property in the islands.

In 1963, Netherlands New Guinea (the Dutch portion of the island of New Guinea) was transferred to Indonesia and renamed West Irian, which became Irian Jaya in 1973 and West Papua in 2000. Hatta and Sukarno, the cofathers of Indonesian independence, split over Sukarno's concept of "guided democracy," and under Sukarno's rule the Indonesian Communist Party (PKI) steadily increased its influence.

Three years later, Sukarno was named president for life. Sukarno enjoyed mass support for his policies, but a growing power struggle between the military and the PKI loomed over his government. After an attempted military coup was put down by army chief of staff General Suharto and officers loyal to him, Suharto's forces killed hundreds of thousands of suspected Communists in a massive purge aimed at undermining Sukarno's rule.

Suharto took over the reins of government and gradually eased Sukarno out of office, completing his consolidation of power in 1967. Under Suharto the military assumed an overarching role in national affairs, and relations with the West were enhanced. Indonesia's economy improved dramatically and

national elections were permitted, although the opposition was so tightly controlled as to virtually choke off dissent.

In 1975, Indonesia invaded the former Portuguese half of the island of Timor and seized the territory in 1976. A separatist movement developed at once. Unlike the rest of Indonesia, which had been a Dutch colony, East Timor was governed by the Portuguese for 400 years, and while 90% of Indonesians are Muslim, the East Timorese are primarily Catholic. More than 200,000 Timorese are reported to have died from famine, disease, and fighting since the annexation. East Timor has received international attention for human rights abuses, and in 1996 two East Timorese resistance activists, Bishop Carlos Filipe Ximenes Belo and José Ramos-Horta, received the Nobel Peace Prize.

In the summer of 1997, Indonesia suffered a major economic setback along with most other Asian economies. Banks failed and the value of Indonesia's currency, the rupiah, plummeted. Antigovernment demonstrations took to the streets and riots broke out, directed mainly at the country's prosperous ethnic Chinese. As the economic crisis deepened, student demonstrators occupied the national Parliament, demanding Suharto's ouster. On May 21, 1998, Suharto stepped down, ending 32 years of rule and handing over power to Vice President B. J. Habibie. The Asian economic crisis hit Indonesia the hardest, and in 1998 one in five jobs was lost. Student unrest continued after Suharto's downfall, although the students' agenda for reform was vague.

June 7, 1999, marked Indonesia's first free parliamentary election since 1955. The ruling Golkar Party took a backseat to the Indonesian Democratic Party-Struggle (PDI-P), led by Megawati Sukarnoputri, the daughter of Sukarno, Indonesia's first president. She had been the head of the PDI in 1994 until Suharto had her removed.

The provinces of Aceh, Ambon (in the Moluccas), Borneo, and Irian Jaya saw rioting and violence in 1999. But nowhere was the violence more brutal and unjust than in East Timor. Habibie at first showed a softening of Indonesia's position on East Timor, unexpectedly announcing in Feb. 1999 that he was willing to hold a referendum on East Timorese independence. Despite the good news, the sudden Indonesian about-face was accompanied by heightened fighting between separatist guerrillas and pro-Indonesian paramilitary forces, who were armed by the Indonesian military. Twice rescheduled because of violence, a UN-organized referendum took place on Aug. 30, 1999, with 79% of the population voting to secede from Indonesia. In the days following the election, pro-Indonesian militias and Indonesian soldiers massacred civilians and forced a third of the population out of the region. Despite repeated assurances that order would be restored to the region, Habibie and the head of the military, General Wiranto, were either unwilling or unable to stop the violent rampage. After enormous international pressure, Indonesia finally agreed to allow UN forces into East Timor on Sept. 12. Led by Australia, an international peacekeeping force began restoring order to the ravaged region.

In a surprising upset, the Indonesian parliament elected Abdurrahman Wahid as the new president of Indonesia on October 20, 1999. Wahid's election over Megawati Sukarnoputri was devastating for the tens of thousands of Indonesian Democratic Party-Struggle supporters. Habibie, the incumbent, dropped out of the race days before the election after losing the confidence of his party when his involvement in a banking scandal was uncovered. Wahid, commonly known as Gus Dur, was a Sufi cleric as well as an adept politician with a reputation for honesty and moderation.

The northern Sumatran province of Aceh became the next troubled region of Indonesia, with Aceh separatists stepping up protests and demands for independence. A devoutly Muslim province of 4.5 million people, Aceh in many ways has more in common with its neighbor Malaysia than it does with Jakarta. President Wahid has proposed a referendum on permitting Islamic law in Aceh, but staunchly refused to discuss independence for the oil-rich province.

Rioting, bombing, and growing unrest continued to plague Indonesia in 2000. In Feb. 2000, President Wahid suspended the powerful General Wiranto from the Indonesian cabinet because he is being investigated for war crimes during the East Timor crisis. On June 4, 2000, separatists declared West Papua (formerly called Irian Jaya) an independent state. Wahid flatly opposed independence for West Papua, which contains sizable copper and gold mines. Unlike East Timor, there is little international support for an independent West Papua. Elsewhere in Indonesia, fighting between Christians and Muslims in the Moluccas Islands has killed 2,500 people since the end of 1998.

In fall 2000, Suharto failed twice to show up in court to face corruption charges of embezzling $570 million in state funds, but his lawyers insisted he was too ill to stand trial. In Sept. 2000 Suharto's playboy son, Hutomo "Tommy" Mandala Putra, was arrested in connection with a spate of bombings, the most serious of which left 15 dead at the Jakarta Stock Exchange.

In the fall of 2000 and winter of 2001, Wahid himself came under increasing criticism for corruption and incompetence. He was blamed for not stopping the continuing ethnic clashes and loss of life in Aceh, West Papua, the Maluku Islands, and especially in Borneo, where the Dayak people turned against Madurese immigrants, slaughtering hundreds. In addition, two financial scandals threatened to implicate Wahid. Thousands of people demonstrated in Jakarta in March 2001 demanding Wahid's resignation. In turn, pro-Wahid demonstrators later took to the streets in Jakarta and East Java. The violence continued economic uncertainty in the recession-plagued country.

In July 2001, Indonesia's legislature forced Wahid from power because of incompetence and corruption, and Vice President Megawati Sukarnoputri assumed the helm. Popular among the poor, Megawati's retiring nature and lack of political experience led some to question her abilities to govern this fledgling democracy beleaguered by separatist movements and continuous violence.

Iran

ISLAMIC REPUBLIC OF IRAN

Chief of State: Ayatollah Khamenei (1989)
President: Mohammad Khatami (1997)
Area: 636,293 sq mi (1,648,000 sq km)
Population (2001 est.): 66,128,965 (average annual rate of natural increase: 1.2%); birth rate: 17.1/1000; infant mortality rate: 29.0/1000; density per sq mi: 104
Capital and largest city (1994 est.): Teheran, 10,400,000 (metro. area). **Largest cities (1994 est.):** Mashad, 1,964,489; Isfahan, 1,220,595; Tabriz, 1,166,203. **Monetary unit:** Rial. **Languages:** Farsi (Persian), Azari, Kurdish, Arabic. **Ethnicity/race:** Persian 51%, Azerbaijani 24%, Gilaki and Mazandarani 8%, Kurd 7%, Arab 3%, Lur 2%, Baloch 2%, Turkmen 2%, other 1%. **Religions:** Shi'ite Muslim 95%, Sunni Muslim 4%. **Literacy rate:** 54% (1990)
Economic summary: GDP/PPP (1999 est.): $347.6 billion; per capita $5,300. **Real growth rate:** 1%. **Inflation:** 30%. **Unemployment:** 25%. **Arable land:** 10%. **Agriculture:** wheat, rice, other grains, sugar beets, fruits, nuts, cotton; dairy products, wool; caviar. **Labor force:** 15.4 million note: shortage of skilled labor; agriculture, 33%; industry, 25%; services, 42% (1997 est.). **Industries:** petroleum, petrochemicals, textiles, cement and other construction materials, food processing (particularly sugar refining and vegetable oil production), metal fabricating, armaments. **Natural resources:** petroleum, natural gas, coal, chromium, copper, iron ore, lead, manganese, zinc, sulfur. **Exports:** $12.2 billion (f.o.b., 1998 est.): petroleum, carpets, fruits, nuts, hides, iron, steel. **Imports:** $13.8 billion (f.o.b., 1998 est.): machinery, military supplies, metal works, foodstuffs, pharmaceuticals, technical services, refined oil products. **Major trading partners:** Japan, Italy, Greece, France, Spain, South Korea, Germany, UAE, UK, Belgium.

Geography Iran, a Middle Eastern country south of the Caspian Sea and north of the Persian Gulf, is three times the size of Arizona. It shares borders with Iraq, Turkey, Azerbaijan, Turkmenistan, Armenia, Afghanistan, and Pakistan.

The Elburz Mountains in the north rise to 18,603 ft (5,670 m) at Mount Damavend. From northwest to southeast, the country is crossed by a desert 800 mi (1,287 km) long.

Government Iran has been an Islamic theocracy since the Pahlavi monarchy regime was overthrown on Feb. 11, 1979.

History The region now called Iran was occupied by the Medes and the Persians in the 1500s B.C., until the Persian king Cyrus the Great overthrew the Medes and became ruler of the Achaemenid (Persian) Empire, which reached from the Indus to the Nile at its zenith in 525 B.C. Persia fell to Alexander in 331–330 B.C., and a succession of other rulers: the Seleucids (312–302 B.C.), the Greek-speaking Parthians (247 B.C.–A.D. 226), the Sasanians, and the Arab Muslims (in 641). By the mid-800s Persia had become an international scientific and cultural center. In the 12th century it was invaded by the Mongols. The Safavid dynasty (1501–1722), under whom the dominant religion became Shi'ite Islam, followed, and was then replaced by the Qajar dynasty (1794–1925).

During the Qajar dynasty, the Russians and the British fought for economic control of the area, and during World War I Iran's neutrality did not stop it from becoming a battlefield for Russian and British troops. A coup in 1921 brought Reza Kahn to power. In 1925 he became shah and changed his name to Reza Shah Pahlavi. He subsequently did much to modernize the country and abolished all foreign extraterritorial rights.

The country's pro-Axis allegiance in World War II led to Anglo-Russian occupation of Iran in 1941 and deposition of the shah in favor of his son, Mohammed Reza Pahlavi. Pahlavi's Westernization programs alienated the clergy, and his authoritarian rule led to massive demonstrations during the 1970s, to which the shah responded with the imposition of martial law in Sept. 1978. The shah and his family fled Iran on Jan. 16, 1979, and the exiled cleric Ayatollah Ruhollah Khomeini returned to establish an Islamic theocracy. Khomeini proceeded with his plans for revitalizing Islamic traditions. He urged women to return to the veil, banned alcohol, Western music, and mixed bathing, shut down the media, closed universities, and eliminated political parties.

Revolutionary militants invaded the U.S. embassy in Teheran on Nov. 4, 1979, seized staff members as hostages, and precipitated an international crisis. Khomeini refused all appeals, even a unanimous vote by the UN Security Council demanding immediate release of the hostages. Iranian hostility toward Washington was reinforced by the Carter administration's economic boycott and deportation order against Iranian students in the U.S., the break in diplomatic relations, and ultimately an aborted U.S. raid in April aimed at rescuing the hostages.

As the first anniversary of the embassy seizure neared, Khomeini and his followers insisted on their original conditions: guarantee by the U.S. not to interfere in Iran's affairs, cancellation of U.S. damage claims against Iran, release of $8 billion in frozen Iranian assets, an apology, and the return of the assets held by the former imperial family. These conditions were largely met and the 52 American hostages were released on Jan. 20, 1980, ending 444 days in captivity.

The sporadic war with Iraq regained momentum in 1982, as Iran launched an offensive in March and regained much of the border area occupied by Iraq in late 1980. The stalemated war with Iraq dragged on well into 1988. Although Iraq expressed its willingness to cease fighting, Iran stated that it would not stop the war until Iraq agreed to pay for war damages, and to punish the Iraqi government leaders involved in the conflict. On July 20, 1988, Khomeini, after a series of Iranian military reverses, agreed to cease-fire negotiations with Iraq. A cease-fire went into effect on Aug. 20, 1988. Khomeini died in June 1989 and Ayatollah Khamenei succeeded him as the supreme leader.

By early 1991 the Islamic revolution appeared to have lost much of its militancy. Attempting to revive a stagnant economy, President Rafsanjani took measures to decentralize the command system and introduce free-market mechanisms.

Mohammad Khatami, a little-known moderate cleric, former newspaperman, and national librarian, won the presidential election with 70% of the vote on May 23, 1997, a stunning victory over the conservative ruling elite. Khatami has supported greater social and political freedoms, and has made overtures for friendlier relations with the West.

His steps at liberalizing the strict clerical rule governing the country has put him at odds with the supreme leader, Ayatollah Khamenei. In 1998, Teheran mayor Gholam-Hossein Karbaschi, a strong supporter of Khatami's liberalization process, was sentenced to prison for embezzlement. Many saw this as a politically motivated attack aimed at Khatami.

In Sept. 1998 Iran deployed thousands of troops on its border with Afghanistan after the Taliban admitted killing eight Iranian diplomats and a journalist. Iran, mainly Shi'ite, supports the rebels fighting against the extremist Sunni Taliban.

Signaling a seismic change in Iran's political environment, reform candidates won the overwhelming majority of seats in Feb. 2000 parliamentary elec-

tions, thereby wresting control from hard-liners, who had dominated the Parliament since the 1979 Islamic revolution. The Parliament's reformist transformation greatly buttressed the efforts of moderate president Mohammad Khatami in constructing what he intends to become a nation of "lasting pluralism and Islamic democracy." Khatami has walked a jittery tightrope between student groups and other liberals pressuring him to introduce bolder freedoms, and Iran's military and conservative clerical elite (including Iran's supreme leader, Ayatollah Khamenei), who have expressed growing impatience with the president's liberalizing measures.

By Oct. 2000, however, the deeply conservative judiciary dampened the reformist impulse by systematically closing down every remaining pro-democracy publication. The new Parliament soon countered by introducing legislation that would limit the judiciary's authority to crack down on the press.

In June 2001 elections, Mohammad Khatami demonstrated the overwhelming popularity of his reforms by winning reelection with 77% of the vote. Khatami's new cabinet, composed of 20 moderates, disappointed liberals who hoped he would step up the pace of reform.

Iraq

REPUBLIC OF IRAQ

National name: Jumhouriyat Al Iraq
President: Saddam Hussein (1979)
Area: 168,753 sq mi (437,072 sq km)
Population (2001 est.): 23,331,985 (average annual rate of natural increase: 2.8%); birth rate: 34.6/1000; infant mortality rate: 60.1/1000; density per sq mi: 138
Capital and largest city (2000 est.): Baghdad, 4,850,000 (metro. area). **Largest cities (est. 1987):** Mosul, 664,221; Irbil, 485,968; Karkuk (Kirkuk), 418,624; Basra, 406,296. **Monetary unit:** Iraqi dinar.
Languages: Arabic (official) and Kurdish. **Ethnicity/race:** Arab 75%–80%, Kurdish 15%–20%, Turkoman, Assyrian, or other 5%. **Religions:** Muslim 97% (Shi'ite 60%–65%, Sunni 32%–37%), Christian or other 3%. **Literacy rate:** 60% (1990)
Economic summary: GDP/PPP (1999 est.): $59.9 billion; per capita $2,700. **Real growth rate:** 13%. **Inflation:** 135%. **Unemployment:** n.a. **Arable land:** 12%. **Agriculture:** wheat, barley, rice, vegetables, dates, cotton; cattle, sheep. **Labor force:** 4.4 million (1989); agriculture, n.a.; industry, n.a.; services, n.a. **Industries:** petroleum, chemicals, textiles, construction materials, food processing. **Natural resources:** petroleum, natural gas, phosphates, sulfur. **Exports:** $12.7 billion (1999 est.): crude oil. **Imports:** $8.9 billion (1999 est.): food, medicine, manufactures. **Major trading partners:** Russia, France, China, Egypt, Vietnam.

Geography Iraq, a triangle of mountains, desert, and fertile river valley, is bounded on the east by Iran, on the north by Turkey, on the west by Syria and Jordan, and on the south by Saudi Arabia and Kuwait. It is twice the size of Idaho. The country has arid desert land west of the Euphrates, a broad central valley between the Euphrates and Tigris, and mountains in the northeast.

Government One-party republic.

History From earliest times Iraq was known as Mesopotamia—the land between the rivers—for it embraces a large part of the alluvial plains of the Tigris and Euphrates Rivers.

An advanced civilization existed by 4000 B.C. Sometime after 2000 B.C. the land became the center of the ancient Babylonian and Assyrian Empires. Mesopotamia was conquered by Cyrus the Great of Persia in 538 B.C., and by Alexander in 331 B.C. After an Arab conquest in A.D. 637–40, Baghdad became capital of the ruling caliphate. The country was cruelly pillaged by the Mongols in 1258, and during the 16th, 17th, and 18th centuries was the object of repeated Turkish-Persian competition.

Nominal Turkish suzerainty imposed in 1638 was replaced by direct Turkish rule in 1831. In World War I, Britain occupied most of Mesopotamia and was given a mandate over the area in 1920. The British renamed the area Iraq and recognized it as a kingdom in 1922. In 1932 the monarchy achieved full independence. Britain again occupied Iraq during World War II because of its pro-Axis stance in the initial years of the war.

Iraq became a charter member of the Arab League in 1945, and Iraqi troops took part in the Arab invasion of Palestine in 1948.

King Faisal II, born on May 2, 1935, succeeded his father, Ghazi I, who was killed in an automobile accident on April 4, 1939. Faisal and his uncle, Crown Prince Abdul-Illah, were assassinated in July 1958 in a swift revolutionary coup that ended the monarchy and brought to power a military junta headed by Abdul Karem Kassim. Kassim reversed the monarchy's pro-Western policies, attempted to rectify the economic disparities between rich and poor, and began to form alliances with Communist countries.

Kassim was overthrown and killed in a coup staged on March 8, 1963, by the Ba'ath Socialist Party. Abdel Salam Arif, a leader in the 1958 coup, staged another coup in Nov. 1963, driving the Ba'ath members of the revolutionary council from power. He adopted a new constitution in 1964. In 1966, he, two cabinet members, and other supporters died in a helicopter crash. His brother, Gen. Abdel Rahman Arif, assumed the presidency, crushed the opposition, and won an indefinite extension of his term in 1967.

His regime was ousted in July 1968 by a junta led by Maj. Gen. Ahmed Hassan al-Bakr of the Ba'ath Party. Bakr and his second-in-command, Saddam Hussein, imposed authoritarian rule in an effort to end the decades of political instability that followed World War II.

One of the world's leading producers of oil, Iraq's oil revenues were used to develop one of the strongest military forces in the region. On July 16, 1979, President Bakr was succeeded by Saddam Hussein, whose regime eventually developed an international reputation for repression, human rights abuses, and terrorism.

A long-standing territorial dispute over control of the Shatt-al-Arab waterway between Iraq and Iran broke into full-scale war on Sept. 20, 1980. Iraqi planes attacked Iranian airfields and the Abadan refinery, and Iraqi ground forces moved into Iran. Despite the smaller size of its armed forces, Iraq took and held the initiative by seizing Abadan and Khurramshahr together with substantial Iranian territory by Dec., and beating back Iranian counterattacks in Jan. In 1982, the Iraqis retreated. The Iraqis clearly wanted to end the war, but the Iranians refused. In Feb. 1986, Iranian forces gained on two fronts; but Iraq retook most of the lost ground in 1988 and a cease-fire took effect that Aug.

In July 1990, President Hussein claimed that Kuwait was flooding world markets with oil and forc-ing down prices; it also made territorial claims on Kuwaiti land. A mediation attempt by Arab leaders failed, and on Aug. 2, 1990, Iraqi troops invaded Kuwait and set up a puppet government. On Jan. 18, 1991, UN forces, under the leadership of U.S. general Norman Schwarzkopf, launched Operation Desert Storm, liberating Kuwait in less than a week.

Despite rebellions by both Shi'ites and Kurds following Iraq's crushing defeat in the Gulf War, Saddam Hussein maintained his draconian grip on Iraq. The UN Security Council imposed sanctions beginning in 1990, which barred Iraq from selling oil except in exchange for food and medicine. Despite the debilitating effects of UN sanctions, Hussein continued to defy the terms of the cease-fire agreement, waging a propaganda campaign that blamed the U.S. for the starvation and poverty suffered by the Iraqi people rather than his own refusal to meet the terms required to remove sanctions.

On Nov. 13, 1997, Iraq expelled the American members of the UN inspections team mandated to ascertain that Iraq had destroyed all its nuclear, chemical, biological, and ballistic arms. Under the 1991 cease-fire resolution, the UN would not lift sanctions until Iraq fully complied. The standoff stretched on over months, and as tensions rose, the U.S. began a military buildup in the Gulf. In Feb. 1998 UN secretary-general Kofi Annan brokered a peaceful solution to the standoff. Over the next months Baghdad continued to impede the UN inspection team, demanding that sanctions be lifted. Finally, in Aug. 1998 Hussein put a complete halt to the inspections. This time, the U.S. opted for diplomatic arm-twisting rather than military threats, and in Sept. the UN Security Council voted unanimously that the lifting of sanctions would not be discussed until cooperation with UN arms inspectors resumed.

On Oct. 31, 1998, the United States and Britain threatened Iraq with the possibility of a military strike if it did not begin cooperating. On Nov. 14 Iraq agreed to unconditional cooperation with the UN inspectors, and the United States and Britain called off planned military action. But on Dec. 15, chief UN weapons inspector Richard Butler reported that Iraq had not lived up to its promise. The following day the United States and Britain began four days of air strikes. The attacks focused on command centers, missile factories, and airfields—targets that the Pentagon believed would damage Iraq's weapons stores. Since then, the U.S. and Britain have waged a steady war of attrition against Iraq, conducting hundreds of air strikes of Iraqi targets within the no-fly zones, which were established after the 1991 Gulf War. The aim of the British and American military appears to be to continue the sustained, low-level warfare in an effort to erode Iraqi military strength and, if fortunate, drive Hussein from power. U.S. and British planes continued to bomb Iraq periodically throughout 2001.

In 2000, the original UN inspections team, UNSCOM, was replaced with UNMOVIC, after the Clinton administration admitted that it had received intelligence reports from UNSCOM's weapons inspectors. In fall 2000, however, Baghdad was still refusing to let the new inspections team into the country.

The sanctions against Iraq have failed to crush its leader but have caused catastrophic suffering among its people—the country's infrastructure is in ruins, and disease, malnutrition, and the infant mortality rate have skyrocketed. The ineffectiveness of the sanctions and the humanitarian crisis left in its wake has turned much of world opinion against sanctions; Britain and the U.S. remain its chief advocates. In 1995 the Security Council voted to ease sanctions somewhat by introducing the "oil for food program," which permitted Iraq to export oil in exchange for food, medicine, and other necessities of life. The U.S. and Britain attempted to tighten sanctions against Iraq in 2001, but their proposed "smart sanctions," meant to eliminate loopholes that permitted Iraq to purchase more than life's necessities, were rejected by the UN Security Council in July.

Ireland

National name: Ireland, or Eire in the Irish language
President: Mary McAleese (1997)
Taoiseach (Prime Minister): Bertie Ahern (1997)
Area: 27,135 sq mi (70,280 sq km)
Population (2001 est.): 3,840,838 (average annual rate of natural increase: 0.7%); birth rate: 14.6/1000; infant mortality rate: 5.5/1000; density per sq mi: 142
Capital: Dublin. **Largest cities (1996):** Dublin, 953,000; Cork, 180,000; Limerick, 79,000; Galway, 57,000.
Monetary units: Irish pound (punt) and euro.
Languages: English, Irish Gaelic. **Ethnicity/race:** Celtic, English. **Religions:** Roman Catholic 93%, Anglican 3%, none 1%, unknown 2%, other 1%.
Literacy rate: 98% (1981)
Economic summary: GDP/PPP (1999 est.): $73.7 billion; per capita $20,300. **Real growth rate:** 8.4%. **Inflation:** 2.2%. **Unemployment:** 5.5%. **Arable land:** 13%. **Agriculture:** turnips, barley, potatoes, sugar beets, wheat; beef; dairy products. **Labor force:** 1.77 million; services, 63%; industry, 28%; agriculture, 9%. **Industries:** food products, brewing, textiles, clothing; chemicals, pharmaceuticals, machinery, transportation equipment, glass and crystal; software. **Natural resources:** zinc, lead, natural gas, barite, copper, gypsum, limestone, dolomite, peat, silver. **Exports:** $66 billion (f.o.b., 1999 est.): machinery and equipment, computers, chemicals, pharmaceuticals; live animals, animal products. **Imports:** $44 billion (c.i.f., 1999 est.): data processing equipment, other machinery and equipment, chemicals; petroleum and petroleum products, textiles, clothing. **Major trading partners:** EU, U.S., Japan, Singapore.

Geography Ireland is situated in the Atlantic Ocean and separated from Great Britain by the Irish Sea. Half the size of Arkansas, it occupies the entire island except for the six counties that make up Northern Ireland. Ireland resembles a basin—a central plain rimmed with mountains, except in the Dublin region. The mountains are low, with the highest peak, Carrantuohill in County Kerry, rising to 3,415 ft (1,041 m). The principal river is the Shannon, which begins in the north-central area, flows south and southwest for about 240 mi (386 km), and empties into the Atlantic.

Government Republic.

History In the Stone and Bronze Ages, Ireland was inhabited by Picts in the north and a people called the Erainn in the south, the same stock, apparently, as in all the isles before the Anglo-Saxon invasion of Britain. About the 4th century B.C., tall, red-haired Celts arrived from Gaul or Galicia. They subdued and assimilated the inhabitants and established a Gaelic civilization. By the beginning of the Christian Era, Ireland was divided into five kingdoms—Ulster, Connacht, Leinster, Meath, and Munster. Saint Patrick introduced Christianity in A.D. 432, and the country developed into a center of Gaelic and Latin learning.

Irish monasteries, the equivalent of universities, attracted intellectuals as well as the pious and sent out missionaries to many parts of Europe and, some believe, to North America.

Norse depredations along the coasts, starting in 795, ended in 1014 with Norse defeat at the Battle of Clontarf by forces under Brian Boru. In the 12th century, the pope gave all of Ireland to the English Crown as a papal fief. In 1171, Henry II of England was acknowledged "Lord of Ireland," but local sectional rule continued for centuries, and English control over the whole island was not reasonably absolute until the 17th century. In the Battle of the Boyne (1690), the Catholic King James II and his French supporters were defeated by the Protestant King William III (of Orange).

By the Act of Union (1801), England and Ireland became the "United Kingdom of Great Britain and Ireland." A steady decline in the Irish economy followed in the next decades. The population had reached 8.25 million when the great potato famine of 1846–48 took many lives and drove more than 2 million people to immigrate to North America.

In the meantime, anti-British agitation continued along with demands for Irish home rule. The advent of World War I delayed the institution of home rule and resulted in the Easter Rebellion in Dublin (April 24–29, 1916), in which Irish nationalists unsuccessfully attempted to throw off British rule. Guerrilla warfare against British forces followed proclamation of a republic by the rebels in 1919. The Irish Free State was established as a dominion on Dec. 6, 1922, with the six northern counties remaining as part of the United Kingdom. The constitution of 1937 changed the nation's name to Éire. Ireland was neutral in World War II.

In 1948, Eamon de Valera, American-born leader of the Sinn Fein, who had won the establishment of the Free State in 1921 in negotiations with Britain's David Lloyd George, was defeated by John A. Costello, who demanded final independence from Britain. The Republic of Ireland was proclaimed on April 18, 1949. It withdrew from the Commonwealth, but in 1955 Ireland entered the United Nations. Throughout the 1960s, two antagonistic currents dominated Irish politics. One sought to bind the wounds of the rebellion and civil war. The other was the effort of the outlawed Irish Republican Army to bring Northern Ireland into the republic.

Under the First Programme for Economic Expansion (1958–63), economic protection was dismantled and foreign investment encouraged. This prosperity brought profound social and cultural changes to what had been one of the poorest and least technologically advanced countries in Europe. Ireland joined the European Economic Community (now the EU) in 1973. In the 1990 presidential election, Mary Robinson was elected the republic's first woman president. The election of a candidate with socialist and feminist sympathies was regarded as a watershed in Irish political life, reflecting the changes taking place in Irish society. Irish voters approved the Maastricht Treaty, which paved the way for the establishment of the EU, by a large majority in a referendum held in 1992. In 1993, the Irish and British governments signed a joint peace initiative (the Downing Street Declaration), in which they pledged to seek mutually agreeable political structures in Northern Ireland and between the two islands. A referendum on allowing divorce under certain conditions—hitherto constitutionally forbidden—was held in Nov. 1995 and narrowly passed.

In 1998 hope for a solution to the troubles in Northern Ireland seemed palpable. A landmark settlement, the Good Friday Accord of April 10, 1998, came after 22 months of intensive negotiations that involved eight of the ten Northern Irish political parties. Chaired by former U.S. senator George Mitchell, the talks were advanced by a high-profile set of mediators, including British prime minister Tony Blair, Irish prime minister Bertie Ahern, and President Bill Clinton. The accord called for Protestants to share political power with the minority Catholics, and gave the Republic of Ireland a voice in Northern Irish affairs. The resounding commitment to the settlement was demonstrated in a dual referendum on May 22: the North approved the accord by a vote of 71% to 29%, and in the Irish Republic 94% favored it.

After numerous stops and starts, the new government was formed on Dec. 2, 2000, when the British government formally transferred governing powers over to the Northern Irish Parliament. But the Good Friday Accord stipulated that the IRA and other paramilitary groups disarm; by May 2000, the deadline for total disarmament, the IRA had still not surrendered a single weapon. Since the formation of the government, Britain has three times rescinded Northern Irish rule because of the IRA's noncompliance.

In June 2001, Ireland voted against expansion of the EU to include other countries. Ireland's rejection of the Nice Treaty came as a shock to the 14 other EU members as well as to the numerous countries aspiring to EU membership—the vote had to be unanimous among the EU partners to move ahead with the expansion.

See also Northern Ireland, under United Kingdom.

Israel

STATE OF ISRAEL

National name: Medinat Yisra'el
President: Moshe Katzav (2000)
Prime Minister: Ariel Sharon (2001)
Area: 8,019 sq mi (20,770 sq km)
Population (2001 est.): 5,938,093[1] (average annual rate of natural increase: 1.3%); birth rate: 19.1/1000; infant mortality rate: 7.7/1000; density per sq mi: 740
Capital[2] and largest city (1993 est.): Jerusalem, 550,500. **Other large cities (1993 est.):** Tel Aviv, 355,900; Haifa, 250,000. **Monetary unit:** Shekel.
Languages: Hebrew (official), Arabic, English.
Ethnicity/race: Jewish 82% (Israel-born 50%, Europe/Americas/Oceania-born 20%, Africa-born 7%, Asia-born 5%), non-Jewish 18% (mostly Arab) (1993 est.). **Religions:** Judaism 82%, Islam 14%, Christian 2%, others 2%. **Literacy rate:** 92% (1983)
Economic summary: GDP/PPP (1999 est.): $105.4 billion; per capita $18,300. **Real growth rate:** 2.1%. **Inflation:** 1.3%. **Unemployment:** 9.1%. **Arable land:** 17%. **Agriculture:** citrus, vegetables, cotton; beef, poultry, dairy products. **Labor force:** 2.3 million (1997); public services, 31.2%; manufacturing, 20.2%; finance and business, 13.1%; commerce, 12.8%; construction, 7.5%; personal and other services, 6.4%; transport, storage, and communications, 6.2%; agriculture, forestry, and fishing, 2.6% (1996).
Industries: food processing, diamond cutting and polishing, textiles and apparel, chemicals, metal products, military equipment, transport equipment, electrical equipment, potash mining, high-technology electronics, tourism. **Natural resources:** copper, phosphates, bromide, potash, clay, sand, sulfur, asphalt, manganese, small amounts of natural gas and crude oil. **Exports:** $23.5 billion (f.o.b., 1999):

machinery and equipment, software, cut diamonds, chemicals, textiles and apparel, agricultural products. **Imports:** $30.6 billion (f.o.b., 1999): raw materials, military equipment, investment goods, rough diamonds, fuels, consumer goods. **Major trading partners:** U.S., UK, Hong Kong, Benelux, Japan, Netherlands, Germany, Italy, Switzerland.

1. Includes West Bank, Gaza Strip, East Jerusalem. 2. Israel proclaimed Jerusalem as its capital in 1950, but the U.S., like nearly all other countries, maintains its embassy in Tel Aviv.

Geography Israel, slightly larger than Massachusetts, lies at the eastern end of the Mediterranean Sea. It is bordered by Egypt on the west, Syria and Jordan on the east, and Lebanon on the north. Northern Israel is largely a plateau traversed from north to south by mountains and broken by great depressions, also running from north to south.

The maritime plain of Israel is remarkably fertile. The southern Negev region, which comprises almost half the total area, is largely a wide desert steppe area. Parts of it have been irrigated and cultivated. The Jordan, the only important river, flows from the north through Lake Hule (Waters of Merom) and Lake Kinneret (Sea of Galilee or Sea of Tiberias), finally entering the Dead Sea, 1,312 ft (400 m) below sea level. This "sea," which is actually a salt lake (394 sq mi; 1,020 sq km), has no outlet, its water balance being maintained by evaporation.

Government Republic.

History Palestine, considered a holy land by Jews, Muslims, and Christians, and homeland of the modern state of Israel, was known as Canaan to the ancient Hebrews. Palestine's name derives from the Philistines, a people who occupied the southern coastal part of the country in the 12th century B.C.

A Hebrew kingdom established in 1000 B.C. was later split into the kingdoms of Judah and Israel; they were subsequently invaded by Assyrians, Babylonians, Egyptians, Persians, Romans, and Alexander the Great of Macedonia. By A.D. 135, few Jews were left in Palestine; most lived in the scattered and tenacious communities of the Diaspora. Palestine became a center of Christian pilgrimage after the emperor Constantine converted to that faith. The Arabs took Palestine from the Byzantine empire in 634–40. Interrupted only by Christian Crusaders, Muslims ruled Palestine until the 20th century. During World War I, British forces defeated the Turks in Palestine and governed the area under a League of Nations mandate from 1923.

As part of the 19th-century Zionist movement, Jews had begun settling in Palestine as early as 1820. This effort to establish a Jewish homeland received British approval in the Balfour Declaration of 1917. During the 1930s, Jews persecuted by the Hitler regime poured into Palestine. The postwar acknowledgment of the Holocaust—Hitler's genocide of 6 million Jews—increased international interest in and sympathy for the cause of Zionism. However, Arabs in Palestine and surrounding countries bitterly opposed prewar and postwar proposals to partition Palestine into Arab and Jewish sectors. The British mandate to govern Palestine ended after the war, and in 1947 the UN voted to partition Palestine. When the British officially withdrew on May 14, 1948, the Jewish National Council proclaimed the State of Israel.

U.S. recognition came within hours. The next day, Arab forces from Egypt, Jordan, Syria, Lebanon, and Iraq invaded the new nation. By the cease-fire on Jan.

7, 1949, Israel had increased its original territory by 50%, taking western Galilee, a broad corridor through central Palestine to Jerusalem, and part of modern Jerusalem. Chaim Weizmann and David Ben-Gurion became Israel's first president and prime minister. The new government was admitted to the UN on May 11, 1949.

The next clash with Arab neighbors came when Egypt nationalized the Suez Canal in 1956 and barred Israeli shipping. Coordinating with an Anglo-French force, Israeli troops seized the Gaza Strip and drove through the Sinai to the east bank of the Suez Canal, but withdrew under U.S. and UN pressure. In the Six-Day War of 1967, Israel made simultaneous air attacks against Syrian, Jordanian, and Egyptian air bases, totally defeating the Arabs. Expanding its territory by 200%, Israel at the cease-fire held the Golan Heights, the West Bank of the Jordan River, Jerusalem's Old City, and all of the Sinai and the east bank of the Suez Canal.

In the face of Israeli reluctance even to discuss the return of occupied territories, the fourth Arab-Israeli War erupted on Oct. 6, 1973, with a surprise Egyptian and Syrian assault on the Jewish high holy day of Yom Kippur. Initial Arab gains were reversed when a cease-fire took effect two weeks later, but Israel suffered heavy losses.

A dramatic breakthrough in the tortuous history of Mideast peace efforts occurred on Nov. 9, 1977, when Egypt's president Anwar Sadat declared his willingness to talk peace. Prime Minister Menachem Begin on Nov. 15 extended an invitation to the Egyptian leader to address the Knesset in Jerusalem. Sadat's arrival in Israel four days later raised worldwide hopes, but a peace agreement between Egypt and Israel was long in coming. On March 14, 1979, the Knesset approved a final peace treaty, and 12 days later Begin and Sadat signed the document, together with President Jimmy Carter, in a White House ceremony. Israel began its withdrawal from the Sinai, which it had annexed from Egypt, on May 25, and the two countries opened their border on May 29.

Although Israel withdrew its last settlers from the Sinai in April 1982, the fragile Mideast peace was shattered on June 9 by a massive Israeli assault on southern Lebanon, where the Palestinian Liberation Organization was entrenched. The PLO had long plagued Israelis with terrorist actions. Israel destroyed PLO strongholds in Tyre and Sidon and reached the suburbs of Beirut on June 10. A U.S.-mediated accord between Lebanon and Israel, signed on May 17, 1983, provided for Israeli withdrawal from Lebanon. Israel eventually withdrew its troops from the Beirut area but kept them in southern Lebanon, where occasional skirmishes would continue. Lebanon, under pressure from Syria, canceled the accord in March 1984.

A continual source of tension has been the relationship between the Jews and the Palestinians living within Israeli territories. Most Arabs fled the region when the state of Israel was declared, but those who remain now make up almost one-fifth of the population of Israel. They are about two-thirds Muslim, as well as Christian and Druze. Palestinians living on the West Bank and the Gaza Strip fomented the riots begun in 1987, known as the *Intifadeh*. Violence heightened as Israeli police cracked down and Palestinians retaliated. Continuing Jewish settlement of lands designated for Palestinians has added to the unrest.

In 1989 the leader of the PLO, Yasir Arafat, reversed decades of PLO polemic by acknowledging Israel's right to exist. He stated his willingness to enter negotiations to create a Palestinian political entity that would coexist with the Israeli state.

In 1991 Israel was struck by Iraqi missiles during the Persian Gulf War. The Israelis did not retaliate in order to preserve the international coalition against Iraq. In 1992 Yitzhak Rabin became prime minister. He halted the disputed Israeli settlement of the occupied territories. Highly secretive talks in Norway resulted in an agreement between the PLO and the Israeli government (the Oslo Agreement, 1993). The accord stipulated a five-year plan in which Palestinians of the West Bank and the Gaza Strip would gradually become self-governing. In 1994 Israel signed a peace treaty with Jordan. Israel has no formal peace agreement with Syria or Lebanon.

On Nov. 4, 1995, Prime Minister Rabin was slain by a Jewish extremist, jeopardizing the tenuous progress toward peace. Shimon Peres succeeded him until May 1996 elections for the Knesset gave Israel a new hard-line prime minister, Benjamin Netanyahu, by a razor-thin margin. Netanyahu reversed or stymied much of the Oslo Agreement, contending that it offered too many concessions too fast and jeopardized Israelis' safety. Elections for seats on the Palestinian Council and for its president took place in Jan. 1996. Yasir Arafat obtained an easy victory as president.

Israeli-Palestinian peace negotiations in 1997 were repeatedly undermined by both sides. Although the Hebron Accord was signed in Jan., calling for the withdrawal of Israeli troops from the city, the construction of new Jewish settlements on the West Bank in March profoundly upset progress toward peace. Some Jews cited the influx of immigration from Russia (since the collapse of the Soviet Union, more than 700,000 Russian Jews have arrived in Israel) as necessitating the additional settlements. Others believe that Netanyahu wished to curb Palestinian expectations raised by the Oslo Agreement.

Terrorism erupted again in 1997 when radical Hamas suicide bombers claimed the lives of more than 20 Israeli civilians. Netanyahu, accusing Palestinian Authority president Arafat of lax security, retaliated with draconian sanctions against Palestinians working in Israel, including the withholding of millions of dollars in tax revenue, a blatant violation of the Oslo Agreement. Netanyahu persisted in authorizing right-wing Israelis to build new settlements in mostly Arab East Jerusalem. Arafat, meanwhile, seemed unwilling or unable to curb the violence of extremist Arabs.

An Oct. 1998 summit at Wye Mills, Md., generated the first real progress in the stymied Middle East peace talks in 19 months, with Israeli prime minister Benjamin Netanyahu and Palestinian president Yasir Arafat settling several important interim issues called for by the 1993 Oslo Peace Accord. The Palestinians agreed to remove language from their founding charter that called for the dismantling of the Jewish state; Israelis agreed to cede an additional 13% of the West Bank.

Although Israel completed the first of three withdrawals from the West Bank on Nov. 20, released 250 Palestinian prisoners, and authorized the opening of the Gaza airport, the peace accord began unraveling almost immediately. Disagreement over the Israeli release of Palestinian prisoners led to violence in the West Bank and Gaza, for which each side blamed the other. To buttress the flagging accord, President Clinton visited the Gaza Strip on Dec. 15, becoming the first American president to set foot on Palestinian-occupied land. The visit coincided with the vote of the Palestine National Council to formally eliminate language from the organization's charter that calls for the destruction of Israel.

Netanyahu found himself attacked from both sides of the political spectrum—the left accused him of intentionally thwarting the peace process and the right accused him of betrayal, having elected him in the belief that he would never give up Israeli territory. In mid-Dec. Parliament voted to dissolve Netanyahu's government and hold elections in the spring, putting the peace negotiations on hold.

By the end of April 1999, Israel had made 41 air raids on Hezbollah guerrillas in Lebanon. The guerrillas were fighting against Israeli troops and their allies, the South Lebanon Army militia, who have occupied a security zone set up in 1985 to guard Israel's borders. Public pressure in Israel to withdraw the troops grew, and the issue dominated the Israeli election campaign in spring 1999. Ehud Barak of the Labour Party won the election with 55.9% of the vote, against 43.9% for incumbent Benjamin Netanyahu of Likud. Yasir Arafat originally planned to declare Palestinian statehood on May 4, but postponed that decision until an undefined time after the election.

Barak created a broad coalition government and on his inauguration (July 6, 1999) announced that "nothing is more important in my view than ... putting an end to the 100-year conflict in the Middle East." By this he meant not only pursuing peace with the Palestinians but establishing relations with Syria and ending the low-grade war in Southern Lebanon with the Iranian-armed Hezbollah guerrillas. Syria has more than 30,000 troops in Lebanon, and Iran uses Syria as its conduit for delivering weapons to Hezbollah.

In Sept. 1999, Israel moved ahead with the 1998 Wye Accord, ceding an additional 7% of territory to the Palestinians.

In Dec. 1999, Israeli-Syrian talks resumed after a nearly four-year hiatus. By Jan. 2000, however, talks had broken down when Syria demanded a detailed discussion of the return of all of the Golan Heights.

In Feb., new Hezbollah attacks on Israeli troops in southern Lebanon led to Israel's retaliatory bombing as well as Barak's decision to pull out of Lebanon. Israeli troops pulled out of Lebanon on May 24, 2000, after 22 years of occupation.

Peace talks in July 2000 at Camp David between Ehud Barak and Yasir Arafat ended unsuccessfully, despite President Clinton's strongest efforts—the status of Jerusalem was the primary sticking point. Clinton blamed Arafat's intransigence, but Palestinian supporters praised his strong stand. Barak, on the other hand, returned to a volatile political situation, with conservatives angered by his concessions and threatening to abandon his fragile parliamentary coalition.

In Sept., Likud leader Ariel Sharon visited the compound called Temple Mount by Jews and Haram al Sharif by Muslims, a fiercely contested site that is sacred to both Jews and Muslims. The visit set off the worst violence in years, killing around 400 people, mostly Palestinians. The violence (dubbed the Al Aska intifada) and the stalled peace process fueled growing concerns about Israeli security, paving the way for Sharon's stunning landslide victory over Barak in Feb. 2001. The 60% turnout was the lowest in Israeli history, an indication of disenchantment with both candidates. Barak was often seen as ineffective and often too willing to make concessions to the Palestinians, while many voters regarded Sharon as a hard-liner whose stance on Israeli security was uncompromising and whose commitment to the peace

process was at best ambivalent. Sharon's victory was greeted with caution in the West and provoked outrage in much of the Arab world. Since then the violence has continued at an alarming rate and no formal peace talks are in place.

Italy

ITALIAN REPUBLIC

National name: Repubblica Italiana
President: Carlo Azeglio Ciampi (1999)
Prime Minister: Silvio Berlusconi (2001)
Area: 116,305 sq mi (301,230 sq km)
Population (2001 est.): 57,679,825 (average annual rate of natural increase: –0.1%); birth rate: 9.1/1000; infant mortality rate: 5.8/1000; density per sq mi: 496
Capital and largest city (1994 est.): Rome, 2,693,383.
Other large cities: Milan, 1,561,438; Naples, 1,204,149; Turin, 952,736; Genoa, 706,754; Palermo, 694,749; Florence, 460,924; Bologna, 394,969; Catania, 372,212; Bari, 355,352; Venice, 306,439.
Monetary units: Lira and euro. **Languages:** Italian; small German-, French-, and Slovene-speaking minorities. **Ethnicity/race:** Italian (includes small clusters of German-, French-, and Slovene-Italians in the north and Albanian-Italians and Greek-Italians in the south), Sicilians, Sardinians. **Religions:** Roman Catholic 98%, other 2%. **Literacy rate:** 97% (1990)
Economic summary: GDP/PPP (1999 est.): $1.212 trillion; per capita $21,400. **Real growth rate:** 1.3%. **Inflation:** 1.7%. **Unemployment:** 11.5%. **Arable land:** 31%. **Agriculture:** fruits, vegetables, grapes, potatoes, sugar beets, soybeans, grain, olives; beef, dairy products; fish. **Labor force:** 23.193 million; services, 61%; industry, 32%; agriculture, 7% (1996). **Industries:** tourism, machinery, iron and steel, chemicals, food processing, textiles, motor vehicles, clothing, footwear, ceramics. **Natural resources:** mercury, potash, marble, sulfur, dwindling natural gas and crude oil reserves, fish, coal, arable land. **Exports:** $242.6 billion (f.o.b., 1998): engineering products, textiles and clothing, production machinery, motor vehicles, transport equipment, chemicals; food, beverages and tobacco; minerals and nonferrous metals. **Imports:** $206.9 billion (f.o.b., 1998): engineering products, chemicals, transport equipment, energy products, minerals and nonferrous metals, textiles and clothing; food, beverages, and tobacco. **Major trading partners:** EU, U.S.

Geography Italy, slightly larger than Arizona, is a long peninsula shaped like a boot bounded on the west by the Tyrrhenian Sea and on the east by the Adriatic. Approximately 600 of Italy's 708 mi (1,139 km) of length are in the long peninsula that projects into the Mediterranean from the fertile basin of the Po River. The Apennine Mountains, branching off from the Alps between Nice and Genoa, form the peninsula's backbone, and rise to a maximum height of 9,560 ft (2,912 m) at the Gran Sasso d'Italia (Corno). The Alps form Italy's northern boundary.

Italy has many northern lakes, lying below the snow-covered peaks of the Alps. The largest are Garda (143 sq mi; 370 sq km), Maggiore (83 sq mi; 215 sq km), and Como (55 sq mi; 142 sq km). The Po, the principal river, flows from the Alps on Italy's western border and crosses the Lombard plain to the Adriatic Sea.

Several islands form part of Italy. Sicily (9,926 sq mi; 25,708 sq km) lies off the toe of the boot, across the Strait of Messina, with a steep and rockbound northern coast and gentler slopes to the sea in the west and south. Mount Etna, an active volcano, rises to

10,741 ft (3,274 m), and most of Sicily is more than 500 ft (3,274 m) in elevation. Sixty-two mi (100 km) southwest of Sicily lies Pantelleria (45 sq mi; 117 sq km), and south of that are Lampedusa and Linosa. Sardinia (9,301 sq mi; 24,090 sq km), which is just south of Corsica and about 125 mi (200 km) west of the mainland, is mountainous, stony, and unproductive.

Government Republic.

History The migrations of Indo-European peoples into Italy probably began about 2000 B.C. and continued down to 1000 B.C. From about the 9th century B.C. until it was overthrown by the Romans in the 3rd century B.C., the Etruscan civilization dominated the area. By 264 B.C. all Italy south of Cisalpine Gaul was under the leadership of Rome. For the next seven centuries, until the barbarian invasions destroyed the western Roman Empire in the 4th and 5th centuries A.D., the history of Italy is largely the history of Rome. From 800 on, the Holy Roman Emperors, Roman Catholic popes, Normans, and Saracens all vied for control over various segments of the Italian peninsula. Numerous city-states, such as Venice and Genoa, whose political and commercial rivalries were intense, and many small principalities flourished in the late Middle Ages. Although Italy remained politically fragmented for centuries, it became the cultural center of the Western world from the 13th to the 16th century.

In 1713, after the War of the Spanish Succession, Milan, Naples, and Sardinia were handed over to the Hapsburgs of Austria, which lost some of its Italian territories in 1735. After 1800, Italy was unified by Napoléon, who crowned himself king of Italy in 1805; but with the Congress of Vienna in 1815, Austria once again became the dominant power in a disunited Italy. Austrian armies crushed Italian uprisings in 1820–21 and 1831. In the 1830s Giuseppe Mazzini, brilliant liberal nationalist, organized the Risorgimento (Resurrection), which laid the foundation for Italian unity. Disappointed Italian patriots looked to the House of Savoy for leadership. Count Camille di Cavour (1810–61), premier of Sardinia in 1852 and the architect of a united Italy, joined England and France in the Crimean War (1853–56), and in 1859, helped France in a war against Austria, thereby obtaining Lombardy. By plebiscite in 1860, Modena, Parma, Tuscany, and the Romagna voted to join Sardinia. In 1860, Giuseppe Garibaldi conquered Sicily and Naples and turned them over to Sardinia. Victor Emmanuel II, king of Sardinia, was proclaimed king of Italy in 1861. The annexation of Venetia in 1866 and of papal Rome in 1870 marked the complete unification of peninsular Italy into one nation under a constitutional monarchy.

Italy declared its neutrality upon the outbreak of World War I on the ground that Germany had embarked upon an offensive war. In 1915, Italy entered the war on the side of the Allies but obtained less territory than it expected in the postwar settlement. Benito ("Il Duce") Mussolini, a former socialist, organized discontented Italians in 1919 into the Fascist Party to "rescue Italy from Bolshevism." He led his Black Shirts in a march on Rome and, on Oct. 28, 1922, became premier. He transformed Italy into a dictatorship, embarking on an expansionist foreign policy with the invasion and annexation of Ethiopia in 1935 and allying himself with Adolf Hitler in the Rome-Berlin Axis in 1936. When the Allies invaded Italy in 1943, Mussolini's dictatorship collapsed; he was executed by Partisans on April 28, 1945, at Dongo on Lake Como. Following the armistice with the Allies (Sept. 3, 1943), Italy joined the war against Germany as a cobelligerent. A June 1946 plebiscite rejected monarchy and a republic was proclaimed. The peace treaty of Sept. 15, 1947, required Italian renunciation of all claims in Ethiopia and Greece and the cession of the Dodecanese to Greece and of five small Alpine areas to France. The Trieste area west of the new Yugoslav territory was made a free territory (until 1954, when the city and a 90-square-mile zone were transferred to Italy and the rest to Yugoslavia).

Italy became an integral member of NATO and the European Economic Community (later the EU) as it successfully rebuilt its postwar economy. A prolonged outbreak of terrorist activities by the left-wing Red Brigades threatened domestic stability in the 1970s, but by the early 1980s the terrorist groups had been suppressed. "Revolving door" governments, political instability, scandal, and corruption characterized Italian politics in 1980s and 1990s.

Italy adopted the euro as its currency in Jan. 1999. Treasury Secretary Carlo Ciampi, who is credited with the economic reforms that permitted Italy to enter the European Monetary Union, was elected president in May 1999.

Italy joined its NATO partners in the Kosovo crisis. Aviano Air Base in northern Italy was a crucial base for launching air strikes into Kosovo and Yugoslavia.

In June 2001, Silvio Berlusconi, the conservative billionaire, was sworn in as prime minister. He pledged to reduce unemployment, cut taxes, revamp the educational system, and reform the bureaucracy. His critics are alarmed by the apparent massive conflict of interest of a prime minister who also owns his country's media empire. He has also been accused of Mafia connections and is currently under indictment for tax fraud and bribery.

Jamaica

Sovereign: Queen Elizabeth II (1952)
Governor-General: Howard F. H. Cooke (1991)
Prime Minister: Percival J. Patterson (1992)
Area: 4,243 sq mi (10,990 sq km)
Population (2001 est.): 2,665,636 (average annual rate of natural increase: 1.3%); birth rate: 18.1/1000; infant mortality rate: 14.2/1000; density per sq mi: 628
Capital and largest city (1991 est.): Kingston, 104,000.
   Monetary unit: Jamaican dollar. **Languages:** English, Jamaican Creole. **Ethnicity/race:** African 76.3%, Afro-European 15.1%, East Indian and Afro-East Indian 3%, white 3.2%, Chinese and Afro-Chinese 1.2%, other 1.2%. **Religions:** Protestant 55.9%, Roman Catholic 5%, other 39.1%. **Literacy rate:** 98% (1990)
Economic summary: GDP/PPP (1999 est.): $8.8 billion; per capita $3,350. **Real growth rate:** –0.5%. **Inflation:** 9.4%. **Unemployment:** 15.5% (1998). **Arable land:** 14%. **Agriculture:** sugarcane, bananas, coffee, citrus, potatoes, vegetables; poultry, goats, milk. **Labor force:** 1.13 million (1998); services, 60%; agriculture, 21%; industry, 19% (1998). **Industries:** tourism, bauxite, textiles, food processing, light manufactures, rum, cement, metal, paper, chemical products. **Natural resources:** bauxite, gypsum, limestone. **Exports:** $1.4 billion (f.o.b., 1999 est.): alumina, bauxite, sugar, bananas, rum. **Imports:** $2.7 billion (f.o.b., 1999 est.): machinery and transport equipment, construction materials, fuel, food, chemicals, fertilizers. **Major trading partners:** U.S., EU, Canada, Caricom countries, Latin America.
Member of Commonwealth of Nations

Geography Jamaica is an island in the West Indies, 90 mi (145 km) south of Cuba and 100 mi (161 km) west of Haiti. It is a little smaller than Connecticut. The island is made up of coastal lowlands, a limestone plateau, and the Blue Mountains, a group of volcanic hills, in the east. Blue Mountain (7,402 ft; 2,256 m) is the tallest peak.

Government Parliamentary democracy.

History Jamaica was inhabited by Arawak Indians when Columbus explored it in 1494 and named it St. Iago. It remained under Spanish rule until 1655, when it became a British possession. Buccaneers operated from Port Royal, also the capital, until it fell into the sea in an earthquake in 1692. Disease decimated the Arawaks, so black slaves were imported to work on the sugar plantations. During the 17th and 18th centuries the British were consistently harassed by the Maroons, armed bands of freed slaves roaming the countryside. Abolition of the slave trade (1807), emancipation of the slaves (1833), and a drop in sugar prices eventually led to a depression that resulted in an uprising in 1865. The following year Jamaica became a Crown colony, and conditions improved considerably. Introduction of bananas reduced dependence on sugar.

On May 5, 1953, Jamaica gained internal autonomy, and in 1958 it led in organizing the West Indies Federation. A nationalist labor leader, Sir Alexander Bustamante, later campaigned to withdraw from the federation. After a referendum, Jamaica became independent on Aug. 6, 1962. Michael Manley, of the socialist People's National Party, became prime minister in 1972.

The Labour Party defeated Manley in 1980 and its capitalist-oriented leader, Edward P. G. Seaga, became prime minister. He encouraged private investment and began an austerity program. Like other Caribbean countries, Jamaica was hard-hit by the 1981–82 recession. Devaluation of the Jamaican dollar made Jamaican products more competitive on the world market and the country achieved record growth in tourism and agriculture. While manufacturing also grew, food prices rose as much as 75% and thousands of Jamaicans fell deeper into poverty.

In 1989, Manley was reelected, but he resigned in 1992 and was replaced by P. J. Patterson. In May 1997 the government signed a "Ship-Rider Agreement," allowing U.S. authorities to enter Jamaican waters and search vessels with the Jamaican government's permission, to fight drug trafficking. In 2001 violence between politically connected gangs escalated in Kingston, promoting fears that the tourist industry could suffer.

Japan

National name: Nippon
Emperor: Akihito (1989)
Prime Minister: Junichiro Koizumi (2001)
Area: 145,882 sq mi (377,835 sq km)
Population (2001 est.): 126,771,662 (average annual rate of natural increase: 0.2%); birth rate: 10.0/1000; infant mortality rate: 3.9/1000; density per sq mi: 869
Capital and largest city (2000 est.): Tokyo, 34,750,000 (metro. area). **Other large cities:** Osaka (2000 est.), 17,800,000 (metro. area); Yokohama, 3,307,136 (part of Tokyo metro. area); Nagoya (2000 est.), 5,100,000 (metro. area); Sapporo, 1,719,000; Kobe, 1,501,000 (part of Osaka metro. area); Kyoto, 1,456,000 (part of Osaka metro. area); Fukuoka, 1,263,000; Kawasaki,

1,196,000 (part of Tokyo metro. area); Hiroshima, 1,099,000. **Monetary unit:** Yen. **Language:** Japanese. **Ethnicity/race:** Japanese 99.4%, other 0.6% (mostly Korean). **Religions:** Shintoist, Buddhist, Christian. **Literacy rate:** 99% (1970)
Economic summary: GDP/PPP (1999 est.): $2.95 trillion; per capita $23,400. **Real growth rate:** 0.3%. **Inflation:** –0.8%. **Unemployment:** 4.7%. **Arable land:** 11%. **Agriculture:** rice, sugar beets, vegetables, fruit; pork, poultry, dairy products, eggs; fish. **Labor force:** 67.76 million (Nov. 1999); trade and services, 65%; industry, 30%; agriculture, forestry, and fishing, 5%. **Industries:** among world's largest and technologically advanced producers of motor vehicles, electronic equipment, machine tools, steel and nonferrous metals, ships, chemicals; textiles, processed foods. **Natural resources:** negligible mineral resources, fish. **Exports:** $413 billion (f.o.b., 1999 est.): motor vehicles, semiconductors, office machinery, chemicals. **Imports:** $306 billion (c.i.f., 1999 est.): fuels, foodstuffs, chemicals, textiles, office machinery. **Major trading partners:** U.S., Taiwan, China, South Korea, Hong Kong, Australia.

Geography An archipelago extending in an arc more than 1,744 mi (2,790 km) from northeast to southwest in the Pacific, Japan is separated from the east coast of Asia by the Sea of Japan. It is approximately the size of Montana.

Japan's four main islands are Honshu, Hokkaido, Kyushu, and Shikoku. The Ryukyu chain to the southwest was U.S.-occupied from 1945 to 1972, when it reverted to Japanese control, and the Kurils to the northeast are Russian-occupied. The surface of the main islands consists largely of mountains separated by narrow valleys.

Located within a geologically active region, Japan sustains approximately 1,000 earthquakes per year, though most are minor. Offshore earthquakes can produce tsunamis, massive ocean waves that can wreak destruction along the Pacific shore. Several of Japan's mountains are active volcanoes.

Government Constitutional monarchy.

History Legend attributes creation of Japan to the sun goddess, from whom the emperors were descended. The first of them was Jimmu, supposed to have ascended the throne in 660 B.C., a tradition that constituted official doctrine until 1945.

Recorded Japanese history begins in approximately A.D. 400, when the Yamato clan, eventually based in Kyoto, managed to gain control of other family groups in central and western Japan. Contact with Korea introduced Buddhism to Japan at about this time. Through the 700s Japan was much influenced by China, and the Yamato clan set up an imperial court similar to that of China. In the ensuing centuries, the authority of the imperial court was undermined as powerful gentry families vied for control.

At the same time, warrior clans were rising to prominence as a distinct class known as samurai. In 1192 the Minamoto clan set up a military government under their leader, Yoritomo. He was designated shogun (military dictator). For the following 700 years, shoguns from a succession of clans ruled in Japan, while the imperial court existed in relative obscurity.

First contact with the West came in about 1542, when a Portuguese ship off course arrived in Japanese waters. Portuguese traders, Jesuit missionaries, and Spanish, Dutch, and English traders followed. Suspicious of Christianity and of Portuguese support of a local Japanese revolt, the shoguns of the Tokugawa period (1603–1867) prohibited all trade with foreign countries; only a Dutch trading post at Nagasaki was permitted. Western attempts to renew trading relations failed until 1853, when Commodore Matthew Perry sailed an American fleet into Tokyo Bay. Trade with the West was forced upon Japan under terms less than favorable to the Japanese. Strife caused by these actions brought down the feudal world of the shoguns. In 1868 the emperor Meiji came to the throne, and the shogun system was abolished.

Japan quickly made the transition from a medieval to a modern power. An imperial army was established with conscription, and parliamentary government was formed in 1889. The Japanese began to take steps to extend their empire. After a brief war with China in 1894–95, Japan acquired Formosa (Taiwan), the Pescadores Islands, and part of southern Manchuria. China also recognized the independence of Korea (Chosen), which Japan later annexed (1910).

In 1904–05, Japan defeated Russia in the Russo-Japanese War, gaining the territory of southern Sakhalin (Karafuto) and Russia's port and rail rights in Manchuria. In World War I Japan seized Germany's Pacific islands and leased areas in China. The Treaty of Versailles then awarded Japan a mandate over the islands.

At the Washington Conference of 1921–22, Japan agreed to respect Chinese national integrity, but in 1931 invaded Manchuria. The following year, Japan set up this area as a puppet state, "Manchukuo," under Emperor Henry Pu-Yi, the last of China's Manchu dynasty. On Nov. 25, 1936, Japan joined the Axis. The invasion of China came the next year, followed by the Pearl Harbor attack on the U.S. on Dec. 7, 1941. Japan won its first military engagements during the war, extending its power over a vast area of the Pacific. Yet after 1942 the Japanese were forced to retreat, island by island, to their own country. The dropping of atomic bombs on the cities of Hiroshima and Nagasaki in 1945 by the United States finally brought the government to admit defeat. Japan surrendered formally on Sept. 2, 1945, aboard the battleship *Missouri* in Tokyo Bay. Southern Sakhalin and the Kuril Islands reverted to the USSR, and Formosa (Taiwan) and Manchuria to China. The Pacific islands remained under U.S. occupation.

Gen. Douglas MacArthur was appointed supreme commander of the U.S. occupation of postwar Japan (1945–52). In 1947 a new constitution took effect. The emperor became largely a symbolic head of state. The U.S. and Japan signed a security treaty in 1951, allowing for U.S. troops to be stationed in Japan. In 1952 Japan regained full sovereignty, and in 1972 the U.S. returned to Japan the Ryuku Islands, including Okinawa.

Japan's postwar economic recovery was nothing short of remarkable. New technologies and manufacturing were undertaken with great success. A shrewd trade policy gave Japan larger shares in many Western markets, an imbalance that caused some tensions with the U.S. The close involvement of Japanese government in the country's banking and industry produced accusations of protectionism. Yet economic growth continued through the 1970s and 1980s, eventually making Japan the world's second-largest economy (after the U.S.).

Japan has also been criticized for hesitation to take an active role in world affairs. Its failure to join the international coalition in the Persian Gulf War in 1991 was a case in point. Japanese prime minister Toshiki Kaifu pledged to provide $9 billion to the U.S. to help defray the expense of the latter's operations in the Persian Gulf. The government attempted to push legislation that would have permitted Japan to send a military contingent to the Gulf in noncombat roles. This was defeated amid public outcry against it.

During the 1990s, Japan has suffered an economic downturn marked by scandals involving government officials, bankers, and leaders of industry. Banks have closed under the weight of bad loans, unemployment has risen, real estate values have dropped, and many businesses have failed. Japan succumbed to the Asian economic crisis in 1998, experiencing its worst recession since World War II. These setbacks led to the resignation of Prime Minister Ryutaro Hashimoto in July 1998. He was replaced by Keizo Obuchi. In 1999 Japan seemed to make slight progress in an economic recovery. The International Monetary Fund reported in Sept. 1999 that "several signals point to a limited recovery of the Japanese economy."

Prime Minister Obuchi died of a stroke in May 2000 and was succeeded by Yoshiro Mori, whose administration was dogged by scandal and blunders from the get-go.

Despite attempts to revive the economy, fears that Japan would slide back into recession increased in early 2001. The embattled Mori resigned in April 2001. He was replaced by Liberal Democrat Junichiro Koizumi—the country's 11th prime minister in 13 years. Koizumi's plans to revitalize the country's tattered economy with painful reforms were buoyed in July elections, when his Liberal Democratic Party and its coalition partners dominated parliamentary elections.

Jordan

THE HASHEMITE KINGDOM OF JORDAN

National name: Al Mamlaka al Urduniya al Hashemiyah
Ruler: King Abdullah II (1999)
Prime Minister: Ali Abu al-Ragheb (2000)
Area: 34,445 sq mi (89,213 sq km) excludes West Bank
Population (2001 est.): 5,153,378 (average annual rate of natural increase: 2.3%); birth rate: 25.4/1000; infant mortality rate: 20.4/1000; density per sq mi: 150
Capital and largest city (1994 est.): Amman, 963,490. **Largest cities (1994 est.):** Zarka, 420,900 (1990); Irbid, 208,201; As-Salt, 187,014. **Monetary unit:** Jordanian dinar. **Languages:** Arabic (official), English. **Ethnicity/race:** Arab 98%, Circassian 1%, Armenian 1%. **Religions:** Islam 92%, Christian 6%, other 2%. **Literacy rate:** 86% (1994)
Economic summary: GDP/PPP (1999 est.): $16 billion (1999 est.); per capita $3,500. **Real growth rate:** 2%. **Inflation:** 3%. **Unemployment:** 15% official rate; actual rate is 25%–30%. **Arable land:** 4%. **Agriculture:** wheat, barley, citrus, tomatoes, melons, olives; sheep, goats, poultry. **Labor force:** 1.15 million; note: in addition, at least 300,000 workers are employed abroad (1997 est.); industry, 11.4%; commerce, restaurants, and hotels, 10.5%; construction, 10%; transport and communications, 8.7%; agriculture, 7.4%; other services, 52% (1992). **Industries:** phosphate mining, petroleum refining, cement, potash, light manufacturing, tourism. **Natural resources:** phosphates, potash, shale oil. **Exports:** $1.8 billion (f.o.b., 1999 est.): phosphates, fertilizers, potash, agricultural products, manufactures. **Imports:** $3.3 billion (c.i.f., 1999 est.): crude oil, machinery, transport equipment, food, live animals, manufactured goods. **Major trading partners:** Iraq, India, Saudi Arabia, EU, Indonesia, UAE, Lebanon, Kuwait, Syria, Ethiopia, Germany, U.S., Japan, UK, Italy, Turkey, Malaysia, China.

Geography The Middle East kingdom of Jordan is bordered on the west by Israel and the Dead Sea, on the north by Syria, on the east by Iraq, and on the south by Saudi Arabia. It is comparable in size to Indiana. Arid hills and mountains make up most of the country. The southern section of the Jordan River flows through the country.

Government Constitutional hereditary monarchy.

History In biblical times, the country that is now Jordan contained the lands of Edom, Moab, Ammon, and Bashan. Together with other Middle Eastern territories, Jordan passed in turn to the Assyrians, the Babylonians, the Persians, and, about 330 B.C., the Seleucids. Conflict between the Seleucids and the Ptolemies enabled the Arabic-speaking Nabataeans to create a kingdom in southeast Jordan. In A.D. 106 it became part of the Roman province of Arabia and in 633–36 was conquered by the Arabs. In the 16th century, Jordan submitted to Ottoman Turkish rule and was administered from Damascus. Taken from the Turks by the British in World War I, Jordan (formerly known as Transjordan) was separated from the Palestine mandate in 1920, and in 1921, placed under the rule of Abdullah ibn Hussein.

In 1923, Britain recognized Jordan's independence, subject to the mandate. In 1946, grateful for Jordan's loyalty in World War II, Britain abolished the mandate. That part of Palestine occupied by Jordanian troops was formally incorporated by action of the Jordanian Parliament in 1950. King Abdullah was assassinated in 1951. His son Talal, who was mentally ill, was deposed the next year. Talal's son Hussein, born on Nov. 14, 1935, succeeded him.

From the beginning of his reign, Hussein had to steer a careful course between his powerful neighbor to the west, Israel, and rising Arab nationalism, frequently a direct threat to his throne. Riots erupted when he joined the Central Treaty Organization (the Baghdad Pact) in 1955, and he incurred further unpopularity when Britain, France, and Israel attacked the Suez Canal in 1956, forcing him to place his army under nominal command of the United Arab Republic of Egypt and Syria. The 1961 breakup of the UAR eased Arab national pressure on Hussein, who was the first to recognize Syria after it reclaimed its independence. Jordan was swept into the 1967 Arab-Israeli War, however, and lost the old city of Jerusalem and all of its territory west of the Jordan River, the West Bank. Embittered Palestinian guerrilla forces virtually took over sections of Jordan in the aftermath of defeat, and open warfare broke out between the Palestinians and government forces in 1970.

Despite intervention of Syrian tanks, Hussein's Bedouin army defeated the Palestinians. The Jordanians drove out the Syrians and 12,000 Iraqi troops who had been in the country since the 1967 war. Ignoring protests from other Arab states, Hussein, by mid-1971, crushed Palestinian strength in Jordan and shifted the problem to Lebanon, where many of the guerrillas had fled. As Egypt and Israel neared final agreement on a peace treaty early in 1979, Hussein met with Yasir Arafat, the PLO leader, on March 17 and issued a joint statement of opposition. Although the U.S. pressed Jordan to break Arab ranks on the issue, Hussein elected to side with the great majority, cutting ties with Cairo and joining the boycott against Egypt.

Jordan's stance during the Persian Gulf War strained relations with the U.S. and led to the termination of U.S. aid. The signing of a national charter by King Hussein and leaders of the main political groups in June 1991 meant political parties were permitted in exchange for acceptance of the constitution and the monarchy. King Hussein's decision to join the Middle East peace talks in mid-1991 helped restore his country's relations with the U.S.

In July 1994 King Hussein and the Israeli prime minister signed a declaration ending the state of belligerency between the two countries. A peace agreement between the two countries was signed on Oct. 26, 1994, although a clause in it calling the king the "custodian" of Islamic holy shrines in Jerusalem angered the PLO. In the wake of the agreement Jordan's relations with the U.S. and with the moderate Arab states, including Saudi Arabia, warmed. In 1997, Jordan began negotiating with the United States about membership in the World Trade Organization, determined to attract foreign investment. On Feb. 7, 1999, King Hussein died of cancer after 46 years on the throne, sending the Middle East and much of the world into mourning for the influential Middle East statesman. Just weeks earlier, on Jan. 26, King Hussein unexpectedly deposed his brother, Prince Hassan, who had been heir apparent for 34 years, and named his eldest son, Abdullah, 37, as the new crown prince. King Abdullah II, a popular military leader with little political experience, became king on Feb. 7, 2000. In June King Abdullah dismissed conservative prime minister Abdul Raouf al-Rawabdeh and replaced him with Ali Abu al-Ragheb, a liberal with strong business ties.

Kazakhstan
REPUBLIC OF KAZAKHSTAN
President: Nursultan A. Nazarbayev (1990)
Prime Minister: Kasymzhomart Tokayev (1999)
Area: 1,049,150 sq mi (2,717,300 sq km)
Population (2001 est.): 16,731,303] (average annual rate of natural increase: 0.7%); birth rate: 17.3/1000; infant mortality rate: 59.2/1000; density per sq mi: 16
Capital (1995 est.): Astana, 280,200 (formerly Aqmola; capital since 1997). **Largest cities (1991):** Almaty (former capital), 1,200,000; Karaganda, 608,600; Shymkent, 438,000; Ust-Kamenogorsk, 332,900; Taraz, 312,300; Astana, 287,000; Aqtöbe, 266,600.
Monetary unit: Tenge. **Languages:** Kazak (Qazaq), official language spoken by over 40% of population; Russian, official language spoken by two-thirds of population and used in everyday business. **Ethnicity/race:** Kazak (Qazaq) 46%, Russian 34.7%, Ukrainian 4.9%, German 3.1%, Uzbek 2.3%, Tatar 1.9%, other 7.1% (1996). **Religions:** Muslim, 47%; Russian Orthodox, 44%; Protestant, 2%; other, 7%. **Literacy rate:** 98% (1989)
Economic summary: GDP/PPP (1999 est.): $54.5 billion; per capita $3,200. **Real growth rate:** 1.7%. **Inflation:** 8.3%. **Unemployment:** 13.7% (1998 est.). **Arable land:** 12%. **Agriculture:** grain (mostly spring wheat), cotton; wool, livestock. **Labor force:** 8.8 million (1997); industry, 27%; agriculture and forestry, 23%; other, 50% (1996). **Industries:** oil, coal, iron ore, manganese, chromite, lead, zinc, copper, titanium, bauxite, gold, silver, phosphates, sulfur, iron and steel, nonferrous metal, tractors and other agricultural machinery, electric motors, construction materials. **Natural resources:** major deposits of petroleum, natural gas, coal, iron ore, manganese, chrome ore, nickel, cobalt, copper, molybdenum, lead, zinc, bauxite, gold, uranium. **Exports:** $5.2 billion (1999 est.): oil, ferrous and nonferrous metals, machinery, chemicals, grain, wool, meat, coal. **Imports:** $4.8 billion (1999 est.): machinery and parts, industrial

materials, oil and gas, vehicles. **Major trading partners:** EU, China, Russia, Ukraine, U.S., Uzbekistan, Turkey, UK, Germany, South Korea.

Geography Kazakhstan lies in the north of the central Asian republics and is bounded by Russia in the north, China in the east, the Kyrgyzstan and Uzbekistan in the south, and the Caspian Sea and part of Turkmenistan in the west. It has almost 1,177 mi (1,894 km) of coastline on the Caspian Sea. Kazakhstan is slightly more than twice the size of Texas. The territory is mostly steppe land with hilly plains and plateaus.

Government Republic.

History The indigenous Kazakhs were a nomadic Turkic people who belonged to several divisions of Kazakh hordes. They grouped together in settlements and lived in dome-shaped tents made of felt called "yurts." Their tribes migrated seasonally to find pastures for their herds of sheep, horses, and goats. Although they had chiefs, the Kazakhs were rarely united as a single nation under one great leader. Their tribes fell under Mongol rule in the 13th century and they were dominated by Tartar khanates until the area was conquered by Russia in the 18th century.

The area became part of the Kirgiz Autonomous Republic formed by the Soviet authorities in 1920, and in 1925 this entity's name was changed to the Kazakh Autonomous Soviet Socialist Republic (Kazakh ASSR). After 1927, the Soviet government began forcing the nomadic Kazakhs to settle on collective and state farms, and the Soviets continued the czarist policy of encouraging large numbers of Russians and other Slavs to settle in the region.

Owing to the region's intensive agricultural development and its use as a testing ground for nuclear weapons by the Soviet government, serious environmental problems developed by the late 20th century. Along with the other central Asian republics, Kazakhstan obtained its independence from the collapsing Soviet Union in 1991. Kazakhstan proclaimed its membership in the Commonwealth of Independent States on Dec. 21, 1991, along with ten other former Soviet republics. In 1993, the country overwhelmingly approved the Nuclear Non-Proliferation Treaty. The president restructured and consolidated many operations of the government in 1997, eliminating a third of the government ministries and agencies. In 1997 the national capital was changed from Almaty, the largest city, to Astana (formerly Aqmola).

In Jan. 1999, Nursultan Nazarbayev was sworn into office for another seven years, although the election was widely criticized because an opposition leader was disqualified from running on a technicality. Despite his authoritarianism, Nazarbayev, who has ruled Kazakhstan since 1989 when it was still part of the Soviet Union, is a widely popular leader. Kazakhstan has the potential for becoming one of central Asia's richest countries because of its huge mineral and oil resources and its liberalized economy, which encourages Western investment. In 2000, oil was discovered in Kazakhstan's portion of the Caspian Sea—it is believed to be the largest oil find in 30 years. In March 2001, a pipeline opened to transport oil from the Tengiz fields to the Russian Black Sea port of Novorossiysk. The 950-mile pipeline has an initial capacity of 560,000 barrels of oil per day. In 2001, Kazakhstan and the governments of Azerbaijan, Georgia, and Turkey signed a memorandum of agreement for an even more ambitious pipeline, which would extend 1,075 mi from Baku, Azerbaijan, to Ceyhan, Turkey, on the Mediterranean.

Kenya

REPUBLIC OF KENYA

National name: Jamhuri ya Kenya
President: Daniel arap Moi (1978)
Area: 224,961 sq mi (582,650 sq km)
Population (2001 est.): 30,765,916 (average annual rate of natural increase: 1.4%); birth rate: 28.5/1000; infant mortality rate: 68.0/1000; density per sq mi: 137
Capital and largest city (1991 est.): Nairobi, 2,000,000.
Other large city: Mombasa, 600,000. **Monetary unit:** Kenyan shilling. **Languages:** English (official), Swahili (national), and several other languages spoken by 25 ethnic groups. **Ethnicity/race:** Kikuyu 22%, Luhya 14%, Luo 13%, Kalenjin 12%, Kamba 11%, Kisii 6%, Meru 6%, Asian, European, and Arab 1%, other 15%. **Religions:** Protestant, 40%; Roman Catholic, 36%; traditional, 6%; Islam, 16%; others, 2%. **Literacy rate:** 69% (1990)
Economic summary: GDP/PPP (1999 est.): $45.1 billion; per capita $1,600. **Real growth rate:** 1.5%. **Inflation:** 6%. **Unemployment:** 50% (1998 est.). **Arable land:** 7%. **Agriculture:** coffee, tea, corn, wheat, sugarcane, fruit, vegetables; dairy products, beef, pork, poultry, eggs. **Labor force:** 9.2 million (1998 est.); agriculture, 75%–80%. **Industries:** small-scale consumer goods (plastic, furniture, batteries, textiles, soap, cigarettes, flour), agricultural products processing; oil refining, cement; tourism. **Natural resources:** gold, limestone, soda ash, salt barites, rubies, fluorspar, garnets, wildlife, hydropower. **Exports:** $2.2 billion (f.o.b., 1999 est.): tea, coffee, horticultural products, petroleum products (1995). **Imports:** $3.3 billion (f.o.b., 1999 est.): machinery and transportation equipment, petroleum products, iron and steel. **Major trading partners:** Uganda, UK, Tanzania, Egypt, Germany, UAE, U.S., Japan, India. **Member of Commonwealth of Nations**

Geography Kenya lies across the equator in east-central Africa on the coast of the Indian Ocean. It is twice the size of Nevada. Kenya borders Somalia to the east, Ethiopia to the north, Tanzania to the south, Uganda to the west, and Sudan to the northwest. In the north, the land is arid; the southwestern corner is in the fertile Lake Victoria Basin; and a length of the eastern depression of the Great Rift Valley separates western highlands from those that rise from the lowland coastal strip. Large game reserves have been developed.

Government Republic.

History Paleontologists believe people may first have inhabited Kenya about 2 million years ago. In the 700s Arab seafarers established settlements along the coast, and the Portuguese took control of the area in the early 1500s. More than 40 ethnic groups reside in Kenya. Its largest group, the Kikuyu, migrated to the region at the beginning of the 18th century.

The land became a British protectorate in 1890 and a Crown colony in 1920, when it went by the name British East Africa. Nationalist stirrings began in 1940s, and in 1952 the Mau Mau movement, made up of Kikuyu militants, rebelled against the government. The fighting lasted until 1956.

On Dec. 12, 1963, Kenya became fully independent. Jomo Kenyatta, a nationalist leader during the independence struggle who had been jailed by the British, became its first president. From 1964 to 1992 the country was ruled as a one-party state by the Kenya African National Union (KANU), first under Kenyatta and then under Daniel arap Moi. Demonstrations and riots pressured Moi to allow for multiparty elections in 1992.

The economy has not flourished under Daniel arap Moi's rule. In the 1990s Kenya's infrastructure began disintegrating and official graft was rampant, contributing to the withdrawal of much foreign aid. In early 1995 President Moi moved against the opposition, and ordered the arrest of anyone who insulted him.

A series of disasters plagued Kenya in 1997 and 1998: severe flooding destroyed roads, bridges, and crops; epidemics of malaria and cholera overwhelmed the ineffectual health care system; and ethnic clashes erupted between the Kikuyu and Kalenjin ethnic groups in the Rift Valley.

On Aug. 7, 1998, the U.S. embassy in Nairobi was bombed by terrorists, killing 243 and injuring more than 1,000. The embassy in neighboring Tanzania was bombed the same day, killing 10.

In a successful effort to win back IMF and World Bank funding, which had been suspended because of Kenya's corruption and poor economic practices, President Moi appointed his high-profile critic and political opponent, Richard Leakey, as head of the civil service. The third-generation white Kenyan, son of paleontologists Louis and Mary Leakey, had been highly effective as head of the Kenya Wildlife Service, introducing a greater amount of efficiency and fairness into the Kenyan government. In his new position as head of the civil service, Leakey made a promising start at cleaning up Kenya's corrupt bureaucracy. But it soon became apparent that the president was not serious about reform, and after 20 months Moi sacked Leakey. Kenya is regularly ranked among the ten most corrupt countries in the world, according to the watchdog group Transparency International.

An anticorruption law, sponsored by the ruling party, failed to pass in Parliament in Aug. 2001 and imperiled Kenya's chances for international aid. Opposition leaders called the law a cynical ploy meant to give the appearance of reform—the proposed law, they contended, was in fact too weak and full of loopholes to make a dent in corruption.

Kiribati

REPUBLIC OF KIRIBATI

President: Teburoro Tito (1994)
Area: 277 sq mi (717 sq km)
Population (2001 est.): 94,149 (average annual growth rate: 2.3%); birth rate: 32.0/1000; infant mortality rate: 54.0/1000; density per sq mi: 340
Capital (1990): Tarawa, 25,154. **Monetary unit:** Australian dollar. **Languages:** English (official), I-Kiribati (Gilbertese). **Ethnicity/race:** Micronesian. **Religions:** Roman Catholic 52.6%, Protestant 40.9%. **Literacy rate:** 90%
Economic summary: GDP/PPP (1999 est.): $74 million, supplemented by a nearly equal amount from external sources; per capita $860. **Real growth rate:** 2.5%. **Inflation:** 2%. **Unemployment:** 2%; underemployment 70% (1992 est.). **Arable land:** 0%. **Agriculture:** copra, taro, breadfruit, sweet potatoes, vegetables; fish. **Labor force:** 7,870 economically active, not including subsistence farmers (1985 est.). **Industries:** fishing, handicrafts. **Natural resources:** phosphate (production discontinued in 1979). **Exports:** $6 million (f.o.b., 1998): copra 62%, seaweed, fish. **Imports:** $37 million (c.i.f., 1998): foodstuffs, machinery and equipment, miscellaneous manufactured goods, fuel. **Major trading partners:** U.S., Australia, New Zealand, Fiji, Japan. **Member of Commonwealth of Nations**

Geography Kiribati, formerly the Gilbert Islands, consists of three widely separated main groups of southwest Pacific islands, the Gilberts on the equator, the Phoenix Islands to the east, and the Line Islands

farther east. Ocean Island, producer of phosphates until it was mined out in 1981, is also included in the 2 million square mi of ocean. Most of the islands of Kiribati are low-lying coral atolls built on a submerged volcanic chain and encircled by reefs.

Government Republic.

History Kiribati was first settled by early Austronesian-speaking peoples long before the 1st century A.D. Fijians and Tongans arrived about the 14th century and subsequently merged with the older groups to form the traditional I-Kiribati Micronesian society and culture. The islands were first sighted by British and American ships in the late 18th and early 19th centuries, and the first British settlers arrived in 1837. A British protectorate since 1892, the Gilbert and Ellice Islands became a Crown colony in 1915–16. Kiritimati (Christmas) Atoll became a part of the colony in 1919, the Phoenix Islands in 1937.

Tarawa and others of the Gilbert group were occupied by Japan during World War II. Tarawa was the site of one of the bloodiest battles in U.S. Marine Corps history when Marines landed in Nov. 1943 to dislodge the Japanese defenders. The Gilbert Islands and Ellice Islands (now Tuvalu) were separated in 1975 and granted internal self-government by Britain. Kiribati became independent on July 12, 1979.

Kiribati's 1995 act of moving the international date line far to the east, so that it encompassed Kiribati's Line Islands group, courted controversy. The move, which fulfilled one of President Tito's campaign promises, was intended to enable Kiribati to become the first country to reach midnight on Dec. 31, 1999, and welcome the new millennium—an event of significance for tourism. In 1999, Kiribati gained UN membership.

Korea, North

DEMOCRATIC PEOPLE'S REPUBLIC OF KOREA

National name: Choson Minjujuui Inmin Konghwaguk
Head of State: Kim Jong II (1994)
Premier: Hong Song Nam (1997)
Area: 46,540 sq mi (120,540 sq km)
Population (2001 est.): 21,968,228 (average annual rate of natural increase: 1.2%); birth rate: 19.1/1000; infant mortality rate: 23.6/1000; density per sq mi: 472
Capital and largest city (1993): Pyongyang, 2,741,260. **Monetary unit:** Won. **Language:** Korean. **Ethnicity/race:** racially homogeneous. **Religions:** Buddhism and Confucianism; religious activities almost nonexistent. **Literacy rate:** 100% (1979)
Economic summary: GDP/PPP (1999 est.): $22.6 billion; per capita $1,000. **Real growth rate:** 1%. **Inflation:** n.a. **Unemployment:** n.a. **Arable land:** 14%. **Agriculture:** rice, corn, potatoes, soybeans, pulses; cattle, pigs, pork, eggs. **Labor force:** 9.6 million; agricultural, 36%; nonagricultural, 64%. **Industries:** military products; machine building, electric power, chemicals; mining (coal, iron ore, magnesite, graphite, copper, zinc, lead, and precious metals), metallurgy; textiles, food processing; tourism. **Natural resources:** coal, lead, tungsten, zinc, graphite, magnesite, iron ore, copper, gold, pyrites, salt, fluorspar, hydropower. **Exports:** $680 million (f.o.b., 1998 est.): minerals, metallurgical products, manufactures (including armaments); agricultural and fishery products. **Imports:** $954 million (c.i.f., 1998 est.): petroleum, coking coal, machinery and equipment; consumer goods, grain. **Major trading partners:** Japan, South Korea, China, Germany, Russia.

Geography Korea is a 600-mile (966 km) peninsula jutting out from Manchuria and China (and a small portion of the USSR) into the Sea of Japan and the Yellow Sea off eastern Asia. North Korea occupies an area slightly smaller than Pennsylvania north of the 38th parallel.

The country is almost completely covered by a series of north-south mountain ranges separated by narrow valleys. The Yalu River forms part of the northern border with Manchuria.

Government Communist dictatorship.

History The ancient history of the Korean peninsula can be traced to the Neolithic Age, when Turkic-Manchurian-Mongol peoples migrated into the region from China. The first agriculturally based settlements appeared around 6000 B.C. Some of the larger communities of this era were established along the Han-gang River near modern-day Seoul, others near Pyongyang and Pusan. According to ancient lore, Korea's earliest civilization, known as Choson, was founded by Tan-gun.

In the 17th century, Korea became a vassal state of China and was cut off from outside contact until the Sino-Japanese War of 1894–95. Following Japan's victory, Korea was granted independence. By 1910 Korea had been annexed by Japan, which developed the country but never won over the Korean nationalists who continued to agitate for independence.

After Japan's surrender at the conclusion of World War II, the Korean peninsula was partitioned into two occupation zones, divided at the 38th parallel. The USSR controlled the north, with the U.S. taking charge of the south. In 1948, the division was made permanent with the establishment of the separate regimes of North and South Korea. The Democratic People's Republic of Korea (North Korea) was established on May 1, 1948, with Kim Il Sung as president.

Hoping to unify the Koreas under a single Communist government, the North launched a surprise invasion of South Korea on June 25, 1950. In the following days, the UN Security Council condemned the attack and demanded an immediate withdrawal.

President Harry S. Truman ordered U.S. air and naval units into action to enforce the UN order. The British government followed suit, and soon a UN multinational command was set up to aid the South Koreans.

The North Korean invaders swiftly seized Seoul and surrounded the allied forces in the peninsula's southeast corner near Pusan. In a desperate bid to reverse the military situation, UN Commander Gen. Douglas MacArthur ordered an amphibious landing at Inchon on Sept. 15 and routed the North Korean army. MacArthur's forces pushed north across the 38th parallel, approaching the Yalu River.

Prompted by this successful counteroffensive, Communist China entered the war, forcing the UN troops into a headlong retreat. Seoul was lost again, then regained; ultimately the war stabilized near the 38th parallel but dragged on for two years while negotiations took place. An armistice was agreed to on July 27, 1953.

By early 1994 tensions had mounted over international inspection of North Korea's nuclear sites. Kim Il Sung's death on July 8, 1994, introduced a period of uncertainty, as his son, Kim Jong Il, assumed the leadership mantle. Negotiations over the country's suspected atomic weapons dragged on, but an agreement was reached in June 1995 that included a provision for providing the North with a South Korean nuclear reactor.

The nuclear crises that characterized the mid-1990s were overshadowed when famine struck the nation's 24 million inhabitants. Two years of floods were followed by severe droughts in 1997 and 1998, causing devastating crop failures. Although international relief programs saved many people, the situation was still considered serious in 1998, with aid agencies warning that North Korea's nationalized food distribution program had virtually shut down, forcing many people to rely on bark and wild plants to sustain themselves. The severity of the famine continued in 1999. Because of lack of fuel and machinery parts, and weather conditions that have encouraged parasites, only 10% of North Korea's rice fields have been worked. Despite the staggering food crisis, hermetic North Korea remains one of the world's few remaining hard-line Communist regimes.

In Sept. 1998 North Korea launched a test missile over Japan, claiming it was simply a scientific satellite. This launch alarmed Japan and much of the rest of the world about North Korea's intentions regarding reentry into the nuclear arms race. In 1999, North Korea agreed to allow the United States to conduct ongoing inspections of a suspected nuclear development site, Kumchangri, which North Korea admits has been devised for "a sensitive military purpose." In exchange, the U.S. would increase food aid and initiate a program for bringing potato production to the country.

Antagonism between North and South Korea erupted into open aggression twice in six months in late 1998 and 1999, with South Korea hitting one North Korean vessel and sinking two others that were discovered trespassing in South Korean waters. In late summer 1999, there were signs that North Korea might test a new version of the long-range rocket it launched over Japan a year earlier.

In the fall of 1999, North Korea's four years of severe famine, which claimed an estimated 2 million to 3 million lives between 1995 and 1998, had begun to wane. Tension with South Korea eased dramatically in June 2000, when South Korea's president, Kim Dae Jung, met with President Kim Jong Il in Pyongyang. The summit marked the first ever meeting of the countries' two leaders. The officials signed a hopeful, yet vague, agreement that outlined plans for unification and peace, reunions of separated families, open communication between the leaders, and a visit to South Korea by Kim Jong Il.

Talks between the two Koreas stalled after the March 2001 meeting between South Korea's president Kim Dae Jung and President George W. Bush. Bush said he was skeptical of Kim Jong Il and would not continue to negotiate with North Korea on its missile program until his administration reviewed the Clinton-era policy on the Communist country. In June, Bush announced that discussions with North Korea would resume, although cross-border dialogue has yet to improve.

Kim visited Russia in late July—the third time he has traveled abroad as president—and repeated his 1999 pledge to suspend the testing of long-range missiles until 2003. Kim and Russian president Vladimir Putin signed the Moscow Declaration, confirming their support of the 1972 Anti-Ballistic Missile Treaty, which President Bush is attempting to modify or abrogate. Despite the thaw in tensions, U.S. military sources report North Korea has fortified its border defenses with artillery and rocket launchers in the past year.

Korea, South

REPUBLIC OF KOREA

National name: Taehan Min'guk
President: Kim Dae Jung (1998)
Prime Minister: Lee Han Dong (2000)
Area: 38,023 sq mi (98,480 sq km)
Population (2001 est.): 47,904,370 (average annual rate of natural increase: 0.9%); birth rate: 14.9/1000; infant mortality rate: 7.7/1000; density per sq mi: 1,260
Capital and largest city (2000 est.): Seoul, 19,850,000 (metro. area). **Other large cities:** Pusan, 3,814,235; Taegu, 2,449,000; Inchon, 2,308,000 (part of Seoul metro. area). **Monetary unit:** Won. **Language:** Korean. **Ethnicity/race:** homogeneous (except for about 20,000 Chinese). **Religions (est. mid-1996):** Christian, 48.2%; Buddhist, 48.8%; Confucianist, 0.8%; Chondogyo (religion of the Heavenly Way), 0.2%; other, 2%. **Literacy rate:** 98% (1995)
Economic summary: GDP/PPP (1999 est.): $625.7 billion; per capita $13,300. **Real growth rate:** 10%. **Inflation:** 0.8%. **Unemployment:** 6.3%. **Arable land:** 19%. **Agriculture:** rice, root crops, barley, vegetables, fruit; cattle, pigs, chickens, milk, eggs; fish. **Labor force:** 22 million (1998); services and other, 68%; mining and manufacturing, 20%; agriculture, fishing, forestry, 12% (1998). **Industries:** electronics, automobile production, chemicals, shipbuilding, steel, textiles, clothing, footwear, food processing. **Natural resources:** coal, tungsten, graphite, molybdenum, lead, hydropower potential. **Exports:** $144 billion (f.o.b., 1999): electronic products, machinery and equipment, motor vehicles, steel, ships; textiles, clothing, footwear; fish. **Imports:** $116 billion (c.i.f., 1999): machinery, electronics and electronic equipment, oil, steel, transport equipment, textiles, organic chemicals, grains. **Major trading partners:** U.S., Japan, China, Hong Kong, Taiwan, Australia, Saudi Arabia.

Geography Slightly larger than Indiana, South Korea lies below the 38th parallel on the Korean peninsula, bordering the East Sea and the Yellow Sea. It is mountainous in the east; in the west and south are many harbors on the mainland and offshore islands.

Government Republic.

History South Korea came into being after World War II, the result of a 1945 agreement reached by the Allies at the Potsdam Conference, making the 38th parallel the boundary between a northern zone of the Korean peninsula to be occupied by the USSR and southern zone to be controlled by U.S. forces. (For details, *see* Korea, North.)

Elections were held in the U.S. zone in 1948 for a national assembly, which adopted a republican constitution and elected Syngman Rhee as the nation's president. The new republic was proclaimed on Aug. 15 and was recognized as the legal government of Korea by the UN on Dec. 12, 1948.

On June 25, 1950, North Korean Communist forces launched a massive surprise attack on South Korea, quickly overrunning the capital, Seoul. U.S. armed intervention was ordered on June 27 by President Harry S. Truman, and on the same day the UN invoked military sanctions against North Korea. Gen. Douglas MacArthur was named commander of the UN forces. U.S. and South Korean troops fought a heroic holding action, but by the first week of Aug. were forced back to a 4,000-square-mile beachhead in southeast Korea. There they stood off superior North Korean forces until Sept. 15, when a major UN amphibious assault was launched deep behind Communist lines at Inchon, the port of Seoul.

By Sept. 30, UN forces were in complete control of South Korea. They then crossed the 38th parallel and pursued retreating Communist forces into North Korea. In late October, as UN forces neared the Sino-Korean border, several hundred thousand Chinese Communist troops entered the conflict, pushing MacArthur's forces back to the border between North and South Korea. By the time truce talks began on July 10, 1951, UN forces had crossed over the parallel again and were driving back into North Korea. Cease-fire negotiations dragged on for two years before an armistice was finally signed at Panmunjom on July 27, 1953, leaving a devastated Korea in need of large-scale rehabilitation. No official peace treaty has ever been signed between the former combatants.

Rhee, after 12 years in office, was forced to resign in 1960 amid rising discontent with his autocratic leadership. Po Sun Yun was elected to succeed him, but political instability continued. In 1961, Gen. Park Chung Hee seized power and subsequently began a program of economic reforms designed to stimulate the nation's economy. The U.S. stepped up military aid, strengthening South Korea's armed forces to 600,000 men. Park's assassination on Oct. 26, 1979, by Kim Jae Kyu, head of the Korean Central Intelligence Agency, brought a liberalizing trend as new president Choi Kyu Hah freed imprisoned dissidents.

The release of opposition leader Kim Dae Jung in Feb. 1980 sparked antigovernment demonstrations that turned into riots, which were brutally suppressed by authorities. Kim, the most visible leader of the opposition, was imprisoned again. Choi resigned on Aug. 16. Chun Doo Hwan, head of a military Special Committee for National Security Measures, was the sole candidate as the electoral college confirmed him as president on Aug. 27. In 1986–87, South Korea's opposition demanded the president be selected by direct popular vote. After weeks of protest and rioting, Chun agreed to the demand. A split in the opposition led to Roh Tae Woo's election on Dec. 16, 1987.

In Aug. of 1996 Roh was convicted on bribery charges and Chun was convicted for bribery as well as his role in the 1979 coup and the 1980 crackdown on rioters. In 1997, an accumulation of corrupt business practices and bad loans led to a series of bankruptcies and a massive devaluation of South Korea's currency. The political instability that followed helped former dissident Kim Dae Jung become the first South Korean president ever to be elected from the political opposition.

In 1998 the Asian economic crisis bottomed out in South Korea, and it began rebounding in 1999—the only sizable Asian economy to do so.

Antagonism between North and South Korea erupted into open aggression twice in six months in late 1998 and 1999, with South Korea hitting one North Korean vessel and sinking two others that were discovered trespassing in South Korean waters. Tensions eased dramatically in June 2000, when President Kim Dae Jung met with the North's president, Kim Jong Il, in Pyongyang. The summit marked the first ever meeting of the countries' leaders.

President Kim Dae Jung won the Nobel Peace Prize in Oct. 2000, for his "Sunshine Policy," which included initiating peace and reconciliation with

North Korea. Cross-border discussions stalled after President George W. Bush told President Kim Dae Jung in a March 2001 meeting that he will not discuss missile negotiations any time soon with North Korea, shelving President Clinton's effort toward normal relations. Bush said in June that he was ready to resume talks with North Korea, though no discussions have occurred.

Kuwait

STATE OF KUWAIT

National name: Dawlat al Kuwayt
Emir: Sheik Jaber al-Ahmad al-Sabah (1977)
Prime Minister: Sheik Saad al-Abdullah Al-Sabah (1978)
Area: 6,880 sq mi (17,820 sq km)
Population (2001 est.): 2,041,961 (average annual rate of natural increase: 1.9%); birth rate: 21.9/1000; infant mortality rate: 11.2/1000; density per sq mi: 297
Capital (1990 est.): Kuwait, 151,060. **Other large city (1993 est.):** as-Salimiyah, 116,104. **Monetary unit:** Kuwaiti dinar. **Languages:** Arabic (official), English. **Ethnicity/race:** Kuwaiti 45%, other Arab 35%, South Asian 9%, Iranian 4%, other 7%. **Religions:** Islam, 85% (Shi'ite 30%, Sunni 45%, other 10%); Christian, Hindu, Parsi, and other, 15%. **Literacy rate:** 73% (1990)
Economic summary: GDP/PPP (1999 est.): $44.8 billion; per capita $22,500. **Real growth rate:** 1.1%. **Inflation:** 2%. **Unemployment:** 1.8% (official 1996 est.). **Arable land:** 0%. **Agriculture:** practically no crops; fish. **Labor force:** 1.3 million (1998 est.); note: 68% of the population in the 15–64 age group is non-national (July 1998 est.); government and social services, 50%; services, 40%; industry and agriculture, 10% (1996 est.). **Industries:** petroleum, petrochemicals, desalination, food processing, construction materials, salt, construction. **Natural resources:** petroleum, fish, shrimp, natural gas. **Exports:** $13.5 billion (f.o.b., 1999 est.): oil and refined products, fertilizers. **Imports:** $8.1 billion (f.o.b., 1999 est.): food, construction materials, vehicles and parts, clothing. **Major trading partners:** Japan, India, U.S., South Korea, Singapore, UK, Germany, Italy.

Geography Kuwait is situated northeast of Saudi Arabia at the northern end of the Persian Gulf, south of Iraq. It is slightly larger than Hawaii. The low-lying desert land is mainly sandy and barren.

Government Kuwait is a constitutional monarchy, governed by the al-Sabah family.

History Kuwait is believed to have been part of an early civilization in the 3rd millennium B.C. and to have traded with Mesopotamian cities. Archeological and historical traces disappeared around the first millennium B.C. At the beginning of the 18th century A.D., the 'Anizah tribe of central Arabia founded Kuwait City, which became an autonomous sheikdom by 1756. 'Abd Rahim of the al-Sabah became the first sheik, and his descendants continue to rule Kuwait today. In the late 18th and early 19th centuries the sheikdom belonged to the fringes of the Ottoman Empire. Kuwait obtained British protection in 1897 when the sheik feared that the Turks would expand their hold over the area. In 1961, Britain ended the protectorate, giving Kuwait independence, but agreed to give military aid on request. Iraq immediately threatened to occupy the area, and the British sent troops to defend Kuwait. Soon afterward the Arab League sent in troops, replacing the British. Iraq's claim was dropped when the Arab League recognized

Kuwait's independence on July 20, 1961. Kuwait typically followed a neutral and mediatory policy among Arab states.

Oil was discovered there in the 1930s, and Kuwait proved to have 20% of the world's known oil resources. Since 1946 it has been the world's second-largest oil exporter. The sheik, who receives half the profits, devotes most of them to the education, welfare, and modernization of his kingdom. In 1966, Sheik Sabah designated a relative, Jaber al-Ahmad al-Sabah, as his successor. By 1968, the sheikdom had established a model welfare state, and it sought to establish dominance among the sheikdoms and emirates of the Persian Gulf.

In July 1990, Iraqi president Hussein blamed Kuwait for falling oil prices. After a failed Arab mediation attempt to solve the dispute peacefully, Iraq invaded Kuwait on Aug. 2, 1990, set up a pro-Iraqi provisional government, and drained Kuwait of its economic resources. A coalition of Arab and Western military forces drove Iraqi troops from Kuwait in a mere four days, from Feb. 23–27, ending the Persian Gulf War. The emir returned to his country from Saudi Arabia in mid-March. Martial law, in effect since the end of the Gulf War, ended in late June. The U.S. sent 2,400 troops to the country in Aug. 1992 as part of a training exercise but this was widely interpreted as a show of strength to Saddam Hussein.

The general election of Oct. 1992 was a success for supporters of a return to Islamic law. A political independent was named speaker of the Parliament, and the opposition held 31 of the 50 seats. Iraqi "training" maneuvers near the Kuwaiti border in Oct. 1994 renewed fears of aggression in the country. A Kuwaiti appeal brought the quick deployment of U.S. and British troops and equipment. In 1999, the emir gave women the right to vote and run for Parliament. Later in 1999, however, Parliament defeated the ruler's decree.

Kyrgyzstan

THE KYRGYZ REPUBLIC

President: Askar Akaev (1990)
Prime Minister: Kurmanbek Bakiyev (2000)
Area: 76,641 sq mi (198,500 sq km)
Population (2001 est.): 4,753,003; (Kyrgyz, 52%; Russian, 21%; Uzbek, 13%; other, 14%) (average annual rate of natural increase: 1.7%); birth rate: 26.2/1000; infant mortality rate: 76.5/1000; density per sq mi: 62
Capital and largest city (1994): Bishkek (formerly Frunze), 631,000. **Other large city (1994):** Osh 213,000. **Monetary unit:** Som. **Languages:** Kyrgyz (official); Russian is de facto second language of communication. **Ethnicity/race:** Kyrgyz 52.4%, Russian 18%, Uzbek 12.9%, Ukrainian 2.5%, German 2.4%, other 11.8%. **Religions:** Muslim, 75%; Russian Orthodox, 20%; other, 5%. **Literacy rate:** 97% (1989)
Economic summary: GDP/PPP (1999 est.): $10.3 billion; per capita $2,300. **Real growth rate:** 3.4%. **Inflation:** 37%. **Unemployment:** 6% (1998 est.). **Arable land:** 7%. **Agriculture:** tobacco, cotton, potatoes, vegetables, grapes, fruits and berries; sheep, goats, cattle, wool. **Labor force:** 1.7 million; agriculture and forestry, 55%; industry, 15%; services, 30% (1999 est.). **Industries:** small machinery, textiles, food processing, cement, shoes, sawn logs, refrigerators, furniture, electric motors, gold, rare earth metals. **Natural resources:** abundant hydropower; significant deposits of gold and rare earth metals; locally exploitable coal, oil, and natural gas; other

deposits of nepheline, mercury, bismuth, lead, and zinc. **Exports:** $515 million (1999 est.): cotton, wool, meat, tobacco; gold, mercury, uranium, hydropower; machinery; shoes. **Imports:** $590 million (1999 est.): oil and gas, machinery and equipment, foodstuffs. **Major trading partners:** Germany, Kazakhstan, Russia, Uzbekistan, China.

Geography Kyrgyzstan (formerly Kirghizia) is a rugged country with the Tien Shan mountain range covering approximately 95% of the whole territory. The mountaintops are covered with perennial snow and glaciers. Kyrgyzstan borders Kazakhstan on the north and northwest, Uzbekistan in the southwest, Tajikistan in the south, and China in the southeast. The republic is the same size in area as the state of Nebraska.

Government Constitutional republic.

History The native Kyrgyz are a Turkic people who in ancient times first settled in the Tien Shan mountains. They were traditionally pastoral nomads. There was extensive Russian colonization in the 1900s and Russian settlers were given much of the best agricultural land. This led to an unsuccessful and disastrous revolt by the Kyrgyz people in 1916. Kyrgyzstan became part of the Soviet Federated Socialist Republic in 1924, and was made an autonomous republic in 1926. It became a constituent republic of the USSR in 1936. The Soviets forced the Kyrgyz to abandon their nomadic culture and brought modern farming and industrial production techniques into their society. It has greatly changed their traditional way of life.

Kyrgyzstan proclaimed its independence from the Soviet Union on Aug. 31, 1991. On Dec. 21, 1991, Kyrgyzstan joined the Commonwealth of Independent States. The country joined the UN and the IMF in 1992 and adopted a shock-therapy economic program. Voters endorsed market reforms in a referendum held in Jan. 1994, and in 1996, referendum voters overwhelmingly endorsed proposed constitutional changes that enhanced the power of the president. Representatives of the country along with those of Russia, China, Kazakhstan, and Tajikistan signed a nonaggression agreement in April 1996. In March 1997, Russian border control was extended until the end of the year as authorities in Kyrgyzstan grew increasingly concerned about the growth of the illegal narcotics trade in the country.

Since 1999, several groups of radical Islamic gunmen, believed to be from Uzbekistan or Tajikistan, have led raids and kidnappings from camps in Kyrgyzstan's mountains.

In elections held Oct. 30, 2000, President Askar Akaev easily won reelection with nearly 75% of the vote. The election, however, was marred by allegations of fraud, diminishing Kyrgyzstan's claim to be the centerpiece of Central Asian democracy. In addition, a requirement that all candidates pass a Kyrgyz language exam to appear on the ballot disqualified seven potential challengers. Most residents speak Russian as their first language after years of Soviet rule.

Laos

LAO PEOPLE'S DEMOCRATIC REPUBLIC

President: Khamtai Siphandon (1998)
Prime Minister: Boungnang Vorachith (2001)
Area: 91,428 sq mi (236,800 sq km)
Population (2001 est.): 5,635,967 (average annual rate of natural increase: 2.5%); birth rate: 37.8/1000; infant

mortality rate: 92.9/1000; density per sq mi: 62
Capital and largest city (1990): Vientiane, 442,000.
Monetary unit: Kip. **Languages:** Lao (official), French, English. **Ethnicity/race:** Lao Loum (lowland) 68%, Lao Theung (upland) 22%, Lao Soung (highland) including the Hmong ("Meo") and the Yao (Mien) 9%, ethnic Vietnamese/Chinese 1%. **Religions:** Buddhist 85%, animist and other 15%. **Literacy rate:** 45% (1988)
Economic summary: GDP/PPP (1999 est.): $7 billion; per capita $1,300. **Real growth rate:** 5.2%. **Inflation:** 140%. **Unemployment:** 5.7% (1997 est.). **Arable land:** 3%. **Agriculture:** sweet potatoes, vegetables, corn, coffee, sugarcane, tobacco; cotton; tea, peanuts, rice; water buffalo, pigs, cattle, poultry. **Labor force:** 1 million–1.5 million; agriculture, 80% (1997 est.). **Industries:** tin and gypsum mining, timber, electric power, agricultural processing, construction, garments. **Natural resources:** timber, hydropower, gypsum, tin, gold, gemstones. **Exports:** $271 million (f.o.b., 1999 est.): wood products, garments, electricity, coffee, tin. **Imports:** $497 million (f.o.b., 1999 est.): machinery and equipment, vehicles, fuel. **Major trading partners:** Vietnam, Thailand, Germany, France, Belgium, Japan, China, Singapore, Hong Kong.

Geography A landlocked nation in Southeast Asia occupying the northwest portion of the Indochinese peninsula, Laos is surrounded by China, Vietnam, Cambodia, Thailand, and Burma. It is twice the size of Pennsylvania.

Laos is a mountainous country, especially in the north, where peaks rise above 9,000 ft (2,800 m). Dense forests cover the northern and eastern areas. The Mekong River, which forms the boundary with Burma and Thailand, flows entirely through the country for 932 mi (1,500 km) of its course.

Government Communist state.

History The Lao people migrated into Laos from southern China from the 8th century onward. In the 14th century the first Laotian state was founded, the Lan Xang kingdom, which ruled Laos until it split into three separate kingdoms in 1713. During the 18th century the three kingdoms came under Siamese (Thai) rule, and in 1893 became a French protectorate. Its territory was incorporated into the union of Indochina. A strong nationalist movement developed during World War II, but France reestablished control in 1946 and made the last of Luang Prabang constitutional monarch of all Laos. France granted semiautonomy in 1949 and then, spurred by the Viet Minh rebellion in Vietnam, full independence within the French Union in 1950.

In 1951, Prince Souphanouvong organized the Pathet Lao, a Communist independence movement, in North Vietnam. Viet Minh and Pathet Lao forces invaded central Laos, and civil war resulted. By the Geneva agreements of 1954 and an armistice of 1955, two northern provinces were given to the Pathet Lao: the rest went to the royal regime. Full sovereignty was given to the kingdom by the Paris agreements of Dec. 29, 1954. In 1957, Prince Souvanna Phouma, the royal premier, and the Pathet Lao leader, Prince Souphanouvong, the premier's half-brother, agreed to reestablishment of a unified government, with Pathet Lao participation and integration of Pathet Lao forces into the royal army. The agreement broke down in 1959, and armed conflict began anew.

In 1960, the struggle became three-way as Gen. Phoumi Nosavan, controlling the bulk of the royal army, set up in the south a pro-Western revolutionary government headed by Prince Boun Gum. General

Phoumi took Vientiane in December, driving Souvanna Phouma into exile in Cambodia. The Soviet bloc supported Souvanna Phouma. In 1961, a cease-fire was arranged and the three princes agreed to a coalition government headed by Souvanna Phouma.

But North Vietnam, the U.S. (in the form of Central Intelligence Agency personnel), and China remained active in Laos after the settlement. North Vietnam used a supply line (Ho Chi Minh Trail) running down the mountain valleys of eastern Laos into Cambodia and South Vietnam, particularly after the U.S.–South Vietnamese incursion into Cambodia in 1970 stopped supplies via Cambodian seaports.

An agreement reached in 1973 revived the coalition government. The Communist Pathet Lao seized complete power in 1975, installing Souphanouvong as president and Kaysone Phomvihane as premier. Since then other parties and political groups have been moribund and most of their leaders have fled the country. The monarchy was abolished on Dec. 2, 1975, when the Pathet Lao ousted a coalition government and King Sisavang Vatthana abdicated.

The Supreme People's Assembly in Aug. 1991 adopted a new constitution that dropped all references to socialism but retained the one-party state. In addition to implementing market-oriented policies, the country has passed laws governing property, inheritance, and contracts.

During 1995 the country began making more diplomatic overtures toward its neighbors. Economic agreements were reached with Burma, and Laos's border disputes with Thailand in the 1980s gave way to warmer relations. The U.S. announced a lifting of its ban on aid to the nation.

By most international estimates, Laos is one of the ten poorest countries in the world. The subsistence farmers who make up more than 80% of the population have been plagued with bad agricultural conditions—alternately flood or drought—since 1993. Since March 2000, Vientiane has been rocked by a series of unexplained blasts. The activity has been widely attributed to a group of Hmong tribesmen based in the north. The anti-Communist rebel group has been protesting the government's reluctance to embrace democratic reforms. Others attribute the bombs to rival factions in the government or military.

In a March 2001 government reshuffle, Finance Minister Boungnang Vorachith replaced Sisavat Keobounphan as prime minister.

Latvia

THE REPUBLIC OF LATVIA

National name: Latvija
President: Vaira Vike-Freiberga (1999)
Prime Minister: Andris Berzins (2000)
Area: 24,938 sq mi (64,589 sq km)
Population (2001 est.): 2,385,231 (average annual rate of natural increase: –0.7%); birth rate: 8.0/1000; infant mortality rate: 15.3/1000; density per sq mi: 96
Capital and largest city (1993 est.): Riga, 874,000.
Other large cities: Daugavpils, 125,000; Liepaja, 108,000. **Monetary unit:** Lats. **Language:** Latvian.
Ethnicity/race: Latvian 51.8%, Russian 33.8%, Belorussian 4.5%, Ukrainian 3.4%, Polish 2.3%, other 4.2%. **Religions:** Lutheran, Catholic, and Baptist.
Literacy: 99% (1989)
Economic summary: GDP/PPP (1999 est.): $9.8 billion; per capita $4,200. **Real growth rate:** 0%. **Inflation:** 3.2%. **Unemployment:** 9.6%. **Arable land:** 27%.
Agriculture: grain, sugar beets, potatoes, vegetables; beef, milk, eggs; fish. **Labor force:** 1.4 million (1997);

agriculture and forestry, 16%; industry, 41%; services, 43% (1990). **Industries:** buses, vans, street and railroad cars, synthetic fibers, agricultural machinery, fertilizers, washing machines, radios, electronics, pharmaceuticals, processed foods, textiles; dependent on imports for energy, raw materials, and intermediate products. **Natural resources:** minimal; amber, peat, limestone, dolomite, hydropower, arable land.
Exports: $1.9 billion (f.o.b., 1999): wood and wood products, machinery and equipment, metals, textiles, foodstuffs. **Imports:** $2.8 billion (f.o.b., 1998): machinery and equipment, chemicals, fuels. **Major trading partners:** Germany, UK, Russia, Sweden, Finland.

Geography Latvia borders Estonia on the north, Lithuania in the south, the Baltic Sea with the Gulf of Riga in the west, Russia in the east, and Belarus in the southeast. Latvia is largely a fertile lowland with numerous lakes and hills to the east.

Government Parliamentary democracy.

History Baltic tribespeople settled along the Baltic Sea, and lacking a centralized government, fell prey to more powerful peoples. In the 13th century they were overcome by the Livonian Brothers of the Sword, a German order of knights whose mission was to conquer and Christianize the Baltic region. The land became part of the state of Livonia until 1561. Germans made up the ruling class of Livonia and Baltic tribes made up the peasantry. German became the official language of the region.

Poland conquered the territory in 1562, until Sweden took over the land in 1629, and ruled over it until 1721. Then the land passed to Russia. From that time until 1918, the Latvians remained Russian subjects, although they preserved their language, customs, and folklore.

The Russian Revolution of 1917 gave them their opportunity for freedom, and the Latvian republic was proclaimed on Nov. 18, 1918. The republic lasted little more than 20 years. Plagued by political instability, Latvia essentially became a dictatorship under President Karlis Ulmanis. It was occupied by Russian troops in 1939 and incorporated into the Soviet Union in 1940. Latvia allied itself with Germany in World War II, and German armies occupied the nation from 1941 to 1943–44. Of the 70,000 Jews living in Latvia during the war, 95% were massacred. In 1944, Russia again took control of Latvia.

Latvia was one of the most economically well-off and industrialized parts of the Soviet Union. When a coup against Soviet president Mikhail Gorbachev failed in 1991, the Baltic nations saw an opportunity to free themselves from Soviet domination and, following the actions of Lithuania and Estonia, Latvia declared its independence on Aug. 21, 1991. European and most other nations quickly recognized their independence, and on Sept. 2, 1991, President Bush announced full diplomatic recognition for Latvia, Estonia, and Lithuania. The Soviet Union recognized Latvia's independence on Sept. 6, and UN membership followed on Sept. 17, 1991.

Because Latvians' ethnic identity had been quashed throughout its history by foreign rulers, the new Latvian republic set up strict citizenship laws, limiting citizenship to ethnic Latvians and to those who had lived in the region before Soviet rule in 1940. This denied about 452,000 of the country's 740,000 ethnic Russians of citizenship.

Latvia's bid to join the European Union was not accepted in talks that began in 1997. In addition to improving its administrative systems, Latvia was told that it had to speed up naturalization of minorities, in particular its large number of Russians. In 1998, a referendum passed, easing the citizenship rules, although it was still necessary to be competent in the Latvian language, which many believe is unreasonable to expect of older or poorly educated ethnic Russians. The EU began negotiations for the admission of Latvia in 1999.

In May 2001, Latvia and eight other central and eastern European countries declared their wish to join NATO in 2002, a "big bang" that would expand NATO to 28 members.

Lebanon

REPUBLIC OF LEBANON

National name: Al-Joumhouriya al-Lubnaniya
President: Émile Lahoud (1998)
Premier: Rafiq al-Hariri (2000)
Area: 4,015 sq mi (10,400 sq km)
Population (2001 est.): 3,627,774 (average annual rate of natural increase: 1.4%); birth rate: 20.2/1000; infant mortality rate: 28.4/1000; density per sq mi: 903
Capital and largest city (1991 est.): Beirut, 1,100,000.
Other large cities: Tripoli, 240,000; Sidon, 100,000.
Monetary unit: Lebanese pound. **Languages:** Arabic (official), French, English. **Ethnicity/race:** Arab 95%, Armenian 4%, other 1%. **Religions:** Islam, 60%; Christian, 40% (17 recognized sects); Judaism, negl. (1 sect). **Literacy rate:** 80% (1990)
Economic summary: GDP/PPP (1999 est.): $16.2 billion; per capita $4,500. **Real growth rate:** 1%. **Inflation:** 4.5%. **Unemployment:** 18% (1997 est.). **Arable land:** 21%. **Agriculture:** citrus, grapes, tomatoes, apples, vegetables, potatoes, olives, tobacco; sheep, goats. **Labor force:** 1.3 million (1999 est.); note: in addition, there are as many as 1 million foreign workers; services, 62%; industry, 31%; agriculture, 7% (1997 est.). **Industries:** banking; food processing; jewelry; cement; textiles; mineral and chemical products; wood and furniture products; oil refining; metal fabricating. **Natural resources:** limestone, iron ore, salt, water-surplus state in a water-deficit region, arable land. **Exports:** $866 million (f.o.b., 1999 est.): foodstuffs and tobacco, textiles, chemicals, metal and metal products, electrical equipment and products, jewelry, paper and paper products. **Imports:** $5.7 billion (f.o.b., 1999 est.): foodstuffs, machinery and transport equipment, consumer goods, chemicals, textiles, metals, fuels, agricultural foods. **Major trading partners:** Saudi Arabia, UAE, France, Syria, U.S., Kuwait, Jordan, Turkey, Italy, Germany, Switzerland, Japan, UK

Geography Lebanon lies at the eastern end of the Mediterranean Sea north of Israel and west of Syria. It is four-fifths the size of Connecticut.

The Lebanon Mountains, which parallel the coast on the west, cover most of the country, while on the eastern border is the Anti-Lebanon range. Between the two lies the Bekaa Valley, the principal agricultural area.

Government Republic.

History After World War I, France was given a League of Nations mandate over Lebanon and its neighbor Syria, which together had previously been a single political unit in the Ottoman Empire. France divided them in 1920 into separate colonial administrations, drawing a border that separated predominantly Muslim Syria from the kaleidoscope of religious communities in Lebanon where Maronite Christians were then dominant. After 20 years of the French mandate regime, Lebanon's independence was proclaimed on Nov. 26, 1941, but full independence came in stages. Under an agreement between representatives of Lebanon and the French National Committee of Liberation, most of the powers exercised by France were transferred to the Lebanese government on Jan. 1, 1944. The evacuation of French troops was completed in 1946.

According to the National Pact, different religious communities are represented in the government by having a Maronite Christian president, a Sunni Muslim prime minister, and a Shi'ite National Assembly speaker. The arrangement worked for two decades. Civil war broke out in 1958, with Muslim factions led by Kamal Jumblat and Saeb Salam rising in insurrection against the Lebanese government headed by President Camille Chamoun, a Maronite Christian favoring close ties to the West. At Chamoun's request, President Eisenhower on July 15 sent U.S. troops to reestablish the government's authority.

Clan warfare between various religious factions in Lebanon goes back centuries. The hodgepodge includes Maronite Christians, who since independence have dominated the government; Sunni Muslims, who have prospered in business and shared political power; the Druze, who hold a faith incorporating close aspects of Islam and Gnosticism; and Shi'ite Muslims.

A new—and bloodier—Lebanese civil war that broke out in 1975 resulted in the addition of still another ingredient in the brew—the Syrians. In the fighting between Lebanese factions, 40,000 Lebanese were estimated to have been killed and 100,000 wounded between March 1975 and Nov. 1976. At that point, a Syrian-dominated Arab Deterrent Force intervened and brought large-scale fighting to a halt.

Palestinian guerrillas staging raids on Israel from Lebanese territory drew punitive Israeli raids on Lebanon and two large-scale Israeli invasions, in 1978 and again in 1982. The Israelis withdrew in June 1978 after the UN Security Council created a 6,000-man peacekeeping force for the area, called UNIFIL. As they departed, the Israelis turned their strongholds over to a Christian militia that they had organized, instead of to the UN force.

The second Israeli invasion came on June 6, 1982, after an assassination attempt by Palestinian terrorists on the Israeli ambassador in London. As a base of the PLO, Lebanon became the Israelis' target. Nearly 7,000 Palestinians were dispersed to other Arab nations, and Israel pulled back some of its forces. The violence seemed to have come to an end when, on Sept. 14, Bashir Gemayel, the 34-year-old president-elect, was killed by a bomb that destroyed the headquarters of his Christian Phalangist Party.

The day after Gemayel's assassination, Israeli troops moved into West Beirut in force. On Sept. 17 it was revealed that Christian militiamen had massacred hundreds of Palestinians in two refugee camps, but Israel denied responsibility. On Sept. 20, Amin Gemayel, older brother of Bashir Gemayel, was elected president by the Parliament.

The massacre in the refugee camps prompted the return of a multinational peacekeeping force. Its mandate was to support the central Lebanese government, but it soon found itself drawn into the struggle for power between different Lebanese factions. During their stay in Lebanon, 260 U.S. Marines and about 60 French soldiers were killed, most of them in suicide bombings of the Marine and French army compounds on Oct. 23, 1983. The multinational force left in the spring of 1984.

In July 1986, Syrian observers took a position in Beirut to monitor a peacekeeping agreement. The agreement broke down and fighting between Shi'ite and Druze militia in West Beirut became so intense that Syrian troops mobilized in Feb. 1987, suppressing militia resistance.

In early 1991 the Lebanese government, backed by Syria, attempted to regain control over the south and disband all private militias, thereby ending the 16-year civil war. These conflicts destroyed much of the infrastructure and industry of Lebanon.

In the general elections of Aug. 1992 most Christians abstained from voting, demanding that Syrian forces first leave the country. The new legislature consisted of mostly pro-Syrian members. The largest Christian party was further weakened when in Jan. 1993 it appeared to split into two factions.

In June 1999, just before Israeli prime minister Benjamin Netanyahu left office, Israel bombed Southern Lebanon, its most severe attack on the country since 1996. In May 2000, the new prime minister, Ehud Barak, withdrew Israeli troops after 22 years of occupation.

In Sept. 2000, opposition party candidates allied with former prime minister Rafiq al-Hariri won a landslide victory in parliamentary elections, in which Lebanon's severe recession was a major issue. Hariri became prime minister a month later.

In the summer of 2001, Syria withdrew nearly all of its 25,000 troops from Beirut and surrounding areas. Troops, however, remain in the countryside.

Lesotho

KINGDOM OF LESOTHO

Sovereign: King Letsie III (1990)
Prime Minister: Pakalitha Mosisili (1998)
Area: 11,720 sq mi (30,355 sq km)
Population (2001 est.): 2,177,062 (average annual rate of natural increase: 1.6%); birth rate: 31.2/1000; infant mortality rate: 82.8/1000; density per sq mi: 186
Capital and largest city (1992): Maseru (1992), 170,000. **Monetary unit:** Loti. **Languages:** English and Sesotho (official); also Zulu and Xhosa. **Ethnicity/race:** Sotho 99.7%, Europeans 1,600, Asians 800.
Religions: Christian, 80%; indigenous beliefs, Muslim, and Bahai. **Literacy rate:** 56% (1966)
Economic summary: GDP/PPP (1998 est.): $4.7 billion; per capita $2,240. **Real growth rate:** −10%. **Inflation:** 8%. **Unemployment:** substantial unemployment and underemployment affecting more than half of the labor force (1999 est.). **Arable land:** 11%. **Agriculture:** corn, wheat, pulses, sorghum, barley; livestock. **Labor force:** 689,000 economically active; 86% of resident population engaged in subsistence agriculture; roughly 35% of the active male wage earners work in South Africa. **Industries:** food, beverages, textiles, handicrafts; construction; tourism. **Natural resources:** water, agricultural and grazing land, some diamonds and other minerals. **Exports:** $235 million (f.o.b., 1998 est.): manufactures 75% (clothing, footwear, road vehicles), wool and mohair, food and live animals (1998). **Imports:** $700 million (f.o.b., 1998 est.): food; building materials, vehicles, machinery, medicines, petroleum products (1995). **Major trading partners:** South African Customs Union, North America, Asia. **Member of Commonwealth of Nations**

Geography Mountainous Lesotho, the size of Maryland, is surrounded by the Republic of South Africa in the east-central part of that country except for short borders on the east and south with two discontinuous units of the Republic of Transkei. The Drakensberg Mountains in the east are Lesotho's principal chain. Elsewhere the region consists of rocky tableland.

Government Constitutional monarchy.

History Lesotho (formerly Basutoland) was constituted a native state under British protection by a treaty signed with the native chief Moshoeshoe in 1843. It was annexed to Cape Colony in 1871, but in 1884 it was restored to direct control by the Crown. The colony of Basutoland became the independent nation of Lesotho on Oct. 4, 1966, with King Moshoeshoe II as sovereign.

In the 1970 elections, Ntsu Mokhehle, head of the Basutoland Congress Party, claimed a victory, but Prime Minister Leabua Jonathan declared a state of emergency, suspended the constitution, and arrested Mokhehle. King Moshoeshoe II returned after a compromise with Jonathan in which the new constitution would name him head of state but forbid his participation in politics.

After the king refused to approve the replacement in Feb. 1990 of individuals dismissed by Justin Metsino Lekhanya, the chairman of the Military Council, the latter stripped the king of his executive power. Then in early March Lekhanya sent the king into exile. In Nov. the king was dethroned, and his son was sworn in as King Letsie III.

Lekhanya was himself forced to resign in April 1991, and Col. Ramaema became the new chairman in May. In Jan. 1995 the crown reverted to the father of Letsie III, Moshoeshoe II. Letsie again became crown prince. In 1996, however, King Moshoeshoe died in an automobile accident, and Letsie again assumed the throne.

In fall 1998, hundreds of demonstrators protested for weeks in front of the king's palace, claiming voting fraud in the May elections that put new Prime Minister Pakalitha Mosisili in power. They demanded that the government step down and hold new elections. Troops from South African and Botswana entered the country to stop the riots and put down an army mutiny.

In Feb. 2000 King Letsie III married a commoner, Karabo Motsoeneng, in a lavish $1.5 million ceremony.

Liberia

REPUBLIC OF LIBERIA

President: Charles Taylor (1997)
Area: 43,000 sq mi (111,370 sq km)
Population (2001 est.): 3,225,837 (average annual rate of natural increase: 3.0%); birth rate: 46.6/1000; infant mortality rate: 132.4/1000; density per sq mi: 75
Capital and largest city (1993 est.): Monrovia, 1,000,000. **Monetary unit:** Liberian dollar.
Languages: English (official) and tribal dialects.
Ethnicity/race: indigenous African tribes 95% (including Kpelle, Bassa, Gio, Kru, Grebo, Mano, Krahn, Gola, Gbandi, Loma, Kissi, Vai, and Bella), Americo-Liberians 5% (descendants of former slaves).
Religions: traditional 70%, Christian 10%, Islam 20%.
Literacy rate: 40% (1990)
Economic summary: GDP/PPP (1999 est.): $2.85 billion; per capita $1,000. **Real growth rate:** 0.5%.
Inflation: 3% (1998 est.). **Unemployment:** 70%.
Arable land: 1%. **Agriculture:** rubber, coffee, cocoa, rice, cassava (tapioca), palm oil, sugarcane, bananas;

sheep, goats; timber. **Labor force:** agriculture, 70%; industry, 8%; services, 22% (1999 est.). **Industries:** rubber processing, palm oil processing, diamonds. **Natural resources:** iron ore, timber, diamonds, gold, hydropower. **Exports:** $39 million (f.o.b., 1998 est.): diamonds, iron ore, rubber, timber, coffee, cocoa. **Imports:** $142 million (f.o.b., 1998 est.): fuels, chemicals, machinery, transportation equipment, manufactured goods; rice and other foodstuffs. **Major trading partners:** Benelux, Norway, Ukraine, Singapore, South Korea, Japan, Italy.

Geography Lying on the Atlantic in the southern part of West Africa, Liberia is bordered by Sierra Leone, Guinea, and Côte d'Ivoire. It is comparable in size to Tennessee.

Most of the country is a plateau covered by dense tropical forests, which thrive under an annual rainfall of about 160 in. a year.

Government Republic.

History Africa's first republic, Liberia was founded in 1822 as a result of the efforts of the American Colonization Society to settle freed American slaves in West Africa. The society contended that the immigration of blacks to Africa was an answer to the problem of slavery as well as to what it felt was the incompatibility of the races. Over the course of forty years, about 12,000 slaves were voluntarily relocated. Originally called Monrovia, the colony became the Free and Independent Republic of Liberia in 1847.

The English-speaking Americo-Liberians, descendants of former American slaves, make up only 5% of the population, but have historically dominated the intellectual and ruling class. Liberia's indigenous population is primarily composed of Mande, Kwa, and Mel peoples.

The government of Africa's first republic was modeled after that of the United States, and Joseph Jenkins Roberts of Virginia was elected the first president. Ironically, Liberia's constitution denied indigenous Liberians equal rights with the lighter-skinned American emigrants and their descendants.

After 1920, considerable progress was made toward opening up the interior, a process that was spurred in 1951 by the establishment of a 43-mile (69-km) railroad from the Bomi Hills from Monrovia. In July 1971, while serving his sixth term as president, William V. S. Tubman died following surgery and was succeeded by his long-time associate, Vice President William R. Tolbert, Jr.

Tolbert was ousted in a military coup carried out April 12, 1980, by Master Sgt. Samuel K. Doe, who was backed by the U.S. government. A rebellion led by Charles Taylor, a former Doe aide, started in Dec. 1989 and, with the help of Côte d'Ivoire and Burkina Faso, took control of Liberia's key population and economic centers by mid-July 1990. His three attempts to take the capital failed, however, and the bloody civil war continued. By mid-April 1996 factional fighting by the country's warlords had destroyed any last vestige of normalcy and civil society.

In what was considered by international observers to be a free election, Charles Taylor won 75.3% of the presidential vote in July 1997. Since then, however, Taylor's government has focused more on armed security rather than reconstruction of the country after its seven-year civil war. While Taylor attempts to fashion himself into a democratic political leader, his behavior remains that of a militia rebel. Taylor supports Sierra Leone's brutal Revolutionary United Front (RUF) in the hopes of toppling his neighbor's

government. Since Sept. 2000, fighting at the junction of the border between Liberia, Sierra Leone, and Guinea has increased between a jumble of warring factions, including the armies of Liberia and Guinea, rebel Guineans and Liberians, and the RUF.

Libya
SOCIALIST PEOPLE'S LIBYAN ARAB JAMAHIRIYA

National name: Socialist People's Libyan Arab Jamahiriya
Head of State: Col. Muammar al-Qaddafi (1969)
Secretary of the General People's Committee: Mubarak Abdallah al-Shamikh (2000)
Area: 679,358 sq mi (1,759,540 sq km)
Population (2001 est.): 5,240,599 (average annual rate of natural increase: 2.4%); birth rate: 27.7/1000; infant mortality rate: 29.0/1000; density per sq mi: 8
Capital: Tripoli. **Largest cities (est. 1988):** Tripoli, 591,062; Benghazi, 446,250. **Monetary unit:** Libyan dinar. **Languages:** Arabic, Italian and English widely understood in major cities. **Ethnicity/race:** Berber and Arab 97%, Greeks, Maltese, Italians, Egyptians, Pakistanis, Turks, Indians, Tunisians. **Religion:** Islam. **Literacy rate:** 64% (1990)
Economic summary: GDP/PPP (1999 est.): $39.3 billion; per capita $7,900. **Real growth rate:** 2%. **Inflation:** 18%. **Unemployment:** 30% (1998 est.). **Arable land:** 1%. **Agriculture:** wheat, barley, olives, dates, citrus, vegetables, peanuts; beef, eggs. **Labor force** (1997 est.): 1.2 million; services and government, 54%; industry, 29%; agriculture, 17%. **Industries:** petroleum, food processing, textiles, handicrafts, cement. **Natural resources:** petroleum, natural gas, gypsum. **Exports:** $6.6 billion (f.o.b., 1998 est.): crude oil, refined petroleum products, natural gas. **Imports:** $7 billion (f.o.b., 1998 est.): machinery, transport equipment, food, manufactured goods. **Major trading partners:** Italy, Germany, Spain, France, Sudan, UK, Tunisia, Belgium.

Geography Libya stretches along the northeast coast of Africa between Tunisia and Algeria on the west and Egypt on the east; to the south are the Sudan, Chad, and Niger. It is one-sixth larger than Alaska. A greater part of the country lies within the Sahara. Along the Mediterranean coast and farther inland is arable plateau land.

Government Military dictatorship.

History The first inhabitants of Libya were Berber tribes. In the 7th century B.C., Phoenicians colonized the eastern section of Libya, called Cyrenaica, and Greeks colonized the western portion, called Tripolitania. Tripolitania was for a time under Carthaginian control. It became part of the Roman Empire from 46 B.C. to A.D. 436, after which it was sacked by the Vandals. Cyrenaica belonged to the Roman Empire from the 1st century B.C. until its decline, after which it was invaded by Arab forces in A.D. 642. Beginning in the 16th century, both Tripolitania and Cyrenaica nominally became part of the Ottoman Empire.

Tripolitania was one of the outposts for the Barbary pirates who raided Mediterranean merchant ships or required them to pay tribute. In 1801 the pasha of Tripoli raised the price of tribute, which led to the Tripolitan war with the United States. When the peace treaty was signed on June 4, 1805, U.S. ships no longer had to pay tribute to Tripoli.

Following the outbreak of hostilities between Italy and Turkey in 1911, Italian troops occupied Tripoli. Italian sovereignty was recognized in 1912. Libyans continued to fight the Italians until 1914, by which time Italy controlled most of the land. Italy formally united Tripolitania and Cyrenaica in 1934 as the colony of Libya.

Libya was the scene of much desert fighting during World War II. After the fall of Tripoli on Jan. 23, 1943, it came under Allied administration. In 1949, the UN voted that Libya should become independent, and in 1951 it became the United Kingdom of Libya. Oil was discovered in the impoverished country in 1958, and eventually transformed its economy.

On Sept. 1, 1969, 27-year-old Col. Muammar al-Qaddafi deposed the king and revolutionized the country, making it a pro-Arabic, anti-Western, Islamic republic with socialist leanings. It was also rabidly anti-Israeli. A notorious firebrand, Qaddafi aligned himself with dictators, such as Uganda's Idi Amin, and fostered anti-Western terrorism.

On Aug. 19, 1981, two U.S. Navy F-14s shot down two Soviet-made SU-22s of the Libyan air force that had attacked them in air space above the Gulf of Sidra. On March 24, 1986, U.S. and Libyan forces skirmished in the Gulf of Sidra, and two Libyan patrol boats were sunk. Qaddafi's troops also supported rebels in Chad but suffered major military reverses in 1987. A two-year-old U.S. covert policy to destabilize the Libyan government ended in failure in Dec. 1990.

On Dec. 21, 1988, a Boeing 747 exploded in flight over Lockerbie, Scotland, the result of a terrorist bomb, killing all 259 people aboard and 11 on the ground. Two Libyan intelligence agents were indicted, but Qaddafi refused to hand them over, leading to UN-approved trade and air traffic embargoes in 1992. On April 5, 1999, after years of negotiations, Libya surrendered the two men. The suspects, Abdel Basset Ali al-Megrahi and Lamen Khalifa Fhimah, were tried in the Netherlands in 2000–2001. Megrahi was found guilty of mass murder; the other defendant was found innocent. As a result of Libya's cooperation, the United Nations lifted sanctions against the nation, which had severely affected the Libyan economy. European companies almost immediately began to court the oil-rich nation once again.

Qaddafi has also sought to play a leading role in African affairs, promoting a united Africa. The policy suffered a severe setback, however, in Sept. 2000 when Libyan resentment over the one million black Africans living in the country of six million people erupted into violence. Rampaging mobs killed hundreds of blacks, prompting several African nations to launch airlifts to repatriate thousands of citizens. Guest workers from other Arab countries were not generally attacked, prompting charges of racism. Qaddafi blamed the violence on opponents of his African initiative.

Liechtenstein

PRINCIPALITY OF LIECHTENSTEIN

Ruler: Prince Hans Adam II (1989)
Head of Government: Otmar Hasler (2001)
Area: 62 sq mi (160 sq km)
Population (2001 est.): 32,528 (average annual growth rate: 0.5%); birth rate: 11.5/1000; infant mortality rate: 5.0/1000; density per sq mi: 527
Capital and largest city (1994): Vaduz, 5,067.
  Monetary unit: Swiss franc. **Languages:** German (official), Alemmanic dialect. **Ethnicity/race:** Alemannic 87.5%; Italian, Turkish, and other 12.5%. **Religions:** Roman Catholic, 80%; Protestant, 6.9%; unknown, 5.6%; other, 7.5%. **Literacy rate:** 100% (1981)
Economic summary: GDP/PPP (1998 est.): $730 million; per capita $23,000. **Real growth rate:** n.a. **Inflation:**

0.5% (1997 est.). **Unemployment:** 1.8% (Feb. 1999). **Arable land:** 24%. **Agriculture:** wheat, barley, corn, potatoes; livestock, dairy products. **Labor force:** 22,891 of which 13,847 are foreigners; 8,231 commute from Austria and Switzerland to work each day; industry, trade, and building, 45%; services, 53%; agriculture, fishing, forestry, and horticulture, 2% (1997 est.). **Industries:** electronics, metal manufacturing, textiles, ceramics, pharmaceuticals, food products, precision instruments, tourism. **Natural resources:** hydroelectric potential, arable land. **Exports:** $2.47 billion (1996): small specialty machinery, dental products, stamps, hardware, pottery. **Imports:** $917.3 million (1996): machinery, metal goods, textiles, foodstuffs, motor vehicles. **Major trading partners:** EU and EFTA countries.

Geography Tiny Liechtenstein, not quite as large as Washington, D.C., lies on the east bank of the Rhine River south of Lake Constance between Austria and Switzerland. It consists of low valley land and Alpine peaks. Falknis (8,401 ft; 2,561 m) and Naafkopf (8,432 ft; 2,570 m) are the tallest.

Government Constitutional monarchy.

History The Liechtensteiners are descended from the Alemanni tribe that came into the region after A.D. 500. Founded in 1719, Liechtenstein was a member of the German Confederation from 1815 to 1866, when it became an independent principality. It abolished its army in 1868 and has managed to stay neutral and undamaged in all European wars since then. Liechtenstein still claims 1,600 sq km of Czech territory (the royal family's ancestral home) confiscated in 1918; the Czech Republic insists that restitution does not go back before Feb. 1948, when the Communists seized power. In a referendum on July 1, 1984, male voters granted women the right to vote in national (but not local) elections—a victory for Prince Hans Adam. A treaty negotiated between EFTA (European Free Trade Association) and the EU linking the two as the European Economic Area was ratified by Liechtenstein in a Dec. 1993 vote, but Switzerland rejected it. After renegotiation the treaty was again subjected to a referendum in April 1995 and approved. Liechtenstein won a special concession limiting immigration.

Blacklisted in 2000 as a center for money laundering by the Financial Action Task Force (FATF), a Paris-based watchdog agency, Liechtenstein toughened its laws and made major efforts to clean up its financial practices.

Lithuania

REPUBLIC OF LITHUANIA

National name: Lietuva
President: Valdas Adamkus (1998)
Prime Minister: Algirdas Brazauskas (2001)
Area: 25,174 sq mi (65,200 sq km)
Population (1998 est.): 3,610,535 (average annual rate of natural increase: –0.3%); birth rate: 10.0/1000; infant mortality rate: 14.5/1000; density per sq mi: 143
Capital and largest city (1993 est.): Vilnius, 590,100.
  Other large cities: Kaunas, 429,000; Klaipéda, 206,400. **Monetary unit:** Litas. **Languages:** Lithuanian (official), Polish, Russian. **Ethnicity/race:** Lithuanian 80.1%, Russian 8.6%, Polish 7.7%, Belorussian 1.5%, other 2.1%. **Religions:** Catholic 85%, others include Lutheran, Russian Orthodox, Protestant, evangelical Christian Baptist, Islam, Judaism. **Literacy:** 98% (1989)
Economic summary: GDP/PPP (1999 est.): $17.3

billion; per capita $4,800. **Real growth rate:** –3%. **Inflation:** 0.3%. **Unemployment:** 10%. **Arable land:** 35%. **Agriculture:** grain, potatoes, sugar beets, flax, vegetables; beef, milk, eggs; fish. **Labor force:** 1.8 million; industry 30%, agriculture 20%, services 50% (1997 est.). **Industries:** metal-cutting machine tools, electric motors, television sets, refrigerators and freezers, petroleum refining, shipbuilding (small ships), furniture making, textiles, food processing, fertilizers, agricultural machinery, optical equipment, electronic components, computers, amber. **Natural resources:** peat, arable land. **Exports:** $3.3 billion (f.o.b., 1999): machinery and equipment, mineral products, textiles and clothing, chemicals, foodstuffs. **Imports:** $4.5 billion (f.o.b., 1999): machinery and equipment, mineral products, chemicals, textiles and clothing, foodstuffs. **Major trading partners:** Russia, Germany, Latvia, Denmark, Belarus.

Geography Lithuania is situated on the eastern shore of the Baltic Sea and borders Latvia on the north, Belarus on the east and south, Poland and the Kaliningrad region of Russia on the southwest. It is a country of gently rolling hills, many forests, rivers and streams, and lakes. Its principal natural resource is agricultural land.

Government Parliamentary democracy.

History The Liths, or Lithuanians, united in the 12th century under the rule of Mindaugas, who became king in 1251. Through marriage, one of the later Lithuanian rulers became the king of Poland (Ladislaus II) in 1386, uniting the countries. In 1410, the Poles and Lithuanians defeated the powerful Teutonic Knights at Tannenberg. From the 14th to the 16th century, Poland and Lithuania made up one of medieval Europe's largest empires, stretching from the Black Sea almost to Moscow. The two countries formed a confederation for almost 200 years, and in 1569 they formally united. Russia, Prussia, and Austria partitioned Poland in 1772, 1792, and 1795. As a consequence, Lithuania came under Russian rule after the last partition. Russia attempted to immerse Lithuania in Russian culture and language, but anti-Russian sentiment continued to grow. Following World War I and the collapse of Russia, Lithuania declared independence (1918), under German protection.

The republic was then annexed by the Soviet Union in 1940. From June 1941 to 1944 it was occupied by German troops, with whom Lithuania served in World War II. Some 240,000 Jews were massacred in Lithuania during the Nazi years. In 1944 the Soviets again annexed Lithuania.

The Lithuanian independence movement reemerged in 1988. In 1990, Vytautas Landsbergis, the non-Communist head of the largest Lithuanian popular movement (Sajudis), was elected president. On the same day, the Supreme Council rejected Soviet rule and declared the restoration of Lithuania's independence, the first Baltic republic to take this action. Confrontation with the Soviet Union ensued along with economic sanctions, but they were lifted after both sides agreed to a face-saving compromise.

Lithuania's independence was quickly recognized by major European and other nations, including the United States. The Soviet Union finally recognized the independence of the Baltic states on Sept. 6, 1991. UN admittance followed on Sept. 17, 1991. Successful implementation of structural and legislative reforms in Lithuania attracted greater foreign direct investments by the mid-1990s.

The EU began negotiations for the admission of Lithuania in 1999. In May 2001, Lithuania and eight other central and eastern European countries declared their wish to join NATO in 2002, a "big bang" that would expand NATO to 28 members.

Luxembourg

GRAND DUCHY OF LUXEMBOURG

National name: Grand-Duché de Luxembourg
Ruler: Grand Duke Henri (2000)
Premier: Jean-Claude Juncker (1995)
Area: 998 sq mi (2,586 sq km)
Population (2001 est.): 442,972 (average annual rate of natural increase: 0.3%); birth rate: 12.3/1000; infant mortality rate: 4.8/1000; density per sq mi: 444
Capital and largest city (1991): Luxembourg, 75,622.
Monetary units: Luxembourg franc and euro.
Languages: Luxermbourgish, French, German.
Ethnicity/race: Celtic base (with French and German blend), Portuguese, Italian, and European (guest and worker residents). **Religions:** Roman Catholic 97%, Protestant and Jewish 3%. **Literacy rate:** 100% (1980)
Economic summary: GDP/PPP (1999 est.): $14.7 billion; per capita $34,200. **Real growth rate:** 4.2%. **Inflation:** 1.1%. **Unemployment:** 2.7%. **Arable land:** 24%. **Agriculture:** barley, oats, potatoes, wheat, fruits, wine grapes; livestock products. **Labor force:** 236,400 (one-third of labor force is foreign workers, mostly from Portugal, Italy, France, Belgium, and Germany) (1998 est.); services, 83.2%; industry, 14.3%; agriculture, 2.5%. **Industries:** banking, iron and steel, food processing, chemicals, metal products, engineering, tires, glass, aluminum. **Natural resources:** iron ore (no longer exploited), arable land. **Exports:** $7.5 billion (f.o.b., 1998): finished steel products, chemicals, rubber products, glass, aluminum, other industrial products. **Imports:** $9.6 billion (c.i.f., 1998): minerals, metals, foodstuffs, quality consumer goods. **Major trading partners:** Germany, France, Belgium, UK, U.S., Netherlands.

Geography Luxembourg is about half the size of Delaware. The Ardennes Mountains extend from Belgium into the northern section of Luxembourg. The rolling plateau of the fertile Bon Pays is in the south.

Government Constitutional monarchy.

History Luxembourg, once part of Charlemagne's empire, became an independent state in 963, when Siegfried, count of Ardennes, became sovereign of Lucilinburhuc ("Little Fortress"). In 1060, Conrad, a descendant of Siegfried, took the title count of Luxembourg. From the 15th to the 18th century, Spain, France, and Austria held the duchy in turn. The Congress of Vienna in 1815 made it a Grand Duchy and gave it to William I, king of the Netherlands. In 1839 the Treaty of London ceded the western part of Luxembourg to Belgium. The eastern part, continuing in personal union with the Netherlands and a member of the German Confederation, became autonomous in 1848 and a neutral territory by decision of the London Conference of 1867, governed by its grand duke. Germany occupied the duchy in World Wars I and II. Allied troops liberated the enclave in 1944.

Luxembourg joined NATO in 1949, the Benelux Economic Union (with Belgium and the Netherlands) in 1948, and the European Economic Community (later the EU) in 1957. In 1961, Prince Jean, son and heir of Grand Duchess Charlotte, was made head of state, acting for his mother. She abdicated in 1964, and Prince Jean became grand duke. Grand Duchess

Charlotte died in 1985. Luxembourg's Parliament approved the Maastricht Accord, paving the way for the economic unity of the EU in July 1992. Crown Prince Henri was sworn in as grand duke in Oct. 2000, replacing his father, Jean, who had been head of state for 26 years.

Macedonia

REPUBLIC OF MACEDONIA[1]

National Name: Republica Makedonija
President: Boris Trajkovski (1999)
Prime Minister: Ljupco Georgievski (1998)
Area: 9,781 sq mi (25,333 sq km)
Population (2001 est.): 2,046,209 (average annual rate of natural increase: 0.6%); birth rate: 13.5/1000; infant mortality rate: 13.0/1000; density per sq mi: 209
Capital and largest city (1994 est.): Skopje, 444,229. **Other large cities:** Bitola, 84,002; Prelep, 70,152; Kumanovo, 68,148. **Monetary unit:** Denar.
Languages: Macedonian, which uses the Cyrillic alphabet, 70%; Albanian, 21%; Turkish, 3%; other, 6%.
Ethnicity/race: Macedonian 65%, Albanian 22%, Turkish 4%, Serb 2%, Rom (Gypsy) 3%, other 4%.
Religions (1994): Eastern Orthodox 67%, Muslim 30%
Economic summary: GDP/PPP (1999 est.): $7.6 billion per capita $3,800. **Real growth rate:** 2.5%. **Inflation:** 1%. **Unemployment:** 35%. **Arable land:** 24%. **Agriculture:** rice, tobacco, wheat, corn, millet, cotton, sesame, mulberry leaves, citrus, vegetables; beef, pork, poultry, mutton. **Labor force:** 673,000 (1995 est.); agriculture, n.a.; industry, n.a.; services, n.a. **Industries:** coal, metallic chromium, lead, zinc, ferronickel, textiles, wood products, tobacco. **Natural resources:** chromium, lead, zinc, manganese, tungsten, nickel, low-grade iron ore, asbestos, sulfur, timber, arable land. **Exports:** $1.2 billion (f.o.b., 1999 est.): food, beverages, tobacco; miscellaneous manufactures, iron and steel. **Imports:** $1.56 billion (f.o.b., 1999 est.): machinery and equipment, chemicals, fuels; food products. **Major trading partners:** Germany, Serbia and Montenegro, U.S., Greece, Italy, Slovenia, Ukraine.

1. The UN recognized the Republic of Macedonia on April 8, 1993, under the temporary name the Former Yugoslav Republic of Macedonia. The U.S. recognized Macedonia as a state in Feb. 1994.

Geography Macedonia is a landlocked state in the heart of the Balkans and is slightly smaller than the state of Vermont. It is a mountainous country with small basins of agricultural land linked by rivers. The three major rivers are the Aliakmon, the Vardar, and the Strymon. The Vardar is the largest and most important river.

Government Republic.

History The Republic of Macedonia occupies the western half of the ancient Kingdom of Macedonia. Historic Macedonia was defeated by Rome and became a Roman province in 148 B.C. After the Roman Empire was divided in A.D. 395, Macedonia was intermittently ruled by the Byzantine Empire until Turkey took possession of the land in 1389. The Ottoman Turks dominated Macedonia for the next five centuries, up until 1913. During the 19th and 20th centuries, there was a constant struggle by the Balkan powers to possess Macedonia for its economic wealth and its strategic military corridors. The Treaty of San Stefano in 1878 ending the Russo-Turkish War gave the largest part of Macedonia to Bulgaria. Bulgaria lost much of its Macedonian territory when it was defeated by the Greeks and Serbs in the Second Balkan War of 1913. Most of Macedonia went to Serbia and the remainder was divided among Greece and Bulgaria.

In 1914, Serbia, which included Macedonia, joined in union with Croatia, Slovenia, and Montenegro to form the kingdom of Serbs, Croats, and Slovenes, which was renamed Yugoslavia in 1929. Bulgaria joined the Axis powers in World War II and occupied parts of Yugoslavia including Macedonia in 1941. During the occupation of their country, Macedonian resistance fighters fought a guerrilla war against the invading troops. The Yugoslavian republic was reestablished after the defeat of Germany in 1945, and in 1946, the government removed Macedonia from Serbian control and made it an autonomous Yugoslavian republic. Later, when President Tito recognized the Macedonian people as a separate nation, the Macedonians strove to develop their own culture and language separate from Bulgaria and Serbia.

In Jan. 1992, Macedonia declared its independence from Yugoslavia and asked for recognition from the European Union nations. It became a member of the UN in 1993 under the provisional name of the Former Yugoslav Republic of Macedonia (FYROM) because Greece vociferously protested Macedonia's right to the name, which is also the name of a large northern province of Greece. To Greece, the use of the name implies Macedonia's interest in territorial expansion into the Greek province. Greece has imposed two trade embargoes against the country as a result.

The Macedonian government, in 1997, urged NATO to extend its peacekeeping role in the Balkans beyond its mid-1998 mandate, saying NATO troops provided a stabilizing role. Ethnic tensions between ethnic Albanians and Macedonians continued to rise during the Kosovo crisis, during which more than 140,000 refugees streamed into the country from neighboring Kosovo. Most of the refugees returned to Kosovo in 2000.

The long-simmering resentment of Macedonia's ethnic Albanians erupted into violence in the winter of 2001, prompting the government to send in troops to the heavily Albanian western section of the country. The rebels sought greater autonomy within Macedonia, including official recognition of the Albanian language. The more radical aspired to create a greater Albania, one that would unite the ethnic Albanians of Macedonia, Kosovo, and Albania proper. After six months of fighting, the rebels and the Macedonian government signed a peace agreement on Aug. 13, 2001, that allowed a British-led NATO force to enter the country and disarm the guerrillas.

Madagascar

REPUBLIC OF MADAGASCAR

National name: Repoblikan'i Madagasikara
President and Head of State: Didier Ratsiraka (1997)
Prime Minister: Tantely Andrianarivo (1998)
Area: 226,656 sq mi (587,040 sq km)
Population (2001 est.): 15,982,563 (average annual rate of natural increase: 3.0%); birth rate: 42.7/1000; infant mortality rate: 83.6/1000; density per sq mi: 71
Capital and largest city (1993 est.): Antananarivo, 1,000,000. **Monetary unit:** Malagasy franc.
Languages: Malagasy and French (both official).
Ethnicity/race: Malayo-Indonesian (Merina and related Betsileo), Cotiers (mixed African, Malayo-Indonesian, and Arab ancestry—Betsimisaraka, Tsimihety, Antaisaka, Sakalava), French, Indian, Creole, Comoran. **Religions:**

traditional 52%, Christian 41%, Islam 7%. **Literacy rate:** 80% (1990)
Economic summary: GDP/PPP (1999 est.): $11.5 billion; per capita $780. **Real growth rate:** 4.5%. **Inflation:** 9.5%. **Unemployment:** n.a. **Arable land:** 4%. **Agriculture:** coffee, vanilla, sugarcane, cloves, cocoa, rice, cassava (tapioca), beans, bananas, peanuts; livestock products. **Labor force:** 7 million (1995). **Industries:** meat processing, soap, breweries, tanneries, sugar, textiles, glassware, cement, automobile assembly plant, paper, petroleum, tourism. **Natural resources:** graphite, chromite, coal, bauxite, salt, quartz, tar sands, semiprecious stones, mica, fish, hydropower. **Exports:** $600 million (f.o.b., 1998 est.): coffee 45%, vanilla 20%, cloves, shellfish, sugar, petroleum products (1995 est.). **Imports:** $881 million (c.i.f., 1998 est.): intermediate manufactures 30%, capital goods 28%, petroleum 15%, consumer goods 14%, food 13% (1995 est.). **Major trading partners:** France, U.S., Germany, Japan, UK, Hong Kong, China, Singapore.

Geography Madagascar lies in the Indian Ocean off the southeast coast of Africa opposite Mozambique. The world's fourth-largest island, it is twice the size of Arizona. The country's low-lying coastal area gives way to a central plateau. The once densely wooded interior has largely been cut down.

Government Multiparty republic.

History The Malagasy are of mixed Malayo-Indonesian and African-Arab ancestry. Indonesians are believed to have migrated about 700. King Andrianampoinimerina (1787–1810) ruled the major kingdom on the island, and his son, Radama I (1810–28) unified much of the island. The French made the island a protectorate in 1885, and then in 1894–95 ended the monarchy, exiling Queen Rànavàlona III to Algiers. A colonial administration was set up, to which the Comoro Islands were attached in 1908, and other territories later. In World War II, the British occupied Madagascar, which retained ties to Vichy France.

An autonomous republic within the French Community since 1958, Madagascar became an independent member of the community in 1960. In May 1973, an army coup led by Maj. Gen. Gabriel Ramanantsoa ousted Philibert Tsiranana, president since 1959. Comdr. Didier Ratsiraka, named president on June 15, 1975, announced that he would follow a socialist course and, after nationalizing banks and insurance companies, declared all mineral resources nationalized. Repression and censorship characterized his regime. Ratsiraka was reelected in 1989 in a suspicious election that led to riots as well as the formation of a multiparty system in 1990. In 1991 Ratsiraka agreed to share power with the democratically minded opposition leader, Albert Zafy, who then overwhelmingly won the presidential elections in Feb. 1993. But Zafy was impeached by Parliament for abusing his constitutional powers during an economic crisis and lost the 1996 presidential election to Ratsiraka, who became president in Feb. 1997.

A succession of violent tropical storms battered Madagascar in the spring of 2000, causing massive flooding and destroying half of the vanilla crop, a major export. More than 40,000 people were left homeless and 1,300 died from a subsequent cholera epidemic. The devastation only added to the increasing environmental degradation of the island. A study released in July 2000 indicated Madagascar's capital, Antananarivo, is the second most polluted city in the world, after Mexico City.

Malawi

REPUBLIC OF MALAWI

President: Bakili Muluzi (1994)
Area: 45,745 sq mi (118,480 sq km)
Population (2001 est.): 10,548,250 (average annual rate of natural increase: 1.5%); birth rate: 37.8/1000; infant mortality rate: 121.1/1000; density per sq mi: 231
Capital (1993 est.): Lilongwe, 260,000. **Largest city (1993 est.):** Blantyre, 399,000. **Monetary unit:** Kwacha. **Languages:** English and Chichewa (both official). **Ethnicity/race:** Chewa, Nyanja, Tumbuko, Yao, Lomwe, Sena, Tonga, Ngoni, Ngonde, Asian, European. **Religions:** Christian 75%, Islam 20%. **Literacy rate:** 49% (1987)
Economic summary: GDP/PPP (1999 est.): $9.4 billion; per capita $940. **Real growth rate:** 4.2%. **Inflation:** 45%. **Unemployment:** n.a. **Arable land:** 34%. **Agriculture:** tobacco, sugarcane, cotton, tea, corn, potatoes, cassava (tapioca), sorghum, pulses; cattle, goats. **Labor force:** 3.5 million; agriculture, 86%; wage earners, 14% (1990 est.). **Industries:** tobacco, tea, sugar, sawmill products, cement, consumer goods. **Natural resources:** limestone, arable land, hydropower, unexploited deposits of uranium, coal, and bauxite. **Exports:** $510 million (f.o.b., 1999): tobacco, tea, sugar, cotton, coffee, peanuts, wood products. **Imports:** $512 million (f.o.b., 1999): food, petroleum products, semimanufactures, consumer goods, transportation equipment. **Major trading partners:** South Africa, U.S., Germany, Netherlands, Japan, Zimbabwe, Zambia, UK **Member of Commonwealth of Nations**

Geography Malawi is a landlocked country the size of Pennsylvania in southeast Africa, surrounded by Mozambique, Zambia, and Tanzania. Lake Malawi, formerly Lake Nyasa, occupies most of the country's eastern border. The north-south Rift Valley is flanked by mountain ranges and high plateau areas.

Government Multiparty democracy.

History Early human inhabitants of what is now Malawi date to 8000–2000 B.C. Bantu-speaking peoples migrated there between the 1st and 4th centuries A.D. A large slave trade took place in the 18th and 19th centuries and brought Islam to the region. At the same time, missionaries introduced Christianity. Several major kingdoms were established in the precolonial period: the Maravi in 1480, the Ngonde in 1600, and in the Chikulamayembe in the 18th century.

The first European to make extensive explorations in the area was David Livingstone in the 1850s and 1860s. In 1884, Cecil Rhodes's British South African Company received a charter to develop the country. The company came into conflict with the Arab slavers in 1887–89. Britain annexed what was then called the Nyasaland territory in 1891 and made it a protectorate in 1892. Sir Harry Johnstone, the first high commissioner, used Royal Navy gunboats to wipe out the slavers.

Between 1951 and 1953 Britain combined Nyasaland with the colonies of Northern and Southern Rhodesia to form a federation, a move protested by black Africans who were wary of alignment with the ultra conservative white-minority rule in South Rhodesia.

On July 6, 1964, Nyasaland became the independent nation of Malawi. Two years later, it became a republic within the Commonwealth of Nations. Dr. Hastings K. Banda became Malawi's first prime minister (a title later changed to president). In his first month as ruler, he declared, "one party, one leader, one government, and no nonsense about it." In 1971 he became president for life, further consolidating his authoritarian rule. In addition to allowing former colonialists to retain considerable power in the country, he maintained warm relations with the white-minority government of South Africa. These policies drew heavy criticism from Malawian citizens and other African nations. In 1992 Banda faced violent protests.

Bakili Muluzi of the United Democratic Front (UDF) won the country's first free election in May 1994, ending Banda's 30-year rule. In 1999 Muluzi was reelected. While Malawi is no longer the repressive society it was under Banda, Muluzi's government has been tainted by corruption scandals. With more than 10% of its adults believed infected, AIDS remains a huge problem. In the summer of 2000 a small bubonic plague outbreak was reported on the Malawi-Mozambique border.

Malaysia

Paramount Ruler: His Majesty Tuanku Salehuddin Abdul Aziz Shah ibni al-Marhum Hisamuddin Alam Shah (1999)
Prime Minister: Mahathir bin Mohamad (1981)
Area: 127,316 sq mi (329,750 sq km)
Population (2001 est.): 22,229,040 (average annual rate of natural increase: 2.0%); birth rate: 24.8/1000; infant mortality rate: 20.3/1000; density per sq mi: 175
Capital and largest city (1991 est.): Kuala Lumpur, 1,145,000. **Largest cities (1991 est.):** Georgetown (Pinang), 220,000; Ipoh, 382,600. **Monetary unit:** Ringgit. **Languages:** Malay (official), Chinese, Tamil, English. **Ethnicity/race:** Malay and other indigenous 59%, Chinese 32%, Indian 9%. **Religions:** Malays (all Muslims), Chinese (predominantly Buddhists), Indians (predominantly Hindus). **Literacy rate:** 78% (1990)
Economic summary: GDP/PPP (1999 est.): $229.1 billion; per capita $10,700. **Real growth rate:** 5%. **Inflation:** 2.8%. **Unemployment:** 3%. **Arable land:** 3%. **Agriculture:** Peninsular Malaysia—rubber, palm oil, rice; Sabah—subsistence crops, rubber, timber, coconuts, rice; Sarawak—rubber, pepper; timber. **Labor force:** 9.3 million; manufacturing, 27%; agriculture, forestry, and fisheries, 16%; local trade and tourism, 17%; services, 15%; government, 10%; construction, 9%. **Industries:** Peninsular Malaysia—rubber and oil palm processing and manufacturing, light manufacturing industry, electronics, tin mining and smelting, logging and processing timber; Sabah—logging, petroleum production; Sarawak—agriculture processing, petroleum production and refining, logging. **Natural resources:** tin, petroleum, timber, copper, iron ore, natural gas, bauxite. **Exports:** $83.5 billion (1999 est.): electronic equipment, petroleum and liquefied natural gas, chemicals, palm oil, wood and wood products, rubber, textiles. **Imports:** $61.5 billion (1999 est.): machinery and equipment, chemicals, food, fuel and lubricants. **Major trading partners:** U.S., Singapore, Japan, Hong Kong, Netherlands, Taiwan, Thailand, South Korea, China. **Member of Commonwealth of Nations**

Geography Malaysia is on the Malay Peninsula in southeast Asia. The nation also includes Sabah and Sarawak on the island of Borneo to the east. Its area slightly exceeds that of New Mexico.

Most of Malaysia is covered by forest, with a mountain range running the length of the peninsula. Extensive forests provide ebony, sandalwood, teak, and other woods.

Government Constitutional monarchy.

History The ancestors of the people that now inhabit the Malaysian peninsula first migrated to the area between 2500 and 1500 B.C. Those living in the coastal regions had early contact with Chinese and Indians; seafaring traders from India brought with them Hinduism, which was blended with the local animist beliefs. As Muslims conquered India, they spread the religion of Islam to Malaysia. In the 15th century A.D., Islam acquired a firm hold on the region when the Hindu ruler of the powerful city-state of Malacca, Parameswara Dewa Shah, was overthrown by his Muslim half-brother, Mudzaffar Shah.

British and Dutch interest in the region grew in the 1800s, with the British East India Company establishing a trading settlement on the island of Singapore. Trade soared, with Singapore's population growing from only 5,000 in 1820 to nearly 100,000 in just 50 years. In the 1880s, Britain formally established protectorates in Malaysia. At about the same time, rubber trees were introduced from Brazil. With the mass production of automobiles, rubber became a valuable export, and laborers were brought in from India to work the rubber plantations.

Following the Japanese occupation of Malaysia during World War II, a growing nationalist movement prompted the British to establish the semi-autonomous Federation of Malaya in 1948. But Communist guerrillas took to the jungles to begin a war of national liberation against the British, who declared a state of emergency to quell the insurgency, which lasted until 1960.

The independent state of Malaysia came into existence on Sept. 16, 1963, as a federation of Malaya, Singapore, Sabah (North Borneo), and Sarawak. In 1965, Singapore withdrew from the federation to become a separate nation. Since 1966, the 11 states of former Malaya have been known as West Malaysia, and Sabah and Sarawak have been known as East Malaysia.

By the late 1960s Malaysia was torn by communal rioting directed against Chinese and Indians, who controlled a disproportionate share of the country's wealth. Beginning in 1968, the government moved to achieve greater economic balance through a national economic policy.

Malaysia was significantly affected in 1978 by the "boat people" fleeing Vietnam. Because the refugees were mostly ethnic Chinese, the government was apprehensive about any increase in a minority that previously had been the source of internal conflict in the country. In April 1988, it announced that within the year it would cease accepting refugees.

In the 1980s, Dr. Mohamed Mahathir succeeded Datuk Hussein as prime minister. Mahathir instituted economic reforms that would transform Malaysia into one of the so-called Asian Tigers. Throughout the 1990s, Mahathir embarked on a massive project to build a new capital from scratch in an attempt to bypass congested Kuala Lumpur.

Beginning in 1997 and continuing through the next year, Malaysia suffered from the Asian currency crisis. Mahathir blamed market speculators for the crisis, and many of his ambitious building projects had to be placed on hold. Instead of following the economic prescriptions of the International Monetary Fund and World Bank, the prime minister opted for fixed exchange rates and capital controls. In late 1999, Malaysia was on the road to economic recovery, and it appeared Mahathir's measures were working.

In Sept. 1998 Mahathir sacked his heir apparent, Anwar Ibrahim, from his posts as deputy prime minister and finance minister, after a disagreement over how to deal with the country's economic problems. In defiance, Anwar launched a reform movement attacking the government. The prime minister then jailed Anwar, who was beaten and charged with trumped-up corruption and sex crimes. Anwar was convicted of sodomy, corruption, and abuse of power in two separate trials and sentenced to a total of 15 years in jail. Five of the charges were dropped in 2001, but Anwar's unusually harsh sentence was not reduced. Malaysia's rigid Internal Security Act, which allows police to detain anyone considered a security risk for up to two years without a trial, was put to the test in Aug. when a judge ruled that four opposition activists—and Anwar supporters—who were jailed under the act could appeal and present exculpatory evidence.

Malaysia's economy stalled in 2001 as the demand for semiconductors and other information technology products slipped worldwide, fueling speculation that the country was headed for recession. The grim economic outlook cast a pall on Mahathir Mohamad's 20th year as prime minister. He assumed the role of finance minister in May, after Daim Zainuddin resigned the post.

Maldives

REPUBLIC OF MALDIVES

President: Maumoon Abdul Gayoom (1978)
Area: 116 sq mi (300 sq km)
Population (2001 est.): 310,764 (average annual rate of natural increase: 3.0%); birth rate: 38.2/1000; infant mortality rate: 63.7/1000; density per sq mi: 2,683
Capital and largest city (1995 census): Malé, 62,973.
Monetary unit: Maldivian Rufiyaa. **Languages:** Dhivehi (official); Arabic, Hindi, and English are also spoken. **Ethnicity/race:** Sinhalese, Dravidian, Arab, African. **Religion:** Islam (Sunni Muslim). **Literacy rate:** 91% (1985)
Economic summary: GDP/PPP (1999 est.): $540 million; per capita $1,800. **Real growth rate:** 7%. **Inflation:** 3%. **Unemployment:** negl. **Arable land:** 10%. **Agriculture:** coconuts, corn, sweet potatoes; fish. **Labor force:** 67,000 (1995); agriculture, 22%; industry, 18%; services, 60% (1995). **Industries:** fish processing, tourism, shipping, boat building, coconut processing, garments, woven mats, rope, handicrafts, coral and sand mining. **Natural resources:** fish. **Exports:** $98 million (f.o.b., 1998): fish, clothing. **Imports:** $312 million (f.o.b., 1998): consumer goods, intermediate and capital goods, petroleum products. **Major trading partners:** U.S., UK, Sri Lanka, Japan, Singapore, India, Canada.

Geography The Republic of Maldives is a group of atolls in the Indian Ocean about 417 mi (671 km) southwest of Sri Lanka. Its 1,190 coral islets stretch over an area of 35,200 square mi (90,000 sq km). With concerns over global warming and the shrinking of the polar ice caps, Maldives feels directly threatened, as none of its islands rises more than six feet above sea level.

Government Republic.

History The Maldives (formerly called the Maldive Islands) were first settled in the 5th century B.C. by Buddhist seafarers from India and Sri Lanka. According to tradition, Islam was adopted in A.D. 1153. Originally the islands were under the suzerainty of Ceylon (now Sri Lanka). They came under British protection in 1887 and were a dependency of the then-colony of Ceylon until 1948. The independence agreement with Britain was signed July 26, 1965. For centuries a sultanate, the islands adopted a republican form of government in 1952, but the sul-

tanate was restored in 1954. In 1968, however, as the result of a referendum, a republic was again established in the recently independent country. Ibrahim Nasir, president since 1968, was removed from office by the Majlis in Nov. 1978 and replaced by Maumoon Abdul Gayoom. President Gayoom was elected to a fifth five-year term in Oct. 1998.

Mali

REPUBLIC OF MALI

National name: République de Mali
President of the Republic: Alpha Oumar Konaré (1992)
Prime Minister: Mande Sidibe (2000)
Area: 478,764 sq mi (1,240,000 sq km)
Population (2001 est.): 11,008,518 (average annual rate of natural increase: 3.0%); birth rate: 48.8/1000; infant mortality rate: 121.4/1000; density per sq mi: 23
Capital and largest city (1992 est.): Bamako, 746,000.
Monetary unit: Franc CFA. **Languages:** French (official), African languages. **Ethnicity/race:** Mande 50% (Bambara, Malinke, Sarakole), Peul 17%, Voltaic 12%, Songhai 6%, Tuareg and Moor 10%, other 5%.
Religions: Islam 90%, traditional 9%, Christian 1%. **Literacy rate:** 32% (1990)
Economic summary: GDP/PPP (1999 est.): $8.5 billion; per capita $820. **Real growth rate:** 5%. **Inflation:** 3%. **Unemployment:** n.a. **Arable land:** 2%. **Agriculture:** cotton, millet, rice, corn, vegetables, peanuts; cattle, sheep, goats. **Labor force:** n.a.; agriculture and fishing, 80% (1998 est.). **Industries:** minor local consumer goods production and food processing; construction; phosphate and gold mining. **Natural resources:** gold, phosphates, kaolin, salt, limestone, uranium, hydropower; note: bauxite, iron ore, manganese, tin, and copper deposits are known but not exploited. **Exports:** $640 million (f.o.b., 1999 est.): cotton 50%, gold, livestock (1998 est.). **Imports:** $650 million (f.o.b., 1999 est.): machinery and equipment, construction materials, petroleum, foodstuffs, textiles. **Major trading partners:** Thailand, Italy, China, Brazil, Côte d'Ivoire, France, EU.

Geography Most of Mali, in West Africa, lies in the Sahara. A landlocked country four-fifths the size of Alaska, it is bordered by Guinea, Senegal, Mauritania, Algeria, Niger, Burkina Faso, and the Côte d'Ivoire. The only fertile area is in the south, where the Niger and Senegal Rivers provide irrigation.

Government Republic.

History Caravan routes have passed through Mali since A.D. 300. The Malinke empire ruled regions of Mali from the 12th to 16th centuries, and the Songhai empire reigned over the Timbuktu-Gao region in the 15th century. Morocco conquered Timbuktu in 1591, and ruled over it for two centuries. Subjugated by France by the end of the 19th century, the land became a colony in 1904 (named French Sudan in 1920) and in 1946 became part of the French Union. On June 20, 1960, it became independent and, under the name of Sudanese Republic, was federated with the Republic of Senegal in the Mali federation. However, Senegal seceded from the Federation on Aug. 20, 1960, and the Sudanese Republic then changed its name to the Republic of Mali on Sept. 22.

In the 1960s, Mali concentrated on economic development, continuing to accept aid from both Soviet bloc and Western nations, as well as international agencies. In the late 1960s, it began retreating from close ties with China. But a purge of conservative opponents brought greater power to President Modibo Keita, and in 1968 the influence of the Chinese and their Malian sympathizers increased. The army overthrew the government on Nov. 19, 1968, and until 1991, Mali was under a military dictatorship. Mali and Burkina Faso fought a brief border war from Dec. 25th to 29th, 1985. Mali's second multiparty national elections took place in May 1997, with President Konaré winning reelection.

Konaré has won international praise for his efforts to revive Mali's faltering economy. His adherence to International Monetary Fund guidelines has increased foreign investment and helped make Mali the second-largest cotton producer in Africa. He is also the chairman of the 15-nation ECOWAS (the Economic Community of West African States), which in recent years has concentrated on brokering peace in Sierra Leone, Liberia, and Guinea.

Malta

MALTA

President: Guido de Marco (1999)
Prime Minister: Eddie Fenech Adami (1998)
Area: 122 sq mi (316 sq km)
Population (2001 est.): 394,583 (average annual rate of natural increase: 0.5%); birth rate: 12.8/1000; infant mortality rate: 5.8/1000; density per sq mi: 3,234
Capital (1992 est.): Valletta, 9,183. **Largest city (est. 1990):** Sliema, 13,541. **Monetary unit:** Maltese lira.
Languages: Maltese and English (both official).
Ethnicity/race: Maltese (descendants of ancient Carthaginians and Phoenicians, with strong elements of Italian and other Mediterranean stock), Spanish, English, Arab. **Religion:** Roman Catholic 98%.
Literacy rate: 88% (1985)
Economic summary: GDP/PPP (1999 est.): $5.3 billion; per capita $13,800. **Real growth rate:** 4%. **Inflation:** 1.8%. **Unemployment:** 5.5% (Sept. 1999). **Arable land:** 38%. **Agriculture:** potatoes, cauliflower, grapes, wheat, barley, tomatoes, citrus, cut flowers, green peppers; pork, milk, poultry, eggs. **Labor force:** 143,700 (Oct. 1997); industry, 24%; services, 71%; agriculture, 5%. **Industries:** tourism; electronics, ship building and repair, construction; food and beverages, textiles, footwear, clothing, tobacco. **Natural resources:** limestone, salt, arable land. **Exports:** $1.8 billion (f.o.b., 1998): machinery and transport equipment, manufactures. **Imports:** $2.7 billion (f.o.b., 1998): machinery and transport equipment, manufactured goods; food, drink, and tobacco. **Major trading partners:** France, U.S., Germany, UK, Italy.
Member of Commonwealth of Nations

Geography The five Maltese islands—Malta, Gozo, Comino, Comminotto, and Filflawith—have a combined land area smaller than Philadelphia. Malta is located in the Mediterranean Sea, about 60 mi (97 km) south of the southeast tip of Sicily.

History The strategic importance of Malta was recognized by the Phoenicians, who occupied it, as did, in turn, the Greeks, Carthaginians, and Romans. The apostle Paul was shipwrecked there in A.D. 60. With the division of the Roman Empire in A.D. 395, Malta was assigned to the eastern portion dominated by Constantinople. Between 870 and 1090, it came under Arab rule. In 1091 the Norman noble Roger I, then ruler of Sicily, came to Malta with a small retinue and defeated the Arabs. The Knights of St. John (Malta), who obtained the three habitable Maltese islands of Malta, Gozo, and Comino from Charles V in 1530, reached their highest fame when they withstood an attack by superior Turkish forces in 1565. Napoléon seized Malta in 1798, but the French forces were ousted by British troops the next year, and British rule was confirmed by the Treaty of Paris in 1814.

Malta was heavily attacked by German and Italian aircraft during World War II but was never invaded by the Axis powers. It became an independent nation on Sept. 21, 1964, and a republic on Dec. 13, 1974, but remained in the British Commonwealth. In 1979, when its alliance with Great Britain ended, Malta sought to guarantee its neutrality through agreements with other countries. Although Malta applied for membership in the European Union, when the Labour Party won the election in Oct. 1996, it froze Malta's EU application and withdrew from the NATO Partnership for Peace program in an effort to maintain its neutrality. When the Nationalist Party won the Sept. 1998 elections, however, it revived the EU accession bid.

Marshall Islands

REPUBLIC OF THE MARSHALL ISLANDS

President: Kessai H. Note (2000)
Total land area: 70 sq mi (181 sq km), includes the atolls of Bikini, Eniwetok, and Kwajalein
Population (2001 est.): 70,822 (average annual rate of natural increase 3.9%); birth rate 45.1/1000; infant mortality rate 39.8/1000; density per sq mi: 1,012
Capital and largest city (1990 est.): Majuro, 20,000.
Languages: Both Marshallese and English are official languages. Marshallese is a language in the Malayo-Polynesian family. **Ethnicity/race:** Micronesian. **Religions:** predominantly Christian, mostly Protestant. **Literacy rate:** 91% (1980)
Economic summary: GDP/PPP (1998 est.): $105 million, supplemented by approximately $65 million annual U.S. aid; per capita $1,670. **Real growth rate:** −5% (1997). **Unemployment:** 16% (1991 est.). **Arable land:** 0%. **Agriculture:** coconuts, cacao, taro, breadfruit, fruits; pigs, chickens. **Labor force:** n.a. **Industries:** copra, fish, tourism, craft items from shell, wood, and pearls, offshore banking (embryonic). **Natural resources:** phosphate deposits, marine products, deep seabed minerals. **Exports:** $28 million (f.o.b., 1997 est.): fish, coconut oil, fish, trochus shells. **Imports:** $58 million (f.o.b., 1997 est.): foodstuffs, machinery and equipment, fuels, beverages, and tobacco. **Major trading partners:** U.S., Japan, Australia, New Zealand, Guam, Singapore.

Geography The Marshall Islands, east of the Carolines, are divided into two chains: the western, or Ralik, group, including the atolls Jaluit, Kwajalein, Wotho, Bikini, and Eniwetok; and the eastern, or Ratak, group, including the atolls Mili, Majuro, Maloelap, Wotje, and Likiep. The islands are of the coral-reef type and rise only a few feet above sea level. The Marshall Islands comprise an area slightly larger than Washington, D.C.

Government Constitutional government in free association with the U.S.

History Micronesian peoples were the first inhabitants of the archipelago. The islands were explored by the Spanish in the 16th century and were named for a British captain in 1788. Germany unsuccessfully attempted to colonize the islands in 1885. Japan claimed them in 1914, but after several battles during World War II, the U.S. seized them from the Japanese. In 1947, the UN made the island group, along with the Mariana and Caroline archipelagos, a U.S. trust territory.

U.S. nuclear testing took place between 1946 and 1958 on the islands of Bikini and Enewetak. The people of Bikini were removed to another island, and a total of 23 U.S. atomic and hydrogen bomb tests were conducted. Despite clean-up attempts, the islands remain uninhabited today because of nuclear contamination. The U.S. paid the islands $183.7 million in damages in 1983. The United States and the Marshall Islands signed a Compact of Free Association in 1986, which meant the islands became self-governing but would receive U.S. military and economic aid. The Marshall Islands were admitted to the UN on Sept. 17, 1991.

In 1997, President Kabua deferred plans for a feasibility study of a controversial proposal to develop Bikini as a commercial nuclear-waste dump for radioactive material produced by Asian power plants. The Compact of Free Association with the U.S. and the associated economic aid are scheduled to expire in 2001. In 1999 the U.S. approved a one-time $3.8-million payment to the relocated people of Bikini atoll.

Mauritania

ISLAMIC REPUBLIC OF MAURITANIA

National name: République Islamique de Mauritanie
President: Col. Maaouye Ould Sidi Ahmed Taya (1984)
Prime Minister: Cheikh El Afia Ould Mohamed Khouna (1996)
Area: 397,953 sq mi (1,030,700 sq km)
Population (2001 est.): 2,747,312 (average annual rate of natural increase: 2.9%); birth rate: 43.0/1000; infant mortality rate: 76.7/1000; density per sq mi: 7
Capital and largest city (1992 est.): Nouakchott, 480,000. **Monetary unit:** Ouguyia. **Languages:** Arabic (official) and French. **Ethnicity/race:** mixed Maur/black 40%, Maur 30%, black 30%. **Religion:** Islam. **Literacy rate:** 34% (1990)
Economic summary: GDP/PPP (1999 est.): $4.9 billion; per capita $1,910. **Real growth rate:** 3.7%. **Inflation:** 9.8% (1998). **Unemployment:** 23% (1995 est.).
Arable land: 0%. **Agriculture:** dates, millet, sorghum, root crops; cattle, sheep; fish products. **Labor force:** 465,000 (1981 est.); 45,000 wage earners (1980); agriculture 47%, services 39%, industry 14%.
Industries: fish processing, mining of iron ore and gypsum. **Natural resources:** iron ore, gypsum, fish, copper, phosphate. **Exports:** $425 million (f.o.b., 1997): fish and fish products, iron ore, gold. **Imports:** $444 million (f.o.b., 1997): machinery and equipment, petroleum products, capital goods, foodstuffs, consumer goods. **Major trading partners:** Japan, Italy, France, Spain, Germany, Benelux.

Geography Mauritania, three times the size of Arizona, is situated in northwest Africa with about 350 mi (592 km) of coastline on the Atlantic Ocean. It is bordered by Morocco on the north, Algeria and Mali on the east, and Senegal on the south. The country is mostly desert, with the exception of the fertile Senegal River valley in the south and grazing land in the north.

Government Military government. The legal system is based on Islam.

History Mauritania was first inhabited by blacks and Berbers, and it became a center for the Berber Almoravid movement, which sought to spread Islam through western Africa. It was first explored by the Portuguese in the 15th century, but by the 19th century the French gained control. They organized the area into a territory in 1904, and made it part of French West Africa.

Mauritania became an independent nation on Nov. 28, 1960, and was admitted to the United Nations in 1961 over the strenuous opposition of Morocco, which claimed the territory. With Moors, Arabs, Berbers, and blacks frequently in conflict, the government in the late 1960s sought to make Arab culture dominant to unify the country.

Mauritania acquired administrative control of the southern part of the former Spanish Sahara when the colonial administration withdrew in 1975, under an agreement with Morocco and Spain. Increased military spending and rising casualties in Western Sahara helped bring down the civilian government of Ould Daddah in 1978. A succession of military rulers followed.

In 1984 Col. Maaouye Ould Sidi Ahmed Taya took control of the government. He relaxed Islamic law, fought corruption, instituted economic reforms urged by the International Monetary Fund, and held the country's first multiparty parliamentary elections in 1986. Although the 1991 constitution set up a multiparty democracy, politics remains based on ethnic and racial lines. The primary conflict is between blacks that dominate southern regions, and the Moorish-Arabic north, which runs the country. Racial tensions reached a peak in 1989 when Mauritania went to war with Senegal in a dispute over the border. As each country repatriated citizens of the other, critics accused Mauritania of taking the opportunity to expel thousands of blacks. Although Mauritania officially abolished slavery in 1980, the nation continues to tolerate the enslavement of blacks by North African Arabs. In 1993, the U.S. State Department estimated that there were more than 90,000 chattel slaves in the country.

In 1992 Taya won the nation's first multiparty presidential election, which opponents charged was rigged. Parliamentary elections were held in 1996 and 1997, with opposition parties winning some seats despite calls for government opponents to boycott the elections. Economically, Mauritania remains hostage to the fluctuating price of iron ore, which provides nearly half its export earnings. The country's first deepwater port opened near Nouakchott in 1986. Taya's attempts to restructure the economy provoke periodic protests, the most serious of which were the bread riots in Nouakchott in 1995. Economic development remains hampered by large-scale deforestation, over exploitation of rich fishing grounds, and chronic water shortages.

Mauritius

President: Cassam Uteem (1992)
Prime Minister: Sir Anerood Jugnauth (2000)
Area: 718 sq mi (1,860 sq km)
Population (2001 est.): 1,189,825 (average annual rate of natural increase: 1.0%); birth rate: 16.5/1000; infant mortality rate: 17.2/1000; density per sq mi: 1,657
Capital and largest city (1993 est.): Port Louis, 134,516. **Monetary unit:** Mauritian rupee.
Languages: English (official), French, Creole, Hindi, Urdu, Hakka, Bojpoori. **Ethnicity/race:** Indo-Mauritian 68%, Creole 27%, Sino-Mauritian 3%, Franco-Mauritian 2%. **Religions:** Hindu 52%, Christian 28.3%, Islam 16.6%, other 3.1%. **Literacy rate:** 81% (1990)
Economic summary: GDP/PPP (1999 est.): $12.3 billion; per capita $10,400. **Real growth rate:** 4%. **Inflation:** 6.8%. **Unemployment:** 2% (1996 est.).
Arable land: 49%. **Agriculture:** sugarcane, tea, corn, potatoes, bananas, pulses; cattle, goats; fish. **Labor**

force: 514,000 (1995); construction and industry 36%, services 24%, agriculture and fishing 14%, trade, restaurants, hotels 16%, transportation and communication 7%, finance 3% (1995). **Industries:** food processing (largely sugar milling), textiles, clothing; chemicals, metal products, transport equipment, nonelectrical machinery; tourism. **Natural resources:** arable land, fish. **Exports:** $1.7 billion (f.o.b., 1999): clothing and textiles, sugar, cut flowers, molasses. **Imports:** $2.1 billion (f.o.b., 1998): manufactured goods, capital equipment, foodstuffs, petroleum products, chemicals (1996). **Major trading partners:** UK, France, U.S., Germany, Italy, South Africa, India, Hong Kong. **Member of Commonwealth of Nations**

Geography Mauritius is a mountainous island in the Indian Ocean east of Madagascar.

Government Republic within the British Commonwealth.

History After a brief Dutch settlement, French immigrants who came in 1715 named the island Île de France and established the first road and harbor infrastructure, as well as the sugar industry, under the leadership of Gov. Mahe de Labourdonnais. Blacks from Africa and Madagascar came as slaves to work in the cane fields. In 1810, the British captured the island and in 1814, by the Treaty of Paris, it was ceded to Great Britain along with its dependencies.

Indian immigration, which followed the abolition of slavery in 1835, rapidly changed the fabric of Mauritian society, and the country flourished with the increased cultivation of sugarcane. The opening of the Suez Canal in 1869 heralded the decline of Mauritius as a port of call for ships rounding the southern tip of Africa, bound for South and East Asia. The economic instability of the price of sugar, the main crop, in the first half of the 20th century brought civil unrest, then economic, administrative, and political reforms. Mauritius became independent on March 12, 1968.

The effects of Cyclone Claudette in 1979, and of falling world sugar prices in the early 1980s, led the government to initiate a vigorous program of agricultural diversification and to develop the processing of imported goods for the export market. The country formally broke ties with the British Crown in March 1992, becoming a republic within the Commonwealth.

In addition to sugar cane, textile production and tourism are the leading industries. Primary education is free, and Mauritius boasts one of the highest literacy rates in sub-Saharan Africa.

Dr. Navinchandra Ramgoolam became prime minister in an unstable coalition government in 1995. The administration has embraced free-market reforms, resulting in an economic expansion through the 1990s. In Sept. 2000 an opposition alliance defeated Ramgoolam, winning 50 of the 70 seats in Parliament. The office of prime minister is to rotate: Ane_rood Jugnath, leader of the Socialist Militant Party, will serve for three years, followed by Paul Berenger, of the Militant Movement. Berenger will be the first non-Hindu to hold office since Mauritius won independence in 1968. With a complicated ethnic mix—about 30% of the population is of African descent, the remainder is of Indian descent, both Hindu and Muslim—racial unrest continues to gnaw at the country.

Mexico

UNITED MEXICAN STATES

Official name: Estados Unidos Mexicanos
President: Vicente Fox Quesada (2000)
Area: 761,602 sq mi (1,972,550 sq km)
Population (2001 est.): 101,879,171 (average annual rate of natural increase: 1.8%); birth rate: 22.8/1000; infant mortality rate: 25.4/1000; density per sq mi: 134
Capital and largest city (2000 est.): Mexico City, 19,750,000 (metro. area). **Other large cities (1995):** Guadalajara, 2,178,000; Monterrey, 1,702,000; Ecatepec, 1,456,438 (part of Mexico City metro. area); Nezahualcóyotl, 1,259,543 (part of Mexico City metro. area); Puebla, 1,222,177. **Monetary unit:** Peso.
Languages: Spanish, Indian languages. **Ethnicity/race:** mestizo (Indian-Spanish) 60%, Amerindian or predominantly Amerindian 30%, Caucasian or predominantly Caucasian 9%, other 1%. **Religions:** nominally Roman Catholic 97%, Protestant 3%.
Literacy rate: 87% (1990)
Economic summary: GDP/PPP (1999 est.): $865.5 billion; per capita $8,500. **Real growth rate:** 3.7%. **Inflation:** 15%. **Unemployment:** 2.5% urban (1998); plus considerable underemployment. **Arable land:** 12%. **Agriculture:** corn, wheat, soybeans, rice, beans, cotton, coffee, fruit, tomatoes; beef, poultry, dairy products; wood products. **Labor force:** 38.6 million (1999); agriculture 24%, industry 21%, services 55% (1997). **Industries:** food and beverages, tobacco, chemicals, iron and steel, petroleum, mining, textiles, clothing, motor vehicles, consumer durables, tourism. **Natural resources:** petroleum, silver, copper, gold, lead, zinc, natural gas, timber. **Exports:** $136.8 billion (f.o.b., 1999), includes in-bond industries (assembly plant operations with links to U.S. companies): manufactured goods, oil and oil products, silver, coffee, cotton. **Imports:** $142.1 billion (f.o.b., 1999), includes in-bond industries (assembly plant operations with links to U.S. companies): metal-working machines, steel mill products, agricultural machinery, electrical equipment, car parts for assembly, repair parts for motor vehicles, aircraft, and aircraft parts. **Major trading partners:** U.S., Canada, Spain, Japan, Venezuela, Chile, Brazil, Germany, South Korea, Italy, France.

Geography Mexico is bordered by the United States to the north, Belize and Guatemala to the southeast; Mexico is about one-fifth the size of the United States. Baja California in the west is an 800-mile (1,287-km) peninsula and forms the Gulf of California. In the east are the Gulf of Mexico and the Bay of Campeche, which is formed by Mexico's other peninsula, the Yucatán. The center of Mexico is a great, high plateau, open to the north, with mountain chains on the east and west and with ocean-front lowlands lying outside of them.

Government Federal republic.

History At least three great civilizations—the Mayas, the Olmecs, and later the Toltecs—preceded the wealthy Aztec empire, conquered in 1519–21 by the Spanish under Hernando Cortés. Spain ruled Mexico as part of the viceroyalty of New Spain for the next 300 years until Sept. 16, 1810, when the Mexicans first revolted. They won independence in 1821.

From 1821 to 1877, there were two emperors, several dictators, and enough presidents and provisional executives to make a new government on the average of every nine months. Mexico lost Texas (1836), and after defeat in the war with the U.S. (1846–48) it lost the area that is now California, Nevada, and Utah, most of Arizona and New Mexico, and parts of Wyoming and Colorado under the Treaty of Guadalupe Hidalgo. In 1855, the Indian patriot Benito Juárez began a series of reforms, including the disestablishment of the Catholic Church, which owned vast property. The subsequent civil war was interrupted by the French invasion of Mexico (1861), and the crowning of Maximilian of Austria as emperor (1864). He was overthrown and executed by forces under Juárez, who again became president in 1867.

The years after the fall of the dictator Porfirio Diaz (1877–80 and 1884–1911) were marked by bloody political-military strife and trouble with the U.S., culminating in the punitive U.S. expedition into northern Mexico (1916–17) in unsuccessful pursuit of the revolutionary Pancho Villa. Since a brief civil war in 1920, Mexico has enjoyed a period of gradual agricultural, political, and social reforms. The Partido Nacional Revolucionario (PNR; National Revolutionary Party), dominated by revolutionary and reformist politicians from northern Mexico, was established in 1929; it continued to control Mexico throughout the 20th century and was renamed the Partido Revolucionario Institucional (PRI; Institutional Revolutionary Party) in 1946. Relations with the U.S. were disturbed in 1938 when all foreign oil wells were expropriated, but a compensation agreement was reached in 1941.

Following World War II, the government emphasized economic growth. During the mid-1970s, under the leadership of President José López Portillo, Mexico became a major petroleum-producer. By the end of Portillo's term, however, Mexico had accumulated a huge external debt because of the government's unrestrained borrowing on the strength of its petroleum revenues. The collapse of oil prices in 1986 cut Mexico's export earnings. In Jan. 1994, Mexico joined Canada and the United States in the North American Free Trade Agreement (NAFTA), which will phase out all tariffs over a 15-year period, and in Jan. 1996, it became a founding member of the World Trade Organization (WTO).

In 1995, the U.S. agreed to prevent the collapse of Mexico's private banks. In return, the U.S. won virtual veto power over much of Mexico's economic policy. In 1997, in what observers called the freest elections in Mexico's history, the PRI lost control of the lower legislative house and the mayoralty of Mexico City in a stunning upset. To increase democracy, President Ernesto Zedillo said in 1999 that he would break precedent and not personally choose the next PRI presidential nominee. Several months later, Mexico held its first presidential primary, which was won by former interior secretary Francisco Labastida, Zedillo's closest ally among the candidates.

In elections held July 2, 2000, the PRI lost the presidency, ending 71 years of one-party rule. Vicente Fox Quesada, of the center-right National Action Party (PAN), took 43% of the vote to Labastida's 36%. Fox vowed tax reform, an overhaul of the legal system, and a reduction in power of the central government. Although PAN picked up seats in the Chamber of Deputies and the Senate, it failed to win a majority in either, forcing it to form coalitions with other parties. In 2001, illegal immigration to the U.S. and disagreements over NAFTA dominated U.S.-Mexican relations.

Micronesia

FEDERATED STATES OF MICRONESIA

President: Leo A. Falcam (1999)
Total area: 271 sq mi (702 sq km). Land area, same (includes islands of Pohnpei, Yap, Chuuk, and Kosrae)
Population (2001 est.): 134,597 (average annual rate of natural increase: 2.1%); birth rate: 27.1/1000; infant mortality rate: 33.5/1000; density per sq mi: 497
Capital: Palikir. **Languages:** English is the official and common language; major indigenous languages are Chukese, Pohnpeian, Yapase, and Kosrean.
Ethnicity/race: nine ethnic Micronesian and Polynesian groups. **Literacy rate:** 85% (1980)
Economic summary: GDP/PPP (1997 est.): $240 million (1997 est.); note: GDP is supplemented by grant aid, averaging perhaps $100 million annually; per capita $2,000. **Real growth rate:** 3%. **Inflation:** 4% (1996 est.). **Unemployment:** 27% (1989). **Arable land:** n.a. **Agriculture:** black pepper, tropical fruits and vegetables, coconuts, cassava (tapioca), sweet potatoes; pigs, chickens. **Labor force:** n.a.; two-thirds are government employees. **Industries:** tourism, construction, fish processing, craft items from shell, wood, and pearls. **Natural resources:** forests, marine products, deep-seabed minerals. **Exports:** $73 million (f.o.b., 1996 est.): fish, garments, bananas, black pepper. **Imports:** $168 million (c.i.f., 1996 est.): food, manufactured goods, machinery and equipment, beverages. **Major trading partners:** Japan, U.S., Guam, Australia.

Geography The Federated States of Micronesia is composed of the island states of Yap, Chuuk (Truk), Pohnpei (Ponape), and Kosrae, all in the Caroline Islands. The islands vary geologically from high mountainous islands to low coral atolls, with volcanic outcroppings on Pohnpei, Kosrae, and Chuuk. They are located 3,200 mi (5,150 km) west-southwest of Hawaii, in the north Pacific Ocean.

Government Constitutional government in free association with the United States since Nov. 1986.

History The islands, inhabited by Micronesian and Polynesian peoples, were colonized by Spain in the 17th century. Germany purchased them from Spain in 1898. They were occupied by the Japanese in 1914, but American forces seized them from the Japanese during World War II. On April 2, 1947, the United Nations Security Council created the Trust Territory of the Pacific Islands. The trust placed the Northern Mariana, Caroline, and Marshall Islands under the administration of the United States.

The Micronesian Federation (F.M.A.) became self-governing in 1979. In 1983, the F.M.A. voted to accept a Compact of Free Association with the U.S., and in Nov. 1986, the U.S. declared the Trust Territory agreements no longer in effect—thereby granting the Federated States of Micronesia full independence.

The F.M.A. was admitted to the United Nations on Sept. 17, 1991. In July 1993, the country became a member of the International Monetary Fund. Micronesia, as well as many other South Pacific countries, is alarmed by the effect continued global warming will have on their islands—the consequent rise in the level of the oceans threatens low-lying islands with flooding and, eventually, with submergence.

Moldova

REPUBLIC OF MOLDOVA

President: Vladimir Voronin (2001)
Prime Minister: Vasile Tarlev (2001)
Area: 13,067 sq mi (33,843 sq km)
Population (2001 est.): 4,431,570 (average annual rate of natural increase: 0.1%); birth rate: 13.4/1000; infant mortality rate: 42.7/1000, density per sq mi: 339
Capital and largest city (1991): Chisinau, 676,700.
Other large cities (1991 est.): Tiraspol, 186,000; Beltsy, 165,000; Bendery (Tighina), 141,500.
Monetary unit: Moldovan Lem. **Languages:** Moldovan (official; virtually the same as Romanian), Russian, Gagauz (a Turkish dialect). **Ethnicity/race:** Moldavian/Romanian 64.5%, Ukrainian 13.8%, Russian 13%, Gagauz 3.5%, Jewish 1.5%, Bulgarian 2%, other 1.7% (1989 figures). **Religions (1991):** Eastern Orthodox 98.5%, Jewish 1.5%, Baptist (only about 1,000 members). **Literacy rate:** 97% (1989)
Economic summary: GDP/PPP (1999 est.): $9.7 billion; per capita $2,200. **Real growth rate:** –4.4%. **Inflation:** 38%. **Unemployment:** 2% (includes only officially registered unemployed; large numbers of underemployed workers) (Sept. 1998). **Arable land:** 53%. **Agriculture:** vegetables, fruits, wine, grain, sugar beets, sunflower seed, tobacco; beef, milk. **Labor force:** 1.7 million (1998); agriculture 40.2%, industry 14.3%, other 45.5% (1998). **Industries:** food processing, agricultural machinery, foundry equipment, refrigerators and freezers, washing machines, hosiery, sugar, vegetable oil, shoes, textiles. **Natural resources:** lignite, phosphorites, gypsum, arable land. **Exports:** $470 million (f.o.b., 1999): foodstuffs, wine, and tobacco 66%; textiles and footwear, machinery (1998). **Imports:** $560 million (f.o.b., 1999): mineral products and fuel 31%, machinery and equipment, chemicals, textiles (1998). **Major trading partners:** Russia. Romania, Ukraine, Germany, Belarus.

Geography Moldova (formerly Moldavia) is a landlocked republic of hilly plains lying west of the Carpathian Mountains between the Prut and Dniester (Dnestr) Rivers. The country is sandwiched between Romania and Ukraine. The area is a very fertile region with rich black soil (chernozem) covering three-quarters of the territory.

Government Democratic republic.

History Most of what is now Moldova was the independent principality of Móldavia in the 14th century. In the 16th century it came under Ottoman Turkish rule. Russia acquired Moldavian territory in 1791, and again in 1812 (the Treaty of Bucharest) when Turkey gave up the province of Bessarabia[1] to Russia. Turkey held the rest of Moldavia but it was passed to Romania in 1918. Russia did not recognize the cession of this territory.

In 1924, the USSR established Moldavia as an Autonomous Soviet Socialist Republic. As a result of the Nazi-Soviet Nonaggression Pact of 1939, Romania was forced to cede all of Bessarabia to the Soviet Union in 1940. The Soviets merged the Moldavia ASSR with the Romanian-speaking districts of Bessarabia to form the Moldavian Soviet Socialist Republic. During World War II, Romania joined Germany in the attack on the Soviet Union and reconquered Bessarabia. But Soviet troops retook the territory in 1944 and reestablished the Moldavian SSR.

For many years, Romania and the USSR disputed each other's territorial claims over Bessarabia. Following the aborted coup against Soviet president Mikhail Gorbachev, Moldavia proclaimed its independence in Sept. 1991, and changed its name to the Romanian spelling, Moldova.

Conflict between ethnic Romanians and the Russian-Ukrainian majority in Trans-Dniester erupted upon independence. Trans-Dniester separatists (primarily ethnic Russians and Ukrainians) fought for independence from Moldova in 1992; progress on resolving the conflict has been slow. In the south, Gagauz, which is composed mostly of Turkic Christians, has also attempted secession.

The Russian financial crisis in fall 1998 severely affected Moldova, which relies on Russia for 60% of its foreign trade. Economic disaster caused an exodus of an estimated 600,000 Moldovans since then— Moldova is considered the poorest country in Europe. In Feb. 2001, the Communist Party won an overwhelming victory in parliamentary elections, and their leader, Vladimir Voronin, became prime minister.

1. The area between the Prut and Dniester Rivers.

Monaco

PRINCIPALITY OF MONACO

National name: Principauté de Monaco
Ruler: Prince Rainier III (1949)
Minister of State: Patrick Leclercq (2000)
Area: 0.75 sq mi (465 acres) (1.95 sq km)
Population (2001 est.): 31,842 (average annual growth rate: –0.3%); birth rate 9.7/1000; infant mortality rate: 5.8/1000; density per sq mi: 42,293
Capital and largest city (1995 est.): Monaco, 30,400.
Monetary unit: French franc. **Languages:** French (official), English, Italian, Monégasque. **Ethnicity/race:** French 47%, Monegasque 16%, Italian 16%, other 21%. **Religion:** Roman Catholic 95%. **Literacy rate:** 99%
Economic summary: GDP/PPP (1999 est.): $870 million; $27,000 per capita. **Real growth rate:** n.a. **Inflation:** n.a. **Unemployment:** 3.1% (1998). **Arable land:** 0%. **Agriculture:** none. **Labor force:** 30,540 (Jan. 1994). **Natural resources:** none. **Exports:** n.a. **Imports:** n.a. Full customs integration with France, which collects and rebates Monegasque trade duties; also participates in EU.

Geography Monaco is a tiny, hilly wedge driven into the French Mediterranean coast; it is 9 mi east of Nice, France.

Government Constitutional monarchy.

History The Phoenicians, and after them the Greeks, had a temple on the Monacan headland honoring Hercules. From *Monoikos,* the Greek surname for this mythological strong man, the principality took its name. After being independent for 800 years, Monaco was annexed to France in 1793 and was placed under Sardinia's protection in 1815. By the Franco-Monegasque treaty of 1861, Monaco went under French guardianship but continued to be independent. A treaty made with France in 1918 contained a clause providing that, in the event that the male Grimaldi dynasty should die out, Monaco would become an autonomous state under French protection.

Monaco has a tourist business that runs as high as 1.5 million visitors a year and is famous for its beaches and casinos. It had gaming tables as early as 1856. Five years later, a 50-year concession to operate the games was granted to François Blanc, of Bad Homburg. This concession passed into the hands of a private company in 1898.

Prince Rainier III, born on May 31, 1923, succeeded his grandfather, Louis II, on the latter's death,

May 9, 1949. Rainier was married, in 1956, to U.S. actress Grace Kelly and they subsequently had three children. Their son, Prince Albert Louis Pierre (b. 1958) is heir to the throne. Immensely popular, Princess Grace died on Sept. 14, 1982, of injuries received in a car accident near Monte Carlo. She was 52.

Monaco's practice of providing a tax shelter for French businessmen resulted in a 1962 dispute between the countries. A compromise was reached by which French citizens with less than five years' residence in Monaco were taxed at French rates, and taxes were imposed on Monegasque companies doing more than 25% of their business outside the principality. In 1967, Rainier took control of the Société des Bains de Mer, operator of the famous Monte Carlo gambling casino, in a program to increase hotel and convention space. The country was admitted to the UN in May 1993, making it the smallest country represented there. The country celebrated the 700th anniversary of the Grimaldi reign during 1997.

Mongolia

MONGOLIA

President: Ntsaagiyn Bagabandi (1997)
Prime Minister: Nambaryn Enkhbayar (2000)
Area: 604,247 sq mi (1,565,000 sq km)
Population (2001 est.): 2,654,999 (average annual rate of natural increase: 1.5%); birth rate: 21.8/1000; infant mortality rate: 53.5/1000; density per sq mi: 4
Capital and largest city (1993 est.): Ulan Bator, 619,000.
Monetary unit: Tugrik. **Languages:** Mongolian, 90%; also Turkic, Russian, and Chinese. **Ethnicity/race:** Mongol 90%, Kazak 4%, Chinese 2%, Russian 2%, other 2%. **Religions:** predominantly Tibetan Buddhist; Islam about 4%. **Literacy rate:** 97% (1989)
Economic summary: GDP/PPP (1999 est.): $6.1 billion; per capita $2,320. **Real growth rate:** 3.5%. **Inflation:** 9.5% (1998). **Unemployment:** 4.5% (1998). **Arable land:** 1%. **Agriculture:** wheat, barley, potatoes, forage crops; sheep, goats, cattle, camels, horses. **Labor force:** 1.256 million (1998); primarily herding/agricultural. **Industries:** construction materials, mining (particularly coal and copper); food and beverages, processing of animal products. **Natural resources:** oil, coal, copper, molybdenum, tungsten, phosphates, tin, nickel, zinc, wolfram, fluorspar, gold. **Exports:** $316.8 million (f.o.b., 1998): copper, livestock, animal products, cashmere, wool, hides, fluorspar, other nonferrous metals. **Imports:** $472.4 million (f.o.b., 1998): machinery and equipment, fuels, food products, industrial consumer goods, chemicals, building materials, sugar, tea. **Major trading partners:** China, Switzerland, Russia, South Korea, U.S., Japan.

Geography Mongolia lies in central Asia between Siberia on the north and China on the south. It is slightly larger than Alaska.

The productive regions of Mongolia—a tableland ranging from 3,000 to 5,000 ft (914 to 1,524 m) in elevation—are in the north, which is well drained by numerous rivers, including the Hovd, Onon, Selenga, and Tula. Much of the Gobi Desert falls within Mongolia.

Government Independent sovereign republic now in transition from Communism.

History Nomadic tribes that periodically plundered agriculturally based China from the west are recorded in Chinese history dating back more than 2,000 years. It was to protect China from these marauding peoples that the Great Wall was con-

structed around 200 B.C. The name *Mongol* comes from a small tribe whose leader, Ghengis Khan, began a conquest that would eventually encompass an enormous empire stretching from Asia to Europe, as far west as the Black Sea and as far south as India and the Himalayas. However, by the 14th century, the kingdom was in serious decline, with invasions from a resurgent China and internecine warfare.

The State of Mongolia was formerly known as Outer Mongolia. It contains the original homeland of the historic Mongols, whose power reached its zenith during the 13th century under Kublai Khan. The area accepted Manchu rule in 1689, but after the Chinese Revolution of 1911 and the fall of the Manchus in 1912, the northern Mongol princes expelled the Chinese officials and declared independence under the Khutukhtu, or "Living Buddha."

In 1921 Soviet troops entered the country, and facilitated the establishment of a republic by Mongolian revolutionaries in 1924. China also made a claim to the region, but was too weak to assert it. Under the 1945 Chinese-Russian Treaty, China agreed to give up Outer Mongolia, which, after a plebiscite, became a nominally independent country.

Allied with the USSR in its dispute with China, Mongolia began mobilizing troops along its borders in 1968 when the two powers became involved in border clashes on the Kazakh-Sinkiang frontier to the west and at the Amur and Ussuri Rivers. A 20-year treaty of friendship and cooperation, signed in 1966, entitled Mongolia to call upon the USSR for military aid in the event of invasion.

In 1989, the Mongolian democratic revolution began, led by Sanjaasurengiyn Zorig. Free elections held in Aug. 1990 produced a multiparty government, though it was still largely Communist. As a result, Mongolia has moved only gradually toward a market economy. With the collapse of the USSR, however, Mongolia was deprived of Soviet aid. Many of the country's factories were forced to shut down, and unemployment rose to 30%. Primarily in reaction to the economic turmoil, the Communist Mongolian People's Revolutionary Party (MPRP) won a significant majority in parliamentary elections in 1992. In 1996, however, the Democratic Alliance, an electoral coalition, defeated the MPRP, breaking with Communist rule for the first time since 1921. But in 1997, a former Communist and chairman of the People's Revolutionary Party, Ntsaagiyn Bagabandi, was elected president, further strengthening the hand of the antireformers.

Disagreement within Mongolia's ruling coalition over the pace and direction of market reforms in April 1998 caused a shakeup that thrust Tsakhiagiyn Elbegdorj, a proreform politician, into the prime minister's position. But parliamentary cross-purposes led to his resignation, and a succession of prime ministers followed.

In July 2000, and again in May 2001, the Mongolian People's Revolutionary Party (formerly the Communist Party) nearly swept parliamentary elections, winning 72 out of 76 seats. Ntsaagiyn Bagabandi was reelected in the 2001 elections, giving the MPRP control of both the presidency and Parliament, as well as a mandate to bolster the sluggish economy and dismal living standards. Former Communists, Bagabandi and the MPRP now support radical reform.

Morocco

KINGDOM OF MOROCCO

National name: al-Mamlaka al-Maghrebia
Ruler: King Muhammad VI (1999)
Prime Minister: Abderrahmane El Youssoufi (1998)
Area: 172,413 sq mi (446,550 sq km)
Population (2001 est.): 30,645,305 (average annual rate of natural increase: 1.8%); birth rate: 24.2/1000; infant mortality rate: 48.1/1000; density per sq mi: 178
Capital (1993 est.): Rabat, 1,220,000. **Largest cities:** Casablanca, 2,943,000; Marrakech, 602,000; Fez, 564,000; Salé, 521,000. **Monetary unit:** Dirham.
Languages: Arabic (official), French, Berber dialects, Spanish. **Ethnicity/race:** Arab-Berber 99.1%, other 0.7%, Jewish 0.2%. **Religions:** Islam 98.7%, Christian 1.1%, Jewish 0.2%. **Literacy rate:** 50% (1990)
Economic summary: GDP/PPP (1999 est.): $108 billion; per capita $3,600. **Real growth rate:** 0%. **Inflation:** 1.9%. **Unemployment:** 19% (1998 est.). **Arable land:** 21%. **Agriculture:** barley, wheat, citrus, wine, vegetables, olives; livestock. **Labor force:** 11 million (1997 est.); agriculture 50%, services 35%, industry 15% (1999 est.). **Industries:** phosphate rock mining and processing, food processing, leather goods, textiles, construction, tourism. **Natural resources:** phosphates, iron ore, manganese, lead, zinc, fish, salt. **Exports:** $7.1 billion (f.o.b., 1998): phosphates and fertilizers, food and beverages, minerals. **Imports:** $9.5 billion (f.o.b., 1998): semiprocessed goods, machinery and equipment, food and beverages, consumer goods, fuel. **Major trading partners:** France, Spain, India, Japan, Italy, U.S., Germany.

Geography Morocco, about one-tenth larger than California, lies across the Strait of Gibraltar on the Mediterranean and looks out on the Atlantic from the northwest shoulder of Africa. Algeria is to the east and Mauritania to the south. On the Atlantic coast there is a fertile plain. The Mediterranean coast is mountainous. The Atlas Mountains, running northeastward from the south to the Algerian frontier, average 11,000 ft (3,353 m) in elevation.

Government Constitutional monarchy.

History Morocco has been the home of the Berbers since the second millennium B.C. In A.D. 46, Morocco was annexed by Rome as part of the province of Mauritania until the Vandals overran this portion of the declining empire in the 5th century. The Arabs invaded circa 685, bringing Islam. The Berbers joined them in invading Spain in 711, but then revolted against the Arabs, resenting their secondary status. In 1086, Berbers took control of large areas of Moorish Spain until they were expelled in the 13th century.

The land was rarely unified and was usually ruled by small tribal states. Conflicts between Berbers and Arabs were chronic. Portugal and Spain began invading Morocco, which helped to unify the land in defense. In 1660 Morocco came under the control of the Alawite dynasty. It is a sherif dynasty—descended from the prophet Muhammad—and rules Morocco to this day.

During the 17th and 18th centuries Morocco was one of the Barbary states, the headquarters of pirates who pillaged Mediterranean traders. European powers became interested in colonizing the country beginning in 1840, and there were frequent clashes with the French and Spanish. Finally, in 1904, France and Spain concluded a secret agreement that divided Morocco into zones of French and Spanish influence, with France controlling almost all of Morocco and Spain controlling the small southwest portion, which became known as Spanish Sahara. Morocco became an even greater object of European rivalry by the turn of the century, leading almost to a European war in 1905 when Germany attempted to gain a foothold in the mineral-rich country. By terms of the Algeciras Conference (1906), the sultan of Morocco maintained control of his lands and France's privileges were curtailed. The conference was a telling indication of what was to come in World War I, with Germany and Austria-Hungary lining up on one side of the territorial dispute, and France, Britain, and the United States on the other.

In 1912, the sultan of Morocco, Moulay Abd al-Hafid, permitted the French protectorate status. Nationalism began to grow during World War II. Sultan Mohammed V was deposed by the French in 1953 and replaced by his uncle, but nationalist agitation forced his return in 1955. On his death on Feb. 26, 1961, his son, Hassan, became king. France and Spain recognized the independence and sovereignty of Morocco in 1956. Sultan Sidi Muhammad formed a constitutional government, and in 1961 Moulay Hassan succeeded his father as Hassan II.

Maintaining excellent relations with the West, King Hassan became the second Arab leader to meet with an Israeli leader when, on July 21, 1986, Prime Minister Shimon Peres came to Morocco. Morocco was also the first Arab state to condemn the 1990 Iraqi invasion of Kuwait. In the 1990s King Hassan promulgated "Hassanian democracy," which allowed for significant political freedom while at the same time retaining ultimate power for the monarch. In Aug. 1999, King Hassan II died after 38 years on the throne and his son, Prince Sidi Muhammad, was crowned King Muhammad VI. Since then Muhammad VI has pledged to make the political system more open, to allow freedom of expression, and to support economic reform. He has also advocated giving more rights to women, which has been opposed by Islamic fundamentalists. The entrenched political elite and the military have also been leery of some reform proposals. With about 20% of the population living in dire poverty, economic expansion is a prime goal.

Morocco's occupation of Western Sahara has been repeatedly criticized by the international community. In the 1970s, tens of thousands of Moroccans crossed the border into Spanish Sahara to back their government's contention that the northern part of the territory was historically part of Morocco. Spain, which had controlled the territory since 1912, withdrew in 1976, creating a power vacuum that was filled by Morocco in the north and Mauritania in the south. When Mauritania withdrew in Aug. 1979, Morocco overran the remainder of the territory. A rebel group, the Polisario Front, has fought against Morocco since 1976 for the independence of Western Sahara on behalf of the indigenous Saharawis. In 1981, King Hassan agreed to a cease-fire with a referendum under international supervision to decide the fate of the Sahara territory, but the dispute remains unresolved.

Mozambique

REPUBLIC OF MOZAMBIQUE

National name: República de Moçambique
President: Joaquim Chissanó (1986)
Prime Minister: Pascoal Mocumbi (1994)
Area: 309,494 sq mi (801,590 sq km)
Population (2001 est.): 19,371,057 (average annual rate

of natural increase: 1.3%); birth rate: 37.2/1000; infant mortality rate: 139.2/1000; density per sq mi: 63
Capital and largest city (1996 est.): Maputo, 1,095,300. **Monetary unit:** Metical. **Languages:** Portuguese (official), Bantu languages. **Ethnicity/race:** indigenous tribal groups 99.6% (Shangaan, Chokwe, Manyika, Sena, Makua, and others), Europeans 0.06%, Euro-Africans 0.2%, Indians 0.08%. **Religions:** traditional 60%, Christian 30%, Islam 10%. **Literacy rate:** 33% (1990)
Economic summary: GDP/PPP (1999 est.): $18.7 billion; per capita $1,000. **Real growth rate:** 10%. **Inflation:** 4%. **Unemployment:** n.a. **Arable land:** 4%. **Agriculture:** cotton, cashew nuts, sugarcane, tea, cassava (tapioca), corn, rice, tropical fruits; beef, poultry. **Labor force:** n.a.; agriculture 81%, industry 6%, services 13% (1997 est.). **Industries:** food, beverages, chemicals (fertilizer, soap, paints), petroleum products, textiles, cement, glass, asbestos, tobacco. **Natural resources:** coal, titanium, natural gas, hydropower. **Exports:** $300 million (f.o.b., 1999 est.): prawns 40%, cashews, cotton, sugar, copra, citrus, coconuts, timber (1997). **Imports:** $1.6 billion (c.i.f., 1999 est.): food, clothing, farm equipment, petroleum, transport equipment (1997). **Major trading partners:** Spain, South Africa, Portugal, U.S., Japan, Malawi, India, Zimbabwe, Saudi Arabia

Geography Mozambique stretches for 1,535 mi (2,470 km) along Africa's southeast coast. It is nearly twice the size of California. Tanzania is to the north; Malawi, Zambia, and Zimbabwe to the west; and South Africa and Swaziland to the south.

The country is generally a low-lying plateau broken up by 25 sizable rivers that flow into the Indian Ocean. The largest is the Zambezi, which provides access to central Africa. The principal ports are Maputo, Beira, and Nacala.

Government Multiparty republic.

History Bantu-speakers migrated to Mozambique in the first millennium, and Arab and Swahili traders settled the region thereafter. It was explored by Vasco da Gama in 1498, and first colonized by Portugal in 1505. By 1510, the Portuguese had control of all the former Arab sultanates on the east African coast. Mozambique was administered as part of Goa, in India, until 1752, when it received its own captain-general. Portuguese colonial rule was repressive.

Guerrilla activity began in 1963 and became so effective by 1973 that Portugal was forced to dispatch 40,000 troops to fight the rebels. A cease-fire was signed in Sept. 1974, and after having been under Portuguese colonial rule for 470 years, Mozambique became independent on June 25, 1975. The first president, Samora Moises Machel, had been the head of the National Front for the Liberation of Mozambique (FRELIMO) in its 10-year guerrilla war for independence. He died in a plane crash on Oct. 19, 1986, and was succeeded by his foreign minister, Joaquim Chissanó.

On Jan. 25, 1985, after a decade of independence, the government was locked in a five-year-old paralyzing war with antigovernment guerrillas, known as the MNR, backed by the white minority government in South Africa. The guerrilla movement weakened President Chissanó's attempts to institute socialism, which he then decided to abandon in 1989. A new constitution was drafted calling for three branches of government and granting civil liberties. A cease-fire agreement was signed in Oct. 1992 between the government and the MNR, ending 16 years of civil war.

In multiparty elections in 1994 President Chissanó won. In Nov. 1995 the country was the first non–former-British colony to become a member of the British Commonwealth. The president's disciplined economic plan has been extremely successful, winning the country foreign confidence and aid. While Mozambique posted some of the world's largest economic growth rates in the late 1990s, it has suffered enormous setbacks because of natural disaster—the enormous damage caused by severe flooding in the winters of 2000 and 2001. Hundreds have died and thousands were displaced by the flooding.

Myanmar

UNION OF MYANMAR

National name: Pyidaungsu Myanmar Naingngandau
Prime Minister: Senior Gen. Than Shwe (1992)
Area: 261,969 sq mi (678,500 sq km)
Population (2001 est.): 41,994,678 (average annual rate of natural increase: 0.8%); birth rate: 20.1/1000; infant mortality rate: 73.7/1000; density per sq mi: 160
Capital: Rangoon (Yangon). **Largest cities (est. 1983):** Rangoon (Yangon), 2,458,712; Mandalay, 532,895.
Monetary unit: Kyat. **Languages:** Burmese, minority languages. **Ethnicity/race:** Burman 68%, Shan 9%, Karen 7%, Rakhine 4%, Chinese 3%, Mon 2%, Indian 2%, other 5%. **Religions:** Buddhist 89.5%, Christian 4.9%, Muslim 3.8%, Hindu 0.05%, Animist 1.3%. **Literacy rate:** 81% (1990)
Economic summary: GDP/PPP (1999 est.): $59.4 billion; per capita $1,200. **Real growth rate:** 4.6%. **Inflation:** 38%. **Unemployment:** 7.1% (official FY97/ 98 est.). **Arable land:** 15%. **Agriculture:** paddy rice, corn, oilseed, sugarcane, pulses; hardwood. **Labor force:** 19.7 million (FY98/99 est.); agriculture, 65%; industry, 10%; services, 25% (1999 est.). **Industries:** agricultural processing; textiles and footwear; wood and wood products; copper, tin, tungsten, iron; construction materials; pharmaceuticals; fertilizer. **Natural resources:** petroleum, timber, tin, antimony, zinc, copper, tungsten, lead, coal, some marble, limestone, precious stones, natural gas, hydropower. **Exports:** $1.2 billion (1998): pulses and beans, prawns, fish, rice; teak, opiates. **Imports:** $2.5 billion (1998): machinery, transport equipment, construction materials, food products. **Major trading partners:** India, China, Singapore, Thailand, Japan, Malaysia.

Geography Slightly smaller than Texas, Myanmar occupies the northwest portion of the Indochinese peninsula. India lies to the northwest and China to the northeast. Bangladesh, Laos, and Thailand are also neighbors. The Bay of Bengal touches the southwest coast. The fertile delta of the Irrawaddy River in the south contains a network of intercommunicating canals and nine principal river mouths.

Government Military regime. In 1989, the military government changed the name of Burma to Myanmar. The U.S. State Department does not recognize the name Myanmar or the military regime that represents it.

History The ethnic origins of modern Myanmar (known historically as Burma) are a mixture of Indo-Aryans, who began pushing into the area around 700 B.C., and the Mongolian invaders under Kublai Khan who penetrated the region in the 13th century. Anawrahta (1044–77) was the first great unifier of Myanmar.

In 1612 the British East India Company sent agents to Burma, but the Burmese doggedly resisted efforts of British, Dutch, and Portuguese traders to establish posts on the Bay of Bengal. Through the Anglo-Burmese War in 1824–26 and two subsequent wars, the British East India Company expanded to the whole of Burma by 1886. Myanmar was annexed to India, then became a separate colony in 1937.

During World War II, Burma was a key battleground; the 800-mile Burma Road was the Allies' vital supply line to China. The Japanese invaded the country in Dec. 1941, and by May 1942 had occupied most of it, cutting off the Burma Road. After one of the most difficult campaigns of the war, Allied forces liberated most of Burma prior to the Japanese surrender in Aug. 1945.

Burma became independent on Jan. 4, 1948. In 1951 and 1952, the socialists achieved power. In 1968, after the government had made headway against communist and separatist rebels, the military regime adopted a "policy of strict nonalignment and set out to follow "the Burmese Way" to socialism. But the insurgents continued to be active.

The civilian government was overthrown in Sept. 1988 by a military junta led by Gen. Saw Maung, an associate of U Ne Win. Virtually the entire country protested the takeover, but demonstrations were brutally quashed. The military government officially changed the name of the country to Myanmar in 1989. When the new government held elections in May 1990, the opposition National League for Democracy (NLD) won in a landslide. But the military, or SLORC (State Law and Order Restoration Council), refused to recognize the election results. The leader of the opposition, Aung San Suu Kyi, was awarded the Nobel Peace Prize in 1991, which focused world attention on SLORC's repressive policies. Daughter of the assassinated general Aung San, who was revered as the father of Burmese independence, Suu Kyi remained under house arrest from 1989 until July 10, 1995. A new constitution was drafted in 1994 that called for an elected executive branch but appeared designed specifically to forbid Suu Kyi from becoming president. Suu Kyi continued to protest against the government, but almost every move she made was answered with a counterblow from SLORC.

Although the ruling junta has maintained a tight grip on Myanmar since 1988, it has not been able to subdue an insurgency in the country's south that has gone on for decades. The ethnic Karen movement has sought an independent homeland along Myanmar's southern border with Thailand. The economy has been in a state of collapse except for the junta-controlled heroin trade, the universities have remained closed, and the AIDS epidemic, unrecognized by the junta, has gripped the country.

In April 1997 the U.S. government imposed sanctions intended to prevent U.S. private investment in Myanmar. In 1998, Suu Kyi's party set a deadline of Aug. 21 for the convening of the 1990 Parliament, which was never allowed to meet after its election. Suu Kyi also challenged the unofficial ban on her leaving the capital, a move that brought retaliation against many of her supporters. Opposition politicians, headed by Suu Kyi, boldly declared in Sept. 1998 that they would act as the country's Parliament and announced that the ruling junta was illegitimate. Thereafter, the government detained hundreds of opposition members and staged several huge artificial demonstrations in which participants called for the deportation of Suu Kyi.

In Sept. 2000 Suu Kyi was placed under house arrest again and thus was prevented from leaving Rangoon to investigate reports that the government was cracking down on her supporters. The ruling military regime and Suu Kyi began landmark talks in Oct. 2000, though signs of democratic reforms remain elusive. The government has, however, extended an olive branch to Suu Kyi, releasing from prison more than 150 members of the National League for Democracy and allowing the NLD to reopen branch offices around Rangoon, the first time since the 1998 government crackdown.

Namibia

REPUBLIC OF NAMIBIA

President: Sam Nujoma (1990)
Prime Minister: Hage Geingob (1990)
Status: Independent Country
Area: 318,694 sq mi (825,418 sq km)
Population (2001 est.): 1,797,677 (average annual growth rate: 1.4%); birth rate: 34.7/1000; infant mortality rate: 71.7/1000; density per sq mi: 6
Capital and largest city (1992 est.): Windhoek, 161,000
Summer capital (est. 1980): Swakopmund, 17,500.
  Monetary unit: Namibian dollars. **Languages:** Afrikaans, German, English (official), several indigenous. **Ethnicity/race:** black 86%, white 6.6%, mixed 7.4%. Note: about 50% of the population belong to the Ovambo tribe and 9% to the Kavangos tribe; other ethnic groups are: Herero 7%, Damara 7%, Nama 5%, Caprivian 4%, Bushmen 3%, Baster 2%, Tswana 0.5%. **Religion:** Predominantly Christian.
  Literacy rate: 38% (1960)
Economic summary: GDP/PPP (1999 est.): $7.1 billion; per capita $4,300. **Real growth rate:** 3%. **Inflation:** 8.5% (1999). **Unemployment:** 30% to 40%, including underemployment (1997 est.). **Arable land:** 1%. **Agriculture:** millet, sorghum, peanuts; livestock; fish. **Labor force:** 500,000; agriculture, 47%; industry, 25%; services, 28% (1999 est.). **Industries:** meatpacking, fish processing, dairy products; mining (diamond, lead, zinc, tin, silver, tungsten, uranium, copper). **Natural resources:** diamonds, copper, uranium, gold, lead, tin, lithium, cadmium, zinc, salt, vanadium, natural gas, hydropower, fish; note: suspected deposits of oil, coal, and iron ore. **Exports:** $1.4 billion (f.o.b., 1999 est.): diamonds, copper, gold, zinc, lead, uranium; cattle, processed fish, karakul skins. **Imports:** $1.5 billion (f.o.b., 1999 est.): foodstuffs; petroleum products and fuel, machinery and equipment, chemicals. **Major trading partners:** UK, South Africa, Spain, France, Japan, Germany, U.S.

Geography Namibia, bounded on the north by Angola and Zambia and on the east by Botswana and South Africa in the south. It is for the most part a portion of the high plateau of southern Africa with a general elevation of from 3,000 to 4,000 ft.

Government Republic.

History The San peoples may have inhabited what is now Namibia more than 2000 years ago. The Bantu-speaking Herero migrated there in the 1600s. The Ovambo, the largest ethnic group today, migrated there in the 1800s.

In the late 15th century, the Portuguese explorer Bartolomeu Dias became the first European to visit Namibia. Formerly called South-West Africa, the territory became a German colony in 1884. In 1908 German troops massacred the majority of the Herero population. The land was taken by South African forces in 1915, becoming a South African mandate by the terms of the Treaty of Versailles in 1920.

South Africa's application for incorporation of the territory was rejected by the UN General Assembly in 1946, and South Africa was invited to prepare a trusteeship agreement instead. By a law passed in 1949, however, the territory was brought into much closer association with South Africa—including representation in its Parliament.

In 1968, the UN called for South Africa's withdrawal from the territory, which was given the name *Namibia*. When South Africa refused, the UN Security Council and the International Court of Justice condemned it. Under a 1974 Security Council resolution, South Africa was required to begin the transfer of power to the Namibians by May 30, 1975, or face UN action. Prime Minister Balthazar J. Vorster rejected UN supervision, claiming that his government was prepared to negotiate Namibian independence, but not with the South-West African People's Organization (SWAPO), the principal black separatist group. Meanwhile, the all-white legislature of South-West Africa eased several laws on apartheid in public places.

Despite international opposition, the Turnhalle Conference in Windhoek drafted a constitution to organize an interim government based on racial divisions, a proposal overwhelmingly endorsed by white voters in the territory in 1977. At the urging of ambassadors of the five Western members of the Security Council, South Africa on June 11 announced rejection of the Turnhalle constitution and acceptance of the Western proposal to include the South-West African People's Organization in negotiations.

As policemen wielding riot sticks charged demonstrators in a black South-West Africa township, South Africa handed over limited powers to a new, multiracial administration in the former German colony on June 17, 1985. Installation of the new government ended South Africa's direct rule, but South Africa retained an effective veto over the new government's decisions along with responsibility for the territory's defense and foreign policy.

An agreement between South Africa, Angola, and Cuba arranged for elections for a constituent assembly in Nov. 1989 to establish a new government. SWAPO won 57% of the vote, a majority but not enough to dictate a constitution unilaterally. In Feb. 1990, SWAPO leader Sam Nujoma was elected president and took office when Namibia became independent on March 21, 1990.

Nujoma was reelected in 1994, and again in 1999, after the constitution was amended to allow him to seek a third term. In Sept. 1999, fighting took place between Namibian troops and separatists from the Caprivi Strip, a narrow corridor jutting out of Namibia that provides the country with access to the Zambezi River.

Nauru
REPUBLIC OF NAURU
President: Rene Harris (2001)
Area: 8 sq mi (21 sq km)
Population (2001 est.): 12,088 (average annual growth rate: 2.0%); birth rate 27.2/1000; infant mortality rate 10.7/1000; density per sq mi: 1,491
Capital (1983): Yaren, 559. **Monetary unit:** Australian dollar. **Languages:** Nauruan (official) and English. **Ethnicity/race:** Nauruan 58%, other Pacific Islander 26%, Chinese 8%, European 8%. **Religions:** Protestant 58%, Roman Catholic 24%, Confucian and Taoist 8%. **Literacy rate:** 99%

Economic summary: GDP/PPP (1993 est.): $100 million; per capita $10,000. **Real growth rate:** n.a. **Inflation:** –3.6%. **Unemployment:** 0%. **Arable land:** 0%. **Agriculture:** coconuts. **Labor force:** employed in mining phosphates, public administration, education, and transportation. **Industries:** phosphate mining, financial services, coconut products. **Natural resources:** phosphates. **Exports:** $25.3 million (f.o.b., 1991): phosphates. **Imports:** $21.1 million (c.i.f., 1991): food, fuel, manufactures, building materials, machinery. **Major trading partners:** Australia, New Zealand, UK, Japan. **Special relationship within the Commonwealth of Nations**

Geography Nauru (pronounced NAH-oo-roo) is an island in the Pacific just south of the equator, about 2,500 mi (4,023 km) southwest of Honolulu.

Government Republic.

History In 1798, a British navigator became the first European to visit the island. Germany annexed it in 1888, and by the turn of the century, phosphate, a lucrative fertilizer, began to be mined. The island was placed under joint Australian, New Zealand, and British mandate after World War I. The Japanese occupied the island during World War II, and forced 1,200 Nauruans—roughly two-thirds of the population—to relocate. In 1947, it became a UN trusteeship administered by Australia. By 1967, the phosphate mining industry finally came under control of the islanders, and on Jan. 31, 1968, Nauru became one of the world's smallest independent republics.

Devastated by almost a century of phosphate stripmining by foreign companies, Nauru appealed to the International Court of Justice. In 1993, Australia offered Nauru an out-of-court settlement for damages, agreeing to pay $2.5 million Australian dollars for 20 years. New Zealand and the UK additionally agreed to pay a one-time settlement of $12 million each. Declining phosphate prices, the high cost of maintaining an international airline, and investments that did not perform well combined to make the economy flounder in the late 1990s. In 1999, Nauru gained membership in the United Nations. In 2000, the U.S. put pressure on the country to review its banking system, which is believed to be used by Russian criminals for money laundering. In 2001 President Bernard Dowiyogo was ousted by Parliament (this had been his fifth, nonconsecutive term), which then reelected former president Rene Harris.

Nepal
KINGDOM OF NEPAL
Ruler: King Gyanendra Bir Bikram Shah Deva (2001)
Prime Minister: Sher Bahadur Deuba (2001)
Area: 54,363 sq mi (140,800 sq km)
Population (2001 est.): 25,284,463 (average annual rate of natural growth: 2.3%); birth rate: 33.4/1000; infant mortality rate: 74.1/1000; density per sq mi: 465
Capital and largest city (1993): Kathmandu, 535,000. **Other large cities:** Lalitpur, 190,000; Biratnagar, 132,000. **Monetary unit:** Nepalese rupee. **Languages:** Nepali (official), Newari, Bhutia, Maithali. **Ethnicity/race:** Newars, Indians, Tibetans, Gurungs, Magars, Tamangs, Bhotias, Rais, Limbus, Sherpas. **Religions:** Hindu 90%, Buddhist 5%, Islam 3%. **Literacy rate:** 38% (1993)
Economic summary: GDP/PPP (1999 est.): $27.4 billion; per capita $1,100. **Real growth rate:** 3.4%. **Inflation:** 11.8% (FY98/99 est.). **Unemployment:** n.a.; substantial underemployment (1999). **Arable land:** 17%. **Agriculture:** rice, corn, wheat, sugarcane, root

crops; milk, water buffalo meat. **Labor force:** 10 million (1996 est.); note: severe lack of skilled labor; agriculture, 81%; services, 16%; industry, 3%. **Industries:** tourism, carpet, textile; small rice, jute, sugar, and oilseed mills; cigarette; cement and brick production. **Natural resources:** quartz, water, timber, hydropower, scenic beauty, small deposits of lignite, copper, cobalt, iron ore. **Exports:** $485 million (f.o.b., 1998), but does not include unrecorded border trade with India: carpets, clothing, leather goods, jute goods, grain. **Imports:** $1.2 billion (f.o.b., 1998): gold, machinery and equipment, petroleum products, fertilizer. **Major trading partners:** India, U.S., Germany, China, Hong Kong, Singapore.

Geography A landlocked country the size of Arkansas, lying between India and the Tibetan Autonomous Region of China, Nepal contains Mount Everest (29,035 ft; 8,850 m), the tallest mountain in the world. Along its southern border, Nepal has a strip of level land that is partly forested, partly cultivated. North of that is the slope of the main section of the Himalayan range, including Everest and many other peaks higher than 8,000 m.

Government In Nov. 1990, King Birendra promulgated a new constitution and introduced a multiparty democracy in Nepal.

History The first civilizations in Nepal, which flourished around the 6th century B.C., were confined to the fertile Kathmandu Valley where the present-day capital of the same name is located. It was in this region that Prince Siddhartha Gautama was born circa 563 B.C. Gautama achieved enlightenment as Buddha, and spawned Buddhist belief.

Nepali rulers' early patronage of Buddhism largely gave way to Hinduism, reflecting the increased influence of India, around the 12th century A.D. Though the successive dynasties of the Gopalas, the Kiratis, and the Licchavis expanded their rule, it was not until the reign of the Malla kings from 1200–1769 that Nepal assumed the approximate dimensions of the modern state.

The kingdom of Nepal was unified in 1768 by King Prithvi Narayan Shah, who had fled India following the Moghul conquests of the subcontinent. Under Shah and his successors Nepal's borders expanded as far west as Kashmir and as far east as Sikkim (now part of India). A commercial treaty was signed with Britain in 1792, and again in 1816 after more than a year of hostilities with the British East India Company.

In 1923, Britain recognized the absolute independence of Nepal. Between 1846 and 1951, the country was ruled by the Rana family, which always held the office of prime minister. In 1951, however, the king took over all power and proclaimed a constitutional monarchy. Mahendra Bir Bikram Shah became king in 1955. After Mahendra died of a heart attack in 1972, Prince Birendra, at 26, succeeded to the throne.

In 1990, a pro-democracy movement forced King Birendra to lift the ban on political parties and appoint an opposition leader to head an interim government as prime minister. The first free election in three decades provided a victory for the liberal Nepali Congress Party in 1991, although the Communists made a strong showing. A small but growing Maoist guerrilla movement seeking to overthrow the constitutional monarchy and install a Communist government has been operating in the countryside since 1996.

In its ten years of democracy, Nepal has been led by seven different prime ministers, as one government after another failed. Parliament has been characterized by fragile alliances and mercurial coalitions. In addition, corruption among MPs has been legion. Because Parliament has been in constant flux, many MPs have lined their pockets as quickly as possible, knowing they may be out of a job at any moment. Voter accountability is nil.

In 1999, the political scene changed when Nepalis gave the majority of the seats in Parliament to the Nepali Congress Party, thereby giving one party enough security to attempt to effectively govern. Krishna Prasad Bhattarai, a famous Nepali freedom fighter who was imprisoned for 14 years by the king's government, became prime minister.

On June 1, 2001, King Birendra was shot and killed by his equally popular son, Dipendra. Crown Prince Dipendra, angered by his family's disapproval of his choice of a bride, also killed his mother and several other members of the royal family before shooting himself. Dipendra was crowned king while in a coma; upon his death on June 4, Prince Gyanendra, the younger brother of Birendra, succeeded him.

The Netherlands

KINGDOM OF THE NETHERLANDS

National name: Koninkrijk der Nederlanden
Sovereign: Queen Beatrix (1980)
Premier: Wim Kok (1994)
Area: 16,036 sq mi (41,532 sq km)
Population (2001 est.): 15,981,472 (average annual rate of natural increase: 0.3%); birth rate: 11.9/1000; infant mortality rate: 4.4/1000; density per sq mi: 997
Capital and largest city (1994 est.): Amsterdam (official), 724,096; The Hague (administrative capital), 445,279. **Other large cities (1994 est.):** Rotterdam, 598,521; Utrecht, 234,106; Eindhoven, 196,130.
Monetary units: Guilder and euro. **Language:** Dutch, Frisian. **Ethnicity/race:** Dutch 96%, Moroccans, Turks, and other 4% (1988). **Religions:** Roman Catholic 34%, Protestant 25%, Muslim 3%, other 2%, unaffiliated 36%. **Literacy rate:** 99% (1979)
Economic summary: GDP/PPP (1999 est.): $365.1 billion; per capita $23,100. **Real growth rate:** 3.4%. **Inflation:** 2.2%. **Unemployment:** 3.5% but generous welfare benefits have prompted large numbers to drop out of the labor market. **Arable land:** 25%. **Agriculture:** grains, potatoes, sugar beets, fruits, vegetables; livestock. **Labor force:** 7 million (1998 est.); services, 73%; industry, 23%; agriculture, 4% (1998 est.). **Industries:** agroindustries, metal and engineering products, electrical machinery and equipment, chemicals, petroleum, construction, microelectronics, fishing. **Natural resources:** natural gas, petroleum, arable land. **Exports:** $169 billion (f.o.b., 1998): machinery and equipment, chemicals, fuels; foodstuffs. **Imports:** $152 billion (f.o.b., 1998): machinery and transport equipment, chemicals, fuels; foodstuffs, clothing. **Major trading partners:** EU, Central and Eastern Europe, U.S.

Geography The Netherlands, on the coast of the North Sea, is twice the size of New Jersey. Part of the great plain of north and west Europe, the Netherlands has maximum dimensions of 190 by 160 mi (360 by 257 km) and is low and flat except in Limburg in the southeast, where some hills rise to 300 ft (92 m). About half the country's area is below sea level, making the famous Dutch dikes a requisite to the use of much land. Reclamation of land from the sea through dikes has continued through recent times. All drainage reaches the North Sea, and the principal rivers—

Rhine, Maas (Meuse), and Schelde—have their sources outside the country.

Government Constitutional monarchy.

History Julius Caesar found the low-lying Netherlands inhabited by Germanic tribes—the Nervii, Frisii, and Batavi. The Batavi on the Roman frontier did not submit to Rome's rule until 13 B.C., and then only as allies.

The Franks controlled the region from the 4th to the 8th century, and it became part of Charlemagne's empire in the 8th and 9th centuries. The area later passed into the hands of Burgundy and the Austrian Hapsburgs, and finally in the 16th century came under Spanish rule.

When Philip II of Spain suppressed political liberties and the growing Protestant movement in the Netherlands, a revolt led by William of Orange broke out in 1568. Under the Union of Utrecht (1579), the seven northern provinces became the United Provinces of the Netherlands. War between the United Provinces and Spain continued into the 17th century, but in 1648 Spain finally recognized Dutch independence.

The Dutch East India Company was established in 1602, and by the end of the 17th century Holland was one of the great sea and colonial powers of Europe.

The nation's independence was not completely established until after the Thirty Years' War (1618–48), when the country's rise as a commercial and maritime power began. In 1688, the English Parliament invited William of Orange, stadtholder, and his wife, Mary Stuart, to rule England as William III and Mary II. William then used the combined resources of England and the Netherlands to wage war on Louis XIV's France. In 1814, all the provinces of Holland and Belgium were merged into one kingdom, but in 1830 the southern provinces broke away to form the kingdom of Belgium. A liberal constitution was adopted by the Netherlands in 1848. The country remained neutral during World War I.

In spite of its neutrality in World War II, the Netherlands was invaded by the Nazis in May 1940, and the Dutch East Indies were later taken by the Japanese. The nation was liberated in May 1945. In 1948, after a reign of 50 years, Queen Wilhelmina abdicated and was succeeded by her daughter Juliana.

In 1949, after a four-year war, the Netherlands granted independence to the Dutch East Indies, which became the Republic of Indonesia. The Netherlands also joined NATO that year. The Netherlands joined the European Economic Community (later, the EU) in 1958. In 1999, it adopted the single European currency, the euro.

In 1963, it turned over the western half of New Guinea to Indonesia, ending 300 years of Dutch presence in Asia. Attainment of independence by Suriname on Nov. 25, 1975, left the Netherlands Antilles and Aruba as the country's only overseas territories.

Although prostitution is legal, the government moved in July 1997 to permit the operation of brothels as a means of regulating the former. Only those with a valid resident's permit would be permitted to be employed in the brothels. In 1999, the Netherlands again defied convention by preparing to legalize euthanasia. In Sept. 2000, the Netherlands became the first nation in the world to legalize same-sex marriages.

Two Libyan intelligence agents accused of the 1988 bombing of Pan Am flight 103 over Lockerbie, Scotland, were tried in the Netherlands in 2000–2001, and the Hague is currently host to the U.N. War Crimes Tribunal for Yugoslavia, which in 2001 began prosecuting former Yugoslavian dictator Slobodan Milosevic, among others.

Netherlands Autonomous Countries

Netherlands Antilles
Status: Part of the Kingdom of the Netherlands
Governor: J. M. Saleh (1990)
Prime Minister: Miguel A. Pourier (2000)
Area: 371 sq mi (960 sq km)
Population (2001 est.): 212,226 (average annual growth rate: 1.0%); birth rate: 16.6/1000; infant mortality rate: 11.4/1000; density per sq mi: 573. **Ethnicity/race:** mixed African 85%, Carib Indian, European, Latin, Asian
Capital and largest city (1993 est.): Willemstad, 197,019. **Literacy rate:** 94% (1981)
Economic summary: GDP/PPP (1998 est.): $2.4 billion; per capita $11,800. **Real growth rate:** –0.3%. **Inflation:** 1.1%. **Unemployment:** 14.9%. **Arable land:** 10%. **Agriculture:** aloes, sorghum, peanuts, vegetables, tropical fruit. **Labor force:** 89,000; agriculture, 1%; industry, 13%; services, 86% (1994 est.). **Industries:** tourism (Curaçao, Sint Maarten, and Bonaire), petroleum refining (Curaçao), petroleum transshipment facilities (Curaçao and Bonaire), light manufacturing (Curaçao). **Natural resources:** phosphates (Curaçao only), salt (Bonaire only). **Exports:** $303 million (f.o.b., 1998): petroleum products. **Imports:** $1.3 billion (c.i.f., 1998): crude petroleum 64%, food, manufactures. **Major trading partners:** U.S., Guatemala, Costa Rica, the Bahamas, Jamaica, Chile, Venezuela, Mexico, Italy, Netherlands, Brazil.

The Netherlands Antilles are composed of two groups of Caribbean islands 500 mi (805 km) apart: Curaçao (173 sq mi; 448 sq km) and Bonaire (95 sq mi; 246 sq km) are located about 40 mi (64 km) off the Venezuelan coast.

Originally inhabited by Arawak Indians, these two islands as well as Aruba were claimed by Spain in 1527, and then by the Dutch in 1643. The Dutch Lesser Antilles to the north—Sint Eustatius, the southern part of Saint Martin (Dutch: Sint Maarten), and Saba—make up the remainder of the island federation. First inhabited by the Carib Indians, Saint Martin was explored by Columbus in 1493. In 1845 the six islands (then including Aruba) officially formed the Netherlands Antilles. In 1994 the islands voted to preserve their federation with the Netherlands.

Aruba
Status: Part of the Kingdom of the Netherlands
Governor: Olindo Koolman (1992)
Prime Minister: Henny Eman (1994)
Area: 75 sq mi (193 sq km)
Population (2001 est.): 70,007; growth rate 0.6%; birth rate: 12.6/1000; infant mortality rate: 6.4/1000; density per sq mi: 939
Capital and largest city (1991 est.): Oranjestad, 20,050. **Ethnicity/race:** mixed European/Caribbean Indian 80%. **Literacy rate:** 95%
Economic summary: GDP/PPP (1998 est.): $1.6 billion; per capita $22,800. **Real growth rate:** 3%. **Inflation:** 2% (1999 est.). **Unemployment:** 0.6% (1996 est.). **Arable land:** 7% aloe plantations included (0.01%). **Agriculture:** aloes; livestock; fish. **Labor force:** 41,501 (1997 est.); most employment is in wholesale and retail trade and repair, followed by hotels and restaurants (1997 est.). **Industries:** tourism, transshipment facilities, oil refining. **Natural**

resources: negl.; white sandy beaches. **Exports:** $1.17 billion (including oil reexports) (1998): transport equipment, live animals and animal products, art and collectibles, machinery and electrical equipment. **Imports:** $1.52 billion (1998): machinery and transport equipment, crude oil for refining and reexport; foodstuffs. **Major trading partners:** U.S., Colombia, Netherlands, Japan.

Aruba, an island slightly larger than Washington, D.C., lies 18 mi (28.9 km) off the coast of Venezuela in the southern Caribbean.

The Arawak Indians were the first inhabitants of Aruba. Spain explored the island in 1499, and more than a century later the Netherlands (1636) claimed the island. After a brief rule by the British, the Dutch again took control of the island in 1816, and it officially became part of the Netherlands Antilles in 1846.

On Jan. 1, 1986, Aruba seceded from the federation, but decided in 1994 to indefinitely postpone the transition to full independence. The Netherlands controls Aruba's defense and foreign affairs, but all internal affairs are handled by an island government directing its own civil service, judiciary, revenue, and currency.

New Zealand

Sovereign: Queen Elizabeth II (1952)
Governor-General: Dame Silvia Cartwright (2001)
Prime Minister: Helen Clark (1999)
Area: 103,737 sq mi (268,680 sq km) (excluding dependencies)
Population (2001 est.): 3,864,129 (average annual growth rate: 0.7%); birth rate: 14.3/1000; infant mortality rate: 6.3/1000; density per sq mi: 37
Capital: Wellington. **Largest cities (est. 1995):** Auckland, 952,600; Wellington, 331,100; Christchurch, 324,400. **Monetary unit:** New Zealand dollar. **Languages:** English (official), Maori. **Ethnicity/race:** European 88%, Maori 8.9%, Pacific Islander 2.9%, other 0.2%. **Religions:** Christian 81%, none or unspecified 18%, Hindu, Confucian, and other 1%. **Literacy rate:** 99% (1980)
Economic summary: GDP/PPP (1999 est.): $63.8 billion; per capita $17,400. **Real growth rate:** 3.1%. **Inflation:** 1.3%. **Unemployment:** 7%. **Arable land:** 9%. **Agriculture:** wheat, barley, potatoes, pulses, fruits, vegetables; wool, beef, dairy products; fish. **Labor force:** 1.86 million (1998): services, 65%; industry, 25%; agriculture, 10% (1995). **Industries:** food processing, wood and paper products, textiles, machinery, transportation equipment, banking and insurance, tourism, mining. **Natural resources:** natural gas, iron ore, sand, coal, timber, hydropower, gold, limestone. **Exports:** $12.2 billion (f.o.b., 1998 est.): dairy products, meat, fish, wool, forestry products, manufactures. **Imports:** $11.2 billion (f.o.b., 1998 est.): machinery and equipment, vehicles and aircraft, petroleum, consumer goods, plastics. **Major trading partners:** Australia, Japan, U.S., UK. **Member of Commonwealth of Nations**

Geography New Zealand, about 1,250 mi (2,012 km) southeast of Australia, consists of two main islands and a number of smaller, outlying islands so scattered that they range from the tropical to the antarctic. The country is the size of Colorado. New Zealand's two main components are the North Island and the South Island, separated by Cook Strait, which varies from 16 to 190 mi (26 to 396 km) in width. The North Island (44,281 sq mi; 115,777 sq km) is 515 mi (829 km) long and volcanic in its south-central part. This area contains many hot springs and beautiful geysers. South Island (58,093 sq mi;

151,215 sq km) has the Southern Alps along its west coast, with Mount Cook (12,283.3 ft; 3,754 m) the highest point. Other inhabited islands include Stewart Island, the Chatham Islands, and Great Barrier Island. The largest of the uninhabited outlying islands are the Auckland Islands (234 sq mi; 606 sq km), Campbell Island (44 sq mi; 114 sq km), the Antipodes Islands (24 sq mi; 62 sq km), and the Kermadec Islands (13 sq mi; 34 sq km).

Government Parliamentary democracy.

History Maoris were the first inhabitants of New Zealand, arriving on the islands in about 1000. Maori oral history maintains the Maoris came to the island in seven canoes from other parts of Polynesia. In 1642 New Zealand was explored by Abel Tasman, a Dutch navigator. British captain James Cook made three voyages to the islands, beginning in 1769. Britain formally annexed the islands in 1840.

The Treaty of Waitangi (Feb. 6, 1840) between the British and several Maori tribes promised to protect Maori land if the Maoris recognized British rule. Encroachment upon the land by European settlers was relentless, however, and skirmishes between the two groups intensified.

From the outset, the country has been in the forefront in instituting social welfare legislation. New Zealand was the world's first country to give women the right to vote (1893). It adopted old age pensions (1898); a national child welfare program (1907); social security for the aged, widows, and orphans, along with family benefit payments; minimum wages; a 40-hour workweek and unemployment and health insurance (1938); and socialized medicine (1941).

New Zealand fought with the Allies in both world wars as well as in Korea. In 1999, it became part of the UN peacekeeping force sent to East Timor.

Cook Islands and Overseas Territories

The Cook Islands (93 sq mi; 241 sq km) were placed under New Zealand administration in 1901. They achieved self-governing status in association with New Zealand in 1965. **Population (2000 est.):** 20,611; growth rate 1.7%; birth rate: 22.2/1000; infant mortality rate: 24.7/1000; density per square mile: 222. The seat of government is on Rarotonga Island. **Languages:** English (official), Maori. **Ethnicity/race:** Polynesian (full blood) 81.3%, Polynesian and European 7.7%, Polynesian and non-European 7.7%, European 2.4%, other 0.9%. **Religions:** Christian (majority belong to the Cook Islands Christian Church). **Economic summary: GDP/PPP** (1998 est.): $112 million; $5,600 per capita. **Exports:** $4.2 million (f.o.b., 1994 est.): copra, fresh and canned citrus fruit, coffee, fish, pearls and pearl shells, clothing. **Imports:** $85 million (c.i.f., 1994): foodstuffs, textiles, fuel, timber, capital goods. **Major trading partners:** New Zealand, Japan, Hong Kong, Italy, Australia.

Niue (100 sq mi; 259 sq km) was formerly administered as part of the Cook Islands. It was placed under separate New Zealand administration in 1901 and achieved self-governing status in association with New Zealand in 1974. The capital is Alofi. **Population (2000 est.):** 2,113 **Languages:** Polynesian, English. **Ethnicity/race:** Polynesian. **Religions:** Ekalesia Niue (Niuean Church—Protestant church closely related to the London Missionary Society) 75%, Latter-Day Saints 10%, other 15% (Roman Catholic, Jehovah's Witnesses, Seventh-Day Adventist). **Economic summary: GDP/PPP** (1994 est.):

$4.5 million; per capita, $2,250. **Exports:** $117,500 (f.o.b., 1989): canned coconut cream, copra, honey, passion fruit products, pawpaw, root crops, limes, footballs, stamps, handicrafts. **Imports:** $4.1 million (c.i.f., 1989): food, live animals, manufactured goods, machinery, fuel, chemicals, lubricants, drugs. **Major trading partners:** New Zealand, Fiji, Cook Islands, Australia, Japan, Samoa, U.S.

The **Ross Dependency** (160,000 sq mi; 414,400 sq km), an Antarctic region, was placed under New Zealand administration in 1923.

Tokelau (3.86 sq mi; 10 sq km) was formerly administered as part of the Gilbert and Ellice Islands colony. It was placed under New Zealand administration in 1925. Its population is 1,458 (2000 est.).

Nicaragua

REPUBLIC OF NICARAGUA

National name: República de Nicaragua
President: Arnoldo Alemán (1997)
Area: 49,998 sq mi (129,494 sq km)
Population (2001 est.): 4,918,393 (average annual rate of natural increase: 2.3%); birth rate: 27.6/1000; infant mortality rate: 33.7/1000; density per sq mi: 98
Capital and largest city (1992 est.): Managua, 974,000. **Monetary unit:** Cordoba. **Language:** Spanish. **Ethnicity/race:** mestizo (mixed Amerindian and white) 69%, white 17%, black 9%, Indian 5%. **Religions:** Roman Catholic 95%, Protestant 5%. **Literacy rate:** 57% (1971)
Economic summary: GDP/PPP (1999 est.): $12.5 billion; per capita $2,650. **Real growth rate:** 6.3%. **Inflation:** 12%. **Unemployment:** 10.5%; considerable underemployment. **Arable land:** 9%. **Agriculture:** coffee, bananas, sugarcane, cotton, rice, corn, tobacco, sesame, soya, beans; beef, veal, pork, poultry, dairy products. **Labor force:** 1.7 million (1999); services, 43%; agriculture, 42%; industry, 15% (1999 est.). **Industries:** food processing, chemicals, machinery and metal products, textiles, clothing, petroleum refining and distribution, beverages, footwear, wood. **Natural resources:** gold, silver, copper, tungsten, lead, zinc, timber, fish. **Exports:** $573 million (f.o.b., 1998 est.): coffee, shrimp and lobster, cotton, tobacco, beef, sugar, bananas; gold. **Imports:** $1.5 billion (c.i.f., 1999 est.): machinery and equipment, raw materials, petroleum products, consumer goods. **Major trading partners:** U.S., Germany, El Salvador, Spain, Costa Rica, France, Venezuela, Mexico.

Geography Largest but most sparsely populated of the Central American nations, Nicaragua borders on Honduras to the north and Costa Rica to the south. It is slightly larger than New York State. Nicaragua is mountainous in the west, with fertile valleys. A plateau slopes eastward toward the Caribbean. Two big lakes—Nicaragua, about 100 mi long (161 km), and Managua, about 38 mi long (61 km)—are connected by the Tipitapa River. The Pacific coast is volcanic and very fertile. The Caribbean coast, swampy and indented, is aptly called the "Mosquito Coast."

Government Republic.

History Nicaragua, which derives its name from the chief of the area's leading Indian tribe at the time of the Spanish Conquest, was first settled by the Spanish in 1522. The country won independence in 1838. For the next century, Nicaragua's politics were dominated by the competition for power between the Liberals, who were centered in the city of León, and the Conservatives, centered in Granada.

To back up its support of the new Conservative government in 1909, the U.S. sent a small detachment of Marines to Nicaragua from 1912 to 1925. The Bryan-Chamorro Treaty of 1916 (terminated in 1970) gave the U.S. an option on a canal route through Nicaragua and naval bases. U.S. Marines were sent again to quell disorder after the 1924 elections. A guerrilla leader, Gen. César Augusto Sandino, fought the U.S. troops from 1927 until their withdrawal in 1933.

After ordering Sandino's assassination, Gen. Anastasio Somoza García was dictator from 1936 until his own assassination in 1956. He was succeeded by his son Luis, who alternated with trusted family friends in the presidency until his death in 1967. He was succeeded by his brother, Maj. Gen. Anastasio Somoza Debayle. The Somozas ruled Nicaragua with an iron fist, reducing its dependence on banana exports, exiling political foes, and amassing a family fortune.

Sandinista guerrillas, leftists who took their name from Sandino, launched an offensive in 1979. After seven weeks of fighting, Somoza fled the country on July 17, 1979. The Sandinistas assumed power two days later. On Jan. 23, 1981, the Reagan administration suspended U.S. aid, charging that Nicaragua, with the aid of Cuba and the Soviet Union, was supplying arms to rebels in El Salvador. The Sandinistas denied the charges. Later that year, Nicaraguan guerrillas known as "Contras," began a war to overthrow the Sandinistas. Elections were finally held on Nov. 4, 1984, with Daniel Ortega, the Sandinista junta coordinator, winning the presidency. The war intensified in 1986–87. Negotiations sponsored by the Contadora (neutral Latin American) nations foundered, but Costa Rican president Oscar Arias promoted a treaty signed by Central American leaders in Aug. 1987.

Violetta Barrios de Chamorro, owner of the opposition paper *La Prensa*, led a broad anti-Sandinista coalition to victory in the 1990 elections, ending 11 years of Sandinista rule. Enthusiasm for Chamorro gradually faded. Business groups were dissatisfied with the pace of reforms; Sandinistas, upset with what they regarded as the dismantling of their earlier achievements, threatened to take up arms again; and many people were disillusioned over governmental corruption and the continuing influence of the Sandinistas on the government and the army. Former Managua mayor and Conservative candidate Arnoldo Alemán won the 1996 election. Ortega was his closest rival.

In 1998, Hurricane Mitch killed more than 9,000 people, left 2 million people homeless, and caused $10 billion in damages. Many people fled to the U.S., which offered Nicaraguans an immigration amnesty program until July 1999.

Nicaragua remains one of the poorest countries in the Western Hemisphere. Property is often caught in a three-way battle between those who owned it before the Sandinistas came to power; cooperatives set up by the Sandinistas; and former Contras who claim they were promised land for joining the anti-Sandinista forces.

In June 2000 Nicaragua did resolve its border dispute with Costa Rica. On Nov. 6, 2000, the Sandinista Party candidate was elected mayor of Managua, defeating the Liberal Party incumbent. Observers said the election indicated disillusionment with the scandal-ridden national government.

Niger

REPUBLIC OF NIGER

National name: République du Niger
President: Tandja Mamadou (1999)
Prime Minister: Hama Amadou (1999)
Area: 489,189 sq mi (1,267,000 sq km)
Population (2001 est.): 10,355,156 (average annual rate of natural increase: 2.8%); birth rate: 50.7/1000; infant mortality rate: 123.6/1000; density per sq mi: 21
Capital and largest city (1988): Niamey, 398,265.
Other large cities: Zinder, 120,900; Maradi, 112,970.
Monetary unit: Franc CFA. **Languages:** French (official); Hausa; Songhai; Arabic. **Ethnicity/race:** Hausa 56%, Djerma 22%, Fula 8.5%, Tuareg 8%, Beri Beri (Kanouri) 4.3%, Arab, Toubou, and Gourmantche 1.2%, about 4,000 French expatriates. **Religions:** Islam 80%, Animist and Christian 20%. **Literacy rate:** 28% (1990)
Economic summary: GDP/PPP (1999 est.): $9.6 billion; per capita $1,000. **Real growth rate:** 2%. **Inflation:** 4.8%. **Unemployment:** n.a. **Arable land:** 3%. **Agriculture:** cowpeas, cotton, peanuts, millet, sorghum, cassava (tapioca), rice; cattle, sheep, goats, camels, donkeys, horses, poultry. **Labor force:** 70,000 receive regular wages or salaries; agriculture, 90%; industry and commerce, 6%; government, 4%. **Industries:** uranium mining, cement, brick, textiles, food processing, chemicals, slaughterhouses. **Natural resources:** uranium, coal, iron ore, tin, phosphates, gold, petroleum. **Exports:** $269 million (f.o.b., 1997): uranium ore 65%, livestock products, cowpeas, onions (1998 est.). **Imports:** $295 million (c.i.f., 1997): consumer goods, primary materials, machinery, vehicles and parts, petroleum, cereals. **Major trading partners:** U.S., Greece, Japan, France, Nigeria, Benin, Côte d'Ivoire, Benelux.

Geography Niger, in West Africa's Sahara region, is four-fifths the size of Alaska. It is surrounded by Mali, Algeria, Libya, Chad, Nigeria, Benin, and Burkina Faso. The Niger River in the southwest flows through the country's only fertile area. Elsewhere the land is semiarid.

Government Republic, emerging from military rule.

History The nomadic Tuaregs were the first inhabitants in the Sahara region. The Hausa (14th century), the Zerma (17th century), the Gobir (18th century), and Fulani also established themselves in the region now called Niger.

Niger was incorporated into French West Africa in 1896. There were frequent rebellions, but when order was restored in 1922, the French made the area a colony. In 1958, the voters approved the French constitution and voted to make the territory an autonomous republic within the French community. The republic adopted a constitution in 1959 but the next year withdrew from the community, proclaiming its independence.

During the 1970s the country's economy flourished from uranium production, but when uranium prices fell in the 1980s, its brief period of prosperity ended. The 1974 army coup ousted President Hamani Diori, who had held office since 1960. An estimated 2 million people were starving in Niger, but 200,000 tons of imported food, half U.S.-supplied, substantially ended famine conditions by the year's end. The new president, Lt. Col. Seyni Kountché, chief of staff of the army, installed a 12-man military government. A predominantly civilian government was formed by Kountché in 1976.

In 1993 the country's first multiparty election resulted in the presidency of Ousmane Mahamane, who was then deposed in a Jan. 1996 coup. In July the military leader of the coup, Ibrahim Baré Maïnassara, was declared president in a rigged election. Considered a corrupt and ineffectual president, Maïnassara was assassinated in April 1999 by his own guards. The National Reconciliation Council, responsible for the coup, kept its promise and held democratic elections; in Nov. 1999, Tandja Mamadou was elected president. As a result, foreign aid, primarily from France, was restored.

The nomadic Tuaregs of the north, of Berber and Arab descent, have a fiercely insular culture and share little affinity with the black African majority of Niger. Conflict between the Tuaregs and the other tribes of Niger first surfaced in the early 20th century. A ceasefire between the government and Tuareg rebels (Revolutionary Armed Forces of the Sahara) went into effect in 1995, and in June 1997, the Democratic Renewal Front, a holdout Tuareg rebel group, also agreed to sign a peace accord. The impoverished Tuaregs have received little of the economic aid they were promised, which is not surprising given Niger's political instability and desperate poverty.

Nigeria

FEDERAL REPUBLIC OF NIGERIA

President: Olusegun Obasanjo (1999)
Area: 356,667 sq mi (923,768 sq km)
Population (2001 est.): 126,635,626 (average annual rate of natural increase: 2.6%); birth rate: 39.7/1000; infant mortality rate: 73.3/1000; density per sq mi: 355
Capital (1995 est.): Abuja, 339,000. **Largest cities:** Lagos (2000 est.), 13,050,000 (metro. area); Ibadan, 1,365,000; Ogbomosho, 711,900; Kano, 657,300.
Monetary unit: Naira. **Languages:** English (official), Hausa, Yoruba, Ibo, and more than 200 others. **Ethnicity/race:** Hausa, Fulani, Yoruba, Ibo, Kanuri, Ibibio, Tiv, Ijaw. **Religions:** Islam 50%, Christian 40%, indigenous 10%. **Literacy rate:** 51% (1990)
Economic summary: GDP/PPP (1999 est.): $110.5 billion; per capita $970. **Real growth rate:** 2.7%. **Inflation:** 12.5%. **Unemployment:** 28% (1992 est.). **Arable land:** 33%. **Agriculture:** cocoa, peanuts, palm oil, corn, rice, sorghum, millet, cassava (tapioca), yams, rubber; cattle, sheep, goats, pigs; timber; fish. **Labor force:** 42.844 million; agriculture, 54%; industry, 6%; services, 40%. **Industries:** crude oil, coal, tin, columbite, palm oil, peanuts, cotton, rubber, wood, hides and skins, textiles, cement and other construction materials, food products, footwear, chemicals, fertilizer, printing, ceramics, steel. **Natural resources:** petroleum, tin, columbite, iron ore, coal, limestone, lead, zinc, natural gas, hydropower, arable land. **Exports:** $13.1 billion (f.o.b., 1999): petroleum and petroleum products 95%, cocoa, rubber. **Imports:** $10 billion (f.o.b., 1999): machinery, chemicals, transport equipment, manufactured goods, food and live animals. **Major trading partners:** U.S., Spain, India, France, Italy, UK, Germany, Netherlands.
Member of Commonwealth of Nations

Geography Nigeria, one-third larger than Texas and the most populous country in Africa, is situated on the Gulf of Guinea in West Africa. Its neighbors are Benin, Niger, Cameroon, and Chad. The lower course of the Niger River flows south through the western part of the country into the Gulf of Guinea. Swamps and mangrove forests border the southern coast; inland are hardwood forests.

Government Multiparty government.

History The first inhabitants of what is now Nigeria were thought to have been the Nok people (500 B.C.– circa A.D. 200). The Kanuri, Hausa, and Fulani peoples subsequently migrated there. Islam was introduced in the 13th century, and the empire of Kanem controlled the area from the end of the 11th century to the 14th.

The Fulani empire ruled the region from the beginning of the 19th century until the British annexed Lagos in 1851 and seized control of the rest of the region by 1886. It formally became the Colony and Protectorate of Nigeria in 1914. During World War I, native troops of the West African frontier force joined with French forces to defeat the German garrison in the Cameroons.

On Oct. 1, 1960, Nigeria gained independence, becoming a member of the Commonwealth of Nations and joining the United Nations. Organized as a loose federation of self-governing states, the independent nation faced an overwhelming task of unifying a country with 250 ethnic and linguistic groups.

Rioting broke out in 1966, and military leaders, primarily of Ibo ethnicity, seized control. In July, a second military coup put Col. Yakubu Gowon in power, a choice unacceptable to the Ibos. Also in that year, the Muslim Hausas in the north massacred the predominantly Christian Ibos in the east, many of whom had been driven from the north. Thousands of Ibos took refuge in the eastern region, which declared its independence as the Republic of Biafra on May 30, 1967. Civil war broke out. In Jan. 1970, after 31 months of civil war, Biafra surrendered to the federal government.

Gowon's nine-year rule was ended in 1975 by a bloodless coup that made Army Brigadier Muritala Rufai Mohammed the new chief of state. The return of civilian leadership was established with the election of Alhaji Shehu Shagari as president in 1979. An oil boom in the 1970s buoyed the economy and by the 1980s Nigeria was considered an exemplar of African democracy and economic well-being.

The military again seized power in 1984, only to be followed by another military coup the following year. Maj. Gen. Ibrahim Babangida announced that the country would be returned to civilian rule, but after the presidential election of June 12, 1993, he voided the results. Nevertheless, Babangida resigned as president in Aug. In Nov. the military, headed by defense minister Sani Abacha, seized power again.

Corruption and notorious governmental inefficiency as well as a harshly repressive military regime characterized Abacha's reign over this oil-rich country. A UN fact-finding mission in 1996 reported that Nigeria's "problems of human rights are terrible and the political problems are terrifying." During the 1970s Nigeria had the 33rd highest per-capita income in the world, but by 1997 it had dropped to the 13th poorest.

As leader of the multination peacekeeping force, ECOMOG, Nigeria has established itself as West Africa's superpower, intervening militarily in the civil wars of Liberia and Sierra Leone. But Nigeria's costly war efforts have been unpopular with its own people, who feel Nigeria's limited economic resources are being unnecessarily drained.

Under military rule for all but ten years since independence from Britain, the military has reneged on its promises to give up power eight times. Despite international pressure to institute democratic rule, the notoriously authoritarian Gen. Sani Abacha, whose formidable security forces kept a tight rein over the country, refused to loosen his absolute grip on political and military power. Abacha's repressive rule turned Nigeria into an international pariah. The hanging of writer Ken Saro-Wiwa in 1995 because he protested against the government was condemned around the world.

Abacha died of a heart attack on June 8, 1998, and was succeeded by another military ruler, Gen. Abdulsalam Abubakar, who pledged to step aside for an elected leader by May 1999. Abubakar's freeing of political prisoners and other gestures of easing the military's iron-clad rule showed signs of hope, but the suspicious death of opposition leader Mashood Abiola, who had been imprisoned by the military ever since he legally won the 1993 presidential election, was a crushing blow to democratic proponents. In Feb. 1999 free presidential elections led to an overwhelming victory for Gen. Olusegun Obasanjo, a former member of the military elite who was imprisoned for three years for criticizing the military rule, and released just eight months before his election. Obasanjo's commitment to democracy, his anti-corruption drives, and his desire to recover billions allegedly stolen by the family and cronies of Abacha initially gained him high praise from the populace as well as the international community. But within two years, the hope of reform seemed doomed as economic mismanagement and rampant corruption persisted. Obasanjo's priorities in 2001 were symbolized by his plans to build a $330 million national soccer stadium, an extravagance that exceeded the combined budget for both health and education.

Nigeria's stability has been repeatedly threatened by fighting between fundamentalist Muslims and Christians over the spread of Islamic law (sharia) across the heavily Muslim north.

Norway

KINGDOM OF NORWAY

National name: Kongeriket Norge
Sovereign: King Harald V (1991)
Prime Minister: Jens Stoltenberg (2000)
Area: 125,181 sq mi (324,220 sq km)
Population (2001 est.): 4,503,440 (average annual growth rate: 0.3%); birth rate: 12.6/1000; infant mortality rate: 3.9/1000; density per sq mi: 36
Capital and largest city (1995): Oslo, 483,401. **Other large cities:** Bergen, 221,717; Trondheim, 142,927; Stavanger, 103,496. **Monetary unit:** Krone.
Languages: Two official forms of Norwegian: Bokmål and Nynorsk. **Ethnicity/race:** Germanic (Nordic, Alpine, Baltic), Lapps (Sami). **Religions:** Evangelical Lutheran 87.8% (state church), other Protestant and Roman Catholic 3.8%, none 3.2%, unknown 5.2%.
Literacy rate: 99% (1976)
Economic summary: GDP/PPP (1999 est.): $111.3 billion; per capita $25,100. **Real growth rate:** 0.8%. **Inflation:** 2.8%. **Unemployment:** 2.9%. **Arable land:** 3%. **Agriculture:** barley, other grains, potatoes; beef, milk; fish. **Labor force:** 2.7 million (1999 est.); services, 74%; industry, 22%; agriculture, forestry, and fishing, 4% (1995). **Industries:** petroleum and gas, food processing, shipbuilding, pulp and paper products, metals, chemicals, timber, mining, textiles, fishing. **Natural resources:** petroleum, copper, natural gas, pyrites, nickel, iron ore, zinc, lead, fish, timber, hydropower. **Exports:** $47.3 billion (f.o.b., 1999 est.): petroleum and petroleum products, machinery and equipment, metals, chemicals, ships, fish. **Imports:** $38.6 billion (f.o.b., 1999 est.): machinery and equipment, chemicals, metals, foodstuffs. **Major trading partners:** EU, U.S., Japan.

Geography Norway is situated in the western part of the Scandinavian peninsula. It extends about 1,100 mi (1,770 km) from the North Sea along the Norwegian Sea to more than 300 mi (483 km) above the Arctic Circle, the farthest north of any European country. It is slightly larger than New Mexico. Nearly 70% of Norway is uninhabitable and covered by mountains, glaciers, moors, and rivers. The hundreds of deep fjords that cut into the coastline give Norway an overall oceanfront of more than 12,000 mi (19,312 km). Galdhø Peak, at 8,100 ft (2,469 m), is Norway's highest point and the Glåma (Glomma) is the principal river, at 372 mi (598 km) long.

Government Constitutional monarchy.

History Norwegians, like the Danes and Swedes, are of Teutonic origin. The Norsemen, also known as Vikings, ravaged the coasts of northwest Europe from the 8th to the 11th century and were ruled by local chieftains. Olaf II Haraldsson became the first effective king of all Norway in 1015 and began converting the Norwegians to Christianity. After 1442, Norway was ruled by Danish kings until 1814, when it was united with Sweden—although retaining a degree of independence and receiving a new constitution—in an uneasy partnership. In 1905, the Norwegian Parliament arranged a peaceful separation and invited a Danish prince to the Norwegian throne—King Haakon VII. A treaty with Sweden provided that all disputes be settled by arbitration and that no fortifications be erected on the common frontier.

When World War I broke out, Norway joined with Sweden and Denmark in a decision to remain neutral and to cooperate in the joint interest of the three countries. In World War II, Norway was invaded by the Germans on April 9, 1940. It resisted for two months before the Nazis took complete control. King Haakon and his government fled to London, where they established a government-in-exile. Maj. Vidkun Quisling, who served as Norway's premier during the war, was the most notorious of the Nazi collaborators. The word for traitor, *quisling,* bears his name. He was executed by the Norwegians on Oct. 24, 1945.

Despite severe losses in the war, Norway recovered quickly as its economy expanded. The country led the world in social experimentation. It entered the North Atlantic Treaty Organization in 1949. In the late 20th century, the Labor Party and the Conservative Party seesawed for control, each sometimes having to lead minority governments. An important debate has been over Norway's membership in the European Union. In an advisory referendum held in Nov. 1994, voters rejected seeking membership for their nation in the EU. The country became the second-largest net oil exporter after Saudi Arabia in 1995. Norway continued to experience rapid economic growth into the new millennium.

In Sept. 2000, Norwegian truckers held a blockade of oil terminals in protest of high gas prices. The blockade failed, however, to gain concessions from the government. Norwegians pay among the highest gas prices in Europe, 70% of which is tax.

Dependencies of Norway

Svalbard (23,957 sq mi; 62,049 sq km), in the Arctic Ocean about 360 mi north of Norway, consists of the Spitsbergen group and several smaller islands, including Bear Island, Hope Island, King Charles Land, and White Island (or Gillis Land). The capital is Longyearbyen. It came under Norwegian adminis-

tration in 1925. Population: 2,416 (2000 est.); growth rate: –3.55%. 62% of the population is Russian and Ukrainian; 38% are Norwegian. Coal mining is the major economic activity. There is also some trapping of seal, polar bear, fox, and walrus. **Bouvet Island** (23 sq mi; 59 sq km), an island nature reserve in the South Atlantic about 1,600 mi south-southwest of the Cape of Good Hope, came under Norwegian administration in 1928. It is uninhabited.

Jan Mayen Island (144 sq mi; 373 sq km), in the Arctic Ocean between Norway and Greenland, came under Norwegian administration in 1929. There are no permanent inhabitants, just workers at the navigation base and weather/radio station. **Peter I Island** (96 sq mi; 249 sq km), lying off Antarctica in the Bellinghausen Sea, came under Norwegian administration in 1931. **Queen Maud Land,** a section of Antarctica, came under Norwegian administration in 1939.

Oman

SULTANATE OF OMAN

National name: Saltonat Uman
Sultan: Qabus ibn Sa'id (1970)
Area: 82,031 sq mi (212,460 sq km)[1]
Population (2001 est.): 2,622,198 (average annual rate of natural increase: 3.4%); birth rate: 38.0/1000; infant mortality rate: 22.5/1000; density per sq mi: 32
Capital and largest city (1991 est.): Muscat, 350,000.
Monetary unit: Omani rial. **Languages:** Arabic (official); also English and Indian languages. **Ethnicity/race:** Arab, Baluchi, South Asian (Indian, Pakistani, Sri Lankan, Bangladeshi), African. **Religion:** Islam 95%.
Literacy rate: 80%
Economic summary: GDP/PPP (1999 est.): $19.6 billion; per capita $8,000. **Real growth rate:** 4%. **Inflation:** –0.07%. **Unemployment:** n.a. **Arable land:** 0%. **Agriculture:** dates, limes, bananas, alfalfa, vegetables; camels; cattle; fish. **Labor force:** 850,000 (1997 est.); agriculture, n.a.; industry, n.a.; services, n.a. **Industries:** crude oil production and refining, natural gas production, construction, cement, copper. **Natural resources:** petroleum, copper, asbestos, some marble, limestone, chromium, gypsum, natural gas. **Exports:** $7.2 billion (f.o.b., 1999 est.): petroleum, reexports, fish, metals, textiles. **Imports:** $5.4 billion (f.o.b., 1999 est.): machinery and transport equipment, manufactured goods, food, livestock, lubricants. **Major trading partners:** Japan, China, Thailand, South Korea, U.S., UAE, UK, Germany.
1. Excluding the Kuria Muria Islands.

Geography Oman is a 1,000-mile-long (1,700-km) coastal plain at the southeast tip of the Arabian peninsula lying on the Arabian Sea and the Gulf of Oman. The interior is a plateau. The country is the size of Kansas.

Government Absolute monarchy.

History Arabs migrated to Oman from the 9th century B.C. onward, and conversion to Islam occurred in the 7th century A.D. Muscat, the capital of the geographical area known as Oman, was occupied by the Portuguese from 1508 to 1648. Then it fell to Ottoman Turks, but in 1741 Ahmad ibn Sa'id forced them out. The descendants of Sultan Ahmad rule Oman today.

Ahmad expanded his empire to East Africa, and for a time the Omani capital was in Zanzibar. After 1861, however, Zanzibar fell from Omani control.

The sultans and imams of Oman clashed continuously throughout the 20th century until 1959, when the last Ibadi imam was evicted from the country. In a palace coup on July 23, 1970, the sultan, Sa'id bin Taimur, who had ruled since 1932, was overthrown by his son, who promised to establish a modern government and use newfound oil wealth to aid the people of this very isolated state. Oman joined the Arab League and the United Nations in 1971.

A long border dispute with Yemen ended in late Oct. 1992 when the sultan signed an agreement with the Yemeni president. In 1997, Oman and Yemen signed maps defining the border between the two countries.

In 1997, Sultan Qabus granted women the right to be elected to the country's consultative body, the Shura Council (Majlis al-Shura). The council has no formal powers, but it advises the sultan on economic matters and public policy. Two women were elected to the council in 1997 as well as in 2000.

Pakistan

ISLAMIC REPUBLIC OF PAKISTAN

President: Gen. Pervez Musharraf (2001)
Area: 310,401 sq mi (803,940 sq km)[1]
Population (2001 est.): 144,616,639 (average annual growth rate: 2.2%); birth rate: 31.2/1000; infant mortality rate: 80.5/1000; density per sq mi: 466
Capital (1981 census): Islamabad, 201,000. **Largest cities:** Karachi (2000 est.), 12,100,000 (metro. area); Lahore (2000 est.), 6,350,000 (metro. area); Faisalabad (Lyallpur), 1,920,000; Rawalpindi, 920,000; Hyderabad, 795,000. **Monetary unit:** Pakistan rupee. **Principal languages:** Punjabi 48%, Sindhi 12%, Siraiki (a Punjabi variant) 10%, Pashtu 8%, Urdu (official) 8%, Balochi 3%, Hindko 2%, Brahui 1%, English, Burushaski, and others. **Ethnicity/race:** Punjabi, Sindhi, Pashtun (Pathan), Baloch, Muhajir (immigrants from India and their descendants). **Religions:** Islam 97%, Hindu, Christian, Buddhist, Parsi. **Literacy rate:** 35% (1990)
Economic summary GDP/PPP (1999 est.): $282 billion; per capita $2,000. **Real growth rate:** 3.1%. **Inflation:** 6%. **Unemployment:** 7% (FY98/99 est.). **Arable land:** 27%. **Agriculture:** cotton, wheat, rice, sugarcane, fruits, vegetables; milk, beef, mutton, eggs. **Labor force:** 38.6 million (1999); note: extensive export of labor, mostly to the Middle East, and use of child labor; agriculture, 44%; industry, 17%; services, 39% (1999 est.). **Industries:** textiles, food processing, beverages, construction materials, clothing, paper products, shrimp. **Natural resources:** land, extensive natural gas reserves, limited petroleum, poor quality coal, iron ore, copper, salt, limestone. **Exports:** $8.4 billion (f.o.b., 1999): cotton, fabrics, and yarn, rice, other agricultural products. **Imports:** $9.8 billion (f.o.b., 1999): machinery, petroleum, petroleum products, chemicals, transportation equipment, edible oils, grains, pulses, flour. **Major trading partners:** U.S., Hong Kong, UK, Germany, UAE, Japan, Malaysia, Saudi Arabia.

1. Excluding Kashmir and Jammu.

Geography Pakistan is situated in the western part of the Indian subcontinent, with Afghanistan and Iran on the west, India on the east, and the Arabian Sea on the south. The name *Pakistan* is derived from the Urdu words *Pak* (meaning pure) and *stan* (meaning country). It is nearly twice the size of California.

The northern and western highlands of Pakistan contain the towering Karakoram and Pamir mountain ranges, which include some of the world's highest peaks: K2 (28,250 ft [8,611 m]) and Nanga Parbat (26,660 ft [8,126 m]). The Baluchistan Plateau lies to the west, and the Thar Desert and an expanse of alluvial plains, the Punjab and Sind, lie to the east. The 1,000-mile-long (1,609 km) Indus River and its tributaries flow through the country from the Kashmir region to the Arabian Sea.

Government Military rule was instituted Oct. 1999; a nominal democracy was declared in June 2001 by the ruling military leader, Pervez Musharraf.

History Pakistan was one of the two original successor states to British India, which was partitioned along religious lines in 1947. For almost 25 years following independence, it consisted of two separate regions, East and West Pakistan, but now is made up only of the western sector. Both India and Pakistan have laid claim to the Kashmir region, and this territorial dispute led to war in 1949, and again in 1965, 1971, and 1999, and remains unresolved today.

What is now Pakistan was in prehistoric times the Indus Valley civilization (c. 2500–1700 B.C.). A series of invaders—Aryans, Persians, Greeks, Arabs, Turks, and others—controlled the region for the next several thousand years. Islam, the dominant religion, was introduced in A.D. 711. In 1526, the land became part of the Mogul Empire, which ruled most of the Indian subcontinent from the 16th to the mid-18th century. By 1857 the British became the dominant power in the region. With Hindus holding most of the economic, social, and political advantages, the Muslim minority's dissatisfaction grew, leading to the formation of the nationalist Muslim League in 1906 by Mohammed Ali Jinnah (1876–1949). The league supported Britain in the Second World War while the Hindu nationalist leaders, Nehru and Gandhi, refused. In return for the league's support of Britain, Jinnah expected British backing for Muslim autonomy. Britain agreed to the formation of Pakistan as a separate dominion within the Commonwealth in Aug. 1947, a bitter disappointment to India's dream of a unified subcontinent. Jinnah became governor-general. The partition of Pakistan and India along religious lines resulted in the largest migration in human history, with 17 million people fleeing across the borders in both directions to escape the sectarian violence accompanying the partition.

Pakistan became a republic on March 23, 1956, with Maj. Gen. Iskander Mirza becoming the first president. Military rule prevailed for the next two decades. Tensions between East and West Pakistan existed from the outset. Separated by more than a thousand miles, the two regions shared few cultural and social traditions other than religion. To the growing resentment of East Pakistan, the West monopolized the country's political and economic power. In 1970, East Pakistan's Awami League, led by the Bengali leader Sheik Mujibur Rahman, secured a majority of the seats in the National Assembly. President Yahya Khan postponed the opening of the National Assembly to skirt East Pakistan's demand for greater autonomy, provoking civil war. The independent state of Bangladesh, or Bengali nation, was proclaimed on March 26, 1971. Indian troops entered the war in its last weeks fighting on the side of the new state. Pakistan was defeated on Dec. 16, 1971, and President Yahya Khan stepped down. Zulfikar Ali Bhutto took over Pakistan and accepted Bangladesh as an independent entity. In 1976 formal relations between India and Pakistan resumed.

Pakistan's first elections under civilian rule took place in March 1977, and the overwhelming victory of Bhutto's Pakistan People's Party (PPP) was denounced as fraudulent. A rising tide of violent protest and political deadlock led to a military takeover on July 5 by Gen. Mohammed Zia ul-Haq. Bhutto was tried and convicted for the 1974 murder of a political opponent, and despite worldwide protests was executed on April 4, 1979, touching off riots by his supporters. Zia declared himself president on Sept. 16, 1978, and ruled by martial law until Dec. 30, 1985, when a measure of representative government was restored. On Aug. 19, 1988, President Zia was killed in a midair explosion of a Pakistani Air Force plane. Elections at the end of 1988 brought longtime Zia opponent Benazir Bhutto, daughter of Zulfikar Bhutto, into office as prime minister.

In the 1990s, Pakistan saw a shaky succession of governments—Benazir Bhutto was prime minister twice and Nawaz Sharif three times, until he was deposed in a coup on Oct. 12, 1999, by Gen. Pervez Musharraf. The Pakistani public, familiar with military rule for 25 of the nation's 52-year history, generally viewed the coup as a positive step, and hoped it would bring a badly needed economic upswing.

Former prime minister Sharif was convicted in April 2000 of hijacking and terrorism and sentenced to two life terms in prison. The charges stemmed from the Oct. 1999 incident in which Sharif refused to allow a passenger plane, which was carrying 198 passengers, including Musharraf, to land in Karachi. In July 2000, the deposed prime minister was sentenced to an additional 14 years in jail on charges of tax evasion. In Dec. Sharif was released from prison and sent with his family to exile in Saudi Arabia. His wife, Kulsoom, had been a leading opponent of Musharraf's regime.

India went ahead with five nuclear tests in May 1998 near Pakistan's borders, which further deteriorated fragile relations between Pakistan and India. In an act of nuclear brinkmanship, Pakistan conducted its own nuclear tests in late May. In the fall of 1998, Pakistan indicated a willingness to sign a nuclear test-ban treaty to rid itself of Western sanctions, which had been imposed since the nuclear testing. Fighting with India again broke out in the disputed territory of Kashmir in May 1999.

In June 2001, a month before a summit with India's prime minister, Atal Behari Vajpayee, Musharraf declared himself president and formal head of state. He promptly assured the country that civilian rule would resume in Oct. 2002, with democratic elections.

Close ties with Afghanistan's Taliban government thrust Pakistan into a difficult position following the Sept. 11, 2001, terrorist bombings of the United States' World Trade Center and the Pentagon. Because Afghanistan has sheltered Osama bin Laden, the suspected mastermind of the bombings, and his Al Qaeda organization, the United States looked to Pakistan, Afghanistan's ally and neighbor, for military and diplomatic support—it sought mediators, intelligence, air space, and the possibility of some ground facilities. But virulent anti-American feeling and strong ties to the Taliban in Pakistan has sparked anger among Islamic fundamentalists and other groups who consider Gen. Musharraf's pro-American stance collaborationist and a betrayal of Islam.

Palau

REPUBLIC OF PALAU

President: Tommy Remengesau (2001)
Total area: 177 sq mi (458 sq km)
Population (2001 est.): 19,092 (average rate of natural increase: 1.2%); birth rate: 19.6/1000; infant mortality rate: 16.7/1000; density per sq mi: 108
Capital and largest city (1995): Koror, 12,299.
Monetary unit: U.S. dollar used. **Languages:** Palauan, English (official). **Ethnicity/race:** Palauans are a composite of Polynesian, Malayan, and Melanesian races. **Religions:** Christian. About one-third of the islanders observe Modekngei religion, indigenous to Palau. **Literacy rate:** 86% (1980)
Economic summary: GDP/PPP (1997 est.): $160 million; note: GDP numbers reflect U.S. spending; per capita $8,800. **Real growth rate:** 10%. **Inflation:** n.a. **Unemployment:** 7%. **Arable land:** n.a. **Agriculture:** coconuts, copra, cassava (tapioca), sweet potatoes. **Labor force:** n.a. **Industries:** tourism, craft items (from shell, wood, pearls), construction, garment making. **Natural resources:** forests, minerals (especially gold), marine products, deep-seabed minerals. **Exports:** $14.3 million (f.o.b., 1996): trochus (type of shellfish), tuna, copra, handicrafts. **Imports:** $72.4 million (f.o.b., 1996): machinery and equipment, fuels. **Major trading partners:** U.S., Japan.

Geography The Palau island chain consists of about 200 islands located in the western Pacific Ocean 528 mi (650 km) southeast of the Philippines. Only eight of the islands are permanently inhabited.

Government Republic.

History The original settlers of Palau are believed to have arrived from Indonesia as early as 2500 B.C. The Palau islands' position on the western threshold of Oceania and their proximity to Southeast Asia have led to the population being a mixture of Malay, Melanesian, Filipino, and Polynesian ancestry.

Explored by the Spanish navigator Ruy López de Villalobos in 1543, the islands remained under nominal Spanish ownership for more than 300 years before Spain sold them to Germany in 1899. Japan occupied Palau during World War I and received a mandate over them from the League of Nations in 1920. They remained in Japanese control and served as an important naval base until the U.S. seized them during World War II. After the war they became a UN trusteeship (1947), administered by the U.S. Palau signed a Compact of Free Association with the U.S. in 1992, requiring the U.S. to provide economic aid in exchange for the right to build and maintain U.S. military facilities in Palau. Palau became a sovereign state in 1994.

Palestinian State (proposed)

WEST BANK AND GAZA STRIP

President: Yasir Arafat (1996)
Area: West Bank: 2,263 sq mi (5,860 sq km); Gaza Strip: 139 sq mi (360 sq km)
Population (2001 est.): West Bank: 2,090,713, Gaza Strip: 1,178,119 (average annual rate of natural increase: West Bank: 3.1%, Gaza Strip: 3.8%); birth rate: West Bank: 35.8/1000, Gaza Strip: 42.5/1000; infant mortality rate: West Bank: 21.8/1,000, Gaza Strip: 25.4/1000; density per sq mi: West Bank: 924, Gaza Strip: 8,476
Capital: Undetermined. **Largest cities (1996 est.):**

Hebron, 294,116; Nablus, 217,935. **Monetary units:** New Israeli shekels, Jordanian dinars, U.S. dollars. **Languages:** Arabic, Hebrew, English, French. **Ethnicity/race:** West Bank: Palestinian Arab and other 83%, Jewish 17%; Gaza Strip: Palestinian Arab and other 99.4%, Jewish 0.6%. **Religions:** West Bank: Muslim 75%, Jewish 17%, Christian and other 8%; Gaza Strip: Muslim 98.7%, Christian 0.7%, Jewish 0.6% **Economic summary: Gaza Strip: GDP/PPP** (1999 est.): $1.17 billion; $1,060 per capita. **Real growth rate:** 4.6%. **Inflation:** 5% (includes West Bank). **Unemployment:** 14.5% (includes West Bank) (1998 est.). **Arable land:** 24%. **Agriculture:** olives, citrus, vegetables; beef, dairy products **Labor force:** n.a.; services, 66%; industry, 21%; agriculture, 13% (1996). **Industries:** generally small family businesses that produce textiles, soap, olive-wood carvings, and mother-of-pearl souvenirs; the Israelis have established some small-scale modern industries in an industrial center. **Natural resources:** arable land. **Exports:** $682 million (includes West Bank) (f.o.b., 1998 est.): citrus, flowers. **Imports:** $2.5 billion (c.i.f., 1998 est.) (includes West Bank): food, consumer goods, construction materials. **Major trading partners:** Israel, Egypt, West Bank. **West Bank: GDP/PPP** (1999 est.): $3.3 billion; $2,050 per capita. **Real growth rate:** 4.6%. **Arable land:** 27%. **Agriculture:** olives, citrus, vegetables; beef, dairy products. **Labor force:** n.a.; agriculture, 13%; industry, 13%; commerce, restaurants, and hotels, 12%; construction, 8%; other services, 54% (1996). **Natural resources:** arable land. **Major trading partners:** Israel, Jordan, Gaza Strip.

Geography The West Bank is mostly composed of limestone hills (conventionally called the Samarian Hills north of Jerusalem and the Judaean Hills south of Jerusalem) having an average height of 2,300 to 3,000 ft (700 to 900 m). The Gaza Strip is located between Israel and Egypt on the Mediterranean coast. It is a flat to rolling sand- and dune-covered coastal plain.

Government The Palestinian Authority (PA), with Arafat its elected leader, took control of the newly non-Israeli-occupied areas, assuming all governmental duties in 1994. Permanent peace talks and implementation of Palestinian self-rule in the West Bank and Gaza Strip are ongoing.

History The history of the proposed modern Palestinian state, which is expected to be formed from the territories of the West Bank and Gaza Strip, began with the British Mandate of Palestine. From Sept. 29, 1923, until May 14, 1948, Britain controlled the region, but by 1947 Britain appealed to the UN to solve the complex problem of competing Palestinian and Jewish claims to the land. In Aug. 1947, the UN proposed dividing Palestine into a Jewish state, an Arab state, and a small international zone. Arabs rejected the idea. As soon as Britain pulled out of Palestine in 1948, neighboring Arab nations invaded, intent on crushing the newly declared State of Israel. Israel emerged victorious, affirming its sovereignty. The remaining areas of Palestine were divided between Transjordan (now Jordan), which annexed the West Bank, and Egypt, which gained control of the Gaza Strip.

Through a series of political and social policies, Jordan sought to consolidate its control over the political future of Palestinians and to become their speaker. Jordan even extended citizenship to Palestinians in 1949—Palestinians constituted about two-thirds of the country's population. In the Gaza Strip, administered by Egypt from 1948–67, poverty and unemployment were high, and most of the Palestinians lived in refugee camps.

In the Arab-Israeli war of 1967, Israel, over a period of six days, defeated the military forces of Egypt, Syria, and Jordan and annexed the territories of East Jerusalem, the Golan Heights, the West Bank, the Gaza Strip, and all of the Sinai peninsula. The Palestinian Liberation Organization (PLO), formed in 1964, was a terrorist organization bent on Israel's annihilation. Palestinian rioting, demonstrations, and terrorist acts against Israelis became chronic. In 1974, PLO leader Yasir Arafat addressed the UN General Assembly, the first stateless government to do so. Violence again escalated in 1987 during the *intifada* ("shaking off"), a new era in Palestinian mass mobilization. In 1988, PLO leader Yasir Arafat proclaimed the independence of the Palestinian State (including the West Bank and Gaza Strip), as a government-in-exile, and publicly eschewed terrorism.

In 1993, highly secretive talks in Norway between the PLO and the Israeli government resulted in the Oslo agreement. The accord stipulated a five-year plan in which Palestinians of the West Bank and the Gaza Strip would gradually become self-governing. On Sept. 13, 1993, Arafat and Israeli prime minister Yitzak Rabin signed the historic "Declaration of Principles." As part of the agreement, Israel pulled out of the Gaza Strip and Jericho in the West Bank in 1994.

The Palestinian Authority (PA), with Arafat as its elected leader, took control of the newly non-Israeli-occupied areas, assuming all governmental duties. Permanent peace talks and implementation of Palestinian self-rule in the West Bank and Gaza Strip are ongoing after seven years. The election in 1999 of Israeli prime minister Ehud Barak was viewed by moderate Palestinians as a positive step toward peace.

But despite intensive negotiations between Barak and Arafat in the summer and fall of 2000, the two leaders remained deadlocked over Israeli-occupied East Jerusalem, which Arafat insists must be the capital of the future Palestinian state. Arafat, however, allowed his Sept. 13 deadline for declaring a Palestinian state to pass in the interest of continued negotiations with Israel. At the end of Sept., however, the stalemate disintegrated into the worst violence between Israelis and Palestinians in years, provoked by Likud hardliner Ariel Sharon's visit to the compound called Temple Mount by Jews and Haram al Sharif by Muslims, a fiercely contested site that is sacred to both Jews and Muslims. The continuing violence, dubbed the Al Aksa intifada, fueled growing concerns about Israeli security, paving the way for the right-wing Sharon's stunning landslide victory over Barak in Feb. 2001, which outraged Palestinians and much of the Arab world. Throughout 2001, violence on both sides continued unabated—about 800 Palestinians and Israelis were killed in the first year of the intifada—and the peace process lost ground.

Panama

REPUBLIC OF PANAMA

National name: República de Panamá
President: Mireya Moscoso (1999)
Area: 30,193 sq mi (78,200 sq km)
Population (2001 est.): 2,845,647 (average annual rate of natural increase: 1.4%); birth rate: 19.1/1000; infant mortality rate: 20.2/1000; density per sq mi: 94
Capital and largest city (1993 est.): Panama City,

450,668. **Other large cities:** San Miguelito, 293,564; Colón, 137,825. **Monetary unit:** Balboa. **Languages:** Spanish (official); many bilingual in English. **Ethnicity/ race:** mestizo (mixed Indian and European ancestry) 70%, West Indian 14%, white 10%, Indian 6%. **Religions:** Roman Catholic over 93%, Protestant 6%. **Literacy rate:** 89% (1990) **Economic summary: GDP/PPP** (1999 est.): $21 billion; per capita $7,600. **Real growth rate:** 4.4%. **Inflation:** 1.5%. **Unemployment:** 13.1% (1997 est.). **Arable land:** 7%. **Agriculture:** bananas, rice, corn, coffee, sugarcane, vegetables; livestock; shrimp. **Labor force:** 1.044 million (1997 est.); note: shortage of skilled labor, but an oversupply of unskilled labor; agriculture, 18%; industry, 18%; services, 64%. **Industries:** construction, petroleum refining, brewing, cement and other construction materials, sugar milling. **Natural resources:** copper, mahogany forests, shrimp, hydropower. **Exports:** $4.7 billion (f.o.b., 1999 est.): bananas, shrimp, sugar, coffee. **Imports:** $6.4 billion (f.o.b., 1999 est.): capital goods, crude oil, foodstuffs, consumer goods, chemicals. **Major trading partners:** U.S., Sweden, Costa Rica, Spain, Benelux, Honduras, Central America and Caribbean, Japan.

Geography   The southernmost of the Central American nations, Panama is south of Costa Rica and north of Colombia. The Panama Canal bisects the isthmus at its narrowest and lowest point, allowing passage from the Caribbean Sea to the Pacific Ocean. Panama is slightly smaller than South Carolina. It is marked by a chain of mountains in the west, moderate hills in the interior, and a low range on the east coast. There are extensive forests in the fertile Caribbean area.

Government   Republic.

History   Visited by Columbus in 1502 on his fourth voyage and explored by Balboa in 1513, Panama was the principal shipping point to and from South and Central America in colonial days. In 1821, when Central America revolted against Spain, Panama joined Colombia, which had already declared its independence. For the next 82 years, Panama attempted unsuccessfully to break away from Colombia. Between 1850 and 1900 Panama had 40 administrations, 50 riots, 5 attempted secessions, and 13 U.S. interventions. After a U.S. proposal for canal rights over the narrow isthmus was rejected by Colombia, Panama proclaimed its independence with U.S. backing in 1903.

For canal rights in perpetuity, the U.S. paid Panama $10 million and agreed to pay $250,000 each year, which was increased to $430,000 in 1933. It was increased again in 1955. In exchange, the U.S. got the Canal Zone—a 10-mile-wide strip across the isthmus—and considerable influence in Panama's affairs.

On Sept. 7, 1974, President Omar Torrijos Herara and President Jimmy Carter signed treaties giving Panama gradual control of the canal, phasing out U.S. military bases, and guaranteeing the canal's neutrality. A Panamanian referendum approved the treaties in Oct. 1974. Despite some opposition, the U.S. Senate approved the treaties in 1978, after requiring several changes.

Nicolas Ardito Barletta, Panama's first directly elected president in 16 years, was inaugurated on Oct. 11, 1984, for a five-year term. He was a puppet of strongman Gen. Manuel Noriega, who replaced him with vice president Eric Arturo Delvalle a year later. In 1988, Noriega was indicted in the U.S. for drug trafficking, but when Delvalle attempted to fire him, Noriega forced the National Assembly to replace Delvalle with Manuel Solis Palma. In Dec. 1989, the assembly named Noriega "maximum leader" and declared the U.S. and Panama to be in a state of war. In Dec. 1989, 24,000 U.S. troops seized control of Panama City in an attempt to capture Noriega after a U.S. soldier was killed in Panama. On Jan. 3, 1990, Noriega surrendered himself to U.S. custody and was transported to Miami, where he was later convicted of drug trafficking. Guillermo Endara, who probably would have won an election suppressed earlier by Noriega, was installed as president.

Ernesto Pérez Balladares of the Democratic Revolutionary Party, whose campaign invoked memories of party founder Torrijos, won the 1994 elections. In May 1999, Panama elected its first woman president, Mireya Moscoso, widow of former president Arnulfo Arias who served in the 1960s.

On Dec. 31, 1999, the U.S. formally handed over control of the Panama Canal to Panama. Meanwhile, Colombian rebels and paramilitary forces have made periodic incursions into Panamanian territory, raising security concerns. Panama has also faced increased drug and arms smuggling.

Panama Canal.   In 1524 King Charles V of Spain ordered a survey of a waterway across the isthmus in consideration of building a canal. In 1878, the Colombian government gave a construction concession to the French Canal Company. The effort ended in bankruptcy nine years later, and the United States ultimately paid the French $40 million for their rights and assets. The U.S. project, built on territory controlled by the United States, began in 1904 and was completed in 1914.

Papua New Guinea

Sovereign: Queen Elizabeth II (1952)
Governor General: Silas Atopare (1997)
Prime Minister: Mekere Morauta (1999)
Area: 178,703 sq mi (462,840 sq km)
Population (2001 est.): 5,049,055 (average annual rate of natural increase: 2.4%); birth rate: 32.2/1000; infant mortality rate: 58.2/1000; density per sq mi: 28
Capital and largest city (1994 est.): Port Moresby, 250,000. **Monetary unit:** Kina. **Languages:** English, Tok Pisin (a Melanesian Creole English), Hiri Motu, and 717 distinct native languages. **Ethnicity/race:** Papuan, Melanesian, Negrito, Micronesian, Polynesian. **Religions:** over half are Christian, remainder indigenous. **Literacy rate:** 50% (1990)
Economic summary: GDP/PPP (1999 est.): $11.6 billion; per capita $2,500. **Real growth rate:** 3.6%. **Inflation:** 16.5%. **Unemployment:** n.a. **Arable land:** 0.1%. **Agriculture:** coffee, cocoa, coconuts, palm kernels, tea, rubber, sweet potatoes, fruit, vegetables; poultry, pork. **Labor force:** 1.941 million; agriculture, n.a.; industry, n.a.; services, n.a. **Industries:** copra crushing, palm oil processing, plywood production, wood chip production; mining of gold, silver, and copper; crude oil production; construction, tourism. **Natural resources:** gold, copper, silver, natural gas, timber, oil, fisheries. **Exports:** $1.9 billion (f.o.b., 1999 est.): oil, gold, copper ore, logs, palm oil, coffee, cocoa, crayfish, and prawns. **Imports:** $1 billion (f.o.b., 1999 est.): machinery and transport equipment, manufactured goods, food, fuels, chemicals. **Major trading partners:** Australia, Japan, Germany, South Korea, Philippines, UK, Singapore, U.S., New Zealand, Malaysia. **Member of Commonwealth of Nations**

Geography Papua New Guinea occupies the eastern half of the island of New Guinea, just north of Australia, and many outlying islands. The Indonesian province of West Papua (Irian Jaya) is to the west. To the north and east are the islands of Manus, New Britain, New Ireland, and Bougainville, all part of Papua New Guinea. About one-tenth larger than California, its mountainous interior has only recently been explored. Two major rivers, the Sepik and the Fly, are navigable for shallow-draft vessels.

Government Parliamentary democracy.

History The first inhabitants of the island New Guinea were Papuan, Melanesian, and Negrito tribes, who altogether spoke more than 700 distinct languages. The eastern half of New Guinea was first explored by Spanish and Portuguese explorers in the 16th century. In 1828, the Dutch formally took possession of the western half of the island (now the province of West Papula [Irian Jaya], Indonesia). In 1885, Germany formally annexed the northern coast and Britain took similar action in the south. In 1906, Britain transferred its rights to British New Guinea to a newly independent Australia, and the name of the territory was changed to the Territory of Papua. Australian troops invaded German New Guinea (called Kaiser-Wilhelmsland) in World War I and gained control of the territory under a League of Nations mandate. New Guinea and some of Papua were invaded by Japanese forces in 1942. After being liberated by the Australians in 1945, it became a United Nations trusteeship, administered by Australia. The territories were combined and called the Territory of Papua and New Guinea.

Australia granted limited home rule in 1951. Autonomy in internal affairs came nine years later, and in Sept. 1975, Papua New Guinea achieved complete independence from Britain.

A violent nine-year secessionist movement took place on the island of Bougainville. In 1989, guerrillas of the Bougainville Revolutionary Army (BRA) shut down the island's Australian-owned copper mine, a major source of revenue for the country. The rebels believed that Bougainville deserved a greater share of the earnings for its copper. In 1990, the BRA declared Bougainville's independence, whereupon the government blockaded the island until Jan. 1991, when a peace treaty was signed. In 1997, Papua New Guinea's government hired South African mercenary soldiers to fight on Bougainville in order to end the long-running crisis, but this action led to massive demonstrations and the mercenary contract was rescinded. In April 1998, a cease-fire was declared.

On July 17, 1998, an earthquake-triggered tsunami (tidal wave) off the northern coast of Papua New Guinea killed at least 1,500 people and left thousands more injured and homeless.

Paraguay

REPUBLIC OF PARAGUAY

National name: República del Paraguay
President: Luis Ángel González Macchi (1999)
Area: 157,046 sq mi (406,750 sq km)
Population (2001 est.): 5,734,139 (average annual rate of natural increase: 2.6%); birth rate: 30.9/1000; infant mortality rate: 29.8/1000; density per sq mi: 37
Capital and largest city (1992): Asunción, 502,426.
Other large cities (1992): Ciudad del Este, 133,893; San Lorenzo, 133,311. **Monetary unit:** Guaraní.
Languages: Spanish (official), Guaraní. **Ethnicity/race:** mestizo (mixed Spanish and Indian) 95%, whites

plus Amerindians 5%. **Religion:** Roman Catholic 90%.
Literacy rate: 90% (1990)
Economic summary: GDP/PPP (1999 est.): $19.9 billion; per capita $3,650. **Real growth rate:** –1%. **Inflation:** 5%. **Unemployment:** 12% (1998 est.).
Arable land: 6%. **Agriculture:** cotton, sugarcane, soybeans, corn, wheat, tobacco, cassava (tapioca), fruits, vegetables; beef, pork, eggs, milk; timber. **Labor force:** 1.7 million (1996); agriculture, 45%. **Industries:** sugar, cement, textiles, beverages, wood products. **Natural resources:** hydropower, timber, iron ore, manganese, limestone. **Exports:** $3.1 billion (f.o.b., 1999 est.): soybeans, feed, cotton, meat, edible oils. **Imports:** $3.2 billion (f.o.b., 1999 est.): road vehicles, consumer goods, tobacco, petroleum products, electrical machinery. **Major trading partners:** Brazil, Argentina, EU, U.S., Uruguay, Hong Kong.

Geography California-size Paraguay is surrounded by Brazil, Bolivia, and Argentina in south-central South America. Eastern Paraguay, between the Paraná and Paraguay Rivers, is upland country with the thickest population settled on the grassy slope that inclines toward the Paraguay River. The greater part of the Chaco region to the west is covered with marshes, lagoons, dense forests, and jungles.

Government Republic.

History Indians speaking Guaraní—the most common language in Paraguay today, after Spanish—were the country's first inhabitants. In 1526 and again in 1529, Sebastian Cabot explored Paraguay when he sailed up the Paraná and Paraguay Rivers. From 1608 until their expulsion from the Spanish dominions in 1767, the Jesuits maintained an extensive establishment in the south and east of Paraguay. In 1811, Paraguay revolted against Spanish rule and became a nominal republic under two consuls.

Paraguay was governed by three dictators during the first 60 years of independence. The third, Francisco López, waged war against Uruguay, Brazil, and Argentina in 1865–70, a conflict in which half the male population was killed. A new constitution in 1870, designed to prevent dictatorships and internal strife, failed to do so, and not until 1912 did a period of comparative economic and political stability begin. The Chaco War (1932–35) with Bolivia won Paraguay more western territory.

After World War II, politics became particularly unstable. Alfredo Stroessner was dictator from 1954 until 1989, during which he was accused of the torture and murder of thousands of political opponents. Despite Paraguay's human rights record, the U.S. continuously supported Stroessner.

Stroessner was overthrown by army leader, Gen. Andres Rodriguez, in 1989. Rodriguez went on to win Paraguay's first multicandidate election in decades. Paraguay's new constitution went into effect in 1992. In 1993, Juan Carlos Wasmosy, a wealthy businessman and the candidate of the governing Colorado Party, won a five-year term in free elections. Raúl Cubas Grau was elected president in May 1998.

In 1999 Cubas was forced from office for his alleged involvement in the assassination of Vice President Luis María Argaña. The vice president had criticized Cubas for refusing to jail his mentor, Gen. Lino Oviedo, who had been convicted of leading a failed 1996 coup against Wasmosy.

The new president, Luis Ángel González Macchi, has undertaken a governmental overhaul, and for the first time since Stroessner was overthrown, political and economic power is no longer entirely within the hands of the corrupt and military-backed Colorado Party. The U.S. has accused the Colorado Party of smuggling, money laundering, trafficking Bolivian cocaine, and supporting international terrorist organizations.

In Aug. 2000 the opposition Liberal Party won its first major victory in more than 50 years with the election of Julio Cesar Franco as vice president. He narrowly defeated the son of the previous vice president, Argaña. Paraguay's government has sought to clean up the political system by bringing to trial political and military figures suspected of human rights violations, corruption, or other crimes.

Peru

REPUBLIC OF PERU

National name: República del Perú
President: Alejandro Toledo (2001)
Prime Minister: Roberto Dañino (2001)
Area: 496,223 sq mi (1,285,220 sq km)
Population (2001 est.): 27,483,864 (average annual rate of natural increase: 1.8%); birth rate: 23.9/1000; infant mortality rate: 39.4/1000; density per sq mi: 55
Capital and largest city (2000 est.): Lima, 7,450,000 (metro. area). **Other large cities:** Arequipa, 939,800; Callao, 648,000; Trujillo, 1,287,000; Chiclayo, 951,000.
Monetary unit: Nuevo Sol (1991). **Languages:** Spanish and Quéchua (both official), Aymara, and other native languages. **Ethnicity/race:** Indian 45%, mestizo (mixed Indian and European ancestry) 37%, white 15%, black, Japanese, Chinese, and other 3%.
Religion: Roman Catholic. **Literacy rate:** 85% (1990)
Economic summary: GDP/PPP (1999 est.): $116 billion; per capita $4,400. **Real growth:** 2.4%. **Inflation:** 5.5%. **Unemployment:** 7.7%; extensive underemployment (1997). **Arable land:** 3%. **Agriculture:** coffee, cotton, sugarcane, rice, wheat, potatoes, plantains, coca; poultry, beef, dairy products, wool; fish. **Labor force:** 7.6 million (1996 est.); agriculture, mining and quarrying, manufacturing, construction, transport, services.
Industries: mining of metals, petroleum, fishing, textiles, clothing, food processing, cement, auto assembly, steel, shipbuilding, metal fabrication. **Natural resources:** copper, silver, gold, petroleum, timber, fish, iron ore, coal, phosphate, potash, hydropower. **Exports:** $5.9 billion (f.o.b., 1999 est.): fish and fish products, copper, zinc, gold, crude petroleum and byproducts, lead, coffee, sugar, cotton. **Imports:** $8.4 billion (c.i.f., 1999 est.): machinery, transport equipment, foodstuffs, petroleum, iron and steel, chemicals, pharmaceuticals. **Major trading partners:** U.S., China, Japan, Switzerland, Germany, UK, Brazil, Colombia, Venezuela, Chile.

Geography Peru, in western South America, extends for nearly 1,500 mi (2,414 km) along the Pacific Ocean. Colombia and Ecuador are to the north, Brazil and Bolivia to the east, and Chile to the south. Five-sixths the size of Alaska, Peru is divided by the Andes Mountains into three sharply differentiated zones. To the west is the coastline, much of it arid, extending 50 to 100 mi (80 to 160 km) inland. The mountain area, with peaks over 20,000 ft (6,096 m), lofty plateaus, and deep valleys, lies centrally. Beyond the mountains to the east is the heavily forested slope leading to the Amazonian plains.

Government Republic.

History Peru was once part of the great Incan empire and later the major vice-royalty of Spanish South America. It was conquered in 1531–33 by Francisco Pizarro. On July 28, 1821, Peru proclaimed its independence, but the Spanish were not finally defeated until 1824. For a hundred years thereafter, revolutions were frequent; a new war was fought with Spain in 1864–66, and an unsuccessful war was fought with Chile from 1879 to 1883 (the War of the Pacific).

Peru emerged from 20 years of dictatorship in 1945 with the inauguration of President José Luis Bustamente y Rivero after the first free election in many decades. But he served for only three years and was succeeded in turn by Gen. Manual A. Odria, Manuel Prado y Ugarteche, and Fernando Belaúnde Terry. On Oct. 3, 1968, Belaúnde was overthrown by Gen. Juan Velasco Alvarado. Velasco nationalized the nation's second-biggest bank and turned two large newspapers over to Marxists in 1970, but he also allowed a new agreement with a copper-mining consortium of four American firms. In 1975, Velasco was replaced in a bloodless coup by his premier, Gen. Francisco Morales Bermudez, who promised to restore civilian government. In elections held on May 18, 1980, Belaúnde Terry, the last previous civilian president and the candidate of the conservative parties that have traditionally governed Peru, was elected president again.

Peru's fragile democracy survived. In 1985, Belaúnde Terry was the first elected president to turn over power to a constitutionally elected successor since 1945. Alberto Fujimori won the 1990 elections. Citing continuing terrorism, drug trafficking, and corruption, Fujimori dissolved Congress, suspended the constitution, and imposed censorship in April 1992. A new constitution was approved in 1993. In Jan. 1995 fighting flared along the disputed border with Ecuador, as it had in 1941 and 1981. In April, Fujimori was reelected, and his party (Change 90–New Majority) won a legislative majority.

In 1997, the disastrous effects of El Niño caused the failure of the fish harvest and a severe drought in Peru. In May 1999, Ecuador and Peru signed a treaty ending the nearly 60-year dispute over a stretch of Amazon jungle.

Fujimori was easily reelected in May 2000 to a third five-year term, after his opponent, Alejandro Toledo, withdrew from the contest, charging fraud. The Organization of American States (OAS) has been investigating voting irregularities. In Sept. 2000, after Fujimori's intelligence chief, Vladimiro Montesinos, was videotaped bribing a congressman, Fujimori called for new elections, declared he would step down, and announced he would dismantle the powerful National Intelligence Service, which has been accused of human rights violations.

Two months later, he stunned his nation by resigning during a trip to Japan. An outraged Congress rejected his resignation and removed him from office on the grounds he was morally unfit to be president. Revelations that Fujimori secretly held Japanese citizenship—and could not be extradited to face corruption charges—enraged popular opinion.

In 2001, the centrist Alejandro Toledo was elected president with 53.1% of the vote, defeating former president Alan García.

The Philippines

REPUBLIC OF THE PHILIPPINES

National name: Republika ng Pilipinas
President: Gloria Macapagal-Arroyo (2001)
Area: 115,830 sq mi (300,000 sq km)
Population (2001 est.): 82,841,518 (average annual rate of natural increase: 2.1%); birth rate: 27.4/1000; infant mortality rate: 28.7/1000; density per sq mi: 715

Capital and largest city (2000 est.): Manila, 13,450,000 (metro. area). **Other large cities:** Quezon City, 1,669,776 (part of Manila metro. area); Cebu, 610,415. **Monetary unit:** Peso. **Languages:** Filipino (based on Tagalog) and English (both official); regional languages: Tagalog, Ilocano, Cebuano, others. **Ethnicity/race:** Christian Malay 91.5%, Muslim Malay 4%, Chinese 1.5%, other 3%. **Religions:** Roman Catholic 84%, Protestant 10%, Islam 5%, Buddhist and other 3%. **Literacy rate:** 94% (1990)
Economic summary: GDP/PPP (1999 est.): $282 billion; per capita $3,600. **Real growth rate:** 2.9%. **Inflation:** 6.8%. **Unemployment:** 9.6% (Oct. 1998). **Arable land:** 19%. **Agriculture:** rice, coconuts, corn, sugarcane, bananas, pineapples, mangoes; pork, eggs, beef; fish. **Labor force:** 32 million (1999 est.); agriculture, 39.8%; government and social services, 19.4%; services, 17.7%; manufacturing, 9.8%; construction, 5.8%, other, 7.5% (1998 est.). **Industries:** textiles, pharmaceuticals, chemicals, wood products, food processing, electronics assembly, petroleum refining, fishing. **Natural resources:** timber, petroleum, nickel, cobalt, silver, gold, salt, copper. **Exports:** $34.8 billion (f.o.b., 1999 est.): electronic equipment, machinery and transport equipment, garments, coconut products. **Imports:** $30.7 billion (f.o.b., 1999 est.): raw materials and intermediate goods, capital goods, consumer goods, fuels. **Major trading partners:** U.S., EU, Japan, Netherlands, Singapore, UK, Hong Kong, South Korea, Taiwan.

Geography The Philippine Islands are an archipelago of over 7,000 islands lying about 500 mi (805 km) off the southeast coast of Asia. The overall land area is comparable to that of Arizona. Only about 7% of the islands are larger than one square mile, and only one-third have names. The largest are Luzon in the north (40,420 sq mi; 104,687 sq km), Mindanao in the south (36,537 sq mi; 94,631 sq km), and Samar (5,124 sq mi; 13,271 sq km). The islands are of volcanic origin, with the larger ones crossed by mountain ranges. The highest peak is Mount Apo (9,690 ft; 2,954 m) on Mindanao.

Government Republic.

History Ferdinand Magellan, the Portuguese navigator in the service of Spain, explored the Philippines in 1521. Twenty-one years later, a Spanish exploration party named the group of islands in honor of Prince Philip, who was later to become Philip II of Spain. Spain retained possession of the islands for the next 350 years.

The Philippines were ceded to the U.S. in 1899 by the Treaty of Paris after the Spanish-American War. Meanwhile, the Filipinos, led by Emilio Aguinaldo, had declared their independence. They initiated guerrilla warfare against U.S. troops that persisted until the capture of Aguinaldo in 1901. By 1902, peace was established except among the Islamic Moros on the southern island of Mindanao.

The first U.S. civilian governor-general was William Howard Taft (1901–04). The Jones Law (1916) provided for the establishment of a Philippine Legislature composed of an elective Senate and House of Representatives. The Tydings-McDuffie Act (1934) provided for a transitional period until 1946, at which time the Philippines would become completely independent. Under a constitution approved by the people of the Philippines in 1935, the Commonwealth of the Philippines came into being with Manuel Quezon y Molina as president.

On Dec. 8, 1941, the islands were invaded by Japanese troops. Following the fall of Gen. Douglas Mac-Arthur's forces at Bataan and Corregidor, Quezon established a government-in-exile that he headed until his death in 1944. He was succeeded by Vice President Sergio Osmeña. U.S. forces under MacArthur reinvaded the Philippines in Oct. 1944 and, after the liberation of Manila in Feb. 1945, Osmeña reestablished the government.

The Philippines achieved full independence on July 4, 1946. Manual A. Roxas y Acuña was elected its first president, succeeded by Elpidio Quirino (1948–53), Ramón Magsaysay (1953–57). Carlos P. García (1957–61), Diosdado Macapagal (1961–65), and Ferdinand E. Marcos (1965–86).

Under Marcos, civil unrest broke out in opposition to the leader's despotic rule. Martial law was declared on Sept. 21, 1972, and Marcos proclaimed a new constitution that ensconced himself as president. Martial law was officially lifted on Jan. 17, 1981, but Marcos and his wife Imelda retained broad powers.

Despite warnings that his life would be endangered, opposition leader Benigno S. Aquino returned to the Philippines from self-exile on Aug. 21, 1983. He was shot to death as he was being escorted from his plane by military police at Manila International Airport. There was widespread suspicion that Marcos had ordered Aquino's assassination. The event became a watershed in modern Filipino political history, acting as a catalyst for opposition groups and the "People Power" movement, led by the late leader's widow, Corazon Aquino.

In an attempt to resecure American support, Marcos set presidential elections for Feb. 7, 1986. With the support of the Catholic Church, Corazon Aquino declared her candidacy. Marcos was declared the official winner, but independent observers reported widespread election fraud and vote-rigging. Anti-Marcos protests exploded in the capital Manila, Defense Minister Juan Enrile and Lt. Gen. Fidel Ramos defected to the opposition, and Marcos lost virtually all support; he was forced to flee into exile and entered the U.S. on Feb. 25, 1986.

The Aquino government survived coup attempts by Marcos supporters and other right-wing elements, including one in Nov. by Enrile. Legislative elections on May 11, 1987, gave pro-Aquino candidates a large majority. Negotiations on renewal of leases for U.S. military bases threatened to sour relations between the two countries. Volcanic eruptions from Mount Pinatubo, however, severely damaged Clark Air Base, and in July 1991 the U.S. decided simply to abandon it.

In elections in May 1992, Gen. Fidel Ramos, who had the support of outgoing Aquino, won the presidency in a seven-way race. In Sept. of that year, the U.S. Navy turned over the Subic Bay naval base to the Philippines, ending a long-standing U.S. military presence. Meanwhile, the separatist Moro National Liberation Front was fighting a protracted war for an Islamic homeland on Mindanao, the southernmost of the two main islands. In 1996, the group agreed to a government plan designed to grant it a greater degree of political autonomy. An administrative body, headed by the former rebel chief, was established to oversee development on the southern islands. Frequent and violent clashes continued into mid-2001, however. The army also battled another rebel group, the Moro Islamic Liberation Front. In August 2001 talks brokered by Malaysia, the Moro Islamic Liberation Front, and the Moro National Liberation Front signed unity agreements with the Philippine government.

Even as the Philippines experienced a somewhat lower rate of growth than many of its Asian neighbors throughout the 1990s, it was spared the brunt of the region's financial crisis following a wave of currency devaluations sparked in July 1997. In May 1998, 61-year-old former action film star Joseph Estrada was elected president of the Philippines, succeeding Fidel Ramos, who declined to contest elections.

In Nov. 2000 the Philippine Senate began to impeach Estrada on corruption charges. Massive street demonstrations and the loss of political support eventually forced Estrada from office. Vice President Gloria Macapagal-Arroyo, daughter of former president Diosdado Macapagal and the holder of a doctorate in economics from Georgetown University, became president in Jan. 2001. In April 2001 the Philippine Supreme Court ruled that Estrada had effectively resigned from office when he stepped down, brushing aside his argument that he was merely on a leave of absence. The ruling confirmed Macapagal-Arroyo as president and stripped Estrada of his presidential immunity, paving the way for his trial on corruption and bribery charges. He was indicted in July on the charge of economic plunder, a capital offense.

Abu Sayyaf, a smaller, separate group of guerrillas that has been fighting since the 1970s for an independent Islamic state and protection of local fishing rights, gained international notoriety throughout 2000 and 2001 with its spree of kidnappings that has resulted in dozens of deaths. Hostages have included several Americans vacationing at beach resorts. The government deployed 5,000 troops in May 2001, but they have been largely ineffective in preventing the kidnappings and liberating hostages.

Poland

REPUBLIC OF POLAND

National name: Rzeczpospolita Polska
President: Aleksander Kwasniewski (1995)
Prime Minister: Leszek Miller (2001)
Area: 120,728 sq mi (312,685 sq km)
Population (2001 est.): 38,633,912 (average annual rate of natural increase: 0.02%); birth rate: 10.2/1000; infant mortality rate: 9.4/1000; density per sq mi: 320
Capital and largest city (1994 est.): Warsaw, 1,642,700. **Other large cities:** Lodz, 833,700; Krakow, 745,100; Wroclaw, 642,300; Poznan, 582,800; Gdansk, 463,100; Szczecin, 417,700. **Monetary unit:** Zloty. **Language:** Polish. **Ethnicity/race:** Polish 97.6%, German 1.3%, Ukrainian 0.6%, Belorussian 0.5% (1990 est.). **Religions:** Roman Catholic 95% (about 75% practicing), Russian Orthodox, Protestant, and other 5%. **Literacy rate:** 98% (1978)
Economic summary: GDP/PPP (1999 est.): $276.5 billion; per capita $7,200. **Real growth rate:** 3.8%. **Inflation:** 8.4%. **Unemployment:** 11%. **Arable land:** 47%. **Agriculture:** potatoes, fruits, vegetables, wheat; poultry, eggs, pork, beef, milk, cheese. **Labor force:** 15.3 million (1998 est.); industry, 25%; agriculture, 25%; services, 50% (1999 est.). **Industries:** machine building, iron and steel, coal mining, chemicals, shipbuilding, food processing, glass, beverages, textiles. **Natural resources:** coal, sulfur, copper, natural gas, silver, lead, salt, arable land. **Exports:** $27.8 billion (f.o.b., 1999): manufactured goods and chemicals, machinery and equipment, food and live animals, mineral fuels (1997). **Imports:** $40.8 billion (f.o.b., 1999): manufactured goods and chemicals, machinery and equipment, mineral fuels, food and live animals (1997). **Major trading partners:** Germany, Italy, Russia, Netherlands, France, Ukraine, UK, U.S.

Geography Poland, a country the size of New Mexico, is in north-central Europe. Most of the country is a plain with no natural boundaries except the Carpathian Mountains in the south and the Oder and Neisse Rivers in the west. Other major rivers, which are important to commerce, are the Vistula, Warta, and Bug.

Government Democratic state.

History Great (north) Poland was founded in 966 by Mieszko I, who belonged to the Piast dynasty. The tribes of southern Poland then united to form Little Poland. In 1047 both Great Poland and Little Poland united under the rule of Casimir I the Restorer. Poland merged with Lithuania by royal marriage in 1386. The Polish-Lithuanian state reached the peak of its power between the 14th and 16th century, scoring military successes against the (Germanic) Knights of the Teutonic Order, the Russians, and the Ottoman Turks.

Lack of a strong monarchy enabled Russia, Prussia, and Austria to carry out a first partition of the country in 1772, a second in 1792, and a third in 1795. For more than a century thereafter, there was no Polish state, just Austrian, Prussian, and Russian sectors, but the Poles never ceased their efforts to regain their independence. The Polish people revolted against Russian, Prussian, and Austrian dominance throughout the 19th century. Poland was formally reconstituted in Nov. 1918, with Marshal Josef Pilsudski as chief of state. In 1919, Ignace Paderewski, the famous pianist and patriot, became the first premier. In 1926, Pilsudski seized complete power in a coup and ruled dictatorially until his death on May 12, 1935.

Despite a 10-year nonaggression pact signed in 1934, Hitler attacked Poland on Sept. 1, 1939. Soviet troops invaded from the east on Sept. 17, and on Sept. 28 a German-Soviet agreement divided Poland between the USSR and Germany. Wladyslaw Raczkiewicz formed a government-in-exile in France, which moved to London after France's defeat in 1940. All of Poland was occupied by Germany after the Nazi attack on the USSR in June 1941. Nazi Germany's occupation policy in Poland was designed to eradicate Polish culture through mass executions and to exterminate the country's large Jewish minority.

The Polish government-in-exile was replaced with the Communist-dominated Polish Committee of National Liberation by the Soviet Union in 1944. Moving to Lublin after that city's liberation, it proclaimed itself the Provisional Government of Poland. Some former members of the Polish government in London joined with the Lublin government to form the Polish Government of National Unity, which Britain and the U.S. recognized. On Aug. 2, 1945, in Berlin, President Harry S. Truman, Joseph Stalin, and Prime Minister Clement Attlee of Britain established a new de facto western frontier for Poland along the Oder and Neisse Rivers. (The border was finally agreed to by West Germany in a nonaggression pact signed on Dec. 7, 1970.) On Aug. 16, 1945, the USSR and Poland signed a treaty delimiting the Soviet-Polish frontier. Under these agreements, Poland was shifted westward. In the east it lost 69,860 square mi (180,934 sq km); in the west it gained (subject to final peace-conference approval) 38,986 square mi (100,973 sq km).

A new constitution in 1952 made Poland a "people's democracy" of the Soviet type. In 1955, Poland became a member of the Warsaw Treaty Organization, and its foreign policy became identical to that of the USSR. The government undertook persecution of the Roman Catholic Church as a remaining source of opposition. Wladyslaw Gomulka was elected leader of the United Workers (Communist) Party in 1956. He denounced the Stalinist terror, ousted many Stalinists, and improved relations with the church. Most collective farms were dissolved, and the press became freer. A strike that began in shipyards and spread to other industries in August 1980 produced a stunning victory for workers when the economically hard-pressed government accepted for the first time in a Marxist state the right of workers to organize in independent unions.

Led by Solidarity, a free union founded by an electrician, Lech Walesa, workers launched a drive for liberty and improved conditions. A national strike for a five-day workweek in Jan. 1981 led to the dismissal of Premier Pinkowski and the naming of the fourth premier in less than a year, Gen. Wojciech Jaruzelski. Martial law was declared on Dec. 13, when Walesa and other Solidarity leaders were arrested. It formally ended in 1984 but the government retained emergency powers. Increasing opposition to the government because of the failing economy led to a new wave of strikes in 1988. Unable to totally quell the dissent, the government relegalized Solidarity and allowed it to compete in elections.

Solidarity members won a stunning victory in 1989, taking almost all the seats in the Senate and all of the 169 seats they were allowed to contest in the Sejm. This gave them substantial influence in the new government. Tadeusz Mazowiecki was appointed prime minister. Lech Walesa won the presidential election of 1990 with 74% of the vote. In 1991, the first fully free parliamentary election since World War II resulted in representation for 29 political parties. In the second democratic parliamentary election of Sept. 1993, voters returned power to ex-Communists and their allies.

Solidarity's popularity and influence, however, began to wane. In 1995, Aleksander Kwasniewski, leader of the successor to the Communist Party, the Democratic Left, won the presidency over Walesa in a landslide.

The pope visited Poland in 1999, which some believe may be his last visit to his homeland. In 1999, Poland became part of NATO, along with the Czech Republic and Hungary. Poland is expected to become the next country accepted into the European Union (EU), though membership is not anticipated before 2004.

In Sept. 2001 parliamentary elections, former communists, reconstituted as the center-left Democratic Left Alliance, won 41% of the vote. The election seemed to mark the demise of Solidarity, which did not win a single seat.

Portugal

REPUBLIC OF PORTUGAL

National name: República Portuguesa
President: Jorge Sampaio (1996)
Prime Minister: Antonio Guterres (1995)
Area: 35,672 sq mi (92,391 sq km)
Population (2001 est.): 10,066,253 (average annual rate of natural increase: 0.1%); birth rate: 11.5/1000; infant mortality rate: 5.9/1000; density per sq mi: 282
Capital and largest city (1991): Lisbon, 677,790. **Other large city (1991):** Oporto, 350,000. **Monetary units:** Escudo and euro. **Language:** Portuguese. **Ethnicity/race:** Homogeneous Mediterranean stock in mainland, Azores, Madeira Islands; citizens of black African

descent who immigrated to mainland during decolonization number less than 100,000. **Religions:** Roman Catholic 97%, 1% Protestant, 2% other. **Literacy rate:** 85% (1991)
Economic summary: GDP/PPP (1999 est.): $151.4 billion; per capita $15,300. **Real growth rate:** 3.2%. **Inflation:** 2.4%. **Unemployment:** 4.6%. **Arable land:** 26%. **Agriculture:** grain, potatoes, olives, grapes; sheep, cattle, goats, poultry, beef, dairy products. **Labor force:** 4.75 million (1998 est.); services, 60%; industry, 30%; agriculture, 10% (1999 est.). **Industries:** textiles and footwear; wood pulp, paper, and cork; metalworking; oil refining; chemicals; fish canning; wine; tourism. **Natural resources:** fish, forests (cork), tungsten, iron ore, uranium ore, marble, arable land, hydro power. **Exports:** $25 billion (f.o.b., 1998): clothing and footwear, machinery, chemicals, cork and paper products, hides. **Imports:** $34.9 billion (f.o.b., 1998): machinery and transport equipment, chemicals, petroleum, textiles, agricultural products. **Major trading partners:** EU, U.S., Japan.

Geography Portugal occupies the western part of the Iberian Peninsula and is slightly smaller than Indiana. The country is crossed by three large rivers that rise in Spain, flow into the Atlantic, and divide the country into three geographic areas. The Minho River, part of the northern boundary, cuts through a mountainous area that extends south to the vicinity of the Douro River. South of the Douro, the mountains slope to the plains around the Tejo River. The remaining division is the southern one of Alentejo. The Azores stretch over 340 mi (547 km) in the Atlantic, and consist of nine islands with a total area of 902 square mi (2,335 sq km). Madeira, consisting of two inhabited islands, Madeira and Porto Santo, and two groups of uninhabited islands, lies in the Atlantic about 535 mi (861 km) southwest of Lisbon.

Government Republic.

History An early Celtic tribe, the Lusitanians are believed to have been the first inhabitants of Portugal. The Roman Empire conquered the region in about 140 B.C. Toward the end of the Roman Empire, the Visigoths had invaded the entire Iberian peninsula.

Portugal won its independence from Moorish Spain in 1143. King John I (1385–1433) unified his country at the expense of the Castilians and the Moors of Morocco. The expansion of Portugal was brilliantly coordinated by John's son, Prince Henry the Navigator. In 1488, Bartolomeu Dias reached the Cape of Good Hope, proving that Asia was accessible by sea. In 1498, Vasco da Gama reached the west coast of India. By the middle of the 16th century, the Portuguese Empire extended to West and East Africa, Brazil, Persia, Indochina, and Malaya.

In 1581, Philip II of Spain invaded Portugal and held it for 60 years, precipitating a catastrophic decline in Portuguese commerce. Courageous and shrewd explorers, the Portuguese proved to be inefficient and corrupt colonizers. By the time the Portuguese monarchy was restored in 1640, Dutch, English, and French competitors began to seize the lion's share of the world's colonies and commerce. Portugal retained Angola and Mozambique in Africa, and Brazil (until 1822).

The corrupt King Carlos, who ascended the throne in 1889, made Joao Franco the premier with dictatorial power in 1906. In 1908, Carlos and his heir were shot dead on the streets of Lisbon. The new king, Manoel II, was driven from the throne in the revolution of 1910, and Portugal became a French-style republic. Traditionally friendly to Britain, Portugal fought in World War I on the Allied side in Africa as well as on the Western Front. Weak postwar governments and a revolution in 1926 brought Antonio Oliveira Salazar to power. As minister of finance (1928–40) and premier (1932–68), Salazar ruled Portugal as a virtual dictator. He kept Portugal neutral in World War II but gave the Allies naval and air bases after 1943. Portugal joined NATO as a founding member in 1949 but did not gain admission to the United Nations until 1955.

Portugal's foreign and colonial policies met with increasing difficulty both at home and abroad beginning in the 1950s—the bloodiest and most protracted wars against colonialism in Africa were fought against the Portuguese. Portugal lost the tiny remnants of its Indian empire—Goa, Daman, and Diu—to Indian military occupation in 1961, the year an insurrection broke out in Angola. For the next 13 years, Salazar, who died in 1970, and his successor, Marcello Caetano, fought independence movements amid growing world criticism. Leftists in the armed forces, weary of a losing battle, launched a successful revolution on April 25, 1974. After the 1974 revolution, the new military junta gave up its territories, beginning with Portuguese Guinea in Sept. 1974, which became the Republic of Guinea-Bissau. The decolonization of the Cape Verde Islands and Mozambique was effected in July 1975. Angola achieved independence later that same year, thus ending a colonial involvement in that continent that had begun in 1415. Full-scale, internationalized civil war, however, followed Portugal's departure from Angola, and Indonesia forcibly annexed independent East Timor. Also in that year, the government nationalized banking, transport, heavy industries, and the media. Portugal continued to experience social, economic, and political upheavals for the next decade.

Portugal was admitted to the European Economic Community (now European Union) on Jan. 1, 1986, and on Feb. 16, Mario Soares became the country's first civilian president in 60 years. Aníbal Cavaço Silva, an advocate of free-market economics and the Social Democratic candidate, was elected as prime minister in 1985, signaling a more politically stable era. General elections in Oct. 1995 went to the Socialist Party, which fell just short of an absolute majority in the assembly. Lisbon mayor Jorge Sampaio, a Socialist, won the race for president in Jan. 1996. Portugal's Socialist government continued to take advantage of rosy economic conditions in 1997, and in 1999 it became a founding member of the European Economic and Monetary Union (EMU). After Portugal's former territory, East Timor, was plunged into violence when its people voted to separate from Indonesia in Aug. 1999, Portugal was in the forefront of urging the UN to send in an armed, international peacekeeping force to protect the East Timorese from pro-Indonesian militia groups.

Portugal gave up its last colony, Macao, on Dec. 20, 1999, turning the small Asian seaport over to China.

In Jan. 2001 elections, incumbent Jorge Sampaio was reelected with 55.8% of the vote.

Qatar

STATE OF QATAR

Emir: Sheik Hamad bin Khalifa al-Thani (1995)
Prime Minister: Abdullah bin Khalifa al-Thani (1996)
Area: 4,416 sq mi (11,437 sq km)
Population (2001 est.): 769,152 (average annual rate of natural increase: 1.2%); birth rate: 15.9/1000; infant mortality rate: 21.4/1000; density per sq mi: 174
Capital (1990 est.): Doha, 300,000. **Monetary unit:** Qatari riyal. **Languages:** Arabic (official); English is also widely spoken. **Ethnicity/race:** Arab 40%, Pakistani 18%, Indian 18%, Iranian 10%, other 14%. **Religion:** Islam 95%. **Literacy rate:** 76% (1986)
Economic summary: GDP/PPP (1999 est.): $12.3 billion; per capita $17,000. **Real growth rate:** 1.5%. **Inflation:** 2% (1999). **Unemployment:** n.a. **Arable land:** 1%. **Agriculture:** fruits, vegetables; poultry, dairy products, beef; fish. **Labor force:** 233,000 (1993 est.). **Industries:** crude oil production and refining, fertilizers, petrochemicals, steel reinforcing bars, cement. **Natural resources:** petroleum, natural gas, fish. **Exports:** $6.7 billion (f.o.b., 1999 est.): petroleum products 80%, fertilizers, steel. **Imports:** $4.2 billion (f.o.b., 1999 est.): machinery and transport equipment, food, chemicals. **Major trading partners:** Japan, Singapore, South Korea, U.S., UAE, UK, France, Italy.

Geography Qatar (pronounced KA-ter) occupies a small peninsula that extends into the Persian Gulf from the east side of the Arabian Peninsula. Saudi Arabia is to the west and the United Arab Emirates to the south. The country is mainly barren.

Government Traditional monarchy.

History Qatar was once controlled by the sheikhs of Bahrain, but in 1867 broke out between the people and their absentee rulers. To keep the peace in the Gulf, the British installed Muhammad ibn Thani Al Thani, head of a leading Qatari family, as the region's ruler. In 1893, the Ottoman Turks made incursions into Qatar, but the emir successfully deflected them. In 1916, the emir agreed to allow Qatar to become a British protectorate.

Oil was discovered in the 1940s, bringing wealth to the country in the 1950s and 1960s. About 85% of Qatar's income from exports comes from oil. Its people have one of the highest per capita incomes in the world. In 1971, Qatar was to join the other emirates of the Trucial Coast to become part of the United Arab Emirates. But both Qatar and Bahrain decided against the merger and instead became independent nations.

Qatar permitted the international forces to use Qatar as a base during the 1991 Persian Gulf War. A border dispute erupted with Saudi Arabia that was settled in Dec. 1992. A territorial dispute with Bahrain over the Hawar Islands remains unresolved, however. In 1994, Qatar signed a defense pact with the U.S., becoming the third Gulf state to do so.

In June 1995 Crown Prince Hamad bin Khalifa al-Thani deposed his father, primarily because the king was out of step with the country's economic reforms. The emir was not stripped of his title, and much of the power was already in his son's hands. The new emir has lifted press censorship and instituted other liberal reforms, including the first democratic election in its history. Although the 1999 election—for the 29-member municipal council—was a minor election, it involved major political change: women were permitted to vote in the election as well as run for office.

Romania

REPUBLIC OF ROMANIA

President: Ion Iliescu (2000)
Prime Minister: Adrian Nastase (2000)
Area: 91,699 sq mi (237,500 sq km)
Population (2001 est.): 22,364,022 (average annual rate of natural increase: –0.1%); birth rate: 10.8/1000; infant mortality rate: 19.4/1000; density per sq mi: 244
Capital and largest city (1992): Bucharest, 2,351,000.
Largest cities (1992): Constanta, 350,476; Iasi, 342,994; Timisoara, 334,278; Cluj-Napoca, 328,008; Galati, 325,788; Brasov, 323,835. **Monetary unit:** Leu.
Languages: Romanian (official); Hungarian- and German-speaking minorities. **Ethnicity/race:** Romanian 89.1%, Hungarian 8.9%, German 0.4%, Ukrainian, Serb, Croat, Russian, Turk, and Gypsy 1.6%. **Religions:** Romanian Orthodox 70%, Roman Catholic 6% (of which 3% are Uniate), Protestant 6%, unaffiliated 18%. **Literacy rate:** 96% (1992)
Economic summary: GDP/PPP (1999 est.): $87.4 billion; per capita $3,900. **Real growth rate:** –4.8%. **Inflation:** 44%. **Unemployment:** 11%. **Arable land:** 41%. **Agriculture:** wheat, corn, sugar beets, sunflower seed, potatoes, grapes; milk, eggs, beef. **Labor force:** 9.6 million (1998 est.); agriculture, 36.5%; industry, 34.4%; services, 29.1% (1994). **Industries:** mining, timber, construction materials, metallurgy, chemicals, machine building, food processing, petroleum production and refining. **Natural resources:** petroleum (reserves declining), timber, natural gas, coal, iron ore, salt, arable land, hydro power. **Exports:** $8.4 billion (f.o.b., 1999 est.): textiles and footwear, metals and metal products, machinery and equipment, minerals and fuels (1998). **Imports:** $9.6 billion (f.o.b., 1999 est.): machinery and equipment, fuels and minerals, chemicals, textiles and footwear (1998). **Major trading partners:** Italy, Germany, France, U.S.

Geography Romania is in southeast Europe, and is slightly smaller than Oregon. The Carpathian Mountains divide Romania's upper half from north to south and connect near the center of the country with the Transylvanian Alps, running east and west. North and west of these ranges lies the Transylvanian plateau, and to the south and east are the plains of Moldavia and Walachia. In its last 190 mi (306 km), the Danube River flows through Romania only. It enters the Black Sea in northern Dobruja, just south of the border with the Ukraine.

Government Republic.

History Most of Romania was the Roman province of Dacia from about A.D. 100 to 271. From the 3rd to the 12th century, wave after wave of barbarian conquerors overran the native Daco-Roman population. Subjection to the first Bulgarian empire (8th–10th century) brought Eastern Orthodox Christianity to the Romanians. In the 11th century, Transylvania was absorbed into the Hungarian empire. By the 16th century, the main Romanian principalities of Moldavia and Walachia had become satellites within the Ottoman Empire, although they retained much independence. After the Russo-Turkish War of 1828–29, they became Russian protectorates. The nation became a kingdom in 1881 after the Congress of Berlin.

At the start of World War I, Romania proclaimed its neutrality, but later joined the Allied side and in 1916 declared war on the Central Powers. The armistice of Nov. 11, 1918, gave Romania vast territories from Russia and the Austro-Hungarian Empire, doubling its size. The areas acquired included Bessarabia, Transylvania, and Bukovina. The Banat, a Hungarian area, was divided with Yugoslavia. King Carol II was crowned in 1930 and transformed the throne into a royal dictatorship. In 1938, he abolished the democratic constitution of 1923. In 1940, the country was reorganized along Fascist lines, and the Fascist Iron Guard became the nucleus of the new totalitarian party. On June 27, the Soviet Union occupied Bessarabia and northern Bukovina. King Carol II dissolved Parliament, granted the new premier, Ion Antonescu, full power, abdicated his throne, and went into exile.

Romania subsequently signed the Axis Pact on Nov. 23, 1940, and the following June joined in Germany's attack on the Soviet Union, reoccupying Bessarabia. About 270,000 Jews were massacred in Fascist Romania. Following the invasion of Romania by the Red Army in Aug. 1944, King Michael led a coup that ousted the Antonescu government. An armistice with the Soviet Union was signed in Moscow on Sept. 12, 1944. A communist-dominated government bloc won elections in 1946, Michael abdicated on Dec. 30, 1947, and in 1955 Romania joined the Warsaw Treaty Organization and the United Nations.

Running a neo-Stalinist police state from 1967–89, Nicolae Ceausescu wound the iron curtain tightly around Romania, turning a moderately prosperous country into one at the brink of starvation. To repay his $10 billion foreign debt in 1982, he ransacked the Romanian economy of everything that could be exported, leaving the country with desperate shortages of food, fuel, and other essentials. An army-assisted rebellion in Dec. 1989 led to Ceausescu's overthrow, trial, and execution.

An ex-Communist, Ion Iliescu of the National Salvation Front, served as president from 1990–95. Emil Constantinescu of the Democratic Convention Party served as president from 1996–2000. The post-Communist governments' conflicted and half-hearted attempts to change to a free-market economy have been largely unrealized. In 2000 former president Iliescu returned to power with a landslide victory, easily defeating a xenophobic nationalist opponent. Discrimination against the Magyars (ethnic Hungarians), and the Roma (gypsies) continues, fueled by several ultra-nationalist political parties.

The country applied for membership in the EU in June 1995, but it is doubtful that Romania will be able to join the Union before at least 2007. Economic reform has proceeded at a glacial pace, and growing dissatisfaction with the government's inefficiencies and economic policies led to a wave of protests by workers, students, and others that peaked in 1997, and again in 1999, when coal miners striked.

Russia

RUSSIAN FEDERATION

President: Vladimir Putin (2000)
Prime Minister: Mikhail Kasyanov (2000)
Area: 6,592,735 sq mi (17,075,200 sq km)
Population (2001 est.): 145,470,197 (average annual rate of natural increase: –0.5%); birth rate: 9.4/1000; infant mortality rate: 20.1/1000; density per sq mi: 22
Capital and largest city (2000 est.): Moscow, 13,200,000 (metro. area). **Other large cities:** St. Petersburg (2000 est.), 5,550,000 (metro. area); Novosibirsk, 1,418,200; Samara, 1,222,500; Chelyabinsk, 1,124,500; Yekaterinburg, 1,347,000; Nizhny Novgorod, 1,424,600; Kazau, 1,092,300; Perm, 1,086,100; Ufa, 1,091,800; Volgograd, 1,000,400.
Monetary unit: Ruble. **Languages:** Russian, others.
Ethnicity/race: Russian 81.5%, Tatar 3.8%, Ukrainian 3%, Chuvash 1.2%, Bashkir 0.9%, Byelorussian 0.8%,

Moldavian 0.7%, other 8.1%. **Religions:** Russian Orthodox, Muslim, others. **Literacy rate:** 98% (1989) **Economic summary: GDP/PPP** (1999 est.): $620.3 billion; per capita $4,200. **Real growth rate:** 3.2%. **Inflation:** 86%. **Unemployment:** 12.4%, plus considerable underemployment. **Arable land:** 8%. **Agriculture:** grain, sugar beets, sunflower seed, vegetables, fruits; beef, milk. **Labor force:** 66 million (1997); agriculture, 15%; industry, 30%; services, 55% (1999 est.). **Industries:** complete range of mining and extractive industries producing coal, oil, gas, chemicals, and metals; all forms of machine building from rolling mills to high-performance aircraft and space vehicles; shipbuilding; road and rail transportation equipment; communications equipment; agricultural machinery, tractors, and construction equipment; electric power generating and transmitting equipment; medical and scientific instruments; consumer durables, textiles, foodstuffs, handicrafts. **Natural resources:** wide natural resource base including major deposits of oil, natural gas, coal, and many strategic minerals, timber; note: formidable obstacles of climate, terrain, and distance hinder exploitation of natural resources. **Exports:** $75.4 billion (1999 est.): petroleum and petroleum products, natural gas, wood and wood products, metals, chemicals, and a wide variety of civilian and military manufactures. **Imports:** $48.2 billion (1999 est.): machinery and equipment, consumer goods, medicines, meat, grain, sugar, semifinished metal products. **Major trading partners:** Ukraine, Germany, U.S., Belarus, Netherlands, China, Kazakhstan, Italy.

Geography The Russian Federation is the largest republic of the Commonwealth of Independent States. It occupies an area about one and four-fifths of the size of the United States and occupies most of eastern Europe and north Asia. Russia stretches from the Baltic Sea in the west to the Pacific Ocean in the east and from the Arctic Ocean in the north to the Black Sea and the Caucasus, the Altai, and Sayan Mountains, and the Amur and Ussuri Rivers in the south. It is bordered by Norway and Finland in the northwest, Estonia, Latvia, Belarus, and Ukraine in the west, Georgia and Azerbaijan in the southwest, and Kazakhstan, Mongolia, and China along the southern border. The federation is composed of 21 republics.

Government Constitutional republic.

History Tradition says the Viking Rurik came to Russia in 862 and founded the first Russian dynasty in Novgorod. The various tribes were united by the spread of Christianity in the 10th and 11th centuries; Vladimir "the Saint" was converted in 988. During the 11th century, the grand dukes of Kiev held such centralizing power as existed. In 1240, Kiev was destroyed by the Mongols, and the Russian territory was split into numerous smaller dukedoms. Early dukes of Moscow extended their dominion over other Russian cities through their office of tribute collector for the Mongols and because of Moscow's role as an administrative and trade center.

In the late 15th century, Duke Ivan III acquired Novgorod and Tver and threw off the Mongol yoke. Ivan IV, the Terrible (1533–84), first Muscovite czar, is considered to have founded the Russian state. He crushed the power of rival princes and boyars (great landowners), but Russia remained largely medieval until the reign of Peter the Great (1689–1725), grandson of the first Romanov czar, Michael (1613–45). Peter made extensive reforms aimed at westernization and, through his defeat of Charles XII of Sweden at the Battle of Poltava in 1709, he extended Russia's

boundaries to the west. Catherine the Great (1762–96) continued Peter's westernization program and also expanded Russian territory, acquiring the Crimea, Ukraine, and part of Poland. During the reign of Alexander I (1801–25), Napoléon's attempt to subdue Russia was defeated (1812–13), and new territory was gained, including Finland (1809) and Bessarabia (1812). Alexander originated the Holy Alliance, which for a time crushed Europe's rising liberal movement.

Alexander II (1855–81) pushed Russia's borders to the Pacific and into central Asia. Serfdom was abolished in 1861, but heavy restrictions were imposed on the emancipated class. Revolutionary strikes, following Russia's defeat in the war with Japan, forced Nicholas II (1894–1917) to grant a representative national body (Duma), elected by narrowly limited suffrage. It met for the first time in 1906, little influencing Nicholas in his reactionary course.

World War I demonstrated czarist corruption and inefficiency, and only patriotism held the poorly equipped army together for a time. Disorders broke out in Petrograd (renamed Leningrad and now St. Petersburg) in March 1917, and defection of the Petrograd garrison launched the revolution. Nicholas II was forced to abdicate on March 15, 1917, and he and his family were killed by revolutionists on July 16, 1918. A provisional government under the successive premierships of Prince Lvov and a moderate, Alexander Kerensky, lost ground to the radical, or Bolshevik, wing of the Socialist Democratic Labor Party. On Nov. 7, 1917, the Bolshevik Revolution, engineered by N. Lenin[1] and Leon Trotsky, overthrew the Kerensky government and authority was vested in a Council of People's Commissars, with Lenin as premier.

The humiliating Treaty of Brest-Litovsk (March 3, 1918) concluded the war with Germany, but civil war and foreign intervention delayed Communist control of all Russia until 1920. A brief war with Poland in 1920 resulted in Russian defeat.

Emergence of the USSR The Union of Soviet Socialist Republics was established as a federation on Dec. 30, 1922. The death of Lenin on Jan. 21, 1924, precipitated an intraparty struggle between Joseph Stalin, general secretary of the party, and Trotsky, who favored swifter socialization at home and fomentation of revolution abroad. Trotsky was dismissed as commissar of war in 1925 and banished from the Soviet Union in 1929. He was murdered in Mexico City on Aug. 21, 1940, by a political agent. Stalin further consolidated his power by a series of purges in the late 1930s, liquidating prominent party leaders and military officers. Stalin assumed the premiership on May 6, 1941.

Soviet foreign policy, at first friendly toward Germany and antagonistic toward Britain and France and then, after Hitler's rise to power in 1933, becoming anti-Fascist and pro–League of Nations, took an abrupt turn on Aug. 24, 1939, with the signing of a nonaggression pact with Nazi Germany. The next month, Moscow joined in the German attack on Poland, seizing territory later incorporated into the Ukrainian and Belorussian SSRs. The Russo-Finnish War (1939–40) added territory to the Karelian SSR set up on March 31, 1940; the annexation of Bessarabia and Bukovina from Romania became part of the

1. N. Lenin was the pseudonym taken by Vladimir Ilich Ulyanov. It is sometimes given as Nikolai Lenin or V. Lenin.

Rulers of Russia Since 1533

Name	Born	Ruled[1]	Name	Born	Ruled[1]
Ivan IV the Terrible	1530	1533–1584	Alexander II	1818	1855–1881
Theodore I	1557	1584–1598	Alexander III	1845	1881–1894
Boris Godunov	c.1551	1598–1605	Nicholas II	1868	1894–1917[7]
Theodore II	1589	1605–1605	**PROVISIONAL GOVERNMENT (PREMIERS)**		
Demetrius I[2]	?	1605–1606	Prince Georgi Lvov	1861	1917–1917
Basil IV Shuiski	?	1606–1610[3]	Alexander Kerensky	1881	1917–1917
"Time of Troubles"	—	1610–1613	**POLITICAL LEADERS OF USSR**		
Michael Romanov	1596	1613–1645	Vladimir Ilyich Lenin	1870	1917–1924
Alexis I	1629	1645–1676	Aleksei Rykov	1881	1924–1930
Theodore III	1656	1676–1682	Vyacheslav Molotov	1890	1930–1941
Ivan V[4]	1666	1682–1689[5]	Joseph Stalin[8]	1879	1941–1953
Peter I the Great[4]	1672	1682–1725	Georgi M. Malenkov	1902	1953–1955
Catherine I	c.1684	1725–1727	Nikolai A. Bulganin	1895	1955–1958
Peter II	1715	1727–1730	Nikita S. Khrushchev	1894	1958–1964
Anna	1693	1730–1740	Leonid I. Brezhnev	1906	1964–1982
Ivan VI	1740	1740–1741[6]	Yuri V. Andropov	1914	1982–1984
Elizabeth	1709	1741–1762	Konstantin U. Chernenko	1912	1984–1985
Peter III	1728	1762–1762	Mikhail S. Gorbachev	1931	1985–1991
Catherine II the Great	1729	1762–1796	**PRESIDENT OF RUSSIA**		
Paul I	1754	1796–1801	Boris Yeltsin	1931	1991–1999
Alexander I	1777	1801–1825	Vladimir Putin	1952	2000–
Nicholas I	1796	1825–1855			

1. For czars through Nicholas II, year of end of rule is also that of death, unless otherwise indicated. 2. Also known as Pseudo-Demetrius. 3. Died 1612. 4. Ruled jointly until 1689, when Ivan was deposed. 5. Died 1696. 6. Died 1764. 7. Killed 1918. 8. General secretary of Communist Party, 1924–53.

new Moldavian SSR on Aug. 2, 1940; and the annexation of the Baltic republics of Estonia, Latvia, and Lithuania in June 1940 created the 14th, 15th, and 16th Soviet republics. The illegal annexation of the Baltic republics was never acknowledged by the U.S. for the 51 years leading up to Soviet recognition of Estonia, Latvia, and Lithuania's independence on Sept. 6, 1991. The Soviet-German collaboration ended abruptly with a lightning attack by Hitler on June 22, 1941, which seized 500,000 sq mi of Russian territory before Soviet defenses, aided by U.S. and British arms, could halt it. The Soviet resurgence at Stalingrad from Nov. 1942 to Feb. 1943 marked the turning point in a long battle, ending in the final offensive of Jan. 1945. Then, after denouncing a 1941 nonaggression pact with Japan in April 1945, when Allied forces were nearing victory in the Pacific, the Soviet Union declared war on Japan on Aug. 8, 1945, and quickly occupied Manchuria, Karafuto, and the Kuril Islands.

The USSR built a cordon of Communist states running from Poland in the north to Albania and Bulgaria in the south, including East Germany, Czechoslovakia, Hungary, and Romania, which composed the territories the Soviet troops occupied at the war's end. With its eastern front solidified, the Soviet Union launched a political offensive against the non-Communist West, moving first to block the Western access to Berlin. The Western powers countered with an airlift, completed unification of West Germany, and organized the defense of western Europe in the North Atlantic Treaty Organization (NATO). Stalin died on March 6, 1953, and was succeeded the next day by G. M. Malenkov as premier.

The new power in the Kremlin was Nikita S. Khrushchev, first secretary of the party. Khrushchev formalized the eastern European system into a Council for Mutual Economic Assistance (Comecon) and a Warsaw Pact Treaty Organization as a counterweight to NATO. The Soviet Union exploded a hydrogen bomb in 1953, developed an intercontinental ballistic missile by 1957, sent the first satellite into space (Sputnik I) in 1957, and put Yuri Gagarin in the first orbital flight around Earth in 1961. Khrushchev's downfall stemmed from his decision to place Soviet nuclear missiles in Cuba and then, when challenged by the U.S., backing down and removing the weapons. He was also blamed for the ideological break with China after 1963. Khrushchev was forced into retirement on Oct. 15, 1964, and was replaced by Leonid I. Brezhnev as first secretary of the party and Aleksei N. Kosygin as premier.

U.S. president Jimmy Carter and Brezhnev signed the SALT II treaty in Vienna on June 18, 1979, setting ceilings on each nation's arsenal of intercontinental ballistic missiles. The U.S. Senate refused to ratify the treaty because of the invasion of Afghanistan by Soviet troops on Dec. 27, 1979. On Nov. 10, 1982, Soviet radio and television announced the death of Leonid Brezhnev. Yuri V. Andropov, who had formerly headed the KGB, became his successor, but died less than two years later, in Feb. 1984. Konstantin U. Chernenko, a 72-year-old party stalwart who had been close to Brezhnev, succeeded him.

In the months following Chernenko's assumption of power, the Kremlin took on a hostile attitude toward the West of a kind rarely seen since the height of the cold war 30 years before. Led by Moscow, all the Soviet bloc countries except Romania boycotted the 1984 Summer Olympic Games in Los Angeles—tit-for-tat for the U.S.-led boycott of the 1980 Moscow Games, in the view of most observers. After 13 months in office, Chernenko died on March 10, 1985. He had been ill much of the time and left only a minor imprint on Soviet history. Chosen to succeed him as Soviet leader was Mikhail S. Gorbachev, who led the Soviet Union in its long-awaited shift to a new generation of leadership. Unlike his immediate predecessors, Gorbachev did not also assume the title of president but wielded power from the post of party general secretary.

The Soviet Union took much criticism in early 1986 over the April 24 meltdown at the Chernobyl nuclear plant and its reluctance to give out any information on the accident.

In June 1987, Gorbachev obtained the support of the Central Committee for proposals that would loosen some government controls over the economy and in June 1988, an unusually open party conference approved several resolutions reforming the Soviet system. These included a shift of some power from the party to local soviets, and a ten-year limit on the terms of elected government and party officials. Gorbachev was elected president in 1989. The elections to the Duma were the first competitive elections in the Soviet Union since 1917. Dissident candidates won a surprisingly large minority although pro-government deputies maintained a strong lock on the Supreme Soviet.

Dissolution of the USSR The possible beginning of the fragmentation of the Communist Party took place when Boris Yeltsin, leader of the Russian SSR who urged faster reform, left the Communist Party along with other radicals. In March 1991, the Soviet people were asked to vote on a referendum on national unity engineered by Gorbachev. The resultant victory for the federal government was tempered by the separate approval in Russia for the creation of a popularly elected presidency of the Russian republics. The bitter election contest for the Russian presidency, principally between Yeltsin and a Communist loyalist, resulted in a major victory for Yeltsin. He took the oath of office for the new position on July 10, 1991.

Reversing his relative hard-line position, Gorbachev together with leaders of nine Soviet republics signed an accord called the Union Treaty, which was meant to preserve the unity of the nation. In exchange the federal government would have turned over control of industrial and natural resources to the individual republics. An attempted coup d'état took place on Aug. 19, 1991, orchestrated by a group of eight senior officials calling itself the State Committee on the State of Emergency. Boris Yeltsin, barricaded in the Russian Parliament building, defiantly called for a general strike. The next day huge crowds demonstrated in Leningrad, and Yeltsin supporters fortified barricades surrounding the Parliament building. On Aug. 21 the coup committee disbanded, and at least some of its members attempted to flee Moscow. The Soviet Parliament formally reinstated Gorbachev as president. Two days later he resigned from his position as general-secretary of the Communist Party and recommended that its Central Committee be disbanded. On Aug. 29 the Parliament approved the suspension of all Communist Party activities pending an investigation of its role in the failed coup. At the time of the attempted coup, the republic's president, Boris Yeltsin, was the most popular political figure in the former Soviet Union. A leading reformer, he became the first directly elected leader in Russian history and received 60% of the vote for president of the Russian Republic.

Yeltsin championed the cause for national reconstruction and the adoption of a Union Treaty with the other republics to create a free-market economic association. On Dec. 12, 1991, the Russian Parliament ratified Yeltsin's plea to establish a new commonwealth of independent nations open to all former members of the Soviet Union. The new union was created with the governments of Ukraine and Belarus who along with Russia were the three original cofounders of the Soviet Union in 1922. After the end of the Soviet Union, Russia and ten other Soviet republics joined in a Commonwealth of Independent States on Dec. 21, 1991.

At the start of 1992, Russia embarked on a series of dramatic economic reforms, including the freeing of prices on most goods, which led to an immediate downturn. A national referendum on confidence in Yeltsin and his economic program took place in April 1993. To the surprise of many, the president and his shock-therapy program won by a resounding margin. In Sept., Yeltsin dissolved the legislative bodies left over from the Soviet era. The impasse between the executive and the legislature resulted in an armed conflict on Oct. 3. Yeltsin prevailed largely through the support of the military and other forces.

The southern republic of Chechnya's president accelerated his region's drive for independence in 1994. In Dec., Russian troops closed the borders and sought to squelch the independence drive. The Russian military forces met firm and costly resistance. In May 1997, the two-year war formally ended with the signing of a peace treaty that adroitly avoided the issue of Chechen independence.

In March 1998 Yeltsin dismissed his entire government and replaced Prime Minister Viktor Chernomyrdin with the young and little known fuel and energy minister Sergei Kiriyenko. On Aug. 28, 1998, amid the Russian stock market's free fall, the Russian government halted trading of the ruble on international currency markets. This financial crisis led to a long-term economic downturn and to political upheaval. President Boris Yeltsin then sacked Prime Minister Kiriyenko and reappointed Chernomyrdin. The Duma rejected Chernomyrdin and on Sept. 11 elected foreign minister Yevgeny Primakov as prime minister. The repercussions of Russia's financial emergency were felt throughout the Commonwealth of Independent States.

Impatient with Yeltsin's chronic illnesses and increasingly erratic behavior, the Duma attempted to impeach him in May 1999 on five charges: provoking the 1991 fall of the Soviet Union, using force to dissolve the Parliament in 1993, starting the ill-conceived 1994–96 war in Chechnya, ruining the nation's military, and impoverishing the Russian people through ruinous economic policies—the charge regarding Chechnya was considered the only one with a chance of approval. But the impeachment motion was quickly quashed and soon Yeltsin was on the ascendancy again. In keeping with his capricious style, Yeltsin dismissed Prime Minister Yevgeny Primakov and replaced him with Interior Minister Sergei Stepashin. Just three months later, however, Yeltsin ousted Stepashin and replaced him with Vladimir Putin on Aug. 9, 1999, announcing that in addition to serving as prime minister, the former KGB agent was his choice as a successor in the 2000 presidential election.

During the Kosovo crisis, Russia sided with its Slavic allies, the Serbs. Regularly calling for a halt to NATO bombing, Yeltsin seemed almost more upset about his marginal role in the conflict than the fact that Serbia was under attack. Russia regularly claimed to be able to finesse a peace deal with the Serbs, yet little diplomatic progress emerged from their efforts.

Just three years after the bloody 1994–96 Chechen-Russian war ended in devastation and stalemate, the fighting started again in 1999, with Russia launching air strikes and following up with ground troops. By the end of Nov., Russian troops had surrounded Chechnya's capital, Grozny, and about 215,000 Chechen refugees had fled to neighboring Ingushetia.

Russia maintained that a political solution was impossible until Islamic militants in Chechnya had been vanquished. In Dec. 2000 the Kremlin issued an ultimatum that all residents of Grozny must evacuate the city. An estimated 10,000–40,000 civilians were virtually trapped in the city, fearful of fleeing Grozny amid the constant barrage of shelling. The ultimatum was eventually softened, in part because of the West's strong condemnation of Russia's handling of Chechnya. Yet Russians themselves remained overwhelmingly in favor of the assault on Chechnya, demonstrated by the strong showing for the pro-government Unity Party in Dec.'s parliamentary elections.

In 1999, the former Russian satellites of Poland, Hungary, and the Czech Republic joined NATO, raising Russia's hackles. The desire of Lithuania, Latvia, and Estonia, all of which were once part of the Soviet Union, to join the organization in the future has further alarmed Russia.

In a decision that took Russia and the world by surprise, Boris Yeltsin resigned on Dec. 31, 1999, and Vladimir Putin became the acting president. One of Putin's first acts was to grant Yeltsin immunity from prosecution (Yeltsin and family members had been accused of corruption and financial misconduct). On March 26, 2000, Putin won the presidential election with about 53% of the vote. Since then Putin has moved to centralize power in Moscow and has attempted to limit the power and influence of both the regional governors and wealthy business leaders. Although Russia remains economically stagnant, Putin has brought his nation a measure of political stability it never had under the mercurial and erratic Yeltsin.

On Feb. 6, 2000, after almost five months of fighting, Russian troops captured Grozny, the Chechen capital. Although the war continues, the control of Grozny is a political as well as a military victory for Putin, whose hard-line stance against Chechnya has greatly contributed to his political popularity.

In Aug. 2000 the Russian government was severely criticized for its handling of the Kursk disaster, a nuclear submarine accident that left 118 sailors dead.

In June 2001, American president Bush attempted to convince a skeptical Putin that the U.S.'s large-scale plans to build an antimissile shield was a purely defensive measure, and was not directed against Russia. The Bush plan would require the U.S. rejection of the Anti-Ballistic Missile Treaty, signed in 1972 with the Soviet Union, which for 30 years has been viewed as a crucial force in keeping the nuclear arms race at bay. Putin and Bush are to continue negotiations.

Rwanda

RWANDESE REPUBLIC

National name: Republika y'u Rwanda
President: Paul Kagame (2000)
Prime Minister: Bernard Makuza (2000)
Area: 10,169 sq mi (26,338 sq km)
Population (2001 est.): 7,312,756 (average annual rate of natural increase: 1.3%); birth rate: 34.0/1000; infant mortality rate: 118.9/1000; density per sq mi: 719
Capital and largest city (1991): Kigali, 232,733.
Monetary unit: Rwanda franc. **Languages:** Kinyarwanda, French, and English (all official).
Ethnicity/race: Hutu 80%, Tutsi 19%, Twa (Pygmoid) 1%. **Religions:** Roman Catholic 56%, Protestant 18%, Islam 1%, Animist 25%. **Literacy rate:** 50% (1990)
Economic summary: GDP/PPP (1999 est.): $5.9 billion; per capita $720. **Real growth rate:** 5.3%. **Inflation:** 10% (1998). **Unemployment:** n.a. **Arable land:** 35%.

Agriculture: coffee, tea, pyrethrum (insecticide made from chrysanthemums), bananas, beans, sorghum, potatoes; livestock. **Labor force:** 3.6 million; agriculture, 90%; government and services, industry and commerce. **Industries:** cement, agricultural products, small-scale beverages, soap, furniture, shoes, plastic goods, textiles, cigarettes. **Natural resources:** gold, cassiterite (tin ore), wolframite (tungsten ore), methane, hydropower, arable land. **Exports:** $70.8 million (f.o.b., 1999 est.): coffee, tea, hides, tin ore. **Imports:** $242 million (f.o.b., 1999 est.): foodstuffs, machinery and equipment, steel, petroleum products, cement and construction material. **Major trading partners:** Brazil, Germany, Belgium, Pakistan, Spain, Kenya, Tanzania, U.S., Benelux, France.

Geography Rwanda, in east-central Africa, is surrounded by Congo, Uganda, Tanzania, and Burundi. It is slightly smaller than Maryland. Steep mountains and deep valleys cover most of the country. Lake Kivu in the northwest, at an altitude of 4,829 ft (1,472 m) is the highest lake in Africa. Extending north of it are the Virunga Mountains, which include the volcano Karisimbi (14,187 ft; 4,324 m), Rwanda's highest point.

Government Republic.

History The original inhabitants of Rwanda were the Twa, a Pygmy people who now make up only 1% of the population. While the Hutu and Tutsi are often considered to be two separate ethnic groups, scholars point out that they speak the same language, have a history of intermarriage, and share many cultural characteristics. Traditionally, the differences between the two groups were occupational rather than ethnic. Agricultural people were considered Hutu, while the cattle-owning elite were identified as Tutsi. Supposedly Tutsi were tall and thin, while Hutu were short and square, but it is often impossible to tell one from the other. The 1933 requirement by the Belgians that everyone carry an identity card indicating tribal ethnicity as Tutsi or Hutu increased the distinction. Since independence, repeated violence in both Rwanda and Burundi has increased ethnic differentiation between the groups.

Rwanda, which became a part of German East Africa in 1890, was first visited by European explorers in 1854. During World War I, it was occupied in 1916 by Belgian troops. After the war, it became a Belgian League of Nations mandate, along with Burundi, under the name of Ruanda-Urundi. The mandate was made a UN trust territory in 1946. Until the Belgian Congo achieved independence in 1960, Ruanda-Urundi was administered as part of that colony. Belgium at first maintained Tutsi dominance but eventually encouraged power sharing between Hutu and Tutsi. Ethnic tensions led to civil war, forcing many Tutsi into exile. When Ruanda became the independent nation of Rwanda on July 1, 1962, it was under Hutu rule.

In Oct. 1990 rebel Tutsi (RPF) in exile in Uganda invaded. Peace accords were signed in Aug. 1993, calling for a coalition government. After the downing of an aircraft in April 1994 carrying the presidents of Rwanda and Burundi, both of whom died in the crash, deep-seated ethnic hatred erupted, and Hutus slaughtered an estimated 800,000 Tutsi civilians. It is believed that the plane was shot down by Hutu extremists who rejected the Hutu-Tutsi power-sharing plan proposed by President Juvénal Habyarimana, a Hutu moderate. Although the genocidal slaughter seemed a spontaneous eruption of hatred, it has in fact been shown to have been carefully orchestrated by the Hutu government. In response, Tutsi rebels swept across the country in a 14-week civil war, routing the largely Hutu government. In the immediate aftermath an estimated 1.7 million Hutu fled across the border into neighboring Zaire (now the Democratic Republic of the Congo), creating an international humanitarian problem. Although the Tutsi rebel force, the Rwandan Patriotic Front, took control of the government, it permitted a Hutu to serve as president, to deflect accusations of a resurgence in Tutsi elitism and foster national unity. Paul Kagame, the Tutsi rebel leader, became vice president and minister of defense.

Amid the legitimate refugees from the genocide were Hutu militiamen who began waging guerrilla warfare from Zaire. The Hutu guerrillas in Zaire, as well as Zaire's threat to exile their own ethnic Tutsi, led to Rwanda's support of rebel forces bent on overthrowing Mobutu Sese Seko's Zaire. But Rwanda's support for the new regime of Laurent Kabila in the Democratic Republic of the Congo soon turned to disenchantment. The Kabila government was not able to prevent the raids from Hutu guerrillas that continued to traumatize the country and destabilize the region. In Aug. 1998, a little more than a year after Kabila took over, a rebellion began against his reign. Despite their denials, it is believed to have been instigated by Rwanda and Uganda.

Refugee problems, continued massacres, and the scars of genocide continued to haunt the national psyche. In Sept. 1998, a UN tribunal sentenced Jean Kambanda, a former prime minister of Rwanda, to life in prison for his part in the 1994 genocide. He became the first person in history to be convicted for the crime of genocide, first defined in the 1948 Genocide Convention after World War II. By 2001, eight others had also been convicted of the same charge. The UN tribunal, however, has been criticized for its inefficiency and slow pace. In Dec. 1999, an independent report, commissioned by the UN, took Kofi Annan and other UN officials to task for not intervening effectively in the genocide.

In April 2000, President Bizimungu resigned and Vice President Paul Kagame became the first Tutsi president of the nation. It was Kagame's rebel force that seized Rwanda's capital and put an end to the genocide in 1994.

St. Kitts and Nevis

FEDERATION OF ST. KITTS AND NEVIS

Sovereign: Queen Elizabeth II (1952)
Governor-General: Sir Cuthbert Sebastian (1996)
Prime Minister: Denzil Douglas (1995)
Area: St. Kitts 65 sq mi (168 sq km); Nevis 36 sq mi (93 sq km)
Population (2001 est.): 38,756 (average annual rate of natural increase: 1.0%); birth rate: 18.8/1000; infant mortality rate: 16.3/1000; density per sq mi: 385
Capital: Basseterre (on St. Kitts), 19,000. **Largest town on Nevis:** Charlestown, 1,771. **Monetary unit:** East Caribbean dollar. **Ethnicity/race:** black African. **Literacy rate:** 98% (1970)
Economic summary: GDP/PPP (1998 est.): $244 million; per capita $6,000. **Real growth rate:** 1.6%. **Inflation:** 1%. **Unemployment:** 4.5% (1997). **Arable land:** 22%. **Agriculture:** sugarcane, rice, yams, vegetables, bananas; fish. **Labor force:** 18,172 (June 1995). **Industries:** sugar processing, tourism, cotton, salt, copra, clothing, footwear, beverages. **Natural resources:** arable land. **Exports:** $42 million (1998):

machinery, food, electronics, beverages, tobacco. **Imports:** $160 million (1998): machinery, manufactures, food, fuels. **Major trading partners:** U.S., UK, Caricom countries.

Geography St. Kitts and Nevis are related physiographically by a volcanic mountain chain that dominates the central core of both islands. St. Kitts is roughly oval in shape except for a long, narrow peninsula to the southeast. St. Kitts's highest point is Mount Liamuiga (3,792 ft [1,156 m]), which has a lake in its forested crater. The Narrows, a 2-mile- (3-kilometer-) wide channel, separates the two islands. The circularly shaped Nevis is surrounded by coral reefs and the island is almost entirely a single mountain, Nevis Peak (3,232 ft [985 m]).

Government Constitutional monarchy.

History When Christopher Columbus visited the islands in 1493, they were inhabited by the Carib people. St. Kitts, formerly St. Christopher, was settled by the British in 1623; Nevis in 1628. The French settled on St. Kitts in 1627, and an Anglo-French rivalry lasted for more than 100 years. After a decisive British victory over the French at Brimstone Hill in 1782, the islands came under permanent British control. The islands, including nearby Anguilla, were united in 1882. They joined the West Indies federation in 1958 and remained in that association until its dissolution in 1962. St. Kitts-Nevis-Anguilla became an associated state of the United Kingdom in 1967. Anguilla seceded in 1980, and St. Kitts and Nevis became independent on Sept. 19, 1983.

A drop in world sugar prices hurt the nation's economy through the mid-1980s, and the government sought to reduce the islands' dependence on sugar production and to diversify the economy, promoting tourism and financial services. In 1990, the premier of Nevis announced that he intended to seek an end to the federation with St. Kitts by 1992, but a local election in June 1992 postponed the idea. In Aug. 1998, 62% of the population voted for Nevis to secede, but the vote fell short of the two-thirds majority required.

St. Lucia

Sovereign: Queen Elizabeth II (1952)
Governor-General: Pearlette Louisy (1997)
Prime Minister: Kenny D. Anthony (1997)
Area: 239 sq mi (620 sq km)
Population (2001 est.): 158,178 (average annual rate of natural increase: 1.6%); birth rate: 21.8/1000; infant mortality rate: 15.2/1000; density per sq mi: 661
Capital and largest city (1992 est.): Castries, 13,600.
Monetary unit: East Caribbean dollar. **Languages:** English (official) and patois. **Ethnicity/race:** African descent 90.3%, mixed 5.5%, East Indian 3.2%, white 0.8%. **Religions:** Roman Catholic 90%, Protestant 7%, Anglican 3%. **Literacy rate:** 67% (1980)
Economic summary: GDP/PPP (1998 est.): $656 million; per capita $4,300. **Real growth rate:** 2.9%. **Inflation:** 3.7%. **Unemployment:** 15% (1996 est.). **Arable land:** 8%. **Agriculture:** bananas, coconuts, vegetables, citrus, root crops, cocoa. **Labor force:** 43,800; agriculture, 43.4%; services, 38.9%; industry and commerce, 17.7% (1983 est.). **Industries:** clothing, assembly of electronic components, beverages, corrugated cardboard boxes, tourism, lime processing, coconut processing. **Natural resources:** forests, sandy beaches, minerals (pumice), mineral springs, geothermal potential. **Exports:** $75 million (1998): bananas 41%, clothing, cocoa, vegetables, fruits, coconut oil. **Imports:** $290 million (1998): food

23%, manufactured goods 21%, machinery and transportation equipment 19%, chemicals, fuels. **Major trading partners:** UK, U.S., Caricom countries, Japan, Canada. **Member of Commonwealth of Nations**

Geography One of the Windward Islands of the eastern Caribbean, St. Lucia lies just south of Martinique. It is of volcanic origin. A chain of wooded mountains runs from north to south, and from them flow many streams into fertile valleys.

Government Parliamentary democracy. A governor-general represents the sovereign, Queen Elizabeth II.

History The first inhabitants of St. Lucia were the Arawak Indians, who were forced off the island by the Caribs. Explored by Spain and then France, St. Lucia became a British territory in 1814 and one of the Windward Islands in 1871. With other Windward Islands, St. Lucia was granted home rule in 1967 as one of the West Indies Associated States. On Feb. 22, 1979, St. Lucia achieved full independence in ceremonies boycotted by the opposition St. Lucia Labour Party, which had advocated a referendum before cutting ties with Britain. The United Workers Party (UWP), then in power, called for new elections and was defeated by the St. Lucia Labour Party (SLP). The UWP was returned to power in the elections of 1982, 1987, and 1992.

Parliamentary elections in May 1997 gave the opposition St. Lucia Labour Party 16 of the 17 seats. The SLP had stressed economic issues and corruption, but the United Workers Party denied the corruption charges.

The 1999 European Union decision to end its preferential treatment of bananas imported from former colonies has led St. Lucia to try to diversify its agricultural crops.

St. Vincent and The Grenadines

Sovereign: Queen Elizabeth II (1952)
Governor-General: Sir Charles Antrobus (1996)
Prime Minister: Dr. Ralph Gonsalves (2001)
Area: 150 sq mi (389 sq km)
Population (2001 est.): 115,942 (average annual rate of natural increase: 1.2%); birth rate: 17.9/1000; infant mortality rate: 16.6/1000; density per sq mi: 772
Capital and largest city (1992 est.): Kingstown, 15,466.
Monetary unit: East Caribbean dollar. **Languages:** English (official), French patois. **Ethnicity/race:** African descent, white, East Indian, Carib Indian. **Religions:** Anglican 47%, Methodist 28%, Roman Catholic 13%. **Literacy rate:** 96% (1970)
Economic summary: GDP/PPP (1999 est.): $309 million; per capita $2,600. **Real growth rate:** 4%. **Inflation:** 2%. **Unemployment:** 22% (1997 est.). **Arable land:** 10%. **Agriculture:** bananas, coconuts, sweet potatoes, spices; small numbers of cattle, sheep, pigs, goats; fish. **Labor force:** 67,000 (1984 est.); agriculture, 26%; industry, 17%; services, 57% (1980 est.). **Industries:** food processing, cement, furniture, clothing, starch. **Natural resources:** hydropower, cropland. **Exports:** $47.8 million (1998 est.): bananas 39%, eddoes and dasheen (taro), arrowroot starch, tennis racquets. **Imports:** $180 million (1998 est.): foodstuffs, machinery and equipment, chemicals and fertilizers, minerals and fuels. **Major trading partners:** Caricom countries, UK, U.S. **Member of Commonwealth of Nations**

Geography St. Vincent, chief island of the chain, is 18 mi (29 km) long and 11 mi (18 km) wide, and is located 100 mi (161 km) west of Barbados. The island is mountainous and well forested. St. Vincent is dominated by the volcano Mount Soufrière, which rises to 4,048 ft (1,234 m). The Grenadines, a chain of nearly 600 islets with a total area of only 17 sq mi (27 sq km), extend for 60 mi (96 km) between St. Vincent and Grenada. The main islands in the Grenadines are Bequia, Balliceau, Canouan, Mayreau, Mustique, Isle D'Quatre, Petit Saint Vincent, and Union Island.

Government Constitutional monarchy.

History The Carib Indians inhabited St. Vincent before the Europeans arrived, and the island still sports a sizable number of Carib artifacts. Explored by Columbus in 1498, and alternately claimed by Britain and France, St. Vincent became a British colony by the Treaty of Paris in 1763. In 1773, the island was divided between the Caribs and the British, but conflicts between the groups persisted. In 1776, the Caribs revolted and were subdued. Thereafter the British deported most of them to islands in the Gulf of Honduras. Sugarcane cultivation brought thousands of African slaves and, later, Portuguese and East Indian laborers.

The islands belonged to the West Indies Federation from 1958 until its dissolution in 1962, won home rule in 1969 as part of the West Indies Associated States, and achieved full independence Oct. 26, 1979. Prime Minister Milton Cato's government quelled a brief rebellion on Dec. 8, 1979, attributed to economic problems following the eruption of La Soufrière in April 1979 (which had caused the evacuation of the northern two-thirds of the island). The eruption, followed by Hurricane Allen in 1980, seriously damaged the nation's economy, particularly the important banana crop, in the 1980s. But by the 1990s the economy had begun to rebound, and the small tourism industry began to grow. In 1996, St. Vincent and the Grenadines signed agreements with the U.S. that allowed U.S. Coast Guard personnel to pursue suspected drug smugglers into their territorial waters and provided for extradition of criminals. In 1997, the country's permanent representative to the Organization of American States assumed the chairmanship of that body's Permanent Council.

With the 1999 decision by the European Union to end its preferential treatment of bananas imported from former colonies, St. Vincent and the Grenadines has sought to diversify its economy, primarily through expanding tourism. In March 2001 elections, the Unity Labour Party (ULP) won a landslide upset, capturing 12 of the 15 contested parliamentary seats. The incumbent New Democrat Party (NDP) won only three seats. Dr. Ralph Gonsalves, a lawyer, became the new prime minister.

Samoa

INDEPENDENT STATE OF SAMOA

Head of State: Malietoa Tanumafili II (1962)
Prime Minister: Tuilaepa Sailele Malielegaoi (1998)
Area: 1,104 sq mi (2,860 sq km)
Population (2001 est.): 179,058 (average annual growth rate: 0.9%); birth rate: 15.6/1000; infant mortality rate: 31.8/1000; density per sq mi: 162
Capital and largest city (1991): Apia, 32,859.
Monetary unit: Tala. **Languages:** Samoan and English. **Ethnicity/race:** Samoan 92.6%, Euronesians 7% (persons of European and Polynesian blood), Europeans 0.4%. **Religion:** Christian 99.7%. **Literacy rate:** 98% (1971)

Economic summary: GDP/PPP (1998 est.): $485 million; per capita $2,100. **Real growth rate:** 1.8%. **Inflation:** 2.2%. **Unemployment:** n.a. **Arable land:** 19%. **Agriculture:** coconuts, bananas, taro, yams. **Labor force:** 82,500 (1991 est.); agriculture:, 65%; services, 30%; industry, 5% (1995 est.). **Industries:** timber, tourism, food processing, fishing. **Natural resources:** hardwood forests, fish, hydropower. **Exports:** $20.3 million (f.o.b., 1998): coconut oil and cream, copra, fish, beer. **Imports:** $96.6 million (f.o.b., 1998): machinery and equipment, foodstuffs. **Major trading partners:** American Samoa, Australia, New Zealand, U.S., Germany, Japan, Fiji.

Geography Samoa, formerly Western Samoa, is in the South Pacific Ocean about 2,200 mi (3,540 km) south of Hawaii. The larger islands in the Samoan chain, Upolu and Savai'i, are mountainous and of volcanic origin. There is little level land except in the coastal areas, where most cultivation takes place.

Government Constitutional monarchy.

History Polynesians, possibly from Tonga, first settled in the Samoan islands about 1000 B.C. Samoa was explored by Dutch and French traders in the 18th century. Toward the end of the 19th century, conflicting interests of the U.S., Britain, and Germany resulted in an 1899 treaty that recognized the paramount interests of the U.S. in those islands west of 171°W (American Samoa) and Germany's interests in the other islands (Western Samoa).

New Zealand seized Western Samoa from Germany in 1914, and in 1946 it became a UN trust territory administered by New Zealand.

A resistance movement to New Zealand rule, known as the *Mau* ("strongly held view") movement, helped to edge the islands toward independence on Jan. 1, 1962. A constitutional monarchy, Samoa has a legislative assembly whose members are from the *matai*, or titled class.

Barraged regularly by cyclones that have wreaked havoc on the country's primarily agrarian economy, Samoa has begun stepping up its tourism industry—not such a difficult undertaking in this archetypical South Pacific paradise.

A referendum in 1990 gave most women the right to vote for the first time. In 1997, a new constitutional amendment changed the country's name to Samoa.

San Marino

MOST SERENE REPUBLIC OF SAN MARINO
National name: Repubblica di San Marino
Captains Regent: Alberto Cecchetti and Gino Giovagnoli (2001)
Area: 24 sq mi (61 sq km)
Population (2001 est.): 27,336 (average annual growth rate 0.3%); birth rate: 10.8/1000; infant mortality rate: 6.2/1000; density per sq mi: 1,161
Capital and largest city (1992 est.): San Marino, 2,397.
Monetary unit: Italian lira. **Language:** Italian.
Ethnicity/race: Sammarinese, Italian. **Religion:** Roman Catholic. **Literacy rate:** 96% (1976)
Economic summary: GDP/PPP (1997 est.): $500 million; per capita $20,000. **Real growth rate:** n.a. **Inflation:** 2%. **Unemployment:** 3.6% (April 1996). **Arable land:** 17%. **Agriculture:** wheat, grapes, corn, olives; cattle, pigs, horses, beef, cheese, hides. **Labor force:** 15,600 (1995); services, 60%; industry, 38%, agriculture, 2% (1998 est.). **Natural resources:** building stone. **Industries:** tourism, banking, textiles, electronics, ceramics, cement, wine. **Exports:** trade data are included with the statistics for Italy: building

stone, lime, wood, chestnuts, wheat, wine, baked goods, hides, ceramics. **Imports:** trade data are included with the statistics for Italy: wide variety of consumer manufactures, food.

Geography One-tenth the size of New York City, San Marino is surrounded by Italy. It is situated in the Apennines, a little inland from the Adriatic Sea near Rimini.

Government Republic.

History According to tradition, San Marino was founded about A.D. 350 and had the good luck for centuries to stay out of the many wars and feuds on the Italian peninsula. It is the oldest republic in the world. San Marino has survived, completely intact, attacks by other self-governing Italian city-states, the Napoleonic Wars, the unification of Italy, and two world wars. Those born in San Marino remain citizens and can vote no matter where they live. Throughout the 1990s San Marino has taken a more active role in international diplomacy, establishing strong diplomatic and economic ties to a host of other countries.

São Tomé and Príncipe

DEMOCRATIC REPUBLIC OF SÃO TOMÉ AND PRÍNCIPE
President: Fradique de Menezes (2001)
Prime Minister: Guilherme Posser da Costa (1999)
Area: 386 sq mi (1,001 sq km)
Population (2001 est.): 165,034 (average annual growth rate: 3.5%); birth rate: 42.7/1000; infant mortality rate: 49.0/1000; density per sq mi: 427
Capital and largest city (1990 est.): São Tomé, 43,420.
Monetary unit: Dobra. **Language:** Portuguese.
Ethnicity/race: mestico, angolares (descendants of Angolan slaves), forros (descendants of freed slaves), servicais (contract laborers from Angola, Mozambique, and Cape Verde), tongas (children of servicais born on the islands), Europeans (primarily Portuguese).
Religions: Roman Catholic, Evangelical Protestant, Seventh-Day Adventist. **Literacy rate:** 57% (1981)
Economic summary: GDP/PPP (1999 est.): $169 million; per capita $1,100. **Real growth rate:** 1.5%. **Inflation:** 10.5% (yearend 1999 est.). **Unemployment:** 50% in the formal business sector (1998 est.). **Arable land:** 2%. **Agriculture:** cocoa, coconuts, palm kernels, copra, cinnamon, pepper, coffee, bananas, papayas, beans; poultry; fish. **Labor force:** n.a.; population mainly engaged in subsistence agriculture and fishing; note: shortages of skilled workers. **Industries:** light construction, textiles, soap, beer; fish processing; timber. **Natural resources:** fish, hydropower. **Exports:** $4.9 million (f.o.b., 1999 est.): cocoa 90%, copra, coffee, palm oil (1997). **Imports:** $19.5 million (f.o.b., 1999 est.): machinery and electrical equipment, food products, petroleum products. **Major trading partners:** Netherlands, Germany, Portugal, France, Angola, Belgium, Japan.

Geography The tiny volcanic islands of São Tomé and Príncipe lie in the Gulf of Guinea about 150 mi (240 km) off West Africa. São Tomé (about 330 sq mi; 859 sq km) is covered by a dense mountainous jungle, out of which have been carved large plantations. Príncipe (about 40 sq mi; 142 sq km) consists of jagged mountains. Other islands in the republic are Pedras Tinhosas and Rolas. About 95% of the population lives on São Tomé.

Government Republic.

History São Tomé and Príncipe, believed to have been originally uninhabited, were explored by Portuguese navigators in 1471 and settled by the end of the century. Intensive cultivation by slave labor made the islands a major producer of sugar during the 17th century but output declined until the introduction of coffee and cacao in the 19th century brought new prosperity. The island of São Tomé was the world's largest producer of cacao in 1908, and the crop is still the most important. Working conditions for laborers, however, were horrendous, and in 1909 British and German chocolate manufacturers boycotted São Tomé cocoa in protest. An exile liberation movement was formed in 1953 after Portuguese landowners quelled labor riots by killing several hundred African workers.

The Portuguese revolution of 1974 brought the end of the overseas empire, and the new Lisbon government transferred power to the liberation movement on July 12, 1975. A former prime minister and dissident, Miguel Trovoada, was elected president in March 1991 after the withdrawal of the two other candidates.

In April 1995 Príncipe became autonomous. In Aug. a bloodless military coup was reversed through Angolan mediation. In Dec. an agreement was struck on forming a coalition government. President Trovoada won reelection in July 1996 against challenger and former president Manuel Pinto da Costa. Protests erupted in April 1997 when the government, in response to its inability to pay for imported oil, raised gasoline prices 140% in order to stem demand. The center-left government made economic improvement a major goal, including the expansion of agriculture and the exploration of potential offshore oil reserves. Businessman Fradique de Menezes won the presidential election in 2001.

Saudi Arabia

KINGDOM OF SAUDI ARABIA

National name: Al-Mamlaka al-'Arabiya as-Sa'udiya
King and Prime Minister: King Fahd bin 'Abdulaziz (1982)
Area: 756,981 sq mi (1,960,582 sq km)
Population (2001 est.): 22,757,092 (average annual rate of natural increase: 3.1%); birth rate: 37.3/1000; infant mortality rate: 51.3/1000; density per sq mi: 30
Capital: Riyadh. **Largest cities (1993):** Riyadh, 3,000,000; Jeddah, 2,500,000; Makkah (Mecca) (1994 est.), 550,000. **Monetary unit:** Riyal. **Languages:** Arabic, English widely spoken. **Ethnicity/race:** Arab 90%, Afro-Asian 10%. **Religion:** Islam 100%. **Literacy rate:** 62% (1990)
Economic summary: GDP/PPP (1999 est.): $191 billion; per capita $9,000. **Real growth rate:** 1.6%. **Inflation:** –1.2% (1999). **Unemployment:** n.a. **Arable land:** 2%. **Agriculture:** wheat, barley, tomatoes, melons, dates, citrus; mutton, chickens, eggs, milk. **Labor force:** 7 million; note: 35% of the population in the 15–64 age group is non-national (July 1998 est.); agriculture, 12%; industry, 25%; services, 63% (1999 est.). **Industries:** crude oil production, petroleum refining, basic petrochemicals, cement, construction, fertilizer, plastics. **Natural resources:** petroleum, natural gas, iron ore, gold, copper. **Exports:** $48 billion (f.o.b., 1999): petroleum and petroleum products 90%. **Imports:** $28 billion (f.o.b., 1999): machinery and equipment, foodstuffs, chemicals, motor vehicles, textiles. **Major trading partners:** Japan, U.S., South Korea, Singapore, India, France, UK, Germany, Italy.

Geography Saudi Arabia occupies most of the Arabian Peninsula, with the Red Sea and the Gulf of Aqaba to the west, and the Arabian Gulf to the east. Neighboring countries are Jordan, Iraq, Kuwait, Qatar, the United Arab Emirates, the Sultanate of Oman, Yemen, and Bahrain, connected to the Saudi mainland by a causeway. Saudi Arabia contains the world's largest continuous sand desert, the Rub Al-Khali, or Empty Quarter. Its oil region lies primarily in the eastern province along the Arabian Gulf.

Government Saudi Arabia was an absolute monarchy until 1992, at which time the Sa'ud royal family introduced the country's first constitution. The legal system is based on the sharia (Islamic law).

History Saudi Arabia is not only the homeland of the Arab peoples—it is thought that the first Arabs originated on the Arabian peninsula—but the homeland of Islam, the world's second-largest religion. Muhammad founded Islam there, and it is the location of the two holy pilgrimage cities of Mecca and Medina. The Islamic calendar begins in 622, the year of the hegira, or Muhammad's flight from Mecca. A succession of invaders attempted to control the peninsula, but by 1517 the Ottoman Empire dominated, and in the middle of the 18th century, it was divided into separate principalities. In 1745 Muhammad ibn 'Abd al-Wahhab began calling for the purification and reform of Islam, and the Wahhabi movement swept across Arabia. By 1811, Wahhabi leaders had waged a jihad—a holy war—against other forms of Islam on the peninsula, and succeeded in uniting much of it. By 1818, however, the Wahhabis had been driven out of power again by the Ottomans and their Egyptian allies.

The kingdom of Saudi Arabia is almost entirely the creation of King Ibn Saud (1882–1953). A descendant of Wahhabi leaders, he seized Riyadh in 1901 and set himself up as leader of the Arab nationalist movement. By 1906 he had established Wahhabi dominance in Nejd and conquered Hejaz in 1924–25. Hejaz and Nejd were merged to form the kingdom of Saudi Arabia in 1932, which was an absolute monarchy ruled by *sharia,* Islamic law. A year later the region of Asir was incorporated into the kingdom.

Oil was discovered in 1936, and commercial production began during World War II. Its wealth allowed the country to provide free health care and education while not collecting any taxes from its people. Saudi Arabia was neutral until nearly the end of the war, but it was permitted to be a charter member of the United Nations. The country joined the Arab League in 1945 and took part in the 1948–49 war against Israel. Saudi Arabia still does not recognize the state of Israel. On Ibn Saud's death in 1953, his eldest son, Saud, began an 11-year reign marked by an increasing hostility toward the radical Arabism of Egypt's Gamal Abdel Nasser. In 1964, the ailing Saud was deposed and replaced by the premier, Crown Prince Faisal, who gave vocal support but no military help to Egypt in the 1967 Arab-Israeli war.

Faisal's assassination by a deranged kinsman in 1975 shook the Middle East, but it failed to alter his kingdom's course. His successor was his brother, Prince Khalid. Khalid gave influential support to Egypt during negotiations on Israeli withdrawal from the Sinai Desert. King Khalid died of a heart attack in 1982, and was succeeded by his half-brother, Prince Fahd bin 'Abdulaziz, who had exercised the real power throughout Khalid's reign. King Fahd, a pro-Western modernist, chose his 58-year-old half-brother, Abdullah, as crown prince.

Saudi Arabia and the smaller, oil-rich Arab states on the Persian Gulf, fearful that they might become Ayatollah Ruhollah Khomeini's next targets if Iran conquered Iraq, made large financial contributions to the Iraqi war effort during the 1980s. At the same time, cheating by other members of the Organization of Petroleum Exporting Countries (OPEC), competition from nonmember oil producers, and conservation efforts by consuming nations combined to drive down the world price of oil. Saudi Arabia has one-third of all known oil reserves, but falling demand and rising production outside OPEC combined to reduce its oil revenues from $120 billion in 1980 to less than $25 billion in 1985, threatening the country with domestic unrest and undermining its influence in the Gulf area.

At the start of 1996, King Fahd passed authority to Crown Prince Abdullah, saying he needed rest. Although not an abdication, it was unclear how long the king would be absent. In 1998 the country's oil income fell by 40% because of a worldwide decline in prices, and entered its first recession in 6 years.

In 2000, Saudi Arabia, along with other OPEC nations experiencing a recession, decided to reduce production to raise oil prices. In 2001, OPEC cut oil production three additional times.

Senegal

REPUBLIC OF SENEGAL

National name: République du Sénégal
President: Abdoulaye Wade (2000)
Prime Minister: Mame Madior Boye (2001)
Area: 75,749 sq mi (196,190 sq km)
Population (2001 est.): 10,284,929 (average annual rate of natural increase: 2.9%); birth rate: 37.5/1000; infant mortality rate: 56.8/1000; density per sq mi: 136
Capital and largest city (1994 est.): Dakar, 1,729,823.
Monetary unit: Franc CFA. **Languages:** French (official); Wolof, Serer, other ethnic dialects. **Ethnicity/race:** Wolof 36%, Fulani 17%, Serer 17%, Toucouleur 9%, Diola 9%, Mandingo 9%, European and Lebanese 1%, other 2%. **Religions:** Islam 92%, indigenous 6%, Christian 2%. **Literacy rate:** 38% (1990)
Economic summary: GDP/PPP (1999 est.): $16.6 billion; per capita $1,650. **Real growth rate:** 5%. **Inflation:** 2%. **Unemployment:** n.a.; urban youth 40%. **Arable land:** 12%. **Agriculture:** peanuts, millet, corn, sorghum, rice, cotton, tomatoes, green vegetables; cattle, poultry, pigs; fish. **Labor force:** n.a.; agriculture, 60%. **Industries:** agricultural and fish processing, phosphate mining, fertilizer production, petroleum refining, construction materials. **Natural resources:** fish, phosphates, iron ore. **Exports:** $925 million (f.o.b., 1998): fish, ground nuts (peanuts), petroleum products, phosphates, cotton. **Imports:** $1.2 billion (f.o.b., 1998): foods and beverages, consumer goods, capital goods, petroleum products. **Major trading partners:** France, other EU countries, Italy, Côte d'Ivoire, Mali, Nigeria, Cameroon, Algeria, U.S., China, Japan.

Geography   The capital of Senegal, Dakar, is the westernmost point in Africa. The country, slightly smaller than South Dakota, surrounds Gambia on three sides and is bordered on the north by Mauritania, on the east by Mali, and on the south by Guinea and Guinea-Bissau.

Senegal is mainly a low-lying country, with a semi-desert area in the north and northeast and forests in the southwest. The largest rivers include the Senegal in the north and the Casamance in the south tropical climate region.

Government   Multiparty democracy.

History   The Toucouleur people, among the early inhabitants of Senegal, converted to Islam in the 11th century, although their religious beliefs retained strong elements of animism. The Portuguese had some stations on the banks of the Senegal River in the 15th century, and the first French settlement was made at Saint-Louis in 1659. Gorée Island became a major center for the Atlantic slave trade through the 1700s, and millions of Africans were shipped from there to the New World. The British took parts of Senegal at various times, but the French gained possession in 1840 and made it part of French West Africa in 1895. In 1946, together with other parts of French West Africa, Senegal became an overseas territory of France. On June 20, 1960, it became an independent republic federated with Mali, but the federation collapsed within four months.

Although Senegal is neither a large nor a strategically located country, it has nonetheless played a prominent role in African politics since its independence. As a black nation that is more than 90% Muslim, Senegal has been a diplomatic and cultural bridge between the Islamic and black African worlds. Senegal has also maintained closer economic, political, and cultural ties to France than probably any other former French African colony.

Senegal's first president, Léopold Sédar Senghor, towered over the country's political life until his voluntary retirement in 1981. He replaced multiparty democracy with an authoritarian regime. Senghor tried to become both French and African, which he discovered was impossible. As an acclaimed poet, Senghor sought to become a "black-skinned Frenchman," a quest he ultimately rejected. An advocate of "African socialism," Senghor increased government involvement in the economy through a series of Four Year plans.

In 1973 Senegal and six other nations created the West African Economic Community. When rising oil prices and fluctuations in the price of peanuts, a major export crop, ruined the economy in the 1970s, Senghor reversed course. He emphasized new industries such as tourism and fishing. Politically, the so-called passive revolution allowed limited opposition.

When the economy continued to stagnate, and with it Senghor's popularity, he resigned after 20 years at the helm in favor of his protégé, Abdou Diouf, who led the country for the next 20 years, initiated further economic and political liberalization, including the sale of government companies and permitting the existence of political parties. In March 2000, opposition party challenger Abdoulaye Wade won 60% of the vote in multiparty elections. Diouf stepped aside in what was hailed as a rare smooth transition of power in Africa. In Jan. 2001, the Senegalese voted in a new constitution that legalized opposition parties and granted women equal property rights with men.

Serbia and Montenegro

SEE YUGOSLAVIA.

Seychelles

REPUBLIC OF SEYCHELLES

President: France-Albert René (1977)
Area: 176 sq mi (455 sq km)
Population (2001 est.): 79,715 (average annual rate of natural increase: 1.1%); birth rate: 17.7/1000; infant mortality rate: 17.3/1000; density per sq mi: 454
Capital and largest city (1993 est.): Victoria, 25,000.
Monetary unit: Seychelles rupee. **Languages:** English and French (both official), and Seselwa (a creole). **Ethnicity/race:** Seychellois (mixture of Asians, Africans, Europeans). **Religions:** Roman Catholic 90%, Anglican 8%. **Literacy rate:** 58% (1971)
Economic summary: GDP/PPP (1999 est.): $590 million; per capita $7,500. **Real growth rate:** 1.8%. **Inflation:** 3% (1999). **Unemployment:** n.a. **Arable land:** 2%. **Agriculture:** coconuts, cinnamon, vanilla, sweet potatoes, cassava (tapioca), bananas; broiler chickens; tuna fish. **Labor force:** 26,000 (1996); industry, 19%; services, 57%; government, 14%; fishing, agriculture, and forestry, 10% (1989). **Industries:** fishing; tourism; processing of coconuts and vanilla, coir (coconut fiber) rope, boat building, printing, furniture; beverages. **Natural resources:** fish, copra, cinnamon trees. **Exports:** $91 million (f.o.b., 1998): fish, cinnamon bark, copra, petroleum products (reexports). **Imports:** $403 million (c.i.f., 1998): machinery and equipment, foodstuffs, petroleum products. **Major trading partners:** France, UK, Netherlands, Italy, China, Germany, Japan, South Africa, Singapore. **Member of Commonwealth of Nations**

Geography Seychelles consist of an archipelago of about 100 islands in the Indian Ocean northeast of Madagascar. The principal islands are Mahé (55 sq mi; 142 sq km), Praslin (15 sq mi; 38 sq km), and La Digue (4 sq mi; 10 sq km). The Aldabra, Farquhar, and Desroches groups are included in the territory of the republic.

Government Socialist multiparty state.

History The Seychelles were uninhabited when the British East India Company became the first visitors to the archipelago in 1609. Thereafter, they became a favorite pirate haven. The French claimed the islands in 1756 and administered them as part of the colony of Mauritius. The British gained control of the islands through the Treaty of Paris (1814), and changed the islands' name from the French Séchelles to the Anglicized Seychelles.

The islands became self-governing in 1975 and independent on June 29, 1976. They have remained a member of the Commonwealth of Nations. Their first president, James Mancham, was overthrown in 1977 by the prime minister, France-Albert René. At first René created a socialist state with a one-party system, but later he reintroduced a multiparty system as well as various reforms.

To increase revenue the government in 1996 quietly initiated an Economic Citizenship Program that provides foreigners with the opportunity to obtain a Seychelles passport upon payment of $25,000. A new law in late 1995 granted immunity from criminal prosecution to anyone investing $10 million in the country.

In elections held in March 1998, President France-Albert René was reelected with 66.6% of the vote.

In Sept. 2001, President René was reelected for another five years, defeating Wavel Ramkalawan, an Anglican priest.

Sierra Leone

REPUBLIC OF SIERRA LEONE

President: Ahmad Tejan Kabbah (1998)
Area: 27,699 sq mi (71,740 sq km)
Population (2001 est.): 5,426,618 (average annual rate of natural increase: 2.6%); birth rate: 45.1/1000; infant mortality rate: 146.5/1000; density per sq mi: 196
Capital and largest city (1994 est.): Freetown, 1,300,000. **Monetary unit:** Leone. **Languages:** English (official), Mende, Temne, Krio. **Ethnicity/race:** 18 native African tribes 99% (Temne 30%, Mende 30%, other 39%), Creole, European, Lebanese, and Asian 1%. **Religions:** Islam 40%, Christian 35%, Indigenous 20%. **Literacy rate:** 21% (1990)
Economic summary: GDP/PPP (1999 est.): $2.5 billion; per capita $500. **Real growth rate:** –10%. **Inflation:** 30%. **Unemployment:** n.a. **Arable land:** 7%. **Agriculture:** rice, coffee, cocoa, palm kernels, palm oil, peanuts; poultry, cattle, sheep, pigs; fish. **Labor force:** 1.369 million (1981 est.); note: only about 65,000 wage earners (1985). **Industries:** mining (diamonds); small-scale manufacturing (beverages, textiles, cigarettes, footwear); petroleum refining. **Natural resources:** diamonds, titanium ore, bauxite, iron ore, gold, chromite. **Exports:** $41 million (f.o.b., 1998): diamonds, rutile, cocoa, coffee, fish. **Imports:** $166 million (f.o.b., 1998): foodstuffs, machinery and equipment, fuels and lubricants, chemicals. **Major trading partners:** Benelux, Spain, U.S., UK, Côte d'Ivoire. **Member of Commonwealth of Nations**

Geography Sierra Leone, on the Atlantic Ocean in West Africa, is half the size of Illinois. Guinea, in the north and east, and Liberia, in the south, are its neighbors. Mangrove swamps lie along the coast, with wooded hills and a plateau in the interior. The eastern region is mountainous.

Government Constitutional democracy.

History The Bulom people were thought to have been the earliest inhabitants of Sierra Leone, followed by the Mende and Temne peoples in the 15th century, and thereafter the Fulani. The Portuguese were the first Europeans to explore the land and gave Sierra Leone its name, which means "lion mountains." Freetown, on the coast, was ceded to English settlers in 1787 as a home for blacks discharged from the British armed forces and also for runaway slaves who had found asylum in London. In 1808 the coastal area became a British colony, and in 1896 a British protectorate was proclaimed over the hinterland.

Sierra Leone became an independent nation on April 27, 1961. A military coup overthrew the civilian government in 1967, which was in turn replaced by civilian rule a year later. The country declared itself a republic on April 19, 1971.

A coup attempt early in 1971 led to then prime minister Siaka Stevens calling in troops from neighboring Guinea's army who remained for two years. Stevens turned the government into a one-party state under the aegis of the All People's Congress Party in April 1978. In 1992 rebel soldiers overthrew Stevens's successor, Joseph Momoh, calling for a return to a multiparty system. In 1996, another military coup ousted the country's military leader and president. Nevertheless, a multiparty presidential election proceeded in 1996, and People's Party candidate Ahmad Tejan Kabbah won with 59.4% of the vote, becoming Sierra Leone's first democratically elected president.

But a violent military coup ousted President Kabbah's civilian government in May 1997. The leader of the coup, Lieut. Col. Johnny Paul Koroma, assumed the title "Head of the Armed Forces Revolutionary Council" (AFRC). Koroma began a reign of terror, destroying the economy and murdering enemies. The Commonwealth of Nations demanded the reinstatement of Kabbah, and ECOMOG, the Nigerian-led peacekeeping force, intervened. On March 10, 1998, after ten months in exile, Kabbah resumed his rule over Sierra Leone. The ousted junta and other rebel forces continued to wage attacks, many of which included the torture, rape, and brutal maimings of thousands of civilians, including countless children—amputation by machete is the horrific signature of the rebels. In addition to political power, the rebels are after control of Sierra Leone's rich diamond fields.

In Jan. 1999, rebels and Liberian mercenaries stormed the capital, demanding the release of the imprisoned Revolutionary United Front (RUF) leader, Foday Sankoh. ECOMOG regained control of Freetown, but President Kabbah later released Sankoh so he could participate in peace negotiations. Pressured by Nigeria and the U.S., among other countries, Kabbah agreed to an untenable power-sharing agreement in July 1999, which made Sankoh vice president of the country—and in charge of the diamond mines. The accord dissolved in May 2000 after the RUF abducted about 500 UN peacekeepers and attacked Freetown. Sankoh was captured and remains in government custody, where he awaits trial for war crimes.

Gen. Issa Sesay, who has taken over RUF command, signed a cease-fire agreement with the government in Nov. 2000. In Sept. 2001, President Kabbah and Sesay met, declaring an end to the war. About 16,000 fighters from various groups, out of a total of 45,000, had disarmed at that time.

Singapore

REPUBLIC OF SINGAPORE

President: S. R. Nathan (1999)
Prime Minister: Goh Chok Tong (1990)
Area: 250 sq mi (648 sq km)
Population (2001 est.): 4,300,419 (average annual rate of natural increase: 0.9%); birth rate: 12.8/1000; infant mortality rate: 3.6/1000; density per sq mi: 17,188
Capital (1996 est.): Singapore, 3,044,000. **Monetary unit:** Singapore dollar. **Languages:** Malay, Chinese (Mandarin), Tamil, English (all official). **Ethnicity/race:** Chinese 76.4%, Malay 14.9%, Indian 6.4%, other 2.3%. **Religions:** Islam, Christian, Buddhist, Hindu, Taoist. **Literacy rate:** 90% (1990)
Economic summary: GDP/PPP (1999 est.): $98 billion; per capita $27,800. **Real growth rate:** 5.5%. **Inflation:** 0.4% (1999). **Unemployment:** 3.2%. **Arable land:** 2%. **Agriculture:** rubber, copra, fruit, vegetables; poultry, eggs, fish, vegetables, orchids, ornamental fish. **Labor force:** 1.932 million (1998); financial, business, and other services, 38%; manufacturing, 21.6%; commerce, 21.4%; construction, 7%; other, 12%. **Industries:** electronics, financial services, oil drilling equipment, petroleum refining, rubber processing and rubber products, processed food and beverages, ship repair, entrepot trade, biotechnology. **Natural resources:** fish, deepwater ports. **Exports:** $114 billion (1999): machinery and equipment (including electronics) 63%, chemicals, mineral fuels (1998). **Imports:** $111 billion (1999): machinery and equipment 57%, mineral fuels, chemicals, foodstuffs (1998). **Major trading partners:** U.S., Malaysia, Hong Kong, Japan, Taiwan, Thailand, UK, China, Germany, Saudi Arabia. **Member of Commonwealth of Nations**

Geography The Republic of Singapore consists of the main island of Singapore, off the southern tip of the Malay Peninsula between the South China Sea and the Indian Ocean, and 58 nearby islands.

Government Republic.

History Inhabitants of the Malaysian peninsula and the island of Singapore first migrated to the area between 2500 and 1500 B.C. (*see* Malaysia). British and Dutch interest in the region grew with the spice trade, and the trading post of Singapore was founded in 1819 by Sir Stamford Raffles. It was made a separate Crown colony of Britain in 1946, when the former colony of the Straits Settlements was dissolved. The other two settlements on the peninsula—Penang and Malacca—became part of the Union of Malaya, and the small island of Labuan was transferred to North Borneo. The Cocos (or Keeling) Islands and Christmas Island were transferred to Australia in 1955 and in 1958, respectively.

Singapore attained full internal self-government in 1959, and Lee Kwan Yew, an economic visionary with an authoritarian streak, took the helm as prime minister. On Sept. 16, 1963, Singapore joined Malaya, Sabah (North Borneo), and Sarawak in the Federation of Malaysia. It withdrew from the Federation on Aug. 9, 1965, and a month later proclaimed itself a republic.

Under Lee, Singapore developed into one of the cleanest, safest, and most economically prosperous cities in Asia. However, Singapore's strict rules of civil obedience also drew criticism from those who said the nation's prosperity was achieved at the expense of individual freedoms. In 1990, Lee stepped down as prime minister but remained "senior minister" with considerable influence over his successor, Goh Chok Tong, who continued to preside over Singapore through difficult economic times in 1998.

The first direct presidential election took place in Aug. 1993. Ong Teng Cheong faced what initially appeared to be only token opposition but which ultimately took 40% of the vote.

In 1998, Singapore and Malaysia's often-strained relations soured again against the backdrop of the Asian financial crisis. Singaporean leaders accused Malaysia of using a newly built $2.3 billion international airport at Kuala Lumpur to supplant the island nation as a regional air hub.

S. R. Nathan was declared president without an election when he was certified as the only candidate eligible to run in the elections originally scheduled for Aug. 28, 1999.

The country announced in July 2001 that it had slipped into recession, the first time since Asia's 1998 economic meltdown. The Trade and Industry Ministry cited slow growth in the United States as a contributing factor in the country's second consecutive quarterly economic decline.

Slovakia

REPUBLIC OF SLOVAKIA

President: Rudolf Schuster (1999)
Prime Minister: Mikulás Dzurinda (1998)
Area: 18,859 sq mi (48,845 sq km)
Population (2001 est.): 5,414,937 (average annual rate of natural increase: 0.1%); birth rate: 10.1/1000; infant mortality rate: 9.0/1000; density per sq mi: 287
Capital and largest city (1993 est.): Bratislava, 446,600. **Other large city (1993 est.):** Kosice, 237,300. **Monetary unit:** Koruna (SKK). **Languages:**

Slovak (official), Hungarian. **Ethnicity/race:** Slovak 85.7%, Hungarian 10.7%, Gypsy 1.5%, Czech 1%, Ruthenian 0.3%, Ukrainian 0.3%, German 0.1%, Polish 0.1%. **Religions:** Roman Catholic 60.3%, atheist 9.7%, Protestant 8.4%, Orthodox 4.1%, other 17.5%. **Literacy rate:** 99%

Economic summary: GDP/PPP (1999 est.): $45.9 billion; per capita $8,500. **Real growth rate:** 1.9%. **Inflation:** 14%. **Unemployment:** 20%. **Arable land:** 31%. **Agriculture:** grains, potatoes, sugar beets, hops, fruit; pigs, cattle, poultry; forest products. **Labor force:** 3.32 million (1997); industry, 29.3%; agriculture, 8.9%; construction, 8%; transport and communication, 8.2%; services, 45.6% (1994). **Industries:** metal and metal products; food and beverages; electricity, gas, coke, oil, nuclear fuel; chemicals and manmade fibers; machinery; paper and printing; earthenware and ceramics; transport vehicles; textiles; electrical and optical apparatus; rubber products. **Natural resources:** brown coal and lignite; small amounts of iron ore, copper and manganese ore; salt; arable land. **Exports:** $10.1 billion (f.o.b., 1999 est.): machinery and transport equipment; intermediate manufactured goods, miscellaneous manufactured goods; chemicals; raw materials (1998). **Imports:** $11.2 billion (f.o.b., 1999 est.): machinery and transport equipment; intermediate manufactured goods; fuels; chemicals; miscellaneous manufactured goods (1998). **Major trading partners:** EU (Germany 29%, Austria 7%), Czech Republic, Poland, Russia.

Geography Slovakia is located in central Europe. The land has rugged mountains, rich in mineral resources, with vast forests and pastures. The Carpathian Mountains dominate the topography of Slovakia, with lowland areas in the southern region. Slovakia is about twice the size of the state of Maryland.

Government Parliamentary democracy.

History Present-day Slovakia was settled by Slavic Slovaks about the 6th century. They were politically united in the Moravian empire in the 9th century. In 907, the Germans and the Magyars conquered the Moravian state, and the Slovaks fell under Hungarian control from the 10th century up until 1918. When the Hapsburg-ruled empire collapsed in 1918 following World War I, the Slovaks joined the Czech lands of Bohemia, Moravia, and part of Silesia to form the new joint state of Czechoslovakia. In March 1939, Germany occupied Czechoslovakia, established a German "protectorate," and created a puppet state out of Slovakia with Monsignor Josef Tiso as premier. The country was liberated from the Germans by the Soviet army in the spring of 1945, and Slovakia was restored to its prewar status and rejoined to a new Czechoslovakian state.

After the Communist Party took power in Feb. 1948, Slovakia was again subjected to a centralized Czech-dominated government, and antagonism between the two republics developed. On Jan. 1969, the nation became the Slovak Socialist Republic of Czechoslovakia.

Nearly 42 years of Communist rule for Slovakia ended when Vaclav Havel became president of Czechoslovakia in 1989 and democratic political reform began. However, with the demise of Communist power, a strong Slovak nationalist movement resurfaced, and the rival relationship between the two states increased. By the end of 1991, discussions between Slovak and Czech political leaders turned to whether the Czech and Slovak republics should continue to coexist within the federal structure or be divided into two independent states.

After the general election in June 1992, it was decided that two fully independent republics would be created. The Republic of Slovakia came into existence on Jan. 1, 1993. The Parliament in February elected Michal Kovac as president.

Vladimir Meciar, who served three times as Slovakia's prime minister, exhibited increasingly authoritarian behavior, and was cited as the reason Slovakia was eliminated from consideration for both the EU and NATO. A referendum in May 1997 on whether the country should join NATO was boycotted by 90% of the electorate after it turned into a showdown between the prime minister and the president, who wanted a question about direct election of the president placed on the ballot. For more than a year, Slovakia was without a president after Michal Kovac finished his term. Finally, the constitution was changed to allow for direct vote, and Rudolf Schuster was elected in May 1999.

Populist prime minister Meciar was unseated in 1998 elections by the reformist government of Mikulás Dzurinda. Meciar has been blamed for Slovakia's very low influx of foreign capital because of his government's lack of transparency. In April 2000 Meciar was arrested and charged with paying illegal bonuses to his cabinet ministers while in office. A three-week standoff with police preceded the arrest, ending only when masked police commandos blew open the door on Meciar's house and seized him. He was also questioned about his alleged involvement in the 1995 kidnapping of the son of Slovakia's former president, Michal Kovac.

Slovakia has again been invited to apply for EU membership and hopes to become part of NATO as well.

Slovenia

REPUBLIC OF SLOVENIA

President: Milan Kucan (1990)
Prime Minister: Janez Drnovsek (2000)
Area: 7,820 sq mi (20,253 sq km)
Population (2001 est.): 1,930,132 (average annual rate of natural increase: –0.1%); birth rate: 9.3/1000; infant mortality rate: 4.5/1000; density per sq mi: 247
Capital and largest city (1996 est.): Ljubljana, 330,000.
Other large city: Maribor, 103,512. **Monetary unit:** Slovenian tolar. **Languages:** Slovenian; most can also speak Serbo-Croatian. **Ethnicity/race:** Slovene 91%, Serbo-Croation 6%, other 3%. **Religions:** Roman Catholic 70.8% (including 2% Uniate), Lutheran 1%, Muslim 1%, other 27.2%. **Literacy rate:** 99%
Economic summary: GDP/PPP (1999 est.): $21.4 billion; per capita $10,900. **Real growth rate:** 3.5%. **Inflation:** 6.3%. **Unemployment:** 7.1% (1997 est.). **Arable land:** 12%. **Agriculture:** potatoes, hops, wheat, sugar beets, corn, grapes; cattle, sheep, poultry. **Labor force:** 857,400; agriculture, n.a.; industry, n.a.; services, n.a. **Industries:** ferrous metallurgy and rolling mill products, aluminum reduction and rolled products, lead and zinc smelting, electronics (including military electronics), trucks, electric power equipment, wood products, textiles, chemicals, machine tools. **Natural resources:** lignite coal, lead, zinc, mercury, uranium, silver, hydropower. **Exports:** $8.4 billion (f.o.b., 1999): manufactured goods, machinery and transport equipment, chemicals, food (1997). **Imports:** $9.7 billion (f.o.b., 1999): machinery and transport equipment, manufactured goods, chemicals, fuels and lubricants, food (1997). **Major trading partners:** Germany, Italy, Croatia, France, Austria, Hungary, Russia.

Geography   Slovenia occupies an area about the size of the state of Massachusetts. It is largely a mountainous republic and almost half of the land is forested, with hilly plains spread across the central and eastern regions. Mount Triglav, the highest peak, rises to 9,393 ft (2,864 m).

Government   Parliamentary democracy.

History   Slovenia was originally settled by Illyrian and Celtic peoples. It became part of the Roman empire in the first century B.C.

The Slovenes were a south Slavic group that settled in the region during the 6th century A.D. During the 7th century, the Slavs established the Slavic state of Samu, which owed its allegiance to the Avars, who dominated the Hungarian plain until Charlemagne defeated them in the late 8th century.

In the 11th century, Slovenia was a separate province of the kingdom of Hungary. When the Hungarians were defeated by the Turks in 1526, Hungary accepted Austrian Hapsburg rule in order to escape Turkish domination. Thus, Slovenia and Croatia became part of the Austro-Hungarian kingdom when the dual-monarchy was established in 1857. Like Croatia and unlike the other Balkan states, it is primarily Roman Catholic.

Following the defeat and collapse of Austria-Hungary in World War I, Slovenia declared its independence. It formally joined with Montenegro, Serbia, and Croatia on Dec. 4, 1918, to form the new nation called the Kingdom of the Serbs, Croats, and Slovenes. The name was later changed to Yugoslavia in 1929.

During World War II, Germany occupied Yugoslavia, and Slovenia was divided among Germany, Italy, and Hungary. For the duration of the war many Slovenes fought a guerrilla war against the Nazis under the leadership of the Croatian-born Communist resistance leader, Marshal Tito. After the final defeat of the Axis powers in 1945, Slovenia was again made into a republic of the newly established Communist nation of Yugoslavia.

In the 1980s, Slovenia agitated for greater autonomy and occasionally threatened to secede. It introduced a multiparty system and in 1990 elected a non-Communist government. Slovenia declared its independence from Yugoslavia on June 25, 1991. The Serbian-dominated Yugoslavian army tried to keep Slovenia in line and some brief fighting took place, but the army then withdrew its forces. Unlike Croatia and Bosnia, Slovenia was able to sever itself from Yugoslavia with relatively little violence. With recognition of its independence granted by the European Community in 1992, the country began realigning its economy and society toward western Europe.

Slovenia is considered one of the most promising candidates for EU admission and expects to join by 2003. In July 2001, Slovenia and Croatia resolved their border dispute, which had persisted since the two countries gained independence from Yugoslavia in 1991.

Solomon Islands

Sovereign: Queen Elizabeth II (1952)
Governor-General: John Lapli (1999)
Prime Minister: Manasseh Sogavare (2000)
Area: 10,985 sq mi (28,450 sq km)
Population (2001 est.): 480,442 (average annual rate of natural increase: 3.0%); birth rate: 34.1/1000; infant mortality rate: 24.5/1000; density per sq mi: 44
Capital and largest city (1990 est.): Honiara (on Guadalcanal), 35,288. **Monetary unit:** Solomon Islands dollar. **Languages:** English, Solomon Pijin (an English pidgin), over 60 indigenous Melanesian languages. **Ethnicity/race:** Melanesian 93%, Polynesian 4%, Micronesian 1.5%, European 0.8%, Chinese 0.3%, other 0.4%. **Religions:** Anglican, Roman Catholic, South Seas Evangelical, Seventh-Day Adventist, United (Methodist) Church, other Protestant. **Literacy rate:** 30%
Economic summary: GDP/PPP (1999 est.): $1.21 billion; per capita $2,650. **Real growth rate:** 3.5%. **Inflation:** 10%. **Unemployment:** n.a. **Arable land:** 1%. **Agriculture:** cocoa, beans, coconuts, palm kernels, rice, potatoes, vegetables, fruit; cattle, pigs; timber; fish. **Labor force:** 26,842. **Industries:** fish (tuna), mining, timber. **Natural resources:** fish, forests, gold, bauxite, phosphates, lead, zinc, nickel. **Exports:** $142 million (f.o.b., 1998 est.): timber, fish, palm oil, cocoa, copra. **Imports:** $160 million (c.i.f., 1998 est.): plant and equipment, manufactured goods, food and live animals, fuel. **Major trading partners:** Japan, Spain, UK, Thailand, Australia, Singapore, New Zealand, U.S. **Member of British Commonwealth**

Geography   A scattered archipelago of mountainous islands and low-lying coral atolls, the Solomon Islands lie east of Papua New Guinea and northeast of Australia in the south Pacific. The islands include Guadalcanal, Malaita, Santa Isabel, San Cristóbal, Choiseul, New Georgia, the Santa Cruz group, and numerous smaller islands.

Government   Parliamentary monarchy.

History   It is thought that people have lived in the Solomon Islands since at least 2000 B.C. Explored in 1568 by Alvaro de Mendana of Spain, the Solomons were not visited again for about 200 years. In 1886, Great Britain and Germany divided the islands between them, but later Britain was given control of the entire territory. The Japanese invaded the islands in World War II, and they became the scene of some of the bloodiest battles in the Pacific theater, most famously the battle of Guadalcanal. The British gained control of the island again in 1945. In 1976 the islands became self-governing, and gained independence in 1978.

Since early 1999, the Isatabus, natives of Guadalcanal, have expelled more than 20,000 Malaitans from the island. The Malaitans had migrated from nearby Malaita, and many secured jobs in the capital, Honiara, stirring resentment among Isatabus that has grown steadily since independence. Ethnic tensions reached their height in June 2000, when the Malaita Eagle Force stole police weapons, forced Prime Minister Bartholomew Ulufa'alu to resign, and seized control of Honiara. The rival groups agreed to a cease-fire in June 2000, barely averting a civil war. Legislators elected opposition leader Manasseh Sogavare prime minister on June 30, 2000.

Somalia
SOMALI DEMOCRATIC REPUBLIC

National name: Al Jumhouriya As-Somalya al-Dimocradia
President: Abdiqasim Salad Hassan (2000)
Prime Minister: Ali Khalif Galaid (2000)
Area: 246,199 sq mi (637,657 sq km)
Population (2001 est.): 7,488,773 (average annual rate of natural increase: 2.9%); birth rate: 47.2/1000; infant mortality rate: 124.0/1000; density per sq mi: 30

Capital and largest city (1990 est.): Mogadishu, 900,000. **Monetary unit:** Somali shilling. **Languages:** Somali (official), Arabic, English, Italian. **Ethnicity/race:** Somali 85%, Bantu, Arabs. **Religion:** Islam (Sunni). **Literacy rate:** 24% (1990)

Economic summary: GDP/PPP (1999 est.): \$4.3 billion; per capita \$600. **Real growth rate:** n.a. **Inflation:** n.a. **Unemployment:** n.a. **Arable land:** 2%. **Agriculture:** bananas, sorghum, corn, sugarcane, mangoes, sesame seeds, beans; cattle, sheep, goats; fish. **Labor force:** 3.7 million (very few are skilled laborers) (1993 est.); agriculture (mostly pastoral nomadism), 71%; industry and services, 29%. **Industries:** a few small industries, including sugar refining, textiles, petroleum refining (mostly shut down). **Natural resources:** uranium and largely unexploited reserves of iron ore, tin, gypsum, bauxite, copper, salt. **Exports:** \$187 million (f.o.b., 1998 est.): livestock, bananas, hides, fish (1997). **Imports:** \$327 million (f.o.b., 1998 est.): manufactures, petroleum products, foodstuffs, construction materials (1995). **Major trading partners:** Saudi Arabia, UAE, Italy, Yemen, Djibouti, Kenya, Belarus, India, Brazil.

Geography Somalia, situated in the Horn of Africa, lies along the Gulf of Aden and the Indian Ocean. It is bounded by Djibouti in the northwest, Ethiopia in the west, and Kenya in the southwest. In area it is slightly smaller than Texas. Generally arid and barren, Somalia has two chief rivers, the Shebelle and the Juba.

Government Between Jan. 1991 and Aug. 2000, Somalia had no working government. A fragile parliamentary government was formed Aug. 22.

History From the 7th to the 10th century, Arab and Persian trading posts were established along the coast of present-day Somalia. Nomadic tribes occupied the interior, occasionally pushing into Ethiopian territory. In the 16th century, Turkish rule extended to the northern coast, and the Sultans of Zanzibar gained control in the south.

After British occupation of Aden in 1839, the Somali coast became its source of food. The French established a coal mining station in 1862 at the site of Djibouti, and the Italians planted a settlement in Eritrea. Egypt, which for a time claimed Turkish rights in the area, was succeeded by Britain. By 1920, a British protectorate and an Italian protectorate occupied what is now Somalia. The British ruled the entire area after 1941, with Italy returning in 1950 to serve as United Nations trustee for its former territory.

By 1960, Britain and Italy granted independence to their respective sectors, enabling the two to join as the Republic of Somalia on July 1, 1960. Somalia broke diplomatic relations with Britain in 1963 when the British granted the Somali-populated Northern Frontier District of Kenya to the Republic of Kenya.

On Oct. 15, 1969, President Abdi Rashid Ali Shermarke was assassinated and the army seized power, dissolving the legislature and arresting all government leaders. Maj. Gen. Mohamed Siad Barre, as president of a renamed Somali Democratic Republic, leaned heavily toward the USSR. In 1977, Somalia openly backed rebels in the easternmost area of Ethiopia, the Ogaden Desert, which had been seized by Ethiopia at the turn of the century. Somalia acknowledged defeat in an eight-month war against the Ethiopians that year, having lost much of its 32,000-man army and most of its tanks and planes. President Siad Barre fled the country in late Jan. 1991. His departure left Somalia in the hands of a number of clan-based guerrilla groups, none of which trusted each other.

Africa's worst drought occurred in 1992, and coupled with the devastation of civil war, Somalia was plunged into a severe famine—an estimated one-third of the population was in danger of dying from starvation. U.S. troops were sent in to protect the delivery of food in Dec. 1992. In May the UN took control of the relief efforts from the U.S. The warlord Mohamed Farah Aidid ambushed UN troops and dragged American bodies through the streets, causing an about-face in America's willingness to involve itself in the fate of this anarchic country. Peace talks in Kenya appeared to be moving slowly but steadily toward an agreement on an interim government, at least in principle, when on March 23, 1994, they collapsed. The last of the U.S. troops left in late March, leaving 19,000 UN troops behind.

Since 1991 Somalia has been engulfed in anarchy. Years of peace negotiations between the various factions have been fruitless, and warlords and militias rule over individual swathes of land. In 1991, a breakaway nation, the Somaliland Republic, proclaimed its independence. Since then several warlords have set up their own ministates— Colonel Abdullahi Yussuf Ahmed is president of breakaway Puntland, and Mohamed "General Morgan" Said Hersi has ruled Jubaland since the fall of 1998. Although internationally unrecognized, these states have been peaceful and stable.

In Aug. 2000, a parliament convened in nearby Djibouti and elected Somalia's first government in nearly a decade. After its first year in office, the new government still controlled only 10% of the country. But it had made significant advances for a country starting over: a national police force and army are in place, half of the 20,000 militias roaming the country had been demobilized, and general violence has subsided.

South Africa
REPUBLIC OF SOUTH AFRICA

National name: Republic of South Africa
President: Thabo Mbeki (1999)
Area: 471,008 sq mi (1,219,912 sq km)
Population (2001 est.): 43,586,097 (average annual rate of natural increase 0.4%); birth rate: 21.1/1000; infant mortality rate: 60.3/1000; density per sq mi: 93
Administrative capital: Pretoria; **Legislative capital:** Cape Town; **Judicial capital:** Bloemfontein. No decision has been made to relocate the seat of government. South Africa is demarcated into nine provinces, consisting of the Gauteng, Northern Province, Mpumalanga, North West, KwaZulu/Natal, Eastern Cape, Western Cape, Northern Cape, and Free State. Each province has its own capital. **Largest metropolitan areas (1995):** Johannesburg (2000 est.), 5,700,000 (metro. area); Cape Peninsula, 2,350,157; East Rand, 1,378,792 (part of Johannesburg metro. area); Durban/Pinetown, 1,137,378; Pretoria, 1,080,187. **Monetary unit:** Rand.
Languages: Xhosa and Zulu (official), English, Afrikaans, Ndebele, Sesotho sa Leboa, Sesotho, Swati, Xitsonga, Setswana, Tshivenda. **Ethnicity/race:** black 75.2%, white 13.6%, Colored 8.6%, Indian 2.6% (1980)
Religions: Christian; Hindu; Islam. **Literacy rate:** 60% (1980)
Economic summary: GDP/PPP (1999 est.): \$296.1 billion; per capita \$6,900. **Real growth rate:** 0.6%. **Inflation:** 5.5%. **Unemployment:** 30%. **Arable land:**

10%. **Agriculture:** corn, wheat, sugarcane, fruits, vegetables; beef, poultry, mutton, wool, dairy products. **Labor force:** 15 million economically active (1997); agriculture, 30%; industry, 25%; services, 45%. **Industries:** mining (world's largest producer of platinum, gold, chromium), automobile assembly, metalworking, machinery, textile, iron and steel, chemicals, fertilizer, foodstuffs. **Natural resources:** gold, chromium, antimony, coal, iron ore, manganese, nickel, phosphates, tin, uranium, gem diamonds, platinum, copper, vanadium, salt, natural gas. **Exports:** $28 billion (f.o.b., 1999 est.): gold, diamonds, other metals and minerals, machinery and equipment. **Imports:** $26 billion (f.o.b., 1999 est.): machinery, foodstuffs and equipment, chemicals, petroleum products, scientific instruments. **Major trading partners:** UK, Italy, Japan, U.S., Germany.

Geography South Africa, on the continent's southern tip, is bordered by the Atlantic Ocean on the west and by the Indian Ocean on the south and east. Its neighbors are Namibia in the northwest, Zimbabwe and Botswana in the north, and Mozambique and Swaziland in the northeast. The kingdom of Lesotho forms an enclave within the southeast part of South Africa, which occupies an area nearly three times that of California.

The southernmost point of Africa is Cape Agulhas, located in the Western Cape Province about 100 mi (161 km) southeast of the Cape of Good Hope.

Government Republic.

History The San people were the first settlers. The Dutch East India Company landed the first European settlers on the Cape of Good Hope in 1652, launching a colony that by the end of the 18th century numbered only about 15,000. Known as Boers or Afrikaners, speaking a Dutch dialect known as Afrikaans, the settlers as early as 1795 tried to establish an independent republic.

After occupying the Cape Colony in that year, Britain took permanent possession in 1814 at the end of the Napoleonic Wars, bringing in 5,000 settlers. Anglicization of government and the freeing of slaves in 1833 drove about 12,000 Afrikaners to make the "great trek" north and east into African tribal territory, where they established the republics of the Transvaal and the Orange Free State.

The discovery of diamonds in 1867 and gold nine years later brought an influx of "outlanders" into the republics and spurred Cape Colony prime minister Cecil Rhodes to plot annexation. Rhodes's scheme of sparking an "outlander" rebellion, to which an armed party under Leander Starr Jameson would ride to the rescue, misfired in 1895, forcing Rhodes to resign. What British expansionists called the "inevitable" war with the Boers eventually broke out on Oct. 11, 1899. The defeat of the Boers in 1902 led in 1910 to the Union of South Africa, composed of four provinces, the two former republics, and the old Cape and Natal colonies. Louis Botha, a Boer, became the first prime minister. Organized political activity among Africans started with the establishment of the African National Congress in 1912.

Jan Christiaan Smuts brought the nation into World War II on the Allied side against Nationalist opposition, and South Africa became a charter member of the United Nations in 1945, but refused to sign the Universal Declaration of Human Rights. Apartheid—racial separation—dominated domestic politics as the Nationalists gained power and imposed greater restrictions on Bantus, Asians, and Coloreds (in South Africa the term meant any nonwhite person). African voters were removed from the voter rolls in 1936.

Afrikaner hostility to Britain triumphed in 1961 with the declaration on May 31 of the Republic of South Africa and the severing of ties with the Commonwealth. Nationalist prime minister H. F. Verwoerd's government in 1963 asserted the power to restrict the freedom of those who opposed rigid racial laws. Three years later, amid increasing racial tension and criticism from the outside world, Verwoerd was assassinated. His Nationalist successor, Balthazar J. Vorster, launched a campaign of conciliation toward conservative black African states, offering development loans and trade concessions.

Elections on May 7, 1987, increased the power of President P. W. Botha's Nationalist Party while enabling the far-right Conservative Party to replace the liberal Progressives as the official opposition. The results of the whites-only vote indicated a strong conservative reaction against Botha's policy of limited reform.

A stroke led Botha to step down as leader of his party in 1989 in favor of F. W. de Klerk. De Klerk accelerated the pace of reform. He removed the ban from the African National Congress, the principal anti-apartheid organization, and released Nelson Mandela, the ANC deputy president, after 27 years of imprisonment. Negotiations between the government and the ANC commenced.

On June 5, 1991, the Parliament scrapped the country's apartheid laws concerning property ownership. On June 17 the Parliament did the same for the Population Registration Act of 1950, which classified all South Africans at birth by race. In Feb. 1993 the ANC approved a plan that would allow minority parties to participate in the government for five years after the end of white rule. Also in February, the first nonwhites entered the cabinet in an apparent bid to broaden the base of the ruling National Party.

The 1994 election, as expected, resulted in a massive victory for Mandela and his ANC. The new government included six ministers from the National Party and three from the Inkatha Freedom Party.

In 1997 the Truth and Reconciliation Commission, chaired by Desmond Tutu, began hearings regarding human rights violations between 1960 and 1993. The commission promised amnesty to those who confessed their crimes under the apartheid system. In 1998 F. W. de Klerk, P. W. Botha, and leaders of the ANC appeared before the commission, and the nation continued to grapple with its enlightened but often painful and divisive process of national recovery.

Nelson Mandela, whose term as president cemented his reputation as one of the world's most enlightened statesmen, retired in 1999. On June 2, 1999, Thabo Mbeki, the pragmatic deputy president of South Africa and leader of the African National Congress, was elected president in a landslide, having already assumed many of Mandela's governing responsibilities.

Spain

KINGDOM OF SPAIN

National name: Reino de España
Ruler: King Juan Carlos I (1975)
Prime Minister: José María Aznar (1996)
Area: 194,896 sq mi (504,782 sq km)[1]
Population (2001 est.): 40,037,995 (average annual growth rate: 0.01%); birth rate: 9.3/1000; infant mortality rate: 4.9/1000; density per sq mi: 205

Capital and largest city (2000 est.): Madrid, 5,050,000 (metro. area). **Other large cities:** Barcelona, 1,630,867; Valencia, 764,293; Seville, 714,148. **Monetary units:** Peseta and euro. **Languages:** Castilian Spanish 74% (official), Catalan 17%, Galician 7%, Basque 2%. **Ethnicity/race:** composite of Mediterranean and Nordic types. **Religion:** Roman Catholic 99%. **Literacy rate:** 95% (1991)
Economic summary: GDP/PPP (1999 est.): $677.5 billion; per capita $17,300. **Real growth rate:** 3.6%. **Inflation:** 2.3%. **Unemployment:** 16%. **Arable land:** 30%. **Agriculture:** grain, vegetables, olives, wine grapes, sugar beets, citrus; beef, pork, poultry, dairy products; fish. **Labor force:** 16.2 million (1997 est.); services, 64%; manufacturing, mining, and construction, 28%; agriculture, 8% (1997 est.).
Industries: textiles and apparel (including footwear), food and beverages, metals and metal manufactures, chemicals, shipbuilding, automobiles, machine tools, tourism. **Natural resources:** coal, lignite, iron ore, uranium, mercury, pyrites, fluorspar, gypsum, zinc, lead, tungsten, copper, kaolin, potash, hydropower, arable land. **Exports:** $112.3 billion (f.o.b., 1999 est.): machinery, motor vehicles; foodstuffs, other consumer goods. **Imports:** $137.5 billion (f.o.b., 1999 est.): machinery and equipment, fuels, chemicals, semifinished goods; foodstuffs, consumer goods (1997). **Major trading partners:** EU, Latin America, U.S., OPEC, Japan.

1. Including the Balearic and Canary Islands.

Geography Spain occupies 85% of the Iberian Peninsula, which it shares with Portugal, in southwest Europe. Africa is less than 10 mi (16 km) south at the Strait of Gibraltar. A broad central plateau slopes to the south and east, crossed by a series of mountain ranges and river valleys. Principal rivers are the Ebro in the northeast, the Tajo in the central region, and the Guadalquivir in the south. Off Spain's east coast in the Mediterranean are the Balearic Islands (1,936 sq mi; 5,014 sq km), the largest of which is Majorca. Sixty mi (97 km) west of Africa are the Canary Islands (2,808 sq mi; 7,273 sq km).

Government Parliamentary monarchy.

History Spain, originally inhabited by Celts, Iberians, and Basques, became a part of the Roman Empire in 206 B.C., when it was conquered by Scipio Africanus. In A.D. 412, the barbarian Visigothic leader Ataulf crossed the Pyrenees and ruled Spain, first in the name of the Roman emperor and then independently. In 711, the Muslims under Tariq entered Spain from Africa and within a few years completed the subjugation of the country. In 732, the Franks, led by Charles Martel, defeated the Muslims near Poitiers, thus preventing the further expansion of Islam in southern Europe. Internal dissension of Spanish Islam invited a steady Christian conquest from the north.

Aragon and Castile were the most important Spanish states from the 12th to the 15th century, consolidated by the marriage of Ferdinand II and Isabella I in 1469. The last Muslim stronghold, Granada, was captured in 1492. Roman Catholicism was established as the official state religion and most Jews (1492) and Muslims (1502) were expelled. In the era of exploration, discovery, and colonization, Spain amassed tremendous wealth and a vast colonial empire through the conquest of Peru by Pizarro (1532–33) and of Mexico by Cortés (1519–21). The Spanish Hapsburg monarchy became for a time the most powerful in the world. In 1588, Philip II sent his invincible Armada to invade England, but its destruction cost Spain its supremacy on the seas and paved the way for

England's colonization of America. Spain then sank rapidly to the status of a second-rate power under the rule of weak Hapsburg kings, and never again played a major role in European politics. The War of the Spanish Succession (1701–14) resulted in Spain's loss of Belgium, Luxembourg, Milan, Sardinia, and Naples. Its colonial empire in the Americas and the Philippines vanished in wars and revolutions during the 18th and 19th centuries.

In World War I, Spain maintained a position of neutrality. In 1923, Gen. Miguel Primo de Rivera became dictator. In 1930, King Alfonso XIII revoked the dictatorship, but a strong antimonarchist and republican movement led to his leaving Spain in 1931. The new constitution declared Spain a workers' republic, broke up the large estates, separated church and state, and secularized the schools. The elections held in 1936 returned a strong Popular Front majority, with Manuel Azaña as president.

On July 18, 1936, a conservative army officer in Morocco, Francisco Franco Bahamonde, led a mutiny against the government. The civil war that followed lasted three years and cost the lives of nearly a million people. Franco was aided by Fascist Italy and Nazi Germany, while Soviet Russia helped the Loyalist side. Several hundred leftist Americans served in the Abraham Lincoln Brigade on the side of the republic. The war ended when Franco took Madrid on March 28, 1939. Franco became head of the state, national chief of the Falange Party (the governing party), and premier and caudillo (leader). In a referendum in 1947, the Spanish people approved a Franco-drafted succession law declaring Spain a monarchy again. Franco, however, continued as chief of state.

In 1969, Franco and the Cortes designated Prince Juan Carlos Alfonso Victor María de Borbón (who married Princess Sophia of Greece on May 14, 1962) to become king of Spain when the provisional government headed by Franco came to an end. Franco died of a heart attack on Nov. 20, 1975, after more than a year of ill health, and Juan Carlos was proclaimed king seven days later.

Under pressure from Catalonian and Basque nationalists, Premier Adolfo Suárez granted home rule to these regions in 1979. Basque separatists committed hundreds of terrorist bombings and kidnappings that continue to the present. With the overwhelming election of Prime Minister Felipe González Márquez and his Spanish Socialist Workers Party in the Oct. 20, 1982, parliamentary elections, the Franco past was finally buried.

Spain entered NATO in 1982. A treaty admitting Spain, along with Portugal, to the European Economic Community, now the European Union, took effect on Jan. 1, 1986. Later that year, Spain voted to remain in NATO but outside of its military command. General elections in March 1996 produced a victory for the conservative Popular Party, which, although lacking an absolute majority in the Cortes, received the backing of regional parties for a coalition government with José María Aznar as prime minister.

On Oct. 16, 1998, Spain issued a warrant for the extradition of former Chilean dictator Augusto Pinochet, charging him with the genocide, torture, and kidnapping of thousands of people, including Spanish nationals, during his 17-year rule. Eventually, Pinochet was returned to Chile where he was deemed unfit to stand trial.

In March 2000, Prime Minister Aznar of the center-right People's Party easily won reelection.

Sri Lanka

DEMOCRATIC SOCIALIST REPUBLIC OF SRI LANKA

President: Chandrika B. Kumaratunga (1994)
Prime Minister: Ratnasiri Wickremanayake (2000)
Area: 25,332 sq mi (65,610 sq km)
Population (2001 est.): 19,408,635 (average annual rate of natural increase: 1.0%); birth rate: 16.6/1000; infant mortality rate: 16.1/1000; density per sq mi: 766
Capitals and largest city (1992 est.): Colombo (official) 1,994,000; Sri Jayawardenepura Kotte (legislative and judicial), 107,000 (1988 est.). **Other large cities (1992 est.):** Gampaha, 1,543,000; Kurunegala, 1,445,000; Kandy, 1,257,000. **Monetary unit:** Sri Lanka rupee.
Languages: Sinhala (official), Tamil, English.
Ethnicity/race: Sinhalese 74%, Tamil 18%, Moor 7%, Burgher, Malay, and Vedda 1%. **Religions:** Buddhist 69%, Hindu 15%, Islam 8%, Christian 8%. **Literacy rate:** 88% (1990)
Economic summary: GDP/PPP (1999 est.): $50.5 billion; per capita $2,600. **Real growth rate:** 3.7%. **Inflation:** 6%. **Unemployment:** 9.5% (1998 est.). **Arable land:** 14%. **Agriculture:** rice, sugarcane, grains, pulses, oilseed, spices, tea, rubber, coconuts; milk, eggs, hides, beef. **Labor force:** 6.6 million (1998); services, 45%; agriculture, 38%; industry, 17% (1998 est.). **Industries:** processing of rubber, tea, coconuts, and other agricultural commodities; clothing, cement, petroleum refining, textiles, tobacco. **Natural resources:** limestone, graphite, mineral sands, gems, phosphates, clay, hydropower. **Exports:** $4.7 billion (f.o.b., 1998): textiles and apparel, tea, diamonds, coconut products, petroleum products. **Imports:** $5.3 billion (f.o.b., 1998): machinery and equipment, textiles, petroleum, foodstuffs. **Major trading partners:** U.S., UK, Middle East, Germany, Japan, India, South Korea, Hong Kong, Taiwan. **Member of Commonwealth of Nations**

Geography An island in the Indian Ocean off the southeast tip of India, Sri Lanka is about half the size of Alabama. Most of the land is flat and rolling; mountains in the south-central region rise to over 8,000 ft (2,438 m).

Government Republic.

History Indo-Aryan emigration from India in the 5th century B.C. came to form the largest ethnic group on Sri Lanka today, the Sinhalese. Tamils, the second-largest ethnic group on the island, were originally from the Tamil region of India, and emigrated between the 3rd century B.C. and A.D. 1200. Until colonial powers controlled Ceylon (the country's name until 1972), Sinhalese and Tamil rulers fought for dominance over the island. The Tamils, primarily Hindus, claimed the northern section of the island and the Sinhalese, who are predominantly Buddhist, controlled the south. In 1505 the Portuguese took possession of Ceylon until the Dutch India Company usurped control (1658–1796). The British took over in 1796, and Ceylon became an English Crown colony in 1802. The British developed coffee, tea, and rubber plantations. On Feb. 4, 1948, after pressure from Ceylonese nationalist leaders (which briefly unified the Tamil and Sinhalese), Ceylon became a self-governing dominion of the Commonwealth of Nations.

S. W. R. D. Bandaranaike became prime minister in 1956 and championed Sinhalese nationalism, making Sinhala the country's only official language and including state support of Buddhism, further marginalizing the Tamil minority. He was assassinated in 1959 by a Buddhist monk. His widow, Sirimavo Bandaranaike, became the world's first female prime minister in 1960. The name *Ceylon* was changed to Sri Lanka on May 22, 1972, which was its original name and means "resplendent island."

The Tamil minority's mounting resentment toward the Sinhalese majority's monopoly on political and economic power, exacerbated by cultural and religious differences, erupted in bloody violence in 1983. The civil war continues today. Tamils make up about 18% of the population in Sri Lanka, whereas approximately three-quarters of Sri Lanka's 18 million people are Sinhalese. Tamil rebel groups, the strongest of which are the Liberation Tigers of Tamil Eelam, or Tamil Tigers, are fighting for a separate nation.

India had sent a peacekeeping force in July 1987 to help maintain an accord granting the Tamil minority limited autonomy. The agreement failed, and Indian troops withdrew at the end of 1989.

President Ranasinghe Premadasa was assassinated at a May Day political rally in 1993, when a Tamil rebel detonated explosives strapped to himself. Tamil extremists have frequently resorted to terrorist attacks against civilians and are renowned for suicide bombers that target government officials. President Kumaratunga was reelected in Dec. 1999, three days after she was wounded by such an attack.

By early 2000, 18 years of war had claimed the lives of more than 64,000, mostly civilians. After routing several military bases at the threshold to the peninsula and closing in on their goal to reclaim Jaffna as their cultural homeland, the Tigers proposed a cease-fire in exchange for the evacuation of government troops from Jaffna. President Kumaratunga refused, despite the possibility of stranding thousands of troops there.

In Aug. 2000, lacking the support of a two-thirds majority in Parliament, Kumaratunga withdrew plans to push through Parliament a new constitution that she hoped would end the protracted civil war by giving broader autonomy to the minority Hindu Tamils.

After her coalition lost control of Parliament in June 2001, President Kumaratunga suspended Parliament for two months and ordered a national referendum on a new constitution. The move was widely viewed as an attempt to block a no-confidence vote against her government. Days later, a group of Tamil Tigers suicide bombers attacked Bandaranaike International Airport and a nearby air force base, destroying or damaging 14 passenger and military planes. Casualties included 14 rebels and 7 soldiers.

Sudan

REPUBLIC OF THE SUDAN

National name: Jamhuryat es-Sudan
President: Lt. Gen. Omar Hassan Ahmad al-Bashir (1993)
Area: 967,493 sq mi (2,505,810 sq km)
Population (2001 est.): 36,080,373 (average annual rate of natural increase: 2.8%); birth rate: 37.9/1000; infant mortality rate: 68.7/1000; density per sq mi: 37
Capital (1993 est.): Khartoum, 924,505. **Largest cities:** Omdurman, 1,267,077; Port Sudan, 305,385.
Monetary unit: Sudanese pound. **Languages:** Arabic (official), English, tribal dialects. **Ethnicity/race:** black 52%, Arab 39%, Beja 6%, foreigners 2%, other 1%. **Religions:** Islam (Sunni) 70%, indigenous 20%, Christian 5%. **Literacy rate:** 27% (1990)
Economic summary: GDP/PPP (1999 est.): $32.6 billion; per capita $940. **Real growth rate:** 3%. **Inflation:** 20%. **Unemployment:** 30% (FY92/93 est.). **Arable land:** 5%. **Agriculture:** cotton, groundnuts

(peanuts), sorghum, millet, wheat, gum arabic, sesame; sheep. **Labor force:** 11 million (1996 est.); note: labor shortages for almost all categories of skilled employment (1983 est.); agriculture, 80%; industry and commerce, 10%; government, 6%; unemployed, 4%. **Industries:** cotton ginning, textiles, cement, edible oils, sugar, soap distilling, shoes, petroleum refining. **Natural resources:** petroleum; small reserves of iron ore, copper, chromium ore, zinc, tungsten, mica, silver, gold, hydropower. **Exports:** $580 million (f.o.b., 1999 est.): cotton, sesame, livestock, groundnuts, oil, gum arabic. **Imports:** $1.4 billion (c.i.f., 1999 est.): foodstuffs, petroleum products, manufactured goods, machinery and transport equipment, medicines and chemicals, textiles. **Major trading partners:** Saudi Arabia, Italy, Germany, Egypt, France, Japan, China, UK, Netherlands, Canada.

Geography The Sudan, in northeast Africa, is the largest country on the continent, measuring about one-fourth the size of the United States. Its neighbors are Chad and the Central African Republic on the west, Egypt and Libya on the north, Ethiopia and Eritrea on the east, and Kenya, Uganda, and Democratic Republic of the Congo on the south. The Red Sea washes about 500 mi of the eastern coast. It is traversed from north to south by the Nile.

Government Military government.

History What is now northern Sudan was in ancient times the kingdom of Nubia, which came under Egyptian rule after 2600 B.C. An Egyptian and Nubian civilization called Kush flourished until A.D. 350. Missionaries converted the region to Christianity in the 6th century, but an influx of Muslim Arabs, who had already conquered Egypt, eventually controlled the area and replaced Christianity with Islam. During the 1500s a people called the Funj conquered much of Sudan, and several other black African groups settled in the south, including the Dinka, Shilluk, Nuer, and Azande. Egyptians again conquered the Sudan in 1874, and after Britain occupied Egypt in 1882, it took over Sudan in 1898, ruling the country in conjunction with Egypt. It was known as the Anglo-Egyptian Sudan between 1898 and 1955.

The 20th century saw the growth of Sudanese nationalism, and in 1953 Egypt and Britain granted the Sudan self-government. Independence was proclaimed on Jan. 1, 1956. Since independence, the Sudan has been ruled by a series of unstable parliamentary governments and military regimes. Under Maj. Gen. Gaafar Mohamed Nimeiri, the Sudan instituted fundamentalist Islamic law in 1983. This exacerbated the rift between the Arab North, the seat of the government, and the black African animists and Christians in the South. Differences in language, religion, ethnicity, and political power erupted in an unending civil war between government forces, strongly influenced by the National Islamic Front (NIF), and the southern rebels, whose most influential faction is the Sudanese People's Liberation Army. Neither side has gained the upper hand, and more than an estimated 1 million people have died in battle or from famines and disease resulting from war. Human rights violations, religious persecution, and allegations that the Sudan has been a safe haven for terrorists have isolated the country from most of the international community. In 1995, the UN imposed sanctions against it.

On Aug. 20, 1998, the United States launched cruise missiles that destroyed a pharmaceutical manufacturing facility in Khartoum that allegedly manufactured chemical weapons. Sudan has close ties with Iraq, which has thwarted the UN inspections of its weapons stockpiles that are thought to include biological weapons. The U.S. contended that the Sudanese factory was financed by the wealthy Islamic militant, Osama bin Laden.

Since 1999 international attention has been focused on evidence that slavery is widespread throughout Sudan. Arab raiders from the north of the country have enslaved thousands of southerners, who are black. The Dinka people have been the hardest hit. Some sources point out that the raids intensified in the 1980s along with the civil war between north and south. Since the early 1990s, several international human rights organizations have engaged in the controversial practice of buying back slaves from the traders. Some contend this may inadvertently encourage slavery since slave redemption has become profitable. The antislavery organizations counter that in the absence of a political solution, buying back slaves is the only hope for thousands of Sudanese.

Ever since Bashir's military coup in 1989, the de facto ruler of Sudan had been Hassan el-Turabi, a cleric and political leader who is a major figure in the pan-Arabic Islamic fundamentalist resurgence. In 1999, however, Bashir ousted Turabi and placed him under house arrest. Since then Bashir has made overtures to the West, and in Sept. 2001, the UN lifted its five-year-old sanctions. The U.S., however, still officially considers it a terrorist state.

Suriname

REPUBLIC OF SURINAME

President: Ronald Venetiaan (2000)
Prime Minister: Jules Ajodhia (2000)
Area: 63,039 sq mi (163,270 sq km)
Population (2001 est.): 433,998 (average annual rate of natural increase: 1.5%); birth rate: 20.5/1000; infant mortality rate: 24.3/1000; density per sq mi: 7
Capital and largest city (1993 est.): Paramaribo, 200,970. **Monetary unit:** Suriname guilder.
  Languages: Dutch (official), Surinamese (lingua franca), English widely spoken. **Ethnicity/race:** Hindustani (also known locally as "East" Indians; their ancestors emigrated from northern India in the latter part of the 19th century) 37%, Creole (mixed European and African ancestry) 31%, Javanese 15.3%, "Bush Black" (also known as "Bush Creole," whose ancestors were brought to the country in the 17th and 18th centuries as slaves) 10.3%, Amerindian 2.6%, Chinese 1.7%, Europeans 1%, other 1.1%. **Religions:** Protestant 25.2%, Roman Catholic 22.8%, Hindu 27.4%, Islam 19.6%, indigenous about 5%. **Literacy rate:** 95% (1990)
Economic summary: GDP/PPP (1999 est.): $1.48 billion; per capita $3,400. **Real growth rate:** –1%. **Inflation:** 170%. **Unemployment:** 20% (1997). **Arable land:** 0%. **Agriculture:** paddy rice, bananas, palm kernels, coconuts, plantains, peanuts; beef, chickens; forest products; shrimp. **Labor force:** 100,000. **Industries:** bauxite and gold mining, alumina and aluminum production, lumbering, food processing, fishing. **Natural resources:** timber, hydropower, fish, kaolin, shrimp, bauxite, gold, and small amounts of nickel, copper, platinum, iron ore. **Exports:** $406.1 million (f.o.b., 1998): alumina, aluminum, crude oil, lumber, shrimp and fish, rice, bananas. **Imports:** $461.4 million (f.o.b., 1998): capital equipment, petroleum, foodstuffs, cotton, consumer goods. **Major trading partners:** Norway, Netherlands, U.S., France, Japan, UK, Trinidad and Tobago, Brazil.

Geography Suriname lies on the northeast coast of South America, with Guyana to the west, French Guiana to the east, and Brazil to the south. It is about one-tenth larger than Michigan. The principal rivers are the Corantijn on the Guyana border, the Marowijne in the east, and the Suriname, on which the capital city of Paramaribo is situated.

Government Republic.

History Suriname's earliest inhabitants were the Surinen Indians, after whom the country is named. By the 16th century they had been supplanted by other South American Indians. Spain explored Suriname in 1593, but by 1602 the Dutch began to settle the land, followed by the English. The English transferred sovereignty to the Dutch in 1667 (the Treaty of Breda) in exchange for New Amsterdam (New York). Colonization was confined to a narrow coastal strip, and until the abolition of slavery in 1863, African slaves furnished the labor for the coffee and sugarcane plantations. Escaped African slaves fled into the interior, reconstituted their western African culture, and came to be called "Bush Negroes" by the Dutch. After 1870, laborers were imported from British India and the Dutch East Indies.

Known as Dutch Guiana, the colony was integrated into the kingdom of the Netherlands in 1948. Two years later Dutch Guiana was granted home rule, except for foreign affairs and defense. After race rioting over unemployment and inflation, the Netherlands granted Suriname complete independence on Nov. 25, 1975. A coup d'état in 1980 brought military rule. During much of the 1980s Suriname was under the control of Lieut. Col. Dési Bouterse, who in late Dec. 1990 resigned as commander of the armed forces. A guerrilla insurgency by the Jungle Commando (a Bush Negro guerrilla group) increased instability, causing some foreign governments to withhold economic aid. Free elections were held on May 25, 1991, depriving the military of much of its political power. In 1992 a peace treaty was signed between the government and several guerrilla groups. In March 1997, the president announced new economic measures, including eliminating import tariffs on most basic goods coupled with strict price controls. Later that year, the Netherlands said it would prosecute Bouterse for cocaine trafficking.

Public discontent over the 70% inflation rate prompted President Jules Wijdenbosch to hold elections in May 2000, one year ahead of schedule. The New Front for Democracy and Development, a coalition led by former President Ronald Venetiaan, defeated Wijdenbosch, winning 33 of the 51 seats in Parliament, one seat short of a two-thirds majority. New Front also beat a coalition led by Bouterse. Venetiaan had served as president from 1991 until 1996, until his defeat by Wijdenbosch.

In 2000, Suriname resolved its dispute with neighboring Guyana over an oil-rich coastal region.

Swaziland

KINGDOM OF SWAZILAND

Ruler: King Mswati III (1986)
Prime Minister: Barnabas Sibusiso Dlamini (1996)
Area: 6,704 sq mi (17,363 sq km)
Population (2001 est.): 1,104,343 (average annual rate of natural increase: 1.8%); birth rate: 40.1/1000; infant mortality rate: 109.2/1000; density per sq mi: 165
Capital and largest city (1990 est.): Mbabane 47,020.
Monetary unit: Lilangeni. **Languages:** English and Swazi (official). **Ethnicity/race:** African 97%, European 3%. **Religions:** Christian 60%, indigenous 40%.
Literacy rate: 70% (1986)
Economic summary: GDP/PPP (1999 est.): $4.2 billion; per capita $4,200. **Real growth rate:** 3.1%. **Inflation:** 6%. **Unemployment:** 22% (1995 est.). **Arable land:** 11%. **Agriculture:** sugarcane, cotton, corn, tobacco, rice, citrus, pineapples, sorghum, peanuts; cattle, goats, sheep. **Labor force:** n.a.; private sector about 70%, public sector about 30%. **Industries:** mining (coal and asbestos), wood pulp, sugar, soft drink concentrates. **Natural resources:** asbestos, coal, clay, cassiterite, hydropower, forests, small gold and diamond deposits, quarry stone, and talc. **Exports:** $825 million (f.o.b., 1999): soft drink concentrates, sugar, wood pulp, cotton yarn, refrigerators, citrus and canned fruit. **Imports:** $1.05 billion (f.o.b., 1999): motor vehicles, machinery, transport equipment, foodstuffs, petroleum products, chemicals. **Major trading partners:** South Africa, EU, Mozambique, U.S., North Korea, Japan, UK, Singapore. **Member of Commonwealth of Nations**

Geography Swaziland, which is about 85% the size of New Jersey, is surrounded by South Africa and Mozambique. The country consists of a high veld in the west and a series of plateaus descending from 6,000 ft (1,829 m) to a low veld of 1,500 ft (457 m).

Government Monarchy.

History Bantu peoples migrated southwest to the area of Mozambique in the 16th century. A number of clans broke away from the main body in the 18th century and settled in Swaziland. In the 19th century these clans organized as a tribe, partly because they were in constant conflict with the Zulu. Their ruler, Mswazi, appealed to the British in the 1840s for help against the Zulu. The British and the Transvaal governments guaranteed the independence of Swaziland in 1881.

South Africa held Swaziland as a protectorate from 1894 to 1899, but after the Boer War, in 1902, Swaziland was transferred to British administration. The paramount chief was recognized as the native authority in 1941. In 1963, the territory was constituted a protectorate, and on Sept. 6, 1968, it became the independent nation of Swaziland.

Since 1986, King Mswati III has ruled as sub-Saharan Africa's last absolute monarch. Political parties are banned and the king appoints 10 of the 65 members of Parliament as well as the prime minister. King Mswati can veto any law passed by the legislature and frequently rules by decree.

With a modern infrastructure, Swaziland boasts one of the largest per capita manufacturing sectors in Africa. It is one of the few countries on the continent never to face an economic crisis severe enough to warrant imposition of a World Bank adjustment program. Many of the businesses in Swaziland moved there from South Africa in the 1980s in an effort to avoid international sanctions against apartheid.

In 2000 AIDS remains a serious threat to Swaziland. An estimated 120,000 people are infected and 50,000 people have died of the disease in the past two years. King Mswati has ordered his subjects to follow the example of himself and his seven wives and undergo routine AIDS tests.

Sweden

KINGDOM OF SWEDEN

National name: Konungariket Sverige
Sovereign: King Carl XVI Gustaf (1973)
Prime Minister: Göran Persson (1996)
Area: 173,731 sq mi (449,964 sq km)
Population (2001 est.): 8,875,053 (average annual rate of natural increase —0.1%); birth rate: 9.9/1000; infant mortality rate: 3.5/1000; density per sq mi: 51
Capital and largest city (1994): Stockholm, 703,627.
Largest cities: Göteborg, 444,553; Malmö, 242,706; Uppsala, 181,191. **Monetary unit:** Krona. **Language:** Swedish. **Ethnicity/race:** white 88%, Lapp (Sami), foreign-born or first-generation immigrants (Finns, Yugoslavs, Danes, Norwegians, Greeks, Turks) 12%.
Religions: Evangelical Lutheran 94%, Roman Catholic 1.5%, Pentecostal 1%, other 3.5%. **Literacy rate:** 99% (1979)
Economic summary: GDP/PPP (1999 est.): $184 billion; per capita $20,700. **Real growth rate:** 3.8%. **Inflation:** 0.4%. **Unemployment:** 5.5% plus about 5% in training programs. **Arable land:** 7%. **Agriculture:** grains, sugar beets, potatoes; meat, milk. **Labor force:** 4.3 million (1996); agriculture; 2%; industry; 24%; services, 74% (1999 est.). **Industries:** iron and steel, precision equipment (bearings, radio and telephone parts, armaments), wood pulp and paper products, processed foods, motor vehicles. **Natural resources:** zinc, iron ore, lead, copper, silver, timber, uranium, hydropower. **Exports:** $85.7 billion (f.o.b., 1999): machinery 35%, motor vehicles, paper products, pulp and wood, iron and steel products, chemicals. **Imports:** $67.9 billion (f.o.b., 1999): machinery, petroleum and petroleum products, chemicals, motor vehicles, iron and steel; foodstuffs, clothing. **Major trading partners:** EU, Norway, U.S.

Geography Sweden, which occupies the eastern part of the Scandinavian peninsula, is the fourth-largest country in Europe, and is one-tenth larger than California. The country slopes eastward and southward from the Kjólen Mountains along the Norwegian border, where the peak elevation is Kebnekaise at 6,965 ft (2,123 m) in Lapland. In the north are mountains and many lakes. To the south and east are central lowlands and south of them are fertile areas of forest, valley, and plain. Along Sweden's rocky coast, chopped up by bays and inlets, are many islands, the largest of which are Gotland and Öland.

Government Constitutional monarchy.

History The earliest historical mention of Sweden is found in Tacitus's *Germania,* where reference is made to the powerful king and strong fleet of the Sviones. In the 11th century, Olaf Sköttkonung became the first Swedish king to be baptized as a Christian. Around 1400, an attempt was made to unite Sweden, Norway, and Denmark into one kingdom, but this led to bitter strife between the Danes and the Swedes. In 1520, the Danish king Christian II conquered Sweden and in the "Stockholm Bloodbath" put leading Swedish personages to death. Gustavus Vasa (1523–60) broke away from Denmark and fashioned the modern Swedish state. He also confiscated property from the Roman Catholic Church in Sweden to pay Sweden's war debts. The king justified his actions on the basis of Martin Luther's doctrines, which were being accepted nationwide with royal encouragement. The Lutheran Swedish church was eventually adopted as the state church.

Sweden played a leading role in the second phase (1630–35) of the Thirty Years' War (1618–48). By the Treaty of Westphalia (1648), Sweden obtained western Pomerania and some neighboring territory on the Baltic. In 1700, a coalition of Russia, Poland, and Denmark united against Sweden and by the Peace of Nystad (1721) forced it to relinquish Livonia, Ingria, Estonia, and parts of Finland. Sweden emerged from the Napoleonic Wars with the acquisition of Norway from Denmark and with a new royal dynasty stemming from Marshal Jean Bernadotte of France, who became King Charles XIV (1818–44). The artificial union between Sweden and Norway led to an uneasy relationship, and the union was finally dissolved in 1905. Sweden maintained a position of neutrality in both world wars.

An elaborate structure of welfare legislation, imitated by many larger nations, began with the establishment of old-age pensions in 1911. Economic prosperity based on its neutralist policy enabled Sweden, together with Norway, to pioneer in public health, housing, and job security programs. Forty-four years of Socialist government were ended in 1976 with the election of a conservative coalition headed by Thorbjörn Fälldin. The Socialists were returned to power in the election of 1982, but Prime Minister Olof Palme, a Socialist, was assassinated by a gunman on Feb. 28, 1986, leaving Sweden stunned. Palme's Socialist domestic policies were carried out by his successor, Ingvar Carlsson. Elections in Sept. 1991 ousted the Social Democrats (Socialists) from power. The new coalition of four conservative parties pledged to reduce taxes and cut back on the welfare state but not alter Sweden's traditional neutrality. In Sept. 1994 the Social Democrats emerged again after three years as the opposition party.

In a 1994 referendum voters approved joining the European Union. Although supportive of a European monetary union, Sweden decided not to adopt the euro when it debuted in 1999.

Switzerland

SWISS CONFEDERATION

National name: Schweiz/Suisse/Svizzera/Svizra
President: Moritz Leuenberger (2001)
Area: 15,942 sq mi (41,290 sq km)
Population (2001 est.): 7,283,274 (average annual rate of natural increase: 0.1%); birth rate: 10.1/1000; infant mortality rate: 4.5/1000; density per sq mi: 457
Capital (1994 est.): Bern, 129,423. **Largest cities:** Zurich, 343,045; Basel, 176,220; Geneva, 171,744; Lausanne, 117,153. **Monetary unit:** Swiss franc.
Languages: German, French, Italian (all official), Romansch. **Ethnicity/race:** German 65%, French 18%, Italian 10%, Romansch 1%, other 6%.
Religions: Roman Catholic 49%, Protestant 40%, other 5%, no religion 8.3%. **Literacy rate:** 99% (1980)
Economic summary: GDP/PPP (1999 est.): $197 billion; per capita $27,100. **Real growth rate:** 1.4%. **Inflation:** 1%. **Unemployment:** 2.8%. **Arable land:** 10%. **Agriculture:** grains, fruits, vegetables; meat, eggs. **Labor force:** 3.8 million (956,000 foreign workers, mostly Italian) (1996 est.); services, 67%; industry, 28%; agriculture and forestry, 5% (1996 est.). **Industries:** machinery, chemicals, watches, textiles, precision instruments. **Natural resources:** hydropower potential, timber, salt. **Exports:** $98.5 billion (f.o.b., 1999): machinery, chemicals, metals, watches, agricultural products. **Imports:** $99 billion (f.o.b., 1999): machinery, chemicals, vehicles, metals; agricultural products, textiles. **Major trading partners:** EU, U.S., Japan.

Geography Switzerland, in central Europe, is the land of the Alps. Its tallest peak is the Dufourspitze at 15,203 ft (4,634 m) on the Swiss side of the Italian border, one of 10 summits of the Monte Rose massif. The tallest peak in all of the Alps, Mont Blanc (15,771 ft; 4,807 m), is actually in France. Most of Switzerland is composed of a mountainous plateau bordered by the great bulk of the Alps on the south and by the Jura Mountains on the northwest. The country's largest lakes—Geneva, Constance (Bodensee), and Maggiore—straddle the French, German-Austrian, and Italian borders, respectively. The Rhine, navigable from Basel to the North Sea, is the principal inland waterway. Switzerland is twice the size of New Jersey.

Government Federal republic.

History Called Helvetia in ancient times, Switzerland in 1291 was a league of cantons in the Holy Roman Empire. Fashioned around the nucleus of three German forest districts of Schwyz, Uri, and Unterwalden, the Swiss Confederation slowly added new cantons. In 1648 the Treaty of Westphalia gave Switzerland its independence from the Holy Roman Empire.

French revolutionary troops occupied the country in 1798 and named it the Helvetic Republic, but Napoleon in 1803 restored its federal government. By 1815, the French- and Italian-speaking peoples of Switzerland had been granted political equality.

In 1815, the Congress of Vienna guaranteed the neutrality and recognized the independence of Switzerland. In the revolutionary period of 1847, the Catholic cantons seceded and organized a separate union called the *Sonderbund*, but they were defeated and rejoined the federation.

In 1848, the new Swiss constitution established a union modeled upon that of the U.S. The federal constitution of 1874 established a strong central government while maintaining large powers of control in each canton. National unity and political conservatism grew as the country prospered from its neutrality. Its banking system became the world's leading repository for international accounts.

Strict neutrality was its policy in both world wars. Geneva was the seat of the League of Nations (later the European headquarters of the United Nations) and of a number of international organizations.

Allegations in the 1990s concerning secret assets of Jewish Holocaust victims deposited in Swiss banks led to international criticism and the establishment of a fund to reimburse them and their families.

Surprisingly, women were not given the right to vote or to hold office until 1971. Switzerland's first woman president—as well as the first Jew to assume the position—was Ruth Dreifuss in 1999.

In Sept. 2000, the Swiss voted against a plan to cut the number of foreigners in the country to 18% of the population (in 2000 foreigners made up 19.3%). Since 1970, four similar anti-immigration plans have failed. With unemployment at 1.8%, the lowest in eight years, few Swiss feel threatened by the economic repercussions of foreign workers.

Syria

SYRIAN ARAB REPUBLIC

National name: Al-Jamhouriya al Arabiya As-Souriya
President: Bashar al-Assad (2000)
Prime Minister: Muhammad Mustafa Miro (2000)
Area: 71,498 sq mi (185,180 sq km)
Population (2001 est.): 16,728,808 (average annual rate of natural increase: 2.5%); birth rate: 30.6/1000; infant mortality rate: 33.8/1000; density per sq mi: 234
Capital (1994 est.): Damascus, 1,549,932. **Largest cities:** Aleppo, 1,591,400; Homs, 644,204; Latakia, 306,535; Hama, 229,000. **Monetary unit:** Syrian pound. **Languages:** Arabic (official), French and English widely understood. **Ethnicity/race:** Arab 90.3%, Kurds, Armenians, and other 9.7%. **Religions:** Islam 90%, Christian 10%. **Literacy rate:** 65% (1990)
Economic summary: GDP/PPP (1999 est.): $42.2 billion; per capita $2,500. **Real growth rate:** 0%. **Inflation:** 2.3%. **Unemployment:** 12%–15% (1998 est.). **Arable land:** 28%. **Agriculture:** wheat, barley, cotton, lentils, chickpeas, olives, sugar beets; beef, mutton, eggs, poultry, milk. **Labor force:** 4.7 million (1998 est.); agriculture; 40%; industry, 20%; services, 40% (1996 est.). **Industries:** petroleum, textiles, food processing, beverages, tobacco, phosphate rock mining. **Natural resources:** petroleum, phosphates, chrome and manganese ores, asphalt, iron ore, rock salt, marble, gypsum, hydropower. **Exports:** $3.3 billion (f.o.b., 1999 est.): petroleum, textiles, manufactured goods, fruits and vegetables, raw cotton, live sheep, phosphates. **Imports:** $3.2 billion (f.o.b., 1999 est.): machinery and equipment, foodstuffs/animals, metal and metal products, textiles, chemicals. **Major trading partners:** Germany, Turkey, Italy, France, Lebanon, Spain, Ukraine, South Korea, Japan, U.S.

Geography Slightly larger than North Dakota, Syria lies at the eastern end of the Mediterranean Sea. It is bordered by Lebanon and Israel on the west, Turkey on the north, Iraq on the east, and Jordan on the south. Coastal Syria is a narrow plain, in back of which is a range of coastal mountains, and still farther inland a steppe area. In the east is the Syrian Desert, and in the south is the Jebel Druze Range. The highest point in Syria is Mount Hermon (9,232 ft; 2,814 m) on the Lebanese border.

Government Republic under a military regime since March 1963.

History Ancient Syria was conquered by Egypt about 1500 B.C., and after that by Hebrews, Assyrians, Chaldeans, Persians, and Alexander the Great of Macedonia. From 64 B.C. until the Arab conquest in A.D. 636, it was part of the Roman Empire except during brief periods. The Arabs made it a trade center for their extensive empire, but it suffered severely from the Mongol invasion in 1260 and fell to the Ottoman Turks in 1516. Syria remained a Turkish province until World War I.

A secret Anglo-French pact of 1916 put Syria in the French zone of influence. The League of Nations gave France a mandate over Syria after World War I, but the French were forced to put down several nationalist uprisings. In 1930, France recognized Syria as an independent republic but still subject to the mandate. After nationalist demonstrations in 1939, the French high commissioner suspended the Syrian constitution. In 1941, British and Free French forces invaded Syria to eliminate Vichy control. During the rest of World War II, Syria was an Allied base. Again in 1945, nationalist demonstrations broke into actual fighting, and

British troops had to restore order. Syrian forces met a series of reverses while participating in the Arab invasion of Palestine in 1948. In 1958, Egypt and Syria formed the United Arab Republic, with Gamal Abdel Nasser of Egypt as president. However, Syria became independent again on Sept. 29, 1961, following a revolution.

In the Arab-Israeli War of 1967, Israel quickly vanquished the Syrian army. Before acceding to the UN cease-fire, the Israeli forces took control of the fortified Golan Heights. Syria joined Egypt in attacking Israel in Oct. 1973 in the fourth Arab-Israeli war, but was pushed back from initial successes on the Golan Heights and ended up losing more land. However, in the settlement worked out by U.S. secretary of state Henry A. Kissinger in 1974, the Syrians recovered all the territory lost in 1973 and a token amount of territory, including the deserted town of Quneitra, lost in 1967.

In the mid-1970s Syria sent some 20,000 troops to support Muslim Lebanese in their armed conflict with Christian militants supported by Israel during the civil war in Lebanon. Syrian troops frequently clashed with Israeli troops during Israel's 1982 invasion of Lebanon and remained thereafter as occupiers of large portions of Lebanon.

The first Arab country to condemn Iraq's invasion of Kuwait, Syria sent troops to help defend Saudi Arabia from possible Iraqi attack. After the Gulf War, hope for peace negotiations between Israel and Arab states, particularly Syria, rose but then foundered. In 1990, President Assad ruled out any possibility of legalizing opposition political parties. In Dec. 1991 voters approved a fourth term for Assad, giving him 99.98% of the vote.

In the 1990s, the slowdown in the Israeli-Palestinian peace process was echoed in the lack of progress in Israeli-Syrian relations. Confronted with a steadily strengthening strategic partnership between Israel and Turkey, Syria took steps to construct a countervailing alliance by improving relations with Iraq, strengthening ties with Iran, and collaborating more closely with Saudi Arabia. The defeat of conservative Israeli prime minister Netanyahu and the election of the Labor Party's Ehud Barak marked a shift in Syrian-Israeli relations. The new Israeli prime minister announced that one of his major goals was to broker peace with Syria and end the low-grade war in Southern Lebanon with the Syrian-backed Hezbollah guerrillas.

In Dec. 1999, Israeli-Syrian talks resumed after a nearly four-year hiatus, with the aging Assad (who would die seven months later) attempting to shore up his legacy. From Syria's point of view, normalization of relations between the two countries largely depended on Israel's withdrawal from the Golan Heights, which was territory that Israel had captured from Syria during the Arab-Israeli War of 1967. From Israel's point of view, relinquishing the Golan Heights, which served as a buffer zone between the two nations, could not occur without a guarantee of Israel's national security. Water rights and the Hezbollah guerrillas fighting Israel in Lebanon—who are essentially controlled by Syria—were also on the agenda. By Jan. 2000, however, talks broke down when Syria demanded a detailed discussion about the return of the entire Golan Heights. Most commentators believe this is only a temporary setback.

On June 10, 2000, President Hafez al-Assad died. He had ruled with an iron fist since taking power in a military coup in 1970. His son, Bashar al-Assad, an ophthalmologist by training, succeeded him.

Taiwan

REPUBLIC OF CHINA

President: Chen Shui-bian (2000)
Prime Minister: Chang Chun-hsiung (2000)
Area: 13,892 sq mi (35,980 sq km)
Population (2001 est.): 22,370,461 (average annual rate of natural increase: 0.8%); birth rate: 14.3/1000; infant mortality rate: 6.9/1000; density per sq mi: 1,610
Capital and largest city (2000 est.): Taipei, 7,700,000 (metro. area). **Largest cities:** Kaohsiung, 1,423,163; Tai Chung, 848,320; Tainan, 705,565; Keelung, 367,668. **Monetary unit:** New Taiwan dollar.
Language: Chinese (Mandarin). **Ethnicity/race:** Taiwanese 84%, mainland Chinese 14%, aborigine 2%. **Religions:** Buddhist 4.86 million, Taoist 3.3 million, Protestant 422,000, Catholic 304,000. **Literacy rate:** 92% (1990).
Economic summary: GDP/PPP (1999 est.): $357 billion; per capita $16,100. **Real growth rate:** 5.5%. **Inflation:** 0.4%. **Unemployment:** 2.9%. **Arable land:** 24%. **Agriculture:** rice, corn, vegetables, fruit, tea; pigs, poultry, beef, milk; fish. **Labor force:** 9.7 million; services, 55%; industry, 37%; agriculture, 8%. **Industries:** electronics, petroleum refining, chemicals, textiles, iron and steel, machinery, cement, food processing. **Natural resources:** small deposits of coal, natural gas, limestone, marble, and asbestos. **Exports:** $121.6 billion (f.o.b., 1999): electronics, electric and machinery equipment 52%, metals, textiles, plastics, chemicals. **Imports:** $101.7 billion (c.i.f., 1999): electronics, electric and machinery equipment 45%, minerals, precision instruments. **Major trading partners:** U.S., Hong Kong, Europe, Japan, Singapore, South Korea, Malaysia.

Geography The Republic of China today consists of the island of Taiwan, an island 100 mi (161 km) off the Asian mainland in the Pacific; two off-shore islands, Kinmen (Quemoy) and Matsu; and the nearby islets of the Pescadores chain. It is slightly larger than the combined areas of Massachusetts and Connecticut. Taiwan is divided by a central mountain range that runs from north to south, rising sharply on the east coast and descending gradually to a broad western plain, where cultivation is concentrated.

Government Multiparty democracy.

History Taiwan was inhabited by aborigines of Malayan descent when Chinese from the areas now designated as Fukien and Kwangtung began settling it in the 7th century, becoming the majority. The Portuguese explored the area in 1590, naming it "the Beautiful" (Formosa). In 1624 the Dutch set up forts in the south, the Spanish in the north. The Dutch forced out the Spanish in 1641 and controlled the island until 1661, when Chinese general Koxinga took it over and established an independent kingdom. The Manchus seized the island in 1683 and held it until 1895, when it passed to Japan after the first Sino-Japanese War. Japan developed and exploited Formosa. It was the target of heavy American bombing during World War II, and at the close of the war the island was restored to China.

After the defeat of its armies on the mainland, the Nationalist government of Generalissimo Chiang Kai-shek retreated to Taiwan in Dec. 1949. Chiang dominated the island, even though only 15% of the population consisted of the 1949 immigrants, the

Kuomintang. He maintained a 600,000-man army in the hope of eventually recovering the mainland. Beijing viewed the Taiwanese government with suspicion and anger, referring to Taiwan as a breakaway province of China.

The UN seat representing all of China was held by the Nationalists for over two decades before being lost in Oct. 1971, when the People's Republic of China was admitted and Taiwan was forced to abdicate its seat to Beijing.

Chiang died at 87 of a heart attack on April 5, 1975. His son, Chiang Ching-kuo, continued as premier and was a dominant figure in the Taipei regime. In April 1991, President Lee Teng-hui formally declared an end to emergency rule, which had existed since Chiang's forces originally occupied the island. In the first full election in many decades, the governing Kuomintang in Dec. 1991 won 71% of the vote, affirming the island's opposition to reunification with China. In Feb. 1993 the president, himself a native Taiwanese, nominated Lien Chan, another native, to be prime minister, marking a further generational shift away from the mainland exiles.

In the island's first free presidential election, voters defied mainland intimidation and gave 54% of the vote to incumbent President Lee Teng-hui. The second-place finisher, with 21%, advocated complete independence from China.

In 1998, Taiwan renewed its push for a separate UN seat—its sixth attempt in recent years. The move has been blocked each time by the Beijing government.

President Lee Teng-hui sorely rankled mainland China by announcing in July 1999 that he was abandoning the longstanding "One China" policy that has kept the peace between the small island and its powerful neighbor, and would from now on deal with China on a "state-to-state basis."

In March 2000 elections—Taiwan's second free presidential elections—voters elected pro-independence candidate Chen Shui-bian of the Democratic Progressive Party, ending more than 50 years of Nationalist rule. China reiterated that "Taiwanese independence, in whatever form, will never be allowed."

Vice Premier Chang Chun-hsiung was named prime minister in Oct. 2000, following the resignation of Tang Fei. While he officially resigned because of ill health, Tang Fei had strongly disagreed with President Chen Shui-bian's decision to halt construction of a $5.5 billion nuclear power plant. The move provoked outrage in Parliament and an ill-fated drive to oust Chen from office. Chen retreated, and construction of the nuclear power plant resumed in Feb. 2001.

Chen's first year in office was marred by the power plant controversy and a plummeting economy that saw the stock market drop nearly 50%, unemployment skyrocket, and the exodus of high-tech workers to China.

Tajikistan

REPUBLIC OF TAJIKISTAN

President: Imomali Rakhmonov (1992)
Prime Minister: Akil Akilov (1999)
Area: 55,251 sq mi (143,100 sq km)
Population (2001 est.): 6,578,681 (average annual rate of natural increase: 2.5%); birth rate, 33.2/1000; infant mortality rate: 116.1/1000; density per sq mi: 119
Capital and largest city (1994 est.): Dushanbe, 524,000.
Other large city: Khodzhent (Leninabad), 164,500.

Monetary unit: Tajik ruble. **Language:** Tajik. **Ethnicity/race:** Tajik 64.9%, Uzbek 25%, Russian 3.5% (declining because of emigration), other 6.6%. **Religion:** Sunni Muslim 80%. **Literacy rate:** 98% (1989)
Economic summary: GDP/PPP (1999 est.): $6.2 billion; per capita $1,020. **Real growth rate:** 2%. **Inflation:** 22%. **Unemployment:** 5.7%; includes only officially registered unemployed; also large numbers of underemployed workers and unregistered unemployed people (Dec. 1998). **Arable land:** 6%. **Agriculture:** cotton, grain, fruits, grapes, vegetables; cattle, sheep, goats. **Labor force:** 1.9 million (1996); agriculture and forestry, 50%; industry, 20%; services, 30% (1997 est.). **Industries:** aluminum, zinc, lead, chemicals and fertilizers, cement, vegetable oil, metal-cutting machine tools, refrigerators and freezers. **Natural resources:** hydropower, some petroleum, uranium, mercury, brown coal, lead, zinc, antimony, tungsten. **Exports:** $634 million (1999 est.): aluminum, electricity, cotton, fruits, vegetable oil, textiles. **Imports:** $770 million (1999 est.): electricity, petroleum products, aluminum oxide, machinery and equipment, foodstuffs. **Major trading partners:** Uzbekistan, Liechtenstein, Russia, Kazakhstan, Netherlands, Switzerland.

Geography Ninety-three percent of Tajikistan's territory is mountainous, and the mountain glaciers are the source of its rivers. Tajikistan is an earthquake-prone area. The republic is bounded by China in the east, Afghanistan to the south, Uzbekistan and Kyrgyzstan to the west and north. The central Asian republic also includes the Gorno-Badakh Shan Autonomous region. Tajikistan is slightly larger than the state of Illinois.

Government Republic.

History The Tajiks, whose language is nearly identical with Persian, were part of the ancient Persian empire that was ruled by Darius I and later conquered by Alexander the Great (333 B.C.). In the 7th and 8th centuries, Arabs conquered the region and brought Islam. The Tajiks were successively ruled by Uzbeks and then Afghans until claimed by Russia in the 1860s. In 1924, Tajikistan was consolidated into a newly formed Tajik Autonomous Soviet Socialist Republic, which was administratively part of the Uzbek SSR until the Tajik ASSR gained full-fledged republic status in 1929.

Tajikistan declared its sovereignty in Aug. 1990. In 1991, the republic's Communist leadership supported the attempted coup against Soviet president Mikhail Gorbachev. Tajikistan joined with ten other former Soviet republics in the Commonwealth of Independent States on Dec. 21, 1991. A parliamentary republic was proclaimed and presidential rule abolished in Nov. 1992. After independence, Tajikistan experienced sporadic conflict as the Communist-dominated government struggled to combat an insurgency by Islamic and democratic opposition forces. Despite continued international efforts to end the civil war, periodic fighting continued. Tajikistan's civil war ended officially on June 27, 1997, with the signing in Moscow of peace accords between the government of President Imomali Rakhmonov and the United Tajik Opposition (UTO), a coalition of largely Islamic groups. Since then, however, peace has been tenuous, marred regularly by killing sprees by various opposition groups.

In 2000, Tajikistan has allowed approximately 25,000 Russian troops into the country to help stem the violence by helping to patrol the border with

Taliban-run Afghanistan. Tajikistan has also agreed to allow for the establishment of a Russian military base in the country.

Tanzania

UNITED REPUBLIC OF TANZANIA

President: Benjamin William Mkapa (1995)
Prime Minister: Frederick Tluway Sumaye (1995)
Area: 364,898 sq mi (945,087 sq km)[1]
Population (2001 est.): 36,232,074 (average annual rate of natural increase: 2.7%); birth rate: 39.7/1000; infant mortality rate: 79.4/1000; density per sq mi: 99
Capitals and largest city (1988): Dar es Salaam (administrative), 1,360,850; Dodoma (official), 45,807 (1978). **Monetary unit:** Tanzanian shilling.
Languages: Swahili and English (both official), local languages. **Ethnicity/race:** mainland: native African (95% Bantu, consisting of well over 100 tribes) 99%, Asian, European, and Arab 1%. Zanzibar: Arab, mixed Arab and native African, native African. **Religions:** Christian 40%, Muslim 33%. **Literacy rate:** 52% (1988)
Economic summary: GDP/PPP (1999 est.): $23.3 billion; per capita $550. **Real growth rate:** 4%. **Inflation:** 8.8%. **Unemployment:** n.a. **Arable land:** 3%. **Agriculture:** coffee, sisal, tea, cotton, pyrethrum (insecticide made from chrysanthemums), cashew nuts, tobacco, cloves (Zanzibar), corn, wheat, cassava (tapioca), bananas, fruits, vegetables; cattle, sheep, goats. **Labor force:** 13.495 million; agriculture, 90%; industry and commerce, 10% (1995 est.). **Industries:** primarily agricultural processing (sugar, beer, cigarettes, sisal twine), diamond and gold mining, oil refining, shoes, cement, textiles, wood products, fertilizer, salt. **Natural resources:** hydropower, tin, phosphates, iron ore, coal, diamonds, gemstones, gold, natural gas, nickel. **Exports:** $828 million (f.o.b., 1999 est.): coffee, manufactured goods, cotton, cashew nuts, minerals, tobacco, sisal (1996). **Imports:** $1.44 billion (f.o.b., 1999 est.): consumer goods, machinery and transportation equipment, industrial raw materials, crude oil. **Major trading partners:** India, Germany, Japan, Malaysia, Rwanda, Netherlands, South Africa, Kenya, UK, Saudi Arabia, China.
Member of Commonwealth of Nations

1. Including Zanzibar.

Geography Tanzania is in East Africa on the Indian Ocean. To the north are Uganda and Kenya; to the west, Burundi, Rwanda, and Congo; and to the south, Mozambique, Zambia, and Malawi. Its area is three times that of New Mexico. Tanzania contains three of Africa's best-known lakes—Victoria in the north, Tanganyika in the west, and Nyasa in the south. Mount Kilimanjaro in the north, 19,340 ft (5,895 m), is the highest point on the continent. The island of Zanzibar is separated from the mainland by a 22-mile channel.

Government Republic.

History Arab traders first began to colonize the area in 700. Portuguese explorers reached the coastal regions in 1500 and held some control until the 17th century, when the sultan of Oman took power. With what are now Burundi and Rwanda, Tanganyika became the colony of German East Africa in 1885. After World War I, it was administered by Britain under a League of Nations mandate and later as a UN trust territory.

Although not mentioned in old histories until the 12th century, Zanzibar was always believed to have had connections with southern Arabia. The Portu-

guese made it one of their tributaries in 1503 and later established a trading post, but they were driven from Oman by Arabs in 1698. Zanzibar was declared independent of Oman in 1861 and, in 1890, it became a British protectorate.

Tanganyika became independent on Dec. 9, 1961; Zanzibar on Dec. 10, 1963. On April 26, 1964, the two nations merged into the United Republic of Tanganyika and Zanzibar. The name was changed to Tanzania six months later.

An invasion by Ugandan troops in Nov. 1978 was followed by a counterattack in Jan. 1979, in which 5,000 Tanzanian troops were joined by 3,000 Ugandan exiles opposed to President Idi Amin. Within a month, full-scale war developed. Tanzanian president Julius Nyerere kept troops in Uganda in open support of former Ugandan president Milton Obote, despite protests from opposition groups, until the national elections in Dec. 1980.

In Nov. 1985, Nyerere stepped down as president. Ali Hassan Mwinyi, his vice president, succeeded him. Running unopposed, Mwinyi was elected president in October. Shortly thereafter plans were announced to study the benefits of instituting a multiparty democracy, and in Oct. 1995 the country's first multiparty elections since independence took place.

On Aug. 7, 1998, the U.S. embassy in Dar es Salaam was bombed by terrorists, killing 10. The same day an even more devastating explosion destroyed the U.S. embassy in neighboring Kenya.

Since taking office in 1995 President Benjamin William Mkapa has sought to increase economic productivity while dealing with serious pollution problems and deforestation. With more than one million people infected with HIV, AIDS care and prevention have been major public health issues. On foreign policy, Tanzania has taken a leading diplomatic role in East Africa, hosting peace talks for the factions fighting in neighboring Burundi. The UN International Criminal Tribunal for Rwanda (ICTR) is located in the town of Arusha. In Oct. 2000, Mkapa was easily reelected.

Thailand

KINGDOM OF THAILAND

Ruler: King Bhumibol Adulyadej (1946)
Prime Minister: Thaksin Shinawatra (2001)
Area: 198,455 sq mi (514,000 sq km)
Population (2001 est.): 61,797,751 (average annual rate of natural increase 0.9%); birth rate: 16.6/1000; infant mortality rate: 30.5/1000; density per sq mi: 311
Capital and largest city (2000 est.): Bangkok, 7,200,000 (metro. area). **Other large cities:** Nonthaburi, 261,335; Chiang Mai, 170,397.
Monetary unit: baht. **Languages:** Thai (Siamese), Chinese, English. **Ethnicity/race:** Thai 75%, Chinese 14%, other 11%. **Religions:** Buddhist 94.4%, Islam 4%, Hindu 1.1%, Christian 0.5%. **Literacy rate:** 93% (1990)
Economic summary: GDP/PPP (1999 est.): $388.7 billion; per capita $6,400. **Real growth rate:** 4%. **Inflation:** 2.4%. **Unemployment:** 4.5% (1998 est.). **Arable land:** 34%. **Agriculture:** rice, cassava (tapioca), rubber, corn, sugarcane, coconuts, soybeans. **Labor force:** 32.6 million (1997 est.); agriculture, 54%; industry, 15%; services, 31% (1996 est.). **Industries:** tourism; textiles and garments, agricultural processing, beverages, tobacco, cement, light manufacturing, such as jewelry; electric appliances and components, computers and parts, integrated circuits, furniture, plastics; world's

second-largest tungsten producer and third-largest tin producer. **Natural resources:** tin, rubber, natural gas, tungsten, tantalum, timber, lead, fish, gypsum, lignite, fluorite, arable land. **Exports:** $58.5 billion (f.o.b., 1999 est.): computers and parts, textiles, rice. **Imports:** $45 billion (f.o.b., 1999 est.): capital goods, intermediate goods and raw materials, consumer goods, fuels. **Major trading partners:** U.S., Japan, Singapore, Hong Kong, Netherlands, UK, Malaysia, China, Taiwan, Germany, Singapore, South Korea, Oman, Indonesia.

Geography Thailand occupies the western half of the Indochinese peninsula and the northern two-thirds of the Malay Peninsula in southeast Asia. Its neighbors are Burma (Myanmar) on the north and west, Laos on the north and northeast, Cambodia on the east, and Malaysia on the south. Thailand is about the size of France.

Government Constitutional monarchy.

History The Thais first began settling their present homeland from the Asian continent in the 6th century, and by the end of the 13th century ruled most of the western portion. During the next 400 years, they fought sporadically with the Cambodians to the east and Burmese to the west. Formerly called Siam, Thailand has never experienced foreign rule. The British gained a colonial foothold in the region in 1824, but by 1896 an Anglo-French accord guaranteed the independence of Thailand. A coup in 1932 demoted the monarchy to titular status and established representative government with universal suffrage.

At the outbreak of World War II, Japanese forces attacked Thailand. After five hours of token resistance Thailand yielded to Japan on Dec. 8, 1941, subsequently becoming a staging area for the Japanese campaign against Malaya. Following the demise of a pro-Japanese puppet government in July 1944, Thailand repudiated the declaration of war it had been forced to make in 1942 against Britain and the U.S.

By the late 1960s the nation's problems largely stemmed from conflicts brewing in neighboring Cambodia and Vietnam. Although Thailand had received $2 billion in U.S. economic and military aid since 1950, and had sent troops (paid by the U.S.) to Vietnam while permitting U.S. bomber bases on its territory, the collapse of South Vietnam and Cambodia in spring 1975 brought rapid changes in the country's diplomatic posture. At the Thai government's insistence, the U.S. agreed to withdraw all 23,000 U.S. military personnel remaining in Thailand by March 1976.

Three years of civilian government ended with a military coup on Oct. 6, 1976. Political parties, banned after the coup, gained limited freedom in 1980. The same year, the National Assembly elected Gen. Prem Tinsulanonda as prime minister. General elections held on April 18, 1983, and July 27, 1986, resulted in Prem continuing as prime minister over a coalition government.

Fleeing from Laos, Vietnam, and the genocidal regime of Cambodia's Pol Pot, refugees flooded into Thailand in 1978 and 1979. Despite efforts by the United States and other Western countries to resettle them, a total of 130,000 Laotians and Vietnamese were living in camps along the Cambodian border in mid-1980.

On April 3, 1981, a military coup against the Prem government failed. Another coup attempt on Sept. 9, 1985, was crushed by loyal troops after 10 hours of fighting in Bangkok. In Feb. 1991 a bloodless putsch led by Gen. Suchinda Kraprayoon overthrew the democratic government on charges of corruption. The new junta declared a state of emergency; under martial law, the houses of Parliament were dismissed and the constitution abolished. Parliamentary elections in March 1992 gave more than half the seats at stake to pro-military parties. In April, the top military commander was appointed prime minister. A scandal over a land-reform program caused the fall of the government in May 1995. The prime minister dissolved Parliament and set a date for new elections. Voters in early July gave the largest number of seats in Parliament to the Thai Nation Party, whose leader moved quickly to form a coalition government. A new draft constitution, calling for cabinet ministers to relinquish their parliamentary seats, came under fire in the early months of 1997 from a number of politicians.

Following several years of unprecedented economic growth, Thailand's economy, once one of the strongest in the region, collapsed under the weight of foreign debt in 1997. The Thai economy's downfall set off a chain reaction in the region, sparking the Asian currency crisis. The Thai government quickly accepted restructuring guidelines as a condition of the International Monetary Fund's $17 billion bailout. Thailand's economy, while far from completely recovered, continued to improve throughout 1998 and 1999. The Thai Rak Thai Party won elections in Jan. 2001 and formed a coalition government with the Chart Thai and New Aspiration Parties. Thaksin Shinawatra became prime minister.

Thailand's Constitutional Court acquitted the hugely popular Thaksin in August of corruption charges. Thaksin, a billionaire telecommunications mogul, was indicted by an anticorruption commission in Dec. 2000 for hiding millions of dollars in asset statements he filed in 1997, when he served briefly as a deputy prime minister.

Togo

REPUBLIC OF TOGO

National name: République Togolaise
President: Gen. Gnassingbé Eyadema (1967)
Prime Minister: Agbeyome Messan Kodjo (2000)
Area: 21,925 sq mi (56,785 sq km)
Population (2001 est.): 5,153,088 (average annual rate of natural increase: 2.6%); birth rate: 37.0/1000; infant mortality rate: 70.4/1000; density per sq mi: 235
Capital and largest city (1983): Lomé, 366,476.
  Monetary unit: Franc CFA. **Languages:** French (official), Ewé, Mina (south), Kabyé, Cotocoli (north), and many dialects. **Ethnicity/race:** native African (37 tribes; largest and most important are Ewe, Mina, and Kabre) 99%, European and Syrian-Lebanese less than 1%. **Religions:** Indigenous beliefs 70%, Christian 20%, Islam 10%. **Literacy rate:** 43% (1990)
Economic summary: GDP/PPP (1999 est.): $8.6 billion; per capita $1,700. **Real growth rate:** 4%. **Inflation:** 3%. **Unemployment:** n.a. **Arable land:** 38%. **Agriculture:** coffee, cocoa, cotton, yams, cassava (tapioca), corn, beans, rice, millet, sorghum; livestock; fish. **Labor force:** 1.538 million (1993 est.); agriculture, 65%; industry, 5%; services, 30% (1998 est.). **Industries:** phosphate mining, agricultural processing, cement; handicrafts, textiles, beverages. **Natural resources:** phosphates, limestone, marble, arable land. **Exports:** $400 million (f.o.b., 1999): cotton, phosphates, coffee, cocoa. **Imports:** $450 million (f.o.b., 1999): machinery and equipment, foodstuffs, petroleum products. **Major trading partners:** Canada, Philippines, Ghana, France, Côte d'Ivoire, China.

Geography Togo, twice the size of Maryland, is on the south coast of West Africa bordering on Ghana to the west, Burkina Faso to the north, and Benin to the east. The Gulf of Guinea coastline, only 32 mi long (51 km), is low and sandy. The only port is at Lomé. The Togo hills traverse the central section.

Government Republic.

History The Voltaic peoples and the Kwa were the earliest known inhabitants. The Ewe followed in the 14th century, and the Ane in the 18th century. The Danish claimed the land in the 18th century, but by 1884 it was established as a German colony (Togoland). The area was split between the British and the French under League of Nations mandates after World War I and subsequently administered as UN trusteeships. The British portion voted for incorporation with Ghana. The French portion became Togo, which declared its independence on April 27, 1960.

Togo's first democratically elected president, Sylvano Olympius, was overthrown in 1963. He was shot by Sgt. Etienne Eyadema while he attempted to scale the walls of the American Embassy to seek asylum. The government of Nicolas Grunitzky was overthrown in a bloodless coup on Jan. 13, 1967, led by Lt. Col. Etienne Eyadema (now called Gen. Gnassingbé Eyadema). A National Reconciliation Committee was set up to rule the country, but in April, Eyadema dissolved the committee and took over as president. He suspended the constitution, banned political parties, and created a cult of personality around his presidency—his official biography describes him as a "force of nature." Under pressure from the West, Eyadema legalized opposition parties in 1993, but the first multiparty presidential election in Aug. 1993 (which gave Eyadema more than 96% of the vote) was considered fraudulent, as was his 1998 reelection. In 2001, Eyadema was the longest-serving ruler in Africa—34 years.

Tonga
KINGDOM OF TONGA

Sovereign: King Taufa'ahau Tupou IV (1965)
Prime Minister: Prince Lavaka Ata Ulukalala (2000)
Area: 289 sq mi (748 sq km)
Population (2001 est.): 104,227 (average annual rate of natural increase: 1.8%; birth rate: 23.6/1000; infant mortality rate: 14.1/1000; density per sq mi: 361
Capital and largest city (1990 est.): Nuku'alofa, 34,000. **Monetary unit:** Pa'anga. **Languages:** Tongan (an Austronesian language), English. **Ethnicity/race:** Polynesian, European (about 300). **Religions:** Christian; Free Wesleyan Church claims over 30,000 adherents. **Literacy rate:** 98.5%
Economic summary: GDP/PPP (1998 est.): $238 million; per capita $2,200. **Real growth rate:** –0.3%. **Inflation:** 3.2%. **Unemployment:** 11.8% (FY93/94). **Arable land:** 24%. **Agriculture:** squash, coconuts, copra, bananas, vanilla beans, cocoa, coffee, ginger, black pepper; fish. **Labor force:** 36,665 (1994); agriculture, 65% (1997 est.). **Industries:** tourism, fishing. **Natural resources:** fish, fertile soil. **Exports:** $8 million (f.o.b., 1998): squash, fish, vanilla beans. **Imports:** $69 million (f.o.b., 1998): foodstuffs, machinery and transport equipment, fuels, chemicals. **Major trading partners:** Japan, U.S., New Zealand, Australia. **Member of Commonwealth of Nations**

Geography Situated east of the Fiji Islands in the South Pacific, Tonga (also called the Friendly Islands) consists of some 150 islands, of which 36 are inhab-

ited. Most of the islands contain active volcanic craters; others are coral atolls.

Government Constitutional monarchy.

History Polynesians have lived on Tonga for at least 3,000 years. The Dutch were the first to explore the islands, landing on Tafahi in 1616. The current royal dynasty of Tonga was founded in 1831 by Taufa'ahau Tupou, who took the name George I. He consolidated the kingdom by conquest and in 1875 granted a constitution. In 1900, his great-grandson, George II, signed a treaty of friendship with Britain, and the country became a British protected state. The treaty was revised in 1959. Tonga became independent on June 4, 1970.

The continuing challenge to the government—largely controlled by the king, his nominees, and a small group of hereditary nobles—posed by the prodemocracy movement was institutionalized in Sept. 1994 with the formation of the Tonga Democratic Party. In March 1997, Cyclone Hina caused damage to crops and buildings, mostly on Tongatapu; one person was reported killed. In 1999, Tonga gained UN membership.

Trinidad and Tobago
REPUBLIC OF TRINIDAD AND TOBAGO

President: Arthur N. R. Robinson (1997)
Prime Minister: Basdeo Panday (2000)
Area: 1,980 sq mi (5,128 sq km)
Population (2001 est.): 1,169,682 (average annual rate of natural increase: 0.5%; birth rate: 13.7/1000; infant mortality rate: 25.0/1000; density per sq mi: 591
Capital and largest city (1995): Port-of-Spain, 52,451. **Monetary unit:** Trinidad and Tobago dollar. **Languages:** English (official), Hindi, French, Spanish. **Ethnicity/race:** black 43%, East Indian (a local term—primarily immigrants from northern India) 40%, mixed 14%, white 1%, Chinese 1%, other 1%. **Religions:** Roman Catholic 33%, Hindu 25%, Anglican 15%, other Christian 14%, Muslim 6%. **Literacy rate:** 95% (1980)
Economic summary: GDP/PPP (1999 est.): $9.41 billion; per capita $8,500. **Real growth rate:** 5%. **Inflation:** 3.5%. **Unemployment:** 14.2% (1998). **Arable land:** 15%. **Agriculture:** cocoa, sugarcane, rice, citrus, coffee, vegetables; poultry. **Labor force:** 558,700 (1998); construction and utilities, 12.4%; manufacturing, mining, and quarrying, 14%; agriculture, 9.5%; services, 64.1% (1997 est.). **Industries:** petroleum, chemicals, tourism, food processing, cement, beverage, cotton textiles. **Natural resources:** petroleum, natural gas, asphalt. **Exports:** $2.4 billion (f.o.b., 1998): petroleum and petroleum products, chemicals, steel products, fertilizer, sugar, cocoa, coffee, citrus, flowers. **Imports:** $3 billion (c.i.f., 1998): machinery, transportation equipment, manufactured goods, food, live animals. **Major trading partners:** U.S., Caricom countries, Central and South America, EU, Japan. **Member of Commonwealth of Nations**

Geography Trinidad and Tobago lie in the Caribbean Sea off the northeast coast of Venezuela. Trinidad, the larger at 1,864 sq mi (4,828 sq km), is mainly flat and rolling, with mountains in the north that reach a height of 3,085 ft (940 m) at Mount Aripo. Tobago, at just 116 sq mi (300 sq km), is heavily forested with hardwood trees.

Government Parliamentary democracy.

History When Trinidad was explored by Columbus in 1498, it was inhabited by the Arawaks; Carib Indians inhabited Tobago. Trinidad remained in Spanish possession, despite raids by other European nations, until it was ceded to Britain in 1802. Tobago passed between Britain and France several times, but it was ultimately given to Britain in 1814. Slavery was abolished in 1834. Between 1845 and 1917, thousands of indentured workers were brought from India to work on sugarcane plantations. In 1889 Trinidad and Tobago were made a single colony.

Partial self-government was instituted in 1925, and from 1958 to 1962 the nation was part of the West Indies Federation. On Aug. 31, 1962, it became independent and on Aug. 1, 1976, Trinidad and Tobago became a republic, remaining within the Commonwealth. While the country is a stable democracy and enjoys the highest living standards in the Caribbean thanks to oil revenue, tension between East Indians and blacks has underlined much of political life. In 1970 rioting and an army mutiny against the East Indian population prompted a state of emergency, which lasted for two years.

Eric Williams, "Father of the Nation" and leader of the People's National Movement (PNM), which is largely supported by blacks, governed from 1956 until his death in 1981. In Dec. 1986 the multiracial National Alliance for Reconstruction (NAR), based in Tobago, won a parliamentary majority, promising to sell most state-owned companies, reorganize the civil service, and reduce dependence on oil.

In 1990, to protest the NAR government, some 100 radical black Muslims blew up the police station in an attempted coup, in which the prime minister and other officials were held hostage for six days. The NAR was defeated in 1991, and the PNM returned to power. In 1995, the East Indian–based party, the United National Congress (UNC), led by Basdeo Panday, formed a coalition government with the NAR. In 2000, Panday narrowly won another term.

Tunisia

REPUBLIC OF TUNISIA

National name: Al-Joumhouria Attunisia
President: Zine al-Abidine Ben Ali (1987)
Prime Minister: Mohamed Ghannouchi (1999)
Area: 63,170 sq mi (163,610 sq km)
Population (2001 est.): 9,705,102 (average annual rate of natural increase: 1.2%); birth rate: 17.1/1000; infant mortality rate: 29.0/1000; density per sq mi: 154
Capital and largest city (1994): Tunis, 887,800.
Monetary unit: Tunisian dinar. **Languages:** Arabic (official), French. **Ethnicity/race:** Arab-Berber 98%, European 1%, Jewish less than 1%. **Religions:** Islam (Sunni) 98%, Christian 1%, Jewish, less than 1%.
Literacy rate: 65% (1990)
Economic summary: GDP/PPP (1999 est.): $52.6 billion; per capita $5,500. **Real growth rate:** 6%. **Inflation:** 2.7%. **Unemployment:** 16.5%. **Arable land:** 19%. **Agriculture:** olives, grain, dairy products, tomatoes, citrus fruit, beef, sugar beets, dates, almonds. **Labor force:** 3 million (1997 est.); note: shortage of skilled labor; services, 55%; industry, 23%; agriculture, 22% (1995 est.). **Industries:** petroleum, mining (particularly phosphate and iron ore), tourism, textiles, footwear, food, beverages. **Natural resources:** petroleum, phosphates, iron ore, lead, zinc, salt, arable land. **Exports:** $5.8 billion (f.o.b., 1999 est.): textiles, mechanical goods, phosphates and chemicals, agricultural products, hydrocarbons. **Imports:** $8.3 billion (c.i.f., 1999 est.): machinery and equipment, hydrocarbons, chemicals, fuel, food. **Major trading partners:** France, Italy, Germany, Belgium, Libya, Spain, U.S.

Geography Tunisia, at the northernmost bulge of Africa, thrusts out toward Sicily to mark the division between the eastern and western Mediterranean Sea. Twice the size of South Carolina, it is bordered on the west by Algeria and by Libya on the south. Coastal plains on the east rise to a north-south escarpment that slopes gently to the west. The Sahara Desert lies in the southernmost part. Tunisia is more mountainous in the north, where the Atlas range continues from Algeria.

Government Republic.

History Tunisia was settled by the Phoenicians in the 12th century B.C. By the sixth and fifth centuries B.C., the great city-state of Carthage (derived from the Phoenician name for "new city") dominated much of the western Mediterranean. The three Punic Wars between Rome and Carthage (the second was the most famous, pitting the Roman general Scipio Africanus against Carthage's Hannibal) led to the complete destruction of Carthage by 146 B.C.

Except for an interval of Vandal conquest in A.D. 439–533, Carthage was part of the Roman Empire until the Arab conquest of 648–69. It was then ruled by various Arab and Berber dynasties until the Turks took it in 1570–74 and made it part of the Ottoman Empire until the 19th century. In the late 16th century, it was a stronghold for the Barbary pirates. French troops occupied the country in 1881, and the bey, the local Tunisian ruler, signed a treaty acknowledging a French protectorate.

Nationalist agitation forced France to recognize Tunisian independence and sovereignty in 1956. The Constituent Assembly deposed the bey on July 25, 1957, declared Tunisia a republic, and elected Habib Bourguiba as president. Bourguiba maintained a pro-Western foreign policy that earned him enemies. Tunisia refused to break relations with the U.S. during the Arab-Israeli War in June 1967. Concerned with Islamic fundamentalist plots against the state, the government stepped up efforts to eradicate the movement, including censorship and frequent detention of suspects.

In 1987, the aged Bourguiba was declared mentally unfit to continue as president and was removed from office. He was succeeded as president by General Zine al-Abidine Ben Ali, whose tenure was marked by a rise in Islamic fundamentalism and growing anti-Western sentiments among the populace.

Ben Ali was reelected in Oct. 1999 with 99% of the vote in an election criticized by many human rights observers. In May 2000 Ben Ali's Constitutional Democratic Assembly Party swept local elections with 92% of the vote, in a contest many opposition leaders boycotted. However, Tunisia's economy continued to improve in the late 1990s, making the country one of the most attractive in Africa for foreign investors.

Turkey

REPUBLIC OF TURKEY

National name: Türkiye Cumhuriyeti
President: Ahmet Necdet Sezer (2000)
Prime Minister: Bülent Ecevit (1999)
Area: 301,382 sq mi (incl. 9,121 in Europe) (780,580 sq km)
Population (2001 est.): 66,493,970 (average annual rate of natural increase 1.2%); birth rate: 18.3/1000; infant mortality rate: 47.3/1000; density per sq mi: 221
Capital (1996 est.): Ankara, 2,890,025. **Largest cities:**

Istanbul (2000 est.), 10,250,000 (metro. area); Izmir, 1,920,807; Adana, 1,010,363; Bursa, 949,810; Gaziantep, 683,557. **Monetary unit:** Turkish lira. **Language:** Turkish. **Ethnicity/race:** Turkish 80%, Kurdish 20%. **Religion:** Islam (mostly Sunni) 98%. Literacy rate: 81% (1990)
Economic summary: GDP/PPP (1999 est.): $409.4 billion; per capita $6,200. **Real growth rate:** –5%. **Inflation:** 65%. **Unemployment:** 7.3% plus underemployment of 6.9% (April 1999 est.). **Arable land:** 32%. **Agriculture:** tobacco, cotton, grain, olives, sugar beets, pulse, citrus; livestock. **Labor force:** 23.8 million (April 1999); note: about 1.5 million Turks work abroad (1994); agriculture, 45.8%; services, 33.7%; industry, 20.5% (April 1999). **Industries:** textiles, food processing, autos, mining (coal, chromite, copper, boron), steel, petroleum, construction, lumber, paper. **Natural resources:** antimony, coal, chromium, mercury, copper, borate, sulfur, iron ore, arable land, hydropower. **Exports:** $26 billion (f.o.b., 1999 est.): apparel, foodstuffs, textiles, metal manufactures. **Imports:** $40 billion (c.i.f., 1999 est.): machinery, semifinished goods, chemicals, transport equipment, fuels. **Major trading partners:** Germany, U.S., UK, Italy, France, Russia.

Geography Turkey is at the northeast end of the Mediterranean Sea in southeast Europe and southwest Asia. To the north is the Black Sea and to the west is the Aegean Sea. Its neighbors are Greece and Bulgaria to the west, Russia and Ukraine to the north (through the Black Sea), Georgia, Armenia, Azerbaijan, and Iran to the east, and Syria and Iraq to the south. The Dardanelles, the Sea of Marmara, and the Bosporus divide the country. Turkey in Europe comprises an area about equal to the state of Massachusetts. It is hilly country drained by the Maritsa River and its tributaries. Turkey in Asia, or Anatolia, is about the size of Texas. Its center is a treeless plateau rimmed by mountains.

Government Parliamentary democracy.

History Anatolia (Turkey in Asia) was occupied in about 1900 B.C. by the Indo-European Hittites and, after the Hittite empire's collapse in 1200 B.C., by Phrygians and Lydians. The Persian Empire occupied the area in the 6th century B.C., giving way to the Roman Empire, then later the Byzantine Empire. The Ottoman Turks first appeared in the early 13th century, subjugating Turkish and Mongol bands pressing against the eastern borders of Byzantium and making the Christian Balkan states their vassals. They gradually spread through the Near East and Balkans, capturing Constantinople in 1453 and storming the gates of Vienna two centuries later. At its height, the Ottoman Empire stretched from the Persian Gulf to western Algeria. Lasting for 600 years, the Ottoman Empire was not only one of the most powerful empires in the history of the Mediterranean region, but it generated a great cultural outpouring of Islamic art, architecture, and literature.

After the reign of Sultan Süleyman I the Magnificent (1494–1566), the Ottoman Empire began to decline politically, administratively, and economically. By the 18th century, Russia was seeking to establish itself as the protector of Christians in Turkey's Balkan territories. Russian ambitions were checked by Britain and France in the Crimean War (1854–56), but the Russo-Turkish War (1877–78) gave Bulgaria virtual independence and Romania and Serbia liberation from their nominal allegiance to the sultan. Turkish weakness stimulated a revolt of young liberals known as the Young Turks in 1909. They

forced Sultan Abdul Hamid to grant a constitution and install a liberal government. However, reforms were no barrier to further defeats in a war with Italy (1911–12) and the Balkan Wars (1912–13). Turkey sided with Germany in World War II, and, as a result, lost territory at the conclusion of the war.

Turkey's current boundaries were drawn in 1923 at the Conference of Lausanne, and Turkey became a republic with Kemal Atatürk as the first president. The Ottoman sultanate and caliphate were abolished, and modernization, reform, and industrialization began under Atatürk's direction. He secularized Turkish society, reducing Islam's dominant role and replacing Arabic with the Latin alphabet for writing the Turkish language. After Atatürk's death in 1938, parliamentary government and a multiparty system gradually took root in Turkey, despite periods of instability and brief intervals of military rule. Neutral during most of World War II, Turkey, on Feb. 23, 1945, declared war on Germany and Japan, but it took no active part in the conflict. Turkey became a full member of NATO in 1952, was a signatory in the Balkan Entente (1953), joined the Baghdad Pact (1955; later CENTO), joined the Organization for European Economic Cooperation (OEEC) and the Council of Europe, and became an associate member of the European Common Market in 1963.

Turkey invaded Cyprus by sea and air on July 20, 1974, following the failure of diplomatic efforts to resolve conflicts between Turkish and Greek Cypriots. Turkey unilaterally announced a ceasefire on Aug. 16, after having gained control of 40% of the island. Turkish Cypriots established their own state in the north on Feb. 13, 1975. In July 1975, after a 30-day warning, Turkey took control of all the U.S. installations except the joint defense base at Incirlik, which it reserved for "NATO tasks alone."

The establishment of military government in Sept. 1980 stopped the slide toward anarchy and brought some improvement in the economy. A Constituent Assembly, consisting of the six-member National Security Council and members appointed by them, drafted a new constitution that was approved by an overwhelming (91.5%) majority of the voters in a Nov. 6, 1982, referendum. Martial law was gradually lifted.

About 12 million Kurds, roughly 20% of Turkey's population, live in the southeast region of Turkey. Turkey, however, does not officially recognize Kurds as a minority group and is therefore exempted from protecting their rights. Oppression of Kurds and Kurdish culture led to the emergence in 1984 of the Kurdistan Workers' Party (PKK), a militant Kurdish terrorist campaign under the leadership of Abdullah Ocalan. Although the guerrilla movement sought independence at first, by the late 1980s the rebel Kurds were willing to accept an autonomous state or a federation with Turkey. In March 1995, Turkish troops moved into northern Iraq seeking to root out Kurdish rebels, who had used Iraq as a base. About 35,000 have died in clashes between the military and the PKK during the 1980s and '90s. On Feb. 16, 1999, Kurd leader and terrorist Abdullah Ocalan was captured, tried, and convicted of treason and separatism on June 2, 1999, and sentenced to death.

On Aug. 17, 1999, western Turkey was devastated by an earthquake (magnitude 7.4) that left more than 17,000 dead and 200,000 homeless. The government was decried for lax control of builders whose faulty construction increased the destruction and added to the death toll. On Nov. 12, another huge earthquake (magnitude 7.2) struck another section of western Turkey, leaving hundreds dead and thousands injured.

The Turkish government hopes an oil pipeline running from Baku, Azerbaijan, to the Mediterranean port city of Ceyhan, Turkey, will bolster the economy. Approved in 1999, the 1,000-mile pipeline will cost some $2.4 billion.

Turkmenistan

TURKMENISTAN

President-for-life: Saparmurad A. Niyazov (1990)
Area: 188,455 sq mi (488,100 sq km)
Population (2001 est.): 4,603,244 (average annual rate of natural increase: 2.0%); birth rate: 28.6/1000; infant mortality rate: 73.3/1000; density per sq mi: 24
Capital and largest city (1994 est.): Ashgabat, 518,000. **Other large cities:** Chardzhou, 166,400; Tashauz, 117,000. **Monetary unit:** Manat.
Languages: Turkmen, 72%; Russian, 12%; Uzbek, 9%. **Ethnicity/race (1995):** Turkmen 77%, Uzbek 9.2%, Russian 6.7%, Kazak 2%, other 5.1%.
Religions: Muslim 89%, Eastern Orthodox 9%, unknown 2%. **Literacy rate:** 98% (1989)
Economic summary: GDP/PPP (1999 est.): $7.7 billion; per capita $1,800. **Real growth rate:** 9%. **Inflation:** 30%. **Unemployment:** n.a. **Arable land:** 3%.
Agriculture: cotton, grain; livestock. **Labor force:** 2.34 million (1996); agriculture and forestry, 44%; industry and construction, 19%; other, 37% (1996).
Industries: natural gas, oil, petroleum products, textiles, food processing. **Natural resources:** petroleum, natural gas, coal, sulfur, salt. **Exports:** $1.1 billion (1999 est.): oil and gas, cotton. **Imports:** $1.25 billion (1999 est.): machinery and equipment, chemicals, foodstuffs. **Major trading partners:** Iran, Turkey, Russia, Kazakhstan, Tajikistan, Azerbaijan, Ukraine, Germany, U.S., Uzbekistan.

Geography Turkmenistan (formerly Turkmenia) is bounded by the Caspian Sea in the west, Kazakhstan in the north, Uzbekistan in the east, and Iran and Afghanistan in the south. About nine-tenths of Turkmenistan is desert, chiefly the Kara-Kum; this is one of the world's largest sand deserts at approximately 138,966 sq mi (360,000 sq km) in area. Many irrigation canals and reservoirs have been built, including the Kara-Kum Canal, which runs from the Amu Darya River westward to the Caspian Sea for a distance of 870 mi (1,400 km).

Government One-party republic.

History Turkmenistan was once part of the ancient Persian Empire. The Turkmen people were originally pastoral nomads and some of them continued this way of life up into the 20th century, living in transportable dome-shaped felt tents. The territory was ruled by the Seljuk Turks in the 11th century. The Mongols of Ghenghis Khan conquered the land in the 13th century and dominated the area for the next two centuries until they were deposed in the late 15th century by invading Uzbeks. Prior to the 19th century, Turkmenia was divided into two lands, one belonging to the khanate of Khiva and the other belonging to the khanate of Bukhara. In 1868, the khanate of Khiva was made part of the Russian empire and Turkmenia became known as the Transcaspia Region of Russian Turkistan. Turkmenistan was later formed out of the Turkistan Autonomous Soviet Socialist Republic, founded in 1922, and was made an independent Soviet Socialist Republic on May 13, 1925. It was the poorest of the Soviet republics.

Turkmenistan declared its sovereignty in Aug. 1990 and became a member of the Commonwealth of Independent States on Dec. 21, 1991, together with ten other former Soviet republics. It established a government more authoritarian than those functioning in the other newly independent central Asian republics. President Saparmurad A. Niyazov, also called the Turkmenbashy (Leader of All Turkmens), has attempted to create a cult of personality through heavy-handed self-promotion. Protests against his authoritarian rule and practices notwithstanding, Niyazov was declared president-for-life in 2000.

In the 1990s, Turkmenistan exported gas through a Russian pipeline, bringing in about $1 billion per year. But in 1993, Russia closed down Turkmenistan's only pipeline because it competed with Russia's own gas exportation. Turkmenistan was limited to exporting gas to its impoverished central Asian neighbors, who were unable to pay their bills. Turkmenistan then opened a pipeline route to Iran, generally agreed to be the most economical route for exporting Caspian oil, and thus ruffled the feathers of Iran's enemy, the U.S. So far, the new plan has not brought in money, and the country is living off loans from Western countries such as Germany who hope to partner with the oil-rich, money-poor country.

Tuvalu

Sovereign: Queen Elizabeth II (1952)
Governor-General: Tomasi Puapua (1998)
Prime Minister: Faimalaga Luka (2001)
Area: 10 sq mi (26 sq km)
Population (2001 est.): 10,991 (growth rate: 1.4%); birth rate: 21.6/1000; infant mortality rate: 22.7/1000; density per sq mi: 1,095
Capital and largest city (1991): Funafuti, 3,839.
Monetary unit: Tuvaluan dollar, Australian dollar.
Languages: Tuvaluan, English. **Ethnicity/race:** Polynesian 96%. **Religion:** Church of Tuvalu (Congregationalist) 97%. **Literacy rate:** less than 50%
Economic summary: GDP/PPP (1995 est.): $7.8 million; per capita $800. **Real growth rate:** 8.7%. **Inflation:** 3.9% (average 1985–93). **Unemployment:** n.a. **Arable land:** 0%. **Agriculture:** coconuts; fish. **Labor force:** n.a.; people make a living mainly through exploitation of the sea, reefs, and atolls and from wages sent home by those working abroad (mostly workers in the phosphate industry and sailors). **Industries:** fishing, tourism, copra. **Natural resources:** fish. **Exports:** $165,000 (f.o.b., 1989): copra. **Imports:** $4.4 million (c.i.f., 1989): food, animals, mineral fuels, machinery, manufactured goods. **Major trading partners:** Fiji, Australia, New Zealand. **Member of Commonwealth of Nations**

Geography Tuvalu consists of nine small islands scattered over 500,000 sq mi of the western Pacific, just south of the equator. The islands include Niulakita, Nukulaelae, Funafuti, Nukufetau, Vaitupu, Nui, Niutao, Nanumaga (Nanumanga), and Nanumea.

Government Constitutional democracy.

History Formerly the Ellice Islands, Tuvalu's first Polynesian settlers were probably Samoans or Tongans. The Ellice Islands became a British protectorate in 1892 and were annexed by Britain in 1915–16 as part of the Gilbert and Ellice Islands Colony. The Ellice Islands were separated from the Gilberts in 1975, given home rule, and renamed Tuvalu. Full independence was granted on Sept. 30, 1978, but it remained part of the Commonwealth. In 1979, the U.S. gave Tuvalu four islands that had been U.S. territory.

In 1997, the government adopted a strong stance on the need to control emissions of greenhouse gases in order to ensure the survival of low-lying island nations, which are threatened by rising sea levels—Tuvalu's highest point is just 16 ft above sea level. In 2000, Tuvalu became a member of the United Nations.

Uganda

REPUBLIC OF UGANDA

President: Yoweri Museveni (1986)
Prime Minister: Apolo Nsibambi (1999)
Area: 91,135 sq mi (236,040 sq km)
Population (2001 est.): 23,985,712 (average annual rate of natural increase: 3.0%); birth rate: 47.5/1000; infant mortality rate: 91.3/1000; density per sq mi: 263
Capital and largest city (1991 est.): Kampala, 773,463.
  Monetary unit: Ugandan shilling. **Languages:** English (official), Swahili, Luganda, Ateso, Luo. **Ethnicity/race:** Baganda 17%, Karamojong 12%, Basogo 8%, Iteso 8%, Langi 6%, Rwanda 6%, Bagisu 5%, Acholi 4%, Lugbara 4%, Bunyoro 3%, Batobo 3%, European, Asian, Arab 1%, other 23%. **Religions:** Christian 66%, Islam 16%. **Literacy rate:** 54% (1991)
Economic summary: GDP/PPP (1999 est.): $24.2 billion; per capita $1,060. **Real growth rate:** 5.5%. **Inflation:** 7% (1999). **Unemployment:** n.a. **Arable land:** 25%. **Agriculture:** coffee, tea, cotton, tobacco, cassava (tapioca), potatoes, corn, millet, pulses; beef, goat meat, milk, poultry. **Labor force:** 8.361 million (1993 est.); agriculture, 82%; industry, 5%; services, 13%. **Industries:** sugar, brewing, tobacco, cotton textiles, cement. **Natural resources:** copper, cobalt, hydropower, limestone, salt, arable land. **Exports:** $471 million (f.o.b., 1999): coffee, fish and fish products, tea; electrical products, iron and steel. **Imports:** $1.1 billion (f.o.b., 1999): vehicles, petroleum, medical supplies; cereals. **Major trading partners:** E.U., Kenya, UK, Japan, India, South Africa.
Member of the Commonwealth of Nations

Geography Uganda, twice the size of Pennsylvania, is in East Africa. It is bordered on the west by Congo, on the north by the Sudan, on the east by Kenya, and on the south by Tanzania and Rwanda. The country, which lies across the equator, is divided into three main areas—swampy lowlands, a fertile plateau with wooded hills, and a desert region. Lake Victoria forms part of the southern border.

Government Multiparty democracy.

History About 500 B.C. Bantu-speaking peoples migrated to the area now called Uganda. By the 14th century, three kingdoms dominated, Buganda (meaning "state of the Gandas"), Bunyoro, and Ankole. Uganda was first explored by Europeans as well as Arab traders in 1844. An Anglo-German agreement of 1890 declared it to be in the British sphere of influence in Africa, and the Imperial British East Africa Company was chartered to develop the area. The company did not prosper financially, and in 1894 a British protectorate was proclaimed. Few Europeans permanently settled in Uganda, but it attracted Indians, Pakistanis, and Goans, who became important players in Ugandan commerce.

Uganda became independent on Oct. 9, 1962, and Sir Edward Mutesa, the king of Buganda (Mutesa II),

was elected the first president and Milton Obote the first prime minister of the newly independent country. With the help of a young army officer, Col. Idi Amin, Prime Minister Obote seized control of the government from President Mutesa four years later.

On Jan. 25, 1971, Colonel Amin deposed President Obote. Obote went into exile in Tanzania. Amin expelled Asian residents and launched a reign of terror against Ugandan opponents, torturing and killing tens of thousands. In 1976, he had himself proclaimed "President for Life." In 1977, Amnesty International estimated that 300,000 may have died under his rule, including church leaders and recalcitrant cabinet ministers.

After Amin held military exercises on the Tanzanian border, angering Tanzania's president Julius Nyerere, a combined force of Tanzanian troops and Ugandan exiles loyal to former president Obote invaded Uganda and chased Amin into exile in Saudi Arabia. After a series of interim administrations, President Obote led his People's Congress Party to victory in 1980 elections that opponents charged were rigged. On July 27, 1985, army troops staged a coup and took over the government. Obote fled into exile. The military regime installed Gen. Tito Okello as chief of state.

The National Resistance Army (NRA), an anti-Obote group led by Yoweri Museveni, kept fighting after it had been excluded from the new regime. It seized Kampala on Jan. 29, 1986, and Museveni was declared president. Museveni has transformed the ruins of Idi Amin and Milton Obote's Uganda into an economic miracle, preaching a philosophy of self-sufficiency and anticorruption. Western countries have flocked to assist him in the country's transformation. Nevertheless, it remains one of Africa's poorest countries. A ban on political parties was lifted in 1996, and the incumbent Museveni won 72% of the vote, reflecting his popularity due to the country's economic recovery.

Uganda continues to battle the extremist Lord's Resistance Army based in Sudan. Close ties with Rwanda (many Rwandan Tutsi exiles helped Museveni come to power) led to the assistance of Uganda and Rwanda in the ousting of Zaire's Mobutu Sese Seko in 1997, and a year later, in efforts to unseat his successor, Laurent Kabila, whom both countries originally supported but from whom they grew estranged. In Aug. 1999, both Uganda and Rwanda signed the Congo peace agreement, along with Kabila, his foreign allies, and the rebel groups who fought against him. But despite the peace agreement, fighting in the Congo soon resumed.

Uganda has waged a successful campaign against AIDS, reducing the rate of new infections through an intensive public health campaign.

Museveni won reelection in March 2001 with 70% of the vote, following a nasty and spirited campaign.

Ukraine

UKRAINE

President: Leonid D. Kuchma (1994)
Prime Minister: Anatoli Kinakh (2001)
Area: 233,089 sq mi (603,700 sq km)
Population (2001 est.): 48,760,474 (average annual rate of natural increase: –0.7%); birth rate: 9.3/1000; infant mortality rate: 21.4/1000; density per sq mi: 209
Capital: Kyiv (Kiev), 2,637,000. **Other large cities:** Kharkiv, 1,622,000; Donetske, 1,121,000; Odessa, 1,104,000; Lviv, 803,000. **Monetary unit:** Hryvnia

(since Sept. 2, 1996). **Language:** Ukrainian.
Ethnicity/race: Ukrainian 73%, Russian 22%, Jewish 1%, other 4%. **Religions:** Orthodox 76%, Ukrainian Catholic (Uniate) 13.5%, Jewish 2.3%, Baptist, Mennonite, Protestant, and Muslim 8.2%. **Literacy rate:** 100% (1979)
Economic summary: GDP/PPP (1999 est.): $109.5 billion; per capita $2,200. **Real growth rate:** −0.4%. **Inflation:** 20%. **Unemployment:** 4.3% officially registered; large number of unregistered or underemployed workers (Dec. 1999). **Arable land:** 58%. **Agriculture:** grain, sugar beets, sunflower seeds, vegetables; beef, milk. **Labor force:** 22.8 million (year-end 1997); industry and construction, 32%; agriculture and forestry, 24%; health, education, and culture, 17%; trade and distribution, 8%; transport and communication, 7%; other, 12% (1996).
Industries: coal, electric power, ferrous and nonferrous metals, machinery and transport equipment, chemicals, food-processing (especially sugar). **Natural resources:** iron ore, coal, manganese, natural gas, oil, salt, sulfur, graphite, titanium, magnesium, kaolin, nickel, mercury, timber, arable land. **Exports:** $11.6 billion (1999 est.): ferrous and nonferrous metals, fuel and petroleum products, machinery and transport equipment, food products. **Imports:** $11.8 billion (1999 est.): energy, machinery and parts, transportation equipment, chemicals. **Major trading partners:** Russia, EU, China, Turkey, U.S.

Geography Located in southeast Europe, the country consists largely of fertile black soil steppes. Mountainous areas include the Carpathians in the southwest and the Crimean chain in the south. There are forest lakes in the north. Ukraine is bordered by Belarus on the north, by Russia on the north, northeast, and east, by the Sea of Azov and the Black Sea on the south, by Moldova and Romania on the southwest, and by Hungary, Slovakia, and Poland on the west.

Government Constitutional republic.

History Ukraine was known as "Kievan Rus" (from which *Russia* is a derivative) up until the 16th century. In the 9th century, Kiev was the major political and cultural center in eastern Europe. Kievan Rus reached the height of its power in the 10th century and adopted Byzantine Christianity, the Church Slavonic written language, and the Cyrillic alphabet during that period. The Mongol conquest in 1240 ended Kievan power. From the 13th to the 16th century, Kiev was under the influence of Poland and western Europe. The negotiation of the Union of Brest-Litovsk in 1596 divided the Ukrainians into Orthodox and Ukrainian Catholic faithful. In 1654, Ukraine asked the czar of Moscovy for protection against Poland, and the Treaty of Pereyasav signed that year recognized the suzerainty of Moscow. The agreement was interpreted by Moscow as an invitation to take over Kiev, and the Ukrainian state was eventually absorbed into the Russian empire.

After the Russian Revolution, Ukraine declared its independence from Russia on Jan. 28, 1918, and several years of warfare ensued with several groups. The Red Army finally was victorious over Kiev, and in 1920 Ukraine became a Soviet republic. In 1922, Ukraine became one of the founders of the United Soviet Socialist Republics. In the 1930s, the Soviet government's enforcement of collectivization met with peasant resistance, which in turn prompted the confiscation of grain from Ukrainian farmers by Soviet authorities; the resulting famine took an estimated 5 million lives. Ukraine was one of the most

devastated Soviet republics during World War II. (For details on World War II, *see* Headline History, World War II.) On April 26, 1986, the nation's nuclear power plant at Chernobyl was the site of the world's worst nuclear accident. On Oct. 29, 1991, the Ukrainian Parliament voted to shut down the reactor within two years' time and asked for international assistance in dismantling it.

When President Leonid Kravchuk was elected by the Ukrainian Parliament in 1990, he vowed to seek Ukrainian sovereignty. Ukraine declared its independence on Aug. 24, 1991. In Dec. 1991, Ukrainian, Russian, and Belorussian leaders cofounded a new Commonwealth of Independent States with the new capital to be situated in Minsk, Belarus. The new country's government was slow to reform the Soviet-era state-run economy, which was plagued by declining production, rising inflation, and widespread unemployment in the years following independence. The U.S. announced in Jan. 1994 that an agreement had been reached with Russia and Ukraine for the destruction of Ukraine's entire nuclear arsenal. In Oct. 1994, Ukraine began a program of economic liberalization and moved to reestablish central authority over Crimea. In 1995, Crimea's separatist leader was removed and the Crimean constitution revoked.

In June 1996, the last strategic nuclear warhead was removed to Russia. Also that month Parliament approved a new constitution that allows for private ownership of land. An agreement was signed in May 1997 on the future of the Black Sea fleet, by which Ukrainian and Russian ships will share the port of Sevastopol for 20 years. Ukraine and Russia also signed a 10-year political treaty three days later, by which, among other provisions, Russia recognized the political and territorial integrity of Ukraine, including the Crimean Peninsula.

The Russian financial crisis in fall 1998 led to severe problems for the Ukrainian economy, which is dependent on Russia for 40% of its foreign trade. Ukraine remains saddled with its Soviet-era economy, and most of its major industries are still under state control. Corruption is rampant, and Western investors have shown only minimal interest. The election of the reform-minded Viktor Yushchenko as prime minister in Dec. 1999, however, was greeted with optimism by the West. He was also highly popular among ordinary Ukrainians. In April of 2001, however, he was dismissed in a no-confidence vote engineered by Communist hardliners and Ukrainian big business.

In the winter of 2001 violent demonstrations rocked Ukraine, with protesters demanding the resignation and impeachment of authoritarian President Leonid Kuchma. Critics accuse Kuchma of involvement in the murder of a journalist critical of government corruption. Kuchma was recorded on tape urging that the journalist be disposed of.

United Arab Emirates

President: Sheikh Zayed Bin Sultan Al-Nahyan (1971)
Prime Minister: Sheikh Maktoum Bin Rashid Al-Maktoum (1990)
Area: 32,000 sq mi (82,880 sq km)
Population (2001 est.): 2,407,460 (average annual rate of natural increase: 1.4%); birth rate: 18.1/1000; infant mortality rate: 16.7/1000; density per sq mi: 75
Capital and largest city (1989 est.): Abu Dhabi, 363,432. **Monetary unit:** U.A.E. dirham. **Languages:** Arabic (official), English as a second language.
Ethnicity/race: Emiri 19%, other Arab and Iranian 23%, South Asian 50%, other expatriates (includes

Westerners and East Asians) 8% (1982). **Religions:** Islam (Sunni 80%, Shi'ite 16%), others 4%. **Literacy rate:** 68% (1980)
Economic summary: GDP/PPP (1999 est.): $41.5 billion; per capita $17,700. **Real growth rate:** 2.5%. **Inflation:** 4%. **Unemployment:** n.a. **Arable land:** 0%. **Agriculture:** dates, vegetables, watermelons; poultry, eggs, dairy products; fish. **Labor force:** 1.38 million (1998 est.); note: 75% of the population in the 15-64 age group is non-national (July 1998 est.); services, 60%; industry, 32%; agriculture, 8% (1996 est.). **Industries:** petroleum, fishing, petrochemicals, construction materials, some boat building, handicrafts, pearling. **Natural resources:** petroleum, natural gas. **Exports:** $34 billion (f.o.b., 1999 est.): crude oil 45%, natural gas, reexports, dried fish, dates. **Imports:** $27.5 billion (f.o.b., 1999 est.): machinery and transport equipment, chemicals, food. **Major trading partners:** Japan, South Korea, India, Singapore, Oman, Iran, U.S., UK, Germany, Italy.

Geography The United Arab Emirates, in the eastern part of the Arabian Peninsula, extends along part of the Gulf of Oman and the southern coast of the Persian Gulf. The nation is the size of Maine. Its neighbors are Saudi Arabia to the west and south, Qatar to the north, and Oman to the east. Most of the land is barren and sandy.

Government Federation formed in 1971 by seven emirates known as the Trucial States—Abu Dhabi (the largest), Dubai, Sharjah, Ajman, Fujairah, Ras al Khaimah, and Umm al-Qaiwain.

History Originally the area was inhabited by a seafaring people who were converted to Islam in the 7th century. Later, a dissident sect, the Carmathians, established a powerful sheikdom, and its army conquered Mecca. After the sheikdom disintegrated, its people became pirates. Threatening the Sultanate of Muscat and Oman early in the 19th century, the pirates provoked the intervention of the British, who in 1820 enforced a partial truce and in 1853 a permanent truce. Thus what had been called the Pirate Coast was renamed the Trucial Coast. The British provided the nine Trucial states with protection but did not formally administer them as a colony.

The British withdrew from the Persian Gulf in 1971, and the Trucial states became a federation called the United Arab Emirates (UAE). Two of the Trucial states, Bahrain and Oman, chose not to join the federation, reducing the number of states to seven.

The country signed a military defense agreement with the U.S. in 1994 and one with France in 1995. In 1997, UAE officials protested Iranian military activities in the Persian Gulf, especially in regard to the ownership of three Gulf islands, which had been the subject of disputes for many years.

In 2000, one of the biggest arms deals in history took place, with the United Arab Emirates buying 80 fighter jets and missiles from Lockheed Martin for nearly $8 billion.

United Kingdom

UNITED KINGDOM OF GREAT BRITAIN AND NORTHERN IRELAND
Sovereign: Queen Elizabeth II (1952)
Prime Minister: Tony Blair (1997)
Area: 94,525 sq mi (244,820 sq km)
Population (2001 est.): 59,647,790 (average annual rate of natural increase: 0.1%); birth rate: 11.5/1000; infant mortality rate: 5.5/1000; density per sq mi: 631

Capital and largest city (2000 est.): London, 11,800,000 (metro. area). **Other large cities:** Birmingham, 1,009,100; Leeds, 721,800; Glasgow, 681,470; Liverpool, 479,000; Bradford, 477,500; Edinburgh, 441,620; Manchester, 434,600; Bristol, 396,600. **Monetary unit:** Pound sterling (£). **Languages:** English, Welsh, Scots Gaelic. **Ethnicity/race:** English 81.5%; Scottish 9.6%; Irish 2.4%; Welsh 1.9%; Ulster 1.8%; West Indian, Indian, Pakistani, and other 2.8%. **Religions:** Church of England (established church), Church of Wales (disestablished), Church of Scotland (established church—Presbyterian), Church of Ireland (disestablished), Roman Catholic, Methodist, Congregational, Baptist, Jewish. **Literacy rate:** 99% (1978)
Economic summary: GDP/PPP (1999 est.): $1.29 trillion; per capita $21,800. **Real growth rate:** 1.9%. **Inflation:** 2.3% (1999). **Unemployment:** 6% (1999). **Arable land:** 25%. **Agriculture:** cereals, oilseed, potatoes, vegetables; cattle, sheep, poultry; fish. **Labor force:** 29.2 million (1999); services, 68.9%; manufacturing and construction, 17.5%; government, 11.3%; energy, 1.2%; agriculture, 1.1% (1996). **Industries:** production machinery including machine tools, electric power equipment, automation equipment, railroad equipment, shipbuilding, aircraft, motor vehicles and parts, electronics and communications equipment, metals, chemicals, coal, petroleum, paper and paper products, food processing, textiles, clothing, and other consumer goods. **Natural resources:** coal, petroleum, natural gas, tin, limestone, iron ore, salt, clay, chalk, gypsum, lead, silica, arable land. **Exports:** $271 billion (f.o.b., 1998): manufactured goods, fuels, chemicals; food, beverages, tobacco. **Imports:** $305.9 billion (f.o.b., 1998): manufactured goods, machinery, fuels; foodstuffs. **Major trading partners:** EU, U.S.

Geography The United Kingdom, consisting of England, Wales, Scotland, and Northern Ireland, is twice the size of New York State. England, in the southeast part of the British Isles, is separated from Scotland on the north by the granite Cheviot Hills; from them the Pennine chain of uplands extends south through the center of England, reaching its highest point in the Lake District in the northwest. To the west along the border of Wales—a land of steep hills and valleys—are the Cambrian Mountains, while the Cotswolds, a range of hills in Gloucestershire, extend into the surrounding shires.

Important rivers flowing into the North Sea are the Thames, Humber, Tees, and Tyne. In the west are the Severn and Wye, which empty into the Bristol Channel and are navigable, as are the Mersey and Ribble.

Government The United Kingdom is a constitutional monarchy and parliamentary democracy, with a queen and a Parliament that has two houses: the House of Lords, with 574 life peers, 92 hereditary peers, 26 bishops, and the House of Commons, which has 651 popularly elected members. Supreme legislative power is vested in Parliament, which sits for five years unless sooner dissolved. The House of Lords was stripped of most of its power in 1911, and now its main function is to revise legislation. In Nov. 1999 hundreds of hereditary peers were expelled in an effort to make the body more democratic. The executive power of the Crown is exercised by the cabinet, headed by the prime minister.

Ruler Queen Elizabeth II, born April 21, 1926, elder daughter of King George VI and Queen Elizabeth, succeeded to the throne on the death of her father on

Feb. 6, 1952. On Nov. 20, 1947, she married Prince Philip, duke of Edinburgh, born June 10, 1921. Their children are Prince Charles[1] (heir apparent), born Nov. 14, 1948; Princess Anne, born Aug. 15, 1950; Prince Andrew, born Feb. 19, 1960; and Prince Edward, born March 10, 1964. Prince William Arthur Philip Louis, son of Prince Charles and the late princess of Wales and second in line to the throne, was born June 21, 1982. A second son, Prince Henry Charles Albert David, was born Sept. 15, 1984, and is third in line.

History Stonehenge and other examples of prehistoric culture are what remains of the earliest inhabitants of Britain. Celtic peoples followed. Roman invasions of the 1st century B.C. brought Britain into contact with continental Europe. When the Roman legions withdrew in the 5th century A.D., Britain fell easy prey to the invading hordes of Angles, Saxons, and Jutes from Scandinavia and the Low Countries. The invasions had little effect on the Celtic peoples of Wales and Scotland. Seven large Anglo-Saxon kingdoms were established, and the original Britons were forced into Wales and Scotland. It was not until the 10th century that the country finally became united under the kings of Wessex. Following the death of Edward the Confessor (1066), a dispute about the succession arose, and William, duke of Normandy, invaded England, defeating the Saxon king, Harold II, at the Battle of Hastings (1066). The Norman conquest introduced Norman French law and feudalism.

The reign of Henry II (1154–89), first of the Plantagenets, saw an increasing centralization of royal power at the expense of the nobles, but in 1215 John (1199–1216) was forced to sign the Magna Carta, which awarded the people, especially the nobles, certain basic rights. Edward I (1272–1307) continued the conquest of Ireland, reduced Wales to subjection, and made some gains in Scotland. In 1314, however, English forces led by Edward II were ousted from Scotland after the Battle of Bannockburn. The late 13th and early 14th centuries saw the development of a separate House of Commons with tax-raising powers. Edward III's claim to the throne of France led to the Hundred Years' War (1338–1453) and the loss of almost all the large English territory in France. In England, the great poverty and discontent caused by the war were intensified by the Black Death, a plague that reduced the population by about one-third. The Wars of the Roses (1455–85), a struggle for the throne between the House of York and the House of Lancaster, ended in the victory of Henry Tudor (Henry VII) at Bosworth Field (1485).

During the reign of Henry VIII (1509–47), the church in England asserted its independence from the Roman Catholic Church. Under Edward VI and Mary, the two extremes of religious fanaticism were reached, and it remained for Henry's daughter, Elizabeth I (1558–1603), to set up the Church of England on a moderate basis. In 1588, the Spanish Armada, a fleet sent out by Catholic King Philip II of Spain, was defeated by the English and destroyed during a storm. During Elizabeth's reign, England became a world power. Elizabeth's heir was a Stuart—James VI of Scotland—who joined the two crowns as James I (1603–25). The Stuart kings incurred large debts and

were forced either to depend on Parliament for taxes or to raise money by illegal means. In 1642, war broke out between Charles I and a large segment of the Parliament; Charles was defeated and executed in 1649, and the monarchy was then abolished. After the death in 1658 of Oliver Cromwell, the lord protector, the Puritan Commonwealth fell to pieces and Charles II was placed on the throne in 1660. The struggle between the king and Parliament continued, but Charles II knew when to compromise. His brother, James II (1685–88), possessed none of his ability and was ousted by the Revolution of 1688, which confirmed the primacy of Parliament. James's daughter, Mary, and her husband, William of Orange, then became the rulers.

Queen Anne's reign (1702–14) was marked by the duke of Marlborough's victories over France at Blenheim, Oudenarde, and Malplaquet in the War of the Spanish Succession. England and Scotland meanwhile were joined by the Act of Union (1707). Upon the death of Anne, the distant claims of the elector of Hanover were recognized, and he became king of Great Britain and Ireland as George I. The unwillingness of the Hanoverian kings to rule resulted in the formation by the royal ministers of a cabinet, headed by a prime minister, which directed all public business. Abroad, the constant wars with France expanded the British Empire all over the globe, particularly in North America and India. This imperial growth was checked by the revolt of the American colonies (1775–81). Struggles with France broke out again in 1793 and during the Napoleonic Wars, which ended at Waterloo in 1815.

The Victorian era, named after Queen Victoria (1837–1901), saw the growth of a democratic system of government that had begun with the Reform Bill of 1832. The two important wars in Victoria's reign were the Crimean War against Russia (1853–56) and the Boer War (1899–1902), the latter enormously extending Britain's influence in Africa. Increasing uneasiness at home and abroad marked the reign of Edward VII (1901–10). Within four years after the accession of George V in 1910, Britain entered World War I when Germany invaded Belgium. The nation was led by coalition cabinets, headed first by Herbert Asquith and then, starting in 1916, by the Welsh statesman David Lloyd George. Postwar labor unrest culminated in the general strike of 1926.

King Edward VIII succeeded to the throne on Jan. 20, 1936, at his father's death, but abdicated on Dec. 11, 1936 (in order to marry an American divorcée, Wallis Warfield Simpson) in favor of his brother, who became George VI.

The efforts of Prime Minister Neville Chamberlain to stem the rising threat of Nazism in Germany failed with the German invasion of Poland on Sept. 1, 1939, which was followed by Britain's entry into World War II on Sept. 3. Allied reverses in the spring of 1940 led to Chamberlain's resignation and the formation of another coalition war cabinet by the Conservative leader, Winston Churchill, who led Britain through most of World War II. Churchill resigned shortly after V-E Day, May 7, 1945, but then formed a "caretaker" government that remained in office until after the parliamentary elections in July, which the Labor Party won overwhelmingly. The new government, formed by Clement R. Attlee, began a moderate socialist program.

In 1951, Churchill again became prime minister at the head of a Conservative government. George VI died on Feb. 6, 1952, and was succeeded by his

---

1. The title Prince of Wales, which is not inherited, was conferred on Prince Charles by his mother on July 26, 1958. The investiture ceremony took place on July 1, 1969. The previous Prince of Wales was Prince Edward Albert, who held the title from 1911 to 1936 before he became Edward VIII.

Rulers of England and Great Britain

Name	Born	Ruled[1]
SAXONS[2]		
Egbert[3]	c. 775	802–839
Ethelwulf	?	839–858
Ethelbald	?	858–860
Ethelbert	?	860–865
Ethelred I	?	865–871
Alfred the Great	849	871–899
Edward the Elder	c. 870	899–924
Athelstan	895	924–939
Edmund I the Deed-doer	921	939–946
Edred	c. 925	946–955
Edwy the Fair	c. 943	955–959
Edgar the Peaceful	943	959–975
Edward the Martyr	c. 962	975–978
Ethelred II the Unready	968	978–1016
Edmund II Ironside	c. 993	1016
DANES		
Canute	995	1016–1035
Harold I Harefoot	c.1016	1035–1040
Hardecanute	c.1018	1040–1042
SAXONS		
Edward the Confessor	c.1004	1042–1066
Harold II	c.1020	1066
HOUSE OF NORMANDY		
William I the Conqueror	1027	1066–1087
William II Rufus	c.1056	1087–1100
Henry I Beauclerc	1068	1100–1135
Stephen of Boulogne	c.1100	1135–1154
HOUSE OF PLANTAGENET		
Henry II	1133	1154–1189
Richard I Coeur de Lion	1157	1189–1199
John Lackland	1167	1199–1216
Henry III	1207	1216–1272
Edward I Longshanks	1239	1272–1307
Edward II	1284	1307–1327
Edward III	1312	1327–1377
Richard II	1367	1377–1399[4]
HOUSE OF LANCASTER		
Henry IV Bolingbroke	1367	1399–1413
Henry V	1387	1413–1422

Name	Born	Ruled[1]
Henry VI	1421	1422–1461[5]
HOUSE OF YORK		
Edward IV	1442	1461–1483[5]
Edward V	1470	1483–1483
Richard III	1452	1483–1485
HOUSE OF TUDOR		
Henry VII	1457	1485–1509
Henry VIII	1491	1509–1547
Edward VI	1537	1547–1553
Jane (Lady Jane Grey)[6]	1537	1553–1553
Mary I ("Bloody Mary")	1516	1553–1558
Elizabeth I	1533	1558–1603
HOUSE OF STUART		
James I[7]	1566	1603–1625
Charles I	1600	1625–1649
COMMONWEALTH		
Council of State	—	1649–1653
Oliver Cromwell[8]	1599	1653–1658
Richard Cromwell[8]	1626	1658–1659[9]
RESTORATION OF HOUSE OF STUART		
Charles II	1630	1660–1685
James II	1633	1685–
		1688[10]
William III[11]	1650	1689–1702
Mary II[11]	1662	1689–1694
Anne	1665	1702–1714
HOUSE OF HANOVER		
George I	1660	1714–1727
George II	1683	1727–1760
George III	1738	1760–1820
George IV	1762	1820–1830
William IV	1765	1830–1837
Victoria	1819	1837–1901
HOUSE OF SAXE-COBURG[12]		
Edward VII	1841	1901–1910
HOUSE OF WINDSOR[12]		
George V	1865	1910–1936
Edward VIII	1894	1936[13]
George VI	1895	1936–1952
Elizabeth II	1926	1952–

1. Year of end of rule is also that of death, unless otherwise indicated. 2. Dates for Saxon kings are still subject of controversy. 3. Became king of West Saxons in 802; considered (from 828) first king of all England. 4. Died 1400. 5. Henry VI reigned again briefly 1470–71. 6. Nominal queen for 9 days; not counted as queen by some authorities. She was beheaded in 1554. 7. Ruled in Scotland as James VI (1567–1625). 8. Lord Protector. 9. Died 1712. 10. Died 1701. 11. Joint rulers (1689–1694). 12. Name changed from Saxe-Coburg to Windsor in 1917. 13. Was known after his abdication as the duke of Windsor, died 1972.

daughter Elizabeth II. Churchill stepped down in 1955 in favor of Sir Anthony Eden, who resigned on grounds of ill health in 1957 and was succeeded by Harold Macmillan and Sir Alec Douglas-Home. In 1964, Harold Wilson led the Labor Party to victory. A lagging economy brought the Conservatives back to power in 1970. Prime Minister Edward Heath won Britain's admission to the European Community. Margaret Thatcher became Britain's first woman prime minister as the Conservatives won 339 seats on May 3, 1979.

An Argentine invasion of the Falkland Islands on April 2, 1982, involved Britain in a war 8,000 mi from the home islands. Although Argentina had long claimed the Falklands, known as the *Malvinas* in Spanish, negotiations were in progress until a month before the invasion. When more than 11,000 Argentine troops on the Falklands surrendered on June 14, 1982, Thatcher declared her intention to garrison the islands indefinitely, together with a naval presence. Although there were continuing economic problems and foreign

policy disputes, an upswing in the economy in 1986–87 led Thatcher to call elections for June 11 in which she won a near-unprecedented third consecutive term. Through much, if not all, of 1990 the Conservatives were losing the confidence of the electorate. The unpopularity of her poll tax together with an uncompromising position toward further European integration eroded support within her own party. When John Major won the Conservative Party leadership in November, Thatcher resigned, paving the way for the queen to ask Mr. Major to form a government.

In the middle of a long recession John Major called a national election for April 1992. Confounding many political observers, the Conservatives won but by a far narrower margin than previously. After months of political maneuvering the UK ratified the Maastrict Treaty in Aug. 1993.

Eighteen years of Conservative rule ended in May 1997 when Tony Blair and the Labour Party triumphed in the British elections. Blair has been compared to U.S. president Bill Clinton for his youthful,

British Prime Ministers Since 1770

Name	Term	Name	Term
Lord North (Tory)	1770–1782	William E. Gladstone (Liberal)	1886–1886
Marquis of Rockingham (Whig)	1782–1782	Marquis of Salisbury (Conservative)	1886–1892
Earl of Shelburne (Whig)	1782–1783	William E. Gladstone (Liberal)	1892–1894
Duke of Portland (Coalition)	1783–1783	Earl of Rosebery (Liberal)	1894–1895
William Pitt, the Younger (Tory)	1783–1801	Marquis of Salisbury (Conservative)	1895–1902
Henry Addington (Tory)	1801–1804	Arthur James Balfour (Conservative)	1902–1905
William Pitt, the Younger (Tory)	1804–1806	Sir H. Campbell-Bannerman (Liberal)	1905–1908
Baron Grenville (Whig)	1806–1807	Herbert H. Asquith (Liberal)	1908–1915
Duke of Portland (Tory)	1807–1809	Herbert H. Asquith (Coalition)	1915–1916
Spencer Perceval (Tory)	1809–1812	David Lloyd George (Coalition)	1916–1922
Earl of Liverpool (Tory)	1812–1827	Andrew Bonar Law (Conservative)	1922–1923
George Canning (Tory)	1827–1827	Stanley Baldwin (Conservative)	1923–1924
Viscount Goderich (Tory)	1827–1828	James Ramsay MacDonald (Labor)	1924–1924
Duke of Wellington (Tory)	1828–1830	Stanley Baldwin (Conservative)	1924–1929
Earl Grey (Whig)	1830–1834	James Ramsay MacDonald (Labor)	1929–1931
Viscount Melbourne (Whig)	1834–1834	James Ramsay MacDonald (Coalition)	1931–1935
Sir Robert Peel (Tory)	1834–1835	Stanley Baldwin (Coalition)	1935–1937
Viscount Melbourne (Whig)	1835–1841	Neville Chamberlain (Coalition)	1937–1940
Sir Robert Peel (Tory)	1841–1846	Winston Churchill (Coalition)	1940–1945
Earl Russell (Whig)	1846–1852	Clement R. Attlee (Labor)	1945–1951
Earl of Derby (Tory)	1852–1852	Sir Winston Churchill (Conservative)	1951–1955
Earl of Aberdeen (Coalition)	1852–1855	Sir Anthony Eden (Conservative)	1955–1957
Viscount Palmerston (Liberal)	1855–1858	Harold Macmillan (Conservative)	1957–1963
Earl of Derby (Conservative)	1858–1859	Sir Alec Frederick Douglas-Home	1963–1964
Viscount Palmerston (Liberal)	1859–1865	(Conservative)	
Earl Russell (Liberal)	1865–1866	Harold Wilson (Labor)	1964–1970
Earl of Derby (Conservative)	1866–1868	Edward Heath (Conservative)	1970–1974
Benjamin Disraeli (Conservative)	1868–1868	Harold Wilson (Labor)	1974–1976
William E. Gladstone (Liberal)	1868–1874	James Callaghan (Labor)	1976–1979
Benjamin Disraeli (Conservative)	1874–1880	Margaret Thatcher (Conservative)	1979–1990
William E. Gladstone (Liberal)	1880–1885	John Major (Conservative)	1990–1997
Marquis of Salisbury (Conservative)	1885–1886	Tony Blair (Labor)	1997–

telegenic personality and centrist views. He produced constitutional reform that partially decentralized the UK, leading to the formation of separate Parliaments in Wales and Scotland by 1999. Britain turned over its colony Hong Kong to China in July 1997.

Blair's controversial meeting in Oct. 1997 with Sinn Fein's president, Gerry Adams, was the first meeting in 76 years between a British prime minister and a Sinn Fein leader. It infuriated numerous factions but was a symbolic gesture in support of the nascent peace talks in Northern Ireland. In 1998 the Good Friday Agreement, strongly supported by Tony Blair, held out the promise of peace between Catholics and Protestants, but talks ran aground in 1999.

Along with the U.S., Britain launched air strikes against Iraq in Dec. 1998 after Saddam Hussein expelled UN arms inspectors. Low-grade bombings of Iraq continued throughout 1999. In the spring of 1999, Britain spearheaded the NATO operation in Kosovo, which resulted in Yugoslavian president Slobodan Milosevic's withdrawal from the territory. British peacekeeping forces remain in Kosovo.

In the fall of 1999, Britain and France argued heatedly about France's refusal to allow the importation of British beef. France remained leery of the possibility of infection from bovine spongiform encephalopathy (BSE), commonly known as mad cow disease, despite the fact that the EU had lifted the three-year ban on British beef in August.

In the fall of 2000 and winter of 2001, Great Britain was beset by a series of problems. In Sept. 2000 rising oil prices prompted protests by truck drivers and farmers who demanded a reduction in the fuel tax. In Nov. 2000, a series of unusually severe rain-

storms and tornados caused high flooding and killed 12 people. In Feb. 2001, foot-and-mouth disease broke out among British livestock, prompting other nations to ban British meat import and forcing the slaughter of thousands of cattle, pigs, and sheep in an effort to stem the highly contagious disease. The outbreak also forced the cancellation of sporting events and prompted travel warnings for rural England. The episode cost farmers and the tourist industry billions of dollars.

In June, 2001, Blair won a second landslide victory, with the Labour Party capturing 413 seats in Parliament. Blair campaigned as a centrist Labour candidate, pledging to improve the health care system and education. He also pledged to submit Britain's adoption of the single European currency, the euro, to a referendum. Led by William Hague, the Conservative Party only picked up one additional seat, for a total of 166 seats. Hague, who had campaigned against Britain's adopting the single European currency, resigned after the election.

Northern Ireland
Status: Part of United Kingdom
Area: 5,452 sq mi (14,121 sq km)
Population (1998 est.): 1,688,600
Capital and largest city (1992): Belfast, 287,500.
   Monetary unit: British pound sterling (£). **Language:** English. **Religions:** Presbyterian, Church of Ireland, Roman Catholic, Methodist.

Geography Northern Ireland is composed of 26 districts, derived from the boroughs of Belfast and Londonderry and the counties of Antrim, Armagh,

Down, Fermanagh, Londonderry, and Tyrone. Together they are commonly called Ulster, though the territory does not include the entire ancient province of Ulster. Predominantly Protestant, it forms the northern part of the island of Ireland, westernmost of the British Isles. It is slightly larger than Connecticut.

Government Northern Ireland is an integral part of the United Kingdom (it has 12 representatives in the British House of Commons), but under the terms of the Government of Ireland Act in 1920, it had a semi-autonomous government. In 1972, however, after three years of sectarian violence between Protestants and Catholics that resulted in more than 400 dead and thousands injured, Britain suspended the Ulster Parliament. The Ulster counties became governed directly from London after an attempt to return certain powers to an elected assembly in Belfast.

As a result of the Good Friday Agreement of 1998, a new coalition government was formed on Dec. 2, 1999, with the British government formally transferring governing power to the Northern Irish Parliament. David Trimble, Protestant leader of the Ulster Unionist Party (UUP) and winner of the 1998 Nobel Peace Prize, became first minister. Britain has suspended the government numerous times, primarily because of the Northern Irish government's disagreements over the decommissioning of weapons. On July 1, 2001, Trimble resigned after giving the IRA an ultimatum on disarming.

History Ulster was part of Catholic Ireland until the reign of Elizabeth I (1558–1603) when, after suppressing three Irish rebellions, the Crown confiscated lands in Ireland and settled the Scots Presbyterians in Ulster. Another rebellion in 1641–51, brutally crushed by Oliver Cromwell, resulted in the settlement of Anglican Englishmen in Ulster. Subsequent political policy favoring Protestants and disadvantaging Catholics encouraged further Protestant settlement in Northern Ireland.

Northern Ireland did not separate from the South until William Gladstone presented, in 1886, his proposal for home rule in Ireland. The Protestants in the North feared domination by the Catholic majority. Industry, moreover, was concentrated in the North and dependent on the British market. When World War I began, civil war threatened between the regions. Northern Ireland, however, did not become a political entity until the six counties accepted the Home Rule Bill of 1920. This set up a semiautonomous Parliament in Belfast and a Crown-appointed governor advised by a cabinet of the prime minister and eight ministers, as well as a 12-member representation in the House of Commons in London.

When the Republic of Ireland gained sovereignty in 1922, relations improved between North and South, although the Irish Republican Army (IRA), outlawed in recent years, continued the struggle to end the partition of Ireland. In 1966–69, rioting and street fighting between Protestants and Catholics occurred in Londonderry, fomented by extremist nationalist Protestants, who feared the Catholics might attain a local majority, and by Catholics demonstrating for civil rights. These confrontations became known as "the Troubles."

The religious communities, Catholic and Protestant, became hostile armed camps. British troops were brought in to separate them, but themselves became a target of Catholics, particularly by the IRA, which by this time had turned into a full-fledged terrorist movement. The goal of the IRA was to eject the British and

unify Northern Ireland with the Irish Republic to the south. The Protestants remained tenaciously loyal to the United Kingdom, and various Protestant terrorist organizations pursued the Unionist cause through violence. Various attempts at representational government and power-sharing foundered during the 1970s, and both sides were further polarized. Direct rule from London and the presence of British troops failed to stop the violence.

In Oct. 1977, the 1976 Nobel Peace Prize was awarded to Mairead Corrigan and Betty Williams, founders of the Community of Peace People, a nonsectarian organization dedicated to creating peace in Northern Ireland. Intermittent violence continued, however, and on Aug. 27, 1979, an IRA bomb killed Lord Mountbatten as he was sailing off southern Ireland, heightening tensions. Catholic protests over the death of IRA hunger striker Bobby Sands in 1981 fueled more violence. Riots, sniper fire, and terrorist attacks killed more than 3,200 people between 1969 and 1998. Among the attempts at reconciliation undertaken during the 1980s was the Anglo-Irish Agreement (1985), which, to the dismay of Unionists, marked the first time the Republic of Ireland had been given an official consultative role in the affairs of the province.

In 1997, Northern Ireland made a significant step in the direction of stemming sectarian strife. The first formal peace talks began on Oct. 6 with representatives of eight major Northern Irish political parties participating, a feat that in itself required three years of negotiations. Two smaller Protestant parties, including hard-liner Ian Paisley's Democratic Unionists, boycotted the talks. For the first time, Sinn Fein, the political wing of the IRA, won two seats in the British Parliament, which went to Sinn Fein president Gerry Adams and second-in-command Martin McGuinness. Although the election strengthened the IRA's political legitimacy, it was the IRA's resumption of the 17-month cease-fire, which had collapsed in Feb. 1996, that gained them a place at the negotiating table.

A landmark settlement, the Good Friday Agreement of April 10, 1998, came after 19 months of intensive negotiations that involved eight of the ten Northern Irish political parties. Chaired by former U.S. senator George Mitchell, the talks were advanced by a high-profile set of mediators, including British prime minister Tony Blair, Irish prime minister Bertie Ahern, and U.S. president Bill Clinton. Two participating groups, the Protestant Ulster Democratic Party and Sinn Fein, were temporarily suspended from the talks because of continued paramilitary activities. The accord called for Protestants to share political power with the minority Catholics, and it gave the Republic of Ireland a voice in Northern Irish affairs. In turn, Catholics were to suspend the goal of a united Ireland—a territorial claim that was the raison d'être of the IRA and was written into the Irish Republic's constitution—unless the largely Protestant North voted in favor of such an arrangement, an unlikely occurrence.

The resounding commitment to the settlement was demonstrated in a dual referendum on May 22, 1998: the North approved the accord by a vote of 71% to 29%, and in the Irish Republic 94% favored it. But the deaths of three Catholic boys in July 1998 during the traditional Protestant marches through Catholic neighborhoods was an appalling reminder of the fragility of peace. In October, the Nobel Peace Prize was awarded to John Hume and David Trimble, leaders of the largest Catholic and Protestant political parties, an incentive for all sides to ensure that this time the peace would last.

In Dec. 1998 the rival Northern Ireland politicians agreed on the organization and contents of the new coalition government, but in June 1999 the peace process again hit an impasse when the IRA refused to disarm prior to the assembly of Northern Ireland's new provincial cabinet. Sinn Fein insisted the IRA would only begin giving up its illegal weapons after the formation of the new government; Unionists demanded disarmament first. As a result, the Ulster Unionists boycotted the assembly session that would have nominated the cabinet to run the new coalition government. The nascent Northern Irish government was stillborn in July 1999.

Subsequent talks on the agreement, which would have ended three decades of direct rule from London, seemed to go nowhere, despite the last-ditch intervention of George Mitchell, who helped engineer the Good Friday Agreement. Finally, at the end of November, David Trimble, leader of the Ulster Unionists, abandoned the seemingly sacrosanct "no guns, no government" position, and took a difficult leap of faith in agreeing to form a government prior to Sinn Fein's disarmament. If the IRA did not begin the destruction of their weapons by Jan. 31, 2000, however, the Ulster Unionists threatened they would withdraw from the Northern Irish Parliament, shutting down the new government. With this compromise in place, the new government was quickly formed, and on Dec. 2, 1999, the British government formally transferred governing power to the Northern Irish Parliament. Two leaders of Sinn Fein, Gerry Adams and Martin McGuinness, received seats in the 4-party, 12-member parliament. By the deadline, Sinn Fein had made little progress toward disarmament, and claimed it had not made any such commitment. As a result, the British government suspended Parliament on Feb. 12, 2000, and once again imposed direct rule. On May 30, 2000, Sinn Fein again pledged to put the IRA's weapons "beyond use," and Britain restored parliamentary powers. While the IRA did allow for the inspection of some of its arms dumps, the months limped by without real progress, and Sinn Fein's commitment to disarmament once again appeared strikingly disingenuous. Finally, David Trimble resigned as first minister of the Northern Ireland Assembly on July 1, 2001, after giving the IRA an ultimatum on disarming. In August the IRA offered another vague disarmament plan, which its supporters hailed as a historic breakthrough. Days later the offer was rescinded.

Some progress, however, has been made on the other key issue of the Good Friday Agreement—reform of the Royal Ulster Constabulary, the notorious and overwhelmingly Protestant Northern Irish police force.

Scotland

Status: Part of United Kingdom
First Minister: Henry McLeish (2000)
Area: 30,414 sq mi (78,772 sq km)
Population (1996 est.): 5,128,000; density per sq mi: 168.6
Capital (1995 est.): Edinburgh, 441,620. **Largest city:** Glasgow, 681,470. **Monetary unit:** British pound sterling (£). **Languages:** English, Scots Gaelic.
Religions: Church of Scotland (established church—Presbyterian), Roman Catholic, Scottish Episcopal Church, Baptist, Methodist

Geography Scotland occupies the northern third of the island of Great Britain. It is bounded by England in the south and on the other three sides by water: by

the Atlantic Ocean on the west and north and by the North Sea on the east. Scotland is divided into three physical regions—the Highlands; the Central Lowlands, containing two-thirds of the population; and the Southern Uplands. The western Highland coast is intersected throughout by long, narrow sea lochs, or fjords. Scotland also includes the Outer and Inner Hebrides and other islands off the west coast and the Orkney and Shetland Islands off the north coast. The famous Scottish Highlands include a series of lochs (or lakes), the largest of which is Loch Ness, famous for its mythical monster.

Government England and Scotland have shared a monarch since 1603 and a Parliament since 1707, but in May 1999, Scotland elected its own Parliament for the first time in three centuries. The new Scottish legislature was in part the result of British prime minister Tony Blair's campaign promise to permit devolution, the transfer of local powers from London to Edinburgh. In a Sept. 1997 referendum, 74% of Scotland voted in favor of their own Parliament, which controls most domestic affairs, including health, education, and transportation, and has powers to legislate and raise taxes. Queen Elizabeth opened the new Parliament on July 2, 1999.

History The first inhabitants of Scotland were the Picts, a Celtic tribe. Between A.D. 82 and A.D. 208, the Romans invaded Scotland, naming it Caledonia. Roman influence over the land, however, was minimal.

The Scots, a Celtic tribe from Ireland, migrated to the west coast of Scotland in about 500. Kenneth McAlpin, King of the Scots, ascended the throne of the Pictish kingdom in about 843, thereby uniting the various Scots and Pictish tribes under one kingdom called Alba. By the 11th century, the monarchy had extended its borders to include much of what is Scotland today.

English influence on the region expanded when Malcolm III, king of Scotland from 1057–93, married an English princess. England's appetite for Scottish land began to grow over the 12th and 13th centuries, and in 1296 King Edward I of England successfully invaded Scotland in 1296. The following year Robert the Bruce led a revolt for independence, was crowned king of Scotland (Robert I) in 1306, and after years of battle defeated the English in 1314 at the Battle of Bannockburn. In 1328 the English finally recognized Scottish independence.

In the 16th century John Knox introduced the Scottish reformation, and the Presbyterian church replaced Catholicism as the official religion. In 1567, Mary, Queen of Scots, a Catholic, was forced to abdicate the Scottish throne, and was later executed by Elizabeth I of England. Mary's son, James VI, was raised as a Protestant, and in 1603 he succeeded Elizabeth on the English throne as King James I of England. James thus became ruler of both Scotland and England, though the countries remained separate. In 1707, after a century of turmoil, Scotland and England passed the Act of Union, which united Scotland, England, and Wales under one rule as the Kingdom of Great Britain. The House of Hanover replaced the Stuart lineage on the throne in 1714, which caused a rebellion among Scots who still supported the Stuarts. The Jacobites, as the rebels were called, led two uprisings, in 1715 and again in 1745.

With the advent of the Industrial Revolution, Scotland, whose chief product had been textiles, began developing the industries of shipbuilding, coal mining, iron, and steel. In the late 20th century Scotland concentrated on electronics and high-tech industries. The North Sea has also become an important source of oil and gas.

In May 1999, Scotland elected its first separate Parliament in three centuries. Labour won the largest number of seats in Parliament, defeating the Scottish National Party (SNP), which supports Scotland's independence from Britain. A year later, however, the new Parliament had not lived up to its new promise—a BBC poll found that only 27% of the populace thought Parliament's performance had been good, and 31% considered it poor. At the same time, however, 62% said they wanted Parliament to have even greater powers.

Wales

Status: Part of United Kingdom
First Secretary: Rhodri Morgan (2000)
Area: 8,019 sq mi (20,768 sq km)
Population (1993 est.): 2,906,500
Capital and largest city (1996 est.): Cardiff, 306,600.
Monetary unit: British pound sterling (£). **Languages:** English, Welsh. **Religions:** Calvinistic Methodist, Church of Wales (disestablished—Anglican), Roman Catholic

Geography Wales lies west of England and is separated from England by the Cambrian Mountains. It is bordered on the northwest, west, and south by the Irish Sea and on the northeast and east by England. Wales is generally hilly; the Snowdon range in the northern part culminates in Mount Snowdon (3,560 ft, 1,085 m), Wales's highest peak.

Government Until 1999, Wales was ruled solely by the UK government and a secretary of state. In the referendum of Sept. 18, 1997, Welsh citizens voted to establish a National Assembly. Wales will remain part of the UK, and the secretary of state for Wales and members of Parliament from Welsh constituencies will continue to have seats in Parliament. Although Wales will control most of its local affairs, unlike Scotland, which in 1999 voted to have its own Parliament, the National Assembly will not be able to legislate and raise taxes. The Welsh assembly officially opened on July 1, 1999.

History The prehistoric peoples of Wales left behind megaliths and other impressive monuments. They were followed by settlements of Celts in the region. The Romans occupied the region from the 1st to the 5th century A.D. Thereafter Angles, Saxons, and Jutes invaded the British island, but they left Wales virtually untouched. Beginning in the 8th century, the various Welsh tribes fought with their Anglo-Saxon neighbors to the east, but the Welsh were able to thwart attempted invasions. After William the Conqueror subdued England in 1066, however, his Norman armies marched into Wales in 1093 and occupied portions of it. By 1282, the English conquest of Wales was complete, and in 1284, the Statute of Rhuddlan formalized England's sovereignty over Wales. In 1301, King Edward I gave his son, who later became Edward II, the title Prince of Wales, a gesture meant to indicate the unity and relationship between the two lands. With the exception of Edward II, all subsequent British monarchs have given this title to their eldest son.

In 1400, the Welsh prince Owen Glendower led a revolt against the English, expelling them from much of Wales in just four years. By 1410, however, his rebellion was crushed. In 1485, Henry VII became king of England. A Welshman and the first in the Tudor line, Henry's reign, and that of subsequent Tudors, made English rule more palatable to the Welsh. His son, King Henry VIII, joined England and Wales under the Act of Union in 1536.

The Industrial Revolution of the 19th century transformed Wales and threatened the traditional livelihood of farmers and shepherds. In the 20th century, the economy of Wales was based primarily on coal production. After World War I, coal prices dropped; this, coupled with the Great Depression, fueled high unemployment rates and economic uncertainty.

In recent years, a resurgence of the Welsh language and culture has demonstrated a stronger national identity among the Welsh, and politically the country moved toward greater self-government (devolution). In 1999, with the strong support of Britain's prime minister Tony Blair, Wales opened the Welsh National Assembly, the first real self-government Wales has had in more than six hundred years.

Dependencies of the United Kingdom

Anguilla

Status: Dependency
Governor: Peter Johnstone (2000)
Chief Minister: Osbourne Fleming (2000)
Area: 35.14 sq mi (91 sq km)
Population (2001 est.): 12,132; average annual rate of natural increase: 1.0%; birth rate: 15.2/1000; infant mortality rate: 24.6/1000; density per sq mi: 345
Capital (1992): The Valley, 1,400. **Monetary unit:** East Caribbean dollar. **Ethnicity/race:** black African. **Literacy:** 95% (1984)
Economic summary: GDP/PPP (1998 est.): $88 million; per capita $7,900. **Real growth rate: 6.5%. Inflation:** 2.5%. **Unemployment:** 7% (1992 est.). **Arable land:** 0%. **Agriculture:** small quantities of tobacco, vegetables; cattle raising. **Labor force:** 4,400 (1992); commerce, 36%; services, 29%; construction, 18%; transportation and utilities, 10%; manufacturing, 3%; agriculture/fishing/forestry/mining, 4%. **Industries:** tourism, boat building, offshore financial services. **Natural resources:** salt, fish, lobster. **Exports:** $4.5 million (1998): lobster, fish, livestock, salt. **Imports:** $57.6 million (1998). **Major trading partners:** n.a.

Anguilla was first colonized in 1650 by English settlers from St. Christopher (St. Kitts) and has since remained a British territory. It was originally part of the West Indies Associated States as a component of the St. Kitts-Nevis-Anguilla Federation. In 1967, Anguilla declared its independence from the federation but Britain did not recognize this action. In Feb. 1969, Anguilla voted to cut all ties with Britain and become an independent republic. In March, Britain landed troops on the island and, on March 30, a truce was signed. In July 1971, Anguilla became a dependency of Britain and two months later Britain ordered the withdrawal of all its troops. A new constitution for Anguilla, effective in Feb. 1976, provided for separate administration and a government of elected representatives. The Associated State of St. Kitts-Nevis-Anguilla ended in 1980, and in 1982 a new Anguillan constitution took effect. In 1997, Anguilla announced that it would build a new airport, with almost double the present runway length, in an effort to increase tourism.

Bermuda

Status: Self-governing dependency
Governor: Thorold Masefield (1997)
Premier: Jennifer Smith (1998)
Area: 23 sq mi (59 sq km)
Population (2001 est.): 63,503; average annual rate of natural increase: 0.5%; birth rate: 12.2/1000; infant mortality rate: 9.6/1000; density per sq mi: 2,797
Capital (1994 est.): Hamilton, 1,100. **Monetary unit:** Bermuda dollar. **Ethnicity/race:** black African 61%, white and other 39%. **Literacy rate:** 98% (1970)
Economic summary: GDP/PPP (1999 est.): $2 billion; per capita $31,500. **Real growth rate:** 2.5%. **Inflation:** 2% (1998 est.). **Unemployment:** negl. (1995). **Arable land:** 6%. **Agriculture:** bananas, vegetables, citrus, flowers; dairy products. **Labor force:** 35,296 (1997); clerical, 23%; services, 22%; laborers, 17%; professional and technical, 17%; administrative and managerial, 12%; sales, 7%; agriculture and fishing, 2% (1996). **Industries:** tourism, finance, insurance, structural concrete products, paints, perfumes, pharmaceuticals, ship repairing. **Natural resources:** limestone, pleasant climate fostering tourism. **Exports:** $32 million (1998 est.): reexports of pharmaceuticals. **Imports:** $624 million (1998 est.): machinery and transport equipment, construction materials, chemicals, food and live animals. **Major trading partners:** UK, U.S., Mexico.

Bermuda is an archipelago of about 360 small islands, 580 mi (934 km) east of North Carolina. The largest is (Great) Bermuda, or Main Island. Explored by Juan de Bermúdez, a Spaniard, the islands were settled in 1612 by an offshoot of the Virginia Company. Bermuda became a Crown colony in 1684.

In 1968, Bermuda was granted a new constitution, its first prime minister, and autonomy, except for foreign relations, defense, and internal security. The predominantly white United Bermuda Party has retained power in four elections against the opposition—the black-led Progressive Labor Party—although Bermuda's population is 61% black. U.S. air and navy bases, which had been leased in 1941 on 99-year terms, closed in 1995, along with Canadian, British army, and Royal Navy bases. In a referendum held in Aug. 1995, nearly three-fourths of those voting opposed independence. The prime minister's unexpected resignation in March 1997 led the ruling United Bermuda Party to name Pamela Gordon the country's first female and youngest premier. She was succeeded in 1998 by Jennifer Smith.

British Antarctic Territory

Status: Dependency
Commissioner: Peter M. Newton (1992)
Area: 500,000 sq mi (1,395,000 sq km)
Population: no permanent residents

The British Antarctic Territory consists of the South Shetland Islands, South Orkney Islands, and nearby Graham Land on the Antarctic continent, largely uninhabited. They are dependencies of the British Crown colony of the Falkland Islands but received a separate administration in 1962, being governed by a British-appointed high commissioner who is governor of the Falklands.

British Indian Ocean Territory

Status: Dependency
Commissioner: John White (1998)
Administrative headquarters: Victoria, Seychelles
Area: 85 sq mi (220 sq km)

This dependency, consisting of the Chagos Archipelago and other small island groups, was formed in 1965 by agreement with Mauritius and the Seychelles. There is no permanent civilian population in the territory. One of its islands, Diego Garcia (17 sq mi), is a joint U.S.-UK refueling and support station that was used during the Persian Gulf War (1991).

British Virgin Islands

VIRGIN ISLANDS
Status: Dependency
Governor: Frank Savage (1998)
Chief Minister: Ralph O'Neal (1995)
Area: 58 sq mi (150 sq km)
Population (2001 est.): 20,812; average annual rate of natural increase: 1.1%; birth rate: 15.2/1000; infant mortality rate: 20.3/1000; density per sq mi: 359
Capital (1991 census): Road Town (on Tortola): 3,983. **Monetary unit:** U.S. dollar. **Literacy rate:** 98% (1970)
Economic summary: GDP/PPP (1999 est.): $287 million; per capita $15,000. **Real growth rate:** 6.8%. **Inflation:** 5.3% (1998). **Unemployment:** 3% (1995). **Arable land:** 20%. **Agriculture:** fruits, vegetables; livestock, poultry; fish. **Labor force:** 4,911 (1980). **Industries:** tourism, light industry, construction, rum, concrete block, offshore financial center. **Natural resources:** negl. **Exports:** $6 million (1998): rum, fresh fish, fruits, animals; gravel, sand. **Imports:** $175 million (1998): building materials, automobiles, foodstuffs, machinery. **Major trading partners:** U.S. Virgin Islands, U.S., Puerto Rico.

Some 36 islands (more than 20 are uninhabited) in the Caribbean Sea northeast of Puerto Rico and west of the Leeward Islands, the British Virgin Islands are economically interdependent with the U.S. Virgin Islands to the south. The principal islands are Tortola, Virgin Gorda, Anegada, and Jost Van Dyke. When Christopher Columbus explored the islands in 1493, he found the Carib people living there. By 1596 most of the Caribs had fled or been killed.

The British Virgin Islands were annexed in 1672. The English planters' slave-based sugar plantations declined after slavery was abolished in the first half of the 19th century. The islands received a separate administration in 1956 as a Crown colony. In 1997, the British Virgin Islands' government decided to spend $25 million on a three-year development plan to increase tourist facilities. Tourism is the islands' mainstay.

Cayman Islands

Status: Dependency
Governor: Peter Smith (1999)
Area: 100 sq mi (259 sq km)
Population (2001 est.): 35,527 average annual rate of natural increase: 0.9%; birth rate: 13.8/1000; infant mortality rate: 10.2/1000; density per sq mi: 355
Capital (1992 est.): George Town (on Grand Cayman), 15,000. **Monetary unit:** Cayman Islands dollar. **Literacy rate:** 98% (1970)
Economic summary: GDP/PPP (1997 est.): $930 million; per capita $24,500. **Real growth rate:** 5%. **Inflation:** 3% (1998). **Unemployment:** 5.1% (1996). **Arable land:** 0%. **Agriculture:** vegetables, fruit; livestock, turtle farming. **Labor force:** 19,820 (1995); agriculture, 1.4%; industry, 12.6%; services, 86% (1995). **Industries:** tourism, banking, insurance and finance, construction, construction materials, furniture. **Natural resources:** fish, climate and beaches that foster tourism. **Exports:** $2.17 million (1997): turtle products, manufactured consumer goods. **Imports:** $432 million (1997): foodstuffs, manufactured goods. **Major trading partners:** U.S., Trinidad and Tobago, UK, Netherlands Antilles, Japan.

The Caymans consist of three islands—Grand Cayman (76 sq mi; 197 sq km), Cayman Brac (22 sq mi; 57 sq km), and Little Cayman (20 sq mi; 52 sq km)—situated about 180 mi (290 km) northwest of Jamaica. They were dependencies of Jamaica until 1959, when they became a unit territory within the Federation of the West Indies. In 1962, upon the dissolution of the federation, the Cayman Islands became a British dependency, and a new constitution approved in 1972 provided for a greater degree of autonomy. Tourism and finance are the Cayman Islands' major industries; tourism increased eightfold between the mid-1970s and the early 1990s, and there are more than 500 licensed banks and trust companies on the islands.

Channel Islands

Status: Crown dependencies
Lieutenant Governor of Jersey: Sir Michael Wilkes (1995)
Lieutenant Governor of Guernsey: Vice Adm. Sir John Coward (1994)
Area: 45 sq mi (116 sq km)
Populations (2000 est.): Jersey, 88,915; Guernsey, 64,080
Capital of Jersey (1991): St. Helier, 28,123
Capital of Guernsey (1991): St. Peter Port, 16,648.
  Monetary units: Guernsey pound; Jersey pound

This group of islands, lying in the English Channel off the northwest coast of France, belonged to the Duchy of Normandy until it passed to the English Crown with the Norman conquest of 1066. It was the only British possession occupied by Germany during World War II. English and French are commonly spoken (though use of the latter is declining), and a Norman-French patois survives.

For administrative purposes, the islands are divided into the Bailiwick of Jersey (45 sq mi; 117 sq km), including the Ecrehous rocks and Les Minquiers, and the Bailiwick of Guernsey (30 sq mi; 78 sq km), including Alderney (3 sq mi; 7.8 sq km); Sark (2 sq mi; 5.2 sq km), Herm, Jethou, Brechou, and other smaller islands. The Channel Islands enjoy tax sovereignty, and their exports are protected by British tariff barriers. Financial services, tourism, market gardening, and dairy farming are important industries.

Falkland Islands and Dependencies

Status: Dependency
Governor: Donald Lamont (1999)
Chief Executive: A. M. Gurr
Area: 4,700 sq mi (12,173 sq km)
Population (July 2000 est.): 2,826
Capital (1991): Stanley (on East Falkland), 1,643.
  Monetary unit: Falkland Island pound
Economic summary: GDP/PPP (2000 est.): $52 million; per capita $24,500. **Real growth rate:** 1%. **Inflation:** 3.6%. **Unemployment:** full employment; labor shortage. **Arable land:** 0%. **Agriculture:** fodder and vegetable crops; sheep, dairy products. **Labor force:** 1,100 (est.); agriculture, 95% (mostly sheepherding and fishing). **Industries:** wool and fish processing; sale of stamps and coins. **Natural resources:** fish, wildlife. **Exports:** $7.6 million (1995): wool, hides, meat. **Imports:** $24.7 million (1995): fuel, food and drink, building materials, clothing. **Major trading partners:** UK, Japan.

This sparsely inhabited dependency consists of a group of islands in the South Atlantic, about 250 mi (402 km) east of the South American mainland. The largest islands are East Falkland and West Falkland. The English captain John Strong made the first recorded landing in the Falklands in 1690. The islands passed between the French, Spanish, and British until 1820, when the Argentine government proclaimed its sovereignty. In 1833 a British force expelled the few remaining Argentine officials from the island without firing a shot, and in 1841 a British civilian lieutenant-governor was appointed for the Falklands. Colonial status was granted to the Falklands in 1892. Argentina, calling the islands *Las Islas Malvinas*, regularly protested Britain's occupation of the islands. On April 2, 1982, Argentina's military government invaded the Falklands. The Falkland Islands war ended 10 weeks later with the surrender of the Argentine forces at Stanley to British troops, who had forcibly reoccupied the islands. Argentina still claims the islands. But an agreement between Argentina and the United Kingdom in 1995 sought to defuse licensing and sovereignty conflicts that would dampen foreign interest in exploiting the Falkland Islands' potential oil reserves.

The Falkland Islands' dependencies are South Georgia Island (1,570 sq mi; 4,066 sq km), the South Sandwich Islands, and other islets. Three former dependencies—Graham Land, the South Shetland Islands, and the South Orkney Islands—were established as a new British dependency, the British Antarctic Territory, in 1962.

Gibraltar

Status: Self-governing dependency
Governor: David Durie (2000)
Chief Minister: Peter Caruana (1996)
Area: 2.51 sq mi (6.5 sq km)
Population (2001 est.): 27,649; average annual rate of natural increase: 0.2%; birth rate: 11.3/1000; infant mortality rate: 5.5/1000; density per sq mi: 11,017.
  Monetary unit: Gibraltar pound. **Literacy rate:** 99%
Economic summary: GDP/PPP (1997 est.): $500 million; per capita $17,500. **Real growth rate:** n.a. **Inflation:** 1.5% (1998). **Unemployment:** 13.5% (1996). **Arable land:** 0%. **Agriculture:** none. **Labor force:** 14,800 (including non-Gibraltar laborers); services, 60%; industry, 40%; agriculture, negl. **Industries:** tourism, banking and finance, shipbuilding and repairing; support to large UK naval and air bases; tobacco, mineral water, beer, canned fish. **Natural resources:** negl. **Exports:** $81.1 million (f.o.b., 1997): (principally reexports) petroleum 51%, manufactured goods 41%, other 8%. **Imports:** $492 million (c.i.f., 1997): fuels, manufactured goods, and foodstuffs. **Major trading partners:** UK, Morocco, Portugal, Netherlands, Spain, U.S., Germany, Japan.

Gibraltar, at the south end of the Iberian Peninsula, is a rocky promontory commanding the western entrance to the Mediterranean. Aside from its strategic importance, it is also a free port, naval base, and coaling station. It was captured by the Moorish leader Tarik, crossing from Africa into Spain in 711, and its name is derived from the Arabic, *Jabal-al-Tarik* (Mount of Tarik). In the 15th century, it passed to the Moorish ruler of Granada and later became Spanish. It was captured by an Anglo-Dutch force in 1704 during the War of the Spanish Succession and passed to Great Britain by the Treaty of Utrecht in 1713. Since then Spain has continually laid claims to it. Most of the inhabitants of Gibraltar are of Spanish, Italian, and Maltese descent, and in 1981 Gibraltarians were granted full British citizenship.

Spanish efforts to recover Gibraltar culminated in a referendum in 1967, in which the residents voted overwhelmingly to retain their link with Britain. In response, Spain sealed Gibraltar's land border between 1969 and 1985. The last British military battalion on the "Rock" was withdrawn in March 1991.

Isle of Man

Status: Self-governing Crown dependency
Lieutenant Governor: Ian David Macfadyen (2000)
Chief Minister: Donald James Gelling (1996)
Area: 221 sq mi (572 sq km)
Population (2001 est.): 73,489; average annual rate of natural increase: –0.03%; birth rate: 11.6/1000; infant mortality rate: 6.4/1000; density per sq mi: 333
Capital (1991): Douglas, 22,214. **Monetary unit:** Isle of Man pound

The Isle of Man is situated in the Irish Sea, equidistant from Scotland, Ireland, and England. Among its earliest inhabitants were Celts, and their language, Manx, which is closely related to Irish and Scottish Gaelic, remained the everyday speech of the people until the first half of the 19th century. Manx now has no native speakers. Norse (Viking) invasions began about 800, and the island was a dependency of Norway until 1266. During this period the Isle of Man came under a Scandinavian system of government that has remained practically unchanged ever since. The island came under the control of England in 1341. After allowing a succession of feudal lords rule the island, the British Parliament purchased sovereignty over the island in 1765. The Isle of Man continues to be administered according to its own laws by a government composed of the lieutenant governor, a legislative council, and a House of Keys, one of the most ancient legislative assemblies in the world.

Leeward Islands

SEE BRITISH VIRGIN ISLANDS; MONTSERRAT.

Montserrat

Status: Dependency
Governor: Tony Longrigg (2001)
Chief Minister: John Osborne (2001)
Area: 39 sq mi (100 sq km)
Population (2001 est.): 7,574; average annual rate of natural increase: 1.0%; birth rate: 17.4/1000; infant mortality rate: 8.2/1000; density per sq mi: 196
Capital (1991 est.): Plymouth, 2,500. **Monetary unit:** East Caribbean dollar
Economic summary: GDP/PPP (1998 est.): $31 million; per capita n.a. **Real growth rate:** –16%. **Inflation:** 5%. **Unemployment:** 20% (1996 est.). **Arable land:** 20%. **Agriculture:** cabbages, carrots, cucumbers, tomatoes, onions, peppers; livestock products. **Labor force:** 4,521 (1992); note—recently lowered by flight of people from volcanic activity; agriculture, n.a; industry, n.a; services, n.a. **Industries:** tourism, rum, textiles, electronic appliances. **Natural resources:** negl. **Exports:** $1.5 million (1998): electronic components, plastic bags, apparel, hot peppers, live plants, cattle. **Imports:** $26 million (1998): machinery and transportation equipment, foodstuffs, manufactured goods, fuels, lubricants, and related materials. **Major trading partners:** U.S., Antigua and Barbuda, UK, Trinidad and Tobago, Japan, Canada.

The island of Montserrat is in the Lesser Antilles of the West Indies. Until 1956, it was a division of the Leeward Islands. In 1958 Montserrat joined the Federation of the West Indies, remaining a member until that organization's dissolution in 1962. Unlike most other British West Indies possessions, Montserrat, with its weak economy, has not vigorously sought independence. The Soufrière Hills volcano began erupting in 1995, and the situation continued to

worsen through 1998, with the capital, Plymouth, destroyed and the southern and central parts of the British colony having been evacuated. Only about 4,000 people were left in the northern "safe zone" in 1998 after thousands had moved to nearby Antigua, Britain, or other parts of the Caribbean.

Pitcairn Island

Status: Dependency
Governor: Martin Williams (nonresident) (1998)
Island Magistrate: Jay Warren (1993)
Area: 18.15 sq mi (47 sq km)
Population (July 2000 est.): 54; density per sq mi: 30
Capital: Adamstown

Pitcairn Island, in the South Pacific about midway between Australia and South America, consists of the island of Pitcairn and the three uninhabited islands of Henderson, Duicie, and Oeno. Pitcairn was settled in 1790 by British mutineers from the ship *Bounty*, commanded by Capt. William Bligh. One of the most remote islands in the world, it was annexed as a British colony in 1838. Overpopulation forced removal of the settlement to Norfolk Island in 1856, but about 40 persons soon returned.

The descendants of First Mate Fletcher Christian, the 8 other mutineers, and the dozen or so Tahitians who accompanied them still inhabit the island. In addition to English, the residents of Pitcairn speak a dialect that is a mixture of Tahitian and 18th-century English.

St. Helena

Status: Dependency
Governor: David Hollamby (1999)
Area: 158 sq mi (410 sq km)
Population (2001 est.): 7,266; average annual rate of natural increase: 0.7%; birth rate: 13.5/1000; infant mortality rate: 22.4/1000; density per sq mi: 46
Capital (1987): Jamestown, 1,332. **Monetary unit:** Pound sterling. **Literacy rate:** 97% (1987)

St. Helena is a remote volcanic island in the South Atlantic about 1,100 mi (1,770 km) from the west coast of Africa. It is famous as Napoleon's place of exile (1815–21). The island was discovered in 1502 by João da Nova, a Spanish navigator in the service of Portugal. It was taken for England in 1659 by the East India Company and was brought under the direct government of the Crown in 1834. After the opening of the Suez Canal, in 1870, St. Helena's importance as a port of call diminished. About two-thirds of the colony's budget is provided by the United Kingdom in the form of a subsidy.

St. Helena has two dependencies: Ascension (34 sq mi; 88 sq km), an island about 700 mi (1,127 km) northwest of St. Helena; and Tristan da Cunha (40 sq mi; 104 sq km), a group of six islands about 1,500 mi (2,414 km) south-southwest of St. Helena.

Turks and Caicos Islands

Status: Dependency
Governor: Mervyn Jones (2000)
Chief Minister: Derek H. Taylor (1995)
Area: 166 sq mi (430 sq km)
Population (2001 est.): 18,122; average annual rate of natural increase: 2.0%; birth rate: 24.9/1000; infant mortality rate: 18.1/1000; density per sq mi: 109
Capital (1990): Cockburn Town, 3,720. **Monetary unit:** U.S. dollar. **Literacy rate:** 98% (1970)
Economic summary: GDP/PPP (1997 est.): $117 million; per capita $7,700. **Real growth rate:** 4%. **Inflation:** 4% (1995). **Unemployment:** 10% (1997 est.). **Arable land:**

2%. **Agriculture:** corn, beans, cassava (tapioca), citrus fruits; fish. **Labor force:** 4,848 (1990 est.); about 33% in government and 20% in agriculture and fishing; significant numbers in tourism, financial, and other services (1997 est.). **Industries:** tourism, offshore financial services. **Natural resources:** spiny lobster, conch. **Exports:** $4.7 million (1993): lobster, dried and fresh conch, conch shells. **Imports:** $46.6 million (1993): food and beverages, tobacco, clothing, manufactures, construction materials. **Major trading partners:** U.S., UK.

These two groups of islands are near the Bahamas in the Caribbean. The principal islands in the Turks group are Grand Turk and Salt Cay; the principal islands in the Caicos group are South Caicos, East Caicos, Middle (or Grand) Caicos, North Caicos, Providenciales, and West Caicos. The islands were not settled by Europeans until 1678, when British colonists from Bermuda established a salt-panning industry. The islands were at first placed under the Bahamas government, but in 1874 they became dependencies of the colony of Jamaica. Following Jamaica's independence, they became a British Crown colony. The salt production industry, the islands' economic mainstay, ceased in 1964 and gave way to tourism, offshore financial services, and fishing.

United States

THE UNITED STATES OF AMERICA

President: George W. Bush (2001)
Vice President: Richard B. Cheney (2001)
Land area (2000): 3,537,441 sq mi (9,161,972.2 sq km)
Population (2000 census): 281,421,906 (change 1990–2000: 13.2%) average annual rate of natural increase (2000): 6.1%; birth rate (1999): 14.5/1000; infant mortality rate (1998): 7.2/1000; density per sq mi: 79.6
Capital (2000 census): Washington, DC, 572,059.
Largest cities (2000 census): New York: city proper, 8,008,278; metro. area, 21,199,865; Los Angeles: city proper, 3,694,820; metro. area, 16,373,645; Chicago, city proper, 2,896,016; metro area, 9,157,540; Houston, 1,953,631; Philadelphia, 1,517,550; Phoenix, 1,321,045; San Diego, 1,223,400; Dallas, 1,188,580; San Antonio, 1,144,646; Detroit, 951,270. **Monetary unit:** dollar. **Languages:** English, sizable Spanish-speaking minority. **Ethnicity/race:** White: 211,460,626 (75.1%); Black: 34,658,190 (12.3%); American Indian and Alaska Native: 2,475,956 (0.9%); Asian: 10,242,998 (3.6%); Native Hawaiian and Other Pacific Islander: 398,835 (0.1%); Other race: 15,359,073 (5.5%); Hispanic origin:[1] 35,305,818 (12.5%); . **Religions:** Protestant, 61%; Roman Catholic, 25%; Jewish, 2%; other, 5%; none, 7%. **Literacy rate:** 97% (1980)
Economic summary: GDP/PPP (1999 est.): $9.255 trillion; per capita $33,900. **Real growth rate:** 4.1%. **Inflation:** 2.2% (1999). **Unemployment:** 4.2% (1999). **Arable land:** 19%. **Agriculture:** wheat, other grains, corn, fruits, vegetables, cotton; beef, pork, poultry, dairy products; forest products; fish. **Labor force:** 139.4 million (includes unemployed) (1999); managerial and professional, 30.3%; technical, sales, and administrative support, 29.2%; services, 13.4%; manufacturing, mining, transportation, and crafts, 24.5%; farming, forestry, and fishing, 2.6% (1999); note: figures exclude the unemployed. **Industries:** leading industrial power in the world, highly diversified and technologically advanced; petroleum, steel, motor vehicles, aerospace, telecommunications, chemicals, electronics, food processing, consumer goods, lumber, mining. **Natural resources:** coal, copper, lead, molybdenum,

phosphates, uranium, bauxite, gold, iron, mercury, nickel, potash, silver, tungsten, zinc, petroleum, natural gas, timber. **Exports:** $663 billion (f.o.b., 1998 est.): capital goods, automobiles, industrial supplies and raw materials, consumer goods, agricultural products. **Imports:** $912 billion (c.i.f., 1998 est.): crude oil and refined petroleum products, machinery, automobiles, consumer goods, industrial raw materials, food and beverages. **Major trading partners:** Canada, Mexico, Japan, UK, Germany, France, Netherlands, China, Taiwan.

1. Persons of Hispanic origin can be of any race.
Government Federal republic.

The president is elected for a four-year term and may be reelected only once. The bicameral Congress consists of the 100-member Senate, elected to a six-year term with one-third of the seats becoming vacant every two years, and the 435-member House of Representatives, elected every two years. The minimum voting age is 18. (*See also* Profile of the United States, U.S. States, U.S. Cities, U.S. Statistics, and U.S. Government and History.)

U.S. Territories and Outlying Areas

Puerto Rico
COMMONWEALTH OF PUERTO RICO

Governor: Sila María Calderón (2001)
Capital and largest city (1990 pop.): San Juan, 437,745. **Other large cities (1990 pop.):** Bayamón, 220,262; Ponce, 190,900; Carolina, 177,806
Land area: 3,515 sq mi (9,104 sq km)
Population (est. 2000): 3,937,316; average annual rate of natural increase: 0.7%; birth rate: 15.3/1000; infant mortality rate: 9.5/1000; density per sq mi: 1,120
Currency: U.S. dollars. **Languages:** Spanish and English (both official). **Ethnicity/race:** Almost entirely Hispanic. **Religions:** Roman Catholic 85%, Protestant denominations and other 15%. **Literacy rate:** 89% (1980)
Economic summary: GDP/PPP (1999 est.): $38.1 billion; per capita $9,800. **Real growth rate:** 4.2%. **Inflation:** 5.2%. **Unemployment:** 13% (FY97/98 est.). **Arable land:** 4%. **Agriculture:** sugarcane, coffee, pineapples, plantains, bananas; livestock products, chickens. **Labor force:** 1.3 million (1996); agriculture, 3%; industry, 20%; services, 77%. **Industries:** pharmaceuticals, electronics, apparel, food products; tourism. **Natural resources:** some copper and nickel; potential for onshore and offshore oil. **Exports:** $34.9 billion (f.o.b., 1999): pharmaceuticals, electronics, apparel, canned tuna, rum, beverage concentrates, medical equipment. **Imports:** $25.3 billion (c.i.f., 1999): chemicals, machinery and equipment, clothing, food, fish, petroleum products. **Major trading partner:** U.S.

The Commonwealth of Puerto Rico is located in the Caribbean Sea, about 1,000 mi east-southeast of Miami, Fla. A possession of the United States, it consists of the island of Puerto Rico plus the adjacent islets of Vieques, Culebra, and Mona. Puerto Rico has a mountainous, tropical ecosystem with very little flat land and few mineral resources.

Puerto Rico's governor is elected directly for a four-year term. A bicameral legislature consists of a 27-member Senate and a 51-member House of Representatives, all elected for four-year terms. From 1940 to 1968, Puerto Rican politics was dominated by a party advocating voluntary association with the U.S. Since then, the New Progressive Party, a party favoring U.S. statehood, has won five of the last eight gubernatorial elections. Puerto Ricans have twice voted to determine their political status. In 1967, the outcome was Commonwealth 60%; statehood 39%; independence 1%. In 1993, Commonwealth dropped to 48.6%; statehood rose to 46.3%; independence polled 4.4%; and 0.6% of the ballots were blank or spoiled.

Under the Commonwealth formula, residents of Puerto Rico lack voting representation in Congress and do not participate in presidential elections. As U.S. citizens, Puerto Ricans are subject to military service and most federal laws. Residents of the Commonwealth pay no federal income tax on locally generated earnings, but Puerto Rico government income-tax rates are set at a level that closely parallels federal-plus-state levies on the mainland.

When Christopher Columbus arrived there in 1493, the island was inhabited by the peaceful Arawak Indians, who were being challenged by the warlike Carib Indians. Puerto Rico remained economically undeveloped until 1830, when sugarcane, coffee, and tobacco plantations were gradually developed. After Puerto Ricans began to press for independence, Spain granted the island broad powers of self-government in 1897. But during the Spanish-American War of 1898 American troops invaded the island and Spain ceded it to the U.S. Since then, Puerto Rico has remained an unincorporated U.S. territory. Its people were granted American citizenship under the Jones Act in 1917; were permitted to elect their own governor, beginning in 1948; and now fully administer their internal affairs under a constitution approved by the U.S. Congress in 1952. In spite of broad popular support for the autonomy of the Commonwealth government and a rapidly modernizing industrial society, there were expressions of dissatisfaction. Puerto Rican extremists dramatized their desire for independence with an attempt to assassinate President Truman on Nov. 1, 1950, and on March 1, 1954, they wounded five congressmen in an attack on the U.S. Capitol.

A self-help program of economic development and social welfare (called "Operation Bootstrap") was forged in the 1940s by four-time governor Luis Muñoz Marín. In a little more than four decades, much of the island's crushing poverty was eliminated. This was done partly through the development of manufacturing and service industries, the latter related to an enormous growth in tourism. Also, many Puerto Ricans migrated to large cities on the mainland U.S.

Puerto Rico is a major hub of Caribbean commerce, finance, tourism, and communications. San Juan is one of the world's busiest cruise-ship ports, and Puerto Rico's standard of living continues to be among the highest in the hemisphere. Its future political status, however, remains unclear. On March 4, 1998, the U.S. House of Representatives passed a bill that called for binding elections in Puerto Rico to decide the island's permanent political status. In 2001, President George Bush decided to end the U.S. Navy's use of a bombing range on the island of Vieques in 2003. However, residents voted overwhelmingly to close the base immediately in a July 2001 referendum.

Guam
TERRITORY OF GUAM

Governor: Carl T. C. Gutierrez (1995)
Capital: Agaña; population (1990) 1,139
Land area: 209 sq mi (541 sq km)
Population (2000 est.): 157,557; average annual rate of natural increase: 2.1%; birth rate: 25.1/1000; infant mortality rate: 6.7/1000; density per sq mi: 754. **1996**

est. net migration: 3 migrants per 1,000 population.
Languages: English and Chamorro; note: most residents are bilingual; Japanese also widely spoken.
Ethnicity/race: Chamorro 47%, Filipino 25%, Caucasian 10%, Chinese, Japanese, Korean, and other, 18%. **Religions:** Roman Catholic 98%, other 2%.
Literacy rate: 96% (1980). **Currency:** U.S. dollars
Economic summary: GDP/PPP (1996 est.): $3 billion; per capita $19,000. **Real growth rate:** n.a. **Inflation:** 4% (1992 est.). **Unemployment:** 2% (1992 est.).
Arable land: 11%. **Agriculture:** fruits, copra, vegetables; eggs, pork, poultry, beef. **Labor force:** 65,660 (1995); federal and territorial government, 31%; private, 69% (trade, 21%; services, 33%; construction, 12%; other, 3%) (1995). **Industries:** U.S. military, tourism, construction, transshipment services, concrete products, printing and publishing, food processing, textiles. **Natural resources:** fishing (largely undeveloped), tourism (especially from Japan).
Exports: $86.1 million (f.o.b., 1992): mostly transshipments of refined petroleum products, construction materials, fish, food and beverage products. **Imports:** $202.4 million (c.i.f., 1992): petroleum and petroleum products, food, manufactured goods. **Major trading partners:** U.S., Japan.

Guam is the largest and southernmost island in the Marianas Archipelago. The island is divided into a northern coralline limestone plateau and a southern chain of volcanic hills. Today Guam is an unincorporated, organized territory of the United States. The people of Guam have been U.S. citizens since 1950. They have been represented in the U.S. Congress since 1973 by a nonvoting delegate, but do not participate in presidential elections. The executive branch includes a popularly elected governor, who serves a four-year term. The legislative branch is a 21-member unicameral legislature whose members are elected every two years.

Guam was probably visited by the Portuguese navigator Ferdinand Magellan (sailing for Spain) in 1521. The island was formally claimed by Spain in 1565, and its people were forced into submission and conversion to Roman Catholicism beginning in 1668. After the Spanish-American War of 1898, Spain ceded Guam to the United States. From 1899 to 1949, the U.S. Navy administered Guam, except during the Japanese occupation from 1941–44. Guam was liberated by American military forces in the summer of 1944. Guam's economy is based on tourism and U.S. military spending (U.S. naval and air force bases occupy one-third of the land on Guam).

U.S. Virgin Islands
VIRGIN ISLANDS OF THE UNITED STATES

Governor: Charles Turnbull (1999)
Capital: Charlotte Amalie (on St. Thomas), population (1990): 12,331
Land area: 136 sq mi (352 sq km)
Population (est. 2000): 122,211; average annual rate of natural increase: 1.0%; birth rate: 15.9/1000; infant mortality rate: 9.4/1000; density per sq mi: 899.
Languages: English (official), but Spanish and French are also spoken. **Ethnicity/race:** West Indian 74% (45% born in the Virgin Islands and 29% born elsewhere in the West Indies), U.S. mainland 13%, Puerto Rican 5%, other 8%, black 80%, white 15%, other 5%, 14% of Hispanic origin. **Religions:** Baptist 42%, Roman Catholic 34%, Episcopalian 17%, other 7%. **Literacy rate:** 90%. **Currency:** U.S. dollars
Economic summary: GDP/PPP (1999 est.): $1.8 billion. **Real growth rate:** n.a; per capita $15,000. **Inflation:**

n.a. **Unemployment:** 4.9% (March 1999). **Arable land:** 15%. **Agriculture:** fruit, vegetables, sorghum; Senepol cattle. **Labor force:** 47,443 (1990 est.); agriculture, 1%; industry, 20%; services, 79% (1990 est.). **Industries:** tourism, petroleum refining, watch assembly, rum distilling, construction, pharmaceuticals, textiles, electronics. **Natural resources:** sun, sand, sea, surf. **Exports:** $n.a.: refined petroleum products. **Imports:** $n.a.: crude oil, foodstuffs, consumer goods, building materials. **Major trading partners:** U.S., Puerto Rico.

The Virgin Islands, consisting of nine main islands and some 75 islets, were explored by Columbus in 1493. They were originally inhabited by the Carib Indians. Since 1666, England has held six of the main islands; the remaining three (St. Croix, St. Thomas, and St. John), as well as about 50 of the islets, were eventually acquired by Denmark, which named them the Danish West Indies. In 1917, these islands were purchased by the U.S. from Denmark for $25 million.

Congress granted U.S. citizenship to Virgin Islanders in 1927. Universal suffrage was given in 1936 to all persons who could read and write English. The governor was elected by popular vote for the first time in 1970; previously he had been appointed by the U.S. president. A unicameral 15-person legislature serves the Virgin Islands, and congressional legislation gave the islands a nonvoting representative in Congress. Residents of the islands substantially enjoy the same rights as those enjoyed by mainlanders, but they may not vote in presidential elections.

Tourism is the primary economic activity, accounting for most of the GDP and 70% of employment. All goods made in the Virgin Islands qualify for duty-free entry into the United States.

American Samoa
TERRITORY OF AMERICAN SAMOA

Governor: Tauese Pita Sunia (1997)
Capital: Pago Pago, population 1990: 3,519
Land area: 77 sq mi (199 sq km)
Population (2001 est.): 67,084; average rate of natural increase: 2.1%; birth rate 24.9/1000; infant mortality rate: 10.4/1000; density per sq mi: 873. **Languages:** Samoan (closely related to Hawaiian and other Polynesian languages) and English; most people are bilingual. **Ethnicity/race:** Samoan (Polynesian) 89%, Tongan 4%, Caucasian 2%, other 6%. **Religions:** Christian Congregationalist 50%, Roman Catholic 20%, Protestant denominations and other 30%. **Literacy rate:** 97% (1980). **Currency:** U.S. dollars
Economic summary: GDP/PPP (1995 est.): $150 million; per capita $2,600. **Real growth rate:** n.a. **Inflation:** n.a. **Unemployment:** 12% (1991). **Arable land:** 5%. **Agriculture:** bananas, coconuts, vegetables, taro, breadfruit, yams, copra, pineapples, papayas; dairy products, livestock. **Labor force:** 13,949 (1996); government, 33%; tuna canneries, 34%; other, 33% (1990). **Industries:** tuna canneries (largely dependent on foreign fishing vessels), handicrafts. **Natural resources:** pumice, pumicite. **Exports:** $313 million (1996): canned tuna 93%. **Imports:** $471 million (1996): materials for canneries 56%, food 8%, petroleum products 7%, machinery and parts 6%. **Major trading partners:** U.S., Japan, New Zealand, Australia, Fiji.

American Samoa, a group of five volcanic islands and two coral atolls located some 2,600 mi south of Hawaii in the South Pacific, is an unincorporated, unorganized territory of the U.S. It includes the eastern Samoan islands of Tutuila, Aunu'u, and Rose; three islands (Ta'u, Olosega, and Ofu) of the Manu'a group; and Swains Island. Around 1000 B.C. Protopolynesians established themselves in the islands, and their descendants are one of the few remaining Polynesian societies. The Dutch navigator Jacob Roggeveen sighted the Manu'a Islands in 1722. American Samoa has been a territory of the United States since April 17, 1900, when the High Chiefs of Tutuila signed the first of two Deeds of Cession for the islands to the U.S. (Congress ratified the Deeds in 1929). Swains Island, which is privately owned, came under U.S. administration in 1925.

Until World War II the United States operated a coaling station and naval base in Pago Pago. During the war, the islands were an important U.S. Marines staging area. In 1960 American Samoa ratified its territorial constitution and has since developed a modern, self-governing political system. American Samoans elect a governor, lieutenant governor, and legislature. The legislature (Fono) consists of two houses: the Senate, selected by village chiefs (matai) for four-year terms, and the House of Representatives, elected by the general population for two-year terms. The people of American Samoa are U.S. nationals, not U.S. citizens, but many have become naturalized American citizens. American Samoa does 80%–90% of its foreign trade with the U.S. Canned tuna is the primary export, earning $300 million annually. Transfers from the U.S. government add substantially to American Samoa's economic well-being.

Northern Mariana Islands
THE COMMONWEALTH OF THE NORTHERN MARIANA ISLANDS, OR CNMI

Governor: Pedro P. Tenorio (1998)
Capital: Chalan Kanoa (on Saipan)
Total area: 184 sq mi (477 sq km)
Population (2001 est.): 74,612; average annual rate of natural increase: 1.8%; birth rate 20.6/1000; infant mortality: 5.7/1000; density per sq mi: 405. Most reside on Saipan, which is also the seat of government; Rota, Agrihan, and Tinian are also inhabited. About half the population are U.S. citizens; the remainder are temporary alien workers. **Languages:** English (official), Chamorro, Carolinian. **Ethnicity/race:** Chamorro, Carolinians, other Micronesians, Caucasian, Japanese, Chinese, Korean. **Religion:** Primarily Roman Catholic. **Literacy rate:** 97% (1980). **Currency:** U.S. dollars
Economic summary: GDP/PPP (1996 est.): $524 million; note: GDP numbers reflect U.S. spending; per capita $9,300. **Real growth rate:** n.a. **Inflation:** 6.5% (1994 est.). **Unemployment:** 14% (residents). **Arable land:** 21%. **Agriculture:** coconuts, fruits, vegetables; cattle. **Labor force:** 6,006 total indigenous labor force; 2,699 unemployed; 28,717 foreign workers (1995); managerial, 20.5%; technical, sales, 16.4%; services, 19.3%; farming, 3.1%; precision production, 13.8%; operators, fabricators, 26.9%. **Industries:** tourism, construction, garments, handicrafts. **Natural resources:** arable land, fish. **Exports:** $1 billion (1998): garments. **Imports:** $n.a.: food, construction equipment and materials, petroleum products. **Major trading partners:** U.S., Japan.

The Northern Mariana Islands, east of the Philippines and south of Japan, include the islands of Rota, Saipan, Tinian, Pagan, Guguan, Agrihan, and Aguijan. Although sighted by Ferdinand Magellan in 1521 as he sailed for Spain, the islands were not settled by Europeans until 1668, when missionaries converted the indigenous Chamorro people to

Catholicism. They were ruled successively by Spain, Germany, and Japan before they became a UN Trusteeship (administered by the U.S.) after World War II. The Commonwealth of the Northern Mariana Islands (CNMI) became part of the United States on Nov. 1986. Spanish cultural traditions remain strong.

In recent years, Saipan's garment industry has been accused of exploiting thousands of Asian immigrants. Saipan's territorial status enables its employers to pay low wages, and while claiming their clothing is "Made in the USA," sidestepping import duties and tariffs.

Midway Islands

Total area: 2 sq mi (5 sq km)
Population (1995 est.): no indigenous inhabitants; 453 U.S. military personnel.

The Midway Islands consist of a circular atoll, 6 mi in diameter, that encloses two islands. Lying about 1,150 mi west-northwest of Hawaii, the islands were first explored by Captain N. C. Brooks on July 5, 1859, in the name of the U.S. The atoll was declared a U.S. possession in 1867, and in 1903 Theodore Roosevelt made it a naval reservation. The island was renamed "Midway" by the U.S. Navy in recognition of its geographic location on the route between California and Japan. Air traffic across the Pacific increased the island's importance in the mid-1930s; the San Francisco–Manila mail route included a regular stop on Midway. Its military importance was soon recognized, and the navy began building an air and submarine base there in 1940. The Battle of Midway, which took place from June 3–6, 1942, was considered a turning point in World War II. After the war, the strategic importance of the island declined; the Midway stop for commercial air traffic was eliminated in 1950, and the air base closed in 1992.

Wake Island

Total area: 2.51 sq mi (6.5 sq km)
Comparative size: about 11 times the size of the Mall in Washington, DC
Population (1995 est.): no indigenous inhabitants; 302 U.S. military personnel and civilian contractors.
Economy: The economic activity is limited to providing services to U.S. military personnel and contractors on the island. All food and manufactured goods must be imported.

Wake Island, about halfway between Midway and Guam, is an atoll consisting of the three islets of Wilkes, Peale, and Wake. They were discovered by the British in 1796 and annexed by the U.S. in 1899. In 1938, Pan American Airways established a seaplane base, and Wake Island was used as a commercial base for several years. On Dec. 8, 1941, it was attacked by the Japanese, who finally took possession on Dec. 23. It was surrendered by the Japanese on Sept. 4, 1945.

Johnston Atoll

Land area: 1.08 sq mi (2.8 sq km); density per sq mi: 1,111
Population (July 1997 est.): no indigenous inhabitants; 1,200 U.S. military and civilian personnel

Johnston is a coral atoll about 700 mi southwest of Hawaii. It consists of four small islands—Johnston Island, Sand Island, Hikina Island, and Akau Island—which lie on a 9-mile-long reef. The atoll was discovered by Capt. Charles James Johnston of HMS *Cornwallis* in 1807. In 1858 it was claimed by Hawaii, and

later became a U.S. possession. Johnston Atoll is a Naval Defensive Sea Area and Airspace Reservation and is closed to the public. In the early 1990s, the U.S. government opened a facility for destroying chemical weapons on Johnston Atoll.

Baker, Howland, and Jarvis Islands

These Pacific islands were claimed by the United States under the Guano Act of 1856 on May 13, 1936. Guano, composed of phosphates, was used as fertilizer in the 19th century, and its collection was highly lucrative. Through the Guano Act the U.S. gained 79 tiny territories around the world; it still controls eight of them. Baker Island is a saucer-shaped atoll with an area of approximately one square mile about 1,650 mi from Hawaii. Howland Island, 36 mi to the northwest, is 1 mile long and half a mile wide. On their round-the-world flight in 1937, Amelia Earhart and Fred J. Noonan were headed for Howland when they disappeared. Jarvis Island is several hundred mi to the east.

Kingman Reef

Kingman Reef, located about 1,000 mi south of Hawaii, was discovered by Capt. E. Fanning in 1798, but named for Capt. W. E. Kingman, who rediscovered it in 1853. Triangular in shape, it is about 9.5 mi long. A U.S. possession since 1922, Kingman Reef is a Naval Defensive Sea Area and Airspace Reservation, and is closed to the public.

Navassa Island

Navassa Island is located in the Caribbean Sea, 99.4 mi (160 km) south of the U.S. naval base at Guantanamo, Cuba, between Cuba, Haiti, and Jamaica. The island has a total area of 2.01 sq mi (5.2 sq km). It was claimed for the U.S. under the Guano Act in 1857. The Navassa Phosphate Company mined the island until 1900, enlisting hundreds of freed American slaves to dig out several tons of guano. Working conditions were so brutal that the laborers finally revolted in 1889, killing their supervisors. The island is also claimed by Haiti.

Palmyra Atoll

Palmyra Atoll is an incorporated territory of the U.S. and privately owned. The atoll has a total area of 4.6 sq mi (11.9 sq km) and is located in the North Pacific Ocean, 994 mi (1,600 km) southwest of Honolulu. It was a U.S. military base during World War II but was not attacked.

Uruguay

ORIENTAL REPUBLIC OF URUGUAY

National name: República Oriental del Uruguay
President: Jorge Batlle (2000)
Area: 68,039 sq mi (176,220 sq km)
Population (2001 est.): 3,360,105 (average annual rate of natural increase: 0.8%); birth rate: 17.4/1000; infant mortality rate: 14.7/1000; density per sq mi: 49
Capital and largest city (1998): Montevideo, 1,330,440.
  Monetary unit: Peso. **Language:** Spanish. **Ethnicity/race:** white 88%, mestizo 8%, black 4%. **Religions:** Roman Catholic 66%, Protestant 2%, Jewish 2%.
  Literacy rate: 96% (1990)
Economic summary: GDP/PPP (1999 est.): $28 billion; per capita $8,500. **Real growth rate:** –2.5%. **Inflation:** 4%. **Unemployment:** 12% (1999). **Arable land:** 7%. **Agriculture:** wheat, rice, barley, corn,

sorghum; livestock; fish. **Labor force:** 1.38 million (1997 est.); agriculture, n.a.; industry, n.a.; services, n.a. **Industries:** food processing, electrical machinery, transportation equipment, petroleum products, textiles, chemicals, beverages. **Natural resources:** arable land, hydropower, minor minerals, fisheries. **Exports:** $2.1 billion (f.o.b., 1999 est.): meat, rice, leather products, vehicles, dairy products, wool, electricity. **Imports:** $3.4 billion (f.o.b., 1999 est.): road vehicles, electrical machinery, metal manufactures, heavy industrial machinery, crude petroleum. **Major trading partners:** Mercosur partners, EU, U.S.

Geography Uruguay, on the east coast of South America south of Brazil and east of Argentina, is comparable in size to Oklahoma. The country consists of a low, rolling plain in the south and a low plateau in the north. It has a 120-mile (193 km) Atlantic shoreline, a 235-mile (378 km) frontage on the Rio de la Plata, and 270 mi (435 km) on the Uruguay River, its western boundary.

Government Republic.

History Prior to European settlement, Uruguay was inhabited by indigenous people, the Charrúas. Juan Díaz de Solis, a Spaniard, visited Uruguay in 1516, but the Portuguese were first to settle it when they founded the town of Colonia del Sacramento in 1680. After a long struggle, Spain wrested the country from Portugal in 1778, by which time almost all of the indigenous people had been exterminated. Uruguay revolted against Spain in 1811, only to be conquered in 1817 by the Portuguese from Brazil. Independence was reasserted with Argentine help in 1825, and the republic was set up in 1828.

A revolt in 1836 touched off nearly 50 years of factional strife, including an inconclusive civil war (1839–51) and a war with Paraguay (1865–70), accompanied by occasional armed intervention by Argentina and Brazil. Uruguay, made prosperous by meat and wool exports, founded a welfare state early in the 20th century under President José Batlle y Ordóñez, who ruled from 1903 to 1929. A decline began in the 1950s as successive governments struggled to maintain a large bureaucracy and costly social benefits. Economic stagnation and left-wing terrorist activity followed.

A military coup ousted the civilian government in 1973. The military dictatorship that followed used fear and terror to demoralize the population, taking thousands of political prisoners. After ruling for 12 years, the brutal military regime permitted election of a civilian government in Nov. 1984 and relinquished rule in March 1985; full political and civil rights were then restored.

Subsequent leaders contended with high inflation and a mammoth national debt. Presidential and legislative elections in Nov. 1994 resulted in a narrow victory for the center-right Colorado Party and its presidential candidate, Julio Sanguinetti Cairolo, who had been president in 1985–90. He pushed for constitutional and economic reforms aimed at reducing inflation and the size of the public sector, including tax increases and privatization. In Nov. 1999 Jorge Batlle, of the center-right Colorado Party, won the presidency. In Aug. 2000 a commission began investigating the disappearances of 160 people who vanished during the military regime.

Uzbekistan

REPUBLIC OF UZBEKISTAN

National name: Uzbekiston Respublikasi
President: Islam A. Karimov (1990)
Prime Minister: Otkir Sultonov (1995)
Area: 172,741 sq mi (447,400 sq km)
Population (2001 est.): 25,155,064 (average annual rate of natural increase: 1.8%); birth rate: 26.1/1000; infant mortality rate: 71.9/1000; density per sq mi: 146
Capital and largest city (1992 est.): Tashkent, 2,106,000. **Other large cities:** Samarkand, 372,000; Andijon, 302,000. **Monetary unit:** Uzbekistani som.
Languages: Uzbek 74.3%, Russian 14.2%, Tajik 4.4%, other 7.1%. **Ethnicity/race (1996 est.):** Uzbek 80%, Russian 5.5%, Tajik 5%, Kazak 3%, Karakalpak 2.5%, Tatar 1.5%, other 2.5%. **Religions:** Muslim (mostly Sunnis) 88%, Eastern Orthodox 9%, other 3%. **Literacy rate:** 99% (1996)
Economic summary: GDP/PPP (1999 est.): $59.3 billion; per capita $2,500. **Real growth rate:** –1%. **Inflation:** 29%. **Unemployment:** 5% plus another 10% underemployed (Dec. 1996 est.). **Arable land:** 9%. **Agriculture:** cotton, vegetables, fruits, grain; livestock. **Labor force:** 11.9 million (1998 est.); agriculture and forestry, 44%; industry, 20%; services, 36% (1995). **Industries:** textiles, food processing, machine building, metallurgy, natural gas. **Natural resources:** natural gas, petroleum, coal, gold, uranium, silver, copper, lead and zinc, tungsten, molybdenum. **Exports:** $2.9 billion (1999 est.): cotton, gold, natural gas, mineral fertilizers, ferrous metals, textiles, food products, automobiles. **Imports:** $3.1 billion (1999 est.): machinery and equipment, chemicals, metals; foodstuffs. **Major trading partners:** Russia, Switzerland, UK, Belgium, Kazakhstan, Tajikistan, South Korea, Germany, U.S., Turkey.

Geography Uzbekistan is situated in central Asia between the Amu Darya and Syr Darya Rivers, the Aral Sea, and the slopes of the Tien Shan Mountains. It is bounded by Kazakhstan in the north and northwest, Kyrgyzstan and Tajikistan in the east and southeast, Turkmenistan in the southwest, and Afghanistan in the south. The republic also includes the Karakalpakstan Autonomous Republic, with its capital, Nukus (1992 est. pop., 182,000). The country is about one-tenth larger in area than the state of California.

Government Republic; authoritarian presidential rule.

History The Uzbekistan land was once part of the ancient Persian empire and was later conquered by Alexander the Great in the 4th century B.C. During the 8th century, the nomadic Turkic tribes living there were converted to Islam by invading Arab forces who dominated the area. The Mongols under Ghengis Khan took over the region from the Seljuk Turks in the 13th century, and it later became part of Tamerlane the Great's empire and that of his successors until the 16th century. The Uzbeks invaded the territory in the early 16th century and merged with the other inhabitants in the area. Their empire broke up into separate Uzbek principalities, the khanates of Khiva, Bukhara, and Kokand. These city-states resisted Russian expansion into the area but were conquered by the Russian forces in the mid-19th century.

The territory was made into the Uzbek Republic in 1924 and became the independent Uzbekistan Soviet Socialist Republic in 1925. Under Soviet rule, Uzbekistan concentrated on growing cotton with the help of irrigation, mechanization, and chemical fertilizers and pesticides, causing serious environmental damage.

In June 1990, Uzbekistan became the first central Asian republic to declare that its own laws had sovereignty over those of the central Soviet government. Uzbekistan became fully independent and joined with ten other former Soviet republics on Dec. 21, 1991, in the Commonwealth of Independent States.

Vozrozhdeniye, an island in the Aral Sea, was a secret test site for biological weapons during the Soviet era. In 1988, the Soviets attempted to bury the evidence on the island, a frightening legacy that Uzbekistan inherited upon independence. U.S. scientists have confirmed that the island contains live anthrax and other deadly poisons.

In Feb. 1992, President Karimov, a former Communist Party boss, affirmed his commitment to democracy and human rights, but he effectively suppressed opposition parties in mid-1993. The criminal code was amended to impose stricter penalties for antigovernment activity. Opposition groups were largely excluded in future elections while the ruling party continued to post decisive victories.

In 1999, the country battled against militant Islamic groups bent on the overthrow of the secular government. In Feb. 1999, a series of bomb blasts killed 16 and injured hundreds in the capital, Tashkent. Militant Islamic gunmen remain stationed across the border in southern Kyrgyzstan, and Uzbek fighter planes have been unable to rout them. In 2000, Russia offered to help Uzbekistan "liquidate" the Islamic extremists, and Russia has also offered to send at least $30 million worth of weapons.

Vanuatu

REPUBLIC OF VANUATU
President: John Bani (1999)
Prime Minister: Edward Natapei (2001)
Area: 5,699 sq mi (14,760 sq km)
Population (2001 est.): 192,910 (average annual rate of natural increase: 1.7%); birth rate: 25.4/1000; infant mortality rate: 61.1/1000; density per sq mi: 34
Capital and largest city (1993 est.): Port Vila; 26,100.
Monetary unit: Vatu. **Languages:** Bislama (a Melanesian pidgin English), English, French (all 3 official). **Ethnicity/race:** indigenous Melanesian 94%, French 4%, Vietnamese, Chinese, other Pacific Islanders. **Religions:** Presbyterian 36.7%, Roman Catholic 15%, Anglican 15%, other Christian 10%, indigenous beliefs 7.6%, other 15.7%. **Literacy rate:** 55% (1979)
Economic summary: GDP/PPP (1999 est.): $245 million; per capita $1,300. **Real growth rate:** n.a. **Inflation:** 3.9% (1998 est.). **Unemployment:** n.a. **Arable land:** 2%. **Agriculture:** copra, coconuts, cocoa, coffee, taro, yams, coconuts, fruits, vegetables; fish, beef. **Labor force:** n.a.; agriculture, 65%; services, 32%; industry, 3% (1995 est.). **Industries:** food and fish freezing, wood processing, meat canning. **Natural resources:** manganese, hardwood forests, fish. **Exports:** $33.8 million (f.o.b. 1998): copra, beef, cocoa, timber, coffee. **Imports:** $76.2 million (f.o.b. 1998): machinery and equipment, foodstuffs, fuels. **Major trading partners:** Japan, Germany, Spain, New Caledonia, Australia, Singapore, New Zealand, France, Fiji.

Geography Vanuatu is an archipelago of 83 islands lying between New Caledonia and Fiji in the South Pacific. Largest of the islands is Espiritu Santo (875 sq mi; 2,266 sq km); others are Efate, Malekula, Malo, Pentecost, and Tanna.

Government Republic.

History The first settlers were believed to have arrived approximately 3,500 years ago from New Guinea and the Solomon Islands by canoe. The islands were sighted by Pedro Fernandes de Queiros of Portugal in 1606 and were charted by the British navigator James Cook in 1774, who named the archipelago New Hebrides, after the northern Scottish islands. Competing British and French claims to the islands led to the formation of a condominium government, allowing for joint British-French rule in 1906. The islands' plantation economy, based on imported Vietnamese labor, was prosperous until the 1920s, when markets for its products declined. Diseases brought by missionaries, sandalwood traders, and others helped reduce the population from approximately 1 million in 1800 to 45,000 in 1935. The islands served as a major Allied base in World War II. After World War II, the indigenous Melanesians began lobbying for independence. In 1980 the country achieved independence and was renamed Vanuatu.

A brief rebellion by French settlers and plantation workers on Espiritu Santo took place in May 1980. Britain, France, and Papua New Guinea sent soldiers, who quelled the revolt, which the new government said was financed by the Phoenix Foundation, a right-wing U.S. group.

Vatican City (Holy See)

National name: Stato della Città del Vaticano
Ruler: Pope John Paul II (1978)
Area: 0.17 sq mi (0.44 sq km)
Population (July 2000 est.): 880; population growth rate: 1.15%; density per sq mi: 5,059. **Monetary unit:** Italian lira. **Languages:** Latin, Italian, and various other languages. **Ethnicity/race:** Italians, Swiss. **Religion:** Roman Catholic.
Labor force: dignitaries, priests, nuns, guards, and 3,000 lay workers who live outside the Vatican.
Budget (1997): Revenues: $209.6 million; expenditures: $209.6 million, including capital expenditures.

Geography The Vatican City State is situated on the Vatican hill, on the right bank of the Tiber River, within the city of Rome.

Government The pope has full legal, executive, and judicial powers. Executive power over the area is in the hands of a commission of cardinals appointed by the pope. The College of Cardinals is the pope's chief advisory body, and upon his death the cardinals elect his successor for life.

History The Vatican City State, sovereign and independent, is the survivor of the papal states that in 1859 comprised an area of some 17,000 sq mi (44,030 sq km). During the struggle for Italian unification, from 1860 to 1870, most of this area became part of Italy. By an Italian law of May 13, 1871, the temporal power of the pope was abrogated, and the territory of the papacy was confined to the Vatican and Lateran palaces and the villa of Castel Gandolfo. The popes consistently refused to recognize this arrangement and, by the Lateran Treaty of Feb. 11, 1929, between the Vatican and the kingdom of Italy, the exclusive dominion and sovereign jurisdiction of the Holy See over the city of the Vatican was again recognized, thus restoring the pope's temporal authority over the area.

The first session of Ecumenical Council Vatican II was opened by John XXIII on Oct. 11, 1962, to plan and set policies for the modernization of the Roman Catholic Church. Pope Paul VI continued the council, opening the second session on Sept. 29, 1963.

On Aug. 26, 1978, Cardinal Albino Luciani was chosen by the College of Cardinals to succeed Paul VI, who had died of a heart attack on Aug. 6. The new pope took the name John Paul I. (For a listing of all the popes, see the table in Religion.) Only 34 days after his election, John Paul I died of a heart attack, ending the shortest reign in 373 years. On Oct. 16, Cardinal Karol Wojtyla, 58, was chosen pope and took the name John Paul II.

On May 13, 1981, a Turkish terrorist shot the pope in St. Peter's Square, the first assassination attempt against the pontiff in modern times. On June 3, 1985, the Vatican and Italy ratified a new church-state treaty, known as a concordat, replacing the Lateran Pact of 1929. The new accord affirmed the independence of Vatican City but ended a number of privileges the Catholic Church had in Italy, including its status as the state religion. The treaty ended Rome's status as a "sacred city." Relations, diplomatic and ecclesiastical, with eastern Europe have improved dramatically with the fall of communism. Relations with Russia, while improving, have not yet reached the ambassadorial level. Diplomatic ties were established in March 1994 with Jordan, and full relations were established with Israel in June. Six months earlier the two nations had accorded each other mutual recognition. The Holy See, calling for closer relations with Orthodoxy, was scheduled to meet with Russian patriarch Alexy II in June 1997, but differences prevented the encounter from taking place. In Jan. 1998, Pope John Paul II made a historic visit to Cuba, hoping to promote religious freedom in that communist nation. Iranian president Mohammad Khatami met with the pope in 1999, the first state visit by an Iranian leader to a western nation since Iran's 1979 Islamic revolution.

In March 2000, the pope issued an apology for sins committed by Catholics over the past 2,000 years, including religious persecutions and discrimination against women. Several groups criticized the vagueness of the apology, wishing the pope had specified the church's particularly egregious sins.

Venezuela

REPUBLIC OF VENEZUELA

National name: Republica de Venezuela
President: Hugo Chavez (1999)
Area: 352,143 sq mi (912,050 sq km)
Population (2001 est.): 23,916,810 (average annual rate of natural increase: 1.6%); birth rate: 20.7/1000; infant mortality rate: 25.4/1000; density per sq mile: 68
Capital: Caracas. **Largest cities (1990 est.):** Caracas, city, 1,824,892, metro area, 2,784,042; Maracaibo, 1,206,726; Valencia, 616,000; Barquisimento, 723,587.
Monetary unit: bolivar. **Languages:** Spanish (official), various indigenous languages in the remote interior.
Ethnicity/race: mestizo 67%, white 21%, black 10%, Amerindian 2%. **Religions:** Roman Catholic 96%, Protestant 2%. **Literacy rate:** 91% (1990)
Economic summary: GDP/PPP (1999 est.): $182.8 billion; per capita $8,000. **Real growth rate:** –7.2%. **Inflation:** 20% (1999). **Unemployment:** 18%. **Arable land:** 4%. **Agriculture:** corn, sorghum, sugarcane, rice, bananas, vegetables, coffee; beef, pork, milk, eggs; fish. **Labor force:** 9.9 million (1999); services, 64%; industry, 23%; agriculture, 13% (1997 est.).

Industries: petroleum, iron ore mining, construction materials, food processing, textiles, steel, aluminum, motor vehicle assembly. **Natural resources:** petroleum, natural gas, iron ore, gold, bauxite, other minerals, hydropower, diamonds. **Exports:** $20.9 billion (f.o.b., 1999): petroleum, bauxite and aluminum, steel, chemicals, agricultural products, basic manufactures (1998). **Imports:** $11.8 billion (f.o.b., 1999): raw materials, machinery and equipment, transport equipment, construction materials (1999). **Major trading partners:** U.S., Puerto Rico, Colombia, Brazil, Japan, Germany, Netherlands, Italy, France, Canada.

Geography Venezuela, a third larger than Texas, occupies most of the northern coast of South America on the Caribbean Sea. It is bordered by Colombia to the west, Guyana to the east, and Brazil to the south. Mountain systems break Venezuela into four distinct areas: (1) the Maracaibo lowlands; (2) the mountainous region in the north and northwest; (3) the Orinoco basin, with the llanos (vast grass-covered plains) on its northern border and great forest areas in the south and southeast; (4) the Guiana Highlands, south of the Orinoco, accounting for nearly half the national territory.

Government Federal republic.

History When Columbus explored Venezuela on his third voyage in 1498, the area was inhabited by Arawak, Carib, and Chibcha Indians. A subsequent Spanish explorer gave the country its name, meaning "Little Venice." Caracas was founded in 1567. Simón Bolívar, who led the liberation of much of the continent from Spain, was born in Caracas in 1783. With Bolívar taking part, Venezuela was one of the first South American colonies to revolt in 1810, winning independence in 1821. Federated at first with Colombia and Ecuador as the Republic of Greater Colombia, Venezuela became a republic in 1830. A period of unstable dictatorships followed. Antonio Guzman Blanco governed from 1870 to 1888, developing an infrastructure, expanding agriculture, and welcoming foreign investment.

Gen. Juan Vicente Gómez was dictator from 1908 to 1935, when Venezuela became a major oil exporter. A military junta ruled after his death. Leftist Dr. Rómulo Betancourt and the Democratic Action Party won a majority of seats in a constituent assembly to draft a new constitution in 1946. A well-known writer, Rómulo Gallegos, candidate of Betancourt's party, became Venezuela's first deomcratically elected president in 1947. Within eight months, Gallegos was overthrown by a military-backed coup led by Marcos Peréz Jiménez, who was ousted himself in 1958. Since 1959, Venezuela has been one of the most stable democracies in Latin America. Betancourt served from 1959–64, while Rafael Caldera Rodríguez, president from 1969 to 1974, legalized the Communist Party and established diplomatic relations with Moscow.

Venezuela benefited from the oil boom of the early 1970s. In 1974, President Carlos Andrés Pérez took office, and in 1976 Venezuela nationalized foreign-owned oil and steel companies, offering compensation. Luis Herrera Campíns took office in 1978. Declining world oil prices sent Venezuela's economy into a tailspin, increasing the country's foreign debt. Pérez was reelected to a nonconsecutive term in 1988 and launched an unpopular austerity program. Military officers staged two unsuccessful coup attempts in 1992, while the following year Congress impeached

Pérez on corruption charges. President Rafael Caldera Rodríguez was elected in Dec. 1993 to face the 1994 collapse of half of the country's banking sector, falling oil prices, foreign debt repayment, and inflation. In 1997, the government announced an expansion of gold and diamond mining to reduce reliance on oil.

Leftist president Hugo Chavez took office in 1999, pledging political and economic reforms to give the poor a greater share of the country's oil wealth. A constituent assembly was formed to rewrite the constitution in July 1999, followed by the creation of a constitutional assembly made up of Chavez's allies that replaced the democratically elected Congress. Chavez's assumption of greater power prompted charges that he is establishing a left-wing dictatorship.

Chavez was reelected to a six-year term in July 2000. Troops were called in to quell serious protests over the election in several cities. In 2000 Chavez visited other OPEC countries, becoming the first foreign head of state to visit Iraq since the 1991 Gulf War. He is close to President Fidel Castro of Cuba, which receives Venezuelan oil at reduced prices.

Vietnam

SOCIALIST REPUBLIC OF VIETNAM

National name: Công Hòa Xa Hôi Chú Nghia Viêt Nam
President: Tran Duc Luong (1997)
Prime Minister: Phan Van Khai (1997)
Area: 127,243 sq mi (329,560 sq km)
Population (2001 est.): 79,939,014 (average annual rate of natural increase: 1.5%); birth rate: 21.2/1000; infant mortality rate: 30.2/1000; density per sq mi: 628
Capital: Hanoi. **Largest cities (1992 est.):** Ho Chi Minh City (Saigon), 3,015,743; Hanoi, 1,073,760. Other large cities (1989): Haiphong, 456,049; Da Nang, 370,670; Nha Trang, 213,687; Qui Nho'n, 160,091; Hué 211,085. **Monetary unit:** Dong. **Languages:** Vietnamese (official), French, English, Khmer, Chinese. **Ethnicity/race:** Vietnamese 85%–90%, Chinese 3%, Muong, Thai, Meo, Khmer, Man, Cham. **Religions:** Buddhist, Roman Catholic, Islam, Taoist, Confucian, Animist. **Literacy rate:** 94% (1995)
Economic summary: GDP/PPP (1999 est.): $143.1 billion; per capita $1,850. **Real growth rate:** 4.8%. **Inflation:** 4%. **Unemployment:** 25% (1995 est.). **Arable land:** 17%. **Agriculture:** paddy rice, corn, potatoes, rubber, soybeans, coffee, tea, bananas; poultry, pigs; fish. **Labor force:** 38.2 million (1998 est.); agriculture, 67%; industry and services, 33% (1997 est.). **Industries:** food processing, garments, shoes, machine building, mining, cement, chemical fertilizer, glass, tires, oil, coal, steel, paper. **Natural resources:** phosphates, coal, manganese, bauxite, chromate, offshore oil and gas deposits, forests, hydropower. **Exports:** $11.5 billion (f.o.b., 1999 est.): crude oil, marine products, rice, coffee, rubber, tea, garments, shoes. **Imports:** $11.6 billion (f.o.b., 1999 est.): machinery and equipment, petroleum products, fertilizer, steel products, raw cotton, grain, cement, motorcycles. **Major trading partners:** Japan, Germany, Singapore, Taiwan, Hong Kong, France, South Korea, U.S., China, Thailand, Sweden.

Geography   Vietnam occupies the eastern and southern part of the Indochinese peninsula in Southeast Asia, with the South China Sea along its entire coast. China is to the north and Laos and Cambodia to the west. Long and narrow on a north-south axis, Vietnam is about twice the size of Arizona. The Mekong River delta lies in the south.

Government   Communist state.

History   The Vietnamese are descendants of nomadic Mongols from China and migrants from Indonesia. According to mythology, the first ruler of Vietnam was Hung Vuong, who founded the nation in 2879 B.C. China ruled the nation then known as Nam Viet as a vassal state from 111 B.C. until the 15th century, an era of nationalistic expansion, when Cambodians were pushed out of the southern area of what is now Vietnam.

A century later, the Portuguese were the first Europeans to enter the area. France established its influence early in the 19th century, and within 80 years conquered the three regions into which the country was then divided—Cochin-China in the south, Annam in the central region, and Tonkin in the north.

France first unified Vietnam in 1887, when a single governor-generalship was created, followed by the first physical links between north and south—a rail and road system. Even at the beginning of World War II, however, there were internal differences among the three regions. Japan took over military bases in Vietnam in 1940, and a pro-Vichy French administration remained until 1945. Veteran Communist leader Ho Chi Minh organized an independence movement known as the Vietminh to exploit the confusion surrounding France's weakened influence in the region. At the end of the war, Ho's followers seized Hanoi and declared a short-lived republic, which ended with the arrival of French forces in 1946.

Paris proposed a unified government within the French Union under the former Annamite emperor, Bao Dai. Cochin-China and Annam accepted the proposal, and Bao Dai was proclaimed emperor of all Vietnam in 1949. Ho and the Vietminh withheld support, and the revolution in China gave them the outside help needed for a war of resistance against French and Vietnamese troops armed largely by a United States worried about cold war Communist expansion.

A bitter defeat at Dien Bien Phu in northwest Vietnam on May 5, 1954, broke the French military campaign and resulted in the division of Vietnam. In the new South, Ngo Dinh Diem, premier under Bao Dai, deposed the monarch in 1955 and made himself president. Diem used strong U.S. backing to create an authoritarian regime that suppressed all opposition but could not eradicate the Northern-supplied Communist Viet Cong.

Skirmishing grew into a full-scale war, with escalating U.S. involvement. A military coup, U.S.-inspired in the view of many, ousted Diem on Nov. 1, 1963, and a kaleidoscope of military governments followed. The most savage fighting of the war occurred in early 1968 during the Vietnamese New Year, known as Tet. Although the so-called Tet Offensive ended in a military defeat for the North, its psychological impact changed the course of the war.

U.S. bombing and an invasion of Cambodia in the summer of 1970—an effort to destroy Viet Cong bases in the neighboring state—marked the end of major U.S. participation in the fighting. Most American ground troops were withdrawn from combat by mid-1971 when the U.S. conducted heavy bombing raids on the Ho Chi Minh Trail—a crucial North Vietnamese supply line. In 1972, secret peace negotiations led by Secretary of State Henry A. Kissinger took place, and a peace settlement was signed in Paris on Jan. 27, 1973.

By April 9, 1975, Hanoi's troops marched within 40 mi of Saigon, the South's capital. South Vietnam's president Thieu resigned on April 21 and fled. Gen. Duong Van Minh, the new president, surrendered

Saigon on April 30, ending a war that claimed the lives of 1.3 million Vietnamese and 58,000 Americans.

In 1977, border clashes between Vietnam and Cambodia intensified, as well as accusations by its former ally Beijing that Chinese residents of Vietnam were being subjected to persecution. Beijing cut off all aid and withdrew 800 technicians.

Hanoi was also preoccupied with a continuing war in Cambodia, where 60,000 Vietnamese troops had invaded and overthrown the country's Communist leader Pol Pot and his pro-Chinese regime. In early 1979, Vietnam was conducting a two-front war: defending its northern border against a Chinese invasion, and supporting its army in Cambodia, which was still fighting Pol Pot's Khmer Rouge guerrillas. Hanoi's Marxist policies combined with the destruction of the country's infrastructure during the decades of fighting devastated Vietnam's economy. However, it started to pick up in 1986 under *do Maui* (economic renovation), an effort at limited privatization. Vietnamese troops began limited withdrawals from Laos and Cambodia in 1988, and Vietnam supported the Cambodian peace agreement signed in Oct. 1991.

The U.S. lifted a Vietnamese trade embargo in Feb. 1994 that had been in place since its involvement in the war. Full diplomatic relations were announced between the two countries in July 1995. In April 1997, a pact was signed with the U.S. concerning repayment of the $146 million wartime debt incurred by the South Vietnamese government, and the following year the nation began a drive to eliminate inefficient bureaucrats and streamline the approval process for direct foreign investment. Efforts of reform-minded officials toward political and economic change have been thwarted by Vietnam's ruling Communist Party. In April 2001, however, reform-minded Nong Duc Manh was appointed general secretary of the ruling Communist Party, succeeding Le Kha Phieu. Even with a reformer at the helm of the party, any change will come slowly and cautiously. Manh previously served as chairman of the National Assembly.

(For a Vietnam War chronology, *see* Headline History.)

Western Sahara

WESTERN SAHARA

Head of State: none
Area: 102,703 sq mi (266,000 sq km)
Population (2000): 250,559; growth rate: 2.9%; birth rate: 45.1/1000; infant mortality rate: 133.6/1000; density per sq mi: 2
Largest cities (1991): El Aaiun (20,010). **Monetary unit:** Moroccan dirham (DH). **Languages:** Hassaniya Arabic, Moroccan Arabic. **Ethnicity/race:** Saharawi, Arab, Berber. **Religion:** Muslim
Economic summary: GDP/PPP (1999 est.): n.a. **Arable land:** 0%. **Agriculture:** fruits and vegetables (grown in the few oases); camels, sheep, goats (kept by nomads). **Labor force:** 12,000; animal husbandry and subsistence farming, 50%. **Industries:** phosphate mining, handicrafts. **Natural resources:** phosphates, iron ore. **Exports:** $n.a.: phosphates 62%. **Imports:** $n.a.: fuel for fishing fleet, foodstuffs. **Major trading partners:** Morocco claims and administers Western Sahara, so trade partners are included in overall Moroccan accounts.

Geography Located in northern Africa on the Atlantic Ocean, Western Sahara is surrounded by Algeria to the east, Morocco to the north, and Mauri-

tania to the south. About the size of Colorado, it is mostly low, flat desert with some small mountains in the south and northeast.

Government Legal status of the territory is disputed and sovereignty unresolved; a UN referendum on the issue is planned. The territory is contested by Morocco and the Polisario Front, which in Feb. 1976 formerly proclaimed a government-in-exile of the Saharawi Arab Democratic Republic, now officially recognized by about 70 countries.

History Little is known about Western Sahara until the 4th century B.C. when trade with Europe began. During the Middle Ages it was occupied first by Berbers and then by the Arabic-speaking Muslim Bedouins. In the 19th century the Spanish laid claim to the southern coastal region, called Rio de Oro, and later occupied the northern interior region, Saguia el Hamra, in 1934. The Spanish formally united the two regions, and it became known as Spanish Sahara in 1958. Both Morocco and Mauritania sought to control the territory, and when the Spanish departed in 1976 they divided the territory between them. In the meantime, the indigenous Saharawis began fighting for independence. In 1976, the insurgents, called the Polisario Front, declared a government-in-exile (the Saharawi Arab Democratic Republic) from their base in Algeria. Mauritania reached a peace agreement with the Polisario in 1979, but Morocco then seized the land given up by Mauritania and now exerts administrative control over the entire region. The Polisario Front fought Morocco to a stalemate, and agreed in Sept. 1991 to a cease-fire, which was contingent on a referendum regarding independence. For the past decade, however, the UN has failed to hold the referendum; disputes over voter eligibility have been the major stumbling block, as well as Morocco's opposition to the referendum. In Aug. 2001, former secretary of state James A. Baker III, special UN envoy to the Western Sahara, proposed that instead of a referendum on independence, Western Sahara consider becoming an autonomous region of Morocco. The Western Sahara government and its ally Algeria rejected the proposal.

Yemen

REPUBLIC OF YEMEN

National name: Al Jumhuriyahal Yamaniyah
President: Ali Abdullah Saleh
Prime Minister: Abdel Qadir Bajamal (2001)
Area: 203,849 sq mi (527,970 sq km)
Population (2001 est.): 18,078,035 (average annual rate of natural increase: 3.4%); birth rate: 43.4/1000; infant mortality rate: 68.5/1000; density per sq mi: 89
Capital (1995): Sanaá, 972,011. **Largest cities (1995):** Tiaz, 2,205,947; Hodiedah, 1,749,944; Aden, 562,162. **Monetary unit:** Rial. **Language:** Arabic. **Ethnicity/race:** predominantly Arab; Afro-Arab concentrations in western coastal locations; South Asians in southern regions; small European communities in major metropolitan areas. **Religion:** Islam (Sunni and Shi'ite). **Literacy rate:** 39% (1990)
Economic summary: GDP/PPP (1999 est.): $12.7 billion; per capita $750. **Real growth rate:** 4%. **Inflation:** 10%. **Unemployment:** 30% (1995 est.). **Arable land:** 3%. **Agriculture:** grain, fruits, vegetables, qat (mildly narcotic shrub), coffee, cotton; dairy products, poultry, beef; fish. **Labor force:** n.a.; most people are employed in agriculture and herding or as expatriate laborers; services, construction; industry, and commerce account for less than one-half of the labor

force. **Industries:** crude oil production and petroleum refining; small-scale production of cotton textiles and leather goods; food processing; handicrafts; small aluminum products factory; cement. **Natural resources:** petroleum, fish, rock salt, marble, small deposits of coal, gold, lead, nickel, and copper, fertile soil in west. **Exports:** $2 billion (f.o.b., 1999 est.): crude oil, cotton, coffee, dried and salted fish. **Imports:** $2.3 billion (f.o.b., 1999 est.): food and live animals, machinery and equipment, manufactured goods. **Major trading partners:** China, South Korea, Thailand, Japan, U.S., UAE, France, Italy, Saudi Arabia.

Geography Formerly divided into two nations, the People's Democratic Republic of Yemen and the Yemen Arab Republic, the Republic of Yemen occupies the southwestern tip of the Arabian Peninsula on the Red Sea opposite Ethiopia, and extends along the southern part of the Arabian Peninsula on the Gulf of Aden and the Indian Ocean. Saudi Arabia is to the north and Oman is to the east. The country is about the size of France. A 700-mile (1,130-km) narrow coastal plain in the south gives way to a mountainous region and then a plateau area. Some of the interior highlands in the west attain a height of 12,000 ft (3,660 m).

Government Parliamentary.

History The history of Yemen dates back to the Minaean (1200–650 B.C.) and Sabaean (750–115 B.C.) kingdoms. Ancient Yemen (centered around the port of Aden) engaged in the lucrative myrrh and frankincense trade. It was invaded by the Romans (1st century A.D.) as well as the Ethiopians and Persians (6th century A.D.). In A.D. 628 it converted to Islam and in the 10th century came under the control of the Rassite dynasty of the Zaidi sect, which remained involved in North Yemeni politics until 1962. The Ottoman Turks nominally occupied the area from 1538 to the decline of their empire in 1918.

The northern portion of Yemen was ruled by imams until a pro-Egyptian military coup took place in 1962. The junta proclaimed the Yemen Arab Republic, and after a civil war in which Egypt's Nasser and the USSR supported the revolutionaries, and King Saud of Saudi Arabia and King Hussein of Jordan supported the royalists, the royalists were finally defeated in mid-1969.

The southern port of Aden, strategically located at the opening of the Red Sea, was colonized by Britain in 1839, and by 1937, with an expansion of its territory, it was known as the Aden Protectorate. In the 1960s the Nationalist Liberation Front (NLF) fought against British rule, which led to the establishment of the People's Republic of Southern Yemen on Nov. 30, 1967. In 1979, under strong Soviet influence, the country became the only Marxist state in the Arab world.

The Republic of Yemen was established on May 22, 1990, when pro-Western Yemen and the Marxist Yemen Arab Republic merged after 300 years of separation to form the new nation. The poverty and decline in Soviet economic support in the South was an important incentive for the merger. The new president, Ali Abdullah Saleh, was elected by the Parliaments of both countries.

Differences over power sharing and the pace of integration between the north and the south came to a head in 1994, resulting in a civil war. The north's superior forces quickly overwhelmed the south in May and early June despite the south's brief declaration of succession. The victorious north presented a

reconciliation plan providing for a general amnesty and pledges to protect political democracy.

The president's party, the General People's Congress, won an enormous victory in the April 1997 parliamentary elections, the first since the civil war. In 1998–99, a militant Islamic group, the Aden-Abyan Islamic Army, kidnapped several groups of Western tourists, which led to the deaths of several during a poorly orchestrated rescue attempt. The group's leader, Zein Al-Abidine al-Mihdar, threatened to continue attacks on tourists and government officials. The goal of the militants is to overthrow the government and turn Yemen into an Islamic state.

On Oct. 12, 2000, 17 Americans died and 37 were wounded when suicide bombers attacked the Navy destroyer *Cole*, which was refueling in Aden, Yemen. The U.S. has had numerous clashes with Yemeni authorities during the investigation of the terrorist act.

Yugoslavia

FEDERAL REPUBLIC OF YUGOSLAVIA

National name: Savezna Republika Jugoslavija
President: Vojislav Kostunica (2000)
Prime Minister: Dragisa Pesic (2001)
Area: 39,517 sq mi (102,350 sq km)
Population (2001 est.): 10,677,290 (Montenegro: 673,981, Serbia: 10,003,309) (average annual rate of natural increase: Montenegro: 0.7%, Serbia: 0.2%); birth rate: Montenegro: 14.8/1000, Serbia: 12.5/1000; infant mortality rate: Montenegro: 10.7/1000, Serbia: 18.0/1000; density per sq mi: 270
Capital and largest city (1994 est.): Belgrade, 1,168,454. **Other large cities:** Novi Sad, 179,626; Nis, 175,391; Pristina, 155,499. **Monetary unit:** Yugoslav new dinar. **Languages:** Serbian 95%, Albanian 5%. What was once known as Serbo-Croatian is now known as Serbian, Croatian, or Bosnian, depending on the speaker's political and ethnic affiliation. It is written in Latin and Cyrillic.
Ethnicity/race: Serbs 63%, Albanians 14%, Montenegrins 6%, Hungarians 4%, other 13%.
Religions: Orthodox 65%, Muslim 19%, Roman Catholic 4%, Protestant 1%, other 11%. **Literacy rate:** 91%
Economic summary: GDP/PPP (1999 est.): $20.6 billion; per capita $1,800. **Real growth rate:** –20%. **Inflation:** 42%. **Unemployment:** 30%. **Arable land:** n.a. **Agriculture:** cereals, fruit, vegetables, tobacco, olives, cattle, sheep, goats. **Labor force:** 1.6 million. **Industries:** machine building (aircraft, trucks, and automobiles; tanks and weapons; electrical equipment; agricultural machinery); metallurgy (steel, aluminum, copper, lead, zinc, chromium, antimony, bismuth, cadmium); mining (coal, bauxite, nonferrous ore, iron ore, limestone); consumer goods (textiles, footwear, foodstuffs, appliances); electronics, petroleum products, chemicals, and pharmaceuticals. **Natural resources:** oil, gas, coal, antimony, copper, lead, zinc, nickel, gold, pyrite, chrome, hydro power. **Exports:** $1.5 billion (1999): manufactured goods, food and live animals, raw materials. **Imports:** $3.3 billion (1999): machinery and transport equipment, fuel and lubricants, manufactured goods, chemicals, food and live animals, raw materials. **Major trading partners:** Bosnia and Herzegovina, Italy, the Former Yugoslav Republic of Macedonia, Germany, Russia.

Geography Serbia and Montenegro are about the size of the state of Kentucky and largely mountainous. The northeastern section of Serbia is part of the rich, fertile Danubian Plain drained by the Danube, Tisa, Sava, and Morava River systems. Montenegro is a jumbled mass of mountains, containing also some grassy slopes and fertile river valleys.

Government The current federation is the third state to call itself by the name Yugoslavia, officially referring to itself as the Federal Republic of Yugoslavia. The United States, however, does not recognize it by that name because the U.S. does not consider the Serbian and Montenegrin federation the successor state of Yugoslavia. Serbia and Montenegro are a federal republic.

History Yugoslavia was formed on Dec. 4, 1918, from the patchwork of Balkan states and territories. World War I began there with the assassination of Archduke Franz Ferdinand of Austria at Sarajevo on June 28, 1914. The new kingdom of Serbs, Croats, and Slovenes included the former kingdoms of Serbia and Montenegro; Bosnia-Herzegovina, previously administered jointly by Austria and Hungary; Croatia-Slavonia, a semiautonomous region of Hungary; and Dalmatia, formerly administered by Austria. King Peter I of Serbia became the first monarch; his son, Alexander I, succeeded him on Aug. 16, 1921. Croatian demands for a federal state forced Alexander to assume dictatorial powers in 1929 and to change the country's name to Yugoslavia. Serbian dominance continued despite his efforts, amid the resentment of other regions. A Macedonian associated with Croatian dissidents assassinated Alexander in Marseilles, France, on Oct. 9, 1934, and his cousin, Prince Paul, became regent for the king's son, Prince Peter.

Paul's pro-Axis policy brought Yugoslavia to sign the Axis Pact on March 25, 1941, and opponents overthrew the government two days later. On April 6 the Nazis occupied the country, and the young king and his government fled. Two guerrilla armies—the Chetniks under Draza Mihajlovic supporting the monarchy, and the Partisans under Tito (Josip Broz) leaning toward the USSR—fought the Nazis for the duration of the war. In 1943, Tito established an Executive National Committee of Liberation to function as a provisional government. Tito won the election held in the fall of 1945, as monarchists boycotted the vote. A new Assembly abolished the monarchy and proclaimed the Federal People's Republic of Yugoslavia, with Tito as prime minister. Tito ruthlessly eliminated the opposition and broke with the Soviet bloc in 1948. Yugoslavia followed a middle road, combining orthodox Communist control of politics and general overall economic policy with a varying degree of freedom in the arts, travel, and individual enterprise. Tito became president in 1953 and president-for-life under a revised constitution adopted in 1963.

After Tito's death on May 4, 1980, a rotating presidency designed to avoid internal dissension was put into effect immediately, and the feared clash of Yugoslavia's multiple nationalities and regions appeared to have been averted. In May 1991 Croatian voters supported a referendum calling for their republic to become an independent nation. A similar referendum passed in December in Slovenia. In June the respective Parliaments in both republics passed declarations of independence. Ethnic violence flared almost immediately. The largely Serbian-led Yugoslav military pounded breakaway Bosnia and Herzegovina, leading the UN Security Council in May 1992 to impose economic sanctions on the Belgrade government.

Despite rampant inflation reaching approximately 3,000% per month in Dec. 1993, the Serbian government of Slobodan Milosevic maintained its effective control over the rump Yugoslavia. Trade sanctions were lifted in Dec. 1995 following the signing of the Dayton Accords. In June 1996, the UN Security Council lifted its heavy weapons embargo. Large groups of demonstrators in 1996–97 engaged in several months of daily protests after Slobodan Milosevic refused to recognize opposition victories in local elections and in elections in Montenegro. Constitutionally barred from another term as president of Serbia, Milosevic became president of the Federal Republic of Yugoslavia (Serbia and Montenegro) in July 1997.

The situation in Serbia's provinces of Montenegro and Kosovo grew divisive in 1997 and 1998. In May 1998, Montenegro elected the reform-minded Milo Djukanovic as president. Not only is he an outspoken critic of Yugoslav president Slobodan Milosevic but he has openly contemplated secession.

Since Feb. 1998 the Yugoslav army and Serbian police have fought against the separatist Kosovo Liberation Army, but their scorched-earth tactics were concentrated on ethnic Albanian civilians—Muslims who make up 90% of Kosovo's population. More than 900 Kosovars were killed in the fighting, and the hundreds of thousands forced to flee their homes were without adequate food and shelter. Although Serbs make up only 10% of Kosovo's population, the region figures strongly in Serbian nationalist mythology.

NATO was reluctant to intervene because Kosovo—unlike Bosnia in 1992—was legally a province of Yugoslavia. The proof of civilian massacres finally gave NATO the impetus to intervene for the first time ever in the dealings of a sovereign nation with its own people. In an Oct. 12, 1998, truce brokered by American diplomat Richard Holbrooke, and under the threat of a military air strike—for which there was little enthusiasm among several NATO countries—Pres. Slobodan Milosevic agreed to the withdrawal of military forces. Fighting continued, however, and neither side accepted Washington's proposal for the province—Kosovars demanded full independence while Serb leaders would agree only to limited autonomy.

After negotiations in February and March 1999 went nowhere, on March 24, 1999, NATO began launching air strikes. Weeks of daily bombings destroyed significant Serbian military targets, yet Milosevic showed no signs of relenting. In fact, Serbian militia stepped up civilian massacres and deportations in Kosovo—by the end of the conflict, the UN high commissioner for refugees estimated that at least 850,000 people had fled Kosovo. The refugee crisis put a heavy burden on neighboring countries such as Albania and Macedonia. Many wondered whether the NATO strikes had actually exacerbated the violence. As effective as NATO airpower might be against Serbian targets, it was utterly helpless in preventing Serb soldiers and paramilitaries from wreaking havoc on Kosovo's civilians.

World opinion was divided over the effectiveness of conducting airstrikes without the support of ground troops, but NATO countries remained reluctant to do so, fearing that the inevitable casualties would dampen the public's support for troops on foreign soil. The initial reason NATO gave for involvement in Kosovo was to avoid a wider Balkan war, but once Serbia began accelerating their campaign of ethnic cleansing in Kosovo, NATO's reason for fighting changed to preventing a human rights calamity. Yet without a concomitant change in military strategy—sending in ground troops—many wondered whether there would be any Kosovars left to save. NATO's hesitation in committing to a land battle—and therefore putting its troops at greater risk—ultimately paid off. Serbia finally agreed to sign a UN-approved peace agreement with NATO on June 3, ending the 11-week war. As Serbian forces withdrew, a five-nation NATO peacekeeping force entered Kosovo and began monitoring the return of refugees. Russia complicated NATO's efforts by demanding a role as a peacekeeper yet refusing to answer to NATO. A new group of refugees, Kosovar's Serbs, began fleeing the province, fearing vengeance from ethnic Albanians. Milosevic, who was indicted as a war criminal by the UN tribunal for the deportation of ethnic Albanians from Kosovo, held fast to the presidency as opposition groups remained disorganized and focused on internecine politics.

In Feb. 2000 fighting broke out between Serbs and Albanians in Mitrovica, Kosovo. NATO peacekeepers struggled to contain the violence.

In Sept. 2000, federal elections in Yugoslavia formally ended the autocratic rule of Slobodan Milosevic, who had entangled his country in almost continuous war, first with the breakaway republics of Croatia and Bosnia (1991–1995) and then in the Serbian province of Kosovo in 1998, which ended with the NATO bombing of 1999. Despite dragging Yugoslavia into economic collapse and relegating it to pariah status throughout much of the world, Milosevic had managed to hold fast to the presidency after the Kosovo debacle—opposition parties remained disorganized and mired in internecine squabbles, and public dissent was sporadic.

In the Sept. 24 elections, Vojislav Kostunica, a constitutional law professor and political outsider, won the presidency in spite of widespread reports of fraud and voter intimidation. When Milosevic refused to honor the results and demanded a runoff election, the country erupted in massive public demonstrations, ultimately forcing Milosevic to step down on Oct. 5. Milosevic's Socialist Party, with its monopoly on political clout, thereafter agreed to share power with the two opposition parties.

The U.S. and the European Union quickly lifted some economic sanctions against Yugoslavia, and the new government was recognized by Russia and China, both of whom had been strong allies of Milosevic's Socialist Party government. But Kostunica was quick to assert himself as a true-believing Serb nationalist with no plans for becoming the darling of the West. He faced a daunting task in revitalizing the nation's shattered economy and in rebuilding the infrastructure destroyed during the NATO bombing.

Milosevic was arrested on April 1, 2001, by Yugoslavian authorities and charged with corruption and abuse of power. The arrest of Milosevic prompted the U.S. to release $50 million in aid to Yugoslavia, which had been withheld pending cooperation on human rights abuses. In June Milosevic was turned over to the United Nations International Criminal Tribunal for the former Yugoslavia in The Hague, where he has been charged with crimes against humanity. The UN Security Council lifted the arms embargo on Yugoslavia in Sept. 2001, removing the last sanction by the international community against the country.

Zaire

SEE CONGO, DEMOCRATIC REPUBLIC OF.

Zambia

REPUBLIC OF ZAMBIA

President: Frederick T. J. Chiluba (1991)
Area: 290,584 sq mi (752,614 sq km)
Population (2001 est.): 9,770,199 (average annual rate of natural increase: 1.9%); birth rate: 41.5/1000; infant mortality rate: 90.9/1000; density per sq mi: 34
Capital: Lusaka. **Largest cities (1997):** Lusaka, 1.6 million (1990 est.); Kitwe, 338,207; Ndola, 376,311; Chingola, 167,954. **Monetary unit:** Kwacha.
Languages: English (official) and local dialects.
Ethnicity/race: African 98.7%, European 1.1%, other 0.2%. **Religions:** Christian 50%–75%, Islam and Hindu 24$–49%, remainder indigenous beliefs.
Literacy rate: 73% (1990)
Economic summary: GDP/PPP (1999 est.): $8.5 billion; per capita $880. **Real growth rate:** 1.5%. **Inflation:** 27.4%. **Unemployment:** 25% (1998). **Arable land:** 7%. **Agriculture:** corn, sorghum, rice, peanuts, sunflower seed, tobacco, cotton, sugarcane, cassava (tapioca); cattle, goats, pigs, beef, pork, poultry, milk, eggs, hides; coffee. **Labor force:** 3.4 million; agriculture, 85%; industry, 6%; services, 9%. **Industries:** copper mining and processing, construction, foodstuffs, beverages, chemicals, textiles, fertilizer. **Natural resources:** copper, cobalt, zinc, lead, coal, emeralds, gold, silver, uranium, hydropower. **Exports:** $900 million (f.o.b., 1999 est.): copper, cobalt, electricity, tobacco. **Imports:** $1.15 billion (f.o.b., 1999 est.): machinery, transportation equipment, foodstuffs, fuels, petroleum products, electricity, fertilizer. **Major trading partners:** Japan, Saudi Arabia, India, Thailand, South Africa, U.S., Malaysia, UK, Zimbabwe.

Geography Zambia, a landlocked country in south-central Africa, is about one-tenth larger than Texas. It is surrounded by Angola, Zaire, Tanzania, Malawi, Mozambique, Zimbabwe, Botswana, and Namibia. The country is mostly a plateau that rises to 8,000 ft (2,434 m) in the east.

Government Republic.

History Early humans inhabited present-day Zambia between one and two million years ago. Today the country is made up almost entirely of Bantu-speaking peoples. Empire builder Cecil Rhodes obtained mining concessions in 1889 from King Lewanika of the Barotse and sent settlers to the area soon thereafter. The region was ruled by the British South Africa Company, which he established, until 1924, when the British government took over the administration.

From 1953 to 1964, Northern Rhodesia was federated with Southern Rhodesia and Nyasaland (now Malawi) in the Federation of Rhodesia and Nyasaland. On Oct. 24, 1964, Northern Rhodesia became the independent nation of Zambia.

Kenneth Kaunda, the first president, kept Zambia within the Commonwealth of Nations. The country's economy, dependent on copper exports, was threatened when Rhodesia declared its independence from British rule in 1965 and defied UN sanctions, which Zambia supported, an action that deprived Zambia of its trade route through Rhodesia. The U.S., Britain, and Canada organized an airlift in 1966 to ship gasoline into Zambia.

In 1972 Kaunda outlawed all opposition political parties. The world copper market collapsed in 1975.

The Zambian economy was devastated—it had been the third-largest miner of copper in the world after the United States and Soviet Union.

With a soaring debt and inflation rate in 1991, riots took place in Lusaka, resulting in a number of killings. Mounting domestic pressure forced Kaunda to move Zambia toward multiparty democracy.

National elections on Oct. 31, 1991, brought a stunning defeat to long-serving President Kaunda and a repudiation of his persistent belief in a one-party state. The newly elected chief executive, Frederick Chiluba, called for sweeping economic reforms, including privatization and the establishment of a stock market. He was reelected in Nov. 1996. Chiluba declared martial law in 1997 and arrested Kaunda following a failed coup attempt. The 1999 slump in world copper prices depressed the economy since copper provides 80% of Zambia's export earnings.

In 2001 Chiluba contemplated changing the constitution to allow him to run for another presidential term. After protests he relented, and selected Levy Mwanawasa, a former vice president with whom he had fallen out, as his successor.

Zimbabwe

REPUBLIC OF ZIMBABWE

President: Robert Mugabe (1987)
Area: 150,803 sq mi (390,580 sq km)
Population (2001 est.): 11,365,366 (average annual rate of natural increase: 0.1%); birth rate: 24.7/1000; infant mortality rate: 62.6/1000; density per sq mi: 75
Capital and largest city (1992): Harare, 1,184,169.
  Other large cities: Bulawayo, 621,000; Chitungwiza, 274,035. **Monetary unit:** Zimbabwean dollar.
  Languages: English (official), Ndebele, Shona (85%).
  Ethnicity/race: African 98% (Shona 71%, Ndebele 16%, other 11%), white 1%, mixed and Asian 1%.
  Religions: Christian 25%, Animist 24%, Syncretic 50%. **Literacy rate:** 80% (1992)
Economic summary: GDP/PPP (1999 est.): $26.5 billion; per capita $2,400. **Real growth rate:** 0%.
  Inflation: 59%. **Unemployment:** 50%. **Arable land:** 7%. **Agriculture:** corn, cotton, tobacco, wheat, coffee, sugarcane, peanuts; cattle, sheep, goats, pigs. **Labor force:** 5 million (1997 est.); agriculture, 66%; services, 24%; industry, 10% (1996 est.). **Industries:** mining (coal, gold, copper, nickel, tin, clay, numerous metallic and nonmetallic ores), steel, wood products, cement, chemicals, fertilizer, clothing and footwear, foodstuffs, beverages. **Natural resources:** coal, chromium ore, asbestos, gold, nickel, copper, iron ore, vanadium, lithium, tin, platinum group metals. **Exports:** $2 billion (f.o.b., 1999 est.): tobacco 23%, gold 14%, ferroalloys 7%, cotton 6% (1997 est.). **Imports:** $2 billion (f.o.b., 1998 est.): machinery and transport equipment 39%, other manufactures 18%, chemicals 15%, fuels 10% (1997 est.). **Major trading partners:** South Africa, UK, Germany, Japan, U.S.

Geography Zimbabwe, a landlocked country in south-central Africa, is slightly smaller than California. It is bordered by Botswana on the west, Zambia on the north, Mozambique on the east, and South Africa on the south.

Government Parliamentary democracy.

History The remains of early humans, dating back 500,000 years, have been discovered in present-day Zimbabwe. The land's earliest settlers, the Khoisan, date back to 200 B.C. After a period of Bantu domination, the Shona people ruled, followed by the Nguni and Zulu peoples. By the mid-19th century the descendants of the Nguni and Zulu, the Ndebele, had established a powerful warrior kingdom.

The first British explorers, colonists, and missionaries arrived in the 1850s, and the massive influx of foreigners led to the establishment of the territory Rhodesia, named after Cecil Rhodes of the British South Africa Company. In 1923, European settlers voted to become the self-governing British colony of Southern Rhodesia. After a brief federation with Northern Rhodesia and Nyasaland (now Malawi) in the post–World War II period, Southern Rhodesia (also known as Rhodesia) chose to remain a colony when its two partners voted for independence in 1963.

On Nov. 11, 1965, the conservative white-minority government of Rhodesia declared its independence from Britain. The country resisted the demands of black Africans, and Prime Minister Ian Smith withstood British pressure, economic sanctions, and guerrilla attacks to uphold white supremacy. On March 1, 1970, Rhodesia formally proclaimed itself a republic. Heightened guerrilla war and a withdrawal of South African military aid in 1976 marked the beginning of the collapse of Smith's 11 years of resistance.

Black nationalist movements were led by Bishop Abel Muzorewa of the African National Congress and Ndabaningi Sithole, who were moderates, and guerrilla leaders Robert Mugabe of the Zimbabwe African National Union (ZANU) and Joshua Nkomo of the Zimbabwe African People's Union (ZAPU), who advocated revolution.

On March 3, 1978, Smith, Muzorewa, Sithole, and Chief Jeremiah Chirau signed an agreement to transfer power to the black majority by Dec. 31, 1978. They constituted themselves an Executive Council, with chairmanship rotating but with Smith retaining the title of prime minister. Blacks were named to each cabinet ministry, serving as coministers with the whites already holding these posts. African nations and rebel leaders immediately denounced the action, but Western governments were more reserved, although none granted recognition to the new regime.

The white minority finally consented to hold multiracial elections in 1980, and Robert Mugabe won a landslide victory. The country achieved independence on April 17, 1980, under the name Zimbabwe. Mugabe eventually established a one-party socialist state, but by 1990 he had instituted multiparty elections and in 1991 deleted all references to Marxism-Leninism and scientific socialism from the constitution. Parliamentary elections in April 1995 gave Mugabe's party a stunning victory with 63 of the 65 contested seats, and in 1996 Mugabe won another six-year term as president.

One-third of Zimbabwe's arable land is owned by 4,000 white farmers. In Feb. 2000 President Mugabe's government lost a referendum on a constitutional amendment that would have allowed the seizure of this land without compensation. Despite the defeat, the government supported the land-taking. Veterans of Zimbabwe's war for independence in the 1970s began squatting on the land and attacking the whites in an effort to reclaim land taken under British colonization. Mugabe's support for the squatters has led to foreign sanctions against Zimbabwe.

United Nations

Preamble of the United Nations Charter

The Charter of the United Nations was adopted at the San Francisco Conference of 1945. The complete text is available on the UN website, www.un.org/aboutun/charter.

We the peoples of the United Nations determined to save succeeding generations from the scourge of war, which twice in our lifetime has brought untold sorrow to mankind, and

To reaffirm faith in fundamental human rights, in the dignity and worth of the human person, in the equal rights of men and women and of nations large and small, and

To establish conditions under which justice and respect for the obligations arising from treaties and other sources of international law can be maintained, and

To promote social progress and better standards of life in larger freedom, and for these ends

To practice tolerance and live together in peace with one another as good neighbors, and

To unite our strength to maintain international peace and security, and

To insure, by the acceptance of principles and the institution of methods, that armed force shall not be used, save in the common interest, and

To employ international machinery for the promotion of the economic and social advancement of all peoples, have resolved to combine our efforts to accomplish these aims.

Accordingly, our respective Governments, through representatives assembled in the city of San Francisco, who have exhibited their full powers found to be in good and due form, have agreed to the present Charter of the United Nations and do hereby establish an international organization to be known as the United Nations.

Principal Organs of the United Nations

Secretariat

This is the directorate on UN operations, apart from political decisions. The staff works under the secretary-general, whom it assists and advises.

Secretaries-General

Kofi Annan, Ghana, Jan. 1, 1997.

Boutros Boutros-Ghali, Egypt, Jan. 1, 1992–Dec. 31, 1996.

Javier Pérez de Cuéllar, Peru, Jan. 1, 1982–Dec. 31, 1991.

Kurt Waldheim, Austria, Jan. 1, 1972–Dec. 31, 1981.

U Thant, Burma (Myanmar), Nov. 3, 1961–Dec. 31, 1971.

Dag Hammarskjöld, Sweden, April 11, 1953–Sept. 17, 1961.

Trygve Lie, Norway, Feb. 1, 1946–April 10, 1953.

General Assembly

The General Assembly is the world's forum for discussing matters affecting world peace and security, and for making recommendations concerning them. It has no power of its own to enforce decisions. It is composed of the 51 original member nations and those admitted since, a total of 189. On important questions including international peace and security, a two-thirds majority of those present and voting is required. Decisions on other questions are made by a simple majority. Emphasis is given on questions relating to international peace and security brought before it by any member, the Security Council, or nonmembers. It also maintains a broad program of international cooperation in economic, social, cultural, educational, and health fields, and for assisting in human rights and freedoms.

Security Council

The Security Council is the primary instrument for establishing and maintaining international peace. Its main purpose is to prevent war by settling disputes between nations. Under the charter, the council is permitted to dispatch a UN force to stop aggression. All member nations undertake to make available armed forces, assistance, and facilities to maintain international peace and security (see p. 897 for list of UN Peacekeeping Operations).

The Security Council has 15 members. There are five permanent members: the United States, the Russian Federation, Britain, France, and China; and 10 temporary members elected by the General Assembly for two-year terms, from five different regions of the world. Voting on procedural matters requires a nine-vote majority to carry. However, on questions of substance, the vote of each of the five permanent members is required. The ten nonpermanent members of the council in 2001 are Singapore (2002), Tunisia (2001), Ukraine (2001), Bangladesh (2001), Colombia (2002), Ireland (2002), Jamaica (2001), Mali (2001), Mauritius (2002), and Norway (2002).

Economic and Social Council

This council is composed of 54 members elected by the General Assembly to 3-year terms. It works closely with the General Assembly as a link with groups formed within the UN to help peoples in such fields as education, health, and human rights.

Agencies of the United Nations

- The International Labor Organization (ILO)
- The Food and Agriculture Organization of the UN (FAO)
- The UN Educational, Scientific and Cultural Organization (UNESCO)
- The World Health Organization (WHO)
- The World Bank
- The International Monetary Fund (IMF)
- The International Civil Aviation Organization (ICAO)
- The Universal Postal Union (UPU)

- The International Telecommunication Union (ITU)
- The World Meteorological Organization (WMO)
- The International Maritime Organization (IMO)
- The World Intellectual Property Organization (WIPO)
- The International Fund for Agricultural Development (IFAD)
- The UN Industrial Development Organization (UNIDO)
- The International Atomic Energy Agency (IAEA)
- The UN and the World Trade Organization (WTO)

UN Peacekeeping Missions

Since 1948 there have been 54 UN peacekeeping operations. Two-thirds (36) of the operations have been established since 1991. Thus far, 118 nations have contributed personnel at various times; 77 are currently providing peacekeepers. As of April 30, 2001, the top contributors of troops to current missions were: Bangladesh (5,739), Nigeria (3,310), Kenya (1,970), Jordan (1,850), Australia (1,692), Ghana (1,649), and Ukraine (1,283). There are currently 15 peacekeeping operations underway.

Current UN Peacekeeping Operations

Region/Country	Duration	Region/Country	Duration
AFRICA		**ASIA**	
Western Sahara	April 1991–present	India/Pakistan	Jan. 1949–present
Sierra Leone	Oct. 1999–present	East Timor	Oct. 1999–present
Democratic Republic of the Congo	Nov. 1999–present	**EUROPE**	
Ethiopia and Eritrea	July 2000–present	Cyprus	March 1964–present
		Georgia	Aug. 1993–present
MIDDLE EAST		Bosnia & Herzegovina	Dec. 1995–present
Middle East	June 1948–present	Croatia	Jan. 1996–present
Golan Heights	June 1974–present	Kosovo	June 1999–present
Lebanon	March 1978–present		
Iraq/Kuwait	April 1991–present		

Completed UN Peacekeeping Operations

Region/Country	Duration	Region/Country	Duration
AFRICA		**AMERICAS**	
Congo	July 1960–June 1964	Dominican Republic	May 1965–Oct. 1966
Angola	Dec. 1988–May 1991	Central America Observer Group	Nov. 1989–Jan. 1992
Namibia	April 1989–March 1990	El Salvador	July 1991–April 1995
Angola	May 1991–Feb. 1995	Haiti	Sept. 1993–June 1996
Somalia	April 1992–March 1993	Haiti	July 1996–July 1997
Mozambique	Dec. 1992–Dec. 1994	Guatemala	Jan.–May 1997
Somalia	March 1993–March 1995	Haiti	Aug.–Nov. 1997
Rwanda/Uganda	June 1993–Sept. 1994	Haiti	Dec. 1997–March 2000
Rwanda	Oct. 1993–March 1996	**ASIA**	
Chad/Libya	May–June 1994	West New Guinea	Oct. 1962–April 1963
Angola	Feb. 1995–June 1997	India/Pakistan	Sept. 1965–March 1966
Angola	June 1997–Feb. 1999	Afghanistan/Pakistan	April 1988–March 1990
Sierra Leone	July 1998–Oct. 1999	Cambodia	Oct. 1991–March 1992
Central African Republic	April 1998–Feb. 2000	Cambodia	March 1992–Sept. 1993
Liberia	Sept. 1993–Sept. 1997	Tajikistan	Dec. 1994–May 2000
MIDEAST		**EUROPE**	
Middle East—1st UN Emergency Force	Nov. 1956–June 1967	Former Yugoslavia	Feb. 1992–Dec. 1995
Lebanon	June–Dec. 1958	Croatia	March 1995–Jan. 1996
Yemen	July 1963–Sept. 1964	Former Yugoslavia Rep. of Macedonia	March 1995–Feb. 1999
Middle East—2nd UN Emergency Force	Oct. 1973–July 1979	Croatia	Jan. 1996–Jan. 1998
Iran/Iraq	Aug. 1988–Feb. 1991	Croatia	Jan. 1998–Oct. 1998

Source: United Nations Dept. of Public Information.

Members of the United Nations (189 nations)

Country	Joined UN[1]	Country	Joined UN[1]	Country	Joined UN[1]
Afghanistan	1946	Germany	1973	Oman	1971
Albania	1955	Ghana	1957	Pakistan	1947
Algeria	1962	Greece	1945	Palau	1994
Andorra	1993	Grenada	1974	Panama	1945
Angola	1976	Guatemala	1945	Papua New Guinea	1975
Antigua and Barbuda	1981	Guinea	1958	Paraguay	1945
Argentina	1945	Guinea-Bissau	1974	Peru	1945
Armenia	1992	Guyana	1966	Philippines	1945
Australia	1945	Haiti	1945	Poland	1945
Austria	1955	Honduras	1945	Portugal	1955
Azerbaijan	1992	Hungary	1955	Qatar	1971
Bahamas	1973	Iceland	1946	Romania	1955
Bahrain	1971	India	1945	Russian Federation	1945
Bangladesh	1974	Indonesia	1950	Rwanda	1962
Barbados	1966	Iran	1945	St. Kitts and Nevis	1983
Belarus	1945	Iraq	1945	St. Lucia	1979
Belgium	1945	Ireland	1955	St. Vincent and the	
Belize	1981	Israel	1949	Grenadines	1980
Benin	1960	Italy	1955	Samoa, Western	1976
Bhutan	1971	Jamaica	1962	San Marino	1992
Bolivia	1945	Japan	1956	São Tomé and Príncipe	1975
Bosnia and Herzegovina	1992	Jordan	1955	Saudi Arabia	1945
Botswana	1966	Kazakhstan	1992	Senegal	1960
Brazil	1945	Kenya	1963	Seychelles	1976
Brunei Darussalam	1984	Kiribati	1999	Sierra Leone	1961
Bulgaria	1955	North Korea	1991	Singapore	1965
Burkina Faso	1960	South Korea	1991	Slovakia[4]	1993
Burma (Myanmar)	1948	Kuwait	1963	Slovenia	1992
Burundi	1962	Kyrgyzstan	1992	Solomon Islands	1978
Cambodia	1955	Laos	1955	Somalia	1960
Cameroon	1960	Latvia	1991	South Africa	1945
Canada	1945	Lebanon	1945	Spain	1955
Cape Verde	1975	Lesotho	1966	Sri Lanka	1955
Central African Republic	1960	Liberia	1945	Sudan	1956
Chad	1960	Libya	1955	Suriname	1975
Chile	1945	Liechtenstein	1990	Swaziland	1968
China[2]	1945	Lithuania	1991	Sweden	1946
Colombia	1945	Luxembourg	1945	Syria	1945
Comoros	1975	Macedonia[3]	1993	Tajikistan	1992
Congo	1960	Madagascar	1960	Tanzania	1961
Congo, Dem. Rep.	1960	Malawi	1964	Thailand	1946
Costa Rica	1945	Malaysia	1957	Togo	1960
Côte d'Ivoire	1960	Maldives	1965	Tonga	1999
Croatia	1992	Mali	1960	Trinidad and Tobago	1962
Cuba	1945	Malta	1964	Tunisia	1956
Cyprus	1960	Marshall Islands	1991	Turkey	1945
Czech Republic[4]	1993	Mauritania	1961	Turkmenistan	1992
Denmark	1945	Mauritius	1968	Tuvalu	2000
Djibouti	1977	Mexico	1945	Uganda	1962
Dominica	1978	Micronesia	1991	Ukraine	1945
Dominican Republic	1945	Moldova	1992	United Arab Emirates	1971
Ecuador	1945	Monaco	1993	United Kingdom	1945
Egypt	1945	Mongolia	1961	United States	1945
El Salvador	1945	Morocco	1956	Uruguay	1945
Equatorial Guinea	1968	Mozambique	1975	Uzbekistan	1992
Eritrea	1993	Namibia	1990	Vanuatu	1981
Estonia	1991	Nauru	1999	Venezuela	1945
Ethiopia	1945	Nepal	1955	Viet Nam	1977
Fiji	1970	Netherlands	1945	Yemen, Republic of	1947
Finland	1955	New Zealand	1945	Yugoslavia[5]	2000
France	1945	Nicaragua	1945	Zambia	1964
Gabon	1960	Niger	1960	Zimbabwe	1980
Gambia	1965	Nigeria	1960		
Georgia	1992	Norway	1945		

1. The UN officially came into existence on Oct. 24, 1945. 2. On Oct. 25, 1971, the UN voted membership to the People's Republic of China, which replaced the Republic of China (Taiwan) in the world body. 3. The General Assembly on April 8, 1993, decided to admit the state provisionally being referred to as "The Former Yugoslav Republic of Macedonia" pending settlement of the difference that has arisen over its name. 4. Czechoslovakia was an original member of the United Nations from Oct. 24, 1945. As of Dec. 31, 1992, it ceased to exist and the Czech Republic and Slovakia as successor states were admitted Jan. 19, 1993. 5. The Socialist Federal Republic of Yugoslavia was a charter member; after its dissolution, the Federal Republic of Yugoslavia was admitted Nov. 1, 2000.

U.S. Representatives to the United Nations

Year	Ambassador	Year	Ambassador
1946	Edward R. Stettinius, Jr.	1975–76	Daniel P. Moynihan
1946–47	Herschel V. Johnson (acting)	1976–77	William W. Scranton
1947–53	Warren R. Austin	1977–79	Andrew Young
1953–60	Henry Cabot Lodge, Jr.	1979–81	Donald McHenry
1960–61	James J. Wadsworth	1981–85	Jeane J. Kirkpatrick
1961–65	Adlai E. Stevenson	1985–89	Vernon A. Walters
1965–68	Arthur J. Goldberg	1989–92	Thomas J. Pickering
1968	George W. Ball	1992–93	Edward J. Perkins
1968–69	James Russell Wiggins	1993–96	Madeleine K. Albright
1969–71	Charles W. Yost	1997–98	Bill Richardson
1971–73	George Bush	1999–2001	Richard Holbrooke
1973–75	John A. Scali	2001–	John D. Negroponte

Selected International Organizations

Arab League (AL)
Members: (21 plus the Palestine Liberation Organization) Algeria, Bahrain, Comoros, Djibouti, Egypt, Iraq, Jordan, Kuwait, Lebanon, Libya, Mauritania, Morocco, Oman, Qatar, Saudi Arabia, Somalia, Sudan, Syria, Tunisia, UAE, Yemen, Palestine Liberation Organization

Association of Southeast Asian Nations (ASEAN)
Members: (10) Brunei, Burma, Cambodia, Indonesia, Laos, Malaysia, Philippines, Singapore, Thailand, Vietnam
Observers: (1) Papua New Guinea
Consultative partners: (2) China, Russia

Big Seven and Group of 7 (G-7)
Members: (7) Big Six (Canada, France, Germany, Italy, Japan, UK) plus the U.S.

Group of 8 (G-8)
Members: (9) Canada, EU (as one member), France, Germany, Italy, Japan, Russia, UK, U.S.

Commonwealth of Nations
Members: (53) Antigua and Barbuda, Australia, the Bahamas, Bangladesh, Barbados, Belize, Botswana, Brunei, Cameroon, Canada, Cyprus, Dominica, Fiji, the Gambia, Ghana, Grenada, Guyana, India, Jamaica, Kenya, Kiribati, Lesotho, Malawi, Malaysia, Maldives, Malta, Mauritius, Mozambique, Namibia, Nauru, New Zealand., Nigeria, Pakistan (suspended), Papua New Guinea, Saint Kitts and Nevis, Saint Lucia, Saint Vincent and the Grenadines, Samoa, Seychelles, Sierra Leone, Singapore, Solomon Islands, South Africa, Sri Lanka, Swaziland, Tanzania, Tonga, Trinidad and Tobago, Uganda, UK, Vanuatu, Zambia, Zimbabwe
Special members: (1) Tuvalu

Commonwealth of Independent States (CIS)
Members: (12) Armenia, Azerbaijan, Belarus, Georgia, Kazakhstan, Kyrgyzstan, Moldova, Russia, Tajikistan, Turkmenistan, Ukraine, Uzbekistan

European Union (EU)
Members: (15) Austria, Belgium, Denmark, Finland, France, Germany, Greece, Ireland, Italy, Luxembourg, Netherlands, Portugal, Spain, Sweden, UK
Membership applicants: (13) Bulgaria, Cyprus, Czech Republic, Estonia, Hungary, Latvia, Lithuania, Malta, Poland, Romania, Slovakia, Slovenia, Turkey

North Atlantic Treaty Organization (NATO)
Members: (19) Belgium, Canada, Czech Republic, Denmark, France, Germany, Greece, Hungary, Iceland, Italy, Luxembourg, Netherlands, Norway, Poland, Portugal, Spain, Turkey, UK, U.S.

Organization of Petroleum Exporting Countries (OPEC)
Members: (11) Algeria, Indonesia, Iran, Iraq, Kuwait, Libya, Nigeria, Qatar, Saudi Arabia, UAE, Venezuela

Foreign Embassies in the United States

Source: U.S. Department of State

Embassy of the Republic of Afghanistan, 2341 Wyoming Ave., N.W., Washington, D.C. 20008. Phone: 202-234-3770.

Embassy of the Republic of Albania, 2100 S St., N.W., Washington, D.C. 20008. Phone: 202-223-4942.

Embassy of the Democratic & Popular Republic of Algeria, 2118 Kalorama Rd., N.W., Washington, D.C. 20008. Phone: 202-265-2800.

Embassy of Andorra, 2 United Nations Plaza, 25th flr. New York, N.Y. 10017. Phone: 212-750-8064.

Embassy of Angola, 1615 M St., N.W., Suite 900, Washington, D.C. 20036. Phone: 202-785-1156.

Embassy of Antigua & Barbuda, 3216 New Mexico Ave., N.W., Washington, D.C. 20016. Phone: 202-362-5211.

Embassy of the Argentine Republic, 1600 New Hampshire Ave., N.W., Washington, D.C. 20009. Phone: 202-238-6400.

Embassy of the Republic of Armenia, 2225 R Street, N.W., Washington, D.C. 20008. Phone: 202-319-1976.

Embassy of Australia, 1601 Massachusetts Ave., N.W., Washington, D.C. 20036. Phone: 202-797-3000.

Embassy of Austria, 3524 International Court, N.W., Washington, D.C. 20008. Phone: 202-895-6700.

Embassy of the Republic of Azerbaijan, 927 15th St., N.W., Suite 700, P.O. Box 28790, Washington, D.C. 20005. Phone: 202-842-0001.

Embassy of the Commonwealth of the Bahamas, 2220 Massachusetts Ave., N.W., Washington, D.C. 20008. Phone: 202-319-2660.

Embassy of the State of Bahrain, 3502 International Dr., N.W., Washington, D.C. 20008. Phone: 202-342-0741.

Embassy of the People's Republic of Bangladesh, 3510 International Drive, N.W., Washington, D.C. 20007. Phone: 202-244-2745.

Embassy of Barbados, 2144 Wyoming Ave., N.W., Washington, D.C. 20008. Phone: 202-939-9200 to 9202.

Embassy of the Republic of Belarus, 1619 New Hampshire Ave., N.W., Washington, D.C. 20009.

Phone: 202-986-1606.

Embassy of Belgium, 3330 Garfield St., N.W., Washington, D.C. 20008. Phone: 202-333-6900.

Embassy of Belize, 2535 Massachusetts Ave., N.W., Washington, D.C. 20008. Phone: 202-332-9636.

Embassy of the Republic of Benin, 2124 Kalorama Road, N.W., Washington, D.C. 20008. Phone: 202-232-6656 to 6658.

Embassy of Bolivia, 3014 Massachusetts Ave., N.W., Washington, D.C. 20008. Phone: 202-483-4410.

Embassy of the Republic of Bosnia and Herzegovina, 2109 E St. N.W., Washington, D.C. 20037. Phone: 202-337-1500.

Embassy of Botswana, 1531–1533 New Hampshire Ave., N.W., Washington, D.C. 20036. Phone: 202-244-4990.

Brazilian Embassy, 3006 Massachusetts Ave., N.W., Washington, D.C. 20008. Phone: 202-238-2700.

Embassy of Brunei Darussalam, 3520 International Court, N.W., Washington, D.C. 20008. Phone: 202-237-1838.

Embassy of the Republic of Bulgaria, 1621 22nd St., N.W., Washington, D.C. 20008. Phone: 202-387-0174.

Embassy of Burkina Faso, 2340 Massachusetts Ave., N.W., Washington, D.C. 20008. Phone: 202-332-5577.

Embassy of the Union of Burma, 2300 S St., N.W., Washington, D.C. 20008. Phone: 202-332-9044.

Embassy of the Republic of Burundi, 2233 Wisconsin Ave., N.W., Suite 212, Washington, D.C. 20007. Phone: 202-342-2574.

Embassy of the Kingdom of Cambodia, 4530 16th St., N.W., Washington, D.C. 20011. Phone: 202-726-7742.

Embassy of the Republic of Cameroon, 2349 Massachusetts Ave., N.W., Washington, D.C. 20008. Phone: 202-265-8790.

Embassy of Canada, 501 Pennsylvania Ave., N.W., Washington, D.C. 20001. Phone: 202-682-1740.

Embassy of the Republic of Cape Verde, 3415 Massachusetts Ave., N.W., Washington, D.C. 20007. Phone: 202-965-6820.

Embassy of Central African Republic, 1618 22nd St. N.W., Washington, D.C. 20008. Phone: 202-483-7800.

Embassy of the Republic of Chad, 2002 R St., N.W., Washington, D.C. 20009. Phone: 202-462-4009.

Embassy of Chile, 1732 Massachusetts Ave., N.W., Washington, D.C. 20036. Phone: 202-785-1746.

Embassy of the People's Republic of China, 2300 Connecticut Ave., N.W., Washington, D.C. 20008. Phone: 202-328-2500 to 2502.

Embassy of Colombia, 2118 Leroy Pl., N.W., Washington, D.C. 20008. Phone: 202-387-8338.

Embassy of the Federal and Islamic Republic of Comoros, c/o Permanent Mission of the Federal and Islamic Republic of Comoros to the United Nations, 420 E. 50th St., New York, N.Y. 10022. Phone: 212-972-8010.

Embassy of the Democratic Republic of Congo, 1800 New Hampshire Ave., N.W., Washington, D.C. 20009. Phone: 202-234-7690.

Embassy of the Republic of Congo, 4891 Colorado Ave., N.W., Washington, D.C. 20011. Phone: 202-726-5500.

Embassy of Costa Rica, 2114 S St., N.W., Washington, D.C. 20008. Phone: 202-234-2945.

Embassy of the Republic of Côte d'Ivoire, 2424 Massachusetts Ave., N.W., Washington, D.C. 20008. Phone: 202-797-0300.

Embassy of the Republic of Croatia, 2343 Massachusetts Ave., N.W., Washington, D.C. 20008. Phone: 202-588-5899.

Cuban Interests Section, 2630 and 2639 16th St., N.W., Washington, D.C. 20009. Phone: 202-797-8518 to 8520.

Embassy of the Republic of Cyprus, 2211 R St. N.W., Washington, D.C. 20008. Phone: 202-462-5772.

Embassy of the Czech Republic, 3900 Spring of Freedom St., N.W., Washington, D.C. 20008. Phone: 202-274-9100.

Royal Danish Embassy, 3200 Whitehaven St., N.W., Washington, D.C. 20008. Phone: 202-234-4300.

Embassy of the Republic of Djibouti, 1156 15th St., N.W., Suite 515, Washington, D.C. 20005. Phone: 202-331-0270.

Embassy of the Commonwealth of Dominica, 3216 New Mexico Ave., N.W., Washington, D.C. 20016. Phone: 202-364-6781/2.

Embassy of the Dominican Republic, 1715 22nd St., N.W., Washington, D.C. 20008. Phone: 202-332-6280.

Embassy of Ecuador, 2535 15th St., N.W., Washington, D.C. 20009. Phone: 202-234-7200.

Embassy of the Arab Republic of Egypt, 3521 International Court, N.W., Washington, D.C. 20008. Phone: 202-966-6342.

Embassy of El Salvador, 2308 California St., N.W., Washington, D.C. 20008. Phone: 202-265-9671.

Embassy of Equatorial Guinea, 2020 16th St., N.W., Washington, D.C. 20009. Phone: 202-518-5700.

Embassy of the State of Eritrea, 1708 New Hampshire Ave., N.W., Washington, D.C., 20009. Phone: 202-319-1991.

Embassy of Estonia, 2131 Massachusetts Ave., Washington, D.C. 20008. Phone: 202-588-0101.

Embassy of Ethiopia, 3506 International Dr., N.W., Washington, D.C. 20008. Phone: 202-364-1200.

Embassy of Fiji, 2233 Wisconsin Ave., N.W., Suite 240, Washington, D.C. 20007. Phone: 202-337-8320.

Embassy of Finland, 3301 Massachusetts Ave., N.W., Washington, D.C. 20008. Phone: 202-298-5800.

Embassy of France, 4101 Reservoir Rd., N.W., Washington, D.C. 20007. Phone: 202-944-6000.

Embassy of the Gabonese Republic, 2034 20th St., N.W., Suite 200, Washington, D.C. 20009. Phone: 202-797-1000.

Embassy of the Gambia, 1155 15th St., N.W., Suite 1000, Washington, D.C. 20005. Phone: 202-785-1399.

Embassy of the Republic of Georgia, 1615 New Hampshire Ave., N.W., Suite 300, Washington, D.C. 20009. Phone: 202-387-2390.

Embassy of Germany, 4645 Reservoir Rd., N.W., Washington, D.C. 20007. Phone: 202-298-4000.

Embassy of Ghana, 3512 International Dr., N.W., Washington, D.C. 20008. Phone: 202-686-4520.

Embassy of Greece, 2221 Massachusetts Ave., N.W., Washington, D.C. 20008. Phone: 202-939-5800.

Embassy of Grenada, 1701 New Hampshire Ave., N.W., Washington, D.C. 20009. Phone: 202-265-2561.

Embassy of Guatemala, 2220 R St., N.W., Washington, D.C. 20008. Phone: 202-745-4952 to 4954.

Embassy of the Republic of Guinea, 2112 Leroy Pl., N.W., Washington, D.C. 20008. Phone: 202-483-9420.

Embassy of the Republic of Guinea-Bissau, 15929 Yunkon Lane, Rockville, Md. 20855. Phone: 301-947-3958.

Embassy of Guyana, 2490 Tracy Pl., N.W., Washington, D.C. 20008. Phone: 202-265-6900.

Embassy of the Republic of Haiti, 2311 Massachusetts Ave., N.W., Washington, D.C. 20008. Phone: 202-332-4090 to 4092.

Apostolic Nunciature of the Holy See, 3339 Massachusetts Ave., N.W., Washington, D.C. 20008. Phone: 202-333-7121.

Embassy of Honduras, 3007 Tilden St., N.W., Suite 4-M, Washington, D.C. 20008. Phone: 202-966-7702.

Embassy of the Republic of Hungary, 3910 Shoemaker St., N.W., Washington, D.C. 20008. Phone: 202-362-6730.

Embassy of Iceland, 1156 15th St., N.W., Suite 1200, Washington, D.C. 20005. Phone: 202-265-6653 to 6655.

Embassy of India, 2107 Massachusetts Ave., N.W., Washington, D.C. 20008. Phone: 202-939-7000.

Embassy of the Republic of Indonesia, 2020 Massachusetts Ave., N.W., Washington, D.C. 20036. Phone: 202-775-5200.

Iranian Interests Section, 2209 Wisconsin Ave., N.W., Washington, D.C. 20007. Phone: 202-965-4990.

Iraqi Interests Section, 1801 P St., N.W., Washington, D.C. 20036. Phone: 202-483-7500.

Embassy of Ireland, 2234 Massachusetts Ave., N.W., Washington, D.C. 20008. Phone: 202-462-3939.

Embassy of Israel, 3514 International Dr., N.W., Washington, D.C. 20008. Phone: 202-364-5500.

Embassy of Italy, 3000 Whitehaven St., N.W., Washington, D.C. 20008. Phone: 202-612-4400.

Embassy of Jamaica, 1520 New Hampshire Ave., N.W., Washington, D.C. 20036. Phone: 202-452-0660.

Embassy of Japan, 2520 Massachusetts Ave., N.W., Washington, D.C. 20008. Phone: 202-238-6700.

Embassy of the Hashemite Kingdom of Jordan, 3504 International Dr., N.W., Washington, D.C. 20008. Phone: 202-966-2664.

Embassy of the Republic of Kazakhstan, (temporary) 1401 16th St., N.W., Washington, D.C. 20036. Phone: 202-232-5488.

Embassy of the Republic of Kenya, 2249 R St., N.W., Washington, D.C. 20008. Phone: 202-387-6101.

Embassy of the Republic of Korea, 2450 Massachusetts Ave., N.W., Washington, D.C. 20008. Phone: 202-939-5600.

Embassy of the State of Kuwait, 2940 Tilden St., N.W., Washington, D.C. 20008. Phone: 202-966-0702.

Embassy of the Kyrgyz Republic, 1732 Wisconsin Ave., Washington, D.C. 20007. Phone: 202-338-5141.

Embassy of the Lao People's Democratic Republic, 2222 S St., N.W., Washington, D.C. 20008. Phone: 202-332-6416.

Embassy of Latvia, 4325 17th St., N.W., Washington, D.C. 20011. Phone: 202-726-8213.

Embassy of Lebanon, 2560 28th St., N.W., Washington, D.C. 20008. Phone: 202-939-6300.

Embassy of the Kingdom of Lesotho, 2511 Massachusetts Ave., N.W., Washington, D.C. 20008. Phone: 202-797-5533 to 5536.

Embassy of the Republic of Liberia, 5201 16th St., N.W., Washington, D.C. 20011. Phone: 202-723-0437.

Embassy of the Republic of Lithuania, 2622 16th St., N.W., Washington, D.C. 20009. Phone: 202-234-5860.

Embassy of Luxembourg, 2200 Massachusetts Ave., N.W., Washington, D.C. 20008. Phone: 202-265-4171.

Embassy of the Republic of Macedonia, 3050 K St., N.W., Suite 210, Washington, D.C. 20007. Phone: 202-337-3063.

Embassy of the Republic of Madagascar, 2374 Massachusetts Ave., N.W., Washington, D.C. 20008.

Phone: 202-265-5525, 5526.

Embassy of Malawi, 2408 Massachusetts Ave., N.W., Washington, D.C. 20008. Phone: 202-797-1007.

Embassy of Malaysia, 2401 Massachusetts Ave., N.W., Washington, D.C. 20008. Phone: 202-328-2700.

Embassy of the Republic of Mali, 2130 R St., N.W., Washington, D.C. 20008. Phone: 202-332-2249.

Embassy of Malta, 2017 Connecticut Ave., N.W., Washington, D.C. 20008. Phone: 202-462-3611.

Embassy of the Republic of the Marshall Islands, 2433 Massachusetts Ave., N.W., Washington, D.C. 20008. Phone: 202-234-5414.

Embassy of the Islamic Republic of Mauritania, 2129 Leroy Pl., N.W., Washington, D.C. 20008. Phone: 202-232-5700.

Embassy of the Republic of Mauritius, 4301 Connecticut Ave., N.W., Suite 441, Washington, D.C. 20008. Phone: 202-244-1491.

Embassy of Mexico, 1911 Pennsylvania Ave., N.W., Washington, D.C. 20006. Phone: 202-728-1600.

Embassy of the Federated States of Micronesia, 1725 N St., N.W., Washington, D.C. 20036. Phone: 202-223-4383.

Embassy of the Republic of Moldova, 2101 S St., N.W., Washington, D.C. 20008. Phone: 202-667-1130, 1131, 1137.

Embassy of Mongolia, 2833 M St., N.W., Washington, D.C. 20007. Phone: 202-333-7117.

Embassy of the Kingdom of Morocco, 1601 21st St., N.W., Washington, D.C. 20009. Phone: 202-462-7979 to 7982, inclusive.

Embassy of the Republic of Mozambique, 1990 M St., N.W., Suite 570, Washington, D.C. 20036. Phone: 202-293-7146.

Embassy of the Union of Myanmar, 2300 S St., N.W., Washington, D.C. 20008. Phone: 202-332-9044.

Embassy of the Republic of Namibia, 1605 New Hampshire Ave., N.W., Washington, D.C. 20009. Phone: 202-986-0540.

Embassy of Nepal, 2131 Leroy Pl., N.W., Washington, D.C. 20008. Phone: 202-667-4550.

Embassy of the Netherlands, 4200 Linnean Ave., N.W., Washington, D.C. 20008. Phone: 202-244-5300; after 6 p.m. 202-494-8594.

Embassy of New Zealand, 37 Observatory Circle, N.W., Washington, D.C. 20008. Phone: 202-328-4800.

Embassy of Nicaragua, 1627 New Hampshire Ave., N.W., Washington, D.C. 20009. Phone: 202-939-6570.

Embassy of the Republic of Niger, 2204 R St., N.W., Washington, D.C. 20008. Phone: 202-483-4224 to 4227, inclusive.

Embassy of the Federal Republic of Nigeria, 1333 16th St., N.W., Washington, D.C. Phone: 202-986-8400.

Royal Embassy of Norway, 2720 34th St., N.W., Washington, D.C. 20008. Phone: 202-333-6000.

Embassy of the Sultanate of Oman, 2535 Belmont Rd., N.W., Washington, D.C. 20008. Phone: 202-387-1980.

Embassy of the Islamic Republic of Pakistan, 2315 Massachusetts Ave., N.W., Washington, D.C. 20008. Phone: 202-939-6200.

Embassy of the Republic of Panama, 2862 McGill Terrace, N.W., Washington, D.C. 20008. Phone: 202-483-1407.

Embassy of Papua New Guinea, 1779 Massachusetts Ave., N.W., Suite 805, Washington, D.C. 20036. Phone: 202-745-3680.

Embassy of Paraguay, 2400 Massachusetts Ave., N.W., Washington, D.C. 20008. Phone: 202-483-6960 to 6962.

Embassy of Peru, 1700 Massachusetts Ave., N.W., Washington, D.C. 20036. Phone: 202-833-9860 to 9869.

Embassy of the Philippines, 1600 Massachusetts Ave., N.W., Washington, D.C. 20036. Phone: 202-467-9300.

Embassy of the Republic of Poland, 2640 16th St., N.W., Washington, D.C. 20009. Phone: 202-234-3800 to 3802.

Embassy of Portugal, 2125 Kalorama Rd., N.W., Washington, D.C. 20008. Phone: 202-328-8610.

Embassy of the State of Qatar, 4200 Wisconsin Ave., N.W., Washington, D.C. 20016. Phone: 202-274-1600.

Embassy of Romania, 1607 23rd St., N.W., Washington, D.C. 20008. Phone: 202-332-4848.

Embassy of the Russian Federation, 2650 Wisconsin Ave., N.W., Washington, D.C. 20007. Phone: 202-298-5700.

Embassy of the Republic of Rwanda, 1714 New Hampshire Ave., N.W., Washington, D.C. 20009. Phone: 202-232-2882.

Embassy of Saint Kitts and Nevis, 3216 New Mexico Ave., N.W., Washington, D.C. 20016. Phone: 202-686-2636.

Embassy of Saint Lucia, 3216 New Mexico Ave., N.W., Washington, D.C. 20016. Phone: 202-364-6792 to 6795.

Embassy of Saint Vincent and the Grenadines, 3216 New Mexico Ave., N.W., Washington, D.C. 20016. Phone: 202-364-6730.

Royal Embassy of Saudi Arabia, 601 New Hampshire Ave., N.W., Washington, D.C. 20037. Phone: 202-342-3800.

Embassy of the Republic of Senegal, 2112 Wyoming Ave., N.W., Washington, D.C. 20008. Phone: 202-234-0540, 0541.

Embassy of the Republic of Seychelles, 800 Second Ave., Suite 400C, New York, N.Y. 10017. Phone: 212-687-9766.

Embassy of Sierra Leone, 1701 19th St., N.W., Washington, D.C. 20009. Phone: 202-939-9261.

Embassy of the Republic of Singapore, 3501 International Pl., N.W., Washington, D.C. 20008. Phone: 202-537-3100.

Embassy of the Slovak Republic, 2201 Wisconsin Ave., N.W., Suite 250, Washington, D.C. 20007. Phone: 202-965-5160.

Embassy of the Republic of Slovenia, 1525 New Hampshire Ave., N.W., Washington, D.C. 20036. Phone: 202-667-5363.

Embassy of the Republic of South Africa, 3051 Massachusetts Ave., N.W., Washington, D.C. 20008. Phone: 202-232-4400.

Embassy of Spain, 2375 Pennsylvania Ave., N.W., Washington, D.C. 20037. Phone: 202-452-0100.

Embassy of Sri Lanka, 2148 Wyoming Ave., N.W., Washington, D.C. 20008. Phone: 202-483-4025 to 4028.

Embassy of the Republic of the Sudan, 2210 Massachusetts Ave., N.W., Washington, D.C. 20008. Phone: 202-338-8565.

Embassy of the Republic of Suriname, 4301 Connecticut Ave., N.W., Suite 460, Washington, D.C. 20008. Phone: 202-244-7488.

Embassy of the Kingdom of Swaziland, 3400 International Drive, N.W., Washington, D.C. 20008.

Phone: 202-362-6683.

Embassy of Sweden, 1501 M St., N.W., Washington, D.C. 20005. Phone: 202-467-2600.

Embassy of Switzerland, 2900 Cathedral Ave., N.W., Washington, D.C. 20008. Phone: 202-745-7900.

Embassy of the Syrian Arab Republic, 2215 Wyoming Ave., N.W., Washington, D.C. 20008. Phone: 202-232-6313.

The Republic of China on Taiwan, 4201 Wisconsin Ave., N.W., Washington, D.C. 20016. Phone: 202-895-1800.

Embassy of the United Republic of Tanzania, 2139 R St., N.W., Washington, D.C. 20008. Phone: 202-939-6125.

Royal Thai Embassy, 1024 Wisconsin Ave., N.W., Washington, D.C. 20007. Phone: 202-944-3600.

Embassy of the Republic of Togo, 2208 Massachusetts Ave., N.W., Washington, D.C. 20008. Phone: 202-234-4212.

Embassy of the Republic of Trinidad and Tobago, 1708 Massachusetts Ave., N.W., Washington, D.C. 20036. Phone: 202-467-6490.

Embassy of Tunisia, 1515 Massachusetts Ave., N.W., Washington, D.C. 20005. Phone: 202-862-1850.

Embassy of the Republic of Turkey, 2525 Massachusetts Ave., N.W., Washington, D.C. 20008. Phone: 202-612-6700.

Embassy of Turkmenistan, 2207 Massachusetts Ave., N.W., Washington, D.C. 20008. Phone: 202-588-1500.

Embassy of the Republic of Uganda, 5911 16th St., N.W., Washington, D.C. 20011. Phone: 202-726-7100.

Embassy of Ukraine, 3350 M St., N.W., Washington, D.C. 20007. Phone: 202-333-0606.

Embassy of the United Arab Emirates, 1255 22nd St., N.W., Suite 700, Washington, D.C. 20007. Phone: 202-955-7999.

United Kingdom of Great Britain & Northern Ireland—British Embassy, 3100 Massachusetts Ave., N.W., Washington, D.C. 20008. Phone: 202-588-6500.

Embassy of Uruguay, 2715 M St., N.W., Washington, D.C. 20007. Phone: 202-331-1313.

Embassy of the Republic of Uzbekistan, 1746 Massachusetts Ave., N.W., Washington, D.C. 20036. Phone: 202-887-5300.

Embassy of the Republic of Venezuela, 1099 30th St., N.W., Washington D.C. 20007. Phone: 202-342-2214.

Embassy of the Socialist Republic of Vietnam, 1233 20th St., N.W., Washington, D.C. 20036. Phone: 202-861-0737.

Embassy of the Republic of Yemen, 2600 Virginia Ave., N.W., Suite 705, Washington, D.C. 20037. Phone: 202-965-4760.

Embassy of the Former S.F. Republic of Yugoslavia, 2410 California St., N.W., Washington, D.C. 20008.

Embassy of the Republic of Zambia, 2419 Massachusetts Ave., N.W., Washington, D.C. 20008. Phone: 202-265-9717.

Embassy of the Republic of Zimbabwe, 1608 New Hampshire Ave., N.W., Washington, D.C. 20009. Phone: 202-332-7100.

Diplomatic Personnel to and from the U.S.

Country	U.S. Representative to[1]	Rank	Representative from[1]	Rank
Albania	Joseph Limprecht	Amb.	Petrit Bushati	Amb.
Algeria	Janet A. Sanderson	Amb.	Idriss Jazairy	Amb.
Andorra	—	—	Juli Minoves Triquell	Amb.
Angola	Joseph G. Sullivan	Amb.	Antonio Dos Santos Franca	Amb.
Antigua and Barbuda[2]	—	—	Lionel Alexander Hurst	Amb.
Argentina	James D. Walsh	Amb.	Guillermo Gonzalez	Amb.
Armenia	Michael Craig Lemmon	Amb.	Arman Kirakossian	Amb.
Australia	Edward W. Grehm, Jr.	Amb.	Michael J. Thawley	Amb.
Austria	Kathryn Walt Hall	Amb.	Dr. Peter Moser	Amb.
Azerbaijan	Ross L. Wilson	Amb.	Hafiz Mir Jalal Pashayev	Amb.
Bahamas	—	—	Joshua Sears	Amb.
Bahrain	Johnny Young	Amb.	Muhammad Abdul Abdallah	Amb.
Bangladesh	Mary Ann Peters	Amb.	Khwaja Mohammad Shehabuddin	Amb.
Barbados[2]	—	—	Courtney N. Blackman	Amb.
Belarus	Michael G. Kozak	Amb.	Valeriy Tsepkalo	Amb.
Belgium	Paul L. Cejas	Amb.	Alexis Reyn	Amb.
Belize	Carolyn Curiel	Amb.	Lisa Shoman	Amb.
Benin	—	—	Lucien Tonoukouin	Amb.
Bolivia	Donna Hrinak	Amb.	Marlene Fernandez Del Granado	Amb.
Bosnia-Herzegovina	Thomas J. Miller	Amb.	Igor Davidovic	Amb.
Botswana	John E. Lange	Amb.	Naomi Ellen Majinda	Amb.
Brazil	Anthony S. Harrington	Amb.	Rubens Antonio Barbosa	Amb.
Brunei	Sylvia Gaye Stanfield	Amb.	Pengiran Anak Dato Puteh	Amb.
Bulgaria	Richard Miles	Amb.	Philip Dimitrov	Amb.
Burkina Faso	Jimmy J. Kolker	Amb.	Bruno Norigoma Zidouemba	Amb.
Burma (Myanmar)	Priscilla A. Clapp	Cd'A	Tin Winn	Amb.
Burundi	Mary C. Yates	Amb.	Thomas Ndikumana	Amb.
Cambodia	Kent M. Wiedemann	Amb.	Roland Eng	Amb.
Cameroon	John M. Yates	Amb.	Jerome Mendouga	Amb.
Canada	Gordon Giffin	Amb.	Raymond Chretien	Amb.
Cape Verde	Michael D. Metelits	Amb.	Amilcar Spencer Lopes	Amb.
Central African Republic	Robert C. Perry	Amb.	Henry Koba	Amb.
Chad	Christopher E. Goldthwait	Amb.	Ahmat Soubiane	Amb.
Chile	John O'Leary	Amb.	Andrew Bigensh	Amb.
China	Joseph W. Prueher	Amb.	Li Zhao Xing	Amb.
Colombia	Curtis W. Kamman	Amb.	Luis Alberto Moreno	Amb.
Comoros	Mark W. Erwin	Amb.	Ahmed Djabir	Amb.
Congo, Dem. Rep. of	William L. Swing	Amb.	Faida Mitifu	Amb.
Congo, Rep. of	David H. Kaeuper	Amb.	Serge Mombouli	Amb.
Costa Rica	Thomas J. Dodd	Amb.	Jaime Daremblum	Amb.
Côte d'Ivoire	George Mu	Amb.	Moise Kaffi Koumove	Amb.
Croatia	Lawrence G. Rossin	Amb.	Miomir Zuzul	Amb.
Cuba	—	—	—	—
Cyprus	Donald Bandler	Amb.	Erato Kozakou-Marcoullis	Amb.
Czech Republic	—	—	Aleksandr Vondra	Amb.
Denmark	Richard Swett	Amb.	Ulrik Andreas Federspiel	Amb.
Djibouti	Lange Schermerhorn	Amb.	Roble Olhaye	Amb.
Dominica[2]	—	—	Dr. Nicholas J. O. Liverpool	Amb.
Dominican Republic	—	—	Roberto B. Saladin Selin	Amb.
Ecuador	Gwen C. Clare	Amb.	Ivonne A-Baki	Amb.
Egypt	Daniel C. Kurtzer	Amb.	M. Nabil Fahmy	Amb.
El Salvador	Anne W. Patterson	Amb.	Rene A. Leon	Amb.
Equatorial Guinea	John M. Yates	Amb.	Pastor Micha Ondo Bile	Amb.
Eritrea	William D. Clarke	Amb.	Selmere Russom	Amb.
Estonia	Melissa Wells	Amb.	Sven Juergenson	Amb.
Ethiopia	Tibor P. Nagy	Amb.		
Fiji [3]	M. Osman Siddique	Amb.	Napoloni Masirewa	Amb.
Finland	Eric Edelman	Amb.	Jaakko Laajava	Amb.
France	—	—	François Bujon de l'Estang	Amb.
Gabon	James V. Ledesma	Amb.	Paul Bunduku-Latha	Amb.
Gambia, The	George W. Haley	Amb.	John Paul Bojang	Amb.
Georgia	Kenneth Spencer Yalowitz	Amb.	Tedo Japaridze	Amb.
Germany	John C. Kornblum	Amb.	Juergen Chrobog	Amb.
Ghana	Kathryn Dee Robinson	Amb.	Kobina A. Koomson	Amb.
Greece	R. Nicholas Burns	Amb.	Alexander Philon	Amb.
Grenada[2]	—	—	Denis G. Antione	Amb.
Guatemala	Prudence Bushnell	Amb.	Ariel Rivera Irias	Amb.
Guinea	Joyce E. Leader	Amb.	Mohamed Aly Thiam	Amb.

Country	U.S. Representative to[1]	Rank	Representative from[1]	Rank
Guinea-Bissau	—	—	Mario Lopes Da Rosa	Amb.
Guyana	James F. Mack	Amb.	Dr. Odeen Ishmael	Amb.
Haiti	Dean Curran	Amb.	Louis Harold Joseph	Cd'A
Holy See	Corrine Claiborne Boggs	Amb.	Gabriel Montalvo	Pap. Nun.
Honduras	Frank Almaguer	Amb.	Dr. Hugo Noe Pino	Amb.
Hong Kong	Michael Klosson	C.G.	—	—
Hungary	Peter F. Tufo	Amb.	Geza Jeszenszky	Amb.
Iceland	Barbara J. Griffiths	Amb.	Jon Baldvin Hannibalsson	Amb.
India	Richard F. Celeste	Amb.	Naresh Chandra	Amb.
Indonesia	Robert S. Gelbard	Amb.	Dr. Dorodjatun Kuntjoro-Jakti	Amb.
Iran	—	—	—	—
Ireland	Michael J. Sullivan	Amb.	Sean O'Huiginn	Amb.
Israel	Martin S. Indyk	Amb.	David Elekana Ivry	Amb.
Italy	Thomas M. Foglietta	Amb.	Ferdinando Salleo	Amb.
Jamaica	—		Dr. Richard Bernal	Amb.
Japan	Thomas S. Foley	Amb.	Shunji Yanai	Amb.
Jerusalem	—	—	—	—
Jordan	William Joseph Burns	Amb.	Marwan Muasher	Amb.
Kazakhstan	Richard Henry Jones	Amb.	Bolat K. Nurgaliyev	Amb.
Kenya	Johnnie Carson	Amb.	Charles M. Kange	Amb.
Kiribati, Republic of	Joan Plaisted	Amb.	—	—
Korea	Stephen W. Bosworth	Amb.	Hong Koo Lee	Amb.
Kuwait	James A. Larocco	Amb.	Muhammed Sabah Al Salim Al Sabah	Amb.
Kyrgyzstan	John M. O'Keefe	Amb.	Baktybek Abdrisaev	Amb.
Laos	—	Amb.	Vang Rattanavong	Amb.
Latvia	James Howard Holmes	Amb.	Aivis Ronis	Amb.
Lebanon	David M. Satterfield	Amb.	Farid Abboud	Amb.
Lesotho	Katherine H. Peterson	Amb.	Dr. Lebohang K. Moleko	Amb.
Liberia	Bismarck Myrick	Amb.	William Bull	Amb.
Lithuania	Keith C. Smith	Amb.	Stasys Sakalauskas	Amb.
Luxembourg	—	—	Arlette Conzemius	Amb.
Macedonia	E. Michael Einik	Amb.	Ljubica Z. Acevska	Amb.
Madagascar	Shirley E. Barnes	Amb.	Zina Andrianarivelo-Razafy	Amb.
Malawi	Roger A. Meece	Amb.	Steven Kandiero	Amb.
Malaysia	B. Lynn Pascoe	Amb.	Dato' Sheikh Abdul Khalid Ghaz-zali	Amb.
Mali	Michael E. Ranneberger	Amb.	Cheick Oumar Diarrah	Amb.
Malta	Kathryn Linda Haycock Proffitt	Amb.	George Saliba	Amb.
Marshall Islands	Joan M. Plaisted	Amb.	Banny de Brum	Amb.
Mauritania	Timberlake Foster	Amb.	Ahmed Ould Kalhisa Ould Jiddou	Amb.
Mauritius	Mark W. Erwin	Amb.	Chitmansing Jesseramsing	Amb.
Mexico	Jeffrey Davidow	Amb.	Jesus F. Reyes-Heroles	Amb.
Micronesia	Diane Edith Watson	Amb.	Jesse B. Marehalau	Amb.
Moldova	Rudolf Vilemk Perina	Amb.	Ceslav Ciobanu	Amb.
Mongolia	John Dinger	Amb.	Jalbuu Choinhor	Amb.
Morocco	Edward M. Gabriel	Amb.	—	—
Mozambique	Sharon Wilkinson	Amb.	Marcos Geraldo Namashulua	Amb.
Namibia	Jeffrey A. Bader	Amb.	Leonard Nangolo Iipumbu	Amb.
Nepal	Ralph Frank	Amb.	Damodar P. Gautam	Amb.
Netherlands	Cynthia P. Schneider	Amb.	Joris M. Vos	Amb.
New Zealand	Carol Moseley Braun	Amb.	James Bolger	Amb.
Nicaragua	Oliver P. Garza	Amb.	Francisco Aguirre-Sacasa	Amb.
Niger	Barbro A. Owens-Kirkpatrick	Amb.	Joseph Diatta	Amb.
Nigeria	Howard Jeter	Amb.	Jibril Muhammad Aminu	Amb.
Norway	Robin Chandler Duke	Amb.	Tom Eric Vraalsen	Amb.
Oman	John Bruce Craig	Amb.	Abdulla Moh'd Aqeel Al Dhahab	Amb.
Pakistan	William B. Milam	Amb.	Dr. Maleeha Lodhi	Amb.
Palau	Allen E. Nugent	CHB	Hersey Kyota	Amb.
Panama	Simon Ferro	Amb.	Guillermo Alfredo Ford Boyd	Amb.
Papua New Guinea	Arma Jane Karaer	Amb.	Nagora Y. Bogan, KBE	Amb.
Paraguay	David N. Greenlee	Amb.	Juan Esteban Aguirre	Amb.
Peru	John R. Hamilton	Amb.	Alfonso Rivero	Amb.
Philippines	Thomas C. Hubbard	Amb.	Ernesto M. Maceda	Amb.
Poland	Christopher R. Hill	Amb.	Przemyslaw Grudzinski	Amb.
Portugal	Gerald S. McGowan	Amb.	Joao Rocha Paris	Amb.
Qatar	Elizabeth D. McKune	Amb.	Saad Muhammad Al-Kubaysi	Amb.
Romania	James Carew Rosapepe	Amb.	Mircea Dan Geoana	Amb.
Russia	James F. Collins	Amb.	Yuriy Viktorovich Ushakov	Amb.
Rwanda	George M. Staples	Amb.	Dr. Richard Sczibera	Amb.

Country	U.S. Representative to[1]	Rank	Representative from[1]	Rank
Saint Kitts and Nevis[2]	—	—	Osbert Liburd	Amb.
Saint Lucia[2]	—	—	Sonia Merlyn Johnny	Amb.
Saint Vincent and the Grenadines[2]	—	—	Kingsley C.A. Layne	Amb.
Samoa, Western	—	—	—	—
Sao Tome and Principe, Dem. Rep. of	James V. Ledesma	Amb.	—	—
Saudi Arabia	Wyche Fowler, Jr.	Amb.	H.R.H. Prince Bandar Bin Sultan	Amb.
Senegal	Harriet L. Elam-Thomas	Amb.	Mamadou Mansour Seck	Amb.
Serbia Montenegro	Richard Miles	Cd'A	—	—
Seychelles	Mark W. Erwin	Amb.	Claude Morel	Amb.
Sierra Leone	Joseph H. Melrose, Jr.	Amb.	John Ernest Leigh	Amb.
Singapore	Steven Jay Green	Amb.	Heng Chee Chan	Amb.
Slovak Republic	Carl Spielvogel	Amb.	Martin Butora	Amb.
Slovenia	Nancy H. Ely-Raphel	Amb.	Marjan Smonig	Amb.
Solomon Islands	Arma Jane Karaer	Amb.	Jeremiah Manele	Cd'A
South Africa	Delano Eugene Lewis, Sr.	Amb.	Sheila Sisulu	Amb.
Spain	Edward L. Romero	Amb.	Javier Ruperez	Amb.
Sri Lanka	Shaun E. Donnelly	Amb.	Dr. Warnasena Rasaputram	Amb.
Sudan	—	—	Mahdi Ibrahim Mohamed	Amb.
Suriname	Dennis K. Hays	Amb.	Arnold Halfhide	Amb.
Swaziland	Gregory L. Johnson	Amb.	Mary Madzandza Kanya	Amb.
Sweden	Lyndon L. Olson, Jr.	Amb.	Rolf Ekeus	Amb.
Switzerland	J. Richard Fredericks	Amb.	Alfred Defago	Amb.
Syria	Ryan C. Crocker	Amb.	Dr. Rostom Al Zoubi	Cd'A
Tajikistan	Robert P. J. Finn	Amb.	—	—
Tanzania	—	Amb.	Mustafa Salim Nyang'anyi	Amb.
Thailand	Richard E. Hecklinger	Amb.	Tej Bunnak	Amb.
Togo	Karl W. Hofmann	Amb.	Pascal Bogjole	Amb.
Trinidad and Tobago	Edward E. Shumaker III	Amb.	Michael A. Arneaud	Amb.
Tunisia	—	Amb.	Noureddine Mejdoub	Amb.
Turkey	Mark Robert Parris	Amb.	Baki Ilkin	Amb.
Turkmenistan	Steven R. Mann	Amb.	Halil Ugur	Amb.
Uganda	Martin G. Brennan	Amb.	Edith Grace Ssempala	Amb.
Ukraine	Carlos E. Pascual	Amb.	Kostyantyn Gryshchenko	Amb.
United Arab Emirates	Theodore E. Kattouf	Amb.	Khalid Khalifa Almvalla	Cd'A
United Kingdom	—	Amb.	Sir Christopher Meyer	Amb.
Uruguay	Christopher C. Ashby	Amb.	Hugo Fernandez Faingold	Amb.
Uzbekistan	John E. Herbst	Amb.	Sadyq Safaev	Amb.
Vanuatu	Arma Jane Karaer	Amb.	—	—
Venezuela	John Francis Maisto	Amb.	Alfredo Toro Hardy	Amb.
Vietnam	Douglas B. Peterson	Amb.	Bang Le	Amb.
Yemen	Barbara K. Bodine	Amb.	Abdulwahab Al-Hajjri	Amb.
Zambia	David B. Dunn	Amb.	Dunstan Weston Kamana	Amb.
Zimbabwe	Thomas McDonald	Amb.	Simbi Yeke Mubako	Amb.

1. As of spring 2000. 2. The U.S. embassy in Barbados currently serves seven independent nations of the Eastern Caribbean (Barbados, Antigua and Barbuda, Dominica, Grenada, St. Kitts and Nevis, St. Lucia, and St. Vincent and the Grenadines) and provides consular services to American citizens in the nearby European dependent territories. 3. Ambassador to Fiji, Nauru, Tonga, and Tuvalu. 4. Head of Interests Section in U.S. 5. Special Representative for Transition in Iraq. NOTE: Amb.=Ambassador; Cd'A=Charge d'Affaires; C.G.=Consul General; Pap. Nun.=Papal Nuncio; P.O.=Principal Officer. *Source:* U.S. Department of State.

Some Milestones in U.S. Diplomatic History

Source: U.S. State Department

Benjamin Franklin was the first U.S. diplomat. He was appointed in 1776 to help gain French support for American independence and later became minister to France (1778). With John Jay and John Adams, he negotiated the peace treaty with Great Britain (Treaty of Paris, Sept. 3, 1783).

The rank of ambassador was first used by the United States in 1893. Thomas F. Bayard was appointed ambassador to Great Britain (March 30) and James B. Eustis became ambassador to France (April 18). Prior to this, the highest-ranking U.S. diplomats were ministers.

Five U.S. ambassadors have been killed by terrorists: John Gordon Mein, Guatemala (August 28, 1968); Cleo A. Noel, Jr., Sudan (March 1, 1973);

Rodger P. Davies, Cyprus (Aug. 19, 1974); Francis E. Meloy, Jr., Lebanon (June 16, 1976); Adolph Dubs, Afghanistan (Feb. 14, 1979).

A number of distinguished writers have held diplomatic or consular posts:
- Washington Irving, Minister to Spain, 1842–46.
- Nathaniel Hawthorne, Consul at Liverpool, 1853–57.
- Bret Harte, Consul at Crefeld, 1878–1880, and at Glasgow, 1880–1885.
- James Russell Lowell, Minister to Spain, 1877–80; to Great Britain, 1880–85.
- James Fenimore Cooper, Consul at Lyon, 1826.
- William Dean Howells, Consul at Venice, 1861–65.
- Archibald MacLeish, Assistant Secretary of State for Public Affairs, 1944–45.

The Olympic Games

1896 Athens, Greece	1948 St. Moritz, Switzerland (W)	1980 Lake Placid, United States (W)
1900 Paris, France	1948 London, Great Britain (S)	1980 Moscow, USSR (S)
1904 St. Louis, United States	1952 Oslo, Norway (W)	1984 Sarajevo, Yugoslavia (W)
1906 Athens, Greece	1952 Helsinki, Finland (S)	1984 Los Angeles, United States (S)
1908 London, Great Britain	1956 Cortina d'Ampezzo, Italy (W)	1988 Calgary, Canada (W)
1912 Stockholm, Sweden	1956 Melbourne, Australia (S)	1988 Seoul, South Korea (S)
1920 Antwerp, Belgium	1960 Squaw Valley, United States (W)	1992 Albertville, France (W)
1924 Chamonix, France(W)	1960 Rome, Italy (S)	1992 Barcelona, Spain (S)
1924 Paris, France (S)	1964 Innsbruck, Austria (W)	1994 Lillehammer, Norway (W)
1928 St. Moritz, Switzerland (W)	1964 Tokyo, Japan (S)	1996 Atlanta, United States (S)
1928 Amsterdam, Netherlands (S)	1968 Grenoble, France (W)	1998 Nagano, Japan (W)
1932 Lake Placid, United States (W)	1968 Mexico City, Mexico (S)	2000 Sydney, Australia (S)
1932 Los Angeles, United States (S)	1972 Sapporo, Japan (W)	2002 Salt Lake City, United States (W)
1936 Garmisch-Partenkirchen,	1972 Munich, Germany (S)	2004 Athens, Greece (S)
Germany (W)	1976 Innsbruck, Austria (W)	2006 Turin, Italy (W)
1936 Berlin, Germany (S)	1976 Montreal, Canada (S)	2008 Beijing, China (S)

(W)—Site of Winter Games. (S)—Site of Summer Games

The first Olympic Games of which there is record were held in 776 B.C., and consisted of one event, a great foot race of about 200 yards held on a plain by the River Alpheus (now the Ruphia) just outside the little town of Olympia in Greece. It was from that date the Greeks began to keep their calendar by "Olympiads," the four-year spans between the celebrations of the famous games.

The modern Olympic Games, which started in Athens in 1896, are the result of the devotion of a French educator, Baron Pierre de Coubertin, to the idea that, since young people and athletics have gone together through the ages, education and athletics might go hand-in-hand toward a better international understanding.

The principal organization responsible for the staging of the Games is the International Olympic Committee (IOC). Other important roles are played by the National Olympic Committees in each participating country, international sports federations, and the organizing committee of the host city.

The Olympic motto is "Citius, Altius, Fortius,"—"Faster, Higher, Stronger." The Olympic symbol is five interlocking circles colored blue, yellow, black, green, and red, on a white background, representing the five continents. At least one of those colors appears in the national flag of every country.

Beginning in 1994, the IOC decided to change the format of having both the Summer and Winter Games in the same year. Summer and Winter Olympics now alternate every two years.

In Feb. 1998 the IOC announced that new sports added to the games must include women's events.

Summer Games: Gold Medals

TRACK AND FIELD–MEN

100-Meter Dash

1896	Thomas Burke, United States	12.00
1900	Francis W. Jarvis, United States	10.80
1904	Archie Hahn, United States	11.00
1906	Archie Hahn, United States	11.20
1908	Reginald Walker, South Africa	10.80
1912	Ralph Craig, United States	10.80
1920	Charles Paddock, United States	10.80
1924	Harold Abrahams, Great Britain	10.60
1928	Percy Williams, Canada	10.80
1932	Eddie Tolan, United States	10.30
1936	Jesse Owens, United States	10.30[1]
1948	Harrison Dillard, United States	10.30
1952	Lindy Remigino, United States	10.40
1956	Bobby Morrow, United States	10.50
1960	Armin Hary, Germany	10.20
1964	Robert Hayes, United States	10.00
1968	James Hines, United States	09.90
1972	Valery Borzow, USSR	10.14
1976	Hasely Crawford, Trinidad and Tobago	10.06
1980	Allan Wells, Britain	10.25
1984	Carl Lewis, United States	09.99
1988	Carl Lewis, United States	09.92[2]
1992	Linford Christie, Great Britain	09.96
1996	Donovan Bailey, Canada	09.84[3]
2000	Maurice Greene, United States	09.87

1. Wind assisted. 2. Lewis was awarded the gold medal when Ben Johnson of Canada, the original winner in 09.79s, was stripped of the medal after testing positive for steroid use. 3. World record.

200-Meter Dash

1900	John Tewksbury, United States	22.20
1904	Archie Hahn, United States	21.60
1908	Robert Kerr, Canada	22.60
1912	Ralph Craig, United States	21.70
1920	Allan Woodring, United States	22.00
1924	Jackson Scholz, United States	21.60
1928	Percy Williams, Canada	21.80
1932	Eddie Tolan, United States	21.20
1936	Jesse Owens, United States	20.70
1948	Melvin E. Patton, United States	21.10
1952	Andrew Stanfield, United States	20.70
1956	Bobby Morrow, United States	20.60
1960	Livio Berruti, Italy	20.50
1964	Henry Carr, United States	20.30
1968	Tommie Smith, United States	19.80
1972	Vallery Borzov, USSR	20.00
1976	Don Quarrie, Jamaica	20.23
1980	Pietro Mennea, Italy	20.19
1984	Carl Lewis, United States	19.80
1988	Joe DeLoach, United States	19.75
1992	Mike Marsh, United States	20.01

1996	Michael Johnson, United States	19.32[1]
2000	Konstantinos Kenteris, Greece	20.09
1. World record.		

400-Meter Dash

1896	Thomas Burke, United States	54.20
1900	Maxwell Long, United States	49.40
1904	Harry Hillman, United States	49.20
1906	Paul Pilgrim, United States	53.20
1908	Wyndham Halswelle, Great Britain (walkover)	50.00
1912	Charles Reidpath, United States	48.20
1920	Bevil Rudd, South Africa	49.60
1924	Eric Liddell, Great Britain	47.60
1928	Ray Barbuti, United States	47.80
1932	William Carr, United States	46.20
1936	Archie Williams, United States	46.50
1948	Arthur Wint, Jamaica, B.W.I.	46.20
1952	George Rhoden, Jamaica, B.W.I.	45.90
1956	Charles Jenkins, United States	46.70
1960	Otis Davis, United States	44.90
1964	Mike Larrabee, United States	45.10
1968	Lee Evans, United States	43.80
1972	Vincent Matthews, United States	44.66
1976	Alberto Juantorena, Cuba	44.26
1980	Viktor Markin, USSR	44.60
1984	Alonzo Babers, United States	44.27
1988	Steve Lewis, United States	43.87
1992	Quincy Watts, United States	43.50
1996	Michael Johnson, United States	43.49
2000	Michael Johnson, United States	43.84

800-Meter Run

1896	Edwin Flack, Australia	2:11.00
1900	Alfred Tysoe, Great Britain	2:01.40
1904	James Lightbody, United States	1:56.00
1906	Paul Pilgrim, United States	2:01.20
1908	Mel Sheppard, United states	1:52.80
1912	Ted Meredith, United States	1:51.90
1920	Albert Hill, Great Britain	1:53.40
1924	Douglas Lowe, Great Britain	1:52.40
1928	Douglas Lowe, Great Britain	1:51.80
1932	Thomas Hampson, Great Britain	1:49.80
1936	John Woodruff, United States	1:52.90
1948	Malvin Whitfield, United States	1:49.20
1952	Malvin Whitfield, United States	1:49.20
1956	Tom Courtney, United States	1:47.70
1960	Peter Snell, New Zealand	1:46.30
1964	Peter Snell, New Zealand	1:45.10
1968	Ralph Doubell, Australia	1:44.30
1972	David Wottle, United States	1:45.90
1976	Alberto Juantorena, Cuba	1:43.50
1980	Steve Ovett, Britain	1:45.40
1984	Joaquin Cruz, Brazil	1:43.00
1988	Paul Ereng, Kenya	1:43.45
1992	William Tanui, Kenya	1:43.66
1996	Vebjoern Rodal, Norway	1:42.58
2000	Nils Schumann, Germany	1:45.08

1,500-Meter Run

1896	Edwin Flack, Australia	4:33.20
1900	Charles Bennett, Great Britain	4:06.00
1904	James Lightbody, United States	4:05.40
1906	James Lightbody, United States	4:12.00
1908	Mel Sheppard, United States	4:03.40
1912	Arnold Jackson, Great Britain	3:56.80
1920	Albert Hill, Great Britain	4:01.80
1924	Paavo Nurmi, Finland	3:53.60
1928	Harry Larva, Finland	3:53.20
1932	Luigi Becali, Italy	3:51.20
1936	Jack Lovelock, New Zealand	3:47.80
1948	Henri Eriksson, Sweden	3:49.80
1952	Joseph Barthel, Luxembourg	3:45.20
1956	Ron Delany, Ireland	3:41.20
1960	Herb Elliott, Australia	3:35.60
1964	Peter Snell, New Zealand	3:38.10
1968	Kipchoge Keino, Kenya	3:34.90

1972	Pekka Vasala, Finland	3:36.30
1976	John Walker, New Zealand	3:39.17
1980	Sebastian Coe, Britain	3:38.40
1984	Sebastian Coe, Britain	3:32.53
1988	Peter Rono, Kenya	3:35.96
1992	Fermin Cacho Ruiz, Spain	3:40.12
1996	Noureddine Morceli, Algeria	3:35.78
2000	Noah Ngeny, Kenya	3:32.07

5,000-Meter Run

1912	Hannes Kolehmainen, Finland	14:36.60
1920	Joseph Guillemot, France	14:55.60
1024	Paavo Nurmi, Finland	14:31.20
1928	Willie Ritola, Finland	14:38.00
1932	Lauri Lehtinen, Finland	14:30.00
1936	Gunnar Hockert, Finland	14:22.20
1948	Gaston Reiff, Belgium	14:17.60
1952	Emil Zatopek, Czechoslovakia	14:06.60
1956	Vladimir Kuts, USSR	13:39.60
1960	Murray Halberg, New Zealand	13:43.40
1964	Bob Schul, United States	13:48.80
1968	Mohamed Gammoudi, Tunisia	14:05.00
1972	Lasse Viren, Finland	13:26.40
1976	Lasse Viren, Finland	13:24.76
1980	Miruts Yifter, Ethiopia	13:21.00
1984	Saud Aouita, Morocco	13:05.59
1988	John Ngugi, Kenya	13:11.70
1992	Dieter Baumann, Germany	13:12.52
1996	Venuste Niyongabo, Burundi	13:07.96
2000	Millon Wolde, Ethiopia	13:35.49

10,000-Meter Run

1912	Hannes Kolehmainen, Finland	31:20.80
1920	Paavo Nurmi, Finland	31:45.80
1924	Willie Ritola, Finland	30:23.20
1928	Paavo Nurmi, Finland	30:18.80
1932	Janusz Kusocinski, Poland	30:11.40
1936	Ilmari Salminen, Finland	30:15.40
1948	Emil Zatopek, Czechoslovakia	29:59.60
1952	Emil Zatopek, Czechoslovakia	29:17.00
1956	Vladimir Kuts, USSR	28:45.60
1960	Peter Bolotnikov, USSR	28:32.20
1964	Billy Mills, United States	28:24.40
1968	Nartali Temu, Kenya	29:27.40
1972	Lasse Viren, Finland	27:38.40
1976	Lasse Viren, Finland	27:40.38
1980	Miruts Yifter, Ethiopia	27:42.70
1984	Alberto Cova, Italy	27:47.50
1988	Mly Brahim Boutaib, Morocco	27:21.46
1992	Khalid Skah, Morocco	27:47.70
1996	Haile Gebrselassie, Ethiopia	27:07.34
2000	Haile Gebrselassie, Ethiopia	21:18.20

Marathon

1896	Spiridon Loues, Greece	2:58:50.00
1900	Michel Teato, France	2:59:45.00
1904	Thomas Hicks, United States	3:28:53.00
1906	William J. Sherring, Canada	2:51:23.65
1908	John J. Hayes, United States	2:55:18.40
1912	Kenneth McArthur, South Africa	2:36:54.80
1920	Hannes Kolehmainen, Finland	2:32:35.80
1924	Albin Stenroos, Finland	2:41:22.60
1928	A.B. El Quafi, France	2:32:57.00
1932	Juan Zabala, Argentina	2:31:36.00
1936	Kitei Son, Japan	2:29:19.20
1948	Delfo Cabrera, Argentina	2:34:51.60
1952	Emil Zatopek, Czechoslovakia	2:23:30.20
1956	Alain Mimoun, France	2:25:00.00
1960	Abebe Bikila, Ethiopia	2:15:16.20
1964	Abebe Bikila, Ethiopia	2:12:11.20
1968	Mamo Wold, Ethiopia	2:20:26.40
1972	Frank Shorter, United States	2:12:19.80
1976	Walter Cierpinski, East Germany	2:09:55.00
1980	Walter Cierpinski, East Germany	2:11:30.00
1984	Carlos Lopes, Portugal	2:09:21.00
1988	Gelindo Bordin, Italy	2:10:47.00

1992	Hwang Young-Cho, South Korea	2:13:23.00
1996	Josia Thugwane, South Africa	2:12:36.00
2000	Gezahgne Abera, Ethiopia	2:10:11.00

110-Meter Hurdles

1896	Thomas Curtis, United States	17.60
1900	Alvin Kraenzlein, United States	15.40
1904	Frederick Schule, United States	16.00
1906	R.G. Leavitt, United States	16.20
1908	Forrest Smithson, United States	15.00
1912	Frederick Kelly, United States	15.10
1920	Earl Thomson, Canada	14.80
1924	Daniel Kinsey, United States	15.00
1928	Sydney Atkinson, South Africa	14.80
1932	George Saling, United States	14.60
1936	Forrest Towns, United States	14.20
1948	William Porter, United States	13.90
1952	Harrison Dillard, United States	13.70
1956	Lee Calhoun, United States	13.50
1960	Lee Calhoun, United States	13.80
1964	Hayes Jones, United States	13.60
1968	Willie Davenport, United States	13.30
1972	Rodney Milburn, United States	13.24
1976	Guy Drut, France	13.30
1980	Thomas Munkelt, East Germany	13.20
1984	Roger Kingdom, United States	13.20
1988	Roger Kingdom, United States	12.98
1992	Mark McCoy, Canada	13.12
1996	Allen Johnson, United States	12.95
2000	Anier Garcia, Cuba	13.00

200-Meter Hurdles

1900	Alvin Kraenzlein, United States	25.40
1904	Harry Hillman, United States	24.60

400-Meter Hurdles

1900	John Tewksbury, United States	57.60
1904	Harry Hillman, United States	53.00
1908	Charles Bacon, United States	55.00
1920	Frank Loomis, United States	54.00
1924	F. Morgan Taylor, United States	52.60
1928	Lord David Burghley, Great Britain	53.40
1932	Robert Tisdall, Ireland	51.80[1]
1936	Glenn Hardin, United States	52.40
1948	Roy Cochran, United States	51.10
1952	Charles Moore, United States	50.80
1956	Glenn Davis, United States	50.10
1960	Glenn Davis, United States	49.30
1964	Rex Cawley, United States	49.60
1968	David Hemery, Great Britain	48.10
1972	John Akii-Bua, Uganda	47.80
1976	Edwin Moses, United States	47.64
1980	Volker Beck, East Germany	48.70
1984	Edwin Moses, United States	47.75
1988	Andre Phillips, United States	47.19
1992	Kevin Young, United States	46.78
1996	Derrick Adkins, United States	47.54
2000	Angelo Taylor, United States	47.50

1. Record not allowed.

2,500-Meter Steeplechase

1900	George Orton, United States	7:34.00
1904	James Lightbody, United States	7:39.60

3,000-Meter Steeplechase

1920	Percy Hodge, Great Britain	10:00.40
1924	Willie Ritola, Finland	09:33.60
1928	Toivo Loukola, Finland	09:21.80
1932	Volmari Iso-Hollo, Finland	10:33.40[1]
1936	Volmari Iso-Hollo, Finland	09:03.80
1948	Thure Sjoestrand, Sweden	09:04.60
1952	Horace Ashenfelter, United States	08:45.40
1956	Chris Brasher, Great Britain	08:41.20
1960	Zdzislaw Krzyskowiak, Poland	08:34.20
1964	Gaston Roelants, Belgium	08:30.80
1968	Amos Biwott, Kenya	08:51.00
1972	Kipchoge Keino, Kenya	08:23.60
1976	Anders Gardervd, Sweden	08:08.02
1980	Bronislaw Malinowski, Poland	08:09.70
1984	Julius Korir, Kenya	08:11.80
1988	Julius Karluki, Kenya	08:05.51
1992	Matthew Birir, Kenya	08:08.84
1996	Joseph Keter, Kenya	08:07.12
2000	Reuben Kosgei, Kenya	08:21.43

1. About 3,450 meters-extra lap by error.

10,000-Meter Walk

1912	George Goulding, Canada	46:28.40
1920	Ugo Frigerio, Italy	48:06.20
1924	Ugo Frigerio, Italy	47:49.00
1948	John Mikaelsson, Sweden	45:13.20
1952	John Mikaelsson, Sweden	45:02.80

20,000-Meter Walk

1956	Leonid Spirin, USSR	1:31:27.40
1960	Vladimir Golubnichy, USSR	1:34:07.20
1964	Ken Mathews, Great Britain	1:29:34.00
1968	Vladimir Golubnichy, USSR	1:33:58.40
1972	Peter Frenkel, East Germany	1:26:42.40
1976	Daniel Bautista, Mexico	1:24:40.60
1980	Maurizio Damilano, Italy	1:23:35.50
1984	Ernesto Conto, Mexico	1:23:13.00
1988	Jozef Pribilinec, Czechoslovakia	1:19:57.00
1992	Daniel Plaza, Spain	1:21:45.00
1996	Jefferson Perez, Ecuador	1:20:07.00
2000	Robert Korzeniowski, Poland	1:18.59.00

50,000-Meter Walk

1932	Thomas W. Green, Great Britain	4:50:10.00
1936	Harold Whitlock, Great Britain	4:30:41.10
1948	John Ljunggren, Sweden	4:41:52.00
1952	Giuseppe Dordoni, Italy	4:28:07.80
1956	Norman Read, New Zealand	4:30:42.80
1960	Donald Thompson, Great Britain	4:25:30.00
1964	Abdon Pamich, Italy	4:11:12.40
1968	Christoph Hohne, East Germany	4:20:13.60
1972	Bern Kannenberg, West Germany	3:56:11.60
1980	Hartwig Guader, East Germany	3:49:24.00
1984	Raul Gonzalez, Mexico	3:37:26.00
1988	Viacheslau Ivanenko, USSR	3:48:29.00
1992	Andrei Perlov, Unified Team[1]	3:50:13.00
1996	Robert Korzeniowski, Poland	3:43:30.00
2000	Robert Korzeniowski, Poland	3:42.22.00

1. Former Soviet Union team.

400-Meter Relay (4x100)

1912	Great Britain	42.40
1920	United States	42.20
1924	United States	41.00
1928	United States	41.00
1932	United States	40.00
1936	United States	39.80
1948	United States	40.60
1952	United States	40.10
1956	United States	39.50
1960	Germany	39.50
1964	United States	39.00
1968	United States	38.20
1972	United States	38.19
1976	United States	38.33
1980	USSR	38.26
1984	United States	37.83
1988	USSR	38.19
1992	United States	37.40[1]
1996	Canada	37.69
2000	United States	37.61

1. World record.

1,600-Meter Relay (4x400)

1912	United States	3:16.60
1920	Great Britain	3:22.20
1924	United States	3:16.00
1928	United States	3:14.20
1932	United States	3:08.20
1936	Great Britain	3:09.00
1948	United States	3:10.40

1952	Jamaica, B.W.I.	3:03.90
1956	United States	3:04.80
1960	United States	3:02.20
1964	United States	3:00.70
1968	United States	2:56.10
1972	Kenya	2:59.80
1976	United States	2:58.65
1980	USSR	3:01.10
1984	United States	2:57.91
1988	United States	2:56.16
1992	United States	2:55.74[1]
1996	United States	2:55.99
2000	United States	2:56.35

1. World record.

Team Race

		Pts
1900	Great Britain (5,000 meters)	26
1904	United States (4 miles)	27
1908	Great Britain (3 miles)	6
1912	United States (3,000 meters)	9
1920	United States (3,000 meters)	10
1924	Finland (3,000 meters)	9

Standing High Jump

1900	Ray Ewry, United States	5 ft. 5 in.
1904	Ray Ewry, United States	4 ft. 11 in.
1906	Ray Ewry, United States	5 ft. 1⅝ in.
1908	Ray Ewry, United States	5 ft. 2 in.
1912	Platt Adams, United States	5 ft. 4⅛ in.

Running High Jump

1896	Ellery Clark, United States	5 ft. 11¼ in.
1900	Irving Baxter, United States	6 ft. 2¾ in.
1904	Samuel Jones, United States	5 ft. 11 in.
1906	Con Leahy, Ireland	5 ft. 9⅞ in.
1908	Harry Porter, United States	6 ft. 3 in.
1912	Alma Richards, United States	6 ft. 4 in.
1920	Richmond Landon, United States	6 ft. 4¼ in.
1924	Harold Osborn, United States	6 ft. 5¹⁵⁄₁₆ in.
1928	Robert W. King, United States	6 ft. 4⅜ in.
1932	Duncan McNaughton, Canada	6 ft. 5⅝ in.
1936	Cornelius Johnson, United States	6 ft. 7¹⁵⁄₁₆ in.
1948	John Winter, Australia	6 ft. 6 in.
1952	Walter David, United States	6 ft. 8¹⁵⁄₁₆ in.
1956	Charles Damas, United States	6 ft. 11¼ in.
1960	Robert Shavlakadze, USSR	7 ft. 1 in.
1964	Valeri Brumel, USSR	7 ft. 1¾ in.
1968	Dick Fosbury, United States	7 ft. 4¼ in.
1972	Yuri Tarmak, USSR	7 ft. 3¾ in.
1976	Jacek Wszola, Poland	7 ft. 4½ in.
1980	Gerd Wessig, East Germany	7 ft. 8¾ in.
1984	Dietmar Mogenburg, West Germany	7 ft. 8½ in.
1988	Guennadi Avdeenko, USSR	7 ft. ½ in.
1992	Javier Sotomayer, Cuba	7 ft. 8½ in.
1996	Charles Austin, United States	7 ft. 10 in.
2000	Sergey Kliugin, Russia	7 ft. 8½ in.

Long Jump

1896	Ellery Clark, United States	20 ft. 9¾ in.
1900	Alvin Kraenzlein, United States	23 ft. 6⅞ in.
1904	Myer Prinstein, United States	24 ft. 1 in.
1906	Myer Prinstein, United States	23 ft. 7½ in.
1908	Frank Irons, United States	24 ft. 6½ in.
1912	Albert Gutterson, United States	24 ft. 11¼ in.
1920	William Petterssen, Sweden	23 ft. 5½ in.
1924	DeHart Hubbard, United States	24 ft. 5⅛ in.
1928	Edward B. Hamm, United States	25 ft. 4¾ in.
1932	Edward Gordon, United States	25 ft. ¾ in.
1936	Jesse Owens, United States	26 ft. 5⁵⁄₁₆ in.
1948	Willie Steele, United States	25 ft. 8 in.
1952	Jerome Biffle, United States	24 ft. 10 in.
1956	Gregory Bell, United States	25 ft. 8¼ in.
1960	Ralph Boston, United States	26 ft. 7¾ in.
1964	Lynn Davies, Great Britain	26 ft. 5¾ in.
1968	Bob Beamon, United States	29 ft. 2½ in.
1972	Randy Williams, United States	27 ft. ½ in.
1976	Arnie Robinson, United States	24 ft. 7¾ in.

1980	Lutz Dombrowski, E. Germany	28 ft. ¼ in.
1984	Carl Lewis, United States	28 ft. ¼ in.
1988	Carl Lewis, United States	28 ft. 7¼ in.
1992	Carl Lewis, United States	28 ft. 5½ in.
1996	Carl Lewis, United States	27 ft. 10¾ in.
2000	Ivan Pedroso, Cuba	28 ft. ¾ in.

Triple Jump

1896	James B. Connolly, United States	45 ft.
1900	Myer Prinstein, United States	47 ft. 4¼ in.
1904	Myer Prinstein, United States	47 ft.
1906	P.G. O'Connor, Ireland	46 ft. 2 in.
1908	Timothy Aherne, Great Britain	48 ft. 1¼ in.
1912	Gustaf Lindblom, Sweden	48 ft. 5⅛ in.
1920	Vilho Tuulos, Finland	47 ft. 6⅞ in.
1924	Archie Winter, Australia	50 ft. 11⅛ in.
1928	Mikio Oda, Japan	49 ft. 10¹³⁄₁₆ in.
1932	Chuhei Nambu, Japan	51 ft. 7 in.
1936	Naoto Tajima, Japan	52 ft. 5⅞ in.
1948	Arne Ahman, Sweden	50 ft. 6¼ in.
1952	Adhemar da Silva, Brazil	53 ft. 2½ in.
1956	Adhemar da Silva, Brazil	53 ft. 7½ in.
1960	Jozef Schmidt, Poland	55 ft. 1¾ in.
1964	Jozef Schmidt, Poland	55 ft. 3¼ in.
1968	Viktor Saneyev, USSR	57 ft. ¾ in.
1972	Viktor Saneyev, USSR	56 ft. 11 in.
1976	Viktor Saneyev, USSR	56 ft. 8¾ in.
1980	Jaak Uudmae, USSR	56 ft. 11⅛ in.
1984	Al Joyner, United States	56 ft. 7½ in.
1988	Hristo Markov, Bulgaria	57 ft. 9¼ in.
1992	Mike Conley, United States	59 ft. 7½ in.
1996	Kenny Harrison, United States	59 ft. 4¼ in.
2000	Jonathan Edwards, Great Britain	58 ft. 1¼ in.

Pole Vault

1896	William Hoyt, United States	10 ft. 9¾ in.
1900	Irving Baxter, United States	10 ft. 9⅞ in.
1904	Charles Dvorak, United States	11 ft. 6 in.
1906	Fernand Gouder, France	11 ft. 6 in.
1908	Alfred Gilbert, United States, and Edward Cook, United States (tie)	12 ft. 2 in.
1912	Harry Babcock, United States	12 ft. 11½ in.
1920	Frank Foss, United States	13 ft. 5 ⁹⁄₁₆ in.
1924	Lee Barnes, United States	12 ft. 11½ in.
1928	Sabin W. Carr, United States	13 ft. 9⅜ in.
1932	William Miller, United States	14 ft. 1⅞ in.
1936	Earle Meadows, United States	14 ft. 3¼ in.
1948	Guinn Smith, United States	14 ft. ¼ in.
1952	Robert Richards, United States	14 ft. 11⅛ in.
1956	Robert Richards, United States	14 ft. 11½ in.
1960	Don Bragg, United States	15 ft. 5⅛ in.
1964	Fred Hansen, United States	16 ft. 8¾ in.
1968	Bob Seagren, United States	17 ft. 8½ in.
1972	Wolfgang Nordwig, East Germany	18 ft. ½ in.
1976	Tadeusz Slusarski, Poland	18 ft. ½ in.
1980	Wladyslaw Kozakiewicz, Poland	18 ft. 11½ in.
1984	Pierre Quinon, France	18 ft. 10¼ in.
1988	Sergei Bubka, USSR	19 ft. 4¼ in.
1992	Maxim Tarassov, Unified Team[1]	19 ft. 0¼ in.
1996	Jean Galfione, France	19 ft. 5¼ in.
2000	Nick Hysong, United States	19 ft. 4¼ in.

1. Former Soviet Union team.

16-lb Shot-Put

1896	Robert Garrett, United States	36 ft. 9¾ in.
1900	Richard Sheldon, United States	46 ft. 3⅛ in.
1904	Ralph Rose, United States	48 ft. 7 in.
1906	Martin Sheridan, United States	40 ft. 4⅘ in.
1908	Ralph Rose, United States	46 ft. 7½ in.
1912	Pat McDonald, United States	50 ft. 4 in.
1920	Ville Porhola, Finland	48 ft. 7⅛ in.
1924	Clarence Houser, United States	49 ft. 2½ in.
1928	John Kuck, United States	52 ft. 11¹¹⁄₁₆ in.
1932	Leo Sexton, United States	52 ft. 6³⁄₁₆ in.
1936	Hans Woellke, Germany	53 ft. 1¾ in.
1948	Wilbur Thompson, United States	56 ft. 2 in.

1952	Parry O'Brien, United States	57 ft. 1½ in.
1956	Parry O'Brien, United States	60 ft. 11 in.
1960	Bill Nieder, United States	64 ft. 6¾ in.
1964	Dallas Long, United States	66 ft. 8¼ in.
1968	Randy Matson, United States	67 ft. 4¾ in.
1972	Wladyslaw Komar, Poland	69 ft. 6 in.
1976	Udo Beyer, East Germany	69 ft. ¾ in.
1980	Vladmir Klselyov, USSR	70 ft. ½ in.
1984	Alessandro Andrei, Italy	69 ft. 9 in.
1988	Uhf Timmerman, East Germany	73 ft. 8¾ in.
1992	Michael Stulze, United States	71 ft. 2½ in.
1996	Randy Barnes, United States	70 ft. 11¼ in.
2000	Arsi Harju, Finland	69 ft. 10¼ in.

Discus Throw

1896	Robert Garrett, United States	95 ft. 7½ in.
1900	Rudolf Bauer, Hungary	118 ft. 2⅞ in.
1904	Martin Sheridan, United States	128 ft. 10½ in.
1906	Martin Sheridan, United States	136 ft. ⅓ in.
1908	Martin Sheridan, United States	134 ft. 2 in.
1912	Armas Taipale, Finland	145 ft. 9/16 in.
1920	Elmer Niklander, Finland	146 ft. 7 in.
1924	Clarence Houser, United States	151 ft. 5¼ in.
1928	Clarence Houser, United States	155 ft. 2⅘ in.
1932	John Anderson, United States	162 ft. 4⅞ in.
1936	Ken Carpenter, United States	165 ft. 7⅜ in.
1948	Adolfo Consolini, Italy	173 ft. 2 in.
1952	Simeon Iness, United States	180 ft. 6½ in.
1956	Al Oerter, United States	184 ft. 10½ in.
1960	Al Oerter, United States	194 ft. 2 in.
1964	Al Oerter, United States	200 ft. 1½ in.
1968	Al Oerter, United States	212 ft. 6 in.
1972	Ludvik Danek, Czechoslovakia	211 ft. 3 in.
1976	Mac Wilkins, United States	221 ft. 5 in.
1980	Viktor Rashchupkin, USSR	218 ft. 8 in.
1984	Rolf Dannenberg, West Germany	218 ft. 6 in.
1988	Jurgen Schult, East Germany	225 ft. 9¼ in.
1992	Romas Ubartas, Lithuania	213 ft. 7¾ in.
1996	Lars Riedel, Germany	227 ft. 8 in.
2000	Virgilijus Alekna, Lithuania	227 ft. 4in.

Javelin Throw

1906	Eric Lemming, Sweden	175 ft. 6 in.
1908	Eric Lemming, Sweden	179 ft. 10½ in.
1912	Eric Lemming, Sweden	198 ft. 11¼ in.
1920	Jonni Myyra, Finland	215 ft. 9¾ in.
1924	Jonni Myyra, Finland	206 ft. 6¾ in.
1928	Eric Lundquist, Sweden	218 ft. 6⅛ in.
1932	Matti Jarvinen, Finland	238 ft. 7 in.
1936	Gerhard Stoeck, Germany	235 ft. 8⁵/₁₆ in.
1948	Kaj Rautavaara, Finland	228 ft. 10½ in.
1952	Cy Young, United States	242 ft.¾ in.
1956	Egil Danielsen, Norway	281 ft. 2¼ in.
1960	Viktor Tsibuelnko, USSR	277 ft. 8⅜ in.
1964	Pauli Nevala, Finland	271 ft. 2¼ in.
1968	Janis Lusis, USSR	295 ft. 7 in.
1972	Klaus Wolfermann, West Germany	296 ft. 10 in.
1976	Miklos Nemeth, Hungary	310 ft. 4 in.
1980	Dainis Kula, USSR	299 ft. 2⅜ in.
1984	Arto Haerkoenen, Finland	284 ft. 8 in.
1988	Tapio Korjus, Finland	276 ft. 6 in.
1992	Jan Zelezny, Czechoslovakia	294 ft. 2 in.
1996	Jan Zelezny, Czech Republic	289 ft. 3 in.
2000	Jan Zelezny, Czech Republic	295 ft. 9½ in.

16-lb Hammer Throw

1900	John Flanagan, United States	167 ft. 4 in.
1904	John Flanagan, United States	168 ft. 1 in.
1908	John Flanagan, United States	170 ft. 4¼ in.
1912	Matt McGrath, United States	179 ft. 7⅛ in.
1920	Pat Ryan, United States	173 ft. 5⅝ in.
1924	Fred Tootell, United States	174 ft. 10¼ in.
1928	Patrick O'Callaghan, Ireland	168 ft. 7½ in.
1932	Patrick O'Callaghan, Ireland	176 ft. 11⅛ in.
1936	Karl Hein, Germany	185 ft. 4 in.
1948	Imre Nemeth, Hungary	183 ft. 11½ in.

1952	Jozsef Csermak, Hungary	197 ft. 11⁹/₁₆ in.
1956	Harold Connolly, United States	207 ft. 2¾ in.
1960	Vasily Rudenkov, USSR	220 ft. 1⅝ in.
1964	Romuald Klim, USSR	228 ft. 9½ in.
1968	Gyula Zsivotzky, Hungary	240 ft. 8 in.
1972	Anatoly Bondarchuk, USSR	247 ft. 8½ in.
1976	Yuri Sedykh, USSR	254 ft. 4 in.
1980	Yuri Sedykh, USSR (81.80m)	268 ft. 4½ in.
1984	Juha Tiainen, Finland	256 ft. 2 in.
1988	Sergei Litvinov, USSR	278 ft. 2½ in.
1992	Andrey Abduvaliyev, Unified Team[1]	270 ft. 9½ in.
1996	Balasz Kiss, Hungary	266 ft. 6 in.
2000	Szymon Ziolkowski, Poland	262 ft. 6 in.

1. Former Soviet Union team.

Decathlon

1912	Jim Thorpe, United States	—
	Hugo Wieslander, Sweden	—
1920	Helge Lovland, Norway	6,804.35 pts.
1924	Harold Osborn, United States	7,710.775 pts.
1928	Paavo Yrjola, Finland	8,053.29 pts.
1932	James Bausch, United States	8,462.23 pts.
1936	Glenn Morris, United States	7,900 pts.[1]
1948	Robert B. Mathias, United States	7,139 pts.
1952	Robert B. Mathias, United States	7,887 pts.
1956	Milton Campbell, United States	7,937 pts.
1960	Rafer Johnson, United States	8,392 pts.
1964	Willi Holdorf, Germany	7,887 pts.[1]
1968	Bill Toomey, United States	8,193 pts.
1972	Nikolai Avilov, USSR	8,454 pts.
1976	Bruce Jenner, United States	8,618 pts.
1980	Daley Thompson, Great Britain	8,495 pts.
1984	Daley Thompson, Great Britain	8,797 pts.
1988	Christian Schenk, East Germany	8,488 pts.
1992	Robert Zmelik, Czechoslovakia	8,611 pts.
1996	Dan O'Brien, United States	8,824 pts.
2000	Erki Nool, Estonia	8,641 pts.

1. Point system revised.

TRACK AND FIELD—WOMEN

100-Meter Dash

1928	Elizabeth Robinson, United States	12.20
1932	Stella Walsh, Poland	11.90
1936	Helen Stephens, United States	11.50
1948	Fanny Blankers-Koen, Netherlands	11.90
1952	Marjorie Jackson, Australia	11.50
1956	Betty Cuthbert, Australia	11.50
1960	Wilma Rudolph, United States	11.00
1964	Wyomia Tyus, United States	11.40
1968	Wyomia Tyus, United States	11.00
1972	Renate Stecher, East Germany	11.07
1976	Annegret Richter, West Germany	11.08
1980	Lyudmila Kondratyeva, USSR	11.06
1984	Evelyn Ashford, United States	10.97
1988	Florence Griffith-Joyner, United States	10.54
1992	Gail Devers, United States	10.82
1996	Gail Devers, United States	10.94
2000	Marion Jones, United States	10.75

200-Meter Dash

1948	Fanny Blankers-Koen, Netherlands	24.40
1952	Marjorie Jackson, Australia	23.70
1956	Betty Cuthbert, Australia	23.40
1960	Wilma Rudolph, United States	24.00
1964	Edith McGuire, United States	23.00
1968	Irena Szewinska, Poland	22.50
1972	Renate Stecher, East Germany	22.40
1976	Baerbel Eckert, East Germany	22.37
1980	Barbara Wockel, East Germany	22.03
1984	Valerie Brisco-Hooks, United States	21.81
1988	Florence Griffith-Joyner, United States	21.34
1992	Gwen Torrence, United States	21.81
1996	Marie-Jose Perec, France	22.12
2000	Marion Jones, United States	21.84

400-Meter Dash

1964	Betty Cuthbert, Australia	52.00
1968	Colette Besson, France	52.00
1972	Monika Zehrt, East Germany	51.08
1976	Irena Szewinska, Poland	49.29
1980	Marita Koch, East Germany	48.88
1984	Valerie Brisco-Hooks, United States	48.83
1988	Olga Bryzguina, USSR	48.65
1992	Marie Jose-Perec, France	48.83
1996	Marie Jose-Perec, France	48.25
2000	Cathy Freeman, Australia	49.11

800-Meter Run

1928	Lina Radke, Germany	2:16.80
1960	Ljudmila Shevcova, USSR	2:04.30
1964	Ann Packer, Great Britain	2:01.10
1968	Madeline Manning, United States	2:00.90
1972	Hildegard Falck, West Germany	1:58.60
1976	Tatiana Kazankina, USSR	1:54.94
1980	Nadezhda Olizarenko, USSR	1:53.50
1984	Doina Melinte, Romania	1:57.60
1988	Sigrun Wodars, East Germany	1:56.10
1992	Ellen Van Langen, Netherlands	1:55.54
1996	Svetlana Masterkova, Russia	1:57.73
2000	Maria Mutola, Mozambique	1:56.15

1,500-Meter Run

1972	Ludmila Bragina, USSR	4:01.40
1976	Tatiana Kazankina, USSR	4:05.48
1980	Tatiana Kazankina, USSR	3:56.60
1984	Gabriella Dorio, Italy	4:03.25
1988	Paula Ivan, Romania	3:53.96
1992	Hassiba Boulmerka, Algeria	3:55.30
1996	Svetlana Masterkova, Russia	4:00.83
2000	Nouria Merah-Benida, Algeria	4:05.10

5,000-Meter Run

1996	Wang, Jun-Xia, China	14:59.88
2000	Gabriela Szabo, Romania	14:40.79

10,000-Meter Run

1992	Derartu Tulu, Ethiopia	31:60.02
1996	Fernanda Ribeiro, Portugal	31:01.63
2000	Derartu Tulu, Ethiopia	30:17.49

80-Meter Hurdles

1932	Mildred Didrikson, United States	11.70
1936	Trebisonda Valla, Italy	11.70
1948	Fanny Blankers-Koen, Netherlands	11.20
1952	Shirley S. de la Hunty, Australia	10.90
1956	Shirley S. de la Hunty, Australia	10.70
1960	Irina Press, USSR	10.80
1964	Karin Balzer, Germany	10.50[1]
1968	Maureen Caird, Australia	10.30

1. Wind assisted.

100-Meter Hurdles

1972	Annelie Ehrhardt, East Germany	12.59
1976	Johanna Schaller, East Germany	12.77
1980	Vera Komisova, USSR	12.56
1984	Benita Fitzgerald-Brown, United States	12.84
1988	Jordanka Donkova, Bulgaria	12.38
1992	Paraskevi Patoulidou, Greece	12.64
1996	Ludmila Engquist, Sweden	12.58
2000	Olga Shishigina, Kazakhstan	12.65

400-Meter Hurdles

1984	Nawai El Moutawakel, Morocco	54.61
1988	Debra Flintoff-King, Australia	53.17
1992	Sally Gunnell, Great Britain	53.23
1996	Deon Hemmings, Jamaica	52.82
2000	Irina Privalova, Russia	53.02

400-Meter Relay

1928	Canada	48.40
1932	United States	47.00
1936	United States	46.90
1948	Netherlands	47.50
1952	United States	45.90
1956	Australia	44.50
1960	United States	44.50
1964	Poland	43.60
1968	United States	42.80
1972	West Germany	42.81
1976	East Germany	42.50
1980	East Germany	41.60
1984	United States	41.65
1988	United States	41.98
1992	United States	42.11
1996	United States	41.95
2000	Bahamas	41.95

1,600-Meter Relay

1972	East Germany	3:23.00
1976	East Germany	3:19.23
1980	USSR	3:20.20
1984	United States	3:18.29
1988	USSR	3:15.18
1992	Unified Team[1]	3:20.20
1996	United States	3:20.91
2000	United States	3:22.62

1. Former Soviet Union team.

10,000-Meter Walk

1992	ChenYue-Lin, China	44:32
1996	Yelena Nikolayeva, Russia	41:49

20,000-Meter Walk

2000	Liping Wang, China	1:29.05

Marathon

1984	Joan Benoit, United States	2:24:52
1988	Rose Mota, Portugal	2:25.40
1992	Valentina Yegorova, Unified Team	2:32.41
1996	Fatuma Roba, Ethiopia	2:26.05
2000	Naoko Takahashi, Japan	2:23.14

Running High Jump

1928	Ethel Catherwood, Canada	5 ft. 3 in.
1932	Jean Shiley, United States	5 ft. 5¼ in.
1936	Ibolya Csak, Hungary	5 ft. 3 in.
1948	Alice Coachman, United States	5 ft. 6⅛ in.
1952	Ester Brand, South Africa	5 ft. 5¾ in.
1956	Mildred McDaniel, United States	5 ft. 9¼ in.
1960	Iolanda Balas, Romania	6 ft. ¾ in.
1964	Iolanda Balas, Romania	6 ft. 2¾ in.
1968	Miloslava Rezkova, Czechoslovakia	5 ft. 11¾ in.
1972	Ulrike Meyfarth, West Germany	6 ft. 3⅝ in.
1976	Rosemarie Ackerman, E. Germany	6 ft. 4 in.
1980	Sara Simeoni, Italy	6 ft. 5½ in.
1984	Ulrike Meyfarth, West Germany	6 ft. 7½ in.
1988	Louise Ritter, United States	6 ft. 8 in.
1992	Heike Henkel, Germany	6 ft. 7½ in.
1996	Stefka Kostadinova, Bulgaria	6 ft. 8¾ in.
2000	Yelena Yelesina, Russia	6 ft. 7 in.

Long Jump

1948	Olga Gyarmati, Hungary	18 ft. 8¼ in.
1952	Yvette Williams, New Zealand	20 ft. 5¾ in.
1956	Elzbieta Krzesinska, Poland	20 ft. 9¾ in.
1960	Vera Krepkina, USSR	20 ft. 10¾ in.
1964	Mary Rand, Great Britain	22 ft. 2 in.
1968	Viorica Ciscopoleanu, Romania	22 ft. 4½ in.
1972	Heidemarie Rosendahl, West Germany	22 ft. 3 in.
1976	Angela Voigt, East Germany	22 ft. ½ in.
1980	Tatiana Kolpakova, USSR	23 ft. 2 in.
1984	Anisoara Stanciu, Romania	22 ft. 10 in.
1988	Jackie Joyner-Kersee, United States	24 ft. 3½ in.
1992	Heike Drechsler, Germany	23 ft. 5¼ in.
1996	Chioma Ajunwa, Nigeria	23 ft. 4½ in.
2000	Heike Drechsler, Germany	22 ft. 11¼ in.

Triple Jump

1996	Inessa Kravets, Ukraine	50 ft. 3½ in.
2000	Tereza Marinova, Belarus	49 ft. 10 ½ in.

Shot-Put

1948	Micheline Ostermeyer, France	45 ft. 1½ in.
1952	Galina Zybina, USSR	50 ft. 1½ in.
1956	Tamara Tishkyevich, USSR	54 ft. 5 in.
1960	Tamara Press, USSR	56 ft. 9⅞ in.

1964	Tamara Press, USSR	59 ft. 6 in.
1968	Margitta Gummel, East Germany	64 ft. 4 in.
1972	Nadezhda Chizhova, USSR	69 ft.
1976	Ivanka Christova, Bulgaria	69 ft. 5 in.
1980	Ilona Sluplanek, East Germany	73 ft. 6 in.
1984	Claudia Losch, West Germany	67 ft. 2¼ in.
1988	Natalya Lisovskaya, USSR	72 ft. 11½ in.
1992	Svetlana Kriveleva, Unified Team[1]	69 ft. 1¼ in.
1996	Astrid Kumbernuss, Germany	67 ft. 5½ in.
2000	Yanina Korolchik, Belarus	67 ft. 5½ in.

1. Former Soviet Union team.

Discus Throw

1928	Helena Konopacka, Poland	129 ft. 11⅞ in.
1932	Lillian Copeland, United States	133 ft. 2 in.
1936	Gisela Mauermayer, Germany	156 ft. 3³⁄₁₆ in.
1948	Micheline Ostermeyer, France	137 ft. 6½ in.
1956	Olga Fikotova, Czechoslovakia	176 ft. 1½ in.
1960	Nina Ponomareva, USSR	180 ft. 8¼ in.
1964	Tamara Press, USSR	187 ft. 10¾ in.
1968	Lia Manoliu, Romania	191 ft. 2½ in.
1972	Faina Melnik, USSR	218 ft. 7 in.
1976	Evelin Schlaak, East Germany	226 ft. 4 in.
1980	Evelin Jahl, East Germany	229 ft. 6½ in.
1984	Ria Stalman, Netherlands	214 ft. 5 in.
1988	Martina Hellmann, East Germany	237 ft. 2¼ in.
1992	Maritza Marten, Cuba	229 ft. 10¼ in.
1996	Ilke Wyludda, Germany	228 ft. 6½ in.
2000	Ellina Zvereva, Belarus	224 ft. 5 in.

Javelin Throw

1932	Mildred Didrikson, United States	143 ft. 4 in.
1936	Tilly Fleischer, Germany	148 ft. 2¾ in.
1948	Herma Bauma, Austria	149 ft. 6 in.
1952	Dana Zatopek, Czechoslovakia	165 ft. 7 in.
1956	Inessa Janzeme, USSR	176 ft. 8 in.
1960	Elvira Ozolina, USSR	183 ft. 8 in.
1964	Mihaela Penes, Romania	198 ft. 7½ in.
1968	Angela Nemeth, Hungary	198 ft.
1972	Ruth Fuchs, East Germany	209 ft. 7 in.
1976	Ruth Fuchs, East Germany	216 ft. 4 in.
1980	Maria Colon, Cuba	224 ft. 5 in.
1984	Tessa Sanderson, Britain	228 ft. 2 in.
1988	Petra Felke, East Germany	245 ft.
1992	Silke Renke, Germany	224 ft. 2½ in.
1996	Heli Rantanen, Finland	222 ft. 11 in.
2000	Trine Hattestad, Norway	226 ft. 1 in.

Hammer Throw

2000	Kamila Skolimowska, Poland	233 ft. 5 ¾ in.

Pole Vault

2000	Stacy Dragila, United States	15 ft. 1 in.

Pentathlon

1964	Irina Press, USSR	5,246 pts.
1968	Ingrid Becker, West Germany	5,098 pts.
1972	Mary Peters, Britain	4,801 pts.
1976	Siegrun Siegl, East Germany	4,745 pts.
1980	Nadyeszhda Tkachenko, USSR	5,083 pts.
1984	Daniele Masala, Italy	5,469 pts.
1988	Jackie Joyner-Kersee, United States	7,291 pts.

Heptathlon

1992	Jackie Joyner-Kersee, United States	7,044 pts.
1996	Ghada Shouaa, Syria	6,780 pts.
2000	Denise Lewis, Great Britain	6,584 pts.

SWIMMING—MEN

50-Meter Freestyle

1988	Matt Biondi, United States	22.14
1992	Alexander Popov, Unified Team[1]	21.91
1996	Alexander Popov, Russia	22.13
2000	Anthony Ervin and Gary Hall, Jr., United States	21.98

1. Former Soviet Union team.

100-Meter Freestyle

1896	Alfred Hajos, Hungary	1:22.20
1904	Zoltan de Halmay, Hungary	1:02.80[1]
1906	Charles Daniels, United States	1:13.00
1908	Charles Daniels, United States	1:05.60
1912	Duke P. Kahanamoku, United States	1:03.40
1920	Duke P. Kahanamoku, United States	1:01.40
1924	John Weissmuller, United States	0:59.00
1928	John Weissmuller, United States	0:58.60
1932	Yasuji Miyazaki, Japan	0:58.20
1936	Ferenc Csik, Hungary	0:57.60
1948	Walter Ris, United States	0:57.30
1952	Clarke Scholes, United States	0:57.40
1956	Jon Henricks, Australia	0:55.40
1960	John Devitt, Australia	0:55.20
1964	Don Schollander, United States	0:53.40
1968	Michael Wenden, Australia	0:52.20
1972	Mark Spitz, United States	0:51.22
1976	Jim Montgomery, United States	0:49.99
1980	Jorg Woithe, East Germany	0:50.40
1984	Rowdy Gaines, United States	0:49.80
1988	Matt Biondi, United States	0:48.63
1992	Alexander Popov, Unified Team[2]	0:49.02
1996	Alexander Popov, Russia	0:48.74
2000	Pieter van den Hoogenband, Netherlands	0:48.30

1. 100 yards. 2. Former Soviet Union team.

200-Meter Freestyle

1900	Frederick Lane, Australia	2:25.20
1904	Charles Daniels, United States	2:44.20[1]
1968	Michael Wenden, Australia	1:55.20
1972	Mark Spitz, United States	1:52.78
1976	Bruce Furniss, United States	1:50.29
1980	Sergei Kopiliakov, USSR	1:49.81
1984	Michael Gross, West Germany	1:47.44
1988	Duncan Armstrong, Australia	1:47.25
1992	Evgueni Sadovyi, Unified Team[2]	1:46.70
1996	Danyon Loader, New Zealand	1:47.63
2000	Pieter van den Hoogenband, Netherlands	1:45.35[3]

1. 220 yards 2. Former Soviet Union team. 3. World record.

400-Meter Freestyle

1896	Paul Neumann, Austria	8:12.60[1]
1904	Charles Daniels, United States	6:16.20[2]
1906	Otto Sheff, Austria	6:23.80
1908	Henry Taylor, Great Britain	5:36.80
1912	George Hodgson, Canada	5:24.40
1920	Norman Ross, United States	5:26.80
1926	John Weissmuller, United States	5:04.20
1928	Albert Zorilla, Argentina	5:01.60
1932	Clarence Crabbe, United States	4:48.40
1936	Jack Medica, United States	4:44.50
1948	William Smith, United States	4:41.00
1952	Jean Boiteux, France	4:30.70
1956	Murray Rose, Australia	4:27.30
1960	Murray Rose, Australia	4:18.30
1964	Don Schollander, United States	4:12.20
1968	Mike Burton, United States	4:09.00
1972	Bradford Cooper, Australia	4:00.27[3]
1976	Brian Goodell, United States	3:51.93
1980	Vladimir Salnikov, USSR	3:51.31
1984	George DiCarlo, United States	3:51.23
1988	Uwe Dassier, East Germany	3:46.95
1992	Evgueni Sadovyi, Unified Team	3:45.00[4]
1996	Danyon Loader, New Zealand	3:47.97
2000	Ian Thorpe, Australia	3:40.59[4]

1. 500 meters. 2. 440 yards. 3. Rich DeMont, United States, won but was disqualified following day for medical reasons. 4. World record.

1,500-Meter Freestyle

1904	Emil Rausch, Germany	27:18.20[1]
1906	Henry Taylor, Great Britain	28:28.00[2]
1908	Henry Taylor, Great Britain	22:48.40
1912	George Hodgson, Canada	22:00.00
1920	Norman Ross, United States	22:23.20

1924	Andrew Charlton, Australia	20:06.60
1928	Arne Borg, Sweden	19:51.80
1932	Kusuo Kitamura, Japan	19:12.40
1936	Noboru Terada, Japan	19:13.70
1948	James McLane, United States	19:18.50
1952	Ford Konno, United States	18:30.00
1956	Murray Rose, Australia	17:58.90
1960	Jon Konrads, Australia	17:19.60
1964	Robert Windle, Australia	17:01.70
1968	Michael Burton, United States	16:38.90
1972	Michael Burton, United States	15:52.58
1976	Brian Goodell, United States	15:02.40
1980	Vladimir Salnikov, USSR	14:58.27
1984	Michael O'Brien, United States	15:05.20
1988	Vladimir Salnikov, USSR	15:00.40
1992	Kieren Perkins, Australia	14:43.48
1996	Kieren Perkins, Australia	14:56.40
2000	Grant Hackett, Australia	14:48.33

1. One mile. 2. 1,600 meters

100-Meter Backstroke

1904	Walter Brack, Germany	1:16.80[1]
1908	Arno Bieberstein, Germany	1:24.60
1912	Harry Hebner, United States	1:21.20
1920	Warren Kealoha, United States	1:15.20
1924	Warren Kealoha, United States	1:13.20
1928	George Kojac, United States	1:08.20
1932	Masaji Kiyokawa, Japan	1:08.60
1936	Adolph Kiefer, United States	1:05.90
1948	Allen Stack, United States	1:06.40
1952	Yoshinobu Oyakawa, United States	1:05.40
1956	David Thiele, Australia	1:02.20
1960	David Thiele, Australia	1:01.90
1968	Roland Matthes, East Germany	0:58.70
1972	Roland Matthes, East Germany	0:56.58
1976	John Naber, United States	0:55.49
1980	Bengt Baron, Sweden	0:56.53
1984	Rick Carey, United States	0:55.79
1988	Daichi Suzuki, Japan	0:55.05
1992	Mark Tewksbury, Canada	0:53.98
1996	Jeff Rouse, United States	0:54.10
2000	Lenny Krayzelburg, United States	0:53.72

1. 100 yards

200-Meter Backstroke

1900	Ernst Hoppenberg, Germany	2:47.00
1964	Jed Graef, United States	2:10.30
1968	Roland Matthes, East Germany	2:09.60
1972	Roland Matthes, East Germany	2:02.82
1976	John Naber, United States	1:59.19
1980	Sandor Wladar, Hungary	2:01.93
1984	Rick Carey, United States	2:00.23
1988	Igor Polianski, USSR	1:59.37
1992	Martin Lopez Zubero, Spain	1:58.47
1996	Brad Bridgewater, United States	1:58.54
2000	Lenny Krayzelburg, United States	1:56.76

100-Meter Breaststroke

1968	Donald McKenzie, United States	1:07.70
1972	Nobutaka Taguchi, Japan	1:04.94
1976	John Hencken, United States	1:03.11
1980	Duncan Goodhew, Britain	1:03.34
1984	Steve Lindquist, United States	1:01.65
1988	Adrian Moorhouse, Great Britain	1:02.04
1992	Nelson Diebel, United States	1:01.50
1996	Fred Deburghgraeve, Belgium	1:00.60[1]
2000	Domenico Fioravanti, Italy	1:00.46

1. World record.

200-Meter Breaststroke

1908	Frederick Holman, Great Britain	3:09.20
1912	Walter Bathe, Germany	3:01.80
1920	Haken Malmroth, Sweden	3:04.40
1924	Robert Skelton, United States	2:56.60
1928	Yoshiyuki Tsuruta, Japan	2:48.80
1932	Yoshiyuki Tsuruta, Japan	2:45.40
1936	Tetsuo Hamuro, Japan	2:41.50

1948	Joseph Verdeur, United States	2:39.30
1952	John Davies, Australia	2:34.40
1956	Masaura Furukawa, Japan	2:34.70
1960	Bill Muliken, United States	2:37.40
1964	Ian O'Brien, Australia	2:07.80
1968	Felipe Munoz, Mexico	2:28.70
1972	John Hencken, United States	2:21.55
1976	David Willkie, Britain	2:15.11
1980	Robertas Zulpa, USSR	2:15.85
1984	Victor Davis, Canada	2:13.34
1988	Jozef Szabo, Hungary	2:13.52
1992	Mike Barrowman, United States	2:10.16
1996	Norbert Rozsa, Hungary	2:12.57
2000	Domenico Fioravanti, Italy	2:10.87

100-Meter Butterfly

1968	Douglas Russell, United States	55.90
1972	Mark Spitz, United States	54.27
1976	Matt Vogel, United States	54.35
1980	Par Arvidsson, Sweden	54.92
1984	Michael Gross, West Germany	53.08
1988	Anthony Nesty, Surinam	53.00
1992	Pablo Morales, United States	53.32
1996	Denis Pankratov, Russia	52.27[1]
2000	Lars Froelander, Sweden	52.00

1. World record.

200-Meter Butterfly

1956	Bill Yorzyk, United States	2:19.30
1960	Mike Troy, United States	2:12.80
1964	Kevin Berry, Australia	2:06.60
1968	Carl Robie, United States	2:08.70
1972	Mark Spitz, United States	2:00.70
1976	Mike Bruner, United States	1:59.23
1980	Sergei Fesenko, USSR	1:59.76
1984	Jon Sieben, Australia	1:57.00
1988	Michael Gross, East Germany	1:56.94
1992	Mel Stewart, United States	1:56.26
1996	Denis Pankratov, Russia	1:56.51
2000	Tom Malchow, United States	1:55.35

200-Meter Individual Medley

1968	Charles Hickcox, United States	2:12.00
1972	Gunnar Larsson, Sweden	2:07.17
1988	Tamas Darnyi, Hungary	2:00.17
1992	Tamas Darnyi, Hungary	2:00.76
1996	Attila Czene, Hungary	1:59.91
2000	Massimiliano Rosolino, Italy	1:58.98

400-Meter Individual Medley

1964	Dick Roth, United States	4:45.40
1968	Charles Hickox, United States	4:48.40
1972	Gunnar Larsson, Sweden	4:31.98
1976	Rod Strachan, United States	4:23.68
1980	Aleksandr Sidorenko, USSR	4:22.80
1984	Alex Baumann, Canada	4:17.41
1988	Tamas Darnyi, Hungary	4:14.75
1992	Tamas Darnyi, Hungary	4:14.23
1996	Tom Dolan, United States	4:14.90
2000	Tom Dolan, United States	4:11.76[1]

1. World record.

400-Meter Freestyle Relay

1964	United States	3:32.20
1968	United States	3:31.70
1972	United States	3:26.42
1988	United States	3:16.52
1992	United States	3:16.74
1996	United States	3:15.41
2000	Australia	3:13.67[1]

1. World record.

800-Meter Freestyle Relay

1908	Great Britain	10:55.60
1912	Australia	10:11.20
1920	United States	10:04.40
1924	United States	09:53.40
1928	United States	09:36.20
1932	Japan	08:58.40

1936	Japan	08:51.50
1948	United States	08:46.10
1952	United States	08:31.10
1956	Australia	08:23.60
1960	United States	08:10.20
1964	United States	07:52.10
1968	United States	07:52.30
1972	United States	07:35.78
1976	United States	07:23.22
1980	USSR	07:23.50
1984	United States	07:16.59
1988	United States	07:12.51
1992	Unified Team[1]	07:11.95
1996	United States	07:14.84
2000	Australia	07:07.05[2]

1. Former Soviet Union team. 2. World record.

400-Meter Medley Relay

1960	United States	4:05.40
1964	United States	3:58.40
1968	United States	3:54.90
1972	United States	3:48.16
1976	United States	3:42.22
1980	Australia	3:45.70
1984	United States	3:39.30
1988	United States	3:36.93
1992	United States	3:36.93
1996	United States	3:34.84
2000	United States	3:33.73[1]

1. World record.

Springboard Dive — **Points**

1908	Albert Zuerner, Germany	85.50
1912	Paul Guenther, Germany	79.23
1920	Louis Kuehn, United States	675.00
1924	Albert White, United States	696.40
1928	Pete Desjardins, United States	185.04
1932	Michael Galitzen, United States	161.38
1936	Richard Degener, United States	163.57
1948	Bruce Harlan, United States	163.64
1952	David Browning, United States	205.59
1956	Robert Clotworthy, United States	159.56
1960	Gary Tobian, United States	170.00
1964	Ken Sitzberger, United States	159.90
1968	Bernard Wrightson, United States	170.15
1972	Vladimir Vasin, USSR	594.09
1976	Phil Boggs, United States	619.05
1980	Alexsandr Portnov, USSR	905.02
1984	Greg Louganis, United States	754.41
1988	Greg Louganis, United States	730.80
1992	Mark Lenzi, United States	676.53
1996	Xiong Ni, China	701.46
2000	Xiong Ni, China	708.72

Platform Dive — **Points**

1904	G.E. Sheldon, United States	12.75
1906	Gottlob Walz, Germany	156.00
1908	Hjalmar Johansson, Sweden	83.75
1912	Erik Adlerz, Sweden	73.94
1920	Clarence Pinkston, United States	100.67
1924	Albert White, United States	487.30
1928	Pete Desjardins, United States	98.74
1932	Harold Smith, United States	124.80
1936	Marshall Wayne, United States	113.58
1948	Samuel Lee, United States	130.05
1952	Samuel Lee, United States	156.28
1956	Joaquin Capilla, Mexico	152.44
1960	Bob Webster, United States	165.56
1964	Bob Webster, United States	148.58
1968	Klaus Dibiasi, Italy	164.18
1972	Klaus Dibiasi, Italy	504.12
1976	Klaus Dibiasi, Italy	600.51
1980	Falk Hoffman, E. Germany	835.65
1984	Greg Louganis, United States	710.91
1988	Greg Louganis, United States	638.61
1992	Sun, Shu-Wei, China	677.31

1996	Dmitri Saoutine, Russia	692.34
2000	Tian Liang, China	724.53

Synchronized 3m Springboard Dive — **Points**

2000	Xiao Hailiang and Xiong Ni, China	365.58

Synchronized 10m Platform Dive — **Points**

2000	Igor Loukachine and Dmitri Saoutine, Russia	365.04

SWIMMING–WOMEN

50-Meter Freestyle

1988	Kristin Otto, East Germany	25.49
1992	Yang, Wen-Yi, China	24.79
1996	Amy Van Dyken, United States	24.87
2000	Inge de Bruijn, Netherlands	24.32

100-Meter Freestyle

1912	Fanny Durack, Australia	1:22.20
1920	Ethelda Bleibtrey, United States	1:13.60
1924	Ethel Lackie, United States	1:12.40
1928	Albina Osipowich, United States	1:11.00
1932	Helene Madison, United States	1:06.80
1936	Hendrika Mastenbroek, Netherlands	1:05.90
1948	Greta Andersen, Denmark	1:06.30
1952	Katalin Szoke, Hungary	1:06.80
1956	Dawn Fraser, Australia	1:02.00
1960	Dawn Fraser, Australia	1:01.20
1964	Dawn Fraser, Australia	0:59.50
1968	Marge Jan Henne, United States	1:00.00
1972	Sandra Neilson, United States	0:58.59
1976	Kornelia Ender, East Germany	0:55.65
1980	Barbara Krause, East Germany	0:54.79
1984	Carrie Steinseifer, United States	0:55.92
1988	Kristin Otto, East Germany	0:54.93
1992	Zhuang Yong, China	0:54.64
1996	Le Jingyi, China	0:54.50
2000	Inge de Bruijn, Netherlands	0:58.83

200-Meter Freestyle

1968	Debbie Meyer, United States	2:10.50
1972	Shane Gould, Australia	2:03.56
1976	Kornelia Ender, East Germany	1:59.26
1980	Barbara Krause, East Germany	1:58.33
1984	Mary Wayle, United States	1:59.23
1988	Heike Friedrich, East Germany	1:57.65
1992	Nicole Haislett, United States	1:57.90
1996	Claudia Poll, Costa Rica	1:58.16
2000	Susie O'Neill, Australia	1:58.24

400-Meter Freestyle

1920	Ethelda Bleibtrey, United States	4:34.00[1]
1924	Martha Norelius, United States	6:02.20
1928	Martha Norelius, United States	5:42.80
1932	Helene Madison, United States	5:28.50
1936	Hendrika Mastenbroek, Netherlands	5:26.40
1948	Ann Curtis, United States	5:17.80
1952	Valerie Gyenge, Hungary	5:12.10
1956	Lorraine Crapp, Australia	4:54.60
1960	Chris von Saltza, United States	4:50.60
1964	Ginny Duenkel, United States	4:43.30
1968	Debbie Meyer, United States	4:31.80
1972	Shane Gould, Australia	4:19.04
1976	Petra Thumer, East Germany	4:09.89
1980	Ines Diers, East Germany	4:08.76
1984	Tiffany Cohen, United States	4:07.10
1988	Janet Evans, United States	4:03.85
1992	Dagmar Hase, Germany	4:07.18
1996	Michelle Smith, Ireland	4:07.25
2000	Brooke Bennett, United States	4:05.80

1. 300 meters.

800-Meter Freestyle

1968	Debbie Meyer, United States	9:24.00
1972	Keena Rothhammer, United States	8:53.68
1976	Petra Thumer, East Germany	8:37.14
1980	Michelle Ford, Australia	8:28.90
1984	Tiffany Cohen, United States	8:24.95
1988	Janet Evans, United States	8:20.20

1992	Janet Evans, Unites States	8:25.52
1996	Brooke Bennett, Unites States	8:27.89
2000	Brooke Bennett, United States	8:19.67

100-Meter Backstroke

1924	Sybil Bauer, United States	1:23.20
1928	Marie Braun, Netherlands	1:22.00
1932	Eleanor Holm, United States	1:19.40
1936	Dina Senff, Netherlands	1:18.90
1948	Karen Harup, Denmark	1:14.40
1952	Joan Harrison, South Africa	1:14.30
1956	Judy Grinham, Great Britain	1:12.90
1960	Lynn Burke, United States	1:09.30
1964	Cathy Ferguson, United States	1:07.70
1968	Kaye Hall, United States	1:06.20
1972	Melissa Belote, United States	1:05.78
1976	Ulrike Richter, East Germany	1:01.83
1980	Rica Reinisch, East Germany	1:00.86
1984	Theresa Andrews, United States	1:02.55
1988	Kristin Otto, East Germany	1:00.89
1992	Krisztina Egerszegi, Hungary	1:00.68
1996	Beth Botsford, United States	1:01.19
2000	Diana Mocanu, Romania	1:00.21

200-Meter Backstroke

1968	Pokey Watson, United States	2:24.80
1972	Melissa Belote, United States	2:19.19
1976	Ulrike Richter, East Germany	2:13.43
1980	Rica Reinisch, East Germany	2:11.77
1984	Jolanda DeRover, Netherlands	2:12.38
1988	Krisztina Egerszegi, Hungary	2:09.29
1992	Krisztina Egerszegi, Hungary	2:07.06
1996	Krisztina Egerszegi, Hungary	2:07.83
2000	Diana Mocanu, Romania	2:08.16

100-Meter Breaststroke

1968	Djurdjica Bjedov, Yugoslavia	1:15.80
1972	Catherine Carr, United States	1:13.58
1976	Hannelore Anke, East Germany	1:11.16
1980	Ute Geweniger, East Germany	1:10.22
1984	Petra Van Staveren, Netherlands	1:09.88
1988	Tainia Dangalakova, Bulgaria	1:07.95
1992	Elena Roudkovskaia, Unified Team	1:08.00
1996	Penny Heyns, South Africa	1:07.73
2000	Megan Quann, United States	1:07.05

200-Meter Breaststroke

1924	Lucy Morton, Great Britain	3:33.20
1928	Hilde Schrader, Germany	3:12.60
1932	Clare Dennis, Australia	3:06.30
1936	Hideko Maehata, Japan	3:03.60
1948	Nel van Vliet, Netherlands	2:57.20
1952	Eva Szekely, Hungary	2:51.70
1956	Ursala Happe, Germany	2:53.10
1960	Anita Lonsbrough, Great Britain	2:49.50
1964	Galina Prozumenschikova, USSR	2:46.40
1968	Sharon Wichman, United States	2:44.40
1972	Beverly Whitfield, Australia	2:41.71
1976	Marina Koshevaia, USSR	2:33.35
1980	Lina Kachushite, USSR	2:29.54
1984	Anne Ottenbrite, Canada	2:30.38
1988	Silke Hoerner, East Germany	2:26.71
1992	Kyoko Iwasaki, Japan	2:26.65
1996	Penny Heyns, South Africa	2:25.41
2000	Agnes Kovacs, Hungary	2:24.35

100-Meter Butterfly

1956	Shelley Mann, United States	1:11.00
1960	Carolyn Schuler, United States	1:09.50
1964	Sharon Stouder, United States	1:04.70
1968	Lynn McClements, Australia	1:05.50
1972	Mayumi Aoki, Japan	1:03.34
1976	Kornelia Ender, East Germany	1:00.13
1980	Caren Metschuck, East Germany	1:00.42
1984	Mary Meagher, United States	0:59.26
1988	Kristin Otto, East Germany	0:59.00
1992	Qian Hong, China	0:58.62
1996	Amy Van Dyken, United States	0:59.13

2000	Inge de Bruijn, Netherlands	0:56.61[1]

1. World record.

200-Meter Butterfly

1968	Ada Kok, Netherlands	2:24.70
1972	Karen Moe, United States	2:15.57
1976	Andrea Pollack, East Germany	2:11.41
1980	Ines Geissler, East Germany	2:10.44
1984	Mary Meagher, United States	2:06.90
1988	Kathleen Nord, East Germany	2:09.51
1992	Summer Sanders, United States	2:06.67
1996	Susan O'Neill, Australia	2:07.76
2000	Misty Hyman, United States	2:05.88

200-Meter Individual Medley

1968	Claudia Kolb, United States	2:24.70
1972	Shane Gould, Australia	2:23.07
1984	Tracy Caulkins, United States	2:12.64
1988	Daniela Hunger, East Germany	2:12.59
1992	Lin Lee, China	2:11.55[1]
1996	Michelle Smith, Ireland	2:13.93
2000	Yana Klochkova, Ukraine	2:10.68

1. World record.

400-Meter Individual Medley

1964	Donna de Varona, United States	5:18.70
1968	Claudia Kolk, United States	5:08.50
1972	Gail Neall, Australia	5:02.97
1976	Ulrike Tauber, East Germany	4:42.77
1980	Petra Schneider, East Germany	4:36.29
1984	Tracy Caulkins, United States	4:39.21
1988	Janet Evans, United States	4:37.76
1992	Krisztina Egerszegi, Hungary	4:36.54
1996	Michelle Smith, Ireland	4:39.18
2000	Yana Klochkova, Ukraine	4:33.59[1]

1. World record.

400-Meter Freestyle Relay

1912	Great Britain	5:52.80
1920	United States	5:11.60
1924	United States	4:58.80
1928	United States	4:47.60
1932	United States	4:38.00
1936	Netherlands	4:36.00
1948	United States	4:29.20
1952	Hungary	4:24.40
1956	Australia	4:17.10
1960	United States	4:08.90
1964	United States	4:03.80
1968	United States	4:02.50
1972	United States	3:55.19
1976	United States	3:44.82
1980	East Germany	3:42.71
1984	United States	3:44.43
1988	East Germany	3:40.63
1992	United States	3:39.46
1996	United States	3:39.29
2000	United States	3:36.61[1]

1. World record.

800-Meter Freestyle Relay

1996	United States	7:59.87
2000	United States	7:57.80

400-Meter Medley Relay

1960	United States	4:41.10
1964	United States	4:33.90
1968	United States	4:28.30
1972	United States	4:20.75
1976	East Germany	4:07.95
1980	East Germany	4:06.67
1984	United States	4:08.34
1988	East Germany	4:03.74
1992	United States	4:02.54
1996	United States	4:02.88
2000	United States	3:58.30[1]

1. World record.

Springboard Dive	Points
1920 Aileen Riggin, United States	539.90
1924 Elizabeth Becker, United States	474.50
1928 Helen Meany, United States	78.62
1932 Georgia Coleman, United States	87.52
1936 Marjorie Gestring, United States	89.27
1948 Victoria M. Draves, United States	108.74
1952 Patricia McCormick, United States	147.30
1956 Patricia McCormick, United States	142.36
1960 Ingrid Kramer, Germany	155.81
1964 Ingrid Kramer Engel, Germany	145.00
1968 Sue Gossick, United States	150.77
1972 Micki King, United States	450.03
1976 Jennifer Chandler, United States	506.19
1980 Irina Kalinina, USSR	725.91
1984 Sylvie Bernier, Canada	530.70
1988 Gao Min, China	580.23
1992 Gao Min, China	572.40
1996 Fu Ming-Xia, China	547.68
2000 Fu Ming-Xia, China	609.42

Platform Dive	Points
1912 Greta Johansson, Sweden	39.90
1920 Stefani Fryland, Denmark	34.60
1924 Caroline Smith, United States	166.00
1928 Elizabeth B. Pinkston, United States	31.60
1932 Dorothy Poynton, United States	40.26
1936 Dorothy Poynton Hill, United States	33.92
1948 Victoria M. Draves, United States	68.87
1952 Patricia McCormick, United States	79.37
1956 Patricia McCormick, United States	84.85
1960 Ingrid Kramer, Germany	91.28
1964 Lesley Bush, United States	99.80
1968 Milena Duchkova, Czechoslovakia	109.59
1972 Ulrika Knape, Sweden	390.00
1976 Elena Vaytsekhovskaia, USSR	406.59
1980 Martina Jaschke, East Germany	596.25
1984 Zhou Ji-Hong, China	435.51
1988 Xu Yan-Mei, China	445.20
1992 Fu Ming-Xia, China	461.43
1996 Fu Ming-Xia, China	521.58
2000 Laura Wilkinson, United States	543.75

Synchronized 3m Springboard Dive	Points
2000 Vera Ilina and Ioulia Pakhalina, Russia	332.64

Synchronized 10m Platform Dive	Points
2000 Li Na and Sang Xue, China	345.12

BASKETBALL–MEN

1904 United States	1972 USSR
1936 United States	1976 United States
1948 United States	1980 Yugoslavia
1952 United States	1984 United States
1956 United States	1988 USSR
1960 United States	1992 United States
1964 United States	1996 United States
1968 United States	2000 United States

BASKETBALL–WOMEN

1976 USSR	1992 Unified Team[1]
1980 USSR	1996 United States
1984 United States	2000 United States
1988 United States	

1. Former Soviet Union team.

BOXING

(U.S. winners only)
NOTE: U.S. boycotted Olympics in 1980.

Flyweight-112 pounds (51 kilograms)

1904	George Finnegan	1952	Nate Brooks
1920	Frank De Genaro	1976	Leo Randolph
1924	Fidel La Barba	1984	Steve McCrory

Bantamweight-119 (54 kg)

1904	O.L. Kirk	1988	Kennedy McKinney

Featherweight-126 pounds (57 kg)

1904	O.L. Kirk	1984	Meldrick Taylor
1924	Jackie Fields		

Lightweight-132 pounds (60 kg)

1904	H.J. Spanger	1976	Howard Davis
1920	Samuel Mosberg	1984	Pernell Whitaker
1968	Ronnie Harris	1992	Oscar De La Hoya

Light Welterweight-140 pounds (63.5 kg)

1952	Charles Adkins	1976	Ray Leonard
1972	Ray Seales	1984	Jerry Page

Welterweight-148 pounds (67 kg)

1904	Al Young	1984	Mark Breland
1932	Edward Flynn		

Light Middleweight-157 pounds (71 kg)

1960	Wilbert McClure	1996	David Reid
1984	Frank Tate		

Middleweight-165 pounds (75 kg)

1904	Charles Mayer	1960	Eddie Cook
1932	Carmen Barth	1976	Michael Spinks
1952	Floyd Patterson		

Light Heavyweight-179 pounds (81 kg)

1920	Edward Eagan	1960	Cassius Clay
1952	Norvel Lee	1976	Leon Spinks
1956	James Boyd	1988	Andrew Maynard

Heavyweight-201 pounds (91 kg)

1904	Sam Berger	1968	George Foreman
1952	Edward Sanders	1984	Henry Tilman
1956	Pete Rademacher	1988	Ray Mercer
1964	Joe Frazier		

Super Heavyweight (unlimited)

1984	Tyrell Biggs

Other 2000 Summer Olympic Games Champions

Archery
Women's individual—Yun Mi-jin, South Korea
Women's team—South Korea
Men's individual—Simon Fairweather, Australia
Men's team—South Korea

Badminton
Men's singles—Ji Xinpeng, China
Men's doubles—Indonesia (Tony Gunawan, Candra Wijaya)
Women's singles—Gong Zhichao, China
Women's doubles—China (Ge Fei, Gu Jun)
Mixed doubles—China (Jun Zhang, Ling Gao)

Baseball
Men—United States

DISTRIBUTION OF MEDALS—2000 SUMMER GAMES

Country	Gold	Silver	Bronze	Total	Country	Gold	Silver	Bronze	Total
United States	39	25	33	97	Iran	3	0	1	4
Russia	32	28	28	88	Turkey	3	0	1	4
China	28	16	15	59	Finland	2	1	1	4
Australia	16	25	17	58	Uzbekistan	1	1	2	4
Germany	14	17	26	57	New Zealand	1	0	3	4
France	13	14	11	38	Argentina	0	2	2	4
Italy	13	8	13	34	Korea	0	1	3	4
Cuba	11	11	7	29	Austria	2	1	0	3
Great Britain	11	10	7	28	Azerbaijan	2	0	1	3
Korea	8	9	11	28	Latvia	1	1	1	3
Romania	11	6	9	26	Yugoslavia	1	1	1	3
Netherlands	12	9	4	25	Estonia	1	0	2	3
Ukraine	3	10	10	23	Thailand	1	0	2	3
Japan	5	8	5	18	Nigeria	0	3	0	3
Hungary	8	6	3	17	Slovenia	2	0	0	2
Belarus	3	3	11	17	Bahamas	1	1	0	2
Poland	6	5	3	14	Croatia	1	0	1	2
Canada	3	3	8	14	Saudi Arabia	0	1	1	2
Bulgaria	5	6	2	13	Moldova	0	1	1	2
Greece	4	6	3	13	Trinidad & Tobago	0	1	1	2
Sweden	4	5	3	12	Costa Rica	0	0	2	2
Brazil	0	6	6	12	Portugal	0	0	2	2
Spain	3	3	5	11	Cameroon	1	0	0	1
Norway	4	3	3	10	Colombia	1	0	0	1
Switzerland	1	6	2	9	Mozambique	1	0	0	1
Ethiopia	4	1	3	8	Ireland	0	1	0	1
Czech Republic	2	3	3	8	Uruguay	0	1	0	1
Kazakhstan	3	4	0	7	Vietnam	0	1	0	1
Kenya	2	3	2	7	Armenia	0	0	1	1
Jamaica	0	4	3	7	Barbados	0	0	1	1
Denmark	2	3	1	6	Chile	0	0	1	1
Indonesia	1	3	2	6	India	0	0	1	1
Mexico	1	2	3	6	Iceland	0	0	1	1
Georgia	0	0	6	6	Israel	0	0	1	1
Lithuania	2	0	3	5	Kyrgyzstan	0	0	1	1
Slovakia	1	3	1	5	Kuwait	0	0	1	1
Algeria	1	1	3	5	Macedonia	0	0	1	1
Belgium	0	2	3	5	Qatar	0	0	1	1
South Africa	0	2	3	5	Sri Lanka	0	0	1	1
Morocco	0	1	4	5	**Total**	**301**	**299**	**328**	**928**
Chinese Taipei	0	1	4	5					

Beach Volleyball
Women—Australia (Natalie Cook, Kerri Pottharst)
Men—United States (Dain Blanton, Eric Fonoimoana)

Boxing
Light flyweight—Brahim Asloum, France
Flyweight—Wijan Ponlid, Thailand
Bantamweight—Guillermo Rigondeaux, Cuba
Featherweight—Bekzat Sattarkhanov, Kazakhstan
Lightweight—Mario Kindelan, Cuba
Light welterweight—Mahamadkadyz Abdullaev, Uzbekistan
Welterweight—Oleg Saitov, Russia
Light middleweight—Yermakhan Ibraimov, Kazakhstan
Middleweight—Jorge Gutierrez, Cuba
Light heavyweight—Alexander Lebziak, Russia
Heavyweight—Felix Savon, Cuba
Super heavyweight—Audley Harrison, Great Britain

Cycling—Men
1 km time trial (track)—Jason Queally, Great Britain
Individual pursuit (track)—Robert Bartko, Germany
Team pursuit (track)—Germany
Individual points race (track)—Juan Llaneras, Spain
Individual sprint (track)—Marty Nothstein, United States
Olympic sprint (track)—France
Madison (track)—Australia
Keirin (track)—Florian Rousseau, France
Mountain bike—Miguel Martinez, France
Individual road race—Jan Ullrich, Germany
Individual time trial (road)—Viacheslav Ekimov, Russia

Cycling—Women
500m time trial (track)—Felicia Ballanger, France
Individual pursuit (track)—Leontien Zijlaard, Netherlands

Sprint (track)—Felicia Ballanger, France
Points race (track)—Antonella Bellutti, Italy
Mountain bike—Paola Pezzo, Italy
Road race—Leontien Zijlaard, Netherlands
Individual time trial (road)—Leontien Zijlaard, Netherlands

Equestrian
Individual three-day—David O'Connor, United States
Three-day team event—Australia
Individual dressage—Anky van Grunsven, Netherlands
Team dressage—Germany
Individual jumping—Jeroen Dubbeldam, Netherlands
Team jumping—Germany

Fencing—Men
Individual epee—Pavel Kolobkov, Russia
Individual foil—Kim Young-ho, South Korea

Individual sabre—Mihai Claudiu
  Covaliu, Romania
Team epee—Italy
Team foil—France
Team sabre—Russia

Fencing—Women
Individual epee—Timea Nagy, Hungary
Individual foil—Valentina Vezzali, Italy
Team epee—Russia
Team foil—Italy

Field Hockey
Men—Netherlands
Women—Australia

Gymnastics—Men
All-around—Alexei Nemov, Russia
Floor exercise—Igors Vihrovs, Latvia
Pommel horse—Marius Urzica,
  Romania
Rings—Szilveszter Csollany, Hungary
Horizontal bar—Alexei Nemov, Russia
Parallel bars—Li Xiaopeng, China
Vault—Gervasio Deferr, Spain
Team—China

Gymnastics—Women
All-around—Simona Amanar, Romania
Uneven bars—Svetlana Khorkina,
  Russia
Balance beam—Liu Xuan, China
Floor exercise—Elena
  Zamolodtchikova, Russia
Vault—Elena Zamolodtchikova, Russia
Team—Romania

Judo—Men
Extra-lightweight (60kg)—Tadahiro
  Nomura, Japan
Half-lightweight (66kg)—Huseyin
  Ozkan, Turkey
Lightweight (73kg)—Giuseppe
  Maddaloni, Italy
Half-middleweight (81kg)—Makoto
  Takimoto, Japan
Middleweight (90kg)—Mark Huizinga,
  Netherlands
Half-heavyweight (100kg)—Kosei
  Inoue, Japan
Heavyweight (100kg+)—David Douillet,
  France

Judo—Women
Extra-lightweight (48kg)—Ryoko
  Tamura, Japan
Half-lightweight (52kg)—Legna
  Verdecia, Cuba
Lightweight (57kg)—Isabel Fernandez,
  Spain
Half-middleweight (63kg)—Severine
  Vandenhende, France
Middleweight (70kg)—Sibelis Veranes,
  Cuba
Half-heavyweight (78kg)—Tang Lin,
  China
Heavyweight (78kg+)—Yuan Hua,
  China

Kayak-Canoe—Men
Canoe singles 500m—Gyorgy Kolonics,
  Hungary
Canoe pairs 500m—Hungary
Kayak singles 500m—Knut Holmann,
  Norway
Kayak pairs 500m—Hungary
Kayak singles 1,000m—Knut Holmann,
  Norway

Canoe singles 1,000m—Andreas
  Dittmer, Germany
Kayak pairs 1,000m—Italy
Canoe pairs 1,000m—Romania
Kayak fours 1,000m—Hungary
Canoe slalom singles—Tony Estanguet,
  France
Canoe slalom pairs—Slovakia
Kayak slalom singles—Thomas
  Schmidt, Germany

Kayak—Women
500m singles—Josefa Idem Guerrini,
  Italy
500m pairs—Germany
500m fours—Germany
Single slalom—Stepanka Hilgertova,
  Czech Republic

Modern Pentathlon
Men—Dmitri Svatkovsky, Russia
Women—Stephanie Cook, Great Britain

Rhythmic Gymnastics
Individual—Yulia Barslukova, Russia
Team—Russia

Rowing—Men
Single sculls—Rob Waddell, New
  Zealand
Lightweight double sculls—Poland
Heavyweight double sculls—Slovenia
Quadruple sculls—Italy
Coxless pair—France
Lightweight coxless four—France
Heavyweight coxless four—Great
  Britain
Eight—Great Britain

Rowing—Women
Single sculls—Ekaterina Karsten,
  Belarus
Lightweight double sculls—Romania
Heavyweight double sculls—Germany
Quadruple sculls—Germany
Coxless pair—Romania
Eight—Romania

Sailing
Open Tornado—Austria
Open 49er—Finland
Open Laser—Ben Ainslie, Great Britain
Open Star—United States
Open Soling—Denmark
Men's Mistral—Christoph Sieber,
  Austria
Men's 470 fleet—Australia
Men's Finn—Iain Percy, Great Britain
Women's Mistral—Alessandra Sensini,
  Italy
Women's 470 fleet—Australia
Women's Europe—Shirley Robertson,
  Great Britain

Shooting—Men
Air pistol—Franck Dumoulin, France
Free pistol—Tanyu Kiriakov, Bulgaria
Rapid fire pistol—Serguei Alifirenko,
  Russia
Trap—Michael Diamond, Australia
Double trap—Richard Faulds, Great
  Britain
Air rifle—Cai Yalin, China
Running target—Yang Ling, China
Rifle prone—Jonas Edman, Sweden
Rifle 3-position—Rajmond Debevec,
  Slovenia

Skeet shooting—Mykola Milchev,
  Ukraine

Shooting—Women
Air pistol—Tao Luna, China
Sport pistol—Maria Grozdeva, Bulgaria
Air rifle—Nancy Johnson, United States
Rifle three position—Renata Maier-
  Rozanska, Poland
Trap—Daina Gudzineviciute, Lithuania
Double trap—Pia Hansen, Sweden
Skeet—Zemfira Meftakhetdinova,
  Azerbaijan

Soccer
Men—Cameroon
Women—Norway

Softball
United States

Synchronized Swimming
Duet—Russia
Team—Russia

Table Tennis
Men's singles—Kong Linghui, China
Men's doubles—China
Women's singles—Wang Nan, China
Women's doubles—China

Taekwondo
Men 58kg—Michail Mouroutsos,
  Greece
Men 68kg—Steven Lopez, United
  States
Men 80kg—Angel Matos Fuentes, Cuba
Men 80kg+—Kim Kyong-hun, South
  Korea
Women 49kg—Lauren Burns, Australia
Women 57kg—Jung Jae-eun, South
  Korea
Women 67kg—Lee Sun-Hee, South
  Korea
Women 67kg+—Chen Zhong, China

Team Handball
Men—Russia
Women—Denmark

Tennis
Men's singles—Yevgeny Kafelnikov,
  Russia
Men's doubles—Canada
Women's singles—Venus Williams,
  United States
Women's doubles—United States

Trampoline
Men—Alexandre Moskalenko, Russia
Women—Irina Karavaeva, Russia

Triathlon
Men—Simon Whitfield, Canada
Women—Brigitte McMahon, Switzer-
  land

Volleyball
Men—Yugoslavia
Women—Cuba

Water Polo
Men—Hungary
Women—Australia

Weightlifting—Men
56kg—Halil Mutlu, Turkey
62kg—Nikolay Pechalov, Croatia

69kg—Galabin Boevski, Bulgaria
77kg—Zhan Xugang, China
85kg—Pyrros Dimas, Greece
94kg—Akakios Kakiasvilis, Greece
105kg—Hossein Tavakoli, Iran
105kg+—Hossein Rezazadeh, Iran

Weightlifting—Women
48kg—Tara Nott, United States
53kg—Yang Xia, China
58kg—Soraya Jimenez, Mexico
63kg—Xiaomin Chen, China

69kg—Lin Weining, China
75kg—Maria Urrutia, Colombia
75kg+—Ding Meiyuan, China

Wrestling—Freestyle
54kg—Namig Abdullayev, Azerbaijan
63kg—Mourad Oumakhanov, Russia
58kg—Alireza Dabir, Iran
69kg—Daniel Igali, Canada
76kg—Alexander Leipold, Germany
85kg—Adam Saitiev, Russia
97kg—Saghid Mourtasaliyev, Russia

130kg—David Moussoulbes, Russia

Wrestling—Greco-Roman
54kg—Sim Kwon Ho, South Korea
58kg—Armen Nazarian, Bulgaria
63kg—Varteres Samourgachev, Russia
69kg—Filiberto Azcuy, Cuba
76kg—Mourat Kardanov, Russia
85kg—Hamza Yerlikaya, Turkey
97kg—Mikael Ljungberg, Sweden
130kg—Rulon Gardner, United States

Winter Games: Gold Medals

FIGURE SKATING—MEN

1908	Ulrich Salchow, Sweden	
1920	Gillis Grafström, Sweden	
1924	Gillis Grafström, Sweden	
1928	Gillis Grafström, Sweden	
1932	Karl Schäfer, Austria	
1936	Karl Schäfer, Austria	
1948	Dick Button, United States	
1952	Dick Button, United States	
1956	Hayes Alan Jenkins, United States	
1960	David Jenkins, United States	
1964	Manfred Schnelldorfer, Germany	
1968	Wolfgang Schwarz, Austria	
1972	Ondrej Nepela, Czechoslovakia	
1976	John Curry, Great Britain	
1980	Robin Cousins, Great Britain	
1984	Scott Hamilton, United States	
1988	Brian Boitano, United States	
1992	Viktor Petrenko, Unified Team*	
1994	Alexei Urmanov, Russia	
1998	Ilia Kulik, Russia	

*Former Soviet Union team.

FIGURE SKATING—WOMEN

1908	Madge Syers, Britain
1920	Magda Julin-Mauroy, Sweden
1924	Herma Planck-Szabó, Austria
1928	Sonja Henie, Norway
1932	Sonja Henie, Norway
1936	Sonja Henie, Norway
1948	Barbara Ann Scott, Canada
1952	Jeanette Altwegg, Great Britain
1956	Tenley Albright, United States
1960	Carol Heiss, United States
1964	Sjoukje Dijkstra, Netherlands
1968	Peggy Fleming, United States
1972	Beatrix Schuba, Austria
1976	Dorothy Hamill, United States
1980	Anett Pötzsch, East Germany
1984	Katarina Witt, East Germany
1988	Katarina Witt, East Germany
1992	Kristi Yamaguchi, United States
1994	Oksana Baiul, Ukraine
1998	Tara Lipinski, United States

SPEED SKATING—MEN

(U.S. winners only)

500 Meters
1924	Charles Jewtraw	44.00
1932	Jack Shea	43.40
1952	Ken Henry	43.20
1964	Terry McDermott	40.10
1980	Eric Heiden	38.03

1,000 Meters
1976	Peter Mueller	1:19.32
1980	Eric Heiden	1:15.18
1994	Dan Jansen	1:12.43[1]

1,500 Meters
1932	Jack Shea	2:57.50
1980	Eric Heiden	1:55.44

5,000 Meters
1932	Irving Jaffee	9:40.80
1980	Eric Heiden	7:02.29

10,000 Meters
1932	Irving Jaffee	19:13.60
1980	Eric Heiden	14:28.13

1. World record.

SPEED SKATING—WOMEN

(U.S. winners only)

500 Meters
1972	Anne Henning	43.33
1976	Sheila Young	42.76
1988	Bonnie Blair	39.10
1992	Bonnie Blair	40.33
1994	Bonnie Blair	39.25

1,000 Meters
1992	Bonnie Blair	1:21.90
1994	Bonnie Blair	1:18.74

1,500 Meters
1972	Dianne Holum	2:20.85

SKIING, ALPINE—MEN

Downhill
1948	Henri Oreiller, France	2:55.00
1952	Zeno Colò, Italy	2:30.80
1956	Toni Sailer, Austria	2:52.20
1960	Jean Vuarnet, France	2:06.00
1964	Egon Zimmermann, Austria	2:18.16
1968	Jean-Claude Killy, France	1:59.85
1972	Bernhard Russi, Switzerland	1:51.43
1976	Franz Klammer, Austria	1:45.73
1980	Leonhard Stock, Austria	1:45.50
1984	Bill Johnson, United States	1:45.59
1988	Pirmin Zurbriggen, Switzerland	1:59.63
1992	Patrick Ortlieb, Austria	1:50.37
1994	Tommy Moe, United States	1:45.75
1998	Jean-Luc Cretier, France	1:50.11

Slalom
1948	Edi Reinalter, Switzerland	2:10.30
1952	Othmar Schneider, Austria	2:00.00
1956	Toni Sailer, Austria	3:14.70
1960	Ernst Hinterseer, Austria	2:08.90
1964	Pepi Stiegler, Austria	2:11.13
1968	Jean-Claude Killy, France	1:39.73
1972	Francisco Ochoa, Spain	1:49.27
1976	Piero Gros, Italy	2:03.29
1980	Ingemar Stenmark, Sweden	1:44.26
1984	Phil Mahre, United States	1:39.41
1988	Alberto Tomba, Italy	1:39.47
1992	Finn Christian Jagge, Norway	1:44.39

1994	Thomas Stangassinger, Austria	2:02.02
1998	Hans-Petter Buraas, Norway	1:49.31

Giant Slalom

1952	Stein Eriksen, Norway	2:25.00
1956	Toni Sailer, Austria	3:00.10
1960	Roger Staub, Switzerland	1:48.30
1964	François Bonlieu, France	1:46.71
1968	Jean-Claude Killy, France	3:29.28
1972	Gustav Thöni, Italy	3:09.62
1976	Heini Hemmi, Switzerland	3:26.97
1980	Ingemar Stenmark, Sweden	2:40.74
1984	Max Julen, Switzerland	2:41.18
1988	Alberto Tomba, Italy	2:06.37
1992	Alberto Tomba, Italy	2:06.98
1994	Markus Wasmeier, Germany	2:52.46
1998	Hermann Maier, Austria	2:38.51

Super Slalom

1988	Frank Piccard, France	1:39.66
1992	Kjetil Andre Aamodt, Norway	1:13.04
1994	Markus Wasmeier, Germany	1:32.53
1998	Hermann Maier, Austria	1:34.84

Men's Combined (Downhill and Slalom)

		Points
1936	Franz Pfnür, Germany	99.25
1948	Henri Oreiller, France	3.27
1952–1984	Not held	
1988	Hubert Strolz, Austria	36.55
1992	Josef Polig, Italy	14.58
		Time
1994	Lasse Kjus, Norway	3:17.53
1998	Mario Reiter, Austria	3:08.06

SKIING, ALPINE–WOMEN

Downhill

1948	Hedy Schlunegger, Switzerland	2:28.30
1952	Trude Jochum-Beiser, Austria	1:47.10
1956	Madeleine Berthod, Switzerland	1:40.70
1960	Heidi Biebl, Germany	1:37.60
1964	Christl Haas, Austria	1:55.39
1968	Olga Pall, Austria	1:40.87
1972	Marie-Theres Nadig, Switzerland	1:36.68
1976	Rosi Mittermaier, West Germany	1:46.16
1980	Annemarie Moser-Pröll, Austria	1:37.52
1984	Michela Figini, Switzerland	1:13.36
1988	Marina Kiehl, West Germany	1:25.86
1992	Kerrin Lee-Gartner, Canada	1:52.55
1994	Katja Seizinger, Germany	1:35.93
1998	Katja Seizinger, Germany	1:28.89

Slalom

1948	Gretchen Fraser, United States	1:57.20
1952	Andrea Mead Lawrence, United States	2:10.60
1956	Renée Colliard, Switzerland	1:52.30
1960	Anne Heggtveit, Canada	1:49.60
1964	Christine Goitschel, France	1:29.86
1968	Marielle Goitschel, France	1:25.86
1972	Barbara Cochran, United States	1:31.24
1976	Rosi Mittermaier, West Germany	1:30.54
1980	Hanni Wenzel, Liechtenstein	1:25.09
1984	Paoletta Magoni, Italy	1:36.47
1988	Vreni Schneider, Switzerland	1:36.69
1992	Petra Kronberger, Austria	1:32.68
1994	Vreni Schneider, Switzerland	1:56.01
1998	Hilde Gerg, Germany	1:32.40

Giant Slalom

1952	Andrea Mead Lawrence, United States	2:06.80
1956	Ossi Reichert, Germany	1:56.50
1960	Yvonne Rügg, Switzerland	1:39.90
1964	Marielle Goitschel, France	1:52.24
1968	Nancy Greene, Canada	1:51.97
1972	Marie-Theres Nadig, Switzerland	1:29.90
1976	Kathy Kreiner, Canada	1:29.13
1980	Hanni Wenzel, Liechtenstein	2:41.66

1984	Debbie Armstrong, United States	2:20.98
1988	Vreni Schneider, Switzerland	2:06.49
1992	Pernilla Wiberg, Sweden	2:12.74
1994	Deborah Compagnoni, Italy	2:30.97
1998	Deborah Compagnoni, Italy	2:50.59

Super Giant Slalom

1988	Sigrid Wolf, Austria	1:19.03
1992	Deborah Compagnoni, Italy	1:21.22
1994	Diann Roffe-Steinrotter, United States	1:22.15
1998	Picabo Street, United States	1:18.02

Combined (Downhill and Slalom)

		Points
1936	Christl Cranz, Germany	97.06
1948	Trude Beiser, Austria	6.58
1952-84	Not held	
1988	Anita Wachter, Austria	29.25
1992	Petra Kronberger, Austria	2.55
		Time
1994	Pernilla Wiberg, Sweden	3:05.16
1998	Katja Seizinger, Germany	2:40.74

ICE HOCKEY

MEN			
1920	Canada	1972	USSR
1924	Canada	1976	USSR
1928	Canada	1980	United States
1932	Canada	1984	USSR
1936	Great Britain	1988	USSR
1948	Canada	1992	Unified Team*
1952	Canada	1994	Sweden
1956	USSR	1998	Czech Republic
1960	United States		**WOMEN**
1964	USSR	1998	United States
1968	USSR		*Former Soviet Union team.

1998 Men's Championship
Czech Republic 1, Russia 0
1998 Women's Championship
United States 3, Canada 1

FREESTYLE SKIING—MEN

Moguls

1992	Edgar Grospiron, France
1994	Jean-Luc Brassard, Canada
1998	Jonny Moseley, United States

Aerials

1994	Andreas Schoenbaechler, Switzerland
1998	Eric Bergoust, United States

FREESTYLE SKIING—WOMEN

Moguls

1992	Donna Weinbrecht, United States
1994	Stine Lise Hattestad, Norway
1998	Tae Satoya, Japan

Aerials

1994	Lina Cherjazova, Uzbekistan
1998	Nikki Stone, United States

1998 UNITED STATES MEDALISTS

Alpine Skiing
Women's Super Giant Slalom—GOLD—Picabo Street, Sun Valley, Idaho

Figure Skating
Women—GOLD—Tara Lipinski, Sugarland, Texas
Women—SILVER—Michelle Kwan, Torrance, Calif.

Freestyle Skiing
Men's Moguls—GOLD—Jonny Moseley, Tiburon, Calif.
Men's Aerials—GOLD—Eric Bergoust, Missoula, Mont.
Women's Aerials—GOLD—Nikki Stone, Westborough, Mass.

Hockey

Women—GOLD—Sara Decosta, Tara Mounsey, Elizabeth Brown, Angela Ruggiero, Colleen Coyne, Karyn Bye, Suzanne Merz, Laurie Baker, Sandra Whyte, Allison Mleczko, Jennifer Schmidgall, Victoria Movsessian, Shelley Looney, Alana Blahoski, Kathryn King, Catherine Granato, Gretchen Ulion, Christina Bailey, Patricia Dunn, Sarah Tueting

Luge

Men's Doubles—SILVER—Chris Thorpe, Marquette, Mich. and Gordy Sheer, Croton, N.Y.

Men's Doubles—BRONZE—Mark Grimmette, Muskegon, Mich. and Brian Martin, Palo Alto, Calif.

Snowboarding

Men's Halfpipe—BRONZE—Ross Powers, South Londonderry, Vt.

Women's Halfpipe—BRONZE—Shannon Dunn, Steamboat Springs, Colo.

Speedskating

Women's 1,000 Meters—SILVER—Chris Witty, West Allis, Wis.

Women's 1,500 Meters—BRONZE—Chris Witty, West Allis, Wis.

DISTRIBUTION OF MEDALS
1998 WINTER OLYMPIC GAMES
(Nagano, Japan)

	Gold	Silver	Bronze	Total
Germany	12	9	8	29
Norway	10	10	5	25
Russia	9	6	3	18
Austria	3	5	9	17
Canada	6	5	4	15
United States	6	3	4	13
Finland	2	4	6	12
Netherlands	5	4	2	11
Japan	5	1	4	10
Italy	2	6	2	10
France	2	1	5	8
China	0	6	2	8
Switzerland	2	2	3	7
South Korea	3	1	2	6
Czech Republic	1	1	1	3
Sweden	0	2	1	3
Belarus	0	0	2	2
Kazakhstan	0	0	2	2
Bulgaria	1	0	0	1
Denmark	0	1	0	1
Ukraine	0	1	0	1
Australia	0	0	1	1
Belgium	0	0	1	1
Great Britain	0	0	1	1

Other 1998 Winter Olympic Games Champions

Biathlon
Men's 10-kilometer—Ole Einar Bjoerndalen, Norway
Men's 20-kilometer—Halvard Hanevold, Norway
Men's 4 × 7.5-kilometer relay—Germany
Women's 7.5-kilometer—Galina Koukleva, Russia
Women's 15-kilometer—Ekaterina Dafovska, Bulgaria
Women's 4 × 7.5-kilometer relay—Germany

Bobsledding
2-man—Canada I and Italy I
4-man—Germany II

Curling
Men—Switzerland
Women—Canada

Figure Skating
Pairs—Oksana Kazakova and Artur Dmitriev, Russia
Ice dancing—Pasha Grishuk and Yevgeny Platov, Russia

Luge
Men's singles—Georg Hackl, Germany
Men's doubles—Stefan Krausse, Jan Behrendt, Germany
Women's singles—Silke Kraushaar, Germany

Skiing, Nordic—Men
Combined team—Norway
Combined—Bjarte Engen Vik, Norway
70-meter jump—Jani Soininen, Finland
90-meter jump—Kazuyoshi Funaki, Japan
Team 120-meter jump—Japan
10-km cross country classical—Bjorn Dählie, Norway
15-km cross country free pursuit—Thomas Alsgaard, Norway
30-km cross country classical—Mika Myllylae, Finland
50-km cross country freestyle—Bjorn Dählie, Norway
4 × 10 kilometer relay—Norway

Skiing, Nordic—Women
5-kilometer classical—Larissa Lazutina, Russia
10-kilometer free pursuit—Larissa Lazutina, Russia
15-kilometer classical—Olga Danilova, Russia
30-kilometer freestyle—Yulia Tchepalova, Russia
4 × 5 kilometer relay—Russia

Snowboarding—Men
Giant slalom—Ross Rebagliati, Canada
Halfpipe—Gian Simmen, Switzerland

Snowboarding—Women
Giant slalom—Karine Ruby, France
Halfpipe—Nicola Thost, Germany

Speed Skating—Men
500m—Hiroyashu Shimizu, Japan
1,000m—Ids Postma, Netherlands
1,500m—Aadne Sondral, Norway
5,000m—Gianni Romme, Netherlands
10,000m—Gianni Romme, Netherlands

Speed Skating—Women
500m—Catriona LeMay-Doan, Canada
1,000m—Marianne Timmer, Netherlands
1,500m—Marianne Timmer, Netherlands
3,000m—Gunda Niemann-Stirnemann, Germany
5,000m—Claudia Pechstein, Germany

Speed Skating, Short Track—Men
500m—Takafumi Nishitani, Japan
1,000m—Kim Dong-sung, South Korea
5,000m relay—Canada

Speed Skating, Short Track—Women
500m—Annie Perreault, Canada
1,000m—Chun Lee-kyung, South Korea
3,000m relay—South Korea

Football

The pastime of kicking around a ball goes back beyond the limits of recorded history. Ancient savage tribes played football of a primitive kind. There was a ball-kicking game played by Athenians, Spartans, and Corinthians 2500 years ago, which the Greeks called *Episkuros*. The Romans had a somewhat similar game called *Harpastum* and are supposed to have carried the game with them when they invaded the British Isles in the first century, B.C.

Undoubtedly the game known in the United States as football traces directly to the English game of rugby, though the modifications have been many. Informal football was played on college lawns well over a century ago, and an annual freshman-sophomore series of "scrimmages" began at Yale in 1840. The first formal intercollegiate football game was the Princeton-Rutgers contest at New Brunswick, N.J., on Nov. 6, 1869, with Rutgers winning by 6 goals to 4.

In those days, games were played with 25, 20, 15, or 11 men on a side. In 1880, there was a convention at which Walter Camp of Yale persuaded the delegates to agree to a rule calling for 11 players on a side.

The first professional game was played in 1895 at Latrobe, Pa. The National Football League was founded in 1921. The All-American Conference went into action in 1946. At the end of the 1949 season the two circuits merged, retaining the name of the older league. In 1960, the American Football League began operations. In 1970, the leagues merged. The United States Football League played its first season in 1983, from March to July. It suspended spring operations after the 1985 season, and planned a 1986 move to fall, but suspended operations again.

In 1991, another effort at spring football was launched, but this time it had the backing of the National Football League. The World League of American Football debuted in March 1991 with ten teams. Three of them were in Europe. The other seven were in North America, including the Montreal Machine in Canada. With television contracts signed with ABC and USA Cable Network, the league seemed to be on sound footing. But after just two seasons, it was suspended. The league returned in 1995, with six teams in Europe. In 1998, it was renamed the NFL Europe League.

College Football

NATIONAL COLLEGE FOOTBALL CHAMPIONS

The "National Collegiate Athletic Association Football Guide" recognizes as unofficial national champion the team selected each year by press association polls of writers and coaches.

1936	Minnesota	1951	Tennessee	1964	Alabama	1975	Oklahoma
1937	Pittsburgh	1952	Mich. State	1965	Alabama and	1976	Pittsburgh
1938	Texas Christian	1953	Maryland		Mich. State	1977	Notre Dame
1939	Texas A & M	1954	Ohio State and	1966	Notre Dame	1978	Alabama and
1940	Minnesota		UCLA	1967	So. Calif.		So. Calif.
1941	Minnesota	1955	Oklahoma	1968	Ohio State	1979	Alabama
1942	Ohio State	1956	Oklahoma	1969	Texas	1980	Georgia
1943	Notre Dame	1957	Auburn and	1970	Texas and	1981	Clemson
1944	Army		Ohio State		Nebraska	1982	Penn State
1945	Army	1958	Louisiana State	1971	Nebraska	1983	Miami
1946	Notre Dame	1959	Syracuse	1972	So. Calif.	1984	Brigham Young
1947	Notre Dame	1960	Minnesota	1973	Notre Dame	1985	Oklahoma
1948	Michigan	1961	Alabama		and U. of Ala.	1986	Penn State
1949	Notre Dame	1962	So. Calif.	1974	Oklahoma and	1987	Miami
1950	Oklahoma	1963	Texas		So. Calif.	1988	Notre Dame

1989	Miami
1990	Colorado and
	Georgia Tech
1991	Miami and
	Washington
1992	Alabama
1993	Florida State
1994	Nebraska
1995	Nebraska
1996	Univ. of Florida
1997	Michigan and
	Nebraska
1998	Tennessee
1999	Florida State
2000	Oklahoma

RECORD OF ANNUAL MAJOR COLLEGE FOOTBALL BOWL GAMES

Rose Bowl (At Pasadena, Calif.)

1902	Michigan 49, Stanford 0	1929	Georgia Tech 8, California 7	1948	Michigan 49, So. Calif. 0
1916	Washington State 14, Brown 0	1930	So. Calif. 47, Pittsburgh 14	1949	Northwestern 20, California 14
1917	Oregon 14, Pennsylvania 0	1931	Alabama 24, Wash. State 0	1950	Ohio State 17, California 14
1918	Mare Island Marines 19, Camp Lewis 7	1932	So. Calif. 21, Tulane 12	1951	Michigan 14, California 6
1919	Great Lakes 17, Mare Island Marines 0	1933	So. Calif. 35, Pittsburgh 0	1952	Illinois 40, Stanford 7
		1934	Columbia 7, Stanford 0	1953	So. Calif. 7, Wisconsin 0
1920	Harvard 7, Oregon 6	1935	Alabama 29, Stanford 13	1954	Michigan State 28, UCLA 20
1921	California 28, Ohio State 0	1936	Stanford 7, So. Methodist 0	1955	Ohio State 20, So. Calif. 7
1922	Washington and Jefferson 0, California 0	1937	Pittsburgh 21, Washington 0	1956	Michigan State 17, UCLA 14
		1938	California 13, Alabama 0	1957	Iowa 35, Oregon State 19
1923	So. Calif. 14, Penn State 3	1939	So. Calif. 7, Duke 3	1958	Ohio State 10, Oregon 7
1924	Navy 14, Washington 14	1940	So. Calif. 14, Tennessee 0	1959	Iowa 38, California 12
1925	Notre Dame 27, Stanford 10	1941	Stanford 21, Nebraska 13	1960	Washington 44, Wisconsin 8
1926	Alabama 20, Washington 19	1942	Oregon State 20, Duke 16[1]	1961	Washington 17, Minnesota 7
1927	Alabama 7, Stanford 7	1943	Georgia 9, UCLA 0	1962	Minnesota 21, UCLA 3
1928	Stanford 7, Pittsburgh 6	1944	So. Calif. 29, Washington 0	1963	So. Calif. 42, Wisconsin 37
		1945	So. Calif. 25, Tennessee 0	1964	Illinois 17, Washington 7
		1946	Alabama 34, So. Calif. 14	1965	Michigan 34, Oregon State 7
		1947	Illinois 45, UCLA 14	1966	UCLA 14, Michigan State 12

1967 Purdue 14, So. Calif. 13
1968 So. Calif. 14, Indiana 3
1969 Ohio State 27, So. Calif. 16
1970 So. Calif. 10, Michigan 3
1971 Stanford 27, Ohio State 17
1972 Stanford 13, Michigan 12
1973 So. Calif. 42, Ohio State 17
1974 Ohio State 42, So. Calif. 21
1975 So. Calif. 18, Ohio State 17
1976 UCLA 23, Ohio State 10
1977 So. Calif. 14, Michigan 6
1978 Washington 27, Michigan 20
1979 So. Calif. 17, Michigan 10
1980 So. Calif. 17, Ohio State 16
1981 Michigan 23, Washington 6
1982 Washington 28, Iowa 0
1983 UCLA 24, Michigan 14
1984 UCLA 45, Illinois 9
1985 So. Calif. 20, Ohio St. 17
1986 UCLA 45, Iowa 28
1987 Arizona State 22, Michigan 15
1988 Michigan State 20, So. Calif. 17
1989 Michigan 22, So. Calif. 14
1990 So. Calif. 17, Michigan 10
1991 Washington 46, Iowa 34
1992 Washington 34, Michigan 14
1993 Michigan 38, Washington 31
1994 Wisconsin 21, UCLA 16
1995 Penn State 38, Oregon 20
1996 So. Calif. 41, Northwestern 32
1997 Ohio State 20, Arizona State 17
1998 Michigan 21, Washington State 16
1999 Wisconsin 38, UCLA 31
2000 Wisconsin 17, Stanford 9
2001 Washington 34, Purdue 24

1. Played at Durham, N.C.

Orange Bowl (At Miami)

1933 Miami (Fla.) 7, Manhattan 0
1934 Duquesne 33, Miami (Fla.) 7
1935 Bucknell 26, Miami (Fla.) 0
1936 Catholic 20, Mississippi 19
1937 Duquesne 13, Mississippi State 12
1938 Auburn 6, Michigan State 0
1939 Tennessee 17, Oklahoma 0
1940 Georgia Tech 21, Missouri 7
1941 Mississippi State 14, Georgetown 7
1942 Georgia 40, Texas Christian 26
1943 Alabama 37, Boston College 21
1944 Louisiana State 19, Texas A & M 14
1945 Tulsa 26, Georgia Tech 12
1946 Miami (Fla.) 13, Holy Cross 6
1947 Rice 8, Tennessee 0
1948 Georgia Tech 20, Kansas 14
1949 Texas 41, Georgia 28
1950 Santa Clara 21, Kentucky 13
1951 Clemson 15, Miami (Fla.) 14
1952 Georgia Tech 17, Baylor 14
1953 Alabama 61, Syracuse 6
1954 Oklahoma 7, Maryland 0
1955 Duke 34, Nebraska 7
1956 Oklahoma 20, Maryland 6
1957 Colorado 27, Clemson 21
1958 Oklahoma 48, Duke 21
1959 Oklahoma 21, Syracuse 6
1960 Georgia 14, Missouri 0
1961 Missouri 21, Navy 14
1962 Louisiana State 25, Colorado 7
1963 Alabama 17, Oklahoma 0

1964 Nebraska 13, Auburn 7
1965 Texas 21, Alabama 17
1966 Alabama 39, Nebraska 28
1967 Florida 27, Georgia Tech 12
1968 Oklahoma 26, Tennessee 24
1969 Penn State 15, Kansas 14
1970 Penn State 10, Missouri 3
1971 Nebraska 17, Louisiana State 12
1972 Nebraska 38, Alabama 6
1973 Nebraska 40, Notre Dame 6
1974 Penn State 16, Louisiana State 9
1975 Notre Dame 13, Alabama 11
1976 Oklahoma 14, Michigan 6
1977 Ohio State 27, Colorado 10
1978 Arkansas 31, Oklahoma 6
1979 Oklahoma 31, Nebraska 24
1980 Oklahoma 24, Florida State 7
1981 Oklahoma 18, Florida State 17
1982 Clemson 22, Nebraska 15
1983 Nebraska 21, Louisiana State 20
1984 Miami (Fla.) 31, Nebraska 30
1985 Washington 28, Oklahoma 17
1986 Oklahoma 25, Penn State 10
1987 Oklahoma 42, Arkansas 8
1988 Miami (Fla.) 20, Oklahoma 14
1989 Miami (Fla.) 23, Nebraska 3
1990 Notre Dame 21, Colorado 6
1991 Colorado 10, Notre Dame 9
1992 Miami (Fla.) 22, Nebraska 0
1993 Florida State 27, Nebraska 14
1994 Florida State 18, Nebraska 16
1995 Nebraska 24, Miami (Fla.) 17
1996 Florida State 31, Notre Dame 26
1997 Nebraska 41, Virginia Tech 21
1998 Nebraska 42, Tennessee 17
1999 Florida 31, Syracuse 10
2000 Michigan 35, Alabama 34
2001 Oklahoma 13, Florida State 2

Sugar Bowl (At New Orleans)

1935 Tulane 20, Temple 14
1936 Texas Christian 3, Louisiana State 2
1937 Santa Clara 21, Louisiana State 14
1938 Santa Clara 6, Louisiana State 0
1939 Texas Christian 15, Carnegie Tech 7
1940 Texas A & M 14, Tulane 13
1941 Boston College 19, Tennessee 13
1942 Fordham 2, Missouri 0
1943 Tennessee 14, Tulsa 7
1944 Georgia Tech 20, Tulsa 18
1945 Duke 29, Alabama 26
1946 Oklahoma A & M 33, St. Mary's (Calif.) 13
1947 Georgia 20, North Carolina 10
1948 Texas 27, Alabama 7
1949 Oklahoma 14, North Carolina 6
1950 Oklahoma 35, Louisiana State 0
1951 Kentucky 13, Oklahoma 7
1952 Maryland 28, Tennessee 13
1953 Georgia Tech 24, Mississippi 7
1954 Georgia Tech 42, West Virginia 19
1955 Navy 21, Mississippi 0
1956 Georgia Tech 7, Pittsburgh 0
1957 Baylor 13, Tennessee 7

1958 Mississippi 39, Texas 7
1959 Louisiana State 7, Clemson 0
1960 Mississippi 21, Louisiana State 0
1961 Mississippi 14, Rice 6
1962 Alabama 10, Arkansas 3
1963 Mississippi 17, Arkansas 13
1964 Alabama 12, Mississippi 7
1965 Louisiana State 13, Syracuse 10
1966 Missouri 20, Florida 18
1967 Alabama 34, Nebraska 7
1968 Louisiana State 20, Wyoming 13
1969 Arkansas 16, Georgia 2
1970 Mississippi 27, Arkansas 22
1971 Tennessee 34, Air Force Academy 13
1972 Oklahoma 40, Auburn 22
1973 Oklahoma 14, Penn State 0
1974 Notre Dame 24, Alabama 23
1975 Nebraska 13, Florida 10
1976 Alabama 13, Penn State 6
1977 Pittsburgh 27, Georgia 3
1978 Alabama 35, Ohio State 6
1979 Alabama 14, Penn State 7
1980 Alabama 24, Arkansas 9
1981 Georgia 17, Notre Dame 10
1982 Pittsburgh 24, Georgia 20
1983 Penn State 27, Georgia 23
1984 Auburn 9, Michigan 7
1985 Nebraska 28, Louisiana State 10
1986 Tennessee 35, Miami (Fla.) 7
1987 Nebraska 30, Louisiana State 15
1988 Syracuse 16, Auburn 16 (tie)
1989 Florida State 13, Auburn 7
1990 Miami (Fla.) 33, Alabama 25
1991 Tennessee 23, Virginia 22
1992 Notre Dame 39, Florida 28
1993 Alabama 34, Miami (Fla.) 13
1994 Florida 41, West Virginia 7
1995 Florida State 23, Florida 17
1996 Virginia Tech 28, Texas 10
1997 Florida 52, Florida State 20
1998 Florida State 31, Ohio State 14
1999 Ohio State 24, Texas A & M 14
2000 Florida State 46, Virginia Tech. 29
2001 Miami (Fla.) 37, Florida 20

Cotton Bowl (At Dallas)

1937 Texas Christian 16, Marquette 6
1938 Rice 28, Colorado 14
1939 St. Mary's (Calif.) 20, Texas Tech. 13
1940 Clemson 6, Boston College 3
1941 Texas A & M 13, Fordham 12
1942 Alabama 29, Texas A & M 21
1943 Texas 14, Georgia Tech 7
1944 Randolph Field 7, Texas 7
1945 Oklahoma A & M 34, Texas Christian 0
1946 Texas 40, Missouri 27
1947 Louisiana State 0, Arkansas 0
1948 So. Methodist 13, Penn State 13
1949 So. Methodist 21, Oregon 13
1950 Rice 27, North Carolina 13
1951 Tennessee 20, Texas 14
1952 Kentucky 20, Texas Christian 7
1953 Texas 16, Tennessee 0
1954 Rice 28, Alabama 6

1955	Georgia Tech 14, Arkansas 6	1990	Tennessee 31, Arkansas 27	1972	Georgia 7, North Carolina 3
1956	Mississippi 14, Texas Christian 13	1991	Miami (Fla.) 46, Texas 3	1973	Auburn 24, Colorado 3
1957	Texas Christian 28, Syracuse 27	1992	Florida State 10, Texas A & M 2	1974	Texas Tech 28, Tennessee 19
1958	Navy 20, Rice 7	1993	Notre Dame 28, Texas A & M 3	1975	Auburn 27, Texas 3
1959	Air Force 0, Texas Christian 0	1994	Notre Dame 24, Texas A & M 21	1976	Maryland 13, Florida 0
1960	Syracuse 23, Texas 14	1995	So. Calif. 55, Texas Tech 14	1977	Notre Dame 20, Penn State 9
1961	Duke 7, Arkansas 6	1996	Colorado 38, Oregon 6	1978	Pittsburgh 34, Clemson 3
1962	Texas 12, Mississippi 7	1997	Brigham Young 19, Kansas State 15	1979	Clemson 17, Ohio State 15
1963	Louisiana State 13, Texas 0	1998	UCLA 29, Texas A & M 23	1980	North Carolina 17, Michigan 15
1964	Texas 28, Navy 6	1999	Texas 38, Mississippi State 11	1981	Pittsburgh 37, South Carolina 9
1965	Arkansas 10, Nebraska 7	2000	Arkansas 27, Texas 6	1982	North Carolina 31, Arkansas 27
1966	Louisiana State 14, Arkansas 7	2001	Kansas State 35, Tennessee 21	1983	Florida State 31, West Virginia 12
1967	Georgia 24, So. Methodist 9			1984	Florida 14, Iowa 6
1968	Texas A & M 20, Alabama 16	**Gator Bowl (At Jacksonville, Fla.)**		1985	Oklahoma State 21, South Carolina 14
1969	Texas 36, Tennessee 13	1953	Florida 14, Tulsa 13	1986	Florida State 34, Oklahoma State 23
1970	Texas 21, Notre Dame 17	1954	Texas Tech 35, Auburn 13		
1971	Notre Dame 24, Texas 11	1955	Auburn 33, Baylor 13	1987	Clemson 27, Stanford 21
1972	Penn State 30, Texas 6	1956	Vanderbilt 25, Auburn 13	1988	Louisiana State 30, South Carolina 13
1973	Texas 17, Alabama 13	1957	Georgia Tech 21, Pittsburgh 14		
1974	Nebraska 19, Texas 3	1958	Tennessee 3, Texas A & M 0	1989	Georgia 34, Mich. State 27
1975	Penn State 41, Baylor 20	1959	Mississippi 7, Florida 3	1990	Clemson 27, West Virginia 7
1976	Arkansas 31, Georgia 10	1960	Arkansas 14, Georgia Tech 7	1991	Michigan 35, Mississippi 3
1977	Houston 30, Maryland 21	1961	Florida 13, Baylor 12	1992	Oklahoma 38, Virginia 14
1978	Notre Dame 38, Texas 10	1962	Penn State 30, Georgia Tech 15	1993	Florida 27, No. Carolina St. 10
1979	Notre Dame 35, Houston 34			1994	Alabama 24, No. Carolina 10
1980	Houston 17, Nebraska 14	1963	Florida 17, Penn State 7	1995	Tennessee 45, Virginia Tech 23
1981	Alabama 30, Baylor 2	1964	No. Carolina 35, Air Force 0	1996	Syracuse 41, Clemson 0
1982	Texas 14, Alabama 12	1965	Florida State 36, Oklahoma 19	1997	North Carolina 20, West Virginia 13
1983	So. Meth. 7, Pittsburgh 3	1966	Georgia Tech 31, Texas Tech 21		
1984	Georgia 10, Texas 9	1967	Tennessee 18, Syracuse 12	1998	North Carolina 42, Virginia Tech 3
1985	Boston College 45, Houston 28	1968	Penn State 17, Florida State 17 (tie)		
1986	Texas A & M 36, Auburn 16			1999	Georgia Tech 35, Notre Dame 28
1987	Ohio State 28, Texas A & M 12	1969	Missouri 35, Alabama 10	2000	Miami (Fla.) 28, Georgia Tech 13
1988	Texas A & M 35, Notre Dame 10	1970	Florida 14, Tennessee 13		
1989	UCLA 17, Arkansas 3	1971	Auburn 35, Mississippi 28	2001	Virginia Tech 41, Clemson 20

RESULTS OF OTHER 2000–2001 BOWL GAMES

Alamo (Dec, 30, 2000)—Nebraska 66, Northwestern 17
Aloha (Dec. 25, 2000)—Boston College 31, Arizona State 17
Citrus (Jan. 1, 2001)—Michigan 31, Auburn 28
Tostitos Fiesta (Jan. 1, 2001)—Tennessee 21, Nebraska 31
GalleryFurniture.com (Dec. 27, 2000)—East Carolina 40, Texas Tech 27
Holiday (Dec. 29, 2000)—Oregon 35, Texas 30
Humanitarian (Dec. 28, 2000)—Boise State 38, Univ. Texas–El Paso 23
Independence (Dec. 31, 2000)—Mississippi State 43, Texas A&M 41
Insight.com (Dec. 28, 2000)—Iowa State 37, Pittsburgh 29
Las Vegas (Dec. 21, 2000)—Univ. Nevada–Las Vegas 31, Arkansas 14

Liberty (Dec. 29, 2000)—Colorado State 22, Louisville 17
MicronPC.com (Dec. 28, 2000)—North Carolina State 38, Minnesota 30
Mobile, Alabama (Dec. 20, 2000)—Southern Mississippi 28, Texas Christian Univ. 21
Motor City (Dec. 27, 2000)—Marshall 25, Cincinnati 14
Music City (Dec. 28, 2000)—West Virginia 49, Mississippi 38
Oahu (Dec. 24, 2000)—Georgia 37, Virginia 14
Outback (Jan. 1, 2001)—South Carolina 24, Ohio State 7
Peach (Dec. 29, 2000)—Louisiana State Univ. 28, Georgia Tech 14
Silicon Valley (Dec. 31, 2000)—Air Force 37, Fresno State 34
Sun (Dec. 29, 2000)—Wisconsin 21, Univ. Calif.–Los Angeles 20

HEISMAN MEMORIAL TROPHY WINNERS

The Heisman Memorial Trophy is presented annually by the Downtown Athletic Club of New York City to the nation's outstanding college football player, as determined by a poll of sportswriters and sportscasters.

1935	Jay Berwanger, Chicago	1949	Leon Hart, Notre Dame	1963	Roger Staubach, Navy
1936	Larry Kelley, Yale	1950	Vic Janowicz, Ohio State	1964	John Huarte, Notre Dame
1937	Clinton Frank, Yale	1951	Dick Kazmaier, Princeton	1965	Mike Garrett, So. Calif.
1938	Davey O'Brien, Texas Christian	1952	Billy Vessels, Oklahoma	1966	Steve Spurrier, Florida
1939	Nile Kinnick, Iowa	1953	Johnny Lattner, Notre Dame	1967	Gary Beban, UCLA
1940	Tom Harmon, Michigan	1954	Alan Ameche, Wisconsin	1968	O.J. Simpson, So. Calif.
1941	Bruce Smith, Minnesota	1955	Howard Cassady, Ohio State	1969	Steve Owens, Oklahoma
1942	Frank Sinkwich, Georgia	1956	Paul Hornung, Notre Dame	1970	Jim Plunkett, Stanford
1943	Angelo Bertelli, Notre Dame	1957	John Crow, Texas A & M	1971	Pat Sullivan, Auburn
1944	Leslie Horvath, Ohio State	1958	Pete Dawkins, Army	1972	Johnny Rodgers, Nebraska
1945	Felix Blanchard, Army	1959	Billy Cannon, Louisiana State	1973	John Cappelletti, Penn State
1946	Glenn Davis, Army	1960	Joe Bellino, Navy	1974-75	Archie Griffin, Ohio State
1947	Johnny Lujack, Notre Dame	1961	Ernie Davis, Syracuse	1976	Tony Dorsett, Pittsburgh
1948	Doak Walker, So. Methodist	1962	Terry Baker, Oregon State	1977	Earl Campbell, Texas

1978	Billy Sims, Oklahoma	1986	Vinny Testaverde, Miami	1994	Rashaan Salaam, Colorado
1979	Charles White, So. Calif.	1987	Tim Brown, Notre Dame	1995	Eddie George, Ohio State
1980	George Rogers, South Carolina	1988	Barry Sanders, Oklahoma State	1996	Danny Wuerffel, Florida
1981	Marcus Allen, So. Calif.	1989	Andre Ware, Houston	1997	Charles Woodson, Michigan
1982	Herschel Walker, Georgia	1990	Ty Detmer, Brigham Young	1998	Ricky Williams, Texas
1983	Mike Rozier, Nebraska	1991	Desmond Howard, Michigan	1999	Ron Dayne, Wisconsin
1984	Doug Flutie, Boston College	1992	Gino Torretta, Miami	2000	Chris Weinke, Florida State
1985	Bo Jackson, Auburn	1993	Charlie Ward, Florida State		

2000 NCAA CHAMPIONSHIP PLAYOFFS

DIVISION I-AA

Quarterfinals
(Dec. 2, 2000)
Montana 34, Richmond 20
Appalachian State 17, Western
  Kentucky 14
Georgia Southern 48, Hofstra 20
Delaware 47, Lehigh 22
Semifinals
(Dec. 9, 2000)
Montana 19, Appalachian State 16
Georgia Southern 27, Delaware 18
Championship
(Dec. 16, 2000)
Georgia Southern 27, Montana 25

DIVISION II

Quarterfinals
(Nov. 25, 2000)
North Dakota State 43,
  Nebraska-Omaha 21
Delta State 20, Catawba 14
Bloomsburg 38, Northwood 14
U.C. Davis 62, Mesa State 18
Semifinals
(Dec. 2, 2000)
Delta State 34, North Dakota State 16
Bloomsburg 58, U.C. Davis 48
Championship
(Dec. 9, 2000)
Delta State 63, Bloomsburg 34

DIVISION III

Quarterfinals
(Dec. 2, 2000)
St. John's (Minn.) 21, Central 18
Hardin-Simmons 33, Trinity (Texas) 30
Mount Union 32, Wittenberg 15
Widener 61, Springfield 27
Semifinals
(Dec. 9, 2000)
Mount Union 70, Widener 30
St. John's (Minn.) 38, Hardin-Simmons
  14
Championship
(Dec. 16, 2000)
Mount Union 10, St. John's (Minn.) 7

2000 NATIONAL ASSOCIATION OF INTERCOLLEGIATE ATHLETICS CHAMPIONSHIPS

Quarterfinals
(Nov. 25, 2000)
Georgetown (Ky.) 37, St. Francis (Ind.) 19
Northwestern Oklahoma State 31, MidAmerica Nazarene
  (Kans.) 27
Northwestern (Iowa) 21, St. Ambrose (Iowa) 14
Carroll (Mont.) 31, Huron (S.D.) 17

Semifinals
(Dec. 2, 2000)
Northwestern Oklahoma State 42, Northwestern (Iowa) 7
Georgetown (Ky.) 28, Carroll (Mont.) 21
Championship
(Dec. 16, 2000)
Georgetown (Ky.) 20, Northwestern Oklahoma State 0

COLLEGE FOOTBALL HALL OF FAME

(P.O. Box 11146, South Bend, Indiana)
NOTE: Date given is player's last year of competition.

Players

Abell, Earl—Colgate, 1915
Agase, Alex—Purdue/Illinois, 1946
Agganis, Harry—Boston Univ., 1952
Albert, Frank—Stanford, 1941
Aldrich, Chas. (Ki)—Texas Christian,
  1938
Aldrich, Malcolm—Yale, 1921
Alexander, Joseph—Syracuse, 1920
Allen, Marcus—So. Calif., 1981
Alworth, Lance—Arkansas, 1961
Ameche, Alan (Horse)—Wisconsin, 1954
Amling, Warren—Ohio State, 1946
Anderson, Dick—Colorado, 1967
Anderson, Donny—Texas Tech, 1965
Anderson, H. (Hunk)—Notre Dame, 1921
Arnett, Jon—So. Calif., 1956
Atkins, Doug—Tennessee, 1952
Babich, Bob—Miami-Ohio, 1968
Bacon, C. Everett—Wesleyan, 1912
Bagnell, Francis (Reds)—Pennsylvania,
  1950
Bailey, Johnny—Texas A&M, 1989
Baker, Hobart (Hobey)—Princeton, 1913
Baker, John—So. Calif., 1931
Baker, Terry—Oregon State, 1962
Ballin, Harold—Princeton, 1914
Banker, Bill—Tulane, 1929
Banonis, Vince—Detroit, 1941
Barnes, Stanley—So. Calif., 1921
Barrett, Charles—Cornell, 1915
Baston, Bert—Minnesota, 1916
Battles, Cliff—W. Va. Wesleyan, 1931
Baugh, Sammy—Texas Christian, 1936
Baughan, Maxie—Georgia Tech, 1959
Bausch, James—Kansas, 1930

Beagle, Ron—Navy, 1955
Beban, Gary—UCLA, 1967
Bechtol, Hub—Texas Tech, 1946
Beck, Ray—Georgia Tech, 1951
Beckett, John—Oregon, 1913
Bednarik, Chuck—Pennsylvania 1948
Behm, Forrest—Nebraska, 1940
Bell, Bobby—Minnesota, 1962
Bellino, Joe—Navy, 1960
Below, Marty—Wisconsin, 1923
Benbrook, A.—Michigan, 1911
Bentrim, Jeff—North Dakota State, 1986
Bertelli, A.—Notre Dame, 1943
Berry, Charlie—Lafayette, 1924
Berwanger, John (Jay)—Chicago, 1935
Bettencourt, Larry—St. Mary's, 1927
Biletnikoff, Fred—Florida State, 1964
Blanchard, Felix (Doc)—Army, 1946
Bock, Ed—Iowa State, 1938
Bomar, Lynn—Vanderbilt, 1924
Bomeisler, Doug (Bo)—Yale, 1913
Booth, Albie—Yale, 1931
Bork, George—Northern Illinois, 1963
Borries, Fred—Navy, 1934
Bosely, Bruce—West Virginia, 1955
Bosseler, Don—Miami (Fla.), 1956
Bottari, Vic—California, 1939
Boynton, Ben—Williams, 1920
Bozis, Al—Georgetown, 1941
Bradshaw, Terry—Louisiana Tech, 1969
Brewer, Charles—Harvard, 1895
Bright, John—Drake, 1951
Brodie, John—Stanford, 1956
Brooke, George—Pennsylvania, 1895
Brosky, Al—Illinois, 1952

Brown, Bob—Nebraska, 1963
Brown, George—Navy/San Diego State,
  1947
Brown, Gordon—Yale, 1900
Brown, Jim—Syracuse, 1956
Brown, John, Jr.—Navy, 1913
Brown, Johnny Mack—Alabama, 1925
Brown, Raymond (Tay)—So. Calif., 1932
Browner, Ross—Notre Dame, 1977
Bruner, Teel—Centre College (Ky.), 1985
Buchanan, Buck—Grambling State,
  1962
Budde, Brad—So. Calif., 1979
Bunker, Paul—Army, 1902
Burford, Chris—Stanford, 1959
Burris, Kurt—Oklahoma, 1954
Burton, Ron—Northwestern, 1956
Butkus, Dick—Illinois, 1964
Butler, Kevin—Georgia, 1984
Butler, Robert—Wisconsin, 1912
Cafego, George—Tennessee, 1939
Cagle, Chris—SW La./Army, 1929
Cain, John—Alabama, 1932
Cameron, Eddie—Wash. & Lee, 1924
Campbell, David C.—Harvard, 1901
Campbell, Earl—Texas, 1977
Cannon, Billy—Louisiana State, 1959
Cannon, Jack—Notre Dame, 1929
Cappelletti, John—Penn State, 1973
Carideo, Frank—Notre Dame, 1930
Caroline, J.C.—Illinois, 1954
Carney, Charles—Illinois, 1921
Carpenter, Bill—Army, 1959
Carpenter, C. Hunter—VPI, 1905
Carroll, Charles—Washington, 1928

Kinard, Terry—Clemson, 1982
Kiner, Steve—Tennessee, 1969
King, Philip—Princeton, 1893
Kinnick, Nile—Iowa, 1939
Kipke, Harry—Michigan, 1923
Kirkpatrick, John Reed—Yale, 1910
Kitzmiller, John—Oregon, 1929
Koch, Barton—Baylor, 1931
Kitner, Malcolm—Texas, 1942
Kramer, Ron—Michigan, 1956
Kroll, Alex—Rutgers, 1961
Krueger, Charlie—Texas A & M, 1957
Kwalick, Ted—Penn State, 1968
Lach, Steve—Duke, 1941
Lane, Myles—Dartmouth, 1927
Lanier, Sr., Willie—Morgan State, 1966
Lattner, Joseph J.—Notre Dame, 1953
Lauricella, Hank—Tennessee, 1952
Lautenschlaeger—Tulane, 1925
Layden, Elmer—Notre Dame, 1924
Layne, Bobby—Texas, 1947
Lea, Langdon—Princeton, 1895
LeBaron, Eddie—Univ. of Pacific, 1949
LeClair, Jim—North Dakota, 1971
Leech, James—Va. Mil. Inst., 1920
Lester, Darrell—Texas Christian, 1935
Lewis, D. D.—Mississippi State, 1968
Lilly, Bob—Texas Christian, 1960
Little, Floyd—Syracuse, 1966
Lio, Augie—Georgetown, 1940
Lockbaum, Gordie—Holy Cross, 1987
Locke, Gordon—Iowa, 1922
Lomax, Neil—Portland (Ore.) State, 1980
Long, Chuck—Iowa, 1985
Long, Mel—Toledo, 1971
Loria, Frank—Virginia Tech, 1967
Lourie, Don—Princeton, 1921
Lucas, Richard—Penn State, 1959
Luckman, Sid—Columbia, 1938
Lujack, John—Notre Dame, 1947
Lund, J.L. (Pug)—Minnesota, 1934
Lynch, Jim—Notre Dame, 1966
MacAfee, Ken—Notre Dame, 1977
Macomber, Bart—Illinois, 1915
MacLeod, Robert—Dartmouth, 1938
Maegle, Dick—Rice, 1954
Mahan, Edward W.—Harvard, 1915
Majors, John—Tennessee, 1956
Mallory, William—Yale, 1893
Mancha, Vaughn—Alabama, 1947
Mann, Gerald—So. Methodist, 1927
Manning, Archie—Mississippi, 1970
Manske, Edgar—Northwestern, 1933
Marinaro, Ed—Cornell, 1971
Markov, Vic—Washington, 1937
Marshall, Robert—Minnesota, 1907
Martin, Jim—Notre Dame, 1949
Matson, Ollie—San Fran. U., 1952
Matthews, Ray—Texas Christian, 1928
Maulbetsch, John—Michigan, 1914
Mauthe, J.L. (Pete)—Penn State, 1912
Maxwell, Robert—Chicago/Swarthmore, 1906
McAfee, George—Duke, 1939
McCauley, Don—North Carolina, 1970
McClung, Thomas L.—Yale, 1891
McColl, William F.—Stanford, 1951
McCormick, James B.—Princeton, 1907
McDonald, Tom—Oklahoma, 1956
McDowall, Jack—No. Carolina State, 1927
McElhenny, Hugh—Washington, 1951
McEver, Gene—Tennessee, 1931
McEwan, John—Minn./Army, 1916
McFadden, J.B.—Clemson, 1939
McFadin, Bud—Texas, 1950
McGee, Mike—Duke, 1959
McGinley, Edward—Pennsylvania, 1924
McGovern, J.—Minnesota, 1910
McGraw, Thurman—Colorado State, 1949
McGriff, Tyrone—Florida A & M, 1979
McKeever, Mike—So. California, 1960
McLaren, George—Pittsburgh, 1918

McMahon, Jim—Brigham Young, 1981
McMillan, Dan—So. Calif./California, 1922
McMillin, A.N. (Bo)—Centre, 1921
McWhorter, Robert—Georgia, 1913
Mercer, Leroy—Pennsylvania, 1912
Meredith, Don—So. Methodist, 1959
Merritt, Frank—Army, 1943
Metzger, Bert—Notre Dame, 1930
Meyland, Wayne—Nebraska, 1967
Michaels, Lou—Kentucky, 1957
Michels, John—Tennessee, 1952
Mickal, Abe—Louisiana State, 1935
Miller, Creighton—Notre Dame, 1943
Miller, Don—Notre Dame, 1925
Miller, Edgar (Rip)—Notre Dame, 1924
Miller, Eugene—Penn State, 1913
Miller, Fred—Notre Dame, 1928
Millner, Wayne—Notre Dame, 1935
Milstead, Century—Wabash/Yale, 1923
Minds, John—Pennsylvania, 1897
Minisi, Anthony—Navy/Pennsylvania, 1947
Modzelewski, Dick—Maryland, 1952
Moffatt, Alex—Princeton, 1884
Molinski, Ed—Tennessee, 1940
Montgomery, Cliff—Columbia, 1933
Montgomery, Wilbert—Abilene Christian, 1976
Moomaw, Donn—UCLA, 1952
Morley, William—Columbia, 1903
Morris, George—Georgia Tech, 1952
Morris, Larry—Georgia Tech, 1954
Morton, Craig—California, 1964
Morton, William—Dartmouth, 1931
Moscrip, Monk—Stanford, 1935
Muller, Harold (Brick)—Calif., 1922
Musso, Johnny—Alabama, 1971
Nagurski, Bronko—Minnesota, 1929
Nevers, Ernie—Stanford, 1925
Newell, Marshall—Harvard, 1893
Newman, Harry—Michigan, 1932
Newsome, Ozzie—Alabama, 1977
Nielsen, Gifford—Brigham Young, 1976
Nobis, Tommy—Texas, 1965
Nomellini, Leo—Minnesota, 1949
Oberland, Andrew—Dartmouth, 1925
O'Brien, Davey—Texas Christian, 1938
O'Brien, Ken—Cal.-Davis, 1982
O'Dea, Pat—Wisconsin, 1899
Odell, Robert—Pennsylvania, 1943
O'Hearn, J.—Cornell, 1915
Olds, Robin—Army, 1942
Oliphant, Elmer—Purdue/Army, 1917
Olsen, Merlin—Utah State, 1961
Onkotz, Dennis—Penn State, 1969
Oosterbaan, Ben—Michigan, 1927
O'Rourke, Charles—Boston College, 1940
Orsi, John—Colgate, 1931
Osgood, W.D.—Cornell/Pennsylvania, 1895
Osmanski, William—Holy Cross, 1938
Outland, John—Kansas/Pennsylvania, 1899
Owen, George—Harvard, 1922
Owens, Jim—Oklahoma, 1949
Owens, Steve—Oklahoma, 1969
Page, Alan—Notre Dame, 1966
Palumbo, Joe—U. of Virginia, 1951
Pardee, Jack—Texas A & M, 1956
Parilli, Vito (Babe)—Kentucky, 1951
Parker, Clarence (Ace)—Duke, 1936
Parker, Jackie—Miss. State, 1953
Parker, James—Ohio State, 1956
Payton, Walter—Jackson State, 1974
Pazzetti, V.J.—Wesleyan/Lehigh, 1912
Peabody, Endicott—Harvard, 1941
Peck, Robert—Pittsburgh, 1916
Pellegrini, Bob—Maryland, 1955
Pennock, Stanley B.—Harvard, 1914
Pfann, George—Cornell, 1923
Phillips, H.D.—Univ. of South, 1904
Phillips, Loyd—Arkansas, 1966
Pingel, John—Michigan State, 1938

Pihos, Pete—Indiana, 1945
Pinckert, Ernie—So. Calif., 1931
Plunkett, Jim—Stanford, 1970
Poe, Arthur—Princeton, 1899
Pollard, Fritz—Brown, 1916
Poole, Barney—Miss./Army, 1947
Powell, Marvin—So. Calif., 1976
Pregulman, Merv—Michigan, 1943
Price, Eddie—Tulane, 1949
Pruitt, Greg—Oklahoma, 1972
Pugh, Larry—Westminster, Pa., 1964
Pund, Henry—Georgia Tech, 1928
Ramsey, Gerrard—Wm. & Mary, 1942
Reasons, Gary—Northwestern State (La.), 1983
Redell, Bill—Occidental, 1963
Redman, Rick—Washington, 1964
Reeds, Claude—Oklahoma, 1913
Reid, Mike—Penn State, 1970
Reid, Steve—Northwestern, 1936
Reid, William—Harvard, 1900
Reifsnyder, Bob—Navy, 1958
Renfro, Mel—Oregon, 1963
Rentner, Ernest—Northwestern, 1932
Ressler, Glenn—Penn State, 1964
Reynolds, Robert—Nebraska, 1952
Reynolds, Robert—Stanford, 1935
Rhome, Jerry—Tulsa, 1964
Richter, Les—California, 1951
Richter, Pat—Wisconsin, 1962
Riley, John—Northwestern, 1931
Rimington, Dave—Nebraska, 1982
Rinehart, Charles—Lafayette, 1897
Ritchie, Richard—Texas A & M, 1977
Ritcher, Jim—No. Carolina St., 1979
Roberts, J.D.—Oklahoma, 1953
Robeson, Paul—Rutgers, 1918
Robinson, Dave—Penn State, 1962
Robinson, Jerry—UCLA, 1978
Rodgers, Ira—West Virginia, 1919
Rodgers, Johnny—Nebraska, 1972
Rogers, Edward L.—Minnesota, 1903
Rogers, George—South Carolina, 1980
Roland, Johnny—Missouri, 1965
Romig, Joe—Colorado, 1961
Rosenberg, Aaron—So. Calif., 1934
Rote, Kyle—So. Methodist, 1950
Routt, Joe—Texas A & M, 1937
Salmon, Louis—Notre Dame, 1904
Sarkisian, Alex—Northwestern, 1948
Sauer, George—Nebraska, 1933
Savitsky, George—Pennsylvania, 1947
Saxon, Jimmy—Texas, 1961
Sayers Gale—Kansas, 1964
Scarbath, Jack—Maryland, 1952
Scarlett, Hunter—Pennsylvania, 1909
Schloredt, Bob—Washington, 1960
Schmidt, Joe—Pittsburgh, 1952
Schoonover, Wear—Arkansas, 1929
Schreiner, Dave—Wisconsin, 1942
Schultz, Adolf (Germany)—Mich., 1908
Schwab, Frank—Lafayette, 1922
Schwartz, Marchmont—Notre Dame, 1931
Schwegler, Paul—Washington, 1931
Scott, Clyde—Arkansas, 1949
Scott, Freddie—Amherst, 1973
Scott, Richard—Navy, 1947
Scott, Tom—Virginia, 1953
Seibels, Henry—Sewanee, 1899
Sellers, Ron—Florida State, 1968
Selmon, Lee Roy—Oklahoma, 1975
Sewell, Harley—Texas, 1952
Shakespeare, Bill—Notre Dame, 1935
Shell, Donnie—So. Carolina St., 1973
Shelton, Murray—Cornell, 1915
Shevlin, Tom—Yale, 1905
Shively, Bernie—Illinois, 1926
Simons, Claude—Tulane, 1934
Sims, Billy—Oklahoma, 1979
Simpson, O.J.—So. Calif., 1968
Singletary, Mike—Baylor, 1980
Sington, Fred—Alabama, 1930
Sinkwich, Frank—Georgia, 1942

Coaches

Professional Football

NATIONAL FOOTBALL LEAGUE FINAL STANDINGS 2000

AMERICAN FOOTBALL CONFERENCE

	W	L	T	Pct	PF	PA
Eastern Division						
Miami Dolphins[1]	11	5	0	.688	323	226
Indianapolis Colts[1]	10	6	0	.625	429	326
New York Jets	9	7	0	.562	321	321
Buffalo Bills	8	8	0	.500	315	350
New England Patriots	5	11	0	.312	276	338
Central Division						
Tennessee Titans[1]	13	3	0	.812	346	191
Baltimore Ravens[2]	12	4	0	.750	333	165
Pittsburgh Steelers	9	7	0	.562	321	255
Jacksonville Jaguars	7	9	0	.438	367	327
Cincinnati Bengals	4	12	0	.250	185	359
Cleveland Browns	3	13	0	.188	161	419
Western Division						
Oakland Raiders[1]	12	4	0	.750	479	299
Denver Broncos[2]	11	5	0	.688	485	369
Kansas City Chiefs	7	9	0	.438	355	354
Seattle Seahawks	6	10	0	.375	320	405
San Diego Chargers	1	15	0	.062	269	440

1. Division champion. 2. Wild card qualifier for playoffs. **Wild card:** Miami 23, Indianapolis, 17; Baltimore 21, Denver 3. **Division:** Oakland 27, Miami 0; Baltimore 24, Tennessee 10. **Conference:** Baltimore 16, Oakland 3.

NATIONAL FOOTBALL CONFERENCE

	W	L	T	Pct	PF	PA
Eastern Division						
New York Giants[1]	12	4	0	.750	328	246
Philadelphia Eagles[2]	11	5	0	.688	351	245
Washington Redskins	8	8	0	.500	281	269
Dallas Cowboys	5	11	0	.312	294	361
Arizona Cardinals	3	13	0	.188	210	443
Central Division						
Minnesota Vikings[1]	11	5	0	.688	397	371
Tampa Bay Buccaneers[2]	10	6	0	.625	388	269
Green Bay Packers	9	7	0	.562	353	323
Detroit Lions	9	7	0	.562	307	307
Chicago Bears	5	11	0	.312	216	355
Western Division						
New Orleans Saints[1]	10	6	0	.625	354	305
St. Louis Rams[2]	10	6	0	.625	540	471
Carolina Panthers	7	9	0	.438	310	310
San Francisco 49ers	6	10	0	.375	388	422
Atlanta Falcons	4	12	0	.250	252	413

1. Division champion. 2. Wild card qualifier for playoffs. **Wild card:** New Orleans 31, St. Louis 28; Philadelphia 21, Tampa Bay 3. **Division:** Minnesota 34, New Orleans 16; New York 20, Philadelphia 10. **Conference:** New York 41, Minnesota 0.

LEAGUE CHAMPIONSHIP—SUPER BOWL XXXV

(Jan. 28, 2001, Raymond James Stadium, Tampa, Fla. Attendance: 71,921. Time: 3:23)

Scoring

	1st Q	2nd Q	3rd Q	4th Q	Final
Baltimore Ravens	7	3	14	10	34
New York Giants	0	0	7	0	7

1st: BAL—Brandon Stokley 38–yd pass from Trent Dilfer (Matt Stover kick), 8P10. Drive: 41 yards in 2 plays. Key play: Jermaine Lewis 43-yd punt return to NYG 22.

2nd: BAL—Stover 47-yd field goal, 13:19. Drive: 59 yards in 7 plays. Key play: Qadry Ismail 44-yd pass from Dilfer to NYG 36.

3rd: BAL—Duane Starks 49-yd interception return (Stover kick), 11:11. NYG—Ron Dixon 97-yd kickoff return (Brad Daluiso kick), 11:29. BAL—Jermaine Lewis 84-yd kickoff return (Stover kick), 11:47.

4th: BAL—Jamal Lewis 3-yd run (Stover kick), 6:15. Drive: 38 yards in 6 plays. Key play: Ben Coates 17-yd pass from Dilfer to NYG 21. BAL—Stover 34-yd field goal, 9:33. Drive: 18 yards in 5 plays. Key play: Robert Bailey recovery of Dixon fumble during kickoff return at NYG 34.

Individual Statistics
Passing: BAL—T. Dilfer 12–25 for 153 yds, T. Banks 0–1. NYG—K. Collins 15–39 for 112 yds.
Receiving: BAL—B. Stokley 3–52, B. Coates 3–30, Q. Ismail 1–44, P. Johnson 1–8, Jermaine Lewis 1–6, S. Sharpe 1–5, Jamal Lewis 1–4, P. Holmes 1–4. NYG—T. Barber 6–26, I. Hilliard 3–30, A. Toomer 2–24, R. Dixon 1–16, H. Cross 1–7, P. Mitchell 1–7, G. Comella 1–2.
Rushing: BAL—Jamal Lewis 27–102, P. Holmes 4–8, Jermaine Lewis 1–1, T. Dilfer 1–0. NYG—T. Barber 11–49, K. Collins 3–12, J. Montgomery 2–5.
Field goals: BAL—M. Stover 2–3.
Punting: BAL—K. Richardson 10–430. NYG—B. Maynard 11–422.
Punt Returns: BAL—Jermaine Lewis 3–34. NYG—I. Hilliard 3–33, T. Barber 2–13.

Interceptions: BAL—D. Starks 1–49, C. McAlister 1–4, J. Sharper 1–4, K. Herring 1–2.

MVP: Ray Lewis, Baltimore linebacker (5 tackles, 4 passes defended).

Statistics of the Game

	Ravens	Giants
First downs	13	11
Rushing	6	2
Passing	6	6
Penalty	1	3
3rd down efficiency	3/16	2/14
4th down efficiency	0/0	1/1
Total offense (net yards)	244	152
Plays	62	59
Average gain	3.9	2.6
Rushes/yards	33/111	16/66
Yards per rush	3.4	4.1
Passing yards (net)	133	86
Times sacked/yards lost	3/20	4/26
Passing yards (gross)	153	112
Completions/attempts	12/26	15/39
Yards per pass	4.6	2.0
Times intercepted	0	4
Return yardage	204	217
Punt returns/yards	3/34	5/46
Kickoff returns/yards	2/111	7/171
Interceptions/yards	4/59	0/0
Fumbles/lost	2/0	2/1
Penalties/yards	9/70	6/27
Punts/average	10/43.0	11/38.4
Punts blocked	0	0
Field goals made/ attempted	2/3	0/0
Time of possession	34:06	25:54

SUPER BOWLS I-XXXIV

Game	Date	Winner	Loser	Site	Attendance
XXXV	Jan. 28, 2001	Baltimore (AFC) 34	New York Giants (NFC) 7	Raymond James Stadium, Tampa, Fla.	71,921
XXXIV	Jan. 30, 2000	St. Louis (NFC) 23	Tennessee (AFC) 16	Georgia Dome, Atlanta, Ga.	72,625
XXXIII	Jan. 31, 1999	Denver (AFC) 34	Atlanta (NFC) 19	Pro Player Stadium, Miami, Fla.	74,803
XXXII	Jan. 25, 1998	Denver (AFC) 31	Green Bay (NFC) 24	Qualcomm Stadium, San Diego, Calif.	68,912
XXXI	Jan. 26, 1997	Green Bay (NFC) 35	New England (AFC) 21	Superdome, New Orleans, La.	72,301
XXX	Jan. 28, 1996	Dallas (NFC) 27	Pittsburgh (AFC) 17	Sun Devil Stadium, Tempe, Ariz.	76,347
XXIX	Jan. 29, 1995	San Francisco (NFC) 49	San Diego (AFC) 26	Joe Robbie Stadium, Miami, Fla.	74,107
XXVIII	Jan. 30, 1994	Dallas (NFC) 30	Buffalo (AFC) 13	Georgia Dome, Atlanta, Ga.	72,817
XXVII	Jan. 31, 1993	Dallas (NFC) 52	Buffalo (AFC) 17	Rose Bowl, Pasadena, Calif.	98,374
XXVI	Jan. 26, 1992	Washington (NFC) 37	Buffalo (AFC) 24	Metrodome, Minneapolis, Minn.	63,130
XXV	Jan. 27, 1991	Giants (NFC) 20	Buffalo (AFC) 19	Tampa Stadium, Tampa, Fla.	73,813
XXIV	Jan. 28, 1990	San Francisco (NFC) 55	Denver (AFC) 10	Superdome, New Orleans	72,919
XXIII	Jan. 22, 1989	San Francisco (NFC) 20	Cincinnati (AFC) 16	Joe Robbie Stadium, Miami, Fla.	75,179
XXII	Jan. 31, 1988	Washington (NFC) 42	Denver (AFC) 10	Jack Murphy Stadium, San Diego, Calif.	73,302
XXI	Jan. 25, 1987	Giants (NFC) 39	Denver (AFC) 20	Rose Bowl, Pasadena, Calif.	101,063
XX	Jan. 26, 1986	Chicago (NFC) 46	New England (AFC) 10	Superdome, New Orleans	73,818
XIX	Jan. 20, 1985	San Francisco (NFC) 38	Miami (AFC) 16	Stanford Stadium, Palo Alto, Calif.	84,059
XVIII	Jan. 22, 1984	Los Angeles Raiders (AFC) 38	Washington (NFC) 9	Tampa Stadium, Tampa, Fla	72,920
XVII	Jan. 30, 1983	Washington (NFC) 27	Miami (AFC) 17	Rose Bowl, Pasadena, Calif.	103,667
XVI	Jan. 24, 1982	San Francisco (NFC) 26	Cincinnati (AFC) 21	Silverdome, Pontiac, Mich.	81,270
XV	Jan. 25, 1981	Oakland (AFC) 27	Philadelphia (NFC) 10	Superdome, New Orleans	75,500
XIV	Jan. 20, 1980	Pittsburgh (AFC) 31	Los Angeles (NFC) 19	Rose Bowl, Pasadena	103,985
XIII	Jan. 21, 1979	Pittsburgh (AFC) 35	Dallas (NFC) 31	Orange Bowl, Miami	79,484
XII	Jan. 15, 1978	Dallas (NFC) 27	Denver (AFC) 10	Superdome, New Orleans	75,583
XI	Jan. 9, 1977	Oakland (AFC) 32	Minnesota (NFC) 14	Rose Bowl, Pasadena	103,424
X	Jan. 18, 1976	Pittsburgh (AFC) 21	Dallas (NFC) 17	Orange Bowl, Miami	80,187
IX	Jan. 12, 1975	Pittsburgh (AFC) 16	Minnesota (NFC) 6	Tulane Stadium, New Orleans	80,997
VIII	Jan. 13, 1974	Miami (AFC) 24	Minnesota (NFC) 7	Rice Stadium, Houston	71,882
VII	Jan. 14, 1973	Miami (AFC) 14	Washington (NFC) 7	Memorial Coliseum, Los Angeles	90,182
VI	Jan. 16, 1972	Dallas (NFC) 24	Miami (AFC) 3	Tulane Stadium, New Orleans	81,591
V	Jan. 17, 1971	Baltimore (AFC) 16	Dallas (NFC) 13	Orange Bowl, Miami	79,204
IV	Jan. 11, 1970	Kansas City (AFL) 23	Minnesota (NFL) 7	Tulane Stadium, New Orleans	80,562
III	Jan. 12, 1969	New York (AFL) 16	Baltimore (NFL) 7	Orange Bowl, Miami	75,389
II	Jan. 14, 1968	Green Bay (NFL) 33	Oakland (AFL) 14	Orange Bowl, Miami	75,546
I	Jan. 15, 1967	Green Bay (NFL) 35	Kansas City (AFL) 10	Memorial Coliseum, Los Angeles	61,946

NOTE: Super Bowls I to IV were played before the American Football League and National Football League merged into the NFL, which was divided into two conferences, the NFC and AFC.

NATIONAL LEAGUE CHAMPIONS

Year	Champion	(W-L-T)	Year	Champion	(W-L-T)	Year	Champion	(W-L-T)
1921	Chicago Bears (Staley's)	(10-1-1)	1926	Frankford Yellow Jackets	(14-1-1)	1930	Green Bay Packers	(10-3-1)
						1931	Green Bay Packers	(12-2-0)
1922	Canton Bulldogs	(10-0-2)	1927	New York Giants	(11-1-1)	1932	Chicago Bears	(7-1-6)
1923	Canton Bulldogs	(11-0-1)	1928	Providence Steamrollers	(8-1-2)			
1924	Cleveland Indians	(7-1-1)						
1925	Chicago Cardinals	(11-2-1)	1929	Green Bay Packers	(12-0-1)			

Year	Eastern Conference winners (W-L-T)	Western Conference winners (W-L-T)	League champion playoff results
1933	New York Giants (11-3-0)	Chicago Bears (10-2-1)	Chicago Bears 23, New York 21
1934	New York Giants (8-5-0)	Chicago Bears (13-0-0)	New York 30, Chicago Bears 13
1935	New York Giants (9-3-0)	Detroit Lions (7-3-2)	Detroit 26, New York 7
1936	Boston Redskins (7-5-0)	Green Bay Packers (10-1-1)	Green Bay 21, Boston 6
1937	Washington Redskins (8-3-0)	Chicago Bears (9-1-1)	Washington 28, Chicago Bears 21
1938	New York Giants (8-2-1)	Green Bay Packers (8-3-0)	New York 23, Green Bay 17
1939	New York Giants (9-1-1)	Green Bay Packers (9-2-0)	Green Bay 27, New York 0
1940	Washington Redskins (9-2-0)	Chicago Bears (8-3-0)	Chicago Bears 73, Washington 0
1941	New York Giants (8-3-0)	Chicago Bears (10-1-1)[2]	Chicago Bears 37, New York 9
1942	Washington Redskins (10-1-1)	Chicago Bears (11-0-0)	Washington 14, Chicago Bears 6
1943	Washington Redskins (6-3-1)[2]	Chicago Bears (8-1-1)	Chicago Bears 41, Washington 21
1944	New York Giants (8-1-1)	Green Bay Packers (8-2-0)	Green Bay 14, New York 7
1945	Washington Redskins (8-2-0)	Cleveland Rams (9-1-0)	Cleveland 15, Washington 14
1946	New York Giants (7-3-1)	Chicago Bears (8-2-1)	Chicago Bears 24, New York 14
1947	Philadelphia Eagles (8-4-0)[2]	Chicago Cardinals (9-3-0)	Chicago Cardinals 28, Philadelphia 21
1948	Philadelphia Eagles (9-2-1)	Chicago Cardinals (11-1-0)	Philadelphia 7, Chicago Cardinals 0
1949	Philadelphia Eagles (11-1-0)	Los Angeles Rams (8-2-2)	Philadelphia 14, Los Angeles 0
1950[1]	Cleveland Browns (10-2-0)[2, 3]	Los Angeles Rams (9-3-0)[2]	Cleveland 30, Los Angeles 28
1951[1]	Cleveland Browns (11-1-0)	Los Angeles Rams (8-4-0)	Los Angeles 24, Cleveland 17
1952[1]	Cleveland Browns (8-4-0)	Detroit Lions (9-3-0)[2]	Detroit 17, Cleveland 7
1953	Cleveland Browns (11-1-0)	Detroit Lions (10-2-0)	Detroit 17, Cleveland 16
1954	Cleveland Browns (9-3-0)	Detroit Lions (9-2-1)	Cleveland 56, Detroit 10

Year	Eastern Conference winners (W-L-T)	Western Conference winners (W-L-T)	League champion playoff results
1955	Cleveland Browns (9-2-1)	Los Angeles Rams (8-3-1)	Cleveland 38, Los Angeles 14
1956	New York Giants (8-3-1)	Chicago Bears (9-2-1)	New York 47, Chicago Bears 7
1957	Cleveland Browns (9-2-1)	Detroit Lions (8-4-0)[2]	Detroit 59, Cleveland 14
1958	New York Giants (9-3-0)[2]	Baltimore Colts (9-3-0)	Baltimore 23, New York 17[4]
1959	New York Giants (10-2-0)	Baltimore Colts (9-3-0)	Baltimore 31, New York 16
1960	Philadelphia Eagles (10-2-0)	Green Bay Packers (8-4-0)	Philadelphia 17, Green Bay 13
1961	New York Giants (10-3-1)	Green Bay Packers (11-3-0)	Green Bay 37, New York 0
1962	New York Giants (12-2-0)	Green Bay Packers (13-1-0)	Green Bay 16, New York 7
1963	New York Giants (11-3-0)	Chicago Bears (11-1-2)	Chicago 14, New York 10
1964	Cleveland Browns (10-3-1)	Baltimore Colts (12-2-0)	Cleveland 27, Baltimore 0
1965	Cleveland Browns (11-3-0)	Green Bay Packers (11-3-1)[2]	Green Bay 23, Cleveland 12
1966	Dallas Cowboys (10-3-1)	Green Bay Packers (12-2-0)	Green Bay 34, Dallas 27
1967	Dallas Cowboys (9-5-0)[2]	Green Bay Packers (9-4-1)[2]	Green Bay 21, Dallas 17
1968	Cleveland Browns (10-4-0)[2]	Baltimore Colts (13-1-0)[2]	Baltimore 34, Cleveland 0
1969	Cleveland Browns (10-3-1)[2]	Minnesota Vikings (12-2-0)[2]	Minnesota 27, Cleveland 7

1. League was divided into American and National Conferences, 1950-52 and again in 1970, when leagues merged. 2. Won divisional playoff. 3. Cleveland Browns and San Francisco 49ers joined league after All-America Football Conference (1946–1949) folded. 4. Won at 8:15 of sudden death overtime period.

NATIONAL CONFERENCE CHAMPIONS

Year	Eastern Division	Central Division	Western Division	Champion
1970	Dallas Cowboys (10-4-0)	Minnesota Vikings (12-2-0)	San Francisco 49ers (10-3-1)	Dallas
1971	Dallas Cowboys (11-3-0)	Minnesota Vikings (11-3-0)	San Francisco 49ers (9-5-0)	Dallas
1972	Washington Redskins (11-3-0)	Green Bay Packers (10-4-0)	San Francisco 49ers (8-5-1)	Washington
1973	Dallas Cowboys (10-4-0)	Minnesota Vikings (12-2-0)	Los Angeles Rams (12-2-0)	Minnesota
1974	St. Louis Cardinals (10-4-0)	Minnesota Vikings (10-4-0)	Los Angeles Rams (10-4-0)	Minnesota
1975	St. Louis Cardinals (11-3-0)	Minnesota Vikings (12-2-0)	Los Angeles Rams (10-4-0)	Dallas[1]
1976	Dallas Cowboys (11-3-0)	Minnesota Vikings (11-2-1)	Los Angeles Rams (10-3-1)	Minnesota
1977	Dallas Cowboys (12-2-0)	Minnesota Vikings (9-5-0)	Los Angeles Rams (10-4-0)	Dallas
1978	Dallas Cowboys (12-4-0)	Minnesota Vikings (8-7-1)	Los Angeles Rams (12-4-0)	Dallas
1979	Dallas Cowboys (11-5-0)	Tampa Bay Buccaneers (10-6-0)	Los Angeles Rams (9-7-0)	Los Angeles
1980	Philadelphia Eagles (12-4-0)	Minnesota Vikings (9-7-0)	Atlanta Falcons (12-4-0)	Philadelphia
1981	Dallas Cowboys (12-4-0)	Tampa Bay Buccaneers (9-7-0)	San Francisco 49ers (13-3-0)	San Francisco
1982[2]				
1983	Washington Redskins (14-2-0)	Detroit Lions (8-8-0)	San Francisco 49ers (10-6-0)	Washington
1984	Washington Redskins (11-5-0)	Chicago Bears (10-6-0)	San Francisco 49ers (15-1-0)	San Francisco
1985	Dallas Cowboys (10-6-0)	Chicago Bears (15-1-0)	Los Angeles Rams (11-5-0)	Chicago
1986	New York Giants (14-2-0)	Chicago Bears (14-2-0)	San Francisco 49ers (10-5-1)	New York
1987	Washington Redskins (11-4-0)	Chicago Bears (11-4-0)	San Francisco 49ers (13-2-0)	Washington
1988	Philadelphia Eagles (10-6-0)	Chicago Bears (12-4-0)	San Francisco 49ers (10-6-0)	San Francisco
1989	New York Giants (12-4-0)	Minnesota Vikings (10-6-0)	San Francisco 49ers (14-2-0)	San Francisco
1990	New York Giants (13-3-0)	Chicago Bears (11-5-0)	San Francisco 49ers (14-2-0)	New York
1991	Washington (14-2-0)	Detroit Lions (12-4-0)	New Orleans Saints (11-5-0)	Washington
1992	Dallas Cowboys (13-3-0)	Minnesota Vikings (11-5-0)	San Francisco 49ers (14-2-0)	Dallas
1993	Dallas Cowboys (12-4-0)	Detroit Lions (10-6-0)	San Francisco 49ers (10-6-0)	Dallas
1994	Dallas Cowboys (12-4-0)	Minnesota Vikings (10-6-0)	San Francisco 49ers (13-3-0)	San Francisco
1995	Dallas Cowboys (12-4-0)	Green Bay Packers (11-5-0)	San Francisco 49ers (11-5-0)	Dallas
1996	Dallas Cowboys (10-6-0)	Green Bay Packers (13-3-0)	Carolina Panthers (12-4-0)	Green Bay
1997	New York Giants (10-5-1)	Green Bay Packers (13-3-0)	San Francisco 49ers (13-3-0)	Green Bay
1998	Dallas Cowboys (10-6-0)	Minnesota Vikings (15-1-0)	Atlanta Falcons (14-2-0)	Atlanta
1999	Washington Redskins (10-6-0)	Tampa Bay Buccaneers (11-5-0)	St. Louis Rams (13-3-0)	St. Louis
2000	New York Giants (12-4-0)	Minnesota Vikings (11-5-0)	New Orleans Saints (10-6-0)	New York

1. Wild card. 2. Schedule reduced to 9 games from usual 16, with no standings kept in Eastern, Central, and Western Divisions, because of 57-day player strike. Washington Redskins won conference title and also had best regular-season record (8-1-0).

AMERICAN LEAGUE CHAMPIONS

Year	Eastern Division (W-L-T)	Western Division (W-L-T)	League champion, playoff results
1960	Houston Oilers (10-4-0)	Los Angeles Chargers (10-4-0)	Houston 24, Los Angeles 16
1961	Houston Oilers (10-3-1)	San Diego Chargers (12-2-0)	Houston 10, San Diego 3
1962	Houston Oilers (11-3-0)	Dallas Texans (11-3-0)	Dallas 20, Houston 17[1]
1963	Boston Patriots (8-6-1)[2]	San Diego Chargers (11-3-0)	San Diego 51, Boston 10
1964	Buffalo Bills (12-2-0)	San Diego Chargers (8-5-1)	Buffalo 20, San Diego 7
1965	Buffalo Bills (10-3-1)	San Diego Chargers (9-2-3)	Buffalo 23, San Diego 0
1966	Buffalo Bills (9-4-1)	Kansas City Chiefs (11-2-1)	Kansas City 31, Buffalo 7
1967	Houston Oilers (9-4-1)	Oakland Raiders (13-1-0)	Oakland 40, Houston 7
1968	New York Jets (11-3-0)	Oakland Raiders (12-2-0)[2]	New York 27, Oakland 23
1969	New York Jets (10-4-0)	Oakland Raiders (12-1-1)	Kansas City 17, Oakland 7[3]

1. Won at 2:45 of second sudden death overtime period. 2. Won divisional playoff. 3. Kansas City defeated New York, 13-6, and Oakland defeated Houston, 56-7, in interdivisional playoffs.

AMERICAN CONFERENCE CHAMPIONS

Year	Eastern Division	Central Division	Western Division	Champion
1970	Baltimore Colts (11-2-1)	Cincinnati Bengals (8-6-0)	Oakland Raiders (8-4-2)	Baltimore
1971	Miami Dolphins (10-3-1)	Cleveland Browns (9-5-0)	Kansas City Chiefs (10-3-1)	Miami
1972	Miami Dolphins (14-0-0)	Pittsburgh Steelers (11-3-0)	Oakland Raiders (10-3-1)	Miami
1973	Miami Dolphins (12-2-0)	Cincinnati Bengals (10-4-0)	Oakland Raiders (9-4-1)	Miami
1974	Miami Dolphins (11-3-0)	Pittsburgh Steelers (10-3-1)	Oakland Raiders (12-2-0)	Pittsburgh
1975	Baltimore Colts (10-4-0)	Pittsburgh Steelers (12-2-0)	Oakland Raiders (12-2-0)	Pittsburgh
1976	Baltimore Colts (11-3-0)	Pittsburgh Steelers (10-4-0)	Oakland Raiders (13-1-0)	Oakland
1977	Baltimore Colts (10-4-0)	Pittsburgh Steelers (9-5-0)	Denver Broncos (12-2-0)	Denver
1978	New England Patriots (11-5-0)	Pittsburgh Steelers (14-2-0)	Denver Broncos (10-6-0)	Pittsburgh
1979	Miami Dolphins (10-6-0)	Pittsburgh Steelers (12-4-0)	San Diego Chargers (12-4-0)	Pittsburgh
1980	Buffalo Bills (11-5-0)	Cleveland Browns (11-5-0)	San Diego Chargers (11-5-0)	Oakland[1]
1981	Miami Dolphins (11-4-1)	Cincinnati Bengals (12-4-0)	San Diego Chargers (10-6-0)	Cincinnati
1982[2]	Miami Dolphins won the conference title, but the Los Angeles Raiders had best regular-season record (8-1-0).			
1983	Miami Dolphins (12-4-0)	Pittsburgh Steelers (10-6-0)	Los Angeles Raiders (12-4-0)	Los Angeles
1984	Miami Dolphins (14-2-0)	Pittsburgh Steelers (9-7-0)	Denver Broncos (13-3-0)	Miami
1985	Miami Dolphins (12-4-0)	Cleveland Browns (8-8)	Los Angeles Raiders (12-4-0)	New England[1]
1986	New England Patriots (11-5-0)	Cleveland Browns (12-4-0)	Denver Broncos (11-5-0)	Denver
1987	Indianapolis Colts (9-6-0)	Cleveland Browns (10-5-0)	Denver Broncos (10-4-1)	Denver
1988	Buffalo Bills (12-4-0)	Cincinnati Bengals (12-4-0)	Seattle Seahawks (9-7-0)	Cincinnati
1989	Buffalo Bills (9-7-0)	Cleveland Browns (9-6-1)	Denver Broncos (11-5-0)	Denver
1990	Buffalo Bills (13-3-0)	Cincinnati Bengals (9-7-0)	Los Angeles Raiders (12-4-0)	Buffalo
1991	Buffalo Bills (13-3-0)	Houston Oilers (11-5-0)	Denver Broncos (12-4-0)	Buffalo
1992	Miami Dolphins (11-5-0)	Pittsburgh Steelers (11-5-0)	San Diego Chargers (11-5-0)	Buffalo[1]
1993	Buffalo Bills (12-4-0)	Houston Oilers (12-4-0)	Kansas City Chiefs (11-5-0)	Buffalo
1994	Miami Dolphins (10-6-0)	Pittsburgh Steelers (12-4-0)	San Diego Chargers (11-5-0)	San Diego
1995	Buffalo Bills (10-6-0)	Pittsburgh Steelers (11-5-0)	Kansas City Chiefs (13-3-0)	Pittsburgh
1996	New England Patriots (11-5-0)	Pittsburgh Steelers (10-6-0)	Denver Broncos (13-3-0)	New England
1997	New England Patriots (10-6-0)	Pittsburgh Steelers (11-5-0)	Kansas City Chiefs (13-3-0)	Denver[1]
1998	New York Jets (12-4-0)	Jacksonville Jaguars (11-5-0)	Denver Broncos (14-2-0)	Denver
1999	Indianapolis Colts (13-3-0)	Jacksonville Jaguars (14-2-0)	Seattle Seahawks (9-7-0)	Tennessee[1]
2000	Miami Dolphins (11-5-0)	Tennessee Titans (13-3-0)	Oakland Raiders (12-4-0)	Baltimore[1]

1. Wild card. 2. Schedule reduced to 9 games from usual 16, with no standings kept in Eastern, Central, and Western Divisions, because of 57-day player strike.

PRO FOOTBALL HALL OF FAME
(National Football Museum, Canton, Ohio)

Teams named are those with which player is best identified; figures in parentheses indicate number of playing seasons.

Adderley, Herb, defensive back, Packers, Cowboys (12)	1961–72
Alworth, Lance, wide receiver, Chargers, Cowboys (12)	1961–72
Atkins, Doug, defensive end, Browns, Bears, Saints (17)	1953–69
Badgro, Morris, end, N.Y. Yankees, Giants, Brooklyn Dodgers (8)	1927, 1930–36
Barney, Lem, defensive back, Lions (11)	1967–78
Battles, Cliff, back, Redskins (6)	1932–37
Baugh, Sammy, quarterback, Redskins (16)	1936–52
Bednarik, Chuck, center-lineback, Eagles (14)	1949–62
Bell, Bert, NFL founder, Eagles and Steelers, NFL Commissioner	1946–59
Bell, Bobby, linebacker, Chiefs (12)	1963–74
Berry, Raymond, end, Colts (13)	1955–67
Bidwell, Charles W., owner, Chicago Cardinals	1933–47
Biletnikoff, Fred, wide receiver, Raiders (14)	1965–78
Blanda, George, quarterback-kicker, Bears, Oilers, Raiders (27)	1949–75
Blount, Mel, cornerback, Pittsburgh Steelers (14)	1970–83
Bradshaw, Terry, quarterback, Pittsburgh Steelers (14)	1970–83
Brown, Jim, fullback, Browns (9)	1957–65
Brown, Paul E., coach, Browns (1946–62), Bengals (1968–75)	1946–75
Brown, Roosevelt, tackle, Giants (13)	1953–65
Brown, Willie, cornerback, Broncos, Raiders (16)	1963–78
Buchanan, Buck, tackle, Chiefs (11)	1963–73
Buoniconti, Nick, linebacker, Patriots, Dolphins (14)	1962–74, 1976
Butkus, Dick, linebacker, Bears (9)	1965–73
Campbell, Earl, running back, Oilers, Saints (8)	1978–85
Canadeo, Tony, back, Packers (11)	1941–52
Carr, Joe, NFL president (18)	1921–39
Chamberlin, Guy, end, 4 teams (9)	1919–27
Christiansen, Jack, defensive back, Lions (8)	1951–58
Clark, Earl (Dutch), quarterback, Spartans, Lions (7)	1931–38
Connor, George, tackle, linebacker, Bears (8)	1948–55
Conzelman, Jimmy, quarterback, 5 teams (10), owner, Detroit Panthers	1921–48
Creekmur, Lou, offensive tackle/guard, Lions (10)	1950–59
Csonka, Larry, back, Dolphins, Giants (11)	1968–79
Davis, Al, owner, Raiders, coach, general manager	1963–
Davis, Willie, defensive end, Packers (10)	1960–69
Dawson, Len, quarterback, Steelers, Browns, Texans, Chiefs (19)	1957–75
Dickerson, Eric, running back, Rams, Colts, Raiders, Falcons (11)	1983–93
Dierdorf, Dan, tackle/center, Cardinals (13)	1971–83
Ditka, Mike, tight end, Bears, Eagles, Cowboys (12)	1961–72
Donovan, Art, defensive tackle, Colts (12)	1950–61
Dorsett, Tony, running back, Cowboys, Broncos (12)	1977–88
Driscoll, John (Paddy), quarterback, Cards, Bears (11)	1919–29
Dudley, Bill, back, Steelers, Lions, Redskins (9)	1942–53
Edwards, Albert Glen (Turk), tackle, Redskins (9)	1932–40
Ewbank, Weeb, coach, Colts, Jets (20)	1954–73
Fears, Tom, end, Rams (9); coach, Saints	1948–56
Finks, Jim, administrator/general manager, Vikings, Bears, Saints	1964–93
Flaherty, Ray, end, Yankees, Giants (9); coach, Redskins, Yankees (14)	1928–49
Ford, Len, end, defensive end, Browns, Packers (11)	1948–58
Fouts, Dan, quarterback, Chargers (15)	1973–87
Fortmann, Daniel J., guard, Bears (8)	1936–43
Gatski, Frank, offensive lineman, Browns (12)	1946–57
George, Bill, linebacker, Bears, Rams (15)	1952–66
Gibbs, Joe, coach, Redskins (11)	1981–92
Gifford, Frank, back, Giants (12)	1952–64
Gillman, Sid, coach, Rams, Chargers, Oilers (18)	1955–70, 73–74
Graham, Otto, quarterback, Browns (10)	1946–55
Grange, Harold (Red), back, Bears, Yankees (9)	1925–34
Grant, Bud, coach, Vikings (18)	1967–85
Greene, Joe, defensive tackle, Steelers (13)	1968–81

NFL INDIVIDUAL LIFETIME, SEASON, AND GAME RECORDS

(American Football League records were incorporated into NFL records after merger of the leagues.)

Players listed in boldface were active during the 2000 season. The NFL does not recognize records from the All-American Football Conference (AAFC) which existed from 1946 to 1949. The 49ers, Browns, and Colts merged with the NFL in 1949.

All-Time Leading Touchdown Scorers (Through 2000)

		Yrs	Rush	Rec	Ret	Total
1	Jerry Rice	16	10	176	1	187
2	Emmitt Smith	11	145	11	0	156
3	Marcus Allen	16	123	21	1	145
4	Jim Brown	9	106	20	0	126
5	Walter Payton	13	110	15	0	125
6	Cris Carter	14	0	123	1	124
7	John Riggins	14	104	12	0	116
8	Lenny Moore	12	63	48	2	113
9	Barry Sanders	10	99	10	0	109
10	Don Hutson	11	3	99	3	105
11	Steve Largent	14	1	100	0	101
12	Franco Harris	13	91	9	0	100
13	Eric Dickerson	11	90	6	0	96
14	Jim Taylor	10	83	10	0	93
15	Tony Dorsett	12	77	13	1	91
	Bobby Mitchell	11	18	65	8	91

All-Time Leading Receivers (Through 2000)

		Yrs	No	Yards	Avg	TD
1	Jerry Rice	16	1,281	19,247	15.0	176
2	Cris Carter	14	1,020	12,962	12.7	123
3	Andre Reed	16	951	13,198	13.9	87
4	Art Monk	16	940	12,721	13.5	68
5	Irving Fryar	17	851	12,785	15.0	84
6	Tim Brown	13	846	12,072	14.3	86
7	Steve Largent	14	819	13,089	16.0	100
8	Henry Ellard	16	814	13,777	16.9	65
9	James Lofton	16	764	14,004	18.3	75
10	Charlie Joiner	18	750	12,146	16.2	65
	Michael Irvin	12	750	11,904	15.9	65
12	Andre Rison	12	743	10,205	13.7	84
13	Gary Clark	11	699	10,856	15.5	65
14	Larry Centers	11	685	5,683	8.3	25
15	Herman Moore	10	666	9,098	13.7	62

All-Time Leading Passers (Minimum 1,500 attempts. Through 2000)

		Yrs	Att	Cmp	Cmp%	Yards	Avg Gain	TD	TD%	Int	Int%	Rating
1	Steve Young	15	4,149	2,667	64.36	33,124	7.98	232	5.6	107	2.6	96.8
2	Joe Montana	15	5,391	3,409	63.2	40,551	7.52	273	5.1	139	2.6	92.3
3	Dan Marino	17	8,358	4,967	59.4	61,361	7.34	420	5.0	252	3.0	86.4
4	Brett Favre	10	4,932	2,997	60.8	34,706	7.04	255	5.2	157	3.2	86.0
5	Peyton Manning	3	1,679	1,014	60.4	12,287	7.32	85	5.1	58	3.5	85.4
6	Mark Brunell	7	2,672	1,608	60.2	19,212	7.19	106	4.0	66	2.5	85.1
7	Brad Johnson	9	1,821	1,126	61.8	12,973	7.12	79	4.3	57	3.1	84.7
8	Jim Kelly	11	4,779	2,874	60.1	35,467	7.42	237	5.0	175	3.7	84.4
9	Roger Staubach	11	2,958	1,685	57.0	22,700	7.67	153	5.2	109	3.7	83.4
10	Neil Lomax	8	3,153	1,817	57.6	22,771	7.22	136	4.3	90	2.9	82.7
11	Sonny Jurgensen	18	4,262	2,433	57.1	32,224	7.56	255	6.0	189	4.4	82.6
12	Len Dawson	19	3,741	2,136	57.1	28,711	7.67	239	6.4	183	4.9	82.5
13	Neil O'Donnell	11	3,121	1,802	57.7	20,938	6.71	116	3.7	65	2.1	81.8
14	Ken Anderson	16	4,475	2,654	59.3	32,838	7.34	197	4.4	160	3.6	81.8
15	Bernie Kosar	12	3,365	1,994	59.3	23,301	6.92	124	3.7	87	2.6	81.8

Note: If the NFL recognized records from the AAFC, **Otto Graham** would rank 4th (after Favre) with the following stats: 10 Yrs; 2,626 Att; 1,464 Comp; 55.8 Comp Pct; 23,584 Yards; 8.98 Avg Gain; 174 TD; 6.6 TD Pct; 135 Int; 5.1 Int Pct; and 86.6 Rating Pts.

All-Time Leading Scorers (Through 2000)

		Yrs	TD	FG	PAT	Total
1	Gary Anderson	19	0	461	676	2,059
2	George Blanda	26	9	335	943	2,002
3	Morten Andersen	19	0	441	615	1,938
4	Norm Johnson	18	0	366	638	1,736
5	Nick Lowery	18	0	383	562	1,711
6	Jan Stenerud	19	0	373	580	1,699
7	Eddie Murray	19	0	352	538	1,594
8	Al Del Greco	17	0	347	543	1,584
9	Pat Leahy	18	0	304	558	1,470
10	Jim Turner	16	1	304	521	1,439
11	Matt Bahr	17	0	300	522	1,422
12	Mark Moseley	16	0	300	482	1,382
13	Jim Bakken	17	0	282	534	1,380
14	Fred Cox	15	0	282	519	1,365
15	Lou Groza	17	1	234	641	1,349

All-Time Leading Rushers (Through 2000)

		Yrs	Car	Yards	Avg	TD
1	Walter Payton	13	3,838	16,726	4.4	110
2	Barry Sanders	10	3,062	15,269	5.0	99
3	Emmitt Smith	11	3,537	15,166	4.3	145
4	Eric Dickerson	11	2,996	13,259	4.4	90
5	Tony Dorsett	12	2,936	12,739	4.3	77
6	Jim Brown	9	2,359	12,312	5.2	106
7	Marcus Allen	16	3,022	12,243	4.1	123
8	Franco Harris	13	2,949	12,120	4.1	91
9	Thurman Thomas	13	2,877	12,074	4.2	65
10	John Riggins	14	2,916	11,352	3.9	104
11	O.J. Simpson	11	2,404	11,236	4.7	61
12	Ricky Watters	9	2,550	10,325	4.1	77
13	Ottis Anderson	14	2,562	10,273	4.0	81
14	Jerome Bettis	8	2,461	9,804	4.0	49
15	Earl Campbell	8	2,187	9,407	4.3	74

Scoring

Most points scored, lifetime—2,059, Gary Anderson, Pittsburgh, 1982–94; Philadelphia, 1995–96; San Francisco, 1997; Minnesota, 1998–2000.

Most points, season—176, Paul Hornung, Green Bay, 1960 (15 td, 41 pat, 15 fg).

Most points, game—40, Ernie Nevers, Chicago Cardinals, 1929 (6 td, 4 pat).

Most touchdowns, lifetime—187, Jerry Rice, San Francisco, 1985–2000.

Most touchdowns, season—26, Marshall Faulk, St. Louis, 2000.

Most points after touchdown, lifetime—943, George Blanda, Chicago Bears, 1949–58; Baltimore, 1950; Houston, 1960–66; Oakland, 1967–75.

Most field goals, lifetime—461, Gary Anderson, Pittsburgh, 1982–94; Philadelphia, 1995–96; San Francisco, 1997; Minnesota, 1998–2000.

Most field goals, season—39, Olindo Mare, Miami, 1999.

Most field goals, game—7, Jim Bakken, St. Louis, 1967; Rich Karlis, Minnesota, 1989; and Chris Boniol, Dallas, 1996.

Longest field goal—63 yards, Tom Dempsey, New Orleans, 1970; Jason Elam, Denver, 1998.

Rushing

Most yards gained, lifetime—16,726, Walter Payton, Chicago Bears, 1975–87.

Most yards gained, season—2,105, Eric Dickerson, Los Angeles, 1984.

Most yards gained, game—278, Corey Dillon, Cincinnati, 2000.

Most touchdowns, lifetime—145, Emmitt Smith, Dallas, 1990–2000.

Most touchdowns, season—25, Emmitt Smith, Dallas, 1995.

Most touchdowns, game—6, Ernie Nevers, Chicago Cardinals, 1929.

Longest run from scrimmage—99 yards, Tony Dorsett, Dallas, 1983.

Receiving

Most pass receptions, lifetime—1,281, Jerry Rice, San Francisco, 1985–2000.

Most pass receptions, season—123, Herman Moore, Detroit, 1995.

Most pass receptions, game—20, Terrell Owens, San Francisco, 2000.

Most yards gained, pass receptions, lifetime—19,247, Jerry Rice, San Francisco, 1985–2000.

Most yards gained, receptions, season—1,848, Jerry Rice, San Francisco, 1995.

Most yards gained, receptions, game—336, Flipper Anderson, Los Angeles Rams, 1989.

Most touchdown receptions, lifetime—176, Jerry Rice, San Francisco, 1985–2000.

Most touchdown pass receptions, season—22, Jerry Rice, San Francisco, 1987.

Most touchdown pass receptions, game—5, Bob Shaw, Chicago Cards, 1950; Kellen Winslow, San Diego, 1981; Jerry Rice, San Francisco, 1990.

Interceptions

Most pass interceptions, lifetime—81, Paul Krause, Washington, 1964-67; Minnesota, 1968–79.

Most pass interceptions, season—14, Richard (Night Train) Lane, Detroit, 1952.

Most pass interceptions, game—4, by 17 players.

Longest pass interception return—104 yards, James Willis, Philadelphia, 1996.

Kicking

Highest average punting, lifetime—45.1 yards, Sammy Baugh, Washington, 1937–52.

Longest punt return—103 yards, Robert Bailey, L.A. Rams, 1994.

Longest kick-off return—106 yards, Roy Green, St. Louis, 1979; Al Carmichael, Green Bay, 1956; Noland Smith, Kansas City, 1967.

Passing

Most touchdown passes, lifetime—420, Dan Marino, Miami, 1983–99.

Most touchdown passes, season—48, Dan Marino, Miami, 1984.

Most touchdown passes, game—7, Sid Luckman, Chicago Bears, 1943; Adrian Burk, Philadelphia, 1954; George Blanda, Houston, 1961; Y. A. Tittle, N.Y. Giants, 1962; Joe Kapp, Minnesota, 1969.

Longest pass completion—99 yards, Frank Filchock (to Andy Farkas), Washington, 1939; George Izo (to Bob Mitchell), Washington, 1963; Karl Sweetan (to Pat Studstill), Detroit, 1966; Sonny Jurgensen (to Gerry Allen), Washington, 1968; Jim Plunkett (to Cliff Branch) L.A. Raiders, 1983; Ron Jaworski (to Mike Quick), Philadelphia, 1985; Stan Humphries (to Tony Martin), San Diego, 1994; Brett Favre (to Robert Brooks), Green Bay, 1995.

Most passes completed, lifetime—4,967, Dan Marino, Miami, 1983–99.

Most passes completed, season—404, Warren Moon, 1991.

Most passes completed, game—45, Drew Bledsoe, New England, 1994.

Most yards gained, lifetime—61,361, Dan Marino, Miami, 1983–99.

Most yards gained, season—5,084, Dan Marino, Miami, 1984.

Most yards gained, game—554, Norm Van Brocklin, Los Angeles, 1951.

NFL REALIGNMENT SET FOR 2002

In May 2001, NFL commissioner Paul Tagliabue announced the division realignment of the league. With the addition of the Houston Texans (formerly the Oilers) in the 2002 season, the National and American Conferences will each have four divisions with four teams per division. Scheduling has also been changed and every team will meet every other team at least once every four years.

The 2002 divisions are:

NFC East: Dallas, New York Giants, Philadelphia, Washington.

NFC South: Atlanta, Carolina, New Orleans, Tampa Bay.

NFC North: Chicago, Detroit, Green Bay, Minnesota.

NFC West: Arizona, St. Louis, San Francisco, Seattle.

AFC East: Buffalo, Miami, New England, New York Jets.

AFC South: Houston, Indianapolis, Jacksonville, Tennessee.

AFC North: Baltimore, Cincinnati, Cleveland, Pittsburgh.

AFC West: Denver, Kansas City, Oakland, San Diego.

Basketball

Basketball may be the one sport whose exact origin is definitely known. In the winter of 1891–92, Dr. James Naismith, an instructor in the YMCA. Training College (now Springfield College) at Springfield, Mass., deliberately invented the game of basketball in order to provide indoor exercise and competition for the students between the closing of the football season and the opening of the baseball season. He affixed peach baskets overhead on the walls at opposite ends of the gymnasium and organized teams to play his new game in which the pur-

pose was to toss an association (soccer) ball into one basket and prevent the opponents from tossing the ball into the other basket. Because Dr. Naismith had eighteen available players when he invented the game, the first rule was: "There shall be nine players on each side." Later the number of players became optional, depending upon the size of the available court, but the five-player standard was adopted when the game spread over the country. U.S. soldiers brought basketball to Europe in World War I, and it soon became a worldwide sport.

College Basketball

NCAA CHAMPIONS

1938	Temple	1953	Indiana	1974	No. Carolina State	1989	Michigan
1939	Oregon	1954	La Salle	1975	UCLA	1990	UNLV
1940	Indiana & USC	1955	San Francisco	1976	Indiana	1991	Duke
1941	Wisconsin	1956	San Francisco	1977	Marquette	1992	Duke
1942	Stanford	1957	North Carolina	1978	Kentucky	1993	North Carolina
1943	Wyoming	1958	Kentucky	1979	Michigan State	1994	Arkansas
1944	Utah	1959	California	1980	Louisville	1995	UCLA
1945	Oklahoma A & M	1960	Ohio State	1981	Indiana	1996	Kentucky
1946	Oklahoma A & M	1961	Cincinnati	1982	North Carolina	1997	Arizona
1947	Holy Cross	1962	Cincinnati	1983	North Carolina State	1998	Kentucky
1948	Kentucky	1963	Loyola (Chicago)	1984	Georgetown	1999	Connecticut
1949	Kentucky	1964	UCLA	1985	Villanova	2000	Michigan State
1950	C.C.N.Y.	1965	UCLA	1986	Louisville	2001	Duke
1951	Kentucky	1966	Texas Western	1987	Indiana		
1952	Kansas	1967–73	UCLA	1988	Kansas		

NATIONAL INVITATION TOURNAMENT (NIT) CHAMPIONS

1938	Temple	1955	Duquesne	1971	North Carolina	1987	So. Mississippi
1939	Long Island U.	1956	Louisville	1972	Maryland	1988	Connecticut
1940	Colorado	1957	Bradley	1973	Virginia Tech	1989	St. John's (N.Y.C.)
1941	Long Island U.	1958	Xavier (Cincinnati)	1974	Purdue	1990	Vanderbilt
1942	West Virginia	1959	St. John's (N.Y.C.)	1975	Princeton	1991	Stanford
1943–44	St. John's (N.Y.C.)	1960	Bradley	1976	Kentucky	1992	Virginia
1945	DePaul	1961	Providence	1977	St. Bonaventure	1993	Minnesota
1946	Kentucky	1962	Dayton	1978	Texas	1994	Villanova
1947	Utah	1963	Providence	1979	Indiana	1995	Virginia Tech
1948	St. Louis	1964	Bradley	1980	Virginia	1996	Nebraska
1949	San Francisco	1965	St. John's (N.Y.C.)	1981	Tulsa	1997	Michigan
1950	C.C.N.Y.	1966	Brigham Young	1982	Bradley	1998	Minnesota
1951	Brigham Young	1967	So. Illinois	1983	Fresno State	1999	California
1952	La Salle	1968	Dayton	1984	Michigan	2000	Wake Forest
1953	Seton Hall	1969	Temple	1985	UCLA	2001	Tulsa
1954	Holy Cross	1970	Marquette	1986	Ohio State		

NCAA DIVISION I INDIVIDUAL CAREER RECORDS

SCORING—TOTAL POINTS

	Yrs	Last	Gm	Pts
Pete Maravich, LSU	3	1970	83	3,667
Freeman Williams, Port. St.	4	1978	106	3,249
Lionel Simmons, La Salle	4	1990	131	3,217
Alphonso Ford, Miss. Val. St.	4	1993	109	3,165
Harry Kelly, Texas Southern	4	1983	110	3,066
Hersey Hawkins, Bradley	4	1988	125	3,008
Oscar Robertson, Cincinnati	3	1960	88	2,973
Danny Manning, Kansas	4	1988	147	2,951
Alfredrick Hughes, Loyola-Ill.	4	1985	120	2,914
Elvin Hayes, Houston	3	1968	93	2,884

SCORING—AVERAGE POINTS

	Yrs	Last	Pts	Avg
Pete Maravich, LSU	3	1970	3,667	44.2
Austin Carr, Notre Dame	3	1971	2,560	34.6
Oscar Robertson, Cinn.	3	1960	2,973	33.8
Calvin Murphy, Niagara	3	1970	2,548	33.1
Dwight Lamar, SW La.	2	1973	1,862	32.7
Frank Selvy, Furman	4	1954	2,538	32.5
Rick Mount, Purdue	3	1970	2,323	32.3
Darrell Floyd, Furman	3	1956	2,281	32.1
Nick Werkman, Seton Hall	3	1964	2,273	32.0
Willie Humes, Idaho St.	2	1971	1,510	31.5

REBOUNDS—TOTAL, SINCE 1973

	Yrs	Last	Gm	No
Tim Duncan, Wake Forest	4	1997	128	1,570
Derrick Coleman, Syracuse	4	1990	143	1,537
Malik Rose, Drexel	4	1996	120	1,514
Ralph Sampson, Virginia	4	1983	132	1,511
Pete Padgett, Nevada-Reno	4	1976	104	1,464
Lionel Simmons, La Salle	4	1990	131	1,429
Anthony Bonner, St. Louis	4	1990	133	1,424
Tyrone Hill, Xavier-Ohio	4	1990	126	1,380
Popeye Jones, Murray St.	4	1992	123	1,374
Michael Brooks, La Salle	4	1980	114	1,372

ASSISTS—TOTAL

	Yrs	Last	Gm	No
Bobby Hurley, Duke	4	1993	140	1,076
Chris Corchiani, N.C. State	4	1991	124	1,038
Ed Cota, N. Carolina	4	2000	138	1,030
Keith Jennings, E. Tenn. St.	4	1991	127	983
Sherman Douglas, Syracuse	4	1989	138	960
Tony Miller, Marquette	4	1995	123	956
Greg Anthony, Portland/UNLV	4	1991	138	950
Doug Gottlieb, ND/Okla St.	4	2000	124	947
Gary Payton, Oregon St.	4	1990	120	938
Orlando Smart, San Fran.	4	1994	116	902

BLOCKED SHOTS—AVERAGE

	Yrs	Last	No	Avg
Keith Closs, Cen. Conn. St.	2	1996	317	5.87
Adonal Foyle, Colgate	3	1997	492	5.66
David Robinson, Navy	2	1987	351	5.24
Shaquille O'Neal, LSU	3	1992	412	4.58
Troy Murphy, Notre Dame	3	2001	425	4.52

Note: minimum 225 blocked shots.

STEALS—AVERAGE

	Yrs	Last	No	Avg
Mookie Blaylock, Oklahoma	2	1989	281	3.80
Ronn McMahon, Eastern Wash	3	1990	225	3.52
Eric Murdock, Providence	4	1991	376	3.21
Van Usher, Tennessee Tech	3	1992	270	3.18
Pepe Sanchez, Temple	4	2000	365	3.15

Note: minimum 225 steals.

NCAA DIVISION I SINGLE-GAME SCORING MARKS

	Year	Pts		Year	Pts
Kevin Bradshaw, US Int'l vs. Loyola-CA	1991	72	Anthony Roberts, Oral Rbts. vs. N.C. A.&T.	1977	66
Pete Maravich, LSU vs. Alabama	1970	69	Scott Haffner, Evansville vs. Dayton	1989	65
Calvin Murphy, Niagara vs. Syracuse	1969	68	Pete Maravich, LSU vs. Kentucky	1970	64
Jay Handlan, Wash. & Lee vs. Furman	1951	66	Johnny Neumann, Ole Miss vs. LSU	1971	63
Pete Maravich, LSU vs. Tulane	1969	66	Hersey Hawkins, Bradley vs. Detroit	1988	63

MEN'S NCAA BASKETBALL CHAMPIONSHIPS, 2001

Division I

First Round—East
Duke 95, Monmouth 52
Georgia 68, Missouri 70
Ohio State 68, Utah State 77 (OT)
UCLA 61, Hofstra 48
Southern California 69, Oklahoma State 54
Boston College 68, Southern Utah 65
Iowa 69, Creighton 56
Kentucky 72, Holy Cross 68

First Round—West
Stanford 89, UNC Greensboro 60
Georgia Tech 62, St. Joseph's 66
Cincinnati 84, Brigham Young 59
Indiana 73, Kent State 77
Wisconsin 49, Georgia State 50
Maryland 83, George Mason 80
Arkansas 61, Georgetown 63
Iowa State 57, Hampton 58

First Round—Midwest
Illinois 96, Northwestern State 54
Tennessee 63, Charlotte 70
Syracuse 79, Hawaii 69
Kansas 99, Cal. State Northridge 75
Notre Dame 83, Xavier 71
Mississippi 72, Iona 70
Wake Forest 63, Butler 79
Arizona 101, Eastern Illinois 76

First Round—South
Michigan State 69, Alabama State 35
California 70, Fresno State 82
Virginia 85, Gonzaga 86
Oklahoma 68, Indiana State 70 (OT)
Texas 65, Temple 79
Florida 69, Western Kentucky 56
Penn State 69, Providence 59
North Carolina 70, Princeton 48

Second Round—East
Duke 94, Missouri 81
Utah State 50, UCLA 75
Southern California 74, Boston College 71
Iowa 79, Kentucky 92

Second Round—West
Stanford 90, St. Joseph's 83
Cincinnati 66, Kent State 43
Georgia State 60, Maryland 79
Georgetown 76, Hampton 57

Second Round—Midwest
Illinois 79, Charlotte 61
Syracuse 58, Kansas 87
Notre Dame 56, Mississippi 59
Butler 52, Arizona 73

Second Round—South
Michigan State 81, Fresno State 65
Gonzaga 85, Indiana State 68
Temple 75, Florida 54
Penn State 82, North Carolina 74

Third Round—East
Duke 76, UCLA 63
Southern California 80, Kentucky 76

Third Round—West
Stanford 78, Cincinnati 65
Maryland 76, Georgetown 66

Third Round—Midwest
Illinois 80, Kansas 64
Mississippi 56, Arizona 66

Third Round—South
Michigan State 77, Gonzaga 62
Temple 84, Penn State 72

Regional Finals
East—Duke 79, Southern California 69
West—Stanford 73, Maryland 87
Midwest—Illinois 81, Arizona 87
South—Temple 62, Michigan State 69

National Semifinals
(March 31, 2001, Minneapolis, Minn.)
Duke 95, Maryland 84
Arizona 80, Michigan State 61

National Final
(April 2, 2001, Minneapolis, Minn.)
Duke 82, Arizona 72

Division II

Semifinals
Kentucky Wesleyan 85, Tampa 84 (OT)
Washburn 96, Western Washington 90

Championship
Kentucky Wesleyan 72, Washburn 63

LEADING NCAA DIVISION I MEN, 2000–2001

SCORING

	TFG	3FG	FT	Pts	Avg
Ronnie McCollum, Centenary	244	85	214	787	29.1
Kyle Hill, Eastern Ill.	250	86	151	737	23.8
DeWayne Jefferson, Miss. Valley State	216	107	98	637	23.6
Tarise Bryson, Illinois State	208	62	207	685	22.8
Henry Domercant, Eastern Ill.	256	79	115	706	22.8
Rashad Phillips, Detroit	232	136	185	785	22.4
Brandon Wolfram, U.T.-El Paso	251	6	206	714	22.3
Rasual Butler, La Salle	231	97	82	641	22.1
Brandon Armstrong, Pepperdine	240	76	128	684	22.1
Marvin O'Connor, St. Joseph	240	99	127	706	22.1

REBOUNDING

	Gm	No	Avg
Chris Marcus, Western Kentucky	31	374	12.1
Reggie Evans, Iowa	35	416	11.9
J. R. VanHoose, Marshall	27	299	11.1
David West, Xavier	29	316	10.9
Eddie Griffin, Seton Hall	30	323	10.8
Jeremy Jefferson, Ark.-Pine Bluffs	23	246	10.7
Brian Carroll, Loyola (Md.)	27	286	10.6
Eric Mann, Va. Military Inst.	28	294	10.5
Joe Breakenridge, Northern Iowa	28	294	10.5
Alvin Jones, Georgia Tech	30	312	10.4

ASSISTS

	Gm	No	Avg
Markus Carr, Cal. St. Northridge	32	286	8.9
Omar Cook, St. John's (N.Y.)	29	252	8.7
Sean Kennedy, Marist	27	219	8.1
Tito Maddox, Fresno State	25	200	8.0
Ashley Robinson, Miss. Valley State	27	201	7.4
Brandon Pardon, Bowling Green	29	204	7.0
Jeremy Stanton, Evansville	26	181	7.0
Kirk Hinrich, Kansas	33	229	6.9
Steve Blake, Maryland	36	248	6.9
Allen Griffin, Syracuse	34	220	6.5

WOMEN'S NCAA CHAMPIONSHIPS, 2001

Division I
First Round—East
Connecticut 101, Long Island 29
Maryland 66, Colorado State 83
Villanova 66, Drake 58
North Carolina State 76, Delaware 57
Texas Christian 77, Penn State 75
Louisiana Tech. 84, Georgia State 48
Wisconsin 68, Missouri 71
Georgia 77, Liberty 48
First Round—Mideast
Tennessee 80, Austin Peay 38
Texas 64, St. Mary's 68
Clemson 54, Chattanooga 49
Xavier 80, Louisville 52
Louisiana State 83, Arizona State 66
Purdue 75, U.C. Santa Barbara 62
Virginia Tech. 77, Denver 57
Texas Tech 100, Pennsylvania 57
First Round—Midwest
Notre Dame 98, Alcorn State 49
Michigan 81, Virginia 71
Utah 79, Fairfield 57
Iowa 89, Oregon 82
Colorado 98, Siena 78
Vanderbilt 83, Idaho State 57
Florida State 72, Tulane 70
Iowa State 100, Howard 61

First Round—West
Duke 96, Wisc.-Milwaukee 63
Baylor 59, Arkansas 68
Southwest Mo. State 89, Toledo 71
Rutgers 80, Stephen F. Austin 43
Washington 67, Old Dominion 65
Florida 84, Holy Cross 52
George Washington 51, Stanford 76
Oklahoma 70, Oral Roberts 64
Second Round—East
Connecticut 89, Colorado State 44
Villanova 64, North Carolina State 68
Texas Christian 59, Louisiana Tech 59
Missouri 78, Georgia 65
Second Round—Mideast
Tennessee 92, St. Mary's 75
Clemson 62, Xavier 77
Louisiana State 70, Purdue 73
Virginia Tech 52, Texas Tech 73
Second Round—Midwest
Notre Dame 88, Michigan 54
Utah 78, Iowa 69
Colorado 59, Vanderbilt 65
Florida State 70, Iowa State 85
Second Round—West
Duke 75, Arkansas 54
Southwest Mo. State 60, Rutgers 53
Washington 86, Florida 75
Stanford 50, Oklahoma 67
Third Round—East
Connecticut 72, North Carolina State 58
Louisiana Tech 78, Missouri 67

Third Round—Mideast
Tennessee 65, Xavier 80
Purdue 74, Texas Tech 72
Third Round—Midwest
Notre Dame 69, Utah 54
Vanderbilt 84, Iowa State 65
Third Round—West
Duke 71, Southwest Mo. State 81
Washington 84, Oklahoma 67
Regional Finals
East—Connecticut 67, Louisiana Tech 48
Mideast—Xavier 78, Purdue 88
Midwest—Notre Dame 72, Vanderbilt 64
West—Southwest Mo. State 104, Washington 67
National Semifinals
(March 30, 2001, St. Louis, Mo.)
Notre Dame 90, Connecticut 75
Purdue 81, Southwest Mo. State 64
National Championship
(April 1, 2001, St. Louis, Mo.)
Notre Dame 68, Purdue 66

Division II
Semifinals
Shippensburg 67, North Dakota 76
Cal Poly Pomona 80, Columbus State 72
Championship
Cal Poly Pomona 87, North Dakota 80

LEADING NCAA DIVISION I WOMEN, 2000–2001

SCORING

	TFG	3FG	FT	Pts	Avg
Jackie Stiles, Southwest Mo. State	365	65	267	1,062	30.3
Deanna Jackson, Univ. Ala.–Birmingham	275	47	180	777	25.1
Janet Holt, Tennessee Tech	236	17	249	738	24.6
LaToya Thomas, Mississippi	276	5	195	752	24.3
Susan Moran, St. Joseph's	230	0	173	633	22.6
Natalie Powers, Western Ky.	225	68	218	736	22.3
Brooke Armistead, Austin Peay	244	42	155	685	22.1
Sheila Lambert, Baylor	242	30	148	662	22.1
Jaynetta Saunders, Texas A&M	240	31	100	611	21.8
Diana Caramanico, Pennsylvania	230	8	139	607	21.7

REBOUNDING

	Gm	No	Avg
Andrea Gardner, Howard	31	439	14.2
Angela Buckner, Wichita State	27	341	12.6
Malveata Johnson, N.C. A&T	29	356	12.3
Schuye LaRue, Virginia	32	379	11.8
Danielle Crockrom, Baylor	30	347	11.6
Deanna Jackson, Univ. Ala.–Birmingham	31	358	11.5
LaQuanda Barksdale, North Carolina	29	334	11.5
Anne Tierney, Lehigh	30	335	11.2
Brenda Abakwue, Sam Houston State	27	297	11.0
Sheena Johnson, Univ. of Texas–Arlington	27	292	10.8

ASSISTS

	Gm	No	Avg
Natasha Pointer, Rutgers	31	257	8.3
Reetta Piipari, Xavier	34	282	8.3
Angela Zampella, St. Joseph's	27	220	8.1
Jamie Lewis, Ohio State	33	257	7.8
Sara Nord, Louisville	29	222	7.7
Reshea Bristol, Arizona	32	242	7.6
Michele Koclanes, Richmond	28	208	7.4
Stacey Dales, Oklahoma	34	248	7.3
Toccara Williams, Texas A&M	28	196	7.0
Misty Garrett, Tennessee Tech	30	209	7.0

OTHER TOURNAMENTS, 2000–2001

MEN

NIT—Tulsa 79, Alabama 60
NAIA Div. I—Faulkner (Ala.) 63, Science and Arts (Okla.) 59
NAIA Div. II—Northwestern 82, MidAmerica Nazarene 78

WOMEN

NIT—Ohio State 62, New Mexico 61
NAIA Div. I—Oklahoma City 69, Auburn Montgomery (Ala.) 52
NAIA Div. II—Northwestern College (Iowa) 77, Albertson College (Idaho) 50

Professional Basketball

NATIONAL BASKETBALL ASSOCIATION CHAMPIONS

The National Basketball Association was originally the Basketball Association of America. It took its current name in 1949 when it merged with the National Basketball League.

Year	Eastern Conference	Western Conference	Winner (Series)
1947	Philadelphia Warriors	Chicago Stags	Philadelphia Warriors (4–1)
1948	Philadelphia Warriors	Baltimore Bullets	Baltimore Bullets (4–2)
1949	Washington Capitols	Minneapolis Lakers	Minneapolis Lakers (4–2)
1950	Syracuse Nationals	Minneapolis Lakers	Minneapolis Lakers (4–2)
1951	New York Knickerbockers	Rochester Royals	Rochester Royals (4–3)
1952	New York Knickerbockers	Minneapolis Lakers	Minneapolis Lakers (4–3)
1953	New York Knickerbockers	Minneapolis Lakers	Minneapolis Lakers (4–1)
1954	Syracuse Nationals	Minneapolis Lakers	Minneapolis Lakers (4–3)
1955	Syracuse Nationals	Ft. Wayne Pistons	Syracuse Nationals (4–3)
1956	Philadelphia Warriors	Ft. Wayne Pistons	Philadelphia Warriors (4–1)
1957	Boston Celtics	St. Louis Hawks	Boston Celtics (4–3)
1958	Boston Celtics	St. Louis Hawks	St. Louis Hawks (4–2)
1959	Boston Celtics	Minneapolis Lakers	Boston Celtics (4–0)
1960	Boston Celtics	St. Louis Hawks	Boston Celtics (4–3)
1961	Boston Celtics	St. Louis Hawks	Boston Celtics (4–1)
1962	Boston Celtics	Los Angeles Lakers	Boston Celtics (4–3)
1963	Boston Celtics	Los Angeles Lakers	Boston Celtics (4–2)
1964	Boston Celtics	San Francisco Warriors	Boston Celtics (4–1)
1965	Boston Celtics	Los Angeles Lakers	Boston Celtics (4–1)
1966	Boston Celtics	Los Angeles Lakers	Boston Celtics (4–3)
1967	Philadelphia 76ers	SF Warriors	Philadelphia 76ers (4–2)
1968	Boston Celtics	Los Angeles Lakers	Boston Celtics (4–2)
1969	Boston Celtics	Los Angeles Lakers	Boston Celtics (4–3)
1970	New York Knickerbockers	Los Angeles Lakers	New York Knickerbockers (4–3)
1971	Baltimore Bullets	Milwaukee Bucks	Milwaukee Bucks (4–0)
1972	New York Knickerbockers	Los Angeles Lakers	Los Angeles Lakers (4–1)
1973	New York Knickerbockers	Los Angeles Lakers	New York Knickerbockers (4–1)
1974	Boston Celtics	Milwaukee Bucks	Boston Celtics (4–3)
1975	Washington Bullets	Golden State Warriors	Golden State Warriors (4–0)
1976	Boston Celtics	Phoenix Suns	Boston Celtics (4–2)
1977	Philadelphia 76ers	Portland Trail Blazers	Portland Trail Blazers (4–2)
1978	Washington Bullets	Seattle SuperSonics	Washington Bullets (4–3)
1979	Washington Bullets	Seattle SuperSonics	Seattle SuperSonics (4–1)
1980	Philadelphia 76ers	Los Angeles Lakers	Los Angeles Lakers (4–2)
1981	Boston Celtics	Houston Rockets	Boston Celtics (4–2)
1982	Philadelphia 76ers	Los Angeles Lakers	Los Angeles Lakers (4–2)
1983	Philadelphia 76ers	Los Angeles Lakers	Philadelphia 76ers (4–0)
1984	Boston Celtics	Los Angeles Lakers	Boston Celtics (4–3)
1985	Boston Celtics	Los Angeles Lakers	Los Angeles Lakers (4–2)
1986	Boston Celtics	Houston Rockets	Boston Celtics (4–2)
1987	Boston Celtics	Los Angeles Lakers	Los Angeles Lakers (4–2)

Year	Eastern Conference	Western Conference	Winner (Series)
1988	Detroit Pistons	Los Angeles Lakers	Los Angeles Lakers (4–3)
1989	Detroit Pistons	Los Angeles Lakers	Detroit Pistons (4–0)
1990	Detroit Pistons	Portland Trail Blazers	Detroit Pistons (4–1)
1991	Chicago Bulls	Los Angeles Lakers	Chicago Bulls (4–1)
1992	Chicago Bulls	Portland Trail Blazers	Chicago Bulls (4–2)
1993	Chicago Bulls	Phoenix Suns	Chicago Bulls (4–2)
1994	New York Knickerbockers	Houston Rockets	Houston Rockets (4–3)
1995	Orlando Magic	Houston Rockets	Houston Rockets (4–0)
1996	Chicago Bulls	Seattle SuperSonics	Chicago Bulls (4–2)
1997	Chicago Bulls	Utah Jazz	Chicago Bulls (4–2)
1998	Chicago Bulls	Utah Jazz	Chicago Bulls (4–2)
1999	New York Knickerbockers	San Antonio Spurs	San Antonio Spurs (4–1)
2000	Indiana Pacers	Los Angeles Lakers	Los Angeles Lakers (4–2)
2001	Philadelphia 76ers	Los Angeles Lakers	Los Angeles Lakers (4–1)

INDIVIDUAL NBA SCORING CHAMPIONS

Season	Player, Team	G	FG	FT	Pts	Avg
1953–54	Neil Johnston, Philadelphia Warriors	72	591	577	1,759	24.4
1954–55	Neil Johnston, Philadelphia Warriors	72	521	589	1,631	22.7
1955–56	Bob Pettit, St. Louis Hawks	72	646	557	1,849	25.7
1956–57	Paul Arizin, Philadelphia Warriors	71	613	591	1,817	25.6
1957–58	George Yardley, Detroit Pistons	72	673	655	2,001	27.8
1958–59	Bob Pettit, St. Louis Hawks	72	719	667	2,105	29.2
1959–60	Wilt Chamberlain, Philadelphia Warriors	72	1,065	577	2,707	37.6
1960–61	Wilt Chamberlain, Philadelphia Warriors	79	1,251	531	3,033	38.4
1961–62	Wilt Chamberlain, Philadelphia Warriors	80	1,597	835	4,029	50.4
1962–63	Wilt Chamberlain, San Francisco Warriors	80	1,463	660	3,586	44.8
1963–64	Wilt Chamberlain, San Francisco Warriors	80	1,204	540	2,948	36.9
1964–65	Wilt Chamberlain, San Francisco Warriors/Phila. 76ers	73	1,063	408	2,534	34.7
1965–66	Wilt Chamberlain, Philadelphia 76ers	79	1,074	501	2,649	33.5
1966–67	Rick Barry, San Francisco Warriors	78	1,011	753	2,775	35.6
1967–68	Dave Bing, Detroit Pistons	79	835	472	2,142	27.1
1968–69	Elvin Hayes, San Diego Rockets	82	930	467	2,327	28.4
1969–70	Jerry West, Los Angeles Lakers	74	831	647	2,309	31.2
1970–71	Lew Alcindor,[1] Milwaukee Bucks	82	1,063	470	2,596	31.7
1971–72	Kareem Abdul-Jabbar, Milwaukee Bucks	81	1,159	504	2,822	34.8
1972–73	Nate Archibald, Kansas City/Omaha Kings	80	1,028	663	2,719	34.0
1973–74	Bob McAdoo, Buffalo Braves	74	901	459	2,261	30.8
1974–75	Bob McAdoo, Buffalo Braves	82	1,095	641	2,831	34.5
1975–76	Bob McAdoo, Buffalo Braves	78	934	559	2,427	31.1
1976–77	Pete Maravich, New Orleans Jazz	73	886	501	2,273	31.1
1977–78	George Gervin, San Antonio Spurs	82	864	504	2,232	27.2
1978–79	George Gervin, San Antonio Spurs	80	947	471	2,365	29.6
1979–80	George Gervin, San Antonio Spurs	78	1,024	505	2,585	33.1
1980–81	Adrian Dantley, Utah Jazz	80	909	632	2,452	30.7
1981–82	George Gervin, San Antonio Spurs	79	993	555	2,551	32.3
1982–83	Alex English, Denver Nuggets	82	959	406	2,326	28.4
1983–84	Adrian Dantley, Utah Jazz	79	802	813	2,418	30.6
1984–85	Bernard King, New York Knicks	55	691	426	1,809	32.9
1985–86	Dominique Wilkins, Atlanta Hawks	78	888	527	2,366	30.3
1986–87	Michael Jordan, Chicago Bulls[2]	82	1,098	833	3,041	37.1
1987–88	Michael Jordan, Chicago Bulls[3]	82	1,069	723	2,868	35.0
1988–89	Michael Jordan, Chicago Bulls[4]	81	966	674	2,633	32.5
1989–90	Michael Jordan, Chicago Bulls[5]	82	1,034	593	2,753	33.6
1990–91	Michael Jordan, Chicago Bulls[6]	82	990	571	2,580	31.5
1991–92	Michael Jordan, Chicago Bulls[7]	80	943	491	2,404	30.1
1992–93	Michael Jordan, Chicago Bulls[8]	78	992	476	2,541	32.6
1993–94	David Robinson, San Antonio Spurs[9]	80	840	693	2,383	29.8
1994–95	Shaquille O'Neal, Orlando Magic[10]	79	930	455	2,315	29.3
1995–96	Michael Jordan, Chicago Bulls[11]	82	916	548	2,491	30.4
1996–97	Michael Jordan, Chicago Bulls[11]	82	920	480	2,431	29.6
1997–98	Michael Jordan, Chicago Bulls[12]	82	881	565	2,357	28.7
1998–99	Allen Iverson, Philadelphia 76ers[13]	48	435	356	1,284	26.8
1999–2000	Shaquille O'Neal, L.A. Lakers	79	956	432	2,344	29.7
2000–01	Allen Iverson, Philadelphia 76ers[14]	71	762	585	2,207	31.1

1. (Kareem Abdul-Jabbar). 2. Also had 12 3-point field goals. 3. Also had 7 3-point field goals. 4. Also had 27 3-point field goals. 5. Also had 92 3-point field goals. 6. Also had 29 3-point field goals. 7. Attempted 27 3-point field goals. 8. Also had 81 3-point field goals. 9. Also had 10 3-point field goals. 10. O'Neal scored no 3-point field goals in 1994–1995. 11. Also had 111 3-point field goals in both 1995–96 and 1996–97. 12. Also had 30 3-point field goals. 13. Also had 58 3-point field goals. 14. Also had 98 3-point field goals.

NBA MOST VALUABLE PLAYERS

1956 Bob Pettit, St. Louis	1975 Bob McAdoo, Buffalo	1991 Michael Jordan, Chicago
1957 Bob Cousy, Boston	1976–77 Kareem Abdul-Jabbar, L.A. Lakers	1992 Michael Jordan, Chicago
1958 Bill Russell, Boston		1993 Charles Barkley, Phoenix
1959 Bob Pettit, St. Louis	1978 Bill Walton, Portland	1994 Hakeem Olajuwon, Houston
1960 Wilt Chamberlain, Philadelphia	1979 Moses Malone, Houston	1995 David Robinson, San Antonio
1961–63 Bill Russell, Boston	1980 Kareem Abdul-Jabbar, L.A. Lakers	1996 Michael Jordan, Chicago
1964 Oscar Robertson, Cincinnati		1997 Karl Malone, Utah
1965 Bill Russell, Boston	1981 Julius Erving, Philadelphia	1998 Michael Jordan, Chicago
1966–68 Wilt Chamberlain, Philadelphia	1982 Moses Malone, Houston	1999 Karl Malone, Utah
1969 Wes Unseld, Baltimore	1983 Moses Malone, Philadelphia	2000 Shaquille O'Neal, L.A. Lakers
1970 Willis Reed, New York	1984 Larry Bird, Boston	2001 Allen Iverson, Philadelphia
1971–72 Lew Alcindor (Kareem Abdul-Jabbar), Milwaukee	1985 Larry Bird, Boston	
1973 Dave Cowens, Boston	1986 Larry Bird, Boston	
1974 Kareem Abdul-Jabbar, Milwaukee	1987 Earvin Johnson, L.A. Lakers	
	1988 Michael Jordan, Chicago	
	1989 Earvin Johnson, L.A. Lakers	
	1990 Earvin Johnson, L.A. Lakers	

NBA LIFETIME LEADERS

(Through 2001 season)

Players in bold face active in 2000–2001 season

POINTS

	Yrs	Gm	Pts	Avg
Kareem Abdul-Jabbar	20	1,560	38,387	24.6
Karl Malone	16	1,273	32,919	25.9
Wilt Chamberlain	14	1,045	31,419	30.1
Michael Jordan	13	930	29,277	31.5
Moses Malone	19	1,329	27,409	20.6
Elvin Hayes	16	1,303	27,313	21.0
Oscar Robertson	14	1,040	26,710	25.7
Dominique Wilkins	15	1,074	26,668	24.8
Hakeem Olajuwon	17	1,177	26,511	22.5
John Havlicek	16	1,270	26,395	20.8

SCORING AVERAGE

Minimum of 400 games or 10,000 points

	Yrs	Gm	Pts	Avg
Michael Jordan	13	930	29,277	31.5
Wilt Chamberlain	14	1,045	31,419	30.1
Shaquille O'Neal	9	608	16,812	27.7
Elgin Baylor	14	846	23,149	27.4
Jerry West	14	932	25,192	27.0
Bob Pettit	11	792	20,880	26.4
George Gervin	10	791	20,708	26.2
Karl Malone	16	1,273	32,919	25.9
Oscar Robertson	14	1,040	26,710	25.7
Dominique Wilkins	15	1,074	26,668	24.8

FIELD GOALS

	Yrs	FG	Att	Pct
Kareem Abdul-Jabbar	20	15,837	28,307	.559
Wilt Chamberlain	14	12,681	23,497	.540
Karl Malone	16	12,102	23,122	.523
Elvin Hayes	16	10,976	24,272	.452
Michael Jordan	13	10,958	21,686	.505
Alex English	15	10,659	21,036	.507
John Havlicek	16	10,513	23,930	.439
Hakeem Olajuwon	17	10,555	20,573	.513
Dominique Wilkins	15	9,963	21,589	.461
Robert Parish	21	9,614	17,914	.537

FREE THROWS

	Yrs	FT	Att	Pct
Karl Malone	16	8,636	11,703	.738
Moses Malone	19	8,531	11,090	.769
Oscar Robertson	14	7,694	9,185	.838
Jerry West	14	7,160	8,801	.814
Dolph Schayes	16	6,979	8,273	.844
Adrian Dantley	15	6,832	8,351	.818
Michael Jordan	13	6,798	8,115	.838
Kareem Abdul-Jabbar	20	6,712	9,304	.721
Charles Barkley	16	6,349	8,643	.734
Bob Pettit	11	6,182	8,119	.761

MOST GAMES PLAYED

		PERSONAL FOULS	
Robert Parish	1,611	Kareem Abdul-Jabbar	4,657
Kareem Abdul-Jabbar	1,560	Robert Parish	4,443
John Stockton	1,340	Buck Williams	4,267
Moses Malone	1,329	**Hakeem Olajuwon**	4,236
Buck Williams	1,307	Elvin Hayes	4,193

BLOCKED SHOTS

		STEALS	
Hakeem Olajuwon	3,740	**John Stockton**	2,976
Kareem Abdul-Jabbar	3,189	Maurice Cheeks	2,310
Mark Eaton	3,064	Michael Jordan	2,306
Patrick Ewing	2,849	Clyde Drexler	2,207
David Robinson	2,703	Alvin Robertson	2,112

REBOUNDS

Wilt Chamberlain	23,924	Robert Parish	14,715
Bill Russell	21,620	Nate Thurmond	14,464
Kareem Abdul-Jabbar	17,440	Buck Williams	14,241
Elvin Hayes	16,279	Wes Unseld	13,769
Moses Malone	16,212	**Hakeem Olajuwon**	13,381

ASSISTS

John Stockton	14,503	Maurice Cheeks	7,392
Magic Johnson	10,141	Lenny Wilkens	7,211
Oscar Robertson	9,887	**Rod Strickland**	7,027
Mark Jackson	9,235	Bob Cousy	6,955
Isiah Thomas	9,061	Guy Rodgers	6,917

NBA INDIVIDUAL RECORDS, GAME

(Through 2000–2001 season)

Most points, game—100, Wilt Chamberlain, Philadelphia vs. New York, 1962

Most free throws, game—28, Wilt Chamberlain, Philadelphia vs. New York, 1962; 28, Adrian Dantley, Utah vs. Houston, 1984

Most field goals, game—36, Wilt Chamberlain, Philadelphia vs. New York, 1962

Most assists, game—30, Scott Skiles, Orlando vs. Denver, 1990

Most rebounds, game—55, Wilt Chamberlain, Philadelphia vs. Boston, 1960

Most 3-pt. field goals, game—11, Dennis Scott, Orlando vs. Atlanta, 1996

Most blocked shots, game—17, Elmore Smith, Los Angeles vs. Portland, 1973

Most steals, game—11, Larry Kenon, San Antonio vs. Kansas City, 1976; 11, Kendall Gill, New Jersey vs. Miami, 1999

NATIONAL BASKETBALL ASSOCIATION FINAL STANDINGS, 2000–2001

EASTERN CONFERENCE
Atlantic Division

	W	L	Pct	GB
Philadelphia 76ers[1]	56	26	.683	—
Miami Heat[2]	50	32	.610	6
New York Knicks[2]	48	34	.585	8
Orlando Magic[2]	43	39	.524	13
Boston Celtics	36	46	.439	20
New Jersey Nets	26	56	.317	30
Washington Wizards	19	63	.232	37

Central Division

	W	L	Pct	GB
Milwaukee Bucks[1]	52	30	.634	—
Toronto Raptors[2]	47	35	.573	5
Charlotte Hornets[2]	46	36	.561	6
Indiana Pacers[2]	41	41	.500	11
Detroit Pistons	32	50	.390	20
Cleveland Cavaliers	30	52	.366	22
Atlanta Hawks	25	57	.305	27
Chicago Bulls	15	67	.183	37

WESTERN CONFERENCE
Midwest Division

	W	L	Pct	GB
San Antonio Spurs[1]	58	24	.707	—
Utah Jazz[2]	53	29	.646	5
Dallas Mavericks[2]	53	29	.646	5
Minnesota Timberwolves[2]	47	35	.573	11
Houston Rockets	45	37	.549	13
Denver Nuggets	40	42	.488	18
Vancouver Grizzlies	23	59	.280	35

Pacific Division

	W	L	Pct	GB
L.A. Lakers[1]	56	26	.683	—
Sacramento Kings[2]	55	27	.671	1
Phoenix Suns[2]	51	31	.622	5
Portland Trail Blazers[2]	50	32	.610	6
Seattle SuperSonics[2]	44	38	.537	12
L.A. Clippers	31	51	.378	25
Golden State Warriors	17	65	.207	39

1. Division champion. 2. Playoff qualifier.

NBA PLAYOFFS, 2001

(All caps denotes home team)

EASTERN CONFERENCE
First Round
(Best of 5)
Charlotte defeated Miami, 3 games to 0
Milwaukee defeated Orlando, 3 games to 1
Philadelphia defeated Indiana, 3 games to 1
Toronto defeated New York, 3 games to 2

Conference Semifinals
(Best of 7)
Milwaukee defeated Charlotte, 4 games to 3
Philadelphia defeated Toronto, 4 games to 3

Conference Finals
(Best of 7)
Philadelphia defeated Milwaukee, 4 games to 3
 May 22—PHILADELPHIA 93, Milwaukee 85
 May 24—Milwaukee 92, PHILADELPHIA 78
 May 26—MILWAUKEE 80, Philadelphia 74
 May 28—PHILADELPHIA 89, Milwaukee 83
 May 30—PHILADELPHIA 89, Milwaukee 88
 June 1—MILWAUKEE 110, Philadelphia 100
 June 2—PHILADELPHIA 108, Milwaukee 91

WESTERN CONFERENCE
First Round
(Best of 5)
L.A. Lakers defeated Portland, 3 games to 0
San Antonio defeated Minnesota, 3 games to 1
Sacramento defeated Phoenix, 3 games to 1
Dallas defeated Utah, 3 games to 2

Conference Semifinals
(Best of 7)
L.A. Lakers defeated Sacramento, 4 games to 0
San Antonio defeated Dallas, 4 games to 1

Conference Finals
(Best of 7)
Los Angeles defeated San Antonio, 4 games to 0
 May 19—Los Angeles 104, SAN ANTONIO 90
 May 21—Los Angeles 88, SAN ANTONIO 81
 May 25—LOS ANGELES 111, San Antonio 72
 May 27—LOS ANGELES 111, San Antonio 82

CHAMPIONSHIP

Los Angeles Lakers defeated Philadelphia 76ers, 4 games to 1
Shaquille O'Neal, Los Angeles, named Finals MVP

June 6—Philadelphia 107, LOS ANGELES 101 (OT)
June 8—LOS ANGELES 98, Philadelphia 89
June 10—Los Angeles 96, Philadelphia 91

June 13—Los Angeles 100, PHILADELPHIA 86
June 15—LOS ANGELES 108, Philadelphia 96

NBA INDIVIDUAL LEADERS, 2000–2001 SEASON

POINTS PER GAME
Minimum of 49 games played

	Gm	Pts	PPG
Allen Iverson, Philadelphia	71	2,207	31.1
Jerry Stackhouse, Detroit	80	2,380	29.8
Shaquille O'Neal, L.A. Lakers	74	2,125	28.7
Kobe Bryant, L.A. Lakers	68	1,938	28.5
Vince Carter, Toronto	75	2,070	27.6
Chris Webber, Sacramento	70	1,898	27.1
Tracy McGrady, Orlando	77	2,065	26.8
Paul Pierce, Boston	82	2,071	25.3
Antawn Jamison, Golden State	82	2,044	24.9
Stephon Marbury, New Jersey	67	1,598	23.9

ASSISTS PER GAME
Minimum of 49 games played

	Gm	Avg	Ast
Jason Kidd, Phoenix	77	9.8	753
John Stockton, Utah	82	8.7	713
Mike Biddy, Vancouver	82	8.4	685
Mark Jackson, New York	83	8.0	661
Andre Miller, Cleveland	82	8.0	657
Gary Payton, Seattle	79	8.1	642
Nick Van Exel, Denver	71	8.5	600
Baron Davis, Charlotte	82	7.3	598
Terrell Brandon, Minnesota	78	7.5	583
Sam Cassell, Milwaukee	76	7.6	580

REBOUNDS PER GAME
Minimum of 49 games played

	Gm	Reb	RPG
Dikembe Mutombo, Philadelphia	75	1,015	13.5
Ben Wallace, Detroit	80	1,052	13.2
Shaquille O'Neal, L.A. Lakers	74	940	12.7
Tim Duncan, San Antonio	82	997	12.2
Antonio McDyess, Denver	70	845	12.1
Kevin Garnett, Minnesota	81	921	11.4
Chris Webber, Sacramento	70	777	11.1
Shawn Marion, Phoenix	79	848	10.7
Antonio Davis, Toronto	78	787	10.1
Elton Brand, Chicago	74	746	10.1

FIELD GOAL PERCENTAGE
Minimum of 288 field goals made

	FGM	FGA	Pct
Shaquille O'Neal, L.A. Lakers	813	1,422	.572
Bonzi Wells, Portland	387	726	.533
Marcus Camby, New York	304	580	.524
Kurt Thomas, New York	314	614	.511
Wally Szczerbiak, Minnesota	469	920	.510
Darius Miles, L.A. Clippers	318	630	.505
John Stockton, Utah	328	651	.504
Donyell Marshall, Utah	427	849	.503
Corliss Williamson, Detroit	325	647	.502
Clarence Weatherspoon, Cleveland	347	692	.501

FREE-THROW PERCENTAGE
Minimum of 120 free throws made

	FTM	FTA	Pct
Reggie Miller, Indiana	323	348	.928
Allan Houston, New York	279	307	.909
Doug Christie, Sacramento	280	312	.897
Steve Nash, Dallas	231	258	.895
Mitch Richmond, Washington	143	160	.894
Steve Smith, Portland	309	347	.890
Ray Allen, Milwaukee	348	392	.888
Darrell Armstrong, Orlando	220	249	.884
Eric Piatkowski, L.A. Clippers	158	181	.873
Terrell Brandon, Minnesota	195	224	.871

3-POINT FIELD GOAL PERCENTAGE
Minimum of 65 3-point field goals made

	3FGM	3FGA	Pct
Brent Barry, Seattle	109	229	.476
John Stockton, Utah	61	132	.462
Shammond Williams, Seattle	61	133	.459
Hubert Davis, Washington	78	171	.456
Danny Ferry, San Antonio	70	156	.449
Toni Kukoc, Atlanta	70	157	.446
Pat Garrity, Orlando	97	224	.433
Ray Allen, Milwaukee	202	467	.433
Rashard Lewis, Seattle	123	285	.432
Dell Curry, Toronto	62	145	.428

BLOCKED SHOTS
Minimum of 49 games played or 96 block shots

	Gm	Blk	BPG
Theo Ratliff, Atlanta	50	187	3.74
Jermaine O'Neal, Indiana	81	228	2.81
Shawn Bradley, Dallas	82	228	2.78
Shaquille O'Neal, L.A. Lakers	74	204	2.76
Dikembe Mutombo, Philadelphia	75	203	2.71
Adonal Foyle, Golden State	58	156	2.69
Raef LaFrentz, Denver	78	206	2.64
David Robinson, San Antonio	80	197	2.46
Tim Duncan, San Antonio	82	192	2.34
Ben Wallace, Detroit	80	186	2.33

STEALS
Minimum of 49 games played or 120 steals

	Gm	Stl	SPG
Allen Iverson, Philadelphia	71	178	2.51
Mookie Blaylock, Golden State	69	163	2.36
Doug Christie, Sacramento	81	183	2.26
Jason Kidd, Phoenix	77	166	2.16
Baron Davis, Charlotte	82	170	2.07
Terrell Brandon, Minnesota	78	161	2.06
Ron Artest, Chicago	76	152	2.00
Darrell Armstrong, Orlando	75	135	1.80
Steve Francis, Houston Rockets	80	141	1.76
Antoine Walker, Boston	81	138	1.70

Women's Professional Basketball

WOMEN'S NATIONAL BASKETBALL ASSOCIATION, 2001 SEASON

Eastern Conference

	W	L	Pct	GB	Home	Road
x-Cleveland Rockers	22	10	.688	—	14–2	8–8
x-New York Liberty	21	11	.656	1	13–3	8–8
x-Miami Sol	20	12	.625	2	10–6	10–6
x-Charlotte Sting	18	14	.563	4	11–5	7–9
Orlando Miracle	13	19	.406	9	10–6	3–13
Indiana Fever	10	22	.313	12	7–9	3–13
Detroit Shock	10	22	.313	12	6–10	4–12
Washington Mystics	10	22	.313	12	8–8	2–14

Western Conference

	W	L	Pct	GB	Home	Road
x-Los Angeles Sparks	28	4	.875	—	16–0	12–4
x-Sacramento Monarchs	20	12	.625	8	12–4	8–8
x-Utah Starzz	19	13	.594	9	9–7	10–6
x-Houston Comets	19	13	.594	9	11–5	8–8
Phoenix Mercury	13	19	.406	15	10–6	3–13
Minnesota Lynx	12	20	.375	16	6–10	6–10
Portland Fire	11	21	.344	17	6–10	5–11
Seattle Storm	10	22	.313	18	5–11	5–11

NOTES: x—clinched playoff qualifier. GB refers to Games Behind leader.

Conference Championship Series (Best of 3)

EASTERN CONFERENCE

Date	Result
Aug. 24	New York 61, Charlotte 57
Aug. 26	Charlotte 62, New York 53
Aug. 27	Charlotte 48, New York 44
	Charlotte wins series, 2–1

WESTERN CONFERENCE

Date	Result
Aug. 24	Los Angeles 74, Sacramento 73
Aug. 26	Sacramento 80, Los Angeles 60
Aug. 27	Los Angeles 93, Sacramento 62
	Los Angeles wins series, 2–1

League Championship Series (Best of 3)
Los Angeles wins championship, 2 games to 0

Date	Result
Aug. 30	Los Angeles 75, Charlotte 66
Sept. 1	Los Angeles 82, Charlotte 54

WNBA ANNUAL AWARDS, 2001 SEASON

Most Valuable Player: Lisa Leslie, Los Angeles
Defensive Player of the Year: Debbie Black, Miami
Sportsmanship Award: Sue Wicks, New York
Coach of the Year: Dan Hughes, Cleveland

Most Improved Player of the Year: Janeth Arcain, Houston
Rookie of the Year: Jackie Stiles, Portland
Shooting Champions: Elena Baranova, Latasha Byears

2001 WNBA LEAGUE LEADERS

POINTS PER GAME

	Gm	Pts	PPG
Katie Smith, Minnesota	32	739	23.1
Lisa Leslie, Los Angeles	31	606	19.5
Tina Thompson, Houston	30	579	19.3
Janeth Arcain, Houston	32	591	18.5
Chamique Holdsclaw, Washington	29	486	16.8

REBOUNDS PER GAME

	Gm	Reb	RPG
Yolanda Griffith, Sacramento	32	357	11.2
Natalie Williams, Utah	31	308	9.9
Lisa Leslie, Los Angeles	31	298	9.6
Chamique Holdsclaw, Washington	29	256	8.8
Tari Phillips, New York	32	257	8.0

ASSISTS PER GAME

	Gm	Ast	APG
Ticha Penicheiro, Sacramento	23	172	7.5
Teresa Weatherspoon, New York	32	203	6.3
Dawn Staley, Charlotte	32	179	5.6
Jennifer Azzi, Utah	32	171	5.3
Kristen Veal, Phoenix	29	125	4.3

BLOCKS PER GAME

	Gm	Blk	BPG
Margo Dydek, Utah	32	113	3.53
Lisa Leslie, Los Angeles	31	71	2.29
Lauren Jackson, Seattle	29	64	2.21
Maria Stepanova, Phoenix	32	64	2.00
Vicky Bullett, Washington	32	58	1.81

STEALS PER GAME

	Gm	Stl	SPG
Debbie Black, Miami	32	82	2.56
Rita Williams, Indiana	32	72	2.25
Nykesha Sales, Orlando	32	70	2.19
Coquese Washington, Houston	32	69	2.16
Yolanda Griffith, Sacramento	32	63	1.97

FIELD GOAL PERCENTAGE

	FGM	FGA	FG%
Latasha Byears, Los Angeles	133	221	.602
Ann Wauters, Cleveland	87	153	.569
Yolanda Griffith, Sacramento	192	368	.522
Rushia Brown, Cleveland	101	195	.518
Tari Phillips, New York	208	410	.507

3-PT. FIELD GOAL PERCENTAGE

	3FGM	3FGA	3FG%
Jennifer Azzi, Utah	38	74	.514
Ukari Figgs, Los Angeles	54	117	.462
Edna Campbell, Sacramento	43	94	.457
Elena Tornikidou, Detroit	22	49	.449
Andrea Stinson, Charlotte	29	65	.446

FREE THROW PERCENTAGE

	FTM	FTA	FT%
Elena Baranova, Miami	66	71	.930
Allison Feaster, Charlotte	58	63	.921
Jennifer Azzi, Utah	88	96	.917
Janeth Arcain, Houston	135	150	.900
Katie Smith, Minnesota	246	275	.895

AMERICAN BASKETBALL LEAGUE

The American Basketball League suspended operations Dec. 22, 1998.

LEAGUE CHAMPIONS

Year	Champions	Head Coach	Series	Runners-up	Head Coach
1997	Columbus Quest	Brian Agler	3-2	Richmond Rage	Lisa Boyer
1998	Columbus Quest	Brian Agler	3-2	Long Beach StingRays	Maura McHugh
1999	league folded				

Sports Personalities

A name in parentheses is the original name or form of name. Localities are places of birth. Dates of birth appear as month/day/year. **Boldface** years in parentheses are dates of **(birth–death)**.

Information has been gathered from many sources, including the individuals themselves. However, the almanac cannot guarantee the accuracy of every individual item.

Aaron, Hank (Henry) (baseball); Mobile, Ala., 2/5/34
Abdul-Jabbar, Kareem (Lewis Ferdinand Alcindor, Jr.) (basketball); New York City, 4/16/47
Affleck, Francis (auto racing) **(1951–1985)**
Agassi, Andre (tennis); Las Vegas, Nev., 4/29/70
Aikman, Troy (football); Henryetta, Okla., 11/21/66
Ali, Muhammad (Cassius Clay) (boxing); Louisville, Ky., 1/18/42
Allen, Dick (Richard Anthony) (baseball); Wampum, Pa., 3/8/42
Allen, George (football) **(1918–1990)**
Allison, Bobby (Robert Arthur) (auto racing); Hueytown, Ala., 12/3/37
Allison, Davey (auto racing); Hueytown, Ala. **(1961–1993)**
Alston, Walter (baseball); Venice, Ohio **(1911–1984)**
Alworth, Lance (football); Houston, 8/3/40
Ameche, Alan (football); Houston, Tex. **(1933–1988)**
Anderson, Sparky (George) (baseball); Bridgewater, S.D., 2/22/34
Andretti, Mario (auto racing); Montona, Trieste, Italy, 2/28/40
Anthony, Earl (bowling); Kent, Wash. **(1939–2001)**
Appling, Luke (baseball); High Point, N.C. **(1907–1990)**
Arcaro, Eddie (George Edward) (jockey); Cincinnati **(1916–1997)**
Armstrong, Lance (bicycling); Plano, Tex., Sept. 18, 1971
Ashe, Arthur (tennis); Richmond, Va. **(1943–1993)**
Ashford, Evelyn (track & field); Shreveport, La., 4/15/57
Austin, Tracy (tennis); Rolling Hills, Calif., 12/2/62
Averill, Earl (baseball); Everett, Wash. **(1915–1983)**
Babashoff, Shirley (swimming); Whittier, Calif., 1/31/57
Baer, Max (boxing); Omaha, Neb. **(1909–1959)**
Bailey, Donovan (track); Canada, 12/16/67
Banks, Ernie (baseball); Dallas, 1/31/31
Bannister, Roger (runner); Harrow, England, 3/24/29
Barkley, Charles (basketball); Leeds, Ala., 2/20/63
Barry, Rick (Richard) (basketball); Elizabeth, N.J., 3/28/44
Bauer, Hank (Henry) (baseball); East St. Louis, Ill., 7/31/22
Baugh, Sammy (football); Temple, Tex., 3/17/14
Baylor, Elgin (basketball); Washington, D.C., 9/16/34
Beamon, Bob (long jumper); New York City, 8/2/46
Becker, Boris (tennis); Leiman, W. Germany, 11/22/67
Bee, Clair (basketball); Cleveland, Ohio **(1896–1983)**
Beliveau, Jean (hockey); Three Rivers, Quebec, Canada, 8/31/31
Belle, Albert (baseball); Shreveport, La., 8/25/66
Beman, Deane (golf); Washington, D.C., 4/22/38
Bench, Johnny (Johnny Lee) (baseball); Oklahoma City, 12/7/47
Berg, Patty (Patricia Jane) (golf); Minneapolis, 2/13/18
Berra, Yogi (Lawrence) (baseball); St. Louis, 5/12/25
Biletnikoff, Frederick (football); Erie, Pa., 2/23/43
Bing, Dave (basketball); Washington, D.C., 11/24/43
Bird, Larry (basketball); French Lick, Ind., 12/7/56
Blaik, Earl H. (football); Detroit **(1897–1989)**
Blanda, George Frederick (football); Youngwood, Pa., 9/17/27
Bledsoe, Drew (football); Walla Walla, Wash., 2/14/72
Blue, Vida (baseball); Mansfield, La., 7/28/49
Bodine, Brett (auto racing); Chemung, N.Y., 1/11/59
Bodine, Geoff (auto racing); Chemung, N.Y., 4/18/49
Boggs, Wade (baseball); Omaha, Neb., 6/15/58
Bonds, Barry (baseball); Riverside, Calif., 7/24/64
Borg, Björn (tennis); Stockholm, Sweden, 6/6/56
Boros, Julius (golf); Fairfield, Conn. **(1920–1994)**
Bossy, Mike (hockey); Montreal, 1/22/57
Boston, Ralph (long jumper); Laurel, Miss., 5/9/39
Bourque, Ray (hockey); Montreal, Que., 12/28/60
Bradley, Bill (William Warren) (basketball); Crystal City, Mo., 7/28/43
Bradley, Pat (golf); Westford, Mass., 3/24/51
Bradshaw, Terry (football); Shreveport, La., 9/2/48
Breedlove, Craig (Norman) (speed driving); Los Angeles, 3/23/38
Brett, George (baseball); Glendale, W. Va., 5/15/53
Brock, Louis Clark (baseball); El Dorado, Ark., 6/18/39
Brown, Jim (football); St. Simon Island, Ga., 2/17/36
Brumel, Valeri (high jumper); Tolbuzino, Siberia, 4/14/42
Bryant, Paul "Bear" (football); Morro Bottom, Ark. **(1913–1983)**
Bryant, Rosalyn Evette (track); Chicago, 1/7/56
Burton, Michael (swimming); Des Moines, Iowa, 7/3/47
Butkus, Dick (Richard Marvin) (football); Chicago, 12/9/42
Calipari, John (basketball); Moon, Pa., 2/10/59
Campanella, Roy (baseball); Homestead, Pa. **(1921–1993)**
Campbell, Earl (football); Tyler, Tex., 3/29/55
Canseco, Jose (baseball); Havana, Cuba, 7/2/64
Caponi, Donna Maria (golf); Detroit, 1/29/45
Cappelletti, Gino (football); Keewatin, Minn., 3/26/34
Capriati, Jennifer (tennis); New York, N.Y., 3/29/76
Carew, Rod (Rodney Cline) (baseball); Gatun, Panama, 10/1/45

Carlos, John (sprinter); New York City, 6/5/45
Carlton, Steven Norman (baseball); Miami, Fla., 12/22/44
Carner, Joanne Gunderson, Mrs. Don (golf); Kirkland, Wash., 3/4/39
Casals, Rosemary (tennis); San Francisco, 9/16/48
Casper, Billy (golf); San Diego, Calif., 6/24/31
Caulkins, Tracy (swimming); Winona, Minn., 1/11/63
Cauthen, Steve (jockey); Covington, Ky., 5/1/60
Chamberlain, Wilt (Wilton) (basketball); Philadelphia **(1936–1999)**
Chandler, A.B. (Happy) (baseball); Louisville, Ky. **(1899–1991)**
Chandler, Spud (baseball); Commerce, Ga. **(1907–1990)**
Chang, Michael (tennis); Hoboken, N.J., 2/22/72
Chapot, Frank (equestrian); Camden, N.J., 2/24/34
Chastain, Brandi (soccer); San Jose, Calif., 7/21/68
Chinaglia, Giorgio (soccer); Carrara, Italy, 1/24/47
Clarke, Bobby (Robert Earle) (hockey); Flin Flon, Manitoba, Canada, 8/13/49
Clemens, Roger (baseball); Dayton, Ohio, 8/4/62
Clemente, Roberto Walker (baseball); Carolina, Puerto Rico **(1934–1972)**
Cobb, Ty (Tyrus Raymond) (baseball); Narrows, Ga. **(1886–1961)**
Cochran, Barbara Ann (skiing); Claremont, N.H., 1/14/51
Cochran, Marilyn (skiing); Burlington, Vt., 2/7/50
Cochran, Robert (skiing); Claremont, N.H., 12/11/51
Coe, Sebastian Newbold (track); London, England, 9/29/56
Coffey, Paul (hockey); Weston, Ont., 6/1/61
Colavito, Rocky (Rocco Domenico) (baseball); New York City, 8/10/33
Coleman, Derrick (basketball); Mobile, Ala., 6/21/67
Comaneci, Nadia (gymnast); Onesti, Romania, 11/12/61
Conigliaro, Tony (baseball); Revere, Mass. **(1945–1990)**
Connors, Jimmy (James Scott) (tennis); East St. Louis, Ill., 9/2/52
Cooper, Cynthia (basketball); Chicago, Ill., 4/14/63
Cordero, Angel (jockey); Santurce, Puerto Rico, 5/8/42
Cosell, Howard (broadcaster); Winston-Salem, N.C. **(1918–1995)**
Courier, Jim (tennis); Sanford, Fla., 8/17/70
Cournoyer, Yvan Serge (hockey); Drummondville, Quebec, Canada, 11/22/43
Court, Margaret Smith (tennis); Albury, New South Wales, Australia, 7/16/42
Cousy, Bob (basketball); New York City, 8/9/28
Crabbe, Buster (swimming); Scottsdale, Ariz. **(1908–1983)**
Crenshaw, Ben (golf); Austin, Tex., 1/11/52
Cronin, Joe (baseball executive); San Francisco **(1906–1984)**
Cruyff, Johan (soccer); Amsterdam, Netherlands, 4/25/47
Csonka, Larry (Lawrence Richard) (football); Stow, Ohio, 12/25/46
Dancer, Stanley (harness racing); New Egypt, N.J., 7/25/27
Dark, Alvin (baseball); Comanche, Okla., 1/7/22
Davenport, Willie (track); Troy, Ala., 6/6/43
Dawson, Andre (baseball); Miami, Fla., 7/10/54
Dawson, Leonard Ray (football); Alliance, Ohio, 6/20/35
Dean, Dizzy (Jay Hanna) (baseball); Lucas, Ark. **(1911–1974)**
DeBusschere, Dave (basketball); Detroit, 10/16/40
De La Hoya, Oscar (boxing); East Los Angeles, Calif., 2/4/73
Delvecchio, Alex Peter (hockey); Fort William, Ontario, Canada, 12/4/31
Demaret, Jim (golf); Houston **(1910–1983)**
Dempsey, Jack (William H.) (boxing); Manassa, Colo. **(1895–1983)**
DeVicenzo, Roberto (golf); Buenos Aires, 4/14/23
Dibbs, Edward George (tennis); Brooklyn, New York, 2/23/51
Dietz, James M. (rowing); New York, N.Y., 1/12/49
DiMaggio, Joe (baseball); Martinez, Calif. **(1914–1999)**
Dionne, Marcel (hockey); Drummondville, Quebec, Canada, 8/3/51
Dorsett, Tony (football); Rochester, Pa., 4/7/54
Dryden, Kenneth (hockey); Hamilton, Ontario, Canada, 8/4/47
Drysdale, Don (baseball); Van Nuys, Calif. **(1936–1993)**
Duran, Roberto (boxing); Panama City, 6/16/51
Durocher, Leo (baseball); West Springfield, Mass. **(1906–1991)**
Durr, Francois (tennis); Algiers, Algeria, 12/25/42
Earnhardt, Dale (auto racing); Concord, N.C. **(1951–2001)**
Eckersley, Dennis (baseball); Oakland, Calif., 10/3/54
Elder, Lee (golf); Dallas, 7/14/34
Elway, John (football); Port Angeles, Wash., 6/28/60
Emerson, Roy (tennis); Kingsway, Australia, 11/3/36
Ender, Kornelia (swimming); Plauen, East Germany, 10/25/58
Erving, Julius ("Dr. J") (basketball); Roosevelt, N.Y., 2/22/50
Esposito, Phil (Philip Anthony) (hockey); Sault Ste. Marie, Ontario, Canada, 2/20/42
Evans, Lee (runner); Mandena, Calif., 2/25/47
Evert, Chris (Christine Marie) (tennis); Fort Lauderdale, Fla., 12/21/54
Ewbank, Weeb (football); Richmond, Ind. **(1907–1998)**

Ewing, Patrick (basketball); Kingston, Jamaica, 8/5/62
Favre, Brett (football); Gulfport, Miss., 10/10/69
Feller, Robert (Bob) (baseball); Van Meter, Iowa, 11/3/18
Feuerbach, Allan Dean (track); Preston, Iowa, 1/12/48
Finley, Charles O. (sportsman); Ensley, Ala. **(1918–1996)**
Fischer, Bobby (chess); Chicago, 3/9/43
Fitzsimmons, Bob (Robert Prometheus) (boxing); Cornwall, England **(1862–1917)**
Fleming, Peggy Gale (ice skating); San Jose, Calif., 7/27/48
Ford, Whitey (Edward) (baseball); New York City, 10/21/28
Foreman, George (boxing); Marshall, Tex., 1/10/49
Fosbury, Richard (high jumper); Portland, Ore., 3/6/47
Fox, Nellie (Jacob Nelson) (baseball); St. Thomas, Pa. **(1927–1975)**
Foxx, James Emory (baseball); Sudlersville, Md. **(1907–1967)**
Foyt, A. J. (auto racing); Houston, 1/16/35
Frazier, Joe (boxing); Beauford, S.C., 1/17/44
Frazier, Walt (basketball); Atlanta, 3/29/45
Freeman, Cathy (track & field); Mackay, Queensland, Australia, 2/16/73
Frick, Ford C. (baseball); Wawaka, Ind. **(1894–1978)**
Furniss, Bruce (swimming); Fresno, Calif., 5/27/57
Gable, Dan (wrestling); Waterloo, Iowa, 10/25/45
Gabriel, Roman (football); Wilmington, N.C., 8/5/40
Gallagher, Michael Donald (skiing); Yonkers, N.Y., 10/3/41
Garvey, Steve (baseball); Tampa, Fla., 12/22/48
Gehrig, Lou (Henry Louis) (baseball); New York City **(1903–1941)**
Gehringer, Charlie (baseball); Fowlerville, Mich. **(1903–1993)**
Geoffrion, "Boom Boom" (Bernie) (hockey); Montreal, 2/14/31
Gerulaitis, Vitas (tennis); Brooklyn, N.Y. **(1954–1994)**
Gervin, George (basketball); Long Beach, Calif., 4/27/52
Giacomin, Ed (hockey); Sudbury, Ontario, Canada, 6/6/39
Giamatti, A. Bartlett (baseball); South Hadley, Mass. **(1938–1989)**
Gibson, Bob (baseball); Omaha, Neb., 11/9/35
Gifford, Frank (football); Santa Monica, Calif., 8/16/30
Gilbert, Rod (Rodrique) (hockey); Montreal, 7/1/41
Gilmore, Artis (basketball); Chipley, Fla., 9/21/49
Glance, Harvey (track); Phenix City, Ala., 3/28/57
Gonzalez, Pancho (tennis); Los Angeles **(1928–1995)**
Goodell, Brian Stuart (swimming); Stockton, Calif., 4/2/59
Gooden, Dwight (baseball); Tampa, Fla., 11/16/64
Goodrich, Gail (basketball); Los Angeles, 4/23/43
Goolagong, Cawley, Evonne (tennis); Griffith, Australia, 7/31/51
Gordon, Jeff (auto racing); Vallejo, Calif., 8/4/71
Gossage, "Goose" (Rich) (baseball); Colorado Springs, Colo., 4/5/51
Graf, Steffi (tennis); Mannheim, W. Germany, 6/14/69
Graham, David (golf); Windson, Australia, 5/23/46
Graham, Otto Everett (football); Waukegan, Ill., 12/6/21
Grange, Red (Harold) (football); Forksville, Pa. **(1904–1991)**
Green, Hubert (golf); Birmingham, Ala., 12/28/46
Greene, Charles E. (sprinter); Pine Bluff, Ark., 3/21/45
Greene, "Mean" (Joe) (football); Temple, Tex., 9/24/46
Gretzky, Wayne (hockey); Brantford, Ont., 1/26/61
Griese, Bob (Robert Allen) (football); Evansville, Ind., 2/3/45
Griffey, Ken, Jr. (baseball); Donora, Pa., 11/21/69
Grove, Lefty (Robert Moses) (baseball); Lonaconing, Md. **(1900–1975)**
Groza, Lou (football); Martins Ferry Ohio, 1/25/24
Guidry, Ronald Ames (baseball); Lafayette, La., 8/28/50
Gwynn, Tony (baseball); Los Angeles, Calif., 5/9/60
Halas, George (football); Chicago **(1895–1983)**
Hall, Gary (swimming); Fayetteville, N.C., 8/7/51
Hamill, Dorothy (figure skating); Chicago, 7/26/56
Hamilton, Scott (figure skating); Bowling Green, Ohio, 8/28/58
Hamm, Mia (soccer); Selma, Ala., 3/17/72
Hammond, Kathy (runner); Sacramento, Calif., 11/2/51
Hardaway, Anfernee (basketball); Memphis, Tenn., 7/18/72
Harding, Tonya (figure skating); Portland, Ore., 11/12/70
Harris, Franco (football); Ft. Dix, N.J., 3/7/50
Hartack, William, Jr. (jockey); Colver, Pa., 12/9/32
Hasek, Dominik (hockey); Pardubice, Czechoslovakia, 1/29/65
Haughton, William (harness racing); Gloversville, N.Y. **(1923–1986)**
Havlicek, John (basketball); Martins Ferry, Ohio, 4/8/40
Hayes, Elvin (basketball); Rayville, La., 11/17/45
Hayes, Woody (football); Upper Arlington, Ohio **(1913–1987)**
Heiden, Eric (speed skating); Madison, Wis., 6/14/58
Hencken, John (swimming); Culver City, Calif., 5/29/54
Henderson, Rickey (baseball); Chicago, 12/25/58
Henie, Sonja (ice skater); Oslo **(1912–1969)**
Herman, Floyd Caves (Babe) (baseball); Buffalo, N.Y. **(1903–1987)**
Hernandez, Keith (baseball); San Francisco, 10/20/53
Hershiser, Orel (baseball); Buffalo, N.Y., 9/16/58
Hickcox, Charles (swimming); Phoenix, Ariz., 2/6/47
Hines, James (sprinter); Dumas, Ark., 9/10/46
Hingis, Martina (tennis); Kosice, Slovakia, 9/30/80
Hodges, Gil (baseball); Princeton, Ind. **(1924–1972)**
Hogan, Ben (golf); Dublin, Tex. **(1912–1997)**
Holmes, Larry (boxing); Cuthert, Ga., 11/3/49
Holyfield, Evander (boxing); Atlanta, Ga., 10/19/62
Hornsby, Rogers (baseball); Winters, Tex. **(1896–1963)**

Hornung, Paul (football); Louisville, Ky., 12/23/35
Houk, Ralph (baseball); Lawrence, Kan., 8/9/19
Howard, Elston (baseball); St. Louis **(1929–1980)**
Howe, Gordon (hockey); Floral, Sask., Canada, 3/31/28
Howell, Jim Lee (football); Lonoke, Ark. **(1914–1995)**
Howser, Dick (baseball); Miami, Fla. **(1937–1987)**
Hubbell, Carl (baseball); Carthage, Mo. **(1903–1988)**
Huff, Sam (Robert Lee) (football); Morgantown, W. Va., 10/4/34
Hull, Bobby (hockey); Point Anne, Ontario, Canada, 1/3/39
Hunter, "Catfish" (Jim) (baseball); Hertford, N.C. **(1946–1999)**
Hutson, Donald (football); Pine Bluff, Ark. **(1913–1997)**
Irwin, Hale (golf); Joplin, Mo., 6/3/45
Jacobs, Helen Hull (tennis); Globe, Ariz. **(1908–1997)**
Jackson, Phil (basketball coach); Deer Lodge, Mont., 9/17/45
Jackson, Reggie (baseball); Wyncote, Pa., 5/18/46
Jagr, Jaromir (hockey); Kladno, Czechoslovakia, 2/15/72
Jeffries, James J. (boxing); Carroll, Ohio **(1875–1953)**
Jenkins, Ferguson Arthur (baseball); Chatham, Ontario, Canada, 12/13/43
Jenner, (W.) Bruce (track); Mt. Kisco, N.Y., 10/28/49
Jezek, Linda (swimming); Palo Alto, Calif., 3/10/60
Johnson, "Magic" (Earvin) (basketball); E. Lansing, Mich., 8/14/59
Johnson, Anthony (rowing); Washington, D.C., 11/16/40
Johnson, Jack (John Arthur) (boxing); Galveston, Tex. **(1876–1946)**
Johnson, Jimmy (football); Port Arthur, Tex., 8/14/43
Johnson, Michael (track); Dallas, Tex., 9/13/67
Johnson, Rafer (decathlon); Hillsboro, Tex., 8/18/35
Johnson, Randy (baseball); Walnut Creek, Calif., 9/10/63
Johnson, Wilham Julius (Judy) (baseball); Wilmington, Del. **(1899–1989)**
Jones, Cobi (soccer); Detroit, Mich., 6/16/70
Jones, Deacon (David) (football); Eatonville, Fla., 12/9/38
Jones, Marion (track & field); Los Angeles, Calif., 10/12/75
Jordan, Michael (basketball); Brooklyn, N.Y., 2/17/63
Joyner, Florence Griffith (sprinter); Mojave Desert, Calif. **(1959–1998)**
Joyner-Kersee, Jackie (track); East St. Louis, Ill., 3/3/62
Juantoreno, Alberto (track); Santiago, Cuba, 12/3/51
Jurgensen, Sonny (football); Wilmington, N.C., 8/23/34
Justice, Dave (baseball); Cincinnati, Ohio, 4/14/66
Kaat, Jim (baseball); Zeeland, Mich., 11/7/38
Kaline, Al (Albert) (baseball); Baltimore, 12/19/34
Keino, Kipchoge (runner); Kapchemoiymo, Kenya, 1/17/40
Kelly, Leroy (football); Philadelphia, 5/20/42
Kelly, Red (Leonard Patrick) (hockey); Simcoe, Ontario, Canada, 7/9/27
Kerrigan, Nancy (figure skating); Woburn, Mass., 10/13/69
Killebrew, Harmon (baseball); Payette, Idaho, 6/29/36
Killy, Jean-Claude (skiing); Saint-Cloud, France, 8/30/43
Kilmer, Bill (William Orland) (football); Topeka, Kan., 9/5/39
King, Bille Jean (Bille Jean Moffitt) (tennis); Long Beach, Calif., 11/22/43
Kinsella, John (swimming); Oak Park, Ill., 8/26/52
Kluszewski, Ted (baseball); Argo, Ill. **(1924–1988)**
Kodes, Jan (tennis); Prague, 3/1/46
Kolb, Claudia (swimming); Hayward, Calif., 12/19/49
Korbut, Olga (gymnast); Grodno, Byelorussia, USSR, 5/16/55
Koufax, Sandy (Sanford) (baseball); Brooklyn, N.Y., 12/30/35
Kramer, Jack (tennis); Las Vegas, Nev., 8/1/21
Kramer, Jerry (football); Jordan, Mont., 1/23/36
Krayzelburg, Lenny (swimming); Odessa, Ukraine, 9/28/75
Kuenn, Harvey (baseball); West Allis, Wis. **(1930–1988)**
Kuhn, Bowie Kent (baseball); Takoma Park, Md., 10/28/26
Kwan, Michelle (figure skating); Torrance, Calif., 7/7/80
Lafleur, Guy Damien (hockey); Thurson, Quebec, Canada, 8/20/51
Laird, Ronald (walker); Louisville, Ky., 5/31/35
Lalas, Alexi (soccer); Birmingham, Mich., 6/1/70
Lamonica, Daryle (football); Fresno, Calif., 7/17/41
Landis, Kenesaw Mountain (1st baseball commissioner); Millville, Ohio **(1866–1944)**
Landry, Tom (football); Mission, Tex. **(1924–2000)**
Landy, John (runner); Australia, 4/4/30
Larrieu, Francie (track); Palo Alto, Calif., 11/28/52
La Russa, Tony (baseball); Tampa, Fla., 10/4/44
Lasorda, Tom (baseball); Norristown, Pa., 9/22/27
Laver, Rod (tennis); Rockhampton, Australia, 8/9/38
Layne, Bobby (football); Lubbock, Texas **(1927–1986)**
Leetch, Brian (hockey); Corpus Christi, Tex., 3/3/68
Lemieux, Mario (hockey); Montreal, Quebec, Canada, 10/5/65
Lendl, Ivan (tennis); Prague, 3/7/60
Leonard, Benny (Benjamin Leiner) (boxing); New York City **(1896–1947)**
Leonard, Sugar Ray (boxing); Wilmington, N.C., 5/17/56
Lewis, Carl (track); Willingboro, N.J., 7/1/61
Lindros, Eric (hockey); London, Ont., 2/28/73
Lipinski, Tara (figure skating); Philadelphia, Pa., 6/10/82
Liquori, Marty (runner); Montclair, N.J., 9/11/49
Little, Lou (football); Leominster, Mass. **(1893–1979)**
Littler, Gene (golf); La Jolla, Calif., 7/21/30

Lobo, Rebecca (basketball); Southwick, Mass., 10/6/73
Lombardi, Vince (football); Brooklyn, N.Y. **(1913–1970)**
Longden, Johnny (horse racing); Wakefield, England, 2/14/07
Lopat, Eddie (baseball); New York, N.Y. **(1918–1992)**
Lopez, Al (baseball); Tampa, Fla., 8/20/08
Lopez, Nancy (golf); Torrance, Calif., 1/6/57
Louis, Joe (Joe Louis Barrow) (boxing); Lafayette, Ala. **(1914–1981)**
Lukas, D. Wayne (horse racing); Antigo, Wis., 9/2/35
Lynn, Frederic Michael (baseball); Chicago, Ill., 2/3/52
Lynn, Janet (figure skating); Rockford, Ill., 4/6/53
Mack, Connie (Cornelius Alexander McGillicuddy) (baseball executive); East Brookfield, Mass. **(1862–1956)**
Mackey, John (football); New York City, 9/24/41
Maddux, Greg (baseball); San Angelo, Texas, 4/15/67
Mahovlich, Frank (Francis William) (hockey); Timmins, Ontario, Canada, 1/10/38
Mahre, Phil (skiing); White Pass, Wash., 5/10/57
Malone, Karl (basketball); Summerfield, La., 7/24/63
Malone, Moses (basketball); Petersburg, Va., 3/23/55
Mandlikova, Hana (tennis); Prague, Czechoslovakia, 2/62
Mann, Carol (golf); Buffalo, N.Y., 2/3/41
Manning, Madeline (runner); Cleveland, 1/11/48
Mantle, Mickey Charles (baseball); Spavinaw, Okla. **(1931–1995)**
Maravich, "Pistol Pete" (Peter) Aliquippa, Pa. **(1948–1988)**
Marble, Alice (tennis); Palm Springs, Calif. **(1913–1990)**
Marciano, Rocky (boxing); Brockton, Mass. **(1923–1969)**
Marichal, Juan (baseball); Laguna Verde, Montecristi, Dominican Republic, 10/20/37
Marino, Dan (football); Pittsburgh, Pa., 9/15/61
Maris, Roger (baseball); Hibbing, Minn. **(1934–1985)**
Martin, Billy (Alfred Manuel) (baseball); Berkeley, Calif. **(1928–1989)**
Martin, Christy (boxing); Mullers, W.Va.,
Martin, Rick (Richard Lionel) (hockey); Verdun, Quebec, Canada, 7/26/51
Mathews, Ed (Edwin) (baseball); Texarkana, Tex. **(1931–2001)**
Mattingly, Don (baseball); Evansville, Ind., 4/20/61
Matson, Randy (shot putter); Kilgore, Tex., 3/5/45
Mays, Willie (baseball); Westfield, Ala., 5/6/31
McAdoo, Bob (basketball); Greensboro, N.C., 9/25/51
McCarthy, Joe (Joseph Vincent) (baseball); Philadelphia **(1887–1978)**
McCovey, Willie Lee (baseball); Mobile, Ala., 1/10/38
McDonald, Lanny (hockey); Hanna, Alberta, Canada, 2/16/53
McDowell, Jack (baseball); Van Nuys, Calif., 1/16/66
McEnroe, John Patrick, Jr. (tennis); Wiesbaden, Germany, 2/16/59
McGraw, John Joseph (baseball); Truxton, N.Y. **(1873–1934)**
McGwire, Mark (baseball); Pomona, Calif., 10/1/63
McLain, Dennis (baseball); Chicago, 3/24/44
McMillan, Kathy Laverne (track); Raeford, N.C., 11/7/57
Merrill, Janice (track); New London, Conn., 6/18/62
Messier, Mark (hockey); Edmonton, Alberta, Canada, 1/18/61
Meyer, Deborah (swimming); Haddonfield, N.J., 8/14/52
Meyers, Anne (basketball); San Diego, Calif., 3/26/55
Middlecoff, Cary (golf); Halls, Tenn. **(1921–1998)**
Mikita, Stan (hockey); Sokolce, Czechoslovakia, 5/20/40
Milburn, Rodney, Jr. (hurdler); Opelousas, La., 5/18/50
Miller, Cheryl (basketball); Riverside, Calif., 1/3/64
Miller, Johnny (golf); San Francisco, 4/29/47
Miller, Reggie (basketball); Riverside, Calif., 8/24/65
Montana, Joe (football); New Eagle, Pa., 6/11/56
Montgomery, Jim (swimming); Madison, Wis., 1/24/55
Moody, Helen Wills (tennis); Centerville, Calif. **(1906–1998)**
Moore, Archie (boxing); Benoit, Miss. **(1916–1998)**
Morgan, Joe Leonard (baseball); Bonham, Tex., 9/19/43
Morrall, Earl (football); Muskegon, Mich., 5/17/34
Morton, Craig L. (football); Flint, Mich., 2/5/43
Mosconi, Willie (pocket billiards); Philadelphia **(1913–1993)**
Moses, Edwin Corley (track); Dayton, Ohio, 8/31/58
Mungo, Van Lingo (baseball); Pageland, S.C. **(1911–1985)**
Munson, Thurman (baseball); Akron, Ohio **(1947–1979)**
Murphy, Calvin (basketball); Norwalk, Conn., 5/9/48
Murray, Eddie (baseball); Los Angeles, Calif., 2/24/56
Musial, Stan (baseball); Donora, Pa., 11/21/20
Myers, Linda (archery); York, Pa., 6/19/47
Naber, John (swimming); Evanston, Ill., 1/20/56
Namath, Joe (Joseph William) (football); Beaver Falls, Pa., 5/31/43
Nastase, Ilie (tennis); Bucharest, 7/19/46
Navratilova, Martina (tennis); Prague, 10/18/56
Nehemiah, Renaldo (track); Newark, N.J., 3/24/59
Nelson, Cindy (skiing); Lutsen, Minn., 8/19/55
Newcombe, John (tennis); Sydney, Australia, 5/23/43
Niekro, Phil (baseball); Lansing, Ohio, 4/1/39
Nicklaus, Jack (golf); Columbus, Ohio, 1/21/40
Norman, Gregory (golf); Mount Isa, Australia, 2/10/55
Oerter, Al (discus thrower); New York City, 9/19/36
Olajuwon, Hakeem (basketball); Lagos, Nigeria, 1/21/63
Oldfield, Barney (racing driver); Fulton County, Ohio **(1878–1946)**
Oliva, Tony (Pedro) (baseball); Pinar Del Rio, Cuba, 7/20/40

Olsen, Merlin Jay (football); Logan, Utah, 9/15/40
O'Malley, Walter (baseball executive); New York City **(1903–1979)**
O'Neal, Shaquille (basketball); Newark, N.J., 3/6/72
Orantes, Manuel (tennis); Granada, Spain, 2/6/49
Orr, Bobby (hockey); Parry Sound, Ontario, Canada, 3/20/48
Ovett, Steve (track); Brighton, England, 10/9/55
Owens, Jesse (track); Decatur, Ala. **(1914–1980)**
Paige, Satchel (Leroy) (baseball); Mobile, Ala. **(1906–1982)**
Palmer, Arnold (golf); Latrobe, Pa., 9/10/29
Palmer, James Alvin (baseball); New York City, 10/15/45
Parcells, Bill (football coach); Englewood, N.J., 8/22/41
Parent, Bernard Marcel (hockey); Montreal, 4/3/45
Park, Brad (Douglas Bradford) (hockey); Toronto, Ontario, Canada, 7/6/48
Parseghian, Ara (football); Akron, Ohio, 5/21/23
Pasarell, Charles (tennis); San Juan, Puerto Rico, 2/12/44
Patterson, Floyd (boxing); Waco, N.C., 1/4/35
Peete, Calvin (golf); Detroit, Mich., 7/18/43
Pelé (Edson Arantes do Nascimento) (soccer); Tres Coracoes, Brazil, 10/23/40
Perry, Gaylord (baseball); Williamston, N.C., 9/15/38
Perry, Jim (baseball); Williamston, N.C., 10/30/36
Pettit, Bob (basketball); Baton Rouge, La., 12/12/32
Petty, Richard Lee (auto racing); Randleman, N.C., 7/2/37
Pincay, Laffit, Jr. (jockey); Panama City, Panama, 12/29/46
Pippen, Scottie (basketball); Hamburg, N.J., 9/25/65
Plager, Barclay (ice hockey); Kirkland Lake, Ontario **(1941–1988)**
Plante, Jacques (hockey); Sahwinigan Falls, Quebec, Canada, 1/17/29
Player, Gary (golf); Johannesburg, South Africa, 11/1/35
Plunkett, Jim (football); San Jose, Calif., 12/5/47
Potvin, Denis Charles (hockey); Hull, Quebec, Canada, 10/29/53
Powell, Boog (John) (baseball); Lakeland, Fla., 8/17/41
Powell, Mike (track); Philadelphia, 11/10/63
Prefontaine, Steve Roland (runner); Coos Bay, Ore. **(1951–1975)**
Prince, Bob (baseball announcer); Pittsburgh **(1917–1985)**
Proell, Annemarie Moser (Alpine skier); Kleinarl, Austria, 3/27/53
Rafter, Patrick (tennis); Brisbane, Australia, 12/28/72
Ralston, Dennis (tennis); Bakersfield, Calif., 7/27/42
Rankin, Judy Torluemke (golf); St. Louis, Mo., 2/18/45
Raschi, Vic (baseball); West Springfield, Mass. **(1919–1988)**
Ratelle, Jean (Joseph Gilbert Yvon Jean) (hockey); St. Jean, Quebec, Canada, 10/29/53
Rawls, Betsy (Elizabeth Earle) (golf); Spartanburg, S.C., 5/4/28
Reed, Willis (basketball); Hico, La., 6/25/42
Reese, Pee Wee (Harold) (baseball); Ekron, Ky. **(1919–1999)**
Resch, Glenn "Chico" (hockey); Moose Jaw, Saskatchewan, Canada, 7/10/48
Rice, Jerry (football); Crawford, Miss., 10/13/62
Richard, Maurice (hockey); Montreal, 8/14/24
Riessen, Martin (tennis); Hinsdale, Ill., 12/4/41
Rigney, William (baseball); Alameda, Calif. **(1918–2001)**
Rios, Marcelo (tennis); Santiago, Chile, 12/26/75
Ripken, Cal, Jr. (baseball); Havre de Grace, Md., 8/24/60
Rizzuto, Phil (baseball); New York City, 9/25/18
Robertson, Oscar (basketball); Charlotte, Tenn., 11/24/38
Robinson, Arnie (track); San Diego, Calif., 4/7/48
Robinson, Brooks (baseball); Little Rock, Ark., 5/18/37
Robinson, David (basketball); Key West, Fla., 8/6/65
Robinson, Frank (baseball); Beaumont, Tex., 8/31/35
Robinson, Jackie (baseball); Cairo, Ga. **(1919–1972)**
Robinson, Larry Clark (hockey); Marvelville, Ontario, Canada, 6/2/51
Robinson, "Sugar" Ray (boxing); Detroit **(1920–1989)**
Rockne, Knute Kenneth (football); Voss, Norway **(1888–1931)**
Rockwell, Martha (skiing); Providence, R.I., 4/26/44
Rodman, Dennis (basketball); Trenton, N.J., 5/13/61
Ronaldo (soccer); Bento Ribeiro, Brazil, 9/22/76
Rono, Harry (track); Kiptaragon, Kenya, 2/12/52
Rooney, Art (football); Pittsburgh, Pa. **(1901–1988)**
Rose, Pete (Peter Edward) (baseball); Cincinnati, 4/14/41
Rosenbloom, Maxie (boxing); New York City **(1904–1976)**
Rosewall, Ken (tennis); Sydney, Australia, 11/2/34
Rote, Kyle (football); San Antonio, 10/27/28
Roush, Edd (baseball); Oakland City, Ind. **(1893–1988)**
Rozelle, Pete (Alvin Ray) (commissioner of National Football League); South Gate, Calif. **(1926–1996)**
Rudolph, Wilma Glodean (sprinter); St. Bethlehem, Tenn. **(1940–1994)**
Russell, Bill (basketball); Monroe, La., 2/12/34
Ruth, Babe (George Herman Ruth) (baseball); Baltimore **(1895–1948)**
Rutherford, Johnny (auto racing); Fort Worth, 3/12/38
Ryan, Nolan (Lynn Nolan, Jr.) (baseball); Refugio, Tex., 1/31/47
Ryon, Luann (archery); Long Beach, Calif., 1/13/53
Ryun, Jim (runner); Wichita, Kan., 4/29/47
Salazar, Alberto (track); Havana, 8/7/58
Sampras, Pete (tennis); Washington, D.C., 8/12/71
Samuels, Howard (horse racing soccer); New York City **(1920–1984)**
Sanders, Barry (football); Wichita, Kan., 7/16/68
Sanders, Deion (baseball/football); Ft. Myers, Fla., 8/9/67

Santana, Manuel (Manuel Santana Martinez) (tennis); Chamartin, Spain, 5/10/38
Sayers, Gale (football); Wichita, Kan., 5/30/43
Schmidt, Mike (baseball); Dayton, Ohio, 9/27/49
Schoendienst, Red (Albert) (baseball); Germantown, Ill., 2/2/23
Schollander, Donald (swimming); Charlotte, N.C., 4/30/46
Scurry, Briana (soccer); Minneapolis, Minn., 9/7/71
Seagren, Bob (Robert Lloyd) (pole vaulter); Pomona, Calif., 10/17/46
Seau, Junior (football); Oceanside, Calif., 1/19/69
Seaver, Tom (baseball); Fresno, Calif., 11/17/44
Seidler, Maren (track); Brooklyn, N.Y., 6/11/62
Seles, Monica (tennis); Novi Sad, Yugoslavia, 12/2/73
Selke, Frank (ice hockey); Canada **(1893–1985)**
Sewell, Joe (baseball); Titus, Ala. **(1898–1990)**
Shepherd, Lee (auto racing) **(1945–1985)**
Shero, Fred (hockey); Camden, N.J. **(1925–1990)**
Shoemaker, Willie (jockey); Fabens, Tex., 8/19/31
Shore, Eddie (ice hockey); Saskatchewan, Canada **(1902–1985)**
Shorter, Frank (runner); Munich, Germany, 10/31/47
Shriver, Pam (tennis); Baltimore, 7/4/62
Shula, Don (Donald Francis) (football); Grand River, Ohio, 1/4/30
Silvester, Jay (discus thrower); Tremonton, Utah, 2/27/37
Simpson, O.J. (Orenthal James) (football); San Francisco, 7/9/47
Sims, Billy (football); St. Louis, 9/18/55
Smith, Bubba (Charles Aaron) (football); Orange, Tex., 2/28/45
Smith, Emmitt (football); Pensacola, Fla., 5/15/69
Smith, Ozzie (baseball); Mobile, Ala., 12/26/54
Smith, Ronnie Ray (sprinter); Los Angeles, 3/28/49
Smith, Stanley Roger (tennis); Pasadena, Calif., 12/14/46
Smith, Tommie (sprinter); Clarksville, Tex., 6/5/44
Smoke, Marcia Jones (canoeing); Oklahoma City, 7/18/41
Snead, Sam (golf); Hot Springs, Va., 5/27/12
Sneva, Tom (auto racing); Spokane, Wash., 6/1/48
Snider, Duke (Edwin) (baseball); Los Angeles, 9/19/26
Solomon, Harold (tennis); Washington, D.C., 9/17/52
Sosa, Sammy (Samuel) (baseball); San Pedro de Macoris, Dominican Republic, 11/12/68
Spahn, Warren (baseball); Buffalo, N.Y., 4/23/21
Speaker, Tristram (baseball); Hubbard City, Tex. **(1888–1958)**
Spencer, Brian (ice hockey); Fort St. James, British Columbia **(1949–1988)**
Spinks, Leon (boxing); St. Louis, 7/11/53
Spitz, Mark (swimming); Modesto, Calif., 2/10/50
Stabler, Kenneth (football); Foley, Ala., 12/25/45
Stagg, Amos Alonzo (football); West Orange, N.J. **(1862–1965)**
Stargell, Willie (Wilver Dornell) (baseball); Earlsboro, Okla. **(1941–2001)**
Starr, Bart (football); Montgomery, Ala., 1/9/34
Staub, "Rusty" (Daniel) (baseball); New Orleans, 4/4/44
Staubach, Roger (football); Cincinnati, 2/5/42
Steinkraus, William C. (equestrian); Cleveland, 10/12/25
Stenerud, Jan (football); Fetsund, Norway, 11/26/42
Stengel, Casey (Charles Dillon) (baseball); Kansas City, Mo. **(1891–1975)**
Stenmark, Ingemar (Alpine skier); Tarnaby, Sweden, 3/18/56
Stevens, Scott (hockey); Completon, New Brunswick, 5/4/66
Stockton, Richard LaClede (tennis); New York City, 2/18/51
Stones, Dwight Edwin (track); Los Angeles, 12/6/53
Strawberry, Darryl (baseball); Los Angeles, 3/12/62
Street, Picabo (skiing); Triumph, Idaho, 4/3/71
Sullivan, John Lawrence (boxing); Boston **(1858–1918)**
Summitt, Pat (basketball); Henrietta, Tenn., 6/14/52
Sutton, Don (Donald Howard) (baseball); Clio, Ala., 4/2/45
Swann, Lynn (football); Alcoa, Tenn., 3/7/52
Swoopes, Sheryl (basketball); Brownfield, Tex., 3/25/71
Tanner, Leonard Roscoe III (tennis); Chattanooga, Tenn., 10/15/51
Tarkenton, Fran (Francis) (football); Richmond, Va., 2/3/40
Tebbetts, Birdie (George R.) (baseball); Nashua, N.H. **(1914–1999)**
Theismann, Joe (football); New Brunswick, N.J., 9/9/46

Thomas, Frank (baseball); Columbus, Ga., 5/27/68
Thomas, Isiah (basketball); Chicago, Ill., 4/30/61
Thomas, Thurman (football); Houston, Texas, 5/16/66
Thompson, David (basketball); Shelby, N.C., 7/13/54
Thorpe, Ian (swimming); Sydney, New South Wales, Australia, 10/13/82
Thorpe, Jim (James Francis) (all-around athlete); nr. Prague, Okla. **(1888–1953)**
Tilden, William Tatem II (tennis); Philadelphia **(1893–1953)**
Tittle, Y. A. (Yelberton Abraham) (football); Marshall, Tex., 10/24/26
Toomey, William (decathlon); Philadelphia, 1/10/39
Trevino, Lee (golf); Dallas, 12/1/39
Trottier, Bryan (hockey); Val Marie, Sask., Canada, 7/17/56
Tunney, Gene (James J.) (boxing); New York City **(1898–1978)**
Tyson, Mike (boxing); Brooklyn, N.Y., 6/30/66
Tyus, Wyomia (runner); Griffin, Ga., 8/29/45
Ueberroth, Peter (baseball); Evanston, Ill., 9/2/37
Unitas, John (football); Pittsburgh, 5/7/33
Unser, Al (auto racing); Albuquerque, N. Mex., 5/29/39
Unser, Bobby (auto racing); Albuquerque, N. Mex., 2/20/34
Valenzuela, Fernando (baseball); Sonora, Mexico, 11/1/60
Valvano, Jim (basketball); New York, N.Y. **(1946–1993)**
Van Brocklin, Norm (football); Eagle Butte, S. Dak. **(1926–1983)**
Vaughn, Mo (baseball); Norwalk, Conn., 12/15/67
Vilas, Guillermo (tennis); Mar del Plata, Argentina, 8/17/52
Viola, Frank (baseball); Hempstead, N.Y., 4/19/60
Viren, Lasse (track); Myrskyla, Finland, 7/12/49
Vitale, Dick (basketball); E. Rutherford, N.J., 6/9/39
Wade, Virginia (tennis); Bournemouth, England, 7/10/45
Wagner, Honus (John Peter Honus) (baseball); Carnegie, Pa. **(1867–1955)**
Waitz, Grete (Andersen) (running); Oslo, Norway, 10/1/53
Walcott, Jersey Joe (Arnold Cream) (boxing); Merchantville, N.J. **(1914–1994)**
Wallace, Rusty (auto racing); St. Louis, Mo., 8/14/56
Walsh, Adam (football) **(1902–1985)**
Walton, Bill (basketball); La Mesa, Calif., 11/5/52
Waterfield, Bob (football); Burbank, Calif **(1921–1983)**
Watson, Martha Rae (track); Long Beach, Calif., 8/19/46
Watson, Tom (golf); Kansas City, Mo., 9/4/49
Weaver, Earl (baseball); St. Louis, 8/14/30
Weiskopf, Tom (golf); Massillon, Ohio, 11/9/42
Weiss, George (baseball executive); New Haven, Conn. **(1895–1972)**
Weissmuller, Johnny (swimmer and actor); Windber, Pa. **(1904–1984)**
West, Jerry (basketball); Cheylan, W. Va., 5/28/38
White, Reggie (football); Chattanooga, Tenn., 12/19/61
White, Willye B. (long jumper); Money, Miss., 1/1/36
Whitworth, Kathy (golf); Monahans, Tex., 9/27/39
Wilkens, Mac Maurice (track); Eugene, Ore., 11/15/50
Wilkins, Lennie (basketball) 11/25/37
Wilkinson, Bud (football); Minneapolis **(1916–1994)**
Williams, Dick (baseball); St. Louis, 5/7/29
Williams, Serena (tennis); Saginaw, Mich., 9/26/81
Williams, Ted (baseball); San Diego, Calif., 8/30/18
Williams, Venus (tennis); Lynnwood, Calif., 6/17/80
Wills, Maury (baseball); Washington, D.C., 10/2/32
Winfield, Dave (baseball); St. Paul, Minn., 10/3/51
Wohlhuter, Richard C. (runner); Geneva, Ill., 12/23/45
Wood, "Smokey Joe" (Joseph) (baseball); Kansas City, Mo. **(1890–1985)**
Woods, Tiger (Eldrick) (golf); Long Beach, Calif., 12/30/75
Wottle, David James (runner); Canton, Ohio, 8/7/50
Wright, Mickey (Mary Kathryn) (golf); San Diego, Calif., 2/14/35
Yarborough, Cale (William Caleb) (auto racing); Timmonsville, S.C., 3/27/39
Yastrzemski, Carl (baseball); Southampton, N.Y., 8/22/39
Young, Cy (Denton True) (baseball); Gilmore, Ohio **(1867–1955)**
Young, Sheila (speed skater, bicycle racer); Detroit, 10/14/50
Young, Steve (football); Salt Lake City, Utah, 10/11/61
Zaharias, Babe Didrikson (golf); Port Arthur, Tex. **(1913–1956)**

Hockey

Ice hockey, by birth and upbringing a Canadian game, is an offshoot of field hockey. Some historians say that the first ice hockey game was played in Montreal in December 1879 between two teams composed almost exclusively of McGill University students, but others assert that earlier hockey games took place in Kingston, Ontario, or Halifax, Nova Scotia. In the Montreal game of 1879, there were fifteen players on a side, who used an assortment of crude sticks to keep the puck in motion. Early rules allowed nine men on a side, but the number was reduced to seven in 1886 and later to six.

The first governing body of the sport was the Amateur Hockey Association of Canada, organized in 1887. In the winter of 1894–1895, a group of college students from the United States visited Canada and saw hockey played. They became enthused over the game and introduced it as a winter sport when they returned home. The first professional league was the International Hockey League, which operated in northern Michigan in 1904–1906.

Until 1910, professionals and amateurs were allowed to play together on "mixed teams," but this arrangement ended with the formation of the first "big league," the National Hockey Association, in eastern Canada in 1910. The Pacific Coast League was organized in 1911 for western Canadian hockey. The league included Seattle and later other American cities. The National Hockey League replaced the National Hockey Association in 1917. Boston, in 1924, was the first American city to join that circuit. The league expanded to include western cities in 1967. The Stanley Cup was competed for by "mixed teams" from 1894 to 1910, thereafter by professionals. It was awarded to the winner of the NHL playoffs from 1926–1967 and now to the league champion.

The World Hockey Association was organized in October 1972 and was dissolved after the 1978–1979 season when the NHL absorbed four of the teams.

Rule changes have been implemented to steer the league from its violent reputation in order to better showcase the world's most talented stars.

Hockey, once considered a cold-weather sport, has taken major strides in increasing its fan base to the southern and western part of the United States as well. In the 1995–1996 season, Florida and Colorado battled in the Stanley Cup Finals, the San Jose Sharks sold out all 41 of their home games, and the second team in two years (Winnipeg) migrated from Canada to the Southwest region of the U.S. (Phoenix).

The league continued to expand when the Nashville Predators joined the league in the 1998–1999 season. The 1999–2000 season included the new Atlanta Thrashers and the 2000–2001 season introduced the Columbus Blue Jackets and the Minnesota Wild.

STANLEY CUP WINNERS

Emblematic of World Professional Championship; NHL Championship after 1967

1893 Montreal A.A.A.	1924 Montreal Canadiens	1956–60 Montreal Canadiens
1894 Montreal A.A.A.	1925 Victoria Cougars	1961 Chicago Blackhawks
1895 Montreal Victorias	1926 Montreal Maroons	1962–64 Toronto Maple Leafs
1896 (Feb.) Winnipeg Victorias	1927 Ottawa Senators	1965–66 Montreal Canadiens
1896 (Dec.) Montreal Victorias	1928 N.Y. Rangers	1967 Toronto Maple Leafs
1897–99 Montreal Victorias	1929 Boston Bruins	1968–69 Montreal Canadiens
1899–1900 Montreal Shamrocks	1930–31 Montreal Canadiens	1970 Boston Bruins
1901 Winnipeg Victorias	1932 Toronto Maple Leafs	1971 Montreal Canadiens
1902 Montreal A.A.A.	1933 N.Y. Rangers	1972 Boston Bruins
1903–05 Ottawa Silver Seven	1934 Chicago Blackhawks	1973 Montreal Canadiens
1906 Montreal Wanderers	1935 Montreal Maroons	1974–75 Philadelphia Flyers
1907 (Jan.) Kenora Thistles	1936–37 Detroit Red Wings	1976–79 Montreal Canadiens
1907 (March) Montreal Wanderers	1938 Chicago Red Hawks	1980–83 N.Y. Islanders
1908 Montreal Wanderers	1939 Boston Bruins	1984–85 Edmonton Oilers
1909 Ottawa Senators	1940 N.Y. Rangers	1986 Montreal Canadiens
1910 Montreal Wanderers	1941 Boston Bruins	1987–88 Edmonton Oilers
1911 Ottawa Senators	1942 Toronto Maple Leafs	1989 Calgary Flames
1912–13 Quebec Bulldogs	1943 Detroit Red Wings	1990 Edmonton Oilers
1914 Toronto Blueshirts	1944 Montreal Canadiens	1991–92 Pittsburgh Penguins
1915 Vancouver Millionaires	1945 Toronto Maple Leafs	1993 Montreal Canadiens
1916 Montreal Canadiens	1946 Montreal Canadiens	1994 N.Y. Rangers
1917 Seattle Metropolitans	1947–49 Toronto Maple Leafs	1995 N.J. Devils
1918 Toronto Arenas	1950 Detroit Red Wings	1996 Colorado Avalanche
1919 No champion	1951 Toronto Maple Leafs	1997–98 Detroit Red Wings
1920–21 Ottawa Senators	1952 Detroit Red Wings	1999 Dallas Stars
1922 Toronto St. Patricks	1953 Montreal Canadiens	2000 N.J. Devils
1923 Ottawa Senators	1954–55 Detroit Red Wings	2001 Colorado Avalanche

NHL CHAMPIONS

Wales Trophy	1958–62 Montreal	1971–72 Boston	1982–84 N.Y.	1993 Montreal
1939–41 Boston	1963 Toronto	1973 Montreal	Islanders	1994 N.Y. Rangers
1942 New York	1964 Montreal	1974 Boston	1985 Philadelphia	1995 New Jersey
1943 Detroit	1965 Detroit	**Eastern Conference[1]**	1986 Montreal	1996 Florida
1944–47 Montreal	1966 Montreal	1975 Buffalo	1987 Philadelphia	1997 Philadelphia
1948 Toronto	1967 Chicago	1976–79 Montreal	1988 Boston	1998 Washington
1948–55 Detroit	**Eastern Division**	1980 Buffalo	1989 Montreal	1999 Buffalo
1956 Montreal	1968–69 Montreal	1981 Montreal	1990 Boston	2000–2001 New
1957 Detroit	1970 Chicago		1991–92 Pittsburgh	Jersey

1. Prior to 1994 was the Wales Conference.

CAMPBELL BOWL

Western Division	1978–79 N.Y. Islanders	1989 Calgary	1995 Detroit
1968–70 St. Louis	1980 Philadelphia	1990 Edmonton	1996 Colorado
1971–73 Chicago	1981 N.Y. Islanders	1991 Minnesota	1997–98 Detroit
1974 Philadelphia	1982–85 Edmonton	1992 Chicago	1999–2000 Dallas
Western Conference[2]	1986 Calgary	1993 Los Angeles	2001 Colorado
1975–77 Philadelphia	1987–88 Edmonton	1994 Vancouver	

2. Prior to 1994 was the Campbell Conference.

NATIONAL HOCKEY LEAGUE YEARLY TROPHY WINNERS

The Hart Trophy—Most Valuable Player

1924 Frank Nighbor, Ottawa
1925 Billy Burch, Hamilton
1926 Nels Stewart, Montreal Maroons
1927 Herb Gardiner, Montreal Canadiens
1928 Howie Morenz, Montreal Canadiens
1929 Roy Worters, N.Y. Americans
1930 Nels Stewart, Montreal Maroons
1931–32 Howie Morenz, Montreal Canadiens
1933 Eddie Shore, Boston
1934 Aurel Joliat, Montreal Canadiens
1935–36 Eddie Shore, Boston
1937 Babe Siebert, Montreal Canadiens
1938 Eddie Shore, Boston
1939 Toe Blake, Montreal Canadiens
1940 Ebbie Goodfellow, Detroit
1941 Bill Cowley, Boston
1942 Tommy Anderson, N.Y. Americans
1943 Bill Cowley, Boston
1944 Babe Pratt, Toronto
1945 Elmer Lach, Montreal Canadiens
1946 Max Bentley, Chicago
1947 Maurice Richard, Montreal Canadiens
1948 Buddy O'Connor, N.Y. Rangers
1949 Sid Abel, Detroit
1950 Chuck Rayner, N.Y. Rangers
1951 Milt Schmidt, Boston
1952–53 Gordie Howe, Detroit
1954 Al Rollins, Chicago
1955 Ted Kennedy, Toronto
1956 Jean Belveau, Montreal Canadiens
1957–58 Gordie Howe, Detroit
1959 Andy Bathgate, N.Y. Rangers
1960 Gordie Howe, Detroit
1961 Bernie Geoffrion, Montreal Canadiens
1962 Jacques Plante, Montreal Canadiens
1963 Gordon Howe, Detroit
1964 Jean Beliveau, Montreal Canadiens
1965–66 Bobby Hull, Chicago
1967–68 Stan Mikita, Chicago
1969 Phil Esposito, Boston
1970–72 Bobby Orr, Boston
1973 Bobby Clarke, Philadelphia
1974 Phil Esposito, Boston
1975–76 Bobby Clarke, Philadelphia
1977–78 Guy Lafleur, Montreal
1979 Bryan Trottier, N.Y. Islanders
1980–87 Wayne Gretzky, Edmonton
1988 Mario Lemieux, Pittsburgh
1989 Wayne Gretzky, Los Angeles
1990 Mark Messier, Edmonton
1991 Brett Hull, St. Louis
1992 Mark Messier, N.Y. Rangers
1993 Mario Lemieux, Pittsburgh
1994 Sergei Fedorov, Detroit
1995 Eric Lindros, Philadelphia
1996 Mario Lemieux, Pittsburgh
1997–98 Dominik Hasek, Buffalo
1999 Jaromir Jagr, Pittsburgh
2000 Chris Pronger, St. Louis
2001 Joe Sakic, Colorado

Vezina Trophy—Leading Goalkeeper

1956–60 Jacques Plante, Montreal
1961 Johnny Bower, Toronto
1962 Jacques Plante, Montreal
1963 Glenn Hall, Chicago
1964 Charlie Hodge, Montreal
1965 Terry Sawchuk—Johnny Bower, Toronto
1966 Gump Worsley—Charlie Hodge, Montreal
1967 Glen Hall—Denis Dejordy, Chicago
1968 Gump Worsley—Rogie Vachon, Montreal
1969 Glenn Hall—Jacques Plante, St. Louis
1970 Tony Esposito, Chicago
1971 Ed Giacomin—Gilles Villemure, N.Y. Rangers
1972 Tony Esposito—Gary Smith, Chicago
1973 Ken Dryden, Montreal
1974 Bernie Parent, Philadelphia and Tony Esposito, Chicago
1975 Bernie Parent, Philadelphia
1976 Ken Dryden, Montreal
1977–79 Ken Dryden—Bunny Larocque, Montreal
1980 Bob Sauve—Don Edwards, Buffalo
1981 Richard Sevigny—Denis Herron—Bunny Larocque, Montreal
1982 Billy Smith, N.Y. Islanders
1983 Pete Peeters, Boston
1984 Tom Barrasso, Buffalo
1985 Pelle Lindbergh, Philadelphia
1986 John Vanbiesbrouck, N.Y. Rangers
1987 Ron Hextall, Philadelphia
1988 Grant Fuhr, Edmonton
1989–90 Patrick Roy, Montreal
1991 Ed Belfour, Chicago
1992 Patrick Roy, Montreal
1993 Ed Belfour, Chicago
1994–95 Dominik Hasek, Buffalo
1996 Jim Carey, Washington
1997–99 Dominik Hasek, Buffalo
2000 Olaf Kolzig, Washington
2001 Dominik Hasek, Buffalo

James Norris Trophy—Defenseman

1954 Red Kelly, Detroit
1955–58 Doug Harvey, Montreal
1959 Tom Johnson, Montreal
1960–62 Doug Harvey, Montreal, N.Y. Rangers (62)
1963–65 Pierre Pilote, Chicago
1966 Jacques Laperriere, Montreal
1967 Harry Howell, N.Y. Rangers
1968–75 Bobby Orr, Boston

1976 Denis Potvin, N.Y. Islanders
1977 Larry Robinson, Montreal
1978–79 Denis Potvin, N.Y. Islanders
1980 Larry Robinson, Montreal
1981 Randy Carlyle, Pittsburgh
1982 Doug Wilson, Chicago
1983–84 Rod Langway, Washington
1985–86 Paul Coffey, Edmonton
1987–88 Ray Bourque, Boston
1989 Chris Chelios, Montreal
1990–91 Ray Bourque, Boston
1992 Brian Leetch, N.Y. Rangers
1993 Chris Chelios, Chicago
1994 Ray Bourque, Boston
1995 Paul Coffey, Detroit
1996 Chris Chelios, Chicago
1997 Brian Leetch, N.Y. Rangers
1998 Rob Blake, Los Angeles
1999 Al MacInnis, St. Louis
2000 Chris Pronger, St. Louis
2001 Nicklas Lidstrom, Detroit

Lady Byng Trophy—Sportsmanship

1960 Don McKenney, Boston
1961 Red Kelly, Toronto
1962–63 Dave Keon, Toronto
1964 Ken Wharram, Chicago
1965 Bobby Hull, Chicago
1966 Alex Delvecchio, Detroit
1967–68 Stan Mikita, Chicago
1969 Alex Delvecchio, Detroit
1970 Phil Goyette, St. Louis
1971 Johnny Bucyk, Boston
1972 Jean Ratelle, N.Y. Rangers
1973 Gilbert Perreault, Buffalo
1974 Johnny Bucyk, Boston
1975 Marcel Dionne, Detroit
1976 Jean Ratelle, N.Y. Rangers, Boston
1977 Marcel Dionne, Los Angeles
1978 Butch Goring, Los Angeles
1979 Bob MacMillan, Atlanta
1980 Wayne Gretzky, Edmonton
1981 Rick Kehoe, Pittsburgh
1982 Rick Middleton, Boston
1983–84 Mike Bossy, N.Y. Islanders
1985 Jari Kurri, Edmonton
1986 Mike Bossy, N.Y. Islanders
1987 Joey Mullen, Calgary
1988 Mats Naslund, Montreal
1989 Joey Mullen, Calgary
1990 Brett Hull, St. Louis
1991–92 Wayne Gretzky, Los Angeles
1993 Pierre Turgeon, N.Y. Islanders
1994 Wayne Gretzky, Los Angeles
1995 Ron Francis, Pittsburgh
1996–97 Paul Kariya, Anaheim
1998 Ron Francis, Pittsburgh
1999 Wayne Gretzky, N.Y. Rangers
2000 Pavol Demitra, St. Louis
2001 Joe Sakic, Colorado

Calder Trophy—Rookie

1962 Bobby Rousseau, Montreal
1963 Kent Douglas, Toronto
1964 Jacques Laperriere, Montreal
1965 Roger Crozier, Detroit
1966 Brit Selby, Toronto

1967 Bobby Orr, Boston
1968 Derek Sanderson, Boston
1969 Danny Grant, Minnesota
1970 Tony Esposito, Chicago
1971 Gilbert Perreault, Buffalo
1972 Ken Dryden, Montreal
1973 Steve Vickers, N.Y. Rangers
1974 Denis Potvin, N.Y. Islanders
1975 Eric Vail, Atlanta
1976 Bryan Trottier, N.Y. Islanders
1977 Willi Plett, Atlanta
1978 Mike Bossy, N.Y. Islanders
1979 Bobby Smith, Minnesota
1980 Ray Bourque, Boston
1981 Peter Stastny, Quebec
1982 Dale Hawerchuk, Winnipeg
1983 Steve Larmer, Chicago
1984 Tom Barrasso, Buffalo
1985 Mario Lemieux, Pittsburgh
1986 Gary Suter, Calgary
1987 Luc Robitaille, Los Angeles
1988 Joe Nieuwendyk, Calgary

1989 Brian Leetch, N.Y. Rangers
1990 Sergei Makarov, Calgary
1991 Ed Belfour, Chicago
1992 Pavel Bure, Vancouver
1993 Teemu Selanne, Winnipeg
1994 Martin Brodeur, N.J. Devils
1995 Peter Forsberg, Quebec
1996 Daniel Alfredsson, Ottawa
1997 Bryan Berard, N.Y. Islanders
1998 Sergei Samsonov, Boston
1999 Chris Drury, Colorado
2000 Scott Gomez, New Jersey
2001 Evgeni Nabokov, San Jose

Art Ross Trophy—Leading Scorer

1955 Bernie Geoffrion, Montreal
1956 Jean Beliveau, Montreal
1957 Gordie Howe, Detroit
1958–59 Dickie Moore, Montreal
1960 Bobby Hull, Chicago
1961 Bernie Geoffrion, Montreal

1962 Bobby Hull, Chicago
1963 Gordie Howe, Detroit
1964–65 Stan Mikita, Chicago
1966 Bobby Hull, Chicago
1967–68 Stan Mikita, Chicago
1969 Phil Esposito, Boston
1970 Bobby Orr, Boston
1971–74 Phil Esposito, Boston
1975 Bobby Orr, Boston
1976–78 Guy Lafleur, Montreal
1979 Bryan Trottier, N.Y. Islanders
1980 Marcel Dionne, Los Angeles
1981–87 Wayne Gretzky, Edmonton
1988–89 Mario Lemieux, Pittsburgh
1990–91 Wayne Gretzky, Los Angeles
1992–93 Mario Lemieux, Pittsburgh
1994 Wayne Gretzky, Los Angeles
1995 Jaromir Jagr, Pittsburgh
1996–97 Mario Lemieux, Pittsburgh
1998–2001 Jaromir Jagr, Pittsburgh

STANLEY CUP PLAYOFFS—2001

NOTE: Home teams are in capitals.

EASTERN CONFERENCE

Quarterfinals
New Jersey Devils defeated Carolina Hurricanes,
    4 games to 2
Toronto Maple Leafs defeated Ottawa Senators,
    4 games to 0
Pittsburgh Penguins defeated Washington Capitals,
    4 games to 2
Buffalo Sabres defeated Philadelphia Flyers,
    4 games to 2

Semifinals
New Jersey Devils defeated Toronto Maple Leafs,
    4 games to 3
Pittsburgh Penguins defeated Buffalo Sabres,
    4 games to 3

Finals
New Jersey Devils defeated Pittsburgh Penguins,
    4 games to 1
May 12—NEW JERSEY 3, Pittsburgh 1
May 15—Pittsburgh 4, NEW JERSEY 2
May 17—New Jersey 3, PITTSBURGH 0
May 19—New Jersey 5, PITTSBURGH 0
May 22—NEW JERSEY 4, Pittsburgh 2

WESTERN CONFERENCE

Quarterfinals
Colorado Avalanche defeated Vancouver Canucks,
    4 games to 0
Los Angeles Kings defeated Detroit Red Wings,
    4 games to 2
St. Louis Blues defeated San Jose Sharks,
    4 games to 2
Dallas Stars defeated Edmonton Oilers,
    4 games to 2

Semifinals
Colorado Avalanche defeated Los Angeles Kings,
    4 games to 3
St. Louis Blues defeated Dallas Stars,
    4 games to 0

Finals
Colorado Avalanche defeated St. Louis Blues,
    4 games to 1
May 12—COLORADO 4, St. Louis 1
May 14—COLORADO 4, St. Louis 2
May 16—ST. LOUIS 4, Colorado 3 (2OT)
May 18—Colorado 4, ST. LOUIS 3 (OT)
May 21—COLORADO 2, St. Louis 1 (OT)

STANLEY CUP CHAMPIONSHIP FINALS

Colorado Avalanche defeated New Jersey Devils, 4 games to 3

May 26—COLORADO 5, New Jersey 0
May 29—New Jersey 2, COLORADO 1
May 31—Colorado 3, NEW JERSEY 1
June 2—NEW JERSEY 3, Colorado 2

June 4—New Jersey 4, COLORADO 1
June 7—Colorado 4, NEW JERSEY 0
June 9—COLORADO 3, New Jersey 1

Conn Smythe Trophy for most valuable player in the playoffs: Patrick Roy, Colorado

OTHER NHL AWARDS—2001

Frank Selke Trophy (Top defensive forward)—John
    Madden, New Jersey
King Clancy Trophy (Humanitarian community
    involvement)—Shjon Podein, Colorado

Jack Adams Award (Coach of the Year)—Bill Barber,
    Philadelphia
Bill Masterson Trophy (Perseverance, sportsmanship, and
    dedication to hockey)—Adam Graves, New York Rangers

NATIONAL HOCKEY LEAGUE FINAL STANDINGS OF THE CLUBS: 2000–2001

EASTERN CONFERENCE
Northeast Division

	W	L	T	Pts	GF	GA
Ottawa Senators[1]	48	21	9	109	274	205
Buffalo Sabres[2]	46	30	5	98	218	184
Toronto Maple Leafs[2]	37	29	11	90	232	207
Boston Bruins	36	30	8	88	227	249
Montreal Canadiens	28	40	8	70	206	232

Atlantic Division

	W	L	T	Pts	GF	GA
New Jersey Devils[1]	48	19	12	111	295	195
Philadelphia Flyers[2]	43	25	11	100	240	207
Pittsburgh Penguins[2]	42	28	9	96	281	256
N.Y. Rangers	33	43	5	72	250	290
N.Y. Islanders	21	51	7	52	185	268

Southeast Division

	W	L	T	Pts	GF	GA
Washington Capitals[1]	41	27	10	96	233	211
Carolina Hurricanes[2]	38	32	9	88	212	225
Florida Panthers	22	38	13	66	200	246
Atlanta Thrashers	23	45	12	60	211	289
Tampa Bay Lightning	24	47	6	59	201	280

1. Division champion. 2. Playoff qualifier.

WESTERN CONFERENCE
Central Division

	W	L	T	Pts	GF	GA
Detroit Red Wings[1]	49	20	9	111	253	202
St. Louis Blues[2]	43	22	12	103	249	195
Nashville Predators	34	36	9	80	186	200
Chicago Blackhawks	29	40	8	71	210	246
Columbus Blue Jackets	28	39	9	71	190	233

Pacific Division

	W	L	T	Pts	GF	GA
Dallas Stars[1]	48	24	8	106	241	187
San Jose Sharks[2]	40	27	12	95	217	192
Los Angeles Kings[2]	38	28	13	92	252	228
Phoenix Coyotes	35	27	17	90	214	212
Anaheim Mighty Ducks	25	41	11	66	188	245

Northwest Division

	W	L	T	Pts	GF	GA
Colorado Avalanche[1]	52	16	10	118	270	192
Edmonton Oilers[2]	39	28	12	93	243	222
Vancouver Canucks[2]	36	28	11	90	239	238
Calgary Flames	27	36	15	73	197	236
Minnesota Wild	25	39	13	68	168	210

NHL LEADING SCORERS: 2000–2001

	Gm	G	A	Pts
Jaromir Jagr, Pittsburgh	81	52	69	121
Joe Sakic, Colorado	82	54	64	118
Patrik Elias, New Jersey	82	40	56	96
Alexei Kovalev, Pittsburgh	79	44	51	95
Jason Allison, Boston	82	36	59	95
Martin Straka, Pittsburgh	82	27	68	95
Pavel Bure, Florida	82	59	33	92
Doug Weight, Edmonton	82	25	65	90
Zigmund Palffy, Los Angeles	73	38	51	89
Peter Forsberg, Colorado	73	27	62	89

NHL LEADING GOALTENDERS: 2000–2001

(Minimum 26 games played)

	Gm	Min	GAA	GA	Shots
Marty Turco, Dallas	26	1,266	1.90	40	532
Roman Cechmanek, Philadelphia	59	3,431	2.01	115	1,464
Manny Legace, Detroit	39	2,136	2.05	73	909
Dominik Hasek, Buffalo	67	3,904	2.11	137	1,726
Brent Johnson, St. Louis	31	1,744	2.17	63	676
Evgeni Nabokov, San Jose	66	3,700	2.19	135	1,582
Patrick Roy, Colorado	62	3,585	2.21	132	1,513
David Aebischer, Colorado	26	1,393	2.24	52	538
Manny Fernandez, Minnesota	42	2,461	2.24	92	1,147
Sean Burke, Phoenix	62	3,644	2.27	138	1,766

NHL CAREER SCORING LEADERS

(Through 2000–2001 season)

		Yrs	Gm	G	A	Pts
1	Wayne Gretzky	20	1,487	894	1,963	2,857
2	Gordie Howe	26	1,767	801	1,049	1,850
3	**Mark Messier**	22	1,561	651	1,130	1,781
4	Marcel Dionne	18	1,348	731	1,040	1,771
5	**Ron Francis**	20	1,489	487	1,137	1,624
6	**Steve Yzerman**	18	1,310	645	969	1,614
7	Phil Esposito	18	1,282	717	873	1,590
8	**Ray Bourque**	22	1,612	410	1,169	1,579
9	**Mario Lemieux**	13	788	648	922	1,570
10	**Paul Coffey**	21	1,409	396	1,135	1,531

Players active during 2000–2001 season in **bold** type.

NHL CAREER GOALTENDING LEADERS

(Through 2000–2001 season)

		Yrs	Gm	W	L	T	Pct
1	**Patrick Roy**	17	903	484	277	110	.619
2	Terry Sawchuk	21	971	447	330	172	.562
3	Jacques Plante	18	837	434	247	146	.614
4	Tony Esposito	16	886	423	306	152	.566
5	Glenn Hall	18	906	407	326	163	.545
6	Grant Fuhr	19	868	403	295	114	.567
7	**Mike Vernon**	18	763	383	264	91	.581
8	Andy Moog	18	713	372	209	88	.622
	J. Vanbiesbrouck	19	877	372	343	119	.517
10	Rogie Vachon	16	795	355	291	127	.541

Players active during 2000–2001 season in **bold** type.

Chess

WORLD CHAMPIONS

1894–	Emanuel Lasker, Germany		1969–71	Boris Spassky, USSR
1921			1972–74	Bobby Fischer, United States
1921–27	Jose R. Capablanca, Cuba		1975	Bobby Fischer, United States[2]; Anatoly
1927–35	Alexander A. Alekhine, USSR			Karpov, USSR
1935–37	Dr. Max Euwe, Netherlands		1976–85	Anatoly Karpov, USSR[3]
1937–46	Alexander A. Alekhine, USSR[1]		1985–	Garry Kasparov, Russia[4]
1948–57	Mikhail Botvinnik, USSR		2000	
1957–58	Vassily Smyslov, USSR		1993–99	Anatoly Karpov, Russia[5]
1958–60	Mikhail Botvinnik, USSR		1999	Alexander Khalifman, Russia[5]
1960–61	Mikhail Tal, USSR		2000	Viswanathan Anand, India[5]
1961–63	Mikhail Botvinnik, USSR			Vladimir Kramnik, Russia[6]
1963–68	Tigran Petrosian, USSR			

1. Alekhine, a French citizen, died while champion. 2. Relinquished title. 3. In 1978, Karpov defeated Viktor Korchnoi 6 games to 5. 4. PCA (Professional Chess Association) world champion after 1993. 5. FIDE (International Chess Federation) world champion. 6. PCA world champion.

UNITED STATES CHAMPIONS

1909–36	Frank J. Marshall, New York		1987	Tie, Nick Defirmian, San Francisco
1936–44	Samuel Reshevsky, New York[1]			Joel Benjamin, Brooklyn, N.Y.
1944–46	Arnold S. Denker, New York		1988	Michael Wilder, Princeton, N.J.
1946	Samuel Reshevsky, Boston		1989	Tie, Stuart Rachels, Birmingham, Ala.
1948	Herman Steiner, Los Angeles			Yasser Seirawan, Seattle, Wash.
1951–52	Larry Evans, New York			Roman Dzindzichashvili, New York, N.Y.
1954–57	Arthur Bisguier, New York		1990–91	Lev Alburt, New York, N.Y.
1958–61	Bobby Fischer, Brooklyn, N.Y.		1992	Gata Kamsky, Brooklyn, N.Y.
1962	Larry Evans, New York			Patrick Wolff, Somerville, Mass.
1963–67	Bobby Fischer, New York		1993	Tie, Alexander Shabalov, Pittsburgh, Pa.
1968	Larry Evans, New York			Alex Yermolinski, Edison, N.J.
1969–71	Samuel Reshevsky, Spring Valley, N.Y.		1994	Boris Gulko, Fairlawn, N.J.
1972	Robert Byrne, Ossining, N.Y.		1995	Patrick Wolff, Somerville, Mass.
1973	Lubomir Kavelek, Washington;		1996	Alex Yurmolinsky, Cleveland, Ohio
	John Grefe, San Francisco		1997	Esther Epstein, Mass. (women)
1974–77	Walter Browne, Berkeley, Calif.			Joel Benjamin, N.Y. (men)
1978–79	Lubomir Kavalek, New York		1998	Irina Krush, Brooklyn, N.Y. (women)
1980	Tie, Walter Browne, Berkeley, Calif.			Nick de Firmian, New York City (men)
	Larry Christiansen, Modesto, Calif.		1999	Anjelina Belakovskaia, Brooklyn, N.Y. (women)
	Larry Evans, Reno, Nev.			Boris Gulko, Fairlawn, N.J. (men)
1981–82[2]	Tie, Walter Browne, Berkeley, Calif.			Marcel Martinez, Miami, Fla. (junior)
	Yasser Seirawan, Seattle, Wash.		2000	Joel Benjamin, New York, N.Y. (men)
1983	Tie, Walter Browne, Berkeley, Calif.			Camilla Baginskaite, Vilnius, Lithuania
	Larry Christiansen, Los Angeles, Calif.,			(women)
	Roman Dzindzichashvili, Corona, N.Y.			Eugene Perelshteyn, Swampscott, Mass.
1984–85	Lev Alburt, New York City			(junior)
1986	Yasser Seirawan, Seattle, Wash.			

1. In 1942, Isaac I. Kashdan of New York was co-champion for a while because of a tie with Reshevsky in that year's tournament. Reshevsky won the play-off. 2. Championship not contested in 1982.

Bowling

The game of bowling in the United States is an indoor development of the more ancient outdoor game that survives as lawn bowling. The outdoor game is prehistoric in origin and probably goes back to primitive man and round stones that were rolled at some target. It is believed that a game something like nine-pins was popular among the Dutch, Swiss, and Germans as long ago as A.D. 1200. The game was played outdoors with an alley consisting of a single plank 12 to 18 inches wide, along which a ball was rolled toward three rows of three pins each placed at the far end of the alley. When the first indoor alleys were built and how the game was modified from time to time are matters of dispute.

It is supposed that the early settlers of New Amsterdam (New York City), being Dutch, brought their two bowling games with them. About a century ago the game of nine-pins was flourishing in the United States but was so corrupted by gambling on matches that it was barred by law in New York and Connecticut. Since the law specifically barred "nine-pins," it was eventually evaded by adding another pin and thus legally making it a new game.

Various organizations were formed to make rules for bowling and supervise competition in the United States but none was successful until the American Bowling Congress, organized Sept. 9, 1895, became the ruling body.

AMERICAN BOWLING CONGRESS CHAMPIONS

Year	Singles	All-events	Year	Singles	All-events
1959	Ed Lubanski	Ed Lubanski	1981	Rob Vital	Rod Toft
1960	Paul Kulbaga	Vince Lucci	1982	Bruce Bohm	Rich Wonders
1961	Lyle Spooner	Luke Karen	1983	Rick Kendrick	Tony Cariello
1962	Andy Renaldo	Billy Young	1984	Bob Antczak and Neal Young (tie)	Bob Goike
1963	Fred Delello	Bus Owalt	1985	Glen Harbison	Barry Asher
1964	Jim Stefanich	Les Zikes, Jr.	1986	Jess Mackey	Ed Marazka
1965	Ken Roeth	Tom Hathaway	1987	Terry Taylor	Ryan Schafer
1966	Don Chapman	John Wilcox	1988	Steve Hutkowski	Rick Steelsmith
1967	Frank Perry	Gary Lewis	1989	Paul Tetreault	George Hall
1968	Wayne Kowalski	Vince Mazzanti	1990	Bob Hochrein	Mike Neumann
1969	Greg Campbell	Eddie Jackson	1991	Ed Deines	Tom Howery
1970	Jake Yoder	Mike Berlin	1992	Bob Youker and Gary Blatchford	
1971	Al Cohn	Al Cohn		(tie)	Mike Tucker
1972	Bill Pointer	Mac Lowry	1993	Dan Bock	Jeff Nimke
1973	Ed Thompson	Ron Woolet	1994	John Weltzien	Thomas Holt
1974	Gene Krause	Bob Hart	1995	Matt Surina	Jeff Kwiatkowski
1975	Jim Setser	Bobby Meadows	1996	Donald Scudder, Jr.	Scott Kurtz
1976	Mike Putzer	Jim Lindquist	1997	John Socha	Jeff Richgels
1977	Frank Gadaleto	Bud Debenham	1998	John Gaines	Chris Barnes
1978	Rich Mersek	Chris Cobus	1999	Dan Winter	Thomas A. Jones
1979	Rick Peters	Bob Basacchi	2000	Garran Hein	Roy Daniels
1980	Mike Eaton	Steve Fehr	2001	Nicholas Hoagland	D. J. Archer

PROFESSIONAL BOWLERS ASSOCIATION

National Championship Tournament

1960	Don Carter	1971	Mike Lemongello	1982	Earl Anthony	1993	Ron Palombi
1961	Dave Soutar	1972	Johnny Guenther	1983	Earl Anthony	1994	David Traber
1962	Carmen Salvino	1973	Earl Anthony	1984	Bob Chamberlain	1995	Scott Alexander
1963	Billy Hardwick	1974	Earl Anthony	1985	Mike Aulby	1996	Butch Soper
1964	Bob Strampe	1975	Earl Anthony	1986	Tom Crites	1997	Rich Steelsmith
1965	Dave Davis	1976	Paul Colwell	1987	Randy Pedersen	1998	Pete Weber
1966	Wayne Zahn	1977	Tommy Hudson	1988	Brian Voss	1999	Tim Criss
1967	Dave Davis	1978	Warren Nelson	1989	Pete Weber	2000	Norm Duke
1968	Wayne Zahn	1979	Mike Aulby	1990	Jim Pencak	2001	Walter Ray Williams,
1969	Mike McGrath	1980	Johnny Petraglia	1991	Mike Miller		Jr.
1970	Mike McGrath	1981	Earl Anthony	1992	Eric Forkel		

BOWLING PROPRIETORS' ASSOCIATION OF AMERICA—MEN

United States Open[1]

1971	Mike Lemongello	1979	Joe Berardi	1987	Del Ballard	1995	Dave Husted
1972	Don Johnson	1980	Steve Martin	1988	Pete Weber	1996	Dave Husted
1973	Mike McGrath	1981	Marshall Holman	1989	Mike Aulby	1997	Not held
1974	Larry Laub	1982	Dave Husted	1990	Ron Palumbi, Jr.	1998	Walter Ray Williams,
1975	Steve Neff	1983	Gary Dickinson	1991	Pete Weber		Jr.
1976	Paul Moser	1984	Mark Roth	1992	Robert Lawrence	1999	Bob Learn, Jr.
1977	Johnny Petraglia	1985	Marshall Holman	1993	Del Ballard, Jr.	2000	Robert Smith
1978	Nelson Burton, Jr.	1986	Steve Cook	1994	Justin Hromek	2001[2]	

1. Replaced All-Star tournament and is rolled as part of BPA tour. 2. 2001 tournament held Dec. 1–9, 2001, after almanac went to press.

WOMEN'S INTERNATIONAL BOWLING CONGRESS CHAMPIONS

Year	Singles	All events	Year	Singles	All events
1959	Mae Bolt	Pat McBride	1969	Joan Bender	Helen Duval
1960	Marge McDaniels	Judy Roberts	1970	Dorothy Fothergill	Dorothy Fothergill
1961	Elaine Newton	Evelyn Teal	1971	Mary Scruggs	Lorrie Nichols
1962	Martha Hoffman	Flossie Argent	1972	D. D. Jacobson	Mildred Martorella
1963	Dot Wilkinson	Helen Shablis	1973	Bobby Buffaloe	Toni Calvery
1964	Jean Havlish	Jean Havlish	1974	Shirley Garms	Judy C. Soutar
1965	Doris Rudell	Donna Zimmerman	1975	Barbara Leicht	Virginia Norton
1966	Gloria Bouvia	Kate Helbig	1976	Bev Shonk	Betty Morris
1967	Gloria Paeth	Carol Miller	1977	Akiko Yamaga	Akiko Yamaga
1968	Norma Parks	Susie Reichley	1978	Mae Bolt	Annese Kelly

Year	Singles	All events	Year	Singles	All events
1979	Betty Morris	Betty Morris	1991	Debbie Kuhn	Debbie Kuhn
1980	Betty Morris	Cheryl Robinson	1992	Patty Ann	Mitsuko Tokimoto
1981	Virginia Norton	Virginia Norton	1993	Karen Collurs and Kari Murph (tie)	Bertha Blackshur and Sharon Davis (tie)
1982	Gracie Freeman	Aleta Rzepecki	1994	Vicki Fifield	Wendy Macpherson-Papanos
1983	Aleta Rzepecki	Virginia Norton			
1984	Freida Gates	Shinobu Saitoh	1995	Beth Owen	Beth Owen
1985	Polly Schwarzel	Aleta Sill	1996	Cindy Berlanga	Lorrie Nichols
1986	Dana Stewart	Robin Romeo and Maria Lewis (tie)	1997	Jean Schmidt	Kendra Cameron
			1998	Nellie Glandon	Liz Johnson
1987	Regi Junak	Leanne Barrette	1999	Maggie Matheson	Marlene Walls
1988	Michelle Meyer-Welty	Lisa Wagner	2000	Cathy Krasner	Carolyn Dorin-Ballard
1989	Lorraine Anderson	Nancy Fehn	2001	Lisa Wagner	Jonquay Armon
1990	Dana Miller-Mackie and Paula Carter (tie)	Carol Norman			

BOWLING PROPRIETORS' ASSOCIATION OF AMERICA—WOMEN

United States Open

1971	Paula Carter	1979	Diana Silva	1987	Carol Nurman	1995	Tish Johnson
1972	Lorrie Nichols	1980	Pat Costello (Calif.)	1988	Lisa Wagner	1996	Liz Johnson
1973	Mildred Martorella	1981	Donna Adamek	1989	Robin Romeo	1997	Not held
1974	Pat Costello (Calif.)	1982	Shinobu Saitoh	1990	Dana Miller-Mackie	1998	Aleta Sill
1975	Paula Carter	1983	Dana Miller	1991	Anne Marie Duggan	1999	Kim Adler
1976	Patty Costello (Pa.)	1984	Karen Ellingsworth	1992	Tish Johnson	2000	Tennelle Grijalva
1977	Betty Morris	1985	Pat Mercatanti	1993	Dede Davidson	2001[1]	
1978	Donna Adamek	1986	Wendy Macpherson	1994	Aleta Sill		

1. 2001 tournament held Dec. 1–9, 2001, after almanac went to press.

WIBC QUEENS TOURNAMENT CHAMPIONS

1961	Janet Harman	1972	Dorothy Fothergill	1983	Aleta Rzepecki	1994	Anne Marie Duggan
1962	Dorothy Wilkinson	1973	Dorothy Fothergill	1984	Kazue Inahashi	1995	Sandy Postma
1963	Irene Monterosso	1974	Judy Soutar	1985	Aleta Sill	1996	Lisa Wagner
1964	D.D. Jacobson	1975	Cindy Powell	1986	Cora Fiebig	1997	Sandra-Jo Shiery-Odom
1965	Betty Kuczynski	1976	Pamela Buckner	1987	Cathy Almeida		
1966	Judy Lee	1977	Dana Stewart	1988	Wendy Macpherson	1998	Lynda Norry
1967	Mildred Martorella	1978	Loa Boxberger	1989	Carol Gianotti	1999	Leanne Barrette
1968	Phyllis Massey	1979	Donna Adamek	1990	Patty Ann	2000	Wendy Macpherson
1969	Ann Feigel	1980	Donna Adamek	1991	Dede Davidson	2001	Carolyn Dorin-Ballard
1970	Mildred Martorella	1981	Katsuko Sugimoto	1992	Cindy Coburn-Carroll		
1971	Mildred Martorella	1982	Katsuko Sugimoto	1993	Jan Schmidt		

PROFESSIONAL BOWLERS ASSOCIATION CHAMPIONSHIP—2001

(Jan. 28–Feb. 4, 2001, Toledo, Ohio)

Winner—Walter Ray Williams, Jr., Ocala, Fla., defeated Jeff Lizzi, Sandusky, Ohio, 258–204 in title match.

3. Tommy Delutz, Jr., Flushing, N.Y.

4. Dave Arnold, Reno, Nev.

5. Chris Hayden, Tampa, Fla.

AMERICAN BOWLING CONGRESS TOURNAMENT—2001

(Feb. 10–June 30, 2001, Reno, Nev.)

Singles—Nicholas Hoagland, Bloomington, Ind.		798
Doubles—Gregg Zicha, Glen Ellyn, Ill., and Bob Udseth, Rolling Meadows, Ill.		1,449
Team—Joliet Town/Country Lanes #2, Joliet, Ill.		3,273
All Events—D. J. Archer, Amarillo, Tex.		2,219

WOMEN'S INTERNATIONAL BOWLING CONGRESS TOURNAMENT—2001

(April 17–June 27, 2001, Ft. Lauderdale, Fla.)

Singles—Lisa Walker, Palmetto, Fla.	756
Doubles—Nancy Fehr, Cincinnati, Ohio, and Lisa Wagner, Palmetto, Fla.	1,412
Team—The Replacements, Fort Worth, Tex.	3,189
All Events—Jonquay Armon, Lake in the Hills, Ill.	2,044

WOMEN'S INTERNATIONAL BOWLING CONGRESS QUEENS TOURNAMENT—2001

(May 13, 2001, Ft. Lauderdale, Fla.)

Winner—Carolyn Dorin-Ballard, N. Richland Hills, Tex., defeated Kelly Kulick, Union, N.J., 213–197 in title match.

3. Kim Terrell, Daly City, Calif.

4. Maxine Nable, Australia

5. Robin Crawford, Hendersonville, Tenn.

Skiing

HISTORY OF SKIING IN THE UNITED STATES

Skis were devised for utility, to aid those who had to travel over snow. The Norwegians, Swedes, Lapps, and other inhabitants of northern lands used skis for many centuries before skiing became a sport. Emigrants from these countries brought skis to the United States with them. The first skier of record in the United States was a mailman by the name of "Snowshoe" Thompson, born and raised in Telemarken, Norway, who came to the United States and, beginning in 1850, used skis through 20 successive winters in carrying mail from Northern California to Carson Valley, Idaho.

Ski clubs sprang up over 100 years ago where there were Norwegian and Swedish settlers in Wisconsin and Minnesota, and ski contests were held in that territory in 1886. On Feb. 21, 1904, at Ishpenning, Mich., a small group of skiers organized the National Ski Association. In 1961 it was renamed the United States Ski Association. In the 1990s it became the United States Ski and Snowboard Association and included freestyle and disabled skiing.

ALPINE SKIING

2001 Chevy Truck U.S. Alpine Championships
(March 23–28, 2001, Big Mountain, Mont.)

Men
Downhill—1. Daron Rahlves, Sugar Bowl, Calif.; 2. Casey Puckett, Aspen, Colo.; 3. Chad Fleischer, Vail, Colo.
Slalom—1. Erik Schlopy, Park City, Utah; 2. Casey Puckett, Aspen, Colo.; 3. Sacha Gros, Vail, Colo.
Super G—1. (tie) Casey Puckett, Aspen, Colo. and Erik Schlopy, Park City, Utah; 3. Daron Rahlves, Sugar Bowl, Calif.
Giant Slalom—Cancelled because of weather.
Combined (3 events)—1. Casey Puckett, Aspen, Colo.; 2. Marco Sullivan, Tahoe City, Calif.; 3. Josh Transue, Hunter, N.Y.

Women
Downhill—1. Kirsten Clark, Raymond, Maine; 2. Picabo Street, Park City, Utah; 3. Jonna Mendes, Heavenly, Calif.
Slalom—1. Sarah Schleper, Vail, Colo.; 2. Tasha Nelson, Mound, Minn.; 3. Pernilla Wiberg, Sweden
Giant Slalom—1. Jonna Mendes, Heavenly, Calif.; 2. Kirsten Clark, Raymond, Maine; 3. Julia Mancuso, Olympic Valley, Calif.
Super G—1. Pernilla Wiberg, Sweden; 2. Jonna Mendes, Heavenly, Calif.; 3. Kirsten Clark, Raymond, Maine
Combined (4 events)—1. Pernilla Wiberg, Sweden; 2. Sarah Schleper, Vail, Colo.; 3. Lindsey C. Kildow, Vail, Colo.

2001 Alpine World Cup Champions

Men	Pts	Women	Pts
Overall—Hermann Maier, Austria	1,618	Overall—Janica Kostelic, Croatia	1,256
Downhill—Hermann Maier, Austria	576	Downhill—Isolde Kostner, Italy	596
Slalom—Benjamin Raich, Austria	545	Slalom—Janica Kostelic, Croatia	824
Giant Slalom—Hermann Maier, Austria	622	Giant Slalom—Sonja Nef, Switzerland	676
Super G—Hermann Maier, Austria	420	Super G—Regine Cavagnoud, France	577
Combined—Lasse Kjus, Norway	100	Combined—Janica Kostelic, Croatia	100

2001 Disabled Alpine World Cup Champions

Men
Downhill—**Blind:** Chris Williamson, Canada; **Sitting:** Martin Braxenthaler, Germany; **Standing:** Michael Milton, Australia
Slalom—**Blind:** Ion Santacana, Spain; **Sitting:** Daniel Wesley, Canada; **Standing:** Rolf Heinzmann, Switzerland
Giant Slalom—**Blind:** Chris Williamson, Canada; **Sitting:** Martin Braxenthaler, Germany; **Standing:** Rolf Heinzmann, Switzerland
Super G—**Blind:** Chris Williamson, Canada; **Sitting:** Martin Braxenthaler, Germany; **Standing:** Rolf Heinzmann, Switzerland
Overall—**Blind:** Chris Williamson, Canada; **Sitting:** Martin Braxenthaler, Germany; **Standing:** Rolf Heinzmann, Switzerland

Women
Downhill—**Blind:** Katerina Tepla, Czech Republic; **Sitting:** Cecilia Paulson, Sweden; **Standing:** Lauren Woolstencroft, Canada
Slalom—**Blind:** Carmen Garcia, Spain; **Sitting:** Muffy Davis, United States; **Standing:** Mary Riddell, United States
Giant Slalom—**Blind:** Carmen Garcia, Spain; **Sitting:** Muffy Davis, United States; **Standing:** Mary Riddell, United States
Super G—**Blind:** Katerina Tepla, Czech Republic; **Sitting:** Sarah Will, United States; **Standing:** Lauren Woolstencroft, Canada
Overall—**Blind:** Carmen Garcia, Spain; **Sitting:** Muffy Davis, United States; **Standing:** Mary Riddell, United States

NORDIC SKIING/SKI JUMPING/CROSS COUNTRY

2001 Chevy Truck U.S. Ski Jumping/Nordic Combined Championships
(March 24–25, 2001, Park City, Utah)

Men

Large Hill (K120m)—1. Alan Alborn, Anchorage, Alaska; 2. Bill Demong, Vermontville, N.Y.; 3. Todd Lodwick, Steamboat Springs, Colo.
Normal Hill (K90m)—1. Bill Demong, Vermontville, N.Y.; 2. Alan Alborn, Anchorage, Alaska; 3. Todd Lodwick, Steamboat Springs, Colo.
Nordic Combined (K90m jumping–10k race)—1. Bill Demong, Vermontville, N.Y.; 2. Todd Lodwick, Steamboat Springs, Colo.; 3. Johnny Spillane, Steamboat Springs, Colo.

Women

Large Hill (K120 m)—1. Lindsay Van, Park City, Utah; 2. Karla Keck, Oconomowoc, Wis.; 3. Liz Szyotori, Saugerties, N.Y.

Normal Hill (K90m)—1. Lindsay Van, Park City, Utah; 2. Liz Szyotori, Saugerties, N.Y.; 3. Karla Keck, Oconomowoc, Wis.

2001 Chevy Truck U.S. Cross Country Championships
(Jan. 3–6, 2001, McCall, Idaho)

Men

Freestyle sprint—Carl Swenson, Boulder, Colo.
10k Classic—Justin Wadsworth, Bend, Ore.
30k Freestyle skate—Justin Wadsworth, Bend, Ore.

Women

Freestyle sprint—Nina Kemppel, Anchorage, Alaska
5k Classic—Nina Kemppel, Anchorage, Alaska
15k Freestyle—Nina Kemppel, Anchorage, Alaska

FREESTYLE SKIING

2001 Freestyle Skiing World Cup Champions
Men

Aerials—Eric Bergoust, United States
Moguls—Mikko Ronkainen, Finland
Overall—Mikko Ronkainen, Finland

Women

Aerials—Jacqui Cooper, Australia
Moguls—Kari Traa, Norway
Overall—Jacqui Cooper, Australia

2001 Chevy Truck U.S. Freestyle Championships
(March 16–18, 2001, Waterville Valley, N.H.)

Men

Aerials—Joe Pack, Park City, Utah
Moguls—Ryan Riley, Steamboat Springs, Colo.
Dual Moguls—Garth Hager, Bothell, Wash.

Women

Aerials—Emily Cook, Belmont, Mass.
Moguls—Hannah Hardaway, Moultonborough, N.H.
Dual Moguls—Shannon Bahrke, Tahoe City, Calif.

SNOWBOARDING

2001 World Cup Snowboard Champions
Men

Giant Slalom—Walter Feichter, Italy
Parallel Slalom—Mathieu Bozzetto, France
Halfpipe—Magnus Sterner, Sweden
Snowboard cross—Jasey Jay Anderson, Canada
Overall—Jasey Jay Anderson, Canada

Women

Giant Slalom—Karine Ruby, France
Parallel Slalom—Carmen Ranigler, Italy
Halfpipe—Sabine Wehr-Hasler, Germany
Snowboard cross—Karine Ruby, France
Overall—Karine Ruby, France

2001 X-Nix U.S. Snowboard Championships
(March 21–26, 2001, Sunday River, Maine)

Men

Slalom—Jeff Greenwood, Hartford, Conn.
Superpipe—Danny Kass, Hamburg, N.J.
Parallel Giant Slalom—Chris Klug, Aspen, Colo.
Snowboard cross—Jasey Jay Anderson, Canada
Overall—Danny Kass, Hamburg, N.J.

Women

Slalom—Rosey Fletcher, Girdwood, Alaska
Superpipe—Kelly Clark, Mt. Snow, Vt.
Parallel Giant Slalom—Rosey Fletcher, Girdwood, Alaska
Snowboard cross—Kelly Clark, Mt. Snow, Vt.
Overall—Kelly Clark, Mt. Snow, Vt.

JAMES E. SULLIVAN MEMORIAL AWARD WINNERS
(Amateur Athlete of the Year Chosen in Amateur Athletic Union Poll)

1930	Robert Tyre Jones, Jr.	Golf	1947	John B. Kelly, Jr.	Rowing
1931	Bernard E. Berlinger	Track and field	1948	Robert B. Mathias	Track and field
1932	James A. Bausch	Track and field	1949	Richard T. Button	Figure skating
1933	Glenn Cunningham	Track and field	1950	Fred Wilt	Track and field
1934	William R. Bonthron	Track and field	1951	Robert E. Richards	Track and field
1935	W. Lawson Little, Jr.	Golf	1952	Horace Ashenfelter	Track and field
1936	Glenn Morris	Track and field	1953	Sammy Lee	Diving
1937	J. Donald Budge	Tennis	1954	Malvin Whitfield	Track and field
1938	Donald R. Lash	Track and field	1955	Harrison Dillard	Track and field
1939	Joseph W. Burk	Rowing	1956	Patricia McCormick	Diving
1940	J. Gregory Rice	Track and field	1957	Bobby Jo Morrow	Track and field
1941	Leslie MacMitchell	Track and field	1958	Glenn Davis	Track and field
1942	Cornelius Warmerdam	Track and field	1959	Parry O'Brien	Track and field
1943	Gilbert L. Dodds	Track and field	1960	Rafer Johnson	Track and field
1944	Ann Curtis	Swimming	1961	Wilma Rudolph Ward	Track and field
1945	Felix (Doc) Blanchard	Football	1962	Jim Beatty	Track and field
1946	Y. Arnold Tucker	Football	1963	John Pennel	Track and field

1964	Don Schollander	Swimming	1983	Edwin Moses	Track and field
1965	Bill Bradley	Basketball	1984	Greg Louganis	Diving
1966	Jim Ryun	Track and field	1985	Joan Benoit-Samuelson	Marathon
1967	Randy Matson	Track and field	1986	Jackie Joyner-Kersee	Heptathlon
1968	Debbie Meyer	Swimming	1987	Jim Abbott	Baseball
1969	Bill Toomey	Decathlon	1988	Florence Griffith-Joyner	Track and field
1970	John Kinsella	Swimming	1989	Janet Evans	Swimming
1971	Mark Spitz	Swimming	1990	John Smith	Wrestling
1972	Frank Shorter	Marathon	1991	Mike Powell	Track and field
1973	Bill Walton	Basketball	1992	Bonnie Blair	Speed skating
1974	Rick Wohlhuter	Track and field	1993	Charles Ward	Football/Basketball
1975	Tim Shaw	Swimming	1994	Dan Jansen	Speed skating
1976	Bruce Jenner	Track and field	1995	Bruce Baumgartner	Wrestling
1977	John Naber	Swimming	1996	Michael Johnson	Track and field
1978	Tracy Caulkins	Swimming	1997	Peyton Manning	Football
1979	Kurt Thomas	Gymnastics	1998	Chamique Holdsclaw	Basketball
1980	Eric Heiden	Speed skating	1999	Kelly and Coco Miller	Basketball
1981	Carl Lewis	Track and field	2000	Rulon Gardner	Wrestling
1982	Mary Decker Tabb	Track and field			

Speed Skating

WORLD SPEED SKATING RECORDS (LONG TRACK)

Distance	Time	Skater	Place	Date
Men				
500 m	34.32	Hiroyasu Shimizu, Japan	Salt Lake City	March 10, 2001
1,000 m	1:08.28	Jeremy Wotherspoon, Canada	Salt Lake City	March 11, 2001
1,500 m	1:45.20	Kyu-Hyuk Lee, Korea	Calgary, Canada	March 15, 2001
3,000 m	3:42.75	Gianni Romme, Netherlands	Calgary, Canada	September 11, 2000
5,000 m	6:18.72	Gianni Romme, Netherlands	Calgary, Canada	Jan. 30, 2000
10,000 m	13:08.71	Gianni Romme, Netherlands	Calgary, Canada	March 29, 1998
Women				
500 m	37.29	Catriona LeMay Doan, Canada	Salt Lake City	March 9, 2001
1,000 m	1:14.13	Monique Garbrecht-Enfeldt, Germany	Salt Lake City	March 10, 2001
1,500 m	1:54.38	Anni Friesinger, Germany	Calgary, Canada	March 4, 2001
3,000 m	3:59.26	Claudia Pechstein, Germany	Calgary, Canada	March 2, 2001
5,000 m	6:52.44	Gunda Niemann-Stirnemann, Germany	Salt Lake City	March 10, 2001

WORLD SPRINT CHAMPIONSHIPS—2001
(Jan. 20–21, 2001, Inzell, Germany)

Men	Times	Women	Times
500 m—Hiroyasu Shimizu, Japan	35.26, 35.65	500 m—Catriona LeMay Doan, Canada	38.71, 39.02
1,000 m—Ådne Søndrål, Norway	1:11.08, 1:11.24	1,000 m—Monique Garbrecht-Enfeldt, Germany	1:17.31, 1:18.23

Overall standings:
1. Michael Ireland, Canada
2. Hiroyasu Shimizu, Japan
3. Jeremy Wotherspoon, Canada

Overall standings:
1. Monique Garbrecht-Enfeldt, Germany
2. Eriko Sanmiya, Japan
3. Catriona LeMay Doan, Canada

WORLD SPEED SKATING CHAMPIONSHIPS—2001
(Feb. 10–11, 2001, Budapest, Hungary)

Men	Time	Women	Time
500 m—Christian Breuer, Germany	37.55	500 m—Anni Friesinger, Germany	39.99
1,500 m—Ids Postma, Netherlands	1:54.12	1,500 m—Anni Friesinger, Germany	2:03.38
5,000 m—Bart Veldkamp, Belgium	6:43.69	3,000 m—Renate Groenewold, Netherlands	4:16.57
10,000 m—Bart Veldkamp, Belgium	13:44.19	5,000 m—Claudia Pechstein, Germany	7:21.68

WORLD SHORT TRACK CHAMPIONSHIPS—2001
(March 30–April 1, 2001, Jeonju City, Republic of Korea)

Men	Time	Women	Time
500 m—JiaJun Li, China	43.433	500 m—Chunlu Wang, China	45.779
1,000 m—JiaJun Li, China	1:32.034	1,000 m—Yang Yang (A), China	1:45.664
1,500 m—Marc Gagnon, Canada	2:20.325	1,500 m—Yang Yang (A), China	2:40.448
3,000 m—Apolo Anton Ohno, United States	5:36.664	3,000 m—Yang Yang (A), China	5:43.454
Relay—United States	7:15.885	Relay—China	4:25.927

Figure Skating

WORLD CHAMPIONS

Men

1960	Alain Giletti, France
1961	No competition
1962	Donald Jackson, Canada
1963	Don McPherson, Canada
1964	Manfred Schnelldorfer, West Germany
1965	Alain Calmat, France
1966–68	Emmerich Danzer, Austria
1969–70	Tim Wood, United States
1971–73	Ondrej Nepela, Czechoslovakia
1974	Jan Hoffman, East Germany
1975	Sergei Yolkov, USSR
1976	John Curry, Britain
1977	Vladimir Kovalev, USSR
1978	Charles Tickner, United States
1979	Vladimir Kovalev, USSR
1980	Jan Hoffman, East Germany
1981–84	Scott Hamilton, United States
1985	Alexandr Fadeev, USSR
1986	Brian Boitano, United States
1987	Brian Orser, Canada
1988	Brian Boitano, United States
1989–91	Kurt Browning, Canada
1992	Viktor Petrenko, Unified Team
1993	Kurt Browning, Canada
1994–95	Elvis Stojko, Canada
1996	Todd Eldredge, United States
1997	Elvis Stojko, Canada
1998– 2000	Alexei Yagudin, Russia
2001	Evgeni Plushenko, Russia

Women

1956–60	Carol Heiss, United States
1961	No competition
1962–64	Sjoukje Dijkstra, Netherlands
1965	Petra Burka, Canada
1966–68	Peggy Fleming, United States
1969–70	Gabriele Seyfert, East Germany
1971–72	Beatrix Schuba, Austria
1973	Karen Magnusson, Canada
1974	Christine Errath, East Germany
1975	Dianne de Leeuw, Netherlands
1976	Dorothy Hamill, United States
1977	Linda Fratianne, United States
1978	Anett Poetzsch, East Germany
1979	Linda Fratianne, United States
1980	Anett Poetzsch, East Germany
1981	Denise Beillmann, Switzerland
1982	Elaine Zayak, United States
1983	Rosalynn Sumners, United States
1984–85	Katarina Witt, East Germany
1986	Debi Thomas, United States
1987–88	Katarina Witt, East Germany
1989	Midori Ito, Japan
1990	Jill Trenary, United States
1991–92	Kristi Yamaguchi, United States
1993	Oksana Baiul, Ukraine
1994	Yuka Sato, Japan
1995	Chen Lu, China
1996	Michelle Kwan, United States
1997	Tara Lipinski, United States
1998	Michelle Kwan, United States
1999	Maria Butyrskaya, Russia
2000– 2001	Michelle Kwan, United States

U.S. CHAMPIONS

Men

1946–52	Richard Button
1953–56	Hayes Jenkins
1957–60	David Jenkins
1961	Bradley Lord
1962	Monty Hoyt
1963	Tommy Liz
1964	Scott Allen
1965	Gary Visconti
1966	Scott Allen
1967	Gary Visconti
1968–70	Tim Wood
1971	John M. Petkevich
1972	Ken Shelley
1973–75	Gordon McKellen
1976	Terry Kubicka
1977–80	Charles Tickner
1981–84	Scott Hamilton
1985–88	Brian Boitano
1989	Christopher Bowman
1990–91	Todd Eldredge
1992	Christopher Bowman
1993–94	Scott Davis
1995	Todd Eldredge
1996	Rudy Galindo
1997–98	Todd Eldredge
1999–2000	Michael Weiss
2001	Timothy Goebel

Women

1943–48	Gretchen Merrill
1949–50	Yvonne Sherman
1951	Sonya Klopfer
1952–56	Tenley Albright
1957–60	Carol Heiss
1961	Laurence Owen
1962	Barbara Roles Pursley
1963	Lorraine Hanlon
1964–68	Peggy Fleming
1969–73	Janet Lynn
1974–76	Dorothy Hamill
1977–80	Linda Fratianne
1981	Elaine Zayak
1982–84	Rosalynn Sumners
1985	Tiffany Chin
1986	Debi Thomas
1987	Jill Trenary
1988	Debi Thomas
1989–90	Jill Trenary
1991	Tonya Harding
1992	Kristi Yamaguchi
1993	Nancy Kerrigan
1994	Tonya Harding
1995	Nicole Bobek
1996	Michelle Kwan
1997	Tara Lipinski
1998–2001	Michelle Kwan

2001 UNITED STATES CHAMPIONSHIPS
(Jan. 14–21, 2001, Boston, Mass.)

Men's singles
1. Timothy Goebel, Rolling Meadows, Ill.
2. Todd Eldredge, Lake Angelus, Mich.
3. Matthew Savoie, Peoria, Ill.

Women's singles
1. Michelle Kwan, Lake Arrowhead, Calif.
2. Sarah Hughes, Great Neck, N.Y.
3. Angela Nikodinov, San Pedro, Calif.

Pairs
1. Kyoko Ina, Guttenberg, N.J., and John Zimmerman, Birmingham, Ala.
2. Tiffany Scott, Hanson, Mass., and Philip Dulebohn, Germantown, Md.
3. Danielle Hartsell and Steve Hartsell, Westland, Mich.

Dance
1. Naomi Lang, Allegan, Mich., and Peter Tchernyshev, St. Petersburg, Russia
2. Tanith Belbin and Benjamin Agosto, Bloomfield Hills, Mich.
3. Jessica Joseph, Bloomfield Hills, Mich., and Brandon Forsyth, Lexington, Mass.

2001 WORLD CHAMPIONSHIPS

(March 19–25, 2001, Vancouver, Canada)

Men's singles
1. Evgeni Plushenko, Russia
2. Alexei Yagudin, Russia
3. Todd Eldredge, United States

Women's singles
1. Michelle Kwan, United States
2. Irina Slutskaya, Russia
3. Sarah Hughes, United States

Pairs
1. Jamie Sale and David Pelletier, Canada
2. Elena Berezhnaya and Anton Sikharulidze, Russia
3. Xue Shen and Hongbo Zhao, China

Dance
1. Barbara Fusar Poli and Maurizio Margaglio, Italy
2. Marina Anissina and Gwendal Peizerat, France
3. Irina Lobacheva and Ilia Averbukh, Russia

Swimming

WORLD RECORDS—MEN

(Through July 29, 2001)

Distance	Record	Holder	Country	Date
Freestyle				
50 m	0:21.64	Alexander Popov	Russia	June 16, 2000
100 m	0:47.84	Pieter van den Hoogenband	Netherlands	Sept. 19, 2000
200 m	1:44.06	Ian Thorpe	Australia	July 25, 2001
400 m	3:40.17	Ian Thorpe	Australia	July 22, 2001
800 m	7:39.16	Ian Thorpe	Australia	July 24, 2001
1,500 m	14:34.56	Grant Hackett	Australia	July 29, 2001
Backstroke				
50 m	0:24.99	Lenny Krayzelburg	United States	Aug. 28, 1999
100 m	0:53.60	Lenny Krayzelburg	United States	Aug. 27, 1999
200 m	1:55.87	Lenny Krayzelburg	United States	Aug. 27, 1999
Breaststroke				
50 m	0:27.39	Ed Moses	United States	March 31, 2001
100 m	0:59.94	Roman Sloudnov	Russia	July 23, 2001
200 m	2:10.16	Mike Barrowman	United States	July 29, 1992
Butterfly				
50 m	0:23.44	Geoff Huegill	Australia	July 27, 2001
100 m	0:51.81	Michael Klim	Australia	Dec. 12, 1999
200 m	1:54.58	Michael Phelps	United States	July 24, 2001
Individual medley				
200 m	1:58.16	Jani Sievinen	Finland	Sept. 11, 1994
400 m	4:11.76	Tom Dolan	United States	Sept. 17, 2000
Medley relay				
400 m	3:33.73	Olympic Team	United States	Sept. 23, 2000
Freestyle relay				
400 m	3:13.67	Olympic Team	Australia	Sept. 16, 2000
800 m	7:04.66	National Team	Australia	July 27, 2001

Approved by the International Swimming Federation (FINA). (FINA discontinued acceptance of records in yards in 1968.) *Source:* FINA.

WORLD RECORDS—WOMEN
(Through July 29, 2001)

Distance	Record	Holder	Country	Date
Freestyle				
50 m	0:24.13	Inge de Bruijn	Netherlands	Sept. 22, 2000
100 m	0:53.77	Inge de Bruijn	Netherlands	Sept. 20, 2000
200 m	1:56.78	Franziska van Almsick	Germany	Sept. 6, 1994
400 m	4:03.85	Janet Evans	United States	Sept. 22, 1988
800 m	8:16.22	Janet Evans	United States	Aug. 20, 1989
1,500 m	15:52.10	Janet Evans	United States	March 26, 1988
Backstroke				
50 m	0:28.25	Sandra Volker	Germany	June 17, 2000
100 m	1:00.16	Cihong He	China	Sept. 10, 1994
200 m	2:06.62	Krisztina Egerszegi	Hungary	Aug. 25, 1991
Breaststroke				
50 m	0:30.83	Penny Heyns	South Africa	Aug. 28, 1999
100 m	1:06.52	Penny Heyns	South Africa	Aug. 23, 1999
200 m	2:22.99	Hui Qi	China	April 13, 2001

Distance	Record	Holder	Country	Date
Butterfly				
50 m	0:25.64	Inge de Bruijn	Netherlands	May 27, 2000
100 m	0:56.61	Inge de Bruijn	Netherlands	Sept. 17, 2000
200 m	2:05.81	Susan O'Neill	Australia	May 17, 2000
Individual medley				
200 m	2:09.72	Yanyan Wu	China	Oct. 17, 1997
400 m	4:33.59	Yana Klochkova	Ukraine	Sept. 16, 2000
Medley relay				
400 m	3:58.30	Olympic Team	United States	Sept. 23, 2000
Freestyle relay				
400 m	3:36.61	Olympic Team	United States	Sept. 16, 2000
800 m	7:55.47	National Team	East Germany	Aug. 18, 1987

Approved by the International Swimming Federation (FINA). (FINA discontinued acceptance of records in yards in 1968.)
Source: FINA.

AMERICAN SWIMMING RECORDS
(Through July 29, 2001)

Distance	Record	Holder	Date	Distance	Record	Holder	Date
MEN				**WOMEN**			
Freestyle				**Freestyle**			
50 m	0:21.76	Gary Hall, Jr.	Aug. 15, 2000	50 m	0:24.63	Dara Torres	Sept. 23, 2000
100 m	0:48.33	Anthony Ervin	July 27, 2001	100 m	0:54.07	Jenny Thompson	Aug. 14, 2000
200 m	1:46.73	Josh Davis	Sept. 18, 2000	200 m	1:57.90	Nicole Haislett	July 27, 1992
400 m	3:47.00	Klete Keller	Sept. 16, 2000	400 m	4:03.85	Janet Evans	Sept. 22, 1988
800 m	7:52.45	Sean Killion	July 27, 1987	800 m	8:16.22	Janet Evans	Aug. 20, 1989
1,500 m	14:56.81	Chris Thompson	Sept. 23, 2000	1,500 m	15:52.10	Janet Evans	March 26, 1988
Backstroke				**Backstroke**			
50 m	0:24.99	Lenny Krayzelburg	Aug. 28, 1999	50 m	0:28.49	Natalie Coughlin	July 23, 2001
100 m	0:53.60	Lenny Krayzelburg	Aug. 27, 1999	100 m	1:00.18	Natalie Coughlin	July 29, 2001
200 m	1:55.87	Lenny Krayzelburg	Aug. 27, 1999	200 m	2:08.60	Betsy Mitchell	June 27, 1986
Breaststroke				**Breaststroke**			
50 m	0:27.39	Ed Moses	March 31, 2001	50 m	0:31.34	Megan Quann	Aug. 11, 2000
100 m	1:00.29	Ed Moses	March 28, 2001	100 m	1:07.05	Megan Quann	Sept. 18, 2000
200 m	2:10.16	Mike Barrowman	July 29, 1992	200 m	2:24.56	Kristy Kowal	Sept. 21, 2000
Butterfly				**Butterfly**			
50 m	0:23.85	Ian Crocker	July 28, 2001	50 m	0:26.50	Dara Torres	Aug. 9, 2000
100 m	0:52.25	Ian Crocker	July 26, 2001	100 m	0:57.58	Dara Torres	Aug. 9, 2000
200 m	1:54.58	Michael Phelps	July 24, 2001	200 m	2:05.88	Misty Hyman	Sept. 20, 2000
Individual medley				**Individual medley**			
200 m	1:59.77	Tom Dolan	Sept. 21, 2000	200 m	2:11.91	Summer Sanders	July 30, 1992
400 m	4:11.76	Tom Dolan	Sept. 17, 2000	400 m	4:37.58	Summer Sanders	July 26, 1992
Medley relay				**Medley relay**			
400 m	3:33.73	U.S. Olympic Team	Sept. 23, 2000	400 m	3:58.30	U.S. Olympic Team	Sept. 23, 2000
Freestyle relay				**Freestyle relay**			
400 m	3:13.86	U.S. Olympic Team	Sept. 16, 2000	400 m	3:36.61	U.S. Olympic Team	Sept. 16, 2000
800 m	7:12.51	U.S. National Team	Sept. 21, 1988	800 m	7:57.61	U.S. National Team	Aug. 26, 1999

Source: United States Swim Team, FINA.

PHILLIPS 66 SUMMER NATIONALS, 2001
(Aug. 14–18, 2001, Fresno, Calif.)

Men	Time	Men	Time
50-m freestyle—Gary Hall, Phoenix SC	0:22.15	200-m breaststroke—Tom Wilkens, Santa Clara Swim	2:14.54
100-m freestyle—Scott Tucker, Novaquatics	0:49.42	100-m butterfly—Michael Phelps, North Baltimore	0:53.15
200-m freestyle—Joshua Davis, Circle C	1:47.13	200-m butterfly—Andrew Livingston, Cypress Fairbank	1:58.08
400-m freestyle—Chad Carvin, Mission Viejo	3:50.04	200-m individual medley—Michael Phelps, North Baltimore	2:00.86
800-m freestyle—Francis Crippen, Germantown AAC	7:59.86	400-m individual medley—Tom Wilkens, Santa Clara Swim	4:19.35
1,500-m freestyle—Christophe Thompson, Club Wolverine	15:16.23	400-m freestyle relay—Circle C "A"	3:19.74
100-m backstroke—Peter Marshall, Stanford Swimming	0:55.57	800-m freestyle relay—Circle C "A"	7:26.97
200-m backstroke—Joshua Davis, Circle C	1:58.58	400-m medley relay—Circle C "A"	3:45.88
100-m breaststroke—Jarrod Marrs, Curl-Burke Swim	1:02.05		

Women	Time	Women	Time
50-m freestyle—Tammie Stone, Texas Aquatics	0:25.43	100-m breaststroke—Megan Quann, Puyallup AC	1:08.61
100-m freestyle—Gabrielle Rose, Novaquatics	0:55.41	200-m breaststroke—Kristen Caverly, Aquazot	2:29.36
200-m freestyle—Lindsay Benko, Trojan Swim Club	2:00.16	100-m butterfly—Dana Kirk, Tacoma Swim Club	1:00.04
400-m freestyle—Ashley Chandler, Sun Devil Aq.	4:13.29	200-m butterfly—Emily Mason, Scottsdale AC	2:10.76
800-m freestyle—Kalyn Keller, Sun Devil Aq.	8:37.14	200-m individual medley—Gabrielle Rose, Novaquatics	2:13.78
1,500-m freestyle—Lauren Costella, Carson Tigershar	16:26.13	400-m individual medley—Kristen Caverly, Aquazot	4:43.09
100-m backstroke—Haley Cope, Cal AQ/Aquajets	1:01.89	400-m freestyle relay—Texas Aquatics "A"	3:43.49
		800-m freestyle relay—Sun Devil Aq. "A"	8:17.38
200-m backstroke—Diana MacManus, Novaquatics	2:12.66	400-m medley relay—Novaquatics "A"	4:09.24

FINA WORLD CHAMPIONSHIPS, 2001

(July 16—29, 2001, Fukuoka, Japan)

Men	Time	Women	Time
50-m freestyle—Anthony Ervin, United States	0:22.09	50-m freestyle—Inge de Brujin, Netherlands	0:24.47
100-m freestyle—Anthony Ervin, United States	0:48.33	100-m freestyle—Inge de Brujin, Netherlands	0:54.18
200-m freestyle—Ian Thorpe, Australia	1:44.06	200-m freestyle—Giaan Rooney, Australia	1:58.57
400-m freestyle—Ian Thorpe, Australia	3:40.17	400-m freestyle—Yana Klochkova, Ukraine	4:07.30
800-m freestyle—Ian Thorpe, Australia	7:39.16	800-m freestyle—Hannah Stockbauer, Germany	8:24.66
1,500-m freestyle—Grant Hackett, Australia	14:34.56	1,500-m freestyle—Hannah Stockbauer, Germany	16:01.02
50-m backstroke—Randall Bal, United States	0:25.34	50-m backstroke—Haley Cope, United States	0:28.51
100-m backstroke—Matt Welsh, Australia	0:54.31	100-m backstroke—Natalie Coughlin, United States	1:00.37
200-m backstroke—Aaron Peirsol, United States	1:57.13	200-m backstroke—Diana Mocanu, Romania	2:09.94
50-m breaststroke—Oleg Lisogor, Ukraine	0:27.52	50-m breaststroke—Xuejuan Luo, China	0:30.84
100-m breaststroke—Roman Sloudnov, Russia	1:00.16	100-m breaststroke—Xuejuan Luo, China	1:07.18
200-m breaststroke—Brendan Hansen, United States	2:10.69	200-m breaststroke—Agnes Kovacs, Hungary	2:24.90
50-m butterfly—Geoff Huegill, Australia	0:23.50	50-m butterfly—Inge de Brujin, Netherlands 1	0:25.90
100-m butterfly—Lars Frolander, Sweden	0:52.10	100-m butterfly—Petria Thomas, Australia	0:58.27
200-m butterfly—Michael Phelps, United States	1:54.58	200-m butterfly—Petria Thomas, Australia	2:06.73
200-m individual medley—Massi Rosolino, Italy	1:59.71	200-m individual medley—Maggie Bowen, United States	2:11.93
400-m individual medley—Alessio Boggiatto, Italy	4:13.15	400-m individual medley—Yana Klochkova, Ukraine	4:36.98
4×100-m medley relay—Australia	3:35.35	4×100-m medley relay—Australia	4:01.50
4×100-m free relay—Australia	3:14.10	4×100-m free relay—Germany	3:39.58
4×200-m free relay—Australia	7:04.66	4×200-m free relay—Great Britain	7:58.69

Boxing

Whether it be called pugilism, prize fighting, or boxing, there is no tracing "the Sweet Science" to any definite source. Tales of rivals exchanging blows for fun, fame, or money go back to earliest recorded history and classical legend. There was a mixture of boxing and wrestling called the "pancratium" in the ancient Olympic Games; in such contests rivals belabored one another with hands fortified by heavy leather wrappings that were sometimes studded with metal. More than one Olympic competitor lost his life in this brutal exercise.

There was little law or order in pugilism until Jack Broughton, one of the early champions of England, drew up a set of rules for the game in 1743. Broughton, called "the father of English boxing," also is credited with having invented boxing gloves. However, these gloves—or "mufflers" as they were called—were used only in teaching "the manly art of self-defense" or in training bouts. All professional championship fights were contested with bare knuckles until 1892, when John L. Sullivan lost the heavyweight championship of the world to James J. Corbett in New Orleans in a bout in which both contestants wore regulation gloves.

The Broughton Rules were superseded by the London Prize Ring Rules of 1838. In 1884 the eighth marquis of Queensberry, with the help of John G. Chambers, put forward the Queensberry Rules, a code that called for gloved contests. Amateurs took to the Queensberry Rules more quickly than the professionals did.

HISTORY OF WORLD HEAVYWEIGHT CHAMPIONSHIP FIGHTS

(Bouts in which a new champion was crowned)

Date	Where held	Winner, weight (age)	Loser, weight (age)	Rounds
Sept. 7, 1892	New Orleans, La.	James J. Corbett, 178 (26)	John L. Sullivan, 212 (33)	21
March 17, 1897	Carson City, Nev.	Bob Fitzsimmons, 167 (34)	James J. Corbett, 183 (30)	KO 14
June 9, 1899	Coney Island, N.Y.	James J. Jeffries, 206 (24)[1]	Bob Fitzsimmons, 167 (37)	KO 11
Feb. 23, 1906	Los Angeles	Tommy Burns, 180 (24)[2]	Marvin Hart, 188 (29)	20
Dec. 26, 1908	Sydney, Australia	Jack Johnson, 196 (30)	Tommy Burns, 176 (27)	KO 14
April 5, 1915	Havana, Cuba	Jess Willard, 230 (33)	Jack Johnson, 205½ (37)	KO 26
July 4, 1919	Toledo, Ohio	Jack Dempsey, 187 (24)	Jess Willard, 245 (37)	KO 3
Sept. 23, 1926	Philadelphia	Gene Tunney, 189 (28)[3]	Jack Dempsey, 190 (31)	10
June 12, 1930	New York	Max Schmeling, 188 (24)	Jack Sharkey, 197 (27)	WF 4
June 21, 1932	Long Island City	Jack Sharkey, 205 (29)	Max Schmeling, 188 (26)	15
June 29, 1933	Long Island City	Primo Carnera, 260½ (26)	Jack Sharkey, 201 (30)	KO 6
June 14, 1934	Long Island City	Max Baer, 209½ (25)	Primo Carnera, 263¼ (27)	KO 11
June 13, 1935	Long Island City	Jim Braddock, 193¾ (29)	Max Baer, 209½ (26)	15
June 22, 1937	Chicago	Joe Louis, 197¼ (23)	Jim Braddock, 197 (31)	KO 8
June 22, 1949	Chicago	Ezzard Charles, 181¾ (27)[4]	Joe Walcott, 195½ (35)	15
Sept. 27, 1950	New York	Ezzard Charles, 184½ (29)[5]	Joe Louis, 218 (36)	15
July 18, 1951	Pittsburgh	Joe Walcott, 194 (37)	Ezzard Charles, 182 (30)	KO 7
Sept. 23, 1952	Philadelphia	Rocky Marciano, 184 (29)[6]	Joe Walcott, 196 (38)	KO13
Nov. 30, 1956	Chicago	Floyd Patterson, 182¼ (21)	Archie Moore, 187¾ (42)	KO 5
June 26, 1959	New York	Ingemar Johansson, 196 (26)	Floyd Patterson, 182 (24)	KO 3
June 20, 1960	New York	Floyd Patterson, 190 (25)	Ingemar Johansson, 194¾ (27)	KO 5
Sept. 25, 1962	Chicago	Sonny Liston, 214 (28)	Floyd Patterson, 189 (27)	KO 1
Feb. 25, 1964	Miami Beach, Fla.	Cassius Clay (Muhammad Ali), 210 (22)[7]	Sonny Liston, 218 (30)	KO 7
March 4, 1968	New York	Joe Frazier, 204½ (24)[8]	Buster Mathis, 243½ (23)	KO 11
April 27, 1968	Oakland, Calif.	Jimmy Ellis, 197 (28)[9]	Jerry Quarry, 195 (22)	15
Feb. 16, 1970	New York	Joe Frazier, 205 (26)[10]	Jimmy Ellis, 188 (29)	KO 5
Jan. 22, 1973	Kingston, Jamaica	George Foreman, 217½ (24)	Joe Frazier, 214 (29)	KO 2
Oct. 30, 1974	Kinshasa, Zaire	Muhammad Ali, 216½ (32)	George Foreman, 220 (26)	KO 8
Feb. 15, 1978	Las Vegas, Nev.	Leon Spinks, 197 (25)	Muhammad Ali, 224½ (36)	15
June 9, 1978	Las Vegas, Nev.	Larry Holmes, 212 (28)[11]	Ken Norton, 220 (32)	15
Sept. 15, 1978	New Orleans	Muhammad Ali, 221 (36)[12]	Leon Spinks, 201 (25)	15
Oct. 20, 1979	Pretoria, S. Africa	John Tate, 240 (24)[13]	Gerrie Coetzee, 222 (24)	15
March 31, 1980	Knoxville, Tenn.	Mike Weaver, 207½ (27)	John Tate, 232 (25)	KO 15
Dec. 10, 1982	Las Vegas, Nev.	Michael Dokes, 216 (24)	Mike Weaver, 209½ (30)	KO 1
Sept. 23, 1983	Richfield, Ohio	Gerrie Coetzee, 215 (28)	Michael Dokes, 217 (25)	KO 10
March 9, 1984	Las Vegas, Nev.	Tim Witherspoon, 220½ (26)[14]	Greg Page, 239½ (25)	12
Aug. 31, 1984	Las Vegas, Nev.	Pinklon Thomas, 216 (26)	Tim Witherspoon, 217 (26)	12
Nov. 9, 1984	Las Vegas, Nev.	Larry Holmes, 221½ (35)[15]	James Smith, 227 (31)	KO 12
Dec. 1, 1984	Sun City, S. Africa	Greg Page, 236 (25)[16]	Gerry Coetzee, 217 (29)	KO 8
April 29, 1985	Buffalo, N.Y.	Tony Tubbs, 229 (26)[16]	Greg Page, 239½ (26)	15
Sept. 21,1985	Las Vegas, Nev.	Michael Spinks, 200 (29)	Larry Holmes, 221 (35)	15
Jan. 17, 1986	Atlanta, Ga.	Tim Witherspoon, 227 (28)	Tony Tubbs, 229 (27)	15
Nov. 23, 1986	Las Vegas, Nev.	Mike Tyson, 217 (20)[17]	Trevor Berbick, 220 (29)	KO 2
Dec. 12, 1986	New York, N.Y.	James Smith, 230 (33)[16]	Tim Witherspoon, 218 (29)	KO 1
March 7, 1987	Las Vegas, Nev.	Mike Tyson, 217 (20)[16]	James Smith, 230 (33)	12
Feb. 10, 1990	Tokyo	James "Buster" Douglas, 231½ (29)[18]	Mike Tyson, (220) (23)	KO 10
Oct. 25, 1990	Las Vegas, Nev.	Evander Holyfield, 208 (28)	James "Buster" Douglas, 246 (30)	KO 3
Nov. 13, 1992	Las Vegas, Nev.	Riddick Bowe,[19] 235 (25)	Evander Holyfield, 205 (30)	12
Nov. 6, 1993	Las Vegas, Nev.	Evander Holyfield, 217 (30)	Riddick Bowe, 246 (26)	12
April 22, 1994	Las Vegas, Nev.	Michael Moorer, 214 (26)	Evander Holyfield,[20] 214 (31)	12
Sept 24, 1994	London	Oliver McCall,[21] 228 (29)	Lennox Lewis, 238 (28)	2
Nov. 5, 1994	Las Vegas, Nev.	George Foreman,[22] 250 (45)	Michael Moorer, 222 (26)	10
April 8, 1995	Las Vegas, Nev.	Bruce Seldon,[23] 232 (28)	Tony Tucker, 238 (36)	7
Dec.9, 1995	Stuttgart, Ger.	Frans Botha,[24] 227 (28)	Axel Schulz, 222 (27)	12
March 16, 1996	Las Vegas, Nev.	Mike Tyson,[25] 220 (29)	Frank Bruno, 247 (34)	3
June 22, 1996	Dortmund, Ger.	Michael Moorer, 222 (28)	Axel Schulz, 222 (27)	12
Sept. 7, 1996	Las Vegas, Nev.	Mike Tyson, 219 (30)	Bruce Seldon, 229 (29)	1
Nov. 9, 1996	Las Vegas, Nev.	Evander Holyfield,[23] 215 (34)	Mike Tyson, 222 (30)	11
Feb. 7, 1997	Las Vegas, Nev.	Lennox Lewis,[25] 251 (31)	Oliver McCall, 237 (30)	5
Nov. 8, 1997	Las Vegas, Nev.	Evander Holyfield,[26] 214 (35)	Michael Moorer, 223 (30)	8
Nov. 13, 1999	Las Vegas, Nev.	Lennox Lewis,[23, 26] 240 (33)	Evander Holyfield, 217 (36)	12
Aug. 12, 2000	Las Vegas, Nev.	Evander Holyfield,[23] 221 (37)	John Ruiz, 224 (24)	12
March 3, 2001	Las Vegas, Nev.	John Ruiz,[23] 227 (27)	Evander Holyfield, 217 (38)	12
Apr. 21, 2001	Carnival City, South Africa	Hasim Rahman, [25, 26] 237 (28)	Lennox Lewis, 253 (35)	KO 5

1. Jeffries retired as champion in March 1905. He named Marvin Hart and Jack Root as leading contenders and agreed to referee their fight in Reno, Nev., on July 3, 1905, with the stipulation that he would term the winner the champion. Hart, 190 (28), knocked out Root, 171 (29), in the 12th round. 2. Burns claimed the title after defeating Hart. 3. Tunney retired as champion after defeating Tom Heeney on July 26, 1928. 4. After Louis announced his retirement as champion on March 1, 1949, Charles won recognition from the National Boxing Association as champion by defeating Walcott. 5. Charles gained undisputed recognition as champion by defeating Louis, who came out of retirement. 6. Retired as champion April 27, 1956.

7. The World Boxing Association (WBA) later withdrew its recognition of Clay as champion and declared the winner of a bout between Ernie Terrell and Eddie Machen would gain its version of the title. Terrell, 199 (25), won a 15-round decision from Machen, 192 (32), in Chicago on March 5, 1965. Clay, 212¼ (25) and Terrell, 212½ (27), met in Houston on Feb. 6, 1967, Clay winning a 15-round decision. 8. Winner recognized by N.Y., Mass., Maine, Ill., Tex. and Pa. to fill vacated title when Clay was stripped of championship for failing to accept U.S. induction. 9. Bout was final of eight-man tournament to fill Clay's place and is recognized by World Boxing Association. 10. Bout settled controversy over title. 11. Holmes won World Boxing Council title after WBC had withdrawn recognition of Spinks, March 18, 1978, and awarded its title to Norton. WBC said Spinks had reneged on agreement to fight Norton. 12. Ali regained World Boxing Association championship. 13. Tate won WBA title after Ali retired and left it vacant. 14. Tim Witherspoon and Greg Page fought for the WBC heavyweight title vacated by Larry Holmes, who could not come to agreement on a deal to fight Page, the No. 1 contender. Holmes declared he would fight under the banner of the International Boxing Federation. Several dates were set and postponed for fights between Holmes and Gerry Coetzee, the WBA champ, the latest being Nov. 16, 1984. 15. First fight under banner of International Boxing Federation. 16. New WBA champion. 17. New WBC champion. 18. New undisputed champion. 19. The WBC stripped Bowe of its version of the title in December 1992 and named Lennox Lewis champion. 20. After the loss, Holyfield retired. 21. New WBC champion. Lennox Lewis had been named champion in 1992 and had won three title defenses before losing to McCall. 22. For combined WBA/IBF titles. Later WBA stripped Foreman of title for failing to fight no. 1 contender Tony Tucker. IBF also stripped Foreman on June 29, 1995. 23. New WBA champion. 24. Botha later tested positive for steroids and was stripped of the title. 25. New WBC champion. 26. New IBF champion. 27. Surrendered WBA title to fight Michael Grant in unsanctioned bout.

OTHER WORLD BOXING TITLEHOLDERS
(Through July 30, 2001)

Light Heavyweight

Year	Champion	Year	Champion	Year	Champion
1903	Jack Root, George Gardner	1980	Matthew Saad Muhammad (WBC), Marvin Johnson (WBA), Eddie (Gregory) Mustafa Muhammad (WBA)	1995	Virgil Hill (WBA), Fabio Tiozzo (WBC), Henry Maske (IBF)
1903–05	Bob Fitzsimmons	1981	Matthew Saad Muhammad (WBC), Eddie Mustafa Muhammad (WBA), Michael Spinks (WBA), Dwight Braxton (WBC)	1996–97	Virgil Hill (WBA), Fabio Tiozzo (WBC), Henry Maske (IBF)
1905–12	Philadelphia Jack O'Brien[1]			1998	Roy Jones (WBA, WBC), Reggie Johnson (IBF)
1912–16	Jack Dillon			1999– 2001	Roy Jones (WBA, WBC, IBF)
1916–20	Battling Levinsky	1982	Dwight Braxton (WBC), Michael Spinks (WBA)		
1920–22	Georges Carpentier	1983	Michael Spinks (undisputed)	**Middleweight**	
1923	Battling Siki	1984	Michael Spinks (undisputed)	1867–72	Tom Chandler
1923–25	Mike McTigue	1985	Michael Spinks (undisputed)[5]	1872–81	George Rooke
1925–26	Paul Berlenbach			1881–82	Mike Donovan[1]
1926–27	Jack Delaney[2]	1986	Marvin Johnson (WBA), Dennis Andries (WBC)	1884–91	Jack (Nonpareil) Dempsey
1927	Mike McTigue	1987	Thomas Hearns (WBC), Virgil Hill (WBA), Bobby Czyz (IBF)	1891–97	Bob Fitzsimmons[2]
1927–29	Tommy Loughran	1988	Charles Williams (IBF), Virgil Hill (WBA), Donny LaLonde (WBC), Sugar Ray Leonard (WBC)	1908	Stanley Ketchel, Billy Papke
1930	Jimmy Slattery			1908–10	Stanley Ketchel[3]
1930–34	Maxie Rosenbloom	1989	Dennis Andries (WBC), Virgil Hill (WBA), Charles Williams (IBF), Jeff Harding (WBC)	1913	Frank Klaus
1934–35	Bob Olin			1913–14	George Chip
1935–39	John Henry Lewis	1990	Virgil Hill (WBA), Charles Williams (IBF), Jeff Harding (WBC), Dennis Andries (WBC)	1914–17	Al McCoy
1939	Melio Bettina			1917–20	Mike O'Dowd
1939–41	Billy Conn[2]	1991	Virgil Hill (WBA), Thomas Hearns (WBA), Dennis Andries (WBC), Charles Williams (IBF)	1920–23	Johnny Wilson
1941	Anton Christoforidis (NBA)			1923–26	Harry Greb
1941–48	Gus Lesnevich	1992	Charles Williams (IBF), James Waring (IBF), Jeff Harding (WBC)	1926	Tiger Flowers
1948–50	Freddie Mills	1993	Virgil Hill (WBA), Jeff Harding (WBC), Henry Maske (IBF)	1926–31	Mickey Walker[2]
1950–52	Joey Maxim	1994	Virgil Hill (WBA), Mike McCallum (WBC), Henry Maske (IBF)	1931–41	Gorilla Jones, Ben Jeby, Marcel Thil, Lou Brouillard, Vince Dundee, Teddy Yarosz, Babe Risko, Freddy Steele, Al Hostak, Solly Krieger, Fred Apostoli, Cerferino Garcia, Ken Overlin, Billy Soose, Tony Zale[4]
1952–61	Archie Moore[3]				
1961–63	Harold Johnson				
1963–65	Willie Pastrano				
1965–66	José Torres			1941–47	Tony Zale
1966–67	Dick Tiger			1947–48	Rocky Graziano
1968	Dick Tiger, Bob Foster			1948	Tony Zale
1969–70	Bob Foster			1948–49	Marcel Cerdan
1971	Vicente Rondon (WBA), Bob Foster (WBC)			1949–51	Jake LaMotta
1972–73	Bob Foster (WBA, WBC)			1951–52	Ray Robinson[1]
1974	John Conteh (WBA), Bob Foster (WBC)[1, 4]			1952	Ray Robinson, Randy Turpin
1975–76	Victor Galindez (WBA), John Conteh (WBC)			1953–55	Carl Olson
1977	Victor Galindez (WBA), John Conteh (WBC),[4] Miguel Cuello (WBC)			1955–57	Ray Robinson[5]
				1957	Gene Fullmer, Ray Robinson
1978	Victor Galindez (WBA), Mike Rossman (WBA), Miguel Cuello (WBC), Mate Parlov (WBC), Marvin Johnson (WBC)			1957–58	Carmen Basilio
				1958–60	Ray Robinson[6]
				1959–60	Gene Fullmer (NBA)
				1960–61	Paul Pender[7]
1979	Mike Rossman (WBA), Victor Galindez (WBA), Marvin Johnson (WBC), Matthew (Franklin) Saad Muhammad (WBC)			1961–62	Terry Downes[1]
				1962	Paul Pender[1]
				1962–63	Dick Tiger
				1963–65	Joey Giardello

1. Retired. 2. Abandoned title. 3. NBA withdrew recognition in 1961, New York Commission in 1962; recognized thereafter only by California and Europe. 4. WBC withdrew recognition. 5. Spinks relinquished title in 1985 to fight for heavyweight title.

1965–66	Dick Tiger
1966	Emile Griffith
1967	Nino Benvenuti, Emile Griffith
1968	Emile Griffith, Nino Benvenuti
1969	Nino Benvenuti
1970	Nino Benvenuti, Carlos Monzon
1971–73	Carlos Monzon
1974–75	Carlos Monzon (WBA), Rodrigo Valdez (WBC)
1976	Carlos Monzon (WBA, WBC), Rodrigo Valdez (WBC)
1977	Carlos Monzon (WBA, WBC),[1] Rodrigo Valdez (WBA, WBC)
1978	Rodrigo Valdez, Hugo Corro
1979	Hugo Corro, Vito Antuofermo
1980	Vito Antuofermo, Alan Minter, Marvin Hagler
1981	Marvin Hagler
1982–86	Marvin Hagler (undisputed)
1987	Marvin Hagler (undisputed), Sugar Ray Leonard (undisputed)
1988	Sumbu Kalambay (WBA), Thomas Hearns (WBC), Iran Barkley (WBC), Frank Tate (IBF), Michael Nunn (IBF), James Kinchen (NABF)
1989	Michael Nunn (IBF), Mike McCallum (WBA), Iran Barkley (WBC), Roberto Duran (WBC)
1990	Michael McCallum (WBA), Michael Nunn (IBF), Iran Barkley (WBC)
1991	Michael Nunn (IBF), James Toney (IBF), Michael McCallum (WBA)
1992	James Toney (IBF), Julian Jackson (WBC), Reggie Johnson (WBA)
1993	Reggie Johnson (WBA), Gerald McClellan (WBA), Roy Jones (IBF)
1994	Julian Jackson (WBA), Gerald McClellan (WBA), Roy Jones (IBF)
1995	Jorge Castro (WBA), Julian Jackson (WBC), Bernard Hopkins (IBF)
1996	William Joppy (WBA), Keith Holmes (WBC), Bernard Hopkins (IBF)
1997	Shinji Takehara (WBA), Quincy Taylor (WBC), Bernard Hopkins (IBF)
1998	William Joppy (WBA), Hassine Cherifi (WBC), Bernard Hopkins (IBF)
1999–	William Joppy (WBA),
2000	Keith Holmes (WBC), Bernard Hopkins (IBF)
2001	Felix Trinidad (WBA), Bernard Hopkins (WBC, IBF)

1. Retired. 2. Abandoned title. 3. Died. 4. National Boxing Association and New York Commission disagreed on champions. Those listed were accepted by one or the other until Zale gained world-wide recognition. 5. Ended retirement in 1954. 6. NBA withdrew recognition. 7. Recognized by New York, Massachusetts, and Europe.

Welterweight

1892–94	Mysterious Billy Smith
1894–96	Tommy Ryan
1896	Kid McCoy[1]
1896– 1900	Mysterious Billy Smith
1900	Rube Ferns
1900–01	Matty Matthews
1901	Ruby Ferns
1901–04	Joe Walcott
1904	Dixie Kid[1]
1904–06	Joe Walcott
1906–07	Honey Mellody
1907	Mike (Twin) Sullivan[1]
1915–19	Ted Lewis
1919–22	Jack Britton
1922–26	Mickey Walker
1926–27	Pete Latzo
1927–29	Joe Dundee
1929–30	Jackie Fields
1930	Young Jack Thompson
1930–31	Tommy Freeman
1931	Young Jack Thompson
1931–32	Lou Brouillard
1932–33	Jackie Fields
1933	Young Corbett 3rd
1933–34	Jimmy McLarnin, Barney Ross
1934–35	Jimmy McLarnin
1935–38	Barney Ross
1938–40	Henry Armstrong
1940–41	Fritzie Zivic
1941–46	Freddie Cochrane
1946	Marty Servo[2]
1946–51	Ray Robinson[1]
1951	Johnny Bratton (NBA)
1951–54	Kid Gavilan
1954–55	Johnny Saxton
1955	Tony DeMarco
1955–56	Carmen Basilio
1956	Johnny Saxton
1956–57	Carmen Basilio[1]
1958	Virgil Akins
1959–60	Don Jordan
1960–61	Benny (Kid) Paret
1961	Emile Griffith
1961–62	Benny (Kid) Paret
1962–63	Emile Griffith, Luis Rodriguez
1963–66	Emile Griffith[1]
1966–69	Curtis Cokes
1969	Curtis Cokes, José Napoles
1970	José Napoles, Billy Backus
1971	Billy Backus, José Napoles
1972–74	José Napoles
1975	José Napoles (WBA, WBC),[3] Angel Espada (WBA), John Stracey (WBC)
1976	Angel Espada (WBA), José Cuevas (WBA), John Stracey (WBC), Carlos Palomino
1977–78	José Cuevas (WBA), Carlos Palomino (WBC)
1979	José Cuevas (WBA), Carlos Palomino (WBC), Wilfredo Benitez (WBC)
1980	José Cuevas (WBA), Ray Leonard (WBC), Roberto Duran (WBC), Thomas Hearns (WBA)
1981	Ray Leonard (WBC), Thomas Hearns (WBA), Ray Leonard (WBC, WBA)
1982	Ray Leonard
1983–85	Donald Curry (WBA), Milton McCrory (WBC)
1985–86	Donald Curry (undisputed)
1987	Mark Breland (WBA), Marlon Starling (WBA), Lloyd Honeyghan (IBF)
1988	Marlon Starling (WBA), Tomas Molinares (WBA), Lloyd Honeyghan (WBC), Simon Brown (IBF)
1989	Mark Breland (WBA), Marlon Starling (WBC), Simon Brown (IBF)
1990	Mark Breland (WBA), Aaron Davis (WBA), Simon Brown (IBF), Marlon Starling (WBC), Maurice Blocker (WBC)
1991	Meldrick Taylor (WBA), Simon Brown (IBF, WBC)
1992	Meldrick Taylor (WBA), James "Buddy" McGirt (WBC), Maurice Blocker (IBF)
1993	Cristianto Espana (WBA), Pernell Whitaker (WBC), Felix Trinidad (IBF)
1994	Ike Quartey (WBA), Pernell Whitaker (WBC), Felix Trinidad (IBF)
1995	Ike Quartey (WBA), Pernell Whitaker (WBC), Felix Trinidad (IBF)
1996–97	Ike Quartey (WBA), Pernell Whitaker (WBC), Felix Trinidad (IBF)
1998	Ike Quartey (WBA), Oscar De La Hoya (WBC), Felix Trinidad (IBF)
1999	James Page (WBA), Oscar De La Hoya (WBC), Felix Trinidad (IBF, WBC)
2000	James Page (WBA), Shane Mosley (WBC), Vacant (IBF)
2001	Andrew Lewis (WBA), Shane Mosley (WBC), Vernon Forrest (IBF)

1. Retired. 2. Abandoned title. 3. WBA withdrew recognition.

Lightweight

1869–99	Kid Lavigne
1899– 1902	Frank Erne
1902–08	Joe Gans
1908–10	Battling Nelson
1910–12	Ad Wolgast
1912–14	Willie Ritchie
1914–17	Freddy Welsh
1917–25	Benny Leonard[1]
1925	Jimmy Goodrich
1925–26	Rocky Kansas
1926–30	Sammy Mandell
1930	Al Singer
1930–33	Tony Canzoneri
1933–35	Barney Ross[2]
1935–36	Tony Canzoneri
1936–38	Lou Ambers
1938–39	Henry Armstrong
1939–40	Lou Ambers
1940–41	Lew Jenkins
1941–42	Sammy Angott[1]
1943–47	Beau Jack (N.Y.), Bob Montgomery (N.Y.), Sammy Angott (NBA), Juan Zurita (NBA), Ike Williams (NBA)
1947–51	Ike Williams
1951–52	James Carter
1952	Lauro Salas

1952–54	James Carter
1954	Paddy DeMarco
1954–55	James Carter
1955–56	Wallace Smith
1956–62	Joe Brown
1962–65	Carlos Ortiz
1965	Ismael Laguna
1965–68	Carlos Ortiz
1968	Teo Cruz
1969	Teo Cruz,
	Mando Ramos
1970	Mando Ramos,
	Ismael Laguna,
	Ken Buchanan
1971	Ken Buchanan (WBA),
	Mando Ramos (WBC),
	Pedro Carrasco (WBC)
1972	Ken Buchanan (WBA),
	Roberto Duran (WBA),
	Pedro Carrasco (WBC),
	Mando Ramos (WBC),
	Chango Carmona (WBC),
	Rodolfo Gonzalez (WBC)
1973	Roberto Duran (WBA),
	Rodolfo Gonzalez (WBC)
1974	Roberto Duran (WBA),
	Rodolfo Gonzalez (WBC),
	Guts Ishimatsu (WBC)
1975	Roberto Duran (WBA),
	Guts Ishimatsu (WBC)
1976	Roberto Duran (WBA),
	Guts Ishimatsu (WBC),
	Esteban De Jesus (WBC)
1977	Roberto Duran (WBA),
	Esteban De Jesus (WBC)
1978	Roberto Duran (WBA,
	WBC)
1979	Roberto Duran,[2]
	Jim Watt (WBC),
	Ernesto Espana (WBA)
1980	Ernesto Espana (WBA),
	Hilmer Kenty (WBA),
	Jim Watt (WBC)
1981	Hilmer Kenty (WBA),
	Sean O'Grady (WBA),
	James Watt (WBC),
	Alexis Arguello (WBC)
	Arturo Frias (WBA)
1982	Arturo Frias (WBA),
	Ray Mancini (WBA),
	Alexis Arguello (WBC)
1983	Edwin Rosario (WBC),
	Ray Mancini (WBA)
1984	Edwin Rosario (WBC),
	Livingstone Bramble
	(WBA)
1985	Jose Luis Ramirez (WBC),
	Hector Camacho (WBC),
	Livingstone Bramble
	(WBA)
1986	Hector Camacho (WBC),
	Livingstone Bramble
	(WBA),
	Jim Paul (IBF)
1987	Edwin Rosario (WBA),
	Jose Luis Ramirez (WBC),
	Greg Haugen (IBF)
1988	Jose Luis Ramirez (WBC),
	Julio Cesar Chavez
	(WBA),
	Greg Haugen (IBF)
	Julio Cesar Chavez (WBC
	& WBA title unified)
1989	Pernell Whitaker (IBF,
	WBC),
	Edwin Rosario (WBA)
1990	Pernell Whitaker (IBF,
	WBC),
	Juan Nazario (WBA)
1991	Pernell Whitaker (IBF,
	WBA, WBC)

1992	Pernell Whitaker (IBF,
	WBA, WBC),[3]
	Joey Gamache (WBA).
1993	Dingaan Thobela (WBC),
	Angel Gonzalez (WBC),
	Freddie Pendleton (IBF)
1994	Orzubek Nazarov (WBA),
	Angel Gonzalez (WBC),
	Rafael Ruelas (IBF)
1995	Orzubek Nazarov (WBA),
	Angel Gonzalez (WBC),
	Oscar De La Hoya (IBF)
1996	Gusshie Nazarov (WBA),
	Jean Baptiste Mendy
	(WBC),
	Phillip Holiday (IBF)
1997	Orzubek Nazarov (WBA),
	Jean Baptiste Mendy
	(WBC),
	Philip Holiday (IBF)
1998	Jean Baptiste Mendy
	(WBA),
	Cesar Bazan (WBC),
	Shane Mosley (IBF)
1999	Stefano Zoff (WBA),
	Stevie Johnston (WBC),
	Paul Spadafora (IBF)
2000	Takanori Hatakeyama
	(WBA), Jose Luis Castillo
	(WBC), Paul Spadafora
	(IBF)
2001	Julien Lorcy (WBA), Jose
	Luis Castillo (WBC), Paul
	Spadafora (IBF)

1. Retired. 2. Abandoned title. 3. Moving up in weight class, so resigned titles.

Featherweight

1889	Dal Hawkins[1]
1890	Billy Murphy
1892–	
1900	George Dixon
1900–01	Terry McGovern
1901	Young Corbett[1]
1901–12	Abe Attell
1912–23	Johnny Kilbane
1923	Eugene Criqui
1923–25	Johnny Dundee[1]
1925–27	Louis (Kid) Kaplan[1]
1927–28	Benny Bass
1928	Tony Canzoneri
1928–29	Andre Routis
1929–32	Battling Battalino[1]
1932	Tommy Paul (NBA),
	Kid Chocolate (N.Y.)
1933–36	Freddie Miller
1936–37	Petey Sarron
1937–38	Henry Armstrong[1]
1938–40	Joey Archibald
1940–41	Harry Jefra,
	Joey Archibald
1941–42	Chalky Wright
1942–48	Willie Pep
1948–49	Sandy Saddler[2]
1949–50	Willie Pep
1950–57	Sandy Saddler
1957–59	Kid Bassey
1959–63	Davey Moore
1963–64	Sugar Ramos
1964–67	Vicente Saldivar[2]
1968	Howard Winstone,
	José Legra,[3]
	Paul Rojas (WBA),
	Sho Saijo (WBA)
1969	Sho Saijo (WBA)
	Johnny Famechon[3]
1970	Sho Saijo (WBA),
	Johnny Famechon,[3]
	Vicente Salvidar,[3]
	Kuniaki Shibata[3]

1971	Sho Saijo (WBA),
	Antonio Gomez (WBA),
	Kuniaki Shibata (WBC)
1972	Antonio Gomez (WBA),
	Ernesto Marcel (WBA),
	Kuniaki Shibata (WBC),
	Clemente Sanchez
	(WBC),
	José Legra (WBC)
1973	Ernesto Marcel (WBA),
	José Legra (WBC),
	Eder Jofre (WBC)
1974	Ernesto Marcel (WBA),[2]
	Ruben Olivares (WBA),
	Alexis Arguello (WBA),
	Eder Jofre (WBC),
	Bobby Chacon (WBC)
1975	Alexis Arguello (WBA),
	Bobby Chacon (WBC),
	Ruben Olivares (WBC),
	David Kotey (WBC)
1976	Alexis Arguello (WBA),[2]
	David Kotey (WBC),
	Danny Lopez (WBC)
1977	Rafael Ortega (WBA),
	Danny Lopez (WBC)
1978	Rafael Ortega (WBA),
	Cecilio Lastra (WBA),
	Eusebio Pedroza (WBA),
	Danny Lopez (WBC)
1979	Eusebio Pedroza (WBA),
	Danny Lopez (WBC)
1980	Eusebio Pedroza (WBA),
	Danny Lopez (WBC),
	Salvador Sanchez (WBC)
1981	Eusebio Pedroza (WBA),
	Salvador Sanchez (WBC)
1982	Eusebio Pedroza (WBA),
	Salvador Sanchez (WBC)[4]
1983	Juan Laporte (WBC),
	Eusebio Pedroza (WBA)
1984	Wilfred Gomez (WBC),
	Eusebio Pedroza (WBA)
1985	Eusebio Pedroza (WBA),
	Barry McGuigan (WBA),
	Azumah Nelson (WBC)
1986	Barry McGuigan (WBA),
	Stevie Cruz (WBA),
	Azumah Nelson (WBC)
1987	Azumah Nelson (WBC),
	Antonio Esparragoza
	(WBA)
1988	Calvin Grove (IBF),
	Jorge Paez (IBF),
	Antonio Esparragoza
	(WBA),
	Jeff Fenech (WBC)
1989	Jorge Paez (IBF),
	Antonio Esparragoza
	(WBA),
	Jeff Fenech (WBC)
1990	Marcos Villasana (WBC),
	Antonio Esparragoza
	(WBA),
	Jorge Paez (IBF)
1991	Yung-Kyun Park (WBA),
	Troy Dorsey (IBF),
	Marcos Villagana (WBC)
1992	Paul Hodkinson (WBC),
	Manuel Medina (IBF),
	Yung-Kyun Park (WBA)
1993	Yung-Kyun Park (WBA),
	Goyo Vargas (WBC),
	Tom Johnson (IBF)
1994	Eloy Rojas (WBA),
	Kevin Kelley (WBC),
	Tom Johnson (IBF)
1995	Eloy Rojas (WBA),
	Alejandro Gonzalez
	(WBC),
	Tom Johnson (IBF)

1996	Wilfredo Vázquez (WBA), Luisito Espinoza (WBC), Tom Johnson (IBF)	
1997	Elroy Rojas (WBA), Luisito Espinoza (WBC), Tom Johnson (IBF)	
1998	Vacant (WBA), Luisito Espinoza (WBC), Manuel Medina (IBF)	
1999	Freddie Norwood (WBA), Cesar Soto (WBC), Manuel Medina (IBF)	
2000	Freddie Norwood (WBA), Guty Espadas (WBC), Paul Ingle (IBF)	
2001	Derrick Gainer (WBA), Erik Morales (WBC), Frankie Toledo (IBF)	

1. Abandoned title. 2. Retired. 3. Recognized in Europe, Mexico, and Orient. 4. Killed in auto accident.

Bantamweight

1890–92	George Dixon[1]
1894–99	Jimmy Barry[2]
1899–	
1900	Terry McGovern[1]
1901	Harry Harris[1]
1902–03	Harry Forbes
1903–04	Frankie Neil
1904	Joe Bowker[1]
1905–07	Jimmy Walsh[1]
1910–14	Johnny Coulon
1914–17	Kid Williams
1917–20	Pete Herman
1920	Joe Lynch
1920–21	Joe Lynch, Pete Herman, Johnny Buff
1922	Johnny Buff, Joe Lynch
1923	Joe Lynch
1924	Joe Lynch, Abe Goldstein, Eddie "Cannonball" Martin
1925	Eddie "Cannonball" Martin, Charlie (Phil) Rosenberg[3]
1927–28	Bud Taylor (NBA)[1]
1929–34	Al Brown
1935	Al Brown, Baltazar Sangchili
1936	Baltazar Sangchili, Tony Marino, Sixto Escobar
1937	Sixto Escobar, Harry Jeffra
1938	Harry Jeffra, Sixto Escobar
1939–40	Sixto Escobar[2]
1940–42	Lou Salica

1942–46	Manuel Ortiz
1947	Manuel Ortiz, Harold Dade
1948–50	Manuel Ortiz
1950–52	Vic Toweel
1952–54	Jimmy Carruthers[2]
1954–55	Robert Cohen
1956	Robert Cohen, Mario D'Agata Raul Macias (NBA)
1957	Mario D'Agata, Alphonse Halimi
1958–59	Alphonse Halimi
1959–60	Jose Becerra[2]
1960–61	Alphonse Halimi[4]
1961–62	Johnny Caldwell[4]
1961–65	Eder Jofre
1965–68	Masahika "Fighting" Harada
1968	Masahika "Fighting" Harada, Lionel Rose
1969	Lionel Rose, Ruben Olivares
1970	Ruben Olivares, Chucho Castillo
1971	Chucho Castillo, Ruben Olivares
1972	Ruben Olivares, Rafael Herrera, Enrique Pinder
1973	Enrique Pinder (WBA), Romeo Anaya (WBA), Arnold Taylor (WBA), Rodolfo Martinez (WBC), Rafael Herrera
1974	Arnold Taylor (WBA), Soo Hwan Hong (WBA), Rafael Herrera (WBC), Rodolfo Martinez (WBC)
1975	Soo Hwan Hong (WBA), Alfonso Zamora (WBA), Rodolfo Martinez (WBC)
1976	Alfonso Zamora (WBA), Rodolfo Martinez (WBC), Carlos Zarate (WBC)
1977	Alfonso Zamora (WBA), Carlos Zarate (WBC), Jorge Lujan (WBA), Carlos Zarate (WBC)
1978	Jorge Lujan (WBA), Carlos Zarate (WBC)
1979	Jorge Lujan (WBA), Carlos Zarate (WBC), Lupe Pintor (WBC)
1980	Jorge Lujan (WBA), Lupe Pintor (WBC), Julian Solis (WBA), Jeff Chandler (WBA)
1981	Lupe Pintor (WBC), Jeff Chandler (WBA)

1982	Lupe Pintor (WBC), Jeff Chandler (WBA)
1983	Jeff Chandler (WBA), Albert Dauila (WBC)
1984	Richie Sandqual (WBA), Albert Dauila (WBC)
1985	Richard Sandoval (WBA), Daniel Zaragoza (WBC), Miguel Lora (WBC)
1986	Richard Sandoval (WBA), Bernardo Pinango (WBA), Jeff Fenech (IBF)
1987	Bernardo Pinango (WBA), Takuya Muguruma (WBA), Miguel Lora (WBC)
1988	Wilfredo Vásquez (WBA), Jibaro Perez (WBC), Moon Sung-gil (WBA), Orlando Canizales (IBF)
1989	Jibaro Perez (WBC), Moon Sung-gil (WBA), Orlando Canizales (IBF), Kaokor Galaxy (WBA), Luis Espinosa (WBA)
1990	Orlando Canizales (IBF), Jibaro Perez (WBC), Luis Espinosa (WBA)
1991	Greg Richardson (WBC), Orlando Canizales (IBF), Luis Espinosa (WBA)
1992	Joichiro Tatsuyoshi (WBC), Victor Manuel Rabanales (WBC), Eddie Cook (WBA), Orlando Gonzales (IBF)
1993	Jorge Julio (WBA), Byun-Jong-il (WBC), Orlando Canizales (IBF)
1994	John Michael Johnson (WBA), Yasuei Yakushiji (WBC), Orlando Canizales (IBF)
1995	Daorun Chuwatang (WBA), Yasuei Yakushiji (WBC), Mbulelo Botile (IBF)
1996–97	Nana Konadu (WBA), Wayne McCullough (WBC), Mbulelo Botile (IBF)
1998	Nana Konadu (WBA), Joichiro Tatsuyoshi (WBC), Tim Austin (IBF)
1999–2001	Paulie Ayala (WBA), Veeraphol Sahaprom (WBC), Tim Austin (IBF)

1. Abandoned title. 2. Retired. 3. Deprived of title for failing to make weight. 4. Recognized in Europe.

Horse Racing

Ancient drawings on stone and bone prove that horse racing is at least 3,000 years old, but thoroughbred racing is a modern development. Practically every thoroughbred in training today traces its registered ancestry back to one or more of three sires that arrived in England about 1728 from the Near East and became known, from the names of their owners, as the Byerly Turk, the Darley Arabian, and the Godolphin Arabian. The Jockey Club (English) was founded at Newmarket in 1750 or 1751 and became the custodian of the Stud Book as well as the court of last resort in deciding turf affairs.

Horse racing took place in this country before the Revolution, but the great lift to the breeding industry came with the importation in 1798, by Col. John Hoomes of Virginia, of Diomed, winner of the Epsom Derby of 1780. Diomed's lineal descendants included such famous 19th-century stars of the American turf as American Eclipse, Sir Archy, and Lexington. From 1800 to the time of the Civil War there were race courses and breeding establishments plentifully scattered through Virginia, North Carolina, South Carolina, Tennessee, Kentucky, and Louisiana.

The oldest stake event in North America is the Queen's Plate, a Canadian fixture that was first run in the Province of Quebec in 1836. The oldest stake event in the United States is the Travers, which was first run at Saratoga in 1864. The gambling that goes with horse racing and trickery by jockeys, trainers, owners, and track officials caused attacks on the sport by reformers and a demand among horse racing enthusiasts for an honest and effective control of some kind, but nothing of lasting value to racing came of this until the formation in 1894 of the Jockey Club (American).

"TRIPLE CROWN" WINNERS IN THE UNITED STATES
(Kentucky Derby, Preakness, and Belmont Stakes)

Year	Horse	Owner	Year	Horse	Owner
1919	Sir Barton	J. K. L. Ross	1946	Assault	Robert J. Kleberg
1930	Gallant Fox	William Woodward	1948	Citation	Warren Wright
1935	Omaha	William Woodward	1973	Secretariat	Meadow Stable
1937	War Admiral	Samuel D. Riddle	1977	Seattle Slew	Karen Taylor
1941	Whirlaway	Warren Wright	1978	Affirmed	Louis Wolfson
1943	Count Fleet	Mrs. John Hertz			

KENTUCKY DERBY
Churchill Downs; 3-year-olds; 1¼ mi.

Year	Winner	Jockey	Wt.	Win val.	Year	Winner	Jockey	Wt.	Win val.
1919	Sir Barton	J. Loftus	112½	$20,825	1961	Carry Back	J. Sellers	126	$120,500
1920	Paul Jones	T. Rice	126	30,375	1962	Decidedly	W. Hartack	126	119,650
1921	Behave Yourself	C. Thompson	126	38,450	1963	Chateauguay	B. Baeza	126	108,900
1922	Morvich	A. Johnson	126	46,775	1964	Northern Dancer	W. Hartack	126	114,300
1923	Zev	E. Sande	126	53,600	1965	Lucky Debonair	W. Shoemaker	126	112,000
1924	Black Gold	J. D. Mooney	126	52,775	1966	Kauai King	D. Brumfield	126	120,500
1925	Flying Ebony	E. Sande	126	52,950	1967	Proud Clarion	R. Ussery	126	119,700
1926	Bubbling Over	A. Johnson	126	50,075	1968	Forward Pass[1]	I. Valenzuela	126	122,600
1927	Whiskery	L. McAtee	126	51,000	1969	Majestic Prince	W. Hartack	126	113,200
1928	Reigh Count	C. Lang	126	55,375	1970	Dust Commander	M. Manganello	126	127,800
1929	Clyde Van Dusen	L. McAtee	126	53,950	1971	Canonero II	G. Avila	126	145,500
1930	Gallant Fox	E. Sande	126	50,725	1972	Riva Ridge	R. Turcotte	126	140,300
1931	Twenty Grand	C. Kurtsinger	126	48,725	1973	Secretariat	R. Turcotte	126	155,050
1932	Burgoo King	E. James	126	52,350	1974	Cannonade	A. Cordero, Jr.	126	274,000
1933	Brokers Tip	D. Meade	126	48,925	1975	Foolish Pleasure	J. Vasquez	126	209,600
1934	Cavalcade	M. Garner	126	28,175	1976	Bold Forbes	A. Cordero, Jr.	126	165,200
1935	Omaha	W. Saunders	126	39,525	1977	Seattle Slew	J. Cruguet	126	214,700
1936	Bold Venture	I. Hanford	126	37,725	1978	Affirmed	S. Cauthen	126	186,900
1937	War Admiral	C. Kurtsinger	126	52,050	1979	Spectacular Bid	R. Franklin	126	228,650
1938	Lawrin	E. Arcaro	126	47,050	1980	Genuine Risk	J. Vasquez	121	250,550
1939	Johnstown	J. Stout	126	46,350	1981	Pleasant Colony	J. Velasquez	126	317,200
1940	Gallahadion	C. Bierman	126	60,150	1982	Gato del Sol	E. Delahoussaye	126	417,600
1941	Whirlaway	E. Arcaro	126	61,275	1983	Sunny's Halo	E. Delahoussaye	126	426,000
1942	Shut Out	W. D. Wright	126	64,225	1984	Swale	L. Pincay, Jr.	126	537,400
1943	Count Fleet	J. Longden	126	60,725	1985	Spend a Buck	A. Cordero, Jr.	126	406,800
1944	Pensive	C. McCreary	126	64,675	1986	Ferdinand	W. Shoemaker	126	609,400
1945	Hoop Jr.	E. Arcaro	126	64,850	1987	Alysheba	C. McCarron	126	618,600
1946	Assault	W. Mehrtens	126	96,400	1988	Winning Colors	G. Stevens	121	611,200
1947	Jet Pilot	E. Guerin	126	92,160	1989	Sunday Silence	P. Valenzuela	126	574,200
1948	Citation	E. Arcaro	126	83,400	1990	Unbridled	C. Perret	126	581,000
1949	Ponde	S. Brooks	126	91,600	1991	Strike the Gold	C. Antley	126	655,800
1950	Middleground	W. Boland	126	92,650	1992	Lil E. Tee	P. Day	126	724,800
1951	Count Turf	C. McCreary	126	98,050	1993	Sea Hero	J. Bailey	126	735,900
1952	Hill Gail	E. Arcaro	126	96,300	1994	Go For Gin	C. McCarron	126	628,800
1953	Dark Star	H. Moreno	126	90,050	1995	Thunder Gulch	G. Stevens	126	707,400
1954	Determine	R. York	126	102,050	1996	Grindstone	J. Bailey	126	869,800
1955	Swaps	W. Shoemaker	126	108,400	1997	Silver Charm	G. Stevens	126	700,000
1956	Needles	D. Erb	126	123,450	1998	Real Quiet	K. Desormeaux	126	738,800
1957	Iron Liege	W. Hartack	126	107,950	1999	Charismatic	C. Antley	126	886,200
1958	Tim Tam	I. Valenzuela	126	116,400	2000	Fusaichi Pegasus	K. Desormeaux	126	888,400
1959	Tomy Lee	W. Shoemaker	126	119,650	2001	Monarchos	J. Chavez	126	812,200
1960	Venetian Way	W. Hartack	126	114,850					

1. Dancer's Image finished first but was disqualified after traces of drug were found in his system.

PREAKNESS STAKES
Pimlico; 3-year-olds; 1³⁄₁₆ mi.

Year	Winner	Jockey	Wt.	Win val.	Year	Winner	Jockey	Wt.	Win val.
1919	Sir Barton	J. Loftus	126	$24,500	1961	Carry Back	J. Sellers	126	$126,200
1920	Man o' War	C. Kummer	126	(¹)	1962	Greek Money	J. Rotz	126	135,800
1921	Broomspun	F. Coltiletti	126	(¹)	1963	Candy Spots	W. Shoemaker	126	127,500
1922	Pillory	L. Morris	126	(¹)	1964	Northern Dancer	W. Hartack	126	124,200
1923	Vigil	B. Marinelli	126	(¹)	1965	Tom Rolfe	R. Turcotte	126	128,100
1924	Nellie Morse	J. Merimee	126	(¹)	1966	Kauai King	D. Brumfield	126	129,000
1925	Coventry	C. Kummer	126	(¹)	1967	Damascus	W. Shoemaker	126	141,500
1926	Display	J. Maiben	126	(¹)	1968	Forward Pass	I. Valenzuela	126	142,700
1927	Bostonian	W. Abel	126	(¹)	1969	Majestic Prince	W. Hartack	126	129,500
1928	Victorian	S. Workman	126	(¹)	1970	Personality	E. Belmonte	126	151,300
1929	Dr. Freeland	L. Schaefer	126	(¹)	1971	Canonero II	G. Avila	126	137,400
1930	Gallant Fox	E. Sande	126	51,925	1972	Bee Bee Bee	E. Nelson	126	135,300
1931	Mate	G. Ellis	126	48,225	1973	Secretariat	R. Turcotte	126	129,900
1932	Burgoo King	E. James	126	50,375	1974	Little Current	M. Rivera	126	156,000
1933	Head Play	C. Kurtsinger	126	26,850	1975	Master Derby	D. McHargue	126	158,100
1934	High Quest	R. Jones	126	25,175	1976	Elocutionist	J. Lively	126	129,700
1935	Omaha	W. Saunders	126	25,325	1977	Seattle Slew	J. Cruguet	126	138,600
1936	Bold Venture	G. Woolf	126	27,325	1978	Affirmed	S. Cauthen	126	136,200
1937	War Admiral	C. Kurtsinger	126	45,600	1979	Spectacular Bid	R. Franklin	126	165,300
1938	Dauber	M. Peters	126	51,875	1980	Codex	A. Cordero	126	180,600
1939	Challedon	G. Seabo	126	53,710	1981	Pleasant Colony	J. Velasquez	126	270,800
1940	Bimelech	F.A. Smith	126	53,230	1982	Aloma's Ruler	J. Kaenel	126	209,900
1941	Whirlaway	E. Arcaro	126	49,365	1983	Deputed			
1942	Alsab	B. James	126	58,175		Testamony	D. Miller	126	251,200
1943	Count Fleet	J. Longden	126	43,190	1984	Gate Dancer	A. Cordero	126	243,600
1944	Pensive	C. McCreary	126	60,075	1985	Tank's Prospect	P. Day	126	423,200
1945	Polynesian	W.D. Wright	126	66,170	1986	Snow Chief	A. Solis	126	411,900
1946	Assault	W. Mehrtens	126	96,620	1987	Alysheba	C. McCarron	126	421,100
1947	Faultless	D. Dodson	126	98,005	1988	Risen Star	E. Delahoussaye	126	413,700
1948	Citation	E. Arcaro	126	91,870	1989	Sunday Silence	P. Valenzuela	126	438,230
1949	Capot	T. Atkinson	126	79,985	1990	Summer Squall	P. Day	126	445,900
1950	Hill Prince	E. Arcaro	126	56,115	1991	Hansel	J. Bailey	126	432,770
1951	Bold	E. Arcaro	126	83,110	1992	Pine Bluff	C. McCarron	126	484,120
1952	Blue Man	C. McCreary	126	86,135	1993	Prairie Bayou	M. Smith	126	471,835
1953	Native Dancer	E. Guerin	126	65,200	1994	Tabasco Cat	P. Day	126	447,720
1954	Hasty Road	J. Adams	126	91,600	1995	Timber Country	P. Day	126	446,810
1955	Nashua	E. Arcaro	126	67,550	1996	Louis Quatorze	P. Day	126	458,120
1956	Fabius	W. Hartack	126	84,250	1997	Silver Charm	G. Stevens	126	488,150
1957	Bold Ruler	E. Arcaro	126	65,250	1998	Real Quiet	K. Desormeaux	126	650,000
1958	Tim Tam	I. Valenzuela	126	97,900	1999	Charismatic	C. Antley	126	650,000
1959	Royal Orbit	W. Harmatz	126	136,200	2000	Red Bullet	J. Bailey	126	650,000
1960	Bally Ache	R. Ussery	126	121,000	2001	Point Given	G. Stevens	126	650,000

1. Data not available.

BELMONT STAKES
Belmont Park; 3-year-olds; 1½ mi.

Run at Jerome Park 1867 to 1890; at Morris Park 1890–94; at Belmont Park 1905–62; at Aqueduct 1963–67. Distance 1⅝ mi prior to 1874; reduced to 1½ mi, 1874; reduced to 1¼ mi, 1890; reduced to 1⅛ mi, 1893; increased to 1¼ mi, 1895; increased to 1⅜ mi, 1896; reduced to 1¼ mi in 1904; increased to 1½ mi, 1926.

Year	Winner	Jockey	Wt.	Win val.	Year	Winner	Jockey	Wt.	Win val.
1919	Sir Barton	J. Loftus	126	$11,950	1930	Gallant Fox	E. Sande	126	$66,040
1920	Man o' War	C. Kummer	126	(¹)	1931	Twenty Grand	C. Kurtsinger	126	58,770
1921	Grey Lag	E. Sande	126	(¹)	1932	Faireno	T. Malley	126	55,120
1922	Pillory	C.H. Miller	126	(¹)	1933	Hurryoff	M. Garner	126	49,490
1923	Zev	E. Sande	126	(¹)	1934	Peace Chance	W.D. Wright	126	43,410
1924	Mad Play	E. Sande	126	(¹)	1935	Omaha	W. Saunders	126	35,480
1925	American Flag	A. Johnson	126	(¹)	1936	Granville	J. Stout	126	29,800
1926	Crusader	A. Johnson	126	(¹)	1937	War Admiral	C. Kurtsinger	126	38,020
1927	Chance Shot	E. Sande	126	(¹)	1938	Pasteurized	J. Stout	126	34,530
1928	Vito	C. Kummer	126	(¹)	1939	Johnstown	J. Stout	126	37,020
1929	Blue Larkspur	M. Garner	126	(¹)	1940	Bimelech	F.A. Smith	126	35,030

Year	Winner	Jockey	Wt.	Win val.	Year	Winner	Jockey	Wt.	Win val.
1941	Whirlaway	E. Arcaro	126	$39,770	1972	Riva Ridge	R. Turcotte	126	$93,540
1942	Shut Out	E. Arcaro	126	44,520	1973	Secretariat	R. Turcotte	126	90,120
1943	Count Fleet	J. Longden	126	35,340	1974	Little Current	M. Rivera	126	101,970
1944	Bounding Home	G.L. Smith	126	55,000	1975	Avatar	W. Shoemaker	126	116,160
1945	Pavot	E. Arcaro	126	56,675	1976	Bold Forbes	A. Cordero, Jr.	126	117,000
1946	Assault	W. Mehrtens	126	75,400	1977	Seattle Slew	J. Cruguet	126	109,080
1947	Phalanx	R. Donoso	126	78,900	1978	Affirmed	S. Cauthen	126	110,580
1948	Citation	E. Arcaro	126	77,700	1979	Coastal	R. Hernandez	126	161,400
1949	Capot	T. Atkinson	126	60,900	1980	Temperence Hill	E. Maple	126	176,220
1950	Middleground	W. Boland	126	61,350	1981	Summing	G. Martens	126	170,580
1951	Counterpoint	D. Gorman	126	82,000	1982	Conquistador			
1952	One Count	E. Arcaro	126	82,400		Cielo	L. Pincay, Jr.	126	159,720
1953	Native Dancer	E. Guerin	126	82,500	1983	Caveat	L. Pincay, Jr.	126	215,100
1954	High Gun	E. Guerin	126	89,000	1984	Swale	L. Pincay, Jr.	126	310,020
1955	Nashua	E. Arcaro	126	83,700	1985	Creme Fraiche	E. Maple	126	307,740
1956	Needles	D. Erb	126	83,600	1986	Danzig			
1957	Gallant Man	W. Shoemaker	126	77,300		Connection	C. McCarron	126	338,640
1958	Cavan	P. Anderson	126	73,440	1987	Bet Twice	C. Perret	126	329,160
1959	Sword Dancer	W. Shoemaker	126	93,525	1988	Risen Star	E. Delahoussaye	126	303,720
1960	Celtic Ash	W. Hartack	126	96,785	1989	Easy Goer	P. Day	126	413,520
1961	Sherluck	B. Baeza	126	104,900	1990	Go And Go	M. Kinane	126	411,600
1962	Jaipur	W. Shoemaker	126	109,550	1991	Hansel	J. Bailey	126	417,480
1963	Chateaugay	B. Baeza	126	101,700	1992	A.P. Indy	E. Delahoussaye	126	458,880
1964	Quadrangle	M. Ycaza	126	110,850	1993	Colonial Affair	J. Krone	126	444,450
1965	Hail to All	J. Sellers	126	104,150	1994	Tabasco Cat	P. Day	126	392,280
1966	Amberoid	W. Boland	126	117,700	1995	Thunder Gulch	G.Stevens	126	415,440
1967	Damascus	W. Shoemaker	126	104,950	1996	Editor's Note	R. Douglas	126	437,880
1968	Stage Door				1997	Touch Gold	C. McCarron	126	432,660
	Johnny	H. Gustines	126	117,700	1998	Victory Gallop	G. Stevens	126	600,000
1969	Arts and Letters	B. Baeza	126	104,050	1999	Lemon Drop Kid	J. Santos	126	600,000
1970	High Echelon	J. Rotz	126	115,000	2000	Commendable	P. Day	126	600,000
1971	Pass Catcher	R. Blum	126	97,710	2001	Point Given	G. Stevens	126	600,000

1. Data not available.

TRIPLE CROWN RACES—2001

Kentucky Derby (Churchill Downs, Louisville, Ky., May 5, 2001). Gross purse: $1,112,000. Distance: 1¼ mi. Order of finish: 1. Monarchos (Chavez), mutuel returns: $23.00, $11.80, $8.80. 2. Invisible Ink (Velazquez), $46.60, $21.20. 3. Congaree (Espinoza), $7.20. 4. Thunder Blitz (Prado). 5. Point Given (Stevens). 6. Jamaican Rum (Delahoussaye). 7. A P Valentine (Nakatani). 8. Express Tour (Flores). 9. Fifty Stars (Meche). 10. Startac (Solis). 11. Millennium Wind (Pincay, Jr.). 12. Arctic Boy (Borel). 13. Songandaprayer (Gryder). 14. Balto Star (Guidry). 15. Dollar Bill (Day). 16. Keats (Melancon). 17. Talk Is Money (Bailey). Winner's purse: $812,000. Margin of victory: 4¾ lengths. Time of race: 1:59.97.

Preakness Stakes (Pimlico, Baltimore, Md., May 19, 2001). Gross purse: $1,000,000. Distance: 1³⁄₁₆ mi. Order of finish: 1. Point Given (Stevens), mutuel returns: $6.60, $5.00, $4.00. 2. A P Valentine (Espinoza), $8.20, $5.20. 3. Congaree (Bailey), $3.40. 4. Dollar Bill (Day). 5. Griffinite (Bridgmohan). 6. Monarchos (Chavez). 7. Marciano (Johnston). 8. Bay Eagle (Dominguez). 9. Percy Hope (Court). 10. Richly Blended (Wilson). 11. Mr. John (Nakatani). Winner's purse: $650,000. Margin of victory: 2¼ lengths. Time of race: 1:55.51.

Belmont Stakes (Belmont Park, Belmont, N.Y., June 9, 2001). Gross purse: $1,000,000. Distance: 1½ mi. Order of finish: 1. Point Given (Stevens), mutuel returns: $4.70, $3.70, $3.00. 2. A P Valentine (Espinoza), $5.00, $3.90. 3. Monarchos (Chavez), $4.20. 4. Dollar Bill (Day). 5. Invisible Ink (Velazquez). 6. Thunder Blitz (Bailey). 7.

Buckle Down Ben (Nakatani). 8. Balto Star (McCarron). 9. Dr. Greenfield (Prado). Winner's purse: $600,000. Margin of victory: 12¼ lengths. Time of race: 2:26.56.

ECLIPSE AWARDS—2000

(Announced Feb. 1, 2001)

Horse of the Year	Tiznow
2-year-old colt or gelding	Macho Uno
2-year-old filly	Caressing
3-year-old colt	Tiznow
3-year-old filly	Surfside
Older colt, horse, or gelding	Lemon Drop Kid
Older filly or mare, 4 and up	Riboletta (Brazil)
Sprinter	Kona Gold
Male turf horse	Kalanisi (Ireland)
Female turf horse	Perfect Sting
Steeplechase	All Gong (Great Britain)
Owner	Frank Stronach/Stronach Stable
Breeder	Frank Stronach/Adena Springs
Trainer	Robert Frankel
Jockey	Jerry Bailey
Apprentice jockey	Tyler Baze

(Based on vote by the Thoroughbred Racing Associations, the *Daily Racing Form*, and the National Turf Writers Association.)

Track and Field

WORLD RECORDS—MEN

(Through Aug. 29, 2001)

Recognized by the International Athletic Federation. The IAAF decided late in 1976 not to recognize records in yards except for the one-mile run.

The IAAF also requires automatic timing for all records for races of 400 meters or less.

Event	Record	Holder	Home country	Where made	Date
Running					
100 m	0:09.79	Maurice Greene	United States	Athens, Greece	June 16, 1999
200 m	0:19.32	Michael Johnson	United States	Atlanta, Ga.	Aug. 1, 1996
400 m	0:43.18	Michael Johnson	United States	Seville, Spain	Aug. 26, 1999
800 m	1:41.11	Wilson Kipketer	Denmark	Köln, Germany	Aug. 24, 1997
1,000 m	2:11.96	Noah Ngeny	Kenya	Rieti, Italy	Sept. 5, 1999
1,500 m	3:26.00	Hicham El Guerrouj	Morocco	Rome, Italy	July 14, 1998
1 mile	3:43.13	Hicham El Guerrouj	Morocco	Rome, Italy	July 7, 1999
2,000 m	4:44.79	Hicham El Guerrouj	Morocco	Berlin, Germany	Sept. 7, 1999
3,000 m	7:20.67	Daniel Komen	Kenya	Rieti, Italy	Sept. 1, 1996
3,000 m steeplechase	7:55.28	Brahim Boulami	Morocco	Brussels, Belgium	Aug. 24, 2001
5,000 m	12:39.36	Haile Gebrselassie	Ethiopia	Helsinki, Finland	June 13, 1998
10,000 m	26:22.75	Haile Gebrselassie	Ethiopia	Hengelo, Netherlands	June 1, 1998
20,000 m	56:55.60	Arturo Barrios	Mexico	La Fleche, France	March 30, 1991
25,000 m	1:13:55.80	Toshihiko Seko	Japan	Christchurch, N.Z.	March 22, 1981
30,000 m	1:29:18.80	Toshihiko Seko	Japan	Christchurch, N.Z.	March 22, 1981
1 hour	21,101 m	Arturo Barrios	Mexico	La Fleche, France	March 30, 1991
Marathon[1]	2:05.42	Khalid Khannouchi	Morocco	Chicago, Ill.	Nov. 24, 1999
Walking					
20,000 m	1:17:25.60	Bernardo Segura	Mexico	Bergen, Norway	May 7, 1994
30,000 m	2:01:44.10	Maurizio Damilano	Italy	Cuneo, Italy	Oct. 3, 1992
50,000 m	3:40:57.90	Thierry Toutain	France	Héricourt, France	Sept. 29, 1996
2 hours	29,572 m	Maurizio Damilano	Italy	Cuneo, Italy	Oct. 3, 1992
Hurdles					
110 m	0:12.91	Colin Jackson	Great Britain	Stuttgart, Germany	Aug. 20, 1993
400 m	0:46.78	Kevin Young	United States	Barcelona, Spain	Aug. 6, 1992
Relay races					
400 m (4 × 100)	0:37.40	National Team	United States	Barcelona, Spain	Aug. 8, 1992
	0:37.40	National Team	United States	Stuttgart, Germany	Aug. 21, 1993
800 m (4 × 200)	1:18.68	Santa Monica T.C.	United States	Walnut, Calif.	April 17, 1994
1,600 m (4 × 400)	2:54.20	National Team	United States	New York, N.Y.	July 22, 1998
3,200 m (4 × 800)	7:03.89	National Team	Britain	London, England	Aug. 30, 1982
6,000 m	14:38.80	National Team	West Germany	Köln, Germany	Aug. 17, 1977
Field events					
High jump	2.45 m	Javier Sotomayor	Cuba	Salamanca, Spain	July 27, 1993
Long jump	8.95 m	Mike Powell	United States	Tokyo, Japan	Aug. 30, 1991
Triple jump	18.29 m	Jonathan Edwards	Great Britain	Goteborg, Sweden	Aug. 7, 1995
Pole vault	6.14 m	Sergey Bubka	Ukraine	Sestriere, Italy	July 31, 1994
Shot-put	23.12 m	Randy Barnes	United States	Los Angeles, Calif.	May 20, 1990
Discus throw	74.08 m	Jürgen Schult	East Germany	Neubrandenburg, E. Germany	June 6, 1986
Hammer throw	86.74 m	Yuriy Sedykh	USSR	Stuttgart, Germany	Aug. 30, 1986
Javelin throw	98.48 m	Jan Zelezny	Czech Republic	Jena, Germany	May 25, 1996
Decathlon	9,026 pts.	Roman Sebrle	Czech Republic	Götzis, Austria	May 27, 2001

1. Not recognized by IAAF as world record, but considered to be "world best performance."

WORLD RECORDS—WOMEN

(Through Aug. 29, 2001)

Event	Record	Holder	Home country	Where made	Date
Running					
100 m	0:10.49	Florence Griffith-Joyner	United States	Indianapolis, Ind.	July 16, 1988
200 m	0:21.34	Florence Griffith-Joyner	United States	Seoul, South Korea	Sept. 29, 1988
400 m	0:47.60	Martina Koch	East Germany	Canberra, Australia	Oct. 6, 1985
800 m	1:53.28	Jarmila Kratochvilova	Czechoslovakia	Munich, W. Germany	July 26, 1983
1000 m	2:28.98	Svetlana Masterkova	Russia	Brussels, Belgium	Aug. 23, 1996
1,500 m	3:50.46	Qu Yunxia	China	Beijing, China	Sept. 11, 1993
1 mile	4:12.56	Svetlana Masterkova	Russia	Zurich, Switzerland	Aug. 14, 1996
2,000 m	5:25.36	Sonia O'Sullivan	Ireland	Edinburgh, Scotland	July 8, 1994
3,000 m	8:06.11	Wang Junxia	China	Beijing, China	Sept. 13, 1993
5,000 m	14:28.09	Jiang Bo	China	Shanghai, China	Oct. 23, 1997

Event	Record	Holder	Home country	Where made	Date
10,000 m	29:31.78	Wang Junxia	China	Beijing, China	Sept. 8, 1993
20,000 m	1:05:26.60	Tegla Loroupe	Kenya	Borgholzhausen, Germany	Sept. 3, 2000
25,000 m	1:29:29.20	Karolina Szabo	Hungary	Budapest, Hungary	April 22, 1988
30,000 m	1:47:05.60	Karolina Szabo	Hungary	Budapest, Hungary	April 22, 1988
1 hour	18.340	Tegla Loroupe	Kenya	Borgholzhausen, Germany	July 8, 1999
3,000 m steeplechase	9:25.31	Justyna Bak	Poland	Nice, France	July 9, 2001
Marathon[1]	2:20:43	Tegla Loroupe	Kenya	Berlin, Germany	Sept. 26, 1999
Walking					
5,000 m	20:13.26	Kerry Saxby-Junna	Australia	Hobart, Australia	Feb. 25, 1996
10,000 m	41:56.23	Nadezhda Ryashkina	Russia	Seattle, Wash.	July 24, 1990
20,000 m	1:29:36.40	Susana Feitor	Portugal	Lisbon, Portugal	July 7, 2001
Hurdles					
100 m	0:12.21	Yordanka Donkova	Bulgaria	Stara Zagora, Bulgaria	Aug. 20, 1988
400 m	0:52.61	Kim Batten	United States	Goteborg, Sweden	Aug. 11, 1995
Relay races					
400 m (4 × 100)	0:41.37	East Germany	E. Germany	Canberra, Australia	Oct. 6, 1985
800 m (4 × 200)	1:27.46	United States "Blue"	United States	Philadelphia, Pa.	April 29, 2000
1,600 m (4 × 400)	3:15.17	USSR	USSR	Seoul, South Korea	Oct. 1, 1988
3,200 m (4 × 800)	7:50.17	USSR	USSR	Moscow, USSR	Aug. 5, 1984
Field events					
High jump	2.09 m	Stefka Kostadinova	Bulgaria	Rome, Italy	Aug. 30, 1987
Pole vault	4.81 m	Stacy Dragila	United States	Palo Alto, Calif.	June 9, 2001
Long jump	7.52 m	Galina Chistyakova	USSR	Leningrad, Russia	June 11, 1988
Triple jump	15.50 m	Inessa Kravets	Ukraine	Goteborg, Sweden	Aug. 10, 1995
Shot-put	22.63 m	Natalya Lisovskaya	USSR	Moscow, Russia	June 7, 1987
Discus throw	76.80 m	Gabriele Reinsch	East Germany	Neubrandenburg, E. Ger.	July 9, 1988
Hammer throw	76.07 m	Mihaela Melinte	Romania	Rüdlingen, Switzerland	Aug. 29, 1999
Javelin throw	71.54 m	Osleidys Menéndez	Cuba	Réthymno, Greece	July 1, 2001
Heptathlon	7,291 pts	Jackie Joyner-Kersee	United States	Seoul, South Korea	Sept. 24, 1988

1. Not recognized by IAAF as world record, but considered to be "world best performance."

AMERICAN RECORDS—MEN

(Through Aug. 29, 2001)

Event	Record	Holder	Where Made	Date
Running				
100 m	0:09.79	Maurice Greene	Athens, Greece	June 16, 1999
200 m	0:19.32	Michael Johnson	Atlanta, Ga.	Aug. 1, 1996
400 m	0:43.18	Michael Johnson	Seville, Spain	Aug. 26, 1999
800 m	1:42.60	Johnny Gray	Koblenz, W. Germany	Aug. 29, 1985
1,000 m	2:13.90	Richard Wohlhuter	Oslo, Norway	July 30, 1974
1,500 m	3:29.77	Sydney Maree	Cologne, W. Germany	Aug. 25, 1985
1 mile	3:47.69	Steve Scott	Oslo, Norway	July 7, 1982
2,000 m	4:52.44	Jim Spivey	Lausanne, Switzerland	Sept. 15, 1987
3,000 m	7:30.84	Bob Kennedy	Monaco	Aug. 8, 1998
5,000 m	12:58.21	Bob Kennedy	Zurich, Switzerland	Aug. 14, 1996
10,000 m	27:20.56	Mark Nenow	Brussels, Belgium	Sept. 5, 1986
20,000 m	58:15.00	Bill Rodgers	Boston, Mass.	Aug. 9, 1977
25,000 m	1:14:11.80	Bill Rodgers	Saratoga, Calif.	Feb. 21, 1979
30,000 m	1:31:49.00	Bill Rodgers	Saratoga, Calif.	Feb. 21, 1979
1 hour	12 mi., 1,351 yds	Bill Rodgers	Boston, Mass.	Aug. 9, 1977
3,000-m steeplechase	8:09.17	Henry Marsh	Koblenz, W. Ger.	Aug. 29, 1985
Marathon	2:07:01	Khalid Khannouchi	Chicago, Ill.	Oct. 22, 2000
Hurdles				
110 m	0:12.92	Roger Kingdom	Berlin, Germany	Aug. 16, 1989
		Allen Johnson	Atlanta, Ga.	June 23, 1996
400 m	0:46.78	Kevin Young	Barcelona	Aug. 6, 1992
Relay races				
400 m (4 × 100)	0:37.40	Olympic Team	Barcelona, Spain	Aug. 8, 1992
		USA National Team	Stuttgart, Germany	Aug. 21, 1993
800 m (4 × 200)	1:18.68	Santa Monica T.C.	Walnut, Calif.	April 17, 1994
1,600 m (4 × 400)	2:54.20	USA National Team	New York, N.Y.	July 22, 1998
3,200 m (4 × 800)	7:06.50	Santa Monica T.C.	Walnut, Calif.	Apr. 26, 1986
6,000 m (4 × 1,500)	14:46.30	National Team	Bourges, France	June 24, 1979
Field events				
High jump	7 ft. 10½ in.	Charles Austin	Zurich, Switzerland	Aug. 7, 1991

Event	Record	Holder	Where Made	Date
Long jump	29 ft. 4½ in.	Mike Powell	Tokyo, Japan	Aug. 30, 1991
Triple jump	59 ft. 4 in.	Kenny Harrison	Atlanta, Ga.	July 27, 1996
Pole vault	19 ft. 9 ¼in.	Jeff Hartwig	Jonesboro, Ark.	June 14, 2000
Shot-put	75 ft. 10¼ in.	Randy Barnes	Los Angeles	May 20, 1990
Discus throw	237 ft. 4 in.	Ben Plucknett	Stockholm, Swe.	July 7, 1981
Javelin throw	285 ft. 10 in.	Tom Pukstys	Jena, Germany	May 25, 1997
Hammer throw	270 ft. 9 in.	Lance Deal	Milan, Italy	July 9, 1996
Decathlon	8,891 pts	Dan O'Brien	Talence, France	Sept. 4–5, 1992

AMERICAN RECORDS—WOMEN

(Through Aug. 29, 2001)

Event	Record	Holder	Where Made	Date
Running				
100 m	0:10.49	Florence Griffith Joyner	Indianapolis, Ind.	July 16, 1988
200 m	21.34	Florence Griffith Joyner	Seoul, South Korea	Sept. 29, 1988
400 m	0:48.83	Valerie Brisco	Los Angeles, Calif.	Aug. 6, 1984
800 m	1:56.40	Jearl Miles-Clark	Zurich, Switzerland	Aug. 11, 1999
1,000 m	2:31.80	Regina Jacobs	Brunswick, Maine	July 3, 1999
1,500 m	3:57.12	Mary Slaney	Stockholm, Sweden.	July 26, 1983
2,000 m	5:32.70	Mary Slaney	Eugene, Ore.	Aug. 3, 1984
1 mile	4:16.71	Mary Decker Slaney	Zurich, Switzerland	Aug. 21, 1985
3,000 m	8:29.69	Mary Decker Slaney	Cologne, Germany	Aug. 25, 1985
5,000 m	14:45.38	Regina Jacobs	Sacramento, Calif.	July 21, 2000
10,000 m	31:19.89	Lynn Jennings	Barcelona, Spain	Aug. 7, 1992
3,000 m steeplechase	9:57.20	Elizabeth Jackson	Sacramento, Calif.	July 17, 2000
Marathon	2:21:21	Joan Samuelson	Chicago, Ill.	Oct. 20, 1985
Hurdles				
100 m	0:12.33	Gail Devers	Sacramento, Calif.	July 23, 2000
400 m	0:52.61	Kim Batten	Gotebörg, Sweden	Aug. 11, 1995
Relay races				
400 m (4 × 100)	41.47	U.S.A. National Team	Athens, Greece	Aug. 9, 1997
800 m (4 × 200)	1:27.46	United States Blue Team	Philadelphia, Pa.	April 29, 2000
1,600 m (4 × 400)	3:15.51	U.S. Olympic Team	Seoul, South Korea	Oct. 1, 1988
Field events				
Pole vault	15 ft 2 ¼ in.	Stacy Dragila	Sacramento, Calif.	July 23, 2000
High jump	6 ft 8 in.	Louise Ritter	Austin, Tex.	July 9, 1988
Long jump	24 ft 7 in.	Jackie Joyner-Kersee	New York, N.Y.	May 22, 1994
Triple jump	47 ft 3½ in.	Sheila Hudson	Stockholm, Sweden	July 8, 1996
Shot-put	66 ft 2½ in.	Ramon Pagel	San Diego, Calif.	June 25, 1988
Discus throw	216 ft 10 in.	Carol Cady	San Jose, Calif.	May 31, 1986
Hammer throw	231 ft 2 in.	Dawn Ellerbe	Philadelphia, Pa.	April 29, 2000
Javelin throw (old)	227 ft 5 in.	Kate Schmidt	Fürth, W. Ger.	Sept. 10, 1977
Javelin throw (new)	192 ft 3 in.	Lynda Blutreich	New Haven, Conn.	July 1, 2000
Heptathlon	7,291 pts	Jackie Joyner-Kersee	Seoul, South Korea	Sept. 23–24, 1988

HISTORY OF THE RECORD FOR THE MILE RUN

(Under 4 minutes) Source: USA Track & Field

Time	Athlete	Country	Year	Location
3:59.4	Roger Bannister	England	1954	Oxford, England
3:58.0	John Landy	Australia	1954	Turku, Finland
3:57.2	Derek Ibbotson	England	1957	London
3:54.5	Herb Elliott	Australia	1958	Dublin
3:54.4	Peter Snell	New Zealand	1962	Wanganui, N.Z.
3:54.1	Peter Snell	New Zealand	1964	Auckland, N.Z.
3:53.6	Michel Jazy	France	1965	Rennes, France
3:51.3	Jim Ryun	United States	1966	Berkeley, Calif.
3:51.1	Jim Ryun	United States	1967	Bakersfield, Calif.
3:51.0	Filbert Bayi	Tanzania	1975	Kingston, Jamaica
3:49.4	John Walker	New Zealand	1975	Goteborg, Sweden
3:49.0	Sebastian Coe	England	1979	Oslo
3:48.8	Steve Ovett	England	1980	Oslo
3:48.53	Sebastian Coe	England	1981	Zurich, Switzerland
3:48.40	Steve Ovett	England	1981	Koblenz, W. Ger.
3:47.33	Sebastian Coe	England	1981	Brussels
3:46.31	Steve Cram	England	1985	Oslo
3:44.39	Noureddine Morceli	Algeria	1993	Rieti, Italy
3:43.13	Hicham El Guerrouj	Morocco	1999	Rome, Italy

TOP TEN WORLD'S FASTEST OUTDOOR MILES

Source: USA Track & Field

Time	Athlete	Country	Date	Location
3:43.13	Hicham El Guerrouj	Morocco	July 27, 1999	Rome, Italy
3:44.39	Nouraddine Morceli	Algeria	Sept. 5, 1993	Rieti, Italy
3:46.31	Steve Cram	England	July 27, 1985	Oslo
3:47.33	Sebastian Coe	England	Aug. 28, 1981	Brussels
3:47.69	Steve Scott	United States	July 7, 1982	Oslo
3:47.79	Jose Gonzalez	Spain	July 27, 1985	Oslo
3:48.40	Steve Ovett	England	Aug. 26, 1981	Koblenz, W. Ger.
3:48.53	Sebastian Coe	England	Aug. 19, 1981	Zurich
3:48.53	Steve Scott	United States	June 26, 1982	Oslo
3:48.8	Steve Ovett	England	July 1, 1980	Oslo

NOTE: Professional marks not included.

TOP TEN WORLD'S FASTEST INDOOR MILES

Source: USA Track & Field

Time	Athlete	Country	Date	Location
3:48.45	Hicham El Guerrouj	Morocco	Feb, 12, 1997	Gent, Netherlands
3:49.78	Eamonn Coghlan	Ireland	Feb. 27, 1983	East Rutherford, N.J.
3:50.6	Eamonn Coghlan	Ireland	Feb. 20, 1981	San Diego
3:50.7	Noureddine Morceli	Algeria	Feb. 20, 1993	Birmingham, England
3:50.94	Marcus O'Sullivan	Ireland	Feb. 13, 1988	East Rutherford, N.J.
3:51.2	Ray Flynn[L]	Ireland	Feb. 27, 1983	East Rutherford, N.J.
3:51.66	Marcus O'Sullivan	Ireland	Feb. 10, 1989	East Rutherford, N.J.
3:51.8	Steve Scott[1]	United States	Feb. 20, 1981	San Diego
3:52.28	Steve Scott[2]	United States	Feb. 27, 1983	East Rutherford, N.J.
3:52.30	Frank O'Mara	Ireland	Feb. 1986	New York

1. Finished second. 2. Finished third.

2001 IAAF WORLD CHAMPIONSHIPS

(Edmonton, Canada, Aug. 3–12, 2001)

Men's Events	Results
100 m—Maurice Greene, United States	9.82
200 m—Konstadínos Kedéris, Greece	20.04
400 m—Avard Moncur, Bahamas	44.64
800 m—André Bucher, Switzerland	1:43.70
1,500 m—Hicham El Guerrouj, Morocco	3:30.68
5,000 m—Richard Limo, Kenya	13:00.77
10,000 m—Charles Kamathi, Kenya	27:53.25
Marathon—Gezahegne Abera, Ethiopia	2:12:42
3,000 m steeplechase—Reuben Kosgei, Kenya	8:15.16
110 m hurdles—Allen Johnson, United States	13:04
400 m hurdles—Felix Sánchez, Dominican Republic	47.49
High jump—Martin Buss, Germany	2.36 m
Pole vault—Dmitri Markov, Australia	6.05 m
Long jump—Iván Pedroso, Cuba	8.40 m
Triple jump—Jonathan Edwards, Great Britain	17.92 m
Shot put—John Godina, United States	21.87 m
Discus throw—Lars Riedel, Germany	69.72 m
Hammer throw—Szymon Ziólkowski, Poland	83.38 m
Javelin throw—Jan Zelezný, Czech Republic	92.80 m
20 km walk—Roman Rasskazov, Russia	1:20:31
50 km walk—Robert Korzeniowski, Poland	3:42:08
4 × 100 m—United States	37.96
4 × 400 m—United States	2:57.54
200 m amputee—Neil Fuller, Australia	23.32
100 m blind—Lorenzo Ricci, Italy	11.71
1,500 m wheelchair—Aaron Gordian, Mexico	3:08.04
Decathlon—Tomás Dvorák, Czech Republic	8,902 pts

Women's Events	Results
100 m—Zhanna Pintusevich-Block, Ukraine	10.82
200 m—Marion Jones, United States	22.39
400 m—Amy Mbacke Thiam, Senegal	49.86
800 m—Maria de Lourdes Mutola, Mozambique	1:57.17
1,500 m—Gabriela Szabo, Romania	4:00.57
5,000 m—Olga Yegorova, Russia	15:03.39
10,000 m—Derartu Tulu, Ethiopia	31:48.81
Marathon—Lidia Simon, Romania	2:26.01
100 m hurdles—Anjanette Kirkland, United States	12.42
400 m hurdles—Nezha Bidouane, Morocco	53.34
High jump—Hestrie Cloete, South Africa	2.00 m
Pole vault—Stacy Dragila, United States	4.75 m
Long jump—Fiona May, Italy	7.02 m
Triple jump—Tatyana Lebedeva, Russia	15.25 m
Shot put—Yanina Korolchik, Belarus	20.61 m
Discus throw—Natalya Sadova, Russia	68.57 m
Hammer throw—Yipsi Moreno, Cuba	70.65 m
Javelin throw—Osleidys Menéndez, Cuba	69.53 m
20 km walk—Olimpiada Ivanova, Russia	1:27:48
4 × 100 m—United States	41.71
4 × 400 m—Jamaica	3:20.65
100 m amputee—Amy Winters, Australia	12.72
200 m blind—Adria Rocha Santos, Brazil	25.76
800 m wheelchair—Louise Sauvage, Australia	1:56.86
Heptathlon—Yelena Prokhorova, Russia	6,694 pts

Tennis

Lawn tennis is a comparatively modern modification of the ancient game of court tennis. Maj. Walter Clopton Wingfield thought that something like court tennis might be played outdoors on lawns, and in Dec., 1873, at Nantclwyd, Wales, he introduced his new game under the name of *Sphairistike* at a lawn party. The game was a success and spread rapidly, but the name was a total failure and almost immediately disappeared when all the players and spectators began to refer to the new game as *lawn tennis*. In the early part of 1874, a young lady named Mary Ewing Outerbridge returned from Bermuda to New York, bringing with her the implements and necessary equipment of the new game, which she had obtained from a British Army supply store in Bermuda. Miss Outerbridge and friends played the first game of lawn tennis in the United States on the grounds of the Staten Island Cricket and Baseball Club in the spring of 1874.

For a few years, the new game went along in haphazard fashion until about 1880, when standard measurements for the court and standard equipment

within definite limits became the rule. In 1881, the U.S. Lawn Tennis Association (whose name was changed in 1975 to the U.S. Tennis Association) was formed and conducted the first national championship at Newport, R.I. The international matches for the Davis Cup began with a series between the British and U.S. players on the courts of the Longwood Cricket Club, Chestnut Hill, Mass., in 1900, with the home players winning.

Professional tennis, which got its start in 1926 when the French star Suzanne Lenglen was paid $50,000 for a tour, received full recognition in 1968. Staid old Wimbledon, the London home of what are considered the world championships, let the pros compete. This decision ended a long controversy over open tennis and changed the format of the competition. The U.S. championships were also opened to the pros and the site of the event, long held at Forest Hills, N.Y., was shifted to the National Tennis Center in Flushing Meadows, N.Y., in 1978. Pro tours for men and women became worldwide in play that continued throughout the year.

DAVIS CUP CHAMPIONSHIPS

No matches in 1901, 1910, 1915–18, and 1940–45

1900 United States 3, British Isles 0	1936 Great Britain 3, Australia 2	1971 United States 3, Romania 2
1902 United States 3, British Isles 2	1937 United States 4, Great Britain 1	1972 United States 3, Romania 2
1903 British Isles 4, United States 1	1938 United States 3, Australia 2	1973 Australia 5, United States 0
1904 British Isles 5, Belgium 0	1939 Australia 3, United States 2	1974 South Africa (Default by India)
1905 British Isles 5, United States 0	1946 United States 5, Australia 0	1975 Sweden 3, Czechoslovakia 2
1906 British Isles 5, United States 0	1947 United States 4, Australia 1	1976 Italy 4, Chile 1
1907 Australasia 3, British Isles 2	1948 United States 5, Australia 0	1977 Australia 3, Italy 1
1908 Australasia 3, United States 2	1949 United States 4, Australia 1	1978 United States 4, Britain 1
1909 Australasia 5, United States 0	1950 Australia 4, United States 1	1979 United States 5, Italy 0
1911 Australasia 5, United States 0	1951 Australia 3, United States 2	1980 Czechoslovakia 4, Italy 1
1912 British Isles 3, Australasia 2	1952 Australia 4, United States 1	1981 United States 3, Argentina 1
1913 United States 3, British Isles 2	1953 Australia 3, United States 2	1982 United States 4, France 1
1914 Australasia 3, United States 2	1954 United States 3, Australia 2	1983 Australia 3, Sweden 2
1919 Australasia 4, British Isles 1	1955 Australia 5, United States 0	1984 Sweden 4, United States 1
1920 United States 5, Australasia 0	1956 Australia 5, United States 0	1985 Sweden 3, West Germany 2
1921 United States 5, Japan 0	1957 Australia 3, United States 2	1986 Australia 3, Sweden 2
1922 United States 4, Australasia 1	1958 United States 3, Australia 2	1987 Sweden 5, India 0
1923 United States 4, Australasia 1	1959 Australia 3, United States 2	1988 West Germany 4, Sweden 1
1924 United States 5, Australasia 0	1960 Australia 4, Italy 1	1989 West Germany 3, Sweden 2
1925 United States 5, France 0	1961 Australia 5, Italy 0	1990 United States 3, Australia 2
1926 United States 4, France 1	1962 Australia 5, Mexico 0	1991 France 3, United States 1
1927 France 3, United States 2	1963 United States 3, Australia 2	1992 United States 3, Switzerland 1
1928 France 4, United States 1	1964 Australia 3, United States 2	1993 Germany 4, Australia 1
1929 France 3, United States 2	1965 Australia 4, Spain 1	1994 Sweden 4, Russia 1
1930 France 4, United States 1	1966 Australia 4, India 1	1995 United States 3, Russia 1
1931 France 3, Great Britain 2	1967 Australia 4, Spain 1	1996 France 3, Sweden 2
1932 France 3, United States 2	1968 United States 4, Australia 1	1997 Sweden 5, United States 0
1933 Great Britain 3, France 2	1969 United States 5, Romania 0	1998 Sweden 4, Italy 1
1934 Great Britain 4, United States 1	1970 United States 5, West	1999 Australia 3, France 2
1935 Great Britain 5, United States 0	Germany 0	2000 Spain 3, Australia 1

FEDERATION CUP CHAMPIONSHIPS

World team competition for women conducted by International Lawn Tennis Federation

1963 United States 2, Australia 1	1971 Australia 3, Britain 0	1979 United States 3, Australia 0
1964 Australia 2, United States 1	1972 South Africa 2, Britain 1	1980 United States 3, Australia 0
1965 Australia 2, United States 1	1973 Australia 3, South Africa 0	1981 United States 3, Britain 0
1966 United States 3, West Germany 0	1974 Australia 2, United States 1	1982 United States 3, West Germany 0
1967 United States 2, Britain 0	1975 Czechoslovakia 3, Australia 0	1983 Czechoslovakia 2, West
1968 Australia 3, Netherlands 0	1976 United States 2, Australia 1	Germany 1
1969 Australia 2, United States 1	1977 United States 2, Australia 1	1984 Czechoslovakia 2, Australia 1
1970 Australia 3, West Germany 0	1978 United States 2, Australia 1	

1985	Czechoslovakia 2, United States 1	1989	United States 3, Spain 0	1995	Spain 3, United States 2
1986	United States 3, Czechoslovakia 0	1990	United States 2, Soviet Union 1	1996	United States 5, Spain 0
1987	West Germany 2, United States 1	1991	Spain 2, United States 1	1997	France 4, Netherlands 1
1988	Czechoslovakia 2, Soviet Union 1	1992	Germany 2, Spain 1	1998	Spain 3, Switzerland 2
		1993	Spain 3, Australia 0	1999	United States 4, Russia 1
		1994	Spain 3, United States 0	2000	United States 5, Spain 0

U.S. NATIONAL AND OPEN CHAMPIONS

SINGLES—MEN

NATIONAL

1881–87	Richard D. Sears	1926–27	Jean Rene Lacoste	1957	Mal Anderson	1977	Guillermo Vilas
1888–89	Henry Slocum, Jr.	1928	Henri Cochet	1958	Ashley Cooper	1978	Jimmy Connors
1890–92	Oliver S. Campbell	1929	Bill Tilden	1959–60	Neale Fraser	1979	John McEnroe
1893–94	Robert D. Wrenn	1930	John H. Doeg	1961	Roy Emerson	1980–81	John McEnroe
1895	Fred H. Hovey	1931–32	Ellsworth Vines	1962	Rod Laver	1982	Jimmy Connors
1896–97	Robert D. Wrenn	1933–34	Fred J. Perry	1963	Rafael Osuna	1983	Jimmy Connors
1898–		1935	Wilmer L. Allison	1964	Roy Emerson	1984	John McEnroe
1900	Malcolm Whitman	1936	Fred J. Perry	1965	Manuel Santana	1985–87	Ivan Lendl
1901–02	William A. Larned	1937–38	Don Budge	1966	Fred Stolle	1988	Mats Wilander
1903	Hugh L. Doherty	1939	Robert L. Riggs	1967	John Newcombe	1989	Boris Becker
1904	Holcombe Ward	1940	Donald McNeill	1968	Arthur Ashe	1990	Pete Sampras
1905	Beals C. Wright	1941	Robert L. Riggs	1969	Rod Laver	1991	Stefan Edberg
1906	William J. Clothier	1942	Fred Schroeder			1992	Stefan Edberg
1907–11	William A. Larned	1943	Joseph Hunt	**OPEN**		1993	Pete Sampras
1912–13	Maurice McLoughlin[1]	1944–45	Frank Parker	1968	Arthur Ashe	1994	Andre Agassi
1914	R. N. Williams II	1946–47	Jack Kramer	1969	Rod Laver	1995	Pete Sampras
1915	William Johnston	1948–49	Richard Gonzales	1970	Ken Rosewall	1996	Pete Sampras
1916	R. N. William II	1950	Arthur Larsen	1971	Stan Smith	1997–98	Patrick Rafter
1917–18	R. Lindley Murray[2]	1951–52	Frank Sedgman	1972	Ilie Nastase	1999	Andre Agassi
1919	William Johnston	1953	Tony Trabert	1973	John Newcombe	2000	Marat Safin
1920–25	Bill Tilden	1954	Vic Seixas	1974	Jimmy Connors	2001	Lleyton Hewitt
		1955	Tony Trabert	1975	Manuel Orantes		
		1956	Ken Rosewall	1976	Jimmy Connors		

1. Challenge Round Abandoned in 1912. 2. Patriotic Tournament in 1917.

SINGLES—WOMEN

NATIONAL

1887	Ellen F. Hansel	1912–14	Mary K. Browne	1948–50	Margaret Osborne duPont	1975–78	Chris Evert
1888–89	Bertha Townsend	1915–18	Molla Bjurstedt	1951–53	Maureen Connolly	1979	Tracy Austin
1890	Ellen C. Roosevelt	1919	Hazel Hotchkiss Wightman	1954–55	Doris Hart	1980	Chris Evert-Lloyd
1891–92	Mabel E. Cahill			1956	Shirley Fry	1981	Tracy Austin
1893	Aline M. Terry	1920–22	Molla Bjurstedt Mallory	1957–58	Althea Gibson	1982	Chris Evert-Lloyd
1894	Helen R. Helwig	1923–25	Helen N. Wills	1959	Maria Bueno	1983–84	Martina Navratilova
1895	Juliette P. Atkinson	1926	Molla B. Mallory	1960–61	Darlene Hard	1985	Hana Mandlikova
1896	Elisabeth H. Moore	1927–29	Helen N. Wills	1962	Margaret Smith	1986–87	Martina Navratilova
1897–98	Juliette P. Atkinson	1930	Betty Nuthall	1963–64	Maria Bueno	1988	Steffi Graf
1899	Marion Jones	1931	Helen Wills Moody	1965	Margaret Smith	1989	Steffi Graf
1900	Myrtle McAteer	1932–35	Helen Jacobs	1966	Maria Bueno	1990	Gabriela Sabatini
1901	Elisabeth H. Moore	1936	Alice Marble	1967	Billie Jean King	1991	Monica Seles
1902	Marion Jones	1937	Anita Lizana	1968–69	Margaret Smith Court[1]	1992	Monica Seles
1903	Elisabeth H. Moore	1938–40	Alice Marble			1993	Steffi Graf
1904	May Sutton	1941	Sarah Palfrey Cooke			1994	Arantxa Sanchez Vicario
1905	Elisabeth H. Moore			**OPEN**			
1906	Helen Homans	1942–44	Pauline Betz	1968	Virginia Wade	1995	Steffi Graf
1907	Evelyn Sears	1945	Sarah Cooke	1969–70	Margaret Court	1996	Steffi Graf
1908	Maud Bargar-Wallach	1946	Pauline Betz	1971–72	Billie Jean King	1997	Martina Hingis
		1947	Louise Brough	1973	Margaret Court	1998	Lindsay Davenport
1909–11	Hazel V. Hotchkiss			1974	Billie Jean King	1999	Serena Williams
						2000–2001	Venus Williams

1. With the inaugural of the Open Tournament in 1968, the United States Lawn Tennis Association held a championship at Longwood, Chestnut Hill, Mass., which barred contract professionals in 1968 and 1969.

DOUBLES—MEN

NATIONAL

1920	Bill Johnston–C. J. Griffin	1923	Bill Tilden–B. I. C. Norton	1925–26	Vincent Richards–R. N. Williams II
1921–22	Bill Tilden–Vincent Richards	1924	H. O. Kinsey–R. G. Kinsey	1927	Bill Tilden–Frank Hunter

1928	G. M. Lott, Jr.–V. Hennessy	1958	Ham Richardson–Alex Olmedo	1981	John McEnroe–Peter Fleming
1929–30	G. M. Lott, Jr.–J. H. Doeg	1959–60	Neale Fraser–Roy Emerson	1982	Kevin Curren–Steve Denton
1931	W. L. Allison–John Van Ryn	1961	Chuck McKinley–Dennis Ralston	1983	John McEnroe–Peter Fleming
1932	E. H. Vines, Jr.–Keith Gledh	1962	Rafael Osuna–Antonio Palafox	1984	John Fitzgerald–Tomas Smid
1933–34	G. M. Lott, Jr.–L. R. Stoefen			1985	Ken Flach–Robert Seguso
1935	W. L. Allison–John Van Ryn	1963–64	Chuck McKinley–Dennis Ralston	1986	Andres Gomez–Slobodan Zivojinovic
1936	Don Budge–Gene Mako	1965–66	Fred Stolle–Roy Emerson	1987	Stefan Edberg–Anders Jarryd
1937	G. von Cramm–H. Henkel	1967	John Newcombe–Tony Roche		
1938	Don Budge–Gene Mako	1968	Stan Smith–Bob Lutz[1]	1988	Sergio Casal–Emilio Sanchez
1939	A. K. Quist–J. E. Bromwich	1969	Richard Crealy–Allan Stone[1]	1989	John McEnroe–Mark Woodforde
1940–41	Jack Kramer–F. R. Schroeder	**OPEN**		1990	Pieter Aldrich–Danie Visser
1942	Gardnar Mulloy–Bill Talbert	1968	Stan Smith–Bob Lutz	1991	John Fitzgerald–Anders Jarryd
1943	Jack Kramer–Frank Parker	1969	Fred Stolle–Ken Rosewall		
1944	Don McNeill–Bob Falkenburg	1970	Nikki Pilic–Fred Barthes	1992	Jim Grabb–Richey Reneberg
1945	Gardnar Mulloy–Bill Talbert	1971	John Newcombe–Roger Taylor	1993	Ken Flach–Rick Leach
1946	Gardnar Mulloy–Bill Talbert			1994	Jacco Hingh–Paul Haarhuis
1947	Jack Kramer–Fred Schroeder	1972	Cliff Drysdale–Roger Taylor	1995–96	Todd Woodbridge–Mark Woodforde
1948	Gardnar Mulloy–Bill Talbert	1973	John Newcombe–Owen Davidson	1997	Yevgeny Kafelnikov–Daniel Vacek
1949	John Bromwich–William Sidwell	1974	Bob Lutz–Stan Smith		
1950	John Bromwich–Frank Sedgman	1975	Jimmy Connors–Ilie Nastase	1998	Sandon Stolle–Cyril Zuk
1951	Frank Sedgman–Ken McGregor	1976	Marty Riessen–Tom Okker	1999	Sebastien Lareau–Alex O'Brien
1952	Vic Seixas–Mervyn Rose	1977	Frew McMillan–Bob Hewitt		
1953	Mervyn Rose–Rex Hartwig	1978	Bob Lutz–Stan Smith	2000	Lleyton Hewitt–Max Mirnyi
1954	Vic Seixas–Tony Trabert	1979	John McEnroe–Peter Fleming	2001	Wayne Black–Kevin Ullyett
1955	Kosei Kamo–Atsushi Miyagi	1980	Stan Smith–Bob Lutz		
1956	Lewis Hoad–Ken Rosewall				
1957	Ashley Cooper–Neale Fraser				

1. With the inaugural of the Open Tournament in 1968, the United States Lawn Tennis Association held a national championship at Longwood, Chestnut Hill, Mass., which barred contract professionals in 1968 and 1969.

DOUBLES—WOMEN

NATIONAL		1962	Darlene Hard–Maria Bueno	1981	Kathy Jordan–Anne Smith
1924	G. W. Wightman–Helen Wills	1963	Margaret Smith–Robyn Ebbern	1982	Rosemary Casals–Wendy Turnbull
1925	Mary K. Browne–Helen Wills	1964	Karen Hantze Susman–Billie Jean Moffitt	1983–84	Martina Navratilova–Pam Shriver
1926	Elizabeth Ryan–Eleanor Goss				
1927	L. A. Godfree–Ermyntrude Harvey	1965	Nancy Richey–Carole Caldwell Graebner	1985	Claudia Khode-Kilsch–Helena Sukova
1928	Hazel Hotchkiss Wightman–Helen Wills	1966	Nancy Richey–Maria Bueno	1986–87	Martina Navratilova–Pam Shriver
		1967	Billie Jean King–Rosemary Casals		
1929	Phoebe Watson–L. R. C. Michell	1968	Margaret Court–Maria Bueno[1]	1988	Gigi Fernandez–Robin White
1930	Betty Nuthall–Sarah Palfrey	1969	Margaret Court–Virginia Wade[1]	1989	Hana Mandlikova–Martina Navratilova
1931	Betty Nuthall–E. B. Wittingstall	**OPEN**		1990	Gigi Fernandez–Martina Navratilova
1932	Helen Jacobs–Sarah Palfrey	1968	Maria Bueno–Margaret Court		
1933	Betty Nuthall–Freda James	1969	Darlene Hard–Francoise Durr	1991	Pam Shriver–Natalia Zvereva
1934	Helen Jacobs–Sarah Palfrey	1970	Margaret Court–Judy Dalton	1992	Gigi Fernandez–Natalia Zvereva
1935	Helen Jacobs–Sarah Palfrey Fabyan	1971	Rosemary Casals–Judy Dalton	1993	Arantxa Sanchez Vicario–Helena Sukova
1936	Marjorie G. Van Ryn–Carolin Babcock	1972	Francoise Durr–Betty Stove		
1937–40	Sarah Palfrey Fabyan–Alice Marble	1973	Margaret Court–Virginia Wade	1994	Jana Novotna–Arantxa Sanchez Vicario
		1974	Billie Jean King–Rosemary Casals	1995	Gigi Fernandez–Natasha Zvereva
1941	Sarah Palfrey Cooke–Margaret Osborne	1975	Margaret Court–Virginia Wade	1996	Gigi Fernandez–Natasha Zvereva
1942–47	A. Louise Brough–Margaret Osborne	1976	Linky Boshoff–Ilana Kloss	1997	Lindsay Davenport–Jana Novotna
1948–50	A. Louise Brough–Margaret O. duPont	1977	Martina Navratilova–Betty Stove	1998	Martina Hingis–Jana Novotna
1951–54	Doris Hart–Shirley Fry	1978	Billie Jean King–Martina Navratilova	1999	Serena Williams–Venus Williams
1955–57	A. Louise Brough–Margaret O. duPont	1979	Betty Stove–Wendy Turnbull	2000	Julie-Halard Decugis–Ai Sugiyama
1958–59	Darlene Hard–Jeanne Arth	1980	Billie Jean King–Martina Navratilova	2001	Lisa Raymond–Renae Stubbs
1960	Darlene Hard–Maria Bueno				
1961	Darlene Hard–Lesley Turner				

1. With the inaugural of the Open Tournament in 1968, the United States Lawn Tennis Association held a national championship at Longwood, Chestnut Hill, Mass., which barred contract professionals in 1968 and 1969.

U.S. OPEN CHAMPIONS—2001
U.S. Open
(Flushing Meadow, N.Y., Aug. 27–Sept. 9, 2001)

Men's singles—Lleyton Hewitt defeated Pete Sampras, 7–6(4), 6–1, 6–1.

Women's singles—Venus Williams defeated Serena Williams, 6–2, 6–4.

Men's doubles—Wayne Black and Kevin Ullyett defeated Don Johnson and Jared Palmer, 7–6(9), 2–6, 6–3.

Women's doubles—Lisa Raymond and Rennae Stubbs defeated Kimberly Po-Messerli and Nathalie Tauziat, 6–2, 5–7, 7–5.

Mixed doubles—Rennae Stubbs and Todd Woodbridge defeated Lisa Raymond and Leander Paes, 6–4, 5–7, 7–6(9).

BRITISH (WIMBLEDON) CHAMPIONS
(Amateur from inception in 1877 through 1967)

SINGLES—MEN

1908–09	Arthur Gore	1933	J. H. Crawford	1959	Alex Olmedo	1983–84	John McEnroe
1910–13	A. F. Wilding	1934–36	Fred Perry	1960	Neale Fraser	1985–86	Boris Becker
1914	N. E. Brookes	1937–38	Don Budge	1961–62	Rod Laver	1987	Pat Cash
1919	G. L. Patterson	1939	Robert L. Riggs	1963	Chuck McKinley	1988	Stefan Edberg
1920–21	Bill Tilden	1946	Yvon Petra	1964–65	Roy Emerson	1989	Boris Becker
1922	G. L. Patterson	1947	Jack Kramer	1966	Manuel Santana	1990	Stefan Edberg
1923	William Johnston	1948	R. Falkenburg	1967	John Newcombe	1991	Michael Stich
1924	Jean Borotra	1949	Fred Schroeder	1968–69	Rod Laver	1992	Andre Agassi
1925	Rene Lacoste	1950	Budge Patty	1970–71	John Newcombe	1993–95	Pete Sampras
1926	Jean Borotra	1951	Richard Savitt	1972	Stan Smith	1996	Richard Krajicek
1927	Henri Cochet	1952	Frank Sedgman	1973	Jan Kodes	1997–	
1928	Rene Lacoste	1953	Vic Siexas	1974	Jimmy Connors	2000	Pete Sampras
1929	Jean Cochet	1954	Jaroslav Drobny	1975	Arthur Ashe	2001	Goran Ivanisevic
1930	Bill Tilden	1955	Tony Trabert	1976–80	Bjorn Borg		
1931	S. B. Wood	1956–57	Lewis Hoad	1981	John McEnroe		
1932	Ellsworth Vines	1958	Ashley Cooper	1982	Jimmy Connors		

SINGLES—WOMEN

1919–23	Suzanne Lenglen	1939	Alice Marble	1964	Maria Bueno	1980	Evonne Goolagong Cawley
1924	Kathleen McKane	1946	Pauline M. Betz	1965	Margaret Smith		
1925	Suzanne Lenglen	1947	Margaret Osborne	1966–68	Billie Jean King	1981	Chris Evert-Lloyd
1926	Kathleen Godfree	1948–50	A. Louise Brough	1969	Ann Jones	1982–87	Martina Navratilova
1927–29	Helen Wills	1951	Doris Hart	1970	Margaret Court	1988–89	Steffi Graf
1930	Helen Wills Moody	1952–54	Maureen Connolly	1971	Evonne Goolagong	1990	Martina Navratilova
1931	Cilly Aussem	1955	A. Louise Brough	1972–73	Billie Jean King	1991–93	Steffi Graf
1932–33	Helen Wills Moody	1956	Shirley Fry	1974	Chris Evert	1994	Conchita Martinez
1934	D. E. Round	1957–58	Althea Gibson	1975	Billie Jean King	1995–96	Steffi Graf
1935	Helen Wills Moody	1959–60	Maria Bueno	1976	Chris Evert	1997	Martina Hingis
1936	Helen Jacobs	1961	Angela Mortimer	1977	Virginia Wade	1998	Jana Novotna
1937	D. E. Round	1962	Karen Susman	1978–79	Martina Navratilova	1999	Lindsay Davenport
1938	Helen Wills Moody	1963	Margaret Smith			2000–	
						2001	Venus Williams

DOUBLES—MEN

1953	K. Rosewall–L. Hoad	1972	Bob Hewitt–Frew McMillan	1986	Joakim Nystrom–Mats Wilander
1954	R. Hartwig–M. Rose	1973	Jimmy Connors–Ilie Nastase		
1955	R. Hartwig–L. Hoad	1974	John Newcombe–Tony Roche	1987	Ken Flach–Robert Seguso
1956	L. Hoad–K. Rosewall			1988	Ken Flach–Robert Seguso
1957	Gardnar Mulloy–Budge Patty	1975	Vitas Gerulaitis–Sandy Mayer	1989	John Fitzgerald–Anders Jarryd
1958	Sven Davidson–Ulf Schmidt	1976	Brian Gottfried–Raul Ramirez	1990	Rick Leach–Jim Pugh
1959	Roy Emerson–Neale Fraser			1991	Anders Jarryd–John Fitzgerald
1960	Dennis Ralston–Rafael Osuna	1977	Ross Case–Geoff Masters		
1961	Roy Emerson–Neale Fraser	1978	Fred McMillan–Bob Hewitt	1992	John McEnroe–Michael Stich
1962	Fred Stolle–Bob Hewitt	1979	Peter Fleming–John McEnroe		
1963	Rafael Osuna–Antonio Palafox	1980	Peter McNamara–Paul McNamee	1993–97	Todd Woodbridge–Mark Woodforde
1964	Fred Stolle–Bob Hewitt	1981	John McEnroe–Peter Fleming	1998	Jacco Eltingh–Paul Haarhuis
1965	John Newcombe–Tony Roche	1982	Paul McNamee–Peter McNamara	1999	Mahesh Bhupathi–Leander Paes
1966	John Newcombe–Ken Fletcher	1983–84	John McEnroe–Peter Fleming	2000	Todd Woodbridge–Mark Woodforde
1967	Bob Hewitt–Frew McMillan	1985	Heinz Gunthardt–Balazs Taroczy	2001	Donald Johnson–Jared Palmer
1968–70	John Newcombe–Tony Roche				
1971	Rod Laver–Roy Emerson				

DOUBLES—WOMEN

1956	Althea Gibson–Angela Buxton	
1957	Althea Gibson–Darlene Hard	
1958	Althea Gibson–Maria Bueno	
1959	Darlene Hard–Jeanne Arth	
1960	Darlene Hard–Maria Bueno	
1961	Karen Hantze–Billie Jean Moffitt	
1962	Karen Hantze Susman–Billie Jean Moffitt	
1963	Darlene Hard–Maria Bueno	
1964	Margaret Smith–Les Turnerley	
1965	Billie Jean Moffitt–Maria Bueno	
1966	Nancy Richey–Maria Bueno	
1967–68	Billie Jean King–Rosemary Casals	
1969	Margaret Court–Judy Tegart	
1970–71	Billie Jean King–Rosemary Casals	
1972	Billie Jean King–Betty Stove	
1973	Billie Jean King–Rosemary Casals	

1974	Evonne Goolagong–Peggy Michel
1975	Ann Kiyomura–Kazuko Sawamatsu
1976	Chris Evert–Martina Navratilova
1977	Helen Cawley–JoAnne Russell
1978	Wendy Turnbull–Kerry Reid
1979	Billie Jean King–Martina Navratilova
1980	Kathy Jordan–Anne Smith
1981	Martina Navratilova–Pam Shriver
1982–84	Pam Shriver–Martina Navratilova
1985	Kathy Jordan–Elizabeth Smylie
1986	Pam Shriver–Martina Navratilova
1987	Claudia Khode-Kilsch–Helena Sukova
1988	Steffi Graf–Gabriela Sabatini

1989	Jana Novotna–Helena Sukova
1990	Jana Novotna–Helena Sukova
1991	Pam Shriver–Natalia Zvereva
1992	Gigi Fernandez–Natalia Zvereva
1993	Gigi Fernandez–Natalia Zvereva
1994	Gigi Fernandez–Natalia Zvereva
1995	Jana Novotna–Arantxa Sanchez Vicario
1996	Martina Hingis–Helena Sukova
1997	Gigi Fernandez–Natasha Zvereva
1998	Martina Hingis–Jana Novotna
1999	Lindsay Davenport–Corina Morariu
2000	Venus Williams–Serena Williams
2001	Lisa Raymond–Rennae Stubbs

OTHER 2001 CHAMPIONS

Wimbledon Open
(Wimbledon, England, June 25–July 8, 2001)
Men's singles—Goran Ivanisevic defeated Patrick Rafter, 6–3, 3–6, 6–3, 2–6, 9–7.
Women's singles—Venus Williams defeated Justine Henin, 6–1, 3–6, 6–0.
Men's doubles—Donald Johnson and Jared Palmer defeated Jiri Novak and David Rikl, 6–4, 4–6, 6–3, 7–6 (8–6).
Women's doubles—Lisa Raymond and Rennae Stubbs defeated Kim Clijsters and Ai Sugiyama, 6–4, 6–3.
Mixed doubles—Leos Friedl and Daniela Hantuchova defeated Mike Bryan and Liezel Huber, 4–6, 6–3, 6–2.

French Open
(Paris, May 28–June 10, 2001)
Men's singles—Gustavo Kuerten defeated Alex Corretja, 6–7 (3–7), 7–5, 6–2, 6–0.
Women's singles—Jennifer Capriati defeated Kim Clijsters, 1–6, 6–4, 12–10.
Men's doubles—Mahesh Bhupathi and Leander Paes defeated Petr Pala and Pavel Vizner, 7–6 (7–5), 6–3.
Women's doubles—Virginia Ruano-Pascual and Paola Suarez defeated Jelena Dokic and Conchita Martinez, 6–2, 6–1.
Mixed doubles—Virginia Ruano-Pascual and Tomas Carbonell defeated Paola Suarez and Jaime Oncins, 7–5, 6–3.

Australian Open
(Melbourne, Australia, Jan. 15–28, 2001)
Men's singles—Andre Agassi defeated Arnaud Clement, 6–4, 6–2, 6–2.
Women's singles—Jennifer Capriati defeated Martina Hingis, 6–4, 6–3.
Men's doubles—Jonas Bjorkman and Todd Woodbridge defeated Byron Black and David Prinosil, 6–1, 5–7, 6–4, 6–4.
Women's doubles—Serena Williams and Venus Williams defeated Lindsay Davenport and Corina Morariu, 6–2, 4–6, 6–4.
Mixed doubles—Ellis Ferreira and Corina Morariu defeated Joshua Eagle and Barbara Schett, 6–1, 6–3.

MEN'S MONEY WINNERS—2001
(through Sept. 23, 2001)

1.	Gustavo Kuerten, Brazil	$2,271,514
2.	Lleyton Hewitt, Australia	1,998,118
3.	Andre Agassi, United States	1,858,616
4.	Patrick Rafter, Australia	1,580,592
5.	Juan Carlos Ferrero, Spain	1,443,221
6.	Yevgeny Kafelnikov, Russia	1,243,699
7.	Pete Sampras, United States	931,281
8.	Goran Ivanisevic, Croatia	925,350
9.	Marat Safin, Russia	882,102
10.	Albert Portas, Spain	752,354
11.	Jan Michael Gambill, United States	746,976
12.	Alex Corretja, Spain	737,112
13.	Andrei Pavel, Romania	721,514
14.	Roger Federer, Switzerland	713,555
15.	Jonas Bjorkman, Sweden	711,596

Source: www.atptour.com.

WOMEN'S MONEY WINNERS—2001
(through Sept. 23, 2001)

1.	Venus Williams, United States	$2,522,610
2.	Jennifer Capriati, United States	2,073,024
3.	Martina Hingis, Switzerland	1,382,029
4.	Serena Williams, United States	1,336,263
5.	Lindsay Davenport, United States	1,154,492
6.	Kim Clijsters, Belgium	994,809
7.	Justine Henin, Belgium	821,004
8.	Amelie Mauresmo, France	794,602
9.	Lisa Raymond, United States	722,085
10.	Jelena Dokic, Yugoslavia	715,891
11.	Nathalie Tauziat, France	603,585
12.	Rennae Stubbs, Australia	536,554
13.	Meghann Shaughnessy, United States	525,926
14.	Monica Seles, United States	503,211
15.	Arantxa Sanchez-Vicario, Spain	478,792

Source: Sanex WTA tour.

Harness Racing

Oliver Wendell Holmes, the famous Autocrat of the Breakfast Table, wrote that the running horse was a gambling toy but the trotting horse was useful and, furthermore, "horse-racing is not a republican institution; horse-trotting is." Oliver Wendell Holmes was a born-and-bred New Englander, and New England was the nursery of the harness racing sport in America. Pacers and trotters were matters of local pride and prejudice in colonial New England, and, shortly after the Revolution, the Messenger and Justin Morgan strains produced many winners in harness racing "matches" along the turnpikes of New York, Connecticut, Rhode Island, Massachusetts, Vermont, and New Hampshire.

There was English thoroughbred blood in Messenger and Justin Morgan, and, many years later, it was blended in Rysdyk's Hambletonian, foaled in 1849. Hambletonian was not particularly fast under harness but his descendants have had almost a monopoly of prizes, titles, and records in the harness racing game. Hambletonian was purchased as a foal with its dam for a total of $124 by William Rysdyk of Goshen, N.Y., and made a modest fortune for the purchaser.

Trotters and pacers often were raced under saddle in the old days, and, in fact, the custom still survives in some places in Europe. Dexter, the great trotter that lowered the mile record from 2:19¾ to 2:17 ¼ in 1867, was said to handle just as well under saddle as when pulling a sulky. But as sulkies were lightened in weight and improved in design, trotting under saddle became less common and finally faded out in this country.

HISTORY OF TRADITIONAL HARNESS RACING STAKES

THE HAMBLETONIAN

Year	Winner	Driver	Best time	Total purse
1967	Speedy Streak	Del Cameron	2:00	$122,650
1968	Nevele Pride	Stanley Dancer	1:59.2	116,190
1969	Lindy's Pride	Howard Beissinger	1:57 .3	124,910
1970	Timothy T.	John Simpson, Jr.	1:58.2[1]	143,630
1971	Speedy Crown	Howard Beissinger	1:57.2	129,770
1972	Super Bowl	Stanley Dancer	1:56.2	119,090
1973	Flirth	Ralph Baldwin	1:57.1	144,710
1974	Christopher T	Billy Haughton	1:58.3	160,150
1975	Bonefish	Stanley Dancer	1:59[2]	232,192
1976	Steve Lobell	Billy Haughton	1:56.2	263,524
1977	Green Speed	Billy Haughton	1:55.3	284,131
1978	Speedy Somolli	Howard Beissinger	1:55[3]	241,280
1979	Legend Hanover	George Sholty	1:56.1	300,000
1980	Burgomeister	Billy Haughton	1:56.3	293,570
1981	Shiaway St. Pat	Ray Remmen	2:01.1[4]	838,000
1982	Speed Bowl	Tommy Haughton	1:56.4	875,750
1983	Duenna	Stanley Dancer	1:57.2	1,000,000
1984	Historic Freight	Ben Webster	1:56.2[5]	1,219,000
1985	Prakas	Bill O'Donnell	1:54.3	1,272,000
1986	Nuclear Kosmos	Ulf Thoresen	1:55.2[6]	1,172,082
1987	Mack Lobell	John Campbell	1:53.3	1,046,300
1988	Armbro Goal	John Campbell	1:54.3	1,156,800
1989	Park Avenue Joe and Probe*	Ron Wayples Bill Fahy	1:54.3	1,131,000
1990	Harmonious	John Campbell	1:54.1	1,346,000
1991	Giant Victory	Jack Moiseyev	1:54.4	1,238,000
1992	Alf Palema	Mickey McNichol	1:56.2[7]	1,288,000
1993	American Winner	Ron Pierce	1:53.1	1,200,000
1994	Victory Dream	Mike Lachance	1:53.4	1,200,000
1995	Tagliabue	John Campbell	1:54.4	1,200,000
1996	Continentalvictory	Mike Lachance	1:52.1	1,200,000
1997	Malabar Man	Malvern Burroughs	1:53.4	1,000,000
1998	Muscles Yankee	John Campbell	1:52.2	1,000,000
1999	Self Possessed	Mike Lachance	1:51.3	1,000,000
2000	Yankee Paco	Travor Ritchie	1:53.2	1,000,000
2001	Scarlet Knight	Stefan Melander	1:53.4	1,000,000

Three-year-old trotters. One mile. Guy McKinney won first race at Syracuse in 1926; held at Goshen, N.Y., 1930–1942, 1944–1956; at Yonkers, N.Y., 1943; at Du Quoin, Ill., 1957–1980. Since 1981, the race has been held at The Meadowlands in East Rutherford, N.J. *Cowinners. Fastest heat won by: 1. By Formal Notice. 2. By Yankee Bambino. 3. By Speedy Somolli and Florida Pro. 4. By Super Juan. 5. Delvin G. Hanover. 6. Royal Prestige. 7. Baltic Sonata.

LITTLE BROWN JUG

Year	Winner	Driver	Best time	Total purse
1967	Best of All	Jim Hackett	1:59[1]	$84,778
1968	Rum Customer	Billy Haughton	1:59.3	104,226
1969	Laverne Hanover	Billy Haughton	2:00.2	109,731
1970	Most Happy Fella	Stanley Dancer	1:57.1	100,110
1971	Nansemond	Herve Filion	1:57.2	102,994
1972	Strike Out	Keith Waples	1:56.3	104,916
1973	Melvin's Woe	Joe O'Brien	1:57.3	120,000
1974	Ambro Omaha	Billy Haughton	1:57	132,630
1975	Seatrain	Ben Webster	1:57[2]	147,813
1976	Keystone Ore	Stanley Dancer	1:56.4[3]	153,799
1977	Governor Skipper	John Chapman	1:56.1	150,000
1978	Happy Escort	William Popfinger	1:55.2[4]	186,760
1979	Hot Hitter	Herve Filion	1:55.3	226,455
1980	Niatross	Clint Galbraith	1:54.4	207,361
1981	Fan Hanover	Glen Garnsey	1:56[5]	243,799
1982	Merger	John Campbell	1:56.3	328,900
1983	Ralph Hanover	Ron Waples	1:55.3	358,800
1984	Colt 46	Norman Boring	1:53.3	366,717
1985	Nihilator	Bill O'Donnell	1:52.1	350,730
1986	Barberry Spur	Bill O'Donnell	1:52.4	407,684
1987	Jaguar Spur	Richard Stillings	1:55.3	412,330
1988	B.J. Scoot	Mike Lachance	1:52.3	486,050
1989	Goalie Jeff	Mike Lachance	1:54.1	500,200
1990	Beach Towel	Ray Remmen	1:53.3	253,049
1991	Precious Bunny	Jack Moiseyev	1:54.1	575,150
1992	Fake Left	Ron Waples	1:54.2	556,210
1993	Life Sign	John Campbell	1:52	465,500
1994	Magical Mike	Mike Lachance	1:52.3	512,830
1995	Nick's Fantasy	John Campbell	1:51.2	543,670
1996	Armbro Operative	Jack Moiyesev	1:52.3	542,220
1997	Western Dreamer	Mike Lachance	1:51.1	605,210
1998	Shady Character	Ron Pierce	1:52.3	566,630
1999	Blissfull Hall	Ron Pierce	1:55.3	543,980
2000	Astreos	Chris Christoforou	1:55.3	547,972
2001	Bettor's Delight	Mike Lachance	1:51.4	646,050

Three-year-old pacers. One Mile. Raced at Delaware County Fair Grounds, Delaware, Ohio. 1. By Nardin's Byrd. 2. By Albert's Star. 3. By Armbro Ranger. 4. By Falcon Almahurst. 5. By Seahawk Hanover.

HARNESS HORSE OF THE YEAR

1959	Bye Bye Byrd, Pacer	1976	Keystone Ore, Pacer	1990	Beach Towel
1960–61	Adios Butler, Pacer	1977	Green Speed, Trotter	1991	Precious Bunny
1962	Su Mac Lad, Trotter	1978	Abercrombie, Pacer	1992	Artsplace
1963	Speedy Scot, Trotter	1979–80	Niatross, Pacer	1993	Staying Together
1964–66	Bret Hanover, Pacer	1981	Fan Hanover, Pacer	1994	Cam's Card Shark
1967–69	Nevele Pride, Trotter	1982–83	Cam Fella, Pacer	1995	CR Kay Suzie
1970	Fresh Yankee, Trotter	1984	Fancy Crown, Trotter	1996	Continentalvictory
1971–72	Albatross, Pacer	1985	Nihilator, Trotter	1997	Malabar Man
1973	Sir Dalrae, Pacer	1986	Forrest Skipper	1998–99	Moni Maker
1974	Delmonica Hanover, Trotter	1987–88	Mack Lobell	2000	Gallo Blue Chip
1975	Savoir, Trotter	1989	Matt's Scooter		

Chosen in poll conducted by U.S. Trotting Association in conjunction with the U.S. Harness Writers Association.

Golf

It may be that golf originated in Holland—historians believe it did—but certainly Scotland fostered the game and is famous for it. In fact, in 1457 the Scottish Parliament, disturbed because football and golf had lured young Scots from the more soldierly exercise of archery, passed an ordinance that "futeball and golf be utterly cryit doun and nocht usit." James I and Charles I of the royal line of Stuarts were golf enthusiasts, whereby the game came to be known as "the royal and ancient game of golf."

The golf balls used in the early games were leather-covered and stuffed with feathers. Clubs of all kinds were fashioned by hand to suit individual players. The great step in spreading the game came with the change from the feather ball to the gutta-percha ball about 1850. In 1860, formal competition began with the establishment of an annual tournament for the British Open championship. There are records of "golf clubs" in the United States as far

back as colonial days but no proof of actual play before John Reid and some friends laid out six holes on the Reid lawn in Yonkers, N.Y., in 1888 and played there with golf balls and clubs brought over from Scotland by Robert Lockhart. This group then formed the St. Andrews Golf Club of Yonkers, and golf was established in this country.

However, it remained a rather sedate and almost aristocratic pastime until a 20-year-old ex-caddy, Francis Ouimet of Boston, defeated two great British professionals, Harry Vardon and Ted Ray, in the United States Open championship at Brookline, Mass., in 1913. This feat put the game and Francis Ouimet on the front pages of the newspapers and stirred a wave of enthusiasm for the sport. The greatest feat so far in golf history is that of Robert Tyre Jones, Jr., of Atlanta, who won the British Open, the British Amateur, the U.S. Open, and the U.S. Amateur titles in one year, 1930.

THE MASTERS TOURNAMENT WINNERS

Augusta National Golf Club, Augusta, Ga.

Year	Winner	Score	Year	Winner	Score	Year	Winner	Score
1934	Horton Smith	284	1958	Arnold Palmer	284	1980	Severiano Ballesteros	275
1935	Gene Sarazen[1]	282	1959	Art Wall, Jr.	284	1981	Tom Watson	280
1936	Horton Smith	285	1960	Arnold Palmer	282	1982	Craig Stadler[1]	284
1937	Byron Nelson	283	1961	Gary Player	280	1983	Severiano Ballesteros	280
1938	Henry Picard	285	1962	Arnold Palmer[1]	280	1984	Ben Crenshaw	277
1939	Ralph Guldahl	279	1963	Jack Nicklaus	286	1985	Bernhard Langer	282
1940	Jimmy Demaret	280	1964	Arnold Palmer	276	1986	Jack Nicklaus	279
1941	Craig Wood	280	1965	Jack Nicklaus	271	1987	Larry Mize[1]	285
1942	Byron Nelson[1]	280	1966	Jack Nicklaus[1]	288	1988	Sandy Lyle	281
1943–45 No Tournaments			1967	Gay Brewer, Jr.	280	1989	Nick Faldo[1]	283
1946	Herman Keiser	282	1968	Bob Goalby	277	1990	Nick Faldo	278
1947	Jimmy Demaret	281	1969	George Archer	281	1991	Ian Woosnam	277
1948	Claude Harmon	279	1970	Billy Casper[1]	279	1992	Fred Couples	275
1949	Sam Snead	282	1971	Charles Coody	279	1993	Bernard Langer	277
1950	Jimmy Demaret	283	1972	Jack Nicklaus	286	1994	Jose Maria Olazabal	279
1951	Ben Hogan	280	1973	Tommy Aaron	283	1995	Ben Crenshaw	274
1952	Sam Snead	286	1974	Gary Player	278	1996	Nick Faldo	276
1953	Ben Hogan	274	1975	Jack Nicklaus	276	1997	Tiger Woods	270
1954	Sam Snead[1]	289	1976	Ray Floyd	271	1998	Mark O'Meara	279
1955	Cary Middlecoff	279	1977	Tom Watson	276	1999	Jose Maria Olazabal	280
1956	Jack Burke	289	1978	Gary Player	277	2000	Vijay Singh	278
1957	Doug Ford	283	1979	Fuzzy Zoeller[1]	280	2001	Tiger Woods	272

1. Winner in playoff.

U.S. OPEN CHAMPIONS

Year	Winner	Score	Where played	Year	Winner	Score	Where played
1895	Horace Rawlins	173	Newport	1911	John McDermott[1]	307	Chicago
1896	James Foulis	152	Shinnecock Hills	1912	John McDermott	294	Buffalo
1897	Joe Lloyd	162	Chicago	1913	Francis Ouimet[1][2]	304	Brookline
1898[3]	Fred Herd	328	Myopia	1914	Walter Hagen	290	Midlothian
1899	Willie Smith	315	Baltimore	1915	Jerome D. Travers[2]	297	Baltusrol
1900	Harry Vardon	313	Chicago	1916	Charles Evans, Jr.[2]	286	Minikahda
1901	Willie Anderson[1]	331	Myopia	1917–18	No tournaments[4]		
1902	Laurie Auchterlonie	307	Garden City	1919	Walter Hagen[2]	301	Brae Burn
1903	Willie Anderson[1]	307	Baltusrol	1920	Edward Ray	295	Inverness
1904	Willie Anderson	303	Glen View	1921	Jim Barnes	289	Columbia
1905	Willie Anderson	314	Myopia	1922	Gene Sarazen	288	Skokie
1906	Alex Smith	295	Onwentsia	1923	R. T. Jones, Jr.[1][2]	296	Inwood
1907	Alex Ross	302	Philadelphia	1924	Cyril Walker	297	Oakland Hills
1908	Fred McLeod[1]	322	Myopia	1925	Willie Macfarlane[1]	291	Worcester
1909	George Sargent	290	Englewood	1926	R. T. Jones, Jr.[2]	293	Scioto
1910	Alex Smith[1]	298	Philadelphia	1927	Tommy Armour[1]	301	Oakmont

Year	Winner	Score	Where played	Year	Winner	Score	Where played
1928	Johnny Farrell[1]	294	Olympia Fields	1968	Lee Trevino	275	Oak Hill
1929	R. T. Jones, Jr.[1][2]	294	Winged Foot	1969	Orville Moody	281	Champions G.C.
1930	R. T. Jones, Jr.[2]	287	Interlachen	1970	Tony Jacklin	281	Hazeltine
1931	Billy Burke[1]	292	Inverness	1971	Lee Trevino[1]	280	Merion
1932	Gene Sarazen	286	Fresh Meadow	1972	Jack Nicklaus	290	Pebble Beach
1933	John Goodman[2]	287	North Shore	1973	Johnny Miller	279	Oakmont
1934	Olin Dutra	293	Merion	1974	Hale Irwin	287	Winged Foot
1935	Sam Parks, Jr.	299	Oakmont	1975	Lou Graham[1]	287	Medinah
1936	Tony Manero	282	Baltusrol	1976	Jerry Pate	277	Atlanta A.C.
1937	Ralph Guldahl	281	Oakland Hills	1977	Hubert Green	278	Southern Hills
1938	Ralph Guldahl	284	Cherry Hills	1978	Andy North	285	Cherry Hills
1939	Byron Nelson[1]	284	Philadelphia	1979	Hale Irwin	284	Inverness
1940	Lawson Little[1]	287	Canterbury	1980	Jack Nicklaus	272	Baltusrol
1941	Craig Wood	284	Colonial	1981	David Graham	273	Merion
1942–45	No tournaments[5]			1982	Tom Watson	282	Pebble Beach
1946	Lloyd Mangrum[1]	284	Canterbury	1983	Larry Nelson	280	Oakmont
1947	Lew Worsham[1]	282	St. Louis	1984	Fuzzy Zoeller[1]	276	Winged Foot
1948	Ben Hogan	276	Riviera	1985	Andy North	279	Oakland Hills
1949	Cary Middlecoff	286	Medinah	1986	Ray Floyd	279	Shinnecock Hills
1950	Ben Hogan[1]	287	Merion	1987	Scott Simpson	277	Olympic Golf Club
1951	Ben Hogan	287	Oakland Hills	1988	Curtis Strange[1]	278	The Country Club
1952	Julius Boros	281	Northwood	1989	Curtis Strange	278	Oak Hill Country Club
1953	Ben Hogan	283	Oakmont				
1954	Ed Furgol	284	Baltusrol	1990	Hale Irwin[1]	280	Medinah C.C.
1955	Jack Fleck[1]	287	Olympic	1991	Payne Stewart[1]	282	Hazeltine
1956	Cary Middlecoff	281	Oak Hill	1992	Tom Kite	285	Pebble Beach
1957	Dick Mayer[1]	298	Inverness	1993	Lee Janzen	272	Baltusrol
1958	Tommy Bolt	283	Southern Hills	1994	Ernie Els	279	Oakmont
1959	Bill Casper, Jr.	282	Winged Foot	1995	Corey Pavin	280	Shinnecock Hills
1960	Arnold Palmer	280	Cherry Hills	1996	Steve Jones	278	Oakland Hills
1961	Gene Littler	281	Oakland Hills	1997	Ernie Els	276	Congressional C.C.
1962	Jack Nicklaus[1]	283	Oakmont	1998	Lee Janzen	280	Olympic Country Club
1963	Julius Boros[1]	293	Country Club				
1964	Ken Venturi	278	Congressional	1999	Payne Stewart	279	Pinehurst
1965	Gary Player[1]	282	Bellerive	2000	Tiger Woods	272	Pebble Beach
1966	Bill Casper[1]	278	Olympic	2001	Retief Goosen	276	Southern Hills
1967	Jack Nicklaus	275	Baltusrol				

1. Winner in playoff. 2. Amateur. 3. In 1898, competition was extended to 72 holes. 4. In 1917, Jock Hutchison, with a 292, won an Open Patriotic Tournament for the benefit of the American Red Cross at Whitemarsh Valley Country Club. 5. In 1942, Ben Hogan, with a 271 won a Hale American National Open Tournament for the benefit of the Navy Relief Society and USO at Ridgemoor Country Club.

U.S. AMATEUR CHAMPIONS

1895	Charles B. Macdonald	1924–25	R. T. Jones, Jr.	1954	Arnold Palmer	1978	John Cook
1896–97	H. J. Whigham	1926	George Von Elm	1955–56	Harvie Ward	1979	Mark O'Meara
1898	Findlay S. Douglas	1927–28	R. T. Jones, Jr.	1957	Hillman Robbins	1980	Hal Sutton
1899	H. M. Harriman	1929	H. R. Johnston	1958	Charles Coe	1981	Nathaniel Crosby
1900–01	Walter J. Travis	1930	R. T. Jones, Jr.	1959	Jack Nicklaus	1982	Jay Sigel
1902	Louis N. James	1931	Francis Ouimet	1960	Deane Beman	1983	Jay Sigel
1903	Walter J. Travis	1932	Ross Somerville	1961	Jack Nicklaus	1984	Scott Verplank
1904–05	H. Chandler Egan	1933	G. T. Dunlap, Jr.	1962	Labron Harris, Jr.	1985	Sam Randolph
1906	Eben M. Byers	1934–35	Lawson Little	1963	Deane Beman	1986	Buddy Alexander
1907–08	Jerome D. Travers	1936	John W. Fischer	1964	Bill Campbell	1987	Bill Mayfair
1909	Robert A. Gardner	1937	John Goodman	1965[2]	Robert Murphy, Jr.	1988	Eric Meeks
1910	W. C. Fownes, Jr.	1938	Willie Turnesa	1966	Gary Cowan[1]	1989	Chris Patton
1911	Harold H. Hilton	1939	Marvin H. Ward	1967	Bob Dickson	1990	Phil Mickelson
1912–13	Jerome D. Travers	1940	R. D. Chapman	1968	Bruce Fleisher	1991	Mitch Voges
1914	Francis Ouimet	1941	Marvin H. Ward	1969	Steven Melnyk	1992	Justin Leonard
1915	Robert A. Gardner	1946	Ted Bishop	1970	Lanny Wadkins	1993	John Harris
1916	Charles Evans, Jr.	1947	Robert Riegel	1971	Gary Cowan	1994–96	Tiger Woods
1919	S. D. Herron	1948	Willie Turnesa	1972	Vinny Giles 3d	1997	Matthew Kuchar
1920	Charles Evans, Jr.	1949	Charles Coe	1973[3]	Craig Stadler	1998	Hank Kuehne
1921	Jesse P. Guilford	1950	Sam Urzetta	1974	Jerry Pate	1999	David Gossett
1922	Jess W. Sweetser	1951	Billy Maxwell	1975	Fred Ridley	2000	Jeff Quinney
1923	Max R. Marston	1952	Jack Westland	1976	Bill Sander	2001	Bubba Dickerson
		1953	Gene Littler	1977	John Fought		

1. Winner in playoff. 2. Tourney switched to medal play through 1972. 3. Return to match play.

U.S. PGA CHAMPIONS

1916	Jim Barnes	1945	Byron Nelson	1965	Dave Marr	1985	Hubert Green
1919	Jim Barnes	1946	Ben Hogan	1966	Al Geiberger	1986	Bob Tway
1920	Jock Hutchison	1947	Jim Ferrier	1967	Don January[1]	1987	Larry Nelson
1921	Walter Hagen	1948	Ben Hogan	1968	Julius Boros	1988	Jeff Sluman
1922–23	Gene Sarazen	1949	Sam Snead	1969	Ray Floyd	1989	Payne Stewart
1924–27	Walter Hagen	1950	Chandler Harper	1970	Dave Stockton	1990	Wayne Grady
1928–29	Leo Diegel	1951	Sam Snead	1971	Jack Nicklaus	1991	John Daly
1930	Tommy Armour	1952	Jim Turnesa	1972	Gary Player	1992	Nick Price
1931	Tom Creavy	1953	Walter Burkemo	1973	Jack Nicklaus	1993	Paul Azinger[1]
1932	Olin Dutra	1954	Chick Harbert	1974	Lee Trevino	1994	Nick Price
1933	Gene Sarazen	1955	Doug Ford	1975	Jack Nicklaus	1995	Steve Elkington
1934	Paul Runyan	1956	Jack Burke, Jr.	1976	Dave Stockton	1996	Mark Brooks[1]
1935	Johnny Revolta	1957	Lionel Hebert	1977	Lanny Wadkins[1]	1997	Davis Love III
1936–37	Denny Shute	1958[2]	Dow Finsterwald	1978	John Mahaffey	1998	Vijay Singh
1938	Paul Runyan	1959	Bob Rosburg	1979	David Graham[1]	1999–	
1939	Henry Picard	1960	Jay Hebert	1980	Jack Nicklaus	2000	Tiger Woods
1940	Byron Nelson	1961	Jerry Barber[1]	1981	Larry Nelson	2001	David Toms
1941	Victor Ghezzi	1962	Gary Player	1982	Ray Floyd		
1942	Sam Snead	1963	Jack Nicklaus	1983	Hal Sutton		
1944	Bob Hamilton	1964	Bobby Nichols	1984	Lee Trevino		

1. Winner in playoff. 2. Switched to medal play.

U.S. WOMEN'S AMATEUR CHAMPIONS

1916	Alexa Stirling	1946	Mildred Zaharias	1965	Jean Ashley	1984	Deb Richard
1919–20	Alexa Stirling	1947	Louise Suggs	1966	JoAnne Gunderson	1985	Michiko Hattori
1921	Marion Hollins	1948	Grace Lenczyk	1967	Lou Dill	1986	Kay Cockerill
1922	Glenna Collett	1949	Mrs. D. G. Porter	1968	JoAnne G. Carner	1987	Kay Cockerill
1923	Edith Cummings	1950	Beverly Hanson	1969	Catherine LaCoste	1988	Pearl Sinn
1924	Dorothy Campbell Hurd	1951	Dorothy Kirby	1970	Martha Wilkinson	1989	Vicki Goetze
		1952	Jacqueline Pung	1971	Laura Baugh	1990	Pat Hurst
1925	Glenna Collett	1953	Mary Lena Faulk	1972	Mary Ann Budke	1991	Amy Fruhwirth
1926	Helen Stetson	1954	Barbara Romack	1973	Carol Semple	1992	Vicki Goetze
1927	Mrs. M. B. Horn	1955	Patricia Lesser	1974	Cynthia Hill	1993	Jill McGill
1928–30	Glenna Collett	1956	Marlene Stewart	1975	Beth Daniel	1994	Wendy Ward
1931	Helen Hicks	1957	JoAnne Gunderson	1976	Donna Horton	1995	Kelli Kuehne
1932–34	Virginia Van Wie	1958	Anne Quast	1977	Beth Daniel	1996	Kelli Kuehne
1935	Glenna Collett Vare	1959	Barbara McIntire	1978	Cathy Sherk	1997	Silvia Cavalleri
1936	Pamela Barton	1960	JoAnne Gunderson	1979	Carolyn Hill	1998	Grace Park
1937	Mrs. J. A. Page, Jr.	1961	Anne Quast Decker	1980	Juli Inkster	1999	Dorothy Delasin
1938	Patty Berg	1962	JoAnne Gunderson	1981	Juli Inkster	2000	Marcy Newton
1939–40	Betty Jameson	1963	Anne Quast Welts	1982	Juli Inkster	2001	Meredith Duncan
1941	Mrs. Frank Newell	1964	Barbara McIntire	1983	Joanne Pacillo		

U.S. WOMEN'S OPEN CHAMPIONS

Year	Winner	Score	Year	Winner	Score	Year	Winner	Score
1946	Patty Berg (match play)	—	1964	Mickey Wright[1]	290	1983	Jan Stephenson	290
			1965	Carol Mann	290	1984	Hollis Stacy	290
1947	Betty Jameson	295	1966	Sandra Spuzich	297	1985	Kathy Baker	280
1948	Mildred D. Zaharias	300	1967	Catherine LaCoste[2]	294	1986	Jane Geddes[1]	287
1949	Louise Suggs	291	1968	Susie Berning	289	1987	Laura Davies[1]	285
1950	Mildred D. Zaharias	291	1969	Donna Caponi	294	1988	Liselotte Neumann	277
1951	Betsy Rawls	293	1970	Donna Caponi	287	1989	Betsy King	278
1952	Louise Suggs	284	1971	JoAnne Carner	288	1990	Betsy King	284
1953	Betsy Rawls[1]	302	1972	Susie Berning	299	1991	Meg Mallon	283
1954	Mildred D. Zaharias	291	1973	Susie Berning	290	1992	Patty Sheehan	280
1955	Fay Crocker	299	1974	Sandra Haynie	295	1993	Lauri Merten	280
1956	Katherine Cornelius[1]	302	1975	Sandra Palmer	295	1994	Patty Sheehan	277
1957	Betsy Rawls	299	1976	JoAnne Carner[1]	292	1995	Annika Sorenstam	278
1958	Mickey Wright	290	1977	Hollis Stacy	292	1996	Annika Sorenstam	272
1959	Mickey Wright	287	1978	Hollis Stacy	289	1997	Alison Nicholas	274
1960	Betsy Rawls	291	1979	Jerilyn Britz	284	1998	Se Ri Pak	290
1961	Mickey Wright	293	1980	Amy Alcott	280	1999	Juli Inkster	272
1962	Murle Lindstrom	301	1981	Pat Bradley	279	2000	Karrie Webb	282
1963	Mary Mills	289	1982	Janet Alex	283	2001	Karrie Webb	273

1. Winner in playoff. 2. Amateur.

BRITISH OPEN CHAMPIONS

(First tournament, held in 1860, was won by Willie Park, Sr.)

Year	Winner	Score	Year	Winner	Score	Year	Winner	Score
1920	George Duncan	303	1952	Bobby Locke	287	1978	Jack Nicklaus	281
1921	Jock Hutchison[1]	296	1953	Ben Hogan	282	1979	Severiano Ballesteros	283
1922	Walter Hagen	300	1954	Peter Thomson	283	1980	Tom Watson	271
1923	A. G. Havers	295	1955	Peter Thomson	281	1981	Bill Rogers	276
1924	Walter Hagen	301	1956	Peter Thomson	286	1982	Tom Watson	284
1925	Jim Barnes	300	1957	Bobby Locke	279	1983	Tom Watson	275
1926	R. T. Jones, Jr.	291	1958	Peter Thomson[1]	278	1984	Severiano Ballesteros	276
1927	R. T. Jones, Jr.	285	1959	Gary Player	284	1985	Sandy Lyle	282
1928	Walter Hagen	292	1960	Kel Nagle	278	1986	Greg Norman	280
1929	Walter Hagen	292	1961	Arnold Palmer	284	1987	Nick Faldo	279
1930	R. T. Jones, Jr.	291	1962	Arnold Palmer	276	1988	Seve Ballesteros	273
1931	Tommy Armour	296	1963	Bob Charles[1]	277	1989	Mark Calcavecchia	275
1932	Gene Sarazen	283	1964	Tony Lema	279	1990	Nick Faldo	270
1933	Denny Shute[1]	292	1965	Peter Thomson	285	1991	Ian Baker-Finch	272
1934	Henry Cotton	283	1966	Jack Nicklaus	282	1992	Nick Faldo	272
1935	A. Perry	283	1967	Roberto de Vicenzo	278	1993	Greg Norman	267
1936	A. H. Padgham	287	1968	Gary Player	289	1994	Nick Price	268
1937	Henry Cotton	290	1969	Tony Jacklin	280	1995	John Daly	282
1938	R. A. Whitcombe	295	1970	Jack Nicklaus[1]	283	1996	Tom Lehman	271
1939	R. Burton	290	1971	Lee Trevino	278	1997	Justin Leonard	272
1940	Sam Snead	290	1972	Lee Trevino	278	1998	Mark O'Meara	280
1947	Fred Daly	294	1973	Tom Weiskopf	276	1999	Paul Lawrie	290
1948	Henry Cotton	283	1974	Gary Player	282	2000	Tiger Woods	269
1949	Bobby Locke[1]	283	1975	Tom Watson[1]	279	2001	David Duval	274
1950	Bobby Locke	279	1976	Johnny Miller	279			
1951	Max Faulkner	285	1977	Tom Watson	268			

OTHER 2001 PGA TOUR WINNERS

(Through Sept. 4, 2001)

Mercedes Championship—Jim Furyk	$630,000
Touchstone Energy Tucson Open—Garrett Willis	540,000
Sony Open in Hawaii—Brad Faxon	720,000
Phoenix Open—Mark Calcavecchia	720,000
AT&T Pebble Beach National Pro-Am—Davis Love III	720,000
Buick Invitational—Phil Mickelson	630,000
Bob Hope Chrysler Classic—Joe Durant	630,000
Nissan Open—Robert Allenby	612,000
Honda Classic—Jesper Parnevik	576,000
Bay Hill Invitational—Tiger Woods	630,000
THE PLAYERS Championship—Tiger Woods	1,080,000
BellSouth Classic—Scott McCarron	594,000
WORLDCOM CLASSIC—Jose Coceres	720,000
Greater Greensboro Chrysler Classic—Scott Hoch	630,000
Compaq Classic of New Orleans—David Toms	720,000
Verizon Byron Nelson Classic—Robert Damron	810,000
MasterCard Colonial—Sergio Garcia	720,000
Kemper Insurance Open—Frank Lickliter	630,000
Memorial Tournament—Tiger Woods	738,000
FedEx St. Jude Classic—Bob Estes	540,000
Buick Classic—Sergio Garcia	630,000
Canon Greater Hartford Open—Phil Mickelson	558,000
Advil Western Open—Scott Hoch	648,000
Greater Milwaukee Open—Shigeki Maruyama	558,000
John Deere Classic—David Gossett	504,000
The INTERNATIONAL Presented by Qwest—Tom Pernice, Jr.	720,000

OTHER 2001 LPGA TOUR WINNERS

(Through Sept. 4, 2001)

YourLife Vitamins LPGA Classic—Se Ri Pak	$150,000
Subaru Memorial of Naples—Sophie Gustafson	150,000
The Office Depot—Grace Park	123,750
Takefuji Classic—Lorie Kane	127,500
Hawaiian Ladies Open—Catriona Matthew	112,500
Welch's-Circle K Championship—Annika Sörenstam	112,500
Nabisco Championship—Annika Sörenstam	225,000
The Office Depot Hosted by Amy Alcott—Annika Sörenstam	120,000
Longs Drugs Challenge—Se Ri Pak	120,000
Kathy Ireland Championship Honoring Harvey Penick—Rosie Jones	135,000
Chick-fil-A Charity Championship—Annika Sörenstam	180,000
Electrolux USA Championship—Juli Inkster	120,000
LPGA Champions Classic—Wendy Doolan'	112,500
Corning Classic—Carin Koch	135,000
Wegmans Rochester International—Laura Davies	150,000
Evian Masters—Rachel Teske	315,000
McDonald's LPGA Championship—Karrie Webb	225,000
ShopRite LPGA Classic—Betsy King	180,000
Jamie Farr Kroger Classic—Se Ri Pak	150,000
Michelob Light Classic—Emilee Klein	120,000
Big Apple Classic—Rosie Jones	142,500
Giant Eagle LPGA Classic—Dorothy Delasin	150,000
Women's British Open—Se Ri Pak	221,650
Wendy's Championship for Children—Wendy Ward	150,000
Bank of Montreal Canadian Women's Open—Annika Sörenstam	180,000

Auto Racing

INDIANAPOLIS 500

Year	Winner	Car	Time	mph	Second place
1911	Ray Harroun	Marmon	6:42:08.000	74.590	Ralph Mulford
1912	Joe Dawson	National	6:21:06.000	78.720	Teddy Tetzloff
1913	Jules Goux	Peugeot	6:35:05.000	75.930	Spencer Wishart
1914	René Thomas	Delage	6:03:45.000	82.470	Arthur Duray
1915	Ralph DePalma	Mercedes	5:33:55.510	89.840	Dario Resta
1916[1]	Dario Resta	Peugeot	3:34:17.000	84.000	Wilbur D'Alene
1919	Howard Wilcox	Peugeot	5:40:42.870	88.050	Eddie Hearne
1920	Gaston Chevrolet	Monroe	5:38:32.000	88.620	René Thomas
1921	Tommy Milton	Frontenac	5:34:44.650	89.620	Roscoe Sarles
1922	Jimmy Murphy	Murphy Special	5:17:30.790	94.480	Harry Hartz
1923	Tommy Milton	H. C. S. Special	5:29:50.170	90.950	Harry Hartz
1924	L. L. Corum-Joe Boyer	Dusenberg Special	5:05:23.510	98.230	Earl Cooper
1925	Peter DePaolo	Dusenberg Special	4:56:39.450	101.130	Dave Lewis
1926[2]	Frank Lockhart	Miller Special	4:10:14.950	95.904	Harry Hartz
1927	George Souders	Dusenberg Special	5:07:33.080	97.540	Earl DeVore
1928	Louis Meyer	Miller Special	5:01:33.750	99.480	Lou Moore
1929	Ray Keech	Simplex Special	5:07:25.420	97.580	Louis Meyer
1930	Billy Arnold	Miller-Hartz Special	4:58:39.720	100.448	Shorty Cantlon
1931	Louis Schneider	Bowes Special	5:10:27.930	96.629	Fred Frame
1932	Fred Frame	Miller-Hartz Special	4:48:03.790	104.144	Howard Wilcox
1933	Louis Meyer	Tydol Special	4:48:00.750	104.162	Wilbur Shaw
1934	Bill Cummings	Boyle Products Special	4:46:05.200	104.863	Mauri Rose
1935	Kelly Petillo	Gilmore Special	4:42:22.710	106.240	Wilbur Shaw
1936	Louis Meyer	Ring Free Special	4:35:03.390	109.069	Ted Horn
1937	Wilbur Shaw	Shaw-Gilmore Special	4:24:07.800	113.580	Ralph Hepburn
1938	Floyd Roberts	Burd Piston Ring Special	4:15:58.400	117.200	Wilbur Shaw
1939	Wilbur Shaw	Boyle Special	4:20:47.390	115.035	Jimmy Snyder
1940	Wilbur Shaw	Boyle Special	4:22:31.170	114.277	Rex Mays
1941	Floyd Davis-Mauri Rose	Noc-Out Hose Clamp Special	4:20:36.240	115.117	Rex Mays
1946	George Robson	Thorne Engineering Special	4:21:26.710	114.820	Jimmy Jackson
1947	Mauri Rose	Blue Crown Special	4:17:52.170	116.338	Bill Holland
1948	Mauri Rose	Blue Crown Special	4:10:23.330	119.814	Bill Holland
1949	Bill Holland	Blue Crown Special	4:07:15.970	121.327	Johnny Parsons
1950[3]	Johnnie Parsons	Wynn's Friction Proof Special	2:46:55.970	124.002	Bill Holland
1951	Lee Wallard	Belanger Special	3:57:38.050	126.244	Mike Nazaruk
1952	Troy Ruttman	Agajanian Special	3:52:41.880	128.922	Jim Rathmann
1953	Bill Vukovich	Fuel Injection Special	3:53:01.690	128.740	Art Cross
1954	Bill Vukovich	Fuel Injection Special	3:49:17.270	130.840	Jim Bryan
1955	Bob Sweikert	John Zink Special	3:53:59.13	128.209	Tony Bettenhausen
1956	Pat Flaherty	John Zink Special	3:53:28.840	128.490	Sam Hanks
1957	Sam Hanks	Belond Exhaust Special	3:41:14.250	135.601	Jim Rathmann
1958	Jimmy Bryan	Belond A-P Special	3:44:13.800	133.791	George Amick
1959	Rodger Ward	Leader Card 500 Roadster	3:40:49.200	135.857	Jim Rathmann
1960	Jim Rathmann	Ken-Paul Special	3:36:11.360	138.767	Rodger Ward
1961	A. J. Foyt	Bowes Special	3:35:37.490	139.130	Eddie Sachs
1962	Rodger Ward	Leader Card Special	3:33:50.330	140.293	Len Sutton
1963	Parnelli Jones	Agajanian Special	3:29:35.400	143.137	Jim Clark
1964	A. J. Foyt	Sheraton-Thompson Spl.	3:23:35.830	147.350	Rodger Ward
1965	Jim Clark	Lotus-Ford	3:19:05.340	150.686	Parnelli Jones
1966	Graham Hill	Red Ball Lola-Ford	3:27:52.530	144.317	Jim Clark
1967[4]	A. J. Foyt	Sheraton-Thompson Coyote-Ford	3:18:24.220	151.207	Al Unser
1968	Bobby Unser	Rislone Eagle-Offenhauser	3:16:13.760	152.882	Dan Gurney
1969	Mario Andretti	STP Hawk-Ford	3:11:14.710	156.867	Dan Gurney
1970	Al Unser	Johnny Lightning P. J. Colt-Ford	3:12:37.040	155.749	Mark Donohue
1971	Al Unser	Johnny Lightning P. J. Colt-Ford	3:10:11.560	157.735	Peter Revson
1972	Mark Donohue	Sunoco McLaren-Offenhauser	3:04:05.540	162.962	Al Unser
1973[5]	Gordon Johncock	STP Eagle-Offenhauser	2:05:26.590	159.036	Bill Vukovich, Jr.
1974	Johnny Rutherford	McLaren-Offenhauser	3:09:10.060	158.589	Bobby Unser
1975[6]	Bobby Unser	Jorgensen Eagle-Offenhauser	2:54:55.080	149.213	Johnny Rutherford
1976[7]	Johnny Rutherford	Hy-gain McLaren-Offenhauser	1:42:52.480	148.725	A. J. Foyt
1977	A. J. Foyt	Gilmore Coyote-Foyt	3:05:57.160	161.331	Tom Sneva
1978	Al Unser	1st Nat'l City Lola-Cosworth	3:05:54.990	161.363	Tom Sneva
1979	Rick Mears	Gould Penske-Cosworth	3:08:27.970	158.899	A. J. Foyt
1980	Johnny Rutherford	Pennzoil Chaparral-Cosworth	3:29:59.560	142.862	Tom Sneva
1981[8]	Bobby Unser	Norton Penske-Cosworth	3:35:41.780	139.029	Mario Andretti
1982	Gordon Johncock	STP Wildcat-Cosworth	3:05:09.140	162.029	Rick Mears
1983	Tom Sneva	Texaco Star March-Cosworth	3:05:03.060	162.117	Al Unser

Year	Winner	Car	Time	mph	Second place
1984	Rick Mears	Pennzoil March-Cosworth	3:03:21.000	162.962	Roberto Guerrero
1985	Danny Sullivan	Miller March-Cosworth	3:16:06.069	152.982	Mario Andretti
1986	Bobby Rahal	Budweiser March-Cosworth	2:55:43.480	170.722	Kevin Cogan
1987	Al Unser, Sr.	Cummins March-Cosworth	3:04:59.147	162.175	Roberto Guerrero
1988	Rick Mears	Pennzoil Penske P.C.17-Chevrolet	3:27:10.204	144.809	Emerson Fittipaldi
1989	Emerson Fittipaldi	Marlboro Penske-Cosworth	2:59:01.040	167.581	Al Unser, Jr.
1990	Arie Luyendyk	Domino's Pizza Lola-Cosworth	2:41:18.248	185.987	Bobby Rahal
1991	Rick Mears	Marlboro Penske-Cosworth	2:50:01.018	176.460	Michael Andretti
1992	Al Unser, Jr.	Valvoline-Chevrolet	3:43.05.148	134.477	Scott Goodyear
1993	Emerson Fittipaldi	Penske-Chevrolet	3:10:49.860	157.207	Arie Luyendyk
1994	Al Unser, Jr.	Penske-Mercedes	3:06:29.006	160.872	Jacques Villeneuve
1995	Jacques Villeneuve	Reynard-Ford	3:15:17.561	156.616	Christian Fittipaldi
1996	Buddy Lazier	Reynard-Ford	3:22:45.753	147.956	Davy Jones
1997	Arie Luyendyk	G Force-Aurora	3:25:43.388	145.827	Scott Goodyear
1998	Eddie Cheever	Dallara-Aurora	3:26:40.524	145.155	Buddy Lazier
1999	Kenny Brack	Dallara-Aurora-Goodyear	3:15:51.182	153.176	Jeff Ward
2000	Juan Montoya	GForce-Aurora-Firestone	2:58:59.431	167.607	Buddy Lazier
2001	Helio Castroneves	Dallara-Aurora-Firestone	3:31:54.180	153.601	Gil de Ferran

1. 300 miles. 2. Race ended at 400 miles because of rain. 3. Race ended at 345 miles because of rain. 4. Race, postponed after 18 laps because of rain on May 30, was finished on May 31. 5. Race postponed May 28 and 29 was cut to 332.5 miles because of rain, May 30. 6. Race ended at 435 miles because of rain. 7. Race ended at 255 miles because of rain. 8. Andretti was awarded the victory the day after the race after Bobby Unser, whose car finished first, was penalized one lap and dropped from first place to second for passing other cars illegally under a yellow caution flag. Unser appealed the decision to the U.S. Auto Club and was upheld. A panel ruled the penalty was too severe and instead fined Unser $40,000, but restored the victory to him.

2001 NASCAR WINSTON CUP RACES

Date	Race	Raceway	Winner
Feb. 18	Daytona 500	Daytona International Speedway	Michael Waltrip
Feb. 25	Dura Lube 400	North Carolina Speedway	Steve Park
March 4	UAW-DaimlerChrysler 400	Las Vegas Motor Speedway	Jeff Gordon
March 11	Cracker Barrel Old Country Store 500	Atlanta Motor Speedway	Kevin Harvick
March 18	Carolina Dodge Dealers 400	Darlington Raceway	Dale Jarrett
March 25	Food City 500	Bristol Motor Speedway	Elliott Sadler
April 1	Harrah's 500	Texas Motor Speedway	Dale Jarrett
April 8	Virginia 500	Martinsville Speedway	Dale Jarrett
April 22	Talladega 500	Talladega Superspeedway	Bobby Hamilton
April 29	NAPA Auto Parts 500	California Speedway	Rusty Wallace
May 5	Pontiac Excitement 400	Richmond International Raceway	Tony Stewart
May 27	Coca-Cola 600	Lowe's Motor Speedway	Jeff Burton
June 3	MBNA Platinum 400	Dover Downs International Speedway	Jeff Gordon
June 10	Kmart 400	Michigan International Speedway	Jeff Gordon
June 17	Pocono 500	Pocono Raceway	Ricky Rudd
June 24	Dodge/Save Mart 350	Sears Point Raceway	Tony Stewart
July 7	Pepsi 400	Daytona International Speedway	Dale Earnhardt, Jr.
July 15	Tropicana 400	Chicagoland Speedway	Kevin Harvick
July 22	New England 300	New Hampshire International Speedway	Dale Jarrett
July 29	Pennsylvania 500	Pocono Raceway	Bobby Labonte
Aug. 5	Brickyard 400	Indianapolis Motor Speedway	Jeff Gordon
Aug. 12	Global Crossing @ The Glen	Watkins Glen International	Jeff Gordon
Aug. 19	Pepsi 400 presented by Meijer	Michigan International Speedway	Sterling Marlin
Aug. 25	Sharpie 500	Bristol Motor Speedway	Tony Stewart
Sept. 2	Mountain Dew Southern 500	Darlington Raceway	Ward Burton
Sept. 8	Chevrolet Monte Carlo 400	Richmond International Raceway	Ricky Rudd
Sept. 23	MBNA Cal Ripken, Jr. 400	Dover Downs International Speedway	Dale Earnhardt, Jr.

NATIONAL ASSOCIATION FOR STOCK CAR AUTO RACING
WINSTON CUP CHAMPIONS

1949	Red Byron	1962–63	Joe Weatherly	1979	Richard Petty	1990	Dale Earnhardt
1950	Bill Rexford	1964	Richard Petty	1980	Dale Earnhardt	1991	Dale Earnhardt
1951	Herb Thomas	1965	Ned Jarrett	1981	Darrell Waltrip	1992	Alan Kulwicki
1952	Tim Flock	1966	David Pearson	1982	Darrell Waltrip	1993	Dale Earnhardt
1953	Herb Thomas	1967	Richard Petty	1983	Bobby Allison	1994	Dale Earnhardt
1954	Lee Petty	1968–69	David Pearson	1984	Terry Labonte	1995	Jeff Gordon
1955	Tim Flock	1970	Bobby Isaac	1985	Darrell Waltrip	1996	Terry Labonte
1956–57	Buck Baker	1971–72	Richard Petty	1986	Dale Earnhardt	1997–98	Jeff Gordon
1958–59	Lee Petty	1973	Benny Parsons	1987	Dale Earnhardt	1999	Dale Jarrett
1960	Rex White	1974–75	Richard Petty	1988	Bill Elliott	2000	Bobby Labonte
1961	Ned Jarrett	1976–78	Cale Yarborough	1989	Rusty Wallace	2001[1]	Jeff Gordon

1. As of Sept.. 23, 2001.

2001 NASCAR LEADING POINT WINNERS
(as of Sept. 23, 2001)

Driver	Pts	Winnings	Driver	Pts	Winnings
1. Jeff Gordon	3,928	$5,627,030	11. Jeff Burton	3,079	2,798,670
2. Ricky Rudd	3,716	3,191,260	12. Mark Martin	3,015	2,713,460
3. Tony Stewart	3,516	2,752,770	13. Bill Elliott	2,990	2,473,240
4. Dale Jarrett	3,507	3,738,440	14. Jimmy Spencer	2,962	1,901,590
5. Sterling Marlin	3,444	2,441,060	15. Matt Kenseth	2,905	1,662,640
6. Dale Earnhardt, Jr.	3,429	3,544,970	16. Steve Park	2,859	2,385,970
7. Kevin Harvick	3,380	2,871,420	17. Ward Burton	2,776	2,503,320
8. Rusty Wallace	3,355	3,433,980	18. Elliott Sadler	2,755	1,988,440
9. Bobby Labonte	3,327	3,075,630	19. Bobby Hamilton	2,742	1,795,530
10. Johnny Benson	3,168	2,057,670	20. Jerry Nadeau	2,726	1,720,630

INDYCAR NATIONAL CHAMPIONS

1910	Ray Harroun	1932	Bob Carey	1959	Rodger Ward	1983	Al Unser
1911	Ralph Mulford	1933	Louis Meyer	1960–61	A. J. Foyt	1984	Mario Andretti
1912	Ralph DePalma	1934	Bill Cummings	1962	Rodger Ward	1985	Al Unser
1913	Earl Cooper	1935	Kelly Petillo	1963–64	A. J. Foyt	1986–87	Bobby Rahal
1914	Ralph DePalma	1936	Mauri Rose	1965–66	Mario Andretti	1988	Danny Sullivan
1915	Earl Cooper	1937	Wilbur Shaw	1967	A. J. Foyt	1989	Emerson Fittipaldi
1916	Dario Resta	1938	Floyd Roberts	1968	Bobby Unser		
1917	Earl Cooper	1939	Wilbur Shaw	1969	Mario Andretti	1990	Al Unser, Jr.
1918	Ralph Mulford	1940–41	Rex Mays	1970	Al Unser	1991	Michael Andretti
1919	Howard Wilcox	1946–48	Ted Horn	1971–72	Joe Leonard	1992	Bobby Rahal
1920	Gaston Chevrolet	1949	Johnnie Parsons	1973	Roger McCluskey	1993	Nigel Mansell
1921	Tommy Milton	1950	Henry Banks	1974	Bobby Unser	1994	Al Unser, Jr.
1922	James Murphy	1951	Tony Bettenhausen	1975	A. J. Foyt	1995	Jacques Villeneuve
1923	Eddie Hearne			1976	Gordon Johncock		
1924	James Murphy	1952	Chuck Stevenson	1977–78	Tom Sneva	1996	Jimmy Vasser
1925	Peter DePaolo	1953	Sam Hanks	1979	Rick Mears	1997–98	Alessandro Zanardi
1926	Harry Hartz	1954	Jimmy Bryan		(CART), A.J. Foyt		
1927	Peter DePaolo	1955	Bob Sweikert		(USAC)[1]	1999	Juan Montoya
1928–29	Louis Meyer	1956–57	Jimmy Bryan	1980	Johnny Rutherford	2000	Gil de Ferran
1930	Billy Arnold	1958	Tony Bettenhausen			2001[2]	Kenny Brack
1931	Louis Schneider			1981–82	Rick Mears		

1. Two separate series were held in 1979. 2. As of Sept. 23, 2001. NOTE: There have been three sanctioning bodies for the series: the Automobile Association of America (1909–1955), the U.S. Auto Club (1956–1979), and the Championship Auto Racing Team (CART), 1979–present.

2001 INDY RACING LEAGUE LEADING POINT WINNERS
(as of Sept. 2, 2001)

Driver	Pts	Driver	Pts	Driver	Pts
1. Sam Hornish, Jr.	451	9. Jeff Ward	232	17. Sarah Fisher	183
2. Buddy Lazier	385	10. Buzz Calkins	222	18. Robby McGehee	180
3. Scott Sharp	315	11. Airton Dare	213	19. Didier Andre	173
4. Felipe Giaffone	295	12. Donnie Beechler	204	20. Greg Ray	169
5. Billy Boat	295	13. Robbie Buhl	202	21. Billy Roe	93
6. Eliseo Salazar	276	14. Shigeaki Hattori	201	22. Jeret Schroeder	77
7. Al Unser, Jr.	259	15. Mark Dismore	198	23. Helio Castroneves	64
8. Eddie Cheever, Jr.	249	16. Jaques Lazier	185	24. Davey Hamilton	54

WORLD GRAND PRIX DRIVER CHAMPIONS

1950	Giuseppe Farina, Italy, Alfa Romeo	1963	Jim Clark, Scotland, Lotus-Ford
1951	Juan Fangio, Argentina, Alfa Romeo	1964	John Surtees, England, Ferrari
1952	Alberto Ascari, Italy, Ferrari	1965	Jim Clark, Scotland, Lotus-Ford
1953	Alberto Ascari, Italy, Ferrari	1966	Jack Brabham, Australia, Brabham-Repco
1954	Juan Fangio, Argentina, Maserati, Mercedes-Benz	1967	Denis Hulme, New Zealand, Brabham-Repco
1955	Juan Fangio, Argentina, Mercedes-Benz	1968	Graham Hill, England, Lotus-Ford
1956	Juan Fangio, Argentina, Lancia-Ferrari	1969	Jackie Stewart, Scotland, Matra-Ford
1957	Juan Fangio, Argentina, Maserati	1970	Jochen Rindt, Austria, Lotus-Ford
1958	Mike Hawthorn, England, Ferrari	1971	Jackie Stewart, Scotland, Tyrrell-Ford
1959	Jack Brabham, Australia, Cooper	1972	Emerson Fittipaldi, Brazil, Lotus-Ford
1960	Jack Brabham, Australia, Cooper	1973	Jackie Stewart, Scotland, Tyrrell-Ford
1961	Phil Hill, United States, Ferrari	1974	Emerson Fittipaldi, Brazil, McLaren-Ford
1962	Graham Hill, England, BRM	1975	Niki Lauda, Austria, Ferrari

1976 James Hunt, Britain, McLaren-Ford	1989 Alain Prost, France, McLaren-Honda
1977 Niki Lauda, Austria, Ferrari	1990 Ayrton Senna, Brazil, McLaren-Honda
1978 Mario Andretti, United States, Lotus	1991 Aryton Senna, Brazil, McLaren-Honda
1979 Jody Scheckter, South Africa, Ferrari	1992 Nigel Mansell, Britain, Williams-Renault
1980 Alan Jones, Australia, Williams-Ford	1993 Alain Prost, France, Williams-Renault
1981 Nelson Piquet, Brazil, Brabham-Ford	1994 Michael Schumacher, Germany, Benetton
1982 Keke Rosberg, Finland, Williams-Ford	1995 Michael Schumacher, Germany, Benetton Renault
1983 Nelson Piquet, Brazil. Brabham-BMW	1996 Damon Hill, Britain, Williams
1984 Nikki Lauda, Austria, McLaren-Porsche	1997 Jacques Villeneuve, Canada, Williams-Renault
1985 Alain Prost, France, McLaren-Porsche	1998 Mika Hakkinen, Finland, McLaren-Mercedes
1986 Alain Prost, France, McLaren-Porsche	1999 Mika Hakkinen, Finland, McLaren-Mercedes
1987 Nelson Piquet, Brazil, Williams-Honda	2000 Michael Schumacher, Germany, Ferrari
1988 Aryton Senna, Brazil, McLaren-Honda	2001 Michael Schumacher, Germany, Ferrari

Yachting

AMERICA'S CUP RECORD

First race in 1851 around Isle of Wight, Cowes, England. First defense and all others through 1920 held 30 miles off New York Bay. Races since 1930 held 30 miles off Newport, R.I. Conducted as one race only in 1851 and 1870; best four-of-seven basis, 1871; best two-of-three, 1876–1887; best three-of-five, 1893–1901; best four-of-seven, since 1930. Figures in parentheses indicate number of races won. The next America's Cup is scheduled to begin Feb. 15, 2003.

Year	Winner and owner	Loser and owner
1851	AMERICA (1), John C. Stevens, U.S.	AURORA, T. Le Marchant, England[1]
1870	MAGIC (1), Franklin Osgood, U.S.	CAMBRIA, James Ashbury, England[2]
1871	COLUMBIA (2), Franklin Osgood, U.S.[3]	LIVONIA (1), James Ashbury, England
	SAPPHO (2), William P. Douglas, U.S.	
1876	MADELEINE (2), John S. Dickerson, U.S.	COUNTESS OF DUFFERIN, Chas. Gifford, Canada
1881	MISCHIEF (2), J. R. Busk, U.S.	ATALANTA, Alexander Cuthbert, Canada
1885	PURITAN (2), J. M. Forbes-Gen. Charles Paine, U.S.	GENESTA, Sir Richard Sutton, England
1886	MAYFLOWER (2), Gen. Charles Paine, U.S.	GALATEA, Lt. William Henn, England
1887	VOLUNTEER (2), Gen. Charles Paine, U.S.	THISTLE, James Bell et al., Scotland
1893	VIGILANT (3), C. Oliver Iselin et al., U.S.	VALKYRIE II, Lord Dunraven, England
1895	DEFENDER (3), C. O. Iselin–W. K. Vanderbilt–E. D. Morgan, U.S.	VALKYRIE III, Lord Dunraven–Lord Lonsdale–Lord Wolverton, England
1899	COLUMBIA (3), J. P. Morgan–C. O. Iselin, U.S.	SHAMROCK I, Sir Thomas Lipton, Ireland
1901	COLUMBIA (3), Edwin D. Morgan, U.S.	SHAMROCK II, Sir Thomas Lipton, Ireland
1903	RELIANCE (3), Cornelius Vanderbilt et al., U.S.	SHAMROCK III, Sir Thomas Lipton, Ireland
1920	RESOLUTE (3), Henry Walters et al., U.S.	SHAMROCK IV (2), Sir Thomas Lipton, Ireland
1930	ENTERPRISE (4), Harold S. Vanderbilt et al., U.S.	SHAMROCK V, Sir Thomas Lipton, Ireland
1934	RAINBOW (4), Harold S. Vanderbilt, U.S.	ENDEAVOUR (2), T. O. M. Sopwith, England
1937	RANGER (4), Harold S. Vanderbilt, U.S.	ENDEAVOUR II, T. O. M. Sopwith, England
1958	COLUMBIA (4), Henry Sears et al., U.S.	SCEPTRE, Hugh Goodson et al., England
1962	WEATHERLY (4), Henry D. Mercer et al., U.S.	GRETEL (1), Sir Frank Packer et al., Australia
1964	CONSTELLATION (4), New York Y.C. Syndicate, U.S.	SOVEREIGN (0), J. Anthony Bowden, England
1967	INTREPID (4), New York Y.C. Syndicate, U.S.	DAME PATTIE (0), Sydney (Aust.) Syndicate
1970	INTREPID (4), New York Y.C. Syndicate, U.S.	GRETEL II (1), Sydney (Aust.) Syndicate
1974	COURAGEOUS (4), New York, N.Y. Syndicate, U.S.	SOUTHERN CROSS (0), Sydney (Aust.) Syndicate
1977	COURAGEOUS (4), New York, N.Y. Syndicate, U.S.	AUSTRALIA (0), Sun City (Aust.) Syndicate
1980	FREEDOM (4), New York, N.Y. Syndicate, U.S.	AUSTRALIA (1), Alan Bond et al, Australia
1983	AUSTRALIA II (4), Alan Bond et al., Australia	LIBERTY, (3) New York, N.Y. Syndicate, U.S.
1987	STARS & STRIPES (4), Dennis Conner et al., United States	KOOKABURRA III (0), Iain Murray et al., Australia
1988[4]	STARS & STRIPES, Dennis Conner, et al., United States	NEW ZEALAND, Michael Fay, et al., New Zealand
1992	AMERICA 3, Bill Koch, et al., United States	IL MORO DI VENEZIA, Paul Cayard, et al., Italy
1995	BLACK MAGIC, Peter Blake, et al., New Zealand	YOUNG AMERICA, Dennis Conner, et al., United States
2000	NEW ZEALAND, Peter Blake, et al., New Zealand	LUNA ROSSA, Patrizio Bertelli, et al., Italy

1. Fourteen British yachts started against America; Aurora finished second. 2. Cambria sailed against 23 U.S. yachts and finished tenth. 3. Columbia was disabled in the third race, after winning the first two; Sappho substituted and won the fourth and fifth. 4. Shortly after Dennis Conner and his 60-foot, twin-hulled catamaran easily defeated the challenge of the New Zealand, a 133-foot, single-hulled yacht in the waters off San Diego in early September 1988, a New York State Supreme Court judge ruled that the Americans did not live up to the America's Cup Deed of Gift, which means competing boats must be similar. The judge ruled that the Americans had an unfair advantage over the monohulled ship, and awarded the Cup to New Zealand. However, an Appeal awarded the Cup to the United States.

Bicycling

TOUR DE FRANCE–2001

(July 7–29, 2001)

	Team	Behind			Team	Behind
1. Lance Armstrong, United States	U.S. Postal	(¹)	6.	François Simon, France	Bonjour	17:22
2. Jan Ullrich, Germany	Deutsche Telekom	06:44	7.	Oscar Sevilla, Spain	Kelme	18:30
3. Joseba Beloki, Spain	O.N.C.E.-Eroski	09:05	8.	Santiago Botero, Colombia	Kelme	20:55
4. Andrei Kivilev, Kazakhstan	Cofidis Credit	09:53	9.	Marcos Serrano, Spain	O.N.C.E.-Eroski	21:45
5. Igor Gonzalez Galdeano, Spain	O.N.C.E.-Eroski	13:28	10.	Michaël Boogerd, Netherlands	Rabobank	22:38

1. Completed course in 86 hours, 17 minutes, 28 seconds.

Marathons

BOSTON MARATHON

(April 16, 2001)

Men	Time	Women	Time
Lee Bong-Ju, Korea	2:09:43	Catherine Ndereba, Kenya	2:23:53
Wheelchair—Ernst Van Dyk, South Africa	1:25:12	Wheelchair—Louise Sauvage, Australia	1:53:54

OTHER 2000–2001 MARATHONS

Tokyo (Feb. 18, 2001)

Men	Time
Kenichi Takahashi, Japan	2:10:50

No women's division

Los Angeles (March 4, 2001)

Men	Time
Steven Ndungu, Kenya	2:13:13
Women	
Elana Paramonova, Russia	2:35:58

Paris (April 8, 2001)

Men	Time
Simon Biwott, Kenya	2:09:40
Women	
Florence Barsosio, Kenya	2:27:52

New York City (Nov. 5, 2000)

Men	Time
Abdelkhader El Mouaziz, Morocco	2:10:09
Women	
Ludmila Petrova, Russia	2:25:45

Little League

LITTLE LEAGUE WORLD SERIES CHAMPIONS

Year	Champion	Runner-up	Score	Year	Champion	Runner-up	Score
1947	Williamsport, Pa.	Lock Haven, Pa.	16–7	1970	Wayne, N.J.	Campbell, Calif.	2–0
1948	Lock Haven, Pa.	St. Petersburg, Fla.	6–5	1971	Tainan, Taiwan	Gary, Ind.	12–3
1949	Hammontown, N.J.	Pensacola, Fla.	5–0	1972	Taipei, Taiwan	Hammond, Ind.	6–0
1950	Houston, Tex.	Bridgeport, Conn.	2–1	1973	Tainan City, Taiwan	Tucson, Ariz.	12–0
1951	Stamford, Conn.	Austin, Tex.	3–0	1974	Kao Hsiung, Taiwan	El Cajon, Calif.	7–2
1952	Norwalk, Conn.	Monongahela, Pa.	4–3	1975	Lakewood, N.J.	Tampa, Fla.	4–3
1953	Birmingham, Ala.	Schenectady, N.Y.	1–0	1976	Tokyo, Japan	Campbell, Calif.	10–3
1954	Schenectady, N.Y.	Colton, Calif.	7–5	1977	Kao Hsiung, Taiwan	El Cajon, Calif.	7–2
1955	Morrisville, Pa.	Merchantville, N.J.	4–3	1978	Pin-Tung, Taiwan	Danville, Calif.	11–1
1956	Roswell, N.M.	Merchantville, N.J.	3–1	1979	Hsien, Taiwan	Campbell, Calif.	2–1
1957	Monterrey, Mex.	LaMesa, Calif.	4–0	1980	Hua Lian, Taiwan	Tampa, Fla.	4–3
1958	Monterrey, Mex.	Kankakee, Ill.	10–1	1981	Tai-Chung, Taiwan	Tampa, Fla.	4–2
1959	Hamtramck, Mich.	Auburn, Calif.	12–0	1982	Kirkland, Wash.	Hsien, Taiwan	6–0
1960	Levittown, Pa.	Ft. Worth, Tex.	5–0	1983	Marietta, Ga.	Barahona, Dom. Rep.	3–1
1961	El Cajon, Calif.	El Campo, Tex.	4–2	1984	Seoul, S. Korea	Altamonte Springs, Fla.	6–2
1962	San Jose, Calif.	Kankakee, Ill.	3–0				
1963	Granada Hills, Calif.	Stratford, Conn.	2–1	1985	Seoul, S. Korea	Mexicali, Mex.	7–1
1964	Staten Island, N.Y.	Monterrey, Mex.	4–0	1986	Tainan Park, Taiwan	Tucson, Ariz.	12–0
1965	Windsor Locks, Conn.	Stoney Creek, Can.	3–1	1987	Hua Lian, Taiwan	Irvine, Calif.	21–1
1966	Houston, Tex.	W. New York, N.J.	8–2	1988	Tai-Chung, Taiwan	Pearl City, Haw.	10–0
1967	West Tokyo, Japan	Chicago, Ill.	4–1	1989	Trumbull, Conn.	Kaohsiung, Taiwan	5–2
1968	Osaka, Japan	Richmond, Va.	1–0	1990	Taipei, Taiwan	Shippensburg, Pa.	9–0
1969	Taipei, Taiwan	Santa Clara, Calif.	5–0				

Year	Champion	Runner-up	Score	Year	Champion	Runner-up	Score
1991	Tai-Chung, Taiwan	San Ramon Valley, Calif.	11–0	1997	Guadalupe, Mexico	South Mission Viejo, Calif.	5–4
1992*	Long Beach, Calif.	Zamboanga, Phil.	6–0	1998	Toms River, N.J.	Kashima, Japan	12–9
1993	Long Beach, Calif.	David Chiriqui, Pan.	3–2	1999	Hirakata, Osaka, Japan	Phenix City, Ala.	5–0
1994	Maracaibo, Venezuela	Northridge, Calif.	4–3				
1995	Tainan, Taiwan	Spring, Texas	17–3	2000	Maracaibo, Venezuela	Bellaire, Tex.	3–2
1996	Kao-Hsuing City, Taipei	Cranston, R.I.	13–3	2001	Tokyo Kitasuna, Tokyo, Japan	Apopka, Fla.	2–1

* Long Beach declared a 6–0 winner after the international tournament committee determined that Zamboanga City had used players that were not within its city limits.

Baseball

The popular tradition that baseball was invented by Abner Doubleday at Cooperstown, N.Y., in 1839 has been enshrined in the Hall of Fame and National Museum of Baseball erected in that town, but research has proved that a game called "Base Ball" was played in this country and England before 1839. The first team baseball as we know it was played at the Elysian Fields, Hoboken, N.J., on June 19, 1846, between the Knickerbockers and the New York Nine. The next fifty years saw a gradual growth of baseball and an improvement of equipment and playing skill.

Historians have it that the first pitcher to throw a curve was William A. (Candy) Cummings in 1867. The Cincinnati Red Stockings were the first all-professional team, and in 1869 they played 64 games without a loss. The standard ball of the same size and weight, still the rule, was adopted in 1872. The first catcher's mask was worn in 1875. The National League was organized in 1876. The first chest protector was worn in 1885. The three-strike rule was put on the books in 1887, and the four-ball ticket to first base was instituted in 1889. The pitching distance was lengthened to 60 feet 6 inches in 1893, and the rules have been modified only slightly since that time.

The American League, under the vigorous leadership of B. B. Johnson, became a major league in 1901. Judge Kenesaw Mountain Landis, by action of the two major leagues, became Commissioner of Baseball in 1921.

MAJOR LEAGUE ALL-STAR GAME

Year	Date	Winning league and manager	Runs	Losing league and manager	Runs	Winning pitcher	Losing pitcher	Site	Paid attendance
1933	July 6	A.L. (Mack)	4	N.L. (McGraw)	2	Gomez	Hallahan	Chicago A.L.	47,595
1934	July 10	A.L. (Cronin)	9	N.L. (Terry)	7	Harder	Mungo	New York N.L.	48,363
1935	July 8	A.L. (Cochrane)	4	N.L. (Frisch)	1	Gomez	Walker	Cleveland A.L.	69,831
1936	July 7	N.L. (Grimm)	4	A.L. (McCarthy)	3	J. Dean	Grove	Boston N.L.	25,556
1937	July 7	A.L. (McCarthy)	8	N.L. (Terry)	3	Gomez	J. Dean	Washington A.L.	31,391
1938	July 6	N.L. (Terry)	4	A.L. (McCarthy)	1	Vander Meer	Gomez	Cincinnati N.L.	27,067
1939	July 11	A.L. (McCarthy)	3	N.L. (Hartnett)	1	Bridges	Lee	New York A.L.	62,892
1940	July 9	N.L. (McKechnie)	4	A.L. (Cronin)	0	Derringer	Ruffing	St. Louis N.L.	32,373
1941	July 8	A.L. (Baker)	7	N.L. (McKechnie)	5	E. Smith	Passeau	Detroit A.L.	54,674
1942	July 6	A.L. (McCarthy)	3	N.L. (Durocher)	1	Chandler	Cooper	New York N.L.	34,178
1943	July 13	A.L. (McCarthy)	5	N.L. (Southworth)	3	Leonard	Cooper	Philadelphia A.L.	31,938
1944	July 11	N.L. (Southworth)	7	A.L. (McCarthy)	1	Raffensberger	Hughson	Pittsburgh N.L.	29,589
1946	July 9	A.L. (O'Neill)	12	N.L. (Grimm)	0	Feller	Passeau	Boston A.L.	34,906
1947	July 8	A.L. (Cronin)	2	N.L. (Dyer)	1	Shea	Sain	Chicago N.L.	41,123
1948	July 13	A.L. (Harris)	5	N.L. (Durocher)	2	Raschi	Schmitz	St. Louis A.L.	34,009
1949	July 12	A.L. (Boudreau)	11	N.L. (Southworth)	7	Trucks	Newcombe	Brooklyn N.L.	32,577
1950	July 11	N.L. (Shotton)	4	A.L. (Stengel)	3[1]	Blackwell	Gray	Chicago A.L.	46,127
1951	July 10	N.L. (Sawyer)	8	A.L. (Stengel)	3	Maglie	Lopat	Detroit A.L.	52,075
1952	July 8	N.L. (Durocher)	3	A.L. (Stengel)	2[2]	Rush	Lemon	Philadelphia N.L.	32,785
1953	July 14	N.L. (Dressen)	5	A.L. (Stengel)	1	Spahn	Reynolds	Cincinnati N.L.	30,846
1954	July 13	A.L. (Stengel)	11	N.L. (Alston)	9	Stone	Conley	Cleveland A.L.	68,751
1955	July 12	N.L. (Durocher)	6	A.L. (Lopez)	5[3]	Conley	Sullivan	Milwaukee N.L.	45,643
1956	July 10	N.L. (Alston)	7	A.L. (Stengel)	3	Friend	Pierce	Washington A.L.	28,843
1957	July 9	A.L. (Stengel)	6	N.L. (Alston)	5	Bunning	Simmons	St. Louis N.L.	30,693
1958	July 8	A.L. (Stengel)	4	N.L. (Haney)	3	Wynn	Friend	Baltimore A.L.	48,829
1959[4]	July 7	N.L. (Haney)	5	A.L. (Stengel)	4	Antonelli	Ford	Pittsburgh N.L.	35,277
	Aug. 3	A.L. (Stengel)	5	N.L. (Haney)	3	Walker	Drysdale	Los Angeles N.L.	55,105
1960[4]	July 11	N.L. (Alston)	5	A.L. (Lopez)	3	Friend	Monbouquette	Kansas City A.L.	30,619
	July 13	N.L. (Alston)	6	A.L. (Lopez)	0	Law	Ford	New York A.L.	38,362
1961[4]	July 11	N.L. (Murtaugh)	5	A.L. (Richards)	4[5]	Miller	Wilhelm	San Francisco N.L.	44,115
	July 31	N.L. (Murtaugh)	1	A.L. (Richards)	1[6]	—	—	Boston A.L.	31,851
1962[4]	July 10	N.L. (Hutchinson)	3	A.L. (Houk)	1	Marichal	Pascual	Washington A.L.	45,480
	July 30	A.L. (Houk)	9	N.L. (Hutchinson)	4	Herbert	Mahaffey	Chicago N.L.	38,359
1963	July 9	N.L. (Dark)	5	A.L. (Houk)	3	Jackson	Bunning	Cleveland A.L.	44,160
1964	July 7	N.L. (Alston)	7	A.L. (Lopez)	4	Marichal	Radatz	New York N.L.	50,850

Year	Date	Winning league and manager	Runs	Losing league and manager	Runs	Winning pitcher	Losing pitcher	Site	Paid attendance
1965	July 13	N.L. (March)	6	A.L. (Lopez)	5	Koufax	McDowell	Minnesota A.L.	46,706
1966	July 12	N.L. (Alston)	2	A.L. (Mele)	1[5]	Perry	Rickert	St. Louis N.L.	49,926
1967	July 11	N.L. (Alston)	2	A.L. (Bauer)	1[7]	Drysdale	Hunter	Anaheim A.L.	46,309
1968	July 9	N.L. (Schoendienst)	1	A.L. (Williams)	0	Drysdale	Tiant	Houston N.L.	48,321
1969	July 23	N.L. (Schoendienst)	9	A.L. (M. Smith)	3	Carlton	Stottlemyre	Washington A.L.	45,259
1970	July 14	N.L. (Hodges)	5	A.L. (Weaver)	4	Osteen	Wright	Cincinnati N.L.	51,838
1971	July 13	A.L. (Weaver)	6	N.L. (Anderson)	4	Blue	Ellis	Detroit A.L.	53,559
1972	July 25	N.L. (Murtaugh)	4	A.L. (Weaver)	3[5]	McGraw	McNally	Atlanta N.L.	53,107
1973	July 24	N.L. (Anderson)	7	A.L. (Williams)	1	Wise	Blyleven	Kansas City A.L.	40,849
1974	July 23	N.L. (Berra)	7	A.L. (Williams)	2	Brett	Tiant	Pittsburgh N.L.	50,706
1975	July 15	N.L. (Alston)	6	A.L. (Dark)	3	Matlack	Hunter	Milwaukee A.L.	51,540
1976	July 13	N.L. (Anderson)	7	A.L. (D. Johnson)	1	R. Jones	Fidrych	Philadelphia N.L.	63,974
1977	July 19	N.L. (Anderson)	7	A.L. (Martin)	5	Sutton	Palmer	New York A.L.	56,683
1978	July 11	N.L. (Lasorda)	7	A.L. (Martin)	3	Sutter	Gossage	San Diego N.L.	51,549
1979	July 17	N.L. (Lasorda)	7	A.L. (Lemon)	6	Sutter	Kern	Seattle A.L.	58,905
1980	July 8	N.L. (Tanner)	4	A.L. (Weaver)	2	Reuss	John	Los Angeles N.L.	56,088
1981[8]	Aug. 9	N.L. (Green)	5	A.L. (Frey)	4	Blue	Fingers	Cleveland A.L.	72,086
1982	July 13	N.L. (Lasorda)	4	A.L. (Martin)	1	Rogers	Eckersley	Montreal N.L.	59,057
1983	July 6	A.L. (Kuenn)	13	N.L. (Herzog)	3	Steib	Soto	Chicago A.L.	43,801
1984	July 11	A.L. (Owens)	3	N.L. (Altobelli)	1	Leg	Steib	San Francisco, N.L.	57,756
1985	July 16	N.L. (Williams)	6	A.L. (Anderson)	1	Hoyt	Morris	Minneapolis, A.L.	54,960
1986	July 15	A.L. (Howser)	3	N.L. (Herzog)	2	Clemens	Gooden	Houston, N.L.	45,774
1987	July 14	N.L. (Johnson)	2	A.L. (McNamara)	0[9]	Smith	Howell	Oakland, A.L.	49,671
1988	July 12	A.L. (Kelly)	2	N.L. (Herzog)	1	Viola	Gooden	Cincinnati, N.L	55,837
1989	July 11	A.L. (LaRussa)	5	N.L. (Lasorda)	3	Ryan	Smoltz	California, A.L.	64,036
1990	July 10	A.L. (LaRussa)	2	N.L. (Craig)	0	Saberhagen	Brantley	Chicago, N.L.	39,071
1991	July 9	A.L. (LaRussa)	4	N.L. (Piniella)	2	Key	Martinez	Toronto, A.L.	52,383
1992	July 14	A.L. (Kelly)	13	N.L. (Cox)	6	Brown	Glavine	San Diego, N.L.	59,372
1993	July 13	A.L. (Gaston)	9	N.L. (Cox)	3	McDowell	Burkett	Baltimore, A.L.	48,147
1994	July 12	N.L. (Fregosi)	8	A.L. (Gaston)	7[5]	Jones	Bere	Pittsburgh, A.L.	59,568
1995	July 11	N.L. (Alou)	3	A.L. (Showalter)	2	Slocumb	Rogers	Texas, A.L.	50,920
1996	July 9	N.L. (Cox)	6	A.L. (Hargrove)	0	Smoltz	Nagy	Philadelphia, N.L.	62,670
1997	July 8	A.L. (Torre)	3	N.L. (Cox)	1	Johnson	Maddux	Cleveland, A.L.	44,916
1998	July 7	A.L. (Hargrove)	13	N.L. (Leyland)	3	Colon	Urbina	Denver, N.L.	51,267
1999	July 13	A.L. (Torre)	4	N.L. (Bochy)	1	P. Martinez	Schilling	Boston, A.L.	34,187
2000	July 11	A.L. (Torre)	6	N.L. (Cox)	3	Baldwin	Leiter	Atlanta, N.L.	51,323
2001	July 10	A.L. (Torre)	4	N.L. (Valentine)	1	Garcia	Park	Seattle, A.L.	47,364

1. Fourteen innings. 2. Five innings, rain. 3. Twelve innings. 4. Two games. 5. Ten innings. 6. Called because of rain after nine innings. 7. Fifteen innings. 8. Game was originally scheduled for July 14, but was put off because of players' strike. 9. Thirteen innings. NOTE: No game in 1945.

NATIONAL BASEBALL HALL OF FAME

Fielders
Cooperstown, N.Y.

Member	Active years	Member	Active years	Member	Active years
Aaron, Henry (Hank)	1954–1976	Chance, Frank	1898–1914	Evers, John	1902–1919
Anson, Adrian (Cap)	1876–1897	Charleston, Oscar[1]	1915–1954	Ferrell, Rick	1929–1947
Aparicio, Luis	1956–1973	Clarke, Fred	1894–1915	Fisk, Carlton	1969–1991
Appling, Lucius (Luke)	1930–1950	Clemente, Roberto	1955–1972	Flick, Elmer	1898–1910
Ashburn, Richie	1948–1962	Cobb, Tyrus	1905–1928	Fox, Nellie	1947–1965
Averill, H. Earl	1929–1941	Cochrane, Gordon (Mickey)	1925–1937	Foxx, James	1925–1945
Baker, J. Frank (Home Run)	1908–1922	Collins, Edward	1906–1930	Frisch, Frank	1919–1937
Bancroft, David	1915–1930	Collins, James	1895–1908	Gehrig, H. Louis (Lou)	1923–1939
Banks, Ernest	1953–1971	Comiskey, Charles	1882–1894	Gehringer, Charles	1924–1942
Beckley, Jacob	1888–1907	Combs, Earle	1924–1935	Gibson, Josh[1]	1929–1946
Bell, James (Cool Papa)[1]	1920–1947	Connor, Roger	1880–1897	Goslin, Leon (Goose)	1921–1938
Bench, John	1967–1983	Crawford, Samuel	1899–1917	Greenberg, Henry (Hank)	1933–1947
Berra, Lawrence (Yogi)	1946–1965	Cronin, Joseph	1926–1945	Hafey, Charles (Chick)	1924–1937
Bottomley, James	1922–1937	Cuyler, Hazen (Kiki)	1921–1938	Hamilton, William	1888–1901
Boudreau, Louis	1938–1952	Dandridge, Ray[1]	1933–1953	Hartnett, Charles (Gabby)	1922–1941
Bresnahan, Roger	1897–1915	Davis, George	1890–1909	Heilmann, Harry	1914–1932
Brett, George	1973–1993	Delahanty, Edward	1888–1903	Herman, William	1931–1947
Brock, Lou	1961–1980	Dickey, William	1928–1946	Hooper, Harry	1909–1925
Brouthers, Dennis	1879–1896	Dihigo, Martin[1]	1923–1945	Hornsby, Rogers	1915–1937
Burkett, Jesse	1890–1905	DiMaggio, Joseph	1936–1951	Irvin, Monford (Monte)[1]	1939–1956
Campanella, Roy	1948–1957	Doby, Larry	1947–1959	Jackson, Reggie	1967–1987
Carew, Rod	1967–1985	Doerr, Bobby	1937–1951	Jackson, Travis	1922–1936
Carey, Max	1910–1929	Duffy, Hugh	1888–1906	Jennings, Hugh	1891–1918
Cepeda, Orlando	1958–1974	Ewing, William	1880–1897	Johnson, William (Judy)[1]	1921–1937
				Kaline, Albert W.	1953–1974

Member	Active years	Member	Active years	Member	Active years
Keeler, William (Wee Willie)	1892–1910	McPhee, John Alexander (Bid)	1882–1899	Slaughter, Enos	1938–1959
Kell, George	1943–1957	Medwick, Joseph (Ducky)	1932–1948	Snider, Edwin D. (Duke)	1947–1964
Kelley, Joseph	1891–1908	Mize, John (The Big Cat)	1936–1953	Speaker, Tristram	1907–1928
Kelly, George	1915–1932	Morgan, Joe	1963–1984	Stargell, Willie	1962–1982
Kelly, Michael (King)	1878–1893	Musial, Stanley	1941–1963	Stearnes, Norman (Turkey)	1921–1942
Killebrew, Harmon	1954–1975	O'Rourke, James	1876–1894	Terry, William	1923–1936
Kiner, Ralph	1946–1955	Ott, Melvin	1926–1947	Thompson, Samuel	1885–1906
Klein, Charles H. (Chuck)	1928–1944	Perez, Tony	1964–1983	Tinker, Joseph	1902–1916
Lajoie, Napoleon	1896–1916	Puckett, Kirby	1984–1995	Traynor, Harold (Pie)	1920–1937
Lazzeri, Tony	1926–1939	Reese, Harold (Pee Wee)	1940–1958	Vaughan, Arky	1932–1948
Leonard, Walter (Buck)[1]	1933–1955	Rice, Edgar (Sam)	1915–1934	Wagner, John (Honus)	1897–1917
Lindstrom, Frederick	1924–1936	Rizzuto, Phil	1941–1956	Wallace, Roderick (Bobby)	1894–1918
Lloyd, John Henry (Pop)[1]	1905–1931	Robinson, Brooks	1955–1977	Waner, Lloyd	1927–1945
Lombardi, Ernie	1932–1947	Robinson, Frank	1956–1976	Waner, Paul	1926–1945
Mantle, Mickey	1951–1968	Robinson, Jack	1947–1956	Ward, John (Monte)	1878–1894
Manush, Henry (Heinie)	1923–1939	Robinson, Wilbert	1886–1902	Wells, Willie	1924–1949
Maranville, Walter (Rabbit)	1912–1935	Roush, Edd	1913–1931	Wheat, Zachariah	1909–1927
Matthews, Edwin	1952–1968	Ruth, Babe	1914–1935	Williams, Billy	1959–1976
Mays, Willie	1951–1973	Schalk, Raymond	1912–1929	Williams, Theodore	1939–1960
Mazeroski, William Stanley (Maz)	1956–1972	Schoendienst, Red	1945–1963	Wilson, Lewis R. (Hack)	1923–1934
McCarthy, Thomas	1884–1896	Schmidt, Mike	1973–1989	Winfield, David Mark	1973–1995
McCovey, Willie	1959–1980	Sewell, Joseph	1920–1933	Yastrzemski, Carl	1961–1983
McGraw, John J.	1891–1906	Simmons, Al	1924–1944	Youngs, Ross (Pep)	1917–1926
		Sisler, George	1915–1930	Yount, Robin	1974–1993

1. Negro League player selected by special committee.

Pitchers

Alexander, Grover	1911–1930	Haines, Jesse	1918–1937	Radbourn, Charles (Hoss)	1880–1891
Bender, Charles (Chief)	1903–1925	Hoyt, Waite	1918–1938	Rixey, Eppa	1912–1933
Brown, Mordecai (3-Finger)	1903–1916	Hubbell, Carl	1928–1943	Roberts, Robert (Robin)	1948–1966
Bunning, Jim	1955–1971	Hunter, Jim (Catfish)	1965–1979	Rogan, Wilber	1920–1938
Carlton, Steve	1965–1988	Jenkins, Ferguson	1965–1983	Ruffing, Charles (Red)	1924–1947
Chesbro, John	1899–1909	Johnson, Walter	1907–1927	Rusie, Amos	1889–1901
Clarkson, John	1882–1894	Joss, Adrian	1902–1910	Ryan, Nolan, Jr.	1966–1973
Coveleski, Stanley	1912–1928	Keefe, Timothy	1880–1893	Seaver, Tom	1967–1986
Day, Leon	1935–1955	Koufax, Sanford (Sandy)	1955–1966	Smith, Hilton Lee	1932–1948
Dean, Jerome (Dizzy)	1930–1947	Lemon, Robert	1946–1958	Spahn, Warren	1942–1965
Drysdale, Don	1956–1969	Lyons, Theodore	1923–1946	Sutton, Don	1966–1988
Faber, Urban (Red)	1914–1933	Marichal, Juan	1960–1975	Vance, Arthur (Dazzy)	1915–1935
Feller, Robert	1936–1956	Marquard, Richard (Rube)	1908–1924	Waddell, Rube	1897–1910
Fingers, Rollie	1968–1985	Mathewson, Christopher	1900–1916	Walsh, Edward	1904–1917
Ford, Edward (Whitey)	1950–1967	McGinnity, Joseph	1899–1908	Welch, Michael (Mickey)	1880–1892
Foster, Andrew (Rube)	1897–1926	Newhouser, Hal	1939–1955	Wilhelm, Hoyt	1952–1972
Foster, Bill	1923–1937	Nichols, Charles (Kid)	1890–1906	Williams, Joseph	1910–1932
Galvin, James (Pud)	1876–1892	Niekro, Phil	1959–1987	Willis, Vic	1898–1910
Gibson, Bob	1959–1975	Paige, Leroy (Satchel)[1]	1926–1965	Wynn, Early	1939–1963
Gomez, Vernon (Lefty)	1930–1943	Palmer, Jim	1965–1984	Young, Denton (Cy)	1890–1911
Griffith, Clark	1891–1914	Pennock, Herbert	1912–1934		
Grimes, Burleigh	1916–1934	Perry, Gaylord	1962–1983		
Grove, Robert (Lefty)	1925–1941	Plank, Edward	1901–1917		

1. Negro League player selected by special committee.

Officials and Others

Alston, Walter[1]	Cummings, William A.[5]	Hulbert, William[2]	McKechnie, William B.[1]
Anderson, Sparky[1]	Durocher, Leo[1]	Johnson, B. Bancroft[2]	Rickey, W. Branch[1][2]
Barlick, Al[4]	Evans, William G.[4][2]	Klem, William[4]	Selee, Frank G.[1]
Barrow, Edward[1][2]	Foster, Rube[2]	Landis, Kenesaw M.[6]	Spalding, Albert G.[4]
Bulkeley, Morgan G.[2]	Frick, Ford C.[6][2]	Lasorda, Tommy[1]	Stengel, Charles D.[7]
Cartwright, Alexander[2]	Giles, Warren C.[2]	Lopez, Alfonso R.[7]	Veeck, Bill[2]
Chadwick, Henry[3]	Hanlon, Ned[2]	Mack, Connie[1][2]	Weaver, Earl[1]
Chandler, A. B.[6]	Harridge, William[2]	MacPhail, Lee, Jr.[2]	Weiss, George M.[2]
Chylak, Nestor, Jr.[4]	Harris, Stanley R.[7]	MacPhail, Leland S.[2]	Wright, George[5]
Comiskey, Charles[1]	Hubbard, R. Calvin[4]	McCarthy, Joseph V.[1]	Wright, Harry[5][1]
Conlan, John[2]	Huggins, Miller J.[1]	McGowan, Bill[4]	Yawkey, Thomas[2]
Connolly, Thomas[4]			

1. Manager. 2. Executive. 3. Writer-statistician. 4. Umpire. 5. Early player. 6. Commissioner. 7. Player-manager.

BASEBALL'S PERFECTLY PITCHED GAMES[1]
(no opposing runner reached base)

Lee Richmond—Worcester vs. Cleveland (N.L.) June 12, 1880 (1–0)

John M. Ward—Providence vs. Buffalo (N.L.) June 17, 1880 (5–0)

Cy Young—Boston vs. Philadelphia (A.L.) May 5, 1904 (3–0)

Addie Joss—Cleveland vs. Chicago (A.L.) Oct. 2, 1908 (1–0)

Ernest Shore[2]—Boston vs. Washington (A.L.) June 23, 1917 (4–0)

Charles Robertson—Chicago vs. Detroit (A.L.) April 30, 1922 (2–0)

Don Larsen[3]—New York (A.L.) vs. Brooklyn (N.L.) Oct. 8, 1956 (2–0)

Jim Bunning—Philadelphia vs. New York (N.L.) June 21, 1964 (6–0)

Sandy Koufax—Los Angeles vs. Chicago (N.L.) Sept. 9, 1965 (1–0)

Jim Hunter—Oakland vs. Minnesota (A.L.) May 8, 1968 (4–0)

Len Barker—Cleveland vs. Toronto (A.L.) May 15, 1981 (3–0)

Mike Witt—California vs. Texas (A.L.) Sept. 30, 1984 (1–0)

Tom Browning—Cincinnati vs. Los Angeles (N.L.) Sept. 16, 1988 (1–0)

Dennis Martinez—Montreal vs. Los Angeles (N.L.) July 28, 1991 (2–0)

Kenny Rogers—Texas vs. California (A.L.) July 28, 1994 (4–0)

David Wells—New York vs. Minnesota (A.L.) May 17, 1998 (4–0)

David Cone[4]—New York (A.L.) vs. Montreal (N.L.) July 18, 1999 (6–0)

1. Harvey Haddix, of Pittsburgh, pitched 12 perfect innings against Milwaukee (N.L.), May 26, 1959, but lost game in 13th on error and hit. 2. Shore, relief pitcher for Babe Ruth who walked first batter before being ejected by umpire, retired 26 batters who faced him and base-runner was out stealing. 3. World Series. 4. Interleague game.

LIFETIME BATTING, PITCHING, AND BASE-RUNNING RECORDS

(Records through 2001. Boldface indicates player active in 2001 season)

Hits (3,000+)

Pete Rose	4,256
Ty Cobb	4,189
Hank Aaron	3,771
Stan Musial	3,630
Tris Speaker	3,514
Carl Yastrzemski	3,419
Cap Anson	3,418
Honus Wagner	3,415
Paul Molitor	3,319
Eddie Collins	3,315
Willie Mays	3,283
Eddie Murray	3,255
Nap Lajoie	3,242
Cal Ripken, Jr.	**3,184**
George Brett	3,154
Paul Waner	3,152
Robin Yount	3,142
Tony Gwynn	**3,141**
Dave Winfield	3,110
Rod Carew	3,053
Lou Brock	3,023
Wade Boggs	3,010
Al Kaline	3,007
Roberto Clemente	3,000
Rickey Henderson	**3,000**

Earned Run Average
(Minimum 1,500 innings pitched)

Ed Walsh	1.82
Addie Joss	1.89
Al Spalding	2.04
Mordecai Brown	2.06
John Ward	2.10
Christy Mathewson	2.13
Tommy Bond	2.14
Rube Waddell	2.16
Walter Johnson	2.17
Ed Reulbach	2.28
Will White	2.28
Ed Plank	2.35
Larry Corcoran	2.36
Ed Cicotte	2.38
Candy Cummings	2.39
Doc White	2.39
Nap Rucker	2.42
George Bradley	2.43
Jim McCormick	2.43

Runs Scored

Rickey Henderson	**2,248**
Ty Cobb	2,246
Hank Aaron	2,174
Babe Ruth	2,174
Pete Rose	2,165
Willie Mays	2,062
Cap Anson	1,996
Stan Musial	1,949
Lou Gehrig	1,888
Tris Speaker	1,882
Mel Ott	1,859
Frank Robinson	1,829
Eddie Collins	1,821
Carl Yastrzemski	1,816
Ted Williams	1,798
Paul Molitor	1,782
Charlie Gehringer	1,774
Jimmie Foxx	1,751
Honus Wagner	1,736
Jim O'Rourke	1,729
Jesse Burkett	1,720
Willie Keeler	1,719
Barry Bonds	**1,713**
Billy Hamilton	1,691
Bid McPhee	1,678
Mickey Mantle	1,677
Dave Winfield	1,669
Joe Morgan	1,650

Strikeouts, Pitching

Nolan Ryan	5,714
Steve Carlton	4,136
Roger Clemens	**3,717**
Bert Blyleven	3,701
Tom Seaver	3,640
Don Sutton	3,574
Gaylord Perry	3,534
Walter Johnson	3,508
Randy Johnson	**3,412**
Phil Niekro	3,342
Ferguson Jenkins	3,192
Bob Gibson	3,117
Jim Bunning	2,855
Mickey Lolich	2,832
Cy Young	2,803
Frank Tanana	2,773
David Cone	**2,655**
Warren Spahn	2,583
Bob Feller	2,581
Tim Keefe	2,564
Jerry Koosman	2,556
Greg Maddux	**2,523**

Home Runs (375+)

Hank Aaron	755
Babe Ruth	714
Willie Mays	660
Frank Robinson	586
Mark McGwire	**583**
Harmon Killebrew	573
Barry Bonds	**567**
Reggie Jackson	563
Mike Schmidt	548
Mickey Mantle	536
Jimmie Foxx	534
Willie McCovey	521
Ted Williams	521
Ernie Banks	512
Eddie Mathews	512
Mel Ott	511
Eddie Murray	504
Lou Gehrig	493
Stan Musial	475
Willie Stargell	475
Dave Winfield	465
Jose Canseco	**462**
Ken Griffey, Jr.	**460**
Carl Yastrzemski	452
Sammy Sosa	**450**

Fred McGriff	**448**
Rafael Palmeiro	**447**
Dave Kingman	442
Andre Dawson	438
Cal Ripken, Jr.	**431**
Billy Williams	426
Darrell Evans	414
Duke Snider	407
Al Kaline	399
Dale Murphy	398
Juan Gonzalez	**397**
Joe Carter	396
Graig Nettles	390
Johnny Bench	389
Dwight Evans	385
Harold Baines	**384**
Frank Howard	382
Jim Rice	382
Albert Belle	**381**
Orlando Cepeda	379
Tony Perez	379
Norm Cash	377
Andres Galarraga	**377**
Carlton Fisk	376

Shutouts

Walter Johnson	110
Grover Alexander	90
Christy Mathewson	79
Cy Young	76
Ed Plank	69
Warren Spahn	63
Nolan Ryan	61
Tom Seaver	61
Bert Blyleven	60
Don Sutton	58
Pud Galvin	57
Ed Walsh	57
Bob Gibson	56
Mordecai Brown	55
Steve Carlton	55
Jim Palmer	53
Gaylord Perry	53
Juan Marichal	52

Strikeouts, Batting

Reggie Jackson	2,597	Chili Davis	1,698	Lance Parrish	1,527	Darrell Evans	1,605
Jose Canseco	**1,942**	**Fred McGriff**	**1,698**	Willie Mays	1,526	Stan Musial	1,599
Willie Stargell	1,936	Dwight Evans	1,697			Pete Rose	1,566
Mike Schmidt	1,883	**Sammy Sosa**	**1,690**	**Walks**		Harmon Killebrew	1,559
Tony Perez	1,867	Dave Winfield	1,686	**Rickey Henderson**	**2,141**	Lou Gehrig	1,508
Andres Galarraga	**1,858**	**Rickey Henderson**	**1,631**	Babe Ruth	2,062	Mike Schmidt	1,507
Dave Kingman	1,816	**Gary Gaetti**	**1,602**	Ted Williams	2,019	Eddie Collins	1,499
Bobby Bonds	1,757	**Mark McGwire**	**1,596**	Joe Morgan	1,865	Willie Mays	1,464
Dale Murphy	1,748	Lee May	1,570	Carl Yastrzemski	1,845	Jimmie Foxx	1,452
Lou Brock	1,730	Dick Allen	1,556	Mickey Mantle	1,733	Eddie Mathews	1,444
Mickey Mantle	1,710	Willie McCovey	1,550	**Barry Bonds**	**1,724**	Frank Robinson	1,420
Harmon Killebrew	1,699	Dave Parker	1,537	Mel Ott	1,708	Wade Boggs	1,412
		Frank Robinson	1,532	Eddie Yost	1,614	Hank Aaron	1,402

RECORD OF WORLD SERIES GAMES
(through 2000)

Figures in parentheses for winning pitchers (WP) and losing pitchers (LP) indicate the game number in the series.

1903—Boston A.L. 5 (Jimmy Collins); Pittsburgh N.L. 3 (Fred Clarke). WP—Boston: Dinneen (2, 6, 8), Young (5, 7); Pittsburgh: Phillippe (1, 3, 4). LP—Boston: Young (1), Hughes (3), Dinneen (7); Pittsburgh: Leever (2, 6), Kennedy (5), Phillippe (7, 8).

1904—No series.

1905—New York N.L. 4 (John J. McGraw); Philadelphia A.L. 1 (Connie Mack). WP—New York: Mathewson (1, 3, 5); McGinnity (4); Phila.: Bender (2). LP—New York: McGinnity (2); Phila.: Plank (1, 4), Coakley (3), Bender (5).

1906—Chicago A.L. 4 (Fielder Jones); Chicago N.L. 2 (Frank Chance). WP—Chicago: A.L.: Altrock (1), Walsh (3, 5), White (6); Chicago: N.L.: Reulbach (2), Brown (4). LP—Chicago A.L.: White (2), Altrock. (4); Chicago: N.L.: Brown (1, 6), Pfeister (3, 5).

1907—Chicago N.L. 4 (Frank Chance); Detroit A.L. 0 (Hugh Jennings). First game tied 3–3, 12 innings. WP—Pfeister (2), Reulbach (3), Overall (4), Brown (5). LP—Mullin (2, 5), Siever (3), Donovan (4).

1908—Chicago N.L. 4 (Frank Chance); Detroit A.L. 1 (Hugh Jennings). WP—Chicago: Brown (1, 4), Overall (2, 5); Det.: Mullin (3). LP—Chicago: Pfeister (3); Det.: Summers (1, 4), Donovan (2, 5).

1909—Pittsburgh N.L. 4 (Fred Clarke); Detroit A.L. 3 (Hugh Jennings). WP—Pittsburgh: Adams (1, 5, 7), Maddox (3); Det.: Donovan (2), Mullin (4, 6). LP—Pittsburgh: Camnitz (2), Leifield (4), Willis (6); Det.: Mullin (1), Summers (3, 5), Donovan (7).

1910—Philadelphia A.L. 4 (Connie Mack); Chicago N.L. 1 (Frank Chance). WP—Phila.: Bender (1), Coombs (2, 3, 5); Chicago: Brown (4). LP—Phila.: Bender (4); Chicago: Overall (1), Brown (2, 5), McIntyre (3).

1911—Philadelphia A.L. 4 (Connie Mack); New York N.L. 2 (John J. McGraw). WP—Phila.: Plank (2), Coombs (3), Bender (4, 6); New York: Mathewson (1), Crandall (5). LP—Phila.: Bender (1), Plank (5); New York: Marquard (2), Mathewson (3, 4), Ames (5).

1912—Boston A.L. 4 (J. Garland Stahl); New York N.L. 3 (John J. McGraw). Second game tied, 6–6, 11 innings. WP—Boston: Wood (1, 4, 8), Bedient (5); New York: Marquard (3, 6), Tesreau (7). LP—Boston: O'Brien (3, 6), Wood (7); New York: Tesreau (1, 4), Mathewson (5, 8).

1913—Philadelphia A.L. 4 (Connie Mack); New York N.L. 1 (John J. McGraw). WP—Phila.: Bender (1, 4), Bush (3), Plank (5); New York: Mathewson (2); LP—Phila.: Plank (2); New York: Marquard (1), Tesreau (4), Demaree (4), Mathewson (5).

1914—Boston N.L. 4 (George Stallings); Philadelphia A.L. 0 (Connie Mack). WP—Rudolph (1, 4), James (2, 3). LP—Bender (1), Plank (2), Bush (3), Shawkey (4).

1915—Boston A.L. 4 (Bill Carrigan); Philadelphia N.L. 1 (Pat Moran). WP—Boston: Foster (2, 5), Leonard (3), Shore (4); Phila.: Alexander (1). LP—Boston: Shore (1); Phila.: Mayer (2), Alexander (3), Chalmers (4), Rixey (5).

1916—Boston A.L. 4 (Bill Carrigan); Brooklyn N.L. 1 (Wilbert Robinson). WP—Boston: Shore (1, 5), Ruth (2), Leonard (4); Brooklyn: Coombs (3). LP—Boston: Mays (3); Brooklyn: Marquard (1, 4), Smith (5), Pfeffer (5).

1917—Chicago A.L. 4 (Clarence Rowland); New York N.L. 2 (John J. McGraw). WP—Chicago: Cicotte (1), Faber (2, 5, 6); New York: Benton (3), Schupp (4), LP—Chicago: Cicotte (3), Faber (4); New York: Sallee (1, 5), Anderson (2), Benton (6).

1918—Boston A.L. 4 (Ed Barrow); Chicago N.L. 2 (Fred Mitchell). WP—Boston: Ruth (1, 4), Mays (3, 6); Chicago: Tyler (2), Vaughn (5). LP—Boston: Bush (2), Jones (5); Chicago: Vaughn (1, 3), Douglas (4), Tyler (6).

1919—Cincinnati N.L. 5 (Pat Moran); Chicago A.L. 3 (William Gleason). WP—Cincinnati: Ruether (1), Sallee (2), Ring (4), Eller (5, 8); Chicago: Kerr (3, 6), Cicotte (7). LP—Cincinnati: Fisher (3), Ring (6), Sallee (7); Chicago: Cicotte (1, 4), Williams (2, 5, 8).

1920—Cleveland A.L. 5 (Tris Speaker); Brooklyn N.L. 2 (Wilbert Robinson). WP—Cleve.: Coveleski (1, 4, 7), Bagby (5), Mails (6); Brooklyn: Grimes (2), Smith (3). LP—Cleve.: Bagby (2), Caldwell (3). Brooklyn: Marquard (1), Cadore (4), Grimes (5, 7), Smith (6).

1921—New York N.L. 5 (John J. McGraw); New York A.L. 3 (Miller Huggins). WP—New York N.L.: Barnes (3, 6), Douglas (4, 7), Nehf (8); New York A.L.: Mays (1), Hoyt (2, 5). LP—New York N.L.: Nehf (2, 5), Douglas (1). New York A.L.: Quinn (3), Mays (4, 7), Shawkey (6), Hoyt (8).

1922—New York N.L. 4 (John J. McGraw); New York A.L. 0 (Miller Huggins). Second game tied 3–3, 10 innings. WP—Ryan (1), Scott (3), McQuillan (4), Nehf (5); LP—Bush (1, 5), Hoyt (3), Mays (4).

1923—New York A.L. 4 (Miller Huggins); New York N.L. 2 (John J. McGraw). WP—New York A.L.: Pennock (2, 6), Shawkey (4), Bush (5); New York N.L.: Ryan (1), Nehf (3). LP—New York A.L.: Bush (1), Jones (3); New York N.L.: McQuillan (2), Scott (4), Bentley (5), Nehf (6).

1924—Washington A.L. 4 (Bucky Harris); New York N.L. 3 (John J. McGraw). WP—Washington: Zachary (2, 6), Mogridge (4), Johnson (7); New York: Nehf (1), McQuillan (3), Bentley (5). LP—Washington: Johnson (1, 5), Marberry (3); New York: Bentley (2, 7), Barnes (4), Nehf (6).

1925—Pittsburgh N.L. 4 (Bill McKechnie); Washington A.L. 3 (Bucky Harris). WP—Pittsburgh: Aldridge (2, 5), Kremer (6, 7); Washington: Johnson (1, 4), Ferguson (3). LP—Pittsburgh: Meadows (1), Kremer (3), Yde (4); Washington: Coveleski (2, 5), Ferguson (6), Johnson (7).

1926—St. Louis N.L. 4 (Rogers Hornsby); New York A.L. 3 (Miller Huggins). WP—St. Louis: Alexander (2, 6), Haines

(3, 7); New York: Pennock (1, 5), Hoyt (4). LP—St. Louis: Sherdel (1, 5), Reinhart (4); New York: Shocker (2), Ruether (3), Shawkey (6), Hoyt (7).

1927—New York A.L. 4 (Miller Huggins); Pittsburgh N.L. 0 (Donie Bush). WP—Hoyt (1), Pipgras (2), Pennock (3), Moore (4). LP—Kremer (1), Aldridge (2), Meadows (3), Miljus (4).

1928—New York A.L. 4 (Miller Huggins); St. Louis N.L. 0 (Bill McKechnie). WP—Hoyt (1, 4), Pipgras (2), Zachary (3). LP—Sherdel (1, 4), Alexander (2), Haines (3).

1929—Philadelphia A.L. 4 (Connie Mack); Chicago N.L. 1 (Joe McCarthy). WP—Phila.: Ehmke (1), Earnshaw (2), Rommel (4), Walberg (5); Chicago: Bush (3). LP—Phila.: Earnshaw (3) Chicago: Root (1), Malone (2, 5), Blake (4).

1930—Philadelphia A.L. 4 (Connie Mack); St. Louis N.L. 2 (Gabby Street). WP—Phila.: Grove (1, 5), Earnshaw (2, 6); St. Louis: Hallahan (3), Haines (4). LP—Phila.: Walberg (3), Grove (4); St. Louis: Grimes (1, 5), Rhem (2), Hallahan (6).

1931—St. Louis N.L. 4 (Gabby Street); Philadelphia A.L. 3 (Connie Mack). WP—St. Louis: Hallahan (2, 5), Grimes (3, 7); Phila.: Grove (1, 6), Earnshaw (4). LP—St. Louis: Derringer (1, 6), Johnson (4); Phila.: Earnshaw (2, 7), Grove (3), Hoyt (5).

1932—New York A.L. 4 (Joe McCarthy); Chicago N.L. 0 (Charles Grimm). WP—Ruffing (1), Gomez (2), Pipgras (3), Moore (4). LP—Bush (1), Warneke (2), Root (3), May (4).

1933—New York N.L. 4 (Bill Terry); Washington A.L. 1 (Joe Cronin.). WP—New York: Hubbell (1, 4), Schumacher (2), Luque (5); Washington: Whitehill (3). LP—New York: Fitzsimmons (3); Washington: Stewart (1), Crowder (2), Weaver (4), Russell (5).

1934—St. Louis N.L. 4 (Frank Frisch); Detroit A.L. 3 (Mickey Cochrane). WP—St. Louis: J. Dean (1, 7), P. Dean (3, 6); Det.: Rowe (2), Auker (4); Bridges (5). LP—St. Louis: W. Walker (2, 4), J. Dean (5); Det.: Crowder (1), Bridges (3), Rowe (6), Auker (7).

1935—Detroit A.L. 4 (Mickey Cochrane); Chicago N.L. 2 (Charles Grimm). WP—Det.: Bridges (2, 6), Rowe (3), Crowder (4); Chicago: Warneke (1, 5); LP—Det.: Rowe (1, 5), Chicago: Root (3, 6), Carleton (4).

1936—New York A.L. 4 (Joe McCarthy); New York N.L. 2 (Bill Terry). WP—New York A.L.: Gomez (2, 6), Hadley (3), Pearson (4); New York N.L.: Hubbell (1), Schumacher (5); LP—New York A.L.: Ruffing (1), Malone (5); New York N.L.: Schumacher (2), Fitzsimmons (3, 6), Hubbell (4).

1937—New York A.L. 4 (Joe McCarthy); New York N.L. 1 (Bill Terry). WP—New York A.L.: Gomez (1, 5), Ruffing (2), Pearson (3); New York N.L.: Hubbell (4). LP—New York A.L.: Hadley (4); New York N.L.: Hubbell (1), Melton (2, 5), Schumacher (3).

1938—New York A.L. 4 (Joe McCarthy); Chicago N.L. 0 (Gabby Hartnett). WP—Ruffing (1, 4), Gomez (2), Pearson (3) LP—Lee (1, 4), Dean (2), Bryant (3).

1939—New York A.L. 4 (Joe McCarthy); Cincinnati N.L. 0 (Bill McKechnie). WP—Ruffing (1), Pearson (2), Hadley (3), Murphy (4). LP—Derringer (1), Walters (2, 4), Thompson (3).

1940—Cincinnati N.L. 4 (Bill McKechnie); Detroit A.L. 3 (Del Baker). WP—Cincinnati: Walters (2, 6), Derringer (4, 7); Det.: Newsom (1, 5), Bridges (3). LP—Cincinnati: Derringer (1), Turner (3), Thompson (5); Det.: Rowe (2, 6), Trout (4), Newsom (7).

1941—New York A.L. 4 (Joe McCarthy); Brooklyn N.L. 1 (Leo Durocher). WP—New York: Ruffing (1), Russo (3), Murphy (4), Bonham (5). LP—Bklyn: Wyatt (2). LP—New York: Chandler (2); Bklyn: Davis (1), Casey (3, 4), Wyatt (5).

1942—St. Louis N.L. 4 (Billy Southworth); New York A.L. 1 (Joe McCarthy). WP—St. Louis: Beazley (2, 5), White (3), Lanier (4); New York: Ruffing (1). LP—St. Louis: Coo-

per (1); New York: Bonham (2), Chandler (3), Donald (4), Ruffing (5).

1943—New York A.L. 4 (Joe McCarthy); St. Louis N.L. 1 (Billy Southworth). WP—New York: Chandler (1, 5), Borowy (3), Russo (4); St. Louis: Cooper (2). LP—New York: Bonham (2); St. Louis: Lanier (1), Brazle (3), Brecheen (4), Cooper (5).

1944—St. Louis N.L. 4 (Billy Southworth); St. Louis A.L. 2 (Luke Sewell). WP—St. Louis N.L.: Donnelly (2), Brecheen (4), Cooper (5), Lanier (6); St. Louis A.L.: Galehouse (1), Kramer (3). LP—St. Louis N.L.: Cooper (1), Wilks (3); St. Louis A.L.: Muncrief (2), Jakucki (4), Galehouse (5), Potter (6).

1945—Detroit A.L. 4 (Steve O'Neill); Chicago N.L. 3 (Charles Grimm). WP—Det.: Trucks (2), Trout (4), Newhouser (5, 7); Chicago: Borowy (1, 6), Passeau (3). LP—Det.: Newhouser (1), Overmire (3), Trout (6); Chicago: Wyse (2), Prim (4), Borowy (5, 7).

1946—St. Louis N.L. 4 (Eddie Dyer); Boston A.L. 3 (Joe Cronin). WP—St. Louis: Brecheen (2, 6, 7), Munger (4); Boston: Johnson (1), Ferriss (3), Dobson (5). LP—St. Louis: Pollet (1), Dickson (3), Brazle (5); Boston: Harris (2, 6), Hughson (4), Klinger (7).

1947—New York A.L. 4 (Bucky Harris); Brooklyn N.L. 3 (Burt Shotton). WP—New York: Shea (1, 5), Reynolds (2), Page (7); Brooklyn: Casey (3, 4), Branca (6). LP—New York: Newsom (3), Bevens (4), Page (6); Brooklyn: Branca (1), Lombardi (2), Barney (5), Gregg (7).

1948—Cleveland A.L. 4 (Lou Boudreau); Boston N.L. 2 (Billy Southworth). WP—Cleve.: Lemon (2, 6), Bearden (3), Gromek (4); Boston: Sain (1), Spahn (5). LP—Cleve.: Feller (1, 5); Boston: Spahn (2), Bickford (3), Sain (4), Voiselle (6).

1949—New York A.L. 4 (Casey Stengel); Brooklyn N.L. 1 (Burt Shotton). WP—New York: Reynolds (1), Page (3), Lopat (4), Raschi (5); Brooklyn: Roe (2). LP—New York: Raschi (2); Brooklyn: Newcombe (1, 4), Branca (3), Barney (5).

1950—New York A.L. 4 (Casey Stengel); Philadelphia N.L. 0 (Eddie Sawyer). WP—Raschi (1), Reynolds (2), Ferrick (3), Ford (4). LP—Konstanty (1), Roberts (2), Meyer (3), Miller (4).

1951—New York A.L. 4 (Casey Stengel); New York N.L. 2 (Leo Durocher). WP—New York A.L.: Lopat (2, 5), Reynolds (4), Raschi (6); New York N.L.: Koslo (1), Hearn (3). LP—New York A.L.: Reynolds (1), Raschi (3); New York N.L.: Jansen (2, 5), Maglie (4), Koslo (6).

1952—New York A.L. 4 (Casey Stengel); Brooklyn N.L. 3 (Chuck Dressen). WP—New York A.L.: Raschi (2, 6), Reynolds (4, 7); Brooklyn: Black (1), Roe (3), Erskine (5). LP—New York: Reynolds (1), Lopat (3), Sain (5); Brooklyn: Erskine (2), Black (4, 7), Loes (6).

1953—New York A.L. 4 (Casey Stengel); Brooklyn N.L. 2 (Chuck Dressen). WP—New York: Sain (1), Lopat (2), McDonald (5), Reynolds (6); Brooklyn: Erskine (3), Loes (4). LP—New York: Raschi (3), Ford (4); Brooklyn: Labine (1, 6), Roe (2), Podres (5).

1954—New York N.L. 4 (Leo Durocher); Cleveland A.L. 0 (Al Lopez). WP—Grissom (1), Antonelli (2), Gomez (3), Liddle (4). LP—Lemon (1, 4), Wynn (2), Garcia (3).

1955—Brooklyn N.L. 4 (Walter Alston); New York A.L. 3 (Casey Stengel). WP—Brooklyn: Podres (3, 7), Labine (4), Craig (5); New York: Ford (1, 6), Byrne (3). LP—Brooklyn: Newcombe (1), Loes (2), Spooner (6); New York: Turley (3), Larsen (4), Grim (5), Byrne (7).

1956—New York A.L. 4 (Casey Stengel); Brooklyn N.L. 3 (Walter Alston). WP—New York: Ford (3), Sturdivant (4), Larsen (5), Kucks (7); Brooklyn: Maglie (1), Bessent (2), Labine (6). LP—New York: Ford (1), Morgan (2), Turley (6); Brooklyn: Craig (3), Erskine (4), Maglie (5), Newcombe (7).

1957—Milwaukee N.L. 4 (Fred Haney); New York A.L. 3 (Casey Stengel). WP—Milwaukee: Burdette (2, 5, 7),

Spahn (4); New York: Ford (1), Larsen (3), Turley (6). LP—Milwaukee: Spahn (1), Buhl (3), Johnson (6); New York: Shantz (2), Grim (4), Ford (5), Larsen (7).

1958—New York A.L. 4 (Casey Stengel); Milwaukee N.L. 3 (Fred Haney). WP—New York: Larsen (3), Turley (5, 7), Duren (6); Milwaukee: Spahn (1, 4), Burdette (2). LP—New York: Duren (1), Turley (2), Ford (4); Milwaukee: Rush (3), Burdette (5, 7), Spahn (6).

1959—Los Angeles N.L. 4 (Walter Alston); Chicago A.L. 2 (Al Lopez). WP—Los Angeles: Podres (3), Drysdale (3), Sherry (4, 6); Chicago: Wynn (1), Shaw (5). LP—Los Angeles: Craig (1), Koufax (5); Chicago: Shaw (2), Donovan (3), Staley (4), Wynn (6).

1960—Pittsburgh N.L. 4 (Danny Murtaugh); New York A.L. 3 (Casey Stengel). WP—Pittsburgh: Law (1, 4), Haddix (5, 7); New York: Turley (2), Ford (3, 6). LP—Pittsburgh: Friend (2, 6), Mizell (3); New York: Ditmar (1, 5), Terry (4, 7).

1961—New York A.L. 4 (Ralph Houk); Cincinnati N.L. 1 (Fred Hutchinson). WP—New York: Ford (1, 4), Arroyo (3), Daley (5); Cincinnati: Jay (2). LP—New York: Terry (2); Cincinnati: O'Toole (1, 4), Purkey (3), Jay (5).

1962—New York A.L. 4 (Ralph Houk); San Francisco N.L. 3 (Al Dark). WP—New York: Ford (1), Stafford (3), Terry (5, 7); San Francisco: Sanford (2), Larsen (4), Pierce (6). LP—New York: Terry (2), Coates (4), Ford (6); San Francisco: O'Dell (1), Pierce (3), Sanford (5, 7).

1963—Los Angeles N.L. 4 (Walter Alston); New York A.L. 0 (Ralph Houk). WP—Koufax (1, 4), Podres (2), Drysdale (3). LP—Ford (1, 4), Downing (2), Bouton (3).

1964—St. Louis N.L. 4 (Johnny Keane); New York A.L. 3 (Yogi Berra). WP—St. Louis: Sadecki (1), Craig (4), Gibson (5, 7); New York: Stottlemyre (2), Bouton (3, 6). LP—St. Louis: Gibson (2), Schultz (3), Simmons (6); New York: Ford (1), Downing (4), Mikkelsen (5), Stottlemyre (7).

1965—Los Angeles N.L. 4 (Walter Alston); Minnesota A.L. 3 (Sam Mele). WP—Los Angeles: Osteen (3), Drysdale (4), Koufax (5, 7); Minnesota: Grant (1, 6), Kaat (3). LP—Los Angeles: Drysdale (1), Koufax (2), Osteen (6); Minnesota: Pascual (3), Grant (4), Kaat (5, 7).

1966—Baltimore A.L. 4 (Hank Bauer); Los Angeles N.L. 0 (Walter Alston). WP—Drabowsky (1), Palmer (2), Bunker (3), McNally (4). LP—Drysdale (1, 4), Koufax (2), Osteen (3).

1967—St. Louis N.L. 4 (Red Schoendienst); Boston A.L. 3 (Dick Williams). WP—St. Louis: Gibson (1, 4, 7), Briles (3); Boston: Lonborg (2, 5), Wyatt (6). LP—St. Louis: Hughes (1), Carlton (5), Lamabe (6); Boston: Santiago (1, 4), Bell (3), Lonborg (7).

1968—Detroit A.L. 4 (Mayo Smith); St. Louis N.L. 3 (Red Schoendienst). WP—Det.: Lolich (2, 5, 7), McLain (6); St. Louis: Gibson (1, 4), Washburn (3), LP—Det.: McLain (1, 4), Wilson (3); St. Louis: Briles (2), Hoerner (5), Washburn (6), Gibson (7).

1969—New York N.L. 4 (Gil Hodges); Baltimore A.L. 1 (Earl Weaver). WP—New York: Koosman (2, 5), Gentry (3), Seaver (4); Baltimore: Cuellar (1). LP—New York: Seaver (1); Baltimore: McNally (2), Palmer (3), Hall (4), Watt (5).

1970—Baltimore A.L. 4 (Earl Weaver); Cincinnati N.L. 1 (Sparky Anderson) 1. WP—Baltimore: Palmer (1), Phoebus (2), McNally (3), Cuellar (5); Cincinnati: Carroll (4). LP—Cincinnati: Nolan (1), Wilcox (2), Cloninger (3), Merritt (5); Baltimore: Watt (4).

1971—Pittsburgh N.L. 4 (Danny Murtaugh); Baltimore A.L. 3 (Earl Weaver). WP—Pittsburgh: Blass (3, 7), Kison (4), Briles (5); Baltimore: McNally (1, 6), Palmer (2). LP—Pittsburgh: Ellis (1), R. Johnson (2), Miller (6); Baltimore: Cuellar (3, 7), Watt (4) McNally (5).

1972—Oakland A.L. 4 (Dick Williams); Cincinnati N.L. (Sparky Anderson) 3. WP—Oakland: Holtzman (1), Hunter (2, 7), Fingers (4); Cincinnati: Billingham (3), Grimsley (5, 6). LP—Oakland: Odom (3), Fingers (5),

Blue (6); Cincinnati: Nolan (1), Grimsley (2), Carroll (4), Borbon (7).

1973—Oakland A.L. 4 (Dick Williams): New York N.L. 3 (Yogi Berra). WP—Oakland: Holtzman (1, 7), Lindblad (3), Hunter (6). New York: McGraw (2), Matlack (4), Koosman (5). LP—Oakland: Fingers (2), Holtzman (4), Blue (5). New York: Matlack (1, 7) Parker (3), Seaver (6).

1974—Oakland A.L. 4 (Al Dark); Los Angeles N.L. 1 (Walter Alston). WP—Oakland: Fingers (1), Hunter (3), Holtzman (4), Odom (5). Los Angeles: Sutton (2). LP—Oakland: Blue (2), Los Angeles: Messersmith (1, 4), Downing (3), Marshall (5).

1975—Cincinnati N.L. 4 (Sparky Anderson); Boston A.L. 3 (Darrell Johnson). WP—Cincinnati: Eastwick (2, 3), Gullett (5), Carroll (7); Boston: Tiant (1, 4), Wise (6). LP—Cincinnati: Gullett (1), Norman (4), Darcy (6); Boston: Drago (3), Willoughby (3), Cleveland (5), Burton (7).

1976—Cincinnati N.L. 4 (Sparky Anderson); New York A.L. 0 (Billy Martin). WP—Gullett (1), Billingham (2), Zachry (3), Nolan (4). LP—Alexander (1), Hunter (2), Ellis (3), Figueroa (4).

1977—New York A.L. 4 (Billy Martin); Los Angeles N.L. 2 (Tom Lasorda). WP—New York: Lyle (1), Torrez (3, 6), Guidry (4); Los Angeles: Hooton (2), Sutton (5). LP—New York: Hunter (2), Gullett (5); Los Angeles: Rhoden (1), John (3), Rau (4), Hooton (6).

1978—New York A.L. 4 (Bob Lemon), Los Angeles N.L. 2 (Tom Lasorda); WP—New York: Guidry (3), Gossage (4); Beattie (5), Hunter (6); Los Angeles: John (1), Hooton (2). LP—New York: Figueroa (1), Hunter (4); Los Angeles: Sutton (3, 6), Welch (4), Hooton (5).

1979—Pittsburgh N.L. 4 (Chuck Tanner), Baltimore A.L. 3 (Earl Weaver); WP—Pittsburgh: D. Robinson (2), Blyleven (5), Candelaria (6), Jackson (7); Baltimore: Flanagan (1), McGregor (3), Stoddard (4). LP—Pittsburgh: Kison (1), Candelaria (3), Tekulve (4); Baltimore: Stanhouse (2), Flanagan (5), Palmer (6), McGregor (7).

1980—Philadelphia N.L. 4 (Dallas Green), Kansas City A.L. 2 (Jim Frey); WP—Philadelphia: Walk (1), Carlton (2), McGraw (5), Carlton (6); Kansas City: Quisenberry (3), Leonard (4). LP—Philadelphia: McGraw (3), Christenson (4); Kansas City: Leonard (1), Quisenberry (2), Quisenberry (5), Gale (6).

1981—Los Angeles N.L. 4 (Tom Lasorda), New York A.L. 2 (Bob Lemon); WP—Los Angeles: Valenzuela (3), Howe (4), Reuss (5), Hooton (6); New York: Guidry (1), John (2). LP—Los Angeles: Reuss (1), Hooton (2); New York: Frazier (3), Frazier (4), Guidry (5), Frazier (6).

1982—St. Louis N.L. 4 (Whitey Herzog), Milwaukee A.L. 3 (Harvey Kuenn); WP—St. Louis: Sutter (2), Andujar (3), Stuper (4), Andujar (7). Milwaukee: Caldwell (1), Slaton (4), Caldwell (5). LP—St. Louis: Forsch (1), Bair (4), Forsch (6). Milwaukee: McClure (2), Vuckovich (3), Sutton (6), McClure (7).

1983—Baltimore A.L. 4 (Joe Altobelli), Philadelphia N.L. 1 (Paul Owens); WP—Baltimore: Boddicker (2), Palmer (3), Davis (4), McGregor (5). Philadelphia: Denny (1).

1984—Detroit A.L. 4 (Sparky Anderson), San Diego N.L. 1 (Dick Williams); WP—Det.: Morris (1,4), Wilcox (3), Lopez (5), San Diego: Hawkins (2). LP—Det.: Petry (2), San Diego: Thurmond (1), Lollar (3), Show (4), Hawkins (5).

1985—Kansas City A.L. 4 (Dick Howser), St. Louis N.L. 3 (Whitey Herzog); WP—KC: Saberhagen (3,7) Quisenberry (6), Jackson (3). St. Louis: Tudor (1,4) Dayley (2). LP—KC: Jackson (1), Leibrandt (2), Black (4); St. Louis: Andujar (3), Forsch (5), Worrell (6), Tudor (7).

1986—New York N.L. 4 (Dave Johnson); Boston A.L. (John McNamara) 3 WP—New York—Ojeda (3), Darling (4), Aguilera (6), McDowell (7), Bos: Hurst (1), (5), Crawford (2). LP—New York Darling (1), Gooden (2, 5).

1987—Minnesota A.L. 4 (Tom Kelly); St. Louis N.L. (Whitey Herzog) 3. WP—Minnesota Viola (1, 7), Blyleven (2),

Schatzeder (6), St. Louis: Tudor (3), Forsch (4), Cox (5). LP—Minnesota Berenguer (3), Viola (4), Blyleven (5); St. Louis: Magrane (1), Cox (2, 7), Tudor (6).

1988—Los Angeles N.L. 4 (Tommy Lasorda); Oakland A.L. (Tony LaRussa) 1. WP—Los Angeles: Hershiser (2, 5), Pena (1), Belcher (4); Oakland: Honeycutt (3). LP—Los Angeles: Howell (3); Oakland: Davis (2, 5), Eckersley (1), Stewart (4).

1989—Oakland A.L. 4 (Tony LaRussa); San Francisco N.L. 0 (Roger Craig). WP—Oakland: Dave Stewart (1, 3), Mike Moore (2, 4). LP—San Francisco: Scott Garrelts (1, 3), Don Robinson (4), Rick Reuschel (2).

1990—Cincinnati N.L. 4 (Lou Piniella); Oakland A.L. 0 (Tony LaRussa). WP—Cincinnati: Jose Rijo (1, 4), Rob Dibble (2), Tom Browning (3). LP—Oakland: Dave Stewart (1, 4), Dennis Eckersley (2), Mike Moore (3).

1991—Minnesota A.L. 4 (Tom Kelly); Atlanta N.L. 3 (Bobby Cox). WP—Minnesota: Morris (1,7), Tapani (2), Aguilera (6). Atlanta: Clancy (3), Stanton (4), Glavine (5). LP—Minnesota: Aguilera (1), Gurhtie (4), Tapani (5). Atlanta: Leibrandt (1, 6), Glavine (2), Pena (7).

1992—Toronto A.L. 4 (Cito Gaston); Atlanta N.L. 2 (Bobby Cox). WP—Toronto: Ward (2, 3), Key (4, 6). Atlanta: Glavine (1), Smoltz (5). LP—Toronto: Morris (1, 5). Atlanta: Leibrandt (6), Reardon (2), Avery (3), Glavine (4).

1993—Toronto A.L. 4 (Cito Gaston); Philadelphia N.L. 2 (Jim Fregosi). WP—Toronto: Leiter (1), Hentgen (3), Castillo (4), Ward (6). Philadelphia: Mullholland (2), Schilling (5). LP—Toronto: Stewart (2), Guzman (5). Philadelphia: Schilling (1), Jackson (3), Williams (4, 6).

1994—World Series cancelled due to players' strike.

1995—Atlanta N.L. 4 (Bobby Cox); Cleveland A.L. 2 (Mike Hargrove). WP—Atlanta: Maddux (1), Glavine (2,6), Avery (4). Cleveland: Mesa (3), Hershiser (5). LP—Atlanta: Pena (3), Maddux (5). Cleveland: Hershiser (1), Martinez (2), Hill (4), Poole (6).

1996—New York A.L. 4 (Joe Torre); Atlanta N.L. 2 (Bobby Cox). WP—New York: Cone (3), Lloyd (4), Pettitte (5), Key (6). Atlanta: Smoltz (1), Maddux (2). LP—New York: Pettitte (1), Key (2). Atlanta: Glavine (3), Avery (4), Smoltz (5), Maddux (6).

1997—Florida N.L. 4 (Jim Leyland); Cleveland A.L. 3 (Mike Hargrove). WP—Florida: Hernandez (1, 5), Cook (3), Powell (7). Cleveland: Ogea (2, 6), Wright (4). LP—Florida: Brown (2, 6), Saunders (4). Cleveland: Hershiser (1, 5), Plunk (3), Nagy (7).

1998—New York A.L. 4 (Joe Torre); San Diego N.L. 0 (Bruce Bochy). WP—New York: Wells (1), Hernandez (2), Mendoza (3), Pettitte (4). LP—San Diego: Wall (1), Ashby (2), Hoffman (3), Brown (4).

1999—New York A.L. 4 (Joe Torre); Atlanta N.L. 0 (Bobby Cox). WP—New York: Hernandez (1), Cone (2), Rivera (3), Clemens (4). LP—Atlanta: Maddux (1), Millwood (2), Remlinger (3), Smoltz (4).

2000—New York Yankees A.L. 4 (Joe Torre); New York Mets N.L. 1 (Bobby Valentine). WP—Yankees: Stanton (1, 5), Clemens (2), Nelson (4). Mets: Franco (3). LP—Wendell (1), Hampton (2), Jones (4), Leiter (5). Yankees: Hernandez (3).

WORLD SERIES CLUB STANDINGS
(through 2000)

	Series	Won	Lost	Pct.
Toronto (A)	2	2	0	1.000
Florida (N)	1	1	0	1.000
Pittsburgh (N)	7	5	2	.714
New York (A)	37	26	11	.703
Oakland (A)	6	4	2	.667
Minnesota (A)	3	2	1	.667
Philadelphia (A)	8	5	3	.625
St. Louis (N)	15	9	6	.600
Boston (A)	9	5	4	.556
Los Angeles (N)	9	5	4	.556
Cincinnati (N)	9	5	4	.556
New York (N-Mets)	4	2	2	.500
Milwaukee (N)	2	1	1	.500
Boston (N)	2	1	1	.500
Chicago (A)	4	2	2	.500
Baltimore (A)	6	3	3	.500
Kansas City (A)	2	1	1	.500

	Series	Won	Lost	Pct.
Detroit (A)	9	4	5	.444
Cleveland (A)	5	2	3	.400
New York (N-Giants)	14	5	9	.357
Washington (A)	3	1	2	.333
Atlanta (N)	5	1	4	.200
Philadelphia (N)	5	1	4	.200
Chicago (N)	10	2	8	.200
Brooklyn (N)	9	1	8	.111
St. Louis (A)	1	0	1	.000
San Francisco (N)	2	0	2	.000
Milwaukee (A)	1	0	1	.000
San Diego (N)	2	0	2	.000

Recapitulation	Won
American League	56
National League	38

LIFETIME WORLD SERIES RECORDS
(through 2000)

Most hits—71, Yogi Berra, New York A.L., 1947, 1949–53, 1955–58, 1960–63.

Most runs—42, Mickey Mantle, New York A.L., 1951–53, 1955–58, 1960–64.

Most runs batted in—40, Mickey Mantle, New York A.L., 1951–53, 1955–58, 1960–64.

Most home runs—18, Mickey Mantle, New York A.L., 1951–53, 1955–58, 1960–64.

Most bases on balls—43, Mickey Mantle, New York A.L., 1951–53, 1955–58, 1960–64.

Most strikeouts—54, Mickey Mantle, New York A.L., 1951–53, 1955–58, 1960–64.

Most stolen bases—14, Eddie Collins, Philadelphia A.L. 1910–11, 13–14; Chicago A.L., 1917, 1919. Lou Brock, St. Louis N.L., 1964, 67–68.

Most victories, pitcher—10, Whitey Ford, New York A.L., 1950, 1953, 1955–58, 1960–64.

Most times member of winning team—10, Yogi Berra, New York A.L., 1947, 1949–53, 1956, 1958, 1961–62.

Most victories, no defeats—6, Vernon Gomez, New York A.L., 1932, 1936(2), 1937(2), 1938.

Most shutouts—4, Christy Mathewson, New York N.L., 1905 (3), 1913.

Most innings pitched—146, Whitey Ford, New York A.L., 1950, 1953, 1955–58, 1960–1964

Most consecutive scoreless innings—33⅔, Whitey Ford, New York A.L., 1960 (18), 1961 (14), 1962 (1⅔).

Most strikeouts by pitcher—94, Whitey Ford, New York A.L., 1950, 1953, 1955–58, 1960–64.

SINGLE GAME AND SINGLE SERIES RECORDS
(through 2000)

Most hits game—5, Paul Molitor, Milwaukee A.L., first game vs. St. Louis N.L., 1982.

Most 4-hit games, series—2, Robin Yount, Milwaukee A.L., first and fifth games vs. St. Louis N.L., 1982.

Most hits inning—2, held by 17 players.

Most hits series—13 (7 games) Bobby Richardson, New York A.L., 1964; Lou Brock, St. Louis N.L., 1968; Marty Barrett, Boston A.L., 1986.

Most home runs, series—5 (6 games) Reggie Jackson, New York A.L., 1977; 4 (7 games) Babe Ruth, New York A.L., 1926; Duke Snider, Brooklyn N.L., 1952, 1955; Hank Bauer, New York A.L., 1958; Gene Tenace, Oakland A.L., 1972; 4 (4 games) Lou Gehrig, New York A.L., 1928; 4 (6 games) Willie Aikens, Kansas City A.L., 1980.

Most home runs, game—3, Babe Ruth, New York A.L., 1926 and 1928; Reggie Jackson, New York A.L., 1977.

Most strikeouts—12 (6 games) Willie Wilson, Kansas City A.L., 1980; 11 (7 games) Ed Mathews, Milwaukee N.L., 1958; Wayne Garrett, New York N.L., 1973; 9 (5 games) Carmelo Martinez, San Diego N.L., 1984; 7 (4 games) Bob Muesel, New York A.L., 1927; Ken Caminiti, San Diego N.L., 1998.

Most stolen bases, game—3, Honus Wagner, Pittsburgh N.L., 1909; Willie Davis, Los Angeles N.L., 1965; Lou Brock, St. Louis N.L., 1967 and 1968.

Most strikeouts by pitcher, game—17, Bob Gibson, St. Louis N.L. 1968.

Most strikeouts by pitcher in succession—6, Horace Eller, Cincinnati N.L., 1919; Moe Drabowsky, Baltimore A.L., 1966.

Most strikeouts by pitcher, series—35 (7 games) Bob Gibson, St. Louis N.L., 1968; 23 (4 games) Sandy Koufax, Los Angeles N.L., 1963; 20 (6 games) Chief Bender, Philadelphia A.L., 1911; 18 (5 games) Christy Mathewson, New York N.L., 1905.

Most bases on balls, series—11 (7 games) Babe Ruth, New York A.L., 1926; Gene Tenace, Oakland A.L., 1973; 9 (6 games) Willie Randolph, New York A.L., 1981; 7 (5 games) James Sheckard, Chicago N.L., 1910; Mickey Cochrane, Philadelphia A.L., 1929; Joe Gordon, New York A.L., 1941; 7 (4 games) Hank Thompson, New York N.L., 1954.

Most consecutive scoreless innings one series—27, Christy Mathewson, New York N.L., 1905.

AMERICAN LEAGUE HOME RUN CHAMPIONS

Year	Player, team	No.	Year	Player, team	No.	Year	Player, team	No.
1901	Nap Lajoie, Philadelphia	13	1937	Joe DiMaggio, New York	46	1970	Frank Howard, Washington	44
1902	Ralph Seybold, Philadelphia	16	1938	Hank Greenberg, Detroit	58	1971	Bill Melton, Chicago	33
1903	Buck Freeman, Boston	13	1939	Jimmie Foxx, Boston	35	1972	Dick Allen, Chicago	37
1904	Harry Davis, Philadelphia	10	1940	Hank Greenberg, Detroit	41	1973	Reggie Jackson, Oakland	32
1905	Harry Davis, Philadelphia	8	1941	Ted Williams, Boston	37	1974	Dick Allen, Chicago	32
1906	Harry Davis, Philadelphia	12	1942	Ted Williams, Boston	36	1975	Reggie Jackson, Oakland;	36
1907	Harry Davis, Philadelphia	8	1943	Rudy York, Detroit	34		George Scott, Milwaukee	
1908	Sam Crawford, Detroit	7	1944	Nick Etten, New York	22	1976	Graig Nettles, New York	32
1909	Ty Cobb, Detroit	9	1945	Vern Stephens, St. Louis	24	1977	Jim Rice, Boston	39
1910	J. Garland Stahl, Boston	10	1946	Hank Greenberg, Detroit	44	1978	Jim Rice, Boston	46
1911	Franklin Baker, Philadelphia	9	1947	Ted Williams, Boston	32	1979	Gorman Thomas, Milwaukee	45
1912	Franklin Baker, Philadelphia	10	1948	Joe DiMaggio, New York	39	1980	Reggie Jackson, New York;	41
1913	Franklin Baker, Philadelphia	12	1949	Ted Williams, Boston	43		Ben Oglivie, Milwaukee	
1914	Franklin Baker, Philadelphia;	8	1950	Al Rosen, Cleveland	37	1981[1]	Tony Armas, Oakland;	22
	Sam Crawford, Detroit		1951	Gus Zernial,	33		Dwight Evans, Boston;	
1915	Robert Roth,	7		Chicago-Philadelphia			Bobby Grich, California;	
	Chicago-Cleveland		1952	Larry Doby, Cleveland	32		Eddie Murray, Baltimore (tie)	
1916	Wally Pipp, New York	12	1953	Al Rosen, Cleveland	43	1982	Gorman Thomas,	39
1917	Wally Pipp, New York	9	1954	Larry Doby, Cleveland	32		Milwaukee; Reggie Jackson,	
1918	Babe Ruth, Boston;	11	1955	Mickey Mantle, New York	37		California	
	Clarence Walker,		1956	Mickey Mantle, New York	52	1983	Jim Rice, Boston	39
	Philadelphia		1957	Roy Sievers, Washington	42	1984	Tony Armas, Boston	43
1919	Babe Ruth, Boston	29	1958	Mickey Mantle, New York	42	1985	Darrell Evans, Detroit	40
1920	Babe Ruth, New York	54	1959	Rocky Colavito, Cleveland;	42	1986	Jesse Barfield, Toronto	40
1921	Babe Ruth, New York	59		Harmon Killebrew,		1987	Mark McGwire, Oakland	49
1922	Ken Williams, St. Louis	39		Washington		1988	Jose Canseco, Oakland	42
1923	Babe Ruth, New York	41	1960	Mickey Mantle, New York	40	1989	Fred McGriff, Toronto	36
1924	Babe Ruth, New York	46	1961	Roger Maris, New York	61	1990	Cecil Fielder, Detroit	51
1925	Bob Meusel, New York	33	1962	Harmon Killebrew,	48	1991	Jose Canseco, Oakland;	44
1926	Babe Ruth, New York	47		Minnesota			Cecil Fielder, Detroit (tie)	
1927	Babe Ruth, New York	60	1963	Harmon Killebrew,	45	1992	Juan Gonzalez, Texas	43
1928	Babe Ruth, New York	54		Minnesota		1993	Juan Gonzalez, Texas	46
1929	Babe Ruth, New York	46	1964	Harmon Killebrew,	49	1994[2]	Ken Griffey, Jr., Seattle	40
1930	Babe Ruth, New York	49		Minnesota		1995	Albert Belle, Cleveland	50
1931	Lou Gehrig, New York; Babe	46	1965	Tony Conigliaro, Boston	32	1996	Mark McGwire, Oakland	52
	Ruth, New York		1966	Frank Robinson, Baltimore	49	1997	Ken Griffey, Jr., Seattle	56
1932	Jimmie Foxx, hiladelphia	58	1967	Carl Yastrzemski, Boston;	44	1998	Ken Griffey, Jr., Seattle	56
1933	Jimmie Foxx, Philadelphia	48		Harmon Killebrew,		1999	Ken Griffey, Jr., Seattle	48
1934	Lou Gehrig, New York	49		Minnesota		2000	Tony Glaus, Anaheim	47
1935	Jimmie Foxx, Philadelphia;	36	1968	Frank Howard, Washington	44	2001	Alex Rodriguez, Texas	52
	Hank Greenberg, Detroit		1969	Harmon Killebrew,	49			
1936	Lou Gehrig, New York	49		Minnesota				

1. Split season because of players' strike. 2. Season ended on Aug. 12 because of players' strike.

AMERICAN LEAGUE BATTING CHAMPIONS

Year	Player, team	Avg.	Year	Player, team	Avg.	Year	Player, team	Avg.
1901	Nap Lajoie, Philadelphia	.422	1935	Buddy Myer, Washington	.349	1969	Rod Carew, Minnesota	.332
1902	Ed Delahanty, Washington	.376	1936	Luke Appling, Chicago	.388	1970	Alex Johnson, California	.329
1903	Nap Lajoie, Cleveland	.355	1937	Charley Gehringer, Detroit	.371	1971	Tony Oliva, Minnesota	.337
1904	Nap Lajoie, Cleveland	.381	1938	Jimmie Foxx, Boston	.349	1972	Rod Carew, Minnesota	.318
1905	Elmer Flick, Cleveland	.306	1939	Joe DiMaggio, New York	.381	1973	Rod Carew, Minnesota	.350
1906	George Stone, St. Louis	.358	1940	Joe DiMaggio, New York	.352	1974	Rod Carew, Minnesota	.364
1907	Ty Cobb, Detroit	.350	1941	Ted Williams, Boston	.406	1975	Rod Carew, Minnesota	.359
1908	Ty Cobb, Detroit	.324	1942	Ted Williams, Boston	.356	1976	George Brett, Kansas City	.333
1909	Ty Cobb, Detroit	.377	1943	Luke Appling, Chicago	.328	1977	Rod Carew, Minnesota	.388
1910	Ty Cobb, Detroit	.385	1944	Lou Boudreau, Cleveland	.327	1978	Rod Carew, Minnesota	.333
1911	Ty Cobb, Detroit	.420	1945	George Sternweiss, New York	.309	1979	Fred Lynn, Boston	.333
1912	Ty Cobb, Detroit	.410				1980	George Brett, Kansas City	.390
1913	Ty Cobb, Detroit	.390	1946	Mickey Vernon, Washington	.353	1981[1]	Carney Lansford, Boston	.336
1914	Ty Cobb, Detroit	.368	1947	Ted Williams, Boston	.343	1982	Willie Wilson, Kansas City	.332
1915	Ty Cobb, Detroit	.369	1948	Ted Williams, Boston	.369	1983	Wade Boggs, Boston	.361
1916	Tris Speaker, Cleveland	.386	1949	George Kell, Detroit	.343	1984	Don Mattingly, New York	.343
1917	Ty Cobb, Detroit	.383	1950	Billy Goodman, Boston	.354	1985	Wade Boggs, Boston	.368
1918	Ty Cobb, Detroit	.382	1951	Ferris Fain, Philadelphia	.344	1986	Wade Boggs, Boston	.357
1919	Ty Cobb, Detroit	.384	1952	Ferris Fain, Philadelphia	.327	1987	Wade Boggs, Boston	.363
1920	George Sisler, St. Louis	.407	1953	Mickey Vernon, Washington	.337	1988	Wade Boggs, Boston	.366
1921	Harry Heilmann, Detroit	.394	1954	Bobby Avila, Cleveland	.341	1989	Kirby Puckett, Minnesota	.339
1922	George Sisler, St. Louis	.420	1955	Al Kaline, Detroit	.340	1990	George Brett, Kansas City	.328
1923	Harry Heilmann, Detroit	.403	1956	Mickey Mantle, New York	.353	1991	Julio Franco, Texas	.341
1924	Babe Ruth, New York	.378	1957	Ted Williams, Boston	.388	1992	Edgar Martinez, Seattle	.343
1925	Harry Heilmann, Detroit	.393	1958	Ted Williams, Boston	.328	1993	John Olerud, Toronto	.363
1926	Heinie Manush, Detroit	.378	1959	Harvey Kuenn, Detroit	.353	1994[2]	Paul O'Neill, New York	.359
1927	Harry Heilmann, Detroit	.398	1960	Pete Runnels, Boston	.320	1995	Edgar Martinez, Seattle	.356
1928	Goose Goslin, Washington	.379	1961	Norman Cash, Detroit	.361	1996	Alex Rodriguez, Seattle	.358
1929	Lew Fonseca, Cleveland	.369	1962	Pete Runnels, Boston	.326	1997	Frank Thomas, Chicago	.347
1930	Al Simmons, Philadelphia	.381	1963	Carl Yastrzemski, Boston	.321	1998	Bernie Williams, New York	.339
1931	Al Simmons, Philadelphia	.390	1964	Tony Oliva, Minnesota	.323	1999	Nomar Garciaparra, Boston	.357
1932	Dale Alexander, Detroit-Boston	.367	1965	Tony Oliva, Minnesota	.321	2000	Nomar Garciaparra, Boston	.372
1933	Jimmie Foxx, Philadelphia	.356	1966	Frank Robinson, Baltimore	.316	2001	Ichiro Suzuki, Seattle	.350
1934	Lou Gehrig, New York	.363	1967	Carl Yastrzemski, Boston	.326			
			1968	Carl Yastrzemski, Boston	.301			

1. Split season because of players' strike. 2. Season ended on Aug. 12 because of players' strike.

NATIONAL LEAGUE HOME RUN CHAMPIONS

Year	Player, team	No.	Year	Player, team	No.	Year	Player, team	No.
1876	George Hall, Philadelphia Athletics	5	1896	Ed Delahanty, Philadelphia; Sam Thompson, Philadelphia	13	1920	Cy Williams, Philadelphia	15
1877	George Shaffer, Louisville	3				1921	George Kelly, New York	23
1878	Paul Hines, Providence	4	1897	Nap Lajoie, Philadelphia	10	1922	Rogers Hornsby, St. Louis	42
1879	Charles Jones, Boston	9	1898	James Colins, Boston	14	1923	Cy Williams, Philadelphia	41
1880	James O'Rourke, Boston; Harry Stovey, Worcester	6	1899	John Freeman, Washington	25	1924	Jacques Fournier, Brooklyn	27
			1900	Herman Long, Boston	12	1925	Rogers Hornsby, St. Louis	39
1881	Dan Brouthers, Buffalo	8	1901	Sam Crawford, Cincinnati	16	1926	Hack Wilson, Chicago	21
1882	George Wood, Detroit	7	1902	Tom Leach, Pittsburgh	6	1927	Hack Wilson, Chicago; Cy Williams, Philadelphia	30
1883	William Ewing, New York	10	1903	James Sheckard, Brooklyn	9			
1884	Ed Williamson, Chicago	27	1904	Harry Lumley, Brooklyn	9	1928	Hack Wilson, Chicago; Jim Bottomley, St. Louis	31
1885	Abner Dalrymple, Chicago	11	1905	Fred Odwell, Cincinnati	9			
1886	Arthur Richardson, Detroit	11	1906	Tim Jordan, Brooklyn	12	1929	Chuck Klein, Philadelphia	43
1887	Roger Connor, New York; Wm. O'Brien, Washington	17	1907	David Brain, Boston	10	1930	Hack Wilson, Chicago	56
			1908	Tim Jordan, Brooklyn	12	1931	Chuck Klein, Philadelphia	31
1888	Roger Connor, New York	14	1909	John Murray, New York	7	1932	Chuck Klein, Philadelphia; Mel Ott, New York	38
1889	Sam Thompson, Philadelphia	20	1910	Fred Beck, Boston; Frank Schulte, Chicago	10			
						1933	Chuck Klein, Philadelphia	28
1890	Tom Burns, Brooklyn; Mike Tiernan, New York	13	1911	Frank Schulte, Chicago	21	1934	Mel Ott, New York; Rip Collins, St. Louis	35
			1912	Henry Zimmerman, Chicago	14			
1891	Harry Stovey, Boston; Mike Tiernan, New York	16	1913	Cliff Cravath, Philadelphia	19	1935	Wally Berger, Boston	34
			1914	Cliff Cravath, Philadelphia	19	1936	Mel Ott, New York	33
1892	Jim Holliday, Cincinnati	13	1915	Cliff Cravath, Philadelphia	24	1937	Mel Ott, New York; Joe Medwick, St. Louis	31
1893	Ed Delahanty, Philadelphia	19	1916	Davis Robertson, New York; Fred Williams, Chicago	12			
1894	Hugh Duffy, Boston; Robert Lowe, Boston	18				1938	Mel Ott, New York	36
			1917	Davis Robertson, New York; Cliff Cravath, Philadelphia	12	1939	John Mize, St. Louis	28
1895	Bill Joyce, Washington	17				1940	John Mize, St. Louis	43
			1918	Cliff Cravath, Philadelphia	8	1941	Dolph Camilli, Brooklyn	34
			1919	Cliff Cravath, Philadelphia	12	1942	Mel Ott, New York	30
						1943	Bill Nicholson, Chicago	29

Year	Player, team	No.	Year	Player, team	No.	Year	Player, team	No.
1944	Bill Nicholson, Chicago	33	1963	Hank Aaron, Milwaukee;	44	1982	Dave Kingman, New York	37
1945	Tommy Holmes, Boston	28		Willie McCovey, San		1983	Mike Schmidt, Philadelphia	40
1946	Ralph Kiner, Pittsburgh	23		Francisco		1984	Mike Schmidt, Philadelphia;	36
1947	Ralph Kiner, Pittsburgh;	51	1964	Willie Mays, San Francisco	47		Dale Murphy, Atlanta	
	John Mize, New York		1965	Willie Mays, San Francisco	52	1985	Dale Murphy, Atlanta	37
1948	Ralph Kiner, Pittsburgh;	40	1966	Hank Aaron, Atlanta	44	1986	Mike Schmidt, Philadelphia	37
	John Mize, New York		1967	Hank Aaron, Atlanta	39	1987	Andre Dawson, Chicago	49
1949	Ralph Kiner, Pittsburgh	54	1968	Willie McCovey, San	36	1988	Darryl Strawberry, New York	39
1950	Ralph Kiner, Pittsburgh	47		Francisco		1989	Kevin Mitchell, San	47
1951	Ralph Kiner, Pittsburgh	42	1969	Willie McCovey, San	45		Francisco	
1952	Ralph Kiner, Pittsburgh;	37		Francisco		1990	Ryne Sandberg, Chicago	40
	Hank Sauer, Chicago		1970	Johnny Bench, Cincinnati	45	1991	Howard Johnson, New York	38
1953	Ed Mathews, Milwaukee	47	1971	Willie Stargell, Pittsburgh	48	1992	Fred McGriff, San Diego	35
1954	Ted Kluszewski, Cincinnati	49	1972	Johnny Bench, Cincinnati	40	1993	Barry Bonds, San Francisco	46
1955	Willie Mays, New York	51	1973	Willie Stargell, Pittsburgh	44	1994²	Matt Williams, San Francisco	43
1956	Duke Snider, Brooklyn	43	1974	Mike Schmidt, Philadelphia	36	1995	Dante Bichette, Colorado	40
1957	Hank Aaron, Milwaukee	44	1975	Mike Schmidt, Philadelphia	38	1996	Andres Galarraga, Colorado	40
1958	Ernie Banks, Chicago	47	1976	Mike Schmidt, Philadelphia	38	1997	Larry Walker, Colorado	49
1959	Ed Mathews, Milwaukee	46	1977	George Foster, Cincinnati	52	1998	Mark McGwire, St. Louis	70
1960	Ernie Banks, Chicago	41	1978	George Foster, Cincinnati	40	1999	Mark McGwire, St. Louis	65
1961	Orlando Cepeda, San	46	1979	Dave Kingman, Chicago	48	2000	Sammy Sosa, Chicago	50
	Francisco		1980	Mike Schmidt, Philadelphia	48	2001	Barry Bonds, San Francisco	73
1962	Willie Mays, San Francisco	49	1981¹	Mike Schmidt, Philadelphia	31			

1. Split season because of players' strike. 2. Season ended on Aug. 12 because of players' strike.

NATIONAL LEAGUE BATTING CHAMPIONS

Year	Player, team	Avg.	Year	Player, team	Avg.	Year	Player, team	Avg.
1876	Roscoe Barnes, Chicago	.404	1914	Jake Daubert, Brooklyn	.329	1954	Willie Mays, New York	.345
1877	Jim White, Boston	.385	1915	Larry Doyle, New York	.320	1955	Richie Ashburn, Philadelphia	.338
1878	Abner Dalrymple, Milwaukee	.356	1916	Hal Chase, Cincinnati	.339	1956	Hank Aaron, Milwaukee	.328
1879	Cap Anson, Chicago	.407	1917	Edd Roush, Cincinnati	.341	1957	Stan Musial, St. Louis	.351
1880	George Gore, Chicago	.365	1918	Zack Wheat, Brooklyn	.335	1958	Richie Ashburn, Philadelphia	.350
1881	Cap Anson, Chicago	.399	1919	Edd Roush, Cincinnati	.321	1959	Hank Aaron, Milwaukee	.355
1882	Dan Brouthers, Buffalo	.367	1920	Rogers Hornsby, St. Louis	.370	1960	Dick Groat, Pittsburgh	.325
1883	Dan Brouthers, Buffalo	.371	1921	Rogers Hornsby, St. Louis	.397	1961	Roberto Clemente,	.351
1884	James O'Rourke, Buffalo	.350	1922	Rogers Hornsby, St. Louis	.401		Pittsburgh	
1885	Roger Connor, New York	.371	1923	Rogers Hornsby, St. Louis	.384	1962	Tommy Davis, Los Angeles	.346
1886	King Kelly, Chicago	.388	1924	Rogers Hornsby, St. Louis	.424	1963	Tommy Davis, Los Angeles	.326
1887	Cap Anson, Chicago	.421	1925	Rogers Hornsby, St. Louis	.403	1964	Roberto Clemente,	.339
1888	Cap Anson, Chicago	.343	1926	Gene Hargrave, Cincinnati	.353		Pittsburgh	
1889	Dan Brouthers, Boston	.373	1927	Paul Waner; Pittsburgh	.380	1965	Roberto Clemente,	.329
1890	John Glasscock, New York	.336	1928	Rogers Hornsby, Boston	.387		Pittsburgh	
1891	William Hamilton,	.338	1929	Lefty O'Doul, Philadelphia	.398	1966	Matty Alou, Pittsburgh	.342
	Philadelphia		1930	Bill Terry, New York	.401	1967	Roberto Clemente,	.357
1892	Dan Brouthers, Brooklyn;	.335	1931	Chick Hafey, St. Louis	.349		Pittsburgh	
	Clarence Childs, Cleveland		1932	Lefty O'Doul, Brooklyn	.368	1968	Pete Rose, Cincinnati	.335
1893	Hugh Duffy, Boston	.378	1933	Chuck Klein, Philadelphia	.368	1969	Pete Rose, Cincinnati	.348
1894	Hugh Duffy, Boston	.438	1934	Paul Waner, Pittsburgh	.362	1970	Rico Carty, Atlanta	.366
1895	Jesse Burkett, Cleveland	.423	1935	Arky Vaughan, Pittsburgh	.385	1971	Joe Torre, St. Louis	.363
1896	Jesse Burkett, Cleveland	.410	1936	Paul Waner, Pittsburgh	.373	1972	Billy Williams, Chicago	.333
1897	Willie Keeler, Baltimore	.432	1937	Joe Medwick, St. Louis	.374	1973	Pete Rose, Cincinnati	.338
1898	Willie Keeler, Baltimore	.379	1938	Ernie Lombardi, Cincinnati	.342	1974	Ralph Garr, Atlanta	.353
1899	Ed Delahanty, Philadelphia	.408	1939	John Mize, St. Louis	.349	1975	Bill Madlock, Chicago	.354
1900	Honus Wagner, Pittsburgh	.381	1940	Debs Garms, Pittsburgh	.355	1976	Bill Madlock, Chicago	.339
1901	Jesse Burkett, St. Louis	.382	1941	Pete Reiser, Brooklyn	.343	1977	Dave Parker, Pittsburgh	.338
1902	Clarence Beaumont,	.357	1942	Ernie Lombardi, Boston	.330	1978	Dave Parker, Pittsburgh	.334
	Pittsburgh		1943	Stan Musial, St. Louis	.357	1979	Keith Hernandez, St. Louis	.344
1903	Honus Wagner, Pittsburgh	.355	1944	Dixie Walker, Brooklyn	.357	1980	Bill Buckner, Chicago	.324
1904	Honus Wagner, Pittsburgh	.349	1945	Phil Cavarretta, Chicago	.355	1981¹	Bill Madlock, Pittsburgh	.341
1905	Cy Seymour, Cincinnati	.377	1946	Stan Musial, St. Louis	.365	1982	Al Oliver, Montreal	.331
1906	Honus Wagner, Pittsburgh	.339	1947	Harry Walker, St.	.363	1983	Bill Madlock, Pittsburgh	.323
1907	Honus Wagner, Pittsburgh	.350		Louis-Philadelphia		1984	Tony Gwynn, San Diego	.351
1908	Honus Wagner, Pittsburgh	.354	1948	Stan Musial, St. Louis	.376	1985	Willie McGee, St. Louis	.353
1909	Honus Wagner, Pittsburgh	.339	1949	Jackie Robinson, Brooklyn	.342	1986	Tim Raines, Montreal	.334
1910	Sherwood Magee,	.331	1950	Stan Musial, St. Louis	.346	1987	Tony Gwynn, San Diego	.370
	Philadelphia		1951	Stan Musial, St. Louis	.355	1988	Tony Gwynn, San Diego	.313
1911	Honus Wagner, Pittsburgh	.334	1952	Stan Musial, St. Louis	.336	1989	Tony Gwynn, San Diego	.336
1912	Henry Zimmerman, Chicago	.372	1953	Carl Furillo, Brooklyn	.344	1990	Willie McGee, St. Louis	.335
1913	Jake Daubert, Brooklyn	.350				1991	Terry Pendleton, Atlanta	.319

Year	Player, team	Avg.	Year	Player, team	Avg.	Year	Player, team	Avg.
1992	Gary Sheffield, San Diego	.330	1996	Tony Gwynn, San Diego	.353	2000	Todd Helton, Colorado	.372
1993	Andres Galarraga, Colorado	.370	1997	Tony Gwynn, San Diego	.372	2001	Larry Walker, Colorado	.350
1994[2]	Tony Gwynn, San Diego	.394	1998	Larry Walker, Colorado	.363			
1995	Tony Gwynn, San Diego	.368	1999	Larry Walker, Colorado	.379			

1. Split season because of players' strike. 2. Season ended on Aug. 12 because of players' strike.

MOST VALUABLE PLAYERS
(Baseball Writers' Association selections)

American League

1931	Lefty Grove, Philadelphia	
1932–33	Jimmie Foxx, Philadelphia	
1934	Mickey Cochrane, Detroit	
1935	Hank Greenberg, Detroit	
1936	Lou Gehrig, New York	
1937	Charlie Gehringer, Detroit	
1938	Jimmie Foxx, Boston	
1939	Joe DiMaggio, New York	
1940	Hank Greenberg, Detroit	
1941	Joe DiMaggio, New York	
1942	Joe Gordon, New York	
1943	Spurgeon Chandler, New York	
1944–45	Hal Newhouser, Detroit	
1946	Ted Williams, Boston	
1947	Joe DiMaggio, New York	
1948	Lou Boudreau, Cleveland	
1949	Ted Williams, Boston	
1950	Phil Rizzuto, New York	
1951	Yogi Berra, New York	
1952	Bobby Shantz, Philadelphia	
1953	Al Rosen, Cleveland	
1954–55	Yogi Berra, New York	
1956–57	Mickey Mantle, New York	
1958	Jackie Jensen, Boston	
1959	Nellie Fox, Chicago	
1960–61	Roger Maris, New York	
1962	Mickey Mantle, New York	
1963	Elston Howard, New York	
1964	Brooks Robinson, Baltimore	
1965	Zoilo Versalles, Minnesota	
1966	Frank Robinson, Baltimore	
1967	Carl Yastrzemski, Boston	
1968	Dennis McLain, Detroit	
1969	Harmon Killebrew, Minnesota	
1970	John (Boog) Powell, Baltimore	
1971	Vida Blue, Oakland	
1972	Dick Allen, Chicago	
1973	Reggie Jackson, Oakland	
1974	Jeff Burroughs, Texas	
1975	Fred Lynn, Boston	
1976	Thurman Munson, New York	
1977	Rod Carew, Minnesota	
1978	Jim Rice, Boston	
1979	Don Baylor, California	
1980	George Brett, Kansas City	
1981	Rollie Fingers, Milwaukee	

1982	Robin Yount, Milwaukee	
1983	Cal Ripken, Jr., Baltimore	
1984	Willie Hernandez, Detroit	
1985	Don Mattingly, New York	
1986	Roger Clemens, Boston	
1987	George Bell, Toronto	
1988	Jose Canseco, Oakland	
1989	Robin Yount, Milwaukee	
1990	Rickey Henderson, Oakland	
1991	Cal Ripken, Jr., Baltimore	
1992	Dennis Eckersley, Oakland	
1993	Frank Thomas, Chicago	
1994	Frank Thomas, Chicago	
1995	Mo Vaughn, Boston	
1996	Juan Gonzalez, Texas	
1997	Ken Griffey, Jr., Seattle	
1998	Juan Gonzalez, Texas	
1999	Ivan Rodriguez, Texas	
2000	Jason Giambi, Oakland	

National League

1931	Frank Frisch, St. Louis	
1932	Chuck Klein, Philadelphia	
1933	Carl Hubbell, New York	
1934	Dizzy Dean, St. Louis	
1935	Gabby Hartnett, Chicago	
1936	Carl Hubbell, New York	
1937	Joe Medwick, St. Louis	
1938	Ernie Lombardi, Cincinnati	
1939	Bucky Walters, Cincinnati	
1940	Frank McCormick, Cincinnati	
1941	Dolph Camilli, Brooklyn	
1942	Mort Cooper, St. Louis	
1943	Stan Musial, St. Louis	
1944	Marty Marion, St. Louis	
1945	Phil Cavarretta, Chicago	
1946	Stan Musial, St. Louis	
1947	Bob Elliott, Boston	
1948	Stan Musial, St. Louis	
1949	Jackie Robinson, Brooklyn	
1950	Jim Konstanty, Philadelphia	
1951	Roy Campanella, Brooklyn	
1952	Hank Sauer, Chicago	
1953	Roy Campanella, Brooklyn	
1954	Willie Mays, New York	
1955	Roy Campanella, Brooklyn	
1956	Don Newcombe, Brooklyn	

1957	Hank Aaron, Milwaukee	
1958–59	Ernie Banks, Chicago	
1960	Dick Groat, Pittsburgh	
1961	Frank Robinson, Cincinnati	
1962	Maury Wills, Los Angeles	
1963	Sandy Koufax, Los Angeles	
1964	Ken Boyer, St. Louis	
1965	Willie Mays, San Francisco	
1966	Roberto Clemente, Pittsburgh	
1967	Orlando Cepeda, St. Louis	
1968	Bob Gibson, St. Louis	
1969	Willie McCovey, San Francisco	
1970	Johnny Bench, Cincinnati	
1971	Joe Torre, St. Louis	
1972	Johnny Bench, Cincinnati	
1973	Pete Rose, Cincinnati	
1974	Steve Garvey, Los Angeles	
1975–76	Joe Morgan, Cincinnati	
1977	George Foster, Cincinnati	
1978	Dave Parker, Pittsburgh	
1979	Willie Stargell, Pittsburgh	
1979	Keith Hernandez, St. Louis	
1980	Mike Schmidt, Philadelphia	
1981	Mike Schmidt, Philadelphia	
1982	Dale Murphy, Atlanta	
1983	Dale Murphy, Atlanta	
1984	Ryne Sandberg, Chicago	
1985	Willie McGee, St. Louis	
1986	Mike Schmidt, Philadelphia	
1987	Andre Dawson, Chicago	
1988	Kirk Gibson, Los Angeles	
1989	Kevin Mitchell, San Francisco	
1990	Barry Bonds, Pittsburgh	
1991	Terry Pendleton, Atlanta	
1992	Barry Bonds, Pittsburgh	
1993	Barry Bonds, San Francisco	
1994	Jeff Bagwell, Houston	
1995	Barry Larkin, Cincinnati	
1996	Ken Caminiti, San Diego	
1997	Larry Walker, Colorado	
1998	Sammy Sosa, Chicago	
1999	Chipper Jones, Atlanta	
2000	Jeff Kent, San Francisco	

CY YOUNG AWARD

1956	Don Newcombe, Brooklyn N.L.	
1957	Warren Spahn, Milwaukee N.L.	
1958	Bob Turley, New York A.L.	
1959	Early Wynn, Chicago A.L.	
1960	Vernon Law, Pittsburgh N.L	
1961	Whitey Ford, New York A.L.	
1962	Don Drysdale, Los Angeles N.L.	
1963	Sandy Koufax, Los Angeles N.L.	
1964	Dean Chance, Los Angeles A.L.	

1965	Sandy Koufax, Los Angeles N.L.	
1966	Sandy Koufax, Los Angeles N.L.	
1967	Jim Lonborg, Boston A.L.;	
	Mike McCormick, San Francisco N.L.	
1968	Dennis McLain, Detroit A.L.;	
	Bob Gibson, St. Louis N.L.	

1969	Mike Cuellar, Baltimore A.L. and	
	Dennis McLain, Detroit A.L.	
	(tied); Tom Seaver, New York N.L.	
1970	Jim Perry, Minnesota A.L.;	
	Bob Gibson, St. Louis N.L.	
1971	Vida Blue, Oakland A.L.;	
	Ferguson Jenkins, Chicago N.L.	
1972	Gaylord Perry, Cleveland A.L.;	
	Steve Carlton, Philadelphia N.L.	

1973	Jim Palmer, Baltimore A.L.; Tom Seaver, New York N.L.	1982	Pete Vuckovich, Milwaukee A.L.; Steve Carlton, Philadelphia N.L.	1990 Bob Welch, Oakland A.L.; Doug Drabek, Pittsburgh N.L.
1974	Catfish Hunter, Oakland A.L.; Mike Marshall, Los Angeles N.L.	1983	LaMarr Hoyt, Chicago A.L.; John Denny, Philadelphia N.L.	1991 Roger Clemens, Boston A.L.; Tom Glavine, Atlanta N.L.
1975	Jim Palmer, Baltimore A.L.; Tom Seaver, New York N.L.	1984	Willie Hernandez, Detroit A.L.; Rick Sutcliffe, Chicago N.L.	1992 Dennis Eckersley, Oakland A.L.; Greg Maddux, Atlanta N.L.
1976	Jim Palmer, Baltimore A.L.; Randy Jones, San Diego N.L.	1985	Bret Saberhagen, Kansas City A.L.; Dwight Gooden, New York N.L.	1993 Jack McDowell, Chicago A.L.; Greg Maddux, Atlanta N.L.
1977	Sparky Lyle, New York A.L.; Steve Carlton, Philadelphia N.L.	1986	Roger Clemens, Boston A.L.; Mike Scott, Houston N.L.	1994 David Cone, Kansas A.L.; Greg Maddux, Atlanta N.L.
1978	Ron Guidry, New York A.L.; Gaylord Perry, San Diego N.L.	1987	Roger Clemens, Boston A.L.; Steve Bedrosian, Philadelphia N.L.	1995 Randy Johnson, Seattle A.L.; Greg Maddux, Atlanta N.L.
1979	Mike Flanagan, Baltimore A.L.; Bruce Sutter, Chicago N.L.	1988	Frank Viola, Minnesota A.L.; Orel Hershiser, Los Angeles, N.L.	1996 Pat Hentgen, Toronto A.L.; John Smoltz, Atlanta N.L.
1980	Steve Stone, Baltimore A.L.; Steve Carlton, Philadelphia N.L.	1989	Bret Saberhagen, Kansas A.L.; Mark Davis, San Diego N.L.	1997 Roger Clemens, Toronto A.L.; Pedro Martinez, Montreal N.L.
1981	Rollie Fingers, Milwaukee A.L.; Fernando Valenzuela, Los Angeles N.L.			1998 Roger Clemens, Toronto A.L.; Tom Glavine, Atlanta N.L.
				1999– Pedro Martinez, Boston A.L.; 2000 Randy Johnson, Arizona N.L.

MAJOR LEAGUE LIFETIME RECORDS

(through 2001)

Wins

		W	L	ERA	G
1	Cy Young	511	316	2.63	906
2	Walter Johnson	417	279	2.17	802
3	Grover Alexander	373	208	2.56	696
4	Christy Mathewson	373	188	2.13	635
5	Pud Galvin	365	310	2.85	705
6	Warren Spahn	363	245	3.09	750
7	Kid Nichols	361	208	2.95	620
8	Tim Keefe	342	225	2.62	600
9	Steve Carlton	329	244	3.22	741
10	John Clarkson	328	178	2.81	531
11	Eddie Plank	326	194	2.35	623
12	Nolan Ryan	324	292	3.19	807
13	Don Sutton	324	256	3.26	774
14	Phil Niekro	318	274	3.35	864
15	Gaylord Perry	314	265	3.11	777
16	Tom Seaver	311	205	2.86	656
17	Old Hoss Radbourn	309	195	2.67	528
18	Mickey Welch	307	210	2.71	565
19	Lefty Grove	300	141	3.06	616
20	Early Wynn	300	244	3.54	691
21	Bobby Mathews	297	248	2.85	578
22	Tommy John	288	231	3.34	760
23	Bert Blyleven	287	250	3.31	692
24	Robin Roberts	286	245	3.41	676
25	Ferguson Jenkins	284	226	3.34	664

Leading Batters, by Batting Average
(Boldface indicates player active in 2001)

		G	AB	H	Avg.
1	Ty Cobb	3,035	11,434	4,189	.366
2	Rogers Hornsby	2,259	8,173	2,930	.358
3	Ed Delahanty	1,835	7,505	2,596	.346
4	Tris Speaker	2,789	10,195	3,514	.345
5	Billy Hamilton	1,591	6,269	2,159	.344
6	Ted Williams	2,292	7,706	2,654	.344
7	Dan Brouthers	1,673	6,711	2,296	.342
8	Harry Heilmann	2,147	7,787	2,660	.342
9	Babe Ruth	2,503	8,399	2,873	.342
10	Willie Keeler	2,123	8,591	2,932	.341
11	Bill Terry	1,721	6,428	2,193	.341
12	Lou Gehrig	2,164	8,001	2,721	.340
13	George Sisler	2,055	8,267	2,812	.340
14	Jesse Burkett	2,066	8,421	2,850	.338
15	**Tony Gwynn**	**2,440**	**9,288**	**3,141**	**.338**
16	Nap Lajoie	2,480	9,589	3,242	.338
17	Al Simmons	2,215	8,759	2,927	.334
18	Cap Anson	2,523	10,278	3,418	.333
19	Eddie Collins	2,826	9,949	3,315	.333
20	Paul Waner	2,549	9,459	3,152	.333
21	Stan Musial	3,026	10,972	3,630	.331
22	Sam Thompson	1,407	5,984	1,979	.331
23	Heinie Manush	2,008	7,654	2,524	.330
24	Wade Boggs	2,440	9,180	3,010	.328
25	Rod Carew	2,469	9,315	3,053	.328

Pitchers Active in 2001

		W	L	ERA	G
1	Roger Clemens	280	145	3.10	545
2	Greg Maddux	257	146	2.84	505
3	Tom Glavine	224	132	3.40	469
4	Orel Hershiser	204	149	3.48	510
5	Randy Johnson	209	101	3.13	401
6	Dwight Gooden	194	112	3.51	430
7	David Cone	193	123	3.44	445
8	Chuck Finley	189	158	3.83	492
9	Kevin Brown	180	118	3.18	402
10	Bret Saberhagen	167	117	3.34	399

Players Active in 2001 (3,000 at-bats minimum)

		G	AB	H	Avg.
1	Tony Gwynn	2,440	9,288	3,141	.338
2	Mike Piazza	1,258	4,638	1,507	.325
3	Derek Jeter	936	3,744	1,199	.320
4	Edgar Martinez	1,672	5,902	1,882	.319
5	Frank Thomas	1,550	5,542	1,770	.319
6	Larry Walker	1,527	5,403	1,702	.315
7	Manny Ramirez	1,109	3,999	1,248	.312
8	Jeff Cirillo	1,084	3,937	1,224	.311
9	Alex Rodriguez	952	3,758	1,167	.311
10	Jason Giambi	953	3,398	1,048	.308

MAJOR LEAGUE ALL-TIME PITCHING RECORDS

(through 2001)

Most Games Won—511, Cy Young, Cleveland N.L., 1890–98, St. Louis N.L., 1899–1900, Boston A.L., 1901–08, Cleveland A.L., 1909–11, Boston N.L., 1911.

Most Games Won, Season—59, Hoss Radbourne, Providence N.L., 1884. (Since 1900—41, Jack Chesbro, New York A.L., 1904.)

Most Consecutive Games Won—24, Carl Hubbell, New York N.L., 1936 (16) and 1937 (8).

Most Consecutive Games Won, Season—19, Tim Keefe, New York N.L., 1888; Rube Marquard, New York N.L., 1912.

Most Years Won 20 or More Games—16, Cy Young, Cleveland N.L., 1891–98, St. Louis N.L., 1899–1900, Boston A.L., 1901–04, 1907–08.

Most Shutouts—113, Walter Johnson, Washington A.L., 1907–27.

Most Shutouts, Season—16, Grover Alexander, Philadelphia N.L., 1916.

Most Consecutive Shutouts—6, Don Drysdale, Los Angeles N.L., 1968.

Most Consecutive Scoreless Innings—59, Orel Hershiser, Los Angeles Dodgers, 1988.

Most Strikeouts—5,714, Nolan Ryan, New York N.L., California A.L., Houston N.L., 1968–1988 Texas, 1989–93.

Most Strikeouts, Season—513, Matthew Kilroy, Baltimore A.A., 1886. (Since 1900—383, Nolan Ryan, California A.L., 1973.)

Most Strikeouts, Game—21, Tom Cheney, Washington A.L., 1962, 16 innings. Nine innings: 20, Roger Clemens, Boston A.L., 1986; Kerry Wood, Chicago N.L., 1998.

Most Consecutive Strikeouts—10, Tom Seaver, New York N.L. vs. San Diego, April 22, 1970.

Most Games, Season—106, Mike Marshall, Los Angeles N.L., 1974.

Most Complete Games, Season—75, William White, Cincinnati N.L., 1879. (Since 1900—48, Jack Chesbro, New York A.L., 1904.)

MAJOR LEAGUE INDIVIDUAL ALL-TIME RECORDS

(through 2001)

Highest Batting Average, Season—.442, James O'Neill, St. Louis, A.A., 1887; .438, Hugh Duffy, Boston N.L., 1894 (Since 1900—.424, Rogers Hornsby, St. Louis N.L., 1924; .422, Nap Lajoie, Phil. A.L., 1901)

Most Times at Bat—14,053, Pete Rose, Cincinnati N.L., 1963–78; Philadelphia N.L., 1979–83; Montreal N.L., 1984; Cincinnati N.L., 1984–86.

Most Years Batted .300 or Better—23, Ty Cobb, Detroit A.L., 1906–26, Philadelphia A.L., 1927–28.

Most Hits—4,256, Pete Rose, Cincinnati 1963–79, Philadelphia 1980–83, Montreal 1984, Cincinnati 1984–86.

Most Hits, Season—257, George Sisler, St. Louis A.L., 1920.

Most Hits in Succession—12, Mike Higgins, Boston A.L., in four games, 1938; Walt Dropo, Detroit A.L., in three games, 1952.

Most Consecutive Games Batted Safely—56, Joe DiMaggio, New York A.L., 1941.

Most Runs—2,248, Rickey Henderson, Oakland A.L., 1979–84, 1989–93, 1994–95, 1998; New York A.L., 1985–89; Toronto A.L., 1993; San Diego N.L., 1996, 1997, 2001; Anaheim A.L., 1997; New York N.L., 1999–2000; Seattle A.L., 2000.

Most Runs, Season—196, William Hamilton, Philadelphia N.L., 1894. (Since 1900—177, Babe Ruth, New York A.L., 1921.)

Most Runs Batted in—2,297, Hank Aaron, Milwaukee N.L., 1954–1965; Atlanta N.L., 1966–74; Milwaukee A.L., 1975–76.

Most Runs Batted in, Season—191, Hack Wilson, Chicago N.L., 1930.

Most Home Runs—755, Hank Aaron, Milwaukee N.L., 1954–1965; Atlanta N.L., 1966–74; Milwaukee A.L., 1975–76.

Most Home Runs, Season—162-game season: 73, Barry Bonds, San Francisco N.L., 2001; 70, Mark McGwire, St. Louis N.L., 1998; 66, Sammy Sosa, Chicago N.L., 1998; 65, Mark McGwire, St. Louis N.L., 1999; 64, Sammy Sosa, Chicago N.L., 2001; 63, Sammy Sosa, Chicago N.L., 1999; 61, Roger Maris, New York A.L., 1961. 154-game season: 60, Babe Ruth, New York A.L., 1927.

Most Home Runs with Bases Filled—23, Lou Gehrig, New York A.L., 1927–39.

Most 2-Base Hits—793, Tris Speaker, Boston A.L., 1907–15, Cleveland A.L., 1916–26, Washington A.L., 1927, Philadelphia A.L., 1928.

Most 2-Base Hits, Season—67, Earl Webb, Boston A.L., 1931.

Most 3-Base Hits—309, Sam Crawford, Cincinnati N.L., 1899–1902, Detroit A.L., 1903–17.

Most 3-Base Hits, Season—36, Owen Wilson, Pittsburgh N.L., 1912.

Most Games Played—3,562, Pete Rose, Cincinnati N.L., Philadelphia N.L., Montreal N.L., 1964–86.

Most Consecutive Games Played—2,632, Cal Ripken, Jr., Baltimore Orioles A.L., 1981–1998.

Most Bases on Balls—2,141, Rickey Henderson, Oakland A.L., 1979–84, 1989–93, 1994–95, 1998; New York A.L., 1985–89; Toronto A.L., 1993; San Diego N.L., 1996, 1997, 2001; Anaheim A.L., 1997; New York N.L., 1999–2000; Seattle A.L., 2000.

Most Bases on Balls, Season—177, Barry Bonds, San Francisco N.L., 2001.

Most Strikeouts, Season—189, Bobby Bonds, San Francisco N.L., 1970.

Most Stolen Bases, Lifetime—1,395, Rickey Henderson, Oakland A.L., 1979–84, 1989–93, 1994–95, 1998; New York A.L., 1985–89; Toronto A.L., 1993; San Diego N.L., 1996, 1997, 2001; Anaheim A.L., 1997; New York N.L., 1999–2000; Seattle A.L., 2000.

Most Stolen Bases, Season—156, Harry Stovey, Phil. A.A., 1888. Since 1900: 130, Rickey Henderson, Oakland A.L., 1982; 118, Lou Brock, St. Louis N.L., 1974.

Most Stolen Bases, Game—7, George Gore, Chicago N.L. 1881; William Hamilton, Philadelphia N.L. 1894. (Since 1900—6, Eddie Collins, Philadelphia A.L., 1912.) and Otis Nixon, Atlanta N.L., 1991.

Most Time Stealing Home, Lifetime—50, Ty Cobb, Detroit-Phil. A.L., 1905–28.

ROOKIE OF THE YEAR
(Baseball Writers' Association selections)

American League

1949 Roy Sievers, St. Louis	1967 Rod Carew, Minnesota	1984 Alvin Davis, Seattle
1950 Walt Dropo, Boston	1968 Stan Bahnsen, New York	1985 Ozzie Guillen, Chicago
1951 Gil McDougald, New York	1969 Lou Piniella, Kansas City	1986 Jose Canseco, Oakland
1952 Harry Byrd, Philadelphia	1970 Thurman Munson, New York	1987 Mark McGwire, Oakland
1953 Harvey Kuenn, Detroit	1971 Chris Chambliss, Cleveland	1988 Walter Weiss, Oakland
1954 Bob Grim, New York	1972 Carlton Fisk, Boston	1989 Gregg Olson, Baltimore
1955 Herb Score, Cleveland	1973 Alonzo Bumbry, Baltimore	1990 Sandy Alomar Jr., Cleveland
1956 Luis Aparicio, Chicago	1974 Mike Hargrove, Texas	1991 Chuck Knoblauch, Minnesota
1957 Tony Kubek, New York	1975 Fred Lynn, Boston	1992 Pat Listach, Milwaukee
1958 Albie Pearson, Washington	1976 Mark Fidrych, Detroit	1993 Tim Salmon, California
1959 Bob Allison, Washington	1977 Eddie Murray, Baltimore	1994 Bob Hamelin, Kansas City
1960 Ron Hansen, Baltimore	1978 Lou Whitaker, Detroit	1995 Marty Cordova, Minnesota
1961 Don Schwall, Boston	1979 Alfredo Griffin, Toronto	1996 Derek Jeter, New York
1962 Tom Tresh, New York	1979 John Castino, Minnesota	1997 Nomar Garciaparra, Boston
1963 Gary Peters, Chicago	1980 Joe Charboneau, Cleveland	1998 Ben Grieve, Oakland
1964 Tony Oliva, Minnesota	1981 Dave Righetti, New York	1999 Carlos Beltran, Kansas City
1965 Curt Blefary, Baltimore	1982 Cal Ripken, Jr., Baltimore	2000 Kazuhiro Sasaki, Seattle
1966 Tommy Agee, Chicago	1983 Ron Kittle, Chicago	

National League

1949 Don Newcombe, Brooklyn	1967 Tom Seaver, New York	1984 Dwight Gooden, New York
1950 Sam Jethroe, Boston	1968 Johnny Bench, Cincinnati	1985 Vince Coleman, St. Louis
1951 Willie Mays, New York	1969 Ted Sizemore, Los Angeles	1986 Todd Worrell, St. Louis
1952 Joe Black, Brooklyn	1970 Carl Morton, Montreal	1987 Benito Santiago, San Diego
1953 Jim Gilliam, Brooklyn	1971 Earl Williams, Atlanta	1988 Chris Sabo, Cincinnati
1954 Wally Moon, St. Louis	1972 Jon Matlack, New York	1989 Jerome Walton, Chicago
1955 Bill Virdon, St. Louis	1973 Gary Matthews, San Francisco	1990 Dave Justice, Atlanta
1956 Frank Robinson, Cincinnati	1974 Bake McBride, St. Louis	1991 Jeff Baguell, Houston
1957 Jack Sanford, Philadelphia	1975 John Montefusco, San Francisco	1992 Eric Karros, Los Angeles
1958 Orlando Cepeda, San Francisco	1976 Pat Zachry, Cincinnati	1993 Mike Piazza, Los Angeles
1959 Willie McCovey, San Francisco	1976 Bruce Metzger, San Diego	1994 Raul Mondesi, Los Angeles
1960 Frank Howard, Los Angeles	1977 Andre Dawson, Montreal	1995 Hideo Nomo, Los Angeles
1961 Billy Williams, Chicago	1978 Bob Horner, Atlanta	1996 Todd Hollandsworth, Los Angeles
1962 Ken Hubbs, Chicago	1979 Rick Sutcliffe, Los Angeles	1997 Scott Rolen, Philadelphia
1963 Pete Rose, Cincinnati	1980 Steve Howe, Los Angeles	1998 Kerry Wood, Chicago
1964 Richie Allen, Philadelphia	1981 Fernando Valenzuela, Los Angeles	1999 Scott Williamson, Cincinnati
1965 Jim Lefebvre, Los Angeles	1982 Steve Sax, Los Angeles	2000 Rafael Furcal, Atlanta
1966 Tommy Helms, Cincinnati	1983 Darryl Strawberry, New York	

MOST HOME RUNS IN ONE SEASON
(45 or More)

HR	Player/Team	Year	HR	Player/Team	Year
73	Barry Bonds, San Francisco (N.L.)	2001	51	John Mize, New York (N.L.)	1947
70	Mark McGwire, St. Louis (N.L.)	1998	51	Willie Mays, New York (N.L.)	1955
66	Sammy Sosa, Chicago (N.L.)	1998	51	Cecil Fielder (A.L.)	1990
65	Mark McGwire, St. Louis (N.L.)	1999	50	Jimmie Foxx, Boston (A.L.)	1938
64	Sammy Sosa, Chicago (N.L.)	2001	50	Albert Belle, Cleveland (A.L.)	1995
63	Sammy Sosa, Chicago (N.L.)	1999	50	Brady Anderson, Baltimore (A.L.)	1996
61	Roger Maris, New York (A.L.)	1961	50	Sammy Sosa, Chicago (N.L.)	2000
60	Babe Ruth, New York (A.L.)	1927	50	Greg Vaughn, San Diego (N.L.)	1998
59	Babe Ruth, New York (A.L.)	1921	49	Babe Ruth, New York (A.L.)	1930
58	Jimmie Foxx, Philadelphia (A.L.)	1932	49	Lou Gehrig, New York (A.L.)	1934
58	Hank Greenberg, Detroit (A.L.)	1938	49	Lou Gehrig, New York (A.L.)	1936
58	Mark McGwire, Oakland (A.L.), St. Louis (N.L.)	1997	49	Ted Kluszewski, Cincinnati (N.L.)	1954
57	Luis Gonzalez, Arizona (N.L.)	2001	49	Willie Mays, San Francisco (N.L.)	1962
56	Hack Wilson, Chicago (N.L.)	1930	49	Harmon Killebrew, Minnesota (A.L.)	1964
56	Ken Griffey, Jr., Seattle (A.L.)	1997	49	Frank Robinson, Baltimore (A.L.)	1966
56	Ken Griffey, Jr., Seattle (A.L.)	1998	49	Harmon Killebrew, Minnesota (A.L.)	1969
54	Babe Ruth, New York (A.L.)	1920	49	Mark McGwire, Oakland (A.L.)	1987
54	Babe Ruth, New York (A.L.)	1928	49	Andre Dawson, Chicago (N.L.)	1987
54	Ralph Kiner, Pittsburgh (N.L.)	1949	49	Ken Griffey, Jr., Seattle (A.L.)	1996
54	Mickey Mantle, New York (A.L.)	1961	49	Larry Walker, Colorado (N.L.)	1997
52	Mickey Mantle, New York (A.L.)	1956	49	Albert Belle, Chicago (A.L.)	1998
52	Willie Mays, San Francisco (N.L.)	1965	49	Barry Bonds, San Francisco (N.L.)	2000
52	George Foster, Cincinnati (N.L.)	1977	49	Shawn Green, Los Angeles (N.L.)	2001
52	Mark McGwire, Oakland (A.L.)	1996	49	Todd Helton, Colorado (N.L.)	2001
52	Alex Rodriguez, Texas (A.L.)	2001	49	Jim Thome, Cleveland (A.L.)	2001
51	Ralph Kiner, Pittsburgh (N.L.)	1947	48	Jimmie Foxx, Philadelphia (A.L.)	1933

HR	Player/Team	Year		HR	Player/Team	Year
48	Harmon Killebrew, Minnesota (A.L.)	1962		46	Babe Ruth, New York (A.L.)	1924
48	Frank Howard, Washington (A.L.)	1969		46	Babe Ruth, New York, (A.L.)	1929
48	Willie Stargell, Pittsburgh (N.L.)	1971		46	Babe Ruth, New York (A.L.)	1931
48	Dave Kingman, Chicago (N.L.)	1979		46	Lou Gehrig, New York (A.L.)	1931
48	Mike Schmidt, Philadelphia (N.L.)	1980		46	Joe DiMaggio, New York (A.L.)	1937
48	Albert Belle, Cleveland (A.L.)	1996		46	Ed Mathews, Milwaukee (N.L.)	1959
48	Ken Griffey, Jr., Seattle (A.L.)	1999		46	Orlando Cepeda, San Francisco (N.L.)	1961
47	Babe Ruth, New York (A.L.)	1926		46	Jim Rice, Boston (A.L.)	1978
47	Ralph Kiner, Pittsburgh (N.L.)	1950		46	Juan Gonzalez, Texas (A.L.)	1993
47	Ed Mathews, Milwaukee (N.L.)	1953		46	Barry Bonds, San Francisco (N.L.)	1993
47	Ernie Banks, Chicago (N.L.)	1958		46	Jose Canseco, Toronto (A.L.)	1998
47	Willie Mays, San Francisco (N.L.)	1964		46	Vinnie Castilla, Colorado (N.L.)	1998
47	Hank Aaron, Atlanta (N.L.)	1971		45	Harmon Killebrew, Minnesota (A.L.)	1963
47	Reggie Jackson, Oakland (A.L.)	1969		45	Willie McCovey, San Francisco (N.L.)	1969
47	George Bell, Toronto (A.L.)	1987		45	Johnny Bench, Cincinnati (N.L.)	1970
47	Kevin Mitchell, San Francisco (N.L.)	1989		45	Gorman Thomas, Milwaukee (A.L.)	1979
47	Andres Galarraga, Colorado (N.L.)	1996		45	Hank Aaron, Milwaukee (N.L.)	1962
47	Juan Gonzalez, Texas (A.L.)	1996		45	Ken Griffey, Jr., Seattle (A.L.)	1993
47	Rafael Palmeiro, Texas (A.L.)	1999		45	Juan Gonzalez, Texas (A.L.)	1998
47	Jeff Bagwell, Houston (N.L.)	2000		45	Manny Ramirez, Cleveland (A.L.)	1998
47	Troy Glaus, Anaheim (A.L.)	2000		45	Chipper Jones, Atlanta (N.L.)	1999
47	Rafael Palmeiro, Texas (A.L.)	2001		45	Greg Vaughn, Cincinnati (N.L.)	1999

MAJOR LEAGUE BASEBALL—2001

AMERICAN LEAGUE FINAL STANDINGS

EASTERN DIVISION

Team	W	L	Pct	GB
New York Yankees	95	65	.594	—
Boston Red Sox	82	79	.509	13.5
Toronto Blue Jays	80	82	.494	16.0
Baltimore Orioles	63	98	.391	32.5
Tampa Bay Devil Rays	62	100	.383	34.0

CENTRAL DIVISION

Team	W	L	Pct	GB
Cleveland Indians	91	71	.562	—
Minnesota Twins	85	77	.525	6.0
Chicago White Sox	83	79	.512	8.0
Detroit Tigers	66	96	.407	25.0
Kansas City Royals	65	97	.401	26.0

WESTERN DIVISION

Team	W	L	Pct	GB
Seattle Mariners	116	46	.716	—
Oakland Athletics	102	60	.630	14.0
Anaheim Angels	75	87	.463	41.0
Texas Rangers	73	89	.451	43.0

AMERICAN LEAGUE LEADERS: 2001

Batting—Ichiro Suzuki, Seattle	.350
Home runs—Alex Rodriguez, Texas	52
Runs batted in—Bret Boone, Seattle	141
Runs—Alex Rodriguez, Texas	133
Hits—Ichiro Suzuki, Seattle	242
Stolen bases—Ichiro Suzuki, Seattle	56
Doubles—Jason Giambi, Oakland	47
Triples—Cristian Guzman, Minnesota	14
Slugging percentage—Jason Giambi, Oakland	.660

A.L. Pitching

Wins—Mark Mulder, Oakland	21
Earned run average—Freddy Garcia, Seattle	3.05
Strikeouts—Hideo Nomo, Boston	220
Innings pitched—Freddy Garcia, Seattle	238.2
Complete games—Steve Sparks, Detroit	8
Shutouts—Mark Mulder, Oakland	4
Saves—Mariano Rivera, New York	50

NATIONAL LEAGUE FINAL STANDINGS

EASTERN DIVISION

Team	W	L	Pct	GB
Atlanta Braves	88	74	.543	—
Philadelphia Phillies	86	76	.531	2.0
New York Mets	82	80	.506	6.0
Florida Marlins	76	86	.469	12.0
Montreal Expos	68	94	.420	20.0

CENTRAL DIVISION

Team	W	L	Pct	GB
Houston Astros	93	69	.574	—
St. Louis Cardinals	93	69	.574	—
Chicago Cubs	88	74	.543	5.0
Milwaukee Brewers	68	94	.420	25.0
Cincinnati Reds	66	96	.407	27.0
Pittsburgh Pirates	62	100	.383	31.0

WESTERN DIVISION

Team	W	L	Pct	GB
Arizona Diamondbacks	92	70	.568	—
San Francisco Giants	90	72	.556	2.0
Los Angeles Dodgers	86	76	.531	6.0
San Diego Padres	79	83	.488	13.0
Colorado Rockies	73	89	.451	19.0

NATIONAL LEAGUE LEADERS: 2001

Batting—Larry Walker, Colorado	.350
Home runs—Barry Bonds, San Francisco	73
Runs batted in—Sammy Sosa, Chicago	160
Runs—Sammy Sosa, Chicago	146
Hits—Rich Aurilia, San Francisco	206
Stolen bases—Juan Pierre, Colorado	46
Doubles—Lance Berkman, Houston	55
Triples—Jimmy Rollins, Philadelphia	12
Slugging percentage—Barry Bonds, San Francisco	.863

N.L. Pitching

Wins—Matt Morris, St. Louis	22
Earned run average—Randy Johnson, Arizona	2.49
Strikeouts—Randy Johnson, Arizona	372
Innings pitched—Curt Schilling, Arizona	256.2
Complete games—Curt Schilling, Arizona	6
Shutouts—Greg Maddux, Atlanta	3
Saves—Robb Nen, San Francisco	45

American League Division Series

New York Yankees defeated Oakland Athletics,
3 games to 2
Oct. 10—Oakland 5, New York 3
Oct. 11—Oakland 2, New York 0
Oct. 13—New York 1, Oakland 0
Oct. 14—New York 9, Oakland 2
Oct. 15—New York 5, Oakland 3

Seattle Mariners defeated Cleveland Indians,
3 games to 2
Oct. 9—Cleveland 5, Seattle 0
Oct. 11—Seattle 5, Cleveland 1
Oct. 13—Cleveland 17, Seattle 2
Oct. 14—Seattle 6, Cleveland 2
Oct. 15—Seattle 3, Cleveland 1

National League Division Series

Atlanta Braves defeated Houston Astros,
3 games to 0
Oct. 9—Atlanta 7, Houston 4
Oct. 10—Atlanta 1, Houston 0
Oct. 12—Atlanta 6, Houston 2

Arizona Diamondbacks defeated St. Louis Cardinals,
3 games to 2
Oct. 9—Arizona 1, St. Louis 0
Oct. 10—St. Louis 4, Arizona 1
Oct. 12—Arizona 5, St. Louis 3
Oct. 13—St. Louis 4, Arizona 1
Oct. 14—Arizona 2, St. Louis 1

AMERICAN LEAGUE AVERAGES–2001

Team Pitching

	W	L	ERA	SHO	SV	R	SO
Anaheim	75	87	4.20	1	43	730	947
Baltimore	63	98	4.67	6	31	829	938
Boston	82	79	4.15	9	48	745	1,259
Chicago	83	79	4.55	7	51	795	921
Cleveland	91	71	4.64	4	42	821	1,218
Detroit	66	96	5.01	2	34	876	859
Kansas City	65	97	4.87	1	30	858	911
Minnesota	85	77	4.51	8	45	766	965
New York	95	65	4.02	9	57	713	1,266
Oakland	102	60	3.59	9	44	645	1,117
Seattle	116	46	3.54	14	56	627	1,051
Tampa Bay	62	100	4.94	6	30	887	1,030
Texas	73	89	5.71	3	37	968	951
Toronto	80	82	4.28	10	41	753	1,041

Team Batting

	Avg.	AB	R	H	HR	RBI
Seattle	.288	5,680	927	1,637	169	881
Cleveland	.278	5,600	897	1,559	212	868
Texas	.275	5,685	890	1,566	246	844
Minnesota	.272	5,560	771	1,514	164	717
Chicago	.268	5,464	798	1,463	214	770
New York	.267	5,577	804	1,488	203	774
Boston	.266	5,605	772	1,493	198	739
Kansas City	.266	5,643	729	1,503	152	691
Oakland	.264	5,573	884	1,469	199	835
Toronto	.263	5,663	767	1,489	195	728
Anaheim	.261	5,551	691	1,447	158	662
Detroit	.260	5,537	724	1,439	139	691
Tampa Bay	.258	5,524	672	1,426	121	645
Baltimore	.248	5,472	687	1,359	136	663

Individual Pitching
(based on 10 decisions)

	W	L	ERA	IP	H	BB	SO
M. Mulder, Oakland	21	8	3.45	229.1	214	51	153
R. Clemens, New York	20	3	3.51	220.1	205	72	213
J. Moyer, Seattle	20	6	3.43	209.2	187	44	119
F. Garcia, Seattle	18	6	3.05	238.2	199	69	163
T. Hudson, Oakland	18	9	3.37	235.0	216	71	181
P. Abbott, Seattle	17	4	4.25	163.0	145	87	118
J. Mays, Minnesota	17	13	3.16	233.2	205	64	123
M. Mussina, New York	17	11	3.15	228.2	202	42	214
C. Sabathia, Cleveland	17	5	4.39	180.1	149	95	171
B. Zito, Oakland	17	8	3.49	214.1	184	80	205
M. Buehrle, Chicago	16	8	3.29	221.1	188	48	126
E. Milton, Minnesota	15	7	4.32	220.2	222	61	157
A. Pettitte, New York	15	10	3.99	200.2	224	41	164
B. Radke, Minnesota	15	11	3.94	226.0	235	26	137
A. Sele, Seattle	15	5	3.60	215.0	216	51	114
B. Colon, Cleveland	14	12	4.09	222.1	220	90	201
S. Sparks, Detroit	14	9	3.65	232.0	244	64	116
C. Lidle, Oakland	13	6	3.59	188.0	170	47	118
H. Nomo, Boston	13	10	4.50	198.0	171	96	220
R. Ortiz, Anaheim	13	11	4.36	208.2	223	76	135

Individual Batting
(based on 300 plate appearances)

	Avg.	AB	R	H	HR	RBI
I. Suzuki, Seattle	.350	692	127	242	8	69
J. Giambi, Oakland	.342	520	109	178	38	120
R. Alomar, Cleveland	.336	575	113	193	20	100
B. Boone, Seattle	.331	623	118	206	37	141
F. Catalanotto, Texas	.330	463	77	153	11	54
J. Gonzalez, Cleveland	.325	532	97	173	35	140
F. McGriff, Tampa Bay	.318	343	40	109	19	61
A. Rodriguez, Texas	.318	632	133	201	52	135
S. Stewart, Toronto	.316	640	103	202	12	60
J. Conine, Baltimore	.311	524	75	163	14	97
D. Jeter, New York	.311	614	110	191	21	74
I. Rodriguez, Texas	.308	442	70	136	25	65
B. Williams, New York	.307	540	102	166	26	94
C. Beltran, Kansas City	.306	617	106	189	24	101
E. Martinez, Seattle	.306	470	80	144	23	116
D. Mientkiewicz, Minnesota	.306	543	77	166	15	74
M. Ramirez, Boston	.306	529	93	162	41	125
M. Ordonez, Chicago	.305	593	97	181	31	113
M. Sweeney, Kansas City	.304	559	97	170	29	99
R. Sanchez, Kansas City	.303	390	46	118	0	28

NATIONAL LEAGUE AVERAGES–2001

Team Pitching

	W	L	ERA	SHO	SV	R	SO		W	L	ERA	SHO	SV	R	SO
Arizona	92	70	3.87	13	34	677	1,297	Milwaukee	68	94	4.64	8	28	806	1,057
Atlanta	88	74	3.59	13	41	643	1,133	Montreal	68	94	4.68	11	28	812	1,103
Chicago	88	74	4.03	6	41	701	1,344	New York	82	80	4.07	14	48	713	1,191
Cincinnati	66	96	4.77	2	35	850	943	Philadelphia	86	76	4.15	7	47	719	1,086
Colorado	73	89	5.29	8	26	906	1,058	Pittsburgh	62	100	5.05	9	36	858	908
Florida	76	86	4.32	11	32	744	1,119	San Diego	79	83	4.52	6	46	812	1,088
Houston	93	69	4.37	6	48	769	1,228	San Francisco	90	72	4.18	8	47	748	1,080
Los Angeles	86	76	4.25	5	46	744	1,212	St. Louis	93	69	3.93	11	38	684	1,083

Individual Pitching (based on 10 decisions)

	W	L	ERA	IP	H	BB	SO
M. Morris, St. Louis	22	8	3.16	216.1	218	54	185
C. Schilling, Arizona	22	6	2.98	256.2	237	39	293
R. Johnson, Arizona	21	6	2.49	249.2	181	71	372
J. Lieber, Chicago	20	6	3.80	232.1	226	41	148
G. Maddux, Atlanta	17	11	3.05	233.0	220	27	173
R. Ortiz, San Francisco	17	9	3.29	218.2	187	91	169
T. Glavine, Atlanta	16	7	3.57	219.1	213	97	116
D. Kile, St. Louis	16	11	3.09	227.1	228	65	179
W. Miller, Houston	16	8	3.40	212.0	183	76	183
J. Vazquez, Montreal	16	11	3.42	223.2	197	44	208
R. Dempster, Florida	15	12	4.94	211.1	218	112	171
C. Park, Los Angeles	15	11	3.50	234.0	183	91	218
R. Person, Philadelphia	15	7	4.19	208.1	179	80	183
M. Hampton, Colorado	14	13	5.41	203.0	236	85	122
D. Hermanson, St. Louis	14	13	4.45	192.1	195	73	123
R. Oswalt, Houston	14	3	2.73	141.2	126	24	144
S. Reynolds, Houston	14	11	4.34	182.2	208	36	102
K. Rueter, San Francisco	14	12	4.42	195.1	213	66	83
O. Daal, Philadelphia	13	7	4.46	185.2	199	56	107
L. Hernandez, San Francisco	13	15	5.24	226.2	266	85	138

Team Batting

	Avg.	AB	R	H	HR	RBI
Colorado	.292	5,690	923	1,663	213	874
Houston	.271	5,528	847	1,500	208	805
St. Louis	.270	5,450	814	1,469	199	768
Arizona	.267	5,595	818	1,494	208	776
San Francisco	.266	5,612	799	1,493	235	775
Florida	.264	5,542	742	1,461	166	713
Cincinnati	.262	5,583	735	1,464	176	690
Chicago	.261	5,406	777	1,409	194	748
Atlanta	.260	5,498	729	1,432	174	696
Philadelphia	.260	5,497	746	1,431	164	708
Los Angeles	.255	5,493	758	1,399	206	714
Montreal	.253	5,379	670	1,361	131	622
San Diego	.252	5,482	789	1,379	161	753
Milwaukee	.251	5,488	740	1,378	209	712
New York	.249	5,459	642	1,361	147	608
Pittsburgh	.247	5,398	657	1,333	161	618

Individual Batting (based on 300 plate appearances)

	Avg.	AB	R	H	HR	RBI
L. Walker, Colorado	.350	497	107	174	38	123
T. Helton, Colorado	.336	587	132	197	49	146
M. Alou, Houston	.331	513	79	170	27	108
L. Berkman, Houston	.331	577	110	191	34	126
C. Jones, Atlanta	.330	572	113	189	38	102
A. Pujols, St. Louis	.329	590	112	194	37	130
B. Bonds, San Francisco	.328	476	129	156	73	137
S. Sosa, Chicago	.328	577	146	189	64	160
J. Pierre, Colorado	.327	617	108	202	2	55
L. Gonzalez, Arizona	.325	609	128	198	57	142
R. Aurilia, San Francisco	.324	636	114	206	37	97
J. Drew, St. Louis	.323	375	80	121	27	73
P. Lo Duca, Los Angeles	.320	460	71	147	25	90
J. Vidro, Montreal	.319	486	82	155	15	59
C. Floyd, Florida	.317	555	123	176	31	103
K. Millar, Florida	.314	449	62	141	20	85
J. Cirillo, Colorado	.313	528	72	165	17	83
G. Sheffield, Los Angeles	.311	515	98	160	36	100
S. Casey, Cincinnati	.310	533	69	165	13	89
B. Giles, Pittsburgh	.309	576	116	178	37	95

AMERICAN LEAGUE CHAMPIONSHIP SERIES—2001

New York Yankees win series, 4 games to 1

1st Game, at Seattle, Oct. 17, 2001

					R	H	E
New York	010	200	001	—	4	9	0
Seattle	000	010	001	—	2	4	0

Pitchers—New York: Pettitte, Rivera. Seattle: Sele, Charlton, Paniagua. Winner: Pettitte. Loser: Sele. Save: Rivera. Attendance: 47,644.

2nd Game, at Seattle, Oct. 18, 2001

					R	H	E
New York	030	000	000	—	3	9	1
Seattle	000	200	000	—	2	6	0

Pitchers—New York: Mussina, Mendoza, Rivera. Seattle: Garcia, Rhodes, Nelson. Winner: Mussina. Loser: Garcia. Save: Rivera. Attendance: 47,791.

3rd Game, at New York, Oct. 20, 2001

					R	H	E
Seattle	000	027	212	—	14	15	0
New York	200	000	010	—	3	7	2

Pitchers—Seattle: Moyer, Paniagua, Halama. New York: Hernandez, Stanton, Wohlers, Witasick. Winner: Moyer. Loser: Hernandez. Attendance: 56,517.

4th Game, at New York, Oct. 21, 2001

					R	H	E
Seattle	000	000	010	—	1	2	0
New York	000	000	012	—	3	4	0

Pitchers—Seattle: Abbott, Charlton, Nelson, Rhodes, Sasaki. New York: Clemens, Mendoza, Rivera. Winner: Rivera. Loser: Sasaki. Attendance: 56,375.

5th Game, at New York, Oct. 22, 2001

					R	H	E
Seattle	000	000	300	—	3	9	1
New York	004	104	030	—	12	13	1

Pitchers—Seattle: Sele, Halama, Pineiro, Paniagua. New York: Pettitte, Mendoza, Stanton, Rivera. Winner: Pettitte. Loser: Sele. Attendance: 56,370.

Series MVP—Andy Pettitte

NATIONAL LEAGUE CHAMPIONSHIP SERIES—2001

Arizona Diamondbacks win series, 4 games to 1

1st Game, at Phoenix, Oct. 16, 2001

					R	H	E
Atlanta	000	000	000	—	0	3	1
Arizona	100	010	00x	—	2	8	0

Pitchers—Atlanta: Maddux, Remlinger, Karsay. Arizona: Johnson. Winner: Johnson. Loser: Maddux. Attendance: 37,729.

2nd Game, at Phoenix, Oct. 17, 2001

					R	H	E
Atlanta	100	000	250	—	8	8	0
Arizona	000	001	000	—	1	5	1

Pitchers—Atlanta: Glavine, Karsay, Smoltz. Arizona: Batista, Morgan, Swindell, Witt, Kim. Winner: Glavine. Loser: Batista. Attendance: 49,334.

3rd Game, at Atlanta, Oct. 19, 2001

					R	H	E
Arizona	002	030	000	—	5	9	1
Atlanta	000	100	000	—	1	4	1

Pitchers—Arizona: Schilling. Atlanta: Burkett, Reed, Remlinger, Ligtenberg, Rudy Seanez, Millwood, Marquis. Winner: Schilling. Loser: Burkett. Attendance: 41,624

4th Game, at Atlanta, Oct. 20 2001

					R	H	E
Arizona	004	200	014	—	11	12	0
Atlanta	110	000	110	—	4	13	4

Pitchers—Arizona: Lopez, Anderson, Morgan, Swindell, Batista, Kim. Atlanta: Maddux, Remlinger, Ligtenberg, Seanez, Karsay, Marquis. Winner: Anderson. Loser: Maddux. Save: Kim. Attendance: 42,291.

5th Game, at Atlanta, Oct. 21, 2001

					R	H	E
Arizona	000	120	000	—	3	6	1
Atlanta	000	100	100	—	2	7	1

Pitchers—Arizona: Johnson, Kim. Atlanta: Glavine, Karsay, Smoltz. Winner: Johnson. Loser: Glavine. Save: Kim. Attendance: 35,652.

Series MVP—Craig Counsell

AMERICAN LEAGUE PENNANT WINNERS

Year	Club	Manager	Won	Lost	Pct	Year	Club	Manager	Won	Lost	Pct
1901	Chicago	Clark C. Griffith	83	53	.610	1941	New York[1]	Joseph V. McCarthy	101	53	.656
1902	Philadelphia	Connie Mack	83	53	.610	1942	New York	Joseph V. McCarthy	103	51	.669
1903	Boston[1]	Jimmy Collins	91	47	.659	1943	New York[1]	Joseph V. McCarthy	98	56	.636
1904	Boston[2]	Jimmy Collins	95	59	.617	1944	St. Louis	Luke Sewell	89	65	.578
1905	Philadelphia	Connie Mack	92	56	.622	1945	Detroit[1]	Steve O'Neill	88	65	.575
1906	Chicago[1]	Fielder A. Jones	93	58	.616	1946	Boston	Joseph E. Cronin	104	50	.675
1907	Detroit	Hugh A. Jennings	92	58	.613	1947	New York[1]	Stanley R. Harris	97	57	.630
1908	Detroit	Hugh A. Jennings	90	63	.588	1948	Cleveland[1]	Lou Boudreau	97	58	.626
1909	Detroit	Hugh A. Jennings	98	54	.645	1949	New York[1]	Casey Stengel	97	57	.630
1910	Philadelphia[1]	Connie Mack	102	48	.680	1950	New York [1]	Casey Stengel	98	56	.636
1911	Philadelphia[1]	Connie Mack	101	50	.669	1951	New York[1]	Casey Stengel	98	56	.636
1912	Boston[1]	J. Garland Stahl	105	47	.691	1952	New York[1]	Casey Stengel	95	59	.617
1913	Philadelphia[1]	Connie Mack	96	57	.627	1953	New York[1]	Casey Stengel	99	52	.656
1914	Philadelphia	Connie Mack	99	53	.651	1954	Cleveland	Al Lopez	111	43	.721
1915	Boston[1]	William F. Carrigan	101	50	.669	1955	New York	Casey Stengel	96	58	.623
1916	Boston[1]	William F. Carrigan	91	63	.591	1956	New York[1]	Casey Stengel	97	57	.630
1917	Chicago[1]	Clarence H. Rowland	100	54	.649	1957	New York	Casey Stengel	98	56	.636
1918	Boston[1]	Ed Barrow	75	51	.595	1958	New York[1]	Casey Stengel	92	62	.597
1919	Chicago	William Gleason	88	52	.629	1959	Chicago	Al Lopez	94	60	.610
1920	Cleveland[1]	Tris Speaker	98	56	.636	1960	New York	Casey Stengel	97	57	.630
1921	New York	Miller J. Huggins	98	55	.641	1961	New York[1]	Ralph Houk	109	53	.673
1922	New York	Miller J. Huggins	94	60	.610	1962	New York[1]	Ralph Houk	96	66	.593
1923	New York[1]	Miller J. Huggins	98	54	.645	1963	New York[1]	Ralph Houk	104	57	.646
1924	Washington[1]	Stanley R. Harris	92	62	.597	1964	New York	Yogi Berra	99	63	.611
1925	Washington	Stanley R. Harris	96	55	.636	1965	Minnesota	Sam Mele	102	60	.630
1926	New York	Miller J. Huggins	91	63	.591	1966	Baltimore[1]	Hank Bauer	97	53	.606
1927	New York[1]	Miller J. Huggins	110	44	.714	1967	Boston	Dick Williams	92	70	.568
1928	New York[1]	Miller J. Huggins	101	53	.656	1968	Detroit[1]	Mayo Smith	103	59	.636
1929	Philadelphia[1]	Connie Mack	104	46	.693	1969	Baltimore[3]	Earl Weaver	109	53	.673
1930	Philadelphia[1]	Connie Mack	102	52	.662	1970	Baltimore[1, 3]	Earl Weaver	108	54	.667
1931	Philadelphia	Connie Mack	107	45	.704	1971	Baltimore[4]	Earl Weaver	101	57	.639
1932	New York[1]	Joseph V. McCarthy	107	47	.695	1972	Oakland[1, 5]	Dick Williams	93	62	.600
1933	Washington	Joseph E. Cronin	99	53	.651	1973	Oakland[1, 6]	Dick Williams	94	68	.580
1934	Detroit	Gordon Cochrane	101	53	.656	1974	Oakland[1, 6]	Alvin Dark	90	72	.556
1935	Detroit[1]	Gordon Cochrane	93	58	.616	1975	Boston[4]	Darrell Johnson	95	65	.594
1936	New York[1]	Joseph V. McCarthy	102	51	.667	1976	New York[7]	Billy Martin	97	62	.610
1937	New York[1]	Joseph V. McCarthy	102	52	.662	1977	New York[1, 7]	Billy Martin	100	62	.617
1938	New York[1]	Joseph V. McCarthy	99	53	.651	1978	New York[1, 7]	Billy Martin and Bob Lemon	100	63	.613
1939	New York[1]	Joseph V. McCarthy	106	45	.702	1979	Baltimore[8]	Earl Weaver	102	57	.642
1940	Detroit	Delmar D. Baker	90	64	.584						

Year	Club	Manager	Won	Lost	Pct
1980	Kansas City[9]	Jim Frey	97	65	.599
1981*	New York[10]	Gene Michael-Bob Lemon	59	48	.551
1982	Milwaukee[11]	Harvey Kuenn	95	67	.586
1983	Baltimore[1, 12]	Joe Altobelli	98	64	.605
1984	Detroit[1, 13]	Sparky Anderson	104	58	.642
1985	Kansas City[1, 14]	Dick Howser	91	71	.562
1986	Boston[11]	John McNamara	95	66	.590
1987	Minnesota[15]	Tom Kelly	85	77	.525
1988	Oakland[16]	Tony LaRussa	104	58	.642
1989	Oakland[1, 17]	Tony LaRussa	99	63	.611
1990	Oakland[18]	Tony LaRussa	103	59	.636

Year	Club	Manager	Won	Lost	Pct
1991	Minnesota[1, 19]	Tom Kelly	95	67	.586
1992	Toronto[1, 10]	Cito Gaston	96	66	.593
1993	Toronto[1, 12]	Cito Gaston	95	67	.586
1994	Strike ended season Aug. 11. No playoffs, no pennant winner.				
1995	Cleveland[20]	Mike Hargrove	100	44	.694
1996	New York[1, 21]	Joe Torre	92	70	.568
1997	Cleveland[6]	Mike Hargrove	86	75	.534
1998	New York[1, 22]	Joe Torre	114	48	.704
1999	New York[1, 23]	Joe Torre	98	64	.605
2000	New York[1, 24]	Joe Torre	87	74	.540
2001	New York[20]	Joe Torre	95	65	.594

*Split season because of players' strike. 1. World Series winner. 2. No World Series. 3. Defeated Minnesota, Western Division winner, in playoff. 4. Defeated Oakland, Western Division Leader, in playoff. 5. Defeated Detroit, Eastern Division winner, in playoff. 6. Defeated Baltimore, Eastern Division winner, in playoff. 7. Defeated Kansas City, Western Division winner, in playoff. 8. Defeated California, Western Division winner, in playoff. 9. Defeated New York, Eastern Division winner, in playoff. 10. Defeated Oakland, Western Division winner, in playoff. 11. Defeated California, Western Division winner, in playoff. 12. Defeated Chicago, Western Division winner, in playoff. 13. Defeated Kansas City, Western Division winner, in playoff. 14. Defeated Toronto, Eastern Division winner, in playoff. 15. Defeated Detroit, Eastern winner, in playoff. 16. Defeated Boston, Eastern division winner, in playoffs. 17. Defeated Toronto, Eastern Division winner, in playoffs. 18. Defeated Boston, Eastern Division winner, in playoffs. 19. Defeated Toronto, Eastern Division winner, in playoffs. 20. Defeated Seattle Mariners, Western Division winner, in playoffs. 21. Defeated Baltimore Orioles, Eastern Division wild-card team, in playoffs. 22. Defeated Cleveland Indians, Central Division winner, in playoffs. 23. Defeated Boston Red Sox, Eastern Division wild-card team, in playoffs. 24. Defeated Seattle Mariners, Western Division wild-card team, in playoffs.

NATIONAL LEAGUE PENNANT WINNERS

Year	Club	Manager	Won	Lost	Pct
1876	Chicago	Albert G. Spalding	52	14	.788
1877	Boston	Harry Wright	31	17	.646
1878	Boston	Harry Wright	41	19	.683
1879	Providence	George Wright	55	23	.705
1880	Chicago	Adrian C. Anson	67	17	.798
1881	Chicago	Adrian C. Anson	56	28	.667
1882	Chicago	Adrian C. Anson	55	29	.655
1883	Boston	John F. Morrill	63	35	.643
1884	Providence	Frank C. Bancroft	84	28	.750
1885	Chicago	Adrian C. Anson	87	25	.777
1886	Chicago	Adrian C. Anson	90	34	.726
1887	Detroit	W. H. Watkins	79	45	.637
1888	New York	James J. Mutrie	84	47	.641
1889	New York	James J. Mutrie	83	43	.659
1890	Brooklyn	Wm. H. McGunnigle	86	43	.667
1891	Boston	Frank G. Selee	87	51	.630
1892	Boston	Frank G. Selee	102	48	.680
1893	Boston	Frank G. Selee	86	44	.662
1894	Baltimore	Edward H. Hanlon	89	39	.695
1895	Baltimore	Edward H. Hanlon	87	43	.669
1896	Baltimore	Edward H. Hanlon	90	39	.698
1897	Boston	Frank G. Selee	93	39	.705
1898	Boston	Frank G. Selee	102	47	.685
1899	Brooklyn	Edward H. Hanlon	88	42	.677
1900	Brooklyn	Edward H. Hanlon	82	54	.603
1901	Pittsburgh	Fred C. Clarke	90	49	.647
1902	Pittsburgh	Fred C. Clarke	103	36	.741
1903	Pittsburgh	Fred C. Clarke	91	49	.650
1904	New York[1]	John J. McGraw	106	47	.693
1905	New York[2]	John J. McGraw	105	48	.686
1906	Chicago	Frank L. Chance	116	36	.763
1907	Chicago[2]	Frank L. Chance	107	45	.704
1908	Chicago[2]	Frank L. Chance	99	55	.643
1909	Pittsburgh[2]	Fred C. Clarke	110	42	.724
1910	Chicago	Frank L. Chance	104	50	.675
1911	New York	John J. McGraw	99	54	.647
1912	New York	John J. McGraw	103	48	.682
1913	New York	John J. McGraw	101	51	.664
1914	Boston[2]	George T. Stallings	94	59	.614
1915	Philadelphia	Patrick J. Moran	90	62	.592
1916	Brooklyn	Wilbert Robinson	94	60	.610
1917	New York	John J. McGraw	98	56	.636
1918	Chicago	Fred L. Mitchell	84	45	.651
1919	Cincinnati[2]	Patrick J. Moran	96	44	.686
1920	Brooklyn	Wilbert Robinson	93	61	.604
1921	New York[2]	John J. McGraw	94	59	.614
1922	New York[2]	John J. McGraw	93	61	.604
1923	New York	John J. McGraw	95	58	.621
1924	New York	John J. McGraw	93	60	.608
1925	Pittsburgh[2]	Wm. B. McKechnie	95	58	.621
1926	St. Louis[2]	Rogers Hornsby	89	65	.578
1927	Pittsburgh	Donie Bush	94	60	.610
1928	St. Louis	Wm. B. McKechnie	95	59	.617
1929	Chicago	Joseph V. McCarthy	98	54	.645
1930	St. Louis	Gabby Street	92	62	.597
1931	St. Louis[2]	Gabby Street	101	53	.656
1932	Chicago	Charles J. Grimm	90	64	.584
1933	New York[2]	William H. Terry	91	61	.599
1934	St. Louis[2]	Frank F. Frisch	95	58	.621
1935	Chicago	Charles J. Grimm	100	54	.649
1936	New York	William H. Terry	92	62	.597
1937	New York	William H. Terry	95	57	.625
1938	Chicago	Gabby Hartnett	89	63	.586
1939	Cincinnati	Wm. B. McKechnie	97	57	.630
1940	Cincinnati[2]	Wm. B. McKechnie	100	53	.654
1941	Brooklyn	Leo E. Durocher	100	54	.649
1942	St. Louis[2]	Wm. H. Southworth	106	48	.688
1943	St. Louis	Wm. H. Southworth	105	49	.682
1944	St. Louis[2]	Wm. H. Southworth	105	49	.682
1945	Chicago	Charles J. Grimm	98	56	.636
1946	St. Louis[2]	Edwin M. Dyer	98	58	.628
1947	Brooklyn	Burton E. Shotton	94	60	.610
1948	Boston	Wm. H. Southworth	91	62	.595
1949	Brooklyn	Burton E. Shotton	97	57	.630
1950	Philadelphia	Edwin M. Sawyer	91	63	.591
1951	New York	Leo E. Durocher	98	59	.624
1952	Brooklyn	Charles W. Dressen	96	57	.630
1953	Brooklyn	Charles W. Dressen	105	49	.682
1954	New York[2]	Leo E. Durocher	97	57	.630
1955	Brooklyn[2]	Walter Alston	98	55	.641

Year	Club	Manager	Won	Lost	Pct
1956	Brooklyn	Walter Alston	93	61	.604
1957	Milwaukee[2]	Fred Haney	95	59	.617
1958	Milwaukee	Fred Haney	92	62	.597
1959	Los Angeles[2]	Walter Alston	88	68	.564
1960	Pittsburgh[2]	Danny Murtaugh	95	59	.617
1961	Cincinnati	Fred Hutchinson	93	61	.604
1962	San Francisco	Alvin Dark	103	62	.624
1963	Los Angeles[2]	Walter Alston	99	63	.611
1964	St. Louis[2]	Johnny Keane	93	69	.574
1965	Los Angeles[2]	Walter Alston	97	65	.599
1966	Los Angeles	Walter Alston	95	67	.586
1967	St. Louis[2]	Red Schoendienst	101	60	.627
1968	St. Louis	Red Schoendienst	97	65	.599
1969	New York[2,3]	Gil Hodges	100	62	.617
1970	Cincinnati[4]	Sparky Anderson	102	60	.630
1971	Pittsburgh[2,5]	Danny Murtaugh	97	65	.599
1972	Cincinnati[4]	Sparky Anderson	95	59	.617
1973	New York[6]	Yogi Berra	82	79	.509
1974	Los Angeles[4]	Walter Alston	102	60	.630
1975	Cincinnati[2,4]	Sparky Anderson	108	54	.667
1976	Cincinnati[7,2]	Sparky Anderson	102	60	.630
1977	Los Angeles[7]	Tom Lasorda	98	64	.605
1978	Los Angeles[7]	Tom Lasorda	95	67	.586
1979	Pittsburgh[2,6]	Chuck Tanner	98	64	.605
1980	Philadelphia[2,8]	Dallas Green	91	71	.562
1981*	Los Angeles[2,9]	Tom Lasorda	63	47	.573
1982	St. Louis[2,3]	Whitey Herzog	92	70	.568
1983	Philadelphia[11]	Paul Owens	90	72	.556
1984	San Diego[12]	Dick Williams	92	70	.568
1985	St. Louis[11]	Whitey Herzog	101	61	.623
1986	New York[2,8]	Dave Johnson	108	54	.667
1987	St. Louis[5]	Whitey Herzog	95	67	.586
1988	Los Angeles[2,10]	Tom Lasorda	94	67	.584
1989	San Francisco[12]	Roger Craig	92	70	.568
1990	Cincinnati[2,4]	Lou Piniella	91	71	.562
1991	Atlanta[4]	Bobby Cox	94	68	.580
1992	Atlanta[4]	Bobby Cox	98	64	.605
1993	Philadelphia[3]	Jim Fregosi	97	65	.599
1994	Strike ended season Aug. 11. No playoffs, no pennant winner.				
1995	Atlanta[2,13]	Bobby Cox	90	54	.625
1996	Atlanta[14]	Bobby Cox	96	66	.593
1997	Florida[2,15]	Jim Leyland	92	70	.568
1998	San Diego[16]	Bruce Bochy	98	64	.605
1999	Atlanta[17]	Bobby Cox	103	59	.636
2000	New York[18]	Bobby Valentine	94	68	.580
2001	Arizona[16]	Bob Brenly	92	70	.568

*Split season because of players' strike. 1. No World Series. 2. World Series winner. 3. Defeated Atlanta, Western Division winner, in playoff. 4. Defeated Pittsburgh, Eastern Division winner, in playoff. 5. Defeated San Francisco, Western Division winner, in playoff. 6. Defeated Cincinnati, Western Division winner, in playoff. 7. Defeated Philadelphia, Eastern Division winner, in playoff. 8. Defeated Houston, Western Division winner, in playoff. 9. Defeated Montreal, Eastern Division winner, in playoff. 10. Defeated New York, Eastern Division winner, in playoff. 11. Defeated Los Angeles, Western Division winner, in playoff. 12. Defeated Chicago, Eastern Division champion, in playoff. 13. Defeated Cincinnati, Central Division winner, in playoff. 14. Defeated St. Louis, Central Division winner, in playoff. 15. Eastern Division wildcard Florida defeated Atlanta, Eastern Division winner, in playoff. 16. Defeated Atlanta, Eastern Division winner, in playoff. 17. Defeated New York, Eastern Division wild card team, in playoff. 18. Eastern Division wild card New York defeated Central Division winner St. Louis in playoff.

WORLD SERIES—2001

Arizona Diamondbacks win series, 4 games to 3
Series co-MVPs—Randy Johnson and Curt Schilling

1st Game—Arizona, Oct. 27
Arizona 9, New York 1

New York (A.L.)	AB	R	H	RBI	Arizona (N.L.)	AB	R	H	RBI
Knoblauch lf	4	0	0	0	Womack ss	4	1	0	0
Stanton p	0	0	0	0	Counsell 2b	4	1	1	1
Jeter ss	3	1	0	0	Gonzalez lf	5	2	2	2
Justice rf-lf	3	0	0	0	Sanders rf	3	2	2	0
Spencer ph	1	0	0	0	Finley cf	4	2	1	1
B. Williams cf	4	0	1	1	M. Williams 3b	3	1	1	1
T. Martinez 1b	3	0	0	0	Grace 1b	3	0	1	2
Posada c	3	0	1	0	Miller c	4	0	2	1
Soriano 2b	3	0	0	0	Schilling p	3	0	0	0
Brosius 3b	3	0	1	0	Bell ph	1	0	0	0
Mussina p	1	0	0	0	Morgan p	0	0	0	0
Choate p	0	0	0	0	Swindell p	0	0	0	0
Wilson ph	1	0	0	0					
Hitchcock p	0	0	0	0					
O'Neill ph-rf	1	0	0	0					
Totals	**30**	**1**	**3**	**1**	**Totals**	**34**	**9**	**10**	**8**

							R	H	E
New York	100	000	000	—			1	3	2
Arizona	104	400	00x	—			9	10	0

2B—New York: B. Williams, Brosius; Arizona: Miller, Gonzalez, Grace. HR—Arizona: Counsell (off Mussina), Gonzalez (off Mussina). S—Arizona: Counsell. SF—Arizona: M. Williams. RBI—New York: B. Williams; Arizona: Counsell, Gonzalez 2, M. Williams, Miller, Finley, Grace 2. E—New York: Justice, Brosius. LOB: New York: 5; Arizona: 6.

New York

	IP	H	R	ER	BB	SO	HR	ERA
Mussina (L, 0–1)	3	6	5	3	1	4	2	9.00
Choate	1	3	4	1	1	1	0	9.00
Hitchcock	3	1	0	0	0	6	0	0.00

	IP	H	R	ER	BB	SO	HR	ERA
Stanton	1	0	0	0	0	0	0	0.00

Arizona

	IP	H	R	ER	BB	SO	HR	ERA
Schilling (W, 1–0)	7	3	1	1	1	8	0	1.29
Morgan	1	0	0	0	0	0	0	0.00
Swindell	1	0	0	0	1	1	0	0.00

IBB—Grace (by Mussina), Sanders (by Choate). HBP—Womack (by Mussina); Jeter (by Schilling). Umpires—HP: Steve Rippley, 1B: Mark Hirschbeck, 2B: Dale Scott, 3B: Ed Rapuano, LF: Jim Joyce, RF: Dana DeMuth. T—2:41. Att.—49,646.

2nd Game—Arizona, Oct. 28
Arizona 4, New York 0

New York (A.L.)	AB	R	H	RBI	Arizona (N.L.)	AB	R	H	RBI
Knoblauch lf	4	0	0	0	Womack ss	4	0	0	0
Velarde 1b	3	0	0	0	Counsell 2b	4	0	0	0
Jeter ss	4	0	0	0	Gonzalez lf	2	0	0	0
B. Williams cf	4	0	0	0	Sanders rf	3	2	1	0
Posada c	3	0	1	0	Bautista cf	3	1	2	1
Spencer rf	3	0	1	0	Finley cf	0	0	0	0
Soriano 2b	3	0	1	0	M. Williams 3b	3	1	2	3
Brosius 3b	3	0	0	0	Grace 1b	3	0	0	0
Pettitte p	2	0	0	0	Miller c	3	0	0	0
Sojo ph	1	0	0	0	Johnson p	3	0	0	0
Stanton p	0	0	0	0					
Totals	**29**	**0**	**3**	**0**	**Totals**	**28**	**4**	**5**	**4**

							R	H	E
New York	000	000	000	—			0	3	0
Arizona	010	030	00x	—			4	5	0

2B—Arizona: Bautista. HR—Arizona: M. Williams. RBI—Arizona: Bautista, M. Williams 3. GIDP—New York: Sojo; Arizona: Miller. DP—New York: 1 (Brosius-Soriano-Velarde); Arizona: 1 (M. Williams-Counsell-Grace). LOB—New York: 3; Arizona: 1.

New York	IP	H	R	ER	BB	SO	HR	ERA
Pettitte (L, 0–1)	7	5	4	4	0	8	1	5.14
Stanton	1	0	0	0	0	0	0	0.00
Arizona								
Johnson (W, 1–0)	9	3	0	0	1	11	0	0.00

HBP—Gonzales (by Pettitte). Umpires—HP: Hirschbeck, 1B: Scott, 2B: Rapuano, 3B: Joyce, LF: DeMuth, RF: Rippley. T—2:35. Att.—49,646.

3rd Game—New York, Oct. 30
New York 2, Arizona 1

Arizona (N.L.)	AB	R	H	RBI	New York (A.L.)	AB	R	H	RBI
Counsell 2b	4	0	0	0	Knoblauch dh	4	0	0	0
Finley cf	2	1	0	0	Jeter ss	4	0	1	0
Gonzalez lf	4	0	1	0	O'Neill rf	4	0	2	0
Sanders rf	3	0	0	0	Bellinger pr-lf	0	0	0	0
Durazo dh	3	0	2	0	B. Williams cf	3	1	1	0
M. Williams 3b	3	0	0	0	T. Martinez 1b	4	0	0	0
Grace 1b	3	0	0	0	Posada c	3	1	1	1
Miller c	3	0	0	0	Spencer lf	1	0	0	0
Womack ss	3	0	0	0	Justice ph-lf-rf	2	0	0	0
					Brosius 3b	3	0	1	1
					Soriano 2b	3	0	1	0
Totals	28	1	3	1	Totals	31	2	7	2

				R	H	E
Arizona	000	100	000	— 1	3	3
New York	010	001	000	— 2	7	1

HR—New York: Posada (off Anderson). SF—Arizona: M. Williams. GIDP—New York: O'Neill. SB—Arizona: Sanders; New York: O'Neill. CS—Arizona: Finley. Picked off—Arizona: Counsell. E—Arizona: Womack, Miller, Grace; New York: Soriano. DP—Arizona: 1 (Counsell-Grace); New York: 1 (Posada-Jeter).

Arizona	IP	H	R	ER	BB	SO	HR	ERA
Anderson (L, 0–1)	5⅓	5	2	1	3	1	1	3.38
Morgan	1⅓	1	0	0	0	1	0	0.00
Swindell	1⅓	1	0	0	0	1	0	0.00
New York								
Clemens (W, 1–0)	7	3	1	1	3	9	1	1.29
Rivera (S, 1)	2	0	0	0	0	4	0	0.00

WP—Anderson, Morgan, Swindell. HBP—Sanders (by Clemens). Umpires—HP: Scott, 1B: Rapuano, 2B: Joyce, 3B: DeMuth, LF: Rippley, RF: Hirschbeck. T—3:26. Att.—55,820.

4th Game—New York, Oct. 31
New York 4, Arizona 3 (10 innings)

Arizona (N.L.)	AB	R	H	RBI	New York (A.L.)	AB	R	H	RBI
Womack ss	4	0	2	0	Jeter ss	5	1	1	1
Counsell 2b	2	0	0	0	O'Neill rf	4	1	1	0
Gonzalez lf	3	1	1	0	B. Williams cf	4	0	1	0
Durazo dh	3	0	1	1	T. Martinez 1b	3	1	1	2
Cummings pr-dh	0	1	0	0	Posada c	3	0	0	0
Bautista ph	1	0	0	0	Justice dh	4	0	1	0
M. Williams 3b	4	0	0	1	Spencer lf	4	1	1	1
Finley cf	4	0	1	0	Brosius 3b	4	0	1	0
Sanders rf	4	0	0	0	Soriano 2b	4	0	0	0
Grace 1b	3	1	1	1					
Miller c	3	0	0	0					
Totals	31	3	6	3	Totals	35	4	7	4

					R	H	E
Arizona	000	100	020	0	3	6	0
New York	001	000	002	1	4	7	0

2B—Arizona: Womack, Durazo; New York: Brosius. HR—Arizona: Grace (off Hernandez); New York: Spencer (off Schilling), Martinez (off Kim), Jeter (off Kim). S—Arizona: Counsell 3. RBI—Arizona: Grace, Durazo, M. Williams; New York: Spencer, Martinez 2, Jeter. GIDP—Arizona: Sanders, Womack; New York: Posada. DP—Arizona: 1 (Counsell-Womack-Grace); New York: 3 (Jeter-Soriano-Martinez, Spencer-Posada, Soriano-Jeter-Martinez).

Arizona	IP	H	R	ER	BB	SO	HR	ERA
Schilling	7	3	1	1	1	9	1	1.29
Kim (L, 0–1)	2⅔	4	3	3	1	5	2	10.12
New York								
Hernandez	6⅓	4	1	1	4	5	1	1.42
Stanton	1	2	2	2	0	0	0	6.00
Mendoza	1⅔	0	0	0	0	1	0	0.00
Rivera (W, 1–0)	1	0	0	0	0	0	0	0.00

HBP—Gonzales (by Henderson), Miller (by Hernandez). Umpires—HP: Rapuano, 1B: Joyce, 2B: DeMuth, 3B: Rippley, LF: Hirschbeck, RF: Scott. T—3:31. Att.—55,863.

5th Game—New York, Nov. 1
New York 3, Arizona 2 (12 innings)

Arizona (N.L.)	AB	R	H	RBI	New York (A.L.)	AB	R	H	RBI
Womack ss	6	0	1	0	Jeter ss	5	0	1	0
Counsell 2b	6	0	0	0	O'Neill rf	3	0	0	0
Gonzalez lf	4	0	0	0	B. Williams cf	4	0	1	0
Bautista lf	1	0	1	0	Martinez 1b	5	0	1	0
Durazo dh	4	0	1	0	Posada c	5	1	1	0
M. Williams 3b	4	0	0	0	Spencer lf	4	0	1	0
Finley cf	4	1	3	1	Justice dh	2	0	0	0
Sanders rf	5	0	0	0	Knoblauch pr	2	1	1	0
Grace 1b	3	0	0	0	Brosius 3b	4	1	1	2
Barajas c	5	1	2	1	Soriano 2b	5	0	2	1
Totals	42	2	8	2	Totals	39	3	9	3

					R	H	E
Arizona	000	020	000	000	2	8	0
New York	000	000	002	001	3	9	1

HR—Arizona: Finley (off Mussina), Barajas (off Mussina); New York: Brosius (off Kim). 2B—New York: Posada. S—Arizona: M. Williams; New York: Brosius. RBI—Arizona: Finley, Barajas; New York: Brosius, Soriano. GIDP—Arizona: Grace; New York: Posada, O'Neill. SB—Arizona: Womack. CS—New York: Soriano. DP—Arizona: 2 (Womack-Counsell-Grace, Counsell-Grace); New York: 1 (Soriano-Jeter-Martinez). E—New York: Posada. LOB—Arizona: 9; New York: 8.

Arizona	IP	H	R	ER	BB	SO	HR	ERA
Batista	7⅔	5	0	0	5	6	0	0.00
Swindell	⅓	0	0	0	0	0	0	0.00
Kim	⅔	2	2	2	0	1	1	13.50
Morgan	2⅓	0	0	0	0	0	0	0.00
Lopez (L, 0–1)	⅓	2	1	1	0	0	0	27.00
New York								
Mussina	8	5	2	2	3	10	2	4.09
Mendoza	1	1	0	0	0	0	0	0.00
Rivera	2	2	0	0	1	0	0	0.00
Hitchcock (W, 1–0)	1	0	0	0	0	0	0	0.00

WP—Batista, Mussina. IBB—Grace (by Mussina), Durazo (by Mussina), Finley (by Rivera). Umpires—HP: Joyce, 1B: DeMuth, 2B: Rippley, 3B: Hirschbeck, LF: Scott, RF: Rapuano. T—4:15. Att.—56,018.

6th Game—Arizona, Nov. 3
Arizona 15, New York 2

New York (A.L.)	AB	R	H	RBI	Arizona (N.L.)	AB	R	H	RBI
Knoblauch lf	3	0	0	0	Womack ss	6	2	3	2
Stanton p	0	0	0	0	Bautista cf	4	0	3	5
Jeter ss	2	0	0	0	Finley ph-cf	1	0	0	0
Wilson ss	2	0	0	0	Gonzalez lf	4	1	2	2
B. Williams cf	2	1	1	0	Dellucci pr-lf	2	0	1	0
Posada c	2	0	0	0	Colbrunn 1b	5	2	2	1
Greene c	2	1	1	0	M. Williams 3b	5	1	3	1
Spencer rf	4	0	1	1	Sanders rf	5	2	4	1
Martinez 1b	2	0	1	0	Bell 2b	5	2	1	1
Sojo 1b	2	0	1	1	Miller c	4	3	2	1
Soriano 2b	4	0	1	0	Barajas c	2	0	0	0
Brosius 3b	4	0	0	0	Johnson p	4	2	1	0
Pettitte p	1	0	1	0	Durazo ph	1	0	0	0
Witasick p	0	0	0	0	Witt p	0	0	0	0
Choate p	1	0	0	0	Brohawn p	0	0	0	0
Bellinger ph-lf	2	0	0	0					
Totals	33	2	7	2	Totals	46	15	22	15

				R	H	E
New York	000	002	000 —	2	7	1
Arizona	138	300	000 —	15	22	0

2B—New York: Greene; Arizona: Womack, Sanders, M. Williams, Gonzalez, Miller. RBI—New York: Spencer, Sojo; Arizona: Bautista 5, Womack 2, Sanders, Bell, Johnson, Gonzalez 2, Colbrunn, M. Williams, Miller. GIDP—New York: Greene; Arizona: Gonzalez. E—New York: Soriano. DP—New York: 1 (Soriano-Martinez-Jeter); Arizona: 1 (M. Williams-Bell-Colbrunn). LOB—New York: 7; Arizona: 10.

New York	IP	H	R	ER	BB	SO	HR	ERA
Pettitte (L, 0–2)	2	7	6	6	2	1	0	10.00
Witasick	1⅓	10	9	9	0	4	0	60.75
Choate	2⅔	4	0	0	0	1	0	2.45
Stanton	2	1	0	0	1	3	0	3.60
Arizona								
Johnson (W, 2–0)	7	6	2	2	2	7	0	1.13
Witt	1	0	0	0	1	1	0	0.00
Brohawn	1	1	0	0	1	0	0	0.00

Pettitte pitched to 2 batters in the 3rd. WP—Witasick. IBB—Miller (by Pettitte). Umpires—HP: DeMuth, 1B: Rippley, 2B: Hirschbeck, 3B: Scott, LF: Rapuano, RF: Joyce. T—3:33. Att.—49,707.

7th Game—Arizona, Nov. 4
Arizona 3, New York 2

New York (A.L.)	AB	R	H	RBI	Arizona (N.L.)	AB	R	H	RBI
Jeter ss	4	1	1	0	Womack ss	5	0	2	1
O'Neill rf	3	0	2	0	Counsell 2b	4	0	1	0
Knoblauch ph-lf	1	0	0	0	Gonzalez lf	5	0	1	1
B. Williams cf	4	0	0	0	M. Williams 3b	4	0	1	0

New York (A.L.)	AB	R	H	RBI	Arizona (N.L.)	AB	R	H	RBI
Martinez 1b	4	0	1	1	Finley cf	4	1	2	0
Posada c	4	0	0	0	Bautista rf	3	0	1	1
Spencer lf-rf	3	0	0	0	Grace 1b	4	0	3	0
Soriano 2b	3	1	1	1	Dellucci pr	0	0	0	0
Brosius 3b	3	0	0	0	Miller c	4	0	0	0
Clemens p	2	0	0	0	Cummings pr	0	1	0	0
Stanton p	0	0	0	0	Schilling p	3	0	0	0
Justice ph	1	0	1	0	Batista p	0	0	0	0
Ricvera p	0	0	0	0	Johnson p	0	0	0	0
					Bell ph	1	1	0	0
Totals	32	2	6	2	**Totals**	37	3	11	3

				R	H	E
New York	000	000	110 —	2	6	3
Arizona	000	001	002 —	3	11	0

2B—New York: O'Neill; Arizona: Bautista, Womack. HR—New York: Soriano (off Schilling). RBI—New York: Martinez, Soriano; Arizona: Bautista, Womack, Gonzalez. CS—Arizona: Womack. E—New York: Clemens, Soriano, Rivera. LOB—New York: 3; Arizona: 11.

New York	IP	H	R	ER	BB	SO	HR	ERA
Clemens	6⅓	7	1	1	1	10	0	1.35
Stanton	⅔	0	0	0	0	0	0	3.18
Rivera (L, 1–1)	1⅓	4	2	1	0	3	0	1.42
Arizona								
Schilling	7⅓	6	2	2	0	9	1	1.69
Batista	⅓	0	0	0	0	0	0	0.00
Johnson (W, 3–0)	1⅓	0	0	0	0	1	0	1.04

HBP—Counsell (by Rivera). Umpires—HP: Rippley, 1B: Hirschbeck, 2B: Scott, 3B: Rapuano, LF: Joyce, RF: DeMuth. T—3:20. Att.—49,589.

ROBERTO CLEMENTE AWARD

The Roberto Clemente Award is presented annually to the Major League Baseball player who combines outstanding baseball skills with work in the community.

1971	Willie Mays, San Francisco Giants
1972	Brooks Robinson, Baltimore Orioles
1973	Al Kaline, Detroit Tigers
1974	Willie Stargell, Pittsburgh Pirates
1975	Lou Brock, St. Louis Cardinals
1976	Pete Rose, Cincinnati Reds
1977	Rod Carew, Minnesota Twins
1978	Greg Luzinski, Philadelphia Phillies
1979	Andre Thornton, Cleveland Indians
1980	Phil Niekro, Atlanta Braves
1981	Steve Garvey, Los Angeles Dodgers
1982	Ken Singleton, Baltimore Orioles
1983	Cecil Cooper, Milwaukee Brewers
1984	Ron Guidry, New York Yankees
1985	Don Baylor, New York Yankees
1986	Garry Maddox, Philadelphia Phillies
1987	Rick Sutcliffe, Chicago Cubs
1988	Dale Murphy, Atlanta Braves
1989	Gary Carter, New York Mets
1990	Dave Stewart, Oakland Athletics
1991	Harold Reynolds, Seattle Mariners
1992	Cal Ripken, Baltimore Orioles
1993	Barry Larkin, Cincinnati Reds
1994	Dave Winfield, Minnesota Twins
1995	Ozzie Smith, St. Louis Cardinals
1996	Kirby Puckett, Minnesota Twins
1997	Eric Davis, Baltimore Orioles
1998	Sammy Sosa, Chicago Cubs
1999	Tony Gwynn, San Diego Padres
2000	Al Leiter, New York Mets
2001	Curt Schilling, Arizona Diamondbacks

Extreme Sports

2001 SUMMER EXTREME GAMES
(Philadelphia, Pa., Aug. 11–22, 2001)

BMX Vert: Dave Mirra

Motocross: Kenny Bartram (big air), Tommy Clowers (step up)

Skateboarding: Matt Dove (vert best trick), Rodil de Araujo, Jr. (park), Tony Hawk and Andy Macdonald (vert doubles), Bob Burnquist (vert), Kerry Getz (street), Rick McCrank (street best trick)

Bicycle stunt: Martti Kuoppa (flatland), Stephen Murray (dirt), Bruce Crisman (park)

Inline: Jaren Grob (men's park), Martina Svobodova (women's park), Taig Khris (men's vert), Fabiola Da Silva (women's vert)

Speed climbing: Maxim Stenkovoy defeated Vladimir Zakharov in 10.430 sec (men), Elena Repko defeated Olga Zakharova in 15.904 sec (women)

Freestyle motocross: Travis Pastrana

Wakeboarding: Danny Harf (men), Dallas Friday (women)

Downhill BMX: Brandon Meadows

Street luge: Dennis Derammelaere (best trick), Brent DeKeyser (super mass downhill)

Soccer

The early history of the sport is uncertain. A form of the game in which a leather ball was dribbled was played in China as early as the 4th century B.C. The Romans played a variation of soccer which eventually spread throughout Europe. British schools and universities played soccer (known as football) during the 1800s, however, each school used different sets of rules and the number of players varied. This difficulty was corrected on Oct. 26, 1863, when the Football Association (FA) was formed in London for the purpose of unifying the rules of the game.

The Federation of International Football Associations (FIFA) was created in 1913 as a world governing body to coordinate all of the national associations in the world. The FIFA held the first World Cup Championship tournament in 1930 in Montevideo, Uruguay. Today, soccer is the world's most popular sport. The first FIFA Women's World Cup was held in 1991 with the United States winning the title.

WORLD CUP
(W) indicates Women's World Cup

1930	Uruguay	1954	West Germany	1978	Argentina	1995	Norway (W)
1934	Italy	1958	Brazil	1982	Italy	1998	France
1938	Italy	1962	Brazil	1986	Argentina	1999	United States (W)
1942	No competition	1966	England	1990	West Germany		
1946	No competition	1970	Brazil	1991	United States (W)		
1950	Uruguay	1974	West Germany	1994	Brazil		

WOMEN'S WORLD CUP—1999

QUARTERFINALS
Norway 3, Sweden 1
China 2, Russia 0
United States 3, Germany 2
Brazil 4, Nigeria 3
   (Brazil won in sudden-death "golden goal" overtime)

SEMIFINALS
United States 2, Brazil 0
China 5, Norway 0
THIRD PLACE
Brazil 0, Norway 0 (Brazil won 5–4 on penalty kicks)
CHAMPIONSHIP
United States 0, China 0 (The United States won 5–4 on penalty kicks)

WORLD CUP—1998

QUARTERFINALS
Denmark 2, Brazil 3
Argentina 1, Netherlands 2
France 0, Italy 0 (France won 4–3 in shootout)
Croatia 3, Germany 0

SEMIFINALS
Netherlands 1, Brazil 1 (Brazil won 4–2 in shootout)
Croatia 1, France 2
THIRD PLACE
Croatia 2, Netherlands 1
CHAMPIONSHIP
France 3, Brazil 0

WORLD CUP
All-Time Top 10

	Points	Matches	Record (W–T–L)	GF	GA		Points	Matches	Record (W–T–L)	GF	GA
1. Brazil	120	80	53–14–13	173	78	6. France	48	41	21–6–14	86	58
2. West Germany	107	78	45–17–16	162	103	7. Spain	42	40	16–10–14	61	48
3. Italy	92	66	38–16–12	105	62	8. Yugoslavia	40	37	16–8–13	60	46
4. Argentina	68	57	29–10–18	100	69	9. Uruguay	38	37	15–8–14	61	52
5. England	53	45	20–13–12	62	42	10. USSR/Russia	38	34	16–6–12	60	40

MAJOR LEAGUE SOCCER 2001 FINAL STANDINGS

The GF and GA columns refer to Goals For and Goals Against in regulation play. The last 10 games of the regular 2001 season were cancelled due to the events of Sept. 11, 2001.

EASTERN CONFERENCE

Team	W	L	T	Pts	GF	GA
Miami Fusion[1]	16	5	5	53	57	36
MetroStars[2]	13	10	3	42	38	35
New England Revolution	7	14	6	27	35	52
DC United	8	16	2	26	42	50

CENTRAL CONFERENCE

Team	W	L	T	Pts	GF	GA
Chicago Fire[1]	16	6	5	53	50	30
Columbus Crew[2]	13	7	6	45	49	36
Dallas Burn[2]	10	11	5	35	48	47
Tampa Bay Mutiny	4	21	2	14	32	68

WESTERN CONFERENCE

Team	W	L	T	Pts	GF	GA	Team	W	L	T	Pts	GF	GA
Los Angeles Galaxy[1]	14	7	5	47	52	36	Kansas City Wizards[2]	11	13	3	36	33	53
San Jose Earthqaukes[2]	13	7	6	45	47	29	Colorado Rapids	5	13	8	23	36	47

1. Conference champions. 2. Playoff qualifiers.

MLS PLAYOFFS

3 points are awarded for a win, and 1 point for a tie. The winner of the series is the first to reach or exceed 5 points.

Quarterfinals
Miami defeated Kansas City, 6 points to 3
San Jose defeated Columbus, 6 points to 0
Los Angeles defeated MetroStars in tie-breaker
Chicago defeated Dallas 7 points to 1

Semifinals
San Jose defeated Miami, 6 points to 3
Los Angeles defeated Chicago, 7 points to 1

MLS CUP
Oct. 21 at Columbus, Ohio
San Jose Earthquakes 2, Los Angeles Galaxy 1

	1st	2nd	OT	Total
San Jose Earthquakes	1	0	1	2
Los Angeles Galaxy	1	0	0	1

Scoring: Los Angeles: Hernandez (Vanney, Hartman), 21st minute. San Jose: Donovan (Russell, Mulrooney) 43rd minute; DeRosario (Ekelund, Ibsen) (96th minute).**MVP:** Dwayne DeRosario, San Jose forward

2001 REGULAR SEASON

LEADING SCORERS

	Gm	G	A	Pts
Alex Pineda Chacon, Miami	25	19	9	47
Diego Serna, Miami	22	15	15	45
John Spencer, Colorado	23	14	7	35
Jeff Cunningham, Columbus	22	10	13	33
John Wilmar Perez, Columbus	25	8	15	31

GOAL SCORING LEADERS

	Gm	No
Alex Pineda Chacon, Miami	25	19
Diego Serna, Miami	22	15
John Spencer, Colorado	23	14
Abdul Thompson Conteh, DC	25	14
Ronald Cerritos, San Jose	25	11
Ariel Graziani, Dallas	25	11

LEADING GOALKEEPERS

	Gm	Shts	Svs	GA	GAA
Zach Thornton, Chicago	27	145	111	30	1.08
Joe Cannon, San Jose	25	134	101	28	1.09
Nick Rimando, Miami	25	155	116	33	1.29
Tim Howard, MetroStars	26	190	146	35	1.33
Tom Presthus, Columbus	25	178	136	35	1.36

ASSIST LEADERS

	Gm	No
Diego Serna, Miami	22	15
John Wilmar Perez, Columbus	25	15
Preki, Miami	24	14
Jeff Cunningham, Columbus	22	13
Ian Bishop, Miami	23	13

WOMEN'S UNITED SOCCER ASSOCIATION 2001 FINAL STANDINGS

The GF and GA columns refer to Goals For and Goals Against in regulation play. 3 points are awarded for a win, and 1 point for a tie.

Team	W	L	T	Pts	GF	GA
Atlanta Beat[1]	10	4	7	37	31	21
Bay Area CyberRays[1,2]	11	6	4	37	27	23
New York Power[1]	9	7	5	32	30	25
Philadelphia Charge[1]	9	8	4	31	35	28
San Diego Spirit	7	7	7	28	29	28
Boston Breakers	8	10	3	27	29	35
Washington Freedom	6	12	3	21	26	35
Carolina Courage	6	12	3	21	28	40

1. Clinched home playoff game. 2. Playoff qualifiers.

WUSA PLAYOFFS

Aug. 18–New York 2, Bay Area 3

Aug. 18—Philadelphia 2, Atlanta 3

Championship
Aug. 25, Foxboro Stadium—Atlanta 3, Bay Area 3 (Atlanta wins on penalty kicks, 4–2)

2001 REGULAR SEASON

POINTS LEADERS

	Gm	G	A	Pts
Tiffeny Milbrett, New York	20	16	3	35
Shannon MacMillan, San Diego	20	12	6	30
Charmaine Hooper, Atlanta	19	12	3	27
Dagny Mellgren, Boston	19	11	4	26
Danielle Fotopoulos, Carolina	21	9	5	23
Maren Meinert, Boston	17	8	7	23

ASSISTS LEADERS

	Gm	Assists
Kristine Lilly, Boston	21	10
Sissi, Bay Area	21	10
Hege Riise, Carolina	18	8
Maren Meinert, Boston	17	7
Cindy Parlow, Atlanta	18	7
Julie Foudy, San Diego	20	7

GOALS LEADERS

	Gm	Goals
Tiffeny Milbrett, New York	20	16
Charmaine Hooper, Atlanta	19	12
Shannon MacMillan, San Diego	20	12
Dagny Mellgren, Boston	19	11
Liu Ailing, Philadelphia	19	10

SHOTS LEADERS

	Gm	Shots
Shannon MacMillan, San Diego	20	86
Kristine Lilly, Boston	21	76
Katia, Bay Area	20	75
Tiffeny Milbrett, New York	20	73
Mia Hamm, Washington	19	61

History of the Income Tax in the United States

Source: Ernst & Young LLP

The nation had few taxes in its early history. From 1791 to 1802, the United States government was supported by internal taxes on distilled spirits, carriages, refined sugar, tobacco and snuff, property sold at auction, corporate bonds, and slaves. The high cost of the War of 1812 brought about the nation's first sales taxes on gold, silverware, jewelry, and watches. In 1817, however, Congress did away with all internal taxes, relying on tariffs on imported goods to provide sufficient funds for running the government.

In 1862, in order to support the Civil War effort, Congress enacted the nation's first income tax law. It was a forerunner of our modern income tax in that it was based on the principles of graduated, or progressive, taxation and of withholding income at the source. During the Civil War, a person earning from $600 to $10,000 per year paid tax at the rate of 3%. Those with incomes of more than $10,000 paid taxes at a higher rate. Additional sales and excise taxes were added, and an "inheritance" tax also made its debut in 1911. In 1866, internal revenue collections reached their highest point in the nation's 90-year history—more than $310 million, an amount not reached again until 1911.

The Act of 1862 established the office of Commissioner of Internal Revenue. The Commissioner was given the power to assess, levy, and collect taxes, and the right to enforce the tax laws through seizure of property and income and through prosecution. His powers and authority remain very much the same today.

In 1868, Congress again focused its taxation efforts on tobacco and distilled spirits and eliminated the income tax in 1872. It had a short-lived revival in 1894 and 1895. In the latter year, the U.S. Supreme Court decided that the income tax was unconstitutional because it was not apportioned among the states in conformity with the Constitution.

In 1913, the 16th Amendment to the Constitution made the income tax a permanent fixture in the U.S. tax system. The amendment gave Congress legal authority to tax income and resulted in a revenue law that taxed incomes of both individuals and corporations. In fiscal year 1918, annual internal revenue collections for the first time passed the billion-dollar mark, rising to $5.4 billion by 1920. With the advent of World War II, employment increased, as did tax collections—to $7.3 billion. The withholding tax on wages was introduced in 1943 and was instrumental in increasing the number of taxpayers to 60 million and tax collections to $43 billion by 1945.

In 1981, Congress enacted the largest tax cut in U.S. history, approximately $750 billion over six years. The tax reduction, however, was partially offset by two tax acts, in 1982 and 1984, that attempted to raise approximately $265 billion.

On Oct. 22, 1986, President Reagan signed into law the Tax Reform Act of 1986, one of the most far-reaching reforms of the United States tax system since the adoption of the income tax. In an attempt to remain revenue neutral, the act called for a $120 billion increase in business taxation and a corresponding decrease in individual taxation over a five-year period.

Following what seemed to be a yearly tradition of new tax acts that began in 1986, the Revenue Reconciliation Act of 1990 was signed into law on Nov. 5, 1990. As with the '87, '88, and '89 acts, the 1990 act, while providing a number of substantive provisions, was small in comparison with the 1986 act. The emphasis of the 1990 act was increased taxes on the wealthy.

On Aug. 10, 1993, President Clinton signed the Revenue Reconciliation Act of 1993 into law. The act's purpose was to reduce by approximately $496 billion the federal deficit that would otherwise accumulate in fiscal years 1994 through 1998.

On Aug. 5, 1997, President Clinton signed the Taxpayer Relief Act of 1997. The act included $152 billion in tax cuts, a cut in capital-gains tax for individuals, a $500 per child tax credit, estate tax relief, tax incentives for education, and a host of revenue-raising and tax-simplification provisions.

On June 7, 2001, President George W. Bush signed the Economic Growth and Tax Relief Reconciliation Act of 2001. The act included a variety of tax cuts and offered benefits to a broad range of taxpayers through relief provisions that included: married couples; families with children, who would receive tax cuts to help pay for education, childcare, and other expenses; single mothers; and seniors. The act also included tax cuts that completely eliminated the entire income tax liability for some families.

Internal Revenue Service

The Internal Revenue Service (IRS), a bureau of the U.S. Treasury Department, is the federal agency charged with the administration of the tax laws passed by Congress. The IRS functions through a national office in Washington, 4 regional offices, 63 district offices, and 10 service centers.

Operations involving most taxpayers are carried out in the district offices and service centers. District offices are organized into Resources Management, Examination, Collection, Taxpayer Service, Employee Plans and Exempt Organizations, and Criminal Investigation. All tax returns are filed with the service centers, where the IRS computer operations are located.

IRS service centers are processing an ever increasing number of returns and documents. Prior to 1987, all tax return processing was performed by hand. This process was time consuming and costly.

Internal Revenue Service

	2000	1996	1995	1994	1993	1970
U.S. population (in thousands)	276,083	266,109	263,730	261,698	259,015	204,878
Number of IRS employees	96,092	102,082	112,023	110,665	113,352	68,683
Cost to govt. of collecting $100 in taxes	$0.39	$0.49	$0.55	$0.58	$0.60	$0.45
Tax per capita	$7,595.24	$5,586.00	$5,216.44	$4,878.00	$4,543.33	$955.31
Collections by principal sources (in thousands of dollars)						
Total IRS collections	$2,096,916,925	$1,486,546,674	$1,375,731,835	$1,276,466,776	$1,176,685,625	$195,722,096
Income and profits taxes						
Individual	$1,137,077,702	$745,313,276	$675,779,337	$619,819,153	$585,774,159	$103,651,585
Corporation	$235,654,894	$189,054,791	$174,422,173	$154,204,684	$131,547,509	$35,036,983
Employment taxes	$639,651,814	$492,365,178	$465,405,305	$443,831,352	$411,510,516	$37,449,188
Estate and gift taxes	$29,721,620	$17,591,817	$15,144,394	$15,606,793	$12,890,965	$3,680,076
Alcohol taxes	(1)	(1)	(1)	(1)	(1)	$4,746,382
Tobacco taxes	(1)	(1)	(1)	(1)	(1)	$2,094,212
Manufacturers' excise taxes	(2)	(2)	(2)	(2)	(2)	6,683,061
All other taxes	$54,810,895	$42,221,611	$44,980,627	$43,004,794	$34,962,476	$2,380,609

NOTE: For fiscal year ending Sept. 30th. 1. Alcohol and tobacco tax collections are now collected and reported by the Bureau of Alcohol, Tobacco, and Firearms. 2. Manufacturers' excise taxes are included in the "All other taxes" amount. *Source:* 2000 IRS Data Book.

In an attempt to improve the speed and efficiency of the manual processing procedure, the IRS began testing an electronic return filing system beginning with the filing of 1985 returns.

The two most significant results of the test were that refunds for the electronically filed returns were issued more quickly and the tax processing error rate was significantly lower when compared to paper returns. Electronic filing of individual income tax returns with refunds became an operational program in selected areas for the 1987 processing year. In 1994 13,510,000 individual returns were filed electronically, compared to 11,143,000 in 1995, and 14,977,123 in 1996.

Auditing Tax Returns

Most taxpayers' contacts with the IRS arise through the auditing of their tax returns. The Service has been empowered by Congress to inquire about all persons who may be liable for any tax and to obtain for review the books and/or records pertinent to those taxpayers' returns. A wide-ranging audit operation is carried out in the 63 district offices by 16,078 revenue agents and 2,831 tax auditors.

The primary method used by the IRS in selecting returns for audits is a computer program that measures the probability of tax error in each return. The higher the score, the greater the tax change potential. Other returns are selected for examination on the basis of claims for refund, multiyear audits, related return audits, and other audits initiated by the IRS as a result of informants' information, special compliance programs, and the information document-matching program.

The Appeals Process

The IRS attempts to resolve tax disputes through an administrative appeals system. Taxpayers who, after audit of their tax returns, disagree with a proposed change in their tax liabilities are entitled to an independent review of their cases. Taxpayers are able to seek an immediate, informal appeal with the Appeals Office. If, however, the dispute arises from a field audit and the amount in question exceeds $10,000, a taxpayer must submit a written protest. Alternatively, the taxpayer can wait for the examiner's report and then request consideration by the Appeals Office and file a protest if necessary. Taxpayers may represent themselves or be represented by an attorney, accountant, or any other adviser authorized to practice before the IRS. Taxpayers can forgo their right to the above process and await receipt of a deficiency notice. At this juncture, taxpayers can either (1) not pay the deficiency and petition the Tax Court by a required deadline or (2) pay the deficiency and file a claim for refund with the District Director's office. If the claim is not allowed, a suit for refund may be brought either in the District Court or the Claims Court within a specified period.

Federal Income Tax Comparisons
Taxes at Selected Rate Brackets After Standard Deductions and Personal Exemptions[1]

Adjusted gross income	Single return listing no dependents					Joint return listing two dependents				
	2000	1999	1998	1995	1975	2000	1999	1998	1995	1975
$10,000	$391	$428	$457	$540	$1,506	$−3,888	$−3,816	$ −5,200	$ −3,110[2]	$ 829
20,000	1,916	1,939	1,858	2,040	4,153	−2,127	−1,965	720	−773	2,860
30,000	3,416	3,439	3,458	3,573	8,018	1,466	1,639	2,200	2,018	5,804
40,000	5,765	4,939	5,595	6,373	12,765	3,214	3,266	3,720	3,518	9,668
50,000	8,593	7,528	6,549	9,173	18,360	4,714	4,766	6,449	5,018	14,260

1. For comparison purposes, tax rate schedules were used. 2. Refund based on a basic earned income credit for families with dependent children.

Federal Individual Income Tax

Tax Brackets—2001 Taxable Income

Joint return	Single taxpayer	Rate
$0–$45,200	$0–$27,050	15.0%
45,201–109,250	27,051–65,550	28.0
109,251–166,500	65,551–136,750	31.0[1]
166,501–297,350[2]	136,751–297,350	36.0[1]
297,351 and up[2]	297,351 and up[2]	39.6[1]

1. The tax rate is effectively increased because total otherwise allowable itemized deductions are reduced by 3% of the taxpayer's adjusted gross income in excess of $128,950. 2. The deduction for personal exemptions is phased out as the taxpayer's gross income exceeds $193,400 for a joint return and $128,950 for single taxpayers.

The federal individual income tax is levied on the worldwide income of U.S. citizens and resident aliens and on certain types of U.S. source income of nonresidents. For a nonitemizer, "tax table income" is adjusted gross income less $2,800 for each personal exemption and the standard deduction. If a taxpayer itemizes, tax table income is adjusted gross income minus total itemized deductions and personal exemptions. In addition, individuals may also be subject to the alternative minimum tax.

Who Must File a Return[1]

If your filing status is:	Age at end of 2000	Gross income at least
Single	Under 65	$7,200
	65 or older	8,300
Married filing jointly	Under 65 (both spouses)	12,950
	65 or older (one spouse)	13,800
	65 or older (both spouses)	14,650
Married filing separately	Any age	2,800
Head of household	Under 65	9,250
	65 or older	10,350
Qualifying widower	Under 65	10,150
	65 or older	11,000

1. In 2001.

Adjusted Gross Income

Gross income consists of wages and salaries, unemployment compensation, tips and gratuities, interest, dividends, annuities, rents and royalties, up to 85% of Social Security benefits if the recipient's income exceeds a base amount, and certain other types of income. Among the items excluded from gross income, and thus not subject to tax, are public assistance benefits and interest on exempt securities (mostly state and local bonds).

Adjusted gross income is determined by subtracting from gross income: alimony paid, penalties on early withdrawal of savings, payments to an IRA (reduced proportionally based upon adjusted gross income levels if taxpayer is an active participant in an employer maintained retirement plan), payments to a Keogh retirement plan, and self-employed health insurance payments and moving expenses.

Itemized Deductions

Taxpayers may itemize deductions or take the standard deduction. The standard deduction amounts for 2000 are as follows: $4,000 for single persons, $6,450 for heads of household, $7,350 for married filing jointly or qualifying widower, and $3,675 for married filing separately. Taxpayers 65 and older or blind are entitled to an additional standard deduction of up to $6,600 for single persons, up to $10,750 for married persons filing jointly or qualifying widowers, up to $7,075 for married persons filing separately, and up to $8,650 for heads of households.

In itemizing deductions, the following are major items that may be deducted in 1998: state and local income and property taxes, charitable contributions, employee moving expenses, medical expenses (exceeding 7.5% of adjusted gross income), casualty losses (only the amount over the $100 floor which exceeds 10% of adjusted gross income), mortgage interest, and miscellaneous deductions (deductible only to the extent by which cumulatively they exceed 2% of adjusted gross income).

Personal Exemptions

Personal exemptions are available to the taxpayer for himself, his spouse, and his dependents. The 2000 amount was $2,800 for each individual. No exemption is allowed to a taxpayer who can be claimed as a dependent on another taxpayer's return.

Credits

Taxpayers can reduce their income tax liability by claiming the benefit of certain tax credits. Each dollar of tax credit offsets a dollar of tax liability. The following are a few of the available tax credits.

Certain low income households may claim an Earned Income Credit. The maximum Earned Income Credit is $353 for taxpayers with no qualifying children, $2,353 for taxpayers with one qualifying child, $3,888 for taxpayers with two or more qualifying children. The maximum credit will be reduced if earned income or adjusted gross income exceeds $12,700 for taxpayers with one or more children, or exceeds $5,800 for taxpayers with no children. For families with no qualifying children, the credit will be zero if earned income or adjusted gross income exceeds $10,700; for families with one qualifying child, the credit will be zero if earned income or adjusted gross income exceeds $27,450; and for taxpayers with two or more qualifying children, the credit will be zero if earned income or adjusted gross income exceeds $31,152. The earned income credit is a refundable credit.

A credit for Child and Dependent Care Expenses is available for amounts paid to care for a qualifying child or other dependent so that the taxpayer can work or look for work. The credit is up to 30% (depending on adjusted gross income) of up to $2,400 of employment-related expenses for one qualifying child or dependent and up to $4,800 of employment-related expenses for two qualifying individuals.

The elderly and those under 65 who are retired under total disability may be entitled to a credit of up to $750 (if single) or $1,125 (if married and filing jointly). No credit is available if the taxpayer is single and has adjusted gross income of $17,500 or more. Similarly, the credit is unavailable to a married couple filing jointly if their adjusted gross income exceeds $25,000.

State Taxes on Individuals

(as of Jan. 1, 2001)

State	Sales/use tax (percent)[1]	Income tax (percent)[2]	State	Sales/use tax (percent)[1]	Income tax (percent)[2]
Alabama	4	2.0 – 5.0	Nebraska	5	2.51 – 6.68
Alaska	none	none	Nevada	6.5	none
Arizona	5	2.87 – 5.04	New Hampshire	none	[6]
Arkansas	5.125	1.0 – 7.0	New Jersey	6	1.4 – 6.37
California	7[3,4]	1.0 – 9.3	New Mexico	5	1.7 – 8.2
Colorado	2.9	4.63	New York	4	4.0 – 6.85
Connecticut	6	3.0 – 4.5	North Carolina	4	6.0 – 7.75
Delaware	none	2.2 – 5.95	North Dakota	5	2.67 – 12.0
Florida	6	none	Ohio	5	0.691 – 6.980
Georgia	4	1.0 – 6.0	Oklahoma	4.5	0.5 – 6.75
Hawaii	4	1.5 – 8.5	Oregon	none	5.0 – 9.0
Idaho	5[5]	2.0 – 8.2	Pennsylvania	6	2.8
Illinois	6.25	3	Rhode Island	7	25.5[7]
Indiana	5	3.4	South Carolina	5	2.5 – 7.0
Iowa	5	0.36 – 8.98	South Dakota	4[5]	none
Kansas	4.9[5]	3.5 – 6.45	Tennessee	6	[6]
Kentucky	6	2.0 – 6.0	Texas	6.25	none
Louisiana	4	2.0 – 6.0	Utah	4.75	2.3 – 7.0
Maine	5	2.0 – 8.5	Vermont	5	24.0[7]
Maryland	5	2.0 – 4.8	Virginia	4.5[3]	2.0 – 5.75
Massachusetts	5	5.6	Washington	6.5	none
Michigan	6	4.2	West Virginia	6	3.0 – 6.5
Minnesota	6.5	5.35 – 7.85	Wisconsin	5	4.6 – 6.75
Mississippi	7	3.0 – 5.0	Wyoming	4[4,5]	none
Missouri	4.225	1.5 – 6.0	District of Columbia	5.75	5.0 – 9.0
Montana	none	2.0 – 11.0			

1. Local and county taxes, if any, are additional. 2. Tax rate for individuals; unless otherwise noted, range denotes progressive structure; higher income pays higher rate. 3. Includes statewide local tax of 1.25% in California and 1% in Virginia. 4. Tax rate may be adjusted annually according to a formula based on balances in the unappropriated general fund and the school foundation fund. 5. Idaho, Kansas, South Dakota, and Wyoming tax food but allow an (income) tax credit to compensate poor households. 6. State income tax is limited to dividends and interest. 7. Percentage of federal tax liability. *Source:* The Federation of Tax Administrators.

Effective for tax years beginning after Dec. 1, 1997, taxpayers who have qualifying children for whom the taxpayer may claim a dependency exemption and who are less than 17 years old as of the close of the tax year are entitled to the child tax credit. The amount of the credit for 2000 was $500. The child credit begins to phase out when AGI reaches $110,000 for joint filers and $75,000 for singles. Taxpayers who have three or more qualifying children may also be entitled to an additional credit.

Federal Estate and Gift Taxes

A Federal Estate Tax Return must generally be filed for the estate of every U.S. citizen or resident whose gross estate, taxable gifts, and specific exemptions exceed $675,000 for decedents dying in 2001, and according to the following table if dying in succeeding years:

Decedent dying in	Exclusion amount
2002 and 2003	$1,000,000
2004 and 2005	1,500,000
2006, 2007, and 2008	2,000,000
2009	3,500,000

A unified credit of $202,050 is available to offset both estate and gift taxes. Any part of the credit used to offset gift taxes is not available to offset estate taxes. As a result, although they are still taxable as gifts, lifetime taxable transfers no longer cushion the impact of progressive estate tax rates. Lifetime transfers and transfers made at death are combined for estate tax rate purposes.

Gift taxes are computed by applying the uniform rate schedule to lifetime taxable transfers (after deducting the unified credit) and subtracting the taxes payable for prior taxable periods. In general, estate taxes are computed by applying the uniform rate schedule to cumulative transfers and subtracting the gift taxes paid. An appropriate adjustment is made for taxes on lifetime transfers—such as certain gifts within three years of death—in a decedent's estate.

Among the deductions allowed in computing the amount of the estate subject to tax are funeral expenditures, administrative costs, claims and bequests to religious, charitable, and fraternal organizations or government welfare agencies, and state inheritance taxes. For transfers made after 1981 during life or death, there is an unlimited marital deduction.

An annual gift tax exclusion is provided that permits tax-free gifts to each donee of $10,000 for each year. A husband and wife who agree to treat gifts to third persons as joint gifts can exclude up to $20,000 a year to each donee. An unlimited exclusion for medical expenses and school tuition both paid directly to the institution for the benefit of any donee is also available in addition to the annual gift tax exclusion.

Federal Corporation Taxes

Corporations are taxed under a graduated tax rate structure. If a corporation has taxable income in excess of $100,000, the amount of tax shall be increased by the lesser of 5% of such excess or $11,750. When a corporation has taxable income in excess of $15,000,000, the amount of tax shall be increased by an additional amount equal to the lesser of 3% of such excess or $100,000.

If the corporation qualifies, it may elect to be an S corporation. If it makes this election, the corporation will not (with certain exceptions) pay corporate tax on its income. Its income is instead passed through and taxed to its shareholders. There are sev-eral requirements a corporation must meet to qualify as an S corporation, including having 75 or fewer shareholders and having only one class of stock.

Corporate Tax Rates

Taxable income	Tax rate
$0–$50,000	15%
$50,001–$75,000	25%
$75,001–$10,000,000	34%
$10,000,001 and up	35%

State Corporation Income and Franchise Taxes

All states except Texas, Nevada, South Dakota, Washington, and Wyoming impose a tax on corporation net income. The majority of states impose the tax at flat rates ranging from 2.3% to approximately 10.75%. Several states have adopted a graduated basis of rates for corporations.

Nearly all states follow the federal law in defining net income. However, many states provide for varying exclusions and adjustments.

A state is empowered to tax all of the net income of its domestic corporations. With regard to non-resident corporations, however, it may only tax the net income on business carried on within its boundaries. Corporations are, therefore, required to apportion their incomes among the states where they do business, and pay a tax to each of these states. Nearly all states provide an apportionment to their domestic corporations, too, in order that they not be unduly burdened. Several states tax unincorporated businesses separately.

Tax Freedom Day

Tax Freedom Day®—the day the average American can expect to quit working for Uncle Sam and his counterparts at the state and local level and begin working for him or herself—arrived on May 3, 2001. It is the 123rd day of the year.

Since 1992, Tax Freedom Day has grown by two weeks, according to Tax Foundation economist Scott Moody. The trend toward later and later Tax Freedom Days is likely to continue. He also said the increase is almost totally due to federal spending, since state and local tax burdens have remained virtually unchanged in the past decade.

However, because the tax burden varies considerably by state, Tax Freedom Day falls on different days. Connecticut has the heaviest tax burden, with Tax Freedom Day arriving May 25. The District of Columbia, May 18; New York, May 14; New Jersey, May 12; Maine, May 11; and Washington State, May 10, also have late Tax Freedom Days.

Alaska has the earliest Tax Freedom Day, April 16, followed by South Dakota, April 21. For West Virginia, Tennessee, South Carolina, Oklahoma, and Alabama, Tax Freedom Day falls on April 23.

Federal Spending by State for Every Tax Dollar Sent to Washington, FY 2000

State	Expenditure	State	Expenditure	State	Expenditure
Total	$1.00	Louisiana	$1.39	Oklahoma	$1.46
Alabama	1.54	Maine	1.32	Oregon	0.93
Alaska	1.68	Maryland	1.32	Pennsylvania	1.06
Arizona	1.18	Massachusetts	0.86	Rhode Island	1.18
Arkansas	1.38	Michigan	0.81	South Carolina	1.27
California	0.86	Minnesota	0.76	South Dakota	1.46
Colorado	0.85	Mississippi	1.78	Tennessee	1.20
Connecticut	0.62	Missouri	1.26	Texas	0.96
Delaware	0.84	Montana	1.59	Utah	1.06
Florida	1.00	Nebraska	1.09	Vermont	1.08
Georgia	0.99	Nevada	0.69	Virginia	1.48
Hawaii	1.56	New Hampshire	0.71	Washington	0.87
Idaho	1.30	New Jersey	0.66	West Virginia	1.75
Illinois	0.74	New Mexico	2.03	Wisconsin	0.83
Indiana	0.92	New York	0.86	Wyoming	1.09
Iowa	1.04	North Carolina	1.06	District of Columbia	6.49
Kansas	1.02	North Dakota	1.86		
Kentucky	1.41	Ohio	0.97		

Source: The Tax Foundation.

In Search of the Best

Each year the editors of TIME name a Man or Woman of the Year—the single person who has done the most in the past 12 months to affect the news of the world, for good or ill. Reflecting the magazine's continuing belief in the power of the individual, TIME's editors embarked on an ambitious project in 2001—to profile the best Americans actively working in a wide variety of fields, from architecture to chemistry to the classroom.

Ultimately, the America's Best series will profile individuals in the following fields: Science and Medicine; Culture and Society; Business and Technology; and Politics and Community. The series was launched with TIME's selection of America's Best Artists and Entertainers—many of them profiled by admiring fellow artists. Excerpts from their appreciations are below. To learn more about the America's Best series, visit Time.com.

America's Best Author
Philip Roth
By Paul Gray

Writers, like the rest of us, are entitled to slow down when they approach retirement age. What Philip Roth did, as he began anticipating the popularly euphemistic Golden Years, was to gun his engine and rev out in rapid succession three of the strongest, most vibrant novels of his long career. *American Pastoral* (1997) examines the fallout from the radical '60s on one New Jersey family, specifically on the suffering father of an unrepentant terrorist daughter. *I Married a Communist* (1998), set during the witch hunts of the late '40s and early '50s, traces that era's devastating effects on a naive radio actor. *The Human Stain* (2000) takes place in 1998, the year that launched Monica Lewinsky and the Clinton impeachment proceedings, and casts a cold eye on the political correctness that unjustly destroys a college professor's career.

Solely on the basis of his output over the past 10 years or so —which also includes the uproarious *Operation Shylock* (1993); the brooding, death-haunted *Sabbath's Theater* (1995); and the terse, erotic *The Dying Animal*, published in May 2001—Roth, 68, would win much support as America's best working novelist. Who else during the same period published so much of such consistently high quality? Even more remarkably, Roth has maintained this elevated standard for more than 40 years, a creative marathon that totals 20 books of fiction. Not all of these are masterpieces, but all are unfailingly ambitious, the products of a mature, demanding artistic conscience.

Roth has tirelessly insisted on the distinction between the raw material of life and the transforming power of fiction, and his energy shows no signs of flagging. His office is a study on his Connecticut property about 60 yards from his house: "I work at my job the way most human beings work at jobs; I start mornings and quit evenings." Bad reviews no longer bother him: "I'm sometimes frustrated by my own efforts but not by the public response. Once a book is out of your hands, readers make of it what they will."

Looking back, Roth sees a pattern to his work: "Ever since *Goodbye, Columbus,* I've been drawn to depicting the impact of place on American lives. *Portnoy's Complaint* is very much the raw response to a way of life that was specific to his American place during his childhood in the '30s and '40s. The link between the individual and his historic moment may be more focused in the recent trilogy, but the interest was there from the start."

Roth is a serious writer who has never been somber in print; his narrative voice is unique, and so is the way he consistently wrings slapstick comedy out of the tics and obsessions of his characters. No one else writing today has been more amusing or more enlightening.

Nancy Crampton/Houghton Mifflin

Paul Gray is a veteran book critic and writer for TIME.

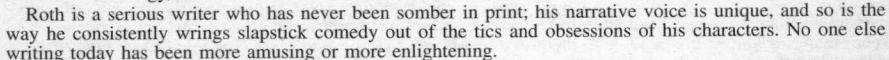

August Wilson

By James Earl Jones

AP/Wide World

It's hard for an actor to go wrong if he's true to the words August Wilson has written. When I played Troy Maxson in *Fences* on Broadway in 1987, the speeches simply guided themselves, they're so well constructed. August was a poet before he became a playwright, and poetry is still part of the language his characters speak. You don't always hear people talk like that in real life, but you wish you could. Like Eugene O'Neill, Tennessee Williams, and Arthur Miller, August didn't just write a great play—he has written volumes of good, better, and best plays. *Fences* was the second in his series about blacks in each decade of the 20th century. But August's plays transcend race. When Carole Shorenstein Hays, who produced *Fences,* saw the play for the first time, she said she was watching a "universal play, and when push comes to shove, families are alike."

Those family confrontations—when the mighty forces that August gathers on the stage clash, either with words or with action—are the scenes that are hard to shake. Just look at Troy. The way he bashes his soul against other souls is illuminating. I always felt he was one of those characters I wish I had really known. August says that when he writes he leaves some blood on the page. You can't get that stuff out of yourself without hurt. It's not therapy; it's more like revelation. He often talks about the pain of writing by quoting Bynum, one of his characters in *Joe Turner's Come and Gone,* who says, "I don't do it lightly. It costs me a piece of myself every time I do." And in doing so, August has earned his place on this list.

James Earl Jones won one of his two Tony Awards for his performance in Fences.

Ang Lee

By Richard Corliss

AP/Wide World

So Ang Lee is America's best director, eh? Best—well, fine—but American? Lee, who was born and raised in Taiwan; who brings a very Mandarin delicacy to his subjects; who has shot most of his features in distant climes (Taipei for *Pushing Hands* and *Eat Drink Man Woman,* rural England for *Sense and Sensibility,* mainland China for *Crouching Tiger Hidden Dragon*); who has never made a movie in Hollywood; and whose name, correctly put, is Lee Ang . . . that Ang Lee? Yes, America gets to claim him—as he claimed it 24 years ago, when he went to college in Illinois. Soon he was in New York City, studying film and assisting another Lee (Spike). Now 46, he still edits his films there and lives in Westchester with his wife, Jane, and their two children.

This dimpled, soft-spoken gent is proving again what has always been true: that American cinema is nourished by the artistry and vision of foreigners (Chaplin and Garbo, Alfred Hitchcock and Billy Wilder). Lately it has been the Asians' turn to show us how films can kick higher or probe deeper. Lee's films do both.

He makes art films that entertain and enthrall. A cosmopolitan chameleon, Lee seems at home in any culture while viewing it with an outsider's ironic acuity. Often his theme is a divided family, or a man estranged from his best instincts. Lee doesn't look for heroes or villains; he finds enough shades of courage and compromise in every heavy heart. Even *Crouching Tiger* is grounded in the ache of unexpressed, unattainable love. Then it explodes like a Chinese firecracker on the Fourth of July. In a career that keeps maturing and surprising, Lee is about to direct his first Hollywood film—*The Incredible Hulk.* An outsider with amazing powers: he could be a very American hero. He could be Ang Lee.

Richard Corliss is a movie critic for TIME.

America's Best Movie Star

Julia Roberts

By Jess Cagle

AP/Wide World

The gods have not only blessed Julia Roberts with a $20 million smile, they've been smiling on her ever since 1985, when she graduated from high school in Smyrna, Ga., and headed to New York City to be with her big sister Lisa. Acting was an afterthought—"something that I could attempt to do in New York"—but fate saw her coming. On the count of three—*Mystic Pizza, Steel Magnolias, Pretty Woman*—Roberts was a star. Now, at age 33, with an Oscar and a recent string of hits that includes the summer of '99 doubleheader *Notting Hill* and *Runaway Bride,* Roberts is flying higher than any full-grown actress (yes, we are aware of Shirley Temple) in history—a salary equal to her male peers and the ability to get behinds the world over into seats on opening weekends.

Since 1990, Roberts has generated nearly $1.5 billion in domestic ticket sales. But even as she has become a regular part of our Friday nights at the movies, she's become an integral part of our weekdays at the water cooler—most recently because of her breakup with actor Benjamin Bratt, her boyfriend of nearly four years. (They actually split not long after the Oscars, but she still calls him "the greatest guy.") We follow her personal travails because we project our dreams onto movie stars, and so we want her to live happily ever after.

Following a mid-'90s career slump, she took the part of a food critic out to steal another woman's fiancé in *My Best Friend's Wedding.* "People told me it was suicide," says Elaine Goldsmith-Thomas, her former agent and now a business partner. But Roberts made the man-hungry heroine lovable with her own gangly appeal, and, she says, the hit 1997 romantic comedy made her realize for the first time that "if I want to [act] for the rest of my life, I will be allowed to, probably." Since then, Roberts has nourished herself with more flawed, challenging characters while still feeding the public the Julia-personas it craves. Rendering the self-righteous crusader of *Erin Brockovich* human with her infectious smile, endearing cackle, and irresistible cleavage, she won the Oscar and our renewed devotion. No star since Katharine Hepburn has employed her personality so effectively on screen.

Jess Cagle, TIME's West Coast senior editor, directs the magazine's coverage of the motion picture industry.

America's Best Actor

Sean Penn

By Dennis Hopper

AP/Wide World

Sean Penn— Never flubs a line.
Goes to where the action is.
Prepares . . . prepares . . . becomes.
Will throw a punch
at a photog
or anyone who provokes him.
Is a stand-up guy.
A man's man.
A trusted friend.
An actor's actor.
A wonderful poet, screenwriter, director.
Father of Dylan and Hopper Jack.
Even sober, the one to party with.
Enjoy the differences in each of his performances.
Dark energy exploding like a sun.
Shows up everyone with his brilliance.
Lives in a moment-to-moment reality.
Uses all his senses in his work.
Makes the accident work for him.
Sean Penn—He is an amazing actor, man, friend.

Dennis Hopper is an actor, writer, and director. He and Penn collaborated in the Hopper-directed film Colors *in 1988 and in Penn's directorial debut,* The Indian Runner, *in 1991.*

Bello
By Bill Irwin

Ringling Bros. & Barnum & Bailey Circus

I like to call him Bello Nock—his clown name and his family name. Although he doesn't act like it, Bello, whose given name is Demetrius, is aristocracy. Members of the Nock family have been circus artists and great clowns for generations. I saw Bello's uncle Pio Nock in the Ringling show when I was 22, and I applied immediately to the Ringling Bros. Clown College. Trained from childhood, Bello, 32, has a grounding in almost every circus skill. He is an incredible acrobat (and one of the strongest men I've ever known), and so when he does a bit about setting up a trampoline, of course he gets in trouble and finds some great gags. He's caught in the springs, first his foot, then his whole body, but he finishes with world-class trampoline work—going breathtakingly high, swooping into a suicide dive, tucking at the last second, then getting caught in the springs again.

There are only a few clowns I love to see again and again, and Bello Nock is one of them. He's really, really good, and he has a really good time; his work fits the circus ring, and he loves the crowd. And his high-layout somersault with his pants falling off just really gets me, it always has.

Bill Irwin is an actor, choreographer, director, performance artist, playwright, and clown.

Susan Stroman
By Mel Brooks

AP/Wide World

Stro—that's what everyone calls Susan Stroman—really understands that theater is about giving the audience a complete show. When she was growing up in Wilmington, Del., her biggest influences were the old black-and-white Fred Astaire movies. Those are movies that really blow the dust off your soul and wake you to the joy of life. It's that sense of joy that is at the very heart of Stro's work, from the classical ballet numbers she choreographed in *Contact* to the finger-snapping swing that filled the stage in *Crazy for You*. In 1998 my collaborator Tom Meehan and I were racking our brains trying to come up with the right director for *The Producers*. Tom suggested Mike Ockrent, Stro's husband, who had directed *Crazy for You*. I told Tom that was the best show I had seen in years. Stro choreographed it. Tom and I were talking to Mike in earnest about directing our show when, tragically, he was found to have leukemia and died. Susan, naturally, was devastated, but we thought it might actually be good for her to take over the reins. We knew she could direct; after all, she had just finished *Contact*. Despite her grief, Stro plunged herself heart and soul into the show. She brought such energy and joy to every rehearsal and really set the tone. She loves pratfalls and pranks, and she encourages comic anarchy. What's not to love?

Comedy writer, performer, and film director, Mel Brooks won three of the record-breaking 12 Tonys awarded to his play The Producers.

David Chase
By Joseph Pistone

Barry Wetcher/HBO

As a former FBI special agent who lived the Mafia lifestyle for six years in deep cover as Donnie Brasco, I can vouch for the authenticity of *The Sopranos,* the HBO phenomenon created by David Chase. I lived day and night with the Bonnano crime family of New York City, interacting with wiseguys and their families, attending Mob weddings, funerals, and family get-togethers. Chase understands their subtleties, from the emphatic hand gestures to their unwritten code of honor. You empathize with Tony Soprano whether he's whacking a guy in the afternoon or arguing with his abrasive Ivy League daughter at dinner, because Chase gets the details right. Chase is an Italian American, and he understands that rich culture with all its ethnic eccentricities, from its love of food to the boisterous ways of communicating. There will inevitably be *Sopranos* knockoffs. But Chase has created an original, and my advice to all others hoping to make a move on *Sopranos* turf: Fuhgeddaboutit!

Joseph Pistone was the subject of the movie Donnie Brasco *and the CBS television series* Falcone.

America's Best Comedian
Chris Rock
By Bruce Handy

AP/Wide World

Chris Rock's voice is a marvel in and of itself, an unlikely fusion of gravel and pipsqueakitude. Always shouting but miraculously never hoarse, he's the bastard vocal son of Redd Foxx and Rosie Perez. And when it comes to American Bestness, Rock may be this project's least controversial selection. After all, TIME has already labeled the 35-year-old comedian "the funniest man in America" in a previous issue. Then again, Rock may be one of this project's more controversial selections; his humor is—defiantly—politically incorrect. But as with all great comedians—which is to say, as with all original thinkers—Rock's insights are beyond tidy labels such as "black," "white," "left," "right," "offensive," or "as harmlessly amusing as *Friends*."

Rock knows the most cathartic laughter springs from a masochistic impulse. (Sadistic laughter, on the other hand, is the junk food of mirth.) Bring the pain—please.

Bruce Handy is a senior editor at TIME.

America's Best Radio Host
Ira Glass
By David Mamet

AP/Wide World

We're blessed, from time to time, with a spontaneous generation of humor and insight. And nowhere is this more exciting than in the emergence or the reinvention of an art form. Ruth Draper did it onstage. She took a parlor turn, the monologue, and turned it into great American drama. Nichols and May took the traditions of the Jewish wedding jester, the commedia dell'arte, and the vaudeville comic and invented improvisational theater. And now here's Ira Glass, 42, who seems to have reinvented radio.

Each week his public radio show *This American Life* chooses a subject and invites writers to expatiate personal stories on that theme. Glass once did three hours on chickens. The pièce de résistance was a memoir of an Israeli chicken kibbutz. The experience not only revealed the storyteller's true sexual orientation, but showed that even immersion in the hell of the mass poultered won't turn one off the bird. "Oh no," he said. "You'll still eat chicken, and you'll chew real slow."

The old Jewish joke goes, "How do you make a Romanian omelet? First, steal two eggs." Glass's programs sound as if their creator began by stealing a microphone. He finds—uncovers—drama and humor in the most pedestrian of places. O thou woods colt of Lord Buckley, out of Diane Arbus. Go thou and conquer.

David Mamet has written numerous films and plays, and he won the Pulitzer Prize in 1984.

America's Best Talk Show Host
Jon Stewart
By Dick Cavett

AP/Wide World

The set is a news desk, and the nice-looking man behind it seems . . . um, troubled. About his life, perhaps? About the news? A touch of indigestion? It's hard to tell, but it becomes clear—and quickly—that he is funny. And smart. Jon Stewart presides over Comedy Central's *The Daily Show,* a blessed wedding of performer and format. Free of the burden of a full stand-up monologue, Stewart is able to put all his energy and wit into the news and guest spots. The word *energy* is almost too strong. Much of Stewart's humor seems to spring from an underlying terrain of world-weariness. The difference between most comic hosts and Stewart is the difference between a brassy sitcom and *The Larry Sanders Show*—for which, in fact, he was a writer and actor. Repeat viewing of Stewart's shows reveals good things you missed the first time—smallish matters of voice shading, inflections, and gestures begun but not completed. If you're a latecomer to his charms, you'll wish your alleged friends had demanded that you start watching a lot sooner. I'd like to see everything he has ever done.

Dick Cavett was the host of The Dick Cavett Show *from 1968 to 1975.*

Martin Puryear
By Robert Hughes

Nigel Parry–CPI

I n art, things go in and out of focus—including beauty. Twenty-five years ago, if an American painter or sculptor, when asked what he wanted to achieve, had replied "Beauty," he might well have earned a double take as a mere decorator. Art was meant to issue political challenges, to confront convention, et cetera. And a lot of truly lousy, polemical art lay in that et cetera. But today the hopes of protest and politically irritant art have gone flat. What count for much more are those stubborn talents to whom the lyrical and the private are likely to be of more value than the collective. To such artists, beauty without cliché is a supreme goal, and there is probably none around who exemplifies this shift better than the sculptor Martin Puryear.

The special intensity of Puryear's work comes from doing everything himself, mainly in wood (though tar, mud, and wire also figure in his repertoire). Through the action of the shaping hand on wood, he brings forth a poetry of material substance that's unique in today's America. Puryear has always been troubled by the art/craft division in American culture. "At bottom it's a class issue really," he says. "Art means thought; craft means manual work. In Japan you'll never see that kind of snobbery; potters and carpenters are honored there as living national treasures."

Puryear's shapes come out of several parallel worlds of form, which, when prolonged, actually do meet. One is industrial—but "obsolete" industrial: the vigorous and noble shapes of what are now antique technologies, such as the carved wooden forms once created by casting patternmakers. Another is folk technology: basket weaving, canoe building, the construction of tents, yurts, and kites. Though he would be the last to deny that in past years the art world, like most things American, has been disfigured by racism, Puryear does not find his own blackness an impediment. "Right from the start, I thought, no one can keep me from being an artist."

Robert Hughes is TIME's art critic.

Sally Mann
By Reynolds Price

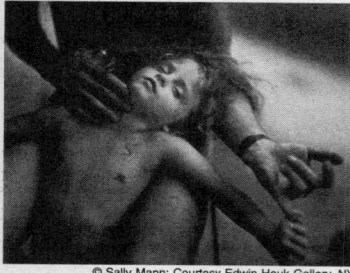

© Sally Mann; Courtesy Edwin Houk Gallery, NY

Last Light, 1990

I n the swarm of artistically minded boomers who matured in the 1970s, there were thousands who hoped to become filmmakers or photographers. Many won a brief success. But three successive decades have drastically winnowed their numbers, and only a few now stand in the ranks of mastery that include such predecessors as Dorothea Lange and Walker Evans. Tall among them is Sally Mann. It was her photographs of her children, published in 1992 as *Immediate Family,* that brought Mann's work to the attention of a wide audience. Mann recorded a combination of spontaneous and carefully arranged moments of childhood repose and revealingly—sometimes unnervingly—imaginative play. What the outraged critics of her child nudes failed to grant was the patent devotion involved throughout the project and the delighted complicity of her son and daughters in so many of the solemn or playful events. No other collection of family photographs is remotely like it, in both its naked candor and the fervor of its maternal curiosity and care.

In this decade Mann has ventured from home more frequently. First, she turned to pictures of her surroundings. More recently, she has taken her incomparably truthful large-frame camera farther south, into Georgia, Mississippi, and Louisiana. From the heart of the Old South's dark history she has returned with eloquent images—devoid of human presence—of the rivers and thickets that continue to harbor our whole country's greatest mystery: how human beings, in the midst of such fecund natural beauty, have continued to be so relentlessly inhuman.

Few photographers of any time or place have matched Sally Mann's steadiness of simple eyesight, her serene technical brilliance, and the clearly communicated eloquence she derives from her subjects, human and otherwise—subjects observed with an ardor that is all but indistinguishable from love.

Reynolds Price is the author of more than 30 books, including Kate Vaiden, *for which he received the National Book Critics Circle Award in 1986.*

America's Best Architect
Steven Holl
By Richard Lacayo

Courtesy Steven Holl Architects
Bellevue Art Museum, Washington State

Most people see buildings as things made of steel and glass, wood and stone. Steven Holl sees them first as things made of space and light. Just as the Moors cultivated the trickle of water everywhere in their desert palaces, Holl, who grew up in the cloudy Pacific Northwest, designs buildings that cherish and supervise every sunbeam. Light gathers in the alcoves of his Bellevue Art Museum in Washington State. It sweeps across the arcs of his Museum of Contemporary Art in Helsinki. It pulses through colored glass in his Chapel of St. Ignatius in Seattle, a building he once described as "seven bottles of light in a stone box."

Holl's other signatures? One is a unique husbandry of space. Each building is not so much a discrete object as a complicated succession of vistas. He called his plan for the Helsinki museum "Chiasma, a Greek word for intertwining." That describes how the museum's curving outer section enfolds a straighter-lined companion structure. It also refers to the complicated lines of sight and movement by which his intricate design reaches out to the surrounding streets. Moving among the museum's 25 galleries, visitors wind between the two portions and upward toward a concluding level of—what else?—sunlight.

After decades of played-out modernist formulas and goofy postmodern replies, we have entered a moment of exciting American architecture. Richard Meier has refined the rules of modernism to high brilliance. Frank Gehry has exploded those same rules to make some of the great buildings of our time. Why should Holl, at 53, be counted the best of them all? Because his buildings epitomize an architecture alert to emotional needs and the spiritual properties of space. Because he conforms his designs so adroitly to their surroundings. Because he knows how to speak through understatement. For all those reasons, his work is more than beautiful. It's illuminating.

Senior writer Richard Lacayo frequently writes on photography and architecture for TIME.

America's Best Fashion Designer
Tom Ford
By Belinda Luscombe

AP/Wide World
Tom Ford design for Yves Saint-Laurent

To do fashion well, one has to master the momentary, to catch time in a bottle-green, double-faced cashmere maxicoat. This is almost harder than making something timeless, because as the moment changes, so must the designer, and he must understand each bank and shoal of time equally well. "The moment of a great dress is a moment," Tom Ford has said. "Not even a week or a month. It's gone at the end of a party."

Ford, 39, born in Texas, raised in New Mexico, and aged in New York City and Europe, has been on the whitecap of—or indeed, his splashes have created—just about every fashion wave since his fall 1995 collection for Gucci. That was the show that brought about a rapprochement between the stylish and the '70s, reacquainting humanity with velvet hip-huggers and satin shirts in a way that allowed us to see an inner beauty or relevance we had somehow overlooked for nigh on two decades. Ford gave that silhouette's androgyny a new spark, suggesting that being located somewhere on a male-female continuum rather than in one gender camp opens up more possibilities.

Ambiguity and transience are perhaps Ford's chief assets as a designer. He won't be nailed down to one look, one sex, one cut, or even one couture house—at least not for long. It's an awkward business, generating desire. Ford has made it into an art form. In his mastery of the now and the new, in his ability to create clothes that grasp and articulate fleeting tastes, Ford is well on his way to securing a lasting place in an ephemeral trade.

Senior writer Belinda Luscombe frequently writes about fashion for TIME.

Lucinda Williams

By Emmylou Harris

Lucinda Williams is a righteous singer. The sound of her voice is so moving that she could sing the phone book and probably give it meaning. But she comes up with extraordinary words for that voice to sing—deceptively simple words like *back steps* or *hairdo*. How do you use the word *hairdo* in a song and make it so poignant that it almost breaks your heart? As a person, Lucinda, who's now 48, doesn't censor herself. She's without guile, and she suffers from that sometimes because people don't know what to make of someone so forthright. They feel as if they want to protect her. But she is a real survivor, and the key to her success as an artist is that she has managed to survive without putting the armor on. Lucinda writes from a very personal standpoint, and that can be difficult. When you go that close to the bone, you are always risking bathos—or being corny or cloying. She plays in dangerous territory, and sometimes you're not sure she's gonna pull it out. Her words take you to another place and make you look at loneliness in a way that you never would have looked at it before.

AP/Wide World

Singer-songwriter Emmylou Harris has recorded since 1967. Her latest album, Red Dirt Girl, *earned her a 10th Grammy Award.*

Cassandra Wilson

By Stanley Crouch

In 1991, after she had been in New York City for almost 10 years, the Mississippi woman known as Cassandra Wilson made a recording titled *Blue Skies* and set herself ahead of all other jazz singers, except for the longtime giants Sarah Vaughan, Ella Fitzgerald, and Betty Carter. With a sensuality too purely adult and far too lyrical to be confused with either the mush or the vulgarity that defines too much popular singing, Wilson remakes standard songs as though none of the lessons laid down by the greats have been lost on her. Wilson knows how to tell a story and how to twist odd sounds out of her throat, which gives the impression that the emotion is so strong it cannot be held in place by a voice or a note. Above all, she doesn't sound like a child or some jaded hussy given to parading self-denigration as a false form of honesty. In her brown beauty, she is a fully grown woman who has high command of the rhythm called swing,

AP/Wide World

which can easily be defined as the sound of the pursuit of happiness. With her thick contralto, Wilson tunes into the wavelengths of romance in all its bounces, its bends, its heights, and its cold-shouldered loneliness. There is no more purely and uncontrived female force in our national music today.

Stanley Crouch's latest book is Don't the Moon Look Lonesome: A Novel of Blues and Swing.

Hilary Hahn

By Terry Teachout

Yes, classical music whiz kids are as common as laid-off dotcom executives, but Hilary Hahn is no robotic virtuoso. Her tone is lean and sweet, her interpretations smart and unshowy; even the hardest-boiled prodigy-hating critics in the business go all mushy when she plays Bach, Beethoven, Barber, and Bernstein. Wait, there's more. She has lovely, wide-set eyes and the figure of a ballerina. And she writes the liner notes for her CDs, as well as an online journal, hilaryhahn.com, illustrated with photos that she takes herself.

Hahn began studying violin at the age of 4, entered Philadelphia's Curtis Institute of Music at 10, and signed an exclusive recording contract with Sony Classical at 16. Yet this wunderkind has paced her career sensibly, steering clear of the pitfalls that await unformed artists who push themselves (or are pushed) too hard. Now, at 21, she is a fully mature musician with a style all her own. Far too many prodigies crash, burn, and vanish, but this remarkable young woman seems here to stay.

Janusz Kawa

Terry Teachout is a contributor to TIME *and the music critic of* Commentary *magazine.*

America's Best Rap Group

The Roots
By Chuck D

Thurston Hopkins/MCA Records

If I have one problem with rap music, and this is one of my only complaints, it's that cats are stuck in the grind of using the same beats per minute all the time. But rhythm and tempo are elements that the Roots always mess around with. They're a great band, and they always go out of their way to experiment and stay responsible to their own point of view. I think their objective is pretty clear: they're trying to bring a true musical aesthetic to rap.

The group—Tariq (Black Thought) Trotter, drummer Ahmir (?uestlove) Thompson, keyboardist Kamal Gray, bassist Leonard (Hub) Hubbard, vocal percussionists Kyle (Scratch) Jones and Rozell (Rahzel) Brown (not pictured), and Malik (Malik B.) Abdul-Bassi—is time tested. In various incarnations, they have been together since 1987. That brings us to the most important part: you've got to be able to perform live, to get in front of the public and sweat for them. Nobody sweats better than the Roots.

Chuck D is a cofounder of the group Public Enemy and of Rapstation.com.

America's Best DJ

DJ Craze
By Christopher John Farley

Brian Smith

DJ Craze, AKA Aristh Delgado, is onstage at the 2000 DMC/Technics World DJ Championships in the Millennium Dome in London, and he's playing the crowd like a video game. Craze, 23, won the world championships in 1998 in Paris; he won again in 1999 in New York City. When Craze spins, it's art—he twists notes in the air the way Jackson Pollock used to drip paint on a canvas. An announcer delivers the judges' decision. . . .

Hold on. Stop the music. How can a guy who just spins records—and mostly records other people recorded—stand beside the likes of Philip Roth and Cassandra Wilson on a list of America's best artists? Well, 75 years ago, many critics thought jazz wasn't an art; 50 years ago, they derided rock; 25 years ago, they went after rap. In the '70s and '80s, DJs such as Kool Herc and Grand Wizard Theodore helped establish DJing as an integral part of hip-hop culture. Craze is taking the genre further. His sets are meticulously planned and carefully executed. Employing a keen ear, he locates the best grooves on a record; sliding his fingers across the vinyl, he nimbly slows down or speeds up the beat; twiddling a cross-fader, he changes the structure of songs by blending the sounds of two records on two different turntables. Craze's work is simultaneously an assault on tradition and a tribute to what's gone before. An announcer delivers the judges' decision: "DJ Craze—the first DJ in history to win one, two, three years consecutively!"

Christopher John Farley is TIME's music critic.

America's Best Rock Band

Sleater-Kinney
By Greil Marcus

Bill Robinson

Sleater-Kinney, composed of Corin Tucker, 28, guitarist-singer Carrie Brownstein, 26, and drummer-singer Janet Weiss, 35, is a punk band because, among other reasons, a sense of exclusion and marginalization is part of what drives its music. That sense is a source of the vehemence in the trio's sound, which has become at once bigger and more agile, harsher and more unpredictable, since the band formed in 1994 in Olympia, Washington. The world is organized so as not to have to listen to songs as frightening and fast as "Youth Decay," and there are thousands of people living in the world desperate to hear a song so unafraid of its own noise, to go to a show precisely to feel unafraid of the noise that they themselves might make. Sleater-Kinney also plays any number of light, happy tunes that don't threaten anybody—that's what one is supposed to say after talking about a song like "Youth Decay," to take the edge off. But with Sleater-Kinney the edge is never off. It's what the band was created to pursue.

Greil Marcus is a columnist for Salon.com and Interview *and author of* Invisible Republic.

The Man of the Year

How "Lucky Lindy"—and a slow week for news— gave birth to a memorable annual tradition

The founders of TIME Magazine, Henry Luce and Briton Haddon, were strong believers in the idea that history is shaped by the deeds of extraordinary men and women. This thesis, most memorably advanced by the British writer Thomas Carlyle, was well-suited to the American vision of the two Yale graduates, since it ran counter to the assertions of Karl Marx and others that history is made by impersonal economic and social forces.

TIME's insistence on the primacy of the individual found its most memorable form in the magazine's annual designation of a Man or Woman of the Year—the person whose actions had most affected the course of the news within the last 12 months. But the magazine's signature annual tribute was not the result of high-level philosophizing: rather, it was driven by something far more important to journalists—a deadline.

The year was 1927; it was the last week in December. During the holiday season, the normal flow of public events had temporarily ebbed to a trickle. Looking to 1928, the editors at TIME were having trouble finding a newsworthy cover subject for the first issue of the new year. At the same time, they realized that they had passed up several opportunities during the year to put aviator Charles Lindbergh on its cover. Since his nonstop flight from New York to Paris in late May, the young pilot had been idolized—yet he had never appeared on the magazine's cover. So the editors came up with a new concept: instead of highlighting a personality of the week, it was decided that the cover for Jan. 2, 1928, would feature Lindbergh, and that beneath his likeness would be the words "Man of the Year."

A year later, the cover for TIME's first issue of 1929 revealed that its editors had named car magnate Walter P. Chrysler as Man of the Year for 1928—and it was obvious that an annual tradition had been born. By the mid-1930s, TIME readers were happily forwarding their suggestions for the Man of the Year to the editors as early as October.

The term "Man of the Year"—redolent of countless Chamber of Commerce dinners—suggests to many people that it is awarded as an accolade. It is not. Rather, it designates the person who, in the editors' opinion, has most affected the course of history in the past twelve months—for good or for ill.

In 1938, for instance, Adolf Hitler completed his Anschluss of Austria and brokered the tragic agreement at Munich that put Czechoslovakia into his hands. However reluctantly, the editors concluded that Hitler's actions had most affected history's course, and he became the 1938 Man of the Year. Similarly, in 1979, Ayatullah Khomeini was named Man of the Year, even while he held Americans hostage in Tehran. TIME received more than 14,000 letters complaining about the choice.

After 75 years, the Man of the Year has become an institution: whereas in one sense it is a sort of intellectual parlor game, it also challenges TIME's editors and readers to reflect on the events of the past year critically, dispassionately, and rigorously. □

1927 Charles Lindbergh	1953 Konrad Adenauer	1977 Anwar Sadat
1928 Walter P. Chrysler	1954 John Foster Dulles	1978 Deng Xiaoping
1929 Owen D. Young	1955 Harlow H. Curtice	1979 Ayatullah Khomeini
1930 Mahatma Gandhi	1956 Hungarian Patriot	1980 Ronald Reagan
1931 Pierre Laval	1957 Nikita Khrushchev	1981 Lech Walesa
1932 Franklin D. Roosevelt	1958 Charles DeGaulle	1982 The Personal Computer
1933 Hugh S. Johnson	1959 Dwight D. Eisenhower	1983 Ronald Reagan and
1934 Franklin D. Roosevelt	1960 U.S. Scientists	Yuri Andropov
1935 Haile Selassie	1961 John F. Kennedy	1984 Peter Ueberroth
1936 Wallis Warfield Simpson	1962 Pope John XXIII	1985 Deng Xiaoping
1937 Gen. and Mrs. Chiang	1963 Rev. Martin Luther King, Jr.	1986 Corazon Aquino
Kai-shek	1964 Lyndon B. Johnson	1987 Mikhail Gorbachev
1938 Adolf Hitler	1965 Gen. William	1988 Endangered Earth
1939 Joseph Stalin	Westmoreland	1989 Mikhail Gorbachev
1940 Winston Churchill	1966 Americans under 25	1990 George Bush
1941 Franklin D. Roosevelt	1967 Lyndon B. Johnson	1991 Ted Turner
1942 Joseph Stalin	1968 Astronauts Anders,	1992 Bill Clinton
1943 Gen. George C. Marshall	Borman, Lovell	1993 The Peacemakers: Rabin,
1944 Gen. Dwight D.	1969 The Middle Americans	Arafat, Mandela, De Klerk
Eisenhower	1970 Willy Brandt	1994 Pope John Paul II
1945 Harry S. Truman	1971 Richard M. Nixon	1995 Newt Gingrich
1946 James F. Byrnes	1972 Richard M. Nixon and	1996 Dr. David Ho
1947 Gen. George C. Marshall	Henry Kissinger	1997 Andrew Grove
1948 Harry S. Truman	1973 Judge John J. Sirica	1998 Bill Clinton and
1949 Winston Churchill	1974 King Faisal	Kenneth Starr
1950 G.I. Joe	1975 American Women	1999 Jeff Bezos
1951 Mohammed Mossadegh	1976 Jimmy Carter	2000 George W. Bush
1952 Queen Elizabeth II		

People in the News, 2001

Danny Almonte, Little League pitching phenom, turned out to be 14, not 12, as his father and coach had claimed. Almonte led his team to the Little League World Series, where he hurled a perfect game. But an investigation in his native Dominican Republic revealed in August that his birth certificate had been falsified, lopping two years off his age to make him eligible for Little League play. The team, the Bronx's Rolando Paulino All-Stars, had to forfeit all victories for the season.

Jessie Arbogast, 8, shark-attack victim, returned to his Mississippi home after a five-week stay at a Pensacola hospital. A 7-foot bull shark bit off the boy's arm in July while he was swimming at Florida's Gulf Islands National Seashore. His arm was reattached, but he remains semiconscious and unable to follow commands.

Lord Jeffrey Archer, novelist and British politician, was found guilty of perjury and perverting justice by a London court in July. The charges against him stemmed from a 1987 libel suit he won against the *Daily Star.* The paper printed that he had an affair with a prostitute, paid her hush money, and falsified records. Outraged at the alleged slander to his good name, Archer sued and won. The paper's allegations were later proved accurate. He was sentenced to four years in jail and fined $250,000.

Lori Berenson, 31, was sentenced to 20 years in prison in Peru after being found guilty in June by a civilian court of "terrorist collaboration" in a 1995 attempt by a Marxist terrorist group to take over the Peruvian Congress. The former New Yorker was first convicted in 1996 by a secret military court and sentenced to life in prison. The military trial was widely condemned as unfair, as her attorneys were not allowed to cross-examine witnesses and the judges presiding over the case were shrouded in hoods. A military tribunal ordered in 2000 that she be retried by a civilian court.

Silvio Berlusconi, Italian politician and media magnate, became prime minister of Italy's 59th postwar "revolving door" government after May elections. Berlusconi is one of the richest men in the world. Allegations of corruption and bribery led to several investigations into his business practices, and he is currently under indictment for tax fraud and bribery.

Osama bin Laden, millionaire Saudi dissident and terrorist, was named as the prime suspect in the horrific September attacks that demolished the World Trade Center towers and caused extensive damage to the Pentagon. More than 5,000 people were reported missing in the tragedy and assumed dead. He denied involvement in the attack but through an aide called it "punishment from Allah." President Bush declared war on terrorism and said he wanted bin Laden "dead or alive." Bin Laden has been implicated in the 1993 World Trade Center bombing, the 1998 bombings at the U.S. embassies in Kenya and Tanzania that killed more than 200, and the 2000 bombing of the USS *Cole* in Yemen.

Barry Bonds, San Francisco Giants left fielder earned the title "home-run king" in October, when he broke Mark McGwire's single-season home-run record (70). Bonds finished the season with 73 dingers.

Veronica "Roni" Bowers, missionary, along with her infant daughter, Charity, was killed in April when Peru's air force shot down the single-engine Cessna in which she was traveling with her family. Her husband, son, and the pilot survived. The air force, working with the crew of an American surveillance plane as part of a joint drug interdiction program, mistook the missionaries for drug traffickers.

David Brock, former conservative journalist, admitted in June that when he was covering the Clarence Thomas confirmation hearings in 1991, he libeled Anita Hill in depicting her as "a little bit nutty and a little bit slutty" and as a liar in *American Spectator* magazine and in his book, *The Real Anita Hill.* He also confessed to embellishing Thomas's reputation.

Linda Chavez, conservative commentator, withdrew her name as President Bush's nominee for secretary of labor in January, after it was revealed that she had sheltered and provided financial assistance to an illegal immigrant in the early 1990s.

Vincent "Buddy" Cianci, Jr., mayor of Providence, Rhode Island, was indicted in April on federal charges of racketeering, conspiracy, extortion, witness tampering, and mail fraud. Several other city officials were also indicted. Cianci is revered in Providence, credited with revitalizing the city's economy and image. Rather than maintaining a low profile after the indictment, Cianci went out of his way to poke fun at the investigation, code-named "Operation Plunder Dome."

Sean Combs (Puff Daddy), entertainment mogul, was acquitted in a Manhattan court in March of four counts of illegal possession of a gun and one count of bribery. The charges stemmed from a December 1999 incident in which three people were shot and injured at a nightclub party in Manhattan. After his legal troubles were behind him, Combs started going by the name P. Diddy.

Gary Condit, 53, Democratic congressman from California, found himself the center of a media frenzy during the summer after former Justice Department Bureau of Prisons intern Chandra Levy, 24, went missing from Washington, DC, in late April. Condit initially denied his relationship with Levy was romantic, as her family had alleged, but later reportedly admitted to police that he had had an affair with her. He has not been identified as a suspect.

Tom Cruise and Nicole Kidman, Hollywood's first couple, shocked the world in February with the news of their separation. In a statement, they cited "difficulties inherent in divergent careers" as the cause for the split. Two days after the announcement, Cruise filed for divorce.

Phoolan Devi, 37, India's "bandit queen," was assassinated by masked gunmen in July. As a teen, she and her lover, Vikram Mallah, led a gang of murderous desperadoes. Eventually some gang members turned on them, killing him and handing her over to a group of upper-caste landowners who, by Devi's account, raped her repeatedly. She spent 11 years in jail for the 1980 revenge-style murders of 22 of her attackers, emerging as a hero of the lower castes. She served in Parliament from 1996 until her death.

Dipendra, 29, crown prince of Nepal, went on a shooting rampage at the family's Kathmandu palace in June, wiping out nearly the entire royal family before turning his revolver on himself. Casualties included his father, King Birendra; his mother, Queen Aiswarya; his sister, Shruti; and his brother, Nirajan. Dipendra temporarily survived the suicide attempt and was enthroned as king as he lay in a coma. Birendra's brother, Gyanendra, became king shortly after Dipendra died. Aiswarya's disapproval of Dipendra's intended bride reportedly prompted her son's homicidal rage.

Ira Einhorn, fugitive, was extradited to the U.S. from France in July to face retrial in the 1977 death of his girlfriend, Holly Maddux. The former antiwar activist and New Age guru was convicted and sentenced to life in prison in absentia in 1993 for beating Maddux to death. He fled the country in 1981 and spent two decades on the lam.

Joseph Ellis, historian and Pulitzer Prize–winning writer, admitted in June that he led his students at Mount Holyoke College to believe that he had served as a paratrooper in Vietnam, when in reality his three years of service had been spent teaching history at the U.S. Military Academy at West Point. He was also accused of embellishing his role in the civil rights and antiwar movements. He was subsequently suspended from Mount Holyoke for one year without pay and stripped of his endowed chair. Ellis won the 2001 Pulitzer Prize for history for *Founding Brothers: The Revolutionary Generation.*

Joseph Estrada, president of the Philippines, resigned in January after the impeachment trial against him collapsed, causing massive street protests and members of his cabinet and senior military officials to withdraw their support. He was accused of receiving $80 million from a gambling-payoff scheme and several more million from tobacco tax kickbacks. Vice President Gloria Macapagal Arroyo, a Harvard-trained economist and the daughter of former president Diosdado Macapagal, succeeded Estrada. In April, Estrada was jailed following his arrest on charges of corruption. He was indicted in July on the capital charge of economic plunder.

Gao Zhan and Qin Guangguang, U.S.-based Chinese scholars, were convicted in July of spying for Taiwan in a Beijing court and sentenced to 10 years in prison. In a related case, Li Shaomin, a naturalized U.S. citizen who taught at a Hong Kong university, was also convicted of spying. He was deported to the U.S. Gao and Qin were granted medical parole weeks later, just before a visit to Beijing by U.S. secretary of state Colin Powell.

Rudolph Giuliani, mayor of New York City, won wide praise for his poised handling of the September 11 terrorist attacks on the World Trade Center towers. He acted with both resolve and compassion, guiding the city through one of its darkest times. Giuliani, prevented from seeking reelection by term-limits laws, offered to extend his term by three months to help with the transition to a new administration.

Thomas Green, proud polygamist, was found guilty on four counts of bigamy and failure to pay child support by a Utah jury in May. A fundamentalist Mormon, Green lives with his five wives and 29 children in Utah. He boasted about his extensive family on national talk shows. In August he was sentenced to five years in prison.

Robert Philip Hanssen, senior FBI agent who specialized in counterintelligence, was indicted in May on charges of spying for Russia. For 15 years, he allegedly handed over to Russia highly sensitive, classified information in exchange for about $1.4 million. In July, as part of a plea agreement, he pleaded guilty to 15 counts of espionage and conspiracy, thus avoiding the death penalty.

Jesse Helms, 79, conservative Republican senator from North Carolina, announced in August that he would not seek reelection in 2002. The darling of the right, Helms has served in the Senate since 1972 and often sparked the ire of moderates and liberals with his archconservatism. He cited failing health for his decision. Pundits immediately began speculating who would run for his seat.

Saad Eddin Ibrahim, sociologist and human rights activist, was convicted in May of defaming Egypt, accepting money from the European Union without authorization, and embezzlement. He was sentenced to seven years in jail by a Cairo, Egypt, court.

Ibrahim—as well as many others throughout Egypt—spoke out against the 1995 elections, which were widely criticized as rigged. In addition, an EU audit reported the funds were used properly, for voter registration. The conviction, which was rendered after only one hour, outraged many human rights groups.

Rev. Jesse Jackson, civil rights activist, admitted in January that he and Karin Stanford had had a child together in 1998, just about the time he was counseling President Clinton during the Lewinsky scandal. Stanford was head of the Washington branch of Jackson's Rainbow/PUSH Coalition.

James Jeffords, U.S. senator from Vermont, sent shockwaves through Washington and beyond in May when he announced he was bolting from the Republican Party to become an Independent. The move stripped Republicans of control of the Senate and gave Democrats the narrowest of majorities (50-49-1). Sen. Tom Daschle become majority leader, the role formerly held by Sen. Trent Lott.

Nkosi Johnson, 12, South African AIDS victim who devoted his short life to fighting discrimination against AIDS victims, died in June. Born with the disease, Johnson far exceeded his life expectancy. He gained international prominence when he delivered a heart-wrenching speech at the 13th International AIDS conference in 2000.

Laurent Kabila, president of the Democratic Republic of Congo, was shot in the presidential palace in Kinshasa in January. He later died from the wounds. Though details are sketchy, many reports indicate that he was shot by a bodyguard. Kabila's son, Maj. Gen. Joseph Kabila, 31, assumed the presidency and inherited a country mired in a bloody civil war and plagued by economic disaster.

Bob Kerrey, former U.S. senator and president of the New School University, was forced to reopen old wounds from the Vietnam War in April when a former Navy SEAL gave an account, which conflicted with Kerrey's, to the *New York Times* and CBS News about a 1969 incident in which several women and children were shot. Kerrey said that his outfit, nicknamed "Kerrey's Raiders," was sent on a mission to kill Viet Cong soldiers meeting in the Mekong Delta. He said his group was fired at and returned fire, only to learn later that they had shot and killed more than a dozen women and children. Fellow SEAL Gerhard Klann told reporters that Kerrey had ordered the unit to round up the civilians and shoot them.

Mohammad Khatami, Iranian politician, was reelected president in June, winning an overwhelming 77% of the vote. The win underscored the populace's desire for reform. Khatami has steadily introduced democratic practices, much to the displeasure of the hard-line clerics who have dominated the country since the 1979 Islamic revolution.

Junichiro Koizumi, Japanese politician, was sworn in as the country's 11th prime minister in 13 years in April, after he was elected president of the ruling Liberal Democratic Party. A reformer, he ran on a platform for change and is faced with revitalizing a tattered economy. Koizumi promptly assembled a cabinet of reformers rather than party stalwarts. He succeeded the immensely unpopular Yoshiro Mori, who stepped down after a year in power.

James Charles Kopp, anti-abortion activist who had been indicted in 1999 in the shooting death of abortion doctor Barnett Slepian, was arrested in March in France. Kopp had been on the lam for more than two years. Authorities traced him to France after investigating other anti-abortion activists.

Radislav Krstic, former Bosnian Serb general, was found guilty of genocide in August by the Hague's international war crimes tribunal and sentenced to 46 years in prison. Krstic was involved in the 1995 massacre in Srebrenica of more than 7,000 unarmed Muslim men and boys and is the first European ever convicted of genocide.

Casey Martin, disabled professional golfer, won the legal right to use a golf cart during competition. In May the U.S. Supreme Court ruled 7–2 in his favor, rejecting the PGA Tour's claim that using a cart would give him an unfair advantage over golfers who have to walk the course. The ruling ended Martin's four-year battle with the PGA.

Ahmed Shah Massoud, legendary guerrilla leader of Afghanistan's Northern Alliance, which has relentlessly challenged the Taliban since 1996, was killed in a September suicide bombing. His attackers, two Algerian terrorists posing as television journalists, are believed to be part of Osama bin Laden's al-Qaeda network. Massoud was an insurmountable resistance leader during the Soviet occupation of Afghanistan in the 1980s.

John McCain and Russell Feingold, determined U.S. senators, shepherded through the Senate in April a sweeping campaign-finance bill that bans soft money, or unlimited contributions to parties; limits advertising by independent groups; increases donations to candidates; and enhances contribution-disclosure rules. The bill, which passed 59–41, survived several amendments and legislative maneuvering intended to water it down or make it constitutionally unsound.

Timothy McVeigh, 33, convicted Oklahoma City bomber, was executed by lethal injection in June for detonating a fertilizer bomb that destroyed the Alfred P. Murrah Federal Building in April 1995 and killed 149 adults and 19 children. It was the first execution by the federal government in 38 years. McVeigh was scheduled to be put to death in May, but the date was postponed when the FBI revealed that it had failed to turn over to the defense thousands of documents related to its investigation.

Megawati Sukarnoputri, Indonesian politician, became president in July, when Abdurraham Wahid was forced to step down amid charges of corruption and incompetence. Megawati, the daughter of Indonesia's first president, Sukarno, inherited a country mired in poverty and ravaged by ethnic unrest in Aceh, Irian Jaya, the Moluccan Islands, and Borneo.

Abdelbaset Ali Mohmed al-Megrahi, Libyan intelligence officer, was found guilty by a Scottish court in January of murder in the 1988 deaths of 270 passengers aboard Pan Am Flight 103 over Lockerbie, Scotland. The court, which was convened in the Netherlands, did not convict a second suspect. The plane was on its way to New York from London when it exploded and fell from the sky.

Emmanuel Milingo, Roman Catholic archbishop, renounced his marriage to Korean acupuncturist Maria Sung in August. The couple had been married in a May multiple wedding ceremony by Rev. Sun Myung Moon, the head of the Unification Church movement. The marriage prompted outrage from the Catholic church, and Milingo was threatened with excommunication unless he dissolved the union. He ultimately chose the church.

Heather Mills, 33, activist and former model, became engaged to former Beatle Paul McCartney in July. Mills lost half of one leg in 1993, when she was hit by a London police motorcycle. She has since devoted her time to helping amputees and victims of land mines. The couple met in 1999.

Slobodan Milosevic, former president of Yugoslavia, was arrested in April after a 26-hour armed standoff with police at his Belgrade home. He was charged with corruption and stealing state funds during his 13-year rule. Milosevic surrendered after Yugoslav officials promised him that he would have a fair trial and would not immediately be turned over to the United Nations war crimes tribunal at the Hague. He

was, however, turned over to the UN in June and will stand trial on charges of committing crimes against humanity during Yugoslavia's crackdown on ethnic Albanians in Kosovo in 1999.

Vladimiro Montesinos, former spy chief of Peru, was captured in Venezuela in June after spending eight months in hiding. He was whisked to Peru, where he faces a laundry list of charges, including bribery, money laundering, arms trafficking, torture, and leading a paramilitary death squad. He fled the country in 2000, after the broadcast of a tape in which he was seen evidently attempting to buy the loyalty of an opposition congressman. The video ended the career of President Alberto Fujimori, who employed Montesinos as a presidential aide, spymaster, and attorney. Since Montesinos fled, thousands of tapes have surfaced that illustrate the corruption rampant during Fujimori's reign.

Robert Mueller III, seasoned prosecutor, was tapped by President Bush to succeed Louis J. Freeh as the director of the FBI. Mueller served as U.S. attorney twice, in Boston from 1982 to 1988 and in San Francisco since 1998. He won easy Senate confirmation in August.

Pervez Musharraf, Pakistani general, declared himself president and formal head of state in June, less than a month before a summit meeting in India with Prime Minister Atal Behari Vajpayee. He promptly assured the country that civilian rule will resume in October 2002, with democratic elections. Musharraf angered Pakistan's Islamic fundamentalists when he agreed to cooperate with the U.S. following September's terrorist attacks.

Richard Myers, four-star general, became the chairman of the Joint Chiefs of Staff, assuming command just weeks after the Sept. 11 terrorist attacks. A 36-year Air Force veteran, Myers served as commander of the U.S. forces in Japan (1993–1996) and commander of the Pacific Air Forces (1997–1998).

Mullah Muhammad Omar, supreme leader of the Taliban, ordered the destruction of all statues in Afghanistan to prevent idol worship. Ancient stone Buddhas, dating back to the 3rd and 5th centuries, were among the artifacts demolished in March, despite international pleas to save the statues. He further incensed much of the world in September, when he defiantly refused to surrender to the U.S. Osama bin Laden, the prime suspect in the terrorist attacks in New York and Washington. Attacks on Afghanistan by U.S. and British forces followed in October.

Shane Osborn, Navy pilot, successfully landed his disabled EP-3 Aries II on China's Hainan Island after colliding in April with a Chinese F-8 fighter over the South China Sea during a surveillance flight. The Chinese jet went down and its pilot, Wang Wei, is presumed dead. The 24 crew members of the U.S. plane were held for 11 days by Chinese authorities, heightening tensions between the U.S. and China.

James Parker, 16, and Robert Tulloch, 17, Vermont teens, were charged in February with first-degree murder for the January stabbing deaths of husband-and-wife Dartmouth College professors, Half and Susanne Zantop. The teens were arrested at an Indiana truck stop two days after fleeing Vermont.

Augusto Pinochet, Chilean general and former president, in July was declared mentally unfit to stand trial on charges of genocide, torture, and kidnapping. The Chilean appeals court said that his ill health resulted in a state of dementia that would make him unable to defend himself. The charges stem from his oppressive rule in Chile from 1973 to 1989.

Julie Ponder and Connell Watkins, Colorado therapists, were convicted in April of child abuse in the death of 10-year-old Candace Newmaker. Newmaker died after undergoing "rebirthing" therapy, in which the therapists wrapped her in a flannel sheet and instructed her to struggle out to simulate birth, thus becoming "reborn" to her adoptive mother. Newmaker spent 70 minutes in the blanket and later died of asphyxiation. Ponder and Watkins were sentenced to 16 years in prison.

Alice Randall, writer, riled the publishing world with her novel, *The Wind Done Gone,* a retelling of Margaret Mitchell's *Gone with the Wind* from the point of view of Scarlett O'Hara's mulatto half-sister. Randall claimed the book was a serious parody and was protected by the First Amendment. In April, a federal judge blocked publication of Randall's novel, citing a copyright infringement. The U.S. Court of Appeals in Atlanta overturned the injunction in May, paving the way for the book's publication. Randall borrowed scenes and dialogue from the original novel.

Dan Rather, *CBS Evening News* anchor, made headlines over the summer for refusing to report the news—or at least what other news outlets deemed newsworthy—about the disappearance of government intern Chandra Levy. He eventually capitulated under pressure from CBS but still devoted much less time to the story than the other networks.

Janet Reno, former U.S. attorney general, announced in September that she will seek the Democratic nomination for governor of Florida. She's looking to unseat Gov. Jeb Bush, the president's brother, whose term ends in 2002.

Marc Rich, fugitive billionaire financier, received a last-minute pardon in January from President Clinton. The move outraged many on both sides of the political aisle. In 1983, Rich and his partner Pincus Green, who was also pardoned, were charged with cheating the government out of nearly $50 million and doing business with Iran during the hostage crisis. Rich fled to Switzerland, where he lived in luxury.

Tom Ridge, former governor of Pennsylvania, was named director of the Office of Homeland Security by President Bush in the wake of September's terrorist attacks. In his cabinet-level position, Ridge is charged with bringing more than 40 federal agencies under one umbrella to prevent future terrorist attacks.

Cal Ripken, Jr., professional baseball player, retired in October, at the end of the 2001 season. Known as the Iron Man of baseball, Ripken spent his entire career with the Baltimore Orioles and in 1998 set a record for the most consecutive games played (2,632).

Hugh Rodham, attorney and brother of Sen. Hillary Rodham Clinton, acknowledged in February that he had been paid $400,000 to represent two convicts, Carlos Vignali, Jr., and Almon Glenn Braswell, who had applied for presidential clemency. Braswell was pardoned for convictions from 1983 on charges of fraud, perjury, and tax evasion. President Clinton commuted the sentence of Vignali, who had been serving time for charges related to trafficking 800 pounds of cocaine. Rodham returned the payments.

Ariel Sharon, right-wing Israeli politician, won a landslide victory over Ehud Barak in the February special prime minister elections. He won 62.6% of the vote to Barak's 37.2%. Sharon said he would work toward peace with the Palestinians only after he brings security to Israel and an end to the violence that has plagued the country since September 1999.

Dmitri Sklyarov, Russian computer programmer, was arrested in July in Las Vegas on charges of violating 1998's Digital Millennium Copyright Act. As an employee of Russia's ElcomSoft, he wrote software that allows users of Adobe eBook to download and distribute copies of electronic books. Programmers and copyright lawyers criticized his arrest and questioned the enforceability of the law.

Nikolay Soltys, 27-year-old Ukrainian immigrant, was arrested in California in August following a 10-day nationwide manhunt. He was accused of stabbing to death his pregnant wife, 3-year-old son, aunt, uncle, and two cousins.

Jane Swift, politician, became Massachusetts's first woman governor in April, when Governor Paul Cellucci, recently confirmed as ambassador to Canada, passed the torch to his second-in-command. Swift, 36, is the youngest governor in the country, and she became the first to give birth while in office when her twins arrived in May.

Lionel Tate, 14, was sentenced to life without parole in March by a Florida court after being found guilty of first-degree murder for killing a 6-year-old girl in 1999. Tate had been practicing wrestling moves when he crushed Tiffany Eunick. His mother rejected a plea bargain in which he would have served three years in a juvenile facility, one year of house arrest, and then 10 years of probation.

Dennis Tito, space tourist, paid $20 million for an eight-day trip to the International Space Station aboard the Russian Soyuz-U booster. Tito, a financial adviser and former NASA engineer, lifted off in April from the Baikonur Cosmodrome in Kazakhstan and returned to Earth in a space capsule, unharmed and buoyant.

John Tobin, Jr., Fulbright scholar, returned to the U.S. in August, after being imprisoned in Russia for six months. He was arrested in January on charges of marijuana possession and was later accused of being a spy-in-training. Tobin denied the accusation and said the marijuana charge was a setup. He was in Russia conducting political research at a university in Voronezh.

Robert Tools received the first self-contained artificial heart in July. The device, the AbioCor, was surgically implanted by doctors at Jewish Hospital in Louisville, Ky. Tools was near death from end-stage heart failure when he underwent the procedure. Doctors said he has "a good future."

David Trimble, Ulster Unionist leader, resigned his post as first minister of the Northern Ireland Assembly in July after the Irish Republican Army once again stalled on disarmament. The move threatened to topple the 1998 Good Friday peace agreement, thus returning governing powers to the British government from the Northern Irish coalition Parliament. Trimble, who won the Nobel Peace Prize in 1998, sought to return to his post in October, after the IRA finally began to dismantle its weapons.

Scott Waddle, commander of the USS *Greeneville,* the submarine that crashed into a Japanese fishing vessel as it emerged in waters off Hawaii, took sole responsibility for the fatal February exercise that claimed the lives of nine Japanese. Waddle acknowledged that mistakes had been made and corners had been cut aboard the 6,900-ton nuclear sub but said his actions were not criminal. He received a reprimand in April and retired from duty.

Fay Weldon, British novelist, raised eyebrows in literary circles when it was announced in September that she had been commissioned to write a novel by the exclusive Italian jeweler Bulgari. *The Bulgari Connection,* to be published by Grove/Atlantic, signals a new trend in literary product placement.

Tina Wesson, diminutive game-show contestant, outwitted, outlasted, and outplayed the 15 other *Survivor II: The Australian Outback* cast members to win $1 million in cash and an amount likely to surpass that in endorsements, commercials, and speaking gigs. Rounding out the final four were custom auto designer and proud Texan Colby Donaldson, gourmet chef Keith Famie, and cute-as-a-button footwear designer Elisabeth Filiarski.

Andrea Pia Yates, Texas mother, was charged in June with capital murder in the deaths of her five children, who ranged in age from 6 months to 7 years. Yates reportedly suffered from postpartum depression. She is accused of methodically drowning the children in the family's bathtub.

2001 Deaths

(through October 26, 2001)

Aaliyah (Aaliyah Haughton), 22: rhythm-and-blues singer and actress who was on the brink of superstardom when she died in a plane crash. Her recent self-titled album reached No. 2 on the Billboard album chart. She appeared in the 2000 film *Romeo Must Die* and in the upcoming *Queen of the Damned.* Aug. 25, 2001

Lionel Abel, 90: playwright, essayist, and novelist who won an Obie Award for his 1956 off-Broadway play *Absalom.* April 19, 2001

Douglas Adams, 49: British author who wrote the *The Hitchhiker's Guide to the Galaxy* series of books, which was adapted for television and stage. His works satirized technology, politics, and bureaucracy. May 11, 2001

Larry Adler, 87: musician whose skill helped to elevate the harmonica to a serious, concert-worthy instrument. He moved to London in 1952, after he was blacklisted in the U.S. He frequently performed with tap dancer Paul Draper. Aug. 7, 2001

Mortimer Adler, 98: philosopher, educator, and writer who helped to devise the Great Book learning program, which included 443 literary classics. His books include *Aristotle for Everybody* (1978) and *Six Great Ideas* (1981). June 28, 2001

Jorge Amado, 88: Brazilian novelist whose political and comic novels have been translated into 50 languages. A former communist, Amado lampooned Brazil's politicians, and as a result spent time in prison and exile. His books include *Gabriela, Clove and Cinnamon* (1958) and *Dona Flor and Her Two Husbands* (1966). Both were made into films starring Sonia Braga. Aug. 6, 2001

A. R. Ammons, 75: award-winning poet whose simple verse often disguised the depth of his work. Ammons wrote nearly 30 books of poetry and won scores of awards, including two National Book Awards, the Bollingen Prize in Poetry, and a National Book Critics Circle Award. His works include *Garbage, Sphere,* and *A Coast of Trees.* Feb. 25, 2001

Poul Anderson, 74: award-winning writer who used his background in physics to craft meticulously accurate works of science fiction. His books include *The Boat of a Million Years* (1989) and *A Midsummer Tempest* (1974). He won seven Hugo Awards and the John W. Campbell Award. July 31, 2001

Earl Anthony, 63: prolific bowling champion of the 1970s and 1980s whose left-handed delivery, crew cut, and glasses became a fixture on the sport's national weekend telecasts. He won 41 national tour titles and eight major tournament titles, more than any other bowler in history, and in 1982 became the first bowler to eclipse the $1 million mark in official PBA earnings. Aug. 14, 2001

Chet Atkins, 77: virtuosic guitar player and record producer who helped to make Nashville the epicenter of country music in the 1950s. Known as the "Country Gentleman," Atkins gained fame in the 1940s, performing with the Carter Family in the Grand Ole Opry. As an executive with RCA, Atkins produced recordings by Hank Snow, Dolly Parton, Waylon Jennings, and Charley Pride. When interest in country music began to wane, Atkins was influential in adapting the genre to appeal to the growing base of rock-and-roll fans. June 30, 2001

Harvey Ball, 79: commercial artist and ad executive who is widely credited with creating the smiley face, the symbol that has been emblazoned on everything from clothing to postage stamps. Ball crafted the bright yellow icon for a Massachusetts insurance company, which paid Ball $45. He never trademarked the icon. April 12, 2001

Balthus (Balthasar Klossowski), 92: French painter known for his portraits, French landscapes, and paintings that often depicted young women in provocative poses. He remains one of Europe's most respected portraitists. His works include *The Mountain* (1937), *The Street* (1933), and *The Guitar Lesson* (1934). Feb. 18, 2001

Christiaan Barnard, 78: South African heart surgeon who made medical history on Dec. 3, 1967, when he performed the first human-to-human heart transplant. Barnard also designed artificial heart valves and developed advanced surgical procedures for organ transplants. He was a vociferous antiapartheid activist who created a frenzy in 1968 when he transplanted the heart of a mixed-race man into a white dentist. Sept. 2, 2001

Abraham Beame, 94: politician who served as mayor of New York City (1974 to 1977). He managed to keep the city financially afloat in 1975 and 1976 amid the city's worst financial crisis. Feb. 10, 2001

King Birendra (Birendra Bir Bikram Shah Deva), 55: King of Nepal who was shot to death by his son, Crown Prince Dipendra, in a massacre that nearly wiped out the entire royal family. His wife, Queen Aiswarya; their daughter, Princess Shruti; and another son, Prince Nirajan, were also killed. Dipendra died of a self-inflicted gunshot wound. Birendra, believed to be the reincarnation of Vishnu, acceded to the throne in 1972. In 1990, a pro-democracy movement led to the first free election in three decades and a new role for Birendra as constitutional monarch. June 1, 2001

Charles Black, Jr., 85: constitutional law expert and professor who helped to write the legal brief for 10-year-old Linda Brown, the plaintiff in the landmark 1954 Supreme Court case, *Brown v. Board of Education.* Black's book, *Impeachment: A Handbook,* was widely referenced during the Watergate scandal and again in 1999 during President Clinton's impeachment. May 5, 2001

Luiz Bonfa, 78: Brazilian guitarist and songwriter who introduced the world to Brazilian bossa nova. His works, noted for samba-based rhythms, were recorded by Stan Getz, Quincy Jones, Frank Sinatra, and other musicians. Jan. 12, 2001

Philip Buchen, 85: attorney who led a group that worked secretly in 1974, making plans for Vice President Gerald Ford's transition to the presidency if President Nixon were to resign. He later advised Ford in his pardon of Nixon. May 21, 2001

Ely Callaway, 82: golf visionary who transformed the Callaway Golf Co. into the world's biggest clubmaker and introduced the "Big Bertha" driver to weekend golfers. After a 30-year career in the textile industry, he bought Hickory Stick, a small golf club company, for $400,000 in 1984. Sales had reached $800 million by 1998. July 5, 2001

Arthur Cantor, 81: prolific Broadway producer who championed the works of Paddy Chayefsky and Herb Gardner. His credits include the Pulitzer Prize—winning plays *All the Way Home* and *The Tenth Man.* April 8, 2001

Howard Clark, 84: business executive who transformed American Express from a young, unstable company into an industry giant. He took over as president and chief executive of the company in 1960 and launched the ad campaign in which celebrities asked, "Do you know me?" He later debuted the "Don't leave home without it" slogan. Clark retired from American Express in 1977. Feb. 2, 2001

Imogene Coca, 92: comedienne whose limitless expressions prompted a million laughs and who hilariously mimicked housewives, divas, and socialites. Coca starred with Sid Caesar on NBC's *Your Show of Shows* from 1950 to 1954. June 2, 2001

Perry Como, 88: Grammy Award–winning crooner known for his laid-back personality and casual song delivery. *The Perry Como Show* was broadcast from 1948 to 1963. His hits included "When You Were 16" and "Catch a Falling Star." May 13, 2001

Gregory Corso, 70: iconoclastic poet and social critic who was a founder of the Beat movement. His poems, including "Elegiac Feelings American," were often intimate and candid, and his criticism was often shocking and provocative. Jan. 17, 2001

Donald Cram, 82: chemist who shared the 1987 Nobel Prize in chemistry for "synthesizing three-dimensional molecules that could mimic the functioning of natural molecules." He also won the National Academy of Science Award in the Chemical Sciences. June 17, 2001

Candida Donadio, 71: literary agent whose first assignment was to sell Joseph Heller's *Catch-22.* The book was originally titled *Catch-18,* but she changed it to avoid confusion with Leon Uris's *Mila 18.* Jan. 20, 2001

Troy Donahue, 65: teen heartthrob who starred in television's *Hawaiian Eye* (1960–62) and *Surfside Six* (1962–63). He made the leap to the big screen in 1957 with *Man Afraid,* and went on to star in *A Summer Place* (1959). Sept. 2, 2001

Morton Downey, Jr., 67: contentious host of the short-lived but popular *Morton Downey, Jr. Show,* a 1980s talk show. Downey had a long and diverse career before he became an icon of the right wing. He had been a singer, record producer, disc jockey, and founder of the American Basketball Association. Pope Paul VI knighted Downey for his humanitarian work in the 1970s. March 12, 2001

Dale Earnhardt, 49: seven-time Winston Cup champion and one of the most beloved drivers in auto racing history. His aggressive racing style earned him the nickname "The Intimidator." He died of injuries sustained in an accident on the final lap of the 2001 Daytona 500. Feb. 18, 2001

Arlene Eisenberg, 66: writer who, with her two daughters, Heidi Murkoff and Sandee Hathaway, wrote the best-selling What to Expect series of pregnancy and child-rearing books. The series includes *What to Expect When You're Expecting* and *What to Expect the First Year.* Feb. 8, 2001

James Ellis, 45: computer scientist who was a creator of Usenet, an international network of electronic discussion groups, and an expert on computer security. He died of non-Hodgkins lymphoma. June 28, 2001

Dale Evans, 88: actress, songwriter, and writer who starred with her husband, Roy Rogers, in several Westerns and on television's *The Roy Rogers Show* (1950–1957). Her big break came in 1944, when she was cast opposite John Wayne in *Old Oklahoma.* Evans wrote several inspirational books, including *Angel Unaware,* which she dedicated to her daughter, Robin, who died as a toddler of complications from Down syndrome. Feb. 7, 2001

Rowland Evans, 79: columnist, pundit, and author who earned the ire of liberals and the praise of conservatives. He cowrote columns and books with Robert Novak. The pair also cohosted *Evans and Novak,* a CNN political talk show. March 23, 2001

Mimi Fariña, 56: folk singer who, in 1974, created Bread and Roses, an organization that stages benefit performances by popular musicians. She was a sister of Joan Baez and was married to singer Richard Fariña, who died in a motorcycle accident in 1966. Their lives are the subject of the recent book, *Positively 4th Street: The Lives and Times of Joan Baez, Bob Dylan, Mimi Fariña, and Richard Fariña,* by David Hajdu. July 18, 2001

Kathleen Freeman, 78: versatile character actress who appeared in dozens of films, TV shows, and Broadway plays. Known for her jowls, Freeman appeared in the films *Singin' in the Rain* (1952), *North to Alaska* (1960), and *The Blues Brothers* (1980). She performed in Broadway's *The Full Monty* days before her death. Aug. 23, 2001

J. C. Furnas, 95: historian and writer known for his in-depth examination of social issues. His article " . . . And Sudden Death" investigated auto-related deaths. The piece led to safer designs of cars and highways. June 3, 2001

Milton Gabler, 90: record producer who started the first independent jazz label, Commodore Records, and ran the Commodore Music Shop, one of New York City's most respected jazz record stores. He recorded jazz greats Billie Holiday, Louis Armstrong, and Ella Fitzgerald. In 1954 he produced "Rock Around the Clock." July 20, 2001

Katharine Graham, 84: newspaper and magazine publisher who transformed the *Washington Post* into one of the most influential newspapers in the country. She took control of the paper in 1963, after the suicide of her husband, Phil Graham. In 1971 she gave her editors the go-ahead to publish the Pentagon Papers after a federal court enjoined the *New York Times* from doing so. Three years later she encouraged reporters Carl Bernstein and Bob Woodward in their relentless investigation of the Watergate scandal. She won a Pulitzer Prize in 1998 for her memoir, *Personal History.* July 17, 2001

Joseph Greenberg, 85: prominent linguist who specialized in classifying the 5,000 languages of the world. He organized Africa's 1,500 languages into four families: Niger-Kordofanian, Afroasiatic, Nilo-Saharan, and Khoisan. May 7, 2001

Jack Haley, Jr., 67: Emmy Award–winning director and producer who helmed the 1974 all-star documentary *That's Entertainment.* He was once married to Liza Minnelli. His father, Jack Haley, played the Tin Man in *The Wizard of Oz.* April 21, 2001

Viktor Hamburger, 100: experimental embryologist who analyzed the developing nervous system. In 1954, he and two colleagues, Rita Levi-Montalcini and Stanley Cohen, discovered the first trophic factor. June 12, 2001

William Hanna, 90: pioneering animator who, with his partner, Joseph Barbera, masterminded the cartoon characters Yogi Bear, Scooby-Doo, and Tom and Jerry. Their *Tom and Jerry* cartoons won seven Oscars, and their film *Anchors Aweigh* (1945) combined animation with live action for the first time. The Hanna-Barbera team won seven Emmy Awards, including the first for an animated series (*The Huckleberry Hound Show*). March 21, 2001

Herblock (Herbert L. Block), 91: famed editorial cartoonist who won three Pulitzer Prizes for his stylized, witty images. In his 50-plus years at the *Washington Post,* he satirized every president from Herbert Hoover to George W. Bush. His targets also included the atomic bomb, Stalin, and the missile-defense program known as "Star Wars." His collections of cartoons include *The Herblock Book* (1952) and *Herblock's State of the Union* (1972). Oct. 7, 2001

William Hewlett, 87: electronics entrepreneur who, with David Packard, scraped together $538 in 1938 and started an electronics company in Palo Alto, Calif. The company, Hewlett Packard, flourished and became the country's second-largest computer maker. Hewlett and Packard are credited with establishing Silicon Valley. Jan. 12, 2001

Clifton Hillegass, 83: publisher who created Cliffs Notes, the popular series of study guides to literature. The yellow-and-black-covered books have been used by millions of students for a concise summary of such classics as *Moby Dick, Wuthering Heights,* and *The Catcher in the Rye.* May 5, 2001

John Lee Hooker, 83: legendary blues musician whose somber lyrics and endless one-chord guitar riffs helped to define boogie blues. He has influenced bands ranging from the Rolling Stones to Carlos Santana to ZZ Top. Hooker won a Grammy Award for "I'm in the Mood," a 1989 duet with Bonnie Raitt, and two more in 1997 for the album *Don't Look Back.* He was inducted into the Rock and Roll Hall of Fame in 1991. June 21, 2001

Frances R. Horwich, 94: matronly host of the 1950s children's educational program *Ding Dong School.* The show inspired *Sesame Street.* She won a 1953 Peabody Award. July 25, 2001

Sir Fred Hoyle, 86: prominent astrophysicist who wrote extensively about cosmological theory, the belief that the universe is in a steady state of time and space. He mockingly coined the term "Big Bang" in the 1940s, ridiculing the theory that the universe originated with an explosion. In 1957 he contributed to groundbreaking papers about the origins of the elements. Aug. 20, 2001

Tove Jansson, 86: Finnish author and artist who wrote and illustrated a series of children's books that featured the Moomins, indefatigable trolls. The books, which include *Comet in Moominland* (1945) and *Moominland Midwinter* (1958), have been translated into more than 30 languages. June 27, 2001

J. J. Johnson, 77: influential jazz musician and composer who is considered the greatest trombonist of all time. He played with such speed and agility that many thought he was playing the valve rather than the slide trombone. He recorded dozens of albums and played with jazz greats Miles Davis, Dizzy Gillespie, and Charlie Parker. Feb. 4, 2001

Pauline Kael, 82: famously influential movie critic whose acerbic wit, vast knowledge of the filmmaking process, and passion for film were widely imitated but never rivaled. She was *The New Yorker's* film critic from 1968 until she retired in 1991, lamenting the disappointing state of cinema. She was especially fond of 1970s films, and championed the works of directors Steven Spielberg, Brian De Palma, and Robert Altman. Sept. 3, 2001

Hank Ketcham, 81: cartoonist who in 1950 created the mischievous character Dennis the Menace, who was based on his own son. June 1, 2001

Hannelore Kohl, 68: wife of former German chancellor Helmut Kohl. She committed suicide after a long bout with a severe, untreatable allergy to sunlight. July 6, 2001

Stanley Kramer, 87: film producer and director whose socially aware films covered such topics as race, juvenile delinquency, and Nazi war crimes and earned him the title "message filmmaker." He remains one of Hollywood's most respected auteurs. His credits include *The Defiant Ones* (1958), *Judgment at Nuremberg* (1961), and *Guess Who's Coming to Dinner* (1967). Feb. 19, 2001

Morris Lapidus, 98: flamboyant postmodern architect who designed several gaudy yet glamorous hotels in South Florida. His work, which shunned the straight line and favored curvy, theatrical elements, was initially derided by critics, who considered his designs kitschy. Opinion of him changed, however, when Miami Beach became a trendy refuge of the jet set. His most famous designs include Miami Beach's Fontainebleau Hilton. Jan. 18, 2001

Tanaquil Le Clercq, 71: French-born, willowy ballerina who frequently and gracefully performed the works of Jerome Robbins and George Balanchine, to whom she was once married. She contracted polio in 1956, at age 27, and became paralyzed from the waist down. In an eerily prescient performance in 1944, Balanchine choreographed a short piece in which he played a character named Polio, and Le Clercq was his victim. Jan. 1, 2001

Jack Lemmon, 76: beloved and versatile actor who excelled at both comic and dramatic roles. In many of his comedies, Lemmon portrayed an Everyman, prone to mishaps and pratfalls. He won two Oscars, one for his supporting role as Ensign Pulver in *Mister Roberts* (1955) and another for his lead role in 1973's *Save the Tiger.* Lemmon starred opposite Walter Matthau in several films, including *The Fortune Cookie* (1966), *The Odd Couple* (1968), and *Grumpy Old Men* (1993). He collaborated with director Billy Wilder in *The Apartment* (1960) and *Some Like It Hot* (1959). Lemmon won an Emmy Award in 2000 for *Tuesdays with Morrie.* June 27, 2001

John Lewis, 80: jazz pianist, composer, and arranger who founded and served as music director of the legendary Modern Jazz Quartet. The MJQ, known for its thoughtfully selected arrangements, combined elements of classical music and bebop and performed from the mid-1950s to the late 1990s. Lewis's compositions include "Django" and "Two Degrees East, Three Degrees West." March 29, 2001

Anne Morrow Lindbergh, 94: lyric writer and aviator who, with her husband, Charles Lindbergh, traveled all over the globe, setting a number of aviational records. She got her glider pilot's license in 1930, becoming the first American woman to do so, and served as her husband's navigator, radio operator, and copilot. They were one of the most high-profile couples of the 1930s, particularly after the tragic kidnapping and murder of their son, Charles Jr., in 1932. Lindbergh wrote more than two dozen critically and commercially successful books, including 1955's *Gift from the Sea.* Feb. 7, 2001

Robert Ludlum, 73: suspense novelist whose fast-paced books about spies and international conspiracies have sold more than 290 million copies and have been translated into 32 languages. Ludlum began his career as an actor and turned to writing at age 42. His books include *Scarlatti Inheritance* and *The Bourne Identity.* March 12, 2001

Peter Maas, 72: writer of gritty nonfiction crime stories that often chronicled the lives of Mafia figures. He collaborated with Mob turncoat Joseph Valachi in *The Valachi Papers* (1969), whistle-blower Marie Ragghianti for *Marie* (1983), and Sammy "The Bull" Gravano for *Underboss* (1997). Aug. 23, 2001

Mike Mansfield, 98: Democrat from Montana who served as Senate majority leader from 1961 to 1977, longer than any other politician. As majority leader, he helped to secure passage of major civil-rights legislation and progressive social programs. He was appointed ambassador to Japan after he left the Senate and served under both Democratic and Republican presidents until his retirement in 1989. Oct. 5, 2001

William H. Masters, 85: human sexuality expert who, with his second wife and co-researcher, Virginia Johnson, studied sexual behavior and demystified the mechanics of sex. Their work focused on the physiological aspects of sex and sought to make it more enjoyable for couples. Masters began studying human sexuality in 1954, and he hired Johnson two years later. They collaborated for 22 years and published several books, including 1966's bestselling *Human Sexual Response.* Feb. 16, 2001

Eddie Matthews, 69: Hall of Fame third baseman and 10-time All-Star who was the only player to suit up for the Braves in Boston, Milwaukee, and Atlanta. He was featured on the first cover of *Sports Illustrated* in Aug. 1954 and was inducted into the Baseball Hall of Fame in 1978. Feb. 18, 2001

Susannah McCorkle, 55: sultry-voiced singer and accomplished writer known for her literary interpretation of jazz standards. Fluent in six languages, McCorkle was particularly fond of translating and performing Brazilian pop songs. She recorded 17 albums and had her fiction published in magazines and the *O. Henry Book of Prize Short Stories.* She committed suicide. May 19, 2001

Al McGuire, 72: former Marquette college basketball coach and television commentator. He coached Marquette from 1964 to 1977, leading the Golden Eagles to 11 consecutive postseason appearances. He won the school's only NCAA championship in 1977. He was elected to the basketball Hall of Fame in 1992. McGuire spent 23 years as a broadcaster, first with NBC and then CBS. Jan. 26, 2001

Dorothy McGuire, 83: distinguished film, stage, and television actress who often portrayed strong but sensitive women. She starred in Broadway's *Claudia* (1941) and in its film adaptation (1943). She made her stage debut at age 13, opposite a young Henry Fonda, in *A Kiss for Cinderella.* Other roles include *A Tree Grows in Brooklyn* (1945) and *Gentleman's Agreement* (1947). Sept. 14, 2001

Jason Miller, 62: playwright and actor who won a Tony Award and Pulitzer Prize in 1973 for *That Champion Season.* He directed the 1982 film adaptation of the play. He received an Oscar nomination for his portrayal of Father Karras in *The Exorcist.* His son is the actor Jason Patric. May 13, 2001

Joseph Moakley, 74: popular politician from Massachusetts who served for 15 terms in the U.S. House of Representatives. A quintessential Boston Irish Democrat, Moakley dedicated his career to his district, securing federal funds to clean up Boston Harbor, to heat the homes of the poor, and to initiate the Big Dig. May 28, 2001

James Myers, 81: songwriter who penned more than 300 songs, including 1954's "Rock Around the Clock," which was recorded by Bill Haley and His Comets. May 9, 2001

R. K. Narayan, 94: prolific Indian writer whose exquisitely crafted novels provided witty and perceptive observations about life in India. His books include *The Printer of Malgudi* (1957) and *The Painter of Signs* (1976). May 13, 2001

John Oakes, 87: iconoclastic editorial-page writer and editor for the *New York Times* who championed liberal causes, notably civil rights, environmentalism, and human rights. He spoke out against the Vietnam War as early as 1965. Oakes began writing editorials for the paper in 1949, and became editor of the page in 1961. He was fired in 1976 by his cousin, the publisher Arthur Ochs Sulzberger, who felt Oakes's views had become too radical. April 5, 2001

Carroll O'Connor, 76: Emmy Award–winning actor who began his career on the stage but will be best remembered for his role as the bigoted yet lovable Archie Bunker on *All in the Family* (1971–79). He won four Emmys for the portrayal and one for his starring turn on *In the Heat of the Night* (1987–1994). His film credits include *Lonely Are the Brave* (1962) and *Return to Me* (2000). June 21, 2001

Victor Paz Estenssoro, 94: politician who served as president of Bolivia three times (1952–56, 1960–64, 1985–89). He was a founder of the National Revolutionary Party and as its leader directed the 1952 revolution, in which tin mines were nationalized, indigenous Bolivians were granted suffrage, and social reforms were instituted. June 7, 2001

John Phillips, 65: folk musician and songwriter whose band, the Mamas and the Papas, spoke to the '60s generation, with breezy songs that epitomized the laid-back, live-and-love attitude of southern California and the hippie lifestyle. The band's success was short-lived, as intraband romantic entanglements and drug use led to its demise. Their hits include "California Dreamin'" and "San Francisco (Be Sure to Wear Flowers in Your Hair)." March 18, 2001

Anthony Quinn, 86: Oscar-winning film and stage actor who is best remembered for his role as an impassioned peasant in the film *Zorba the Greek* (1964). He won Academy Awards for his performances in *Viva Zapata!* (1952) and *Lust for Life* (1956). June 3, 2001

Francisco Rabal (Paco Rabal), 75: popular Spanish film and stage actor who won the Best Actor award at the 1984 Cannes Film Festival for *The Holy Innocents.* His other credits include *Tie Me Up, Tie Me Down* (1989). Aug. 29, 2001

Alan Rafkin, 73: Emmy Award–winning television director whose credits include *M*A*S*H, The Dick Van Dyke Show,* and *Murphy Brown.* Aug. 6, 2001

Joey Ramone (Jeffrey Hyman), 49: Unconventional musician who founded the Ramones, a pioneering punk band whose influence extends from the Sex Pistols and the Clash to U2 and Nirvana. The band recorded 21 albums. Its hits include "Teenage Lobotomy" and "Rock 'n' Roll High School." He died of lymphatic cancer. April 15, 2001

Simon Raven, 73: British novelist whose acerbic novels skewered England's upper crust. He is best known for *Alms for Oblivion,* a 10-book series that follows a group of men from their days as students at an elite school through the 1970s. May 12, 2001

Maureen Reagan, 60: political activist and daughter of President Ronald Reagan. She ran unsuccessfully for the U.S. Senate in 1982 and Congress in 1992. She died of melanoma. Aug. 8, 2001

James Rhodes, 91: four-term Republican governor of Ohio who sent national guardsmen to Kent State in 1970 during a Vietnam War protest. Soldiers killed four students during the unrest. March 4, 2001

Mordecai Richler, 70: Canadian novelist and critic whose unflinchingly sarcastic yet brilliant works were typically set within the Canadian Jewish community. He reserved his most potent barbs for proponents of the Quebec separatist movement. His books include *The Apprenticeship of Duddy Kravitz* (1959), which was adapted for the big screen in 1974, and *St. Urbain's Horseman* (1971). July 4, 2001

Robert Rimmer, 84: novelist who wrote 1966's controversial *The Harrad Experiment,* about three men and three women who were roommates at an exclusive college. His other works also dealt with complicated sexual relationships. Aug. 1, 2001

Michael Ritchie, 62: filmmaker who directed the films *Downhill Racer, The Candidate,* and *The Bad News Bears.* He also helmed the television movie *The Positively True Adventures of the Alleged Texas Cheerleader-Murdering Mom.* April 16, 2001

William P. Rogers, 87: lawyer and diplomat who served as secretary of state under President Richard Nixon (1969–1973) and attorney general for President Eisenhower (1957–1961). Jan. 2, 2001

Herbert Ross, 74: choreographer who used his expertise in dance to helm the mainstream Hollywood hits *The Turning Point* (1977) and *Footloose* (1984). He also directed *The Goodbye Girl* (1977) and *Steel Magnolias* (1989). He created several dances for the American Ballet Theater. Oct. 9, 2001

Edward "Big Daddy" Roth, 69: car customizer and cartoonist whose outrageous designs—of both hot rods and cartoon characters—have been elevated to high art. His most famous character was Rat Fink, a hairy rat with yellow teeth and eyes that was often called Mickey Mouse's evil twin. April 4, 2001

James St. Clair, 80: leading Boston trial lawyer who represented President Richard Nixon in 1974 during the Watergate scandal. He also defended Yale University chaplain Rev. William Sloane Coffin, who was accused of encouraging draft evasion, and represented the Boston School Committee in its battle against mandatory busing. March 10, 2001

Clifford Shull, 85: former M.I.T. professor who shared a 1994 Nobel Prize in Physics for helping to "answer the question of where atoms are." He developed a technique, called neutron scattering, to study the molecular structure of materials by bouncing neutrons off them. March 31, 2001

Herbert A. Simon, 84: polymath who won several awards, including the 1978 Nobel Prize in Economics, for his theory on decision making and his groundbreaking research and work on artificial intelligence. He was awarded the National Medal of Science in 1986 and was inducted into the Chinese Academy of Sciences in 1994, one of only 14 foreign scientists to be so honored. Feb. 9, 2001

David Spedding, 58: spymaster, known as C, who headed Britain's Secret Intelligence Service (MI6) from 1994 to 1999. He specialized in Middle East issues and in 1984 helped to prevent an assassination attempt by Abu Nidal on Queen Elizabeth II during her visit to Jordan. June 13, 2001

Floyd Spence, 73: Republican from South Carolina who served in the U.S. House of Representatives from 1970 until his death. Spence was chairman of the House Armed Services Committee from 1995 to 2001. Aug. 16, 2001

Kim Stanley, 76: versatile actress who bewitched Broadway audiences as a tomboy in *Picnic,* a spent chanteuse in *Bus Stop,* and a young single mother in *The Traveling Lady.* She earned Oscar nominations for *Séance on a Wet Afternoon* (1964) and *Frances* (1982). Aug. 20, 2001

Willie Stargell, 61: one of baseball's greatest home run hitters and the intimidating but amicable leader of the Pittsburgh Pirates teams of the 1970s. Most of his 475 career home runs were colossal, game-altering blasts. He was inducted into the Baseball Hall of Fame in 1988. April 9, 2001

Harold E. Stassen, 93: politician who was known as the "boy wonder" of politics. He was elected governor of Minnesota in 1938 at age 31. Stassen unsuccessfully sought the Republican presidential nomination nine times. March 4, 2001

Isaac Stern, 81: Soviet-born concert violinist who was considered one of the world's leading virtuosos of the 20th century. Stern was a prolific performer, touring relentlessly around the world. In 1960 he led a successful drive to save Carnegie Hall from demolition. The building's main concert hall was named in his honor in 1997. He made his debut at age 11 with the San Francisco Symphony Orchestra and first appeared in New York in 1937. In 1994 Sony Classical released *Isaac Stern: A Life in Music,* a 44-disc collection of his works. Sept. 22, 2001

Jerry Sterner, 62: playwright who wrote the off-Broadway hit *Other People's Money.* He penned seven plays while working the overnight shift for the New York City Transit Authority. June 11, 2001

Beatrice Straight, 86: actress who won a Best Supporting Actress Oscar in 1977 for her performance in *Network* and a Tony Award in 1953 for her role as Elizabeth Proctor in *The Crucible.* April 7, 2001

Korey Stringer, 27: Minnesota Vikings Pro Bowl offensive tackle who died of heat stroke during the team's preseason training camp. He had started the last 65 straight games at right tackle for the Vikings and had played in 91 of a possible 93 regular season games in his six seasons. Aug. 1, 2001

Rev. Leon Sullivan, 78: civil rights leader and Baptist pastor whose Sullivan Principles, guidelines that outlined how U.S. companies should operate their businesses in South Africa, contributed to the end of apartheid. April 25, 2001

Ron Towson, 68: singer who was a founding member of the Grammy-winning band the Fifth Dimension. The band's hits include "Aquarius/Let the Sun Shine In" and "Wedding Bell Blues." Aug. 2, 2001

Dame Dorothy Tutin, 71: versatile British actress who won wide praise for her performances in plays by Shakespeare, Ibsen, and Harold Pinter. Aug. 6, 2001

Arturo Uslar Pietri, 94: Venezuelan novelist and essayist who is considered one of the most influential Latin American writers. His most famous work was also his first, the historical novel *Las Lanzas Coloradas* (1931), which chronicles Venezuela's fight for independence from Spain. His other works include *The Road from El Dorado* (1947), a biography of Lope de Aguirre. Feb. 26, 2001

Ninette de Valois, 102: choreographer and dance teacher who founded England's Royal Ballet, one of the world's most respected ballet companies. Her dances include *Job* (1931) and *Bar aux Folies-Bergère* (1934). March 8, 2001

Duong Van Minh, 85: Vietnamese army officer and political leader who served as a military adviser to President Diem and then led the 1963 coup that ousted him. He is believed to have given the order to execute Diem. Van Minh was head of government in 1963, before going into exile. He returned and served as president in 1975, until the North Vietnamese took over the country. Aug. 6, 2001

Nguyen Van Thieu, 76: former president of South Vietnam (1967–75) who led the country during most of the war against North Vietnam. He began his military career with the Vietminh, but later joined the South Vietnamese National Army. He led the coup that ousted President Diem in 1963 and was elected president in 1967 and again in 1971's controversial election. Van Thieu resigned and fled the country in 1975, when the North Vietnamese troops marched into Saigon. Sept. 29, 2001

Henry Wade, 86: Dallas County, Texas, district attorney (1951–1987) who led the prosecution that won the 1964 conviction of Jack Ruby. He was also the Wade in the landmark 1973 Supreme Court case *Roe v. Wade.* In 1970 a pregnant woman challenged the Texas law that prohibited abortion except to save a woman's life. Wade's office defended the state law at trial, where the law was declared unconstitutional. The Supreme Court affirmed a woman's right to abortion. March 1, 2001

Ray Walston, 86: versatile, eccentric actor who won a Tony Award for his role as the Devil in Broadway's *Damn Yankees.* He may have in fact sold his soul to Satan when he signed on to play the titular extraterrestrial in television's *My Favorite Martian* solely for the paycheck. Jan. 1, 2001

Auberon Waugh, 61: iconoclastic British journalist, satirist, and critic who unapologetically unleashed his vituperation in *The New Statesman, Private Eye,* and the *Daily Telegraph.* Jan. 16, 2001

Eudora Welty, 92: Pulitzer Prize–winning writer whose lyrical short stories, which were usually set in the South, centered on families and their attendant issues, squabbles, and eccentricities. Her keen flair for language and sharp wit earned her several other awards, including the National Book Award and six O. Henry Awards. The email program Eudora is named after her. Her short-story collections include *A Curtain of Green* (1941) and *The Bride of Innisfallen* (1955). July 23, 2001

Leonard Woodcock, 89: president of the United Auto Workers who led a 67-day strike against auto giant General Motors in 1970, which resulted in higher wages and pensions. As President Carter's envoy to China, he negotiated with Chinese officials to reestablish diplomatic ties with the U.S. Jan. 16, 2001

Elizabeth Yates, 95: prolific author of children's books. Her book *Amos Fortune, Free Man* (1950) won the Newbery Medal. July 29, 2001

See first page of book for additional tabs.